American and British Theatrical Biography:

A Directory

by

J. P. WEARING

The Scarecrow Press, Inc.

Metuchen, N.J. & London

1979

Library of Congress Cataloging in Publication Data

Wearing, J   P
   American and British theatrical biography.

   1. Theater--United States--Biography--Dictories.
2. Theater--Great Britain--Biography--Directories.
I. Title.
PN2285.W42   792'.0295   78-31162
ISBN 0-8108-1201-0

INTRODUCTION

This directory is intended as a reference tool to locate biographical information about figures connected with the American and British theatre. For each person the following information is provided: name (with cross-references to stage names, pseudonyms, etc.), dates of birth and death, nationality, theatrical occupation(s), and a code to the source(s) containing fuller biographical information.

It should be noted that a person might not appear under the same name in each source. Sometimes a person changed names in the course of his or her career; this is particularly true of women in earlier centuries, who would perform under their maiden names until they married, and who would then perform under their married names. In some cases, some female performers were known by several names, since they married two or three times. In these instances I have listed such people under the name by which they were best known, with cross-references to their other names. Thus, in locating such people in various sources, users should be aware that the person may appear under the various names I have given (as additional information in square brackets), and not necessarily under the main name-entry in the directory. Also, some sources have the practice of dealing with all members of the same theatrical family under a single entry; hence, such entries may have to be scanned to locate the information indicated by this directory. Users should also check any appendices or addenda which may contain the relevant information. And while the directory is alphabetized strictly on a letter-by-letter basis, such may not be the case with all the sources surveyed; thus, for example, I make no alphabetical distinction between "Mac" and "Mc", while a specific source may list these prefixes separately. (I have attempted to resolve all variant spellings of names, but I am conscious that some inadvertant duplications may still remain. Users should, therefore, check similar spellings of names: for example, Abbott, Abbot, Abott, or, Smith, Smythe, etc.)

The question of birth (and occasionally death) dates is vexed, to say the least. I have attempted to give the best consensus of such dates; when there is no such consensus I provide all dates given in the various sources. Where the age at death is known (but the birth year is not), I provide the age at death in square brackets after the year of death: for example, (d. 1977 [49]).

While the focus of the directory is on American and British figures, I have also included "foreign" personalities when the sources surveyed make some mention of their contribution to the American or British theatre. In addition, the directory embraces the spheres of ballet, opera, music, circus, music-hall and the like to the extent that some figures from those spheres are included in the sources surveyed, and might be considered to have contributed to "the theatre" in the widest sense of that word.

I have also thought it useful to include basic information derived from necrologies which sometimes form part of some of the volumes surveyed: such information is designated by the appropriate code and an asterisk (*). In every instance, users will find it worthwhile to consult such necrologies, since all kinds of information are buried therein.

I would be grateful if users would bring to my attention any errors or omissions, as well as suggestions for additional sources which might be surveyed for future editions of this directory.

I am grateful to the staffs of the British Library, London, and of the several libraries which have furnished books via the interlibrary loan program. I owe a special debt of thanks to the staff of the Central Reference Department of the University of Arizona Library who helped make my task easier than it would otherwise have been. My research assistant, Miss Paula Pranka, provided help with parts of the bibliography of sources and with some of the proofreading, for which I am grateful. As ever, I remain indebted to my friends who have materially helped me during the preparation of this book--

in particular Mr. Peter Turnbull and Miss Lesley Whitbourn
of London, England.

J. P. Wearing
University of Arizona
April 1978

SOURCES INDEXED

AAS   Robin May. A Companion to the Theatre: The Anglo-American
Stage from 1920. Guildford & London: Lutterworth, 1973.

BD   Philip H. Highfill, Jr., et al. A Biographical Dictionary of Actors, Actresses, Musicians, Dancers, Managers, & Other
Stage Personnel in London, 1660-1800. 4 vols. to date. Car-
bondale: Southern Illinois University Press, 1973- .

BE   Walter Rigdon, ed. The Biographical Encyclopedia and Who's
Who of the American Theatre. New York: Heinemann, 1966.

BP/1   John Chapman and Garrison P. Sherwood, eds. The Best Plays
of 1894-1899. New York: Dodd, Mead, 1955.

BP/2   Burns Mantle and Garrison P. Sherwood, eds. The Best Plays
of 1899-1909 and the Year Book of the Drama in America.
New York: Dodd, Mead, 1944.

BP/3   and   . The Best Plays of 1909-1919 and the
Year Book of the Drama in America. New York: Dodd, Mead,
1933.

BP/4   Burns Mantle, ed. The Best Plays of 1919-20 and the Year Book
of the Drama in America. Boston: Small, Maynard, 1920.

BP/5   . The Best Plays of 1920-21 and the Year Book of the
Drama in America. Boston: Small, Maynard, 1921.

BP/6   . The Best Plays of 1921-22 and the Year Book of the
Drama in America. Boston: Small, Maynard, 1922.

BP/7   . The Best Plays of 1922-23 and the Year Book of the
Drama in America. Boston: Small, Maynard, 1923.

BP/8   . The Best Plays of 1923-24 and the Year Book of the
Drama in America. Boston: Small, Maynard, 1924.

BP/9   . The Best Plays of 1924-25 and the Year Book of the
Drama in America. Boston: Small, Maynard, 1925.

BP/10   . The Best Plays of 1925-26 and the Year Book of the
Drama in America. New York: Dodd, Mead, 1926.

BP/11   . The Best Plays of 1926-27 and the Year Book of the
Drama in America. New York: Dodd, Mead, 1928.

BP/12   . The Best Plays of 1927-28 and the Year Book of the
Drama in America. New York: Dodd, Mead, 1928.

1

BP/13   _____ . The Best Plays of 1928-29 and the Year Book of the Drama in America. New York: Dodd, Mead, 1929.

BP/14   _____ . The Best Plays of 1929-30 and the Year Book of the Drama in America. New York: Dodd, Mead, 1931.

BP/15   _____ . The Best Plays of 1930-31 and the Year Book of the Drama in America. New York: Dodd, Mead, 1931.

BP/16   _____ . The Best Plays of 1931-32 and the Year Book of the Drama in America. New York: Dodd, Mead, 1932.

BP/17   _____ . The Best Plays of 1932-33 and the Year Book of the Drama in America. New York: Dodd, Mead, 1933.

BP/18   _____ . The Best Plays of 1933-34 and the Year Book of the Drama in America. New York: Dodd, Mead, 1934.

BP/19   _____ . The Best Plays of 1934-35 and the Year Book of the Drama in America. New York: Dodd, Mead, 1935.

BP/20   _____ . The Best Plays of 1935-36 and the Year Book of the Drama in America. New York: Dodd, Mead, 1937.

BP/21   _____ . The Best Plays of 1936-37 and the Year Book of the Drama in America. New York: Dodd, Mead, 1937.

BP/22   _____ . The Best Plays of 1937-38 and the Year Book of the Drama in America. New York: Dodd, Mead, 1938.

BP/23   _____ . The Best Plays of 1938-39 and the Year Book of the Drama in America. New York: Dodd, Mead, 1939.

BP/24   _____ . The Best Plays of 1939-40 and the Year Book of the Drama in America. New York: Dodd, Mead, 1940.

BP/25   _____ . The Best Plays of 1940-41 and the Year Book of the Drama in America. New York: Dodd, Mead, 1941.

BP/26   _____ . The Best Plays of 1941-42 and the Year Book of the Drama in America. New York: Dodd, Mead, 1942.

BP/27   _____ . The Best Plays of 1942-43 and the Year Book of the Drama in America. New York: Dodd, Mead, 1943.

BP/28   _____ . The Best Plays of 1943-44 and the Year Book of the Drama in America. New York: Dodd, Mead, 1944.

BP/29   _____ . The Best Plays of 1944-45 and the Year Book of the Drama in America. New York: Dodd, Mead, 1945.

BP/30   _____ . The Best Plays of 1945-46 and the Year Book of the Drama in America. New York: Dodd, Mead, 1946.

BP/31   _____ . The Best Plays of 1946-47 and the Year Book of the Drama in America. New York: Dodd, Mead, 1947.

BP/32   John Chapman, ed. The Burns Mantle Best Plays of 1947-48 and the Year Book of the Drama in America. New York: Dodd, Mead, 1948.

BP/33   . The Burns Mantle Best Plays of 1948-49 and the Year Book of Drama in America. New York: Dodd, Mead, 1949.

BP/34   . The Burns Mantle Best Plays of 1949-50 and the Year Book of Drama in America. New York: Dodd, Mead, 1950.

BP/35   . The Burns Mantle Best Plays of 1950-51 and the Year Book of the Drama in America. New York: Dodd, Mead, 1951.

BP/36   . The Burns Mantle Best Plays of 1951-52 and the Year Book of the Drama in America. New York: Dodd, Mead, 1952.

BP/37   Louis Kronenberger, ed. The Burns Mantle Yearbook. The Best Plays of 1952-1953. New York & Toronto: Dodd, Mead, 1953.

BP/38   . The Burns Mantle Yearbook: The Best Plays of 1953-1954. New York & Toronto: Dodd, Mead, 1954.

BP/39   . The Burns Mantle Yearbook: The Best Plays of 1954-1955. New York & Toronto: Dodd, Mead, 1955.

BP/40   . The Burns Mantle Yearbook: The Best Plays of 1955-1956. New York & Toronto: Dodd, Mead, 1956.

BP/41   . The Burns Mantle Yearbook: The Best Plays of 1956-1957. New York & Toronto: Dodd, Mead, 1957.

BP/42   . The Burns Mantle Yearbook: The Best Plays of 1957-1958. New York & Toronto: Dodd, Mead, 1958.

BP/43   . The Burns Mantle Yearbook: The Best Plays of 1958-1959. New York & Toronto: Dodd, Mead, 1959.

BP/44   . The Burns Mantle Yearbook: The Best Plays of 1959-1960. New York & Toronto: Dodd, Mead, 1960.

BP/45   . The Burns Mantle Yearbook: The Best Plays of 1960-1961. New York & Toronto: Dodd, Mead, 1961.

BP/46   Henry Hewes, ed. The Burns Mantle Yearbook: The Best Plays of 1961-1962. New York & Toronto: Dodd, Mead, 1962.

BP/47   . The Burns Mantle Yearbook: The Best Plays of 1962-1963. New York & Toronto: Dodd, Mead, 1963.

BP/48   . The Burns Mantle Yearbook: The Best Plays of 1963-1964. New York & Toronto: Dodd, Mead, 1964.

BP/49   Guernsey, Otis L., Jr. The Burns Mantle Yearbook: The Best Plays of 1964-1965. New York & Toronto: Dodd, Mead, 1965.

BP/50   . The Burns Mantle Yearbook: The Best Plays of 1965-1966. New York & Toronto: Dodd, Mead, 1966.

BP/51   <u>   </u>. <u>The Burns Mantle Yearbook: The Best Plays of 1966-
<u>1967.</u> New York & Toronto: Dodd, Mead, 1967.</u>

BP/52   <u>   </u>. <u>The Burns Mantle Yearbook: The Best Plays of 1967-
<u>1968.</u> New York & Toronto: Dodd, Mead, 1968.</u>

BP/53   <u>   </u>. <u>The Burns Mantle Yearbook: The Best Plays of 1968-
<u>1969.</u> New York & Toronto: Dodd, Mead, 1969.</u>

BP/54   <u>   </u>. <u>The Burns Mantle Yearbook: The Best Plays of 1969-
<u>1970.</u> New York & Toronto: Dodd, Mead, 1970.</u>

BP/55   <u>   </u>. <u>The Burns Mantle Yearbook: The Best Plays of 1970-
<u>1971.</u> New York & Toronto: Dodd, Mead, 1971.</u>

BP/56   <u>   </u>. <u>The Burns Mantle Yearbook: The Best Plays of 1971-
<u>1972.</u> New York & Toronto: Dodd, Mead, 1972.</u>

BP/57   <u>   </u>. <u>The Burns Mantle Yearbook: The Best Plays of 1972-
<u>1973.</u> New York & Toronto: Dodd, Mead, 1973.</u>

BP/58   <u>   </u>. <u>The Burns Mantle Yearbook: The Best Plays of 1973-
<u>1974.</u> New York & Toronto: Dodd, Mead, 1974.</u>

BP/59   <u>   </u>. <u>The Burns Mantle Yearbook: The Best Plays of 1974-
<u>1975.</u> New York & Toronto: Dodd, Mead, 1975.</u>

BP/60   <u>   </u>. <u>The Burns Mantle Yearbook: The Best Plays of 1975-
<u>1976.</u> New York & Toronto: Dodd, Mead, 1976.</u>

BS   <u>The Biography of the British Stage: Being Correct Narratives of
the Lives of all the Principal Actors & Actresses at Drury-
Lane, Covent-Garden, the Haymarket, the Lyceum, the Surrey,
the Coburg, and the Adelphi Theatres.</u> London: Sherwood,
Jones, 1824.

BTR/74   Eric Johns, ed. <u>British Theatre Review 1974.</u> Eastbourne:
Vance-Offord, 1975.

CB   <u>Current Biography.</u> New York: Wilson, 1940-1976. [Annual.]

CD   James Vinson, ed. <u>Contemporary Dramatists.</u> 2nd ed. London:
St. James Press; New York: St. Martin's Press, 1977.

CDP   Lillian Arvilla Hall. <u>Catalogue of Dramatic Portraits in the The-
atre Collection of the Harvard College Library.</u> 4 vols. Cam-
bridge, Mass.: Harvard University Press, 1930-1934.

CH   Michael Anderson, et al. <u>Crowell's Handbook of Contemporary
Drama.</u> New York: Crowell, 1971.

COC   Phyllis Hartnoll, ed. <u>The Concise Oxford Companion to the The-
atre.</u> London: Oxford University Press, 1972.

CP/1   David E. Baker. <u>The Companion to the Play-House; or, An His-
torical Account of all the Dramatic Writers (and their works)
that have appeared in Great Britain and Ireland, from the Com-
mencement of our Theatrical Exhibitions, down to the Present
Year, 1764.</u> 2 vols. London: Becker & Dehondt, 1764.

CP/2   Isaac Reed. Biographica Dramatica; or, A Companion to the Playhouse. 2 vols. London: Rivington, 1782. [A revision of CP/1.]

CP/3   Stephen Jones. Biographica Dramatica; or, A Companion to the Playhouse. 3 vols. London: Longman, Hurst, et al., 1812. [A revision of CP/1, CP/2.]

DA   Edwin Nungezer. A Dictionary of Actors and of Other Persons Associated with the Public Representation of Plays in England before 1642. New Haven, Conn.: Yale University Press, 1929.

DAB   Dictionary of American Biography. 20 vols. & 4 suppls. New York: Scribner's, 1928-74.

DD   W. Davenport Adams. A Dictionary of the Drama: A Guide to the Plays, Playwrights, Players, and Playhouses of the United Kingdom and America from the Earliest Times to the Present. London: Chatto & Windus, 1904. [Only vol. 1., A-G, published.]

DNB   Dictionary of National Biography. 22 vols., & 7 suppls. London, 1885-1971.

DP   Erskine Reid & Herbert Compton. The Dramatic Peerage, 1891: Personal Notes and Professional Sketches of the Actors and Actresses of the London Stage. London: General Publishing Co. [1891].

EA/68-   The Era Almanack and Annual. Published annually 1868-1919 by
EA/19   The Era office, London. [EA/68-EA/99 indicates the almanacks for the years 1868-1899; EA/00-EA/19 indicates the almanacks for 1900-1919.]

EAP   Oscar Wegelin. Early American Plays 1714-1830. New York: Dunlap Society, 1900.

ES   Enciclopedia dello spettacolo. 10 vols., & suppl. Rome: Casa Editrice le Maschere, 1954-1966.

FGF   Frederick Gard Fleay. A Biographical Chronicle of the English Drama 1559-1642. 2 vols. London: Reeves & Turner, 1891.

GC   William L. Keese. A Group of Comedians. New York: Dunlap Society, 1901.

GRB/1   Bampton Hunt, ed. The Green Room Book, or, Who's Who on the Stage: An Annual Biographical Record of the Dramatic, Musical and Variety World, 1906. London: T. Sealey Clark, 1906.

GRB/2   John Parker, ed. The Green Room Book or Who's Who on the Stage, 1907. London: T. Sealey Clark, 1907.

GRB/3   _____. The Green Room Book or Who's Who on the Stage, 1908. London: T. Sealey Clark, 1908.

GRB/4   _____. The Green Room Book or Who's Who on the Stage,
              1909. London: T. Sealey Clark, 1909.

GT   Thomas Gilliland. The Dramatic Mirror: Including a Biograph-
              ical and Critical Account of all the Dramatic Writers and Per-
              formers and a History of the Country Theatres in England,
              Ireland and Scotland. 2 vols. London: Chapple, 1808.

HAS   T. Allston Brown. History of the American Stage: Containing
              Biographical Sketches of Nearly Every Member of the Pro-
              fession that has appeared on the American Stage, from 1773
              to 1870. New York: Dick & Fitzgerald, 1870.

HJD   James D. Hart. The Oxford Companion to American Literature.
              4th ed. New York: Oxford University Press, 1965.

HP   Sir Paul Harvey, ed. The Oxford Companion to English Litera-
              ture. 4th ed. Rev. Dorothy Eagle. Oxford: Clarendon
              Press, 1967.

MD   Siegfried Melchinger. The Concise Encyclopedia of Modern
              Drama. New York: Horizon, 1964.

MH   McGraw-Hill Encyclopedia of World Drama. 4 vols. New York:
              McGraw-Hill, 1972.

MWD   Myron Matlaw. Modern World Drama: An Encyclopedia. New
              York: Dutton, 1972.

NTH   Bernard Sobel, ed. The New Theatre Handbook and Digest of
              Plays. New York: Crown, 1959.

NYM   Harrison Grey Fiske, ed. The New York Mirror Annual and Di-
              rectory of the Theatrical Profession for 1888. New York:
              New York Mirror, 1888.

OAA/1   Charles Eyre Pascoe, ed. The Dramatic List: A Record of the
              Principal Performances of Living Actors and Actresses of the
              British Stage; With Criticisms from Contemporary Journals.
              1st ed. London: Hardwicke & Bogue, 1879.

OAA/2   _____. Our Actors and Actresses: The Dramatic List: A
              Record of the Performances of Living Actors and Actresses of
              the British Stage. 2nd ed. London: David Bogue, 1880.

OC/1   Phyllis Hartnoll, ed. The Oxford Companion to the Theatre. 1st
              ed. London: Oxford University Press, 1951.

OC/2   _____. The Oxford Companion to the Theatre. 2nd ed. Lon-
              don: Oxford University Press, 1957.

OC/3   _____. The Oxford Companion to the Theatre. 3rd ed. Lon-
              don: Oxford University Press, 1967.

OX   William Oxberry. Oxberry's Dramatic Biography and Histrionic
              Anecdotes. London: George Virtue, 1825-27. [Title and im-
              print varies.]

PDT   John Russell Taylor. The Penguin Dictionary of the Theatre. Rev. ed. Harmondsworth: Penguin, 1970.

PP/1   John Bouve Clapp and Edwin Francis Edgett. Players of the Present. Pt. 1. New York: Dunlap Society, 1899.

PP/2   _____. Players of the Present. Pt. 2. New York: Dunlap Society, 1900.

PP/3   _____. Players of the Present. Pt. 3. New York: Dunlap Society, 1901.

RE   John Gassner and Edward Quinn, eds. The Reader's Encyclopedia of World Drama. New York: Crowell, 1969.

RJ   James Rees. The Dramatic Authors of America. Philadelphia: G. B. Zieber, 1845.

SR   Robert L. Sherman. Actors and Authors with Composers who helped make them famous: A Chronological Record and Brief Biography of Theatrical Celebrities from 1750 to 1950. Chicago: The Author, 1951.

TD/1   The Thespian Dictionary; or, Dramatic Biography of the Eighteenth Century: Containing Sketches of the Lives, Productions, &c. of All the Principal Managers, Dramatists, Composers, Commentators, Actors, and Actresses, of the United Kingdom: Interspersed with Several Original Anecdotes; and Forming a Concise History of the English Stage. London: T. Hurst, 1802.

TD/2   The Thespian Dictionary ... of the English Stage. 2nd ed. London: James Cundee, 1805.

TW/1   Daniel Blum, ed. Theatre World (1944-45 Season). Vol. 1. New York: Blum, 1945.

TW/2   _____. Theatre World (1945-46 Season). Vol. 2. New York: Blum, 1946.

TW/3   _____. Theatre World (1946-47 Season). Vol. 3. New York: Blum, 1947.

TW/4   _____. Theatre World (1947-48 Season). Vol. 4. New York: Blum, 1948.

TW/5   _____. Theatre World (1948-49 Season). Vol. 5. New York: Greenberg, 1950.

TW/6   _____. Theatre World (1949-50 Season). Vol. 6. New York: Greenberg, 1950.

TW/7   _____. Theatre World (1950-51 Season). Vol. 7. New York: Greenberg, 1951.

TW/8   _____. Theatre World (1951-52 Season). Vol. 8. New York: Greenberg, 1952.

TW/9   _____ . Theatre World (1952-53 Season).   Vol. 9.   New York: Greenberg, 1953.

TW/10   _____ . Theatre World (1953-54 Season).   Vol. 10. New York: Greenberg, 1954.

TW/11   _____ . Theatre World (1954-55 Season).   Vol. 11. New York: Greenberg, 1955.

TW/12   _____ . Theatre World (1955-56 Season).   Vol. 12. New York: Greenberg, 1956.

TW/13   _____ . Theatre World (1956-57 Season).   Vol. 13. New York: Greenberg, 1957.

TW/14   _____ . Theatre World (1957-58 Season).   Vol. 14. Philadelphia: Chilton, 1958.

TW/15   _____ . Theatre World (1958-59 Season).   Vol. 15. Philadelphia: Chilton, 1959.

TW/16   _____ . Theatre World (1959-60 Season).   Vol. 16. Philadelphia: Chilton, 1960.

TW/17   _____ . Theatre World (1960-61 Season).   Vol. 17. Philadelphia: Chilton, 1961.

TW/18   _____ . Theatre World (1961-62 Season).   Vol. 18. Philadelphia: Chilton, 1962.

TW/19   _____ . Theatre World (1962-63 Season).   Vol. 19. Philadelphia: Chilton, 1963.

TW/20   _____ . Theatre World (1963-64 Season).   Vol. 20. Philadelphia: Chilton, 1964.

TW/21   John Willis, ed. Theatre World (1964-65 Season).   Vol. 21. New York: Crown, 1965.

TW/22   _____ . Theatre World (1965-66 Season).   Vol. 22. New York: Crown, 1966.

TW/23   _____ . Theatre World (1966-67 Season).   Vol. 23. New York: Crown, 1967.

TW/24   _____ . Theatre World (1967-68 Season).   Vol. 24. New York: Crown, 1968.

TW/25   _____ . Theatre World (1968-69 Season).   Vol. 25. New York: Crown, 1969.

TW/26   _____ . Theatre World (1969-70 Season).   Vol. 26. New York: Crown, 1970.

TW/27   _____ . Theatre World (1970-71 Season).   Vol. 27. New York: Crown, 1971.

TW/28   _____ . Theatre World (1971-72 Season).   Vol. 28. New York: Crown, 1973.

TW/29   _____. Theatre World (1972-73 Season). Vol. 29. New
                York: Crown, 1974.

TW/30   _____. Theatre World (1973-74 Season). Vol. 30. New
                York: Crown, 1975.

WWA/H   Who Was Who in America: Historical Volume 1607-1896. Chi-
                cago: Marquis, 1963.

WWA/1   Who Was Who in America: Vol. 1: 1897-1942. Chicago: Mar-
                quis, 1966.

WWA/2   Who Was Who in America: Vol. 2: 1943-1950. Chicago: Mar-
                quis, 1966.

WWA/3   Who Was Who in America: Vol. 3: 1951-1960. Chicago: Mar-
                quis, 1966.

WWA/4   Who Was Who in America: Vol. 4: 1961-1968. Chicago: Mar-
                quis, 1968.

WWA/5   Who Was Who in America: Vol. 5: 1969-1973. Chicago: Mar-
                quis, 1973.

WWM   Dixie Hines and Harry Prescott Hanaford, eds. Who's Who in
                Music and Drama. New York: H. P. Hanaford, 1914.

WWS   Walter Browne and E. de Roy Koch. Who's Who on the Stage
                1908: The Dramatic Reference Book and Biographical Diction-
                ary of the Theatre: Containing Careers of Actors, Actresses,
                Managers and Playwrights of the American Stage. New York:
                Dodge, 1908.

WWT/1   John Parker, ed. The New Dramatic List: Who's Who in the
                Theatre: A Biographical Record of the Contemporary Stage.
                1st ed. London: Pitman, 1912.

WWT/2   _____. The New Dramatic List: Who's Who in the Theatre:
                A Biographical Record of the Contemporary Stage: With a
                Foreword by Sir Herbert Beerbohm Tree. 2nd ed. London:
                Pitman, 1914.

WWT/3   _____. The New Dramatic List: Who's Who in the Theatre:
                A Biographical Record of the Contemporary Stage. 3rd ed.,
                rev. London: Pitman, 1916.

WWT/4   _____. The New Dramatic List: Who's Who in the Theatre:
                A Biographical Record of the Contemporary Stage. 4th ed.,
                rev. London: Pitman, 1922.

WWT/5   _____. The Dramatic List: Who's Who in the Theatre: A
                Biographical Record of the Contemporary Stage. 5th ed., rev.
                London: Pitman, 1925.

WWT/6   _____. The Dramatic List: Who's Who in the Theatre: A
                Biographical Record of the Contemporary Stage. 6th ed., rev.
                London: Pitman, 1930.

WWT/7   . The Dramatic List: Who's Who in the Theatre: A
Biographical Record of the Contemporary Stage. 7th ed., rev.
London: Pitman, 1933.

WWT/8   . The Dramatic List: Who's Who in the Theatre: A
Biographical Record of the Contemporary Stage. 8th ed., rev.
London: Pitman, 1936.

WWT/9   . The Dramatic List: Who's Who in the Theatre: A
Biographical Record of the Contemporary Stage. 9th ed., rev.
London: Pitman, 1939.

WWT/10   . The Dramatic List: Who's Who in the Theatre: A
Biographical Record of the Contemporary Stage. 10th ed.,
rev. London: Pitman, 1947.

WWT/11   . The Dramatic List: Who's Who in the Theatre: A
Biographical Record of the Contemporary Stage. 11th ed.,
rev. London: Pitman, 1952.

WWT/12   . Who's Who in the Theatre: A Biographical Record of
the Contemporary Stage. 12th ed. London: Pitman, 1957.

WWT/13 Freda Gaye, ed. Who's Who in the Theatre: A Biographical
Record of the Contemporary Stage. 13th ed. London: Pitman, 1961.

WWT/14   . Who's Who in the Theatre: A Biographical Record of
the Contemporary Stage. 14th ed. London: Pitman, 1967.

WWT/15 Who's Who in the Theatre: A Biographical Record of the Contemporary Stage. 15th ed. London: Pitman, 1972.

WWT/16 Ian Herbert, ed. Who's Who in the Theatre: A Biographical
Record of the Contemporary Stage. 16th ed. London: Pitman; Detroit: Gale Research, 1977.

WWW/1 Who Was Who: Vol. 1: 1897-1915. 5th ed. London: Black,
1967.

WWW/2 Who Was Who: Vol. 2: 1916-1928. 4th ed. London: Black,
1967.

WWW/3 Who Was Who: Vol. 3: 1929-1940. 2nd ed. London: Black,
1967.

WWW/4 Who Was Who: Vol. 4: 1941-1950. 3rd ed. London: Black,
1964.

WWW/5 Who Was Who: Vol. 5: 1951-1960. 2nd ed. London: Black,
1964.

WWW/6 Who Was Who: Vol. 6: 1961-1970. London: Black, 1972.

A., R. (fl early 17th cent) drama-
tist CP/2-3
AARON, David (b 1947) American
actor TW/29-30
AARON, Jack (b 1933) American
actor TW/26-30
AARONOFF, Alma S. (d 1969
[53]) public relations BP/54*
AARONS, Alexander A. (d 1943
[52]) producing manager SR,
WWT/6-8
AARONS, Alfred E. (d 1936
[71]) American producing
manager, composer SR,
WWS, WWT/6-8
AARONSON, Irving (d 1963 [68])
composer, bandleader BE*
AARONSON, Rudolph (d 1919)
manager WWT/14*
AASEN, John (d 1938 [51]) per-
former BE*
ABA, Marika (d 1972) publicist
BP/57*
ABALDO, Joseph American actor
TW/30
ABARBANELL, Jacob Ralph
(1852-1922) American drama-
tist WWA/1
ABARBANELL, Lina (1880-1963)
German actress, singer ES,
TW/19, WWM, WWS, WWT/
1-2, 6-9
ABBA, Marta (b 1900/07) Italian
actress ES, WWT/9
ABBAS, Hector (1884-1942) Dutch
actor WWT/6-8
ABBE, Charles Smith (d 1932
[73]) American actor PP/1
ABBE, Josephine A. CDP
ABBEY, Henry Eugène (1846-96)
American manager CDP,
COC, DAB, OC/1-3, SR,
WWA/H
ABBEY, Mrs. Henry Eugène see

Girard, Florence
ABBEY, May Evers [Mrs. George
Lessey] (d 1952 [80]) American
performer BE*
ABBOT, Elizabeth Bradshaw see
Abbott, Mrs. William
ABBOT, John (d 1744) singer BD
ABBOT, Marie singer CDP
ABBOT, William see Abbott,
William
ABBOT, Mrs. William see Ab-
bott, Mrs. William
ABBOTT, Mr. (fl 1718-19) numberer
BD
ABBOTT, Mr. (fl 1799) instrumen-
talist BD
ABBOTT, Al (d 1962 [78]) perform-
er BE*
ABBOTT, Alf (d 1887 [40]) variety
artist EA/88*
ABBOTT, Amy (d 1904) music-hall
performer EA/05*
ABBOTT, Annie ["The Georgia Mag-
net"; Priscilla Rawlinson]
(1868-1943) American perform-
er SR
ABBOTT, Anthony Duke (fl 1795-
99) English musician BD
ABBOTT, Bessie Pickens (1878-
1919) American singer GRB/1-
2, SR, WWA/1, WWM, WWS
ABBOTT, Betty (b 1924) American
actress TW/4
ABBOTT, Bud [William] (1900-74)
American comedian CB, ES,
SR, TW/30
ABBOTT, C. (d 1817 [89]) performer BE*
ABBOTT, Charles (fl second half
19th cent) actor SR
ABBOTT, Charles (d 1874 [32])
pantomimist EA/75*
ABBOTT, Clara Barnes (d 1956
[82]) musical director BE*

---

*An asterisk indicates that information appears in a necrology portion of the
book cited.

ABBOTT, Dolly (d 1955 [68])
American performer BE*
ABBOTT, Dorothy L. (d 1937
[51]) American performer
BE*
ABBOTT, Edward B. (d 1932
[50]) performer BE*
ABBOTT, Edward S. [né Sanders]
(d 1936 [22]) American per-
former BE*
ABBOTT, Emma (1850-91) Amer-
ican singer CDP, DAB, ES,
SR, WWA/H
ABBOTT, Frank (d 1899 [25])
descriptive vocalist EA/00*
ABBOTT, George (fl 1740) mu-
sician BD
ABBOTT, George Francis (b 1887)
American actor, dramatist,
producer, director AAS, BE,
CB, CD, COC, ES, HJD,
MD, MH, MWD, NTH, OC/
1-3, PDT, SR, TW/2-8,
WWT/6-16
ABBOTT, Harriet (d 1874) dancer
EA/75*
ABBOTT, Harry (1861-1942)
press representative, actor
SR
ABBOTT, Henry (fl 1762-84)
stage doorkeeper BD
ABBOTT, John (b 1905) English
actor BE, ES, TW/2, 6,
13, WWT/9-11
ABBOTT, Judith American cast-
ing director, director, actress
BE
ABBOTT, Marion (1866-1937)
American performer SR
ABBOTT, Michael Ann (d 1972
[44]) performer BP/57*
ABBOTT, Nancy Ann (d 1964
[63]) American actress BE*
ABBOTT, Paul (d 1872) panto-
mimist EA/73*
ABBOTT, Percy (d 1960 [74])
Australian magician BE*
ABBOTT, Philip (b 1924) Amer-
ican actor BE, TW/16
ABBOTT, Richard (b 1899) Bel-
gian/American actor BE
ABBOTT, T. (fl 1788?-1821?)
actor, singer BD
ABBOTT, William (1789-1843)
English actor, dramatist BS,
CDP, COC, DD, DNB, ES,
HAS, OC/1-3, SR, WWA/H
ABBOTT, Mrs. William [née Bu-

loid; Mrs. William Bradshaw]
(c. 1820-58) American actress
CDP, DD, HAS, SR
ABBOTT, Yarnell (d 1938 [67])
American writer BE*
ABDULLAH, Achmed (1881-1945)
Syrian dramatist CB, SR
ABDUSHELLI, Zurab (1913-57) Rus-
sian announcer BE*
A'BECKET, Thomas (1808-90) Eng-
lish actor, singer, composer,
musician HAS, SR
A BECKETT, Arthur William (1844-
1909) English dramatist DD,
DNB, WWW/1
A BECKETT, Gilbert Abbott (1811-
56) English dramatist DD, DNB,
ES, HP
A BECKETT, Gilbert Arthur (1837-
91) English dramatist DD, DNB,
HP, SR
ABEGG, Mrs. (fl 1758-63) actress,
singer BD
ABEGGLEN, Homer N. (b 1901)
American educator, director
BE
ABEL, Alfred (d 1937 [72]) actor
BE*
ABEL, George (d 1916 [46]) Irish?
lessee EA/18*
ABEL, Grover Cleveland (d 1972
[79]) dance teacher BP/57*
ABEL, Harry Nelson (d 1882) ad-
vance agent EA/83*
ABEL, Karl Friedrich (1723-87)
German instrumentalist, com-
poser BD, CDP, DNB
ABEL, Lionel (b 1910) American
dramatist, critic ES, MD,
MWD
ABEL, Mala (d 1905) EA/07*
ABEL, Neal (d 1952 [70]) perform-
er BE*
ABEL, Walter (b 1898) American
actor BE, ES, SR, TW/2-8,
14-15, 17, 19, 24, WWT/7-16
ABEL, William Henry (d 1887 [53])
EA/88*
ABELES, Edward S. (1869-1919)
American actor GRB/2-4, SR,
WWM, WWS, WWT/1-3
ABELES, Joseph (b 1911) American
theatrical photographer BE
ABELES, Julian T. (d 1973 [80])
lawyer BP/57*
ABELL, Edith (d 1926 [78]) singer
CDP
ABELL, John (1650?-1724?) Scottish

singer, instrumentalist BD, DNB

ABELL, Kjeld (1901-61) Danish dramatist, designer COC, ES, MWD, OC/1-3

ABELL BROTHERS (fl 1726-27) house servants? BD

ABELMAN, Lester (d 1972 [58]) critic BP/56*

ABELS, Gregory (b 1941) American actor TW/28, 30

ABELS, Marcella Ruth see Cisney, Marcella

ABELSON, Hope (b 1919) American producer BE

ABEND, Sheldon (b 1929) American literary representative BE

ABERCROMBIE, Lascelles (1881-1938) English critic, dramatist DNB, ES, OC/1, WWT/2-8, WWW/3

ABERDEIN, Mr. (fl 1782-96) Scottish actor, singer BD

ABERDEIN, Mr. (fl 1783-1819) dresser, scene man? BD

ABERT, Johann Joseph (1832-1915) Bohemian composer, conductor ES

ABINGDON, Marie [Mrs. Charles Glenny] (d 1898 [39]) actress EA/99*, WWT/14*

ABINGDON, William (1888-1959) English director WWT/6-12

ABINGDON, W[illiam] L. (1859-1918) English actor DD, DP, EA/95, GRB/1-4, WWM, WWS, WWT/1-3

ABINGDON, Mrs. W[illiam] L. see Fernandez, Bijou

ABINGTON, Frances see Abington, Mrs. James

ABINGTON, James (d 1806) trumpeter, singer BD

ABINGTON, Mrs. James [Frances Barton] (1737-1815) English actress BD, CDP, COC, DD, DNB, ES, GT, NTH, OC/2-3, TD/1-2

ABINGTON, Joseph (d 1744) violinist BD

ABINGTON, Leonard (d 1767) violinist, trumpeter, composer, singer? BD

ABINGTON, Leonard Joseph (fl 1794) singer BD

ABINGTON, William (fl 1774-94) composer, instrumentalist BD

ABLAMOWICZ, Anna singer CDP

ABLE, Frank [J. H. R. Penrose] (d 1893) EA/94*

ABLE, Will B. (b 1923) American actor, singer, dancer, comedian, mimist, choreographer BE, TW/25-26

ABLEMAN, Paul (b 1927) English dramatist CD

ABORN, Louis H. (b 1912) American executive BE

ABORN, Milton (1864-1933) American manager DAB, SR, WWA/1, WWM, WWT/7

ABORN, Sargent (1866-1956) American impresario SR, WWM

ABOS, Gerolamo (1700-60) Italian composer ES

ABOTT, Bessie Pickens see Abbott, Bessie Pickens

ABOUCHAR, Joan (b 1937) Chinese/American children's theatre manager BE

ABRAHALL, Mr. (fl 1700) musician BD

ABRAHAM, Mr. (fl 1793) presenter BD

ABRAHAM, F. Murray (b 1939) American actor TW/24-30

ABRAHAM, John (fl 1688) instrumentalist BD

ABRAHAM, Louis (d 1975 [51]) producer/director/choreographer BP/60*

ABRAHAM, Paul (1892-1960) composer ES, WWT/8-10

ABRAHAMS, A. E. (1873-1966) English proprietor WWT/6-10

ABRAHAMS, Barney (d 1969 [62]) manager BP/54*

ABRAHAMS, David Bramah (1775-1837) English violist, violinist, singer BD

ABRAHAMS, Doris Cole (b 1925) American producing manager WWT/15-16

ABRAHAMS, Elizabeth (d 1906) EA/07*

ABRAHAMS, Frederick (d 1912 [90]) music-hall proprietor EA/13*

ABRAHAMS, John (fl 1775-79) house servant? BD

ABRAHAMS, Joseph B. (d 1969 [84]) designer BP/54*

ABRAHAMS, Louis William (d 1890 [33]) EA/91*

ABRAHAMS, Mrs. M. (d 1870 [29]) EA/71*

ABRAHAMS, Morris (d 1915 [84])
manager WWT/14*
ABRAHAMS, Mrs. Morris (d 1885)
EA/87*
ABRAHAMSOHN, Otto see
Brahm, Otto
ABRAM, Lancelot Arthur (d 1899)
musical director EA/00*
ABRAM, Launcelot Sharpe see
Sharpe, L.
ABRAMS, Bill (b 1943) American
actor TW/27
ABRAMS, Charles (fl 1794) Vio-
loncellist BD
ABRAMS, Eliza (b 1763?) singer
BD
ABRAMS, Flora (fl 1778) singer
BD
ABRAMS, Miss G. (fl 1778-80)
singer, actress BD
ABRAMS, Harriet (1760-1825?)
singer, composer BD,
CDP
ABRAMS, Jane (fl 1799) singer?
BD
ABRAMS, Theodosia [Mrs.
Thomas Fisher; Mrs. Joseph
Garrow] (c 1761-1849)
singer BD
ABRAMS, William (fl 1794) vio-
linist, violist BD
ABRAMSON, Charles H. (b 1902)
American producer BE
ABRAVANEL, Maurice (b 1903)
Greek/American musical
director, conductor, educa-
tor BE, ES
ABRUZZO, Raffaella Julia Thérésa
see Allen, Rae
ABSE, Dannie (b 1923) Welsh
dramatist CD
ABT, Frank (d 1885 [65]) com-
poser EA/86*
ABUD, Charles J. (d 1926 [71])
manager WWT/14*
ABUZA, Sophie see Tucker,
Sophie
ABYNGDON, Henry (fl 1455-78)
master of the Chapel Royal
DA
ACE, Jane (d 1974 [74]) actress
BP/59*, WWT/16*
ACHARD, Marcel (1900-74) French
dramatist, director BE,
BTR/74, MWD
ACHENBACH, Maximilian see
Alvary, Max
ACHILLE, Mons. (fl 1827)

French dancer HAS
ACHILLE, Mme. (b 1797) French
dancer CDP, HAS
ACHMAN, Mr. actor TD/2
ACHMET, Mrs. [Mrs. William
Cairns; Catherine Ann Egan]
(b 1766) actress BD, DD,
TD/1-2
ACHMET, Miss (fl 1794) actress
BD
ACHURCH, Janet [née Janet Achurch
Sharp; Mrs. Charles Charring-
ton] (1864-1916) English actress,
COC, DD, DP, EA/95, ES,
GRB/1-4, OC/1-3, WWT/1-3,
WWW/2
ACHURCH, Thomas (d 1771) actor
BD
ACHURCH, Mrs. [Thomas?] (fl
1734) actress BD
ACKER, Iris American actress
TW/30
ACKER, Mabel actress TW/1, 3
ACKERILL, Mr. (fl 1793-95) slack-
wire dancer, equestrian, tum-
bler BD
ACKERILL, Master (fl 1793-95)
slack-wire dancer, violinist
BD
ACKERMAN, Al (d 1971 [90])
performer BP/56*
ACKERMAN, Floyd F. (b 1927)
American producer, personal
manager, theatre representative
BE
ACKERMAN, Irene (d 1916 [45])
American actress CDP, WWS
ACKERMAN, Irving (d 1970 [85])
theatre owner BP/55*
ACKERMAN, Loni Zoe (b 1949)
American actress TW/26-30
ACKERMAN, P. Dodd, Sr. (d
1963 [87]) American designer
BE*
ACKERMANN, Charlotte (1757-74)
actress BE*
ACKERMANN, Dorothea (1752-1821)
actress BE*
ACKERMANN, Konrad Ernst (1710-
71) actor, manager BE*,
WWT/14*
ACKERY, Mr. (fl 1787) actor BD
ACKERY, Cecil (d 1963 [70]) magi-
cian BE*
ACKLAND, Henry (d 1900 [52])
singer EA/01*
ACKLAND, Joss (b 1928) English
actor AAS, WWT/15-16

ACKLAND, Rodney (b 1908) English actor, dramatist AAS, BE, CD, ES, PDT, WWT/7-15
ACKMAN, Mrs. (fl 1779) house servant? BD
ACKMAN, Ellis (d 1774) actor BD
ACKROYD, David (b 1940) American actor TW/28, 30
ACKTE, Aino (1876-1944) Finnish singer ES, WWM
ACOSTA, Rodolfo (d 1974 [54]) performer BP/59*
ACTE, Aino see Ackté, Aino
ACTMAN, Irving (d 1967 [60]) composer/lyricist BP/52*
ACTON-BOND, Acton see Bond, Acton
ACTON-PHILLIPS, Sophia Matilda (d 1900) EA/01*
ADAIR, Alice (d 1895) EA/97*
ADAIR, Jean (d 1953 [80]) Canadian actress TW/1, 6-7, 9, WWT/8-11
ADAIR, Robert (d 1954 [54]) actor WWT/14*
ADAIR, Yvonne (b 1925) American singer, dancer, actress BE
ADAM, Adolph (d 1856 [53]) composer EA/72*
ADAM, Noelle (b 1933) French dancer, actress BE, TW/19
ADAM, Ronald (b 1896) English actor, manager, dramatist AAS, WWT/8-16
ADAM, V. equestrian performer CDP
ADAM, William (d 1879 [18]) violinist EA/80*
ADAMBERGER, Valentin (1743-1804) German singer BD
ADAMOV, Arthur (1908-70) Russian/French dramatist CH, COC, MH, OC/3
ADAMS (d 1887 [82]) aeronaut EA/88*
ADAMS, Mr. equestrian performer CDP
ADAMS, Mr. (fl 1669-73) actor BD
ADAMS, Mr. (fl 1728) actor BD
ADAMS, Mr. (fl 1736-48) dancer, actor BD
ADAMS, Mr. (fl 1763-70?) singer BD
ADAMS, Mr. (fl 1782-1800) bird imitator, tumbler, equestrian BD
ADAMS, Mr. (fl 1788) actor BD
ADAMS, Mrs. (fl 1731) actress BD
ADAMS, Mrs. (fl 1748) dancer/actress BD
ADAMS, Mrs. (fl 1750) actress, singer BD
ADAMS, Mrs. (fl 1798-1800) box-office keeper BD
ADAMS, Master (fl 1763-66) singer BD
ADAMS, Master (fl 1795) bird imitator BD
ADAMS, Miss see Barrymore, Mrs. William
ADAMS, Abigail (d 1955 [37]) actress BE*
ADAMS, Mrs. A. A. see Duff, Mary
ADAMS, Albert F. (d 1965 [82]) performer BP/50*
ADAMS, Alice (d 1877) EA/78*
ADAMS, Alice Baldwin [Mrs. Burton Adams] (d 1936 [83]) actress BE*
ADAMS, Anna Matilda (fl 1800?-08?) dancer, actress? BD
ADAMS, Annie [Mrs. H. Wall] (d 1905 [61]) variety artist CDP, ES, GRB/1, SR
ADAMS, Annie (d 1916 [69]) actress WWT/14*
ADAMS, Arthur Henry (1872-1936) New Zealand dramatist WWW/3
ADAMS, Augustus A. see Addams, Augustus A.
ADAMS, Bert (d 1904) manager EA/05*
ADAMS, Blake (d 1913) Scottish actor GRB/2-3
ADAMS, Bob (d 1948 [74]) comedian WWT/14*
ADAMS, Bret (b 1930) American producer, talent representative BE
ADAMS, Mrs. Burton see Adams, Alice Baldwin
ADAMS, Caroline (d 1889) actress EA/90*
ADAMS, Casey see Showalter, Max
ADAMS, C. F. (d 1854) American actor HAS
ADAMS, Mrs. C. F. (fl 1850) American actress HAS
ADAMS, Charles (fl c. 1745-51) actor BD

ADAMS, Charles (d 1880 [52])
circus manager EA/82*

ADAMS, Charles R. (1834-1900)
American singer CDP, DAB,
ES, WWA/H

ADAMS, Claire (fl 1920s) actress
ES

ADAMS, Constance see De Mille,
Mrs. Cecil

ADAMS, Diana (b 1926) American
dancer CB, ES

ADAMS, Dick (b 1889) Irish manager WWT/2

ADAMS, Miss E. (fl 1800-08)
dancer, singer BD

ADAMS, Earl P. actor SR

ADAMS, Edie American actress,
entertainer BE, WWT/16

ADAMS, Edith [Edith Enke] (b
1927) American singer,
actress CB, TW/9-19

ADAMS, Edwin (1834-77) Ameri-
can actor CDP, COC, DAB,
DD, ES, HAS, OC/1-3, SR,
WWA/H

ADAMS, Mrs. Edwin (fl c1820s)
American actress, dancer
HAS

ADAMS, Frances Sale (d 1969
[77]) performer BP/54*

ADAMS, Mrs. Francis (d 1972
[86]) performer BP/57*

ADAMS, Frank Ramsay (1883-
1963) American dramatist
WWA/4

ADAMS, Frank Steward (d 1964
[79]) organist BE*

ADAMS, Franklin Pierce (1881-
1960) American performer,
writer BE*

ADAMS, Franklin R. dramatist
SR

ADAMS, George (fl 1729) dramatist CP/1-3, DD, GT

ADAMS, George (1777-1810)
English instrumental musician BD

ADAMS, George (d 1870 [47])
actor EA/71*

ADAMS, George Frederick (d
1917 [40]) EA/18*

ADAMS, George H. (1853-1935)
English clown CDP

ADAMS, G. G., the Elder (d
1853) American actor HAS,
SR

ADAMS, Miss H. (fl 1800-08)
dancer, singer BD

ADAMS, Ida (d 1960 [72]) actress
WWT/4-5

ADAMS, Isabel [Mrs. Ernest Clif-
ton] (d 1893 [62]) actress
EA/94*, WWT/14*

ADAMS, Jack (fl 1667?) clown BD

ADAMS, James (b c.1771) violinist,
organist BD

ADAMS, James Blake (b c.1749)
organist, violoncellist, violinist
BD

ADAMS, Jill (d 1964 [41]) dancer
BE*

ADAMS, Joey (b 1911) American
comedian, producer, toastmaster
BE

ADAMS, John (fl 1576-91) actor
DA

ADAMS, John (fl 1739) musician
BD

ADAMS, John (fl 1739) musician
BD [sic]

ADAMS, John (fl 1794) horn player,
organist BD

ADAMS, John (d 1873) minstrel
EA/74*

ADAMS, John B. (1830-63) American
actor HAS, SR

ADAMS, John Cranford (b 1903)
American writer, educator BE

ADAMS, John F. American actor
HAS

ADAMS, John Jay (fl 1822) American
actor DD

ADAMS, Joseph Quincy (1881-1946)
American scholar CB, DAB,
OC/1-2, WWA/2

ADAMS, J. P. (d 1853) American
comedian HAS, SR

ADAMS, Julian (d 1887 [62]) conductor EA/88*

ADAMS, Justin actor, dramatist
SR

ADAMS, Kathryn (d 1959 [65])
American actress BE*

ADAMS, Lee (b 1924) American
lyricist BE

ADAMS, Leslie (1887-1936) American actor SR

ADAMS, Lionel (d 1952 [86]) actor
TW/9

ADAMS, Margaret (d 1873 [63])
EA/74*

ADAMS, Margie [Mrs. H. Wilmot
Young] (1881-1937) Canadian
actress BE*

ADAMS, Mason (b 1919) American
actor TW/16, 26-28, 30

ADAMS, Maude [Maude Kiskadden] (1872-1953) American actress ES, GRB/2-4, HJD, NTH, OC/1-3, PP/1, SR, TW/10, WWA/3, WWM, WWS, WWT/1-11

ADAMS, Milward (b 1857) American manager WWM

ADAMS, Miriam (b 1907) English actress WWT/7-9

ADAMS, Nicholas [Nathan Anspach] (d 1935 [64]) American actor BE*

ADAMS, Nick (d 1968 [36]) performer BP/52*

ADAMS, Rebecca (d 1865) American actress HAS

ADAMS, Robert British Guianan actor WWT/10-11

ADAMS, Robert K. (b 1909) American producer, director, actor BE, ES

ADAMS, Roger (b 1917) English composer BE

ADAMS, Ronald (b 1896) English manager ES, WWT/7

ADAMS, Miss S. (fl 1800-08) dancer, singer BD

ADAMS, Mrs. Sam see Nott, Cicely

ADAMS, Samuel (d 1893 [55]) lessee EA/94*

ADAMS, Samuel Hopkins (1871-1958) American writer BE*

ADAMS, Sarah Ann see Nott, Cicely

ADAMS, Selby (1872-1943) American actor, showboat manager SR

ADAMS, Sheila K. (b 1950) American actress TW/30

ADAMS, Stanley (b 1907) American lyricist, executive BE

ADAMS, Stephen see Maybrick, Michael

ADAMS, Suzanne (1872/73-1953) American singer SR, WWS, WWA/5

ADAMS, Thomas (b 1783) oboist, organist BD

ADAMS, Trude (b 1931) American actress TW/22

ADAMS, Virginia (d 1975 [62]) performer BP/59*

ADAMS, William (d 1897) business manager EA/98*

ADAMS, Mrs. William (d 1877) EA/78*

ADAMS, William Davenport (1851-1904) English critic, scholar DNB, WWW/1

ADAMS, William Henry Davenport (1828-91) English scholar DNB

ADAMS, William P. (d 1972 [85]) actor TW/29

ADAMS, W. J. singer CDP

ADAMSON, Mr. (fl 1816) English actor SR

ADAMSON, John (fl 1808) translator CP/3, DD

ADAMSON, Owen (d 1672) singer BD

ADAMSON, Patrick (fl 1572) dramatist FGF

ADAMSON, Richard (fl 1661) singer BD

ADCOCK, Mr. (d 1753) English actor DD, SR

ADCOCK, Mr. (fl 1794?-1803?) actor, singer?, manager? BD

ADCOCK, Miss (fl 1782-83) singer BD

ADCOCK, Miss see Wilson, Mrs.

ADCOCK, Abraham (d 1773) trumpeter, organist, violinist, organ builder BD

ADCOCK, William (fl 1752-72) English actor BD, HAS

ADCOCK, Mrs. William [Mary Palmer] (d 1773) BD

ADDAMS, Augustus A. (d 1851) American actor CDP, DD, HAS, SR

ADDAMS, Dawn (b 1930) English actress ES, WWT/15-16

ADDAMS, John dramatist RJ

ADDAMS, Mrs. J. P. see Provost, Mary

ADDERLEY, James (d 1917) EA/18*

ADDERSLEY, T. G. (d 1879 [28]) agent EA/80*

ADDIE, Harriet Frances [Fanny Hamilton] (1816-75) actress DD

ADDINGTON, Sir William (d 1811 [83]) dramatist CP/3

ADDINSELL, Richard Stewart [or Stuart] (1904-77) English composer BE, ES, WWT/7-16

ADDIS, George actor TW/24-25

ADDIS, John B. (b 1804) English actor, stage manager HAS, SR

ADDISON, Mrs. (fl 1747-52)

dancer BD
ADDISON, Mrs. (fl 1796) singer
TD/1-2
ADDISON, Anne see Howard,
Anne
ADDISON, Carlotta [Mrs. Charles
La Trobe] (1849/50-1914)
English actress DD, DP,
EA/95, GRB/1-4, OAA/1-2,
WWT/1-2
ADDISON, Edward Phillips (1808-
74) actor DD
ADDISON, Fanny (b 1847) English
actress DD, OAA/1-2
ADDISON, Col. Henry Robert
(1805-76) dramatist DD,
EA/68
ADDISON, John (d 1799) musician
BD
ADDISON, John (c.1766-1844)
English double bass player,
violoncellist, composer BD,
DD, DNB, ES
ADDISON, John English composer
BE
ADDISON, Mrs. John [Elizabeth
Willems] (fl 1785?-1840)
BD, DD
ADDISON, Joseph (1672-1719)
English dramatist CDP,
COC, CP/1-3, DD, DNB,
ES, GT, HP, MH, NTH,
OC/1-3, SR, TD/1-2
ADDISON, Laura (1822-52) Eng-
lish actress CDP, DD,
DNB, ES, HAS
ADDISON, R. (d 1868 [71]) music
publisher EA/69*
ADDISON, Thomas dramatist SR
ADDISON, Victoria (d 1971 [92])
performer BP/55*
ADDY, Wesley (b 1912/13) Amer-
ican actor BE, TW/2-4, 6-
7, 10-18, 26, 29, WWT/11-16
ADE, George (1866-1944) American
dramatist CB, COC, DAB,
ES, GRB/2-4, HJD, MH,
MWD, NTH, OC/1-3, SR,
WWA/2, WWM, WWS,
WWT/1-9
ADEANE, Mr. (fl 1786) dancer ?
BD
ADELAIDE, Mlle. (fl 1788-89)
dancer BD
ADELAIDE, Mary see Whytal,
Mrs. Russ
ADELINE, Mlle. (fl 1840-50)
dancer HAS

A'DELL, E. (b 1875) English actor
GRB/1
ADESON, Beatrice (d 1917) EA/18*
ADESON, Martin (d 1936) actor
WWT/14*
ADESON, Stephen (d 1945) actor
WWT/14*
ADINY-MILLET, Ada [Addie Chap-
man] (1855-1924) French singer
ES
ADIX, Vern (b 1912) American edu-
cator, director, designer BE
ADKIN, Elizabeth A. (d 1892 [53])
actress EA/93*
ADKINS, Gilbert (d 1967) comedian,
singer TW/24
ADKINS, Morton (b 1877) American
singer WWM
ADKINSON, Will (fl 1625) actor
DA
ADLER, Adolph J. (d 1961 [77])
theatre owner-manager BE*
ADLER, Allen A. (d 1964 [47])
American producer, writer
BE*
ADLER, Benjamin (d 1974 [84])
theatrical backer TW/30
ADLER, Celia (b 1898) American
actress TW/11
ADLER, Eleanor (d 1974 [34]) per-
former BP/59*
ADLER, Felix (1897-1960) American
clown BE*
ADLER, Frances (1891-1964) Amer-
ican actress, teacher BE,
TW/21
ADLER, Harriet (d 1974 [55]) per-
former BP/58*
ADLER, Harry (d 1973 [66]) per-
sonal manager, agent BP/57*
ADLER, Hyman (d 1945 [62]) actor,
producer WWT/14*
ADLER, Jacob (d 1974 [101])
dramatist BP/59*
ADLER, Jacob P. (1855-1926)
Russian actor ES, GRB/3-4,
NTH, SR, WWT/1-5
ADLER, Larry (b 1914) American
musician, composer, performer
BE, CB, SR
ADLER, Luther (b 1903) American
actor, director AAS, BE, ES,
SR, TW/1-9, 12-13, 16, 20-
26, WWT/8-16
ADLER, Richard (b 1921) American
composer, lyricist, director,
producer AAS, BE, ES, WWT/
15-16

ADLER, Sarah (d 1953 [45])
American actress NTH
ADLER, Stella (b 1902) American
actress, director, teacher
BE, ES, TW/2-7, WWT/
8-16
ADMIRE, Jere American actor
TW/26-27
ADOLPHUS, John (d 1845 [79])
barrister EA/72*
ADOREE, Renée [Renée de la
Fointe] (1902-33) French
actress BE*
ADRIAN, G[ilbert] (1903-58)
American costume designer
WWA/3
ADRIAN, James American actor
TW/28
ADRIAN, Max (1903-73) English
actor, director AAS, BE,
ES, TW/13, 15-17, 24, 29,
WWT/10-15
ADRIANA, Cora (fl 1871) Amer-
ican dancer CDP
ADRIANI, Mr. (fl 1765-67)
dancer BD
ADRIENNE, Jean (b 1905) Indian/
English actress, singer,
dancer WWT/7-11
ADSON, F. (fl 1634) actor DA
ADYE, Algernon (d 1897 [36])
actor EA/97*
ADYE, Harriette see Howard,
Inez
ADYE, Oscar (d 1914 [55]) Eng-
lish actor GRB/3-4, WWT/
1-2
A. E. [George William Russell]
(1867-1935) Irish dramatist
COC, MH, MWD, OC/2-3
AENEA [Mrs. Letitia Dando]
English dancer GRB/1
AESCHYLUS (525-456 B. C.)
Greek dramatist ES
AFFELDER, Paul B. (d 1975
[59]) critic BP/59*
AFINOGENOV, Alexander Niko-
laevich (1904-41) Russian
dramatist COC, MWD,
OC/1-3
AFRICAN, The (fl 1793-95)
equestrian, tumbler BD
AFRIQUE [Alexander Watkin]
(d 1961 [54]) South African
performer BE*
AFTON, Effie American actress
TW/8, 10
AGAOGLU, Adalet (b 1929)

Turkish dramatist RE
AGAR, Mr. actor CDP
AGAR, Dan (b 1881) English actor
WWT/4-7
AGAR, Grace Hale (d 1963 [74])
actress BE*
AGATE, James Evershed (1877-
1947) English critic AAS,
COC, DNB, ES, NTH, OC/1-3,
PDT, WWT/5-10, WWW/4
AGATE, May (1892-1960) English
actress COC, ES, OC/2-3,
WWT/6-10
AGGAS, Robert (c. 1619-79) English
scene painter BD, COC, DD,
DNB, ES, OC/1-3
AGGAS, Robert (fl 1662-79) drum-
mer BD
AGLGAZE, Julia Cohn (d 1975 [73])
lawyer BP/59*
AGNESI, Luigi (1838-75) Belgian
composer, singer ES
AGNETTA, Signora (fl 1747-51)
singer BD
AGNEW, Beatrice actress GRB/
3-4, WWT/1
AGOSTINELLI-QUIROLI, Adelina
(b 1882) Italian singer ES
AGOUST [William Bridge] (d 1894)
circus clown EA/95*
AGRATI, Signora (d 1887) actress
EA/88*
AGRESS, Ted (b 1945) American
actor TW/25, 28
AGUE, James W. (d 1975 [75])
performer BP/60*
AGUGLIA-FERRAU, Mimi (1884-
1970) Italian actress ES,
WWT/3
AGUIARI, Lucrezia [Mme. Giuseppe
Colla] (1743-83) Italian singer
BD
AGUS, Joseph (fl 1763?) violinist,
composer? BD
AGUS, Joseph (1749-1803?) violin-
ist, composer? BD
AHEARNE, Tom (1904-69) American
actor TW/22-23, 25
AHERNE, Brian (b 1902) English
actor AAS, BE, CB, ES, SR,
TW/1-8, 10-18, WWT/6-15
AHERNE, Patrick (d 1970 [69])
performer BP/55*
AHLERS, Anny (1906-33) German
actress, singer NTH, WWT/7
AHLERT, Fred E. (1892-1953)
American composer BE*
AHMED, Raju (d 1972 [35])

performer BP/57*
AHRENDT, Carl Frederick William (1842-1909) German actor BE*
AICARD, Jean (1848-1921) French dramatist GRB/2-4
AICKIN, Elinor (d 1914 [80]) actress DD, EA/95
AICKIN, Francis (d 1805) Irish actor BD, CDP, DD, DNB, ES, TD/1-2
AICKIN, Graves (d 1799) actor BD
AICKIN, Mrs. Graves (1770-1814) actress BD
AICKIN, James (c. 1735-1803) Irish actor BD, CDP, DD, DNB, TD/1-2
AIDE, Hamilton (1826-1906) French/English dramatist DD, DNB, GRB/1, WWW/1
AIDMAN, Charles (b 1925) American actor, director BE
AIDOO, Ama Ata (b 1942) Ghanian dramatist CD
AIKEN, Albert W. (1846-94) American actor, singer, dramatist CDP, HAS
AIKEN, Conrad (1889-1973) American poet, dramatist MD, MWD
AIKEN, Frank Eugene (1840-1910) American actor, manager CDP, HAS, PP/1, SR, WWA/1, WWS
AIKEN, George L. (1830-76) American actor, dramatist COC, DAB, DD, ES, HAS, HJD, MH, NTH, OC/1-3, RE, SR, WWA/H
AIKEN, Peter (d 1876) comic singer EA/77*
AIKEN, Mrs. Peter (d 1869 [32]) EA/70*
AILEY, Alvin (b 1931) American actor, dancer, choreographer, director, dance coach BE, CB, ES, TW/14, 19
AIME, Mlle. (fl 1791) dancer BD
AIMEE, Kirsten (b 1969) American actor TW/29
AIMEE, Marie [Marie Trochon] (1852-87) French actress, singer CDP, DD, NYM, SR
AINLEY, Beatrice (d 1939) actress WWT/14*
AINLEY, Henry Hinchliffe (1879-

1945) English actor AAS, COC, DNB, ES, GRB/1-4, OC/1-3, SR, TW/2, WWT/1-9, WWW/4
AINLEY, Mrs. Henry Hinchliffe see Sheldon, Suzanne
AINLEY, Richard (1910-56) English actor ES, WWT/7-14
AINLEY, Mrs. Thomas (d 1884) EA/85*
AINSLEE, Adra (d 1963 [87]) actress BE*
AINSLEY, Mary (d 1906) EA/07*
AINSLEY, Paul (b 1945) American actor TW/28-29
AINSWORTH, Mr. (fl 1788-90) house servant BD
AINSWORTH, Frank K. (d 1879) American business manager, advance agent EA/80*
AINSWORTH, George dramatist FGF
AINSWORTH, Helen Shumate (d 1961 [59]) American performer, talent representative BE*
AINSWORTH, Sydney (d 1922 [50]) English actor WWM
AIRE, James (fl 1794) singer BD
AISTON, Arthur C. (1868-1924) American producer SR
AITCHISON, Ivy see St. Helier, Ivy
AITKEN, Alice (d 1868 [25]) singer EA/69*
AITKEN, Grover Robert see Dale, Grover
AITKEN, James (d 1891 [38]) advance agent EA/92*
AITKEN, Kate (d 1971 [81]) performer BP/56*
AITKEN, Margaret Edith [Margaret Edith Bunten] (d 1909) elocutionist EA/10*
AITKEN, Maria (b 1945) Irish actress WWT/16
AITKEN, William (d 1882 [55]) dramatist, actor EA/83*
AITKIN, John (fl 1764-1774) singer BD
AITKINS, Anna (fl 1851) actress HAS
AITKINS, Edward (d 1883 [64]) comedian EA/84*
AKAR, John (d 1975 [48]) performer BP/60*
AKBAR (d 1911) gymnast EA/12*
AKED, Muriel (1887-1955) English actress WWT/7-11
AKEMAN, David (d 1973 [57])

performer BP/58*
AKEROYDE, Samuel (b c.1650)
English composer, instru-
mentalist BD
AKERS, Andra (b 1946) American
actress TW/28, 30
AKERSTROM, Ullie (fl 1890s)
actress, dramatist SR
AKERY, Mr. (fl 1767-88) house
servant? BD
AKHURST, Herbert George (d
1888 [38]) actor EA/89*
AKHURST, Walter James (d 1880
[24]) actor EA/81*
AKHURST, William (d 1878 [55])
English/Australian dramatist
EA/79*
AKID, Everard (d 1879 [65])
musician EA/80*
AKIMOV, Nikolai (d 1968 [67])
producer/director/choreog-
rapher BP/53*
AKINS, Zoe (1886-1958) American
dramatist COC, ES, HJD,
MD, MH, MWD, NTH,
OC/3, SR, TW/14, WWA/3,
WWT/5-12
AKSENFELD, Israel (1787-1866)
Russian dramatist ES
AKST, Harry (1894-1963) song-
writer BE*, BP/47*
ALABASTER, William (1567-
1640) English dramatist
CP/2-3, DD, FGF
ALAINO, Caroline (b 1832)
Italian actress, singer
HAS, SR
ALARCON Y MENDOZA, Juan
Ruiz de (c.1581-1639)
Mexican dramatist COC
ALBA, Alney (b 1910) American
actor TW/9
ALBAN, Jean-Pierre (d 1973
[38]) performer BP/57*
ALBANESE, Francesco (b 1912)
Italian singer ES
ALBANESE, Licia (b 1913/14)
Italian singer CB, ES
ALBANESI, Meggie (1899-1923)
English actress AAS, WWT/4
ALBANI, Mme. [Marie Louise
Emma Cecile Albani-Gye]
(1852-1930) Canadian singer
CDP, DNB, ES, GRB/1-4,
WWA/3-4, WWS, WWW/3
ALBANI-GYE, Marie Louise
Emma Cecile see Albani,
Mme.

ALBAUGH, John W. (1837-1909)
American actor, manager CDP,
DD, HAS, PP/1, SR, WWA/1,
WWS
ALBAUGH, John W., Jr. (1867-
1910) American actor, manager
WWS
ALBAUGH, Mrs. John W., Jr. see
May, Olive
ALBEE, Edward [Franklin] (b 1928)
American dramatist, producer
AAS, BE, CB, CD, CH, COC,
ES, HJD, MD, MH, MWD,
OC/3, PDT, RE, WWT/14-16
ALBEE, Edward Franklin (1857-
1930) American manager DAB,
ES, OC/1-3, SR, WWA/1,
WWS
ALBEE, Portia (b 1860) American
actress PP/1
ALBENIZ, Isaac (1860-1909) Spanish
composer, pianist ES
ALBER, David O. (d 1969 [59])
public relations BP/53*
ALBERG, Mildred Freed (b 1920)
Canadian producer BE
ALBERGHETTI, Anna Maria (b
1936) Italian singer BE, CB,
TW/14, 18
ALBERGHETTI, Carla (b 1939)
Italian singer BE
ALBERGOTTI, Vittoria (fl 1713)
Italian singer BD
ALBERNI, Luis (d 1962 [75]) Spanish
actor BE*
ALBERS, Henry (1866-1926) Dutch/
French singer ES
ALBERT (1789-1865) French dancer,
choreographer ES
ALBERT, Arthur comedian, singer
CDP
ALBERT, Ben English comedian
CDP
ALBERT, Mrs. C. S. see Traux,
Sarah
ALBERT, Eddie (b 1908) American
actor BE, CB, ES, TW/29,
WWT/16
ALBERT, Eugène d' (1864-1932)
Scottish pianist, composer ES
ALBERT, Frank [J. J. Hughes] (d
1902 [68]) EA/03*
ALBERT, Fred English singer,
composer CDP
ALBERT, Margot (b 1943) American
actress TW/26
ALBERT, Mark [Mark Albert Bing-
ham] (d 1890) vocal comedian

EA/91*
ALBERT, Rose [Mrs. Fred
Evans] (d 1903 [32]) music-
hall performer EA/04*
ALBERT, Wil (b 1930) American
actor TW/30
ALBERT, William (1863-1941)
West Indian business manager
WWT/4-7
ALBERTA, Laura actress CDP
ALBERTARELLI, Francesco (fl
1788-92) Italian singer BD
ALBERTAZZI, Emma [Emma
Howson] (1813/14-47) singer
CDP, DD, DNB, ES
ALBERTAZZI, Giorgio (b 1923)
Italian actor ES
ALBERTIERI, Luigi (1860-1930)
Italian dancer, choreographer
ES
ALBERTINE, Hannah [Hannah
Manchester] (1831-89)
actress, dancer CDP, HAS
ALBERTINI, Mme. (fl 1859)
singer CDP
ALBERTO, Thomas (d 1871 [31])
music-hall performer?
EA/72*
ALBERTSON, Frank (1909-64)
American actor TW/8-11,
20
ALBERTSON, Jack (b 1910?)
American actor CB, TW/6,
8, 20, 29-30, WWT/16
ALBERTSON, Lillian (d 1962
[81]) American actress,
producer TW/19
ALBERY, Sir Bronson James
(1881-1971) English manager
ES, OC/1-3, WWA/5,
WWT/5-14
ALBERY, Donald Arthur Rolleston
(b 1914) English producer
BE, OC/3, WWT/10-16
ALBERY, James (1838-89) Eng-
lish dramatist DD, DNB,
ES, OC/1-3, SR
ALBIN, J. (d 1886) bicycle
performer EA/87*
ALBINI, Lieut. [Frederick Baxter
Ewing] (b 1849) English illu-
sionist, humorist GRB/1
ALBONE, James (fl 1740) singer
BD
ALBONI, Mme. Marietta [Mme.
Zeiger, Countess Pepoli]
(1824-94) Italian singer
CDP, ES, HAS, SR

ALBRECHT, Caterina K. (d 1896)
pianist EA/97*
ALBRECHT, Johanna (b 1940) Amer-
ican actress TW/27
ALBRICI, Bartolomeo (b c.1630)
Italian instrumentalist, singer,
composer BD
ALBRICI, Leonora (fl 1662-71)
Italian singer BD
ALBRICI, Vincenzo (1631-96) Italian
instrumentalist, singer, com-
poser BD
ALBRIGHT, Bob (d 1971 [87]) per-
former BP/55*
ALBRIGHT, Hardie (1903-75) Amer-
ican actor WWT/7-11
ALBRIGHT, H. Darkes (b 1907)
American educator, writer,
editor BE
ALBU, Annie (fl 1881-90) English
singer, actress CDP, DD, DP
ALBUZIO, Mr. (fl 1753-54) singer
BD
ALCALDE, Mario (b 1926) American
actor TW/10-12, 21
ALCHORNE, Mrs. (1683-87) strong
woman BD
ALCIDOR [Philippe Toubel] (fl 1662-
68) actor BD
ALCOCK, Mr. (fl 1714) actor BD
ALCOCK, Mrs. (fl 1714) actress
BD
ALCOCK, Merle (d 1975 [85]) per-
former BP/59*
ALCORN, M. (d 1912) sketch per-
former EA/13*
ALCOTT, Mrs. Margaret see
Leighton, Margaret
ALDA, Alan (b 1936) American actor
BE, TW/20-24, WWT/15-16
ALDA, Frances [Frances Davis]
(1883-1952) New Zealand singer
ES
ALDA, Robert (b 1914) American
actor AAS, BE, ES, TW/7-8,
13, 21-22, 25-26, WWT/15-16
ALDAY, Paul (1764-1835?) French
violinist, composer BD
ALDEN, Hortense (b 1903) American
actress BE, WWT/9-10
ALDEN, John (d 1962 [55]) Australian
actor, director WWT/14*
ALDEN, Mary Maguire (d 1946
[63]) American actress BE*
ALDERMAN, John (b 1937) American
actor TW/16, 21
ALDERSON, Clifton (1864-1930)
English actor EA/97, WWT/3-6

ALDERSON, Mrs. Clifton see
Thorne, May
ALDERSON, William (fl 1509-13)
member of the Chapel Royal
DA
ALDERSON, William (b 1935)
American actor TW/25
ALDERTON, John (b 1940) English actor WWT/15-16
ALDIN, Arthur (b 1872) English
manager WWT/3
ALDINI, Mme. (fl 1857) singer
HAS
ALDOUS, Lucette (b 1938) New
Zealand dancer ES
ALDREDGE, Theoni V. Greek
costume designer BE,
WWT/15-16
ALDREDGE, Thomas (b 1928)
American actor, producer,
director BE, TW/22-30,
WWT/16
ALDRICH, Louis [Louis Lyon]
(1843-1901) American actor
CDP, COC, DAB, ES,
OC/1-3, PP/1, SR, WWA/H
ALDRICH, Mariska (b 1881)
American singer ES, WWM
ALDRICH, Perley Dunn (b 1863)
American vocal teacher
WWM
ALDRICH, Richard (1863-1937)
American critic BE*,
BP/21*
ALDRICH, Richard Stoddard
(b 1902) American manager,
producer BE, CB, ES,
TW/2-8, WWT/9-15
ALDRICH, Thomas Baily (1836-
1907) American writer ES,
HJD, WWW/1
ALDRIDGE, Mr. (d 1768) performer? BD
ALDRIDGE, Mr. (fl 1790) performer? BD
ALDRIDGE, Arthur (b 1879)
English singer WWM
ALDRIDGE, Carrie [Carrie
Southall] (d 1907) EA/08*,
GRB/3*
ALDRIDGE, Ira (d 1886 [24])
pianist EA/87*
ALDRIDGE, Ira Frederick (1804-
67) American actor CDP,
COC, DAB, DD, ES, HAS,
OC/1-3, PDT, WWA/H
ALDRIDGE, John Franklin (d
1899 [54]) actor EA/00*

ALDRIDGE, John Stratten (d 1973
[59]) critic BP/58*
ALDRIDGE, Michael (b 1920) English actor AAS, WWT/11-16
ALDRIDGE, Robert (d 1793) dancer,
ballet master BD
ALDWIN, Mr. (fl 1741) singer BD
ALEDORE (fl 1711) singer? BD
ALEICHEM, Sholom (1859-1916)
Russian/American dramatist
COC, OC/1-3, PDT
ALETTER, Frank (b 1926) American
actor TW/12-13, 16
ALEWORTH, Jeoffrey (d 1687) instrumentalist, singer BD
ALEWORTH, William (fl 1662-69)
violinist BD
ALEXANDER, Mr. (fl 1666-67)
actor BD
ALEXANDER, Mr. (fl 1849) actor
HAS
ALEXANDER, Master (fl 1759)
actor BD
ALEXANDER, Miss (fl 1864-69)
American actress HAS
ALEXANDER, Ada music-hall singer
CDP
ALEXANDER, Mrs. Adam see
Blake, Joanna
ALEXANDER, Annie Emma [Mrs.
A. Bradley] (d 1908) EA/09*
ALEXANDER, Arthur (d 1899 [45])
comedian EA/01*
ALEXANDER, Augustine (d 1907
[46]) EA/08*
ALEXANDER, Ben (d 1969 [58])
performer BP/54*
ALEXANDER, Benjamin (fl 1794-95)
violinist BD
ALEXANDER, Brandy (b 1943)
American actress TW/25
ALEXANDER, Charles K. (b 1919/
20/23) Egyptian actor BE,
TW/3, 27-28
ALEXANDER, Cris (b 1920) American actor, photographer BE,
TW/1-3, 9-11, 13, 16, 22
ALEXANDER, David (d 1973 [65])
critic BP/57*
ALEXANDER, Franz (d 1910) EA/
11*
ALEXANDER, George (d 1813)
"Spotted Boy" CDP
ALEXANDER, Sir George [George
Alexander Gibb Samson] (1858-
1918) English actor, manager
COC, EA/96, DD, DNB, DP,
ES, GRB/1-4, NTH, OC/1-3,

SR, WWS, WWT/1-3, WWW/2
ALEXANDER, Hugh (b 1939) Canadian actor TW/26
ALEXANDER, James (d 1962 [46]) musical comedian TW/18
ALEXANDER, James (b 1941) American actor TW/25, 30
ALEXANDER, Jane (b 1939) American actress TW/25, 29-30, WWT/16
ALEXANDER, Janet (d 1961) English actress GRB/1-4, WWT/2-6
ALEXANDER, J. F. (d 1876 [58]) EA/88*
ALEXANDER, John (1796-1851) Scottish manager, actor DD
ALEXANDER, John (b 1897) American actor BE, ES, TW/4-7, 10-20, WWT/9-16
ALEXANDER, Katherine (b 1901) American actress BE, ES, TW/2-7, WWT/7-13
ALEXANDER, Lois (d 1968 [77]) performer BP/52*
ALEXANDER, Mara (d 1965) performer BP/49*
ALEXANDER, Muriel [Muriel Marsh] (1898-1975) Irish actress WWT/5-8
ALEXANDER, Rod (b 1919/22) American educator, actor, director BE, TW/4, 6
ALEXANDER, Rod (b 1920) American dancer, choreographer, director BE
ALEXANDER, Ronald (b 1917) American dramatist, actor BE
ALEXANDER, Ross [Ross Alexander Smith] (1907-37) American actor BE*, BP/21*
ALEXANDER, Sidney (1845-1911) actor SR
ALEXANDER, S. King [W. B. Codrington Ball] Irish manager GRB/1-2
ALEXANDER, Terence (b 1923) English actor WWT/15-16
ALEXANDER, Terry (b 1947) American actor TW/28, 30
ALEXANDER, William, Earl of Stirling (1567/68-1640) dramatist CP/1-3, DD, ES, FGF
ALEXANDRA, Ada (d 1907)

Dutch/English comedienne EA/08*, GRB/3*
ALEXANDRE [Alexander Vattenmare] (1796-1864) French ventriloquist, impersonator CDP, DAB, HAS, WWA/H
ALEXANDRE, Mme. (fl 1859) tight-rope dancer HAS
ALEXANDRE, Rene (d 1946) French actor SR
ALEXANDRE, W. B. (d 1878) ventriloquist EA/79*
ALEXANDRINA dancer CDP
ALEXIS, Mr. (fl 1794) violinist BD
ALFASA, Joe (b 1914) American actor TW/23-26
ALFIERI, Vittorio Amedeo (1749-1803) Italian dramatist ES, OC/1-3
ALFORD, Fred (d 1878) comic singer EA/79*
ALFORD, Walter (b 1912) Canadian press representative BE
ALFORD-MASON, T. (b 1877) English actor, singer, mimic, hypnotist, mesmerist GRB/1
ALFRED, Edward (d 1793) actor, house servant, singer BD
ALFRED, William (b 1922) American scholar, dramatist CD, CH, MH
ALFRIEND, Edward Morrisson (b 1843) American dramatist WWA/4
ALGERANOFF, Harcourt [Harcourt Essex] English dancer ES
ALGERANOVA, Claudie Italian dancer ES
ALI, George (d 1947 [81]) animal impersonator WWT/14*
ALIAS, Charles (d 1921) costumier WWT/14*
ALIAS, Sarah Anne (d 1897) costumier EA/98*
ALICE, Mary (b 1941) American actress TW/24, 26, 28-30
ALINDER, Dallas (b 1941) American actor TW/30
ALISON, George (1866-1936) English actor SR, WWM
ALIVE AND TRUCKING THEATRE CO., The theatre collective CD
ALIX, Mina [Florence Exton] (d 1904) cyclist EA/05*
ALIZA, Ben (b 1938) American actor TW/21

ALKER, Theo (d 1906) comedian
EA/07*
ALKOK, John (fl 1554) actor DA
ALLABY, William (fl 1641-62)
musician BD
ALLAN, Mrs. (d 1909) dancing
teacher EA/10*
ALLAN, Alexander (b 1806)
dramatist CDP
ALLAN, Alf (d 1902 [49]) come-
dian WWT/14*
ALLAN, Alfred Thomas see
Perry, Alf
ALLAN, Andrew (d 1974 [66])
performer BP/58*
ALLAN, Charles G. (1852-1911)
English actor DD, EA/97,
GRB/1-4
ALLAN, Christopher (d 1973
[46]) agent BP/58*
ALLAN, Dot (d 1964) dramatist
BP/49*
ALLAN, Elizabeth (b 1910)
English actress ES, WWT/
7-14
ALLAN, Emily (d 1889) EA/90*
ALLAN, Ernest (d 1903 [33])
pianist, composer EA/04*
ALLAN, Jed (b 1938) American
actor TW/23
ALLAN, John, Jr. (d 1878 [24])
musical director EA/79*
ALLAN, Louise Rosalie [née
Despréaux] (1810-56) actress
BE*
ALLAN, Maud (1879-1956) Cana-
dian dancer ES, GRB/4,
WWT/1-11, WWW/5
ALLAN, Oswald (d 1893 [45])
dramatist EA/94*
ALLAN, Ted (b 1916) Canadian
dramatist CD
ALLAN, Watty (d 1903 [35])
comedian WWT/14*
ALLAN CARADORI, Mme. (d
1865 [65]) singer HAS, SR
ALLANDALE, Fred [Frederick
Arnold] (1872-1921) English
actor, singer GRB/1-3
ALLANO clown CDP
ALLANSON, Charles (fl 1691-96)
singer BD
ALLARD, Sieur (fl 1702) French
dancer BD
ALLARDICE, James (d 1966 [46])
dramatist BP/50*
ALLARDICE, Robert Barclay
(1779-1854) pedestrian CDP

ALLDEN, Mr. S. (fl 1794) violinist
BD
ALLEGRANTI, Teresa Maddalena
[Mrs. Harrison] (c. 1750-c. 1802)
Italian singer BD
ALLEGRET, Marc (d 1973 [73])
producer/director/choreographer
BP/58*
ALLEGRO, Anita (d 1964) actress
BE*
ALLEN, Mr. (fl 1732-33) actor BD
ALLEN, Mr. (fl 1733-34) treasurer
BD
ALLEN, Mr. (fl 1737-40) house
servant BD
ALLEN, Mr. (fl 1746-57) actor
BD
ALLEN, Mr. (fl 1761-74?) house
servant? BD
ALLEN, Mr. (fl 1764-65) dresser
BD
ALLEN, Mr. (fl 1764-98) dramatist
CP/3
ALLEN, Mr. (fl 1793) dancer BD
ALLEN, Mr. (fl 1828) American
actor HAS
ALLEN, Mrs. (fl 1746-67) house
servant? BD
ALLEN, Mrs. (fl 1789-92) BD
ALLEN, Adrianne (b 1907) English
actress BE, ES, TW/3, 5-6,
13, WWT/7-14
ALLEN, A. Hylton (b 1879) English
actor ES, WWT/4-12
ALLEN, Alfred (1866-1947) Ameri-
can dramatist WWA/2, WWM
ALLEN, Andrew Jackson (1776-
1853) American actor, cos-
tumier CDP, DD, HAS, SR,
WWA/H
ALLEN, Ann (fl 1742-69) actress,
house servant? BD
ALLEN, Mrs. Annie (d 1893) EA/
94*
ALLEN, Mme. Caradori see
Allan Caradori, Mme.
ALLEN, Charles Leslie (1830-1917)
American actor GRB/3-4,
PP/1, WWM, WWS, WWT/1-3
ALLEN, Chesney [William E. Allen]
(b 1896) English music-hall
comedian COC, WWT/10-11
ALLEN, Mrs. Clarissa [Mrs. La-
combe or La Coomb] (d 1851)
American actress DD, HAS,
SR
ALLEN, C. Leslie (b 1830) Ameri-
can actor HAS

ALLEN, Mrs. C. Leslie [Sarah Lyon] (fl c. 1850s) English actress HAS

ALLEN, David (d 1903 [72]) theatrical printer EA/04*

ALLEN, Deborah (b 1950) American actress TW/30

ALLEN, Dennis R. (b 1940) American actor TW/25

ALLEN, Dion (b 1922) American actor TW/7-8

ALLEN, Dorothy (d 1970 [74]) performer BP/55*

ALLEN, Mrs. Edwin (d 1905 [51]) EA/06*

ALLEN, Elizabeth [Elizabeth Ellen Gillease] (b 1934) American actress, singer BE, TW/16-17, 21-23, WWT/15-16

ALLEN, Emily Louisa (d 1905 [45]) EA/06*

ALLEN, Mrs. F. (d 1874) EA/75*

ALLEN, Frank (b 1851) English manager, proprietor GRB/1-4, WWT/1-2

ALLEN, Fred [John Florence Sullivan] (1894-1956) American actor ES, NTH, SR, TW/12

ALLEN, Frederick (d 1879) circus proprietor EA/80*

ALLEN, G. (d 1870) circus proprietor? EA/71*

ALLEN, George (d 1877) singer EA/78*

ALLEN, Gracie (1905-64) American comedienne CB, ES, SR, TW/21, WWA/4

ALLEN, Harry actor CDP

ALLEN, Harry (d 1876) equestrian EA/77*

ALLEN, Harry (d 1906 [24]) music-hall comedian EA/07*

ALLEN, Henry (d 1867 [48]) comedian EA/68*

ALLEN, Henry Robinson (1809-76) Irish singer ES

ALLEN, H. Marsh English actor GRB/3-4, WWT/1-6

ALLEN, Horace (d 1896 [40]) actor EA/97*

ALLEN, Inglis (1879-1943) English dramatist WWW/4

ALLEN, Jack (b 1907) English actor WWT/9-16

ALLEN, James (fl 1732) singer BD

ALLEN, Mrs. James see Grahame, Cissy

ALLEN, James Lane (1849-1915) American dramatist WWM, WWW/2

ALLEN, Jay (b 1922) American dramatist MH

ALLEN, Jeremy (fl 1640) actor DA

ALLEN, Jerrard Grant (b 1878) English manager GRB/2-4, WWT/1

ALLEN, J. H. American actor DD

ALLEN, Mrs. J. H. see Allen, Louise

ALLEN, Mrs. J. H. see Vaidis, Lizzie

ALLEN, John (1570?-93?) actor DA

ALLEN, John (d 1722) violinist BD

ALLEN, John (fl 1761) musician? BD

ALLEN, Johnny [George Erb] (1844-85) minstrel CDP

ALLEN, John Piers (b 1912) English principal of the Central School of Speech and Drama WWT/16

ALLEN, Jonelle (b 1944) American actress TW/28-30

ALLEN, Jonny (b 1962) American actor TW/26

ALLEN, Joseph (1840-1917) English actor SR

ALLEN, Joseph (d 1952 [80]) American actor TW/9

ALLEN, Joseph, Jr. (d 1963 [44]) American actor BE*

ALLEN, Joyce (b 1926) American actress TW/3

ALLEN, Judith (fl 1933-50) American actress ES

ALLEN, Judy (b 1945) American actress TW/24, 28

ALLEN, Kelcey (1875-1951) American critic NTH, TW/8, WWT/7-11

ALLEN, Kenneth (d 1976 [72]) performer BP/60*

ALLEN, Leslie (fl 1759-61) English actor SR

ALLEN, Mrs. Leslie (fl 1759-61) English actress SR

ALLEN, Lester (d 1949 [58]) comedian TW/6

ALLEN, Lewis (b 1905) English actor ES

ALLEN, Lewis (b 1922) American

producer BE
ALLEN, Louise [Mrs. J. H.
Allen] (fl 1856) American?
actress CDP
ALLEN, Louise [Mrs. William
Collier] (d 1909 [36]) Amer-
ican actress GRB/2-4, WWS
ALLEN, Marc, III (b 1943) Amer-
ican actor TW/26-27
ALLEN, Marie [Mrs. Wilkinson]
(d 1880 [27]) actress EA/81*
ALLEN, Marsh see Allen,
H. Marsh
ALLEN, Michael K. (b 1940)
American actor TW/24
ALLEN, Neal (d 1974 [22]) com-
poser/lyricist BP/58*
ALLEN, Norman (b 1939) English
actor TW/21-23, 25-26,
28-29
ALLEN, Patrick (b 1927) actor
WWT/16
ALLEN, Paul Hastings (b 1883)
American composer ES
ALLEN, Percy (d 1959 [86])
critic WWT/14*
ALLEN, Rae [Raffaella Julia
Thérésa Abruzzo] (b 1926)
American actress BE, TW/
16, 21-23, 25-27, 29,
WWT/14-16
ALLEN, Ralph Donkin (d 1906
[69]) EA/07*
ALLEN, Reginald (b 1905) Amer-
ican administrator, writer
BE
ALLEN, Richard (fl 1609-13)
actor DA
ALLEN, Rita (d 1968 [56])
producer BE, TW/25
ALLEN, Robert (b 1906) Amer-
ican actor TW/1-3, 13, 16
ALLEN, Robert H. (d 1912)
EA/13*
ALLEN, Mrs. Robert W. (1865-
91) actress SR
ALLEN, Seth (b 1941) American
actor TW/25-26, 28-30
ALLEN, Sheila (b 1932) English
actress WWT/14-16
ALLEN, Steve (b 1921) American
comedian, composer, writer
BE
ALLEN, Susan Westford (d 1944
[79]) performer TW/1
ALLEN, Theodore singer CDP
ALLEN, Thomas (1696?-1738)
house servant, pugilist BD

ALLEN, Thomas (b c.1757) dwarf
BD, CDP
ALLEN, Thomas (fl 1794) musician
BD
ALLEN, Tomasso (d 1898 [37])
equestrian EA/99*
ALLEN, Vera (b 1897) American
actress BE, TW/2-3, 10-11,
WWT/10-14
ALLEN, Viola [Mrs. Peter Duryea]
(1869-1948) American actress
COC, DAB, ES, GRB/2-4,
NTH, OC/1-3, PP/1, SR,
TW/4, WWA/2, WWM, WWS,
WWT/1-10
ALLEN, Mrs. Vivian Beaumont (d
1962 [70]) philanthropist BE*,
BP/47*
ALLEN, Vivienne (d 1963 [42])
performer BP/48*
ALLEN, W. (fl 1794) musician BD
ALLEN, Walter (b 1940) actor
TW/25
ALLEN, Walter C. (d 1903) music-
hall comedian EA/04*
ALLEN, W. H. (d 1884) pedestal
clog dancer EA/85*
ALLEN, William (d 1647) English
actor COC, DA, DD, ES,
OC/1-3
ALLEN, William E. see Allen,
Chesney
ALLEN, Woody (b 1935) American
comedian, writer CB, TW/25-
26, WWT/16
ALLENBY, Frank (1898-1953) Tas-
manian actor ES, TW/4,
WWT/7-12
ALLENBY, Peggy [Eleanor Byrne
Fox] (1905-67) American
actress WWT/7-8
ALLENSON, Mr. (fl 1669-70) actor?
BD
ALLENTUCK, Max (b 1911) Ameri-
can business manager, manager
BE
ALLERS, Mr. (fl 1793) actor BD
ALLERS, Franz (b 1905) Czech
conductor BE
ALLESTREE, Mary [Geraldine Ed-
dowes] (d 1912) English actress
GRB/1
ALLEYN, Annie [Mrs. Charles
Bernard] (1860-96) English
actress DD
ALLEYN, Edward (1566-1626) Eng-
lish actor CDP, COC, DA, DD,
DNB, ES, GT, HP, NTH,

OC/1-3, PDT
ALLEYN, Hilda (d 1897 [18])
singer EA/98*
ALLEYN, John (1556/57-96)
actor DA
ALLEYN, Richard (d 1601) actor
DA
ALLEYN, W. (d 1895) comedian
EA/96*
ALLEYNE, Miss [?=Muriel
Alleyne] actress DD
ALLEYNE, J. M. (d 1874 [40])
music-hall chairman EA/75*
ALLEYNE, Muriel [Flora Mid-
dleton Stanley] English
actress GRB/1
ALLEYNE-BARRETT, Elise Bar-
bara see Craven, Elise
ALLEYN'S BOY (fl 1600-01)
actor DA
ALLFORD, Mrs. Emma (d 1871)
EA/72*
ALLFORD, Mary (d 1875) EA/
76*
ALLGOOD, Sara (1883-1950)
Irish actress COC, ES,
OC/1-3, TW/2-7, WWT/
2-10
ALLIN, Norman (b 1885) English
singer, chorus master ES
ALLINGHAM, Mr. (fl 1798)
house servant BD
ALLINGHAM, John (fl 1636)
actor DA
ALLINGHAM, John Till (fl 1799-
1810) English dramatist
CDP, CP/3, DD, DNB,
ES, GT, TD/1-2
ALLINGHAM, Maria Caroline
[Mrs. Samuel Ricketts] (d
1811) English actress BD
ALLINGHAM, William (1828-89)
dramatist DD
ALLINSON, Mrs. (fl 1699) singer
BD
ALLINSON, Michael English
actor BE, TW/22-23, 26-
27, WWT/16
ALLIO, René (b 1921) French
scene designer, costume
designer ES
ALLISON, Mr. (fl 1735) actor
BD
ALLISON, Mr. (fl 1788-92)
dancer BD
ALLISON, Mrs. (fl 1703-05)
actress BD
ALLISON, Miss (b 1819) see

Seymour, Mrs.
ALLISON, Betty (fl 1693-97) actress
BD
ALLISON, George (d 1936 [70])
actor WWT/14*
ALLISON, James (d 1890) Australian
manager EA/91*
ALLISON, Laura (d 1879 [59])
actress, manager CDP
ALLISON, Maria (fl 1698-99)
actress, singer BD
ALLISON, Ralph (fl 1690s) singer
BD
ALLISTER, Claud (1891-1967/70)
English actor ES, TW/4,
WWT/7-13
ALLITEN, Mary Frances (d 1912
[63]) composer EA/13*
ALLMON, Clinton (b 1941) Ameri-
can actor TW/25-26
ALLNUTT, Alfred (d 1867 [17])
singer? EA/68*
ALLNUTT, Eugénie (d 1901) ballet
mistress, actress EA/02*
ALLNUTT, Sarah (d 1887 [80])
EA/88*
ALLSBROOKE, Bill (b 1945) Amer-
ican actor TW/26-28
ALLWOOD, Frederick William (d
1903) composer, conductor
EA/04*
ALLWOOD, Thomas (d 1886) actor,
composer EA/88*
ALLYN, Adam (d 1768) actor BD,
HAS
ALLYN, Mrs. Adam (fl 1759-61) HAS
ALLYN, Alyce (d 1975) performer
BP/60*
ALLYN, William (b 1927) American
actor TW/3
ALLYSON, June (b 1923/26) Amer-
ican actress CB, ES, TW/26
ALMAR, C. Norman (d 1900 [33])
advance agent EA/01*
ALMAR, George (b 1802) actor,
dramatist, manager CDP, DD
ALMAR, Joe (d 1897) gymnast
EA/98*
ALMA-TADEMA, Sir Lawrence
(1836-1912) Dutch/English de-
signer, painter COC, DNB,
OC/1-3, WWW/1
ALMERS, Walter (d 1916) EA/17*
ALMOND, Emma [Miss E. Romer]
(1814-68) English singer
CDP, DD
ALMOND, John (d 1885) comedian,
scenic artist EA/86*

ALMOND, R. P. (d 1878 [54])
theatrical and musical caterer
EA/79*
ALMONTE, Charlie [Charles
Frederick Burgess] (d 1892
[48]) founder of the Almonte
Troupe EA/93*
ALMONTE, Marie A. (d 1973)
performer BP/58*
ALMONTE, William [William Bur-
gess] (d 1900 [43]) pantomim-
ist EA/01*
ALMONTI, Ada Burgess (d 1899)
EA/00*
ALMORAVIDS, Tchaka (b 1939)
American actor TW/26
ALONSO, Alicia (b 1921) Cuban
dancer CB, ES
ALONSO, Fernando (b 1914)
Cuban dancer ES
ALONSO, Master [of the Tre-
maine Family] CDP
ALPAR, Gita (b 1900) Hungarian
actress, singer WWT/8-10
ALPERN, Morris Mark (b 1940)
American actor TW/23
ALPERN, Susan (b 1955) Amer-
ican actress TW/24
ALPERSON, Edward L. (d 1969
[73]) producer/director/
choreographer BP/54*
ALPORT, Sidney (d 1906 [59])
manager EA/07*
ALSEDGER, Mr. (fl 1794) musi-
cian BD
ALSKA, Daisy (d 1892) EA/93*
ALSKA, Walter [Walter Pollard]
(d 1896) variety performer
EA/97*
ALSOP, Mrs. Frances (d 1821)
English actress CDP, DD,
HAS, SR
ALSWANG, Ralph (b 1916) Amer-
ican designer, director,
producer BE, TW/2-8,
WWT/12-16
ALT, Natalie American singer,
actress WWT/4-5
ALTEMUS, J. K. (d 1854) actor
HAS
ALTEMUS, Mrs. J. K. (fl 1842)
actress HAS
ALTER, Lottie (fl 1890-1900)
American actress WWM,
WWS
ALTER, Martha (b 1904) Amer-
ican composer ES
ALTGLASS, Max Mayer (1895-

1952) Polish singer WWA/3
ALTHOFF, Charles R. (d 1962 [72])
actor BE*
ALTHOUSE, Earl F. (d 1971 [78])
performer BP/55*
ALTHOUSE, Paul Shearer (1889-
1954) American singer ES,
WWA/3
ALTIER, William B. (d 1971)
founder of the first dinner
theatre BP/56*
ALTIERE, Guiditta singer CDP
ALTMAN, Charles American stage
lighting executive BE
ALTMAN, Frieda (b 1904) American
actress BE, ES, TW/2-6
ALTMAN, Richard (b 1932) Ameri-
can director, actor BE, ES
ALTMAN, Ruth American actress,
singer BE, WWT/8-10
ALTON, George (d 1875 [48]) singer
EA/76*
ALTON, Robert (d 1957 [54]) Amer-
ican director, choreographer
TW/13
ALVA, Mme. [Mrs. Hettie St. John
Brenon] (d 1904) lyric artist
EA/05*
ALVAREZ [Albert Raymond Gour-
ron] (1861-1933) French singer
ES, GRB/1-4, WWS
ALVAREZ, Anita (b 1920) American
actress TW/3-4, 6
ALVAREZ, Carmen American
dancer, singer, actress BE,
TW/24-26, 29-30
ALVAREZ, Julio (d 1969 [63])
performer BP/54*
ALVAREZ, Luis (b 1872) Spanish
singer GRB/3
ALVAREZ, Marguerite d' (b c.1886)
English singer ES
ALVAREZ QUINTERO, Joaquin
(1873-1944) Spanish dramatist
CB, COC, MWD, OC/2-3,
PDT
ALVAREZ QUINTERO, Serafin
(1871-1938) Spanish dramatist
COC, MWD, OC/2-3, PDT
ALVARY, Lorenzo (b 1909) Amer-
ican singer ES
ALVARY, Max [Maximilian Achen-
bach] (1856-98) German singer
ES
ALVO, Henry [Henry Thorpe] (d
1901 [43]) circus proprietor
EA/02*
ALVORD, Ned (d 1970 [87])

publicist BP/55*
ALZAR, Mme. [Mrs. T. Stevens]
(d 1907 [43]) costumier EA/
08*, GRB/3*
AMADEI, Alexander (fl 1684)
mountebank BD
AMADEI, Filippo (b c.1683)
Italian instrumentalist,
composer BD
AMADI, Mme. [Annie Tremaine]
actress, singer DD
AMALIA, Miss (fl. 1869-88)
actress DD, OAA/2
AMAN, John American actor
TW/25, 28
AMANTINI, Sig. (fl 1778) singer
BD
AMATO, Pasquale (1879-1942)
Italian singer CB, ES, WWA/2
AMAYA, Carmen (1913-63)
Spanish dancer, choreographer
ES, TW/20
AMBER, Mabel (1866-1945) Amer-
ican actress SR
AMBER, Maude (d 1938 [66])
American actress BE*
AMBER, Norton (fl 1744-54)
patentee, banker, pit-door-
keeper BD
AMBERG, George H. (1901-71)
critic, curator ES
AMBERG, Gustave (1844-1921)
manager BP/5*, WWT/14*
AMBIENT, Mark (1860-1937)
English dramatist, actor
DD, GRB/1-3, WWT/2-7
AMBLER, Mr. (fl 1661) singer
BD
AMBLER, Johnson (d 1873)
manager EA/74*
AMBRE, Emilie (d 1898) singer
CDP
AMBROISE, Antonio (fl 1752-78)
puppet-showman BD
AMBROSE, Mr. (fl 1735-36)
house servant BD
AMBROSE, Mrs. [Mrs. Jona]
(fl c.1739-1813) actress
BD
AMBROSE, Mrs. (fl 1735-36)
house servant? BD
AMBROSE, Mrs. [née Mahon]
(fl 1770-89) singer BD
AMBROSE, Miss (fl 1731-32)
dancer BD
AMBROSE, Miss [Mrs. Kelf;
Mrs. Egerton] (fl 1739-
1813) Gibraltan actress

BD, DD
AMBROSE, Miss E. (fl 1756-87)
actress BD
AMBROSE, John (b 1763) English
instrumentalist, composer BD
AMBROSE, Kay English critic ES
AMBROSINI, Antonia (fl 1754)
singer BD
AMBURGH, Van see Van Am-
burgh, Isaac A.
AMCOTTS, Vincent (d 1881) drama-
tist, manager DD
AMECHE, Don [Dominic Felix Am-
ici] (b 1908) American actor
CB, SR, TW/24, WWT/15-16
AMENDOLIA, Don (b 1945) Ameri-
can actor TW/28
AMERICAN WOMAN, The (fl 1781)
dwarf? BD
AMERIS, Giovanna (d 1891) singer
EA/92*
AMES, Adrienne (d 1947 [39])
American actress TW/2-3
AMES, Amy (d 1916) actress SR
AMES, Cindy American actress
TW/26, 28
AMES, Ed (b 1929) American actor
TW/20
AMES, Emma see Girdlestone,
Amy
AMES, Florenz (b 1884) American
actor, singer TW/1, 8, WWT/
10-12
AMES, Gerald (1881-1933) English
actor ES, WWT/4-7
AMES, Harry (d 1969 [76]) per-
former BP/54*
AMES, Leon (b 1903) American
actor BE, TW/24, WWT/10-11
AMES, Michael see Andrews, Tod
AMES, Percy (d 1936 [62]) English
actor SR
AMES, Robert (1893-1931) American
actor ES, WWT/5-6
AMES, Rosemary (b 1906) American
actress WWT/8-9
AMES, Winthrop (1871-1937) Amer-
ican manager COC, DAB, ES,
NTH, OC/1-3, SR, WWA/1,
WWT/3-8
AMHERST, G. A. see Amherst,
J. H.
AMHERST, J. H. [or G. A.] (1776-
1851) English actor, dramatist
DD, HAS, SR
AMIC, Henry (d 1929 [75]) drama-
tist BE*
AMICA, V. (fl 1848) chorus

master HAS
AMIC-ANGELO, Andrew (b 1943)
American actor TW/24, 27
AMICI, Dominic Felix see
Ameche, Don
AMICONI, Jacopo (c. 1675-1752)
Italian scene painter BD
AMIEL, Josette (b 1933) French
dancer ES
AMMIDON, Hoyt (b 1909) Ameri-
can executive BE
AMNER, Ralph (c. 1584-1664)
English singer BD
AMODIO, Alessandro (fl 1855)
singer CDP
AMORE, James (d 1974 [27])
performer BP/58*
AMORETTI, Giustina (fl 1748-49)
Italian singer BD
AMOREVOLI, Angelo (1716-98)
Italian singer BD, ES
AMOS, Ruth American actress
TW/4
"AMOS AND ANDY" see Gosden,
Charles Freeman
AMPHLETT, Mr. (fl 1802)
dramatist CP/3
AMRAM, David Werner (b 1930)
American composer, con-
ductor, musician BE, CB
AMSDEN, Minneola (d 1962 [75])
performer BE*
AMSTEL, Jane (d 1949 [48])
actress WWT/14*
ANALEAU, Mr. (fl 1687-88)
singer? BD
ANANIA, John (b 1923) Italian
actor TW/26-28
ANATO, Marie (d 1889) EA/90*
ANATO, Nina see Melbourne,
Mrs. Walter
ANATO, Palmyra equestrienne
CDP
ANCEY, Georges (1860-1926)
dramatist BE*
ANCHUTZ, Miss see Zimmer-
man, Mlle.
ANCLIFFE, Charles (d 1953
[72]) composer WWT/14*
ANCONA, Mario (1860-1931) Italian
singer ES
ANCOT, Jean (1779-1848) violinist,
pianist, composer CDP
ANDERMAN, Maureen (b 1946)
American actress TW/27-29
ANDERS, Glenn (b 1890) American
actor BE, ES, TW/1-18,
WWT/6-14

ANDERS, Katie (b 1942) American
actress TW/25, 28
ANDERSEN, Gerald (b 1910) English
actor TW/3
ANDERSEN, Hans Christian (1805-
75) Danish dramatist BE*
ANDERSEN, Lale (d 1972 [59]) per-
former BP/57*
ANDERSON, Mr. (d 1767) actor
BD
ANDERSON, Mr. (fl 1794) musician
BD
ANDERSON, Mr. (fl 1850s) English
prompter HAS
ANDERSON, Mrs. (fl 1743?-50)
actress BD
ANDERSON, Mrs. see Hill, Mrs.
ANDERSON, Miss (fl 1733-37)
dancer BD
ANDERSON, Miss (fl 1782) actress
BD
ANDERSON, Addie (1844/58-84)
American actress HAS
ANDERSON, A. G. (d 1904) pro-
prietor EA/05*
ANDERSON, Alfred (d 1876 [28])
pianist EA/77*
ANDERSON, Anne Renée (b 1920)
American actress TW/5
ANDERSON, Beverly (b 1932) Amer-
ican talent representative BE
ANDERSON, Bronco Billy (d 1971
[88]) performer BP/55*
ANDERSON, Mrs. Caroline Amelia
Sophia (d 1868) EA/69*
ANDERSON, Cecil (d 1968 [62])
composer/lyricist BP/53*
ANDERSON, Christian Oscar (d
1876 [59]) EA/77*
ANDERSON, Clair Mathes (d 1964
[68]) American actress BE*
ANDERSON, Dallas (d 1934 [60])
Scottish performer BE*, BP/
19*, WWT/14*
ANDERSON, Daphne (b 1922) English
actress, singer WWT/11-16
ANDERSON, David (fl 1874-82)
critic DD
ANDERSON, David C. (1813-84)
American actor CDP, DD,
HAS, SR
ANDERSON, Mrs. David C. (d
1840) actress DD, HAS, SR
ANDERSON, David-Rhys (b 1945)
Welsh actor TW/23
ANDERSON, Douglas (b 1948)
American actor TW/30
ANDERSON, E. Abbot see

Aynesworth, E. Allan
ANDERSON, Edith (b 1816) American actress SR
ANDERSON, Elizabeth (d 1887) EA/89*
ANDERSON, Elizabeth see Thomas, Mrs. Jacob Wonderly, I
ANDERSON, Flora (d 1870 [17]) EA/71*
ANDERSON, Florence (d 1962 [80]) English wardrobe mistress, performer BE*, BP/47*
ANDERSON, Fred see Sutherland, Fred
ANDERSON, Garland (d 1939 [53]) American dramatist BE*, WWT/14*
ANDERSON, George composer CDP
ANDERSON, George Frederick (d 1876 [83]) violinist EA/78*
ANDERSON, G. H. (d 1867 [36]) comedian, singer EA/68*
ANDERSON, G. H. (b 1861) actor SR
ANDERSON, Gwen actress TW/1
ANDERSON, Harry English comedian, singer CDP
ANDERSON, Harry (d 1918) EA/19*
ANDERSON, Mrs. Henry see Macfarren, Alice
ANDERSON, Hugh (d 1965 [75]) dramatist BP/50*
ANDERSON, James (fl 1820s) American? actor, prompter CDP, DD, HAS
ANDERSON, James (d 1893) Irish actor EA/94*
ANDERSON, James (d 1969) performer BP/54*
ANDERSON, James P. (1837-1911) American circus performer and manager SR
ANDERSON, James Robertson (1811-95) Scottish actor CDP, DD, DNB, ES, HAS, OAA/1-2, SR, WWA/H
ANDERSON, Mrs. James Robertson (fl 1831) English actress HAS
ANDERSON, Jane see Germon, Mrs. C. G.
ANDERSON, J. F. R. (d 1905) journalist EA/06*
ANDERSON, J. Grant (b 1897)

Scottish actor, producer WWT/11-16
ANDERSON, Mrs. J. H. see Levey, Nellie
ANDERSON, John (b 1922) American actor TW/13
ANDERSON, John Hargis (1896-1943) American critic, dramatist CB, NTH, SR, WWA/2, WWT/9
ANDERSON, John Henry [Wizard of the North] (1815-74) Scottish magician, actor CDP, DNB, SR
ANDERSON, John Henry (d 1878 [34]) EA/79*
ANDERSON, John Murray (1886-1954) Canadian producer, lyricist, dancer, ES, TW/2-8, 10, WWA/3, WWT/5-11
ANDERSON, Josephine [née Bartolozzi] (1807-48) English actress CDP, DD, HAS
ANDERSON, Joshua R. (fl 1831) actor, singer CDP, DD, SR
ANDERSON, Dame Judith (b 1898) Australian/American actress AAS, BE, CB, COC, ES, NTH, OC/1-3, PDT, SR, TW/2-21, 23, 27, WWT/6-16
ANDERSON, Julia (d 1950 [86]) Danish/American dramatist, actress BE*, BP/36*
ANDERSON, Katherine American actress TW/8
ANDERSON, Lawrence (1893-1939) English actor WWT/5-8
ANDERSON, Lee (d 1889 [41]) manager EA/91*
ANDERSON, Leroy (1908-75) American composer, conductor BE, CB
ANDERSON, L. G. Abbot see Goodrich, Louis
ANDERSON, Linda (d 1975 [36]) producer/director/choreographer BP/60*
ANDERSON, Lindsay Gordon (b 1923) English director AAS, CB, COC, PDT, WWT/14-16
ANDERSON, Lizzie (d 1878 [16]) EA/79*
ANDERSON, Louise (d 1877) American actress EA/78*
ANDERSON, Lucy (1790-1878) pianist CDP
ANDERSON, Maggie (d 1876 [36]) EA/78*

ANDERSON, Marian (b 1908)
American singer CB, SR
ANDERSON, Marie (d 1900)
actress EA/97
ANDERSON, Mary [Mme. de
Navarro] (1859-1940) American actress CB, CDP,
COC, DAB, DD, ES, GRB/1,
3, NTH, OC/1-3, PP/1,
SR, WWA/4, WWM, WWS,
WWT/4-9
ANDERSON, Mary American
actress TW/11
ANDERSON, Max (d 1943) manager SR
ANDERSON, Maxwell (1888-1959)
American dramatist AAS,
CB, CH, COC, ES, HJD,
MD, MH, MWD, NTH,
OC/1-3, PDT, RE, SR,
TW/14, WWA/3, WWT/6-
12, WWW/5
ANDERSON, Millar (b 1880)
Irish actor GRB/1-2
ANDERSON, Ophelia [née Pelby]
(1813-52) American actress
DD, HAS, SR
ANDERSON, P. August (1839-
1919) actor SR
ANDERSON, Paul American
actor TW/5-6
ANDERSON, Percy (d 1928 [77])
designer WWT/14*
ANDERSON, Phyllis Stohl (d
1956 [49]) American literary
representative BE*, BP/41*
ANDERSON, Reddick (d 1907)
English actor CDP
ANDERSON, Richard (b 1926)
American actor BE
ANDERSON, Robert W. (d 1971
[31]) performer BP/55*
ANDERSON, Robert W[oodruff]
(b 1917) American dramatist
AAS, BE, CB, CD, CH, ES,
HJD, MD, MWD, PDT,
WWT/13-16
ANDERSON, Robina (d 1900 [54])
actress EA/01*
ANDERSON, Rona (b 1928) Scottish actress WWT/12-16
ANDERSON, Ruth (d 1975 [64])
performer BP/60*
ANDERSON, Sara (b 1920)
American actress TW/4
ANDERSON, Sherwood (1876-1941)
American dramatist DAB,
NTH, WWW/4

ANDERSON, Stuart [Stuart Newman]
(d 1911 [25]) box-office keeper
EA/12*
ANDERSON, Thomas (d 1891 [70])
musician EA/92*
ANDERSON, Thomas (b 1906) American actor TW/25-29
ANDERSON, T. J. (d 1897) stage
manager EA/98*
ANDERSON, Victoria (d 1875) wirewalker EA/76*
ANDERSON, Weldon see Atherstone, Weldon
ANDERSON, Will (d 1869 [34])
music-hall performer? EA/70*
ANDERSON, William (d 1869) American actor DD
ANDERSON, Mrs. William (d 1831)
American actress DD, HAS,
SR
ANDERTON, Mr. actor CDP
ANDERTON, Sarah [née Coxer]
(d 1869) English actress DD,
HAS
ANDES, Keith (b 1920) American
actor, singer BE, TW/3-9
ANDETON, Mr. actor CDP
ANDO, Flavio Italian actor, manager WWT/2-3
ANDOGA, Victor (d 1969 [91])
producer/director/choreographer
BP/54*
ANDRA, Fern (d 1974 [80]) performer BP/58*
ANDRE, Frank (b 1942) American
actor TW/24-26
ANDRE, Gaby (d 1972) performer
BP/57*
ANDRE, Gwili (d 1959 [51]) Danish
actress BE*
ANDRE, Joan (b 1929) American
actress TW/3
ANDRE, Mjr. John (1751-80) English designer NTH, SR
ANDRE, Theodore see Van Griethuysen, Ted
ANDREA, Sieur (fl 1781) whistler
BD
ANDREAE, Otto Stuart see
Stuart, Otto
ANDREAS, Miss (fl 1779-80) dancer
BD
ANDREE, Emilie see D'Alençon,
Emilienne
ANDREEV, Leonid Nikolaevich see
Andreyev, Leonid Nikolaivich
ANDREINI, Isabella (1562-1604)
actress, singer CDP

ANDREONI, Mr. (fl 1739-42)
Italian singer BD
ANDRES, Barbara (b 1939) American actress TW/26
ANDRESEN, Hans (b 1869) German actor, manager GRB/4, WWT/1-2
ANDREWE, Henry (fl 1509-11) member of the Chapel Royal DA
ANDREWES, Richard (fl 1584) actor DA
ANDREWS, Mr. (fl 1752) actor BD
ANDREWS, Mr. (fl 1792-99?) dresser, house servant BD
ANDREWS, Mr. (fl 1794) music porter BD
ANDREWS, Mr. (fl 1794) singer BD
ANDREWS, Mrs. (fl 1696-97) actress BD
ANDREWS, Mrs. (d 1907) "coon" singer EA/08*
ANDREWS, Miss (fl 1796-98) singer, actress BD, DD, TD/1-2
ANDREWS, Miss actress HAS
ANDREWS, A. [né Isaacs] (b 1807) Jamaican actor DD, HAS
ANDREWS, Adora (d 1956 [84]) American actress BE*
ANDREWS, Albert Garcia (d 1950 [93]) American actor OAA/1-2, TW/7
ANDREWS, Ann (b 1895) American actress BE, TW/3-8, WWT/7-11
ANDREWS, Bobbie (b 1894) English actor WWT/1-4
ANDREWS, Charles Bond (d 1899 [42]) composer, conductor EA/00*
ANDREWS, Dana (b 1912) American actor BE, CB, ES, WWT/14-16
ANDREWS, Mr. E. (fl 1760-70?) singer BD
ANDREWS, E. A. (d 1893 [28]) EA/94*
ANDREWS, Edward (b 1914) American actor TW/5, 8, 17
ANDREWS, Elizabeth (1821-1910) English actress BE*, WWT/14*
ANDREWS, George H. (1798-1866) English actor CDP, DD, HAS, SR
ANDREWS, George Lee (b 1942) American actor TW/28-30
ANDREWS, Harry (b 1911) English actor AAS, ES, TW/2, 8, WWT/11-16
ANDREWS, Henry (d 1890) actor EA/91*
ANDREWS, James Glen (d 1880 [40]) actor EA/81*
ANDREWS, James Petit (d 1797) English dramatist CP/3, DD
ANDREWS, Jane (d 1883 [50]) EA/84*
ANDREWS, Jane see Germon, Mrs. Greene C.
ANDREWS, Jane A. singer CDP
ANDREWS, Julie [Julia Elizabeth Wells] (b 1935) English actress, singer AAS, BE, CB, ES, TW/11-20, WWT/11-15
ANDREWS, Lois (d 1968 [44]) actress TW/24
ANDREWS, Louise [Mrs. Arthur Baer] (d 1950) performer BE*
ANDREWS, Lyle D. (d 1950 [79]) American proprietor, manager BE*, BP/34*, WWT/14*
ANDREWS, Maidie English actress WWT/6-14
ANDREWS, Marie American actress TW/27
ANDREWS, Maxene American actress TW/30
ANDREWS, Miles Peter (c. 1750-1814) English dramatist CDP, CP/2-3, DD, DNB, ES, GT, TD/1-2
ANDREWS, Nancy (b 1924) American actress, singer BE, TW/6-9, 11-21, 26-27, WWT/14-16
ANDREWS, Richard Hoffman (d 1891 [88]) composer EA/92*
ANDREWS, Robert (1895-1976?) English actor ES, WWT/5-13
ANDREWS, Robert C. (fl 1789-1819) scene painter, proprietor BD
ANDREWS, Stanley (d 1969 [77]) performer BP/54*
ANDREWS, Tod [Michael Ames] (1914/20-72) American actor BE, TW/1-3, 5-13, 16, 29, WWT/12-15
ANDREWS, Walter English comedian CDP
ANDREWS, W. C. (fl 1878)

American actor SR
ANDREWS, William (d 1878 [42])
Australian comedian EA/79*
ANDREWS, W. S. (fl 1860s)
actor HAS
ANDREYEV, Leonid Nikolaivich
(1871-1919) Russian dramatist
COC, MWD, OC/1-3, PDT
ANDRIESSEN, Pelagie (b 1863)
Austrian singer ES
ANDROWES, George (fl 1608)
theatre share-holder DA
ANDRUSS, Mrs. Albert see
Herndon, Agnes
ANELLO, Jerome (b 1939) American actor TW/28
ANEREAU, John (fl 1794-97)
singer BD
ANFOSSI, Pasquale (1727-97)
Italian composer, musical
director BD
ANGEL, Mr. (fl 1720-32) Harper
BD
ANGEL, Edward (fl 1660-73)
English actor BD, COC,
DD, ES, OC/1-3
ANGEL, Heather (b 1909) English
actress ES, WWT/7-10
ANGEL, Lou (b 1940) American
actor TW/23-24
ANGEL, Morris (d 1941) costumier WWT/14*
ANGELA, June (b 1959) American
actress TW/27
ANGELELLI, Augusta [Mrs. Vittorio Correr; Augusta Wynne]
(fl 1798) singer BD
ANGELES, Aimee [Mrs. George
Considine] (b 1880) actress,
dancer WWS
ANGELES, Victoria de los [Victoria Gamez Cima] (b 1923)
Spanish singer CB
ANGELI, Francesco (fl 1678-79)
Italian actor BD
ANGELI, Pier (d 1971 [39]) performer BP/56*
ANGELICA, Mrs. (fl 1785) singer
BD
ANGELINA (fl 1827) actress
CDP
ANGELINA, La Petite American?
dancer CDP
ANGELINA, Giuseppi (d 1916)
conductor SR
ANGELIQUE, Mlle. (fl 1828)
dancer HAS
ANGELL, Edythe (d 1966 [68])

performer BP/51*
ANGELL, George (fl 1736-39) musician BD
ANGELL, Victor (d 1874) gymnast
EA/75*
ANGELL, W. H. (d 1872 [74])
comedian, manager EA/72*
ANGELO, Mme. [Margaret Ann
Ashworth] (d 1911 [40]) performer EA/12*
ANGELO, Sig. (d c.1663) musician
BD
ANGELO, Sig. (fl 1723-24) scene
painter? BD
ANGELO, Signora (fl 1714-15)
singer? BD
ANGELO, Henry (1760-1839?)
fencing-master CDP, DNB
ANGELOU, Maya [Marguerite Johnson] (b 1928) American writer,
entertainer CB
ANGELUS, Muriel (b 1909/12) English actress WWT/7-10
ANGER, Al (d 1966 [65]) performer
BP/50*
ANGERS, Avril (b 1922) English
actress, singer WWT/11-16
ANGIER, Mr. (fl 1784-85) singer
BD
ANGLER, Mr. (fl 1786) performer
BD
ANGLIN, Margaret (1876-1958)
Canadian/American actress
COC, ES, GRB/2-4, NTH,
OC/1-3, SR, TW/2-3, 5-7,
15, WWA/5, WWM, WWS,
WWT/1-11
ANGOLD, Edith (d 1971 [76]) performer BP/56*
ANGRASINI, Sig. (fl 1831) singer
HAS
ANGRASINI, Signorina (fl 1825)
singer HAS
ANGUS, J. Keith (b 1848) Scottish
dramatist DD
ANKRUM, Morris (d 1964 [68])
performer BP/49*
ANNA, Signora (fl 1703) singer BD
ANNABELLA [Suzanne Georgette
Charpentier] (b 1912/13)
French actress TW/3, WWT/10
ANNALS, Michael (b 1938) English
designer AAS, WWT/15-16
ANNATO, Palmyre equestrienne
CDP
ANNEGAN, J. B. (b 1944) American
actor TW/26
ANNESLEY, Mr. (fl 1800)

manager? BD
ANNESLEY, Mrs. (fl 1744-49)
dancer BD
ANNESLEY, Lady Constance see
O'Niel, Colette
ANNIBALI, Domenico (1705-79?)
Italian singer BD
ANOUILH, Jean (b 1910) French
dramatist BE, CB, COC,
ES, HP, MH, MWD, NTH,
OC/1-3, PDT
ANSALDO, Pericle (b 1889) Italian
stage manager ES
ANSANI, Giovanni (1744-1826)
Italian singer, composer BD
ANSCHUTZ, Carl Friedrich Niko-
laus (1813/15/18-70) German
conductor CDP, ES, WWA/H
ANSEIMI, Rosina (d 1965 [85])
performer BP/49*
ANSELL, Mr. (fl 1785) dancer
BD
ANSELL, Mr. (fl 1827) English
actor HAS
ANSELL, Mrs. (fl 1788-91) house
servant? BD
ANSELL, Mrs. (fl 1800) actress
DD
ANSELL, Miss (fl 1787-88) house
servant? BD
ANSELL, Albert E. (d 1912)
advance manager EA/13*
ANSELL, Eva (d 1894 [22])
serio-comic EA/95*
ANSELL, John (fl 1761-88) box-
keeper BD
ANSELL, John (1874-1948) Eng-
lish composer, conductor
GRB/4, WWT/1-10, WWW/4
ANSELL, Mary (d 1950 [83])
actress DD
ANSELL, Thomas (d 1788) house
servant BD
ANSELL, William (fl 1762-90)
house servant, bill-sticker
BD
ANSELMO, Mr. (fl 1786-1803)
house servant BD
ANSELMO, Mrs. (fl 1794-1804)
dresser BD
ANSERMET, Ernest Alexandre
(1883-1969) Swiss conductor
CB
ANSKY [Solomon Rappoport]
(1863-1920) dramatist COC,
OC/1-3
ANSLEY, Abraham (d 1662)
trumpeter BD

ANSLEY, Edmond [Buster Brown]
(d 1972 [84]) midget BP/57*
ANSON, A. E. (1879-1936) English
actor SR, WWT/1-8
ANSON, Barbara American actress
TW/25
ANSON, Carlotta [Mrs. Wilson
Howard] English actress GRB/1
ANSON, Cecile E. [Mrs. John H.
R. Penrose] English actress
GRB/1
ANSON, C. W. (d 1944) actor
WWT/14*
ANSON, E. (fl 1833) actress HAS
ANSON, Frank (d 1897 [39]) actor
EA/98*
ANSON, George William (1847-1920)
Scottish actor DD, EA/95,
GRB/3-4, OAA/2, WWT/1-3
ANSON, John William (1817-81)
English actor DD, OAA/1-2
ANSON, Reginald F. (d 1919) actor
WWT/14*
ANSPACH, Elizabeth, Margravine
of (1750-1828) English dramatist
CDP, CP/3, DD, DNB, GT,
TD/1-2
ANSPACH, Nathan see Adams,
Nicholas
ANSPACHER, Florence S. (d 1971
[84]) patron BP/56*
ANSPACHER, Louis Kaufman (1878-
1947) American dramatist ES,
SR, WWA/2, WWM, WWS,
WWT/4-7
ANSPACHER, Mrs. Louis Kaufman
see Kidder, Kathryn
"ANSTEY, F."[Thomas Anstey
Gutherie] (1856-1934) English
dramatist DD, ES, GRB/2-4,
HP, WWM, WWT/1-7, WWW/3
ANSTEY, Percy [Percy Page-Phil-
lips] (1876-1920) French actor
GRB/1-3, WWW/2
ANSTISS, Jessie (d 1881) actress
EA/82*
ANSTRUTHER, Harold [Harold Ed-
ward Archer] English actor
WWT/4-6
ANTHEIL, George (1900-59) Amer-
ican composer CB, ES,
WWA/3
ANTHES, Georg (1863-1922) German
singer ES
ANTHONY, Mr. (fl 1733) French
horn player BD
ANTHONY, Carl (d 1930 [52]) actor
BE*, BP/15*, WWT/14*

ANTHONY, C. F. (d 1871) Eng-
lish musician EA/72*
ANTHONY, C. L. see Smith,
Dodie
ANTHONY, Edward (d 1971 [76])
author BP/56*
ANTHONY, Jack [John Anthony
Herbertson] (d 1962 [61])
Scottish performer BE*
ANTHONY, John J. (d 1970)
performer BP/55*
ANTHONY, Joseph [né Deuster]
(b 1912) American director,
actor, dramatist BE, ES,
TW/8-9, 23, WWT/14-16
ANTHONY, Michael (b 1943)
Australian actor TW/26
ANTHONY, Peter (fl 1672-73)
trumpeter BD
ANTHONY, Robert (b 1941)
American actor TW/25,
27-29
ANTINORI, Luigi (fl 1726) singer
BD
ANTLEY, George (d 1910) actor
EA/11*
ANTOGNINI, Cirillo (fl 1843)
Italian singer CDP
ANTOINE, André (1858-1943)
French actor, producer,
manager COC, GRB/1-4,
NTH, OC/1-3, WWT/1
ANTOINE, Josephine Louise
(1908-71) American singer
CB
ANTOINE, Robert (b 1932)
American actor TW/5
ANTOINE, Theophil (d 1891 [70])
EA/91*
ANTON, Pauline see Marvel,
Pauline
ANTONELLI, Sig. (d 1895) con-
ductor EA/96*
ANTONET [Umberto Guillaume]
(1872-1935) Italian clown ES
ANTONIADOU, Koula (b 1945)
Cypriot actor TW/28
ANTONIE, Mons. (d 1732) actor,
acrobat BD
ANTONINO, Teresa dancer CDP
ANTONIO [Antonio Ruiz Soler]
(b 1921/23) Spanish dancer,
choreographer CB, ES,
WWT/12
ANTONIO, Carl horse trainer
CDP
ANTONIO, Lou (b 1934) American
actor, director BE,

TW/14-15, 17-21
ANTONOVA, Helene A. (d 1973
[75]) performer BP/58*
ANTONY, Hilda (b 1886) Chilean
actress GRB/4, WWT/1-10
ANTOON, A. J. (b 1944) American
director WWT/16
ANTRIM, Harry (d 1967 [72]) actor
TW/23
ANTROBUS, John (b 1933) English
actor, dramatist AAS, CD,
WWT/15-16
ANUNCIATI, Signora (fl 1766-67)
singer BD
AP ARTHUR, Jeffrey (fl 1759)
dancer BD
APFEL, Oscar (d 1938) American
producer, director ES
APILEUTTER, Christopher (fl 1615)
actor DA
APLIN, Emma H. (d 1965 [48])
executive BP/50*
APLON, Boris American actor
TW/26-29
APOTHEOLA Indian chief CDP
APPEL, Anna (d 1963 [75]) Rumani-
an actress TW/20
APPELBAUM, Gertrude (b 1918)
American business manager
BE
APPELL, Don American librettist,
producer, director, actor BE,
CD
APPERLEY, John (fl 1613-20)
musician DA
APPLEBY, Mr. (fl 1696-99) acrobat
BD
APPLEBY, Mr. (fl 1792) puppet-
show man BD
APPLEBY, Master (fl 1798-1819)
dancer BD
APPLEBY, Dorothy (b 1908) Amer-
ican actress WWT/8-19
APPLEBY, Mrs. Emma (d 1885
[59]) EA/86*
APPLEBY, Louie (d 1902 [40])
actress EA/03*
APPLEBY, Thomas Bilton (d 1892
[47]) English actor, lessee
DD, OAA/2
APPLEBY, William (fl 1787-1818)
messenger, porter BD
APPLETON, Master (fl 1790-93?)
musician BD
APPLETON, George J. (d 1926
[82]) manager BE*, BP/11*,
WWT/14*
APPLEWHITE, Eric Leon (d 1973

[76]) performer BP/58*
APPLEYARD, Beatrice (b 1918)
English dancer, choreographer
ES
APPLIN, Arthur (d 1949 [76])
English actor GRB/1-4
APPLIN, Mrs. Arthur see
Olive, Edyth
APPLIN, George (d 1949 [76])
dramatist BE*
APPY, Henry (b 1828) violinist
CDP
APSTEIN, Theodore (b 1918)
Russian/American dramatist
BE
APTHORP, William Foster (b
1848) American critic WWA/
4, WWM
APTOMMAS, John S. (d 1917
[20]) EA/18*
APTOMMAS, Priscilla (d 1907)
harpist EA/08*
AQUILANTI, Chiaretta (fl 1742-
63) dancer BD
ARBAN, Mr. (d 1889 [63]) con-
ductor EA/90*
ARBEIT, Herman (b 1925) Amer-
ican actor TW/29
ARBENINA, Stella (1887-1976)
Russian actress WWT/5-10
ARBOS, Enrique Fernández
(1863-1939) Spanish musical
director, composer, violinist
ES
ARBUCKLE, Maclyn (1866-1931)
American actor ES, GRB/
3-4, SR, WWA/1, WWM,
WWS, WWT/1-6
ARBUCKLE, Matthew (1828-83)
musician, bandmaster CDP
ARBUCKLE, Minta Durfee (d
1975 [85]) performer BP/60*
ARBUCKLE, Roscoe [Fatty]
(1887-1933) American actor,
director BE*, BP/18*, ES
ARBURY, Guy (d 1972 [65])
actor TW/29
ARBUTHNOT, Dr. John (d 1735)
Scottish dramatist CP/3
ARBUZOV, Aleksei Nikolayevich
(b 1908) Russian dramatist
COC, PDT
ARCARO, Flavia (1876/82-1937)
American actress WWM
ARCE, Juan F. Acosts (d 1968
[78]) composer/lyricist
BP/53*
ARCEDECKNE, Mrs. see

Elsworthy, Miss
ARCHELL, Mr. (fl 1794) trumpeter
BD
ARCHER, Mr. (fl 1735-42) actor
BD
ARCHER, Mr. (fl 1786-1803) Scot-
tish actor DD, TD/1-2
ARCHER, Mrs. (fl 1848) actress
HAS
ARCHER, Alexander (1757?-1817)
actor BD
ARCHER, Belle (1860-1900) Ameri-
can actress WWA/1
ARCHER, Charles (1861-1941)
Scottish writer WWW/4
ARCHER, Charles George (d 1901
[41]) EA/02*
ARCHER, C. J. (d 1905) manager
EA/06*
ARCHER, Elisha (1760-1800) Eng-
lish violinist BD
ARCHER, Eugene (d 1973 [42])
critic BP/57*
ARCHER, Frank [Frank Bishop
Arnold] (d 1917 [72]) English
actor DD, OAA/1-2
ARCHER, Mrs. Frederick see
Pritchard, Marie
ARCHER, Harold Edward see
Anstruther, Harold
ARCHER, Harry (1888-1960) Amer-
ican composer BE*, BP/44*
ARCHER, Joe English comedian
CDP
ARCHER, John (1835-1921) English
actor DD, OAA/1-2
ARCHER, John B. (b 1915) Ameri-
can actor BE, TW/1-8, WWT/
11-13
ARCHER, Osceola American actress
TW/24, 28
ARCHER, Richard (fl 1603) actor
DA
ARCHER, Thomas (1789-1848)
English comedian, dramatist,
BS, CDP, DD, DNB, ES, HAS
ARCHER, Thomas (d 1851) English
singer HAS, SR
ARCHER, Mrs. Thomas American
actress DD
ARCHER, William (1856-1924)
Scottish critic, dramatist
COC, DD, DNB, ES, GRB/1-4,
HP, MD, MWD, NTH, OC/1-3,
PDT, WWT/1-4, WWW/2
ARCHEVEQUE, Mr. (fl 1773-74)
box-office keeper BD
ARCHEY, Mr. (fl 1708) house

servant BD
ARCHIBALD, Mrs. (fl 1856)
actress HAS
ARCHIBALD, Douglas (b 1919)
Trinidadian dramatist CD
ARCHIBALD, William (1915/24-70)
West Indian dramatist, director, singer, dancer BE, ES,
MH, TW/1-3, 6-7, 27
ARCHIPOVA, Irina Konstantinovna
(b 1925) Russian singer ES
ARDEN, Edwin Hunter Pendleton
(1864-1918) American dramatist, actor, manager DAB,
ES, GRB/3-4, SR, WWA/1,
WWM, WWS, WWT/2-3
ARDEN, Eliza (fl 1850s) actress
DD
ARDEN, Eve [Eunice Quedens]
(b 1912) American actress
BE, CB, ES, TW/23, WWT/
10-16
ARDEN, H. T. see Arnold,
Henry Thomas
ARDEN, Jane Welsh dramatist,
actress CD
ARDEN, John (b 1930) English
dramatist, director AAS,
CD, CH, COC, ES, MD,
MWD, OC/3, PDT, RE,
WWT/14-16
ARDEN, Milly see Chaplin,
Amelia
ARDEN, Victor (d 1962 [69])
composer BP/47*
ARDEN, Wallace (d 1903) actor
EA/04*
ARDITI, Luigi (1822-1903) Italian
composer, conductor, musician CDP, DNB, ES, WWW/1
ARDITI, Virginia (d 1909) EA/10*
ARDREY, Robert (b 1908) American dramatist BE, CB, CD,
ES, MD, MWD, WWT/9-14
ARDRON, Samuel singer, composer CDP
ARENA, Giuseppe (fl 1738-46)
Italian composer ES
ARENT, Arthur (1904/05/06-72)
American dramatist BE,
ES, MD, MH, MWD
ARGENTINA [Antonia Mercé]
(1890-1936) Argentinian dancer,
choreographer ES, WWT/8
ARGENTINITA [Encarnación López
Julves] (1905-45) Argentinian
dancer CB, ES, TW/2
ARGO, Allison (b 1953) American

actress TW/30
ARGYLE, Fanny Austin (d 1917)
American actress SR
ARGYLE, Gertrude [Gertrude F.
DeVingut] (fl 1861) actress
HAS
ARGYLE, Pearl [Pearl Wellman]
(1910-47) South African dancer
ES, SR, WWT/8-10
ARIMONDI, Vittorio (1861-1928)
Italian singer ES
ARIOSTI, Attilio Malachia (d 1666)
Italian composer, violist BD
ARIS, Ben (b 1937) English actor
TW/25
ARISHIMA, Takeo (1878-1923)
Japanese dramatist ES
ARISTIPPE [Félix Bernier de Maligny] (d 1865) French actor
ES
ARKELL, Elizabeth English actress
WWT/5-9
ARKELL, Monique see Berendt,
Rachel
ARKELL, Reginald (1882-1959)
English dramatist, lyricist
WWT/4-12, WWW/5
ARKELL, Rosy (d 1897 [28]) EA/
98*
ARKIN, Alan (b 1934) American
actor, writer, composer BE,
CB, ES, TW/19-22, WWT/15-16
ARKINSTALL, Beatrice K. [Beatrice
K. Court] (d 1917) EA/18*
ARKINSTALL, John (fl 1603) actor
DA
ARLEN, Bill (b 1951) American
actor TW/30
ARLEN, Harold [Hyman Arluck] (b
1905) American composer BE,
CB, ES, PDT, WWT/15-16
ARLEN, Jerry American musical
director BE
ARLEN, Michael (1895-1956) Bulgarian/English dramatist
DNB, WWT/6-10, WWW/5
ARLEN, Richard (1899-1976) American actor TW/1
ARLEN, Stephen Walter [né Badham]
(1913-72) English manager,
director WWT/15
ARLING, Joyce (b 1911) American
actress BE, WWT/9-11
ARLINGTON, Billy (1835-91) minstrel SR
ARLINGTON, Billy (b 1873) American actor WWT/6
ARLINGTON, Mrs. Eddie [née

Nettie Bowne] (1877-1947)
actress SR
ARLINGTON, Eleanor (d 1973)
performer BP/58*
ARLINGTON, Maggie [Margaret
Ryerson] (1853-77) American
actress NYM
ARLINGTON, May (b 1847) Amer-
ican actress HAS
ARLINGTON, William [né Burnell]
American comedian HAS
ARLISS, Dimitra American actress
TW/27
ARLISS, Florence Montgomery
(d 1950 [77]) English actress
TW/6
ARLISS, George (1868-1946)
English actor CB, DAB,
DNB, ES, GRB/3-4, NTH,
OC/1-3, SR, TW/2, WWA/
2, WWM, WWS, WWT/1-9,
WWW/4
ARLISS, Mrs. George see
Montgomery, Florence
ARLUCK, Hyman see Arlen,
Harold
ARMALENA, Mr. (fl 1777) musi-
cian? BD
ARMAND, Joseph (b 1833) Amer-
ican actor HAS
ARMAND'ARY, Mlle. French
singer CDP
ARMBRUSTER, Carl (1846-1917)
German musical director
ES
ARMBRUSTER, Violet actress
EA/95
ARMEN, Johnny (b 1938) Ameri-
can actor TW/27-29
ARMENDARIZ, Pedro (d 1963)
Mexican actor BE*
ARMETTA, Henry (1888-1945)
Italian actor TW/2
ARMIGER, Edward (d 1635) actor
DA
ARMIN, Robert (c.1568-c.1611)
English clown, actor, drama-
tist CDP, COC, CP/1-3,
DA, DD, DNB, ES, FGF,
GT, NTH, OC/1-3
ARMISTEAD, Horace (b 1898)
English scene designer ES
ARMITAGE, Bessie (d 1918)
EA/19*
ARMITAGE, Buford (b 1898)
American manager, stage
manager, actor BE
ARMITAGE, Merle (b 1893)

American impresario ES
ARMITAGE, R. A. see Gay, Noel
ARMITAGE, Sarah (d 1913) EA/14*
ARMITAGE, Walter W. (d 1953
[46]) South African actor, pro-
ducer BE*, BP/37*
ARMONDOS, George (d 1965 [64])
performer BP/50*
ARMOUR, A. C. (d 1893 [38])
comedian EA/95*
ARMOUR, William Alexander (d
1916 [44]) EA/17*
ARMSTEAD, Mrs. [Elizabeth Brid-
get Blane; Mrs. Charles James
Fox] (1750-1842) English actress
BD
ARMSTRONG, Mr. (fl 1717-19)
singer BD
ARMSTRONG, Mr. (fl 1722) dancer
BD
ARMSTRONG, Mr. (fl 1726)
trumpeter BD
ARMSTRONG, Anna (1863-1948)
actress, trapezist SR
ARMSTRONG, Anthony (1897-1976)
Canadian/English dramatist
AAS, ES, WWT/7-14
ARMSTRONG, Mrs. Charles see
Melba, Nellie
ARMSTRONG, Charlotte (d 1969
[64]) dramatist BP/54*
ARMSTRONG, Charlotte Eva (d
1901) EA/02*
ARMSTRONG, Clara [Mrs. Felix
Pitt] (d 1894 [39]) actress
EA/95*
ARMSTRONG, Mjr. Edwin H. (1890-
1954) American inventor, engi-
neer BE*
ARMSTRONG, Elizabeth [Kitty Ann
Worlock; Mrs. John Moody, II]
(1763-1846) English dancer BD
ARMSTRONG, Eunice B. (d 1971
[84]) dramatist BP/56*
ARMSTRONG, Gordon E. (d 1965
[64]) critic BP/50*
ARMSTRONG, Harry (1879-1951)
American songwriter BE*,
BP/35*
ARMSTRONG, Sir Harry Gloster
(d 1938 [77]) English actor
BE*, WWT/14*
ARMSTRONG, Helen (fl 1858)
actress HAS
ARMSTRONG, Henry (d 1877 [62])
actor EA/78*
ARMSTRONG, John (fl 1769) pro-
prietor BD

ARMSTRONG, Dr. John (c.1709-79) English dramatist CP/2-3, DD, GT

ARMSTRONG, John (1893-1973) English scene designer ES

ARMSTRONG, John A. (d 1974 [60]) theatre operator BP/59*

ARMSTRONG, Louis (1900-71) American musician CB, ES

ARMSTRONG, Ned (d 1961 [55]) press representative BE*, BP/46*

ARMSTRONG, Paul (1869-1915) American dramatist DAB, ES, GRB/3-4, OC/1-3, SR, WWA/1, WWM, WWS, WWT/1-2

ARMSTRONG, Robert (1896-1973) American actor ES, TW/1, 29, WWT/6-10

ARMSTRONG, Sydney [Mrs. W. G. Smyth] American actress WWM, WWS

ARMSTRONG, Mr. W. (fl 1708-13) violist BD

ARMSTRONG, Will H. (d 1943 [74]) performer BE*

ARMSTRONG, William [William D'Alvini; "Jap of Japs"] (d. 1889 [42]) EA/90*

ARMSTRONG, William (d 1895) clown EA/96*

ARMSTRONG, William [William M. Devine] (d 19--?) American performer BE*

ARMSTRONG, Sir William (1882-1952) Scottish actor, producer, director AAS, COC, DNB, ES, OC/1-3, WWT/4-11, WWW/5

ARMSTRONG, William Dawson (1868-1936) American composer ES, WWM

ARMSTRONG, Will Steven (1930-69) American designer BE, ES, TW/26, WWT/14

ARMUS, Sidney (b 1924) American actor TW/11, 17, 21-24

ARMYTAGE, Grace [Mrs. Campbell Bradley] (d 1907) actress EA/08*, GRB/3*

ARMYTAGE, Seul (d 1897 [21]) music-hall performer EA/98*

ARNATT, John (b 1917) English actor WWT/12-16

ARNAUD, Yvonne Germaine (1892-1958) French actress,

singer AAS, COC, ES, OC/3, TW/14, WWT/2-12, WWW/5

ARNAULD, Mons. (fl 1764-70) dancer BD

ARNAUT, John (d 1965 [65]) performer BP/50*

ARNAZ, Desi (b 1917) Cuban musician CB

ARNDT, Felix (1889-1918) American composer BE*

ARNE, Miss (fl 1795) singer DD, TD/1-2

ARNE, Cecilia see Arne, Mrs. Thomas Augustine

ARNE, Michael (c.1740-86) composer, singer, musician BD, DD, DNB, ES

ARNE, Mrs. Michael, II [Elizabeth Wright] (1751?-69) singer BD

ARNE, Mrs. Michael, III [Ann Venables] (fl 1772-1820) singer BD

ARNE, Richard (b 1719) English singer, actor BD

ARNE, Susanna Maria see Cibber, Mrs. Theophilus, II

ARNE, Thomas (1682-1736) English box-numberer, manager? BD

ARNE, Dr. Thomas Augustine (1710-78) English composer BD, CDP, CP/1-3, DD, DNB, ES, TD/1-2

ARNE, Mrs. Thomas Augustine [Cecilia Young] (1711-89) English singer BD, DNB

ARNEEL, Eugen (d 1972 [52]) critic BP/57*

ARNELL, Nydia (d 1970 [74]) musical comedian TW/26

ARNELL, Patricia (b 1950) American actress TW/29

ARNELL, Richard (b 1917) English composer ES

ARNESS, James (b 1923) American actor CB

ARNO, Sig. (1895-1975) German actor, singer, director BE, TW/1-2, 16-17

ARNO, Owen G. (d 1969 [35]) dramatist BP/54*

ARNOLD, Mr. (fl 1696-1702) actor BD

ARNOLD, Mr. (fl 1771-85?) proprietor BD

ARNOLD, Mrs. singer DD, HAS

ARNOLD, Mrs. see Belfille, Mrs.

ARNOLD, Miss (fl 1794-96) actress

BD
ARNOLD, Charles (1854-1905)
Swiss/English actor, singer
DD, GRB/1
ARNOLD, Charles (d 1917 [77])
actor EA/18*
ARNOLD, Cornelius (fl 1757)
dramatist CP/2-3, DD, GT
ARNOLD, Doris (d 1969 [61])
producer/director/choreograph-
er BP/54*
ARNOLD, Eddie (d 1962 [34])
performer BE*
ARNOLD, Eddy (b 1918) Ameri-
can singer CB
ARNOLD, Edward [Gunther
Schneider] (1890-1956)
American actor ES, TW/12,
WWA/3, WWT/8-10
ARNOLD, Elizabeth (fl 1797-
1809) actress, singer, dancer
SR
ARNOLD, Elizabeth see Clen-
dining, Mrs. William
ARNOLD, Emily C. (d 1900
[40]) descriptive singer
EA/01*
ARNOLD, Frank Bishop see
Archer, Frank
ARNOLD, Franz (1878-1960)
German dramatist WWT/
11-12
ARNOLD, Frederick see
Allandale, Fred
ARNOLD, G. J. (fl 1846) actor
HAS
ARNOLD, Mrs. Henry [Elizabeth
Smith; Mrs. Charles Tubbs]
(fl 1784-c.1799) actress,
singer BD
ARNOLD, Henry C. English come-
dian CDP
ARNOLD, Henry Thomas [H. T.
Arden] (1840-76) dramatist
DD
ARNOLD, H. Somerfield (d 1900)
actor EA/01*
ARNOLD, J. (d 1878) Negro
artist EA/79*
ARNOLD, Jack [Arnold Jack
Gluck] (d 1962 [59]) per-
former BE*
ARNOLD, James A. (d 1905)
singer, actor, manager
GRB/1
ARNOLD, Jeanne American
actress TW/26-28, 30
ARNOLD, Jonas (d 1975 [72])

publicist BP/60*
ARNOLD, Laura (d 1963 [c.73])
American actress, talent repre-
sentative BE*
ARNOLD, Lilian (d 1974 [69]) pro-
ducer/director/choreographer
BP/59*
ARNOLD, Lilian American talent
representative BE
ARNOLD, Madison (b 1935) Ameri-
can actor TW/25, 27
ARNOLD, Mary Sophia see
Bailey, Mrs. William
ARNOLD, Mat [Charles Kerr] (d
1894) pantomimist, comedian
EA/95*
ARNOLD, Matthew (1822-88) English
critic, dramatist COC, DD,
ES, HP, NTH, OC/1-3
ARNOLD, Maurice (b 1865) Ameri-
can composer WWA/4, WWM
ARNOLD, Phil (d 1968 [55]) per-
former BP/52*
ARNOLD, Phyl (d 1941 [38]) actress
WWT/7-8
ARNOLD, Priscilla (d 1898) EA/99*
ARNOLD, Reggie (d 1963 [43]) per-
former BE*
ARNOLD, Dr. Samuel (1740-1802)
English composer, conductor,
manager, organist, musical
editor BD, CDP, DD, DNB,
ES, TD/1-2
ARNOLD, Samuel James (1774-1852)
English manager, dramatist
CP/3, DD, DNB, ES, GT,
TD/1-2
ARNOLD, Seth (d 1955 [70]) English/
American actor TW/1, 6-7
ARNOLD, T. (fl 1799) proprietor
BD
ARNOLD, Tom (d 1969 [72]) mana-
ger WWT/9-14, WWW/6
ARNOLD, Victor (b 1936) American
actor TW/22-26, 28, 30
ARNOLD, Wade (d 1975) producer/
director/choreographer BP/59*
ARNOLD, W. H. dramatist DD
ARNOLDI, Sig. (fl 1848) singer
HAS
ARNOLDSON, Sigrid (1861-1943)
Swedish singer ES, WWA/5
ARNOT, Edwin (d 1885) actor
EA/86*
ARNOT, Louise [Mrs. Mary Louise
Gunn] (d 1919 [76]) actress
BE*
ARNOTT, Emma (d 1891 [47])

EA/93*
ARNOTT, Peter Douglas (b 1931)
English educator, puppeteer
BE
ARNOULD, Mr. (fl 1687-88)
singer BD
ARNOULD, Sophie (1740-1802)
French actress, singer BE*,
WWT/14*
ARNOULD-PLESSY, Mme. (d 1897
[78]) actress WWT/14*
ARNSTEIN, Alexander (d 1895)
musician EA/96*
ARNULL, Mr. (fl 1784-1817)
musician BD
ARON, Robert (fl 1702) mounte-
bank BD
ARONS, Morris (d 1877 [29])
advance agent EA/78*
ARONSON, Boris Solomon (b
1900/04) American designer
AAS, BE, COC, ES, OC/3,
WWT/11-16
ARONSON, Edward (d 1888 [29])
American actor EA/89*
ARONSON, Rudolph (1856-1919)
American composer, mana-
ger CDP, SR, WWA/1,
WWS
ARONSTEIN, Martin (b 1936)
American lighting designer
WWT/16
AROVA, Sonia (b 1927) Bulgarian/
English dancer ES
ARPER, Mrs. Clarence F.
see Atwood, Lorena E.
ARPINO, Gerald (b 1929) Amer-
ican dancer, choreographer
ES
ARQUETTE, Cliff[ord] (1905-74)
American comedian CB
ARRABAL, Fernando [Fernando
Arrabal Téran] (b 1932)
Spanish dramatist CB, CH,
COC, RE, WWT/15-16
ARRANDALE, Gilbert (d 1908
[39]) EA/09*
ARRIGHI, Mel (b 1933) American
actor TW/18
ARRIGONI, Carlo (b 1697) Italian
composer, band leader,
musician BD
ARRINGTON, Lillie see Bur-
roughs, Marie
ARROWSMITH, Mr. (fl 1673)
dramatist CP/1-3
ARROWSMITH, Daniel (fl 1783-
94) singer, composer BD

ARROWSMITH, William (fl 1673)
dramatist DD
ARROWSMITH, William (b 1924)
American translator, editor,
educator BE
ARROYO, Martina (b 1936?) Amer-
ican singer CB
ARTAUD, Antonin (1896-1948)
French actor, theorist CH,
COC, PDT
ARTAUD, Stephen (d 1886 [71])
actor EA/87*
ARTELL, R. F. [Robert Frederick
Corson] (d 1885) gymnast
EA/86*
ARTHUR, Beatrice (b 1926?) Amer-
ican actress BE, CB, TW/15,
21-24, WWT/16
ARTHUR, Carol (b 1935) American
actress, singer, comedienne
BE, TW/22
ARTHUR, Daniel V. (d 1939 [72])
manager WWT/14*
ARTHUR, Daphne (b 1925) English
actress WWT/11-13
ARTHUR, George K. [George Brest]
(b 1899) Scottish actor ES
ARTHUR, Hartney J. (b 1917) Aus-
tralian producer, director,
actor BE
ARTHUR, Helen (d 1939 [60]) Amer-
ican press representative BE*
ARTHUR, Hope American actress
TW/24
ARTHUR, Jean [Gladys Green] (b
1905/08) American actress
BE, CB, ES, TW/6-7, WWT/
8-12
ARTHUR, John (1708?-72) English
actor, machinist, manager,
dramatist BD, CDP, CP/2-3
DD, GT, TD/1-2
ARTHUR, John (d 1916 [44]) actor,
stage manager WWT/14*
ARTHUR, Mrs. John, II [Grace
Read; Mrs. Daniel Williams]
(fl 1760-74) actress, singer
BD
ARTHUR, Johnny American actor
ES, TW/5
ARTHUR, Joseph (1848-1906) Amer-
ican dramatist BE*, WWT/14*
ARTHUR, Julia [Mrs. B. P. Chen-
ey, Jr.] (1869-1950) Canadian
actress ES, GRB/2-4, PP/1,
SR, TW/6, WWA/5, WWS,
WWT/1-9
ARTHUR, Lee American agent,

dramatist SR
ARTHUR, Paul (1856/59-1928)
American actor GRB/2-4,
WWS, WWT/1-5
ARTHUR, Phil (b 1923) American
actor TW/3, 6-18
ARTHUR, Robert (d 1929 [73])
manager GRB/4, WWT/1-5
ARTHUR, Roger (fl 1669) musi-
cian BD
ARTHUR, Sam [Sam Geary] (d
1908 [39]) EA/09*
ARTHUR, Thomas dramatist
FGF
ARTHUR, Thomas (fl 1528-29)
actor DA
ARTHUR, Wallis English come-
dian CDP
ARTHUR-JONES, Winifred [Mrs.
Leslie Faber] (b 1880)
English actress GRB/3-4,
WWT/1-6
ARTHURS, George (1875-1944)
English lyricist, librettist
WWT/4-9
ARTHURSON, Mr. (fl 1847)
Singer CDP, HAS
ARTIMA, Baldassare (fl 1669-71)
scenekeeper BD
ARTINGSTALL, William (d 1868
[36]) musician EA/68*
ARTOIS, Jack (d 1910 [34])
acrobat EA/12*
ARUNDALE, Grace [Grace Kelly]
actress GRB/2-4, WWT/1-5
ARUNDALE, Sybil [Sybil Kelly]
(1879/82-1965) English
actress ES, GRB/1-4,
WWT/1-11
ARUNDEL, Honor (d 1973) drama-
tist BP/58*
ARUNDELL, Dennis (b 1898)
English actor, producer,
musician, composer, director
AAS, ES, WWT/9-15
ARVOLD, Alfred G. (1882-1957)
American educator, little
theatre initiator BE*
ARZSCHAR, Robert (fl 1608-1616)
English actor DA
ASBRIDGE, John (1725-1800)
musician BD
ASBURY, Mr. pantaloon CDP
ASCH, Sholom (1880-1957)
Polish/American dramatist
MH, MWD, NTH, OC/1-3,
RE, WWW/5
ASCHE, Oscar [John Stanger

Heiss] (1871-1936) Australian/
English actor COC, DNB,
ES, GRB/1-4, NTH, OC/1-3,
WWT/1-8, WWW/3
ASCHE, Mrs. Oscar see Brayton,
Lily
ASCHER, Anton (d 1884) composer
EA/85*
ASCHER, Joseph (d 1869 [39])
pianist EA/70*
ASCHER, Leo (1880-1942) Austrian
composer CB
ASCOUGH, Charles Edward (d
1779) dramatist CP/2, GT,
TD/1-2
ASH, Arty (d 1954 [61]) comedian
WWT/14*
ASH, Gordon (d 1929 [52]) actor
WWT/4-5
ASH, Ingram (d 1974 [55]) executive
BP/59*
ASH, Joe (fl 1680s?) boxkeeper
BD
ASH, Maie (1888-1923) English
actress, dancer GRB/1-4,
WWT/1-2
ASH, Paul R. (d 1958 [57]) band-
leader BE*
ASHBEE, Ashton (d 1898 [29])
actor EA/99*
ASHBORNE, Edward (fl 1624) actor
DA
ASHBUNY, Mr. (fl 1689) house ser-
vant? BD
ASHBURTON, Lady [Frances Bel-
mont] (b 1884) American
actress GRB/1
ASHBURY, Mr. (fl 1767-69) house
servant? BD
ASHBURY, John (fl 1690-1700) fifer
BD
ASHBURY, Joseph (1638-1720)
English actor, manager DD,
DNB, ES
ASHCROFT, Dame Peggy (b 1907)
English actress AAS, BE,
CB, COC, ES, OC/2-3, PDT,
TW/5-7, WWT/7-16
ASHCROFT, William E. (d 1906)
EA/07*
ASHCROFT, W. J. (d 1918 [73])
EA/19*
ASHE, Andrew (c. 1759-1838) Irish
musician BD
ASHE, Martin (b 1909) American
actor TW/13
ASHE, Warren (d 1947 [44]) Amer-
ican actor TW/1

ASHER, Mrs. (d 1899) EA/00*
ASHER, Angelo Andrew musical
director GRB/1
ASHER, Jane (b 1946) English
actress TW/23, 27, WWT/
15-16
ASHER, Max (d 1957 [77]) actor
BE*
ASHER, Morris (d 1895) EA/96*
ASHERMANN, Otto (b 1903) Aus-
trian educator, director BE
ASHERSON, Renée (b 1915) Eng-
lish actress AAS, ES, WWT/
10-16
ASHFORD, Charles (1850-1903)
English actor DD, OAA/2
ASHFORD, Daisy (d 1972 [90])
dramatist BP/56*
ASHFORD, Harry (d 1903 [40])
variety comedian EA/05*
ASHFORD, Harry (1858-1926)
English actor SR
ASHFORD, Tom (d 1887) music-
hall artist EA/88*
ASHLEY, Annie (d 1947 [82])
American actress BE*,
WWT/14*
ASHLEY, Barbara American
singer, actress BE, TW/7-
19
ASHLEY, Celeste American theatre
librarian BE
ASHLEY, Charles (d 1888) acting
manager EA/89*
ASHLEY, Charles Jane (c. 1773-
1843) musician BD, DNB
ASHLEY, Charles Milton (d
1910) proprietor EA/11*
ASHLEY, Gen. Christopher (1767-
1818) English violinist BD
ASHLEY, Elizabeth [née Cole]
(b 1939) American actress
BE, TW/18, 20, 28, WWT/
15-16
ASHLEY, Esther Potter [née
McCormac] (d 1887) Ameri-
can actress NYM
ASHLEY, Helen [Mrs. Clarence
S. Spencer; née Hurt] (d
1954 [75]) actress, writer
BE*
ASHLEY, Henry Jeffries (d 1890
[59]) English actor, singer
CDP, DD, DP, OAA/1-2
ASHLEY, Iris (b 1909) Irish
actress, singer WWT/8-9
ASHLEY, Jane (1740-1809) bas-
soonist BD

ASHLEY, Jane Jeffries (d 1909)
EA/11*
ASHLEY, J. B. [Henry Thomas Buz-
zard] (d 1892 [36]) actor EA/
93*
ASHLEY, Mrs. J. B. see Uns-
worth, Evelyn
ASHLEY, Joel American actor
TW/1
ASHLEY, John (1734-1805) bassoon-
ist, oratorio manager BD,
DNB
ASHLEY, John James (1771-1815)
English musician, composer
BD, DNB
ASHLEY, Minne [Mrs. William Astor
Chanler] (1875-1945) American
actress, singer, dancer WWM,
WWS
ASHLEY, Richard Godfrey (1774-
1836) English musician BD,
DNB
ASHLEY, Stephen W. (fl 1863)
actor CDP
ASHLEY, Ted American talent rep-
resentative BE
ASHLEY, William (fl 1672) musi-
cian BD
ASHMER, James G. [né Gollicker]
(1826-63) English actor HAS
ASHMORE, Basil (b 1915) English
producer WWT/11-16
ASHMORE, Dorothy (d 1892) EA/
93*
ASHMORE, Joseph (fl 1794) singer
BD
ASHMORE, Peter (b 1916) English
director, actor BE, WWT/11-
14
ASHTON, Mr. (fl 1624-25?) actor
DA
ASHTON, Mr. (fl 1698) actor BD
ASHTON, Amelia (d 1868) EA/69*
ASHTON, Florence (d 1973 [69])
performer BP/58*
ASHTON, Frederick (b 1906) English
dancer, choreographer CB,
ES, OC/1-2, WWT/8-12
ASHTON, George (d 1935 [82])
agent GRB/2-4
ASHTON, Gordon (d 1874) actor
EA/75*
ASHTON, Henrietta [Mrs. Walter
Ashton] (d 1912) EA/13*
ASHTON, Robert (fl 1675-79) vio-
linist BD
ASHTON, Robert (fl 1727) Irish
dramatist CP/2, DD, TD/1

ASHTON, Sylvia (d 1940 [60])
American actress BE*
ASHTON, Thomas (fl 1673)
musician BD
ASHTON, Thomas (fl 1737-58)
musician BD
ASHTON, Mrs. Walter see
Ashton, Henrietta
ASHTON, Winifred see Dane,
Clemence
ASHWELL, Charles (d 1916 [34])
EA/17*
ASHWELL, Lena [Mrs. Arthur
Playfair] (1872-1957) English
actress COC, DNB, EA/96,
ES, GRB/1-4, OC/1-3,
WWM, WWS, WWT/1-12,
WWW/5
ASHWIN, Mr. (fl 1795-1813?)
tailor, actor, dancer? BD
ASHWORTH, John Henry (d 1916
[50]) advance manager EA/
17*
ASHWORTH, Margaret Ann see
Angelo, Mme.
ASHWYNNE, Muriel [Muriel
Walker] English actress
GRB/3-4
ASKAM, Perry (d 1961 [60])
American singer, actor TW/
18
ASKEN, Aaron (fl 1627-40)
dancer DA
ASKER, Mrs. (fl 1782-84) actress,
equestrienne? BD
ASKER, Mrs. Catherine (d 1867)
actress EA/68*
ASKEW, John (d 1895) violin
maker EA/96*
ASKEW, Mary Jane (d 1909)
EA/10*
ASKEY, Mr. (fl 1794) singer
BD
ASKEY, Arthur Bowden (b 1900)
English comedian ES,
WWT/10-16
ASKIN, Harry (d 1934 [67])
American manager, producer
BE*, BP/19*
ASKINS, Mr. (fl 1796) ventrilo-
quist BD
ASKWIN, Mr. (fl 1793) scene
painter BD
ASPEY, Mr. (fl 1742-44) singer,
actor BD
ASPINALL, T. H. (d 1897) pro-
prietor EA/98*
ASPINALL, Mrs. W. E. see

Mason, Kitty
ASPINWALL, Stanhope (d 1771)
dramatist CP/2-3
ASPLAND, George V. (d 1911)
showman EA/10*
ASPULL, George (1813-32) pianist
CDP, DNB
ASQUITH, Anthony (1902-68) English
actor, producer ES, WWT/10,
WWW/6
ASQUITH, Lady Cynthia Mary Evelyn
(1887-1960) English dramatist
DNB
ASQUITH, Mary (d 1942 [69])
actress BE*, WWT/14*
ASSELIN, Mr. (fl 1772-75) dancer
BD
ASSELIN, Mlle. (fl 1759-66) dancer
BD
ASSONI, Sig. (d 1860) singer HAS
ASTAIRE, Adele (b 1898) American
actress, dancer BE, SR,
WWT/5-11
ASTAIRE, Ann Geilus (d 1975 [96])
BP/60*
ASTAIRE, Fred (b 1899/1900)
American actor, dancer AAS,
BE, CB, ES, SR, WWT/5-11
ASTAR, Ben Palestinian actor
TW/10-11
ASTHER, Nils (b 1901) Swedish
actor ES
ASTLEY, Miss (fl 1773) equestri-
enne, actress? BD
ASTLEY, Edward (fl 1782-93) door-
keeper, bill-sticker, hostler
BD
ASTLEY, Hannah Waldo (fl 1820s)
equestrienne CDP
ASTLEY, Hugh F. L. (d 1910 [78])
chairman EA/11*
ASTLEY, Jessie Marion (d 1880)
EA/82*
ASTLEY, John English actor WWT/
4-6
ASTLEY, John Philip Conway (1767-
1821) equestrian, actor, mana-
ger, dramatist BD, CDP
ASTLEY, Philip (1742-1814) English
equestrian, manager BD, CDP,
DD, DNB, ES, HP, OC/3
ASTLEY, Mrs. Philip [Patty Jones]
(d 1794) equestrienne BD
ASTON, Anthony (c. 1682-c.1753)
English actor, singer, dancer,
manager, composer, dramatist
BD, CDP, COC, CP/1-3, DD,
DNB, ES, GT, HJD, NTH,

OC/1-3, SR, TD/1-2,
WWA/H
ASTON, Mrs. Anthony (fl 1704-
35?) actress BD
ASTON, Frank (b 1897) American
critic NTH
ASTON, Joseph (1762-1844) Eng-
lish dramatist DD
ASTON, Kate CDP
ASTON, Mrs. Knight see Brent,
Mabel
ASTON, Robert Irish dramatist
TD/2
ASTON, Walter (fl 1733) drama-
tist CP/2-3, DD, GT
ASTON, Walter (c.1706-c.39)
actor BD
ASTOR, Adelaide [Mrs. George
Grossmith] (d 1951) English
actress BE*, WWT/14*
ASTOR, George (d 1970 [77])
performer BP/55*
ASTOR, June (d 1967 [49]) per-
former BP/52*
ASTOR, Mary (b 1906) American
actress, writer BE, CB,
TW/1
ASTOR, Richard (b 1927) Ameri-
can talent representative
BE
ASTREDO, Humbert Allen Amer-
ican actor TW/24, 27-28
ASTROP, Maggie (d 1882) singer
EA/83*
ASTRUC, Gabriel (1864-1938)
French impresario ES
ATCHESON, Mr. (fl 1722) actor
BD
ATCHINSON-ELY, Edgar English
comedian CDP
ATCHISON, Prof. D. L. (d 1878)
American aeronaut EA/79*
ATCHLEY, Hooper (d 1943 [57])
actor BE*
ATES, Roscoe (d 1962 [67])
American actor BE*,
BP/46*
ATHAS, Nick (b 1937) American
actor TW/23-24
ATHAY, W. (d 1874) musician
EA/75*
ATHERLEY, Frank actor GRB/
1-3
ATHERSTONE, Weldon [Weldon
Anderson] (d 1910) actor
EA/11*
ATHERTON, Miss (fl 1732-44)
dancer, singer, actress BD

ATHERTON, Miss (fl 1790-91)
actress BD
ATHERTON, Alice [Mrs. Willie
Edouin] (1854-99) actress,
singer CDP, DD
ATHERTON, Daisy (d 1961 [80])
English actress BE*
ATHERTON, Gertrude American
dramatist WWM
ATHERTON, James (d 1898 [54])
animal trainer EA/99*
ATHERTON, Joshua (fl 1745-94?)
musician BD
ATHERTON, Mary (d 1877) EA/79*
ATHERTON, William (b 1947)
American actor TW/28-29
ATHEY, Bertha (d 1897) singer
EA/98*
ATHOL, Katherine Phoebe Mary
see Seymour, Katie
"ATHOL FORBES" see Phillips,
Rev. Forbes Alexander
ATHYA, Cpt. F. see Solomon,
Solomon
ATIENZA, Edward (b 1924) English
actor AAS, BE, TW/16, 19,
22-23, WWT/15-16
ATKIN, Charles (b 1910) English
stage manager, director, actor
BE
ATKIN, David (d 1917) EA/18*
ATKIN, John A. (d 1907 [49])
actor, manager GRB/3
ATKIN, Mrs. John A. see Nelson,
Florence
ATKIN, Nancy (b 1904) English
actress WWT/5-6
ATKINS, Mr. (d 1725?) pit door-
keeper BD
ATKINS, Mr. (fl 1783-92) house
servant BD
ATKINS, Mr. (fl late 18th cent)
actor, manager DD, TD/2
ATKINS, Mrs. (fl 1722?-39) box-
keeper BD
ATKINS, Mrs. (fl 1797) actress,
singer DD
ATKINS, Mrs. (d 1886) actress
EA/87*
ATKINS, Alfred (d 1941 [41]) actor
WWT/14*
ATKINS, Charles (d 1775) dancer,
singer, actor BD
ATKINS, Edward (1819-83) actor
CDP, DD
ATKINS, Eileen (b 1934) English
actress AAS, TW/23-24, 28
WWT/14-16

ATKINS, Eliza (fl 1797-1806)
actress CDP
ATKINS, James (fl 1794) singer
BD
ATKINS, John (d 1671) composer,
violinist BD
ATKINS, Michael (fl 1755-75)
singer, actor BD
ATKINS, Michael (c. 1747-1812)
actor, manager, scene
painter, dancer, composer,
singer BD
ATKINS, Norton (d 1903 [39])
songwriter EA/04*
ATKINS, Robert (1886-1972)
English actor, director
AAS, COC, ES, OC/1-3,
WWT/4-14
ATKINS, Mrs. Selenear (d 1892)
EA/93*
ATKINS, Thomas C. (d 1968
[80]) dramatist BP/53*
ATKINS, Tom American actor
TW/24-26, 28-30
ATKINS, Will (d 1912 [58])
vocal comedian EA/13*
ATKINS, William (1763-1831)
singer, actor BD
ATKINS, Mrs. William [Eliza
Warrell; Mrs. Hill] (fl
1787-1808?) singer, actress
BD, TD/1-2
ATKINSON, Mr. (fl 1747-51)
doorkeeper BD
ATKINSON, Mr. (fl 1750) actor
BD
ATKINSON, Mr. (fl 1781) actor
BD
ATKINSON, Mrs. (d 1887) EA/88*
ATKINSON, Master (fl 1783)
dancer BD
ATKINSON, Miss (fl 1771-82)
actress BD
ATKINSON, Miss [The pig-faced
lady] CDP
ATKINSON, Miss (fl 1853-64)
actress DD
ATKINSON, Alex (d 1962 [45])
dramatist WWT/14*
ATKINSON, Brooks see Atkinson,
Justin Brooks
ATKINSON, Charles H. (d 1909
[72]) minstrel BE*
ATKINSON, Clinton (b 1927)
actor TW/25
ATKINSON, David (b 1921) Cana-
dian actor, singer BE,
TW/12-13, 15-17, 23-30

ATKINSON, Elizabeth (d 1880 [70])
EA/81*
ATKINSON, E. Philip (d 1902 [46])
manager EA/03*
ATKINSON, Frank (d 1963 [72])
performer BE*
ATKINSON, Frederick (d 1879 [36])
proprietor EA/80*
ATKINSON, George Aytoun see
Aytoun, George
ATKINSON, Mrs. George Aytoun
(d 1888) EA/89*
ATKINSON, George H. (d 1955 [75])
press representative BE*
ATKINSON, Harry [Harry Atkinson
Fitts] (b 1866) Australian vari-
ety artist GRB/1
ATKINSON, Howard T. (d 1975
[75]) performer BP/60*
ATKINSON, Isabella (d 1898)
actress EA/99*
ATKINSON, James Henry (d 1916)
actor EA/17*
ATKINSON, John B. (d 1868 [35])
musician EA/69*
ATKINSON, Joseph (1743-1818)
Irish dramatist CP/3, DD,
DNB, GT, TD/1-2
ATKINSON, Justin Brooks (b 1894)
American critic AAS, BE,
CB, COC, ES, HJD, NTH,
OC/1-3, PDT, WWT/6-16
ATKINSON, L. (fl 1848) actor
HAS
ATKINSON, Matthew (b 1963) Amer-
ican actor TW/27
ATKINSON, Peggy [Peggy Longo]
(b 1943) American actress
TW/30
ATKINSON, Rosalind (b 1900) New
Zealand/English actress AAS,
BE, ES, WWT/9-16
ATKINSON, Thomas (1600-39) Eng-
lish dramatist DD, FGF
ATLAS (fl 1787) strong man BD
ATLAS, Leopold (1907-54) Ameri-
can dramatist BE*
ATLEE, Howard (b 1926) American
press representative BE
ATOM, Willie [William Henry War-
ren] (b 1875) English actor
GRB/1
ATTAWAY, Ruth American actress
BE
ATTENBOROUGH, Sir Richard (b
1923) English actor ES, WWT/
10-16
ATTERBURY, Luffman (d 1796)

musician BD, DNB
ATTERIDGE, Harold Richard
(1886-1938) American drama-
tist ES, SR, WWA/1-2,
WWT/5-8
ATTERINO, Sig. (fl 1754) dancer
BD
ATTERSOLL, Mrs. (d 1893 [66])
EA/94*
ATTEWELL, George (fl 1590-95)
actor DA, DD
ATTIE, Paulette (b 1936) Ameri-
can actress TW/27
ATTLE, John C. American actor
TW/24-30
ATTLES, Joseph (b 1903) Amer-
ican actor TW/25-26, 28-29
ATTWELL, Hugh (d 1621) English
actor DA, DD, DNB, ES,
OC/1-3
ATTWELLS, Frank (d 1892 [49])
lessee EA/93*
ATTWOOD, Mr. (fl 1784) vio-
linist BD
ATTWOOD, Miss (fl 1794) musi-
cian BD
ATTWOOD, Francis (b 1775)
musician BD
ATTWOOD, Herbert (d 1911)
EA/12*
ATTWOOD, Thomas (b 1737)
musician BD
ATTWOOD, Thomas (1765-1838)
English singer, composer,
violoncellist BD, DD,
DNB, ES, TD/1-2
ATWATER, Edith (b 1911) Amer-
ican actress BE, TW/3-8,
WWT/10-15
ATWELL, Ben H. (d 1951 [74])
American manager, press
agent WWM
ATWELL, Grace [Mrs. Edwin
Mordant] American actress
WWM
ATWELL, Hugh see Attwell,
Hugh
ATWELL, Roy (1880-1962) Amer-
ican comedian TW/18, WWM
ATWILL, Lionel (1885-1946)
English actor CB, ES, SR,
TW/2, WWA/2, WWT/3-9
ATWOOD, Mr. (fl 1734-35)
house servant? BD
ATWOOD, Alban [Alban Gwynne
Atwood] English actor GRB/
1-4
ATWOOD, Alban Gwynne see

Atwood, Alban
ATWOOD, Donna (b 1926) American
dancer, ice skater CB
ATWOOD, G. C. (fl 1858) American
actor HAS
ATWOOD, Mrs. G. C. (fl 1854)
actress HAS
ATWOOD, John (fl 1735) musician?
BD
ATWOOD, Lorena E. [Mrs. Clar-
ence F. Arper] (d 1947) Amer-
ican actress WWS
ATWOOD, Neill (fl 1850s) comedian
HAS
ATWOOD, Roland (d 1903) actor
EA/04*
AUBE, Mrs. C. L. (d 1894 [23])
EA/95*
AUBER, Daniel François Esprit
(1782-1871) French composer
DD, ES
AUBERJONOIS, René (b 1940)
American actor TW/25-30,
WWT/15-16
AUBERT, Mrs. (fl 1719) dramatist
CP/3, DD
AUBERT, Mons. (fl 1 715-1725)
dancer BD
AUBERT, Isabella (fl 1715-20)
singer, author BD
AUBERT, Jeanne (b 1906) French
actress, singer WWT/8-9
AUBERT, John (fl 1695-1716) oboist
BD
AUBIN, Mrs. (fl 1730) dramatist
CP/3, DD
AUBIN, Mrs. (fl 1724-29) orator
BD
AUBREY, Bob (d 1903) music-hall
performer? EA/04*
AUBREY, Georges (d 1975 [47])
performer BP/60*
AUBREY, Mrs. James see Hen-
derson, Marie
AUBREY, Kate (fl 1874) English
actress DD, OAA/1-2
AUBREY, Lizzie [Mrs. Charles
Dodsworth] (d 1900) EA/01*
AUBREY, Madge [Marjorie Alex-
andra Witham] (1902-70) Eng-
lish actress WWT/8-9
AUBREY, Mrs. W. [Mrs. W.
Aubrey Chandler] (b 1838) Eng-
lish actress GRB/1
AUBUCHON, Jacques (b 1924) Amer-
ican actor TW/9-10
AUCKLAND, Marie [Mrs. Charles
Herrick Jennings] English

actress GRB/1
AUDE, Joseph (1755-1841)
    dramatist BE*
AUDEN, W[ystan] H[ugh] (1907-
    73) English/American drama-
    tist AAS, BE, CB, COC,
    ES, HJD, HP, MD, MH,
    MWD, NTH, OC/1-3, PDT,
    WWT/9-15
AUDLEY, Joseph (d 1896 [65])
    EA/97*
AUDLEY, Maxine (b 1923) English
    actress AAS, WWT/12-16
AUDLEY, Sarah (d 1898) EA/00*
AUDRAN, Alfred (d 1884 [35])
    singer EA/85*
AUDRAN, Edmond (1917-51)
    French dancer ES
AUDRE, Olga [Mrs. Mabel Win-
    penny] (d 1917 [49]) actress
    EA/18*
AUDREY, May (d 1909) actress
    EA/10*
AUER, Florence (d 1962 [82])
    actress TW/18
AUER, Mischa (1905-67) Russian
    actor TW/3, 23
AUERBACH, Artie (d 1957 [54])
    American performer BE*
AUERBACH, George (d 1973
    [68]) dramatist BP/58*
AUERBACH, Leonard stage
    manager BE
AUERBACH-LEVY, William (d
    1961 [75]) caricaturist,
    artist BE*
AUG, Edna (1878-1938) American
    performer BE*, BP/23*
AUGARDE, Adrienne (d 1913)
    actress, singer GRB/1-4,
    WWS, WWT/1
AUGARDE, Amy (1868-1959)
    English actress DD,
    GRB/2-4, WWT/1-9
AUGARDE, Gertrude [Mrs.
    George Henry Trader] (d
    1959) actress BE*
AUGER, Mr. (fl 1783) dancer
    BD
AUGER, Genevieve see Gene-
    vieve
AUGUST, Edwin (d 1964 [81])
    actor, director BE*
AUGUST, Harold (d 1909) clown
    EA/11*
AUGUSTA, Mlle. (1806-1901)
    French dancer CDP, HAS,
    SR

AUGUSTA, Mlle. [Augusta Rabineau]
    (1848-63) American HAS
AUGUSTE, Mlle. M. (fl 1741-53)
    dancer BD
AUGUSTEN, William (fl 1595-97)
    actor DA
AULICK, W. W. (b 1873) American
    press representative WWM
AULISI, Joseph G. costume designer
    WWT/16
AULT, Marie (1870-1951) English
    actress ES, WWT/5-11
AUMONT, Jean-Pierre (b 1909/13)
    French actor TW/5-6, 12, 15,
    19, 26, 28, WWT/15-16
AURELIUS, Mary American actress
    TW/6-7
AURETTI, Anne (1742-54) dancer
    BD, CDP
AURETTI, Janneton (fl 1742-63)
    dancer BD
AURIOL, Mme. (d 1862 [33]) EA/
    72*
AURIOL, Francesca dancer CDP
AURIOL, Jean Baptiste (d 1881
    [76]) clown, acrobat CDP
AURTHUR, Robert Alan (b 1922)
    American dramatist, producer
    BE
AUSTA, Amber [Mrs. William
    Haines] (d 1910 [27]) variety
    comedienne EA/11*
AUSTEN, Mr. (fl 1744) actor BD
AUSTEN-LEE, Cyril (b 1870) Eng-
    lish actor GRB/1-4
AUSTIN, Mr. (fl late 18th cent)
    actor, manager DD
AUSTIN, Mr. (fl 1757-67) scene
    painter, candle snuffer BD
AUSTIN, Mr. (fl 1794) singer BD
AUSTIN, Mr. (fl 1794) violinist
    BD
AUSTIN, Mr. (fl 1830s) English
    actor, musician HAS
AUSTIN, Miss (fl 1766-67) actress
    BD
AUSTIN, Miss (fl 1794) pianist BD
AUSTIN, Miss (fl 1846) singer HAS
AUSTIN, Albert English actor ES
AUSTIN, Alfred (1835-1913) English
    dramatist DNB, ES, WWW/1
AUSTIN, Anslow J. (d 1939) honor-
    ary secretary of Actors'
    Orphanage WWT/14*
AUSTIN, Billy (d 1967 [59]) per-
    former BP/51*
AUSTIN, Charles (1878-1944) Eng-
    lish music-hall performer

COC, OC/1-3
AUSTIN, Charles (fl 1967) actor
TW/24
AUSTIN, Charlotte Stuart (d
1900) EA/01*
AUSTIN, Edgar [William Edgar
Piercey] (d 1893) "The
Lightning Cartoonist" EA/
94*
AUSTIN, Elizabeth (fl 1827) Eng-
lish actress, singer CDP,
DD, HAS
AUSTIN, Emma (d 1900 [62])
EA/01*
AUSTIN, Ernest Collier (d 1916
[23]) composer EA/17*
AUSTIN, F. (d 1904 [36])
comedian EA/05*
AUSTIN, Frederic (1872-1952)
English singer, composer
WWW/5
AUSTIN, Frederick Britten (1885-
1941) English dramatist CB,
WWW/4
AUSTIN, Gene (d 1972 [71])
singer, composer BP/52*,
WWWT/16*
AUSTIN, George (d 1905 [80])
EA/06*
AUSTIN, George [Ross Johnstone
Smith] (b 1879) Indian/
English actor GRB/1
AUSTIN, G. H. (d 1907 [28])
comedian EA/08*
AUSTIN, Henry [né Oates] (d
1912) EA/14*
AUSTIN, Jennie [Mrs. Joseph
Hurtig] (d 1938) performer
BE*
AUSTIN, José (d 1881) circus
performer EA/82*
AUSTIN, Joseph (1735-1821)
actor, manager BD
AUSTIN, J. W. (d 1905) musical
director EA/06*
AUSTIN, Kenneth S. (d 1898)
EA/00*
AUSTIN, Lizzie (d 1892) EA/93*
AUSTIN, Louis Frederick (d
1905) critic, dramatist
WWT/14*
AUSTIN, Lyn (b 1922) American
producer BE
AUSTIN, Mary (d 1880 [75])
EA/81*
AUSTIN, Mary [née Hunter]
(1868-1934) American drama-
tist ES, WWA/1

AUSTIN, Mary Elizabeth (d 1898)
EA/99*
AUSTIN, Mrs. Noel [Louisa Crad-
dock] (d 1869 [21]) burlesque
actress EA/70*
AUSTIN, Rumbo [Thomas William
Rumbo] (d 1917 [59]) EA/18*
AUSTIN, Samuel (d 1886 [77])
EA/87*
AUSTIN, S. H. (d 1918 [62]) EA/
19*
AUSTIN, Sumner Francis (b 1888)
English singer, impresario
ES
AUSTIN-LEIGH, Mrs. see
O'Reilly, Emmie
AUSTIN-LEIGH, Anthony (b 1860)
English actor-manager GRB/1
AUSTIN-MORTIMER (d 1911 [29])
EA/12*
AUSTRAL, Florence (1894-1968)
Australian singer WWW/6
AUSTRALIAN CHILDREN CDP
AVALOS, Luis (b 1946) Cuban actor
TW/26-30
AVEDON, Doe (b 1925) American
TW/5-7
AVELING, Mrs. H. see Willett,
Miss W.
AVELLONI, Casimiro (fl 1721)
musician BD
AVELLONI, Signora Casimiro see
Durastanti, Margherita
AVENEL, Mlle. (d 1857) actress
HAS
AVERAY, Robert (fl 1756) dramatist
CP/2-3, DD, GT
AVERELL, Robert see Averill,
Robert
AVERILL, Robert (d 1913) actor
WWT/14*
AVERY, Brian (b 1940) American
actor TW/23
AVERY, Madge (d 1909) actress
EA/11*
AVERY, Phyllis (b 1924) American
actress BE, TW/2
AVERY, Thomas (fl 1768) master
carpenter BD
AVERY, Val (b 1924) American
actress TW/26
AVES, Dreda (d 1942) American
singer WWA/2
AVES, Rosetta (d 1883 [70]) EA/
84*
AVISON, Charles (1709-70) English
musician, composer BD, DNB
AVOGLIO, Christina Maria (fl

1740-44) Italian singer BD
AVOLA, Little (d 1886 [11])
   EA/87*
"AVOLINA" see Chadwick,
   Sophia
AVONDALE, Mrs. Walter (d
   1886 [35]) EA/87*
AVONE, Thomas L. (d 1912
   [60]) music-hall artist EA/
   13*
AVORY, Mr. (fl 1738) house
   servant? BD
AVRIL, Suzanne [Suzanne Dela-
   roche] French actress
   WWT/2-3
AWAD, Jacqueline (b 1941)
   actress TW/25-26
AXELROD, George (b 1922)
   American dramatist, pro-
   ducer, director AAS, BE,
   CD, MD, MH
AXELROD, Jack (b 1930) Amer-
   ican actor TW/27
AXEN, Robert (fl 1631-35) actor
   DA
AXER, Erwin (b 1917) Polish
   actor ES
AXT, John Mitchell (fl 1748)
   kettle drummer BD
AXT, William L. (d 1959 [71])
   composer, conductor BE*
AXWORTHY, Geoffrey (b 1923)
   English director of drama
   WWT/15-16
AYCKBOURN, Alan (b 1939)
   English dramatist, director,
   actor AAS, CD, WWT/15-
   16
AYED, Aly Ben (d 1972 [40])
   performer BP/56*
AYER, Harriet Hubbard adapter
   DD
AYER, Nat D. (d 1952 [65])
   American composer WWT/
   4-6
AYERS, Agnes (1896-1940)
   American actress BE*
AYERS, Christine American
   actress TW/1
AYERS, David H. (b 1924)
   American executive, direc-
   tor, educator BE
AYERS, Lemuel (1915-55)
   American scene designer,
   costumier, producer ES,
   TW/2-8, 12, WWA/3
AYERS, Shirley Osborn (d 1967
   [50]) actress, producer,

costume designer TW/24
AYERTON, Randle (1869-1940)
   English performer BE*
AYLETT, Mr. (fl 1726-29) gallery
   doorkeeper BD
AYLETT, Mrs. (fl 1716-26) gallery
   doorkeeper BD
AYLEWORTH, Mr. (fl 1721) dancer
   BD
AYLEWORTH, Jonathan (fl 1739)
   musician BD
AYLEWORTH [Joseph?] (fl 1708-10)
   violinist BD
AYLIFF, Mrs. (fl 1690-97) singer,
   actress BD, DD
AYLIFF, Henry Kiell (1872-1949)
   South African actor, producer,
   director AAS, WWT/5-10,
   WWW/4
AYLIFFE, John (1803-47) comedian
   DD
AYLING, W. L. (1816-57) American
   actor HAS
AYLING, Mrs. W. L. (b 1819)
   American actress HAS
AYLMER, Christopher (fl 1662)
   musician BD
AYLMER, David (d 1964 [31]) actor
   BE*, BP/49*
AYLMER, Sir Felix (b 1889) English
   actor AAS, BE, ES, WWT/5-
   15
AYLMER, George (fl 1787-1801)
   singer, actor BD
AYLWARD, Emily (d 1895) EA/96*
AYLWARD, Theodore (1730-1801)
   English singer, organist, com-
   poser BD, DNB
AYLWYN, Jean (1885-1964) Scottish
   actress GRB/4, WWT/1-6
AYMAR, William T. (d 1883) clown
   CDP
AYME [Mr. ?] (fl 1726-27) house
   servant BD
AYME, Marcel (1902-67) French
   dramatist BE, MWD
AYNESWORTH, E. Allan [E. Abbot
   Anderson] (1865-1959) English
   actor DD, DP, EA/96, ES,
   GRB/1-4, WWT/1-11
AYNSCOMB, Mr. (fl 1761-62)
   singer BD
AYNSTEY, Howard (b 1864) English
   musical director GRB/1
AYNSWORTH, John (d 1581) actor
   DA
AYRE, William (fl 1737-40) trans-
   lator CP/1-3, DD, GT

AYRES, Miss (fl 1840s) English
actress HAS
AYRES, Ames (d 1872 [23])
trapezist EA/72*
AYRES [James?] (fl 1729-44)
actor, dramatist? BD,
CP/1-3, DD, GT
AYRES, Matthew (fl 1702) actor
BD
AYRES, Philip Bernard Chinery
(d 1899) EA/00*
AYRES, Robert (d 1968 [54])
performer BP/53*
AYRTON, Edmund (1734-1808)
English organist, composer,
concert organizer, singer
BD, DNB
AYRTON, Edward Edmund (fl
1784-94) singer, organist
BD
AYRTON, Michael (1921-75)
English scene designer ES
AYRTON, Norman (b 1924) Eng-
lish principal of the London
Academy of Music and
Dramatic Art WWT/15-16
AYRTON, Randle (1869-1940)
English actor AAS, WWT/
4-9
AYRTON, Robert (d 1924) actor
BE*, WWT/14*
AYRTON, William (1777-1858)
English singer, music critic,
manager BD, DD, DNB,
ES
AYRTON, William Francis Mor-
rall (1778-1850) English
singer, organist BD, DD
AYRTOUN, Margaret (fl 1884)
actress CDP, DD
AYSCOUGH, Cpt. George Edward
(d 1779) dramatist CDP,
CP/3, DD, DNB
AYSCOUGH, Samuel (1745-1804)
scholar DD, DNB
AYTON, Fanny (b 1806?) English
singer CDP, ES
AYTON, Richard (1786-1823)
English dramatist DD, DNB
AYTOUN, George [George Aytoun
Atkinson] Scottish dramatic
and variety agent GRB/1
AYTOUN, Mrs. George see
Sipple, Rosina
AYTOUN, William Edmonstoune
(1813-65) dramatist DD,
DNB
AZA, Bert (d 1953 [70]) agent

WWT/14*
AZITO, (b 1948) American actor
TW/30
AZNAVOUR, Charles (b 1924)
French singer, composer, actor
CB
AZTEC CHILDREN [Bartola (b 1840);
Maximo (b 1832)] CDP, HAS
AZUMA IV, Tokuho Japanese dancer
CB
AZZARA, Candy (b 1945) American
actress TW/25-26

- B -

B., G. (fl 1704) dramatist CP/3
B., H. H. (fl 1659) dramatist
CP/3
B., J. dramatist CP/1
B., J. (fl 1809) dramatist CP/3
B., P. see Belon, Peter
B., R. [?=Richard Bower, q.v.]
English dramatist FGF
B., W. (fl 1717-18) dramatist
CP/1-3
BABB, Mrs. (fl 1706-07) actress
BD
BABBINI, Matteo (1754-1816) Italian
singer BD
BABCOCK, Barbara actress TW/26
BABCOCK, Edward Chester see
Van Heusen, James
BABEL, Charles (fl 1697-1716)
instrumentalist BD
BABEL, Isaak (1894-1941) Russian
dramatist MWD
BABEL, William (c.1690-1723)
English composer, instrumental-
ist BD
BABER, Jane (d 1873) actress
EA/74*
BABHAM, Christopher (fl 1632)
English actor DA
BABILEE, Jean [né Guttman] (b
1923) French dancer, choreog-
rapher ES
BABIN, Victor (d 1972 [63]) com-
poser/lyricist BP/56*
BABNIGG, Emma (d 1904 [80])
singer EA/05*
"BABY BENSON" see Fish, Mar-
guerite
BACALL, Lauren [Betty Joan
Perske] (b 1924) American
actress AAS, BE, CB, ES,
TW/22-25, 27-28, WWT/15-16
BACCALA, Dona (b 1945) American

actress TW/22-23
BACCALONI, Salvatore (1900-69)
Italian singer CB, TW/26,
WWA/5
BACCELLI, Giovanna (b 1801)
Italian dancer BD, CDP
BACCELY, Mrs. (b.c.1730)
English actress SR
BACCHELLI, Signorina see
Corri, Signora Domenico
BACCHUS, Mrs. Reginald see
Bowman, Isa
BACH, Fernand (d 1953 [72])
comedian WWT/14*
BACH, Johann Christian (1735-82)
German composer, instru-
mentalist, entrepreneur
BD, ES
BACH, Johann Christoph (b 1764)
German musician, teacher
BD
BACH, Leonhard Emil (1849-
1902) German musician,
composer ES
BACH, Dr. Otto (d 1893 [60])
conductor EA/94*
BACH, Reginald (1886-1941)
English actor, producer
CB, WWT/4-9
BACHARACH, Burt (b 1929)
American composer CB
BACHE, Walter (d 1888 [45])
pianist EA/89*
BACKER, George (d 1974 [70s])
dramatist BP/58*
BACKINGTON, Miss (fl 1734)
actress BD
BACKSTEAD, Will see Bark-
sted, William
BACKSTER, Richard see
Baxter, Richard
BACKUS, Charles (1831-83)
American minstrel CDP,
HAS, SR
BACKUS, E. Y. (d 1914 [62])
American actor, stage mana-
ger BE*
BACKUS, George (1857-1939)
American actor, dramatist
WWM
BACKUS, Richard (b 1945)
American actor TW/27-30,
WWT/16
BACLANOVA, Olga (1899-1974)
Russian actress ES, TW/
2-3, 6-7, WWT/8-10
BACON, Mr. (fl 1784) singer
BD

BACON, Catherine (b 1947) Ameri-
can actress TW/26, 28
BACON, Charles (d 1886) sculptor
EA/87*
BACON, David Gaspar, Jr. (1914-
42) American actor BE*
BACON, Delia Salter (1811-59)
American dramatist, writer
DD, HJD, WWA/H
BACON, Elizabeth see Poole,
Elizabeth
BACON, Ernst (b 1898) American
composer, pianist, conductor
ES
BACON, Faith (d 1956 ⌈c.45])
performer BE*
BACON, Sir Francis (1561-1626)
English dramatist FGF, NTH
BACON, Frank (1864-1922) Ameri-
can actor, dramatist, manager
COC, DAB, ES, MWD, NTH,
OC/1-3, SR, WWA/1, WWT/4
BACON, James (fl 1795) dramatist
CP/3, DD
BACON, James (1821-58) American
actor HAS, SR
BACON, Jane (d 1956 ⌈89]) actress
BE*
BACON, Jane (b 1894/95) English
actress ES, WWT/6-9
BACON, Job [or John] (fl 1624-25)
actor DA
BACON, John see Bacon, Job
BACON, Lloyd (b 1890) American
actor ES
BACON, Mai (b 1897) English
actress WWT/5-14
BACON, Max (d 1969 [65]) per-
former BP/54*
BACON, Dr. Phanuel (1700-83)
English dramatist CP/2-3,
DD, DNB, GT
BACON, Walter Scott (d 1973 [82])
producer/director/choreographer
BP/58*
BADA, Angelo (1875-1941) Italian
singer CB
BADCOCK, [Mr. ?] (fl 1796-99)
house servant BD
BADDELEY, Jr. (fl 1781) actor
BD
BADDELEY, Angela (1904-76) Eng-
lish actress AAS, COC, ES,
WWT/6-16
BADDELEY, Clinton (d 1918 [46])
EA/19*
BADDELEY, Hermione (b 1906)
English actress AAS, BE,

COC, TW/18-19, 24-25,
WWT/5-16
BADDELEY, Richard (fl 1661-62)
sub-treasurer BD
BADDELEY, Robert (1732-94)
English actor BD, CDP,
COC, DD, DNB, ES, GT,
OC/1-3, TD/1-2
BADDELEY, Mrs. Robert see
Baddeley, Sophia
BADDELEY, Sophia ⌈Mrs. Robert
Baddeley; née Snow] (1745-
86) English actress BD,
CDP, DD, DNB, OC/1-3,
TD/1-2
BADDELEY, W. St. Clair (fl
1878-79) dramatist DD
BADDOW (d 1911) ventriloquist
EA/13*
BADEL, Alan Fernand (b 1923)
English actor, director,
producer AAS, BE, COC,
ES, TW/20, WWT/11-16
BADEL, Sarah (b 1943) English
actress WWT/15-16
BADER, Merwin O. (d 1975
⌈80]) theatre builder BP/
60*
BADERNA, Maria (b 1830)
Italian dancer ES
BADHAM, Stephen see Arlen,
Stephen
BADIA, Leopold (b 1905) Spanish
actor TW/3
BADIA, Luigi (1819-99) Italian
composer, singing master
ES
BADIALI, Cesare (1810-65)
Italian singer CDP, ES,
HAS
BADILAI, Signora Frederic
(b c.1817) actress, singer
SR
BADINI, Signora (fl 1792) singer
BD
BADINI, Carlo Francesco (fl
1770-93) Italian librettist,
manager BD
BADLEY, Robert A. (1865-
1918) producer SR
BADLOWE, Richard (fl 1594)
actor DA
BADY, Berthe (d 1921 [49])
actress WWT/14*
BAER, Mr. (fl 1774) clarinetist
BD
BAER, Mrs. Arthur see
Andrews, Louise

BAER, Marian (b 1926) American
actress TW/29
BAER, Max (1909-59) American
boxer, performer TW/16
BAER, Richard see Barr, Richard
BAERWITZ, Sam (d 1974 ⌈82])
producer/director/choreographer
BP/59*
BAETTY, Mr. (fl 1795-97) house
servant? BD
BAFF, Reggie (b 1949) American
actress TW/26
BAFF, Regina American actress
TW/30
BAGDASARIAN, Ross S. (d 1972
[52]) composer/lyricist BP/56*
BAGG, Mr. (fl 1767-69) doorkeeper
BD
BAGGOT, King (1880-1948) Ameri-
can actor ES, TW/5
BAGGS, Zachary (fl 1685-1710)
treasurer BD
BAGLEY, Ben (b 1933) American
producer, director BE
BAGLEY, Caroline ⌈Mrs. Edgar
Bagley] (d 1908) EA/09*
BAGLEY, Mrs. Edgar see Bagley,
Caroline
BAGLEY, Eleanore (b 1924) Amer-
ican actress TW/4
BAGLEY, Sam (d 1968 [65]) per-
former BP/53*
BAGNAGE, Mr. (fl 1716-17) pit-
keeper BD
BAGNAL, Mrs. (fl 1764-65) candle-
woman BD
BAGNALL, Mr. (fl 1734) harpsi-
chordist BD
BAGNALL, Joshua L. (d 1894 [69])
EA/95*
BAGNALL, Sam (d 1885) singer,
composer CDP
BAGNALL, Walter Wilcock (d 1885
⌈33]) EA/86*
BAGNOLD, Enid [Lady Roderick
Jones] (b 1889) English drama-
tist AAS, BE, CB, CD, COC,
MD, MWD, PDT, WWT/14-16
BAGNOLESI, Anna [Giovanni Battista
Pinacci] (fl 1731-32) singer
BD
BAGOT, A. G. (fl 1885-90) drama-
tist DD
BAGSTARE, Richard (fl 1636) actor
DA
BAGWELL, Marsha (b 1946) Amer-
ican actress TW/30
BAHN, Chester B. (d 1962 [68])

English journalist, editor
BE*
BAHR-MILDENBURG, Anna (1872-
1947) Austrian singer ES
BAILDON, Joseph (1727-74) Eng-
lish composer, organist,
singer BD
BAILDON, Thomas (d 1760)
English singer, composer
BD
BAILDON, Thomas (d 1762) Eng-
lish singer, composer BD
BAILEY, Mr. (fl 1800) actor
HAS
BAILEY, Mrs. [née Watson]
(b 1815) English actress
HAS
BAILEY, Abraham (fl 1667) drama-
tist CP/1-3, DD
BAILEY, Alison (d 1965 [51])
performer BP/49*
BAILEY, Bill (d 1966 [80])
performer BP/50*
BAILEY, Bryan (1922-60) Eng-
lish actor, manager COC,
OC/3
BAILEY, Charles (d 1903 [36])
EA/04*
BAILEY, Consuela (fl 1905-11)
actress WWM
BAILEY, Francis (d 1902 [65])
EA/03*
BAILEY, Frankie (1859-1953)
American showgirl TW/10
BAILEY, Frank J. (d 1971 [32])
producer/director/choreog-
rapher BP/56*
BAILEY, Gordon (b 1875) English
actor GRB/1-2, WWT/2-6
BAILEY, Hackaliah (1770-1845)
circus performer SR
BAILEY, H. C. (1878-1961)
English critic WWT/2-3
BAILEY, Henry (d 1893 [75])
marionette proprietor EA/94*
BAILEY, Prof. James (d 1890
[58]) EA/92*
BAILEY, James Anthony (1847-
1906) American circus owner
and manager, showman
CDP, DAB, ES, SR, WWA/1
BAILEY, Dr. John (d 1746) Eng-
lish dramatist CP/1
BAILEY, John Cann (1864-1931)
critic DNB
BAILEY, Joseph (d 1972 [61])
lawyer BP/57*
BAILEY, Lilian [Mrs. Georg

Henschel] (1860-1901) singer
CDP
BAILEY, Margery (1891-1963)
American scholar BE*
BAILEY, Mary [née Nellie de Vere]
(d 1878 [25]) EA/79*
BAILEY, Mary (d 1902) EA/04*
BAILEY, Mildred (d 1951 [48])
American singer BE*
BAILEY, Pearl (b 1918) American
actress, singer BE, CB,
TW/2, 6-8, 11-12, 24-26,
WWT/15-16
BAILEY, Robin (b 1919) English
actor AAS, BE, TW/20, WWT/
11-16
BAILEY, Ruth American producer,
actress BE
BAILEY, Samuel (fl 1694-1707)
actor BD
BAILEY, Mrs. Thomas [Charlotte
Watson] (b 1815) actress
CDP, SR
BAILEY, William [William O'Reilly]
(d 1791) English actor, manager
BD
BAILEY, William (d 1927 [82])
manager WWT/14*
BAILEY, Mrs. William [Mrs. Wil-
liam O'Reilly; née Mary Sophia
Arnold] (fl 1778-82) actress,
singer BD
BAILEY, William H. (b 1826)
American actor HAS
BAILEY, William N. (d 1962 [76])
American director, actor BE*
BAILHE, Edilou see Claire, Ludi
BAILLIE, Joanna (1762-1851) Scot-
tish dramatist CDP, CP/3,
DD, DNB, ES, HP
BAILLIE, John (fl 1736) Scottish
lawyer, dramatist CP/3, DD
BAILLIE, Dr. John (d 1743) drama-
tist CP/2-3, DD, GT
BAILY, Mrs. (fl 1742-46) actress
BD
BAILY, Georgina F. [Mrs. Har-
rington Baily] (d 1909 [54])
manager EA/11*
BAILY, Harrington (d 1908) mana-
ger, agent EA/10*, GRB/3*
BAILY, Mrs. Harrington see
Baily, Georgina F.
BAIN, Conrad (b 1923) Canadian
actor BE, TW/14, 21-30,
WWT/15-16
BAIN, Donald (b 1922) English actor
TW/3

BAIN, W. J. (d 1895) elocution-
ist EA/96*
BAINBRIDGE, A. E. (fl 1900)
manager, agent SR
BAINBRIDGE, Cecil J. W. (d
1944) manager WWT/14*
BAINBRIDGE, Clement actor,
manager SR
BAINBRIDGE, Julian (d 1969
[91]) performer BP/53*
BAINBRIDGE, Mrs. Richard see
Fayne, Kate
BAINBRIDGE, Richard Bousfield
(d 1904) lessee EA/05*,
WWT/14*
BAINES, Florence (1877-1918)
English actress GRB/2-4,
WWT/1
BAINES, Mary Lavinia (d 1910
[59]) actress EA/11*
BAINES, Richard Thomas jour-
nalist GRB/2-3
BAINI, Cecilia (fl 1763-64) singer
BD
BAINTER, Fay (1892-1968) Amer-
ican actress BE, ES, TW/
2-16, 24, WWA/5, WWT/4-14
BAINTON, Edgar Leslie (b 1880)
English composer ES
BAIRD, Bill (b 1904) American
puppeteer, writer, designer
BE, CB, ES
BAIRD, Claribel (b 1904) Amer-
ican educator, director,
actress BE, TW/22-23
BAIRD, Cora (1912-67) American
puppeteer, actress BE, CB,
TW/24, WWA/5
BAIRD, Dorothea [Mrs. H. B.
Irving] (1875-1933) English
actress CDP, COC, GRB/
1-4, OC/1-3, WWS, WWT/
1-6, WWW/3
BAIRD, Ethel English actress
WWT/3-7
BAIRD, Leah (d 1971 [60]) per-
former BP/56*
BAIRD, Stewart (d 1947 [66])
American singer, actress
TW/4
BAIRD, Tom (d 1976) composer/
lyricist BP/60*
BAIRNSFATHER, Bruce (1887-
1959) English dramatist
BE*
BAJOR, Gisi (d 1951 [55])
actress WWT/14*
BAKER, Mr. (fl 1683) actor BD

BAKER, Mr. (fl 1729-30) singer
BD
BAKER, Mr. (fl 1732) dancer, actor
BD
BAKER, Mr. (fl 1740) actor BD
BAKER, Mr. (fl 1742-45) pit door-
keeper BD
BAKER, Mr. (fl 1744-45) singer
BD
BAKER, Mr. (fl 1749-50) singer
BD
BAKER, Mr. (fl 1752-57) house
servant BD
BAKER, Mr. (fl 1760-61) box-office
keeper BD
BAKER, Mr. (fl 1760-69?) dancer,
actor BD
BAKER, Mr. (fl 1770) singer BD
BAKER, Mr. (fl 1775) actor BD
BAKER, Mr. (fl 1776-77) actor
BD
BAKER, Mr. (fl 1794) actor CDP
BAKER, Mr. (fl 1820) actor DD
BAKER, Mr. (fl 1821) actor CDP
BAKER, Mr. (d 1897 [41]) entre-
preneur EA/98*
BAKER, Mrs. (d 1760?) singer,
actress, dancer BD
BAKER, Mrs. (fl 1770) puppeteer
BD
BAKER, Mrs. (fl 1780) actress
BD
BAKER, Mrs. (b 1800) English
actress BS
BAKER, Mrs. manager, dancer
DD
BAKER, Mrs. (d 1899 [87]) custo-
dian of Anne Hathaway's cottage
EA/00*
BAKER, Miss (fl 1746-47) dancer
BD
BAKER, [Miss?] (fl 1766-67)
singer BD
BAKER, Miss (fl 1828) see
Nichols, Mrs. Horace F.
BAKER, Alexina [Mrs. John Lewis]
(1821-87) American actress
CDP, DD, HAS, NYM, SR
BAKER, Mrs. Alfred see Wright,
Nelly
BAKER, Ann (1761-1817) actress
BD
BAKER, Arthur (d 1911 [31]) per-
former EA/12*
BAKER, Bartholomew (fl 1615?-
1679) actor BD
BAKER, Basil (d 1859 [54]) come-
dian EA/72*, WWT/14*

BAKER, Belle (d 1957 [67])
American vaudevillian
TW/13
BAKER, Benjamin (fl 1730-36)
kettle-drummer BD
BAKER, Benjamin A. (1818-90)
American actor, manager,
dramatist CDP, COC,
DAB, DD, ES, HAS, HJD,
OC/1-3, SR
BAKER, Benny (b 1907) Ameri-
can actor TW/28-30,
WWT/10-11
BAKER, Berkley (fl 1775-1805)
actor, manager BD, TD/1-2
BAKER, Bertha Kunz (d 1943)
American dramatic reader
WWA/2
BAKER, Blanche CDP
BAKER, Carroll (b 1931) Amer-
ican actress BE, ES,
TW/10, 12-13, 19
BAKER, Charles (fl 1758-70)
gallery office keeper BD
BAKER, Charles (d 1844)
comedian EA/72*
BAKER, Clara L. [Mrs. George
L. Baker] (d 1858) singer?
HAS
BAKER, Mrs. C. W. see
Baker, Matilda
BAKER, Daniel E. (d 1939 [78])
American performer BE*
BAKER, David (b 1926) Ameri-
can composer, pianist BE
BAKER, David Lionel Erskine
(1730-67?) English actor,
dramatist, historian BD,
CDP, CP/2-3, DD, DNB,
ES, GT, TD/1-2
BAKER, Mrs. David Lionel
Erskine [née Elizabeth Clen-
don] (d 1778) English actress
BD
BAKER, Dorothy (1907-68) Amer-
ican dramatist BE, CB,
HJD, WWA/5
BAKER, Elizabeth (1879-1962)
English dramatist ES,
NTH, WWT/2-11
BAKER, Ellis (b 1898) American
actor TW/2-3, 6-7
BAKER, Elsie (d 1971 [78]) per-
former BP/56*
BAKER, Emma Mabella singer
CDP
BAKER, Fay American actress
TW/3

BAKER, Fletcher (d 1879) singer,
composer EA/80*
BAKER, Frances (fl 1677) actress
BD
BAKER, Francis (fl 1670-90) actor
BD
BAKER, Frank (d 1909 [23]) proper-
ty master EA/10*
BAKER, Frederick (d 1888) singer,
actor EA/89*
BAKER, George (1773?-1847) Eng-
lish musician, composer BD,
DNB
BAKER, George (1885-1976) English
actor, singer, script-writer
WWT/9-15
BAKER, George (b 1931) Bulgarian/
English actor, director, pro-
ducer TW/15, WWT/14-16
BAKER, George E. singer CDP
BAKER, Mrs. George L. see
Baker, Clara L.
BAKER, George Pierce (1866-1935)
American dramatist, scholar
COC, DAB, ES, HJD, MH,
NTH, OC/1-3, WWT/6-7
BAKER, G. T. Howard, Jr. (d
1886) performer EA/88*
BAKER, Harry (fl 1592) actor DA
BAKER, Henrietta see Chanfrau,
Henrietta
BAKER, Henry Barton (d 1906 [60])
historian, actor DD
BAKER, Henry Chichester see
Chichester, Henry
BAKER, Howard (d 1907 [53]) EA/
08*
BAKER, Howard (b 1905) American
dramatist, educator BE
BAKER, Iris (b 1901) Indian/English
actress ES, WWT/7-13
BAKER, Jane King (d 1971 [75])
performer BP/56*
BAKER, Janet (b 1933) English
singer CB
BAKER, Job (fl 1709-44) kettle-
drummer BD
BAKER, John (d 1679) trumpeter
BD
BAKER, John E. (d 1966) director
BP/51*
BAKER, [John] Lewis (d 1873 [50])
American actor CDP, HAS,
SR, WWA/H
BAKER, Josephine (1906-75) Amer-
ican performer BE, CB, ES,
SR, WWT/15-16
BAKER, Josephine Turck (d 1942)

American dramatist WWA/2
BAKER, J. S. (fl 1787-1800)
actor, manager BD
BAKER, J. S. (b 1830) American
actor HAS, SR
BAKER, Mrs. J. S. (fl 1785-
1800) actress, singer, dancer
BD
BAKER, Mrs. J. S. [née Porter]
(fl 1838) American actress
HAS, SR
BAKER, Katherine (d 1729)
actress BD
BAKER, Kenny (b 1912) Ameri-
can singer, actor BE
BAKER, Lee (1880-1948) Amer-
ican actor ES, SR, TW/4,
WWT/4-10
BAKER, Lenny (b 1945) Amer-
ican actor TW/25-27, 30
BAKER, Lewis see Baker,
John Lewis
BAKER, Lewis J. (d 1962 [79])
Russian/American performer
BE*
BAKER, Mark (b 1946) American
actor TW/28-30
BAKER, Matilda [Mrs. C. W.
Baker] (b 1801) actress
CDP, OX
BAKER, Norah see Baring,
Norah
BAKER, Paul (b 1911) American
producer, director, educator
BE
BAKER, Peter F. (fl 1886)
actor CDP, SR
BAKER, Phil (1898-1963) Amer-
ican comedian SR, TW/20,
WWA/4
BAKER, R. (fl 1737) see
Baker, Robert
BAKER, Ray (d 1976 [35]) pro-
ducer/director/choreographer
BP/60*
BAKER, Richard (fl 1778-79)
singer, actor BD
BAKER, Mrs. Richard see
D'Elmar, Camille
BAKER, Robert (fl 1574) actor
DA
BAKER, Robert (fl 1737) drama-
tist CP/2-3, DD, GT
BAKER, Sarah [née Wakelin]
(1736-1816) English pro-
prietor, manager, dancer,
actress BD, COC, OC/2-3
BAKER, Sir Stanley (1928-76)

Welsh actor ES, TW/8
BAKER, Tarkington (d 1924 [45])
press representative, critic
BE*, BP/8*
BAKER, Thomas (fl 1700-09) Eng-
lish dramatist CP/1-3, DD,
DNB, GT, TD/1-2
BAKER, Thomas (c. 1686-1745)
singer BD
BAKER, Thomas (fl 1745-85?) act-
or, singer, dancer BD
BAKER, Thomas (c. 1765-1801)
actor, singer BD, TD/1-2
BAKER, Thomas (fl 1832-50) Eng-
lish musician, conductor, com-
poser CDP, HAS, SR
BAKER, Mrs. Thomas [née Eliza-
beth Miller] (fl 1761-92)
actress, singer, dancer BD
BAKER, Walter see Bray, Walter
BAKER, W. F. (d 1899 [60])
singer EA/00*
BAKER, William (fl 1784-96) singer
BD
BAKER, William (d 1879 [42])
singer EA/80*
BAKER, William K. (d 1976 [50])
critic BP/60*
BAKER, W. J. see Fleming,
William J.
BAKER, Word (b 1923) American
producer, director BE
BAKEWELL, [Mary] (fl 1771-87)
actress BD
BAKLANOFF, Georges (1882-1938)
Russian singer WWA/1
BAKST, Léon (1866-1924) Russian
costume designer COC
BALABAN, A. J. (d 1962 [73])
American executive BE*
BALABAN, Emanuel (1895-1973)
American conductor WWA/5
BALABAN, Robert (b 1945) Amer-
ican actor TW/24-26, 28-29
BALANCHINE, George (b 1904)
Russian/American choreograph-
er BE, CB, ES, TW/2-8,
WWT/10-16
BALATRI, Filippo (1676-1756)
Italian singer BD
BALBI, Rosina (fl 1748-60) Italian
dancer BD
BALBIRNIE, Robert T. G. de Vaux
see Gore, Ivan Pat
BALCH, Marston (b 1901) American
educator, director BE
BALDASSARI, Benedetto (fl 1712-
25) singer BD

BALDAUFF, Patrick (b 1938)
American actor TW/24, 26
BALDERSTON, John Lloyd (1889-
1954) American dramatist
ES, MD, MH, MWD, NTH,
SR, WWT/7-11, WWW/5
BALDI, Antonio (fl 1726-28)
Italian singer BD, ES
BALDIE, Dacre (d 1907 [70])
actor EA/08*, GRB/3*
BALDUCCI, Sig. (fl 1739) ma-
chinist BD
BALDWIN, Mr. (fl 1774-75)
actor BD
BALDWIN, Annie actress EA/97
BALDWIN, Caroline (d 1896)
EA/98*
BALDWIN, Earl (d 1970 [69])
dramatist BP/55*
BALDWIN, J. (fl 1783-94)
music-porter, musician?
BD
BALDWIN, James Arthur (b
1924) American dramatist
CD, CH, ES, HJD, MH,
MWD
BALDWIN, Joseph (1787-1820)
English actor DD, HAS, SR
BALDWIN, Joseph B. (b 1918)
American educator, drama-
tist BE
BALDWIN, Mary (fl 1703-06)
singer BD
BALDWIN, Robert (d 1866)
actor HAS
BALDWIN, Silas (1825-67)
American contortionist,
musician, juggler HAS, SR
BALDWIN, Thomas Scott (b
1857) American acrobat
SR
BALE, Edwin (d 1912) EA/13*
BALE, Emma (d 1897 [43])
EA/99*
BALE, Frank (d 1899) music-
hall performer EA/01*
BALE, John (1495-1563) Irish
dramatist CP/1-3, DD,
ES, FGF, HP, MH, OC/1-3
BALE, W. (d 1916) EA/17*
BALELLI, Antonio (fl 1786-89)
Italian singer BD
BALENTYNE, James [or James
Valentine] (d 1889) wire-
walker, juggler EA/90*
BALES, William (b 1915) Ameri-
can dancer, choreographer,
dance master ES

BALETTI, Sig. (fl 1755-56) dancer
BD
BALFE, Lizzie (d 1890) EA/91*
BALFE, Louise (b 1864) actress,
singer SR
BALFE, Michael William (1808-70)
Irish composer, singer CDP,
DD, DNB, ES, SR
BALFE, Victoria [Duchesse de
Frias] (d 1871 [34]) singer
CDP
BALFOUR, Betty (b 1903) English
actress ES
BALFOUR, Ethel [Ethel Alice Win-
ton] (b 1885) English actress
GRB/1
BALFOUR, Thomas (b 1849) English
actor OAA/2
BALFOUR, William (d 1964 [89])
actor BE*
BALHATCHET, Bob (b 1944) Amer-
ican actor TW/30
BALICOURT, Simon (fl 1735-48)
flutist BD
BALIEFF, Nikita (1877-1936)
Russian compere, cabaret de-
viser COC, OC/1-3
BALIN, Ina (b 1937) American
actress BE, TW/14-17
BALIN, Mireille (d 1968 [59]) per-
former BP/53*
BALL, Mr. (fl 1799-1804) house
servant BD
BALL, Mrs. (fl 1789) singer BD
BALL, Miss (fl 1781) actress BD
BALL, Miss see Bass, Mrs.
Charles
BALL, Donald I. (d 1974 [69])
producer/director/choreographer
BP/58*
BALL, Edmund (fl 1778) dramatist
CP/3, DD
BALL, Edward see Fitzball, Ed-
ward
BALL, Eleanor [Mrs. Meredith
Ball] (d 1903) EA/05*
BALL, Ernest R. (1878-1927)
American composer SR, WWM
BALL, Frank see Thornton,
Frank
BALL, Harry [William Henry
Powles] (d 1888) singer EA/89*
BALL, James (d 1889) proprietor
EA/90*
BALL, J. H. (d 1885) EA/86*
BALL, J. Meredith (d 1915 [77])
conductor, composer BE*
BALL, Joseph (d 1906)

proprietor EA/07*
BALL, Lewis (1820-1905) Welsh
actor DD, GRB/1
BALL, Mrs. Lewis see Ball,
Margaret
BALL, Lucille (b 1911) Ameri-
can actress, producer BE,
CB
BALL, Margaret [Mrs. Lewis
Ball] (d 1880 [56]) EA/81*
BALL, Matilda Powles (d 1901
[58]) EA/02*
BALL, Mrs. Meredith see
Ball, Eleanor
BALL, Robert Hamilton (b 1902)
American educator, historian
BE
BALL, Sarah (d 1904) EA/05*
BALL, Suzan (1933-55) American
actress BE*
BALL, Mr. W. (d. 1869 [84])
composer EA/70*
BALL, W. B. Codrington see
Alexander, S. King
BALL, Wilfred (d 1897 [49])
musical director EA/98*
BALL, William (b 1931) Amer-
ican actor, director, pro-
ducer AAS, BE, CB, ES,
WWT/15-16
BALLANGER, G. N. (d 1916
[48]) American manager
EA/17*
BALLANTINE, Edward (d 1971
[84]) composer/lyricist
BP/56*
BALLANTINE, E. J. (d 1968
[80]) actor, director TW/25
BALLANTYNE, Paul (b 1909)
American actor BE, TW/
9-20, 25, 27, WWT/15-16
BALLARD, Sig. (fl 1752-53)
Italian animal trainer BD
BALLARD, Florence (d 1976
[32]) performer BP/60*
BALLARD, Frederick (1884-1957)
American dramatist ES
BALLARD, J. G. dramatist SR
BALLARD, Jonathan (fl 1755-62)
treasurer BD
BALLARD, Kaye (b 1926) Amer-
ican actress, singer BE,
CB, TW/9, 11-12, 17-23,
30, WWT/16
BALLARD, Lucinda (b 1908)
American designer BE,
ES, TW/2-8
BALLARD, Sarah see Terry,

Sarah Ballard
BALLARD, Thomas (d 1908) scene
artist EA/09*
BALLARINI, Mr. (fl 1778) puppet-
show man BD
BALLERINO, Virginia (d 1974)
performer BP/58*
"BALLETINO, Sig." (fl 1753-54)
dancer? BD
"BALLETINO, Signora" (fl 1753-54)
dancer? BD
BALLEW, Leighton M. (b 1916)
American educator BE
BALLIN, Hugo (d 1956 [76]) Ameri-
can producer, director, painter
BE*, BP/41*
BALLIN, Mrs. Hugo Ballin see
Ballin, Mabel
BALLIN, Mabel [Mrs. Hugo Ballin]
(d 1958 [73]) American actress
BE*
BALLOCH, George S. (d 1971 [46])
producer/director/choreographer
BP/56*
BALLS (fl 1631) actor DA
BALLS, Mrs. CDP
BALLS, John S. (1799-1844) English
actor CDP, DD, HAS, SR
BALMAIN, Andrew (d 1893 [75])
EA/94*
BALMAIN, Rollo (186?-1920) Scot-
tish actor, manager GRB/1-4
BALMAIN, Mrs. Rollo see
Mignon, Sara
BALMAT, Mr. (fl 1785-87) acrobat
BD
BALMER, Edwin (1883-1959) Amer-
ican writer WWA/3
BALMFORTH, [John?] (fl 1784)
singer BD
BALON, Jean (fl 1698-99) dancer
BD
BALPH, Mme. (fl 1784) equestri-
enne BD
BALSAM, Martin (b 1919) American
actor AAS, BE, TW/12-14,
22-24, WWT/15-16
BALSHAW, Jarvis (fl 1794) singer
BD
BALSHAW, Peter (fl 1794) singer
BD
BALTHAZAR, Mr. (fl 1760-63)
dancer BD
BALTIMORE, Jake (d 1898) singer
EA/99*
BALTZAR, Thomas (c.1630-63)
Swedish violinist BD, DNB
BAMATTRE, Martha (d 1970 [78])

performer BP/55*
BAMBER, Willis (d 1878) master
carpenter EA/79*
BAMBERGER, Theron (d 1953
[59]) American producer,
press agent TW/10
BAMBOSCHEK, Giuseppe (1890/
91-1969) Italian conductor
ES, WWA/5
BAMBRIDGE, Mr. (fl 1731-43)
actor BD
BAMBRIDGE, Mrs. (fl 1731-38)
actress BD
BAMBRIDGE, Mrs. (fl 1749)
house servant? BD
BAMBRIDGE, Mrs. (fl 1757-67)
dancer BD
BAMBRIDGE, Thomas (d 1867
[82]) musician EA/68*
BAMBRIDGE, William Herbert
(d 1917 [28]) singer, actor
EA/18*
BAMFIELD, Mr. (fl 1671) actor,
dancer BD
BAMFIELD, Edward (1732-68)
giant BD
BAMFORD, Mr. (fl 1847) actor
HAS
BAMPTON, Rose (b 1908) Amer-
ican singer ES
BANASTER, Gilbert (fl 1478-84?)
master of the Chapel Royal
DA
"BANBAREGINES, Sig." (fl 1752-
54) dancer BD
BANBERRY, Mr. (fl 1746) actor,
singer, dancer BD
BANBURY, Frith (b 1912) Eng-
lish director, actor, manager
AAS, COC, ES, WWT/10-16
BANCKER, James W. (1790-1866)
American? equestrian mana-
ger, actor, circus performer
HAS, SR
BANCROFT, Anne [née Italiano]
(b 1931) American actress
AAS, BE, CB, ES, TW/14-
22, 24-25, WWT/13-16
BANCROFT, Charles (d 1969
[58]) performer BP/54*
BANCROFT, George (1882-1956)
American actor ES, TW/13
BANCROFT, George P. see
Pleydell, George
BANCROFT, John (d 1969) Eng-
lish dramatist CP/1-3, DD,
GT
BANCROFT, Lady Marie [Marie

Effie Wilton] (1839-1921) Eng-
lish actress, manager CDP,
COC, DD, DNB, ES, GRB/1-4,
NTH, OAA/1-2, OC/1-3, SR,
WWT/1-3, WWW/2
BANCROFT, Sir Squire Bancroft
(1841-1926) English actor,
manager CDP, COC, DD,
DNB, DP, ES, GRB/1-4,
OAA/1-2, OC/1-3, WWT/1-5,
WWW/2
BAND, Thomas see Bond, Thomas
BANDEL, Emma Frederick (d 1969
[3]) performer BP/54*
BANDIERA, Anna (fl 1756) singer
BD
BANDMANN, Daniel Edward (1840-
1905) German actor CDP, DD,
HAS, OAA/1-2, SR, WWA/1
BANDMANN, Maurice E. (d 1922
[49]) manager WWT/14*
BANDMANN-PALMER, Mrs. [née
Millicent Palmer] (d 1926 [81])
English actress CDP, DD,
EA/96, GRB/1-4, OAA/1-2
BANDURRIA, George [né Haydock]
(d 1907 [69]) musician EA/09*
BANE, Paula American actress
TW/2-3
BANFORD, Mr. (fl 1728) box keeper
BD
BANG, Herman Joachim (1857-1912)
dramatist BE*
BANGS, Frank C. (1833-1908)
American actor CDP, DAB,
DD, ES, GRB/3-4, HAS,
OC/1-3, PP/1
BANGS, John Kendrick (1862-1922)
American dramatist DAB,
GRB/2-4, WWA/1, WWS,
WWT/1-4, WWW/2
BANIM, John (1798-1842) Irish
dramatist CDP, DD, DNB,
ES, HP
BANISTER, Mr. (fl c.1676) dancer
BD
BANISTER, Ella (fl 1886-90) Amer-
ican actress DP
BANISTER, James (fl 1676-86)
violinist BD
BANISTER, Rev. James (fl 1780)
translator CP/3
BANISTER, Jeoffrey (1641-84)
violinist BD
BANISTER, John (1630?-79) English
instrumentalist, composer,
impresario BD, DD, DNB,
ES

BANISTER, John (1662-1736)
English violinist BD
BANISTER, John (b 1686) English flutist BD
BANISTER, Thomas (fl 1673) musician BD
BANKES, William (fl 1635) actor DA
BANKHEAD, Tallulah Brockman (1903-68) American actress AAS, BE, CB, COC, ES, NTH, PDT, SR, TW/1-21, 25, WWA/5, WWT/5-14
BANKS, Mr. (fl 1588-1637) Scottish equestrian CDP, DNB
BANKS, Mr. (fl 1723) actor BD
BANKS, Mr. (fl 1746-49?) actor BD
BANKS, Mr. (d 1752) doorkeeper, office keeper BD
BANKS, Mr. (fl 1780) carver? actor BD
BANKS, Mr. (fl 1789) actor BD
BANKS, Mr. (fl 1800-27) dancer, actor BD
BANKS, Mrs. (fl 1789) actress BD
BANKS, Aaron (d 1883) minstrel EA/84*
BANKS, Bertram (d 1916 [39]) child impersonator EA/17*
BANKS, "Billy" (d 1886) minstrel EA/87*
BANKS, Charles Eugene (1852-1932) American dramatist WWA/1
BANKS, Clara (d 1891 [34]) EA/92*
BANKS, Emily [Mrs. James Banks] (d 1882 [29]) EA/83*
BANKS, Ern (d 1893) actor EA/95*
BANKS, George Linnaeus (1821-81) dramatist DD
BANKS, Henry (1744-1829) tailor, wardrobe keeper BD
BANKS, Mrs. James see Banks, Emily
BANKS, Joe singer CDP
BANKS, John (c.1650-1706) English dramatist COC, CP/1-3, DD, DNB, ES, GT, OC/1-3
BANKS, Leslie James (1890-1952)

English actor AAS, COC, DNB, ES, OC/3, TW/6-8, WWT/4-11, WWW/5
BANKS, Louisa see Brower, Mrs. Frank
BANKS, Monty (1897-1950) French actor, director BE*
BANKS, Nathaniel P. (fl 1839) American actor HAS, SR
BANKS, Thomas (1756-1810) English scene painter, dancer, actor BD
BANKS, W. (fl 1796-1812?) actor, singer, dancer BD
BANKS, Walter (d 1903 [42]) humorist EA/05*
BANKS, William (d 1776) dancer, actor, designer BD
BANNEN, Ian (b 1928) Scottish actor AAS, WWT/13-16
BANNER, Mr. (d 1800?) doorkeeper BD
BANNER, Mr. (fl 1801) doorkeeper BD
BANNER, Mr. (fl 1801) sweeper BD
BANNER, Jack (d 1974 [67]) journalist, publicist BP/58*
BANNER, John (1910-73) Polish/American actor TW/29, WWA/5
BANNERMAN, Celia (b 1946) English actress WWT/15-16
BANNERMAN, Mrs. G. L. see Evelyne, Alma
BANNERMAN, Kay (b 1919) English dramatist, actress ES, WWT/10-16
BANNERMAN, Margaret (1896-1976) Canadian actress BE, TW/1, 3, WWT/4-15
BANNISTER, Mr. (fl 1790-97) puppet-showman BD
BANNISTER, Mrs. (fl 1793-94?) actress BD
BANNISTER, Charles (1741-1804) English actor, singer BD, CDP, DD, DNB, ES, OC/1-3, TD/1-2
BANNISTER, Harry (1893-1961) American actor TW/5-11, 13, 17, WWT/11-13
BANNISTER, Master J. (fl 1773) actor BD
BANNISTER, J. (fl 1879-80) actor DD
BANNISTER, James (fl 1771-83) actor BD

BANNISTER, John see
Banister, John
BANNISTER, John (d 1725) vio-
linist CDP
BANNISTER, John (1760-1836)
English actor BD, CDP,
COC, DD, DNB, ES, GT,
OC/1-3, OX, TD/1-2
BANNISTER, Mrs. John [née
Elizabeth Harper] (1757-
1849) English actress BD,
CDP, COC, TD/1-2
BANNISTER, Matilda (d 1879
[62]) EA/80*
BANNISTER, Nathaniel Harring-
ton (1813-47) American
actor, dramatist DAB, DD,
ES, HAS, HJD, OC/1-3,
RJ, SR, WWA/H
BANNISTER, Mrs. Nathaniel
Harrington [née Amelia
Green] (fl 1817-53) American
actress DD, HAS
BANNISTER, T. B. (fl 1871-93)
dramatist DD
BANSON, Richard (fl 1777-94)
scene painter BD
BANTI, Signora (fl 1756-58)
dancer BD, CDP
BANTI, Signora (fl 1860) Spanish
singer HAS
BANTI, Felicita (fl 1777-88?)
dancer BD
BANTI, Zaccaria (fl 1758?-1802)
dancer BD
BANTI, Signora Zaccaria [née
Brigitta Giorgi] (c. 1756-
1806) Italian singer BD,
CDP, ES
BANTI-GIORGI, Brigida see
Banti, Signora Zaccaria
BANTOCK, Sir Granville Ran-
some (1868-1946) English
composer DNB, ES, WWW/4
BANTOCK, Leedham (d 1928
[58]) dramatist, actor BE*,
WWT/14*
BANVARD, Fifi (d 1962) Aus-
tralian actress WWT/14*
BANVARD, John (1820-91) ex-
hibitor CDP
BANWELL, Louisa (d 1891
[43]) EA/92*
BANYAI, George (b 1905) Hun-
garian/American general
manager, house manager
BE
BANYARD, Mr. (fl 1785) actor

BD
BAPTIST, Mr. (fl 1691) oboist BD
BAPTIST, Mr. (fl 1784-85) dancer
BD
BAPTISTE, Mr. (fl 1724) flutist
BD
BAPTISTE, Mr. (fl 1782) clown,
equestrian, tumbler BD
BARA, Theda (1890-1955) Ameri-
can actress TW/11
BARAGREY, John (1918-75) Ameri-
can actor BE, TW/6-8, 22-
23, 28
BARAGWANATH, John G. (d 1965
[76]) dramatist BP/50*
BARAKA, Imamu Amiri [Leroi
Jones] (b 1934) American
dramatist, educator, adminis-
trator CB, CD, CH, HJD,
MH, MWD, WWT/16
BARAL, Robert (b 1910) American
writer BE
BARAS, Charles (1826-73) American
actor, dramatist SR
BARASCH, Norman (b 1922) Ameri-
can dramatist BE
BARATOW BEN-ZWI [Paul Brenner]
(1878-1952) Russian actor ES
BARATTI, Francesco (fl 1754-55)
Italian singer BD
BARBALONGA, Signor (d 1911)
singer EA/13*
BARBANDT, Charles (fl 1754-61)
musician, composer, teacher
BD
BARBARINA see Campanini,
Barbarina
BARBAT, Percy D. (d 1965 [82])
performer BP/50*
BARBEAU, Adrienne (b 1945) Amer-
ican actress TW/27-29
BARBEE, Richard (b 1887) Ameri-
can actor WWT/5-8
BARBER, Miss see Mason, Mrs.
BARBER, [Mr. ?] (fl 1708) house
servant BD
BARBER, Mr. (fl 1725-28) house
servant? BD
BARBER, Mr. (fl 1780) actor BD
BARBER, Mr. (fl 1784?-94) violist
BD
BARBER, Mrs. Charles J. see
Newton, Elizabeth Blanche
BARBER, Samuel (b 1910) American
composer, conductor CB, ES,
HJD
BARBER, William Charles (d 1912
[58]) journalist EA/13*

"BARBERINI, La" see Campanini, Barbarina
BARBERRE, Mons. (fl 1827-31) French dancer HAS
BARBERRE, Mme. (fl 1825) French singer HAS
BARBETTE, Yander (d 1973 [68]) performer BP/58*
BARBIER, George W. (1866-1945) American actor CB, ES, SR
BARBIER, Jane (d 1757) singer BD
BARBIERE, M. G. (fl 1827) French dancer CDP
BARBIERI, Fedora (b 1919/20) Italian singer CB, ES
BARBILI, Signorina (fl 1848) Italian singer SR
BARBIROLLI, Sir John (1899-1970) English conductor ES
BARBOR, H. R. (1893-1933) English journalist WWT/6-7
BARBOTT, Mr. (fl 1794) violinist, dancing master? BD
BARBOUR, Edwin (b 1841) actor, dramatist SR
BARBOUR, Joyce (b 1901) English actress ES, WWT/5-15
BARBOUR, Oliver (d 1968 [63]) actor, director, producer TW/24
BARBOUR, Robert MacDermot see MacDermot, Robert
BARBOUR, Thomas (b 1921) American actor TW/22, 24-27, 29-30
BARBOUR, William (d 1910 [47]) electrician EA/11*
BARCAVELLE [Mrs.?] (fl 1786) dancer? house servant? BD
BARCELLA, Ernest L. (d 1974 [63]) publicist BP/58*
BARCLAY, Mr. (fl 1741-44) actor BD
BARCLAY, Arthur J. English manager GRB/1-3
BARCLAY, Caroline [Mrs. Caroline Whalley] (fl 1792-94) actress BD, CDP, TD/1-2
BARCLAY, Delancey (d 1917) American actor SR
BARCLAY, Don Van Tassel (d 1975 [83]) performer BP/60*
BARCLAY, James M. (fl 1836) dramatist DD
BARCLAY, Jered American

actor TW/23, 26
BARCLAY, Sir William see Berkley, Sir William
BARCOCK, Mr. (fl 1730-33) actor BD
BARCROFT, Judith American actress TW/23
BARD, Wilkie [Billie Smith] (1870-1944) English music-hall artist CDP, COC, OC/1-3, SR
BARDIN, Peter (d 1773) actor BD
BARDOLEAU, Mr. (1794-1801?) singer BD
BARDOLY, Dr. Louis S. (d 1969 [75]) dramatist BP/54*
BARDON, Henry (b 1923) Czech actor WWT/15-16
BARDSLEY, John (d 1916 [33]) singer WWT/14*
BARE, Carl (d 1975 [15]) performer BP/60*
BARE, Thomas (d 1908) EA/09*
BARER, Marshall (b 1923) American lyricist, director, dramatist BE
BARETTA, Mlle. (fl 1869-79) dancer CDP
BARETTI, Giuseppe Marc Antonio (1719-89) Italian writer CDP, ES
BARFIELD, Mr. (fl 1784) actor BD
BARFIELD, Roger (fl 1606) actor DA
BARFOOT, Mrs. see Bates, Miss
BARFOOT, Harry (d 1870) comedian EA/71*
BARFORD, Mr. (fl 1794) musician, music seller, actor? BD
BARFORD, Richard (fl 1729) dramatist CP/1-3, DD, GT
BARGE, Fred (d 1900) actor EA/01*
BARGE, Gillian (b 1940) English actress WWT/16
BARGY, Roy (d 1974 [79]) composer/lyricist BP/58*
BARI, Lenny (b 1955) American actor TW/28
BARILI, Clotida (fl 1847-48) singer CDP, HAS
BARING, Hon. Maurice (1874-1945) dramatist WWT/2-7
BARING, Norah [Norah Baker] English actress ES
BARK, John Daly (c.1775-1808) Irish dramatist WWA/H
BARKANY, Marie (b 1862) German

actress WWT/2
BARKENTIN, Marjorie (d 1974
[83]) dramatist TW/30
BARKER (fl 1603) actor DA
BARKER, Mr. (fl 1690) English
dramatist CP/1-3
BARKER, Mr. (fl 1752) actor
BD
BARKER, Mrs. see Grattan,
Mrs. Henry P.
BARKER, Annie A. (d 1908)
actress EA/09*
BARKER, Bernard (d 1917) EA/
18*
BARKER, Carrie [Carrie Ender-
son] (d 1887) EA/88*
BARKER, Clive (b 1931) English
actor, director, dramatist
WWT/15-16
BARKER, Felix English critic
AAS
BARKER, George (d 1876 [64])
singer, composer EA/77*
BARKER, George see Murray,
G. W.
BARKER, Harley Granville see
Granville-Barker, Harley
BARKER, Henry Aston (fl 1787?-
1823) panorama exhibitor
BD
BARKER, Howard (b 1946) Eng-
lish dramatist CD, WWT/
16
BARKER, Jack (d 1950 [55])
musical comedy actor TW/7
BARKER, James Nelson (1784-
1858) American dramatist
COC, DAB, DD, EAP, ES,
HJD, MH, OC/1-3, RE,
RJ, SR, WWA/H
BARKER, John (d 1897) round-
about proprietor EA/98*
BARKER, Joseph (b 1862)
Scottish actor GRB/1
BARKER, Lex (d 1973 [53])
performer BP/57*
BARKER, Margaret (b 1908)
American actress TW/5-12
BARKER, Mike (d 1976 [60])
executive BP/60*
BARKER, Mrs. R. see
Cruise, Marie
BARKER, Reginald (1886-1937)
Scottish actor ES
BARKER, Reginald (1895-1945)
American? actor, manager
SR
BARKER, Richard (d 1903 [69])

actor, stage manager BE*,
EA/04*, WWT/14*
BARKER, Robert (c.1739-1806)
panorama exhibitor BD, CDP
BARKER, Ronnie (b 1929) English
actor WWT/15-16
BARKER, Thomas (fl 1620) drama-
tist CP/1-3
BARKER, William H. (d 1863)
American minstrel HAS
BARKHURST, Mr. (fl 1691-92)
musician BD
BARKOW, Arthur A. (d 1972 [58])
stage manager BP/56*
BARKSHIRE, Percy E. (b 1882)
English singer GRB/1
BARKSTED, William (fl 1606-11)
English dramatist, actor CP/
1-3, DA, DD, DNB, FGF
BARKSTEED see Barksted, Wil-
liam
BARKWELL, Mr. (fl 1686) musician
BD
BARKWORTH, Peter (b 1929) Eng-
lish actor WWT/14-16
BARLETTE, Sophie [Mrs. W.
Bryant] (d 1905) music-hall
performer EA/06*
BARLEY-CLARKE, Lily (b 1886)
English actress GRB/1
BARLEY-CLARKE, Marion [Mrs.
Albert H. Clarke] (d 1917 [56])
EA/18*
BARLING, Violet see Brandon,
Violet
BARLOG, Boleslaw (b 1906) German
director WWT/14
BARLOW ["The Great Australian
Vocalist"] singer CDP
BARLOW, Mr. (fl 1745-46) actor,
singer BD
BARLOW, Billie (1862/65-1937)
English actress, singer CDP,
WWT/4-6
BARLOW, Edward (fl 1785-1800)
treasurer BD
BARLOW, Harriet (d 1878 [22])
actress EA/79*
BARLOW, H. J. (1892-1970) Eng-
lish manager WWT/11-14
BARLOW, Howard (1892-1972)
American conductor CB
BARLOW, Milt G. (1843-1904)
minstrel performer and manager
CDP, SR
BARLOW, Nevett (d 1973 [39])
composer/lyricist BP/58*
BARLOW, Reginald (1867?-1943)

American actor CB, SR
BARLOW, Samuel L. M. (b
1892) American composer,
conductor ES
BARLOW, Seaghan (d 1972 [80s])
member of the National
Dramatic Society BP/57*
BARMAN, Mr. (fl 1735-36) actor?
house servant? BD
BARMORE, S. Wesley see
Harris, Samuel
BARNABE, Bruno (b 1905) Eng-
lish actor ES, WWT/10-16
BARNABEE, Henry Clay (1833-
1917) American actor,
singer CDP, DAB, ES,
NTH, SR, WWA/1, WWM,
WWS
BARNARD, Mr. (fl 1744-48) actor
BD
BARNARD, Mr. (fl 1750-54)
house servant BD
BARNARD, Mrs. (fl 1744) actress
BD
BARNARD, Mrs. (fl 1779-85)
actress BD
BARNARD, Miss (fl 1783) actress
BD
BARNARD, Amelia (d 1891)
EA/93*
BARNARD, Annie (d 1941)
actress BE*
BARNARD, Barney (d 1924 [46])
American comedian BP/8*
BARNARD, Bert (d 1917 [31])
variety agent EA/18*
BARNARD, Mrs. C. (d 1869)
composer EA/70*
BARNARD, Cecil (d 1896 [31])
performer EA/97*
BARNARD, Charles (1838-1920)
American dramatist ES,
WWA/1
BARNARD, Mrs. Charles (d
1911) EA/12*
BARNARD, Daniel (d 1879)
proprietor EA/80*
BARNARD, Edward (fl 1741-57)
dramatist CP/2-3, GT
BARNARD, Henry (b 1921)
American actor TW/2-6, 9
BARNARD, Henry see Guinard,
John
BARNARD, Ivor (1887-1953)
English actor ES, WWT/6-11
BARNARD, Sir John (fl 1722-37)
parliamentarian TD/1-2
BARNARD, John (d 1773?)

musician BD
BARNARD, John (1812-95) musical
director, composer DD
BARNARD, Mollie (b 1830) English
actress HAS
BARNARD, Sophye (b 1888) Ameri-
can singer WWM
BARNAY, Ludwig (b 1842) German
manager GRB/4, WWT/1-2
BARNBY, Sir Joseph (1838-96)
principal of Guildhall School of
Music EA/97*
BARNE, Will (fl 1602) actor DA
BARNES, Mr. (fl 1721) actor BD
BARNES, Mr. (fl 1743?-59) door-
keeper BD
BARNES, Mr. (fl 1757-60) constable
BD
BARNES, Mr. (fl 1777-82) actor
BD
BARNES, Mr. (fl 1795-98) dancer
BD
BARNES, Mrs. (fl 1782-1808?)
actress BD, CDP
BARNES, Mrs. (d 1916) EA/17*
BARNES, Miss (fl 1781-92) actress,
singer, dancer BD
BARNES, Barnaby (1569-c.1609)
English dramatist CP/1-3,
ES, FGF, RE
BARNES, Barry K. (1906-65) Eng-
lish actor ES, WWT/9-12,
WWW/6
BARNES, Billy (b 1927) American
lyricist, composer, singer BE
BARNES, Binnie [Gertrude Maude
Barnes] (b 1905/08) English
actress ES, TW/8, WWT/7-9
BARNES, Charles (d 1711) singer
BD
BARNES, Charlotte Mary Sanford
(1818-63) American actress,
dramatist COC, DAB, ES,
HJD, OC/1-3, RJ, SR, WWA/H
BARNES, Clive (b 1927) English
critic AAS, CB, WWT/16
BARNES, Djuna (b 1892) American
dramatist, actress CD, HJD,
MD
BARNES, Edward (d c.1703) rope-
dancer, booth operator BD
BARNES, Mrs. Edward (fl 1704-11)
fair booth operator BD
BARNES, Elliott (b 1843) dramatist
SR
BARNES, Emily Jane (d 1911)
equestrienne EA/12*
BARNES, E. S. (d 1905)

music-hall manager EA/06*
BARNES, F. E. (d 1880) actor,
musician EA/81*
BARNES, Fred singer CDP
BARNES, Fred (d 1917) EA/18*
BARNES, George (d 1878) pro-
prietor EA/79*
BARNES, Howard (1904-68) Eng-
lish critic TW/24, WWA/5,
WWT/10-13
BARNES, James (d 1838 [51])
actor CDP, DD
BARNES, James (d 1888) clown
EA/89*
BARNES, J. H. see Barnes,
John H.
BARNES, Joe (d 1964 [59]) per-
former BE*
BARNES, John (1761-1841)
English actor CDP, COC,
DD, HAS, SR
BARNES, Mrs. John (d 1841)
English actress SR,
WWA/H
BARNES, John H. (1850/52-
1925) English actor DD,
EA/96, GRB/1-4, OAA/2,
SR, WWS, WWT/1-5
BARNES, Joshua (1654-1712)
English translator, dramatist
CP/3
BARNES, Kempster (b 1923)
South African actor TW/3
BARNES, Sir Kenneth Ralph
(1878-1957) English prin-
cipal of the Royal Academy
of Dramatic Art, dramatist
COC, DNB, ES, OC/1-3,
WWT/4-12, WWW/5
BARNES, Mabel Thomas (d
1962) performer BE*
BARNES, Mae (b 1907) Ameri-
can singer, dancer, actress
BE, TW/10-12
BARNES, Margaret Ayer (1886-
1967) American dramatist
HJD, TW/24
BARNES, Mary (1780-1864)
English actress DD, HAS
BARNES, Mary (d 1869 [51])
actress? EA/70*
BARNES, Peter (b 1931) Eng-
lish dramatist, director
AAS, CD, WWT/15-16
BARNES, Price [John Price
Burnham] (d 1877 [31])
singer EA/78*
BARNES, Richard (fl 1675-91)

actor, singer BD
BARNES, Sidney (d 1889) actor,
singer CDP
BARNES, Thomas (fl 1629) actor
DA
BARNES, Thomas (1785-1841) Eng-
lish critic COC, OC/1-3
BARNES, T. Roy (d 1937 [56])
English actor BE*, BP/21*
BARNES, Verona actress TW/25-
26, 28, 30
BARNES, William A. (fl 1870)
dramatist SR
BARNES, William Augustus (1826-
68) actor CDP, HAS, SR
BARNES, Winifred (1892/94-1935)
actress, singer WWT/3-7
BARNET, Mr. (fl 1778-1845?)
actor BD
BARNET, Mrs. (fl 1795) singer
BD
BARNET, Mrs. (fl 1848) actress
HAS
BARNET, Master (fl 1750) actor
BD
BARNET, Jarvis (fl 1748-50) actor
BD
BARNET, Robert Ayers (1850/53-
1933) American dramatist,
librettist WWM
BARNETT, Mrs. (fl 1729) actress
BD
BARNETT, Mrs. (d 1905) EA/06*
BARNETT, Alice [Mrs. Dickins]
(d 1901) actress, singer DD
BARNETT, Benjamin (fl c.1855)
actor DD
BARNETT, Catherine (fl 1786-1800)
actress, singer BD
BARNETT, Chester A. (d 1947
[62]) actor TW/4
BARNETT, C. Z. (d 1890 [88])
dramatist, librettist, performer
DD
BARNETT, Domenico J. (d 1911
[70]) professor of music EA/
13*
BARNETT, Mrs. E. F. Kemble (d
1895) EA/96*
BARNETT, Emma (d 1877) actress
EA/78*
BARNETT, Mrs. Frances (d 1870
[71]) actress EA/71*
BARNETT, Henry (d 1868 [76])
manager EA/68*
BARNETT, Humphrey (d 1874 [62])
acting manager EA/75*
BARNETT, John (fl 1794) bass

viol-player BD
BARNETT, John (1802-90) English composer, singer, musical director CDP, DD, DNB, ES
BARNETT, John Francis (1838-1916) composer, pianist DD
BARNETT, Millie see Soutten, Mme.
BARNETT, Morris (1800-56) French?/English actor, dramatist CDP, DD, DNB
BARNETT, Orlando (b 1867) English actor GRB/1
BARNETT, R. A. (b c.1860) dramatist SR
BARNETT, Richard (d 1892 [21]) actor, singer EA/94*
BARNETT, Mrs. Richard (d 1873) actress, singer EA/75*
BARNETT, Thomas (fl 1794) musician BD
BARNEY, Jay (b 1918) American actor, stage manager BE, TW/12-15, 22, 24-25, 28
BARNEY, Ludwig (b 1845) actor SR
BARNEY, Phil (d 1975 [81]) critic BP/60*
BARNHARD, Lawrence C. (d 1975 [71]) producer/director/choreographer BP/59*
BARNHART, Franklin (d 1976 [49]) union executive BP/60*
BARNHILL, James (b 1922) American educator, actor, director BE
BARNS, Mr. (fl 1794-95) house servant BD
BARNS, Mrs. (fl 1725) actress? BD
BARNSHAW, John (fl 1768-83) actor, singer BD
BARNUM, Bush (d 1971 [60]) publicist BP/56*
BARNUM, George William (1853-1937) American actor WWM
BARNUM, John (fl 1876) actor, singer CDP
BARNUM, Phineas Taylor (1810-91) American circus showman CDP, COC, DAB, DD, ES, HAS, HJD, HP, NTH, OC/1-3, PDT, SR, WWA/H
BARNWELL, Mr. (fl 1794-95)

dresser BD
BARON, Mr. (fl 1800) singer BD
BARON, Louis [or Lewis] (d 1920 [62]) actor BE*, WWT/14*
BARON, Milton (d 1972 [76]) producer/director/choreographer BP/57*
BARON, Robert (b 1630) English dramatist CP/1-3, DD, DNB, FGF
BARON, Robert Alex (b 1920) American company manager, general manager, director, press representative BE
BARON, Sandy (b 1938) American actor TW/22-24, 28-29
BARON, Sheldon (b 1935) American actor TW/23
"BARONESS, The" [Joanna Maria Lindelheim] (fl 1703-17) Italian singer BD
BARONOVA, Irina (b 1919) Russian dancer ES, TW/1, WWT/9-12
BAROWBY, Miss (fl 1766) actress, dancer BD
BARR, Mr. (fl 1749-50) stage doorkeeper BD
BARR, Mr. (fl 1788-95) actor BD
BARR, Benjamin (fl 1794) bass viol player? BD
BARR, Byron Ellsworth see Young, Gig
BARR, Geoffrey (b 1924) American personal manager, actor BE, TW/7
BARR, Ida (d 1967 [85]) performer BP/52*
BARR, Jeanne (d 1967 [35]) actress TW/24
BARR, Margaret English dancer, choreographer ES
BARR, Olive (d 1912 [88]) EA/13*
BARR, Patrick (b 1908) Indian/English actor WWT/10-16
BARR, Richard [né Baer] (b 1917) American producer, director BE, WWT/14-16
BARR, Richard M. (d 1972 [64]) publicist BP/57*
BARRACLOUGH, Sydney (1869/71-1930) English actor, singer GRB/1-4
BARRAND, William (fl 1793) bass viol player? BD
BARRAS, Charles M. (1826-73) American actor, dramatist BE*
BARRAS, Joseph (fl 1756)

proprietor BD
BARRASFORD, Elizabeth (d 1894
[32]) EA/95*
BARRASFORD, Thomas (1860-
1910) English manager
GRB/1
BARRASFORD, Mrs. [Thomas;
Maude D'Almaine] English
singer GRB/1
BARRAT, Mr. (d 1795) actor
TD/1
BARRAT, Robert (1891-1970)
American actor ES, TW/26
BARRATT, Mr. (fl 1784?-94)
bass viol player BD
BARRATT, Augustus English
composer, lyricist WWT/
4-6
BARRATT, Walter Augustus (d
1947 [73]) Scottish com-
poser, producer, conductor
BE*
BARRATT, Watson (1884-1962)
American scene designer
ES, TW/2-8, WWT/7-13
BARRAUD, George (b 1893)
English actor ES
BARRAUD, Mark H. (d 1887
[39]) scene artist EA/89*
BARRAULT, Jean-Louis (b 1910)
French director, actor BE,
CB, COC, ES, NTH, OC/3,
WWT/11-14
BARRE, Mons. (fl 1796-98)
choreographer, dance director
BD
BARRE, Mlle. (fl 1795-96)
dancer BD
BARRE, Albert (d 1910 [54])
dramatist BE*, WWT/14*
BARRE, George (d 1892) EA/93*
BARRE, Mrs. [Joseph?; née
Groce] (fl 1768-97?) actress,
singer BD
BARREM, Mr. (fl 1795) house
servant? BD
BARRERA, José (b 1929) Spanish
dancer TW/26
BARRERE, Jean (b 1918) Ameri-
can stage manager, director
BE
BARRESFORD, Mrs. see
Bulkeley, Mrs. George
BARRET, Mr. (fl 1730-32) actor
BD
BARRET, Mr. (fl 1789) actor,
manager TD/2
BARRET, John (fl 1635) actor DA

BARRET, R. (fl 1784-85) actor BD
BARRETT, Mr. (fl 1722) actor BD
BARRETT, Mr. (fl 1736-37) musi-
cian? BD
BARRETT, Mr. (fl 1776-1805?)
box-keeper, constable BD
BARRETT, Mr. (d 1777?) actor
BD
BARRETT, Mr. (fl 1784-94) double-
bass player BD
BARRETT, Mr. (fl 1797-1800) vio-
linist BD
BARRETT, Mrs. (fl 1776) actress
BD
BARRETT, Mrs. (fl 1790-1816)
actress, dancer, singer BD
BARRETT, Mrs. (fl 1797) BD
BARRETT, Miss (fl 1776) actress/
singer BD
BARRETT, Miss (fl 1784) actress
BD
BARRETT, Ann Jane (1801-53)
actress CDP, HAS
BARRETT, Edith (1906-77) American
actress ES, WWT/7-10
BARRETT, Eliza [Mrs. Oscar
Barrett] (d 1908) EA/10*
BARRETT, Ellen Anna (d 1892)
EA/93*
BARRETT, George (1869-1935)
English actor DP, GRB/3-4,
WWT/1-7
BARRETT, Mrs. George [Mrs.
Henry] (1801-53) American
actress DD
BARRETT, Mrs. George see
Vincent, Nellie
BARRETT, George Edward (1849-94)
English actor DD, OC/1-3
BARRETT, George Horton (1794-
1860) American/English actor
CDP, COC, DAB, DD, ES,
HAS, OC/1-3, SR, WWA/H
BARRETT, Mrs. George Horton
[née Stockwell; Mrs. Drum-
mond; Mrs. Henry] (d 1857
[55]) actress HAS, SR
BARRETT, Georgianna (b 1829)
American actress HAS
BARRETT, Giles Linnett (1744-
1809) actor, manager BD,
CDP, DD, HAS
BARRETT, Mrs. Giles Linnett
[née Ranoe; Mrs. Rivers;
Mrs. Belfield] (d 1832) actress
BD, DD, HAS
BARRETT, Henry J. (d 1908) EA/
09*

BARRETT, Henry Michael (d
1872 [68]) English actor
BE*, EA/73*
BARRETT, Ivy Rice (d 1962
[64]) performer BE*
BARRETT, Jane (d 1969) per-
former BP/54*
BARRETT, J. H. (b 1831) Amer-
ican actor HAS
BARRETT, Mrs. J. H. [Emily
Viola Crocker] (d 1869)
American actress HAS
BARRETT, Jimmie (d 1964
[80]) performer BE*
BARRETT, John (c.1674-c.1720)
organist, composer BD
BARRETT, John (d 1795) actor
BD, TD/2
BARRETT, [John?] (fl 1799)
actor BD
BARRETT, John L. (d 1874
[50]) comedian EA/75*
BARRETT, John Peter (b 1937)
American actor TW/30
BARRETT, J. Pritchard (d
1900) scene artist EA/01*
BARRETT, Laurinda (b 1931)
American actress TW/13,
24, 30
BARRETT, Lawrence (1838-91)
American actor, producer
CDP, COC, DAB, DD, ES,
HAS, NTH, OC/1-3, SR,
WWA/H
BARRETT, Leslie (b 1919)
American actor TW/23-
24, 30
BARRETT, Lester (fl 1894)
singer CDP
BARRETT, Lester (d 1970 [68])
performer BP/55*
BARRETT, Lillian Foster (1884-
1963) American dramatist
WWA/4
BARRETT, Louis F. (1843-96)
American actor SR
BARRETT, Mary Anne (d 1893)
EA/94*
BARRETT, Minnette (d 1964
[80]) actress TW/21
BARRETT, Nora Cunneen (d
1965 [65]) performer BP/50*
BARRETT, Oscar, Sr. (d 1941
[95]) composer, conductor,
producer BE*
BARRETT, Oscar, Jr. (1875-
1943) English manager DD,
WWT/3-9

BARRETT, Mrs. Oscar see Bar-
rett, Eliza
BARRETT, Raina (b 1941) American
actress TW/26-29
BARRETT, Ray (d 1973 [65]) per-
former BP/57*
BARRETT, Reginald (1861-1940)
English composer WWA/1,
WWM
BARRETT, Robert Reville see
Reville, Robert
BARRETT, Roger (d 1968 [47])
performer BP/53*
BARRETT, Sidney Harrison (d 1901
[36]) comedian EA/02*
BARRETT, T. A. see Stuart,
Leslie
BARRETT, T. W. singer, com-
poser CDP
BARRETT, Viola Crocker see
Barrett, Mrs. J. H.
BARRETT, W. A. (fl 1882) libret-
tist DD
BARRETT, Walter (fl 1623) actor
DA
BARRETT, Wilson (1846-1904) Eng-
lish actor, manager CDP,
COC, DD, DNB, DP, EA/96,
ES, GRB/1, OAA/2, OC/1-3,
SR, WWA/1, WWW/1
BARRETT, Wilson (b 1900) English
actor, manager WWT/9-13
BARRETT, Mrs. Wilson see
Heath, Caroline
BARREY, Lodowick see Barry,
Lodowick
BARRIE, Amanda [née Broadhurst]
(b 1939) English actress WWT/
14-16
BARRIE, Barbara (b 1931) American
actress TW/25-30, WWT/16
BARRIE, Frank (b 1940) English
actor TW/23
BARRIE, Sir James Matthew (1860-
1937) Scottish dramatist AAS,
COC, DD, DNB, ES, GRB/1-4,
HP, MD, MH, MWD, NTH,
OC/1-3, PDT, RE, SR, WWS,
WWT/1-8, WWW/3
BARRIE, Mona (b 1909) English
actress ES
BARRIE, Wendy (b 1912) English
actress ES
BARRIERE, Hippolite (fl 1823-24)
theatre owner WWA/H
BARRINGER, Ned (d 1976 [87])
performer BP/60*
BARRINGTON, Mr. (fl 1783) actor,

singer BD
BARRINGTON, Mrs. (fl 1732-33)
actress? BD
BARRINGTON, Henry Harding
(d 1908) actor EA/09*,
GRB/4*
BARRINGTON, John (1715-73)
Irish actor BD
BARRINGTON, Mrs. John [née
Ann Hallam (fl 1733-73)
actress BD
BARRINGTON, Josephine (d 1973)
performer BP/57*
BARRINGTON, Pattie [Mary Kay]
(d 1906 [22]) EA/07*
BARRINGTON, Roland (d 1893
[40]) actor EA/94*
BARRINGTON, Rutland [George
Rutland Fleet] (1853-1922)
English actor CDP, DD,
DNB, DP, EA/95, ES,
GRB/1-4, OAA/2, WWT/1-4
BARRIS, Harry (d 1962 [57])
American composer, per-
former BE*
BARRISCALE, Bessie (d 1965
[81]) performer BP/50*
BARRISFORD, Mrs. Ebenezer
see Bulkley, Mrs. George
BARRISON, Mabel (1882-1912)
actress CDP
BARROIS, Mons. (fl 1754-55)
dancer BD
BARRON, [Mrs.?] (fl 1760-61)
charwoman BD
BARRON, Mlle. (d 1852) dancer
HAS
BARRON, Carter Tate (1905-50)
American executive WWA/3
BARRON, Charles (1840-1918)
American actor CDP, HAS,
SR, PP/1
BARRON, Elwyn Alfred (1855-
1929) American dramatist
GRB/2-3, SR, WWA/1,
WWM, WWW/3
BARRON, John (fl 1784-94)
singer, pianist, violinist?
BD
BARRON, Madge Douglas [Mrs.
Charles Harley] (d 1900
[35]) EA/01*
BARRON, Marcus (1925-44)
actor WWT/8-9
BARRON, Mark (1905-60) Amer-
ican critic NTH, WWA/4
BARRON, Muriel (b 1906) Scot-
tish actress, singer

WWT/10-12
BARRON, William (d 1890) EA/91*
BARRON, William Augustus (fl
1760?-94) violoncellist BD
BARROW, Bernard (b 1927) Ameri-
can educator, director, actor
BE
BARROW, D. (fl 1850) actor HAS
BARROW, James O. see Barrows,
James O.
BARROW, Janet (d 1965?) English
actress TW/7
BARROW, John (d 1904) stage
manager EA/05*
BARROW, Julia Bennet (b 1824)
English actress, manager
CDP, HAS
BARROW, Thomas (1722?-89)
Welsh singer, harpsichord
teacher BD
BARROW, William (d 1902 [36])
music-hall manager EA/04*
BARROWS, James O. (1857-1925)
American actor PP/1, SR,
WWS
BARRS, Georgina (d 1902) EA/03*
BARRS, Norman (b 1917) English
actor TW/4, 6, 13, 20, 22-
24, 26-28, 30
BARR-SMITH, A. (b 1905) Australian
actor ES
BARRY, Mr. (fl 1699) actor? BD
BARRY, Mr. (fl 1799) actor BD
BARRY, Ann see Barry, Mrs.
Spranger
BARRY, Bob [Oscar Mills] (d 1918)
EA/19*
BARRY, Bobby (1887-1964) Ameri-
can actor TW/3
BARRY, Charles Whittle (d 1889)
actor EA/90*
BARRY, Christine [Grace Under-
wood] (b 1911) Welsh actress
WWT/9-10
BARRY, David Loring (d 1610)
lessee DA
BARRY, Donna American actress
TW/26
BARRY, Edwin (fl 1879) singer
CDP
BARRY, Elaine (d 1948) dancer
TW/4
BARRY, Elizabeth (1658-1713) Eng-
lish actress BD, CDP, COC,
DD, DNB, ES, HP, NTH,
OC/1-3
BARRY, Elizabeth (d 1873 [68])
EA/74*

BARRY, Fred (d 1964) English
dancer TW/1
BARRY, Frederick (b 1876)
American composer WWM
BARRY, Gene (b 1919) American
actor TW/2-3, 6-8
BARRY, H. C. [F. W. Russell]
(d 1909) singer, composer
CDP
BARRY, Helen [Mrs. Alexander
Rolls] (d 1904 [51]) English
actress CDP, DD, OAA/
1-2, SR
BARRY, Joan (b 1901/02/03)
actress WWT/4-8
BARRY, John (b 1915) American
singer TW/1-3
BARRY, John D. (b 1866) Amer-
ican dramatist WWM
BARRY, Leonard (fl 1890s) singer
CDP
BARRY, Leonard (d 1972 [50])
performer BP/57*
BARRY, Lodowick [Lodowick
Barrey] (fl c.1620) English
dramatist CP/1-3, DD,
DNB, FGF
BARRY, Lydia [Mrs. George
Felix] (d 1932 [56]) American
vaudevillian CDP, SR,
WWM
BARRY, Mary (fl 1698) actress
BD
BARRY, Mary Ann (d 1891 [85])
EA/92*
BARRY, Matthew (b 1962) Amer-
ican actor TW/29
BARRY, Pat (d 1879 [29]) Irish
comedian EA/80*
BARRY, Philip (1896-1949)
American dramatist AAS,
COC, DAB, ES, HJD, MD,
MH, MWD, NTH, OC/1-3,
PDT, RE, SR, TW/6,
WWA/1, WWT/6-10
BARRY, Shiel (1842/43-97) Irish
actor DD, DP, OAA/1-2
BARRY, Shiel (1882-1916) Eng-
lish actor GRB/4, WWT/
1-3
BARRY, Mrs. Shiel see Minto,
Dorothy
BARRY, Spranger (1719-77) Irish
actor, manager BD, CDP,
COC, DD, DNB, ES, GT,
NTH, OC/1-3, TD/1-2
BARRY, Mrs. Spranger [née
Ann Street; Mrs. William

Dancer; Mrs. Thomas Craw-
ford] (1734-1801) English act-
ress BD, CDP, DD, DNB,
ES, GT, TD/1-2
BARRY, Thomas (c.1743-68) Irish
actor BD
BARRY, Thomas (d 1857 [47])
clown, actor CDP, DD, HAS,
SR
BARRY, Thomas (1798-1876) Eng-
lish actor, manager CDP
BARRY, Mrs. Thomas (fl 1766-74)
actress BD
BARRY, Mrs. Thomas (d 1854)
actress DD, HAS
BARRY, Mrs. Thomas see
Biddles, Clara S.
BARRY, Mrs. Thomas see
Redmund, Clara S.
BARRY, Tom (d 1857 [47]) clown
BE*, WWT/14*
BARRY, Tom (d 1931 [47]) Ameri-
can dramatist BE*
BARRY, Viola (d 1964 [70]) actress
BE*
BARRY, W. H. (d 1893) mana-
ger EA/94*
BARRY, William (d 1780) actor,
treasurer BD
BARRY, Mrs. William [née Jane
Osborne] (1739-71) English
actress BD
BARRY, William J. (d 1898 [38])
EA/99*
BARRY AND FAY actors, variety
performers SR
BARRYMORE, Miss (fl 1785) actress
BD
BARRYMORE, Earl of (1769-93)
English actor, patron CDP,
COC, DD, OC/1-3
BARRYMORE, Ann (d 1862 [62])
actress CDP
BARRYMORE, Diana (1921-60)
American actress ES, TW/1,
3-16, WWT/10-12
BARRYMORE, Ethel (1879-1959)
American actress AAS, CB,
COC, ES, GRB/2-4, NTH,
OC/1-3, PTD, SR, TW/1-15,
WWA/3, WWM, WWS, WWT/
1-12, WWW/5
BARRYMORE, Georgiana Emma
Drew (1856-93) American actress
DAB, ES, NTH, OC/1-3,
WWA/H
BARRYMORE, John (1882-1942)
American actor AAS, CB,

COC, DAB, ES, GRB/3-4,
NTH, OC/1-3, PDT, SR,
WWA/2, WWT/1-9, WWW/4
BARRYMORE, Lionel (1878-1954)
English actor AAS, CB,
COC, ES, NTH, OC/1-3,
PDT, SR, TW/11, WWA/3,
WWT/1-11, WWW/5
BARRYMORE, Mrs. Lionel see
Rankin, Doris
BARRYMORE, Maurice [Herman
Blythe] (1847-1905) American
actor, dramatist COC, DAB,
DD, ES, GRB/1, NTH,
OC/1-3, PP/1, SR, WWA/1
BARRYMORE, William (1759-
1830) English actor, drama-
tist, manager BD, COC,
GT, OC/1-3, TD/1
BARRYMORE, Mrs. William
[Miss Adams] (d 1862)
actress DD, HAS, SR
BARRYMORE, William Henry
(d 1845) actor, dramatist
CDP, DD, HAS, SR,
OC/1-3
BARSACQ, André (1909-73)
French scene designer ES
BARSANTI, Francesco (b
c.1690) Italian instrumen-
talist, composer BD
BARSANTI, Jane [Mrs. John
Richard Kirwan Lyster;
Mrs. Richard Daly; Mrs.
Lisley] (d 1795) actress,
singer BD, CDP, DD
BARSBY, Mrs. E. A. [Mrs.
Frank Barsby] (d 1906)
EA/07*
BARSBY, Frank (d 1892) actor
EA/93*
BARSBY, Mrs. Frank see
Barsby, Mrs. E. A.
BARSTOW, Edith (d 1960)
American choreographer
WWA/3
BARSTOW, James S., Jr. (d
1968 [49]) critic BP/53*
BART, Jan (d 1971 [52]) com-
poser/lyricist BP/56*
BART, Lionel (b 1930) English
composer, lyricist, drama-
tist, director AAS, BE,
CD, PDT, WWT/14-16
BARTEESKE, John (fl 1660)
drummer BD
BARTELL, Bob (d 1903) music-
hall artist EA/04*

BARTELL, Jerry (b 1942) American
actor TW/30
BARTELL, Richard (d 1967 [69])
performer BP/52*
BARTELLE, Jennie Dickerson
[née Maude Dickerson] (1856-
1943) singer SR
BARTELMAN, Mrs. (fl 1767) singer
BD
BARTELS, Louis John (1896-1932)
American actor SR
BARTENIEFF, George (b 1933)
German actor TW/3, 22-28
BARTET, Jeanne Julia (1854-1941)
French actress GRB/1-4,
WWT/1-4
BARTH, Alice (d 1910 [61]) singer
EA/11*
BARTH, Belle (d 1971 [59]) per-
former BP/55*
BARTH, Cecil [Cecil Walenn]
(d 1949 [84]) manager GRB/
1-3, WWT/4-7
BARTHELEMON, Master (fl 1783-
84) singer BD
BARTHELEMON, Cecilia Maria
[Mrs. Henslowe] (b 1770?)
singer, musician BD
BARTHELEMON, François Hippolyte
(1741-1808) French musician,
bandleader, composer BD,
DNB, ES, TD/1-2
BARTHELMESS, Richard Semler
(1895-1963) American actor
TW/20
BARTHOLDI, Fred (d 1961 [58])
manager BE*
BARTHOLOMAE, Phillip H. (1880-
1947) American dramatist,
librettist, manager SR, WWT/
5-9
BARTHOLOMEW, Mrs. (d 1891 [80])
composer, pianist EA/92*
BARTHOLOMEW, Anne Charlotte
[née Fayermann] (d 1862)
dramatist DD
BARTHOLOMEW, John (fl 1794)
dramatist CP/3
BARTHOLOMEW, John see Barty,
Jack
BARTHOLOMEW, William H. (1830-
1917) American actor, circus
performer CDP, SR
"BARTHOLOMEW FAIR MUSICIAN,
The" CDP
BARTHOLOMON, J. (fl 1786) actor
BD
BARTHROPE, Mr. (fl 1775-86)

house servant BD
BARTLE, Colin (d 1973 [58])
theatre club founder BP/
58*
BARTLE, Marion Elizabeth see
De Roos, Marie
BARTLE, Onye [?] (fl 1603)
actor DA
BARTLEMAN, James (1769-1821)
English singer BD, CDP,
DNB
BARTLEMAN, Thomas (d 1879)
singer EA/80*
BARTLET, Joseph (b 1763) Amer-
ican dramatist RJ
BARTLETT, Mr. (fl 1735-41)
musician? BD
BARTLETT, Mr. (fl 1794) Eng-
lish actor HAS
BARTLETT, Sir Basil (b 1905)
English actor ES, WWT/
8-13
BARTLETT, Bonnie (b 1929)
American actress TW/26
BARTLETT, Charles (b 1941)
American actor TW/29-30
BARTLETT, Clifford (1903-36)
Welsh actor WWT/8
BARTLETT, D'Jamin American
actress TW/30
BARTLETT, Elise [Elise Porter]
actress WWT/7-9
BARTLETT, Fred (d 1912)
actor, manager EA/13*
BARTLETT, Mme. Gordon (d
1894) singer EA/95*
BARTLETT, Homer Newton
(b 1845) American com-
poser WWA/4, WWM
BARTLETT, James J. (d 1880)
actor EA/81*
BARTLETT, J. J. English actor
GRB/1-3
BARTLETT, John (1820-1905)
American writer WWA/1
BARTLETT, Josephine (d 1910
[48]) American performer
BE*
BARTLETT, Lucinda (d 1904)
EA/05*
BARTLETT, Mrs. M. A. (d
1917) EA/18*
BARTLETT, Martine American
actress BE, TW/14
BARTLETT, Michael (b 1901)
American actor, singer
TW/27-29, WWT/9-10
BARTLETT, Peter (b 1942)

American actor TW/30
BARTLEY, Mr. (fl 1800-22) English
actor BS, TD/2
BARTLEY, Mrs. see Bartley,
Mrs. George
BARTLEY, George (1782-1858)
English actor CDP, DD,
DNB, ES, GT, HAS, OX, SR
BARTLEY, Mrs. George [née Wil-
liamson] (1783-1850) English
actress BS, CDP, DD, DNB,
HAS, SR
BARTLEY, Sarah see Bartley,
Mrs. George
BARTLEY, Sir William see
Berkley, Sir William
BARTOLETTI, Bruno (b 1926) Italian
conductor ES
BARTOLINI, Sig. (d 1894 [72])
singer EA/95*
BARTOLINI, Vincenzio (fl 1782-92)
singer BD
BARTOLOMEO, Noreen (b 1947)
American actress TW/28
BARTOLOMICI, Luigi (d 1800)
dancer BD
BARTOLOTTI, Girolamo (fl 1731)
trumpeter BD
BARTOLOZZI, Josephine see
Anderson, Josephine
BARTOLOZZI, Lucia Elizabeth see
Vestris, Mme.
BARTON, Mr. (fl 1721) dancer BD
BARTON, Mr. (fl 1736) actor BD
BARTON, Mr. (fl 1791-92) house
servant? actor? BD
BARTON, Mr. (d 1848) English
actor DD, HAS
BARTON, Andrew (fl 1767) Ameri-
can dramatist, librettist EAP,
WWA/H
BARTON, Charles (b 1902) American
actor ES
BARTON, Donald (b 1928) American
actor TW/15
BARTON, Dora [Dora Brockbank]
(d 1966) English actress GRB/
1-4, WWT/1-10
BARTON, Frances see Abington,
Mrs. James
BARTON, Gary (b 1947) American
actor TW/24
BARTON, Grace (fl 1900-06) Amer-
ican actress WWS
BARTON, H. Reyner (d 1966)
actor BP/50*, WWT/14*
BARTON, James (d 1848) English
actor, stage manager WWA/H

BARTON, James (1890-1962)
American actor ES, TW/
2-16, 18, WWT/8-13

BARTON, John (d 1875 [68])
actor EA/76*

BARTON, John (1870-1946)
American actor TW/3,
SR

BARTON, John (b 1928) English
director, dramatist AAS,
COC, WWT/14-16

BARTON, Julia see MacMillan,
Mrs.

BARTON, Lucy (b 1891) American costume designer, educator BE

BARTON, Margaret (b 1926)
English actress ES, WWT/
10-13

BARTON, Mary [Mrs. J. B.
Brockbank] (d 1970) English
actress ES, GRB/1-2,
WWT/4-10

BARTON, Onesiphorus (d 1608)
actor DA

BARTON, Reyner see Barton,
H. Reyner

BARTON, Sam (d 1941 [46])
performer BE*

BARTON, Susan (fl 1849) fat
woman CDP

BARTON, Ward J. (d 1963
[87]) performer BE*

BARTON, William (d 1778?)
musician, pleasure garden
proprietor BD

BARTON, William (d 1900 [71])
EA/01*

BARTON, Gen. William B. (d
1891) American actor EA/
92*

BARTON, Arthur (b 1935) American actor TW/27

BARTSCH, Hans (d 1952 [68])
German producer, literary
representative BE*

BARTY, Jack [John Bartholo-
mew] (1888-1942) English
actor WWT/9

BARWELL, Thomas (fl 1677-
1700) trumpeter BD

BARWICK, Edwin (d 1928 [70])
singer, comedian, composer
CDP

BARWICK, Mary Ann (d 1904
[69]) EA/05*

BARYSHNIKOV, Mikhail (b 1948)
Russian dancer CB

BARZELL, Wolfe (d 1969 [72])
performer BP/53*

BARZIN, Leon Eugene (b 1900)
Belgian/American conductor
CB

BASCOMB, Henry (b 1833) American actor HAS

BASCOMB, Mrs. Henry L. see
Skerrett, Mrs. George

BASECU, Elinor (b 1927) American
actress TW/30

BASEHART, Richard (b 1914/19)
American actor BE, ES, TW/
1-2, 14-18, 24, WWT/15-16

BASELEON, Michael American actor
TW/20, 22-23, 26

BASHALL, James A. (d 1905 [68])
EA/06*

BASHALL, Joseph (d 1883) singer
EA/84*

BASIL, Mr. (fl 1778) fair booth
proprietor BD

BASIL, Arthur John (d 1873 [25])
composer, author EA/74*

BASIL, George (d 1873 [26]) comedian EA/74*

BASING, S. Herberte (d 1898 [40])
actor, manager WWT/14*

BASKCOMB, A. W. (1880-1939)
English actor GRB/2-4, WWT/
1-9

BASKCOMB, Lawrence (1883-1962)
English actor WWT/7-11

BASKER, Thomas (fl 1620) English
dramatist CP/1-2

BASQUETTE, Lina (b 1909) American dancer ES

BASRIER, Mr. (fl 1675) violinist
BD

BASS, Mr. (fl 1778-84) actor BD

BASS, Alfred (b 1921) English actor
WWT/11-16

BASS, Charles (1803-63) English
actor CDP, DD, HAS

BASS, Mrs. Charles [Miss Ball]
(d 1852) Canadian actress
HAS

BASS, Emory American actor
TW/23, 25-26, 29-30

BASS, Helen Kennedy (d 1973) performer BP/59*

BASS, Kate (d 1894 [36]) EA/95*

BASS, Rochelle see Owens,
Rochelle

BASS, Tom (d 1913) singer, composer CDP

BASS, Will (d 1917) EA/18*

BASSAN, Mr. (fl 1766-84) house

servant BD
BASSAN, Miss (fl 1773-80)
dancer BD
BASSANO, Henry (d 1665) musician BD
BASSE, Joe (d 1972 [71]) performer BP/56*
BASSE, Thomas (fl 1611-19) actor DA
BASSERMAN, Albert (1867-1952) German actor COC, OC/1-3, TW/1, 8
BASSERMAN, Else (d 1961 [83]) actress TW/1
BASSERMANN, Dr. August (1848-1931) German manager COC, GRB/4, OC/1-3, WWT/1-2
BASSET, Serge (d 1917) dramatist, critic BE*
BASSETT, Mr. (fl 1794) bass viol player BD
BASSETT, Adelaide (d 1895) parachutist EA/96*
BASSETT, James see Bertram, Charles
BASSETT, John (d 1787) instrumentalist BD
BASSETT, Leon (b 1870) English musical director GRB/1
BASSETT, Russell (d 1918 [72]) American actor BE*
BASSETT, W. S. (d 1910 [38]) conductor EA/11*
BASSHE, Emjo (c. 1899-1939) American dramatist MD
BASSI, Amedeo (1874/76-1949) Italian singer ES, WWA/5, WWM
BASSIE, Joan (b 1939) American actress TW/23, 27-29
BASSINGWHITE, [John?] (fl 1779) actor BD
BASSMAN, George (b 1914) American musical director, composer, conductor, actor BE
BASTAR, Mrs. [née Green] (fl 1800) actress TD/1-2
BASTEE (d 1747) dancer BD
BASTER, Mrs. John [née Eleanor Green] (fl 1799-1809?) actress, singer BD
BASTIANINI, Ettore (d 1967) Italian singer WWA/4
BASTON, Mrs. (fl 1735-36) dresser BD
BASTON, Miss (fl 1732-35) dancer, harpsichordist BD

BASTON, John (fl 1709-39) flutist, composer BD
BASTON, Robert dramatist CP/3
BASTON, Thomas (fl 1709-20) musician BD
BASTOW, George (fl late 19th cent) actor, singer CDP
BASTOW, Louis (d 1886) advance agent EA/87*
BATAGLIO, Matteo (fl 1662?-70) musician BD
BATAILLE, Henry (d 1922 [49]) dramatist WWT/14*
BATCHELDER, Marjorie [Mrs. Paul McPharlin] (b 1903) American marionettist ES
BATCHELLER, Jennie (d 1966 [70]) performer BP/51*
BATCHELLER, Joseph D. (b 1915) American educator, director BE
BATCHELOR, Miss (fl 1750-54) dancer BD
BATCHELOR, Mrs. D. S. (d 1884) EA/85*
BATCHELOR, Nelly [Nelly Ethair] (d 1882) characteristic singer EA/83*
BATE, Mr. (fl 1779) actor BD
BATE, Henry see Dudley, Sir Henry Bate
BATEMAN, Mr. (fl 1782) actor BD
BATEMAN, Mrs. (fl 1730) actress? BD
BATEMAN, Ellen Douglas (1844-1936) American actress CDP, COC, DD, ES, HAS, OC/1-3, SR
BATEMAN, Frank (d 1906 [42]) actor EA/07*
BATEMAN, Harold L. (d 1878 [28]) EA/79*
BATEMAN, Hezekiah Linthicum (1812-75) American manager COC, DD, DNB, ES, OC/1-3, SR
BATEMAN, Isabel Emilie (1854-1934) American actress CDP, COC, DD, ES, OAA/1-2, OC/1-3
BATEMAN, Jessie (b 1877) actress GRB/3-4, WWT/1-9
BATEMAN, John (fl 1667) actor? BD
BATEMAN, Kate Josephine [Mrs. Crowe] (1843-1917) American actress CDP, COC, DAB, DD, ES, GRB/1-4, HAS, OAA/1-2,

OC/1-3, SR, WWT/1-3
BATEMAN, Leah [Leah Bateman-
Hunter] (b 1892) English
actress WWT/1-8
BATEMAN, Mrs. [Mary?] (1765?-
1829) actress, fencer, singer
BD
BATEMAN, Richard (d 1874)
actor EA/75*
BATEMAN, Sidney Frances
Cowell (1823-81) American
actress, dramatist COC,
DAB, DD, DNB, ES, HJD,
NTH, OC/1-3, WWA/H
BATEMAN, Thomas (fl 1660-69)
actor BD
BATEMAN, Mrs. Thomas (d
1900) EA/01*
BATEMAN, Victory (1866-1926)
American actress SR,
WWM, WWS
BATEMAN, Virginia Frances
[Mrs. Edward Compton]
(1853-1940) American actress,
manager DD, ES, GRB/1-4,
OAA/1-2, OC/1-3, WWT/
1-8
BATEMAN, Zillah (1900-70)
English actress WWT/7-8
BATEMAN-HUNTER, Leah see
Bateman, Leah
BATES, Mr. (fl 1749) actor BD
BATES, Mrs. (fl 1678) actress
BD
BATES, Miss [Mrs. Barfoot]
(fl 1793-1820?) dancer,
singer BD
BATES, Alan Arthur (b 1934)
English actor AAS, BE,
CB, COC, ES, TW/14, 18,
21, 29, WWT/13-16
BATES, Barbara (d 1969 [43])
performer BP/53*
BATES, Blanche (1873-1941)
American actress CB,
COC, DAB, ES, GRB/2-4,
NTH, OC/1-3, SR, WWA/
1-2, WWM, WWS, WWT/
1-9
BATES, Florence (1888-1954)
American actress BE*
BATES, F. M. (d 1879) Aus-
tralian actor EA/80*
BATES, Mrs. F. M. (d 1908)
actress SR
BATES, Frank M. (fl 1858-68)
actor, manager HAS
BATES, Guy (d 1968 [92])

performer BP/52*
BATES, J. (fl 1722) actor? BD
BATES, J. (fl 1794) singer BD
BATES, Jacob (fl 1760?-70?) Eng-
lish equestrian BD, CDP, ES
BATES, James (d 1784) actor BD
BATES, Mrs. James [née Patty Ann
Scrase] (d 1787) actress BD
BATES, James W. (d 1853) manager
HAS
BATES, Joah (1740-99) conductor,
organist BD
BATES, Mrs. Joah [née Sarah Har-
rop] (d 1811) English singer,
actress BD
BATES, John (fl 1685) singer BD
BATES, John (fl 1846-56) theatre
owner WWA/H
BATES, Jonathan (d 1967 [42])
dramatist BP/52*
BATES, Lulu American singer,
actress BE
BATES, Marie (d 1923 [70]) Amer-
ican actress CDP, SR
BATES, Mary see Dibdin, Mrs.
Charles Isaac Mungo
BATES, Michael (b 1920) Indian/
English actor AAS, WWT/15-
16
BATES, Cpt. M. V. giant CDP
BATES, Mrs. M. V. giant CDP
BATES, Robert (d 1786) actor BD
BATES, Sally (b 1907) American
actress WWT/8-9
BATES, Sarah (d 1811) singer
CDP, DNB
BATES, Thomas (d 1679) violist,
teacher BD
BATES, Thorpe (1883-1958) English
actor, singer WWT/4-11,
WWW/5
BATES, Wilbur M. (b 1861) Amer-
ican representative GRB/3-4
BATES, William (d 1813?) actor,
dancer, singer, machinist,
manager BD, DD, HAS
BATES, William Joseph (d 1901
[44]) proprietor EA/02*
BATES, William Oscar (1852-1924)
American dramatist WWA/1
BATESON, Timothy (b 1926) English
actor AAS, WWT/15-16
BATESSEN, [Mr.?] (fl 1783-84)
performer? BD
BATH, Albert J. (d 1964 [85])
performer BE*
BATH, Hubert (b 1883) English
composer, conductor ES,

WWT/4-9
BATH, James (d 1909 [73]) publisher EA/10*
BATHURST, Charles Bradsworth (d 1889 [43]) music-hall performer EA/90*
BATIE, Frank (d 1949 [69]) American actor BE*, BP/34*
BATIERE, Mrs. (fl 1784) actress BD
BATIST, John (d 1875 [56]) proprietor EA/76*
BATIST, Mrs. John (d 1875) EA/76*
BATLEY, Dorothy (b 1902) English actress WWT/5-10
BATLEY, Mrs. Ernest G. [Ethel Gordon Mussay] (d 1917 [38]) EA/18*
BATLEY, Isaac see Hicken, Isaac George
BATLEY, Ralph Cecil (d 1917) EA/18*
BATLEY, Mrs. Ralph Cecil see Terry-Lewis, Mabel
BATSON, Mr. (fl 1774) actor BD
BATSON, Mrs. (fl 1774) actress BD
BATSON, George (b 1918) American dramatist BE
BATT, Mr. (fl 1734) actor BD
BATT, Madeline (d 1975 [80]) BP/60*
BATTALINI, Luis (fl 1847) singer HAS
BATTEN, Mrs. Louis see Wilton, Jenny
BATTERSBY, Harry (d 1917) proprietor EA/18*
BATTERSBY, Mrs. Henry (d 1902 [45]) manager EA/03*
BATTIS, Emery (b 1915) American actor TW/25
BATTISHILL, Jonathan (1738-1801) instrumentalist, singer, composer BD
BATTISHILL, Mrs. Jonathan see Davies, Elizabeth
BATTLE, Ralph (1649-1713) organist BD
BATTLE, Robert C. (d 1965 [34]) performer BP/50*
BATTLE, William (fl 1691-1711) singer BD
BATTLES, John (b 1921) American actor, singer BE, TW/1, 4, WWT/11-12

BATTLES, Marjorie (b 1939) American actress TW/22-24
BATTLEY, Thomas (d 1880 [26]) gymnast EA/81*
BATTY, Archibald (1887-1961) English actor WWT/8-13
BATTY, George (d 1867 [64]) proprietor ES
BATTY, Thomas (d 1903 [71]) equestrian, circus manager CDP, ES
BATTY, Mrs. Thomas (d 1875) EA/76*
BATTY, William (d 1868 [67]) equestrian manager, proprietor ES
BATTY, Mrs. William (d 1879 [69]) EA/80*
BAU, Gordon R. (d 1975 [68]) make up artist BP/60*
BAUCARDE, Carlo (1825-83) Italian singer ES, HAS
BAUDOUIN, Mons. (fl 1734-45) dancer BD
BAUEMANN, E. O. see Royelle, Charles
BAUER, David (d 1973 [55]) performer BP/57*
BAUERSMITH, Paula (b 1909) American actress BE, TW/14-20, 23-24, WWT/14-16
BAUGH, Mrs. Fred see Harvey, Alice
BAUGHAN, Edward Algernon (1865-1938) English critic GRB/2-4, WWT/1-8, WWW/3
BAUGHMAN, Eliza (d 1901 [49]) gunman EA/02*
BAUM, Harry (d 1974 [58]) performer BP/58*
BAUM, Mrs. H. William (d 1970 [88]) performer BP/54*
BAUM, Kurt (b 1908) Czech singer CB, ES
BAUM, Lyman Frank (1856-1919) American dramatist DAB, ES, HJD, SR, WWA/1, WWM, WWS
BAUM, Martin (b 1924) American talent representative BE
BAUM, Morton (d 1968 [62]) lawyer BP/52*
BAUM, Vicki (1898-1960) Austrian dramatist, librettist ES, NTH, WWA/4, WWW/5
BAUMANN, Kathryn (b 1946) American actress TW/26, 30
BAUMGARTEN, Karl Friedrich

(1740-1824) musician, composer, teacher BD
BAUMGARTEN, Samuel (fl 1752-92) bassoonist BD
BAUMGARTNER, Mr. (fl 1742) actor? BD
BAUMGARTNER, Bertha (d 1888) wild animal trainer EA/90*
BAUR, Franklyn (d 1950 [46]) singer TW/6
BAUSMAN, Nellie Dutton (d 1974 [85]) performer BP/58*
BAUX, Julien (b c.1789) violinist BD
BAVAAR, Tony (b 1921) American actor, singer TW/7, 9-14
BAVAN, Yolande (b 1942) Ceylonese actress TW/24, 26-28
BAVIER, Frances (b 1905) American actress TW/1, 3-9
BAWCOMBE, Fred (d 1895) comedian EA/96*
BAWCOMBE, Maria (d 1892) EA/93*
BAWN, Harry (fl late 18th cent) singer CDP
BAWTREE, Arthur actor GRB/1
BAWTREE, Charles Frederick (d 1911) manager EA/12*
BAX, Clifford (1886-1962) English dramatist COC, ES, MH, NTH, OC/3, WWT/5-13, WWW/6
BAXLEY, Barbara (b 1925/27) American actress BE, TW/9-12, 19-21, 23, 25-26, WWT/14-16
BAXTER, Mrs. (fl 1706-11) actress BD
BAXTER, Mrs. (fl 1741) actress BD
BAXTER, Sir A. Beverley (1891-1964) Canadian critic WWT/10-13
BAXTER, Alan (1908-76) American actor BE, ES, TW/2-15, WWT/11-15
BAXTER, Anne (b 1923) American actress BE, CB, ES, TW/14, 28, 30, WWT/16
BAXTER, Barry (1894-1922) Welsh actor WWT/4
BAXTER, Beryl (b 1926) English actress WWT/12-15
BAXTER, Sir Beverley see Baxter, Sir A. Beverley
BAXTER, Charles (b 1924)

American actor TW/20, 24
BAXTER, Eleanor (fl 1799-1801) performer BD
BAXTER, Frank (b 1922) American actor TW/2-3, 5-11
BAXTER, Gladys (d 1972) performer BP/56*
BAXTER, Jane (b 1909) German/English actress AAS, ES, TW/3, WWT/7-16
BAXTER, Mrs. J. Emmett see Corcoran, Jane
BAXTER, John (fl 1663-70) scenekeeper BD
BAXTER, Keith [née Baxter-Wright] (b 1933/35) Welsh actor BE, TW/18-19, 24, 27-29, WWT/15-16
BAXTER, Lora (d 1955 [47]) performer BE*, BP/40*
BAXTER, Phil (d 1972 [75]) composer/lyricist BP/57*
BAXTER, Richard (1593-1666?) English actor DA, OC/1-3
BAXTER, Richard (1618-c.1666) English actor BD, OC/3
BAXTER, Richard (d 1747) English dancer BD
BAXTER, Robert (fl 1600-13) actor DA
BAXTER, Stanley (b 1926) Scottish actor WWT/13-16
BAXTER, Warner (1893-1951) American actor ES, TW/7, WWA/3
BAXTER, William J. (d 1873 [31]) singer, actor EA/74*
BAXTER-DILLON, F. (b 1880) English actor GRB/1
BAXTER-WRIGHT, Keith see Baxter, Keith
BAY, Mr. (fl 1724) gallery keeper BD
BAY, Howard (b 1912) American designer BE, ES, TW/2, 5-8, WWT/10-16
BAYES, Nora [Dora Goldberg] (1880-1928) American actress, singer CDP, ES, SR, WWT/4-5
BAYFIELD, St. Clair [J. St. Clair Roberts] (1875-1967) English actor GRB/1, TW/1, 5-6, 23
BAYLEY, Mr. (fl 1749) house servant BD
BAYLEY, Mr. (fl 1783-85) box and lobby keeper BD
BAYLEY, Mrs. (fl 1780-81) singer BD
BAYLEY, Caroline (b 1890) Irish

actress WWT/2-5
BAYLEY, Eric (fl 1882) actor
  CDP
BAYLEY, George (fl 1662) actor,
  manager BD
BAYLEY, Hilda (d 1971) English
  actress WWT/3-13
BAYLEY, James G. (d 1887
  [37]) actor EA/88*
BAYLEY, John (fl 1798) drama-
  tist CP/3
BAYLIES, Edmund (b 1904)
  American actor, stage mana-
  ger, director BE
BAYLIS, Christina (d 1898 [70])
  music-hall proprietor EA/
  99*
BAYLIS, Donald (d 1920) business
  manager WWT/14*
BAYLIS, James S. (d 1870) pro-
  prietor EA/71*
BAYLIS, John (fl 1804) translator
  CP/3
BAYLIS, Lilian Mary (1874-1937)
  English manager, impresario
  AAS, COC, DNB, ES, OC/
  1-3, PDT, WWT/4-8, WWW/3
BAYLIS, Mary (d 1902) EA/03*
BAYLISS, Jacob (d 1901) EA/02*
BAYLISS, John (d 1906 [59])
  musical director EA/07*
BAYLISS, Peter actor WWT/
  15-16
BAYLY, Ada Ellen see Lyall,
  Edna
BAYLY, Caroline English actress
  WWT/9-10
BAYLY, Edward (fl 1628) actor
  DA
BAYLY, Thomas (fl 1581) actor
  DA
BAYLY, Thomas Haines (1797-
  1839) English dramatist
  CDP, DD, HP
BAYLYE (fl 1582) actor DA
BAYMAN, Annie see Bayman,
  Mary Anne
BAYMAN, Mary Anne [Annie
  Bayman] (d 1882 [37])
  EA/83*
BAYNE, Mr. (fl 1777-90) house
  servant BD
BAYNE, Beverly (b 1896) Amer-
  ican actress TW/2-11
BAYNE, Mrs. Milton H. see
  Dubois, Gene
BAYNE, Robert actor GRB/1
BAYNE, Walter McPherson (d

1859 [64]) scene artist, actor
  HAS
BAYNES, Mr. (fl 1797-1800) actor,
  singer BD
BAYNHAM, Thomas (d 1882 [87])
  EA/83*
BAYNHAM, Walter (fl 1853-92)
  actor, critic DD
BAYNHAM, Mrs. Walter [Fanny
  Maskell] (d 1919 [90]) actress
  DD
BAYNTON, Henry (1892-1951) Eng-
  lish actor, manager WWT/4-10
BAYZAND, William (d 1802)
  dancer, actor BD
BAYZAND, Mrs. William [née
  Elizabeth Taylor] (fl 1792-96)
  singer BD
BAZON, [Mr.?] (fl 1784-85) house
  servant? BD
BAZZINI, Antonio (d 1897 [78])
  Italian composer EA/98*
BEACH, Ann (b 1938) English
  actress WWT/14-16
BEACH, Charles E. (fl 1854) Amer-
  ican actor HAS
BEACH, Gary (b 1947) American
  actor TW/29-30
BEACH, George B. (fl 1856-63)
  actor HAS
BEACH, Hugh D. (d 1975 [61])
  producer/director/choreographer
  BP/59*
BEACH, Lewis (c.1807-27) Ameri-
  can dramatist EAP, RJ, SR
BEACH, Rex (1877-1949) American
  dramatist WWA/2
BEACH, W. E. (fl 1890) actor
  SR
BEACH, William (1874-1926) actor
  SR
BEACH AND BOWERS (fl 1892)
  minstrels, managers SR
BEACHNER, Louis (b 1923) Ameri-
  can actor TW/26, 29
BEADEMORE, Mr. (fl 1786?-94)
  singer BD
BEADON, Phyllis (b 1889) Indian/
  English actress GRB/1-2
BEAGLE, G. H. (d 1908) manager
  EA/09*
BEAL, Jerry (b 1946) American
  actor TW/30
BEAL, John (b 1909) American
  actor, director BE, ES, TW/
  2-20, 23, 25-28, WWT/8-16
BEAL, Royal (1899-1969) American
  actor BE, TW/1-8, 12-14,

25, WWA/5

BEAL, Scott (d 1973 [83]) performer BP/58*

BEALBY, George [George Edward Wright] (1877-1931) English actor GRB/1-3, WWT/4-6

BEALE, Mr. (fl 1796-1815?) instrumentalist BD

BEALE, Charles (d 1905 [85]) EA/06*

BEALE, Charles James (d 1882 [63]) chorus master EA/83*

BEALE, Elizabeth (d 1891 [70]) actress EA/92*

BEALE, Felix C. (d 1879 [36]) violinist EA/80*

BEALE, Franklin Parkes (1874-1947) vaudevillian SR

BEALE, Harold G. W. (d 1911 [27]) variety manager EA/12*

BEALE, Simon (d c.1695) trumpeter BD

BEALE, Thomas Willert ["Walter Maynard"] (1831-94) musician DD

BEALE, Thurley (d 1897) singer EA/98*

BEALL, Thomas (fl 1794-1803?) singer BD

BEALS, Margaret American actress TW/23

BEAN, Joseph (d 1881 [74]) musician EA/82*

BEAN, Orson (b 1928) American actor BE, CB, TW/8, 10-15, 18-21, 23-24, 26, WWT/14-16

BEAN, Reathel (b 1942) American actor TW/25, 27-28, 30

BEANE, Fanny (b 1853) dancer, singer, actress CDP

BEANE, George A., Sr. (d 1893) American actor SR

BEANLAND, Mrs. R. W. (d 1875) EA/76*

BEARD, Charles (b 1945) American actor TW/26

BEARD, James American actor TW/25-27

BEARD, John (c.1716-91) English singer, actor, manager, patentee BD, CDP, DD, DNB, ES, GT, OC/1-3, TD/1-2

BEARD, Dr. Thomas (fl 1631)

dramatist CP/3

BEARD, Mrs. Thomas, Jr. see Conquest, Lizzie

BEARDA, T. (fl 1794) violinist BD

BEARDSLEY, Alice (b 1927) American actress TW/25, 28-29

BEARDWELL, John (fl 1671) musician BD

BEARNES, Hugh (fl 1794) bass viol player BD

BEART, Rudolf (fl 1608) actor DA

BEASLEY, Byron (1872-1927) actor SR

BEASLEY, Edward [Richard de Freyne Jones] (d 1899) actor EA/00*

BEASLEY, Harry (d 1890 [27]) music-hall performer EA/91*

BEASLEY, William Manton (d 1908) EA/09*

BEATON, Sir Cecil (b 1904) English designer AAS, BE, CB, ES, PDT, TW/3, WWT/10-16

BEATRICE, Mlle. [Marie Beatrice Binda] (1839-78) Italian actress CDP, DD, OAA/1-2

BEATTIE, Dorothy American actress TW/5-6

BEATTIE, Nancy (d 1908 [61]) lessee EA/09*

BEATTY, Bessie (1886-1947) American dramatist WWA/2

BEATTY, George (d 1971 [76]) performer BP/56*

BEATTY, Harcourt actor WWT/4-5

BEATTY, May (d 1945 [64]) New Zealand actress, singer WWT/4-9

BEATTY, Raymond (d 1973 [70]) performer BP/58*

BEATTY, Robert (b 1909) Canadian actor ES, WWT/10-16

BEATTY, Roberta (b 1891) American actress WWT/8-9

BEATTY, Sophia Elizabeth (d 1900 [73]) EA/01*

BEATTY, Warren (b 1937) American actor BE, CB, ES

BEATTY-KINGSTON, W. (fl 1884-92) librettist DD

BEAUCARDE, Carlo see Baucardé, Carlo

BEAUCHAMP, George [né Patrick Sarsfield Beauchamp] (d 1900 [38]) music-hall comedian CDP

BEAUCHAMP, Mrs. George
see Lingard, Nellie
BEAUCHAMP, John (d 1921 [70])
actor DD, EA/95, GRB/
3-4, WWT/1-3
BEAUCHAMP, Patrick Sarsfield
see Beauchamp, George
BEAUCHAMP, Richard John (d
1898 [21]) actor EA/00*
BEAUCHENE BEAUDOIN, Louise
(1817-94) French actress ES
BEAUDET, Louise (1865-1948)
French/Spanish actress,
singer CDP, DD, TW/4
BEAUFIELD, Mrs. (fl 1784)
actress BD
BEAUFORD, Mr. (fl 1741) actor
BD
BEAUFORT, [Miss?] (fl 1794-
95) singer BD
BEAUFORT, G. H. (d 1885 [41])
actor EA/86*
BEAUFORT, Grace [Mrs. Frank
Lister] (d 1896 [27]) actress
EA/97*
BEAUFORT, John (b 1912) Cana-
dian critic WWT/13-16
BEAUFORT, Leslie [T. Smyth
Nicolson] English actor
GRB/1
BEAULIEU, Mrs. (fl 1783-85)
figure dancer BD
BEAULIEU, Miss (fl 1785) figure
dancer BD
BEAUMONT, Dr. (fl 1777) actor
HAS
BEAUMONT, Mr. (fl 1731-47)
dancer, actor BD
BEAUMONT, Mr. (fl 1794) stage
door-keeper BD
BEAUMONT, Mrs. (fl 1769-73?)
singer BD
BEAUMONT, Mrs. [Mrs. Ixon]
(fl 1800-02) actress BD
BEAUMONT, Mrs. (fl 1810)
actress HAS
BEAUMONT, Allen (fl 1880)
actor DD, OAA/2
BEAUMONT, Alma see Odiva
BEAUMONT, Annie (d 1882)
actress, singer CDP
BEAUMONT, Arthur [A. B.
Collins] (d 1890 [28]) EA/91*
BEAUMONT, Cyril William
(1891-1976) English critic
WWT/12-14
BEAUMONT, Mrs. De Jersey
(fl 1810-14) actress DD

BEAUMONT, Diana (1909-64) Eng-
lish actress WWT/7-13
BEAUMONT, E. R. (b 1865) English
producer, stage manager, actor
GRB/1
BEAUMONT, Sir Francis (c.1584-
1616) English dramatist CDP,
COC, CP/1-3, DD, DNB,
ES, FGF, HP, MH, NTH,
OC/1-3, PDT, RE
BEAUMONT, Harry (b 1888) Amer-
ican actor ES
BEAUMONT, Henry (d 1791) violin-
ist? BD
BEAUMONT, Hugh (1908-73) mana-
ger AAS, TW/29, WWT/8-15
BEAUMONT, John (b 1902) English
manager WWT/11-15
BEAUMONT, Mrs. M. R. (d 1878
[56]) housekeeper EA/79*
BEAUMONT, Muriel [Mrs. Gerald
du Maurier] (1881-1957) actress
COC, GRB/1-4, OC/3, WWT/
1-6
BEAUMONT, Nellie (d 1938 [68])
actress, singer CDP
BEAUMONT, Ralph (b 1926) Amer-
ican choreographer, dancer
BE
BEAUMONT, Roma (b 1914) English
actress, dancer WWT/9-11
BEAUMONT, Rose (d 1938) actress
BE*
BEAUMONT, Walter [Walter Bret-
tell] (1872-1910) English actor
GRB/1-2
BEAUMONT, William Alexander
(d 1895 [26]) Negro lion tamer
EA/97*
BEAUPINS, Mons. (fl 1672-75)
singer BD
BEAUPRE, Mons. (fl 1788-89)
dancer BD
BEAVEN, Mrs. (d 1905) EA/06*
BEAVERS, Louise (d 1962 [60])
actress BE*, BP/47*
BEAW, Mr. (fl 1730-35) box-keeper
BD
BEAZLEY, Samuel (1786-1851)
English architect, designer
COC, DD, OC/1-3
BEAZLEY, Samuel, Jr. (fl 1811)
dramatist CP/3
BEBAN, George (1873-1928) English
actor, producer ES, SR,
WWA/1
BECCELEY, Mrs. (fl 1753) actress
DD, HAS

BECHER, Lady see O'Neill,
Eliza
BECHER, Albert J. see Becher-
vaire, Albert J.
BECHER, John C. (b 1915) Amer-
ican actor BE, TW/25-26
BECHER, Martin (fl 1870)
dramatist DD
BECHER, Thomas costume de-
signer BE
BECHER, Ulrich (b 1910) German
dramatist CH, MD
BECHERVAIRE, Albert J. (d
1883 [28]) EA/84*
BECHET, Sidney (1897-1959)
American musician WWA/4
BECHI, Gino (b 1913) Italian
singer ES
BECHTEL, William (1858-1930)
German/American actor SR
BECK, Don (d 1967 [31]) per-
former BP/52*
BECK, Gordon (b 1929) American
educator, editor, director
BE
BECK, James (d 1973 [41]) per-
former BP/58*
BECK, Julian (b 1925) American
director, scene designer,
actor, producer BE, COC,
ES, WWT/15-16
BECK, Lethbridge (d 1897 [86])
actor EA/98*
BECK, Martin (1869-1940) Czech/
American producer, mana-
ger, actor CB, DAB, NTH,
SR, WWA/4
BECK, Mrs. Martin (b 1889)
American executive BE
BECK, Philip (d 1889 [35]) actor
EA/91*
BECK, Rolly (b 1918) American
actor TW/3
BECK, Stanley (b 1936) American
actor TW/19, 21, 29
BECK, Thomas (b 1909) Ameri-
can actor TW/3
BECK, William (1869-1925) Hun-
garian singer WWA/1
BECKER, Bruce (b 1925) Amer-
ican producer, theatre owner
BE
BECKER, Edward American
actor TW/24-27
BECKER, John C. (d 1963 [81])
scene designer BE*
BECKER, Nan Brennan (d 1965)
performer BP/50*

BECKER, Ned M. (d 1975 [82])
performer BP/60*
BECKER, Pierre (d 1893) circus
performer EA/94*
BECKER, Ray (b 1934) American
actor TW/26-28
BECKER, William (b 1927) Ameri-
can theatre executive, actor,
director BE
BECKERMAN, Bernard (b 1921)
American educator, director
BE
BECKER-THEODORE, Lee (b 1933)
American choreographer,
dancer, actress BE
BECKET, Andrew (fl 1806) writer
CP/3, DD
BECKETT, Clara Bates (d 1869)
EA/70*
BECKETT, Fred (d 1892 [46])
EA/94*
BECKETT, George (d 1876 [37])
comedian EA/77*
BECKETT, G. F. (d 1891) EA/92*
BECKETT, Harry (1839-80) English
actor, comedian CDP, DD
BECKETT, J.G. (1839-87) English
actor HAS
BECKETT, Mrs. J. G. see
Desmond, Maggie
BECKETT, Mary (d 1886) EA/87*
BECKETT, May Ada Ivy (d 1917
[3]) EA/18*
BECKETT, Phillip (fl 1660-74) in-
strumentalist BD
BECKETT, Samuel Barclay (b 1906)
Irish dramatist, director AAS,
BE, CB, CD, CH, COC, ES,
HP, MD, MH, MWD, NTH,
OC/3, PDT, RE, WWT/13-16
BECKETT, Scotty (d 1968 [38])
performer BP/52*
BECKETT, Thomas William (d
1874 [61]) actor, pantomimist
EA/75*
BECKETT, Walter (d 1887 [33])
bandmaster EA/88*
BECKHAM, Mr. (fl 1731-49) actor,
prompter BD
BECKHAM, Mrs. (fl 1735-49)
actress BD
BECKHAM, Mrs. (fl 1776-77)
candle woman BD
BECKHAM, Willard (b 1948) Amer-
ican actor TW/30
BECKHARD, Arthur J. producer,
manager WWT/8
BECKINGHAM, Charles (1699-1731)

English dramatist CP/1-3,
DD, DNB, GT, TD/1-2
BECKINGTON, Miss (fl 1734)
actress BD
BECKLEY, Beatrice Mary (b
1885) English actress WWT/
4-6
BECKMAN, David (b 1944) Amer-
ican actor TW/28
BECKMAN, Henry (b 1921) Cana-
dian actor TW/7
BECKWITH, Charles Alfred (d
1898 [33]) tank performer
EA/99*
BECKWITH, Frederick E. (d
1898 [76]) swimmer EA/99*
BECKWITH, J. W. (d 1908)
business manager GRB/4
BECKWITH, Linden [Mrs. Spencer
J. Johnson, Jr.] (b 1885)
American singer, vaude-
villian WWM
BECKWITH, Lizzie (d 1905)
swimmer EA/06*
BECKWITH, Reginald (1908-65)
English actor, dramatist
ES, WWT/10-13
BECKWITH, William (d 1892 [36])
swimmer EA/94*
BEDDOE, Alfred (d 1892 [45])
actor, manager EA/93*
BEDDOES, Thomas Lovell
(1803-49) English dramatic
poet DD, DNB, ES, HP,
NTH
BEDELIA, Bonnie (b 1948) Amer-
ican actress TW/22-23
BEDELLS, James actor DD
BEDELLS, Phyllis (b 1893)
English dancer, choreog-
rapher ES, WWT/4-10
BEDFORD, Arthur George Sharpe
(d 1899 [22]) actor EA/00*
BEDFORD, Brian (b 1935) Eng-
lish actor AAS, BE, TW/
19-21, 23-30, WWT/14-16
BEDFORD, Charles John Abbott
(d 1879 [37]) stage manager
EA/81*
BEDFORD, E. A. see Vasco
BEDFORD, Edward (fl 1667-71)
manager BD
BEDFORD, Harry singer, com-
poser CDP [see also next
two entries]
BEDFORD, Harry (d 1870 [70])
singer EA/71*
BEDFORD, Harry (d 1939 [66])

comedian BE*
BEDFORD, Henry (d 1923 [77])
actor, dramatist DD, DP
BEDFORD, Herbert (1867-1945)
English composer WWW/3
BEDFORD, Mrs. Herbert see
Lehmann, Liza
BEDFORD, Mary Anne (d 1875 [52])
box-office keeper EA/76*
BEDFORD, Mary Sophia (d 1886)
EA/87*
BEDFORD, Patrick (b 1932) Irish
actor TW/22, 26, 29
BEDFORD, Paul John (c.1792-1871)
English actor, singer CDP,
DD, DNB, ES, OC/1-3
BEDFORD, Mrs. Paul John see
Greene, Elizabeth
BEDINI, Signora (fl 1787-88) dancer
BD
BEDINI, Mlle. (fl 1793) dancer BD
BEDINI, Jean (d 1956 [85]) producer
BE*, BP/41*
BEDLOE, Cpt. William (d 1680)
English dramatist CP/1-2,
DD, GT
BEDOUIN ARABS (fl 1838) CDP
BEDOWE, Elis (fl 1635) actor DA
BEDSMORE, Thomas (d 1881) actor?
organist EA/82*
BEDWELL, Mr. (fl 1726-27) house
servant? BD
BEDWELL, Stanley (d 1916) EA/17*
BEE, William (fl 1599-1624) actor
DA
BEEBE, Henrietta (b 1844) singer
CDP
BEEBE, Lucius (d 1966 [63]) jour-
nalist BP/50*
BEEBE, Mary (fl 1885) singer
CDP
BEECHAM, Charles (d 1912 [41])
music-hall manager EA/13*
BEECHAM, E. T. (d 1901 [30])
singer EA/02*
BEECHAM, Sir Joseph (d 1916 [68])
producer BE*, WWT/14*
BEECHAM, Sir Thomas (1879-1961)
English conductor, composer
CB, ES, TW/17, WWW/6
BEECHER, Janet (1884-1955) Amer-
ican actress TW/1-3, 5-7,
12, WWM, WWT/4-11
BEECHER, William G., Jr. (d
1973 [69]) composer/lyricist
BP/58*
BEECHEY, A. B. (fl 1850) actor
HAS

BEECROFT, G. A. (d 1873)
composer EA/74*
BEEHLER, Dave (d 1968 [87])
agent BP/52*
BEEKMAN, John K. (fl 1802-21)
American? theatre owner
WWA/H
BEELAND, Ambrose (fl 1624-72)
violinist BD
BEEMS, Patricia Jane (d 1973
[46]) performer BP/57*
BEER, Henry see Henry, Basil
BEERBOHM, Clarence Evelyn
(d 1917 [32]) English actor
WWT/1-3
BEERBOHM, Julius (d 1906 [53])
EA/07*, GRB/2*
BEERBOHM, Sir Max (1872-1956)
English critic, dramatist
COC, DD, DNB, ES, GRB/
1-4, HP, MD, MWD, NTH,
OC/1-3, TW/12, WWA/3,
WWT/1-11, WWW/5
BEERBOHM, W. Julius Ewald
(d 1892 [82]) EA/93*
BEERE, Mrs. Bernard [Mrs.
H. C. S. Olivier] (1856-
1915) English actress CDP,
DD, DP, GRB/1-4, OAA/2,
WWT/1-2
BEERS, Francine American
actress TW/29
BEERS, Robert (d 1972 [51])
performer BP/56*
BEERY, Lee [or Leigh] American
actress TW/26, 29-30
BEERY, Noah (1882-1946) Amer-
ican actor TW/1-2
BEERY, Wallace (1885-1949)
American actor DAB, ES,
SR, WWA/2, WWW/4
BEESLEY, Mr. (fl 1780) actor
BD
BEESON, Mr. (fl 1729-31) house
servant? BD
BEESTON, (fl 1560-61) actor
DA
BEESTON, Mr. (fl 1708-12) vio-
linist BD
BEESTON, Mr. (fl 1782-84)
house servant? BD
BEESTON, Christopher (1570?-
1638) English actor, mana-
ger COC, DA, ES, OC/1-3
BEESTON, George (fl 1660?-75)
actor BD
BEESTON, Robert (fl 1603-17)
actor DA

BEESTON, William (1606?-82) Eng-
lish actor, manager BD, COC,
DA, DD, OC/1-3
BEET, Alice (d 1931) English act-
ress GRB/1-4, WWT/1-6
BEET, Fanny (d 1886 [40]) EA/87*
BEETLESTONE, W. M. actor CDP
BEETON, Mr. (fl 1794-1803)
house servant BD
BEFUS, Roy (d 1973 [44]) stage
manager BP/58*
BEGG, Mrs. William see Bentley,
Florence
BEGGARS THEATRE theatre collec-
tive CD
BEGGS, Lee (1870-1943) actor SR
BEGLEY, Ed (1901-70) American
actor BE, CB, TW/3-8, 11-
18, 25-26, WWA/5, WWT/14
BEHAN, Brendan (1923-64) Irish
dramatist AAS, BE, CB, CD,
CH, COC, ES, MD, MH,
MWD, PDT, RE, TW/20,
WWA/4, WWT/13, WWW/6
BEHEL, Jacob see Pedel, Jacob
BEHIN (d 1843 [36]) Belgian giant
EA/72*
BEHMANN, Edward (d 1888 [28])
manager EA/89*
BEHN, Mrs. Aphra (1640-89) Eng-
lish dramatist CDP, COC,
CP/1-3, DD, DNB, ES, GT,
HP, MH, NTH, OC/1-3
BEHN, Harry (d 1973 [74]) drama-
tist BP/58*
BEHN, Noel (b 1928) American
producer BE
BEHNKE, Emil (d 1892) teacher,
writer EA/93*
BEHREND, Henrietta (d 1859)
singer HAS
BEHRMAN, Samuel Nathaniel (1893-
1973) American dramatist
AAS, BE, CB, CH, COC, ES,
HJD, MD, MH, MWD, NTH,
OC/1-3, PDT, RE, SR, TW/
30, WWT/6-15
BEHYMER, Lynden Ellsworth
(1862-1947) American impres-
ario WWA/2
BEHYMER, Minetta S. (d 1958 [93])
impresario BE*
BEILBY, Mr. (fl 1784-94) musician
BD
BEIN, Albert (b 1902) Rumanian/
American dramatist BE, ES,
HJD, MD, MWD
BEINHORN, Nat (d 1974 [55])

investor BP/58*
BEITH, John Hay see Hay, Ian
BEJARD, Mons. (fl 1675) musician BD
BEJART, Maurice (b 1927)
French choreographer CB,
ES
BELA, Nicholas (d 1963 [63])
Hungarian dramatist BE*,
BP/48*
BELAFONTE, Harry (b 1924/27)
American singer, actor BE,
CB, ES, TW/10-16
BELANGER, Joanne (b 1945)
American actress TW/30
BELARSKY, Sidor (d 1975 [77])
performer BP/60*
BELASCO, Anne Margaret (d
1895) EA/96*
BELASCO, David [né Valasco]
(1853-1931) American manager, dramatist COC, DAB,
DD, ES, GRB/2-4, HJD,
MH, MWD, NTH, OC/1-3,
PDT, RE, SR, WWA/1,
WWM, WWS, WWT/1-6,
WWW/3
BELASCO, Edward (1874-1937)
American producer SR
BELASCO, Frederick (d 1920
[59]) manager, producer
SR
BELASCO, Genevieve (d 1956
[84]) English actress BE*,
BP/41*
BELASCO, George (d 1896 [60])
EA/97*
BELASCO, Jacques (d 1973 [56])
composer/lyricist BP/58*
BELASCO, Juliet Crosby (d
1907 [30]) American actress
GRB/3*
BELASCO, Leon (b 1902) Russian/American actor BE
BELASCO, Ruby Hamilton actress, singer GRB/1-2
BELASCO, Will [né Sutherland]
(d 1911) music-hall performer
EA/12*
BELASCO, William (d 1976 [41])
producer/director/choreographer BP/60*
BELCHAM, Henry (d 1917 [67])
journalist EA/18*
BELCHER, Frank (1869-1947)
actor, singer SR
BELCHER, Marjorie Celeste
see Champion, Madge

BELCHIER, Dawbridge-Court (1580?-
1621) English dramatist CP/1-
3, DD, DNB, FGF
BELCOUR, Mrs. (fl 1830) actress
HAS
BELDEN, N. B. see Clarke,
N. B.
BELDING, Henry (d 1908) actor
EA/09*, GRB/4*
BELDING, Mrs. Henry see King,
Lottie
BELDON, Edwin (fl 1899) American
actor WWS
BELDON, Eileen (b 1901) English
actress AAS, WWT/4-16
BELENGER, Mr. (fl 1794-95) scene
designer BD
BELFIELD, Mrs. see Barrett,
Mrs. Giles Linnett
BELFIELD, Frederick H. (b 1901)
American executive BE
BELFILLE, Mrs. [Mrs. Arnold;
née Burdett] (d 1789) English
actress BD, DD
BELFORD, Mr. (fl 1849) actor
HAS
BELFORD, Mrs. (d 1887) EA/88*
BELFORD, William Rowles (1824-
81) English actor DD, OAA/2
BELFORT, Mrs. (fl 1760-61)
dancer BD
BELFOUR, Hugo John (1802-27)
dramatist DD
BELFRAGE, Bruce (1901-74) English actor BTR/74, WWT/11-
12
BELFRY, May (d 1902 [25]) actress
EA/03*
BELFRY, Venie [Mrs. C. Foster
Marner] (d 1910) comedienne
EA/11*
BELGADO, Mario (d 1969 [63])
performer BP/54*
BEL GEDDES, Barbara see
Geddes, Barbara Bel
BEL GEDDES, Edith Lutyens (b
1916) costume designer, costumier, producer BE
BEL GEDDES, Norman see
Geddes, Norman Bel
BELKNAP, Edwin Star (fl 1883-94)
American dramatist WWA/1,
WWM
BELL, Mr. (fl 1750-51) singer,
actor? BD
BELL, Mr. (fl 1785-91) equestrian,
dancer, tumbler BD
BELL, Mrs. (fl 1791) dancer BD

BELL, Master (fl 1785-86)
tumbler BD
BELL, Ann (b 1939) English
actress WWT/15-16
BELL, Archie (d 1943 [65])
critic, dramatist BE*
BELL, Armstrong (d 1910) act-
ing manager EA/11*
BELL, Benjamin John see
Dashwood, Harry
BELL, Brian see Murray,
Brian
BELL, Mr. C. (d 1888) EA/89*
BELL, Dr. Campton (d 1963
[58]) educator BE*
BELL, Christopher (fl 1628-61)
musician BD
BELL, Clarence F. (d 1963
[66]) press representative
BE*
BELL, Daniel W. (b 1891)
American executive BE
BELL, Diana (d 1964) performer
BP/49*
BELL, Mrs. Digby see Joyce,
Laura
BELL, Digby Valentine (1851-
1917) American actor, singer
CDP, GRB/2-4, SR, WWA/
1, WWM, WWS, WWT/1-3
BELL, D. V. (fl 1829) Ameri-
can dramatist EAP
BELL, Mrs. Edward M. see
Harrison, Maud
BELL, Eliza [Mrs. Robert Bell]
(d 1879) EA/80*
BELL, Emil (d 1902 [19]) circus
performer EA/03*
BELL, Enid (b 1888) English
actress WWT/2-5
BELL, Eva [Mrs. Charles Rod-
ney] (d 1901 [34]) actress,
singer CDP
BELL, Dame Florence Evelyn
Eleanore (1851-1930) drama-
tist NTH
BELL, Frank (b 1843) dancer,
minstrel CDP
BELL, Frank Eddington (d 1882
[52]) manager EA/83*
BELL, Gaston (1877-1963)
American actor WWS
BELL, Mrs. George Hamilton
see Hamilton, Georgina
BELL, Hillary (1857-1903) Irish
critic WWA/1
BELL, Mrs. Hugh (1851-1930)
French dramatist DD

BELL, Isabell (d 1870) EA/71*
BELL, J. (d 1884 [43]) circus
clown EA/84*
BELL, James (d 1917) lessee EA/
18*
BELL, James (b 1891) American
actor BE, WWT/8-11
BELL, Mrs. James (d 1891) EA/
92*
BELL, John (1745-1831) English
publisher, bookseller COC,
DNB, OC/1-3
BELL, John Joy (1871-1938) Scot-
tish dramatist OC/1-3, WWW/3
BELL, John Keble see Howard,
Keble
BELL, Joseph (d 1918) EA/19*
BELL, Joseph Henry (d 1890 [35])
EA/91*
BELL, Kittie English actress,
dancer GRB/1
BELL, Laura Joyce (1858-1904)
English comic opera singer
WWA/1
BELL, Leslie R. (d 1962 [55])
conductor, composer BE*
BELL, Louisa (d 1891) EA/92*
BELL, Mrs. M. (d 1873 [37]) EA/
74*
BELL, Marie (b 1905) French act-
ress TW/20
BELL, Marion American singer
TW/3-7
BELL, Mary (b 1904) American
actress TW/14, 19, 24, 28-
29
BELL, Mary Hayley (b 1914)
Chinese/English actress,
dramatist BE, WWT/10-14
BELL, Minnie (fl 1881-92) actress,
dramatist DD
BELL, Nolan D. (d 1976 [55]) per-
former BP/60*
BELL, Percy (1848-1913) English
actor OAA/1-2
BELL, Rex (d 1962 [58]) American
actor BE*
BELL, Richard (d 1672) actor BD
BELL, Richard (d 1881?) circus
proprietor EA/82*
BELL, Robert (1800-67) Irish
dramatist DD
BELL, Robert (d 1902 [66]) music-
hall proprietor EA/03*
BELL, Mrs. Robert see Bell,
Eliza
BELL, Robert Stanley Warren (1871-
1921) English dramatist WWW/2

BELL, Rose see Saroni, Rose
BELL, Stanley (1881-1952) English director, actor TW/1, 12-13, WWT/4-11
BELL, Stuart Henry (d 1896) scene painter, manager EA/97*
BELL, Thomas (d 1743) singer BD
BELL, Thomas (d 1815) actor, dancer BD
BELL, William (d 1874 [21]) Negro artist EA/75*
BELL, William (d 1891) EA/92*
BELL, William Henry (1873-1946) English composer ES
BELLA, Rose see Vining, Mrs. A.
BELLAIR, Ellen Amelia Frances (d 1880) actress, singer EA/81*
BELLAIR, Jenny see Warden, Mrs. J. F.
BELLAIR, John (d 1879 [76]) actor EA/80*
BELLAIR, Mary Ann [Mrs. Collie] (d 1881) actress EA/82*
BELLAM, [Mr.?] (fl 1730) dancer BD
BELLAMY, Mr. (fl 1761) singer BD
BELLAMY, Mrs. [Mrs. Walter; née Seal] (d 1771) English actress BD
BELLAMY, Ada [Mrs. Howard Talbot] (d 1895) actress EA/96*
BELLAMY, B. P. (fl 1797) actor BD
BELLAMY, Daniel, Sr. (b 1687) English dramatist CP/1-3, DD
BELLAMY, Daniel, Jr. (d 1788) English dramatist CP/1-3, DD
BELLAMY, Frank see Denton, Frank
BELLAMY, Franklyn (b 1886) English actor WWT/5-9
BELLAMY, George Anne (c. 1727-88) English actress BD, CDP, COC, DD, DNB, ES, GT, NTH, OC/1-3, TD/1-2
BELLAMY, George E. (1866-1944) English actor GRB/1-2

BELLAMY, Henry Ernest (d 1932 [70]) English producer BE*, WWT/14*
BELLAMY, Ralph (b 1904) American actor BE, CB, ES, SR, TW/2-19, WWT/10-14
BELLAMY, Richard (1743?-1813) chorus master, composer BD, DNB
BELLAMY, Somers (fl 1877-89) dramatist DD
BELLAMY, Thomas (1745-1800) English dramatist CP/3, DD
BELLAMY, Thomas Ludford (1771-1843) singer, proprietor, choir master BD, CDP, DNB, GT
BELLAMY, William (d 1843 [74]) singer EA/72*
BELLAMY, William Hoare (1800-66) Irish actor DD, HAS, SR
BELLAMY, Mrs. William Hoare [Mrs. A. W. Penson] (d 1857) Scottish actress HAS
BELLANI, Mons. (fl 1794) dancer HAS
BELLARINA, Bella (d 1969 [72]) performer BP/53*
BELLAVER, Harry (b 1905) American actor BE, TW/22-23, 29-30
BELLE, Marjorie (b 1921) American actress TW/1
BELLERS, Fettiplace (1687-1750?) English dramatist CP/2-3, DD, DNB, GT
BELLETTI, Giovanni (b 1813) singer CDP
BELLEVERE see Hill, Mrs. George
BELLEW, Alfred (d 1932) director WWT/14*
BELLEW, Eugenie (d 1903) actress EA/04*
BELLEW, Harold Kyrle (1855-1911) English actor, dramatist DD, DNB, DP, ES, GRB/1-4, OAA/2, OC/1-3, SR, WWA/1, WWM, WWS
BELLEW, John Chippendale Mortesquieu (1824-74) English dramatic reader CDP
BELLEW, Kyrle (1887/90-1948) English actress TW/4, WWT/4-9
BELLEW, Mrs. Kyrle see Legrande, Eugénie
BELLEZZA, Vincenzo (1888-1964) Italian conductor WWA/4

BELLGUARD, Mr. (fl 1738)
actor BD
BELLIN, Mr. (fl 1794) bass
viol player BD
BELLIN, Olga [née Bielinski]
(b 1932/25) American
actress BE, TW/12-13,
18-20
BELLING, Tom (fl 1850-77)
American clown ES
BELLINGHAM, Mr. (fl 1775)
actor BD
BELLINGHAM, Henry (fl 1864-
95) dramatist DD
BELLINI, Cal American actor
TW/22-25
BELLINI, Laura (d 1975 [73])
performer BP/59*
BELLINI, Vincenzio (1802-35)
Italian composer CDP
BELLMORE, Bertha (b 1882)
English actress TW/3,
WWT/8
BELLOC, Teresa (1784-1855)
singer CDP
BELLOLI, Marianna (fl 1793)
singer BD
BELLOMO, Joe (b 1938) Amer-
ican actor TW/28-30
BELLONINI, Edna (b 1903)
English actress, singer
WWT/6
BELLONINI, Walter (d 1943 [87])
comedian BE*
BELLOW, Alexander (d 1976
[63]) composer/lyricist
BP/60*
BELLOW, Saul (b 1915) Cana-
dian/American dramatist
CD, HJD
BELLOWS, Henry Whitney (b
1814) American writer DD
BELLOWS, Jean American
actress TW/3
BELLOWS, Johnson McClure
(1870-1949) American im-
presario, critic WWA/2
BELLOWS, Phyllis (b 1934)
American literary agent
BE
BELL-PORTER, Lillian (b 1874)
English singer GRB/1
BELL-PORTER, W. E. (b
1868) English musical
director, composer GRB/1
BELLUGI, Piero (b 1924) Italian
conductor ES
BELLWOOD, Bessie [Elizabeth

Ann Katherine Mahoney] (1847-
96) English music-hall perform-
er CDP, COC, OC/1-3
BELLWOOD, George (d 1894) come-
dian EA/95*
BELMAS, Mons. (d 1878) trapezist
EA/79*
BELMONT, Mr. (fl 1792) actor BD
BELMONT, Frances see Ashbur-
ton, Lady
BELMONT, Mrs. George (d 1900)
EA/01*
BELMONT, Harry (d 1888) music-
hall performer EA/89*
BELMONTE, Herman (d 1975 [84])
performer BP/60*
BELMORE, Alfred (d 1918) EA/19*
BELMORE, Alice (d 1919 [29])
actress WWT/14*
BELMORE, Alice (1870?-1943) Eng-
lish actress CB, DD, SR
BELMORE, Bertha (1882-1953)
English actress ES, TW/1-2,
5-10, WWT/9-11
BELMORE, Daisy (d 1954 [80])
English actress TW/1, 11
BELMORE, Edward (d 1918) EA/
19*
BELMORE, George [George Ben-
jamin Garstin] (d 1875 [47])
actor CDP, DD
BELMORE, George (d 1898 [35])
actor EA/99*
BELMORE, George (d 1956) actor
BE*, WWT/14*
BELMORE, Mrs. George (d 1911)
EA/12*
BELMORE, Herbert (d 1952 [77])
actor BE*, WWT/14*
BELMORE, Lily [or Lillie; Mrs.
Claude Wallace] (d 1901 [29])
actress DD, EA/96
BELMORE, Lionel (d 1953 [86])
English actor, stage manager
BE*, BP/37*
BELMORE, Paul (d 1907 [34]) actor
EA/08*, GRB/3*
BELOID, Mme. (1803-56) actress
SR
BELON, Peter (fl 1690) dramatist
CP/1-3, GT
BELOT, Adolph French dramatist
SR
BELSON, Edward (d 1975 [77])
performer BP/60*
BELT, Elmer (b 1893) American
curator BE
BELT, T. (fl 1590) actor DA

BELT AND BRACES ROADSHOW
CO. LTD. theatre collective
CD
BELTON, F. Elizabeth (d 1867)
EA/68*
BELTON, Phoebe [Mrs. Charles
Rider-Noble] (d 1899) EA/
00*
BELTRAM, Sydney [né Bustin]
(d 1911 [60]) actor EA/12*
BELTRAM, Mrs. Sydney see
Engel, Nina
BELVERSTONE, Sarah (d 1867
[80]) EA/68*
BELVERSTONE, Mr. W. (d 1867
[71]) EA/68*
BELVISO, Thomas Henry (1896-
1967) American composer,
conductor WWA/4
BELWIN, Alma (d 1924 [29])
performer BE*, BP/8*
BELZONI, Antonio (b 1780)
Italian actor ES
BELZONI, Giovanni Baptista
(1778-1823) Italian actor
DNB, ES
BEN, Miss (fl 1720) actress BD
BENADERET, Bea (d 1968 [62])
performer BP/53*
BEN-AMI, Jacob (1890-1977)
Russian/American actor,
director, producer BE,
ES, NTH, TW/3, 5-7, 13-
16, 24, 29, WWT/5-10
BENARDIN, Estelle (fl 1828)
French dancer HAS
BENATZKY, Ralph (d 1957 [73])
Moravian composer BP/42*
BENAVENTA, Jacinto (1866-
1954) Spanish dramatist CB,
ES, OC/1-3, RE, WWT/
2-4, WWW/5
BENBROOK, E. J. (d 1888 [43])
business manager EA/89*
BENCE, Mr. (fl 1750-57) fair
booth operator BD
BENCHLEY, Marie Bucklin
singer CDP
BENCHLEY, Nathaniel (b 1915)
American writer BE, CB
BENCHLEY, Robert Charles
(1889-1945) American critic,
actor CB, DAB, ES, HJD,
NTH, OC/1-3, SR, TW/2
WWA/2, WWT/8-9
BENCKI, Mr. (fl 1751) violon-
cellist BD
BENCRAFT, James (d 1765)

actor, dancer, singer BD
BENDA, Mme. (fl 1790-92) singer
BD
BENDA, Georges K. [Georges
Kugelmann] French scene de-
signer ES
BENDA, Wladyslaw Theodor (d
1948 [75]) Polish artist BE*,
BP/33*
BENDALL, Ernest Alfred (1846-
1924) English critic, examiner
of plays DD, GRB/2-4,
WWT/1-4, WWW/2
BENDER, Mr. (fl c.1839) actor
CDP
BENDER, Charles (d 1857 [44])
call boy EA/72*
BENDER, Dr. Milton (d 1964 [69])
actors' business manager BE*
BENDER, Paul (1875-1947) German
singer ES
BENDER, Russell (d 1969 [59])
performer BP/54*
BENDIX, Doreen (d 1931 [25])
actress BE*
BENDIX, Max (1866-1945) American
conductor WWA/2, WWM
BENDIX, William (1906-64) Ameri-
can actor BE, CB, ES, TW/
21, WWA/4
BENDLER, Salomon (1683-1724)
German singer BD
BENDON, Bert (d 1964) Scottish
performer, writer BE*
BENECH, Rudolf F. (d 1975 [59])
producer/director/choreographer
BP/59*
BENEDETTI, Sesto (fl 1848-50)
Italian singer CDP, HAS
BENEDICT, Sir Julius (1804-85)
English conductor, composer
CDP, DD, DNB, ES
BENEDICT, Leon (b 1926) Ameri-
can actor TW/25
BENEDICT, Lew (1839-1920) Amer-
ican actor, minstrel CDP,
HAS, SR
BENEDICTUS, David (b 1938) Eng-
lish director, dramatist WWT/
15-16
BENEDIX, Roderick German drama-
tist DD
BENELLI, Antonio Peregrino (1771-
1830) Italian singer, composer
BD
BENELLI, Sem (1875-1949) Italian
dramatist MWD, OC/1-3,
TW/6, WWT/4

BENESH, Joan Dorothy [née Rothwell] (b 1920) English choreographer CB

BENESH, Rudolf Frank (1916-75) English musician CB

BENET, Harry (d 1948 [71]) producer, director BE*

BENET, Stephen Vincent (1898-1943) American dramatist, librettist ES, HJD, HP

BENEUX, L. R. (1842-69) American actor HAS

BENEVENTANO, G. F. (b 1824) Italian singer CDP

BENFIELD, Robert (d 1649) English actor DA, ES, GT, OC/1-3

BENFORD, Austin (fl 1674-85) singer BD

BENGE, Mr. (fl 1794) equestrian? BD

BENGOUGH, Henry (d 1825) actor CDP, TD/2

BENHAM, Arthur (d 1895 [23]) dramatist DD

BENHAM, Earl (d 1976 [89]) performer BP/60*

BENHAM, Emily [Mrs. George Benham] (d 1910 [50]) EA/12*

BENHAM, George (d 1911 [64]) clown EA/12*

BENHAM, Mrs. George see Benham, Emily

BENHAM, Mrs. George see Benham, Margaret

BENHAM, Margaret [Mrs. George Benham] (d 1882) EA/83*

BENIADES, Ted American actor TW/26

BENIGNI, Guiseppe (fl 1790-91) singer BD

BENINI, Anna [Signora Bernardo Mengozzi] (fl 1784-c.1791) Italian singer BD

BENION, John (fl 1661-77) actor BD

BENJAMIN, Arthur (b 1893) Australian composer ES

BENJAMIN, C. B. (d 1951 [65]) manager BE*

BENJAMIN, Fred (b 1944) American actor TW/26-28

BENJAMIN, Julius (d 1888 [60]) pianist EA/89*

BENJAMIN, Morris Edgar (b 1881) English manager

WWT/7-9

BENJAMIN, Park (b 1809) American writer DD, RJ

BENJAMIN, Richard (b 1938) American actor TW/23-24, 28

BENLINE, Arthur J. (b 1902) American architect, engineer BE

BENNALD, Mr. (fl 1736) actor BD

BENNEE, William Jacob (d 1888 [46]) actor EA/89*

BENNELL, Peter (d c.1775) musician BD

BENNET, Mr. (fl 1749-51) house servant BD

BENNET, Mr. (fl 1784-89) actor BD

BENNET, Mrs. (fl 1783-85) dresser BD

BENNET, Master (fl 1748) actor BD

BENNET, Clarissa Ann see Conquest, Mrs. Benjamin Oliver

BENNET, Elizabeth (1714-91) actress, singer BD

BENNET, John (fl 1744?-72?) instrumentalist BD

BENNET, Philip (d c.1752) dramatist CP/1-3, DD, GT

BENNETT, Mr. (fl 1795-1816?) box-keeper BD

BENNETT, Mr. (fl 1823) English actor BS

BENNETT, Mr. (fl 1831) Scottish actor HAS

BENNETT, Mrs. (fl 1883) actress DD

BENNETT, Miss see Esten, Mrs.

BENNETT, Alan (b 1934) English dramatist, actor AAS, BE, CD, WWT/15-16

BENNETT, Annie Maria (d 1893 [24]) EA/95*

BENNETT, Arnold (1867-1931) English dramatist, manager DNB, ES, HP, MD, MH, MWD, NTH, OC/1-3, SR, WWM, WWT/1-6, WWW/3

BENNETT, Barbara (d 1958 [52]) American actress BE*, BP/43*

BENNETT, Belle (1883-1932) American actress SR

BENNETT, Billy (d 1942) comedian WWT/14*

BENNETT, Charles (d 1892 [48]) manager EA/94*

BENNETT, Charles (b 1889/99) English dramatist ES, WWT/

7-10
BENNETT, Charles H. (d 1889
[36]) musical director
EA/90*
BENNETT, Clarence (1858-1930)
actor, dramatist, manager
SR
BENNETT, Compton (d 1974 [74])
producer/director/choreog-
rapher BP/59*
BENNETT, Constance (1905-65)
American actress, producer,
director BE, ES, TW/22,
WWA/4
BENNETT, Edward (d 1880)
manager EA/81*
BENNETT, Eliza Frances see
Foster, Eliza Frances
BENNETT, [Ellis?] see Ben-
nett, James
BENNETT, Enid (1895-1969)
Australian actress ES
BENNETT, Faith [Margaret
Riddick] actress WWT/8
BENNETT, Fanny [Mrs. Cull]
(d 1874 [22]) actress
EA/76*
BENNETT, Fran (b 1935) Amer-
ican actress TW/25
BENNETT, George (d 1970
[53]) publicist BP/55*
BENNETT, George John (1800-
79) English actor, drama-
tist CDP, DD, DNB
BENNETT, Mrs. Harry (d 1905)
EA/06*
BENNETT, H. G. Dudley (d
1918 [52]) EA/19*
BENNETT, Hywel (b 1944)
Welsh actor WWT/15-16
BENNETT, James [or Ellis?]
(fl 1799) box-keeper BD
BENNETT, James (d 1885) actor
CDP, DD
BENNETT, Jane (fl 1850)
actress BD
BENNETT, Jane Sperry see
Connell, Jane
BENNETT, Jill (b 1931) English
actress AAS, WWT/14-16
BENNETT, Joan (b 1910) Amer-
ican actress BE, ES, SR,
TW/14-15, WWT/15-16
BENNETT, Joe (d 1967 [78])
vaudevillian TW/24
BENNETT, John (fl 1665)
scene-keeper BD
BENNETT, Johnstone (1870-1906)

actor WWA/1
BENNETT, Mrs. Johnstone Ameri-
can actress SR
BENNETT, Joseph (d 1911 [79])
dramatist, librettist DD
BENNETT, Mrs. Joseph (d 1943
[84]) actress BE*, WWT/14*
BENNETT, Julia (d 1903 [79]) Eng-
lish actress DD, SR
BENNETT, Kate (d 1917) EA/18*
BENNETT, Leila actress WWT/6-7
BENNETT, Lily [Mrs. Paddy Wood]
(d 1879) music-hall performer
EA/80*
BENNETT, Linda (b 1942) American
actress TW/21, 23-24
BENNETT, Maria (fl 1752) singer
BD
BENNETT, Meg (b 1948) American
actress TW/29-30
BENNETT, Michael choreographer,
director CD, WWT/16
BENNETT, Peter (b 1917) English
actor TW/3, WWT/10-16
BENNETT, Raymond (d 1969 [68])
performer BP/53*
BENNETT, Richard (1870/72/73/
75-1944) American actor CB,
DAB, ES, GRB/3-4, SR, TW/
1, WWA/2, WWM, WWS,
WWT/1-9
BENNETT, R. M. (d 1886 [52])
journalist EA/87*
BENNETT, Robert Russell (b 1894)
American composer, conductor
BE, CB, ES
BENNETT, Rosa (fl 1852) actress
DD
BENNETT, Stellar English actress
TW/26
BENNETT, Stephen (fl 1825) actor
CDP
BENNETT, Thomas (d 1872) actor
WWT/14*
BENNETT, Vivienne (b 1905) Eng-
lish actress AAS, ES, WWT/
8-16
BENNETT, Warner (fl 1741-68?)
dancer, singer, actor BD
BENNETT, Wilda (1894-1967)
American actress TW/24,
WWT/4-8
BENNETT, Will A. (b 1874) Cana-
dian press representative
GRB/1-2
BENNETT, William (d 1875) actor,
secretary EA/76*
BENNETT, William (d 1911 [76])

proprietor EA/12*
BENNETT, Mrs. William (d
1907) EA/08*, GRB/3*
BENNETT, William Mineard
(1778-1858) singer CDP
BENNETT, William Sterndale
(1816-75) English composer
CDP, DNB
BENNETTS, R. T. (d 1888)
EA/89*
BENNIE, Mr. (fl 1841) actor
HAS
BENNISON, Louis (d 1929 [46])
American actor BE*, BP/
13*
BENNY, Jack (1894-1974) Amer-
ican comedian BTR/74,
CB, SR
BENOIS, Nadia (1896-1974) Rus-
sian scene designer, cos-
tume designer ES
BENOIT see Tourniaire, Benoit
BENOIT, Denise (d 1973 [53])
performer BP/58*
BENOIT, Patricia (b 1927)
American actress TW/8-
9, 12-16
BENONE, Alfred (d 1908)
music-hall manager EA/09*
BENONVILLE, Mr. (fl 1774)
machinist? BD
BENRIMO, Joseph Henry McAlpin
(1871/74-1942) American
dramatist, director CB,
SR, WWA/1, WWT/4-9
BENSER, John Daniel (d 1785)
instrumentalist, composer
BD
BENSLEY, Robert (1742-1817)
English actor BD, CDP,
DD, DNB, ES, GT, OC/
1-3, TD/1-2
BENSON, Mr. (fl 1735) actor BD
BENSON, Mr. (fl 1776-86)
actor BD
BENSON, Mrs. (fl 1675) singer
BD
BENSON, Mrs. (fl 1728-31)
actress BD
BENSON, Mrs. (fl 1784-86)
actress, singer BD
BENSON, Alex (d 1974 [46])
producer/director/choreog-
rapher BP/58*
BENSON, Arthur (d 1917) EA/
18*
BENSON, Chris (d 1889 [39])
singer EA/90*

BENSON, Ellen see Yates, Ellen
BENSON, Eric William (d 1916
[29]) EA/17*
BENSON, Sir F[rank] R[obert] (1858-
1939) English actor, manager
AAS, DD, DNB, DP, ES,
GRB/1-4, OC/1-3, PDT,
WWM, WWT/1-9, WWW/3
BENSON, Lady F[rank] R[obert;
Constance Featherstonhaugh]
(1860-1946) actress GRB/2-4,
OC/1-3, WWT/1-9
BENSON, George (d 1908 [83])
actor GRB/4*
BENSON, George (b 1911) Welsh
actor AAS, BE, TW/4, WWT/
9-16
BENSON, G. H. (d 1885 [23]) actor
EA/87*
BENSON, Harry (d 1916) EA/17*
BENSON, Harry A. (d 1902 [36])
EA/04*
BENSON, Robby (b 1956) American
actor TW/25, 27-28
BENSON, Robert (1765-96) English
actor, dramatist BD, CP/3,
DD, TD/1-2
BENSON, Mrs. Robert [née Susanna
Satchell] (1758-1814) English
actress BD
BENSON, Ruth [Mrs. Holbrook
Blinn] (1873-1948) American
actress GRB/3-4, WWT/1-5
BENSON, Sally (1897/1900-1972)
American dramatist BE, CD,
HJD, TW/29, WWA/5
BENSON, Tony (d 1891) music-hall
artist EA/92*
BENSON, Mrs. T. W. see
Weston, Emmeline Montague
Falconer
BENSON, William (d 1869) wardrobe
keeper EA/70*
BENSON, William (d 1887) EA/88*
BENSTEAD, Fabbie (d 1970) per-
former BP/55*
BENT, Mr. (fl 1793-1805) gallery
doorkeeper BD
BENT, Buena (1890-1957) English
actress WWT/4-12
BENT, Georgia (fl c.1874) singer
CDP
BENT, Horace (d 1907 [70]) come-
dian EA/08*, GRB/3*
BENT, Marion [Mrs. Pat Rooney]
(1879-1940) American performer
SR
BENT, William Richard (d 1913)

EA/14*
BENTHALL, Michael Pickersgill
(1919-74) English director
AAS, BE, BTR/74, ES,
PDT, WWT/11-15
BENTHAM, Frederick (b 1911)
lighting designer, inventor
WWT/15-16
BENTHAM, Josephine American
dramatist BE
BENTHAM, Samuel (c.1653-c.
1730) English singer BD
BENTINCK, A. Gow (d 1902)
actor EA/03*
BENTLEY, Mrs. (d 1916 [63])
EA/18*
BENTLEY, Mrs. Arthur [Clara
Hayward] (d 1868 [21])
dancer EA/69*
BENTLEY, Dave (d 1912 [30])
comedian EA/13*
BENTLEY, Doris (d 1944)
actress BE*, WWT/14*
BENTLEY, Eric (b 1916)
English/American critic,
director, dramatist AAS,
BE, CD, ES, NTH, PDT,
WWT/14-16
BENTLEY, Florence [Mrs. Wil-
liam Begg] (b 1862) Italian/
English actress GRB/1-2
BENTLEY, Grendon (1877-1956)
English actor WWT/2-3
BENTLEY, Herschel American
actor TW/5-6
BENTLEY, Irene [Mrs. Henry
B. Smith] (d 1940 [70])
American actress, singer
GRB/3-4, WWA/1, WWS,
WWT/1-5
BENTLEY, John (c.1553-85)
actor DA
BENTLEY, John (fl 1803) drama-
tist CP/3, DD
BENTLEY, Joseph (d 1912)
EA/13*
BENTLEY, Laura see Linden,
Mrs. Henry
BENTLEY, Muriel (b 1922)
American dancer ES
BENTLEY, Richard (1708-82)
dramatist CP/1-3, DD,
GT, TD/1-2
BENTLEY, Spencer (d 1963)
actor BE*
BENTLEY, Thomas see
Bentley, Richard
BENTLEY, Walter (1849-1927)

Scottish actor DD, OAA/1-2
BENTON, Charles (d 1758) musi-
cian BD
BENTON, Mrs. Fred see Har-
rison-Tate, A.
BENTONELLI, Joseph (d 1975 [74])
performer BP/59*
BENUCCI, Francesco [Pietro?]
(c.1745-1824) Italian singer BD
BENUCCI, [Pietro?] see Benucci,
Francesco
BENWELL, Archibald (d 1918)
EA/19*
BEN-ZALI, Sidney (b 1945) Bra-
zilian actor TW/27-28
BENZELL, Mimi (1924-70) Amer-
ican singer, actress BE,
TW/27
BENZON, Otto (1856-1927) drama-
tist BE*
BERARD, Christian (1902-49)
French designer ES, TW/5
BERARD, Peter (fl 1808) drama-
tist CP/3
BERARDI, Signor (fl 1763-65)
dancer BD
BERBERIAN, Cathy (b 1925) Ameri-
can singer ES
BERCHER, Jean see D'Auberval,
Jean
BERDEEN, Robert American actor
TW/26-28
BERDESHEVSKY, Margo Ann (b
1945) American actress TW/
23, 25, 28-29
BERECLOTH, Mr. (fl 1788-1814)
door-keeper BD
BERECLOTH, Mrs. (fl 1794-95)
dresser BD
BEREK, Augustus see Burt,
Frank A.
BERENDT, Rachel [Monique Arkell]
(d 1957) French actress WWT/
8-9
BERENSTADT, Gaetano (fl 1717-24)
singer BD
BERENY, Mrs. Henry see Wiehe,
Charlotte
BERESFORD, Bernard (d 1893)
singer EA/94*
BERESFORD, Blanche (d 1874 [20])
actress EA/75*
BERESFORD, George singer CDP
BERESFORD, Harry (1867-1944)
English actor TW/1, WWA/2,
WWT/5-8
BERESFORD, Hugh (d 1905 [21])
EA/06*

BERESFORD, J. Cooke (b 1870)
actor GRB/1-2
BERG, Dale (b 1931) American
actress TW/26
BERG, Ellen [Mrs. Robert Ede-
son] (d 1906 [32]) actress
BE*, WWT/14*
BERG, George (fl 1753-71)
instrumentalist, composer
BD
BERG, Gertrude (1899-1966)
American actress, dramatist
BE, CB, TW/23, WWA/4,
WWT/13-14
BERG, Harold C. (d 1973 [73])
composer/lyricist BP/58*
BERG, Nancy (b 1931) American
actress BE, TW/13
BERGAN, Harry (d 1917 [48])
actor EA/18*
BERGANZA, Teresa (b 1934)
Spanish singer ES
BERGE, Irénée (1870-1926)
French director, composer
WWA/1
BERGEL, John Graham (1902-41)
English critic WWT/7-9
BERGEN, Betty (d 1964 [34])
aerialist BE*
BERGEN, Edgar John (b 1903)
American ventriloquist
CB, ES
BERGEN, Fanny Dickerson (b
1846) American dramatist
WWA/4
BERGEN, Nella [Mrs. De Wolf
Hopper] (1873-1919) Amer-
ican singer, actress GRB/
3-4, WWM, WWS, WWT/
2-3
BERGEN, Polly (b 1930) Amer-
ican actress, singer BE,
CB, TW/11-13
BERGER, Anna (fl c.1873)
singer, musician CDP
BERGER, Augustin (b 1861)
Czech ballet master WWA/4
BERGER, Bob (b 1922) Ameri-
can actor TW/24-25
BERGER, Bill (b 1928) Aus-
trian/American actor,
director BE
BERGER, Henning (b 1872)
Swedish dramatist WWT/
3-4
BERGER, Henrietta Newman
(1856-1943) American act-
ress, bell-ringer SR

BERGER, Herbert L. (d 1968)
executive BP/52*
BERGER, Rosetta Jane (d 1911)
EA/12*
BERGER, Sam (d 1972 [63]) mana-
ger BP/57*
BERGER, Victoria Sherry (d 1975
[67]) performer BP/60*
BERGER, William (fl 1840) Amer-
ican dramatist RJ
BERGERAC, Savinien de Cyrano de
(1619-55) French dramatist
OC/1-3
BERGERE, Lee American actor
TW/29
BERGERE, Ouida [Mrs. Louis
Weadock] (b 1887) Spanish
actress WWM
BERGERE, Valerie (1872-1938)
French actress WWM, WWS,
WWT/7-8
BERGER FAMILY (fl 1850s) per-
formers SR
BERGERSEN, Baldwin (b 1914)
Australian/American composer,
musical director, musician
BE
BERGH, Arthur (d 1962) American
composer WWA/4
BERGHOF, Herbert (b 1900/09)
Austrian/American actor, di-
rector BE, TW/1, 3-17,
25-26, WWT/11-16
BERGIN, Pat (d 1893) music-hall
artist EA/94*
BERGLUND, Joel (b 1903) Swedish
singer ES
BERGMAN, Benedict (fl 1792-94)
violinist BD
BERGMAN, Carl see Bergmann,
Carl
BERGMAN, Gladys (d 1965 [82])
performer BP/49*
BERGMAN, Henry (d 1962 [75])
performer BE*
BERGMAN, Hjalmar Frederik
(1883-1931) Swedish dramatist
COC, ES, MH
BERGMAN, Ingrid (b 1917) Swedish
actress BE, SR, TW/3-6,
24, 28, WWT/11-16
BERGMANN, Alan American actor
TW/22, 26
BERGMANN, Carl (1821-76) Ger-
man conductor DAB
BERGMANN, Eugene J. (d 1975
[77]) performer BP/59*
BERGNER, Elisabeth (b 1900)

Austrian actress AAS, BE, NTH, SR, TW/1-7, WWT/ 8-16

BERGONZI, Carlo (b 1924) Italian singer ES

BERGSON, Michael (d 1898) composer EA/99*

BERINGER, Esmé (1875-1972) English actress COC, DD, EA/96-97, GRB/1-4, OC/3, WWT/1-14

BERINGER, Mrs. Oscar [Aimée Daniell] (1856-1936) American dramatist DD, GRB/1-4, WWT/1-8, WWW/3

BERINGER, Vera (1879-1964) English actress COC, DD, DP, EA/97, GRB/2-4, OC/3, WWT/1-13

BERIO, Luciano (b 1925) Italian composer CB, ES

BERIOSOVA, Svetlana (b 1932) Lithuanian/English dancer CB, ES

BERK, Ernest (b 1909) English choreographer, dancer ES

BERKELEY, Mrs. (fl 1765) house servant? BD

BERKELEY, Miss (fl 1761-76) house servant BD

BERKELEY, Arthur (d 1962 [66]) actor BE*

BERKELEY, Ballard (b 1904) English actor ES, WWT/9-13

BERKELEY, Busby [né Busby Berkeley William Enos] (1895-1976) American director, producer, actor BE, CB, ES, WWT/15-16

BERKELEY, George Monck (1763-93) English dramatist CP/3, DD

BERKELEY, Gertrude [Mrs. Wilson Enos] (fl 1900-08) American actress WWS

BERKELEY, Lennox (b 1903) English composer ES

BERKELEY, Reginald Cheyne (1890-1935) English dramatist ES, WWT/4-7

BERKELEY, Sir William see Berkley, Sir William

BERKELEY, Wilma Australian actress, singer WWT/7-8

BERKELY, Mr. (fl 1766-67) property man BD

BERKELY, Miss (fl 1776-77)

actress BD

BERKEY, Ralph (b 1912) American dramatist BE

BERKLEY [or Barclay, or Bartley], Sir William (d 1677) English dramatist CP/1-3, DD, FGF

BERKOWITZ, Sol (b 1922) American composer, writer BE

BERKOWSKY, Paul B. (b 1932) American manager BE

BERKSON, Michael (b 1939) American actor TW/23

BERLE, Frank (d 1973 [70]) manager BP/57*

BERLE, Milton [né Berlinger] (b 1908) American actor, producer, lyricist, writer BE, CB, ES, TW/1-2, 5-8, 25, WWT/10-16

BERLEIN, Annie Mack (1850-1935) Irish actress SR

BERLIN, Alexandra American actress TW/24

BERLIN, Elaine see May, Elaine

BERLIN, Irving (b 1888) Russian/ American composer, lyricist AAS, BE, CB, ES, HJD, MH, NTH, PDT, WWT/4-16

BERLIN, J. Norman (d 1943 [67]) actor BE*

BERLINGER, Milton see Berle, Milton

BERLINGER, Warren (b 1937) American actor BE, TW/10-19, WWT/14-16

BERLYN, Alfred (1860-1936) English dramatist GRB/2-4, WWT/1-8, WWW/3

BERLYN, Mrs. Alfred (d 1943) critic, journalist WWW/4

BERLYN, Ivan [Ivan Emanuel Julian von Berlin] (1874-1934) English actor GRB/1-4

BERMAN, A. L. (1890-1975) American attorney BE

BERMAN, Eugene (1899-1972) Russian scene designer CB, ES

BERMAN, Harry (d 1974 [76]) performer BP/58*

BERMAN, Max (d 1972 [88]) costumier BP/57*, WWT/16*

BERMAN, Shelley (b 1926) American comedian, actor BE

BERMANGE, Barry (b 1933) English dramatist CD

BERN, Chris V. [Robinson Byrne] (b 1872) English variety artist GRB/1

BERN, Paul (1889-1932) American

actor, director ES, WWA/1
BERNACCHI, Antonio Maria
(1685-1756) Italian singer
BD
BERNAGE, George [né Burnidge]
(d 1903 [47]) actor EA/04*
BERNAL, Mr. (fl 1796) puppeteer
BD
BERNARD, Mr. (fl 1750) actor
BD
BERNARD, Mrs. (fl 1824) actress
CDP
BERNARD, Mons. (fl 1790-93)
machinist BD
BERNARD, Mrs. Albert see
Stafford, Emily
BERNARD, Anthony (1891-1963)
English conductor, composer
ES, WWW/6
BERNARD, Anthony W. (d 1879
[61]) American musician
EA/80*
BERNARD, Barney (1877-1924)
American actor SR, WWT/4
BERNARD, Caroline E. (fl 1853-
62) actress HAS
BERNARD, Charles minstrel
CDP
BERNARD, Charles (d 1895)
actor, singer, manager,
dramatist DD, SR
BERNARD, Mrs. Charles see
Alleyn, Annie
BERNARD, Mrs. Charles [née
Tilden] (d c.1870) actress
DD, HAS
BERNARD, Charles S. (1816-
74) American actor, secre-
tary of the American Drama-
tic Fund CDP, HAS
BERNARD, Charles W. (d 1917)
performer? SR
BERNARD, Dick (d 1925 [60])
actor BE*, WWT/14*
BERNARD, Dorothy [Mrs. A.
H. Van Beuren] (1890-1955)
actress TW/1, 12
BERNARD, Ed (b 1939) American
actor TW/26
BERNARD, James (d 1973 [43])
performer BP/57*
BERNARD, Jean-Jacques (b
1888) French dramatist
COC, OC/1-3
BERNARD, John (1756-1828)
English actor, manager,
author BD, CDP, DAB,
DD, DNB, ES, HAS,

OC/3, SR, TD/2, WWA/H
BERNARD, Mrs. John, I [Mrs.
Cooper; née Roberts] (1750-92)
actress BD, DD, TD/1-2
BERNARD, Mrs. John, II [née
Fisher] (d 1805) actress DD
BERNARD, Kenneth (b 1930) Amer-
ican dramatist, director CD
BERNARD, Kitty (d 1962) performer
BE*
BERNARD, Leon (d 1935 [58]) actor
BE*, WWT/14*
BERNARD, Lionel (1818-62) Ameri-
can actor DD, HAS
BERNARD, Paul see Bernard,
Tristan
BERNARD, Richard (1566/67-1641)
dramatist CP/1-3, DD
BERNARD, Sallie (d 1878 [12])
actress EA/79*
BERNARD, Sam (1863-1927) English
actor GRB/2-4, SR, WWA/1,
WWS, WWT/1-5
BERNARD, Sam (d 1950 [61]) actor
BE*
BERNARD, Mrs. S. E. see
Stanley, Laura
BERNARD, Tristan [Paul Bernard]
(1866-1947) French dramatist
COC, OC/1-3, WWT/3-4
BERNARD, Vivian (d 1913) actress
SR
BERNARD, William Bayle (1807-75)
American dramatist DAB, DD,
DNB, EA/68, ES, HJD, SR,
WWA/H
BERNARD, William H. (1833-90)
American minstrel HAS, SR
BERNARDI, Signora (fl 1720)
singer BD
BERNARDI, Master (fl 1783-85)
call boy BD
BERNARDI, Boris (d 1974 [70])
manager BP/59*
BERNARDI, Helen (d 1971 [89])
performer BP/57*
BERNARDI, Herschel (b 1923)
American actor TW/25-26
BERNARDO, [Mr.?] (fl 1688) musi-
cian BD
"BERNARDO" (d 1880) female im-
personator, minstrel CDP
BERNASCHINA, Antonio (d 1876
[62]) ballet master EA/77*
BERNASCHINA, Marianna (d 1870)
actress EA/71*
BERNASCONI, Antonia (b c.1740)
German singer BD, ES

BERNAT, Julie see Judith, Mlle.

BERNATO, Mlle. [Mrs. Charles Romaine] (d 1877) pantomimist? EA/78*

BERNAUER, Rudolph (d 1953 [73]) Hungarian dramatist, librettist, producer BE*, WWT/14*

BERNERS, Lord see Bourchier, John

BERNERS, Lord [Gerald Hugh Tyrwhitt Wilson Berners] (1883-1950) English composer, painter, writer ES, WWW/4

BERNERS, Gerald Hugh Tyrwhitt Wilson see Berners, Lord

BERNES, Mark (d 1969 [57]) performer BP/54*

BERNET, Mr. (fl 1797) scene painter BD

BERNEY, William (d 1961 [40]) dramatist BE*, BP/46*

BERNEYOSKI, Hans (fl 1661-68) drummer BD

BERNHARDT, Mrs. Curtis see Argyle, Pearl

BERNHARDT, Maurice (d 1928 [65]) producer, manager BE*, WWT/14*

BERNHARDT, Melvin American director WWT/15-16

BERNHARDT, Sarah Henriette Rosine (1845-1923) French actress, manager CDP, COC, DP, ES, GRB/1-4, HP, NTH, OC/1-3, PDT, SR, WWA/1, WWM, WWS, WWT/1-4

BERNHEIM, Shirl (b 1921) American actress TW/27-38

BERNICAT, Firmin (d 1883 [33]) composer EA/84*

BERNIE, Ben (1891?-1943) American actor, musician CB, SR

BERNIE, Dick (d 1971 [60]) performer BP/55*

BERNSTEIN, Aline [née Frankhau] (1881/82-1955) American designer COC, ES, NTH, OC/1-3, TW/3, 5-8, 12, WWT/7-12

BERNSTEIN, Henri (1876-1953) French dramatist MWD, TW/10

BERNSTEIN, Herman (d 1963 [58]) American executive, production manager BE*, BP/48*, WWT/14*

BERNSTEIN, Karl American press representative BE

BERNSTEIN, Leonard (b 1918) American composer, conductor AAS, BE, ES, HJD, MH, NTH, PDT, WWT/13-16

BERNSTEIN, Sidney (d 1966 [56]) producer TW/23

BERNSTEIN, Stephen (b 1944) American actor TW/24

BEROLZHEIMER, Hobart F. (b 1921) American librettist BE

BERR, Georges (d 1942 [74]) actor, dramatist BE*, WWT/14*

BERR DU TURIQUE, Julien (d 1923 [60]) dramatist BE*, WWT/14*

BERRIAN, Bill see Berrian, William

BERRIAN, William (b 1929) American actor TW/5, 25, 29

BERRIDGE, Mr. (fl 1794) bass viol player BD

BERRIMAN, Joseph (d 1730) actor BD

BERRINGTON, Mary (d 1888) EA/89*

BERRISFORD, [Robert?] (fl 1745-77) house servant BD

BERRY, Aline (d 1967 [62]) actress TW/23

BERRY, [Ann?] (fl 1749) actress BD

BERRY, Bill see Berry, William Henry

BERRY, Catherine see D'Egville, Mrs. James Harvey

BERRY, Mrs. Charles see Darling, Bessie

BERRY, Charles W. (fl 1870-90) actor, dramatist SR

BERRY, C[hristopher?] (fl 1776-81) actor BD

BERRY, Edward (1697-1750) actor CDP

BERRY, Edward (1706-60) actor, singer, dancer BD, DD

BERRY, Eric (b 1913) English actor AAS, BE, TW/11, 16-18, 20, 22, 27-30, WWT/11-16

BERRY, James (1883-1918) English actor WWT/2

BERRY, James J. (d 1969 [54]) performer BP/53*

BERRY, John (d 1821) actor BD

BERRY, John American actor
TW/28
BERRY, Ken (b 1933) American
actor TW/16-17
BERRY, Mary (1763-1852)
dramatist DD
BERRY, Sidney N. (d 1975 [66])
producer/director/choreog-
rapher BP/59*
BERRY, Thomas (d 1701?) actor
BD
BERRY, Thomas (fl 1737) actor
BD
BERRY, Wallace (d 1949 [60])
actor TW/5
BERRY, Mrs. W. H. see
Hanson, Kitty
BERRY, William Henry (1872-
1951) English actor, singer
ES, GRB/4, WWT/1-11
BERSELLI, Matteo (fl 1719-21)
singer BD
BERSON, William (d 1916)
EA/17*
BERT, Frederic (1844-1911)
American minstrel, manager
SR
BERTE, Charles [Grant Bryant]
(1875-1908) English drama-
tist GRB/1-4
BERTEAU, Mons. (fl 1675)
dancer BD
BERTENSHAW, Betty Jane (d
1975) performer BP/60*
BERTHIER, Jacques (b 1916)
French actor ES
BERTI, Ettore (1870-1940)
Italian actor ES
BERTIE, Mr. (fl 1708) manager?
BD
BERTIN, Mr. (fl 1793) pianist
BD
BERTIN, Emile (b 1878) French
scene designer ES
BERTIN, Josephine (fl 1849)
dancer CDP, HAS
BERTIN, Pierre (b 1895) French
actor TW/9
BERTINI, Ambrose (d 1894 [28])
composer, pianist EA/96*
BERTLES, Miss see Dighton,
Mrs. Robert
BERTOLDI, Ena [Beatrice Mary
Spink] (d 1906 [28]) gymnast
EA/07*
BERTOLLI, Francesca (fl 1729-
37) singer BD
BERTON, Pierre (d 1912 [70])

actor, dramatist BE*, WWT/
14*
BERTONI, Ferdinando Giuseppe
(1725-1813) Italian composer
BD, ES
BERTRAM, Alexander Brown (d
1867) actor? EA/68*
BERTRAM, Arthur (1860-1955)
English business manager
GRB/1-4, WWT/1-5
BERTRAM, Bert (b 1893) Australian
actor TW/25
BERTRAM, Charles (fl 1794) horn
player BD
BERTRAM, Charles [James Bas-
sett] (d 1907 [53]) conjuror
EA/08*, GRB/3*
BERTRAM, Ellen see Walters,
Mrs. W. H.
BERTRAM, Eugene (1872-1941)
English business manager
WWT/4-6
BERTRAM, Eva [Ethel Brierley]
English actress GRB/1-2
BERTRAM, Frank (d 1941 [70])
actor BE*, WWT/14*
BERTRAM, Helen [née Lulu May
Burt; Mrs. E. J. Morgan] (b
1869) American actress, singer
WWA/5, WWS
BERTRAM, Henry (d 1898) actor
EA/99*
BERTRAM, Lily [Mrs. T. W. Raw-
son] English actress GRB/1
BERTRAM, Lucy see Hadaway,
Mrs. Thomas H.
BERTRAM, William [Benjamin
Switzer] (b 1880) Canadian
actor, director ES
BERTRAND (d 1883) singer EA/84*
"BERTRAND" see Dove, Mark
BERTRAND, E. C. (c.1842-87)
English dramatist, manager
DD, NYM
BERTRAND, Henry (d 1898) circus
manager EA/99*
BERTRAND, Kate Emma (d 1889
[33]) EA/90*
BERUH, Joseph (b 1924) American
producer, company manager,
general manager, director
BE, WWT/16
BERWICK, Mrs. (fl 1765) dresser
BD
BERYL, H. Cecil (d 1931) manager
WWT/14*
BERYL, Mrs. H. Cecil see
Eversfield, Miss

BERYL, Sara (d 1897) singer,
actress EA/98*
BERYL, William (d 1903 [22])
EA/04*
BESANT, Sonya (d 1970 [40])
performer BP/55*
BESANT, Sir Walter (1836-1901)
writer, dramatist DD
BESEMERES, John see Daly,
John
BESFORD, Mr. (fl 1759) mes-
senger BD
BESFORD, Mr. (fl 1766-68)
actor BD
BESFORD, Mr. (1767-89) lamp
man BD
BESFORD, Esther (b c.1757)
English actress, dancer BD
BESFORD, Joseph (d 1789)
property man BD
BESFORD, Mrs. [Joseph?] (fl
1767-68) dancer BD
BESFORD, Samuel (fl 1763-91)
actor, dancer BD
BESIER, Rudolf (1878-1942)
Dutch/English dramatist
ES, MH, MWD, NTH, SR,
WWT/2-9, WWW/4
BESLEY, Henry (d 1902) actor,
dramatist EA/03*
BESOYAN, Rick (1924-70)
American composer, lyricist,
librettist, director, producer
BE
BESOZZI, Antonio (1714-81)
oboist BD
BESOZZI, Carlo (b c.1738)
Italian oboist BD
BESOZZI, Gaetano (1727-98)
Italian oboist BD
BESSIN, Henrietta (d 1850 [26])
singer HAS
BESSLE, Elizabeth (d 1906)
actress, dramatist DD
BESSMERTNOVA, Natalija (b
1941) Russian dancer ES
BESSON, George (d 1905 [47])
EA/06*
BEST, Mr. (fl 1779-85) actor
BD
BEST, Mrs. Charles see
Lalo, Louise Dorothy
BEST, Edna (1900-74) English
actress BE, BTR/74,
CB, ES, TW/8-16, WWT/
4-13
BEST, Paul (b 1908) German
actor TW/1-3

BEST, William (fl 1862-95) drama-
tist DD
BEST, Willie (d 1962 [46]) actor
BE*
BEST, W. T. (d 1897 [71]) organ-
ist EA/98*
BESTIC, Charles M. (d 1909) actor
EA/10*
BESTOR, Don (d 1970 [80]) com-
poser/lyricist BP/54*
BESTOW, William (d 1873 [84])
EA/74*
BESTRY, Harry (d 1969 [80]) agent
BP/54*
BESWICK, Mrs. (fl 1787) dancer
BD
BESWICK, Miss (fl 1726) house ser-
vant? BD
BESWICK, Miss (fl 1787) dancer
BD
BESWICK, Harriette Emily see
Everard, Harriette Emily
BESWICK, William [William Cres-
wick] (d 1883 [54]) EA/84*
BESWICKE, Mrs. Darley see
Everard, Harriette Emily
BESWORTH, [Mr.?] (fl 1761) ward-
robe assistant BD
BETHELL, William (fl 1784-c.94)
singer BD
BETHEN, Charles (d 1876 [56])
actor? EA/77*
BETHENCOURT, Francis (b 1924/
26) English actor, writer BE,
TW/13, 18, 22-23, 26, 29
BETHUN, Mr. (fl 1733-38) dancer
BD
BETHUNE, Mr. (fl 1746) house
servant? BD
BETJEMANN, George Stanley (d
1899 [63]) EA/00*
BETJEMANN, Gilbert R. (d 1896
[31]) musician EA/97*
BETON, Miss (fl 1798) actress
BD
BETTANY, F. G. (d 1942 [73])
critic BE*, WWT/14*
BETTELHEIM, Edwin Sumner (1865-
1938) American critic WWM,
WWT/2-5
BETTENHAM, George (d 1694)
singer BD
BETTERTON, John (d 1816) actor
BD
BETTERTON, Julia see Glover,
Julia
BETTERTON, Mary see Betterton,
Mrs. Thomas

BETTERTON, Thomas (1635?-
1710) English actor, mana-
ger, dramatist BD, CDP,
COC, CP/1-3, DD, DNB,
ES, GT, HP, NTH, PDT,
OC/1-3, TD/1-2
BETTERTON, Mrs. Thomas [née
Mary Saunderson] (b c.1637-
1712) English actress BD,
COC, CP/1-3, DD, DNB,
ES, HP, NTH, OC/1-3
BETTERTON, Thomas William
(d 1834) Irish actor BD,
HAS, SR, TD/1-2
BETTERTON, William (1644-61)
English actor BD, DD
BETTGER, Lyle (b 1915) Amer-
ican actor TW/2-6
BETTI, Ugo (1892-1953) Italian
dramatist COC, MWD,
NTH, PDT, OC/2-3
BETTINI, Signor (fl 1850-52)
singer HAS
BETTINI, Signora (fl 1744-45)
dancer BD
BETTINI, Geremia (1823-65)
Italian singer CDP
BETTIS, Valerie Elizabeth
(b 1919) American dancer,
choreographer, actress,
director BE, CB, ES, TW/
4-9, WWT/15-16
BETTMANN, Otto L. (b 1903)
German/American archivist
BE
BETTON, George (d 1969) per-
former BP/54*
BETTS, Mr. (fl 1748) actor BD
BETTS, Mr. (fl 1797-99) actor,
singer BD
BETTS, Arthur (1776-1847) Eng-
lish violinist, composer BD
BETTS, Edward (c.1773?-c.1806)
English musician, instrument
maker BD
BETTS, Edward William (b 1881)
English journalist, critic
WWT/5, 9-11
BETTS, Ernest (1896-1975?)
English critic ES, WWT/
10-11
BETTS, John [Edward?] (1755-
1823) English violin maker,
teacher, musician BD
BETTS, Richard (fl 1669) musi-
cian? BD
BETTY, Mrs. (d 1872 [80])
EA/74*

BETTY, Ann Starkie (d 1904 [60])
EA/05*
BETTY, Henry (1819-97) English
actor CDP, DD
BETTY, William Henry West (1791-
1874) English actor CDP,
COC, DD, DNB, ES, GT, HP,
NTH, OC/1-3, OX, TD/2
BEUF, Augusto (b 1887) Italian
singer ES
BEULER, Jacob (d 1873) comic song
writer EA/74*
BEVAN, Billy (d 1957 [70]) Aus-
tralian actor BE*
BEVAN, Donald (b 1920) American
dramatist BE
BEVAN, Faith (b 1896) Welsh act-
ress, singer WWT/4-7
BEVAN, Frank (b 1903) American
educator, costume designer BE
BEVAN, Fred (d 1893) music-hall
artist EA/94*
BEVAN, Isla (b 1910) English act-
ress WWT/7-8
BEVANS, Lionel (d 1965 [81]) per-
former BP/49*
BEVANS, Philippa (1916/17-68)
English actress BE, TW/9-16,
24
BEVAN-SLATOR, Mrs. see
Crawford, Amy
BEVERIDGE, Mrs. (d 1887) EA/
88*
BEVERIDGE, Charles (d 1884)
EA/85*
BEVERIDGE, Mrs. Charles see
Clarke, Fanny M.
BEVERIDGE, Glen (1886-1947)
American actor SR
BEVERIDGE, J[ames] D. (1844-
1926) Irish actor DD, DP,
EA/97, GRB/1-4, OAA/1-2,
WWS, WWT/1-5
BEVERIDGE, Mrs. James D. see
Beveridge, Jenny
BEVERIDGE, Jenny (d 1898) EA/
99*
BEVERIDGE, Kuhne American act-
ress WWM
BEVERIDGE, Ray [Mrs. Madison
Seliger] (b 1887) American
actress WWM
BEVERLEY, E. D. (d 1880 [42])
singer EA/81*
BEVERLEY, George Augustus (d
1890) EA/91*
BEVERLEY, Henry (fl 1800-26)
English actor DD, GT, TD/1

BEVERLEY, Mrs. Henry (fl 1801) actress DD
BEVERLEY, Henry Roxby (1796-1863) comedian CDP, DD, DNB
BEVERLEY, Hilda (d 1942) actress BE*, WWT/14*
BEVERLEY, Maude (fl c.1885) singer CDP
BEVERLEY, Percy Charles (d 1903 [54]) actor EA/04*
BEVERLEY, W. G. (d 1867 [86]) actor EA/68*
BEVERLEY, William [Roxby] (d 1842 [69]) manager, producer DD
BEVERLEY, William Roxby (c. 1814-89) English scene painter CDP, COC, DD, DNB, OC/1-3
BEVERLEY, Mrs. William Roxby (d 1851 [75]) actress, manager BE*, WWT/14*
BEVERLY, Henry Roxby (d 1873) author, actor EA/74*
BEVERLY, John (fl 1794?) double-bass player BD
BEVIGNANI, Enrico (1841-1903) Italian conductor, composer ES
BEVIL, Mr. (fl 1729-31) box keeper BD
BEW, Charles (fl 1791-1837) actor BD
BEWES, Rodney (b 1937) English actor WWT/15-16
BEWLEY, Mr. (fl 1715) housekeeper BD
BEWLEY, Elizabeth (fl 1716-21) house servant? BD
BEWLEY, John (fl 1724-36) stage doorkeeper BD
BEWLEY, William (fl 1724-36) gallerykeeper, boxkeeper BD
BEY, Rafic (b 1948) Moroccan actor TW/29-30
BEYER, Elsie manager WWT/11-13
BEZANSON, Philip (d 1975 [59]) composer/lyricist BP/59*
BHASKAR [Roy Chowhury] (b 1930) Indian actor, dancer, choreographer, singer BE, TW/16-17
BIAGGINI, Sig. (fl 1783) exhibitor BD
BIAL, Rudolf (1834-81) violinist,

conductor, composer CDP
BIANCARDI, Sig. (fl 1720) musician? BD
BIANCHI, Sig. (fl 1769-70) singer BD
BIANCHI, Francesco (fl 1748-49) singer BD
BIANCHI, Francesco (c.1751-1810) Italian composer, musician BD, ES, TD/1
BIANCHI, Mrs. Francesco [née Jane Jackson; Mrs. John Lacy] (1776-1858) English singer BD
BIANCHI, Giovanni Battista (fl 1780-82) Italian conductor, composer BD
BIANCHI, John C. M. (1775-1802) violinist, composer BD
BIANCHINI, Mr. (fl 1743-47) house servant BD
BIBB, Joe (d 1893 [48]) clown EA/95*
BIBBY, Mr. (fl 1746) actor, singer BD
BIBBY, Mr. (fl 1815-16) actor DD
BIBBY, Charles (1878-1917) English actor WWT/1-3
BIBERMAN, Herbert (d 1971 [71]) director TW/28
BIBO, Irving (d 1962 [72]) composer BE*
BIBSON, Miss (fl 1781) actress BD
BICK, James (d 1712?) ventriloquist, imitator BD, CDP
BICKEL, Frederick McIntyre see March, Fredric
BICKEL, George L. (1863?-1941) American comedian CB
BICKERDIKE, A. W. (d 1889 [39]) pianist EA/90*
BICKERDIKE, Mary (d 1882) EA/83*
BICKERSTAFF, Miss (d c.1724) actress BD
BICKERSTAFF, Agnes (d 1893 [66]) EA/94*
BICKERSTAFF, Isaac (1735-1812) Irish dramatist COC, CP/1-3, DD, DNB, ES, GT, HP, MH, OC/1-3, PDT, TD/1-2
BICKERSTAFF, John (d c.1724) English actor BD
BICKERSTAFFE, Henry (d 1873 [50]) scene artist EA/74*
BICKERTON, Joseph P., Jr. (d 1936 [58]) manager, producer WWT/14*
BICKFORD, Charles A. (1891-1967)

American actor BE, ES, TW/24, WWT/7-9
BICKFORD, Melville G. T. (d 1913) EA/14*
BICKHAM, Mr. (fl 1733) actor? BD
BICKHAM, Mrs. (fl 1779) candle-woman BD
BICKLEY, Mrs. Harry see Bickley, Thirza
BICKLEY, Thirza [Mrs. Harry Bickley] (d 1916) EA/17*
BICKLEY, Tony American actor TW/3-6
BICKNELL, Mr. (fl 1794) bassoonist BD
BICKNELL, Mrs. (fl 1755) singer BD
BICKNELL, Alexander (fl 1788) dramatist CP/3, DD
BICKNELL, George James (d 1874 [35]) pianist EA/75*
BICKNELL, Margaret [née Younger] (c.1680-1723) Scottish actress, dancer BD, DD, DNB
BIDDALL, George Freeman (d 1909) illusionist EA/10*
BIDDALL, Mrs. William (d 1892) EA/93*
BIDDLE, Barnaby American dramatist RJ
BIDDLE, Edward (fl 1717) dramatist CP/3, DD
BIDDLE, George see Edgar, George
BIDDLE, Mrs. Harry see Onzalo, Elise
BIDDLES, Mrs. Adelaide see Calvert, Mrs. Charles
BIDDLES, Clara S. [Mrs. Thomas Barry] (fl 1854-84) English actress HAS, PP/1, SR
BIDDLES, J. (fl 1856) actor HAS
BIDDY, Mrs. (fl 1728-29) dancer BD
BIDEAUX, Gustave (b 1830) French minstrel HAS
BIDLAKE, Rev. John (fl 1800) dramatist CP/3, DD
BIDOTTI, Mons. (fl 1788-94) dancer, actor BD
BIDOU, Henri (d 1943 [70]) critic BE*, WWT/14*
BIDWELL, Mr. (fl 1778-79) actor BD
BIDWELL, Barnabas (1763-1833)

American dramatist EAP
BIDWELL, Charles E. (b 1831) American actor HAS
BIDWELL, Mrs. Charles E. see Bidwell, Dollie
BIDWELL, David (1820-89) American manager SR
BIDWELL, Dollie [Mrs. Charles E. Bidwell] (b 1843) American actress CDP, HAS
BIEBER, Margarete (b 1879) German/American educator, writer BE, ES
BIEL, Jacob see Pedel, Jacob
BIELINSKI, Olga see Bellin, Olga
BIEN, Robert Taylor see Warwick, Robert
BIENFAIT, Mons. (fl 1756) dancer BD
BIERDEMANN, Augustino (d 1880) musician EA/81*
BIERDT, Burchart (fl 1612) English actor DA
BIFFIN, Miss (d 1850 [66]) freak EA/72*
BIGARI, Francesco (fl 1766-72) scene painter, machinist BD
BIGELOW, Charles A. (1862-1912) American actor SR, WWS
BIGELOW, Joe (d 1976 [66]) dramatist BP/60*
BIGELOW, Otis (b 1920) American actor TW/18
BIGFORD, Mary (fl 1727) candle-woman BD
BIGG, John (b 1777) English musician, teacher BD
BIGGERS, Earl Derr (1884-1933) American dramatist DAB, ES, SR, WWA/1, WWT/4-7
BIGGS, Mr. (fl 1737) actor BD
BIGGS, Mr. (fl 1794-97) singer BD
BIGGS, Mrs. (fl 1719-20) actress BD
BIGGS, Miss (fl 1798) BD
BIGGS, Anne [Mrs. Samuel Young] (1775-1825) English actress, singer BD, TD/1
[B]IGGS, James (fl 1669) scene keeper BD
BIGGS, James (1771-98) English actor, singer BD, TD/1-2
BIGGS, John (fl 1667?-89) actor BD
BIGGS, John (fl 1731-39) violoncellist? BD
BIGI, Giacinta (fl 1791-96) Italian

singer BD
BIGLEY, Isabel (b 1928) American actress, singer BE,
TW/7-12
BIGNAL, Mr. (fl 1732) actor
BD
BIGNAL, Mrs. (fl 1732) actress
BD
BIGNARDI, Sig. (fl 1857) singer
CDP, HAS
BIGNELL, Mr. (fl 1830-31)
prompter HAS
BIGNELL, Charles (fl late 19th
cent) singer CDP
BIGNELL, Robert Richard (d
1888 [76]) proprietor EA/
89*
BIGNEY, Mrs. Dibden see
Bigney, Edith
BIGNEY, Edith [Mrs. Dibden
Bigney] (d 1890 [24]) actress
EA/91*
BIGNY, George (d 1889) property
master EA/90*
BIGONZI, Sig. (fl 1724) singer
BD
BIGWOOD, George Barnes (d
1913 [84]) actor BE*, EA/
14*, WWT/14*
BIGWOOD, Mrs. G[eorge]
B[arnes] (d 1893) EA/95*
BIHIN, Mons. (b 1808) Belgian
giant CDP
BIJOU, Bert (fl c.1903) singer,
comedian CDP
BIJOU, Mrs. Peter (d 1911)
performer EA/12*
BIKEL, Theodore (b 1924)
Austrian actor, musician,
singer BE, CB, TW/11-17,
22-23, WWT/14-16
BILBROOKE, Lydia (b 1888)
English actress WWT/1-6
BILETTA, Emanuele (1825-90)
Italian composer ES
BILKINS, Taylor (fl 1871)
dramatist DD
BILL-BELOTSERKOVSKY, Vladimir Naumovich (1884-1970)
Russian dramatist COC,
MWD, OC/3
BILLERS, William dramatist
CP/1
BILLETDOUX, François (b
1927) French dramatist
PDT
BILLING, H. Chiswell (1881-1934)
Welsh business manager

WWT/4-7
BILLINGESLEY, John (fl 1572)
payee DA
BILLINGS, A. D. (d 1882 [36])
actor EA/83*
BILLINGS, "Josh" [Henry W. Shaw]
(1818-85) writer SR
BILLINGS, Mary [Mrs. G. Robinson] (d 1877) actress EA/78*
BILLINGS, William (1746-1800)
American composer BE*
BILLINGTON, Adeline (1825-1917)
actress DD, GRB/2-4, OAA/
2, WWT/1-3
BILLINGTON, Elizabeth see
Billington, Mrs. James
BILLINGTON, Fred (d 1917 [63])
actor, singer BE*, EA/18*,
WWT/14*
BILLINGTON, James (1756-94)
English double-bass player BD
BILLINGTON, Mrs. James [née
Elizabeth Weichsel] (1765/68-
1818) English singer, actress,
composer BD, CDP, DD,
DNB, ES, GT, OX, TD/1-2
BILLINGTON, John (1830-1904)
actor CDP, DD, DP, OAA/
1-2
BILLINGTON, Mrs. John see
Billington, Adeline
BILLINGTON, Lee (b 1932) American actress TW/25
BILLINGTON, Michael (b 1939)
English critic, actor, author
WWT/16
BILLINGTON, Thomas (c.1754-
1832) English musician, singer,
teacher, composer BD, DNB
BILLIONI, Mons. (fl 1749-51)
dancer BD
BILLOE, Miss (fl 1741) actress
BD
BILLSBURY, John H. (d 1964 [78])
producer, theatre operator,
agent, singer BE*
BILLY-HADEN (fl 19th cent) English
clown ES
BILOWIT, Ira J. (b 1925) American
producer BE
BILSINGHAM, Miss (fl 1786) dancer
BD
BILTON, Belle see Clancarty,
Countess of
BILTON, Florence actress CDP
BIMBONI, Alberto (b 1888) Italian
conductor, composer ES
BIMKO, Fiszl [or Fishel]

(1890-1965) Polish/American
dramatist ES
BIMOLLE, Arcangelo (fl 1763)
Italian violinist BD
BINCKS, Mrs. (fl 1735-c.1740)
dresser BD
BINDA, Marie Beatrice see
Beatrice, Mlle.
BINDER, Fred (d 1963) American
performer BE*
BINDER, Marguerite (d 1870)
singer EA/71*
BINDIGER, Emily (b 1955) Amer-
ican actress TW/30
BINDLEY, (b 1869) actress,
musician CDP, SR
BINETY, Anna (fl 1761-63) dancer
BD
BINETY, Giorgio (fl 1761-63)
dancer BD
BING, Gus (d 1967 [74]) per-
former BP/52*
BING, Herman (d 1947 [57])
German actor BE*
BING, Rudolf (b 1902) Austrian
impresario CB, ES
BING, Suzanne (b 1885) French
actress, translator ES
BINGE, John (d 1878 [74]) singer
EA/79*
BINGHAM, Mr. (fl 1778) actor
BD
BINGHAM, Amelia [Mrs. Lloyd
Bingham] (1869-1927) Amer-
ican actress DAB, ES,
GRB/2-4, SR, WWA/1,
WWM, WWS, WWT/1-5
BINGHAM, Bob (b 1946) Ameri-
can actor TW/28-29
BINGHAM, Clifton (b 1859)
English librettist GRB/1
BINGHAM, Ernest (d 1907) busi-
ness manager EA/08*,
GRB/3*
BINGHAM, George (fl 1689-97)
violinist? BD
BINGHAM, George (d 1967 [74])
actor, singer TW/24
BINGHAM, J. Clarke (d 1962
[65]) English actor BE*
BINGHAM, Leslie [Mrs. Joseph
Byton Totten] (d 1945 [61])
American actress TW/1
BINGHAM, Lionel John (1878-
1911) English critic, jour-
nalist WWW/2
BINGHAM, Lloyd (d 1915) press
agent, manager SR

BINGHAM, Mrs. Lloyd see
Bingham, Amelia
BINGHAM, Mark Albert see Al-
bert, Mark
BINGHAM, Ralph (b 1870) American
performer WWM
BINGHAM, Tom (d 1892) Yankee
comedian EA/93*
BINGLEY, Isaac Charles see
Durand, Charles
BINGLEY, Vason I. (d 1898 [32])
circus musical director EA/
99*
BINGNER, Mr. (fl 1766-67) lobby
doorkeeper BD
BINKS, Maria (d 1894) EA/95*
BINLEY, [Mr. ?] (fl 1792) singer
BD
BINNER, Margery (b 1908) English
actress WWT/8-9
BINNEY, Constance (b 1900) Amer-
ican actress ES, WWT/5-8
BINNEY, Frank singer, composer
CDP
BINNS, Edward (b 1916) American
actor TW/4-6, 16
BINNS, Jennie (d 1900) music-hall
artist EA/01*
BINT, Sidney W. (d 1910) EA/11*
BINT, Mrs. W. see Leamar, Kate
BINT, William singer CDP
BINYON, Laurence (1869-1946) Eng-
lish dramatist DNB, ES, GRB/
3-4, NTH, OC/1-3, WWA/2,
WWT/1-9, WWW/4
BIOLETTI, Mrs. (d 1899 [84])
EA/01*
BION, Victor (d 1908 [66]) variety
performer EA/09*
BIOW, Milton R. (d 1976 [83]) ad-
vertising agency executive
BP/60*
BIRABEAU, André (b 1890) French
dramatist MWD
BIRCH, Mr. (fl 1737) actor BD
BIRCH, Mr. (fl 1766) actor BD
BIRCH, Mr. (fl 1794) singer? BD
BIRCH, Emma (d 1891) EA/92*
BIRCH, Frank (1889-1956) English
producer, actor ES, WWT/
6-10
BIRCH, George (b c.1498) court
interluder DA
BIRCH, George (fl 1619-24) actor
DA
BIRCH, John (fl 1547-56) court
interluder DA
BIRCH, Joseph (d 1879) actor?

EA/80*
BIRCH, Patricia choreographer,
    director WWT/16
BIRCH, Paul (b 1912) American
    actor TW/10-11
BIRCH, Peter (b 1922) American
    actor TW/1-3, 6-9
BIRCH, Samuel (1757-1841) Eng-
    lish dramatist CDP, CP/3,
    DD, DNB, GT, TD/1-2
BIRCH, Walter (d 1892 [41])
    minstrel EA/94*
BIRCH, William (1831-97) Amer-
    ican minstrel CDP, HAS,
    SR
BIRCH, William Alfred (d 1887)
    EA/88*
BIRCHALL, Miss actress TD/2
BIRCHALL, Robert (d 1819)
    publisher, impresario BD
BIRCHALL, William John [W.
    J. Seymour] (d 1871) come-
    dian EA/72*
BIRCHENOUGH, Agnes [Mrs.
    Fawcett Lomax] (d 1891)
    actress EA/92*
BIRCHENOUGH, Bella [Mrs.
    George Blythe] (d 1891)
    music-hall artist EA/93*
BIRCHENOUGH, Mrs. Ellen (d
    1874) EA/75*
BIRCHENSHA, John (d 1681)
    theorist, teacher, violist
    BD
BIRCHILL, Miss see Vincent,
    Mrs.
BIRCH-PFEIFFER, Mme. (d
    1867) dramatist EA/68*
BIRD, Mr. (fl 1732-34) actor
    BD
BIRD, Miss [Mrs. W. Jukes]
    (d 1885 [49]) actress EA/
    85*
BIRD, Miss (fl 1784-85) actress
    BD
BIRD, Charles A. (d 1925 [70])
    American manager BE*,
    BP/10*
BIRD, David (b 1907) English
    actor WWT/10-16
BIRD, James (1788-1839) English
    dramatist DNB
BIRD, John (fl 1702) mountebank
    BD
BIRD, John (b 1936) English
    actor, dramatist WWT/16
BIRD, John Woodall (d 1917
    [25]) actor WWT/14*

BIRD, Joseph (b 1926) American
    actor TW/22-25
BIRD, Rhymus (fl 1702) mountebank
    BD
BIRD, Richard (b 1894) English
    actor AAS, ES, WWT/5-15
BIRD, Robert Montgomery (1806-54)
    American dramatist CDP,
    COC, DAB, DD, ES, HJD,
    MH, OC/1-3, RE, RJ, SR,
    WWA/H
BIRD, Theophilus (1608-64) English
    actor BD, COC, DD, ES,
    OC/1-3
BIRD [or Bourne], Theophilus (d
    1682?) actor BD, DA
BIRD, Will (d 1910 [28]) music-hall
    stage manager EA/12*
BIRD [or Bourne], William (d 1624)
    English actor COC, DA, ES,
    FGF, OC/1-3
BIRIMISA, George (b 1924) Ameri-
    can dramatist, director, actor
    CD
BIRKETT, Viva (1887-1934) English
    actress WWT/1-7
BIRKHEAD, Matthew (d 1722) sing-
    er, dancer BD
BIRMINGHAM, George A. [Rev. J.
    O. Hannay] (1865-1950) Irish
    dramatist WWT/2-10
BIRNEY, David (b 1939) American
    actor TW/24-29
BIRNIE, Mr. (fl 1796-97) house
    servant BD
BIRO, Lajos (b 1948 [68]) Hungarian
    dramatist BE*, WWT/14*
BIRON, Gerald (d 1906) actor EA/
    07*
BIRREL, Andrew (fl 1802) drama-
    tist CP/3, DD
BIRRELL, Francis (d 1935 [44])
    critic, dramatist BE*, WWT/
    14*
BIRT, [Mr.?] (fl 1791-92) house
    servant? BD
BIRT, Miss S. [Mme. Frederic]
    (fl 1791-1813) dancer BD
BIRTCHNELL, Arthur J. (d 1869
    [31]) professor of music EA/
    70*
BISBEE, Noah, Sr. (fl 1808) Amer-
    ican dramatist EAP
BISCACCIANTI, Elise (1824?-96)
    American singer, actress
    CDP, ES, HAS
BISCARDI, Luigi (d 1876) composer,
    organist EA/77*

BISCHOF, Maria Anna see
Brandt, Marianne
BISHOP, Mr. (fl 1735) singer
BD
BISHOP, Mr. (fl 1738-44) gallery
keeper BD
BISHOP, Mr. (fl 1741) actor BD
BISHOP, Mr. (fl 1776-77) dancer
BD
BISHOP, Mr. (fl 1797-1803) box
keeper BD
BISHOP, Mr. (d 1871) actor
EA/72*
BISHOP, Mrs. (fl 1741-42)
dancer, actress, singer BD
BISHOP, Mrs. (fl 1776-78?)
actress BD
BISHOP, Mrs. (d 1886) EA/87*
BISHOP, A. C. (d 1893 [29])
EA/94*
BISHOP, Alfred (d 1910 [44])
comedian EA/11*
BISHOP, Alfred (1841/43/45-
1928) English actor DD,
GRB/1-4, WWT/1-5
BISHOP, Ann [Mrs. John Bishop]
(d 1892) EA/93*
BISHOP, Ann[a]; née Rivière]
(1814-84) English singer,
actress CDP, DD, DNB,
ES, HAS, SR
BISHOP, Arthur (d 1904 [26])
actor EA/05*
BISHOP, Charles B. (1833-89)
American actor, manager
CDP, SR
BISHOP, Charles E. (d 1889)
actor EA/90*
BISHOP, Charlotte (d 1883)
EA/84*
BISHOP, David (1857-1921) singer
SR
BISHOP, Mrs. George E. (d
1891) EA/92*
BISHOP, George Walter (1886-
1965) English critic COC,
OC/3, WWT/6-13, WWW/6
BISHOP, Harry W. see Robin-
son, Harry
BISHOP, Henry (fl 1784-90)
violinist, dancing master,
dancer? BD
BISHOP, Sir Henry Rowley
(1786-1855) English com-
poser CDP, DD, DNB,
ES, SR
BISHOP, James (d 1881 [88])
showman EA/82*

BISHOP, Jane (d 1969) performer
BP/53*
BISHOP, Jane Mary (d 1900) EA/
01*
BISHOP, Joe (b 1931) American
actor TW/13-16
BISHOP, Joey [Joseph Abraham
Gottlieb] (b 1919) American
comedian CB
BISHOP, Mrs. John see Bishop,
Ann
BISHOP, Kate (1847-1923) actress
DD, GRB/3-4, OAA/2, WWT/
1-4
BISHOP, Laura S. (fl 1859) drama-
tic reader HAS
BISHOP, Lilian (d 1917) EA/18*
BISHOP, Louisa (fl 1863-64) act-
ress HAS
BISHOP, Richard (1898-1956)
American actor TW/1-3, 12
BISHOP, Robert (fl 1677) trumpeter
BD
BISHOP, Robert H., III (1916-63)
American producer, attorney
BE
BISHOP, Ronald (b 1923) American
actor TW/23-24, 27, 30
BISHOP, Rose see Egan, Rose
BISHOP, Sallie American actress
HAS
BISHOP, Samuel (1731-95) English
dramatist CP/3, DD
BISHOP, T. Brigham CDP
BISHOP, Thomas (fl 1837-52) Eng-
lish singer CDP, DD, HAS,
SR
BISHOP, Tom (d 1872) singer EA/
73*
BISHOP, Ward (d 1966 [66]) stage
manager TW/23
BISHOP, Washington Irving (d 1889
[41]) mind reader CDP
BISHOP, Will (1867-1944) English
dancer, ballet master, producer
GRB/1-4, WWT/1-5
BISHOP, William (1918-59) Ameri-
can actor BE*
BISPHAM, David Scull (1857-1921)
American singer DAB, DD,
ES, GRB/1-4, SR, WWA/1,
WWM, WWS, WWW/2
BISSELL, Richard (1913-77) Amer-
ican dramatist BE
BISSETT, Mr. (fl 1791) actor HAS
BISSETT, Donald J. (b 1930) Amer-
ican educator BE
BISSHOPP, Mrs. C. H. (d 1916)

EA/17*
BISSON, Mary Ann (d 1877 [64])
actress EA/78*
BISTEGHI, Achille Scipione see
Brizzi, Sig.
BITHMERE, Mme. (fl 1784-87)
French dancer BD
BITHMERE, A[ugustin?] (fl 1783)
French dancer BD
BITHMERE, Augustine Louis (fl
1784-87) French dancer BD
BITHMERE, Marie Françoise
(fl 1784-88) French dancer,
actress BD
BITTI, Alexander (fl 1715-30)
violinist BD
BITTLESTONE, George (d 1869
[50]) machinist EA/70*
BITTNER, Jack (b 1938) Amer-
ican actor TW/4-5, 29
BIVENS, Burke (d 1967 [64])
composer/lyricist BP/52*
BIXBY, Bill (b 1934) American
actor TW/23
BIXBY, Frank (fl 1890s) drama-
tist SR
BIZET, Georges (1838-75)
French composer ES
BJOERLING, Jussi (1911-60)
Swedish singer CB, ES,
WWA/4, WWW/5
BJÖNER, Ingrid (b 1932) Nor-
wegian singer ES
BJORKMAN, Edwin August
(1866-1951) critic, trans-
lator BE*
BJÖRLING, Sigurd (b 1907)
Swedish singer ES
BJÖRNSON, Björnstjerne (1832-
1910) Norwegian dramatist
COC, GRB/1-4, OC/1-3
BLACHER, Boris (d 1975 [72])
composer/lyricist BP/59*
BLACK, Alfred (b 1913) Eng-
lish manager WWT/11-15
BLACK, Arthur John (1855-
1936) English painter
WWW/3
BLACK, David (b 1931) Amer-
ican producer BE, WWT/
15-16
BLACK, Donna Olivia (b 1948)
American actress TW/27
BLACK, Dorothy (b 1899) South
African actress ES,
WWT/6-13
BLACK, Eugene R. (b 1898)
American executive BE

BLACK, George (1890-1945) English
manager, producer COC, ES,
OC/1-3, WWT/9
BLACK, George (1911-70) English
manager WWT/11-14
BLACK, Jean Ferguson (d 1969
[68]) dramatist BP/54*
BLACK, Jessica (b 1884) English
actress GRB/1-2
BLACK, J. Moreton (d 1892 [31])
dramatist EA/93*
BLACK, Karen (b 1942) American
actress CB
BLACK, Kenneth (b 1856) Scottish
actor GRB/1-2
BLACK, Mrs. Kenneth see Kirk,
Jessie
BLACK, Kitty (b 1914) South African
dramatist WWT/11-16
BLACK, Lew (d 1971 [60]) performer
BP/55*
BLACK, Maggie (d 1898) EA/99*
BLACKBURN, Mr. (fl 1780) actor
BD
BLACKBURN, Aubrey (d 1974 [74])
agent BTR/74
BLACKBURN, Clarice American
actress TW/12, 21
BLACKBURN, Dorothy American
actress BE, TW/30
BLACKBURN, John ["Cleo"] (d
1887 [34]) EA/88*
BLACKBURN, Joseph (d 1841)
American clown HAS, SR
BLACKBURN, Robert (b 1925)
American actor TW/13-18, 28
"BLACK DICK" (fl 1597) actor DA
BLACKER, Mr. (fl 1773) English
actor HAS
BLACKER, Henry (b 1724) giant
BD, CDP
BLACKET, Joseph (d 1810 [c. 24])
dramatist CP/3
BLACKFORD, Mr. (fl 1791-92)
house servant? BD
BLACKHAM, Olive English marion-
ettist ES
BLACKIE, Gregory Watt ["G. W.
Blake"] (d 1868 [39]) stage
manager EA/69*
BLACKLER, Betty (b 1929) English
actress WWT/10-14
BLACKLOCK, Dr. Thomas (1721-
91) Scottish dramatist CP/3
BLACKLY, Mr. (fl 1715) singer
BD
BLACKMAN, Eugene J. (b 1932)
American educator BE

BLACKMAN, Fred J. (1879-
1951) English producer
WWT/5-9
BLACKMAN, Honor actress
WWT/15-16
BLACKMER, Sidney (1894/95/
98-1973) American actor,
producer, director BE,
TW/1-17, 20, 30, WWT/
6-15
BLACKMERE, Sydney see
Blackmer, Sidney
BLACKMORE, Mr. (fl 1786-1804)
scene painter BD
BLACKMORE, Mr. (fl 1790)
puppeteer BD
BLACKMORE (d 1838) tight-rope
dancer EA/72*
BLACKMORE, Mrs. (fl 1791)
rope dancer BD
BLACKMORE, Master (fl 1798-
1807?) dancer, rope dancer,
actor, singer, esquestrian BD
BLACKMORE, Arthur (d 1894
[30]) agent EA/95*
BLACKMORE, Herbert (d 1938
[77]) agent WWT/14*
BLACKMORE, Peter (b 1909)
English dramatist WWT/
12-15
BLACKMORE, Robert (d 1879
[45]) agent EA/80*
BLACKMORE, Master T. (fl
1798-1807) dancer, rope
dancer, actor, singer,
equestrian BD
BLACKMORE, William (fl 1754-
70) tailor BD
"BLACK PRINCE, The" (fl 1700)
dwarf BD
"BLACK STORM, The" see
Collins, W. J.
BLACKTON, Jack (b 1938)
American actor TW/25-28,
30
BLACKTON, Jay (b 1909) Amer-
ican musical director, con-
ductor, composer BE
BLACKWAGE, William (fl 1594)
actor? servant? DA
BLACKWELL, Carlyle (1888-
1955) American actor ES,
TW/12
BLACKWELL, Carlyle, Jr. (d
1974 [61]) performer BP/
59*
BLACKWELL, Earl (b 1914)
American publisher BE

BLACKWELL, Henry (fl 1698)
fencing master? BD
BLACKWELL, Henry see Court-
ney, Baron
BLACKWOOD, George (b 1904)
American actor TW/3-6
BLACKWOOD, Thomas (fl 1592-
1603) actor DA
"BLADDERBRIDGE, Mr." (fl 1774)
musician BD
BLADEN, Martin (d 1746) English
dramatist CP/1-3, DD, GT
BLAGDEN, Mr. (fl 1760-67?)
dancer BD
BLAGDEN, Mr. (fl 1765-77) dresser
BD
BLAGDEN, [Mr.?] (fl 1776-77)
dresser BD
BLAGDEN, Master (fl 1755-59)
dancer BD
BLAGDEN, Miss (fl 1759-62)
dancer BD
BLAGDEN, Nicholas (fl 1660-68)
actor BD
BLAGOI, George (d 1971 [73])
performer BP/56*
BLAGRAVE, John (fl 1683-94)
musician BD
BLAGRAVE, Robert (fl 1660-69)
instrumentalist BD
BLAGRAVE, Thomas (d 1688)
English instrumentalist, singer
BD, DNB
BLAGROVE, Henry Gamble (d 1872
[61]) violinist EA/74*
BLAGROVE, Richard Manning (d
1895 [69]) musician EA/96*
BLAGROVE, Thomas master of
the Revels COC, OC/3
BLAGROVE, William (fl 1624-35)
deputy to the master of the
Revels DA
BLAIKE, Ben (fl 1826) actor CDP,
HAS
BLAINE, Jimmy (d 1967 [42]) pro-
ducer, writer, actor TW/23
BLAINE, Vivian [née Stapleton]
(b 1923) American actress,
singer AAS, BE, TW/7-16,
19, 23, 28, WWT/12-16
BLAIR, Mr. (fl 1772-91) actor
BD
BLAIR, Mr. (d 1823) actor HAS
BLAIR, Barbara (b 1944) American
actress TW/30
BLAIR, Betsy (b 1923) American
actress BE, ES
BLAIR, David (1932-76) English

dancer, choreographer CB,
ES
BLAIR, Eugenie (d 1922 [54])
American actress SR,
WWA/5
BLAIR, George (d 1970 [64])
producer/director/chore-
ographer BP/54*
BLAIR, Helen Bowen (d 1972
[82]) patron BP/57*
BLAIR, Isla (b 1944) Indian/
English actress WWT/16
BLAIR, Janet American
actress, singer, dancer
BE
BLAIR, Joan [Mrs. A. S.
Homewood] English actress
GRB/1-2
BLAIR, John (d 1948 [73])
actor WWT/14*
BLAIR, Joyce [née Ogus]
(b 1932) English actress,
dancer WWT/15-16
BLAIR, Lionel [né Ogus] (b
1931) Canadian/English
dancer, choreographer,
actor WWT/15-16
BLAIR, Mary (d 1947 [52])
American actress TW/4
BLAIR, Phyllis [Mrs. J. E.
Vedrenne] English actress
GRB/1-4
BLAIR, William (d 1891)
actor EA/92*
BLAIR, William (b 1896)
American house manager,
press representative BE
BLAISDELL, John W. (1840-
1911) American actor,
manager SR
BLAISDELL, William (1867-
1930) actor SR
BLAK, John (fl 1624) lessee
DA
BLAKE, Mr. (fl 1753?-98?)
dancer, ballet master BD
BLAKE, Mr. (fl 1760-61)
dancer BD
BLAKE, Mrs. (fl 1761) dancer
BD
BLAKE, Miss (fl 1821) singer
DD
BLAKE, Annie (b 1849) Amer-
ican actress HAS
BLAKE, Benjamin (1751-1827)
English musician, composer,
teacher BD
BLAKE, Betty (b 1920)

American publisher BE
BLAKE, Brandon English actor,
dramatist, general manager
GRB/2
BLAKE, Caroline (1798-1881)
actress CDP
BLAKE, Charles (fl 1868) writer
DD
BLAKE, Eubie (b 1883) American
composer, lyricist CB
BLAKE, F. J. (d 1874) treasurer
EA/76*
BLAKE, Flora [Mrs. Harry Blake]
(d 1910) EA/11*
BLAKE, George see Redmond,
Charles
"BLAKE, G. W." see Blackie,
Gregory Watt
BLAKE, Mrs. Harry see Blake,
Flora
BLAKE, James (fl 1794-1802?)
singer BD
BLAKE, Joanna [Mrs. Adam Alex-
ander] (d 1895) actress, singer
EA/96*
BLAKE, John (d 1849 [58]) Ameri-
can? treasurer CDP
BLAKE, John (d 1878 [26]) actor
EA/79*
BLAKE, Madge (d 1969) performer
BP/53*
BLAKE, Maria Louisa Aylmer (d
1876) EA/77*
BLAKE, Minnie (d 1908) EA/09*
BLAKE, Orlando (b 1832) American
actor HAS
BLAKE, Mrs. Orlando [Julia Wes-
ton] (b 1840) American actress
HAS
BLAKE, Robert (b 1933) American
actor CB
BLAKE, Robert (d 1975) manager
BP/59*
BLAKE, Sydney (b 1951) Italian/
American actor TW/30
BLAKE, Thomas (fl 1798) musician
BD
BLAKE, Thomas G. dramatist DD
BLAKE, Violet Fisher (d 1967 [70])
performer BP/51*
BLAKE, William (1757-1827) English
dramatist CP/3
BLAKE, William (d 1866) gymnast
HAS
BLAKE, William Rufus (1805-63)
Canadian actor, impresario
CDP, DAB, DD, ES, GC, HAS,
SR, WWA/H

BLAKE, Mrs. William Rufus
[Caroline Placide] (1798-
1881) American actress DD,
HAS
BLAKELEY, James (1873-1915)
English actor GRB/1-4,
WWS, WWT/1-3
BLAKELEY, Thomas see
Blakely, Thomas H.
BLAKELEY, Tom S. (b 1790)
actor, composer SR
BLAKELEY, William S. (1830-
97) actor DD, DNB, DP
BLAKELOCK, Denys (1901-70)
English actor WWT/6-14,
WWW/6
BLAKELY, Colin (b 1930) Irish
actor AAS, WWT/14-16
BLAKELY, Don F. (d 1976
[49]) producer/director/
choreographer BP/60*
BLAKELY, Gene (b 1922)
American actor BE, TW/
2-3, 6-8, 11-19, 24
BLAKELY, Thomas H. (fl 1782-
1840) American actor DD,
HAS
BLAKELY, William see
Blakeley, William
BLAKEMORE, Michael (b
1928) Australian actor,
director AAS, WWT/15-16
BLAKENEY, Olive (b 1899)
American actress WWT/
7-12
BLAKES, Mr. (fl 1698) actor?
booth operator BD
BLAKES, Mr. (fl 1761) fire
eater BD
BLAKES, Charles (d 1763)
actor, singer BD, CDP,
TD/2
BLAKEY, Mr. (fl 1743-63)
actor BD
BLAKISTON, Clarence (1864-
1943) English actor GRB/
1-4, WWT/1-9
BLAKISTON, Sydney (d 1917
[47]) professor of music
EA/18*
BLAMAUER, Karoline see
Lenya, Lottie
BLAME, Mr. (fl 1794) singer
BD
BLAMEY, Frederick (d 1944
[58]) actor, singer WWT/14*
BLAMIRE, William (d 1868)
scene artist, property man

EA/69*
BLAMPHIN, Charles (d 1895 [64])
harpist, composer EA/96*
BLANC, Ernest (b 1923) French
singer ES
BLANCH, Rev. John (b 1650?)
dramatist CP/1-3, DD, GT
BLANCH, William see Woodhull,
Fred
BLANCHAR, Pierre (d 1963 [67])
performer BP/48*
BLANCHARD, Mr. (fl 1819) actor
CDP
BLANCHARD, The Misses (fl 1789-
91) dancers BD
BLANCHARD, Amy (d 1910 [66])
burlesque artist EA/11*
BLANCHARD, Ann [Mrs. S. B.
Blanchard] (d 1874) EA/75*
BLANCHARD, Blanche (d 1893 [17])
trapezist EA/94*
BLANCHARD, Cecilia [Mrs. William
Blanchard] (d 1869 [89]) actress
HAS
BLANCHARD, Edward Leman (1820-
89) English dramatist, critic
CDP, COC, DD, EA/68, ES,
OC/1-3
BLANCHARD, Mrs. Edward Leman
(d 1907 [86]) GRB/3*
BLANCHARD, Edwin H. (d 1973
[78]) journalist, publicist BP/58*
BLANCHARD, Elizabeth Walker
see Charles, Elizabeth Walker
BLANCHARD, Jane (d 1903) EA/
05*
BLANCHARD, Jean-Pierre (b 1753)
French balloonist, exhibitor BD,
CDP
BLANCHARD, J. H. S. (d 1874
[43]) comic singer EA/75*
BLANCHARD, Kitty [Mrs. Arthur
McKee Rankin] (1847-1911)
American actress CDP, COC,
OC/2-3, PP/3
BLANCHARD, Lillian (d 1966 [91])
performer BP/50*
BLANCHARD, Mari (d 1970) per-
former BP/54*
BLANCHARD, Sarah (d 1875 [89])
EA/76*
BLANCHARD, Mrs. S. B. see
Blanchard, Ann
BLANCHARD, Thomas (fl 1766-87)
actor BD
BLANCHARD, Thomas (1760-97)
English actor BD, COC, DD,
OC/1-3, TD/1-2

BLANCHARD, Thomas (d 1859 [72]) actor CDP, COC, OC/1-3

BLANCHARD, Mrs. Thomas [Charlotte Wright] (b 1761) English singer, actress BD

BLANCHARD, William (1769-1835) English actor BS, CDP, COC, DD, DNB, ES, HAS, OC/1-3, OX, SR, TD/1-2

BLANCHARD, Mrs. William see Blanchard, Cecilia

BLANCHE, Mme. [Millie Catherine Nelson] (d 1896 [64]) circus performer EA/97*

BLANCHE, Mlle. (d 1892) rope dancer EA/93*

BLANCHE, Ada (1862/68-1953) English actress, singer CDP, DD, GRB/1-4, WWT/1-6

BLANCHE, Belle [Blanche Minzesheimer] (1891-1963) American actress, mimic WWS

BLANCHE, Edith (d 1929 [63]) actress WWT/14*

BLANCHE, Marie (b 1893) English actress, singer WWT/3-9

BLANCHFIELD, Charles E. (d 1971 [83]) performer BP/56*

BLANCK, Nicholas (d 1778) musician BD

BLAND, Mr. (fl 1790) actor CDP

BLAND, Mr. see Welson, Mr.

BLAND, Alan (1897-1946) English press representative WWT/7-9

BLAND, Charles (fl 1826-34) singer DD

BLAND, George (d 1753) actor BD

BLAND, George (d 1807) English actor BD, COC, OC/1-3, TD/1-2

BLAND, Mrs. George [née Maria Theresa Catherine Tersi; sometimes called Romani, Romanzini] (1770-1838) singer, actress BD, CDP, DD, DNB, EA/92, GT, OC/1-3, OX, TD/1-2

BLAND, Georgina (d 1881 [78])

EA/83*

BLAND, Harcourt (d 1875 [64]) actor BE*, EA/76*, WWT/14*

BLAND, Harry [Henry Clifford] (d 1888) actor EA/89*

BLAND, Humphrey (1812-69) English actor HAS

BLAND, Mrs. Humphrey [née Emily Lewis] (d 1880 [41]) American actress HAS

BLAND, Mrs. Humphrey see Faucit, Harriet

BLAND, James (fl 1784-1815) Scottish actor BD

BLAND, James (1798-1861) English actor, singer CDP, DD, OC/1-3

BLAND, James A. (1854-1911) American composer, minstrel HJD, SR

BLAND, John (d 1788) dramatist CP/2-3, DD, DNB

BLAND, Joyce (1906-63) Welsh actress ES, WWT/7-10

BLAND, Maria Theresa Romanzini see Bland, Mrs. George

BLAND, Robert Henderson (d 1941) actor, dramatist GRB/1-2

BLAND, Thomas Beckford (d 1870 [51]) duologue artist EA/71*

BLAND, W. Humphrey see Bland, Humphrey

BLAND, Zoe (d 1883) actress EA/84*

BLANDE, Edith (d 1923 [64]) actress DD

BLANDE, Sarah Ann (d 1901 [76]) EA/02*

BLANDFORD, Mr. (fl 1789) actor BD

BLANDFORD, F. W. (d 1879 [24]) actor EA/80*

BLANDFORD, Margaret (d 1884) EA/85*

BLANDFORD, Percy (fl 1880s) singer, actor OAA/2

BLANDWICK, Clara (d 1962 [81]) American actress WWM

BLANDY, Mr. (fl 1781-87) constable BD

BLANE, Elizabeth Bridget see Armstead, Mrs.

BLANE, Ralph [né Hunsecker] (b 1914) American composer, actor, singer, producer, director, dramatist BE

BLANEY, Miss (fl 1781-82) actress BD

BLANEY, Charles Edward
(1868-1944) American manager, dramatist GRB/2-4,
SR, WWT/1-6

BLANEY, Harry Clay (b 1874/
78) American actor WWM,
WWS

BLANEY, H. Clay (1908-64)
American producer BE

BLANEY, John (fl 1609-26)
actor DA

BLANEY, Norah (b 1896) English actress, composer, pianist WWT/5-8, 14-15

BLANFIELD, Mr. (fl 1 767)
pyrotechnist BD

BLANGY, Hermine (fl 1846)
dancer CDP, HAS

BLANK, William Alexander (fl
1605) Scottish dancer DA

BLANKENSHIP, Vicki (b 1941)
American actress TW/23

BLANKFORT, Michael (b 1907)
American dramatist BE

BLANKSHINE, Robert (b 1948)
American actor TW/29

BLANT, Mr. (fl 1788) house
servant? BD

BLASINI, Elisa (b 1848) Austrian
dancer HAS

BLASIS, Carlo (1795-1878)
Italian dancer, choreographer,
ballet master ES

BLASS, Robert (b 1867) American singer WWM

BLASTOCK, Mr. (fl 1735-36)
actor BD

BLATCHLEY, W. E. (d 1889)
actor EA/91*

BLATT, Edward A. (b 1905)
American producer, director,
manager BE

BLAU, Bela (d 1940 [44]) Hungarian producer BE*, BP/
25*

BLAU, Herbert (b 1926) American director, educator,
producer, dramatist BE,
ES

BLAUVELT, Lilian [Mrs. William F. Pendleton] (1874-
1947) American singer
GRB/1, WWA/2, WWM,
WWS

BLAVIS, Joseph Henry (d 1894
[55]) EA/95*

BLAYNEY, May (1875-1953)
English actress TW/9,
WWT/1-6

BLECHMAN, Marcus (d 1975 [67])
producer/director/choreographer
BP/60*

BLECKNER, Jeff American director
WWT/16

BLEDSOE, Earl (d 1962) performer
BE*

BLEDSOE, Jules C. (1898-1943)
American singer, actor, composer CB

BLEECK, John (d 1963 [83]) restaurateur BP/47*

BLEEZARDE, Gloria (b 1940)
American actress TW/20, 23-
24, 26

BLENDEL, Mr. (fl 1772) actor BD

BLENKINSOP-COULSON, H. B.
see Conway, H. B.

BLENNOW, Alexandre (d 1892)
horse trainer EA/93*

BLESSINGTON, Murrough Boyle,
Lord (d 1702 [93]) dramatist
CP/1-3, GT

BLEWITT, C. (fl 1785-88) singer
BD

BLEWITT, Jonas (d 1805) organist,
composer BD

BLEWITT, Jonathan (1782-1853)
English musician, writer, com-
poser, musical director CDP,
DNB

BLEWITT, William (d 1884 [43])
music-hall performer EA/85*

BLEY, Maurice (b 1910) American
community theatre director,
producer BE

BLICK, Newton (1899-1965) actor
WWT/14

BLIEDEN, Ivan Lawrence see
Blyden, Larry

BLIGHT, John J. T. (d 1876 [75])
musician EA/77*

BLINCOE, Edward (d 1967 [28])
performer BP/51*

BLIND, Eric (d 1916) actor EA/
18*

BLINK, George (fl 1837) dramatist
DD

BLINN, Holbrook (1872-1928) Amer-
ican actor DAB, ES, GRB/1-4,
SR, WWA/1, WWM, WWS,
WWT/1-5

BLINN, Mrs. Holbrook see
Benson, Ruth

BLINN, Nellie Holbrook (d 1909)
actress BE*, WWT/14*

BLISS, Mr. (fl 1757) actor BD

BLISS, Anthony A. (b 1913)
American lawyer BE
BLISS, Sir Arthur (1891-1975)
English composer ES
BLISS, Hebe (d 1956 [79])
actress BE*, WWT/14*
BLISS, Helena [née Helen
Louise Lipp] (b 1917/19)
American actress, singer
BE, TW/1-6, 10-13, WWT/
11-16
BLISS, Herbert (b 1923) Amer-
ican dancer ES
BLISS, Imogene (b 1918) Amer-
ican actress TW/23-26, 30
BLISSET, Francis (1773-1850)
actor CDP
BLISSETT, Mr. (fl 1797-1821)
actor DD, TD/2
BLISSETT, Francis (1742?-
1824) English actor BD,
CDP, SR
BLITZ, Antonio (1810-77) Eng-
lish magician CDP, SR,
WWA/H
BLITZSTEIN, Marc (1905-64)
American composer, librettist
AAS, BE, ES, MD, MH,
MWD, NTH, TW/20, WWA/4
BLOCH, Bertram (b 1892)
American dramatist BE
BLOCH, Ernest (1880-1959)
Swiss/American composer
ES
BLOCH, Rosine (d 1891 [41])
singer EA/92*
BLOCK, Chad (b 1938) Ameri-
can actor TW/23-24, 26-29
BLOCK, Larry (b 1942) Amer-
ican actor TW/28
BLOCK, Ralph (d 1974 [84])
dramatist BP/58*
BLOCK, Sheridan (fl 1900s)
American actor WWS
BLOCK, Steven (b 1928) Amer-
ican talent representative
BE
BLOCK, William Norris see
Norris, William
BLOCK, William J. (d 1932
[63]) American manager
WWS
BLOCKER, Dan (d 1972 [43])
performer BP/56*
BLODGET, Alden S. (d 1964
[80]) American producer,
manager BE*
BLOFSON, Richard (b 1933)

American stage manager, pro-
ducer, lighting designer BE
BLOGG, Mr. (fl 1739-48) singer BD
BLOIS, Eustace (d 1933 [52]) im-
presario WWT/14*
BLOMFIELD, Charles William see
Marlow, Harry
BLOMFIELD, Derek (1920-64) Eng-
lish actor WWT/10-13
BLOMQUIST, Allen (b 1928) Ameri-
can director, educator BE
BLONDEL, Mons. (fl 1742) dancer
BD
BLONDELL, Joan (b 1909/12)
American actress BE, ES, TW/
28, WWT/15-16
BLONDIN, Charles [Emile Gravele]
(1824-97) tight-rope walker,
acrobat CDP
BLONDIN, Charlotte Lawrence (d
1888) EA/90*
BLOOD, Adele [Mrs. Edward
Davis] (1886-1936) American
actress WWM
BLOOD, J. J. (fl 1885-91) drama-
tist DD
BLOODGOOD, Clara Sutton (1870-
1907) American actress GRB/
2-3, SR, WWA/1
BLOODGOOD, Harry [Carlos Mauran]
(d 1886 [41]) comedian, minstrel
CDP
BLOOM, Claire (b 1931) English
actress AAS, BE, CB, ES,
TW/13-16, 27-28, WWT/11-16
BLOOM, Norton L. (d 1972 [45])
producer/director/choreographer
BP/57*
BLOOM, Rube (d 1976 [73]) com-
poser/lyricist BP/60*
BLOOM, Sol (b 1870) American
actor, songwriter SR
BLOOM, Verna American actress
TW/23, 28
BLOOMER, Mr. (fl 1784) singer
BD
BLOOMFIELD, Mr. (fl 1787-92)
actor BD
BLOOMGARDEN, Kermit (1904-76)
American producer, manager
BE, CB, WWT/11-16
BLORE, Eric (1887-1959) English
actor ES, TW/15, WWT/5-10
BLOSSOM, Henry Martyr, Jr.
(1866-1919) American dramatist
GRB/3-4, SR, WWA/1, WWS,
WWT/1-3
BLOUNT, Arthur (b 1877) English

actor GRB/1

BLOUNT, Helon (b 1929) American actress, singer TW/
29, WWT/16

BLOW, John (1649-1708) English
composer, organist, teacher
BD, CDP, DNB, ES

BLOW, Mark (d 1921 [49]) English actor, manager GRB/2

BLOW, Sydney [Jellings-Blow]
(1878-1961) English actor,
dramatist GRB/1-2, WWT/
2-11, WWW/6

BLOWER, Mr. (fl 1777?-91)
puppeteer, actor? BD

BLOWER, Miss A. (fl 1782)
actress? BD

BLOWER, Elizabeth (b 1763)
actress, singer BD

BLOWITZ, William F. (d 1964
[48]) American press representative BE*

BLUDRICK, Mr. (fl 1780) actor
BD

BLUE, Ben (d 1975 [73]) actor,
comedian BP/59*, WWT/
16*

BLUE, Monte (d 1963 [73])
American actor, press
representative BE*, BP/
47*

BLUE, Rita Hassan (d 1973
[68]) actress, producer,
critic TW/30

BLUETT, Gus (d 1936 [32])
actor, singer WWT/14*

BLUM, Daniel (1900-65)
American writer, producer
BE, ES, TW/21, WWA/4

BLUM, Edward (b 1928)
American casting director
BE

BLUM, Gustav (d 1963 [76])
producer TW/20

BLUM, Martin A. (d 1972
[36]) publicist BP/57*

BLUM, William (b 1901)
American manager BE

BLUM, William David see
Darrid, William

BLUMB, Mr. (fl 1792) imitator,
pianist BD

BLUMBERG, Harold D. (b
1922) American costumier
BE

BLUME, Mr. (fl 1783-85) box
keeper BD

BLUME, Mrs. (fl 1783-85)

dresser BD

BLUME, Heinrich (1788-1856)
German singer ES

BLUMENFELD, Robert [Robert
Fields] (b 1943) American actor,
singer TW/27

BLUMENTHAL, George (1863?-1943)
producer, manager CB

BLUMENTHAL, Jacques (1829-1908)
German/English songwriter DNB

BLUMENTHAL, Oscar (1852-1917)
German dramatist GRB/4,
WWT/1-2

BLUMENTHAL, Richard M. (d 1962
[55]) French producer BE*

BLUMENTHAL-TAMARINA, Maria
(d 1938 [79]) actress BE*,
WWT/14*

BLUNDELL, James (d 1786) violoncellist, composer, singer BD

BLUNDIVILLE, John (fl 1665) singer
BD

BLUNKALL, Ervin (1875-1943)
actor SR

BLUNT, Mr. (fl 1689) actor BD

BLUNT, Mr. (fl 1744) actor BD

BLUNT, Mrs. (fl 1729-30) actress
BD

BLUNT, Arthur Cecil see Cecil,
Arthur

BLUNT, T. (fl 1794) violinist BD

BLURTON, James (b 1756) dancer,
actor, singer BD

BLURTON, Mrs. James [Mary] (fl
1793-1800) actress, singer BD

BLY, Dan (d 1973 [37]) stage manager TW/29

BLYDE, Frederick (d 1887) EA/88*

BLYDEN, Larry [né Ivan Lawrence
Blieden] (1925-75) American act-
or, director, producer BE,
TW/23-25, 28-29, WWT/15-16

BLYTHE, Betty (d 1972 [72]) actress
BP/56*, WWT/16*

BLYTHE, Bobby (b 1894) Australian
actor, singer WWT/5-7

BLYTHE, Charles M. (d 1886 [58])
actor EA/87*

BLYTHE, Coralie (1880-1928)
actress GRB/1-4, WWT/1-5

BLYTHE, Mrs. G. see Blythe, M.

BLYTHE, George (d 1892 [56])
EA/93*

BLYTHE, Mrs. George see
Birchenough, Bella

BLYTHE, Herman see Barrymore,
Maurice

BLYTHE, Mrs. James S. see

Hodson, Sylvia
BLYTHE, John (b 1921) English
actor WWT/16
BLYTHE, Mrs. John S. see
Hodson, Sylvia
BLYTHE, J. S. (d 1918) EA/
19*
BLYTHE, M. [Mrs. G. Blythe]
(d 1875 [32]) EA/76*
BLYTHE, Stephen (d 1889)
musical director EA/90*
BLYTHE, T. Gordon (d 1974
[85]) actor BTR/74
BLYTHE, Violet actress, singer
WWT/4-13
BLYTH-PRATT, Violet actress
WWT/5-6
BOADEN, James (1762-1839)
English dramatist, critic
CDP, COC, CP/3, DD, ES,
GT, OC/1-3, TD/1-2
BOAG, William (d 1939 [72])
American actor, manager
BP/23*
BOAK, Alfred Brydone see
Brydone, Alfred
BOAK, Eliza Brydone (d 1913
[76]) EA/14*
BOARDMAN, Lillian [Mrs. Lil-
lian Boardman Smith] (d
1953 [60]) actress BE*,
BP/38*
BOARDMAN, Virginia True (d
1971 [82]) performer BP/
56*
BOARER, Beatrice (d 1954)
actress WWT/14*
BOAZ, Charles (b 1919) Amer-
ican actor TW/8-10, 21
BOBADILLA, Pepita [née Nelly
Burton] Ecuadorian actress
WWT/4-5
BOBBIE, Walter (b 1945)
American actor TW/28-30
BOCCHINI, Sig. (fl 1773-74)
dancer BD
BOCHERT, Charles G. (d 1971
[92]) publicist BP/56*
BOCHSA, Robert-Nicholas-
Charles (1789-1856) French
harpist, composer ES
BOCK, Jerry (b 1928) American
composer AAS, BE, WWT/
15-16
BOCKELMANN, Rudolf (b 1892)
German singer ES
BODANZKY, Arthur (1877-1939)
Austrian conductor DAB,

ES, WWA/1
BODDA, Louisa Fanny see Pyne,
Louisa Fanny
BODDAPYNE, Louisa Fanny see
Pyne, Louisa Farry
BODDEN, James (d 1885) advance
agent EA/86*
BODDINGTON, Ernest Fearby (b
1873) English/American dramatist
WWA/5
BODDY, Edward (d 1918) EA/19*
BODE, Allan (d 1975 [69]) performer
BP/60*
BODE, Milton (1860/63-1938) Eng-
lish manager, actor GRB/4,
WWT/1-8
BODEL, Burman (d 1969 [58]) per-
former BP/54*
BODEN, Rosa Augusta (d 1888 [78])
actress EA/89*
BODENHAM, Mr. (fl 1672) musician
BD
BODENHAM, Estelle D'Arcy see
Yelland, Estelle D'Arcy
BODENHEIM, Maxwell (1893-1954)
American performer BE*
BODENS, Cpt. Charles (fl 1732-60)
dramatist CP/1-3, GT, TD/2
BODIE, Jack [Pat Murphy] (d 1917)
comedian, dancer EA/18*
BODIE, Jeannie (d 1909) EA/10*
BODIN, Mr. (fl 1742) rope dancer,
tumbler BD
BODKIN, Thomas V. (d 1974 [87])
manager BP/58*
BODLEY, Ellen (d 1969) dramatist
BP/54*
BODOM, Borghild (b 1908) Norwegian
actress, singer WWT/7
BODWIN, Mr. (fl 1784) bassoonist
BD
BODY, W. (fl 1742-45) proprietor
BD
BOEHM, Gustav (b 1854) Austrian/
American dramatist WWM
BOEHNEL, Molly (d 1963 [56])
dramatist BP/47*
BOESE, Joachim (d 1971 [38])
performer BP/55*
BOESEN, William (d 1972 [48])
performer BP/56*
BOETTCHER, Henry F. (b 1903)
American educator, director BE
BOGAERDE, Derek van den see
Bogarde, Dirk
BOGARD, Travis (b 1918) American
educator BE
BOGARDE, Dirk [Derek van den

Bogaerde] (b 1920/21) English
actor CB, ES, WWT/11-14

BOGARDUS, Cpt. A. N. (d 1913)
American marksman SR

BOGART, Andrew (b 1874)
American actor WWS

BOGART, David (d 1964 [81])
singer, actor BE*

BOGART, Humphrey DeForest (1899-
1957) American actor, producer
CB, ES, SR, TW/13, WWA/3,
WWT/8-10, WWW/5

BOGDANOFF, Leonard (d 1975
[50]) financier BP/60*

BOGDANOFF, Rose (d 1957
[53]) American designer BE*

BOGEL, Alexandra (d 1879 [35])
singer EA/80*

BOGERT, William (b 1936) American actor TW/24-25, 28-30

BOGGETTI, Victor (b 1895)
English actor WWT/10-12

BOGGS, Gail (b 1951) American
actress TW/29

BOHAM, Mr. (fl 1741) actor BD

BOHEE, George B. (b 1857) Canadian variety artist GRB/1

BOHEE, James Douglas (d 1897
[53]) comedian EA/99*

BOHEME, Anthony (d 1731)
actor BD, DD

BOHEME, Mrs. Anthony, II
(fl 1730) actress BD

BOHM, Joseph (1795-1876)
violinist, composer CDP

BOHM, Karl (b 1894) Austrian
conductor CB

BOHNEN, Michael (b 1888)
German ES

BOHNEN, Roman (1901-49) American actor ES, TW/5, WWT/10

BOIELDIEU, Adrien (d 1883
[67]) composer EA/84*

BOIMAISON, Mr. (fl 1788-96)
actor BD

BOIMAISON, Mrs. (fl 1793-96)
actress, singer BD

BOISEY, Michael see Boissy,
Michael

BOISGERARD, Mons. (fl 1791-1820)
dancer, choreographer BD

BOISGERARD, Mme. (fl 1791)
dancer BD

BOISSET (d 1901 [34]) gymnast,
pantomimist EA/03*

BOISSET, Fred (d 1895 [32]) gymnast, pantomimist EA/96*

BOISSY [or Boisey], Michael (fl 1752)

French dramatist CP/2-3, GT

BOITAR, Beatrice (fl 1729) actress
BD

BOITO, Arrigo (1842-1919) Italian
composer, librettist ES

BOKER, George Henry (1823-90)
American dramatist CDP, COC,
DAB, DD, ES, HJD, MH, OC/
1-3, RE

BOKOR, Margit (b 1909) Hungarian
singer WWA/3

BOLADO, Maria Margharita see
Margo

BOLAM, F. W. (d 1913 [50]) EA/14*

BOLAM, James (b 1938) English
actor WWT/15-16

BOLAN, Jeanne (d 1976 [49]) performer BP/60*

BOLAND, Bridget (b 1913) English
dramatist CD, PDT

BOLAND, Clay A. (d 1963 [59])
composer BP/48*

BOLAND, Eddie (b 1885) American
actor ES

BOLAND, Mary (1885-1965) Ameri-
can actress BE, ES, GRB/3-4,
TW/2-16, 22, WWA/4, WWM,
WWT/1-13

BOLAND, William (d 1953 [69])
singer WWT/14*

BOLASNI, Saul (b 1923) American
costume designer BE

BOLENDER, Todd (b 1914) American
dancer, choreographer, ballet
master ES

BOLENO, Emma (d 1867 [35])
actress EA/68*

BOLENO, Gardiner (d 1891) EA/92*

BOLENO, Harry (d 1875) clown CDP

BOLENO, Mrs. H. G. (d 1875) EA/
76*

BOLENO, Mrs. H. G. (d 1888) EA/
89*

BOLENO, Samson (d 1872) music-
hall performer EA/73*

BOLENO MARSH see Tolkein,
Alfred

BOLERO [Wilson Storey] (d 1910
[33]) acrobat, clown EA/12*

BOLES, Athena Lorde (d 1973
[57]) performer BP/58*

BOLES, John (1900-69) American
actor, singer BE, ES, TW/1,
25, WWT/7-12

BOLESLAVSKY, Richard (1889-1937)
Polish producer, director ES,
NTH, WWT/6-8

BOLEY, May (d 1963 [81]) musical

comedy actress TW/19

BOLEYN, Richard Smith (fl 1870-80) English actor OAA/1-2

BOLEYN, Mrs. Richard Smith see Brough, Fanny Whiteside

BOLGER, Ray[mond Wallace] (b 1904/06) American actor, dancer AAS, BE, CB, ES, TW/2-20, 25, WWT/9-16

BOLGER, Robert (d 1969 [32]) performer BP/54*

BOLIN, Shannon (b 1917) American actress, singer BE, TW/20, 22, 26

BOLINGBROKE, Mrs. (fl 1777) actress BD

BOLINI, Horace (d 1892) singer EA/93*

BOLITHO, W. (d 1892) EA/93*

BOLLA, Maria (fl 1799-1804) Italian singer, actress BD

BOLLAERT, James (d 1869 [57]) costumier EA/70*

BOLLARD, Robert Gordon (d 1964 [44]) musical director BP/49*

BOLLER, Robert O., Sr. (d 1962 [75]) architect BE*

BOLLINGER, Anne (d 1962 [39]) singer TW/19

BOLM, Adolph (1884/87-1951) Russian dancer, choreographer ES, TW/7, WWT/4, 9-11

BOLOGNA, Sig. (fl 1662-88) puppeteer BD

BOLOGNA, Barbara (fl 1786-1804) dancer BD

BOLOGNA, John Peter (1775-1846) Italian harlequin, dancer, tumbler, machinist BD, CDP

BOLOGNA, Louis (d 1808) Italian tumbler, clown, dancer, singer BD

BOLOGNA, Mrs. Louis (fl 1799-1800) dancer BD

BOLOGNA, Pietro (fl 1786-1814) Italian clown, rope dancer BD

BOLOGNA, Mrs. Pietro (fl 1786-98?) Italian tumbler, dancer, singer BD

BOLSTER, Anita (b 1900) Irish actress TW/2-6

BOLSTER, Stephen (b 1933) American actor TW/24, 27

BOLT, Carol (b 1941) Canadian dramatist CD

BOLT, H. P. (d 1884 [68]) pro-prietor EA/85*

BOLT, Robert Oxton (b 1924) English dramatist AAS, BE, CB, CD, CH, COC, ES, MH, MWD, OC/3, PDT, RE, WWT/13-16

BOLTON, Mr. (fl 1730-31) house servant? BD

BOLTON, Mr. (fl 1773) actor BD

BOLTON, Mrs. (fl 1789-1801) house servant BD

BOLTON, Mrs. (d 1913) EA/14*

BOLTON, A. J. (d 1917) manager EA/18*

BOLTON, Caroline (d 1871 [28]) actress? EA/72*

BOLTON, Edwin L. (d 1971 [53]) critic BP/56*

BOLTON, Eliza (fl 1809) actress CDP

BOLTON, G. Benson (d 1917 [27]) musician EA/18*

BOLTON, George (d 1868 [43]) actor, manager EA/69*, WWT/14*

BOLTON, Guy Reginald (b 1881/84/86) English dramatist, librettist AAS, BE, CD, ES, MWD, PDT, SR, WWT/4-16

BOLTON, Jack (d 1962 [60]) talent representative BE*

BOLTON, Lavinia, Duchess of (1708-60) actress CDP, GT

BOLTON, Mary [Lady Thurlow] (1790-1830) actress CDP, EA/79

BOLTON, Sam (d 1879 [32]) pantomimist EA/80*

BOLTON, Sarah (d 1893) writer EA/94*

BOLTON, Thomas (d 1895) actor EA/96*

BOLTON, Whitney (1900-69) American critic BE, NTH, TW/26

BOMAN, Mr. (b c. 1695?) English actor BD

BOMAN, Mrs. (fl 1716-56) singer, dancer, actress BD

BOMAN [or Bowman], John (c. 1651?-1739) English actor, singer BD, DD

BOMAN, Mrs. John [née Elizabeth Watson] (1677?-1707?) English actress, singer BD

BOMBARDIN, Mr. (fl 1751) bassoonist BD

"BOMBASTINI, Sig." (fl 1759) musician BD

"BOMBASTINI, Signora" (fl 1759) dancer? BD

"BOMBASTO, Sig." (fl 1751-60)

singer, musician, dancer BD

"BOMBAZEENO, Sig." (fl 1752-54) dancer BD

BONACCI, Anna (fl 20th cent) Italian dramatist ES

BONACICH, Walter Adey (d 1892 [44]) agent EA/93*

BONANOVA, Fortunio (d 1969 [73]) performer BP/53*

BONARELLI DELLA ROVERE, Guidobaldo (1563-1608) Italian dramatist COC, OC/1-3

BONARIUS, Harold (d 1917) musician EA/18*

BONASERA, Eftichios (1865-1928) Greek actor ES

BONCI, Alessandro (1870-1940) Italian singer ES, WWA/5

BOND, Mr. (fl 1784) singer BD

BOND, Professor (fl c. 1849) musician CDP

BOND, Acton (d 1941 [80]) Canadian actor, dramatist DD, GRB/1-4, WWT/1-6

BOND, Bert [Herbert Rowley] (d 1964 [81]) performer BE*

BOND, Carrie Jacobs (1862-1946) American composer BE*

BOND, C[hristopher] G[odfrey] (b 1945) English dramatist, actor CD

BOND, Edward (b 1935) English dramatist AAS, CD, CH, COC, PDT, WWT/15-16

BOND, Emmanuel (d 1874) music-hall performer EA/75*

BOND, Frederic Drew (1859/61-1914) American actor PP/1, WWS, WWT/1-2

BOND, Mrs. Frederick see Rose, Annie

BOND, Gary (b 1940) English actor TW/20, WWT/15-16

BOND, Henry Charles (d 1873 [41]) prompter EA/74*

BOND, Herbert (d 1869 [31]) singer EA/70*

BOND, Jean see Guillemen, Louis Charles

BOND, Jessie (1853-1942) English actress, singer CB, DD, DP, EA/95, OAA/2, SR, WWT/6-9

BOND, John (fl 1784-1807?) singer BD

BOND, Lilian (b 1910) English actress WWT/8-9

BOND, Ridge (b 1923) American actor TW/8

BOND, Rudy (b 1913/15) American actor, director BE, TW/4, 8, 23-25, 28-30

BOND, Sheila (b 1928) American actress, dancer, singer BE, TW/3-16, WWT/11-14

BOND, Sudie (b 1928) American actress, dancer BE, TW/22-27, 29-30, WWT/15-16

BOND, Thomas (d 1635) English actor CDP, DA, OC/1-3

BOND, Ward (d 1960 [c. 56]) American actor BE*

BOND, William (d 1735) English dramatist, actor CP/2-3, DD, DNB, GT, TD/1-2

BONDI, Beulah (b 1892) American actress BE, ES, WWT/7-9

BONDS, Margaret (d 1972 [59]) composer/lyricist BP/56*

BOND-SAYERS, Arthur (d 1912) musical director EA/13*

BONDY, Ed (b 1932) American talent representative BE

BONEFACE, George C. see Boniface, George C.

BONEFACE, George C., Jr. (d 1917) actor SR

BONEHILL, Mrs. (d 1904) EA/06*

BONEHILL, Bessie (d 1902) English actress, singer, music-hall comedienne CDP, SR

BONEHILL, Elias (d 1900 [75]) EA/02*

BONEHILL, Henry (d 1877 [30]) EA/88*

BONEHILL, Jane (d 1886 [35]) EA/87*

BONEHILL, Jessie (d 1884 [23]) singer, dancer EA/85*

BONEHILL, Marian (d 1874 [25]) singer EA/75*

BONELLE, Dick (b 1936) American actor TW/26, 28-30

BONELLI, William actor, dramatist SR

BONEMAN, Frederick (1833-1911) German singer SR

BONEN, William (fl 1623) English dramatist FGF

BONERZ, Peter (b 1938) American actor TW/27

BONEWAY, Mlle. (fl 1746) actress BD

BONFANTI, Luigi (fl 1794-98) singer BD

BONFANTI, Marietta (1847-1921) Italian/American dancer CDP, ES

BONFILS, Helen (d 1972 [82])
American producer, actress,
publisher BE, TW/29, WWT/15
BONGARD, Hal (d 1967 [61]) exe-
cutive BP/52*
BONHAM, Melville (d 1876) drama-
tic reader EA/78*
BONI, Daniela (b 1942) Italian ac-
tress TW/10
BONIFACE, George C. (1833-1912)
American actor CDP, PP/1, SR
BONIFACE, Mrs. George C. (d
1883) actress BE*, WWT/14*
BONIFACE, George C., Jr. see
Boneface, George C., Jr.
BONIME, Abby (b 1932) American
actress TW/4
BONINSEGNA, Celestina (1877-
1947) Italian singer ES
BONITA [Mrs. Lew Hearn] (b 1885)
American comedienne WWM,
WWS
BONN, Ferdinand (d 1933 [71])
actor WWT/14*
BONNAIRE, Mme. (d 1863 [28])
trapezist EA/69*
BONNAIRE, Henri (b 1869) French
composer, journalist WWT/4
BONNELL, Jay (b 1932) Amer-
ican actor TW/27
BONNER, [Mrs.?] (fl 1791) ac-
tress BD
BONNER, Geraldine (fl 1887) Amer-
ican critic, dramatist WWM
BONNER, Isabel (d 1955 [47])
American actress TW/8, 12
BONNET, [Mr.?] (fl 1757-58)
house servant? BD
BONNET, Eliza F. see White,
Mrs. Cool
BONNET, James (b 1938) Amer-
ican actor TW/14-16
BONNEVAL, Mlle. (fl 1741-44)
French dancer BD
BONNHEIM, Byron A. (d 1972
[54]) publicist BP/56*
BONNIE, Beatrice (d 1918 [35])
EA/19*
BONNOR, Charles (fl 1777-1829?)
English actor, dramatist BD,
CP/3, DD, DNB
BONOMI, Giac[inta?] (fl 1757-
59) dancer BD
BONOCINI, Giovanni (1670-1747)
Italian violoncellist, composer
BD, CP/1, ES
BONSALL, Bessie (d 1963 [92])
performer BE*

BONSOR, Mr. (fl 1793-1810) door-
keeper BD
BONSTELLE, Jessie (1872-1932)
American actress, manager, pro-
ducer DAB, ES, NTH, OC/1-3,
SR
BONTEMPS, Arna (d 1973 [70])
dramatist BP/58*
BONUS, Ben producer, dramatist,
actor WWT/16
BONVILLE, Mr. [E. N. Morgan] (fl
1787-89) actor, singer BD
BONWICK, Miss (fl 1794) organist,
singer BD
BONYNGE, Leta (b 1917) American
actress TW/25-26
BOOKE, Sorrell (b 1930) American
actor TW/23, 25, WWT/16
BOOKER, George [né Dingle] (d
1908 [49]) American comedian
EA/09*
BOOKMAN, Leo (b 1932) American
talent representative BE
BOOMAR, Mr. (fl 1719) singer BD
BOON, "Blind" Negro musician SR
BOONE, Lizzie [Mrs. P. L. Rose]
(d 1897) actress, singer EA/98*
BOONE, Richard (b 1917) American
actor, director BE, CB
BOONE, William (d 1891) EA/92*
BOOR, Frank (d 1938 [73]) Brazili-
an/English agent, manager
GRB/1-2, WWT/4-8
BOORDE, Andrew (1490?-1549)
English actor CDP
BOORN, Alfred (d 1886 [25]) eques-
trian EA/87*
BOORN, Benjamin, Jr. (d 1876
[25]) equestrian EA/77*
BOORN, James (d 1893 [73]) circus
proprietor EA/94*
BOORNE, George (d 1893) equestrian
EA/94*
BOOSE, Mr. C. (d 1868 [53]) band-
master EA/69*
BOOSEY, Charles (d 1905 [78])
publisher EA/06*
BOOSEY, John (d 1893) concert or-
ganiser EA/94*
BOOSEY, Philip Harold see Cun-
ingham, Philip
BOOSEY, William (d 1933 [69]) pro-
ducer, publisher BE*, WWT/14*
BOOT, Gladys (d 1964 [74]) English
actress WWT/13
BOOTE, Rosie [Marchioness of
Headfort] (1878-1958) English
actress COC, GRB/1, OC/3

BOOTH, Mr. (fl 1762-71) actor BD
BOOTH, Mr. (fl 1780-82) actor BD
BOOTH, Mr. (fl 1784) singer BD
BOOTH, Mrs. (fl 1740-41) actress
    BD
BOOTH, Mrs. (fl 1778) actress,
    dramatist CP/3
BOOTH, Miss (fl 1715) singer BD
BOOTH, Agnes [Marian Agnes Land
    Rookes] (1846-1910) Australian/
    American actress CDP, DAB,
    DD, ES, PP/1, SR, WWA/1
BOOTH, Arthur E. (d 1898 [29])
    gymnast EA/99*
BOOTH, Barton (1679?/81-1733)
    English actor, manager, dramatist
    BD, CDP, COC, CP/1-3,
    DNB, ES, GT, OC/1-3, TD/1-2
BOOTH, Mrs. Barton, II [née
    Hester Santlow] (c. 1690-1773)
    English actress, dancer BD,
    CDP, DNB
BOOTH, Blanche de Bar (d 1930
    [86]) actress BE*, WWT/14*
BOOTH, Carol (b 1941) English
    actress TW/21
BOOTH, Charles (fl 1660?-82?)
    prompter BD
BOOTH, Cockran Joseph (d
    1789) actor, singer BD
BOOTH, Mrs. Cockran Joseph
    (fl 1774-91) actress BD
BOOTH, Edwin Thomas (1833-
    93) American actor CDP,
    COC, DAB, DD, DP, ES,
    HAS, HJD, NTH, OC/1-3,
    PDT, SR, WWA/H
BOOTH, Mrs. Edwin Thomas
    [Mary Devlin] (1840-62)
    American dancer HAS
BOOTH, Helen (d 1971) per-
    former BP/55*
BOOTH, Hope [Mrs. Rennold Wolf]
    (1872-1933) Canadian actress
    WWS
BOOTH, James [né Geeves-
    Booth] (b 1933) English actor
    AAS, WWT/14-16
BOOTH, J. H. English actor GRB/1
BOOTH, John (d 1779) perform-
    er? BD
BOOTH, John (fl 1780-96) tailor BD
BOOTH, Mrs. John [Ursula Agnes]
    (1740-1803) actress, singer BD
BOOTH, John E. (b 1919) Amer-
    ican writer BE
BOOTH, John Hunter (d 1971
    [85]) dramatist TW/28

BOOTH, John Wilkes (1838-65) Amer-
    ican actor CDP, COC, DAB, DD,
    ES, HAS, HJD, NTH, OC/1-3,
    PDT, SR, WWA/H
BOOTH, Joseph [né Martin] (d 1797)
    English actor, exhibitor BD
BOOTH, J. S. (1821-58) comedian
    HAS
BOOTH, Junius (d 1912 [c. 45])
    American actor GRB/1-2
BOOTH, Junius Brutus (1796-1852)
    English actor CDP, COC, DAB,
    DD, DNB, ES, HAS, HJD, NTH,
    OC/1-3, OX, PDT, RJ, SR,
    WWA/H
BOOTH, Junius Brutus, Jr. (1821-
    83) actor CDP, COC, DD, ES,
    HAS, OC/1-3, PDT, SR
BOOTH, Junius Brutus, III (b 1868)
    American actor SR
BOOTH, Mrs. Junius Brutus, Jr., I
    [née DeBar] (b 1810) Irish actress
    HAS
BOOTH, Mrs. Junius Brutus, Jr.,
    II [née Harriet Mace] (d 1859)
    actress HAS
BOOTH, Mrs. Junius Brutus, Jr.,
    III HAS
BOOTH, Mary (1840-62) actress
    CDP
BOOTH, Mary (d 1881) actress
    CDP
BOOTH, Nellie (d 1973 [84]) per-
    former BP/57*
BOOTH, Nesdon (d 1964 [45]) actor
    BE*
BOOTH, Rachel (d 1868 [55]) EA/69*
BOOTH, Rita (d 1892) actress SR
BOOTH, Rosalie Ann (d 1889 [65])
    EA/90*
BOOTH, Miss S. (b 1794) English
    actress BS
BOOTH, Sallie (d 1902 [63]) actress
    BE*, EA/03*, WWT/14*
BOOTH, Sarah (1793-1867) English
    actress CDP, DD, DNB, EA/92,
    OX
BOOTH, Shirley [née Thelma Booth]
    (b 1907) American actress AAS,
    BE, CB, ES, NTH, SR, TW/1-
    3, 5-19, 26-28, WWT/9-16
BOOTH, Sydney Barton (1873-1937)
    actor CDP, COC, OC/1-3, WWM
BOOTH, T. G. (d 1855) actor
    CDP, HAS
BOOTH, Thelma see Booth, Shirley
BOOTH, T[homas] B[ennett] (d 1872)
    actor SR

BOOTH, Webster (b 1902) English actor, singer WWT/10-13

BOOTHBY, Mr. (fl 1735-36) actor BD

BOOTHSBY, Sir Brooke (1743-1824) English dramatist CP/3, DD

BOOTHBY, Mrs. Frances (fl c. 1665) dramatist CP/1-3, GT

BOOTHE, Clare (b 1902/03) American dramatist CB, ES, HJD, MH, MWD, NTH, ST, WWT/9-12

BOQUET, Louis-René (1717-1814) French designer, decorator BD

BORAH, Leo Arthur (1889-1959) American editor WWA/4

BORANI, Charles [Henry Charles Moss] (d 1900 [37]) pantomimist EA/01*

BORCH, Gaston (b 1871) French composer, conductor WWM

BORCHARD, Mme. Comte (d 1866) singer, pianist HAS

BORCHERS, Gladys (b 1891) American educator BE

BORDEN, Olive (1907-47) American actress BE*

BORDO, Ed (b 1931) American actor TW/26, 28

BORDOGNI, Louisa (fl 1833) Italian singer CDP, ES

BORDONI, Irene (1895-1953) French actress, singer SR, TW/3, 5-9, WWT/4-11

BORDONI-HASSE, Faustina (1693-1781) Italian singer ES

BOREE, Albert (d 1910) German comedian EA/11*

BOREL, Louis see Borell, Louis

BORELL [or Borel], Louis (1906-73) Dutch actor TW/3, 29, WWT/9-14

BORELLA, Arthur James (1868-1947) American circus clown SR

BOREO, Emile (d 1951 [66]) Polish performer BE*, BP/36*

BORETZ, Allen (b 1900) American dramatist, composer BE

BORG, Veda Ann (d 1973 [58]) actress BP/58*, WWT/16*

BORGE, Victor (b 1909) Danish/American performer BE, CB

BORGHESA, Eufrasia (fl 1841-44) Italian singer CDP, HAS

BORGHI, Luigi (fl 1772-94) violinist, composer, manager BD

BORGHI, Signora Luigi [née Anna Casentini] (fl 1790-97) singer BD

BORGHI-MAMO, Adelaide (1829-1901) Italian singer CDP, ES

BORGIOLI, Dino (b 1891) Italian singer ES

BORGNINE, Ernest (b 1917) American actor CB, ES

BORI, Lucrezia (1889-1960) Spanish singer ES, TW/16, WWA/4

BORIS, Ruthanna (b 1918) American dancer, choreographer ES

BORLIN, Jean (1893-1930) Swedish dancer, choreographer ES

BORNAL, Mr. (fl 1796) puppeteer BD

BORNE, Constantine (fl 1768) freak BD

BORNE, Theophilus see Bird, Theophilus

BORNE, William see Bird, William

BOROMEO, Sig. (fl 1742-43) dancer BD

BOROSINI, Francesco (b c. 1690) Italian singer BD

BOROWSKY, Marvin S. (b 1907) American educator, writer BE

BORRANI, Sig. (fl 1854) singer CDP, HAS

BORRELLI, Jim (b 1948) American actor TW/27-30

BORRI, Pasquale (1820-84) Italian dancer, choreographer ES

BORROW, Sarah (d 1875 [76]) EA/76*

BORROW, William (d 1872 [74]) EA/73*

BORSELLI, Elisabetta see Borselli, Signora Fausto

BORSELLI, Fausto (fl 1789-90) singer BD

BORSELLI, Signora Fausto [Elisabetta] (fl 1789-90) singer BD

BORTHWICK, A. T. (d 1943 [65]) critic, journalist BE*, WWT/14*

BORUFF, John (b 1910) American actor, dramatist BE

BORUP, Doan (1875-1944) actor SR

BORUWLASKI, Joseph (1739-1837) Polish dwarf, musician BD, CDP, DNB

BORWELL, Montague (b 1866) English singer GRB/1

BORWICK, A. F. (d 1917?) EA/18*

BORZAGE, Daniel (d 1975 [78]) performer BP/60*

BORZAGE, Lew (d 1974 [71]) producer/director/choreographer BP/59*

BOSAN, Alonzo (b 1886) American actor TW/8

BOSANECK, Herr (d 1871)
musical director EA/72*
BOSCAWEN, Mr. (fl 1735)
actor BD
BOSCAWEN, Hon. Kathleen
Pamela see Carme,
Pamela
BOSCH, Frederick (fl 1739-43)
musician BD
BOSCHETTI, Leonilda (fl 1866)
French singer HAS
BOSCHETTI, Signora Mengis
(fl 1770-72) singer BD
BOSCHI, Giuseppe Maria (fl
1710-28) Italian singer
BD, ES
BOSCHI, Signora Giuseppe
Maria [née Francesca Vanini]
(fl 1710-11) Italian singer
BD
BOSCO (d 1906 [72]) magician
EA/07*
BOSCO, Leotard (d 1895 [45])
manager EA/96*
BOSCO, Mrs. Leotard see
Bosco, Mary
BOSCO, Mary (d 1897 [46])
EA/99*
BOSCO, Philip (b 1930) Amer-
ican actor AAS, BE, TW/
23-30, WWT/15-16
BOSEGRAVE, George (fl 1623-
24) lessee DA
BOSGRAVE, George see
Bosegrave, George
BOSILLO, Nick (d 1964 [80])
performer BE*
BOSIO, Angiolina (1830-59)
Italian singer CDP, ES,
HAS, SR
BOSKOTIN, Mr. (fl 1732) actor
BD
BOSLEY, Tom (b 1927) Ameri-
can actor BE, TW/21-24,
WWT/15-16
BOSSERT, Mr. magician CDP
BOSSI, Cesare (d 1802) com-
poser, instrumentalist BD
BOSSI, Mme. Cesare see
Del Caro, Mlle.
BOSSICK, Bernard B. (d 1975
[57]) performer BP/60*
BOSSY, Frederick (fl 1794)
violinist BD
BOSTOCK, Mr. (fl 1742-50)
actor BD
BOSTOCK, Mrs. [née Wombwell]
(d 1904 [70]) EA/06*

BOSTOCK, Edward H. (d 1940 [81])
circus proprietor BE*, WWT/
14*
BOSTOCK, Frank (d 1898) conductor
EA/99*
BOSTOCK, Frank C. (1866-1912)
English circus and show propri-
etor ES, SR
BOSTOCK, Harry (d 1917) EA/18*
BOSTOCK, James (d 1878 [63])
proprietor EA/79*
BOSTOCK, N. C. ["The Comic
King"] (d 1916 [66]) EA/18*
BOSTOCK, Thomas H. (b 1899)
English manager WWT/9-10
BOSTOCK, Mrs. W. B. [née Kloet]
(d 1907) EA/08*
BOSTON, Nelroy Buck (d 1962
[51]) actress BE*
"BOSTON GEORGE" see Pablo
BOSTWICK, Barry (b 1945) Ameri-
can actor TW/25-30
BOSTWICK, Emma Gillingham (fl
1850s) singer CDP
BOSTWICK, Harold American actor,
pianist TW/3
BOSWELL, Mr. (fl 1788-95) house
servant? BD
BOSWELL, Mrs. (d 1898 [84])
circus performer? EA/99*
BOSWELL, A. P. [Arthur A.
Palmer] (d 1912 [55]) comedian
EA/13*
BOSWELL, Mrs. A. P. see
Hayes, Florence
BOSWELL, David (d 1865 [34])
actor HAS
BOSWELL, Edith [Mrs. Henry Luigi
Boswell] (d 1902) circus per-
former EA/04*
BOSWELL, Mrs. Henry Luigi see
Boswell, Edith
BOSWELL, James (fl 1821) scholar
DD
BOSWELL, James Clement (1826-
59) English clown ES
BOSWELL, Joseph H. (fl 1835-43)
American actor HAS
BOSWORTH, Agnes Ellinor [Nelly
Danvers] (d 1883 [31]) EA/84*
BOSWORTH, Henry Alexander (d
1893) scene artist, athlete
EA/84*
BOSWORTH, Hobart Van Zandt
(1867-1943) American actor CB,
ES, WWA/2
BOSWORTH, Patricia (b 1933)
American actress TW/13

BOSWORTH, Robart (1867-1943)
American actor, dramatist,
director SR

BOTARELLI, Mrs. (fl 1778-84)
singer BD

BOTELLI, Sig. (fl 1717) Italian
singer BD

BOTHAM, Benjamin William (d
1877) proprietor EA/79*

BOTHAM, Clayton (d 1907)
music-hall director EA/08*,
GRB/3*

BOTHAM, Ellen (d 1882 [51])
proprietor EA/83*

BOTHAM, William (fl 1663)
actor? BD

BOTHMAN, Fay (d 1975) agent
BP/59*

BOTHMAR, Mr. [Baron?] (fl
1734) oboist BD

BOTHNER, Gustave (1858-1933)
manager SR

BOTLY, Mrs. [née Fanny Chap-
man] (d 1874 [29]) pianist
EA/75*

BOTSFORD, Mrs. (fl 1830)
American dramatist EAP

BOTT, Alan (b 1894) English
critic WWT/8-9

BOTT, Mrs. Barrington (d
1894) EA/95*

BOTT, [Richard?] (fl 1785-87)
house servant? BD

BOTT, William (d 1882 [56])
performer? manager? EA/
83*

BOTTERO, Alessandro (1831-
92) Italian singer ES

BOTTESINI, Giovanni (1822-89)
Italian singer, composer,
conductor ES

BOTTESINI, Pietro (d 1874)
musician EA/75*

BOTTING, Mr. (d 1887) EA/
88*

BOTTING, Robert F. (d 1892)
proprietor EA/94*

BOTTOMLEY, Gordon (1874-
1948) English dramatist
COC, DNB, OC/1-3, WWT/
5-10, WWW/4

BOTTOMLEY, Robert Maude
(1886-1968) English actor
GRB/1-2

BOTTOMLEY, Roland (1879-
1947) English actor GRB/
1-2, SR, TW/3

BOUCHELLE, Mme. Wallace

singer CDP

BOUCHER, Anthony (fl 1689-96)
actor BD

BOUCHER, F. T. (d 1913) EA/14*

BOUCHER, Thomas (d 1755) dancer,
prompter, boxkeeper, sub-treasurer BD

BOUCHEZ, Arthur (d 1965 [77])
performer BP/49*

BOUCHIER, Chili [née Dorothy
Bouchier] (b 1909) English
actress WWT/10-16

BOUCHIER, Dorothy see Bouchier,
Chili

BOUCHIER, Josias (d 1695) English
singer BD

BOUCICAULT, Aubrey (1869-1913)
English actor, dramatist DD,
DP, ES, GRB/1-4, OC/3, SR,
WWM, WWS, WWT/1-2

BOUCICAULT, Mrs. Aubrey see
Boucicault, Ruth Baldwin Holt

BOUCICAULT, Dion Clayton (1878-
1937) dramatist ES, OC/3

BOUCICAULT, Dion George (1859-
1929) American actor, manager
COC, DD, DNB, ES, GRB/1-4,
OC/1-3, WWA/1, WWT/1-5,
WWW/3

BOUCICAULT, Mrs. Dion George
see Vanbrugh, Irene

BOUCICAULT, Dion Lardner (1820/
22-90) Irish dramatist, actor
CDP, COC, DAB, DD, DNB,
EA/68, ES, HAS, HJD, HP,
MH, NTH, OAA/1-2, OC/1-3,
PDT, RE, SR, WWA/H

BOUCICAULT, Mrs. Dion Lardner
[Agnes Kelly Robertson] (1833-
1916) Scottish actress CDP,
COC, DD, EA/97, ES, GRB/1-4,
HAS, OAA/1-2, OC/1-3, PP/3,
WWT/1-3

BOUCICAULT, Mrs. Dion Lardner,
II see Thorndyke, Louise

BOUCICAULT, Dion William (d
1876 [22]) EA/77*

BOUCICAULT, Donald (1888-1940)
actor ES, OC/3

BOUCICAULT, Eva [Mrs. John Clay-
ton] actress ES, OC/3

BOUCICAULT, Nina [Mrs. E. H.
Kelly] (1867-1950) English actress
COC, DD, ES, GRB/1-4, OC/
2-3, SR, TW/7, WWT/1-10

BOUCICAULT, Ruth Baldwin Holt
[Mrs. Aubrey Boucicault] (fl 1895-
1920) American actress WWA/5

BOUCICAULT, W. S. (d 1881
[62]) EA/82*
BOUDET, Mons. (fl 1726) French
dancer BD
BOUDET, Mme. (fl 1726) French
dancer BD
BOUDET, Mlle. (fl 1726) French
dancer BD
BOUDINOT, Annie [Annie Sendel-
beck] (d 1887 [50]) actress
NYM
BOUDINOT, Frank B. (d 1864)
minstrel HAS
BOUDROW, Joseph Hart see
Hart, Joseph
BOUFFE, Hugues-Marie-Désiré
(1800-88) French actor ES
BOUGH, Sam (d 1878 [57]) scene
painter EA/79*
BOUGHNER, Daniel E. (d 1974
[65]) historian BP/58*
BOUGHTON, J. W. (d 1914)
manager WWT/14*
BOUGHTON, Rutland (1878-1960)
English composer DNB, ES,
WWT/5-11, WWW/5
BOUGHTON, Walter (b 1918)
American educator, director
BE
BOUGIER, Mlle. (fl 1791) dancer
BD
BOUHY, Jacques-Joseph-André
(1848-1929) Belgian singer ES
BOULAN, Alice (d 1877) EA/78*
BOULANGER, Mr. actor CDP
BOULARD, Sig. (fl 1840-51)
American actor, singer HAS
BOULARD, Sig. (fl 1848) singer
HAS
BOULARD, James M. singer
CDP
BOULD, Beckett (b 1880) English
actor WWT/11-13
BOULDING, J. W. (fl 1882-97)
dramatist DD
BOULE, Philip [Jean Philippe?]
(1697?-1744?) French?
scene painter BD
BOULLIMIER, Tony (d 1917)
manager EA/18*
BOULOINGE, Mr. (fl 1799)
house servant? BD
BOULT, Sir Adrian [Cedric]
(b 1889) English conductor
CB
BOULT, Mrs. Charles see
Boult, Gertrude
BOULT, Ernest (d 1909 [71])

manager EA/10*
BOULT, Gertrude [Mrs. Charles
Boult] (d 1903 [32]) EA/04*
BOULTBY, Mrs. (fl 1740-41)
actress BD
BOULTER, Rosalyn (b 1916) English
actress WWT/9-12
BOULTER, Stanley (d 1917) EA/18*
BOULTING, Sydney see Cotes,
Peter
BOULTON, Mr. (fl 1794) house
servant BD
BOULTON, Christian Harold Ernest
(d 1917 [20]) dramatist, writer
EA/18*
BOULTON, Guy Pelham (b 1890)
English actor WWT/7-10
BOULTON, Thomas (fl 1768) English
dramatist CP/2-3, GT
BOUNDY, Alice (d 1897) dancer
EA/98*
BOUNTY, William (d 1687?)
trumpeter BD
BOUQUET, James (fl 1794) violinist
BD
BOUQUETON, Mons. (fl 1775-76)
ballet master BD
BOURBON, Ray (d 1971 [78]) Amer-
ican actor TW/1, 28
BOURBONNEL, Jules Alphonse (d
1897) circus manager EA/98*
BOURCHIER, Arthur (1863-1927)
English actor, manager, drama-
tist COC, DD, DNB, EA/95,
ES, GRB/1-4, OC/2-3, SR,
WWM, WWT/1-5, WWW/2
BOURCHIER, Mrs. Arthur see
Vanbrugh, Violet
BOURCHIER, John, Lord Berners
(d 1532 [63]) English dramatist
CP/2-3, DD
BOURDET, Edouard (1877-1945)
French dramatist MH, OC/1-3
BOURDIN, Roger (b 1900) French
singer ES
BOURDON, Mr. [Gabriel?] (fl 1700-
37?) singer BD
BOURGEOIS, Mlle. (fl 1793) dancer
BD
BOURGEOIS, Benjamin (fl 1765)
dramatist CP/2-3, GT
BOURGEOIS, Jeanne see Mistin-
guett
BOURGET, Paul (1852-1935) drama-
tist, critic BE*, WWT/14*
BOURK, William (fl 1780-97) dancer
BD
BOURK, Mrs. William [née

Elizabeth Bradshaw] (fl 1779-
93) dancer BD
BOURKE, E. (d 1869) actor
EA/70*
BOURKE, George Arlington (d
1908 [48]) EA/09*
BOURN, Emma (d 1907) circus
performer EA/08*
BOURNE, Adeline (d 1965 [92])
Indian/English actress WWT/
1-5
BOURNE, [Barnard?] (fl 1733-
60) actor BD
BOURNE, Barnard (b c.1745)
musician BD
BOURNE, Joseph H. (d 1877
[50]) actor EA/78*
BOURNE, Nettie see Arlington,
Mrs. Eddie
BOURNE, Reuben (fl 1692)
dramatist CP/1-3, DNB,
GT
BOURNE, Theophilus see
Bird, Theophilus
BOURNE, Thomas (fl 1635)
actor DA
BOURNE, William see Bird,
William
BOURNE, William Payne (d
1972 [36]) performer BP/
57*
BOURNEUF, Philip (b 1912)
American actor BE, TW/
2-14, 16, WWT/11-16
BOURNONVILLE, Antoine (1760-
1843) French dancer BD
BOURRELIER, Mr. (fl 1785-
90) house servant BD
BOURSKAYA, Ina (1888-1955)
Russian singer WWA/3
BOURVIL (d 1970 [57]) per-
former BP/55*
BOUSET, John see Sackville,
Thomas
BOUSFIELD, Elizabeth Hudson
(d 1876) EA/77*
BOUTEL, Mrs. (fl 1663-96)
actress DD, DNB
BOUTELL, Henry (fl 1687-89)
actor BD
BOUTET, [Mons.?] (fl 1675)
instrumentalist BD
BOUTFLOWER, Mr. (fl 1784)
violinist BD
BOUTON, Miss (fl 1784) actress
BD
BOUVERIE, Mark (d 1895) music-
hall director EA/96*

BOUVET, Maximilien-Nicolas (1854-
1943) French singer ES
BOUVIER, Corinne (d 1973 [31])
performer BP/58*
BOUWMEESTER, Louis (1842-1925)
Dutch actor ES, WWT/3-4
BOUWMEESTER, Theo (b 1873)
Dutch actor GRB/1
BOUXARY, Mons. (fl 1848) dancer
HAS
BOVA, Joseph (b 1924) American
actor BE, TW/20, 23-26, 28-
30, WWT/15-16
BOVAL, [Mons.?] (fl 1714-70?)
French dancer BD
BOVAL, William (fl 1739) musician
BD
BOVASSO, Julie (b 1930) American
actress, director, dramatist,
producer AAS, BE, CD, TW/
12-14, 22, 26, 28, WWT/15-16
BOVETT, La Petite (fl 1854)
actress HAS
BOVEY, Mrs. A. (d 1882) costumier
EA/83*
BOVILL, Charles H. (1878-1918)
Indian/English lyricist, librettist
WWT/2-3
BOWAN, Mr. (fl 1780) actor BD
BOWAN, Sibyl American actress
TW/25-26
BOWATER, Mr. actor CDP
BOWDEN, Mrs. (fl 1699-1704)
actress BD
BOWDEN, Charles (b 1913) Ameri-
can producer, director, actor
BE, WWT/15-16
BOWDEN, Wright (1752-1823) Eng-
lish singer, actor BD, CDP,
TD/1-2
BOWDLER, Thomas (1754-1825)
English editor DNB, HP
BOWDOIN, Harriet S. (d 1965 [60])
critic BP/49*
BOWEN, Mr. (fl 1734-35) actor
BD
BOWEN, Mr. (fl 1784) singer BD
BOWEN, Cyril see Moncrieff, R.
Scott
BOWEN, Daniel (c.1760-1856)
American? showman WWA/H
BOWEN, Frances C. (b 1905)
American educator BE
BOWEN, Jemmy (b c.1685) singer
BD
BOWEN, John (b 1924) Indian/English
dramatist, director, actor AAS,
CD, CH, WWT/15-16

BOWEN, Mr. W. (d 1886)
EA/87*
BOWEN, William (1666-1718)
Irish actor BD, DD
BOWER, Mrs. (fl 1721) singer
BD
BOWER, Miss E. [Mrs. Saphrini]
(d 1891) EA/92*
BOWER, Henry (fl 1664-67)
wardrobe keeper BD
BOWER, Marian (d 1945) drama-
tist WWT/4-9
BOWER, Richard (fl 1545-61)
master of the Chapel Royal
DA [see also B., R.]
BOWERING, Adelaide [Mrs. J.
B. Steele] (d 1899) actress
EA/00*
BOWERS, Mr. (fl 1757-73)
boxkeeper BD
BOWERS, Charles (b 1847) actor
SR
BOWERS, David P. (1822-57)
American actor HAS
BOWERS, Mrs. David P. see
Bowers, Elizabeth Crocker
BOWERS, Dun (d 1859) singer
HAS
BOWERS, Edward (d 1865 [38])
minstrel HAS
BOWERS, Elizabeth Crocker
(1830-95) American actress,
manager CDP, DAB, DD,
ES, HAS, SR, WWA/H
BOWERS, Faubion (b 1917)
American author BE
BOWERS, George Vining (1835-
78) American comedian DD,
HAS
BOWERS, John Valentine (fl
1834-50) English actor HAS
BOWERS, Kathleen see Bowers,
Lally
BOWERS, Kenny (b 1923) Amer-
ican actor TW/2-4
BOWERS, Lally [née Kathleen
Bowers] (b 1917) English
actress AAS, TW/23,
WWT/12-16
BOWERS, Richard (fl 1636)
actor DA
BOWERS, Robert Hood (1877-
1941) American composer
WWA/1, WWT/5-7
BOWERS, Viola [Mrs. Viola
Bowers Simmons] (d 1962
[79]) American performer
BE*

BOWES, Alice (d 1969 [79]) English
actress WWT/4-9
BOWES, Mjr. Edward E. (1874-
1946) American manager, pro-
moter SR
BOWES, Mary Eleanor, Countess
of Strathmore (d 1800) dramatist
CP/3
BOWFORD, Mr. (fl 1733) dancer
BD
BOWICK, Ellen reciter GRB/1-2
BOWINGTON, Mr. (fl 1737) actor
BD
BOWKETT, Sidney (d 1937 [69])
dramatist BE*
BOWLER, Annie Kemp (d 1876)
singer EA/77*
BOWLES, Miss (fl 1779) actress
BD
BOWLES, George (d 1968 [78])
composer/lyricist BP/52*
BOWLES, Mrs. George see
Rodney, Babette
BOWLES, Mrs. Henry Robert see
Aickin, Mrs. Graves
BOWLES, Jane (1917-73) American
dramatist BE
BOWLES, Paul Frederic (b 1910)
American composer, writer
BE, ES, HJD
BOWLES, Robert (1748-1806) English
actor, singer BD
BOWLEY, Mr. (fl 1792-1820) box-
keeper, officekeeper BD
BOWLEY, Mrs. (fl 1746-47) house
servant? BD
BOWLEY, Flora Juliet (fl 1900s)
American actress WWS
BOWLEY, Robert Kanzow (d 1870
[57]) manager EA/71*
BOWLING, J. P. (d 1886 [35])
principal EA/87*
BOWLING, Tom (d 1889 [72]) EA/
91*
BOWMAN, Mr. (fl 1792-94) actor
BD, TD/2
BOWMAN, Althea Olive see West,
Olive
BOWMAN, Empsie English actress
GRB/1-2
BOWMAN, Helen see Bowman,
Nellie
BOWMAN, Isa [Mrs. Reginald Bac-
chus] English actor GRB/1-3
BOWMAN, John see Boman, John
BOWMAN, John (b 1816) actor HAS
BOWMAN, John J. (d 1966 [57])
treasurer BP/50*

BOWMAN, Laura (d 1957 [76])
actress TW/13
BOWMAN, Lee (b 1914) Ameri-
can actor BE, ES
BOWMAN, Maggie [Mrs. Tom
J. Morton] English actor
GRB/1-2
BOWMAN, Mattie (d 1947 [68])
actress WWT/14*
BOWMAN, Nellie [Helen Bow-
man] (b 1878) English actress
GRB/1-4, WWT/1-4
BOWMAN, Ross (d 1926) Amer-
ican stage manager BE
BOWMAN, Sarah (d 1892)
EA/93*
BOWMAN, T. C. (d 1907 [65])
actor EA/08*, GRB/3*
BOWMAN, Walter P. (b 1910)
American educator, writer
BE
BOWMAN, Wayne (b 1914)
American educator, writer,
director, designer ES
BOWMER, Angus L. (b 1904)
American producer, director,
educator BE
BOWN, Mrs. Clifford see
Cross, Jessie
BOWN, George (d 1910 [90])
actor EA/11*
BOWN, William Paul (d 1889
[35]) American singer,
comedian EA/90*
BOWNE, Owen O. (d 1963 [84])
dancer BE*
BOWRING, George (fl 1574)
actor DA
BOWRINGE, Gregory (fl 1582)
actor DA
BOWRON, William A. actor
GRB/1
BOWSKILL, Jack (d 1904) actor
EA/05*
BOWTELL, Mrs. Barnaby [née
Elizabeth Ridley] (fl 1662?-
97) actress BD
BOWYER, Mrs. (fl 1798-99)
singer BD
BOWYER, Frederick (d 1936
[87]) dramatist, songwriter
BE*, WWT/14*
BOWYER, Michael (d 1645)
English actor DA, OC/1-3
BOX, Muriel (b 1905) English
dramatist ES
BOX, Sidney (b 1907) English
dramatist ES

BOXER, John (b 1909) English actor
WWT/9-16
BOXHORN, Jerome (d 1975 [55])
designer BP/60*
BOXLEY, Edward (fl 1773) musician
BD
BOYACK, Mr. (fl 1766-76) actor,
singer BD
BOYAR, Ben A. (1895-1964) Ameri-
can producer, general manager
BE
BOYAR, Monica Dominican Republi-
can actress, singer BE
BOYCE, Miss (fl 1807) English
actress BS, CDP, GT
BOYCE, Mrs. Charles (d 1864 [44])
actress EA/72*
BOYCE, Frank (d 1904 [47]) lessee
EA/05*
BOYCE, John (fl 1701-10) actor
BD
BOYCE, John T. (1829-67) Ameri-
can minstrel HAS
BOYCE, Samuel (d 1775) dramatist
CP/2-3, DNB, GT
BOYCE, Thomas (d 1793) English
dramatist CP/3, DNB
BOYCE, Thomas (d 1794) English
dancer, actor BD
BOYCE, Mrs. Thomas (fl 1790-96)
dancer BD
BOYCE, William (1710-79) English
composer, organist, teacher,
conductor BD, CDP, DNB, ES
BOYCE, William (1764-1823?) Eng-
lish double-bass player BD
BOYD, Alastair (d 1970 [50]) pub-
licist BP/55*
BOYD, Alexander (d 1883 [53])
proprietor EA/84*
BOYD, Anna (d 1916) actress
WWT/14*
BOYD, Archie (1852-1914) American
actor SR, WWM
BOYD, Belle (1843-1900) American
actress SR, WWA/H
BOYD, Billie (1831-69) American
imitator HAS
BOYD, Charles A. (b 1864) actor
SR
BOYD, Mrs. Edwin (d 1913) EA/
14*
BOYD, Elisse American lyricist,
composer BE
BOYD, Elizabeth (fl 1739) dramatist
CP/2-3, GT
BOYD, Ernest (1887-1946) Irish
dramatist WWW/4

BOYD, Frank M. (b 1863) Scottish critic GRB/1-4, WWT/1-5

BOYD, Mrs. Frank M. see Hewitt, Agnes

BOYD, Harold E. (d 1965 [72]) performer BP/50*

BOYD, Harry Hutcheson (b 1869) Irish dramatist WWA/5, WWM

BOYD, Henry (fl 1793) Irish dramatist CP/3

BOYD, Jeanne (d 1968 [78]) composer/lyricist BP/53*

BOYD, J. M. (d 1887) EA/88*

BOYD, Richard (b 1937) American community theatre administrator BE

BOYD, Sam, Jr. (b 1915) American educator BE

BOYD, Stephen [William Millar] (1928-77) Irish/American actor CB

BOYD, Sydney (b 1901) Scottish actor TW/2-3

BOYD, William (d 1972 [74]) performer BP/57*

BOYD, William Henry (d 1935 [45]) American actor ES, SR

BOYDE, Edwin (d 1909 [39]) comedian EA/10*

BOYDE, Elizabeth dramatist CP/1

BOYDE, Hesther see Colles, Mrs. Joseph

BOYD-JONES, Ernest (d 1904) actor EA/05*, WWT/14*

BOYDSTON, Hazel Allen (d 1969) performer BP/54*

BOYER, Mr. (fl 1789-94?) singer BD

BOYER, Mrs. [Miss Percy Lorraine] (d 1888 [29]) American actress EA/89*

BOYER, Abel (1667-1729) French dramatist CP/1-3, GT

BOYER, Charles (b 1899) French actor BE, CB, ES, SR, TW/6, 8-11, 15, 19-20, WWT/15

BOYER, Ken (b 1934) American actor TW/14-15

BOYER, Rachel (d 1935 [70]) actress BE*, WWT/14*

BOYES, Mr. (d 1791) actor BD

BOYLAN, Mary American

actress TW/2-4, 28-30

BOYLE, Anna (b 1862) actress CDP

BOYLE, Billy (b 1945) Irish actor WWT/16

BOYLE, Charles, Earl of Orrery (1676-1731) English dramatist CP/2-3, GT

BOYLE, E. Roger (b 1907) American educator, director BE

BOYLE, Frank (d 1892) singer EA/93*

BOYLE, Herbert (d 1908) EA/09*

BOYLE, John Francis (1863-1918) singer SR

BOYLE, Murrough see Blessington, Murrough Boyle, Lord

BOYLE, Ray (b 1925) American director, producer, actor BE, TW/7

BOYLE, Roger see Orrery, Lord

BOYLE, William (fl 1529) dramatist CP/3

BOYLE, William (1853-1923) Irish dramatist COC, ES, MH, NTH, OC/1-3, WWT/2-4

BOYNE, Clifton (1874-1945) actor WWT/4-5

BOYNE, Eva Leonard (d 1960 [74]) English actress TW/16

BOYNE, Leonard (1853-1920) Irish actor DD, DP, EA/96, GRB/1-4, SR, WWT/1-3

BOYT, John (b 1921) American designer, producer, writer BE

BOYTLER, Arcadu (b 1895) Russian choreographer, dancer, actor ES

BOZ, Sig. [John Weston] (d 1880) conjurer EA/81*

BOZEMAN, Beverly (b 1927) American actress TW/12

BOZYK, Max (1900-70) Polish actor TW/23, 26

BOZYK, Rose (b 1914) Polish actress TW/23, 26-27

BRABAN, Harvey (b 1883) English actor WWT/7-9

BRABANT, Francis (fl 1669-90) kettledrummer BD

BRABAZON, T. B. English actor GRB/1

BRABAZON, Mrs. T. B. see Murray, Lillian

BRABOURNE, John (d 1908) actor EA/10*, GRB/4*

BRACCO, Roberto (1861-1943) Italian dramatist MH

BRACEGIRDLE, Anne (1663?-1748)

English actress BD, CDP,
COC, DD, DNB, ES, GT,
HP, NTH, OC/1-3, PDT,
TD/1-2
BRACEWELL, Ethel Australian
actress GRB/1
BRACEWELL, Joe (d 1909 [71])
English actor GRB/1
BRACKEN, Eddie (b 1920)
American actor, director,
writer, singer BE, CB,
ES, TW/22-25, WWT/15-16
BRACKENBURY, Richard (fl
1598) actor DA
BRACKENRIDGE, Hugh Henry
(1748-1816) American drama-
tist ES, OC/1-3
BRACKER, Milton (d 1964 [54])
critic BP/48*
BRACKETT, Charles (d 1969
[76]) critic BP/53*
BRACKMAN, Marie L. (d 1963
[90]) singer BE*
BRACY, Mr. (fl 1677) gallery-
keeper BD
BRACY, Henry (d 1917) actor,
singer DD
BRADA, Ede (b 1879) Austrian
dancer, choreographer, bal-
let teacher ES
BRADA, Rezso (b 1906) Hun-
garian dancer, choreographer
ES
BRADBURY, Mr. C. (d 1869
[65]) equestrian EA/70*
BRADBURY, Charles W. (d
1905) music-hall artist EA/
06*
BRADBURY, James H. (1857-
1940) American actor WWM,
WWT/4-8
BRADBURY, John W. (fl 1879-
84) actor DD
BRADBURY, Ray (b 1920) Amer-
ican dramatist HJD
BRADBURY, Robert (1774-1831)
English clown CDP, DD
BRADDOCK, Edward (d 1708)
singer BD
BRADDOCK, Hugh (fl 1679)
singer BD
BRADDON, Mary Elizabeth
(1837-1915) dramatist DD,
EA/69, HP, WWW/1
BRADE, James (d 1870 [27])
actor EA/71*
BRADEL, John F. (d 1962 [79])
stage manager, union executive

BE*
BRADEN, Bernard (b 1916) Canadian
actor, producer, director WWT/
12-15
BRADEN, Frank (d 1962 [76]) press
representative BE*
BRADEN, Waldo W. (b 1911) Amer-
ican educator BE
BRADFIELD, Axford (fl 1794)
singer BD
BRADFIELD, W. Louis (1866-1919)
English actor, singer GRB/1-4,
WWT/1-3
BRADFORD, Mrs. (fl 1775) singer?
BD
BRADFORD, Dora see Stuart,
Dora
BRADFORD, Edith [Mrs. Charles
Meakins] (b 1884) American
singer WWM
BRADFORD, Gamaliel (1863-1932)
American dramatist DAB
BRADFORD, Dr. Jacob (d 1897)
music-hall director EA/98*
BRADFORD, James M. (d 1933
[89]) American performer BE*,
BP/17*
BRADFORD, Joseph (1843-86) Amer-
ican actor, dramatist DAB, ES,
WWA/H
BRADFORD, Lane (d 1973 [50])
performer BP/58*
BRADFORD, Marshall (d 1971 [75])
performer BP/55*
BRADFORD, Reuben A. (d 1975 [82])
performer BP/60*
BRADFORD, Roark (1896-1948)
American dramatist WWA/2
BRADFORD, [Thomas?] (fl 1778-84?)
violoncellist BD
BRADFORD, Thomas (d 1908 [63])
music-hall proprietor EA/09*,
GRB/4*
BRADIE, Pat (d 1888 [22]) EA/89*
BRADLEY, Mrs. A. see Alex-
ander, Annie Emma
BRADLEY, Albert Davis (fl 1849)
American actor HAS
BRADLEY, Alice M. (fl 1915)
dramatist SR
BRADLEY, Andrew Cecil (1851-1935)
English critic DNB, ES, HP,
WWW/3
BRADLEY, Buddy (1913-72) Ameri-
can choreographer, dancer,
director, producer BE, WWT/
10-12
BRADLEY, Mrs. Campbell see

Armytage, Grace
BRADLEY, Mrs. Dave see
Bradley, Mary Ann
BRADLEY, E. Campbell (d 1889)
EA/90*
BRADLEY, Harry C. [H. B.
Cockrill] (fl 1886-1912) Amer-
ican actor WWM
BRADLEY, Herbert Davies (1878-
1934) dramatist WWW/3
BRADLEY, James Knott (d 1896)
comedian EA/97*
BRADLEY, J. Kenneth (d 1969
[66]) trustee of the American
Shakespeare Festival BP/54*
BRADLEY, John (fl 1673) tailor
BD
BRADLEY, John (b 1829) Amer-
ican actor HAS
BRADLEY, John (d 1910 [46])
proprietor EA/11*
BRADLEY, J. W. (d 1887) act-
ing manager EA/88*
BRADLEY, Leonora (d 1935
[80]) American actress BE*,
BP/19*
BRADLEY, Lilian Trimble (b
1875) American dramatist,
producer WWT/6-11
BRADLEY, Lovyss (d 1969 [63])
performer BP/54*
BRADLEY, Mrs. M. (fl 1772-
77) singer BD
BRADLEY, Mary Ann [Mrs.
Dave Bradley] (d 1881) EA/
82*
BRADLEY, Michael J. (d 1888
[29]) American comedian,
dancer EA/89*
BRADLEY, Oscar (d 1948 [55])
English conductor BE*,
BP/33*
BRADLEY, Richard (fl 1694-
1700) musician BD
BRADLEY, Thomas (d 1829)
actor CDP
BRADLEY, Truman (d 1974 [69])
performer BP/59*
BRADLEY, Will (b 1868) Ameri-
can dramatist WWA/4
BRADNEY, Mr. (fl 1775) actor
BD
BRADNUM, Frederick dramatist
CD
BRADS, Charles (fl 1794) vio-
linist BD
BRADSHAW, Mr. (fl 1680s?)
boxkeeper BD

BRADSHAW, Mrs. (fl 1785) per-
former BD
BRADSHAW, Mrs. [Mrs. Hauton-
ville; Mrs. Cross] (fl 1831-52)
actress HAS
BRADSHAW, Ann Maria [née Tree]
(1801-62) English actress, singer
BS, CDP, DNB, OX
BRADSHAW, Elizabeth see Bowk,
Mrs. William
BRADSHAW, Fanny (1900-73) Amer-
ican director, teacher BE,
TW/30
BRADSHAW, John (1812-76) actor
CDP, DD
BRADSHAW, John J. (d 1855)
American actor HAS
BRADSHAW, Justin (d 1974 [59])
performer BP/59*
BRADSHAW, Leslie Havergal (d
1950) English manager WWA/3
BRADSHAW, Lucretia [Mrs. Martin
Folkes] (d c.1755) actress, singer
BD, DNB
BRADSHAW, Mary see Bradshaw,
Mrs. [William?]
BRADSHAW, Richard (fl 1595-1633)
actor DA
BRADSHAW, [William?] (fl 1735-45)
boxkeeper, box bookkeeper BD
BRADSHAW, Mrs. [William?;
Mary] (d 1780) actress BD
BRADSHAW, Mrs. William see
Abbott, Mrs. William
BRADSTREET, John (d 1618) actor
DA
BRADT, Clifton E. (d 1961 [62])
American critic BE*
BRADWELL, Edmund (d 1871 [72])
decorator EA/72*
BRADWELL, William (d 1849) ma-
chinist DD
BRADY, Mr. (fl 1774-75?) actor
BD
BRADY, Mr. (fl 1795) actor BD
BRADY, Master (fl 1785) dancer
BD
BRADY, Alice (1892-1939) American
actress, singer DAB, ES, NTH,
OC/1-3, SR, WWA/1, WWT/4-9
BRADY, Barbara (b 1927) American
actress TW/6-7
BRADY, Charles (fl 1783-85) stage
doorkeeper BD
BRADY, E. F. (d 1893 [58]) EA/
94*
BRADY, Eleanor (d 1971 [73])
actress TW/27

BRADY, Grace George see
George, Grace
BRADY, Hugh (d 1921 [40])
actor BE*, BP/5*
BRADY, Mrs. James [Marie
France] (d 1900) variety
artist EA/01*
BRADY, John Albert (d 1913)
EA/14*
BRADY, Kenneth Darryl (d 1974
[27]) performer BP/58*
BRADY, Leo B. (b 1917) Amer-
ican educator, dramatist,
director BE
BRADY, Mary (d 1968) per-
former BP/53*
BRADY, Dr. Nicholas (1659-
1726) Irish dramatist CP/
1-3, GT
BRADY, Pat (d 1972 [57]) per-
former BP/56*
BRADY, Patrick (fl 1779-1816)
barber, hair dresser BD
BRADY, Terence (b 1939) Eng-
lish actor, dramatist WWT/
15-16
BRADY, Thomas (fl 1686) kettledrummer BD
BRADY, Veronica (1890-1964)
Irish actress, singer WWT/
5-11
BRADY, William Aloysius (1863-
1950) American manager,
actor COC, DAB, ES,
GRB/2-4, NTH, OC/1-3,
SR, TW/6, WWA/2, WWM,
WWS, WWT/1-10
BRADY, William A[loysius], Jr.
(1900-35) American producer,
manager SR, WWT/6-7
BRADY, Mrs. William A[loysius]
see George, Grace
BRAE, June (b 1918) English
dancer ES, WWT/10-12
BRAGAGLIA, Marinella Italian
actress WWT/2-3
BRAGDON, Claude Fayette (d
1946 [80]) American de-
signer, architect BE*,
BP/31*
BRAGG, Bernard (b 1928) Amer-
ican actor TW/25-26
BRAGHETTI, Prospero (fl
1793-1810) singer BD
BRAGNOLI, Sig. (fl 1856) singer
SR
BRAHA, Herb [Herb Simon] (b
1946) American actor TW/

28-30
BRAHAM, Albert (fl 1861) English
actor HAS
BRAHAM, Amelia Georgina [Mrs.
Carl Robarts] (d 1903 [50])
EA/05*
BRAHAM, Augustus (fl 1850) Eng-
lish singer CDP, HAS
BRAHAM, Charles (d 1884) singer
CDP
BRAHAM, David (1838-1905) Eng-
lish/American composer ES
BRAHAM, Hamilton (d 1862) singer
EA/72*
BRAHAM, Harry (d 1923 [73]) Eng-
lish actor CDP, SR
BRAHAM, Horace (1896-1955) Eng-
lish actor TW/2-3, 12, WWT/
7-11
BRAHAM, John (1777-1856) English
singer, composer, manager
BD, BS, CDP, DD, DNB, ES,
GT, HAS, OX, SR, TD/2
BRAHAM, Josef (d 1877 [50])
musician EA/78*
BRAHAM, Leonora (1853-1931)
actress, singer DD, DP, EA/
97, WWT/6
BRAHAM, Lionel (d 1947 [68])
English actor TW/4, WWT/7-10
BRAHAM, Philip (1881-1934) English
composer, conductor WWT/4-7
BRAHAM, Sarah (d 1883 [96])
EA/84*
BRAHAM, Cpt. W. (d 1877) ama-
teur actor EA/78*
BRAHM, Otto [né Abrahamsohn]
(1856-1912) performer, manager
BE*, WWT/14*
BRAHMS, Caryl dramatist, critic,
librettist CD, WWT/15-16
BRAID, George Ross (1812-78)
actor DD
BRAIDWOOD, Margaret (b 1924)
English actress TW/27
BRAINERD, Anna see Granger,
Maude
BRAINERD, Maria S. (fl c. 1886)
singer CDP
BRAITHWAITE, Mr. (d 1773) master
tailor BD
BRAITHWAITE, Mr. (fl 1776-77)
dresser BD
BRAITHWAITE, Ann (fl 1775-90)
actress, dancer BD
BRAITHWAITE, Dame Lilian [Mrs.
Gerald Lawrence] (1873-1948)
English actress AAS, COC, DD,

DNB, ES, GRB/1-4, OC/
1-3, SR, TW/5, WWT/
1-10, WWW/4
BRAITHWAITE, Richard (1588-
1673) English dramatist
CP/3, FGF
BRAITHWAITE, Warwick (1898-
1971) New Zealand composer,
conductor ES
BRAMAH, Miss see McCor-
mack, Mrs. M.
BRAMAH, Marie [Mrs. John
Hudspeth] (d 1908 [64])
EA/09*, GRB/4*
BRAMALL, Eric (b 1922) English
marionettist ES
BRAMBELL, Wilfrid (b 1912)
Irish actor WWT/15-16
BRAMBILLA, Linda CDP
BRAMBILLA, Marietta (1807-75)
Italian singer CDP, ES
BRAMBILLA, Veronica Graziella
(d 1894) singer EA/95*
BRAMBLE, Mrs. actress TD/2
BRAME, Henry W. (d 1906 [46])
actor EA/07*
BRAMHALL, Mrs. (d 1886 [46])
EA/87*
BRAMHALL, Mrs. Walter [née
Tilly Wilbraham] (d 1878 [22])
actress EA/80*
BRAMHALL, William (d 1890
[61]) comedian EA/91*
BRAMLEY, Raymond (b 1891)
American actor BE, TW/3,
5-6, 8, 13
BRAMMER, Lily English singer
GRB/1
BRAMPTON, Lady [Miss Rey-
nolds] (d 1907) actress
GRB/3
BRAMPTON, John (fl 1423)
actor DA
BRAMSBOTTOM, Abraham (fl
1794) musician BD
BRAMSON, Karen (d 1936)
dramatist BE*, WWT/14*
BRAMSON, Sam (d 1962 [60])
American talent representative
BE*
BRAMSTON, Mr. (fl 1752)
actor? BD
BRAMWELL, Mr. (fl 1794-1804)
singer BD
BRAMWELL, Georgiana (fl
1791-1804) singer, actress
BD
BRAN, Mary (d 1972 [73])

producer/director/choreographer
BP/57*
BRANCA, Guglielmo (1849-1928)
Italian conductor, composer
ES
BRANCH, Eileen (b 1911) English
actress WWT/7-8
BRANCH, Phyllis (d 1972 [48])
performer BP/57*
BRAND, Miss (fl 1780) actress
BD
BRAND, Barbarina, Lady Dacre
(1768-1854) English dramatist
DNB
BRAND, Deane (d 1899 [39])
singer, actor DD
BRAND, George (d 1898 [50])
singer? EA/99*
BRAND, Hannah (d 1821) English
actress, dramatist BD, CP/3,
DD, DNB, GT, TD/1-2
BRAND, Mike (d 1975 [27]) per-
former BP/59*
BRAND, Neville (1895-1951) Eng-
lish dramatist WWW/5
BRAND, Oswald (d 1909 [52])
dramatist, manager DD
BRAND, Phoebe (b 1907) American
actress, director, teacher BE
BRAND, Tita English actress
GRB/1-3
BRANDANE, John [John MacIntyre]
(1869-1947) Scottish dramatist
ES, OC/1-3
BRANDE, Thomas (fl 1574) actor
DA
BRANDEAUX, Palmere (d 1965
[64]) choreographer BP/49*
BRANDEIS, Frederic (1835-91)
Austrian musician WWA/H
BRANDEIS, Ruth (b 1942) Ameri-
can actress TW/24
BRANDES, Marthe (1862-1930)
French actress GRB/1-4
BRANDFON, Martin (b 1949)
American actor TW/28
BRANDI, Gaetano (fl 1784-1818?)
musician? BD
BRANDIES, Bob (d 1973 [71])
performer BP/58*
BRANDO, Jocelyn (b 1919) Amer-
ican actor TW/4-8, 29-30
BRANDO, Marlon (b 1924) Amer-
ican actor, director, producer
BE, CB, ES, TW/1-14
BRANDON, Mr. (fl 1848) actor
HAS
BRANDON, Arthur F. (d 1975

[50]) composer/lyricist BP/
60*
BRANDON, Bella see Forge,
Mrs. R.
BRANDON, Bill (b 1944) Amer-
ican actor TW/24-25
BRANDON, Daisy (d 1899 [20])
actress EA/00*
BRANDON, Dorothy dramatist
WWT/5-11
BRANDON, Edith actress CDP
BRANDON, Florence [Mrs.
Harold Perry] (d 1961 [82])
English actress GRB/1
BRANDON, Henry (b 1912)
German/American actor
TW/6-9, 13-15
BRANDON, Isaac (fl 1808)
dramatist CP/3
BRANDON, James W. treasurer
CDP
BRANDON, James William
(1754-1825) English box book-
keeper, housekeeper BD
BRANDON, Jocelyn (d 1948
[82]) dramatist BE*, WWT/
14*
BRANDON, John (fl 1789-1813)
treasurer BD
BRANDON, [Martha?] (1727?-
98) concessionaire BD
BRANDON, Michael (b 1945)
American actor TW/25
BRANDON, Olga (1865-1906)
Australian actress CDP,
DD, DP
BRANDON, Peter (b 1926)
German/American actor
BE, TW/8-15, 18-20, 23, 29
BRANDON, Samuel (fl 1598)
English dramatist CP/1-3,
FGF
BRANDON, Violet [née Barling]
(d 1903 [26]) actress EA/04*
BRANDON-THOMAS, Amy Mar-
guerite (1890-1974) English
actress BTR/74, WWT/
1-11
BRANDON-THOMAS, Jevan
(b 1898) English actor,
dramatist WWT/6-15
BRANDRAM, Julia (d 1907 [77])
actress, singer WWT/14*
BRANDRAM, Rosina [Moult]
(d 1907) English actress,
singer DD, EA/95, GRB/
1-3, WWW/1
BRANDRAM, Samuel (d 1892

[68]) reciter EA/93*, WWT/
14*
BRANDRAM, Mrs. Samuel see
Murray, Julia
BRANDRETH, H. B. (d 1921)
manager WWT/14*
BRANDT, Alvin (b 1922) American
executive, editor, writer BE
BRANDT, George (1916-63) Amer-
ican producer BE*, BP/48*
BRANDT, Mrs. Harry N. (d 1973
[68]) co-chairman of the Amer-
ican Theatre Wing Club BP/
57*
BRANDT, Ivan [Roy Francis Cook]
(b 1903) English actor ES,
WWT/8-12
BRANDT, Lou (d 1971 [56]) pro-
ducer/director/choreographer
BP/56*
BRANDT, Marianne [Maria Anna
Bischof] (1842-1921) Austrian
singer ES
BRANDT, Martin (b 1908) German
actor TW/3
BRANDT, Max (b 1925) German
actor TW/30
BRANGIN, Mr. (fl 1781-91) house
servant? BD
BRANGIN, Rhoda [Mrs. James
Spriggs] (fl 1779-91) actress
BD
BRANMAN, Mr. (fl 1795) watch-
man BD
BRANNAN, Miss E. C. (fl 1866)
singer HAS
BRANNIGAN, Bob (d 1973 [75])
stagehand BP/57*
BRANNIGAN, Desmond (d 1918)
EA/19*
BRANNIGAN, Owen (1908-73) Eng-
lish singer ES
BRANNUM, Tom (b 1941) Ameri-
can actor TW/25-26, 29
BRANON, John (b 1939) American
actor TW/24, 26, 29
BRANSBY, Astley (d 1789) actor
BD, TD/2
BRANSCOMB, J. (d c. 1815) ma-
chinist BD
BRANSCOMBE, Mrs. (d 1891)
EA/92*
BRANSCOMBE, Arthur (d 1924)
dramatist DD
BRANSCOMBE, Maud (fl 1876)
actress CDP
BRANSON, Mr. (fl 1767-84) house
servant? BD

BRANSON, Mrs. (fl 1767-84) actress BD
BRANSON, Margaret (d 1868 [38]) EA/69*
BRANSON, May (b 1867) actress, singer CDP
BRANSON, William Scholes (d 1884 [74]) actor, manager EA/85*
BRANT, Luke (d 1888 [35]) American vaudevillian EA/89*
BRANTON, Fred (d 1890) music-hall stage manager EA/91*
BRANZELL, Karin Maria (1891-1974) Swedish singer CB, ES
BRAS, Hermans (fl c. 1819) Prussian fat boy CDP
BRASINGTON, Alan American actor TW/25-26, 30
BRASLAU, Sophie (1892-1935) American singer DAB, WWA/1, WWW/3
BRASMER, William (b 1921) American educator, director BE
BRASSELL, Peter minstrel CDP
BRASSEUR, Albert Jules (1862-1932) French actor WWT/2-4
BRASSEUR, Jules (d 1890 [61]) actor, producer BE*, WWT/14*
BRASSEUR, Pierre (d 1972 [66]) actor, dramatist BP/57*, WWT/16*
BRASSEY, Mr. (fl 1728-48) actor BD
BRASSINGTON, William Salt (1859-1939) English curator WWW/3
BRASWELL, Charles (d 1974 [49]) American actor TW/23-24, 26-28, 30
BRATT, William (d 1871 [55]) proprietor EA/72*
BRATTON, John Walter (1867-1947) American lyricist, dramatist, manager SR, WWA/4, WWS
BRAUN, Carl (1888-1946) German singer ES
BRAUN, Eric (d 1970 [46]) performer BP/55*
BRAUN, Eugene (d 1965 [77]) electrician, lighting designer BP/49*

BRAUN, Felix (b 1885) Austrian dramatist CH
BRAUN, Roger (b 1941) American actor TW/26
BRAUNSTEIN, Alan (b 1947) American actor TW/27-29
BRAVILLE, Mr. (fl 1776-77) puppeteer BD
BRAVO, Nino (d 1973 [28]) performer BP/57*
BRAWN, John P. (1872-1943) producer SR
BRAY, Mr. (fl 1689-85) dancer, dancing master BD
BRAY, Mrs. (d 1752) proprietor, actress BD
BRAY, Alice [Mrs. Charles Fanshawe Everest] (d 1889) actress EA/90*
BRAY, Antony (fl 1635) actor DA
BRAY, John (1782-1822) dramatist, actor, composer EAP, HAS, RJ
BRAY, Walter [né Baker] (d 1891) minstrel CDP
BRAY, Will H. actor CDP
BRAYBROOK, Marie see Henderson, Marie
BRAYFIELD, George W. (d 1968) secretary, treasurer BP/52*
BRAYNE, Harry (b 1865) English actor GRB/1
BRAYTON, Lily [Mrs. Oscar Asche] (1876-1953) English actress ES, GRB/1-4, OC/1-3, WWT/1-11
BRAZONG, Mr. (fl 1691) musician BD
BREAD AND PUPPET THEATRE theatre collective CD
BREAKSTON, George P. (d 1972 [65]) performer BP/57*
BREARLEY, Mr. (fl 1783-85) boxkeeper, lobby keeper BD
BRECHER, Egon (1885-1946) Czech actor, producer SR, TW/3, WWT/7-9
BRECHT, Bertolt Friedrich (1898-1956) German dramatist CH, COC, ES, MH, MWD, NTH, OC/2-3, PDT, RE, WWA/4
BRECHT, George dramatist CD
BRECK, Charles (1782-1822) American dramatist EAP, RJ
BRECKENRIDGE, Hugh Henry (1748-1816) Scottish/American dramatist EAP
BREEDING, Guinevare (b 1939)

American actress TW/23
BREEN, Helen (b 1902/05)
English actress, singer
WWT/7-11
BREEN, May Singhi (d 1970
[76]) performer BP/55*
BREEN, Robert (b 1914) Amer-
ican director, actor, pro-
ducer BE
BREEN, T. D. (d 1882) Irish?
prompter EA/83*
BREESE, Edmund (1871-1936)
American actor ES, GRB/
3-4, SR, WWA/1, WWM,
WWS, WWT/1-8
BREEZE, Mabel [Mrs. W. Per-
cival] (d 1896 [31]) music-
hall artist EA/97*
BREIL, Joseph Carl (1870-1926)
American composer ES,
WWA/1, WWM
BREILLAT, George (fl 1794)
singer BD
BREIT, Harvey (1913-68) Amer-
ican dramatist, editor BE,
TW/24
BREL, Jacques (b 1929) Belgian
composer, lyricist, singer
CB
BRELSFORD, Joseph P. (d 1854)
American actor HAS
BREMA, Marie (1856-1925)
English singer ES, WWW/2
BREMAN, Edward (d 1870 [33])
scene artist EA/71*
BREMAURE, Mrs. Gabriel see
Kiralfy, Amalia
BREMERS, Beverly Ann (b
1950) American actress
TW/26-28
BREMS, Else (b 1908) Danish
singer ES
BREMSETH, Lloyd (b 1948)
American actor TW/27, 30
BRENAN, Mr. (fl 1756) Irish?
dramatist CP/2-3, GT
BRENDEL, El (d 1964 [73])
American actor TW/20
BRENDERS, Stan (d 1969 [65])
composer/lyricist BP/54*
BRENLIN, George (b 1930)
American actor TW/14
BRENNAN, Mrs. (d 1891)
EA/92*
BRENNAN, Denis (b 1927)
Irish actor TW/4
BRENNAN, Eileen (b 1935)
American actress BE

BRENNAN, Frederick Hazlitt (d
1962 [60]) dramatist BP/47*
BRENNAN, James J. (d 1965 [80])
executive BE/49*
BRENNAN, Jay (d 1961 [78]) per-
former TW/17
BRENNAN, J. Keirn (d 1948 [74])
composer BE, BP/32*
BRENNAN, Maggie (d 1913 [74])
actress DD, OAA/1-2
BRENNAN, Maude (1855-1915)
English actress DD, OAA/1-2
BRENNAN, Maureen (b 1952)
American actress TW/30
BRENNAN, Walter (d 1974 [80])
performer BP/59*
BRENNEN, Anna American actress
TW/28-29
BRENNER, A. minstrel CDP
BRENNER, Paul see Baratow
Ben-Zwi
BRENON, Edward St. John (d
1917) EA/18*
BRENON, Mrs. Hettie St. John
see Alva, Mme.
BRENT, Mr. (fl 1797) actor BD
BRENT, Mrs. (fl 1787-97) actress
BD
BRENT, Bessie [Eliza Travers]
(d 1871) actress EA/72*
BRENT, Charles (1693-1770)
singer, fencing master BD
BRENT, Charlotte [Mrs. Pinto]
(d 1802) English singer, actress
DD, DNB, ES, TD/1-2
BRENT, Evelyn [Elizabeth Riggs]
(1899-1975) American actress
ES
BRENT, George (b 1904) Irish
actor ES
BRENT, Mabel [Mrs. Knight Aston]
(d 1874 [25]) actress EA/75*
BRENT, Marian [Mary Wentworth
Elroy] (1853-1887) American
actress NYM
BRENT, Romney [Rómulo Larralde]
(1902-76) Mexican actor, drama-
tist, director BE, ES, TW/
1-9, WWT/8-15
BRENTANO, Felix (d 1961 [52])
Austrian producer BE*, BP/
46*
BRENTANO, Lowell (d 1950 [55])
American dramatist BE*,
BP/35*
BRENTON, Howard (b 1942) Eng-
lish dramatist, actor CD,
WWT/16

BREON, Edmond (1882-1951)
Scottish actor WWT/5-10
BRERELY, Mr. (fl 1777) actor
BD
BRERETON, Mr. (fl 1771-88)
house servant BD
BRERETON, Alice (d 1896 [19])
singer EA/97*
BRERETON, Austin (1862-1922)
English critic, manager DD,
GRB/1-4, WWT/1-4, WWW/2
BRERETON, Stella (fl 1879-88)
actress DD
BRERETON, Thomas (1691-1722)
English dramatist CP/1-3,
DD, DNB, GT
BRERETON, William (fl 18th
cent) master of ceremonies
CDP
BRERETON, William (1751-87)
English actor BD, CDP,
DD, TD/1-2
BRESCHARD (fl 1809-12) eques-
trian, circus manager
WWA/H
BRESIL, Marguerite (b 1880)
French actress GRB/4,
WWT/1-4
BRESLAW, Philip (1726-1803)
German conjurer BD, CDP
BRESLIN, Tommy (b 1946)
American actor TW/24,
26-27, 29-30
BRESLOW, Rosalind American
actress TW/27
BREST, George see Arthur,
George K.
BRETHERTON, Dorothea (d
1976 [79]) performer BP/60*
BRETON, Cecil (d 1916) busi-
ness manager WWT/14*
BRETON, Nicholas (fl 1605)
dramatist CP/1-3, FGF
BRETT, Mr. (fl 1740-50)
singer, actor BD
BRETT, Master (fl 1750) actor?
BD
BRETT, Mrs. (fl 1795-1803)
actress HAS
BRETT, Miss see King, Mrs.
BRETT, Anne [Mrs. F. Brett]
(d 1899 [71]) EA/91*
BRETT, Anne see Chetwood,
Mrs. William Rufus, II
BRETT, Arabella (d 1803)
actress BE* [?= Mrs. John
Hodgkinson, q. v.]
BRETT, Mrs. Dawson [née

Elizabeth Cibber] (b 1701) Eng-
lish dancer, actress BD
BRETT, Edwin J. (b 1867) English
actor GRB/1
BRETT, Mrs. F. see Brett,
Anne
BRETT, Frances R. see Chap-
man, Mrs. George
BRETT, Hannah see Brett, Mrs.
William
BRETT, Harry (d 1918) EA/19*
BRETT, Mrs. Harry J. (d 1916)
EA/17*
BRETT, Jeremy [né Huggins] (b
1933/35) English actor AAS,
TW/13, 20, WWT/14-16
BRETT, John G. (d 1899 [33])
actor EA/00*, WWT/14*
BRETT, Stanley (1879-1923) Eng-
lish actor GRB/1-4, WWT/1-4
BRETT, William (d 1789) singer,
actor BD
BRETT, William (fl 1773-82)
singer BD
BRETT, Mrs. William [Hannah]
(d c. 1804) actress, singer BD
BRETTELL, Walter see Beau-
mont, Walter
BRETTEN, William (fl 1546) mem-
ber of the Chapel Royal DA
BRETTINGHAM, Elsa English
actress GRB/1
BREVAL, Cpt. John Durant (d
1738/39) English dramatist
CP/1-3, GT, TD/1-2
BREVAL, Lucienne [Berthe-Agnès-
Lisette Schilling] (1869-1935)
German singer ES, GRB/1-4
BREW, Anthony (fl 1619-22) actor
DA [see also: Brewer,
Anthony]
BREWER, Anthony (fl 1630-55)
English dramatist CP/1-3,
DD, DNB, FGF
BREWER, George (b 1766) English
dramatist CP/3, DD, GT,
TD/1-2
BREWER, George (d 1907 [50])
showman EA/08*
BREWER, George, Jr. (1899-1968)
American dramatist, producer,
director, executive BE
BREWER, Joseph W. (d 1860 [38])
gymnast HAS
BREWER, Sherri "Peaches"
American actress TW/24
BREWER-MOORE, Cathy (b 1948)
American actress TW/30

BREWERTON, Alice (d 1875
[24]) actress EA/76*
BREWMAN, Mr. (fl 1789)
actor BD
BREWSTER, Charles H. (d
1893) EA/94*
BREWSTER, Henry (c1747-88)
musician, singer, composer
BD
BREWSTER, John E. (d 1912
[58]) banjo troupe proprietor
EA/13*
BREYER, Mrs. J. E. [née
Eliza Walsh] (d 1864 [67])
actress HAS
BREYER, John F. (fl 1857-68)
Scottish actor HAS
BREYER, M. V. (fl 1851)
Scottish actor HAS
BREZANY, Eugene (b 1945)
American actor TW/28
BRIAN, Donald (1877-1948)
Canadian actor, singer CDP,
ES, SR, TW/2-3, 5, WWA/
2, WWM, WWS, WWT/1-10
BRIAN, J. F. (d 1890) singer,
dancer EA/91*
BRIAN, Mrs. J. F. singer
CDP
BRIAN, Mrs. J. F. (d 1895
[56]) actress EA/96*
BRIANSKY, Oleg (b 1929) Bel-
gian dancer, choreographer
ES
BRIANT, August W. (d 1970
[82]) performer BP/54*
BRIANT, Gertrude see Davies,
Gertrude
BRICE, Mr. (fl 1793-1801)
house servant BD
BRICE, Miss (fl 1782) actress
BD
BRICE, Elizabeth (d 1965)
singer, dancer TW/21
BRICE, Fanny (1891-1951)
American actress, singer
CB, ES, NTH, TW/7,
WWA/3, WWT/7-11
BRICE, Monte (d 1962 [71])
American producer, director
BE*
BRICHTA, Mme. (fl 1831)
singer HAS
BRICKELL, Susan (b 1950)
American actress TW/28
BRICKER, Hershel (b 1905)
American educator, director,
writer BE

BRICKLAYER, Miss (fl 1756-57)
singer BD
BRICKLER, Miss (fl 1758-67)
singer BD
BRICKWELL, H. T. (1858-1928)
English manager GRB/1
BRICKWELL, William (d 1893 [33])
manager, director EA/94*
BRIDA, Luigi (fl 1794-95) singer
BD
BRIDA, Marie Catherine see
Dorival à Corifet
BRIDE, Mr. (fl 1741?-61) scene
shifter BD
BRIDE, Mrs. (fl 1765) dresser
BD
BRIDE, Elizabeth [Mrs. Lefevre;
Mrs. Samworth?] (d 1826)
actress, dancer BD, DD, TD/
1-2
BRIDEKIRK, John (d 1879 [63])
actor? EA/80*
BRIDEL, Edmund Philip (fl 1807)
dramatist CP/3
BRIDER, Miss (fl 1765) dancer
BD
BRIDGE, John (d 1893 [72]) EA/
94*
BRIDGE, Peter (b 1925) English
producer WWT/14-16
BRIDGE, Thomas (d 1872) singer
EA/73*
BRIDGE, William see Agoust
BRIDGEMAN, Mr. (fl 1794) house
servant? BD
BRIDGEMAN, John V. (fl 1860-64)
dramatist DD [see also:
Bridgman, John V.]
BRIDGES, Mr. (fl 1690-92) actor
BD
BRIDGES, Mr. (fl 1728?-51) actor
BD
BRIDGES, Mr. (fl 1752-61) actor
BD
BRIDGES, Mrs. equestrienne
CDP
BRIDGES, Mrs. (fl 1744-49)
actress, singer BD
BRIDGES, Anthony O'Neil (d 1879)
equestrian EA/80*
BRIDGES, Beau (b 1941) American
actor TW/22
BRIDGES, Eloise (fl 1853) Amer-
ican actress CDP, HAS
BRIDGES, Gertrude Agnes [Mrs.
Charles Wincott] (d 1881 [41])
EA/89*
BRIDGES, Lloyd (b 1913) American

actor TW/10, 24
BRIDGES, Paul Francis (fl
1660-73) musician BD
BRIDGES, Robert Seymour (1844-
1930) English dramatist DD,
DNB, HP, WWW/3
BRIDGES, Mrs. Selim see
Organ, Harriet
BRIDGES, Thomas (fl 1759-75)
English dramatist CP/2-3,
DD, DNB, GT, TD/1-2
BRIDGES-ADAMS, William
(1889-1965) English director,
designer, author BE, COC,
ES, WWT/4-13, WWW/6
BRIDGETOWER, George Augustus
Polgreen (1778-1860) violinist
BD
BRIDGEWATER, John William
Stevenson see Kove, Kenneth
BRIDGEWATER, Leslie (1893-
1974) English composer, con-
ductor WWT/9-15
BRIDGEWATER, Mr. R. (d
1869 [55]) singer EA/70*
BRIDGMAN, Mr. (fl 1742) actor
BD
BRIDGMAN, Mrs. (fl 1794)
actress BD
BRIDGMAN, Cunningham (fl
1873-92) dramatist, libret-
tist DD
BRIDGMAN, F. W. (d 1892)
EA/94*
BRIDGMAN, John V. (d 1889
[69]) journalist, librettist
EA/90* [see also: Bridgman,
John V.]
BRIDGMAN, Louisa (d 1909)
EA/10*
BRIDGMAN, William (fl 1684)
musician? BD
BRIDGMAN, William (d 1903)
variety artist EA/04*
BRIDGWATER, Roger (d 1754)
actor, dancer BD, DD
BRIDIE, James [Osborne
Henry Mavor] (1888-1951)
Scottish dramatist AAS,
CH, COC, DNB, ES, HP,
MD, MH, MWD, NTH,
OC/1-3, PDT, RE, TW/7,
WWT/7-11, WWW/5
BRIEF, [Mr. ?] (fl 1734) actor
BD
BRIEN, Alan (b 1925) English
critic WWT/14-16
BRIERCLIFFE, Nellie (d 1966)

actress, singer WWT/4-8
BRIERLEY, Alfred (d 1916) EA/
17*
BRIERLEY, David (b 1936) English
general manager WWT/16
BRIERLEY, Ethel see Bertram,
Eva
BRIERLEY, Jack (d 1900) comedian
EA/01*
BRIERS, Richard (b 1934) English
actor AAS, WWT/14-16
BRIESEMEISTER, Otto (1866-1910)
German singer ES
BRIEUX, Eugène (1858-1932)
French dramatist COC, GRB/
1-4, HP, MD, MWD, OC/1-3,
RE, SR, WWT/1
BRIGG, Mr. (fl 1781-1803) dancer
BD
BRIGG, Mrs. (fl 1790-1802) dancer
BD
BRIGGS, Mr. (fl 1776-77) door-
keeper BD
BRIGGS, Mr. (fl 1781) actor BD
BRIGGS, Mr. (fl 1784) singer BD
BRIGGS, Bunny (b 1923) American
actress TW/2
BRIGGS, Don (b 1911) American
actor TW/8
BRIGGS, Harlan (d 1952 [72])
American actor BE*, BP/36*
BRIGGS, Hedley (1907-68) English
actor, producer, designer,
dancer WWT/9-12
BRIGGS, Matt (d 1962 [79]) Amer-
ican actor TW/1, 19
BRIGGS, Millard (d 1967 [59])
performer BP/51*
BRIGGS, Oceana (b 1928) vaude-
villian, actress TW/24
BRIGGS, Wallace Neal (b 1914)
American educator, director
BE
BRIGGS, William A. (b 1915)
American architect BE
BRIGHAM, William Stanhope (b
1938) American manufacturer
BE
BRIGHOUSE, Harold (1882-1958)
English dramatist AAS, COC,
ES, MD, MH, MWD, NTH,
OC/3, PDT, WWT/2-11, WWW/5
BRIGHT, Mr. (fl 1711) musician?
BD
BRIGHT, Mr. (fl 1733) actor,
singer BD
BRIGHT, Mrs. (fl 1750) actress
BD

BRIGHT, Addison (d 1906)
critic EA/07*, WWT/14*
BRIGHT, Mrs. Augustus (d
1906) dramatist DD
BRIGHT, Bella actress CDP
BRIGHT, Edward (1721-50)
English fat man CDP
BRIGHT, George (fl c. 1677-
1707) actor BD
BRIGHT, John Holloway see
Sargano
BRIGHT, Molly (fl 1783-85)
wardrobe keeper BD
BRIGHT, R. Golding (d 1941
[67]) agent WWT/14*
BRIGHT, Mrs. R. Golding
see Egerton, George
BRIGHT, Richard (b 1937) Amer-
ican actor TW/24, 27-28
BRIGHT, William (fl 1794)
singer? BD
BRIGHTEN, Charles R. (d 1899)
music-hall manager EA/00*
BRIGHTLING, Lotta see
Wynne, Evelyne
BRIGHTMAN, Stanley (1888-1961)
English producing manager,
dramatist WWT/7-13
BRIGHTON Charles (d 1896 [29])
actor, singer, composer CDP
BRIGHTSTAIN, Annie singer
CDP
BRIGHTWELL, Peter (fl 1689)
actor BD
BRIGNOLI, Mlle. (b 1844) Amer-
ican musician HAS
BRIGNOLI, Ortolani (d 1884)
singer HAS
BRIGNOLI, Pasquale (1823-84)
Italian singer CDP, HAS
BRILA, Mons. (fl 1742) acrobat
BD
BRILA, Mme. (fl 1742) acrobat
BD
BRILA, Fils (b c. 1739) acrobat
BD
BRILL, Daniel (d 1898 [81])
EA/99*
BRILL, Fran (b 1946) American
actress TW/25
BRILL, Gene (d 1970 [38])
executive BP/55*
BRILLIANSO, Charles (d 1896
[29]) circus performer EA/97*
BRILLIANT, Marie [Jeanne Le
Maignen] (1724-67) French
actress ES
BRILLIANT, Paul (c. 1824-64)

French dancer, ballet master
CDP, HAS, SR
BRINCKERHOFF, Burt (b 1936)
American actor, producer
BE, TW/24
BRINDLEY, Madge (d 1968) per-
former BP/53*
BRINDLEY, Thomas Tait (d 1892
[48]) actor? EA/93*
BRINK, Robert (b 1944) American
actor TW/26-27
BRINKEROFF, Clara M. (b 1828)
singer CDP
BRINKLEY, John D. (d 1972 [65])
performer BP/57*
BRINLEY, Matthew (fl 1671-77)
scenekeeper BD
BRINSLEY, Mr. (fl 1781-82) actor
BD
BRINSMEAD, John (d 1908 [93])
piano maker EA/09*
BRIQUET, Jean (1864-1936) Ger-
man composer, dramatist,
actor BE*
BRISCOE, Herbert (d 1902 [26])
actor, stage manager EA/03*
BRISCOE, Johnson (d 1969 [86])
agent, historian BP/53*
BRISCOE, Lottie [Mrs. Harry
Mountford] (d 1950 [67]) Amer-
ican actress TW/6
BRISCOE, Olive (b 1887) American
vaudevillian WWM
BRISMAN, Chaim (d 1970 [67])
performer BP/55*
BRISSON, Carl (1895-1958) Danish
actor ES, TW/2-3, 15, WWT/
5-12
BRISSON, Cleo (d 1975 [81]) per-
former BP/60*
BRISSON, Frederick (b 1913)
Danish producer BE, WWT/15-
16
BRISTOL, Earl of see Digby,
George
BRISTOW, Mr. (d 1848) English
actor HAS
BRISTOW, Miss (fl 1807) actress,
dancer CDP
BRISTOW, Mrs. [Mrs. Robert
Skinner] (fl 1797-1804) singer
BD
BRISTOW, Charles (b 1928) Eng-
lish lighting designer WWT/
15-16
BRISTOW, George (fl 1671) actor
BD
BRISTOW, George Frederick

(1825-98) American violinist,
composer, conductor, organist CDP, DAB, ES,
WWA/H
BRISTOW, James (fl 1597-1603)
actor DA
BRISTOWE, Agnes (d 1898)
actress EA/99*
BRISTOWE, Francis (fl 1635)
translator CP/3
BRITAIN, Mr. (fl 1675-78) pit
keeper BD
BRITEN, Mr. (fl 1661-64) actor
BD
BRITT, Elton (d 1972 [59]) composer/lyricst BP/57*
BRITT, Jacqueline (d 1974 [29])
actress, singer TW/30
BRITTEN, Benjamin (1913-76)
English composer, conductor
CB, ES, HP, NTH
BRITTENHAM, Robert (fl 1838-
39) American actor HAS
BRITTENHAM, Mrs. Robert (fl
1839) actress HAS
BRITTINGHAM, Miss (fl 1852)
American actress HAS
BRITTLEBANK, Mrs. (d 1891
[60]) EA/92*
BRITTLEBANK, William (d
1897 [66]) lessee EA/98*
BRITTON, Mrs. (fl 1729-31)
actress, dancer BD
BRITTON, Clifton (d 1963 [52])
director BE*
BRITTON, Don (b 1937) American actor TW/13-14
BRITTON, Ethel (d 1972 [57])
performer BP/56*
BRITTON, Gary (b 1943)
American actor TW/23-24
BRITTON, George (b 1910)
American actor TW/8-9
BRITTON, Hutin [Mrs. Matheson Lang] (1876-1965) English actress COC, ES,
OC/1-3, WWT/1-11
BRITTON, Leonhard (b 1942)
American actor TW/25
BRITTON, Lillian [Mrs. Jefferson Egan] (fl 1900s)
American singer WWS
BRITTON, Pamela (d 1974 [51])
actress BP/59*, WWT/16*
BRITTON, Mrs. Robert see
Weber, Liza
BRITTON, Thomas (1644-1714)
English instrumentalist,

impresario BD, CDP
BRITTON, Tony (b 1924) English
actor AAS, WWT/15-16
BRITTON, Wallace (d 1872) actor
EA/73*
BRIZZI, Sig. [Achille Scipione
Bisteghi] (d 1884 [74]) singer
EA/85*
BROAD, Mr. (fl 1754-69) boxkeeper BD
BROAD, Mr. (fl 1760-61) doorkeeper BD
BROAD, Mrs. (fl 1735-36) house
servant BD
BROAD, George (b 1777) English
musician, composer BD
BROADBENT, Amanda see
Barrie, Amanda
BROADBENT, Dora see Bryan,
Dora
BROADBENT, Olive Ormond (d
1899 [17]) dancer EA/00*
BROADBRIDGE, Grace (d 1898
[23]) EA/99*
BROADFOOT, Alexander (d 1847)
actor, stage manager EA/72*
BROADFOOT, William (d 1852)
performer? EA/72*
BROADHEAD, W. H. (d 1931 [81])
manager WWT/14*
BROADHEAD, William Birch (d
1907 [34]) proprietor GRB/3
BROADHURST, Mr. (fl 1811)
singer BS
BROADHURST, Miss (fl 1773-96)
actress, singer CDP, HAS,
TD/1-2
BROADHURST, Miss (b c. 1775)
singer, actress BD
BROADHURST, George Howells
(1866-1952) English/American
dramatist DD, ES, GRB/2-4,
MWD, NTH, OC/1-3, SR, TW/
9, WWA/3, WWM, WWT/1-11,
WWW/5
BROADHURST, Kent (b 1940)
American actor TW/25, 30
BROADHURST, Thomas W. (1858-
1936) English dramatist SR
BROADHURST, William (d 1869
[82]) actor CDP
BROADLEY, Edward (d 1947) English actor, stage manager
SR
BROADWAY, James (d 1889) billposter SR
BROADWOOD, Henry Fowler (d
1893 [82]) instrument maker

EA/94*
BROBSTON, Miss see Wilson,
Mrs. Alexander
BROCAS, Mr. (fl 1755) actor
BD
BROCHU, James (b 1946) Amer-
ican actor TW/26-27
BROCK, Mr. equestrian CDP
BROCK, Adam see Williams,
E. B.
BROCK, Eliza (d 1893 [74])
EA/95*
BROCK, Fanny (d 1883 [30])
EA/84*
BROCK, James (b 1727) pyro-
technist BD
BROCK, John (d 1720) pyro-
technist BD
BROCK, John (b 1700) pyro-
technist BD
BROCK, Thomas (1756-1819)
English pyrotechnist BD
BROCK, William (b 1752) Eng-
lish pyrotechnist BD
BROCK, William (1779-1849)
pyrotechnist BD
BROCKBANK, Dora see
Barton, Dora
BROCKBANK, Harrison (1867-
1947) English actor, singer
GRB/1-4
BROCKBANK, Mrs. Harrison
(d 1894) EA/95*
BROCKBANK, Mrs. J. B. see
Barton, Mary
BROCKBANK, John Benn (d
1896) EA/97*
BROCKETT, O. G. (b 1923)
American educator, writer
BE
BROCKIN, Mr. (fl 1776-90)
dresser BD
BROCKIN, Mrs. (fl 1765)
dresser BD
BROCKMAN, James (d 1967
[80]) performer BP/51*
BROCKSMITH, Roy (b 1945)
American actor TW/28-30
BROCKWELL, Benjamin (fl
1665) musician BD
BROCKWELL, Henry (fl 1661-
88) violinist BD
BRODAS, Mr. (fl 1750) tailor
BD
BRODER, Jane talent repre-
sentative BE
BRODERICK, Mr. (fl 1771-76)
actor, singer BD

BRODERICK, Emma (1864-1948)
singer SR
BRODERICK, Helen (1891-1959)
American actress, singer ES,
TW/16, WWT/7-10
BRODERICK, James (b 1928)
American actor TW/22, 24,
26-27, 29
BRODIE, Matthew (1863-1908)
Scottish actor DD, EA/95,
GRB/1, 4
BRODIE, Mrs. Matthew see
Rees, Alice
BRODIE, Steve singer CDP
BRODIE, Mrs. William (d 1886)
EA/88*
BRODKIN, Herbert scene designer
TW/4-5
BRODRIBB, John Henry see
Irving, Sir Henry
BRODSZKY, Nicholas (b 1905)
Russian/English composer ES
BRODY, Estelle (b 1904) Canadian
actress ES
BROEDER, Ray (b 1898) Austro-
Hungarian manager BE
BROEKMAN, David Hendrines
(1899-1958) Dutch composer,
conductor WWA/3
BROGDEN, Mr. (fl 1730) actor
BD
BROGDEN, Mrs. Arthur, Sr.
see Brogden, Dorothy
BROGDEN, Mrs. Arthur see
LeButt, Ada
BROGDEN, Dorothy [Mrs. Arthur
Brogden, Sr.] (d 1911 [34])
singer EA/12*
BROGDEN, Gwendoline (b 1891)
English actress, singer WWT/
3-6
BROGDEN, Paddy (d 1878) Irish
singer EA/79*
BROHAN, Madeleine (d 1900 [66])
actress WWT/14*
BROHAN, Suzanne (d 1887 [80])
actress WWT/14*
"BROILEAU, The Mlles. " (fl
1753) performers BD
BROKAW, Charles (d 1975 [77])
actor BP/60*, WWT/16*
BROKE, Charles Frederick Tucker
see Brooke, Charles Frederick
Tucker
BROMBERG, J. Edward (1904-51)
Hungarian actor ES, TW/3,
5-8, WWT/8-11
BROME, Alexander (1620-66)

English dramatist CP/1-3,
DD, DNB, FGF
BROME, Richard (c. 1590-1653)
English dramatist CP/1-3,
DD, DNB, ES, FGF, HP,
MH, NTH, OC/1-3, RE
BROME, Richard (fl 1628)
actor DA
BROMEFILD, Richard (fl 1628)
actor DA
BROMEHAM (fl 1582) actor DA
BROMELOW, John see Little
Gulliver
BROMFIELD, Louis (1896-1956)
American dramatist ES,
NTH, WWA/3, WWW/5
BROMFIELD, William (fl 1755)
dramatist CP/3
BROMHEAD, H. H. (d 1889
[29]) acting manager EA/91*
BROMLEY, Master (fl 1763-82)
harpist BD
BROMLEY, Charles (d 1902)
proprietor EA/03*
BROMLEY, Emily (d 1860 [31])
actress, singer WWT/14*
BROMLEY, John (fl 1778-1802)
scene painter BD
BROMLEY, Nelly (d 1939 [89])
actress DD, OAA/2
BROMLEY, Thomas (fl 1603)
lessee DA
BROMLEY Thomas (d 1841
[68]) actor EA/72*
BROMLEY, William (fl 1780-
1803) scene painter BD
BROMLEY, William (d 1887)
property master EA/88*
BROMLEY, Mrs. William
(d 1880 [51]) EA/81*
BROMLEY-DAVENPORT, Arthur
(1867-1946) English actor
WWT/4-10
BROMWICH, Frederick Dudman
(1873-1942) English actor,
manager GRB/1
BRON, Eleanor English actress
WWT/16
BRONNER, Edwin (b 1926)
American dramatist, his-
torian BE
BRONSON, Betty (d 1971 [64])
actress BP/56*, WWT/
16*
BRONSON, Charles (b 1922?)
American actor CB
BRONSON, James (b 1921)
American actor TW/8

BRONSON, Lillian (b 1902) Amer-
ican actress TW/4
BRONSON-HOWARD, George (b
1884) American critic WWM
BROOK, Clive (1887-1974) English
actor AAS, BTR/74, ES,
TW/7, WWT/5-15
BROOK, Edward Harcourt see
Brooke, Edward James Mac-
donald
BROOK, Faith (b 1922) English
actress TW/4, WWT/11-16
BROOK, Sir Fulk Greville (1554-
1628) English dramatist CP/1
BROOK, J. (fl 1722-23) house
servant? BD
BROOK, Joseph (d 1868 [65])
singer EA/69*
BROOK, Lesley (b 1917) English
actress WWT/10-11
BROOK, Lyndon (b 1927) American
actor TW/8
BROOK, Peter Stephen Paul (b
1925) English producer, direc-
tor, designer AAS, BE, CB,
CH, COC, ES, OC/2-3, PDT,
WWT/11-16
BROOK, Sara costume designer
WWT/16
BROOK, Thomas Graven Hodgkin-
son (d 1889 [36]) actor EA/90*
BROOKAM, Mrs. (fl 1779) dresser
BD
BROOKE, Mr. (fl 1788-89) actor
BD
BROOKE, Miss (fl 1781-89)
actress BD
BROOKE, Miss (fl 1789) dramatist
CP/3
BROOKE, Arthur (d 1563) writer
DD
BROOKE, C. [Mrs. Richard
Brooke] (d 1874 [32]) EA/75*
BROOKE, C. (d 1889) scene artist
EA/90*
BROOKE, Charles Frederick Tuck-
er (1883-1946) American scholar
DAB
BROOKE, Cynthia [Mrs. F. G.
Latham] (1875-1949) Australian
actress GRB/1, WWT/3-6
BROOKE, Edward James Mac-
donald [Edward Harcourt Brook]
(d 1884 [41]) actor EA/85*
BROOKE, E. H. (1843-84) actor
DD
BROOKE, E. H. (d 1929 [53])
English actor, stage manager

GRB/1-4
BROOKE, Mrs. E. H. (d 1915
[80]) actress DD, GRB/
3-4, WWT/1-3
BROOKE, Emily (d 1953) actress
WWT/4-5
BROOKE, Fergus (d 1882)
secretary EA/83*
BROOKE, Frances [née Moore]
(1724-89) English dramatist,
proprietor, actress BD,
CP/2-3, DD, DNB, GT,
TD/1-2
BROOKE, Frederick G. (d 1909)
sketch producer EA/10*
BROOKE, Gustavus Vaughan
(1818-66) English actor CDP,
COC, DD, DNB, ES, HAS,
OC/1-3
BROOKE, Mrs. Gustavus Vaughan
see Jones, Avonia
BROOKE, Harold (b 1910) Eng-
lish dramatist WWT/15-16
BROOKE, Harry (fl 1898-1913)
English scene designer ES
BROOKE, Henry (1703?-83)
Irish dramatist CDP, CP/
1-3, DD, ES, GT, HP,
NTH, TD/1-2
BROOKE, H. Sullivan (d 1923)
composer, conductor BE*,
WWT/14*
BROOKE, Iris (b 1908) English
educator, writer, costume
designer BE
BROOKE, James (fl 1773-84)
proprietor BD
BROOKE, James (d 1872 [36])
proprietor EA/73*
BROOKE, Mrs. John see
Brooke, Frances
BROOKE, Marie [Mrs. D.
Scott-Dalgleish] (d 1907)
composer EA/08*, GRB/3*
BROOKE, Paul (b 1944) Eng-
lish actor TW/30
BROOKE, Ralph (b 1920)
American actor TW/1, 3
BROOKE, Richard (fl 1672-73)
actor BD
BROOKE, Mrs. Richard see
Brooke, C.
BROOKE, Sarah (b 1875)
Indian/English actress
GRB/1-4, WWT/1-6
BROOKE, Walter American actor
TW/5, 8-9
BROOKES, Mr. (fl 1778) actor

BD
BROOKES, Mrs. [née Moore]
dramatist CP/1
BROOKES, Miss (fl 1774-75?)
dancer BD
BROOKES, George (1834-69) Eng-
lish actor HAS
BROOKES, George (d 1967 [68])
performer BP/51*
BROOKES, George see Verlino,
Charles
BROOKES, Mrs. George (fl 1861)
American actress HAS
BROOKES, Harriet Morton (d 1868
[55]) actress WWT/14*
BROOKES, Jacqueline (b 1930)
American actress AAS, BE,
TW/11-20, 22-23, 26-30, WWT/
15-16
BROOKES, L. DeGarmo American
actor, choreographer CDP
BROOKES, Mrs. Moreton (d 1868
[55]) actress EA/68*
BROOKES, R. (fl 1737) English
dramatist CP/2-3, GT
BROOKES, Robert (fl 1702) actor
BD
BROOKES, Dr. Samuel (fl 1613-15)
dramatist CP/3, FGF
BROOKFIELD, Mrs. (d 1895)
EA/97*
BROOKFIELD, Charles Hallam
Elton (1857-1913) English actor,
examiner of plays, dramatist
COC, DD, DP, GRB/1-4, SR,
WWT/1-2, WWW/1
BROOKFIELD, Sydney F. (d 1916)
journalist EA/17*, WWT/14*
BROOKHOUSER, Frank (d 1975
[63]) journalist BP/60*
BROOKING, Cecil (d 1940) actor
WWT/14*
BROOK-JONES, Elwyn (1911-62)
English actor WWT/10-13
BROOKLYN, Jessie (d 1886)
EA/87*
BROOKLYN, May English actress
SR
BROOKS, The Masters (fl 1737-
39) dancers BD
BROOKS, Mr. (d 1750) house ser-
vant, actor? BD
BROOKS, Mr. (fl 1774) animal
trainer? BD
BROOKS, Mr. (fl 1783-85) con-
stable BD
BROOKS, [Mr. ?] (fl 1794) actor?
BD

BROOKS, Mr. (fl 1839-40) actor, dancer HAS

BROOKS, Mrs. (fl 1760-67) charwoman BD

BROOKS, Mrs. [Miss Watson] (fl 1786-94) actress BD, DD, TD/1-2

BROOKS, Mrs. (fl 1798) actress BD

BROOKS, Mrs. (fl 1840) actress HAS

BROOKS, Miss see Pickup, Mrs.

BROOKS, Anita (fl c. 1855) singer CDP

BROOKS, Arreline (d 1879) dancer EA/80*

BROOKS, Beatrice (b 1925) American actress TW/23

BROOKS, Charles William Shirley (1815-74) dramatist DD, EA/68

BROOKS, Constance Ida (d 1901 [36]) EA/02*

BROOKS, David (b 1917-20) American actor, singer, director, producer BE, TW/1-6, 19-20, 26, 28

BROOKS, Donald (b 1928) American costume designer BE, CB

BROOKS, Edgar Oswald (b 1880) English manager GRB/1

BROOKS, Edith (d 1902) parachute proprietor EA/03*

BROOKS, Fred Emerson (1850-1923) American dramatist WWA/1

BROOKS, George singer, actor CDP

BROOKS, Geraldine (1925-77) American actress BE, ES, TW/3, 9-12, 26

BROOKS, Harvey O. (d 1968 [69]) composer/lyricist BP/53*

BROOKS, Helen (d 1971 [60]) actress TW/27

BROOKS, Helen M. (d 1912) EA/13*

BROOKS, Hugh (d 1974 [67]) impresario BP/59*

BROOKS, Mrs. Irving see Von Hatzfeldt, Olga

BROOKS, Jack (d 1971 [59]) performer BP/56*

BROOKS, James (fl 1749) house servant? BD

BROOKS, James (1760-1809) English band leader BD

BROOKS, James (d 1911 [49]) actor EA/12*

BROOKS, Joseph (d 1916 [68]) American manager SR

BROOKS, Lawrence (b 1912) American actor, singer BE, TW/1-3, 5-6, 22

BROOKS, Louise (b 1900) American dancer, actress ES

BROOKS, Maria Gowen (c. 1794-1845) American dramatist HJD

BROOKS, Martin (b 1925) American actor TW/7-18, 20

BROOKS, Maude (d 1971 [92]) theatre owner BP/56*

BROOKS, May K. (d 1963 [68]) performer BE*

BROOKS, Mel (b 1926?) American dramatist, writer BE, CB

BROOKS, Nat (d 1877 [39]) singer EA/78*

BROOKS, Neil (d 1975 [62]) general manager BP/60*

BROOKS, Phyllis (b 1914) American actress TW/1

BROOKS, Quintus H. (d 1916 [58]) manager WWT/14*

BROOKS, Ralph Turner (d 1963 [43]) producer, director BE*

BROOKS, Shelton L. (d 1975 [89]) composer/lyricist BP/60*

BROOKS, Shirley see Brooks, Charles William Shirley

BROOKS, Thomas (d 1878 [83]) cashier EA/79*

BROOKS, Virginia Fox see Vernon, Virginia

BROOKS, Mrs. Watson (fl 1786) actress CDP

BROOKS, Wilson (1914-66) American actor TW/6-7, 23

BROOKSBANK, Miss (fl 1785) actress BD

BROOKYN, May [Mrs. King] (d 1894 [35]) actress EA/95*

BROOM, Frank (d 1899 [29]) comedian, acrobat EA/00*

"BROOMSTICKADO, Mynheer Von Poop-Poop" (fl 1757-60) bassoonist BD

BROONES, Martin (b 1892) American composer WWT/8-11

BROPHY, Annie [Mrs. A. K. Thomas] (d 1910 [51]) actress EA/11*

BROPHY, Bridget (b 1929) English

dramatist CD
BROPHY, Edward (d 1960 [65])
American actor BE*
BROTHERSON, Eric (b 1911)
American actor TW/2-3,
6-12, WWT/11-16
BROTHERTON, Thomas J. R.
(d 1969 [77]) treasurer
BP/54*
BROUETT, Albert French actor
WWT/7
BROUGH, Mrs. Barnabas see
Brough, Fanny
BROUGH, Fanny [Mrs. Barnabas
Brough] (d 1897 [94]) EA/98*
BROUGH, Fanny Whiteside [Mrs.
Richard Smith Boleyn] (1854-
1914) French/English actress
COC, DD, DP, EA/95, ES,
GRB/1-4, OAA/1-2, OC/1-3,
WWT/1-2
BROUGH, Lionel (1836-1900)
Welsh actor CDP, COC, DD,
DNB, DP, ES, GRB/1-4,
OAA/1-2, OC/1-3, WWW/1
BROUGH, Mrs. Lionel see
Brough, Margaret Rose
BROUGH, Margaret (d 1901)
actress EA/02*
BROUGH, Margaret Rose [Mrs.
Lionel Brough] (d 1901 [60])
EA/02*
BROUGH, Mary Bessie (1863-
1934) English actress AAS,
COC, ES, GRB/4, OC/1-3,
WWT/1-7, WWW/3
BROUGH, Robert (d 1906 [49])
actor, manager, singer
CDP, DD
BROUGH, Mrs. Robert [Florence
Trevelyan] (d 1932 [73])
actress WWT/4-5
BROUGH, Robert Barnabas (1828-
60) English dramatist COC,
DD, DNB, ES, OC/1-3
BROUGH, Sarah Ann (d 1877)
pianist EA/78*
BROUGH, Sydney (1868-1911)
English actor DD, DP,
EA/95, ES, GRB/1-4,
OC/1-3
BROUGH, William (1826-70)
English dramatist COC, DD,
DNB, EA/68, ES, OC/1-3
BROUGH, Mrs. William see
Romer, Anne
BROUGH, William Francis (1798-
1867) Irish actor, singer

CDP, HAS, SR
BROUGHAM, Emma see Robert-
son, Emma
BROUGHAM, John (1810-80) Irish/
American dramatist, actor,
manager CDP, COC, DAB,
DD, DNB, EA/68, ES, GC,
HAS, HJD, NTH, OAA/1-2,
OC/1-3, SR, WWA/H
BROUGHAM, Mrs. John, I [Ann-
ette Nelson; Mrs. Coppleson
Hodges] (fl 1828-37) actress
HAS
BROUGHAM, Mrs. John, II [née
Williams] (fl 1836-42) actress
HAS
BROUGHAM, W. (d 1885 [48])
conjuror, singer EA/86*
BROUGHAM, W. H. (d 1916 [65])
actor EA/18*
BROUGHTON, Emma (d 1926)
actress, dancer WWT/14*
BROUGHTON, Frederick W. (1851-
94) dramatist DD
BROUGHTON, Henry James (d
1876 [29]) actor EA/77*
BROUGHTON, James (d 1887 [52])
musician EA/88*
BROUGHTON, Jessie (b 1885)
English vocalist GRB/1-4,
WWT/1-2
BROUGHTON, John (1705-89) Eng-
lish? pugilist DNB
BROUGHTON, Mrs. John, I (d
1870) actress CDP
BROUGHTON, Phyllis (d 1926 [64])
actress, dancer, singer DD,
DP, EA/96, GRB/2-4, WWT/
1-5
BROUGHTON, Simon J. (d 1964
[80]) performer BE*
BROUGHTON, Thomas (1704-74)
English dramatist CP/2-3,
DD, GT
BROUN, Heywood Campbell (1888-
1939) American critic NTH,
WWT/5-9
BROUN, Heywood Hale (b 1918)
American actor BE, TW/10-12,
22-23
BROUNOFF, Platon (1863-1924)
Russian composer WWA/1
BROUS, Mr. (fl 1708) tailor BD
BROUSIL, Alois (d 1888 [42])
musical director, violinist
EA/89*
BROUWENSTIJN, Gré (b 1915)
Dutch singer ES

BROWER, Frank (1820-74) American comedian CDP, HAS

BROWER, Mrs. Frank [Louisa Banks] (fl 1851) performer HAS

BROWN, Mr. (fl 1708) box-keeper BD

BROWN, Mr. (fl 1718) drama-tist CP/2-3

BROWN, Mr. (fl 1719-29) box-keeper or officekeeper BD

BROWN, Mr. (fl 1724) actor BD

BROWN, Mr. (fl 1748-51) actor, dancer, singer BD

BROWN, Mr. (fl 1763-64) actor BD

BROWN, Mr. (fl 1768?-1817?) singer BD

BROWN, Mr. (fl 1770?-1808?) actor BD

BROWN, Mr. (fl 1771) equestrian BD

BROWN, Mr. (fl 1776-77) dresser BD

BROWN, [Mr.?] (fl 1776-77) performer BD

BROWN, Mr. (fl 1791) exhibitor BD

BROWN, Mr. (fl 1794) singer? BD

BROWN, Mr. (fl 1796) CP/3

BROWN, Mr. (fl 1798-99) actor BD

BROWN, Mr. ["Big Brown"] (d 1836) actor HAS

BROWN, Mrs. (fl 1662) actress BD

BROWN, Mrs. (fl 1707) actress BD

BROWN, Mrs. (fl 1708) dresser BD

BROWN, Mrs. (fl 1736-51) actress BD

BROWN, Mrs. (fl 1764) actress BD

BROWN, Mrs. (fl 1776-78) dresser BD

BROWN, Mrs. (fl 1786) per-former? BD

BROWN, Mrs. (fl c. 1786-87) singer BD

BROWN, Mrs. (fl 1790-97) actress, singer BD

BROWN, Mrs. [née Biggs] (fl 1798-1801) actress BD

BROWN, Miss (fl 1767-78) dancer, actress BD

BROWN, Miss (fl 1782) actress BD

BROWN, Miss (fl 1791) actress BD

BROWN, Abraham (fl 1739-68) violinist, composer BD

BROWN, Mrs. A. H. see Robson, May

BROWN, Albert O. (d 1945 [73]) American producer BE*, BP/29*

BROWN, Alice (1857-1948) Ameri-can dramatist WWA/2

BROWN, Ann see Cargill, Mrs. R.

BROWN, Anthony (fl 1739) drama-tist CP/1-3, DD, GT, TD/1-2

BROWN, Archibald (d 1916) EA/18*

BROWN, Bertrand (d 1964 [75]) American songwriter, press representative BE*

BROWN, Bessie Greenwood (d 1973 [92]) performer BP/57*

BROWN, Buster see Ansley, Edmond

BROWN, Carrie Clarke Ward (1862-1926) American performer SR

BROWN, Chamberlain (d 1955 [67]) agent TW/12

BROWN, Charles Armitage (fl 1814) librettist DD

BROWN, Charles Brockden (1771-1810) American dramatist EAP

BROWN, Charles D. (d 1948 [60]) American actor TW/5

BROWN, Charles E. (1862-1947) magician, ventriloquist SR

BROWN, Clark (1877-1943) Ameri-can manager SR

BROWN, Dan (d 1875 [39]) minstrel EA/76*

BROWN, Daniel (b 1947) American actor TW/29

BROWN, Danny (d 1976 [63]) pro-ducer/director/choreographer BP/60*

BROWN, David Paul (1795-1875) American dramatist CDP, DAB, EAP, NTH, RJ

BROWN, DeMarcus (b 1900) Amer-ican educator, director BE

BROWN, Dennis (d 1969 [55]) producer/director/choreographer BP/54*

BROWN, Miss E. (fl 1797-98)
actress BD
BROWN, Edith Ann see
Heron-Brown, Edith
BROWN, Mrs. Edwin see
Kelly, Kate
BROWN, Elizabeth (d 1885 [84])
EA/86*
BROWN, Elizabeth (d 1906)
EA/07*
BROWN, Elizabeth American
actress TW/26
BROWN, Ellen (d 1895) EA/97*
BROWN, Fanny (b 1837) Ameri-
can actress HAS
BROWN, Firman H., Jr. (b
1926) American educator,
director BE
BROWN, Florrie (d 1892 [19])
EA/93*
BROWN, Fred (d 1899) musician
EA/01*
BROWN, Frederick (d 1871)
pianist EA/72*
BROWN, Frederick (d 1901 [51])
entrepreneur EA/03*
BROWN, Master Frederick (fl
1805) juvenile prodigy CDP
BROWN, Frederick Charles see
Seel, Charles
BROWN, George Anderson (d
1920 [81]) actor BE*, BP/5*
BROWN, Georgia [née Klot] (b
1933) English actress, singer
AAS, BE, WWT/14-16
BROWN, G. H. (d 1881 [26])
musician EA/82*
BROWN, Gilmor (d 1960 [73])
American producer, director
CB, ES, TW/16
BROWN, Graham (b 1924) Amer-
ican actor TW/24-27, 29-30
BROWN, Harry singer CDP
BROWN, Harry Joe (d 1972 [78])
producer/director/choreograph-
er BP/56*
BROWN, Helen (b 1902) Ameri-
can community theatre direc-
tor BE
BROWN, Helen see Hayes,
Helen
BROWN, Henry (d 1720) actor
BD
BROWN, Henry (d 1902 [87])
jester EA/03*
BROWN, Henry C. (d 1970 [44])
agent BP/54*
BROWN, Hubert Sydney (1898-

1949) English composer, writer
WWW/4
BROWN, I. H. actor CDP
BROWN, Irene (d 1965 [72]) per-
former BP/50*
BROWN, Irving (b 1922) American
educator, director BE
BROWN, Ivor (1891-1974) English
critic, dramatist AAS, BE,
BTR/74, OC/1-3, PDT, WWT/
6-15
BROWN, J. (d 1818) actor, acro-
bat, singer BD
BROWN, J. (fl 1819) writer DD
BROWN, Mrs. J. [Mrs. William
Ross; née Mills] (d 1823)
actress, singer BD, CDP, DD
BROWN, James (fl 1783) dramatist
CP/3
BROWN, James (fl 1794) trumpeter
BD
BROWN, James H. (d 1930) actor,
manager SR
BROWN, James Henry (d 1873 [66])
secretary EA/74*
BROWN, J. B. elocution teacher
CDP
BROWN, Jessie (d 1892) actress
EA/93*
BROWN, Joe (d 1883) minstrel
CDP
BROWN, Joe (b 1830) American
dancer, comedian HAS
BROWN, Joe E. (1892-1973) Amer-
ican actor, comedian BE, CB,
ES, SR, TW/2-8, 30, WWA/5,
WWT/7-15
BROWN, Dr. John (1715-66) Eng-
lish dramatist CP/3, DD
BROWN, John (fl 1732-36) singer,
actor BD
BROWN, John Mason (1900-69)
American critic AAS, BE, CB,
COC, ES, HJD, NTH, OC/1-3,
PDT, TW/25, WWT/6-14,
WWW/6
BROWN, John Mills (d 1859 [77])
English actor CDP, HAS
BROWN, Johnnie ["Lord Tom
Doddy"] (d 1898 [16]) comedian
EA/00*
BROWN, Johnny Mack (d 1974
[70]) actor BP/59*, WWT/16*
BROWN, John Russell (b 1923)
English director, scholar
WWT/15-16
BROWN, Josephine actress TW/1,
13-14

BROWN, J. Purdy (d 1834)
manager HAS
BROWN, Kay (b 1902) American
talent representative, pro-
ducer BE
BROWN, Kelly (b 1928) American
dancer BE, TW/15-16
BROWN, Kenneth H. (b 1936)
American dramatist CD
BROWN, Kermit (b 1937) Amer-
ican actor TW/24-25, 28
BROWN, Lawrence (d 1972 [79])
composer/lyricist BP/57*
BROWN, Lew (1893/99-1958)
American lyricist, librettist,
producer, manager WWT/
8-11
BROWN, Lillian actress CDP
BROWN, Lillian (d 1969 [83])
actress, singer, male im-
personator TW/26
BROWN, Lionel (1888-1964)
Irish dramatist WWT/9-13
BROWN, Louise actress, singer
WWT/6-7
BROWN, L. Slade (b 1922)
American producer BE
BROWN, Lyman C. (d 1961
[60]) American talent repre-
sentative BE*
BROWN, Martin (d 1891 [50])
proprietor EA/92*
BROWN, Martin (1885-1936)
Canadian dramatist, dancer,
actor SR, WWT/5-8
BROWN, Mollie equestrienne
CDP
BROWN, Nacio Herb (d 1964
[68]) composer/lyricist BP/
49*
BROWN, Nella F. reader CDP
BROWN, Nellie [Mrs. Ellen
Alice Holt] (d 1892 [31])
music-hall artist EA/93*
BROWN, [Owen?] (fl 1794)
actor BD
BROWN, Pamela Mary (1917-75)
English actress AAS, BE,
ES, TW/3, 6-8, 14-16,
WWT/10-14
BROWN, Pendleton (b 1948)
American actor TW/28
BROWN, Percy (1883-1918) actor
SR
BROWN, R. see Persivani
BROWN, Reed, Jr. (d 1962 [63])
American actor TW/19
BROWN, R. G. (b 1933)

American actor TW/18, 25-27
BROWN, Robert ["Buster"] see
Ansley, Edmond
BROWN, Rose M. (d 1965 [61])
performer BP/49*
BROWN, Rowland C. (d 1963 [62])
director BE*
BROWN, Russ (d 1964 [72]) singer,
actor TW/21
BROWN, Russ (d 1971 [56]) com-
poser/lyricist BP/55*
BROWN, Samuel (d 1917) EA/18*
BROWN, Samuel Edwin (1826-69)
American actor HAS
BROWN, Sarah (1757-1806) dancer
BD
BROWN, Sedley (1856-1928) Amer-
ican director WWM
BROWN, Susan (d 1932) American
actress TW/23
BROWN, Tally (b 1934) American
actress TW/25-26, 28-29
BROWN, Thomas (1663-1704) Eng-
lish dramatist CP/3, DD, GT
BROWN, Thomas (fl 1715-40)
violinist, composer BD
BROWN, Thomas (fl 1794) singer
BD
BROWN, Thomas (d 1865) property
man HAS
BROWN, Thomas Allston (1836-
1918) American historian, agent,
manager CDP, DD, SR, WWA/
4, WWM
BROWN, Tom (b 1913) American
actor ES
BROWN, Vincent (fl 1901) drama-
tist DD
BROWN, Wally (d 1961 [57]) actor
BE*, BP/46*
BROWN, Walter P. (b 1926)
American actor TW/22, 24, 30
BROWN, William (fl 1789-94)
violoncellist BD
BROWN, William (d 1870 [31])
singer? EA/71*
BROWN, William B. singer,
humorist, composer, comedian
CDP
BROWN, William F. dramatist
CD
BROWN, William Ruddle (b 1868)
English actor GRB/1
BROWN, Mrs. William Ruddle
see Howitt, Nellie
BROWN, Winifred Colleano (d 1973
[75]) performer BP/57*
BROWNBILL, Thomas Robson see

Robson, Frederick
BROWNE (fl 1596) actor DA
BROWNE, Mr. (fl 1749-56)
house servant? BD
BROWNE, Mr. (fl 1787) Amer-
ican? actor TD/1-2
BROWNE, Mr. (fl 1823) actor
BS
BROWNE, Brineta (b 1885)
English actress GRB/1-2
BROWNE, Campbell (d 1903 [39])
singer EA/04*
BROWNE, Charles (fl 1739)
musician BD
BROWNE, Charles Farrar ["Art-
emus Ward"] (1834-67) Amer-
ican entertainer, comedian
CDP, HAS, SR
BROWNE, Mrs. Chris see
Browne, Leonora Mary
BROWNE, Coral (b 1913)
Australian actress AAS,
BE, CB, TW/12, 20, 22,
WWT/9-16
BROWNE, David (d 1871 [28])
actor EA/72*
BROWNE, Edward (fl 1584-1603)
actor DA
BROWNE, Edward (d 1916 [69])
circus musician EA/17*
BROWNE, E. Martin (b 1900)
English producer, actor,
director AAS, BE, COC,
ES, OC/1-3, PDT, WWT/9-16
BROWNE, Frederick (d 1838)
English actor, manager HAS
BROWNE, Mrs. Frederick [née
De Camp] see De Camp,
Sophia
BROWNE, George F. (b 1833)
American actor HAS
BROWNE, G. H. (d 1877 [51])
proprietor EA/78*
BROWNE, Mrs. Graham see
McIntosh, Madge
BROWNE, G. Walter (b 1856)
actor, singer, dramatist DD
BROWNE, Henry (fl 1583) actor
DA
BROWNE, Irene (1896-1965)
English actress BE, ES,
TW/22, WWT/4-13
BROWNE, James S. (1791-1869)
English actor HAS
BROWNE, John (fl 1551-63) court
interluder DA
BROWNE, John (fl 1608) actor
DA

BROWNE, Dr. John (1715-66)
English dramatist CP/1-2, GT,
TD/1-2
BROWNE, K. R. G. (d 1940 [45])
librettist WWT/14*
BROWNE, Laidman (1896-1961)
English actor ES, WWT/9-10
BROWNE, Leonora Mary [Mrs.
Chris Browne] (d 1905) EA/06*
BROWNE, Lewis Allen (1876-1937)
American dramatist WWA/1
BROWNE, Louise American act-
ress, singer, dancer WWT/8-9
BROWNE, Marjorie (b 1913) Eng-
lish actress, singer WWT/9-13
BROWNE, Matthew Campbell (fl
1778-1806) actor BD
BROWNE, Maurice (1881-1955)
English actor, manager, drama-
tist COC, ES, MWD, NTH,
OC/3, WWA/3, WWT/6-11,
WWW/5
BROWNE, Moses (1703-87) drama-
tist CP/1-3, DD
BROWNE, Nellie see Taylor,
Mrs. C. R.
BROWNE, Old (fl 1602) actor DA
BROWNE, Pattie (b 1869) Australian
actress GRB/1-4, WWT/1-5
BROWNE, Porter Emerson (1879-
1934) American dramatist SR,
WWA/1, WWM, WWT/1-7
BROWNE, Rachell (fl 1666-70)
tirewoman BD
BROWNE, Richard (fl 1670-75)
violinist BD
BROWNE, Robert (fl 1583-1620/40)
English actor COC, DA, ES,
OC/1-3
BROWNE, Roscoe Lee (b 1925)
American actor BE, WWT/15-
16
BROWNE, Solomon James (1791-
1869) English actor CDP, DD,
OX
BROWNE, Stella (b 1906) English
actress, singer WWT/7-9
BROWNE, Thomas (d 1704) English
dramatist CP/2
BROWNE, Thomas (fl 1675-83)
violinist BD
BROWNE, Thomas (b 1906) English
dramatist WWT/10-14
BROWNE, Tom (d 1884) musician,
composer EA/85*
BROWNE, Tom (d 1899) songwriter
EA/00*
BROWNE, Walter (1856-1911)

English actor, dramatist,
singer WWS
BROWNE, Walter E. dramatist
SR
BROWNE, W. Graham (1870/75-
1937) Irish actor COC, GRB/
1-4, WWT/1-8
BROWNE, William (fl c. 1600-32)
actor DA
BROWNE, William (1590-1645)
English writer CP/3, DD,
FGF
BROWNE, Wynyard Barry (1911-
64) English dramatist AAS,
PDT, WWT/11-13
BROWNELL, Mabel (b 1888)
American actress WWM
BROWNING, Mr. (fl 1785-86)
house servant? bassoonist?
BD
BROWNING, Miss (fl 1785-86)
singer, dancer BD
BROWNING, Bonnie (d 1918)
EA/19*
BROWNING, Edith (d 1926 [51])
actress, singer BE*, BP/
10*
BROWNING, Harry G. (b c. 1863)
actor SR
BROWNING, Robert (1812-89)
English dramatist DD, DNB,
ES, HP, NTH, OC/1-3,
PDT, RE
BROWNING, Robert (b 1942)
American actor TW/26, 29
BROWNING, Rod (b 1942) Amer-
ican actor TW/29
BROWNING, Susan (b 1941)
American actress, singer
TW/24, 26-30, WWT/16
BROWNING, Tod (d 1962 [82])
director BP/47*
BROWNLEE, Brian American
actor TW/29-30
BROWNLEE, Dell French/
American actor TW/27-29
BROWNLEE, John Donald Mac-
kenzie (1901-69) Australian
executive, singer BE, ES,
WWW/6
BROWNLOW, Wallace (d 1919)
actor, singer WWT/14*
BROWN-POTTER, Cora Urquhart
see Potter, Cora Urquhart
BROWNSMITH, John (fl 1751-79)
prompter, actor BD, DD
BROWNSTONE, Joseph (1920-70)
American stage manager,

director, producer BE
BROXUP, Katherine [née Studt]
(d 1906) EA/07*
BRUBACH, Gary (b 1950) Ameri-
can actor TW/30
BRUCATO, Jimmy (d 1973 [55])
producer/director/choreographer
BP/57*
BRUCE, Mr. actor CDP
BRUCE, Mr. (fl 1794-95) door-
keeper BD
BRUCE, Mrs. (fl 1705-06) dancer
BD
BRUCE, Allan (b 1930) Scottish
actor TW/22
BRUCE, Betty (1921/25-74) Amer-
ican dancer, singer, comedienne
BE, TW/1-7, WWT/10-11
BRUCE, Brenda (b 1918) English
actress AAS, ES, WWT/10-16
BRUCE, Carol (b 1919) American
actress, singer BE, TW/1,
5-7, 21-22, 24, WWT/10-16
BRUCE, Charles (d 1877 [32])
minstrel EA/78*
BRUCE, Charley (d 1890 [35])
EA/91*
BRUCE, Clifford [Clifford B.
Scott] (b 1884) Canadian actor
WWM
BRUCE, David (d 1976 [60]) per-
former BP/60*
BRUCE, Edgar (d 1901 [56]) actor,
manager, proprietor DD, DP,
OAA/2
BRUCE, Mrs. Edgar see Bruce,
Lucy Sybil
BRUCE, Edgar K. (1893-1971)
English actor WWT/8-15
BRUCE, Edith (d 1925) actress
DD, OAA/2
BRUCE, Geraldine (d 1953 [72])
actress TW/10
BRUCE, Mrs. H. A. see
Bruce, Mary Ann
BRUCE, Harry actor, producer,
stage manager, manager GRB/1
BRUCE, Henry Alexander (d 1901
[69]) managing director EA/02*,
WWT/14*
BRUCE, Katherine (b 1941) Amer-
ican actress TW/23, 29
BRUCE, Lucy Sybil [Mrs. Edgar
Bruce] (d 1901 [28]) EA/02*
BRUCE, Hon. Mrs. Lyndhurst
Henry see Clifford, Camille
BRUCE, Mary Ann [Mrs. H. A.
Bruce] (d 1908) EA/09*,

GRB/4*
BRUCE, Nigel (1895-1953)
American actor ES, TW/
10, WWT/5-11
BRUCE, Paul (d 1971) performer
BP/55*
BRUCE, Samuel (b 1936) Cana-
dian actor TW/28
BRUCE, Sybil Etonia see
Bruce, Tonie Edgar
BRUCE, Tonie Edgar [Sybil
Etonia Bruce] (1892-1966)
English actress WWT/5-11
BRUCE, Tony (d 1937 [27])
actor BE*, WWT/14*
BRUCE, William (fl 1730-51)
musician BD
BRUCE-POTTER, Hilda (b 1888)
English actress WWT/2-12
BRUCKER, Mr. (fl 1795) house
servant? BD
BRUCKNER, Ferdinand [Theodor
Tagger] (1891-1958) Austrian/
American dramatist, director
CH, MH, MWD, OC/3
BRUDNAL, Mr. (fl 1753) actor
BD
BRUFORD, Rose Elizabeth (b
1904) English college prin-
cipal WWT/14-16
BRUGNER, Mr. (fl 1766-67)
lobby doorkeeper BD
BRUGUIER, Anthony (fl 1786-
98) dancing master BD
BRUGUIER, Sophia (fl 1798-99)
dancer BD
BRUGUIER, Susan (fl 1798-99)
dancer BD
BRUHN, Erik Belton Evers (b
1928) Danish dancer,
choreographer CB, ES
BRUKERWICH, Mrs. see Stoll,
Blanche
BRULE, André (1879-1953)
French actor, manager ES,
WWT/4, 10
BRULL, Anton (d 1911 [74])
EA/12*
BRULL, Joseph [Pepi] (d 1908
36]) EA/10
BRUMEN, Miss (fl 1794) singer
BD
BRUMMEL, David (b 1942)
American actor TW/30
BRUMMELL, William (fl 1785?)
performer? BD
BRUNATTI, Antonio (fl 1663-67)
scene keeper BD

BRUNDAGE, John Herbert see
Herbert, John
BRUNDAGE, Mary Anne (fl 1815-
20) actress HAS
BRUNDIN, Bo (b 1937) Swedish
actor TW/23
BRUNE, Adrienne [Phyllis Caro-
line Brune] (b 1892/97)
Australian actress, singer
WWT/5-11
BRUNE, Clarence M. (b 1870)
Scottish actor WWT/1
BRUNE, Gabrielle (b 1912) Eng-
lish actress, singer WWT/10-
12
BRUNE, Minnie Tittell (b 1883)
American actress WWT/1-5
BRUNE, Phyllis Caroline see
Brune, Adrienne
BRUNEAU, Alfred (1857-1934)
French composer GRB/1-4,
WWM
BRUNEL, Adrian (b 1892) English
actor ES
BRUNETTE, Miss (fl 1734-42)
actress, dancer BD
BRUNETTI, Gaetano (d 1758)
scene painter BD
BRUNETTS, Mons. (fl 1675)
manager? BD
BRUNI, Domenico (fl 1793) singer
BD
BRUNING, Albert (1863-1929)
German actor WWM
BRUNING, Francesca (b 1907)
American actress BE, TW/3,
WWT/8-14
BRUNN, Mr. (fl 1775-78) pup-
peteer, dancer BD
BRUNO, Anthony J. (d 1976 [82])
photographer BP/60*
BRUNO, Giordano (1548-1600)
Italian dramatist COC, OC/
1-3
BRUNO, Jean (b 1926) American
actress TW/27-30
BRUNO, Mrs. W. Lee see
Garratt, Jessie
BRUNORO, Sig. (fl 1742) dancer
BD
BRUNOT, Andre (d 1973 [93])
performer BP/58*
BRUNS, Edna (d 1960 [80]) per-
former BE*, BP/45*
BRUNS, Julia (1895-1927) Amer-
ican actress WWT/4-5
BRUNS, Mona American actress
TW/2-3

BRUNS, Philip (b 1931) Amer-
ican actor TW/23, 25-27, 29
BRUNSDON, John (fl 1774-81)
actor BD, CDP
BRUNSWICK, Mark (d 1971
[69]) composer/lyricist
BP/55*
BRUNTON, Anna (b 1773)
dramatist CP/3, DD
BRUNTON, Ann[e; Anne Merry;
Mrs. Robert Merry] (1768-
1808) English actress CDP,
COC, DAB, ES, HAS, OC/
1-3, SR, TD/1-2, WWA/H
BRUNTON, Annie (fl 1880)
actress DD
BRUNTON, Dorothy (1893-1977)
Australian actress, singer
WWT/4-10
BRUNTON, Miss E. [Mrs.
Diver] (d 1893] actress EA/
94*
BRUNTON, Elizabeth [Mrs.
Peter Columbine] (c. 1772-99)
English actress BD, TD/1-2
BRUNTON, Elizabeth (d 1893)
actress WWT/14*
BRUNTON, Elizabeth see
Yates, Elizabeth
BRUNTON, Garland Lewis (d
1975 [72]) performer BP/60*
BRUNTON, John (1741-1822)
English actor, manager BD,
DD, ES, OC/1-3, TD/1-2
BRUNTON, John (1775-1848) English
actor CDP, DD, GT, OC/1-3,
TD/1-2
BRUNTON, John (d 1909 [62])
scene artist EA/10*
BRUNTON, Mrs. John [Anna
Ross] (b 1773) English act-
ress, dramatist BD
BRUNTON, Louisa [Countess
Craven] (1779-1860) English
actress CDP, COC, DD,
ES, GT, OC/1-3
BRUNTON, Watty (d 1904 [76])
comedian EA/05*, WWT/14*
BRUNTON, Mrs. Watty, Sr.
(d 1893 [57]) singer, actress
EA/94*
BRUNTON, W. H. (fl 1836)
English actor HAS
BRUNTON, Mrs. W. H. [née
Helen Matthews] (b 1827)
Irish actress HAS, SR
BRUODIN, Mr. (fl 1749) actor BD
BRUSCANTINI, Sesto (b 1919)

Italian singer ES
BRUSH, Clinton E., III (b 1911)
American architect BE
BRUSH, Mrs. Clinton E. [née
Martha Hughes Stockton] (b
1911) American actress, edu-
cator BE
BRUSKIN, Perry (b 1916) Ameri-
can producer, director, stage
manager, actor BE
BRUSTEIN, Robert Sanford (b 1927)
American actor, director,
critic AAS, BE, CB, WWT/
15-16
BRUTON, James (d 1867 [52])
writer EA/68*
BRUYLANTS, Francine (d 1974 [75])
performer BP/59*
BRYAN, Mr. (fl 1713?-26) musi-
cian BD
BRYAN, Mr. (fl 1750) actor? BD
BRYAN, Mr. (fl 1784) singer BD
BRYAN, Daniel (fl 1670) scene
keeper BD
BRYAN, Dora [née Broadbent] (b
1924) English actress AAS,
WWT/12-16
BRYAN, [Frederick?] (d 1770?)
prompter BD
BRYAN, George (fl 1586-1613)
English actor DA, GT, NTH
BRYAN, Hal [Johnson Clark] (1891-
1948) English actor WWT/10
BRYAN, Herbert George (d 1948)
English producer WWT/9-10
BRYAN, Jackson L. (d 1964 [55])
performer BP/49*
BRYAN, John (d 1769) musician
BD
BRYAN, John (d 1969 [58]) pro-
ducer/director/choreographer
BP/54*
BRYAN, Julien H. (d 1974 [75])
producer/director/choreographer
BP/59*
BRYAN, Marian Knighton (d 1974
[74]) dance teacher BP/59*
BRYAN, Mary (fl 1624) lessee DA
BRYAN, Peggy (b 1916) English
actress WWT/9-11
BRYANT, Billy (1888-1948) actor,
showboat manager SR
BRYANT, Cpt. Billy (d 1968 [79])
showboat captain BP/52*
[?=preceding entry, q. v.]
BRYANT, Charles E. (1879-1948)
English actor ES, TW/5,
WWT/1-10

BRYANT, Dan [Daniel Webster O'Bryan] (1833-75) American comedian, minstrel, manager CDP, HAS, SR

BRYANT, George (d 1889) marionette proprietor EA/90*

BRYANT, Grant see Berte, Charles

BRYANT, Jerry [né O'Brien] (1828-61) American minstrel CDP, HAS

BRYANT, John (d 1868 [30]) singer EA/69*

BRYANT, John (b 1916) American actor TW/2

BRYANT, J. V. (1889-1924) English actress WWT/2-4

BRYANT, Mardi (b 1924) American actress TW/2

BRYANT, Margaret C. (b 1908) American educator BE

BRYANT, Marshall F. (d 1971 [79]) critic BP/56*

BRYANT, Mary (b 1936) American press representative, actress BE

BRYANT, Michael (b 1928) English actor AAS, WWT/14-16

BRYANT, Nana (d 1955 [67]) American actress TW/3, 12

BRYANT, Neil [Cornelius A. O'Brien] (1835-1902) minstrel CDP

BRYANT, Robin (d 1976 [50]) performer BP/60*

BRYANT, Sam (1855-1948) actor, showboat manager SR

BRYANT, Mrs. W. see Barlette, Sophie

BRYANT, Willie (d 1964 [56]) actor BE*, BP/48*

BRYARS, Mr. (fl 1723-24) boxkeeper BD

BRYCE, Edward (b 1921) American actor TW/4-16

BRYDEN, Bill (b 1942) Scottish director, dramatist WWT/16

BRYDEN, Ronald (b 1927) English critic AAS, WWT/15-16

BRYDGE, Matilda [Mrs. T. B. Brydge] (d 1882) EA/83*

BRYDGE, T. B. (d 1917) music-hall performer EA/18*

BRYDGE, Mrs. T. B. see Brydge, Matilda

BRYDON, W. B. (b 1933) English actor TW/24-25, 29-30

BRYDONE, Alfred [Alfred Brydone Boak] (1863-1920) Scottish actor GRB/1-4, WWT/1-3

BRYER, Vera (1905-67) English actress, singer TW/24, WWT/7-9

BRYER, William Frederick see Edouin, Willie

BRYERS, Mr. (fl 1716) boxkeeper BD

BRYGGMAN, Larry (b 1938) American actor TW/25-27, 30

BRYLAWSKI, Fulton (d 1973 [88]) lawyer BP/58*

BRYNING, John (b 1913) English actor WWT/10-14

BRYNNER, Yul (b 1917) Japanese/Swiss actor, director CB, ES, TW/7-15

BRYSON, Lyman Lloyd (b 1888) American dramatist CB

BRYTON, Frederick (d 1902) American actor CDP, SR

BUBB, [Elizabeth?] (fl 1723-27) dresser BD

BUBB, George (d 1878 [55]) EA/79*

BUBBLES, John (b 1902) American performer, actor TW/24

BUCALOSSI, Brigata (d 1924) composer, conductor BE*, WWT/14*

BUCALOSSI, Ernest (d 1933 [69]) composer, conductor BE*, WWT/14*

BUCALOSSI, Procida (d 1918 [86]) composer, conductor BE*, WWT/14*

BUCHAN, Mr. (d 1800) watchman, sweeper BD

BUCHAN, Mrs. (fl 1789-94) dresser BD

BUCHAN, Annabelle Whitford (d 1961 [83]) performer BE*

BUCHAN, D. B. see Young, D. B.

BUCHANAN, Mr. (fl 1724) actor BD

BUCHANAN, Mrs. Charles [Elizabeth] (d 1736) actress BD, DD

BUCHANAN, Charles L. (d 1962 [77]) critic BE*

BUCHANAN, Elizabeth see Buchanan, Mrs. Charles

BUCHANAN, George (1506-82) Scottish dramatist ES

BUCHANAN, Mrs. J. [née Sarah Vivash] (d 1871) actress EA/72*

BUCHANAN, Jack (1890-1957) Scottish actor, producer, manager AAS, DNB, ES, TW/4-7, 14, WWT/4-12, WWW/5

BUCHANAN, McKean (1823-72) American actor CDP, DD, HAS, SR

BUCHANAN, Margaret (d 1970) performer BP/55*

BUCHANAN, Maud actress WWT/4-5

BUCHANAN, Robert actor, manager SR

BUCHANAN, Robert Williams (1841-1901) English dramatist DD, DNB, HP, SR, WWW/1

BUCHANAN, Thompson (1877-1937) American dramatist SR, WWM, WWT/1-8

BUCHANAN, Virginia Ellen (1846/66-1931) American actress CDP, HAS

BUCHANAN, Walter John see Buchanan, Jack

BUCHANAN, William Insco (1852-1909) American manager DAB

BUCHHOLZ, Horst (b 1933) German actor BE, CB, TW/16-19

BUCHINGER, Mr. (fl 1735) flutist BD

BUCHINGER, Mathew see Buckinger, Matthew

BUCHMAN, Sidney (d 1975 [73]) dramatist BP/60*

BUCHNER, Georg (1813-37) German dramatist COC, NTH, OC/1-3, PDT

BUCHS, Julio (d 1973 [46]) producer/director/choreographer BP/57*

BUCHTRUP, Bjarne (b 1942) Danish actor TW/30

BUCHWALD, Julius (d 1970 [61]) composer/lyricist BP/55*

BUCK, [Mr. ?] (fl 1760-61) doorkeeper BD

BUCK, [Mr. ?] (fl 1761) property man BD

BUCK, David (b 1936) English actor WWT/15-16

BUCK, Dudley (d 1909) composer, organist EA/10*

BUCK, Mrs. Frank Pacey see Sale, Sara

BUCK, Gene (1885-1957) American librettist, producer, songwriter NTH, SR, TW/13

BUCK, Sir George (d 1622) master of the Revels COC, DD, OC/3

BUCK, Henry (d 1879) master of ceremonies EA/81*

BUCK, Inez (d 1957 [67]) actress TW/14

BUCK, Paul (fl 1592) dramatist CP/2-3 [see also: Bucke, Paul]

BUCK, Pearl S. (1892-1973) American writer BE

BUCK, Timothy (d 1741) swordsman, actor BD

BUCK, William (d 1777) actor BD

BUCKE, Charles (1781-1846) English dramatist DD, DNB

BUCKE, Paul (fl 1580-99) actor DA [see also; Buck, Paul]

BUCKEREDGE, Edward (fl 1594) actor DA

BUCKHAM, Bernard (1882-1963) English critic WWT/7-11, WWW/6

BUCKHAM, William (d 1887 [35]) drummer EA/88*

BUCKHOLTZ, Mr. (fl 1791-1801) music copyist BD

BUCKHURST, Lord see Sackville, Thomas

BUCKINGER, Miss (fl 1761-69) dancer BD

BUCKINGER, Joseph (fl 1784-1805) musician BD

BUCKINGER, Matthew (b 1674) German musician, painter, inventor, freak BD, CDP

BUCKINGHAM, Fannie Louise (fl 1877) actress CDP, SR

BUCKINGHAM, George Villiers, 2nd Duke of (1628-87) English dramatist CDP, COC, CP/1-3, DD, DNB, ES, GT, HP, OC/1-3, PDT

BUCKINGHAM, James (fl 1784-94) singer BD

BUCKINGHAM, John Sheffield, Duke of (1648-1721) English dramatist CP/1-3, DD, DNB, MH

BUCKINGHAM, Leicester Silk (1825-67) English dramatist DD, DNB

BUCKINGHAM, Robert (d 1895)
box office keeper EA/96*
BUCKINGHAM, Thomas (d 1847
[52]) actor, singer CDP
BUCKLAND, George singer
CDP
BUCKLAND, George (fl 1773)
musician BD
BUCKLAND, George (d 1884
[63]) musical entertainer
EA/85*
BUCKLAND, Mrs. John W.
[Kate Horn] (c. 1826-96)
actress CDP, HAS, SR
BUCKLAW, Alfred actor DD,
EA/95, WWT/2-6
BUCKLER, Mrs. (fl 1789-97)
actress BD
BUCKLER, Augustin (fl 1682)
trumpeter BD
BUCKLER, Edward (fl c. 1677?)
singer BD
BUCKLER, Hugh C. (d 1936
[66]) English actor WWT/
4-8
BUCKLER, John (d 1936 [40])
English actor BE*, BP/
21*
BUCKLER, Percy (d 1897)
actor EA/98*
BUCKLER, Mrs. Sidney see
Fairbrother, Sydney
BUCKLES, Ann American
actress TW/8, 30
BUCKLEY, Mr. (fl 1742) door-
keeper BD
BUCKLEY, Annie (1872-1916)
American actress SR, WWS
BUCKLEY, Betty (b 1947) Amer-
ican actress TW/25-27,
29-30
BUCKLEY, Charles T. (d 1920)
manager BE*, BP/5*
BUCKLEY, E. J. (fl 1870s)
actor SR
BUCKLEY, Elizabeth see
Buckley, Mrs. Richard
BUCKLEY, Floyd (d 1956 [82])
American actor TW/13
BUCKLEY, Frank (d 1909)
musical clown EA/10*
BUCKLEY, F. Rawson (1866-
1943) English actor GRB/1
BUCKLEY, Frederick [Master
Ole Bull] (1833-64) English
minstrel, composer, violin-
ist CDP, HAS
BUCKLEY, George (d 1884 [37])

minstrel EA/85*
BUCKLEY, George Swayne ["Young
Sweeney"] (1829-79) English
minstrel, banjoist CDP, HAS
BUCKLEY, Hal (b 1937) American
actor TW/23
BUCKLEY, J. (d 1867 [27]) comic
singer EA/68*
BUCKLEY, James K. [James
Burke] (1803-72) minstrel
CDP
BUCKLEY, Joe [Timothy Clancy]
(1835-84) minstrel CDP
BUCKLEY, Joe (d 1897) minstrel
comedian EA/98*
BUCKLEY, John (d 1805) musician
BD
BUCKLEY, John William (d 1869
[45]) box bookkeeper EA/70*
BUCKLEY, Kay (b 1921) American
actress TW/4
BUCKLEY, May [May Uhl] (b 1875)
American actress GRB/4,
WWS, WWA/5, WWT/1-11
BUCKLEY, R. Bishop [J. C.
Rainer] (1826-67) American
minstrel CDP, HAS
BUCKLEY, Richard (fl 1694-1716)
actor BD
BUCKLEY, Mrs. Richard [Eliza-
beth] (fl 1694-1700) actress
BD
BUCKLEY, [Thomas?] (fl 1784?-
94) violoncellist BD
BUCKLEY, Tim (d 1975 [28]) per-
former BP/60*
BUCKLEY, Mrs. W. H. [née
Fanny Moore] (d 1879 [34])
actress? EA/80*
BUCKLEY, William (d 1875 [35])
musician EA/76*
BUCKLEY, William ["Billy"] (d
1894) minstrel CDP
BUCKMAN, Rosina (d 1948) New
Zealand singer WWW/4
BUCKMASTER, John (b 1915)
English actor TW/3-8, WWT/
9-12
BUCKNALL, H. W. (d 1895 [33])
circus manager EA/96*
BUCKNALL, Thomas (fl 1739-46?)
musician BD
BUCKSTONE, Isabella see
Copeland, Isabella
BUCKSTONE, John Baldwin (1802-
79) English dramatist, actor,
manager CDP, COC, DD,
DNB, EA/68, ES, HAS,

OAA/1-2, OC/1-3, OX, SR, WWA/H

BUCKSTONE, Mrs. John Baldwin see Copeland, Isabella

BUCKSTONE, John Copeland (1858-1924) English actor DD, EA/96, GRB/3-4, OAA/2, WWT/1-4

BUCKSTONE, Lucy Isabella (1859-93) actress CDP, DD, DP, OAA/1-2

BUCKSTONE, Rowland (1860-1922) English actor GRB/3-4, WWS, WWT/1-4

BUCKTON, Florence (b 1893) English actress WWT/5-8

BUCKY, Frida Sarsen (d 1974) composer/lyricist BP/59*

BUD, Mrs. (fl 1697-1701) actress BD

BUDD, Mrs. (d 1894) EA/95*

BUDD, Master (fl c. 1745-50) singer BD

BUDD, Benjamin Richard (fl 1794) violinist, composer BD

BUDD, George see Langley, Charles

BUDD, Herbert (d 1913 [51]) EA/14*

BUDD, Jake (d 1888) American actor EA/89*

BUDD, Nelson H. (d 1974 [74]) critic BP/59*

BUDD, Norman (b 1914) English actor TW/24

BUDD, Thomas (b c. 1751) English musician BD

BUDD, Thomas (c. 1761-89) musician BD

BUDD, Thomas (fl 1774-94?) musician BD

BUDGELL, Anne Eustace (c. 1726-c. 55) actress, singer BD

BUDWORTH, James H. (b 1831) American minstrel HAS

BUEHLER, Arthur (d 1962 [68]) actor BE*

BUER, Minnie (d 1883 [25]) EA/84*

BUETT, Hugh (fl 1651-62) musician BD

BUFANO, Remo (1894-1948) Italian/American marionettist ES

"BUFFALO BILL" see Cody, William Frederick

BUFFETT, Kenny (b 1926) American actor TW/4

BUFFINGTON, Adele (d 1973 [73]) dramatist BP/58*

BUFFON, [Mons.?] (fl 1734-35) actor BD

BUFMAN, Zev (b 1930) Israeli producer, actor BE, WWT/15-16

BUFTON, Eleanor [Mrs. Arthur Swanborough] (1840-93) Welsh actress CDP, DD, DNB, ES, OAA/1-2

BUFTON, Esther (d 1883 [71]) EA/84*

BUGBY, John (fl 1401) grammar master of the children of the Chapel Royal DA

"BUG-NOSE" (fl 1754) dancer BD

BUGIANI, Sig. (fl 1753-54) dancer BD

BUGIANI, Elizabetta (fl 1752-57) dancer BD

BUHER, Mr. (fl 1683) actor BD

BUHLER, Richard (d 1925 [48]) American actor BE*, BP/9*

BUISLAY FAMILY, The gymnasts, pantomimists HAS

BUIST, W[alter] Scott (b 1860) English actor DD, EA/97, GRB/3-4, WWT/1-3

BUJONES, Fernando (b 1955) American dancer CB

BUKA, Donald (b 1921) American actor TW/1-6, 22-23, 27

BUKLANK, Alexander (fl 1624) musician? DA

BULFINCH, Charles (1763-1844) architect BE*

BULGAKOV, Barbara Russian actress BE

BULGAKOV, Leo (1889-1948) Russian actor, producer NTH, TW/5, WWT/7-10

BULGAKOV, Mikhael Afanaseyev (1891-1940) Russian dramatist COC, OC/1-3

BULGER, Harry (1872-1926) actor, singer CDP, SR

BULIFANT, Joyce (b 1938) American actress TW/15-18, 23

BULING, Hans (fl 1670) Dutch mountebank, actor BD, CDP

BULKELEY, Mrs. (fl 1769) equestrienne BD

BULKELY, Mr. (fl 1742-43) actor BD

BULKLEY, Mr. (fl 1709) musician

BD
BULKLEY, Mr. (fl 1713)
musician? BD
BULKLEY, George (d 1784)
violinist BD
BULKLEY, Mrs. George [Mary
Wilford; Mrs. Ebenezer Bar-
risford] (1748-92) English
actress, dancer BD, CDP,
DD, TD/1-2
BULL, Mr. (fl 1797) actor BD
BULL, Charles (d 1890) drama-
tist EA/91*
BULL, George (d 1916) jour-
nalist EA/17*, WWT/14*
BULL, John (fl 1572-86) actor,
musician DA
BULL, Master Ole see Buck-
ley, Frederick
BULL, Ole Bornemann (1810-
80) Norwegian violinist CDP,
ES, HAS, HJD, SR
BULL, Peter (b 1912) English
actor, producer AAS, BE,
TW/20, 22-24, WWT/11-15
BULL, Thomas (fl 1579-80)
actor DA
BULL, Thomas (fl 1794) musi-
cian BD
BULL, William (fl 1666-1700)
trumpeter, instrument maker
BD
BULLARD, John (fl 1690-92)
kettledrummer BD
BULLBRICK, George (fl 1750-57)
actor, dancer BD
BULLEN, Arthur Henry (fl
1881-87) scholar DD
BULLEN, Julia [Mrs. George
Lewis] (d 1891) burlesque
and music-hall artist EA/93*
BULLER, Lady Yarde eques-
trienne CDP
BULLEY, Moses (d 1880 [22])
trapezist EA/81*
BULLIN, G. W. (d 1890 [38])
advance agent EA/91*
BULLINS, Ed. (b 1935) American dramatist CD, CH, WWT/
16
BULLOCH, John (1805-82)
scholar DNB
BULLOCH, John Malcolm (1867-
1938) Scottish critic GRB/
1-4, WWT/1-8, WWW/3
BULLOCK, Mrs. (d 1890) EA/91*
BULLOCK, Miss (fl 1777-78)
dancer BD

BULLOCK, Christopher (c. 1690-
1722) English actor, dramatist
BD, CP/1-3, DD, DNB, TD/
1-2
BULLOCK, Mrs. Christopher
[Jane Rogers] (d 1739) English
actress BD, DD, TD/2
BULLOCK, Elizabeth Villiers see
Villiers, Lizzie
BULLOCK, Harriet see Dyer,
Mrs. Michael
BULLOCK, Henrietta Maria [Mrs.
John Ogden] (fl 1719-48?)
dancer, actress BD
BULLOCK, Henry C. (d 1893 [37])
EA/94*
BULLOCK, Hildebrand (d 1733)
English actor BD
BULLOCK, Mrs. Hildebrand [Ann
Russell] (fl 1714-48) dancer
BD
BULLOCK, Phoebe (d 1888) EA/
89*
BULLOCK, W. (d 1882) marionet-
tist EA/83*
BULLOCK, William (c. 1667-1742)
English actor, booth manager
BD, CDP, DD, DNB
BULLOCK, William (d 1733 [c. 83])
English actor BD
BULLOUGH, Mrs. John see
Darrell, Maudi
BULLS, Mr. (fl 1782) actor BD
"BULL SPEAKER" see Amner,
Ralph
BULMER, Mr. (fl 1772-74)
scourer BD
BULOFF, Joseph (b 1907) Lithuan-
ian actor, director BE, TW/
1-3, 6-8, 15, 29, WWT/12-16
BULOID, Elizabeth see Abbott,
Mrs. William
BULOS, Yusef (b 1940) Palestinian
actor TW/28
BULTEEL, John (d 1669) dramatist
GT
BULWER-LYTTON, Edward see
Lytton, Edward George Earle
Lytton Bulwer-Lytton, Lord
BUMBRY, Grace Ann (b 1937)
American singer CB
BUNCE, Alan (d 1965 [62]) Amer-
ican actor BE, TW/14-15,
18, 21, WWT/8-10
BUNCE, Oliver Bell (1828-90)
American dramatist HJD
BUNCH, Boyd (d 1969) composer/
lyricist BP/53*

BUNDY, Robert M. (d 1974)
agent BP/59*
BUNKER, Ralph (d 1966 [77])
actor TW/22
BUNN, Alfred (1798-1860)
English manager CDP,
DD, DNB, ES, HAS, OC/
1-3
BUNN, Margaret Agnes Somer-
ville (1799-1883) English
actress BS, CDP, DD,
DNB, OC/2-3, OX
BUNNAGE, Avis English actress
AAS, WWT/14-16
BUNNING, Herbert (1863-1937)
English composer, conductor
GRB/1-4, WWW/3
BUNNY, John (1863-1915) Amer-
ican actor ES, SR
BUNSBY, Jack see Vanden-
burgh, Theodore H.
BUNSTON, Herbert (1870-1935)
English actor WWT/4-7
BUNT, George (b 1942) Ameri-
can actor TW/25
BUNTEN, Margaret Edith see
Aitken, Margaret Edith
BUNTH, H. see Sutton, Charles
BUNTING, Emma actress SR
BUNTLINE, Ned actor, drama-
tist, manager SR
BUNYAN, John (1628-88) English
writer ES, NTH
BUR, Mr. (fl 1742) actor BD
BURANI, Michelette (d 1957
[73]) actress TW/14
BURBAGE, Mr. (fl 1794) singer
BD
BURBAGE, Cuthbert (c. 1566-
1636) English actor DA, ES,
NTH, OC/1-3
BURBAGE, James (c. 1530-97)
English actor COC, DA, DD,
DNB, ES, HP, NTH, OC/
1-3
BURBAGE, Richard (c. 1567-
1619) English actor CDP,
COC, DA, DD, DNB, ES,
GT, HP, NTH, OC/1-3, PDT
BURBECK, Frank (1857-1930)
American actor SR, WWM
BURBIDGE, Douglas (1895-1959)
English actor WWT/5-10
BURBRIDGE, Edward scene de-
signer WWT/16
BURCH, Mr. (fl 1708) dresser
BD
BURCH, John George (d 1886

[24]) gymnast EA/87*
BURCHARD, Pepin (b 1775) Amer-
ican circus performer & mana-
ger SR
BURCHELL, Clara [Mrs. J. C.
Smith] (d 1911 [78]) actress
EA/12*
BURCHETT, Mr. (fl 1794) singer?
BD
BURCHILL, William (d 1930) Eng-
lish actor, business manager,
producer GRB/1-2, WWT/2-6
BURDE, John (fl 1554) actor DA
BURDE, Simon (fl 1554) actor
DA
BURDEN, Hugh (b 1913) English
actor, dramatist AAS, WWT/
10-16
BURDEN, Jahaziel (fl 1794) singer
BD
BURDEN, John Jabez (fl 1794)
singer BD
BURDEN, Kitty [nêe White] (fl
1757-83) actress, singer BD,
GT, TD/1-2
BURDEN, W. (fl 1768-94) actor,
singer BD
BURDETT, Miss see Belfille,
Mrs.
BURDETT, A. H. (d 1910) mana-
ger EA/11*
BURDETT, Frank (d 1903 [62])
property master EA/04*
BURDETT, James (fl 1794) instru-
mentalist, singer? BD
BURDETT, Osbert (1885-1936)
English dramatist WWW/3
BURDETTE, Harry (d 1918) EA/
19*
BURDETTE, Henry (d 1903 [36])
actor? EA/04*
BURDON, Mr. (fl 1795-1806?)
singer BD
BURDON, Albert (b 1900) English
actor WWT/8-11
BUREAU, Joseph Grêgoir (fl 1749)
musician BD
BURELL, Mr. (fl 1778) pit & box
office keeper BD
BURETTE, Pauline see Nanton,
Mrs. Lewis
BURFORD, Mr. (fl 1670-72)
actor, dancer BD
BURFORD, Charles Henry (d 1899
[77]) actor EA/00*
BURFORD, Robert (d 1861 [70])
artist, proprietor EA/72*
BURGANI, Mr. (fl 1786-87) house

servant? BD
BURGE, James (b 1943) Amer-
ican actor TW/26
BURGE, Robert (d 1901 [55])
proprietor, manager EA/02*
BURGE, Mrs. S. A. (d 1901
[56]) proprietor EA/02*
BURGE, Stuart (b 1918) Eng-
lish actor, director WWT/
14-16
BURGEN, Henry (fl 1667-70)
scene keeper BD
BURGES, Sir James Bland (b
1752) English dramatist
CP/3
BURGES, Robert (d 1559) actor
DA
BURGESS, Mr. (fl 1852-65)
actor HAS
BURGESS, Col. minstrel,
manager SR
BURGESS, Master (fl 1738-39)
actor BD
BURGESS, Master (fl 1789-90)
house servant BD
BURGESS, Mrs. (fl 1780) drama-
tist CP/2-3, DD, GT, TD/
1-2
BURGESS, Anthony (b 1917)
English writer CB
BURGESS, Charles Frederick
see Almonte, Charlie
BURGESS, Colin ["Cool Burgess"]
(1840-1905) minstrel, manager
CDP
BURGESS, Earl actor, manager
SR
BURGESS, [Elizabeth?] (fl 1735-
42) actress BD
BURGESS, Fred (d 1893 [66])
minstrel CDP
BURGESS, Mrs. Frederick (d
1882) EA/83*
BURGESS, Hazel (d 1973 [63])
performer BP/58*
BURGESS, Henry (d 1765)
musician BD
BURGESS, Henry (fl 1738-65)
musician, composer BD
BURGESS, Mr. J. (d 1868 [40])
proprietor EA/69*
BURGESS, John (fl 1794) singer
BD
BURGESS, Lydia (d 1887 [81])
EA/88*
BURGESS, Neil (1846/51?-1910)
American actor CDP, DAB,
DD, PP/1, SR, WWS

BURGESS, Walter (b 1934) Cana-
dian actor TW/15
BURGESS, William (d 1871 [35])
comedian EA/72*
BURGESS, William see Almonte,
William
BURGESSE, Charles (fl 1686)
trumpeter BD
BURGESSE, Robert (fl 1662-69)
trumpeter BD
BURGETTE, William L. (d 1976
[64]) performer BP/60*
BURGHALL, J. E. (fl 1778-97)
actor, fencing & dancing master
BD
BURGHCLERE, Lord see Gard-
ner, Herbert
BURGHER, Fairfax (1895/1908-
1965) American actor TW/11-
13
BURGHERSH, Lord (1784-1859)
English composer ES
BURGHOFF, Gary (b 1943) Amer-
ican actor TW/23-24
BURGIS, Mrs. (fl 1740-47?) house
servant? BD
BURGIS, Kathleen (b 1907) English
actress, singer WWT/7-9
BURGOYNE, Mr. (d 1895) EA/96*
BURGOYNE, Mrs. E. A. (d 1916)
EA/17*
BURGOYNE, John (1722-92) Eng-
lish dramatist CDP, CP/2-3,
DD, DNB, EAP, ES, GT,
HJD, HP, TD/1-2
BURGOYNE, Virginia see
Rizareli, Virginia
BURIAN, Jarka M. (b 1927) Amer-
ican educator, director, actor
BE
BURK, Amy (b 1944) American
actress TW/26
BURK, John Daly (c. 1775-1808)
Irish/American dramatist DAB,
EAP, ES, HJD, RJ
BURKE, Mr. (fl 1751-52) house
servant? BD
BURKE, Mr. (fl 1765-77) dresser
BD
BURKE, Mr. (fl 1797-1807) house
servant? BD
BURKE, Miss (fl 1793) Irish
dramatist CP/3
BURKE, Alfred (b 1918) English
actor WWT/16
BURKE, Billie (1885-1970) Ameri-
can actress AAS, BE, COC,
ES, GRB/1-4, SR, TW/2-16,

26, WWA/5, WWM, WWS,
WWT/1-14
BURKE, Bonnie (d 1971 [71])
performer BP/56*
BURKE, Charles A. (1822?-54?)
American singer, composer
CDP, HAS
BURKE, Mrs. Charles A. [Mar-
garet Murcoyne] (1818-49)
American actress HAS
BURKE, Mrs. Charles A., II
actress HAS
BURKE, Charles Saint Thomas
(1822-54) American actor,
dramatist CDP, COC, DAB,
DD, HAS, OC/3, SR, WWA/H
BURKE, Cornelius G. (d 1973
[70]) critic BP/57*
BURKE, Daniel (1867-1943)
dancer SR
BURKE, David (b 1934) English
actor WWT/16
BURKE, Edwin (b 1889) Ameri-
can dramatist, actor ES,
SR
BURKE, Georgia (b 1906/08)
American actress BE, TW/
1-3, 6-9, 22
BURKE, Ione (fl 1870) actress
CDP, DD, HAS
BURKE, James (d 1968) per-
former BP/52*
BURKE, James see Buckley,
James K.
BURKE, John D. (fl 1797) writer
DD
BURKE, John J. (fl c. 1895)
actor, singer CDP, SR
BURKE, John M. (d 1880 [30])
Irish actor, singer, com-
poser CDP
BURKE, Johnny (1908-64) Amer-
ican composer, lyricist, pro-
ducer, publisher BE
BURKE, Joseph ["The Irish
Roscius"] (b 1818) Irish
actor, violinist CDP, DD,
HAS, SR
BURKE, Kevin (d 1969 [25])
composer/lyricist BP/54*
BURKE, Margaret (1818-49)
actress CDP
BURKE, Marie (b 1894) Eng-
lish actress, singer AAS,
WWT/6-15
BURKE, Maurice (b 1902) Amer-
ican actor, singer TW/1-3
BURKE, Myra (d 1944 [79])

actress BE*, WWT/14*
BURKE, Patricia (b 1917) Italian
actress WWT/8-16
BURKE, Thomas (d 1825) English
actor CDP, DD, HAS
BURKE, Mrs. Thomas see
Jefferson, Mrs. Joseph
BURKE, Tobias John (d 1878 [30])
actor EA/79*
BURKE, Tom (1890-1969) English
actor, singer WWT/6-11
BURKE, W. (fl 1806) dramatist
CP/3
BURKE, W. (fl 1832) actor? HAS
BURKE, Walter actor TW/1-3,
7-8, 13
BURKE, W. E. (d 1906 [63])
music-hall performer EA/07*
BURKE, William (d 1970 [74])
executive BP/54*
BURKE, William E. clown CDP
BURKE, William J. (1856-1915)
minstrel SR
BURKHARDT, Adison (fl 1911)
dramatist SR
BURKHEAD, Henry (fl 1641) Eng-
lish dramatist CP/1-3, GT
BURKITT, Thomas (fl 1776-90)
singer BD
BURKS, Donnie [or Donny] Ameri-
can actor TW/24-26, 30
BURLEIGH, John (fl 1729) per-
former? BD
BURLES, W. J. (d 1873) actor
EA/74*
BURLEY, Johnny see Butterly,
John Thomas
BURLING, Mr. (fl 1785-88) singer
BD
BURLINGHAME, Lloyd designer
WWT/16
BURLINGTON, Mr. (fl 1784) singer
BD
BURMAN, Borah Z. (d 1964 [34])
critic BP/49*
BURMAN, S. D. (d 1975 [76])
composer/lyricist BP/60*
BURME, Jef Van (d 1965 [58])
composer/lyricist BP/49*
BURN, Miss (fl 1759) actress,
dancer BD
BURNABY, Charles (fl 1700-03)
dramatist CP/1-3, GT
BURNABY, G. Davy (1881-1949)
English actor, dramatist COC,
WWT/4-10, WWW/4
BURNAND, Sir Francis Cowley
(1836-1917) English dramatist,

actor CDP, DD, DNB,
EA/68, ES, GRB/1-4, HP,
OC/1-3, PDT, SR, WWM,
WWT/1-3, WWW/2
BURNAND, Mrs. F[rancis]
C[owley; Cecilia Ranoe] (d
1870 [27]) EA/71*
BURNAND, Lily (fl 1893) singer
CDP
BURNARD, Fred (d 1912) EA/
13*
BURNARD, Joseph (fl 1794)
singer? BD
BURNARD, Thomas (fl 1739)
musician BD
BURNE, Arthur (1873-1945)
English actor GRB/1,
WWT/9
BURNE, Nancy (1912-54) English
actress, dancer, singer
WWT/9-11
BURNEL, Henry (fl 1641) Irish?
dramatist CP/1-3, DNB,
FGF, GT
BURNELL, Mr. (fl 1719) box-
keeper BD
BURNELL, Buster (d 1964 [41])
dancer, choreographer BE*
BURNELL, Harry [Henry Wil-
liams Jee] (d 1906 [24])
music-hall performer EA/
07*
BURNELL, Henry see Burnel,
Henry
BURNELL, William see Arling-
ton, William
BURNET, Mrs. (fl 1749) actress
BD
BURNET, Dana (d 1962 [74])
dramatist BE*
BURNET, [Richard?] (fl 1728-
55?) actor, dancer BD
BURNET, Mrs. Walter
Randall, Pollie
BURNETT, Mr. (fl 1772-81)
actor BD
BURNETT, Mrs. (fl 1772)
actress BD
BURNETT, Miss (fl 1783-1822)
singer, actress BD
BURNETT, Ada singer, actress
CDP
BURNETT, Al (d 1973 [67])
performer BP/57*
BURNETT, Alfred (1824-84)
American humorist CDP,
HAS
BURNETT, Mrs. Arnold see

Pearce, Lizzie
BURNETT, Carol (b 1935) Ameri-
can actress, comedienne, singer
BE, CB, ES, TW/16-21, WWT/
14-16
BURNETT, Charles A. (d 1974
[86]) performer BP/59*
BURNETT, Chester A. (d 1976
[65]) performer BP/60*
BURNETT, Elizabeth (d 1903)
EA/04*
BURNETT, Frances Hodgson [Mrs.
Stephen Townsend] (1849-1924)
English dramatist DD, ES,
GRB/2-4, HJD, HP, SR,
WWA/1, WWM, WWS, WWT/
1-4, WWW/2
BURNETT, Gertrude actress
GRB/1-4
BURNETT, Mr. H. (d 1893 [81])
singer EA/94*
BURNETT, Henry (fl 1607) actor
DA
BURNETT, James G. (1819-70)
comedian CDP
BURNETT, J. N. (d 1916) EA/17*
BURNETT, Joan (d 1908) English
actress GRB/1-4
BURNETT, J. P. (d 1917 [71])
dramatist, actor DD
BURNETT, Mrs. J. P. see
Lee, Jennie
BURNETT, Olive American actress
TW/25
BURNETT, Sally [Sarah A. John-
son] (d 1868) actress? HAS
BURNETT, William (c. 1742-c. 97)
kettledrummer BD
BURNETT, Mrs. [William?] (d
c. 1822?) actress, singer BD
BURNETTE, Amy (fl 1871-80)
English actress OAA/1-2
BURNETTE, Clarence (d 1906)
actor EA/07*, WWT/14*
BURNETTE, George Charles see
Byrne, Gerald
BURNEY, Mr. (fl 1718-31) actor
BD
BURNEY, Mr. (fl 1730) harpsi-
chordist BD
BURNEY, Miss [Mrs. W. Holman]
(d 1903) actress EA/04*
BURNEY, Charles (1726-1814)
English organist, composer,
historian BD, CDP, CP/2-3,
ES, GT
BURNEY, Charles Rousseau (1747-
1819) English harpsichordist BD

BURNEY, Mrs. Charles Rousseau [Esther Burney] (1749-
1832) English harpsichordist
BD

BURNEY, Estelle (fl 1891)
actress, dramatist CDP, DD

BURNEY, Esther see Burney,
Mrs. Charles Rousseau

BURNEY, Fanny [Mme. D'Arblay]
(1752-1840) English dramatist
CP/3, DD

BURNEY, Thomas (fl 1726-32)
dancer, dancing master BD

BURNHAM, Lord (d 1916 [82])
newspaper proprietor EA/
17*

BURNHAM, Barbara (b 1900)
English dramatist WWT/
9-11

BURNHAM, Charles C. (1858-
1938) American manager,
producer WWM, SR

BURNHAM, John Price see
Barnes, Price

BURNIDGE, George see
Bernage, George

BURNLEIGH, Lena actress
WWT/2-4

BURNLEY, Mr. (fl 1725-32)
house servant? BD

BURNLEY, Curtis [Mrs. Chris-
tian E. Railing] (b 1880)
American impersonator
WWM

BURNLEY, Fred (d 1975 [41])
producer/director/choreog-
rapher BP/60*

BURNOT, Agnes (d 1893 [51])
EA/94*

BURNOT, Walter (d 1905)
dramatist, songwriter EA/
06*

BURNS, Alfred (d 1874 [34])
actor? EA/75*

BURNS, Anne K. (d 1968 [82])
dramatist BP/53*

BURNS, Bart (b 1918) American actor TW/8

BURNS, Bob (1890-1956) American comedian TW/12, WWA/
3

BURNS, Catherine (b 1945)
American actress TW/24,
26

"BURNS, Corrie" see Righton,
Edward

BURNS, David (1902-71) American actor AAS, BE, TW/5-9,

13-27, WWA/5, WWT/9-15

BURNS, Edward (d 1970) performer BP/55*

BURNS, Eileen American actress
TW/29

BURNS, George (b 1896) American
comedian CB, ES

BURNS, Georgina (fl 1878) singer
CDP

BURNS, James (d 1796) ventriloquist BD, CDP

BURNS, J. C. (d 1889) American
singer, dancer EA/90*

BURNS, Jerry (d 1962 [73]) performer BE*

BURNS, John (d 1894 [35]) manager EA/95*

BURNS, Nat (d 1962 [75]) American actor TW/19

BURNS, Noel (d 1966 [67]) singer
TW/23

BURNS, Orney (d 1838) circus
performer HAS

BURNS, Ralph (b 1922) American
orchestrator BE

BURNS, Robert Emmett (d 1974
[62]) agent BP/59*

BURNS, Thomas (d 1893 [31])
high diver EA/98*

BURNSIDE, Jean (fl 1873) actress, dramatist, manager
CDP

BURNSIDE, Mortimer B. (d 1971
[81]) investor BP/56*

BURNSIDE, R. H. (1870-1952)
English/American dramatist,
director NTH, SR, WWT/4-12

BURNSIDE, Tom (d 1899) manager
EA/00*

BURNSIDE, William, Jr. (d 1976
[49]) performer BP/60*

BURNUM, Mr. (fl 1729) actor
BD

BURONI, Signora (fl 1777) singer
BD

BURR, Mrs. (fl 1694) singer BD

BURR, Ann[e] (b 1920) American
actress TW/1-3, 9, WWT/
11-13

BURR, Bessie Fisher (d 1974
[82]) performer BP/59*

BURR, Courtney (d 1961 [70])
producer TW/18

BURR, Courtney (b 1948) American actor TW/30

BURR, Donald (b 1907) American
actor, director BE

BURR, Lonnie (b 1943) American

actor TW/30
BURR, Marion (d 1976 [67])
performer BP/60*
BURR, Raymond William
Stacy (b 1917) Canadian
actor CB, ES
BURR, Robert American actor
TW/20-24, 27-28, WWT/16
BURR, Simon (fl 1654-71)
musician BD
BURRA, Edward (b 1905)
English scene designer ES
BURRAGE, Alfred McLelland
(1889-1956) English drama-
tist WWW/5
BURRELL, Miss (b 1795)
singer, actress CDP
BURRELL, Daisy (b 1893)
English actress, singer
WWT/4-6
BURRELL, Fred (b 1936)
American actor TW/23-24
BURRELL, John (1910-72) Eng-
lish director, producer
AAS, ES, TW/29, WWT/
10-13
BURRELL, Pamela (b 1945)
American actress TW/24
BURRELL, Sheila (b 1922)
English actress AAS,
WWT/11-16
BURRELL, Sophia, Lady (1750?-
1882) English dramatist CP/
3, DNB
BURRILL, Ena (b 1908) Uru-
guayan actress WWT/8-13
BURRIS, Robert (d 1907)
scene artist EA/08*,
GRB/3*
BURRIS-MEYER, Harold (b 1902)
American director, educator,
consultant BE
BURROUGHES, Mr. (fl 1646)
dramatist CP/2-3, FGF, GT
BURROUGHS, Mr. (fl 1771-81)
house servant BD
BURROUGHS, Mrs. (fl 1671-73)
actress BD
BURROUGHS, Mrs. see Emery,
Miss
BURROUGHS, Claud de Blenau
(1848-76) American actor
CDP, HAS
BURROUGHS, John (d 1878 [69])
actor EA/80*
BURROUGHS, Judyth (b 1940)
American actress TW/5
BURROUGHS, Marie [Little

Arrington] (1866-1926) American
actress DD, SR, WWA/4,
WWM, WWS
BURROUGHS, Robert C. (b 1923)
American educator BE
BURROUGHS, Watkins (1790?-
1869) English actor, stage
manager, manager CDP, HAS,
SR
BURROUGHS, William F. (d 1898
[58]) actor CDP
BURROW, Robert Samuel see
Faulkner, Robert
BURROWES, James (d 1926 [84])
actor BE*
BURROWS, Mr. (fl 1746) house
servant? BD
BURROWS, Abe (b 1910) American
dramatist, director BE, CB,
CD, ES, HJD, MWD, PDT,
WWT/12-16
BURROWS, Charles (1864-1947)
actor SR
BURROWS, Mrs. Harriett see
Palmerston, Minnie
BURROWS, James (fl 1796-1825)
singer, actor, instrumentalist?
BD
BURROWS, James (1842-1926)
actor SR
BURROWS, John (b 1945) English
dramatist, director, actor
CD
BURROWS, Robert (fl 1794)
singer? BD
BURROWS, Tom (d 1917) EA/18*
BURROWS, Vinie (b 1928) Ameri-
can actress TW/12, 25, 28-
29
BURROWS, William Frederick (d
1894 [34]) music-hall artist
EA/96*
BURRUS, Ron (b 1944) American
actor TW/26
BURRY, Solen (1902-53) Russian
actor TW/2
BURSLEM, Ashworth (d 1969 [55])
critic BP/54*
BURSLEM, Charles (d 1886 [28])
dramatist, journalist EA/87*
BURSTEIN, Mike (b 1945) Ameri-
can actor TW/25-26
BURSTON, Reginald (d 1968)
producer/director/choreographer
BP/52*
BURSTYN, Ellen (b 1932) Ameri-
can actress CB
BURT, Mr. (fl 1745) actor BD

BURT, Mr. (fl 1777-85) clown BD

BURT, Benjamin Hapgood (b 1876) American composer, lyricist WWM

BURT, Cecil (d 1916 [64]) EA/17*

BURT, Frank (b 1862) American manager WWA/4

BURT, Frank A. [Augustus Berek] (d 1964 [82]) performer BE*

BURT, Frederick (d 1943 [67]) American actor BE*, WWT/14*

BURT, Harriet (1885-1935) American actress WWS

BURT, J. Norman (d 1888) EA/89*

BURT, Laura [Mrs. H. B. Stanford] (1875-1952) English actress GRB/3-4, WWM, WWS, WWT/1-7

BURT, Lulu May see Bertram, Helen

BURT, Nicholas (fl c. 1635-90) actor BD, DA, DD

BURT, William P. (d 1955 [88]) actor, director BE*, BP/39*

BURTOFT, [William?] (fl 1781-87) housekeeper, box book-keeper BD

BURTON, Mr. (fl 1722-27) numberer BD

BURTON, Mr. (fl 1792-94) singer BD

BURTON, Mrs. (fl 1722-30) boxkeeper BD

BURTON, Miss (d 1771?) actress BD

BURTON, Anthony (fl 1628) actor DA

BURTON, Charles (d 1897 [64]) transformation dancer EA/98*

BURTON, David (1890-1963) Russian/American director ES

BURTON, Edmund (d 1772) actor BD

BURTON, Edward (d 1896 [72]) actor EA/97*

BURTON, Elizabeth (1751-71) English actress BD

BURTON, F. D. (d 1894 [69]) manager EA/95*

BURTON, Frederick (b 1871)

American actor GRB/3-4, WWT/1-9

BURTON, Frederick Charles (d 1917 [95]) actor EA/18*

BURTON, Frederick Russell (1861-1909) American composer DAB

BURTON, George (d 1784) singer BD

BURTON, Henry D. (d 1895 [52]) comedian EA/96*

BURTON, Mrs. Henry D. see Williams, Emma

BURTON, Henry K. (1886-1947) actor SR

BURTON, Herschell American actor TW/26

BURTON, Jessie singer CDP

BURTON, John English actor GRB/1

BURTON, John (1730-82) English musician, composer BD

BURTON, John (1763-97?) English actor BD, CDP, TD/1-2

BURTON, John (d 1872 [38]) conductor EA/73*

BURTON, Lancelot (fl 1776-86?) actor? house servant? BD

BURTON, Langhorne (1872-1949) English actor GRB/1, WWT/3-7

BURTON, Maud [née Rankin] (d 1911 [49]) actress EA/12*

BURTON, Nellie (d 1868 [19]) actress EA/69*

BURTON, Nelly see Bobadilla, Pepita

BURTON, Percy (1878-1948) English manager, business manager WWT/2-10

BURTON, Philip (b 1904) Welsh director, teacher BE

BURTON, Philippina [Mrs. Hill?] (fl 1770-88?) actress, dramatist BD, CP/2-3

BURTON, Polly [née Kiddie] (d 1911 [42]) actress EA/13*

BURTON, Richard [né Richard Walter Jenkins] (b 1925) Welsh actor AAS, BE, CB, COC, ES, PDT, TW/7-21, WWT/11-16

BURTON, Richard P. see Burton, Percy

BURTON, Robert (fl 1784-1800) proprietor BD

BURTON, Robert (d 1878 [62]) proprietor EA/79*

BURTON, Robert (d 1879 [30])

proprietor EA/80*
BURTON, Robert (d 1955 [46])
actor TW/12
BURTON, Robert J. (d 1965
[51]) executive BP/49*
BURTON, Sarah [Mrs. T. D.
Burton] (d 1882 [41]) EA/83*
BURTON, Sarah (b 1912) English actress TW/3-5
BURTON, Mrs. T. D. see
Burton, Sarah
BURTON, Thomas Bowman (d
1899) EA/00*
BURTON, W. minstrel CDP
BURTON, W. (d 1774) English
comedian CDP
BURTON, Warren (b 1944)
American actor TW/24-26
BURTON, William (fl 1596)
dramatist FGF
BURTON, William (1575-1645)
English dramatist CP/3
BURTON, William (d 1813?)
actor BD
BURTON, Mrs. William E.
see Hill, Jane
BURTON, William Evans (1804-
60) English/American actor,
manager, dramatist CDP,
COC, DAB, DD, DNB, ES,
HAS, HJD, OC/1-3, SR,
WWA/H
BURTON, William H. (1843?-
1926) English actor SR
BURTONYA, Clee (b 1932)
American actor TW/25
BURTT, Mr. (fl 1784) actor
BD
BURTWELL, Frederick (d 1948)
actor BE*, WWT/14*
BURVILLE, Alice (fl 1874-80)
actress, singer DD, OAA/2
BURY, Mons. (fl 1675) musician BD
BURY, Mr. (fl 1720-21) performer? BD
BURY, Miss (fl 1783-89) dancer
BD
BURY, John (b 1925) Welsh designer AAS, ES, WWT/14-16
BURY, Samuel L. (d 1909)
variety agent EA/10*
BUSBY, Amy (d 1957 [85])
American actress TW/14,
SR
BUSBY, James (d 1871 [45])
comic singer EA/72*
BUSBY, John (1755-1838)

English composer, musician,
singer BD
BUSCH, Constance (d 1898 [48])
EA/99*
BUSCH, Fritz (1890-1951) German
conductor CB, WWA/3
BUSCH, Lydia English actress
GRB/2-4
BUSCH, Mae [Mrs. Thomas C.
Tate] (1897-1946) Australian
actress ES, TW/2
BUSH, Mr. (fl 1779) actor, singer
BD
BUSH, Alan Dudley (b 1900) English composer, conductor ES
BUSH, Amyas (fl 1758) dramatist
CP/1-3, GT
BUSH, Anita (d 1974) performer,
theatre company founder BP/
58*
BUSH, Mrs. Charles see
Charles, Florence
BUSH, Frances Cleveland (d 1967
[78]) musical-comedy singer
TW/24
BUSH, Frank (d 1927 [71]) monologist BE*, BP/12*
BUSH, Fred [né Frederick Taylor]
(d 1903/04) variety artist EA/
04*, EA/05*
BUSH, Norman (b 1933) American
actor TW/26-28
BUSHBY, Mr. (fl 1784) singer
BD
BUSHE, Amyas see Bush, Amyas
BUSHEL, Robert (fl 1766-94)
gallerykeeper, treasurer BD
BUSHELL, Anthony (b 1904) English actor ES, WWT/6-13
BUSHELL, Frederick (d 1872 [38])
EA/73*
BUSHELL, Leonard O. (d 1976
[78]) voice teacher BP/60*
BUSH-FEKETE, Leslie (b 1896)
Hungarian dramatist BE
BUSHMAN, Francis X. (b 1885)
American actor ES
BUSHNELL, Arthur (d 1967 [50])
performer BP/52*
BUSHNELL, Catherine Hayes (d
1861 [36]) EA/72*
BUSLEY, Jessie [Mrs. Ernest
Joy] (1869-1950) American
actress GRB/3-4, SR, TW/
2-3, 5-6, WWT/1-10
BUSNACH, William (d 1907 [75])
dramatist BE*, WWT/14*
BUSS, Harry (b 1874) English

actor GRB/1

BUSS, Mary Ann (d 1907) comedian EA/08*

BUSS, Robert William (1804-75) theatrical portrait painter DNB

BUSSE, Margaret [Margaret Bussey] actress GRB/3-4, WWT/1-5

BUSSELL, Jan (b 1909) English marionettist ES

BUSSER, Henri (d 1973 [101]) composer/lyricist BP/58*

BUSSEY, Hank (d 1971 [80]) performer BP/55*

BUSSEY, Margaret see Bussé, Margaret

BUSSLEY, Oliver James see Cox, Harry

BUSSY, René (b 1879) French actor GRB/4, WWT/1-3

BUSTIN, Sydney see Beltram, Sydney

BUSTLER, Mr. (fl 1742-43) actor BD

BUSWELL, John (1733-63) English musician, composer BD

BUTCHER, Master (fl 1746) singer BD

BUTCHER, Mr. (fl 1724-28) actor BD

BUTCHER, Mrs. (fl 1724-25) actress BD

BUTCHER, Mrs. (fl 1746-48) house servant? BD

BUTCHER, Ernest (b 1885) English actor, singer WWT/9-10

BUTCHER, Harry (d 1895 [23]) dog trainer EA/96*

BUTCHER, John (d 1869 [36]) musician EA/70*

BUTCHER, Robert see Butler, Robert

BUTE, Henry (d 1917 [50]) EA/18*

BUTE, Olive (d 1900) actress EA/01*

BUTLER, Mr. (fl 1720) house servant? BD

BUTLER, Mr. (fl 1734-48) actor BD

BUTLER, Mr. (fl 1770-79) actor BD

BUTLER, Mr. (fl c. 1772) organist BD

BUTLER, Mrs. (fl 1746-50)

actress BD

BUTLER, Albert W. (d 1973 [84]) publicist BP/58*

BUTLER, Alfred Joline see Butler, Fred J.

BUTLER, Alice [Mrs. Charles W. Butler] (1868-1919) English actress WWS

BUTLER, Gen. Benjamin F. (1818-93) American agent SR

BUTLER, Benjamin H. (d 1888 [41]) American manager EA/89*

BUTLER, Charles (d 1920 [64]) actor BE*, BP/5*

BUTLER, Mrs. Charles see Long, Harriet C.

BUTLER, Mrs. Charles W. see Butler, Alice

BUTLER, Charlotte (fl 1673-95) actress, singer, dancer BD

BUTLER, David (b 1894) American actor ES

BUTLER, Edward (1882-1947) actor SR

BUTLER, E. H. (fl 1839) actor CDP

BUTLER, Elizabeth (d 1748) actress BD, DD

BUTLER, Mrs. Fanny see Kemble, Fanny

BUTLER, Fred J. [Alfred Joline Butler] (b 1867) American actor WWS

BUTLER, Henry J. (d 1909 [63]) stage manager EA/10*

BUTLER, Mrs. Henry J. see Tremayne, Bella

BUTLER, Horace (d 1906) proprietor EA/07*

BUTLER, James (fl 1732-39) singer BD

BUTLER, James (d 1892) stage manager EA/93*

BUTLER, James H. (b 1908) American educator BE

BUTLER, John (fl 1773-88) gallery office keeper BD

BUTLER, John (fl 1840) dramatist RJ

BUTLER, John (d 1864) minstrel HAS

BUTLER, John (b 1920) American choreographer, director, dancer BE, CB, ES, TW/2-3

BUTLER, John Dale (d 1882 [52]) manager EA/83*

BUTLER, John Davies see

Gaunt, David
BUTLER, John Pearce (d 1906 [54]) circus advance agent EA/07*
BUTLER, Michael see Esmond, Wilfred
BUTLER, Nellie [née Chute] (fl 1894-1912) American actress WWM
BUTLER, Philip (d 1786) master carpenter BD
BUTLER, Pierce CDP
BUTLER, Pierce J. [?= Pierce Butler] (d 1868 [74]) actor EA/69*
BUTLER, Rachel Barton (d 1920) dramatist BE*, BP/5*
BUTLER, Ralph (d 1969 [82]) composer/lyricist BP/53*
BUTLER, Rhoda (b 1949) American actress TW/30
BUTLER, Richard William (1844-1928) English dramatist, critic DD, GRB/3-4, WWT/1-5
BUTLER, Robert [né Butcher] (b 1832) clown CDP, HAS
BUTLER, Mrs. Robert [Amelia Wells] (b 1833) American circus performer, singer, actress, dancer HAS
BUTLER, Royal (d 1973 [80]) performer BP/58*
BUTLER, Sam actor, manager TD/2
BUTLER, Samuel (1612-80) English dramatist CP/3
BUTLER, Samuel (d 1812) theatre builder COC
BUTLER, Samuel (d 1945 [48]) actor WWT/14*
BUTLER, Samuel S. W. (1797-1845) English actor CDP, COC, DD, HAS, SR
BUTLER, Mrs. Samuel S. W. (fl 1841) actress HAS
BUTLER, Thomas Hamley (d 1823) composer DD
BUTLER, Todd (b 1936) American actor TW/25
BUTLER, W. actor TD/2
BUTLER, W. George (d 1882) comedian, pantomimist EA/83*
BUTLER, William (fl 1780-1817?) dancer, house servant? BD
BUTLER, William see Clancent,

William
BUTLER, Mrs. William (fl 1789-1812) singer BD
BUTLER, Mrs. William (d 1872) EA/73*
BUTLIN, Jan (b 1940) English director, dramatist WWT/16
BUTSOVA, Hilda (d 1976 [78]) performer BP/60*
BUTT, Sir Alfred (1878-1962) English manager, producer COC, GRB/3-4, NTH, WWT/1-9
BUTT, Dame Clara [Mrs. Kennerley Rumford] (1873-1936) English singer DNB, GRB/1, WWW/3
BUTT, George (1741-95) English dramatist CP/3
BUTTERFIELD, Everett (d 1925 [40]) American actor BE*, BP/9*
BUTTERFIELD, Isabel (d 1870) singer EA/71*
BUTTERFIELD, Walter S. (fl 1900s) American actor, dramatist, manager SR
BUTTERFIELD, Walton (d 1966 [68]) performer BP/51*
BUTTERLY, John Thomas [Johnny Burley] (d 1888 [32]) clown, comedian EA/89*
BUTTERSBY, Mrs. [Mrs. Stickney] (fl 1823-35) actress HAS
BUTTERWORTH, Annie (d 1885) singer EA/87*
BUTTERWORTH, Charles E. (1896-1946) American actor ES, SR, TW/2-3, WWT/8-9
BUTTERWORTH, Clara English singer, actress WWT/4-7
BUTTERWORTH, Walter T. (d 1962 [69]) actor BE*
BUTTERWORTH, William (d 1896 [72]) minstrel manager EA/98*
BUTTERY, Miss see Cleland, Miss
BUTTERY, Henry (d 1876 [30]) property master EA/77*
BUTTON, Dick (b 1929) American producer, actor BE, TW/13-15
BUTTONS, Red [Aaron Chwatt] (b 1919) American actor CB, TW/3-6
BUTTRAM, Jan (b 1946) American actress TW/30
BUXTON, Mr. (fl 1782) actor BD
BUXTON, Mr. (fl c. 1812) actor

CDP
BUXTON, Bertha (d 1881) actress EA/82*
BUXTON, Charles Henry (d 1894 [49]) EA/95*
BUXTON, Frederick F. (d 1858) English actor HAS, SR
BUXTON, Jedidiah (1707-72) illiterate calculating genius CDP, DNB
BUXTON, John see Zambra
BUXTON, Maria (fl 1837-52) American dancer HAS
BUZARGLO, Mr. (fl 1792-97) scene painter BD
BUZARGLO, Louis (fl 1793-95) scene painter BD
BUZILARICO, Sig. (fl 1786) ventriloquist BD
BUZO, Alexander (b 1944) Australian dramatist, director, actor CD, WWT/16
BUZZARD, Henry Thomas see Ashley, J. B.
BUZZELL, Edward [Edie] (b 1897) American actor ES, WWT/7-10
BUZZELL, Eugene (d 1973 [68]) public relations director BP/57*
BUZZI, Ruth (b 1936) American actress TW/22-24
BYAL, Carl (d 1972 [83]) performer BP/57*
BYARS, Thomas (d 1896) music-hall stage manager EA/97*
BYATT, Henry (fl 1877-94) dramatist DD
BYDE, Alfred J. (d 1916) actor EA/17*
BYERLEY, John Scott ["John Scott Ripon"] (fl 1803) English dramatist CP/3
BYERLEY, Vivienne English press representative WWT/11-16
BYERLY, Mr. (fl 1769) actor HAS
BYERS, Catherine American actress TW/30
BYERS, Charles A. (d 1975 [72]) producer/director/choreographer BP/60*
BYFIELD, Miss (fl 1828) actress CDP
BYFORD, George actor, singer, composer CDP

BYFORD, Roy (1873-1939) English actor WWT/4-8
BYFORD, Mrs. Roy see Hunt, Doris
BYINGTON, Spring (1893-1971) American actress BE, CB, ES, TW/28, WWA/5, WWT/8-11
BYLAND, Ambrose (fl 1624) actor DA
BYLES, Bobby (d 1969 [38]) performer BP/54*
BYNAM, Mr. J. (fl 1797-1820) house servant BD
BYNG, David (d 1881 [72]) EA/83*
BYNG, Mrs. David B. see Byng, Jane Buckley
BYNG, Douglas (b 1893) English actor, entertainer AAS, BTR/74, TW/13, WWT/8-16
BYNG, George W. conductor, composer WWT/4-7
BYNG, Jane Buckley [Mrs. David B. Byng] (d 1881) EA/82*
BYNNER, Witter (1881-1968) American dramatist WWA/5, WWM, WWW/6
BYRAM, John (1901-77) American press representative, editor, producer BE
BYRAM, Marian (b 1904) American press representative BE
BYRD, Carl (b 1935) American actor TW/27
BYRD, Sam[uel Armanie] (1908-55) American actor, producer CB, TW/3, 12, WWT/9-11
BYRN, [Mrs.?] (fl 1760-66) charwoman BD
BYRN, James (1756-1845) dancer, choreographer BD, DD
BYRN, John (fl 1794) singer? BD
BYRN, Oscar (c. 1795-1867) dancer BD
BYRNE, Mr. (d 1780) dancer BD
BYRNE, Mr. (fl 1783-90) box-keeper, lobby keeper BD
BYRNE, Mrs. (d 1782) dancer BD
BYRNE, Mrs. (fl c. 1785-1800) singer, dancer, actress BD
BYRNE, Miss (fl 1784-87) dancer BD
BYRNE, Cecily English actress WWT/4-12
BYRNE, Charles (1761-83) giant BD
BYRNE, Charles (d 1871 [27])

actor EA/72*
BYRNE, Charles Alfred (1848-
1909) English/American
dramatist DD, WWA/1
BYRNE, Eleanor (fl 1817)
actress CDP
BYRNE, Francis M. (1875-1923)
American actor WWM, WWS
BYRNE, Gaylea American act-
ress TW/25-29
BYRNE, George J. (d 1966 [62])
performer BP/51*
BYRNE, Gerald [George Charles
Burnette] (d 1917) actor
EA/18*
BYRNE, James see Byrn,
James
BYRNE, James A. (1868-1927)
American actor, acrobat,
dramatist SR
BYRNE, John J. (d 1968) drama-
tist BP/53*
BYRNE, John Keyes see Leonard,
Hugh
BYRNE, Kate Oscar English act-
ress, singer GRB/1
BYRNE, Oscar (1795-1867)
ballet master DD, DNB,
GT, HAS
BYRNE, Mrs. Oscar (fl 1793)
English actress HAS
BYRNE, Patsy (b 1933) English
actress WWT/14-16
BYRNE, Peter (b 1928) English
actor WWT/15-16
BYRNE, Peter C. (d 1867 [44])
actor HAS
BYRNE, Robinson see Bern,
Chris V.
BYRNE, [William?] (1743-1805?)
scene painter BD
BYRNE, William (d 1916 [21])
EA/17*
BYRNES, Mrs. [Mrs. Ferrers]
(fl 1836) English actress
HAS
BYRNES, Burke (b 1937) Amer-
ican actor TW/25-26
BYRNES, Maureen (b 1944)
American actress TW/26-29
BYRON, Alfred (d 1891) EA/
92*
BYRON, Arthur W[illiam] (1872-
1943) American actor CB,
ES, GRB/3-4, NTH, SR,
WWS, WWT/1-9
BYRON, Mrs. Arthur see
Mapleson, Laura

BYRON, Mrs. E. M. [Mrs. Henry
James Byron] (d 1889 [40])
actress EA/90*
BYRON, Fred (fl c. 1876) singer
CDP
BYRON, George Gordon, Lord
(1788-1824) English dramatist
COC, DD, DNB, ES, HP, MH,
OC/1-3, PDT, RE, SR
BYRON, H. (d 1884 [80]) EA/85*
BYRON, Henrietta [Mrs. Barney
Fagan] (d 1924) performer
BE*, BP/8*
BYRON, Mrs. Henry (d 1876 [44])
EA/77*
BYRON, Henry James (1834-84)
English dramatist, actor CDP,
COC, DD, DNB, EA/68, ES,
NTH, OAA/1-2, OC/1-3
BYRON, Mrs. Henry James see
Byron, Mrs. E. M.
BYRON, John (b 1912) Chinese/
English actor, dancer WWT/
10-12
BYRON, Kate see Byron, Mrs.
Oliver Doud
BYRON, Marie Josephine (d 1900
[70]) EA/01*
BYRON, Oliver Doud (1842-1920)
American actor CDP, NTH,
PP/1, SR, WWM, WWS
BYRON, Mrs. Oliver Doud [Kate
Crehan] (1846-1920) Irish act-
ress PP/1, SR
BYRON, Paul (b 1888) American
actor TW/2
BYRON, Terence (d 1936 [49])
actor, manager WWT/14*
BYRT, Wilfred Clarence (d 1908
[32]) music-hall performer?
EA/09*

- C -

C., J. (fl 1620) dramatist CP/1-3
C., J. (fl 1739) dramatist CP/3
C., R. (fl 1621) dramatist CP/
1-3, FGF
CAAN, James (b 1939) American
actor CB
CABAL, Alan (b 1953) American
actor TW/23
CABALLE, Montserrat (b 1933)
Spanish singer CB
CABAN, Rose Evangeline (d 1902)
circus performer EA/04*
CABANEL, Mons. (fl 1789-1804?)

dancer? actor? pyrotechnist
BD
CABANEL, Eliza (fl 1792-1800)
dancer BD
CABANEL, Harriot [later Mrs.
Helme] (fl 1791-1806) dancer
BD
CABANEL, Rudolphe (1763-
1839) French architect, ma-
chinist, inventor, pyrotechnist
BD
CABANEL, Victoire (fl 1792-93)
dancer BD
CABANES, Mr. (fl 1784) violinist
BD
CABEL, Marie (d 1885 [48])
singer EA/86*
CABELL, Mr. (fl 1760) dresser
BD
CABLE, Mrs. (d 1767) house
servant? BD
CABLE, Christopher (b 1930)
American actor TW/27
CABOT, Bruce (d 1972 [67/68])
performer BP/56*, WWT/
16*
CABOT, Eliot (1899-1938) Amer-
ican actor SR, WWT/7-8
CACCIALANZA, Gisella (b 1914)
American dancer ES
CACEY, Dorothy (b 1882) Eng-
lish actress GRB/1
CACOYANNIS, Michael (b 1922)
Cypriot director CB
CADDICK, Thomas (d 1877 [37])
comedian EA/78*
CADELL, Jean (1884-1967)
Scottish actress AAS, TW/3,
24, WWT/3-14
CADEMAN, Philip (b c. 1643)
actor BD
CADET, Mr. (fl 1707-11) musi-
cian BD
CADET, Mr. (fl 1708) house
servant BD
CADLE, Albert Henry (d 1907
[34]) agent EA/08*
CADLE, Ernest (b 1871) English
agent GRB/1
CADLE, Henry (b 1873) English
agent GRB/1
CADMAN, Charles Wakefield
(1881-1946) American com-
poser DAB, ES, HJD,
WWA/2
CADMAN, Ethel (b 1886) Eng-
lish actress, singer WWM,
WWT/2-8

CADMAN, Robert (d 1740) rope-
walker BD
CADWALADER, Jessica [Mrs.
Robert Ryan] (d 1972 [57]) per-
former BP/56*
CADWALADR, Llewelyn (1860-
1909) Welsh singer GRB/1
CADWELL, Mr. (fl 1776-77)
dresser BD
CADY, Mr. (fl 1773) hairdresser
BD
CAEDES, Auguste (d 1884) com-
poser EA/85*
CAESAR, Irving (b 1895) American
lyricist, librettist BE, WWT/
6-16
CAESAR, Sid (b 1922) American
actor, comedian, musician
BE, CB, ES, TW/19, 27,
WWT/15-16
CAFFARELLI, Sig. [Gaetano
Maiorano] (1710-83) Italian
singer BD
CAFFREY, Stephen (d 1902 [54])
actor EA/03*, WWT/14*
CAFFRY, John [Frank Fleming]
(d 1883) actor? EA/84*
CAGE, John (b 1912) American
composer CD, ES
CAGE, Ruth (b 1923) American
press representative BE
CAGNEY, James (b 1904) American
actor BE, CB, ES, WWT/7-10
CAGNEY, Jeanne (b 1919) Ameri-
can actress BE, TW/1, 3,
WWT/11-13
CAHILL, Albert Joseph Simmons
(d 1916) EA/17*
CAHILL, James (b 1940) American
actor TW/23, 25-26, 28, 30
CAHILL, Lily (1885/91-1955) Amer-
ican actress TW/2-6, 12,
WWT/6-11
CAHILL, Marie [Mrs. Daniel V.
Arthur] (1870-1933) American
actress, singer ES, GRB/2-4,
NTH, SR, WWA/1, WWS,
WWT/1-7
CAHILL, Paul (d 1974 [42]) pro-
ducer/director/choreographer
BP/59*
CAHILL, William B. (d 1906 [77])
manager WWT/14*
CAHLMAN, Robert (b 1924) Amer-
ican director, producer, lectur-
er, publicist BE
CAHN, Julius (d 1921) manager
BE*, BP/5*

CAHN, Sammy (b 1913) American actor, songwriter CB, TW/30, WWT/16

CAHUSAC, William Maurice (fl 1794-1829) musician, publisher, instrument maker, singer? BD

CAIL, Harold J. (d 1968 [66]) critic BP/53*

CAILLOT, François (fl 1771-93) pyrotechnist BD

CAIN, Mr. (fl 1799) English actor HAS

CAIN, Andrew (fl 1620-44) English actor COC, ES, OC/1-3

CAIN, James Mallahan (1892-1977) American dramatist BE, CB, ES, HJD

CAIN, Patrick J. (d 1949 [70]) American scenery warehouse operator BE*, BP/33*

CAIN, Perry (d 1975 [49]) performer BP/59*

CAIN, Robert (d 1954 [67]) actor BE*

CAINE, Derwent Hall (b 1892) English actor, manager WWT/2-5

CAINE, Georgia (d 1964 [88]) actress BE*

CAINE, Henry (1888-1962) English actor WWT/4-13

CAINE, John (d 1904 [83]) EA/05*

CAINE, Lily Hall (d 1914) actress DD, GRB/2-4, WWT/1-2

CAINE, Michael (b 1933) English actor CB

CAINE, Richard (b 1940) American actor TW/27

CAINE, Sir Thomas Henry Hall (1853-1931) English dramatist DD, ES, GRB/2-4, HP, SR, WWM, WWS, WWT/1-6, WWW/3

CAIRD, Mr. see D'Arcy, Mr.

CAIRD, Dora [Mrs. Graham Good] (d 1910) actress EA/11*

CAIRD, Laurence (d 1955 [88]) actor WWT/14*

CAIRNS, Angus (1910-75) American actor TW/26-27

CAIRNS, Fred (d 1896) music-hall comedian EA/97*

CAIRNS, Mrs. William see

Achmet, Mrs.

CAIRNS-JAMES, Lewis Scottish actor GRB/1-4

CAJANUS, Mynheer (fl 1734) actor BD

CAJANUS, Daniel (1703-49) German giant BD

CALBES, Eleanor (b 1940) Filipino actress TW/24, 27

CALCAGNI, Mr. (fl 1790) singer BD

CALCOTT, John F. (d 1895) conductor EA/96*

CALCRAFT, Granby (d 1855) actor, manager EA/72*, WWT/14*

CALCRAFT, Mrs. Grandby see Love, Emma Sarah

CALCRAFT, John William [né Cole] (d 1870) actor, dramatist CDP, DD

CALDARA, Orme (1875-1925) American actor SR, WWM

CALDER, John Richard (d 1875 [25]) comedian EA/76*

CALDER, King (d 1964 [65]) American actor TW/8, 21

CALDERISI, David (b 1940) Canadian actor, director, producer WWT/15-16

CALDER-MARSHALL, Anna (b 1947) English actress WWT/15-16

CALDERON, George (1868-1915) English dramatist DNB, ES, HP, WWT/2-3, WWW/1

CALDERON DE LA BARCA, Pedro (1600-81) Spanish dramatist DD, OC/1-3, PDT

CALDICOT, Jonas (fl 1661) singer BD

CALDICOT, Richard (b 1908) English actor WWT/16

CALDICOTT, Alfred James (1842-97) musician, conductor DD, DNB

CALDUCCI, Sig. (fl 1781-82) singer BD

CALDWELL, Anne (1869-1936) American dramatist, composer SR, WWT/4-8

CALDWELL, Bryan (d 1969 [54]) public relations BP/54*

CALDWELL, Erskine (b 1903) American writer CB

CALDWELL, Gisela American actress TW/30

CALDWELL, Henry (d 1961 [42])

producer, actor BE*
CALDWELL, J. (d 1880) lessee,
proprietor EA/81*
CALDWELL, James H. (1793-
1863) English actor, manager,
dramatist CDP, DD, ES,
HAS, RJ, SR, WWA/H
CALDWELL, Marianne [Mari-
anne Lipsett] (d 1933 [67])
West Indian/English actress
GRB/1-4, WWT/1-5
CALDWELL, Orville (1896-1967)
American actor BE, TW/24
CALDWELL, Sarah (b 1928)
American conductor CB
CALDWELL, Zoe (b 1933/34)
Australian actress AAS,
CB, TW/23-26, 29-30,
WWT/14-16
CALEF, Jennie [née Murphy]
dancer, actress CDP
CALEF, Lillian [née Murphy]
actress, singer CDP
CALFHILL, James (d 1570)
English dramatist CP/3,
FGF
CALHAEM, Emilie (d 1943 [73])
actress WWT/14*
CALHAEM, Mrs. Francis Emily
[Mrs. Stanislaus Calhaem]
(d 1911 [68]) actress EA/
12*, WWT/14*
CALHAEM, Stanislaus (d 1901
[78]) actor DD, OAA/2
CALHAEM, Mrs. Stanislaus
see Calhaem, Francis Emily
CALHERN, Louis (1895-1956)
American actor AAS, CB,
ES, TW/1-8, 12, WWA/3,
WWT/7-11
CALHOUN, Eleanor (1862-1957)
American actress DD
CALHOUN, Mrs. Fred G. see
Thorndyke, Louise
CALHOUN, Robert (b 1930)
American technical director,
production supervisor, stage
manager BE
CALICE, Myron (d 1908 [61])
actor CDP
"CALIFORNIA DIAMOND, The"
see Dauvray, Helen
CALIN, Mickey (b 1935) Ameri-
can actor TW/12, 15-16
CALKIN, Mr. (fl 1790-1817)
gallery doorkeeper BD
CALKIN, Arthur (d 1974 [80s])
performer BP/60*

CALKIN, Joseph (fl 1781-1815)
musician BD
CALKIN, Joseph (1781-1846) Eng-
lish musician, bookseller BD
CALKINS, Michael (b 1948) Amer-
ican actor TW/30
CALL, John (1915-73) American
actor TW/1, 3, 16, 22-24,
27, 29
CALLADINE, C. (1822-61) actor
HAS, SR
CALLADINE, Mrs. C. see
Calladine, Eliza
CALLADINE, Eliza [née Eberle]
(1834-54) American actress
HAS, SR
CALLAGHAN, J. (d 1910 [39])
musical director EA/11*
CALLAGHAN, J. Dorsey (d 1975
[80]) critic BP/60*
CALLAGHAN, T. C. (d 1917 [64])
comedian EA/18*
CALLAHAN, Bill (b 1926) Ameri-
can actor TW/2-10
CALLAHAN, Billy (d 1964 [53])
performer BE*
CALLAHAN, Charles E. (1843-1917)
actor, dramatist SR
CALLAHAN, Charles S. (d 1964
[73]) performer BP/49*
CALLAHAN, Emmett (d 1965 [72])
performer BP/50*
CALLAHAN, James T. (b 1930)
American actor TW/30
CALLAHAN, Kristina American
actress TW/26
CALLAHAN, T. C. singer CDP
CALLAN, Chris (b 1944) American
actor TW/30
CALLAN, Henry J. (d 1905 [34])
English acting manager GRB/1
CALLAN, John (d 1909) minstrel
comedian EA/11*
CALLAN, William (b 1918) Amer-
ican actor TW/22
CALLAND, S. (d 1877) pianist
EA/78*
CALLAS, Maria (1923-77) Ameri-
can singer CB
CALLAWAY, Paul (b 1909) Ameri-
can conductor, musician, edu-
cator BE
CALLAWAY, Tod singer CDP
CALLCOTT, Albert (d 1888 [53])
scene artist EA/89*
CALLCOTT, Albert W. (d 1901
[30]) scene artist EA/02*
CALLCOTT, Augustus Wall

(1779-1844) English painter,
singer BD

CALLCOTT, John Wall (1766-
1821) English musician,
composer, singer, teacher
BD, DNB

CALLCOTT, William (fl 1790-
1800) English musician BD

CALLCOTT, William (d 1878
[78]) musician, composer
EA/79*

CALLCOTT, William John (d
1900 [77]) scene painter
EA/01*

CALLEAR, Herbert (d 1917)
EA/18*

CALLEGA, Joseph (d 1975 [78])
performer BP/60*

CALLEIA, Joseph [né Spurin-
Calleia] (b 1897) Maltese
actor BE, WWT/11-13

CALLENDER, Charles (d 1897
[70]) manager CDP, SR

CALLENDER, E. Romaine (fl 1875-
82) actor, dramatist DD

CALLENDER, Mrs. E. Romaine (d
1890) actress EA/91*

CALLIGAN, Edward O. (d 1962 [64])
talent representative BE*

CALLOWAY, Cab (b 1907) American actor, musician, composer ES, TW/30, WWT/16

CALMOUR, Alfred Cecil (d 1912
[55]) dramatist, actor DD,
GRB/2-4, WWT/1

CALORI, Angiola (1732-c. 90)
Italian singer BD

CALTHROP, Dion Clayton (1878-
1937) English dramatist, designer WWT/2-8, WWW/3

CALTHROP, Donald (1888-1940)
English actor ES, WWT/2-9

CALTHROP, Gladys E. English
designer ES, WWT/8-14

CALTHROP, John Alfred Clayton
see Clayton, John

CALVE, Emma (1858/64-1942)
Spanish singer CB, ES,
GRB/1, 4, SR, WWA/1,
WWS, WWW/4

CALVERLEY, Thomas (fl 1665-
67) actor? BD

CALVERLY, Joseph (fl 1794)
singer BD

CALVERT, Mrs. (fl 1772) singer
BD

CALVERT, Adelaide Helen (1837-
1921) English actress CDP,

OC/1-3

CALVERT, Alexander (d 1917)
English actor GRB/1-4

CALVERT, Catherine (1890-1971)
American actress TW/27,
WWM, WWT/5-6

CALVERT, Cecil G. (b 1871)
English actor GRB/3-4, WWT/
1-5

CALVERT, [Charles?] (fl 1784-86)
actor BD

CALVERT, Charles Alexander
(1828-79) English actor, manager CDP, DD, DNB, ES, OC/
1-3

CALVERT, Mrs. Charles Alexander
[Adelaide Biddles] (1837-1921)
English actress DD, GRB/1-4,
HAS, WWT/1-3, WWW/2

CALVERT, E. H. (fl 1900-36)
American actor ES

CALVERT, Frank (d 1913) EA/14*

CALVERT, Frederick Baltimore
(1793-1877) actor DNB

CALVERT, George Henry (1803-
89) American dramatist HJD

CALVERT, Henry (b 1920) American actor TW/23, 25-27

CALVERT, Leonard Charles English actor GRB/1-4

CALVERT, Louis (1859-1923)
English actor COC, DD, GRB/
1-4, OC/1-3, SR, WWT/1-4

CALVERT, Mrs. Louis see
Roberts, Rose

CALVERT, Patricia (b 1908) English actress WWT/8-11

CALVERT, Phyllis (b 1915) English actress AAS, ES, WWT/
10-16

CALVERT, Thomas (d 1901 [67])
professor of music EA/01*

CALVERT, William (fl 1877-92)
director, actor, dramatist
DD, EA/95

CALVERTO, J[ames] F[erguson]
English agent GRB/1

CALVESI, Vincenzo (fl 1786-88)
singer BD

CALVESI, Teresa (fl 1783-92)
singer BD

CALVIN, Henry (1918-75) American
actor TW/3-5, 10-12, 22

CALZOLARI, Enrico (1823-88)
singer CDP

CAMANO, Mrs. (fl 1733) actress
BD

CAMARGO, Marie Anne de Cupis

de (1710-70) dancer BD,
CDP, ES, OC/1-2

CAMBELL, Mr. dramatist CP/
2-3

CAMBER, Susan (b 1947) American dancer TW/24

CAMBERT, Robert (c. 1628-77)
French composer, impresario,
band leader BD

CAMBLOS, Charles S. (d 1887)
actor NYM

CAMBLOS, Mrs. Charles S.
see Conway, Lillian

CAMBRIA, Frank (d 1966 [83])
designer BP/51*

CAMBRIDGE, Mr. (fl 1827)
actor HAS

CAMBRIDGE, Arthur (b c. 1840)
manager, agent, dramatist?
SR

CAMBRIDGE, Godfrey (b 1933)
American actor, comedian
CB

CAMBRIDGE, Harry (d 1892)
vocal comedian EA/94*

CAMBURINI, Sig. singer CDP

CAMEL, Tom (fl 1785) equestrian BD

CAMELINAT, Hermine see
French, Hermene

CAMEO, Frank (d 1902 [27])
music-hall performer EA/
03*

CAMERON, Mr. (fl 1797) actor
BD

CAMERON, Mr. (d 1800) boxkeeper BD

CAMERON, Beatrice see
Mansfield, Beatrice

CAMERON, Charles E. F. (d
1917 [45]) EA/18*

CAMERON, Donald (d 1868)
musician EA/69*

CAMERON, Donald (d 1955 [66])
actor TW/12, WWT/7-11

CAMERON, Ewin (d 1892 [82])
EA/93*

CAMERON, Frances (b 1886)
American singer WWM

CAMERON, Hugh (1879-1941)
American actor CB, SR

CAMERON, Kathryn (d 1954
[71]) actress TW/1, 10

CAMERON, Marlene (b 1935)
American actress TW/6-7

CAMERON, Mary Agnes (b 1838)
Irish? actress HAS, SR

CAMERON, Retta (d 1975 [49])

performer BP/60*

CAMERON, Sylvia (b 1881) English
singer GRB/1

CAMERON, Violet [Mrs. De Ben-
saude] (1862-1919) actress,
singer CDP, DD, DP, GRB/
1-4, OAA/2, WWT/1-3

CAMERON, Walter M. (d 1909
[53]) EA/10*

CAMERY, Mr. (fl 1777-78) actor
BD

CAMILLE, Master (fl 1712) dancer
BD

CAMILLO, Mary (fl 1796-97)
posture maker BD

CAMMANS, Jan (d 1976 [84])
performer BP/60*

CAMP, Frank E. (1870-1943)
musician, dramatist? SR

CAMP, Harry Squire see Godfrey,
H. S.

CAMP, Jack (d 1907 [40]) comic
singer EA/08*

CAMP, Richard (b 1923) American
actor TW/2-3

CAMP, Sheppard (b 1876) American composer, actor WWM

CAMPAGNOLI, Bartolommeo (1751-
1827) violinist, musical director, composer CDP

CAMPANA, Fabio (1819-82) Italian
composer, singing master ES

CAMPANARI, Giuseppe (1858-1927)
Italian singer CDP, WWA/1

CAMPANELLA, Joseph (b 1925/27)
American actor BE, TW/19

CAMPANELLA, Philip (b 1948)
American actor TW/28-30

CAMPANINI, Barbarina (1721-99)
Italian dancer BD, ES

CAMPANINI, Cleofonte (1860-1919)
Italian musical director ES,
WWA/1

CAMPANINI, Italio (1845-96)
Italian singer CDP, ES, SR

CAMPANINI, Miriamne see
Domitilla, Miriamne

CAMPBELL, Mr. (fl 1732-36)
actor BD

CAMPBELL, Mr. (fl 1804) actor
TD/2

CAMPBELL, Mr. (fl early 19th
cent) actor CDP

CAMPBELL, Mr. (d 1882 [67])
EA/83*

CAMPBELL, [Mrs. ? Miss?] (fl
1722-24) actress BD

CAMPBELL, Mrs. (fl 1751) singer,

actress BD
CAMPBELL, Mrs. [née Wallis]
(fl 1789-1814) English actress
CDP, DNB, GT, TD/1-2
CAMPBELL, Miss (fl 1779)
actress BD
CAMPBELL, Miss [Mrs. J.
Gunning] (fl 1799-1806?)
actress BD, TD/1-2
CAMPBELL, A. H. (1826-65)
English actor HAS, SR
CAMPBELL, Alan (d 1917)
dramatist EA/18*
CAMPBELL, Alan (d 1963 [58])
actor TW/20
CAMPBELL, Lady Archibald
Scottish dramatist GRB/1-3
CAMPBELL, A. V. see
Voullaire, Andrew Leonard
CAMPBELL, Bartley (1843-88)
American dramatist, manager
CDP, COC, DAB, DD, ES,
HJD, OC/1-3, SR, WWA/H
CAMPBELL, Charles (1905-64)
American actor TW/6-7
CAMPBELL, Clifford [Frederick
Hankins] (d 1901 [41]) actor
EA/03*
CAMPBELL, Colin Scottish
actor ES
CAMPBELL, Colin see Carle-
ton, Royce
CAMPBELL, Craig (b 1884)
Canadian actor, singer WWM
CAMPBELL, Denis (d 1909 [48])
Irish comedian EA/10*
CAMPBELL, Douglas (b 1922)
Scottish actor, director AAS,
BE, CB, WWT/12-16
CAMPBELL, Duncan (d 1898
[46]) actor EA/99*
CAMPBELL, Mrs. Edmund V.
see Campbell, Mary
CAMPBELL, Edmund Vaullaire
(d 1910 [75]) actor EA/11*,
WWT/14*
CAMPBELL, Ellen (fl 1810)
actress CDP
CAMPBELL, Eric (d c. 1917)
Scottish actor ES
CAMPBELL, E. V. see
Campbell, Edmund Vaullaire
CAMPBELL, Flora American
actress TW/1, 20
CAMPBELL, Frances (d 1948)
actress BE*, WWT/14*
CAMPBELL, Sir Francis J.
(1832-1914) American musician

SR
CAMPBELL, Frank singer, com-
poser CDP
CAMPBELL, Gabrielle Margaret
Vere see Preedy, George R.
CAMPBELL, Gary (b 1938) Amer-
ican actor TW/23
CAMPBELL, Herbert (1844-1904)
English actor, music-hall per-
former CDP, COC, DD, DP,
GRB/1, OC/1-3
CAMPBELL, Mrs. Herbert (d
1891 [33]) EA/92*
CAMPBELL, Mrs. Herbert see
Campbell, Lizzie
CAMPBELL, Howard (d 1896 [42])
comedian EA/97*
CAMPBELL, J. (d 1802) actor
BD
CAMPBELL, Mrs. J. A. see
Fulton, Mary
CAMPBELL, James (d 1893)
singer EA/94*
CAMPBELL, J. C. [né George
Keller St. John] (d 1875 [31])
comedian, minstrel CDP
CAMPBELL, John (fl 1868) Amer-
ican carpenter HAS
CAMPBELL, John actor TW/1,
23
CAMPBELL, Judy (b 1916) English
actress AAS, ES, WWT/10-16
CAMPBELL, Katherine Roger
see Fawcett, Marion
CAMPBELL, Lily Bess (1883-1967)
American scholar BE, WWA/4
CAMPBELL, Lizzie [Mrs. Herbert
Campbell] (d 1884) EA/85*
CAMPBELL, Margaret (b 1894)
English actress, singer WWT/
4-8
CAMPBELL, Mary [Mrs. Edmund
V. Campbell] (d 1896) EA/97*
CAMPBELL, Mary see Law-
rence, Mrs. Arthur
CAMPBELL, Maurice (d 1942 [74])
manager WWT/14*
CAMPBELL, Oscar James, Jr.
(d 1970 [90]) scholar BP/55*
CAMPBELL, Mrs. Patrick [Bea-
trice Stella Tanner] (1865-1940)
English actress COC, DD,
DNB, EA/95-96, ES, GRB/1-4,
NTH, OC/1-3, PDT, SR, WWA/
1, WWM, WWS, WWT/1-9,
WWW/3
CAMPBELL, Patton (b 1926) Amer-
ican designer BE, WWT/15-16

CAMPBELL, Sandy (b 1924)
American actor TW/2, 4
CAMPBELL, S. C. [né Sherwood A. Coan] (1829-74)
singer, minstrel CDP, HAS
CAMPBELL, Stella Patrick
(b 1886) English actress
GRB/3-4, WWT/1-9
CAMPBELL, Thomas (1777-1844) writer BD
CAMPBELL, Violet (1892-1970)
English actress WWT/4-8
CAMPBELL, Walter George
see Lucy, Arnold
CAMPBELL, Webster (d 1972
[79]) performer BP/57*
CAMPBELL, William (fl 1784-1810?) musician BD
CAMPBELL, William (d 1870
[48]) comedian EA/71*
CAMPBELL, William (d 1878
[26]) Scottish giant EA/79*
CAMPEAU, Frank (1864-1943)
American actor SR
CAMPEAU, Jane Harrison (d 1974
[48]) performer BP/58*
CAMPIAN, Edmund (1540-81)
English dramatist CP/3
CAMPINA, Fidela (b 1897)
Spanish singer ES
"CAMPIOLI" [Antonio Gualandi]
(fl 1708-32) German singer
BD
CAMPION, Alfred (d 1896 [25])
EA/97*
CAMPION, Cyril (1894-1961)
English dramatist WWT/6-13
CAMPION, Edmond (fl 1654)
dramatist FGF
CAMPION, Maria Ann [Mrs.
Alexander Pope] (1775/77-1803) Irish actress DD,
DNB, ES, GT, TD/1-2
CAMPION, Mary Anne (c. 1687-1706) singer, dancer, harpsichordist BD
CAMPION, Thomas (1567-1620)
English musician COC, CP/
2-3, DD, DNB, ES, FGF,
HP, OC/1-3
CAMPION, Thomas (d 1905)
EA/06*
CAMPION, William E. (d 1973
[61]) musician BP/58*
CAMPIONI, Sig. (fl 1744-70?)
dancer, ballet master BD
CAMPIONI, Signora (fl 1744-54?)
dancer BD

CAMPKIN, Reginald E. (d 1918)
EA/19*
CAMPLOS, Lilian Conway (d 1891
[32]) EA/92*
CAMPOLINI, Signora (fl 1767-68)
singer BD
CAMPORA, Giuseppe (b 1923)
Italian singer CB
CAMPORESE, Violante (1785-1839)
Italian singer, actress CDP,
ES
CAMPTON, David (b 1924) English
dramatist, director, actor CD,
CH, ES, MH, PDT
CAMRYN, Walter American dancer,
choreographer ES
CAMUS, Albert (1913-60) French
dramatist OC/3, WWW/5
CAN, Betty (b 1933) American
actress TW/15
CANADINA (fl 1761-66) house servant, constable BD
CANAVAN, Eliza Louisa see
Plunkett, Mrs. Charles
CANBY, Albert H. (1860-1940)
American manager CB, CDP,
GRB/2-4
CANDELIN, Susan Mary Charlotte
see Vaughan, Susie
CANDELON, Catherine see
Vaughan, Kate
CANDIDES, William (1840-1910)
singer CDP
CANDLER, James (fl 1569) actor
DA
CANDLER, Peter (b 1926) American general manager, educator,
lighting designer BE
CANDRIX, Fud (d 1974 [65]) musician BP/58*
CANE, Andrew (fl 1622-54?) actor
DA, DD
CANE, Harry (b 1849) actor DD
CANEGATA, Leonard Lionel
Cornelius see Lee, Canada
CANEMAKER, John (b 1943)
American actor TW/25, 29
CANETTI, Elias (b 1905) Austrian
dramatist CH
CANFIELD, Curtis (b 1903) American educator, director BE
CANFIELD, Eugene (1851-1904)
comedian, minstrel CDP
CANFIELD, Mary Grace (b 1926)
American actress TW/21
CANFIELD, William F. (d 1925
[64]) performer BE*, BP/9*
CANGALOVIC, Miroslav (b 1921)

Yugoslavian singer ES
CANIGLIA, Maria (b 1906)
Italian singer ES
CANLETS, Master (fl 1785)
actor BD
CANNAN, Denis (b 1919) English
dramatist, actor AAS, CD,
CH, PDT, WWT/11-16
CANNAN, Gilbert (1884-1955)
English dramatist ES, WWT/
2-7, WWW/5
CANNELL, William (d 1882 [32])
administrator EA/84*
CANNING, Effie J. composer
CDP
CANNING, Mrs. George [née
Mary Ann Costello; Mrs.
Samuel Reddish, II; Mrs.
Richard Hunn] (1747?-1827)
English actress BD, DD
CANNING, James J. (b 1946)
American actor TW/28-30
CANNINGE, George (b 1846)
actor DD
CANNON, Anthony see Hart,
Tony
CANNON, Charles James (1800-
60) American dramatist
CDP, HJD, WWA/H
CANNON, Esma (d 1972) Aus-
tralian actress WWT/10
CANNON, Frances Ann see
Dougherty, Frances Ann
CANNON, Hughie (1840-1912)
minstrel, composer SR
CANNON, J. D. (b 1922) Amer-
ican actor BE
CANNON, Jimmy (d 1973 [63])
journalist BP/58*
CANNON, Maureen (b 1926)
American actress TW/1-3
CANNON, Nicholas (fl 1662-65)
drummer BD
CANNON, Raymond American
actor ES
CANOLL, James (1817-67) Amer-
ican actor HAS
CANONGE, Louis Placide (1822-
93) American dramatist DAB
CANSINO, Eduardo, Jr. (d 1974
[54]) performer BP/58*
CANSINO, Gabriel (d 1963 [50])
dancer, teacher BE*
CANTELO, H. (d 1797) musician?
BD
CANTELO, Hezekiah (d 1811)
instrumentalist BD
CANTELO, Thomas (1774-1807)

instrumentalist, teacher BD
CANTER, Mr. (fl 1773-74) dancer
BD
CANTER, James (fl 1768-83) scene
painter, machinist, landscape
painter BD
CANTOR, Mrs. (fl 1838-48) Eng-
lish actress HAS
CANTOR, Arthur (b 1920) Ameri-
can producer, press representa-
tive BE, WWT/15-16
CANTOR, David L. (d 1968 [68])
publicist BP/52*
CANTOR, Eddie (1892-1964) Amer-
ican actor, singer, producer
BE, CB, ES, NTH, SR, TW/
2-8, 21, WWA/4, WWT/5-13,
WWW/6
CANTOR, Mrs. Eddie see
Cantor, Ida
CANTOR, Ida (d 1962 [70]) BP/
47*
CANTOR, Moss see Cinders,
Ettie
CANTOR, Nat (d 1956 [59]) actor
TW/12
CANTRELL, Mrs. (fl 1716-37)
actress, singer BD
CANTRELL, Miss (fl 1736-39)
dancer, actress BD
CANTRELL, Miss (fl 1766?-71)
singer BD
CANTRELL, Miss [Mrs. John
Morris] (d 1876) singer EA/77*
CANTRELL, Nick (b 1943) Ameri-
can actor TW/26
CANZI, Caterina (1805-40) Italian
singer ES
CAPALBO, Carmen (b 1925) Amer-
ican director, producer BE
CAPDEVILLE, Miss (fl 1762)
dancer BD
CAPDEVILLE, Mlle. (fl 1754-71)
dancer, proprietor BD
CAPE, Mr. (fl 1758-73) dresser
BD
CAPE, Fred (d 1893 [44]) comedian
EA/94*, WWT/14*
CAPE, Frederick Damer (d 1882
[52]) journalist, lecturer EA/
83*
CAPE, T. Ireby (b 1873) English
actor, stage manager GRB/1
CAPEK, Josef (1887-1945) Czech
dramatist COC
CAPEK, Josef Horymír (1860-1932)
musical director ES
CAPEK, Karel (1890-1938) Czech

dramatist COC, OC/2-3
CAPELL, Edward (1713-81)
English scholar CDP, CP/
2-3, DD, DNB, GT, HP,
TD/1-2
CAPERON, Nicholas (fl 1660-68)
trumpeter BD
CAPERS, Virginia (b 1925)
American actress TW/30
CAPET, Helen actress CDP
CAPITANI, Master (fl 1760)
dancer BD
CAPITANI, [John?] (fl 1743-63)
singer BD
CAPITANI, Polly (fl 1759-66)
dancer BD
CAPLE, [John?] (d 1860 [40])
actor, manager CDP, EA/
72*
CAPLIN, Gertrude (b 1921)
American producer BE
CAPO, Bobby, Jr. (b 1950)
Puerto Rican actor TW/25
CAPOCCI, Guerino C. (d 1973
[79]) musician BP/57*
CAPODILUPO, Tony (b 1940)
American actor TW/23-25
CAPON, Mr. (fl 1789) actor BD
CAPON, William (1757-1827)
English architect, scene de-
signer, artist BD, CDP,
COC, DNB, ES, OC/1-3
CAPORALE, Andrea Francisca
(d c. 1757) violoncellist,
composer BD
CAPOTE, Truman (b 1924)
American dramatist BE,
CB, CD, ES, HJD, MD,
MWD
CAPOUL, Joseph Amédee Victor
(b 1839) singer, actor CDP
CAPOUL, Victor (1839-1924)
French singer ES
CAPPELL, Mrs. (fl 1847)
actress HAS
CAPPELL, Cordelia (fl 1850)
actress HAS
CAPPELLETTI, [Petronio?
Giuseppe?] (fl 1791-96?) sing-
er, composer BD
CAPPELLETTI, Theresa Poggi (fl
1791) singer BD
CAPPER, Miss (fl 1798-1810?)
singer BD
CAPPERVILLA, Ellen see
Coppervilla, Ellen
CAPPONI, Sig. (d 1880) singer
EA/81*

CAPPY, Ted American choreog-
rapher, director BE
CAPRICE, June (1899-1936) Amer-
ican actress BE*
CAPTAIN EDDIE [Edward Henry
Knipschield] (d 1964 [57])
aerialist BE*
"CAPUCHINO, Sig. " (fl 1746)
dancer BD
"CAPUCHINO, Signora" (fl 1746)
dancer BD
CAPURRO, Alfred see Drake,
Alfred
CAPUS, Alfred (1858-1922) French
dramatist GRB/1-4
CAPUZZI, Giuseppe Antonio (1755-
1818) Italian violinist, composer
BD
CARA, Irene (b 1959) American
actress TW/26-30
CARABALDI, Sig. (fl 1773-74?)
singer BD
CARABO, Jacques (fl 1796-97)
posture maker BD
CARACOL, Manolo (d 1973 [62])
performer BP/57*
CARADIMAS, Lana (b 1945) Amer-
ican actress TW/29-30
CARADORI, Anna (b 1822) singer
HAS, SR
CARADORI-ALLEN, Maria Caterina
Rosalbina (1800-65) Italian singer
CDP, DNB
CARAFA, Sig. (d 1872 [85]) com-
poser EA/73*
CARANTI, Signora Luigia (fl 1857)
singer HAS
CARARA, Signora Antonio (fl
1768?-78) singer BD
CARATHA, Mahomet (fl 1819)
Turkish equilibrist CDP
CARATTA, Mahomet (fl 1747-51)
Turkish equilibrist, manager
BD
CARAVEN, Nora (d 1894 [24])
actress EA/95*
CARAVOGLIA, Charles [Charles
F. Caravoglia-Buckmaster]
(b 1868) English actor, stage
manager GRB/1-2
CARAVOGLIA-BUCKMASTER,
Charles F. see Caravoglia,
Charles
CARBERRY, Joseph (b 1948) Amer-
ican actor TW/30
CARBONE, Bobby (d 1964 [77])
performer BP/49*
CARBONELLI, Giovanni Steffano

(c. 1700-72) Italian violinist,
bandleader, composer BD
CARBREY, John (d 1962 [77])
performer BE*
CARCARES, Ernie (d 1971 [69])
musician BP/55*
CARD, Andrew (fl 1683-1707)
concessionaire BD
CARD, Kathryn (d 1964 [71])
actress BE*
CARDARELLI, Sig. (fl 1775-
76) singer BD
CARDEN, James (b 1837) Irish
actor HAS, SR
CARDEN, Mrs. James see
Leigh, Miss Marston
CARDEN, William (b 1947)
American actor TW/30
CARDER, Emmeline (d 1961)
actress BE*
CARDI, Signora (fl 1773-74)
singer BD
CARDINALE, Mr. (fl 1789)
singer BD
CARDON, Louis (1747-1805)
French harpist BD
CARDOW, Charles composer,
author CDP
CARDOWNIE, J. W. (d 1900)
dancer EA/01*
CARDUS, Sir Neville (d 1975
[85]) critic BP/59*
CARDWELL, Carolyn Y. (b
1938) American actress TW/
24
CARELESS, Elizabeth (d 1752)
singer BD
CARELL, Annette (d 1967) per-
former BP/52*
CARELL, John see Caryl,
John
CARESTINI, Giovanni (1705-60)
Italian singer BD, CDP,
ES
CAREW, Lady Elizabeth (fl 1613)
dramatist CP/1-3, FGF
CAREW, Helen American actress
BE, TW/11-12
CAREW, James (1875-1938)
American actor COC, GRB/
2-4, SR, WWA/1, WWM,
WWS, WWT/1-8
CAREW, John (fl 1660-63) house
servant BD
CAREW, Margaret Felicité Anne
(b 1799) actress, singer
CDP, OX
CAREW, Ora (d 1955 [62])

actress BE*
CAREW, Peter (b 1922) American
actor TW/27-28
CAREW, Thomas (1595?-1639?)
English masque writer, lyricist
CP/1-3, DD, DNB, FGF, HP
CAREWE, Edwin (1883-1940)
American actor ES
CAREY, Mr. (fl 1714-16) singer
BD
CAREY, Mr. (fl 1754) violinist
BD
CAREY, Miss (fl 1755-62) actress
BD
CAREY, Ann (d 1833) CDP
CAREY, Charles (d 1901) comedian
EA/03*
CAREY, Charles English actor,
manager GRB/1
CAREY, David (b 1945) American
actor TW/27
CAREY, Denis (b 1909) English
director, actor AAS, BE,
WWT/12-16
CAREY, Edna actress CDP
CAREY, Eleanor (1852-1915)
Chilean actress CDP, WWS
CAREY, Elizabeth [Mrs. Tom
Carey] (d 1876) EA/77*
CAREY, Francis Clive Savill (b
1883) English singer, director
ES
CAREY, Frank (b 1934) American
actor TW/26, 28-30
CAREY, George Saville (1743-1807)
English actor, monologuist,
dramatist BD, CDP, CP/3,
DD, DNB, GT, TD/1-2
CAREY, Mrs. George Saville [née
Gillo] (fl 1789-98) BD
CAREY, Giles (fl 1609-13) actor
DA
CAREY, Harriett [Mrs. Tom
Carey] (d 1868) EA/69*
CAREY, Harry (1878-1947) Amer-
ican actor ES, TW/4
CAREY, Henry (1690-1743) English
musician, dramatist CDP,
CP/1-3, DD, DNB, ES, GT,
HP, NTH, TD/1-2
CAREY, Henry Lucius, Lord Vis-
count Falkland (d 1663) drama-
tist CP/1-3, DD
CAREY, Joseph A. (d 1964 [81])
actor BE*
CAREY, Joseph P. actor, singer
CDP
CAREY, Joyce (b 1898) English

actress, dramatist BE,
COC, ES, WWT/4-16
CAREY, Macdonald (b 1913)
American actor BE, ES,
TW/10
CAREY, May (d 1966) producer,
director BP/50*
CAREY, Pat (d 1912 [53]) Irish
comedian EA/13*
CAREY, Mrs. Pat see Howard,
Lizzie
CAREY, Ron (b 1935) American
actor TW/25
CAREY, Rev. Thomas F. (1904-
72) American director, pro-
ducer BE, TW/28
CAREY, Mrs. Tom see Carey,
Elizabeth
CAREY, Mrs. Tom see Carey,
Harriett
CAREY, T. P. (fl 1865) Irish
singer HAS
CARFAX, Bruce (1905-70) Eng-
lish actor, singer WWT/
7-13
CARGILL, Ann see Cargill,
Mrs. R.
CARGILL, Judith American
actress TW/3
CARGILL, Patrick (b 1918)
English actor, dramatist
WWT/14-16
CARGILL, Mrs. R. [née Ann
Brown] (c. 1759-84) English
actress, singer BD, CDP,
DNB, TD/1-2
CARHART, Georgiana (d 1959
[93]) singer TW/15
CARHART, James L. (1843-
1937) American actor WWS
CARINGTON, Dorothy (b 1872)
English actress GRB/1
CARIOLI, Claudine (fl 1857-58)
singer HAS
CARIOU, Leonard (b 1939)
Canadian actor AAS, TW/
25-30, WWT/15-16
CARLE, Alice actress, singer
CDP
CARLE, Pietro (d 1899) bird
performer EA/00*
CARLE, Richard [Charles
Nicholas Carleton] (1871-
1941) American actor, drama-
tist CB, CDP, GRB/2-4,
SR, WWA/1, WWM, WWS,
WWT/1-9
CARLELL, Lodowick (fl 1629-

64) dramatist CP/1-3, DD,
DNB, FGF, GT
CARLES, Mr. actor GT, TD/2
CARLES, Henry (d 1858 [48])
actor, singer WWT/14*
CARLETON, Mr. (d 1783) house
servant BD
CARLETON, Mr. (fl 1765-90)
lobby doorkeeper BD
CARLETON, Miss (fl 1785) actress
BD
CARLETON, Billie [Florence
Lenora Stewart] (d 1918 [22])
actress EA/19*, WWT/14*
CARLETON, Charles Nicholas
see Carle, Richard
CARLETON, Claire [or Clare] (b
1913) American actress TW/
6-7, WWT/9-13
CARLETON, Henry Guy (1856?-
1910) American dramatist DAB,
DD, GRB/2-4, HJD, SR,
WWA/1, WWS
CARLETON, John (fl 1662-64)
actor? BD
CARLETON, Laurie (d 1899)
EA/00*
CARLETON, Lloyd B. American
actor, director ES
CARLETON, Marjorie (d 1964)
dramatist BE*
CARLETON, Nicholas (fl c. 1580)
actor DA
CARLETON, Royce [Colin Camp-
bell] (1860-95) Scottish actor
DD, DP
CARLETON, William (1827-85)
Irish actor, dramatist, singer
CDP, DD, HAS
CARLETON, William P. (d 1947
[74]) actor, singer WWT/14*
CARLETON, William T. (fl 1873)
singer, manager CDP
CARLETON, William T. (d 1930)
producer WWT/14*
CARLETON, W. T. (d 1922)
actor, singer WWT/14*
CARLI, Miss (fl 1762-70) singer
BD
CARLIER, Madeleine (d 1935 [57])
actress WWT/14*
CARLILE, Mrs. Frank see
Gerard, Ethel
CARLILE, James (d 1691) English
dramatist, actor CP/3, DD,
DNB
CARLIN, Charles (d 1908 [49])
performer? EA/09*

CARLIN, Chet (b 1918) Amer-
ican actor TW/28-30
CARLIN, Cynthia (d 1973)
actress TW/28
CARLIN, Herbert (d 1967 [70])
press agent BP/51*
CARLIN, Roger (d 1974 [62])
producer/director/choreog-
rapher BP/58*
CARLIN, Thomas (b 1928)
American actor TW/12-13,
15-16, 20
CARLINI, Rosa (fl 1758-59)
dancer BD
CARLINO, Lewis John (b 1932)
American dramatist CD
CARLINO, Sieur (fl 1777)
tumbler BD
CARLISLE, Earl of see
Howard, Frederic
CARLISLE, Mrs. (fl 1745) act-
ress BD
CARLISLE, Miss (fl 1869-80)
actress DD
CARLISLE, Alexandra [Alexandra
Swift] (1886-1936) English
actress GRB/3-4, SR,
WWT/1-8
CARLISLE, Frank (d 1918) EA/
19*
CARLISLE, Frederic Howard,
Earl of see Howard, Fred-
eric
CARLISLE, James (d 1691)
English actor, dramatist
BD, CP/1-2, GT
CARLISLE, James (d 1864)
circus performer HAS
CARLISLE, Joseph (d 1896 [66])
comedian EA/97*
CARLISLE, Kitty (b 1914/15)
American actress, singer
BE, TW/5-13, 15-16, WWT/
9-16
CARLISLE, Margaret (b 1905)
American actress, singer
WWT/7-10
CARLISLE, Sybil (b 1871)
South African/English act-
ress DD, GRB/1-4, WWT/
1-8
CARLO (fl 1803) performing
dog CDP
CARLO, Mr. (fl 1785-86) singer
BD
CARLO, Harry acrobat CDP
CARLO, Monte (1883-1967)
Danish lyricist, composer,

publisher BE, TW/24
CARLO, Phoebe (fl 1883-86) act-
ress CDP, DD
CARLO FAMILY, The (fl 1850)
HAS
CARLOMAN, Mrs. (d 1875 [44])
EA/77*
CARLOS, Fred (d 1904) actor
EA/05*, WWT/14*
CARLOS, Mrs. Fred see
D'Lonra, Annie
CARLSBERG, Gotthold (1838-81)
musician, orchestra leader
CDP
CARLSEN, John A. (1915-75)
Canadian representative WWT/
11-14
CARLSON, Keith (d 1975 [34])
producer/director/choreographer
BP/59*
CARLSON, Ken (d 1973 [53])
performer BP/57*
CARLSON, Leslie (b 1933) Amer-
ican actor TW/25-26
CARLSON, Richard (1912-77)
American actor ES
CARLTON, Mr. (fl 1729) dancer
BD
CARLTON, Sir Arthur Roscoe
(1865-1931) English actor,
manager, proprietor GRB/1-4
CARLTON, Mrs. Charles see
Carlton, Lizzie
CARLTON, Henry singer CDP
CARLTON, Henry see Cavendish,
Henry Frederick Compton
CARLTON, Henry F. (d 1973 [80])
dramatist BP/57*
CARLTON, James (d 1890) circus
performer EA/91*
CARLTON, Kathleen (d 1964 [65])
actress BE*
CARLTON, Lizzie [Mrs. Charles
Carlton] (d 1906) EA/07*
CARLTON, Louis H. (b 1863)
English dramatist, manager
GRB/1
CARLTON, Neil (d 1912 [58])
actor? EA/13*
CARLTON, Peter (fl 1673-77)
actor BD
CARLTON, T. S. (d 1892 [45])
manager EA/93*
CARLTON, William (d 1973 [50])
musician BP/58*
CARLTON, William T. (fl 1870s)
English singer SR
CARLYLE, Francis (d 1916 [48])

actor WWT/14*
CARLYLE, Richard (b 1920)
Canadian actor TW/6-8,
11-12
CARLYON, Eunice Nowlan (d
1904 [81]) EA/05*
CARLYON, Frank (d 1908 [36])
manager EA/09*
CARLYON, Kate (d 1924 [75])
actress WWT/14*
CARMAN, Mrs. [née Conway]
(fl 1848) actress HAS
CARMAN, Miss dancer HAS
CARMAN, Allan (d 1969 [72])
performer BP/54*
CARMAN, Jerry (d 1975 [75])
agent BP/60*
CARME, Pamela [Hon. Kathleen
Pamela Boscawen] (b 1902)
English actress WWT/6-8
CARMEL, Eddie (d 1972 [36])
circus giant BP/57*
CARMENCITA Spanish dancer
SR
CARMICHAEL, Ian (b 1920)
English actor AAS, WWT/
12-16
CARMICHAEL, Thomas (fl
1737-79) prompter BD
CARMICHAEL, Thomas Percy
see Percy, A. C.
CARMIGNANI, Giovanni (fl
1762-63) singer BD
CARMIGNANI, Signora Giovanni?
(fl 1763) singer? BD
CARMINATI, Tullio (1894-1971)
Italian actor ES, TW/27,
WWT/7-10
CARMINES, Al composer, lyri-
cist, performer, director,
producer WWT/16
CARMODY, Jay (d 1973 [72])
American critic BE
CARNABY, James (fl 1701?-13)
actor BD
CARNCROSS, John L. (b c.1834)
American minstrel, singer
CDP
CARNE, Mrs. (fl 1793-95)
actress BD
CARNE, Miss (fl 1781-82)
actress BD
CARNE, Miss (fl 1799-1802)
dancer BD
CARNE, Elizabeth see Carne,
Mrs. John
CARNE, John (fl 1740-68) house
servant BD

CARNE, Mrs. John [Elizabeth]
(fl c. 1762-83) house servant
BD
CARNE, Joseph (fl 1877-96) actor
DD, EA/97
CARNE, Judy (b 1939) English
actress TW/26
CARNEGIE, Douglas John (d 1913)
EA/14*
CARNEGIE, Gordon (d 1916) EA/
17*
CARNELIA, Craig (b 1949) Amer-
ican actor TW/25-26
CARNEVALE, Pietro (fl 1782?-91)
Italian? musician, deputy mana-
ger, proprietor BD
CARNEVALE, Signora Pietro (fl
1783-92) singer, actress BD
CARNEY, Mr. (fl 1733-45) dancer,
actor BD
CARNEY, Annie [Mrs. Tom Car-
ney] (d 1910 [52]) EA/11*
CARNEY, Art (b 1918) American
performer, actor BE, CB,
TW/15-16, 19, 21-22, 25, 28-
30, WWT/15-16
CARNEY, Frank (b 1904) Irish
dramatist, actor, producer BE
CARNEY, George (1887-1947)
English actor WWT/9-10
CARNEY, Kate (1868-1950) English
music-hall artist CDP, COC,
ES, OC/1-3
CARNEY, Kay American actress
TW/26
CARNEY, Pat [James Sullivan]
(d 1893) music-hall artist
EA/94*
CARNEY, Tom [Henry Penny] (d
1911 [52]) Irish comedian EA/
13*
CARNEY, Mrs. Tom see
Carney, Annie
CARNEY, William (d 1972 [73])
journalist BP/56*
CARNEY, "Yankee" Henri (d 1902)
music-hall performer EA/03*
CARNOVSKY, Morris (b 1897/98)
American actor AAS, BE, ES,
TW/4-8, 12-18, WWT/9-16
CARO, Warren (b 1907) American
executive, actor BE, WWT/16
CAROL, J. C. (d 1899) manager
EA/00*
CAROL, John (d 1968 [58]) per-
former BP/53*

CAROLA, Mme. (d 1900 [37])
circus performer EA/01*
CAROLINA TWINS freaks CDP
CAROLINE, Mlle. (fl 1842)
equestrienne CDP
CARON, Leon (d 1905 [55])
composer, conductor EA/
06*
CARON, Leslie (b 1931) French
dancer, actress CB, COC,
ES, WWT/13-14
CAROZZI, Carlotta (fl 1864)
Italian singer HAS
CARPENTER, Mr. (fl 1736)
actor BD
CARPENTER, Mr. (fl 1838)
actor HAS
CARPENTER, Mrs. (fl 1851)
actress HAS
CARPENTER, Carleton [or
Carlton] (b 1926) American
actor, composer BE, TW/
10-17, 22-23, 26, 30,
WWT/16
CARPENTER, Claude E. (d
1976 [71]) designer BP/60*
CARPENTER, Constance (b
1906) English actress, singer
BE, WWT/7-16
CARPENTER, Edward Childs
(1871/72-1950) American
dramatist TW/7, WWA/5,
WWT/4-10
CARPENTER, Mrs. E. J.
see Evans, Millicent
CARPENTER, Ernest (1868-1909)
manager GRB/3-4
CARPENTER, Freddie (b 1908)
Australian dancer, director
WWT/10-16
CARPENTER, Frederick (d
1904 [63]) lessee EA/05*
CARPENTER, John Alden
(1876-1951) American com-
poser CB, ES, HJD,
WWA/3
CARPENTER, Joseph Edwards
(1813-85) English dramatist
DD, EA/68
CARPENTER, Louisa d'A. (d
1976 [68]) producer/director/
choreographer BP/60*
CARPENTER, Mary Ann (d
1877 [29]) EA/78*
CARPENTER, Maud (d 1967)
manager WWT/8-10
CARPENTER, Paul (d 1964 [43])
Canadian actor BE*

CARPENTER, Richard (fl 1623-70)
dramatist CP/1-3, DD
CARPENTER, Robert (1748-85)
actor, singer BD
CARPENTER, Thelma (b 1922)
American singer BE, TW/11,
25-26
CARPENTER, Tyler (b 1917)
American actor TW/4
CARPENTER, William (fl 1611-25)
actor DA
"CARPENTIER, Mr." (fl 1754)
actor? BD
CARR (fl 1805) actor? dramatist
CP/3
CARR, Mr. (d 1797) actor, eques-
trian, tumbler BD
CARR, Mr. (fl 1797) watchman
BD
CARR, Mrs. (fl 1741) dancer BD
CARR, Mrs. (fl 1789) American
dramatist EAP
CARR, Alexander (1878-1946)
Russian/American actor CB,
ES, GRB/3-4, SR, TW/3,
WWA/2, WWM, WWS, WWT/
1-9
CARR, Anthony (b 1924) American
actor TW/2-3
CARR, A. Selby (d 1974 [70])
agent BP/59*
CARR, Ben (d 1916) EA/17*
CARR, Benjamin (1768-1831) Eng-
lish composer, publisher, musi-
cian, singer BD, CDP, DAB,
ES, HAS, WWA/H
CARR, Eric Marcus (d 1916 [20])
EA/17*
CARR, F. Osmond (1858-1916)
English composer DD, ES,
GRB/3-4, WWT/1-3
CARR, George actor, singer CDP
CARR, George (d 1962 [69]) actor
WWT/6-9
CARR, Georgia (d 1971 [46]) per-
former BP/56*
CARR, Gina (d 1972 [35]) actress
TW/29
CARR, Howard (1880-1960) English
composer, conductor WWT/
4-7, WWW/5
CARR, I. N. (d 1866) pantomimist
HAS
CARR, Isabella (d 1867 [49])
actress? HAS
CARR, Jane [Rita Brunström]
(1909-57) English actress
WWT/9-12

CARR, John (fl 1631) actor
DA
CARR, Sir John (b 1772) English
dramatist CP/3
CARR, Rev. Dr. John (d 1807
[76]) dramatist CP/2-3, GT
CARR, Sir John (fl 1804) drama-
tist CP/3, DD
CARR, Joseph W. Comyns (1849-
1916) English dramatist,
critic, manager DD, ES,
GRB/1-4, NTH, WWT/1-3,
WWW/2
CARR, Kenneth (b 1943) Ameri-
can actor TW/22-26, 30
CARR, Lawrence (1916-69)
American producer BE,
TW/25, WWA/5, WWT/
14-15
CARR, Leon (d 1976 [65])
composer/lyricist BP/60*
CARR, Louisa [Mrs. Peach]
(fl 1821-23) actress CDP
CARR, Lucy (d 1897) English
equestrienne EA/98*
CARR, Mary (fl 1856) actress
HAS
CARR, Mary (d 1973 [99]) per-
former BP/58*
CARR, Mickey (d 1973) musi-
cian BP/58*
CARR, Mildred [Mrs. James
Willard] Welsh actress
GRB/1
CARR, Oliver (fl 1741-69)
actor, manager BD
CARR, Philip (1874-1957) Eng-
lish dramatist, critic, jour-
nalist DD, WWT/11-12
CARR, Philip (d 1969 [38])
performer BP/54*
CARR, Richard (fl 1684) musi-
cian, publisher BD
CARR, Robert (fl 1674-96)
violist BD
CARR, Robert (fl 1766) drama-
tist CP/3, DD
CARR, R. P. (d 1872) agent
EA/73*
CARR, Samuel (fl 1770) drama-
tist CP/2, GT
CARR, Sarah (d 1907 [70])
EA/08*
CARR, Tom (d 1906 [58]) musi-
cian EA/07*
CARRA, Lawrence (b 1909)
Italian director, educator
BE

CARRADINE, David (b 1940)
American actor TW/22-23,
25, 27
CARRADINE, John (b 1906) Amer-
ican actor AAS, BE, ES, TW/
5-7, WWT/11-16
CARR-COOK, Madge (1856-1933)
English actress GRB/3-4,
NTH, WWT/1-7
CARRE, Ada [Mrs. Oscar Carré]
(d 1897 [27]) EA/98*
CARRE, Adolph (d 1881 [31])
EA/82*
CARRE, Mrs. Adolf see Carré,
Mrs. M. P.
CARRE, Albert (1852-1938) French
dramatist GRB/1, 3-4, WWT/
1
CARRE, Anthony see Fawcett,
Anthony
CARRE, Marguerite (d 1947 [75])
singer WWT/14*
CARRE, Marie-Thérèse (b 1757)
French dancer BD
CARRE, Mrs. M. P. [Mrs. Adolf
Carré] (d 1877) EA/78*
CARRE, Mrs. Oscar see Carré,
Ada
CARREIRE, Victor (d 1966 [70])
performer BP/50*
CARRENO, Teresa (1853-1917)
pianist, composer, singer,
conductor CDP
CARRICK, Edward [Edward
Anthony Craig] (b 1905) English
designer ES, OC/1-2, WWT/
8-14
CARRICK, Hartley (1881-1929)
dramatist WWT/3-6
CARRICK, Tom [Alban Thomas
Steet] (b 1868) English actor
GRB/1
CARRIDEN, William (d 1911) actor
EA/12*
CARRIER, Mrs. (fl 1743) actress
BD
CARRIGAN, Thomas J. (d 1941
[55]) American actor BE*,
WWT/14*
CARRILLO, Leo (1881-1961)
American actor ES, TW/18,
WWT/7-10
CARRINGTON, Abbie Beeson (fl
1880) singer CDP
CARRINGTON, A. R. drummer,
composer CDP
CARRINGTON, Ethel (1889-1962)
English actress WWT/4-7

CARRINGTON, Eva see De Clifford, Lady

CARRINGTON, Evelyn (d 1942 [66]) actress BE*, WWT/14*

CARRINGTON, Frank (1901-75) American producer, director BE

CARRINGTON, Helen (d 1963 [68]) performer BP/48*

CARRINGTON, Katherine (d 1953 [43]) American actress BE*, BP/37*

CARRINGTON, Murray (1885-1941) English actor WWT/4-9

CARRODUS, John Tiplady (1836-95) English musician DNB

CARROLL, Adam (d 1974 [76]) composer TW/30

CARROLL, Albert (1898-1956) American actor TW/1, 3, 6-7, 13

CARROLL, Clifford A. (d 1970 [69]) journalist BP/54*

CARROLL, Daniel Patrick see La Rue, Danny

CARROLL, Danny (b 1940) American actor TW/21-25

CARROLL, Diahann (b 1935) American singer, actress BE, CB, TW/11, 18-20

CARROLL, Earl (1892/93-1948) American manager, producer, dramatist COC, DAB, ES, NTH, OC/3, SR, TW/5, WWA/2, WWT/5-10

CARROLL, Edward (d 1869 [27]) equestrian EA/70*

CARROLL, Edward (d 1879 [37]) prompter EA/80*

CARROLL, Edward Linus (d 1975 [68]) producer/director/choreographer BP/60*

CARROLL, E. J. (d 1931 [62]) manager WWT/14*

CARROLL, Frederick (d 1889 [67]) novelty traveller EA/90*

CARROLL, Garnet H. (d 1964 [61]) producer, theatre owner, actor BE*, WWT/14*

CARROLL, Gene (d 1972 [74]) performer BP/56*

CARROLL, Harry (d 1962 [70]) composer BE*, BP/47*

CARROLL, Helena Scottish actress, producer BE, TW/22-24, 26-30

CARROLL, James (b 1817) American actor SR

CARROLL, Jean (d 1972 [63]) performer BP/57*

CARROLL, Jimmy (d 1972 [59]) composer/lyricist BP/56*

CARROLL, John actor, singer CDP

CARROLL, John (d 1880 [39]) comedian, dancer EA/81*

CARROLL, John Edward (d 1916) EA/17*

CARROLL, John W. (1837-81) American actor CDP, HAS

CARROLL, June American singer, actress, lyricist BE, TW/8-10

CARROLL, Mrs. J. W. [née Jennie Melville] (b 1843) American actress HAS

CARROLL, Katie actress, singer CDP

CARROLL, Lawrence W. (d 1963 [65]) manager BE*

CARROLL, Leo G. (1892-1972) English actor AAS, BE, ES, TW/1-17, 29, WWA/5, WWT/5-14

CARROLL, Louise (d 1975) performer BP/60*

CARROLL, Madeleine (b 1906) English actress BE, CB, ES, TW/5-6, WWT/6-12

CARROLL, Marie Elise equestrienne CDP

CARROLL, Nancy [Ann La Hiff] (1906-65) American actress BE, ES, TW/5-6, 22, WWT/7-10

CARROLL, Nicholas Cahill (d 1871) comedian, pantaloon EA/72*

CARROLL, Pat (b 1927) American actress BE

CARROLL, Patrick (1902-65) American librarian BE

CARROLL, Paul Vincent (1900-68) Irish dramatist AAS, BE, COC, ES, MD, MH, MWD, NTH, OC/1-3, PDT, RE, SR, TW/25, WWA/5, WWT/9-14, WWW/6

CARROLL, Richard actor CDP

CARROLL, Richard Field (1864-1925) American actor CDP, SR, WWS

CARROLL, R. M. (1831-69) minstrel, female impersonator CDP

CARROLL, Robert (b 1920)

American actor TW/4-8,
10-13, 15

CARROLL, Sydney W. [George
Frederick Carl Whiteman]
(1877-1958) Australian critic,
dramatist, manager COC,
OC/3, WWT/7-11

CARROLL, Vinette (b 1922)
American actress, director,
administrator AAS, BE,
TW/18, WWT/15-16

CARROLL, William B. (d 1889
[74]) American circus performer EA/90*

CARROLL, William J. (1853-96)
minstrel, banjoist CDP

CARRON, George (d 1970 [40])
performer BP/54*

CARRUTH, Richard (d 1973
[53]) producer/director/
choreographer BP/58*

CARRUTHERS, James (b 1931)
American actor TW/29

CARRY, George D. (d 1970 [57])
musician BP/55*

CARSELL, Susette (d 1946)
musician SR

CARSEY, Mary (d 1973 [35])
performer BP/58*

CARSOIN, Mrs. (d 1893) EA/
95*

CARSON, Charles (b 1885) English actor TW/13, WWT/5-16

CARSON, Charles L. (d 1901)
publisher BE*, WWT/14*

CARSON, Mrs. Charles L.
[Kittie Claremont] (1879-1919)
English actress GRB/1-4,
WWT/1-3

CARSON, Cora Youngblood (1886-
1943) American entertainer,
bandleader SR

CARSON, Cyrus (fl 1850) American actor HAS

CARSON, David (b 1837) American? actor HAS, SR

CARSON, Doris (b 1910) actress,
singer WWT/9

CARSON, Emma actress CDP

CARSON, Frances (b 1895) American actress BE, TW/1-3,
WWT/4-13

CARSON, Jack (1910-63) Canadian actor ES, TW/8

CARSON, Jeannie (b 1925/29)
English actress, singer BE,
TW/5-8, 10-19, WWT/12-16

CARSON, J. Harold (b 1885)

English actor GRB/1

CARSON, John (b 1927) Ceylonese
actor TW/24

CARSON, Kate (fl 1857-65) actress
DD

CARSON, Lionel [Lionel Courtier-
Dutton] (1873-1937) editor
GRB/3-4, WWT/1-7, WWW/3

CARSON, Mindy (b 1926) American
actress, singer BE

CARSON, Murray (1865-1917) English actor, dramatist DD,
EA/95, GRB/1-4, WWS, WWT/
1-3, WWW/2

CARSON, William G. B. (b 1891)
American educator, dramatist
BE

CARSONI, Marie [Mrs. Walter
Thompson] (d 1898 [44]) musician EA/99*

CARSWELL, Mr. (d 1905 [68])
EA/06*

CARTE, Blanche [Mrs. Richard
D'Oyly Carte] (d 1885 [70])
EA/86*

CARTE, Charles (b 1870) actor,
manager GRB/1

CARTE, Lucas D'Oyly (d 1906)
EA/08*

CARTE, Richard (d 1891 [83])
composer, musician EA/92*

CARTE, Richard D'Oyly see
D'Oyly Carte, Richard

CARTE, Mrs. Richard D'Oyly
see Carte, Blanche

CARTE, Mrs. Richard D'Oyly
see D'Oyly Carte, Mrs.
Richard

CARTE, Rupert D'Oyly see
D'Oyly Carte, Rupert

CARTEN, Audrey (b 1900) English
actress WWT/5-9

CARTER, [Mr. ?] (fl c. 1661-62)
performer BD

CARTER, Mr. (fl 1746) actor BD

CARTER, Mr. (fl 1760-61) candle-
man BD

CARTER, Mr. (fl 1800) puppeteer
BD

CARTER, "Little" (d 1850 [81])
treasurer EA/72*

CARTER, Mrs. (fl 1719-26)
dresser BD

CARTER, Mrs. (fl 1728-36)
singer BD

CARTER, Mrs. (d 1910) EA/11*

CARTER, Miss (fl 1741-42) actress,
singer BD

CARTER, Miss (fl 1759-65)
singer BD
CARTER, Amanda see Fyffe,
Kitty
CARTER, Andrew (d 1669)
singer BD
CARTER, Mrs. B. (d 1887)
EA/88*
CARTER, Bere (d 1917) EA/18*
CARTER, Billy (b 1834) min-
strel, banjoist CDP
CARTER, Caroline Louise Dud-
ley see Carter, Mrs.
Leslie
CARTER, Carvel (d 1967 [31])
performer BP/51*
CARTER, Charles Thomas
(c. 1735-1804) Irish musician,
composer BD, DD, DNB,
TD/1-2
CARTER, Charlton see
Heston, Charlton
CARTER, Desmond (d 1939)
English lyricist, dramatist
WWT/6-8, WWW/3
CARTER, Don (b 1933) American
actor TW/30
CARTER, Elizabeth (d 1916
[52]) EA/17*
CARTER, Elizabeth Clegg (d
1890 [65]) EA/91*
CARTER, Elliott (b 1908) Amer-
ican composer ES
CARTER, Ernest (b 1886) Amer-
ican composer ES
CARTER, Frank (d 1920 [32])
comedian BE*, BP/4*
CARTER, Frederick (d 1970
[70]) English manager WWT/
14
CARTER, Helen E. H. (fl 1881)
singer CDP
CARTER, Henry Lee (d 1862
[37]) EA/72*
CARTER, Herbert (d 1918)
EA/19*
CARTER, Hubert Edward (d
1934 [65]) English actor
WWT/1-7
CARTER, Huntly (b 1874) Eng-
lish actor GRB/1
CARTER, J. (fl 1787) dramatist
CP/3, DD
CARTER, J. (fl 1794) singer
BD
CARTER, Jack (1917-67) Eng-
lish choreographer, dancer
ES

CARTER, James (1812/14-47)
English actor ES, HAS
CARTER, James (d 1899) wax-
works proprietor EA/00*
CARTER, Janis American actress
ES
CARTER, J. Heneage (b 1826)
English lecturer, singer, actor
HAS
CARTER, John (d 1871 [35])
musician EA/72*
CARTER, John (d 1907 [87]) actor
DD, GRB/3
CARTER, Mrs. John (d 1891)
actress DD
CARTER, Mrs. John (d 1908 [53])
actress GRB/4*
CARTER, John Richard (d 1885
[34]) manager EA/86*
CARTER, J. P. (fl 1843) minstrel,
banjoist CDP
CARTER, Leslie (d 1921 [48])
actor BE*, WWT/14*
CARTER, Mrs. Leslie [Caroline
Louise Dudley] (1862-1937)
American actress COC, DAB,
DD, ES, GRB/1-4, NTH, OC/
1-3, PP/1, SR, WWA/1,
WWM, WWS, WWT/1-8
CARTER, Lincoln J. (1865-1926)
dramatist SR
CARTER, Lloyd (b 1935) American
actor TW/25
CARTER, Lonnie (b 1942) Ameri-
can dramatist CD
CARTER, Margaret English actress
WWT/5-9
CARTER, Myra (b 1930) American
actress TW/29
CARTER, Nell (1894-1965) actress
WWT/2-13
CARTER, Ralph (b 1961) American
actor TW/29-30
CARTER, Richard (fl 1728-43)
musician BD
CARTER, Thomas (1768-1800)
singer BD
CARTER, Thomas see Carter,
Charles Thomas
CARTER-BROWN, T. (d 1893 [44])
manager EA/94*
CARTER-EDWARDS, James [James
Edwards] (1840-1930) English
actor DD, OAA/2, WWT/2-6
CARTERET, Anna [née Wilkinson]
(b 1942) Indian/English actress
WWT/15-16
CARTINI, Albert [Albert Ware]

(d 1894) equestrian comedian
EA/95*

CARTINI, Fred (d 1899 [29])
circus performer EA/00*

CARTLITCH, John G. (1793-
1875) actor, manager CDP,
HAS

CARTON, James E. (d 1879
[25]) American comedian
EA/80*

CARTON, R[ichard] C[laude;
né Critchett] (1856-1928)
English actor, dramatist
COC, DD, EA/97, ES,
GRB/1-4, NTH, OAA/1-2,
OC/1-3, WWS, WWT/1-5,
WWW/2

CARTOON ARCHETYPICAL
SLOGAN THEATRE theatre
collective CD

CARTWRIGHT, Mr. (fl 1710)
doorkeeper BD

CARTWRIGHT, Mr. (fl 1740-
51?) actor BD

CARTWRIGHT, Mr. (fl 1785)
actor BD

CARTWRIGHT, Mrs. (fl 1671)
actress BD

CARTWRIGHT, Mrs. (fl 1772)
singer BD

CARTWRIGHT, Mrs. (fl 1785)
actress BD

CARTWRIGHT, Mrs. (d 1792)
actress BD

CARTWRIGHT, Master (b
c. 1750) dancer BD

CARTWRIGHT, Miss (fl 1800)
musical glasses player BD

CARTWRIGHT, Charles [Charles
Morley] (1855-1916) actor
DD, EA/96, GRB/2-4, SR,
WWS, WWT/1-2

CARTWRIGHT, George (fl 1661)
dramatist CP/1-3, DD,
DNB, FGF, GT

CARTWRIGHT, John (1756-1824)
musical glasses player BD,
TD/1

CARTWRIGHT, Peggy (b 1912)
Canadian actress, dancer
WWT/7

CARTWRIGHT, Thomas (d 1875)
musician EA/76*

CARTWRIGHT, William (d 1650?)
actor DA, DD, OC/3

CARTWRIGHT, William (c. 1606-
86) actor BD, CDP, COC,
DA, DD, DNB, ES, OC/1-3

CARTWRIGHT, William (1611-43)
English dramatist CDP, COC,
CP/1-3, DD, DNB, ES, FGF,
GT, HP, RE

CARTWRIGHT, William (d 1869)
musician EA/70*

CARUS, Emma [Mrs. Harry James
Everall] (1879-1927) German
singer, actress CDP, WWA/1,
WWS, WWT/4-5

CARUSO, Mr. (fl 1748-56) musician BD

CARUSO, Enrico (1873-1921)
Italian singer CDP, DAB,
ES, HP, SR, WWA/1

CARVALHO-MIOLAN, Caroline
Marie Felix (1827-95) singer
CDP

CARVER, Kathryn (d 1947 [41])
actress BE*

CARVER, Louise (d 1956 [87])
actress TW/12

CARVER, Lynne (d 1955 [38])
actress BE*

CARVER, Norman (b 1899) American manager BE

CARVER, Robert (d 1791) scene
painter, artist BD

CARVER, Robert (d 1971) performer BP/56*

CARVER, W. F. ["Doctor"]
champion rifle shot CDP

CARVER, William (fl 1624) actor
DA

CARVIL, Bert Forrest (b 1880)
Canadian actor WWS

CARVIL, Harry (b 1880) Canadian
actor WWS

CARVILL, Henry J. (d 1941 [74])
English actor GRB/1-4

CARVILLE, Frederick (d 1881
[28]) EA/82*

CARY, Annie Louise (1841/42-
1921) American singer CDP,
DAB, ES, WWA/1, WWM

CARY, Falkland L. (b 1897) Irish
dramatist WWT/11-16

CARY, Mary (fl 1865) actress
CDP

CARYL, John (fl 1667-1717) English? dramatist CP/1-3, GT

CARYLL, Ivan [John or Felix
Tilkin] (1861-1921) Belgian
composer, conductor DD, ES,
GRB/1-4, SR, WWT/1-3,
WWW/2

CARYLL, John (1625-1711) dramatist DD

CARYLLON, Ethel L. [Mrs.
Ralph Roberts] English
actress GRB/1
CARYSFORT, Earl of see
Proby, John Joshua
CASADESUS, Mathilde (d 1965
[44]) performer BP/50*
CASAIA, Miss (fl 1766-67)
dancer BD
CASALI, Luigi (fl 1791) dancer
BD
CASALIS, Jeanne de (1898-1966)
actress, dramatist WWW/6
CASANOVA, Gaetano Giuseppe
Giacomo (fl c. 1719-27) actor
BD
CASANOVA, Signora Gaetano
Giuseppe Giacomo [née
Zanetta Farusi] (fl c. 1719-
27) actress BD
CASARINI, Signora (fl 1746-48)
Italian singer BD
CASARTELLI, Gabrielle (b 1910)
English actress WWT/5-10
CASAUBON, Frances Anne (d
1885 [37]) performer? EA/
86*
CASAZZA, Elvira (b 1887)
Italian singer ES
CASE, Master (fl 1737-39) dancer
BD
CASE, Allen American actor
TW/14, 16, 22-23
CASE, Charley (d 1916) mono-
logist SR
CASE, Ethel L. (d 1971 [87])
founder of Long Beach Com-
munity Players BP/56*
CASE, Nelson (d 1976 [66])
performer BP/60*
CASELLI, Signora (fl 1743-44)
singer BD
CASELLI, T. (d 1883) comedian
EA/84*
CASENTINI, Anna see Borghi,
Signora Luigi
CASEY [Master] (fl 18th cent)
squinting beggar boy CDP
CASEY, Mr. (fl 1748) actor BD
CASEY, Mrs. (fl 1783-85)
actress BD
CASEY, Ethel (d 1971 [49])
performer BP/55*
CASEY, John (d c. 1792) actor
BD
CASEY, Kenneth (d 1965 [66])
composer/lyricist BP/50*
CASEY, Pat (d 1962 [87])

American talent representative
BE*
CASEY, Polly (fl 1741) singer BD
CASEY, Rosemary (1904-76) Amer-
ican dramatist BE
CASEY, William Francis (b 1884)
Irish dramatist ES
CASH, Dan (d 1973 [53]) producer/
director/choreographer BP/57*
CASH, Edith May [Mrs. George
Cash] (d 1917) EA/18*
CASH, Mrs. George see Cash,
Edith May
CASH, Morny singer CDP
CASH, Rosalind (b 1938) American
actress TW/24-28, 30, WWT/
16
CASH, William F. (d 1963) per-
former BE*
CASHAN, Patrick Martin (d 1899
[56]) music-hall singer EA/00*
CASHELL, Oliver (d 1747) actor
BD
CASHMAN, Betty American act-
ress, director, coach BE
CASHMORE, John Garrett (d 1876)
harpist EA/77*
CASHMORE, Thomas Isaac (d
1886) equestrian clown EA/87*
CASIMERE, Mons. (fl 1785-87)
tumbler, ropedancer BD
CASIMERE, Mme. (fl 1787) dancer
BD
CASIMERE, Fils (fl 1785-87)
tumbler BD
CASON, Mr. (fl 1726?-61) dresser
BD
CASON, Barbara (b 1933) Ameri-
can actress TW/25, 27-30
CASPARY, Vera (b 1904) Ameri-
can dramatist BE, CB
CASPER, Richard (b 1949) Ameri-
can actor TW/29
CASS, Frank singer CDP
CASS, Henry (b 1902) English
actor, producer AAS, WWT/
8-16
CASS, H. Marie (d 1969 [77])
BP/54*
CASS, John (d 1890 [60]) perform-
er? EA/91*
CASS, Peggy (b 1924/26) American
actress BE, TW/13-20, 24-27,
WWT/14-16
CASS, Ronald (b 1923) Welsh com-
poser WWT/14-16
CASSANI, Giuseppe (fl 1708-12)
singer BD

CASSAVETES, John (b 1929) American actor CB

CASSEL, Irwin (d 1971 [84]) composer/lyricist BP/56*

CASSEL, Rita Allen (d 1968 [56]) director? choreographer? BP/53*

CASSICK, Jack (d 1918) EA/19*

CASSIDAY, Rose (fl 1851) actress HAS

CASSIDY, Claudia American critic BE, CB

CASSIDY, G. W. (d 1887) manager, architect EA/88*

CASSIDY, Jack (1927-76) American actor, singer, dancer BE, TW/12-13, 15-16, 19-22, 26, WWT/14-16

CASSIDY, James (d 1869) musician EA/70*

CASSIDY, John (d 1907 [40]) manager EA/08*

CASSIDY, J. Rice (d 1927 [66]) actor BE*, WWT/14*

CASSIM, James (d 1879 [28]) American clown EA/80*

CASSMORE, Judy (b 1942) American actress TW/21

CASSON, Ann (b 1915) English actress WWT/6-14

CASSON, Charles Henry (d 1886) EA/87*

CASSON, Christopher (b 1912) English actor WWT/11-14

CASSON, Ezra (d 1887) EA/88*

CASSON, John (b 1909) English actor, producer WWT/11-12

CASSON, Sir Lewis Thomas (1875-1969) English actor, director AAS, BE, COC, ES, OC/1-3, TW/13, 15, 25, WWT/2-14, WWW/6

CASSON, Louis (d 1950) actor, producer, manager BE*, WWT/14*

CASSON, Margaret (b c. 1775) harpsichordist BD

CASSON, Mary (b 1914) English actress WWT/6-9

CASSON, Walter (d 1905 [44]) actor EA/06*

CASTANET, Mons. (d 1888) gymnast EA/89*

CASTANG, Veronica (b 1938) English actress TW/30

CASTANOS, Luz (b 1935) American actor TW/28-29

CASTEL, Albert R. (d 1972 [67]) musician BP/57*

CASTELL, Thomas (d 1730) doorkeeper BD

CASTELLAN, Anaide see Castellan-Giampietro, Jeanne Anais

CASTELLAN-GIAMPIETRO, Jeanne Anais (b 1819) French singer CDP, HAS

CASTELLANO, Richard (b 1933) American actor TW/23-26

CASTELLE, Mrs. [Mrs. Castelli] (fl 1787-1804) singer BD

CASTELLI, Mr. (fl 1783-84) dog trainer BD

CASTELLI, Mrs. see Castelle, Mrs.

CASTELLI, Anna (fl 1754-55) Italian singer BD

CASTELLO, Mr. (fl 1793-1803) doorkeeper BD

CASTELLO, John (b 1924) American actor TW/4

CASTELMARY, Armand see Castlemary, Armand

CASTIGLIONE, Master (fl 1771) dancer BD

CASTIGLIONE, Mr. (fl 1734-36) dancer BD

CASTILE, Lynn (d 1975 [77]) singer, actress BP/59*, WWT/16*

CASTLE, Mrs. (fl 1734) actress BD

CASTLE, Betty (d 1962 [47]) performer BE*

CASTLE, Egerton (1858-1920) French/English dramatist WWM, WWW/2

CASTLE, Harry Gilbert singer, composer, minstrel CDP

CASTLE, Irene (d 1969 [75]) American dancer ES, SR, TW/25

CASTLE, John (b 1940) English actor WWT/15-16

CASTLE, Nick (d 1968 [56]) producer, director BP/53*

CASTLE, Peggy (d 1973 [47]) performer BP/58*

CASTLE, Richard (d 1779) actor BD

CASTLE, Roy (b 1932) English actor, singer, dancer TW/22

CASTLE, Thomas (fl 1608-10) actor DA

CASTLE, Vernon Blythe (1887-1918) English actor, dancer CDP, DAB, ES, SR, WWA/4, WWM

CASTLE, William (1836-1909) English singer CDP, WWA/1

CASTLEMAN, Richard (fl 1711-39) treasurer BD

CASTLEMARY, Armand (1834-97) Italian singer CDP, ES

CASTLES, Mr. (fl 1734) house servant? BD

CASTLES, Amy (b 1884) Australian singer GRB/1

CASTLETON, Kate (d 1892 [35]) actress SR

CASTLETON, Robert [Robert Ellis] (b 1872) Mauritian actor, dramatist GRB/1

CASTLING, Will (d 1876) comedian EA/78*

CASTO, Jean actress TW/1, 3, 6-7

CASTON, George (d 1893) bandmaster EA/94*

CASTRUCCI, Pietro (1679-1752) Italian violinist, composer, bandleader BD

CASTRUCCI, Prospero (d 1760) violinist BD

CATALANI, Angelica (1779?/82-1849) Italian singer CDP, GT

CATANEO, Sig. (fl c. 1735-62) musician, teacher BD

CATCHPOLE, Mr. (fl 1799) puppeteer BD

CATENACCI, Maria (fl 1783-86) singer BD

CATER, Percy (d 1971 [73]) critic BP/55*

CATERINA, Signora (fl 1756) wire dancer BD

CATES, Mr. (fl 1746) actor BD

CATES, Frank (d 1896 [43]) actor EA/97*

CATES, Gilbert (b 1934) American producer, director BE

CATES, Gordon (d 1970 [63]) musician BP/55*

CATES, Joseph (b 1924) American producer, director BE

CATES, Madlyn (b 1925) American actress TW/26

CATESBY, Mr. (fl 1741) actor BD

CATHCART, Charles (d 1912 [56]) actor EA/14*, WWT/14*

CATHCART, Mrs. Charles (d 1884) EA/85*

CATHCART, Mrs. Jack see Gumm, Suzanne

CATHCART, James Faucit (1828-1902) actor DD

CATHCART, James Leander (d 1865 [65]) actor WWT/14*

CATHCART, Jane (d 1875) actress EA/76*

CATHCART, Maud (fl 1878) English actress DD, OAA/1-2

CATHCART, Mrs. R. (d 1875) EA/76*

CATHCART, Rolleston William George (d 1896 [64]) actor EA/97*

CATHCART, Rowley (1832-96) English dramatist, actor DD, OAA/1

CATHERWOOD, Caroline (d 1889) EA/90*

CATHIE, Mrs. Leslie Roy see Cathie, Nina

CATHIE, Nina [Mrs. Leslie Cathie] (d 1904 [20]) EA/04*

CATLETT, Mary Jo (b 1938) American actress TW/23-30

CATLETT, Walter (1889-1960) American actor TW/17, WWT/4-11

CATLEY, Ann [Mrs. Francis Lascelles] (1745-89) English actress, singer, dancer BD, CDP, DD, DNB, ES, GT, TD/1-2

CATLIN, Edward N. musician, composer CDP

CATLIN, Faith (b 1949) American actress TW/29-30

CATLING, Thomas (1838-1920) English critic GRB/2-4, WWT/1-3

CATLING, Thomas Thurgood (1863-1939) English critic GRB/2-4

CATMUR, Caroline (d 1916) EA/18*

CATON, Mr. (fl 1796-1804) box keeper BD

CATON, Edward (b c. 1900) American dancer, choreographer ES

CATRANI, Catrano (d 1974 [61]) producer/director/choreographer BP/59*

CATT, Mrs. S. H. (d 1916 [39])

EA/17*
CATTANES (fl 1602-03) actor?
DA
CATTANI, Joseph (fl 1739)
musician BD
CATTLEY, Cyril (1876-1937)
English actor, stage manager
WWT/8
CATTO, John (d 1902 [40])
acrobat EA/03*
CATTO, Max (b 1907) English
dramatist WWT/9-14
CATTON, Charles (1728-98)
English artist, decorator,
scene painter? BD
CATTON, Charles (1756-1819)
English artist, scene painter
BD
CAUBAYE-BERNHARDT, Suzanne
(b 1897) French actress
TW/1
CAUBISENS, Henri stage manager
BE
CAUFFMAN, Frank Guernsey
(b 1850) American musician
WWA/4
CAUFIELD, Betty (b 1925)
American actress TW/1
CAULFIELD, James (1764-1826)
print seller, author CDP
CAULFIELD, Joan (b 1922)
actress CB
CAULFIELD, John (fl 1794-1819)
singer BD
CAULFIELD, John (d 1879)
musical director EA/80*
CAULFIELD, John see Caul-
field, Thomas
CAULFIELD, Mrs. John see
Caulfield, Louisa
CAULFIELD, Mrs. John see
Loseby, Constance
CAULFIELD, Louisa [Mrs.
John Caulfield] (1822-70)
actress DD
CAULFIELD, Thomas [or John]
(1766-1815) English actor
BD, CDP, DD, HAS,
TD/1-2
CAUN, Susanna (fl 1729) actress
BD
CAUSE, Miss H. see Fiddes,
Harriet Catherine
CAUSTON, Mr. (fl 1720-46)
house servant? BD
CAUTE, David (b 1936)
Egyptian/English dramatist
CD

CAUTHERLEY, Samuel (d 1805)
actor BD, DD, TD/1-2
CAUTLEY, Lawrence (d 1899 [37])
actor DD, DP, EA/95
CAUX, Marquis de (d 1889) EA/
91*
CAVALHO, Sylvia actress GRB/2
CAVALIERI, Lina (1874-1944)
Italian singer ES, WWA/5
CAVALLAZI-MAPLESON, Mme.
Italian ballet director GRB/
1-4
CAVALLERIZZO, Claudio (fl 1576)
Italian actor DA
CAVAN, Jack (d 1972 [64]) musi-
cian BP/57*
CAVAN, Marie (1889-1968) Amer-
ican singer WWA/5, WWM
CAVANA, Mr. (fl 1789-92) singer
BD
CAVANAGH, Elizabeth (d 1884)
EA/85*
CAVANAGH, James actor, singer
CDP
CAVANAGH, Lilian (d 1932) Eng-
lish actress WWT/3-7
CAVANAGH, Paul (b 1895) English
actor ES, WWT/6-10
CAVANAGH, W. B. (b 1833) Irish
actor HAS
CAVANAH, John (d 1901) manager
EA/02*
CAVANAUGH, Fannie (d 1975 [83])
performer BP/59*
CAVANAUGH, Hobart (d 1950 [63])
American actor TW/6
CAVANAUGH, James (d 1967 [75])
composer/lyricist BP/52*
CAVANAUGH, Michael American
actor TW/26-29
CAVANIA, Margaret [Mrs. Basil
Gill] English actress GRB/1-3
CAVANNA, Elise [Mrs. James
Welton] (d 1963 [61]) actress
BE*
CAVE, George (d 1877 [49]) treas-
urer EA/78*
CAVE, Mrs. Henry see Cave,
Marie Louise
CAVE, J. H. minstrel, banjoist
CDP
CAVE, John (d 1664) singer BD
CAVE, Joseph Arnold (1823-1912)
English actor, manager, pro-
prietor, music-hall performer
CDP, COC, DD, GRB/1-4,
OC/1-3
CAVE, Marie Louise [Mrs. Henry

Cave] (d 1891) EA/92*
CAVELL, Will (fl 1671-72) per-
former BD
CAVELLA, Harry singer, com-
poser CDP
CAVENDER, Glenn W. (d 1962
[78]) performer BE*
CAVENDER, Leona (fl 1869)
actress CDP
CAVENDISH, Ada [Mrs. Frank
Marshall] (1847-95) English
actress CDP, DD, DNB,
DP, ES, OAA/1-2
CAVENDISH, Harry (d 1888)
music-hall artist EA/89*
CAVENDISH, Henry Frederick
Compton [Henry Carlton]
(d 1886) actor EA/87*
CAVENDISH, Mrs. H. S. H.
see Jay, Isabel
CAVENDISH, June (d 1976)
performer BP/60*
CAVENDISH, Margaret, Duchess
of Newcastle (d 1673) English
dramatist CP/1-3, GT, HP
CAVENDISH, Milly (d 1867)
English singer HAS
CAVENDISH, Rose [Mrs. Leo-
pold Cohen] (d 1897 [32])
actress EA/98*
CAVENDISH, William, Duke of
Newcastle (1592-1676) Eng-
lish dramatist CP/1-3,
FGF, GT
CAVENS, Albert (b 1921) Bel-
gian actor TW/24
CAVETT, Dick (b 1936) Ameri-
can actor CB
CAVETT, Dick (d 1973 [67])
dramatist BP/57*
CAVRAN, Georgia (fl 1880-82)
actress CDP
CAWARDEN, Sir Thomas (fl
1545) master of the Revels
COC, OC/2-3
CAWBRAEST, Walter (fl 1665)
drummer BD
CAWDELL, James (d 1800)
dramatist, manager, come-
dian CP/3, DD, DNB
CAWDER, Jo (fl 1760-61)
sweeper BD
CAWDERY, George (d 1898 [68])
carpenter EA/99*
CAWLEY, Master (fl 1757-59)
dancer, actor BD
CAWOOD, Martin (d 1867)
secretary EA/68*

CAWSE, Harriet (fl 1832) singer,
actress CDP
CAWSTON, Mr. (fl 1789-97) house
servant BD
CAWTHORN, Joseph (1867/68-1949)
American actor CDP, GRB/
3-4, SR, TW/5, WWA/2, WWS,
WWT/1-10
CAWTHORN, Lily [Mrs. Arthur
Waller] (d 1894 [28]) actress
EA/95*
CAXTON, Mr. (fl 1747) painter
BD
CAYFORD, Mr. (fl 1735) house
servant? BD
CAYVAN, Georgia (c. 1858-1906)
American actress DAB, PP/1,
SR, WWA/1
CAYWORTH, John (fl 1636) drama-
tist FGF
CAZALY, James (d 1904 [48])
EA/06*
CAZAURAN, Augustus R. (1820-
89) French/American dramatist
DD, SR
CAZENEUVE, Bernard Marius (b
1839) magician CDP
CAZMAN, Henri (d 1917) conjurer,
illusionist EA/18*
CEBALLOS, Larry actor, singer
CDP
CECCHETTI, Enrico (1847-1928)
Italian dancer, maître de ballet
ES, WWT/4-5
CECIL (fl 1614-15) dramatist
CP/3, FGF
CECIL, Arthur [Arthur Cecil Blunt]
(1843-96) English actor CDP,
DD, DNB, DP, OAA/1-2
CECIL, Henry [né Henry Cecil
Leon] (1902-76) dramatist
WWT/15-16
CECIL, Mrs. John see Leslie,
Minnie
CECIL, Mary (1885-1940) actress
CB
CECIL, Phyllis [Phyllis Ponsford]
English actress GRB/1
CECIL, Sylvia (b 1906) English
actress, singer WWT/11-12
CECIL, Tom English actor GRB/1
CECILL see Cecil
CEDA, William (d 1873 [47]) min-
strel EA/73*
CEDAR, Hugh (d 1916) music-hall
comedian EA/17*
CEDERSTROM, Baroness see
Patti, Adelina

CEDRIC, Mrs. (d 1917) EA/
18*
CEFALO, Pietro (fl 1670)
musician BD
"CELEBRATED GRIMACIER,
The" (fl c. 1790) clown BD
CELESIA, Dorothea (1738-90)
English dramatist DNB
CELESTE, Céline (1814-82)
French actress, dancer
CDP, COC, DD, DNB, ES,
HAS, OAA/1-2, OC/1-3,
SR
CELESTE, La Petite (fl 1837-
40) dancer HAS
CELESTE, Rosa (b 1848) Amer-
ican tight-rope performer
HAS
CELESTIN, Jack (b 1894) Irish
dramatist WWT/7-9
CELESTINO, Eligio (c. 1737-
1812) Italian violinist, com-
poser BD
CELESTINO, Signora Eligio (fl
1780-92) singer BD
CELISIA, Mrs. (d 1790) drama-
tist CP/2-3, DD, GT
CELLARIUS, Sig. dancer CDP
CELLI, Faith (1888-1942) Eng-
lish actress WWT/4-7
CELLI, Frank H. (d 1904 [63])
singer, actor, dramatist
DD
CELLI, Mrs. Frank H. see
Pyne, Susan
CELLI, Vincenzo (b 1905) Italian
dancer, choreographer, teacher
ES
CELLIER, Alfred (1844-91)
English composer, conductor
CDP, DD, DNB, ES
CELLIER, Antoinette (b 1913)
English actress WWT/8-13
CELLIER, Francois (1850-1914)
French musical director,
composer DD, SR
CELLIER, Frank (1872/84-1948)
English actor, manager ES,
GRB/2, TW/5, WWT/3-10
CELLIER, Marguerite (b 1880)
English actress GRB/1-2
CELLINI, Mme. singer CDP
CELLINI, Renato (1912-67)
Italian conductor WWA/4
CELOTTI, Ziuliana (fl 1705-
14) singer BD
CELSON, Miss (fl 1798) singer
BD

CEMMITT, Miss (fl 1785-91)
singer BD
CENTLIVRE, Joseph (fl 1715-39)
organist BD
CENTLIVRE, Susannah (1667-1723)
English actress, dramatist
CDP, COC, CP/1-3, DD, DNB,
ES, GT, HP, MH, NTH, OC/
1-3, TD/1-2
CERAIL, Mlle. (d 1723) French?
dancer, singer BD
CERISSA, Mlle. (d 1871 [21])
trapezist EA/72*
CERITO, Ada singer CDP
CERRITO, Fanny (1817/21-c. 1899/
1909) Italian dancer CDP, ES,
OC/2
CERVANTES SAAVEDRA, Miguel
de (1547-1616) Spanish drama-
tist COC
CERVETTO, Giacobbe (1682-1783)
Italian violoncellist, composer
BD, TD/1-2
CERVETTO, James (1749-1837)
English violoncellist, composer
BD, DNB
CERVI, Gino (d 1974 [72]) per-
former BP/58*, WWT/16*
CESANA, Renzo (d 1970) performer
BP/55*
CHABERT, Ivan Ivanetz (fl c. 1818?)
"fire king phenomenon" CDP
CHABERT, Julien Xavier (1791-
1859) French "fire king"
CDP, HAS, SR
CHABOT, Marie-Louise see
De Verneuil, Mme. Louis
François Joseph
CHABOUD, Pietro (fl 1707-25)
instrumentalist, composer BD
CHABRAN, Charles (b c. 1723)
Italian violinist BD
CHABRAN, Francesco [Felice?]
(c. 1757-1829) English? musi-
cian, composer BD
CHACE, Dorothy American actress
TW/24, 26, 28-30
CHADAL, Georges (b 1875) French
singer WWM
CHADBON, Tom (b 1946) English
actor WWT/15-16
CHADWICK, (d 1889 [46]) English
clown EA/90*
CHADWICK, George Whitefield
(1854-1931) American composer
ES, HJD
CHADWICK, James see Olmar,
Mons.

CHADWICK, John (d 1972 [65])
performer BP/57*
CHADWICK, John Henry (d
1917 [60]) EA/18*
CHADWICK, Sophia [Mrs. H.
Valdo; "Avolina"] (d 1886)
performer? EA/87*
CHADWICK, Thomas (d 1908)
EA/09*
CHADWICK, William Thorpe
(d 1908 [57]) EA/09*
CHAFFE, Christopher (fl 1794)
musician BD
CHAGRIN, Francis (d 1972 [67])
conductor BP/57*
CHAGRIN, Julian (b 1940) Eng-
lish actor, mimist WWT/
15-16
CHAIGNEAU, William (1709-81)
Irish dramatist DNB
CHAIKIN, Joseph (b 1935) Amer-
ican actor, director, pro-
ducer WWT/16
CHAIKIN, Shami (b 1931) Amer-
ican actress TW/29-30
CHALBAUD, Esteban (b 1945)
Venezuelan actor TW/29
CHALET, William (d 1868 [38])
manager EA/89*
CHALIAPIN, Feodor (1873-
1938) Russian singer ES,
WWA/1
CHALIF, Frances Robinson (d
1971) performer BP/56*
CHALKLEY, Ann (b 1922)
English actress TW/3
CHALLENGER, Rudy (b 1928)
American actor TW/24,
26
CHALLENOR, Bromley (1884-
1935) English actor, manager
WWT/6-7
CHALLIS, Edith (d 1883) actress
OAA/2
CHALLIS, Emma [Mrs. Rass
Challis] (d 1892) EA/93*
CHALLIS, Mrs. Rass see
Challis, Emma
CHALLONER, Neville Butler
(b 1784) English instru-
mentalist, bandleader,
teacher, composer, music
seller BD
CHALMERS, Alexander (1759-
1834) writer DD
CHALMERS, F. S. (d 1806)
English actor SR
CHALMERS, James (d 1810)

actor, dancer BD, CDP, HAS,
TD/1-2
CHALMERS, Mrs. James [née
Eleanor Mills] (d 1792) actress,
singer BD
CHALMERS, [Mrs. James, Sarah?]
(fl 1754-85?) actress BD
CHALMERS, [Sarah?] see
Chalmers, [Mrs. James, Sarah?]
CHALMERS, Thomas Hardie (1884-
1966) American singer, actor
BE, TW/3, 5-7, 10-13, 15-16,
23, WWA/4
CHALMERS, William (d c. 1806)
scene painter BD
CHALONER, William (d 1868 [38])
performer? EA/69*
CHALZEL, Leo (d 1953 [52])
American actor WWT/10-11
CHAMBERLAIN, Charlie (d 1972
[61]) performer BP/57*
CHAMBERLAIN, George (1891-
1976) English manager WWT/
10-14
CHAMBERLAIN, John S. (d 1916)
actor, producer, comedian
EA/17*, WWT/14*
CHAMBERLAIN, Mrs. J. S. see
Chamberlain, Lizzie
CHAMBERLAIN, Lizzie [Mrs. J.
S. Chamberlain] (d 1884 [32])
EA/85*
CHAMBERLAIN, Richard (b 1935)
American actor AAS, CB,
WWT/16
CHAMBERLAIN, Robert (b 1607)
English dramatist CP/1-3,
DD, FGF
CHAMBERLAINE, Frances see
Sheridan, Frances
CHAMBERLAINE, Robert see
Chamberlain, Robert
CHAMBERLAYNE, Mr. (fl 1674)
performer? BD
CHAMBERLAYNE, William (1619-
89) dramatist CP/1-3, DD,
DNB, GT, HP
CHAMBERLIN, Ione (b 1880)
American actress WWS
CHAMBERLIN, Riley (b 1854)
American actor WWM
CHAMBERS, Mr. (fl 1758) stage-
hand? BD
CHAMBERS, Mr. (fl 1777-79)
actor BD
CHAMBERS, Mr. actor TD/2
CHAMBERS, Miss (fl 1805) drama-
tist CP/3, DD

CHAMBERS, A. A. (fl 1785-97) actor, singer BD
CHAMBERS, Charles (fl 1771) actor BD
CHAMBERS, Charles Haddon (1860-1921) Australian dramatist DD, GRB/1-4, SR, WWM, WWS, WWT/1-3, WWW/2
CHAMBERS, Sir Edmund Kercheever (1866-1954) English historian DNB, ES, HP
CHAMBERS, Emma (d 1933 [85]) actress, singer CDP, DD, OAA/2, WWT/1-3
CHAMBERS, Harriet [née Harriet Dyer; Mrs. William Taplin] (d 1804) actress BD
CHAMBERS, H. Kellett (1867-1935) Australian dramatist GRB/3-4, WWM, WWS, WWT/1-5
CHAMBERS, Isabella (fl 1722-41) singer, actress BD
CHAMBERS, James (d 1871 [44]) actor? EA/72*
CHAMBERS, John (fl 1702) mountebank BD
CHAMBERS, John (d 1880 [62]) actor EA/81*
CHAMBERS, Lucy (d 1894) Australian singer EA/95*
CHAMBERS, Lyster (1876-1947) American actor SR
CHAMBERS, McCall singer, actor CDP
CHAMBERS, Margaret (d 1880) actress EA/81*
CHAMBERS, Mary (d 1903 [71]) EA/04*
CHAMBERS, Mary see Kean, Mrs. Edmund
CHAMBERS, Norma (d 1953) American actress BE*, BP/37*
CHAMBERS, Ralph (d 1968 [76]) actor TW/24
CHAMBERS, Robert W. (1865-1933) American dramatist HJD
CHAMBERS, Mrs. Stephen see Corelli, Cecilia
CHAMBERS, Sydney (d 1871) comedian EA/72*
CHAMBERS, Thomas (d 1883 [59]) actor EA/84*
CHAMBERS, William (fl 1624) actor DA

CHAMBERS, William (b 1910) American stage manager, director, actor BE
CHAMBERS, Mrs. William [née Elizabeth Davis?] (d 1792) singer, actress BD
CHAMLEE, Mario (1892-1966) American singer WWA/4
"CHAMPION, Mr." (fl 1738) actor BD
CHAMPION, Ada Welsh actress GRB/1
CHAMPION, George (d 1871 [60]) professor of music EA/72*
CHAMPION, Gower (b 1920/21) American choreographer, director AAS, BE, CB, ES, TW/5-8, WWT/14-16
CHAMPION, Harry (1866-1942) English music-hall performer CDP, COC, OC/1-3, PDT
CHAMPION, Madge [née Marjorie Celeste Belcher] (b 1923/25) American actress, dancer BE, CB, ES
CHAMPION, William [William Rooles Lonnen] (d 1890 [57]) EA/91*
CHAMPNESS, Masters (fl 1794) singers BD
CHAMPNESS, Samuel Thomas (d 1803) singer, actor BD
CHAMPNESS, Thomas Weldon (fl 1794-1803) singer BD
CHAMPNESS, Weldon (fl 1758-98) singer BD
CHAMPVILLE, Gabriel-Léonard Hervé de Bus de (fl 1748-89) French actor BD
CHAN, Peter (d 1969 [68]) actor, entertainer TW/25
CHANCELLOR, Betty Irish actress WWT/9-10
CHANCELLOR, Joyce (b 1906) Irish actress WWT/7-10
CHANDLER, Christine (d 1975 [30]) performer BP/60*
CHANDLER, Douglas (1917-70) American actor TW/1
CHANDLER, George W. see Garrison, George W.
CHANDLER, Helen (1906/09-65) American actress BE, TW/21, WWT/6-11
CHANDLER, Jeff (d 1961 [42]) American actor BE*
CHANDLER, Joan actress TW/1
CHANDLER, Leah (b 1950)

American actress TW/29-30
CHANDLER, Lennox (d 1905
[30]) singer EA/06*
CHANDLER, Mildred (b 1902)
American actress TW/24
CHANDLER, Thelma (d 1968
[64]) stage manager TW/25
CHANDLER, Thomas (d 1893
[36]) stage manager EA/94*
CHANDLER, W. Aubrey (d 1909
[72]) actor EA/10*
CHANDLER, Mrs. W. Aubrey
see Aubrey, Mrs. W.
CHANDOS, Alice actress CDP
CHANEY, John (d 1895) music-
hall proprietor EA/96*
CHANEY, Lon (1883-1930)
American actor DAB, ES,
SR, WWA/4
CHANEY, Lon, Jr. (d 1973
[67]) performer BP/58*,
WWT/16*
CHANEY, Stewart (1905/10-69)
American scene designer
BE, ES, TW/2-8, 26, WWT/
10-14
CHANFRAU, Francis S. (1824-
84) American actor CDP,
COC, DAB, DD, ES, HAS,
OC/1-3, SR, WWA/H
CHANFRAU, Mrs. Francis S.
see Chanfrau, Henrietta
CHANFRAU, Henrietta [Henri-
etta Baker; Jeanette Davis]
(1837-1909) American actress
CDP, COC, DAB, DD, HAS,
OC/1-3, SR
CHANFRAU, Henry Trenchard
(1858-1901) actor CDP
CHANG (d 1893 [46]) Chinese
giant CDP
CHANG, Tisa Chinese actress
TW/27-28
CHANIN, Henry (d 1973 [79])
theatre builder BP/57*
CHANLER, Mrs. William Astor
see Ashley, Minnie
CHANNEL, Luke (fl 1653-91?)
dancing master BD
CHANNING, Carol (b 1921)
American actress, singer
AAS, BE, CB, ES, TW/
5-8, 10-24, 27, 29-30,
WWT/11-16
CHANNING, William (d 1877)
scene artist EA/78*
CHANNOUVEAU, Jean (fl 1661-
67) actor, manager BD

CHANTRELL, Prof. (d 1879) acro-
bat EA/80*
CHANTRELL, Annie (d 1888)
EA/89*
CHANTRELL, Clara [Mrs. H. J.
Charlton] (d 1887) EA/88*
CHAPEL, Eugenia (d 1964 [52])
actress, executive BE*
CHAPENDER, Martin (d 1905)
conjurer, illusionist EA/06*
CHAPIN, Alice (d 1934 [76])
American actress GRB/1-2
CHAPIN, Anne Morrison (d 1967)
actress, dramatist TW/23
CHAPIN, Benjamin Chester (1874-
1918) American dramatist WWA/
1
CHAPIN, Harold (1886-1915) Amer-
ican actor, stage manager,
dramatist ES, GRB/2-3, MD,
MWD, NTH, WWT/2-3, WWW/1
CHAPIN, Louis Le Bourgeois (b
1918) American critic WWT/
14-16
CHAPIN, Schuyler G. (b 1923)
American manager CB
CHAPIN, Victor actor TW/1
CHAPLIN, Amelia [Mrs. G. H.
Chaplin; Milly Arden] (d 1887
[47]) EA/88*
CHAPLIN, Charles (d 1901) music-
hall comedian EA/02*
CHAPLIN, Charles, Jr. (1925-68)
American actor TW/6-7
CHAPLIN, Sir Charles Spencer
(1889-1977) English actor CDP,
CB, ES, GRB/1, HJD, NTH,
SR, WWT/4-11
CHAPLIN, Ellen see Fitzwilliam,
Mrs. Edward Francis
CHAPLIN, George (d 1881) lessee
EA/82*
CHAPLIN, George D. [né Inglis]
(b 1837) actor CDP
CHAPLIN, Geraldine (b 1944)
American actress TW/24
CHAPLIN, Mrs. G. H. see
Chaplin, Amelia
CHAPLIN, Henry (d 1789) actor,
singer BD
CHAPLIN, Sydney (1885-1965)
South African actor ES
CHAPLIN, Sydney (b 1926) Ameri-
can actor BE, TW/13-22
CHAPMAN, Mr. (fl 1674) actor
BD
CHAPMAN, Mr. (fl 1756-72)
musician BD

CHAPMAN, Mr. (fl 1775) actor
BD
CHAPMAN, Mr. (fl 1776-1817?)
house servant BD
CHAPMAN, Mr. (fl 1794) vio-
linist BD
CHAPMAN, Mr. (fl 1799-1804?)
dancer? BD
CHAPMAN, Mr. (fl 1805) actor
TD/2
CHAPMAN, Mr. (fl 1805) actor
BS, GT
CHAPMAN, Mr. actor CDP
CHAPMAN, Miss (d 1805) Amer-
ican actress CDP, TD/1-2
CHAPMAN, Ada Blanche (b
1820) English actress SR
CHAPMAN, Ada Blanche (1851-
1941) American actress
CB, CDP, HAS
CHAPMAN, Addie see Adiny-
Millet, Ada
CHAPMAN, Alonzo see Parks,
Alonzo
CHAPMAN, Barnet [Charles
Robinson] (d 1870 [31]) actor
EA/71*
CHAPMAN, Blanche see
Chapman, Ada Blanche
CHAPMAN, Caroline (1818-76)
actress CDP, ES, HAS
CHAPMAN, Caroline (fl 1864)
actress HAS
CHAPMAN, Catherine [Mrs. John
Chapman] (d 1906) EA/07*
CHAPMAN, Mrs. Charles E.
see Chapman, Harriet Ethel
CHAPMAN, Charlotte Jane [Mrs.
Morton] (1762-1805) Ameri-
can/English actress, singer
BD
CHAPMAN, Christopher (d 1681)
singer BD
CHAPMAN, Constance (b 1912)
English actress WWT/15-16
CHAPMAN, David (d 1904 [39])
proprietor EA/05*
CHAPMAN, Edward (b 1901)
English actor AAS, ES,
WWT/7-15
CHAPMAN, Edythe [Mrs. James
Neill] (1863-1948) actress
SR, TW/5
CHAPMAN, Elizabeth [née Jeffer-
son; Mrs. Samuel Chapman;
Mrs. Augustus Richardson;
Mrs. Charles J. B. Fisher]
(1810-90) American actress

CDP, ES, SR
CHAPMAN, Ella (fl 1876-90) act-
ress, singer, musician CDP,
DD
CHAPMAN, Fanny see Botly,
Mrs.
CHAPMAN, Frank (d 1966 [66])
singer TW/23
CHAPMAN, Frank M. manager
CDP
CHAPMAN, George (c. 1560-1634)
English dramatist CDP, COC,
CP/1-3, DD, DNB, ES, FGF,
HP, MH, NTH, OC/1-3, PDT,
RE
CHAPMAN, [George?] (fl 1792-
1804?) exhibitor, treasurer
BD
CHAPMAN, George (fl 1830-51)
actor ES, HAS
CHAPMAN, George (d 1896 [64])
music-hall performer, manager
EA/97*
CHAPMAN, George (d 1902 [62])
musical director EA/04*
CHAPMAN, Mrs. George [née
Frances R. Brett] (d 1804)
actress, singer BD, TD/1-2
CHAPMAN, Mrs. George (d 1894)
EA/95*
CHAPMAN, Mrs. George see
Mandlebert, Kate
CHAPMAN, Gilbert W. (b 1902)
American executive BE
CHAPMAN, Hannah see Chap-
man, Mrs. Thomas
CHAPMAN, Harriet Ethel [Mrs.
Charles E. Chapman] (d 1904
[27]) EA/05*
CHAPMAN, Harry (1822-65) Eng-
lish actor HAS, SR
CHAPMAN, Harry (d 1888 [84])
showman EA/89*
CHAPMAN, Henry (b 1910) English
dramatist PDT
CHAPMAN, James Fitzjames Rock
(d 1876 [69]) actor EA/77*
CHAPMAN, J. M. (d 1906 [70])
EA/07*
CHAPMAN, John (d 1895 [59])
Negro comedian EA/96*
CHAPMAN, John (1900-72) Ameri-
can critic BE, NTH, TW/28,
WWT/10-15
CHAPMAN, Mrs. John see
Chapman, Catherine
CHAPMAN, John Jay (1862-1933)
American dramatist HJD

CHAPMAN, John Kemble (d
1852 [47/57[) manager
EA/72*, WWT/14*
CHAPMAN, John R. (b 1927)
English dramatist, actor
AAS, WWT/14-16
CHAPMAN, Mrs. J. W. see
Chapman, Martha
CHAPMAN, Lina (d 1967 [37])
performer BP/51*
CHAPMAN, Lonny (b 1920)
American actor, director,
dramatist BE
CHAPMAN, Martha [Mrs. T.
W. Chapman] (d 1906 [48])
EA/07*
CHAPMAN, Nathan (d 1871)
boxkeeper EA/72*
CHAPMAN, Pattie (d 1912 [82])
actress WWT/14*
CHAPMAN, Richard (fl 1787-
c. 1795?) instrumentalist,
composer BD
CHAPMAN, Robert (fl 1796)
violinist BD
CHAPMAN, Robert H. (b 1919)
American director, drama-
tist, educator BE
CHAPMAN, Mrs. Robert W.
see Desmond, Maggie
CHAPMAN, Mrs. Samuel see
Chapman, Elizabeth
CHAPMAN, Samuel Henry (1799-
1830) English/American actor,
dramatist EAP, ES, HAS,
RJ, SR
CHAPMAN, Thomas (c. 1683-
1747) actor BD
CHAPMAN, Mrs. Thomas
[Hannah] (d c. 1756) actress,
dancer BD
CHAPMAN, Mr. W. (d 1868
[68]) actor EA/69*
CHAPMAN, Mrs. W. H. (d
1879 [62]) American actress
EA/80*
CHAPMAN, William (1764-1839)
American showboat manager
COC, ES, HAS, OC/1-3
CHAPMAN, [William?] (fl 1770?-
1820?) actor, singer BD
CHAPMAN, William (fl 1829)
actor DD
CHAPMAN, William (d 1871
[41]) musical director EA/
72*
CHAPMAN, William (b 1923)
American actor TW/17

CHAPMAN, William A. (d 1857)
English actor ES, HAS, SR
CHAPMAN, Mrs. William A.
[Mrs. Trowbridge; Mrs. Josiah
Silsbee] (d 1880 [67]) English
actress HAS, SR
CHAPMAN, William Adams (fl
1839) actor CDP
CHAPMAN, William B. (1799-1857)
English actor, manager HAS,
SR
CHAPMAN, William S. (1769-1839)
English actor SR
CHAPMAN-HUSTON, W. M. see
Raleigh, Desmond Mountjoy
CHAPPELL, Mr. (fl 1690-91)
actor BD
CHAPPELL, Charles (b 1860)
English business manager
GRB/1
CHAPPELL, Fred (b 1943) Ameri-
can actor TW/25
CHAPPELL, James (d 1899 [61])
manager EA/00*
CHAPPELL, James (d 1907 [78])
clown, music-hall manager
EA/08*
CHAPPELL, John (fl 1600-01)
member of the Chapel Royal
DA
CHAPPELL, William (d 1888 [78])
antiquarian society founder
EA/89*
CHAPPELL, William (b 1908)
English dancer, designer, direc-
tor ES, WWT/9-16
CHAPPELL, William Francis (d
1886 [67]) equestrian clown
EA/87*
CHAPPELLE, Frederick W. (b
1895) English composer WWT/
4-9
CHAPPIEL, Richard (1774-1830)
English musician BD
CHAPPINGTON, Mr. (fl 1735-36)
constable BD
CHAPUY, Leonard Louis (d 1906
[41]) actor? EA/07*
CHAPUY, Louis (d 1908 [72])
professor of elocution EA/09*
CHARD, Kate (d 1942 [80]) Eng-
lish actress, singer CDP, DD,
DP, EA/96
CHARDIN, Mr. (fl 1729) actor
BD
CHARELL, Erik (1895-1974) Ger-
man producer WWT/7-9
CHARIG, Phil (d 1960 [58])

composer BE*
CHARINI, Mr. (fl 1786) equestrian? BD
CHARISSE, Zan (b 1951) American actress TW/28
CHARKE, Catharine Maria [Mrs. Harman] (1730-73) actress BD
CHARKE, Charlotte see Charke, Mrs. Richard
CHARKE, Richard (d c. 1738) violinist, singer, composer, actor, dancer BD
CHARKE, Mrs. Richard [née Charlotte Cibber; Mrs. John Sacheverell] (1713-60) English actress, manager, puppeteer, author BD, CDP, COC, CP/1-3, DD, DNB, ES, OC/1-3, TD/1-2
CHARLAP, Mark ["Moose"] (d 1974 [45]) composer BE
CHARLES, Mons. (fl 1733-56) musician BD
CHARLES, Mr. (fl 1740-41) dancer BD
CHARLES, Mr. (fl 1744-55) actor BD
CHARLES, Mr. (fl 1784-85) stage door keeper BD
CHARLES, Prof. (d 1917) EA/18*
CHARLES, Master (fl 1748) BD
CHARLES, Master (fl 1780) actor BD
CHARLES, Elizabeth Walker [née Blanchard; Mrs. Thomas S. Hamblin] (d 1849) actress CDP, HAS
CHARLES, Florence [Mrs. Charles Bush] (d 1907) EA/08*
CHARLES, Fred (d 1904 [75]) actor DD
CHARLES, G. C. (fl 1855) Irish comedian HAS
CHARLES, G. F. [George Imbert] (d 1891 [69]) lessee, manager EA/92*
CHARLES, H. R. (d 1876 [25]) actor EA/78*
CHARLES, Jacques (d 1971 [89]) talent scout, producer, dramatist BP/56*, WWT/16*
CHARLES, James S. (1808-65) American actor HAS, SR

CHARLES, John (fl 1671-72) scene keeper BD
CHARLES, Leonard (d 1886 [43]) music-hall artist EA/87*
CHARLES, Lucile (d 1965 [64]) performer BP/49*
CHARLES, Marie (d 1864) columbine EA/72*
CHARLES, Mary Ann (fl 1855-58) actress CDP, HAS
CHARLES, Meroe actress CDP
CHARLES, Michael (d 1967 [26]) performer BP/51*
CHARLES, Pamela [née Foster] (b 1932) English actress, singer WWT/15-16
CHARLES, Paul (b 1947) American actor TW/23, 26
CHARLES, Thomas W. (d 1895) manager, musician, conductor DD
CHARLES, Walter (b 1945) American actor TW/30
CHARLES, William (d 1910) scene artist EA/11*
CHARLES, Zachary A. (b 1943) American actor TW/2
CHARLESON, Mary (d 1961 [76]) actress BE*
"CHARLES THE MERRY TRUMPETER" (fl 1729-33?) horn player, dancer, actor BD
CHARLESWORTH, Dr. G. H. (d 1916) EA/17*
CHARLIP, Morris I. (d 1974 [45]) composer WWT/16*
CHARLOT, André Eugene Maurice (1882-1956) French/English manager AAS, COC, DNB, PDT, TW/12, WWT/4-11, WWW/5
CHARLOT, Mrs. André see Gladman, Florence
CHARLTON, Mr. (fl 1729-31) box keeper BD
CHARLTON, Mr. (fl 1794-98) violinist BD
CHARLTON, Alethea (d 1976 [43]) performer BP/60*
CHARLTON, Archer (d 1880) assistant acting manager EA/81*
CHARLTON, Harold C. (d 1954) actor BE*, WWT/14*
CHARLTON, Henry (d 1888 [25]) circus performer EA/89*
CHARLTON, Mrs. H. J. see Chantrell, Clara

CHARLTON, Loudon (b 1869)
American impresario WWM
CHARLTON, Nathaniel Daniel
(d 1889) equestrian clown
EA/90*
CHARLTON, Randal (d 1931)
critic WWT/14*
CHARLTON, Mrs. Richard see
Charlton, Sarah
CHARLTON, Sarah (d 1879)
EA/80*
CHARLTON, Will (d 1916)
EA/17*
CHARMAN, W. , Jr. (d 1870
[18]) actor EA/71*
CHARNEY, Jordan American
actor TW/22-24, 26-30
CHARNIN, Martin (b 1934)
American lyricist, actor,
director, producer BE,
WWT/15-16
CHARNLEY, Lucy (d 1905 [64])
EA/06*
CHARNOCK, John (1756-1807)
dramatist CP/3, DD
CHARON, Mme. (fl 1755-56)
dancer BD
CHARON, Jacques (d 1975 [55])
actor, director BP/60*,
WWT/16*
CHARPENTIER, Mme. (fl 1734-
35) dancer? BD
CHARPENTIER, Suzanne Georg-
ette see Annabella
CHARREL, Erik (d 1974 [80])
producer/director/choreog-
rapher BP/59*
CHARRINGTON, Charles (d 1926)
actor, lessee, dramatist DD
CHARRINGTON, Mrs. Charles
see Achurch, Janet
CHARSTONE, W. (d 1886) con-
ductor EA/88*
CHART, Mr. (fl 1794-95) car-
penter BD
CHART, Ellen Elizabeth [née
Rollason] (d 1892) actress?
EA/93*
CHART, F. B. (d 1878 [49])
treasurer, acting manager
EA/79*
CHART, Henry Nye (1822-76)
lessee, actor, manager DD,
ES
CHART, Henry Nye (1868-1934)
English actor DD, ES, WWT/
3-5
CHART, Mrs. Henry Nye

(d 1892) manager ES
CHART, Thomas (d 1875) treasurer
EA/76*
CHART, William (d 1910 [78]) re-
freshment contractor EA/11*
CHARTERS, John (d 1917 [53])
EA/18*
CHARTERS, Spencer (1864-1943)
American actor CB, SR
CHARTOFF, Melanie (b 1948)
American actress TW/29
CHARVAY, Robert [Adrien Lefort]
(1858-1926) French dramatist
GRB/4, WWT/3
CHASE, Cleveland B. (d 1975 [71])
producer/director/choreographer
BP/59*
CHASE, Edna (b 1888) American
actress WWS
CHASE, Ilka (1900/05-78) Ameri-
can actress BE, CB, ES,
TW/1-8, 22-23, WWT/8-16
CHASE, Jo Flores American actor
TW/24
CHASE, Lucia dancer, ballet com-
pany manager CB
CHASE, Mary Coyle (b 1907) Amer-
ican dramatist BE, CB, CD,
ES, HJD, MD, MH, MWD,
WWT/16
CHASE, Pauline (1885-1962) Amer-
ican actress, dancer ES,
GRB/1-4, WWM, WWS, WWT/
1-9
CHASE, Sallie Marshall (d 1965
[55]) performer BP/50*
CHASE, Stanley (b 1928) American
producer BE
CHASE, Stephen (b 1902) Ameri-
can actor TW/2-4, 6-7, 10-12
CHASE, Tommy (d 1969 [62])
musician BP/54*
CHASE, William comedian, min-
strel CDP
CHASE, William B. (d 1948 [76])
American critic BE*, BP/33*,
WWT/14*
CHASEN, Dave (d 1973 [74])
vaudevillian, actor TW/30
CHASEN, Heather (b 1927) English
actress WWT/15-16
CHATEAUNEUF, Mons. (fl 1748-49)
dancer, manager BD
CHATEAUNEUF, Marie (b 1721)
French dancer, singer, mana-
ger BD
CHATER, Geoffrey [né Robinson]
(b 1921) English actor

WWT/15-16
CHATHAM, Pitt (d 1923 [37])
actor, singer BE*, WWT/
14*
CHATILLION, Mons. (fl 1735)
dancer BD
CHATIN, Marienne (d 1972 [68])
executive BP/56*
CHATRIEN, Louis Gratien
Charles Alexandre see
Erckmann-Chatrian
CHATTAWAY, Miss M. (d 1891
[77]) custodian of Shake-
speare's birthplace EA/92*
CHATTAWAY, Thurland com-
poser CDP
CHATTERLEY, Mr. (fl c.
1812?) actor CDP
CHATTERLEY, Mrs. see
Chatterley, Louisa
CHATTERLEY, Miss (fl 1791-
98) actress, singer BD
CHATTERLEY, J. (fl 1795?-
1803?) dancer, actor BD
CHATTERLEY, Louisa [Mrs.
William Simmonds Chatterley;
née Simeon] (1797-1866)
English actress BS, CDP,
DD, OX
CHATTERLEY, Robert E. (fl
1792-1818) messenger,
prompter, actor BD
CHATTERLEY, Mrs. Robert
E. (1795-1819) actress BD
CHATTERLEY, William Sim-
monds (1787-1821) English
actor, dancer BD, CDP,
DD, DNB
CHATTERLEY, Mrs. William
Simmonds see Chatterley,
Louisa
CHATTERS, Frank (d 1868)
Negro artist EA/69*
CHATTERS, Kate [Mrs. Flower-
day] (d 1897) variety per-
former EA/98*
CHATTERTON, Mrs. Balsir
see Kinton, Swaine
CHATTERTON, Charles (d 1894)
secretary EA/95*
CHATTERTON, E. A. (d 1875
[65]) EA/77*
CHATTERTON, Edward Keble
English critic GRB/2-3
CHATTERTON, Eliza D. [Mrs.
John Balsir Chatterton] (d
1877 [70]) EA/78*
CHATTERTON, Frederick Balsir

(1834-86) manager, actor
CDP, DD
CHATTERTON, Mrs. Frederick
Balsir see Chatterton, Mary
Ann
CHATTERTON, Lady Georgiana
(d 1876) dramatist DD
CHATTERTON, John Balsir (d
1871 [66]) musician EA/72*
CHATTERTON, Mrs. John Balsir
see Chatterton, Eliza D.
CHATTERTON, Mary (d 1899 [42])
musician EA/00*
CHATTERTON, Mary Ann [Mrs.
Frederick Balsir Chatterton]
(d 1909 [77]) EA/10*
CHATTERTON, Ruth (1893-1961)
American actress ES, SR,
TW/2-8, 10-16, 18, WWA/4,
WWT/4-13
CHATTERTON, Thomas (1752-70)
English dramatist CDP, CP/
2-3, DNB, GT, HP, TD/1-2
CHATTERTON, Vivienne (d 1974)
actress BTR/74
CHATTON, Sydney (d 1966 [48])
performer BP/51*
CHATWIN, Margaret (d 1937 [56])
English actress WWT/5-8
CHAUCHOIN, Lily see Colbert,
Claudette
CHAUNDLER, George (fl 1669)
manager? BD
CHAUVENET, Virginia (d 1949
[65]) American actress TW/5
CHAVCHAVADZE, Paul (d 1971
[72]) actor BP/56*
CHAVES, A. (fl 1705) dramatist
CP/1-3, DD
CHAVEZ, Carlos (b 1899) Mexi-
can composer, conductor ES
CHAVIGNY, Mons. (fl 1720-21)
actor BD
CHAVIGNY, Mme. (fl 1720-21)
actress BD
CHAYEFSKY, Paddy [Sidney] (b
1923) American dramatist,
producer, director AAS, BE,
CB, CD, CH, COC, ES, HJD,
MD, MH, MWD, PDT, WWT/
14-16
CHAZAL, Mrs. see De Gam-
barini, Elisabetta
CHAZEL, Leo (d 1953 [52]) actor
TW/10
CHEATHAM, Kitty (1864?-1946)
American actress CB, WWM,
WWS

CHECCHI, Andrea (d 1974 [57])
performer BP/58*
CHECCO, Al (b 1922) American
actor TW/5-6
CHEEKE, Henry (fl 1561) drama-
tist CP/1-3, FGF
CHEER, Miss (fl 1767-93) actress
CDP, HAS, WWA/H
CHEESE, Mr. (fl 1784) singer
BD
CHEESEMAN, Peter (b 1932)
English director WWT/15-16
CHEESMAN, William (1860-
1907) English actor EA/96,
GRB/1, 3
CHEETHAM, Leonard see
Mudie, Leonard
CHEEVERS, Joseph E. (b 1848)
dancer, minstrel CDP
CHEKHOV, Anton Pavlovich
(1860-1904) Russian dramatist
COC, MD, OC/1-3
CHEKHOV, Michael [Alexandro-
vich] (1891-1955) Russian
actor, director ES, NTH,
OC/3, WWT/10-11
CHEKINI, Mr. English dancer
HAS
CHELLERI, Sig. (fl 1725) bass
viol player BD
CHELSUM, James (c. 1700-43)
singer BD
CHELTNAM, Charles Smith (b
1823) English dramatist,
critic DD, EA/68
CHELTON, Nick (b 1946) Eng-
lish lighting designer WWT/
16
CHEMBINI, Mr. (fl 1784-85)
singer? BD
CHEMONT, Mons. (fl 1742)
dancer BD
CHEN, Kitty Chinese actress
TW/30
CHEN, Tina Chinese actress
TW/28, 30
CHENAL, Marthe (d 1947 [62])
actress, singer WWT/14*
CHENERY, Arthur English actor,
variety artist GRB/1
CHENERY, Herbert (d 1928)
business manager WWT/14*
CHENERY, James William (d
1907 [28]) EA/08*
CHENEY, Master (fl 1770)
singer BD
CHENEY, Miss see Gardiner,
Mrs.

CHENEY, Arthur (1837-78) mana-
ger CDP
CHENEY, Mrs. B. P., Jr. see
Arthur, Julia
CHENEY, Sheldon (b 1886) Ameri-
can writer BE, ES, WWT/10-
11
CHENG, Stephen Chinese actor
TW/28
CHENOWETH, Emily [Emily
Ernest] (d 1881 [20]) actress
EA/82*
CHERB, George W. (d 1974 [50])
musician BP/58*
CHERENSI, B. Frere (fl 1796)
French dramatist CP/3
CHERI, Rose [Rose-Marie Cizos]
(1824-61) French actress OC/
1-3
CHERIE, Adelaide actress CDP
CHERIN, Robert (b 1936) American
house manager BE
CHERINGTON, Richard (fl 1678-
85) singer BD
CHERITON, David (c. 1707-58)
singer BD
CHERKASOV, Nicolai (d 1966 [63])
actor WWT/14
CHERNUCK, Dorothy American
producer, director, educator
BE
CHERRELL, Gwen (b 1926) English
actress AAS, WWT/11-16
CHERRIER, Miss (fl 1708) dancer
BD
CHERRIER, René (fl 1699-1708)
dancer, choreographer BD
CHERRINGTON, Harriet Eastman
(d 1965 [81]) performer BP/
49*
CHERRINGTON, John (fl 1676)
singer BD
CHERRY, Miss (fl 1814) actress
CDP
CHERRY, Addie (1859?-1942)
American performer CB, ES
CHERRY, Andrew (1762-1812)
Irish actor CDP, CP/3, DD,
DNB, ES, GT, TD/1-2
CHERRY, Charles (1872/74-1931)
English actor WWA/5, WWS,
WWT/1-6
CHERRY, Effie (d 1944 [66])
American actress, singer TW/1
CHERRY, Elizabeth [Mrs. J. W.
Cherry] (d 1886) EA/87*
CHERRY, Fred English actor
GRB/1

CHERRY, Harriet (d 1880 [84])
actress? EA/81*
CHERRY, Helen (b 1915) Eng-
lish actress WWT/10-11
CHERRY, Jessie (d 1903 [67])
American performer ES
CHERRY, John (d 1968 [80])
actor TW/1, 24
CHERRY, J. W. (d 1889)
songwriter EA/90*
CHERRY, Mrs. J. W. see
Cherry, Elizabeth
CHERRY, Lizzie (d 1936 [67])
American performer ES
CHERRY, Malcolm (1878-1925)
English actor, dramatist
WWT/1-5
CHERRY, V. Ewing (d 1969
[76]) performer BP/53*
CHERRY, Wal (b 1932) Australian
director, educator WWT/16
CHERRYMAN, Rex (d 1928 [30])
American actor BE*, BP/
13*, WWT/14*
CHERRY SISTERS ES
CHESKIN, Irving (b 1915) Amer-
ican executive BE, WWT/16
CHESLOCK, Louis (b 1899)
English/American composer
ES
CHESNEY, Arthur (d 1949 [67])
English actor WWT/3-10
CHESSMAN, Edward (d 1891)
comedian EA/92*
CHESSON, Thomas (fl 1580?)
actor DA
CHESTER, Mrs. Alfred see
Chester, Marie
CHESTER, Betty (1895/96-1943)
English actress WWT/4-7
CHESTER, Eddie (d 1964 [67])
performer BP/49*
CHESTER, Edith (d 1894 [33])
actress DD
CHESTER, Elsie (d 1937)
actress WWT/14*
CHESTER, Eliza (b 1799) Eng-
lish actress BS, CDP, DD,
OX
CHESTER, Francis (d 1881 [70])
architect EA/83*
CHESTER, George Randolph
(1869-1924) American drama-
tist WWA/1
CHESTER, Harry (d 1869) come-
dian EA/70*
CHESTER, John (d 1878) actor
EA/79*

CHESTER, Kate actress CDP
CHESTER, Marie [Mrs. Maitland;
Mrs. Alfred Chester] (d 1889)
music-hall artist EA/90*
CHESTER, Roland (d 1916) EA/
17*
CHESTER, Mrs. Sam (d 1918)
American actress SR
CHESTER, S. K. [S. C. Knapp]
(1836-1921) American actor
HAS
CHESTER, Mrs. S. K. (b 1843)
American actress HAS
CHESTERTON, Gilbert K. (1874-
1936) English dramatist ES
CHESTNEY, Josephine (fl 1861)
American actress HAS
CHETHAM-STRODE, Warren
(1897-1974) English dramatist
WWT/9-14
CHETTLE, Mr. (fl 1740-48?)
actor, dancer, singer BD
CHETTLE, Henry (c. 1560-1607)
English dramatist COC, CP/3,
DD, DNB, ES, FGF, HP,
NTH, OC/1-3, RE
CHETWOOD, Richabella [Mrs.
Tobias Gemea] (fl 1738-71)
actress BD
CHETWOOD, William Rufus (d
1766) prompter, dramatist,
actor BD, CDP, CP/1-3, DD,
DNB, GT, TD/1-2
CHETWYN, Robert [né Suckling]
(b 1933) English actor, director
WWT/15-16
CHEVALIER, Mons. (fl 1784) ex-
hibitor BD
CHEVALIER, Albert (1861-1923)
English actor, music-hall per-
former CDP, COC, DD, DNB,
DP, ES, GRB/1-4, OC/1-3,
PDT, SR, WWS, WWT/1-4,
WWW/2
CHEVALIER, Albert (d 1959 [60])
actor WWT/14*
CHEVALIER, Gus (d 1947 [56])
performer BE*, WWT/14*
CHEVALIER, Marcelle actress
WWT/2-4
CHEVALIER, Maurice (1888-1972)
French actor, singer BE, CB,
COC, ES, NTH, OC/3, SR,
TW/3, 5-7, 21, 28, WWA/5,
WWT/7-15
CHEVALIER, May (d 1940) actress
BE*, WWT/14*
CHEVALIER, Pierre (fl 1780-88)

dancer, choreographer BD
CHEVALIER, Thomas (fl 1694-99)
oboist BD
CHEVALLIER, Zara dancer CDP
CHEVIGNY, Mr. (fl 1797-98)
dancer? BD
CHEVRIER, [Mons.?] (fl 1726-
27) dancer BD
CHEW, Virgilia R. (b 1905)
American actress TW/23,
25-26
CHEYNE, Mr. (fl 1794-1806)
carpenter, machinist BD
CHIARELL, Luigi (1880/84-
1947) Italian dramatist
COC, MWD, OC/3
CHIARINA, Sig. (d 1897 [82])
circus proprietor EA/98*
CHIARINI, Mme. (fl 1854)
equestrienne HAS
CHICHESTER, Henry [Henry
Chichester Baker] (1864-
1908) English actor GRB/1
CHICKINGHAM, Mr. (fl 1799)
actor BD
CHICOINE, Randal (b 1944)
actor TW/30
CHIDLEY, Mrs. Sidney (d 1889)
EA/90*
CHIESI, Amy [Mrs. Arthur
Chiesi] (d 1888) EA/89*
CHIESI, Mrs. Arthur see
Chiesi, Amy
CHIESI, Giuseppe (d 1887)
proprietor EA/88*
CHILD, Mr. (fl 1732) actor BD
CHILD, Mr. (fl 1794-95) dresser
BD
CHILD, Mrs. (fl 1773?-82) ac-
tress BD
CHILD, Miss see Webb, Mrs.
CHILD, Ann see Seguin, Mrs.
Arthur Edward Shelden
CHILD, Anne (fl 1666-68)
actress? BD
CHILD, Harold Hannyngton
(1869-1945) English critic
DNB, ES, WWT/2-9, WWW/4
CHILD, Marilyn American
actress TW/24, 27, 30
CHILD, Thomas (fl 1714) actor
BD
CHILD, Rev. Thomas (d 1906
[66]) EA/07*
CHILD, William (1606-97) singer,
composer, instrumentalist
BD, DNB
CHILDE, Henry Langdon (d

1874 [92]) inventor EA/75*
CHILDERS, Naomi (d 1964 [71])
actress BE*
CHILDRESS, Alice (b 1920) Amer-
ican actress, dramatist, direc-
tor CD, TW/1
CHILDS, Gilbert (d 1931) actor
WWT/4-6
CHILIBY (fl 1783) performing horse
BD
CHIMENTI, Margherita (fl 1736-
38) singer BD
CHINA, Mr. (fl 1724) horn player
BD
CHING LING LOO [Will E. Robin-
son] magician SR
CHINN, Lori American actress
TW/29
CHINNALL, Mr. (fl 1764-75)
doorkeeper, checktaker BD
CHINOY, Helen Krich (b 1922)
American educator, director
BE
CHIPCHASE, Elizabeth (d 1892)
EA/93*
CHIPP, Mr. (fl 1822) actor HAS
CHIPP, Mrs. (fl 1822) actress
HAS
CHIPP, Dr. Edmund Thomas (d
1886 [63]) organist EA/88*
CHIPP, Thomas Paul (1793-1870)
English musician DNB
CHIPPENDALE, Alfreda [née
Schoolcraft] (d 1887 [42])
American actress DD, NYM
CHIPPENDALE, Arthur A. see
Lynn
CHIPPENDALE, Henry (d 1878
[29]) agent EA/79*
CHIPPENDALE, Johann (d 1910)
actor EA/12*
CHIPPENDALE, Mary Jane [Mary
J. Snowdon] (1837?-88) English
actress CDP, DD, DNB,
OAA/1-2
CHIPPENDALE, Thomas (1782-99)
callboy BD
CHIPPENDALE, Mrs. W. B. (fl
1863) actress HAS
CHIPPENDALE, William (fl 1793-
1835?) actor BD
CHIPPENDALE, Mrs. William (fl
1797-1820?) singer BD
CHIPPENDALE, William Henry
(1801-88) English actor CDP,
DD, DNB, ES, HAS, OAA/1-2,
SR
CHIPPENDALE, Mrs. William

Henry see Chippendale,
Mary Jane
CHIRGWIN, Edward (d 1882 [72])
EA/83*
CHIRGWIN, George H. (1854-
1922) English variety artist
CDP, COC, GRB/1-4,
OC/1-3
CHIRGWIN, Mrs. George H. (d
1892 [37]) EA/93*
CHIRGWIN, John (d 1882) EA/
83*
CHIRINGHELLI, Signora (fl
1774) dancer BD
CHISE, Mme. (fl 1757) dancer
BD
CHISHOLM, Eric (b 1904) Scot-
tish musical director, com-
poser ES
CHISHOLM, James D. (d 1907
[75]) EA/08*
CHISHOLM, Robert (1898-1960)
Australian actor, singer
TW/1-4, 6-7, WWT/7-12
CHISHOLM, Samuel Robertson
(d 1900 [67]) proprietor
EA/01*
CHISHOLM, Mrs. S. R. (d
1886 [53]) EA/87*
CHISNEL, John (d 1867) circus
performer? EA/68*
CHISWELL, Melville (d 1918
[32]) EA/19*
CHISWICK, William (b 1813)
English actor SR
CHITTLE, Samuel (fl 1715-20)
singer BD
CHIVERS, Thomas Holley
(1809-58) American drama-
tist HJD, WWA/H
CHLUMBERG, Hans (1897-1930)
Austrian dramatist MWD
CHOATE, Edward (1908-75)
American manager, producer
BE
CHOBANIAN, Haig (b 1937)
American actor TW/24, 26
CHOBER, Cora Lena [Mrs. M.
E. Coudelle] (d 1877) singer
NYM
CHOCA, Mrs. (fl 1734) actress
BD
CHOCK, Alexander (fl 1666-67)
scene keeper BD
CHOCK, Dennis (b c. 1689)
actress BD
CHOCKE, George (fl 1698-99)
musician BD

CHODOROV, Edward (b 1904)
American dramatist, director,
producer, scenarist BE, CB,
ES, HJD, MD, MWD, WWT/
10-14
CHODOROV, Jerome (b 1911)
American dramatist, director
BE, CD, COC, ES, HJD, MH,
MWD, WWT/10-16
CHOFE, Robert (fl 1554) actor
DA
CHOLLET, Mons. (d 1892 [95])
singer EA/93*
CHOLLET, Constance (fl 1771)
dancer BD
CHORLEY, Henry Fothergill (1808-
72) English dramatist, critic
DD, DNB
CHORLEY, John Rutter (1807?-67)
English scholar, dramatist
DNB
CHORPENNING, Ruth (b 1905)
American actress WWT/8-10
CHOSE, Mr. (fl 1734-35) dancer
BD
CHOTZINOFF, Samuel (d 1964 [74])
Russian/American dramatist,
critic BE*, BP/48*
CHOW, Caryn Ann (b 1957) Amer-
ican actress TW/24
CHOWHURY, Roy see Bhaskar
CHRIS, Marilyn (b 1939) American
actress TW/27-30
CHRISMAN, Carolyn American
actress TW/27, 29
CHRISTENSEN, Harold (b 1902)
American dancer, teacher ES
CHRISTENSEN, Lew (b 1906/09)
American choreographer, dancer
BE, ES
CHRISTENSEN, William F. (b
1902) American choreographer,
dancer, educator BE, ES
CHRISTI, Vito (b 1924) American
actor TW/1-7
CHRISTIAN, Mr. (fl 1750-53)
dancer BD
CHRISTIAN, Mrs. [née Vaughan]
(fl 1730-33) actress BD
CHRISTIAN, Miss (fl 1784) actress
BD
CHRISTIAN, Benjamin (fl 1794)
violinist BD
CHRISTIAN, Charles (fl c. 1700)
singer BD
CHRISTIAN, Edward (fl 1784?-94)
singer BD
CHRISTIAN, Frances Ann [née

Fanny Waldron] (d 1874 [83])
EA/76*
CHRISTIAN, Frank J. (d 1973
[86]) musician BP/58*
CHRISTIAN, Robert (b 1939)
American actor TW/23,
25-28, 30
CHRISTIAN, Thomas (1810-67)
minstrel HAS, SR
CHRISTIAN, Thomas see
Christmas, Thomas
CHRISTIAN, Thomas Berry (d
1874 [90]) EA/76*
CHRISTIAN, Mrs. Thomas
Berry see Christian,
Frances Ann
CHRISTIAN, Lieut. T. P. (fl
1790-91) dramatist CP/3,
DD
CHRISTIAN, William (d 1699)
singer BD
CHRISTIANS, Mady (1900-51)
Austrian actress CB, ES,
TW/1-8, WWT/8-11
CHRISTIANS, Rudolf (1869-
1921) German actor, manager
WWT/2
CHRISTIE, Dame Agatha Mary
Clarissa [née Miller] (1890/
91-1976) English dramatist
AAS, BE, CB, CD, COC,
ES, HP, PDT, WWT/10-16
CHRISTIE, Al (1886-1951)
Canadian producer, director,
actor ES
CHRISTIE, Audrey (b 1911/12)
American actress BE,
TW/1-19, WWT/9-16
CHRISTIE, Campbell (1893-1963)
Indian/English dramatist
AAS, WWT/12-13
CHRISTIE, Charles H. (d 1955
[75]) producer BE*
CHRISTIE, Dorothy [née Dorothy
Casson Walker] (b 1896) Eng-
lish dramatist AAS, WWT/
12-14
CHRISTIE, George (1873-1949)
American actor WWT/8-10
CHRISTIE, John (d 1962 [80])
impresario BE*
CHRISTIE, Julie (b 1941) Indian/
English actress CB, TW/
29-30
CHRISTMAS, Mrs. (fl c. 1673-
75) actress? BD
CHRISTMAS, David (b 1942)
American actor TW/25-26

CHRISTMAS, John (d c. 1677)
trumpeter BD
CHRISTMAS, Thomas (fl 1663)
trumpeter BD
CHRISTMAS, Thomas (fl 1692-96)
singer BD
CHRISTOFF, George see Chris-
topher, George
CHRISTOPHER, George [George
Christoff] (d 1881 [c. 55]) tight-
rope artist EA/82*
CHRISTOPHER, Jordan (b 1940)
American actor TW/29
CHRISTOPHER, Thom (b 1940)
American actor TW/29-30
CHRISTOPHERSON, John (fl 1546)
dramatist CP/3
CHRISTY, Dave (1853-1926) min-
strel SR
CHRISTY, E. Byron (d 1866 [28])
minstrel? HAS
CHRISTY, Edwin P. (1815-62)
singer, banjoist, founder of
Christy's Minstrels CDP, HAS,
HJD, SR, WWA/H
CHRISTY, Floyd (d 1962 [55])
performer BE*
CHRISTY, George N. [né Harring-
ton] (1827-68) American min-
strel CDP, HAS, SR
CHRISTY, George Washington (d
1975 [86]) circus owner BP/
60*
CHRISTY, Ken (d 1962 [67]) actor
BE*
CHRISTY, William A. (d 1862
[23]) minstrel HAS
CHRONEGK, Ludwig (1837-91)
actor COC
CHUDLEIGH, Arthur (1858-1932)
English manager GRB/4,
WWT/1-6
CHUDLEIGH, John (fl 1669-74)
actor? BD
CHUJOY, Anatole (d 1969 [74])
critic BP/53*
CHUMBLEY, Mr. (fl 1797-1802)
boxkeeper BD
CHUNG LING SOO [Williams Ells-
worth Robinson] (d 1918 [56])
EA/19*
CHURCH, Mr. (fl 1744) house ser-
vant? BD
CHURCH, Mr. (fl 1752-53) musi-
cian BD
CHURCH, Mr. (fl 1770) actor,
singer BD
CHURCH, Mrs. (d 1877 [74])

actress? EA/78*
CHURCH, Charles (d 1872 [69])
actor? EA/73*
CHURCH, Esmé (1893-1972)
English actress, director
AAS, ES, WWT/7-14
CHURCH, George (d 1871)
musician EA/72*
CHURCH, George (b 1912)
American actor TW/11-
12, 20
CHURCH, Harry (d 1890 [58])
chairman EA/91*
CHURCH, John (1675-1741)
English singer, composer
BD, DNB
CHURCH, Maria (d 1887)
EA/88*
CHURCH, Samuel (fl 1792) per-
former BD
CHURCH, Samuel Harden
(1858-1943) dramatist CB
CHURCH, Sandra American
actress BE
CHURCH, Tom (d 1872 [37])
pianist EA/73*
CHURCH, Tony (b 1930) English
actor AAS, TW/24, WWT/
15-16
CHURCH, William (fl 1666-70)
scenekeeper BD
CHURCHILL, Miss (fl 1782)
actress BD
CHURCHILL, Allen (b 1911)
American writer BE
CHURCHILL, Berton (1876-1940)
Canadian actor CB, ES, SR,
WWT/7-9
CHURCHILL, Caryl (b 1938)
English dramatist CD
CHURCHILL, Charles (1731-64)
poet CDP
CHURCHILL, Diana (b 1913)
American actress AAS,
ES, WWT/8-15
CHURCHILL, Donald dramatist
CD
CHURCHILL, Prof. J. Edwin
American actor HAS
CHURCHILL, John (fl 1699-
1700) carpenter BD
CHURCHILL, J. W. singer
CDP
CHURCHILL, Marguerite (b
1910) American actress ES,
WWT/7-9
CHURCHILL, Sarah (b 1914)
English actress CB, ES,

TW/7-8, WWT/10-16
CHURCHILL, William (1760?-1812)
musician BD
CHURCHILL, William James (d
1893 [49]) music-hall artist
EA/94*
CHURCHILL, Winston (1871-1947)
American dramatist GRB/2-4,
WWT/1-3
CHURCHMAN, Mr. (fl 1715) actor
BD
CHURTON, Mr. (fl 1796) manager?
actor? BD
CHURTON, Mrs. (fl 1792) actress
BD
CHUTE, Charles Kean (d 1905
[46]) actor EA/06*
CHUTE, George Macready (d 1888
[37]) manager EA/89*, WWT/
14*
CHUTE, James H. (d 1878 [68])
proprietor, manager EA/79*,
WWT/14*
CHUTE, Mrs. James H. (d 1878
[54]) EA/79*
CHUTE, James Macready (d 1912
[55]) manager, proprietor EA/
13*, WWT/14*
CHUTE, John Coleman (d 1913
[94]) manager WWT/14*
CHUTE, Marchette (b 1909) Amer-
ican dramatist BE
CHUTE, Stephen Macready (d 1899
[47]) EA/00*
CHUTE, William Charles Macready
(d 1908 [25]) EA/09*
CHWATT, Aaron see Buttons,
Red
CIACCHI, Sig. (fl 1746-48) singer
BD
CIANCHETTINI, Pio ["Mozart
Britannicus"] (1799-1851) Eng-
lish composer CDP
CIANELLI, Alma (d 1968 [76])
performer BP/53*
CIANNELI, Eduardo (1889-1969)
Italian/American actor ES,
TW/26
CIAPARELLI, Gina (fl 1897-1911)
Italian singer WWM
CIARDINI, Domenico (fl 1763)
singer BD
"CIAVARTINO, Sig." (fl 1754)
musical performer? BD
CIBBER, Charlotte see Charke,
Mrs. Richard
CIBBER, Colley (1671-1757) Eng-
lish actor, manager, dramatist

BD, CDP, COC, CP/1-3,
DD, DNB, ES, GT, HP,
MH, NTH, OC/1-3, PDT,
SR, TD/1-2
CIBBER, Mrs. Colley [née
Katherine Shore] (c. 1669-
1734) singer, actress BD
CIBBER, Elizabeth see
Brett, Mrs. Dawson
CIBBER, Jane (b 1730) English
actress BD
CIBBER, Susanna Maria see
Cibber, Mrs. Theophilus, II
CIBBER, Theophilus (1703-58)
English actor, dancer,
dramatist, manager BD,
CDP, COC, CP/1-3, DD,
DNB, ES, GT, OC/1-3,
TD/1-2
CIBBER, Mrs. Theophilus, I
[née Jane Johnson] (1706-33)
actress, singer BD
CIBBER, Mrs. Theophilus, II
[née Susanna Maria] (1714-66)
English actress, singer,
dramatist BD, CDP, CP/
1-3, DD, DNB, ES, GT,
NTH, OC/1-3, TD/1-2
CICERI, Charles (fl 1793-1800)
Italian scene painter, ma-
chinist BD
CICERI, Leo (1928-70) Canadian
actor TW/12, 27
CIECA, Io (1710-11) singer BD
CIEPLINSKI, Jan (d 1972 [71])
producer/director/choreog-
rapher BP/56*
CIGADA, Francesco (b 1878)
Italian singer ES
CIGNA, Gina Italian singer ES
CILENTO, Diane (b 1933)
Australian actress AAS,
BE, TW/12-15, WWT/14-16
CIMA, Victoria Gamez see
Angeles, Victoria de los
CIMADOR, Giovanni Battista
(1761-1805) Italian musician,
composer BD, ES
CIMADORI, Giovanni Andrea
(d c. 1684) Italian actor BD
CIMBER, Matt (b 1936) Ameri-
can producer, director BE
CIMINI, Pietro (d 1971 [97])
conductor BP/56*
CINDERS, Ettie [Miss Cantor]
English actress GRB/1
CINKO, Paula (b 1950) actress
TW/29-30

CINQUEVALLI, Adelina [Mrs.
Paul Cinquevalli] (d 1908)
EA/09*
CINQUEVALLI, Paul (1859-1918)
Polish juggler OC/1-3
CINQUEVALLI, Mrs. Paul see
Cinquevalli, Adelina
CINTI, Mlle. see Damoreau,
Laure Cinthie
CIOCCA, Signora (fl 1847) dancer
HAS
CIOFFI, Charles (b 1935) American
actor TW/25-27
CIOLLI, Augusta (d 1967 [65])
actress TW/23
"CIPERINI, Sig. " (fl 1759) singer
BD
CIPRANDI, Ercole (fl 1754-91?)
singer BD
CIPRIANI, Giovanni Battista (1727-
85) Italian scene painter, en-
graver, historical painter BD
CIPRIANI, Lorenzo Angelo (fl 1791-
96) singer BD, CDP
CIPRICO, George M. (b 1847)
American actor CDP, DD,
HAS
CIRKER, Mitchell (d 1953 [70])
American set designer BE*,
BP/37*
CIRRI, Giovanni Battista (b c. 1740)
Italian violoncellist, composer
BD
CISNEROS, Eleanora de (1878-
1934) American singer ES
CISNEY, Marcella [Marcella
Ruth Abels] American adminis-
trator, director, actress BE
CISSEL, Chuck (b 1948) American
actor TW/29-30
CITKOWITZ, Israel (d 1974 [65])
composer/lyricist BP/58*
CIZO, Mr. (fl 1790) singer BD
CIZOS, Rose-Marie see Chéri,
Rose
CLABBURN, Mr. (fl 1794) singer
BD
CLACY, Frederick (d 1874 [30])
dwarf pantomimist EA/75*
CLAGGET, Charles (1740?-1820?)
Irish violinist, inventor, com-
poser BD, DNB
CLAGGET, Walter (1742-98) Irish
instrumentalist, composer,
proprietor BD
CLAGGETT, Crispus (fl 1795-97)
impresario, lessee BD
CLAIR, Cissie [Mrs. H. Buckstone

Clair] (d 1901) EA/02*
CLAIR, Mrs. H. Buckstone
see Clair, Cissie
CLAIR, Lionel (d 1891) actor
EA/92*
CLAIR, Lucy [Mrs. Watty Clair]
(d 1882) EA/83*
CLAIR, Mavis (b 1916) English
actress WWT/8-10
CLAIR, Richard (b 1935)
American actor TW/14,
17-18
CLAIR, Mrs. Watty see
Clair, Lucy
CLAIRBERT, Clara (b 1899)
Belgian singer ES
CLAIRE, Attalie (fl 1890-97)
Canadian singer, actress
DD, DP
CLAIRE, Helen (1911-74) Amer-
ican actress BE, TW/1,
30, WWT/9-11
CLAIRE, Ina (b 1892/95) Amer-
ican actress, singer AAS,
BE, CB, ES, NTH, SR,
TW/2-8, 10-16, WWT/3-14
CLAIRE, Ludi [née Edilou
Bailhé] (b 1922) American
actress BE, TW/14-17,
27, 30
CLAIRVILLE, Charles (d 1918
[63]) librettist WWT/14*
CLAMAKIN, Mrs. (fl 1731)
dancer BD
CLAMAN, Julian (d 1969 [51])
dramatist BP/53*
CLAMP, John (d 1907 [74])
banjo maker EA/08*
CLANCARTY, Countess of
[Belle Bilton; Lady Dunlo]
(d 1906 [38]) English actress
CDP, GRB/1
CLANCENT, William [William
Butler] (d 1893 [53]) EA/95*
CLANCEY, Jean (d 1893) sand
dancer EA/94*
CLANCY, Deirdre (b 1943)
English designer WWT/16
CLANCY, James (b 1912) Amer-
ican director, educator BE
CLANCY, Laura (d 1884) actress
CDP
CLANCY, Michael (fl c. 1700-
c. 50) Irish? dramatist, actor
CP/1-3, DD, GT
CLANCY, Timothy see Buck-
ley, Joe
CLANCY, Tom (b 1926) Irish

actor TW/16, 29-30
CLANCY, Venie (d 1882) actress
CDP
CLANFIELD, Mr. (fl 1775-76)
boxkeeper BD
CLANFIELD, Mr. (fl 1794) singer?
musician BD
CLANFIELD, Samuel (fl 1750-
1800) pyrotechnist, proprietor
BD
CLANTON, Ralph (b 1914) Amer-
ican actor TW/1-8, 10-12,
24, 28-29, WWT/12-13, 16
CLAPHAM, Mrs. (fl 1786) actress
BD
CLAPHAM, Charles (d 1959 [65])
performer BE*, WWT/14*
CLAPP, C. C. (fl 1856) actor
HAS
CLAPP, Charles (d 1962 [63])
American songwriter BE*
CLAPP, Charles Edwin, Jr. (d
1957 [57]) American producer
BE*, BP/41*
CLAPP, Henry Austin (d 1904
[62]) critic WWT/14*
CLAPP, Philip Greeley (1888-
1954) American composer
WWA/3
CLAPP, William W. (1826-91)
journalist CDP
CLAPTON, John (d 1872) pro-
prietor EA/73*
CLARA, Mlle. equestrienne CDP
CLARA, Mlle. (fl 1828) dancer
HAS
CLARANCE, Lloyd (d 1939 [90])
actor, manager WWT/14*
CLARE, Ada actress EA/97
CLARE, Ada [née Jane McEthenrey;
Mrs. Frank P. Noyes; Agnes
Stansfield] (1836-74) actress
CDP, HAS
CLARE, Bridget [Mrs. Edward
Clare] (d 1887 [46]) EA/88*
CLARE, Dickie [Richard Clare
Robinson] (b 1871) English actor
GRB/1
CLARE, Edward (d 1869 [51])
professor of music EA/70*
CLARE, Mrs. Edward see
Clare, Bridget
CLARE, Mary (1892/94-1970)
English actress AAS, ES,
WWT/3-14, WWW/6
CLARE, Phyllis (d 1947 [42/62])
English actress BE*, WWT/
14*

CLAREMONT, Kittie see
Carson, Mrs. Charles L.
CLAREMONT, Lizzie [Mrs.
Henry Spry] (d 1904 [62])
actress EA/05*, WWT/
14*
CLAREMONT, William (d 1832)
English actor BD, BS
CLARENCE, George D. (d
1904 [60]) actor EA/06*
CLARENCE, James (d 1906
[35]) performer? EA/07*
CLARENCE, O[liver] B. (1870-
1955) English actor ES,
GRB/3-4, WWT/1-11
CLARENCE, Nellie actress
GRB/1-2
CLARENDON, Miss (fl 1742)
actress BD
CLARENDON, Miss (fl 1841)
actress, manager HAS
CLARENDON, Charles (d 1899
[34]) comic singer EA/00*
CLARENDON, J. Hayden (b
1879) Irish actor WWS
CLARENS, Elsie (d 1917)
actress EA/18*
CLAREY, H. O. (d 1906)
comedian EA/07*
CLARGES, Verner (d 1911 [65])
English actor PP/1, SR
CLARIDGE, John (fl 1766-90)
lobby doorkeeper, supernum-
erary BD
CLARIDGE, Norman (b 1903/05)
English actor WWT/8-16
CLARISSA (b 1924) American
actress TW/2-3
CLARK, Mr. (fl 1731) actor
BD
CLARK, Mr. (fl 1792-1819?)
singer BD
CLARK, Mr. (fl 1800) puppeteer
BD
CLARK, Mr. (fl 1800-06) scene
painter BD
CLARK, Mr. (d 1812) waxworks
exhibitor BD
CLARK, Mr. (d 1881) EA/83*
CLARK, Mrs. (fl 1695-1723?)
actress, singer, dancer BD
CLARK, Mrs. (fl 1760-1814?)
waxworks exhibitor? BD
CLARK, Mrs. (fl 1789) singer
BD
CLARK, Mrs. ["Naneys Gown"]
(d 1884 [70]) giant EA/85*
CLARK, Master (fl 1724-30)

dancer BD
CLARK, Miss (fl 1736) actress,
singer BD
CLARK, Miss (fl 1736-47?) act-
ress, singer BD
CLARK, Miss (fl 1787) actress
BD
CLARK, Miss see Isherwood,
Mrs.
CLARK, Alexander (d 1932 [66])
American comedian BE*,
BP/17*
CLARK, Alexander (b 1901/04)
American actor BE, TW/8,
19, 21, 23-26
CLARK, Alfred Indian/English
actor WWT/4-9
CLARK, Allan (d 1908) bandmaster
EA/09*
CLARK, Barrett H. (1890-1953)
Canadian critic, actor, director
ES, HJD, NTH, WWA/3, WWT/
7-13
CLARK, Bobby (1888-1960) Amer-
ican actor CB, ES, SR, TW/
1-8, 10-13, 15-16, WWA/3,
WWT/7-12
CLARK, Brian dramatist CD
CLARK, Buddy (1911-49) American
singer TW/6
CLARK, Mrs. C. [Mrs. T. G.
Clark] (d 1890) EA/91*
CLARK, Charles (d 1919 [64])
manager WWT/14*
CLARK, Charles Dow (d 1959
[89]) actor TW/15
CLARK, Charles William (1865-
1925) American singer WWA/1
CLARK, Cuthbert (1869-1953)
English musical director, com-
poser BE*
CLARK, D. (fl 1784?-94) violinist
BD
CLARK, Dane (b 1913) American
actor ES
CLARK, Dorothy L. English act-
ress, singer GRB/1
CLARK, Dort (b 1917) American
actor BE, TW/1, 3-8, 10-18,
26
CLARK, Edward (d 1789) singer,
organist BD
CLARK, Edward (d 1894 [62])
architect EA/95*
CLARK, Edwin A. (b 1871) Amer-
ican actor WWS
CLARK, E. Holman (1864-1925)
English actor DD, EA/96,

GRB/2-4, WWT/1-5
CLARK, Elsie (d 1966 [67])
performer BP/50*
CLARK, Ernest (b 1912) Eng-
lish actor AAS, TW/6, 11,
WWT/12-16
CLARK, Ethel Schneider (d
1964 [48]) actress BE*
CLARK, F. Donald (b 1913)
American educator BE
CLARK, Mrs. Frank Pierce
see Hughes, Lizzie
CLARK, Fred (1914-68) Ameri-
can actor BE, TW/13-16,
25, WWA/5, WWT/14
CLARK, Mrs. Fred (d 1909)
EA/10*
CLARK, Frederick (d 1916)
stage manager EA/17*
CLARK, Garner (d 1971 [56])
musician BP/56*
CLARK, Harry (d 1956 [45])
actor TW/12
CLARK, Henri (d 1905 [65])
music-hall comedian CDP
CLARK, Mrs. Henri (d 1881)
EA/82*
CLARK, Herbert F. (d 1920
[60]) dramatist WWT/14*
CLARK, Hugh (d 1653) English
actor DA, OC/1-3
CLARK, Israel see De Luré
CLARK, Jerman (d 1705)
dancing master BD
CLARK, Jerry American actor
TW/28
CLARK, John (fl 1793-1803)
scene painter BD
CLARK, John (fl 1794) violinist
BD
CLARK, Johnny (d 1967) per-
former BP/52*
CLARK, John Pepper (b 1935)
Nigerian dramatist CD
CLARK, John Richard (b 1932)
Australian director WWT/16
CLARK, John Sleeper see
Clarke, John Sleeper
CLARK, Johnson see Bryan,
Hal
CLARK, Joseph (d 1696?) posture
maker BD, CDP, DNB
CLARK, Kendall (b 1912) Amer-
ican actor BE, TW/3, 8,
10-16
CLARK, Lillian actress CDP
CLARK, Louise Hamilton (d
1900 [26]) comedienne EA/01*

CLARK [or Clarke], Marguerite
(1882/87-1940) American singer,
actress CB, ES, GRB/3-4,
SR, WWA/1, WWM, WWS,
WWT/1-6
CLARK, Marilyn American actress
TW/23
CLARK, Marjory (b 1900) English
actress WWT/7-10
CLARK, Norman (b 1887) Ameri-
can critic BE
CLARK, Oliver (b 1939) American
actor TW/23-27
CLARK, Peggy (b 1915) American
designer BE
CLARK, Phillip (b 1941) American
actor TW/23, 26
CLARK, Richard (b 1780) singer,
pianist, violinist BD
CLARK, Roger actor TW/1, 3, 5
CLARK, Rose Francis Langdon
(d 1962 [80]) performer BE*
CLARK, Rosie Amy (d 1897)
EA/98*
CLARK, Sill (fl 1600-41?) actor?
stage-attendant? DA
CLARK, Sylvia (d 1970) performer
BP/54*
CLARK, T. G. (d 1894) actor?
EA/95*
CLARK, Mrs. T. G. see Clark,
Mrs. C.
CLARK, Thomas (fl 1670-91?)
actor BD
"CLARK, Thornton" see Carson,
Murray
CLARK, T. Sealey (d 1909 [59])
publisher BE*, EA/10*, WWT/
14*
CLARK, Wallis (1888/89-1961)
English actor TW/2-3, 17,
WWT/7-11
CLARK, W. H. (c. 1863-1913)
Canadian singer SR
CLARK, William (fl 1784-88)
singer BD
CLARK, William (fl 1794) singer
BD
CLARK, William (1816-87) actor,
musician DD, NYM
CLARK, William (d 1899 [65])
EA/00*
CLARK, William (d 1909) showman
EA/10*
CLARK, William (d 1917) actor
EA/18*
CLARK, William George (1821-78)
English? scholar DNB

CLARK, William H. (d 1887
[71]) actor WWT/14*
CLARK, William T. (d 1925
[62]) actor BE*, BP/10*
CLARK, Willis Gaylord (1810-
41) American author CDP
CLARK, Wyndham (d 1872 [35])
Scottish singer EA/73*
CLARKE, Mr. (fl 1675) French?
dancer BD
CLARKE, Mr. (fl 1724-26)
dancer? BD
CLARKE, Mr. (fl 1726-28)
dancer BD
CLARKE, Mr. (fl 1729) singer
BD
CLARKE, Mr. (fl 1743) actor
BD
CLARKE, Mr. (fl 1760-62)
house servant BD
CLARKE, Mr. (fl 1765) singer
BD
CLARKE, Mr. (fl 1778-79)
actor BD
CLARKE, Mr. (fl 1786-90?)
actor BD
CLARKE, Mr. (fl 1793-95)
doorkeeper BD
CLARKE (fl 1797) actor BD
CLARKE, Mr. actor CDP
CLARKE, Mrs. (fl 1765) singer
BD
CLARKE, Mrs. (fl 1786) actress
BD
CLARKE, Mrs. [Mrs. W. S.
Forrest] (1831-52) actress
HAS
CLARKE, Mrs. (d 1879) EA/
81*
CLARKE, Master (fl 1781-83)
dancer BD
CLARKE, Miss (fl 1829) tight-
rope performer CDP
CLARKE, Miss (fl 1847)
actress HAS
CLARKE, A. (d 1889) manager
EA/90*
CLARKE, Adele (fl 1868)
actress HAS
CLARKE, Albert (d 1971 [73])
performer BP/55*
CLARKE, Albert H. (b 1851)
English actor GRB/1
CLARKE, Mrs. Albert H.
see Barley-Clarke, Marion
CLARKE, Alfred (d 1883)
scene artist EA/84*
CLARKE, Alfred Claude (d

1899 [48]) manager EA/00*
CLARKE, Algernon (b 1864) Eng-
lish musical director, composer
GRB/1
CLARKE, Annie M. (1845-1902)
American actress CDP, PP/1,
SR
CLARKE, Mrs. Asia Booth [Mrs.
John Sleeper Clarke] (1838-88)
writer DD
CLARKE, Austin (1896-1974) Irish
dramatist ES, MD
CLARKE, Bryan see Forbes,
Bryan
CLARKE, Burt G. (1847-1913)
actor SR
CLARKE, C. A. (fl 1875-94)
dramatist DD
CLARKE, Mrs. C. A. (d 1900
[66]) EA/01*
CLARKE, Sir Campbell (1835-
1902) dramatist DD, WWW/1
CLARKE, Celenia [Mrs. George
Clarke] (d 1901) EA/02*
CLARKE, Charles (d 1875 [55])
box book-keeper EA/76*
CLARKE, Charles A. (d 1876
[48]) manager EA/77*
CLARKE, Charles A. (d 1913)
EA/14*
CLARKE, Charles Cowden (1787-
1877) writer DD
CLARKE, Mrs. Charles Cowden
see Clarke, Mary Cowden
CLARKE, Conrad B. (d 1859)
actor HAS
CLARKE, Constantia (1825-53)
English actress HAS
CLARKE, Corson W. (1814-67)
American actor CDP, HAS
CLARKE, Creston (1865-1910)
American actor DD, GRB/3-4,
PP/1, WWA/1, WWS
CLARKE, Mrs. Creston see
Prince, Adelaide
CLARKE, Cuthbert (1869-1953)
English musical director, com-
poser GRB/4, WWT/1-6
CLARKE, David (b 1908) American
actor BE, TW/26
CLARKE, Della [Mrs. J. F. Sulli-
van] (b 1878) American actress,
dramatist WWM
CLARKE, Eden (d 1869 [26])
comic singer EA/70*
CLARKE, Edward see Clarke,
Nathaniel
CLARKE, E. Holman see

Clark, E. Holman
CLARKE, Ellen (d 1903) EA/
04*
CLARKE, Elsie (d 1917 [19])
actress EA/18*
CLARKE, Ernie [Tommy Dodd]
(d 1898 [62]) comedian EA/
99*
CLARKE, Eugene singer, sing-
ing teacher CDP
CLARKE, Fanny M. [Mrs.
Charles Beveridge] (d 1890)
EA/92*
CLARKE, Florence [Mrs. L. S.
Dewar] (d 1890 [28]) EA/91*
CLARKE, Francis (d 1907
[31]) EA/08*
CLARKE, Frederick (fl 1851)
actor HAS
CLARKE, Frederick see
Victor, Frederick
CLARKE, Gage (1905-64) Amer-
ican actor TW/6-7, 21
CLARKE, George (1886-1946)
English actor WWT/6-10
CLARKE, Mrs. George see
Clarke, Celenia
CLARKE, George H. (1840-
1906?) American actor CDP,
DD, HAS, PP/1
CLARKE, George P. (1824-60)
American actor HAS
CLARKE, George Somers (fl
1790) dramatist CP/3,
DD
CLARKE, Gordon B. (1906-72)
American actor TW/23, 28
CLARKE, Hamilton (1840-1912)
composer, conductor DD
CLARKE, Harry Corson (d
1923 [62]) American come-
dian, agent WWS
CLARKE, Henry Savile (1841-
93) dramatist, critic DD
CLARKE, Holman see Clark,
E. Holman
CLARKE, Isaac (fl 1660-64)
musician BD
CLARKE, James W. (d 1880
[40]) dancer EA/81*
CLARKE, Jeremiah (1673?-1707)
English singer, organist,
composer BD, DNB, ES
CLARKE, J. Hamilton see
Clarke, Hamilton
CLARKE, J. I. C. see
Clarke, Joseph Ignatius
Constantine

CLARKE, J. L. (fl 1784?-1811?)
musician BD
CLARKE, John (fl 1608) member
of the Chapel Royal DA
CLARKE, John (fl 1671-1701)
theatre keeper BD
CLARKE, [John?] (fl 1770-1836?)
singer BD
CLARKE, John (d 1879 [c. 50])
actor DD, DNB, OAA/1-2
CLARKE, John (d 1974 [69])
performer BP/59*
CLARKE, Mrs. John see Fur-
tado, Terese Elizabeth
CLARKE, John H. (1788-1838)
English actor DD, HAS, SR
CLARKE, John H. (d 1910) actor?
EA/11*
CLARKE, John Sleeper (1833-99)
American actor, manager
CDP, COC, DAB, DD, DNB,
ES, HAS, OAA/1-2, OC/1-3,
PP/1, SR, WWA/1
CLARKE, Mrs. John Sleeper see
Clarke, Mrs. Asia Booth
CLARKE, John Woodruff (fl 1794-
1800) actor BD
CLARKE, Joseph Ignatius Constan-
tine (1846-1925) Irish/American
dramatist DAB, GRB/3-4,
WWA/1, WWM
CLARKE, Josiah (d 1907 [70])
EA/08*
CLARKE, Lydia (b 1923) American
actress TW/6-8, 10-11
CLARKE, Mae (b 1907/10) Ameri-
can actress, dancer ES, WWT/
8-9
CLARKE, Marcus Andrew Hislop
(1846-81) English dramatist
DNB, HP
CLARKE, Marion [Mrs. Fred Pol-
lard] (d 1898 [32]) actress
EA/99*
CLARKE, Marlande (d 1892 [34])
actor EA/93*
CLARKE, Mary [alias Wood] (fl
1603) actress? DA
CLARKE, Mary Anne (1776-1852)
English actress? DNB
CLARKE, Mary Bayard Devereux
(1827-86) American librettist
WWA/H
CLARKE, Mary Victoria Cowden
(1809-98) English scholar DD,
DNB, HP
CLARKE, Matthew (d 1786) actor
BD, CDP, DD

CLARKE, Nathaniel (1699-1783) actor, dancer BD
CLARKE, Mrs. [Nathaniel?] (fl 1727-47) actress, singer BD
CLARKE, N. B. [né Belden] (b 1810) American actor, stage manager, dramatist HAS, SR
CLARKE, Nigel (1895-1976) English actor WWT/10-12
CLARKE, Philip (b 1904) English actor TW/2
CLARKE, Richard (fl 1730-60?) violinist BD
CLARKE, Richard (fl 1889-95) singer, actor, dramatist DD
CLARKE, Richard (b 1933) English actor TW/24, 27
CLARKE, Robert (fl 1617-24) actor DA
CLARKE, Robert (1777-1853) dancer BD
CLARKE, Robert (fl 1844) acting manager CDP
CLARKE, Sir Rupert (1865-1926) manager WWT/1-5
CLARKE, Stephen (fl 1809) dramatist CP/3, DD
CLARKE, Thomas (fl 1572) actor DA
CLARKE, Thomas (d 1866 [24]) comedian HAS
CLARKE, Thomas [Tom Griffiths] (d 1904 [32]) comedian EA/05*
CLARKE, Walter (d 1903 [27]) circus performer EA/04*
CLARKE, Mrs. W. H. see Leatitia, Mme.
CLARKE, Wilfred (1867-1945) American actor DD, SR, WWM
CLARKE, William Hutchinson (b 1865) Canadian actor, singer WWS
CLARKE-JERVOISE, Lady Florence (d 1912) dramatist EA/13*
CLARKE-SMITH, Douglas A. (1888-1959) Scottish actor WWT/5-12
CLARKE-TRAVERS, Sarah Ada (d 1916) EA/17*
CLARKSON, Mr. (fl 1723-28) pit office keeper BD
CLARKSON, Mr. (fl 1750-65) actor BD, HAS

CLARKSON, Mr. (fl 1778) booth proprietor BD
CLARKSON, Mrs. (fl 1752-53) actress HAS
CLARKSON, George (d 1908) manager EA/09*
CLARKSON, Joan (b 1903) actress WWT/6-10
CLARKSON, John (b 1932) English actor TW/28-30
CLARKSON, Louisa see Wall, Mrs. Harry
CLARKSON, W. H. (d 1878 [58]) perruquier EA/79*
CLARKSON, William (1865-1934) English costumier, perruquier GRB/1, WWT/2-7
CLARY, Mr. (fl 1791-95) costume designer BD
CLARY, Mme. (fl 1757-58) dancer BD
CLARY, Robert [né Widerman] (b 1926) French actor, singer BE
CLARY, Roy (b 1939) Canadian actor TW/24
CLASON, Mr. (d 1830 [32]) actor HAS
CLATTEN, Lilian see Mayo, Margaret
"CLATTERBANE" (fl 1774) musician BD
CLAUDE, Mrs. [Miss Hogg] (fl 1798) American actress HAS
CLAUDE, Angelina (fl 1873-76) actress DD
CLAUDE, John (fl 1804) actor HAS
CLAUDEL, Paul (1868-1955) French dramatist COC, OC/1-3
CLAUGHTON, Susan English actress WWT/4-5
CLAUSEN, Constance (b 1925) American actress TW/9
CLAUSSEN, Johanna (b 1842) German actress HAS
CLAUSSEN, Joy (b 1938) American actress, singer BE
CLAUSSEN, Julia (1879-1941) Swedish singer CB, WWA/1
CLAVERDON, Jennie (d 1900) music-hall performer EA/01*
CLAVERING, Marie (b 1869) actress GRB/2
CLAVERING-WARDELL, Anna Maria [née Kelly] (d 1875) EA/76*
CLAWOOD, Robert (fl 1765)

musician BD
CLAWSON, Mrs. Isaac S. see
Holman, Mrs. Joseph George
CLAXTON, Mr. (fl 1703-07)
dancer BD
CLAXTON, Mr. (fl 1703-07)
dancer, composer BD
CLAXTON, Kate (1848-1924)
American actress CDP,
COC, DAB, DD, ES, OC/
1-3, PP/1, SR, WWA/1,
WWM
CLAXTON, Tom (d 1916) vari-
ety agent EA/18*
CLAY, Cecil (d 1920 [73])
dramatist BE*, WWT/14*
CLAY, Mrs. Cecil see
Vokes, Rosina
CLAY, Edwin (d 1908 [56])
EA/09*
CLAY, Frederick (1839-89)
French/English musician,
composer DD, DNB, ES
CLAY, Henry (fl 1624-26?)
actor DA
CLAY, Joseph (fl 1709-10)
musician BD
CLAY, Lila (d 1899) actress,
composer, director EA/00*
CLAY, Louise (b 1938) Amer-
ican actress TW/26, 29-30
CLAY, Nathaniel (fl 1618-29)
actor DA
CLAY, Samuel (fl 1784?-94)
singer? instrumentalist?
music copyist BD
CLAY, Tom [né Thomas
Lindsay Clay] (d 1892) song
& pantomime writer EA/93*
CLAY, William (fl 1784-94)
singer BD
CLAYBURGH, Alma (d 1958 [77])
singer TW/15
CLAYBURGH, Jill (b 1944)
American actress TW/25-
27, 29-30
CLAYDEN, Pauline (b 1922)
English dancer ES
CLAYSACK, S. (fl 1794) musi-
cian BD
CLAYTON, Master (fl 1763)
dancer BD
CLAYTON, Bessie (1870-1948)
American vaudevillian ES,
TW/5
CLAYTON, Dorine (d 1917 [4])
EA/18*
CLAYTON, Ella see Tannyhill,

Mrs. Francis A.
CLAYTON, Estelle (1867-1917)
American actress, dramatist
CDP, DD, SR
CLAYTON, Ethel (d 1966 [82])
American actress ES, TW/23
CLAYTON, Frank H. composer
CDP
CLAYTON, Harold (d 1971 [68])
producer, director BP/56*
CLAYTON, Hazel [Mrs. Mack
Hilliard] (d 1963 [77]) actress
BE*
CLAYTON, Herbert (1876-1931)
English actor, singer, producer,
manager GRB/1-4, WWT/5-6
CLAYTON, Jan (b 1917) American
actress, singer BE, TW/1-2,
12-16, 29
CLAYTON, John (fl 1762-78) scene
painter BD
CLAYTON, John [John Alfred Clay-
ton Calthrop] (1845-88) English
actor CDP, COC, DD, DNB,
ES, OAA/1-2
CLAYTON, Mrs. John see
Boucicault, Eva
CLAYTON, Lou (d 1950 [63])
actor, manager TW/7
CLAYTON, Thomas (1673-1725?)
English composer, impresario,
violinist? BD, CP/1, DD,
DNB, ES
CLAYTON, Una (d 1968 [92])
actress WWS
CLAYTON, William (c. 1636-97)
instrumentalist, singer BD
CLAYTON, William (d 1867 [21])
musician EA/68*
CLAYTONE, Richard (fl 1623)
actor DA
CLEAR, Richard (fl 1659-62)
carver BD
CLEARY, Mr. (fl 1811) actor HAS
CLEARY, Edwin (d 1922 [64])
actor, manager, journalist
WWT/14*
CLEARY, Maurice G. (d 1973
[78]) actors' business manager
BP/57*
CLEARY, Peggy (d 1972 [80]) per-
former BP/56*
CLEATER, Mrs. (fl 1745-65)
dresser BD
CLEATHER, Gordon (b 1872)
Italian/English actor, singer
GRB/3-4, WWT/1-5
CLEAVE, Arthur (b 1884) English

actor WWT/4-5
CLEAVELY [or Clevly], Price
(fl 1732) singer BD
CLEETER, Mr. (fl 1708) bill
carrier BD
CLEGG, Miss see Davis, Mrs.
CLEGG, Charles Albert (d 1893
[29]) actor? EA/94*
CLEGG, John (1714-50?) Irish
violinist BD, DNB
CLEGG, Joseph (d 1880 [35])
actor? EA/81*
CLEGG, Marie [Mrs. Hodgkin-
son] (d 1893 [34]) actress?
EA/94*
CLEGG, Sarah (d 1890 [54])
actress? EA/91*
CLEGG, Tom (d 1897 [48]) Negro
comedian EA/98*
CLEGG, William (fl 1784?-94) singer,
actor? BD
CLEGHORN, William see
Yates, George
CLEIN, Ed (b 1944) American
actor TW/25-26
CLELAND, Miss [Miss Buttery]
(b 1762) actress BD, TD/2
CLELAND, John (1709-89) Eng-
lish dramatist CP/1-3, DD,
DNB
CLEMENS, Henry Cameron (d
1932 [66]) actor SR
CLEMENS, Le Roy (b 1889)
American dramatist WWT/
6-9
CLEMENT, Clay (1863-1910)
American actor, dramatist
WWA/1
CLEMENT, Clay (1888/89-1956)
American actor SR, TW/
13, WWT/6-7
CLEMENT, Donald (d 1970 [29])
American actor TW/26-27
CLEMENT, Dora actress TW/1
CLEMENT, Edmond (1871-1928)
French singer WWA/1, WWM
CLEMENT, Elfrida English actress
GRB/1-4, WWT/1-2
CLEMENT, Frank (d 1937)
critic BE*, WWT/14*
CLEMENT, Franz (1780-1842)
Austrian violinist, composer,
conductor BD
CLEMENT, John (fl 1660-88?)
singer, therbo player BD
CLEMENT, John Maurice (d
1912 [71]) proprietor EA/13*

CLEMENT, Tom Henri (d 1872)
skater, singer EA/73*
CLEMENT, William (fl 1550)
actor DA
CLEMENTI, Sig. (fl 1739) singer
BD
CLEMENTI, Muzio (1752-1832)
Italian musician, composer,
conductor BD
CLEMENTINA, Sobieska (fl 1772)
equestrienne BD
CLEMENTINE, Sig. (fl 1699)
singer BD
CLEMENTS, Arthur (fl 1876-84)
dramatist DD
CLEMENTS, Charles see Rix,
John
CLEMENTS, Colin (1894-1948)
American dramatist SR, TW/
4, WWA/2
CLEMENTS, Dudley (d 1947 [58])
actor TW/4
CLEMENTS, Florence Ryerson (d
1965 [70]) dramatist BP/50*
CLEMENTS, Frank (1844-86?)
Scottish actor OAA/1-2
CLEMENTS, Harry (d 1970) musi-
cian BP/55*
CLEMENTS, H. C. (b 1880) Eng-
lish manager GRB/1
CLEMENTS, Sir John Selby (b
1910) English actor, manager,
producer AAS, COC, ES,
PDT, WWT/9-16
CLEMENTS, Larry (d 1916) EA/
17*
CLEMENTS, Miriam actress GRB/
3-4, WWT/1-6
CLEMENTS, Neva West (d 1965)
performer BP/50*
CLEMENTS, William (d 1906)
fireman EA/07*
CLEMENT-SCOTT, Joan (1907-69)
English actress WWT/5-7
CLEMMENTS, George (d 1907
[67]) circus musical director
EA/08*
CLEMSON, Charles (d 1909 [41])
variety performer? EA/10*
CLENDINING, Miss (fl 1798)
actress BD
CLENDINING, Mrs. William [née
Elizabeth Arnold] (1768-99)
English actress, singer BD,
TD/1-2
CLENDON, Elizabeth see
Baker, Mrs. David Lionel

Erskine
"CLEO" see Blackburn, John
CLERC, Elise (d 1925) dancer
WWT/14*
CLERICI, Roberto (fl 1711-48)
scene painter BD
CLERICUS, Joseph see Clark,
Joseph
CLERK, Mr. (fl 1784) singer
BD
CLERKE, Shadwell see Hamund,
St. John
CLERKE, William (fl 1662-63)
actor, dramatist CP/3, DD
CLERKE, William (d 1663)
musician BD
CLEUGH, Dennis (b 1881) actor
GRB/1
CLEVA, Fausto (1902-71) Italian
conductor WWA/5
CLEVELAND, Mr. (fl 1728)
dancer BD
CLEVELAND, Mr. (fl 1796) actor
HAS
CLEVELAND, Mrs. (fl 1796)
actress HAS
CLEVELAND, Miss see Stirling,
Mrs. Arthur
CLEVELAND, Anna (fl 1900s)
American actress WWM
CLEVELAND, Charles Edward
(1864-1914) minstrel, circus
manager, agent SR
CLEVELAND, George (d 1957
[71]) actor BE*
CLEVELAND, Jean (b 1903)
American actress TW/2
CLEVELAND, Louie (d 1899)
actress EA/00*
CLEVELAND, Thomas (fl
1792-99) actor BD
CLEVERE, Amy singer CDP
CLEVERMAN, M. (d 1875 [45])
conjuror EA/76*
CLEVLY, Price see Cleavely,
Price
CLEWES, Winston (1906-57)
dramatist WWW/5
CLEWLOW, F. D. (d 1957 [72])
director BE*, WWT/14*
CLEY, Henry see Clay, Henry
CLEZY, Cool (d 1893) comedian
EA/94*
CLIBURN, Mrs. J. F. see
Ware, Irene
CLIFF, Laddie (1891/92-1937)
English actor, manager,
dancer ES, SR, WWM,

WWT/4-8
CLIFF, Oliver (b 1918) American
actor TW/2-8
CLIFFE, Alice Belmore see
Belmore, Alice
CLIFFE, H. Cooper (1862-1939)
English actor DD, EA/97,
GRB/2-4, WWS, WWT/1-8
CLIFFORD, Mr. (fl 1781-94?)
actor BD
CLIFFORD, Mr. (fl 1792-93)
singer BD
CLIFFORD, Mr. (fl 1796) actor
BD
CLIFFORD, Mr. (fl 1799) manager
BD
CLIFFORD, Mrs. [née Robins;
Mrs. George Sims] (fl 1779-
1809?) actress BD
CLIFFORD, Mrs. (fl 1799) actress
BD
CLIFFORD, Mrs. see Price,
Mrs.
CLIFFORD, Lady see De La
Pasture, Mrs. Henry
CLIFFORD, Miss see Harrison,
Mrs.
CLIFFORD, B. (d 1884) actor
EA/85*
CLIFFORD, Bessie (d 1967) per-
former BP/51*
CLIFFORD, Billy "Single" (1869-
1930) American minstrel, circus
performer SR
CLIFFORD, Camille [Hon. Mrs.
Lyndhurst Henry Bruce] Danish/
American actress GRB/1, 3-4,
WWT/1-6
CLIFFORD, Charles (d 1908 [39])
actor GRB/4*
CLIFFORD, Charles [Sir Charles
William Woolfe Clifton-Browne]
(1867-1943) English actor,
manager GRB/1
CLIFFORD, Mrs. Charles (d 1877)
actress EA/78*
CLIFFORD, Miss E. [Mrs. Talbot]
(d 1891) actress EA/92*
CLIFFORD, Ed (1845-95) American
actor SR
CLIFFORD, Edmund see Junot,
W. E. D.
CLIFFORD, Edwin (fl 1867-76)
English actor OAA/1-2
CLIFFORD, Elizabeth [Miss Mc-
Ginty] (d 1889) actress, ballet
mistress EA/90*
CLIFFORD, Ellen actress CDP

CLIFFORD, Frank see Watts, Francis Walter
CLIFFORD, Gervan (d 1886) actor EA/87*
CLIFFORD, Gordon (d 1968 [65]) composer BP/53*
CLIFFORD, Harry (d 1897 [65]) actor CDP
CLIFFORD, Harry singer CDP
CLIFFORD, Henry see Bland, Harry
CLIFFORD, Mrs. Henry Marston see Clifford, Rose
CLIFFORD, Herbert (d 1874) actor? EA/76*
CLIFFORD, Jack (d 1956 [76]) dancer, actor TW/13
CLIFFORD, John (b 1947) American dancer, choreographer CB
CLIFFORD, Kathleen (1887-1962) American actress, singer TW/19, WWT/4-6
CLIFFORD, Margaret Ellen (1908-71) American director, actress, educator BE
CLIFFORD, Maria (1794?-1850) actress CDP
CLIFFORD, Marie [Mrs. R. J. Seaton] (d 1906) entertainer EA/07*
CLIFFORD, Martin (fl 1671-77) writer DD
CLIFFORD, Nat singer, composer CDP
CLIFFORD, Rose [Mrs. Henry Marston Clifford] (d 1909) EA/10*
CLIFFORD, Thomas E. singer CDP
CLIFFORD, Mrs. William (1791-1850) English actress DD
CLIFFORD, Mrs. W. K. (d 1929) dramatist DD, GRB/3-4, WWM, WWT/1-5, WWW/3
CLIFT, Ernest Paul (1881-1963) English manager, dramatist WWT/4-13
CLIFT, Montgomery (1920-66) American actor BE, CB, ES, TW/1-7, 10-13, 23, WWA/4, WWT/10-11
CLIFTON, Mr. (fl 1852) actor HAS
CLIFTON, Ada (fl 1855-67) English actress CDP, HAS

CLIFTON, Augusta (d 1882 [55]) actress EA/83*
CLIFTON, Bernard (1902-70) actor, singer WWT/10-14
CLIFTON, Elmer (d 1949 [59]) actor, director BE*
CLIFTON, Mrs. Ernest see Adams, Isabel
CLIFTON, Ethel [Mrs. Herbert Ralland] (d 1897) actress EA/98*
CLIFTON, Fanny see Stirling, Mrs.
CLIFTON, Frederic (b 1844) actor OAA/1-2
CLIFTON, George (d 1876 [35]) comic singer EA/77*
CLIFTON, Harriett (d 1910 [63]) actress EA/11*, WWT/14*
CLIFTON, Harry (1832-72) English music-hall performer CDP, OC/1-3
CLIFTON, Howard singer, composer CDP
CLIFTON, John (d 1880 [40]) actor EA/81*
CLIFTON, Joseph [né Dilks] (b 1858) American dramatist, actor SR
CLIFTON, Josephine [née Miller; Mrs. Robert Place] (1813-47) American actress CDP, DAB, ES, HAS, SR, WWA/H
CLIFTON, Lina [Miss P. Weldon] (d 1890 [27]) American singer EA/91*
CLIFTON, Marion P. (1833-1917) English actress SR
CLIFTON, Thomas (fl 1600) actor DA
CLIFTON, W. (d 1875) stage manager EA/76*
CLIFTON, William Rumball (d 1877) actor, stage manager EA/79*
CLIFTON-BROWNE, Sir Charles William Woolfe see Clifford, Charles
CLIMENHAGA, Joel Ray (b 1922) South African educator BE
CLINCH, Mr. (c. 1663-1734) imitator BD
CLINCH, Charles Powell (1797-1880) American dramatist CDP, EAP, RJ, WWA/H
CLINCH, Herbert (fl 1697) musician BD
CLINCH, J. H. (d 1916) EA/17*

CLINCH, Lawrence (d 1812)
Irish actor BD, CDP, DD,
TD/1-2
CLINE, Andre (fl 1828-62)
English tight-rope dancer
HAS
CLINE, John (d 1886) tight-rope
performer CDP
CLINE, Maggie (1857-1934)
American actress, singer
CDP, NTH, SR
CLINE, Rose see Merryfield,
Rose
CLINE, Thomas S. (fl 1835)
English actor HAS
CLINETOP, Lucie (b 1849)
American dancer CDP, HAS
CLINETOP, Sallie (b 1851)
American dancer CDP, HAS
CLINFORD, Mr. (fl 1792) actor
BD
CLINGO, Mr. (fl 1759-63) pit
doorkeeper BD
CLINTON, Mr. [né Hamblin]
(fl 1856) actor HAS
CLINTON, Master (fl 1763-65)
dancer BD
CLINTON, Arthur (d 1869)
prompter EA/70*
CLINTON, Dudley [Ernest Gil-
lame] (1868-1908) English
actor GRB/4
CLINTON, Edward (b 1948)
American actor TW/26
CLINTON, Ella [Mrs. Frances
H. France] (d 1898) actress
EA/99*
CLINTON, Henry see Gilligan,
Joseph
CLINTON, James (d 1897 [43])
musician EA/98*
CLINTON, J. W. (d 1880)
actor EA/81*
CLINTON, Kate (d 1935) actress
BE*, WWT/14*
CLINTON, Kitty CDP
CLINTON-BADDELEY, Constance
(d 1901) EA/02*
CLINTON-BADDELEY, Victor
Clinton (1900-70) English
actor ES
CLITHEROE, Jimmy (d 1973
[50s] performer BP/58*
CLITHEROW, Benjamin (fl c.
1740-74) pyrotechnist BD
CLITHEROW, W. F. (b 1848)
English actor GRB/1-2
CLIUTMAS, Harry F. (d 1964

[83]) performer BE*
CLIVE, Colin (1900-37) French/
English actor ES, SR, WWT/
6-8
CLIVE, David J. (b 1923) Ameri-
can stage manager, producer,
director BE
CLIVE, Edward E. (1876-1940)
English actor, producer CB,
SR
CLIVE, Franklin (d 1924) singer
WWT/14*
CLIVE, F. Wybert [Frederic W.
Maclachlan] (b 1879) English
dramatist, actor GRB/1-2
CLIVE, Mrs. George see
Clive, Kitty
CLIVE, Kitty [née Catherine
Raftor; Mrs. George Clive]
(1711-85) English actress,
singer BD, CDP, COC, CP/
1-3, DD, DNB, ES, GT, HP,
OC/1-3, TD/1-2
CLIVE, Vincent (d 1943) English
actor WWT/1-7
CLIVE, Wybert (d 1892 [32])
actor, dramatist EA/93*
CLODOCHE, Mons. (fl 1869)
dancer CDP
CLOFULLIA, Josephine [née
Rebecca Westgate] (1824-80)
bearded lady CDP
CLOGG, Hallye (d 1965 [86])
chorus girl TW/22
CLOSE, Elizabeth (d 1869) EA/
70*
CLOSE, Ivy (d 1968 [78]) perform-
er BP/53*
CLOSE, W. R. (d 1875 [39])
lessee EA/76*
CLOSS, William F. (d 1908)
musical director EA/09*
CLOSSER, Louise see Hale,
Louise
CLOSSON, Mr. (fl 1738-55) actor,
dancer, animal imitator BD
CLOSSON, Mlle. (fl 1740) dancer
BD
CLOTHIER, Devereux (fl 1662-99)
drummer BD
CLOTHIER, John (d 1753) drum-
mer BD
CLOUGH, Mrs. (fl 1670-73) act-
ress BD
CLOUGH, Miss (fl 1748) actress
BD
CLOUGH, Thomas (d 1770) actor
BD, CDP

CLOVELLY, Cecil (d 1965 [74])
English actor TW/21
CLOW, William E. , II (d 1970
[40]) production assistant
BP/54*
CLOWES, Louisa Jane (d 1884)
marionettist? EA/86*
CLOWES, Richard (b 1900)
English representative, mana-
ger WWT/8, 10
CLOZEL, Mlle. (fl 1828) act-
ress? HAS
CLUBLEY, John Sherwood (d
1964) actor, director BE*
CLUCAS, Charles (d 1905 [39])
manager GRB/1
CLUCHEY, Rich (b 1933) Amer-
ican dramatist, director,
actor CD
CLUN, Walter (d 1664) actor
BD, DA, DD
CLUNES, Alec S. (1912-70)
English actor AAS, COC,
ES, WWT/9-14, WWW/6
CLURMAN, Edith (d 1973 [55])
dancer BP/57*
CLURMAN, Harold Edgar (b
1901) American director,
manager, critic AAS, BE,
CB, COC, ES, OC/3, PDT,
TW/2-8, WWT/10-16
CLUTSAM, George H. (1866-
1951) Australian composer
ES, WWW/5
CLYDE, Amy [Mrs. J. Dobson
Clyde] (d 1917) EA/18*
CLYDE, Mrs. J. Dobson see
Clyde, Amy
CLYDE, Jean (d 1962 [73])
actress BE*, WWT/14*
CLYDE, Jeremy (b 1941) Eng-
lish actor TW/27
CLYDE, John (d 1917) EA/18*
CLYDE, June (b 1909) American
actress WWT/8-11
CLYNDES, J. H. (d 1927 [86])
actor DD
CO, Ja. (fl 17th cent?) drama-
tist FGF
COAD, Emily (fl 1839-51)
English singer CDP
COAD, Harry (1825-87) actor
NYM
COAD, Oral Sumner (b 1887)
American historian, educator
ES
COAKLEY, Marion actress
WWT/7

COAN, Caryll [Crickett] American
actress TW/28, 30
COAN, John (1728-64) English
dwarf BD
COAN, Sherwood A. see Camp-
bell, S. C.
COATES, Mr. (fl 1793-1803)
doorkeeper BD
COATES, Mr. (fl 1799) proprietor
BD
COATES, Mrs. (fl 1797-1822?)
singer, actress BD
COATES, Albert (1882-1953)
Russian/English composer,
conductor ES, WWW/5
COATES, Arthur see Coates,
Fred
COATES, Carolyn (b 1930) Ameri-
can actress TW/22-28, WWT/
15-16
COATES, Edith (b 1908) English
singer ES
COATES, Elizabeth (fl 1788?-
1830) actress BD
COATES, Emma Anne [Mrs.
Robert Coates] (fl c. 1830?)
CDP
COATES, Fred [Arthur Coates]
(b 1867) English actor GRB/1
COATES, Mrs. James S. (d 1875
[28]) EA/76*
COATES, John (1865-1941) English
actor, singer CB, DD, EA/96
COATES, Robert ["Romeo"] (1772-
1848) English actor CDP, COC,
DD, DNB, OC/1-3
COATES, Mrs. Robert see
Coates, Emma Anne
COATES, Mrs. W. H. (d 1870
[65]) actress EA/71*
COATS, Mrs. (fl 1796) actress
TD/1-2
COATS, Miss (fl 1779-80) singer
BD
COBB, Charles Edward see
Ross, Charles
COBB, Edmund (d 1974 [82]) per-
former BP/59*
COBB, George (d 1877 [90]) pro-
prietor EA/79*
COBB, Gerard Francis (d 1904)
composer EA/05*
COBB, Gladys (b 1892) English
costumier ES
COBB, Irvin S. (1876/77-1944)
American actor, dramatist
CB, SR, WWM
COBB, James (d 1697) singer,

composer BD
COBB, James (1756-1818)
dramatist CDP, CP/2-3,
DD, DNB, ES, GT, TD/1-2
COBB, John S. (d 1969 [37])
producer, director BP/53*
COBB, Lee J. (1911-76)
American actor AAS, BE,
ES, TW/5, 25-26, WWT/
10-13
COBB, Richard see Temple,
Richard
COBB, Tiger (d 1965) performer
BP/49*
COBBE, John (d 1891) acting
manager EA/92*
COBHAM, Mr. (fl 1769) per-
former? BD
COBHAM, Charles (1774-1819)
English violinist, violist BD
COBHAM, Thomas (1779/86-
1842) English actor CDP,
DD, DNB, OX
COBORN, Mr. (d 1886 [87])
EA/88*
COBORN, Mrs. (d 1905 [93])
EA/06*
COBORN, Charles [Colin Whitton
McCallum] (1852-1945) Eng-
lish actor, singer, librettist
CDP, COC, ES, GRB/1-3,
OC/1-3
COBORNE, Edward (fl 1616)
actor DA
COBRA, Frederic Walter (d
1886 [25]) acrobat EA/87*
COBURN, Mrs. Charles D.
see Coburn, Ivah
COBURN, Charles Douville
(1877-1961) American actor,
manager CB, COC, ES,
NTH, OC/1-3, SR, TW/1,
3, 5-7, 18, WWA/4, WWM,
WWT/4-13
COBURN, Ivah [Ivah Wills]
(1882-1937) American act-
ress, manager NTH, OC/
1-3, WWM
COBURN, Joan actress TW/11
COBURN, John Arthur (1869-
1943) minstrel SR
COCA, Imogene (b 1908/09)
American actress BE,
CB, ES, TW/2-3, 5-7, 30,
WWT/15-16
COCCHI, Gioacchino (1715-
1804) Italian composer,
musical director, conductor BD

"COCHININO, Sig. " (fl 1754)
musician BD
COCHOIS, Francis H. (fl 1734-35)
dancer, actor BD
COCHOIS, Michel (fl 1719-35)
actor BD
COCHOIS, Mme. Michel [née
Moylin] (fl 1719-35) actress
BD
COCHOY, Michel see Cochois,
Michel
COCHRAN, Sir Charles Blake
(1873-1951) English manager,
agent AAS, CB, COC, DNB,
ES, GRB/1-2, NTH, OC/1-3,
PDT, TW/7, WWT/2-11,
WWW/5
COCHRAN, Eddie (d 1975) per-
former BP/60*
COCHRAN, Mrs. Howard see
Jenoure, Aida
COCHRAN, Steve (1917-65) Ameri-
can actor, director, producer
BE, ES, TW/22
COCHRANE, Frank (1882-1962)
English actor WWT/4-11
COCHRANE, George (d 1917)
EA/18*
COCHRANE, Howard (b 1873)
English actor GRB/2
COCHRANE, Jeanetta (b 1883)
English costumier ES
COCHRANE, June (d 1967 [64])
actress TW/24
COCK, J. Lamborn (d 1891 [82])
publisher, treasurer EA/92*
COCKAIN, Sir Aston see
Cokayne, Sir Aston
COCKBURN, Mr. (fl 1784-85)
actor BD
COCKBURN, Catharine [née Trot-
ter] (1679-1749) English drama-
tist CP/1-3, DD, DNB, GT,
TD/1-2
COCKBURN, George W. (b 1869)
English actor GRB/1
COCKBURN, John M. (d 1964
[66]) critic BE*, BP/49*
COCKBURN, Mrs. Peter see
Dyer, Lizzie
COCKERILLE, Lili American
actress TW/29
COCKETTES, The theatre collec-
tive CD
COCKING, Robert (d 1837) aero-
naut CDP
COCKINGS, George (d 1802) Eng-
lish dramatist CP/2-3, DNB,

EAP, GT

COCKLIN, Mr. (fl 1764-65) violinist BD

COCKRAM, Master (d 1878) musician EA/79*

COCKRAM, William Edward [Leigh Wilson] (d 1870 [34]) singer EA/71*

COCKRILL, H. B. see Bradley, Harry C.

COCKRILL, Helen (d 1880) EA/81*

COCKSHUTT, Stanislaus (d 1969 [66]) performer BP/55*

COCKYE, Miss (fl 1685-91) actress BD

COCO [Thomas Cox] (d 1899) music-hall performer EA/01*

COCO, Antony (fl 1796) acrobat? BD

COCO, Concetto (fl 1796-97) posture maker BD

COCO, James (b 1929/30) American actor CB, TW/22-27, WWT/15-16

COCROFT, Thoda (1893-1943) American actress, agent SR

COCTEAU, Jean Maurice (1889-1963) French dramatist COC

CODBOLT, Lightfoot (fl 1607) actor DA

CODBOLT, Thomas (fl 1607) actor DA

CODE, Grant (1896-1974) American actor, dramatist TW/28

CODE, Reginald F. (d 1975 [78]) producer/director/choreographer BP/60*

CODECASA, Mme. Giovanni (d 1869) singer EA/70*

CODESACA, Mme. [Saporiti] (d 1870 [101]) singer EA/71*

"CODGERINO, Sig." (fl 1752) dancer BD

"CODGERINO, Signora" (fl 1752) dancer BD

CODMAN, Louie (d 1947 [84]) actress WWT/14*

CODONA, W. (d 1873 [27]) circus performer EA/74*

CODRINGTON, Ann (b 1895) Indian/English actress WWT/9-13

CODRINGTON, Robert (1601-65?) English dramatist CP/1-3, DD

CODRON, Michael (b 1930) English manager, producer WWT/13-16

CODY, Ethel (d 1957 [62]) American actress, singer TW/14

CODY, Frank (d 1917) EA/18*

CODY, Lew (1887-1934) American actor ES

CODY, William Frederick (1846-1917) American showman CDP, DAB, ES, HP, HJD, NTH, OC/1-3, SR

COE, Mr. (fl 1719-23) pit office keeper BD

COE, Mr. (fl 1855-64) actor DD

COE, Fred H. (b 1914) American producer, director BE, CB, WWT/15-16

COE, Isabelle (d 1919) actress SR

COE, John (b 1925) American actor TW/24-26, 28-29

COE, Peter (b 1929) English director AAS, BE, WWT/14-16

COE, Richard L. (b 1916) American critic BE

COE, Thomas (d 1886) actor, stage manager EA/87*

COERNE, Louis Adolphe (1870-1922) American composer DAB, ES

COFFEE, Andrew J. (d 1975 [74]) performer BP/60*

COFFEE, Lenore J. (b 1895) American dramatist ES

COFFEY, Charles (d 1745) Irish dramatist CP/1-3, DD, DNB, ES, GT, TD/1-2

COFFEY, Denise (b 1936) English actress WWT/15-16

COFFIELD, Peter (b 1945) American actor TW/25-29

COFFIN, C. Hayden (1862-1935) English actor, singer CDP, DD, DP, ES, GRB/1-4, WWT/1-7, WWW/3

COFFIN, Emily (fl 1887-92) dramatist DD

COFFIN, Francis (fl 1595-1602) actor DA

COFFIN, Frederick (b 1943) American actor TW/27-30

COGAN, David J. (b 1923) American producer, theatre owner, representative BE

COGAN, Jane [Mrs. William R.

Cogan] (d 1886) EA/87*
COGAN, John (d c. 1673) actor
BD
COGAN, Mrs. William R. see
Cogan, Jane
COGERT, Jed (d 1961 [80])
actor BE*
COGGIN, Barbara American
actress TW/28, 30
COGHILL, Nevill Henry Ken-
dal Aylmer (b 1899) Irish
producer, director, adapter
CD, COC, WWT/15-16
COGHLAN, Charles F. (1842-
99) English actor CDP, DD,
ES, NTH, OAA/2, OC/1-3,
PP/1, SR, WWA/1
COGHLAN, Charles F. (d
1972 [25]) director? chore-
ographer? BP/56*
COGHLAN, Eily (d 1900)
actress EA/01*, WWT/
14*
COGHLAN, Gertrude [Mrs.
Augustus Pitou, Jr.]
(1879-1952) English actress
GRB/2-4, TW/9, WWS,
WWT/1-6
COGHLAN, Lewis (d 1888 [30])
actor EA/89*
COGHLAN, Rosalind (d 1937
[51]) American actress
WWM
COGHLAN, Rose (1851?-1932)
English actress CDP,
COC, DAB, DD, GRB/
2-4, NTH, OAA/2, OC/
1-3, PP/1, SR, WWA/1,
WWM, WWS, WWT/1-6
COGILL, Charles W. (d 1903
[53]) actor, dancer CDP
COGILL, Harry (d 1903) min-
strel EA/04*
COGNIARD, Hippolyte (d 1882
[74]) dramatist, director
EA/83*
COHAN, Cal (1859-1944) min-
strel SR
COHAN, George Michael (1878-
1942) American actor, drama-
tist, composer, manager
AAS, CB, COC, DAB, ES,
GRB/2-4, HJD, MD, MH,
MWD, NTH, OC/1-3, PDT,
SR, WWA/1, WWM, WWS,
WWT/1-9, WWW/4
COHAN, Mrs. George Michael
(d 1972 [89]) dancer BP/57*

COHAN, Georgette (b 1900) Amer-
ican actress SR, WWT/4-7
COHAN, Helen Frances Costigan
(1854-1928) actress BE*,
BP/13*, WWT/14*
COHAN, Henry (d 1975 [75])
manager, agent BP/59*
COHAN, Jere J. (1848-1917)
American actor SR
COHAN, Josephine (1876-1916)
American performer BE*,
WWT/14*
COHAN, Robert (b 1929) American
dancer TW/13
COHAN, Timothy (1846-1914) Irish
actor SR
COHAN, William (d 1976 [66])
producer/director/choreographer
BP/60*
COHEN, Mr. (fl 1770) musician
BD
COHEN, Abe (d 1974 [76]) com-
pany manager BP/58*
COHEN, Al (b 1939) American
actor TW/25-26
COHEN, Alexander (b 1920) Amer-
ican producer AAS, BE, CB,
WWT/14-16
COHEN, Alfred J. see Dale,
Alan
COHEN, Angelina (d 1893) EA/94*
COHEN, Betty see Comden,
Betty
COHEN, Frederick (1904-67) Ger-
man/American director, com-
poser, actor, musical director,
producer, educator BE, TW/
23
COHEN, Gustave (1879-1958)
French scholar COC, OC/1-3
COHEN, Harold (d 1969 [63])
critic BP/54*
COHEN, Harry I. (b 1891) New
Zealand manager WWT/6
COHEN, Isaac (d 1910 [77]) mana-
ger, producer EA/11*, WWT/
14*
COHEN, Mrs. Isaac see Har-
rison, Fanny
COHEN, Katie (d 1946 [82])
actress BE*, WWT/14*
COHEN, Kip (b 1940) American
casting director, production as-
sociate BE
COHEN, Mrs. Leopold see
Cavendish, Rose
COHEN, Margery (b 1947) Ameri-
can actress TW/26-30

COHEN, Martin B. (b 1923)
American producer, director
BE
COHEN, Max (d 1968) manager
BP/52*
COHEN, Max A. (d 1971 [75])
theatre owner BP/56*
COHEN, Morris (d 1973 [66])
performer BP/57*
COHEN, Nathan (1923-71)
Australian critic BE
COHEN, Octavus Roy (1891-
1959) American dramatist
BE*, BP/43*
COHEN, Sammy (b 1902) Amer-
ican actor ES
COHEN, Sara B. (d 1963 [82])
performer BE*
COHEN, Selma Jeanne (b 1920)
American writer, editor BE
COHEN, Sidney I. (d 1973 [64])
consultant BP/58*
COHN, Harry (1891-1958) per-
former, producer BE*
COHN, Janet American literary
representative BE
COINDE, Mr. (fl 1788-89)
ballet master BD
COIT, Dorothy (b 1889) Amer-
ican dramatist, educator
ES
COKAIN, Sir Aston see
Cokayne, Sir Aston
COKAYNE, Sir Aston (1608-84)
English poet CDP, CP/1-3,
DD, FGF
COKAYNE, Mary (fl 1753-75)
actress BD
COKE, Mr. (fl 1784) singer
BD
COKE, Peter (b 1913) English
actor, dramatist WWT/9-15
COKE, Richard (fl 1547-56)
actor DA
COKE, Richard (d 1955 [63])
actor BE*, WWT/14*
COKER, Mr. (fl 1715-21) actor
BD
COKER, Mr. (fl 1733) dancer
BD
COKER, Mrs. (fl 1731-39)
actress BD
COKER, Master Richard CDP
COLAS, Stella (d 1913 [65])
French actress CDP, DD
COLBERT, Claudette [née Lily
Chauchoin] (b 1905/07)
French actress AAS, BE,

CB, ES, SR, TW/14, 16, 20,
30, WWT/6-16
COLBIN, Rod (b 1923) American
actor, fencing master BE
COLBORNE, John (fl 1775-84)
boxkeeper BD
COLBOURNE, Maurice (1894-1965)
English actor, manager WWT/
7-14
COLBRAN, Isabella (1785-1845)
Spanish singer ES
COLBRAND, Edward (fl 1610-13)
actor DA
COLBRON, Grace Isabel (d 1943)
American dramatist GRB/3-4,
WWT/1
COLBY, Barbara (1940-75) Amer-
ican actress TW/22, 28
COLBY, Ethel [née Duckman] (b
1908) American actress, singer,
critic BE, NTH
COLBY, Marion (b 1923) American
actress TW/3
COLBY, Sidney J. (d 1970 [42])
manager BP/55*
COLCHESTER, Enrique (d 1896)
proprietor EA/97*
COLCLOUGH, Mr. musician CDP
COLE, Mr. (d 1730) harpsichordist
BD
COLE, Mr. (fl 1749) house ser-
vant? BD
COLE, Mr. (fl 1760-61) billsticker
BD
COLE, Mr. (fl 1761) dresser BD
COLE, Mr. (fl 1784) violinist BD
COLE, Mr. (fl 1785?-94) violist
BD
COLE, Mr. (fl 1795-99) boxkeeper
BD
COLE, Mrs. (fl 1696) actress BD
COLE, Mrs. (fl 1838) actress
HAS
COLE, Miss (b 1729) English act-
ress, dancer, singer BD
COLE, Alonzo Deen (d 1971 [74])
producer, director BP/55*
COLE, Belle (d 1905 [60]) Ameri-
can singer CDP, GRB/1
COLE, Blanche (d 1888) singer,
actress CDP, DD
COLE, Bob (1869-1912) librettist,
lyricist BE*
COLE, Brian (d 1972 [28]) musi-
cian BP/57*
COLE, Charles H. (d 1916) EA/
17*
COLE, David (b 1936) English

actor TW/13
COLE, Dennis (b 1943) American
actor TW/28
COLE, E. D. (fl 1707-41) actor,
dancer, prompter BD
COLE, Eddie (d 1969 [59]) per-
former BP/55*
COLE, Edith (1870-1927) actress
WWT/2-5
COLE, Edward C. (b 1904)
American educator BE
COLE, Elizabeth see Ashley,
Elizabeth
COLE, George (b 1925) English
actor AAS, WWT/10-16
COLE, Hazel B. (d 1974 [79])
business manager BP/59*
COLE, Horace (d 1916 [41])
manager EA/17*
COLE, Mr. J. (fl 1785?-94)
singer BD
COLE, Jack (1914-74) American
choreographer, dancer, direc-
tor BE, TW/30
COLE, Jacob (d 1868 [73])
comic songwriter EA/69*
COLE, Mrs. James (d 1881
[73]) EA/82*
COLE, Janet see Hunter, Kim
COLE, Jennie (d 1908) EA/09*
COLE, Jessie (d 1877 [28])
EA/78*
COLE, John (d 1901 [85])
EA/02*
COLE, John William see
Calcraft, John William
COLE, Kay (b 1948) American
actress TW/28-30
COLE, Laurence (d 1883 [32])
comedian EA/84*
COLE, Maggie Porter (1857-
1942) singer SR
COLE, Mary Keith (d 1975
[61]) performer BP/59*
COLE, Maurice (d 1965 [72])
performer BP/50*
COLE, Owen Blayney (d 1886
[78]) EA/87*
COLE, Robert (1865-1911)
American comedian SR
COLE, Rose C. [Mrs. Walter
Cole] (d 1890 [35]) EA/91*
COLE, Toby (b 1916) American
talent & literary representa-
tive BE
COLE, Walter ventriloquist,
entertainer CDP
COLE, Mrs. Walter see

Cole, Rose C.
COLE, Wendall (b 1914) American
educator BE
COLE, William Washington (b
1847) American manager SR
COLE, W. J. (d 1870) manager,
actor EA/71*
COLEBY, Wilfred T. (b 1865)
dramatist WWT/2-3
COLEMAN, Mr. (fl 1670s?) im-
presario BD
COLEMAN, Mr. (fl 1749-50) actor
BD
COLEMAN, Alexander see
Sandy, Little
COLEMAN, Alice performer CDP
COLEMAN, Amy English actress
GRB/1
COLEMAN, Carole (d 1964 [42])
American performer BE*
COLEMAN, Charles (c. 1595-1664)
English instrumentalist, singer,
composer BD, DNB, ES
COLEMAN, Charles (d 1694) musi-
cian BD
COLEMAN, Clara performer CDP
COLEMAN, Cornelius J. (d 1973
[44]) musician BP/57*
COLEMAN, Cy composer BE
COLEMAN, David (d 1882) variety
agent EA/83*
COLEMAN, Deborah (b 1919)
American representative BE
COLEMAN, E. B. [E. Coles] (b
1838) English actor HAS, SR
COLEMAN, Edward (d 1669) sing-
er, composer BD, DNB
COLEMAN, Edward (b 1840) Eng-
lish actor HAS
COLEMAN, Emil (d 1965 [72])
conductor BP/49*
COLEMAN, Fanny (1840-1919)
actress DD, GRB/2-4, WWT/
1-3
COLEMAN, Fay R. (b 1918) Amer-
ican puppeteer BE
COLEMAN, Frank, III (d 1970 [35])
singer, actor TW/27
COLEMAN, Frank J. American
actor ES
COLEMAN, Helen (b 1843) Ameri-
can actress HAS, SR
COLEMAN, Irene see Murdock,
Ann
COLEMAN, James (d 1868) scene
artist EA/69*
COLEMAN, Jane (b 1810) American
actress HAS

COLEMAN, J. J. (b 1860)
American actor, agent,
manager SR
COLEMAN, John (fl 1668)
musician BD
COLEMAN, John (1831-1904)
actor, manager, dramatist
CDP, DD
COLEMAN, Mrs. John see
Davies, Maria Jane
COLEMAN, John A. CDP
COLEMAN, Laurina [Mrs. Sandy
Coleman] (d 1882 [30]) EA/
83*
COLEMAN, Leo (b 1919) Amer-
ican actor TW/3
COLEMAN, Lonnie (b 1920)
American dramatist BE
COLEMAN, Louie performer
CDP
COLEMAN, Maggie [Mrs. J.
O'Gorman] (d 1898 [30])
dancer? EA/99*
COLEMAN, Maria Jane see
Davies, Maria Jane
COLEMAN, Millicent American
actress TW/1
COLEMAN, Nancy (b 1914)
American actress BE, ES,
TW/12-13, 25-26
COLEMAN, Robert, Jr. (1900-
74) American critic BE,
NTH, WWT/11-14
COLEMAN, Sam (d 1883 [36])
comedian EA/84*
COLEMAN, Mrs. Sandy see
Coleman, Laurina
COLEMAN, Shepard (b 1924)
American musical director
BE
COLEMAN, Warren R. (d 1968
[67]) actor TW/24
COLEMAN, William (1766-1829)
American journalist, author
CDP
COLEMAN, William (fl 1794)
violinist BD
COLEMAN, William (d 1885)
equestrian EA/86*
COLENO, Florrie (d 1889 [18])
male impersonator EA/90*
COLENO, Mrs. Tom (d 1894
[41]) EA/95*
COLERIDGE, Amy (d 1951 [85])
actress CDP
COLERIDGE, Ethel (1883-1976)
English actress WWT/5-11
COLERIDGE, Samuel Taylor

(1772-1834) English critic,
dramatist COC, CP/3, DD,
DNB, ES, HP, NTH, OC/1-3
COLERIDGE, Sylvia (b 1909/12)
Indian/English actress WWT/
9-16
COLERIDGE-TAYLOR, Samuel
(1875-1912) English composer
DNB
COLES, A. J. see Stewer, Jan
COLES, Charles (fl 1760-70)
house servant? BD
COLES, C. Mortimer (d 1896)
actor EA/97*
COLES, E. see Coleman, E. B.
COLES, John (d 1800) violinist
BD
COLES, Robert (fl 1598-99) actor
DA
COLES, William (fl 1784-94)
oboist BD
COLES, Zaida (b 1933) American
actress TW/24-27, 29
COLETTI, Ferdinand (d 1876 [32])
pianist EA/77*
COLETTI, Filippo (1811-94)
Italian singer CDP, ES
COLETTI, Frank (d 1968 [68])
actor, singer, stage manager
TW/25
COLEY, John (d 1870 [25]) comic
singer EA/71*
COLEY, Thomas (b 1917/18)
American actor TW/3, 26-27
COLGAN, Michael (d 1870 [35])
musician EA/71*
COLICOS, John (b 1928) Canadian
actor AAS, TW/22, 24, WWT/
16
COLIN, Jean (b 1905) English act-
ress, singer WWT/6-12
COLIN, Saul (d 1967 [58]) director,
critic TW/23
COLINA, Fernando (d 1969 [37])
producer, director BP/53*
COLL, Owen (b 1887) Canadian
actor TW/3
COLLA, Mme. Giuseppe see
Aguiari, Lucrezia
COLLARD, Mr. (fl 1736) dancer
BD
COLLARD, Archangello Corelli
(b 1772) musician BD
COLLARD, Henry ["Pocket Sims
Reeves"] (d 1888) singer EA/
89*
COLLEANO, Bonar, Sr. (d 1957
[60+]) performer BE*,

WWT/14*
COLLEANO, Bonar, Jr. (1923-58) American actor WWT/10-12
COLLEANO, Con (d 1973 [73]) performer BP/58*
COLLENS, Gina American actress TW/23
COLLES, Mrs. Joseph [née Hesther Boyde] (fl 1776-80) actress, singer BD
COLLET, Mr. (fl 1729-34) actor BD
COLLET, Mr. (fl 1770-71) actor BD
COLLET, Mr. (fl 1785-1822?) dancer, singer, equestrian, machinist? BD
COLLET, Mrs. [Ann?] (fl 1765-71) actress, singer BD
COLLET, Catherine [Mrs. Tetherington] (fl 1767-1800) dancer, actress BD
COLLET, John (fl 1754?-70) violinist BD
COLLET, Osmond (d 1881 [78]) proprietor EA/82*
COLLET, Richard (fl 1737-67) violinist BD
COLLET, Richard (1885-1946) English manager NTH, SR, WWT/4-9
COLLET, Thomas (fl 1739-43) musician BD
COLLETT, Catherine see Collet, Catherine
COLLETT, Dan (d 1904) music-hall performer EA/05*
COLLETT, John (fl 1806) dramatist CP/3
COLLETT, John (d 1888 [77]) actor EA/89*
COLLETT, Thomas George [Wilfred Roxby] (d 1887 [42]) music-hall artist EA/88*
COLLETTE, Charles Henry (1842-1924) English actor, singer CDP, DD, DP, GRB/1-4, OAA/1-2, WWT/1-4, WWW/2
COLLETTE, Mary (fl 1889-91) actress DD
COLLETTI, Sig. (b 1820) Italian singer HAS, SR
COLLEWELL, Richard (fl 1633) actor DA
COLLEY, Mr. (fl 1774-84) house servant BD
COLLEY, Edward (d 1883 [45])

EA/84*
COLLEY, Edward (d 1890 [31]) music-hall agent EA/91*
COLLEY, Mrs. Edward see Leonie, Annie
COLLIE, Mrs. see Bellair, Mary Ann
COLLIER, Mr. (fl 1725?-31) actor, dancer BD
COLLIER, Cecil (d 1975 [67]) performer BP/60*
COLLIER, Constance (1878-1955) English actress CB, COC, DD, EA/97, ES, GRB/1-4, NTH, OC/1-3, SR, TW/11, WWM, WWT/1-11, WWW/5
COLLIER, Freddie (d 1965 [70]) performer BP/49*
COLLIER, Gaylan Jane (b 1924) American educator BE
COLLIER, Sir George (fl 1762-84) dramatist CP/2-3, GT
COLLIER, Hal (1859-1931) English actor GRB/1
COLLIER, Isabel M. Field (b 1881) English actress GRB/1-4
COLLIER, J. (fl 1702) orator BD
COLLIER, James Walter (1836-98) American actor, manager CDP, HAS, SR
COLLIER, Mrs. James W[alter] dancer CDP
COLLIER, Jeremy (1656-1726) English writer CDP, COC, DD, HP, NTH, OC/1-3, PDT
COLLIER, Joel [George Veal] (fl 18th cent) musician DNB
COLLIER, John Payne (1789-1883) English critic COC, DD, DNB, ES, HP, OC/1-3
COLLIER, J. W. (d 1868) pantomimist EA/69*
COLLIER, J. Walter (d 1920 [60]) manager BP/5*
COLLIER, Lizzie (d 1914) actress WWT/14*
COLLIER, Lizzie Hudson (d 1924 [60]) actress BE*, WWT/14*
COLLIER, Luiza Leopoldina (d 1891 [70]) EA/92*
COLLIER, Marie Elizabeth (1927-71) Australian singer WWA/5
COLLIER, Patience [née Rene Ritcher] (b 1910) English actress AAS, WWT/13-16
COLLIER, William (fl 1709-14) proprietor, manager BD, TD/1-2

COLLIER, William (1866-1944) American actor, dramatist CB, DD, ES, GRB/2-4, NTH, SR, WWA/2, WWM, WWS, WWT/1-9

COLLIER, Mrs. William see Allen, Louise

COLLIER, William C. (b 1903) American dramatist ES

COLLIGAN, James (d 1974 [70]) producer/director/choreographer BP/58*

COLLINGBOURNE, Mr. (fl 1824) actor HAS

COLLINGBOURNE, Miss (fl 1840) actress HAS

COLLINGBOURNE, Florence English actress GRB/1-2

COLLINGBOURNE, William E. (d 1862) American? prompter HAS

COLLINGE, Patricia (1894-1974) Irish actress BE, ES, NTH, SR, TW/2-19, 30, WWT/4-14

COLLINGHAM, G. G. (d 1923) dramatist BE*, WWT/14*

COLLINGS, Mr. (fl 1792-1804) actor, scene painter BD

COLLINGS, W. H. (d 1890 [63]) English/American actor, stage manager EA/91*

COLLINGS, W. Jesse (b 1887) English critic WWT/7-8

COLLINGWOOD, Dr. dramatist CP/3

COLLINGWOOD, Lawrence Arthur (b 1887) English composer, conductor ES

COLLINGWOOD, Lester (d 1910 [54]) actor, manager, dramatist, proprietor EA/11*, WWT/14*

COLLINGWOOD, S. (fl 1794) singer BD

COLLINGWOOD, William (fl 1793-94) singer BD

COLLINI, Signora (fl early 19th cent) singer CDP

COLLINS, Mr. (fl 1771) actor BD

COLLINS, Mr. (fl 1774-81) doorkeeper, supernumerary BD

COLLINS, Mr. (fl 1794) actor HAS

COLLINS, Mrs. (fl 1771) actress BD

COLLINS, Mrs. (fl 1794)

actress HAS

COLLINS, A. B. see Beaumont, Arthur

COLLINS, A. Greville (b 1896) English manager WWT/5-7

COLLINS, Allen Frederick (b 1915) American stage manager, actor, bookseller BE

COLLINS, Anthony (b 1893) English conductor, composer ES

COLLINS, Mrs. Arthur see Collins, Elizabeth

COLLINS, Arthur Pelham (1863-1932) English manager DD, ES, GRB/1-4, SR, WWM, WWT/1-6, WWW/3

COLLINS, Barry (b 1941) English dramatist CD

COLLINS, Bert (d 1962 [63]) performer BE*

COLLINS, Bill (b 1935) American actor TW/30

COLLINS, Blanche (b 1918) American actress TW/2-6, 22-23, 25-26

COLLINS, C. E. (fl 1868) dancer HAS, SR

COLLINS, Cecil A[rthur] (b 1874) English actor GRB/1-2

COLLINS, Charles (fl 1667-70) scene keeper BD

COLLINS, Charles (b 1880) American actor CDP, SR

COLLINS, Charles (d 1964 [83]) critic BE*, BP/48*

COLLINS, Charles (b 1904) American actor TW/2, WWT/8-11

COLLINS, Charles (b 1942) American actor TW/29

COLLINS, Charles James (1820-64) dramatist DNB

COLLINS, Clementina [née Hayward?; Mrs. Thomas Woodfall] (fl 1776-1837) actress BD

COLLINS, Dan W. actor, singer CDP

COLLINS, David (d 1917) manager EA/18*

COLLINS, Dorothy (b 1927) Canadian actress TW/28-29

COLLINS, Mrs. E. [Mrs. William Collins] (d 1874) EA/75*

COLLINS, Edward (fl 1636) actor DA

COLLINS, Edwin J. (b 1875) English actor GRB/1

COLLINS, Eli Whitney (b 1880) American actor, dramatist SR

COLLINS, Elizabeth [Mrs. Arthur Collins] (d 1898 [30]) EA/99*

COLLINS, Elizabeth see Ripon, Mrs. George

COLLINS, Elizabeth Eayrs see Larkelle, Lillie

COLLINS, Emma (fl 1853) singer HAS

COLLINS, Ernest H. (d 1948 [89]) business manager WWT/14*

COLLINS, Ernest S. (d 1975 [84]) producer/director/ choreographer BP/60*

COLLINS, Frank (d 1917 [20]) EA/18*

COLLINS, Frank (1878-1957) English actor, producer GRB/3-4, WWT/5-12

COLLINS, Fred (d 1916) EA/17*

COLLINS, Grace (d 1892) EA/93*

COLLINS, Dr. G. T. (d 1866) treasurer HAS

COLLINS, Horace (1875-1964) English secretary of the Society of West-end Theatre Managers WWT/10-13

COLLINS, Hubert (d 1868) comedian, pantomimist EA/69*

COLLINS, Isaac (1797-1871) violinist CDP

COLLINS, J. (fl 1763-92) actor, carpenter BD, TD/2

COLLINS, Mrs. J. (fl 1770-96) actress BD

COLLINS, Janet (b 1923) American dancer ES

COLLINS, Jeffery (fl 1624) actor DA

COLLINS, Jem see Lennox, James

COLLINS, Jennie Higham [Mrs. Wildon Collins] (d 1917) EA/18*

COLLINS, Jerry (d 1976 [50]) performer BP/60*

COLLINS, John (c. 1725-c. 57) scene painter BD, DNB

COLLINS, John (1741-97) English scholar DNB

COLLINS, John (1742-1808) English monologuist, actor, singer, poet, publisher BD, DD, DNB, TD/1-2

COLLINS, John (1811-74)

Irish comedian CDP, HAS, SR

COLLINS, John Churton (1848-1908) critic HP

COLLINS, John H. (d 1860) singer, minstrel CDP

COLLINS, John J. (d 1903 [37]) showman EA/04*

COLLINS, John R. (b 1878) English actor GRB/1

COLLINS, José (1887-1958) English actress, singer DNB, OC/1-3, TW/15, WWT/4-11

COLLINS, Joshua (fl 1819-20) theatre builder, manager WWA/H

COLLINS, Laura (d 1868) actress EA/69*

COLLINS, Lewis D. (b 1899) American actor ES

COLLINS, Lottie (1866-1910) English music-hall performer CDP, COC, DD, OC/1-3, PDT

COLLINS, Marie actress, singer CDP

COLLINS, Marty (d 1968 [72]) performer BP/53*

COLLINS, May (d 1955 [49]) actress TW/11

COLLINS, O. B. (b 1830) American actor CDP

COLLINS, Mrs. O. B. see Raymond, Kate

COLLINS, Olive (c. 1871-87) American actress NYM

COLLINS, Patrick (1859-1943) English showman WWW/4

COLLINS, Paul (b 1937) English actor TW/22-24

COLLINS, Pauline (b 1940) English actress WWT/15-16

COLLINS, Peter (d 1973) musician BP/58*

COLLINS, Ray (d 1965 [75]) actor TW/22

COLLINS, Rosina (fl 1853) singer HAS

COLLINS, Russell (1897-1965) American actor BE, ES, TW/1-20, 22, WWT/9-14

COLLINS, Sam [né Vagg] (1826-65) Irish music-hall performer CDP, COC, OC/2-3

COLLINS, Sewell (1876-1934) American producer, dramatist NTH, WWM, WWT/5-7

COLLINS, Stephen (b 1947) American actor TW/28-30

COLLINS, Strangways Churton

see Lesmere, Henry
COLLINS, Ted (d 1964 [64])
personal manager BP/48*
COLLINS, Thomas (1775-1806)
actor CDP, DD, TD/2
COLLINS, Thomas (d 1877)
musician EA/78*
COLLINS, Thomas Francis (d
1904 [40]) music-hall per-
former EA/05*
COLLINS, Thomas W. (fl 1836)
dramatist RJ
COLLINS, Una (d 1964 [45])
actress BE*
COLLINS, Viotti (d 1899 [77])
musician EA/00*
COLLINS, Walter E. (d 1917
[31]) conductor EA/18*
COLLINS, W. H. (fl 1863)
actor HAS
COLLINS, Mrs. Wildon see
Collins, Jennie Higham
COLLINS, Wilkie (1824-89)
English dramatist CDP,
COC, DD, DNB, EA/69, ES
COLLINS, William (d 1763)
actor, dancer BD
COLLINS, William (d 1898 [39])
variety performer EA/99*
COLLINS, Mrs. William see
Collins, Mrs. E.
COLLINS, William P. see
Pearson, William C.
COLLINS, Winnie (b 1896)
English actress, singer
WWT/6-9
COLLINS, W. J. ["The
Black Storm"] (d 1876)
comedian EA/77*
COLLINSON, Annie (d 1869)
actress EA/70*
COLLINSON, Laurence (b 1925)
English dramatist CD
COLLIS, [Francis?] (fl 1777-
84?) house servant? super-
numerary? BD
COLLIS, Mrs. [Francis? née
Susanna Richardson] (fl
1777-84) house servant? BD
COLLIS, John (fl 1672) musician
BD
COLLIS, Thomas W. (d 1873)
musician EA/74*
COLLISON, Wilson (1892/93-
1941) American dramatist
CB, SR, WWA/1, WWT/4-8
COLLOM, Ida M. (d 1879)
singer EA/80*

COLLS, J. H. (fl 1795-1805)
dramatist, actor CP/3
COLLUM, John (d 1962 [36]) actor
BE*
COLLYER, Bud (d 1969 [61]) actor
TW/26
COLLYER, Dan (d 1918) performer
BE*
COLLYER, Eve (b 1927) American
actress TW/22
COLLYER, June (d 1968 [61]) per-
former BP/52*
COLMACK, John (fl 1699) musi-
cian BD
COLMAN, Mr. (fl 1749) actor,
singer BD
COLMAN, Benjamin (1673-1747)
American dramatist EAP
COLMAN, Booth (b 1923) American
actor TW/2-6
COLMAN, George, the Elder
(1732-94) English dramatist,
manager BD, CDP, COC,
CP/1-3, DD, DNB, ES, GT,
HP, MH, NTH, OC/1-3, PDT,
SR, TD/1-2
COLMAN, George, the Younger
(1762-1836) English dramatist,
manager, examiner of plays
BD, CDP, COC, CP/3, DD,
DNB, ES, GT, HP, NTH,
OC/1-3, PDT, SR, TD/1-2
COLMAN, Mrs. George, the
Younger see Colman, Mary
COLMAN, Mary [née Logan; Mrs.
Gibbs] (1770-1844) English act-
ress BS, CDP, DD, DNB,
GT, OC/1-3, OX, TD/1-2
COLMAN, Ronald (1891-1958)
English actor CB, ES, SR,
TW/14, WWT/6-11, WWW/5
COLMAN, William (fl 1509-26?)
member of the Chapel Royal
DA
COLMER, Albert Ernest (d 1906)
music-hall assistant manager
EA/07*
COLMER, Graham John see
John, Graham
COLNAGHI, C. P. (fl 1891) actor,
dramatist DD
COLOMBA, Giovanni Battista Inno-
cenzo (1717-93) Italian scene
painter, machinist, costume de-
signer BD
COLOMBATI, Elisabetta (fl 1791-
1811) Italian singer BD
COLOMBE, Emilie (fl 1788-89)

COLOMBIER 234

dancer BD
COLOMBIER, Marie (c. 1842-
1910) French actress OC/
1-3
COLOMBO, Vera (b 1931) Italian
dancer ES
COLON, Alex (b 1941) Puerto
Rican actor TW/27
COLON, Jenny (1808-42) French
actress OC/3
COLON, Miriam (b 1945) Puerto
Rican actress, producer,
director TW/28-29, WWT/
16
COLONA, Edgardo (d 1904 [58])
actor EA/05*
COLONNE, Edouard (d 1910)
conductor EA/11*
COLONY, Alfred T. (d 1964)
actor BE*
"COLOSSUS" (fl 1745) giant
BD
COLPI, Sig. (fl 1764-89)
posture maker, ropedancer
BD
COLPI, Signora (fl 1777) rope-
dancer BD
COLPI, Signorino (fl 1767-77)
ropedancer BD
COLQUHOUN, Jessie [Mrs. R.
M. Colquhoun] (d 1899) EA/
00*
COLQUHOUN, Mrs. R. M. see
Colquhoun, Jessie
COLRIEN, Harriet (d 1909)
EA/10*
COLSON, C. David (b 1941)
American actor TW/26-
29
COLSON, Lizzie [née Richmond]
(1861-1887) American actress
NYM
COLSON, Pauline (1833-84)
singer CDP, HAS, SR
COLSTON, C. I. (d 1932 [95])
secretary of the Actors'
Benevolent Fund WWT/14*
COLT, Alvin (b 1915/16)
American designer BE, ES,
TW/8, WWT/13-16
COLT, Phyllis (d 1971 [52])
performer BP/55*
COLTMAN, Mr. (fl 1794)
organist BD
COLTON, Cheri American actor
TW/25-30
COLTON, Jacque Lynn (b 1939)
American actress TW/25

COLTON, John B. (1889-1946)
English/American dramatist
ES, HJD, MH, TW/3, WWT/
6-11
COLUM, Padraic (1881-1972) Irish
dramatist COC, ES, MD, MH,
MWD, OC/1-3, RE, WWA/5
COLUMBINE, Mrs. Peter see
Brunton, Elizabeth
COLUMBUS, Tobie (b 1951)
American actress TW/30
COLVERD, Edward Fred (d 1910
[37]) EA/11*
COLVERD, Joseph (d 1903) comic
singer EA/04*
COLVILL (fl 1779) singer BD
COLVILLE, Samuel (1825-86)
Irish manager, actor CDP,
SR
COLWELL, Claire [Mrs. Wedg-
wood Nowell] (b 1882) American
actress WWM
COLYER, Austin (b 1935) Ameri-
can actor TW/24-26, 30
COMANNI, Mr. (fl 1734) dancer
BD
COMBE, Mrs. George (d 1868)
EA/69*
COMBER, Mrs. (d 1908) EA/09*
COMBER, Bobbie [né Edmund]
(1886-1942) English actor WWT/
8-9
COMBER, Edmund see Comber,
Bobbie
COMBERMERE, Edward (b 1888)
English actor WWT/4-5
COMBES, William (fl 1594) actor
DA
COMDEN, Betty [née Cohen] (b
1918/19) American librettist,
lyricist, dramatist, actress
AAS, BE, CB, CD, ES, TW/
1-3, WWT/14-16
COMEGYS, Kathleen (b 1895) Amer-
ican actress BE, TW/3, 11-12
COMELATI, Mr. (fl 1735-41)
singer? BD
COMELLI, Attilio (1858-1925)
Italian/English designer ES
COMER, Mr. (fl 1813-19) actor
DD
COMER, Amelia (fl 1861) English
actress HAS
COMER, Bobbie see Comber,
Bobbie
COMER, Charles A. (d 1971 [73])
community theatre founder
BP/56*

COMER, George (fl 1865-99)
dramatist DD
COMER, Henry (fl 1660-76)
violinist BD
COMER, John (d 1886 [86])
singer EA/87*
COMER, Samuel M. (d 1974
[81]) designer BP/59*
COMER, Thomas (1790-1862)
English actor, musician
CDP, HAS, SR
COMERFORD, Mr. (fl 1789-94)
prompter's assistant, actor
BD
COMERFORD, Henry (d 1718)
actor BD
COMERFORD, Maurice (d 1903
[49]) publisher, editor EA/
04*, BE*, WWT/14*
"COMIC KING, The" see
Bostock, N. C.
COMINGORE, Dorothy (d 1971)
performer BP/56*
COMINS, Mr. (fl 1784) singer
BD
COMMANO, Giovanni Giuseppe
(fl 1730-32) singer BD
COMO, Professor [Percy James
Harley] (d 1892) sleight-of-
hand performer EA/93*
COMO, Antonio (fl 1770-76)
dancer, ballet master BD
COMO, Signora Antonio (fl 1775)
dancer BD
COMORN, Mlle. dancer CDP
COMPANY OF FOUR, The
producing managers WWT/
11
COMPANY THEATRE, The
theatre collective CD
COMPSON, Betty (1897-1974)
American actress ES
COMPTON, Betty (d 1944 [37])
actress SR, TW/1
COMPTON, Charles (d 1897 [37])
music-hall comedian EA/
98*
COMPTON, Charles G. (d 1911)
dramatist, critic, writer DD
COMPTON, Edward (1854-1918)
English actor COC, DD,
EA/96, GRB/1-4, OAA/2,
OC/1-3, WWT/1-3
COMPTON, Mrs. Edward see
Bateman, Virginia
COMPTON, Elizabeth [Mrs.
Henry Compton] (d 1881 [34])
EA/83*

COMPTON, Emmeline Catherine
[Mrs. Henry Compton] (d 1910)
EA/12*
COMPTON, Fay (b 1894) English
actress, singer AAS, BE,
COC, ES, OC/1-3, WWT/3-15
COMPTON, Francis (b 1885/90-
1964) English actor BE, TW/
8-16, 19-21
COMPTON, Henry [né Charles
Mackenzie] (1805-77) English
actor CDP, COC, DD, DNB,
ES, OC/1-3
COMPTON, Mrs. Henry see
Compton, Elizabeth
COMPTON, Mrs. Henry see
Compton, Emmeline Catherine
COMPTON, H. L. (d 1916 [54])
EA/17*
COMPTON, John (b 1923) Ameri-
can actor TW/2
COMPTON, June-Lynn (b 1942)
American actress TW/23
COMPTON, Katharine Mackenzie
(1853-1928) English actress
DD, ES, GRB/1-4, OAA/1-2,
OC/1-3, WWT/1-5
COMPTON, Madge (d 1970) actress
WWT/4-14
COMPTON, Percy (d 1910) actor
DD
COMPTON, Rouse (fl 1784-94)
violinist BD
COMPTON, Sydney (d 1938) English
actor GRB/1-4
COMPTON, Mrs. Sydney see
Osborne, Theresa
COMPTON, Viola (1886-1971) Eng-
lish actress GRB/3-4, WWT/
1-9
COMPTON, W. H. (b 1843) Eng-
lish actor SR
COMPTON, Wilfred (b 1877) Eng-
lish actor GRB/1
COMSTOCK, Anthony (1844-1915)
American reformer NTH
COMSTOCK, F. Ray (1880-1949)
American manager TW/6,
WWA/2, WWT/4-10
COMSTOCK, Mrs. F. Ray (d 1970
[80]) manager BP/55*
COMSTOCK, Martin (b 1864)
American manager GRB/1
COMSTOCK, Nanette [Mrs. Frank
Burbeck] (1871/73-1942) Amer-
ican actress DD, GRB/2-4,
SR, WWM, WWS, WWT/1-6
COMYN, Henry (d 1880 [46])

actor? EA/81*

CON, Jim see Gillespy, James

CONAWAY, Donald F. union
executive BE

CONAWAY, Jeff (b 1950) American actor TW/30

CONCANEN, Edward (d 1879
[32]) actor EA/80*

CONCANEN, Matthew (1701-49)
Irish dramatist CP/1-3,
DNB

CONCEPCION, Cesar (d 1974
[64]) musician BP/58*

CONCHAS, Paul (d 1916) EA/
17*

CONCHITA (d 1940 [79]) actress
BE*, WWT/14*

CONDELL, Charlotte (d 1759)
actress BD

CONDELL, Henry (d 1627) Eng-
lish actor COC, DA, DD,
DNB, ES, NTH, OC/1-3,
PDT

CONDELL, Henry (c. 1757-1824)
English musician, composer
BD, DD, DNB

CONDELL, John (d 1779) boxkeeper, concessionaire BD

CONDELL, John (fl 1779-84)
boxkeeper BD

CONDELL, T. (d 1876) manager
EA/77*

CONDO, Alice Maud (d 1901)
"Japanese performer" EA/
02*

CONDON, Eddie (1905-73)
musician CB

CONDON, Eva actress TW/1,
11

CONDOS, Dimo (b 1932) American actor TW/25-28

CONDUIT, Mrs. Mauvaise [née
Ribbon; Mrs. DeBar] (1805-
41) English actress HAS,
SR

CONE, Thomas George (d 1976
[85]) performer BP/60*

CONE, Spencer Houghton (1785-
1855) actor CDP, HAS, SR

CONEGLIANO, Emanuele see
Da Ponte, Lorenzo

CONELLY, Patrick C. (1842-
74) actor CDP

CONFORTI, Gino (b 1932) American actor TW/22-24

CONFREY, Zez (d 1971 [76])
composer/lyricist BP/56*

CONGDON, David (b 1943)

American actor TW/25

CONGO, William (d 1908) equestrian EA/09*

CONGOR, Pauline (fl 1867) actress
HAS

CONGREVE, William (1670-1729) English dramatist CDP, COC, CP/1-
3, DD, DNB, ES, GT, HP, MH,
NTH, OC/1-3, PDT, RE, SR

CONGREVE, W. La Touche (d
1916) EA/17*

CONHEIM, Mrs. Hermann see
Morton, Martha

CONIBEAR, Elizabeth Jenkins (d
1965 [86]) performer BP/49*

CONINGHAM, Mr. (fl 1768-72)
equestrian BD

CONINGSBY, Gilbert (fl 1674-82)
singer BD

CONINX, Louis Joseph (d 1876
[72]) flautist EA/77*

CONKEY, Thomas (1882-1927) singer
SR

CONKLE, E[llsworth] P[routy]
(b 1899) American dramatist,
educator BE, ES, HJD, MD,
MWD, NTH, SR

CONKLIN, Chester (1888-1971)
American circus clown ES

CONKLIN, George circus performer, animal trainer SR

CONKLIN, James (d 1971 [71])
theatre owner BP/56*

CONKLIN, John (d 1838) American
circus performer HAS

CONKLIN, Peggy (b 1912) American actress BE, SR, TW/1-9,
WWT/8-15

CONKLIN, Peter (b 1842) American
minstrel, tumbler HAS, SR

CONKLING, Charles A. (d 1964
[57]) dancer BE*

CONLAN, Frank (d 1955 [81])
actor TW/12

CONLEY, Eugene (b 1908/18)
American singer CB, ES

CONLEY, Harry J. (d 1975 [90])
performer BP/60*

CONLEY, Tom (d 1903 [31])
music-hall comedian EA/04*

CONLIN, Bernard see Florence,
William Jermyn

CONLIN, Jimmy (d 1962 [77])
actor BE*

CONLIN, Ray, Sr. (d 1964 [73])
performer BE*

CONLON, Edward Jerrold (d 1912
[61]) secretary EA/13*

CONLOW, Peter (b 1929) American actor TW/8-20
CONLY, George A. (1845-82) singer CDP
CONN, Maurice H. (d 1973 [67]) producer/director/choreographer BP/58*
CONN, Stewart (b 1936) Scottish dramatist, director CD
CONNARD, Miss (fl 1794) actress, singer BD
CONNEAUX, Arthur F. (d 1902 [16]) EA/03*
CONNEL, Henry (fl 1668-69) barber BD
CONNELL, David (b 1935) American actor TW/25-26, 28-30
CONNELL, E. (d 1801) singer, actor BD
CONNELL, Mrs. E. [Maria] (fl 1785-93?) ticket seller, boxkeeper, actress BD
CONNELL, F. Norreys (1874-1948) Irish dramatist WWT/2-10
CONNELL, Gordon (b 1923) American actor, musician, coach BE, TW/23-24, 28-29
CONNELL, Horatio (b 1876) American singer WWM
CONNELL, James W. (d 1969 [56]) musician BP/54*
CONNELL, Jane [née Jane Sperry Bennett] (b 1925) American actress BE, TW/13, 22-25, 27-29, WWT/15-16
CONNELL, John (b 1923) American actor TW/12-13
CONNELL, Leigh (b 1926) American producer BE
CONNELLY, Mr. (fl 1793-95) doorkeeper BD
CONNELLY, [Miss?] (fl 1724) house servant? BD
CONNELLY, Miss (fl 1799) dancer BD
CONNELLY, Celia Logan (1837-1904) American dramatist WWA/1
CONNELLY, Edward J. (d 1928 [73]) American actor GRB/3-4, WWM, WWT/1-2
CONNELLY, Fanny [Mrs. Michael Connelly] (d 1888) EA/89*
CONNELLY, Marc[us Cook]

(b 1890) American dramatist, director, actor, educator, producer AAS, BE, CB, CD, COC, ES, HJD, MD, MH, MWD, NTH, PDT, RE, SR, WWT/5-16
CONNELLY, Michael (d 1911) musical director EA/12*
CONNELLY, Mrs. Michael see Connelly, Fanny
CONNER, Charlotte Mary Sanford Barnes [Mrs. Edmon S. Conner] (d 1863) actress CDP
CONNER, Edmon S. (1809-91) American actor CDP, SR
CONNER, Mrs. Edmon S. see Conner, Charlotte Mary Sanford Barnes
CONNER, Nadine (b 1913) American singer CB
CONNERS, Barry (1883-1933) American dramatist, actor WWT/6-7
CONNERS, James L. (d 1970 [72]) journalist BP/55*
CONNERY, Sean (b 1930) Scottish actor CB, ES
CONNESS, Robert (1867?-1941) American actor CB
CONNIFORD, T. P. (d 1900 [38]) actor EA/01*
CONNOLLEY, Denise (b 1951) American actress TW/30
CONNOLLY, Mr. (fl 1736) dramatist GT
CONNOLLY, Bobby (d 1944 [49]) dance director BE*, WWT/14*
CONNOLLY, Charles (d 1969 [90]) manager of the Players BP/54*
CONNOLLY, George (b 1944) American actor TW/25-26, 29
CONNOLLY, Gus (d 1900) Irish comedian EA/01*
CONNOLLY, J. (fl 1847) Irish actor HAS
CONNOLLY, James Smith (d 1874) singer EA/75*
CONNOLLY, Maria [Mrs. Mary Anne Lowrey] (d 1890 [26]) EA/91*
CONNOLLY, Michael (d 1911 [80]) composer BE*, WWT/14*
CONNOLLY, Patricia (b 1933) actress TW/24-25, 29-30
CONNOLLY, Patrick (b 1842) English/American fight arranger, actor, gas boy, engineer HAS

CONNOLLY, Sadie (fl 1875-
1906) American actress
WWS
CONNOLLY, T. (d 1884) musical
director EA/85*
CONNOLLY, Thomas American
actor TW/22-23, 27
CONNOLLY, Walter (1887-1940)
American actor CB, ES,
SR, WWT/7-9
CONNOR, Mr. (fl 1741?-50)
house servant? BD
CONNOR, Mr. (fl 1788) actor
BD
CONNOR, Allen (d 1973 [75])
talent agent BP/58*
CONNOR, Charles (d 1826)
Irish actor BS, CDP, DD,
DNB, OX
CONNOR, Edmund Sheppard
(1809-91) American actor,
manager HAS
CONNOR, Mrs. Edmund Shep-
pard (d 1863) actress HAS
CONNOR, Frank J. (d 1902)
manager EA/03*
CONNOR, H. (d 1887) EA/88*
CONNOR, James (1824-67)
Irish actor HAS, SR
CONNOR, John, Sr. (d 1880
[86]) scene artist EA/81*
CONNOR, John (d 1911 [78])
scene artist EA/12*
CONNOR, Kaye (b 1925) Cana-
dian actress TW/3
CONNOR, Patrick (d 1897)
Irish comedian EA/98*
CONNOR, Thomas L. (d 1878)
American actor EA/79*
CONNOR, Whitfield (b 1916)
Irish actor BE, TW/4-19,
24-26
CONOLLY, Mr. (fl 1736) Irish
dramatist CP/1-3
CONOLLY, Patricia see
Connolly, Patricia
CONOR, Harry (d 1931 [75])
performer BE*, BP/15*
CONOVER, Anna (fl 1886)
actress, lessee, manager
CDP, DD
CONQUEST, Mr. (fl 1830) singer
CDP
CONQUEST, Arthur (1875-1945)
English actor, gymnast ES,
GRB/1-4, OC/2-3, WWT/
1-9
CONQUEST, Benjamin Oliver

(1805-72) English actor, propri-
etor DD, ES, OC/1-3
CONQUEST, Mrs. Benjamin Oliver
[Clarissa Ann Bennett] (1802-67)
ballet mistress, dancer ES
CONQUEST, Clara see Dillon,
Mrs. Charles
CONQUEST, Daisy (d 1889 [16])
EA/91*
CONQUEST, Elizabeth Oliver (d
1890 [50]) EA/92*
CONQUEST, Fred (1871-1941)
English actor, gymnast ES,
GRB/2-4, OC/2-3, WWT/1-9
CONQUEST, George (d 1901 [64])
proprietor, pantomimist EA/02*
CONQUEST, George (1858-1926)
English actor, manager, drama-
tist CDP, DD, DP, ES, GRB/
1-4, OAA/2, OC/2-3, WWT/
1-5
CONQUEST, Mrs. George (d 1890
[50]) ballet mistress, dancer
WWT/14*
CONQUEST, George Augustus (1837-
1901) English actor, manager,
acrobat COC, DD, DNB, OAA/
2, OC/1-3
CONQUEST, Ida (1870/76-1937)
American actress GRB/2-4,
WWA/1, WWS, WWT/1-6
CONQUEST, Lizzie [Mrs. Thomas
Beard, Jr.] (d 1876 [17/18])
actress EA/77*, WWT/14*
CONRAD, Barbara see Hoffe,
Barbara
CONRAD, Con (1890/91-1938)
American composer ES, WWT/
6-8
CONRAD, Eugene J. (d 1964 [69])
American dramatist BE*, BP/
48*
CONRAD, John (d 1888 [58]) musi-
cian EA/90*
CONRAD, Joseph (1857-1924)
Polish/English writer MD, MWD
CONRAD, Robert Taylor (1810-58)
American dramatist CDP, DAB,
ES, HJD, MH, NTH, RJ
CONRAD, William (d 1891) German
clown CDP
CONRAN, William Sansfield (d 1867
[56]) musician EA/68*
CONRIED, Hans (b 1917) actor
WWT/16
CONRIED, Heinrich (1855-1909)
Austrian manager DAB, ES,
GRB/3-4, WWS

CONROY, Constance (d 1888
[25]) actress EA/89*
CONROY, Frank (1890-1964)
English actor, manager
ES, SR, TW/1-20, WWT/
5-13
CONROY, Jean (d 1964 [29])
performer BP/49*
CONROY, Mrs. Peter S. (d
1879) EA/80*
CONROY, Thom (d 1971 [60])
performer BP/56*
CONS, Emma (d 1912 [74])
manager WWT/14*
CONSIDINE, Bob (d 1975 [68])
journalist BP/60*
CONSIDINE, Mrs. George
see Angeles, Aimee
CONSIDINE, John (1862-1943)
American showman SR
CONSTABLE, Mr. (fl 1749-
1803) house servant BD
CONSTABLE, Francis editor
CP/1
CONSTABLE, Mrs. Fred H.
see Stanley, Rose
CONSTABLE, James M. (d
1974 [68]) producer/director/
choreographer BP/59*
CONSTANCE, Mlle. (fl 1784-
87) dancer BD
CONSTANDUROS, Mabel (d
1957 [77]) English actress
WWT/8-12, WWW/5
CONSTANT, Yvonne [née
Coronakis] (b 1935) French
actress, singer, dancer
BE, TW/23
CONSTANTINE, Michael (b 1927)
American actor BE, TW/15
CONSTANTINI, Sig. (fl 1741-
42) dancer BD
CONSTANTINI, Signora (fl 1726-
27) dancer BD
CONSTANTIN-WEYER, Maurice
(d 1964 [83]) dramatist
BP/49*
CONTANDIN, Ferdinand Joseph
Desire see Fernandel
CONTAT, Louise (d 1813 [52])
actress WWT/14*
CONTE, John (b 1915) American
actor, singer BE, WWT/
11-12
CONTE, Richard (d 1975 [65])
actor WWT/16*, BP/59*
CONTI, Anna (fl 1754-55)
dancer BD

CONTI, Italia (1874-1946) English
actress, teacher COC, ES,
GRB/1-3, OC/1-3, PDT, WWT/
4-9, WWW/4
CONTI, Vincenzo (fl 1766-96) scene
painter BD
CONTINI, Giovanna (fl 1742-43)
singer BD
CONVERSE, Frank B. (b 1837)
American banjoist, minstrel
HAS, SR
CONVERSE, Frederick S[hepherd]
(1871-1940) American composer
CB, DAB, HJD, WWM
CONVILLE, Mrs. Alec (d 1900 [27])
actress EA/01*
CONVILLE, David (b 1929) English
actor, director AAS, WWT/15-
16
CONVY, Bert (b 1936) American
actor BE, TW/14, 20-26,
WWT/15-16
CONWAY, Mr. Irish piper, dancer
CDP
CONWAY, Miss see Carman, Mrs.
CONWAY, Bert (d 1910) EA/11*
CONWAY, Billy (d 1892 [38])
comedian, minstrel CDP
CONWAY, Curt (1915-74) American
actor, director, teacher BE,
TW/16, 30
CONWAY, Diane (b 1944) American
actress TW/24-26
CONWAY, E. H. (fl 1825-32) Eng-
lish dancer, ballet master, teach-
er CDP, HAS
CONWAY, Mrs. E. H. (fl 1825-55)
English dancer CDP, HAS
CONWAY, Frederick Bartlett (1819-
74) English actor, manager
CDP, DAB, HAS, OC/1-3, SR,
WWA/H
CONWAY, Mrs. Frederick Bartlett
see Conway, Sarah G.
CONWAY, George [John Foot] (d
1908 [27]) musical director
EA/09*
CONWAY, George W. (d 1919)
actor SR
CONWAY, Harold (b 1906) English
press representative, critic
WWT/8-14
CONWAY, Harry (d 1905) Negro
comedian EA/06*
CONWAY, H. B. [Blenkinsop-Coul-
son] (1850-1909) English actor
CDP, DD, DP, GRB/1, OAA/
1-2

CONWAY, Helen [Mrs. Herbert H. Spencer] (d 1901) EA/ 02*

CONWAY, Henry Seymour (1720-95) dramatist CP/3, GT, TD/1-2

CONWAY, H. J. (1800-60) English prompter HAS, SR

CONWAY, Mrs. H. J. (d 1839) English actress HAS, SR

CONWAY, Hugh [F. J. Fargus] (1848-85) dramatist DD

CONWAY, Jack (1887-1952) American actor, director ES

CONWAY, J. H. dramatist RJ

CONWAY, John American actor TW/1, 3

CONWAY, John (b 1922) Canadian marionettist ES

CONWAY, John Ashby (b 1905) American educator BE

CONWAY, J. Rudolph (d 1973 [80]) associated with circuses BP/58*

CONWAY, Kevin Bryan (b 1942) American actor TW/26-30

CONWAY, Lillian [Mrs. Charles S. Camblos] (d 1891) actress CDP

CONWAY, Lizzie (d 1916) actress WWT/14*

CONWAY, Marianne see Tearle, Marianne

CONWAY, Minnie see Tearle, Marianne

CONWAY, Neal (d 1888 [36]) American acrobat EA/89*

CONWAY, Norbert (d 1965 [76]) executive BP/50*

CONWAY, Russ (b 1913) Canadian actor TW/12

CONWAY, Sarah [née Crocker; Mrs. Frederick B. Conway] (1834-75) English actress CDP, HAS, OC/1-3, SR, WWA/H

CONWAY, Shirl [née Shirley Elizabeth Crosman] (b 1916) American actress BE, TW/11-13

CONWAY, Tom (d 1916) music-hall performer EA/17*

CONWAY, W. (fl 1836) English actor HAS

CONWAY, William (d 1950 [36]) manager WWT/14*

CONWAY, William Augustus

[né Rugg] (1789-1828) English actor CDP, COC, DD, DNB, ES, HAS, OC/1-3, SR

CONWY, Mr. (fl 1797) actor BD

CONY, Barkham ["The Dog Star"] (1802-58) English actor, performer CDP, HAS, SR

CONY, B. B. (d 1867) actor HAS

CONY, Thomas (d 1866) actor HAS

CONYERS, Mr. (fl 1744-52) singer, actor BD

CONYERS, Addie (fl 1884-88) actress DD

CONYERS, Charles (d 1896 [35]) singer EA/97*, WWT/14*

CONYERS, Charles Harold (d 1905 [21]) EA/06*

CONYERS, Joseph (d 1920 [60]) actor BE*, BP/5*

CONYNGHAM, Fred (b 1909) Australian actor WWT/7-11

COOGAN, Richard actor TW/1, 11-12

COOGRAN, Gene B. (d 1972) performer BP/56*

COOK, Mr. (fl 1694-1718) singer, violinist? BD

COOK, Mr. (fl 1716-32) dancer BD

COOK, Mr. (fl 1718-50?) dancer BD

COOK, Mr. (d 1731) boxkeeper BD

COOK, Mr. (fl 1735) musician BD

COOK, Mr. (fl 1765) singer BD

COOK, Mr. (fl 1785) tumbler BD

COOK, Mr. (fl 1793-1800) singer BD

COOK, Mr. (fl 1794) singer BD

COOK, Mr. (fl 1795) costumier BD

COOK, Mr. (fl 1829) actor HAS

COOK, Mrs. (fl 1718) performer BD

COOK, Mrs. (fl 1726-37) boxkeeper BD

COOK, Mrs. (fl 1730) actress BD

COOK, Mrs. (fl 1740-41) dancer BD

COOK, Mrs. (fl 1748) actress BD

COOK, Mrs. (fl 1763) actress BD

COOK, Master (fl 1737) singer, harpsichordist BD

COOK, Alice Aynsley (fl 1873) actress, singer DD

COOK, Alton F. (d 1967 [62]) critic BP/52*

COOK, Arthur (fl 1794) violinist BD

COOK, Augustus (1859-1904)

Scottish actor SR
COOK, Mrs. Aynsley (d 1880
[48]) actress, singer EA/81*
COOK, Barbara (b 1927) Amer-
ican actress, singer BE,
CB, TW/8, 11-23, 28-29,
WWT/14-16
COOK, Charles Emerson (d 1941
[71]) American agent, pro-
ducer, director BE*, BP/
25*, WWT/14*
COOK, Dan (d 1894) singer, clown
EA/95*
COOK, Dan (1901-61) American
actor CB, ES, TW/1-16,
18, WWA/4, WWT/10-13
COOK, Edward Dutton (1829-83)
English critic COC, DD,
DNB, ES, OC/1-3
COOK, Elisha, Jr. (b 1902/06)
American actor BE, WWT/
8-11
COOK, Francis Edward ["Zeno"]
(d 1881 [22]) gymnast EA/82*
COOK, Furneaux see Cook,
John Furneaux
COOK, George (fl 1830) actor
HAS
COOK, George Cram (1873-
1924) American dramatist,
producer ES, HJD, MD,
MWD, NTH
COOK, James (fl 1863) see
Cooke, James
COOK, James (b 1937) American
actor TW/24-25, 27, 29
COOK, James A. (d 1908)
EA/09*
COOK, James M. (b 1825)
English actor HAS, SR
COOK, Jean Lawrence (d 1976
[76]) composer/lyricist
BP/60*
COOK, Joe (1890-1959) American
actor ES, SR, TW/15,
WWT/6-11
COOK, John (fl 1599-1604)
see Cooke, John
COOK, John (fl 1767-1801)
puppeteer, exhibitor BD
COOK, John (d 1881) equestrian
EA/82*
COOK, John Furneaux (d 1903
[63]) actor, singer DD
COOK, John Russell (1911-64)
American theatre librarian BE*
COOK, Joseph (fl 1702) per-
former BD

COOK, Kattie (d 1890) EA/92*
COOK, Ken (d 1963 [49]) actor
BE*
COOK, Layton (fl 1794) singer BD
COOK, Madge Carr see Carr-
Cook, Madge
COOK, Michael (b 1933) English/
Canadian dramatist CD
COOK, Patrick (b 1949) American
actor TW/26
COOK, Peter (b 1937) English
actor, writer BE, TW/30,
WWT/16
COOK, Roderick (b 1932) English
actor TW/26, 29-30
COOK, Roy Francis see Brandt,
Ivan
COOK, Mr. [S?] (fl 1797-1819)
doorkeeper? BD
COOK, Sarah see Cooke, Sarah
COOK, Thomas (fl 1766-68) house
servant BD
COOK, Thomas Aynsley (1832-94)
actor, singer DD
COOK, William (d 1824) Irish
dramatist, writer CDP, CP/3,
DD, DNB
COOK, William Henry (d 1891 [27])
EA/92*
COOK, Will Marion (1869-1944)
American composer DAB
COOKE, Mr. actor CDP
COOKE, Mr. (fl 1719) musician BD
COOKE, Mr. (fl 1751-70) equilibrist
BD
COOKE, Mr. (fl 1758) harpsichordist
BD
COOKE, Mr. (fl 1761-62) actor BD
COOKE, Mr. (fl 1782-84) actor BD
COOKE, Mr. (fl 1796-97) singer
BD
COOKE, Mrs. (fl 1735-36) dresser
BD
COOKE, Mrs. (d 1745) see
Cooke, Mary
COOKE, Mrs. (fl 1756-57) actress?
BD
COOKE, Mrs. (fl 1852) actress
HAS
COOKE, Abell (fl 1606-07) actor
DA
COOKE, A[dam] M[oses] E[manuel;
né Thomas] (fl 1762-71) English
dramatist CP/2-3, GT
COOKE, Alexander (d 1614) English
actor DA, ES, GT, NTH
COOKE, Arthur (fl 1669) musician
BD

COOKE, Benjamin (d c. 1743)
musician, music seller, pub-
lisher BD
COOKE, Benjamin (1734-93)
English organist, composer,
choirmaster, conductor BD,
CDP, DNB
COOKE, Charles (d 1900 [70])
actor EA/01*
COOKE, Mrs. Charles (d 1881)
EA/82*
COOKE, Charles J. (b 1857)
English scene painter, pro-
perty man GRB/1
COOKE, Mrs. Charles P.
see Cooke, Emma
COOKE, Eddie (1869-1942) Amer-
ican manager, press agent
SR
COOKE, Edward (fl 1509-11)
member of the Chapel Royal
DA
COOKE, Edward (fl 1678)
dramatist CP/1-3, DD, DNB
COOKE, Ellen equestrienne
CDP
COOKE, Emma [Mrs. Charles
P. Cooke] (d 1904) EA/05*
COOKE, Mrs. Eugene see
Cooke, Helena
COOKE, Frank (d 1869 [67])
actor? EA/70*
COOKE, Fred (d 1905 [59])
actor EA/06*
COOKE, G. A. (d 1905) illu-
sionist GRB/1
COOKE, George (1807/11-63)
English actor CDP, DD,
DNB
COOKE, Mrs. George (d 1877
[74]) EA/78*
COOKE, George A. (d 1905
[79]) vaudevillian? EA/06*,
WWT/14*
COOKE, George Frederick
(1756-1812) English actor
BD, CDP, COC, DD, DNB,
ES, GT, HAS, NTH, OC/
1-3, OX, SR, TD/1-2
COOKE, Mrs. George Frederick,
II see Daniels, Alicia
COOKE, Harry (d 1958 [56])
American performer BE*,
BP/42*
COOKE, Harry Welby (d 1882)
circus proprietor EA/83*
COOKE, Helena [Mrs. Eugene
Cooke] (d 1890 [43]) EA/91*

COOKE, Henry (c. 1616-72) English
singer, composer, teacher BD,
DNB, ES
COOKE, Henry (d 1898 [71]) actor
EA/99*
COOKE, H. Michael Angelo Gratton
(d 1889) musician EA/90*
COOKE, James (fl 1791-1825)
singer, actor BD
COOKE, James (fl 1863) English
clown, manager CDP, ES, HAS
COOKE, James (d 1869) equestrian
EA/70*
COOKE, James (d 1899) actor
EA/00*
COOKE, Mrs. James (d 1875 [61])
EA/76*
COOKE, Mrs. James [Bessie Walt-
ers] (d 1887) actress? EA/88*
COOKE, James Henry (d 1879 [43])
actor EA/80*
COOKE, Jemima (d 1882 [74])
EA/83*
COOKE, J. M. see Maguire,
James
COOKE, Mrs. J. M. see Jones,
Mrs. W. G.
COOKE, Jo (fl 1614) dramatist
DNB
COOKE, John (fl 1599-1604) drama-
tist CP/1-3, DD, FGF
COOKE, John (d 1887 [66]) EA/88*
COOKE, John (d 1900 [40]) music-
hall agent, songwriter EA/01*
COOKE, John Corbet (d 1879)
manager EA/80*
COOKE, John Esten (1830-86)
American writer OC/1-2
COOKE, John Henry (d 1901 [87])
proprietor EA/02*
COOKE, John Henry (d 1917 [80]?)
equestrian CDP
COOKE, John P. (1820-65) English
composer, conductor HAS, SR
COOKE, Mrs. John P. see
Weston, Lottie
COOKE, Julia CDP
COOKE, J. Y. F. (d 1918) EA/19*
COOKE, Kate equestrienne CDP
COOKE, Lionel (fl 1583-88) actor
DA
COOKE, Mrs. M. A. (d 1868 [85])
EA/69*
COOKE, Marjorie Benton (d 1920
[44]) monologist BE*, BP/4*
COOKE, Mary (1666?-1745) actress,
singer BD
COOKE, Mary Anne equestrienne

HAS
COOKE, Matthew (fl 1780-1800?)
instrumentalist, singer, com-
poser BD
COOKE, Philip (fl 1739-55)
dancing master BD
COOKE, Philip (d 1755) dancer
BD
COOKE, Richard P. (b 1904)
American critic BE, NTH
COOKE, Robert (1768-1814)
English organist, composer,
singer BD
COOKE, Rosa actress, singer
CDP
COOKE, Sander (d 1614) actor
WWT/14*
COOKE, Sarah (d 1688) actress
BD
COOKE, Stanley (1868-1931)
English actor WWT/2-5
COOKE, Steve (d 1909 [47])
music-hall comedian EA/10*
COOKE, Thomas (fl 1583-84)
actor DA
COOKE, Thomas (c.1702-56)
English dramatist CP/1-3,
DD, GT
COOKE, Thomas (1722-83)
English dramatist DNB
COOKE, Thomas (b c.1752)
English circus performer
ES
COOKE, Thomas (d 1939 [65])
American actor BE*
COOKE, Thomas Coffin (d 1939
[65]) actor BP/23*
COOKE, Thomas Edwin circus
performer ES
COOKE, Thomas Potter (1786-
1864) English actor BS,
CDP, COC, DD, DNB, ES,
OC/1-3, OX
COOKE, Thomas Simpson (1782-
1848) Irish actor, singer,
composer BS, CDP, DD,
DNB, ES, OX
COOKE, Thomas Taplin (1782-
1866) English circus per-
former ES
COOKE, Cpt. Tom (d 1901)
musical performer EA/02*
COOKE, William (fl 1608-35)
share-holder, actor DA
COOKE, William (fl 1763-1800)
deputy treasurer BD
COOKE, William (d 1824) see
Cook, William

COOKE, William (fl 19th cent?)
circus manager CDP
COOKE, William (d 1886) eques-
trian manager, clown ES
COOKE, William (d 1895 [45])
conductor EA/96*
COOKE, Mrs. William (d 1874)
EA/75*
COOKMAN, Anthony Victor (1894-
1962) English critic AAS,
COC, ES, OC/1-3, WWT/10-13,
WWW/6
COOKSEY, Curtis (1892-1962)
American actor TW/3-4, 6
COOKSON, Georgina (b 1918)
English actress TW/3, WWT/
12-15
COOKSON, Peter (b 1913/15)
American actor, producer BE,
TW/3-16
COOKSON, S. A. (d 1947 [78])
actor BE*, WWT/14*
COOLEY, Dennis (b 1948) American
actor TW/29
COOLEY, Hollis Eli (1859-1918)
American manager WWA/1,
WWM
COOLEY, Spade (d 1969 [59])
musician BP/54*
COOLIDGE, Philip (1908-67) Amer-
ican actor BE, TW/1, 3, 5-13,
15-16, 23
COOLING, John (fl 1640?) actor
DA
COOMBE, Carol [Gwendoline Alice
Coombe] (1911-66) Australian
actress WWT/8-12
COOMBE, Gwendoline Alice see
Coombe, Carol
COOMBES, Mr. (fl 1789-1805)
property man, actor, singer
BD
COOMBES, Miss (fl 1795-1802)
dancer BD
COOMBS, Arthur actor, singer
CDP
COOMBS, Jane (b 1842) actress
CDP, HAS, SR
COOMBS, Martin B. (fl 1852) actor
HAS
COON, Gene L. (d 1973 [48]) pro-
ducer/director/ choreographer
BP/58*
COONAN, Sheila (b 1922) Canadian
actress TW/25-28
COONEY, Dennis (b 1938) American
actor TW/18-20, 22, 24, 29
COONEY, Laurette see Taylor,

Laurette
COONEY, Ray (b 1932) English
dramatist, actor, director
WWT/15-16
COONS, Johnny (d 1975 [58])
performer BP/60*
COOP, Colin (d 1937) actor
BE*, WWT/14*
COOPE, James E. (d 1892)
circus proprietor EA/93*
COOPER, Mr. (fl 1695-1701)
singer BD
COOPER, Mr. (fl 1729-46)
boxkeeper BD
COOPER, Mr. (fl 1749) actor
BD
COOPER, Mr. (fl 1767) per-
former BD
COOPER, Mr. (fl 1781) dancer
BD
COOPER, Mr. (fl 1795) scene
painter, machinist BD
COOPER, Mr. (fl 1795-1803)
actor TD/1-2
COOPER, Mr. (fl 1798) actor
BD
COOPER, Mr. (d 1809) actor
BD
COOPER, Dr. (fl 1822) drama-
tist EAP
COOPER, Mrs. (fl 1722-34)
actress BD
COOPER, Mrs. (fl 1775-77?)
wardrobe assistant? BD
COOPER, Mrs. (d 1868)
EA/69*
COOPER, Mrs. see Bernard,
Mrs. John, I
COOPER, Mrs. (d 1906) see
Lina, Mme.
COOPER, Master (fl 1795) actor
BD
COOPER, Miss (fl 1785-87?)
dancer BD
COOPER, Miss (fl 1793) singer,
actress BD
COOPER, Mrs. A. M. Garratt
(d 1916) EA/17*
COOPER, Anna (fl 1851) actress
HAS
COOPER, Anthony Kemble (b
1908) English actor BE,
TW/1-3, 6, 8, 20, 22-23,
WWT/7-15
COOPER, Ashley (d 1952 [70])
Australian actor BE*, BP/36*
COOPER, Charles (d 1876 [56])
organist EA/77*

COOPER, Charles Kemble (d 1923
[69]) actor BE*, WWT/14*
COOPER, Christine (b 1946) Amer-
ican actress TW/26
COOPER, Clancy (d 1975 [68])
actor BP/60*, WWT/16*
COOPER, Clarence (d 1974 [53])
performer BP/59*
COOPER, Clifford (d 1895 [76])
actor BE*, EA/96*, WWT/14*
COOPER, Mrs. Clifford [Agnes
Kemble] (1823-95) actress BE*,
EA/96*, WWT/14*
COOPER, Dulcie (b 1907) American
actress TW/2-3
COOPER, Edward (d 1956) actor
BE*, WWT/14*
COOPER, Edward W. (d 1912)
variety performer EA/13*
COOPER, Elizabeth (fl 1737) drama-
tist CP/1-3, DD, DNB, GT
COOPER, Emil (b 1877) English/
Russian conductor ES
COOPER, Enid (b 1902) English
actress WWT/7
COOPER, Ernest George (d 1894
[40]) EA/95*
COOPER, Evelyne Love (d 1968)
composer/lyricist BP/53*
COOPER, Eward (d 1945 [40])
actor, entertainer WWT/14*
COOPER, Fannie [Mrs. Sidney
Cooper] (d 1909) EA/10*
COOPER, Fanny see Cooper,
Frances
COOPER, F. Fox see Cooper,
Frederick Fox
COOPER, F. Harwood (d 1905 [78])
actor WWT/14*
COOPER, Frances [Mrs. Thomas
Haines Lacy] (1819-72) actress
CDP, DD, DNB
COOPER, Francis (fl 1671) musi-
cian BD
COOPER, Frank talent representative
BE
COOPER, Frank J. (d 1875 [35])
proprietor EA/76*
COOPER, Frank Kemble (1857-1918)
English actor DD, EA/96, GRB/
1-4, OAA/2, WWT/1-3
COOPER, Frank Staunton (d 1885
[30]) actor EA/86*
COOPER, Fred actor, dancer CDP
COOPER, Fred (d 1909 [50]) humor-
ist EA/10*
COOPER, Frederick (1890/97-1945)
English actor WWT/5-8

COOPER, Frederick Fox (1806-79) dramatist, manager DD

COOPER, Frederick Harwood (d 1905 [78]) actor EA/06*

COOPER, George (fl 1794) musician BD

COOPER, George A. (d 1889) proprietor EA/90*

COOPER, Giles (1918-66) English dramatist AAS, CD, CH, WWT/14, WWW/6

COOPER, Dame Gladys (1888-1971) English actress AAS, BE, CB, COC, ES, TW/2-8, 12-16, 28, WWA/4, WWT/1-15

COOPER, G. Melville (1896-1973) English actor AAS, BE, ES, TW/1-10, 22-23, 27, 29, WWT/7-15

COOPER, Greta Kemble actress WWT/7-8

COOPER, Harwood (d 1943 [74]) actor DD, OAA/2

COOPER, Henry (fl 1790?-1819?) musician BD

COOPER, Henry C. (1807/19-81) English musician, manager HAS, SR

COOPER, Herbert B. see Treherne, Bernard

COOPER, Herman E. lawyer BE

COOPER, Jackie (b 1922) American actor, producer, director BE, ES, TW/5-16

COOPER, James (d 1882 [83]) EA/83*

COOPER, John (1790-1870) actor BS, CDP, DD, DNB, EA/92, OX

COOPER, John Wilbye (d 1885) singer EA/86*

COOPER, Joseph (fl 1794) singer? BD

COOPER, Joseph (d 1886) music-hall artist EA/87*

COOPER, Lillian Kemble (1891-1977) actress WWT/6-8

COOPER, Lizzie (b 1844) American actress HAS

COOPER, Margaret (d 1922) performer BE*, WWT/14*

COOPER, Marian (fl 1940s) American actress SR

COOPER, Marilyn (b 1935) American singer, actress, dancer BE, TW/18, 23-24, 26-28

COOPER, Melville see Cooper, G. Melville

COOPER, Merian C. (d 1973 [78]) producer/director/choreographer BP/57*

COOPER, Milroy (d 1917 [69]) actor EA/18*

COOPER, Peggy (b 1931) American actress TW/27-28

COOPER, Priscilla Elizabeth (d 1889) actress HAS, SR

COOPER, Ralph (fl 1763) singer BD

COOPER, Ray (b 1930) English actor TW/24-25

COOPER, Reynaud (d 1892 [35]) actor EA/93*

COOPER, Richard (fl 1794) singer? BD

COOPER, Richard (1893-1947) English actor WWT/7-8

COOPER, Mrs. Sidney see Cooper, Fannie

COOPER, Thomas Abthorpe (1776-1849) English actor, manager BD, CDP, COC, DAB, DD, ES, HAS, OC/1-3, SR, WWA/H

COOPER, Thomas Clifford (1819-95) English actor DD, OAA/2

COOPER, Violet Kemble (1886/89-1961) English actress NTH, TW/18, WWT/4-9

COOPER, Wilbye (d 1907 [47]) musician, music-hall manager EA/09*

COOPER, William (d 1868) actor EA/69*

COOPER, Wyatt (b 1927) American actor TW/16

COOPER-CLIFFE, Henry see Cliffe, H. Cooper

COOTE, Bert (1868-1949) English manager, actor COC, GRB/1-2, SR, WWT/4-8

COOTE, Carrie see Pearce, Lady

COOTE, Charles (d 1880 [71]) musician EA/81*

COOTE, Charles (1858-97) actor CDP, DD

COOTE, Lizzie (1862-86) actress CDP, DD

COOTE, Louie see Mills, Mary Louisa

COOTE, Robert (d 1888 [54]) musical director, composer CDP

COOTE, Robert (b 1909) English actor BE, TW/9, 12-16,

WWT/13-16
COOTON, Mrs. Frank see
Spence, Beatrice
COOTS, J. Fred (b 1897) Amer-
ican composer BE
COPE, Mrs. (fl 1770-71) dancer
BD
COPE, Patricia (b 1943) Ameri-
can actress TW/26, 29
COPEAU, Jacques (1878-1949)
French actor, manager, pro-
ducer COC, MWD, NTH,
OC/1-3, PDT, WWT/9-10,
WWW/4
COPELAN, Sheila (d 1966 [30])
performer BP/50*
COPELAND, Mrs. (fl 1729)
dancer BD
COPELAND, Miss (b 1801)
actress EA/92
COPELAND, Alfred (d 1872)
harpist EA/73*
COPELAND, Bella see Cope-
land, Isabella
COPELAND, Fanny Elizabeth
see Fitzwilliam, Mrs. Ed-
ward
COPELAND, Mrs. Harry see
Copeland, Margaret
COPELAND, Isabella [Mrs. J.
B. Buckstone] (d 1912 [73])
actress DD
COPELAND, Joan [née Joan
Maxine Miller] (b 1922)
American actress, singer
BE, TW/5-7, 21, 25, 27-28,
WWT/15-16
COPELAND, J. T. (d 1882)
journalist EA/83*
COPELAND, Margaret [Mrs.
Harry Copeland] (d 1894)
EA/95*
COPELAND, Mary Dowell (d
1963 [48]) American per-
former BE*, BP/47*
COPELAND, William R. (1799-
1867) manager, actor, lessee
DD
COPELAND, Mrs. William R.
(d 1863) actress WWT/14*
COPEN, Elizabeth see Copin,
Mrs. Roger
COPERARIO, Giovanni (d 1626)
composer DNB
COPIN, Mrs. Roger [Elizabeth]
(fl 1733-73) actress, singer
BD
COPINGER, May Irene see

Howard, Kathryn
COPLAND, Mr. (fl 1756) boxkeeper
BD
COPLAND, Mr. (fl 1789-91) house
servant BD
COPLAND, Aaron (b 1900) American
composer CB, ES, HJD
COPLAND, Charles (fl 1891) singer
DD
COPLAND, H. (fl 1859) actor HAS
COPLANDE, Robert (fl 16th cent)
English writer ES
COPLEY, Ada Mary see Morgan,
Ada
COPLEY, Joan (d 1969 [69]) per-
former BP/53*
COPLEY, Peter (b 1915) English
actor AAS, WWT/11-16
COPLEY, Mrs. Walter see
Morgan, Ada
COPLEY, Mrs. Walter see
Oakley, Ada
COPPEE, François (1842-1908)
French dramatist GRB/1-4
COPPEL, Alec (d 1972) Australian
dramatist BE, WWT/11
COPPEN, Hazel (d 1975 [50])
performer BP/59*
"COPPER CAPTAIN" see Brown,
Henry
COPPERVILLA, Ellen (d 1852)
dancer HAS
COPPIN, Elizabeth J. (d 1873 [85])
EA/74*
COPPIN, Hon. George Selth (1818/
19-1906) Australian actor, mana-
ger DNB, GRB/1, HAS
COPPING, Bernard (b 1871) English
actor GRB/1
COPPINGER, Matthew (d 1685)
actor BD
COPPINI, Ettore (d 1935 [91])
maître de ballet WWT/14*
COPPOLA, Anton (b 1918) American
musical director BE
COPPOLA, Frank (b 1944) American
actor TW/28, 30
COPPOLA, Giuseppe (fl 1777-79)
singer BD
COPPOLA, Nora American actress
TW/27
COPPOLA, Sam J. (b 1935) Amer-
ican actor TW/27, 29
COPRARIO, Giovanni see Coper-
ario, Giovanni
COQUELIN, Constant-Benoît (1841-
1909) French actor CDP, GRB/
1-4, OC/3, WWA/4

COQUELIN, Ernest-Alexandre-
Honoré [cadet] (1848-1909)
French actor GRB/1-4
COQUELIN, Jean (1865-1944)
French actor, manager GRB/
1-4, OC/3, WWT/1-4
CORADINI, Sig. (fl 1767-68?)
dancer BD
CORADINI, Mlle. see Kruger,
Annie
"CORALLINA" see Costantini,
Domenica
CORBALLY, Miss (fl 1732)
actress BD
CORBET, Hamilton (d 1885)
Scottish singer EA/86*
CORBET, [Neeves?] (d 1761?)
singer BD
CORBET, Symon (b 1675?)
singer BD
CORBETT, Mr. (fl 1780) actor
BD
CORBETT, Gretchen (b 1947)
American actress TW/25-
29, WWT/16
CORBETT, Harry H. (b 1925)
Burmese/English actor WWT/
14-16
CORBETT, James John (1866-
1933) American actor, fighter
DAB, SR, WWS
CORBETT, Leonora (1908-1960)
English actress TW/2-7,
17, WWT/7-11
CORBETT, Mary (fl 1670?-82?)
actress BD
CORBETT, Mary (d 1974 [48])
performer BP/58*
CORBETT, Thalberg see Thal-
berg, T. B.
CORBETT, William (1680-1748)
English violinist, composer
BD, DNB
CORBETTA, Francesco (c.1620-
81) guitar player BD
CORBIN, Barry (b 1940) Amer-
ican actor TW/26, 28-29
CORBIN, John (1870-1959)
American critic GRB/2-4,
WWT/1-9, WWW/5
CORBY, Mr. (fl 1847) dancer
CDP
CORBY, Mlle. (fl 1828-35)
actress HAS
CORBYN, Master (fl 1785) dancer
BD
CORBYN, H. W. (d 1880) agent
EA/81*

CORBYN, Wardle (d 1880) agent
EA/81*
CORCORAN, Jane [Mrs. J. Em-
mett Baxter] American actress
GRB/3-4, WWM, WWT/1-9
CORCORAN, Katharine see
Herne, Mrs. James A.
CORCORAN, Leslie (d 1891) EA/
92*
CORCY, Diancinto (fl 1669-71)
scene keeper BD
CORDELL, Cathleen [née Kelly]
(b 1916/17) American actress
BE, TW/4, WWT/9-13
CORDELL, Thomas (fl 1663-70)
scene keeper BD
CORDEN, George (fl 1640) actor
DA
CORDER, Bruce English manager
BE
CORDER, Frederick (1852-1932)
English composer ES, WWW/3
CORDIER, Angiolina (fl 1862)
French singer CDP, HAS
CORDNER, Blaine (b 1901) Ameri-
can actor TW/1, 3-10, 27
CORDNER, W. J. (d 1870) musi-
cian EA/71*
CORDON, Norman (d 1964 [60])
American singer, teacher BE*
CORDONA, Cpt. Thomas Bridgman
(d 1891) lion tamer EA/92*
CORDONI, Sig. (fl 1760) violinist
BD
CORELLI, Sig. (fl 1849) musician?
HAS
CORELLI, Alfonso (d 1970 [70])
conductor BP/55*
CORELLI, Blanche singer, actress
CDP
CORELLI, Cecilia [Mrs. Stephen
Chambers] (d 1886) EA/87*
CORELLI, Franco (b 1924?) Italian
singer CB
CORELLI, Kathryn (d 1970 [70])
performer BP/54*
COREN, Leo (d 1974 [73]) talent
booker BP/59*
COREY, John (fl c.1699-1735)
actor, dramatist BD, CP/1-3,
DD, DNB, GT, TD/2
COREY, John (d c.1721) dramatist
CP/1-3, GT, TD/1
COREY, Mrs. John [née Katherine
Mitchell] (b c.1635) actress BD
COREY, Joseph (d 1972 [45]) per-
former BP/57*
COREY, Madison (b 1873) American

manager WWM
COREY, Mrs. Madison see
Wilber, Mabel
COREY, Sidney A. actor CDP
COREY, Mrs. W. E. see
Gillman, Mabelle
COREY, Wendell (1914-68) Amer-
ican actor BE, ES, TW/2-3,
6, 13, 25, WWA/5, WWT/
11-14
COREY, William (d c.1664?)
actor BD
CORFE, Mr. (b 1718) singer BD
CORFE, Arthur Thomas (1773-
1863) English musician, sing-
er, composer BD
CORFE, James (fl 1735-50)
musician, composer BD
CORFE, John (b 1769) musician
BD
CORFE, Joseph (1740-1820)
English singer, organist,
composer BD
CORI, Angelo Italian musician,
composer CP/1 [see also:
Corri, Angelo]
CORINNE [Corinne Belle De
Brion] (1873-1937) American
actress CDP, WWM, WWS
CORKE, Norman (d 1889 [20])
actor EA/90*
CORKERY, Daniel (1878-1964)
Irish dramatist ES
CORLESSE, Mrs. E. C. see
Taylor, Annie
CORLEY, Robert A. (d 1971)
performer BP/56*
CORMACK, Mr. actor CDP
CORMACK, John (d 1890) ballet
master EA/91*
CORN, Alfred Jacob see
Ryder, Alfred
CORNACCHINI, Emanuele (fl
1759-60) singer BD
CORNE, Mr. (fl 1782) actor BD
CORNEILLE, [Mons.?] (fl 1675)
harpsichordist BD
CORNEILLE, Mons. (fl 1735-
36) acrobat BD
CORNEILLE, Pierre (1606-84)
French dramatist DD, OC/
1-3
CORNEL, Master (fl 1745-47)
singer BD
CORNELIUS, Mr. (fl 1675)
violinist BD
CORNELIUS, Peter (1865-1934)
Danish singer ES

CORNELL, John (1913-69) American
stage manager BE, TW/25
CORNELL, Katharine (1893/98-
1974) German/American actress
AAS, BE, BTR/74, CB, ES,
HJD, NTH, OC/2-3, PDT, SR,
TW/1-21, WWT/4-15
CORNELYS, Mrs. (fl 1781) actress,
dramatist CP/3
CORNELYS, Miss (fl 1791-1801)
actress BD
CORNELYS, John (1735-1818)
Irish? actor, singer BD,
CDP, TD/1-2
CORNELYS, Mrs. John [Margaret]
(1723-97) actress BD
CORNELYS, Margaret see
Cornelys, Mrs. John
CORNELYS, Teresa [née Imer]
(1723-97) Italian singer, entre-
preneur BD, DNB
CORNER, Julia (1798-1875) English
dramatist DNB
CORNES, James (d 1874) musician
EA/76*
CORNET, Sig. (fl 1726-27) dancer
BD
CORNEWALL-WALKER, Thomas
James Raglan see Raglan,
James
CORNEY, Mr. (fl 1661) singer BD
CORNEY, Arthur singer, composer
CDP
CORNILLE, Marguerite CDP
CORNISH, James (d 1804) oboist
BD
CORNISH, James John (1767-1803)
musician BD
CORNISH, John (fl 1501) gentleman
of the Chapel Royal, pageant-
master DA
CORNISH, Kit (fl 1508) actor DA
CORNISH, Thomas (fl 1794-1818)
oboist BD
CORNISH, William (fl 1479-80)
master of song school DA
CORNISH, William (fl 1509-23)
master of the Chapel Royal
DA, ES
CORNOCK, J. R. see Crauford,
J. R.
CORNUE, Virginia (b 1945) Ameri-
can actress TW/30
CORNWALL, Mr. (d c.1724) scene
painter BD
CORNWALL, Anna (d 1872 [93])
pianist EA/73*
CORNWALL, Barry see Proctor,

Bryan Walter
CORNWALL, Mr. H. (d 1869
[59]) equestrian? EA/70*
CORNWELL, David (fl c.1700-
13?) acrobat, conjurer, ex-
hibitor BD
CORNWELL, Judy (b 1942)
English actress WWT/15-16
CORNYSSHE, William (d 1524?)
musician DNB
CORONA SABOLINI, Teresa
see Costantini, Signora
Giovanni Battista
CORONAKIS, Yvonne see Con-
stant, Yvonne
CORPORA, Sig. (fl 1722) vio-
linist BD
CORRE, Joseph (fl 1800) manager
WWA/H
CORREL, Gladis (d 1962 [70])
performer BE*
CORRELL, Charles J. (1890-
1972) actor CB, TW/29
CORRER, Mrs. Vittorio see
Angelelli, Augusta
CORREY, Elizabeth (d 1912 [63])
EA/13*
CORRI, Adrienne (b 1932) Scot-
tish actress TW/8
CORRI, Angelo (fl 1739) mana-
ger? BD
CORRI, Charles Montague (b
1861) English conductor
WWT/5-9
CORRI, Clarence (fl 1899)
composer, musical director
DD
CORRI, Domenico (1746-1825)
Italian composer DNB, ES
CORRI, Signora Domenico
[née Bacchelli] (fl 1771-
1810) Italian singer BD
CORRI, Dussek (d 1870) actor,
singer DD
CORRI, Mrs. E. Dussek see
Thirlwall, Annie
CORRI, Francesca (b 1795)
actress, singer ES
CORRI, Ghita [Mrs. Neville
Lynn] Scottish singer GRB/1
CORRI, Haydn (1785-1860)
musician DD
CORRI, Haydn (1842-76) actor,
singer DD, ES
CORRI, Mrs. Haydn (d 1867
[67]) singer EA/68*
CORRI, Henry (1824-88) actor,
singer DD, ES

CORRI, Ida Gillies (d 1908 [67])
singer EA/09*
CORRI, Kathleen (fl 1880) actress,
singer DD
CORRI, Monte (1784-1849) com-
poser, musical director DD
CORRI, Pat (1820-76) actor, singer
CDP, DD, ES
CORRI, Rupert (d 1876) scene artist
EA/77*
CORRI, Sophia see Dussek, Mrs.
Jan Ladislav
CORRI, Mrs. V. [née Annie Parker]
(d 1870 [29]) actress EA/71*
CORRI, William (d 1932 [73]) musi-
cian WWT/14*
CORRIE, D. T. actor, singer,
composer CDP
CORRIE, Joe (1894-1968) Scottish
dramatist OC/1-3
CORRIGAN, Charles (d 1966 [72])
performer BP/50*
CORRIGAN, Emmett (1868/71-1932)
Dutch/American actor SR, WWS,
WWT/4-6
CORRIGAN, Helen (d 1887) EA/88*
CORRIGAN, Lloyd (d 1969 [69])
performer BP/54*
CORRIGAN, Robert W. (b 1927)
American educator BE
CORRUCCINI, Roberto (1859-1926)
Italian singer WWA/1
CORRY, A. D. (d 1902 [43]) mana-
ger EA/03*
CORRY, Eliza (d 1877) EA/79*
CORRY, Mrs. T. C. S. see
Corry, Eliza
CORRY, Walter Frederick Stewart
(d 1893) singer EA/94*
CORSARO, Frank (b 1924) American
director, dramatist, actor,
teacher BE, CB, WWT/14-16
CORSETTI, Guiseppe (fl 1833)
singer HAS
"CORSICAN FAMILY, The" see
Teresia, Mme.
CORSON, Richard American actor,
writer, educator BE
CORSON, Robert Frederick see
Artell, R. F.
CORT, Alex (b 1939) American
dancer TW/23-24
CORT, Harry Linsley (d 1937 [44])
producer, author BE*, BP/21*
CORT, John (1859-1929) American
manager SR
CORTES, Mr. (fl 1790-91) rope
walker, dancer, tumbler BD

CORTESI, Adelaide (1828-89)
Italian singer CDP, ES,
HAS
CORTESI, Antonio (1796-1879)
Italian dancer, choreographer
ES
CORTEZ, Leon (d 1970 [72])
performer BP/55*
CORTHELL, Herbert (1875/78-
1947) American actor SR,
TW/3, WWM, WWS
CORTIS, Antonio (1892-1952)
Italian singer ES
CORTO, Diana (b 1942) Ameri-
can actress TW/25
CORUM, Paul (b 1943) Ameri-
can actor TW/27
CORWIN, Norman [Lewis] (b
1910) American dramatist,
director, producer BE,
CB, HJD
CORY, Mr. (fl 1675) actor BD
CORY, Kenneth (b 1941) Ameri-
can actor TW/28-29
CORY, Thomas (fl 1791-1808?)
actor BD, TD/1-2
CORY-THOMAS, Lambert (d
1908) English actor GRB/1
CORZATTE, Clayton (b 1927)
American actor TW/22-25
COSBY, Bill (b 1938) American
comedian CB
COSBY, Thomas (fl 1663-70)
rope dancer, booth operator
BD
COSBY, Mrs. Thomas (fl 1663-
64) rope dancer BD
COSGROVE, Marie [Mrs. Charles
Pateman] (d 1892 [34]) actress
EA/93*
COSHAM, Ernest (d 1910 [44])
actor GRB/3-4
COSIO, Rosita (b 1933) Puerto
Rican actress TW/2
COSLOW, Jacqueline (b 1943)
American actress TW/28
COSMAN, Lydia (d 1900)
music-hall singer EA/01*
COSNETT, T. (d 1871 [27])
comic singer EA/72*
COSSA, Sig. (fl 1785) tumbler
BD
COSSART, Ernest (1876-1951)
English actor TW/2-7,
WWT/7-11
COSSART, Valerie (b 1910)
English actress WWT/9-12
COSSINS, W. (fl 1734-35)

boxkeeper BD
COSSIRA, Emile (1857-1923) French
singer ES
COSTA, Carlo (d 1888 [62]) music
teacher EA/89*
COSTA, Davide (fl 1843-64) Italian
dancer, choreographer ES
COSTA, Gioacchino (fl 1790) singer
BD
COSTA, Sir Michael (1810-84)
Italian/English composer, con-
ductor CDP, DNB, ES
COSTA, Raphael (d 1892 [76])
EA/93*
COSTAIN, Mr. (fl 1764-95) dresser,
caller, concessionaire? BD
COSTANTINI, Signora (fl 1726)
singer BD
COSTANTINI, Costantino (b c.1634)
Italian actor, musician BD
COSTANTINI, Domenica (fl 1674-
86) Italian actress BD
COSTANTINI, Giovanni Battista
(d 1720) Italian actor, musician
BD
COSTANTINI, Signora Giovanni
Battista [née Teresa Corona
Sabolini] (d 1730) Italian actress
BD
COSTANZA, Signora (fl 1742-43)
dancer BD
COSTELL, Mary Anne see Can-
ning, Mrs. George
COSTELLA, Michael (d 1896)
"jester" EA/97*
COSTELLO, Miss (fl 1780) actress
BD
COSTELLO, Charles (d 1973 [83])
stage manager BP/58*
COSTELLO, Helene (d 1957 [53])
American actress BE*
COSTELLO, Joseph (d 1888 [56])
musical director EA/89*
COSTELLO, Lou (1906-59) Ameri-
can vaudevillian ES, TW/15,
WWA/3
COSTELLO, Mariclare American
actress TW/25-26, 29
COSTELLO, Mary Anne see
Canning, Mrs. George
COSTELLO, Maurice (1877-1950)
American actor ES, TW/7
COSTELLO, Michael (d 1883 [39])
music-hall artist EA/84*
COSTELLO, Philip (d 1901) EA/02*
COSTELLO, Tom (1863-1945) Eng-
lish music-hall performer CDP,
COC, OC/1-3

COSTELLO, Mrs. Tom (d 1912
[49]) EA/13*
COSTELLO, William A. (d 1971
[73]) performer BP/56*
COSTELLOW, Thomas (fl 1775-
1815?) composer, singer,
teacher BD
COSTENTENUS, Cpt. Greek/
Albanian tattoed man CDP
COSTER, Nicholas (b 1934)
English actor TW/18-20,
24-25, 27-30
COSTETOMEPOLITAN, Mr.
(fl 1772-82) Greek acrobat,
slack-rope walker, clown,
equestrian BD
COSTIGAN, James (b 1926/28)
American dramatist, actor
BE, ES
COSTIGAN, Josephine see
Pardey, Mrs. George
COSTIL, William, Jr. (d 1976
[63]) producer/director/
choreographer BP/60*
COSTIN, Mr. (fl 1746-72) box-
keeper BD
COSTOLLO, Patrick (d 1766)
actor BD
COTA, Keith (b 1931) American
actor TW/25
COTES, Mr. (fl 1767) singer
BD
COTES, Charles Greville (d
1905 [31]) songwriter EA/07*
COTES, Peter [né Sydney
Boulting] (b 1912) English
actor, manager, producer,
director AAS, WWT/10-16
COTON, A. V. (d 1969 [63])
critic BP/54*
COTOPOULI, Marika (d 1954 [68])
Greek actress TW/11
COTSHALL, Mr. (fl 1758) actor
BD
COTSOPOULOS, Thanos (b 1911)
Greek actor TW/9
COTSWORTH, Staats (b 1908)
American actor BE, TW/
10-11, 21-24, 26, 28, WWT/
14-16
COTT, Ted (d 1973 [55]) direc-
tor/producer/choreographer
BP/58*
COTTAM, Kent (b 1935) actor
TW/30
COTTE, Edward (d 1906 [70])
singer, actor DD
COTTELL, Lansdowne (d 1909

[73]?) singer GRB/1
COTTELL, Victor Lansdowne (d
1912) professor of music EA/
13*
COTTEN, Joseph (b 1905) American
actor AAS, BE, ES, TW/14,
16, 19, WWT/14-16
COTTER, George Sackville (1755-
1831) translator, writer DD
COTTER, Jayne see Meadows,
Jayne
COTTER, Patrick [alias O'Brien]
(1761?-1806) Irish giant CDP,
DNB
COTTEREAU, Symon (fl 1670)
musician BD
COTTEREL, Miss (fl 1750) singer
BD
COTTIN, Mr. (fl 1700-06) dancer
BD
COTTINET, Edmond (d 1895 [71])
dramatist EA/96*
COTTON, Mr. (fl 1782) actor BD
COTTON, Mrs. (fl 1708) dresser
BD
COTTON, A. Benjamin (1829-1908)
American minstrel manager and
performer CDP, HAS
COTTON, Charles (1630-87) English
dramatist CP/1-3, DD, GT
COTTON, Fred Ayres (d 1964 [57])
American actor, executive TW/
2-3, 20
COTTON, George (d 1975 [72])
performer BP/60*
COTTON, John (fl 1794-1800) vio-
linist BD
COTTON, John (1886-1946) Ameri-
can dramatist SR
COTTON, Lucy (d 1948 [57]) act-
ress TW/5
COTTON, Robert F. English actor
BE*
COTTON, Wilfred (b 1873) English
actor, manager GRB/1-4,
WWT/1-6
COTTON, Mrs. Wilfred see
Reeve, Ada
COTTRELL, Miss (d 1866 [25])
actress, singer EA/72*
COTTRELL, Cherry (b 1909) Eng-
lish actress WWT/9-12
COTTRELL, Richard (b 1936) Eng-
lish director, manager, drama-
tist AAS, WWT/15-16
COTTRELL, Richard (b 1944)
American actor TW/25-26
COTTRELL, Thomas (d 1867 [52])

musician EA/68*
COTTRELL, William (b 1918)
American actor TW/25-26
COTTRELLY, Mathilde (1851-
1933) German singer, act-
ress CDP, SR
COTTS, Campbell (1902-64)
South African actor TW/9
COTZ, Peter (fl 1818-29)
equestrian HAS
COUCH, Mr. (fl 1710-21?)
impresario, dancing master?
violinist? BD
COUDELLE, Mrs. M. E. see
Chober, Cora Lena
COUGHLIN, Bill T. (d 1974
[81]) performer BP/59*
COUGHLIN, Kevin (1945-76)
American actor TW/15
COUGHTREE, Rosa Ann [Marie
Leslie] (d 1882) actress
EA/83*
COULDOCK, Charles Walter
(1815-98) English/American
actor CDP, DAB, DD, ES,
HAS, OC/1-3, SR, WWA/H
COULDOCK, Eliza (fl 1853)
actress HAS
COULDOCK, Louisa (d 1877
[60]) English actress HAS
COULON, Anne Jacqueline
[Mme. Pierre Gabriel
Gardel, I] (fl 1787-92)
French dancer BD
COULON, Eugene (fl 1787-1830)
dancing master CDP
COULOURIS, George (b 1903)
English actor AAS, BE,
ES, TW/2-7, 21-22, WWT/
9-16
COULSEY, Charles (d 1881
[13]) performer EA/82*
COULSON, Robert F. (d 1909
[35]) lessee EA/10*
COULSONE, Harry (d 1887
[40]) variety entertainer
EA/88*
COULSON-MAYNE, E. W.
(d 1917 [20]) EA/18*
COULTER, Frazer (1848-1937)
Canadian actor CDP,
WWM, WWS
COULTER, Kay actress TW/1
COULTER, Philip Frazer see
Coulter, Frazer
COULTER, Mrs. Robert Porter
see Millard, Evelyn
COULTON, Mr. (fl 1789-90)

house servant? BD
COUNCIL, Richard (b 1947) Ameri-
can actor TW/30
COUNSELL, John (b 1905) English
director, manager, actor AAS,
COC, OC/3, WWT/10-16
COUNTER, Frederick Stanhope see
Stanhope, Frederick
COUNTISS, Cathrine (fl 1900s)
American actress WWM, WWS
COUNTS, Mr. (fl 1794) musician
BD
COUP, William Cameron (1833-95)
American circus & theatrical
manager CDP, ES
COUPE, Diane (b 1939) English
actress TW/23-26
COUPER, Barbara (b 1903) English
actress WWT/8-14
COURCO, Mr. see Curco, Mr.
COURT, Beatrice K. see Arkin-
stall, Beatrice K.
COURT, Bob (d 1970 [68]) per-
former BP/55*
COURT, Geraldine (b 1942) Ameri-
can actress TW/29
COURTAINE, Harry (d 1899) actor
CDP
COURTE, Mrs. Henry see
Courte, Louisa
COURTE, Louisa [Mrs. Henry
Courte] (d 1906 [82]) EA/07*
"COURTE, S. X." (fl 1894-98)
dramatist DD
COURTELINE, Georges [Georges
Moinaux] (1858-1929) French
dramatist MWD, WWT/3
COURTENAY, Mr. (fl late 18th
cent) actor CDP
COURTENAY, Miss [Miss Crawley]
(fl 1777) actress, singer BD
COURTENAY, Denis (1760-94)
Irish piper BD
COURTENAY, Edward (d 1884)
EA/85*
COURTENAY, Eliza [Mrs. Lindo
Courtenay] (d 1906 [64]) EA/08*
COURTENAY, Eveline [Mrs. John
Hay] (d 1898) actress EA/00*
COURTENAY, Foster (d 1909) actor
EA/11*
COURTENAY, Dr. Fred (d 1910)
proprietor? EA/11*
COURTENAY, Lindo (d 1896 [65])
lessee, manager EA/97*
COURTENAY, Mrs. Lindo (d 1885)
EA/86*
COURTENAY, Mrs. Lindo see

Courtenay, Eliza
COURTENAY, Tom (b 1937)
English actor AAS, CB,
ES, WWT/14-16
COURTENAY, Vera (fl 1900s)
American singer WWM
COURTENAY, William (1875-
1933) American actor WWS,
WWT/1-7
COURTENAY, William J. (d
1908) EA/09*
COURTENEY, Fay (d 1943 [65])
American actress BE*,
BP/28*
COURTEVILLE, Raphael (d
1675) singer BD
COURTEVILLE, Raphael (d
c.1735) organist, composer,
singer BD, DNB
COURTEVILLE, Raphael (d
1772) organist BD
COURTICE, Thomas [Sydney
W. Curtiss] (b 1872) Eng-
lish business manager
GRB/1-2
COURTICE, Mrs. Thomas
see Curtiss, Alice May
COURTIER-DUTTON, Lionel
see Carson, Lionel
COURTLEIGH, Edna (d 1962 [77])
actress BE*
COURTLEIGH, William Louis
(1869-1930) Canadian actor
ES, GRB/2-4, SR, WWA/1,
WWS, WWT/1-6
COURTLY, Thomas J. (d 1934
[67]) business manager
WWT/14*
COURTNAY, Denis see Cour-
tenay, Denis
COURTNEIDGE, Charles (d 1935)
actor BE*, WWT/14*
COURTNEIDGE, Dame Cicely
(b 1893) Australian actress
AAS, COC, NTH, TW/4-11,
WWT/1-16
COURTNEIDGE, Robert (1859-
1939) Scottish manager,
dramatist GRB/4, WWT/
1-8
COURTNEIDGE, Mrs. Robert
[Rosie Nott] (d 1914 [46])
actress BE*, WWT/14*
COURTNEIDGE, Rosaline (1903-
26) English actress WWT/5
COURTNEY, Mr. (fl 1749-62)
singer BD
COURTNEY, Mr. (fl 1773-75)

actor, singer BD
COURTNEY, Alexander (b 1940)
American actor TW/24-26
COURTNEY, Baron [Henry Black-
well] (d 1901 [66]) music-hall
chairman EA/02*
COURTNEY, C. C. librettist CD
COURTNEY, Denis see Courtenay,
Denis
COURTNEY, Elizabeth (d 1974 [69])
designer BP/59*
COURTNEY, Fay (1868-1943) Amer-
ican actress SR
COURTNEY, F. C. (d 1890) actor
EA/91*
COURTNEY, Gordon (1895-1964)
English composer, producer,
manager, press representative,
business manager WWT/9-10
COURTNEY, Harry (d 1872) pianist
EA/73*
COURTNEY, Inez (d 1975 [67])
performer BP/59*
COURTNEY, James (b 1924) Amer-
ican actor TW/6
COURTNEY, James J. (d 1888
[43]) proprietor EA/89*
COURTNEY, John (1813-65) actor,
dramatist DD
COURTNEY, Mary (d 1874 [65])
EA/76*
COURTNEY, Maud actress, singer
CDP
COURTNEY, Oscar W. (d 1963 [85])
performer BE*
COURTNEY, Paul (d 1906) comedian,
sketch artist EA/08*
COURTNEY, William (1876-1933)
American actor SR
COURTNEY, William Leonard
(1850-1928) Indian/English
dramatist, critic DD, ES,
GRB/2-4, WWT/1-5, WWW/2
COURTRIGHT, Clyde (d 1967 [82])
performer BP/52*
COURTS, Mr. (fl 1760-61) singer
BD
COURVILLE, Albert de see De
Courville, Albert
COUSENS, Robert (1818-67) English
actor HAS
COUSINS, Mr. (fl 1748) fair booth
proprietor BD
COUSINS, Charles (d 1890) musical
director EA/91*
COUSINS, Rosie [Mrs. Fred Street]
(d 1908 [31]) EA/09*
COUSTOS, Mr. (fl 1747-50) singer

BD

COUSTUP, George (fl 1785-99)
musician BD

COUTCHEE, Noyai (fl 1795-96)
performer BD

COUTTS, Miss (fl 1779) actress
BD

COUTTS, Compton (d 1910 [60])
actor EA/11*, WWT/14*

COUTTS, Harriot see Mellon,
Harriot

COUTTS, Henri (d 1910 [42])
quick-change artist EA/11*

COVE, Augusta (d 1903) actress? EA/04*

COVENEY, George (d 1918
[60]) EA/19*

COVENEY, H. (1790-1881) actor
CDP, DD

COVENEY, Mrs. H. (d 1854 [67])
actress WWT/14*

COVENEY, Harriett [Mrs. Charles
A. Jecks] (1828-92) actress
DD, DP, OAA/2

COVENEY, Jane [Mrs. Larkins]
(1824-1900) actress CDP,
DD

COVENTRY, Rev. Francis (d
c.1759) dramatist CP/3

COVENTRY, Lucy (d 1918) EA/
19*

COVER, Franklin Edward (b
1928) American actor TW/
23, 25-27, 30

COVERDALE, Ernest Charles
see Prescott, Walter

COVERT, Mr. singer CDP

COVILL, Mr. (fl 1786-94)
singer, dancer? BD

COWAN, Adam (d 1908) manager
EA/09*

COWAN, Clara (d 1907) EA/08*

COWAN, Grant (b 1935) Canadian actor TW/27-28

COWAN, Irene (b 1914) American actress TW/8

COWAN, Jerome (1897-1972)
American actor BE, TW/28

COWAN, John F. actor CDP

COWAN, Lynn F. (d 1973)
musician BP/58*

COWAN, Maurice A. (b 1891)
English manager WWT/6

COWARD, Edward Fales (1862-
1933) American dramatist
WWA/1, WWM

COWARD, James (1824-80) English musician DNB

COWARD, Sir Noel Pierce (1899-
1973) English actor, dramatist,
composer, producer AAS, BE,
CB, CH, COC, ES, HP, MD,
MH, MWD, NTH, OC/1-3,
PDT, RE, SR, TW/15-16, 29,
WWA/5, WWT/4-15

COWCHER, Mr. (fl 1781) actor
BD

COWDEN, Irene (d 1961) actress
BE*

COWDERY, Mrs. [née Bessie Ed-
wards] (d 1878) actress EA/79*

COWDERY, Charles (d 1878) actor
EA/79*

COWE, Charlotte (d 1905) EA/06*

COWELL, Mrs. [née Sheppard] (b
1801) English actress HAS

COWELL, Anna [née Cruise] (b
1824) Irish singer, actress
HAS, SR

COWELL, Emilie Marguerite [Mrs.
Sam Cowell] (d 1899 [80]) EA/
00*

COWELL, Florence see Tapping,
Mrs. Alfred B.

COWELL, Henry Dixon (b 1897)
American composer ES

COWELL, Joseph (d before 1870)
English scene painter ES, HAS

COWELL, Joseph Leathley [Hawkins
Witchett] (1792-1863) English act-
or CDP, COC, DD, DNB, ES,
HAS, OC/1-3, SR, WWA/H

COWELL, Lydia (fl 1876-91)
actress DD

COWELL, Mrs. Sam see Cowell,
Emilie Marguerite

COWELL, Samuel Houghton (1820-
64) English/American music-hall
performer CDP, COC, DD,
DNB, ES, HAS, OC/1-3

COWELL, Sidney Frances see
Bateman, Sidney Frances

COWELL, Sydney (1846-1925)
English actress CDP, ES, OC/
1-3, PP/1

COWELL, Sydney (1872-1941) see
Fairbrother, Sydney

COWELL, William (1820-68) Irish
business manager, writer, actor?
HAS, SR

COWELS, Charles O. (1861-1916)
actor SR

COWELS, Eugene (1860-1948) Canadian composer, actor SR

COWEN, Emily (d 1910 [89]) EA/
11*

COWEN, Sir Frederick Hymen (1852-1935) Jamaican/English composer, conductor DD, DNB, ES, GRB/1, WWW/3

COWEN, Henrietta (fl 1891-99) actress DD

COWEN, Lawrence (1865-1942) English dramatist WWW/2-7

COWEN, Louis (d 1925 [69]) critic, dramatist BE*, WWT/14*

COWEN, Ron (b 1944) American dramatist CD

COWEN, William Joyce (d 1964 [76]) dramatist BE*

COWIE, Laura (1892-1969) Scottish actress ES, WWT/1-11

COWIE, Robert, Sr. (d 1877 [67]) proprietor EA/78*

COWIE, Robert G. W. (d 1963 [49]) press officer BP/48*

COWL, Jane (1884/90-1950) American actress, dramatist COC, DAB, ES, NTH, SR, TW/2-7, WWA/3, WWM, WWT/4-10

COWLE, William (d 1885 [84]) actor EA/86*

COWLES, Chandler (b 1917) American producer, actor BE, TW/2-6

COWLES, Eugene (1860-1948) Canadian singer, actor TW/5, WWA/4, WWS

COWLES, Matthew (b 1944) American actor TW/22, 24-26, 30

COWLES, M. B. (1843-87) American advance agent NYM

COWLEY, Abraham (1618-67) English dramatist COC, CP/1-3, DD, DNB, ES, FGF, GT, HP, OC/1-3

COWLEY, Albert (d 1876 [35]) singer EA/77*

COWLEY, Eric (1886-1948) English actor WWT/7-10

COWLEY, Francis Laurence (fl 1739) musician BD

COWLEY, Hannah [née Parkhouse] (1743-1809) English dramatist CDP, COC, CP/2-3, DD, DNB, ES, GT, HP, NTH, OC/1-3, TD/1-2

COWLEY, Richard (d 1619)

English actor COC, DA, GT, NTH, OC/1-3

COWLEY-POLHILL, R. (b 1844) English business manager, actor GRB/1

COWPER, Mr. (fl 1785-94) singer BD

COWPER, Mrs. (fl 1748-60) actress BD

COWPER, Miss (fl 1771-80?) singer BD

COWPER, Clara (d 1917) actress DD, EA/95

COWPER, Edward Alfred (d 1893) EA/94*

COWPER, John Curtis (1827-85) actor CDP, DD

COWRAN, Clay (d 1972 [58]) critic BP/56*

COWSLADE, Miss (fl 1755) actress BD

COX, Mr. (fl 1729-30) house servant BD

COX, Mr. (fl 1732-36) dancer BD

COX, Mr. (fl 1741) actor BD

COX, Mr. (fl 1761) actor BD

COX, Mr. (fl 1781-89) house servant BD

COX, Mr. (fl 1788-92) actor, singer BD

COX, Mrs. (fl 1760) singer BD

COX, Mrs. (fl 1781-82) singer, actress BD

COX, Mrs. (fl 1783-85) dresser BD

COX, Mrs. (fl 1798) dancer? BD

COX, Miss (fl 1795-1804) actress, dancer, singer? BD

COX, Brian (b 1946) Scottish actor WWT/16

COX, C. Douglas (d 1904 [60]) manager, actor EA/05*, WWT/14*

COX, Charles B. (d 1889 [48]) proprietor EA/90*

COX, Constance (b 1912) English dramatist AAS, WWT/11-16

COX, Dorothy Isobel see Wynyard, Diana

COX, Douglas see Cox, C. Douglas

COX, Elizabeth (c.1639?-88?) actress BD

COX, Faulkner (d 1906) actor EA/08*

COX, Gabriel (1747-92) master carpenter, machinist BD

COX, Garnet Wolseley (d 1904 [32])

composer EA/05*

COX, George William [George Lupriel] (d 1886 [59]) circus performer EA/88*

COX, Harry [Oliver James Bussley] (1841-82) actor DD

COX, Henry Blackford (d 1880 [43]) EA/82*

COX, Hugh (1731-63) singer, harpsichordist BD

COX, [John?] (fl 1751-64?) singer, publisher, instrument maker BD

COX, John George (d 1758) oboist, dancing master BD

COX, Nellie singer CDP

COX, Ray (fl 1900s) American actress, singer CDP, WWM

COX, Richard (b 1948) American actor TW/28, 30

COX, Robert (d 1655) English actor, dramatist COC, CP/1-3, DD, OC/1-3

COX, Robert (d 1974 [79]) performer BP/59*

COX, Susannah (fl 1702-15) actress BD

COX, Thomas see Coco

COX, Wally (1924-73) American actor CB, TW/29, WWA/5

COX, W. Herbert English actor GRB/1

COXE, Louis O. (b 1918) American educator, dramatist BE

COXER, Sarah see Anderton, Sarah

COXEY, William Douglas (1883/84-1943) American writer SR, WWM

COX-IFE, William (d 1968) producer/director BP/52*

COY, Walter (b 1913) American actor TW/4-6

COYLE, Mr. (fl 1784) musician BD

COYLE, Mr. (fl 1832) English/American manager HAS

COYLE, Mrs. Frank see Drew, Nelly

COYLE, George (d 1876) singer EA/77*

COYLE, Mrs. George see Coyle, Mary Ann

COYLE, Joe (d 1973 [56]) performer BP/58*

COYLE, John E. (d 1909 [40]) variety comedian EA/10*

COYLE, John E. (d 1964 [70]) singer, actor CDP

COYLE, Mary Ann [Mrs. George Coyle] (d 1877) EA/78*

COYLE, Matilda (d 1889) EA/91*

COYLE, Miles (1714-96?) singer, musician BD

COYLE, S. (d 1889) EA/90*

COYNE, Alice M. Rawlinson [Mrs. Fred Coyne] (d 1884 [35]) EA/85*

COYNE, Anne [Mrs. Joseph Stirling Coyne] (d 1880) EA/81*

COYNE, Edmund Stirling (d 1902 [52]) dramatist EA/03*

COYNE, Elizabeth [Mrs. J. Dennis Coyne] (d 1892 [46]) EA/94*

COYNE, Frank singer, actor CDP

COYNE, Frank (d 1882) music-hall artist EA/83*

COYNE, Frank (d 1906 [30]) variety comedian EA/07*

COYNE, Fred singer, actor CDP

COYNE, Fred (d 1886 [39]) comedian EA/87*

COYNE, Mrs. Fred see Coyne, Alice M. Rawlinson

COYNE, Gardiner [Henry Andrew Gardiner] (d 1900) Irish actor CDP, HAS

COYNE, Mrs. J. Dennis see Coyne, Elizabeth

COYNE, Joseph (1867/70-1941) American actor ES, GRB/2-4, WWS, WWT/1-9

COYNE, Joseph Stirling (1803/05-68) Irish dramatist CDP, DD, DNB, EA/68, ES

COYNE, Mrs. Joseph Stirling see Coyne, Anne

COYNE, Kathleen (b 1945) American actress TW/26

[COYSH, Miss?] (fl 1682) actress BD

COYSH, John (fl 1667-c. 97) actor, manager BD

COYSH, Mrs. John [Dorothy?] (fl 1668-79) actress BD

CRABBE, Mrs. see Herbert, Louisa

CRABTREE, Charles [Charles Lestree] (d 1917) comedy juggler EA/18*

CRABTREE, Charlotte see Lotta

CRABTREE, Don (b 1928) American actor TW/26

CRABTREE, Paul (b 1918) American director, actor, producer BE,

TW/1, 3, 6-8
CRACE, Mr. (fl 1789-1803)
scene painter BD
CRACRAFT, Tom Adrian (d
1963 [58]) scene designer
BP/48*
CRADDOCK, John (d 1873 [43])
actor? EA/74*
CRADDOCK, Joseph (fl 1771)
dramatist GT
CRADDOCK, Louisa see
Austin, Mrs. Noel
CRADOCK, Joseph (1742-1826)
English dramatist CDP,
CP/2-3, DD, DNB
CRADOCK, William (fl 1669)
musician BD
CRAFT, Roy (d 1965 [75])
performer BP/49*
CRAFT, Thomas (b 1937) Eng-
lish actor TW/26
CRAFTS, Charley (d 1974 [78])
performer BP/58*
CRAFTS, Griffin (d 1973 [73])
performer BP/58*
CRAFTS, William (1787-1826)
American critic, dramatist
EAP, HJD
CRAGEN, William (d 1972 [62])
actor, director TW/29
CRAGG, Amanda [Mrs. J. W.
Cragg] (d 1909) acrobat
EA/10*
CRAGG, Billy (d 1918) EA/19*
CRAGG, Mrs. J. W. [Alice
Daly] (d 1889) EA/90*
CRAGG, Mrs. J. W. see
Cragg, Amanda
CRAGGS, Mr. (fl 1744) actor
BD
CRAIG, Master (fl 1792) singer
BD
CRAIG, [Adam?] (d 1741) vio-
linist BD
CRAIG, Adam H. (d 1911)
EA/13*
CRAIG, Casey American actor
TW/29
CRAIG, Clavering [Graham
Daviss] (d 1916 [44]) actor,
musical director EA/17*
CRAIG, David (b 1923) American
lyricist, librettist, coach BE
CRAIG, Edith Geraldine Ailsa
(1869-1947) English actress,
director GRB/1-4, OC/1-3,
SR, TW/3, WWS, WWT/1-10
CRAIG, Edward Anthony see

Carrick, Edward
CRAIG, Edward Gordon (1872-1966)
English actor, producer, scene
designer BE, COC, DD, DP,
ES, GRB/1-4, NTH, OC/1-3,
PDT, TW/23, WWT/1-14
CRAIG, George Wymark (d 1898
[64]) manager EA/99*
CRAIG, Hardin (1875-1968) Ameri-
can scholar BE
CRAIG, Helen (b 1912/14) American
actress, teacher BE, ES, TW/
2-11, 22-24, WWT/10-16
CRAIG, Joel American actor TW/
29
CRAIG, John (d 1890 [62]) EA/91*
CRAIG, John (1868-1932) American
actor SR
CRAIG, Laura (1880-1947) American
actress SR
CRAIG, May (d 1972 [83]) Irish
actress TW/28
CRAIG, Michael [né Gregson] (b
1929) Indian/English actor
WWT/15-16
CRAIG, Miriam (d 1971 [54])
performer BP/55*
CRAIG, Noel American actor TW/
26-30
CRAIG, Phyllis (b 1936) English
actress TW/24-26
CRAIG, Robert H. (b 1842) Ameri-
can actor HAS
CRAIG, Walter (d 1972 [71]) singer,
dancer, actor TW/29
CRAIG, Walter James (d 1885)
EA/86*
CRAIG, Wendy (b 1934) English
actress WWT/14-16
CRAIG, William C. (b 1908) Amer-
ican educator, director BE
CRAIG, William James (1843-1906)
Irish scholar DNB
CRAIGIE, Mrs. Pearl Mary Teresa
see Hobbes, John Oliver
CRAIN, Harold (b 1911) American
educator BE
CRAMER, Miss [Mrs. Plumer] (fl
1828) actress CDP
CRAMER, Charles (d 1799) violinist
BD
CRAMER, Edd (d 1963 [39]) actor
BE*
CRAMER, Fanny [Mrs. William
Danvers; Mrs. Nagle] (fl 1852-
59) actress? HAS
CRAMER, Franz (1772-1848) German
violinist, impresario BD, CDP,

DNB
CRAMER, Mrs. H. [Miss M.
E. Poole] (1803-68) English
actress HAS
CRAMER, Henry (d 1877) musi-
cian EA/78*
CRAMER, Johann Baptist (1771-
1858) German musician,
composer, publisher BD,
CDP, DNB
CRAMER, M. E. (1803-68)
actress CDP
CRAMER, Wilhelm (1745-99)
German violinist, composer,
impresario BD, CDP, DNB
CRAMERER, Mlle. (fl 1779-80)
dancer BD
CRAMPTON, Charlotte (b 1816)
actress CDP, HAS, SR
CRAMPTON, Victoire, Lady
(1837-71) French/English
singer DNB
CRANDALL, Edward (1904-68)
American actor TW/1-3,
6, 24
CRANDALL, Jashf (b 1900)
American dancer, choreog-
rapher, maître de ballet ES
CRANDELL, David Miller (b
1914) American executive
BE
CRANDELL, R. F. (d 1974 [72])
journalist BP/59*
CRANE, Mrs. (fl 1761) actress
HAS
CRANE, Dean (b 1932) American
dancer, choreographer, direc-
tor, aerialist, costume de-
signer BE, TW/25-27
CRANE, D. H. see Howard,
Dan
CRANE, Edith (1865/75-1912)
American actress SR, WWS
CRANE, Edward (fl 1761) drama-
tist CP/2-3, GT
CRANE, Ellen (d 1963 [78])
performer BP/48*
CRANE, Emily (d 1901) actress
EA/02*
CRANE, Gardner (b 1874)
American vaudevillian WWM
CRANE, Mrs. Gardner (b 1875)
American vaudevillian WWM
CRANE, Harold (b 1975) English
actor, singer WWM
CRANE, Harry T. English actor
GRB/1
CRANE, Jessie [Mrs. Harry

J. Crane] (d 1908) EA/09*
CRANE, Mrs. Harry J. see
Crane, Jessie
CRANE, John (fl 1550) actor DA
CRANE, Lillian Marie (d 1916 [14])
EA/17*
CRANE, Norma (d 1973 [42]) act-
ress TW/30
CRANE, Ralph (c. 1550/60-after
1621) English player copier DA,
OC/1-3
CRANE, Richard (b 1944) English
dramatist WWT/16
CRANE, William (fl 1523-45)
master of the Chapel Royal
DA, DNB
CRANE, William Henry (1845-1928)
American actor CDP, COC,
DAB, DD, ES, GRB/1-4, OC/
1-3, PP/1, SR, WWA/1, WWM,
WWS, WWT/1-5
CRANFIELD, Mr. (fl 1780-1800?)
dancer, actor BD
CRANFIELD, Mrs. (fl 1790-98)
dancer BD
CRANFIELD, T. (fl 1796-1805?)
dancer BD
CRANFORD, Miss (fl 1784-94)
singer, actress BD
CRANKE (d 1783) dramatist CP/3
CRANKO, John (1927-73) American
choreographer, ballet director
CB, ES
CRANMER, Arthur (d 1954 [69])
singer WWT/14*
CRANWIGGE, James (fl 1598)
actor? DA
CRAPEAU [or Crapo], Marion H.
[Mrs. W. W. Pearce] (fl 1859)
actress HAS
CRAPO, Marion H. see Crapeau,
Marion H.
CRASTON, Mrs. see Durant,
Marie
CRASTON, Annie [Mrs. W. Walton]
(d 1908) actress EA/09*
CRASTON, William (d 1902 [33])
manager EA/03*
CRATER, Allene (d 1957 [77])
singer, actress TW/14
CRATHORN, Mr. (fl 1776-94)
English violoncellist, composer
BD
CRAUFORD, Mrs. (fl 1765) dancer
BD
CRAUFORD, Ellen Elizabeth [Mrs.
W. R. Crauford] (d 1873) EA/
74*

CRAUFORD, J. R. [J. R.
Cornock] (1847/48/50-1930)
English actor OAA/2,
WWT/1-6
CRAUFORD, Mrs. J. R. see
Ingram, Alice
CRAUFORD, Lane (d 1928 [44])
historian, actor WWT/14*
CRAUFORD, Louise (d 1892)
actress EA/93*
CRAUFORD, W. R. (d 1874
[45]) actor? EA/75*
CRAUFORD, Mrs. W. R.
see Crauford, Ellen Elizabeth
CRAUFURD, David (fl 1700-04)
Scottish dramatist CP/1-3,
DD
CRAUFURD, Russell actor EA/
96
CRAUFURD, Mrs. Russell see
Poole, Annie
CRAVEN, Mr. (fl 1749) actor,
singer BD
CRAVEN, Miss (fl 1771-73)
actress BD
CRAVEN, Countess see Brun-
ton, Louisa
CRAVEN, Alicia singer CDP
CRAVEN, Arthur [John Edward
Davies] (d 1894) clown, come-
dian EA/95*
CRAVEN, Arthur Scott (d 1917)
actor, dramatist GRB/3-4,
WWT/1-3
CRAVEN, Elise [Elise Barbara
Alleyne-Barrett] (b 1898)
English actress, dancer
WWT/1-7
CRAVEN, Lady Elizabeth (fl
1767-80) dramatist CP/2
CRAVEN, Frank (1875-1945)
American actor, dramatist,
producer CB, DAB, ES,
NTH, OC/1-3, SR, TW/2,
WWA/2, WWT/3-9
CRAVEN, Gemma (b 1950) Irish
actress WWT/16
CRAVEN, Hawes [Henry Hawes
Craven Green] (1837-1910)
English scene painter COC,
DD, DNB, ES, OC/1-3
CRAVEN, Henry Thornton (1818/
21-1905) English dramatist,
actor CDP, DD, DNB, EA/
68, GRB/1, OAA/1-2
CRAVEN, Mrs. H[enry] T[horn-
ton] see Nelson, Eliza
CRAVEN, Jane [Mrs. Will Craven]

(d 1884) EA/85*
CRAVEN, Robin (b 1906/10) Eng-
lish actor BE, TW/3-16
CRAVEN, Ruby (d 1964 [76/77])
Australian actress BE*, WWT/
14*
CRAVEN, Tom (1868-1919) English
actor, manager, dramatist DD,
WWT/2-3
CRAVEN, Walter Stokes (fl 1894-
97) actor, singer, dramatist
DD, SR
CRAVEN, Mrs. Will see Craven,
Jane
CRAVEN, William (fl 1770-74)
proprietor BD
CRAVES, H. (fl 1705) dramatist
GT
CRAWCOUR, David (d 1891 [43])
EA/92*
CRAWFORD, Mr. actor, manager
TD/1-2
CRAWFORD, Mrs. (fl 1760-61)
dancer BD
CRAWFORD, Mrs. (fl 1857) actress
HAS
CRAWFORD, Miss (fl 1770-71)
actress BD
CRAWFORD, Miss (fl 1785?-94?)
singer BD
CRAWFORD, Adelaide actress?
singer? CDP
CRAWFORD, Alice (b 1882) Aus-
tralian actress GRB/3-4, WWT/
1-7
CRAWFORD, Amy [Mrs. Bevan-
Slator] (d 1898) actress EA/99*
CRAWFORD, Anne (1920-56) Pales-
tinian/English actress ES,
WWT/12
CRAWFORD, Anne see Barry,
Mrs. Spranger
CRAWFORD, Bertie actress, singer
CDP
CRAWFORD, Boyd (b 1914) American
actor TW/4-6
CRAWFORD, Broderick (b 1911)
American actor BE, CB, ES
CRAWFORD, Charles (d 1969 [44])
critic BP/54*
CRAWFORD, Cheryl (b 1902) Amer-
ican producer, director, manager
AAS, BE, CB, COC, ES, TW/
2-8, WWT/10-16
CRAWFORD, Clifton (1870-1920)
Scottish actor SR
CRAWFORD, Dorothy (d 1976 [90])
theatre founder BP/60*

CRAWFORD, Dorothy Maude
[née Gabain] (b 1885) li-
brarian BE
CRAWFORD, F. Marion (1854-
1909) American writer,
dramatist DD, ES
CRAWFORD, Howard M. (d 1969
[55]) performer BP/54*
CRAWFORD, Jack Randall (b
1878) American educator BE
CRAWFORD, Joan (1908-77)
American actress CB
CRAWFORD, Mary (b 1940)
American actress TW/24
CRAWFORD, Michael (b 1942)
English actor TW/23,
WWT/16
CRAWFORD, Mimi (d 1966 [61])
English actress, singer,
dancer WWT/5-8
CRAWFORD, Nan (d 1975 [82])
actress BP/60*, WWT/16*
CRAWFORD, Peter (d 1793)
treasurer, manager BD
CRAWFORD, Thomas (1750-94)
English actor, musician,
manager BD, GT
CRAWFORD, Mrs. Thomas
see Barry, Mrs. Spranger
CRAWFORD, William (d 1916)
comedian EA/18*
CRAWLEY, Mr. (fl 1695-c.
1727) puppeteer BD
CRAWLEY, Mr. (fl 1784) singer
BD
CRAWLEY, Miss see Cour-
tenay, Miss
CRAWLEY, Dan (d 1912 [40])
Irish comedian CDP, EA/
13*
CRAWLEY, J. Sayre see
Crawley, Sayre
CRAWLEY, Robert (b 1917)
American actor TW/4-5, 23
CRAWLEY, Sayre (1870-1948)
English actor SR, TW/4
CRAWSHAW, John (d 1871 [35])
musician EA/72*
CRAWSHAW, William James
(d 1913 [43]) EA/14*
CRAYFORD, Mrs. see Thorne,
Alice
CRAYTHORNE, James ["Rus-
sell"] (d 1887 [37]) music-
hall artist EA/88*
CREAMER, Harry (d 1894)
minstrel EA/95*
CREAMER, Henry (d 1891)

EA/92*
CREAN, Mrs. John see Rogers,
Maggie
CREBER, Theophilus (d 1902) pro-
prietor EA/03*
CRECRAFT, Elizabeth (d 1917 [97])
travelling show-woman EA/18*
CREE, Mrs. Douglas see Rorke,
Kate
CREED, Mr. (fl 1794-95) singer
BD
CREED [or Creede], Thomas (d
1616?) stationer DNB
CREEDON, John Barry (d 1900)
comedian EA/01*
CREEK, Thomas (fl 1668-70?)
actor? BD
CREEL, Frances (d 1957 [43])
actress TW/13
CREESE, D. (d 1917 [33]) manager
EA/18*
CREESE, René see Ray, René
CREESE, T. A. (fl 1860-66) Amer-
ican actor HAS
CREESE, Mrs. T. A. [née Eliza-
beth Perry] (b 1843) American
dancer, singer, actress HAS
CREGAN, David (b 1931) English
dramatist CD, WWT/15-16
CREGAR, Samuel Laird (1916-44)
American actor TW/1
CREHAN, Ada see Rehan, Ada
CREHAN, Joseph (d 1966 [82])
performer BP/50*
CREHAN, Kate see Byron, Mrs.
Oliver Doud
CREIGHTON, Anthony (b 1923)
Scottish actor, dramatist PDT
CRELIN, Mrs. E. W. see
D'Arville, Camille
CRELLIN, Herbert see Standing,
Herbert
CREMLIN, F. Canadian actor
GRB/1
CREMONINI, Clementina (fl 1763-
66) Italian singer BD
CREMONINI, Domenico (fl 1784-87)
Italian singer BD
CREMONINI, Giuseppe (1866-1903)
Italian singer ES
CREPE, Mlle. see D'Auberval,
Mme. Jean
CRESCENTINI, Girolamo (1762-
1846) Italian singer BD
CRESCIMANO, Mlle. (fl 1859)
singer HAS
CRESPI, Signora (fl 1773-86)
dancer BD

CRESPIN, Régine (b 1927)
French singer ES
CRESPION, Stephen (c. 1649-
1711) singer BD
CRESSALL, Maud (1886-1962)
English actress WWT/1-8
CRESSEA, Mrs. (fl 1698) im-
presario BD
CRESSETT, John (fl in Restora-
tion) impresario BD
CRESSON, James (b 1935)
American actor TW/18-19
CRESSWELL, Mr. (fl 1780-
1809?) actor BD
CRESSWELL, Helen (fl 1880)
actress DD
CRESSWELL, John (fl 1796-1814)
carpenter, scene painter,
machinist, chorus singer?
BD
CRESSWELL, Thomas (fl 1660-
79) trumpeter BD
CRESSY, Mrs. Will M. see
Dayne, Blanche
CRESSY, Will Martin (1863/65-
1930) American actor SR,
WWA/1, WWM, WWS
CREST, Robert (b 1938) Ameri-
can actor TW/28
CRESWELL, Helen (d 1949 [103])
actress BE*, WWT/14*
CRESWELL, Saylor (b 1939)
American actor TW/24, 30
CRESWICK, Charles Edward (d
1885 [35]) EA/86*
CRESWICK, Elizabeth [Mrs.
William Creswick] (d 1876
[67]) EA/77*
CRESWICK, Janette (d 1900)
EA/01*
CRESWICK, Mr. [W.?] (d 1792)
actor BD, TD/2
CRESWICK, William (1813-88)
English actor CDP, DD,
DNB, ES, HAS, OAA/1-2
CRESWICK, William see
Beswick, William
CRESWICK, Mrs. William see
Creswick, Elizabeth
CRETA, Joachim Frederic (fl
1729) horn player BD
CREVELLI, Signorina (fl 1825)
singer HAS
CREW, Mr. (d 1871) publisher
EA/72*
CREWE, Mr. (fl 1792) actor BD
CREWE, Bertie (d 1937 [74])
architect BE*, WWT/14*

CREWES, Jeremiah (fl 1630-65?)
drummer BD
CREWS, Laura Hope (1880-1942)
American actress CB, ES, SR,
WWS, WWT/1-9
CRIBARAI, Joe (d 1971 [51]) com-
poser/lyricist BP/56*
CRIBBINS, Bernard (b 1928) Eng-
lish actor WWT/15-16
CRICHTON, Haldane (d 1938 [85])
manager WWT/14*
CRICHTON, Kyle S. (1896-1960)
American dramatist BE*
CRICHTON, Madge (b 1881) English
actress GRB/1-4, WWS, WWT/
1-6
CRICK, Edmund (d 1886) EA/87*
CRIDER, Ethel Osborne (d 1975)
composer/lyricist BP/59*
CRIDLAND, Mr. (fl 1761-73)
boxkeeper BD
CRIDLAND, Howard (d 1917 [46])
EA/18*
CRIEVE, Mrs. (d 1787?) sweeper
BD
CRIGHTON, James (d 1902 [59])
steam circus proprietor EA/03*
CRIPPEN, Mr. (fl 1784) singer
BD
CRIPPEN, George [George Dele-
vanti] (d 1887 [39]) somersault
rider EA/88*
CRISAFULLI, Henri (d 1900 [72])
dramatist EA/01*
CRISCUOLO, Louis (b 1934) Amer-
ican actor TW/29
CRISHAM, Walter (b 1906) Ameri-
can actor, dancer WWT/9-14
CRISP, Mrs. (fl 1787) actress BD
CRISP, Miss (fl 1799) actress BD
CRISP, Charles (fl 1799-1821?)
actor, manager BD
CRISP, Donald (d 1974 [93]) per-
former BP/58*, WWT/16*
CRISP, Henry (fl 1754) dramatist
CP/1-3, GT, TD/1-2
CRISP, Henry (1844-82) actor CDP
CRISP, Henry (d 1906 [53]) actor
EA/07*, WWT/14*
CRISP, John (fl 1799-1819?) actor,
manager BD
CRISP, Samuel (1707-68) actor BD
CRISP, Samuel (d 1783 [76]) drama-
tist DD, DNB
CRISP, Mrs. Samuel [née Henrietta
Maria Tollett] (1709-80) actress,
dancer, singer BD
CRISP, W.H. (fl 1848) Irish actor

HAS, SR

CRISPE, Samuel see Crisp, Samuel

CRISPI, Signora see Crespi, Signora

CRISPI, Ida (fl 1900s) English actress, singer WWS

CRIST, Bainbridge (1883-1969) American composer WWA/5

CRISTIANI, Ernesto (d 1973 [91]) associated with circuses BP/58*

CRITCHETT, R. C. see Carton, R. C.

"CROAKER, Alley" (fl 1759) singer BD

CROCKER, Emerson (d 1971 [60]) producer/director/choreographer BP/56*

CROCKER, Emily Viola see Barrett, Mrs. J. H.

CROCKER, Henry (d 1937 [62]) producer, manager BE*, WWT/14*

CROCKER, John (d 1853) American actor HAS

CROCKER, Mrs. John (d 1853) HAS

CROCKER, John Paul (d 1869 [35]) minstrel proprietor & performer CDP

CROCKER, Sarah see Conway, Sarah

CROCKETT, James (1835-65) English circus performer HAS

CROCKETT, Sarah (d 1901 [78]) EA/03*

CROFT, Annie [or Anne] (1896-1959) English actress, singer WWT/5-10

CROFT, Henry (fl 1771-72) actor BD

CROFT, Michael (b 1922) English actor, Founder of British National Youth Theatre, director COC, ES, WWT/15-16

CROFT, Nita (b 1902) English actress, singer WWT/10-14

CROFT, Paddy English actress TW/25-30, WWT/16

CROFT, William (1678-1727) English organist, composer BD, DNB

CROFTON, Cecil (d 1935 [76]) actor, dramatist DD

CROFTON, Charles (d 1883)

actor EA/84*

CROFTS, Mr. (fl 1740-57?) actor, dancer? BD

CROFTS, Mrs. (fl 1680-87) actress BD

CROFTS, Mrs. (d 1778) BD

CROFTS, Miss (fl 1786-90) equestrienne, dancer, actress, singer BD

CROFTS, Mary (fl 1740-41) lamp woman BD

CROISETTE, Sophie (d 1901 [54]) actress WWT/14*

CROKE, Wentworth (1871-1930) English manager GRB/4, WWT/1-6

CROKER, John Wilson (1780-1857) writer DD

CROKER, T. F. Dillon (1831-1912) English dramatic journalist GRB/3-4, WWT/1

CROKER, Thomas Crofton (1798-1854) dramatist DD

CROKER-KING, C. H. (1873-1951) English actor GRB/1, WWT/4-9

CROLL, Don (b 1947) American actor TW/28

CROLY, George (1780-1860) Irish critic, dramatist DD, DNB, HP, NTH

CROME, Mrs. Michael Sharp see Crome, Teresa

CROME, Robert (fl c.1745-c.65) violinist, composer BD

CROME, Teresa [Mrs. Michael Sharp Crome] (d 1881) EA/82*

CROMMELYNCK, Fernand (1888-1970) Belgian dramatist COC

CROMPTON, Reginald (d 1945 [75]) English actor, singer GRB/1-3

CROMPTON, William H. (1843-1909) English actor CDP, GRB/3-4, PP/1

CROMWELL, Mr. (fl 1799-c.1860) actor HAS

CROMWELL, Cecil [Miss Pym] (d 1913) English actress GRB/1-4

CROMWELL, George Reed (d 1899) lecturer CDP

CROMWELL, John (b 1887/88) American actor, producer, producing manager AAS, BE, ES, TW/8-12, 28, WWT/6-16

CROMWELL, J. T. (b 1935) American actor TW/27-28

CROMWELL, Richard (d 1960 [50]) actor TW/17

CROMWELL, William Oliver
(d 1890 [55]) actor, acting
manager EA/91*
CRONE, Adeline (d 1962 [70])
performer BE*
CRONIN, Jane (b 1936) Ameri-
can actress TW/22, 29-30
CRONIN, John (d 1898) circus
musical director EA/99*
CRONIN, William (d 1911)
actor, dancer CDP
CRONIN, William Francis (1905-
65) American executive
WWA/4
CRONIN-SMYTHE (d 1889 [29])
singer, writer EA/90*
CRONYN, Carrie [Mrs. Frank
Curzon] Irish actress GRB/1
CRONYN, George William
(1888-1969) American
dramatist WWA/5
CRONYN, Hume (b 1911) Cana-
dian actor, director, writer
AAS, BE, CB, ES, TW/8-
23, 26, 28-30, WWT/12-16
CRONYN, Lizzie singer CDP
CRONYN, Tandy (b 1945) Amer-
ican actress TW/26-27, 29
CROOK, Miss (fl 1747-48)
actress BD
CROOK, John (d 1922) com-
poser, conductor DD, GRB/
1-4, WWT/1-4
CROOKE, Miss see Mason,
Mrs.
CROOKE, C. (d 1882 [57])
proprietor EA/83*
CROOKE, John (d 1882) musi-
cal director EA/84*
CROOKS, Alexander Richard
(d 1972 [72]) American
singer WWA/5
CROOME, Mr. (fl 1667) booth
operator BD
CROPPER, Roy (1898-1954)
American actor, singer
TW/10, WWT/9-11
CROPPONI, Mr. (fl 1733-34)
dancer, actor BD
CROSBIE, Richard (fl 1793)
Irish aeronaut CDP
CROSBY, Mr. (fl 1786) house
servant BD
CROSBY, Miss (fl 1800) singer
BD
CROSBY, Bing (1904-77) Amer-
ican singer CB
CROSBY, Charles A. manager

CDP
CROSBY, Edward Harold (d 1934
[75]) American dramatist, critic
BE*, BP/19*, WWT/14*
CROSBY, Edward John (d 1973 [73])
publicist BP/58*
CROSBY, Hazel (d 1964 [74]) per-
former BE*
CROSBY, James (d 1930) minstrel
SR
CROSBY, J. H. (b 1830) American
manager SR
CROSBY, John (d 1724) actor BD
CROSBY, Joseph (b 1922) American
executive BE
CROSBY, Juliette (d 1969 [73])
actress TW/25
CROSBY, L. V. H. (d 1884 [60])
singer, composer, minstrel
CDP
CROSBY, Sir Richard (fl 1793)
Irish actor HAS
CROSBY, Wade (d 1975 [65]) per-
former BP/60*
CROSBY-BELASCO, Juliet (d 1907
[30]) actress WWT/14*
CROSDILL, John (1751?-1825)
English musician BD, DNB
CROSDILL, Richard (1698-70)
violoncellist BD
CROSE, Mr. (fl 1794) double-bass
player BD
CROSLAND, Mrs. W. H. see
Rutland, Ruth
CROSMAN, Mr. (fl 1762) viola
d'amore player BD
CROSMAN, Henrietta [Mrs. Maurice
Campbell] (1865-1944) American
actress ES, GRB/2-4, WWA/2,
WWM, WWS, WWT/1-9
CROSMAN, Shirley Elizabeth see
Conway, Shirl
CROSMOND, Hélène see Turner,
Helena
CROSS, Mr. (fl c.1745?) animal
tamer BD
CROSS, Mr. (fl 1772-91?) actor
BD
CROSS, Mrs. see Bradshaw, Mrs.
CROSS, Miss (fl 1740-41) actress?
BD
CROSS, Alfred B. (d 1910 [56])
actor EA/96
CROSS, Mrs. Alfred B. see
Cross, Mary
CROSS, Mrs. A. W. see Gold,
Belle
CROSS, Benjamin (1786-1857) CDP

CROSS, Beverley (b 1931) English dramatist, director, actor AAS, CD, WWT/14-16

CROSS, Douglas (d 1975 [54]) composer/lyricist BP/59*

CROSS, Edward (d 1854 [81]) menagerie proprietor EA/72*

CROSS, Emily (d 1884) actress CDP

CROSS, Emily [Mrs. M. E. Jobling] (d 1904) actress, singer DD

CROSS, George (d 1800?) violinist? BD

CROSS, Jack (d 1904) comedian EA/05*

CROSS, James C. (d c.1810) English actor, proprietor, acting manager, dramatist CP/3, DD, ES, GT, TD/1-2

CROSS, Jessie [Mrs. Clifford Bown] (d 1903) actress EA/04*

CROSS, Joan (b 1900) English singer, director ES

CROSS, John Cartwright (d 1809) actor, dramatist, manager BD

CROSS, Mrs. [John Cartwright? Mrs. Gilbert Hamilton] (fl 1790-93) singer, actress BD

CROSS, Joseph C. (d 1877) singer EA/78*

CROSS, Julian (1851-1925) English actor, dramatist DD, GRB/1-4, WWT/1-5

CROSS, Mrs. Julian see Cross, Sophie

CROSS, Letitia (c.1677-1737) singer, dancer BD

CROSS, Margaret (d 1913) EA/14*

CROSS, Marie ["George Eliot"] (d 1880 [57]) EA/82*

CROSS, Mary [Mrs. Alfred B. Cross] (d 1904) EA/05*

CROSS, Max (d 1900) scene artist EA/01*

CROSS, Richard (fl c.1695?-1725) actor BD

CROSS, Richard (d 1760) prompter, actor, dancer BD, TD/1-2

CROSS, Richard (fl 1748-60) actor, dancer, violinist BD

CROSS, Mrs. Richard [née Frances Shireburn] (1707-81) actress, singer BD

CROSS, Sophia (d 1884 [73]) actress EA/85*

CROSS, Sophie [Mrs. Julian Cross] (d 1910) EA/11*

CROSS, Thomas (b c.1630) treasurer BD

CROSS, Thomas (d 1737) numberer BD

CROSS, Wellington (d 1975 [88]) performer BP/60*

CROSS, William (d 1900 [57]) wild animal importer EA/01*

CROSS, Mrs. William (d 1891) EA/92*

CROSSAN, Mrs. W. H. (d 1880) actress EA/81*

CROSSARO, Signor (fl 1787-89) Italian dancer BD

CROSSE, Edward (d 1907 [56]) musical director, composer EA/08*

CROSSE, Mrs. Edward see Crosse, Mary

CROSSE, Gay S. (d 1971 [54]) musician BP/55*

CROSSE, Mary [Mrs. Edward Crosse] (d 1911 [50]) EA/12*

CROSSE, Nicholas (fl 1607) actor DA

CROSSE, Rupert (d 1973 [45]) performer BP/57*

CROSSE, Samuel (fl 1594?-1623?) actor DA, GT

CROSSFIELD, Mr. (fl 1698-99) singer BD

CROSSLAND, Maggie [Mrs. Victor Gouriet] (d 1904) EA/05*

CROSSLEY, Ada [Mrs. Muecke] Australian singer GRB/1

CROSSLEY-TAYLOR, E. W. (d 1963 [68]) manager BE*

CROSSLING, Tom (d 1873) Negro minstrel EA/74*

CROSSMAN, Master (fl 1785-93) equestrian BD

CROSSMAN, Harriet (d 1875 [35]) actress EA/76*

CROSSMAN, Henrietta (1865-1944) American actress SR, TW/1

CROSSMAN, John (fl 1787-1817) equestrian, dancer BD

CROSWELL, Anne [née Mary Ann Pearson] American lyricist, writer BE

CROSWELL, Joseph (fl 1802?) American? dramatist EAP

CROTCH, William (1775-1847) English musician, composer, teacher BD, CDP, DNB

CROTHERS, Rachel (1878-1958) American dramatist, producing manager AAS, COC, ES, GRB/3-4, HJD, MD, MH, MWD, NTH, OC/2-3, RE, SR, TW/15, WWA/3, WWM, WWT/1-11

CROTTY, Leslie (d 1903 [50]) singer EA/04*, WWT/14*

CROUCH, Mr. (fl 1743) actor BD

CROUCH, Mrs. [née S. Phillips] (fl 1834) actress HAS

CROUCH, Anna Maria see Crouch, Mrs. Rawlings Edward

CROUCH, Frederick William Nichols (1808-96) English musician SR

CROUCH, Harry (d 1893) comedian EA/94*

CROUCH, Jack H. (b 1918) American educator BE

CROUCH, John (fl 1679-1710?) violinist, dancing master? BD

CROUCH, John (1762-93) instrumentalist BD

CROUCH, Mrs. Rawlings Edward [née Anna Maria Phillips] (1763-1805) English actress, singer BD, CDP, DD, DNB, OX, TD/1-2

CROUCH, William (1749-1833) instrumentalist BD

CROUESTE, Edwin (1841-91) English circus clown HAS

CROUESTE, George John Coney (d 1881 [18]) EA/82*

CROUESTE, Harry ["Queen's Jester"] (d 1891) circus clown EA/92*

CROUSE (fl 17th cent?) dramatist FGF

CROUSE, Russel (1893-1966) American dramatist, producer, writer BE, CB, COC, ES, HJD, MH, MWD, NTH, SR, TW/2-8, 22, WWT/10-14, WWW/6

CROUTA, Mr. (fl 1837) American actor HAS

CROW (fl 1740) Irish? porter CDP

CROWDEN, Graham (b 1922) Scottish actor AAS, WWT/15-16

CROWDEN, Roy see Royston, Roy

CROWDER, Charles (d 1887 [69]) EA/88*

CROWDER, Mrs. Charles (d 1893 [56]) EA/94*

CROWDER, Charles S. (d 1889) proprietor EA/90*

CROWDER, Jack (b 1939) American actor TW/24-26

CROWDER, John (d 1674) trumpeter BD

CROWDY, James (d 1909 [61]) proprietor EA/10*

CROWE, Mrs see Bateman, Mrs.

CROWE, Charles Henry (d 1900 [65]) EA/01*

CROWE, [Eleanor?] (fl 1796-1801) actress BD

CROWE, Ellen Beatrice (d 1974 [78]) performer BP/58*

CROWE, George (d 1889 [47]) EA/90*

CROWE, Gillian (b 1934) English executive BE

CROWE, Gwyllym (d 1894) conductor EA/95*

CROWE, Sidney (b 1871) English actress DD, EA/97, GRB/1-2

CROWE, William (fl 1792-96) dancer BD

CROWE, Mrs. William [née Jane Rowson] (fl 1791-99) dancer BD

CROWHURST, Alfred (d 1878 [33]) equestrian director EA/79*

CROWHURST, Charles (d 1891 [60]) EA/93*

CROWHURST, Charles (d 1892) EA/94*

CROWHURST, Mary (d 1886 [79]) EA/87*

CROWLEY, Mr. (fl 1845) actor HAS

CROWLEY, Alice (d 1972 [88]) co-founder of the Neighbourhood Playhouse BP/56*

CROWLEY, Ann (b 1929) American actress TW/3-11

CROWLEY, Dick (b 1929) American actor TW/26

CROWLEY, Edward (b 1926) American actor TW/24-26, 28, 30

CROWLEY, Mart (b 1935) American dramatist CD, MH, WWT/16

CROWLEY, Pat (b 1934) American actress TW/7-11

CROWNE, John (1640?-1703/04/

12/14) English dramatist
COC, CP/1-3, DAB, DD,
DNB, ES, GT, HP, MH,
OC/1-3, WWA/H
"CROWQUILL, Alfred" see For-
rester, Alfred Henry
CROWSON, Will (d 1905) EA/
06*
CROWTHER, Mr. (fl 1782) actor
BD
CROWTHER, Amelia Augusta
[Mrs. T. H. Crowther] (d
1890) EA/91*
CROWTHER, Mrs. Benjamin
see Vincent, Eliza
CROWTHER, F. C. (d 1884 [34])
journalist EA/85*
CROWTHER, John (d 1879 [37])
promoter EA/80*
CROWTHER, Leslie (b 1933)
English actor WWT/15-16
CROWTHER, Richard (d 1871
[21]) clog dancer EA/72*
CROWTHER, Mrs. T. H. see
Crowther, Amelia Augusta
CROX, Elvia [Mrs. T. Q.
Seabrooke] (d 1911) actress
WWT/14*
CROXALL, Dr. Samuel (d 1752)
English dramatist CP/2-3,
GT
CROXTON, Arthur (b 1868)
English manager WWT/4-5
CROXTON, Darryl (b 1946)
American actor TW/26
CROYDON, Joan (b 1908) Amer-
ican actress TW/11
CROZA, John Francis (fl 1748-
50) manager BD
CROZIER, Miss (fl 1742)
dancer, singer BD
CROZIER, Charles (b 1852)
English dramatist, actor,
acting manager GRB/1-2
CROZIER, Eric (b 1904) English
librettist, director ES
CROZIER, Robert American
actor TW/7
CROZIER, Temple Edgcumbe
(d 1896 [24]) actor EA/97*
CRUDDAS, Audrey (b 1914)
South African designer ES
CRUDGE, Alexander (d 1759)
doorkeeper, housekeeper BD
CRUFT, Mrs. (d 1858) English?
HAS
CRUICKSHANK, Andrew (b 1907)
Scottish actor AAS, TW/8,

WWT/9-16
CRUICKSHANK, Gladys (b 1902)
English actress, singer WWT/
6-7
CRUICKSHANK, Jessie [Mrs. Wil-
liam C. Cruickshank] (d 1892)
EA/93*
CRUICKSHANK, Mrs. William C.
see Cruickshank, Jessie
CRUIKSHANK, A. Stewart (1877-
1949) Scottish manager WWT/
7-10
CRUIKSHANK, Stewart (1908-66)
Scottish manager WWT/10-14
CRUIKSHANK, Victor (d 1882)
actor EA/83*
"CRUIKSHANK OF AMERICA, The"
see Johnson, David
CRUIKSHANKS, Charles (1844-1928)
actor WWT/3-5
CRUIKSHANKS, Charles C. (d 1904
[39]) actor EA/05*
CRUIKSHANKS, William C. (d 1902
[57]) clown, jester EA/03*
CRUISE, Anna see Cowell, Anna
CRUISE, Mrs. Henry (d 1884)
pianist EA/86*
CRUISE, John H. (d 1906 [46])
performer? EA/07*
CRUISE, Marie [Mrs. R. Barker]
(d 1887 [56]) actress EA/88*
CRUMMIT, Frank (1889-1943)
American actor, songwriter
CB, SR
CRUSE, Annie [née Dashwood] (d
1868 [23]) singer EA/69*
CRUTCHLEY, Rosalie (b 1921)
English actress WWT/10-15
CRUTCHLOW, F. E. [Mrs. Thomas
Crutchlow] (d 1899 [51]) EA/00*
CRUTCHLOW, Mrs. Thomas see
Crutchlow, F. E.
CRUTTWELL, Hugh (b 1918) Eng-
lish director, principal of the
Royal Academy of Dramatic Art
WWT/14-16
CRUVELLI, Mlle. (fl 1859) singer
HAS
CRUVELLI, Marie (d 1868) EA/69*
CRUYS, Francis (fl 1673-1700)
violinist BD
CRUYS, Samuel CDP
CRUZE, James (1884-1942) Ameri-
can actor ES
CRYER, Charles Henry [Vitelo] (d
1916 [24]) weight-lifter EA/17*
CRYER, David (b 1936) American
actor, singer TW/20, 24-30,

WWT/16

CRYER, Gretchen (b 1935) American actress, librettist CD, TW/24, 30

CSIRSCU, Eugene (d 1970 [53]) musician BP/55*

CUBAS, Isabella (1831-64) Spanish dancer CDP, HAS

CUBIT, Mr. (fl 1794-1807) musician BD

CUBITT, Miss see Jackson, Charlotte

CUBITT, Marie Caroline (b 1800) actress BS, CDP, OX

CUBITT, William (fl 1775-1830?) actor, singer, violinist, dancer? BD, TD/1-2

CUCKOW, Mr. see Curco, Mr.

CUDD, Leslie (d 1916) EA/17*

CUDDY, Edward flautist CDP

CUDMORE, Richard (1787-1840) English instrumentalist, composer BD, DNB

CUDWORTH, Mr. (fl c.1675-91) actor BD

CUDWORTH, Mr. (fl 1794) violinist BD

CUENCA, Pedro Fernandez (d 1940) actor BE*, WWT/14*

CUERTON, Mr. (fl 1800-04) dancer, whistler BD

CUKA, Frances (b 1936) English actress AAS, WWT/13-16

CUKOR, George (b 1899) American director BE, CB, ES, SR

CULBERTSON, Ernest H. (d 1972 [86]) executive BP/57*

CULCUP, The Misses (fl 1797) actresses BD

CULEEN, James Edward (d 1909 [29]) business manager EA/10*

CULHANE, Will E. actor, manager SR

CULL, Mrs. see Bennett, Fanny

CULL, Cecil (d 1875 [33]) singer EA/76*

CULLEN, Mr. (fl c.1810?) actor CDP

CULLEN, Bernard (d 1883) actor EA/84*

CULLEN, Edward L. (1899-1964) American actor BE

CULLEN, Richard Limmere (d 1900 [45]) scene artist EA/02*

CULLEN, Rose [Mrs. Albert Tuck] (d 1888) actress DD

CULLENFORD, George Everett (d 1881 [57]) actor EA/82*

CULLENFORD, Thomasin Catherine [Mrs. William Cullenford] (d 1890 [82]) EA/91*

CULLENFORD, William (d 1874 [77]) secretary of the Royal General Theatrical Fund EA/75*, WWT/14*

CULLENFORD, Mrs. William see Cullenford, Thomasin Catherine

CULLEY, Frederick (1879-1942) English actor WWT/8-9

CULLEY, Jane (b 1943) American actress TW/29

CULLIFORD, C. J. (d 1893) printer EA/94*

CULLINAN, Ralph (d 1950 [68]) actor TW/6

CULLING, Mrs. Greek/English actress GRB/1

CULLING, Ada Clare [Mrs. Otto C. Culling] (d 1903 [31]) EA/05*

CULLING, Mrs. Otto C. see Culling, Ada Clare

CULLIS, Brian (d 1969 [41]) performer BP/53*

CULLMAN, Howard S. (1891-1972) American investor, executive BE, TW/29

CULLMAN, Marguerite [née Sanders] author, investor BE

CULLUM, Mrs. (fl 1775) dramatist CP/3

CULLUM, Jim, Sr. (d 1973 [59]) musician BP/58*

CULLUM, John (b 1930) American actor, singer TW/22-30, WWT/16

CULMER, Lee (d 1965) performer BP/50*

CULP, Robert (b 1930) American actor TW/13

CULVER, Mr. (fl 1772-94) singer BD

CULVER, D. Jay (1902-68) American journalist, photographer BE

CULVER, Roland (b 1900) English actor AAS, BE, ES, TW/22-23, WWT/9-16

CUMBER, John (fl 1616-23) actor DA

CUMBERBIRCH, Lilian (d 1903 [20]) musician EA/05*

CUMBERLAND, Gerald (1879-1926)

English critic, dramatist
WWT/2-5, WWW/2

CUMBERLAND, John (1787-1866)
publisher DD

CUMBERLAND, John (b 1880)
Canadian actor WWT/4-8

CUMBERLAND, Richard (1732-
1811) English dramatist
CDP, COC, CP/1-3, DD,
DNB, ES, GT, HP, MH,
NTH, OC/1-3, SR, TD/1-2

CUMMENS, Ellen [Nellie] (d
1905 [54]) American actress
CDP

CUMMING, Gordon (d 1866
[47]) "lion hunter" EA/72*

CUMMING, Ruth (d 1967 [63])
actress, singer TW/24

CUMMINGS, Arthur see Cum-
mings, Richard

CUMMINGS, Bob (b 1910) American actor, producer BE

CUMMINGS, Clara (d 1894 [15])
singer EA/95*

CUMMINGS, Constance [née
Halverstadt] (b 1910) Amer-
ican actress AAS, BE, ES,
TW/1-7, 25-26, WWT/8-16

CUMMINGS, Cyril (d 1912 [39])
EA/13*

CUMMINGS, E. E. (1894-1962)
American dramatist HJD,
MD, MH, MWD

CUMMINGS, Irving (1889-1959)
American actor ES, TW/15

CUMMINGS, Jennie see Dreher,
Virginia

CUMMINGS, Minnie actress
CDP

CUMMINGS, Richard (d 1872)
singer EA/73*

CUMMINGS, Richard (d 1916)
EA/17*

CUMMINGS, Robert (b 1910)
American actor CB, ES,
TW/8, 22-23

CUMMINGS, Vicki (1913-69)
American actress BE, TW/
1-17, 23-24, 26, WWT/11-14

CUMMINS, Mr. actor TD/2

CUMMINS, Alexander (fl 1818)
manager WWA/H

CUMMINS, Geraldine Dorothy
(1890-1969) dramatist WWW/6

CUMMINS, Margaret (d 1879)
EA/80*

CUMMINS, Peggy (b 1925) Welsh
actress ES, WWT/10-11

CUNARD, Grace (d 1967 [73]) performer BP/51*

CUNARD, James (d 1912) performer? EA/13*

CUNARD, Lance (b 1910) American
actor TW/22-23, 25-26

CUNDALL, Henry (d 1627) actor
GT

CUNDELL, Edric (d 1961 [67])
director WWT/14*

CUNINGHAM, Peter (d 1869 [53])
critic WWT/14*

CUNINGHAM, Philip [Philip Harold
Boosey] (1865-1928) English actor
GRB/1-4, WWT/1-5

CUNINGHAME, Charles [Charles
John Cuninghame Minney] (b
1850) English actor, agent
GRB/1

CUNLIFFE, Jerry (b 1935) American actor TW/28

CUNLIFFE, John William (1865-1946)
English scholar WWW/4

CUNNINGHAM, Annie (d 1916 [64])
EA/17*

CUNNINGHAM, Arthur (1869-1944)
Canadian singer SR

CUNNINGHAM, Arthur (d 1955 [67])
musical comedy actor TW/12

CUNNINGHAM, Claude (b 1880)
English singer WWM

CUNNINGHAM, Dan (b 1917) English
actor TW/8

CUNNINGHAM, Edward (d 1880)
comic vocalist EA/81*

CUNNINGHAM, Francis (1820-75)
scholar DNB

CUNNINGHAM, George (d 1962 [58])
actor, choreographer, director
BE*

CUNNINGHAM, Harry (d 1878) actor,
agent EA/79*

CUNNINGHAM, James see Seymour, James

CUNNINGHAM, John (1729-73) Irish
actor, dramatist CDP, CP/2-3,
DD, DNB, GT, HP, TD/1-2

CUNNINGHAM, John (b 1932) American actor TW/24-28

CUNNINGHAM, Josias (fl 1765)
dramatist CP/2-3, GT

CUNNINGHAM, Merce (b 1922)
American choreographer, dancer
CB, CD, ES

CUNNINGHAM, Minnie (1853-1924)
actress CDP

CUNNINGHAM, Paul (1890-1960)
American composer WWA/4

CUNNINGHAM, Peter (fl c.
1852?) writer DD
CUNNINGHAM, Peter C. (fl
1836-60) Scottish actor
CDP, HAS
CUNNINGHAM, Mrs. Peter C.
see Cunningham, Virginia
CUNNINGHAM, Richard D. (fl
1861) American actor HAS
CUNNINGHAM, Robert (b 1866)
Tasmanian actor, singer
WWT/6-8
CUNNINGHAM, Robert (b 1921)
American actor TW/6-8
CUNNINGHAM, Ronnie (b 1923)
American actor TW/2-3,
23
CUNNINGHAM, Ruby Hale White
(d 1971 [79]) performer
BP/55*
CUNNINGHAM, Sarah (b 1918)
American actress TW/22-
23, 26, 29
CUNNINGHAM, [Thomas?] (fl
1795-1817?) actor BD
CUNNINGHAM, Virginia [Mrs.
Peter C. Cunningham; Mrs.
Charles Pope; Mrs. John D.
German] (1834-74) actress
CDP
CUNNINGHAM, W. (fl 1733-54?)
dancer, singer, actor BD
CUNNINGHAM, Zamah (d 1967
[74]) American actress TW/
1, 22, 24
CUNNINGTON, Phillis writer
BE
CUOZZO, Alberta American
actress TW/25-26
CUPER, Boyder (fl c.1691)
proprietor BD
CUPER, John (fl 1717) proprietor
BD
CURCO, Mr. (fl 1687-1700)
singer BD
CURIONI, Rosa (fl 1754-62)
Italian singer BD
CURKAW, Mr. see Curco, Mr.
CURLL, Edmund (d 1747 [72])
publisher WWT/14*
CURNOCK, Richard (b 1922)
English actor TW/26, 28-29
CURNOW, Allen (b 1911) New
Zealand dramatist CD
CURRAH, Brian (b 1929) English
designer WWT/15-16
CURRAN, Homer F. (d 1952)
American producer BE*,

BP/37*
CURRAN, Paul (b 1913) English
actor AAS
CURRANS, Mrs. J. W. (d 1904)
EA/06*
CURRER, Elizabeth (fl 1673-1743?)
actress BD
CURRIE, Clive (1877-1935) English
actor, producer WWT/5-7
CURRIE, Finlay (1878-1968) Scot-
tish actor ES, WWT/8-14
CURRIE, Thomas A. (b 1929)
American talent representative
BE
CURRIER, Frank (d 1928 [71])
actor BE*, BP/12*
CURRY, Mr. (fl 1708-16) boxkeeper
BD
CURRY, Henry J. (d 1907 [61])
entertainment director EA/08*
CURRY, Mrs. Henry James see
Curry, Selina
CURRY, Mason (b 1906/08) Cana-
dian actor TW/2, 7-8
CURRY, Selina [Mrs. Henry James
Curry] (d 1887 [39]) EA/88*
CURRY, Thomas (b 1855) English
organist GRB/1
CURRY, Winnie Garland (d 1973)
performer BP/57*
CURRYER, Mr. (fl 1744-47) office-
keeper BD
CURTEEN, Mr. (fl 1772-95) box-
keeper BD
CURTEN, Miss (fl 1791-95) house
servant? performer? BD
CURTET, Pierre (fl 1762-74)
dancer BD
CURTEYS, James (fl 1509-11)
member of the Chapel Royal
DA
CURTI, Carlos musical director,
composer CDP
CURTIES, Mr. (fl 1794-1801), actor,
singer BD
CURTIN, Phyllis (b 1922?) American
singer CB
CURTIS, Alan (d 1953 [43]) Ameri-
can actor BE*
CURTIS, Allen (d 1861 [84]) actor
BE*
CURTIS, Arthur John Powles (d
1916) actor EA/17*
CURTIS, Beatrice see White,
Beatrice
CURTIS, Donald (b 1915) American
actor TW/5-7
CURTIS, Donna (b 1938) American

actress TW/24, 29
CURTIS, G. W. P. (1824-92)
American dramatist SR
CURTIS, Jack (d 1970 [44])
performer BP/55*
CURTIS, Jackie (b 1947) American dramatist, director, actor CD
CURTIS, Keene (b 1923) American actor, production stage manager BE, TW/22-29, WWT/15-16
CURTIS, King (d 1971 [37]) musician BP/56*
CURTIS, May singer CDP
CURTIS, M. B. (1851-1921?) actor CDP, SR
CURTIS, Samuel (d 1906 [23]) singer? EA/07*
CURTIS, Samuel J. (b 1867) American singer, vaudevillian CDP, WWM
CURTIS, Tony (b 1925) American actor CB
CURTIS, Walter (d 1910) entertainer EA/11*
CURTIS, W. H. (b 1809) American actor HAS
CURTISS, Alice May [Mrs. Thomas Courtice] (d 1917) EA/18*
CURTISS, Charles M. (d 1899) EA/00*
CURTISS, George [Robert J. H. de Courcy] English actor GRB/1
CURTISS, Sydney (d 1916 [8]) EA/17*
CURTISS, Sydney W. see Courtice, Thomas
CURTIZ, David (d 1962 [68]) Hungarian actor BE*
CURTO, Gregorio (1805-87) Spanish singer, composer NYM
CURTZ, Mlle. (fl 1769-76) dancer BD
CURVIN, Jonathan W. (b 1911) American educator BE
CURWEN, John Spencer (d 1916 [68]) EA/17*
CURWEN, Patric (1884-1949) English actor WWT/6-10
CURZ, Mlle. see Curtz, Mlle.
CURZON, Frank A. (1868-1927) English manager, lessee, actor ES, GRB/1-4, WWT/1-5, WWW/2

CURZON, Mrs. Frank [A.] see Cronyn, Carrie
CURZON, George (1898-1976) English actor TW/6, WWT/6-14
CUSACK, Cyril (b 1910) South African/Irish actor, manager AAS, BE, ES, WWT/11-16
CUSACK, Philip (b 1934) American actor TW/23, 26, 28
CUSHING, Catherine Chisholm (d 1952) American dramatist SR, WWT/4-10
CUSHING, Charles C. S. see Cushing, Tom
CUSHING, Henry W. (d 1899 [56]) EA/00*
CUSHING, John (1719-90) actor BD
CUSHING, Mrs. John (fl 1743-51) actress, singer BD
CUSHING, Mary W. (d 1974 [80s]) critic BP/59*
CUSHING, Peter (b 1913) English actor AAS, ES, WWT/11-16
CUSHING, Tom (1879-1941) American dramatist CB, WWA/1, WWT/5-9
CUSHING, Winnifred American actress TW/5-7
CUSHMAN, Alice (b 1861) American actress HAS
CUSHMAN, Asa (b 1833) American actress HAS
CUSHMAN, Charles Augustus (d 1896 [78]) EA/97*
CUSHMAN, Charlotte Saunders (1816-76) American actress CDP, COC, DAB, DD, ES, HAS, HJD, NTH, OC/1-3, SR, WWA/H
CUSHMAN, Corlene [Mrs. Ike Jones] (d 1894) singer EA/96*
CUSHMAN, Emma (fl 1856) English? actress HAS
CUSHMAN, Frank (1853-1907) minstrel CDP
CUSHMAN, Nancy (b 1913) American actress BE, TW/9, 21-23, 29
CUSHMAN, Major Pauline (1833-93) American actress CDP, DAB, HAS, WWA/H
CUSHMAN, Reuben Adcock (d 1906 [63]) Negro performer EA/07*
CUSHMAN, Sadie actress CDP
CUSHMAN, Susan Webb (1822-59) American actress CDP, DAB, HAS, OC/1-3, SR, WWA/H
CUSICK, Polly [Mrs. Charles Rezene] (d 1903 [37]) seriocomic EA/04*

CUSINS, Sir William George (d 1893 [60]) master of the Queen's music EA/94*

CUSSANS, Mrs. [Mrs. Higginson; Mrs. Egerson] (fl 1797-1800) actress BD

CUSSANS, John P. (fl 1797-1803) actor, singer BD, TD/1-2

CUSSANS, William see Cussans, John P.

CUSTANCE, Richard L. (d 1873) musician EA/74*

CUSTIS, George Washington Parke (1781-1857) American dramatist DAB, EAP, ES, HJD, RJ, WWA/H

CUSTONELLI, Signora (fl 1752) singer BD

CUTHBERT, Mr. (fl 1743-55) actor BD

CUTHBERT, Mrs. (fl 1708-26) dresser BD

CUTHBERT, Mrs. (fl 1743-55) actress BD

CUTHBERT, Agnes [Mrs. Alfred Cuthbert] (d 1891) EA/92*

CUTHBERT, Mrs. Alfred see Cuthbert, Agnes

CUTHBERT, Edmund (d 1908) actor? EA/09*

CUTHBERT, Henry John (d 1888 [78]) scene artist EA/89*

CUTHBERT, Ian Holm see Holm, Ian

CUTHBERT, Maud see Robini, Mrs. Alf

CUTHBERT, Mrs. P. G. (d 1878 [83]) actress EA/79*

CUTHBERT, Robert Arthur (d 1903 [33]) EA/04*

CUTHBERT, Thomas (d 1737) violinist, copyist BD

CUTHBERTSON, Miss (fl 1793) dramatist CP/3

CUTHBERTSON, Iain (b 1930) Scottish actress, director WWT/15-16

CUTLER, James (fl c.1605) member of the Chapel Royal DA

CUTLER, James (fl 1678-83) singer BD

CUTLER, Kate [Mrs. Sydney Ellison] (1870-1955) English actress, singer DD, GRB/1-4, WWT/1-11

CUTLER, Lucy A. (fl 1849-54)

American actress HAS

CUTLER, Peggy [Mrs. Douglas Furber] (d 1945) actress BE*, WWT/14*

CUTLER, Robert Frye (d 1976 [75]) producer/director/choreographer BP/60*

CUTLER, William Henry (b 1792) English musician DNB

CUTNER, Sidney B. (d 1971 [68]) composer/lyricist BP/56*

CUTTER, Mrs. George Albert (b 1873) American composer WWA/5

CUTTER, William F. (d 1866) comedian HAS

CUTTI, Bertha (1887-1948) Italian singer SR

CUTTING, Master (b 1718) singer BD

CUTTS, G. W. (d 1916) EA/17*

CUTTS, John (fl 1745) dramatist CP/1-3, GT

CUTTS, John English actor TW/28

CUTTS, Patricia (1931-74) English actress BE, TW/22-23

CUVILLIER, Charles (b 1879) French composer WWT/4

CUYLER, Margaret [Mrs. Dominic Rice] (1758-1814) English actress BD, CDP, TD/1-2

CUZZONI, Francesca [Signora Pietro Giuseppe Sandoni; Signora San-Antonio Ferre] (c. 1700-70) Italian singer BD, CDP

CWIKOWSKI, Bill (b 1945) American actor TW/29

CYMBER, Miss (fl 1747) actress BD

CYPHER, Jon (b 1932) American actor TW/22-23, 25-27, 30

CYPKIN, Diane (b 1948) German actress TW/27, 29-30

CZAJOWSKI, Maryan see Lester, The Great

CZAKO, Glenn R. (b 1949) American actor TW/27

CZETTEL, Ladislaus (1894/1904-1949) Hungarian/American costume designer CB, TW/2-5

CZILLAG, Rose (d 1892) singer EA/93*

CZINNER, Paul (d 1972 [82]) producer/director/choreographer BP/57*

- D -

D., Jr., Mr. (fl 1766-67) pro-
perty man BD
D., D. (fl 1633) dramatist
CP/1-3
D., I. dramatist CP/1-2
D., J. (fl 1640-74) dramatist
CP/3, FGF
D., R. dramatist CP/1
D., T. dramatist CP/1
DAB see Dob
DABBS, Dr. G. H. R. (d 1913)
dramatist DD
DABDOUB, Jack American actor
TW/25-29
DABELL, Mr. (fl 1772) actor
BD
DABNEY, Kathleen (b 1942)
American actress TW/24, 28
DABOLL, William S. (d 1892)
actor CDP
DABORNE, Robert (d 1628)
dramatist, patentee CP/1-3,
DA, DD, DNB, FGF
DABOVILLE, Mons. (d 1883)
pianist EA/84*
DACE, Mr. (fl 1735) dancer
BD
D'ACE, Annie [Mrs. Charles
D'Ace] (d 1894 [39]) EA/95*
D'ACE, Mrs. Charles see
D'Ace, Annie
DA COSTA, Mrs. [née Kent;
Mrs. H. Knight] (fl 1837-52)
English actress HAS
DACOSTA, Albert Lloyd (1928-
67) American singer WWA/5
DA COSTA, Morton [né Morton
Tecosky] (b 1914) American
director, actor, producer
BE, TW/2, 6-9, WWT/13-16
DACRE, Lady see Brand,
Barbarina
DACRE, Arthur [né Culver
James] (d 1895) actor CDP,
DD, DP
DACRE, Mrs. Arthur see
Roselle, Amy
DACRE, Harry composer CDP
DACRE, Helena actress EA/97
DACRE, H. S. (d 1918 [68])
EA/19*
DACRES, Mr. (fl 1661) actor
BD
DACRES, Andrew (d 1669)
painter BD
DACROY, Owen (b 1859) English

actor, acting manager GRB/1
DADSWELL, Pearl (d 1963 [47])
performer BE*
DAGGETT, Robert True (d 1975
[71]) performer BP/60*
DAGLISH, Master (fl 1790) actor
BD
DAGLISH, Thomas (fl 1776-94)
music copyist, house servant
BD
DAGMAR, Anna Lang Wolseley
(d 1917) EA/18*
DAGMAR, James (d 1903 [76])
circus performer EA/04*
DAGMAR, Marie (d 1925) actress
EA/97
DAGNALL, Mr. (fl 1661) singer
BD
DAGNALL, Ells (1863/68-1935)
English actor, producer, stage
manager GRB/1, WWT/1-7
DAGNALL, Thomas C. (d 1926
[46]) manager WWT/5
D'AGOSTINO, Albert (b 1893) Amer-
ican scene designer ES
D'AGUILAR, Rose (fl 1799?) trans-
lator CP/3
DAHL, Arlene American actress
TW/10
DAHMEN, Hermanus (1755-1830)
Dutch horn player BD
DAHMEN, Wilhelm (b 1769) Dutch
horn player BD
DAHURON, [Francis?] (fl 1719-28)
flutist, singer BD
DAI, Lin (d 1964 [33]) actress BE*
DAILEY, Dan (b 1915) American
actor, singer, dancer TW/22-
23, 25-26, WWT/16
DAILEY, Irene (b 1920) American
actress, teacher BE, TW/19-
22, 24, WWT/15-16
DAILEY, Jack (b 1883) American
actor TW/2
DAILEY, J. W. (d 1976 [74])
publicist BP/60*
DAILEY, Peter (1868-1908) Ameri-
can actor NTH, WWS
DAILING, David American dramatist
RJ
DAINE, Lois (b 1941) English act-
ress TW/22
DAINTON, Marie (1877/80/81/83-
1938) English actress GRB/1-4,
WWT/1-8
DAIPER, H. W. (d 1911) EA/12*
DAIROLLES, Adrienne (fl 1888-97)
actress DD

DALBERG, Camilla (b 1880) German actress, singer GRB/1-4

D'ALBERG, Rose singer CDP

DALBERG, Baron Wolfgang Heribert von (1750-1806) producer BE*

D'ALBERT, George (d 1884) comedian EA/86*

D'ALBERT, George (d 1949 [71]) singer, performer CDP

D'ALBERTE, Albert David (d 1903) high-rope walker EA/04*

D'ALBERTE, Julia (d 1912 [57]) operatic dancer EA/13*

D'ALBERTE, Theodore (d 1871) dancer EA/72*

DALBEY, Cynthia (b 1944) American actress TW/25-26

DALBY, Mr. (fl 1785-90) house servant BD

DALBY, Miss [Mrs. Hulme] (d 1906) gymnast EA/07*

DALBY, Louisa see Simpson, Mrs. (d 1872)

DALE, Mr. (fl 1784) singer BD

DALE, Mr. (fl 1794) violinist BD

DALE, Al. (d 1969 [48]) talent agent BP/54*

DALE, Alan [Alfred J. Cohen] (1861-1928) English dramatist, critic GRB/2-4, WWA/1, WWM, WWT/1-5

DALE, Brian (d 1907) comedian EA/08*

DALE, Charles (1883-1971) American variety artist ES, TW/28

DALE, E. J. (d 1900) magician CDP

DALE, Elise see Jones, Mrs. Herbert B.

DALE, Esther (d 1961 [75]) American actress TW/1, 18

"DALE, Felix" see Merivale, H. C.

DALE, Georgiana singer CDP

DALE, Gretchen [Mrs. Howard Estabrook] (b 1886) American actress WWS

DALE, Grover [né Grover Robert Aitken] (b 1935/36) American singer, dancer BE, TW/21-23

DALE, Harold S. (d 1974 [84])

performer BP/59*

DALE, Mrs. Harry see Monti, Gertie

DALE, James Littlewood (b 1886/ 87) English actor ES, WWT/4-14

DALE, J. Baldwin (d 1874 [37]) comedian EA/75*

DALE, Jim [né Smith] (b 1935/36) English actor AAS, TW/30, WWT/15-16

DALE, John (1803-72) actor CDP, EA/73*

DALE, Joseph (1750-1821) instrumentalist, music seller BD, ES

DALE, Margaret (1880-1972) American actress GRB/2-4, TW/2-7, 28, WWM, WWS, WWT/1-11

DALE, Margaret (b 1922) English dancer WWT/10-12

DALE, Margie [Mrs. Nicholas Rinaldo] (d 1962 [54]) performer BE*

DALE, Pat (d 1970 [57]) performer BP/55*

DALE, Thomas (fl c.1699) booth operator BD

DALE, Welton (b 1867/69) English actor GRB/2-4

DALE, William (fl 1774-1805?) box keeper BD

DALE, William (d 1807) boxkeeper BD

D'ALENCON, Emilienne [Emilie Andrée] French variety artist GRB/1

DALES, Harry (d 1903 [64]) Negro comedian EA/04*

DALES, John L. (b 1907) American lawyer, executive BE

DALEY, Miss actress CDP

DALEY, Cass (d 1975 [59]) actress BP/59*, WWT/16*

DALEY, Guilbert A. (b 1923) American educator BE

DALEY, Mary Patricia (b 1932) American educator, director BE

D'ALFREDS, Mrs. Edward see D'Alfreds, Jemima

D'ALFREDS, Jemima [Mrs. Edward D'Alfreds] (d 1883) EA/84*

DALL, Miss (fl 1776-94) singer, actress, composer BD, TD/1-2

DALL, John (1916-71) American actor TW/1, 5-7, 11-12, 27

DALL, Nicholas Thomas (d 1776) Dutch scene painter, painter BD

DALL' ABACO, Giuseppe Marie

Clement (1710-1805) Dutch
violoncellist, composer BD
DALLA RIZZA, Gilda (d 1975
[82]) performer BP/60*
DALLAS, Mrs. E. S. see
Dallas, Isabelle
DALLAS, George (d 1905)
musical director EA/06*
DALLAS, Henry (d 1917 [51])
comedian, manager EA/
18*
DALLAS, Isabelle see Glyn,
Isabelle
DALLAS, Mrs. James see
Varden, Dorothy
DALLAS, J. J. (1853-1915)
actor, singer CDP, DD,
DP, GRB/1-4, WWT/1-2
DALLAS, John (fl 1780-87)
scene painter BD
DALLAS, Letitia Marion [Miss
Darragh] (d 1917) actress
EA/18*
DALLAS, Meredith (b 1916)
American educator, actor,
director BE
DALLAS, Mervyn (d 1911 [87])
English actor SR
DALLAS, Robert Charles
(1754-1824) English drama-
tist CP/3, DD
DALLIMORE, Maurice (d 1973
[70s]) performer BP/57*
D'ALMAINE, Mrs. (d 1906)
EA/07*
D'ALMAINE, Mrs. Ernest see
D'Almaine, Mary
D'ALMAINE, Mary [Mrs. Ernest
D'Almaine] (d 1909) singer
EA/10*
D'ALMAINE, Maude see
Barrassford, Mrs.
DAL MONTE, Toti (d 1975
[81]) performer BP/59*
DALMORES, Charles (1871-
1939) French singer WWA/
1, WWS
D'ALROY, Evelyn (d 1915 [33])
English actress WWT/1-2
DALRYMPLE, Mrs. (fl 1782-
83) house servant? BD
DALRYMPLE, Jean (b 1910)
American producer, director,
publicist AAS, BE, CB,
TW/3-8, WWT/11-16
DALTON, Mr. (fl 1759-63)
ticket taker BD
DALTON, Mrs. (d 1891) EA/92*

DALTON, Miss (fl 1791) actress
BD
DALTON, Amy (fl 1664-67) actress
BD
DALTON, Charles (1864-1942) Eng-
lish actor CB, DD, EA/95,
GRB/2, 4, SR, WWS, WWT/1-9
DALTON, Charles see Bethen,
Charles
D'ALTON, Curtis (d 1911 [51])
singer EA/12*
D'ALTON, Mrs. Curtis see
D'Alton, Emma
DALTON, Doris (b 1910/12) Amer-
ican actress TW/3-11, WWT/
10-11
DALTON, Dorothy (1893/94-1972)
American actress ES, TW/28,
WWT/4-6
D'ALTON, Emma [Mrs. Curtis
D'Alton] (d 1893) EA/95*
DALTON, Harry (d 1906) EA/07*
DALTON, Harry (d 1909) manager
EA/10*
DALTON, Helen (d 1893) singer
EA/94*
DALTON, Mrs. James T. [Sally
Holman] (1852-88) American
actress, singer CDP
D'ALTON, Jessie (d 1911) actress
EA/12*
DALTON, John (1709-63) English
dramatist CP/1-3, GT, TD/1-2
DALTON, John (fl 1775) dramatist
CP/2-3, GT
DALTON, Kate [Mrs. George Elli-
son] (d 1912 [62]) singer EA/13*
D'ALTON, Marion [Mrs. Charles
Sullivan] (d 1900 [36]) EA/01*
DALTON, Mrs. Sam (d 1895) EA/
96*
DALTON, Shirley English actress
GRB/1
DALTON, Test (1875-1945) American
dramatist WWA/2
DALTON, Will singer CDP
DALTON, William see Eltinge,
Julian
DALTRA, Marie [Mrs. Lionel Rig-
nold] (d 1932 [84]) Welsh actress
GRB/1
DALTRAY, Thomas (d 1889 [39])
gymnast EA/90*
D'ALTROY, Walter (d 1875) acrobat
EA/76*
D'ALVERA, Marie (d 1902) actress
EA/03*
D'ALVINI, William see

Armstrong, William
DALY, Mr. (fl 1732) actor BD
DALY, Mr. (fl 1779) actor BD
DALY, Mr. (fl 1856) actor HAS
DALY, Mrs. (fl 1756?-63)
actress BD
DALY, Miss CDP
DALY, Alice see Cragg, Mrs.
J. W.
DALY, Arnold (1875-1927)
American actor, producer
COC, ES, GRB/2-4, NTH,
OC/1-3, SR, WWA/1,
WWM, WWS, WWT/1-5
DALY, Augustin (1839-99) Amer-
ican dramatist, manager,
critic CDP, COC, DAB,
DD, ES, HJD, MH, MWD,
NTH, OC/1-3, RE, SR,
WWA/1, WWW/1
DALY, Mrs. Augustin (d 1907
[58]) GRB/3*
DALY, Cpt. Bill see Daly,
William
DALY, Blyth (b 1902) American
actress WWT/6-8
DALY, Brian (d 1923 [60])
actor, lyricist WWT/14*
DALY, Carroll John (1889-
1958) American manager
WWA/3
DALY, Claude (d 1892) marks-
man EA/93*
DALY, Dan (1858-1904) actor
BE*, BP/2*, WWT/14*
DALY, Dixie (d 1963 [66])
performer BE*
DALY, Ellen [Mrs. Frederick
L. Phillips] (1815-90)
actress CDP
DALY, Miss H. see O'Grady,
Mrs. F.
DALY, Henry F. (b 1828) actor
SR
DALY, James (b 1918) American
actor BE, CB, TW/7-15,
20, WWT/14-16
DALY, John (d 1867 [63]) actor
EA/68*
DALY, John [John Besemeres]
(fl 1850-74) dramatist DD,
EA/69
DALY, Julia [Mrs. Wayne Ol-
wine; Mrs. Warren Edgarton]
(1833-87) actress CDP, HAS,
NYM, SR
DALY, Lawrence (d 1900 [38])
actor, producer, manager

BE*, EA/01*, WWT/14*
DALY, Lillian Moran (d 1894 [18])
EA/95*
DALY, Lizzie Derious (1876-1913)
actress, dancer, singer CDP,
SR
DALY, Mae (d 1962 [70]) performer
BE*
DALY, Maria (d 1905 [75]) actress
EA/06*, WWT/14*
DALY, Mark (1887-1957) Scottish
actor WWT/6-11
DALY, Mrs. Michael H. see
Nolan, Pattie
DALY, Peter Christopher Arnold
(1875-1927) American actor
DAB
DALY, Richard (1758-1813) Irish
actor, manager BD, CDP,
DD, DNB, TD/1-2
DALY, Mrs. Richard see Bar-
santi, Jane
DALY, Robert (d 1889) American
actor EA/90*
DALY, Tom (1855-92) minstrel
CDP
DALY, Vinie dancer, singer CDP
DALY, William ["Captain Bill"]
minstrel CDP
DALY, William (d 1857 [61]) actor
WWT/14*
DALY, William, Jr. (d 1974 [67])
performer BP/59*
DALY, Mrs. William (d 1883 [79])
actress EA/84*, WWT/14*
DALYA, Jacqueline (b 1919) Amer-
ican actress TW/2, 6
DALZELL, Allan C. [né Allan
Cameron Pfeifer] (1896-1972)
American press representative,
manager BE
DALZELL, Davidson (b 1858) Eng-
lish actor SR
DALZELL, William (b 1917) Amer-
ican actor TW/4
DALZIEL, May (d 1969 [68]) per-
former BP/54*
DAM, Henry J. W. (d 1906 [48])
American dramatist DD, WWA/1
DAM, Mrs. Henry J. W. see
Dorr, Dorothy
DAMALA, Jacques (d 1889 [40])
actor BE*, WWT/14*
DAMASCENE, Alexander (d 1719)
French singer, composer BD,
DNB
DAMASZEK, Marvin see Deems,
Mickey

D'AMBOISE, Jacques (b 1934)
American dancer, choreog-
rapher CB, ES
D'AMBROSIA, Angela American
actress TW/24
DAME, Mr. (fl 1783) musician
BD
D'AMELI, Eugene see Eugene,
Master
DAMEN, Henry Alban (d 1891)
EA/92*
DAMER, Frank [Edward F.
Dawson] (d 1911) stage mana-
ger EA/12*
DAMEREL, George (d 1936 [57])
American singer BE*, BP/
21*
DAMES, Harry L. (d 1971 [82])
performer BP/55*
DAMIANI, Vitale (fl 1799-1800)
Italian singer BD
DAMON, Cathryn American act-
ress TW/21-22, 25-30
DAMON, Les (d 1962 [53])
actor BE*
DAMON, Stuart [né Stuart
Michael Zonis] (b 1937) Amer-
ican actor, singer BE, TW/
16, 18-22, WWT/15-16
DAMOREAU, Laure Cinthie
[Mlle. Cinti] (1801-63) singer
CDP
DAMPIER, Alfred (b 1842)
actor, manager DD, GRB/
2-4
DAMPIER, Claude (d 1955 [76])
music-hall comedian WWT/
14*
DAMPORT, Edward (fl 1633)
actor DA
DAMROSCH, Frank Heino (1859-
1937) German/American
chorus master DAB
DAMROSCH, Walter Johannes
(1862-1950) Prussian com-
poser, conductor CB, DAB,
ES, HJD, SR, WWA/3,
WWM, WWW/4
DANA, Barbara (b 1940) American actress TW/22, 26, 30
DANA, Henry (1855-1921) English manager GRB/2-4,
WWT/1-3
DANA, Leora (b 1923) American
actress BE, TW/6-16,
20-26, 28-29, WWT/15-16
DANA, Marie Louise (d 1946
[70]) actress TW/3

DANA, Viola (b 1898) American
actress ES
DANBURY, Ethel [Mrs. Harry
Starr] (d 1905) actress EA/07*
DANBY, Master (fl 1792-1814?)
singer BD
DANBY, Charles (fl 1776-1814?)
actor, singer BD
DANBY, Charles (1857-1906) Eng-
lish actor, singer CDP, DD,
GRB/1
DANBY, Frank (d 1912) actor EA/
13*
DANBY, Humphrey (fl 1709-39)
flutist BD
DANBY, John (1757-98) singer,
composer BD, DNB
DANCE, Miss (fl 1821) actress
CDP
DANCE, Charles (1794-1863) drama-
tist DD, DNB
DANCE, Sir George (1858/65-1932)
English dramatist, manager
COC, DD, ES, GRB/1-4, OC/
1-3, SR, WWT/1-6, WWW/3
DANCE, James [alias Love] (1722-
74) English? comedian, manager,
dramatist CDP, CP/2-3, DD,
DNB, GT, TD/1-2
DANCE, Reginald [Francis Reginald
Dance Scroggs] (b 1867) English
actor GRB/1
DANCE, William (1755-1840) musi-
cian, composer BD, DNB
DANCER, Mrs. (fl 1766) house
servant? BD
DANCER, Miss (fl 1782-88) actress
BD
DANCER, Ann see Barry, Mrs.
Spranger
DANCER, John (fl 1660-75) Irish?
dramatist CP/1-3, DD, DNB,
GT
DANCER, John Wimperis (d 1790)
actor, singer BD
DANCER, William (d 1759) actor
BD
DANCER, Mrs. William see
Barry, Mrs. Spranger
DANCEY, Mr. (fl 1734) dancer?
BD
DANCEY, Mrs. (fl 1732-39) actress,
dancer BD
DANCEY, Miss (fl 1731-40) actress,
dancer BD
DANDO, Letitia see Aenea
DANDO, W[alter] P[feffer] (1852-
1944) English theatrical

engineer GRB/1
DANDO, William (d 1878 [30])
comedian EA/79*
DANDRE, Victor (d 1944 [74])
ballet impresario WWT/
14*
D'ANDRIA, Giorgio (d 1972
[72]) producer/director/
choreographer BP/57*
DANDRIDGE, Dorothy (d 1965)
singer, actress WWA/4
DANDY, Jess [Jesse A.
Danzig] (1871-1923) American come-
dian WWM
DANE, Clemence [Winifred Ash-
ton; Diana Portis] (1888-1965)
English dramatist, actress
AAS, BE, COC, ES, MD,
MH, MWD, NTH, OC/3,
SR, TW/21, WWA/4, WWT/
5-13, WWW/6
DANE, Essex (d 1962 [96])
English actress GRB/1-4,
WWS
DANE, Ethel actress WWT/2-5
DANE, Marjorie (b 1898) actress
WWT/2-3
DANEEL, Sylvia [née Sylvia
Jadviga Lakomska] (b
1930/31) Polish actress BE,
TW/13-16, 30
DANEMAN, Paul (b 1925) Eng-
lish actor AAS, WWT/12-16
DANEMORE, A. [Augustus
Yorke] (d 1891) EA/92*
DANESE, Connie American
actress TW/29-30
DANEY, Mr. (fl 1766) house
servant? BD
DANFORTH, Edward W. (d 1857)
prompter HAS
DANFORTH, William (1867-1941)
actor, singer CB, SR,
WWT/7-9
D'ANFOY, Mr. (fl 1730) dancer
BD
D'ANGELIS, Mr. American
actor HAS
D'ANGELIS, Sally see Fulton,
Sarah
D'ANGELO, Carlo (d 1973 [54])
performer BP/58*
DANGERFIELD, Mr. (fl 1791-
1804) boxkeeper BD
DANGERFIELD, Frederick (d
1904 [53]) scene artist EA/
05*
DANGEVILLE, Mons. (fl 1720)

dancer BD
DANGLE, Steven (fl 1794) violinist
BD
DANGLER, Anita American actress
TW/12, 23-24, 29-30
D'ANGRI, Eléna (b 1824) Italian
singer CDP, HAS
DANIEL, Mr. (fl 1782-89) actor
BD
DANIEL, Billy (d 1962 [50]) chore-
ographer BE*
"DANIEL, Dapper" see "Dapper
Daniel"
DANIEL, George (1789-1864) Eng-
lish critic, dramatist CDP,
DD, DNB
DANIEL, John (fl 1615-24) musi-
cian, patentee DA, DNB
DANIEL, Mark (fl 1794-1802?)
singer BD
DANIEL, Mary see Daniel, Mrs.
William
DANIEL, Rita (d 1951) actress
BE*, WWT/14*
DANIEL, Samuel (c.1563-1619)
English dramatist CP/1-3,
DA, DD, DNB, FGF, HP, NTH,
OC/1-3, RE
DANIEL, William (fl 1621-37) actor
DA
DANIEL, William (d 1755) actor
BD
DANIEL, Mrs. William [Mrs.
Charles Somerset Woodham]
(fl 1742-56) actress, dancer
BD
DANIELE, Graciela (b 1939) Brazilian
actress TW/25-29
DANIELEWSKI, Tad (b 1921) Polish
director, producer, scenarist
BE
DANIELIAN, Leon (b 1920) American
dancer ES
DANIELL, Aimée see Beringer,
Mrs. Oscar
DANIELL, Henry (1894-1963) English
actor ES, TW/2-11, 20, WWT/
4-13
DANIELOVITCH, Issure see
Douglas, Kirk
DANIELS, Mr. (fl 1850-60) Ameri-
can actor HAS
DANIELS, Miss singer? CDP
DANIELS, Alfred (d 1964 [81]) per-
former BP/49*
DANIELS, Alicia [Mrs. George
Frederick Cooke, II. Mrs. Wind-
sor] (d 1826) singer, actress

BD, CDP

DANIELS, Bebe (1901-71) American actress, singer ES, WWT/10-14

DANIELS, Becky [Mrs. E. Gaertner] (d 1907 [26]) circus performer EA/08*

DANIELS, Bill (b 1927) American actor TW/9

DANIELS, Carolan (b 1940) American actress TW/21-22

DANIELS, Carrie E. actress, musician CDP

DANIELS, Charlotte (d 1973 [44]) performer BP/57*

DANIELS, Danny (b 1924) American choreographer, dancer, director BE, TW/2-4, 6-8

DANIELS, David (b 1927) American singer, actor BE, TW/11-20, 25-26

DANIELS, Edgar (b 1932) American actor TW/19-20, 22-24

DANIELS, Frank Albert (1856/60-1935) American actor, singer DAB, GRB/2-4, OC/1-3, SR, WWA/1, WWS, WWT/1-7

DANIELS, Harold (d 1971 [68]) producer/director/choreographer BP/56*

DANIELS, Mo (d 1890 [60]) musical clown EA/92*

DANIELS, Mrs. Moses see Daniels, Rotana

DANIELS, Rotana [Mrs. Moses Daniels] (d 1881 [48]) EA/82*

DANIELS, Walker (b 1943) American actor TW/24-25

DANIELS, William (b 1927) American actor BE, TW/18-20, 22-28, 30

DANILOVA, Alexandra (b 1904/07) Russian dancer, choreographer BE, ES, TW/14, WWT/9-12

DANJURO, Ichikawa (d 1903) actor, manager WWT/14*

DANK, David [né Zweibelsharf] (b 1895) Russian actor BE

D'ANKA, Cornélie (fl 1871) actress, singer DD

DANKS, Hart Pease (1834-1903) American composer BE*

DANKS, John (fl 1723-24) violinist BD

DANNELL, Mr. (fl 1784) actor BD

DANNER, Blythe American actress TW/25-28, WWT/16

DANNER, John (fl 1629) actor DA

DANNREUTHER, Edward George (1844-1905) German pianist ES, GRB/1

D'ANNUNZIO, Gabriele (1864-1938) Italian dramatist GRB/3

D'ANNUNZIO, Lola (d 1956 [26]) actress TW/13

DANO, Royal (b 1922) American actor TW/8

DANOIGERS, Oscar (d 1976 [74]) producer/director/choreographer BP/60*

DANSEY, Herbert (1870-1917) Italian actor GRB/3-4, WWT/1-3

DANSON, George (d 1881 [82]) scene artist EA/82*

DANSON, Thomas (d 1893 [64]) scene artist EA/95*

DANTE (1883-1955) Danish magician TW/12

DANTE, Ethel (d 1954 [92]) actress BE*, WWT/14*

DANTE, Lionel (d 1974 [67]) performer BP/59*

DANTER, John (d 1908 [64]) showman EA/09*

DANTER, William (d 1902 [65]) amusement caterer EA/03*

DANTINE, Helmut (b 1918) Austrian actor TW/3

D'ANTONAKIS, Fleury (b 1939) Greek actress TW/21-22

D'ANTONIE, Elise dancer CDP

DANTZIG, Eli (d 1968 [70]) conductor BP/53*

DANVERS, Billy (d 1964) English actor BE*

DANVERS, Edward (d 1906) comedian EA/08*

DANVERS, Edwin (d 1906) actor DD

DANVERS, Frank B. (d 1896 [42]) actor EA/97*

DANVERS, Mrs. Fred see Rainbird, Marie

DANVERS, George (d 1917 [39]) comedian EA/18*

DANVERS, H. dramatist DD

DANVERS, John composer, lyricist, minstrel CDP

DANVERS, Johnny (1860/70-1939) English actor OC/1-3, WWT/4-7

DANVERS, Nelly see Bosworth,

Agnes Ellinor
DANVERS, Thomas Ramsay
(d 1895 [37]) actor EA/96*
DANVERS, Mrs. William
see Cramer, Fanny
DANVIL, Maud [Mrs. Dan
Leeson] (d 1898) music-hall
performer EA/00*
DANZI, Muriel Chapman (d 1973
[62]) performer BP/57*
DANZIG, Jesse A. see Dandy,
Jess
DANZIGER, Maia (b 1950) ac-
tress TW/30
D'APOLITO, Alfred (d 1965
[54]) executive, journalist
BP/50*
DA PONTE, Lorenzo [Emanuele
Conegliano] (1749-1838)
Italian librettist, impresario,
teacher BD, COC, EAP,
ES, WWA/H
DA PONTE, Lorenzo L. (d
1840) dramatist EAP
"DAPPER DANIEL" (fl 1699)
fencer BD
DARBIE, Richard (fl 1602) actor
DA
D'ARBLAY, Frances see
Burney, Fanny
DARBY, Mr. (fl 1760) house
servant? BD
DARBY, Mr. (fl 1769) actor
HAS
DARBY, Aaron (fl 1688-89)
actor BD
DARBY, Fred (d 1898 [37])
comic singer EA/99*
DARBY, Mary see Robinson,
Mary
DARBY, William [Pablo Fanque]
(d 1871 [67]) circus propri-
etor EA/72*
DARBYSHIRE, Iris (b 1905)
English actress WWT/8-9
DARBYSHIRE, Taylor (1875-
1943) English critic WWW/4
D'ARC, Lambert (d 1893 [69])
waxworks proprietor EA/
94*
D'ARC, Nellie (d 1901 [32])
marionettist EA/02*
D'ARCY, Mr. [Mr. Caird] (fl
· 1797-1802?) singer, actor
BD, TD/1-2
D'ARCY, Miss (fl 1770-71)
actress BD
D'ARCY, Belle (d 1936 [64])

American actress GRB/1,
WWM, WWS
D'ARCY, George see Yelland,
Willie
D'ARCY, Hugh Antoine (d 1925
[82]) French actor, manager
BE*, BP/10*
DARCY, James (fl 1732-49) Irish
dramatist CP/1-3, GT, TD/
1-2
D'ARCY, Roy (1894-1969) Ameri-
can actor ES, TW/26
DARCY, Stafford (fl 1660-62)
singer BD
DARDEN, Norma Jean American
actress TW/24, 27, 30
DARE, Cyrus singer, composer,
lyricist CDP
DARE, Daphne English designer
WWT/16
DARE, Dulcie [Mrs. Dan Thomas]
(d 1904) music-hall performer
EA/05*
DARE, Ernest (d 1969 [87]) per-
former BP/54*
DARE, Eva (d 1931) actress BE*,
WWT/14*
DARE, Frank H. acrobat CDP
DARE, Leona (1855-1922) trapezist
CDP
DARE, Phyllis (1890-1975) actress
GRB/2-4, WWT/1-12
DARE, Richard (d 1964 [41]) actor
BE*
DARE, Stuart (d 1902) gymnast,
athlete EA/03*
DARE, Thomas S. acrobat CDP
DARE, Virginia (d 1962) actress
BE*
DARE, Zena (1887-1975) English
actress ES, GRB/2-4, WWT/
1-14
DAREMONT, A. (b 1862) French
actor, dramatist SR
DAREWSKI, Herman (1883-1947)
Russian composer WWT/4-10,
WWW/4
DAREWSKI, Max (1894-1929) Eng-
lish composer, conductor, pian-
ist WWT/4-6
DARGAN, Olive Thomas (fl 1904-
47) dramatist HJD
DARGON, Augusta C. (d 1902) ac-
tress CDP
DARIMATE, Mlle. see Durancy,
Mme.
DARK, Christopher (d 1971) per-
former BP/56*

DARK, Frederick (d 1917) comedian EA/18*

DARK, Sidney (1874-1947) English critic GRB/2-4, WWT/1-4, WWW/4

DARK, Stanley (b 1874) English actor WWS

DARKE, Rebecca (b 1935) American actress TW/23

DARKIN, Joseph (fl 1794) singer BD

DARLEY, Mr. see Darley, John

DARLEY, Mrs. [nèe Ellen Westray] (d 1849) English actress HAS

DARLEY, Anne see Darley, Mrs. William [John?]

DARLEY, George (1795-1846) Irish critic, dramatist DD, DNB, HP

DARLEY, John (d 1819) English actor HAS, SR

DARLEY, John, Jr. (1775/79-1853) actor HAS, SR

DARLEY, John Edward (d 1878 [37]) master carpenter EA/79*

DARLEY, William [John?] (c. 1756-1809) English singer, actor BD, CDP, TD/1-2

DARLEY, Mrs. William [John?; Anne] (1758?-1838?) singer, actress BD, CDP

DARLING, Mr. (fl 1785) actor BD

DARLING, Bessie [Mrs. Charles Berry] actress CDP

DARLING, Candy (d 1974 [26]) American actress TW/30

DARLING, Daisy (d 1974 [67]) actress TW/30

DARLING, David dramatist EAP

DARLING, Jean [nèe Dorothy Jean LeVake] (b 1925) American singer, actress BE, TW/1-5

DARLING, Joan [nèe Kugell] (b 1935/40) American actress, director BE, TW/24

DARLING, May (d 1971 [83]) performer BP/55*

DARLING, William (fl 1794) singer BD

DARLINGTON, William Aubrey (b 1890) English critic,

dramatist AAS, BE, COC, OC/1-3, PDT, WWT/4-16

DARLOE, Richard see Darlowe, Richard

DARLOWE, Richard (fl c. 1590-1602) actor DA

DARMOND, Grace (d 1963 [65]) performer BP/48*

D'ARMOND, Isabell (b 1887) American actress, singer WWM

DARNEL, Hale (d 1969 [44]) producer/director/choreographer BP/53*

DARNELL, Linda (d 1965 [43]) performer BP/49*

DARNELL, Nellie (d 1905 [21]) EA/06*

DARNELL, Robert (b 1929) American actor TW/26, 28-29

DARNLEY, Alice [Mrs. J. H. Darnley] (d 1908) EA/09*

DARNLEY, Herbert (d 1947 [75]) English actor, dramatist GRB/1-3

DARNLEY, Herbert Blundell (d 1917) actor EA/18*

DARNLEY, J. H. (d 1938 [81]) actor, dramatist DD

DARNLEY, Mrs. J. H. see Darnley, Alice

DARNLEY, Wilfred (d 1916 [37]) EA/17*

DARNTON, Charles (d 1950 [80]) critic BE*, BP/34*, WWT/14*

DARRAGH, Miss see Dallas, Letitia Marion

DARRAGH, Miss F. (d 1917) actress GRB/3-4, WWT/1-3

DARRANT, Symon (fl 1672) violinist BD

DARRELL, Mr. (fl 1708) house servant BD

DARRELL, Bennett (d 1907) performer? EA/08*

DARRELL, Charles (1858-1932) English dramatist, actor GRB/1-3

DARRELL, Mrs. Charles see Tempest, Amy

DARRELL, Fred (d 1898) actor, variety agent EA/99*

DARRELL, Mrs. George see Peachey, Catherine

DARRELL, J. Stevan (d 1970 [65]) actor TW/27

DARRELL, Maisie (b 1901) English actress WWT/6-10

DARRELL, Maudi [Mrs. John

Bullough] (1882-1910) English
actress GRB/1-4
DARRELL, Peter (b 1929) Eng-
lish choreographer, dancer
ES
DARRID, William [né William
David Blum] (b 1923) Ameri-
can producer BE
DARRIEUX, Danielle (b 1917)
French actress TW/29
DARROCH, Joseph (d 1917)
EA/18*
DARROW, Richard American
actor TW/26
DARROW, Stephen (d 1892 [74])
Australian actor EA/93*
DARTON, Mrs. H. see
Sloman, Mrs. John
DARVAS, Lili (1902/06-74)
Hungarian/American actress
BE, ES, TW/1-7, 9-19,
24-25, 27, WWT/13-15
DARVI, Bella (d 1971 [44])
performer BP/56*
DARVILE, Mr. (fl 1784) singer
BD
DARVILE, Jr., Mr. (fl 1784)
singer BD
D'ARVILLE, Camille [Mrs. E.
W. Crelin] (1863-1932)
Dutch actress, singer CDP,
DD, DP, GRB/2-4, SR,
WWA/1, WWM, WWS, WWT/
1-5
DARWELL, Jane (d 1967 [87])
American actress ES, TW/24
DARYL, Julian (d 1880 [36])
actor EA/81*
DARZIN, Diana (b 1953) Amer-
ican actress TW/30
DASH, Pauly (d 1974 [55])
performer BP/58*
DASH, Thomas R. (b 1897)
Russian/American critic
NTH
DASHIELL, Willard (1868?-
1943) actor CB
DASHINGTON, James J. (d
1962 [84]) performer BE*
DASHWAY, Mrs. Charles (d
1886) EA/87*
DASHWOOD, Annie see
Cruse, Annie
DASHWOOD, Mrs. A. P. see
Delafield, E. M.
DASHWOOD, Edmée Elizabeth
Monica see Delafield, E. M.
DASHWOOD, Harry [Benjamin

John Bell] (d 1900 [35]) comic
singer EA/01*
DASHWOOD, [John?] (fl 1799-
1813) doorkeeper BD
DA SILVA, Howard [né Silverblatt]
(b 1909) American actor, di-
rector, producer BE, TW/25-
28, WWT/13-16
DASSIN, Jean [or Jules] (b 1911)
American director BE, ES
D'ASTE, Lottie (d 1878 [26])
gymnast EA/79*
DATE, Keshavrao (d 1971 [32])
performer BP/56*
D'AUBAN, Mrs. (d 1867 [47])
EA/68*
D'AUBAN, Emma (d 1910) dancer
EA/11*, WWT/14*
D'AUBAN, Ernest (d 1941 [67])
director BE*, WWT/14*
D'AUBAN, John (d 1922 [80]) stage
manager, dancer WWT/14*
D'AUBAN, Mariette (d 1906 [60])
ballet mistress EA/07*
DAUBENY, Sir Peter Lauderdale
(1921-75) English impresario,
manager AAS, COC, OC/3,
WWT/10-15
D'AUBERVAL, Jean [Jean Bercher]
(1742-1806) French dancer,
ballet master, choreographer
BD, ES
D'AUBERVAL, Mme. Jean [née
Crêpé; Mme. Théodore] (d
1798) dancer BD
DAUBRAY, Mons. (d 1892 [55])
actor EA/93*
DAUFEL, Andre (d 1975 [56])
performer BP/59*
D'AUNAY, Josias? (fl 1635) French
actor DA
DAUNCEY, Sylvanus (1864-1912)
dramatist DD
DAUNT, William (1893-1938) Irish
actor WWT/8
DAUPHIN, Claude [né Claude Maria
Eugent LeGrand] (b 1903/04)
French actor, writer, director
BE, TW/3, 6-8, 12-16, 18,
WWT/12-16
DAUSE, Mrs. (fl 1760) dancer BD
D'AUVIGNE, Mons. (fl 1773) ballet
master BD
DAUVRY, Helen [née Nellie Wil-
liams; "Little Nell, the Calif-
ornia Diamond"] (b 1858) Eng-
lish actress, singer CDP, DD,
SR

DAVALOS, Richard (b 1930)
American actor   TW/12-16
DAVANT, Henrick (fl 1685-1716)
trumpeter BD
DAVENANT, Alexander (b c. 1658)
treasurer, proprietor BD
DAVENANT, Charles (1656-1714)
proprietor, producer, inspec-
tor of plays, dramatist BD,
CP/1-3, DD
DAVENANT, Henrietta Maria du
Tremblay (d 1691) French?
proprietor BD
DAVENANT, Nicholas (b c. 1665)
lessee BD
DAVENANT, Ralph (c. 1659-98)
treasurer BD
DAVENANT, Thomas (b 1664)
English manager BD
DAVENANT, W. (fl 1857) Eng-
lish actor HAS
DAVENANT, Sir William (1606-
68) English dramatist, mana-
ger BD, CDP, COC, CP/
1-3, DA, DD, DNB, ES,
FGF, HP, MH, NTH, OC/
1-3, PDT, RE
DAVENCOURT, Mons. (fl 1705)
dancer BD
DAVENPORT, Mr. (fl 1729-58?)
dancer, actor, dancing master
BD
DAVENPORT, Mr. (fl 1776?-79)
actor BD
DAVENPORT, Mr. (fl 1795-1803)
actor TD/1-2
DAVENPORT, Mrs. (fl 1733-41)
dancer, actress BD
DAVENPORT, Adolphus H. [né
Hoyt] (1828-73) American
actor CDP, DD, HAS, SR
DAVENPORT, Alice [Mrs. Harry
Bryant Davenport] (b 1864)
actress ES
DAVENPORT, Mrs. Arthur
Bromley (d 1917) actress
EA/18*
DAVENPORT, Blanche [Bianca
Lablanche] singer, actress
CDP
DAVENPORT, Butler (1871-
1958) American actor,
dramatist, producer NTH,
TW/14
DAVENPORT, Clara (d 1908
[68]) actress GRB/4*
DAVENPORT, Davis (d 1975 [42])
performer BP/60*

DAVENPORT, Dorothy (b 1895)
American actress ES
DAVENPORT, Edgar Longfellow
(1862-1918) American actor
COC, ES, OC/1-3, PP/1
DAVENPORT, Edward Loomis
(1815-77) American actor
CDP, COC, DAB, DD, ES,
HAS, NTH, OC/1-3, SR,
WWA/H
DAVENPORT, Mrs. Edward
Loomis see Davenport, Fanny
Elizabeth
DAVENPORT, Elizabeth (fl 1664?-
75?) actress BD
DAVENPORT, Eva [Mrs. Neil
O'Brien] (d 1932 [74]) English
actress WWS
DAVENPORT, Fanny Elizabeth
[née Vining; Mrs. Edward
Loomis Davenport] (1829-91)
English actress CDP, COC,
DD, ES, HAS, OC/1-3, SR
DAVENPORT, Fanny Lily Gipsy
(1850-98) English actress
CDP, COC, DAB, ES, HAS,
NTH, OC/1-3, WWA/H
DAVENPORT, Frances (fl 1664-68)
actress BD
DAVENPORT, George Gosling (c.
1758-1814) actor, manager BD,
DD, GT
DAVENPORT, Mrs. George Gos-
ling [née Mary Ann Harvey]
(1759-1843) English actress,
singer BD, BS, CDP, DD,
DNB, GT, OX
DAVENPORT, G. Victor (d 1899
[30]) actor EA/00*
DAVENPORT, Mrs. Harry see
Rankin, Phyllis
DAVENPORT, Harry Bryant (1866-
1949) American actor COC,
ES, OC/1-3, TW/6, WWS,
WWT/7-10
DAVENPORT, Mrs. Harry Bryant
see Davenport, Alice
DAVENPORT, Henry (d 1880 [36])
manager, lessee EA/81*
DAVENPORT, Hester [Countess of
Oxford; Mrs. Peter Hoet] (1641?-
1717) actress BD
DAVENPORT, Ira (1839-1911)
American magician SR
DAVENPORT, Jane (fl 1667-68)
actress BD
DAVENPORT, Jean (1826-1903)
actress, dramatist SR

DAVENPORT, Jean Margaret see Lander, Mrs. Frederick W.

DAVENPORT, John (fl 1689) musician BD

DAVENPORT, Julia [Mrs. Lewis Davenport] (d 1909 [27]) EA/11*

DAVENPORT, Mrs. Lewis see Davenport, Julia

DAVENPORT, Lily (d 1878) American actress EA/79*

DAVENPORT, Lizzie see Mathews, Mrs. Charles James

DAVENPORT, Louise see Sheridan, Mrs. William Edward

DAVENPORT, Mary (d 1916? [65]) actress CDP

DAVENPORT, Mary Ann see Davenport, Mrs. George Gosling

DAVENPORT, May (1856-1927) American actress COC, ES, OC/1-3, PP/1

DAVENPORT, Millia (b 1895) American costume designer BE

DAVENPORT, Nigel (b 1928) English actor WWT/14-16

DAVENPORT, N. T. [né Deven] (fl 1849-50) actor HAS

DAVENPORT, Orrin B. (d 1962 [77]) equestrian BE*

DAVENPORT, Pembroke (b 1911) American musical director, composer, lyricist, actor BE

DAVENPORT, Robert (fl 1623) English dramatist CP/1-3, DD, DNB, FGF, NTH

DAVENPORT, Ruth [Mrs. Wilson] actress, singer GRB/1

DAVENPORT, Thomas Donald (1792-1851) English actor, manager COC, DD, HAS

DAVENPORT, William Henry Harrison (1841-77) American illusionist WWA/H

DAVENTRY, George (d 1904 [45]) actor EA/05*

DAVES, Delmer (1904-77) American actor ES

DAVEY, George (d 1909 [71]) EA/10*

DAVEY, Leon G. (b 1904)

English scene designer ES

DAVEY, Nuna [née Margaret Symonds] (b 1902) Indian/English actress WWT/10-14

DAVEY, Peter (1857-1946) English agent, manager GRB/1-4, WWT/1-9

DAVEY, Richard (d 1870 [69]) property master EA/71*

DAVEY, Richard (fl 1886-93) dramatist DD

DAVEY, Samuel (fl 1737-39) Irish dramatist CP/1-3, GT

DAVEY, Thomas W. actor, manager SR

DAVID, Mr. (fl 1791) Czech musician BD

DAVID, Clifford (b 1932/33) American actor BE, TW/16-19, 22-23, 25-28

DAVID, Jean (b 1931) American actress TW/26-27, 29-30

DAVID, Jeff (b 1940) American actor TW/24, 26-28

DAVID, Mack (b 1912) American composer, lyricist BE

DAVID, Pete (d 1974 [80]) performer BP/58*

DAVID, Ross singer CDP

DAVID, Thayer (b 1927) American actor TW/12-13, 19-20, 22-23, 27, 29-30

DAVID, Virginia (d 1973 [47]) performer BP/58*

DAVID, William (d 1965 [83]) performer BP/49*

DAVID, Worton (d 1940) dramatist, composer WWT/4-9

DAVIDE, Giacomo (1750-1820) Italian singer BD

DAVIDGE, Mr. (fl 1792) puppeteer BD

DAVIDGE, George B. (1793-1842) actor, manager CDP, DD, OX

DAVIDGE, J. H. (d 1874 [49]) property master EA/75*

DAVIDGE, William (d 1899) English actor CDP, HAS

DAVIDGE, Mrs. William (d 1892 [74]) comedian HAS?, EA/93*

DAVIDGE, Mrs. William see Harold, Maggie

DAVIDGE, William Pleater (1814-88) English actor, dramatist CDP, DAB, DD, ES, HAS, SR, WWA/H

DAVIDOFF, Frances Mack (d 1967 [60]) performer BP/52*

DAVIDS, Joseph (fl 1783) house
servant? BD
DAVIDSON, Mrs. (d 1870 [67])
equestrian EA/71*
DAVIDSON, Rev. Anthony (fl
1805) Scottish dramatist
CP/3
DAVIDSON, Bill (b 1918) Amer-
ican writer BE
DAVIDSON, Cecil (d 1974 [69])
producer/director/choreograph-
er BP/59*
DAVIDSON, Doré (1847-1930)
actor, dramatist SR
DAVIDSON, Frederick Lewis
Maitland (d 1936) critic
WWW/3
DAVIDSON, Gordon (b 1933)
American producer, director
WWT/16
DAVIDSON, Jack (d 1903 [22])
actor? EA/04*
DAVIDSON, Jack (b 1936) Amer-
ican actor TW/25, 28
DAVIDSON, John (1857-1909)
Scottish dramatist DD, DNB,
GRB/1-4, HP, WWW/1
DAVIDSON, John (b 1941) Amer-
ican actor, singer CB, TW/
20, 22
DAVIDSON, Lorraine (b 1945)
American actress TW/30
DAVIDSON, Maitland (d 1936
[62]) critic BE*, WWT/14*
DAVIDSON, Margaret Miller
(1823-38) American actress,
dramatist WWA/H
DAVIDSON, Milton editor BE
DAVIDSON, Norris West (d
1975 [69]) producer/director/
choreographer BP/60*
DAVIDSON, Richard (b 1918)
American lawyer BE
DAVIES, Mr. (fl 1716-17) music
copyist BD
DAVIES, Mr. (fl 1783-1817)
constable BD
DAVIES, Mr. (fl 1796-99)
dancer BD
DAVIES, Master (fl 1779) dancer
BD
DAVIES, Miss (fl 1794-95)
singer BD
DAVIES, Acton (1870-1916)
Canadian critic GRB/2-4,
WWA/1, WWM, WWT/1-3
DAVIES, A. Gardner (d 1939
[32]) producer WWT/14*

DAVIES, Alfred (b 1856) English
stage manager, manager GRB/1
DAVIES, Anna [Mrs. Emanuel
Samuel] (fl 1786-1836) actress
BD
DAVIES, Ben[jamin Grey] (1858-
1943) Welsh singer, actor DD,
DP, ES, GRB/1-4, WWT/1-9,
WWW/4
DAVIES, Betty-Ann (1910-55) Eng-
lish actress, singer TW/8, 11,
WWT/10-11
DAVIES, Brian (b 1912) American
actor, singer BE
DAVIES, Brian (b 1938/39) Welsh
actor, singer BE, TW/30
DAVIES, Cecilia (1753?-1836)
English singer BD, DNB, ES
DAVIES, Charles see Stirling,
Charles
DAVIES, Charles J. (d 1910 [74])
secretary of the Royal General
Theatrical Fund EA/11*
DAVIES, Denis (d 1900 [21]) actor
EA/01*
DAVIES, D. R. (d 1870 [41]) pro-
prietor EA/71*
DAVIES, E. D. (d 1896 [76])
ventriloquist CDP
DAVIES, Edna (b 1905) Welsh
actress WWT/6-8
DAVIES, Elizabeth [Mrs. Jonathan
Battishill; Mrs. Anthony Web-
ster] (d 1777) actress, singer
BD
DAVIES, Elizabeth see Davies,
Mrs. William
DAVIES, George [George Smythe]
(d 1885 [33]) EA/86*
DAVIES, Mrs. George see
O'Malley, Alice Mary
DAVIES, Harry Parr (1914-55)
Welsh composer WWT/10-11
DAVIES, Hubert Henry (1869-1917)
English dramatist ES, GRB/1-4,
NTH, WWT/1-3, WWW/2
DAVIES, Hugh (fl 1742-43?) actor
BD
DAVIES, Jack (d 1946 [57]) mana-
ger, agent WWT/14*
DAVIES, Jessie Gordon (d 1913)
EA/14*
DAVIES, John Edward see
Craven, Arthur
DAVIES, Katie see Deane, Bar-
bara
DAVIES, "Kiddy" see Davies,
William

DAVIES, Lew (d 1968 [57])
composer/lyricist BP/53*
DAVIES, Lilian (d 1910) ac-
tress EA/12*
DAVIES, Lilian (1895-1932)
Welsh actress, singer WWT/
5-6
DAVIES, Maria Jane [Mrs. John
Coleman] (d 1893) actress
EA/94*, WWT/14*
DAVIES, Marianne (1744-1816?)
singer, instrumentalist BD,
DNB
DAVIES, Marion (1897-1961)
American actress ES, TW/
18, WWA/4, WWT/7-10
DAVIES, Phoebe (d 1912) Amer-
ican actress WWM, WWS
DAVIES, Phoebe see Davis,
Phoebe
DAVIES, Robert (d 1896 [65])
circus proprietor EA/97*
DAVIES, Robertson (b 1913)
Canadian dramatist, actor,
educator CD, MH, RE
DAVIES, Susannah see Davies,
Mrs. Thomas
DAVIES, Richard (d 1773) flutist,
composer BD
DAVIES, Thomas (c. 1712-85)
Scottish? actor, bookseller,
printer, proprietor BD,
CDP, DD, DNB, ES, TD/1
DAVIES, Mrs. Thomas [née
Susannah Yarrow] (1723-1801)
actress BD
DAVIES, Thomas C. (d 1881
[33]) comedian EA/82*
DAVIES, Tudor (d 1958) Welsh
singer WWW/5
DAVIES, Valentine (1905-61)
American dramatist WWA/4
DAVIES, W. G. (d 1909) EA/
10*
DAVIES, W. H. (d 1883 [76])
EA/84*
DAVIES, William (1751-1809)
English singer BD
DAVIES, William (fl 1786)
dramatist CP/3
DAVIES, William (d 1907 [47])
song composer, professor of
music EA/08*
DAVIES, Mrs. William [Eliza-
beth] (d 1782) actress BD
DAVIES, Mrs. William (d 1873
[72]) EA/75*
DAVIES, William Cadwalader

(d 1905 [57]) EA/06*
DAVILA, Diana (b 1947) American
actress TW/24-26, 28-29
DAVIN, John A. see Pell,
Johnny
DAVIN-POWER, Maurice (d 1975
[66]) dramatist BP/60*
DAVIOT, Gordon [Elizabeth Mac-
kintosh] (1896-1952) Scottish
dramatist ES, WWT/8-11,
WWW/5
DAVIS, Mr. (fl 1696) actor BD
DAVIS, Mr. (fl 1722-23) actor
BD
DAVIS, Mr. (fl 1733-35) singer,
actor BD
DAVIS, Mr. (fl 1736-52) dancer
BD
DAVIS, Mr. (fl 1754-61) violinist
BD
DAVIS, Mr. (fl 1780) actor BD
DAVIS, Mr. (fl 1787-95?) singer,
dancer BD
DAVIS, Mr. (fl 1787-1803) cos-
tume designer BD
DAVIS, Mr. (fl 1794) singer BD
DAVIS, Mrs. [née Clegg] (fl 1726-
45) singer BD
DAVIS, Mrs. (fl 1741) actress
BD
DAVIS, [Mrs. ?] (fl 1793-1814)
dresser BD
DAVIS, Mrs. (fl 1795) singer?
dancer? BD
DAVIS, Mrs. (fl 1799?-1803)
singer, actress BD
DAVIS, Mrs. [Miss Williams] (fl
1799-1803) costume designer
BD
DAVIS, Master (fl 1792) dancer
BD
DAVIS, Miss (b c. 1736) Irish
harpsichordist BD
DAVIS, Miss (fl 1739-62?) actress,
dancer, singer? BD
DAVIS, Miss (fl 1789-91) eques-
trienne BD
DAVIS, Miss (fl 1794) singer BD
DAVIS, Miss (fl 1799) actress BD
DAVIS, Prof. Alexander ventrilo-
quist CDP
DAVIS, Alfred (d 1916 [88]) EA/
17*
DAVIS, Mrs. Alfred (d 1869 [32])
EA/70*
DAVIS, Allan (b 1913) English
producer, director WWT/11-16
DAVIS, Andrew Jackson (1826-

1910) lecturer CDP
DAVIS, Ann (d 1961 [68]) actress
TW/18
DAVIS, Arthur (d 1894 [67])
comedian, manager EA/95*
DAVIS, Bessie McCoy (d 1931)
actress, singer WWT/14*
DAVIS, Bette [Ruth Elizabeth]
(b 1908) American actress
BE, CB, ES, WWT/16
DAVIS, Blevins (d 1971 [68])
producer, dramatist TW/28
DAVIS, Bob (d 1971 [61]) stand-
in BP/56*
DAVIS, Boyd (1885-1963) Amer-
ican actor WWT/7-10
DAVIS, Buster [Carl Estes
Davis] (b 1920) American
arranger, musical director
BE
DAVIS, Carl (b 1936) American
composer WWT/16
DAVIS, Caroline (fl 1853) actress
HAS
DAVIS, Charles Belmont (d
1926 [60]) American critic
BE*, BP/11*, WWT/14*
DAVIS, Charles Lindsay (b 1849)
American producer SR
DAVIS, Cherry American actress
TW/27-29
DAVIS, Clatie Polk (d 1975)
performer BP/60*
DAVIS, Clifton American actor
TW/26-30
DAVIS, David (fl 1799-1815?)
musician, instrument maker
BD
DAVIS, Dibble see Davis,
Thomas Dibble
DAVIS, Dick ["Fixer"] (d 1892
[43]) sketch artist EA/93*
DAVIS, Donald (b 1928) Cana-
dian actor, director, producer
BE
DAVIS, Dora (d 1967 [92]) actress
WWT/15*
DAVIS, E. D. see Davies,
E. D.
DAVIS, Eddie (d 1958 [58]) Amer-
ican writer BE*, BP/43*
DAVIS, Edward Dean (1806-87)
English manager, lessee,
actor DD, NYM
DAVIS, Edwards (b 1873) Amer-
ican actor, dramatist, pro-
ducer WWM
[DAVIS?], Elizabeth see

Chambers, Mrs. William
DAVIS, Emma J. see Nichols,
Emma J.
DAVIS, Eugene C. (d 1969) pro-
ducer/director/choreographer
BP/54*
DAVIS, Evelyn (b 1906) American
actress TW/2-3, 11-12
DAVIS, F. (fl 1768) actor BD
DAVIS, Fay [Mrs. Gerald Law-
rence] (1872-1945) American
actress COC, DD, ES, GRB/
1-4, WWA/2, WWS, WWT/1-9
DAVIS, Fitzroy (b 1912) American
actor, writer, singer, director,
critic BE
DAVIS, Flora (b 1883) English
actress GRB/1
DAVIS, Florence (b 1876) American
actress WWM
DAVIS, Freeman (d 1974 [71])
performer BP/59*
DAVIS, Garry (b 1921) American
actor TW/7-8
DAVIS, Rev. Gary (d 1972 [76])
performer BP/56*
DAVIS, Gilbert (b 1899) South
African actor WWT/7-10
DAVIS, Gussie L. comedian, au-
thor CDP
DAVIS, Hallie Flanagan (1890-1969)
American director, educator
BE, COC, TW/26, WWA/5
DAVIS, Hannah [Mrs. J. W.
Davis] (d 1893) EA/94*
DAVIS, Harry composer CDP
DAVIS, Harry E. (b 1905) Amer-
ican educator, director BE
DAVIS, Henry (fl 1756) doorkeeper
BD
DAVIS, Henry (d 1865) American
Ethiopian performer HAS
DAVIS, Mrs. Henry [née Nash]
(d 1868 [30]) actress? EA/69*
DAVIS, Horace (d 1910) EA/11*
DAVIS, Hugh (fl 1594-1603) actor?
DA
DAVIS, Irving Kaye (d 1965 [65])
dramatist, press agent TW/22
DAVIS, J. (fl c. 1824?) actor CDP
DAVIS, J. (fl 1837) English actor
HAS
DAVIS, Mrs. J. (d 1894) EA/95*
DAVIS, James see Hall, Owen
DAVIS, Jeanette see Chanfrau,
Henrietta
DAVIS, Jed H. (b 1921) American
educator, director BE

DAVIS, Jessie Bartlett (1859/61-1905) American singer, actress CDP, SR

DAVIS, "Jew" (fl 1795?-1819) singer, actor BD

DAVIS, Joan (b 1906) English dancer, director, producer WWT/12-15

DAVIS, Joan (1912-61) American comedienne CB, TW/17, WWA/4

DAVIS, Joe (b 1912) English lighting designer WWT/15-16

DAVIS, John (fl 1700-05) singer BD

DAVIS, John (fl 1771-1813?) actor BD

DAVIS, John (d 1793) proprietor BD

DAVIS, John (c. 1780-c. 1838) French/American manager DAB, WWA/H

DAVIS, John (1821-75) English actor, manager CDP, HAS

DAVIS, John B. (d 1970 [76]) critic BP/54*

DAVIS, John Francis (fl c. 1730?-53) composer, flutist? BD

DAVIS, Josephine singer, actress CDP

DAVIS, Mrs. J. W. see Davis, Hannah

DAVIS, Mrs. K. (fl 1789-92) dancer BD

DAVIS, Katherine (fl 1681-91) actress BD

DAVIS, "Kiddy" see Davies, William

DAVIS, Lee (d 1973) performer BP/58*

DAVIS, Lew (d 1878) American minstrel, comedian EA/79*

DAVIS, Luther (b 1916) American dramatist, producer BE

DAVIS, Mary [Mrs. James Paisible] (fl 1660-98) actress, dancer, singer BD, CDP, DD, DNB

DAVIS, Meyer (1896-1976) American musician, actor, producer BE

DAVIS, Mildred (d 1969 [68]) performer BP/54*

DAVIS, "Moll" see Davis, Mary

DAVIS, Nancy (b 1921) American actress TW/2

DAVIS, Lieut.-Col. Newnham see Newnham-Davis, Lieut.-Col. Nathaniel

DAVIS, Ossie (b 1917) American actor, dramatist, producer, director BE, CB, CD, ES, TW/22, 28, WWT/15-16

DAVIS, Owen (1874-1956) American dramatist COC, ES, MD, MH, MWD, NTH, OC/1-3, SR, TW/13, WWT/5-12

DAVIS, Owen, Jr. (1907-49) American actor TW/5, WWT/8-10

DAVIS, Peter (d 1974 [80]) producer/director/choreographer BP/59*

DAVIS, Peter (d 1974 [78]) general manager BP/59*

DAVIS, Phil (d 1974 [78]) performer BP/58*

DAVIS, Phoebe (b 1864/65) Welsh actress PP/1, WWT/1

DAVIS, Ray C. actor, dancer WWT/16

DAVIS, Richard (1697-1785) box office keeper BD

DAVIS, Richard American actor TW/1-3

DAVIS, Richard Harding (1864-1916) American dramatist ES, GRB/2-4, WWA/1, WWM, WWS, WWT/1-3, WWW/2

DAVIS, Mrs. Richard Harding see McCoy, Bessie

DAVIS, Robert (d 1906) actor? EA/07*

DAVIS, Mrs. Robert see Fernandez, Rose

DAVIS, Robert H[obart] (1869-1942) American dramatist CB, WWA/2, WWM

DAVIS, Rufe (d 1974 [66]) performer BP/59*

DAVIS, Sammy, Jr. (b 1925/26) American performer, dancer, singer, actor BE, CB, ES, TW/13, 21-22, WWT/14-16

DAVIS, Sarah see Davis, Mrs. William [Sarah]

DAVIS, Sidney (d 1883 [70]) actor EA/84*

DAVIS, Sidney [Alfred Earl Sidney Davis] (b 1867) English acting manager GRB/1

DAVIS, Solomon (fl 1785) musician BD

DAVIS, Thomas (fl 1702) stroller BD

DAVIS, Thomas (fl 1739-c. 1778)

composer, instrumentalist?
BD
DAVIS, Thomas (fl c. 1760-68)
watchman, dresser BD
DAVIS, Thomas (d 1874 [48])
minstrel EA/75*
DAVIS, Thomas Dibble (d 1795)
actor, manager BD
DAVIS, Mrs. [Thomas Dibble,
I?; Elizabeth] (fl 1758?-68)
actress BD
DAVIS, Mrs. Thomas Dibble,
V (fl 1785-1813?) actress
BD
DAVIS, Thomas H. (1859-1911)
American actor, manager SR
DAVIS, Tom Buffen (1867-1931)
English manager GRB/3-4,
WWT/1-6
DAVIS, Uriel (d 1971 [80]) com-
poser/lyricist BP/56*
DAVIS, W. (fl 1817-24) eques-
trian CDP
DAVIS, Mrs. W. A. see
Murray, Thomasina Pringle
DAVIS, Will (b 1914) American
actor TW/6
DAVIS, William (fl 1685) singer
BD
DAVIS, William (fl 1789-1824)
equestrian, manager BD
DAVIS, William (fl 1794) singer
BD
DAVIS, William (d 1868) Irish
actor HAS
DAVIS, Mrs. William [Sarah] (d
1797) actress, singer BD
DAVIS, William Boyd (b 1885)
American actor WWT/4-6
DAVIS, William G. (d 1889 [45])
American acting manager
EA/90*
DAVIS, Willis J. (d 1963 [76])
American manager BE*
DAVIS, Will J. (1844/47/54-
1919) American manager
SR, WWA/1, WWM, WWS
DAVISON, Mr. (fl 1788) actor
BD
DAVISON, Charles (d 1871) min-
strel, comedian EA/72*
DAVISON, James W. (d 1885
[71]) critic EA/86*
DAVISON, Maria Rebecca [née
Duncan] (1783-1858) English
actress BS, CDP, DD, DNB,
GT, OX
DAVISON, Mary (fl 1718?-25)

actress BD
DAVISON, Robert (b 1922) Ameri-
can designer ES, TW/2-4
DAVISON, Will (d 1905) EA/06*
DAVISS, Graham see Craig,
Clavering
DAVITS, Mary see Davis, Mary
DAVY, Master (fl 1741) dancer
BD
DAVY, Charles (d 1797 [75])
dramatist CP/3
DAVY, John (1763-1824) English
composer, instrumentalist BD,
CDP, DNB, ES, TD/1-2
DAVY, Samuel see Davey, Sam-
uel
DAVYS, Mary (fl 1725/56) Irish
dramatist CP/1-3, DNB, GT
DAW, Miss (fl 1760-68) dancer
BD
DAW, Evelyn (d 1970 [58]) per-
former BP/55*
DAWE, Carlton (d 1935 [69])
dramatist BE*, WWT/14*
DAWE, Thomas F. (1881-1928)
Irish manager WWT/4-5
DAWE, William (fl 1792-95) car-
penter, sceneman BD
DAWE, William Henry (d 1898
[51]) actor EA/99*
DAWES, Mr. (fl 1791-92) singer
BD
DAWES, Mrs. (fl 1777-79) actress
BD
DAWES, Mrs. (fl 1799) canvas
worker BD
DAWES, Miss see Daw, Miss
DAWES, Ezekiel H. (1817-50)
American actor HAS
DAWES, Gertrude [née Briant] (b
1835) American actress, dancer
HAS
DAWES, Robert (fl 1610-14) actor
DA
DAWES, Rufus (1803-59) American
dramatist HJD, RJ
DAWISON, Bogumil (fl 1866-67)
German actor HAS
DAWLEY, Herbert M. (d 1970
[90]) performer BP/55*
DAWLEY, J. Searle American ac-
tor ES
DAWN, Hazel (b 1891/94) American
actress, singer BE, ES, WWT/
3-8
DAWN, Hazel, Jr. (b 1929) Amer-
ican actress TW/5-8
DAWN, Isabel (d 1966 [62])

actress TW/23
DAWN, J. R. (d 1872 [23])
singer EA/73*
DAWSON, Mr. actor, manager
TD/1-2
DAWSON, Mr. (d 1748) actor
BD
DAWSON, Mr. (fl 1767) bill-
sticker BD
DAWSON, Mr. (fl 1776-82)
tumbler, ropedancer BD
DAWSON, Mr. (fl 1789-97)
actor BD
DAWSON, Miss (fl 1779-82)
actress, singer BD
DAWSON, Anna actress WWT/
16
DAWSON, Anthony (b 1916)
Scottish actor TW/9
DAWSON, Beatrice (1908-76)
English costume designer
WWT/15-16
DAWSON, Mrs. Charles see
Robins, Gertrude L.
DAWSON, Curt (b 1941) Amer-
ican actor TW/26-27, 30
DAWSON, Edward F. see
Damer, Frank
DAWSON, Elide Webb (d 1975
[79]) performer BP/59*
DAWSON, Forbes (b 1860) Eng-
lish actor, dramatist DD,
DP, GRB/1-4, WWT/1-8
DAWSON, Mrs. Forbes see
Harcourt, Lottie
DAWSON, George comedian,
dancer, ballet master TD/1
DAWSON, George (d 1876)
scholar EA/77*
DAWSON, Gladys (d 1969 [71])
performer BP/53*
DAWSON, Grattan (fl 1857)
actor HAS
DAWSON, Ivo (d 1934 [54]) actor
BE*, WWT/14*
DAWSON, James (d 1878 [79])
actor EA/79*
DAWSON, Jane [Mrs. Randal
Lingham] (d 1909 [86])
EA/10*
DAWSON, Jenny (d 1936) actress
EA/97
DAWSON, John (fl 1607) actor
DA
DAWSON, Jon (b 1910) American
actor TW/3-6
DAWSON, Joseph Morrison
(1818-67) English actor HAS

DAWSON, Mark (b 1920) American
actor, singer BE, TW/3-20,
23, 28-29
DAWSON, Nancy (c. 1730?-67)
English dancer BD, CDP, DD,
DNB, ES
DAWSON, Nancy (fl 1785) dancer
BD
DAWSON, Peter (1882-1961)
Australian singer WWW/6
DAWSON, Richard (fl 1739-66)
house servant BD
DAWSON, Stewart (d 1896) actor
EA/97*, WWT/14*
DAWSON, Mrs. William V. (d
1896) EA/97*
DAY, Mr. (fl 1742) dancer BD
DAY, Mr. (fl 1759-61) pyrotech-
nist BD
DAY, Mr. (fl 1852-53) actor HAS
DAY, Mr. (d 1873) carpenter
EA/75*
DAY, Mrs. (fl 1744) singer BD
DAY, Anna (b 1884) American
actress WWS
DAY, Charles (fl 1767) house ser-
vant? BD
DAY, Charles Ernest David (d
1911 [36]) EA/12*
DAY, Clarence [Shepard] (1874-
1935) writer HJD
DAY, Connie (b 1940) American
actress TW/28, 30
DAY, Cyrus L. (d 1968 [67])
teacher BP/53*
DAY, Dinah (b 1945) American
actress TW/28
DAY, Dorothy [née Ettlinger]
(1898-1975) American actress,
dramatist, critic BE
DAY, Edith (1896-1971) American
actress, singer TW/27, WWT/
4-11
DAY, Edmund (1860/66/67-1923)
American dramatist SR, WWA/
1, WWM
DAY, Ellen [Mrs. James Day] (d
1892) EA/93*
DAY, Frances [Frances Victoria
Schenk] (b 1908/12) American/
English actress, singer ES,
WWT/7-11
DAY, [George?] (fl 1762?-99?)
actor BD
DAY, Mrs. [George?] (fl 1770?-
1800?) actress BD
DAY, George D. (fl 1895-99)
dramatist DD

DAY, George D. (d 1911) mana-
ger EA/13*
DAY, Harry (d 1898) music-hall
proprietor EA/99*
DAY, Harry (d 1939 [59]) pro-
prietor, manager WWT/14*
DAY, Mrs. Harry (d 1886 [38])
actress EA/87*
DAY, Harry T. (d 1900) acro-
bat, pantomimist EA/01*
DAY, James (d 1868 [18]) Cana-
dian circus performer HAS
DAY, James (d 1876 [64]) pro-
prietor EA/77*
DAY, James (d 1883 [47]) pro-
prietor EA/84*
DAY, Mrs. James see Day,
Ellen
DAY, Jane [Mrs. John Day]
(d 1884 [52]) EA/85*
DAY, Janet (b 1938) American
actress TW/24
DAY, John (d 1584) dramatist
BE*, WWT/14*
DAY, John (c. 1574-c. 1640)
English dramatist, diarist
COC, CP/1-3, DD, DNB,
FGF, HP, NTH, OC/1-3,
RE
DAY, John (fl 1600-04) actor
DA
DAY, John (d 1888) menagerie
proprietor EA/89*
DAY, John (d 1905 [75]) musician
EA/06*
DAY, Mrs. John see Day,
Jane
DAY, John T. (fl 1897-98)
dramatist DD
DAY, Julietta (d 1957 [63])
actress TW/14
DAY, Laraine (b 1920) American
actress ES
DAY, Marie Elizabeth see
Santley, Marie
DAY, Marjorie (b 1889) New
Zealand actress WWT/2-6
DAY, May (b 1887) English
actress GRB/1
DAY, Nora [Mrs. Julian Royce]
(d 1898) actress EA/99*
DAY, Percy Leng English
journalist GRB/1-2
DAY, Philip (d 1887 [42]) actor
DD
DAY, Richard Digby (b 1940)
Welsh director WWT/15-16
DAY, Roy (d 1963 [75]) actor,

librarian BE*, BP/47*
DAY, Thomas (fl 1600-37) actor,
musician, organist, master of
the Chapel Royal DA
DAY, William (fl 1673) musician
BD
DAY, William (d 1894 [50]) lessee
EA/95*
DAY, William Charles (d 1895
[73]) actor EA/96*
DAY, William H. (1854-1927) Eng-
lish actor DD, EA/95
DAYKARHANOVA, Tamara (b 1892/
94) Russian actress, teacher
BE, TW/9-10
DAYLEY, Maggie (fl 1864) actress
HAS
DAYNE, Blanche [Mrs. Will M.
Cressy] (d 1944 [73]) American
vaudevillian WWM
DAYNES-GRASSOT, Brigitte (d
1926 [93]) actress WWT/14*
DAYRELL, Ada see Fowler,
Mrs. Montague
DAYTON, E. Mans (d 1907) acro-
bat EA/08*
DAYTON, June American actress
TW/3, 5-7
DAZEY, Charles Turner (1853-
1938) American dramatist ES,
GRB/2-4, SR, WWA/1, WWM,
WWS, WWT/1-8
DAZEY, Francis Mitchell (d 1970
[78]) dramatist BP/55*
DAZIE, Mlle. [née Daisy Peterkin]
(1882-1952) American dancer
TW/9, WWT/4-5, WWM, WWS
D'BAINVILLE, [Mons.] (fl 1733)
dancer BD
DEACON, James (d 1871 [68])
music-hall proprietor EA/72*
DEACON, James William (d 1896)
music-hall proprietor EA/97*
DEACON, Mrs. J. W. see
Deacon, Mary Ann
DEACON, Mary Ann [Mrs. J. W.
Deacon] (d 1879 [42]) EA/80*
DEACON, Richard (b 1922) Amer-
ican actor TW/26
DE ACOSTA, Mercedes (d 1968
[75]) dramatist BP/52*
DEACY, Jane talent representative
BE
DEADRICK, Louisa (fl 1864) ac-
tress HAS
DEAGON, Arthur (1873-1927)
Canadian actor WWS
DEAKIN, James (d 1879) EA/80*

DE ALBELA, Pedro (d 1877)
music teacher EA/78*
DEALY, James (d 1965 [85])
performer BP/50*
DE AMICIS, Domenico (fl 1759-
63) Italian singer BD
DE AMICIS, Signora Domenico,
Anna Lucia (fl c. 1755-89)
Italian singer, dancer BD, ES
DEAN, Mr. (fl 1761) trumpeter
BD
DEAN, Mr. (fl 1799) lamplighter
BD
DEAN, Alexander (1893-1939)
American director WWA/1
DEAN, Alfred (b 1830) SR
DEAN, Basil (1888-1971) Eng-
lish actor, director, drama-
tist, manager AAS, COC,
ES, MWD, OC/3, WWT/2-14
DEAN, Mrs. Benjamin F. see
Jones, Mrs. W. G.
DEAN, Benjamin John (d 1879)
musician EA/80*
DEAN, Doris (b 1889) English
actress, singer, dancer,
mimic GRB/1-4
DEAN, Edwin (b 1805) actor,
manager SR
DEAN, Fabian (d 1971 [41]) per-
former BP/55*
DEAN, Fanny [Mrs. Henry P.
Halsey] (d 1859) Canadian
actress CDP, HAS
DEAN, Georgie see Spaulding,
Georgie Dean
DEAN, Henry (fl 1794) musician
BD
DEAN, Isabel (b 1918) English
actress WWT/10-16
DEAN, Ivor (d 1974 [57]) per-
former BP/59*
DEAN, James (d 1867) Negro
delineator EA/68*
DEAN, James (1931-55) Ameri-
can actor ES, TW/10-12,
WWA/4
DEAN, John W. (d 1950 [75])
American actor BE*, BP/
35*, WWT/14*
DEAN, Joseph (d 1867) clown
EA/68*
DEAN, Joseph (d 1880 [29])
equestrian EA/81*
DEAN, Julia (1830-68) American
actress CDP, COC, DAB,
DD, ES, HAS, OC/1-3, SR,
WWA/H

DEAN, Julia (1880-1952) American
actress SR, TW/9, WWM,
WWT/4-6
DEAN, Kate singer CDP
DEAN, Laura (b 1963) American
actress TW/30
DEAN, Matthew (d 1878) singer,
banjoist EA/79*
DEAN, Milton (d 1962 [63]) press
agent BP/47*
DEAN, Priscilla (b 1896) American
actress ES
DEAN, Thomas (fl 1701-31) instru-
mentalist, composer BD, DNB
DEAN, Thomas (fl 1707-08) in-
strumentalist, singer, composer
BD
DEAN, Thomas ["The Royal Punch
Man"] (d 1887 [37]) EA/88*
DEAN, Thomas (d 1901) proprietor
EA/02*
DEAN, William (d 1885 [47]) con-
ductor EA/86*
DeANDA, Peter (b 1940) American
actor TW/22-24, 26
DEANE, Barbara [Katie Davies;
Mrs. Basil Loder] (b 1886)
Welsh actress, singer GRB/
1-4, WWT/5-7
DEANE, Charles (d 1910 [44])
variety comedian EA/11*
DEANE, Charles singer CDP
DEANE, Doris (d 1974 [73]) per-
former BP/58*
DEANE, Henry (d 1897) actor
EA/98*
DEANE, Henry (d 1917) EA/18*
DEANE, Julia A. see Jones,
Mrs. W. G.
DEANE, Lucie (b 1842) American
actress HAS
DEANE, Richard (fl 1661-73?)
trumpeter BD
DEANE, Tessa actress, singer
WWT/7-12
DEANE, Vivian (d 1893 [10]) actor
EA/94*
DEANE, William (d 1910 [45])
conductor EA/11*
DE ANGELIS, Mme. singer CDP
DE ANGELIS, Jefferson (1859-
1933) American actor, singer
DAB, DD, ES, GRB/2-4, OC/
1-3, SR, WWA/1, WWM, WWS,
WWT/1-7
DE ANGELO, Carlo (d 1962 [66])
actor, director BE*
DEANI, Herr (d 1888 [60]) con-

tortionist EA/89*
DEANS, Charlotte (1768-1859)
actress HAS
DEANS, F. Harris (1886-1961)
English critic, dramatist
WWT/4-13, WWW/6
DEAR, Peter see Dearing,
Peter
DEARBORN, Dalton (b 1930)
American actor TW/14-15, 23
DEARDEN, Audrey American
actress TW/9
DEARDEN, Basil (b 1911) English
dramatist, actor ES
DEARDEN, Harold (1882-1962)
English dramatist WWT/6-11
DEARDORFF, David (b 1947)
American actor TW/30
DEARING, Edgar (d 1974) per-
former BP/59*
DEARING, Peter [Peter Dear]
(b 1912) actor, producer
WWT/9-13
DEARING, Rose singer, actress
CDP
DEARING, William H. (d 1859)
actor HAS
DEARL, Mrs. (fl 1765) singer
BD
DEARLE, Mr. (fl c. 1755-c. 80)
singer BD
DEARLOVE, Charles Henry (d
1896 [63]) EA/97*
DEARLOVE, Mark William (d
1880 [78]) musician EA/81*
DEARLOVE, Mrs. Richard see
Dearlove, Sarah
DEARLOVE, Richard H. (d 1894)
musical director EA/95*
DEARLOVE, Sarah [Mrs. Richard
Dearlove] (d 1873) EA/74*
DEARLY, Max (1875-1943)
French actor, singer GRB/
4, WWT/1-4
DEARMER, Jessie Mabel see
Dearlove, Mrs. Percy
DEARMER, Mrs. Percy [Jessie
Mabel] (1872-1915) dramatist
WWW/1
DEARTH, Harry (1876-1933) Eng-
lish actor, singer WWT/2-7
DEASE, Mr. (fl 1732) actor BD
DEATH, Thomas (1739-1802)
English actor, lecturer BD,
CDP, TD/1-2
DE AUBRY, Diane (d 1969 [79])
performer BP/54*
DEAVEN, John Bruce (b 1947)

American actor TW/30
DEAVES, Mr. (fl 1848) actor HAS
DEAVES, Ada (d 1920 [64]) per-
former BE*, BP/5*
DEAVES, Walter Eugene (1854-
1919) American marionettist
ES
DE BANZIE, Brenda English ac-
tress BE, TW/13-14, WWT/
12-15
DeBAR, Mrs. see Conduit, Mrs.
Mauvaise
DEBAR, Miss see Booth, Mrs.
Junius Brutus, Jr. , I
DEBAR, Benedict (1812-77) Amer-
ican actor, manager CDP,
HAS, SR
DE BAR, Mrs. Benedict [Henrietta
Vallee] (b 1828) American
dancer, actress HAS
DE BAR, Blanche Booth (b 1844)
American actress CDP, HAS
DE BASIL, Wassily (1880-1951)
Russian impresario ES, WWT/
9-11
DE BATHE, Lady see Langtry,
Lily
DE BAUDIN, Baptiste (fl c. 1787)
dancer BD
DE BEAR, Archibald (1889-1970)
English producer, manager,
critic WWT/5-13
DE BEER, Gerrit (b 1935) Dutch
actor TW/23-25, 30
DE BEGNIS, Claudine (1800-53)
singer CDP
DE BEGNIS, Giuseppe (1793-1849)
singer CDP
DE BEGNIS, Signora Giuseppe
see De Begnis, Claudine
DE BELLEVILLE, Frederick (1857-
1923) Belgian actor CDP, GRB/
2-4, WWA/1, WWM, WWS,
WWT/1-4
DE BELOCCA, Anna (b 1854)
Russian singer CDP
DEBENHAM, Cicely (1891-1955)
English actress, singer WWT/
4-8
DE BENSAUDE, Mrs. see
Cameron, Violet
DE BENSAUDE, David (d 1897)
EA/98*
DE BERIOT, Charles Auguste (d
1870 [68]) musician EA/71*
DEBIN, Nat[han] (b 1911) American
talent representative BE
DE BLASIO, Gene (d 1971 [30])

performer BP/56*

DE BLASIS, James (b 1931)
American educator, director
BE

DEBLIN, Miss (fl 1825) dancer
CDP

DE BLOIS, Mons. (fl 1732)
dancer BD

DE BOER VAN RIJK, Esther
(d 1937 [84]) actress WWT/
14*

DEBON, Mme. (fl 1742) performer BD

DEBONAY, John L. (b 1848)
actor HAS

DE BRAHAM, Miss see Greene,
Emma Marie

DE BRAY, Henry (1889-1965)
French actor, singer WWT/
4-8

DE BREAME, Maxent (fl 1675-
78) oboist BD

DE BRECOURT, Sieur [Guil-
laume Marcoureau] (fl 1674)
French manager BD

DE BRENNER, Harry (d 1903)
minstrel EA/04*

DE BRESMES, Maxent see
De Breame, Maxent

DE BRION, Corinne Belle see
Corinne

DEBROC, Mons. (fl 1720-43)
acrobat, dancer BD

DEBROKE, Mons. see Debroc,
Mons.

DEBUIN, Henry (fl 1794) singer
BD

DE BURGH, Aimée (d 1946)
Scottish actress WWT/2-6

DE BURGH, Frank (d 1909 [63])
tattooed man EA/10*

DEBUSKEY, Merle (b 1923)
American press representative
BE

DE CAMP, Mons. (fl 1727) dancer
BD

DECAMP, Anne Theresa actress,
dancer TD/1-2

DE CAMP, Adelaide (1780-1834)
French actress, dancer BD,
TD/2

DE CAMP, George Louis (1752-
87) flutist BD

DE CAMP, Sophia (fl 1776-77)
dancer BD

DE CAMP, Sophia [Mrs. Frederick Browne] (1785-1841)
English actress, dancer BD,

HAS

DE CAMP, Vincent (1779-1839)
English actor, singer BD,
CDP, GT, HAS, TD/1

DE CARLO, Yvonne (b 1922/24)
Canadian dancer ES, TW/27-29

DE CARMO, Pussy (d 1964 [63])
Portuguese performer BE*

DE'CARO see Del Caro

DE CASALIS, Jeanne (1897-1966)
South African actress ES,
WWT/5-13

DE CASTAN, Armand see
Castelmary, Armand

DE CASTREJON, Blanca (d 1969
[53]) performer BP/54*

DE CASTRO, Mrs. A. see De
Castro, Caroline

DE CASTRO, Caroline [Mrs. A.
De Castro] (d 1884) EA/85*

DE CASTRO, Frances (fl 1795)
equestrienne? BD

DE CASTRO, James (1758-1835)
English actor, monologist,
mimic, singer BD, CDP

DE CASTRO, Mrs. James (fl 1791-
95) singer, actress BD

DECASTRO, John (d 1758) actor
WWT/14*

DECATERS-LABLACHE, Mme.
La Baronne (d 1881) EA/82*

DECATUR, Emmett Daniel (1815-
1904) musician WWA/H

DECAYNE, Andrew see Cane,
Andrew

DE CISNEROS, Eleonora (1878-
1934) American singer WWA/
1, WWM

DECKARD, Diane American actress TW/28

DECKER, Nelson W. (b 1841)
American actor HAS

DE CLEVE, Vincent (d 1827)
treasurer BD

DE CLIFFORD, Lady [Eva Car-
rington] (b 1886) English actress
GRB/1

DE CORDOBA, Pedro (1881-1950)
American actor ES, TW/7,
WWM, WWT/4-10

DE CORDOVA, Mr. (fl 1824) West
Indian actor HAS

DE CORDOVA, Arturo (d 1973
[66]) performer BP/58*

DE CORDOVA, Rudolph (1860-
1941) Jamaican actor, dramatist DD, GRB/3-4, NTH,
WWM, WWT/1-9, WWW/4

DECOURCELLE, Adrien (d 1892
[69]) dramatist EA/93*
DECOURCELLE, Pierre (1856-
1926) French dramatist
GRB/1-4
DECOURCY, Ellie see Mack-
worth, Patti
DE COURCY, Robert J. H. see
Curtiss, George
DE COURCY, William (d 1917)
EA/18*
DECOURSEY, Nellie (d 1964 [95])
vaudevillian BE*, WWT/14*
DE COURVILLE, Albert P.
(1887-1960) English manager,
producer COC, ES, NTH,
OC/3, TW/2, WWT/4-12
DEE, Blanche (b 1936) American
actress TW/23, 26, 29
DEE, Danny (d 1970 [48]) per-
former BP/55*
DEE, Frances (b 1907) American
actress TW/2
DEE, Ruby [née Ruby Ann Wal-
lace] (b 1923) American ac-
tress BE, CB, ES, TW/26-
27, 29, WWT/15-16
DEEBANK, Felix (b 1920) Eng-
lish actor TW/9-10
DEEBLE, Mr. (fl 1767-94)
singer BD
DEEBLE, Deborah (b 1945)
American actress TW/25,
28-29
DEEKS, Barbara see Windsor,
Barbara
DEEMS, Mickey [né Marvin
Damaszek] (b 1925) American
actor, writer BE, TW/19,
30
DEEN, Nedra (d 1975) performer
BP/60*, WWT/16*
DEERING, Nathaniel (1791-1881)
American dramatist DAB,
EAP, ES, HJD
DEERING, Olive actress TW/
2-4, 20, 24, WWT/16
DEERING, Olly (d 1906) actor
EA/07*
DEERING, Rebekah [Mrs. Ernest
Stevens] (d 1906 [51]) EA/07*
DEERS, Harry (d 1906) minstrel
EA/07*
DEETER, Jasper (1893-1972)
American producer, director,
actor, teacher BE, ES, TW/
28
DEEVY, Teresa (d 1963 [60])

dramatist BE*
DE FABECK, Arthur Charles
Rock see Rock, Charles
DE FABEES, Richard (b 1947)
American actor TW/30
DE FAIBER, Ernestine (b 1843)
dancer HAS
DE FELICE, Aurelia American
actress TW/30
DE FERAUDY, Maurice (1859-
1932) French actor, dramatist
GRB/1, 3-4, WWT/1-3
DE FERRIS, Lola (d 1974 [81])
performer BP/59*
DE FESCH, William (1687-1761)
Dutch musician, composer BD
DE FESCH, Mrs. [William?] (fl
1732) singer BD
DEFFENBACH, F. (fl 1821?)
American dramatist EAP, RJ
DE FILIPPO, Eduardo (b 1900)
Italian actor, dramatist NTH,
OC/3
DE FILIPPO, Peppino (b 1903)
Italian actor, dramatist COC,
OC/3
DE FILIPPO, Titina (1898-1963)
Italian actress, dramatist OC/3
DE FIVAS, Sidney see Glover,
Augustus
DE FLERS, Robert (d 1927 [56])
dramatist BE*, WWT/14*
DE FLORENCE, Ferdinand (fl 1663-
65) musician BD
DEFOE, Alice (b 1883) English
actress GRB/1
DeFOE, Louis Vincent (1869-1922)
American critic WWA/1, WWM,
WWT/4
DE FOMPRE, Mons. (fl 1724-36)
Italian? actor, dancer BD
DE FOMPRE, Mme. (fl 1734-35)
actress, dancer BD
DE FORE, Don (b 1916/17) Amer-
ican actor, producer BE, ES
DE FOREST, Marian (d 1935 [70])
American dramatic editor WWM
DE FORRESTER, F. Claude see
De Haven, F. Claude
DE FRANCESCO, Giuseppe Venuto
(d 1892 [54]) ballet master
EA/93*
DE FRANCESCO, Louis (d 1974
[87]) composer/lyricist BP/59*
DE FRANO, Mlle. (fl 1737) dancer
BD
DE FRECE, Henry (d 1931 [96])
proprietor, manager WWT/14*

DE FRECE, Hettie [Mrs. Jack De Frece] (d 1908 [33]) EA/10*

DE FRECE, Isaac (d 1902) music-hall agent EA/03*

DE FRECE, Mrs. Jack see De Frece, Hettie

DE FRECE, Lauri (1880-1921) English actor GRB/2-4, WWT/1-3

DE FRECE, Sir Walter (1870-1935) English manager GRB/2-4

DE FRECE, Mrs. Walter see Tilley, Vesta

DEFRERE, Désiré (1888-1964) Belgian singer, director BE*

DE FRIES, Mr. (fl 1859) actor HAS

DEFRIES, Violet English singer GRB/1

DeGAETANI, Thomas (b 1929) American technician, educator BE

DEGAMAR, Mr. (fl 1760s?) actor BD

DE GAMBARINI, Elisabetta [Mrs. Chazal] (b 1731?) singer, composer, organist BD

DEGENER, Claire S. [née Sweeney] (b 1928) American literary representative BE

DeGHELDER, Stephan (b 1945) American actor TW/25

DEGHELDERODE, Michel see Ghelderode, Michel de

DE GIOVANNI, Pasquale (fl 1796-1820) Italian singer BD

DE GLORION, William [Watkin Wyatt Wynne] (d 1898) circus entrepreneur EA/99*

DE GOGORZA, Emilio Eduardo (1874-1949) American singer WWA/3

DEGOTTI, Mr. (fl 1797-98) scene painter BD

DE GRAFT, Joe Ghanaian dramatist CD

DE GRANGER, Claude (fl 1663) musician BD

DE GRASSE, Sam (d 1953 [78]) actor BE*

DE GREMONT, Mlle. (fl 1720) performer? BD

DE GRESAC, Fred (d 1943 [75]) dramatist, librettist BE*, WWT/14*

DE GREY, Marie [Ellen Washington Preston] (d 1897) actress DD

DE GRIMBERGUE, Jean-Baptiste (d 1722) Belgian manager BD

DE GROACH, Mrs. (fl 1852) actress HAS

DE GROOT, Gerry (d 1975) performer BP/60*

DE GROOT, Sara Irish actress GRB/1-4

DE GROOT, Walter (b 1896) English press representative WWT/9

DE GUERBEL, Countess see Ward, Genevieve

D'EGVILLE, Master (fl 1794) singer BD

D'EGVILLE, Miss (fl 1794) singer BD

D'EGVILLE, Mons. (fl 1794) violinist BD

D'EGVILLE, Fanny (fl 1779-1800) dancer BD

D'EGVILLE, George (fl 1786-1806) dancer, dancing master BD

D'EGVILLE, James Harvey (c. 1770-1836) dancer, choreographer BD, CDP, GT, TD/1-2

D'EGVILLE, Mrs. James Harvey [née Catherine Berry] (fl 1791-1802) dancer BD

D'EGVILLE, Lewis (fl 1792-99) dancer BD

D'EGVILLE, Peter (fl 1768-94) dancer, ballet master, choreographer BD

D'EGVILLE, Mme. Peter (fl 1772-96) dancer BD

D'EGVILLE, Sophia (fl 1791-95) dancer BD

DE HAGA, John (d 1872) singer EA/73*

DEHALLE, Samuel (d 1887 [50]) EA/88*

DE HALSALLE, Henry (b 1872) dramatist, critic GRB/1

DE HARTOG, Jan (b 1914) Dutch dramatist BE, MD

DE HAVEN, Carter (1886-1977) American actor ES, WWM

DE HAVEN, F. Claude [F. Claude De Forrester] (b 1846) American banjoist, singer, ventriloquist, magician, actor HAS

DE HAVEN, Gloria (b 1925) American actress, singer BE, TW/24

DE HAVEN, Rose (d 1972 [91])

performer BP/57*
DE HAVILLAND, Olivia (b 1916)
American actress BE, CB,
ES, TW/7-9
DE HENNEY, [Mme. ?] (fl 1753)
dancer BD
DeHETRE, Katherine (b 1946)
American actress TW/28
DE HIGHTREHIGHT, Mr. (fl 1718)
Swiss fire-eater BD
DEHN, Paul (1912-76) English
dramatist, lyricist, critic
WWT/12-16
DEIGHTON, Mr. actor TD/1-2
DEIGHTON, Marga Ann Indian/
English actress TW/5-11
DEITCH, Dan (b 1945) American
actor TW/30
DE JACQUES, Eulallean see
Lorraine, Lilian
DE JARDIN, Mons. (fl 1750-51)
dancer BD
DEJAZET, Eugene (d 1880 [60])
composer EA/81*
DEJAZET, Pauline Virginie (1798-
1875) French actress COC,
OC/1-3
DE JONG, Frank (d 1903) mana-
ger EA/05*
DEKARO (d 1916 [86]) juggler
EA/18*
DEKKER, Albert (1905-68) Amer-
ican actor, director BE, ES,
TW/22, 24, WWA/5, WWT/
13-14
DEKKER, Thomas (c. 1572-c. 1632)
English dramatist CDP, COC,
CP/1-3, DD, DNB, ES, FGF,
HP, MH, NTH, OC/1-3, PDT,
RE
DEKOLTA, Joseph B. (b 1845)
French magician SR
DE KORPONAY, Gabriel (fl 1884)
dancer CDP
DE KOVEN, Reginald (1859/61-
1920) American conductor,
composer DAB, DD, ES,
GRB/3-4, HJD, SR, WWA/1,
WWM, WWS, WWT/1-3
DeKOVEN, Roger (b 1907) Amer-
ican actor BE, TW/3, 22,
24, 26-27
DE KOWA, Victor (d 1973 [69])
performer BP/57*
DE KRUIF, Paul (1890-1971)
American writer BE
DELACEY, Kate (fl 1852) singer
HAS

DE LA CHAPELLE, Mons. (fl
1791-92) French dancer BD
DE LA COINTRIE, Mons. (fl 1751-
53) dancer BD
DE LA COINTRIE, Mme. (fl 1749-
52) dancer BD
DE LA COUR, W. (fl 1740-63)
scene painter BD
DEL'ACQUA, Teresa (fl 1790)
singer BD
DE LA CROIX, Mlle. (fl 1790-99)
dancer BD
DE LACY, Valerie English actress,
singer GRB/1-2
DE LACY, Walter (d 1874) musi-
cian EA/75*
DELAFIELD, E. M. [née Edmée
Elizabeth de la Pasture; Mrs.
A. P. Dashwood] (1890-1943)
English dramatist DNB, WWT/
8-9
DE LA FOINTE, Renée see
Adoree, Renée
DE LA FOND, Mr. (fl 1716) im-
presario BD
DELAFORCE, Augustus Edward (d
1900 [86]) EA/02*
DELAGAR, Mr. (fl 1775) dancer
BD
DELAGARDE, [Charles?] (fl 1705-
36) dancer, choreographer,
dancing master BD
DELAGARDE, Mrs. [Charles?] (fl
1710-11) dancer BD
DELAGARDE, Charles (fl 1718-34)
dancer BD
DELAGARDE, J. (fl 1718-50)
dancer BD
DELAGARDE, Mrs. J. [née Oates]
(fl 1730-51) English actress,
dancer BD
DE LA GRANGE, Mons. (fl 1738)
dancer BD
DE LA GRANGE, Mlle. (fl 1738)
dancer BD
DE LA GRANGE, Anna (b 1825)
French singer HAS
DE LA GRANGE, Sophie (fl 1865)
pianist HAS
DE LA HAY, Mons. (fl 1707)
dancer BD
DE LA HAY, Mr. (fl 1736-38)
dancer BD
DE LA HAYE, Ina (1906-72) Russian actress, singer WWT/10-
15
DELAHOY, [Master?] (fl 1799)
dancer BD

DELAHOYDE, Mr. (fl 1745-50)
   musician BD
DELAINE, Jack (d 1918) EA/19*
DELAIR, Paul (d 1894 [52])
   dramatist BE*, WWT/14*
DE LAITRE, Mons. (fl 1752-59)
   dancer BD
DELAMAINE, Henry (fl 1733-55?)
   dancer, choreographer BD
DELAMANO, William (fl 1850s)
   artist WWA/H
DE LA MARCA, Raffaello (b
   1871) Italian singer WWM
DELAMAYNE, Thomas (fl 1742)
   dramatist CP/2-3, GT
DE LA MOTTE, Marguerite
   (1902-50) actress BE*
DELAN, [B. ?] (fl 1797) house
   servant? BD
"DE LA NASH, Mme. " see
   Fielding, Henry
DELAND, Annie [Mrs. George
   Finnegan] (1842-93) American
   actress CDP, HAS
"DELANE" see Huntley, Thomas
   L.
DELANE, Dennis (d 1750) Irish
   actor BD, DD, DNB
DELANEY, Arthur (d 1899 [31])
   comic singer EA/00*
DELANEY, Charles (d 1959
   [67]) actor BE*
DELANEY, J. S. (d 1884) come-
   dian EA/86*
DELANEY, Maureen (d 1961
   [73]) Irish actress BE*, BP/
   45*, WWT/14*
DELANEY, Shelagh (b 1939)
   English dramatist AAS, BE,
   CB, CD, CH, ES, MD, MH,
   MWD, PDT, WWT/14-16
DELANEY, Tom (d 1905 [36])
   music-hall comedian EA/06*
DE LANGE, Herman (1851-1929)
   Dutch/English actor DD,
   WWT/2-5
DE LANGE, Mrs. Herman see
   Hill, Annie
DELANNOY, Edmond (d 1888
   [71]) actor WWT/14*
DELANO, Fanny actress CDP
DELANO, Jeppe actor CDP
DELANO, Paul tattoed man CDP
DELANOY, Edmond (d 1888 [71])
   actor BE*
DE LANTY, Virginia see
   Powys, Stephen
DELANY, Maureen (d 1961 [73])

Irish actress TW/17
DELANY, Richard see Guido,
   Frank
DELAP, John (1725-1812) English
   dramatist CP/1-3, DD, DNB,
   GT, TD/1-2
DE LA PASTURE, Edmée Eliza-
   beth Monica see Delafield,
   E. M.
DE LA PASTURE, Mrs. Henry
   [Lady Clifford] (1866-1945)
   Italian dramatist GRB/2-4,
   NTH, WWT/1-7, WWW/4
DELAPORTE, Agnes (fl 1886-90)
   actress, singer DD
DELAPORTE, Eleanor (d 1917)
   EA/18*
DE LA PORTE, [Gérard?] (fl
   1660s?) violinist BD
DE LAPPE, Gemze (b 1921/22/25)
   American dancer, actress,
   choreographer BE, ES, TW/
   8-9, 15, 21
DE LARA, Isidore (d 1935) com-
   poser WWW/3
DELARO, Elma singer, actress
   CDP
DE LA ROCHE, Mazo (d 1961
   [82]) dramatist WWT/14*
DELAROCHE, Suzanne see
   Avril, Suzanne
DE LA ROCHE-GUILHEN, Mme.
   (fl 1677) director, dramatist
   BD
DE LAROUX, Hugues (d 1925)
   dramatist WWT/14*
DE LA ROVERE, Luigi (fl 1790-
   91) scene painter BD
DELARUE, Mr. (fl 1827) actor
   HAS
DE LA SALLE, Michel Joseph
   ["Old Joe"] (d 1887) actor,
   critic NYM
DELASCEY, Mr. (fl 1757) dancer
   BD
DE LASCO, Maude singer CDP
DE LA TORRE, Claudio (d 1973
   [77]) dramatist BP/57*
DE LA TOUR, Alexander (fl 1689-
   1700) violinist? BD
DE LA TOUR, Frances (b 1944)
   English actress WWT/16
DELAUNAY, Louis (d 1903 [77])
   actor WWT/14*
DELAVAL, Frances actress EA/97
DE LAVALLADE, Carmen (b 1931)
   American dancer, actress BE,
   CB

DE LA VALLE, Mme. (fl 1790-
96) musician BD
DELAVANTI, Rose (d 1883 [47])
EA/84*
DE LA VOLEE, Jean (fl 1633)
French musician BD
DELAWN, Mr. (fl 1734) dancer
BD
DELBERT, Robert (b 1946) Amer-
ican actor TW/26, 30
DEL CAMPO, Thomazio Alegro
(fl 1718) Italian acrobat BD
DEL CARO, Mlle. [Mme. Cesare
Bossi] (fl 1794-1803) dancer
BD
DEL CARO, Mlle. (fl 1790-1815)
dancer BD
DELCY, Catharine (fl c. 1845)
English actress CDP, HAS
DELDERFIELD, R. F. (1912-72)
English dramatist AAS,
WWT/10-14
DELEGALL, Bob (b 1945) Amer-
ican actor TW/27-28
DE LEGH, Kitty (b 1887/95)
English actress WWT/7-11
DELEHANTY, Thornton W. (d
1971 [77]) critic BP/56*
DELEHANTY, William H. (1846-
80) American singer, com-
poser, choreographer, min-
strel CDP, HAS, SR
DE LEON, Jack (1897-1956)
Panamanian manager WWT/
6-12
DE LEON, Millie (d 1922 [52])
dancer BE*, BP/7*
DE LEON, Thomas Cooper
(1839-1914) American writer
WWA/1
DE LEON, Walter American
actor ES
DE LEPINE, Mr. (fl 1719)
machinist BD
DE L'EPINE, Francesca
Margherita [Mrs. John Chris-
topher Pepusch] (d 1746)
singer BD
DE LETRAZ, Jean (d 1954 [57])
dramatist WWT/14*
DELEVANTE, Frederick (d
1889) musical director EA/
90*
DELEVANTI, Cyril (d 1975 [86])
performer BP/60*
DELEVANTI, George see
Crippen, George
DELEVANTI, John (d 1908 [83])

acrobat, clown EA/09*
DELEVINE, Minnie (d 1911) per-
former? EA/12*
DELF, Harry (d 1964 [71]) come-
dian, dramatist, director TW/
20
DELF, Juliet (d 1962 [74]) vaude-
villian TW/18
DELFEVRE, Mme. (fl 1786-87)
dancer BD
DELFONT, Bernard [né Barnet
Winogradsky] (b 1909) Russian/
English producer, manager
BE, WWT/10-16
DELGADO, Roger (d 1973 [53])
performer BP/58*
DEL GRANDE, Gertrude (d 1894
[20]) singer EA/95*
DELIA, Mlle. French actress
CDP
DE LIAGRE, Alfred, Jr. (b 1904)
American producer, director,
manager BE, TW/2-8, WWT/
15-16
DE LIAS, R. J. (d 1883) manager
EA/84*
DELICATI, Luigi (fl 1789) singer
BD
DELICATI, Signora Luigi [Margher-
ita] (fl 1789) singer BD
DELICATI, Margherita see
Delicati, Signora Luigi
DELIGHT, June (d 1975 [77])
performer BP/60*
DELIGNY, Louise (fl 1791) dancer
BD
DELILLE, Octavia (fl 1851) French
singer CDP
DELIMA, Margaret Linley (d 1969
[67]) performer BP/54*
DE LISLE, Mons. (fl 1675)
dancer BD
DELISLE, Mons. (fl 1734-35)
French actor, dancer BD
DELISLE, Mlle. (c. 1684-1758)
French actress BD
DE L'ISLE, Mlle. (fl 1735-36)
dancer BD
DE LISSALE, Mr. (fl 1742) house
servant? BD
DE LIURY, Mlle. (fl 1720) per-
former? BD
DELL, Mr. (fl 1760-61) horn
player BD
DELL, African (d 1899 [37])
ventriloquist EA/00*
DELL, Floyd (1887-1969) Ameri-
can dramatist ES, WWT/7-9

DELL, Gabriel [né del Vecchio] (b 1923/30) West Indian actor TW/20-25, 28, 30, WWT/15-16

DELL, Henry (fl 1756-66) dramatist CP/2-3, DNB, GT, TD/1-2

DELL, James (d c. 1774) musician BD

DELL, Jeffrey (b 1899) English dramatist WWT/8-9

DELLA CASA, Lisa (b 1921) Swiss singer CB, ES

DELLA CHIESA, Vivian (b 1915) American singer CB

DELL AGATA, Michele (fl 1758-63) dancer BD

DELLA PORTA, Giambattista (1538-1613) Italian dramatist COC

DELLA ROVERE see De La Rovere

della SORTE, Joseph (b 1940) American actor TW/25, 27-28, 30

DELLENBAUGH, Harriet Rogers Otis (d 1930) American actress, dramatic reader WWA/1

DELLINGER, Miss (fl 1817) English actress HAS

DELLO JOIO, Norman (b 1913) American composer CB, ES

DELMAN, Mr. actor HAS

D'ELMAR, Camille [Mrs. Richard Baker] (d 1902) actress EA/03*

DELMAR, Emily (d 1881) EA/83*

DELMAR, Georgina [Mrs. H. Winsloe Hall] English actress, vocalist GRB/1-4

DEL MEDICO, Michael (b 1933) American actor TW/26-27, 30

DELMONTE, Jack (d 1973 [84]) actor TW/30

DELMORE, George E. (b 1874) American vaudevillian WWM

DELMORE, Ralph (1853-1923) American actor SR, WWM, WWS

DELNA, Marie (1875-1932) French singer ES

DELON, Jack (d 1970 [42]) actor, singer TW/27

DELONEY, The Messrs. (fl 1675) guitar players BD

DE LONG, Mons. dancing teacher

CDP

DELORME, Mme. (fl 1730-37) dancer BD

DELORME, Mlle. (fl 1730-37) dancer, actress BD

DE LORNE, Blanche (d 1911) actress EA/12*

DE LOS ANGELES, Victoria see Angeles, Victoria de los

DE LOSSKING (d 1890) American comedian EA/91*

DELOTTO, Joseph (d 1899) circus clown, comedian EA/00*

DE LOUTHERBOURG, Philip James [Philippe Jacques] (1740-1812) German scene designer, painter BD, COC, ES, OC/1-3

DELPINI, Carlo Antonio (1740-1828) Italian actor, dancer, choreographer, singer BD, CDP, DNB, ES, TD/1-2

DELPINI, Signora Carlo Antonio (fl 1784-1828) actress, singer BD

DELPIT, Albert (b 1849) American/French dramatist DD

DEL PUENTE, Giuseppe (1843-1900) Italian singer ES

DELROY, Irene (b 1898) American actress, dancer WWT/7-8

DELROY, Maurice (d 1917) illusionist EA/18*

DE LUCA, Giuseppe (1876-1950) Italian singer CB, ES, WWA/3

DE LUCE, Virginia [née Virginia de Luce Wilson] (b 1921) American actress, singer, dancer BE, TW/8-19

De LUISE, Dom (b 1933) American actor TW/20

DE LUNGO, Tony (b 1892) Italian actor WWT/7-10

DE LURE [Israel Clark] (d 1900) illusionist EA/01*

DE LUSSAN, Zelie (c. 1865-1949) American singer CDP, GRB/1-4, WWS

DEL VAL, Jean (d 1975 [83]) performer BP/59*

DEL VECCHIO, Gabriel see Dell, Gabriel

DELVERD, Thomas ["Japanese Tommy"] (d 1887) minstrel EA/88*

D'ELVILLE, Rinallo (fl 1813) dramatist EAP

DELYLE, Alda (d 1927 [33]) prima donna BE*, BP/12*

DELYSIA, Alice (b 1885/89/91)
French actress, singer
COC, OC/1-3, WWT/4-12
DEMAIMBRAY [Stephen Triboudet?]
(fl 1735?-44) machinist BD
DeMAIO, Peter American actor
TW/26, 29-30
DE MAJO, Signor (fl 1766) singer?
BD
DEMAR, Mons. (fl 1736) dancer
BD
DE MAR, Carrie (d 1963 [87])
performer BE*
DE MARCHI, Emilio (1861-1917)
Italian singer ES
DEMARCO, Norman (b 1910)
American educator BE
DE MARCO, Tony (d 1965 [67])
dancer TW/22
DEMAREST, Rubin (d 1962 [76])
actor BE*
DEMAREST, William (b 1892)
American actor ES
DEMARIA, Mr. (fl 1773-75)
dancer? BD
DEMARIA, J. (fl 1793?-1814)
scene painter BD
DE MARNEY, Derrick (b 1906)
English actor ES, WWT/8-14
DE MARNEY, Terence (1909-71)
English actor WWT/8-14
DeMARTIN, Imelda [née Imelda
Italia deMartin di Fabbro]
(b 1936) Italian actress,
dancer, singer BE, TW/20-
21
DEMAS, Carole (b 1940) Ameri-
can actress TW/20, 24-25,
28-30
DE MATTOS, A. T. (1865-1921)
translator DD
DE MAX, Edouard (d 1924 [55])
actor WWT/14*
DeMAY, Sally (b 1922) American
actress TW/28
DEMEMBRAY see Demaimbray
DE MENDOZA, Don Fernando
Diaz (d 1930) actor, manager
WWT/14*
DEMERA, Signora (fl 1771)
singer BD
DEMEREST, G. W. minstrel
CDP
DE MERODE, Cléo French
dancer GRB/1-4
DE MEYER, Leopold pianist
CDP
DE MICHELI, Mr. (fl 1783-85)

boxkeeper BD
DE MICHELI, Leopoldo (fl 1761-
91) singer, music copyist BD
DE MICHELI, Signora Leopoldo
[Mary Ann] (fl 1775-78) singer
BD
DE MICHELI, Mary Ann see
De Micheli, Signora Leopoldo
DE MILLE, Agnes (b 1908) Amer-
ican dancer, choreographer,
director AAS, BE, CB, ES,
NTH, TW/2-8, WWT/10-16
DeMILLE, Beatrice M. (d 1923)
talent representative BE*,
BP/8*
DE MILLE, Mrs. Cecil [Constance
Adams] (d 1960 [87]) American
actress BE*
DE MILLE, Cecil Blount (1881-
1959) American actor, drama-
tist, producer ES, GRB/3-4,
NTH, SR, TW/15, WWA/5,
WWT/1-9, WWW/5
DE MILLE, Henry Churchill
(1850-93) American dramatist
CDP, DAB, DD, SR, WWA/H
DE MILLE, William Churchill
(1878/83-1955) American drama-
tist, actor ES, GRB/3-4,
NTH, SR, TW/11, WWA/3,
WWM, WWT/1-9
DEMING, Mrs. L. L. singer,
composer, lyricist CDP
DEMING, Will H. (1870/71-1926)
American actor SR, WWM
DE MINIL, Renée (d 1941) actress
BE*, WWT/14*
DE MIRA, Signora (fl 1793-1800)
singer BD
DE MIRAIL see Dumirail
DEMODORE, Mr. (fl 1715) flutist
BD
DE MOE, William (d 1874) musi-
cal director, composer EA/
75*
DE MOLAS, Nicholas (d 1944)
Russian/American scene de-
signer ES
DE MOND, Willy (d 1976 [72])
hosier BP/60*
DE MONDION, Edmund [Edmund
Pilletts] (fl 1866-67) actor
HAS
DEMONT, Charles (d 1976 [84])
performer BP/60*
DE MONTI (d 1910 [42]) skater
EA/11*
DE MOOR, Teda (b 1915) South

African dancer, choreographer
ES
DEMOREST, Vienna singer,
composer CDP
DeMOTT, John A. (d 1975 [63])
performer BP/59*
DeMOTTE, Warren (d 1970
[60]) critic BP/55*
DEMOURIER, Mr. (fl 1774-75?)
dancer BD
DEMPSEY, Clifford (d 1938 [73])
American actor BE*, BP/23*
DEMPSEY, Jerome (b 1929)
American actor TW/28
DEMPSEY, Mark (b 1936) Amer-
ican actor TW/26-28
DEMPSEY, Mary Ellen (d 1905
[25]) EA/06*
DEMPSEY, W. P. singer CDP
DEMPSTER, Hugh (b 1900) Eng-
lish actor WWT/11-15
DEMPSTER, John Hugh (d 1901)
manager EA/02*
DEMPSTER, Robert (b 1883)
American actor WWM
DEMPSTER, William R. (1808-
71) composer CDP
DE MURSKA, Ilma (d 1889 [53])
singer EA/90*
DEMUTH, Norman (1898-1968)
English composer, conductor
ES
DE NAVARRO, Mary see
Anderson, Mary
DENBY, Mr. (fl 1784) violinist
BD
DENBY, Edwin (b 1903) Amer-
ican dancer, choreographer
ES
DENBY, William (fl 1842-46)
English actor HAS
DENCE, Marjorie (d 1966) ac-
tress WWT/15*
DENCH, Judi (b 1934/35) English
actress AAS, COC, WWT/
14-16
DENE, Dorothy (d 1899) actress
DD, DP, EA/96
DENE, Ruyston (d 1911 [52])
actor, sketch artist EA/12*
DE NEERGAARD, Beatrice [née
Flood] (b 1908/10) American
actress BE, TW/2-3
DENENHOLZ, Reginald (1913-73)
American press representative
BE, TW/30
DENES, Oscar (b 1893) Hungarian
actor, singer WWT/8-9

DENGEL, Jake (b 1933) American
actor TW/25, 27, 29-30
DENGEL, Roni (b 1942) American
actor TW/27
DENHAM, Mr. (d 1832) actor
CDP
DENHAM, Miss see Durham,
Miss
DENHAM, Fanny actress CDP
DENHAM, George W. (d 1907
[62]) American actor GRB/3*,
WWT/14*
DENHAM, Isolde (b 1920) English
actress WWT/10-11
DENHAM, Sir John (1615-68/69)
Irish/English dramatist CP/
1-3, DD, FGF, HP
DENHAM, June Catherine Church
see St. Denis, Teddie
DENHAM, Mary Anne (d 1855)
American actress HAS
DENHAM, Maurice (b 1909) Eng-
lish actor WWT/11-16
DENHAM, Reginald (b 1894) Eng-
lish actor, producer, director
AAS, BE, ES, TW/2-8, WWT/
5-16
DENHAM, Robert (c. 1723-82)
singer BD
DENIER, John (b 1838) American
pantomimist, gymnast, tight-
rope performer HAS
DENIER, Tony (1839-1917) clown,
manager CDP, SR
DENIN, Kate (1837-1907) Ameri-
can actress CDP, HAS, SR
DENIN, Susan (1835-75) American
actress CDP, HAS, SR
DE NIRO, Robert (b 1943) Amer-
ican actor CB, TW/27-28
DENIS, Charles (d c. 1772) drama-
tist CP/2-3, GT
DENIS, Ruth see St. Denis,
Ruth
DENISON, A. M. (d 1891) actor
EA/92*
DENISON, Merrill (b 1893) Cana-
dian dramatist MH, RE
DENISON, Michael (b 1915) Eng-
lish actor AAS, ES, WWT/
11-16
DENISON, Robert G. (b 1937)
American actor TW/29
DENKER, Henry (b 1912) Ameri-
can dramatist, director, pro-
ducer BE, ES, MD
DENLEY, Mrs. (d 1875) EA/76*
DENMAN, Edmund (c. 1754-1827)

English? instrumentalist
BD
DENMAN, Henry (1774-1816)
English singer, actor, in-
strumentalist BD
DENMAN, William (1766-1806)
actor, singer BD, GT, TD/
1-2
DENMARK, L. Kirk (b 1916)
American educator BE
DENNEN, Barry (b 1938) Amer-
ican actor TW/28-29
DENNER, Mr. (fl 1758) violinist
BD
D'ENNERY, Adolphe Philippe
(1812-99) French dramatist
DD
DENNET, Mr. (fl 1753) actor
BD
DENNETT, Miss B. (fl 1799?-
1820?) dancer, actress?
BD, DD
DENNETT, Eliza [Mrs. Robert
O'Neill] (fl 1799?-1820?)
dancer, actress? BD, DD
DENNETT, Miss F. (fl 1799?-
1820?) dancer, actress?
BD, DD
DENNING, Thomas (1790-1821)
actor CDP
DENNING, Will H. (d 1926 [55])
actor BE*
DENNIS, Mr. (fl 1725-31) per-
former? BD
DENNIS, Mr. (fl 1752-80?)
singer, dancer BD
DENNIS, Mr. (fl 1779) actor BD
DENNIS, Mrs. (fl 1720) singer
BD
DENNIS, Mrs. (fl 1752-70?)
singer, dancer BD
DENNIS, Arthur (b 1870) English
actor GRB/1-2
DENNIS, Dorian (d 1970 [47])
performer BP/55*
DENNIS, John (1657-1733/34)
English critic, dramatist
CDP, CP/1-3, DD, ES, GT,
HP, NTH, TD/1-2
DENNIS, Nick actor TW/4
DENNIS, Nigel (b 1912) English
dramatist, critic AAS, CD,
MD, MWD, PDT
DENNIS, Roland (b 1944) Amer-
ican actor TW/25, 27, 29
DENNIS, Dr. Russell (d 1964
[48]) actor BE*
DENNIS, Sandy (b 1937) American

actress AAS, BE, CB, TW/24,
27, 29, WWT/15-16
DENNIS, Will [Stephen Townesend]
(1859-1914) English actor DD,
EA/95, GRB/1-4
DENNISON, Mr. (d 1756) dancer
BD
DENNISON, Mr. Irish actor HAS
DENNISON, Mrs. (fl 1752) singer,
dancer BD
DENNISON, Frank (d 1964 [63])
English actor, conductor BE*
DENNISTON, Reynolds (1881-1943)
New Zealand actor CB, SR
DENNISTOUN, J. (d 1898 [39])
manager EA/99*
DENNON, T. J. (d 1889 [28])
business manager EA/90*
DENNY, Mr. (fl 1757-68) door-
keeper BD
DENNY, Mr. (fl 1784) violoncellist
BD
DENNY, Mrs. (fl 1783-85) dresser
BD
DENNY, Ernest (1869-1943) Eng-
lish dramatist GRB/4, WWT/
1-9
DENNY, Frances Ann (1798-1875)
actress COC
DENNY, George V. (b 1899) actor
SR
DENNY, Henry (fl 1783-91) car-
penter BD
DENNY, Reginald (1891-1967)
English actor, singer BE, ES,
TW/24, WWA/4, WWT/7-14
DENNY, Mrs. W. H. (d 1902
[41]) EA/03*
DENNY, William Henry [William
Henry Dugmore] (1853-1915)
English actor DD, DP, EA/
97, GRB/1-4, WWM, WWS,
WWT/1-2
DENNY, W. R. (d 1896 [32])
dramatist EA/97*
DENOYE see Denoyer
DENOYER, [G. ? Philip?] (d 1788)
dancer, choreographer BD
DENT, Alan (b 1905) Scottish
critic ES, WWT/9-16
DENT, Bert music-hall manager
GRB/1
DENT, G. Calvert (d 1904 [51])
acting manager EA/05*
DENT, John (fl 1782-95) dramatist
CP/3, GT, TD/1-2
DENT, Lizzie [Mrs. Jack Seebold]
(d 1897) EA/99*

DENT, Richard (fl c. 1714-28)
  barber BD
DENTON, Mrs. (fl 1749-67?)
  actress BD
DENTON, Crahan (d 1966 [52])
  American actor BE, TW/23
DENTON, C. St. John see
  Denton, St. John C.
DENTON, Frank [Frank Bellamy]
  (1878-1945) English actor
  WWT/1-6
DENTON, John see Denton,
  "Thomas"
DENTON, Percy singer CDP
DENTON, St. John C. (d 1933
  [76]) English agent, manager
  GRB/1-4
DENTON, "Thomas" [John] (d
  1789) English artificer, ex-
  hibitor BD
DENTS, [Master?] (fl 1723)
  dancer BD
DENTS, [Miss?] (fl 1723) dancer
  BD
DENTS, De Long (fl 1723)
  dancer BD
DENVIL, Alice (d 1908) actress
  EA/09*, WWT/14*
DENVIL, Clara (d 1867 [18])
  EA/68*, WWT/14*
DENVIL, Mrs. Henry see
  Denvil, Marianne
DENVIL, Henry Gaskell (1804-66)
  English actor CDP, DD,
  HAS
DENVIL, Horace Gaskin (d 1878
  [25]) actor EA/79*
DENVIL, Marianne [Mrs. Henry
  Denvil] (d 1889 [79]) EA/91*
DENVIL, Rachel [Mrs. Rachel
  Finney Troy] (d 1885) actress
  CDP
DENVILLE, Alfred (1876-1955)
  English actor, manager WWT/
  7-11
DENVILLE, Charles (d 1876 [25])
  actor EA/77*
DENYER, James (d 1972 [46])
  publicist BP/57*
DENYGTEN, Thomas see Dow-
  ton, Thomas
DENZER, Jacob (d 1863) gymnast
  HAS
DENZIL, Madge [Mrs. Alec F.
  Frank] (d 1897) actress EA/
  98*
DEODORE, Peter (fl 1674) per-
  former? BD

D'EON DE BEAUMONT, Charles
  Geneviève Louis Auguste André
  Timothée (1728-1810) French
  swordsman, impresario, diplo-
  matist BD, CDP
DE ORDUNA, Juan (d 1974 [67])
  producer/director/choreographer
  BP/58*
DE OSTA, Mrs. John (d 1891
  [37]) EA/92*
DE PAOLI, Gaetano (fl 1795)
  singer BD
DE PAOLIS, Alessio (1893-1964)
  Italian singer ES, WWA/4
"DE PARIS, Mlle. à la mode" (fl
  1731) dancer BD
DE PARRAVICINI, S. A. (d 1893)
  agent EA/94*
DE PASQUALI, Bernice (d 1925)
  American singer WWM
DE PAUL, Gene (b 1919) Ameri-
  can composer, pianist BE
DE PINNA, David (d 1908) mana-
  ger EA/09*
DEPORT, Mr. (fl 1749) wigmaker
  BD
DE POUGY, Liane (b 1873) French
  variety artist GRB/1-4
DEPPE, Hans (d 1969 [71]) pro-
  ducer/director/choreographer
  BP/54*
DER ABRAHMIAN, Arousiak (d
  1973 [82]) performer BP/58*
DERBY, Mr. (fl 1757-62) office
  keeper BD
DERBY, Countess of see Farren,
  Elizabeth
DERBY, Edward Smith-Stanley
  (1752-1834) CDP
DE REEDER, Louis (d 1910)
  musical director EA/12*
DE REES, James (d 1908) fit-up
  proprietor EA/10*
DE RENZIE, Leonard (d 1974
  [73]) manager BP/58*
DE RESZKE, Edouard (1853-1917)
  Polish singer ES, SR, WWA/1
DE RESZKE, Jean (1850-1925)
  Polish singer ES, SR, WWA/2
DE RETZSKE, Josefina (1855-91)
  singer ES
DE REYES, Consuelo (1893-1948)
  English director, dramatist
  WWT/8-10
DERHAM, Miss see Durham,
  Miss
D'ERINA, Rosa singer CDP
DERIOUS, Lizzie singer CDP

DERIVIS, Maria (fl 1882) singer
CDP
D'ERLANGER, Frederic A.
(1868-1943) composer WWW/4
DERLE see Dearle
DERMAN, Lou (d 1976 [61])
dramatist BP/60*
DERMONT, Paul (d 1970 [54])
performer BP/55*
DERMOT, Garrett (1830-63)
comedian HAS
DERN, Bruce (b 1936) American
actor TW/15
D'ERNE, Frances Mabel see
Newcombe, Mabel
DeROCHER, L. E. (b 1912)
Canadian manager BE
DEROISEY, Lucien (d 1972 [60])
producer/director/choreog-
rapher BP/57*
DEROISSI, Miss (fl 1763) dancer
BD
DE ROOS, Marie [Marion Eliza-
beth Battle] English actress
GRB/1
DE ROSA, Sig. (d 1871 [90])
singer EA/72*
DE ROSA, Mlle. (fl 1868) dancer
CDP
DE ROSE, Peter (1896-1953)
American songwriter BE*,
BP/37*
DE ROSSENAW, Ninetta (fl 1754-
55) actress BD
DERR, Richard (b 1917) Ameri-
can actor BE, TW/5-19,
WWT/12-14
DERRICK, Joseph (fl 1880-86)
dramatist DD
DERRICK, Samuel (1724-69)
Irish translator CP/1-3,
GT, TD/1-2
DE RUSSO, Richard (b 1946)
American actor TW/29
DERWENT, Clarence (1884-1959)
English actor, producer,
dramatist CB, COC, OC/3,
TW/1-8, 12-16, WWA/3,
WWT/8-12
DERWENT, Elfrida (d 1958
[80+]) English actress BE*,
BP/43*
DERWOOD, Mrs. Charles E.
see Wynter, Florrie
DE SABATA, Victor (b 1892)
Italian conductor ES
DESABAYE, Mr. (fl 1687-1711)
musician BD

DESAGULIERS, [Dr. ?] (fl 1740)
pyrotechnist BD
DE ST. LEU, Mr. (fl 1794) flutist
BD
DeSAL, Frank (b 1943) American
actor TW/25
DE SANCTIS, Alfredo Italian actor
WWT/2-4
DE SANTIS, Joe (b 1909) Ameri-
can actor TW/9
DESBARQUES, Mons. (fl 1705-08)
dancer BD
DESBARQUES, Mme. (fl 1708)
dancer BD
DESBARQUES, Mlle. (fl 1707)
dancer BD
DESBOROUGH, Juliet [Mrs. F.
W. Irish] (d 1892 [54]) actress
EA/93*, WWT/14*
DESBOROUGH, Philip (b 1883)
English actor WWT/5-6
DESCHALLIEZ, Louise [Louise
Deschalliez de Vaurenville]
(fl 1720-22) dancer BD
DESCHAMPS, Emile (d 1871 [79])
composer EA/72*
DESCOATE, John (fl 1695)
trumpeter BD
DESCOMBES, Mrs. [Fraulein
Laura] (d 1904 [73]) high-wire
performer EA/05*
DESDECHINA, Signora (fl 1749)
dancer BD
DE SELINCOURT, Hugh (1878-1951)
English critic WWT/1-5
DE SHADE, Mons. (fl 1743) dancer
BD
DESHALN, Mr. (fl 1737) house
servant? BD
DES HAYES, André J. J. (fl
1797?-1811) dancer, chore-
ographer BD
DESHAYES [Jean Baptiste Fran-
çois] (1705-79?) actor, chore-
ographer? BD
DESHAYES, Paul (d 1891 [57])
actor BE*, WWT/14*
DE SHIELDS, Andre (b 1946)
American actor TW/29-30
DE SICA, Vittorio (d 1974 [73])
performer BP/59*
DE SILVA, David (b 1936) Ameri-
can talent representative BE
DE SILVA, Frank (d 1968 [78])
actor TW/24
DE SILVA, Nina [Angelita Helena]
(1868/69-1949) actress COC,
WWT/1-10

DeSIMONE, B. J. (b 1939)
American actor TW/24-27
DE SISLEY, Mme. (fl 1794)
singer BD
DESJARDINS, Pauline (fl 1844)
dancer CDP, HAS
DESKINS, Mervyn (b 1937) American actor TW/30
DESLANDES, Raymond (d 1890 [64]) manager WWT/14*
DESLYS, Gaby (1881/84-1920)
French actress, dancer ES, OC/1-3, SR, WWT/3
DESMOND, Bob (d 1901 [42])
Negro comedian EA/01*
DESMOND, Florence (b 1905/07)
English actress, singer AAS, ES, WWT/7-14
DESMOND, Maggie [Mrs. J. G. Beckett; Mrs. Robert W. Chapman] (1848-72) Irish actress CDP, HAS
DESMOND, Mona actress, singer CDP
DESMOND, Patrick American actor TW/25-26
DESMOND, Shaw (1877-1960)
Irish dramatist WWW/6
DESMOND, William (1878-1949)
Irish/American actor ES, TW/6
DESMOULINS, John (fl 1778)
house servant? BD
DESMOULINS, Mrs. [John?]
(fl 1778) house servant? BD
DESNOYE see Denoyer
DESNOYER see Denoyer
DE SOLLA, Barton (d 1899 [66])
actor EA/00*
DE SOLLA, B. M. (d 1894 [77])
professor of music EA/95*
DE SOLLA, Rachel (d 1920)
actress BE*, WWT/14*
DESORMES, Mons. (fl 1749)
actor BD
DE SOUSA, May (1887-1948)
American actress, singer
GRB/2-4, TW/5, WWT/1-5
DESPLACES, Henri (d 1877 [53]) singer EA/78*
DESPO (b 1922) Greek performer TW/23, 27-30
DESPREAUX, Louise Rosalie see Allan, Louise Rosalie
DESPRES, Suzanne (1875-1951)
French actress GRB/4, WWT/1-3
DESPREZ, Frank (1853-1916)

English dramatist, critic DD, WWT/1-3
DESSE, Mons. (fl 1735-61) dancer BD
DESSE, Mr. (fl 1761) dancer BD
D'ESSER, Mr. (fl 1748) dancer BD
DESSESSARS, Mons. (fl 1734-35) actor BD
DESSESSARS, Mme. (fl 1734-35) actress BD
"DES SINGES, Le Chevalier" (fl 1767-68) performing monkey BD
DESSUSLEFOUR, Françoise-Marie see Durancy, Mme. Jean-François
DE STAINER, Marguerite [Mrs. James Guidery] (d 1911 [25]) EA/12*
D'ESTE, Emmie see Warner, Mrs. H.
DESTINN, Emmy (1878-1930)
Bohemian singer WWA/1
DESTOUCHES, Philippe Néricault (1680-1754) French dramatist OC/1-3
DESTRADE, [Francis?] (d 1754)
dancer, actor BD
DE SURLIS, Jean (fl 1663-1707)
actor, manager BD
DE SWIRSKY, Countess Thamara (b 1888) Russian dancer WWM
DE SYLVA, Brown G. (1896-1950)
American librettist, lyricist
AAS, CB, DAB, ES, TW/7, WWA/3, WWT/6-10
DE SYLVA, Buddy see De Sylva, Brown G.
DE SYLVA, Henderson American librettist, lyricist AAS
DETCHON, Adelaide actress CDP
DE TOLLY, Deena (d 1976) performer BP/60*
DETOY, Charles (b 1897) American executive BE
DE TREVILLE, Yvonne (1881-1954) American singer WWA/3, WWM
DETTEY, Miss (fl 1794) singer BD
DETTMAR, Lottie (d 1902) actress, dancer EA/03*
DETTMER, Roger (b 1927) American critic BE
DE TURA, Gennaro (1880-1939)
Italian singer ES
DEULIN, Herr [Isaac Dowling] (d

1860 [43]) EA/72*
DEULIN, Paul (d 1878 [37])
comedian EA/79*
DEULIN, Mrs. Paul (d 1879
[38]) EA/80*
DEUSTER, Joseph see Anthony,
Joseph
DEUTSCH, Ernst (1890-1969)
Austrian actor ES, TW/25
DEUTSCH, Milt (d 1974 [56])
manager, agent BP/58*
DEVAL, Jacques (1890-1972)
French dramatist BE, MWD,
WWT/9
DE VALOIS, Dame Ninette [Edris
Stannus] (b 1898) Irish dancer
CB, ES, OC/1-2, WWT/5-12
DEVANT, Anthony (fl 1669) musi-
cian? BD
DEVANT, David [David Wighton]
(1863-1941) English illusionist
GRB/1-4
DE VASCO, Mlle. (d 1886)
trapezist EA/87*
DE VAURENVILLE, Louise
Deschalliez see Deschalliez,
Louise
DE VAUX, Renée (d 1961 [80])
actress WWT/14*
D'EVELYN, Miss (fl 1797-98)
actress, singer BD
DEVEN, N. T. see Davenport,
N. T.
DE VERA, Cris (d 1974 [49])
performer BP/59*
DE VERE, Charles (1823-68)
American circus performer
HAS
DE VERE, Clementine Duchene
(d 1954 [89]) singer WWT/14*
DE VERE, Mrs. E. see De
Vere, Stella
DEVERE, Francesca (d 1952
[61]) American actress BE*,
BP/37*
DE VERE, Frederick (d 1910)
EA/11*
DE VERE, George F. (d 1910
[75]) actor BE*, WWT/14*
DE VERE, Nellie see Bailey,
Mary
DE VERE, Nora (d 1905) serio-
comic EA/06*
DEVERE, Sam (d 1907 [65])
minstrel, banjoist CDP
DE VERE, Stella [Mrs. E. De
Vere] (d 1893) music-hall
performer EA/94*

DEVEREAUX, Jack (d 1958 [76])
actor TW/14
DEVEREAUX, Mrs. Jack see
Drew, Louise
DEVEREAUX, Louise Drew see
Drew, Louise
DEVERELL, John W. (1880-1965)
actor WWT/3-13
DEVERELL, Mrs. M. (fl 1792)
English? dramatist CP/3
DEVEREUX, Ernest (d 1908 [29])
actor EA/10*
DEVEREUX, John (d 1890) musical
director EA/91*
DEVEREUX, John Drew (b 1918)
American actor TW/5-11
DEVEREUX, Robert, Earl of Es-
sex (1566-1601) English masque
writer DNB
DEVEREUX, William (d 1945 [75])
actor, dramatist GRB/3-4,
WWT/1-9
DE VERNEUIL, [Louis François
Joseph?] (fl 1718-35) actor
BD
DE VERNEUIL, [Mme. Louis
François Joseph; née Marie-
Louise Chabot] (fl 1718-35)
actress BD
DE VERNEUIL, Mimi (fl 1733-35)
dancer, actress? BD
DEVIENNE, Mr. (fl 1797-98)
flutist BD
DE VILLABOS, Guadeloupe Velez
see Velez, Lupe
DEVIN, William (d 1917 [50])
musician EA/18*
DEVINE, Claire (d 1973 [82])
singer, actress TW/29
DEVINE, George Alexander (1910-
66) English actor, producer,
manager AAS, BE, CH, COC,
ES, OC/2-3, PDT, WWT/9-14,
WWW/6
DEVINE, William M. see
Armstrong, William
DEVINGUT, Gertrude F. see
Argyle, Gertrude
DEVISSE, Mons. (fl 1750-54)
dancer BD
DEVLIN, Jay (b 1929) American
actor TW/26
DEVLIN, John (b 1937) American
actor TW/21, 23, 25, 28-29
DEVLIN, Mary see Booth, Mrs.
Edwin Thomas
DEVLIN, William (b 1911) Scottish
actor AAS, TW/4, WWT/8-14

DEVNEY, Mrs. M. A. (d
1890 [61]) EA/91*
DE VOLA, Robert (d 1886 [37])
acrobat EA/87*
"DE VOLTORE, Mons. " (fl 1734)
acrobat BD
DEVON, Pru (d 1973) performer
BP/57*
DEVONO, Prof. (d 1909) con-
jurer EA/10*
DEVONSHIRE, Mr. (fl 1795)
exhibitor BD
DEVOTO, Mr. (fl 1778-84)
house servant? BD
DEVOTO, Anthony (fl c. 1662-67)
puppeteer BD
DEVOTO, John (fl 1672-76)
property man, manager BD
DEVOTO, John (fl 1708-52)
scene painter BD
DE VOY, Mrs. Albert see
De Voy, Sarah
DE VOY, George (d 1896) EA/97*
DE VOY, Sam (d 1907 [64])
Negro comedian EA/08*
DE VOY, Sarah [Mrs. Albert
De Voy] (d 1893) EA/94*
DE VOYE, James (d 1906) ani-
mal trainer EA/08*
DEVRIENT, Eduard (1801-77)
producer, actor BE*, WWT/
14*
DEVRIENT, Emil (1803-72)
German actor OC/1-3
DEVRIENT, Karl (1797-1872)
actor BE*
DEVRIENT, Ludwig (d 1832 [48])
actor, manager WWT/14*
DEVRIENT, Max (1857-1929)
actor BE*, WWT/14*
DE VRIES, Peter (b 1910) Amer-
ican dramatist BE
DE VRIES, Rosa (fl 1850) singer
CDP, HAS
DEW, Edward (b 1909) American
actor TW/2-3
DEW, John Henry see Drew,
Harry
DE WALDEN, T. B. (b 1811)
English actor, dramatist DD,
HAS, SR
DEWAR, Fred (fl 1860-77) actor
DD
DEWAR, Frederick C. (d 1878
[46]) actor EA/79*, WWT/
14*
DEWAR, J. A. (d 1897 [64])
actor WWT/14*

DEWAR, Mrs. James see
Dewar, Rose Eliza
DEWAR, John A. (d 1897 [60])
actor EA/98*
DEWAR, L. S. (d 1885) actor
EA/86*
DEWAR, Mrs. L. S. see
Clarke, Florence
DEWAR, Rose Eliza [Mrs. James
Dewar] (d 1867 [70]) EA/68*
DE WARFAZ, George (1889-1959)
actor WWT/4-10
DE WEERTH, Ernest (d 1967 [62])
designer TW/23
DEWELL, Michael (b 1931) Amer-
ican producer BE, WWT/16
DEWELL, Nicholas (fl 1689-99)
trumpeter BD
DEWEY, James G. (d 1964 [86])
composer/lyricist BP/49*
DEWEY, Kenneth S. G. (d 1972
[37]) theatre founder BP/57*
DEWEY, Pat (d 1892 [34]) EA/
93*
DEWEY, Rufus Hosmer (b 1881)
American press representative
WWM
DeWHARTON, Barbara Lee (d
1972 [48]) performer BP/56*
DEWHURST, Colleen (b 1926?)
Canadian actress AAS, BE,
CB, TW/14-20, 24, 26-30,
WWT/14-16
DEWHURST, Elizabeth [Mrs. J.
Dewhurst] (d 1885 [36]) EA/86*
DEWHURST, Frances Clara [Mrs.
Jonathan Dewhurst] (d 1912
[50]) EA/13*
DEWHURST, J. (fl 1871-84) actor
DD
DEWHURST, Mrs. J. see
Dewhurst, Elizabeth
DEWHURST, Mrs. J. D. see
Dewhurst, Mrs. M. M.
DEWHURST, Jonathan (d 1913)
actor BE*, EA/14*, WWT/14*
DEWHURST, Mrs. Jonathan see
Dewhurst, Frances Clara
DEWHURST, Keith (b 1931) Eng-
lish dramatist CD
DEWHURST, Mrs. M. M. [Mrs.
J. D. Dewhurst] (d 1874 [33])
EA/75*
DEWICK, Dawson English actor
GRB/1
DE WILD, Gene (b 1929) Ameri-
can educator, director, actor
BE

DE WILDE, Brandon (1942-72)
American actor TW/9, 21,
29, WWA/5
DE WILDE, Frederic (b 1914)
American stage manager,
actor, director BE
DE WILHORST, Cora (fl 1857)
singer CDP
DeWINDT, Hal (b 1933) Ameri-
can actor TW/18
DEWINNE, Henri (d 1897 [64])
ballet master EA/98*
DE WINTON, Alice English ac-
tress DD, EA/96, GRB/1-4,
WWT/1-5
DE WINTON, Stewart (b 1879)
Scottish actor GRB/1
DE WITT, Fay (b 1935) Ameri-
can actress, singer BE
DEWITZ, Ursula (d 1975 [60])
theatre owner BP/60*
DE WOLFE, Billy [né William
Andrew Jones] (1907-74)
American actor BE, BTR/
74, TW/10-11, 13, 30, WWT/
14-15
DE WOLFE, Elsie (1865-1950)
American actress DAB,
GRB/2-4, SR, TW/7, WWM,
WWS, WWT/1-4
DEWS, Peter (b 1929) English
director AAS, WWT/16
DE WYNNE, Charles (d 1902)
juggler EA/03*
DEXTER, Aubrey [Douglas Peter
Jonas] (1898-1958) English
actor WWT/9-12
DEXTER, Brad (b 1917) Ameri-
can actor TW/5-6
DEXTER, Elliott (1870-1941)
American actor ES
DEXTER, John (1726-64) Irish
actor BD
DEXTER, John (b 1925) English
director AAS, CB, ES,
PDT, WWT/14-16
DEYMAN, Mrs. (fl 1714) actress
BD
DeYOUNG, Cliff (b 1945) Amer-
ican actor TW/28-29
D'FERROU VILLE, Mons. (fl
1732) dancer BD
D'HERBAGE, Mons. (fl 1736)
actor BD
D'HERVIGNI, Mlle. (fl 1735-36)
dancer BD
DHERY, Robert [né Fourrey] (b
1921) actor, director BE

D'HIVER, Marian (d 1882) EA/
83*
DHOTRE, Damoo (d 1973 [72])
performer BP/57*
DIACOFF, Mrs. Tom see
Shelton, Laura Blanche
DIAGHILEV, Serge (1872-1929)
Russian impresario COC, ES,
OC/1-3, WWT/4-5
DIAMOND, Mr. (fl 1660) acrobat
BD
DIAMOND, Mr. (fl 1784-90) actor
BD
DIAMOND, Alf (d 1917 [24]) come-
dian EA/18*
DIAMOND, Charles singer, min-
strel CDP
DIAMOND, David (b 1915) Ameri-
can composer CB
DIAMOND, Frank (d 1888) minstrel
EA/89*
DIAMOND, Harry (d 1906 [40])
EA/07*
DIAMOND, Mrs. Harry see
Stanley, Nelly
DIAMOND, John (1823-57) Ameri-
can dancer HAS
DIAMOND, Lillian (d 1962 [73])
performer, wardrobe mistress
BE*
DIAMOND, Margaret (b 1916)
English actress WWT/11-16
DIAMOND, Matthew (b 1951)
American actor TW/28
DIAMOND, Michael (b 1945) Amer-
ican actor TW/27-29
DIAMOND, Neil (b 1941) American
singer TW/29
DIAMOND, William see Dimond,
William Wyatt
DIAMOND, Zelda see Fichandler,
Zelda
"DIANA" see Constantini, Signora
Giovanni Battista
"DIANA, Signora" (fl 1726-27)
actress BD
DIANI, Ermissilde (b 1848) Italian
dancer HAS
DIANTA [Auguste Offroy] (d 1900
[41]) acrobat EA/01*
DI ASPINO, Diego (fl 1744-45)
singer BD
"DIAVOLINO, Signor" (fl 1754)
musician BD
DIBBLE, Robert (fl 1793-1817)
singer BD
DIBBLE, Thomas see Davis,
Thomas Dibble

DIBDIN, Miss (fl 1799-1804)
dancer BD
DIBDIN, Ann see Dibdin, Mrs.
Thomas John
DIBDIN, Anne CDP
DIBDIN, Charles (1745-1814)
English dramatist, actor,
lyricist, singer, pianist BD,
CDP, COC, CP/2-3, DD,
DNB, ES, GT, HP, OC/1-3,
PDT, SR, TD/1-2
DIBDIN, Charles Isaac Mungo
[né Pitt] (1768-1833) English
dramatist, actor, singer,
manager BD, CDP, COC,
CP/3, DD, DNB, ES, OC/
1-3
DIBDIN, Mrs. Charles Isaac
Mungo [née May Bates] (1782-
1816) actress, singer BD,
CDP
DIBDIN, Henry Edward (1813-66)
English musician DNB
DIBDIN, Mary see Dibdin,
Mrs. Charles Isaac Mungo
DIBDIN, Thomas John [né Pitt]
(1771-1841) English actor,
scene painter, dramatist,
manager BD, CDP, COC,
CP/3, DD, DNB, ES, GT,
OC/1-3, TD/1-2
DIBDIN, Mrs. Thomas John
[née Ann Hilliar] (1775-1828)
actress, singer BD, CDP
Di BLASIO, Joe (d 1973 [62])
producer/director/choreograph-
er BP/58*
DICK, Mr. (fl 1790-1805) tailor
BD
DICK, Mrs. (fl 1797) house ser-
vant? BD
DICK, C. G. Cotsford (1846-
1911) English composer,
dramatist DD, GRB/1-4,
WWW/1
DICK, E. [Dutton's Boy] (fl
1597) actor DA
DICKENS, Miss (fl 1855) actress
HAS
DICKENS, Charles (1812-70) Eng-
lish writer CDP, COC, DD,
DNB, EA/69, ES, OC/1-3
DICKENS, Charles (d 1896 [59])
EA/97*
DICKENS, C. Stafford (1896-
1967) English dramatist, pro-
ducer, actor TW/24, WWT/
8-14

DICKENS, Edward Buller Lytton
(d 1902 [50]) EA/03*
DICKENS, Fanny (d 1895) actress
EA/96*
DICKENS, Mary (fl 1883-86) ac-
tress DD
DICKENSON, Mrs. (fl 1746-65)
boxkeeper BD
DICKENSON, G. K. (d 1863) actor
WWT/14*
DICKENSON, [Samuel?] (fl 1784-
1810) oboist BD
DICKER, Maitland (1858-1917)
English actor, stage manager,
manager GRB/4
DICKERSON, Mr. (fl 1794) violin-
ist BD
DICKERSON, Maude see Bart-
elle, Jennie Dickerson
DICKESON, Herbert (b 1875) Eng-
lish actor GRB/1
DICKEY, Anna Mary actress TW/1
DICKEY, Paul (1884/85-1933)
American dramatist WWT/6-7
DICKINS, Mr. (fl 1705-06) actor
BD
DICKINS, Mrs. see Barnett,
Alice
DICKINS, John Thanet (d 1896
[61]) EA/97*
DICKINSON, Albert (d 1908) per-
former? EA/09*
DICKINSON, Anna Elizabeth (1842-
1932) American actress, lectur-
er, dramatist CDP, DAB
DICKINSON, Genevieve [née
Giesen] (b 1909) American edu-
cator, director BE
DICKINSON, George acting mana-
ger GRB/1
DICKINSON, G. K. (d 1863) Eng-
lish actor HAS
DICKINSON, Isabel (fl 1848) ac-
tress DD
DICKINSON, John (fl 1745-79) gal-
lery office keeper BD
DICKINSON, Maggie (d 1949) ac-
tress, singer BE*, WWT/14*
DICKINSON, Thomas Herbert (b
1877) American critic ES
DICKONS, Maria [née Poole]
(1770?-1833) English singer,
actress CDP, DD, DNB
DICKSON, Charles (1862-1927)
American actor, dramatist,
manager SR
DICKSON, Donald (d 1972 [61])
performer BP/57*

DICKSON, Dorothy (b 1896)
American actress, dancer
AAS, BE, ES, WWT/4-13
DICKSON, Gloria (d 1945 [28])
actress BE*
DICKSON, James (b 1949) Amer-
ican actor TW/29
DICKSON, James A. (1774-1853)
English actor HAS
DICKSON, J. W. (fl 1858) actor
HAS
DICKSON, Lamont (d 1944)
actor BE*, WWT/14*
DICKSON, Lydia (d 1928 [40])
comedienne BE*, BP/12*
DICKSON, Walter (d 1918)
EA/19*
"DICK WHITTINGTON" see
Colman, George, the Elder
DIDCOTT, Hugh Jay (d 1909
[73]) variety agent EA/10*
DIDDEAR, Charles Bannister
(1801-59) actor CDP, DD
DIDDEAR, Harriet Elizabeth
[Mrs. John Saville Faucit;
Mrs. William Farren, the
Younger] (1789-1857) English
actress BD, BS, DD, OX
DIDDEAR, [John? Charles?]
(1761-1841) manager, actor
BD
DIDELOT, Charles-Louis (1767-
1837) Swedish dancer, chore-
ographer BD
DIDELOT, Mme. Charles-Louis
[née Marie-Rose Paul] (d
1803) dancer BD
DIDIEE, Nantier (fl 1855) singer
CDP, HAS
DIDIER, Abraham J. (1739-1823)
actor BD, TD/1-2
DIDIER, Mrs. Abraham J. [née
Margaret Evans] (1741-1829)
actress, singer BD
DIDIER, Kate (d 1901) EA/02*
DIDO, Mrs. Tony see James,
Lil
DIDRING, Ernest (1868-1931)
Swedish dramatist WWT/2-3
DIDSBURY, Robert (fl 1787-94)
singer BD
DIEG, Alfred (d 1901) music-
hall producer EA/02*
DIENER, Joan (b 1934) Ameri-
can actress, singer BE,
TW/10-12, 22-24, 26, 28-29,
WWT/15-16
DIERKES, John (d 1975 [69])

performer BP/59*
DIERLAM, Robert J. (b 1917)
American educator, director
BE
DIERS, Eugene (d 1970 [70s])
performer BP/55*
DIERS, Hank (b 1931) American
educator BE
DIESEL, Leota American critic
BE
DIESEY, Mr. (fl 1767) dancer
BD
DIETERLE, Charlotte (d 1968
[72]) performer BP/52*
DIETERLE, William (d 1972 [79])
producer/director/choreographer
BP/57*
DIETRICH, Christian (d 1760)
bass player BD
DIETRICH, Dena (b 1928) Ameri-
can actress TW/23-24, 28-30
DIETRICH, John E. (b 1913)
American educator BE
DIETRICH, Marlene (b 1900/04)
German performer TW/24-25,
WWT/16
DIETRICH, Rene (b 1886) Ameri-
can singer WWM
DIETRICHSTEIN, Leo (fl 1893)
actor, dramatist DD
DIETZ, Claude see Garry,
Claude
DIETZ, Eileen American actress
TW/27-28, 30
DIETZ, Ella (fl 1872) actress
CDP
DIETZ, Howard (b 1896) American
lyricist, librettist, dramatist
CB, CD, MWD, NTH, WWT/
8-16
DIETZ, Linda (d 1920) American
actress, singer CDP, DD,
OAA/2
DIEUPART, Charles (d c.1740)
French musician, composer,
impresario BD
DIEY, Mrs. Alf see Diey, Annie
DIEY, Annie [Mrs. Alf Diey] (d
1874) EA/75*
DI FABBRO, Imelda Italia de
Martin see DeMartin, Imelda
D'IFFANGER, Thomas Howard
Paul ["Valentine"] (d 1886 [42])
comedian EA/87*
DIFFEN, Ray (b 1922) English
costume designer, costumier
BE
DIFILIPPI, Arturo (d 1972 [78])

performer BP/57*
DIGBY, Mr. (fl 1781) actor,
singer BD
DIGBY, George, Earl of Bristol
(d 1676) dramatist CP/1-3,
GT
DIGBY, Maude English actress
EA/97, GRB/1
DIGBY, Robert (d 1963 [50])
manager WWT/14*
DIGGES, Dudley (1879/80-1947)
Irish actor, producer, director
COC, DAB, NTH, OC/1-3,
SR, TW/1-4, WWA/2, WWT/
6-10
DIGGES, Mrs. Dudley see
Digges, Mary
DIGGES, Dudley West (1720-86)
English actor, singer, mana-
ger BD, CDP, COC, DD,
DNB, ES, OC/1-3, TD/1-2
DIGGES, Ernest (d 1970) per-
former BP/55*
DIGGES, Mary [Mrs. Dudley
Digges; née Mary Quinn] (d
1947) Irish actress SR
DIGGES, Richard Evered (d 1889)
EA/91*
DIGGORY, William Thomas (d
1882 [27]) actor EA/84*
DIGGS, Richard (d 1727) actor
BD
DIGHTON, Mr. (fl 1733-48)
actor BD
DIGHTON, John (b 1909) English
dramatist AAS, WWT/12-16
DIGHTON, Robert (c. 1752-1814)
actor, singer, dramatist,
scene painter BD, CDP
DIGHTON, Mrs. Robert [Miss
Bertles] (fl 1787-94) singer
BD
DIGNAM, Mr. (fl 1743) house
servant? BD
DIGNAM, Mark (b 1909) English
actor AAS, WWT/9-16
DIGNUM, Charles (c. 1765-1827)
English singer, actor, com-
poser BD, CDP, DD, DNB,
GT, TD/2
DI GRAZIO, Randy (b 1952)
American actor TW/30
DIL, Mr. (fl 1796) house servant?
BD
DILBERGLUE, Mrs. see
Anderton, Sarah
DILKE, Charles Wentworth (1789-
1864) critic DNB

DILKE, Thomas (d c. 1698) English
dramatist CP/1-3, DD, GT
DILKS, Joseph see Clifton,
Joseph
DILL, Max M. (d 1949 [71])
comedian TW/6
DILLER, Mons. (fl 1788) pyro-
technist BD
DILLER, Phyllis (b 1917) Ameri-
can actress, comedienne CB,
TW/26
DILLEY, Joseph J. (b 1838)
dramatist DD, EA/69
DILLIGH, Avni (d 1971 [62]) per-
former BP/56*
DILLINGHAM, Anna E. (fl 1859-
68) actress HAS
DILLINGHAM, Charles Bancroft
(1868-1934) American manager
DAB, NTH, OC/1-3, SR,
WWA/1, WWM, WWT/2-7
DILLMAN, Bradford (b 1930)
American actor BE, CB, ES,
TW/13-19
DILLON, Alexander see Macin-
doe, Alexander
DILLON, Baron (fl 1784) singer
BD
DILLON, Charles (1819-81) Eng-
lish actor, manager CDP, DD,
ES, HAS, OAA/1-2
DILLON, Mrs. Charles [Clara
Conquest] (d 1888 [63]) actress
DD
DILLON, Charles E. (d 1964 [76])
actor BE*
DILLON, Clara (d 1898 [53])
dramatist, actress DD
DILLON, Enrica Clay (b 1780)
singer SR
DILLON, Fanny (1881-1947) Amer-
ican composer WWA/2
DILLON, Frances (d 1947 [75])
actress GRB/3-4, WWT/1-7
DILLON, James (d 1889) actor
EA/90*
DILLON, John [né John Daily
Marum] (1831-1913) Irish actor
CDP, SR
DILLON, Melinda (b 1939) Ameri-
can actress BE, TW/19-20,
23-27
DILLON, Thomas Patrick (d 1962
[66]) performer BE*
DILLON, Tom see Spence, Tom
DILLON, Will (d 1966 [89]) com-
poser/lyricist BP/50*
DILMEN, Güngör (b 1930) Turkish

dramatist RE

DI LORENZO, Tina (d 1930 [57])
actress BE*, WWT/14*

DILWORTH, Gordon (b 1913)
American actor, singer BE,
TW/22-23

DIMITRIEW, Vladimir (d 1964
[78]) ballet school founder
BP/49*

DIMKNELL, Mr. (fl 1799) house
servant BD

DIMMOCK, Mr. (fl 1758-62)
doorkeeper, billsticker BD

DIMMOCK, Master (fl 1739)
actor BD

DIMOND, William H. (1832-57)
American actor? HAS

DIMOND, William Wyatt (d 1812
[62]) actor, manager, dramatist BD, CDP, CP/3, DD,
GT, TD/1-2

DI MURSKA, Ilma (1843-89)
singer CDP

DIN, Dulce S. (d 1975 [39])
performer BP/60*

DINE, Jim painter CD

DINEHART, Alan (1890-1944)
American actor, producer
CB, SR, TW/1, WWA/2,
WWT/5-9

DING----, Mr. (fl 1661-62)
actor BD

"DINGDONG" (fl 1774) musician
BD

DINGEON, Helen actress CDP

DINGLE, Charles (1887-1956)
American actor TW/10-12

DINGLE, George see Booker,
George

DINGLE, Tom (d 1925 [38])
dancer BE*, BP/10*

DINGLEY, Joseph (fl 1766)
proprietor BD

DINGWALL, Alexander W. (d
1918 [60]) producer BE*,
WWT/14*

DINNEFORD, William (d 1852)
English actor, manager HAS

DINSMORE, O. A. (b 1849)
American actor HAS

DIPAOLA, Earlamae (d 1972 [44])
performer BP/57*

DIPLOCK, Dr. (d 1892) EA/93*

DIPLOCK, F. Bramah (d 1898)
acting manager EA/99*

DIPPEL, Andreas (1866-1932)
German singer, manager ES,
SR, WWA/1, WWM

DIPPLE, George (d 1909) pantomimist EA/10*

DIRCKS, Rudolf (b 1875) English
dramatist, critic GRB/2-4

DI RHIGINI, Countess see
Russell, Ella

DI RHONA, Albina (fl 1860) actress, dancer CDP

DIRKENS, Annie (1870-1942) German actress, singer ES

DISHER, Maurice Willson (1893-
1969) English critic AAS, ES,
WWT/4-14, WWW/6

DISHLEY see Distle

DISHY, Bob actor WWT/16

DISKIN, Marshall (d 1975 [62])
producer/director/choreographer
BP/60*

DISNEY, Thomas (fl 1671-98)
actor BD

DISTIN, John (d 1863 [74]?) musician CDP

DISTIN, Theodore (d 1893 [69])
singer, composer EA/94*

DISTIN, Mrs. Theodore [Sarah
Connor] (d 1863 [33]) singer
EA/72*

DISTIN FAMILY musicians CDP

DISTLE (fl 1610-36?) actor DA

DISTLEY see Distle

DISWELL, Mr. (fl 1794-95) puppeteer BD

DITCHER, Mr. (fl 1797-1813)
doorkeeper BD

DITHMAR, Edward Augustus (1854-
1917) American critic WWM

DITRICHSTEIN, Leo (1858/65-
1928) Austrian actor, dramatist DAB, ES, GRB/2-4, SR,
WWA/1, WWM, WWS, WWT/
1-5

DITSON, Lenny (d 1975 [63]) performer BP/60*

DITTINI, Mme. (d 1904 [45])
actress EA/05*

DITTMAR, Heinrich (d 1910)
musician EA/11*

DIVENY, Mary American actress
TW/5

DIVER, Mrs. see Brunton,
Miss E.

DIX, Beulah Marie (1876-1970)
American dramatist GRB/2-4,
WWM, WWS, WWT/1-3

DIX, Dorothy (1892-1970) English
actress WWT/1-10

DIX, Frank (d 1949 [78]) pantomime author BE*, WWT/14*

DIX, J. Airlie (d 1911) song
composer EA/13*
DIX, Lillian (d 1922 [58]) actress
BE*, BP/7*
DIX, Richard (1894-1949) Ameri-
can actor ES, TW/6
DIXEY, E. Freeman (1833-1904)
minstrel CDP
DIXEY, Henry E. (1859-1943)
American actor CB, CDP,
GRB/2-4, NTH, PP/1, SR,
WWA/2, WWS, WWT/1-9
DIXEY, Phyllis (d 1964 [50])
performer BE*
DIXON, Mr. (fl 1762-71) door-
keeper BD
DIXON, Adèle (b 1908) English
actress WWT/6-14
DIXON, Aland (d 1976 [65]) per-
former BP/60*
DIXON, Mrs. B. [Mme. Purcell]
(d 1869 [30]) singer EA/70*
DIXON, Campbell (1895-1960)
Tasmanian dramatist, critic
WWT/9-12, WWW/5
DIXON, Charlotte [Mrs. G.
H. Dixon] (d 1891) EA/93*
DIXON, Clara Ann [Mrs. Smith;
Mrs. Sterling] (fl 1795-1822)
singer, actress BD, CDP,
TD/1-2
DIXON, Cliff (d 1968 [79]) per-
former BP/52*
DIXON, Conway (d 1943 [69]) ac-
tor BE*, WWT/14*
DIXON, Cornelius (fl 1770-1821)
scene painter, architect BD
DIXON, Mrs. [Cornelius?] (fl
1787) dancer BD
DIXON, Denver (d 1972 [82])
performer BP/57*
DIXON, Dorothy (1875-1947)
actress SR
DIXON, Edwin (d 1871 [42])
comedian EA/72*
DIXON, George Washington (1795-
1861) American actor, black-
face performer CDP, HAS,
SR
DIXON, Gerald (d 1879) drama-
tist DD
DIXON, Mrs. G. H. see
Dixon, Charlotte
DIXON, Harland (d 1969 [83])
vaudevillian TW/26
DIXON, James (fl 1660-62) actor
BD
DIXON, Jean (b 1896/1905)

American actress BE, TW/1-9,
14-17, WWT/8-14
DIXON, J. L. (d 1888 [47]) come-
dian EA/89*
DIXON, Lee (1914-53) American
actor, dancer TW/1, 9
DIXON, Lillian B. (d 1962 [69])
performer BE*
DIXON, MacIntyre (b 1931) Ameri-
can actor TW/22, 25, 27-30
DIXON, Madelyn (d 1975 [81]) per-
former BP/60*
DIXON, Paul (d 1974 [53]) per-
former BP/59*
DIXON, Mrs. Robert (d 1911)
EA/12*
DIXON, Thomas (fl 1794) violinist
BD
DIXON, Thomas (1864-1946) Amer-
ican actor, dramatist, manager
SR, WWA/2, WWM, WWS
DIXON, W. (d 1872) singer? EA/
73*
DIXON, William (fl 1792-96?)
singer, music engraver, copyist
BD
DIXON, William Jerrold (d 1879)
dramatist EA/80*
DIZENZO, Charles (b 1938) Amer-
ican dramatist CD
D'JALMA, Prince Sadi (d 1891)
"fire king" CDP
DJURY, Vladimir (d 1972 [60])
specialist BP/57*
D'LEGARD, [Charles?] see
Delagarde, [Charles?]
D'LONRA, Annie [Mrs. Fred Car-
los] (d 1900) serio-comic?
EA/01*
DMITRI, Richard American actor
TW/25, 29
DOANE, Joseph (fl 1793-94) singer
BD
DOANE, Samantha (b 1946) Amer-
ican actress TW/27
DOB (fl 1598-1601) actor DA
DOBBIN, Mrs. Francis Le Fanu
(d 1895) EA/96*
DOBBS, Mr. actor CDP
DOBBS, Francis (fl 1774) Irish
dramatist, producer CP/2-3,
GT, TD/1-2
DOBBS, Mattiwilda (b 1925) Amer-
ican singer CB, ES
DOBE see Dob
DOBELL, Elizabeth Rothwell
[Mrs. Frederic Dobell] (d 1877
[24]) EA/78*

DOBELL, Mrs. Frederic see Dobell, Elizabeth Rothwell

DOBELL, William L. (d 1932) manager, actor WWT/14*

DOBIE, Alan English actor AAS, WWT/14-16

DOBLE, Frances (1902-69) Canadian actress WWT/5-9

DOBLER, Herr (d 1904 [65]) wizard EA/05*

DOBNEY, Ann (c. 1670-1760) proprietor BD

DOBREE, Hugh Leslie (b 1884) English actor GRB/1-2

DOBRITSCH, Al (d 1971 [60]) performer BP/55*

DOBSON, Mr. (fl 1728-34) violoncellist BD

DOBSON, Mr. (fl 1792) actor BD

DOBSON, Benjamin (fl 1664-69) fencing master, manager? BD

DOBSON, Franklin B. (1838-87) manager, banjoist NYM

DOBSON, James (b 1923) American actor TW/2, 5-9

DOBSON, John (fl 1626) actor DA

DOBSON, John (d 1904) comedian EA/05*

DOBSON, Marjorie (d 1911 [43]) actress EA/12*

DOBSON, Oswald Harry (d 1917 [24]) actor EA/18*

DOCKRILL, Eliza [Mrs. R. H. Dockrill] equestrienne CDP

DOCKRILL, R. H. equestrian CDP

DOCKRILL, Mrs. R. H. see Dockrill, Eliza

DOCKSTADER, Lew (1856-1924) American minstrel, manager CDP, DAB, ES, OC/3, SR

DOCTOR, Joseph (fl 1787-1800) clown, equilibrist, tumbler, actor BD, HAS

DOCTOR, Mrs. [Joseph] (fl 1799) actress HAS

DODD, Alice (d 1869) actress EA/70*

DODD, Alice singer, actress CDP

DODD, Claire (d 1973 [50+]) actress TW/30

DODD, Emily (d 1944) actress TW/1

DODD, Henry (d 1867 [53])

EA/68*

DODD, James Solas (1721-1805) English actor, lecturer BD, CP/2-3, DNB, GT, TD/1-2

DODD, James William (1734-96) English actor, singer, manager BD, CDP, COC, DD, ES, GT, OC/1-3, TD/1-2

DODD, Mrs. James William (d 1769) actress, singer BD

DODD, John (fl 1784?-94) singer BD

DODD, Ken (b 1929) English comedian WWT/14-16

DODD, Lee Wilson (1879-1933) American dramatist DAB, OC/1-3, SR, WWA/1, WWM, WWT/4-7

DODD, Martha see Dodd, Mrs. James William

DODD, Tommy see Clarke, Ernie

DODD, William (1729-77) English dramatist CP/3, GT

DODD, William (d 1908) circus agent EA/09*

DODDRIDGE, Joseph (1769-1826) American dramatist EAP

DODDS, Jack (d 1962 [35]) dancer BE*

DODDS, Jamieson (1884-1942) English actor, singer WWT/4-9

DODDS, William American stage manager BE

"DODDY, Lord Tom" see Brown, Johnny

DODGE, Mrs. see Watson, Mrs.

DODGE, Henry Irving (1861-1934) American critic, dramatist WWT/4-6

DODGE, Jerry (1937-74) American actor TW/24-25, 28-30

DODGE, Ossian E. (b 1820) American singer CDP

DODGE, Roger Pryor (d 1974 [76]) performer BP/59*

DODGE, Shirlee American choreographer, teacher, director BE

DODGE, Wendell P. (d 1976 [92]) producer/director/choreographer BP/60*

DODGSON, Henry (d 1876 [39]) harpist EA/77*

DODIMEAD, David (b 1919) English actor WWT/15-16

DODIMEAR, Mr. (fl 1793)

dancer BD
DODSLEY, James (d 1797 [73])
publisher BE*, WWT/14*
DODSLEY, Robert (1703-64)
English dramatist CDP,
COC, CP/1-3, DD, DNB,
ES, GT, HP, OC/1-3, TD/
1-2
DODSON, Mr. (fl 1731-34) sing-
er, actor BD
DODSON, Mrs. (fl 1740-49)
actress, singer BD
DODSON, Miss (fl 1740-42)
actress, dancer BD
DODSON, Mrs. Alfred D. see
Dodson, Clare
DODSON, Clare [Mrs. Alfred
D. Dodson] (d 1908) EA/09*
DODSON, John E. (1857-1931)
English actor DD, GRB/2-4,
PP/1, SR, WWA/1, WWM,
WWS, WWT/1-5
DODSON, Mrs. John E. see
Irish, Annie
DODSON, Lamott (d 1975) per-
former BP/59*
DODSON, Owen (b 1914) Ameri-
can educator, dramatist,
director BE
DODSWORTH, Charles (d 1920)
actor DD
DODSWORTH, Mrs. Charles
see Aubrey, Lizzie
DODWORTH, Allen composer,
musician CDP
DODWORTH, Harvey B. (1822-
91) bandmaster CDP
DOE, Miss (fl 1772) actress BD
DOE, Edith (d 1905) EA/06*
DOE, John (fl 1766-1804) house
servant, actor BD
DOEL, James (1803/04-1902)
actor DD, WWW/1
"DOGE OF DRURY, The" see
Steele, Richard
DOGGET, Mr. (fl 1748) actor
BD
DOGGET, James (fl 1794) singer
BD
DOGGETT, Gertrude (fl 1866)
actress HAS
DOGGETT, Thomas (c. 1670-
1721) English actor, singer,
manager, dramatist BD,
CDP, COC, CP/1-3, DD,
DNB, ES, GT, HP, OC/1-3,
TD/1-2
DOGGETT, Thomas (fl 1791)

actor, dancer BD
"DOG STAR, The" see Cony,
Barkham
DOHERTY, Brian (d 1974 [68])
dramatist BP/59*
DOHERTY, Charlotte Ellen see
Grant, Nellie
DOHERTY, Chester (d 1975 [71])
performer BP/59*
DOHMAN, Dennis (b 1945) Ameri-
can actor TW/30
DOIGE, Mr. (fl 1810) actor HAS
DOILE, Ann (fl 1797) house ser-
vant? BD
DOILE, Margaret (fl 1797-1800)
house servant? BD
D'OISLY, Maurice (1882-1949)
English singer WWW/4
DOLAN, Mary [née Mary Rebecca
Goettling] (b 1919) American
talent representative BE
DOLAN, Michael J. (d 1954 [70])
actor BE*, WWT/14*
DOLAN, Robert Emmett (1908-72)
American composer, conductor
BE, TW/29, WWA/5
DOLARO, Hattie (d 1941 [80])
actress, singer BE*, WWT/
14*
DOLARO, Selina (1853-89) singer,
actress CDP, DD, OAA/2
DOLBIER, Maurice (b 1912) Amer-
ican actor CB
DOLBY, Charlotte Helen CDP
DOLBY, Henry Gray (d 1913 [59])
EA/14*
DOLENZ, George (d 1963 [55])
Italian actor BE*
DOLIN, Anton [Patrick Healey-
Kay] (b 1904) English dancer,
choreographer CB, ES, OC/2,
TW/3, WWT/6-13
DOLIVE, William (b 1943) Amer-
ican actor TW/24
DOLL, Bill (b 1910) American
press representative BE
DOLLAR, William (b 1907) Amer-
ican dancer, choreographer
ES
"DOLL COMMON" see Corey,
Mrs. John
DOLLY, Jennie (1892-1941) Hun-
garian dancer CB, ES, WWT/
4-9
DOLLY, Rosie (1892-1970) Hun-
garian dancer ES, TW/26,
WWT/4-9
DOLMAN, Frederick William see

Dolman, Richard
DOLMAN, John (1824/30?-95)
American actor, lawyer
CDP, HAS
DOLMAN, Richard [Frederick
William Dolman] (b 1895)
English actor WWT/7-12
DOMBRE, Barbara (d 1973 [28])
performer BP/57*
DOME, Mrs. Zoltan see
Nordica, Mme.
DOMINGO, Placido (b 1941)
Spanish singer CB
DOMINGUEZ, Alberto (d 1975
[73]) composer/lyricist BP/
60*
DOMINIC, Mr. (fl 1726) scene
painter BD
"DOMINICHINO" see Annibali,
Domenico
DOMINIQUE, Mons. (fl 1742-51)
actor, acrobat, manager BD
DOMINIQUE, Mme. (fl 1748)
singer, dancer BD
DOMINIQUE, Ivan (d 1973 [45])
performer BP/57*
DOMINIQUE, Polly (b 1741)
performer BD
DOMITILLA, Miriamne [née
Campanini] (fl 1741-48)
dancer BD
DON, Lady Emilia Eliza [née
Emily Saunders] (d 1875)
English actress HAS
DON, Laura actress, dramatist
CDP
DON, Sir William Henry (1826-
62) English actor CDP, DD,
DNB, HAS
DONADIEU, Miss (fl 1775) singer
BD
DONAGH, Emily (d 1891) chorister
EA/92*
DONAGHEY, Frederick (1870-1937)
American dramatist, manager
WWS
DONAHUE, Jack (1892-1930)
American actor, singer SR,
WWT/6
DONAHUE, Vincent (d 1976 [58])
executive BP/60*
DONALD, James (b 1917) Eng-
lish actor AAS, WWT/10-15
DONALD, John (b 1856) English
manager GRB/1-4
DONALD, Mrs. John see
Temple, Rose
DONALDSON, Mr. (fl 1772)

actor BD
DONALDSON, Alexander (d 1794)
printer, bookseller, treasurer
BD
DONALDSON, Anne Maria see
Faulkner, Anne Maria
DONALDSON, Arthur (1869-1955)
Swedish actor, singer TW/12,
WWS
DONALDSON, Donella see Hay-
don, Julie
DONALDSON, Jack (d 1975 [65])
performer BP/60*
DONALDSON, Muriel Pollock (d
1971) composer/lyricist BP/
56*
DONALDSON, Walter (1893-1947)
American songwriter BE*
DONALDSON, Walter A. (b 1832)
American actor HAS
DONALDSON, Walter Alexander
(d 1877 [84]) actor EA/79*,
WWT/14*
DONALDSON, William B. (1822-
73) minstrel CDP, HAS
DONALLAN, Mr. (fl 1798-1819)
sweeper, watchman BD
DONAT, Peter (b 1928) Canadian
actor BE, TW/13-20, 28
DONAT, Robert (1905-58) English
actor AAS, COC, DNB, ES,
OC/3, WWA/3, WWT/7-12
DONATH, Ludwig (1907-67) Aus-
trian actor, coach BE, TW/
24, WWT/14
DONATO (d 1865) dancer EA/72*,
WWT/14*
DONATO, Josephine Lucchese (d
1974 [78]) performer BP/59*
DONAVON, Lucy [Mrs. Thomas
Donavon] (d 1887) EA/88*
DONAVON, Mrs. Thomas see
Donavon, Lucy
DONDELL, Sprackling (fl 1712)
musician? BD
DONE, Dr. William (d 1895 [80])
conductor, musician EA/96*
DONEGAN, James E. (d 1916)
proprietor EA/17*
DONEGAN, Martin (b 1931) Irish
actor TW/25, 30
DONEHUE, Vincent J. (1916/20/
22-66) American director BE,
TW/22, WWA/4, WWT/13-14
DONELLY, Henry V. see
Donnelly, Henry V.
DONER, Maurice (d 1971 [66])
performer BP/55*

DONHOWE, Gwyda (b 1933)
American actress TW/26-28
DONISTHORPE, G. Sheila (1898-1946) English dramatist WWT/9
DONIZETTI, Gaetano (1797-1848) composer CDP
DONLAN, Yolande (b 1920) American actress AAS, WWT/11-16
DONLEAVY, J. P. (b 1926) American dramatist AAS, CD, HJD, MD, MWD, WWT/14-16
DONLEVY, Brian (1903-72) Irish actor BE, ES, TW/28, WWT/9-10
DONMAN, Mr. (fl 1785-89) bassoonist BD
DONN, Marie (d 1973 [74]) performer BP/58*
DONNAHEY, Edith see Vaughan, Ada
DONNAY, Maurice (1862-1945) French dramatist GRB/1, 3-4
DONNE, Mary (d 1866) dancer HAS
DONNE, William Bodham (1807-82) English examiner of plays DNB
DONNELL, E. T. (d 1879 [32]) actor? musician? EA/81*
DONNELL, Martin (d 1891 [35]) EA/93*
DONNELL, Patrick (b 1916) Irish actor, administrator WWT/14-16
DONNELLY, Charles (d 1875) comedian EA/76*
DONNELLY, Mrs. Charles see Donnelly, Mrs. R.
DONNELLY, Donal (b 1931) English actor TW/23-24, 29, WWT/15-16
DONNELLY, Dorothy Agnes (1880-1928) American actress, dramatist. GRB/3-4, WWA/1, WWM, WWS, WWT/1-5
DONNELLY, Henry V. (d 1910 [49]) actor, vaudevillian CDP
DONNELLY, H. Grattan (fl 1898) American? dramatist DD, SR
DONNELLY, Jamie actress TW/24
DONNELLY, Leo (1878-1935)

American actor, dramatist SR
DONNELLY, Michael (d 1882) stage manager EA/84*
DONNELLY, Mrs. R. [Mrs. Charles Donnelly] (d 1898) EA/00*
DONNELLY, Ruth (b 1896) American actress BE, TW/29
DONNELLY, Thomas Lester (1832-80) actor, manager CDP
DONNELLY, Tom (d 1976 [57]) critic BP/60*
DONNER, Clive (b 1926) English director WWT/16
DONNOLLY, R. J. (d 1908 [45]) American critic GRB/4*
DONOGHUE, William (d 1872 [30]) singer EA/72*
DONOHUE, Jack (b 1908) American actor, dancer, director, choreographer BE, WWT/9-16
DONOVAN, Master (fl 1739-41) actor BD
DONOVAN, Alice Dougan (d 1971 [90]) dramatist BP/55*
DONOVAN, Frank R. (d 1975 [69]) producer/director/choreographer BP/60*
DONOVAN, Josephine [Mrs. W. H. Donovan] (d 1894 [25]) EA/95*
DONOVAN, Walter (d 1964 [75]) American performer, composer BE*
DONOVAN, Warde (b 1919) American actor, singer TW/3-4
DONOVAN, Mrs. W. H. see Donovan, Josephine
DONSTALL, James see Tunstall, James
DONSTONE, James see Tunstall, James
DONWALT, Mr. (fl 1767) musician BD
DONZELLI, Domenico (1790-1873) Italian singer ES
DOOLEY, Gordon (d 1930 [31]) comedian BE*, BP/14*
DOOLEY, James (d 1949 [69]) vaudevillian TW/5
DOOLEY, Jed (d 1973 [89]) performer BP/58*
DOOLEY, Johnny (d 1928 [41]) Scottish comedian BE*, BP/12*, WWT/14*
DOOLEY, Paul (b 1928) American actor TW/25-26
DOOLEY, Ray [Rachel Rice

Dooley] (b 1896/1903) Scottish actress, singer, dancer BE, TW/4-7, WWT/6-9

DOOLEY, Robert (d 1922 [52]) comedian BE*, BP/7*

DOOLEY, William (d 1921 [39]) acrobatic comedian BE*, BP/6*

DOOLEY, Willian G. (d 1975 [70]) critic BP/59*

DOOLITTLE, James (b 1914) American executive, producer BE

DOONAN, George (d 1973 [76]) performer BP/57*

DOONAN, J. P. (d 1900) Irish comedian EA/01*

DOONE, Neville (fl 1891-98) actor, dramatist DD

DOONE, Rupert (1904-66) director COC

DOONER, James (d 1910 [70]) showman EA/11*

DOORESCOURT, John (fl 1689-99) trumpeter BD

DOORLEY, Frank M. (d 1966 [80]) performer BP/50*

DOORSMING, Mr. (fl 1748) singer BD

DORAN, Charles (1877-1964) Irish actor, manager WWT/3-13

DORAN, James see Vane, W. H.

DORAN, John (1807-78) English writer CDP, DD, DNB, ES

DORATI, Antal (b 1906) Hungarian conductor CB

DORCASE, Mr. (fl 1675) singer BD

DORE, Mrs. (fl 1785) actress BD

DORE, Alexander (b 1923) English director, actor WWT/15-16

DORE, Hezekiah (d 1874 [34]) manager EA/75*

DOREE, Ada (fl 1888) actress, singer DP

DORELL, Miss (fl 1797) actress BD

DORELLI, Signor (fl 1791-95) singer BD

DOREMUS, Mrs. C. A. American? dramatist DD

DOREMUS, Mrs. Thomas C. see Wilton, Ellie

DORFMAN, Irvin (b 1924) American press representative, producer BE

DORFMAN, Nat (b 1895) American press representative, dramatist BE

DORGERE, Arlette French actress, singer WWT/4

DORI, Alison (d 1909) EA/10*

DORIA, Clara see Rogers, Clara Kathleen

DORIEN, Mr. (fl 1773) actor BD

DORIN, Phoebe (b 1940) American actress TW/26, 29-30

DORIN, Rube (d 1965 [48]) critic BP/49*

DORION, Mr. (fl 1784-95) singer BD

DORIS, John B. (fl 1863-86) circus performer SR

DORIS, Lily (d 1906) performer? EA/07*

DORIVAL, Anne Marguerite (d 1788) dancer BD

DORIVAL, Georges (d 1939 [78]) actor BE*, WWT/14*

DORIVAL A CORIFET [Marie Catherine Brida] (b c. 1754) French dancer BD

DORKIN, Jack (d 1975 [81]) performer BP/60*

DORKIN, Millie Morgan (d 1972 [77]) performer BP/57*

DORLAG, Arthur H. (b 1922) American educator, director BE

DORMAN, Mr. (fl 1740) dramatist CP/1-3

DORMAN, Mr. (fl 1740-41) house servant? BD

DORMAN, John (b 1922) American actor TW/15, 22-23, 25

DORMAN, Ridley (fl 1752-73?) violinist BD

DORMAN, Mrs. Ridley [née Elizabeth Young] (d 1773) singer, actress BD

D'ORME, Aileen (1877-1939) English actress, singer WWT/4-7

D'ORME, Josephine [née Ordz] (1830-81) singer CDP

DORMER, Mr. (fl 1805) actor CDP

DORMER, Daisy (d 1947 [64]) singer CDP

D'ORMY, Martini (fl 1854) singer HAS

DORN, Dolores [née Dorn-Heft] (b 1935) American actress BE

DORN, Lily Austrian singer
WWM
DORN, Philip (d 1975 [75])
Dutch actor TW/3
DORNAN, John (d 1918 [71])
EA/19*
DORNEY, Louis (1876-1940)
singer CB
DORNEY, Richard (1620-81)
violinist BD
DORNEY, Richard (d 1921 [79])
manager BE*, BP/5*
DORN-HEFT, Dolores (b 1936)
American actress TW/25
DORNTON, Agnes (d 1901)
EA/02*
DORNTON, Charles (d 1900)
actor, manager DD
DORNTON, Mrs. Charles see
Dornton, Louisa
DORNTON, Harold (d 1891)
EA/92*
DORNTON, Louisa [Mrs. Charles
Dornton; née Louisa Robertson]
(d 1881) EA/82*
DORO, Marie (1882-1956) Amer-
ican actress ES, GRB/2-4,
TW/13, WWM, WWS, WWT/
1-6
DORR, Dorothy [Mrs. H. J.
W. Dam] (b 1867) American
actress DD, GRB/2-4,
WWM, WWS, WWT/1-5
DORREE, Bobbie (d 1974 [68])
performer BP/58*
DORRELL, William (d 1896
[86]) composer, musician
EA/98*
DORRILL, Charles C. (d 1912
[51]) manager, director EA/
13*
DORRILL, John (d 1974 [44])
managing director BTR/74
D'ORSAY, Fifi (b 1904) Cana-
dian actress TW/27-29
D'ORSAY, Lawrance [Dorset
William Lawrence] (1853/60-
1931) actor DD, EA/95,
GRB/1-4, SR, WWM, WWS,
WWT/1-6
DORSET, Earl of see Sack-
ville, Thomas
DORSEY, Sandra [Sandy Ellen]
(b 1939) American actress
TW/29
DORSION, Mlle. (fl 1792) dancer
BD
D'ORTA, Rachele [Signora

Giorgi] (fl 1784-85) singer BD
D'ORTA, Rosina (fl 1784) singer
BD
DORTOR, Joseph see Doctor,
Joseph
DORUS-GRAS, Julie Aimée Josèphe
(1805-96) singer CDP
DORVAL, Max (d 1902) manager
WWT/14*
D'ORVAL-VALENTIONO, E. L.
(d 1885 [32]) singer EA/86*
DORZIAT, Gabrielle French ac-
tress GRB/4, WWT/1-4
DOSEL, [William?] (fl 1788-96)
doorkeeper BD
DOSER, Mr. (fl 1789) house ser-
vant? BD
DOS PASSOS, John (1896-1970)
American dramatist BE, CB,
ES, HJD, HP, MD, MWD,
WWW/6
DOSSIE, Robert (d 1777) dramatist
CP/2-3, GT, TD/1-2
DOSTOIEVSKY, Feodor Milhailovich
(1821-81) Russian writer COC,
OC/2-3
DOT, Doreen (d 1969 [70]) per-
former BP/54*
DOTHWAIT, Mr. (fl 1794) flutist
BD
DOTRICE, Roy (b 1923/25) English
actor AAS, COC, TW/24,
WWT/14-16
DOTTI, Anna (fl 1724-27) singer
BD
DOTTRIDGE, Mrs. (d 1886) EA/
87*
DOTTRIDGE, Dolly [Mrs. C. H.
Longden] (d 1909 [47]) EA/10*
DOTTRIDGE, Joseph William (d
1896 [78]) EA/98*
DOUBLEDAY, Richard (d 1975
[52]) producer/director/chore-
ographer BP/59*
DOUBLEDAY, Thomas (1790-1870)
English dramatist DNB
DOUBTON, Thomas see Down-
ton, Thomas
DOUCE, Francis (1775-1834)
writer DD
DOUCET, Catherine Calhoun (d
1958 [83]) American actress
TW/1-3, 14, WWT/8-9
DOUGHARTY, Hougline (1844-1919)
minstrel SR
DOUGHERTY, Mr. (fl c. 1870)
actor HAS
DOUGHERTY, Frances Ann [née

Cannon] American producer
BE
DOUGHERTY, Hughey (b 1844)
American minstrel CDP,
HAS
DOUGHERTY, M. J. (fl 1854)
actor HAS
DOUGHERTY, Walter Hampden
see Hampden, Walter
DOUGHTON, Thomas (fl 1628-34)
actor DA
DOUGHTY, Charles Montagu
(1843-1926) dramatist HP
DOUGHTY, Henry actor GRB/1
DOUGHTY, James (1819-1913)
clown DD
DOUGLAS, Mr. (fl 1770) actor
BD
DOUGLAS, Mr. (fl 1776-1817)
house servant BD
DOUGLAS, Rev. (fl 1784?)
dramatist CP/3
DOUGLAS, Miss (fl 1777) actress
BD
DOUGLAS, Alexander (fl 1672-
73) actor? BD
DOUGLAS, Belle [Emma Ducklin]
(d 1907) actress EA/08*
DOUGLAS, Byron (d 1935 [70])
actor BE*, BP/19*, WWT/
14*
DOUGLAS, Daphne (d 1917)
EA/18*
DOUGLAS, David (b c.1730)
English actor, theatre builder
HAS, SR
DOUGLAS, Mrs. David see
Hallam, Mrs. Lewis
DOUGLAS, Dorothea (d 1962 [79])
performer BE*
DOUGLAS, Felicity [née Tomlin]
(b 1910) English dramatist
WWT/15-16
DOUGLAS, Fred (d 1892 [42])
actor EA/93*
DOUGLAS, G. R. [G. Douglas
Robertson] (d 1882) dramatist
DD
DOUGLAS, Helen Gahagan see
Gahagan, Helen
DOUGLAS, Mrs. Jack (d 1911)
EA/12*
DOUGLAS, Jeff (d 1975 [32])
critic BP/60*
DOUGLAS, Johanna (b 1917)
American actress TW/23-26
DOUGLAS, John (d 1872) pro-
prietor EA/73*

DOUGLAS, Kenneth [Kenneth
Savory] (d 1923 [49/52]) English
actor GRB/3-4, WWT/1-4
DOUGLAS, Mrs. Kenneth see
Lane, Grace
DOUGLAS, Kirk [né Issure Daniel-
ovitch] (b 1916/20) American
actor BE, CB, ES, TW/1-3
DOUGLAS, Larry (b 1914) Amer-
ican actor, singer BE, TW/
4-12, 25-26
DOUGLAS, Lewis W. (b 1894)
American executive BE
DOUGLAS, Maggie St. Clair see
Hampton, Mrs. Henry
DOUGLAS, Marie Booth (d 1932
[75]) actress BE*, WWT/14*
DOUGLAS, Melvyn [Melvyn Hes-
selberg] (b 1901) American
actor, director, producer
AAS, BE, CB, ES, SR, TW/
5-19, 24, WWT/7-16
DOUGLAS, Michael (b 1944) Amer-
ican actor TW/27
DOUGLAS, Milton (1901-70) Amer-
ican actor TW/2-3
DOUGLAS, Paul (1907-59) Ameri-
can actor ES, TW/2-5, 13-14,
16
DOUGLAS, R. H. (d 1935) actor
BE*, WWT/14*
DOUGLAS, Richard see Doug-
lass, Richard
DOUGLAS, Robert (b 1909/10)
English actor AAS, BE, ES,
WWT/8-13
DOUGLAS, Mrs. Stephen A. see
Shattuck, Truly
DOUGLAS, Susan (b 1926) Hun-
garian/English actress TW/2-5
DOUGLAS, T. B. (fl 1851) Amer-
ican actor HAS
DOUGLAS, Tom (b 1903) American
actor WWT/5-9
DOUGLAS, Torrington (b 1901)
English press representative
WWT/11-16
DOUGLAS, Valerie (d 1969 [31])
performer BP/53*
DOUGLAS, Wallace (b 1911) Cana-
dian producer, director WWT/
11-16
DOUGLAS, William (fl 1720-45)
trumpeter BD
DOUGLAS, William Budd (d 1867)
actor HAS
DOUGLAS-BARBOR, Dorothy Eng-
lish actress GRB/1

DOUGLASS, Albert (1864-1940) manager WWT/7-9

DOUGLASS, Amy (b 1902) American actress TW/5-6

DOUGLASS, Bertie Richard (d 1904 [26]) EA/05*

DOUGLASS, Bill Henry (b 1951) American actor TW/29-30

DOUGLASS, Mrs. Byron (d 1905) EA/06*

DOUGLASS, David (d 1786) American actor, manager COC, ES, NTH, OC/1-3

DOUGLASS, Edwin Herbert (b 1867) American singer WWA/4

DOUGLASS, George Samuel (1853-1909) English music-hall manager GRB/1

DOUGLASS, Jane Isabella [Mrs. John Douglass] (d 1881 [65]) EA/82*

DOUGLASS, John (1814-74) proprietor, actor, manager DD

DOUGLASS, John (d 1917 [76]) manager, dramatist, producer DD

DOUGLASS, Mrs. John see Douglass, Jane Isabella

DOUGLASS, Margaret (d 1949 [53]) American actress TW/1-6

DOUGLASS, P. American actor TW/28

DOUGLASS, R. H. (d 1935?) actor, monologist GRB/1-4

DOUGLASS, Richard (d 1911 [67]) scene artist BE*, EA/12*, WWT/14*

DOUGLASS, Stephen [né Fitch] (b 1921) American actor, singer, director AAS, BE, TW/7-8, 10-17, 20, 22-23, WWT/11-16

DOUGLASS, Thomas Mace (d 1906 [83]) EA/07*

DOUGLASS, Vincent (1900-26) English dramatist WWT/5

DOULENS, Roger B. (d 1972 [57]) publicist BP/57*

DOURIF, Brad (b 1950) American actor TW/30

D'OUVILLY, George Gerbier (fl 1661) Dutch? dramatist CP/1-3, DNB

DOVA, Nina (b 1926) English actress TW/11, 25, 27-29

DOVE, Elizabeth see Dove, Mrs. Michael

DOVE, Henry (fl 1674-78?) violinist BD

DOVE, Mark ["Bertrand"] (d 1867 [18]) gymnast EA/68*

DOVE, Michael (d 1747) actor, dancer BD

DOVE, Mrs. Michael (fl 1731-47) actress, dancer BD

DOVE, Owen (d 1893 [48]) dramatist, actor EA/94*

DOVER, Antony (fl 1635) actor DA

DOVER, John (d 1725) dramatist CP/1-3, DNB, GT

DOVEY, Mr. (fl 1724-27) house servant BD

DOVEY, Alice (1885-1969) American actress, singer WWT/4-6

DOW, Ada (d 1926 [79]) actress BE*, BP/10*, WWT/14*

DOW, Alexander (d 1779) Scottish dramatist CDP, CP/2-3, DNB, GT, TD/1-2

DOW, Clara (1883-1969) English actress, singer GRB/4, WWT/1-3

DOW, Emily (fl 1854) singer HAS

DOW, R. A. (b 1941) American actor TW/27, 29-30

DOWD, Harrison (b 1897) American actor BE

DOWD, M'el American actress BE, TW/22-29, WWT/15-16

DOWDELL, Mr. (fl c. 1710) bass player BD

DOWDELL, Robert (b 1932) American actor TW/14

DOWDEN, Edward (1843-1913) Irish critic DD, DNB

DOWDING, Mr. (fl 1784) singer BD

DOWELL, Anthony (b 1943) English dancer CB

DOWELL, Horace (d 1974 [70]) composer/lyricist BP/59*

DOWER, E. (fl 1738) dramatist CP/1-3, GT

DOWGHTON, Thomas see Downton, Thomas

DOWLAND, Robert see Dulandt, Robert

DOWLE, Rowland (fl 1636) actor DA

DOWLER, Mrs. (fl 1794-95) dresser BD

DOWLING, Mr. prompter HAS

DOWLING, Constance (d 1969 [49]) actress TW/26

DOWLING, Eddie [né Joseph
Nelson Goucher] (1894?-1976)
American actor, dramatist,
producer AAS, CB, ES,
NTH, SR, TW/1-9, WWT/7-15
DOWLING, Edward Duryea (d
1967 [63]) director, producer
TW/24
DOWLING, Isaac see Deulin,
Herr
DOWLING, Joan (1928-54) Eng-
lish actress WWT/11
DOWLING, Joseph (b 1850)
dramatist, actor SR
DOWLING, Maurice G. (fl 1834-
37) dramatist DD
DOWLING, Richard (1846-98)
dramatist DD
DOWLING, Robert W. (1895-1973)
American theatre owner, execu-
tive BE, TW/30
DOWLING, Vincent (b 1922)
American actor TW/24
DOWN, Mr. (fl 1731) house ser-
vant? BD
DOWN, Mrs. (d 1881 [90])
EA/82*
DOWN, Oliphant (d 1917) drama-
tist EA/18*
DOWNER, Alan S. (1912-70)
American scholar BE, WWA/5
DOWNER, J. W. (d 1893 [56])
manager EA/94*
DOWNES, Mr. (fl 1729) actor
BD
DOWNES, Cpt. (fl 1733) drama-
tist CP/3
DOWNES, Edward Ray (d 1968
[63]) stage manager BP/52*
DOWNES, John (fl 1661-1719)
English writer, prompter,
actor BD, COC, DD, DNB,
ES, OC/1-3
DOWNES, W. H. singer CDP
DOWNES, Wilhelmina [Mrs.
William Downes] (d 1917 [34])
EA/18*
DOWNES, Mrs. William see
Downes, Wilhelmina
DOWNEY, Morton (b 1902)
American singer CB
DOWNHAM, Hugh (fl 1779)
dramatist CP/2, GT, TD/1-2
DOWNIE, Alex (b 1806) Ameri-
can clown, equestrian, trampo-
linist HAS
DOWNIE, Louise (b 1841) Amer-
ican? drummer girl HAS

DOWNIE, William M. (d 1911)
EA/12*
DOWNING, Adelaide see Lewis,
Mrs. G.
DOWNING, David (b 1943) Ameri-
can actor TW/24-29
DOWNING, George (d 1780) actor,
dramatist BD, CP/2-3, DD,
GT, TD/1-2
DOWNING, Joe (b 1904) American
actor TW/2-3
DOWNING, Robert (1914-75) Amer-
ican actor, stage manager,
director, dramatist, historian
BE, TW/23
DOWNING, Robert L. (1857-1944)
American actor GRB/2-3,
PP/1, SR, WWA/2, WWM,
WWS
DOWNING, Russell (d 1968 [67])
executive BP/53*
DOWNING, Sam (d 1967 [82])
performer BP/52*
DOWNING, Virginia American ac-
tress TW/26, 29
DOWNMAN, Mr. (fl 1788) scene
painter BD
DOWNMAN, Hugh (d 1809) English
dramatist CP/3, DD
DOWNES, Johnny see Downs,
Johnny
DOWNS, Jane English actress
WWT/14-16
DOWNS, Johnny American actor
TW/2-6
DOWNS, Margaret see Rogers,
Mrs. Ben G.
DOWNS, Will (d 1918) EA/19*
DOWNTON, Thomas (fl 1593?-
1622?) actor, dramatist CP/
3, DA
DOWNTON'S BOY (fl 1600-02)
actor DA
DOWSE, Mr. (d 1783) singer BD
DOWSE, Thomas Edward Fugion
(d 1897 [44]) actor EA/98*
DOWSETT, Ellen [Mrs. Vernon
Dowsett] (d 1907 [45]) EA/08*
DOWSETT, Mrs. Vernon see
Dowsett, Ellen
DOWSING, Emma Ada [Mrs.
Thomas C. Howitt] (d 1884)
EA/85*
DOWSING, John (fl 1678) singer
BD
DOWSON, Mr. (fl 1777) actor BD
DOWSON, Mrs. H. M. (fl
1680) see Filippi, Rosina

DOWSON, Ann (fl c. 1765-74)
singer BD
DOWSON, John (fl 1680) dancing
master BD
DOWTEN, Thomas see Down-
ton, Thomas
DOWTON, Emily (d 1924 [84])
actress BE*, WWT/14*
DOWTON, Harry (d 1889 [29])
singer EA/90*
DOWTON, Henry (b 1798) actor
DNB
DOWTON, Thomas see Down-
ton, Thomas
DOWTON, William (1764-1851)
English actor, manager BD,
BS, CDP, COC, DD, DNB,
ES, GT, HAS, OC/1-3, OX,
SR, TD/1-2
DOWTON, William Paton (d
1883 [88]) actor DNB
DOYLE, Mr. (fl 1800-09) house
servant? BD
DOYLE, Mr. English actor
HAS
DOYLE, Mrs. (fl 1789-1801)
house servant? BD
DOYLE, Sir Arthur Conan (1859-
1930) Scottish dramatist DD,
DNB, ES, GRB/2-4, WWM,
WWT/1-6, WWW/3
DOYLE, C. W. (d 1901 [79])
musician EA/02*
DOYLE, Edward (d 1905) EA/
06*
DOYLE, Frank Q. (b 1872)
American singer, actor, agent
WWM
DOYLE, Gene [né Eugene Tauben-
haus] (b 1909) American actor,
lyricist BE
DOYLE, James (fl 1794) singer?
BD
DOYLE, James (d 1927 [38])
American dancer BE*,
BP/11*
DOYLE, John (d 1794) singer,
actor BD
DOYLE, John T. (d 1935 [62])
American actor BE*, BP/20*
DOYLE, Kathleen (b 1947) Amer-
ican actress TW/27
DOYLE, Len (d 1959 [66]) actor
TW/16
DOYLE, Lila [Mrs. Harry Mills]
(d 1908) EA/09*
DOYLE, Margaret (d 1793) BD
DOYLE, Michael (d 1890 [45])

manager EA/91*
DOYLE, Miriam (d 1962) actress,
producer BE*
DOYLE, Moya see Mannering,
Moya
DOYLE, Paddy (d 1873) comic
singer EA/74*
DOYLE, Paddy (d 1895) Irish
comedian EA/96*
D'OYLY CARTE, Richard (1844-
1901) English impresario COC,
DD, DNB, ES, NTH, OC/1-3,
PDT, SR, WWW/1
D'OYLY CARTE, Mrs. Richard
[née Couper Black] (d 1913)
manager GRB/2-4, ES, WWT/1
D'OYLY CARTE, Rupert (1876-
1948) English manager CB,
NTH, TW/5, WWT/4-10, WWW/
4
DOYNE, Jennie [Mrs. John Henry
Doyne] (d 1894) EA/95*
DOYNE, John H. (d 1893) stage
manager EA/94*
DOYNE, Mrs. J[ohn?] H. (d 1879)
EA/80*
DOYNE, Mrs. John Henry see
Doyne, Jennie
DRACO, Mrs. Pan E. (d 1906
[24]) EA/07*
DRAGHI, Giovanni Battista (b c.
1640) Italian musician, com-
poser, librettist BD, DNB
DRAGO, Cathleen (d 1938) actress
BE*, WWT/14*
"DRAGON" (fl 1775) performing
dog BD
DRAGONETTI, Domenico (1763-
1846) double-bass player, com-
poser BD, DNB
DRAKE, Mr. (fl 1799-1802) dancer
BD
DRAKE, Mrs. (fl 1799) dancer
BD
DRAKE, Miss (fl 1798-1801)
dancer, singer BD
DRAKE, Alexander (1800-93) Eng-
lish actor, manager HAS, SR
DRAKE, Mrs. Alexander see
Drake, Frances Ann
DRAKE, Alfred [né Capurro] (b
1914) American actor, singer,
director AAS, BE, CB, ES,
TW/1-24, 30, WWT/10-16
DRAKE, Christopher (b 1929)
American actor TW/15-18
DRAKE, Fabia (b 1904) English
actress WWT/6-11

DRAKE, Frances Ann [Mrs. Alexander Drake] (1797-1875) American actress CDP, DAB, DD, HAS, WWA/4

DRAKE, Harry (d 1971 [70]) agent BP/56*

DRAKE, Dr. James (1667-1706/07) English dramatist CP/1-3, DD, GT

DRAKE, Jonas Hardcastle (d 1901 [66]) Diorama proprietor EA/02*

DRAKE, Mrs. Jonas Hardcastle see Drake, Rebecca

DRAKE, Julia (fl 1800-15) English actress DD, HAS, SR

DRAKE, Julia [Mrs. George Edwards?] (d 1888 [32]) actress SR

DRAKE, Rebecca [Mrs. Jonas Hardcastle Drake] (d 1901 [67]) EA/02*

DRAKE, Robert (fl 1550) actor DA

DRAKE, Ronald (b 1928) English actor BE

DRAKE, Samuel (1768/69-1854) English actor COC, DAB, DD, ES, OC/2, SR, WWA/4

DRAKE, Tom (b 1915) American actor ES

DRAKE, William A. (1899-1965) American dramatist WWT/9-13

DRAKEUP, Daniel (d 1879 [44]) musician EA/80*

DRANGE, Emily (d 1961 [63]) performer BE*

DRANSFIELD, Jane (b 1875) American dramatist, actress WWA/5

DRAPER, Mr. (fl 1776) singer BD

DRAPER, Miss (fl 1776-82) singer BD

DRAPER, Anne (b 1938) American actress BE, TW/24

DRAPER, Don (b 1929) American actor TW/28

DRAPER, J. F. (d 1876) burlesque writer EA/77*

DRAPER, Joseph (d 1962 [55]) performer BE*

DRAPER, Marcus (d 1917 [32]) actor, manager WWT/14*

DRAPER, Margaret (b 1922) American actress TW/5

DRAPER, Mark Denman (d 1917

[32]) actor, manager EA/18*

DRAPER, Matthew (fl 1731) dramatist CP/2-3, DD, GT

DRAPER, Paul (b 1913) Italian dancer BE, CB

DRAPER, Ruth (1884-1956) American monologist COC, ES, HP, NTH, OC/3, PDT, TW/13, WWA/3, WWT/8-12, WWW/5

DRAPER, Stephen (b 1906) American talent representative BE

DRASIN, Tamara see Tamara

DRATLER, Jay (d 1968 [57]) dramatist BP/53*

DRAYCOTT, Charles (d 1917 [44]) lessee EA/18*

DRAYCOTT, Wilfred (b 1848) actor GRB/1-4, WWT/4-6

DRAYLIN, Paul (d 1970 [56]) performer BP/55*

DRAYSON, Edith (d 1926 [37]) actress BE*, WWT/14*

DRAYTON, Alfred (1881-1949) English actor AAS, ES, WWT/4-10

DRAYTON, Edwin (d 1885) actor EA/86*

DRAYTON, Henry (d 1871) American singer CDP, HAS

DRAYTON, Mrs. Henry [née Susanna Lowe] (fl 1853) singer HAS

DRAYTON, Michael (1563-1631) English dramatist, share-holder CP/1-3, DA, DD, ES, FGF, MH

DRAYTON, W. H. (d 1874 [38]) actor EA/75*

DRAZ, Francis K. (d 1974 [79]) designer BP/59*

DREGHORN, Lord see MacLaurin, John

DREHER, Konrad (b 1859) German actor, manager WWT/2

DREHER, Mrs. Paul see Dreher, Virginia

DREHER, Virginia [née Jennie Cummings; Mrs. Paul Dreher] (d 1898) actress CDP

DREHER, Walter Arthur (d 1962 [61]) Argentinian/American actor BE*

DREIER, John T. (b 1913) American designer, director, educator BE

DREISER, Edward M. (d 1958 [84]) actor BE*, BP/42*

DREISER, Theodore (1871-1945)

American dramatist ES, MD,
MWD, NTH, WWT/6-9
DREMAK, W. P. American actor
TW/24, 29
DRENCH, Master (fl 1795) actor
BD
DRESDEL, Sonia [née Lois Obee]
(1909-76) English actress
AAS, ES, WWT/10-16
DRESSER, Louise (1882-1965)
American actress ES, TW/
21, WWA/4, WWT/1-8
DRESSER, Paul (1857-1911) Amer-
ican composer, lyricist, actor,
manager CDP, SR
DRESSLER, Eric (b 1896/1900)
American actor BE, ES,
WWT/7-10
DRESSLER, John (fl 1777-1808)
musician, composer BD
DRESSLER, Marie [Lelia Koerber]
(1869/71-1934) Canadian ac-
tress, singer DAB, ES,
GRB/3-4, NTH, OC/1-3, SR,
WWA/1, WWM, WWS, WWT/
1-7
DREUSSART, Mr. (fl 1707) pro-
prietor? BD
DREVER, Constance (d 1948 [68])
Indian singer, actress GRB/
1-4, WWT/1-7
DREW, Mr. (fl 1722-23) actor
BD
DREW, Adine (d 1888) American
actress EA/89*
DREW, Frank Nelson (1831-1903)
Irish actor CDP, HAS, SR
DREW, Mrs. Frank Nelson
[Fanny Gribbles; Mrs. C. L.
Stone] (b 1831) American ac-
tress HAS
DREW, George (b 1929) Ameri-
can actor TW/8
DREW, Georgiana (1856-93)
actress DD, ES
DREW, Harry [John Henry Dew]
(b 1865) Welsh singer GRB/1
DREW, James H. see Sum-
merville, Hamilton S.
DREW, John (1827-62) Irish/
American actor CDP, DAB,
DD, ES, HAS, HJD, NTH,
OC/1-3, SR, WWA/H
DREW, John (1853-1927) Ameri-
can actor CDP, COC, DAB,
DD, DP, ES, GRB/1-4,
NTH, OC/1-3, PP/1, SR,
WWA/1, WWM, WWS,

WWT/1-5
DREW, Mrs. John [Louisa Lane]
(1820-97) English/American
actress CDP, COC, DD, ES,
HAS, NTH, OC/1-3, WWA/H
DREW, Louisa D. (1846-94?) ac-
tress ES, HAS
DREW, Louise (d 1954 [72]) Amer-
ican actress TW/10, WWM
DREW, Lucille McVey (d 1925
[35]) actress BE*, BP/10*
DREW, Nelly [Mrs. Frank Coyle]
(d 1892 [29]) comedian, dancer
EA/93*
DREW, Sidney [Sidney White]
(1868-1919/20) American actor
ES, OC/1-3, SR
DREW, Thomas Henry (d 1891)
costumier EA/92*
DREW, William (d 1871) singer
EA/72*
DREWE, Bartholomew (fl 1614)
actor DA
DREWE, Thomas (fl 1616-53?)
actor, dramatist CP/2-3, DA,
DD, DNB, FGF
DREWITT, Stanley (b 1874/78)
English actor, director GRB/
2, WWT/2-11
DREYFUSS, Henry (1904-72) Amer-
ican designer WWT/7-12
DREYFUSS, Jane [née Jane Dever-
eux Philbin] (b 1924) American
talent representative BE
DREYFUSS, Michael (d 1960 [32])
actor TW/16
DREYFUSS, Richard (b 1947) Amer-
ican actor CB
DREYSCHOCK, Alexander (1818-69)
pianist CDP
DRIDGE, Mr. (fl 1740) dancer?
BD
DRIESBACH, Jacob (d 1877) lion
tamer CDP
DRINKWATER, Albert Edwin (d
1923 [71]) English actor, drama-
tist, manager EA/96, GRB/1-4,
WWT/2-4
DRINKWATER, John (1882-1937)
English dramatist, actor AAS,
COC, DNB, ES, HP, MD,
MH, MWD, NTH, OC/1-3,
PDT, SR, WWT/4-8, WWW/3
DRISCHELL, Ralph (b 1927) Amer-
ican actor TW/24-27, 30
DRISCOLL, Mr. (fl 1745-56) house
servant BD
DRISCOLL, Arthur F. (d 1967 [82])

lawyer BP/51*

DRISCOLL, H. C. D. (d 1917)
EA/18*

DRISCOLL, Lawrason (b 1946)
American actress TW/30

DRIVAS, Robert (b 1938) American actor, director BE,
TW/14-15, 19-21, 25, 28,
30, WWT/16

DRIVER, Donald actor, director,
dramatist CD, WWT/16

DRIVER, Harry (d 1973 [46])
dramatist BP/58*

DRIVER, John (b 1947) American
actor TW/30

DRIVER, Tom F. (b 1925) American critic, educator BE

DRIVER, W. (d 1870) clown
EA/71*

DROESHOUT, Martin (fl 1620-51)
English engraver NTH

"DROGHIERINA, La" see
Chimenti, Margherita

DROHAN, Benjamin V. (d 1972
[77]) composer/lyricist BP/56*

"DROLLELO, Mynheer" (fl 1746)
dancer BD

DROM, Thomas (fl 1600-01) actor
DA

DROMAT, [Marianne?] (fl 1792-
95) dancer BD

DROMGOOLE, Patrick (b 1930)
Chilean director WWT/15-16

DROUET, Mlle. (fl 1852) French
dancer CDP, HAS

DROUET, Louis (d 1873 [81])
flautist EA/74*

DROUET, Robert (1870-1914)
American actor, dramatist
GRB/3-4, WWA/1, WWS,
WWT/1-2

DROUVILLE, Mons. (fl 1771-73)
dancer BD

DROY, Frank (d 1973 [64])
performer BP/57*

DROZ, Henri Louis Jaquet
(1752-91) exhibitor, mechanician BD

DRUCE, Duncan (d 1916 [37])
actor, stage manager, producer EA/17*

DRUCE, Herbert (1870-1931)
English actor, producer
GRB/4, WWT/1-6

DRUCKER, Frances (d 1970 [69])
producer TW/26

DRUE, Thomas see Drewe,
Thomas

DRULIE, Sylvia (b 1928) American
producer, executive BE

DRUM, Leonard American actor
TW/23

DRUMMOND, Mr. (fl 1738-69)
proprietor BD

DRUMMOND, Mr. (fl 1756) actor
BD

DRUMMOND, Mrs. see Barrett,
Mrs. George Horton

DRUMMOND, Alexander M. (1884-
1956) American educator BE*

DRUMMOND, Alice (b 1929) American actress TW/21-23, 26-
28, 30

DRUMMOND, Dolores [Mrs.
Sprague] (1834/38/40-1926)
English actress DD, GRB/1-4,
OAA/1-2, WWT/1-5

DRUMMOND, Mary (d 1837 [77])
actress HAS

DRUMMOND, Thomas George (d
1873) actor EA/74*

DRUMMOND, W. C. (fl 1810-50)
English actor, stage manager,
dancing master HAS

DRURY, John (d 1916) EA/17*

DRURY, Robert (fl 1732-41) dramatist, actor BD, CP/1-3,
DD, GT

DRURY, Thomas see Drury,
Robert

DRURY, William (fl 1618-41)
dramatist CP/3, DNB, FGF

DRURY, William Henry (d 1896
[48]) scene artist EA/97*

DRURY, Lieut.-Col. William
Price (1861-1949) dramatist
GRB/4, WWT/1-9, WWW/4

DRUSIANO see Martinelli

DRY, Mr. actor CDP

DRYCE, John Pete (d 1892) comedian EA/93*

DRYDEN, James (d 1913) EA/14*

DRYDEN, John (1631-1700) English
dramatist, critic CDP, COC,
CP/1-3, DD, DNB, ES, GT,
HP, MH, NTH, OC/1-3, PDT,
RE

DRYDEN, John, Jr. (1667/68-
1701) English dramatist CP/
1-3, DD, GT

DRYDEN, J. P. (d 1911) actor,
sketch proprietor EA/12*

DRYDEN, Leo singer, composer
CDP

DRYDEN, Mrs. Leo see Tyler,
Marie

DRYDEN, Vaughan (b 1875) English critic, dramatist WWT/6

DRYE, John W., Jr. (b 1900) American lawyer BE

DRYSDALE, Learmont (1866-1909) Scottish composer DNB, ES

DUANE, Frank [né Frank Duane Rosengren] (b 1926) American dramatist BE

DUBAS, Marie (d 1972 [78]) performer BP/56*

DUBE, Marcel (b 1930) Canadian dramatist MH

DUBELLAMY, Charles Clementine [John Evans] (d 1793) actor, singer BD, CDP, TD/1-2

DUBELLAMY, Mrs. Charles Clementine, I [Frances Maria] (d 1773) actress, singer BD

DUBELLAMY, Margaret see Didier, Mrs. Abraham J.

DUBERMAN, Martin B. (b 1930) American historian, dramatist CD, CH

DUBEY, Matt [né Matthew David Dubinsky] (b 1928) American lyricist BE

DUBIN, Al (d 1945 [54]) Swiss lyricist BE*

DUBINSKY, Matthew David see Dubey, Matt

DU BOIS, [Mons.?] (fl 1730) dancer? BD

DUBOIS, Mr. (fl 1859-60) actor HAS

DUBOIS, Baptiste see Dubois, Jean Baptiste

DUBOIS, Camille (fl 1875) actress DD

DU BOIS, Charles (fl 1792-1807) dancer BD

DUBOIS, Dorothea (d 1774) dramatist CP/2-3, DD, GT, TD/1-2

DUBOIS, Frank (fl 1696) actor BD

DUBOIS, Gene [Mrs. Milton H. Bayne] (d 1962 [61]) actress BE*

DUBOIS, Jack (d 1908 [16]) EA/09*

DUBOIS, James [Alfonso Maillard] (d 1907 [36]) animal impersonator EA/08*

DUBOIS, Jean Baptiste (1762-1817) clown, acrobat, dancer, actor, singer BD, TD/1-2

DUBOIS, M. (fl 1796) dancer HAS

DUBOIS, P. B. (fl 1726) translator CP/3

DU BOIS, Raoul Pene (b 1914) American designer WWT/10-16

DUBOISON, Mr. (fl 1795) performer? BD

DUBOSC, Gaston (d 1941 [81]) actor WWT/14*

DUBOURG, Augustus W. (d 1910 [80]) dramatist DD

DUBOURG, Matthew (1703-67) English violinist, composer BD, DNB

DUBRAWSKI, Frank (d 1972 [46]) BP/57*

DU BREIL, Mons. (fl 1711) dancer BD

DUBREUIL, Mons. (fl 1721-22) actor? dancer? BD

DUBREUIL, Mme. (fl 1721-22) actress? dancer? BD

DUBREUIL, Ernest (d 1886 [55]) librettist EA/87*

DUBREUL, Sig. (fl 1848) singer HAS

DU BROCQ, Mons. see Debroc, Mons.

DUBRUCQ, Jean Batiste (d 1893 [63]) musician EA/94*

DUBUISSON, Mons. (fl 1734-42) dancer, actor BD

DU CANE, Augusta (d 1909 [69]) EA/10*

DUCE, R. W. (d 1916) music-hall manager EA/17*

DUCHEMIN, [Mlle.?] (fl 1789) dancer BD

DUCHESNE, Mons. (fl 1791-92) dancer BD

DUCHESNE, Mme. (fl 1791) dancer BD

DUCK, Mr. (fl 1735-44) doorkeeper BD

DUCK, William (d 1892 [72]) manager EA/93*, WWT/14*

DUCKENFIELD, Mrs. George (d 1878) EA/79*

DUCKENFIELD, John (d 1875) proprietor EA/76*

DUCKLIN, Emma see Douglas, Belle

DUCKMAN, Ethel see Colby, Ethel

DUCKWORTH, Mr. (fl 1792-93) manager BD

DUCKWORTH, Mr. (fl 1794)

violinist BD
DUCKWORTH, Mrs. W. M. (d
1912 [67]) actress EA/13*
DUCRAST, Mme. (fl 1794) singer
BD
DUCROW, Miss equestrienne
CDP
DUCROW, Andrew (1793-1842)
English equestrian, ropedancer,
equilibrist, manager BD,
CDP, DD, DNB, ES, HP, OX
DUCROW, Mrs. Andrew see
Woolford, Miss
DUCROW, John (d 1834) eques-
trian, clown BD, CDP
DUCROW, Peter (d 1814) strong
man, acrobat, manager BD
DUCY-BARRE, Louise (fl 1850)
French dancer CDP
DUDA, Andrea (b 1945) American
actress TW/29-30
DUDDY, John (fl 1794) singer BD
DUDDY, Thomas (fl 1794) instru-
mentalist BD
DUDGEON, Thomas (d 1880)
scene artist EA/81*
DUDLAY, Adeline (1859-1934)
actress CDP
DUDLEY, Mr. (fl 1794) singer
BD
DUDLEY, Mr. (fl 1800-12) house
servant BD
DUDLEY, Miss (fl 1778-83) ac-
tress, dancer BD
DUDLEY, Arthur F. (d 1916
[37]) EA/17*
DUDLEY, Arthur W. see
Ward, Henry
DUDLEY, Bide (1877-1944) Amer-
ican critic, dramatist CB,
WWA/2, WWT/6-9
DUDLEY, Carl (d 1973 [63])
producer/director/choreograph-
er BP/58*
DUDLEY, Caroline Louise see
Carter, Mrs. Leslie
DUDLEY, Ethel M. (d 1968 [76])
performer BP/52*
DUDLEY, Henry (d 1873) actor
EA/74*
DUDLEY, Sir Henry Bate (1745-
1814) English dramatist CP/
2-3, DD, DNB, GT, TD/1-2
DUDLEY, J. (fl 1794) singer BD
DUDLEY, John S. (d 1966 [72])
lawyer BP/50*
DUDLEY, Raymond see Turner,
Montague

DUDLEY, S. (fl 1794) singer BD
DUDLEY, Mrs. Sam (d 1876)
EA/78*
DUDLEY, Samuel (d 1882 [36])
music-hall artist EA/83*
DUDLEY, Sara English actress
GRB/1
DUDLEY, William (b 1947) English
designer WWT/16
DUDLEY-BENNETT, H. G. (d
1918 [52]) manager WWT/14*
DUEL, Mr. (fl 1724-27) house
servant BD
DUEL, Peter (d 1971 [31]) per-
former BP/56*
DUELL, William (b 1923) Ameri-
can actor TW/23-28
DUERR, Edwin (b 1906) American
director, educator BE
DUERRENMATT, Friedrich see
Dürrenmatt, Friedrich
DUFAINANAS, Miss (fl 1799)
house servant? BD
DUFF, Charles St. Lawrence
(1894-1966) Scottish dramatist
WWW/6
DUFF, Gordon (d 1975 [66]) pro-
ducer/director/choreographer
BP/60*
DUFF, Harry (d 1890 [85]) actor?
EA/91*
DUFF, J. C. (d 1928 [73]) mana-
ger WWT/14*
DUFF, John A. (d 1889) American
actor, manager EA/90*, WWT/
14*
DUFF, John R. (1787-1831) Irish
actor CDP, COC, DD, HAS,
SR
DUFF, Mrs. John R. see
Duff, Mary Ann
DUFF, Mary [Mrs. A. A. Adams;
Mrs. Joseph Gilbert; Mrs. J.
G. Porter] (d 1852) Irish ac-
tress HAS, SR
DUFF, Mary Ann [née Dyke; Mrs.
John R. Duff] (1794-1857) Eng-
lish/American actress CDP,
COC, DAB, DD, HAS, OC/1-3,
SR, WWA/H
DUFF, Sarah see Halliday, Mrs.
Andrew
DUFF, Thomas (d 1892 [69])
American actor HAS
DUFF, William (b 1927) American
actor TW/6-7
DUFFEE, F. Harold American
dramatist RJ

DUFFELL, Bee (d 1974) Irish actress BTR/74

DUFFET, Thomas (fl 1678) dramatist CP/1-3, DD, DNB, ES, GT

DUFFEY, Peter (fl 1768-1805) singer, actor BD, TD/1-2

DUFFIELD, Mrs. (d 1854) actress HAS

DUFFIELD, Caesar (fl 1669-1707) violinist BD

DUFFIELD, Harry S. actor CDP

DUFFIELD, John (fl 1720-22) dancer BD

DUFFIELD, Kate [Kate Wemyss] (b 1821) American actress HAS

DUFFIELD, Kenneth (b 1885) Australian composer, producing manager WWT/8-11

DUFFIELD, Saunders B. (d 1879) actor, manager EA/80*

DUFF-MacCORMICK, Cara Canadian actress TW/26, 28-30

DUFFOUR, Mr. (fl 1777-97) property man? BD

DUFFRY, Thomas (d 1889 [45]) musician EA/90*

DUFFY, Anne (d 1913 [60]) EA/14*

DUFFY, Barney (d 1906) performer? EA/07*

DUFFY, Bernard (d 1858) actor HAS

DUFFY, Henry (d 1961 [71]) producer, actor, theatre owner TW/18

DUFFY, Herbert (d 1952) actor BE*, BP/37*

DUFFY, James (d 1972 [56]) circus manager BP/57*

DUFFY, John (d 1909 [55]) circus proprietor EA/10*

DUFFY, Maureen (b 1933) English dramatist CD

DUFFY, Patrick James (d 1890 [63]) gymnast EA/91*

DUFFY, William (1801-36) American actor, manager HAS

DUFLOS, Raphael (d 1946 [88]) actor BE*, WWT/14*

DUFOUR, Mr. (fl 1760-63) dancer BD

DUFOUR, Camilla [Mrs. Jacob Henry Sarratt] (fl 1796-1809) singer, actress BD, TD/2

DUFOUR, Val (b 1928) American actress TW/8-14

DUFRANNE, Hector French singer WWM

DUGAN, Dennis (b 1946) American actor TW/28

DUGAN, Johnny (d 1972 [50]) performer BP/56*

DUGANNE, Augustine Joseph Hickey (1823-84) dramatist HJD

DUGARD, Mark John (d 1882 [40]) performer EA/84*

DUGAY, Mons. (fl 1741-48) dancer, slackrope dancer BD

DUGDALE, Mr. (fl 1779) actor BD

DUGGAN, Andrew (b 1923) American actor BE, TW/10-13

DUGGAN, Edmund (d 1938 [72]) producer, actor BE*, WWT/14*

DUGGAN, Maggie (d 1919 [59]) actress, singer CDP

DUGGAN, Mary (fl 1886-92) actress, singer DD

DUGGAN, Tom (d 1903) EA/04*

DUGMORE, William Henry see Denny, William Henry

DUGRANDE, Mons. (fl 1743) dancer BD

DUIGNAN, Thomas (d 1910) music-hall manager EA/12*

DUILL, Mrs. John Lewis [née Catherine Mary Satchell; Mrs. John Taylor, I] (d 1789) actress BD

DUJONCEL, Mons. (fl 1749-62?) French dancer BD

DUKAS, James (b 1926) American actor TW/22-24, 26

DUKE, Mr. see Dyke, Mr.

DUKE, Ivy (b 1896) English actress WWT/6-7

DUKE, John (fl 1590-1617) actor DA

DUKE, N. see Dukes, N.

DUKE, Patty (b 1946) American actress BE, CB, TW/18-19

DUKE, Robert (b 1917) American actor BE, TW/7-20

DUKE, Vernon [Vladimir Dukelsky] (1903-69) Russian composer, lyricist BE, CB, TW/25, WWA/5, WWT/6-11

DUKES, Ashley (1885-1959) English dramatist, manager, critic COC, DNB, ES, NTH, OC/1-3, PDT, WWT/4-12, WWW/5

DUKES, Mrs. Ashley see Rambert, Marie

DUKES, Charles William [Charles Wilford] (d 1887 [42]) performer? EA/88*

DUKES, N. (fl 1730-55) dancer BD

DUKINFIELD, William Claude see Fields, W[illiam] C[laude]

DULAC, Arthur (d 1962 [52]) French actor BE*

DULAC, Odette [Jeanne Latrilhe] singer GRB/1-4

DULANDT, Robert (fl 1623) musician DA

DULCKEN, Louise (1811-50) pianist CDP

DULEY, John Henry (1835-64) American comedian HAS

DULIN, [Mons.] (fl 1767) dancer BD

DULISSE, Mme. (fl 1757-58) dancer BD

DULISSE, Mlle. (fl 1757-59) dancer BD

DULLEA, Keir (b 1936?) American actor CB, TW/15, 24, 26, WWT/16

DULLIN, Charles (1885-1949) French actor, producer OC/1-3

DULLZELL, Paul (1879-1961) American actor, director, administrator WWT/10-13

DULO, Jane (b 1918) American actress TW/2

DULONDEL, Mons. (fl 1720) actor BD

DUMAI, D. (fl 1756-83) dancer BD

DUMAS, Alexandre (1803-70) French dramatist SR

DU MAURIER, Daphne (b 1907) English dramatist BE, COC, ES, OC/3, WWT/10-14

DU MAURIER, George Louis Palmella Busson (1834-96) English artist, writer DNB, NTH, OC/1-3

DU MAURIER, Sir Gerald Hubert Edward Busson (1873-1934) English actor AAS, COC, DD, DNB, ES, GRB/1-4, NTH, OC/1-3, PDT, SR, WWT/1-7, WWW/3

DU MAURIER, Mrs. Gerald see Beaumont, Muriel

DU MAURIER, Guy (1865-1916) English dramatist OC/1-3

DU MAURIER, Muriel see Beaumont, Muriel

DUMAYNE, Norma (d 1910) EA/11*

DUMBRILLE, Douglass (d 1974 [84]) Canadian actor TW/30

DUMENEY, Mrs. (fl 1709-17?) actress BD

DUMENY, Camille (d 1920 [62]) actor BE*, WWT/14*

DUMILATRE, Adele (fl c. 1840?) dancer CDP

DU MINIL, Renée (b 1868) French actress GRB/4, WWT/1-4

DUMIRAIL, Mons. (fl 1674-1716) French dancer BD

DUMIRAIL, fils (fl 1716) French dancer BD

DUMKE, Ralph (d 1964 [64]) comedian TW/20

DUMONT, Mons. (fl 1734-35) scene keeper BD

DUMONT, Mons. (fl 1737-50) dancer BD

DUMONT, Mme. (fl 1724-25) actress BD

DUMONT, Mme. (fl 1738-48) dancer BD

DUMONT, Mrs. (fl 1799-1800) singer BD

DUMONT, Mlle. (fl 1748) dancer BD

DUMONT, Mlle. (fl 1781) dancer BD

DUMONT, Frank (d 1918) American minstrel, dramatist, actor, manager CDP, SR

DUMONT, J. B. (fl 1824) American dramatist EAP, RJ

DUMONT, Louise (d 1932) actress BE*, WWT/14*

DUMONT, Margaret (d 1965 [75]) actress, singer TW/21

DUMORIER, Mr. (fl 1792-93) scene painter? BD

DUMPHEY, Mrs. (d 1782) actress BD

DUNANT, Mr. (fl 1799) actor BD

DUNAWAY, Faye (b 1941) American actress CB, TW/22-23, WWT/16

DUNBAR, Mr. (d c. 1762) boxkeeper BD

DUNBAR, E. C. actor, singer CDP [see also following]

DUNBAR, Edward Charles (d 1900 [58]) actor, singer, musician EA/01* [see also previous

DUNBAR, Erroll (fl 1905) American actor WWA/1, WWS
DUNBAR, George (d 1887) actor EA/88*
DUNBAR, Joan Pauline (d 1913) EA/14*
DUNBAR, Joe (d 1894) EA/96*
DUNBAR, John (b 1877) English actor, business manager GRB/1
DUNCA, Kenney (d 1972 [69]) performer BP/56*
DUNCALFE, Henry (fl 1732-39) musician BD
DUNCAN, Angus (b 1912) American executive BE, WWT/13-16
DUNCAN, Archie (b 1914) Scottish actor WWT/15-16
DUNCAN, Augustin (1873-1954) American actor, producer ES, TW/2-4, 10, WWT/7-11
DUNCAN, Charles H. see Keston, C. B.
DUNCAN, David (d 1874 [48]) musician EA/75*
DUNCAN, Emily (d 1889) actress CDP, DD
DUNCAN, Ged (fl 1798) dramatist CP/3
DUNCAN, Isadora (1878-1927) American dancer DAB, ES, HJD, NTH, OC/1-2, PDT, WWA/4, WWT/4-5
DUNCAN, Lisa (d 1976 [76]) performer BP/60*
DUNCAN, Malcolm (1881-1942) American actor CB, WWS, WWT/7-9
DUNCAN, Maria Rebecca see Davison, Maria Rebecca
DUNCAN, Mary (b 1903/05) American actress ES, WWT/5-8
DUNCAN, Pamela (b 1934) American actress TW/25
DUNCAN, Raymond (d 1966 [91]) actor, dancer TW/23
DUNCAN, Ronald (b 1914) English dramatist, director AAS, CD, CH, ES, MD, MWD, PDT, WWT/11-16
DUNCAN, Rosetta (d 1959 [63]) American actress TW/16, WWT/6-11
DUNCAN, Sandy (b 1946) American actress TW/23-27,

WWT/16
DUNCAN, Sophie (d 1894 [28]) American? variety performer EA/95*
DUNCAN, Thomas R. (d 1865) actor HAS
DUNCAN, Thomas W. (b 1905) American dramatist CB
DUNCAN, Timothy (d 1801) Irish? actor BD
DUNCAN, Mrs. Timothy [née Legg] (fl 1778-1801) actress BD
DUNCAN, Todd (b 1900/03) American actor, singer BE, CB, WWT/10-11
DUNCAN, Vivian American actress WWT/6-11
DUNCAN, William (d 1961 [81]) actor BE*
DUNCAN, William see Rowley, Cpt.
DUNCAN, William Cary (1874-1945) American librettist WWT/5-11
DUNCAN, William H. American actor ES
DUNCAN, William James (d 1917) EA/18*
DUNCOMB, Mr. (fl 1784-94) singer BD
DUNCOMBE, John (fl 1710-16) singer BD
DUNCOMBE, William (d 1769 [80]) dramatist CP/1-3, DD
DUNCOMBE, Mrs. William see Eldéf, Lilian
DUNDAS, Henry [Arthur Harrison] (d 1907 [47]) manager, actor GRB/3
DUNDAS, Lilian (d 1911) actress EA/12*
DUNDAS-SLATER, Charles (d 1912) music-hall manager EA/13*
DUNDY, Elmer S. (d 1907 [45]) American manager GRB/3*, WWT/14*
DUNEMBRAY see Demaimbray
DUNFEE, Ethelyne (b 1937) American actress TW/23-24
DUNFEE, Jack (b 1901) manager, agent WWT/9-15
DUNFEE, Katharine (b 1948) American actress TW/27
DUNGAN, Andrew (d 1887) journalist EA/88*
DUNHAM, Joanna (b 1936) English

actress TW/18, WWT/15-16
DUNHAM, Katherine (b 1910/12)
American dancer, choreograph-
er, producer, actress BE,
CB, ES, TW/2-8, WWT/11-
16
DUNHAM, S. S. (b 1819?) Amer-
ican actor, singer HAS
DUNHILL, Thomas Frederick
(1877-1946) English composer
DNB, ES
DUNKEL, Eugene (d 1972 [81])
designer BP/56*
DUNKELS, Dorothy (b 1907)
English actress WWT/7-10
DUNKELS, Marjorie (b 1916)
English actress, impersonator
WWT/12-13
DUNKLEY, Theophilus (d 1909
[65]) theatrical undertaker
EA/10*
DUNLAP, Louis M. (d 1976
[64]) composer, lyricist
BP/60*
DUNLAP, William (1766-1839)
American dramatist, manager
CDP, COC, CP/3, DAB, DD,
EAP, ES, HAS, HJD, MH,
NTH, OC/1-3, RE, RJ, SR,
WWA/H
DUNLO, Lady see Clancarty,
Countess of
DUNLOP (fl 1789) dramatist
CP/3
DUNLOP, Frank (b 1927) English
director AAS, WWT/15-16
DUNLOP, John see Langtry,
Paul
DUNN, Arthur (1866-1932) Amer-
ican comedian WWM
DUNN, Dick (d 1903 [55]) comic
singer EA/04*
DUNN, Edwin Wallace (d 1931
[73]) American press repre-
sentative WWM
DUNN, Emma (1875-1966) Eng-
lish actress SR, TW/23,
WWT/4-10
DUNN, Geoffrey (b 1903) English
actor, singer, producer,
director ES, WWT/10-16
DUNN, Gregg (d 1964 [48]) actor
BE*
DUNN, Henry (d 1876 [21]) vio-
linist EA/77*
DUNN, James (1905/06-67) Amer-
ican actor BE, ES, TW/24
DUNN, James Colgan (1818-91)

actor, singer CDP
DUNN, James Phillip (1884-1936)
American composer WWA/1
DUNN, J. Malcolm (d 1946 [70])
actor TW/3
DUNN, [John?] (fl 1745-62?) vio-
linist, composer? BD
DUNN, John (fl 1844) actor CDP,
DD, HAS, SR
DUNN, John (d 1875) comedian
EA/76*
DUNN, John Benjamin (b 1812)
actor CDP
DUNN, Joseph (d 1851) comedian
HAS
DUNN, Joseph Barrington (d 1920
[58]) American actor BE*
DUNN, Liam (d 1976 [59]) per-
former BP/60*
DUNN, Michael [né Gary Neil
Miller] (1934-73) American ac-
tor, singer BE, TW/25, 28,
30
DUNN, Ralph (b 1900/02) American
actor BE, TW/15
DUNN, Sinclair (d 1911 [64]) Scot-
tish singer EA/12*
DUNN, William Nathaniel (1782-
1855) treasurer BD
DUNNE, Eithne Irish? actress
TW/3
DUNNE, Irene (b 1904) American
actress, singer BE, CB, ES,
WWT/7-11
DUNNETT, Walter A., III (b 1941)
American actor TW/23
DUNNING, Mr. (fl 1747-48) actor
BD
DUNNING, Alice (b 1847) English
singer HAS, SR
DUNNING, A. T. (d 1886) Aus-
tralian manager EA/87*
DUNNING, Harriet Sarah see
Lingard, Dickey
DUNNING, Philip Hart (1890-1968)
American actor, dramatist,
producer, director BE, ES,
MD, MH, MWD, NTH, SR,
WWA/5, WWT/6-11
DUNNING, Ruth (b 1911) Welsh
actress WWT/9-16
DUNNINGER, Joseph (1892-1975)
American magician CB
DUNNOCK, Mildred (b 1900) Amer-
ican actress AAS, BE, CB,
TW/1-13, 20-23, 26-27, WWT/
11-16
DUNOYER see Denoyer

DUNPHIE, Charles J. (d 1908
[87]) critic BE*, WWT/14*
DUNROBIN, L. Race [Lionel
Claude Race Procter] Mada-
gascan/English? actor GRB/
1-4
DUNSANY, Lord [Edward John
Moreton Drax Plunkett] (1878-
1957) Irish dramatist AAS,
COC, ES, HP, MD, MH,
MWD, NTH, OC/1-3, RE,
WWT/1-11, WWW/5
DUNSTALL, John (1717-78) actor,
singer BD, CDP, DD
DUNSTALL, Mrs. John [Mary]
(d 1758) actress, singer BD
DUNSTALL, Mary see Dun-
stall, Mrs. John
DUNSTER, Charles (fl 1785)
translator CP/3, DD
DUNSTONE, Mrs. (fl 1735) ac-
tress BD
DUNTHORNE, Henry (d 1883)
singer EA/84*
DUNVILLE, Mrs. Fred see
Rehan, Meg
DUNVILLE, T. E. [T. E. Wallon]
(c. 1870-1924) English music-
hall performer CDP, COC,
OC/1-3
"DUODECIMO" see Dodd, James
William
DU PAIN, [Mlle. ?] (fl 1789)
dancer BD
DU PARK, Miss (fl 1800)
harpist BD
DUPEE, William (fl 1794) music
porter BD
DU PERIER, François du Mouriez
(c. 1650-1723) French manager,
actor BD
DUPIN, Mons. (fl 1661-63) actor
BD
DUPLAISIR, Lewis see Duples-
sis, Lewis
DUPLANY, Claude Marius see
Marius, Claude
DUPLESSEY, Lewis see Duples-
sis, Lewis
DUPLESSIS, Lewis (fl 1724-76?)
dancer BD
DUPLISSY, Lewis see Duples-
sis, Lewis
DUPONT, Charlotte Louise (b
1791) French actress CDP
DU PONT, Paul (d 1957 [51])
American costume designer
BE*, BP/41*

DUPORT, Miss (fl 1770) singer
BD
DUPORT, Jean Pierre (1741-1818)
French violoncellist, composer
BD
DUPRATO, Jules (d 1892 [65])
composer EA/93*
DUPRE, Mons. (fl 1679-1705)
lutenist BD
DUPRE, Mons. (fl 1715-1717)
dancer BD
DUPRE, Mons. (d c. 1735) dancer,
choreographer BD
DUPRE, Mr. (fl 1754) singer BD
DUPRE, Mme. (fl 1735-55) dancer?
BD
DUPRE, Eléonore [Caroline?] (fl
1776-87) dancer BD
DUPRE, James (fl 1725-51) dancer
BD
DUPRE, Louis (c. 1690/95-c. 1774)
French dancer, choreographer
ES
DUPREE, Miss (fl 1797) harpist
BD
DUPREE, Josie see Zanfretta,
Josephine
DUPREE, Minnie (1873/75-1947)
American actress GRB/3-4,
SR, TW/1-3, WWM, WWS,
WWT/1-10
DUPRES, Mr. (fl 1761) dancer
BD
DUPRET, Mr. (fl 1800) chore-
ographer BD
DUPREZ, Mr. (fl 1776-82) dancer
BD
DUPREZ, Charles H. minstrel
manager HAS
DUPREZ, Fred (1884-1938) Amer-
ican actor WWT/4-8
DUPREZ, John Louis Philippe
(d 1899 [54]) illusionist EA/00*
DUPREZ, June (b 1918) English
actress ES, TW/3, WWT/11
DUPREZ, Louis Gilbert (1806-96)
singer CDP
DUPREZ, May Moore (d 1946
[57]) music-hall performer
BE*, WWT/14*
DUPREZ-VANDEN HEUVEL, Mme.
(d 1876) singer EA/76*
DUPUIS, Mons. (fl 1757-59)
dancer BD
DUPUIS, Mr. (fl 1797-1800)
watchman BD
DUPUIS, Adolphe (d 1891 [67])
actor BE*, WWT/14*

DUPUIS, Charles (fl 1794-1804)
organist, singer? BD
DUPUIS, Thomas Sanders (1733-
96) English organist, com-
poser BD
DUPUIS, Thomas Skelton (fl
1789) dramatist CP/3
DUPUY, Louis T. see Leyton,
Edgar
DU QUA, Mrs. (fl 1697) actress
BD
DUQUESNE, Edmond [Edmond
Lockard] (b 1855) French actor
GRB/4, WWT/1-3
DUQUESNEY, Mons. (fl 1784-86)
dancer BD
DUQUESNEY, Jacques Alexandre
(fl 1756?-91) dancer BD
DUQUETTE, Tony (b 1918) Amer-
ican designer BE
DURANCI, Mr. (d 1793) actor,
swordsman? BD
DURANCY, Mons. [Jean-Fran-
çois Fienzal] (fl 1746-66)
actor BD
DURANCY, Mme. [Mme. Jean-
François Fienzal; née Fran-
çoise-Marie Dessuslefour]
(fl 1746-62) actress BD
DURAND, Mlle. (fl 1791) dancer
BD
DURAND, Charles [Isaac Charles
Bingley] (1827-1904) singer,
manager DD
DURAND, Charles [né Spring-
meyer] (b 1912) American
stage manager, director, actor
BE
DURAND, Edouard (d 1926 [55])
French actor BE*, BP/11*
DURAND, Rosalie [née Durang]
(1829-66) American singer,
actress CDP, DD, HAS
DURANDEAU, Augustus E. (d
1893) songwriter EA/94*
DURANG, Augustus F. (b 1800)
American actor HAS, SR
DURANG, Caroline (fl 1785)
dancer ES
DURANG, Catharine American
actress HAS, SR
DURANG, Charles (b 1794)
American actor, stage mana-
ger, prompter, ballet master
ES, HAS
DURANG, Charles (1796-1870)
historian BE*
DURANG, Mrs. Charles [née

Mary White] (b 1802) English
actress ES, HAS
DURANG, Charlotte (1803-24)
American actress ES, HAS,
SR
DURANG, Mrs. F. [née Plane]
actress HAS
DURANG, Ferdinand (1796-1831)
American actor CDP, HAS,
SR
DURANG, John (1786-1822) Amer-
ican dancer ES, HAS, SR
DURANG, Juliet Catharine see
Godey, Mrs.
DURANG, Mary (fl c. 1812) dancer
ES
DURANG, Richard F. (1796-1831)
American actor SR
DURANG, Rosalie see Durand,
Rosalie
DURANT, Marie [Mrs. Craston]
(d 1900) actress EA/01*
DURANTE, Jimmy (b 1893) Amer-
ican actor, singer BE, CB,
SR, WWT/9-11
DURAS, Marguerite [née Donna-
dieu] (b 1914) French dramatist
COC, MWD, WWT/15-16
DURASTANTI, Margherita [Signora
Casimiro Avelloni] (b c. 1685)
Italian singer BD
DURBIN, Maud [Mrs. Otis Skinner]
(d 1936 [66]) American actress
BE*, BP/21*, WWT/14*
DURBRIDGE, Mr. (fl 1783-85)
box & lobby keeper BD
DU REE, Meurisse (d 1970 [37])
producer/director/choreographer
BP/55*
DURET, Marie (d 1881) actress
CDP, DD, HAS
DUREVIDGE, J. E. (1813-61)
American actor, dramatist SR
D'URFEY, Thomas (1653-1723)
English dramatist, lyricist,
singer, composer, actor? BD,
CDP, COC, CP/1-3, DD,
DNB, ES, GT, HP, NTH, OC/
1-3
DURGIN, Cyrus W. (1907-62)
American critic, editor BE*,
BP/47*
DURHAM, Mr. (fl 1714) actor
BD
DURHAM, Miss (fl 1757-58) dancer
BD
DURHAM, Edward P. (b 1881)
English actor GRB/1

DURHAM, Richard (d 1969 [80])
composer/lyricist BP/54*
DURIE, Mrs. [née Hanna] (fl
1827) actress HAS
DURIEUX, Tilla (d 1971 [90])
German actress TW/27
DURIUSSEL, Mons. (fl 1828)
French dancer HAS
DURIVAGE, Francis Alexander
(1814-81) American dramatist
DAB
DURIVAGE, John (d 1869) actor
HAS
DURIVAGE, O. E. American
dramatist, actor HAS
DURKIN, James (1876-1934)
Canadian actor WWM
DURLAND, Sig. (d 1916 [82])
proprietor, caterer EA/17*
DURNING, Charles (b 1933)
American actor TW/24-28,
30
DURRANT, John Rowland (d 1853)
founder of Garrick Club EA/
72*
DURRAVAN, Malachy (fl 1772-
83) actor BD
DURRELL, Lawrence (b 1912)
English dramatist CD, MD,
MWD
DURRELL, Michael actor TW/
24-25, 29-30
DÜRRENMATT, Friedrich (b
1921) Swiss dramatist BE,
CB, COC, MH, MWD, OC/3,
WWT/14-16
DURRIVAGE, John E. (1813-
61) American actor HAS
DURSTON, Zoe singer CDP
DURU, Alfred (d 1889 [60])
dramatist BE*, WWT/14*
DU RUEL, Mons. (fl 1703-06)
dancer BD
DU RUEL, Mme. (fl 1704-06)
dancer BD
DURUSET, Mr. (b 1776) English
actor BS
DURUSET, John (1796-1843)
singer CDP, DD
DURYEA, Dan (1907-68) Amer-
ican actor ES, TW/25,
WWA/5
DURYEA, George (b 1904) Amer-
ican actor ES
DURYEA, May (d 1949 [80])
actress TW/6
DURYEA, Mrs. Peter see
Allen, Viola

DUSCHNITZ, Marco (1827-87)
Hungarian singer NYM
DUSE, Eleonora (1859-1924) Italian
actress COC, ES, GRB/1-4,
NTH, OC/1-3, SR, WWA/4,
WWM, WWS, WWT/1-4
DUSER, Mons. (fl 1775?-90?)
clown, tumbler BD
DUSONI, George (d 1895 [70])
animal trainer EA/96*
DU SOUCHET, H. A. (1852-1922)
American dramatist DD, GRB/
2-4, SR, WWM, WWT/1-4
DUSSAULT, Nancy (b 1936) Amer-
ican singer, actress BE, TW/
17-23, 27, 29, WWT/15-16
D'USSEAU, Arnaud (b 1916) Amer-
ican dramatist BE, CB, ES,
WWT/10-14
DUSSEAU, Joanne (b 1942) Amer-
ican actress TW/27
DUSSEK, Jan Ladislav (1760-1812)
Bohemian musician, composer
BD, ES
DUSSEK, Mrs. Jan Ladislav [née
Sophia Giustina Corri; Mrs.
John Alvis Moralt] (1775-c.
1830) Scottish singer, harpist,
pianist, composer BD, DNB,
ES
DUTAC, Mons. (fl 1724-25) actor
BD
DU TERREAUX, Louis Henry
(1841-78) dramatist DD
DUTFIELD, William Rochez (d
1905 [70]) EA/06*
DUTNALL, Martin (d 1867 [29])
pantomime writer EA/68*
DUTTON, Mr. (fl 1730) actor BD
DUTTON, Mrs. (fl 1730) actress
BD
DUTTON, Alice (b 1851) American
pianist HAS
DUTTON, Dolie dwarf CDP
DUTTON, Edward (fl 1597-1600)
actor DA
DUTTON, Frederick (fl 1768-85)
actor BD
DUTTON, John (fl 1575-91) actor
DA
DUTTON, Lawrence (fl 1561-92)
actor DA
DUTTON, Thomas (fl c. 1799)
dramatist CP/3
DUTTON, Thomas (d 1893 [67])
managing director EA/94*
DUVAL, Mr. (fl 1742) dancer BD
DUVAL, Mr. (fl 1764-67) dancer

BD
DUVAL, Mme. (fl 1741-45)
dancer BD
DUVAL, Mlle. (fl 1740-44)
dancer BD
DU VAL, Charles (d 1889)
monologuist EA/90*
DU VAL, Charles H. composer,
mimic, singer CDP
DUVAL, Charles Henry see
Scholes, Charles Henry
DUVAL, Clifton gymnast CDP
DUVAL, Elizabeth (d 1904)
EA/05*
DUVAL, Eugene gymnast CDP
DUVAL, Frederick James (d
1913 [27]) EA/14*
DUVAL, Georges (d 1919 [72])
dramatist BE*, WWT/14*
DUVAL, Heaton (d 1888) ventrilo-
quist EA/89*
DUVAL. Livingston gymnast
CDP
DuVAL, John (fl 1730) dancer
BD
DUVAL, Marie Nina de Harven
see Stella, Nina
DUVAL, Paul (d 1900 [53]) actor
EA/01*
DUVARD, Mrs. Primogene (d
1877 [53]) dramatist EA/78*
DUVERNAY, C. B. (d 1873)
EA/74*
DUVERNAY, Pauline Yolande
Marie Louise [Mrs. Lyne
Stephens] (1813-94) dancer
CDP
DUX, Emilienne (b 1874) French
actress WWT/2-3
DUXBURY, Elspeth (1909-67)
Indian/English actress WWT/
8-10
DVONCH, Frederick (b 1914)
American conductor, musical
director BE
DWIGHT, Mrs. (d 1892) EA/93*
DWIGHT, Christine (d 1889)
music-hall performer EA/90*
DWIGHT, Henry Charles (d
1889 [60]) proprietor EA/90*
DWIGHT, Henry James (d 1875
[27]) Negro artist EA/76*
DWIGHT, Mrs. J. see St.
John, Miss J.
DWIGHT, James (d 1892) EA/93*
DWIGHT, John (d 1903 [40])
comic acrobat EA/04*
DWIGHT, Ogden G. (d 1970 [55])

critic BP/55*
DWORSHAK, Mr. (fl 1791) musi-
cian BD
DWYER, Mr. (d 1817) actor CDP,
DD, TD/2
DWYER, Ada [Mrs. Harold Rus-
sell] (d 1952 [89]) American
actress GRB/3-4, TW/9,
WWM, WWS, WWT/1-6
DWYER, Frank (b 1945) American
actor TW/29-30
DWYER, James (d 1888 [60])
EA/89*
DWYER, Jimmy (d 1965 [72]) per-
former BP/50*
DWYER, John Hambury (d 1843)
Irish singer, actor CDP, HAS
DWYER, Leslie (b 1906) English
actor WWT/11-15
DWYER, Michael (d 1926 [72])
actor, singer DD
DWYER, P. W. dramatist CP/3,
DD
DWYER, Tim (d 1903 [42]) actor
EA/04*
DYALL, Franklin (1874-1950)
English actor, producer ES,
GRB/2-4, WWT/1-10, WWW/4
DYALL, Valentine (b 1908) English
actor WWT/11-16
DYAS, Ada (1843-1908) English
actress CDP, DD, GRB/4,
OAA/2, WWA/4
DYAS, Ann Ada [Mrs. E. Dyas]
(d 1871 [48]) EA/72*, WWT/
14*
DYAS, Mrs. E. see Dyas, Ann
Ada
DYAS, Edward (1815-77) actor
DD
DYBAS, James (b 1944) American
actor TW/21-22, 24-25, 29
DYBLE, Richard (fl 1672) musi-
cian BD
DYCE, Rev. Alexander (1798-1869)
editor, critic DD
DYCKE, Marjorie L. [née Platt]
(b 1916) American educator
BE
DYE, Carol Finch (d 1962 [31])
American actress BE*
DYELL, Mr. (fl 1776) actor BD
DYER, Mr. (fl 1716?-20?) singer
BD
DYER, Mr. (fl 1732-34) actor BD
DYER, Mr. (fl c. 1752) actor
TD/1
DYER, Mrs. (fl 1692-93) singer

BD
DYER, Mrs. (fl 1733-34) actress
BD
DYER, Arthur Edwin (d 1902
[58]) composer, musician
EA/03*
DYER, [Benjamin? John?] (fl
1675) dancer BD
DYER, Charles Raymond (b 1928)
English dramatist, actor,
director AAS, BE, CD, CH,
WWT/14-16
DYER, Deb (d 1973 [69]) per-
former BP/57*
DYER, Edward (fl 1672-86) vio-
linist, composer BD
DYER, Harriet see Chambers,
Harriet
DYER, James (fl 1770) dancer
BD
DYER, Jane (d 1881 [82]) actress
EA/82*
DYER, Lizzie [Mrs. Peter Cock-
burn] (d 1906) singer EA/07*
DYER, Michael (d 1774) actor,
singer BD
DYER, Mrs. Michael [née Harriet
Bullock] (b 1721?) actress,
dancer BD
DYER, Robert (fl 1833) writer
DD
DYER, Teddy (d 1912 [67])
gymnast EA/13*
DYER, William (fl 1726?-39)
musician BD
DYETT, Walter Fairman (b 1873)
American actor WWS
DYKE, Mr. (fl c. 1661-62) actor
BD
DYKE, Mr. (fl 1754) bassoonist
BD
DYKE, Mr. (fl 1819) actor HAS
DYKE, John (fl 1789?-1814?)
actor, singer, dancer BD
DYKE, Mary Ann see Duff,
Mary Ann
DYKE, Winifred Hart English
actress, dancer GRB/1-4
DYKES, Mr. (fl 1710-25) box
keeper BD
"DYKWYNKYN". see Keene,
Richard Wynne
DYMOCK (fl c. 1602-c. 33) trans-
lator CP/3
DYMOV, Ossip (1878-1959) Rus-
sian dramatist COC, MWD
DYNE, John (d 1788) singer,
composer BD

DYNE, Richard (fl c. 1760-76)
singer BD
DYNELEY, Peter English actor
TW/9
DYOTT, John (d 1876) Irish actor
CDP, DD, HAS
DYOTT, Mrs. John (d 1876) ac-
tress HAS
DYRENFORTH, James (d 1973)
American actor, dramatist
WWT/6-8
DYSART, Florence (fl 1886-91)
actress, singer DD
DYSART, Richard A. actor WWT/
16
DYSON, Sir George (d 1964 [81])
composer/lyricist BP/49*
DYSON, Joshua (d 1910 [58]) per-
former? EA/11*
DYSON, Laura (d 1950 [80]) ac-
tress BE*, WWT/14*

- E -

EACHARD, Lawrence see Echard,
Lawrence
EADEN, Henry (d 1880) actor
EA/81*
EADES, Dr. Richard (1571-1604)
English dramatist FGF
EADIE, Dennis (1869/75-1928)
Scottish actor, manager ES,
WWT/1-5, WWW/2
EAGAN, Louis (d 1919) American?
actor, stage manager SR
EAGELS, Jeanne (1894-1929) Amer-
ican actress DAB, ES, NTH,
SR, WWA/1, WWT/4-6
EAGER, Edward (d 1964 [53])
composer/lyricist BP/49*
EAGER, Helen (d 1952) American
critic WWA/3
EAGER, Johnny (d 1963 [38]) per-
former BP/48*
EAGLE, George Barnardo (d 1858
[41]) "Wizard of the South"
EA/72*
EAGLE, Jeff (b 1947) American
actor TW/28
EAGLESFIELD, Tom (d 1874)
music-hall performer? EA/76*
EAGLESON, Thomas Wallace see
Keene, Thomas Wallace
EAGON, Joel (b 1941) American
actor TW/29
EAKER, Ira (b 1922) American
publisher BE

EAMES, Clare (1896-1930)
American actress ES, WWT/
5-6

EAMES, Emma [Mrs. Julian
Story] (1867-1949) American
singer ES, GRB/1, SR,
WWA/3

EAMES, Ethelbert Richard (d
1897 [22]) singer EA/98*

EARDLEY-WILMOT, May (d
1970 [86]) composer/lyricist
BP/55*

EARL, Donna (d 1965 [63])
performer BP/50*

EARL, Josephine (d 1972) pro-
ducer/director/choreographer
BP/56*

EARLE [Richard Williams] (d
1906) musician EA/08*

EARLE, Clara [Mrs. George
Howard] English actress
GRB/1

EARLE, Edward Canadian actor
ES

EARLE, Evalyn [née Emerson]
American actress WWA/5

EARLE, Fred actor, singer
CDP

EARLE, J. (d 1917 [19]) EA/18*

EARLE, Jackson (d 1971 [69])
performer BP/55*

EARLE, John (fl 1640) actor
DA

EARLE, Lilias [Mrs. Nevill
Graham] (d 1935 [62]) English
actress GRB/1

EARLE, Mattie actress CDP

EARLE, Mrs. Robert see
Johnstone, Clara

EARLE, Virginia (1875-1937)
American actress, singer
GRB/2-4, SR, WWS, WWT/
1-5

EARLE, William, Jr. (fl 1799)
dramatist CP/3

EARLESMERE, Florence Helena
see Evers, Adeline

EARNFRED, Thomas (b 1915)
American press representative
BE

EASON, Myles (b 1915) Australian
actor WWT/11-16

EAST, Mr. (d 1880) Negro performer EA/81*

EAST, Charles A. (d 1914 [51])
actor, producer WWT/14*

EAST, James Gully (d 1900 [37])
actor EA/01*, WWT/14*

EAST, John M. (d 1924 [63]) actor
BE*, WWT/14*

EAST, Joseph Samuel (d 1896)
singer EA/97*

EAST, Patrick (d 1969 [48]) agent,
publicist BP/54*

EASTCOTT, Mrs. (fl 1848?) singer
CDP

EASTLAKE, Mary (d 1911 [55])
actress DD, DP

EASTLAKE, Wallace (d 1909 [35])
actor EA/10*

EASTMAN, Barrett (1869-1910)
American critic WWA/1

EASTMAN, Carl (d 1970 [61/62])
press agent TW/26

EASTMAN, Frederick (1859-1920)
English actor GRB/2-4, WWT/
1-3

EASTMAN, Helen (fl 1864) American actress HAS

EASTMAN, Jimmy (d 1904 [19])
acrobat EA/05*

EASTMAN, Joan (d 1969 [32])
performer BP/54*

EASTON, Edward (b 1942) American actor TW/23, 28-29

EASTON, Florence (1884-1955)
English singer ES, TW/12

EASTON, Richard (b 1933) Canadian actor AAS, BE, TW/24-
25, 28, WWT/14-16

EASTWOOD, F. (d 1909 [34])
musical director EA/10*

EASTWOOD, Irene Frances see
Ziegler, Anne

EASTWOOD, Lillian (d 1917)
EA/18*

EATON, Miss (fl 1837) actress
HAS

EATON, Charles (d 1903 [45])
actor EA/04*

EATON, Charles Henry (1813-43)
American actor CDP, HAS,
SR, WWA/H

EATON, Dorothy actress TW/3

EATON, Edwin (d 1890) EA/91*

EATON, Jack (d 1903 [24]) actor?
singer? EA/04*

EATON, Mary (1902-48) American
actress, singer, dancer SR,
TW/5, WWT/6-8

EATON, N. W. (fl 1809?) American? dramatist EAP

EATON, Sally (b 1947) American
actress TW/27

EATON, Thomas Davis see
Vose, Val

EATON, Wallas (b 1917) English actor WWT/11-16
EATON, Walter Prichard (1878-1957) American critic ES, WWT/10-12
EATON, Will D. (fl 1878-97) American dramatist SR
EATON, William (fl 1622) actor DA
EAVES, George (d 1899) proprietor EA/90*
EAVES, Hilary (b 1914) English actress WWT/9-10
EBB, Fred (b 1933) American lyricist CD, WWT/15-16
EBERG, Victor (d 1972 [47]) performer BP/56*
EBERHART, Constance American singer BE
EBERHART, Richard (b 1904) American dramatist, educator BE
EBERLE, Annie see Sefton, Mrs. Joseph
EBERLE, Charles (d 1840) American actor HAS
EBERLE, David (1804-64) American actor HAS
EBERLE, Eliza see Calladine, Eliza
EBERLE, Elizabeth see Kent, Mrs. William
EBERLE, Eugene A. (1840-1917) American actor WWS
EBERLE, Henry (d 1842) American actor HAS
EBERLE, Mrs. Henry (fl 1840) actress HAS
EBERLE, Robert M. (1840-1912) American actor, manager SR
EBERLE, Sophia see La Forrest, Mrs.
EBERS, John (1785?-1830?) English manager DNB
EBERT, Joyce [née Womack] (b 1933) American actress BE, TW/28, WWT/16
EBI, Earl (d 1973 [69]) producer/director/choreographer BP/57*
EBOR, Little see Silbon, Fred
EBSEN, Buddy actor TW/2-3
EBSWORTH, Joseph (1788-1868) dramatist DD
EBSWORTH, Mrs. Joseph see Ebsworth, Mary Emma
EBSWORTH, Mary Emma [Mrs. Joseph Ebsworth] (1794-1881)

English dramatist DD, DNB
EBURNE, Margaret see Eburne, Mrs. W[illiam?] H[awthorne?]
EBURNE, Maude (d 1960 [85]) actress TW/17
EBURNE, William Hawthorne (d 1874) actor EA/75*, WWT/14*
EBURNE, Mrs. W[illiam?] H[awthorne?] (d 1903 [73]) actress WWT/14*
ECCLES, Ambrose (d 1809) Irish dramatist, scholar CP/3, DD, DNB
ECCLES, Donald (b 1908) English actor WWT/12-16
ECCLES, Janet (1895-1966) English actress TW/13, WWT/6-8
ECCLES, John (c. 1668-1735) English composer DD, DNB, ES
ECCLES, Joseph Bruce (d 1882 [37]) scene artist EA/83*
ECCLESHALL, James (d 1875 [37]) stage manager EA/76*
ECCLESTON, William (d 1625/52?) English actor DA, DNB, ES, GT, NTH, OC/1-3
ECCLESTONE, Edward (fl 1679) dramatist CP/1-3, GT
ECHARD, Lawrence (1671-1730) English dramatist CP/1-3, DD, GT
ECHEGARAY, José (1832/33-1916) Spanish dramatist COC, GRB/1-4, NTH, OC/1-3, WWT/1
ECKART, Jean [née Jean Levy] (b 1921) American designer, producer BE, ES, WWT/12-16
ECKART, William Joseph (b 1920) American designer, producer BE, ES, WWT/12-16
ECKER, I. Elmer (d 1975 [77]) lawyer BP/60*
ECKERLIN, Fanny actress CDP
ECKERT, George (b 1927) American stage manager, director BE
ECKERT, Johanna see Holm, Hanya
ECKERT, Karl Anton Florian (1820-79) composer CDP
ECKLES, Robert (d 1975 [55]) performer BP/60*
ECKSTEIN, Louis (d 1935 [70]) American patron BP/20*
ECKSTEIN, Maxwell (d 1974 [69]) composer/lyricist BP/58*
eda-YOUNG, Barbara (b 1945) American actress TW/26, 28-30

EDDIE, El Nino (b 1855) American rope dancer HAS

EDDINGER, Wallace (1881-1929) American actor WWA/1, WWM, WWT/2-5

EDDINGTON, Paul (b 1927) English actor WWT/14-16

EDDISON, Robert (b 1908) Japanese/English actor AAS, ES, WWT/9-16

EDDLEMAN, Jack (b 1933) American actor TW/22

EDDOWES, Geraldine see Allestree, Mary

EDDY, Edward (1822-75) American actor CDP, COC, HAS, OC/1-3, SR

EDDY, Jim (d 1975 [50]) publicist BP/60*

EDDY, Nelson (1901-67) American actor, singer CB, ES, SR, WWA/4, WWT/9-10

EDE, Mr. actor CDP

EDE, George (b 1931) American actor TW/29-30

EDELMAN, Louis F. (d 1976 [75]) producer/director/choreographer BP/60*

EDELSTEIN, Gertrude see Berg, Gertrude

EDELSTEIN, Ray (b 1937) American actor TW/27-29

EDELSTEIN, Rose (d 1969) production manager BP/54*

EDELSTEN, Mrs. E. H. see Edelsten, Eliza

EDELSTEN, Eliza [Mrs. E. H. Edelsten] (d 1897) EA/98*

EDEN, Guy E. Morton (d 1954) dramatist WWW/5

EDEN, Tony (b 1927) American actress TW/1-3, 5

EDENS, Roger (d 1970 [64]) producer/director/choreographer BP/55*

EDESON, Robert (1868-1931) American actor COC, DAB, GRB/2-4, OC/1-3, SR, WWA/1, WWM, WWS, WWT/1-6

EDESON, Mrs. Robert see Berg, Ellen

EDGAR, Alfred (d 1881) EA/82*

EDGAR, Alice [Mrs. J. Thorp] (d 1907) actress EA/08*

EDGAR, Alice see Marriott, Alice

EDGAR, Charles (d 1905 [44]) music-hall comedian EA/06*

EDGAR, David (b 1948) English dramatist CD

EDGAR, Edward Fisher (d 1884 [56]) actor, manager, lessee CDP, DD, OAA/2

EDGAR, Mrs. Edward Fisher see Edgar, Eliza

EDGAR, Eliza [Mrs. Edward Fisher Edgar] (d 1901 [87]) EA/02*

EDGAR, George [né Biddle] (d 1899 [68]) actor CDP

EDGAR, Howard Tripp (d 1927) English actor GRB/1

EDGAR, John W. (d 1909 [67]) music-hall manager EA/10*

EDGAR, Marriott (1880-1951) Scottish actor, dramatist WWT/8-10

EDGAR, Maud (d 1890 [21]) EA/91*

EDGAR, Mrs. R. see Marriott, Alice

EDGAR, Mrs. Richard [Jennie Taylor] (d 1937 [81]) actress BE*, WWT/14*

EDGAR, Richard Horatio (1848-94) actor, manager DD

EDGAR, Robert (d 1870) manager, lessee DD

EDGAR, Stuart (d 1903) actor EA/04*

EDGAR, Thomas (d 1874 [62]) musician EA/75*

EDGARTON, Mrs. Warren see Daly, Julia

EDGCUMBE, Richard (1764-1839) English composer, writer DNB, ES

EDGE, Mrs. T. A. see Tuplin, Lily

EDGETT, Edwin Francis (1867-1946) American historian, critic WWT/9

EDGEWORTH, Jane (b 1922) English actress, administrator WWT/14-16

EDGINTON, May (1883-1957) dramatist WWT/5-11

EDISON, Thomas Alva (1847-1931) American lighting designer BE*

EDISS, Connie (1871/77-1934) English actress CDP, ES, GRB/1-4, WWM, WWS, WWT/1-7

EDLIN, Tubby [Henry] (b 1882) English actor WWT/5-7

EDLOE (b 1943) American actress TW/26, 29
EDMEAD, Miss (fl 1795) dramatist CP/3
EDMISTON, Miss (b 1801) Irish actress BS, CDP
EDMONDS, Mrs. see Yeomans, Mrs. Thomas
EDMONDS, Charles (fl 1855-65) Irish actor HAS
EDMONDS, Mrs. Charles (fl 1852-68) Canadian actress HAS
EDMONDS, Connie [Priscilla Mary Grant] (d 1897 [29]) actress EA/98*
EDMONDS, E. (d 1907 [70]) stage manager EA/08*
EDMONDS, Emma (fl 1854) singer? HAS
EDMONDS, Georgie (d 1883 [27]) singer EA/84*
EDMONDS, Mrs. H. [Mrs. J. Edmonds] (d 1890) EA/92*
EDMONDS, Mrs. J. see Edmonds, Mrs. H.
EDMONDS, James (d 1871 [66]) menagerie proprietor EA/73*
EDMONDS, Mrs. Joe see Robina, Lilian
EDMONDS, John (d 1634?) actor DA
EDMONDS, Lily (d 1902 [17]) EA/03*
EDMONDS, Louis (b 1923) American actor TW/13-19, 25, 30
EDMONDS, Mitchell (b 1940) American actor TW/25, 29
EDMONDS, T. W. [Thomas Edmond Wharton] (d 1874) prompter EA/75*
EDMONDSON, Edward E. (d 1976 [65]) performer BP/60*
EDMONSTON, R. S. (d 1917) EA/18*
EDMONSTON, W. S. (d 1917) EA/18*
EDMUNDA, Prof. (d 1904) ventriloquist EA/05*
EDMUNDS, Edmund (d 1872) comedian EA/73*
EDMUNDS, Mrs. Edmund see Macready, Caroline
EDMUNDS, Lydia (d 1889) EA/90*
EDMUNDS-HEMINGWAY, Clara (1878-1958) American singer, composer, dramatist WWA/3

EDNEY, Florence (1879-1950) English actress TW/2-3, 7, WWT/8-10
EDOUARD, Louis (d 1887 [43]) scene artist EA/88*
EDOUIN, May (d 1944) actress BE*, WWT/14*
EDOUIN, Rose (1844-1925) English actress WWT/4-5
EDOUIN, Willie [William Frederick Bryer] (1841/46-1908) English actor, manager, dramatist CDP, COC, DD, DNB, DP, GRB/1-4, OC/1-3
EDOUIN, Mrs. Willie see Atherton, Alice
EDRIAN, Fanny [née Parks] (d 1867) actress HAS
EDROFF, William (d 1870) musical director EA/71*
EDSON, Calvin ["The Living Skeleton"] (1789-1833) American freak HAS
EDSON, Elie (d 1971 [89]) publicist BP/56*
EDSON, Marjory (b 1943) American actress TW/26
EDSTROM, Katherine (d 1973 [72]) performer BP/58*
EDVINA, Marie Louise Lucienne Juliette (1885?-1948) Canadian singer ES, WWW/4
EDWARD, Georgiana see Pauncefort, Mrs. George
EDWARD, John (d 1882 [76]) actor? EA/83*
EDWARDES, Conway Theodore Marriott (d 1880) dramatist DD
EDWARDES, Mjr. D'Arcy (d 1916) EA/17*
EDWARDES, Felix (d 1954 [83]) English producer WWT/6-11
EDWARDES, George (1852-1915) English manager COC, ES, GRB/1-4, OC/1-3, PDT, WWS, WWT/1-3, WWW/1
EDWARDES, George D'Arcy (d 1917) EA/18*
EDWARDES, Olga (b 1917) South African actress WWT/11-13
EDWARDES, Paula (b 1878) American actress, singer GRB/2-4, WWS, WWT/1-5
EDWARDES, Richard (c. 1523-66) English dramatist DD, FGF
EDWARDS, Mrs. (fl 1780-89) actress CDP, TD/1-2
EDWARDS, Miss (fl 1781) drama-

tist CP/3
EDWARDS, A. C. (b 1909) Amer-
ican educator, publisher BE
EDWARDS, Alan (d 1954 [61])
actor TW/10
EDWARDS, Arthur (d 1910)
singer? EA/11*
EDWARDS, Ben [né George Ben-
jamin] (b 1916) American de-
signer BE, WWT/15-16
EDWARDS, Bessie see Cow-
dery, Mrs.
EDWARDS, Bruce (d 1927 [54])
Scottish manager BE*, BP/
11*
EDWARDS, Clara (d 1974 [95])
composer/lyricist BP/58*
EDWARDS, Cliff (d 1971 [76])
actor, singer, vaudevillian
TW/28
EDWARDS, Darrell Darwin (d
1975 [56]) composer/lyricist
BP/60*
EDWARDS, David (d 1900)
music-hall comedian EA/01*
EDWARDS, Emily Frances
[Mrs. George Edwards] (d
1885) EA/87*
EDWARDS, E. W. (fl 1854)
actor HAS
EDWARDS, Fanny actress CDP
EDWARDS, Fred (b 1860) Eng-
lish actor, stage manager
WWS
EDWARDS, George actor? CDP
EDWARDS, Mrs. George see
Drake, Julia
EDWARDS, Mrs. George see
Edwards, Emily Frances
EDWARDS, George Henry (d
1908 [81]) actor EA/09*
EDWARDS, G. Spencer (d 1916
[79]) English critic CDP,
DD, GRB/1-4, WWT/1-3
EDWARDS, Gus (1881?-1945)
German/American actor, pro-
ducer, songwriter CB, NTH,
SR, TW/2
EDWARDS, Harry (d 1891 [66])
actor EA/92*
EDWARDS, Harry (d 1917) stage
manager EA/18*
EDWARDS, Harry D. (d 1969
[82]) producer/director/chore-
ographer BP/54*
EDWARDS, Henry (1824/30-91)
English actor, manager CDP,
HAS

EDWARDS, Henry (1882/83-1952)
English actor, dramatist, mana-
ger ES, WWT/6-11
EDWARDS, Henry Sutherland (1829-
1906) English writer, dramatist
DD, ES
EDWARDS, Hilton (b 1903) English
actor, producer, director COC,
ES, OC/3, TW/4-7, WWT/8-16
EDWARDS, James (d 1970 [48])
actor TW/26
EDWARDS, James see Carter-
Edwards, James
EDWARDS, J. Gordon (d 1925)
Canadian actor, director ES
EDWARDS, Joan (b 1919) American
singer, songwriter CB
EDWARDS, John actor, singer
TD/2
EDWARDS, John (fl 1808) Irish
dramatist CP/3
EDWARDS, John (d 1911 [67])
actor EA/12*
EDWARDS, J. P. see Swinburne,
John
EDWARDS, Julia (d 1976 [93])
performer BP/60*
EDWARDS, Julian (1855-1910) Eng-
lish composer, actor, manager
DAB, DD, ES, GRB/2-4, SR,
WWS
EDWARDS, Margaret (d 1891 [69])
actress? EA/92*
EDWARDS, Nate (d 1972 [70]) pro-
ducing manager BP/57*
EDWARDS, Neely (d 1965 [82])
performer BP/50*
EDWARDS, Osman (1864-1936)
English critic, translator DD,
GRB/2-4, WWT/1-6
EDWARDS, P. H. (fl 1808) drama-
tist CP/3
EDWARDS, Richard (1523-66) Eng-
lish dramatist, master of the
Chapel Royal CP/1-3, DA,
DNB, ES, HP
EDWARDS, Richard (d 1604 [81])
dramatist BE*, WWT/14*
EDWARDS, Ronnie Claire (b 1933)
American actor TW/27-29
EDWARDS, Sarah (d 1965 [82])
performer BP/49*
EDWARDS, Sarah Ann (d 1870)
EA/71*
EDWARDS, Sherman (b 1919) Amer-
ican composer, lyricist AAS,
WWT/15-16
EDWARDS, Susie (d 1963 [65])

performer BE*, BP/48*

EDWARDS, T. Mills see Mills, T. E.

EDWARDS, Tommy (d 1969 [47]) composer/lyricist BP/54*

EDWARDS, Prof. Vaughan (d 1891) musician EA/92*

EDWARDS, Vincent (b 1928) American actor CB

EDWARDS, Virginia [Mrs. William Hunter] (d 1964) actress, dramatist BE*

EDWARDS, Welsh [né Edward Welsh] (1832-83) actor CDP

EDWARDS, W. H. (d 1891 [59]) panoramist EA/92*

EDWARDS, Mrs. W. H. see Edwards, Sarah Anne

EDWARDS, Will actor, singer CDP

EDWARDS-MINOR, George English acting manager GRB/1-2

EDWARD THE SIXTH English dramatist CP/2-3

EDWIN, Mr. (d 1842) English actor HAS

EDWIN, Benjamin W. [né Huggins] (b 1794) English actor CDP, OX

EDWIN, Elizabeth Rebecca [Elizabeth Rebecca Richards] (c. 1771-1854) English actress CDP, DD, DNB, OC/1-3, OX, TD/1-2

EDWIN, Grace English actress GRB/1

EDWIN, J. H. [De Vere Hayes] (b 1878) Irish actor GRB/1

EDWIN, John, the Elder (1749-90) English actor CDP, COC, DD, DNB, ES, GT, OC/1-3, TD/1-2

EDWIN, Mrs. John, the Elder (d 1794) actress WWT/14*

EDWIN, John, the Younger (1768-1803) English actor CDP, DD, DNB, ES, OC/1-3, TD/1-2

EDWIN, Mrs. John, the Younger (d 1805 [37]) actress WWT/14*

EDWIN, Lina (d 1883) actress, manager CDP, DD

EDWIN, Ruth (d 1909) actress EA/10*

EDWIN, Sophie (b c. 1838) Australian actress HAS

EDWIN, T. Emery (d 1951 [79]) actor BE*

EDWIN, Walter (d 1899 [61]) stage manager EA/00*

EDWIN, William (fl 1836) actor CDP

EDZARD, George (d 1885) EA/86*

EEDES, Richard (d 1604) English dramatist CP/2-3

EEKHOFF, Isaac (d 1874 [64]) musician EA/75*

EFFRAT, John (1908-65) American stage manager, producer, director, actor BE, TW/2, 21

EGAN, Catherine Ann see Achmet, Mrs.

EGAN, F. B. (1818-77) actor, manager DD

EGAN, Frank C. (d 1927 [55]) American producer BE*, BP/11*

EGAN, Jane (d 1893) EA/94*

EGAN, Jefferson (fl 1902-06) American actor, singer WWS

EGAN, Mrs. Jefferson see Britton, Lillian

EGAN, Jenny American actress TW/25

EGAN, Michael (1896-1956) Irish dramatist ES, WWT/8-12

EGAN, Miska (d 1964 [73]) actor BE*

EGAN, Pierce (1772-1849) English journalist, dramatist COC, OC/1-3

EGAN, Rose [Rose Bishop] (fl 1870s) English actress DD, OAA/2

EGAN, Mrs. Thomas W. see Gordon, Marie

EGAN, William (d 1785) actor TD/1-2

EGAN, William, the Younger (d 1822 [60]) actor WWT/14*

EGBERT, Albert (d 1942) comedian BE*, WWT/14*

EGBERT, Tom E. see Tennyck, Egbert Fairchild

EGBUNA, Obi (b 1938) Nigerian dramatist CD

EGERSON, Mrs. see Cussans, Mrs.

EGERTON, Mrs. see Ambrose, Miss

EGERTON, Daniel (1772-1835) English actor, manager BS, CDP, DD, DNB, OX, TD/1-2

EGERTON, Mrs. Daniel see Egerton, Sarah

EGERTON, Frank composer CDP

EGERTON, Frank [W. F. Hughes] (d 1905) music-hall agent & manager EA/06*

EGERTON, Mrs. Frank [Leonora Grey] (d 1887) EA/88*

EGERTON, George (d 1880) acting manager EA/81*

EGERTON, George [Mrs. R. Golding Bright] (d 1945 [86]) Australian dramatist WWT/3-7

EGERTON, Percy (d 1905 [31]) musician EA/06*

EGERTON, Sarah [née Fisher] (1782-1847) English actress BS, CDP, DD, DNB, OX

EGERTON, Mrs. Walter see Scott, Frances Emily

EGGAR, Jack (b 1904) South African manager WWT/9-10

EGGERTH, Marta (b 1912/15/16) Hungarian actress, singer BE, CB, ES, TW/2, WWT/10

EGGINGTON, Arthur Gostling see Willerby, Arthur

EGGINTON, R. (d 1917) EA/18*

EGINTON, Walter see Lilo, Toby

EGLETON, Mrs. actress CDP

EGLEVSKY, André (1917-77) Russian dancer CB

EGLI, Joseph E. (d 1974 [74]) producer/director/choreographer BP/59*

EHRENBERG, Alexandra (d 1896 [33]) musician, singer EA/97*

EHRENSPERGER, Harold (b 1897) American educator BE

EICHBERG, Julius (1824-93) German musician, composer CDP, DAB, WWA/H

EICHBERGER, Wilhelm see Esmond, Carl

EICHELBAUM, Stanley (b 1926) American critic BE

EICHELIN (fl 1604) actor DA

EICHLER, C. H. musician CDP

EIGSTI, Karl (b 1938) American designer WWT/16

EINFELD, S. Charles (d 1974 [73]) producer/director/choreographer BP/59*

EINSTEIN, Harry (d 1958 [54]) performer BE*

EISELE, Lou (b 1912) American costume designer TW/2-5

EISEN, Max American press representative BE

EISENSTAT, Jacob (d 1975 [33]) producer/director/choreographer BP/60*

EISFELDT, Mrs. Kurt see Irwin, May

EISINGER, Irene (b 1906) Austrian actress, singer WWT/9-11

EISLER, Hanns (1898-1962) German composer CB

EISLEY, Fred (b 1925) American actor TW/12

EKHOF, Conrad (d 1778 [58]) actor WWT/14*

EKINS, John R. W. (d 1917 [18]) actor EA/18*

ELBA [Albert Edward Fenton] (d 1900 [34]) trapezist EA/01*

ELBIN, Thomas (d 1907 [64]) acrobat EA/08*

ELCAR, Dana (b 1927) American actress BE, TW/23

ELCOCK, Mary (d 1908 [53]) EA/09*

ELDEE, Lilian (d 1904 [34]) singer, dramatist WWT/14*

ELDEF, Lilian [Mrs. William Duncombe] (d 1904 [34]) actress EA/05*

ELDER, Eldon (b 1924) American designer BE, WWT/12-16

ELDER, Lonne, III (b 1931) American dramatist, actor CD, WWT/15-16

ELDERSHAW, Albert (d 1917) EA/18*

ELDERTON, Joseph (fl 1746) dramatist CP/3

ELDERTON, William (d 1592?) actor, dramatist DA, DNB, FGF

ELDON, Bob (d 1916) EA/17*

ELDRED, Arthur (d 1942 [66]) English actor GRB/3-4, WWT/1-2

ELDRED, Gill (d 1885 [72]) animal trainer, equestrian EA/86*

ELDRED, Ida (d 1918) EA/19*

ELDRED, Joseph (1843-84) English actor CDP, DD, OAA/2

ELDRED, Mrs. Joseph (d 1883) actress EA/84*

ELDRIDGE, Elaine American actress TW/27

ELDRIDGE, Florence (b 1901) American actress BE, CB, TW/3-9, 13-16, WWT/7-15

ELDRIDGE, Lillie (b 1852) American actress HAS

ELDRIDGE, Louisa [nêe Harwood] (d 1905 [76]) American actress DD, HAS, PP/1

ELDRIDGE, Preston W. (d 1925 [71]) American minstrel BE*, BP/10*

ELEN, Ernest Augustus see Elen, Gus

ELEN, Gus [Ernest Augustus Elen] (1862-1940) English actor CDP, COC, GRB/1-3, OC/1-3 WWS

ELEN, Mercy (d 1896 [65]) EA/97*

ELENA, Signorina (fl 1861) singer HAS

ELEY, Douglas N. (d 1911 [44]) EA/12*

ELFORD, Richard (d 1714) singer DNB

ELGAR, Avril [nêe Williams] (b 1932) English actress WWT/15-16

ELGAR, Sir Edward (1857-1934) English composer ES

ELGAR, Henry (d 1917 [84]) musician EA/18*

ELIAS, Ellen (b 1950) American actress TW/26

ELIAS, Hector Argentinian actor TW/28-29, WWT/16

ELIAS, Rosalind (b 1931) American singer CB

ELIC, Josip (b 1921) American actor TW/27

ELINORE, Kate [Mrs. Samuel Goldberg] (1876-1924) American actress WWM

ELINORE, May [Mrs. Robert Franckin] (fl 1912-13) American vaudevillian WWM

ELIOT, Arthur (d 1936 [62]) dramatist, producer BE*, WWT/14*

"ELIOT, George" see Cross, Marie

ELIOT, Max [Mrs. Granville Alden Ellis] (d 1911) American critic GRB/2-4

ELIOT, T[homas] S[tearns] (1888-1965) American/English dramatist AAS, BE, CB, CH, COC, ES, HJD, HP, MD, MH, MWD, NTH, OC/1-3, PDT, RE, TW/21, WWA/4, WWT/9-13, WWW/6

ELISCU, Fernanda (1878/82-1968) Rumanian actress WWM,

WWT/1-11

ELISE, Mlle. (fl 1867?) dancer CDP

ELITZ, Jenny see Van Zandt, Mrs.

ELIZABETH, Mrs. see Mason, Mrs.

ELIZABETH, Queen see Queen Elizabeth I

ELIZONDO, Hector (b 1936) American actor TW/25-27, 29-30, WWT/16

ELKAN, Emil (d 1917) EA/18*

ELKINS, Edward B. see Fielding, Edward

ELKINS, Flora American actress TW/24, 30

ELKINS, Hillard (b 1929) American producer WWT/15-16

ELKINS, Marie Louise (d 1961 [71]) producer BE*

ELLA, Miss [Petronella Jensen] (b 1870) German lion tamer & trainer GRB/1

ELLA, John (1802-88) Scottish musician, musical director DNB, ES

ELLABY, J. N. (d 1895 [45]) reciter EA/96*

ELLAR, Thomas (1782-1842) harlequin CDP

ELLA ZOYARA, Miss [Olmaz or Omar Kingsley] (1830-79) American equestrian CDP, ES

ELLEN, Sany see Dorsey, Sandra

ELLERBE, Harry (b 1905) American actor, director BE, TW/1-17

ELLERTON, Alfred, Jr. (d 1910 [20]) composer EA/11*

ELLERTON, J. L. (d 1873) composer EA/74*

ELLERTON, John A. (d 1911) EA/12*

ELLERTON, William (fl 1858-69) English actor HAS

ELLERY, John English actor, business manager, stage manager GRB/1

ELLIN, David (b 1925) Canadian actor TW/2, 24, 26-27, 29-30

ELLINGER, Désirée (1893/95-1951) English actress, singer TW/7, WWT/4-10

ELLINGTON, Duke (1899-1974) American composer, musician BE, CB, TW/30

ELLINGTON, Evie Ellis (d 1976

[64]) performer BP/60*

ELLIOT, Miss actress TD/2

ELLIOT, Arthur (d 1936 [78])
Indian/English? actor BE*,
BP/20*

ELLIOT, Drew American actor
TW/23

ELLIOT, George [Anderson Mc-
Dowell] (b 1899) English press
representative WWT/9-11

ELLIOT, Jane (b 1947) American
actress TW/22-24

ELLIOT, Samuel (fl 1800) American? dramatist EAP

ELLIOT, Stephanie (b 1931) American actress TW/25-26

ELLIOT, W. G. (fl 1882-1900)
actor DD, EA/95

ELLIOT, William (d 1931 [52])
actor, manager BE*

ELLIOTT, Mr. actor CDP

ELLIOTT (d 1883 [63]) acrobat
EA/84*

ELLIOTT, Alonzo (d 1964 [73])
American composer, lyricist
BE*

ELLIOTT, Ann (1743-69) actress
CDP

ELLIOTT, Ann [Mrs. Will Elliott]
(d 1886 [27]) EA/87*

ELLIOTT, Augustus (d 1904)
acrobat EA/06*

ELLIOTT, Bob (b 1923) American
actor TW/27

ELLIOTT, Cecil (b 1900) American actor TW/2

ELLIOTT, Charles (d 1881) acrobat EA/82*

ELLIOTT, Charlotte [Mrs. Tom
E. Smale] (d 1906) comedienne
EA/07*, WWT/14*

ELLIOTT, Denholm (b 1922) English actor AAS, BE, ES,
TW/23, WWT/11-16

ELLIOTT, Dick (d 1961 [75])
actor BE*

ELLIOTT, Don (b 1926) American
musician, composer, singer,
actor BE

ELLIOTT, E. P. [E. Green] (d
1874 [60]) actor? EA/75*

ELLIOTT, George (d 1903) comic
singer EA/04*

ELLIOTT, Mrs. George see
Scott, Nellie

ELLIOTT, George Henry (1884-
1962) English/American music-
hall performer COC, OC/1-3

ELLIOTT, Gertrude [Mrs. J.
Forbes-Robertson] (1874-1950)
American actress COC, DD,
GRB/1-4, OC/1-3, TW/7,
WWA/3, WWM, WWS, WWT/1-10

ELLIOTT, G. H. (d 1962 [78])
English performer BE*, WWT/
14*

ELLIOTT, Gus (d 1910 [30]) comic
acrobatic juggler EA/11*

ELLIOTT, James (d 1876 [35])
actor EA/77*

ELLIOTT, Mme. James (d 1888)
EA/89*

ELLIOTT, James B. (d 1906)
EA/07*

ELLIOTT, James S. (b 1924) American actor, producer TW/1-4

ELLIOTT, Jeannie see Venoi,
Jeannie

ELLIOTT, John H. (d 1889 [34])
manager EA/90*

ELLIOTT, John Tiffany (d 1963
[48]) literary representative
BE*

ELLIOTT, Julia (fl 1858-60) actress HAS

ELLIOTT, Lizzie (d 1889 [33])
dancer EA/91*

ELLIOTT, Louie (d 1886 [26])
transformation dancer EA/87*

ELLIOTT, Madge (1896/98-1955)
English actress, dancer TW/
12, WWT/6-11

ELLIOTT, Maxine [Mrs. Nat Good-
win] (1868/71/73-1940) American
actress CB, COC, DAB, DD,
ES, GRB/1-4, NTH, OC/1-3,
SR, WWA/1, WWM, WWS,
WWT/1-9

ELLIOTT, Michael (b 1931) English
director AAS, WWT/14-16

ELLIOTT, Otto (d 1895) acrobatic
comedian EA/96*

ELLIOTT, Patricia (b 1942) American actress, singer TW/25-30,
WWT/16

ELLIOTT, Paul (b 1941) English
producing manager WWT/16

ELLIOTT, Percy (b 1870) English
violinist, composer, conductor
GRB/1

ELLIOTT, Ralph (d 1909 [68])
EA/10*

ELLIOTT, Ruth (d 1971 [81]) performer BP/55*

ELLIOTT, Sarah Barnwell (1848-
1928) American dramatist DAB

ELLIOTT, Stephen actor WWT/16

ELLIOTT, Sumner Locke (b 1917) Australian dramatist, actor BE

ELLIOTT, Thomas (d 1889) agent EA/90*

ELLIOTT, Timothy James (d 1877 [28]) clown EA/78*

ELLIOTT, Topsy (d 1902) dancer EA/03*

ELLIOTT, Mrs. Will see Elliott, Ann

ELLIOTT, William (1885-1932) American actor, producer WWT/4-6

ELLIOTT, William A. (d 1905) actor EA/07*, WWT/14*

ELLIOTT, Zo (d 1964 [73]) composer/lyricist BP/49*

ELLIS, Mrs. (fl 1809?) American? dramatist EAP, RJ

ELLIS, Amy (d 1911) music-hall comedienne EA/12*

ELLIS, Anita (b 1926) Canadian singer, actress BE

ELLIS, Anthony Louis (1873-1944) English critic, manager GRB/2-4, WWT/1-9, WWW/4

ELLIS, Sir Arthur E. (d 1907) comptroller of the Lord Chamberlain's department EA/08*

ELLIS, Bert (d 1917) EA/18*

ELLIS, Brandon (d 1916 [87]) dramatist BE*, EA/17, WWT/14*

ELLIS, Carrie [Mrs. Leslie Beaufort] English actress GRB/1

ELLIS, Charles (d 1976 [83]) performer BP/60*

ELLIS, Charles T. actor, singer, composer CDP

ELLIS, Clara (d 1850) English actress CDP, HAS

ELLIS, Edith (d 1960 [86]) American dramatist TW/17, WWT/6-11

ELLIS, Edward (1872-1952) American actor, dramatist TW/9, WWM, WWT/7-9

ELLIS, Edwin (1844-78) musician, musical director, composer DNB

ELLIS, Evelyn (1894?/1900-1958) American actress TW/9, 14

ELLIS, George (d 1871 [54]) professor of music EA/72*

ELLIS, George (d 1900 [59])

music-hall comedian EA/01*

ELLIS, George see Raeburn, Sam

ELLIS, George Cressall [or Cresswell] (d 1875 [65]) manager, director EA/76*, WWT/14*

ELLIS, Mrs. Granville Alden see Eliot, Max

ELLIS, Harold dramatist DD

ELLIS, Harvey (fl 1850) actor HAS

ELLIS, Havelock (1859-1939) English writer DD, HP

ELLIS, Mrs. Havelock (d 1916) writer EA/17*

ELLIS, James (d 1874 [61]) manager EA/75*

ELLIS, James R. (d 1895 [65]) manager EA/96*

ELLIS, John B. (d 1873 [34]) musician EA/74*

ELLIS, John Somerville (b 1870) Scottish musical director GRB/1

ELLIS, Larry (b 1939) American actor TW/28-29

ELLIS, Lionel English manager, actor GRB/1

ELLIS, Lottie see Langlois, Caroline

ELLIS, Louis (d 1887) pantomimist EA/88*

ELLIS, Marie English actress GRB/1

ELLIS, Marion (b 1942) American actress TW/29

ELLIS, Mary (d 1884 [41]) EA/85*

ELLIS, Mary (b 1900) American actress, singer AAS, BE, ES, WWT/6-16

ELLIS, Maurice (b 1905) American actor TW/11

ELLIS, Max (d 1964 [50]) production executive BE*

ELLIS, Michael (b 1917) American producer BE

ELLIS, Patricia (d 1970 [49]) performer BP/54*

ELLIS, Percy (d 1905 [29]) acting manager GRB/1

ELLIS, Richard George (d 1868) comic singer EA/69*

ELLIS, Robert see Castleton, Robert

ELLIS, Vivian (b 1904) English composer, lyricist AAS, ES, WWT/6-16

ELLIS, Walter L. G. dramatist, critic DD

ELLIS, Walter W. (1874-1956) English dramatist WWT/4-11

ELLIS, Will (d 1896 [43]) music-
hall chairman EA/97*
ELLIS, William (fl 1839) actor,
theatre builder HAS
ELLIS, William (d 1858) American
actor HAS
ELLIS, William Henry (d 1869
[43]) actor EA/70*
ELLIS-FERMOR, Una (1894-1958)
critic BE*
ELLISON, Ada (d 1969) production
manager BP/54*
ELLISON, Mrs. George see
Dalton, Kate
ELLISON, James (fl 1812?) Amer-
ican? dramatist EAP, RJ
ELLISON, James (b 1910) Amer-
ican actor TW/1
ELLISON, Joseph Roy (b 1875)
American manager WWA/5
ELLISON, Sydney (d 1930 [61])
director BE*, WWT/14*
ELLISON, William (d 1903 [60])
circus musical director EA/
04*
ELLISSEN, Isabel see Raleigh,
Mrs. Cecil
ELLISTON, Charles (d 1909 [44])
manager EA/10*
ELLISTON, Daisy (b 1894) Eng-
lish actress, dancer WWT/
4-7
ELLISTON, Grace [Grace Rutter]
(1881-1950) American actress
GRB/3-4, TW/7, WWA/3,
WWM, WWS, WWT/1-6
ELLISTON, Louise [Sarah Stone]
(d 1899) EA/00*
ELLISTON, Robert William (1774-
1831) English actor, lessee,
manager BS, CDP, COC,
CP/3, DD, DNB, ES, GT,
OC/1-3, OX, TD/1-2
ELLISTON, W. (d 1893) manager
EA/94*
ELLISTON, William Henry (d
1901 [66]) EA/02*
ELLMENREICH, Franziska (1850-
1931) German actress WWT/2
ELLMORE, Thomas see Saxon,
Thomas A.
ELLSLER, Effie see Ellsler,
Mrs. John A.
ELLSLER, Effie (1858-1942)
American actress CDP, SR,
WWA/1
ELLSLER, John A. (1821/22-
1903) American actor, manager

CDP, HAS, PP/1
ELLSLER, Mrs. John A. [née
Euphemia Murray] (1824-1918)
American actress HAS
ELLSLER, Therese see Elssler,
Therese
ELLSTEIN, Abraham (d 1963 [56])
composer, conductor BE*,
BP/47*
ELLSWORTH, Arley B. (d 1971
[74]) performer BP/56*
ELLSWORTH, Elinor American
actress TW/28
ELMER, Bessie English actress
GRB/1
ELMO, Cloe (b 1910) Italian singer
ES
ELMORE, Mrs. actress CDP
ELMORE, Miss (fl 1850) actress
HAS
ELMORE, Annie [Mrs. James El-
more] (d 1898) EA/00*
ELMORE, James (d 1901 [61]) actor
EA/02*, WWT/14*
ELMORE, Mrs. James see El-
more, Annie
ELMORE, Marcus (d 1872) Eng-
lish? actress HAS
ELMORE, Mrs. Marcus (d 1899)
actress HAS
ELMORE, Marion [Mrs. Frank
Losee] actress CDP
ELMORE, Mary Hannah see El-
more, Mrs. Marcus
ELMORE, Maud actress CDP
ELMORE, Steve (b 1936) American
actor TW/30
ELMORE-FRITH, Mrs. H. see
Liston, Effie
"ELM ORTON" see Pomeroy,
Louise
ELMY, Mary (1712-92) English
actress ES, TD/2
ELPHICK, Michael (b 1946) English
actor TW/25
ELPHINSTONE, Mr. actor CDP
ELPHINSTONE, Miss (fl 1834-36)
English actress HAS
ELPHINSTONE, Annie [Mrs. James
Elphinstone] (d 1900) EA/01*
ELPHINSTONE, Mrs. Charles G.
(d 1904) EA/06*
ELPHINSTONE, Douglas (d 1909
[26]) manager EA/10*
ELPHINSTONE, Emma Marian
Maria [Mrs. James Sheridan
Knowles] (d 1888 [81]) actress
CDP

ELPHINSTONE, Mrs. James see
Elphinstone, Annie
ELPHINSTONE, James H. (d 1892)
manager EA/93*
ELPHINSTONE, Montague (b 1880)
English actor GRB/1-4
ELRINGTON, Francis (d 1746
[54]) actor WWT/14*
ELRINGTON, Thomas (1688-1732)
English actor, manager DD,
DNB, ES
ELROY, Mary Wentworth see
Brent, Marian
ELSER, Frank B. (d 1935 [50])
American dramatist BE*,
BP/19*
ELSGOOD, Mr. (fl 1839?) actor
CDP
ELSIE, Lily (1886-1962) English
actress ES, GRB/1-4, TW/19,
WWT/1-11
ELSIE, Marie actress, singer
CDP
ELSLER, Herminie (fl 1838)
dancer CDP
ELSNER, Marie E. (b 1856)
American singer HAS
ELSOM, Isobel (b 1893) English
actress, singer BE, ES, TW/
1, 6-11, 13-15, WWT/3-14
ELSON, Anita (b 1898) English
actress WWT/5-7
ELSSLER, Fanny (1810-84) Aus-
trian dancer CDP, ES, HAS,
OC/1-2, SR
ELSSLER, Theodore dancer CDP
ELSSLER, Therese (d 1878 [70])
dancer CDP
ELSTON, Robert (b 1934) Amer-
ican actor BE, TW/20, 23-
25, 28-29
ELSWORTH, Thomas (d 1895 [55])
lessee EA/96*
ELSWORTHY, Agnes (fl 1850-56)
English actress CDP, HAS
ELSWORTHY, Maria [Mrs. Arche-
deckne] (1825-79) actress DD
ELTINGE, Julian [William Dalton]
(1883-1941) American actor
CB, COC, ES, OC/3, SR,
WWA/1, WWT/3-9
ELTON, Miss (fl 1836) actress
HAS
ELTON, Caroline (d 1901/02
[68]) actress EA/03*, WWT/
14*
ELTON, Edward S. (d 1884 [53])
actor EA/85*

ELTON, Edward William (1794-
1843) English actor CDP, DD,
DNB, OC/1-3
ELTON, Frank (d 1874) comic song-
writer EA/75*
ELTON, Frank (d 1954 [73]) actor
BE*, WWT/14*
ELTON, Fred (fl 1904?) composer
CDP
ELTON, George (1875-1942) English
actor WWT/4-9
ELTON, Henry (d 1874 [32]) actor
EA/75*
ELTON, Jenny see Lane, Jane
ELTON, William (d 1843 [49]) actor
WWT/14*
ELTON, William (1850-1903) actor
DD
ELVEY, Gwladys (d 1972) perform-
er BP/56*
ELVEY, Maurice [William Seward
Folkard] (1887-1967) English ac-
tor, director ES, WWT/2-11,
WWW/6
ELVIDGE, June (d 1965 [59]) per-
former BP/49*
ELVIN, Mrs. [Charlotte Elizabeth
Keegan] (d 1916) actress EA/
17*
ELVIN, Joe (1862-1935) English
music-hall performer OC/1-3
ELVIN, Violetta (b 1925) Russian/
English dancer ES, WWT/12
ELVIN, Will (d 1893) music-hall
performer EA/94*
ELWELL, Herbert (d 1974 [75])
critic BP/58*
ELWELL, Isaac (d 1890) circus
clown EA/92*
ELWELL, Joe (d 1910 [80]) clown,
animal trainer EA/11*
ELWOOD, Arthur (d 1903 [53]) ac-
tor DD
ELY, Lyn American producer BE
ELZE, Karl critic DD
ELZY, Ruby (1910?-43) singer CB
EMANUEL, Lauren (d 1887) EA/
88*
EMANUEL, Samuel (d 1887) music-
hall performer? EA/88*
EMCH, George (b 1927) Polish ac-
tor TW/29
EMDEN, Henry (1852-1930) English
scene designer ES
EMDEN, Margaret (d 1946) actress
BE*, WWT/14*
EMDEN, T. Walter L. (b 1847)
architect DD

EMDEN, William Samuel (d 1872
[71]) manager, dramatist DD
EMDEN, Mrs. William Samuel
actress DD
EMERALD, Connie (d 1959 [68])
actress WWT/6-9
EMERICK, Robert (d 1973 [57])
performer BP/58*
EMERSON, Mr. singer, variety
performer CDP
EMERSON, Billy [né Redmond]
(1846-1902) singer, minstrel
CDP
EMERSON, Edward (d 1975 [65])
performer BP/59*
EMERSON, Evalyn see Earle,
Evalyn
EMERSON, Faye (b 1917) Amer-
ican actress BE, CB, TW/
4-19, WWT/14-15
EMERSON, George A. (d 1963
[59]) animal trainer BE*
EMERSON, Hope (d 1960 [62])
American actress TW/1,
3-4, 16
EMERSON, James Curtis (d 1904)
manager, actor EA/05*
EMERSON, John (1874-1956)
American actor, dramatist,
director ES, NTH, TW/12,
WWM, WWT/5-11
EMERSON, Mary (d 1921) actress
BE*, BP/5*
EMERSON, Mort (b 1853) singer,
dancer, minstrel CDP
EMERSON, Walter actor, singer
CDP
EMERSON, Walter (d 1893) Amer-
ican musician CDP
EMERSON, William P. [né Wil-
liam E. Redman] (1836/46-
1932) Irish minstrel HAS, SR
EMERTON, Roy [Hugh Fitzroy
Emerton] (1892-1944) English
actor WWT/9
EMERY, Miss [Mrs. Burroughs]
(d 1832) English actress CDP,
HAS
EMERY, Ann [Mrs. John Emery]
(d 1870 [89]) EA/71*, WWT/
14*
EMERY, Edward (1861-1938)
English actor ES, WWS
EMERY, Mrs. Edward see
Farr, Florence
EMERY, Mrs. Edward see
Waldron, Georgia
EMERY, Edwin T. (d 1951 [79])

actor TW/8
EMERY, Frances A. (fl 1846) ac-
tress HAS
EMERY, Frank (d 1910) actor
EA/11*, WWT/14*
EMERY, Frederick (d 1930 [65])
actor BE*, WWT/14*
EMERY, Gilbert [Gilbert Emery
Bensley Pottle] (1875-1945)
American actor, dramatist
HJD, WWT/5-9
EMERY, Isabella Mackle (d 1827
[72]) actress WWT/14*
EMERY, John (1777-1822) English
actor CDP, COC, DD, DNB,
ES, GT, OC/1-3, OX, TD/1-2
EMERY, John (d 1874) comedian
EA/75*
EMERY, John (c. 1905-64) actor
BE, ES, TW/21, WWT/9-13
EMERY, Mrs. John see Emery,
Ann
EMERY, Katherine (b 1908) Amer-
ican actress BE, WWT/9-11
EMERY, Louise [or Louie] (d 1943)
actress BE*, WWT/14*
EMERY, Mackle (d 1825 [85])
actor DD
EMERY, Philip (d 1859 [44]) actor
WWT/14*
EMERY, Pollie (1875-1958) English
actress GRB/1-4, WWT/1, 4-
11
EMERY, Rose (d 1912 [61]) EA/
14*
EMERY, Rose (d 1934 [89]) actress
BE*, WWT/14*
EMERY, Mrs. S. A. see
Meates, Mrs. Arthur E.
EMERY, Mrs. Samuel (d 1886)
EA/87*, WWT/14*
EMERY, Samuel Anderson (1817-
81) English actor CDP, COC,
DD, DNB, ES, HAS, OAA/1-2,
OC/1-3
EMERY, Winifred [Mrs. Cyril
Maude] (1862-1924) English ac-
tress CDP, COC, DD, DP,
EA/95-96, ES, GRB/1-4, OC/
1-3, WWT/1-4, WWW/2
EMHARDT, Robert (b 1916) Amer-
ican actor, director BE, TW/
5-8, 12-16, WWT/14
EMIL-BEHNKE, Kate (d 1957 [86])
drama instructor BE*, WWT/
14*
EMILE, Robert (d 1889) clown
EA/90*

EMMERSON, Aggie [Mrs. Frederick Renad] (d 1894) EA/95*
EMMERSON, Alfred T. (d 1917) musical director EA/18*
EMMERSON, Dorothy L. Japanese/American actress TW/26
EMMET, Alfred (b 1908) English director WWT/15-16
EMMET, Katherine (d 1960 [78]) actress TW/17
EMMETT, Bessie [Mrs. Richard Temple] (d 1875 [28]) EA/76*
EMMETT, Bobbie [W. J. McNeill] (d 1898 [37]) music-hall performer EA/00*
EMMETT, Daniel Decatur (1815-1904) American minstrel, composer CDP, DAB, HJD, SR, WWA/H
EMMETT, Joseph Kline (1841-91) American actor, manager CDP, DD, HAS, SR
EMMETT, Nat (d 1910) variety artist EA/11*
EMMETT, Robert (b 1921) American actor TW/9-10
EMMONS, Lizzie (d 1863) actress HAS
EMMOTT, Mrs. Elizabeth see Herbert, Miss Emmott
EMNEY, Fred (1865-1917) English actor COC, GRB/1-4, OC/1-3, WWT/1-3
EMNEY, Fred (b 1900) English actor COC, OC/1-3, WWT/8-16
EMNEY, Joan Fred actress WWT/9-10
EMORY, Carl (d 1966 [59]) actor TW/23
EMPY, Cleo see Mayfield, Cleo
EMPY, Guy (d 1963 [79]) songwriter, actor, director BE*
EMSON, Mr. singer, minstrel CDP
ENDERSBY, Paul (d 1968 [69]) performer BP/53*
ENDERSON, Carrie see Barker, Carrie
ENDERSSOHN, Harry (d 1877 [49]) clown EA/78*
ENDORE, Guy (d 1970 [69]) dramatist BP/54*
ENDRES, Augusta actress? CDP
ENDREY, Eugene (d 1967 [76]) producer/director/choreographer BP/52*
ENGEL, Carl (d 1893) EA/94*

ENGEL, Jennie (fl 1858?) actress CDP
ENGEL, Josephine [Mrs. Leo Engel] (d 1888 [31]) EA/89*
ENGEL, Lehman (b 1910) American composer, conductor BE
ENGEL, Mrs. Leo see Engel, Josephine
ENGEL, Nina [Mrs. Sidney Beltram] (d 1917) EA/18*
ENGEL, Robert (b 1948) American actor TW/27
ENGEL, Susan (b 1935) Austrian actress WWT/15-16
ENGELBACH, E. C. (d 1916 [69]) lessee EA/17*, WWT/14*
ENGELHARDT, Wallace (b 1923) American actor TW/26
ENGELS, George (d 1907 [61]) dramatist, actor BE*, WWT/14*
ENGELS, M. (fl 1838) musician CDP
ENGLAND, Barry (b 1934) English dramatist CD
ENGLAND, Daisy (d 1943 [81]) actress EA/97
ENGLAND, James Sharp (fl 1809?) performer? CDP
ENGLAND, Paul (1893-1968) English actor, singer WWT/6-7
ENGLANDER, Ludwig (1859/82-1914) Austrian conductor, composer DD, GRB/3-4, SR, WWS, WWT/1-2
ENGLE, Billy (d 1966 [77]) performer BP/51*
ENGLEFIELD, Violet (d 1946 [60]) actress BE*, WWT/14*
ENGLER, Alvina (d 1913) EA/14*
ENGLISH, Mr. (d 1875 [39]) agent, manager EA/76*
ENGLISH, D. G. (d 1893) EA/94*
ENGLISH, George (d 1911) music-hall proprietor EA/12*
ENGLISH, Mrs. George (d 1894 [40]) EA/95*
ENGLISH, George Griffiths (d 1907 [38]) EA/08*
ENGLISH, Granville (d 1968 [73]) composer/lyricist BP/53*
ENGLISH, John (fl 1494-1531) actor DA
ENGLISH, Paul Allen (d 1972 [44]) performer BP/57*
ENGLISH, Ralph (d 1970 [59]) performer BP/55*
ENGLISH, Thomas Dunn (1819-1902)

American dramatist DAB, RJ
ENGLISH, William B. (d 1864
[52]) manager HAS
ENGLISH DWARF (b 1709) CDP
ENGLISH STAGE COMPANY LTD.
producing managers WWT/
13-14
ENGLUND, George (b 1926) Amer-
ican actor TW/8
ENGLUND, Maude Beatrice Gal-
braith (d 1962 [71]) singer BE*
ENGSTROM, Arthur Hamilton
see Revelle, Arthur Hamilton
ENKE, Edith see Adams, Edith
ENLOE, William G. (d 1972 [70])
manager BP/57*
ENNIS, Charles (b 1917) American
choirmaster BE
ENOCH, Frederick (d 1905) lyricist
GRB/1
ENOS, Busby Berkeley William
see Berkeley, Busby
ENOS, Mrs. Wilson see Berkeley,
Gertrude
ENRIGHT, Josephine (d 1976 [72])
performer BP/60*
ENRIGHT, Sara (d 1963 [75]) ac-
tress, talent representative
BE*, BP/47*
ENSERRO, Michael (b 1918) Amer-
ican actor TW/20-24, 26, 28-
29
ENSON, Fanny (d 1897) actress
DD
ENSSLEN, Dick (b 1926) American
actor TW/24-25, 30
ENTEN, Boni (b 1947) American
actress TW/25-26, 28-29
ENTERS, Angna (b 1907) American
mime actress BE, CB, COC,
ES, OC/3
ENTERS, Warren (b 1927) Amer-
ican director BE
ENTHOVEN, Gabrielle (1868-
1950) English historian, drama-
tist COC, ES, OC/1-3, WWT/
6-10, WWW/4
ENTWISTLE, Mr. (fl 1804-14)
actor HAS
ENTWISTLE, Mrs. see Mason,
Mrs.
ENTWISTLE, Ethel (d 1918)
EA/19*
ENTWISTLE, Lillian Millicent
(d 1932) actress BE*
ENTWISTLE, William (d 1869
[35]) music-hall proprietor
EA/71*

ENZER, Jack (d 1917) performer?
EA/18*
EPAILLY, Jules (d 1967 [80s])
performer BP/51*
EPHRAIM, Lee (1877-1953) Ameri-
can manager WWT/6-11
EPHRON, Henry (b 1912) American
dramatist BE
EPHRON, Phoebe [née Wolkind]
(1916-71) American dramatist
BE, TW/28
EPITAUX, Fred (d 1913) actor
WWT/14*
EPLETT, Kate (d 1905) EA/06*
EPLETT, Tom (d 1905) EA/06*
EPPERSON, Don (d 1973 [35])
performer BP/57*
EPSTEIN, Alvin (b 1925) American
actor AAS, BE, ES, TW/15-
16, 18-20, 22-23, 26-27, WWT/
14-16
EPSTEIN, Brian (d 1967 [32]) pro-
ducing manager WWT/15*
EPSTEIN, Howard (d 1969 [51])
lawyer BP/54*
EPSTEIN, Julius (b 1909) American
dramatist, producer BE
EPSTEIN, Philip G. (d 1952 [42])
American dramatist BE*, BP/
36*
EPSTEIN, Pierre (b 1930) French
actor TW/28, 30
ERANION, Henry E. (d 1905) con-
jurer EA/06*
ERATO, Carl John Bergstrom (d
1885 [52]) Swedish gymnast
EA/86*
ERB, George see Allen, Johnny
ERCKMANN, Emile see Erck-
mann-Chatrian
ERCKMANN-CHATRIAN [Emile
Erckmann (1822-99), & Louis
Gratien Charles Alexandre
Chatrian (1826-90) French
dramatists COC, ES, HP,
NTH, OC/1-3
ERDMAN, Jean (b 1917) Hawaiian
dancer, choreographer CB,
TW/23, 29
ERDMAN, Nikolai R. (d 1970 [68])
dramatist BP/55*
ERHARDT, Thomas (b 1928) Amer-
ican literary & talent repre-
sentative BE
ERIC, Elspeth American actress
TW/1
ERIC, Fred (d 1935 [61]) American
actor WWT/1-7

ERICHS, Harold (d 1976 [74])
editor BP/60*
ERICKSON, Ed (b 1931) American actor TW/24
ERICKSON, John (d 1972 [74]) composer/lyricist BP/57*
ERICKSON, Leif (b 1911) American actor BE
ERICSON, John (b 1926) German/ American actor BE, TW/9
ERIVEN, Stuart (d 1967 [64]) actor WWT/15*
ERK, Ludwig (d 1883 [77]) musical director EA/84*
ERLANGER, Abraham Lincoln (1860-1930) American manager DAB, ES, GRB/2-4, NTH, SR, WWA/1, WWM, WWT/1-6
ERLANGER, Frederic [Ferdinand Regnal] (1868-1943) French/ English composer ES
ERLE, T. W. (fl 1880) writer DD
ERMINIE, Mlle. (fl 1857) singer? HAS
ERMOLIEFF, Joseph N. (d 1962 [72]) Russian producer BE*
ERNE, Vincent (b 1884) English actor WWT/5-7
ERNEST, Charles (d 1897) singer, minstrel CDP
ERNEST, Emily see Chenoweth, Emily
ERNEST, Lily see Mansel, Lady
ERNESTINE, Mme. (d 1890) dancer EA/91*
ERNO, George (d 1905) EA/06*
ERNO, Harry (d 1890 [35]) music-hall performer EA/91*
ERNST, Earle (b 1911) American educator, director BE
ERNST, Leila (b 1922) American actress TW/3-4
ERNST, Phillip (1792-1868) German musician HAS
ERNSTONE, Helena Cecile [née Schott] (fl 1863-79) German actress DD, OAA/2
ERON, Kate (d 1885 [24]) EA/86*
ERRANI, Achille (d 1897 [73]) singer CDP, HAS
ERRINGTON, Bertha (d 1889) actress? EA/90*
ERRINGTON, Richard (fl 1622-36) manager, actor DA
ERRIS, Fanny actress GRB/1
ERROL, Leon (1881-1951) Australian actor ES, SR, TW/8,

WWT/4-11
ERROLLE, Ralph [né Ralph Errolle Smith] (1887-1973) American singer WWM
ERSKIN, Chester (b 1903) Austrian producer, manager, actor WWT/7-11
ERSKINE, Hon. Andrew (fl 1764) dramatist CP/3
ERSKINE, Sir David (1772-1837) dramatist DD, DNB
ERSKINE, Howard (b 1926) American producer, director, actor BE, WWT/14-16
ERSKINE, James see Rosslyn, Earl of
ERSKINE, John (1879-1951) American librettist WWW/5
ERSKINE, Mrs. Steuart (d 1948) dramatist WWW/4
ERSKINE, Wallace (d 1943 [81]) English actor WWM, WWS
ERVINE, St. John Greer (1883-1971) Irish dramatist, critic AAS, COC, ES, MD, MH, MWD, NTH, OC/1-3, PDT, RE, SR, TW/27, WWA/5, WWT/2-14
ERWIN, Barbara (b 1937) American dancer TW/29-30
ERWIN, Stuart (1902/03-67) American actor BE, ES, TW/24
ESCAMO [Charles Waldon] (d 1901 [35]) conjuror EA/03*
ESCANDE, Maurice (d 1973 [80]) actor WWT/16*
ESCOTT, Lucy (fl 1858-60) singer, dancer CDP, HAS
ESCOTT, Thomas Hay Sweet (d 1924) writer WWW/2
ESDAIL, Arthur (b 1857) actor GRB/1
ESDAILE, Florence (b 1875) Australian singer GRB/1-3
ESDEN, Alice English actress GRB/1
ESHER, Lord (d 1963 [82]) chairman of London Theatre Council WWT/14*
ESKENAS, Linda (b 1950) American actress TW/30
ESLER, Lemist (1888-1960) dramatist, actor, educator BE*
ESMOND, Annie (1873-1945) actress WWT/6-9
ESMOND, Carl [Wilhelm Eichberger] (b 1905/08) Austrian actor TW/14, WWT/9-10
ESMOND, Henry Vernon [H. V.

Jack] (1869-1922) English actor,
dramatist COC, DD, DNB,
EA/95, ES, GRB/1-4, OC/1-3,
WWS, WWT/1-4, WWW/2

ESMOND, Mrs. Henry Vernon
see Moore, Eva

ESMOND, Jill (b 1908) English
actress WWT/6-12

ESMOND, Wilfred [Michael Butler]
(1849-1913) Irish singer, manager GRB/1

ESMONDE, Lewis (d 1877 [32])
lessee EA/78*

ESMONDE, Teresa (fl 1853) actress HAS

ESMOND-MOORE, Jill see
Esmond, Jill

ESPINDA, David (d 1975 [61])
performer BP/60*

ESPINOSA, Mme. (d 1933 [84])
dancer WWT/14*

ESPINOSA, Clarence (b 1961)
American actor TW/25

ESPINOSA, Edouard (1872-1950)
English dancer, maître de
ballet, choreographer ES,
WWT/6-10

ESPINOSA, Judith (d 1949 [72])
dancer BE*, WWT/14*

ESPINOSA, Leon (fl 1850-51)
dancer CDP, HAS

ESPLA, Oscar (d 1976 [96])
composer/lyricist BP/60*

ESPOSITO, Giancarlo (b 1958)
Danish actor TW/29-30

ESPOSITO, Michele (1855-1929)
Italian composer WWW/3

ESSEN, Viola (b 1925) American
dancer TW/1, 5-6

ESSER, Peter (d 1970 [84])
performer BP/55*

ESSEX, Dowager Countess of
see Stephens, Catherine

ESSEX, Earl of see Devereux,
Robert

ESSEX, George, Sr. (d 1871 [55])
singer EA/72*

ESSEX, Harcourt see Algeranoff,
Harcourt

ESSEX, Harold (d 1973 [68])
performer BP/57*

ESSEX, John (d 1744) English
dancer, choreographer ES

ESSEX, Tony (d 1975 [49])
producer/director/choreographer
BP/60*

ESSLER, Fred (d 1973 [77]) performer BP/57*

ESSLIN, Martin (b 1918) Hungarian
critic BE, WWT/16

ESSMAN, Manuel (b 1898) American
scene designer ES

ESTABROOK, Howard (b 1884)
American actor ES, WWM,
WWT/4-8

ESTABROOK, Mrs. Howard see
Dale, Gretchen

ESTCOURT, Dick (1668-1712) English actor COC, CP/1-3, DD,
DNB, GT, OC/1-3, TD/1-2

ESTCOURT, Frank (d 1893 [46])
music-hall chairman? EA/94*

ESTCOURT, Richard see Estcourt, Dick

ESTELLE, Mr. (d 1829) American
actor HAS

ESTELLE, Caroline (d 1874) dancer
EA/75*

ESTEN, Harriet Pye [née Bennett;
Mrs. Scott-Waring] (1768?-1868)
actress CDP, GT, TD/1-2

ESTERMAN, Laura (b 1945) American actress TW/26-27, 29-30

ESTEVEZ, Ramon see Sheen,
Martin

ESTEY, Suellen American actress
TW/28-30

ESTHER, Mlle. (b 1816) French
dancer HAS

ESTOTEVILLE, George (fl 1640)
actor DA

ESTY, Alice (d 1935 [71]) American singer DD, GRB/1-4

ESTY, Annah B. (d 1912) EA/13*

ETCHELLS, Will (d 1878) comic
singer EA/79*

ETHAIR, Emily [Mrs. A. Scott]
(d 1878 [27]) singer, actress
EA/79*

ETHAIR, Nelly see Batchelor,
Nelly

ETHAIR, Rose (d 1870) equestrienne EA/71*

ETHAIR, Uncle Steve [Stephen
Etheridge] (d 1891 [72]) EA/92*

ETHARDO, Steve (d 1911 [76])
spiral ascensionist EA/12*

ETHEL, Agnes (1852-1903) American? actress, manager? CDP,
DD, HAS, WWA/H

ETHERDO [John Johnson] (d 1916
[82]) clown, pantomimist EA/
17*

ETHERDO, Mary Ann [Emily Man-
fred] (d 1882) EA/83*

ETHERDO, Thomas (d 1902 [49])

acrobat EA/03*
ETHERDO, William (d 1893) gymnast EA/95*
ETHEREGE, Sir George (1634-91) English dramatist COC, CP/1-3, DD, DNB, ES, GT, HP, MH, NTH, OC/1-3, PDT, RE
ETHERIDGE, May (d 1935) actress WWT/14*
ETHERIDGE, Stephen see Ethair, Uncle Steve
ETHERINGTON, James (d 1877 [46]) pantomimist EA/78*
ETHERINGTON, James (1902-48) English actor, singer WWT/10
ETHLO, Maggie [Mrs. Fred Stokes] (d 1897 [20]) dancer EA/98*
ETLER, Alvin D. (d 1973 [60]) composer/lyricist BP/58*
ETTING, Ruth (b 1907) American actress, singer WWT/7-9
ETTLINGER, Dorothy see Day, Dorothy
EUGENE, Marvellous [Alfred Eugene Godolphin Cooke] (d 1900 [55]) equestrian EA/01*
EUGENE, Master [Eugene D'Ameli] (1836-1907) female impersonator, minstrel CDP
EUGENE, Max (d 1917) singer EA/18*
EUGENE, Thomas (d 1911 [52]) acrobat, gymnast EA/12*
EUNSON, Dale (b 1904) American dramatist BE
EUNSON, Katherine Albert (d 1970 [68]) dramatist BP/55*
EURARDO, Sig. see Rowley, Joseph
EURIPIDES (480-406 B. C.) Greek dramatist ES
EUSTACE, Edward J. (d 1971) dramatist BP/56*
EUSTACE, Jennie A. (1865/66-1936) American actress WWM, WWS
EUSTAPHIEVE, Alexis (fl 1814?) American? dramatist EAP
EUSTREL, Antony (b 1904) English actor WWT/10-13
EVAIN, W. H. (fl 1850) actor HAS
EVANKO, Ed Canadian actor TW/25-26, 28, 30
EVANS, Mr. actor, singer CDP
EVANS, Alice (b 1939) American actress TW/24

EVANS, Alison Ridley (b 1929) English producer BE
EVANS, Amy Rosalind [Mrs. Fred Evans] (d 1885) EA/86*
EVANS, Anne [Mrs. George Evans] (d 1877 [26]) EA/78*
EVANS, Bob (d 1903 [34]) one-legged singer, dancer EA/04*
EVANS, Caradoc (d 1945 [70]) Welsh dramatist WWT/6-9, WWW/4
EVANS, Charles E. (1856/57-1945) American actor, manager CDP, SR, WWS
EVANS, Charles Smart (1778-1849) singer DNB
EVANS, Clifford (b 1912) Welsh actor ES, WWT/9-10, 14
EVANS, Damon [Dickie Evans] (b 1950) American actor TW/27-30
EVANS, Dickie see Evans, Damon
EVANS, Dillon (b 1921) English actor TW/28-29
EVANS, Douglas (d 1968 [64]) performer BP/52*
EVANS, Dame Edith Mary (1888-1976) English actress AAS, CB, COC, ES, OC/1-3, PDT, TW/7-15, WWT/4-16
EVANS, Edwin, Jr. (1874-1945) English critic ES
EVANS, Eliza (d 1908) EA/09*
EVANS, Evan E. (d 1962 [73]) performer BE*
EVANS, Frank J. (fl 1865) actor CDP
EVANS, Fred comedian CDP
EVANS, Fred (d 1909 [69]) clown BE*, EA/10*, WWT/14*
EVANS, Mrs. Fred (d 1904 [83]) EA/05*
EVANS, Mrs. Fred see Albert, Rose
EVANS, Mrs. Fred see Evans, Amy Rosalind
EVANS, George (1870-1915) Welsh minstrel BE*
EVANS, Mrs. George see Evans, Anne
EVANS, George F. actor HAS
EVANS, George S. (d 1911) scene artist EA/12*
EVANS, Geraint (b 1922) Welsh singer ES
EVANS, Gouldwais (fl 1629) musician DA
EVANS, Greek Harry (d 1967 [77]) singer TW/23

EVANS, Harry (d 1905) comedian
EA/06*
EVANS, Harvey (b 1941) American actor TW/26-30
EVANS, Helen Hartz (d 1974 [77]) performer BP/58*
EVANS, Henry (fl 1582-1603) Welsh lessee DA
EVANS, J. (d 1879) minstrel?
EA/80*
EVANS, Jane (d 1898) EA/99*
EVANS, Jessie (b 1918) Welsh actress AAS, WWT/10-16
EVANS, J. H. (d 1865) dramatist HAS
EVANS, Joe (d 1973 [57]) performer BP/58*
EVANS, John (1693?-1734?) Irish? actor, manager DNB
EVANS, John (d 1878) gymnast EA/79*
EVANS, John see Dubellamy, Charles Clementine
EVANS, John see Pasco
EVANS, John D. (d 1887) circus performer NYM
EVANS, Johnny (b 1946) American actor TW/25
EVANS, Judith American actress TW/29
EVANS, Julia [Mrs. Thomas Evans] (d 1910 [83]) EA/11*
EVANS, Madge (b 1909) American actress BE, ES, TW/5-7, WWT/7-11
EVANS, Margaret see Didier, Mrs. Abraham J.
EVANS, Mary (d 1892 [49]) EA/93*
EVANS, Mary Jane (b 1923) American educator BE
EVANS, Maurice Herbert (b 1901) English actor, producer AAS, BE, CB, COC, ES, NTH, OC/1-3, SR, TW/2-21, WWT/7-16
EVANS, May [Mrs. W. Horne] (d 1911) music-hall comedian EA/12*
EVANS, Michael (b 1922/26) English actor BE, TW/8, WWT/14-15
EVANS, Michele (b 1942) American actress TW/23
EVANS, Millicent [Mrs. E. J. Carpenter] (fl 1900s) American actress WWM
EVANS, Nancy (b 1915) English

actress, singer WWT/10-14
EVANS, Nathaniel (1742-67) American dramatist EAP
EVANS, Norman (d 1962 [61]) performer BE*
EVANS, Pat (b 1940) American actress TW/28
EVANS, Ray (b 1915) American songwriter BE
EVANS, Redd L. (d 1972 [60]) composer/lyricist BP/57*
EVANS, Renee (d 1971 [63]) performer BP/56*
EVANS, Rex (1903-69) English actor TW/3, 5-9, 25
EVANS, Reynolds (d 1967 [72]) actor TW/1, 8, 10-15, 20, 24
EVANS, Rose (d 1875 [25]) actress EA/76*
EVANS, Ross (d 1967 [51]) dramatist BP/52*
EVANS, Rothbury (d 1944 [81]) actor BE*, WWT/14*
EVANS, Susan (d 1888) EA/89*
EVANS, T. E. (d 1894) lessee EA/95*
EVANS, Tenniel (b 1926) Kenyan actor WWT/15-16
EVANS, T. F. (d 1876 [58]) music-hall proprietor EA/77*
EVANS, Thomas (d 1881) singer EA/82*
EVANS, Thomas (d 1887 [62]) animal impersonator EA/88*
EVANS, Mrs. Thomas see Evans, Julia
EVANS, Tom (d 1903) scene artist EA/04*
EVANS, Wilbur (b 1905/08) American singer, actor, director BE, TW/1-6, 10-12, 23-24
EVANS, Will (1873/75-1931) English actor CDP, COC, GRB/1-3 OC/1-3, WWT/4-6
EVANS, Mrs. Will see Luxmore, Ada
EVANS, William C. (fl 1822) actor CDP
EVANS, Winifred (b 1890) English actress WWT/7-14
EVARART, E. (d 1889) deputy manager EA/90*
EVARD, Mr. (fl 1842-50) actor, manager HAS
EVARTS, William H. (1867-1940) American actor SR
EVATT, Mr. (fl 1798-99) actor TD/1-2

EVELEIGH, Corp. Harold West-
lake (d 1916 [19]) EA/17*
EVELEIGH, Lawrence Westlake
(d 1917 [21]) EA/18*
EVELING, Stanley (b 1925) Eng-
lish dramatist CD, WWT/
15-16
EVELYN, Clara (b 1886) English
actress, singer WWT/1-7
EVELYN, Ernest Evelyn (d 1892)
EA/93*
EVELYN, John (1620-1706) drama-
tist DD
EVELYN, Judith (1913-67) Amer-
ican actress BE, TW/2-18,
23, WWA/4, WWT/10-14
EVELYN, T. H. (d 1879) lessee
EA/80*
EVELYNE, Alma [Mrs. G. L.
Bannerman] English actress
GRB/1
EVENNETT, Wallace (b 1888)
English actor WWT/6-10
EVERALL, Mrs. Harry James
see Carus, Emma
EVERARD, Miss see Everard,
Harriette Emily
EVERARD, Edward Cape (b
1755) actor DD
EVERARD, George (d 1907 [34])
songwriter EA/08*
EVERARD, H. (fl 1870s) actress
OAA/2
EVERARD, Harriette Emily [Mrs.
Darley Beswicke] (1844-82)
actress, singer DD
EVERARD, James E. (d 1879
[38]) stage hand? EA/80*
EVERARD, Margaret Ada Clegg
see Lundberg, Ada
EVERARD, Tom L. (d 1896)
music-hall singer EA/97*
EVERARD, W. (d 1884) EA/85*
EVERARD, Walter (d 1924 [74])
actor BE*, WWT/14*
EVEREST, Barbara (1890-1968)
English actress TW/2-6,
WWT/3-14
EVEREST, Mrs. Charles Fan-
shawe see Bray, Alice
EVERETT, David (1770-1813)
American dramatist EAP
EVERETT, Ethel (d 1973 [63])
performer BP/56*
EVERETT, George (d 1881 [57])
actor WWT/14*
EVERETT, Jake (b 1946) Amer-
ican actor TW/30

EVERETT, Sophie (d 1963 [88])
performer BE*
EVERETT, Timmy (b 1938/39)
American actor, dancer, direc-
tor, choreographer BE, TW/
14-17, 20
EVERETTE, Lily (d 1891) skater
EA/92*
EVERHART, Rex (b 1920) American
actor AAS, BE, TW/22-28, 30,
WWT/15-16
EVERILL, Frederick Augustus
(1829-1900) English actor DD,
OAA/1-2
EVERITT (1779-80) gigantic infant
CDP
EVERLEIGH, Kate (d 1926 [62])
actress BE*, WWT/14*
EVERS, Adeline [Florence Helena
Earlesmere] (d 1896) actress
EA/97*
EVERS, Herbert (b 1922) American
actor TW/5-11, 14-15
EVERSFIELD, Miss [Mrs. H. Cecil
Beryl] (d 1885) EA/86*
EVERSFIELD, Harry (d 1896) actor
DD, EA/95
EVERSLEIGH, Clara (d 1918) EA/
19*
EVERSLEIGH, Flo [Mrs. Harry
Kirk] (d 1910) actress EA/12*
EVERSLEIGH, Harry (d 1906) actor
EA/07*
EVERSLEY, H. A. [C. H. James]
(d 1899) professor of music
EA/00*
EVERSMAN, Alice M. (d 1974 [88])
critic BP/58*
EVERTON, Paul (1868/70-1948)
American actor TW/4, WWM,
WWS
EVESEED, Henry (d 1614?) member
of the Chapel Royal DA
EVESSON, Isabelle [Mensing] (1863-
1914) American actress DD,
GRB/3-4, SR, WWS
EVETT, Robert (1874-1949) English
actor, singer, manager GRB/
1-4, WWT/1-10
EVETT, Robert (d 1974 [52]) com-
poser/lyricist BP/59*
EVILL, Henry (d 1916 [91]) director
of the Royal General Theatrical
Fund EA/17*
EVISON, Fred G. (b 1871) English
actor GRB/1
EWART, Stephen T. (b 1869) English
actor WWT/4-5

EWELL, Caroline Elizabeth (d
1909 [69]) actress BE*, EA/
10*, WWT/14*
EWELL, Lois (b 1885) American
singer WWM
EWELL, Tom (b 1909) American
actor AAS, BE, CB, TW/
3-6, 14-17, 22, WWT/11-16
EWER, Donald (b 1923) English
actor TW/27-28
EWING, Aileen see Grey, Anne
EWING, Frederick Baxter see
Albini, Lieut.
EWING, Cpt. Peter (fl 1792?)
dramatist CP/3
EWING, Robert W. (fl 1825-26)
dramatist, critic EAP, RJ
EWING, Sherman (d 1975 [73])
producer/director/choreog-
rapher BP/59*
EWINS, Harry (d 1901 [39]) clown,
pantomimist EA/02*
EWINS, Mrs. Harry see
Tyrrell, Kittie
EXTON, Clive (b 1930) English
dramatist CD, PDT
EXTON, Florence see Alix,
Mina
EXTON, Winifred see Fraser,
Winifred
EYDTWARTT, John (fl 1627)
actor DA
EYEN, Tom (b 1941) American
dramatist, director CD,
WWT/15-16
EYLAND, Henry (d 1881 [78])
composer EA/82*
EYRE, Edmund John (1767-1816)
English actor, dramatist CP/
3, GT, TD/1-2
EYRE, Gerald (d 1885) actor
BE*, EA/86*, WWT/14*
EYRE, John Edmund (d 1816
[48]) dramatist BE*, WWT/
14*
EYRE, Laurence (1881-1959)
American dramatist, actor
ES, WWA/3, WWT/4-11
EYRE, Lyttleton (d 1902 [26])
actor EA/04*
EYRE, Peter (b 1942) American
actor WWT/16
EYRE, Richard (b 1943) English
director WWT/16
EYRE, Ronald (b 1929) English
director, dramatist AAS,
WWT/15-16
EYRE, Sophie [née Ryan] (1853-

92) Irish actress CDP, DD, DP
EYSSELINCK, Walter (b 1931) Bel-
gian director, dramatist WWT/
15-16
EYTHE, William (1918-57) Ameri-
can actor, producer TW/5-9,
13, WWT/11-12
EYTINGE, Harry (1822-1902) actor
CDP
EYTINGE, Rose [Mrs. Cyril Searle]
(1835/38-1911) American actress
DAB, DD, ES, HAS, PP/1,
WWA/1, WWM, WWS
EYTINGE, Samuel D. (d 1859)
American actor HAS
EYTON, Frank (1894-1962) English
lyricist, dramatist WWT/9-13,
WWW/6

- F -

FABBRI, Diego (b 1911) Italian
dramatist OC/3
FABBRI, Flora dancer CDP
FABBRI, Guerrina (1868-1946)
Italian singer ES
FABBRI, Inez (fl 1860) German
singer CDP, HAS
FABELL, Peter (fl 15th cent)
magician DNB
FABER, Beryl [Mrs. Cosmo Ham-
ilton] (d 1912) English actress
GRB/1-4, WWT/1
FABER, Leslie (1879-1929) English
actor ES, GRB/3-4, WWT/1-5
FABER, Mrs. Leslie see Arthur-
Jones, Winifred
FABER, Myrtie Bedell (d 1896)
actress EA/97*
FABIAN, Mons. (d 1876) equestrian
clown EA/77*
FABIAN, Madge (b 1880) English
actress WWT/1-7
FABIAN, Olga Austrian actress
TW/3, 6, 8-9
FABIAN, Simon (d 1970 [71]) theatre
builder BP/55*
FABIAN, Thomas (fl 1735) drama-
tist CP/1-3, GT
FABIAN, Thomas (d 1896) circus
performer? EA/97*
FABIANI, Aurelio (1895-1973)
Italian manager WWA/5
FABRAY, Nanette (b 1920/22)
American actress, singer BE,
CB, TW/2-13, 19-20, 29,
WWT/11-16

FABRE, Emil (d 1955 [86])
French dramatist BP/40*
FABRI, Annibale Pio (1697-1760)
Italian singer, composer ES
FABRICUS, Jan (d 1964 [93])
dramatist BP/49*
FABRIS, Armanda (fl 1886) singer
CDP
FABRIZI, Mario (d 1963 [38])
performer BE*
FACCIO, Franco (d 1891 [51])
conductor, composer EA/92*
FADEL, Yvan (d 1971 [78]) per-
former BP/56*
FAGAN, Barney (d 1937 [87])
American actor BE*, BP/21*
FAGAN, Mrs. Barney see
Byron, Henrietta
FAGAN, Irene (d 1971 [86])
costumier BP/55*
FAGAN, James Bernard (1873-
1933) English dramatist, pro-
ducer, manager, actor COC,
DNB, ES, GRB/3-4, OC/1-3,
WWT/1-7, WWW/3
FAGAN, Mrs. James Bernard
see Kirby, Elisabeth
FAGAN, Joan (b 1934) American
singer, actress BE
FAGAN, Myron C. dramatist,
producer, manager WWT/
6-13
FAHEY, Myrna (d 1973 [34])
performer BP/57*
FAIN, Sammy (b 1902) American
composer BE
FAINE, Hy (b 1910) Russian/
American executive BE
FAIR, Adrah (b 1897) American
actress, singer WWT/6-7
FAIR, Elinor (b 1904) American
actress ES
FAIR, May (d 1971 [67]) per-
former BP/55*
FAIR, William B. (1851-1909)
music-hall performer CDP,
COC, OC/1-3
FAIR, Mrs. William D. (fl 1863)
actress HAS
FAIRBANKS, Albert L. (d 1971
[65]) performer BP/56*
FAIRBANKS, Douglas, Sr. (1883-
1939) American actor DAB,
ES, SR, WWA/1, WWM,
WWT/3-9, WWW/3
FAIRBANKS, Douglas, Jr. (b
1909) American actor CB,
ES, SR, WWT/8-11, 16

FAIRBANKS, Robert (d 1908) actor?
singer? EA/09*
FAIRBROTHER, Benjamin Smith (d
1878 [74]) actor? EA/79*
FAIRBROTHER, Louisa [Mrs. Fitz-
George] (1816-90) actress
CDP, DD
FAIRBROTHER, Robert (d 1841
[72]) prompter CDP
FAIRBROTHER, Sydney [Sydney
Cowell; Mrs. Sidney Buckler]
(1872-1941) actress COC, DD,
EA/97, GRB/2-4, OC/1-3,
WWT/1-9
FAIRBURN, George (d 1918 [54])
EA/19*
FAIRCHILD, Mr. (d 1852) comedian
HAS
FAIRCHILD, Charlotte (b 1930)
American actress TW/28-30
FAIRCHILD, Edgar (d 1975 [76])
composer/lyricist BP/59*
FAIRCHILD, J. L. (fl 1826) actor
HAS
FAIRCLOUGH, Boothroyd (d 1911
[86]) American actor CDP, HAS
FAIRFAX, Lance (1899-1974) New
Zealand actor, singer BTR/74,
WWT/8-10
FAIRFAX, Lettice (1876-1948) ac-
tress DD, GRB/3-4, WWT/1-8
FAIRFAX, Marion [Mrs. Tully
Marshall] (b 1879) American
dramatist WWM, WWT/3-7
FAIRFIELD, Miss see McClean,
Mrs.
FAIRFIELD, Sumner Lincoln (1803-
44) American dramatist, actor
EAP, HJD, WWA/H
FAIRHURST, Edwin (d 1973) per-
former BP/57*
FAIRHURST, James (d 1907 [87])
music-hall proprietor EA/08*
FAIRLAMB, James Remington
(1838-1908) American composer
DAB
FAIRLEIGH, Paget [Arthur Paget
Ford] (d 1885) EA/86*
FAIRLEY, Dorothy [Mrs. Charles
Locke] (d 1907) actress EA/08*
FAIRLEY, Mrs. M. A. [Mrs. P.
G. Fairley] (d 1916) EA/17*
FAIRLEY, Mrs. P. G. see
Fairley, Mrs. M. A.
FAIRMAN, Austin (1892-1964) Eng-
lish actor WWT/8-11
FAIRMAN, Michael (b 1934) Amer-
ican actor TW/22-24

FAIRS, Gilbert see Hare, Gilbert
FAIRS, John see Hare, John
FAIRWEATHER, David Carnegy (b 1899) English editor, press representative WWT/9-16
FAIRWEATHER, Virginia (b 1922) English press representative WWT/14-16
FAIRY QUEEN [Eliza Nestel] CDP
FAITHFULL, Emily (d 1895 [60]) dramatic reader EA/96*
FAITHFULL, Marianne (b 1946) English actress WWT/15-16
FALASCO, Donald (d 1965 [38]) performer BP/50*
FALCK, Lionel (1889-1971) English manager WWT/11
FALCON, Cornélie see Falcon, Marie Cornélie
FALCON, Marie Cornélie (1812-97) singer CDP
FALCONER, Mrs. see Lambert, E. A.
FALCONER, Edmund (1813/14/25-79) Irish actor, manager, dramatist DNB, EA/68, HAS, OAA/1-2, SR
FALCONER, Mrs. Edmund (d 1864) actress WWT/14*
FALCONER, Helen (d 1968) actress TW/25
FALGI, Nick (d 1973 [40+]) performer BP/58*
FALK, Peter (b 1927) American actor BE, CB, TW/20, 28-30
FALK, Richard (b 1912) American press representative, producer BE
FALK, Sawyer (1898-1961) American educator BE*
FALKENHAIN, Patricia (b 1926) American actress BE
FALKLAND, Lord Viscount see Carey, Henry Lucius
FALKLAND, Amelia, Lady actress CDP
FALLON, Richard (b 1923) American educator, director BE
FALLS, Gregory A. (b 1922) American educator, director, actor BE
FANCHETTE, Amy [Amy Vaile] (b 1861) English actress GRB/1
FANCHETTE, Kate [Mrs. John Russell] (d 1896) EA/97*

FANCK, Arnold (d 1974 [85]) producer/director/choreographer BP/59*
FANCOURT, Darrell (1888-1953) English actor, singer TW/4, 10, WWT/5-11
FANCOURT, Mrs. Tom see Rubie, Jennie
FANCY, Richard (b 1943) American actor TW/30
FANE, Blanche (d 1858) actress CDP, DD
FANE, Sir Francis, Jr. (d 1689?) English dramatist CP/1-3, DNB, GT
FANN, Albert (b 1933) American actor TW/27
FANNIN, Joseph T. (fl 1850) actor HAS
FANNIN, Paddy (d 1888 [48]) comic singer CDP
FANNING, James Francis (d 1883) professor of music EA/84*
FANNING, Lillie (d 1892 [39]) EA/94*
FANNING, Win (b 1918) American journalist BE
FANQUE, Pablo see Darby, William
FANSHAW, Sir Richard (1607-66) English dramatist CP/1-3
FANSHAWE, H. A. W. (d 1917) EA/18*
FANT, Lou (d 1931) American actor TW/25-26
FANT, Roy actor TW/1
FANTI, Clementina (fl 1833) singer CDP
FARADAY, Philip Michael (1875-1944) English manager, composer WWT/1-8
FARAGOH, Francis Edwards (d 1966 [71]) dramatist TW/23
FARBAR, Bernard (b 1935) American actor TW/23
FAREBROTHER, Miss see Fairbrother, Louisa
FAREBROTHER, Violet (1888-1969) English actress TW/3, WWT/4-14
FARENTINO, James (b 1938) American actor TW/29-30
FARGUS, R. J. see Conway, Hugh
FARIA, Arthur (b 1944) American actor TW/28-29
FARINI ["Lulu"] (fl 1871-86) female impersonator CDP

FARJEON, Benjamin Leopold (d 1903 [65]) dramatist BE*, EA/04*, WWT/14*

FARJEON, Eleanor (1881-1965) English dramatist NTH, WWW/6

FARJEON, Herbert (1887-1945) English critic, dramatist NTH, OC/1-3, WWT/6-9, WWW/4

FARJEON, Joseph Jefferson (1883-1955) dramatist NTH, WWT/6-11, WWW/5

FARKAS, Karl (d 1971 [77]) performer BP/55*

FARKOA, Maurice (1864/67-1916) Egyptian/English? actor, singer GRB/1-4, WWS, WWT/1-3

FARLEIGH, Lynn (b 1942) English actress WWT/15-16

FARLEY, Mr. (fl 1797-1801) actor, prompter TD/1-2

FARLEY, Charles (1771-1859) English actor, dramatist, machinist BS, CDP, DD, DNB, GT

FARLEY, James (d 1887 [46]) musical director EA/88*

FARLEY, Mary Ann see Vincent, Mrs. James R.

FARLEY, Morgan (b 1901) American actor WWT/6-10

FARLOW, Mary Ann see Vincent, Mrs. James R.

FARMER, Elizabeth (d 1890 [78]) EA/91*

FARMER, Frances (d 1970 [56]) actress TW/27

FARMER, Henry (d 1891) composer EA/92*

FARMER, John (fl 1554) actor DA

FARMER, John (d 1874 [83]) singer EA/75*

FARMER, John (1835-1901) composer DNB

FARMER, Lucia Eliza [Mrs. James Harwood] (d 1898 [62]) actress EA/00*

FARNABY, Richard (fl 1623-24) musician DA

FARNELL, Jack (d 1976 [61]) producer/director/choreographer BP/60*

FARNIE, Henry Brougham (d 1899) Scottish dramatist, journalist DD

FARNOL, Lynn (d 1963 [63]) American press representative BE*, BP/47*

FARNSWORTH, Harry (d 1916) EA/17*

FARNUM, Dustin (1871/74/75/76-1929) American actor DAB, ES, GRB/3-4, SR, WWA/1, WWM, WWS, WWT/1-5

FARNUM, Franklyn (d 1961 [83]) American actor BE*

FARNUM, G. Dustin (d 1912 [65]) actor WWT/14*

FARNUM, William (1875-1953) American actor ES, SR, TW/10, WWT/3-9

FARQUHAR, George (1678-1707) English dramatist CDP, COC, CP/1-3, DD, DNB, ES, GT, HP, MH, NTH, OC/1-3, PDT, RE, SR

FARQUHAR, Gilbert (1850-1920) English actor DD, DP, EA/97, GRB/1-4, WWW/2

FARQUHAR, Malcolm (b 1924) Welsh director, actor WWT/15-16

FARQUHAR, Robroy (b 1916) English director, actor, manager BE

FARQUHARSON, Alexander (d 1904 [43]) actor EA/05*

FARQUHARSON, Robert (d 1880 [59]) singer EA/80*

FARQUHARSON, Robert (1877-1966) English actor WWT/5-9

FARQUHARSON, Wilfred (d 1916) EA/17*

FARR, "Chick" (d 1948) comedian BE*, WWT/14*

FARR, Derek (b 1912) English actor WWT/11-16

FARR, Florence [Mrs. Edward Emery] (1860-1917) English actress, producer, manager COC, DD, OC/3, WWT/1-3

FARR, Kimberly (b 1948) American actress TW/29-30

FARRAH, Abd'Elkader (b 1926) Algerian designer AAS, WWT/15-16

FARRANT, Richard (fl 1564-80) master of the Children of Windsor, lessee DA

FARRAR, Geraldine (1882-1967) American singer ES, SR, TW/23, WWA/4, WWW/6

FARRAR, Gwen (1879-1944)

English actress, singer WWT/
5-9
FARREL, Charles (d c.1795
[c.97] actor TD/2
FARRELL, Alfred (d 1907) variety
comedian EA/08*
FARRELL, Anthony B. (1899-
1970) producer, investor BE
FARRELL, Brian American actor
TW/29-30
FARRELL, Catherine F. (d 1964
[73]) performer BE*
FARRELL, Charles (d 1970 [78])
producer/director/choreograph-
er BP/55*
FARRELL, Charles (b 1901/02/
06) Irish actor ES, WWT/
8-16
FARRELL, Eileen (b 1920) Amer-
ican singer CB
FARRELL, Eve (d 1972) per-
former BP/56*
FARRELL, Glenda (1904-71)
American actress BE, TW/1,
5-7, 11-16, 25, 27, WWA/5,
WWT/8-15
FARRELL, Henry (d 1878 [43])
actor EA/79*
FARRELL, John (d 1848 [57])
actor, dramatist, manager
CDP
FARRELL, John J. (fl 1884)
American actor WWS
FARRELL, Josephine (d 1972
[87]) performer BP/56*
FARRELL, Margaret [Mrs. Ken-
nedy] (d 1793) actress CDP
FARRELL, Marguerite (d 1951
[62]) actress TW/7
FARRELL, Mary (b 1912) Amer-
ican actress, director BE,
TW/13
FARRELL, M. J. [née Mary
Nesta Skrine] (b 1905) drama-
tist WWT/10-14
FARRELL, Nellie [or Nelly]
(d 1889) singer CDP
FARRELL, Paul (1893-1975)
Irish actor WWT/8-14
FARRELL, Sarah Ann (d 1906)
show girl EA/08*
FARRELL, Suzanne (b 1945)
American dancer CB, ES
FARREN, Miss see Knight,
Mrs. Thomas
FARREN, Babs [Clara Bianca
Rouhan Farren] (b 1904)
actress WWT/4-5, 7

FARREN, Clara Bianca Rouhan
see Farren, Babs
FARREN, Elizabeth (1759-1829)
English actress CDP, COC,
DD, DNB, GT, OC/1-3, TD/1-2
FARREN, Ellen [Mrs. Robert
Soutar; Nellie Farren] (1848-1904)
English actress CDP, COC,
DD, DNB, DP, ES, OAA/1-2,
OC/1-3
FARREN, Fanny Fitz (fl 1859)
actress HAS
FARREN, Florence (d 1878 [25])
actress EA/79*, WWT/14*
FARREN, Fred (d 1956 [82]) Eng-
lish actor, dancer WWT/2-8
FARREN, George Francis (d 1935
[74]) American actor BE*,
BP/19*
FARREN, George Percy (d 1861
[53]) Irish actor CDP, HAS,
WWA/H
FARREN, Mrs. George Percy [née
Mary Ann Russell] (d 1894 [76])
actress CDP, HAS, WWA/H
FARREN, Mrs. Harry see Win-
slow, Kate
FARREN, Henry (1826-60) English
actor DD, DNB, ES, HAS,
OC/1-3
FARREN, Mary Ann see Farren,
Mrs. George Percy
FARREN, Nellie see Farren,
Ellen
FARREN, Percival (1784-1843)
English actor DD, ES, OC/1-3
FARREN, William (1725-95) English
actor CDP, DD, ES, OC/1-3,
TD/1-2
FARREN, William (1786-1861) Eng-
lish actor, manager BS, CDP,
DD, DNB, ES, OC/1-3, OX
FARREN, William, Sr. (1825-1908)
English actor CDP, DD, DNB,
DP, ES, GRB/1-4, OAA/1-2,
OC/1-3
FARREN, William, Jr. (1853-1937)
English actor, dramatist DD,
DP, ES, GRB/1-4, OC/1-3,
WWT/1-6, WWW/3
FARREN, Mrs. William, the
Younger see Diddear, Harriet
Elizabeth
FARRER, Mr. (fl 1790) dramatist
CP/3
FARRER, Ann (b 1916) English ac-
tress WWT/11-14
FARRISSEY, Dan (d 1880) Irish

comedian EA/80*
FARRON, Thomas J. actor CDP
FARROW, John (b 1904) Australian
dramatist ES
FARROW, Mia (b 1946) American
actress CB, WWT/16
FARTHING, Maud [Mrs. Christie
Simonsens] (d 1907) singer
EA/08*
FARUSI, Zanetta see Casanova,
Signora Gaetano Giuseppe Gia-
como
FASCIANO, Richard (b 1943)
American actor TW/27-29
FASCIOTTI, Signorina (fl 1849)
singer HAS
FASSETT, Jay (b 1889) American
actor BE, TW/3-6
FATTY ARBUCKLE see Ar-
buckle, Roscoe
FAUCIT, Mrs. (fl 1811) drama-
tist CP/3
FAUCIT, Edmund Saville (1811-
57) actor DD
FAUCIT, Harriet [Mrs. Humphrey
Bland] (1789/99-1847/57) ac-
tress CDP, DD
FAUCIT, Helen [Helena Saville;
Mrs. Theodore Martin] (1817-
98) English actress CDP,
COC, DD, DNB, ES, OAA/
1-2, OC/1-3, WWW/1
FAUCIT, John Saville (d 1853
[70]) actor, dramatist, mana-
ger DD
FAUCIT, Mrs. John Saville see
Diddear, Harriet Elizabeth
FAUE, Mrs. James see Faue,
Mary Anne
FAUE, Mary Anne [Mrs. James
Faue] (d 1907) EA/08*
FAUGERES, Margaretta Bleecker
(1771-1801) American dramatist
EAP, RJ
FAUGHMAN, Richard (d 1962
[29]) acrobat BE*
FAULKLAND, Mary [née Field-
ing] (d 1879 [48]) actress
EA/80*
FAULKNER, Mr. (fl 1800s?)
actor TD/2
FAULKNER, Anne Maria [Mrs.
Donaldson] (fl 18th cent)
singer CDP
FAULKNER, Edith Jane (d 1975
[81]) performer BP/60*
FAULKNER, Fanny (d 1871)
actress EA/72*

FAULKNER, Robert [Robert Samuel
Burrow] (b 1879) English actor
GRB/1
FAULKNER, Seldon (b 1929) Amer-
ican educator BE
FAULKNER, Thomas (1775-1847)
Irish actor HAS
FAULKNER, William (1897-1962)
American dramatist CH, ES,
MD, MWD, WWW/6
FAUST, Edwin (d 1910 [69]) EA/
11*
FAUST, Lotta [Mrs. Richie Ling]
(1880/81-1910) American actress
GRB/3-4, WWS
FAVANTI, Rita (d 1867) singer
EA/68*
FAVART, Mme. (d 1772 [44])
actress WWT/14*
FAVART, Edmée (d 1941) actress,
singer WWT/14*
FAVART, Maria (d 1908 [75]) ac-
tress WWT/14*
FAVERO, Mafalda (b 1905) Italian
singer ES
FAVERSHAM, Edith Campbell (d
1945 [61]) actress TW/1
FAVERSHAM, Julie Opp see
Opp, Julie
FAVERSHAM, William (1868-1940)
English/American actor, mana-
ger CB, COC, DAB, ES,
GRB/2-4, NTH, OC/1-3, SR,
WWA/1, WWM, WWS, WWT/1-9
FAVERSHAM, Mrs. William see
Opp, Julie
FAVORITE, Harriet Leaf (d 1972
[76]) patron BP/57*
FAVRE, John (d 1876 [36]) property
master EA/77*
FAWCETT, Mr. (fl 1760-92) actor
TD/1-2
FAWCETT, Mr. (fl 1795) English
actor HAS
FAWCETT, Mrs. [Miss Miles] (d
1797) actress WWT/14*
FAWCETT, Anthony [Carré] (b
1869) English actor GRB/1
FAWCETT, Charles (d 1867) Eng-
lish actor, dramatist HAS
FAWCETT, Charles S. (1855-1922)
actor, dramatist DD, DP,
WWT/4
FAWCETT, Edgar (1847-1904) Amer-
ican dramatist DD, HJD
FAWCETT, Eric (1904-72) English
actor, singer WWT/9-10
FAWCETT, George (1860/61-1939)

American actor, manager
GRB/3-4, WWA/1, WWM,
WWT/1-8
FAWCETT, Mrs. George see
Haswell, Percy
FAWCETT, John (d 1793) actor,
singer, musician DD, DNB
FAWCETT, John (1768/69-1837)
English actor, dramatist,
singer BS, CDP, CP/3,
DNB, GT, OX, TD/1-2
FAWCETT, Mrs. John [née
Moore] (d 1797) English ac-
tress TD/1-2
FAWCETT, L'estrange English
critic WWT/7-9
FAWCETT, Marion [Katherine
Roger Campbell] (1886-1957)
Scottish actress, producer
WWT/8-12
FAWCETT, Owen S. (1838-1904)
English actor CDP, HAS,
PP/1, WWA/1
FAWCETT, William (d 1916)
EA/17*
FAWDON, Walter see Vokes,
Walter
FAWKES, Mr. (fl early 18th
cent) conjuror CDP
FAWN, James (1850-1923) actor,
singer CDP, DD, WWT/4
FAWSITT, Amy [Mrs. Menzies]
(d 1876 [30]) American? ac-
tress CDP, DD
FAX, Max [Fred C. Wilson] (b
1867) English actor, dramatist
GRB/1
FAX, Reuben (d 1908 [46]) actor
GRB/4*
FAY, Abby (fl 1858?) singer
CDP
FAY, Anna Eva (1863-1927)
American mind reader SR
FAY, Bertha singer CDP
FAY, Brendan (d 1975 [54])
American actor TW/24-26,
28-30
FAY, Edward M. (d 1964 [88])
theatre owner, manager BE*
FAY, Frank (1897-1961) Ameri-
can actor, singer CB, SR,
TW/1-8, 18, WWT/7-12
FAY, Frank J. [or G.] (1870-
1931) Irish actor COC, OC/
1-3
FAY, Hugh (d 1895 [43]) actor
CDP
FAY, Léontine CDP

FAY, Maude (fl 1900s) American
singer WWM
FAY, Terry American casting di-
rector BE
FAY, William George (1872-1949)
Irish actor, manager COC,
DNB, ES, GRB/4, OC/1-3,
TW/4, WWT/1-10
FAYE, Irma (d 1976 [63]) performer
BP/60*
FAYE, Joey [né Joseph Antony Pal-
ladino] (b 1910) American actor,
comedian BE, TW/8, 11, 25-
27, 30, WWT/15-16
FAYERMANN, Anne Charlotte see
Bartholomew, Anne Charlotte
FAYME, T. B. (d 1906) comedian
EA/07*
FAYNE, Greta actress, singer
WWT/6-11
FAYNE, Kate [Mrs. Richard Bain-
bridge] (d 1903) actress EA/04*
FAYOLLE, Berthe (d 1934 [68])
actress BE*, WWT/14*
FAYRE, Eleanor [née Eleanor Mary
Tydfil Smith-Thomas] (b 1910)
Welsh actress WWT/10
FAZAN, Eleanor (b 1930) Kenyan
director, choreographer, actress
WWT/14-16
FAZENDA, Louise [Mrs. Hal Wal-
lis] (d 1962 [67]) American ac-
tress BE*
FEALY, Maude [Mrs. Louis F.
Sherwin] (1883-1971) American
actress GRB/2-4, WWM, WWS,
WWT/1-8
FEARL, Clifford American actor
TW/25-26
FEARNLEY, John (b 1914) American
director BE
FEARON, Mr. (fl 1803) actor TD/2
FEARON, George Edward (b 1901)
English press representative
WWT/9-15
FEARON, James (d 1789 [43])
actor CDP, TD/1-2
FEATHER, Ike (b 1949) American
actor TW/28
FEATHER, Lorraine (b 1948) Amer-
ican actress TW/25
FEATHER, Ruth (d 1965 [77]) per-
former BP/49*
FEATHERSTON, Eddie (d 1965)
performer BP/50*
FEATHERSTON, Vane (1864-1948)
English actress DD, EA/95,
GRB/1-4, WWT/1-9

FEATHERSTONE, Miss actress
CDP
FEATHERSTONE, Bessie (d 1907)
variety comedian, actress
GRB/3
FEATHERSTONE, Edward George
(d 1893) music-hall proprietor
EA/94*
FEATHERSTONE, Edward George,
Jr. (d 1893) musician EA/94*
FEATHERSTONE, Isabella see
Paul, Mrs. Howard
FEATHERSTONE, Kevin (b 1958)
American actor TW/23
FEATHERSTONE, Mrs. S. (d
1889 [78]) EA/90*
FEATHERSTONHAUGH, Constance
see Benson, Mrs. F. R.
FECHTER, Mrs. Charles (d
1894 [74]) EA/96*
FECHTER, Charles Albert (1824-
79) English actor, dramatist
CDP, COC, DAB, DD, DNB,
ES, NTH, OAA/1-2, OC/1-3,
SR, WWA/H
FECHTER, Paul (d 1888) EA/89*
FECTOR, William (b 1764) actor
CDP
FEDER, Abe (b 1909) American
lighting & scene designer,
producer BE, WWT/16
FEDER, A. H. see Feder, Abe
FEDER, Joseph (d 1970 [69])
business manager BP/55*
FEDER, Sabina (d 1975) per-
former BP/59*
FEDERICI, Frederick (d 1888)
singer WWT/14*
FEDOROVA, Alexandra (d 1972
[83]) dancer, choreographer
BP/57*, WWT/1*
FEDOROVITCH, Sophie (1893-
1953) designer COC, OC/3
FEELEY, Clara (d 1889) acrobat
EA/90*
FEELEY, Mattie [Mrs. Michael
Feeley] (d 1887) EA/88*
FEELEY, Michael (d 1889 [49])
EA/90*
FEELEY, Mrs. Michael see
Feeley, Mattie
FEELY, Terence John (b 1928)
English dramatist WWT/15-
16
FEENEY, Emma [Mrs. Patrick
Feeney] (d 1888) EA/89*
FEENEY, Patrick (d 1883 [82])
showman EA/84*

FEENEY, Patrick (d 1889 [38])
Irish comedian, singer EA/90*
FEENEY, Mrs. Patrick see
Feeney, Emma
FEIFFER, Jules (b 1929) American
dramatist AAS, CD, CH, MH,
WWT/15-16
FEIGAY, Paul (b 1920) American
producer BE, TW/2-5
FEILD, Edward A. (d 1891) singer,
musician EA/93*
FEILDE, Matthew (d 1796) drama-
tist CP/3, DD
FEILER, Herta (d 1970 [54]) per-
former BP/55*
FEIN, Maria (d 1965 [73]) actress
WWT/14*
FEINBERG, Abe I. (d 1962 [71])
talent representative BE*
FEINBERG, Joe (d 1975 [73]) agent
BP/60*
FEINER, Marjorie Lynne (b 1948)
American actress TW/27
FEINMAN, Sigmund (d 1909 [52])
actor BE*, WWT/14*
FEINSTEIN, Alan (b 1941) American
actor TW/22, 25, 30
FEINSTEIN, Laurence [Alan Yorke]
see Feinstein, Alan
FEIST, Catherine (d 1876 [78])
actress EA/77*
FEIST, Gene (b 1930) American
director, producer WWT/15-16
FELD, Eliot (b 1942) American
dancer, choreographer CB
FELD, Israel S. (d 1972 [61]) cir-
cus owner BP/57*
FELD, Leo (d 1896 [39]) conductor
EA/97*
FELDARY, Eric (d 1968 [48]) per-
former BP/52*
FELDER, Clarence (b 1938) Amer-
ican actor TW/30
FELDMAN, Andrea (d 1972) per-
former BP/57*
FELDMAN, David (d 1895 [17])
acrobat EA/96*
FELDMAN, Edythe A. (d 1971 [58])
performer BP/55*
FELDMAN, Erwin (d 1972 [67])
lawyer BP/56*
FELDMAN, Gladys (1899-1974)
actress BE, TW/30
FELDMAN, Laurence (1926-67)
American producer, director
BE, TW/23
FELDMAN, Maurice (d 1976 [66])
publicist BP/60*

FELDMAN, Shellie American
actress TW/23-24

FELDSTEIN, Robert D. (d 1969
[42]) producer/director/
choreographer BP/54*

FELEKY, Leslie (d 1971 [59])
composer/lyricist BP/56*

FELGATE, Peter (b 1919) English actor, dancer, singer
WWT/12-15

FELIX, Adeline M. [Mrs. Tony
Felix] (d 1908) EA/09*

FELIX, Charlotte [Mrs. Fred
Felix] (d 1890) EA/91*

FELIX, Elisa see Rachel

FELIX, Mrs. Fred see Felix,
Charlotte

FELIX, George (b 1866) American vaudevillian WWM

FELIX, Mrs. George see
Barry, Lydia

FELIX, Hugo (1866-1934) composer WWT/2-7

FELIX, Lena [Mrs. Toney
Felix] (d 1891) EA/92*

FELIX, Raphael (d 1872 [46])
director EA/73*

FELIX, Sarah (d 1877 [59]) actress BE*, WWT/14*

FELIX, Mrs. Toney see Felix,
Lena

FELIX, Tony [Thomas Green]
(d 1911) clown EA/12*

FELIX, Mrs. Tony see Felix,
Adeline M.

FELL, C. C. (d 1907 [64])
museum proprietor EA/08*

FELL, Charles Tasker (d 1894
[58]) acting manager EA/95*

FELL, Talbot (d 1898 [24]) actor
EA/99*

FELLMAN, Mons. (fl 1828)
French dancer HAS

FELLOWES, Amy [Mrs. William
Terriss] (d 1898) actress
COC

FELLOWES, Rockcliffe (d 1950
[65]) Canadian actor BE*

FELLOWES-ROBINSON, Dora
(d 1946) Mauritian/English
business manager, producer
WWT/4-5

FELLOWS, Dexter William (d
1937 [66]) American press
representative BE*, BP/22*

FELLOWS, Don (b 1922) American actor TW/6-8, 21-23,
27-28

FELLOWS, Edith (b 1923) American
actress TW/2-7, 13

FELLOWS, Frances Ethel (d 1882)
actress EA/83*

FELLOWS, J. B. (fl 1852?) minstrel manager CDP

FELSENSTEIN, Walter (d 1975
[74]) producer/director/chore-
ographer BP/60*

FELSTED, Beatrice English actress
GRB/1

FELTON, Happy (d 1964 [56]) performer BP/49*

FELYNE, Renée (d 1910 [26]) actress BE*, WWT/14*

FENDALL, Percy (d 1917) dramatist DD

FENDER, Doris (d 1975 [75]) performer BP/60*

FENELON, E. (d 1863) musical
director HAS

FENN, Ezekiel (b 1620) English
actor DA, COC, OC/1-3

FENN, Frederick (1868-1924)
English dramatist DD, GRB/
2-4, WWT/1-4, WWW/2

FENN, George Manville (d 1909
[78]) dramatist DD

FENN, Peggy American actress
BE

FENNELL, James (1766-1816) Eng-
lish actor, dramatist CDP,
COC, CP/3, DAB, DD, DNB,
EAP, HAS, OC/1-3, RJ, SR,
TD/1-2, WWA/H

FENNELL, James, Jr. (fl 1812)
actor HAS

FENNER, H. Wolcott (d 1972 [61])
circus executive BP/57*

FENNESSY, John (b 1946) American
actor TW/27

FENNO, Ada V. (d 1975 [90]) pro-
ducer/director/choreographer
BP/60*

FENNO, Richard F. (d 1967 [40])
composer/lyricist BP/52*

FENNO, Will (b 1948) American
actor TW/28

FENNO, William Augustus (b 1814)
American actor, lecturer, dramatist HAS, RJ

FENTON, Albert Edward see
Elba

FENTON, Mrs. C. H. see
Hodson, Kate

FENTON, Charles (d 1877 [56])
actor, scene artist DD

FENTON, Mrs. Charles [Caroline

Parkes] (d 1887) actress EA/
88*
FENTON, Mrs. Charles see
Hodson, Kate
FENTON, Elijah (1683-1730) English dramatist CP/1-3, DD,
GT, TD/1-2
FENTON, Elizabeth [Mrs. John
Fenton] (d 1874 [32]) EA/76*
FENTON, Frank (b 1868) English
actor, manager GRB/1-4
FENTON, Frank (d 1957 [51])
American actor BE*, BP/42*
FENTON, Frederick Gill (1817-
98) English scene designer
ES
FENTON, Harry (d 1868 [33])
actor? EA/69*
FENTON, James Gill (d 1877
[83]) actor? EA/78*
FENTON, Mrs. John T. see
Fenton, Rosina Ruth
FENTON, Kitty [Mrs. Harry
Roxbury] (d 1902 [32]) actress
EA/03*
FENTON, Lavinia (1708-60) English actress CDP, COC, DD,
DNB, ES, OC/1-3
FENTON, Lucille (d 1966 [50s])
performer BP/51*
FENTON, Mabel (1872-1931)
American actress SR, WWS
FENTON, Ralph D. (b 1883)
English assistant manager
GRB/1
FENTON, Rosina Ruth [Mrs.
John T. Fenton] (d 1892)
EA/93*
FENTUM, John (d 1879) performer? EA/81*
FENTUM, Jonathan (fl 1784?)
musician? CDP
FENWICK, Harry see Hardie,
W. R.
FENWICK, Irene (1887-1936)
American actress CDP,
WWT/4-8
FENWICK, John (fl 1800) dramatist CP/3
FENWICKE, Arthur (d 1895)
actor EA/96*
FENZL, Franz dancer CDP
FENZL, John dancer, acrobat
CDP
FENZL, Sophie dancer CDP
FEODOROVNA, Vera (d 1910)
actress WWT/14*
FERAL, Roger (d 1964 [60])

dramatist BP/49*
FERBER, Bernie (d 1965 [59])
manager BP/50*
FERBER, Edna (1887-1968) American dramatist AAS, BE, COC,
HJD, MD, MH, MWD, NTH,
OC/3, TW/24, WWT/6-14,
WWW/6
FERDINAND, Annie [Mrs. George
Ferdinand] (d 1872 [37]) EA/73*
FERDINAND, Mrs. George see
Ferdinand, Annie
FERGUSON, Miss actress CDP
FERGUSON, Anna E. (fl 1858) actress HAS
FERGUSON, Barney (d 1924 [71])
performer BE*, BP/9*
FERGUSON, Catherine (b 1895)
English actress, singer WWT/
5-7
FERGUSON, Elizabeth [Mrs. R.
Ferguson] (d 1876) EA/77*
FERGUSON, Elsie (1883/85/86-
1961) American actress CB,
SR, TW/2-6, 18, WWA/4,
WWM, WWT/1-11
FERGUSON, Frank (d 1937 [74])
American dramatist, actor
WWM
FERGUSON, Howard (d 1974 [78])
performer BP/58*
FERGUSON, John (d 1867 [70])
comedian EA/68*
FERGUSON, John (d 1887 [70])
music-hall performer? EA/88*
FERGUSON, Mrs. R. see Ferguson, Elizabeth
FERGUSON, Rachel (1893-1957)
English dramatist WWW/5
FERGUSON, Robert V. (c.1860-
1913) Scottish actor SR, WWS
FERGUSON, William Jason (1849-
1930) American actor DAB,
PP/1, SR, WWA/1, WWM,
WWS
FERGUSSON, Francis (b 1904)
American critic BE
FERLINGHETTI, Lawrence (b 1911)
American dramatist CD, CH
FERN, Sable (d 1942 [66]) comedienne, singer WWT/14*
FERNALD, Chester Bailey (1869-
1938) American dramatist
GRB/3-4, HJD, NTH, WWA/1,
WWT/1-8, WWW/3
FERNALD, John Bailey (b 1905)
American producer, principal of
the Royal Academy of Dramatic

Art, director AAS, OC/2-3, WWT/7-16

FERNANDEL [Ferdinand Joseph Desire Contandin] (1903-71) French actor WWA/5

FERNANDEZ, Mrs. (d 1880 [76]) EA/81*

FERNANDEZ, A. B. (d 1909 [68]) EA/10*

FERNANDEZ, Bijou [Mrs. W. L. Abingdon] (1877-1961) American actress GRB/3-4, TW/10-11, 18, WWM, WWS, WWT/1-5

FERNANDEZ, James (1835-1915) Russian/English actor DD, GRB/1-4, OAA/1-2, WWT/1-2

FERNANDEZ, Jose (b 1948) Cuban actor TW/26-28, 30

FERNANDEZ, Rose [Mrs. Robert Davis] (d 1900 [30]) equestrian EA/01*

FERNE, Fred (d 1953 [61]) manager WWT/14*

FERNLEY, Henry (d 1918) EA/19*

FERNS, Katie (d 1900 [34]) actress EA/01*

FERON, Elizabeth (1793/97-1853) English singer, actress CDP, DD, HAS, WWA/H

FERRABOSCO, Alfonso (fl 1562-78) Italian actor DA

FERRAND, Henry (d 1892) actor EA/93*

FERRANI, Frederick (d 1888) singer EA/89*

FERRANTI, Pietro (d 1896) composer, singer CDP

FERRAR, Ada (1867-1951) English actress DD, GRB/2-4

FERRAR, Beatrice (d 1958 [82]) English actress DD, GRB/3-4, WWT/1-6

FERRAR, John (fl 1765) Irish? dramatist CP/3

FERRAR, Thomas H. (d 1917) EA/18*

FERRARD, Grace (d 1965 [100]) performer BP/49*

FERRARI-FONTANA, Edoardo (1878-1936) Italian singer WWA/1

FERRARIS, Amalia (1828-1904) Italian dancer ES

FERRE, Signora San-Antonio see Cuzzoni, Francesca

FERRELL, Conchata (b 1943) American actress TW/29-30

FERRER, José (b 1909/12) Puerto Rican actor, producer, director AAS, BE, CB, ES, NTH, TW/1-21, 23-26, WWT/10-16

FERRER, Mel (b 1917) American actor, director, producer BE, ES, TW/10

FERRER, Melchior singer TW/2

FERRERS, Mr. (d 1841) Scottish prompter HAS

FERRERS, Mrs. see Byrnes, Mrs.

FERRERS, Edward (d c.1564) dramatist CP/2-3

FERRERS, George (1500?-79) dramatist, Master of the King's Pastimes DD, FGF

FERRERS, Helen (d 1943 [77]) English actress EA/96, GRB/1-4, WWT/1-8

FERRET, James (fl 1635) actor DA

FERRI, Gaetano (1816-81) singer CDP, HAS

FERRIAR, Dr. John (fl 1788) dramatist CP/3, DD

FERRIER, Jessie see Lindon, Louie

FERRIER, Kathleen (1912-53) English singer CB, DNB, ES, WWA/4, WWW/5

FERRIER, Paul (d 1920 [77]) dramatist WWT/14*

FERRIS, Barbara (b 1943) English actress TW/24, WWT/15-16

FERRIS, David (fl 1629) actor DA

FERRIS, John (b 1839) American actor HAS

FERRISS, Joseph (d 1885) comedian EA/86*

FERRO, Beth H. (d 1974 [49]) producer/director/choreographer BP/59*

FERRUGIO, Richard (b 1949) American actor TW/29

FERRUSAC, La Comtesse de (fl 1859) American singer HAS

FERRY, Robert (d 1890 [70]) musician EA/91*

FESCO, Michael (b 1936) American actor TW/16-19

FESSENDEN, William H. (fl 1879?) singer CDP

FEST, J. (fl 1845) actor HAS

FETHERSON, William (fl 1612) actor DA

FETTER, Selena see Royle,
Selena Fetter
FEUCHTWANGER, Lion (1884-
1958) German dramatist
MWD, NTH
FEUER, Cy (b 1911) American
producer, director BE, WWT/
14-16
FEUILLERE, Edwige (b 1907)
French actress OC/3, TW/
13-14
FEUILLET, Octave (1821-90)
French dramatist DD
FEUSSNER, Alfred (d 1969 [33])
performer BP/54*
FEYDEAU, Georges (1862-1921)
French dramatist COC, MD,
MWD, OC/3, PDT
FEYGHINE, Julie (d 1882) ac-
tress EA/83*
FFOLKES, David (b 1912) Eng-
lish designer ES, TW/3-8,
WWT/11-13
FFOLLIOTT, Gladys (d 1928
[69]) Irish actress WWT/4-5
FFRANGCON-DAVIES, David
(1850-1918) Welsh singer
WWW/2
FFRANGCON-DAVIES, Gwen (b
1896) English actress, singer
AAS, ES, WWT/5-16
FIAN, Robbee (b 1951) American
dancer TW/30
"FIBBER McGEE" see Jordan,
James E.
FICE, E. S. (d 1875) musician
EA/76*
FICHANDLER, Zelda [née Dia-
mond] (b 1924) American pro-
ducer, director AAS, BE,
WWT/15-16
FICKETT, Mary American actress
BE, TW/14-17, 20
FIDDES, Harriet Catherine [Miss
H. Cause] (d 1889 [77]) EA/
90*
FIDDES, Josephine (d 1923 [85])
English actress HAS
FIDGE, William (fl 1571) actor
DA
FIEDLER, John (b 1925) Ameri-
can actor BE, TW/10, 21-
23, 26
FIELD dramatist EAP
FIELD, Mrs. (d 1881 [61]) drama
coach? EA/82*
FIELD, Miss (fl 1777) actress
CDP

FIELD, Alexander (1892-1971) Eng-
lish actor WWT/7-13
FIELD, Al. G. (d 1921 [72]) Amer-
ican minstrel BE*, WWT/14*
FIELD, Barron (d 1846 [59]) critic
WWT/14*
FIELD, Ben (d 1939 [61]) actor
WWT/4-9
FIELD, Benjamin (d 1897) manager
EA/98*
FIELD, Mrs. Benjamin see
Field, Sarah Fawcett
FIELD, Betty (1918-73) American
actress AAS, BE, CB, TW/1-
20, 22, 27, 30, WWT/9-16
FIELD, Edward Salisbury (d 1936
[56]) American dramatist WWT/
4-8
FIELD, Francis (d 1968 [75])
dramatist BP/52*
FIELD, Henry (fl 1635) actor DA
FIELD, Henry (d 1889) EA/90*
FIELD, Jean see Kent, Jean
FIELD, J. K. (d 1842) Irish actor
HAS
FIELD, John (b 1921) English
dancer, ballet master ES
FIELD, Jonathan (b 1912) English
actor, producer, composer
WWT/11-14
FIELD, Joseph M. (1810-56) Eng-
lish/American actor, editor,
manager, dramatist CDP, DAB,
HAS, HJD, RJ, WWA/H
FIELD, Julian dramatist DD
FIELD, Kate see Field, Mary
Katherine Kemble
FIELD, Leonard (b 1908) American
producer, director BE
FIELD, Lila (d 1954) dramatist
BE*, WWT/14*
FIELD, Margaret St. John see
Field, Virginia
FIELD, Mary Katherine Kemble
(1838-96) American actress,
dramatist, singer CDP, DAB,
DD, WWA/H
FIELD, Matthew see Feilde,
Matthew
"FIELD, Michael" dramatist DD,
HP, WWW/1
FIELD, Nathaniel (1587-1620) Eng-
lish actor, dramatist CDP,
COC, CP/1-3, DA, DNB, ES,
FGF, GT, HP, NTH, OC/1-3,
RE
FIELD, Rachel Lyman (1894-1942)
children's dramatist CB, HJD,

WWA/2

FIELD, Richard Montgomery (1834-1902) manager CDP

FIELD, Robert (b 1916) American actor TW/1-3

FIELD, Robin (b 1947) American actor TW/28-29

FIELD, Ron choreographer, director WWT/16

FIELD, Roswell Martin (1851-1919) critic HJD

FIELD, Sarah Fawcett [Mrs. Benjamin Field] (d 1883 [40]) EA/80*

FIELD, Shirley Ann (b 1936) English actress ES

FIELD, Sid (1904-50) English comedian TW/6, WWT/10

FIELD, Sylvia [Harriett Johnson] (b 1901/02) American actress BE, TW/5-8, WWT/7-13

FIELD, T. M. American writer DD

FIELD, Virginia [née Margaret St. John Field] (b 1917) English actress TW/5, WWT/10-12

FIELD, William H. (d 1971 [56]) producer/director/choreographer BP/56*

FIELDE, Matthew see Feilde, Matthew

FIELDEN, Lionel (d 1974 [78]) producer/director/choreographer BP/59*

FIELDHOUSE, Harry (d 1909 [43]) musician EA/11*

FIELDING, Mr. (fl 1825) English actor HAS

FIELDING, Anne (b 1936) American actress TW/15

FIELDING, Anne (b 1943) American actress TW/26

FIELDING, Ben (d 1893 [44]) singer, actor CDP

FIELDING, Mrs. C. (d 1886) EA/87*

FIELDING, Dora (d 1898) seriocomic EA/99*

FIELDING, Edward [Edward B. Elkins] (1875-1945) American actor WWM

FIELDING, Fenella (b 1934) English actress WWT/14-16

FIELDING, Harold English producer WWT/15-16

FIELDING, Henry (1707-54) English dramatist, writer CDP,

COC, CP/1-3, DD, DNB, ES, GT, HP, MH, NTH, OC/1-3, RE, SR, TD/1-2

FIELDING, John actor CDP

FIELDING, Maggie actress CDP

FIELDING, Marjorie (1892-1956) English actress WWT/8-12, WWW/5

FIELDING, Mary see Faulkland, Mary

FIELDING, Sarah (1710/14-68) English dramatist CP/2-3, GT, HP

FIELDING, Timothy (d 1738) actor COC, OC/3

FIELDING, William J. (d 1874 [48]) singer EA/75*

FIELDING, W. J. actor? CDP

FIELDS, A. G. (b 1851) circus manager, actor, singer, minstrel SR

FIELDS, Benny (d 1959 [65]) American vaudevillian TW/16

FIELDS, Dorothy (1905-74) American librettist, lyricist BE, CB, COC, NTH, TW/30, WWT/10-15

FIELDS, Frank (d 1869) equestrian EA/70*

FIELDS, Frank Gaskin (d 1969 [59]) composer/lyricist BP/53*

FIELDS, Gracie [née Stansfield] (b 1898) English actress, singer CB, COC, ES, OC/3, SR, WWT/5-11

FIELDS, Harry D. (d 1961 [65]) performer BE*

FIELDS, Herbert (1897/98-1958) American librettist CB, COC, NTH, TW/14, WWT/7-12

FIELDS, John F. (b 1853) minstrel CDP

FIELDS, Joseph (1895-1966) American dramatist AAS, BE, COC, MD, MH, MWD, NTH, TW/22, WWT/10-14

FIELDS, Joseph H. (1798-1856) English/American actor, manager, dramatist SR

FIELDS, Judy American actress TW/29

FIELDS, Kate (d 1896) American actress SR

FIELDS, Lew [Lewis Maurice Fields] (1867-1941) American actor, manager CB, COC, ES, GRB/3-4, NTH, SR, WWA/1, WWM, WWS, WWT/1-9

FIELDS, Robert (b 1938) American

actor TW/23

FIELDS, Robert see Blumenfeld, Robert

FIELDS, Sid (d 1975 [77]) comedian, dramatist BP/60*, WWT/16*

FIELDS, Stanley (1884?-1941) actor CB

FIELDS, William (d 1961 [62]) press agent TW/17

FIELDS, W[illiam] C[laude; né Dukinfield] (1879/80-1946) American actor COC, DAB, ES, OC/3, SR, TW/3, WWA/ 2, WWM, WWT/7-10

FIENNES, Sydney [Cowley Polhill] (b 1877) English actor GRB/1

FIENZAL, Jean-François see Durancy, Mons.

FIENZAL, Mme. Jean-François see Durancy, Mme. Jean-François

FIFE, Bobby (d 1972 [70]) performer BP/56*

FIFE, Evelyn Henderson (d 1969 [81]) performer BP/53*

FIFE, George (d 1902) manager EA/03*

FIFIELD, Elaine (b 1930) Australian dancer WWT/12

FIGETTE, Ada (d 1904 [21]) EA/05*

FIGG, James (d 1734) English pugilist DNB

FIGGINS, Jane see Wenham, Jane

FIGMAN, Max (1868-1952) Austrian actor, director WWS, WWT/1-2

FIGMAN, Oscar (d 1930 [48]) actor BE*, BP/15*, WWT/ 14*

FIGNER, Nikolai Nikolaevich (1857-1918) Russian singer ES

FIGUERORA, Laura (b 1948) Puerto Rican actress TW/26

FILDES, Audrey (b 1922) English actress WWT/10-13

FILIPPI, Rosina [Mrs. H. M. Dowson] (1866-1930) Italian actress, dramatist DD, GRB/1-4, WWT/1-6

FILKINS, Grace (d 1962 [97]) American actress TW/19, WWS, WWT/2-7

FILLIS, Annie (b 1866) English circus performer ES

FILLIS, Annie (1869-1951) English acrobat, circus performer ES

FILLIS, Charles (b 1839) English acrobat, equestrian ES

FILLIS, Frank (d 1927) English equestrian ES

FILLIS, Mrs. Frank E. see Fillis, Lizzie

FILLIS, Harry (d 1873 [23]) equestrian EA/74*

FILLIS, Henry (d 1869 [41]) EA/ 70*

FILLIS, James (1834-1913) English circus performer ES

FILLIS, Lizzie [Mrs. Frank E. Fillis] (d 1890) EA/91*

FILLIS, Thomas (d 1876 [45]) equestrian EA/77*

FILLIS, Thomas English equestrian, clown ES

FILMER, A. E. producer, actor WWT/6-10

FILMER, Edward (fl 1675-1707) dramatist CP/1-3, DNB, GT

FILMORE, Lewis (fl 1841-82) dramatist, translator DD

FILOMENA, Josefina (b 1853) Chilean pianist HAS

FIMBERG, Harold A. (d 1974 [67]) dramatist BP/58*

FINA, Jack (d 1970) composer/ lyricist BP/54*

FINCH, Anne, Countess of Winchilsea (d 1720) English dramatist CP/1-3, GT

FINCH, Flora (1869-1940) English actress ES

FINCH, Henry (d 1901 [62]) lessee EA/02*

FINCH, John dramatist CD

FINCH, Mrs. Jones see Finch, Sarah

FINCH, Peter (1916-77) English actor AAS, CB, ES, WWT/11-15

FINCH, Sarah [Mrs. Jones Finch] (d 1877) EA/78*

FINCK, Herman [Herman von der Finck] (1869/72-1939) English conductor, composer GRB/1, WWT/4-8, WWW/3

FINDLATER, Adam S. (d 1911) music-hall director EA/12*

FINDLATER, Richard (b 1921) critic AAS

FINDLAY, Ruth (d 1949 [45]) actress TW/6

FINDLAY, Thomas B. (1871-1941) Canadian actor WWM

FINDON, B. W. (1859-1943)
English dramatist, critic DD,
GRB/2-4, WWT/1-8, WWW/4
FINE, Aaron (d 1963 [46]) drama-
tist BE*
FINE, Hank (d 1975 [72]) publi-
cist BP/60*
FINE, Larry (d 1975 [73]) come-
dian BP/59*, WWT/16*
FINE, Marshall H. (d 1975
[48]) executive BP/59*
FINE, Max (d 1974 [74]) theatri-
cal display creator BP/59*
FINEBERG, Isaac (d 1903 [85])
music-hall proprietor EA/
04*
FINEGAN, James (d 1916 [49])
agent EA/18*
FINEMAN, Vivian (b 1951) Amer-
ican actress TW/30
FINGER, Godfrey (c.1685-1717)
Moravian composer DD, DNB
FINGER, Simeon Woolfe (d 1916
[42]) musician EA/17*
FINKELSTEIN, Sidney (d 1974
[64]) critic BP/58*
FINKELSTONE, George N. (d
1966 [74]) performer BP/50*
FINKLEHOFFE, Fred F. (1911-
77) American producer,
dramatist BE
FINLAY, Edward J. (d 1912)
actor EA/13*
FINLAY, Frank (b 1926) English
actor AAS, WWT/14-16
FINLAY, P. (d 1875) scene
artist EA/76*
FINLEY, Patte American actress
TW/22-23
FINN, Arthur actor WWT/8-9
FINN, Frank S. (fl 1857) actor
HAS
FINN, George H. (d 1854) Amer-
ican actor HAS
FINN, Henry James (1785/87/
90-1840) American actor,
dramatist CDP, COC, DAB,
EAP, HAS, OC/1-3, RJ, SR,
WWA/H
FINN, H. W. (fl 1850) actor HAS
FINN, Jonathan (d 1971 [87])
dramatist BP/56*
FINNEGAN, Edward (d 1971 [72])
performer BP/55*
FINNEGAN, Mrs. George see
Deland, Annie
FINNEGAN, James F. (d 1972
[64]) publicist BP/57*

FINNELL, Carrie (d 1963 [70])
American performer BE*, BP/
48*
FINNERTY, Warren (d 1974 [40/49])
actor BP/59*, WWT/16*
FINNEY (fl 1783) dramatist CP/3
FINNEY, Albert (b 1936) English
actor AAS, BE, CB, COC, ES,
PDT, TW/20, 24, WWT/13-16
FINNEY, Jameson Lee (1863/68-
1911) American actor GRB/3-4,
WWS
FINNEY, Martha (d 1889) EA/90*
FINNEY, Mary (1906-73) American
actress BE, TW/9-15, 29
FINNEY, May see Fortescue,
May
FINNEY, William (d 1903) diver
EA/04*
FIORE, Frank (b 1953) American
actor TW/26-27
FIORENTINI, Claudina (fl 1853)
singer CDP
FIORILLO, Tiberio (1608-94) Italian
actor OC/1-3
FIRE, Richard (b 1945) American
actor TW/29
FIREHOUSE THEATRE, The theatre
collective CD
FIRESTONE, Eddie (b 1920) Amer-
ican actor, director BE, TW/
10-11
FIRESTONE, Scott (b 1962) Ameri-
can actor TW/29
FIRMIN, Dorothy (b 1888) English
actress, singer, dancer GRB/1
FIRTH, Anne (b 1918) English ac-
tress WWT/9-11
FIRTH, Edwin (b 1869) English ac-
tor GRB/1
FIRTH, Elizabeth (b 1884) American
actress, singer GRB/4, WWT/
1-5
FIRTH, Henry (d 1884 [58]) musician EA/85*
FIRTH, Henry Redfern (d 1916 [1])
EA/17*
FIRTH, Tazeena (b 1935) English
designer WWT/16
FISCALL, Martha (d 1880) equestrian EA/81*
FISCHER, Alice [Mrs. William Har-
court] (1869-1947) American ac-
tress GRB/2-4, TW/4, WWM,
WWS, WWT/1-9
FISCHER, Bob (d 1972 [36]) per-
former BP/57*
FISCHER, Charlotte Andrews (d

1968 [58]) performer BP/53*
FISCHER, Clifford C. (d 1951
[69]) Belgian producer BE*,
BP/36*
FISCHER, Emil Friedrich August
(1838-1914) German singer
DAB, ES
FISCHER, Harry (d 1908) actor
EA/09*, WWT/14*
FISCHER, Mrs. Harry see
Searle, Kate
FISCHER, Jane (b 1930) American
dancer TW/4
FISCHER, Max (d 1974 [65]) per-
former BP/59*
FISCHER, Robert E. (b 1923)
American architect BE
FISCHER, Ruth (b 1895) Rumani-
an/American press representa-
tive BE
FISCHER, Ruth (b 1919) American
press representative BE
FISH, Mrs. A. F. see Fish,
Eliza Rachel
FISH, Charles W. (fl 1877)
equestrian CDP
FISH, Eliza Rachel [Mrs. A. F.
Fish] (d 1910) EA/11*
FISH, Fred C. (d 1900 [43])
variety comedian EA/02*
FISH, Jenny (b 1852) actress,
dancer CDP
FISH, Marguerite [Mrs. Charles
Warren; "Baby Benson"] (d
1903 [34]) actress CDP
FISHBOURNE, Mr. dramatist
CP/1-3
FISHER (fl 1798?) dramatist
CP/3
FISHER, Miss see Bernard,
Mrs. John, II
FISHER, A. (d 1875) acting
manager EA/76*
FISHER, Alexander (d 1893 [71])
American actor EA/94*,
WWT/14*
FISHER, Alexina CDP
FISHER, Alfred (d 1975 [68])
performer BP/59*
FISHER, Mrs. Alice see Rams-
dale, Alice
FISHER, Allan (d 1917 [23]) ac-
tor EA/18*
FISHER, Amelia (fl 1827-29)
English actress HAS
FISHER, Carl (1909-74) American
business manager, general
manager BE

FISHER, Charles (1795-1869) actor,
manager, musician DD
FISHER, Charles (1815/16-91)
English actor CDP, DD, ES,
GC, HAS, WWA/H
FISHER, Charles (d 1916) actor
WWT/14*
FISHER, Charles J. B. (1804-59)
actor HAS
FISHER, Mrs. Charles J. B. see
Chapman, Elizabeth
FISHER, Clara (1811-98) English
actress, singer BS, CDP,
COC, DAB, DD, HAS, OC/1-3,
WWA/H
FISHER, Clara, Little (b 1853)
American actress HAS
FISHER, David (1760/61-1832)
English singer, manager DD,
ES
FISHER, David, the Elder (1788-
1858) English actor CDP, DD,
DNB, ES
FISHER, David, the Younger (1816-
87) English actor DD, DNB,
ES, NYM, OAA/1-2
FISHER, Mrs. David see Fisher,
Mary
FISHER, Douglas (b 1934) American
actor TW/27, 29-30
FISHER, Fred (d 1875) scene painter
EA/76*
FISHER, Fred (1875-1942) German
composer BE*
FISHER, Gail (b 1939) American
actress TW/22
FISHER, George (d 1864) agent
EA/72*
FISHER, Harry E. (d 1923 [55])
English performer BE*, BP/7*
FISHER, Irving (d 1959 [73]) actor,
singer TW/15
FISHER, Irving (d 1964 [60]) per-
former BP/49*
FISHER, James B. (d 1887) Amer-
ican journalist, dramatist EA/
88*
FISHER, Jane [Mrs. George Ver-
non] (d 1869) actress BE*
FISHER, Dr. Jasper (fl 1607-31)
English dramatist CP/2-3,
FGF
FISHER, J. B. (fl 1808) dramatist
CP/3
FISHER, J. B. S. (1804-59) English
actor, manager SR
FISHER, John (fl 1622) lessee DA
FISHER, John (d 1848) English

actor HAS

FISHER, John (d 1885) lessee EA/86*

FISHER, John Abraham (1744-1806) English musician, composer DNB

FISHER, John C. (d 1921 [67]) American manager, producer BE*, BP/6*, WWT/14*

FISHER, John R. (d 1868) actor HAS

FISHER, Jules (b 1937) American lighting designer BE, WWT/16

FISHER, Kate (1823/40-1918) American actress CDP, HAS

FISHER, Lewis T. (b 1915) American producer, actor BE

FISHER, Lilian May see Ramsdale, Lilian

FISHER, Lola (1896-1926) American actress SR, WWT/5

FISHER, Lola American singer, actress BE

FISHER, Mary [Mrs. David Fisher] (d 1879) EA/80*

FISHER, Nelle (b 1914) American dancer, choreographer, director BE, TW/1, 4

FISHER, Oceana (fl 1838-68) actress HAS

FISHER, Palmer (d 1827) English actor HAS

FISHER, Mrs. Palmer see Thayer, Mrs. Edward

FISHER, Perkins D. (1860-1930) American actor, manager SR

FISHER, Ruth H. (d 1974 [60s]) performer BP/59*

FISHER, Sallie (d 1950 [69]) American actress TW/7, WWM

FISHER, Sarah see Egerton, Sarah

FISHER, Mrs. Thomas see Abrams, Theodosia

FISHER, Thomas Alexander [né Thomas Smith] (fl 1847) actor HAS

FISHER, Walter David (1845-89) English actor, manager ES

FISHER, Walter H. (fl 1873-79) English actor DD, OAA/2

FISHMAN, Henry (d 1964 [76]) Russian/American actor BE*

FISHMAN, Melvin A. (d 1976 [46]) producer/director/choreographer BP/60*

FISK, Edith (d 1976 [67]) performer BP/60*

FISK, James, Jr. (d 1872) manager WWT/14*

FISKE, Harrison Grey (1861-1942) American dramatist, manager DAB, DD, GRB/2-4, SR, WWA/2, WWM, WWS, WWT/1-9

FISKE, Mrs. Harrison Grey see Fiske, Minnie Maddern

FISKE, James B. (1835-72) American manager, impresario CDP, HAS, SR

FISKE, Marian [Mrs. Thomas J. Martin] (d 1896) actress CDP

FISKE, Mary H. (d 1889) American dramatist, journalist EA/90*

FISKE, Minnie Maddern [Mrs. Harrison Grey Fiske] (1865-1932) American actress CDP, COC, DAB, ES, GRB/2-4, HJD, NTH, OC/1-3, PP/1, SR, WWA/1, WWM, WWS, WWT/1-6

FISKE, Moses W. (1830-87) American actor, manager CDP, HAS, NYM

FISKE, Stephen (1840-1916) American dramatist, critic CDP, DAB, GRB/2-4, WWA/1, WWM, WWT/1-3

FITCH, Clyde (1865-1909) American dramatist COC, DAB, DD, ES, GRB/2-4, HJD, MD, MH, MWD, NTH, OC/1-3, RE, WWA/1, WWS, WWW/1

FITCH, Haidee (b 1892) English actress, dancer GRB/1

FITCH, Joseph (b 1921) American educator, director BE

FITCH, Robert (b 1934) American actor TW/30

FITCH, Stephen see Douglass, Stephen

FITCH, William Clyde see Fitch, Clyde

FITCHETT, Henry (d 1877 [40]) musician EA/78*

FITCHETT, H. W. (d 1877) musician EA/78*

FITE, Mrs. E. M. S. (fl 1890s-1900s) American agent WWM

FITT, Mrs. (d 1892 [53]) EA/93*

FITTS, Dudley (1903-68) American educator, translator BE

FITTS, Harry Atkinson see Atkinson, Harry

FITZ, Charles E. (d 1920) actor BE*, BP/5*

FITZ, Erica (b 1942) American
actress TW/24
FITZBALL, Edward (1792-1873)
English dramatist CDP,
COC, DD, DNB, EA/68, OC/
1-3
FITZGEORGE, Mrs. see Fair-
brother, Louisa
FITZGERALD, Mr. actor CDP
FITZGERALD, Alexander (fl
1858-68) actor HAS
FITZGERALD, Aubrey Whitestone
(b 1876) Irish actor GRB/1,
WWT/1-5
FITZGERALD, Barry [né William
Joseph Shields] (1888-1961)
Irish actor CB, ES, TW/17,
WWA/4, WWT/10-11
FITZGERALD, Cissy (1873?-1941)
English actress CB
FITZGERALD, Daniel (d 1906
[46]) circus proprietor EA/07*
FITZGERALD, Dorothy (d 1899)
EA/01*
FITZGERALD, Eddie see Foy,
Eddie
FITZGERALD, Edith (d 1968
[75]) dramatist BP/52*
FITZGERALD, Edward (1809-83)
translator, dramatist DD, HP
FITZGERALD, Edward (b 1876)
Irish actor, business manager
GRB/1-4, WWS, WWT/3-4
FITZGERALD, Ellie Teresa
[Mrs. John G. Fitzgerald]
(d 1886 [28]) EA/87*
FITZGERALD, Florence Irene
(d 1962 [72]) actress BE*
FITZGERALD, F. Scott (1896-
1940) American dramatist
MD
FITZGERALD, Geraldine (b 1914)
Irish actress BE, CB, TW/
27-28, WWT/15-16
FITZGERALD, John (d 1912 [74])
musical director EA/13*
FITZGERALD, Mrs. John G.
see Fitzgerald, Ellie Teresa
FITZGERALD, Leo William (d
1968 [78]) agent BP/52*
FITZGERALD, Lillian (d 1947)
actress, singer TW/4
FITZGERALD, M. (fl 1792)
dramatist CP/3
FITZGERALD, Michael see
Robinson, James
FITZGERALD, Neil (b 1898)
Irish actor TW/9, 19, 23,

25-28, 30, WWT/16
FITZGERALD, Percy Hetherington
(1834-1925) Irish historian,
dramatist DD, WWT/1-5
FITZGERALD, Randle Hannaford
(d 1890 [26]) actor EA/91*
FITZGERALD, Richard (d 1889)
American agent EA/90*
FITZGERALD, S. J. Adair (1859-
1925) dramatist DD, WWT/3-5,
WWW/2
FITZGERALD, Thomas (1819-91)
American dramatist DAB,
WWA/H
FITZGERALD, Tom (d 1910) EA/
11*
FITZGERALD, Walter (1896-1976)
English actor AAS, BE, TW/
12, WWT/9-15
FITZGERALD, William C. (d 1969
[53]) critic BP/53*
FITZGIBBON, Gerald singer CDP
FITZGIBBON, H. B. see Gibbon,
H. B.
FITZGIBBON, Louis A. (d 1961
[81]) performer BE*
FITZGIBBONS, John Joseph (1890-
1966) American executive WWA/4
FITZHARRIS, Coralie (d 1973 [74])
performer BP/58*
FITZHARRIS, Edward (d 1974 [84])
performer BP/59*
FITZHENRY, Mrs. [née Flannigan]
(d 1790) actress CDP, DNB,
GT, TD/1-2
FITZHUGH, Mrs. (d 1905) EA/06*
FITZJAMES, Louise dancer CDP
FITZ-JAMES, Nathalie (fl 1851)
dancer CDP
FITZMAURICE, Mrs. see Hip-
pisley, E.
FITZMAURICE, George (1877-1963)
Irish dramatist MH, MWD, RE
FITZMAURICE, Michael T. (d 1967
[59]) performer BP/52*
FITZPATRICK, Emma (d 1868)
English actress CDP, DD, HAS
FITZPATRICK, Mrs. J.H. see
Josephs, Patti
FITZPATRICK, Kelly (b 1937)
American actor TW/27, 30
FITZPATRICK, P. (d 1884 [42])
musician EA/85*
FITZPATRICK, Thomas J. (d 1971
[89]) publicist BP/56*
FITZ-RENHARD, Mr. (d 1880)
ventriloquist EA/81*
FITZROY, F. R. (d 1888) actor

EA/89*
FITZROY, J. B. (d 1879 [72])
actor EA/80*
FITZROY, Kate [Mrs. A. R.
Fitzroy] (d 1887) actor EA/88*
FITZROY, Thomas (d 1918)
EA/19*
FITZSIMMONS, Robert Prometheus
(1862-1917) English pugilist,
actor DAB
FITZWARREN, Fanny (fl 1859)
actress CDP
FITZWILLIAM, Mr. (fl 1821)
actor EA/92
FITZWILLIAM, Edward (1788-
1852) English actor BS, CDP,
DD, DNB, OX
FITZWILLIAM, Mrs. Edward
[Fanny Elizabeth Copeland]
(1802-54) English actress BS,
CDP, DD, DNB, HAS, OX,
WWA/H
FITZWILLIAM, Edward Francis
(1824-57) English composer,
musical director DD, DNB
FITZWILLIAM, Mrs. Edward
Francis [Ellen Chaplin] (1822-
80) actress DD, DNB
FITZWILLIAM, Fanny Elizabeth
see Fitzwilliam, Mrs. Edward
FITZWILLIAM, Kathleen Mary
[Mrs. C. Withall] (1826-94)
actress, singer CDP, DD,
OAA/1-2
FITZWILLIAMS, Edwin (d 1857)
composer HAS [? = Fitzwil-
liam, Edward Francis, q.v.]
FITZWILLIAMS, Fanny see
Fitzwilliam, Mrs. Edward
FIX, Ress Jenkins (d 1975 [81])
performer BP/59*
"FIXER" see Davis, Dick
FLACK, Nanette (d 1971) per-
former BP/56*
FLACKS, Niki (b 1943) American
actress TW/23
FLAGEOLET, Mons. (fl 1869)
dancer CDP
FLAGSTAD, Kirsten (1895-1962)
Norwegian singer CB, ES,
TW/19, WWA/4, WWW/6
FLAHERTY, Pat. J., Sr. (d
1970) performer BP/55*
FLAKEY, James (d 1907) acrobat
EA/08*
FLAMM, Donald (b 1899) Ameri-
can producer BE
FLANAGAN, Ann (d 1975 [60s])

performer BP/60*
FLANAGAN, Bud [né Robert Winth-
rop] (1896-1968) English comedian
COC, WWT/10-14
FLANAGAN, Charles [Charles
Knowles] (d 1887 [65]) musician
EA/89*
FLANAGAN, Dick (d 1970 [56])
publicist BP/55*
FLANAGAN, Fionnuala (b 1941)
Irish actress TW/25, 28, 30
FLANAGAN, Florence see Forde,
Florrie
FLANAGAN, Hallie (1890-1969)
American director of Federal
Theatre Project of America
W.P.A., historian COC, NTH,
OC/1-3, WWT/9-14
FLANAGAN, Neil (b 1934) American
actor TW/29-30
FLANAGAN, Pauline (b 1925) Irish
actress TW/27-29
FLANAGAN, Richard (d 1917 [68])
manager WWT/2-3
FLANAGAN, Walter (b 1928) Amer-
ican actor TW/24-26, 29-30
FLANAGAN, William, Jr. (d 1969
[46]) composer/lyricist BP/54*
FLANDERS, Christian (b 1929)
Dutch actor TW/15
FLANDERS, Ed (b 1934) American
actor TW/30
FLANDERS, Michael Henry (1922-
75) English actor, lyricist, en-
tertainer BE, CB, COC, ES,
OC/3, TW/23, WWT/13-15
FLANGE, Dora [Mrs. George Vil-
liers] (d 1901) actress EA/02*
FLANNIGAN, Miss see Fitzhenry,
Mrs.
FLASTER, Karl (d 1965 [59]) com-
poser/lyricist BP/49*
FLAVIN, James (d 1976 [69]) per-
former BP/60*
FLAVIN, Martin (1883-1967) Amer-
ican dramatist BE, CB, HJD,
MD, MH, MWD, NTH, TW/24,
WWA/4, WWT/7-13
FLAWS, Mary (d 1888 [60]) EA/89*
FLEAY, F. Gard (1831-1909) his-
torian, critic DD, DNB
FLEBBE, Beulah Marie Dix (b
1876) American dramatist
WWA/5
FLECKER, James Elroy (1884-1915)
English dramatist COC, DNB,
ES, HP, MH, OC/1-3, PDT
FLECKNOE, Richard (fl 1654-67)

dramatist CP/1-3, DD, GT
FLEET, Mrs. George see
Gillette, Florence .
FLEET, George Rutland see
Barrington, Rutland
FLEETWOOD, Charles (d c.1745)
English manager CDP, COC,
OC/1-3, TD/1-2
FLEETWOOD, John Gerard (d
1776) actor WWT/14*
FLEETWOOD, Susan (b 1944)
Scottish actress AAS, WWT/
16
FLEISCHMAN, Mark (b 1935)
American actor TW/15-20
FLEISCHMAN, Maurice L. (d
1963 [79]) theatre owner BE*
FLEISCHMANN, Julius (1900-68)
producer BE
FLEMING, Miss [Mrs. Stanley]
(1796?-1861) actress DNB
FLEMING, Alice (d 1952 [70])
actress TW/9
FLEMING, Brandon (b 1889)
English dramatist WWT/6-10
FLEMING, Eric (1924-66) Amer-
ican actor TW/9, 11, 23
FLEMING, Frank see Caffry,
John
"FLEMING, George" see
Fletcher, Constance
FLEMING, Ian (1888-1969) Aus-
tralian actor WWT/5-13
FLEMING, Lucy (b 1947) English
actress WWT/15-16
FLEMING, Nita (d 1876 [15])
singer EA/77*
FLEMING, Noel (d 1950 [67])
actor BE*, WWT/14*
FLEMING, Rhonda (b 1922) Amer-
ican actress TW/29
FLEMING, Robert, Jr. (fl 1691)
dramatist CP/3
FLEMING, Tom (b 1927) Scottish
actor, director AAS, WWT/
14-16
FLEMING, William J. [W. J.
Baker] (1839-1921) American
actor HAS
FLEMING, William Maybury
(1817-66) American actor,
manager CDP, DAB, HAS,
WWA/H
FLEMING, Mrs. William M[ay-
bury?] (d 1859) actress HAS
FLEMMING, Claude (1884-1952)
Australian actor, singer
WWT/2-9

FLEMMING, Herbert (1856-1908)
actor, manager DD, EA/97
FLEMYNG, Robert (b 1912) English
actor AAS, BE, TW/3-4, 6-9,
11-17, WWT/8-16
FLERS, P. L. (d 1932 [65]) drama-
tist BE*, WWT/14*
FLERS, Robert de (1872-1927)
French dramatist MWD
FLESCH, Ella (d 1957 [55]) Hun-
garian singer TW/13
FLETCHER, Mr. (fl 1856) American
actor HAS
FLETCHER (d 1893) waxworks pro-
prietor EA/94*
FLETCHER, Mrs. [née Greer] (fl
1826) actress HAS
FLETCHER, Allen (b 1922) Ameri-
can director AAS, BE, WWT/
15-16
FLETCHER, Bramwell (b 1904/06)
English actor BE, TW/1, 3-16,
19, 22, WWT/8-16
FLETCHER, C. C. (b 1833) scene
artist CDP
FLETCHER, Constance ["George
Fleming"] (b 1858) dramatist
DD, GRB/2-4, WWA/4, WWT/
1-8, WWW/3
FLETCHER, Mrs. E. (d 1890)
EA/91*
FLETCHER, Edward (d 1896 [59])
proprietor EA/97*
FLETCHER, Mrs. Edward see
Fletcher, Elizabeth
FLETCHER, Elizabeth [Mrs. Ed-
ward Fletcher] (d 1899) EA/00*
FLETCHER, Emily Payne [Mrs.
Payne Fletcher] (d 1895 [46])
EA/96*
FLETCHER, George (fl 1847)
critic DD
FLETCHER, Ifan Kyrle (d 1969)
historian WWT/15*
FLETCHER, Jack (b 1921) Ameri-
can actor TW/7, 22-26, 29-30
FLETCHER, John (1579-1625) Eng-
lish dramatist CDP, COC, CP/
1-3, DD, DNB, ES, FGF, HP,
MH, NTH, OC/1-3, PDT, RE
FLETCHER, John (b 1809) English
actor HAS
FLETCHER, John C. (d 1886 [45])
property master EA/87*
FLETCHER, Lawrence (d 1608?)
actor DA, GT
FLETCHER, Lawrence (1902/04-70)
American actor TW/1-7, 13-15,

26
FLETCHER, Payne (d 1916 [69])
EA/18*
FLETCHER, Mrs. Payne see
Fletcher, Emily Payne
FLETCHER, Percy (1879-1932)
English composer, conductor
WWT/4-6
FLETCHER, Phineas (1582-1650)
English dramatist CP/1-3,
DD, DNB, FGF, HP
FLETCHER, Robert (d 1972 [87])
composer/lyricist BP/57*
FLETCHER, Robert [né Robert
Fletcher Wyckoff] (b 1923)
American designer AAS, BE,
WWT/15-16
FLETCHER, W. (d 1873 [29])
comic singer EA/74*
FLEXMORE, Ann (d 1869 [88])
EA/71*
FLEXMORE, Richard [R. F.
Geater] (1824-60) English
pantomimist CDP, DD, DNB
FLEXNER, Anne Crawford (1874-
1955) American dramatist
WWA/3, WWT/5-10
FLICKER, Theodore (b 1930)
American director, dramatist,
actor, producer BE
FLINDT, Flemming (b 1936)
Danish dancer, choreographer
ES
FLINN, Kate Irish singer GRB/1
FLINT, Ettie (d 1904) music-hall
performer EA/05*
FLINT, Helen (d 1967 [69]) ac-
tress TW/24
FLINT-SHIPMAN, Veronica (b
1931) English producing mana-
ger WWT/16
FLIPPEN, Jay C. (d 1971 [70])
actor TW/27
FLIPPIN, Lucy Lee (b 1943)
American actress TW/27, 30
FLOCKTON, Mr. conjuror CDP
FLOCKTON, Charles P. (d 1904
[76]) actor DD, OAA/2
FLOOD, Ann (b 1932) American
actress TW/13
FLOOD, Beatrice see De Neer-
gaard, Beatrice
FLOOD, Brean Stewart (d 1917)
EA/18*
FLOOD, John (d 1865) actor?
HAS
FLOOD, John (d 1924) actor
BE*, BP/9*

FLOOD, Susan (d 1879 [40]) Amer-
ican actress EA/80*
FLOOD, W. H. (d 1900) musical
director EA/01*
FLOOD-PORTER, Gertrude Mary
(d 1911) EA/12*
FLOOD-PORTER, Matilda Grace
(d 1911) EA/12*
FLOOK, Richard actor CDP
FLORADOR, Minnie (d 1902) bur-
lesque artiste EA/03*
FLORANCE, Cassius (d 1975 [65])
producer/director/choreographer
BP/59*
FLORENCE, Katherine (fl 1890s)
English actress PP/1, WWS
FLORENCE, Tom (d 1908) showman
EA/10*
FLORENCE, William Jermyn [né
Bernard Conlin] (1831-91) Amer-
ican actor CDP, COC, DAB,
DD, HAS, NTH, OC/1-3, SR,
WWA/H
FLORENCE, Mrs. William Jermyn
[Mrs. Joseph Littell; née Malvina
Pray] (1834-1906) actress, mana-
ger, dancer CDP, COC, HAS,
NTH, SR, WWA/1
FLORENE, Nellie (d 1904) EA/
05*
FLORIDA, Pietro (b 1860) Italian
composer WWA/1, WWM
FLORIDOR [Josias de Soulas, Sieur
de Primefosse] (1608-72) French
actor DA, OC/1-3
FLORIDOR, Josias see Lau,
Hurfries de
FLORINGTON, Jane Hinton [Mrs.
John Hinton Florington] (d 1886
[73]) EA/87*
FLORIO, C. M. (fl 1800-01) English
composer TD/1-2
FLORY, Julia McClune (d 1971
[89]) designer BP/55*
FLORY, Regine (1894-1926) actress,
dancer WWT/4-5
FLORY, Mrs. Walter (d 1971 [89])
theatre founder BP/55*
FLOSSOW, Al (d 1976 [80]) per-
former BP/60*
FLOTOW, Frederich (1812-88) Ger-
man composer SR
FLOURY, Antoine (d 1894 [59])
manager EA/95*
FLOWER, (fl 1600) actor DA
FLOWER, Sir Archibald (d 1950
[85]) English executive BE*,
WWT/14*

FLOWER, Charles E. (d 1892) founder of Shakespeare Memorial EA/93*

FLOWER, Sir Fordham (d 1966 [62]) patron, executive BP/51*, WWT/15*

FLOWER, Sara (d 1865) actress, singer EA/72*, WWT/14*

FLOWER, Thomas (d 1839) actor CDP

FLOWERDAY, Mrs. see Chatters, Kate

FLOWERTON, Consuelo (d 1965 [65]) actress, singer TW/22

FLOYD, Carlisle (b 1926) American composer CB

FLOYD, Gwendoline (d 1950 [80]) actress WWT/4-10

FLOYD, Sara (d 1972 [78]) actress TW/29

FLOYD, William Rudolph (1832-80) American actor, manager CDP, HAS

"FLYING PIEMAN, The" see England, James Sharp

FLYNN, Miss (fl 19th cent) actress HAS

FLYNN, Errol (1909-59) actor TW/16

FLYNN, George H. (d 1854) actor? HAS

FLYNN, Harry (d 1905) actor EA/06*

FLYNN, Hazel (d 1964 [65]) journalist, press representative BE*, BP/48*

FLYNN, J. D. [John Phelton, Jr.] (d 1889 [40]) comedian EA/90*

FLYNN, Joe (d 1974 [49]) performer BP/59*

FLYNN, Thomas (1798-1849) English actor, stage manager, manager HAS, WWA/H

FLYNN, Mrs. Thomas [née Twybell] (d 1851) American actress HAS

FLYNN, Thomas F. (b 1946) American actor TW/27-28

FOCH, Dirk (d 1973 [87]) composer/lyricist BP/57*

FOCH, Nina (b 1924) Dutch actress BE, TW/3-4, 6-9, 13-14, 16, WWT/11-16

FODOR, Joleen (b 1939) American actress TW/21-22, 26

FODOR, Josephine (1793-1870) singer CDP

FODOR, Ladislaus (b 1898) Hungarian dramatist WWT/8-14

FOGARTY, Frank (d 1925 [50]) vaudevillian BP/9*

FOGARTY, Jan (d 1969 [65]) performer BP/54*

FOGARTY, Dr. J. S. (d 1893 [34]) EA/94*

FOGERTY, Elsie (1866-1945) English founder of Central School of Speech Training and Dramatic Art, actress COC, DNB, OC/1-3, WWT/7-9, WWW/4

FOGERTY, Joseph (d 1887 [83]) proprietor EA/88*

FOGERTY, Mrs. Joseph (d 1888) EA/89*

FOGERTY, Robert (d 1907 [63]) proprietor EA/08*

FOGLER, Gertrude (d 1970 [91]) diction coach BP/55*

FOKINA, Vera (d 1958 [69]) dancer TW/15

FOKINE, Alexander Russian/American dancer, choreographer ES

FOKINE, Leon (d 1973 [68]) performer BP/58*

FOKINE, Michel (1880-1942) Russian dancer, choreographer, maître de ballet CB, DAB, ES, NTH, WWA/2, WWT/4-9

FOLEY, Allen James see Foli, Allen James

FOLEY, Michael (b 1848) American comedian HAS

FOLEY, Paul A. (b 1905) American stage manager, director, actor BE

FOLEY, Red (d 1968 [58]) performer BP/53*

FOLGER, Henry Clay (1857-1930) American philanthropist COC, OC/1-3

FOLGER, Mrs. John H. see Macmillan, Violet

FOLI, Allen James [né Foley] (1842-99) singer CDP

FOLKARD, William Seward see Elvey, Maurice

FOLKES, Mrs. Martin see Bradshaw, Lucretia

FOLLAND, Mr. (d 1856) agent HAS

FOLLAND, Minnie see Montez, Minnie

FOLLET, John (d 1799 [32]) actor CDP, TD/1-2

FOLLIS, Dorothy (1892-1923)

American actress BE*, BP/8*

FOLLOWS, John (d 1888) actor?
EA/89*

FOLTZ, Jane (d 1975) performer
BP/60*

FOLWELL, Denis (d 1971 [66])
performer BP/55*

FONDA, Henry (b 1905) American
actor AAS, BE, CB, ES, SR,
TW/4-20, 22-23, 26, 30,
WWT/9-16

FONDA, Jane (b 1937) American
actress BE, CB, ES, TW/
16-20, WWT/14-16

FONDA, Peter (b 1939) American
actor TW/18-20

FONSECA, Joseph (d 1974 [49])
performer BP/59*

FONTAINE, Joan (b 1917) American actress BE, ES, TW/13

FONTAINE, Lillian (d 1975 [88])
performer BP/59*

FONTAINE, Tony (d 1974) performer BP/59*

FONTANNE, Lynn (b 1887?)
English actress BE, CB,
COC, ES, HJD, NTH, OC/
1-3, PDT, SR, TW/2-21,
WWT/3-16

FONTENELLE, Miss see Wil-
liamson, Mrs. J. Brown

FONTEYN, Margot [née Margaret
Hookham] (b 1919) English
dancer CB, ES, WWT/9-12

FOOT, Jesse (fl 1811) dramatist
CP/3

FOOT, John see Conway,
George

FOOT, John Forester dramatist
EAP, RJ

FOOTE, Mr. (fl 1802) actor
TD/2

FOOTE, Commodore [Charles W.
Nestel] (b 1848) dwarf CDP

FOOTE, Mr. (d 1882) actor EA/
83*

FOOTE, Miss see Harrington,
Maria, Dowager Countess of

FOOTE, Miss see Lytton, Miss

FOOTE, Barrington see Foote,
Vere Cecil

FOOTE, Gene (b 1936) American
actor TW/29-30

FOOTE, Horton (b 1916) American dramatist BE, ES, PDT,
WWT/14-16

FOOTE, John Forrester (fl 1822)
actor CDP, HAS

FOOTE, John S. (d 1882) comedian,
proprietor, actor, manager,
lessee DD

FOOTE, John Taintor (1881-1950)
American dramatist WWA/2

FOOTE, Lydia Alice (1844-92) English actress DD, DNB, OAA/
1-2, OC/1-3

FOOTE, Maria (c.1797-1867) English actress BS, CDP, COC,
DD, DNB, OC/1-3, OX

FOOTE, Samuel (1720-77) English
actor, dramatist CDP, COC,
CP/1-3, DD, DNB, ES, GT,
HP, MH, NTH, OC/1-3, SR,
TD/1-2

FOOTE, Samuel (fl 1796-98) actor,
manager TD/1-2

FOOTE, Vere Cecil [Barrington
Foote] (d 1910) singer EA/11*

FOOTE, W. S. (d 1882) actor
EA/82*

FOOTIT, George (b 1864) English
clown GRB/1

FOOTTIT, George (d 1875) circus
proprietor EA/76*

FORAN, Anna E. (d 1969 [77])
dancer BP/54*

FORAN, Arthur F. (d 1967 [55])
performer BP/51*

FORAN, Thomas F. (d 1970 [79])
performer BP/55*

"FORBES, Athol" see Phillips,
Rev. Forbes Alexander

FORBES, Billy see Randall, W.

FORBES, Brenda (b 1908/09) English actress AAS, BE, TW/1-4,
13-14, 23-24, 30, WWT/10-16

FORBES, Bryan [né Clarke] (b
1926) English actor WWT/13-14

FORBES, Donna Liggitt (b 1947)
American actress TW/29

FORBES, Earle (d 1970 [73]) performer BP/55*

FORBES, Edward (1889-1969?)
American actor TW/2

FORBES, Fred (d 1899 [35]) music-
hall acting manager EA/00*

FORBES, Freddie (1895-1952) English actor WWT/7-9

FORBES, James (1871/72-1938)
Canadian manager, dramatist,
actor GRB/3-4, HJD, MWD,
SR, WWA/1, WWM, WWT/1-8

FORBES, Kenneth (b 1920) American actor TW/5-7

FORBES, Mary (1880-1964?) actress TW/21, WWT/2-9

FORBES, Meriel (b 1913) English actress BE, WWT/8-16
FORBES, Norman [Forbes-Robertson] (1858/59-1936) Scottish actor DD, GRB/1-4, OC/1-3, WWT/1-6
FORBES, Ralph (1902/05-51) English actor TW/1-7, WWT/6-11
FORBES, Scott (b 1921) English actor TW/9-12
FORBES, William C. (d 1868 [61]) actor, manager HAS, WWA/H
FORBES, Mrs. William C. [née Fannie Marie Gee] (d 1865) actress HAS
FORBES, William Nathaniel (d 1900 [75]) EA/01*
FORBES-ROBERTSON, Beatrice (1883-1967) English actress GRB/3-4, WWT/1-8
FORBES-ROBERTSON, Eric (1865-1935) English actor OC/1-3
FORBES-ROBERTSON, Frances (d 1902 [75]) EA/04*
FORBES-ROBERTSON, Frank (1885-1947) actor WWT/6-10
FORBES-ROBERTSON, Ian see Robertson, Ian
FORBES-ROBERTSON, J., Sr. (d 1903 [81]) EA/04*
FORBES-ROBERTSON, Jean (1905-62) English actress AAS, COC, OC/1-3, TW/19, WWT/6-13, WWW/6
FORBES-ROBERTSON, Sir Johnston (1853-1937) English actor, manager CDP, COC, DNB, DP, EA/97, ES, GRB/1-4, NTH, OAA/1-2, OC/1-3, PDT, SR, WWA/1, WWM, WWS, WWT/1-8, WWW/3
FORBES-ROBERTSON, Mrs. Johnston see Elliott, Gertrude
FORBES-ROBERTSON, Norman see Forbes, Norman
FORCE, Joan American actress TW/23
FORCER, Francis, the Elder (1650?-1705?) composer, lessee DNB
FORD, Miss see Johnson, Mrs.
FORD, Arthur Paget see Fairleigh, Paget
FORD, Audrey [Mrs. James Welch] English actress GRB/3-4, WWT/1-6
FORD, Constance American actress BE, TW/22, 30
FORD, Corey (d 1969 [67]) performer BP/54*
FORD, David (b 1929) American actor TW/11, 21, 25-28
FORD, Edward H. (d 1970 [82]) vaudevillian TW/26
FORD, Ernest (1858-1919) composer, conductor DD, WWW/2
FORD, Francis (d 1953 [71]) actor BE*
FORD, Frank (b 1916) American producer BE
FORD, George D. (d 1974 [94]) producer/director/choreographer BP/59*
FORD, Gipsy (d 1907) variety performer EA/09*
FORD, Glenn (b 1916) Canadian/American actor CB, ES
FORD, Harriet (d 1949 [86]) American dramatist TW/6, WWA/3, WWT/4-9
FORD, Harrison (d 1957 [73]) actor TW/14
FORD, Harry (d 1883 [36]) musician EA/84*
FORD, Harry (d 1894) comedian, singer CDP
FORD, Helen American actress, singer BE, WWT/6-11
FORD, Hugh (fl 1898-1917) American actor, manager WWA/5
FORD, Mrs. Jack see Morgan, Violet
FORD, John (1586-1639) English dramatist COC, CP/1-3, DD, DNB, ES, FGF, HP, MH, NTH, OC/1-3, PDT, RE
FORD, John (d 1963 [81]) performer BE*
FORD, John (d 1973 [78]) producer/director/choreographer BP/58*
FORD, Mrs. John see Gehrue, Mayme
FORD, John Thomson (1829-94) American manager, actor? CDP, COC, DAB, DD, HAS, OC/1-3, SR, WWA/H
FORD, Julia Ellsworth (b 1859) American dramatist WWA/5
FORD, Mrs. Martin [Jeannie Scott] (d 1874) actress EA/75*
FORD, Millie (d 1911 [32]) actress EA/12*

FORD, Olivia (d 1884) EA/85*
FORD, Paul [né Paul Ford
Weaver] (1901-76) American
actor BE, TW/2-4, 10-12,
15-17, 19-22, 24, 26, 28,
WWT/14-16
FORD, Philip (d 1976 [73]) pro-
ducer/director/choreographer
BP/60*
FORD, Rosetta (d 1912 [56])
EA/13*
FORD, Ruth (b 1920) American
actress, dramatist AAS, BE,
TW/4-9, 12, 15, 23-24, 28-
30, WWT/14-16
FORD, Sydney (b 1938) English
actor TW/27
FORD, Thomas (fl 1660) English
dramatist CP/1-3, GT
FORD, Thomas W. (d 1909)
EA/10*
FORD, W. (d 1890) EA/91*
FORD, Wallace (1898-1966)
English actor BE, TW/23,
WWT/9-11
FORD, Wilton (d 1908 [57]) vari-
ety manager EA/09*
FORDE, Master (fl 1837?) actor
CDP
FORDE, Blanche see Sennett,
Mrs. Thomas
FORDE, Brownlow (fl 1771) actor,
dramatist CP/2-3, GT
FORDE, Catherine Maria (b
1805) actress, singer CDP
FORDE, Emmie [Mrs. Edward
A. Ryleston] (d 1889) actress
EA/90*
FORDE, Florrie [Florence Flana-
gan] (1876-1940) Australian
music-hall performer CDP,
COC, OC/1-3
FORDE, George (d 1872 [60])
singer EA/73*
FORDE, Hal (d 1955 [78]) Irish
actor, singer TW/12
FORDE, H. Athol actor EA/96
FORDE, Mrs. H. Athol see
Forde, Kathleen
FORDE, Mrs. H. Athol see
Protheroe, May
FORDE, J. G. (d 1873 [42])
patter singer, actor CDP
FORDE, Kathleen [Mrs. H.
Athol Forde] (d 1908) EA/09*
FORDE, Stanley Hamilton (b
1878) American actor WWS
FORDE, Thomas (fl 1660) drama-

tist FGF
FORDHAM, Edward King (b 1881)
English actor GRB/1-4
FORDHAM, Fred (d 1909 [55])
music-hall manager EA/10*
FORDIN, Hugh G. (b 1935) Ameri-
can producer BE
FORDRED, Dorice (b 1902) South
African actress WWT/8-13
FORDYCE, Marie D. (d 1976 [83])
performer BP/60*
FORDYCE, Vera actress GRB/1
FOREMAN, Elliot S. (d 1971 [87])
advance man BP/55*
FOREMAN, Richard (b 1937) Amer-
ican dramatist, director CD
FOREPAUGH, Adam (1831-90)
American circus manager CDP,
DAB, SR, WWA/H
FOREPAUGH, John A. (d 1895)
producer BE*, WWT/14*
FOREST, Charles (d 1871) actor
EA/72*
FOREST, Lillian (d 1887) actress
NYM
FOREST, Lucy (d 1903 [34]) variety
performer EA/04*
FOREST, Theophilus see For-
rest, Theophilus
FORGE, Mrs. R. [née Bella Bran-
don] (d 1868 [19]) singer EA/69*
FORGEOT, Eliza (fl 1845) French
actress CDP
FORIOSE, The Sisters (fl 1829)
tight-rope performers HAS
FORLOW, Ted (b 1931) American
actor TW/25-29
FORMAN, Arthur Edmund (b 1918)
American actor TW/27, 30
FORMAN, George Frederick (1811-
52) actor CDP
FORMAN, Justus Miles (1875-1915)
American dramatist WWW/1
FORMAN, Simon (1552-1611) writer
DD
FORMBY, George (1905-61) English
comedian, performer CDP,
COC, ES, OC/3, WWW/6
FORMES, Carl [or Karl] (1810/16/
18-89) German singer CDP,
HAS, ES, WWA/H
FORMES, Theodor (d 1874) singer
EA/75*
FORMIDO, Sir Cornelius (fl 1653)
dramatist CP/3, FGF
FORNASARI, Luciano (fl 1833)
singer CDP, HAS
FORNES, Maria Irene (b 1930)

Cuban/American dramatist, director CD

FORNIA, Rita (1876-1922) American singer WWA/1

FORREST, Anne (b 1897) Danish actress WWT/7-8

FORREST, Arthur (d 1908 [50]) music-hall comedian CDP

FORREST, Arthur (d 1933 [74]) German actor BE*, BP/17*

FORREST, Mrs. Arthur see Rhodes, Pollie

FORREST, Catharine Norton [Mrs. Edwin Forrest] (1818-91) actress CDP

FORREST, Edwin (1806-72) American actor CDP, COC, DAB, DD, ES, HAS, HJD, NTH, OC/1-3, SR, WWA/H

FORREST, Mrs. Edwin see Forrest, Catharine Norton

FORREST, Mrs. Edwin see Sinclair, Caroline N.

FORREST, Ella [Mrs. John Soden] (d 1908) performer EA/09*

FORREST, Fred (b 1936) American actor TW/26

FORREST, George (b 1915) American lyricist, composer BE

FORREST, Milton Earl (b 1946) American actor TW/27

FORREST, Paul (b 1923) American actor TW/26

FORREST, Rebecca CDP

FORREST, Sam (1870-1944) American producer, dramatist, actor SR, WWT/6-9

FORREST, Theodosius [or Theophilus] (1728-84) English dramatist CP/2-3, DNB, GT, TD/1-2

FORREST, Col. Thomas (1747-1825) American? dramatist EAP, ES [see also Barton, Andrew]

FORREST, William (b 1800) American actor, manager SR

FORREST, W. S. (d 1868 [62]) actor, manager HAS

FORREST, Mrs. W. S. see Clarke, Mrs.

FORRESTAL, Josephine Ogden (d 1976 [76]) investor BP/60*

FORRESTER, Alfred Henry ["Alfred Crowquill"] (d 1872 [67]) EA/73*

FORRESTER, Frederick C. (d

1952 [80]) actor TW/9

FORRESTER, Henry (1797-1840) actor CDP, DD

FORRESTER, Henry [Henry Frost] (1827-82) English actor DD

FORRESTER, Jack (d 1963 [59]) performer BE*

FORRESTER, Maude actress CDP

FORRESTER, N. C. (fl 1848) actor HAS

FORRESTER, Mrs. N. C. (fl 1850) actress HAS

FORRESTER, William (d 1885) actor EA/86*

FORSLUND, Connie (b 1950) American actress TW/29-30

FORSTER, Mrs. (d 1873) EA/75*

FORSTER, Mrs. Edwin (d 1893 [67]) EA/94*

FORSTER, E. M. (1879-1970) English librettist, dramatist WWA/5, WWW/6

FORSTER, Emily Rachel see Hinton, Mary

FORSTER, Harry (d 1885) comic singer EA/87*

FORSTER, John (1812-76) English historian CDP, DD, DNB, GT, OC/1-3

FORSTER, Robert (d 1888 [64]) manager EA/89*

FORSTER, Robert (b 1941) American actor TW/22, 29-30

FORSTER, Rudolf (d 1968 [84]) performer BP/53*

FORSTER, Wilfred (1872-1924) English actor GRB/2-4, WWT/1-4

FORSTER, William Pateman (d 1917) EA/18*

FORSTER, W. R. (d 1887) musician EA/88*

FORSTER-BOVILL, W. B. (b 1871) Welsh business manager WWT/5

FORSYTH, Bertram (d 1927 [40]) actor, dramatist BE*, WWT/14*

FORSYTH, Bruce [né Bruce Forsyth Johnson] (b 1928) English actor WWT/15-16

FORSYTH, Clara Fisher [Mrs. Francis Forsyth] (d 1884) EA/85*

FORSYTH, Mrs. Francis see Forsyth, Clara Fisher

FORSYTH, Gerald (d 1971 [90]) designer BP/55*

FORSYTH, Helen (d 1901) actress CDP, DD, EA/95

FORSYTH, James (b 1913) Scottish dramatist BE, CD, MD, MWD, PDT

FORSYTH, Lina Dalrymple [Mrs. Robert Forsyth] (d 1886) EA/87*

FORSYTH, Matthew (1896-1954) English actor, producer WWT/8-11

FORSYTH, Neil (1866-1915) manager GRB/1-3, WWT/1-2, WWW/1

FORSYTH, Mrs. Robert see Forsyth, Lina Dalrymple

FORSYTHE, Charles (b 1928) American stage manager, director, actor BE

FORSYTHE, Henderson (b 1917) American actor, director BE, TW/14, 21-24, 26-30, WWT/15-16

FORSYTHE, John [né John Lincoln Freund] (b 1918) American actor BE, CB, TW/10-12, WWT/12-13, 15-16

FORT, Hank (d 1973 [59]) composer/lyricist BP/57*

FORT, Robert (d 1901) proprietor EA/02*

FORT, Syvilla (d 1975 [58]) performer BP/60*

FORTENBERRY, Beth (b 1948) American actress TW/28

FORTESCUE, Florence (d 1917 [63]) EA/18*

FORTESCUE, George K. (1846?-1914) actor CDP

FORTESCUE, Gulia H. (fl 19th cent) singer CDP

FORTESCUE, Julia [Lady Gardner] (d 1899) actress DD

FORTESCUE, May [May Finney] (1862-1950) English actress CDP, DD, DP, GRB/1-4, WWT/1-9

FORTESCUE, Viola (d 1953 [78]) American actress TW/10

FORTH, Eric [Fred Osterstock] (d 1908) EA/09*

FORTI, Giuseppe (fl 1849) singer CDP

FORTI, Marietta dancer CDP

FORTIER, Frank (d 1974) showman BP/58*

FORTUNE, Henry (d 1877 [55]) actor EA/78*

FORTUNE, Richard (d 1880) musician EA/81*

FORTUS, Daniel (b 1953) American actor TW/30

FORWOOD, Harry (d 1967 [62]) press agent TW/23

FOSBERG, Harold (d 1888) American actor EA/89*

FOSBROOKE, Sophia Louisa actress CDP

FOSBROOKE, Thomas Leopold (d 1871) pantomimist EA/72*

FOSBROOKE, William (1835-98) actor DD

FOSS, Charles see Fulton, Charles

FOSS, George R. (1859-1938) English producer, actor GRB/1-4, WWT/5-7

FOSS, Mrs. George R. see Fraser, Winifred

FOSS, Lukas (b 1922) German/American composer ES

FOSSE, Bob (b 1927) American director, choreographer, dancer, actor BE, CB, CD, TW/6, WWT/15-16

FOSSETT, Alfred Francis (d 1896 [33]) circus performer EA/97*

FOSSETT, Emma (d 1912 [84]) circus proprietor EA/13*

FOSTER dramatist EAP, RJ

FOSTER, Mr. (fl 1831?) actor CDP

FOSTER, Miss see Young, Mrs. Charles

FOSTER, Alexander (fl 1611-29) actor DA

FOSTER, Barry (b 1927) American actor AAS, TW/20, WWT/14-16

FOSTER, Basil S. (1882-1959) English actor, singer WWT/2-10

FOSTER, Betty (d 1970) performer BP/55*

FOSTER, Charles American actor, dramatist DD

FOSTER, Charles B. (d 1887) actor? NYM

FOSTER, Charles Hubbs (d 1895 [61]) American dramatist EA/96*

FOSTER, Charles J. (1827-64) English dancer? actor CDP, HAS

FOSTER, Claiborne (b 1896/98/1900) American actress TW/13, WWT/6-8

FOSTER, Donald (1894?-1969) American actor TW/1, 4, 8-9, 26

FOSTER, Dudley (d 1973 [48])

actor BP/57*

FOSTER, Edward (1876-1927) Irish manager, actor GRB/1, WWT/4-5

FOSTER, Eliza Frances [née Bennett] (b 1829) American actress HAS

FOSTER, Fanny (fl 1872) actress CDP

FOSTER, F. Carlton (d 1912 [29]) singer EA/13*

FOSTER, Frances American actress TW/25-30

FOSTER, Fred (d 1880 [30]) music-hall performer, actor CDP, EA/81*

FOSTER, Gloria (b 1936) American actress TW/22-23, 28-29, WWT/16

FOSTER, Gus (d 1901 [53]) music-hall manager EA/02*

FOSTER, Herbert (b 1936) Canadian actor TW/25-27

FOSTER, John (b 1830) American clown HAS

FOSTER, John (d 1917) actor EA/18*

FOSTER, Joseph (d 1974 [69]) critic BP/59*

FOSTER, Julia (b 1942) English actress WWT/15-16

FOSTER, Lewis R. (d 1974 [75]) producer/director/choreographer BP/59*

FOSTER, Lillian (d 1949 [63]) actress TW/5

FOSTER, Marie (b 1927) American actress TW/4

FOSTER, Matthew (d 1868 [43]) musician EA/69*

FOSTER, M. P. (d 1882 [49]) actor? EA/83*

FOSTER, Norman (1900/03-76) American actor WWT/7-10

FOSTER, Pamela see Charles, Pamela

FOSTER, Paul (b 1931) American dramatist CD, WWT/16

FOSTER, Phoebe (b 1896) American actress WWT/7-11

FOSTER, Preston (d 1970 [69]) performer BP/55*

FOSTER, S. actor CDP

FOSTER, Sidney (d 1870) equestrian? actor? EA/71*

FOSTER, Stephen Collins (1826-64) American composer CDP, DAB, HAS, HJD, WWA/H

FOSTER, Thomas Cooke (d 1891 [78]) critic, journalist EA/92*

FOSTER, Vivian [Foster Hall] English humorist, ventriloquist, conjuror GRB/1

FOSTER, Mrs. W. see Lauri, Charlotte

FOSTER, William Miles (b 1811) American actor HAS

FOSTER, W. M. (d 1872) conductor EA/74*

FOSTER, Mrs. W. M. (d 1869) EA/70*

FOSTER, Mrs. W. M. see White, Mrs. Cool

FOTHERGILL, Edwin Frederick (d 1903 [64]) music-hall comedian EA/04*

FOTTERAL, James Irish actor TD/1-2

FOUCART, M. (d 1896) balloonist EA/97*

FOUCH, Richard (fl 1631) actor DA

FOULDS, J. E. (d 1892) musician EA/93*

FOULGER, Byron (d 1970 [70]) performer BP/54*

FOULKROD, Emily Virginia (fl 1852-57) American dancer HAS

FOUNTAIN, John (d c. 1669) English? dramatist CP/1-3, GT

FOUNTAIN, Joseph (d 1887 [60]) scene artist EA/88*

FOURREY, Robert see Dhery, Robert

FOWKES, Conrad (b 1933) American actor TW/23-24, 26-28

FOWLER, Bruce (d 1973 [80]) producer/director/choreographer BP/58*

FOWLER, Edward (d 1883) actor EA/85*

FOWLER, Eliza (d 1896) EA/98*

FOWLER, Elsie (d 1916) performer? EA/17*

FOWLER, Emily [Mrs. John C. Pemberton] (1849-96) English actress CDP, DD, OAA/1-2

FOWLER, Gene (1890-1960) American dramatist BE*

FOWLER, Gertrude (d 1935 [42]) actress BE*, BP/19*

FOWLER, Henry J. (d 1899) actor? EA/00*

FOWLER, Manly B. (fl 1821?) American? dramatist EAP, RJ

FOWLER, Mrs. Montague [Ada

Dayrell] (d 1911) dramatist
EA/12*

FOWLER, Richard (d 1643) English actor DA, OC/1-3

FOWLER, William (d 1871 [25])
musician EA/72*

FOWLES, Derek (b 1937) English actor TW/20

FOWLIE, Wallace (b 1908) American educator, writer BE

FOX, Mr. (fl 1797-99) actor
HAS

FOX, Mr. (d 1803) actor TD/2

FOX, Adèle [Mrs. C. H. Fox]
(d 1896 [33]) EA/97*

FOX, Caroline see Howard,
Mrs. George Cunnibell

FOX, Mrs. C. H. see Fox,
Adèle

FOX, Charles, Sr. (d 1882)
scene artist EA/83*

FOX, Charles (d 1888) music-hall artist EA/89*

FOX, Charles (d 1893) manager
EA/94*

FOX, Charles H. (1828-64)
American comedian, musician
CDP, HAS

FOX, Charles H. (d 1893 [35])
perruquier EA/94*, WWT/
14*

FOX, Mrs. Charles James see
Armstead, Mrs.

FOX, Charles Kemble (1833-75)
American actor, manager
CDP, DAB, HAS, OC/1-3,
SR, WWA/H

FOX, Colin (b 1938) Canadian
actor TW/25

FOX, Della [Mrs. J. Levy]
(1871/72-1913) American actress, singer GRB/2-4, SR,
WWA/1, WWS, WWT/1

FOX, Eddie (b 1848) minstrel,
composer CDP

FOX, Eleanor Byrne see Allenby, Peggy

FOX, Emma [Mrs. Thompson]
(d 1893) EA/94*

FOX, Ernest singer, minstrel
CDP

FOX, Franklyn (d 1967 [73])
actor TW/24

FOX, Fred (d 1913 [51]) EA/14*

FOX, Frederick (b 1910) American designer BE, ES, TW/3-8, WWT/10-15

FOX, George (d 1902 [54]) com-

poser, singer DD

FOX, George Washington Lafayette
(1825-77) American actor CDP,
COC, DAB, DD, HAS, OC/1-3,
WWA/H

FOX, Gilbert (1776-1807?) English
actor, singer DAB, WWA/H

FOX, Harry (d 1876) music-hall
chairman EA/77*

FOX, Harry (d 1959 [77]) vaudevillian TW/16

FOX, Mrs. Harry (d 1872) EA/
73*

FOX, Herbert Henry (d 1916) EA/
17*

FOX, Imro (d 1910 [60]) EA/11*

FOX, James (1843-87) American
comedian NYM

FOX, James A. (b 1827) American
actor HAS

FOX, Janet American actress
TW/6, 23

FOX, John, Jr. (fl 1890s-1900s)
writer WWM

FOX, John S. (d 1881) comedian
EA/82*

FOX, Joseph (b 1852) comedian,
minstrel CDP

FOX, Mary H. [née Mary Hewins]
(b 1842) American actress HAS

FOX, Melvin J. (d 1968 [53])
theatre owner BP/52*

FOX, Phil (d 1972) performer
BP/56*

FOX, Mrs. Polly see Phillips,
Mabel

FOX, Robin (1913-71) English producer WWT/14

FOX, Sidney (1910-42) American
actress CB, WWT/7-9

FOX, Stuart (d 1951 [57]) American
performer BE*, BP/36*

FOX, W. (d 1891) athlete EA/92*

FOX, Will H. (b 1858) American
vaudevillian WWM

FOX, Mrs. Will H. (d 1902 [33])
EA/03*

FOX, William (b 1911) Philippino/
English actor WWT/8-16

FOXWORTH, Robert (b 1941)
American actor TW/28

FOY, Bertha variety artist CDP

FOY, Eddie [Eddie Fitzgerald]
(1854/56-1928) American actor
COC, DAB, GRB/3, OC/1-3,
SR, WWA/1, WWM, WWS,
WWT/1-5

FOY, Eddie, Jr. (b 1905) Ameri-

can actor, dancer BE, TW/2-
19, WWT/15-16
FOY, Ida variety artist CDP
FOY, Richard (d 1947 [42]) vaude-
villian, manager TW/3
FOY, Tom (d 1917 [51]) comedian
EA/18*
FOY SISTERS see Foy, Bertha;
Foy, Ida
FRACCI, Carla (b 1936) Italian
dancer CB, ES
FRAGANZA, Trixie see Friganza,
Trixie
FRAGSON, Harry [Harry Potts]
(1869-1913) English variety
artist, composer COC, ES,
GRB/1-4, OC/1-3
FRAINE, Mr. CDP
FRAME, Mrs. W. F. (d 1890)
EA/91*
FRAMPTON, Charles H. (d 1911
[63]) scene artist EA/12*
FRAMPTON, Eleanor (d 1973
[77]) performer BP/58*
FRAMPTON, Mrs. F. see
Frampton, M. K. P.
FRAMPTON, Fred (d 1884 [68])
manager, pantomimist, ballet
master, dancer EA/85*,
WWT/14*
FRAMPTON, M. K. P. [Mrs. F.
Frampton] (d 1896 [83]) EA/
97*
FRANCA, Celia (b 1921) English
dancer, choreographer CB,
ES
FRANCE, Mrs. (fl 1853) actress
HAS
FRANCE, Abbie (d 1907) EA/08*
FRANCE, Alexis (b 1906) Rhode-
sian actress WWT/8-14
FRANCE, Alf (d 1917) EA/18*
FRANCE, Anna see Wheelock,
Mrs. J. F.
FRANCE, Caesar (d 1890 [67])
professor of music EA/91*
FRANCE, Charles Vernon (1868-
1949) English actor GRB/3-4,
WWT/1-10
FRANCE, Charlotte see Hale,
Mrs. Charles B.
FRANCE, Mrs. Frank H. see
Clinton, Ella
FRANCE, Marie see Brady,
Mrs. James
FRANCE, Richard (b 1930) Amer-
ican actor, singer, dancer,
choreographer BE, TW/10,

12, 20-23, 25
FRANCE, Shirley Henry (1839-79)
English actor, prompter HAS
FRANCE, Sidney C. (1838-95)
actor, dramatist CDP
FRANCE, Thomas (d 1909 [77])
EA/10*
FRANCI, Benvenuto (b 1891)
Italian singer ES
FRANCIA, Leopoldo (b 1875)
Italian singer GRB/1
FRANCINE, Anne (b 1917) Ameri-
can actress, singer BE, TW/
2, 10-11, 25-26
FRANCIOSA, Anthony [né Papaleo]
(b 1928) American actor BE,
CB, ES, TW/12-15
FRANCIS (fl 1792) dramatist
CP/3, GT, TD/1-2
FRANCIS, Mrs. (d 1911 [78])
circus proprietor EA/12*
FRANCIS, Alfred (b 1909) English
manager WWT/15-16
FRANCIS, Ann (d 1800) translator
CP/3
FRANCIS, Arlene (b 1908) Ameri-
can actress BE, CB, TW/1-7,
10-16, 21-23, 30, WWT/10-16
FRANCIS, Dick (d 1949 [59])
comedian BE*, WWT/14*
FRANCIS, Doris (b 1903) English
actress, singer WWT/10
FRANCIS, Edmonstone (d 1880
[41]) actor, acting manager
EA/81*
FRANCIS, Emma (d 1889 [15])
EA/90*
FRANCIS, Gerald G. (b 1950)
American actor TW/28-30
FRANCIS, Harry (d 1901) Negro
comedian EA/02*
FRANCIS, Ivor (b 1918) Canadian
actor TW/23
FRANCIS, Jack (d 1917) EA/18*
FRANCIS, James (d 1886 [46])
minstrel proprietor, singer
CDP
FRANCIS, James (d 1897 [67])
actor EA/98*
FRANCIS, Mrs. James see
Francis, Mary Ann
FRANCIS, Mrs. James A. see
Francis, Louisa
FRANCIS, Jane F. (d 1876 [41])
actress? EA/77*
FRANCIS, Jean (b 1923) American
actress TW/25
FRANCIS, J. O. (d 1956 [74])

Welsh dramatist BE*, WWT/
14*

FRANCIS, John (d 1893) musician
EA/94*

FRANCIS, Kay (1899/1905-1968)
American actress ES, TW/
2-7, 25, WWA/5, WWT/7-13

FRANCIS, Louisa [Mrs. James
A. Francis] (d 1894 [27])
EA/95*

FRANCIS, Mary Ann [Mrs. James
Francis] (d 1881 [40]) EA/82*

FRANCIS, M. E. (d 1930 [72])
Irish dramatist WWT/1-6

FRANCIS, Nelson (b 1852) English manager GRB/1-2

FRANCIS, Philip (d 1773) Irish
dramatist CP/2-3, DD, GT,
TD/1-2

FRANCIS, Robert (d 1955 [25])
actor BE*

FRANCIS, Virginia see Bateman, Virginia Francis

FRANCIS, W. (d 1892) aerial
performer EA/93*

FRANCIS, William (d 1826 [69])
English dancer, circus performer? actor CDP, HAS

FRANCIS, William (d 1908 [62])
performer? EA/09*

FRANCIS, Mrs. William (d 1834)
English actress? circus performer? CDP, HAS

FRANCIS, Mrs. William (d 1888)
EA/89*

FRANCISQUY, Mons. (fl 1796)
French dancer HAS

FRANCK, C. Harry (b 1844)
American actor HAS

FRANCK, Celestine (fl 1850-51)
dancer HAS

FRANCK, Henry (d 1880 [28])
actor? EA/81*

FRANCK, Victorine (fl 1850-51)
dancer HAS

FRANCKIN, Mrs. Robert see
Elinore, May

FRANCKLIN, Dr. Thomas (1721-
84) dramatist CP/2-3, DD,
GT, TD/1-2

FRANCKS, Don (b 1932) Canadian
actor TW/22, 25

FRANCOIS, Annie (d 1878) tight-
rope artist EA/79*

FRANCONI [John Measey] (d 1894)
EA/95*

FRANCONI, Henri Adolphe (b
1801) equestrian CDP

FRANCONI, Laurent (1776-1849)
circus owner, equestrian CDP

FRANK, Mrs. Alec F. see
Denzil, Madge

FRANK, Arlyne (b 1930) American
singer, actress BE

FRANK, Bruno (1887-1945) German
dramatist COC, OC/1-3, WWT/
8

FRANK, Carl (d 1972 [63]) actor
TW/29

FRANK, Dorothy [or Dottie] (b
1942) American actress TW/
26, 28, 30

FRANK, Jim American actor
TW/28

FRANK, John C. (d 1910) EA/11*

FRANK, Judy (b 1936) American
actress TW/24

FRANK, Marvin (d 1974 [48])
publicist BP/58*

FRANK, Mary K. (b 1911) American producer BE

FRANKAU, Aline see Bernstein,
Aline

FRANKAU, Ronald (1894-1951)
English actor, entertainer
WWT/10-11

FRANKEL, Benjamin (d 1973
[67]) composer/lyricist BP/57*

FRANKEL, Gene (b 1923) American director ES, WWT/15-16

FRANKEL, Kenneth (b 1941) American actor TW/23

FRANKEL, Lou (d 1974 [63])
journalist BP/59*

FRANKEN, Rose (b 1895/98)
American dramatist, producer
CB, MD, MWD, WWT/10-11

FRANKENBERG, Lloyd F. (d
1975 [67]) critic BP/59*

FRANKENHEIMER, John (b 1930)
American director CB

FRANKFORT MOORE, Grace (d
1901) EA/02*

FRANKISS, Betty (b 1912) English
actress, singer WWT/9-13

FRANKLEIN, Lucy (d 1903 [59])
singer EA/04*

FRANKLIN, Mr. actor CDP

FRANKLIN, Alberta (d 1976 [79])
performer BP/60*

FRANKLIN, Andrew (fl 1785-1804)
Irish dramatist CP/3, DD,
GT, TD/1

FRANKLIN, Benjamin F. (d 1963
[88]) minstrel BE*

FRANKLIN, Bonnie (b 1944)

American actress TW/26-30
FRANKLIN, Clara (fl 1889?)
 singer CDP
FRANKLIN, Daniel (b 1940) American actor TW/23, 25
FRANKLIN, Frederic (b 1914) English dancer CB, ES
FRANKLIN, Gertrude singer CDP
FRANKLIN, Mrs. H. (d 1874 [43]) EA/75*
FRANKLIN, Harold B. (1890-1941) American manager WWT/8
FRANKLIN, Henry (d 1877 [62]) advance agent EA/78*
FRANKLIN, Hugh (b 1916) American actor TW/4, 22-24, 26, 28-29
FRANKLIN, Irene (1876-1941) American actress CB, SR, WWT/7-9
FRANKLIN, J. C. (d 1879) American pantomimist EA/80*
FRANKLIN, Lidija (b 1922) Russian actress TW/3-4
FRANKLIN, Nancy American actress TW/26-27
FRANKLIN, Nony (d 1965 [40]) performer BP/50*
FRANKLIN, Roger American actor TW/25
FRANKLIN, William (b 1906) American actor TW/2
FRANKLYN, Beth (d 1956 [83]) actress TW/12
FRANKLYN, Charles (d 1891 [39]) stage manager EA/92*
FRANKLYN, Irwin (d 1966 [62]) publicist, actor TW/23
FRANKLYN, Leo (1897-1975) English actor AAS, WWT/9-15
FRANKLYN-LYNCH, Grace (fl 1893-1907) American actress WWS
FRANKS, Mrs. Arthur B. see Hunt, Maggie
FRANKS, Hannah Louisa (d 1892 [28]) EA/93*
FRANKS, Jerry (d 1971 [63]) producer/director/choreographer BP/56*
FRANKS, Laurie (b 1929) American actress TW/25-26
FRANKS, Leo W. (d 1968 [62]) performer BP/52*
FRANKS, Lorraine (d 1976 [58]) producer/director/choreographer BP/60*

FRANKS, Ollie (d 1976 [56]) performer BP/60*
FRANKS, Percy (d 1976 [83]) performer BP/60*
FRANKS, Sydney [Frank Sylvester] (d 1900 [58]) actor, singer CDP
FRANKS, Wilfred (b 1872) English manager, business manager, stage manager GRB/1-4
FRANMORE, Ida (d 1913) EA/14*
FRANZ, Adele American literary representative BE
FRANZ, Eduard (b 1902) American actor TW/1-4, 14-15, 23, 25-26, WWT/16
FRANZ, Joy (b 1944) American actress TW/29-30
FRARY, Mrs. (fl 1848) English actress HAS
FRASCA, Mary (d 1973) performer BP/58*
FRASCHINI, Gaetano (d 1887 [72]) singer EA/88*
FRASER, Agnes [Mrs. Walter Passmore] (d 1968 [90]) Scottish actress GRB/1-4, WWT/1-6
FRASER, Alec (1884-1956) Scottish actor, singer WWT/4-9
FRASER, Bill (b 1908) Scottish actor WWT/11-16
FRASER, Claude Lovat (1890-1921) English artist, stage designer COC, DNB, ES, OC/1-3, PDT
FRASER, Constance (d 1973 [63]) performer BP/57*
FRASER, Eddie (d 1972 [61]) producer/director/choreographer BP/56*
FRASER, Fred (d 1879 [63]) actor, scene artist EA/80*
FRASER, Mrs. John see Vincent, Ruth
FRASER, John James see Frazer, John James
FRASER, Kate [The Little Wonder] (d 1868 [18]) EA/69*
FRASER, Keith (d 1915 [41]) actor WWT/14*
FRASER, Lovat (b 1908) Scottish manager WWT/11-13
FRASER, Lydia [Lydia Bashall] (d 1898) actress EA/99*
FRASER, Margaret Campbell actress GRB/1-2
FRASER, Marie (fl 1886-91) actress DD

FRASER, Moyra (b 1923) Australian actress, dancer WWT/12-16

FRASER, Robert (d 1878 [45]) singer EA/79*

FRASER, Robert (1842-96) actor, dramatist CDP, SR

FRASER, Shelagh English actress WWT/15-16

FRASER, Winifred [Mrs. George R. Foss; née Exton] (b 1868/72) English actress DD, GRB/2-4, WWT/1-7

FRASER-BRUNNER, Queenie [Lizzie Webb] English actress GRB/1

FRASER-SIMSON, Harold (1878-1944) English composer WWT/4-9

FRATELLINI, Paul (d 1940) clown CB

FRATTI, Mario (b 1927) Italian/American dramatist, educator CD, MWD

FRAUNCE, Abraham (fl 1590-91) dramatist CP/1-3

FRAWLEY, T. Daniel (1864-1936) American actor, manager SR

FRAWLEY, William (1893-1966) American actor, singer, dancer TW/22, WWA/4

FRAYN, Michael (b 1933) English dramatist AAS, CD, WWT/16

FRAYNE, Frank (fl 1870-90) dramatist, manager SR

FRAYNE, Frankie marksman CDP

FRAYNE, Frank Ives (1836-91) actor, marksman CDP

FRAYNE, Mrs. Frank Ives markswoman CDP

FRAYNE, Matthew (d 1887) actor EA/88*

FRAYNE, Viola actress TW/1

FRAZEE, Harry Herbert (1880-1929) American manager WWA/1, WWT/4-5

FRAZER, E. see Rogers, E.

FRAZER, Henry (d 1892 [70]) actor EA/93*

FRAZER, I. J. (fl 1844) singer CDP

FRAZER, John J[ames] (d 1863 [59]) actor, singer CDP

FRAZIER, Charlotte (b 1939) American actress TW/27

FRAZIER, Mattie see Herndon, Agnes

FREAR, "Billy" (d 1888) American minstrel EA/90*

FREAR, Fred (fl 1879-1908) American actor WWS

FREDA, Mlle. (d 1917) EA/18*

FREDERIC, Mme. see Birt, Miss S.

FREDERICI, Blanche (d 1933 [55]) actress BE*, WWT/14*

FREDERICI, Mme. Himmer (fl 1864) singer HAS

FREDERICK [Antoine-Louis-Prosper Lemaître] (1800-76) French actor COC

FREDERICK, Helena (d 1926 [44]) prima donna BE*, BP/11*

FREDERICK, James (d 1888) EA/89*

FREDERICK, Pauline (1884/85-1938) American actress, singer ES, GRB/3-4, SR, WWA/1, WWM, WWS, WWT/1-8

FREDERICK, Walter (d 1885) actor EA/86*

FREDERICKS, Mons. (fl 1845) dancer HAS

FREDERICKS, Albert (d 1901 [61]) proprietor BE*, EA/02*, WWT/14*

FREDERICKS, Charles (1918-70) American actor, singer TW/2, 4-8, 26

FREDERICKS, Emily [Mrs. Fred Fredericks] (d 1901 [61]) EA/02*

FREDERICKS, Mrs. F. see Vaul, Polly

FREDERICKS, Fred [F. L. O'Leary] (d 1894) actor? EA/95*

FREDERICKS, Fred (d 1939 [75]) producer, manager BE*, WWT/14*

FREDERICKS, Mrs. Fred see Fredericks, Emily

FREDERICKS, George (d 1891 [45]) music-hall performer EA/92*

FREDERICKS, Louise (d 1870) dancer EA/71*

FREDERICKS, Sam (d 1922 [46]) producer, manager BE*, WWT/14*

FREDERICKS, W. H. (d 1897) manager EA/98*

FREDERICKS, William Hamlet (d 1897 [27]) actor? EA/98*

FREDERICKS, William Sheridan

(1799-1878) Irish actor CDP, HAS

FREDMAN, Alice (d 1950 [71]) founder of theatre societies BE*, WWT/14*

FREDRIK, Burry (b 1925) American producer, stage manager, director BE

FREDRO, Aleksander (1793-1876) Polish dramatist COC, OC/3

FREE, John (fl 1757) dramatist CP/3

FREEAR, Albert (d 1905) minstrel comedian EA/06*

FREEAR, Charles Thomas Wood (d 1906 [59]) entertainer EA/07*

FREEAR, Harriett [Mrs. Charles T. W. Freear] (d 1893) EA/94*

FREEAR, Louie (1871/73-1939) English actress CDP, COC, DD, GRB/1-4, WWT/1-8

FREE BERTHYSER, Dora (d 1867) dancer HAS

FREEBORN, Cassius (d 1954 [76]) composer, musical director BE*

FREECE, Mrs. de (d 1881 [78]) EA/82*

FREED, Mr. dramatist RJ

FREED, Arthur (d 1973 [78]) composer/lyricist, producer/director/choreographer BP/57*

FREED, Barboura M. (d 1975 [43]) performer BP/60*

FREED, Bert (b 1919) American actor TW/2, 4

FREED, Fred (d 1974 [53]) producer/director/choreographer BP/58*

FREED, Isadore (1900-60) Russian/American composer WWA/4

FREED, Sam (b 1948) American actor TW/30

FREEDLEY, George Reynolds (1904-67) American historian AAS, BE, CB, COC, ES, NTH, OC/2-3, WWT/10-14

FREEDLEY, Vinton (1891-1969) American managing producer, actor BE, NTH, TW/3-8, 26, WWA/5, WWT/6-14

FREEDMAN, Bill (b 1929) Canadian producing manager WWT/16

FREEDMAN, Gerald (b 1927)

American director, producer, composer, dramatist WWT/16

FREEDMAN, Harold (d 1966 [69]) Scottish literary representative BE

FREEDMAN, Leonore (d 1964) actress BE*

FREEDMAN, Zac (d 1968 [61]) publicist BP/52*

FREEHOLD, The theatre collective CD

FREEL, Alira (d 1935 [28]) American actress BE*, BP/20*

FREELAND, Frank [Joseph Mulligan] (b 1847) English actor, singer GRB/1

FREELAND, Joseph (d 1909 [61]) manager EA/10*

FREELAND, Louie (d 1910) actress EA/11*

FREEMAN, Al, Jr. (b 1934) American actor TW/25-26, 29-30, WWT/16

FREEMAN, Ann [Mrs. Harry Freeman] (d 1885 [25]) EA/86*

FREEMAN, Ann English actress TW/24, 27

FREEMAN, Arny (b 1908) American actor TW/22-24, 26, 28-30, WWT/16

FREEMAN, Charles (d 1881) proprietor EA/82*

FREEMAN, Charles J. (d 1964 [82]) agent BE*

FREEMAN, Charles K. (b 1900/05) English critic, director BE, TW/2, 4

FREEMAN, David (b 1945) Canadian dramatist CD

FREEMAN, Edward Urquhart (d 1902) musical director EA/03*

FREEMAN, Elijah (d 1887 [70]) lion-tamer EA/88*

FREEMAN, Frances (b 1923) American actress TW/5

FREEMAN, Frank (1892-1962) English actor WWT/6-7

FREEMAN, H. A. (d 1929) producer, manager BE*, WWT/14*

FREEMAN, Harry actor, singer CDP

FREEMAN, Mrs. Harry see Freeman, Ann

FREEMAN, Henry Charles (d 1887) scene artist EA/88*

FREEMAN, Howard (d 1967) American actor, director BE,

TW/24

FREEMAN, Isabella (fl 1860) American actress, reader HAS

FREEMAN, Leonard (d 1974 [53]) producer/director/choreographer BP/58*

FREEMAN, Mark (fl 1733) English dramatist CP/2-3

FREEMAN, Max (d 1912) German actor, stage manager WWS

FREEMAN, Morgan (b 1937) American actor TW/24, 26, 28

FREEMAN, Ralph (d 1655) dramatist CP/1-3, DD, FGF

FREEMAN, Stella (1910-36) English actress WWT/6-8

FREEMAN, Thomas (d 1874 [60]) costumier EA/75*

FREEMAN, Valdo Lee (d 1972 [72]) producer/director/choreographer BP/57*

FREEMANTLE, George (d 1894) musical director EA/95*

FREER, Charles (d 1857 [55]) Maltese actor CDP, DD, HAS

FREER, John Charles see Freer, Charles

FREESE, Marie (d 1905) EA/06*

FREE SOUTHERN THEATRE, The theatre collective CD

FREEZER, Herbert J. (d 1963 [61]) investor BE*

FREGOLI, Leopold (d 1936 [69]) Protean artist BE*, WWT/14*

FREIMAN, Louis (d 1967 [75]) actor, dramatist TW/23

FREITAG, Dorothea (b 1914) American composer, arranger, musical director BE

FREMAN, Maurice (d 1912) German/American actor, stage manager, director SR

FREMSTAD, Olive (d 1951 [83]) Swedish singer CDP, TW/7, WWA/3, WWM

FRENCH, Col. see French, Mjr.

FRENCH, Mjr. (fl 18th cent) actor CDP

FRENCH, Anne Warner see Warner, Anne

FRENCH, Arthur American actor TW/24-30

FRENCH, Arthur W., III (b 1965) American actor TW/28

FRENCH, Bruce (b 1945) American actor TW/28

FRENCH, David (b 1939) Canadian dramatist, actor CD

FRENCH, Edie [Mrs. Edith Smith] (d 1902) music-hall performer EA/03*

FRENCH, Eleanor (d 1975 [59]) performer BP/59*

FRENCH, Elizabeth (d 1913) EA/14*

FRENCH, Elizabeth English actress, singer WWT/10-13

FRENCH, Elsie actress WWT/7-12

FRENCH, Eva (fl 1883?) actress CDP

FRENCH, Fred (d 1899 [68]) comic singer, actor CDP

FRENCH, Mrs. Fred see French, Mary Ann

FRENCH, George (d 1911 [65]) proprietor EA/12*

FRENCH, G. H. (d 1873) actor EA/74*

FRENCH, Harold (b 1897/1900) English actor, producer, director AAS, WWT/4-16

FRENCH, Henri, the Great (b 1876) Belgian vaudevillian WWM

FRENCH, Herbert C. (d 1924 [33]) dancer, director BE*, BP/8*

FRENCH, Hermene [née Hermine Camelinat] (b 1924) English actress, dancer, singer WWT/11-13

FRENCH, Hugh (b 1910) English actor, singer WWT/10-11

FRENCH, James Murphy (d 1758) dramatist CP/3

FRENCH, La Verne (b 1923) American actor TW/6-7

FRENCH, Lena G. actress CDP

FRENCH, Leslie (b 1904) English actor, singer, dancer, director AAS, WWT/7-16

FRENCH, Lizzie (d 1911) EA/12*

FRENCH, Marie (d 1918) EA/19*

FRENCH, Mary Amelia [Mrs. Samuel French] (d 1887 [60]) EA/88*

FRENCH, Mary Ann [Mrs. Fred French] (d 1904 [75]) EA/05*

FRENCH, Minnie (d 1899) actress CDP

FRENCH, Park M. (d 1974 [93]) designer BP/58*

FRENCH, Pauline American actress GRB/1, WWS
FRENCH, Samuel (d 1898 [76]) publisher DD
FRENCH, Mrs. Samuel see French, Mary Amelia
FRENCH, Stanley J. (1908-64) English business manager, producing manager WWT/ 10-13
FRENCH, Sydney (d 1878 [42]?) dramatist, critic DD
FRENCH, T. Henry (d 1902) producer, publisher, manager BE*, WWT/14*
FRENCH, Tom see Leak, Thomas
FRENCH, Valerie [née Harrison] (b 1932) English actress TW/ 22-23, 25, 27, 30, WWT/15-16
FRENCH, Windsor B., II (d 1973 [68]) critic BP/57*
FRENCH GIANT (b 1800?) CDP
FRENCH OPERA TROUPE (fl 1845) HAS
FRENI, Mirella (b 1935) Italian singer ES
FRERE, Gladys Bartle English actress GRB/1
FRERE, John Hookham (1769-1846) translator DD
FRESNAY, Pierre [Pierre Laudenbach] (1897-1975) French actor, director BE, CB, PDT, WWT/ 8-14
FREUD, Sigmund (1856-1939) Austrian psychologist NTH
FREUND, John C. (b 1848) English dramatist WWM
FREUND, John Lincoln see Forsythe, John
FREUND, Kim (b 1955) American actress TW/24
FREY, Leonard (b 1938) American actor TW/28, 30
FREY, Nathaniel (1913-70) American actor BE, TW/8-13, 15, 19, 21-24, 27, WWT/14-15
FREYERBOTT, Bartholomeus (fl 1615) actor DA
FREZZOLINI, Ermine (1818-84) Italian singer CDP, ES, HAS
FRIAS, Duchess de see Balfe, Victoria
FRIEBUS, Florida (b 1909) American actress, dramatist BE, TW/5, 22

FRIED, Walter (1910-75) American producer, manager BE, TW/ 3, 6-7
FRIEDBERG, Dr. Charles K. (d 1972 [64]) dramatist BP/57*
FRIEDERICH, W. J. (b 1916) American educator, director BE
FRIEDLAND, Anatole (1888-1938) Russian composer, performer BE*
FRIEDLANDER, Jane (b 1939) American producer BE
FRIEDLANDER, William B. (d 1968 [83]) dramatist, composer, producing manager TW/24, WWT/6-11
FRIEDMAN, Bruce Jay (b 1930) American dramatist, director CD
FRIEDMAN, Leo B. producer BE
FRIEDMAN, Leon (b 1872) American agent WWM
FRIEDMAN, Lillian see Weber, Mrs. Joe
FRIEDMAN, Max (d 1964 [76]) songwriter, performer BE*, BP/49*
FRIEDMAN, Phil (d 1974 [83]) producer/director/choreographer BP/58*
FRIEDMAN, Phil (b 1921) American business manager BE
FRIEDMAN, Samuel J. (1912-74) American press representative BE, TW/30
FRIEDMANN, Shraga (d 1970 [47]) performer BP/55*
FRIEL, Brian (b 1929) Irish dramatist CB, CD, MWD, RE, WWT/15-16
FRIEND, Cliff (d 1974 [80]) composer/lyricist BP/59*
FRIEND, Philip (b 1915) English actor TW/8
FRIEND, Violet (d 1906) actress, singer, manager CDP
FRIEND, Wilton (d 1912 [76]) music-hall manager EA/13*, WWT/14*
FRIENDLY, Dan (d 1972 [59]) treasurer BP/56*
FRIERSON, Monte L. (b 1930) American manager, producer BE
FRIES, Helen Warnow (d 1970 [44]) performer BP/55*
FRIES, Mrs. Wulf [née Gann]

(d 1853) actress? HAS
FRIESEN, Norman actor TW/23
FRIGANZA, Trixie [Delia O'Cal-
laghan] (1870-1955) American
actress, singer GRB/2-4,
TW/11, WWM, WWS, WWT/
1-9
FRIMBLEY, Frederick (d 1871)
actor? EA/72*
FRIMBLY, Mr. actor CDP
FRIML, Charles Rudolf (1879/
81/84-1972) Czech composer
AAS, BE, PDT, TW/29,
WWA/5, WWT/4-14
FRINGS, Ketti [née Katherine
Hartley] American dramatist
BE
FRINK, Robert (b 1937) American
actor TW/25
FRISBIE, Noah, Jr. (b 1758)
American dramatist EAP
FRISBY, Terence (b 1932) Eng-
lish actor, director, dramatist
AAS, CD, WWT/15-16
FRISCH, Albert (d 1976 [60])
composer/lyricist BP/60*
FRISCH, Max Rudolf (b 1911)
Swiss dramatist BE, CB,
COC, MWD, OC/3, WWT/
14-16
FRISCO, Joe (d 1958 [68]) vaude-
villian TW/15
FRISWELL, Hain (d 1878) co-
founder of Urban Club EA/79*
FRITCH, Letitia Louise singer
CDP
FRITH, Edward (d 1875 [38])
music-hall lessee EA/76*
FRITH, J. Leslie (1889-1961)
English actor, dramatist
WWT/10-13
FRITH, Mary (fl 1610) DA
FRITH, Walter (d 1941) English
dramatist DD, WWW/4
FRITSCH, Willy (d 1973 [72])
performer BP/58*
FRITSCHY, Walter A. (d 1972
[91]) producer/director/chore-
ographer BP/57*
FRITZ, Mrs. Edward (d 1883
[36]) EA/85*
FRITZ, Jack (d 1901) music-hall
performer EA/02*
FRIZZELL, William Orville (d
1975 [47]) performer BP/60*
FRODSHAM, Bridge (1734-68)
English actor CDP, DD,
DNB

FROELICH, William J. (d 1963
[60]) American performer BE*
FROGGATT, R. H. (d 1877 [45])
musician EA/78*
FROHMAN, Bert (d 1974 [74])
performer BP/59*
FROHMAN, Charles (1860-1915)
American manager CDP, COC,
DAB, DD, ES, GRB/1-4, HJD,
NTH, OC/1-3, SR, WWA/1,
WWM, WWS, WWT/1-2, WWW/1
FROHMAN, Daniel (1850/51/53-
1940) American manager CB,
CDP, COC, DAB, DD, ES,
GRB/2-4, HJD, NTH, OC/1-3,
SR, WWA/1, WWM, WWS,
WWT/1-9
FROHMAN, Gustave (1855-1930)
American manager COC, OC/
1-3
FROME, Barbara (d 1976 [54])
performer BP/60*
FROME, Lawrence (d 1916) EA/
17*
FROME, Samuel Blake (fl 1809)
dramatist? librettist? lyricist?
CP/3
FRONANI, Angelo (d 1918 [44])
EA/19*
FROSCH, Aaron R. (b 1924) Amer-
ican lawyer BE
FROST, Alice American actress
TW/12-13
FROST, Edith [Mrs. H. L. War-
ren] American actress WWM
FROST, Henry see Forrester,
Henry
FROST, Mrs. J. C. (fl 1852) ac-
tress HAS
FROST, John (fl 1600) actor DA
FROWDE, Philip (d 1738) drama-
tist CP/1-3, DD, DNB, GT,
TD/1-2
FRUIN, J. J. (d 1907 [44]) secre-
tary of Music Hall Home EA/
08*
FRY, Charles (d 1928 [83]) per-
former, director BE*, WWT/
14*
FRY, Christopher [né Harris] (b
1907) English dramatist, direc-
tor, actor AAS, BE, CB, CD,
CH, COC, ES, GT, MD, MH,
MWD, NTH, OC/1-3, PDT,
WWT/11-16
FRY, Horace (d 1942 [67]) business
manager WWT/14*
FRY, Ray (b 1923) American actor

TW/24-30.
FRY, Roy H. (d 1905) actor EA/
06*
FRY, William Henry (1815-64)
American composer DAB,
WWA/H
FRYER, J. C. manager CDP
FRYER, Peg (fl late 17th &
early 18th cents) actress DD
FRYER, Robert (b 1920) American
producer BE, WWT/14-16
FRYERS, Austin (fl 1883-99)
dramatist DD
FUCHS, Dick (b 1944) American
actor TW/28-29
FUCHS, Leo (b 1911) Polish actor
BE, TW/30
FUCHS, Theodore (b 1904) Amer-
ican educator BE
FUDGE, Alan (b 1944) American
actor TW/24-25
FUE, Charles (d 1965 [80]) drama-
tist BP/50*
FUELL, Emelia [Milly Seymour;
Mrs. J. C. Fuell] (d 1878) ac-
tress EA/79*
FUELL, J. C. (d 1882) EA/83*
FUELL, Mrs. J. C. see Fuell,
Emelia
FUERHEERD, Josephine B. (d
1976 [84]) performer BP/60*
FUERTES, Dolores Adios see
Menken, Adah Isaacs
FUGARD, Athol (b 1932) South
African dramatist, actor, di-
rector AAS, CB, CD, WWT/
15-16
FUJI-KO (1883-1912) Japanese
dancer, pantomimist WWM
FULCHER, Florence (d 1917 [25])
singer EA/18*
FULDA, Dr. Ludwig (1862-1939)
German dramatist DD, GRB/
1, 3-4
FULFORD, David (b 1925) Amer-
ican director, actor, producer
BE
FULLAM, Michael (d 1825) actor
CDP
FULLER, Mr. (fl 1838) American
actor HAS
FULLER, Alfred (d 1844 [37])
clown EA/72*
FULLER, Ben (d 1894) diver
EA/95*
FULLER, Sir Benjamin John (b
1875) English manager WWT/
5-9

FULLER, Caroline Macomber (b
1873) American dramatist
WWA/5
FULLER, Dean (b 1922) American
composer, dramatist BE
FULLER, Frances (b 1907/08)
American actress BE, WWT/
9-10
FULLER, Frank (d 1908 [64]) ac-
tor EA/09*
FULLER, Mrs. Frank see
Howard, Constance
FULLER, Isaac (1606-72) English
scene painter COC, OC/1-3
FULLER, John, Sr. (d 1909 [60])
EA/10*
FULLER, John G. (b 1913) Amer-
ican dramatist BE
FULLER, Leslie (d 1948 [57])
comedian BE*, WWT/14*
FULLER, Loie (1870-1928) Amer-
ican actress, dancer CDP,
DAB, DD, ES, GRB/1-4,
WWA/1, WWS, WWT/1-5
FULLER, Margaret Hastings (d
1916 [40]) EA/17*
FULLER, Mollie (d 1933 [68])
American actress BE*
FULLER, Penny (b 1940) American
actress TW/26-28
FULLER, Rosalinde (b 1901) Eng-
lish actress COC, OC/3,
WWT/6-16
FULLERTON, Richard (d 1802)
actor HAS
FULLERTON, William (d 1888)
composer DD
FULLFORD, Mrs. Robert see
Pixley, Annie
FULMER, Ray (b 1933) American
actor TW/14-15
FULTON, Charles J. [Charles
Foss] (1857-1938) English actor
GRB/2-4, WWT/1-5
FULTON, Eileen American ac-
tress, singer BE
FULTON, Mary [Mrs. J. A.
Campbell] actress GRB/1
FULTON, Maude (1881-1950)
American dramatist, actress
TW/7, WWT/5-9
FULTON, Reuben (d 1891 [55])
proprietor EA/92*
FULTON, Richard S. (d 1916)
EA/17*
FULTON, Sarah [Sally D'Angelis]
(d 1882) actress EA/83*
FULWEL, Ulpian (b 1556) English

dramatist CP/1-3, DD, FGF
FUNKE, Lewis (b 1912) American
editor BE
FUQUA, Charles (d 1971 [60])
performer BP/56*
FURBER, Douglas (1885-1961)
English actor, dramatist
WWT/5-13, WWW/6
FURBER, Mrs. Douglas see
Cutler, Peggy
FURBISH, Charles E. (1846-81)
American manager CDP
FURLEY, Shelagh (d 1951) ac-
tress BE*, WWT/14*
FURNESS, Betty (b 1916) Ameri-
can actress CB
FURNESS, Horace Howard (1833-
1912) American critic DD,
HJD, WWA/1, WWM
FURNISS, Grace Livingstone (d
1938 [74]) American dramatist
GRB/3-4, WWM, WWT/1-2
FURNIVAL, Henry [W. Henry
Parr] (b 1862) English actor,
manager GRB/1
FURNIVALL, Frederick James
(1825-1910) English critic DD,
HP, WWW/1
FURR, James (d 1897) equestrian
EA/98*
FURRER, Urs B. (d 1975 [41])
producer/director/choreographer
BP/60*
FURRY, Edna see Hopper,
Hedda
FURSCH-MADI, Amy (d 1894
[46]) singer CDP
FURSE, Douglas (b 1903) English
designer WWT/9
FURSE, Jill (d 1944 [28]) actress
BE*, WWT/14*
FURSE, Judith (1912-74) English
actress, producer WWT/10-14
FURSE, Margaret (d 1974 [63])
designer BP/59*
FURSE, Roger (1903-73) English
designer AAS, ES, WWT/
10-15
FURST, William American drama-
tist DD
FURST, William Wallace (d 1917
[65]) composer BE*
FURTADO, Charles Knox (d 1891)
acting manager EA/92*
FURTADO, Teresa Elizabeth
[Mrs. John Clarke] (1845-77)
actress CDP, DD
FURTH, George actor, dramatist

CD, WWT/16
FURTWANGLER, Wilhelm (1886-
1954) German conductor ES,
WWA/3
FUSSELLE, Kate (d 1911 [50])
singer EA/12*
FYFE, Alexander (fl 1705-09)
dramatist CP/1-3, GT
FYFE, H. Hamilton (1869-1951)
English critic CB, DNB,
GRB/2-4, WWT/1-6, WWW/5
FYFE, Isaac (d 1964) performer
BP/49*
FYFFE, Charles J. (1830-1910)
American actor HAS
FYFFE, Kitty [Amanda Carter]
(fl 1865) comedienne HAS
FYFFE, Will (1885-1947) Scottish
music-hall performer TW/4,
OC/1-3
FYLES, Franklin (1847-1911)
American critic, dramatist
DD, GRB/2-4, SR
FYNE, Elizabeth (d 1913) EA/14*
FYNES, Richard (d 1892) propri-
etor, manager EA/93*

- G -

GABAIN, Dorothy Maude see
Crawford, Dorothy Maude
GABEL, June (b 1945) American
actress TW/25-30
GABEL, Martin (b 1912) American
actor AAS, BE, TW/12-15,
19, 26, WWT/9-16
GABLE, Christopher (b 1940) Eng-
lish dancer ES
GABLE, Clark (1901-60) American
actor CB, ES, TW/17, WWA/
4, WWT/7-10, WWW/5
GABLER, Carl (b 1932) American
actor TW/23
GABOR, Eva (b 1925/26) Hungarian
actress BE, CB, TW/12-14
GABOR, Zsa Zsa (b 1923) Hun-
garian actress TW/27
GABRIEL, Ethel (d 1967 [78])
actress WWT/15*
GABRIEL, Gilbert W. (1890-1952)
American critic NTH, TW/9,
WWT/6-9
GABRIEL, Gus (d 1973 [63]) show-
man BP/58*
GABRIEL, Virginia [Mary Ann
Virginia March] (1825-77) Eng-
lish composer CDP, DD, DNB

GABRIELLI, Caterina (1730-96) Italian singer ES

GABUSSI, Vincenzo (1800-46) Italian singer, singing teacher ES

GACHET, Alice (d 1960) actress, director, teacher BE*, WWT/ 14*

GADD, Renée (b 1908) Argentinian actress, dancer WWT/7-11

GADEMANN, Elsa (b 1881) German actress GRB/4, WWT/ 1-2

GADES, Antonio (b 1936) Spanish dancer, choreographer CB

GADSBY, C. Rivers (d 1961 [73]) actor WWT/14*

GADSBY, Henry R. (d 1907) composer EA/08*

GADSDEN, Lionel (d 1965 [86]) actor WWT/14*

GADSKI, Bertha (d 1907) actress WWT/14*

GADSKI, Johanna (1871-1932) German singer CDP, ES, WWA/1

GAERTNER, Mrs. E. see Daniels, Becky

GAERTNER, Jenny (d 1894) EA/95*

GAFFIGAN, Catherine American actress TW/23

GAFFNEY, Mrs. John see Gaffney, Laura

GAFFNEY, Laura [Mrs. John Gaffney] (d 1903) EA/04*

GAFFNEY, Liam (b 1911) Irish actor WWT/11-14

GAGE, Richard N. (1905-72) American director BE

GAGER, William (fl 1574-1610) dramatist CP/1-3, DD, FGF

GAGLIANO, Frank (b 1931) American dramatist CD, WWT/15-16

GAHAGAN, Helen (b 1900) American actress, singer BE, CB, SR, WWT/5-13

GAIGE, Crosby (1882-1949) American producing manager NTH, TW/5, WWA/2, WWT/ 6-10

GAIGE, Truman [né Stanley Ruhland] American actor BE

GAIL, Zoë [née Zoë Margaret Stapleton] (b 1920) South African actress, dancer WWT/ 10-13

GAINES, Richard American actor TW/9

GAINSBOROUGH, Monta (fl 1869-78) English actress DD, OAA/ 1-2

GAITES, Joseph M. (d 1940 [67]) American producer, director BE*, BP/25*, WWT/14*

GALA, Frank (d 1911 [37]) performer? EA/12*

GALARNO, Bill (b 1938) American actor TW/20

GALDOS, Benito Pedro (b 1845) Spanish dramatist GRB/1, 3-4

GALE, Lieut. (d 1850 [54]) aeronaut EA/72*

GALE, Adeona (1842-61) Irish dancer CDP, HAS

GALE, Chet W. (d 1970 [52]) performer BP/55*

GALE, Florence (b 1881) American actress WWM

GALE, Fred (d 1902 [43]) music-hall performer EA/03*

GALE, George (1800-50) English/ American actor CDP, HAS, SR

GALE, George (fl 1890s?) singer CDP

GALE, Mrs. George (fl 1831-61) actress HAS

GALE, Hannah (1839-61) Irish dancer CDP, HAS

GALE, John (b 1929) English producer WWT/14-16

GALE, Joseph T. (d 1976 [70]) entertainment pioneer BP/60*

GALE, Mrs. J. W. (d 1892) EA/ 93*

GALE, Matilda (d 1880 [75]) EA/ 81*

GALE, Minna [Minna Gale Haynes; Mrs. Archibald C. Haynes] (1867/69-1944?) American actress PP/1, SR, WWA/5, WWM

GALE, Moe (d 1964 [65]) agent BP/49*

GALE, Richard (b 1921) English actor TW/7

GALE, Ruth (b 1846) English dancer HAS

GALE, Sarah Ann see Rouse, Mrs.

GALE, Mrs. William Charles see Rouse, Mrs.

GALE, Zelia (b 1844) English equestrienne, tight-rope per-

former HAS
GALE, Zona (1874-1938) American dramatist MD, MH, MWD, NTH, WWT/6-8, WWW/3
GALEFFI, Carlo (b 1885) Italian singer ES
GALEOTTI, Vincenzo (1733-1916) Italian/Danish dancer, choreographer ES
GALER, Mrs. Elliot see Reeves, Fanny
GALER, Elliot John Norman (1828-1901) proprietor, singer, manager, dramatist DD
GALE SISTERS, The HAS
GALICI, Vincent Michael (b 1945) American actor TW/28
GALIK, Denise (b 1951) American actress TW/29
GALINDO, Mrs. [née Gough] actress CDP, TD/1-2
GALIPAUX, Felix (1860-1931) French dramatist, actor WWT/1
GALLACHER, Tom Scottish dramatist CD
GALLAGHER, Mr. (fl 1846) actor HAS
GALLAGHER, Dan (d 1973) performer BP/58*
GALLAGHER, Helen (b 1926) American actress, singer BE, TW/22-29, WWT/14-16
GALLAGHER, Jack singer, actor CDP
GALLAGHER, James Lancaster (1817-87) American actor, stage manager NYM
GALLAGHER, John (d 1879 [39]) equestrian director EA/80*
GALLAGHER, Mjr. John (d 1912 [79]) manager EA/13*
GALLAGHER, John (b 1947) American actor TW/27
GALLAGHER, Mrs. John see Gallagher, Mary
GALLAGHER, Mary [Mrs. John Gallagher] (d 1904 [71]) EA/06*
GALLAGHER, Richard (1896/1900-55) American actor WWT/6-10
GALLAGHER, Robert (b 1920) American actor TW/10
GALLAGHER, Skeets (1896-1955) American actor TW/1, 3, 11
GALLAHER, Donald (b 1895) Irish actor WWT/7-10

GALLAND, Bertha (1876/77-1932) American actress GRB/2-4, WWM, WWS, WWT/1-3
GALLATIN, Alberta (d 1948 [87]) American actress TW/5
GALLAWAY, Marian (b 1903) American educator, director BE
GALLET, Sébastien (b c. 1750) French dancer, choreographer ES
GALLETTI, Annetti (fl 1858-69) French dancer CDP, HAS
GALLETTI GIANOLI, Isabella (1835-1901) Italian singer ES
GALLEY, Arthur English giant CDP
GALLI, Richard (b 1942) American actor TW/30
GALLI, Rosina (d 1940 [45]) dancer BE*, BP/24*, WWT/14*
GALLIARD, John Ernest (1687?-1749) composer DD, DNB
GALLI-CURCI, Amelita (1889-1963) Italian singer ES, SR, TW/20, WWA/4, WWW/6
GALLIER, Charles H. (b 1878) English actress GRB/1
GALLIER, Elizabeth (d 1894) EA/95*
GALLI-MARIE DE L'ISLE, Célestine (1840-1905) French singer ES
GALLIMORE, Catherine (d 1962 [57]) performer BE*, BP/47*
GALLIMORE, Florrie singer CDP
GALLIMORE, Henry (d 1885) EA/86*
GALLIMORE, Mary (d 1898) EA/99*
GALLINI, Giovanni Andrea Battista (1728-1805) dancing master CDP
GALLISON, Joseph (b 1939) American actor TW/24-26
GALLO, Alberto (d 1964 [75]) choreographer, teacher BE*
GALLO, Fortune (1878-1970) Italian impresario CB, NTH, WWA/5
GALLO, Lew (b 1928) American actor TW/12
GALLO, Sofia (1888-1948) American singer SR
GALLON, Nellie Tom (d 1938) actress BE*, WWT/14*
GALLON, Tom (1866-1914) English dramatist WWW/1

GALLONE, Carmine (d 1973 [87]) producer/director/choreographer BP/57*

GALLOP, Sammy (d 1971 [55]) composer/lyricist BP/55*

GALLOTT, John (d 1852) English actor CDP, HAS

GALLOWAY, B. T. (d 1916) EA/17*

GALLOWAY, Don (b 1937) American actor TW/18-19

GALLOWAY, Mrs. F. see Le Grand, Mlle.

GALLOWAY, George (fl 1802-06) dramatist CP/3

GALLOWAY, George (b 1834) American actor, singer HAS

GALLOWAY, Hunter (d 1969 [59]) performer BP/53*

GALLOWAY, Louise (d 1949 [70]) American actress TW/6

GALLUP, Bonnie (b 1945) American actress TW/29-30

GALMAN, Peter W. (b 1945) American actor TW/26

GALPHIN, Martha American actress TW/26

GALSWORTHY, John (1867-1933) English dramatist AAS, COC, DNB, GRB/3-4, ES, HP, MD, MH, MWD, NTH, OC/1-3, PDT, RE, SR, WWM, WWT/1-7, WWW/3

GALT, John (d 1839 [59]) writer BE*, WWT/14*

GALT, William R. (d 1972 [91]) vaudeville agent BP/57*

GALTON, Blanche (fl 1868) actress? CDP, HAS

GALTON, Mary Pyne (fl 1868) actress? HAS

GALTON, Susan (b 1849) English singer, actress CDP, HAS

GALVANI, Dino (1890-1960) Italian actor WWT/6-10

GALVIN, Gene (b 1917) American actor TW/24-25

GALVIN, George see Leon, Dan

GALVIN, James (b 1933) American actor TW/29

GALVIN, Sydney Paul [Dan Leno, Jr.] (1892-1962) dancer, comedian COC, OC/3

GAM, Rita (b 1928) American actress BE, TW/24, 29

GAMBLE, Ralph (d 1966 [64]) performer BP/50*

GAMBLE, Theodore Roosevelt (1906-61) American executive WWA/4

GAMBLE, Tom (1898-1946) English comedian WWT/10

GAMBLE, Warburton (d 1945 [62]) actor BE*, WWT/14*

GAMBLING, John B. (d 1974 [77]) performer BP/59*

GAMBOA, Marcelo (b 1939) Argentinian actor TW/25-26, 28

GAMBOLD, John (d 1771) Welsh dramatist CP/2-3, DD, GT

GAMBON, Michael (b 1940) Irish actor WWT/16

GAMLIN, Lionel James (1903-67) actor WWW/6

GAMMON, Percy (d 1917) EA/18*

GAMMON, William (b 1943) American actor TW/30

GAMPEL, Chris see Gampel, C. M.

GAMPEL, C. M. (b 1921) Canadian actor TW/14, 25-26, 30

GAMPEL, Morison see Gampel, C. M.

GANDY, Sidney (d 1912 [47]) ventriloquist EA/13*

GANEY, David J. (d 1887) actor NYM

GANIMAN, Charles "Chick" (b 1926) American actor TW/26

GANN, Miss see Fries, Mrs. Wulf

GANN, James (fl 1844) English actor HAS

GANN, Louisa M. A. (b 1826) actress, singer CDP, HAS

GANNE, Louis (b 1862) French composer GRB/1

GANNON, Charles A. (d 1972 [78]) performer BP/57*

GANNON, Elenor [Mrs. T. R. Gannon] (d 1893) EA/94*

GANNON, James (d 1974 [73]) composer/lyricist BP/56*

GANNON, Liam Irish actress TW/26

GANNON, Martha Ann (d 1906) EA/07*

GANNON, Mary (1829-68) American actress CDP, DD, HAS, SR

GANNON, Thomas (d 1917) variety agent EA/18*

GANNON, Mrs. T. R. see Gannon, Elenor

GANNON, W. (d 1891) EA/92*

GANON, James American actor
TW/1, 3
GANS, Sidney (d 1972 [60])
critic BP/57*
GANT, William George (d 1881)
EA/82*
GANT, William George see
Ross, Charlie
GANTHONY, Nellie [Mrs. Arthur
Sykes] English entertainer
GRB/1-4
GANTHONY, Richard (d 1924
[67]) dramatist, actor BE*,
WWT/14*
GANTHONY, Robert (d 1931 [82])
dramatist, performer BE*,
WWT/14*
GANTILLON, Simon (1887-1961)
French dramatist COC
GANTRY, Donald (b 1936) Amer-
ican actor TW/28, 30
GANTY, Little singer, actor
CDP
GANZ, Herr (d 1869 [74]) musi-
cian EA/70*
GANZ, Moritz (d 1868 [64])
musician EA/69*
GANZ, Wilhelm (1833-1914)
Austrian conductor, composer,
musician GRB/1, WWW/1
GAPPER, H. B. M. see
Gascoigne, Henry
GARBANATI, Mr. (fl 1850) actor
HAS
GARBER, Victor (b 1949) Cana-
dian actor TW/29
GARBIN, Eduardo (1865-1943)
Italian singer ES
GARBOIS, Sophie Charlotte
see Neville, Charlotte
GARBOIS, Mrs. W. H. see
Neville, Charlotte
GARCIA, Sig. (1778-1836) Spanish
singer HAS
GARCIA, Edward (d 1893) lessee
EA/94*
GARCIA, Henry (d 1970 [66])
performer BP/55*
GARCIA, Manuel (1805-1906)
Spanish singer, singing teacher
ES
GARD, Robert E. (b 1910) Amer-
ican educator, director BE
GARDE, Betty (b 1905) American
actress BE, TW/5-8, 23-24,
WWT/10-11, 15-16
GARDEL, Mme. Pierre Gabriel,
I see Coulon, Anne Jacqueline

GARDELLA, Tess (d 1950 [52])
American singer, comedienne
TW/6
GARDEN, David (b 1932) Ameri-
can actor TW/2
GARDEN, Edmund (1822-80) actor
DD
GARDEN, E[dmund] W[illiam]
(1845-1939) English actor DD,
DP, GRB/1-4, OAA/1-2, WWT/
1-9
GARDEN, Mary (1874/76/77-1967)
Scottish singer ES, GRB/1,
SR, TW/23, WWA/4, WWW/6
GARDENER, Julian see Royce,
Julian
GARDENER, Shayle (b 1890) New
Zealand actor WWT/5-6
GARDENIA, Vincent [né Scogna-
miglio] (b 1922/23) Italian/
American actor BE, TW/25-
30, WWT/16
GARDER, Ann American actress
TW/25
GARDIE, Mme. (d 1798) actress
HAS
GARDIN, Vladimir (1877-1965)
Russian actor OC/3
GARDINER, Mrs. [née Cheney]
(fl 1763-82) actress, dramatist
CP/2, GT, TD/1-2
GARDINER, Cyril (b 1897) English
actor WWT/10
GARDINER, E. W. (d 1899 [37])
actor DD, DP, EA/96
GARDINER, Henry Andrew see
Coyne, Gardiner
GARDINER, John (d 1884 [46])
actor EA/86*
GARDINER, John (d 1889 [24])
EA/90*
GARDINER, John (d 1897 [74])
circus manager EA/99*
GARDINER, Matthew (fl 1740-41)
Irish? dramatist CP/1-3, GT
GARDINER, Patrick (d 1970 [44])
performer BP/55*
GARDINER, Reginald (b 1903) Eng-
lish actor BE, TW/12, WWT/
7-10
GARDINER, William (fl 1806)
dramatist CP/3
GARDINER, Willie Elslice (d
1917 [7]) EA/18*
GARDNER, Lady see Fortesque,
Julia
GARDNER, Mrs. [Miss Cheney] (d
1790) actress, dramatist CDP,

CP/3, DD, DNB
GARDNER, Master CDP
GARDNER, Archibald M. (d 1972
[65]) critic BP/57*
GARDNER, Cecil (d 1901 [25])
variety manager EA/02*
GARDNER, Charles A. (c. 1848-
1924) actor, composer, singer
CDP, SR
GARDNER, David (b 1928) Cana-
dian actor TW/12
GARDNER, Ed (1905-63) Ameri-
can producer, writer CB,
WWA/4
GARDNER, Eliza (d 1911) EA/12*
GARDNER, Godfrey Derman (d
1916 [34]) EA/17*
GARDNER, Harry (d 1917) clown
EA/18*
GARDNER, Helen Louise (d
1968) performer BP/53*
GARDNER, Herb (b 1934) drama-
tist BE
GARDNER, Herbert [Lord Burgh-
clere] (fl 1875-85) dramatist
DD
GARDNER, Jack (d 1950 [77])
singer, actor CDP, TW/7
GARDNER, John (d 1851 [49])
actor EA/72*
GARDNER, Mrs. John see
Gardner, Ruth
GARDNER, Katie see Sawin,
Mrs. George Arthur
GARDNER, Peter H. (d 1917)
actor EA/18*
GARDNER, Renée (d 1973 [43])
performer BP/58*
GARDNER, Rita actress, singer
BE
GARDNER, Ruth [Mrs. John
Gardner] (d 1892) EA/93*
GARDNER, Shayle (1890-1945)
New Zealand actor WWT/7-9
GARDNER, Thomas (d 1867 [55])
proprietor EA/68*
GARDNER, William (d 1870)
actor EA/71*
GARDNER, William Henry (1865-
1932) American composer
WWA/1
GARDNER, William John (d 1912
[41]) EA/14*
GARDONI, Sig. (d 1882 [61])
singer EA/83*
GAREY, James R. (1861-1947)
actor, dramatist SR
GAREY, Peter (b 1917) American

actor TW/6-7
GARFEIN, Jack (b 1930) Czech/
American director BE, ES
GARFIELD, Allen (b 1939) Ameri-
can actor TW/26
GARFIELD, Benjamin dramatist
CP/3, FGF
GARFIELD, David (b 1941) Amer-
ican actor TW/26-29
GARFIELD, John [né Julius Gar-
finkle] (1913-53) American ac-
tor AAS, CB, ES, TW/5-8,
WWT/11
GARFIELD, Julie (b 1946) Ameri-
can actress TW/25, 27, 30
GARFIELD, Kurt (b 1931) Ameri-
can actor TW/26, 28
GARFINKLE, Julius see Gar-
field, John
GARGAN, Edward F. (d 1964 [62])
actor BE*, BP/48*
GARGAN, William (b 1905) Amer-
ican actor WWT/8-10
GARLAND, Geoff (b 1932) English
actor TW/23, 25-29
GARLAND, Hamlin (1860-1940)
American dramatist WWA/1
GARLAND, Mrs. Herbert see
McKenzie, Florence
GARLAND, Herbert Theodore see
Trevor, Theodore
GARLAND, John (fl 1583-1616)
actor DA
GARLAND, Judy [née Gumm]
(1922-69) American actress,
singer, dancer CB, TW/26,
WWA/5
GARLAND, Patrick director,
dramatist AAS, WWT/15-16
GARLAND, Robert (1895-1955)
American critic NTH, TW/12,
WWT/8-12
GARLICK (fl c. 1610) actor DA
GARMAN, Mr. G. (d 1867 [48])
singer EA/68*
GARNER, Mr. (d 1843) singer
HAS
GARNER, Arthur (b 1851) English
actor DD, OAA/1-2
GARNER, Mrs. Arthur [Blanche
Stammers] (d 1883) actress
EA/84*
GARNER, James (b 1928) Ameri-
can actor CB
GARNER, Martin (b 1927) Ameri-
can actor TW/28, 30
GARNER, Peggy Ann (b 1932)
American actress TW/6-8,

11-12

GARNER, William Henry (d 1916 [74]) EA/17*

GARNERIN, André Jae (1769-1823) French aeronaut CDP

GARNETT, Constance (1862-1948) translator NTH

GARNETT, Edward (1868-1937) dramatist NTH, WWT/1-8, WWW/3

GARNETT, Louise Ayres (d 1937) American composer WWA/1

GARNIER, Mr. (d 1884) EA/85*

GARNIER, Leon (d 1905 [49]) French songwriter GRB/1

GARON, Norm (d 1975 [41]) performer BP/59*

GAROZZO, Nella (d 1972 [50+]) publicist BP/57*

GARR, Eddie (d 1940) comedian WWT/14*

GARR, Eddie (d 1956 [56]) American vaudevillian TW/13

GARRARD, Mr. (d 1878 [46]) musician EA/79*

GARRATT, Adah (d 1898) actress EA/00*

GARRATT, Jessie [Mrs. W. Lee Bruno] (d 1896 [44]) actress EA/97*

GARRATT, John (d 1871) clown EA/72*

GARRATT, Mary Annie (d 1886 [90]) EA/87*

GARRETT, Arthur (1869-1941) English manager WWT/2-9

GARRETT, Betty (b 1919/20) American actress, singer BE, TW/1-6, 20-21, WWT/11, 14-16

GARRETT, Bob (b 1947) American actor TW/29-30

GARRETT, George (d 1878 [46]) musician EA/79*

GARRETT, John (fl 1619) actor DA

GARRETT, Joy (b 1945) American actress TW/26-28

GARRETT, Kelly (b 1948) American actress TW/29-30

GARRETT, Oliver H. P. (d 1952 [54]) American dramatist BE*, BP/36*

GARRETT, William H. (d 1888 [49]) actor, manager EA/89*

GARRICK, Mrs. [née Gray] (d c. 1844) actress CDP

GARRICK, Beulah (b 1921) English actress TW/27, 30

GARRICK, David (1717-79) English actor, dramatist, manager CDP, COC, CP/1-3, DD, DNB, ES, GT, HP, MH, NTH, OC/1-3, OX, PDT, SR, TD/1-2

GARRICK, Mrs. David see Violetti, Eva Maria

GARRICK, Eva Marie see Violetti, Eva Maria

GARRICK, Gus (fl 1890s?) singer, actor CDP

GARRICK, Helen Collier (d 1954 [87]) actress TW/11

GARRICK, Henry Walter (b 1871) English press manager GRB/1-3

GARRICK, Jack (d 1917 [19]) comedian EA/18*

GARRICK, John (b 1902) English actor, singer WWT/7-11

GARRICK, Nathan David (d 1876 [67]) EA/77*

GARRICK, P. CDP

GARRICK, Richard T. (d 1962 [83]) actor BE*

GARRICK, Sarah Jane (d 1859 [76]) actress EA/72*

GARRISON, George W. [né Chandler] (fl 1867) actor HAS

GARRISON, Mabel (d 1963 [77]) American singer TW/20, WWA/4

GARRISON, Michael (d 1966 [43]) performer BP/51*

GARRISON, Sean (b 1937) American actor TW/16, 18-20, 22

GARROD, W[alter] V[incent] (b 1879) Irish actor, manager GRB/1

GARROW, Mrs. Joseph see Abrams, Theodosia

GARRY, Charles (d 1939 [68]) actor BE*, WWT/14*

GARRY, Claude [Claude Dietz] (1877-1918) French actor WWT/3

GARSI, Ginlia (b 1822) Italian singer SR

GARSIDE, John (1887-1958) English actor, designer WWT/6-12

GARSIDE, Thomas (d 1881 [44]) conductor EA/82*

GARSON, Greer (b 1908) Irish actress CB, ES, SR, WWT/8-11

GARSON, T. E. (fl 1838) American actor HAS

GARSTIN, George Benjamin see

Belmore, George

GARSTONE, Kate (d 1885) music-
hall performer EA/86*

GARTEN, H. F. [né Koenigsgar-
ten] (b 1904) Austrian librettist,
educator BE

GARTER, Thomas (fl 1578) dramatist CP/1-3, FGF

GARTHORNE, C. W. [Charles
Warlhouse Grimston] (d 1900
[54]) actor DD, OAA/2

GARTON, Flo [Mrs. F. Heath]
(d 1907) variety performer
EA/08*

GARTSIDE, Henry see Neville,
Henry

GARTSIDE-NEVILLE, Mrs.
George see Neville, Mary
C. H.

GARVEY, Miss (fl 1849) actress
HAS

GARVICE, Charles (d 1920)
dramatist WWW/2

GARVIE, Edward (1870-1939)
American actor WWM

GARY, David (b 1946) American
actor TW/26

GARY, Harold (b 1910) American
actor TW/3, 23-25, 28-30

GARY, Sid (d 1973 [72]) performer BP/57*

GASCOIGNE, Bamber (b 1935)
English critic, lyricist AAS,
WWT/14-16

GASCOIGNE, Charles [Charles
Sullivan] (d 1887 [39]) Irish
comedian EA/88*

GASCOIGNE, George (c. 1535-
77) English scholar, dramatist
CDP, COC, CP/1-3, DD,
DNB, ES, FGF, HP, MH,
OC/1-3, PDT, RE

GASCOIGNE, George (d 1916)
assistant manager EA/17*

GASCOIGNE, Henry [H. B. M.
Gapper] (d 1894 [44]) actor,
manager, dramatist, lessee
DD

GASCOIGNE, William (fl 1589)
actor DA

GASCON, Edward E. (d 1965
[93]) performer BP/49*

GASCON, Jean (b 1921) Canadian
actor, director AAS, WWT/
13-16

GASCOYNE, William (fl 1624-31)
actor DA

GASELLI, Silva see Gassell,

Sylvia

GASKELL, Clarence (1892-1948)
composer, musical director
SR

GASKILL, William (b 1930) English
director, stage manager, actor
AAS, COC, ES, PDT, WWT/
14-16

GASNIER, Louis (d 1963 [87])
French actor, director BE*

GASPARONI, Sig. (fl 1856) singer
HAS

GASPARRE, Dick (d 1971 [72])
composer/lyricist BP/56*

GASPER, Edd K. (b 1937) American actor TW/25-26

GASSELL, Sylvia [Silva Gaselli]
(b 1923) American actress
TW/9, 20, 24-27

GASSIER, Louis Edward (1822-71)
singer CDP, HAS

GASSIER, Mme. Louis Edward (fl
1855-58) singer CDP, HAS

GASSIER, Pepita see Gassier,
Mme. Louis Edward

GASSMAN, Josephine (d 1962 [82])
performer BE*

GASSNER, John (1903-67) Hungari-
an/American critic, historian,
dramatist BE, CB, COC, ES,
NTH, TW/23, WWT/11-14

GASTELLE, Stella (d 1936) actress, singer BE*, WWT/14*

GASTON, E. B. (d 1858 [35]) actor WWT/14*

GASTON, George (1843-1937)
American actor BE*, WWT/14*

GASTON, Penny (b 1942) Canadian
actress TW/23

GATAKER, Thomas (fl 1730)
dramatist CP/3

GATES, Mrs. (d 1870 [72]) actress EA/71*

GATES, Eleanor (1875-1951) American dramatist TW/7, WWT/
4-9

GATES, James (d 1868 [39]) scene
artist EA/69*

GATES, Larry (b 1915) American
actor BE, TW/8-12, 20, 24,
WWT/12-16

GATES, Ruth (1888-1966) American
actress BE, TW/1, 22

GATES, William F. (d 1843) American actor CDP, HAS

GATES AND MORANGE American
scene designer ES

GATESON, Marjorie (1891/97-

1977) American actress, singer BE, TW/3-7, 10-14, WWT/11-14

GATHERCOLE, John (d 1895 [42]) manager EA/96*

GATLEY, T. (d 1886) proprietor EA/87*

GATTI, Agostino (d 1897 [55]) proprietor EA/98*, WWT/14*

GATTI, Carlo (d 1878 [61]) music-hall proprietor EA/79*, WWT/14*

GATTI, Sir John Maria (1872-1929) English manager WWT/1-6

GATTI, Rocco J. S. (d 1950 [76]) proprietor WWT/14*

GATTI, Stefano (d 1906 [61]) proprietor, manager EA/07*, GRB/2*

GATTI-CASAZZA, Giulio (1869-1940) Italian impresario DAB, ES, WWA/1, WWM

GATTIE, A. W. (d 1925 [69]) dramatist BE*, WWT/14*

GATTIE, Henry (1774-1844) English actor, singer BS, CDP, DD, DNB, EA/92, OX

GATTY, Alfred Scott singer, composer CDP

GATTY, Nicholas Comyn (1874-1946) composer WWW/4

GAUDIN, Thomas (d 1889 [78]) EA/90*

GAUDRY, Joseph actor TD/1-2

GAUDSCHMIDT, Max (d 1972 [83]) performer BP/56*

GAUDY, Miss (b c. 1780) actress TD/2

GAUGE, Alexander (1914-60) Chinese/English actor TW/3

GAUGIN, Lorraine (d 1974 [50]) performer BP/59*

GAUL, George (1885-1939) American actor WWT/7-8

GAUL, Patricia American actress TW/29

GAUNT, David [John Davies Butler] (d 1883 [20]) actor EA/84*

GAUNT, Elsie (d 1910) actress EA/11*

GAUNT, Percy (1852-96) American songwriter BE*

GAUNT, Picton see Roxborough, Picton

GAUNT, William Clifford (d

1942 [69]) proprietor WWT/14*

GAUNTIER, Gene (d 1966 [80s]) performer BP/51*

GAUNTLETT, Dr. (d 1876) musician EA/77*

GAUNTLETT, Hilary Sebastian (d 1911 [24]) musician EA/12*

GAUTHIER, Eva (1885-1958) Canadian singer WWA/3

GAUTIER, Eugene (d 1878 [56]) composer EA/79*

GAUTIER, Leonard (d 1948 [56]) dog trainer TW/4

GAVER, Jack (1906-74) American editor, critic BE, NTH

GAVIN, John (b 1935) American actor TW/30

GAVON, Igors (b 1937) Latvian actor TW/23-29

GAWTHORNE, Peter A. (1884-1962) Irish actor WWT/4-10

GAXIOLA, Arturo see Gaxton, William

GAXTON, William [Arturo Gaxiola] (1893-1963) American actor AAS, TW/1-14, 19, WWT/7-11

GAY, Mr. (fl 1831-33) English actor HAS

GAY, Mrs. (d 1889) EA/91*

GAY, John (1685-1732) English dramatist CDP, COC, CP/1-3, DNB, ES, GT, HP, MH, NTH, OC/1-3, PDT, RE, SR, TD/1-2

GAY, Joseph see Breval, Cpt. John Durant

GAY, Maisie (1883-1945) English actress, singer TW/2, WWT/4-9, WWW/4

GAY, Maria (1879-1943) Spanish singer ES

GAY, Noel [R. M. Armitage] (1898-1954) English composer WWT/6-11

GAY, Ralph George (d 1890 [27]) EA/91*

GAY, Walter (d 1936 [73]) actor BE*, WWT/14*

GAYARRE, Julian (1844-90) Spanish singer ES

GAYE, Albie (d 1965) performer BP/50*

GAYE, Freda (b 1907) English actress, editor, curator BE, WWT/13-15

GAYER, Echlin (1878-1926) actor SR

GAYLE, Tim (d 1970 [57]) publicist BP/55*

GAYLER, Charles (1820-92) American dramatist, actor CDP, DAB, SR, WWA/H

GAYLOR, Bobbie (b c. 1861) actor, dramatist, producer SR

GAYLORD, Julia (d 1894) actress, singer CDP

GAYLORD, Lowrenzo (1836-78) minstrel, manager CDP

GAYNES, Edmund (b 1947) American actor TW/25-28

GAYNES, George [George Jongeyans] (b 1917) Finnish actor, singer BE, TW/7, 9-15, 19-23, 30, WWT/16

GAYNOR, Charles (1909-75) American lyricist, composer BE

GAYTHORNE, Pamela (b 1882) actress WWT/2-6

GAYTIE, Fred A. [Frederick Augustus Hetherington] (b 1862) English actor GRB/1

GAYTON, Edmund dramatist CP/3

GAZE, George (d 1904 [72]) proprietor EA/05*

GAZE, Mrs. Leslie see Gorton, Belle

GAZZANIGA, Marietta (c. 1824-84) Sardinian singer CDP, HAS

GAZZARA, Ben (b 1930) American actor AAS, BE, CB, ES, TW/10-21, WWT/12-16

GAZZO, Michael V. (b 1923) American dramatist, actor, director BE, MH

GAZZOLO, Frank A. P. (b 1873) American manager, producer, agent SR

GEAR, Luella (b 1897/99) American actress BE, TW/1-8, 10-15, WWT/5-15

GEAR, Robert (d 1893 [73]) performer? EA/94*

GEARY, Sam see Arthur, Sam

GEARY, Samuel (d 1889 [46]) EA/90*

GEATER, R. F. see Flexmore, Richard

GeBAUER, Gene (b 1934) American actor TW/27-30

GEBERT, Ernst (d 1961 [59]) German conductor BE*

GECKS, Mr. (d 1888) bandmaster EA/89*

GEDDA, Nicolai (b 1925) Swedish singer CB, ES

GEDDES, Dr. (fl 1582?) dramatist FGF

GEDDES, Barbara Bel (b 1922/23) American actress AAS, BE, CB, COC, ES, OC/3, TW/2-20, 22-24, 29-30, WWT/11-16

GEDDES, George E. (d 1973 [68]) theatre founder BP/58*

GEDDES, Norman Bel (1893-1958) American scene designer, producer, director CB, COC, ES, NTH, OC/1-3, PDT, SR, TW/14, WWA/3, WWT/7-11, WWW/5

GEDGE, John Kerr (d 1876) singer EA/77*

GEE, Caroline Eliza [Mrs. Palmer] (d 1887 [71]) actress? EA/88*

GEE, Caroline Eliza Palmer (d 1871 [19]) actress EA/72*

GEE, Fannie Marie see Forbes, Mrs. W. C.

GEE, George (d 1959 [64]) actor WWT/6-12

GEE, Jack (d 1973 [84]) manager BP/58*

GEE, John (d 1902) actor? EA/03*

GEER, Ellen (b 1941) American actress BE

GEER, Seth (d 1866) actor HAS

GEER, Will (b 1902/05) American actor AAS, BE, TW/1-6, 10-14, 22-23, 25, 27, WWT/10-16

GEEVES-BOOTH, James see Booth, James

GEFFREY, John dramatist CP/2-3

GEHMAN, Richard (1921-72) American writer BE

GEHRI, Alfred (d 1972 [76]) performer, dramatist BP/56*, WWT/16*

GEHRUE, Mayme [Mrs. John Ford] (b 1883) American actress WWM

GEIRINGER, Jean (d 1962 [62]) Austrian librettist, lyricist BE*

GEIS, Wayne (b 1945) American actor TW/26

GEIST, Irving (d 1970 [70]) backer BP/55*

GEISTINGER, Marie (1836-1903) German singer, actress CDP, ES

GEISWEILER, Maria (fl 1799)

translator CP/3
GEIWITZ, Emma C. (c. 1820-1915)
German actress SR
GELB, Arthur (b 1924) American
editor, critic BE
GELB, James stage manager,
director BE
GELBART, Larry S. (b 1923)
American librettist BE
GELBER, Eugene (d 1974 [46])
producer/director/choreographer
BP/58*
GELBERT, Jack Allen (b 1932)
American dramatist, director
AAS, BE, CD, CH, COC,
ES, MD, MH, MWD, PDT,
RE, WWT/15-16
GEL'CER, Ekaterina Vasil'evna
(b 1876) Russian dancer ES
GELDARD, Mrs. R. see Gel-
dard, Sarah Ann
GELDARD, Sarah Ann [Mrs. R.
Geldard] (d 1878) EA/79*
GELDERD, James (d 1918) EA/
19*
GELFAND, Carol (b 1937) Amer-
ican actress TW/26-28
GELLMAN, Jacob see Gilford,
Jack
GELLNER, Julius (b 1899)
Bohemian director, actor
WWT/15-16
GELTZER, Catherine (fl 1871-
1914) dancer OC/1-2
GEMEA, Mrs. Tobias see
Chetwood, Richabella
GEMIER, Firmin (d 1933 [68])
French actor, producer BP/
18*
GEMIGNANI, Rhoda (b 1940)
American actress TW/25, 30
GEMMELL, Don (b 1903) Scottish
director, manager, actor
WWT/14-16
GEMMILL, William D. (d 1882
[37]) manager CDP
GENDRON, Pierre (d 1956 [60])
actor BE*
GENEE, Dame Adeline (1878-
1970) Danish dancer CDP, ES,
GRB/1-4, OC/1-2, WWM,
WWS, WWT/1-12, WWW/6
GENEE, Alexander (d 1938 [88])
dancer, director BE*, WWT/
14*
GENEE, Ottilie (fl 1865) German
actress CDP
GENEST, Edmond (b 1943) Amer-

ican actor TW/28-29
GENEST, John (1764-1839) scholar
HP
GENET, Jean (b 1909/10) French
dramatist CB, COC, OC/3,
PDT, WWT/14-16
GENET, Pauline (d 1856) English
dancer HAS
GENEVIEVE [née Genevieve Auger]
(b 1930) French singer, actress
BE
GENGE, George (d 1863 [42])
singer EA/72*
GENIAT, Marcelle [née Eugenie
Martin] (d 1959 [80]) Russian/
French actress WWT/4, 10
GENIN, John H. (d 1878 [59])
American? merchant CDP
GENISE, Livia (b 1949) American
actress TW/29-30
GENN, Edward P. (d 1947 [50])
producer BE*, WWT/14*
GENN, Leo (1905-78) English ac-
tor AAS, BE, ES, TW/3-6,
13-14, 20, 24, WWT/9-16
GENNARO, Peter (b 1924?) Amer-
ican choreographer, dancer
BE, CB, ES, TW/13-15
GENT, George (d 1974 [49]) jour-
nalist BP/59*
GENTELE, Goeran (1917-72)
Swedish manager, director CB,
WWA/5
GENTILE, Gerard L. (d 1973
[62]) designer BP/58*
GENTLE, Alice (1885-1958) Amer-
ican singer TW/14, WWA/3,
WWM
GENTLEMAN, Francis (1728-84)
Irish critic, actor, dramatist
COC, CP/1-3, DNB, GT, OC/
1-3, TD/1-2
GENTLES, Avril (b 1929) Ameri-
can actress TW/25-27, 29-30
GENTRY, Amelia (d 1963 [40])
performer BE*
GENTRY, Bob (b 1940) American
actor TW/17-20
GENZMER, Hertha (d 1971 [74])
performer BP/55*
GEOFFREY, Mr. dramatist CP/3
GEOGHEGAN, Frederick (d 1868
[28]) professor of music EA/
69*
GEOGHEGAN, J. B. (d 1889)
music-hall manager, songwriter
EA/90*
GEOGHEGAN, Mrs. J. B. (d 1889)

EA/90*

GEOLY, Andrew (b 1907) costumier BE

GEORGE, Mr. (fl 1800s) actor TD/2

GEORGE, Miss (d c. 1803?) actress TD/1-2

GEORGE, Mlle. [Marguerite-Josephine Weymer] (1787-1867) French actress COC

GEORGE, Miss see Tuson, Isabella

GEORGE, A. E. (1869-1920) English actor GRB/1-4, WWT/1-3

GEORGE, Alfred (d 1906) musichall comedian EA/07*

GEORGE, Amelia Angelica (b 1803) English singer, actress CDP, HAS, OX

GEORGE, Collin (b 1929) Welsh director, actor WWT/15-16

GEORGE, Mrs. E. [née Lottie Moreton] (d 1873 [28]) actress EA/74*

GEORGE, Mrs. Edward J. see George, Emily

GEORGE, Edward John (b 1842) English actor OAA/2

GEORGE, Emily [Mrs. Edward J. George] (d 1901 [45]) actress EA/02*

GEORGE, G. H. (d 1875) dramatist, actor? EA/76*

GEORGE, Mrs. G. H. see Hadwin, Ann

GEORGE, Gladys (1904-54) American actress TW/5-6, 11, WWT/8-11

GEORGE, Gorgeous (d 1963 [48]) performer BP/48*

GEORGE, Grace [Mrs. William A. Brady] (1879-1961) American actress COC, GRB/2-4, OC/1-3, SR, TW/2-9, 17, WWM, WWS, WWT/1-12

GEORGE, Harry (d 1904) EA/05*

GEORGE, Henry (d 1908 [60]) actor, manager GRB/4

GEORGE, Joseph H. (fl 1851) American actor HAS

GEORGE, Marie (1879-1955) American actress GRB/1-4, WWS, WWT/1-8

GEORGE, Muriel (1883-1965) English actress WWT/9-12

GEORGE, Sam J. (d 1969) manager BP/54*

GEORGE, William (d 1896 [50]) hosier EA/97*

"GEORGE FLEMING" see Fletcher, Constance

GEORGER, Alfred M. (d 1974 [85]) treasurer BP/59*

GEORGES, Katherine (d 1973) performer BP/58*

GEORGI, Yvonne (d 1975 [77]) dancer, choreographer BP/59*, WWT/16*

"GEORGIA MAGNET, The" see Abbott, Annie

GERACI, Robert (b 1939) American actor TW/26, 28-30

GERAGHTY, Pat (d 1898) Irish comedian EA/99*

GERALD, Ara (1900-57) Australian actress WWT/8-10

GERALD, Florence (d 1942 [84]) American actress BE*, WWT/14*

GERALD, Frank (1855-1942) English actor BE*, WWT/14*

GERARD, Dorothy (d 1908) EA/09*

GERARD, Florence (fl 1878-83) actress DD

GERARD, John (d 1886) circus performer? EA/87*

GERARD, Linda (b 1938) American actress TW/28

GERARD, Manny (d 1973 [47]) designer BP/58*

GERARD, Richard see Husch, Richard J.

GERARD, Teddie (b 1892) Argentinian actress WWT/4-7

GERAY, Steve (b 1904) Hungarian actor WWT/8-10

GERBER, Alex (d 1969 [74]) composer/lyricist BP/53*

GERBER, Ella (b 1916) American director, actress BE

GERBER, Henry W. (d 1967 [85]) producer/director/choreographer BP/52*

GERBER, Jay (b 1929) American actor TW/24

GERBER, Morton (d 1975 [60]) executive? BP/59*

GERDLER, Adam (fl 1635) actor DA

GERHARD, Karl (d 1964 [73]) performer BP/48*

GERLACH, Robert American actor TW/25-26

GERLE, Theodolinda (fl 1847)

singer HAS

GERMAN, Sir Edward (1862-1936) English composer DD, DNB, ES, GRB/1-4, WWS, WWT/ 1-8, WWW/3

GERMANOVA, Maria Nikolaevna (1884-1940) Russian actress COC, OC/3

GERMAN-REED, Mrs. Alfred (d 1916) EA/18*

GERMON, Euphemia [Effie] (1845/47-1914) American actress CDP, HAS, PP/1, SR, WWS

GERMON, Francis (fl 1844) minstrel CDP

GERMON, Greene C. (d 1854) actor CDP, HAS

GERMON, Mrs. Greene C. [Jane Anderson or Andrews] (fl 1839-58) actress DD, HAS, SR

GERMON, Jane (d 1909 [87]) actress WWT/14*

GERMON, John (fl 1857) actor HAS

GERMON, Mrs. John D. see Cunningham, Virginia

GEROLD, Arthur (b 1923) American costumier, producer, manager BE

GERRARD, Ethel [Mrs. Frank Carlile] (d 1903) actress EA/04*

GERRARD, Gene (1892-1971) English actor WWT/5-11

GERRARD, John Francis (d 1907 [54]) actor GRB/2*

GERRARD, Teddie (1892-1942) Argentinian actress BE*

GERRING, Mrs. Charles (d 1887) EA/88*

GERRINGER, Robert (b 1926) American actor BE

GERRISH, Sylvia (d 1906 [48]) American actress, singer CDP

GERRY (fl 1607) actor DA

GERSHWIN, George (1898-1937) American composer AAS, DAB, ES, HJD, MH, NTH, PDT, SR, WWA/1, WWT/5-8, WWW/3

GERSHWIN, Ira (b 1896) American lyricist BE, CB, ES, HJD, WWT/7-14

GERSTAD, John [né Gjerstad] (b 1924/25) American actor, producer, director, dramatist

BE, TW/1, 24-28, WWT/13-16

GERSTEN, Bernard (b 1923) American producer, director, stage manager BE, WWT/16

GERSTEN, Berta (d 1972 [78]) Polish actress TW/29

GERSTER, Etelka (1855/57-1920) Hungarian singer CDP, ES

GERSTLE, Frank (d 1970 [53]) performer BP/54*

GERSTMAN, Felix G. Austrian impresario, producer BE

GERUSSI, Bruno actor WWT/14-15

GERVASE, Charles (d 1901) actor EA/02*

GERVILLE-REACHE, Jeanne [Mme. George Gibier Rambaud] (fl 1900s) French singer WWM

GESENSWAY, Louis (d 1976 [70]) composer/lyricist BP/60*

GESSNER, Adrienne Austrian actress TW/1, 24

GEST, Morris (1881-1942) Russian manager CB, DAB, NTH, SR, WWA/2, WWT/4-9

GETCHELL, Dr. Charles Munro (1909-63) American educator BE*

GETCHELL, Franklin (b 1947) American actor TW/30

GETHING, William Henry (d 1904 [45]) musical director EA/06*

GETTY, Talitha Pol (d 1971) performer BP/56*

GETZ, Johnnie G. (d 1964 [84]) American performer BE*

GEVA, Tamara (b 1907) Russian actress, dancer BE, TW/9, 11, 21, WWT/9-15

GEW (fl late 16th cent) actor? DA

GHELDERODE, Michel de (1898-1962) Belgian dramatist OC/3, PDT

GHEON, Henri (1875-1943) French dramatist COC, OC/1-3

GHEUSI, Pierre B. (b 1865) French dramatist GRB/4

GHIONI, Mlle. (fl 1858) singer HAS

GHOSTLEY, Alice (b 1926) American actress TW/9-19, 21-22, WWT/14-16

GIACHETTI, Fosco (d 1974 [70]) performer BP/59*

GIACOMINO (1884-1956) Italian clown ES

GIACOSA, Giuseppe (1847-1906) Italian dramatist OC/1-3, RE

GIANNINI, Olga Italian actress
WWT/3-4
GIBB, Margaret (d 1967 [54])
performer BP/51*
GIBB, Mary (d 1967 [54]) per-
former BP/51*
GIBBERSON, William (b 1919)
American actor BE
GIBBES, George (fl 1628) actor
DA
GIBBON, Charles (d 1917) act-
ing manager EA/18*
GIBBON, H. B. [FitzGibbon] (b
1873) English actor, producer,
business manager GRB/1-2
GIBBON, James Deverell (1779-
1852) actor CDP
GIBBONS, Mr. (fl 1845) actor
HAS
GIBBONS, Mrs. (fl 1845) actress
HAS
GIBBONS, Alfred (d 1900) EA/01*
GIBBONS, Mrs. Alfred see
Mario, Dot
GIBBONS, Arthur (1871-1935)
English actor, manager WWT/
6-7
GIBBONS, Barney (d 1876 [46])
Irish singer EA/77*
GIBBONS, Carroll (d 1954 [51])
musician WWT/14*
GIBBONS, Edyth (fl 1899-1904)
English vaudevillian WWM
GIBBONS, Frank A. trapezist
CDP
GIBBONS, Irene (1907-62) Amer-
ican costume designer BE*
GIBBONS, Nellie Isabella [Mrs.
Walter Gibbons] (d 1911 [28])
EA/12*
GIBBONS, Rod (b 1949) American
actor TW/29
GIBBONS, Rose (d 1964 [78])
actress BE*, BP/49*
GIBBONS, Mrs. Walter see
Gibbons, Nellie Isabella
GIBBORNE, Thomas (fl 1624)
lessee DA
GIBBS (fl 1602) actor DA
GIBBS, Mrs. see Colman,
Mary Logan
GIBBS, Mrs. see Gibbs, P.
GIBBS, Abigail (d 1907 [80])
EA/08*
GIBBS, Mrs. Alexander see
Gibbs, P.
GIBBS, Andrew (d 1873) comedian
EA/74*

GIBBS, Ann American actress
TW/26-27
GIBBS, Charles (d 1910) coon
artist EA/11*
GIBBS, Cora (d 1966 [65]) treas-
urer BP/50*
GIBBS, Cosmo see Hamilton,
Cosmo
GIBBS, John (d 1870) property
master EA/71*
GIBBS, John see Gilbert, John
GIBBS, Maria see Colman,
Mary
GIBBS, Nancy (d 1956 [63]) Welsh
singer, actress WWT/4-7
GIBBS, P. [Mrs. Alexander Gibbs;
née Graddon] (1804-54?) English
actress CDP, DD, DNB, HAS,
OX
GIBBS, Robert Paton (d 1940 [81])
American actor BE*, BP/25*
GIBBS, Robert Weston (d 1891
[51]) circus agent EA/92*
GIBBS, Robert Wilkes (d 1871
[51]) pantomimist EA/72*
GIBBS, Robert Wilkes see Har-
rison, Robert
GIBBS, Sheila (b 1947) American
actress TW/29
GIBBS, Thomas (d 1869) singer
EA/70*
GIBBS, Wolcott (1902-58) Ameri-
can critic COC, NTH, OC/1-3,
TW/15, WWA/3
GIBES, Antony (fl 1628) actor DA
GIBNEY, Frank (b 1924) American
journalist BE
GIBSON, Mr. (d 1771) actor TD/
1-2
GIBSON, Alfred (d 1920 [60]) ac-
tor, singer CDP
GIBSON, Brenda (b 1870) actress
WWT/1-5
GIBSON, Chloë (b 1899) English
producer WWT/11-15
GIBSON, Clara (d 1882) actress
EA/83*
GIBSON, Don (b 1917) American
actor TW/1-3
GIBSON, Edward see Lyle,
Lyston
GIBSON, Ernest (d 1917) EA/18*
GIBSON, Florrie (d 1917) EA/18*
GIBSON, Francis (fl 1800) drama-
tist CP/3
GIBSON, Frank (1853-87) American
agent NYM
GIBSON, H. (fl c. 1620) actor DA

GIBSON, Hoot (1892-1962) Amer-
ican actor BE*, BP/47*
GIBSON, James Rhind (1842-87)
Scottish actor DD, OAA/1-2
GIBSON, Judy (b 1947) American
actress TW/27-30
GIBSON, Mrs. L. (d 1866) ac-
tress HAS
GIBSON, Madeline (b 1909) Eng-
lish actress WWT/8-10
GIBSON, Preston (1879-1937)
American dramatist WWA/1
GIBSON, Richard (fl 1494-1508)
actor DA
GIBSON, Virginia American ac-
tress TW/13-14
GIBSON, William (b 1914) Amer-
ican dramatist AAS, BE, CD,
ES, MD, MWD, PDT, WWT/
14-16
.GIBSON, Wynne (b 1905) American
actress, singer BE, WWT/7-
10
GIDDENS, George (1845-1920)
English actor CDP, DD, DP,
EA/95, GRB/1-4, OAA/2,
WWS, WWT/1-3, WWW/2
GIDE, André (1871-1951) French
dramatist OC/3
GIDEON (fl 1602) actor DA
GIDEON, Johnny (d 1901 [78])
dramatist, historian BE*,
EA/02*, WWT/14*
GIDEON, Melville J. (1884-1933)
American composer WWT/4-7
GIEHSE, Therese (d 1975 [76])
performer BP/59*
GIELGUD, Sir John (b 1904) Eng-
lish actor, producer AAS, BE,
CB, COC, ES, NTH, OC/1-3,
PDT, TW/3-23, 27, WWT/5-16
GIELGUD, Val (b 1900) English
dramatist, producer ES,
WWT/9-14
GIERASCH, Stefan (b 1926) Amer-
ican actor TW/15, 23, 26-27,
29-30
GIESEN, Genevieve see Dickin-
son, Genevieve
GIESLER, Jerry (d 1962 [75])
American lawyer BE*
GIFFARD, Mrs. (fl 1786) Eng-
lish actress CDP, HAS
GIFFARD, Henry (1694-1772)
English actor, manager CP/
3, OC/1-3, TD/1-2
GIFFARD, Mary Agnes (fl 1871-
83) actress DD

GIFFEN, Robert Lawrence (d 1946
[73]) American producer, di-
rector, authors' representative
BE*, BP/30*
GIFFORD, Elizabeth (d 1893) EA/
94*
GIFFORD, Frances [Mrs. S. L.
Gifford] (d 1892 [64]) EA/94*
GIFFORD, Gordon (d 1962 [48])
performer BE*
GIFFORD, Hazen (b 1928) Canadian
actor TW/23
GIFFORD, John actor TW/1
GIFFORD, Samuel L. (d 1896)
manager EA/97*
GIFFORD, Mrs. S. L. see
Gifford, Frances
GIFFORD, William (1756/57-1826)
English dramatist CP/3, DD
GIFFORD, William (d 1886) EA/
87*
GIFTOS, Elaine (b 1945) American
actress TW/24
GIGLI, Benjamino (1890-1957) Italian
singer ES, TW/14, WWW/5
GIGLIO, A. Gino American mana-
ger BE
GILBART, Eleanor [Ena Graham]
(d 1909) English actress GRB/1
GILBERT, Mr. dancer CDP
GILBERT, Miss see Norton,
Mrs.
GILBERT, Anne Jane see Gil-
bert, Mrs. George Henry
GILBERT, Barbara American ac-
tress TW/29
GILBERT, Benjamin A. (1904-72)
American physician BE, TW/29
GILBERT, Billy (1894-1971) Amer-
ican actor, director BE, TW/
3, 28
GILBERT, Bobby (d 1973 [75])
performer BP/58*
GILBERT, Edmond (d 1869) pro-
prietor EA/70*
GILBERT, Eliza M. (d 1873)
dancer, ballet mistress EA/74*
GILBERT, Fred (d 1903) song-
writer EA/04*
GILBERT, George Hartley (d 1878
[28]) American actor EA/79*
GILBERT, George Henry (1821-66)
English dancer, stage manager
CDP, HAS
GILBERT, Mrs. George Henry
[Ann Hartley] (1821-1904)
American actress CDP, COC,
DAB, DD, HAS, NTH, OC/1-3,

PP/1, SR, WWA/1

GILBERT, Henry (d 1868 [47])
scene artist EA/69*

GILBERT, Henry Franklin Belknap
(1868-1928) American composer
DAB, WWA/1

GILBERT, H. Pomeroy (d 1891
[54]) actor EA/92*

GILBERT, Jean [M. Winterfield]
(1879-1943) German composer
WWT/5-9

GILBERT, Jody (b 1916) American actress TW/3

GILBERT, John [John Gibbs]
(1810-89) American actor
CDP, COC, DAB, DD, HAS,
NTH, OC/1-3, WWA/H

GILBERT, John (1897/98-1936)
American actor SR, WWA/1

GILBERT, Mrs. John (1806-66)
American actress CDP, HAS

GILBERT, Mrs. Joseph see
Duff, Mary

GILBERT, Kate actress CDP

GILBERT, Lizzie [Mrs. E. G.
Savage] (d 1904 [75]) ballet
mistress EA/04*

GILBERT, Lou [né Gitlitz] (b
1909) American actor AAS,
BE, TW/5-8, 10-14, 23,
25-27, 29-30, WWT/15-16

GILBERT, Louis Wolfe (1886-
1970) Russian/American
vaudevillian, songwriter,
journalist WWA/5

GILBERT, Maria (d 1904 [73])
EA/05*

GILBERT, Marian (d 1872)
dancer EA/73*

GILBERT, Mercedes (d 1952
[58]) American actress TW/2,
8

GILBERT, Michael George (d
1908 [77]) EA/09*

GILBERT, Olive Welsh actress,
singer AAS, WWT/9-16

GILBERT, Paul (d 1976 [58])
performer BP/60*

GILBERT, Ray (d 1976 [63])
composer/lyricist BP/60*

GILBERT, Ronnie American actor
TW/25

GILBERT, Vivian (b 1881) English actor GRB/1

GILBERT, Walter (d 1947 [60])
American actor TW/3

GILBERT, William (d 1871 [23])
musician EA/72*

GILBERT, William (1804-90)
dramatist, librettist DD

GILBERT, William G. (d 1868
[25]) comedian EA/69*

GILBERT, Sir William Schwenck
(1836-1911) English dramatist
CDP, COC, DD, DNB, EA/69,
ES, GRB/1-4, HP, MH, MWD,
NTH, OC/1-3, PDT, RE, SR,
WWS, WWW/1

GILBERT, Willie (b 1916) American dramatist BE

GILBERT, Mrs. W. J. see
Mostyn, Annie

GILBEY, George singer, actor
CDP

GILBEY, Tom [Tom J. Kildare]
(d 1916) music-hall performer
EA/17*

GILBIRT, Bert singer, actor CDP

GILBURNE, Samuel (fl 1605) actor
DA, GT, NTH

GILCHRIST, Connie [Countess of
Orkney] (1865-1946) English ac-
tress CDP, COC, DD, GRB/1,
OC/1-3

GILCHRIST, James (d 1894 [62])
musician EA/95*

GILCHRIST, James Walt see
Kelvin, James

GILCHRIST, Rubina (d 1956) actress BE*, WWT/14*

GILDAY, Charles (1859-89) actor,
minstrel CDP

GILDEA, Mary (d 1957 [70]) actress TW/13

GILDER, Jeanette (d 1916 [66])
critic, dramatist BE*, WWT/
14*

GILDER, Rosamond (b 1900)
American critic BE, CB,
COC, ES, NTH, OC/1-3, WWT/
9-11, 14-16

GILDON, Charles (1665-1724)
English dramatist CP/1-3,
DD, GT, TD/1-2

GILES, Arthur (d 1904 [48])
manager EA/05*

GILES, Harriet Gilleno see Onra

GILES, John (d 1868) conductor
EA/69*

GILES, John S. (1799-1881) theatre
owner CDP

GILES, Nathaniel (fl 1595-1634)
master of the Children of the
Chapel Royal DA

GILES, Paul Kirk (1895-1976)
American actor, executive BE

GILES, Thomas (fl 1585-1613)
master of the Children of
Paul's DA

GILES'S BOY (fl 1602) actor DA

GILFERT, Charles (1787-1829)
German/American manager,
composer, conductor DD,
HAS, SR

GILFERT, Mrs. Charles [née
Agnes Holman] (1793-1833)
English actress CDP, HAS

GILFORD, Jack [né Jacob Gell-
man] American actor AAS,
BE, TW/13-18, 23-24, 26-30,
WWT/15-16

GILKES, William (d 1868) scene
artist EA/69*

GILKEY, Stanley (b 1900) American producer BE

GILL, Basil (1877-1955) English
actor GRB/1-4, TW/11,
WWT/1-11

GILL, Mrs. Basil see Cavania,
Margaret

GILL, Brendan (b 1914) American
critic, dramatist BE, WWT/
15-16

GILL, Mr. C. (d 1869 [72])
lessee EA/70*

GILL, Mrs. C. (d 1869) EA/70*

GILL, Harry (d 1893 [42]) comic
singer EA/94*

GILL, Henry (d 1954 [55])
singer WWT/14*

GILL, Mrs. J. B. see Gill,
Mary

GILL, John (d 1868 [50]) singer?
EA/69*

GILL, John (d 1971 [41]) comic
singer EA/72*

GILL, Joseph (d 1870) music-hall
manager EA/71*

GILL, Mary [Mrs. J. B. Gill]
(d 1911) EA/12*

GILL, Paul (d 1934) actor WWT/
6-7

GILL, Peter (b 1939) Welsh
director, dramatist, actor
CD, WWT/15-16

GILL, Thomas (d 1894) EA/96*

GILL, Tom (b 1916) English
actor WWT/10-16

GILL, William Fearing (1844-
1917) American dramatist
DD, WWA/1

GILLAIN, Maurice (d 1971 [80])
actor WWT/16*

GILLAME, Ernest see Clinton,
Dudley

GILLARS, Mildred E. (b 1900)
American actress SR

GILLEASE, Elizabeth Ellen see
Allen, Elizabeth

GILLENO, Albert Edward (d 1899)
clown EA/00*

GILLENO, Henry William (d 1874)
circus proprietor EA/75*

GILLENO, Janet (d 1894) EA/95*

GILLENO, Tom (d 1905) EA/06*

GILLESPIE, Jean (b 1923) American actress TW/4-5

GILLESPIE, Joseph (fl 1897)
singer, actor CDP

GILLESPIE, Marie (d 1969) performer BP/54*

GILLESPIE, Richard Henry (1878-
1952) English manager WWT/
4-11

GILLESPIE, T. (d 1883) actor
EA/84*

GILLESPIE, W. F. (b 1830)
American actor HAS

GILLESPY, James [Jim Con] (d
1898) proprietor EA/99*

GILLETT, Eric (b 1893) English
critic WWT/14

GILLETT, Margaret (d 1876 [61])
dramatist EA/77*

GILLETTE, Anita [née Luebben]
(b 1936) American actress,
singer BE, TW/19-21, 23-27,
WWT/14-16

GILLETTE, A. S. (b 1904) American educator, scene designer
BE

GILLETTE, Florence [Mrs. George
Fleet] (d 1900) actress CDP

GILLETTE, Priscilla (b 1925)
American actress TW/6-16

GILLETTE, Ruth (b 1907) American singer, actress BE, TW/
27

GILLETTE, Viola (fl 1898-1912)
American singer, actress
WWM, WWS

GILLETTE, William (1855-1937)
American actor, dramatist
CDP, COC, DAB, DD, ES,
HJD, GRB/2-4, MH, MWD,
NTH, OC/1-3, PP/1, SR,
WWA/1, WWM, WWS, WWT/
1-8, WWW/3

GILLETTE, Mrs. William (d
1888) EA/89*

GILLIAN, Kay (b 1932) American
actress TW/29

GILLIAN, Maurice (d 1971 [80])
performer BP/56*

GILLIE, Jean (1915-49) English
actress, singer WWT/9-10

GILLIES, Robert (d 1876 [24])
musician EA/77*

GILLIES, Robert Pearse (1788-
1858) translator DD

GILLIGAN, Joseph [Henry Clinton]
(d 1871) comedian EA/73*

GILLILAND, Helen (1897-1942)
Irish actress, singer WWT/
5-9

GILLILAND, Thomas (d c. 1816)
historian CDP, DD, DNB

GILLIN, Delia (d 1908) ventriloquist EA/09*

GILLINGHAM, Miss E. singer
CDP

GILLINGHAM, George (fl 1797)
musician CDP

GILLIS, Thomas C. (d 1972
[58]) fund raiser BP/56*

GILLMAN, Mabelle [Mrs. W. E.
Corey] (b 1880) American
actress, singer CDP, GRB/
2-4, WWM, WWS, WWT/1-6

GILLMORE, Frank (1867-1943)
American actor CB, CDP,
DD, EA/96, GRB/2-4, NTH,
SR, WWA/2, WWM, WWS,
WWT/1-9

GILLMORE, Mrs. Frank see
McGilvray, Laura

GILLMORE, Margalo (b 1897)
English actress AAS, BE,
TW/2-16, WWT/5-14

GILLO, Miss see Carey, Mrs.
George Saville

GILLUM, William (d 1797)
dramatist CP/3

GILMAN, Ada (d 1921 [67]) actress CDP, PP/1

GILMAN, Henry (d 1902 [59])
manager EA/04*

GILMAN, Larry (b 1950) American actor TW/30

GILMAN, Lawrence (1878-1939)
American critic WWA/1

GILMAN, Mabelle see Gillman,
Mabelle

GILMER, Mlle. (d 1903 [79])
dancer EA/04*

GILMER, Albert (d 1917 [56])
manager GRB/2-4

GILMER, Albert Hatton (1878-
1950) American dramatist,
educator WWA/3

GILMER, William J. (d 1899 [72])
EA/01*

GILMORE, Barney (b 1867) American singer, comedian WWS

GILMORE, Douglas (d 1950 [47])
actor TW/7

GILMORE, Edward G. (d 1908
[69]) American manager CDP,
GRB/4

GILMORE, Mrs. Harry (d 1912
[41]) EA/13*

GILMORE, Janette (b 1905) actress, singer WWT/6-8

GILMORE, Patrick Sarsfield
(1829-92) Irish bandmaster
CDP, DAB, SR

GILMORE, Paul (fl 1896) actor
SR

GILMORE, Peter (b 1931) actor,
singer WWT/15-16

GILMORE, Ruth (d 1976) performer BP/60*

GILMORE, Thomas (d 1892 [35])
scene artist EA/93*

GILMORE, Virginia (b 1919)
American actress BE, TW/1-4,
WWT/10-14

GILMORE, W. H. producer, actor
WWT/6-7

GILMOUR, Brian (1894-1954) actor
WWT/6-8

GILMOUR, Gordon (d 1962 [48])
actor, dramatist BE*

GILMOUR, J. H. (d 1922 [65])
Canadian actor, producer
WWS

GILPIN, Charles Sidney (1878-
1930) American actor COC,
DAB, ES, OC/1-3, SR, WWA/
1, WWT/5-6

GILPIN, John (b 1930) English
dancer ES

GILROY, Frank D. (b 1925)
American dramatist CB, CD,
CH, ES, HJD, MH, MWD,
WWT/15-16

GILSON, Lottie (1867-1912) actress CDP, SR

GILTINAN, Donal (d 1976 [67])
dramatist BP/60*

GILTON, Miss (d 1880) music-
hall performer EA/81*

GIM, Asa (b 1945) Korean actress
TW/28-29

GIMBEL, Norman (b 1927) American lyricist, composer BE

GINASTERA, Alberto (b 1916)
Argentinian composer CB

GINGOLD, Hermione Ferdinanda
(b 1897) English actress AAS,
BE, CB, COC, ES, TW/10-
21, 29-30, WWT/9-16
GINISTY, Paul (d 1932 [66])
dramatist, critic BE*, WWT/
14*
GINNER, Ruby (b 1886) French
dancer WWT/5-9
GINNES, Abram S. (b 1914)
dramatist BE
GINNETT, Albert George (d 1894)
EA/95*
GINNETT, Amelia [Mrs. Claude
Ginnett] (d 1896 [31]) EA/97*
GINNETT, Claude (d 1911 [54])
circus proprietor EA/13*
GINNETT, Mrs. Claude see
Ginnett, Amelia
GINNETT, Ellen [Mrs. William
Ginnett] (d 1910 [67]) EA/11*
GINNETT, Florence [Mrs. Fred
Ginnett] (d 1898) circus pro-
prietor EA/99*
GINNETT, Mrs. Fred see
Ginnett, Florence
GINNETT, George (d 1907) circus
proprietor EA/08*
GINNETT, John Frederick (d
1892) circus proprietor EA/
93*
GINNETT, Mrs. J. P. (d 1877
[75]) EA/78*
GINNETT, William (d 1888 [49])
circus proprietor EA/89*
GINNETT, Mrs. William see
Ginnett, Ellen
GINSBERG, Ernest (d 1964 [61])
performer BP/49*
GINSBERG, Sol see Violinsky
GINSBURG, Allen (b 1926) Amer-
ican actor TW/29
GINSBURY, Norman (b 1903)
English dramatist BE, WWT/
9-16
GINTY, Elizabeth Beall (d 1949
[86]) American dramatist
BE*, BP/34*
GINTY, Robert (b 1948) American
actor TW/29
GINZLER, Robert (d 1962 [53])
orchestrator BP/47*
GIOI, Vivi (d 1975 [58]) per-
former BP/60*
GIONI, J. M. (fl 1854) actor
HAS
GIORDANI, Thomaso (fl 1783-1804)
composer, manager TD/1-2

GIORDANO, Frank American actor
TW/26, 30
GIORDMAINE, John (d 1974 [75])
performer BP/58*
GIORGI, Signora see D'Orta,
Rachele
GIORGI, Leonard (d 1871 [30])
musician EA/72*
GIORZA, Paolo (1832-1914) Italian
composer ES
GIOVANELLI, Edward (d 1881
[57]) manager WWT/14*
GIPSON, Fred (d 1973 [65])
dramatist BP/58*
GIRARD, Donald (b 1953) Ameri-
can actor TW/25-26
GIRARD, Eddie (b 1858) minstrel,
vaudevillian CDP
GIRARD, Mrs. Emile see
Girard, Kate
GIRARD, Florence [Mrs. Henry
E. Abbey] (fl 1877) actress
CDP
GIRARD, Kate [Mrs. George Faw-
cett Rowe] (d 1885) actress
CDP
GIRARD, Kate [Mrs. Emile Gir-
ard] (d 1897 [36]) pantomimist
EA/99*
GIRARD, Oscar (d 1899) Ameri-
can comedian EA/00*
GIRARDEAU, Frank (b 1942)
American actor TW/29
GIRARDELLI, Josephine (fl 1820)
fire-eater CDP
GIRARDOT, Mlle. (fl 1829)
French actress HAS
GIRARDOT, Etienne (1856-1939)
English/American actor SR,
WWM, WWS
GIRARDOT, Isabelle English ac-
tress WWS
GIRAUDOUX, Jean (1882-1944)
French dramatist COC, MD,
OC/1-3
GIRDLESTONE, Amy [née Emma
Ames] (fl 1868) actress HAS
GIRDLESTONE, Madge English
actress GRB/1-2
GIROFLI, Mme. John (d 1893)
ballet mistress EA/94*
GISH, Dorothy (1898-1968) Amer-
ican actress BE, CB, ES,
NTH, SR, TW/2-21, 25, WWT/
6-14
GISH, Lillian (b 1896/99) Ameri-
can actress BE, CB, ES,
NTH, SR, TW/2-22, 24, 29-30,

WWT/7-16
GISH, Mary R. (c. 1860-1948)
actress SR
GITANA, Gertie [Gertrude Mary
Ross] (1889-1957) American
music-hall performer COC,
OC/3
GITLITZ, Lou see Gilbert, Lou
GITTINS, Mary (d 1906) EA/07*
GIUBELEI, Mr. (d 1851) singer
HAS
GIUBILEI, Augustine (d 1848)
dancer CDP, HAS
GIUBILEI, Theodore Victor (1801-
45) English actor, singer CDP,
HAS
GIUGLINI, Antonio (1827-65)
Italian singer ES
GIULINI, Carlo Maria (b 1914)
Italian conductor ES
GIVENS, Jimmie (d 1964 [47])
performer BE*
GIVLER, Mary Louise [Mrs.
Oscar Shaw] (d 1964 [77])
American performer BE*
GIVNEY, Kathryn American ac-
tress TW/1-4
GJERSTAD, John see Gerstad,
John
GLADDING, R. H. (fl 1858)
actor HAS
GLADHILL, John (d 1874) actor,
scene painter EA/75*
GLADMAN, Florence [Mrs.
André Charlot] (d 1956 [66])
performer, producer BE*,
WWT/14*
GLADSTANE, Mary (b 1830)
English actress CDP, HAS
GLADSTONE, W. H. (d 1900
[80]) actor EA/01*, WWT/14*
GLAGOLIN, Boris (d 1948 [70])
actor BE*, WWT/14*
GLANVILLE, Maxwell (b 1918)
West Indian actor TW/25-26,
29-30
GLAPTHORNE, Henry (fl 1634-
40) dramatist CP/1-3, DD,
DNB, FGF
GLASER, Darrel (b 1957) Amer-
ican actor TW/25-26
GLASER, Joseph G. (d 1969
[72]) agent BP/54*
GLASER, Lulu [Mrs. R. C.
Herz] (1874/76-1958) Amer-
ican actress, singer CDP,
DD, GRB/2-4, SR, TW/15,
WWA/3, WWS, WWT/1-7

GLASER, Paul (d 1974 [50]) exe-
cutive BP/57*
GLASER, Vaughan actor TW/2
GLASKIN, T. J. (d 1890) EA/91*
GLASPELL, Susan (1882-1948)
American dramatist COC,
DAB, ES, HJD, MD, MH,
MWD, NTH, OC/1-3, TW/5,
WWT/5-10, WWW/4
GLASS, Dudley (b 1899) Australian
composer WWT/9-14
GLASS, Montague (1877-1934)
English dramatist NTH, WWT/
4-7
GLASSER, Lulu see Glaser,
Lulu
GLASSFORD, Andrew L. (d 1918)
actor, manager SR
GLASSFORD, David (1866-1935)
Australian actor SR, WWM,
WWT/7
GLASSINGTON, Mr. prompter
TD/2
GLASSMAN, William (b 1945)
American actor TW/25
GLAUM, Louise (d 1970 [70])
performer BP/55*
GLAZER, Barney (d 1975 [66])
columnist BP/59*
GLAZER, Benjamin (1887-1956)
Irish/American dramatist ES
GLAZER, Maurice (d 1971 [51])
producer/director/choreographer
BP/56*
GLAZIER, Marie (b 1881) Ameri-
can actress, vaudevillian
WWM
GLEASON, Frederic Grant (1848-
1903) American composer
DAB, WWA/1
GLEASON, Jackie (b 1916) Amer-
ican comedian, composer BE,
ES, TW/1, 5-6
GLEASON, James (1886-1959)
American actor, dramatist,
manager TW/15, WWA/3,
WWT/6-10
GLEASON, John (b 1941) American
lighting designer WWT/16
GLEASON, Lucille Webster (1888-
1947) American actress SR,
TW/3
GLEASON, Ralph J. (d 1975 [58])
critic BP/60*
GLEASON, Russell (d 1945 [36])
actor TW/2
GLEASON, Thomas (b 1915)
American actor TW/5-10

GLEN, Archie (d 1966 [77])
performer BP/50*
GLENDINNING, Ernest (1884-
1936) English actor SR,
WWM, WWT/4-8
GLENDINNING, Ethel (b 1910)
Scottish actress WWT/7, 9
GLENDINNING, John (1857-1916)
English actor GRB/3-4,
WWS, WWT/1-3
GLENDINNING, Mrs. John see
Millward, Jessie
GLENGALL, Lord dramatist DD
GLENISTER, Frank (1860-1945)
manager WWT/4-9
GLENN, Alice (b 1941) American
actress TW/23
GLENN, Bette (b 1946) American
actress TW/27
GLENN, Cynda (d 1968 [59]) per-
former BP/53*
GLENN, Frederick (b 1939)
American actor TW/26
GLENN, Raymond [Bob Custer]
(d 1974 [76]) performer BP/
59*
GLENN, Roy, Sr. (d 1971 [56])
performer BP/55*
GLENN, Samuel W. (1828-1903)
American actor CDP, HAS
GLENN, Scott (b 1942) American
actor TW/22-24
GLENNEY, Bessie [Elizabeth
Alice Graham] (d 1903) ac-
tress EA/04*
GLENNEY, Charles see Glenny,
Charles H.
GLENNEY, Thomas H. see
Glenny, Thomas H.
GLENNIE, Brian (b 1912) Eng-
lish actor WWT/6-8
GLENNIE, Dora English actress
GRB/1-2
GLENNIE, Miss G. (d 1876
[23]) actress EA/77*
GLENNIE, Herbert [George
Holiday] (d 1890) EA/91*
GLENN-SMITH, Michael (b 1945)
American actor TW/25-26,
30
GLENNY [or Glenney], Charles
H. (1857-1922) Scottish actor
DD, DP, EA/95, GRB/1-4,
OAA/2, WWT/1-4
GLENNY, Mrs. Charles see
Abingdon, Marie
GLENNY, Mrs. Charles Hall
see Glenny, Isabella Jane

GLENNY, Isabella Jane [Mrs.
Charles Hall Glenny] (d 1891
[32]) EA/93*
GLENNY, Thomas H. (d 1891
[60]) actor CDP, DD
GLENROY, William Cruikshanks
(d 1911) manager EA/12*
GLENVILLE, Harry (d 1910 [62])
actor EA/11*
GLENVILLE, Peter (b 1913) Eng-
lish actor, director, producer,
dramatist BE, COC, ES,
PDT, TW/7-8, WWT/8-16
GLENVILLE, Philip Irish actor
TD/1-2
GLENVILLE, Shaun (1884-1968)
Irish actor COC, WWT/4-13
GLICK, Carl (1889-1971) Ameri-
can dramatist, director NTH,
WWA/5
GLICK, Joseph (1880-1943) Amer-
ican actor, manager SR
GLICKMAN, Will (b 1910) Amer-
ican librettist BE
GLINDON, Mr. singer, songwrit-
er CDP
GLOSE, Augusta [Mrs. Charles
S. Leeds] (fl 1900s) American
vaudevillian WWM
GLOSSOP, Mme. Feron (d 1853)
singer EA/72*
GLOSSOP, Joseph (d 1835) actor,
producer BE*, WWT/14*
GLOSSOP, Mrs. Joseph see
Feron, Elizabeth
GLOSSOP, Maria Elizabeth see
Harris, Maria
GLOSSOP, Mary Ann see
Harris, Mary Ann
GLOSSOP-HARRIS, Florence
(1883-1931) English actress,
producer BE*, WWT/14*
GLOUCHEVITCH, Barbara (d 1974
[46]) performer BP/59*
GLOVER, Mrs. (d 1871) EA/72*
GLOVER, Mrs. see Glover,
Julia
GLOVER, Annie (d 1910) EA/11*
GLOVER, Augustus [Sidney De
Fivas] (1846-1903) Scottish
actor DD, OAA/1-2
GLOVER, Bessie (d 1911 [50])
actress EA/12*
GLOVER, Bruce (b 1932) American
actor TW/17-20
GLOVER, Carrie (d 1976 [49])
performer BP/60*
GLOVER, Charles William (1806-

63) English composer, musician DD, DNB

GLOVER, David (b 1927) English actor TW/26

GLOVER, Edmund (1813-60) English manager, actor DD, DNB, OC/1-3

GLOVER, Edmund Samuel (d 1884 [24]) property master EA/85*

GLOVER, Eleanor [Mrs. George Harvey] (d 1908 [25]) actress EA/09*

GLOVER, Ferdinand (d 1859 [23]) singer EA/72*

GLOVER, Frederick (fl 1869-74) actor DD

GLOVER, Halcott (1877-1949) English dramatist WWT/8-9, WWW/4

GLOVER, Howard W. (d 1875) composer EA/76*

GLOVER, James Mackey (1861-1931) Irish conductor, composer, managing director DD, GRB/1-4, WWT/1-6, WWW/3

GLOVER, John (b 1944) American actor TW/27-30

GLOVER, Mrs. John (d 1881) EA/82*

GLOVER, Julia [née Betterton] (1779/81/83-1850) English actress BS, CDP, DD, DNB, ES, GT, OC/1-3, OX

GLOVER, Julian (b 1935) English actor WWT/15-16

GLOVER, Lyman Beecher (1846-1915) American manager WWA/1, WWM

GLOVER, Phillis Frances Agnes (1807-31) actress CDP, OX

GLOVER, Phyllis (fl 1870) actress DD

GLOVER, Richard (1712-85) dramatist CP/1-3, DD, TD/1-2

GLOVER, Stephen (d 1869 [58]) composer EA/71*

GLOVER, Thomas J. (d 1971) performer BP/55*

GLOVER, William (d 1916 [83]) manager, scene artist, lessee DD

GLOVER, William (b 1911) American critic BE

GLOVER, William Howard (1819-75) English composer, conductor, musician DD, DNB, WWA/H

GLUCK, Alma (1884-1938) Rumanian singer DAB, WWA/1

GLUCK, Arnold Jack see Arnold, Jack

GLUCKMAN, Leon (b 1922) South African actor, director, producing manager WWT/16

GLYN, Gertrude (d 1908 [52]) composer EA/09*

GLYN, Isabella [Mrs. E. S. Dallas] (1823-89) Scottish actress CDP, DD, DNB, ES, OAA/1-2

GLYN, Neva Carr (d 1975) performer BP/60*

GLYNN, Golly see Green (d 1916)

GLYNNE, Angela (b 1933) English actress WWT/10-12

GLYNNE, Ella Florentia (d 1904 [20]) EA/06*

GLYNNE, Howell (d 1969 [64]) performer BP/54*

GLYNNE, Mary (1898-1954) Welsh actress WWT/2-11

GLYNNE, Olivia (b 1888) English actress GRB/2

GNATT, Poul (b 1923) Danish dancer, dancing teacher ES

GNONE, Sig. (fl 1859) actor HAS

GOAD, Christopher (fl 1629-35) actor DA

GOBBI, Tito (b 1913/15) Italian singer CB, ES

GOBERMAN, Max (d 1962 [51]) American conductor BE*

GOBLE, Diana (b 1946) American actress TW/26

GODARD, Benjamin (d 1895) composer EA/96*

GODD, Barbara (d 1944) actress BE*

GODDARD, Mrs. [Katie Hamilton] (d 1883 [42]) Scottish singer EA/84*

GODDARD, Miss (fl 1850) actress CDP

GODDARD, Alfred (d 1908 [57]) proprietor EA/09*

GODDARD, Arabella (b 1836) pianist CDP

GODDARD, Charles W. (1879-1951) American dramatist WWA/3, WWT/5-11

GODDARD, Percy (d 1917 [33])

musician EA/18*
GODDARD, Willoughby (b 1926)
English actor WWT/14-16
GODDEN, Jimmy (1879-1956)
English actor WWT/5-11
GODDERIS, Albert (d 1971 [89])
performer BP/55*
GODEFROID, Felix (d 1897 [79])
musician, composer EA/98*
GODEY, Mrs. [née Juliet Cath-
erine Durang] (1804-49) Amer-
ican dancer, actress HAS
GODEY, Howard (d 1894 [29])
EA/95*
GODFREY, Charles [Paul Lacey]
(1851-1900) English music-
hall singer CDP, OC/1-3
GODFREY, Mrs. Charles see
Godfrey, Maude
GODFREY, Mrs. Daniel God-
frey (d 1890) EA/92*
GODFREY, Derek (b 1924) Eng-
lish actor AAS, WWT/14-16
GODFREY, Frederick (d 1882)
bandmaster EA/83*
GODFREY, Fred W. (d 1912
[43]) EA/13*
GODFREY, George (d 1974
[80+]) talent scout BP/58*
GODFREY, George William (1844-
97) dramatist DD
GODFREY, Henry (d 1879 [43])
equestrian EA/80*
GODFREY, H. S. [Harry Squire
Camp] (b 1877) English vari-
ety artist GRB/1
GODFREY, Maude [Mrs. Charles
Godfrey] (d 1897 [30]) EA/
98*
GODFREY, Peter (1899-1970)
English actor, manager, pro-
ducer COC, WWT/6-11
GODFREY, Renee Haal (d 1964
[44]) performer BE*
GODFREY, Thomas (1736-63)
American dramatist COC,
CP/3, DAB, DD, DNB, EAP,
ES, NTH, OC/1-3, RJ,
WWA/H
GODFREY-TURNER, L. [Leopold
McClintock Turner] English
critic WWT/1-4
GODKIN, Paul (b 1918) American
actor TW/4
GODMOND, Christopher (fl 1836-
40?) dramatist DD
GODOWSKY, Dagmar (d 1975
[78]) actress WWT/16*

GODREAU, Miguel (b 1946) Puerto
Rican actor TW/25
GODRICH, Thomas (d 1887 [50])
music-hall proprietor EA/88*
GODWIN, Arthur J. (d 1892 [39])
musician, musical director
EA/93*
GODWIN, Edward William (1833-
86) English architect, designer
COC, DD, OC/1-3
GODWIN, Harold (d 1917 [42])
EA/18*
GODWIN, Harry (d 1902) manager
EA/03*
GODWIN, Richard (fl 1631) actor
DA
GODWIN, Will (fl 1890s?) singer,
composer CDP
GODWIN, William (1756-1836)
dramatist CP/3, DD
GOEKEL, Fred (b 1936) American
actor TW/23
GOETHE, Johann Wolfgang von
(1749-1832) German dramatist
COC
GOETTLING, Mary Rebecca see
Dolan, Mary
GOETZ, Augustus (d 1957 [56])
American dramatist BE*,
BP/42*, WWT/14*
GOETZ, E. Ray (d 1954 [68])
English producer, songwriter
TW/11
GOETZ, Ruth Goodman (b 1912)
American dramatist WWT/13-
16
GOETZ, Theo (d 1972 [78]) Austri-
an actor TW/29
GOETZL, Dr. Anselm (d 1923
[44]) composer BP/7*
GOFF, Mr. actor CDP
GOFF, Mr. see Goiffee, Mons.
GOFF, Lewin (b 1919) American
educator BE
GOFFE, Alexander see Goughe,
Alexander
GOFFE, Robert see Goughe,
Robert
GOFFE, Thomas (1591-1629) Eng-
lish dramatist CP/1-3, DD,
FGF
GOFFIN, Cora (b 1901/02) actress
WWT/3-11
GOFFIN, Peter (1906-74) English
designer BTR/74, WWT/9-14
GOFORTH, Frances American
actress, dramatist BE, TW/1
GOFTON, E. Story (d 1939 [92])

actor BE*, WWT/14*

GOGOL, Nikolai Vasilievich
(1809-52) Russian dramatist
COC, OC/2-3

GOIFFEE, Mons. [né Goff] (fl
1831) English actor, pantomimist HAS

GOIFFEE, Mme. (fl 1832) English? actress HAS

GOIMBAULT, Odette (b 1901)
French actress WWT/3

GOING, Frederica American actress TW/1

GOLD, Belle [Mrs. A. W.
Cross] (b 1882) American
actress WWM, WWS

GOLD, Ben (d 1918) EA/19*

GOLD, David (b 1929) American
dancer TW/24

GOLD, Jimmy (d 1967 [81/87])
comedian BP/52*, WWT/
15*

GOLD, Joey (d 1966) ticket broker
BP/51*

GOLD, Michael (1893-1967) American dramatist HJD, MD,
MWD

GOLD, Sid (d 1974 [67]) performer BP/58*

GOLD, Zisha (b 1910) American
actress TW/25

GOLDBECK, Robert (1839-1908)
Prussian composer DAB

GOLDBERG, Dora see Bayes,
Nora

GOLDBERG, Isaac (1887-1938)
American writer WWA/1

GOLDBERG, J. P. (d 1890 [65])
professor of music EA/92*

GOLDBERG, Marcus see Lyle,
Kenyon

"GOLDBERG, Max" (fl 1895-98)
dramatist DD

GOLDBERG, Miles M. (b 1882)
American critic WWM

GOLDBERG, Nathan (d 1961
[74]) Austrian actor, producer
BE*

GOLDBERG, Rose (d 1966 [78])
actress TW/23

GOLDBERG, R[ubin?] L. (1883-
1974?) American vaudevillian
WWM

GOLDBERG, Mrs. Samuel see
Elinore, Kate

GOLDBLATT, Charles see
Vance, Charles

GOLDBLATT, Harold M. (d 1966

[75]) lawyer BP/51*

GOLDBLATT, Martin (d 1968
[43]) publicist BP/52*

GOLDBOGEN, Michael see
Todd, Michael

GOLDEN, Bartholomew (d 1897
[54]) proprietor EA/99*

GOLDEN, Edward (b 1917) Irish
actor TW/4

GOLDEN, Edward J., Jr. (b 1934)
American director, actor, educator BE

GOLDEN, George Fuller (1868-
1912) American singer, dancer,
monologist CDP

GOLDEN, Grace (fl 1889) American actress WWA/5

GOLDEN, John (1874/75-1955)
American dramatist, composer,
producer CB, COC, NTH,
SR, TW/2-8, 12, WWA/3,
WWT/5-11

GOLDEN, John (d 1972 [68]) com-
poser/lyricist BP/57*

GOLDEN, Joseph (b 1928) American educator, dramatist BE

GOLDEN, Michael (b 1913) Irish
actor WWT/10-16

GOLDEN, Richard (1853/54-1909)
American actor, singer DD,
GRB/3-4, SR, WWA/1, WWS

GOLDEN, Mrs. Richard see
Wiley, Dora

GOLDER, Jennie (d 1928 [34])
actress BE*, WWT/14*

GOLDER, Lew (d 1962 [78]) producer BE*

GOLDFADEN, Abraham (1840-
1908) Russian dramatist COC,
ES, MWD, OC/1-3, RE

GOLDGRAN, Henry (d 1972 [58])
producer/director/choreographer
BP/57*

GOLDHARDT, William (d 1967
[72]) treasurer BP/52*

GOLDIE, F. Wyndham (1897/98-
1957) English actor WWT/8-12

GOLDIE, Horace (d 1939 [65])
magician BE*

GOLDIE, Hugh (b 1919) English
director, actor WWT/15-16

GOLDIE, Sydney E. (d 1974 [73])
journalist BP/59*

GOLDIN, Elias (d 1972 [59]) pro-
ducer/director/choreographer
BP/56*

GOLDIN, Horace (1873-1939)
Russian/American illusionist

DAB, GRB/1-3, SR

GOLDINA, Miriam (b 1898) Russian actress, director, translator BE

GOLDING (fl 1640?) actor DA

GOLDING, Arthur (d 1570) dramatist CP/2-3, DD

GOLDING, George (d 1907 [47]) comedian EA/08*

GOLDING, William (b 1911) English dramatist CB, MWD

GOLDINGHAM, William dramatist CP/3, FGF

GOLDMAN, Edwin Franks (1878-1956) American conductor, composer BE*

GOLDMAN, Irving (b 1909) American executive BE

GOLDMAN, Isaac (d 1973 [80]) performer BP/58*

GOLDMAN, James (b 1927) American dramatist, lyricist BE, CD, MH

GOLDMAN, Milton (b 1914) American talent representative BE

GOLDMAN, Nannie English actress GRB/1

GOLDMAN, Theodore see Mann, Theodore

GOLDMAN, William (b 1931) American dramatist BE, CD

GOLDMANN, Max see Reinhardt, Max

GOLDNER, Charles (1900-65) Austrian actor, producer WWT/10-11

GOLDONI, Carlo (1707-93) Italian dramatist OC/1-3

GOLDOVSKY, Boris (b 1908) Russian director, conductor CB

GOLDOWSKY, Dagmar (d 1975 [78]) performer BP/59*

GOLDRICH, Fred (b 1947) American actor TW/29

GOLDSACK, Daisy (fl 1900?) singer CDP

GOLDSCHMID, Otto (fl 1851) actor? singer? HAS

GOLDSCHMIDT, Otto (d 1907 [77]) composer EA/08*

GOLDSMID, Lionel (fl 1856) English actor HAS

GOLDSMITH, Edith see Oliver, Edith

GOLDSMITH, Eleanor (b 1923) American costume designer

TW/5

GOLDSMITH, Francis (d 1655) dramatist CP/1-3, DD

GOLDSMITH, George American talent representative BE

GOLDSMITH, Ina (d 1915 [56]) actress EA/96

GOLDSMITH, Mary (fl 1803-04) dramatist CP/3

GOLDSMITH, Merwin (b 1937) American actor TW/24, 26, 28-30

GOLDSMITH, Oliver (1730-74) English dramatist CDP, COC, CP/2-3, DD, DNB, ES, GT, HP, MH, NTH, OC/1-3, PDT, RE, SR, TD/1-2

GOLDSMITH, R. G. (d 1887 [67]) manager EA/88*

GOLDSMITH, Ted (b 1909) American press representative BE

GOLDSON, Belinda see Groshon, Belinda

GOLDSTEIN, Becky (d 1971 [94]) actress BP/55*, WWT/16*

GOLDSTEIN, Braham see Murray, Braham

GOLDSTEIN, Elliott see Gould, Elliott

GOLDSTEIN, Jennie (1899-1960) American actress TW/9-11, 16

GOLDSTEIN, Robert (d 1974 [70]) producer/director/choreographer BP/58*

GOLDSTON, James Mayer see Mokana

GOLDSTONE, Nat (d 1966 [62]) producer/director/choreographer BP/51*

GOLDTHWAIT, Jennie (fl 1887) American actress SR

GOLDTWAITE, Dora (d 1922) actress CDP

GOLENPAUL, Dan (d 1974 [73]) producer/director/choreographer BP/58*

GOLLANCZ, Israel scholar DD

GOLLICKER, James G. see Ashmer, James G.

GOLLMER, Benjamin (1865-1947) circus manager SR

GOLONKA, Arlene (b 1936) American actress BE

GOLSWORTHY, Arnold (1865-1939) dramatist, writer WWW/3

GOLTERMANN, Julius (d 1876) composer, musician EA/77*

GOLUB, Harry (d 1970 [74])
performer BP/55*
GOMBELL, Minna (1893-1973)
American actress TW/29,
WWT/7-10
GOMERSAL, Mr. (fl 1850s) actor
DD
GOMERSAL, Alexander Edward
(1788-1862) English actor,
manager CDP, DD
GOMERSAL, Amy [Mrs. William
Gomersal] (d 1903 [43]) EA/
04*
GOMERSAL, Maria [Mrs. Wil-
liam Gomersal] (d 1871 [26])
EA/72*
GOMERSAL, Robert (1600-46?)
English dramatist CP/1-3,
DD, DNB, FGF
GOMERSAL, William (d 1902
[70]) lessee EA/03*
GOMERSAL, Mrs. William
see Gomersal, Amy
GOMERSAL, Mrs. William
see Gomersal, Maria
GOMERSALL, E. W. (d 1863)
English actor, lessee, mana-
ger HAS
GOMERSALL, William (fl 1863-
68) English actor, singer
HAS
GOMERSALL, Mrs. William
(fl 1863-68) English actress,
singer HAS
GOMEZ, Alice (d 1922) Indian
singer WWW/2
GOMEZ, Gene (fl 1910?) singer
CDP
GOMEZ, Jerry (d 1974 [73])
producer/director/choreographer
BP/59*
GOMEZ, Thomas (1905-71) Amer-
ican actor BE, TW/28
GOMPERTZ, Mrs. (d 1878 [63])
EA/79*
GONCHAROV, George (d 1954
[50]) ballet master WWT/14*
GONCHAROVA, Nathalie (1881-
1962) Russian scene designer
COC
GONDOLFO, Lucia Rosita (d
1891 [19]) lion tamer EA/92*
GONNE, Lillian (fl 1910?)
singer CDP
GONZALES, Mary F. (fl 1854)
actress HAS
GONZALEZ, Nilda (b 1929)
Puerto Rican educator BE

GOOCH, Harriet (d 1895 [79])
proprietor EA/96*
GOOCH, Henry (d 1873 [62])
music-hall proprietor EA/74*
GOOCH, Steve (b 1945) English
dramatist, director CD
GOOD, Mrs. Graham see Caird,
Dora
GOOD, Karen (b 1948) American
actress TW/29
GOOD, Kip (d 1964 [45]) actor,
production assistant BE*,
BP/48*
GOOD, William (d 1911) manager,
journalist EA/12*
GOODALE, Baptiste (fl 1589) actor
DA
GOODALE, George Pomeroy (1843-
1919) American critic WWA/1
GOODALE, Thomas (fl 1581-93)
actor DA
GOODALL, Mrs. [née Stanton]
see Goodall, Charlotte
GOODALL, Miss (b 1801?) singer
CDP
GOODALL, Anne (1847-77) actress
DD
GOODALL, Bella (1852-84) actress
DD
GOODALL, Charlotte [née Stanton]
(1765-1830) actress CDP, DD,
DNB, GT, TD/1-2
GOODALL, Edyth (1886-1929)
Scottish actress WWT/2-5
GOODALL, Elizabeth (d 1884
[75]) EA/85*
GOODALL, Isabella (b 1851) Eng-
lish actress OAA/1-2
GOODALL, James see Goodhall,
James
GOODALL, M. A. [Mrs. Maltheus
Goodall] (d 1889) EA/90*
GOODALL, Mrs. Maltheus see
Goodall, M. A.
GOODALL, Rose (fl 1879) actress
CDP
GOODALL, Thomas (b 1767) Eng-
lish dramatist CP/3
GOODALL, Thomas (d 1881) mu-
sician EA/82*
GOODALL, William (fl 1740)
dramatist CP/2-3, GT
GOODALL, William R. (1831-56)
American actor CDP, HAS
GOODALL, Mrs. William R. [née
Fanny L. Riley] (1834-58)
American actress HAS
GOODBODY, Buzz (d 1975 [28])

director BP/59*, WWT/16*

GOODCHILD, Edward (d 1878
[63]) proprietor EA/79*

GOODCHILD, George (1888-1969)
English dramatist WWW/6

GOODE, Jack (d 1971 [63]) actor,
singer TW/28

GOODENOUGH, Richard Josceline
(d 1781) dramatist CP/2-3,
GT

GOODENOW, Miriam C. see
Robb, Mariam G.

GOODES, Cpt. (d 1916) reciter,
teacher EA/17*

GOODFRIEND, Lynda (b 1950)
American actress TW/28

GOODHALL, James (fl c. 1754-
72) English? dramatist CP/
2-3, GT

GOODHALL, Mathew (d 1897)
music-hall performer EA/98*

GOODHART, Charles (d 1910
[41]) actor EA/12*

GOODING, R. A. (d 1881)
spiritualist EA/82*

GOODLIFFE, John Herbert [Sig.
Trippello] (d 1917) EA/18*

GOODLIFFE, Michael (1914-76)
English actor AAS, WWT/
12-16

GOODMAN, Mr. (fl 18th cent)
American actor NTH

GOODMAN, Mr. (fl 1772) English? actor HAS

GOODMAN, Alfred (1890-1972)
Russian musical director,
composer BE, TW/28

GOODMAN, Arthur (d 1965 [74])
dramatist BP/49*

GOODMAN, Bernard R. (d 1975
[64]) producer/director/chore-
ographer BP/60*

GOODMAN, Cardell [or Cardonnel]
(c. 1649-99) English actor
COC, DD, OC/1-3

GOODMAN, Dody American actress BE, TW/22, 25-26,
29-30, WWT/15-16

GOODMAN, Edward (d 1962 [74])
American dramatist, producer,
director TW/19

GOODMAN, Frank (d 1897) business manager EA/98*

GOODMAN, Frank (b 1916) American press representative BE

GOODMAN, Gladys B. see
Unger, Gladys B.

GOODMAN, Harry (d 1970) com-

poser/lyricist BP/55*

GOODMAN, John Spellman (1838-
68) American actor HAS

GOODMAN, Jules Eckert (1876-
1962) American dramatist MH,
NTH, WWA/4, WWM, WWT/
4-11

GOODMAN, Kenneth Sawyer (1883-
1918) American dramatist
DAB

GOODMAN, Lillian Rosedale (d
1972 [84]) performer BP/56*

GOODMAN, Paul (1911-72) American dramatist WWA/5

GOODMAN, Philip (d 1940 [55])
American producer, manager
WWT/6-7

GOODMAN, Randolph (b 1908)
American educator, dramatist
BE

GOODMAN, Richard (d 1881) actor, scene artist EA/82*

GOODMAN, Robyn (b 1947) American actress TW/30

GOODNER, Carol (b 1904) American actress BE, TW/2-11,
18, WWT/6-14

GOODRICH, Arthur F. (1878-1941)
American dramatist CB, WWA/
1, WWT/5-9

GOODRICH, Edna [Mrs. Nat C.
Goodwin] (b 1883) American
actress GRB/3-4, SR, WWM,
WWS, WWT/1-7

GOODRICH, Frances (b 1891?)
American dramatist BE, MH

GOODRICH, Frank Boott (1826-94)
American dramatist DAB

GOODRICH, Louis [L. G. Abbot
Anderson] (d 1945 [72]) English
actor GRB/1-4, WWT/4-9

GOODRICH, Sallie B. (fl 1863-68)
actress, lecturer HAS

GOODROW, Garry (b 1938) American actor TW/29-30

GOODSELL, Comfort (d 1868 [40])
comedian HAS

GOODSELL, G. Dean (b 1907)
American educator, director,
choreographer BE

GOODSON, Lennie (d 1917 [15])
EA/18*

GOODWIN, Bonnie (d 1907) coon
impersonator EA/08*

GOODWIN, Clara (d 1903 [85])
dancer EA/04*

GOODWIN, Ewart (b 1907) American executive BE

GOODWIN, George K. (1830-82)
manager CDP
GOODWIN, J. Cheever (1850-
1912) American dramatist DD,
GRB/3-4, SR, WWA/1, WWS,
WWT/1
GOODWIN, John (d 1883) EA/84*
GOODWIN, John (b 1921) English
press representative WWT/
11-16
GOODWIN, Louise (d 1968 [86])
performer BP/52*
GOODWIN, Michael American
actor TW/29
GOODWIN, Myra (1867-92) Amer-
ican actress CDP
GOODWIN, Nat Carl (1857-1919)
American actor CDP, COC,
DAB, GRB/2-4, OC/3, PP/1,
SR, WWA/1, WWM, WWS,
WWT/1-3, WWW/2
GOODWIN, Mrs. Nat Carl see
Elliott, Maxine
GOODWIN, Mrs. Nat Carl see
Goodrich, Edna
GOODWIN, Mrs. Nat Carl see
Weathersby, Eliza
GOODWIN, T. (fl 1779) dramatist
CP/2-3, GT
GOODWIN, W. R. see Linyard,
W. K.
GOODYER, Percy R. (b 1884)
English actor GRB/1
GOOLD, Charles (d 1907 [53])
actor EA/08*
GOOLD, William (d 1889) EA/
90*
GOOLDEN, Richard (b 1891/95)
English actor AAS, WWT/8-16
GOOSSENS, Eugene (d 1906 [60])
conductor EA/08*
GOOSSENS, Sir Eugene (1893-
1962) English conductor CB,
ES, WWA/4, WWW/6
GOOSTRY, Mrs. Charles see
Sedgwick, Amy
GOPAL, Ram (b 1917) Indian
dancer, choreographer WWT/
11-12
GORALL, Leslie (d 1971 [54])
producer/director/choreographer
BP/55*
GORBEA, Carlos (b 1938) Puerto
Rican actor TW/30
GORCEY, Bernard (d 1955 [67])
actor BE*, BP/40*
GORCEY, Leo (d 1969 [52]) actor
TW/26

GORCHAKOV, Nicolai Mikhailovich
(1899-1958) Russian producer
COC
GORDANI, Nina (d 1966 [64]) per-
former BP/50*
GORDIN, Jacob (1853-1909) Ukran-
ian dramatist COC, DAB, ES,
MWD, OC/1-3, RE
GORDON, Mr. (fl 1752) translator
CP/2-3
GORDON, Miss actress CDP
GORDON, Alexander (fl 1731)
dramatist CP/3
GORDON, Amy actress? CDP
GORDON, Archibald D. (1835-95)
Ceylonese dramatist WWA/H
GORDON, Barry (b 1948) Ameri-
can singer, actor BE
GORDON, Bernard (d 1912 [39])
singer? EA/13*
GORDON, Bert (d 1974 [76])
performer BP/59*
GORDON, Bobby (d 1973 [69])
performer BP/57*
GORDON, Bruce (b 1916) American
actor BE, TW/8
GORDON, Carl (b 1932) American
actor TW/28-30
GORDON, Cecil [Thomas John-
stone] (d 1902) minstrel EA/
03*
GORDON, Charles Kilbourn (b
1888) American producer,
manager, dramatist WWT/6-9
GORDON, Cliff (b 1880) Austrian/
American actor, manager
WWM
GORDON, Cliff (d 1964 [44]) per-
former BP/49*
GORDON, Colin (1911-72) Ceylon-
ese actor AAS, WWT/12-15
GORDON, Douglas (1871-1935)
English actor, producer GRB/
1, 3-4, WWT/1-7
GORDON, Edith Althoff (d 1970
[65]) performer BP/55*
GORDON, Fanny (fl 1850) actress
HAS
GORDON, Frank Odell (d 1973
[95]) performer BP/58*
GORDON, Gavin (1901-70) Scottish
actor, singer, composer TW/
4-8, 27, WWT/9-14
GORDON, George G. (d 1917)
singer? EA/18*
GORDON, George Lash (1851-95)
English actor, dramatist DD,
OAA/2

GORDON, George W. W. (d 1887 [32]) EA/88*

GORDON, Gloria (d 1962) actress BE*

GORDON, Grant (d 1972 [64]) performer BP/57*

GORDON, G. Swayne (d 1949 [69]) American actor BE*, BP/34*

GORDON, Harriett (d 1869 [35]) actress DD

GORDON, Hayes (b 1920) American director, producer, actor BE, TW/6-8, WWT/16

GORDON, Huntley (d 1956 [69]) actor BE*

GORDON, James M. (d 1944 [86]) actor, director BE*, WWT/14*

GORDON, J. B. (d 1914) actor WWT/14*

GORDON, Mrs. J. B. see Scobie, Lizzie

GORDON, Joseph William (d 1893) lessee EA/94*

GORDON, Mrs. J. W. (d 1884) actress EA/85*

GORDON, Kitty [Hon. Mrs. W. W. Horsley-Beresford] (1878-1974) English actress, singer CDP, GRB/3-4, TW/30, WWM, WWT/1-7

GORDON, Leon (1884-1960) English actor, dramatist WWT/ 5-11

GORDON, Lizzie (d 1866) actress HAS

GORDON, L. S. dramatist DD

GORDON, Mack (d 1959 [54]) Polish lyricist, performer BE*

GORDON, Mrs. M. A. M. [Mrs. T. Gordon] (d 1875) EA/76*

GORDON, Marie [née Marie Eugenie Phillips; Mrs. Thomas W. Egan; Mrs. John T. Raymond] (d 1891) actress CDP

GORDON, Marjorie (b 1893) English actress, singer WWT/ 4-10

GORDON, Mark American actor TW/22

GORDON, Martha (d 1909) EA/ 10*

GORDON, Max (b 1892) American manager, producer BE, CB, NTH, SR, TW/2-8, WWT/8-14

GORDON, Michael (b 1909) American director, actor BE, TW/2

GORDON, Nellie English actress GRB/1

GORDON, Nelly see Gourlay, Helen Lawson

GORDON, Noele (b 1923) English actress, singer WWT/11-13

GORDON, Oliver (d 1970 [67]) performer BP/55*

GORDON, Pamela (b 1918) English actress TW/3

GORDON, Paul (d 1929 [43]) American actor BE*, BP/13*

GORDON, Paul Vincent (d 1965 [45]) drama coach BP/50*

GORDON, Peggy (b 1949) American actress TW/27-30

GORDON, Riki (d 1973 [38]) performer BP/57*

GORDON, Robert (d 1971 [76]) performer BP/56*

GORDON, Robert H. (d 1963 [58]) director BP/48*

GORDON, Rose M. (d 1973) performer BP/58*

GORDON, Ruth (b 1896) American actress, dramatist AAS, BE, CB, ES, NTH, SR, TW/1-23, WWT/7-16

GORDON, Scott (b 1951) American actor TW/30

GORDON, Stanley S. (b 1870) English actor GRB/1

GORDON, Mrs. T. see Gordon, Mrs. M. A. M.

GORDON, Vera (1886-1948) Russian actress TW/4

GORDON, Walter [William Aylmer Gowing] (1823-92) English actor DD, EA/69

GORDON, Walter (d 1901 [30]) variety comedian EA/03*

GORDON, Walter Lewis (d 1888) musician EA/89*

GORDON, William (fl 1731) dramatist CP/2, GT

GORDON, William (d 1874 [73]) scene artist EA/76*

GORDONA, Adelaide equestrienne CDP

GORDONE, Charles (b 1925/27) American dramatist, actor, director CD, MH, TW/26, WWT/16

GORDON-LEE, Kathleen English actress WWT/4-6

GORDON-LENNOX, Mrs. C.

Cosmo see Tempest, Marie Susan

GORDON-LENNOX, Cosmo Stuart Charles see Stuart, Cosmo

GORDON-MADDICK, Frank (d 1906 [48]) EA/07*

GORE, Catherine Grace Frances [née Moody] (1799-1861) English dramatist DD, DNB, HP

GORE, Ivan Pat [Robert T. G. de Vaux Balbirnie] English actor GRB/1

GORE, Larry (d 1973 [50]) publicist BP/58*

GORE, Walter (b 1910) English dancer, choreographer ES

GORE-BROWNE, Robert (b 1893) English dramatist WWT/9-14

GOREE, Frederick [Frank Musgrave] (d 1876 [28]) musician EA/77*

GOREE, George, Sr. (d 1876) musician EA/77*

GORELIK, Mordecai (b 1899) Russian/American designer, director, educator BE, ES, NTH, TW/3-4, WWT/15-16

GORHAM, Maurice (d 1975 [73]) producer/director/choreographer BP/60*

GORIN, G. T. (d 1889) EA/90*

GORIN, Igor (b 1909) Russian/American singer CB

GORING, Charles (fl 1687?-1708) dramatist CP/1-3, GT

GORING, Marius (b 1912) English actor AAS, ES, WWT/9-16

GORKY, Maxim (1868-1936) Russian dramatist COC, MWD, OC/1-3

GORMAN, Bob (b 1928) American actor TW/24, 26

GORMAN, Cliff (b 1936) American actor TW/24, 27-29, WWT/16

GORMAN, Edward (d 1915) American actor SR

GORMAN, Eric (d 1971 [85]) actor BP/56*, WWT/16*

GORMAN, Frederick E. (d 1972 [89]) performer BP/56*

GORMAN, Mari (b 1944) American actress TW/29-30

GORMAN, Tom (d 1971 [63]) actor TW/28

GORME, Eydie American actress, singer TW/24

GORNEY, Jay (b 1896) Russian composer, director, producer, executive BE

GORNEY, Karen (b 1945) American actress TW/28

GORNO, Jimmy (d 1969 [65]) designer BP/54*

GORR, Rita (b 1926) Belgian singer ES

GORSKI, Virginia (b 1926) American actress TW/4-5

GORST, Mrs. Harold (1869-1926) dramatist WWW/2

GORST, Richard (d 1896 [65]) executive EA/97*

GORTON, Belle [Mrs. Leslie Gaze] (d 1912 [28]) actress EA/13*

GORTON, Francis G. (d 1894) music-hall director EA/96*

GORTON, Joseph (fl 1880s-1890s) American minstrel SR

GORWIN, Peter (b 1948) American actor TW/28

GOSCH, Martin A. (d 1973 [62]) producer/director/choreographer BP/58*

GOSDEN, Charles Freeman ["Amos" of "Amos & Andy"] actor SR

GOSE, Carl see McKay, Scott

GOSFIELD, Maurice (1913-64) American actor TW/7, 21

GOSHEN, Col. Ruth (d 1889) giant CDP

GOSLING, Harold (b 1897) English business manager WWT/7-13

GOSNAY, Francis (d 1899) acting manager EA/00*

GOSS, Barry (b 1961) American actor TW/30

GOSS, Sir John (d 1880 [79]) composer, musician EA/81*

GOSS, Joseph (d 1892) EA/93*

GOSSE, Edmund (1849-1928) English writer DD, NTH

GOSSETT, Louis (b 1936) American actor, singer BE, TW/10, 12, 20, 22-24, 28

GOSSIN, Harry W. (1832-66) actor HAS

GOSSIN, John American clown HAS

GOSSMAN, Irving (d 1964 [63]) American actor, producer BE*

GOSSON, Stephen (1554-1623) English dramatist, actor CP/2-3, DA, DD, FGF, HP, NTH

GOTH, Trudy (d 1974) performer
BP/58*
GOTHIE, Bob (b 1930) American
actor TW/13
GOTT, Barbara (d 1944) actress
WWT/4-9
GOTTESFELD, Chone (d 1964
[73]) Russian dramatist BE*,
BP/48*
GOTTFRIED, Martin (b 1933)
American critic BE
GOTTHOLD, J. Newton (d 1888)
American actor CDP, HAS
GOTTLIEB, Arthur (d 1962
[63]) American producer BE*
GOTTLIEB, David (d 1962 [81])
costumier BE*
GOTTLIEB, Joseph Abraham
see Bishop, Joey
GOTTLIEB, Morton (b 1921)
American producer, manager
BE, WWT/15-16
GOTTLIEB, Polly Rose (d 1971)
performer BP/55*
GOTTSCHALK, Ferdinand (1858/
69-1944) English actor, drama-
tist, producer GRB/3-4,
PP/1, SR, TW/1, WWM,
WWT/1-9
GOTTSCHALK, Louis Moreau
(1829-69) American pianist,
composer CDP, DAB, HAS,
WWA/H
GOUDGE, Elizabeth (b 1900)
English dramatist CB
GOUFFE, Mons. (fl 1831) actor
CDP
GOUGENHEIM, Adelaide (b 1828)
English actress CDP, HAS,
SR
GOUGENHEIM, Josephine (fl
1850-60) American actress
CDP, DD, HAS
GOUGH, Miss see Galindo,
Mrs.
GOUGH, Alexander (b 1614)
English actor DA, OC/1-3
GOUGH, J. G. (fl 1640) drama-
tist CP/2-3, FGF
GOUGH, John (d 1968 [74]) per-
former BP/53*
GOUGH, John Robert (d 1899
[64]) musician EA/00*
GOUGH, Lloyd actor TW/2-3,
10, 14
GOUGH, Michael (b 1917)
Malaysian/English actor
AAS, WWT/11-16

GOUGH, Minnie (d 1891) music-
hall performer CDP
GOUGH, Robert (d 1625) English
actor COC, DA, DD, GT,
NTH, OC/1-3
GOUGH, Thomas (d 1879 [37])
actor? EA/80*
GOUGHE, Alexander see Gough,
Alexander
GOUGHE, Robert see Gough,
Robert
GOUGHE, Thomas (fl 1572) actor
DA
GOULD, Mr. (fl 1737) dramatist
CP/1
GOULD, Mrs. Irish actress HAS
GOULD, Bernard [né Partridge]
(1861-1945) English actor DD,
GRB/1-4
GOULD, Billy (d 1950 [81]) actor
TW/6
GOULD, Dave (d 1969 [70]) dance
director BP/54*
GOULD, Diana (b 1913) actress,
dancer WWT/10-11
GOULD, Edith (c. 1861-1921) ac-
tress SR
GOULD, Edward (d 1893) manager
EA/95*
GOULD, Elliott [né Goldstein] (b
1938) American actor BE,
CB, TW/18, 22-24, WWT/15-16
GOULD, Fred (d 1902) EA/03*
GOULD, Fred (d 1917 [75/76])
actor, dramatist, producer
BE*, EA/18*, WWT/14*
GOULD, Fred (d 1918) EA/19*
GOULD, Mrs. George J. see
Kingdon, Edith
GOULD, Gordon (b 1930) American
actor TW/22-25, 27, 30
GOULD, Gypsy (d 1966 [64]) per-
former BP/50*
GOULD, Harold (d 1952 [78])
American performer BE*, BP/
36*
GOULD, Harold (b 1923) American
actor TW/26-27
GOULD, Harry E. , Sr. (d 1971
[72]) showman, theatre owner
BP/55*
GOULD, Howard (1863/67-1938)
American actor PP/1, SR,
WWA/1, WWM, WWS
GOULD, James Nutcombe see
Gould, Nutcombe
GOULD, John (d 1974 [37]) drama-
tist BP/59*

GOULD, John (b 1940) English composer, performer WWT/16

GOULD, Julia (1824/27-93) English actress CDP, HAS

GOULD, Lita singer CDP

GOULD, Marguerite (b 1923) American actress TW/8

GOULD, Morton (b 1913) American composer, conductor BE

GOULD, Napoleon W. (fl 1819-81) singer, composer, musician CDP

GOULD, Nutcombe (1849-99) actor DD, EA/95, WWW/1

GOULD, Prissie (d 1892 [22]) EA/93*

GOULD, Robert (fl 1696-1737) dramatist CP/1-3, DNB, GT

GOULD, Mrs. S. M. (d 1880) EA/81*

GOULD, William (fl 1900?) comedian, singer CDP

GOULDEN, Mrs. Edmund B. see Goulden, Mary

GOULDEN, Mary [Mrs. Edmund B. Goulden] (d 1895) EA/96*

GOULDING, Alfred (d 1972 [76]) performer BP/56*

GOULDING, Edmund (1891/92-1959) English actor, dramatist, composer ES, WWT/5-10

GOULET, Robert (b 1933) Canadian/American actor, singer BE, CB, TW/17-20, 24, WWT/16

GOULSTONE, James (d 1852) balloonist EA/72*

GOURIET, Mrs. Victor see Crossland, Maggie

GOURLAY, Corbet Ryder (d 1897 [50]) advertiser, entrepreneur EA/98*

GOURLAY, Haggie see Gourlay, Maggie

GOURLAY, Helen Lawson [Nelly Gordon] (d 1872 [26]) actress EA/73*, WWT/14*

GOURLAY, Jenny (fl 1858-68) actress HAS

GOURLAY, John actor CDP

GOURLAY, Maggie (1847-68) Scottish actress HAS, SR

GOURLAY, Minnie (d 1889) actress EA/90*

GOURLAY, William (d 1882) actor DD

GOURLAY, William Cameron (d 1883 [65]) Scottish comedian EA/84*

GOURRON, Albert Raymond see Alvarez

GOUVY, Ludwig Theodore (d 1898 [79]) composer EA/99*

GOVELL, R. dramatist CP/3, FGF

GOVER, Mrs. Charles see Hanbury, Pattie

GOVEY, Alfred (d 1889 [67]) actor EA/90*

GOW, James (d 1879 [85]) Scottish actor EA/80*

GOW, James (1907-52) American dramatist CB, ES, TW/8, WWT/10

GOW, Ronald (b 1897) English dramatist AAS, CD, WWT/8-16

GOWARD, Miss see Keeley, Mary Ann

GOWARD, Annie [Mrs. Charles Fawcett] (d 1907 [48]) actress GRB/3

GOWARD, Mary Ann see Keeley, Mary Ann

GOWER, James (d 1917 [67]) EA/18*

GOWER, Rose (d 1891) music-hall performer EA/93*

GOWING, Emilia Julia [Mrs. William Aylmer Gowing] (d 1905) EA/06*

GOWING, William Aylmer see Gordon, Walter

GOWING, Mrs. William Aylmer see Gowing, Emilia Julia

GOZ, Harry G. (b 1932) American actor TW/27-30

GOZZI, Carlo (1720-1806) Italian dramatist COC, NTH, OC/2-3

GRABLE, Betty (1916-73) American actress, singer, dancer TW/22-24, 30, WWA/5, WWT/15

GRACE, Amy [Mrs. Leonard Rayne] (1876-1945) English actress GRB/1-4

GRACE, Carol actress BE, TW/15

GRACE, Charity (d 1965 [86]) actress TW/22

GRACE, Edmund (d 1908 [62]) actor EA/10*

GRACE, Francis (fl 1610-23) actor DA

GRACE, James Delmon (1827-76) American actor CDP, HAS

GRACE, Jean (d 1972 [85]) agent BP/56*

GRACE, Jessica (fl 1900?) singer, actress CDP

GRACE, Richard (d 1627?) actor DA

GRACIE, Sally American actress BE, TW/12-14, 25, 30

GRADDON, Miss see Gibbs, P.

GRADWELL, Henry (fl 1631) actor DA

GRADY, Alfred (d 1918) EA/19*

GRAEVER, Madeline (fl 1858) pianist HAS

GRAF, Herbert (1903-73) Austrian director CB, WWA/5

GRAFF, Edward (d 1893 [46]) variety agent EA/94*

GRAFF, George (d 1973 [86]) composer/lyricist BP/57*

GRAFF, Wilton (1903-69) American actor BE, TW/25

GRAFTON, Cecil [Constance M. Smith] (d 1904) actress EA/05*

GRAFTON, Jane [Mrs. Stafford Grafton] actress CDP

GRAFTON, Mrs. Stafford see Grafton, Jane

GRAHAM, Alma (d 1884) EA/85*

GRAHAM, Annie (fl 1855) American actress CDP, HAS

GRAHAM, Caroline (d 1910 [74]) EA/11*

GRAHAM, Colin (b 1931) English director ES

GRAHAM, Daphne see Sheridan, Mary

GRAHAM, Elizabeth Alice see Glenney, Bessie

GRAHAM, Ena see Gilbart, Eleanor

GRAHAM, Ernest (d 1945 [67]) actor BE*, WWT/14*

GRAHAM, Frank (d 1862 [32]) actor? HAS

GRAHAM, Frank (d 1867 [26]) comedian EA/68*

GRAHAM, Mrs. Frank (b 1842) English actress HAS

GRAHAM, Mrs. Fred see Graham, Lucinda

GRAHAM, Fred W. (d 1916 [42]) comedian EA/17*

GRAHAM, Genine (b 1925) English actress TW/9

GRAHAM, George (d 1767) dramatist CP/2-3, DNB

GRAHAM, George (d 1847) English actor HAS, SR

GRAHAM, George (d 1869) property man EA/70*

GRAHAM, George (1875-1939) English actor SR

GRAHAM, Mrs. George see George, Mary Stuart

GRAHAM, George St. Casse (d 1893 [28]) scene artist EA/94*

GRAHAM, Gertrude [Mrs. Fred Temple] (d 1908) actress EA/09*

GRAHAM, Harry (1874-1936) English dramatist NTH, WWT/4-8

GRAHAM, Irvin (b 1909) American composer, lyricist BE

GRAHAM, J. F. (d 1933 [82]) actor, producer BE*, WWT/14*

GRAHAM, John (fl 1812-17) American actor HAS

GRAHAM, John [née G. Monro] (d 1863 [46]) actor CDP

GRAHAM, John Somerville (d 1907) EA/08*

GRAHAM, Joseph (d 1976 [83]) performer BP/60*

GRAHAM, J. P. (d 1904) music-hall performer EA/05*

GRAHAM, June F. American actress TW/25, 27

GRAHAM, Kenneth L. (b 1915) American educator BE

GRAHAM, Lillie (fl 1855) American actress HAS

GRAHAM, Lionel (d 1893 [42]) actor EA/94*

GRAHAM, Lucinda [Mrs. Fred Graham] (d 1906) EA/07*

GRAHAM, Ly [Graham Lobb] (d 1883 [27]) actor EA/84*

GRAHAM, Malcolm Harry (d 1889 [24]) actor EA/90*

GRAHAM, Martha (b 1900/02) American dancer, choreographer BE, CB, ES, NTH, WWT/11-12

GRAHAM, Mary Ann see Yates, Mary Ann

GRAHAM, Mary Anne (fl 1856) actress HAS

GRAHAM, Mary Stuart [Mrs. George Graham] (d 1880) EA/81*

GRAHAM, Morland (1891-1949)

Scottish actor WWT/8-10
GRAHAM, Nevill English actor,
stage manager, business
manager GRB/1
GRAHAM, Mrs. Nevill see
Earle, Lilias
GRAHAM, Richard (b 1915)
American actor TW/26, 30
GRAHAM, Richard Elliott (fl
1850) actor CDP
GRAHAM, Richard L. (d 1851)
Scottish actor HAS
GRAHAM, Robert Emmet (b
1858) American actor CDP,
WWM, WWS
GRAHAM, Ronald (1913-50)
Scottish actor TW/1, 3, 7
GRAHAM, Ronny (b 1919) Amer-
ican actor, director, lyricist,
composer BE, TW/8-19, 21,
WWT/15-16
GRAHAM, Shad E. (d 1969 [72])
designer BP/53*
GRAHAM, Tom (d 1897 [28])
music-hall comedian, com-
poser CDP
GRAHAM, Violet (1890-1967)
actress WWT/4-8
GRAHAM, Virginia (d 1964
[45]) actress BE*
GRAHAM, Mrs. Walter (d 1867)
EA/68*
GRAHAM, William (d 1974 [74])
producer/director/choreographer
BP/59*
GRAHAME, Cissy [Mrs. James
Allen] (b 1862) English actress,
manager DD, DP, EA/95,
GRB/1, OAA/2
GRAHAME, Emmie [Mrs. Kerbey
D. Bowen] (d 1917) EA/18*
GRAHAME, Gloria (b 1925)
American actress ES
GRAHAME, Gracie actress,
singer CDP
GRAHAME, James (fl 1807)
dramatist CP/3
GRAHAME, J.. G. (d 1907) actor
DD, GRB/3, OAA/2
GRAHAME, J. Lynward (b 1881)
Irish actor GRB/1
GRAHAME, Margot (b 1911)
English actress WWT/7-11
GRAHN, Lucile (1819/25-1907)
Danish dancer CDP, ES
GRAHN, Mary (b 1901) librarian
BE
GRAIN, Richard Corney (1844-95)

English actor, composer, singer
CDP, DD
GRAINER, Ron (b 1922) Australian
composer WWT/15-16
GRAINGER, Gawn (b 1940) Irish
actor TW/23-24, WWT/16
GRAINGER, George Pugh (d 1879
[64]) actor EA/80*
GRAINGER, Mrs. W. P. (d 1886)
actress EA/87*
GRAJALES, Fernando Felix (d
1975 [32]) producer/director/
choreographer BP/60*
GRAMM, Donald (b 1927) American
singer CB
GRAMMANI, W. H. (d 1855 [55])
pantomimist CDP
GRANACH, Alexander (1890-1945)
Russian actor BE*
GRANBY, Cornelius W. (d 1886
[82]) actor, producer BE*,
WWT/14*
GRANBY, Joseph (d 1965 [80])
performer BP/50*
GRANDIN, Elmer (d 1933 [72])
actor BE*
GRANDJEAN, Louise (d 1934 [64])
actress BE*, WWT/14*
GRANDY, Fred (b 1948) American
actor TW/29-30
GRANGER, Miss see Jones,
Mrs.
GRANGER, Farley (b 1925) Amer-
ican actor BE, TW/15-18, 20
GRANGER, John (b 1924) American
actor TW/10-13, 28
GRANGER, Maude [Anna Brainerd]
(b 1851?) actress CDP
GRANGER, Stewart [né James
Lablache Stewart] (b 1913)
English actor ES, WWT/10-12
GRANIER, Jeanne (d 1939 [88])
French actress GRB/1-4,
WWT/1-4
GRANLUND, Nils T. (d 1957
[65]) Finnish? producer BP/41*
GRANNELL, Denis (d 1896) mana-
ger, lessee EA/97*
GRANNELL, William (b 1929)
American actor TW/25
GRANT, Mr. see Raymond, Mr.
GRANT, Prof. (d 1900 [48]) ven-
triloquist EA/01*
GRANT, Miss see Saville, Mrs.
E. F.
GRANT, Alexander (b 1925) New
Zealand/English dancer ES
GRANT, Barney (d 1962 [50])

performer BE*

GRANT, Billy (d 1971) performer BP/55*

GRANT, Bob (b 1932) English actor, dramatist WWT/15-16

GRANT, Burt (fl 1893?) dancer CDP

GRANT, Cary (b 1904) English/ American actor CB, ES, SR

GRANT, Charles (b 1865) English actor GRB/1

GRANT, Earl (d 1970) performer BP/55*

GRANT, Elspeth (d 1975 [60s]) critic BP/60*

GRANT, Francis Thomas Hope (d 1887) EA/88*

GRANT, James Edward (d 1966 [61]) dramatist BP/50*

GRANT, James M. (fl 1805) dramatist CP/3

GRANT, Lee (b 1927/29?) American actress BE, CB, TW/ 5-9, 13-15, 28-30

GRANT, Maxwell (d 1961 [39]) sketch writer BE*

GRANT, Micki American actress TW/22, 26-30

GRANT, Neil (b 1882) Scottish dramatist WWT/6-14

GRANT, Nellie [Charlotte Ellen Doherty] (d 1911 [31]) actress EA/12*

GRANT, Pauline (b 1915) English dancer, choreographer, director WWT/10-16

GRANT, Priscilla Mary see Edmonds, Connie

GRANT, Sydney (1873-1953) American vaudevillian TW/10, WWM

GRANT, Thomas (d 1881 [25]) EA/82*

GRANT, Mrs. W. Christie (d 1910) EA/11*

GRANT, W. F. (d 1923) actor BE*, WWT/14*

GRANTHAM, John (d 1882) actor EA/83*

GRANTHAM, Louisa (d 1884) EA/85*

GRANTHAM, Wilfred (b 1898) English actor WWT/9-14

GRANTZOW, Adele (d 1877 [36]) dancer EA/78*

GRANVAL, Jean-Pierre (b 1923) French actor TW/9

GRANVILLE, Audrey (d 1972

[62]) performer BP/56*

GRANVILLE, Bernard (1886-1936) American actor, dancer WWT/ 4-8

GRANVILLE, Charlotte [née Stuart; Mrs. Synge] (b 1863) actress DD, EA/96, GRB/2-4, WWM, WWT/1-9

GRANVILLE, Edgar (d 1909 [54]) music-hall comedian, composer CDP

GRANVILLE, Edward (d 1917) EA/18*

GRANVILLE, Fred [Ralph Haines Watson] (d 1894 [35]) singer EA/95*

GRANVILLE, George, Lord Lansdown (1667-1735) English dramatist CP/1-3

GRANVILLE, H. Such (fl 1868-80) dramatist DD

GRANVILLE, Louise (d 1968 [73]) performer BP/53*

GRANVILLE, Millicent [Millicent Granville Smith] (b 1884) English actress GRB/1

GRANVILLE, Sydney (d 1959 [79]) English actor, singer TW/16, WWT/5-11

GRANVILLE-BARKER, Harley (1877-1946) English actor, dramatist, manager AAS, COC, DD, DNB, ES, GRB/1-4, HP, MD, MH, MWD, NTH, OC/1-3, PDT, RE, SR, WWS, WWT/1-9, WWW/4

GRANVILLE-BARKER, Helen (d 1950) dramatist WWT/6-8, WWW/4

GRAPEWIN, Charles (1869-1956) American vaudevillian, actor TW/12

GRASS, Gunter (b 1927) German dramatist COC

GRASSAN, Adeline see Hind, Mrs. Thomas James

GRASSINI, Giuseppina (1773-1850) Italian singer ES

GRASSLE, Karen American actress TW/25, 28-29

GRASSMAN, Daniel see Mason, Dan

GRASSO, Giovanni (1875-1930) Italian actor COC, OC/1-3, WWT/3

GRASSOT, Paul (d 1860 [59]) actor WWT/14*

GRATTAN, Miss see Harris,

Mrs.
GRATTAN, Emily (fl 1875-77)
actress CDP
GRATTAN, Emma (fl 1854-69)
English actress CDP, HAS
GRATTAN, Harry (1867?-1951)
English actor, dramatist
CDP, DD, GRB/1-4, WWT/
3-9
GRATTAN, Henry Plunkett (1808-
89) Irish actor, dramatist
CDP, DD, HAS
GRATTAN, Mrs. Henry P[lunkett;
Mrs. Barker; Mrs. Madison]
(1810-76) English actress
CDP, HAS
GRATTAN, Kittie [Mrs. Edward
Lytton] (b 1874) English ac-
tress GRB/1-4
GRATTAN, Lawrence (d 1941
[71]) American actor, drama-
tist SR
GRATTON, Fred (1894-1966)
English press representative
WWT/11-14
GRAU, Jacob F. (1817-77) Aus-
trian impresario CDP, SR
GRAU, Maurice (1849-1907)
Austrian manager DAB, ES,
GRB/2-3, WWA/1, WWW/1
GRAU, Robert (d 1916) writer,
producer, manager BE*,
WWT/14*
GRAUMAN, Sid (1879-1950)
American executive BE*
GRAUNGER, John (fl 1509-11)
member of the Chapel Royal
DA
GRAUPNER, Mr. (fl 1796) actor
HAS
GRAUPNER, Mrs. [Miss Heelyer]
(fl 1794) actress HAS
GRAVELE, Emile see Blondin,
Charles
GRAVENSTEIN, Wynand (d 1886)
musician EA/87*
GRAVER, J. Adams (b 1835)
American actor HAS
GRAVES, Mr. (d 1869) scene
artist EA/70*
GRAVES, Alfred Percival (b
1846) dramatist DD
GRAVES, Clotilde Inez Mary
(1863-1932) Irish dramatist
DD, GRB/2-4, WWT/1-6,
WWW/3
GRAVES, Elsie Elizabeth (d 1969
[78]) performer BP/54*

GRAVES, Ernest (b 1919) Ameri-
can actor TW/3-4, 22, 24
GRAVES, George (1876-1949) Eng-
lish actor DNB, GRB/1-4,
TW/5, WWT/1-10
GRAVES, J. (d 1869) scene artist
WWT/14*
GRAVES, Kate (d 1898 [24]) ac-
tress EA/00*
GRAVES, Laura (d 1925 [55])
actress BE*, WWT/14*
GRAVES, Maud actress CDP
GRAVES, Peter (b 1911) English
actor, singer AAS, WWT/10-16
GRAVES, Richard (1715-1804)
English dramatist CP/3
GRAVET, Fernand (1905-70) Bel-
gian actor TW/21, 27
GRAVEUR, Emma (d 1899) EA/00*
GRAVEY, Fernand see Gravet,
Fernand
GRAY, Mr. (fl 1798) singer, actor
TD/1-2
GRAY, Dr. (fl 1822) dramatist
EAP
GRAY, Mrs. (fl 1791) actress
HAS
GRAY, Mrs. see Garrick, Mrs.
GRAY, Ada [Mrs. Charles A.
Watkins; Mrs. Charles S. Tin-
gay] (1834-1902) actress CDP
GRAY, Alice (b 1833) American
actress HAS
GRAY, Beatrice (b 1924) American
actress TW/4
GRAY, Charles [né Donald Mar-
shall Gray] (b 1928) English
actor BE, TW/13, 21-22,
WWT/15-16
GRAY, Dolores (b 1924) American
actress, singer AAS, BE,
TW/2-3, 6-11, 15-18, 23,
WWT/11-16
GRAY, Donald Marshall see
Gray, Charles
GRAY, Dora English actress
GRB/2
GRAY, Dulcie (b 1919) Malaysian/
English actress WWT/10-16
GRAY, Duncan (d 1969 [76]) per-
former BP/54*
GRAY, Edith (d 1898) actress
EA/99*
GRAY, Mrs. Edward (d 1905
[27]) EA/06*
GRAY, Edward Earl ["Monsewer
Eddie Gray"] (d 1969 [71])
performer BP/54*

GRAY, Elaine (d 1969) performer
BP/54*
GRAY, Elspet (b 1929) Scottish
actress WWT/15-16
GRAY, Eve (b 1904) English
actress, singer WWT/6-9
GRAY, Florence [Mrs. David
Collins] (d 1904) EA/06*
GRAY, Gilda (d 1959 [60])
Polish actress, singer TW/
16
GRAY, Ida M. (d 1942 [84])
actress BE*, WWT/14*
GRAY, Jack (b 1927) American/
Canadian dramatist, director
CD
GRAY, Jackson (1796-1837) Amer-
ican actor HAS
GRAY, James see Stuart, Ed-
ward Patrick
GRAY, Jennifer (1916-62)
Chinese/English actress WWT/
10-13
GRAY, Joan American actress
TW/5, 10-11
GRAY, John (d 1873 [56]) scene
artist EA/74*
GRAY, John (fl 1890) dramatist
DD
GRAY, John (d 1903) actor?
EA/04*
GRAY, Lawrence (d 1970 [71])
performer BP/54*
GRAY, Leonard (d 1964 [50])
performer BE*
GRAY, Leslie A. (d 1916 [25])
EA/17*
GRAY, Linda (b 1910) English
actress, singer WWT/10-16
GRAY, Madge (d 1965 [58]) per-
former BP/49*
GRAY, Margaret (fl 1623-24)
lessee DA
GRAY, Margery American ac-
tress, singer, dancer BE
GRAY, Nicholas Stuart (b 1919)
Scottish dramatist, actor,
director WWT/13-16
GRAY, Paul (b 1930) American
educator, director, editor
BE
GRAY, Richard (b 1896) English
actor WWT/9
GRAY, Robert (b 1940) Ameri-
can actor TW/24
GRAY, Robert S. (b 1911) Amer-
ican educator BE
GRAY, Sally [nee Constance

Vera Stevens] (b 1916) English
actress WWT/10-11
GRAY, Simon (b 1936) English
dramatist AAS, CD, WWT/15-
16
GRAY, Terence (b 1895) English
producer COC, ES, OC/3,
WWT/6-10
GRAY, Thomas (d 1768 [100+])
clown EA/72*
GRAY, Thomas (1716-72) English
dramatist CP/2-3
GRAY, Thomas J. (1888-1924)
American writer WWM
GRAY, Timothy American per-
former, director BE
GRAY, William (d 1875) lessee
EA/76*
GRAY, William (d 1896 [60])
actor EA/97*
GRAY, William (d 1943 [83])
actor, dramatist BE*
GRAY, Winifred see Russell,
Countess
GRAYDON, J. L. music-hall
proprietor & manager GRB/1-3
GRAYSON, Bette [Mrs. Clifford
Odets] (d 1954 [32]) actress
BE*
GRAYSON, Helen singer CDP
GRAYSON, Richard (b 1925) Amer-
ican manager, stage manager,
actor, director BE
GREANEY, Mary (b 1944) Irish
actress TW/23
GREASLEY, Alice Georgina [Mrs.
T. H. Greasley] (d 1892) EA/
94*
GREASLEY, Emily [Mrs. T. G.
Greasley] (d 1888 [25]) EA/89*
GREASLEY, Mrs. T. G. see
Greasley, Emily
GREASLEY, Mrs. T. H. see
Greasley, Alice Georgina
GREATHEED, Bertie (1759-1826)
English dramatist CP/3, DNB,
TD/1-2
GREATOREX, George (d 1916
[28]) magician EA/18*
"GREAT RAYMOND, The" see
Raymond, Maurice
GREAVES, John (fl 1572) actor
DA
GREAVES, Thomas (d 1877 [37])
secretary, treasurer EA/78*
GREAVES, Thomas (d 1908 [71])
musical director EA/09*
GREAZA, Walter N. (1897/1900-

1973) American actor BE,
TW/1-6, 29, WWT/9-11
GREBANIER, Bernard (b 1903)
American educator, director,
writer BE
GREBER, Giacomo dramatist
CP/1
GRECO, Francis (d 1909) EA/10*
GRECO, José (b 1918) Italian
dancer, choreographer CB
GREDULE, Mons. (fl 1850)
dancer HAS
GREE, Mrs. (fl 1845) actress
HAS
GREEN, Gen. dwarf CDP
GREEN (d 1916 [27]) EA/17*
GREEN, Miss see Bastar, Mrs.
GREEN, Mrs. [Jane Hippisley]
see Green, Jane
GREEN, Abel (1900-73) American
editor, writer NTH, TW/29,
WWT/15
GREEN, Adolph (b 1915/18)
American librettist, lyricist,
entertainer AAS, BE, CB,
ES, TW/1, WWT/14-16
GREEN, Alexander (fl 1663)
dramatist CP/1-3, GT
GREEN, Amelia see Bannister,
Mrs. Nathaniel Harrington
GREEN, Anna Katherine [Anna
K. G. Rohlfs] (b 1846)
American dramatist WWA/1,
WWM
GREEN, Belle (b 1881) Indian/
English entertainer GRB/1
GREEN, Bernard (d 1975 [66])
composer BP/60*, WWT/
16*
GREEN, Dr. Carleton (d 1962
[52]) educator BE*
GREEN, Charles (1785-1870)
aeronaut CDP
GREEN, Daniel Harding (d 1877
[70]) actor EA/78*
GREEN, Del (b 1938) American
actress TW/23, 28
GREEN, Denis (1903-54) English
actor, dramatist TW/5-6
GREEN, Dorothy (1886-1961)
English actress AAS, ES,
WWT/4-13
GREEN, Dorothy [Mrs. Norman
November] (d 1963 [71]) ac-
tress BE*
GREEN, E. see Elliott, E. P.
GREEN, Eleanor see Baster,
Mrs. John

GREEN, Elizabeth (d 1909) EA/
10*
GREEN, Frank (d 1891) actor
EA/93*
GREEN, Frank W. (d 1884) drama-
tist CDP, DD
GREEN, George (d 1876 [38])
clown EA/77*
GREEN, George Smith (d 1762)
English? dramatist CP/1-3
GREEN, George Thomas (d 1877)
musical director EA/78*
GREEN, Gladys see Arthur, Jean
GREEN, Harry (1892-1958) Amer-
ican actor TW/14, WWT/4-12
GREEN, Henry Hawes Craven
see Craven, Hawes
GREEN, Hernandez (d 1902 [73])
acrobat EA/03*
GREEN, H. J. see Kemble,
H. J.
GREEN, Howard (b 1936) American
actor TW/24, 27, 29
GREEN, Isadore (d 1963 [59])
journalist BE*
GREEN, J. (d 1910 [47]) stage
manager EA/11*
GREEN, James Burton (d 1922
[48]) songwriter, musician BE*
GREEN, Jane [née Hippisley] (d
1791) actress CDP, DD, DNB
GREEN, Janet (b 1914) English
dramatist, actress BE, WWT/
12-14
GREEN, Jeanette F. (d 1970 [71])
artists' representative BP/55*
GREEN, J. Edwin (b 1834) Amer-
ican singer, proprietor, imi-
tator HAS
GREEN, John musician CDP
GREEN, John? (fl 1606-27) Eng-
lish actor COC, DA, OC/1-3
GREEN, John (1801-74) American
actor, manager, singer DNB,
SR
GREEN, John H. (b 1915) Ameri-
can educator BE
GREEN, Johnny (b 1908) American
composer, musical director
BE
GREEN, Julien (b 1900) American
dramatist MD, MH, MWD
GREEN, Leonard (d 1917 [2])
EA/18*
GREEN, Lizzie (d 1906) actress
EA/07*
GREEN, Mabel (b 1887/90) English
actress GRB/1-3, WWT/5-7

GREEN, Marion (1890-1956)
American actor, singer TW/1,
12, WWT/8-11
GREEN, Martyn [William Martyn-
Green] (1899-1975) English ac-
tor, singer BE, CB, TW/4-9,
12-19, 23-25, 27-28, WWT/8-
16
GREEN, Mary-Pat (b 1951) Amer-
ican actress TW/30
GREEN, Mitzi (1920-69) American
actress TW/2-6, 25, WWT/
9-11
GREEN, Morris (d 1963 [73])
producer BE*, BP/47*
GREEN, Paul Eliot (b 1894)
American dramatist AAS,
BE, CD, COC, ES, HJD,
MD, MH, MWD, NTH, OC/
1-3, RE, SR, WWT/6-11,
15-16
GREEN, Richard (d 1884 [52])
comic singer EA/85*
GREEN, Richard (d 1914 [49])
English singer, actor DD,
GRB/1-4
GREEN, Robert musician CDP
GREEN, Robert (d 1882) singer
CDP
GREEN, Rupert (fl 1777) drama-
tist CP/2-3, GT
GREEN, Ruth (d 1976 [72])
executive BE
GREEN, Stanley (b 1923) Amer-
ican publicist, writer BE
GREEN, Thomas (1786-1859)
actor DD
GREEN, Thomas (fl 1847?) scene
painter CDP
GREEN, Thomas see Felix,
Tony
GREEN, Thomas C. (1832-66)
American actor HAS
GREEN, Tom (b 1852) English
actor, stage manager GRB/1
GREEN, William (d 1816) actor,
manager CDP
GREEN, William A. (d 1917)
EA/18*
GREENBANK, Harry Hewetson
(1866-99) dramatist, librettist,
lyricist DD
GREENBANK, Percy (1878-1968)
English librettist, lyricist
WWT/5-14, WWW/6
GREENBANK, T. K. (fl 1832)
actor HAS
GREENBAUM, Hyam (b 1910)

English conductor, composer
WWT/8
GREENBERG, Ben (d 1972 [70])
manager BP/56*
GREENE, Mr. (d 1816) actor
HAS
GREENE, Mrs. [Miss Willems]
(d 1827) actress HAS
GREENE, Billy M. (d 1973 [76])
performer BP/58*
GREENE, Charles (d 1849) Amer-
ican actor HAS
GREENE, Mrs. Charles (d 1838)
American actress HAS
GREENE, Mrs. Charles C. see
Tiffany, Annie Ward
GREENE, Clay M. (1850-1933)
American dramatist DD, GRB/
2-4, SR, WWA/1, WWM,
WWS, WWT/1-7
GREENE, Edith Elizabeth see
Greene, Eric
GREENE, Elizabeth [Mrs. Paul
John Bedford] (d 1833) actress
CDP
GREENE, Emma Marie [Miss De
Braham] (d 1889) actress EA/
90*
GREENE, Eric [née Edith Eliza-
beth] (1876-1917) English actress
BE*
GREENE, Ethel Frances (b 1887)
English actress GRB/1
GREENE, Evie [Mrs. Richard
Temple, Jr.] (1876/87-1917)
English actress, singer CDP,
DD, GRB/1-4, WWS, WWT/1-3
GREENE, Gene (b 1881) American
vaudevillian WWM
GREENE, Mrs. Gene (d 1913)
EA/14*
GREENE, Graham (b 1904) English
dramatist AAS, BE, CB, CD,
COC, ES, HP, MD, MH,
MWD, OC/3, PDT, WWT/13-16
GREENE, G. W. (fl 1848) Ameri-
can actor HAS
GREENE, Herbert (b 1921) Amer-
ican producer, conductor, com-
poser, actor BE
GREENE, H. Plunket (1865-1936)
Irish singer CDP, DNB, GRB/
1, WWW/3
GREENE, James (b 1926) Ameri-
can actor TW/22-25, 27-30
GREENE, Jeanne (d 1975 [69])
actress BP/59*, WWT/16*
GREENE, John (d 1860) American

actor, manager HAS
GREENE, Mrs. John [Anne
Nuskay] (1800-62) American
actress HAS
GREENE, Lorne (b 1915) Cana-
dian actor BE, CB
GREENE, Marty (b 1909) Amer-
ican actor TW/25, 27
GREENE, Mary (d 1970) pro-
ducer/director/choreographer
BP/55*
GREENE, Maxine (b 1945) Amer-
ican actress TW/24
GREENE, Milton American mu-
sical director, actor, com-
poser BE
GREENE, Norman (d 1945 [66])
actor, singer BE*, WWT/
14*
GREENE, Patterson (1898-1968)
American critic, dramatist
BE, WWA/5
GREENE, Reuben (b 1938)
American actor TW/24-27
GREENE, Richard (b 1946)
American actor TW/28
GREENE, Robert (c. 1560-92)
English dramatist COC,
CP/1-3, DA, DD, DNB, ES,
FGF, HP, MH, NTH, OC/
1-3, PDT, RE
GREENE, Thomas (d c. 1612/14)
comedian CDP, DA
GREENE, Walter (d 1963 [69])
journalist BE*
GREENE, William (d 1970 [43])
actor, executive TW/26
GREENER, Dorothy (1917-71)
English actress BE, TW/16-
19, 25, 28, WWT/15
GREENFIELD (fl 1790) dramatist
CP/3
GREENFIELD, Elizabeth T.
(1826-76) singer CDP, HAS
GREENFIELD, Felix (d 1974
[57]) performer BP/59*
GREENHILL, Mrs. Thomas see
Richards, Mrs.
GREENHOUSE, Martha American
actress TW/17-21, 25, 27-29
GREENLAW, Nora (d 1909)
actress EA/10*
GREENLEAF, Raymond (1892-1963)
American actor BE*
GREENLEES, Leslie M. (d 1975
[68]) critic BP/60*
GREENSHIELDS, Charles (d 1907
[61]) EA/08*

GREENSTREET, Sydney (1879/80-
1954) English actor CB, SR,
TW/10, WWM, WWT/9-11
GREENWALD, Joseph (c. 1878-
1938) American actor SR,
WWT/6-8
GREENWALD, Milton see Kidd,
Michael
GREENWALL, Henry W. (1832-
1913) manager SR
GREENWAY, Teresa [Mrs. George
Prestwich] (d 1876) singer
EA/77*
GREENWOOD, Anne [Mrs. Thomas
Greenwood] (d 1882 [31]) ac-
tress EA/83*
GREENWOOD, Charlotte (b 1893)
American actress BE, ES,
TW/5-9, WWT/7-13
GREENWOOD, Ethel (d 1970 [72])
performer BP/55*
GREENWOOD, Jane (b 1934) Eng-
lish designer WWT/15-16
GREENWOOD, Joan (b 1919/21)
English actress AAS, BE,
CB, ES, TW/10-12, 23, WWT/
11-16
GREENWOOD, Lyndon (b 1873)
English actor, business mana-
ger GRB/1
GREENWOOD, Reginald Charles
see Payne, Reginald
GREENWOOD, Thomas, Sr. (d
1797) English scene designer
ES
GREENWOOD, Thomas (1779-1822)
English scene artist DD, ES
GREENWOOD, Mrs. Thomas see
Greenwood, Anne
GREENWOOD, Thomas Longdon
(1806-79) manager, dramatist
DD, ES
GREENWOOD, Tom (d 1909 [71])
showman EA/10*
GREENWOOD, Walter (1903-74)
English dramatist AAS, BTR/
74, WWT/10-15
GREENWOOD, William see
McCoy, W.
GREER, Miss see Fletcher,
Mrs.
GREER, Howard (d 1974 [78])
designer BP/58*
GREER, Michael (b 1943) Ameri-
can actor TW/26
GREET, Ben see Greet, Sir
Philip Ben
GREET, Clare (1871-1939) actress

WWT/4-8

GREET, Maurice (d 1951 [70])
English actor BE*, BP/35*

GREET, Mildred C. (d 1964
[64]) actress BE*, BP/49*

GREET, Sir Philip Ben (1857-
1936) English actor, manager
AAS, COC, DD, DNB, EA/
96, ES, GRB/1-4, NTH,
OC/3, SR, WWS, WWT/1-8,
WWW/3

GREET, William (d 1914 [63])
manager WWT/14*

GREET, Mrs. William (fl 1890s)
dramatist DD

GREEVEN, Alix Augusta see
Greveen, Alice Augusta

GREEY, E. (d 1888 [52]) dramatist, manager EA/89*

GREG, Sir Walter Wilson (1875-
1959) English scholar DNB,
ES, HP, WWW/5

GREGG, Everley (1903-59)
English actress WWT/9-12

GREGG, Hubert (b 1914/16)
English actor, lyricist, composer WWT/8-16

GREGG, Julie (b 1944) American
actress TW/24

GREGG, Mitchell (b 1921) American actor TW/16-20

GREGG, Peter (b 1913) American
actor TW/2

GREGG, Robert (d 1909 [88])
EA/10*

GREGOR, Nora (d 1949) actress
BE*, WWT/14*

GREGORI, Mercia (b 1901) South
African actress WWT/6

GREGORY, Andre producer,
director WWT/16

GREGORY, Arthur William (d
1887) EA/88*

GREGORY, Lady Augusta (1852-
1932) Irish dramatist, director
COC, DNB, ES, HP, MH,
MWD, NTH, OC/1-3, PDT,
RE, WWT/1-4, WWW/3

GREGORY, Barnard (1796-1852)
actor, journalist DD

GREGORY, Bobby (d 1971 [71])
composer/lyricist BP/55*

GREGORY, Lady Charles see
Stirling, Mrs.

GREGORY, Dora (1872-1954)
English actress WWT/5-11

GREGORY, Elizabeth [Mrs. J.
C. Gregory] (d 1872 [42])

EA/73*

GREGORY, Fanny [Mrs. Thomas
Gregory] (d 1894) EA/95*

GREGORY, Frank (b 1884) English
manager WWT/7-10

GREGORY, George (d 1808) Irish
dramatist CP/3

GREGORY, Hilda (d 1917) actress
EA/18*

GREGORY, Jack (fl 1602) actor
DA

GREGORY, James (d 1912 [76])
manager EA/13*

GREGORY, James (b 1911) American actor BE, TW/6-12

GREGORY, Jay (b 1939) American
actor TW/23, 26

GREGORY, Mrs. J. C. see
Gregory, Elizabeth

GREGORY, John (d 1907 [61])
musical director EA/09*

GREGORY, Joseph (d 1882) proprietor EA/83*

GREGORY, Paul (b 1920) American producer, actor, talent
representative BE

GREGORY, Sara (b 1921) Australian actress, singer WWT/11-14

GREGORY, Susan (d 1970 [25])
assistant stage manager BP/
54*

GREGORY, Thomas (d 1899 [80])
showman EA/01*

GREGORY, Mrs. Thomas see
Gregory, Fanny

GREGORY, W. A. (b 1923)
American producer, director
BE

GREGORY, Walner (d 1911 [43])
manager EA/11*

GREGORY, Will (b 1928) Scottish
actor TW/23, 25-26

GREGSON, Frederick Holgate (d
1895) actor EA/97*

GREGSON, James R. (b 1889)
English dramatist, producer,
actor WWT/5-14

GREGSON, John (d 1975 [55])
actor BP/59*, WWT/16*

GREGSON, Michael see Craig,
Michael

GREHAN, Samuel (d 1880 [44])
comic singer EA/81*

GREIG, Andrew (d 1887) secretary
EA/88*

GREIG, Florence see St. John,
Florence

GREIG, George Taffey (d 1913

[34]) EA/14*

GREIN, J[acob] T[homas] (1862-1935) Dutch critic COC, DD, ES, GRB/1-4, NTH, OC/1-3, WWT/1-7, WWW/3

GREIN, Mrs. J[acob] T[homas] see Greveen, Alice Augusta

GRENE, David (b 1913) American educator BE

GRENEKER, Claude P. (d 1949 [68]) American press agent TW/5

GRENFELL, Joyce Irene (b 1910) English diseuse, actress AAS, BE, CB, COC, OC/3, PDT, TW/12, WWT/10-16

GRENICH, B. (fl 1840) dancer HAS

GRENVILLE, Mr. (fl 1767) actor HAS

GRENVILLE, Arthur actor EA/96

GRESAC, Mme. Fred French dramatist WWT/1, 6-7

GRESHAM, Alfred (d 1912 [49]) actor EA/13*

GRESHAM, Edith American actress TW/4

GRESHAM, Herbert (d 1921 [68]) English actor, director BE*, BP/5*, WWT/14*

GREVE, Dora singer CDP

GREVEEN, Alice Augusta ["Michael Orme"; Mrs. J. T. Grein; Alix Augusta Greeven] dramatist, producer, translator GRB/2-4, WWT/4-9

GREVILLE, Mr. (fl 1767) actor WWA/H

GREVILLE, Mrs. (d 1802) actress CDP

GREVILLE, Mrs. Arthur see Oram, Mona K.

GREVILLE, Clara (b 1792) actress CDP

GREVILLE, Curtis (fl 1622-34) actor DA

GREVILLE, Eden (fl 1891) dramatist DD

GREVILLE, Sir Fulke, Lord Brooke (1554-1628) English dramatist CP/2-3, DD, DNB, FGF, HP, RE

GREVILLE, Isabella (d 1882) EA/83*

GREVILLE, Mabel [Mrs. W. H. Webster] (b 1882) English actress, singer GRB/1

GREVILLE, Lady Mercy see Parson, Nancie

GREVILLE, Lady Violet (fl 1890-94) dramatist DD

GREW, Mary (1902-71) English actress WWT/6-15

GREY, Mr. (d 1884) EA/85*

GREY, Alice (1833-90) actress CDP

GREY, Anne [née Aileen Ewing] (b 1907) English actress WWT/8

GREY, Beryl (b 1925/27) English dancer ES, WWT/11-12

GREY, Caroline Edith [Mrs. Lytton Grey] (d 1887) EA/88*

GREY, Charles Oscar (d 1885 [25]) EA/86*

GREY, Christian (b 1938) American actor TW/29-30

GREY, Clifford (1887-1941) English lyricist, dramatist, actor CB, WWT/4-9, WWW/4

GREY, Edwin (d 1873 [39]) actor EA/74*

GREY, Elise (d 1889 [32]) actress EA/90*

GREY, Ellen Martha Colfield (d 1884) EA/85*

GREY, Eve English actress, singer WWT/5

GREY, Frank Herbert (d 1951 [67]) composer, conductor BE*, WWT/14*

GREY, Jane (1883-1944) American actress SR, TW/1, WWM, WWT/4-9

GREY, Jane Susan Mary (d 1899 [61]) actress EA/00*

GREY, Joel (b 1932) American actor, singer, entertainer CB, TW/12, 23-26, WWT/15-16

GREY, Katherine (1873-1950) American actress GRB/3-4, SR, TW/6, WWM, WWS, WWT/1-10

GREY, Leonora see Egerton, Mrs. Frank

GREY, Lily (d 1898) actress EA/99*

GREY, Lytton (d 1931 [80]) actor BE*, WWT/14*

GREY, Mrs. Lytton see Grey, Caroline Edith

GREY, Marie de [Ellen Washington Preston] (d 1897) actress BE*, EA/98*, WWT/14*

GREY, Marion (d 1949 [74]) actress BE*

GREY, Mary (d 1974 [96]) actress BTR/74, WWT/4-11
GREY, Nina (d 1905 [25]) actress EA/06*
GREY, Stanley (fl 1891) singer, actor CDP
GREY, Sylvia (d 1958 [92]) actress, dancer DD, DP
GREY, William (d 1877) musician EA/78*
GRIBBIN, Daniel (d 1884) musical director, composer EA/85*
GRIBBLE, George Dunning (1882-1956) dramatist WWT/6-10
GRIBBLE, Harry Wagstaff (b 1896) English dramatist, producer, actor BE, CB, TW/2, 5, WWT/6-11
GRIBBLES, Fanny see Drew, Mrs. Frank Nelson
GRIBBON, Eddie T. (d 1965 [75]) performer BP/50*
GRIBBON, Harry (d 1961 [75]) American actor TW/1
GRIBOV, Alexei Nikolaevich (b 1902) Russian actor WWT/13-14
GRICE, C. E. (fl 1816?) American? dramatist EAP, RJ
GRICE, Wayne (b 1942) American actor TW/24
GRICE, W. H. (d 1896) singer EA/97*
GRIDLEY, James Lawrence (d 1901 [42]) actor, manager EA/03*
GRIEBLING, Otto (d 1972 [75]) performer BP/56*
GRIEG, Florence see St. John, Florence
GRIEG, Nordahl (1902-43) dramatist BE*
GRIERSON, Robert (b 1810) American actor HAS
GRIERSON, Thomas (fl 1827-28) English actor HAS
GRIESBACH, George Adolphus (d 1875 [74]) musician EA/76*
GRIESBACH, John Henry (d 1875) composer EA/76*
GRIEVE, John Henderson (1770-1845) English scene painter COC, DD, ES, OC/1-3
GRIEVE, Thomas (1799-1882) English scene artist COC, DD, DNB, ES, OC/1-3

GRIEVE, Thomas Walford (1841-82) English scene artist COC, ES, OC/1-3
GRIEVE, William (1800-44) English scene painter COC, DD, DNB, ES, OC/1-3
GRIFF [Henry Hadden Griffiths] (b 1864) English juggler, ventriloquist GRB/1
GRIFF, George (d 1916) EA/17*
GRIFFEN, Dr. Hamilton (d 1893) EA/94*
GRIFFIES, Ethel (1878-1975) English actress BE, CB, TW/4-7, 22-23, WWT/11-15
GRIFFIN (fl 1597) actor DA
GRIFFIN, Mr. (fl 17th cent) actor CDP
GRIFFIN, Arbid (d 1974 [60]) producer/director/choreographer BP/59*
GRIFFIN, Arthur (d 1953 [75]) American actor BE*, BP/37*
GRIFFIN, Benjamin (1680-1740) English actor, dramatist CDP, CP/1-3, DD, DNB, GT, TD/1-2
GRIFFIN, Elsie English actress, singer WWT/5-9
GRIFFIN, Fred Seeley (d 1904 [32]) music-hall comedian EA/05*
GRIFFIN, George (d 1875 [62]) equestrian tent maker EA/76*
GRIFFIN, Gerald (1803-40) Irish dramatist CDP, DD, DNB, HP
GRIFFIN, Gerald (d 1962 [70]) American actor, singer, songwriter BE*
GRIFFIN, G. W. H. (1829-79) American minstrel, manager CDP, HAS
GRIFFIN, Hayden (b 1930) American talent & literary representative BE
GRIFFIN, Hayden (b 1943) South African designer WWT/16
GRIFFIN, James Warren (d 1903) musician EA/04*
GRIFFIN, John David (d 1973 [45]) critic BP/58*
GRIFFIN, Norman (b 1887) Welsh actor, singer WWT/5-7
GRIFFIN, Mrs. Tony see Ralf, Emily
GRIFFIS, William (b 1917) American actor TW/22-23, 26, 30

GRIFFITH, Andy (b 1926) American actor BE, CB, ES, TW/12-17
GRIFFITH, David Wark (1875/80-1948) American director, dramatist ES, NTH, WWA/2, WWT/4-10
GRIFFITH, Donald M. (b 1947) American actor TW/29-30
GRIFFITH, Ed (b 1938) American actor TW/19
GRIFFITH, Elizabeth (1720?-93) dramatist, actress CDP, CP/2-3, DD
GRIFFITH, Frank Carlos (1851-1939) American actor, manager CDP, WWA/1
GRIFFITH, George H. (b 1822) English actor HAS
GRIFFITH, Mrs. George H. (fl 1854) actress HAS
GRIFFITH, Hubert (1896-1953) English critic, dramatist COC, OC/1-3, WWT/5-11
GRIFFITH, Hugh (b 1912) Welsh actor AAS, BE, TW/8, 19, WWT/11-16
GRIFFITH, John (b 1868/69) Canadian actor SR, WWA/5
GRIFFITH, Linda (d 1949 [65]) actress BE*
GRIFFITH, Lydia Elizabeth (1832-97) actress COC
GRIFFITH, Peter (b 1933) American actor TW/3
GRIFFITH, Raymond (d 1957 [70]) actor, producer BE*
GRIFFITH, Richard (d 1788) dramatist CP/3, DD
GRIFFITH, Richard (d 1969 [57]) critic BP/54*
GRIFFITH, Robert E. (d 1961 [54]) American producer, stage manager, actor TW/18
GRIFFITH, Samuel (d 1883) equestrian EA/84*
GRIFFITH, Thomas (d 1744 [63]) actor WWT/14*
GRIFFITHS, Mr. (d c.1804) prompter, actor TD/1-2
GRIFFITHS, Mrs. (d 1895 [75]) EA/96*
GRIFFITHS, Derek (b 1946) English actor WWT/16
GRIFFITHS, Doris (b 1970 [68]) performer BP/54*
GRIFFITHS, Dorothy see Scott, Dorothy

GRIFFITHS, Elizabeth (fl 1765-79) dramatist GT, TD/1-2
GRIFFITHS, George H. (d 1888 [65]) actor EA/89*
GRIFFITHS, Henry Hadden see Griff
GRIFFITHS, James (d 1850) actor HAS
GRIFFITHS, Jane (b 1930) English actress WWT/12-15
GRIFFITHS, Joe (d 1901 [49]) music-hall acrobat, clown EA/02*
GRIFFITHS, John (d 1880 [59]) equestrian clown EA/81*
GRIFFITHS, R. (d 1877) music-hall musical director EA/79*
GRIFFITHS, Robert (d 1881 [69]) musician EA/82*
GRIFFITHS, Tom see Clarke, Thomas
GRIFFITHS, Trevor (b 1935) English dramatist WWT/16
GRIFFITHS, W. H. (d 1923) manager WWT/14*
GRIFFITHS, William (d 1908 [77]) musician EA/09*
GRIGAS, John (b 1930) American actor TW/27-29
GRIGGS, John (1908-58) American actor TW/9, 23
GRILLO, John (b 1942) English dramatist, actor CD
GRIMALD, Nicholas (1519-62) English dramatist CP/3, DD
GRIMALDI, Denis (b 1947) American actor TW/27
GRIMALDI, George H. (d 1951 [58]) dramatist BE*, WWT/14*
GRIMALDI, Giuseppe (1713-88) ballet master COC, DD
GRIMALDI, Joseph (1778-1837) English clown BS, CDP, COC, DD, DNB, ES, HP, NTH, OC/1-3, OX, PDT, TD/1-2
GRIMALDI, Joseph Samuel (1802-63) clown CDP, COC, DD, DNB, ES, GT
GRIMALDI, Marion (b 1926) English actress, singer WWT/15-16
GRIMALDI, Nicolini Italian composer, director? CP/1
GRIMANI, Miss (fl 1803) actress TD/2
GRIMANI, Cecilia (fl 1822?) actress CDP
GRIMANI, Julia [Mrs. Charles Wayne Young] (d 1806 [21])

actress BE*, WWT/14*
GRIMBALL, Elizabeth Berkeley
(d 1953) American producer
WWA/3
GRIME, Edward (d 1907 [50])
proprietor EA/08*
GRIMES, Mr. (fl 1712) drama-
tist CP/2-3
GRIMES, Arthur (fl 1625-26)
actor DA
GRIMES, Daryl (b 1931) Ameri-
can actor TW/12
GRIMES, Frank (b 1947) Irish
actor TW/26
GRIMES, Margaret (d 1912) EA/
13*
GRIMES, Tammy (b 1934) Amer-
ican actress, singer AAS,
BE, CB, TW/12-21, 24, 26,
WWT/14-16
GRIMM, Harry E. (d 1970 [72])
performer BP/55*
GRIMSHAW, Nicholas (d 1970
[69]) performer BP/55*
GRIMSTON, Charles W. see
Garthorne, C. W.
GRIMSTON, Dorothy May English
actress GRB/3-4, WWT/1-5
GRIMSTON, Harold Robertson
(d 1930) conductor WWT/14*
GRIMSTON, William, Lord
Viscount (c. 1692-1756) Irish?
dramatist CP/1-3, GT
GRIMSTON, William Hunter
see Kendal, William Hunter
GRIMWOOD, Herbert (1875-1929)
English actor GRB/2-4,
WWT/1-7
GRINDALL, Annie Elizabeth
[Mrs. Harry E. Grindall]
(d 1883) EA/84*
GRINDALL, Mrs. Harry E.
see Grindall, Annie Elizabeth
GRINDALL, Henry Rupert (d
1905 [57]) EA/06*
GRINDALL, William (d 1879
[74]) costumier EA/80*
GRINER, Barbara (b 1934)
American producer, theatre
owner BE
GRINER, Geunie (d 1975 [47])
performer BP/60*
GRINGLE, Arthur E. (fl 1900s)
American actor, editor,
reader, lecturer WWM
GRISDALE, Walter (d 1883 [59])
actor EA/84*
GRISEL, Louis Racine (b 1849)

American actor WWS
GRISI, Carlotta (1819-99) Italian
dancer, singer CDP, ES,
OC/1-2
GRISI, Giuditta (1805-40) Italian
singer ES
GRISI, Guilia (1811-69) Italian
singer CDP, ES, HAS, SR
GRISMAN, Sam H. producer,
manager WWT/9-11
GRISMER, Joseph Rhode (1849-
1922) American actor, drama-
tist, manager CDP, GRB/3-4,
SR, WWA/1, WWM, WWS,
WWT/1-4
GRIST, Mr. actor TD/1-2
GRIST, Harriet (fl 1792) actress
CDP
GRIST, Thomas (fl 18th cent)
author CDP
GRIST, William (1840-96) libret-
tist, dramatist DD
GRISWOLD, Gertrude (c. 1860-
1912) American singer SR
GRISWOLD, Grace (d 1927 [55])
American actress, dramatist
GRB/4, WWM, WWT/1-5
GRIZZARD, George (b 1928)
American actor AAS, BE,
CB, TW/11-26, 28-30, WWT/
14-16
GROCE, [Catherine?] see
Barre, Mrs. [Joseph?]
GROCK [Adrien Wettach] (1880-
1959) Swiss clown COC,
NTH, OC/2-3, PDT, TW/16
GRODIN, Charles (b 1935) Amer-
ican actor, director TW/19,
27, WWT/16
GROENINGS, Franz (d 1902 [63])
musical director EA/03*
GROH, David (b 1939) American
actor TW/30
GROODY, Louise (1897-1961)
American actress, singer TW/
18, WWT/6-11
GROOM, Philip (d 1917 [26])
dancer, ballet master EA/18*
GROOME, Reginald (b 1861) Irish
singer GRB/1
GROOME, Mrs. Samuel W. see
Haslam, Maud
GROOMS, Red painter CD
GROPPER, Milton Herbert (1896/
97-1955) American dramatist
WWT/6-11
GROS, Edward (d 1901 [19]) EA/
02*

GROS, Eugene (d 1902 [23])
EA/03*
GROS, Henri (d 1910 [60])
music-hall managing director
EA/11*
GROS, Mrs. Henri see Gros,
Isabella
GROS, Isabella [Mrs. Henri Gros]
(d 1909 [61]) EA/10*
GROS, Louise (d 1902 [81])
EA/03*
GROSBARD, Ulu (b 1929) Bel-
gian director BE, WWT/
15-16
GROSBAYNE, Benjamin (d 1976
[82]) critic BP/60*
GROSETTE, Henry William (fl
1810) dramatist CP/3
GROSHON, Belinda (d 1822) Eng-
lish actress HAS
GROSS, Edward (b 1897) Amer-
ican producer TW/2
GROSS, Edwin (d 1866) comedian
HAS
GROSS, Gene (b 1920) American
actor TW/24-26
GROSS, Jesse (b 1929) American
theatre reporter BE
GROSS, Seymour (d 1970 [56])
stage manager, actor BP/54*
GROSS, Shelly (b 1921) American
producer BE, WWT/16
GROSSI, Mlle. (d 1873) singer
EA/75*
GROSSI, Enrico (1828-66) Italian
singer HAS
GROSSKURTH, Kurt (d 1975 [66])
performer BP/60*
GROSSMAN, George (d 1972 [67])
publicist BP/56*
GROSSMAN, Suzanne Swiss ac-
tress TW/22, 24-26
GROSSMITH, Mrs. (d 1882)
EA/83*
GROSSMITH, Ena (1896-1944)
English actress WWT/4-9
GROSSMITH, George (d 1880)
reader, entertainer, dramatist
DD
GROSSMITH, George, Sr. (1847-
1912) English actor CDP,
COC, DD, DNB, DP, EA/95,
ES, GRB/1-4, OC/1-3, OAA/
2, PDT, SR, WWM, WWT/1,
WWW/1
GROSSMITH, George, Jr. (1874-
1935) English actor, dramatist
CDP, COC, DD, DNB, ES,

GRB/1-4, OC/1-3, PDT, WWS,
WWT/1-7, WWW/3
GROSSMITH, Mrs. George see
Astor, Adelaide
GROSSMITH, Mrs. George see
Grossmith, Rosa
GROSSMITH, Lawrence (1877-1944)
English actor COC, ES, GRB/
1-4, OC/1-3, WWS, WWT/1-9
GROSSMITH, Rosa [Mrs. George
Grossmith] (d 1905 [57]) EA/06*
GROSSMITH, Weedon (1852-1919)
English actor COC, DD, DNB,
DP, EA/95, GRB/1-4, OC/1-3,
PDT, WWM, WWS, WWT/1-3,
WWW/2
GROSSMITH, Mrs. Weedon see
Palfrey, May Lever
GROSSMITH, William Robert (b
c. 1827) actor CDP
GROSVENOR, Annie (d 1891) music-
hall performer EA/92*
GROSVENOR, Henry (d 1892) EA/
93*
GROSVENOR, Joseph (fl 1840-57)
English actor HAS
GROSVENOR, Laura (d 1879)
singer EA/80*
GROSVENOR, William H. see
Hamilton, William Henry
GROTO, Luigi (1541-85) Italian
dramatist COC
GROTOWSKI, Jerzy (b 1933) Polish
director CB, COC
GROUT, James David (b 1927)
English actor, director TW/21,
30, WWT/15-16
GROUT, Philip (b 1930) English
director WWT/15-16
GROVE, Mr. (fl 1793-1803) actor
CDP, GT, TD/2
GROVE, Miss (fl 1837) Scottish
actress HAS
GROVE, Miss see Yarnold, Mrs.
Edwin
GROVE, Florence C. (d 1902)
dramatist DD
GROVE, Fred [F. Grove Palmer]
(1851-1927) English actor
GRB/1, 4, WWT/1-5
GROVE, Sir George (d 1900 [80])
director of the Royal College of
Music EA/01*
GROVE, Joseph (d 1764) publisher
CP/2-3
GROVE, W. (fl 1782) dramatist
CP/3
GROVER, Edward (b 1932) Ameri-

can actor TW/22

GROVER, J. Holmes (b 1838)
American dramatist, actor
DD

GROVER, Leonard (1835-1926)
American actor, manager,
dramatist CDP, HAS, SR

GROVER, Leonard, Jr. (1859-
1947) actor SR

GROVER, Myrtle (d 1970) performer BP/55*

GROVER, Russell singer, actor
CDP

GROVER, Stanley (b 1926) American actor, singer BE, TW/
17-20, 23-24, 26-28, 30

GROVES, Charles (1843-1909)
Irish actor DD, GRB/1-4,
OAA/2

GROVES, Charles (1875-1955)
English actor WWT/5-11

GROVES, Eliza [née Smith] (fl
1834) American actress HAS

GROVES, Fred (1880-1955) English actor WWT/6-11

GROVES, John (d 1887 [70])
property master EA/88*

GROVES, Johnny (d 1912) comedian EA/13*

GROVES, Richard (d 1879 [21])
property master EA/80*

GROVES, Walter (d 1906 [41])
comedian EA/07*

GRUBB, John (fl 1795) share-
holder TD/1-2

GRUBB, Lily (d 1890) American
actress, singer CDP

GRUBE, Carl (b 1866) German
actor, stage manager GRB/4,
WWT/1-2

GRUBE, Max (d 1934 [80]) actor,
dramatist BE*, WWT/14*

GRUENBERG, Louis (1884-1964)
Russian/American composer
HJD

GRUET, Allan (b 1945) American
actor TW/27-28

GRUN, Bernard (1901-72) Czech
composer, conductor WWT/
10-14

GRÜNDGENS, Gustaf (1899-1963)
German actor, producer COC,
OC/3

GRUNDMAN, Clare (b 1913)
American composer, actor
BE

GRUNDY, Lily English actress
GRB/3-4, WWT/1-5

GRUNDY, Sydney (1848-1914) Eng-
lish dramatist COC, DD, ES,
GRB/1-4, MH, NTH, OC/1-3,
SR, WWM, WWS, WWT/1-2,
WWW/1

GRUNEISEN, Charles Lewis (1806-
79) English critic, director
DNB

GRUNWALD, Alfred (d 1951 [67])
Austrian librettist BE*, BP/35*

GRUSKIN, George (d 1975 [65])
agent BP/60*

GRUVER, Elbert A. (d 1962 [57])
stage manager BE*

GRYMES, Anthony (fl 1628) actor
DA

GRYMES, Thomas (fl 1600-01)
member of the Chapel Royal
DA

GRYMMESBY, John (fl 1423)
member of the Chapel Royal
DA

GRYNES (fl 1633) actor DA

GRYZBOWSKI, Walter (d 1976
[58]) personal manager BP/60*

GUALANDI, Antonio see "Campioli"

GUARALDI, Vince (d 1976 [47])
composer/lyricist BP/60*

GUARD, Kit (d 1961 [67]) actor
BE*

GUARD, William J. (d 1932 [70])
Irish press representative BE*,
BP/16*

GUARDINO, Harry (b 1925) American actor BE, ES, TW/20,
23-24

GUARE, John (b 1938) American
dramatist AAS, CD, WWT/16

GUARINI, Giovanni Battista (1537-
1612) Italian dramatist OC/1-3

GUARRINO, Sig. (d 1876) ballet
master EA/77*

GUBER, Lee (b 1920) American
producer BE, WWT/16

GUEDALLA, Mrs. Herbert see
Hanbury, Lily

GUEDEN, Hilde (b 1923) Austrian
singer CB

GUENTHER, Dorothee (d 1975
[79]) producer/director/chore-
ographer BP/60*

GUENTHER, Ruth (d 1974 [64])
performer BP/59*

GUERIN, Michael (d 1884) agent
EA/85*

GUERINT, Sebastian Francis (d
1870 [79]) acting manager

EA/71*
GUERITE, Laura (fl 1900?) sing-
er, actress CDP
GUERRABELLA, Mme. (fl 1859-
62) singer HAS
GUERRERO, Danny (b 1945)
American actor TW/24, 27-29
GUERRERO, Maria (1868-1928)
Spanish actress GRB/2-4
GUEST, Christopher Haden (b
1948) American actor TW/26,
28-30
GUEST, Ellis (fl 1625-34) actor
DA
GUEST, James W. (d 1879) Amer-
ican? prompter EA/80*
GUEST, Jean H. (b 1921) Amer-
ican executive BE
GUEST, Rosa Annie (d 1908
[58]) EA/09*
GUETARY, Georges [né Lambros
Worloou] (b 1917) Egyptian ac-
tor, singer WWT/11-15
GUETTEL, Henry (b 1928) Amer-
ican producer BE
GUGGISBERG, Mrs. see Moore,
Decima
GUHLKE, Antoinette (b 1925)
American actress TW/5
GUIDERY, Mrs. James see
De Stainer, Marguerite
GUIDI, Sig. (d 1857) singer HAS
GUIDI, Clementina Noel (b 1841)
Italian singer HAS
GUIDO, Frank [Richard Delany]
(d 1893) musician EA/94*
GUILBERT, Ann (b 1928) Amer-
ican actress TW/16
GUILBERT, Yvette [Mrs. Max
Schiller] (1868/69-1944) French
singer CDP, COC, GRB/1-4,
NTH, OC/1-3, SR, WWA/4,
WWM, WWS, WWT/1-9,
WWW/4
GUILFORD, Earl of see North,
Francis
GUILFOYLE, Paul (d 1961 [58])
American actor, director BE*
GUILLAMORE, Joseph (d 1890)
EA/91*
GUILLAUME, Robert (b 1937)
American actor TW/29-30
GUILLAUME, Umberto see
Antonet
GUILLEMEN, Louis Charles
[Jean Bond] (d 1870) antipodean
artist EA/71*
GUILMAN, Robert (fl 1628-29)

actor DA
GUILMETTE, Charles (fl 1856)
singer CDP
GUINAN, Texas (d 1933) American
actress BE*, BP/18*
GUINARD, John [Henry Barnard]
(d 1883 [26]) singer EA/84*
GUINNESS, Sir Alec (b 1914) Eng-
lish actor AAS, BE, CB,
COC, ES, OC/2-3, PDT, TW/
6-9, 20-21, WWT/9-16
GUINNESS, Arthur D'Esterre (d
1893) actor EA/94*
GUION, Daniel (d 1896 [39]) EA/
97*
GUION, John (d 1906) EA/08*
GUION, Netta (fl 1892) actress
CDP
GUION, Raymond see Raymond,
Gene
GUITERMAN, Arthur (1871-1943)
dramatist CB
GUITRY, Lucien-Germain (1860-
1925) French actor GRB/1-4,
NTH, WWT/2, 4
GUITRY, Sacha (1885-1957) Rus-
sian dramatist, actor, manager
COC, NTH, OC/1-3, TW/14,
WWT/8-12
GUITRY, Yvonne Printemps (b
1895) French actress OC/2-3
GUITTARD, Laurence (b 1939)
American actor TW/29-30
GUITTON, Frances Eleanor [Mrs.
Jules Guitton] (d 1881 [48])
EA/82*
GUITTON, Jean (d 1973 [86])
dramatist BP/57*
GUITTON, Mrs. Jules see
Guitton, Frances Eleanor
GUIVER, James (d 1894) actor
EA/96*
GULBRANDSEN, Charles (d 1974
[83]) designer BP/58*
GULLAN, Campbell (d 1939) Scot-
tish actor, producer WWT/3-9
GULLIFER, A. F. (d 1916) EA/
17*
GULLIVER, Charles (1882-1961)
English manager WWT/4-10
GULLIVER, Joseph Henry (d 1884)
Negro comedian EA/86*
GULLY, John (1783-1863) boxer
CDP
GUMBERT, Ferdinand (d 1896 [78])
composer, critic EA/97*
GUMM, Mary Jane see Gumm,
Suzanne

GUMM, Suzanne [Mrs. Jack
Cathcart; née Mary Jane
Gumm] (d 1964 [48]) performer
BE*
GUNDUNAS, Lewis (b 1930)
American actor TW/25
GUNDY, George (d 1880) mana-
ger EA/81*
GUNG'L, Josef (d 1889 [78])
composer, conductor EA/90*
GUNN, Miss see Wulfries,
Mrs.
GUNN, Archie (b 1863) English
artist, designer WWM
GUNN, Haidee (1882/83-1961)
English actress GRB/1-4,
WWT/1-7
GUNN, James (d 1895) EA/96*
GUNN, John (d 1878 [46]) actor?
EA/79*
GUNN, John (d 1909 [38]) pro-
prietor, manager EA/10*,
WWT/14*
GUNN, Mrs. John see Gunn,
Mary Frances
GUNN, Judy (b 1914) English
actress WWT/8-11
GUNN, Mary Frances [Mrs.
John Gunn] (d 1894) EA/95*
GUNN, Mary Louise see Arnot,
Louise
GUNN, Michael (d 1901 [61])
proprietor, manager EA/02*,
WWT/14*
GUNN, Michael Louis (d 1886
[19]) EA/87*
GUNN, Moses (b 1929) American
actor, director TW/23-28,
WWT/15-16
GUNN, Vincenetta (b 1944) Amer-
ican actress TW/29
GUNNELL, John (b 1911) Amer-
ican educator, director BE
GUNNELL, Richard (d 1634) Eng-
lish actor, dramatist, manager
DA, FGF, OC/1-3
GUNNING, Miss (fl 1803) drama-
tist CP/3
GUNNING, Mrs. J. see Camp-
bell, Miss
GUNNING, Louise (1879-1960)
actress, singer TW/17,
WWT/1-5
GUNTER, Archibald Clavering
(1847-1907) English dramatist
CDP, DAB, DD, GRB/3,
HJD, SR, WWA/1, WWW/1
GURIE, Sigrid (d 1969 [58])

performer BP/54*
GURIN, Ellen (d 1972 [24]) per-
former BP/57*
GURN, James C. see Marlowe,
James C.
GURNER, Mrs. (fl 1834-37) Eng-
lish actress SR
GURNETT, Ursula (fl 1890s?) sing-
er CDP
GURNEY, A. R., Jr. (b 1930)
American dramatist CD
GURNEY, Claud (1897-1946)
English producer WWT/9
GURNEY, Dennis (b 1897) English
actor, director BE
GURNEY, Edmund (d 1925 [73])
actor BE*, BP/9*, WWT/14*
GURNEY, Rachel English actress
WWT/13-16
GURTLER, Arnold B., Jr. execu-
tive BE
GUSS, Louis (b 1918) American
actor BE, TW/18-19, 24-25,
27-28
GUSTAFSON, Carol (b 1925) Amer-
ican actress BE
GUSTAFSON, William (b 1887)
American singer WWA/1
GUSTAVE, George (d 1896) Ethiopi-
an minstrel EA/97*
GUTHERIE, Thomas Anstey see
Anstey, F.
GUTHRIE, Lady (d 1972 [67])
dramatist BP/57*
GUTHRIE, Robert Graham (d 1898)
EA/99*
GUTHRIE, Thomas J. (d 1899
[32]) actor, sketch artist EA/
00*
GUTHRIE, Sir Tyrone (1900-71)
English producer, actor, direc-
tor, dramatist AAS, BE, CB,
COC, ES, NTH, OC/1-3, PDT,
TW/27, WWA/5, WWT/7-15
GUTHRIE, William (d 1885 [53])
acting manager EA/86*
GUTSKOW, Karl (d 1878 [67])
dramatist, singer EA/80*
GUTTMANN, Jean see Babilée,
Jean
GUTZKOW, Karl Ferdinand (1811-
78) German dramatist OC/2-3
GUY, Cooper (d 1887 [34]) EA/88*
GUY, George G. (d 1872 [33])
box-keeper EA/73*
GUY, Horace (d 1900 [34]) actor
EA/01*
GUY, John William (d 1902 [32])

music-hall stage manager
EA/03*

GUY, W. E. (d 1876 [65]) actor
EA/77*

GUYNES, Charles (d 1971 [37])
dramatist BP/56*

GUYON, Albert (d 1913 [45])
EA/14*

GUZMAN, Richard (d 1972 [29])
performer BP/57*

GWALTER, William (fl 1622-23)
lessee DA

GWENN, Edmund (1875-1959)
Welsh actor CB, ES, GRB/
4, NTH, TW/2-7, 16, WWT/
1-11

GWENN, Mrs. Edmund see
Terry, Minnie

GWENT, Gwilym (d 1891) composer CDP

GWILLIM, Jack (b 1915) English
actor TW/28, 30

GWILYM, Mike (b 1949) Welsh
actor WWT/16

GWINNE, Matthew (d 1627/39)
dramatist CP/2-3, FGF

GWINNET, Richard (d 1717) English dramatist CP/2-3, GT

GWYNN, Michael (1916-76) English actor WWT/12-16

GWYNN, Nell (1650-87) English
actress CDP, COC, DD,
DNB, ES, GT, NTH, OC/
1-3, PDT

GWYNNE, Emma [Mrs. Edward
Sass] actress CDP

GWYNNE, Fanny (fl 1864-71)
actress DD

GWYNNE, Fred (b 1926) American actor TW/8, 29-30,
WWT/16

GWYNNE, Jack (d 1969 [74])
performer BP/54*

GWYNNE, Jennie [Mrs. Arthur
Rodney] (d 1889) actress
EA/90*

GWYNNE, Julia (d 1934 [78])
actress DD

GWYNNE, Neil (d 1903 [34])
serio-comic CDP

GWYTHER, Geoffrey Matheson
(1890-1944) actor, singer,
composer WWT/6-9

GYDE, Margaret (d 1909) EA/
10*

GYE, Frederick (d 1869 [88])
manager WWT/14*

GYE, Frederick (1810-78) English

proprietor, director CDP, DNB

GYLLOME, Foke (fl 1581) actor
DA

GYNGELL, G. ? (d 1833) magician
CDP

GYNT, Greta (b 1916) Norwegian
actress, dancer WWT/9-13

GYRDLER, Russell (fl 1598) member of the Children of Paul's
DA

GYRKE, Richard (fl 1550) actor
DA

- H -

H., C. (fl 1800) dramatist CP/3

H., Eleanor (fl 1803) dramatist
CP/3

H., W. (fl 1737) dramatist CP/3

HAAGA, Agnes (b 1916) American
educator BE

HAAS, Dolly (b 1910) German actress BE

HAAS, Hugo (b 1902) Czech actor
TW/5

HAAS, Mabel (fl 1885?) singer
CDP

HABBERTON, John (1842-1921)
American? dramatist WWW/2

HABELMANN, Theodore (fl 1864)
German singer CDP

HABERFIELD, Graham (d 1975
[34]) performer BP/60*

HABERSTROTH, Alex (d 1973 [67])
producer/director/choreographer
BP/58*

HABINGTON, William (1605-54)
English dramatist CP/1-3,
DNB, FGF, HP

HACHE, Mlle. [Julia Wideman]
(d 1892) actress EA/93*

HACK, Signe (d 1973 [74]) performer BP/57*

HACKER, Maria (d 1963) actress
BE*

HACKET, Dr. John (1592-1670)
English dramatist CP/2-3,
FGF

HACKETT, Albert (b 1900) American dramatist, actor BE,
HJD, MWD

HACKETT, Arthur (1884-1969)
American singer WWA/5

HACKETT, Buddy (b 1924) American actor BE, CB, TW/21-22,
24

HACKETT, Charles (1889-1942)

American singer CB, WWA/1

HACKETT, Charles M. (d 1970 [61]) journalist BP/55*

HACKETT, Clara C. [Mrs. James Henry Hackett, II] (1834-1909) actress CDP

HACKETT, Florence (d 1954 [72]) actress BE*

HACKETT, Hal (1924-67) American actor TW/13-16, 24

HACKETT, James Henry (1800-71) American actor, manager CDP, COC, DAB, ES, HAS, NTH, OC/1-3, SR, WWA/H

HACKETT, Mrs. James Henry [Catharine Lee Sugg] (1797-1848) actress CDP, COC, HAS, OC/3

HACKETT, Mrs. James Henry, II see Hackett, Clara C.

HACKETT, James Ketelas (1869-1926) Canadian actor, manager CDP, COC, DAB, GRB/2-4, OC/1-3, PP/1, SR, WWA/1, WWM, WWS, WWT/1-5

HACKETT, Mrs. James Ketelas see Mannering, Mary

HACKETT, Joan American actress BE, TW/17-21, 26, 28-29

HACKETT, Lillian (d 1973) performer BP/57*

HACKETT, Maria (d 1874 [91]) EA/75*

HACKETT, Norman Honore (b 1874) Canadian actor GRB/3-4, WWT/1-6

HACKETT, Raymond (1902-57) American actor TW/2, 15, WWT/6-9

HACKETT, Walter (1876-1944) American dramatist COC, SR, WWT/3-9, WWW/4

HACKMAN, Gene (b 1931) American actor CB, TW/24

HACKMAN, William H. (d 1973 [62]) performer BP/58*

HACKNEY, Mabel [Mrs. Laurence Irving] (d 1914) actress GRB/3-4, WWT/1-2

HACKURT, Mr. (fl 1844) actor HAS

HACKURT, Mrs. (fl 1846) actress HAS

HACON, Harry (d 1892) sketch artist EA/93*

HADAWAY, Polly (fl 1836) actress HAS

HADAWAY, Mrs. Thomas [Lucy Bertram] (d 1834) actress, singer HAS, SR

HADAWAY, Thomas H. (1801-92) English actor CDP, HAS, SR

HADDOCK, J. (d 1887 [65]) treasurer EA/88*

HADDON, Archibald (1871-1942) English critic WWT/4-9, WWW/4

HADDON, Peter (1898-1962) English actor WWT/5-13

HADDRICK, Ron (b 1929) Australian actor AAS, WWT/14-16

HADFIELD, Annie [Mrs. Samuel Hadfield] (d 1912 [58]) EA/13*

HADFIELD, James (1772-1841) lunatic/assassin CDP

HADFIELD, Mrs. Samuel see Hadfield, Annie

HADGE, Michael (b 1932) American actor TW/22-24, 26, 28-29

HADING, Jane [Jeanette Hadingue] (1859-1933) French actress CDP, GRB/1, 3-4, SR, WWA/4, WWT/1-3

HADING, Jane [Jeanne Alfredine Trefouret] (d 1941 [81]) French actress BE*, WWT/14*

HADINGUE, Jeanette see Hading, Jane

HADLEY, Henry Kimball (1871-1937) American composer, conductor DAB, ES

HADLEY, Reed (d 1974 [63]) performer BP/59*

HADWIN, Ann [Mrs. G. H. George] (d 1877 [58]) actress EA/78*

HAEMANN, F. W. (d 1899) conjuror EA/00*

HAERTING, Edward (fl 1866) manager CDP

HAFFNER, Frank see Heywood, Charles

HAGAN, James B. (1888-1947) American actor, dramatist, manager SR

HAGAN, John (d 1887 [28]) music-hall proprietor EA/89*

HAGEMAN, Larry see Hagman, Larry

HAGEMAN, Richard (1882-1966) Dutch composer, conductor WWA/4

HAGEN, Reigh (b 1936) American actor TW/26

HAGEN, Uta (b 1919) German actress AAS, BE, CB, ES, TW/1, 3-17, 19-20, 24, WWT/10-16

HAGEN, Mrs. Warner see
Woodward, Grace
HAGENBECK, Carl (d 1887 [78])
EA/88*
HAGGAR, Charles (d 1904 [87])
lion tamer EA/05*
HAGGAR, Sarah [Mrs. W. Haggar] (d 1909 [58]) EA/10*
HAGGAR, Mrs. W. see Haggar,
Sarah
HAGGARD, Stephen (1911-43)
Guatemalan actor AAS, COC,
WWT/8-9
HAGGIN, Ben Ali (1882-1951)
American scene designer
NTH, TW/8
HAGGITT, Rev. John (fl 1794)
dramatist CP/3
HAGGOTT, John Cecil (d 1964
[50]) American producer,
director BE*, BP/49*
HAGLEY, Miss (fl 1788) actress
TD/1-2
HAGMAN, Larry [Hageman] (b
1931) American actor TW/
7-8, 15-20
HAGUE, Albert (b 1920) German
composer BE, WWT/15-16
HAGUE, Charles (1769-1821)
music professor CDP
HAGUE, Clarence [James M.
Hague] Welsh actor GRB/1-3
HAGUE, James M. see Hague,
Clarence
HAGUE, Mary (d 1894) EA/95*
HAGUE, Pauline (b 1884) English
actress, singer GRB/1
HAGUE, Mrs. Sam (d 1879)
EA/80*
HAGUE, Samuel (1829-1901) English clog dancer, manager,
minstrel CDP, HAS
HAID, Charles (b 1943) American
actor TW/28
HAIG, Emma (1898-1939) American actress, singer WWT/
6-8
HAIG, Peter (b 1939) American
actor TW/26
HAIGH, Mme. (d 1899) singer
EA/00*
HAIGH, Henry (b 1832) English
singer CDP, HAS, SR
HAIGH, Kenneth (b 1932) English
actor AAS, BE, TW/14-17,
24, PDT, WWT/13-16
HAIGH, Winter singer, minstrel
CDP

HAIGH, Mrs. Winter (d 1890 [53])
EA/91*
HAIGHT, George (b 1905) American
producer, dramatist BE, WWT/
9
HAILES, Lord (1726-92) Scottish
dramatist CP/3
HAILEY, Marion (b 1941) American actress TW/23-24, 26-29
HAILEY, Oliver (b 1932) American
dramatist CD, WWT/15-16
HAIM, Matti (d 1967 [56]) performer BP/52*
HAINES, A. Larry (b 1917) American actor TW/22-23, 25-29
HAINES, Edmund (d 1974 [59])
composer/lyricist BP/59*
HAINES, Herbert E. (1880-1923)
English composer, conductor
WWT/2-4
HAINES, John Thomas (1799?-
1843) actor, dramatist CDP,
DNB
HAINES, Joseph (d 1701) English
actor CDP, COC, CP/1-3,
DNB, ES, GT, OC/1-3
HAINES, Mervyn, Jr. (b 1933)
American actor TW/25-27
HAINES, Rhea (d 1964 [69])
actress BE*
HAINES, Robert Terrel (1870-1943)
American actor GRB/3-4, SR,
WWA/5, WWM, WWS, WWT/1-9
HAINES, William (d 1973 [73])
performer BP/58*
HAINES, Mrs. William see
Austa, Amber
HAINES, William Wister (b 1908)
American dramatist BE, MWD
HAIRE, Wilson John (b 1932) Irish
dramatist CD
HAITE, J. J. (d 1874) composer
EA/75*
HAIZINGER, Amalie (1800-84)
German singer, actress ES
HAJOS, Mitzi (b 1891) Hungarian
actress CDP, TW/2-3, WWM,
WWT/9-11
HALASZ, Laszlo (b 1905) Hungarian
musical director CB
HALDON, Lady English actress
GRB/1
HALE (fl 17th cent) piper CDP
HALE, Mr. (d 1746?) actor TD/
1-2
HALE, Alan (1892-1950) American
actor TW/6
HALE, Barnaby (d 1964 [37])

performer BP/49*

HALE, Binnie [Beatrice Mary Hale-Munro] (b 1899) English actress, singer WWT/4-14

HALE, Charles B. (1819-76) English actor CDP, HAS

HALE, Mrs. Charles B. (1830-65) English actress HAS

HALE, Dorothy (d 1938 [33]) American actress BE*, BP/23*

HALE, Edward Everett, III (d 1953 [46]) American actor BE*

HALE, Frank (d 1972 [72]) theatre owner BP/57*

HALE, George (d 1956 [55]) American choreographer TW/13

HALE, Helen (fl 1902-07) American actress WWS

HALE, John (fl 1852) actor HAS

HALE, John (d 1947 [88]) actor, manager SR, TW/3

HALE, John (b 1926) English dramatist, director CD

HALE, J. Robert (1874-1940) English actor, singer CDP, WWT/2-9

HALE, Lionel (b 1909) English critic, dramatist WWT/8-16

HALE, Louise [née Closser; Mrs. Walter Hale] (1872-1933) American actress, dramatist DAB, GRB/3-4, NTH, OC/1-3, WWA/1, WWM, WWT/1-7

HALE, Malcolm (d 1968 [27]) performer BP/53*

HALE, Mary Beale (fl 1860) actress HAS

HALE, Norman (d 1916 [26]) entertainer EA/17*

HALE, Philip (1854-1934) American critic DAB, WWA/1

HALE, Randolph (d 1974 [65]) performer BP/59*

HALE, Ruth (d 1934 [48]) American critic, press representative BE*, BP/19*

HALE, Sarah Josepha (1788-1879) dramatist HJD

HALE, Sonnie [John Robert Hale-Munro] (1902-59) English actor TW/15, WWT/5-12

HALE, S. T. (b 1899) English press representative WWT/7-10

HALE, Walter (b 1869) American actor GRB/3, WWM

HALE, Mrs. Walter see Hale, Louise

HALE, William Palmer (d 1871 [46]) burlesque writer EA/72*

HALE-MUNRO, Beatrice Mary see Hale, Binnie

HALE-MUNRO, John Robert see Hale, Sonnie

HALES, Charles (1810-65) English actor SR

HALES, F. David (d 1976 [55]) publicist BP/60*

HALES, Henry (d 1874 [52]) costumier EA/75*

HALES, John (d 1873) singer, comedian EA/74*

HALES, Jonathan (b 1937) English dramatist, director WWT/16

HALES, Martha [Mrs. T. Gardiner Hales] (d 1909 [65]) EA/10*

HALES, Richard (d 1892 [48]) actor? EA/93*

HALES, Richard King (d 1887 [65]) EA/88*

HALES, Robert (d 1863 [43]) giant HAS

HALES, Rose [Mrs. Fred Hibernia] (d 1895) variety performer, singer EA/96*

HALES, T. Gardiner (d 1913) EA/14*

HALES, Mrs. T. Gardiner see Hales, Martha

HALES, Thomas (1740?-80) English/French dramatist DNB, NTH

HALEVY, Ludovic (1834-1908) French dramatist GRB/1-4

HALEY, Jack (b 1901/02) American actor BE, TW/2-8, WWT/8-11

HALFORD, J. actor CDP

HALFORD, John (d 1904 [84]) actor EA/05*

HALFPENNY, Tony (b 1913) English actor WWT/7-10

HALIWELL, Edward (fl 1532) dramatist CP/3

HALL, Abraham Oakey (1826-98) dramatist, actor CDP

HALL, Adelaide (b 1910) American actress, singer BE

HALL, Adrian (b 1928) American director BE

HALL, Albert (d 1907 [43]) songwriter EA/08*

HALL, Albert (b 1937) American

actor TW/27-30

HALL, Alfred (d 1917 [79]) comedian, entertainer EA/18*

HALL, Anmer [Alderson Burrell
Horne] (1863-1953) English
producer, manager, actor
COC, WWT/6-11, WWW/5

HALL, Artie [Mrs. Robert Ful-
gora] (fl 1890?) singer, actress CDP

HALL, Benjamin M., III (d 1970
[46]) editor BP/55*

HALL, Bettina (b 1906) American
actress, singer WWT/7-10

HALL, Bob (d 1970 [83]) performer BP/55*

HALL, Bob (b 1907) American
theatre owner, manager, producer BE

HALL, Brian (b 1959) American
actor TW/28

HALL, Bruce (b 1919) American
actor TW/25-26, 29

HALL, Charles (d 1867) scene
artist EA/68*

HALL, Charles (d 1874 [58])
conductor EA/75*

HALL, Charles (d 1907 [69])
Australian actor EA/08*

HALL, Charles King (d 1895
[50]) musician EA/96*

HALL, Clay (b 1940) American
actor TW/11

HALL, Cliff (d 1972 [78])
vaudevillian TW/29

HALL, Clinton (d 1880 [63])
lessee EA/81*

HALL, David (b 1929) English
producer, actor WWT/14-15

HALL, David S. (d 1965 [76])
performer BP/49*

HALL, Dorothy (d 1953 [47])
American actress TW/9,
WWT/7-10

HALL, Ed (b 1931) American actor
TW/20, 22, 26

HALL, Edward dramatist RJ

HALL, Edwin S. (d 1973 [54])
sound technician BP/58*

HALL, Emma (fl 1856) actress
HAS

HALL, Everard American? dramatist EAP

HALL, Foster see Foster, Vivian

HALL, Frank singer, song composer CDP

HALL, Frank (d 1898 [62]) comedian EA/99*

HALL, Frederick (d 1898) manager
EA/99*

HALL, George (d 1893) EA/94*

HALL, George (b 1907/16) Canadian actor TW/2-3, 5-7, 24,
26, 28, 30

HALL, Mrs. George see Kelton,
Aggie

HALL, George D. (d 1894 [28])
EA/95*

HALL, Geraldine (d 1970 [65])
performer BP/55*

HALL, Grayson actress WWT/16

HALL, Harry [or Henry] (1804-58)
Irish actor, stage manager
CDP, HAS

HALL, Henry (d 1893 [55]) steam
circus proprietor EA/94*

HALL, Henry Tudor (d 1887 [46])
EA/88*

HALL, Mrs. H. Winsloe see
Delmar, Georgina

HALL, Jacob (fl 1668) rope dancer
CDP, DNB

HALL, James (fl 1834) American
actor HAS

HALL, James (1900-40) American
actor CB

HALL, J. Clinton (1840-89) actor,
manager CDP

HALL, Jeanette F. (d 1976 [77])
performer BP/60*

HALL, J. H. (d 1850) actor HAS

HALL, J. M. (d 1877 [36]) actor
EA/78*

HALL, John actor TD/2

HALL, John C., Jr. (b 1929)
American union representative
BE

HALL, Josephine (d 1920) American actress WWA/1

HALL, Juanita [née Long] (d 1968
[66]) American actress, singer
BE, TW/5-9, 11-18, 24, WWA/4

HALL, J. W. (fl c. 1900?) actor,
singer, song composer CDP

HALL, Laura Nelson [Mrs. Frederick Truesdell] (b 1876) American actress GRB/3-4, WWM,
WWT/1-6

HALL, Lillian (b 1850) American
actress HAS

HALL, Lois Ann (b 1947) American actress TW/28

HALL, Margaret American actress
TW/19-20, 22-26

HALL, Mark (b 1955) American
actor TW/26-27

HALL, Michael (b 1927) American actor TW/4

HALL, Natalie (b 1904) American actress, singer WWT/7-11

HALL, Owen [James Davis] (1853-1907) English dramatist, librettist GRB/1-3, WWS, WWW/1

HALL, Pamela (b 1946/47) American actress TW/25, 27-30

HALL, Pauline (1860-1919) American actress, singer CDP, SR, WWA/1, WWM, WWS, WWT/1-3

HALL, Sir Peter Reginald Frederick (b 1930) English producer, manager, director AAS, BE, CB, COC, ES, OC/3, PDT, WWT/13-16

HALL, Porter (d 1953 [65]) actor TW/10

HALL, Richard (b 1938) American actor TW/25

HALL, Mrs. R. J. see Hayes, Mabel

HALL, Robert (fl 1779) dramatist CP/3

HALL, Robert (d 1901 [56]) music-hall lessee EA/02*

HALL, Mrs. S. C. (d 1881 [81]) dramatist BE*, WWT/14*

HALL, Thurston (1882-1958) American actor TW/14, WWS, WWT/5-10

HALL, Mrs. Tom (d 1899 [37]) EA/00*

HALL, William (fl 1632) actor DA

HALL, Willis (b 1929) English dramatist AAS, CD, CH, MD, MWD, PDT, WWT/14-16

HALLAM, Mrs. (fl 1752-53) actress HAS

HALLAM, Mrs. [née Hattie Sheppard] (d 1874) actress EA/75*

HALLAM, A. (fl 1750) translator CP/3

HALLAM, A. (fl 1752-95) actor HAS

HALLAM, Adam (d 1738) actor BE*, WWT/14*

HALLAM, Ann (d 1740) actress BE*, WWT/14*

HALLAM, Ann see Barrington, Mrs. John

HALLAM, Basil (1889-1916) English actor, singer WWT/3

HALLAM, Frederick (d 1920 [60]) Canadian comedian BE*, BP/4*

HALLAM, Isabella (1746-1826) English actress OC/1-3

HALLAM, John (d 1829) English actor HAS

HALLAM, Mrs. John [née Stannard] (d 1838) English actress HAS

HALLAM, Lewis, Sr. (1714-56) English actor, manager COC, HAS, OC/1-3, SR

HALLAM, Lewis, Jr. (1740-1808) English/American actor, manager CDP, COC, DAB, HAS, ES, OC/1-3, SR, WWA/H

HALLAM, Mrs. Lewis [Mrs. David Douglas] (d 1773) English actress CDP, HAS

HALLAM, Mrs. Lewis, II [née Tuke] (fl 1785) actress CDP, HAS

HALLAM, Mirvan (1771-1811) West Indian actor HAS

HALLAM, Nancy (fl 1759-61) actress BE*

HALLAM, Sarah (fl 1770-75) actress BE*

HALLAM, Thomas (d 1735) actor CDP

HALLAM, William (d 1758 [46]?) actor, manager HAS, SR

HALLANDE, Miss (d 1832) English actress BS, CDP

HALLARD, Charles Maitland (1865-1942) Scottish actor GRB/3-4, WWT/1-9

HALLATT, Henry (1888-1952) English actor WWT/6-11

HALLATT, May (b 1878) English actress TW/13

HALLATT, W. H. (d 1927 [80]) actor, producer BE*, WWT/14*

HALLATT, Mrs. W. H. see Hope, Carrie Sydney

HALLAWAIE, "The Younger" (fl 1580) actor DA

HALL-CAINE, Lily see Caine, Lily Hall

HALLE, C. (fl 1859) pantomimist, comedian HAS

HALLE, Sir Charles (1819-95) conductor, musician CDP

HALLE, Lady Charles (d 1911 [72]) EA/12*

HALLE, Cliff (d 1976 [57]) performer BP/60*

HALLEAN, Mme. American?
bearded lady CDP
HALLECK, Daniel (b 1946)
American actor TW/25
HALLEN, Mrs. Fred [Enid Hart]
(d 1889 [32]) American actress
EA/90*
HALLEN, Molly Fuller (fl 1894?)
singer, actress CDP
HALLER, Tobias (b 1951) Amer-
ican actor TW/29
HALLET, Benjamin (b 1744?)
musician CDP
HALLETT, Jack (b 1948) Ameri-
can actor TW/28
HALLETT, Louis (b 1870) Amer-
ican manager, agent WWM
HALLETT, Mrs. W. H. see
Hope, Carrie Sydney
HALLEWELL, F. J. (d 1899 [53])
singer EA/00*
HALLEY, Mandane Phillips (d
1967 [87]) performer BP/51*
HALLEY, Richard (fl 1636) actor
DA
HALLIDAY, Andrew (1830/31-77)
Scottish dramatist CDP, DNB,
EA/68
HALLIDAY, Mrs. Andrew [Sarah
Duff] (d 1879) EA/80*
HALLIDAY, Charles (d 1886
[34]) musician EA/87*
HALLIDAY, Charles (d 1901 [58])
musical director EA/02*
HALLIDAY, Gardner (b 1966 [56])
performer BP/51*
HALLIDAY, Hildegarde (1907-77)
American actress TW/1, 3,
5-9
HALLIDAY, James (d 1917)
EA/18*
HALLIDAY, John (1880-1947)
American actor TW/4,
WWT/6-10
HALLIDAY, Lena (d 1937) actress
WWT/1-8
HALLIDAY, Richard (1905-73)
American producer BE, TW/29
HALLIDAY, Robert (b 1893) Scot-
tish actor, singer TW/8,
WWT/6-10
HALLING, Daisy (b 1881) English
actress GRB/1
HALLING, Sydney (d 1904 [49])
actor EA/05*
HALLIWELL, David (b 1936/37)
English dramatist, producer
AAS, CD, CH, WWT/15-16

HALLIWELL, Edward (fl 1532)
dramatist FGF
HALLIWELL-PHILLIPS, James
Orchard (1820-89) writer CDP,
DNB, HP
HALLOR, Edith (d 1971 [75])
performer BP/56*
HALLORAN, L. H. ["Philo-Nauti-
cus"] (fl 1801) dramatist CP/3
HALLOW, John (b 1924) American
actor TW/23-26
HALLOWS, Edward Noble (d 1887)
actor EA/88*
HALLOWS, Mrs. Sydney L. see
Rigden, Maud
HALLS, William (d 1893 [35])
"A Jackley Wonder" EA/94*
HALMAN, Ella (b 1906) English
actress TW/4
HALPERIN, Michael (d 1974 [71])
lawyer BP/58*
HALPERIN, Nan (d 1963 [65])
performer BE*, BP/48*,
WWT/14*
HALPERN, Leivick see Leivick,
H.
HALPERN, Morty stage manager,
actor BE
HALPIN, Frank (d 1917) EA/18*
HALPIN, John (d 1916 [41]) EA/
17*
HALPRIN, Ann choreographer CD
HALSEY, Mrs. Henry P. see
Dean, Fanny
HALSTAN, Margaret [Mrs. John
Hartman Morgan] (b 1879/80)
English actress GRB/1-4,
WWT/1-14
HALSTEAD, Byron C. (d 1963
[62]) performer BP/48*
HALSTEAD, David (d 1890 [51])
EA/91*
HALSTEAD, William P. (b 1906)
American educator BE
HALTINER, Fred (d 1973 [37])
Swiss actor BP/58*, WWT/16*
HALTON, Charles American actor
TW/6
HALTON, Mrs. P. W. (d 1894)
EA/95*
HALVERSTADT, Constance see
Cummings, Constance
HAM, Isabella C. (d 1910) EA/11*
HAMAN, Catharine Maria (d 1773)
English actress HAS
HAMAR, Clifford E. (b 1914)
American educator, director
BE

HAMBLETON, Mrs. (d 1851)
Australian actress HAS
HAMBLETON, Anne B. C. (d
1962 [24]) BE*, BP/46*
HAMBLETON, T. Edward (b
1911) American producer,
director BE, WWT/13-16
HAMBLETON, William (d 1879
[81]) actor EA/80*
HAMBLIN, Mr. see Clinton,
Mr.
HAMBLIN, Bessie (fl 1838-57)
English actress HAS
HAMBLIN, Thomas Sowerby
(1800-53) American actor,
manager CDP, COC, DAB,
HAS, OC/1-3, SR, WWA/H
HAMBLIN, Mrs. Thomas Sowerby
see Charles, Elizabeth Walker
HAMBLIN, Mrs. Thomas Sowerby,
IV see Shaw, Mrs.
HAMBLIN, Mrs. Thomas Sowerby
see Shaw, Mary
HAMBLIN, William H. (b 1827)
American actor HAS
HAMBLIN, Mrs. William H.
(b 1833) American dancer,
actress HAS
HAMBLING, Arthur (b 1888) Eng-
lish actor WWT/9-13
HAMELIN, Clement (d 1957)
actor BE*, WWT/14*
HAMER, Gerald (d 1972 [86])
performer BP/57*
HAMER, Joseph (b 1932) Amer-
ican actor TW/25-26, 30
HAMER, Mrs. R. J. see
Pearce, Lottie
HAMER, Robert (d 1963 [52])
director BE*
HAMERTON, Henry (fl 1635)
groom DA
HAMES, Jack (b 1880) English
actor GRB/1
HAMID, George Abou (1896-1971)
Lebanese circus executive
WWA/5
HAMILL, Mary (b 1943) American
actress TW/25, 27, 29-30
HAMILTON, Col. (fl 1823?)
American? dramatist EAP,
RJ
HAMILTON, Mrs. (fl 1745-72)
actress DNB, GT, TD/1-2
HAMILTON, Mrs. [née Peters]
(fl 1800) actress TD/1-2
HAMILTON, Mrs. (d 1834) ac-
tress HAS

HAMILTON, Mrs. (d 1907) EA/08*
HAMILTON, Miss (fl 1830) actress
HAS
HAMILTON, Alfred H. (d 1906)
EA/07*
HAMILTON, Allen (b 1935) Amer-
ican actor TW/25
HAMILTON, Caroline [Mrs. Josiah
Hamilton] (d 1904 [70]) EA/05*
HAMILTON, Charles (fl 1784?)
translator CP/3
HAMILTON, Cicely [née Cicely
Mary Hammill] (1872-1952)
dramatist, actress GRB/4,
NTH, WWT/1-11, WWW/5
HAMILTON, Claude (b 1831) Amer-
ican actor HAS
HAMILTON, Mrs. Claude [Hattie]
(fl 1862-64) English actress
HAS
HAMILTON, Clayton (1881-1946)
American critic, dramatist
CB, DAB, SR, WWA/2, WWT/
7-9
HAMILTON, Cosmo [Cosmo Gibbs]
(1872?-1942) dramatist CB,
GRB/3-4, NTH, WWT/1-9,
WWW/4
HAMILTON, Mrs. Cosmo see
Faber, Beryl
HAMILTON, David (d 1908) EA/
09*
HAMILTON, Diana (1898/1900-
1951) English actress WWT/
5-11
HAMILTON, Dorothy (b 1897) Eng-
lish actress WWT/7-11
HAMILTON, Edward H. (d 1837)
English actor HAS
HAMILTON, Eric (b 1954) Ameri-
can actor TW/25
HAMILTON, Fanny see Addie,
Mrs.
HAMILTON, Gavin J. (d 1911 [58])
actor EA/12*
HAMILTON, George Sinclair (d
1899) EA/00*
HAMILTON, Georgina [Mrs.
George Hamilton Bell] (b 1869)
English actress GRB/1
[HAMILTON, Mrs. Gilbert?] see
Cross, Mrs. [John Cartwright?]
HAMILTON, Gloria American ac-
tress TW/8
HAMILTON, Grace see Russell,
Mrs.
HAMILTON, Grosvenor Herbert (d
1916) EA/17*

HAMILTON, Hale [Hale Rice Hamilton] (1880-1942) American actor CB, SR, WWT/2-9

HAMILTON, Hale Rice see Hamilton, Hale

HAMILTON, Hattie see Hamilton, Mrs. Claude

HAMILTON, Henry (d 1918 [65]) English dramatist, actor GRB/3-4, OAA/1-2, WWT/1-3, WWW/2

HAMILTON, Henry Bishop (b 1810) English actor, manager SR

HAMILTON, Jeffrey (b 1957) American actor TW/26

HAMILTON, John (b 1940) American actor TW/27

HAMILTON, John Angus (d 1913) EA/14*

HAMILTON, John F. (1893-1967) American actor BE, TW/24

HAMILTON, Joseph (d 1892) panorama exhibitor EA/93*

HAMILTON, Joseph (d 1894) EA/95*

HAMILTON, Mrs. Josiah see Hamilton, Caroline

HAMILTON, Karen Sue (d 1969 [23]) performer BP/54*

HAMILTON, Kate (d 1893) dancer, dancing teacher EA/94*

HAMILTON, Katie see Goddard, Mrs.

HAMILTON, Lance producer BE

HAMILTON, Lindisfarne (b 1910) English actress WWT/9-10

HAMILTON, Mahlon (d 1960 [77]) actor BE*

HAMILTON, Margaret (d 1963 [95]) critic BP/47*

HAMILTON, Margaret (b 1902) American actress BE, TW/8, 13-17, 22-23, 25-26, 30, WWT/14-16

HAMILTON, Murray American actor BE, TW/25-26

HAMILTON, Myron actor TD/2

HAMILTON, Nancy (b 1908) American dramatist, lyricist, actress, producer BE

HAMILTON, Neil (b 1897/99) American actor BE, ES, TW/1-8, 10-12, WWT/11-14

HAMILTON, Newburgh (fl 1715-43) dramatist CP/1-3, GT, TD/1-2

HAMILTON, Patrick (1904-62)

English dramatist MD, PDT, WWT/7-13

HAMILTON, Peter (b 1915) American actor TW/4-8

HAMILTON, Robert (fl 1836-49) Scottish actor CDP, HAS

HAMILTON, Mrs. Robert [née Sarah Johannot; Mrs. Rowbotham] (d 1838) English actress HAS

HAMILTON, Roger (b 1928) American actor TW/24, 27-30

HAMILTON, Rose (d 1897) actress, singer EA/98*

HAMILTON, Roy (d 1969 [40]) performer BP/54*

HAMILTON, R. P. (b 1874) English actor GRB/1

HAMILTON, Sidney [Percy T. F. Kingsmill] (b 1885) English entertainer GRB/1

HAMILTON, Sidney (d 1974 [78]) performer BP/59*

HAMILTON, Theodore (1830/36-1916) American actor CDP, HAS, PP/1, SR, WWS

HAMILTON, William actor TD/2

HAMILTON, William (d 1907 [69]) proprietor EA/08*

HAMILTON, William Bishop (1810-68) English actor, lessee, manager HAS

HAMILTON, William Henry [William H. Grosvenor] (1829-64) English actor HAS

HAMILTON, Willie (d 1894 [22]) EA/95*

HAMLET, T. (d 1853 [84]) theatre builder EA/72*

HAMLETT, Dilys (b 1928) English actress WWT/15-16

HAMLETT, Robert (fl 1611-25) actor DA

HAMLEY-CLIFFORD, Molly (d 1956) actress BE*, WWT/14*

HAMLIN, George (d 1923) American singer BE*, BP/7*

HAMLIN, George (b 1920) American director, producer, educator, actor BE

HAMLIN, Mrs. George Wright (d 1964 [93]) dramatist BE*, BP/49*

HAMLIN, John A. (d 1908 [73]) manager GRB/4*, WWT/14*

HAMLUC, W. (fl c. 1625) actor DA

HAMMER, Ben (b 1925) American

actor TW/22-23, 28

HAMMER, Mark (b 1937) American actor TW/29

HAMMER, Will (d 1957 [69]) impresario BE*, WWT/14*

HAMMERLEE, Patricia (b 1929) American actress TW/9, 12-13

HAMMERSLEY, Mrs. (d 1906) EA/07*

HAMMERSLEY, Miss (fl 1818-24) English actress BS, CDP

HAMMERSLY, Robert (d 1964 [29]) magician BE*

HAMMERSTEIN, Arthur (1872/ 73/76-1955) American manager ES, NTH, TW/12, WWT/6-11

HAMMERSTEIN, Elaine (1898-1948) actress TW/5

HAMMERSTEIN, James (b 1931) American producer, director, stage manager BE, WWT/16

HAMMERSTEIN, Oscar (1847-1919) German manager, dramatist, composer, theatre designer CDP, COC, ES, GRB/ 2-4, HJD, NTH, SR, WWA/1, WWS, WWT/1-3, WWW/2

HAMMERSTEIN, Oscar, II (1895-1960) American librettist, lyricist AAS, CB, COC, DAB, ES, HJD, MH, MWD, NTH, OC/3, PDT, TW/2-8, 17, WWA/4, WWT/5-12, WWW/5

HAMMERSTEIN, Theodore M. (d 1973 [72]) producer/director/choreographer BP/58*

HAMMERSTEIN, William (1874-1914) American impresario ES

HAMMERTON, Mr. Irish actor TD/1-2

HAMMERTON, Stephen (fl 1630-47) English actor DA, OC/ 1-3

HAMMIL, John (b 1948) American actor TW/30

HAMMILL, Cicely Mary see Hamilton, Cicely

HAMMOND, Mr. (fl 1791) actor HAS

HAMMOND, Mr. (fl 1800) Welsh actor HAS

HAMMOND, Aubrey (1893-1940) English designer ES, WWT/ 6-9, WWW/3

HAMMOND, Bert E. (b 1880) English business manager WWT/ 4-12

HAMMOND, Caroline [Mrs. W. Hammond] (d 1894) EA/95*

HAMMOND, Dorothy (d 1950 [76]) English actress WWT/4-5

HAMMOND, Edward (d 1895) actor EA/96*

HAMMOND, Felix (d 1885) actor EA/86*

HAMMOND, Jessie (d 1868 [33]) musician EA/69*

HAMMOND, John (fl 1494) actor DA

HAMMOND, Kay [Dorothy Katherine Standing] (b 1909) English actress AAS, COC, ES, WWT/7-14

HAMMOND, Percy (1873-1936) American critic AAS, COC, DAB, NTH, OC/3, WWA/1, WWT/5-8

HAMMOND, Peter (b 1923) English actor WWT/11-14

HAMMOND, Ruth (b 1905) actress TW/1, 3, 5-7

HAMMOND, Mrs. T. see Hammond, Caroline

HAMMOND, Virginia (d 1972 [82]) American actress BE, TW/28

HAMMOND, William (fl 1740) dramatist CP/1-3, GT

HAMMOND, William James (1797-1848) actor, manager CDP

HAMMONDE, Frank (d 1909) actor EA/11*

HAMOND (fl 1565) actor DA

HAMPDEN, Walter [Walter Hampden Dougherty] (1879-1956) American actor CB, COC, ES, GRB/1-4, NTH, OC/1-3, SR, TW/1-12, WWA/3, WWM, WWS, WWT/1-11

HAMPER, Genevieve (d 1971 [82]) actress TW/27

HAMPSHIRE, Susan (b 1941?/42) English actress, stage manager CB, WWT/14-16

HAMPSON, Ernie (d 1909 [35]) EA/10*

HAMPSON, Harry (d 1906 [30]) EA/07*

HAMPSON, Oscar (d 1906) comedian EA/08*

HAMPTON, Mr. (d 1871 [72]) aeronaut EA/72*

HAMPTON, Christopher (b 1946) English dramatist AAS, CD,

CH, COC, WWT/15-16
HAMPTON, Henry (d 1895 [45])
actor EA/96*
HAMPTON, Mrs. Henry [Maggie
St. Clair Douglas] (d 1902)
actress EA/03*
HAMPTON, Louise (1876-1954)
English actress WWT/5-11
HAMPTON, Mary (d 1931 [63])
American actress BE*,
BP/15*
HAMPTON, Myra (d 1945 [44])
actress BE*, WWT/14*
HAMPTON, Wade skeleton CDP
HAMRICK, Burwell (d 1970
[64]) designer BP/55*
HAMUND, St. John [Shadwell
Clerke] (1869-1929) English
actor GRB/1
HANAKO, Mme. (b 1882) Japanese
actress GRB/4, WWT/1-4
HANAU, Stella (d 1972 [81])
publicist BP/56*
HANBURY, Elizabeth (d 1916)
EA/17*
HANBURY, Lily [Mrs. Herbert
Guedalla] (1874-1908) English
actress EA/96, GRB/1-4,
WWW/1
HANBURY, Pattie [Mrs. Charles
Gover] (d 1908) actress EA/
09*
HANCHETT, David (b 1823)
American actor, manager
HAS, SR
HANCHETT, Emma (d 1879 [60])
American actress EA/80*
HANCOCK, Christopher (b 1928)
English actor WWT/15-16
HANCOCK, Myrtle J. (d 1948
[65]) American minstrel BE*,
BP/33*
HANCOCK, Sheila (b 1933) Eng-
lish actress AAS, TW/22,
WWT/14-16
HANCOCK, Tony (1924-68) Eng-
lish actor WWW/6
HANCOX, Daisy (b 1898) Eng-
lish actress, singer WWT/4-5
HANDEL, George Frederick
(1685-1759) German composer
CDP, DNB, ES, HP, TD/1-2
HANDFORD, Henry (d 1888 [64])
EA/89*
HANDKE, Peter (b 1942) Austrian
dramatist CB
HANDL, Irene (b 1901/12) Eng-
lish actress AAS, WWT/9-16

HANDLEY, J. W. actor EA/97
HANDLEY, Tommy (1896-1949)
English performer WWW/4
HANDMAN, Wynn (b 1922) director,
producer, teacher BE, WWT/
15-16
HANDS, Terry (b 1941) English
director AAS, WWT/15-16
HANDWERKER, Nathan (d 1974
[83]) BP/58*
HANDY, William Christopher
(1873-1958) American composer
BE*, BP/42*
HANDYSIDE, Clarence (d 1931
[77]) Canadian actor BE*,
BP/16*, WWT/14*
HANDZIC, Jean (d 1963 [41])
singer TW/20
HANEY, Carol (1924-64) American
actress TW/10-20, WWA/4
HANEY, Felix (b 1861) American
actor WWM
HANEY, J. Francis (d 1964) per-
former BE*
HANEY, Sonja (b 1943) American
actress TW/28-29
HANFORD, Charles Barnum (1859/
64-1926) American actor,
manager PP/1, SR, WWA/1,
WWM
HANFORD, Edwin (fl 1889?) sing-
er, actor, song composer CDP
HANKIN, St. John (1869-1909)
English dramatist COC, DNB,
ES, GRB/2-4, MD, MH, MWD,
NTH, OC/1-3, RE, WWW/1
HANKINS, Frederick see Camp-
bell, Clifford
HANKINSON, James B. (d 1873
[35]) musician EA/74*
HANKS, Charles (d 1870) comedian
EA/71*
HANKS, John singer, song com-
poser, minstrel CDP
HANLEY, Ellen (b 1926) American
actress TW/3-20, 26-28
HANLEY, Jack (d 1973 [50]) per-
former BP/58*
HANLEY, James (1892-1942) com-
poser CB
HANLEY, James (b 1901) Irish
dramatist CD
HANLEY, J. G. (1822?-1869)
American actor, manager,
stage manager HAS, SR
HANLEY, Jimmy (1918-70) actor
WWT/13-14
HANLEY, Katie (b 1949) American

actress TW/28-30
HANLEY, Martin (b 1820) Irish
  actor, manager SR
HANLEY, Martin W. (d 1905)
  manager WWT/14*
HANLEY, Ted (fl 1898?) singer,
  actor CDP
HANLEY, William (b 1931)
  American dramatist BE,
  CD, CH, ES, MWD, WWT/
  15-16
HANLON, Bert (d 1972) com-
  poser/lyricist BP/56*
HANLON, Bob (d 1907 [46])
  gymnast GRB/3
HANLON, Daniel E. (b 1877)
  American actor WWM
HANLON, Dick (d 1905) acrobat
  EA/06*
HANLON, Frederick (b 1848)
  acrobat, pantomimist CDP,
  ES
HANLON, Jane [Mrs. Thomas
  Hanlon] (d 1894) EA/95*
HANLON, Thomas (d 1880 [69])
  EA/81*
HANLON, Mrs. Thomas see
  Hanlon, Jane
HANLON, William A. (d 1969)
  performer BP/54*
HANLON BROTHERS, The HAS
HANLON-LEES, Alfred (b 1844)
  acrobat CDP, ES, HAS
HANLON-LEES, Edward (1854-
  1931) English acrobat CDP,
  COC, ES, OC/1-3
HANLON-LEES, George (1839-
  1926) English acrobat CDP,
  COC, ES, HAS, OC/1-3, SR
HANLON-LEES, Thomas (1838-
  68) English acrobat CDP, SR
HANLON-LEES, William (1844-
  1923) English acrobat CDP,
  COC, ES, HAS, OC/1-3, SR
HANLY, Richard (fl 1628) actor
  DA
HANMER, Don (b 1919) American
  actor TW/5-9, 12-13
HANMER, Sir Thomas (1677-
  1746) writer CDP
HANN, Charles R. (b 1868) Eng-
  lish actor GRB/1
HANN, Thomas R. (d 1878 [57])
  English actor HAS
HANN, Walter (1838-1922) English
  scene artist WWT/1-3
HANNA, Mrs. (fl 1821) actress
  HAS

HANNA, Miss see Durie, Mrs.
HANNAFIN, Daniel P. (b 1933)
  American actor TW/22, 24
HANNAH, Rose Ann (d 1887)
  EA/89*
HANNAN, Philip see Phillips,
  Frederick
HANNAY, Rev. J. O. see
  Birmingham, George
HANNEFORD, Mr. (d 1889) cir-
  cus performer EA/90*
HANNEFORD, Mrs. (d 1889) cir-
  cus performer EA/90*
HANNEN, Hermione (b 1913)
  English actress WWT/9-10,
  12-13
HANNEN, Nicholas James (1881-
  1972) English actor, producer
  AAS, NTH, TW/2, WWT/4-14
HANNING, Geraldine American
  actress TW/28
HANNOCH, Dan (d 1974 [69])
  performer BP/58*
HANRAY, Lawrence (1874-1947)
  English actor WWT/4-10
HANSARD, J. B. (d 1908 [68])
  actor, scene artist EA/09*
  WWT/14*
HANSBERRY, Lorraine (1930-65)
  American dramatist AAS, BE,
  CB, CD, CH, ES, MH, MWD,
  PDT, TW/21, WWA/4
HANSELL, Thomas (d 1895 [41])
  acting manager EA/96*
HANSEN, Al painter CD
HANSEN, Hans (d 1962 [76]) Ger-
  man actor TW/19
HANSEN, Harold I. (b 1914)
  American educator BE
HANSEN, Juanita (d 1961 [66])
  actress BE*
HANSEN, Laura (d 1914) English
  actress GRB/1
HANSEN, Lawrence William (d
  1968) composer/lyricist BP/
  52*
HANSEN, Ronn (b 1939) American
  actor TW/26, 28
HANSEN, William (1911-75) Amer-
  ican actor TW/3, 8, 10-12,
  19
HANSON, Gladys (1887-1973)
  American actress TW/29,
  WWT/4-10
HANSON, Harry (1895-1972) South
  African actor, manager AAS,
  WWT/10-13
HANSON, Harry L. [Harry L.

Parker] (b 1856) American minstrel, vaudevillian WWM

HANSON, Howard (b 1896) American composer CB, HJD

HANSON, Isadora (fl 1847) American actress HAS

HANSON, John [né Watts] (b 1922) Canadian singer, actor AAS, WWT/15-16

HANSON, Johnny (d 1907 [64]) clown, comedian BE*, EA/08*, WWT/14*

HANSON, Kitty [Mrs. W. H. Berry] (d 1947 [76]) actress BE*, WWT/14*

HANSON, Lars (d 1965 [78]) Swedish actor TW/21

HANSON, M. H. (b 1864) Danish impresario WWM

HANSON, Nicholas (fl 1623-28) actor DA

HANSON, Peter (b 1921) American actor TW/9

HANSON, Philip (b 1924) American actor TW/27

HANSON, Preston (b 1921) American actor TW/7-9

HANSON, Mr. T. (d 1868 [29]) stage manager EA/69*

HANSON, Winnie see Lightner, Winnie

HANTON, John Dee (d 1906 [18]) EA/07*

HANZEL, Carol (b 1945) American actress TW/29

HAPGOOD, Elizabeth Reynolds (1894-1974) American translator BE

HAPGOOD, Hutchins (1869-1944) American critic WWA/2

HAPGOOD, Norman (1868-1937) American critic GRB/2-3, NTH

HARA, Mary American actress TW/26, 30

HARARI, Ezra (d 1970 [76]) producer/director/choreographer BP/54*

HARBACH, Otto A. (1873-1963) American dramatist, librettist, lyricist CB, TW/19, WWA/4, WWT/4-11, WWW/6

HARBACH, William (fl c. 1785) dramatist CP/3

HARBAGE, Alfred (1901-76) American scholar BE

HARBEN, Hubert (1878-1941) English actor WWT/3-9

HARBEN, Joan (1909-53) English actress WWT/7-11

HARBON, William James (d 1884) EA/85*

HARBORD, Carl English actor WWT/7-9

HARBORD, Gordon (b 1901) English manager WWT/8-10

HARBURG, Edgar Y. (b 1898) American lyricist, dramatist BE, CD, WWT/15-16

HARBURY, Charles (d 1928 [85]) actor BE*, BP/12*, WWT/14*

HARBY, George Washington dramatist RJ

HARBY, Isaac (1788-1828) American dramatist DAB, EAP, RJ, WWA/H

HARCOURT, Charles (d 1880 [42]) actor OAA/1-2

HARCOURT, Cissie (d 1916) comedian EA/18*

HARCOURT, Cyril (d 1924 [52]) actor, dramatist WWT/3-4

HARCOURT, Francis (d 1884 [35]) actor EA/85*

HARCOURT, Fred (d 1906) magician EA/07*

HARCOURT, G. Bees (fl 1871?) singer, song composer, minstrel CDP

HARCOURT, Mrs. George see Harcourt, Mrs. M.

HARCOURT, James (1873-1951) English actor WWT/8-11

HARCOURT, Leonard (d 1880) actor EA/81*

HARCOURT, Leslie (b 1890) English actor, producer WWT/8-9

HARCOURT, Lottie [Mrs. Forbes Dawson] (d 1893) actress EA/94*

HARCOURT, Mrs. M. [Mrs. George Harcourt] (d 1888 [31]) EA/89*

HARCOURT, Marie [Miss Hart] Scottish actress GRB/1

HARCOURT, Robert Vernon (1878-1962) English dramatist GRB/1-4, WWT/1-4

HARCOURT, Sidney (d 1905 [49]) comedian EA/06*

HARCOURT, Mrs. William see Fischer, Alice

HARDACRE, Agnes Denby (d 1911 [39]) actress EA/12*

HARDACRE, Esther (d 1896 [60]) EA/97*

HARDACRE, John Pitt (1855-1933)

English actor, manager WWT/
3-7
HARDENBERG, Frank (1829-89)
American actor CDP
HARDHAM, John (d 1772) English
dramatist CP/1-3, GT
HARDIE, A. C. (d 1939) actor
BE*, WWT/14*
HARDIE, Mrs. J. M. see
Von Ler, Sarah
HARDIE, James M. (d 1905)
managing director EA/06*
HARDIE, James W. (d 1912) ac-
tor, manager SR
HARDIE, Russell (1904/06-73)
American actor BE, TW/1-
20, 30, WWT/10-14
HARDIE, Sarah Blanche (d 1884)
EA/85*
HARDIE, W. R. [Harry Fenwick]
(d 1884) actor? EA/85*
HARDIMAN, Terrence (b 1937)
English actor WWT/15-16
HARDIN, John A. (d 1976 [88])
theatre supply company exe-
cutive BP/60*
HARDING, Mr. (fl 1839?) actor
CDP
HARDING, Miss see Marshall,
Mrs. G.
HARDING, Alfred (d 1945) Eng-
lish actor GRB/1
HARDING, Alfred (d 1969 [77])
editor BP/54*
HARDING, Ann (b 1902/04)
American actress BE, ES,
WWT/6-15
HARDING, Bert (d 1917 [31])
musician, composer EA/18*
HARDING, Charles (d 1895
[50]) singer EA/96*
HARDING, Mrs. Charles see
Sutherland, Annie
HARDING, D. Lyn [David
Llewellyn Harding] (1867-
1952) Welsh actor GRB/2-4,
TW/9, WWM, WWT/1-11
HARDING, Florence R. (d 1913
[26]) EA/14*
HARDING, Frank (d 1911 [47])
actor EA/12*
HARDING, John (b 1948) English
actor, dramatist CD, WWT/
16
HARDING, Joseph (d 1881 [51])
proprietor EA/82*
HARDING, Joseph R. W. (d 1880
[58]) EA/81*

HARDING, June (b 1940) American
actress TW/17-20
HARDING, Nannie Welsh singer
GRB/1
HARDING, Rudge (d 1932 [70])
English actor EA/97, GRB/1-4,
WWT/1-4
HARDING, Samuel (1618-c. 40)
English dramatist CP/2-3,
DNB, FGF
HARDING, W. (d 1909) actor?
EA/10*
HARDINGE, Mr. (fl 1797-1802)
English actor HAS, TD/2
HARDINGE, Mrs. actress HAS
HARDINGE, Emma (fl 1855) ac-
tress CDP, HAS
HARDINGE, Fanny (fl 1854) ac-
tress HAS
HARDINGE, H. C. M. dramatist
WWT/4-7
HARDMAN, W. H. (d 1886)
comedian EA/87*
HARDMUTH, Paul (d 1962 [73])
German actor BE*
HARDS, Ira (1872-1938) American
producer WWT/6-8
HARDWICK, James (d 1886 [71])
comic songwriter EA/87*
HARDWICK, Paul (b 1918) English
actor AAS, WWT/14-16
HARDWICKE, Sir Cedric Webster
(1893-1964) English actor, di-
rector AAS, BE, CB, COC,
ES, NTH, OC/1-3, TW/2-16,
18-19, 21, WWA/4, WWT/5-13,
WWW/6
HARDWICKE, Clarice (b 1900)
Australian actress WWT/5-10
HARDWICKE, Edward (b 1932)
English actor WWT/15-16
HARDY, Prof. (d 1899 [30]) ven-
triloquist EA/00*
HARDY, Arthur F. (b 1870) Eng-
lish manager WWT/1-11
HARDY, A. S. (d 1901) Negro
comedian EA/02*
HARDY, Betty (b 1904) English
actress WWT/7-10
HARDY, Charles Edward (d 1906
[50]) manager EA/07*
HARDY, Cherry (1897-1963) Eng-
lish actress TW/4-6
HARDY, James (d 1877) musician
EA/78*
HARDY, Joseph (b 1918) American
actor TW/28, 30
HARDY, Joseph (b 1929) American

director WWT/15-16
HARDY, Nelson (b 1861) English
ventriloquist GRB/1
HARDY, Oliver (1892-1957)
vaudevillian, actor TW/14
HARDY, Robert (b 1925) English
actor AAS, TW/14, WWT/
14-16
HARDY, Sam B. (1883-1935)
American actor WWS
HARDY, Sarah (b 1940) American
actress TW/30
HARDY, Silva giantess CDP
HARDY, Thomas (1840-1928)
English dramatist DNB, ES,
HP, MWD, NTH, PDT,
WWW/2
HARE, Betty (b 1900) English ac-
tress, singer WWT/8-15
HARE, David (b 1947) English
dramatist AAS, CD, WWT/16
HARE, Doris (b 1905) Welsh
actress, singer WWT/8-16
HARE, Ernest Dudley (b 1900)
English actor AAS, WWT/9-16
HARE, Francis Lumsden see
Hare, Lumsden
HARE, Mrs. Francis Lumsden
see Ruttledge, Frances
HARE, Gilbert [Fairs] (1869-
1951) English actor ES, GRB/
1-3, WWT/4-8
HARE, J. (d 1909 [87]) agent
EA/10*
HARE, Sir John [Fairs] (1844-
1921) English actor, manager
CDP, COC, DNB, DP, ES,
GRB/1-4, NTH, OAA/1-2,
OC/1-3, SR, WWS, WWT/1-3,
WWW/2
HARE, J. Robertson (b 1891)
English actor COC, WWT/
6-16
HARE, Kate (d 1957 [83]) actress
BE*, WWT/14*
HARE, Lumsden (1875-1964) Irish
actor BE, GRB/1-2, TW/21
HARE, Mrs. Lumsden see
Ruttledge, Frances
HARE, Mollie (d 1971) performer
BP/55*
HARE, Reginald (d 1888) acting
manager EA/89*
HARE, Rene Vivian (d 1969 [72])
performer BP/54*
HARE, Will (b 1919) American
actor TW/1-7, 10-14, 20,
23-24, 28-30, WWT/16

HARE, Winifred (b 1875) English
actress, singer CDP, GRB/
3-4, WWT/1-8
HARENS, Dean (b 1921) American
actor TW/3-7, 9-11
HAREWOOD, Earl of (b 1923)
English director, executive
CB
HARFORD, Miss see Hoper,
Mrs.
HARFORD, W. scene artist WWT/
1-7
HARGRAVE, Mr. (fl 1796-1804)
actor TD/1-2
HARGRAVE, Roy (b 1908) Ameri-
can actor, director, dramatist
WWT/10-13
HARGREAVES, Mrs. Albert [Kitty
Page] (d 1916 [35]) EA/17*
HARGREAVES, Anthony (d 1969)
composer/lyricist BP/54*
HARGREAVES, Frank (d 1886)
music-hall manager EA/87*
HARGREAVES, Mrs. J. (d 1908)
EA/09*
HARGREAVES, William (1841-1919)
English actor GRB/1
HARKER, Mrs. (d 1916 [90]) EA/
17*
HARKER, Mrs. Allen (d 1933)
English dramatist WWW/3
HARKER, Frederick (d 1941 [79])
actor BE*, WWT/14*
HARKER, George (d 1875) prompter
EA/76*
HARKER, Mrs. George see
Wynter, Amy
HARKER, George H. English actor
EA/96
HARKER, Gordon (1885-1967) Eng-
lish actor ES, WWT/6-14,
WWW/6
HARKER, Joseph (b 1892) English
scene artist WWT/9-12
HARKER, Joseph C. (1855-1927)
English scene artist ES,
WWT/1-5, WWW/2
HARKEY, James (b 1934) Ameri-
can actor TW/28
HARKINS, Daniel H. (1835/36-1902)
American actor, manager
CDP, HAS, PP/1, SR
HARKINS, Jim (d 1970 [82]) per-
former BP/55*
HARKINS, Marion (d 1962 [68])
performer BE*
HARKINS, William S. (1856-1945)
manager SR

HARKNESS, Rebekah (b 1915)
American dance patron, com-
poser CB
HARLAM, Macey (d 1924) actor
BP/8*
HARLAN, Otis (1865-1940)
American actor CB, GRB/
3-4, WWA/1, WWM, WWS,
WWT/1-9
HARLAN, Russell B. (d 1974
[70]) performer BP/58*
HARLAND, Ada (b 1847) English
actress CDP, HAS
HARLAND, Alec (d 1965) per-
former BP/50*
HARLAND, Fred [William R.
Russ] (d 1912) actor EA/13*
HARLAND, Julia [née Wallack;
Mrs. W. Haskins] actress,
singer CDP
HARLEY, Charles (d 1916) Eng-
lish actor GRB/1
HARLEY, Mrs. Charles see
Barron, Madge Douglas
HARLEY, Edwin (fl 1885) sing-
er, minstrel CDP
HARLEY, Frederick (d 1867)
comic singer, composer CDP
HARLEY, George Davies (1762-
1811) English actor CDP,
DNB, GT, TD/1-2
HARLEY, Henry (d 1891) musi-
cian EA/92*
HARLEY, John Pritt (1786/90?-
1858) English actor, singer
BS, CDP, DNB, OX
HARLEY, Kate singer, actress
CDP
HARLEY, Percy James see
Como, Professor
HARLEY, Rex [Reginald Ernest
Page] (d 1909 [40]) mimic
EA/10*
HARLEY, Violet (d 1903 [35])
serio-comic, singer EA/04*
HARLEY, Violet M. English
actress GRB/1
HARLEY, Walter (d 1909 [63])
magician, showman EA/11*
HARLING, William Franke
(1887-1958) English composer
WWA/3
HARLINGTON, Grace [Mrs. F.
R. Gwyn Richardson] (b 1883)
English actress GRB/1
HARLOW, Edward (d 1890 [35])
circus clown EA/91*
HARLOW, Elizabeth (fl 1789)

dramatist CP/3
HARLOW, Gertrude (d 1947 [73])
actress BE*, WWT/14*
HARLOW, Richard (1872-1920)
comedian BE*, BP/4*
HARLOW, Tom (d 1901) comedian
EA/02*
HARLOWE, Mrs. see Harlowe,
Sarah
HARLOWE, Sarah [Mrs. Francis
G. Waldron] (1765-1852) English
actress BS, CDP, DNB, GT,
OX, TD/1-2
HARMAN, Mrs. see Clarke,
Catharine Maria
HARMAN, Billy (d 1913) EA/14*
HARMAN, Homer H. (d 1971) pub-
licity director BP/55*
HARMAN, Lindsay (b 1865) English
actor, singer, stage manager
GRB/1
HARMAN, W. (d 1888) music-hall
performer EA/89*
HARMER, Dolly (d 1956 [89]) Eng-
lish actress, variety artist
CDP, GRB/1
HARMER, Margaret (d 1902) ac-
tress EA/03*
HARMER, Peter (d 1894 [68])
EA/95*
HARMON, Charlotte American pro-
ducer, editor BE
HARMON, Irving (d 1973 [66]) ac-
tor, singer TW/29
HARMON, Jennifer (b 1943) Ameri-
can actress TW/28, 30
HARMON, Jill (b 1949) American
actress TW/27-29
HARMON, Joy (b 1940) American
actress TW/15
HARMON, Lee (d 1972 [41]) per-
former BP/57*
HARMON, Lewis (b 1911) American
press representative, producer,
manager BE
HARMSTON, W. (d 1881 [71]) cir-
cus manager, architect EA/82*
HARMSTON, William Batty (d 1893
[49]) circus proprietor EA/94*
HARNED, Virginia [Mrs. E. H.
Sothern] (1872-1946) American
actress CDP, GRB/2-4, TW/2,
WWA/2, WWM, WWS, WWT/1-6
HARNEY, Ben (b 1952) American
actor TW/28-30
HARNEY, Benjamin Robertson
(1872-1938) composer, performer
BE*

HARNICK, Jay (b 1928) American director, producer BE
HARNICK, Sheldon (b 1924) American lyricist, composer BE
HAROLD, Henry (d 1871 [44]) actor EA/72*
HAROLD, John Danvers (d 1868) musician EA/69*
HAROLD, Lizzie (fl 1872) singer, actress CDP
HAROLD, Maggie [Mrs. William Davidge] (1852-1907) singer, actress CDP
HAROLDE, Ralf (d 1974 [75]) performer BP/59*
HARPER, Mr. (fl 1733-34) actor GT, TD/1-2
HARPER, Mr. (d 1813) West Indian actor HAS
HARPER, Mrs. actress HAS
HARPER, David H. (d 1969 [41]) union executive BP/54*
HARPER, Elizabeth see Bannister, Mrs. John
HARPER, Fanny (d 1875 [22]) statue performer EA/76*
HARPER, Fred (d 1963 [60]) performer BE*
HARPER, George T. (d 1974 [72]) performer BP/59*
HARPER, Gerald (b 1929) English actor WWT/15-16
HARPER, John (d 1742) actor CDP, DNB
HARPER, Ron (b 1936) American actor TW/29
HARPER, Samuel (fl 1737) dramatist CP/2-3, GT
HARPER, Thomas (1787-1853) English musician DNB
HARPER, Thomas (d 1892) EA/93*
HARPER, Valerie (b 1940?) American actress, dancer CB
HARPLEY, T. (fl 1790) dramatist CP/3
HARRADINE, Archie (d 1974 [76]) actor BTR/74
HARRIGAN, Edward (1845-1911) American actor, dramatist, manager CDP, COC, DAB, GRB/2-4, HJD, MH, MWD, NTH, OC/1-3, PP/1, RE, SR, WWA/1, WWS
HARRIGAN, Nedda [Grace Harrigan] (b 1902) American actress BE, WWT/8-11
HARRIGAN, William (1893/94-

1966) American actor BE, OC/1-3, TW/1-8, 11-15, 22, WWT/6-13
HARRINGTON, Mr. actor TD/1-2
HARRINGTON, Mr. (fl 1837-41) English actor HAS
HARRINGTON, Mrs. (fl 1837) actress HAS
HARRINGTON, Dowager Countess of see Foote, Maria
HARRINGTON, Alice (d 1954 [81]) American actress BE*, BP/39*
HARRINGTON, Charles English actor, manager GRB/1
HARRINGTON, Charles Stanhope (1780-1851) CDP
HARRINGTON, Donal (b 1905) American educator BE
HARRINGTON, Florence (d 1942 [80]) actress BE*, WWT/14*
HARRINGTON, George A. (d 1859) minstrel CDP
HARRINGTON, George N. see Christy, George N.
HARRINGTON, Herschel R. (d 1975 [75]) producer/director/choreographer BP/59*
HARRINGTON, James (d 1906 [22]) stage manager EA/07*
HARRINGTON, James A. (d 1908 [88]) actor GRB/4*
HARRINGTON, John Patrick (b 1865) English composer, dramatist GRB/1-3
HARRINGTON, Prof. Jonathan (b 1809) American ventriloquist HAS
HARRINGTON, Kate American actress TW/19, 23, 30
HARRINGTON, Maria see Foote, Maria
HARRINGTON, Pat, Sr. (1900-64) Canadian actor BE, TW/22
HARRINGTON, William (1804-35) American equestrian CDP, HAS
HARRIOTT, Mrs. F. C. see Morris, Clara
HARRIS, Mrs. [Miss Grattan] (d 1856) actress? HAS
HARRIS, Alexander (b 1927) English actor TW/7
HARRIS, Audrey Sophia (1901-66) English designer WWT/8-14 [see also: Motley]
HARRIS, Augustus Glossop (1825-73) English manager, actor COC, DNB, OC/1-3
HARRIS, Sir Augustus Henry Glossop

(1852-96) French/English actor,
manager, producer, dramatist
CDP, DNB, NTH, OAA/1-2,
OC/1-3
HARRIS, Averell (d 1966) actor
TW/23
HARRIS, Bagnall (b 1907) Cana-
dian/English designer ES
HARRIS, Barbara (b 1935/37)
American actress BE, CB,
ES, TW/22-24, 26, WWT/15-16
HARRIS, Bennie Michel (d 1975
[54]) performer BP/59*
HARRIS, Charlene (b 1925) Amer-
ican actress TW/7
HARRIS, Charles (d 1897 [42])
stage manager, producer
EA/98*, WWT/14*
HARRIS, Charles A. "Honey" (d
1962 [75]) performer BE*
HARRIS, Charles Kassell (1865-
1930) American songwriter
DAB, WWS
HARRIS, Charles L. (1854-92)
actor CDP
HARRIS, Christopher see Fry,
Christopher
HARRIS, Clare (d 1949 [59])
actress WWT/5-10
HARRIS, Cynthia American ac-
tress TW/28-30
HARRIS, Dru (b 1952) American
actress TW/30
HARRIS, Mrs. E. see Rose,
Mlle.
HARRIS, Elmer Blaney (1878-
1966) dramatist TW/23,
WWT/4-11
HARRIS, Mrs. F. J. (d 1893)
EA/95*
HARRIS, Flora [Mrs. Sheridan
Moore] (d 1910 [80]) Australian
actress EA/11*
HARRIS, Florence Glossop (b
1883) English actress GRB/
3-4, WWT/1-6
HARRIS, Frank (1855-1931)
Irish writer MD, NTH,
WWW/3
HARRIS, Fred Orrin (b 1901)
American educator BE
HARRIS, George, II American
actor TW/25-26
HARRIS, George W. (d 1895
[63]) actor, manager EA/96*
HARRIS, George W. (d 1929
[49]) scene designer & artist
BE*, WWT/14*

HARRIS, Georgiana see Kenny,
Mrs. George
HARRIS, G. F. (d 1867 [70]) pro-
fessor of music EA/68*
HARRIS, Gus (fl 1914?) singer
CDP
HARRIS, Mrs. G. W. (d 1869)
EA/70*
HARRIS, Mrs. G. W. (d 1873)
EA/74*
HARRIS, Henry (c. 1634-1704) Eng-
lish actor COC, OC/1-3
HARRIS, Henry B. (1866-1912)
American manager GRB/2-4,
SR, WWA/1, WWM, WWS,
WWT/1
HARRIS, Herbert H. (c. 1896-1948)
American producer TW/3-5
HARRIS, Hildred (1898-1944) ac-
tress SR
HARRIS, Howard (d 1878) music-
hall chairman EA/79*
HARRIS, James (1709-80) English
dramatist CP/2-3, GT
HARRIS, Jed [Jed Horowitz] (b
1899/1900) American producing
manager BE, NTH, TW/2-8,
WWT/6-14
HARRIS, John (fl 1635) actor DA
HARRIS, John (d 1874) lessee
EA/75*
HARRIS, John H. (d 1969 [70])
showman BP/53*
HARRIS, Jonathan (b 1914) Ameri-
can actor TW/6-9
HARRIS, Joseph? (fl 1661-81) actor
DNB
HARRIS, Joseph (fl 1661-1702) ac-
tor, dramatist CDP, CP/1-3,
DNB
HARRIS, Joseph manager BE
HARRIS, Julie (b 1925) American
actress AAS, BE, CB, ES,
NTH, TW/5-23, 25-30, WWT/
14-16
HARRIS, Leland B. (b 1912) Amer-
ican union executive BE
HARRIS, Leonore (d 1953 [74])
American actress TW/3-7, 10
HARRIS, Leslie (fl 1895?) singer,
musician, actor CDP
HARRIS, Lizzie (fl 1864) actress
HAS
HARRIS, Margaret F. (b 1904)
English designer WWT/9-16
[see also: Motley]
HARRIS, Maria [Maria Elizabeth
Glossop] (1851-1904) English

actress CDP, OAA/1-2
HARRIS, Mary Ann [née Glossop]
(d 1892) EA/93*
HARRIS, Mary Ann (d 1900 [25])
EA/01*
HARRIS, Mildred (1901-44) American actress BE*
HARRIS, Mitchell (d 1948 [65])
performer BE*
HARRIS, Morris O. (d 1974 [59])
performer BP/59*
HARRIS, Nelly [Mrs. Horace
Sedger] (d 1897) actress CDP
HARRIS, Patience Glossop (d
1901 [44]) EA/03*
HARRIS, Raymond (d 1971 [86])
dramatist BP/55*
HARRIS, Renée (d 1969 [93])
producer TW/26
HARRIS, Richard (b 1933) Irish
actor CB, ES, WWT/14-15
HARRIS, Robert (b 1900) actor
AAS, WWT/5-16
HARRIS, Robert H. (b 1911) American actor TW/22
HARRIS, Rosemary (b 1930) English actress AAS, BE, CB,
TW/9, 15-23, 28-30, WWT/
12-16
HARRIS, Sadie (b 1888) American
actress WWS
HARRIS, Sam H. (1872-1941)
American manager, producer
CB, DAB, NTH, SR, WWA/1,
WWM, WWS, WWT/1-9
HARRIS, Samuel E. [S. Wesley
Barmore] (1825-58) actor
CDP, HAS
HARRIS, Stacy (d 1973 [54]) performer BP/57*
HARRIS, Sylvia (d 1966 [60])
producer TW/23
HARRIS, T. C. see O'Callan,
Thomas
HARRIS, Thomas (d 1820 [82])
proprietor TD/1-2
HARRIS, William (1839/42-1916)
American actor, manager,
producer CDP, HAS, SR,
WWM
HARRIS, William, Jr. (1884-
1946) American producer,
manager CB, TW/3, WWA/2,
WWT/6-9
HARRIS, Will J. (d 1967 [73])
producer/director/choreographer
BP/52*
HARRISBURG, J. C. M. drama-

tist RJ
HARRISON, Mr. (fl 1824) actor?
CDP
HARRISON, Mrs. [née Clifford] (d
1842) English actress HAS
HARRISON, Mrs. see Allegranti,
Teresa Maddalena
HARRISON, Miss see Powell,
Mrs. Snelling
HARRISON, Mrs. A. [Mrs. C.
Harrison] (d 1875) EA/77*
HARRISON, Agnes (d 1868 [87])
EA/69*
HARRISON, Alice Maud (1849/50-
96) American actress CDP, HAS,
SR
HARRISON, Arthur see Dundas,
Henry
HARRISON, Austin (1873-1928)
critic, dramatist WWT/1-5
HARRISON, Bob [Bayard Patterson]
(1842-1912) minstrel CDP
HARRISON, Mrs. C. see Harrison, Mrs. A.
HARRISON, C. B. (d 1862) actor?
HAS
HARRISON, Charles (d 1870) actor?
EA/71*
HARRISON, Charles Lancelot (d
1917) EA/18*
HARRISON, Charles Samuel (d 1891
[37]) singer EA/93*
HARRISON, Clifford (d 1903) elocutionist EA/05*
HARRISON, Cyril (b 1866) English
actor GRB/1
HARRISON, Dennis see Patrick,
Dennis
HARRISON, Duncan (d 1934 [72])
Canadian dramatist, manager
BE*, BP/18*
HARRISON, Mjr. Duncan B. dramatist, song composer CDP
HARRISON, Mrs. E. C. [Mrs.
William Harrison] (d 1889) EA/
90*
HARRISON, Edward (d 1912 [44])
music-hall manager EA/13*
HARRISON, Elizabeth (fl 1756)
dramatist CP/3
HARRISON, E. T. (d 1889 [70])
circus architect EA/90*
HARRISON, Evelyn [Mrs. Walter
Maxwell] (d 1903 [28]) actress
EA/04*
HARRISON, Fanny [Mrs. Isaac
Cohen] (d 1909 [70]) actress,
singer BE*, EA/10*, WWT/14*

HARRISON, Frances actress
CDP
HARRISON, Frank (b 1869) Eng-
lish stage manager, producer
GRB/1-3
HARRISON, Mrs. Frank see
Kay, Ethel
HARRISON, Frederick (d 1904)
variety performer EA/05*
HARRISON, Frederick (d 1926
[72]) English lessee, manager
GRB/1-4, WWT/1-5, WWW/2
HARRISON, Gabriel (1818-1902)
American actor, dramatist,
manager CDP, DAB
HARRISON, George (d 1886)
EA/87*
HARRISON, George (d 1887) cos-
tumier EA/88*
HARRISON, George (d 1887)
manager EA/88*
HARRISON, Mrs. Gulielma
[Mrs. Robert Harrison] (d
1870 [31]) EA/71*
HARRISON, Harriet (d 1881 [62])
costumier EA/82*
HARRISON, Harry P. (1878-
1968) American manager
WWA/5
HARRISON, H. T. (d 1899)
singer EA/00*
HARRISON, James G. (d 1890)
EA/91*
HARRISON, Jay S. (d 1974 [47])
critic BP/59*
HARRISON, J. N. (d 1870 [79])
president of the Sacred Har-
monic Society EA/71*
HARRISON, John (fl 1602) actor
DA
HARRISON, John (d 1878 [59])
costumier EA/79*
HARRISON, John (b 1924) Eng-
lish director, dramatist,
actor CD, WWT/16
HARRISON, Kathleen (b 1898)
English actress AAS, WWT/
7-16
HARRISON, Lee (d 1916 [50])
singer, actor CDP
HARRISON, Leo (1850-1916)
actor SR
HARRISON, Louis (1859-1936)
American actor, dramatist,
manager CDP, SR
HARRISON, Maud [Mrs. Edward
M. Bell] (1854-1907) Ameri-
can actress CDP, WWS

HARRISON, Michael (b 1945) Amer-
ican actor TW/25
HARRISON, Mona (d 1957) Scottish
actress GRB/2-4, WWT/1-12
HARRISON, Nell (d 1973 [93])
American actress TW/1, 30
HARRISON, Lieut. Nicholas Bacon
(fl 1789) dramatist CP/3
HARRISON, Percy (d 1917 [71])
concert director EA/18*
HARRISON, Peter Basil see
Markham, David
HARRISON, Ray American actor
TW/1
HARRISON, Rex (b 1908) English
actor AAS, BE, CB, ES, TW/
5-18, 29, WWT/9-16
HARRISON, Richard (fl 1617) actor
DA
HARRISON, Richard Berry (1864-
1935) American actor, lecturer
COC, DAB, OC/1-3, SR, WWA/1
HARRISON, Robert [Robert Wilkes
Gibbs] (d 1885 [22]) acrobat
EA/86*
HARRISON, Robert (d 1953 [68])
American actor BE*, BP/37*
HARRISON, Mrs. Robert see
Harrison, Gulielma
HARRISON, Rowley (d 1898) come-
dian EA/99*
HARRISON, Samuel (1760-1812)
singer CDP
HARRISON, Susan (b 1938) Ameri-
can actress TW/14
HARRISON, Thomas (fl 1727-29)
dramatist CP/2-3, GT
HARRISON, Thomas (d 1879 [34])
musician EA/80*
HARRISON, Valerie see French,
Valerie
HARRISON, W. (d 1847) English
actor HAS
HARRISON, Mrs. W. see Majil-
ton, Flo
HARRISON, W[ilbur] Vernon (1879-
1929) American manager WWA/1
HARRISON, William (fl 1583) li-
censee, actor? DA
HARRISON, William (fl 1701) drama-
tist CP/1-3, GT
HARRISON, William (1813-68) Eng-
lish actor, singer, manager
CDP, DNB, HAS, SR
HARRISON, Mrs. William see
Harrison, Mrs. E. C.
HARRISON, William Bristow (1812-
81) English actor, manager

CDP, HAS, SR
HARRISON-TATE, A. [Mrs.
Fred Benton] English actress
GRB/1
HARRISS, Sophie Australian
actress GRB/1
HARRITY, Richard (b 1907) Amer-
ican dramatist, actor BE
HARROD, W. (fl 1753-69) Eng-
lish dramatist CP/2-3, GT
HARROLD, J. (d 1908) EA/09*
HARROLD, Jack (b 1920) Amer-
ican actor TW/27
HARROLD, Orville (d 1933 [55])
American singer WWA/1
HARRON, Donald (b 1924) Cana-
dian actor BE, TW/11-20
HARRON, Robert (1894-1920)
actor BE*, BP/5*
HARROP, Sarah (d 1890 [85])
EA/91*
HARROP, Sarah see Bates,
Mrs. Joah
HARROWAY, John (d 1857 [47])
composer, musical director
EA/72*
HARRY (fl 1710) raree showman
CDP
HART, Mrs. actress TD/2
HART, Miss see Harcourt,
Marie
HART, Annie [Mrs. William
Lester] (d 1947 [87]) singer,
actress CDP, TW/4
HART, Arthur (d 1911 [54])
dramatic agent EA/12*
HART, Bernard (1911-64) Amer-
ican producing manager, stage
manager BE, TW/2-8, 21,
WWT/11-13
HART, Billy (b 1864) American
vaudevillian WWM
HART, Mrs. Billy see Marie,
La Belle
HART, Charles (d 1683) English
actor COC, DA, DNB, ES,
NTH, OC/1-3
HART, Charles (fl 1754) Scottish
dramatist CP/2-3, GT
HART, Diane (b 1926) English
actress WWT/15-16
HART, Dolores (b 1930) Ameri-
can actress TW/15-16
HART, Dora Jane (d 1890 [66])
EA/91*
HART, E. A. actor, singer,
song composer CDP
HART, Enid see Hallen, Mrs.

Fred
HART, Everett L. (d 1973 [51])
producer/director/choreographer
BP/57*
HART, Fred (d 1894) manager
EA/95*
HART, Gabriel (d 1905) EA/06*
HART, George (d 1891 [52]) musi-
cian EA/92*
HART, Henry (d 1909 [81]) music-
hall proprietor CDP
HART, Henry (b 1917) American
actor TW/6-7
HART, Jack (d 1974 [102]) performer
BP/59*
HART, Jerry (d 1908 [23]) EA/09*
HART, John (1833-1904) comedian,
minstrel manager, performer
CDP
HART, John (d 1937) producer,
executive, manager BE*, WWT/
14*
HART, Joseph [Joseph Hart Boud-
row] (1858/62-1921) American
comedian, producer, manager
WWM, WWS
HART, Joseph Binns (1794-1844)
English composer, musician,
chorus-master DNB
HART, Josh [J. Jones] (b 1834)
American prop-man, actor HAS
HART, Leolyn (d 1911 [59]) scene
artist EA/12*
HART, Leonard (d 1917 [37]) musi-
cian EA/18*
HART, Lorenz (1895-1943) Ameri-
can lyricist AAS, CB, DAB,
ES, MH, PDT, WWA/4, WWT/6-9
HART, Marie see Marie, La Belle
HART, M. Blair (b 1907) American
educator, director BE
HART, Moss (1904-61) American
librettist, dramatist, director
AAS, CB, COC, ES, HJD, MD,
MH, MWD, NTH, OC/2-3,
PDT, RE, SR, TW/18, WWA/4,
WWT/8-13, WWW/6
HART, Nicholas (b 1684) the great
sleeper CDP
HART, Richard (1915-51) American
actor TW/1-7
HART, Teddy (1897-1971) American
actor BE, TW/27, WWT/10-11
HART, Tony [Anthony Cannon]
(1857-91) female impersonator
CDP, COC, NTH, OC/2-3, SR
HART, Vivian actress, singer
WWT/7-10

HART, Walter (d 1973 [67]) pro-
ducer, director TW/30
HART, William (fl 1634-36)
actor DA
HART, William Griffith see
Melville, Harry
HART, William Matthew (d 1905
[42]) manager GRB/1
HART, William S. (1870?-1946)
American actor CB, CDP,
DAB, ES, SR, TW/3, WWM,
WWT/4-9
HARTE, Francis Bret (1839-1902)
American dramatist NTH
HARTFORD, Huntington (b 1911)
American producer, publisher,
patron BE, CB
HARTFORD, W. S. (b 1879)
Scottish actor GRB/1
HARTIG, Mary (b 1935) American
actress TW/9
HARTIG, Michael Frank (b 1936)
American talent representative
BE
HARTILL, Willie [Horrox] (b
1872) English stage manager
GRB/1
HARTKE, Rev. Gilbert (b 1907)
American educator BE
HARTLAND, Frank (1783-1852)
actor CDP [see also following
entry]
HARTLAND, Frederick (d 1852
[70]) pantomimist EA/72*
[see also previous entry]
HARTLEY, Ann see Gilbert,
Mrs. George
HARTLEY, Charles William
see Harley, Charles
HARTLEY, Elizabeth [née White]
(1751-1824) English actress
CDP, COC, DNB, OC/1-3,
OX
HARTLEY, Frederick Charles
(d 1891 [28]) animal trainer
EA/93*
HARTLEY, Henry (d 1868 [41])
professor of music EA/69*
HARTLEY, J. H. (d 1901 [49])
Negro comedian EA/02*
HARTLEY, Katherine see
Frings, Ketti
HARTLEY, Neil (b 1919) Amer-
ican producer BE
HARTLEY, Randolph (b 1870)
American dramatist, librettist
WWM
HARTLEY, Mrs. Randolph see

Wakeman, Emily
HARTLEY, Vivian Mary see
Leigh, Vivien
HARTLEY-MILBURN, Julie (1904-
49) English actress WWT/5-7
HARTMAN, Elek (b 1922) American
actor TW/24-25
HARTMAN, Ferris (fl 1894?) sing-
er, actor CDP
HARTMAN, Grace (1907-55) Amer-
ican dancer CB, TW/4-7, 12
HARTMAN, Jonathan William (d
1965 [90]) performer BP/50*
HARTMAN, M. (d 1900 [95]) com-
poser EA/01*
HARTMAN, Paul (1904-73) Ameri-
can dancer, actor, magician,
singer BE, CB, TW/4-18, 30
HARTMANN, Helene (d 1898)
Australian actress EA/99*
HARTNELL, William (1908-75)
English actor WWT/11-15
HARTNOLL, Phyllis (b 1906) Eng-
lish scholar, historian, drama-
tist AAS, BE
HARTREE, Walter D. (d 1907
[49]) acting manager EA/08*
HARTSON, Hall (d 1773) Irish
dramatist CP/2-3, GT, TD/1-2
HARTWIG, Brigitta see Zorina,
Vera
HARTWIG, Walter (d 1941 [61])
American producer BE*, BP/
25*
HARTY, Mrs. Hamilton see
Nicholls, Agnes
HARTZ, Mr. (d 1903 [66]) ventrilo-
quist, conjuror CDP
HARTZ, M. magician CDP
HARTZELL, Willard C. (d 1970
[60]) performer BP/55*
HARUM, Avind (b 1944) Norwegian
actor TW/25
HARVEN, Jane (d 1969 [50]) per-
former BP/54*
HARVEY (fl 1597) actor DA
HARVEY, Mr. actor CDP
HARVEY, Miss see Lewis, Mrs.
Henry
HARVEY, Alice [Mrs. Fred Baugh]
(d 1908 [43]) comedian EA/09*
HARVEY, Catherine (d 1899) EA/
01*
HARVEY, Dennis (d 1902) EA/03*
HARVEY, Don C. (d 1963 [51])
performer BE*
HARVEY, Edward (d 1906) music-
hall performer EA/07*

HARVEY, Edward (d 1975 [82])
performer BP/60*
HARVEY, Mrs. E. M. [Mrs.
Frank Harvey] (d 1907) EA/
08*
HARVEY, Forrester (d 1945
[55]) actor BE*, WWT/14*
HARVEY, Frank (1842-1903)
English actor, dramatist
OAA/2
HARVEY, Frank (1885-1965)
English actor, dramatist
WWT/7-13
HARVEY, Mrs. Frank see
Harvey, Mrs. E. M.
HARVEY, Frank, Jr. (b 1912)
English actor, dramatist,
producer WWT/11-16
HARVEY, Fred (d 1895 [39])
singer, actor CDP
HARVEY, Mrs. George see
Glover, Eleanor
HARVEY, Georgette (d 1952 [69])
American actress TW/8
HARVEY, Georgia (d 1960 [85])
Canadian actress TW/16
HARVEY, Helen (b 1916) Amer-
ican literary representative
BE
HARVEY, James Clarence (b
1859) American dramatist
WWM
HARVEY, J. B. (d 1862 [70])
manager EA/72*
HARVEY, Joan (b 1935) Ameri-
can actress TW/17-18
HARVEY, John (d 1901) EA/02*
HARVEY, John (d 1908 [62])
EA/10*
HARVEY, John (d 1970 [53])
actor, talent representative
TW/27
HARVEY, John (b 1917) Ameri-
can talent representative BE
HARVEY, Mrs. John see
Zerbini, Carlotta
HARVEY, Sir John Martin (1863-
1944) English actor, manager
COC, DNB, GRB/1-4, NTH,
OC/1-3, WWT/1-9, WWW/4
HARVEY, Lady John Martin
see De Silva, Nina
HARVEY, Kenneth (b 1918) Cana-
dian actor TW/11-12
HARVEY, Laurence [né Skikne]
(1928-73) Lithuanian actor
AAS, BE, CB, ES, TW/12-
18, 30, WWT/13-15

HARVEY, Lilian (1906-68) English
actress, singer, dancer ES
HARVEY, Mary Ann see Daven-
port, Mrs. George Gosling
HARVEY, May [Mrs. Charles T.
H. Helmsley] (d 1930) English
actress GRB/1-4
HARVEY, Michael (b 1917) Ameri-
can actor TW/6-8
HARVEY, Morris (1877-1944) Eng-
lish actor WWT/4-9
HARVEY, Patsey J. (d 1890 [27])
EA/91*
HARVEY, Paul (d 1955 [71]) Amer-
ican actor TW/12
HARVEY, Peter (b 1933) Guate-
malan/American designer WWT/
15-16
HARVEY, Rose [Mrs. W. Lindsay]
(d 1899) actress? singer? EA/
00*
HARVEY, Rupert (1887-1954) Eng-
lish actor WWT/4-9
HARVEY, Susie [Susannah Elizabeth
Matthews; Mrs. Theodore Mat-
thews] (d 1893) EA/94*
HARVEY, Walter (d 1905) actor?
EA/06*
HARVEY, W. H. (d 1889 [56])
clown EA/90*
HARVEY, Mrs. Will see Holt,
Hettie
HARVEY, William (d 1856 [43])
harlequin EA/72*
HARVEY, William (d 1907) music-
hall comedian EA/08*
HARVEY, William François (d
1899 [49]) equestrian EA/00*
HARVUOT, Inez see Manning,
Irene
HARVYE, William (fl 1628) actor
DA
HARWOOD, Mr. (fl 1822?) actor
CDP
HARWOOD, Mrs. [née Julia Wade]
(d 1876) EA/77*
HARWOOD, Miss (d 1888) dramatist
EA/89*
HARWOOD, Florence actress
GRB/3-4
HARWOOD, George (d 1903 [61])
music-hall proprietor EA/04*
HARWOOD, George Julian (d 1909)
musical director EA/10*
HARWOOD, Harold Marsh (1874-
1959) English dramatist, mana-
ger COC, OC/3, WWT/4-12
HARWOOD, Harry (d 1926 [78])

American actor BE*, BP/11*
HARWOOD, H. R. (d 1898) Aus-
tralian actor EA/99*
HARWOOD, Mrs. H. R. (d 1887)
EA/88*
HARWOOD, Isabella (1840?-88)
dramatist DNB
HARWOOD, Isabella see Neil,
Ross
HARWOOD, James (d 1900 [83])
actor EA/01*, WWT/14*
HARWOOD, James see Farmer,
Lucia Eliza
HARWOOD, John (1876-1944)
English actor, stage manager,
director GRB/4, WWT/1-9
HARWOOD, John Edmund (1771-
1809) American actor CDP,
COC, HAS, OC/1-3, SR,
WWA/H
HARWOOD, Louisa see Eldridge,
Louisa
HARWOOD, Lucia actress CDP
HARWOOD, Robb (d 1910 [40])
English actor GRB/1-4
HARWOOD, Thomas (fl 1787)
dramatist CP/3
HASCALL, Lon (d 1932 [60])
American actor BE*, BP/17*,
WWT/14*
HASELDEN, T. J. (d 1895) pro-
fessor of music EA/96*
HASELMAYER, Louis (b 1839)
Austrian magician HAS
HASHIM, Edmund (d 1974 [42])
performer BP/59*
HASKELL, Arnold Lionel (b 1903)
English critic ES
HASKER, James John (d 1906 [88])
Australian actor EA/07*
HASKINS, Douglas N. (d 1973
[45]) performer BP/58*
HASKINS, Mrs. W. see Har-
land, Julia
HASLAM, James (d 1891 [33])
step-dancer EA/92*
HASLAM, John (d 1892 [37])
EA/94*
HASLAM, Maud [Mrs. Samuel
W. Groome] (d 1899 [30])
actress CDP
HASLAM, Rene (d 1918) EA/19*
HASLEM, Bert (d 1903) actor,
dancer BE*, EA/04*
HASSALL, Christopher (1912-63)
English actor, dramatist,
lyricist WWT/9-13, WWW/6
HASSAN, Prince (d 1908) wire-

walker EA/09*
HASSELL, George (d 1937 [56])
English actor BE*, BP/21*,
WWT/14*
HASSELMANS, Louis (1878-1957)
French conductor WWA/3
HASSELQUIST, Jenny Swedish
dancer WWT/4
HASSETT, Michael (d 1972) per-
former BP/56*
HASSLER, Simon (1832-1901) musi-
cian, composer WWA/1
HASSO, Signe [née Larssen] (b
1910/15/18) Swedish actress
BE, TW/12-16, 24, WWT/11-16
HASTINGS, Alice [Mrs. Roland
Reed] (d 1888 [32]) American
actress EA/90*
HASTINGS, Annie [née Wilmot] (d
1891 [45]) EA/92*
HASTINGS, Basil Mcdonald (1881-
1928) English dramatist WWT/
2-5
HASTINGS, Christopher (b 1948)
American actor TW/30
HASTINGS, Fred (d 1891) comedian,
stage manager EA/92*
HASTINGS, Mrs. Frederick (d 1880
[51]) actress EA/82*
HASTINGS, Gilbert see MacDer-
mott, The Great
HASTINGS, H. (d 1894 [41]) mana-
ger EA/95*
HASTINGS, Harold (d 1973 [56])
musical director, composer BE,
TW/29
HASTINGS, Helen [Mrs. T. H.
Smith] (d 1895 [28]) actress
CDP
HASTINGS, Hugh (b 1917) Australian
actor, dramatist TW/30, WWT/
11-16
HASTINGS, Kate [Mrs. W. C.
Phillips] (d 1890) actress EA/
91*
HASTINGS, Michael (b 1938) Eng-
lish dramatist AAS, CD, PDT
HASTINGS, Mortimer S. (d 1899
[53]) actor EA/00*
HASTINGS, Sir Patrick (1880-1952)
dramatist WWT/7-11
HASTINGS, William T. (d 1972
[65]) manager BP/57*
HASWELL, Percy [Mrs. George
Fawcett] (d 1945 [74]) American
actress GRB/3-4, PP/1, TW/
2, WWM, WWS, WWT/1-8
HATCH, Eric (d 1973 [71]) drama-

tist BP/58*
HATCH, Frank (d 1938 [74])
American actor, dramatist,
director BE*, BP/23*
HATCH, Henry (d 1885 [69])
proprietor EA/86*
HATCH, Ike (d 1961 [69]) Amer-
ican performer BE*
HATCH, James V. (b 1928)
American dramatist, educator
BE
HATCHER, Tom (b 1933) Amer-
ican actor TW/13-15
HATCHETT, William (fl 1730-41)
dramatist, actor CP/1-3,
GT, TD/1-2
HATCHMAN, Emily (d 1903)
EA/04*
HATCHMAN, Henry C. (d 1903)
EA/04*
HATCHMAN, Henry William (d
1916) actor EA/17*
HATFIELD, Hurd (b 1920) Amer-
ican actor BE
HATFIELD, Lansing (d 1954)
American singer TW/1,
WWA/3
HATHAWAY, Miss actress HAS
HATHERTON, Arthur (d 1924)
actor WWT/4
HATHOL (d 1890) boy acrobat
EA/91*
HATHWAY, Richard (fl 1598-
1602) dramatist CP/2-3,
DNB, FGF
HATHWELL, Mr. English actor
HAS
HATHWELL, Henrietta American
actress HAS
HATHWELL, Louisa (fl 1822)
American actress HAS
HATHWELL, Matilda English
dancer, actress HAS
HATLEN, Theodore (b 1911)
American educator BE
HATT, W. [W. Rousillion] (d
1887) trapezist EA/88*
HATTON, Mr. (fl 1801-03)
actor TD/1-2
HATTON, A. C. (d 1883 [34])
actor EA/84*
HATTON, Adele Bradford (d
1957 [76]) actress BE*,
WWT/14*
HATTON, Alfred (d 1917) musi-
cian EA/18*
HATTON, Ann Julia (fl 1794)
dramatist EAP, RJ

HATTON, Bessie English actress
CDP, DP, GRB/1-3
HATTON, Fanny [Fanny Locke] (d
1939 [69]) American dramatist
WWT/4-9
HATTON, Frederick H. (1879-1946)
American dramatist, critic
WWT/4-9
HATTON, John Liptrot (1809-86)
English composer, conductor
DNB
HATTON, Joseph (b 1801) American
dramatist SR
HATTON, Joseph (1841-1907) Eng-
lish dramatist DNB, GRB/1-3,
WWW/1
HATTON, Louisa (d 1901 [56])
actress EA/02*
HATTON, Raymond (d 1971 [84])
actor BP/56*, WWT/16*
HATTON, Walter [Thomas Spurway]
(d 1903 [54]) lessee EA/04*
HATTON, William (d 1916) EA/17*
HATTORI, Raymond (d 1973 [65])
composer/lyricist BP/58*
HAUCK, Minnie see Hauk, Minnie
HAUERBACH, Otto (b 1873) Amer-
ican dramatist WWM
HAUGER, George (b 1921) English
educator BE
HAUGHTON, Miss actress TD/1-2
HAUGHTON, Hugh (fl 1634) actor
DA
HAUGHTON, William (1578-1603)
dramatist CP/3, DNB, FGF
HAUK, Minnie (1852?-1929) Amer-
ican singer CDP, DAB, ES,
HAS, SR, WWA/2, WWM
HAUPT, William A. (fl 1863) actor
HAS
HAUPT, William Ayers see
Mestayer, William A.
HAUPTMAN, Laurent (d 1870)
musician, composer EA/71*
HAUPTMANN, Carl (d 1921) drama-
tist BE*, WWT/14*
HAUPTMANN, Gerhart (1862-1946)
German dramatist COC, GRB/
1-4, OC/3, WWM, WWT/1-2
HAUPTMANN, John (fl 1815) dwarf
CDP
HAUSER, Frank (b 1922) Welsh
director AAS, COC, WWT/13-
16
HAUSER, Miska (1822-87) musician
CDP
HAUSMAN, Howard L. (b 1914)
American talent representative

BE
HAUSTED, Peter (d 1645) English
dramatist CP/1-3, DNB,
FGF
HAUTONVILLE, Mrs. see
Bradshaw, Mrs.
HAVANA ITALIAN OPERA
TROUPE HAS
HAVARD, William (d 1778 [68])
actor, dramatist CDP, CP/
1-3, DNB, GT, TD/1-2
HAVEL, Arthur (d 1965 [68])
performer BP/49*
HAVENS, John F. (b 1912) Amer-
ican attorney BE
HAVER, Phyllis (d 1960 [60])
American actress BE*
HAVERGAL, Giles (b 1938) Scot-
tish director WWT/15-16
HAVERLAND, Anna (fl 1892)
singer CDP
HAVERLY, Jack H. (1837-1901)
American manager CDP,
DAB, SR, WWA/H
HAVESON, Jimmy (b 1924) Amer-
ican actor TW/26
HAVEZ, Jean (d 1925 [55]) song-
writer BE*, BP/9*
HAVILAND, Augusta (d 1925)
actress BE*, WWT/14*
HAVILAND, William (1860-1917)
English actor, manager GRB/
2-4, WWT/1-3
HAVILAND, Mrs. William see
Latimer, Edyth
HAVLIN, John H. (d 1924 [77])
American manager, treasurer
SR
HAVOC, June [née Hovick] (b
1916) American actress, sing-
er, director AAS, BE, TW/
1-19, 23, WWT/10-16
HAWES, David (b 1919) Ameri-
can educator, director BE
HAWES, Maria B. [Mrs. J. D.
Merest] (d 1886) singer
EA/87*
HAWES, William (1785-1846)
English singer, composer,
manager DNB
HAWK, Harry (1837-1916) actor
CDP
HAWK, Jeremy (b 1916) South
African actor WWT/15-16
HAWKER, Essex (fl 1729) actor,
performer CP/2-3, GT,
TD/1-2
HAWKES, John (b 1925) American

dramatist, educator CD, CH
HAWKES, Kirkby (d 1970 [67])
dramatist BP/54*
HAWKES, Thomas (d 1902) music-
hall manager EA/03*
HAWKESWORTH (fl 1636) dramatist
CP/3, FGF
HAWKESWORTH, John (1716-73)
dramatist CP/1-3, DNB, GT,
TD/1-2
HAWKESWORTH, Walter (d 1606)
dramatist DNB
HAWKINS, Alexander (fl 1601) les-
see, patentee DA
HAWKINS, Anthony Hope (1863-
1933) English dramatist DNB,
GRB/1, 4, HP, WWW/3
HAWKINS, Erick (b 1915/17) Amer-
ican dancer, choreographer
CB, ES
HAWKINS, Erskine (b 1914) Amer-
ican musician CB
HAWKINS, Etta (d 1945 [80]) ac-
tress BE*, WWT/14*
HAWKINS, Harry Stuart see
Stuart, Harry
HAWKINS, Henry (d 1878 [52])
musician EA/79*
HAWKINS, Iris (b 1893) English
actress GRB/2-4, WWT/1-6
HAWKINS, Jack (1910-73) English
actor AAS, CB, ES, TW/7-15,
30, WWA/5, WWT/7-14
HAWKINS, Micah (fl 1825?) drama-
tist EAP, RJ
HAWKINS, Michael American actor
TW/24, 26
HAWKINS, Robert (d 1875) actor
EA/76*
HAWKINS, Stockwell (1874-1927)
Welsh actor WWT/5
HAWKINS, Trish (b 1945) American
actress TW/29-30
HAWKINS, W. (fl 1780-86) drama-
tist CP/3
HAWKINS, William (fl 1627-34)
dramatist CP/1-3, FGF
HAWKINS, William (d 1801) drama-
tist CP/2-3, GT
HAWKINS, William see Roselle,
W. H.
HAWKS, Mr. dramatist CP/1
HAWKS, Wells (1870-1941) Ameri-
can theatrical representative
GRB/3-4, WWM
HAWLEY, Dudley (d 1941 [62])
English actor BE*, BP/25*,
WWT/14*

HAWLEY, Emma Cox [Mrs. Fred Hawley] (d 1898 [67]) EA/99*

HAWLEY, Esther (d 1968 [62]) performer BP/53*

HAWLEY, Mrs. Fred see Hawley, Emma Cox

HAWLEY, Frederick (1827-89) English scholar, actor, dramatist DNB, OAA/2

HAWLEY, H. Dudley (1879?-1941) English actor CB

HAWLEY, Ida (fl 1897-1908) Canadian actress WWS

HAWLEY, Richard (fl 1636) actor DA

HAWLEY, Stanley (d 1916) EA/17*

HAWLEY, Thomas (b 1935) American actor TW/19

HAWLING, Francis (fl 1723-51) dramatist CP/2-3, GT

HAWORTH, Don dramatist CD

HAWORTH, Joseph (1855/58-1903) American actor CDP, DAB, PP/1, SR, WWA/1

HAWORTH, Lawrence (d 1868 [25]) manager EA/69*

HAWTHORNE, Alice (fl 1855?) song composer CDP

HAWTHORNE, Charles J. (1809-87) scene artist NYM

HAWTHORNE, David (d 1942) actor WWT/8-9

HAWTHORNE, Georgiana (b 1811) English dancer, singer? actress? HAS

HAWTHORNE, Grace (d 1922 [62]) actress, lessee, producer CDP, DP

HAWTHORNE, Lil American variety artist CDP, GRB/1-2

HAWTHORNE, Lola singer, actress CDP

HAWTHORNE, Louise [née Mary Timmons; Mrs. George Morton] (d 1876 [29]) actress CDP

HAWTHORNE, Nellie actress, singer CDP

HAWTHORNE, Nigel (b 1929) English actor WWT/15-16

HAWTIN, Miss (fl 1770) freak CDP

HAWTREY, Anthony (1909-54) English actor, manager WWT/9-11

HAWTREY, Charles (b 1914) English actor WWT/9-13

HAWTREY, Mrs. Charles see Hawtrey, Madeline Harriet

HAWTREY, Sir Charles Henry (1858-1923) English actor, manager CDP, COC, DNB, DP, EA/97, ES, GRB/1-4, NTH, OC/1-3, SR, WWA/1, WWM, WWS, WWT/1-4, WWW/2

HAWTREY, Edward M. (d 1916) EA/17*

HAWTREY, George P[roctor] (d 1910 [64]) actor, dramatist BE*, EA/11*, WWT/14*

HAWTREY, Madeline Harriet [Mrs. Charles Hawtrey] (d 1905 [47]) EA/06*

HAWTREY, Marjory (b 1900) English actress WWT/11-14

HAWTREY, William Francis (1856-1914) English actor DP, WWM

HAWTRY, Anthony see Hawtrey, Anthony

HAY, Mrs. Charles see Saker, Rose

HAY, Harriett see Litchfield, Harriett

HAY, Ian [John Hay Beith] (1876-1952) English dramatist COC, DNB, NTH, OC/3, WWT/4-11

HAY, Joan (b 1894) actress, singer WWT/5-9

HAY, Mrs. John see Courtenay, Eveline

HAY, John M. (b 1868) English actor, singer GRB/1

HAY, Mary (1901-57) American actress, singer TW/13, WWT/6-7

HAY, Valerie (b 1910) English actress, singer WWT/8-11

HAY, Will (1888-1949) actor WWW/4

HAYAKAWA, Sessue (1890-1973) Japanese actor CB

HAYDEN, Bob (d 1974 [49]) performer BP/59*

HAYDEN, Louis (d 1971 [56]) performer BP/55*

HAYDEN, Madoline Mary (d 1908 [34]) EA/09*

HAYDEN, Martin (fl 1892) actor CDP

HAYDEN, Maud [Mrs. Heath Saunders] (d 1910 [38]) EA/11*

HAYDEN, Melissa (b 1922/28) Canadian dancer CB, ES

HAYDEN, Terese (b 1921) American producer, director, actress

BE, WWT/15-16

HAYDOCK, George see Bandurria, George

HAYDON, Ethel [Mrs. George Robey] (1876/78-1954) Australian actress CDP, GRB/1-4, WWT/1-6

HAYDON, Florence (d 1918 [80]) English actress WWT/1-3

HAYDON, John S. (d 1907 [70]) actor BE*, EA/08*, WWT/14*

HAYDON, Mrs. J[ohn] S. see Haydon, Mary Ann

HAYDON, Julie [Donella Donaldson] (b 1910) American actress BE, NTH, TW/1-12, WWT/8-12

HAYDON, Mary Ann [Mrs. John S. Haydon] (d 1887) EA/88*

HAYE, Helen (1874-1957) Indian/English actress COC, ES, GRB/1, OC/3, TW/14, WWT/1-12

HAYES, Miss (d 1881) actress EA/82*

HAYES, Ada (d 1962 [87]) performer BE*

HAYES, Barbara American actress TW/24-25

HAYES, Ben American actor TW/19-20

HAYES, Benjamin (b 1842) American comedian, minstrel HAS

HAYES, Bernadene American actress TW/1

HAYES, Beverly (b 1940) American actress TW/25

HAYES, Bill (b 1925) American actor, singer BE, TW/9-10, 24

HAYES, Blanche [Mrs. Fred Rutt] (d 1889 [38]) actress EA/90*

HAYES, Catharine (1825-61) Irish singer CDP, DNB, ES, HAS

HAYES, Clarence E. singer CDP

HAYES, De Vere see Edwin, J. H.

HAYES, Elton (d 1917) performer? EA/18*

HAYES, Florence [Mrs. A. P. Boswell] (d 1908 [52]) music-hall performer EA/09*

HAYES, Frank (fl 1907?) actor, singer CDP

HAYES, F. W. (d 1918 [70])

dramatist BE*, WWT/14*

HAYES, George (1888-1967) English actor AAS, BE, TW/3, WWT/4-13

HAYES, Mrs. George see May, Eva

HAYES, Helen [née Brown] (b 1900) American actress AAS, BE, CB, COC, ES, NTH, OC/1-3, PDT, SR, TW/1-26, WWT/4-16

HAYES, Henry (d 1891) singer EA/92*

HAYES, Henry J. (d 1905) music-hall manager EA/06*

HAYES, Hubert (d 1964) dramatist BE*, BP/49*

HAYES, James (d 1975 [60]) producer/director/choreographer BP/59*

HAYES, Joseph (b 1918) American dramatist, producer, director BE

HAYES, Laurence C. (d 1974 [71]) performer BP/59*

HAYES, Louis [Louis de Vere Hayes] American actor GRB/1

HAYES, Mabel [Mrs. R. J. Hall] (d 1892 [43]) actress EA/93*

HAYES, Margaret [Maggie] (1924-77) American actress BE, TW/1-3, 20

HAYES, Maurice (fl 1900?) singer, actor CDP

HAYES, Milton (d 1940 [56]) performer BE*, WWT/14*

HAYES, Patricia (b 1909) English actress WWT/9-10

HAYES, Paul (d 1969 [86]) performer BP/54*

HAYES, Percy (d 1908 [42]) music-hall manager EA/09*

HAYES, Peter Lind (b 1915) American actor BE, CB, TW/25

HAYES, Reginald (d 1953) actor, singer BE*, WWT/14*

HAYES, Samuel (b 1749) dramatist CP/2-3, GT

HAYES, Samuel (d 1892) entrepreneur EA/93*

HAYES, Sydney see Page, James Augustus

HAYES, Tim (1841-77) Irish clog dancer HAS

HAYESON, Jimmy (b 1924) American actor TW/28-29

HAYLE, Douglas (b 1942) American actor TW/25, 27, 30

HAYLEY, George see Stayley,

George
HAYLEY, William (1745-1820)
English dramatist CDP, CP/
3, GT, TD/1-2
HAYM, Nicholas dramatist CP/1
HAYMAN, Alf (1865-1921) American producer BE*, BP/5*,
WWT/14*
HAYMAN, Alfred (d 1917 [67])
American manager GRB/2-4,
WWA/1, WWT/1-3
HAYMAN, Arthur (d 1901 [39])
actor EA/02*
HAYMAN, Leonard (d 1962 [61])
English performer BE*
HAYMAN, Lillian (b 1922) American actress, singer WWT/16
HAYMEN, Helen Violet Carolyn
see Lynne, Carole
HAYMES, Thomas (fl 1789-1800)
English actor TD/1-2
HAYNES, Alfred W. (d 1924
[63]) American performer
BE*, BP/9*
HAYNES, Mrs. Archibald C.
see Gale, Minna
HAYNES, F. (fl 1830s) dramatist
RJ
HAYNES, Henry D. (d 1971
[51]) performer BP/56*
HAYNES, Henry S. (d 1885 [45])
comedian EA/86*
HAYNES, Mrs. Henry S. (d
1885) actor EA/86*
HAYNES, Hilda American actress
TW/29-30
HAYNES, Jennie [Mrs. Harry
Wenburn] (d 1904/06) EA/05*,
EA/07*
HAYNES, Mrs. Joe see Haynes,
Louisa
HAYNES, Joseph (d 1909 [59])
music-hall manager EA/10*
HAYNES, Joseph see Haines,
Joseph
HAYNES, Joseph see Stanley,
Jean
HAYNES, Louisa [Mrs. Joe
Haynes] (d 1907 [53]) music-hall manager EA/08*
HAYNES, Mel (b 1921) American
actor TW/21
HAYNES, Michael (d 1879 [26])
Irish comic singer EA/81*
HAYNES, Minna Gale see
Gale, Minna
HAYNES, Rosetta [Mrs. T. P.
Haynes] (d 1908) actress

GRB/4*
HAYNES, T[homas] P[ercival] (d
1915 [65]) English actor EA/96,
OAA/1-2
HAYNES, Mrs. T[homas] P[ercival]
see Haynes, Rosetta
HAYNES, Tiger (b 1907) actor
TW/23, 30
HAYS, Mr. (fl 1821) actor HAS
HAYS, Alfred (d 1899 [61]) librarian
EA/00*
HAYS, Bill (b 1938) English director
WWT/15-16
HAYS, David (b 1930) American
designer BE, ES, WWT/15-16
HAYS, Jack (d 1975 [76]) producer/
director/choreographer BP/60*
HAYS, William Shakespeare (1837-
1907) American songwriter,
journalist BE*
HAYSELL, George (fl 1583-84)
actor DA
HAYTER, James (b 1907) Indian/
English actor WWT/9-16
HAYTER, William (d 1904 [67])
EA/06*
HAYTHORNE, Joan (b 1915) English
actress WWT/10-16
HAYTON, Lennie (d 1971 [63])
composer, lyricist BP/55*
HAYTOR, Arthur (d 1909) variety
comedian EA/10*
HAYWARD, Mr. (d 1860) American
actor HAS
HAYWARD, Beatrice Herford (d
1952 [84]) actress WWT/14*
HAYWARD, Caroline Mary see
Rignold, Kate
HAYWARD, Clara see Bentley,
Mrs. Arthur
[HAYWARD?], Clementina see
Collins, Clementina
HAYWARD, Mrs. E. (d 1888 [26])
EA/89*
HAYWARD, George (d 1869 [52])
musical director EA/70*
HAYWARD, Henry (d 1884) musician EA/85*
HAYWARD, Leland (1902-71) American manager, agent BE, CB,
TW/2-8, 27, WWT/10-15
HAYWARD, William (d 1896) music-hall chairman EA/97*
HAYWELL, Frederick see Hawley, Frederick
HAYWOOD, Eliza (1693?-1756)
actress, dramatist CP/1-3,
GT, HP, TD/1-2

HAYWOOD, Hetty (fl 1896?)
singer, actress CDP
HAYWORTH, Vinton (d 1970 [64])
performer BP/54*
HAZARD, Mr. (d 1831) actor
HAS
HAZARD, Mrs. (fl 1839) actress
HAS
HAZARD, Joseph (fl 1767) drama-
tist CP/2-3, GT
HAZELL, Francis Nalder (d 1913
[59]) EA/14*
HAZELL, Hy (1922-70) English
actress WWT/12-14
HAZELTINE, William (b 1866)
American actor WWS
HAZLEHURST, Jack (d 1908 [19])
EA/09*
HAZLETON, George Cochrane
(1868-1921) American drama-
tist, actor DAB, SR, WWS
HAZLETON, Mrs. Victor (d
1883) EA/84*
HAZLEWOOD, Colin Henry (d
1875 [52]) dramatist EA/69
HAZLEWOOD, Eliza (d 1876)
dancer EA/77*
HAZLEWOOD, Henry Colin (d
1897 [59]) manager EA/98*
HAZLITT, William (1778-1830)
English critic CDP, COC,
DNB, ES, HP, NTH, OC/1-3,
PDT
HAZZARD, Alice Dovey (d 1969
[84]) performer BP/53*
HAZZARD, John E. (1881-1935)
American actor WWA/1,
WWM, WWT/4-7
HEAD, Charles (d 1889 [61])
proprietor EA/90*
HEAD, Henry C. S. see Henry,
S. Creagh
HEAD, Richard (d 1678) Irish
dramatist CP/1-3, GT
HEADFORT, Marchioness of
see Boote, Rosie
HEADLAM, Rev. Stewart Duck-
worth (b 1847) English minis-
ter GRB/2-4
HEADLAND, T. (d 1888 [82])
secretary EA/89*
HEAL, Joan (b 1922) English
actress, singer WWT/12-16
HEALEY, J. R. (d 1877 [45])
American actor EA/78*
HEALEY, Thomas A. (d 1872)
actor EA/73*
HEALEY-KAY, Patrick see

Dolin, Anton
HEALY, Dan (d 1969 [80]) actor,
singer TW/30
HEALY, Gerald (d 1963 [45]) per-
former, dramatist, producer
BE*, BP/47*
HEALY, Jack (d 1972 [68]) perform-
er BP/57*
HEALY, John see Le Hay, John
HEALY, Mary (b 1918/20) Ameri-
can actress, singer BE, TW/
1-3, 14-15
HEALY, Robert (b 1922) American
actor TW/2
HEAP, Swinnerton (d 1900 [53])
composer EA/01*
HEAPHY, Mr. Irish manager TD/
1-2
HEAPHY, Thomas M. (b 1891)
American actor TW/3
HEARD, Mr. (fl 1797) actor HAS
HEARD, Miss (fl 1801) actress
CP/3, TD/1-2
HEARD, Elizabeth (d 1797 [47])
actress CDP
HEARD, William (d c. 1776 [34])
dramatist, bookseller CP/2-3,
DNB, GT
HEARD, Mrs. William (d 1799) ac-
tress CP/3
HEARN, Bert (d 1898) music-hall
performer EA/99*
HEARN, Dennis (b 1949) American
actor TW/30
HEARN, George (b 1934) American
actor TW/25, 29
HEARN, James S. (1873-1913) Eng-
lish actor GRB/2-4, WWT/1-2
HEARN, Julia Knox (d 1976 [92])
performer BP/60*
HEARN, Lew (b 1882) Polish actor,
singer WWT/6-11
HEARN, Mrs. Lew see Bonita
HEARN, Sam (d 1964 [75]) per-
former BP/49*
HEARNE, George (d 1909 [78])
EA/10*
HEARNE, Mrs. George (d 1901
[45]) EA/02*
HEARNE, Richard (b 1909) English
actor WWT/8-14
HEARNE, Thomas (fl 1597) actor
DA
HEARTWELL, Henry (fl 1799)
dramatist CP/3, GT, TD/1-2
HEATH, Bob (b 1948) American
actor TW/29-30
HEATH, Boxley (d 1882) enter-

tainer EA/83*
HEATH, Caroline [Mrs. Wilson Barrett] (1837-87) actress CDP, NYM, OAA/1-2
HEATH, Dody (b 1928) American actress TW/7-8
HEATH, Eira (b 1940) English actress WWT/15-16
HEATH, Mrs. F. see Garton, Flo
HEATH, Frank (d 1908 [52]) treasurer EA/10*
HEATH, Frederic (d 1900 [43]) music-hall performer EA/01*
HEATH, Frederick (d 1874 [29]) musician EA/76*
HEATH, George (b 1852) American actor, minstrel WWS
HEATH, Gordon (b 1918) American actor, director BE, TW/2, 26
HEATH, Ida (d 1950 [77]) performer BE*, WWT/14*
HEATH, Lily (d 1913) EA/14*
HEATH, Marie (b 1866) singer, actress CDP
HEATH, Rosée singer, actress CDP
HEATH, Thomas (d 1889 [63]) scene artist EA/91*
HEATH, Thomas Kurton (1852/53-1938) American comedian, minstrel DAB, SR, WWM
HEATH, William (d 1868 [48]) actor? EA/69*
HEATH, Mrs. William (d 1898 [23]) EA/99*
HEATHCOTE, A. M. (d 1934 [87]) dramatist BE*, WWT/14*
HEATHCOTE, Ernest (fl 1895) actor, dancer, singer CDP
HEATHCOTE, Kate (fl 1871) actress CDP
HEATHER, Jerrold (b 1874) English actor GRB/1
HEATHERLEY, Clifford (1888-1937) English actor WWT/4-8
HEATHERTON, Ray (b 1910) American actor, singer BE
HEATON, Percy (1894-1971) American actor WWA/5
HEATON, Theodore (d 1880) conductor EA/81*
HEAVENS, Mrs. J. (d 1873) EA/74*
HEAVER, Mrs. W. (d 1910) EA/12*

HEAVER, William (d 1906) EA/07*
HEAVER, Rev. William (d 1912) EA/13*
HEBDEN, John (fl 1740) musician CDP
HEBDEN, Will (fl 1890?) singer, actor CDP
HEBERLE, Teresa dancer CDP
HEBERT, Fred (1911-72) American producer, director, manager BE, TW/28
HEBERTOT, Jacques (d 1970 [84]) producer/director/choreographer BP/55*
HECHT, Albert (b 1903) American actor TW/4-7
HECHT, Ben (1894-1964) American dramatist AAS, CB, ES, HJD, MD, MH, MWD, NTH, PDT, SR, TW/20, WWA/4, WWT/8-13
HECHT, Edward (d 1887 [54]) musician, conductor EA/88*
HECHT, Jenny (b 1943) American actress TW/9
HECHT, Paul (b 1941) English actor TW/23-29
HECHT, Ted (d 1969 [61]) actor TW/26
HECK, Howard (d 1969 [73]) treasurer BP/54*
HECKART, Eileen (b 1919) American actress AAS, BE, CB, TW/9-27, 30, WWT/12-16
HECKLE, Emma singer CDP
HECKROTH, Hein (d 1970 [69]) designer BP/55*
HECKSCHER, August (b 1913) American journalist, writer, executive BE
HECTOR, "Little" [Tom Hector Walsh] (d 1893) music-hall performer EA/94*
HEDGES BROTHERS (fl 1912?) variety artists CDP
HEDISON, Al (b 1929) American actor TW/12-15
HEDLEY, H. B. (d 1931 [41]) composer, lyricist WWT/6
HEDLEY, John (d 1890) lessee EA/91*
HEDMAN, Martha (b 1888) Swedish actress WWT/3-6, 10
HEDMONT, E. C. (1857-1940) American singer GRB/1-4
HEELEY, Desmond designer AAS, WWT/15-16
HEELEY, Frank (d 1895) clown EA/96*

HEELY, Mr. (fl 1794) actor HAS
HEELY, Mrs. (fl 1794) actress
HAS
HEELYER, Miss see Graupner,
Mrs.
HEENAN, Mrs. John C. see
Stevens, Sara
HEFFERNAN, John (b 1934) American actor BE, TW/22, 24-30,
WWT/15-16
HEFFERNAN, Mary (d 1908) EA/
09*
HEFFERNON, E. M. (d 1876 [64])
manager EA/77*
HEFFNER, Hubert (b 1901) American educator, writer BE
HEFFRON, J. C. singer, actor
CDP
HEFLIN, Emmet Evan see
Heflin, Van
HEFLIN, Frances (b 1922/24)
American actress BE, TW/1,
21, WWT/10-11
HEFLIN, Marta (b 1945) American
actress TW/24-29
HEFLIN, Martin (d 1972) publicist
BP/56*
HEFLIN, Nora (b 1950) American
actress TW/29
HEFLIN, Van [né Emmet Evan
Heflin] (1909/10-71) American
actor BE, TW/20, 28,
WWA/5, WWT/10
HEGGEN, Thomas O. (1919-49)
American writer MH, TW/5
HEGGIE, O. P. (1879-1936)
Australian actor WWT/1-8
HEGLON, Meyriane Belgian
singer GRB/1-2
HEGNER, Otto (b 1876) musician, composer CDP
HEHL, Walter (d 1890) manager,
treasurer EA/91*
HEIDEGGER, John James (1659?-
1749) Swiss manager CDP,
CP/1, DNB
HEIDT, Joseph (d 1962 [52])
American press representative
BE*, BP/47*
HEIGHLEY, Bruce (b 1939) English actor TW/26, 29
HEIGHT, Bob (d 1881) comedian
EA/82*
HEIJERMANS, Herman (1864-
1924) Dutch dramatist COC,
GRB/1-4, NTH, WWT/3
HEILBRONN, Marie (d 1886) actress, singer CDP

HEILBRONN, William (b 1879)
English actor WWT/9-11
HEIMAN, Marcus (b 1886) American executive SR
HEIMER, Mel (d 1971 [55]) critic
BP/55*
HEIN, Silvio (1879-1928) American
composer WWM, WWT/4-6
HEINE, Albert (1867-1949) German
actor, manager GRB/4, WWT/
1-2
HEINEL, Anne Frédérique (1752-
1808) German dancer OC/1-2
HEINEMAN, William (d 1974 [74])
producer/director/choreographer
BP/59*
HEINEMANN, Eda (b 1900) Japanese
actress BE, TW/1, 13-15, 19
HEINEMANN, William (1863-1920)
English publisher, dramatist
WWW/2
HEININGER, Francis (d 1973 [62])
dramatist BP/58*
HEINLEIN, Mary Virginia (d 1961
[58]) American educator BE*
HEINRICH JULIUS, Duke of Brunswick (1564-1613) German dramatist OC/1-3
HEINRICH, Rudolf (d 1975 [49])
designer BP/60*
HEINZ, Gerard (1904-72) German
actor WWT/11-15
HEIR, Robert (d 1868) actor EA/
69*
HEISKELL, Josephine see Louisette, Josephine
HEISS, John Stanger see Asche,
Oscar
HEISTER, George scene artist
CDP
HEIT, Michael (b 1943) American
actor TW/23-24
HELBURN, Theresa (1887-1959)
American dramatist, manager
CB, COC, TW/2-8, 16, WWA/3,
WWT/7-12
HELD, Anna [Mrs. Florenz Ziegfeld] (1873-1918) French actress,
singer CDP, COC, ES, GRB/
2-4, NTH, SR, WWM, WWS,
WWT/1-3
HELD, Dan (b 1948) American actor TW/29-30
HELENA, Mme. see Sleap, Ellen
Caroline
HELENA, Edith (b 1876) American
actress, singer WWS
HELENE [Rose Hélène Winter] (d

1912) variety performer EA/13*
HELENE, Eily (fl 1902?) singer
CDP
HELFEND, Dennis (b 1939) American actor TW/29-30
HELLE, John (fl 1597) clown
DA
HELLER, Claire (b 1929) American producer BE
HELLER, Haidée performer CDP
HELLER, Jeanne (d 1908) actress
BE*, WWT/14*
HELLER, Joseph (b 1923) American dramatist CB, CD
HELLER, Robert see Heller, Robert Palmer
HELLER, Robert see Palmer, William Henry
HELLER, Robert P. (d 1975 [60]) producer/director/choreographer BP/60*
HELLER, Robert Palmer (1833-78) American magician, pianist
CDP, HAS, SR
HELLER, Stephen (d 1888 [72]) musician, composer EA/89*
HELLINGER, Mark (1903/04-47) American writer SR
HELLIWELL, Hubert J. (d 1917)
EA/18*
HELLMAN, Lillian (b 1905) American dramatist, director
AAS, BE, CB, CD, CH, COC, ES, HJD, MD, MH, MWD, NTH, OC/1-3, PDT, RE, SR, WWT/9-16
HELLMER, Kurt (b 1909) German literary representative
BE
HELM, Anne (b 1938) Canadian actress TW/14
HELM, Frances American actress BE
HELM, Peter (b 1941) Canadian actor TW/16
HELME, Mr. (fl 1801) actor
CDP
HELME, Mrs. see Cabanel, Harriot
HELMERS, June (b 1941) American actress TW/23, 26-27, 29
HELMOND, Katherine American actress TW/27-29
HELMORE, Arthur (d 1941 [83]) actor EA/95
HELMORE, Tom (b 1912/16) English actor BE, TW/6-16,

22, 24
HELMS, Alan (b 1938) American actor TW/17-19
HELMSLEY, Charles Thomas Hunt (1865-1940) English manager, actor GRB/2-4, WWT/1-7
HELMSLEY, Mrs. Charles Thomas Hunt see Harvey, May
HELPMANN, Sir Robert Murray (b 1909) Australian actor, dancer, choreographer AAS, BE, CB, COC, ES, OC/1-3, TW/8, WWT/8-16
HELPS, Sir Arthur (1813-75) dramatist HP
HELSCHER, Fern (d 1974 [73]) publicist BP/58*
HELTAI, Jenö (1871-1957) Hungarian dramatist COC, OC/1-3
HELTON, Alf (d 1937 [78]) English actor BE*, BP/21*
HELTON, Mrs. George see Zaraza
HELTON, Percy (d 1971 [77]) vaudevillian, actor TW/28
HELY, R. W. (d 1881) EA/83*
HEMING, Fred (d 1908) actor
EA/09*
HEMING, Percy (b 1885) English actor, singer WWT/5-11
HEMING, Violet (b 1893/95) English actress BE, TW/1-3, WWM, WWT/4-14
HEMINGE, John (1556-1630) English actor COC, DA, DNB, ES, GT, HP, NTH, OC/1-3, PDT
HEMINGE, William (b 1602) English dramatist CP/1-3, DNB, FGF, GT
HEMINGWAY, Ernest (1899-1961) American dramatist ES, HJD, MD, MWD
HEMINGWAY, Marie (1893-1939) English actress WWT/3-7
HEMLEY, Jesse (d 1970 [63]) lawyer BP/55*
HEMMERDE, Edward George (1871-1948) English dramatist WWT/1-10
HEMMING, Miss see Walton, Elsie
HEMMING, Alfred (d 1942 [91]) singer, composer, actor CDP
HEMMING, Henry (1805-49) actor
CDP
HEMMING, Richard Walton (d 1909) comedian EA/10*
HEMMINGS, William (d 1874) circus

performer? EA/75*

HEMPEL, Frieda (1884-1955)
German singer ES, TW/12,
WWA/3, WWW/5

HEMPLE, Samuel (b 1833) American comedian HAS

HEMSLEY, Estelle (1892-1968)
American actress BE, TW/25

HEMSLEY, Harry May (d 1951
[73]) child impersonator BE*,
WWT/14*

HEMSLEY, Margaret (d 1918)
EA/19*

HEMSLEY, Sherman (b 1938)
American actor TW/25-29

HEMSLEY, Winston DeWitt (b
1947) American actor TW/28

HEMSLEY, W. T. (1850-1918)
English scene artist WWT/
1-3

HENABERY, Joseph E. (d 1976
[88]) producer/director/chore-
ographer BP/60*

HENDERSON, A. see Hender-
son, Andrew

HENDERSON, Alexander (1823/
29-86) manager CDP, COC

HENDERSON, Mrs. Alexander
see Thompson, Lydia

HENDERSON, Alex F. (1866/68-
1933) English manager
WWT/2-7

HENDERSON, Andrew (fl 1752?)
Scottish dramatist CP/1-3,
GT

HENDERSON, Annie (d 1878 [27])
dancer EA/79*

HENDERSON, Archibald (b 1877)
American critic NTH

HENDERSON, Bessie [Mrs. H.
F. Young] (d 1885) actress
EA/86*

HENDERSON, Mrs. C. E. T.
see Horwood, Lena

HENDERSON, Charles (fl 1854)
actor HAS

HENDERSON, David (1853-1908)
Scottish manager, producer
GRB/4, SR, WWS

HENDERSON, Del (d 1956 [79])
actor, director BE*

HENDERSON, Dickie (b 1922)
American actor, music-hall
comedian WWT/12-16

HENDERSON, Elvira (b 1903)
Cuban actress WWT/7-10

HENDERSON, Ettie see Hen-
derson, Mrs. William

HENDERSON, Florence (b 1934)
American actress, singer BE,
CB, WWT/15-16

HENDERSON, Frank (d 1907) musician? EA/08*

HENDERSON, Grace (d 1944 [84])
American actress BE*, WWT/
14*

HENDERSON, Henrietta (d 1887)
actress NYM

HENDERSON, J. (d 1916 [63])
dramatist, producer EA/18*

HENDERSON, Jack (d 1957 [79])
actor TW/13

HENDERSON, John (1747-85) Eng-
lish actor CDP, COC, DNB,
ES, GT, NTH, OC/1-3, OX,
TD/1-2

HENDERSON, John (d 1867 [45])
equestrian director CDP

HENDERSON, John Raymond (d
1937 [48]) American press
representative BE*, BP/22*

HENDERSON, Laura (d 1944 [80])
producer BE*, WWT/14*

HENDERSON, Lizzie (d 1917)
EA/18*

HENDERSON, Lucius (d 1947 [86])
American actor, producer
TW/3

HENDERSON, Mrs. Lucius see
Lyons, Gretchen

HENDERSON, Luther (b 1919) composer, musical director BE

HENDERSON, Marcia (b 1929)
American actress TW/6-9

HENDERSON, Marie [Mrs. James
Aubrey] (d 1882) actress EA/83*

HENDERSON, Marie [Mrs. George
Rignold; Marie Braybrook] (d
1902 [58]) actress BE*, EA/
03*, WWT/14*

HENDERSON, Melanie (b 1957)
American actress TW/26-28

HENDERSON, Ray (d 1937 [48])
press representative WWT/14*

HENDERSON, Ray (1896-1970)
American composer BE, TW/
27, WWT/6-11

HENDERSON, Robert (b 1904)
American producer, manager,
director, actor WWT/11-16

HENDERSON, Thomas (d 1970 [81])
composer/lyricist BP/54*

HENDERSON, William (fl 1821-55)
actor, manager HAS

HENDERSON, William (1824-89)
actor, manager CDP

HENDERSON, William (d 1908)
manager EA/09*
HENDERSON, Mrs. William
[Henrietta Lewis] (1835-1909)
American? actress HAS
HENDERSON, Willie (b 1839)
American actor HAS
HENDL, Walter (b 1917) Amer-
ican conductor CB
HENDON, Agnes actress SR
HENDRICKS, Ben F. (1868-1930)
American actor WWM
HENDRIE, Ernest (1859-1929)
actor, dramatist WWT/2-5
HENDRY, Thomas (b 1929)
Canadian dramatist CD
HENDRY, Tiffany (b 1942)
American actress TW/26, 29
HENEKER, David (b 1906) Eng-
lish composer, lyricist
WWT/15-16
HENGLER, Herr see Severn, A.
HENGLER, Mrs. Charles see
Hengler, Mary Ann Frances
HENGLER, Edward Henry (d
1865 [45]) equestrian EA/72*
HENGLER, F. C. (d 1889 [34])
EA/90*
HENGLER, Frederick Charles
(d 1887 [67]) circus proprietor
BE*, EA/88*, WWT/14*
HENGLER, Julia Fanny (d 1879
[21]) EA/80*
HENGLER, Mary Ann Frances
[Mrs. Charles Hengler] (d
1902 [74]) EA/03*
HENGLER, T[homas] M. (1844/
45-88) American minstrel,
actor CDP, HAS
HENGST, Marilyn (b 1946) Amer-
ican actress TW/27
HENIE, Sonja (d 1969 [57]) per-
former BP/54*
HENKENS, Harry [né Hincken]
(1809-53) American actor
HAS
HENLEY, Anthony (d 1711) Eng-
lish? dramatist CP/2-3
HENLEY, Drewe English actor
TW/23
HENLEY, Edward J[ohn] (1861-
98) English actor CDP, SR
HENLEY, Herbert James (1882-
1937) English critic WWT/
5-7
HENLEY, Joan (b 1904) Irish
actress WWT/7-15
HENLEY, Josephine [Mrs.

Charles H. Reid] (d 1908) bur-
lesque artist EA/09*
HENLEY, William Ernest (1849-
1903) English dramatist DNB,
HP, WWW/1
HENNECART, Maria (fl 1859)
Italian dancer CDP, HAS
HENNEQUIN, F. C. (d 1917 [41])
monologist EA/18*
HENNESIER, Samuel (d 1870) min-
strel EA/71*
HENNESSEY, May (fl 1901?) singer,
actress CDP
HENNESSY, Roland Burke (1870-
1939) American critic GRB/2-4,
WWM, WWT/1-2
HENNIGER, Rolf (b 1925) German
actor WWT/14
HENNING, Doug (b 1947) Canadian
magician, actor CB, TW/30
HENNING, Pat (d 1973 [62]) per-
former BP/56*
HENNINGS, Betty (d 1939 [89])
actress BE*, WWT/14*
HENNIS, Bob (d 1893) comedian
EA/94*
HENO, Prof. (d 1907 [56]) conjuror
EA/08*
HENRADE, Mary (d 1876 [34])
actress EA/77*
HENREID, Paul (b 1908) Italian ac-
tor CB, TW/29
HENRI, Blanche see Macklin,
Mrs. Francis Mary
HENRI, Blanche Marian (fl 1870-
79) English actress OAA/1-2
HENRI, Charles [né Montague] (d
1865) actor HAS
HENRI, Mrs. Charles (d 1879
[48]) actress EA/80*
HENRI, Jack (d 1917) EA/18*
HENRI, Louie (d 1947 [84]) actress
BE*, WWT/14*
HENRIQUES, Madelaine (1841-1929)
American actress CDP, HAS
HENRITZE, Bette American actress
TW/23-30, WWT/16
HENRY, Mr. actor HAS
HENRY, Mr. performer CDP
HENRY, Mr. (fl 1820) conjuror
CDP
HENRY, Mrs. performer CDP
HENRY, Mrs. see Barrett, Mrs.
George Horton
HENRY, Annie K. (d 1907 [30])
EA/08*
HENRY, Basil [Henry Beer] (d
1893) actor EA/94*

HENRY, Chaplin singer CDP
HENRY, Charles (d 1910) performer EA/11*
HENRY, Charles (1890-1968) English dramatist, producer WWT/6-14
HENRY, Creagh see Henry, S. Creagh
HENRY, David (d 1903 [64]) EA/04*
HENRY, Mrs. David Skene (d 1912) EA/13*
HENRY, Dick (d 1971 [82]) agent BP/55*
HENRY, Mrs. E. Bayle (d 1871) actress EA/72*
HENRY, George B. (d 1869) actor HAS
HENRY, George H. (b 1903) American educator, director BE
HENRY, Hiram (d 1920 [76]) minstrel BE*, BP/4*
HENRY, Jo-Ann (d 1972 [49]) performer BP/56*
HENRY, John (1738-94) American actor, manager, dramatist CDP, COC, CP/3, DAB, EAP, HAS, OC/1-3, RJ, SR, WWA/H
HENRY, Mrs. John, I [Miss Storer] (fl 1765) actress HAS
HENRY, Mrs. John, II (fl 1786) actress HAS
HENRY, Little minstrel CDP
HENRY, Mabel (d 1904) actress EA/05*
HENRY, Martha (b 1938) American actress TW/27-28
HENRY, Martin (1872-1942) English manager, actor WWT/5-8
HENRY, Patrick, II (b 1935) American educator, director BE
HENRY, Roland (fl 1909?) singer, song composer CDP
HENRY, Sam H. (d 1968) performer BP/53*
HENRY, S. Creagh [Henry C. S. Head] (1863-1946) English actor, dramatist GRB/1-4
HENRY, Shirley (d 1972 [47]) composer/lyricist BP/56*
HENRY, Thomas (b 1815) actor CDP
HENRY, Victor (b 1943) English actor TW/23, WWT/15

HENRY, William (b c. 1800) English actor SR
HENRY, William (fl 1831-37) English actor HAS
HENRY, Mrs. William (b c. 1800) English actress HAS, SR
HENSCHEL, Sir Georg (1850-1934) composer, singer CDP, WWA/2, WWW/3
HENSCHEL, Mrs. Georg see Bailey, Lilian
HENSHAW, James Ene (b 1924) Nigerian dramatist CD
HENSHAW, Thomas E. (d 1914) actor SR
HENSHAW, Thomas H. (d 1868 [87]) professor of music EA/69*
HENSHAW, William (d 1879 [29]) bill poster EA/80*
HENSLER, Elise (1832-1929) actress, singer CDP, HAS
HENSLOWE, Mrs. see Barthélemon, Cecilia Maria
HENSLOWE, Francis (fl 1590) actor DA
HENSLOWE, Philip (d 1616) English proprietor, manager COC, DA, DNB, GT, HP, NTH, OC/1-3, PDT
HENSON, Gladys (b 1897) Irish actress WWT/9-16
HENSON, J. W. (d 1916) EA/17*
HENSON, Leslie (1891-1957) English actor, producing manager AAS, COC, DNB, ES, OC/3, TW/14, WWT/4-12, WWW/5
HENSON, Nicky (b 1945) English actor WWT/15-16
HENTON, Thomas (d 1883 [20]) equestrian? EA/84*
HENTSCHEL, Carl (d 1930 [65]) club founder BE*, WWT/14*
HENTSCHEL, Irene (b 1891) English producer WWT/8-14
HENTZ, Caroline Lee (fl 1833?) dramatist RJ
HENZE, Hans Werner (b 1926) German composer CB
HEPBURN, Audrey (b 1929) Belgian/English actress BE, CB, ES, TW/8-16
HEPBURN, Katharine Houghton (b 1909) American actress AAS, BE, CB, COC, ES, NTH, SR, TW/2-21, 26-27, WWT/8-16
HEPBURNE, George (d 1880) scene artist, property master EA/81*
HEPENSTALL, Hazel see

Hughes, Hazel
HEPPELL, Albert H. (d 1912)
high diver EA/13*
HEPPLE, Jeanne (b 1936) English
actress TW/22-23, 27-30,
WWT/14-16
HEPPLE, Peter (b 1927) English
editor WWT/16
HEPPNER, Rosa (b 1905) English
press representative WWT/
10-16
HEPTON, William Thomas [Frank
Williams] (d 1872 [38]) EA/73*
HEPWORTH, Mrs. Cecil M. (d
1917) EA/18*
HEPWORTH, Joseph (d 1868)
singer EA/69*
HEPWORTH, William Henry (d
1886 [24]) musician EA/87*
HERAUD, Mrs. (d 1867) EA/68*
HERAUD, Edith (fl 1851-70)
English actress OAA/2
HERAUD, John A. (1799-1887)
English dramatist EA/68,
NYM
HERBECK, Johann (d 1877 [46])
composer EA/78*
HERBERT, Mr. (fl 1752) English
actor HAS
HERBERT, Mr. (fl 1802-04) actor,
dramatist CP/3
HERBERT, Mrs. [Helen Kent]
(fl 1829-51) English actress
HAS
HERBERT, Mrs. [Agnes Michell]
(d 1877) actress EA/78*
HERBERT, Miss see Taylor,
Mrs. Charles
HERBERT, Sir Alan Patrick
(1890-1971) English dramatist
AAS, PDT, WWT/6-15
HERBERT, Annie [Mrs. George
Townway] (d 1885) singer
EA/87*
HERBERT, Arthur (d 1906 [36])
EA/07*
HERBERT, Diana (b 1928) Amer-
ican actress TW/8-17
HERBERT, Don American pro-
ducer BE
HERBERT, Eliza (d 1878) EA/
79*
HERBERT, Miss Emmott [Eliza-
beth Emmott] (d 1895 [30])
actress EA/96*
HERBERT, Ethel (d 1904) ac-
tress EA/05*
HERBERT, Evelyn (b 1898) Amer-

ican actress, singer WWT/7-10
HERBERT, F. Hugh (1897-1958)
English dramatist MH, TW/14,
WWA/3, WWT/10-12
HERBERT, Fred (fl 1891?) singer
CDP
HERBERT, Fred (d 1972 [60])
producer/director/choreographer
BP/56*
HERBERT, Mrs. Fred see Her-
bert, Janie
HERBERT, Galwey English actor
GRB/1
HERBERT, George (d 1891 [26])
EA/92*
HERBERT, Sir Henry (1596-1673)
English Master of the Revels
COC, OC/1-3
HERBERT, Henry (1879-1947) Eng-
lish actor SR, TW/3, WWT/6-
10
HERBERT, Holmes (d 1956 [28])
actor BE*
HERBERT, Hugh (1887-1952) Amer-
ican actor TW/2
HERBERT, Janie [Mrs. Fred Her-
bert] (d 1890 [24]) EA/91*
HERBERT, Jocelyn (b 1917) English
designer AAS, ES, WWT/14-16
HERBERT, John (d 1835) English
actor HAS
HERBERT, John (d 1852 [38/40])
actor EA/72*, WWT/14*
HERBERT, John [John Herbert
Brundage] (b 1926) Canadian
dramatist, director, actor,
dancer CD
HERBERT, John, Jr. (1803-64)
English actor CDP, HAS
HERBERT, Joseph (d 1923 [56])
English comedian, librettist
BE*, BP/7*, WWT/14*
HERBERT, Kate see Lewis, Mrs.
W.
HERBERT, Lew (d 1968 [65]) per-
former BP/53*
HERBERT, Louisa [Mrs. Crabbe]
(d 1921 [89]) actress OAA/1-2
HERBERT, Mary, Countess of
Pembroke (d 1621) translator
CP/1-3
HERBERT, Tim actor TW/1
HERBERT, Victor (1859-1924) Irish
composer, conductor DAB, ES,
GRB/3-4, HJD, MH, NTH,
PDT, SR, WWA/1, WWS, WWT/
1-4
HERBERT, William (1844-96) In-

dian/English actor CDP,
OAA/1-2
HERBERTE, Mrs. E. B. see
Herberte, Elizabeth
HERBERTE, Elizabeth [Mrs.
E. B. Herberte] (d 1883 [32])
EA/84*
HERBERTSON, John Anthony
see Anthony, Jack
HERCAT, Prof. (d 1913) EA/14*
HERCZEG, Geza (d 1954 [65])
Hungarian dramatist BP/38*
HERENDEEN, Fred (d 1962 [68])
dramatist BE*
HERFORD, Beatrice (d 1952 [84])
English actress, monologist
TW/9, WWA/5
HERGET, Bob (b 1924) American
choreographer, director, dancer
BE, TW/5
HERIAT, Philippe (d 1971 [73])
critic BP/56*
HERIG, Maria freak CDP
HERING, Doris American critic
BE
HERIOT, Henry (fl 1547-52) actor
DA
HERIOT, Wilton (d 1913) actor,
stage manager, dramatist EA/
14*
HERIOT, Mrs. Wilton [Flossie
Wilkinson] (d 1905) EA/06*
HERKO, Fred (d 1964 [29])
choreographer BP/49*
HERLEIN, Lillian (d 1971) per-
former BP/55*
HERLIE, Eileen (b 1920) Scottish
actress AAS, BE, TW/12-21,
24, 29, WWT/10-16
HERLIHY, Ed American actor
TW/24, 30
HERLIHY, James Leo (b 1927)
American dramatist, actor,
director BE, CB, CD
HERMAN, Al (d 1967 [84]) per-
former BP/52*
HERMAN, Cynthia (b 1947) Amer-
ican actress TW/30
HERMAN, Henry (1832-94) drama-
tist DNB
HERMAN, Jerry (b 1933) Ameri-
can composer, lyricist BE,
CB, WWT/16
HERMAN, John producer BE
HERMAN, La Rosa (d 1920 [79])
actress BP/5*
HERMAN, Lewis (b 1905) English
director, producer BE

HERMAN, Marguerite (b 1914)
American director, producer,
actress BE
HERMAN, Maxine (b 1948) Ameri-
can actress TW/26-27
HERMAN, Selma American actress
WWS
HERMAN, Tom (d 1972 [63]) per-
former BP/56*
HERMANN, Prof. (b 1821) German
magician HAS
HERMANN, Agnes M. [Mrs. Louis
Hermann] (d 1909) EA/10*
HERMANN, Alexander (d 1896 [52])
conjuror EA/98*
HERMANN, David (1876-1930) di-
rector, actor, producer COC
HERMANN, Leon (d 1909 [42])
conjuror EA/10*
HERMANN, Louis (d 1884 [73])
actor EA/85*
HERMANN, Mrs. Louis see
Hermann, Agnes M.
HERMANN, Phil (fl 1890?) singer,
actor CDP
HERMANN, Theodore (d 1874) con-
ductor EA/75*
HERMANT, Abel (d 1950 [86])
dramatist, critic BE*, WWT/
14*
HERMES, Alice American speech
teacher BE
HERNANDEZ, Juano (d 1970 [74])
actor TW/27
HERNDON, Agnes [née Mattie
Frazier; Mrs. Joseph A. Jessel;
Mrs. Albert Andruss] (d 1920)
American actress CDP
HERNDON, Richard G. (d 1958
[85]) French producing manager
WWT/6-9
HERNDON, T. J. (b 1833) Ameri-
can actor HAS
HERNE, Chrystal see Herne,
Katherine Chrystal
HERNE, James A. (1839-1901)
American actor, dramatist
CDP, COC, DAB, ES, HAS,
HJD, MH, MWD, NTH, OC/1-3,
PP/1, RE, SR, WWA/1
HERNE, Mrs. James A. [Katharine
Corcoran] (1839-1901) actress
COC, PP/1, WWA/H
HERNE, John F. (d 1888 [41])
American actor EA/88*
HERNE, Julie (1881-1955) American
actress, dramatist TW/11,
WWM, WWS

HERNE, Katherine Chrystal (1882/83-1950) American actress DAB, GRB/3-4, TW/7, WWM, WWS, WWT/1-10
HERNE, Katherine Corcoran see Herne, Mrs. James A.
HERO, Maria (b 1942) American actress TW/25
HERON, Agnes see Natali, Agnes
HERON, Bijou see Miller, Mrs. Henry
HERON, Dalziel (d 1911) actor BE*, EA/12*, WWT/14*
HERON, Fanny see Natali, Fanny
HERON, James (d 1918) EA/19*
HERON, Joyce (b 1916) Egyptian/English actress WWT/10-16
HERON, Mary Ann (fl 1848) actress HAS
HERON, Matilda Agnes (1830-77) American actress CDP, COC, DAB, HAS, OC/1-3, WWA/H
HERON, Philip (d 1911 [23]) actor EA/12*
HERON, Robert (c. 1760-1807) Scottish dramatist CP/3
HERON-BROWN, Edith [Edith Anne Brown] English actress GRB/1-2
HERR, Melvin (b 1916) American administrator, business manager BE
HERRAND, Marcel (d 1953 [55]) actor, producer WWT/14*
HERRIDGE, Frances American critic, editor BE
HERRING, Mrs. (fl 1836) actress HAS
HERRING, Fanny (1832-1906) English actress CDP, HAS
HERRING, Paul (d 1878 [78]) clown CDP
HERRMANN, Alexander (1844-96) German magician CDP, SR, WWA/H
HERRMANN, Bernard (d 1975 [64]) composer/lyricist BP/60*
HERRMANN, Prof. Carl (d 1887) conjurer EA/88*
HERRMANN, Compar (1815-87) German magician NYM, SR
HERRMANN, Edward (b 1943) American actor TW/27-28, 30
HERRMANN, Priscilla (d 1893) EA/94*
HERRON, Mark (b 1930) American actor TW/13

HERRON, Randy (b 1946) American actor TW/29
HERSCHER, Sylvia (b 1913) American literary representative, producer, agent, manager BE
HERSEE, Henry (d 1896 [76]) librettist EA/97*
HERSEE, Rose (fl 1867-69) singer CDP, HAS
HERSEY, David (b 1939) American lighting designer WWT/16
HERSHEY, Burnet (1896-1971) Rumanian dramatist BE
HERSHOLT, Jean (1886-1956) Danish actor BE*, BP/41*, WWT/14*
HERSKOVITS, Bela (d 1974 [54]) performer BP/58*
HERTER, William (b 1947) American actor TW/24
HERTZ, Alfred (1872-1942) German conductor CB, DAB, WWA/2, WWM, WWW/4
HERTZ, Carl (d 1924 [64]) magician BE*, WWT/14*
HERTZ, Henrik (1798-1870) Danish dramatist COC, OC/1-3
HERTZ, Ida (fl 1870-79) English actress OAA/1-2
HERVEY, Miss (fl early 19th cent) albino CDP
HERVEY, Arthur (1855-1922) French/English? composer WWW/2
HERVEY, Grizelda (b 1901) English actress WWT/6-11
HERVEY, Irene American actress TW/1
HERVEY, Joe (d 1899) singer EA/00*
HERVEY, John, Lord (1696-1743) English dramatist CP/2-3
HERVEY, Rose actress, singer DP
HERVIEU, Paul (1857-1915) French dramatist GRB/1-4
HERWYN, W. G. (d 1877 [32]) stage manager EA/78*
HERZ, Andrew (d 1972 [25]) dramatist BP/57*
HERZ, Ralph C. (1878-1921) French actor CDP, GRB/3-4, WWM, WWS, WWT/1-3
HERZ, Mrs. Ralph C. see Glaser, Lulu
HESLEWOOD, Tom (1868-1959) English actor, costume designer GRB/1-4, WWT/1-7
HESLOP, Mr. (d 1854) actor CDP

HESLOP, Charles (1883-1966)
English actor, singer WWT/
8-14
HESS, Cort (b 1838) American
actor HAS
HESS, Jack J. (d 1970 [78]) pub-
licist BP/55*
HESS, Rodger (b 1938) American
talent representative BE
HESSELTINE, Stark (b 1929)
American talent & literary
representative BE
HESSER, Jupiter Z. K. M. (fl
1851?) composer CDP
HESSLEGRAVE, Mrs. H. see
Riley, Eliza
HESTER, Sally American actress
TW/5
HESTON, Charlton [né Carter]
(b 1921/22/23/24) American
actor BE, CB, ES, TW/6-11,
13-16, WWT/13-16
HESTOR, George (1877-1925)
English actor WWT/2-5
HETHERINGTON, Frederick
Augustus see Gaytie, Fred A.
HETON, Robert (fl 1635-37)
manager, actor? DA
HEUER, George (d 1887) treas-
urer NYM
HEUMAN, Barbara (b 1944) Amer-
ican actress TW/28-29
HEWER, John (b 1922) English
actor TW/11
HEWERDINE, William (fl 1790)
singer CDP
HEWES, Henry (b 1917) American
critic, dramatist BE, COC,
NTH, OC/3, WWT/13-16
HEWETSON, W. B. (fl 1808)
dramatist CP/3
HEWETT, Christopher English
actor, director BE, WWT/
12-16
HEWETT, Dorothy (b 1923) Aus-
tralian dramatist CD
HEWETT, J. H. (fl 1831?)
American? dramatist RJ
HEWETT, Molly (d 1970) per-
former BP/56*
HEWINS, Mary see Fox, Mary
H.
HEWITT, Agnes [Mrs. Frank M.
Boyd] (d 1924 [61]) Indian/
English actress DP, GRB/
3-4, WWT/1-4
HEWITT, Alan (b 1915) American
actor, director BE, TW/4-8,

10-13
HEWITT, Alice (d 1973 [102]) per-
former BP/58*
HEWITT, Barnard Wolcott (b 1906)
American educator BE
HEWITT, Henry C. (1885/86-1968)
English actor WWT/5-14
HEWITT, James (1770-1827) Eng-
lish composer, conductor DAB,
HJD
HEWITT, John (fl 1729-34) drama-
tist CP/1-3, GT, TD/1-2
HEWITT, John Hill (1801-90) Amer-
ican songwriter, journalist BE*
HEWITT, John Q. (b 1881) Ameri-
can actor TW/2
HEWITT, John S. (d 1881) actor
EA/82*
HEWITT, Robert (b 1922) Australian
actor TW/22, 25-27
HEWLETT, Mr. (fl 1821) actor
CDP
HEWLETT, Maurice (1861-1923)
English dramatist GRB/2-4,
WWT/1-4
HEWSE, Richard (fl 1554) actor
DA
HEWSON, J. James (d 1923 [71])
dramatist, journalist BE*,
WWT/14*
HEWSON, John Thomas (d 1880
[26]) comic singer EA/81*
HEY, Richard (fl 1782-96) drama-
tist CP/3
HEYBURN, Weldon (d 1951 [46])
actor TW/7
HEYDT, Louis Jean (1905-60)
American actor TW/1, 3-6,
16, WWT/10-12
HEYES, Herbert (1889-1958) Amer-
ican actor TW/2
HEYL, Lewis J. (d 1839) American
actor HAS
HEYLIN, Peter (1599-1662) English
dramatist CP/2-3, FGF
HEYMAN, Barton (b 1937) Ameri-
can actor TW/26-30
HEYSE, Paul Johann Ludwig (1830-
1914) German dramatist GRB/
1-4
HEYSHAM, William Sayre Ameri-
can? dramatist RJ
HEYWARD, Dorothy (1890-1961)
American dramatist ES, MWD,
TW/18, WWA/4, WWT/9-13
HEYWARD, Du Bose (1885-1940)
American dramatist DAB, ES,
HJD, MD, MH, MWD, NTH,

WWT/9, WWW/3-4

HEYWOOD, Charles [né Frank Haffner] (b 1848) singer, female impersonator CDP

HEYWOOD, Eliza see Haywood, Eliza

HEYWOOD, Frank (d 1874) actor EA/75*

HEYWOOD, Jasper (1535-98) English dramatist CP/1-3

HEYWOOD, John (c. 1497-1580) English dramatist COC, CP/1-3, DA, DNB, ES, HP, MH, OC/1-3, PDT, RE

HEYWOOD, Joseph (d 1877 [44]) equestrian clown EA/78*

HEYWOOD, Matthew dramatist CP/1-3

HEYWOOD, Thomas (c. 1570-1641) English actor, dramatist COC, CP/1-3, DA, DNB, ES, FGF, HP, MH, NTH, OC/1-3, PDT, RE

HIAM, Frank (d 1899 [58]) conjuring apparatus manufacturer EA/01*

HIAM, Henry (d 1900 [35]) conjuring apparatus manufacturer EA/01*

HIBBARD, Edna (1895-1942) American actress CB, WWT/7-9

HIBBERD, Jack (b 1940) Australian dramatist, director CD

HIBBERT, Geoffrey (d 1969 [48]) performer BP/53*

HIBBERT, Henry George (1862-1924) English critic GRB/2-3, WWT/4

HIBBERT, Louise (b 1855) Spanish/English actress OAA/1-2

HIBBS, Elizabeth (d 1896) music-hall performer EA/97*

HIBBS, Thomas (d 1894) music-hall performer EA/95*

HIBERNIA, Fred (d 1893) music-hall performer? EA/94*

HIBERNIA, Mrs. Fred see Hales, Rose

HICHENS, Robert Smythe (1864-1950) English dramatist GRB/1-4, NTH, SR, WWT/1-10, WWW/4

HICHINS, H. J. (d 1911 [67]) manager GRB/1

HICKEN, Edward (d 1887 [85]) equestrian EA/88*

HICKEN, Isaac George [Isaac Batley] (d 1890 [34]) EA/91*

HICKEN, Thomas see Battley, Thomas

HICKEY, Hiram Phineas (b 1824) American actor HAS

HICKEY, William American actor, director BE, TW/27-30

HICKIN, Jacques (d 1904 [49]) acrobat EA/05*

HICKLEY, Richard Barkley (d 1904) EA/06*

HICKLIN, Margery (b 1904) English actress WWT/5-8

HICKLIN, Ralph (d 1970 [48]) critic BP/54*

HICKMAN, Alfred (d 1931 [57]) actor CDP

HICKMAN, Charles (b 1905) English actor, director AAS, WWT/7-16

HICKMAN, Howard (d 1949 [69]) actor TW/6

HICKMAN, James (b 1932) American actor TW/12

HICKMAN, J. Hampton (b 1937) American theatre owner, producer BE

HICKS, Agnes Rosa (d 1886 [36]) singer EA/87*

HICKS, Annie [Mrs. W. R. Hicks] (d 1873 [28]) EA/74*

HICKS, Betty Seymour (b 1905) English actress WWT/6-7

HICKS, C. Carroll (fl 1858) actor HAS

HICKS, Cecil (d 1888) musician EA/89*

HICKS, Sir Edward Seymour (1871-1949) English actor, manager, dramatist AAS, CDP, COC, DNB, EA/96, ES, GRB/1-4, NTH, OC/1-3, SR, TW/5, WWS, WWT/1-10, WWW/4

HICKS, Mrs. Edward Seymour see Terriss, Ellaline

HICKS, Henry Douglas (d 1902 [60]) actor EA/03*

HICKS, Jack (d 1974 [60]) producer/director/choreographer BP/59*

HICKS, Julian (d 1882) scene artist EA/84*, WWT/14*

HICKS, Julian (1858-1941) English scene artist WWT/1-6

HICKS, Leonard M. (d 1971 [53]) actor TW/28

HICKS, Newton Tree (d 1873 [62]) actor CDP

HICKS, Patricia (b 1921) English

actress TW/7

HICKS, Richard (d 1900) Irish comedian EA/02*

HICKS, Russell (1895-1957) American actor TW/10-11, 13

HICKS, Thomas Reid Strachan see Trelawney, R. S.

HICKS, Tommy see Steele, Tommy

HICKS, Walter (d 1917 [28]) comedian EA/18*

HICKS, Mrs. W. R. see Hicks, Annie

HICKSON, Henry (d 1887) EA/88*

HICKSON, Joan (b 1906) English actress WWT/9-16

HICKWORTH, John (1815-58) actor, manager HAS

HIDALGO, Elvira de (b 1892?) Spanish singer ES

HIELD, Mrs. (fl 1836) English actress SR

HIELD, Anne [née Scholey] (fl 1832-55) English actress HAS

HIELD, C. W. (fl 1834-38) actor HAS

HIELD, Mrs. C. W. (fl 1834-38) actress HAS

HIELD, William (d 1877 [71]) actor EA/78*

HIELD, William, Jr. (d 1858) English actor HAS

HIFFERNAN, Paul (1719-77) Irish dramatist CP/1-3, GT, TD/ 1-2

HIFFERT, Caroline (fl 1844) German singer, actress CDP

HIFFERT, Catherine (fl 1849-58) German actress, singer HAS

HIGDEN, Henry (fl 1693) dramatist CP/1-3, GT

HIGDEN, Ralph (fl 1328) dramatist CP/3

HIGGIE, Thomas Henry (d 1893 [85]) actor, dramatist BE*, EA/94*, WWT/14*

HIGGINBOTTOM, Frances Ann [Fanny Smith] (d 1868 [22]) dancer EA/69*

HIGGINS, Prof. (d 1891 [34]) aeronaut EA/92*

HIGGINS, Albert (d 1975 [32]) performer BP/59*

HIGGINS, David (d 1936 [78]) American actor, dramatist BE*, BP/21*

HIGGINS, Dennis (b 1942) American actor TW/27

HIGGINS, Dick performer? CD

HIGGINS, Frederick Robert (1896-1941) Irish manager, dramatist CB

HIGGINS, Michael (b 1922) American actor, director BE, TW/ 2-3, 7, 13-15, 21, 28-30

HIGGINS, Norman (1898-1974) English manager BTR/74, WWT/ 11-15

HIGGINS, Robert (b 1932) American actor TW/13-14

HIGGINSON, Mrs. see Cussans, Mrs.

HIGGONS, Bevil (c. 1670-1735) dramatist CP/1-3, GT

HIGH, Bolen (b 1945) American actor TW/26-28

HIGHAM, Fred (d 1918 [63]) EA/ 19*

HIGHLAND, George A. (d 1954) producer, director BE*, WWT/ 14*

HIGHLEY, Reginald (1884-1942) English manager WWT/6-7

HIGHMORE, John (fl 1731) manager CDP, TD/1-2

HIGHT, Mrs. B. F. see Hight, Lizzie

HIGHT, Fred (fl 1853) American actor HAS

HIGHT, Lizzie [Mrs. T. M. Hunter; Mrs. B. F. Hight] (1843-1927) actress CDP

HIGHTOWER, Marilyn (b 1923) American dancer WWT/11-13

HIGHTOWER, Rosella (b 1920) American dancer, choreographer ES

HIGNELL, Rose (b 1896) English actress, singer WWT/6-9

HIGNETT, H. R. (1870-1959) English actor GRB/4, WWT/1-11

HIKEN, Gerald (b 1927) American actor, director BE, TW/14, 21, 29, WWT/14-16

HIKEN, Nat (1914-68) American dramatist, director BE

HILARIOT, Antonia see Hilariot, Mrs. Charles

HILARIOT, Charles (fl 1851) French dancer HAS

HILARIOT, Mrs. Charles (fl 1851) dancer CDP, HAS

HILARY, Jennifer (b 1942) English actress TW/23-24, WWT/14-16

HILARY, Ruth (d 1968 [61]) performer BP/53*

HILDEBRANDT, F. (d 1870)
pantomimist EA/71*
HILDON, Chester see Hildon,
Rochester L.
HILDON, Rochester L. [Chester
Hildon] (d 1886) acting manager
EA/87*
HILDRETH, Mr. (fl 1851) actor
HAS
HILDRETH, Miss (d 1847) actress
HAS
HILDRETH, Albert (d 1969 [64])
box office treasurer BP/53*
HILDRETH, Sarah (b 1810) Amer-
ican actress HAS, SR
HILDYARD, Walter (d 1901 [78])
clown EA/02*
HILL, Mrs. (fl 1724-34) BD
HILL, Mrs. [Mrs. Stanley] (d
1834) English actress HAS
HILL, Mrs. (d 1906) EA/07*
HILL, Mrs. see Atkins, Mrs.
William
HILL, Mrs. see Burton,
Philippina
HILL, Aaron (1685-1750) English
dramatist CDP, COC, CP/
1-3, DNB, GT, HP, NTH,
OC/3, TD/1-2
HILL, Abram (b 1911) American
director, dramatist CB
HILL, Ann (b 1921) American
children's theatre executive
BE
HILL, Anne Russell (fl 1840-52)
English actress HAS
HILL, Annie [Mrs. Herman de
Lange] (d 1943) actress CDP,
DP
HILL, Arthur (b 1922) Canadian
actor AAS, BE, ES, TW/14-
15, 19-22, 24, WWT/14-16
HILL, Barton (d 1911 [82]) actor
WWT/14*
HILL, Benson (d 1845 [49]) actor,
dramatist BE*, EA/72*,
WWT/14*
HILL, Billie English actress,
singer WWT/6-8
HILL, Billy (1899-1940) Ameri-
can songwriter BE*
HILL, Brownlow (d 1872) actor
EA/73*
HILL, Caroline L. Brook English
actress OAA/1-2
HILL, Charles John (1805-74)
actor CDP
HILL, Charles John Barton

(1828/30-1911) English actor
CDP, HAS, PP/1
HILL, Mrs. Charles John Barton
(fl 1851) actress HAS
HILL, Charles Walter Blencoe (d
1869 [31]) actor? EA/70*
HILL, Charlotte (d 1872 [40]) per-
former? EA/73*
HILL, Ellen (d 1866 [63]) actress
EA/72*
HILL, Emily Caroline [Mrs. Frank
Hill] (d 1912) EA/13*
HILL, Errol (b 1921) Trinidadian
dramatist, director, educator
CD
HILL, Mrs. Frank see Hill,
Emily Caroline
HILL, Frederic Stanhope (1805-51)
American actor, dramatist
DAB, HAS, RJ, WWA/H
HILL, Mrs. F. Wilbur see
Whitaker, Willette
HILL, George (d 1878 [35]) musi-
cian EA/79*
HILL, Mrs. George [Bellevere] (d
1879 [25]) actress? EA/80*
HILL, George Handel ["Yankee"]
(1798-1849) American actor
CDP, DAB, HAS, HJD, SR,
WWA/H
HILL, George Ray (b 1922) Ameri-
can director BE, ES, WWT/
14-16
HILL, Gus (1860-1940) American
actor, dramatist, manager SR,
WWM
HILL, Hamilton (fl 1900?) Australian
singer CDP
HILL, Harriet [Mrs. T. Hill] (fl
early 19th cent) actress, singer
CDP
HILL, Helen Oursler (d 1968) per-
former BP/52*
HILL, Holly American actress
TW/24
HILL, Miss J. (fl 1847-52) actress
HAS
HILL, James (d 1817) English ac-
tor, singer CDP, DNB, GT,
TD/1-2
HILL, Jane [Mrs. William E. Bur-
ton] (d 1863 [39]) actress CDP
HILL, Jane (d 1975 [95]) performer
BP/60*
HILL, Jenny [Jane Woodley] (1851-
96) English music-hall performer
CDP, COC, OC/1-3
HILL, Jerome (d 1972 [67]) pro-

ducer/director/choreographer
BP/57*

HILL, J. M. (d 1912) manager
SR

HILL, Sir John (c. 1716/17-75)
dramatist CDP, CP/1-3,
GT, TD/1-2

HILL, John Henry [John Wilson]
(d 1887 [31]) property man
EA/88*

HILL, John Henry (d 1893 [35])
conductor EA/94*

HILL, John J. (d 1962 [70]) press
representative BE*

HILL, John T. (d 1900) music-
hall proprietor EA/01*

HILL, June (d 1975 [95]) actress
WWT/16*

HILL, Lawrence (b 1912) American producer BE

HILL, Lucienne [née Palmer]
English dramatist BE, WWT/
14-16

HILL, Martha American educator
BE

HILL, Percy (d 1912 [34]) acrobat EA/13*

HILL, Peter Murray (b 1908)
English actor WWT/9-11

HILL, Phyllis (b 1925) American
actress TW/9-12

HILL, Ralston (b 1927) American
actor TW/25-28

HILL, Reuben (fl 1899?) singer,
actor CDP

HILL, Richard (fl 1778) dramatist CP/2-3, GT

HILL, Richard (d 1890) actor
EA/91*

HILL, Ronnie (b 1911) English
composer, lyricist, journalist
WWT/12-16

HILL, Rose (b 1914) English actress, singer WWT/12-16

HILL, Ruby (b 1922) American
actress TW/2

HILL, Sinclair [Gerard Arthur
Lewin Sinclair-Hill] (1896-
1945) English producer WWT/
8-9

HILL, Mrs. Stephen see Hoban,
Lilian

HILL, Steven (b 1922) American
actor TW/4-11, 17-19

HILL, Mrs. T. see Hill, Harriet

HILL, Thomas see Hill, Tom

HILL, Thomas see Hilson,
Thomas

HILL, Thomas Bentley Lilwall (d
1902 [21]) actor EA/03*

HILL, Thomas Henry Weist (d 1891
[63]) principal of Guildhall
School of Music EA/93*

HILL, Tom (d 1851 [57]) clown
CDP

HILL, Walter (d 1879) comedian
EA/80*

HILL, Walter Osborn (d 1963 [87])
actor BE*

HILL, Wesley (d 1930 [55]) American actor BE*, BP/15*

HILL, William see Maynard,
Ambrose

HILL, William J. (1834-88) actor
CDP

HILLARY, Ann (b 1931) American
actress BE

HILLER, Ferdinand (d 1885 [74])
composer EA/86*

HILLER, Dame Wendy (b 1912)
English actress AAS, BE, CB,
ES, TW/4-8, 18, WWT/8-16

HILLERY, Mable (d 1976 [46]) performer BP/60*

HILLHOUSE, James Abraham (1789-
1841) American dramatist EAP,
HJD, RJ

HILLIAR, Ann see Dibdin, Mrs.
Thomas John

HILLIARD, Bob (1918-71) American
songwriter, producer, publisher
BE

HILLIARD, Harry (d 1890) sketch
artist EA/91*

HILLIARD, Harry S. (d 1895 [34])
actor EA/96*

HILLIARD, Harry S. (d 1966) performer BP/50*

HILLIARD, Hazel (d 1971 [83])
performer BP/56*

HILLIARD, Kathlyn (1896-1933)
Scottish actress, singer WWT/
6-7

HILLIARD, Mack C. (d 1965 [89])
producer/director BP/50*

HILLIARD, Patricia (b 1916) Indian/
English actress WWT/8-13

HILLIARD, Peter (d 1974 [37])
performer BP/59*

HILLIARD, Robert C. (1857-1927)
American actor, dramatist
CDP, GRB/2-4, SR, WWA/1,
WWM, WWS, WWT/1-5

HILLIAS, Peg (b 1914) American
actress TW/6-7

HILLIE, Edward (d 1975 [56])
producer/director/choreographer
BP/60*
HILLIER, Alice May (d 1873 [19])
actress EA/74*
HILLIER, Emily [Mrs. William
Hillier] (d 1917) EA/18*
HILLIER, James (d 1874 [34])
actor, comic singer CDP
HILLIER, Mrs. William see
Hillier, Emily
HILLIGSBERG, Mme. (fl 1801)
dancer CDP
HILLIS, Margaret (b 1921) Amer-
ican conductor CB
HILLMAN, George (b 1906) Amer-
ican actor TW/24-25
HILLMAN, Lori (b 1951) Ameri-
can actress TW/29
HILLMAN, Michael (1902-41)
South African actor, manager
WWT/9
HILLYARD, Mr. actor, manager
TD/2
HILSON, Ellen see Hilson,
Mrs. Thomas
HILSON, Thomas [né Hill] (1784-
1834) English actor CDP,
HAS
HILSON, Mrs. Thomas [Ellen
Augusta Johnson] (1801-37)
actress CDP, HAS
HILTON, A. T. (d 1908 [67])
EA/09*
HILTON, Daisy (d 1969 [60])
performer BP/53*
HILTON, Hilda (d 1888 [35])
actress EA/89*, WWT/14*
HILTON, James (d 1954 [54])
English writer BE*, BP/39*
HILTON, J. W. (d 1871 [35])
Negro minstrel EA/72*
HILTON, Marie American singer
SR
HILTON, Tessy [Mrs. Widdell]
(d 1879 [25]) actress EA/80*
HILTON, Violet (d 1969 [60])
performer BP/53*
HILTON, William (fl 1776) drama-
tist CP/3
HILYARD, Maud (d 1926) actress
BE*, WWT/14*
HIME, Edward Lawrence (d 1900
[77]) composer EA/01*
HINCHMAN, Mr. (fl 1849) actor
HAS
HINCKEN, Harry see Henkens,
Harry

HINCKLEY, Alfred (b 1920) Amer-
ican actor TW/23, 25, 27
HINCKLEY, Allen (1877-1954)
American singer WWA/3,
WWM
HINCKLEY, Dorothy (d 1972) ac-
tress TW/29
HINCKLEY, Isabella (1840-62)
American singer CDP, HAS
HINCKLEY, Sallie A. (b 1841)
American actress HAS
HIND, Adeline see Hind, Mrs.
Thomas James
HIND, Benjamin Nash (d 1873 [40])
singer EA/74*
HIND, Horace (d 1917 [21]) EA/18*
HIND, Thomas James (b 1815)
English actor CDP, HAS
HIND, Mrs. Thomas James [née
Adeline Grassan; Mrs. Stephen
Knight] (b 1813) American ac-
tress CDP, HAS
HINDELL, Gus singer CDP
HINDERER, Mrs. (d 1893) EA/94*
HINDES, Mr. manager TD/2
HINDLE, Annie (fl 1869?) singer,
male impersonator CDP
HINDLE, James A. (d 1917) EA/
18*
HINDLE, Winifred (d 1969) per-
former BP/54*
HINDLEY, John (d 1867 [47]) pro-
fessor of music EA/68*
HINDLEY, John W. (d 1878 [26])
musician EA/79*
HINDS, Michael (d 1892 [66]) cir-
cus performer? EA/93*
HINE, Frederick (d 1879 [70])
treasurer EA/80*
HINE, Hubert (d 1950 [59]) actor,
director, stage manager BE*,
WWT/14*
HINE, Jack (d 1899 [40]) actor?
EA/00*
HINES, Dixie (d 1928 [56]) press
representative BE*, BP/13*
HINES, Elizabeth (1899-1971)
American actress, singer TW/
27, WWT/5-7
HINES, Harry (d 1967 [78]) per-
former BP/51*
HINES, Jerome (b 1921) American
singer CB, ES
HINES, Mimi (b 1933) Canadian
actress TW/22-23
HINES, Patrick (b 1930) American
actor, director BE, TW/22,
29-30, WWT/15-16

HINES, Timothy Edwin see Hines, William E.

HINES, William (d 1889 [22]) American clog dancer EA/90*

HINES, William E. [Timothy Edwin Hines] (b 1859) American actor WWM

HINGLE, Pat (b 1923) American actor BE, CB, TW/11-22, 24-28, 30, WWT/13-16

HINGSTON, Edward Peron (d 1876 [52]) acting manager EA/77*

HINGSTON, Hannah [Mrs. P. Hingston] (d 1895 [77]) EA/96*

HINGSTON, James (d 1902 [75]) EA/03*

HINGSTON, Lilian actress CDP

HINGSTON, Mrs. P. see Hingston, Hannah

HINKEL, Cecil E. (b 1913) American educator BE

HINKLEY, Del (b 1930) American actor TW/23, 25, 27

HINKSON, Mary (b 1930) American dancer BE

HINNANT, Bill (b 1935) American actor TW/18-19, 23-24, 26-30

HINNANT, Skip (b 1940) American actor TW/23-25

HINRICHS, Gustav (1850-1942) German conductor CB

HINSHAW, William W. (1867-1947) American singer, conductor, producer SR, WWA/2, WWM

HINSON, Bonnie (b 1946) American actress TW/26-27, 30

HINSTOCK, Robert (fl 1538-51) actor DA

HINT, Robert (fl 1629) actor DA

HINTON, Charles (d 1917) EA/18*

HINTON, Henry L. (b 1840) American actor HAS

HINTON, Mary [Emily Rachel Forster] (b 1896) actress WWT/9-14

HIPPISLEY, E. [Mrs. Fitzmaurice] (fl 1741-66) actress DNB

HIPPISLEY, Jane see Green, Jane

HIPPISLEY, John (d 1748) actor, dramatist CDP, CP/1-3, DNB, GT, TD/1-2

HIPPISLEY, John (d 1767) actor,

dramatist DNB

HIPPLE, Hugh see Marlowe, Hugh

HIPWORTH, Mr. (d 1795) actor HAS

HIRD, James William (d 1871 [43]) musician EA/72*

HIRD, Thora (b 1916) English actress WWT/11-16

HIROSE, George (d 1974 [75]) performer BP/59*

HIRSCH, John Stephan (b 1930) Hungarian director AAS, WWT/15-16

HIRSCH, Judd (b 1935) American actor TW/24-25, 29-30

HIRSCH, Louis Achille (1881/87-1924) American composer WWT/4

HIRSCH, Max (d 1925 [61]) executive BE*, BP/10*

HIRSCH, Samuel (b 1917) American educator, director, actor BE

HIRSCHBEIN, Peretz (1880-1948) Russian dramatist DAB, MH, MWD, NTH, RE

HIRSCHFELD, Al (b 1903) American artist BE

HIRSCHFELD, Guido (d 1889) manager EA/90*

HIRSCHFELD, Kurt (d 1964 [62]) producer/director BP/49*

HIRSON, Alice (b 1929) American actress TW/23, 30

HISHIN, Bernard (d 1944 [59]) manager WWT/14*

HISLOP, Joseph (b 1887) Scottish actor, singer WWT/8-10

HISSAM-DEMOSS, Mary (fl 1890-1910) American singer WWM

HITCHCOCK, Edward (1793-1864) American dramatist EAP

HITCHCOCK, Flora Zabelle (d 1968 [88]) performer BP/53*

HITCHCOCK, Fordyce (fl 1844-48) manager CDP

HITCHCOCK, Pat (b 1930) English actress TW/1

HITCHCOCK, Raymond (1865-1929) American actor CDP, DAB, GRB/3-4, SR, WWM, WWS, WWT/1-6

HITCHCOCK, Robert (d 1809) actor, prompter, dramatist CP/2-3, DNB, GT, TD/1-2

HITCHENER, W. H. (fl 1808) dramatist CP/3

HITCHINS, Harry J. (d 1911)

EA/12*
HITCHINS, H. J. manager GRB/
2-4
HITE, Mabel (1883/85-1912)
American actress CDP, SR,
WWS
HIVNOR, Robert (b 1916) Amer-
ican dramatist CD, CH
HIX, Don (d 1964) performer
BP/49*
HIXON, Frank G. (d 1973 [82])
promoter BP/57*
HO, Wai Ching (b 1943) British
actor TW/25, 27
HOADLY, Benjamin (1706-57)
English dramatist COC, CP/
1-3, DNB, GT, HP, OC/1-3,
SR, TD/1-2
HOADLY, Dr. John (1711-76)
English dramatist CP/2-3,
DNB, GT, TD/1-2
HOAG, Mitzi (b 1932) American
actress TW/15
HOAGLAND, Harland (d 1971 [75])
performer BP/55*
HOARE, Miss see Ward, Mrs.
HOARE, Douglas (b 1875) English
dramatist WWT/3-11
HOARE, Prince (1755-1834) Eng-
lish dramatist CDP, CP/3,
DNB, GT, TD/1-2
HOARE, Ryton (d 1908 [24])
EA/09*
HOBAN, Agnes E. (d 1962 [73])
performer BE*
HOBAN, Lilian [Mrs. Stephen
Hill] (d 1890) EA/91*
HOBAN, Michael see Hoban,
James Brown
HOBART, Doty (d 1958 [72])
dramatist BE*, BP/43*
HOBART, George V. (1867-1926)
Canadian/American dramatist
GRB/2-4, SR, WWA/1, WWS,
WWT/1-5
HOBART, Rose (b 1906) American
actress BE, WWT/7-11
HOBBES, Halliwell, Jr. English
actor TW/4
HOBBES, Herbert Halliwell (1877-
1962) English actor GRB/1,
TW/1, 3-4, 11-12, 18, WWT/
1-13
HOBBES, John Oliver [Mrs.
Craigie] (1867-1906) American
dramatist DNB, GRB/1, HP,
WWA/1, WWW/1
HOBBES, Thomas (fl 1610-31)

actor DA
HOBBS, Mr. (d 1877) singer EA/
78*
HOBBS, Billy (d 1917) actor, sing-
er CDP
HOBBS, Carleton (b 1898) English
actor WWT/7-8
HOBBS, Frederick (1880-1942)
New Zealand actor, singer
WWT/4-9
HOBBS, Jack (1893-1968) English
actor WWT/3-12
HOBBS, William (b 1939) English
fight arranger, actor WWT/15-16
HOBGOOD, Burnet (b 1922) Ameri-
can educator, director BE
HOBIN, Thomas (d 1911) singer
EA/12*
HOBSON, Cpt. A. P. (d 1885)
manager EA/86*
HOBSON, Fred see Leslie, Fred
HOBSON, Harold (b 1904) English
critic AAS, BE, CH, COC,
PDT, WWT/11-16
HOBSON, James (b 1938) Canadian
actor TW/27
HOBSON, John (d 1887) musical
director EA/88*
HOBSON, Joseph (d 1892 [69]) pro-
prietor EA/93*
HOBSON, Mrs. Joseph (d 1886)
EA/87*
HOBSON, Martin (d 1880 [47])
conductor EA/82*
HOBSON, Maud (d 1913) actress
BE*, WWT/14*
HOBSON, May (b 1889) English ac-
tress, singer WWT/4-6
HOBSON, Valerie (b 1917) Irish
actress ES
HOBY, Mrs. Charles J. see
Lynde, Flo
HOCHHUTH, Rolf (b 1931) German
dramatist CB, CH, COC, ES,
MH, MWD, PDT, RE, WWT/14-
16
HOCHULI, Paul (d 1964 [60]) jour-
nalist BE*
HOCHWÄLDER, Fritz (b 1911)
Austrian/Swiss dramatist COC,
PDT
HOCKENHULL, John Charles (d
1892 [41]) musician EA/93*
HOCKER, David (b 1911) American
talent representative BE
HOCKRIDGE, Edmund (b 1919)
Canadian actor, singer WWT/
12-15

HOCTOR, Harriet (b 1907) American dancer BE, WWT/8-10
HOCTOR, Robin (b 1953) American actor TW/29
HODAPP, Ann (b 1946) American actress TW/26-30
HODGDON, Samuel K. (d 1922 [69]) American vaudeville manager BE*, BP/6*
HODGE, Francis Richard (b 1915) American educator, director BE
HODGE, Merton [Horace Emerton Hodge] (1904-58) New Zealand dramatist WWT/8-11
HODGE, William Thomas (1874-1932) American actor, dramatist COC, DAB, OC/1-3, SR, WWA/1, WWM, WWT/3-6
HODGES, Ann American actress TW/28
HODGES, Ann Elizabeth (d 1871 [29]) singer EA/72*
HODGES, Mrs. Coppleson see Brougham, Mrs. John, I
HODGES, Eddie (b 1947) American actor, singer BE
HODGES, Horace (1865-1951) actor WWT/1-11
HODGES, J. A. (fl 1856) Canadian actor HAS
HODGES, Mrs. J. A. English actress HAS
HODGES, James (d 1881 [38]) journalist EA/82*
HODGES, Joy American actress TW/1-6, 29
HODGES, Nicholas (d 1884 [56]) manager EA/85*
HODGES, Thomas see Hogini, T.
HODGINS, Earle (d 1964 [65]) actor BE*
HODGKINSON, Frances see Hodgkinson, Mrs. John
HODGKINSON, John (c. 1765-1805) English actor, dramatist CDP, COC, DAB, EAP, HAS, OC/1-3, RJ, SR, WWA/H
HODGKINSON, Mrs. John [née Brett; ?= Arabella Brett, q. v.] (d 1803 [32]) English actress CDP, HAS
HODGKINSON, Marie see Clegg, Marie
HODGSON, Albert (d 1897) music-hall stage manager EA/98*
HODGSON, Alfred G. P. see

Paumier, Alfred
HODGSON, A. R. (d 1896 [47]) actor EA/98*
HODGSON, E. Miles (b 1889) English actor GRB/1
HODGSON, John (d 1888 [71]) EA/89*
HODGSON, William Wilson (d 1904) EA/05*
HODIAK, John (1914-55) American actor TW/8-10, 12
HODSON, Charles Henry see Stanley, Hodson
HODSON, George A. (d 1869 [47]) comedian, singer CDP
HODSON, Georgina Rosa (b 1830) Irish actress, singer CDP, HAS
HODSON, Henrietta [Mrs. Henry Labouchere] (1841-1910) English actress CDP, COC, DNB, OC/1-3, OAA/2
HODSON, James Landsdale (d 1956 [65]) English dramatist BE*, WWT/14*
HODSON, Kate [Mrs. Charles Fenton] (d 1917) actress OAA/2
HODSON, Nellie (d 1940) actress BE*, WWT/14*
HODSON, Sylvia [Mrs. John S. Blythe] (d 1893) actress BE*, EA/94*, WWT/14*
HODSON, William (fl 1775-83) dramatist CP/2, GT, TD/1-2
HOELBURG, Franz (d 1965 [79]) performer BP/49*
HOENY, A. Winfield American actor TW/1
HOERLE, Helen (d 1966 [65]) press agent BP/50*
HOET, Mrs. Peter see Davenport, Hester
HOEY, Dennis [Samuel David Hyams] (1893-1960) English actor, singer WWT/8-12
HOEY, Iris (b 1885) English actress WWT/1-13
HOEY, James F. (1851-1924) actor, minstrel CDP
HOEY, Mrs. John [Josephine Shaw] (1822/24-96) English actress CDP, HAS, SR
HOEY, Josephine see Hoey, Mrs. John
HOEY, W. H. (d 1970 [76]) performer BP/55*
HOEY, William F. (1855-97) actor, performer CDP, SR
HOFER, Chris (d 1964 [44]) Amer-

ican press representative,
actor BE*

HOFF, Louise (b 1921) American
actress, singer, dancer BE

HOFF, Robin (b 1952) American
actress TW/30

HOFFE, Barbara [Barbara Con-
rad] actress WWT/4-9

HOFFE, Monckton [Reaney
Monckton Hoffe-Miles] (1880-
1951) Irish dramatist, actor
WWT/2-11, WWW/5

HOFFE-MILES, Reaney Monckton
see Hoffe, Monckton

HOFFMAN, Aaron (1880-1924)
American dramatist WWM,
WWT/4

HOFFMAN, Bill (d 1962 [44])
American dramatist BE*

HOFFMAN, Charles H. (d 1972
[60]) producer/director/
choreographer BP/56*

HOFFMAN, Dustin (b 1937)
American actor AAS, CB,
TW/23, 25, WWT/15-16

HOFFMAN, Ferdi actor TW/1,
4, 18, 21, 23

HOFFMAN, Frederick (d 1887)
music-hall proprietor EA/88*

HOFFMAN, Gertrude (d 1966
[80]) Canadian dancer TW/23

HOFFMAN, Howard R. (d 1969
[76]) performer BP/54*

HOFFMAN, Irving (d 1968 [59])
critic BP/53*

HOFFMAN, Jane American actress BE, TW/2, 13, 19-21,
25-29, WWT/15-16

HOFFMAN, Lloyd (d 1973 [62])
publicist BP/57*

HOFFMAN, Maud American
actress GRB/1-4, WWS,
WWT/1-5

HOFFMAN, Max (d 1963 [88])
German musical director
TW/19

HOFFMAN, Max, Jr. (d 1945
[c. 42]) American actor TW/1

HOFFMAN, Theodore (b 1922)
American educator, dramatist
BE

HOFFMAN, William M. (b 1939)
American dramatist, director,
actor CD

HOFFMANN, Hermine H. (d
1971 [47]) performer BP/56*

HOFFMANN, Mrs. Maurice H.
see Irving, Sydney

HOFLICH, Lucie (d 1956 [73]) actress BE*, WWT/14*

HOFMAN, Elsbeth (b 1918) American actress TW/2

HOFMANN, Josef (b 1877) musician
CDP

HOFMEISTER, Caroline CDP

HOFPAUER, Max (fl 1890) German
actor CDP

HOGAN, Babette Hilda see Warren, Betty

HOGAN, Charlie (d 1970 [67])
agent BP/55*

HOGAN, John P. (b 1847) dancer,
minstrel CDP

HOGAN, Jonathan (b 1951) American
actor TW/29-30

HOGAN, Michael (b 1898) English
actor WWT/7-10

HOGARTH, George (d 1870 [86])
writer EA/71*

HOGARTH, Lionel (1874-1946)
American actor TW/2

HOGARTH, Vladimir [A. E. Moore]
(b 1876) English singer GRB/1

HOGARTH, William (d 1899 [55])
singer, manager BE*, EA/00*,
WWT/14*

HOGG, Miss see Claude, Mrs.

HOGG, Curly (d 1974 [57]) performer BP/59*

HOGG, Ian (b 1937) English actor
AAS, WWT/15-16

HOGG, John (1770-1813) English
actor HAS

HOGG, Mrs. John [Ann Storer] (d
1816 [67]) actress HAS

HOGG, Mary Anne [Mrs. Wentworth
Hogg] (d 1907 [58]) EA/08*

HOGG, Mrs. Wentworth see
Hogg, Mary Anne

HOGGAN-ARMADALE, E. (d 1917)
actor, dramatist EA/18*

HOGGETT, Henry (d 1881 [55])
acrobat EA/82*

HOGINI, Mrs. Harry (d 1895)
EA/96*

HOGINI, T. [Thomas Hodges] (d
1893) acrobat EA/94*

HOHLER, Thomas Theobald (d
1892) singer EA/93*

HOHNSTOCK, Adele (fl 1849) actress HAS

HOHNSTOCK, Charles (fl 1849)
actor HAS

HOIER, Thomas P. (d 1951 [74])
Danish performer BE*, BP/36*

HOKER, John (d c. 1548) dramatist

CP/2-3
HOLBERG, Ludvig (1684-1754)
Norwegian dramatist COC
HOLBROOK, Ann Catherine (1780-1837) actress DNB
HOLBROOK, E. G. C. (d 1943)
business manager WWT/14*
HOLBROOK, Hal (b 1916/25)
American actor AAS, BE,
CB, TW/18-25, 28, WWT/15-16
HOLBROOK, Joseph Charles (d 1870 [41]) circus proprietor
EA/71*
HOLBROOK, Louise actress
WWT/1-7
HOLBROOK, Ruby (d 1975 [63])
performer BP/60*
HOLBROOK, William (d 1971
[70s]) performer BP/56*
HOLBROOKE, Josef (1878-1958)
English musician WWW/5
HOLCOMB, Marion actress,
singer HAS
HOLCOMBE, Herbert (d 1908)
singer, vaudevillian CDP
HOLCOMBE, Ray Edward (b 1898)
American educator, director,
dramatist BE
HOLCOMBE, Thomas (d 1625?)
actor DA
HOLCROFT, Thomas (1744-1809)
English dramatist, actor
CDP, COC, CP/2-3, DNB,
ES, GT, HP, NTH, OC/1-3,
TD/1-2
HOLDEN, Mr. (fl 1662-65) dramatist CP/2-3
HOLDEN, Mr. (fl 1799) dramatist
CP/3
HOLDEN, Fay (d 1973 [79]) performer BP/58*, WWT/16*
HOLDEN, Hal (b 1938) American
actor TW/25
HOLDEN, James (b 1923) American actor TW/4, 10-12
HOLDEN, Jan [née Wilkinson] (b
1931) English actress WWT/
15-16
HOLDEN, John (d 1879 [63])
marionette exhibitor EA/80*
HOLDEN, John (d 1899 [58])
marionette proprietor EA/00*
HOLDEN, John (d 1967) producer/director/choreographer
BP/52*
HOLDEN, Mrs. John see
Holden, Louisa
HOLDEN, Louisa [Mrs. John

Holden] (d 1891) EA/92*
HOLDER, G. B. see Howard,
Rollin
HOLDER, Geoffrey (b 1930/31)
West Indian dancer, choreographer, singer BE, CB, WWT/
16
HOLDER, Henry (d 1880 [69])
music-hall proprietor EA/81*
HOLDER, Owen (b 1921) English
actor TW/4, WWT/12-16
HOLDRIDGE, Barbara (b 1929)
American producer BE
HOLDSWORTH, Camilla (d 1897
[43]) sketch artist EA/98*
HOLE, Rev. Donald (d 1947 [79])
WWT/14*
HOLE, Richard (fl 1526-30) actor
DA
HOLFORD, Mrs. M. (fl 1799)
dramatist CP/3
HOLGATE, Ronald (b 1937) American actor TW/17, 22-23, 25-28
HOLGMAN, Benjamin (d 1963 [72])
press agent BP/47*
HOLIDAY, Dr. Barten (d 1661)
English dramatist CP/1-3, FGF
HOLIDAY, Billie (d 1959 [44])
American singer BE*
HOLIDAY, George see Glennie,
Herbert
HOLL, Henry (d 1884 [73]) actor,
dramatist CDP
HOLLAND, Mr. actor TD/2
HOLLAND, Mr. (fl early 19th
cent) actor CDP
HOLLAND, Aaron (fl 1605) theatre
builder DA
HOLLAND, Alice (fl 1868?) CDP
HOLLAND, Anthony (b 1912) English designer WWT/14-16
HOLLAND, Anthony (b 1933) American actor BE, TW/25-28
HOLLAND, Betty Lou (b 1931)
American actress BE, TW/2-4
HOLLAND, Charles (1733-69) English actor CDP, DNB, GT,
TD/1-2
HOLLAND, Charles (1768-1849?)
English actor DNB, GT, TD/1
HOLLAND, C. Maurice (d 1974)
producer/director/choreographer
BP/59*
HOLLAND, Edmund Milton (1848-
1913) English actor CDP, DAB,
GRB/2-4, OC/1-3, PP/1,
WWA/1, WWM, WWS, WWT/
1-2

HOLLAND, Edwin Clifford (1794-1824) American dramatist EAP, RJ

HOLLAND, Mrs. E. M. see Seward, Emily

HOLLAND, Fanny [Mrs. Arthur Law] (1847-1931) English actress, singer CDP, GRB/1-3, WWW/3

HOLLAND, George (1791-1870) English actor, promoter CDP, COC, DAB, GC, HAS, OC/1-3, SR, WWA/H

HOLLAND, George (d 1910 [63/64]) American actor BE*, EA/11*, WWT/14*

HOLLAND, John (fl 1590) actor DA

HOLLAND, Joseph Jefferson (1860-1926) English actor DAB, OC/1-3, SR, WWA/1

HOLLAND, J. Talbot (b 1928) American actor TW/12

HOLLAND, Mildred (1869-1944) actress CDP, GRB/3-4, SR, WWM, WWT/1-3

HOLLAND, R. V. (b 1916) American educator BE

HOLLAND, Samuel (fl 1656) dramatist CP/2-3

HOLLAND, Theodore (1878-1947) composer WWW/4

HOLLAND, Vyvyan (d 1967 [80]) dramatist BP/52*

HOLLAND, W. A. (fl 1806) dramatist CP/3

HOLLAND, William (d 1895 [58]) manager, caterer EA/97*, WWT/14*

HOLLANDER, Frederick (d 1976 [79]) composer BP/60*

HOLLANDER, Jack (b 1918) American actor TW/22-26, 29-30

HOLLENDER, Count Max (d 1906 [51]) director EA/07*

HOLLES, Antony (1901-50) English actor WWT/4-10

HOLLES, Robert dramatist CD

HOLLES, William (1867-1947) English actor, producer, manager GRB/1-3, WWT/4-8

HOLLICK, W. F. (d 1899) music-hall stage manager EA/00*

HOLLIDAY, Bob (b 1932) American actor TW/22-23

HOLLIDAY, David (b 1937) American actor TW/25-28

HOLLIDAY, Judy (1921/22/23-65) American actress, singer BE, CB, ES, TW/1-20, 22, WWA/4, WWT/11-13

HOLLIDAY, Marjorie (d 1969 [49]) performer BP/54*

HOLLIDAY, Polly American actress TW/29

HOLLINGSHEAD, Austin (d 1941 [64]) business manager WWT/14*

HOLLINGSHEAD, Bessie (d 1915) actress CDP

HOLLINGSHEAD, John (1827-1904) English dramatist, manager CDP, COC, DNB, EA/69, GRB/1, OC/1-3, WWW/1

HOLLINGSHEAD, Mrs. John see Hollingshead, Mrs. M.

HOLLINGSHEAD, John Edward (d 1902 [44]) acting manager, treasurer, business manager EA/03*

HOLLINGSHEAD, Mrs. M. [Mrs. John Hollingshead] (d 1890 [67]) EA/91*

HOLLINGSWORTH, Mr. (fl 1788) actor TD/1-2

HOLLINGSWORTH, Alfred (d 1926 [52]) actor BE*, BP/11*

HOLLINGSWORTH, Mrs. C. S. [Mrs. T. R. Hollingsworth] (d 1875) EA/76*

HOLLINGSWORTH, George (d 1892 [63]) EA/93*

HOLLINGSWORTH, Mrs. T. R. see Hollingsworth, Mrs. C. S.

HOLLINS, Henry Harrison (d 1882 [50]) bandmaster EA/83*

HOLLINS, Mabel (b 1887) English actress WWS

HOLLIS, John (d 1878) Negro comedian EA/79*

HOLLISTER, Louis (b 1921) American actor TW/5-7

HOLLISTER, Paul M. (d 1970 [79]) publicist BP/55*

HOLLISTER, Walter (d 1905 [44]) acting manager GRB/1

HOLLMAN, Carl (d 1879 [23]) musician, composer EA/81*

HOLLOWAY, Miss (fl 1804) actress TD/2

HOLLOWAY, Baliol (1883-1967) English actor AAS, WWT/4-11, WWW/6

HOLLOWAY, Catherine [Mrs. Henry Holloway] (d 1880 [34]) EA/81*

HOLLOWAY, Edmund (d 1906 [85])

Australian actor EA/07*

HOLLOWAY, Mrs. Edmund (d 1887) Australian actress EA/88*

HOLLOWAY, Mrs. Henry see Holloway, Catherine

HOLLOWAY, James (d 1879 [60]) actor CDP

HOLLOWAY, Jean (b 1929) American actress TW/13-14

HOLLOWAY, John (d 1871) actor EA/72*

HOLLOWAY, John (d 1878 [24]) clown, vaulter EA/79*

HOLLOWAY, John J. (d 1890 [22]) EA/91*

HOLLOWAY, Stanley (b 1890) English actor, singer AAS, BE, CB, ES, TW/12-14, WWT/6-16

HOLLOWAY, Sterling American actor BE

HOLLOWAY, W. E. (1885-1952) Australian actor WWT/9-11

HOLLOWAY, William (d 1893) clown EA/94*

HOLLOWAY, William Edward (d 1903 [37]) circus performer EA/04*

HOLLOWAY, W. J. (d 1913) English actor, producer GRB/1-4

HOLLY, Ellen (b 1931) American actress BE, TW/29-30

HOLLY, John (b 1944) American actor TW/30

HOLLYWOOD, Daniel (b 1914) Irish producer, literary representative BE

HOLM, Cecil (b 1904) American actor, dramatist WWT/9-11

HOLM, Celeste (b 1919) American actress, singer AAS, BE, TW/1-20, 24-26, WWT/10-16

HOLM, Dolores (d 1976 [69]) designer BP/60*

HOLM, Hanya [née Johanna Eckert] (b 1898) German/American dancer, choreographer, director BE, CB, ES, TW/5-8, WWT/15-16

HOLM, Ian [né Ian Holm Cuthbert] (b 1931) English actor AAS, WWT/14-16

HOLM, John Cecil (b 1904) American actor, dramatist, director BE, MD, MWD,

TW/20, 22-23, 25-27, WWT/12-16

HOLM, Klaus (b 1920) German designer BE

HOLMAN, Agnes see Gilfert, Mrs. Charles

HOLMAN, Benjamin (d 1864 [22]) comedian HAS

HOLMAN, George (fl 1836) American singer HAS

HOLMAN, Mrs. George [Harriet Phillips] (fl 1838) American singer HAS

HOLMAN, Gertrude [Mrs. Sydney Smith] (d 1912) EA/13*

HOLMAN, Joseph George (1764-1817) English actor, dramatist CDP, CP/3, DNB, GT, HAS, TD/1-2

HOLMAN, Mrs. Joseph George [Miss Lattimer] (d 1859) English actress CDP, HAS

HOLMAN, Julia (d 1879 [31]) American singer, actress CDP

HOLMAN, Libby (1906-71) American actress, singer BE, TW/2-3, 28, WWT/9-11

HOLMAN, Mary see Holman, Mrs. Joseph George

HOLMAN, Sally see Dalton, Mrs. James T.

HOLMAN, Sandra (b 1928) American actress TW/2

HOLMAN, Sonja (b 1949) American actress TW/25

HOLMAN, Thomas (fl 1629) actor DA

HOLMAN, Mrs. W. see Burney, Miss

HOLME, Constance (d 1955) dramatist WWW/5

HOLME, Myra [Lady A. W. Pinero] (d 1919) actress OAA/2

HOLME, Stanford (b 1904) French actor, producer WWT/8-13

HOLME, Thea (b 1907) English actress WWT/7-16

HOLMES, Alfred (d 1876) composer EA/77*

HOLMES, Alfred Miles (d 1917) door-keeper EA/18*

HOLMES, Basil Ralph Gardiner (d 1917) actor EA/18*

HOLMES, Brenda (b 1954) American actress TW/30

HOLMES, Burton (1870-1958) American lecturer TW/15

HOLMES, Charles W. (b 1846)

American actor HAS
HOLMES, E. B. (b 1840) Ameri-
can actor HAS
HOLMES, Edward (d 1885 [48])
music-hall manager EA/86*
HOLMES, Florence (d 1917)
EA/18*
HOLMES, Helen (1892-1950)
American actress WWT/4-7
HOLMES, Henry (d 1883) music-
hall performer? EA/85*
HOLMES, Jack (b 1932) American
composer, lyricist, musical
director, conductor, singer
BE
HOLMES, Jerry (b 1938) Ameri-
can actor TW/23
HOLMES, Mrs. John see
Holmes, Sarah Eliza
HOLMES, Mjr. Know (d 1893
[85]) actor EA/94*
HOLMES, Morrice [James Mor-
rice Orr] (d 1909 [59]) EA/10*
HOLMES, Phillips (1909-42)
American actor CB, WWA/2
HOLMES, Ralph (d 1945 [30])
American actor TW/2
HOLMES, Robert (1899-1945)
English actor WWT/6-9
HOLMES, Sarah Eliza [Mrs.
John Holmes] (d 1890 [54])
EA/91*
HOLMES, S. F. R. (d 1847)
actor HAS
HOLMES, Stuart (d 1971 [87])
performer BP/56*
HOLMES, Taylor (1872/78-1959)
American actor TW/2-7, 16,
WWM, WWT/6-11
HOLMES, Thomas (b 1816) actor
CDP
HOLMES, Mrs. Thomas (d 1893
[69]) EA/94*
HOLMES, T. W. (d 1887 [28])
EA/88*
HOLMES, Wendell (d 1962 [47])
actor BE*
HOLMES, William (1840-66)
American comic singer HAS
HOLMES, W. M. (d 1888 [72])
EA/90*
HOLMES-GORE, Arthur (1871-
1915) English actor WWT/1-3
HOLMES-GORE, Dorothy (1896-
1977) English actress WWT/
4-9
HOLSTON, William (d 1876 [45])
English actor HAS

HOLT, Abe (d 1904 [42]) comedian
EA/05*
HOLT, Alice [Mrs. Clarance H.]
(d 1895 [44]) actress EA/96*
HOLT, Clarance (1826-1903) Eng-
lish actor OAA/2
HOLT, Mrs. Clarance (d 1878) ac-
tress EA/79*
HOLT, Mrs. Clarance H. see
Holt, Alice
HOLT, Clarence (d 1920) actor
BE*, BP/5*
HOLT, Elise (1847-73) English
dancer, actress CDP, HAS
HOLT, Elizabeth Ruth (d 1912)
actress? EA/13*
HOLT, Ellen Alice see Brown,
Nellie
HOLT, Francis Ludlow (fl 1805-10)
dramatist CP/3
HOLT, Harold (d 1953 [67]) im-
presario BE*, WWT/14*
HOLT, Hettie [Mrs. Will Harvey]
(d 1911 [34]) EA/12*
HOLT, Issy [Mrs. H. F. Tyrrell]
(d 1893 [26]) music-hall per-
former EA/94*
HOLT, Jack (1888-1951) American
actor BE*
HOLT, James (fl 1603-19) actor
DA
HOLT, John (fl 1561) actor DA
HOLT, John (d 1901 [57]) director
EA/02*
HOLT, Marshall (d 1917) performer
EA/18*
HOLT, Maud see Tree, Maud
Beerbohm
HOLT, Nat (d 1971 [78]) manager
BP/56*
HOLT, Richard (d 1867 [41]) pro-
fessor of music EA/68*
HOLT, Richard (1867-1931) Ameri-
can critic WWA/1
HOLT, Stella (d 1967 [50]) Ameri-
can producer, manager BE,
TW/24
HOLT, Tim (d 1973 [54]) performer
BP/57*
HOLTUM (fl 1875?) cannon-ball
catcher CDP
HOLTZ, Lou (b 1898) American
actor BE, WWT/9-11
HOLTZMANN, David Marshall (1908-
65) American producer, lawyer
BE
HOLZAGER, Toni Ward (d 1973
[66]) designer BP/58*

HOLZER, Adela producer WWT/
16
HOLZHEW, Behrendt (fl 1614-15)
actor DA
HOLZMAN, Benjamin F. (d 1963
[72]) talent representative,
press representative BE*
HOLZMAN, Samuel (d 1972 [80])
amusement park operator
BP/57*
HOMAN, David (b 1907) Norwegian
designer WWT/9-13
HOMAN, Gertrude (d 1951 [71])
actress TW/8
HOME, Rev. John (1722-1808)
Scottish dramatist CDP, COC,
CP/1-3, DNB, ES, GT, HP,
OC/1-3, SR, TD/1-2
HOME, North Dalrymple (d
1887 [30]) singer EA/88*
HOME, William Douglas (b 1912)
Scottish dramatist, actor
AAS, BE, CD, CH, COC,
ES, MD, MWD, PDT, WWT/
11-16
HOMER, Benjamin (d 1975 [57])
composer/lyricist BP/59*
HOMER, Louise Dilworth Beatty
(1871-1947) American singer
DAB, TW/3, WWA/2, WWW/4
HOMEWOOD, A[shley] S[pencer]
(b 1869) English actor GRB/
1-2
HOMEWOOD, Mrs. A[shley]
S[pencer] see Blair, Joan
HOMFRAY, Emma Sophia see
Sterling, Ella
HOMFREY, Gladys (d 1932 [83])
actress WWT/2-5
HOMOLKA, Oscar (b 1898/1903)
Austrian actor BE, TW/1-6,
WWT/8-14
HONE, Mary (d 1909) EA/10*
HONE, Mary (b 1904) American
actress WWT/7-10
HONER, Mary (b 1914) English
dancer WWT/9-11
HONEY, George (d 1905 [40])
actor GRB/1, OAA/1-2
HONEY, George Alfred (1822/
23-80) actor, singer CDP,
DNB
HONEY, Laura (1816?-43) actress,
singer CDP, DNB
HONEY, Laura (fl 1858) English
actress HAS
HONEY, Sam see Sherar, John
HONIG, Edwin (b 1919) American

educator, translator, critic BE
HONIG, Gale (b 1956) American ac-
tress TW/24
HONNAN, Richard (fl 1640) actor
DA
HONNER, Adele (fl 1852?) singer
CDP
HONNER, Maria see Honer,
Mrs. Robert William
HONNER, Robert William (1809-52)
English actor CDP
HONNER, Mrs. Robert William
(1808/12-70) Irish actress CDP,
DNB
HONNOR, Mrs. R. see Morton,
Mrs. F.
HONRI, Percy [Percy Harry Thomp-
son] (1874-1953) English musical
entertainer CDP, GRB/1
HONYMAN, John (1613-36) English
actor DA, OC/1-3
HONYMAN, Richard (b 1618) Eng-
lish actor OC/1-3
HOOD, Cpt. Basil (1864-1917) Eng-
lish dramatist GRB/1-4, WWT/
1-3, WWW/2
HOOD, Henry Lionel (d 1879 [45])
actor EA/80*
HOOD, John (b 1831) American
actor HAS
HOOD, John D. (fl 1900) singer,
minstrel CDP
HOOD, Marion (d 1912 [59]) ac-
tress, singer DP
HOOD, Sydney Paxton see
Paxton, Sydney
HOOK, Miss (fl 1782) actress
TD/1-2
HOOK, Alfred H. (b 1879) English
acting manager GRB/1
HOOK, Mrs. Alfred H. see
Kearns, Rosie
HOOK, James (1746-1827) English
musician, composer, musical
director CDP, ES
HOOK, Rev. Dr. James (fl 1795-
97) dramatist CP/3, GT, TD/
1-2
HOOK, Mrs. James [née Madden]
(d 1805) dramatist CP/3
HOOK, Nellie (d 1966 [80]) per-
former BP/50*
HOOK, Theodore Edward (1788-
1842) dramatist CDP, CP/3,
GT
HOOKER, Brian (1880-1946) Amer-
ican actor, librettist HJD,
TW/3, WWM

HOOKHAM, Margaret see Fonteyn, Margot

HOOKS, David (b 1920) American actor, director BE, TW/28-29

HOOKS, Robert (b 1937) American actor, producer, director CB, TW/22-24, 26, 30, WWT/16

HOOLE, Charles (1610-66) English dramatist CP/2-3

HOOLE, John (1727-1803) English dramatist CP/2-3, GT, TD/1-2

HOOLEY, Richard M. (1822-93) Irish musician, manager CDP, HAS, SR

HOOPE, Richard (fl 1595?) actor? DA

HOOPER, Edward (d 1865 [70]) actor, lessee, manager CDP

HOOPER, Ewan (b 1935) Scottish actor, director, manager AAS, WWT/15-16

HOOPER, F. Pitman (d 1892 [31]) EA/93*

HOOVER, Richard A. (d 1973 [59]) BP/58*

HOPE, Adele Blood (d 1936 [50]) actress, promoter BE*, BP/21*

HOPE, Anthony [Anthony Hawkins] (1863-1933) English dramatist GRB/2, WWM, WWT/1-7

HOPE, Bob (b 1903) English/American actor, producer BE, CB, ES, SR, WWT/9-10

HOPE, Carrie Sydney [Mrs. W. H. Hallatt] (d 1887) actress NYM

HOPE, Charlotte [Charlotte Elizabeth Young] (d 1891 [26]) EA/92*

HOPE, Douglas (d 1975 [82]) performer BP/60*

HOPE, Eric see Yarmouth, Earl of

HOPE, Ethel [Mrs. E. B. Norman] (d 1899 [49]) actress CDP

HOPE, Evelyn (d 1966) English actress WWT/6-9

HOPE, Francis James (d 1975 [84]) performer BP/60*

HOPE, Henry Jenner (d 1897 [55]) musician EA/98*

HOPE, Mabel Ellams (d 1937) dramatist BE*, WWT/14*

HOPE, Maidie (1881-1937) English actress WWT/2-8

HOPE, Mrs. Stanley see Thearle, Nellie

HOPE, Vida (1918-63) English actress, singer WWT/11-13

HOPER, Mrs. [née Harford] (fl 1748-49) dramatist CP/1-3, GT, TD/1-2

HOPE-WALLACE, Philip A. (b 1911) critic AAS, WWT/11-16

HOPKINS, Mr. (fl 1799) actor HAS

HOPKINS, Mrs. (d 1801) actress CDP, TD/1-2

HOPKINS, Miss (fl 1771?) actress CDP, TD/1-2

HOPKINS, Miss see Kemble, Mrs. John Philip

HOPKINS, Albert (d 1889 [35]) gymnast EA/90*

HOPKINS, Anthony (b 1937) Welsh actor AAS, WWT/15-16

HOPKINS, Arthur (1878-1950) American manager, dramatist, producer CB, NTH, TW/2-6, WWT/4-10

HOPKINS, Bob (d 1962 [44]) actor BE*

HOPKINS, Bruce (b 1948) American actor TW/30

HOPKINS, Charles (d c.1700) English dramatist CP/1-3, GT

HOPKINS, Charles (1884-1953) American actor, producing manager TW/9, WWT/6-11

HOPKINS, Cherry Preisser (d 1964 [46]) performer BP/49*

HOPKINS, Henry C. (d 1876 [32]) equestrian agent EA/77*

HOPKINS, Joan (b 1915) English actress WWT/11

HOPKINS, John (b 1931) English dramatist CD

HOPKINS, Miriam (1902/04-72) American actress BE, ES, NTH, TW/1-8, 29, WWA/5, WWT/6-14

HOPKINS, Richard (d 1881) actor EA/82*

HOPKINSON, Francis (1737-91) American dramatist EAP

HOPKINSON, Thomas (1709-51) English/American dramatist EAP

HOPPER, Bernhard (d 1877) composer EA/78*

HOPPER, Charles H. (d 1916 [53]) actor, singer CDP

HOPPER, De Wolf (1858-1938)

American actor, singer CDP,
COC, DAB, GRB/2-4, NTH,
OC/1-3, SR, WWA/1, WWM,
WWS, WWT/1-7

HOPPER, Mrs. De Wolf see
Bergen, Nella

HOPPER, Edna Wallace (1864/74-
1959) American actress, singer
CDP, GRB/2-4, NTH, TW/16,
WWA/3, WWM, WWS, WWT/
1-7

HOPPER, E. Mason (d 1967
[82]) performer BP/51*

HOPPER, Hedda [née Edna Furry]
(1890-1966) American actress,
singer SR, TW/22

HOPPER, Rika (d 1963 [86]) actress BE*

HOPPER, Victoria (b 1909) Canadian actress, singer WWT/
8-14

HOPPER, William (d 1970 [55])
performer BP/54*

HOPWOOD, Avery (1882-1928)
American dramatist DAB,
GRB/3-4, HJD, MH, MWD,
WWA/1, WWM, WWT/1-5,
WWW/2

HORAN, Edward (b 1898) American composer WWT/10-13

HORD, John (d 1876 [64]) actor,
manager EA/77*

HORDE, Thomas, Jr. (fl 1769-
84) dramatist CP/2-3, GT

HORDEN, Hildebrand (d 1696)
actor, dramatist CP/1-3,
GT, WWT/11-16

HORDERN, Michael (b 1911) English actor AAS, WWT/11-16

HOREN, Bob (b 1925) American
actor TW/25-26

HOREN, Leah (b 1942) American
actress TW/25, 28

HORGAN, Patrick (b 1929) English actor TW/30

HORINE, Kathryn Kunkel (d 1965
[56]) performer BP/50*

HORITZ, Joseph F. (d 1961
[87]) performer BE*

HORKHEIMER, Herbert M. (d
1962 [80]) producer BE*

HORMAN, Nora (d 1916) EA/17*

HORMAN, W. E. (d 1875 [48])
EA/76*

HORMANN, Nicholas (b 1944)
American actor TW/30

HORN, Charles Edward (1786-
1849) English actor, singer,

composer BS, CDP, HAS, OX,
WWA/H

HORN, Mrs. Charles Edward, I
see Horn, Matilda

HORN, Mrs. Charles E[dward], II
[Miss Horton] (d 1887 [76]?)
English actress CDP, HAS

HORN, Eph (1818-77) American
minstrel CDP, HAS, SR

HORN, H. C. (fl 1842) composer,
conductor SR

HORN, James (fl 1625) actor DA

HORN, Mrs. James see Reeve,
Joey

HORN, Kate see Buckland, Mrs.
John W.

HORN, Leonard (d 1975 [48]) pro-
ducer/director/choreographer
BP/60*

HORN, Mary (b 1916) Scottish actress WWT/11-12

HORN, Mary Ann see Horn,
Mrs. Charles Edward

HORN, Matilda [Mrs. Charles
Edward Horn, I] (b 1790) English actress CDP, OX

HORNBLOW, Arthur (1865/68-1942)
English writer CB, ES, GRB/
3, SR, WWA/2

HORNBLOW, Juliette Crosby (d
1969 [73]) performer BP/53*

HORNBY, Kate see Phillips,
Harriett

HORNCASTLE, Henry see Horncastle, James Henry

HORNCASTLE, James Henry (1801-
69) English actor, singer CDP,
HAS

HORNE, Alderson Burrell see
Hall, Anmer

HORNE, A. P. business manager,
actor WWT/6-8

HORNE, David (d 1869 [27]) scene
artist EA/70*

HORNE, David (1898-1970) English
actor WWT/6-14

HORNE, F. Lennox (d 1874 [67])
dramatist EA/75*

HORNE, Geoffrey (b 1933) Argen-
tinian/American actor BE

HORNE, John (fl 1677) dramatist
CP/3

HORNE, Kenneth (1900-75) English
dramatist AAS, WWT/8-15

HORNE, Lena (b 1917) American
performer BE, CB

HORNE, Marilyn (b 1934) American
singer CB, ES

HORNE, Richard Hengist (1803-84) English dramatist CDP, HP
HORNE, Rev. Thomas (d 1918 [68]) EA/19*
HORNE, Mrs. W. see Evans, May
HORNE, William actor TW/1
HORNER, Harry (d 1917 [44]) EA/18*
HORNER, Harry (b 1910/12) Czech/American director, scene designer BE, ES, TW/3-5
HORNER, James (d 1892 [43]) EA/93*
HORNER, Jed (b 1922) American director BE
HORNER, Lottie (d 1964) talent representative BE*
HORNER, Richard (b 1920) American manager, producer BE, WWT/16
HORNIMAN, Annie Elizabeth Fredericka (1860-1937) English manager AAS, COC, DNB, ES, GRB/4, HP, NTH, OC/1-3, PDT, WWT/1-8, WWW/3
HORNIMAN, Roy (1872-1930) English dramatist GRB/4, WWT/1-6, WWW/3
HORNSBY, Nancy (1910-58) English actress WWT/8-11
HORNUNG, E. W. (b 1866) English dramatist WWM
HOROVITZ, Israel (b 1939) American dramatist, director CD, CH, WWT/15-16
HORREY, Frederick (b 1921) English actor TW/3
HORRIGAN, John P. (d 1973 [47]) publicist BP/58*
HORROCKS, Joseph R. (d 1912 [45]) scene artist EA/13*
HORROX, John (d 1868 [47]) proprietor EA/69*
HORROX, Willie see Hartill, Willie
HORSFALL, John Thomas (d 1902 [52]) musician, composer EA/03*
HORSFORD, Anna Maria (b 1947) American actress TW/26, 30
HORSFORD, Arthur J. (d 1877) scene artist EA/78*
HORSLEY, Charles Edward (d 1876 [51]) musician EA/77*
HORSLEY, William (1774-1858) musician, composer CDP
HORSLEY-BERESFORD, Hon. Mrs. W. W. see Gordon, Kitty
HORSMAN, Charles (1825-86) Welsh actor OAA/1-2
HORSMAN, Mrs. Charles see Horsman, Charlotte
HORSMAN, Charlotte [Mrs. Charles Horsman] (d 1878 [50]) actress EA/79*
HORSNELL, Horace (1882/83-1949) English critic, dramatist WWT/9-10, WWW/4
HORSPOOL, J. (b 1856) English composer GRB/1-3
HORST, Louis (1884-1964) American composer, dance teacher WWA/4
HORTON, Mrs. (fl 1713) actress TD/2
HORTON, Miss see Horn, Mrs. Charles E[dward], II
HORTON, Bessie see Love, Bessie
HORTON, Christiana (1696?-1756?) actress DNB
HORTON, Claude English actor TW/8, 28
HORTON, Edward (fl 1630) actor DA
HORTON, Edward Everett (1886/87-1970) American actor, manager, producer BE, CB, TW/7-8, 22, 27, WWA/5, WWT/7-14
HORTON, F. C. (d 1867 [52]) musical librarian EA/68*
HORTON, George (d 1888 [66]) professor of music EA/89*
HORTON, George (d 1908 [83]) professor of music EA/09*
HORTON, James (d 1879 [25]) advance agent EA/80*
HORTON, Jane [Mrs. Walter Horton] (d 1892) EA/93*
HORTON, J. W. (d 1889 [49]) librarian EA/90*
HORTON, Lester (1906-53) American dancer, choreographer ES
HORTON, Priscilla see Reed, Priscilla
HORTON, Robert (b 1870/76) English actor WWT/5-8
HORTON, Russell (b 1941) American actor TW/24, 27
HORTON, Mrs. Walter see Horton, Jane
HORTON, W. F. (1817-87) singer NYM
HORTON, William (d 1892 [39])

musical director EA/93*

HORTON, William Charles (d 1894 [73]) actor EA/95*

HORTOP, Jack (d 1970 [57]) tour manager BP/55*

HORWIN, C. Jerome (d 1954 [49]) American dramatist BE*, BP/38*

HORWITT, Arnold B. (b 1918) American lyricist, sketch writer BE

HORWITZ, Charles (b 1864) American dramatist WWM

HORWOOD, Lena [Mrs. C. E. T. Henderson] (d 1905 [27]) EA/06*

HORWOOD, Thomas (d 1878) musical black clown EA/79*

HOSKING, Arthur (d 1970 [96]) composer/lyricist BP/55*

HOSKINS, Ben (d 1876 [36]) comic singer EA/77*

HOSKINS, Bob (b 1942) English actor WWT/16

HOSKINS, Maurice (d 1917) musician EA/18*

HOSKINS, William (d 1886 [70]) actor CDP

HOSKWITH, Arnold K. (b 1917) American talent representative BE

HOSMER, Adele (fl 1852?) singer CDP

HOSMER, Jean [Jean Stanley] (1842-90) American actress CDP, HAS

HOSMER, William Henry Cuyler (1814-77) American dramatist EAP

HOTCHKISS, Mrs. Sterne (fl 1859) actress HAS

HOTINE, Mrs. (d 1890 [99]) EA/92*

HOTINE, John (d 1904 [64]) animal trainer EA/05*

HOTINE, Mary (d 1890) EA/91*

HOTTENTOT VENUS exhibit CDP

HOTVEDT, Phyllis Shaw (d 1964 [53]) actress BE*

HOTZ, Mr. (fl 1829) American singer HAS

HOUDIN, Robert (d 1871 [66]) conjuror EA/72*

HOUDINI, Harry (1872-1926) American magician NTH, SR, WWA/1

HOUGH, Mrs. G. A. (d 1854

[36]) actress? HAS

HOUGH, J. (fl 1778) dramatist CP/2-3, GT

HOUGH, Lotty (fl 1862-63) actress, singer HAS

HOUGH, W. actor, prompter TD/2

HOUGH, Mrs. W. H. (b 1833) American actress HAS

HOUGH, William (fl 1806?) tutor CDP

HOUGH, Will M. (d 1962 [80]) librettist, lyricist BE*, BP/47*

HOUGHTON, Belle (d 1964 [95]) performer BE*

HOUGHTON, Charles G. (d 1869) manager EA/70*

HOUGHTON, Genevieve (d 1974 [78]) actress, singer, vaudevillian BP/59*, WWT/16*

HOUGHTON, Rev. George C. (d 1923) BP/7*

HOUGHTON, Katharine (b 1945) American actress TW/22, 25-26

HOUGHTON, Mary Anne (d 1916 [86]) EA/18*

HOUGHTON, Norris (b 1909) American director, producer, designer AAS, BE, WWT/13-16

HOUGHTON, Robert (fl 1633) actor DA

HOUGHTON, Stanley (1881-1913) English dramatist COC, DNB, HP, MD, MH, MWD, OC/1-3, PDT, WWT/2, WWW/1

HOUGHTON, T. C. see Howard, T. Charles

HOUK, Norman C. (d 1970 [73]) critic BP/54*

HOULTON, Robert (fl 1784-1800) English composer, lyricist, dramatist CP/3, DNB, GT, TD/1-2

HOUPT, Charles J. (d 1851) American actor HAS

HOUPT, Mrs. Charles J. [Emily Mestayer] (fl 1822) American actress HAS

HOUSE, Billy (d 1961 [71]) comedian TW/18

HOUSE, Eric Canadian actor AAS, WWT/14-16

HOUSE, Jane (b 1946) Panamanian actress TW/28-29

HOUSE, Ron American actor TW/29-30

HOUSEHOLDER, Cyril (d 1969 [73]) performer BP/54*

HOUSEMAN, John (b 1902) Rumanian/American manager, director, producer AAS, BE, COC, TW/2, WWT/13-16

HOUSER, Mervin (d 1976 [65]) performer BP/60*

HOUSLEY, Gracie (d 1902 [24]) actress EA/03*

HOUSMAN, Laurence (1865-1959) English dramatist AAS, COC, DNB, ES, GRB/2-4, HP, MD, MH, MWD, NTH, OC/3, WWA/3, WWT/1-12, WWW/5

HOUSSEIN, Lassar (d 1917) acrobat EA/18*

HOUSTON, Billie (d 1972 [66]) performer BP/57*

HOUSTON, Donald (b 1923) Welsh actor WWT/11-16

HOUSTON, George F. (d 1944 [45]) American actor TW/1

HOUSTON, Grace (b 1916) American costume designer TW/2-3, 6-7

HOUSTON, Jane American actress WWT/4-7

HOUSTON, Josephine (b 1911) American actress, singer WWT/9-10

HOUSTON, Renée (b 1902) Scottish actress WWT/11-16

HOUSTON, T. (fl 1803) dramatist CP/3

HOUSTON, Lady Thomas (d 1780) dramatist CP/3

HOVELER, Audrey (d 1974 [48]) producer/director/choreographer BP/59*

HOVELL, William (fl 1615) actor DA

HOVEY, Richard (1864-1900) American dramatist HJD

HOVHANESS, Alan (b 1911) American composer CB

HOVICK, June see Havoc, June

HOVICK, Rose Louise see Lee, Gypsy Rose

HOVIS, Joan (b 1932) American actress TW/14-16

HOWARD, Mme. (d 1890 [52]) costumier EA/91*

HOWARD, Alan (b 1937) English actor AAS, WWT/15-16

HOWARD, Alan (b 1951) American actor TW/22, 24, 28

HOWARD, Andrée (1910-68) English dancer, choreographer ES, WWT/10-12, WWW/6

HOWARD, Anne [née Addison; Mrs. Welmhurst] English actress HAS

HOWARD, Art (d 1963 [71]) performer BE*

HOWARD, Bart (b 1915) American composer, lyricist BE

HOWARD, Bella (d 1886) actress EA/87*

HOWARD, Bronson (1842-1908) American dramatist CDP, COC, DAB, ES, GRB/2-4, HJD, MH, MWD, NTH, OC/1-3, RE, SR, WWA/1, WWS, WWW/1

HOWARD, Bruce (b 1963) American actor TW/30

HOWARD, Carrie [Mrs. H. Sweet] (d 1883) performer? EA/85*

HOWARD, Cecil (d 1895 [59]) critic, historian BE*, EA/96*, WWT/14*

HOWARD, Charles (d 1898) lecturer EA/99*

HOWARD, Charles actor TW/1

HOWARD, Mrs. Charles see Watkins, Mrs. Henry

HOWARD, Charles D. A. (1855-87) actor NYM

HOWARD, Charles D. S. (1800/05-53/58) English actor CDP, HAS, SR

HOWARD, Charles Thomas see Williams, Charles

HOWARD, Constance [Mrs. Frank Fuller] (d 1881) actress EA/82*

HOWARD, Cordelia (1848-1941) American actress CDP, HAS

HOWARD, Dan [D. H. Crane] (d 1877) American banjoist EA/78*

HOWARD, David S. (b 1928) American actor TW/23

HOWARD, Eddy (d 1963 [54]) composer/lyricist BP/47*

HOWARD, Edward (fl 1668-78) dramatist CP/1-3, DNB

HOWARD, Edward (d 1900 [55]) ghost illusion proprietor EA/01*

HOWARD, Emma (d 1900 [62]) EA/01*

HOWARD, Esther (d 1965 [72]) performer BP/49*

HOWARD, Eugene (1880/81-1965) American actor, singer BE, TW/22, WWT/7-11

HOWARD, Florence (b 1879) American actress WWS

HOWARD, Florence Emily (d 1907) actress EA/08*

HOWARD, Francis (b 1835) Canadian actress HAS

HOWARD, Francis see Howerd, Frankie

HOWARD, Frank (fl 1870?) song composer CDP

HOWARD, Frank (1850-1915) American minstrel SR

HOWARD, Frederic, Earl of Carlisle (1748-1826) dramatist CP/3, DD

HOWARD, Frederick (d 1882 [26]) comedian EA/83*

HOWARD, Mrs. G. C. (d 1908 [79]) actress GRB/4*

HOWARD, Sir George dramatist FGF

HOWARD, George (d 1921 [55]) English actor, manager GRB/1

HOWARD, Mrs. George see Earle, Clara

HOWARD, George Bronson (1884-1922) American dramatist WWA/1

HOWARD, George Cunnibell (1820-87) Canadian actor CDP, HAS, NYM, WWA/H

HOWARD, Mrs. George Cunnibell [née Caroline Fox] (1829-1908) American actress CDP, GRB/4, HAS

HOWARD, George Edmund (d 1786) dramatist CP/2-3, GT, TD/1-2

HOWARD, G. W. (fl 1851) American actor HAS

HOWARD, Harold (b 1875) American actor WWS

HOWARD, Henry [Henry Howard Moffatt] (d 1890 [42]) diorama proprietor EA/91*

HOWARD, Henry John (1812-53) English actor HAS

HOWARD, Inez [Harriette Adye] (d 1901) EA/02*

HOWARD, Jack (b 1889) American actor TW/2

HOWARD, James (fl 1672-74) dramatist CP/1-3, DNB

HOWARD, James (1808-48) English actor HAS

HOWARD, James Brown [Michael Hoban] (d 1895 [54]) actor, producer, proprietor BE*, EA/96*, WWT/14*

HOWARD, J. B. (d 1879 [35]) American comedian EA/80*

HOWARD, Mrs. J. B. see

Howard, Sarah

HOWARD, J. Bannister (1867-1946) English manager WWT/3-9

HOWARD, J. C. (d 1892 [58]) actor EA/93*

HOWARD, Johnny (d 1976 [70s]) performer BP/60*

HOWARD, Joseph (1868-1961) American composer, vaudevillian SR, TW/17

HOWARD, Joseph E. (fl 1890s?) singer, vaudevillian CDP

HOWARD, Kathleen (d 1956 [77]) Canadian/American singer TW/13, WWA/3

HOWARD, Kathryn [May Irene Copinger] American dramatic editor WWM

HOWARD, Keble [John Keble Bell] (1875-1928) English dramatist GRB/2-4, WWT/1-5, WWW/2

HOWARD, Ken (b 1944) American actor TW/25-27, 29-30, WWT/15-16

HOWARD, Leslie (1893-1943) English actor AAS, CB, DAB, DNB, ES, NTH, SR, WWT/4-9, WWW/4

HOWARD, Lionel G. (d 1917) EA/18*

HOWARD, Lisa (b 1930) American actress TW/15

HOWARD, Lizzie [Mrs. Pat Carey] (d 1901 [37]) singer, actress CDP

HOWARD, Louisa (fl 1854) English actress HAS

HOWARD, Mabel (b 1884) American actress WWS

HOWARD, May C. (b 1845) American actress CDP, HAS, SR

HOWARD, Milly actress, singer CDP

HOWARD, Moe (d 1975 [78]) comedian BP/59*, WWT/16*

HOWARD, Norah (1901-68) English actress TW/4, 9, WWT/6-14

HOWARD, Paul Mason (d 1975 [84]) composer/lyricist BP/59*

HOWARD, Peter (b 1927) American conductor, composer, musician BE

HOWARD, Rance (b 1928) American actor TW/13

HOWARD, Sir Robert (1626-98) dramatist CP/1-3, DNB

HOWARD, Roger (b 1938) English dramatist CD

HOWARD, Rollin [G. B. Holder] (1840-79) female impersonator CDP, HAS

HOWARD, Russell (b 1918) English actor TW/8

HOWARD, Sam (d 1877 [32]) Negro comedian EA/78*

HOWARD, Sam (d 1964 [61]) talent representative, performer BE*

HOWARD, Sam (d 1972 [88]) performer BP/57*

HOWARD, Sarah [Mrs. J. B. Howard] (d 1912 [84]) EA/13*, WWT/14*

HOWARD, Sarah Martin (d 1902 [83]) EA/03*

HOWARD, Selby (b 1874) English actor GRB/1

HOWARD, Seth C. (d 1860 [38]) minstrel HAS

HOWARD, Shemp (d 1955 [60]) comedian TW/12

HOWARD, Sidney Coe (1891-1939) American dramatist AAS, COC, ES, HJD, MD, MH, MWD, NTH, OC/1-3, PDT, RE, WWT/6-8

HOWARD, Sydney (1885-1946) English actor TW/3, WWT/6-9

HOWARD, Sydney Lester (d 1908) EA/09*

HOWARD, T. Charles [T. C. Houghton] (b 1845) American actor HAS

HOWARD, Thomas (fl 1598) actor DA

HOWARD, Thomas (d 1894) circus performer? EA/95*

HOWARD, Thomas Martin (b 1859) English entertainer, illusionist GRB/1

HOWARD, Tom (1885-1955) Irish comedian TW/11

HOWARD, Trevor (b 1916) English actor AAS, CB, ES, WWT/10-16

HOWARD, Virginia (b 1834) American actress HAS

HOWARD, Walter (d 1905 [58]) singer, minstrel CDP

HOWARD, Walter (1866-1922) English actor, manager, dramatist WWT/3-4, WWW/2

HOWARD, Mrs. Walter (d 1903) EA/04*

HOWARD, William Chouet (d 1871 [65]) actor EA/72*

HOWARD, William Jason (d 1871 [62]) actor EA/72*

HOWARD, William W. (d 1963 [65]) American executive BE*

HOWARD, Willie (1883/86-1949) American actor, singer CDP, DAB, NTH, TW/2-5, WWA/3, WWT/7-10

HOWARD, Wilson actor GRB/1

HOWARD, Mrs. Wilson see Anson, Carlotta

HOWARTH, Donald (b 1931) English dramatist, director, actor AAS, CD, WWT/15-16

HOWE, Elizabeth [Mrs. H. Howe] (d 1875) EA/76*

HOWE, Elizabeth Sophia (d 1886) EA/87*

HOWE, Fred (d 1885) music-hall performer EA/86*

HOWE, George (b 1900) Chilean actor, director AAS, BE, TW/9, WWT/7-16

HOWE, Mrs. H. see Howe, Elizabeth

HOWE, Harry (b 1866) English actor, singer, dancer GRB/1

HOWE, Helen (1905-75) American monologist CB

HOWE, Henry [Henry Howe Hutchinson] (1812-96) English actor CDP, DNB, DP, OAA/1-2, OC/1-3, SR

HOWE, Henry A. H. (d 1894 [61]) critic EA/95*

HOWE, Illa Cameron (b 1948) American actress TW/28

HOWE, J. Burdette (1828-1908) English actor, manager CDP, GRB/4, HAS, SR

HOWE, Julia Ward (1819-1910) American dramatist WWW/1

HOWE, Katharine B. (fl 1889?) singer CDP

HOWE, Leonard (b 1875) English actor, business manager GRB/1

HOWE, Lizzie (d 1902) actress EA/03*

HOWE, Mary (fl 1891?) singer CDP

HOWE, Molly (d 1890 [15]) music-hall performer EA/91*

HOWE, Walter (b 1860) English actor, manager GRB/1

HOWE, Willard American actor WWS

HOWELL, Mr. singer CDP

HOWELL, Mr. (fl 1811-12) actor

CDP
HOWELL, Alfred (d 1862 [53])
costumier HAS
HOWELL, Arthur (d 1885 [49])
musician EA/86*
HOWELL, Edward (d 1898 [54])
musician EA/99*
HOWELL, Eric American actor
TW/28
HOWELL, Miss F. (fl 1800)
singer TD/1-2
HOWELL, Fred A. (d 1886 [46])
singer EA/87*
HOWELL, J. A. (d 1895) actor
EA/96*
HOWELL, James (1594-1666)
Welsh dramatist CP/1-3
HOWELL, James (d 1877) min-
strel EA/78*
HOWELL, Jane director WWT/
15-16
HOWELL, John (1888-1928)
Welsh actor WWT/4-5
HOWELL, John Daggett (b 1911)
American director BE
HOWELL, Margaret (b 1947)
American actress TW/26,
28
HOWELL, Matthew (d 1873 [76])
harlequin EA/74*
HOWELL, Miriam American
literary representative BE
HOWELL, Stephanus (fl 1423)
actor DA
HOWELL-POOLE, William (d
1894 [37]) actor, dramatist
EA/95*
HOWELLS, Fanny (fl 1800) ac-
tress CDP
HOWELLS, Ursula (b 1922) Eng-
lish actress TW/7, WWT/
11-16
HOWELLS, William Dean (1837-
1920) American dramatist,
critic ES, HJD, HP, MH,
MWD, NTH, SR, WWA/1,
WWW/2
HOWERD, Frankie [né Francis
Howard] (b 1921) English actor
TW/25, WWT/14-16
HOWERTON, Clarence (d 1975
[62]) performer BP/60*
HOWES, Basil (b 1901) English
actor, singer WWT/6-8
HOWES, Bobby (1895-1972) Eng-
lish actor AAS, WWT/6-15
HOWES, Frank (d 1974 [82])
critic BP/59*

HOWES, John F. (d 1968 [54]) per-
former BP/52*
HOWES, Oliver (fl 1628) actor DA
HOWES, Sally Ann (b 1930) English
actress, singer BE, TW/20-21,
WWT/12-16
HOWES, Seth B. (1815-1901) Amer-
ican circus manager SR
HOWITT, Belle (fl 1869) actress
CDP
HOWITT, Nellie [Mrs. W. Ruddle
Brown] Scottish actress GRB/1
HOWITT, T. C. (d 1886) EA/88*
HOWITT, Mrs. Thomas C. see
Dowsing, Emma Ada
HOWLAND, Alan (d 1946 [47])
actor BE*, WWT/14*
HOWLAND, Beth (b 1941) American
actress TW/26-28
HOWLAND, Jobyna (1880-1936)
American actress WWT/6-8
HOWLAND, Olin (d 1959 [63]) actor
TW/16
HOWLE, William J. (d 1907) EA/
08*
HOWLETT, Carl (d 1907 [48])
marionette proprietor EA/08*
HOWLETT, Noel (b 1901) English
actor WWT/9-16
HOWROYDE, Mrs. (d 1911) EA/12*
HOWS, J. W. S. (fl 1834) actor
HAS
HOWSON, Albert S. (b 1881) Amer-
ican actor WWM
HOWSON, Charles Edwin (d 1907
[59]) treasurer EA/08*
HOWSON, Charles Edwin (d 1916)
actor SR
HOWSON, Emma (1844-1928) Tas-
manian singer, actress CDP,
OAA/2
HOWSON, Emma see Albertazzi,
Emma
HOWSON, Frank (1817-69) English
singer, musician, manager,
director, producer HAS
HOWSON, Frank A. (d 1945 [66])
actor BE*, WWT/14*
HOWSON, John (1844-87) Tasmanian
actor, singer CDP, NYM,
OAA/2
HOY, Mr. manager TD/1-2
HOYLE, Edgar (d 1917) manager
EA/18*
HOYLE, Fanny (d 1874) singer?
EA/75*
HOYM, Eliza actress CDP
HOYM, Otto (fl 1854) manager CDP

HOYT, Adolphus H. see Daven-
port, Adolphus H.
HOYT, Caroline Miskel [Mrs.
Charles H. Hoyt] (d 1898
[25]) American actress BE*,
EA/99*, WWT/14*
HOYT, Mrs. Charles H. see
Hoyt, Caroline Miskel
HOYT, Charles Hale (1860-1900)
American dramatist CDP,
COC, DAB, HJD, MWD, NTH,
OC/1-3, RE, WWA/1
HOYT, Mrs. Charles Hale [Flora
Walsh] (d 1893) actress BE*,
WWT/14*
HOYT, Edward N. (b 1859)
American actor WWS
HOYT, Eileen (d 1970 [67]) per-
former BP/55*
HOYT, Harlowe R. (d 1970)
critic BP/55*
HOYT, Howard (1913-71) Amer-
ican producer, manager,
artists' representative BE
HOYT, Julia (d 1955 [58]) Amer-
ican actress TW/12
HROSWITHA (fl 10th cent) Ger-
man dramatist COC
HRUBY, Norbert J. (b 1918)
American producer, educator,
director BE
HSIUNG, Shih I. (b 1902) Chinese
dramatist BE, WWT/9-14
HUBAN, Eileen (1895-1935)
Irish actress WWT/4-7
HUBBARD, Christiana (d 1893)
EA/94*
HUBBARD, Didrikke (d 1974)
performer BP/58*
HUBBARD, Elbert (b 1856)
American dramatist, enter-
tainer, lecturer WWM
HUBBARD, Elizabeth American
actress TW/24, 28
HUBBARD, Frances Virginia
American composer WWA/5
HUBBARD, Lilian (fl 1880?)
singer CDP
HUBBARD, Lorna (b 1910) ac-
tress, singer WWT/7-10
HUBBARD, Lulu Mae (d 1966
[59]) actress TW/23
HUBBARD, Robert F. (d 1909
[72]) EA/10*
HUBBELL, Kyra Deakin (d 1965
[63]) performer BP/50*
HUBBELL, Raymond (1879-1954)
American composer WWA/3,

WWT/4-11
HUBER, Ann Elizabeth (d 1905)
EA/06*
HUBER, Gusti (b 1914) Austrian
actress BE, TW/8-15, WWT/
12-13
HUBER, Harold (d 1959 [49]) Amer-
ican actor BE*, BP/44*
HUBER, Paul (b 1895) American
actor TW/10
HUBER, Richard M. (d 1965 [84])
publisher BP/49*
HUBERT (fl 1631) actor DA
HUBERT, George (d 1963 [82])
performer BE*
HUBERT, Marcie Japanese/Ameri-
can actress TW/23
HUBY, John, Jr. (d 1880) master
carpenter EA/81*
HUBY, Roberta actress, singer
WWT/10-14
HUDD, Walter (1898-1963) English
actor, producer AAS, WWT/
8-13, WWW/6
HUDDART, Mr. (fl 1798) actor
TD/1-2
HUDDART, Fanny [Mrs. John Rus-
sell] (d 1880) singer, actress
CDP
HUDDART, John F. (fl 1869?)
song composer CDP
HUDDART, Mary Amelia see
Warner, Mary Amelia
HUDDART, Thomas (d 1831) actor
WWT/14*
HUDDLE, Elizabeth (b 1940) Amer-
ican actress TW/22-23, 27
HUDMAN, Wesley (d 1964 [48])
actor BE*
HUDSMITH, William Henry (d 1889)
music-hall chairman EA/90*
HUDSON, Mr. (fl 1849-50) Irish
comedian HAS
HUDSON, Alfred (1879-1914) actor
SR
HUDSON, Charles (d 1897), actor,
dramatist BE*, EA/98*, WWT/
14*
HUDSON, Charles (b 1931) Ameri-
can actor TW/22, 27, 30
HUDSON, Edward (b 1924) Ameri-
can actor TW/2
HUDSON, Eric (1861-1918) English
actor GRB/1
HUDSON, Harry B. [né Hunter] (b
1839) Canadian actor CDP,
HAS
HUDSON, James (1811-78) Irish

comedian CDP
HUDSON, Jeffrey (1619-82) dwarf
CDP
HUDSON, John (b 1921) American
actor TW/3
HUDSON, Leo (1839-73) English
equestrienne CDP, HAS
HUDSON, Richard (fl 1612) actor
DA
HUDSON, Rochelle (d 1972 [57])
performer BP/56*, WWT/16*
HUDSON, Thomas (d 1844 [50])
comic songwriter & singer
EA/72*
HUDSON, T. P. (d 1909 [57]) per-
former EA/10*
HUDSPETH, Henrietta [Mrs. Ed-
mund Phelps] (fl 1859) actress
OAA/2
HUDSPETH, John (d 1866 [59])
actor CDP
HUDSPETH, Mrs. John (d 1891
[84]) EA/93*
HUDSPETH, Mrs. John see
Bramah, Marie
HUDSPETH, John Henry (d 1903
[63]) comedian EA/04*
HUESTON, John (d 1865) Amer-
ican actor HAS
HUFF, Alexander F. (d 1965
[70]) performer BP/49*
HUFF, Forrest (1876-1947) actor,
singer SR, TW/4
HUFF, Louise (d 1973 [77]) per-
former BP/58*
HUFFMAN, David (b 1945) Amer-
ican actor TW/28-30
HUFFMAN, Jessie C. (d 1935
[66]) director, producer BE*,
WWT/14*
HUGGINS, Mr. (d 1800) actor
HAS
HUGGINS, Benjamin W. see
Edwin, Benjamin W.
HUGGINS, Jeremy see Brett,
Jeremy
HUGGINS, William (d 1761)
dramatist CP/2-3
HUGHES, Mr. (fl 1794-1824)
actor HAS
HUGHES, Mr. (fl 1794) actor
CDP
HUGHES, Mr. (fl 1834) actor
CDP
HUGHES, Mrs. (fl 1784-90)
dramatist CP/3
HUGHES, Mrs. (fl 1794) actress
CDP

HUGHES, Mrs. (fl 1794-1824) ac-
tress HAS
HUGHES, Mrs. [Mrs. Young] (fl
1846) actress HAS
HUGHES, Miss (fl 1831) actress
HAS
HUGHES, Adelaide (d 1937 [20])
American performer BE*
HUGHES, Adelaide (d 1960 [70])
dancer TW/16
HUGHES, Andy actor, song com-
poser CDP
HUGHES, Anna May (b 1918) Amer-
ican educator BE
HUGHES, Annie [Mrs. Edmund
Maurice] (1869-1954) English ac-
tress CDP, DP, EA/95, GRB/
1-4, WWS, WWT/1-11
HUGHES, Archie (d 1860?) actor
NTH
HUGHES, Barnard (b 1915) Amer-
ican actor TW/24-30, WWT/16
HUGHES, Beaumont (d 1906 [76])
actor EA/07*
HUGHES, Mrs. Beaumont see
Hughes, Margaret Hackett
HUGHES, Mrs. C. H. see
Hughes, Mary
HUGHES, Daisy (d 1893) serio-
comic EA/94*
HUGHES, David (d 1973 [43]) per-
former BP/57*
HUGHES, Del American stage
manager, director, actor BE
HUGHES, Edwin (d 1867 [54])
equestrian EA/68*
HUGHES, Elinor (b 1906) American
critic BE, NTH
HUGHES, Elizabeth (fl 1831) ac-
tress, singer CDP
HUGHES, Ernest (d 1962 [82]) per-
former, historian BE*
HUGHES, Esther (fl 1812) actress
CDP
HUGHES, Fanny [Mrs. Julio Henry
Hughes] (d 1880 [66]) EA/81*
HUGHES, Fanny (d 1888 [45]) ac-
tress BE*, WWT/14*
HUGHES, Fanny see Swanborough,
Fanny
HUGHES, Mrs. Frederic see
Hughes, Sarah Jane
HUGHES, Frederick (d 1883 [41])
comedian EA/84*
HUGHES, Gareth (d 1965 [71])
Welsh actor TW/22
HUGHES, Glenn (1894-1964) Ameri-
can educator, dramatist BE

HUGHES, Gordon (fl 1894?)
singer CDP
HUGHES, Harry (d 1897) comedian EA/98*
HUGHES, Hatcher (1883-1945)
American dramatist CB,
HJD, MD, MWD, NTH, SR,
WWA/2, WWT/8-11
HUGHES, Hazel [née Hepenstall]
(1913-74) South African actress BTR/74, WWT/15
HUGHES, Henry (d 1872 [62])
actor CDP
HUGHES, Henry (1828-1914)
American minstrel SR
HUGHES, James American press
representative, manager BE
HUGHES, Jennie (fl 1873) actress, singer CDP
HUGHES, J. J. see Albert,
Frank
HUGHES, John (1677-1719) English dramatist CDP, CP/
1-3, GT, SR, TD/1-2
HUGHES, John (d 1887) Welsh
writer EA/88*
HUGHES, John Charles (1789-
1840) actor CDP
HUGHES, Julio Henry (d 1872
[62]) actor EA/73*
HUGHES, Mrs. Julio Henry
see Hughes, Fanny (d 1880)
HUGHES, Langston (1902-67)
American dramatist BE,
CB, CH, ES, MD, MH,
MWD, TW/23, WWA/4
HUGHES, Lizzie [Mrs. Frank
Pierce Clark] actress CDP
HUGHES, Lloyd (d 1958 [61])
actor BE*
HUGHES, Margaret (1643?-1719)
English actress CDP, DNB,
NTH
HUGHES, Margaret Hackett [Mrs.
Beaumont Hughes] (d 1877)
EA/79*
HUGHES, Mary [Mrs. C. H.
Hughes] (d 1876 [35]) EA/77*
HUGHES, Matt (d 1882 [61])
scene artist EA/83*
HUGHES, Morfa [Ethel Margaret
Morfa-Hughes] (b 1876) English actress, singer GRB/1
HUGHES, R. see Newcomb,
Bobby
HUGHES, Richard (1789-1814)
English actor, manager BS,
TD/1-2

HUGHES, Richard (1900-76) dramatist HP
HUGHES, Roddy (b 1891) Welsh
actor WWT/10-13
HUGHES, R. S. (d 1893) Welsh
song composer EA/94*
HUGHES, Ruey (d 1871 [23]) dancer,
minstrel CDP
HUGHES, Rupert (1872-1956) American dramatist GRB/3-4, HJD,
WWA/3, WWM, WWS, WWT/1-
11
HUGHES, Sarah Jane [Jennie Kelsey; Mrs. Frederic Hughes]
(d 1880) EA/82*
HUGHES, T. Harris (1806-91)
magician SR
HUGHES, Thomas (fl 1587) dramatist CP/3, DNB, FGF
HUGHES, Thomas (d 1857 [49])
actor EA/72*, WWT/14*
HUGHES, Tom (b 1932) American
producer BE
HUGHES, Tresa (b 1929) American
actress TW/17, 21-30
HUGHES, W. F. see Egerton,
Frank
HUGHES, W. H. (d 1905 [58])
manager EA/06*
HUGHES, William (b 1924) American actor TW/21
"HUGH MORTON" see McLellan,
C. M. S.
HUGHSON, Matthew (d 1879 [28])
Negro comedian EA/80*
"HUGO see Oxford, Mr.
HUGO, Emil (b 1836) German actor
HAS
HUGO, Lawrence (b 1917) American
actor BE, TW/24, 27, 30
HUGO, Mauritz (d 1974 [65]) performer BP/59*
HUGO, Victor (1802-85) French
dramatist SR
HUGO, William (d 1896) minstrel
EA/97*
HUGUENET, Felix (1858-1926)
French actor WWT/1-2
HUGUES, Clovis (d 1907 [56])
dramatist EA/08*
HUISH, Robert (fl 1809) translator
CP/3
HULBERT, Claude (1900-64) English actor WWT/5-13, WWW/6
HULBERT, Jack (b 1892) English
actor, dramatist, manager,
producer AAS, ES, WWT/3-16
HULBURD, H. L. (d 1973) per-

former BP/57*

HULBURT, John W. (b 1907) American educator BE

HULET, Charles (1701-36) actor DNB

HULETT, Mr. (fl 1753) English dancer, violinist HAS

HULEY, Pete (d 1973 [80]) performer BP/57*

HULINE, James (d 1890 [74]) pantomimist, clown BE*, EA/91*, WWT/14*

HULINE, James (d 1904 [54]) EA/06*

HULINE, John Alfred (d 1904 [35]) EA/06*

HULINE, W. (d 1890 [74]) actor, clown CDP

HULL, Charles (b 1936) Austrian/American actor TW/24-25

HULL, Henry (1890-1977) American actor, dramatist BE, TW/1-16, WWT/5-14

HULL, John (fl 1600) actor DA

HULL, Josephine [née Sherwood] (1886-1957) American actress CB, TW/1-13, WWA/3, WWT/10-12

HULL, Maryann (d 1970 [39]) performer BP/54*

HULL, Shelley (d 1919 [35]) American actor WWM

HULL, Thomas (1728-1808) English actor, manager, dramatist CDP, CP/2-3, DNB, GT, TD/1-2

HULL, Tom American actor TW/26

HULL, Warren (d 1974 [71]) performer BP/59*

HULLEY, Bernard (d 1917 [49]) musical director EA/18*

HULLEY, Will (d 1878 [28]) comic singer EA/79*

HULLIN, Mme. (fl 1820s?) dancer CDP

HULL TRUCK theatre collective CD

HULME, Mrs. see Dalby, Miss

HULSKAMP, Victoria S. (fl 1885?) singer CDP

HULTMAN, Robert L. (b 1927) American actor TW/29

HUMBY, Anne (fl 1818-49) actress CDP, DNB

HUME, Benita (1906-68) English actress WWT/6-10

HUME, Ernest (d 1910) singer? EA/11*

HUME, Fergus (d 1932 [73]) dramatist BE*, WWT/14*

HUME, J. (d 1892) Negro comedian EA/94*

HUME, Kenneth (d 1967 [41]) dramatist BP/52*

HUMIERES, Robert D' (d 1916) dramatist WWT/14*

HUMISTON, William Henry (1869-1923) American musician, conductor, composer DAB

HUMMERT, James (b 1944) American actor TW/29-30

HUMPERDINCK, Engelbert (1854-1921) German composer WWM

HUMPHREY, Cavada American actress BE, TW/22-24, 26, 29, WWT/14-16

HUMPHREY, Doris (1895-1958) American dancer, choreographer CB, ES, TW/15, WWA/3

HUMPHREYS, Mr. (d c. 1738 [c. 40]) dramatist CP/2-3

HUMPHREYS, Mrs. (fl 1803) actress CDP

HUMPHREYS, Cecil (1883-1947) English actor TW/2-4, WWT/4-10

HUMPHREYS, Col. David (1753-1818) American dramatist CP/3, EAP, RJ

HUMPHREYS, George (d 1911 [32]) variety acting manager EA/12*

HUMPHREYS, Griffith (fl 1895?) singer, song composer CDP

HUMPHREYS, John D. (d 1906) circus advance agent EA/07*

HUMPHREYS, Rex (d 1911 [28]) actor EA/12*

HUMPHRIES, Mr. (d 1867) musician EA/68*

HUMPHRIES, Miss (fl 1797) actress TD/1-2

HUMPHRIES, John (d 1927 [63]) actor WWT/4-5

HUMPHRIES, Mrs. John see Innes, Isabel

HUMPHRIS, Gordon (b 1921) English actor, dancer WWT/11

HUNDON, Mrs. T. J. [Clara Goldsby Wilton] (d 1889) American actress EA/90*

HUNEKER, Erick H. (d 1971 [77]) designer BP/55*

HUNEKER, James Gibbons (1857/60-1921) American critic COC,

DAB, ES, HJD, NTH, OC/1-3,
WWA/1, WWM, WWW/2
HUNN, Richard see Canning,
Mrs. George
HUNNICUTT, Arthur American
actor TW/1-3
HUNNIS, William (fl 1566-97)
master of the Chapel Royal
DA, FGF
HUNSECKER, Ralph Uriah see
Blane, Ralph
HUNT, Al (d 1964 [45]) press
representative BE*
HUNT, Arabella (d 1705) singer
CDP
HUNT, Betty Lee (b 1920) Amer-
ican press representative BE
HUNT, Carl (b 1941) American
actor TW/27-28
HUNT, Mrs. Charles [née Ann
Jeannette Kerr] (b 1816) Eng-
lish actress HAS
HUNT, Charles Henry (d 1879
[33]) music-hall proprietor
EA/80*
HUNT, Charles W. (d 1855) actor
HAS
HUNT, Doris [Mrs. Roy Byford]
(d 1911 [39]) actress EA/12*
HUNT, Miss E. (d 1893) EA/94*
HUNT, Eliza (d 1889) EA/90*
HUNT, George W. "Jingo" (d
1904) composer EA/05*
HUNT, Henry B. (d 1854 [60])
English actor, singer CDP,
HAS
HUNT, Hugh Sydney (b 1911)
English producer, director,
critic AAS, COC, WWT/8-16
HUNT, John (d 1894) EA/95*
HUNT, Mrs. John see Hunt,
Mary Ann
HUNT, Julia A. (fl 1881?) singer,
actress CDP
HUNT, Leigh (1784-1859) English
critic COC, ES, HP, OC/1-3
HUNT, Maggie [Mrs. Arthur B.
Franks] (d 1904 [44]) actress
EA/05*
HUNT, Marsha (b 1917) American
actress BE, TW/5-8, 23,
WWT/11
HUNT, Martita (1900-69) Argen-
tinian/English actress AAS,
BE, COC, ES, TW/5-6, 26,
WWT/6-14, WWW/6
HUNT, Mary Ann [Mrs. John
Hunt] (d 1875) EA/76*

HUNT, Nathaniel (d 1891) manager
EA/92*
HUNT, Peter (b 1938) American
director, lighting designer
WWT/15-16
HUNT, Peter H. (d 1970 [55]) pro-
ducer/director/choreographer
BP/55*
HUNT, Phil (b 1868) American
manager, actor WWS
HUNT, Ralph (d 1900) minstrel?
EA/01*
HUNT, Reginald (d 1916 [19]) actor?
EA/17*
HUNT, Robert (fl 1631) actor DA
HUNT, Thomas (fl 1597-1611) actor
DA
HUNT, William (fl 1713) dramatist
CP/1-3, GT
HUNT, William (d 1827) gymnast
HAS
HUNT, William E. (b 1923) Ameri-
can producer, director, actor
BE
HUNT, William Henry (d 1894 [42])
composer EA/96*
HUNTEN, Franz (1793-1878) com-
poser CDP
HUNTER, Mr. (fl 1829-39) eques-
trian HAS
HUNTER, Agnes Emma (d 1908 [52])
actress EA/09*
HUNTER, Frederick J. (b 1916)
American educator BE
HUNTER, George M. (fl 1794)
dramatist CP/3
HUNTER, Glenn (1896-1945) Ameri-
can actor CB, TW/2, WWT/5-9
HUNTER, Govenor see Hunter,
[Robert]
HUNTER, Harriet see Seymour,
Mrs. Guilfoyle
HUNTER, Harrison (d 1923) English
actor BE*, BP/7*, WWT/14*
HUNTER, Harry (d 1881) actor
CDP
HUNTER, Harry (d 1906 [65]) min-
strel EA/07*
HUNTER, Harry B. see Hudson,
Harry B.
HUNTER, Ian (1900-75) South Afri-
can actor AAS, ES, TW/5-6,
WWT/5-14
HUNTER, Ivory Joe (d 1974 [63])
composer/lyricist BP/59*
HUNTER, Jackie (d 1951 [50])
Canadian actor BE*, WWT/14*
HUNTER, James (d 1887) EA/88*

HUNTER, James (d 1890) circus custodian EA/91*

HUNTER, James (b 1943) English actor TW/24

HUNTER, J. D. (d 1916) comedian, pantomime director EA/18*

HUNTER, Jeffrey (d 1969 [42]) performer BP/54*

HUNTER, John (1763-1801) English dramatist CP/3

HUNTER, Kenneth (b 1882) South African actor WWT/7-10

HUNTER, Kermit (b 1910) American dramatist, educator BE, CB, MWD

HUNTER, Kim [née Janet Cole] (b 1922) American actress BE, CB, TW/7-15, 23-24, 26, 29-30, WWT/12-16

HUNTER, Lavinia Ernestine (d 1909 [59]) dramatist EA/10*

HUNTER, Maria (fl 1782) actress CDP

HUNTER, Mary American director TW/5-6

HUNTER, Mary see Austin, Mary

HUNTER, Norman Charles (1908-71) English dramatist AAS, CD, CH, COC, MD, PDT, WWT/9-15

HUNTER, Mrs. Parke see Price, Lillah

HUNTER, Richard (fl 1699-1702) actor WWA/H

HUNTER, Richard (d 1962 [87]) actor BE*

HUNTER, [Robert] (d 1734) English dramatist CP/1-3, EAP, GT

HUNTER, Ruth (d 1976 [74]) wardrobe supervisor BP/60*

HUNTER, Susan (d 1976 [39]) performer BP/60*

HUNTER, Mrs. T. M. see Hight, Lizzie

HUNTER, T. Marvin (fl 1860) actor HAS

HUNTER, Victor William (b 1910) English manager WWT/15-16

HUNTER, William (d 1886 [42]) Ethiopian comedian EA/87*

HUNTINGDON, Mr. (fl 1807) actor HAS

HUNTINGTON, Agnes (fl 1889) singer, actress DP

HUNTINGTON, Catharine (b 1889) American actress, director, producer BE

HUNTINGTON, Harry (1832-60) American agent, circus performer? HAS

HUNTINGTON, Nathaniel (d 1970 [87]) performer BP/54*

HUNTLEY, Mr. (b 1787) English actor BS

HUNTLEY, Dick (fl 1592) actor? prompter? DA

HUNTLEY, Francis (1787-1831) English actor CDP, DNB, OX

HUNTLEY, Francis Walter [Frank Huntley] (d 1885 [56]) actor EA/86*, WWT/14*

HUNTLEY, Frank see Huntley, Francis Walter

HUNTLEY, Mrs. Frank (d 1895) actress EA/96*, WWT/14*

HUNTLEY, George (b 1826) actor CDP

HUNTLEY, George Frederick (d 1913 [54]) EA/14*

HUNTLEY, George Patrick (1868-1927) Irish actor GRB/1-4, WWT/1-5

HUNTLEY, Mrs. George Patrick see Kelly, Eve

HUNTLEY, G[eorge] P[atrick], Jr. (b 1904) American actor WWT/7-9

HUNTLEY, Grace (d 1896) actress BE*, EA/97*, WWT/14*

HUNTLEY, Mrs. James H. see Kennedy, Florence

HUNTLEY, John (b 1805) English prompter, actor, manager HAS

HUNTLEY, Marion (d 1899 [36]) actress EA/00*

HUNTLEY, Raymond (b 1904) English actor AAS, TW/7, WWT/9-16

HUNTLEY, Thomas L. ["Delane"] (d 1865) tight-rope walker HAS

HUNTLEY, Tim (b 1904) American actor WWT/10

HUNTLEY-WRIGHT, Betty (b 1911) actress, singer WWT/10-15

HUNTLEY-WRIGHT, José (b 1918) English actress WWT/10-11

HUOT, Denise (b 1936) American actress TW/23-25

HUPFELD, Herman (d 1951 [57]) American songwriter BE*, BP/36*

HUPPELER, Cindia (b 1951) American actress TW/29

HURDLE, Jack (d 1971 [62])
producer/director/choreographer
BP/56*
HURGINI, Herr (d 1900) juggler
EA/01*
HURGON, Austen A. (d 1942
[74]) actor, dramatist, pro-
ducer WWT/3-7
HURLBUT, W. J. (b 1883) Amer-
ican dramatist SR, WWT/1-11
HURLEY, Alec (1863/71-1913)
English actor GRB/1-3, OC/
1-3, WWS
HURLEY, Dunlea (d 1973 [64])
dramatist BP/58*
HURLEY, Jerry (d 1901 [38])
gymnast EA/02*
HURLEY, Laurel (b 1927) Amer-
ican singer CB, TW/10
HURLEY, Michael (d 1879) Amer-
ican scene artist EA/80*
HURLSTONE, Thomas (fl 1792-
94) dramatist CP/3, TD/1-2
HURN, Douglas (d 1974 [49])
performer BP/59*
HURNDALL, Richard (b 1910)
English actor WWT/15-16
HURNEY, Kate American actress
TW/23, 29
HUROK, Sol (1888-1974) Russian/
American impresario AAS,
BE, CB, ES, TW/30, WWT/
13-15
HURRAN, Dick (b 1911) English
director WWT/12-16
HURRELL, John D. (b 1924)
English educator BE
HURRY, Leslie (b 1909) English
designer AAS, COC, ES,
OC/3, PDT, WWT/11-16
HURST, Mr. actor TD/1-2
HURST, Agnes (d 1869 [75])
EA/70*
HURST, Brandon (d 1947 [81])
English actor BE*, BP/32*,
WWT/14*
HURST, David (b 1926) German
actor, director BE
HURST, Fannie (1889-1968) Amer-
ican dramatist HJD, WWT/
5-10
HURST, J. H. (d 1905) comic
singer, mimic EA/06*
HURST, Joseph (d 1899 [66])
box office manager EA/00*
HURST, Lew (d 1975 [57]) de-
signer BP/59*
HURST, Robert (fl 1725) drama-

tist CP/1-3, GT, TD/1-2
HURST, Will (d 1911) Negro come-
dian EA/12*
HURST, Mrs. William (d 1887)
actress EA/88*
HURST, William George (d 1905
[47]) acrobat EA/06*
HURSTBOURNE, Walter (d 1917)
EA/18*
HURT, Helen see Ashley, Helen
HURT, John (b 1940) English actor
WWT/15-16
HURTIG, Mrs. Joseph see Austin,
Jennie
HURTIG, Louis (d 1924 [53]) pro-
ducer BE*, BP/9*
HURWITCH, Moses (1844-1910)
dramatist BE*
HURWITZ, Mr. B. (d 1868) decor-
ator EA/69*
HUSBANDS, J. W. (d 1917) critic
EA/18*
HUSCH, Richard J. [Richard Ger-
ard] (d 1948 [72]) American
lyricist BE*, BP/33*
HUSK, James (d 1879 [68]) singer
EA/80*
HUSMANN, Ron (b 1937) American
actor, singer BE, TW/17-20,
27-30, WWT/16
HUSSEY, Dyneley (d 1972 [79])
critic BP/57*
HUSSEY, Frank (b 1834) comedian,
minstrel CDP
HUSSEY, Jimmy (1891-1930) Amer-
ican actor WWT/5-6
HUSSEY, John George (d 1881)
EA/82*
HUSSEY, Ruth (b 1914) American
actress BE, TW/2-7, WWT/
10-11
HUSTING, Lucille (d 1972 [70s])
performer BP/57*
HUSTON, James (b 1941) American
actor TW/30
HUSTON, John (b 1906) American
actor, dramatist CB, ES
HUSTON, Martin (b 1941) American
actor TW/22-23, 26
HUSTON, Philip (b 1908/10) Amer-
ican actor, director BE, TW/
1-12, 27
HUSTON, Walter (1884-1950) Cana-
dian actor AAS, CB, DAB, ES,
NTH, SR, TW/2-6, WWA/4,
WWT/6-10
HUTCHESON, David (1905-76)
Scottish actor WWT/8-16

HUTCHESON, LaVerne American
actor, singer BE
HUTCHINGS, William (fl 1827)
English actor HAS
HUTCHINGS, W. S. ["The Light-
ning Calculator"] (b 1832)
American actor HAS
HUTCHINS, Fred B. (b 1911)
American educator BE
HUTCHINS, G. T. (d 1917) musi-
cal director EA/18*
HUTCHINSON, Abby J. (1829-92)
singer CDP
HUTCHINSON, Ann [Mrs. David
Hutchinson] (d 1878 [66]) EA/
79*
HUTCHINSON, Mrs. David see
Hutchinson, Ann
HUTCHINSON, Dorothy (d 1962
[80]) American singer BE*
HUTCHINSON, Emma (d 1917
[72]) actress, manager WWT/3
HUTCHINSON, George H. (d
1869) actor HAS
HUTCHINSON, George P. (d 1898
[70]) circus proprietor EA/99*
HUTCHINSON, Gerald (d 1897
[29]) actor EA/98*
HUTCHINSON, Harry (b 1892)
Irish actor WWT/9-16
HUTCHINSON, Henry Howe see
Howe, Henry
HUTCHINSON, Jessie singer
CDP
HUTCHINSON, Jody (d 1973 [57])
composer/lyricist BP/58*
HUTCHINSON, John W. singer
CDP
HUTCHINSON, Joseph (d 1871
[44]) proprietor EA/72*
HUTCHINSON, Joseph (d 1890)
circus proprietor EA/91*
HUTCHINSON, Josephine (b 1904)
American actress BE, WWT/
6-9
HUTCHINSON, Kathryn (fl 1900s)
American actress WWS
HUTCHINSON, Laurie (b 1945)
American actress TW/27
HUTCHINSON, Leslie (d 1969
[69]) performer BP/54*
HUTCHINSON, Mary (d 1887)
EA/88*
HUTCHINSON, Willie A. (d 1887
[18]) EA/88*
HUTCHINSON BROTHERS acro-
bats CDP, SR
HUTCHINSON SCOTT, Jay (b

1924) English designer WWT/
13-14
HUTCHISON, Emma see Hutchi-
son, Mrs. James George
HUTCHISON, Mrs. James George
[Emma Hutchison] (d 1917) ac-
tress, manager EA/18*
HUTCHISON, Muriel (d 1975 [60])
American actress WWT/10-11
HUTCHISON, Percy (1875-1945)
English actor, manager WWT/
1-9
HUTCHISON, Ronald Macdonald
see Tate, Henry
HUTH, Mrs. Frank see Moore,
Bertha
HUTH, Harold (1892-1967) English
actor WWT/7-9
HUTT, William (b 1920) Canadian
actor, director AAS, TW/24,
WWT/13-16
HUTTO, Jack (b 1928) American
literary representative BE
HUTTON, Mons. (fl 1827) French
dancer HAS
HUTTON, Mme. (fl 1827) French
dancer HAS
HUTTON, Betty (b 1921) American
singer, actress BE, CB, ES
HUTTON, Joseph (1787-1828)
American dramatist EAP, NTH,
RJ
HUTTON, Joseph (fl 1812) actor
HAS
HUTTON, June (d 1973) performer
BP/57*
HUTTON, Lawrence (1843-1904)
American? critic CDP, HJD
HUTTON, Mary (d 1898 [37]) singer
EA/99*
HUXLEY, Aldous (1894-1963) Eng-
lish dramatist ES, MD, MWD
HUY, John (d 1891 [57]) acting
manager EA/92*
HYACINTH, Mlle. (fl 1828) dancer
HAS
HYAMS, Barry (b 1911) American
press representative, producer,
critic BE
HYAMS, Harry (d 1965 [84]) pro-
ducer/director BP/50*
HYAMS, Samuel David see Hoey,
Dennis
HYATT, George F. (fl 1825-32)
actor CDP, HAS
HYATT, Herman (d 1968 [62]) per-
former BP/52*
HYDE, A. J. (d 1917) EA/18*

HYDE, Bruce (b 1941) American actor TW/23, 25

HYDE, Douglas (1860-1949) Irish dramatist COC, MWD, WWW/4

HYDE, Florence Mary (d 1879 [18]) singer EA/80*

HYDE, Henry, Lord Hyde & Cornbury (d 1758) dramatist CP/2-3, GT

HYDE, Herman (d 1967 [69]) performer BP/52*

HYDE, Mariette English actress GRB/1

HYDE, Marion [Mrs. M. J. White] (d 1911) actress EA/12*

HYDE, Tom (d 1893) actor EA/94*

HYDE, Walter (d 1951) English singer WWW/5

HYDES, J. P. (fl 1859) Australian comedian HAS

HYDES, Marcus John (d 1902) manager EA/03*

HYDE-WHITE, Wilfrid (b 1903) English actor AAS, BE, TW/29, WWT/14-16

HYEM, Constance Ethel (1874-1928) English actress, singer GRB/4, WWT/1-5

HYER, W. G. (fl c. 1820?) dramatist EAP, RJ

HYETT, Robert (b 1873) English actor, singer GRB/2

HYLAN, Donald (d 1968 [69]) performer BP/53*

HYLAND, Augustin Allen (d 1963 [58]) performer BE*

HYLAND, Diana (1936-77) American actress BE

HYLAND, Frances (b 1927) Canadian actress WWT/12-16

HYLAND, William (fl 1746) dramatist CP/2-3, GT

HYLES, Ann (d 1884 [61]) music-hall proprietor EA/85*

HYLES, Edwin Charles (d 1885 [35]) music-hall proprietor EA/86*

HYLES, George (d 1879) music-hall proprietor EA/80*

HYLES, William (d 1878 [35]) music-hall proprietor EA/79*

HYLL, Nicholas (fl 1423) member of the Chapel Royal DA

HYLTON, C. Barry (d 1916) performer? EA/17*

HYLTON, Jack (1892-1965) Eng-lish conductor, composer, manager TW/21, WWT/9-13, WWW/6

HYLTON, Millie (1868-1920) English actress CDP, WWT/3

HYLTON, Richard (1920-62) American actor TW/1, 4-7, 18, WWT/11

HYMAN, Earle (b 1926) American actor AAS, BE, TW/1, 9-16, 18-20, 22, 24, 27, 29-30, WWT/14-16

HYMAN, Elaine American actress TW/23, 27-28

HYMAN, Joseph M. (1901-77?) American producing manager BE, TW/3-6, WWT/11

HYMAN, Maurice A. (d 1907 [63]) music-hall director EA/08*

HYMAN, Prudence English dancer WWT/12

HYMAN, Walter A. (d 1973 [51]) producer/director/choreographer BP/58*

HYMER, John B. (d 1953 [77]) American dramatist WWT/6-11

HYMER, Warren (d 1948 [42]) actor BE*

HYND, Colin (d 1970 [84]) performer BP/55*

HYNES, Katherine English? actress TW/13

HYNICKA, Rudolph Kelker (1859-1927) American executive WWA/1

HYSLOP, Alfred (b 1925) American actor TW/5

HYSON, Dorothy (b 1915/16) American actress WWT/8-11

HYTOWN, Noel (d 1965 [66]) performer BP/50*

- I -

IACANGELO, Peter (b 1948) American actor TW/30

IBBOT, Miss (fl 1760-87) actress TD/1-2

IBRAHIM, Ada (d 1893) equilibrist EA/94*

IBSEN, Henrik (1828-1906) Norwegian dramatist COC, ES, GRB/1, OC/1-3, RE

IDA, Mr. acrobat CDP

IDALENE actress, singer CDP

IDE, Patrick (b 1916) English manager WWT/11-16

IDEN, Rosalind (b 1911) English

actress TW/3-4, WWT/10-14
IDZIKOWSKI, Stanislas (d 1977)
Polish dancer WWT/9-11
IFERD, Alice (d 1868) dancer
HAS
IGLESIAS, Roberto (b 1927)
Guatemalan dancer, choreog-
rapher CB
IGNATOV, Johnna (b 1941) Amer-
ican actress TW/30
IHNAT, Steve (d 1972 [37]) per-
former BP/56*
IKELHEIMER, Desire (fl 1848)
Belgian singer? HAS
ILES, Samuel (d 1872 [27]) musi-
cian EA/73*
ILIFF, Edward Henry (fl 1788)
actor TD/1-2
ILIFF, Mrs. Edward Henry ac-
tress TD/1-2
ILLING, Meta (d 1909 [37]) ac-
tress EA/11*, WWT/14*
ILLING, Peter (1905-66) Austrian
actor WWT/13-14
ILLINGTON, Margaret [Mrs.
Daniel Frohman] (1879/81-
1934) American actress DAB,
GRB/2-4, OC/1-3, SR, WWA/1,
WWM, WWS, WWT/1-7
ILLINGTON, Marie [Mrs. Gordon
Maddick] (d 1927 [71]) English
actress CDP, GRB/1-3,
OAA/2, WWT/1-5
ILLINGWORTH, Elsie (d 1973
[87]) performer BP/58*
ILLINGWORTH, Prunella see
Scales, Prunella
IMANO, Gertrude [Mrs. H. M.
Imano] (d 1899) singer EA/
00*
IMANO, Mrs. H. M. see
Imano, Gertrude
IMBERT, George see Charles,
G. F.
IMBODEN, David C. (d 1974
[87]) performer BP/58*
IMER, Teresa see Cornelys,
Teresa
IMESON, George L. (d 1918 [65])
EA/19*
IMESON, John (d 1885 [61])
manager EA/86*
IMHOF, Roger (d 1958 [83])
American vaudevillian TW/14
IMPERT, Margaret (b 1946)
American actress TW/30
IMRIE, Cuthbert (d 1908 [27])
actor? EA/09*

INCE, Alexander (1892-1966) Hun-
garian producer, publisher BE,
TW/22
INCE, Annette (fl 1849-57) dancer,
actress HAS
INCE, Edith see Melvin, Mrs.
A. Douglas
INCE, Emma (b 1828) American
dancer HAS
INCE, John E. (d 1909 [68]) come-
dian EA/10*
INCE, Ralph W. (d 1935 [50])
American actor, director BE*,
BP/21*
INCE, Thomas Harper (1882-1924)
American actor ES
INCH, William (d 1888 [44]) musi-
cian EA/90*
INCHBALD, Elizabeth [née Simpson]
(1753-1821) English actress,
dramatist CDP, COC, CP/3,
DNB, ES, GT, HP, OC/1-3,
SR, TD/1-2
INCHBALD, Joseph (d 1779) actor
BE*, WWT/14*
INCHINDI, Sig. (d 1876 [78]) singer
EA/77*
INCLEDON, Benjamin Charles
(1757/63-1826) English singer,
actor? CDP, DNB, GT, HAS,
OX, TD/1-2
INCLEDON, Charles (d 1826 [63])
WWT/14*
INCLEDON, Charles (1791-1865)
actor, singer DNB
INCLEDON, John (d 1826 [69])
singer EA/72*
INESCORT, Elaine (d 1964 [86])
English actress GRB/3-4,
WWT/1-8
INESCORT, Frieda (1901/05-76)
Scottish actress TW/1-7,
WWT/6-11
INFANT LYRA, The (fl 1825?)
musician CDP
ING, Alvin (b 1938) American actor
TW/27-28, 30
INGALS, Miles (d 1974 [71]) agent
BP/58*
INGE, Benson (d 1970 [61]) drama-
tist BP/54*
INGE, William (1913-73) American
dramatist AAS, CB, CD, CH,
COC, HJD, MD, MH, MWD,
NTH, OC/3, PDT, RE, TW/30,
WWA/5, WWT/12-15
INGELAND, Thomas (fl 1560s)
dramatist CP/1-2, FGF

INGERSOLL, Charles Jared (1782-1862) American dramatist EAP, RJ, SR

INGERSOLL, David (d 1847) American actor CDP, HAS, SR

INGERSOLL, William (d 1936 [76]) actor BP/20*, WWT/14*

INGHAM, Barrie (b 1932/42) English actor AAS, WWT/15-16

INGHAM, John dramatist EAP, RJ

INGHRAM, Rose American actress TW/2

INGLE, Charles (d 1940 [77]) composer WWT/14*

INGLEBY, Clement Mansfield (d 1886 [63]) Shakespearean commentator EA/87*

INGLESBY, Mona (b 1918) English dancer, choreographer WWT/10-12

INGLIS, George D. see Chaplin, George D.

INGLIS, Phil (d 1917) EA/18*

INGRAHAM, Prentiss (1843-1904) dramatist HJD

INGRAM, Alice [Mrs. J. R. Crauford] actress OAA/2

INGRAM, Beatrice [Mrs. Charles Borland] (fl 1890-1900) American actress WWM

INGRAM, Mrs. Clyde Rapp (d 1974 [75]) designer BP/58*

INGRAM, Fred (d 1916) comedian EA/17*

INGRAM, Gwladys (d 1911 [24]) actress EA/12*

INGRAM, Jack (d 1969 [66]) performer BP/53*

INGRAM, James (d 1890) "Late of Wall's Phantoscope Company" EA/91*

INGRAM, Rex (1896-1969) American actor BE, TW/2-6, 26, WWT/9-11

INKERSALL, J. G. (d 1867 [44]) singer EA/68*

INMAN, Bessie (d 1907) EA/08*

INMAN, Edward Frederick (d 1898 [69]) EA/99*

INMAN, Mary (d 1892) EA/93*

INNES, Isabel [Mrs. John Humphries] English actress GRB/1

INNESS-BROWN, Virginia Royall (b 1901) American executive BE

INTER-ACTION TRUST theatre collective CD

INTROPODI, Ethel (d 1946 [50]) American actress SR, TW/3

INTROPODI, Josie (d 1941 [75]) American actress BE*, BP/26*, WWT/14*

INVERARITY, Elizabeth see Martyn, Mrs. Charles

IONESCO, Eugène (b 1912) Rumanian/French dramatist BE, CB, COC, OC/3

IOOR, William (c. 1780-c. 1830) American dramatist DAB, EAP, HJD, RJ, WWA/H

IRELAND, Anthony (1902-57) Peruvian/English actor TW/7-8, 14, WWT/7-12

IRELAND, John (b 1916) Canadian actor, director BE

IRELAND, Joseph Norton (1817-98) American writer CDP, WWA/H

IRELAND, Kenneth (b 1920) Scottish administrator WWT/14-16

IRELAND, Thomas (d 1873 [65]) actor? EA/75*

IRELAND, William Henry (1775-1835) English forger, dramatist CDP, COC, CP/3, DNB, HP, OC/1-3, TD/1-2

IRISH, Annie [Mrs. J. E. Dodson] (1862/65-1947) English actress DP, GRB/2-4, WWS, WWT/1-5

IRISH, Frederick William (b 1835) English actor OAA/1-2

IRISH, Mrs. Frederick William see Desborough, Juliet

"IRISH ROSCIUS, The" see Burke, Joseph

IRMA, Mlle. (fl 1868) French actress CDP

IRSCHICH, Magda (fl 1866) German actress CDP

IRTON, Mrs. see Russell, Edith

IRVIN, John (d 1918) EA/19*

IRVINE, Harry (d 1951 [77]) English actor TW/1, 4, 8

IRVINE, John (d 1968 [55]) performer BP/52*

IRVINE, Richard F. (d 1976 [65]) designer BP/60*

IRVINE, Robin (1901-33) English actor WWT/7

IRVING, Ben (1919-68) American union executive BE

IRVING, Daisy (d 1938) Irish actress, singer WWT/3-7

IRVING, Elizabeth (b 1904) English actress WWT/4-6

IRVING, Ellis (b 1902) Australian
actor WWT/9-16
IRVING, Ernest (d 1953 [75])
composer, conductor WWT/14*
IRVING, Ethel [Mrs. Gilbert Por-
teous] (1869-1963) actress
GRB/1-4, WWT/1-11
IRVING, Frederick R. (d 1969
[75]) performer BP/54*
IRVING, George (1874-1914)
American actor WWA/1, WWS
IRVING, George S. [né George
Irving Shelasky] (b 1922)
American actor, singer BE,
TW/5-6, 9-10, 13-14, 16,
19-30, WWT/15-16
IRVING, Henrietta (1855-91)
American actress CDP, HAS,
SR
IRVING, Sir Henry [John Henry
Brodribb] (1838-1905) English
actor, manager CDP, COC,
DNB, DP, ES, GRB/1, HP,
NTH, OAA/1-2, OC/1-3,
PDT, SR, WWA/1, WWW/1
IRVING, H[enry] B[rodribb] (1870-
1919) English actor CDP,
COC, EA/97, ES, GRB/1-4,
NTH, OC/1-3, SR, WWS,
WWT/1-3, WWW/2
IRVING, Mrs. H[enry] B[rodribb]
see Baird, Dorothea
IRVING, Isabel [Mrs. W. H.
Thompson] (1871-1944) Amer-
ican actress GRB/2-4, PP/2,
SR, TW/1, WWA/2, WWM,
WWS, WWT/1-8
IRVING, John (d 1867 [63]) pro-
fessor of music EA/68*
IRVING, John (b 1927) English
actor TW/17
IRVING, Mrs. Joseph (d 1925
[80]) actress BE*, WWT/14*
IRVING, Joseph Henry (d 1870
[31]) English comedian HAS
IRVING, Jules [né Jules Israel]
(b 1925) American director,
producer BE, CB, WWT/
15-16
IRVING, K. Ernest (1878-1953)
English composer, conductor
WWT/9-11
IRVING, Laurence Henry Forster
(b 1897) English designer,
writer AAS, COC, ES,
OC/3, WWT/6-14
IRVING, Laurence Sidney Brod-
ribb (1871-1914) English actor,

dramatist COC, ES, GRB/1-4,
NTH, OC/1-3, SR, WWT/1-2,
WWW/1
IRVING, Mrs. Laurence Sidney
Brodribb see Hackney, Mabel
IRVING, Roy (b 1911) English actor
TW/4, 9
IRVING, Sydney [Mrs. Maurice H.
Hoffmann] (d 1900) EA/01*
IRVING, Washington (1783-1859)
American dramatist COC, ES,
OC/3
IRWIN, Charles Irish actor TW/1
IRWIN, Edward (1867-1937) English
actor, dramatist WWT/5-8
IRWIN, Eyles (b 1751) Indian/Irish
dramatist CP/3
IRWIN, Felix (d 1950 [57]) actor
BE*, WWT/14*
IRWIN, Flo (d 1930 [71]) Canadian
actress BE*, BP/15*
IRWIN, Kathleen (fl 1868-77) Eng-
lish actress, singer OAA/1-2
IRWIN, Margaret (d 1967) writer
WWW/6
IRWIN, Max (d 1864) American
comedian HAS
IRWIN, May [Mrs. Kurt Eisfeldt]
(1862-1938) Canadian actress
DAB, GRB/2-4, PP/2, SR,
WWA/1, WWM, WWS, WWT/1-8
IRWIN, Percy G. (d 1917) actor?
EA/18*
IRWIN, Selden (b 1833) American
actor HAS, SR
IRWIN, Mrs. Seldon (b 1834)
American actress HAS
IRWIN, Wallace (1875-1959) Amer-
ican dramatist WWA/3
IRWIN, Will (b 1907) American
musician, musical director,
composer BE
IRWIN, William Henry (1873-1948)
American dramatist WWA/2
ISAAC (c. 1655-c. 1720) English bal-
let master ES
ISAAC, Arthur (d 1890) actor EA/
91*
ISAAC, John (1791-1839) actor
CDP
ISAACS, Mr. (b 1791) singer BS
ISAACS, Miss see Millar, Mrs.
S. A.
ISAACS, A. see Andrews, A.
ISAACS, Edith J. R. (1878-1956)
American theatrical journalist,
critic, historian AAS, COC,
ES, NTH, OC/1-3, TW/12,

WWA/3, WWT/7-11
ISAACS, P. B. (1831-65) Eng-
lish minstrel HAS, SR
ISAACS, Rebecca [Mrs. Thomas
Roberts] (d 1877 [47]) actress,
singer CDP
ISAACSON, Carl L. (b 1920)
American educator BE
ISDELL, Miss (fl 1811) Irish
dramatist CP/3
ISHAM, Frederick S. (d 1922
[57]) dramatist BE*, BP/7*
ISHAM, Sir Gyles (1903-76) Eng-
lish actor WWT/6-11
ISHERWOOD, Mr. American actor
HAS
ISHERWOOD, Mrs. [Miss Clark]
(d 1841) American actress
HAS
ISHERWOOD, Christopher (b 1904)
English dramatist CB, CD,
HJD, HP, MD, MH, MWD,
NTH, PDT, WWT/9-11
ISHERWOOD, Harry (d 1840) ac-
tor, scene painter SR
ISHERWOOD, William (d 1841)
American actor HAS
ISHII, Kan (d 1972 [71]) performer
BP/56*
ISIDORA, Don (d 1876) actor
EA/77*
ISLIPP, Adam (fl 1622) share-
holder DA
ISOLA, Emile (d 1945 [85])
manager BE*, WWT/14*
ISOLA, Vincent (d 1947 [85])
manager BE*, WWT/14*
ISRAEL, Jules see Irving,
Jules
ITALIANO, Anne see Bancroft,
Anne
ITKIN, Bella (b 1920) Russian
director BE
ITO, Yuji (d 1963 [66]) scene
designer BP/48*
IT'S ALL RIGHT TO BE WOMAN
THEATRE theatre collective
CD
IVAN, Rosalind (d 1959 [75])
English actress TW/15
IVANOFF, Nicholas (1809-80)
singer CDP
IVANS, Elaine (b 1900) American
actress TW/2-3
IVERS, Miss see Orger, Mrs.
Thomas
IVES, Alice E. (1883-1930)
American dramatist SR, WWM

IVES, Anne American actress
TW/27-30
IVES, Burl (b 1909) American ac-
tor, singer BE, CB, ES, TW/
1, 6-7, 10-13, 24, WWT/15-16
IVES, George (b 1922) American
actor TW/6-7
IVES, G. H. (d 1862) Irish magi-
cian HAS, SR
IVES, Joe (d 1917) EA/18*
IVES, Robert (d 1879) singer EA/
80*
IVO, Alexander actor TW/1
IVOR, Frances Scottish actress
EA/96, GRB/3-4, WWT/1-7
IVORY, Thomas (1709-79) architect
DNB
IXON, Mrs. see Beaumont, Mrs.
IZANT, Robert J. (d 1971 [84])
critic BP/56*
IZARD, Alfred E. (d 1910 [47])
musician EA/11*
IZENOUR, George (b 1912) Ameri-
can theatre designer BE
IZON, Ada (d 1889) EA/90*
IZON, Thomas (d 1900 [55]) music-
hall comedian EA/01*
IZUMI, Edward I. (d 1975 [63])
performer BP/60*

- J -

J., B. (fl 1661) dramatist CP/1-3
J., T. (fl 1654) dramatist CP/3
JACCHIA, Agide (1875-1932) Italian
musical director WWA/1
JACK, Edwin Booth (b 1863) actor
HAS
JACK, H. V. see Esmond, Henry
V.
JACK, John Henry (b 1836) Ameri-
can actor, manager CDP, HAS,
PP/2
JACK, Rosalie (b 1855) American
actress HAS
JACK, Sam T. (d 1899 [46]) mana-
ger CDP
JACK, Walter C. (d 1888 [27])
American actor EA/89*
JACKLEY, George (d 1950 [65])
comedian BE*, WWT/14*
JACKMAN, H. (d 1873) musician
EA/74*
JACKMAN, Henry Wilson (d 1879)
treasurer EA/80*
JACKMAN, Isaac (fl 1777-95)
Irish dramatist CP/2-3, DNB,

GT, TD/1
JACKMAN, W. (d 1852 [70])
manager EA/72*
JACKSON (fl c. 1629) actor DA
JACKSON, Mr. (fl 1714) trans-
lator CP/2-3
JACKSON, Miss (fl 1775) actress
CDP
JACKSON, Abram Wilbur (1806-
66) American actor, theatre
builder, manager CDP, HAS
JACKSON, Al (d 1975 [39]) com-
poser/lyricist BP/60*
JACKSON, Albert (d 1913) Eng-
lish actor SR
JACKSON, Alfred Graham (d
1965 [72]) dramatist BP/50*
JACKSON, Ann see Jackson,
Anne (b 1926)
JACKSON, Anne (1782-1869)
actress COC
JACKSON, Anne (b 1926) Amer-
ican actress BE, ES, TW/
5-24, 26-28, 30, WWT/11-16
JACKSON, Sir Barry Vincent
(1879-1961) English manager,
dramatist AAS, COC, ES,
OC/1-3, PDT, WWT/4-13,
WWW/6
JACKSON, C. D. (b 1902) Amer-
ican publisher BE
JACKSON, Charles (fl 1857)
American actor HAS
JACKSON, Charles (d 1873)
music-hall chairman EA/74*
JACKSON, Charles (d 1968 [65])
dramatist BP/53*
JACKSON, Charlotte [Miss Cubitt]
(d 1870) singer? musician?
EA/71*
JACKSON, Dorothea American
actress TW/3
JACKSON, Edward (fl 1622) les-
see DA
JACKSON, Ella (fl 1862) actress
HAS
JACKSON, Ernestine American
actress TW/30
JACKSON, Ethel (1877-1957)
American actress, singer
TW/14, WWT/1-10
JACKSON, Freda (b 1909) Eng-
lish actress AAS, WWT/9-16
JACKSON, Frederic (1886-1953)
American dramatist WWT/
4-11
JACKSON, George (d 1871 [24])
music-hall chairman EA/72*

JACKSON, George James William
(d 1896) professor of music
EA/98*
JACKSON, Glenda (b 1936) English
actress AAS, CB, WWT/15-16
JACKSON, Gordon (b 1923) Scottish
actor WWT/15-16
JACKSON, Harry (fl 1865) Australian
actor, circus clown HAS, SR
JACKSON, Harry (d 1885 [49]) ac-
tor, stage manager EA/86*,
WWT/14*
JACKSON, Harry (b 1923) American
actor TW/10-12
JACKSON, Mrs. Harry [Annie Lock-
hart] (fl c. 1865) actress HAS,
SR
JACKSON, Mrs. Harry see
Jackson, Marie Louise
JACKSON, Hart (d 1882 [47]) drama-
tist, manager CDP
JACKSON, Henry Conrad (d 1973
[46]) performer BP/58*
JACKSON, Horace Bertie (d 1908)
showman EA/09*
JACKSON, Isabella [Mrs. T. Jack-
son] (d 1871 [26]) EA/72*
JACKSON, James (fl 1789?) singer
CDP
JACKSON, Jane see Bianchi,
Mrs. Francesco
JACKSON, Jennie (d 1976 [54]) per-
former BP/60*
JACKSON, Jenny (d 1899 [27])
male impersonator EA/00*
JACKSON, Joe (d 1942 [62]) Austrian
comedian CB
JACKSON, John (1742-1806) English
actor, manager, dramatist CDP,
CP/2-3, DNB, GT
JACKSON, John (1769-1845) English
pugilist CDP, DNB
JACKSON, John [né McIllway] (d
1843) American slack-rope per-
former HAS
JACKSON, John (d 1892) music-hall
proprietor EA/94*
JACKSON, John Enderby (d 1903
[76]) manager EA/04*
JACKSON, John George (d 1879
[35]) professor of music EA/81*
. JACKSON, John Sidney (d 1859)
HAS
JACKSON, Leonard [L. Errol
Jaye] (b 1928) American actor
TW/26-29
JACKSON, Lizzie see Mathews,
Mrs. Charles James

JACKSON, Marie Louise [Mrs. Harry Jackson] (d 1903) EA/04*

JACKSON, Mary (b 1915) American actress TW/26

JACKSON, Minnie (fl 1859-69) actress HAS

JACKSON, Nelson (b 1870) English entertainer GRB/1-3

JACKSON, Phebe (d 1891) EA/92*

JACKSON, Mrs. T. see Jackson, Isabella

JACKSON, Theodore (b 1838) American actor, minstrel HAS, SR

JACKSON, Theodore John (d 1891 [58]) musical director EA/92*

JACKSON, Thomas (d 1798) actor TD/2

JACKSON, Thomas (d 1967 [81]) performer BP/52*

JACKSON, W. F. (d 1896 [63]) singer EA/97*

JACKSON, William (1730-1803) English dramatist, composer, performer CDP, CP/3, GT, TD/1-2

JACKSON, William (d 1876) musician EA/77*

JACOB, Giles (1686-1744) dramatist CP/1-3, GT

JACOB, Sir Hildebrand (fl 1664) English dramatist CP/1-3, GT

JACOB, Naomi (1889-1964) English actress WWT/10-11

JACOBI, Derek (b 1938) English actor AAS, WWT/15-16

JACOBI, Frederick (1891-1952) American composer WWA/3

JACOBI, Georges (1840-1906) German composer, conductor GRB/1, WWW/1

JACOBI, Lou (b 1913) Canadian actor BE, TW/23-26, 28, 30, WWT/15-16

JACOBI, Maurice (d 1939) musical director BE*, WWT/14*

JACOBI, Victor (1883-1921) Hungarian composer BE*, BP/6*, WWT/14*

JACOBS, Mr. (d 1870) wizard EA/71*

JACOBS, Miss (fl 1792) singer TD/1-2

JACOBS, Arthur P. (d 1973 [51]) producer/director/choreographer BP/58*

JACOBS, Austin Lewis see Parker, Lew

JACOBS, Carl (b 1916) American actor TW/24

JACOBS, Charles (fl 1857) singer HAS

JACOBS, E. M. (d 1966 [85]) booking agent BP/51*

JACOBS, G. W. musician CDP

JACOBS, Helen (d 1974 [53]) producer/director/choreographer BP/59*

JACOBS, Jim (b 1942) American actor, librettist CD, TW/28

JACOBS, Max William (b 1937) American actor TW/22

JACOBS, Morris (b 1906) American business manager BE

JACOBS, Sally [née Rich] (b 1932) English designer AAS, WWT/15-16

JACOBS, Steven (d 1969 [32]) talent scout BP/54*

JACOBS, Thomas (d 1976 [73]) stand in BP/60*

JACOBS, Will (b 1945) American actor TW/29

JACOBS, William Wymark (1863-1943) English dramatist WWM, WWT/1-9

JACOBSEN, L. H. (d 1941 [81]) critic BE*

JACOBSON, Mr. singer, musician CDP

JACOBSON, Barbara Scott (d 1972 [57]) performer BP/56*

JACOBSON, Clarence (d 1971 [84]) manager BP/56*

JACOBSON, Irving (b 1905) American actor, producer BE

JACOBSON, Lisa Japanese/American actress TW/30

JACOBSON, Sam (d 1964 [89]) performer BE*

JACOBSON, Sol (b 1912) American press representative BE

JACOBY, Scott (b 1955) American actor TW/24, 26

JACQUEMOT, Ray American actor TW/3-7

JACQUES, Mrs. Edgar F. see Jacques, Fanny Lavinia

JACQUES, Fanny Lavinia [Mrs. Edgar F. Jacques] (d 1911 [81]) EA/12*

JACQUES, Frederic (b 1864) English actor GRB/1

JACQUES, Mrs. Frederic see Rayner, Minnie Gray

JACQUES, Hattie [née Josephine Edwina] (b 1924) English actress WWT/13-16

JACQUES, Josephine Edwina see Jacques, Hattie

JACQUES, Rosa (d 1857) singer HAS

JACQUIN, Maurice (d 1974 [74]) producer/director/choreographer BP/59*

JADEN, Donna Mae see Paige, Janis

JAELL, Alfred (1832-82) musician, composer CDP

JAFFE, Carl (d 1974 [72]) actor, producer BP/58*, WWT/16*

JAFFE, Herb English literary representative BE

JAFFE, Michael (d 1976 [71]) performer BP/60*

JAFFE, Sam (b 1893/97/98) American actor AAS, BE, TW/2-8, 10-15, WWT/8-16

JAFFE, Teri (d 1975 [58]) charity organiser BP/60*

JAGGARD, William (1568-1623) English printer, publisher NTH

JAGGER, Dean (b 1904) American actor TW/4-6, WWT/10-11

JAGO, Richard (1715-81) English dramatist CP/3

JAHN, Marie Léonie Eugénie see Yahne, Mlle.

JAKEWAY, Samuel John (d 1887) singer EA/88*

JALKIO, Maj-Lis (b 1945) actress TW/30

JALLAND, Henry (1861-1928) English business manager WWT/2-4

JAMES, Albert (fl 1868-90) actor, singer CDP, DP

JAMES, Amelia Jane see Smythson, Miss Montague

JAMES, Aphie [Mrs. Louis James] (b 1875) American actress WWA/5, WWM

JAMES, C. (fl 1787) translator CP/3

JAMES, Cairns see James, Lewis Cairns

JAMES, Mrs. Cairns see Moore, Jessie

JAMES, C. H. see Eversley, H. A.

JAMES, Mrs. Charles see James, Sarah

JAMES, Charles A. (d 1917) proprietor EA/18*

JAMES, Charles James (d 1888 [83/84]) scene artist, producer, lessee BE*, EA/89*, WWT/14*

JAMES, Charles S. (d 1868 [35]) scene artist EA/69*

JAMES, Charlotte Varian (fl 1859) American singer? HAS

JAMES, Clifton (d 1963 [65]) actor BE*

JAMES, Clifton (b 1921) American actor BE, TW/14, 19, 21-22, 24

JAMES, C. Stanfield (d 1868 [35]) scene artist, manager WWT/14*

JAMES, Culver see Dacre, Arthur

JAMES, Cyril (d 1975 [63]) producer/director/choreographer BP/60*

JAMES, David (1839-93) English actor CDP, COC, DNB, DP, OAA/1-2, OC/1-3

JAMES, Mrs. David (d 1881 [38]) EA/82*

JAMES, David, Jr. (d 1917) actor, director BE*, WWT/14*

JAMES, Dorothy Dorian American actress TW/28

JAMES, Edwin F. (fl 1865) actor HAS

JAMES, Emrys (b 1930) Welsh actor AAS, WWT/15-16

JAMES, Eric (b 1943) American actor TW/25-26

JAMES, Mrs. E. W. see James, Florrie

JAMES, Florence (1857-1929) English dramatist WWW/3

JAMES, Florrie [Mrs. E. W. James] (d 1911 [28]) EA/12*

JAMES, Francesca American actress TW/30

JAMES, Francis (b 1907) Australian actor WWT/7-10

JAMES, Frankie (d 1974 [72]) actress, singer TW/30

JAMES, Frazer singer CDP

JAMES, George (d 1898 [76]) comedian EA/99*

JAMES, Gerald (d 1964 [77]) actor, manager BE*, WWT/14*

JAMES, Gerald (b 1917) Welsh actor AAS, WWT/15-16

JAMES, Hal (d 1971 [58]) producer TW/28

JAMES, Hattie (1845-61) English dancer HAS

JAMES, Haydn (d 1916) musical director, composer EA/17*

JAMES, Henry (1843-1916) American dramatist COC, DNB, ES, HJD, HP, MD, MWD, OC/1-3, PDT, RE

JAMES, Horace D. (d 1925 [72]) actor BE*, BP/10*

JAMES, Jessie (d 1974 [38]) performer BP/59*

JAMES, John (d 1900) acrobat EA/01*

JAMES, John Albert (d 1906 [33]) minstrel, comedian EA/07*

JAMES, John Edward (d 1885 [54]) EA/86*

JAMES, Johnny Painter (d 1881) step-dancer EA/82*

JAMES, Julia (1890-1964) English actress WWT/2-5

JAMES, Kate (d 1913 [57]) actress CDP

JAMES, Lewis Cairns (1865-1946) Scottish actor, singer, stage manager, producer WWW/4

JAMES, Lil [Mrs. Tony Dido] (d 1904) music-hall performer EA/05*

JAMES, Lithgow (d 1900) singer EA/01*, WWT/14*

JAMES, Louis (1842-1910) American actor COC, DAB, GRB/2-4, OC/1-3, PP/2, SR, WWA/1, WWS

JAMES, Mrs. Louis see James, Aphie

JAMES, Mary American actress TW/2-7, 9

JAMES, Michael see Jayston, Michael

JAMES, Millie [Mrs. Edgar Seidenberg] (b 1876) actress GRB/2, WWS

JAMES, Peter (b 1940) English director WWT/16

JAMES, Philip (d 1975 [85]) composer/lyricist BP/60*

JAMES, Polly English actress (b 1941) English actress TW/21, WWT/16

JAMES, Mrs. P. R. see Smythson, Miss Montague

JAMES, Rian (d 1953 [53]) dramatist BE*, BP/37*

JAMES, Richard Jones's Boy (fl 1599) actor? DA

JAMES, Sarah [Mrs. Charles James] (d 1905 [47]) EA/06*

JAMES, Sidney (d 1976 [62]) actor BP/60*

JAMES, Skip (d 1969 [67]) performer BP/54*

JAMES, William (b 1938) American actor TW/29

JAMESON, House (1902-71) American actor BE, TW/15, 19-20, 22-24, 27

JAMESON, Jo Anne (b 1944) American actress TW/23

JAMESON, Joyce (b 1932) American actress BE

JAMESON, Pauline (b 1920) English actress AAS, WWT/11-16

JAMES-TAYLOR, Jeremy (b 1948) English actor TW/30

JAMIESON, Carrie (d 1892) American actress EA/93*

JAMIESON, George (1812-68) American actor, dramatist CDP, HAS, RJ

JAMIESON, William L. (1835-68) American actor HAS

JAMIN, Georges (d 1971 [64]) performer BP/55*

JAMIN-BARTLETT, D. (b 1948) American actress TW/29

JAMISON, Alexander (d 1880 [84]) musician EA/81*

JAMISON, Bob (1799-1868) English actor HAS

JAMISON, Judith (b 1944) American dancer CB

JAMISON, Marshall (b 1918) American producer, director, actor BE

JAMROG, Joe (b 1932) American actor TW/30

JANAUSCHEK, Francesca Romana Magdalena (1830-1904) Czech actress CDP, COC, DAB, HAS, OC/1-3, PP/2, WWA/1

JANCOWSKI, Elizabeth (d 1904) EA/05*

JANES, Kenneth H. English educator, director, actor, dramatist BE

JANIS, Chelle (d 1974 [71]) performer BP/59*

JANIS, Conrad (b 1928) American actor, musician BE, TW/1-2, 8-16, 18-20, 25-26, 29, WWT/15-16

JANIS, Elsie (1889-1956) American actress, mimic COC, GRB/3-4,

NTH, SR, TW/12, WWA/3,
WWS, WWT/1-11
JANIS, Percy (d 1907) American
actor GRB/3*
JANISCH, Antonie (fl 1868) Aus-
trian actress CDP
JANNEY, Ben (b 1927) American
director, stage manager BE
JANNEY, Leon (b 1917) American
actor BE, TW/5-6, 10-16,
18, 20-21, 26
JANNEY, Russell (1884-1963)
American manager CB, TW/
20, WWA/4, WWT/6-9
JANNINGS, Emil (1886-1950)
American/German actor NTH
JANNINGS, Orin (d 1966 [48])
actor, dramatist TW/23
JANS, Harry (d 1962 [62]) per-
former BE*
JANSEN, Jim (b 1945) American
actor TW/30
JANSEN, Marie (1864-1914) Amer-
ican actress, singer CDP, SR,
WWA/1, WWS
JANSSEN, Herbert (b 1895) Ger-
man singer ES
JANVIER, Emma (d 1924) come-
dienne BE*, BP/9*, WWT/14*
"JAPANESE TOMMY" see
Delverd, Thomas
JAQUES, Eliza (d 1893 [71])
EA/94*
JAQUES, Francis (fl 1642) drama-
tist CP/2-3, FGF
JAQUET, Catharine (b 1760)
actress CDP
JARBEAU, Vernona (d 1914 [53])
actress CDP
JARDINE, Betty [Elizabeth Mc-
Kittrick Jardine] (d 1945) Eng-
lish actress WWT/9
JARDON, Dorothy (d 1966 [83])
performer BP/51*
JARKOWSKY, Andrew American
actor TW/30
JARMAN, Anthony (fl 1622)
lessee DA
JARMAN, Frances Eleanor
see Ternan, Mrs. Thomas
JARMAN, Herbert (1871-1919)
actor GRB/3-4, WWT/1-3
JARMAN, Peter (d 1969) critic
BP/54*
JARNAC, Dorothy American ac-
tress TW/2, 5-7, 10
JARRATT, Edward (d 1885 [86])
EA/86*

JARRELL, Randall (d 1965 [51])
dramatist BP/50*
JARRETT, Asbury Bond (d 1894
[62]) American manager EA/95*
JARRETT, Bella (b 1931) American
actress TW/29
JARRETT, Henry C. (d 1886)
manager BE*
JARRETT, Henry C. (1827/28-1903)
American actor, manager CDP,
HAS, SR
JARRETT, Jerry (b 1918) American
actor TW/25-29
JARRY, Alfred (1873-1907) French
dramatist COC, OC/3
JARVICE (fl 1635) musician DA
JARVIS, Ernest Herbert (d 1908)
showman's manager EA/09*
JARVIS, Graham (b 1930) Canadian
actor TW/23-25, 30
JARVIS, Henry (d 1871 [44]) actor
EA/72*
JARVIS, J. H. (1845-87) English
actor NYM
JARVIS, Robert C. (d 1971 [79])
director, actor, singer TW/28
JASLOW, Annette Schein (d 1967
[79]) publicity agent BP/51*
JASON, Harvey (b 1940) English
actor TW/22-23
JASON, Rick (b 1926) American ac-
tor TW/6-9
JASON, Will (d 1970 [69]) com-
poser/lyricist BP/54*
JASPER, Zina (b 1939) American
actress TW/24, 26-27
JAY, David (b 1961) American actor
TW/28, 30
JAY, Don American actor TW/30
JAY, Dorothy (b 1897) English ac-
tress, singer WWT/4-5
JAY, Ernest (1893-1957) English
actor WWT/9-12
JAY, Harriett (1863-1932) English
dramatist DP, GRB/4, WWT/
1-6, WWW/3
JAY, Isabel [Mrs. H. S. H. Caven-
dish] (1879-1927) English actress,
singer GRB/1-4, WWT/1-5
JAY, John Herbert (1871-1942)
English business manager,
manager WWT/1-9
JAY, William (b 1935) American
actor TW/24-29
JAYE, L. Errol see Jackson,
Leonard
JAYSTON, Michael [né James] (b
1936) English actor WWT/15-16

JEAKINS, Dorothy (b 1914) American costume designer BE

JEAN, Jess [John William Quick] (d 1908 [55]) EA/09*

JEANMAIRE, Zizi [Renée] (b 1924) French dancer, singer, actress BE, CB, ES, TW/10-11, 21

JEANNETTE, Gertrude (b 1918) American actress TW/25-26

JEANS, Frederick see Lennox, Fred J.

JEANS, Isabel (b 1891) English actress AAS, NTH, WWT/5-16

JEANS, Ronald (1887-1973) English dramatist AAS, WWT/4-14

JEANS, Ursula (1906-73) Indian/English actress AAS, NTH, TW/29, WWT/6-15

JEAYES, Allan (1885-1963) English actor WWT/4-13

JECKS, Mrs. Charles A. see Coveney, Harriett

JECKS, Charles Albert (d 1895) business manager, manager EA/96*, WWT/14*

JECKS, Clara (d 1951 [94]) actress DP, EA/97, GRB/3-4, OAA/2, WWT/1-6

JEDD, Gerry (d 1962 [37]) American actor TW/16, 19

JEE, Mrs. Albert (d 1906 [24]) EA/07*

JEE, Henry Williams see Burnell, Harry

JEE, James Henry (d 1906 [57]) acrobat, circus proprietor EA/07*

JEE, Joseph (d 1890 [49]) musical performer? EA/91*

JEE, Joseph (d 1911) music-hall performer EA/12*

JEE, Mrs. Joseph, Sr. (d 1887) EA/88*

JEE, William (d 1885 [40]) musical grotesque EA/86*

JEFF (d 1899) music-hall performer EA/00*

JEFFERIES, Mr. dramatist CP/1

JEFFERIES, Mr. (fl 1812) actor CDP

JEFFERIES, Douglas (1884-1959) English actor WWT/5-12

JEFFERIMI, Mr. (fl 1835) actor CDP

JEFFERS, Doug (b 1942) American actor TW/29

JEFFERS, John Robinson (1887-1962) American dramatist ES, HJD, HP, MD, MH, MWD, TW/18

JEFFERSON, Mr. actor TD/2

JEFFERSON, Mrs. Arthur see Metcalfe, Madge

JEFFERSON, Charles Burke (1851-1908) American actor, manager OC/1-3

JEFFERSON, Cornelia (b 1835) American actress HAS, SR

JEFFERSON, Cornelia Frances [Cornelia Frances Thomas] (1796-1849) actress, singer CDP, HAS, OC/1-3, SR, WWA/H

JEFFERSON, Elizabeth see Chapman, Elizabeth

JEFFERSON, Euphemia American? actress? ES

JEFFERSON, Herbert, Jr. (b 1946) American actor TW/29

JEFFERSON, Hester (d c. 1845) American? actress? ES

JEFFERSON, John (d 1831) American actor ES, HAS, SR

JEFFERSON, Joseph (1774-1832) English/American actor CDP, DAB, ES, HAS, OC/1-3, SR, WWA/H

JEFFERSON, Joseph (1804-42) American actor, scene painter CDP, ES, HAS, OC/1-3, SR

JEFFERSON, Joseph (1829-1905) American actor CDP, COC, DAB, GRB/1, HAS, HJD, NTH, OAA/1-2, OC/1-3, PP/2, SR, WWA/1, WWW/1

JEFFERSON, Joseph (1869-1919) American actor WWA/1

JEFFERSON, Mrs. Joseph [née Thomas; Mrs. Thomas Burke] (1796-1850) American singer, actress? ES, HAS

JEFFERSON, Mrs. Joseph, I [Miss Lockyer] (1832-61) English actress HAS

JEFFERSON, Mary Anne American? actress? ES

JEFFERSON, Maude [Mrs. Edward P. Durham] (b 1885) American actress GRB/1

JEFFERSON, Thomas (1732-1807) English actor, manager CDP, ES, OC/1-3

JEFFERSON, Thomas (d 1824) American actor ES, HAS

JEFFERSON, Thomas (d 1932 [76]) actor BE*, BP/16*, WWT/14*

JEFFERSON, William Winter (d
1946 [70]) English actor BE*,
BP/30*, WWT/14*
JEFFERY, Daniel Smith (d 1904
[44]) singer EA/05*
JEFFERYE, William (d 1889
[60]) proprietor EA/90*
JEFFES, Anthony (fl 1597-1612)
actor DA
JEFFES, Humphrey (d 1618) actor
DA
JEFFORD, Barbara (b 1930) Eng-
lish actress AAS, BE, WWT/
11-16
JEFFREY, John dramatist? FGF
JEFFREY, Peter (b 1929) English
actor WWT/16
JEFFREY, Robert (b 1934) Cana-
dian actor TW/18-19
JEFFREYS, Ann (b 1923/28)
American actress, singer
BE, TW/3-11, 22, WWT/11-16
JEFFREYS, Ellis [Mrs. Herbert
Sleath Skelton] (1868/72-1943)
Irish actress GRB/1-4, SR,
WWS, WWT/1-9
JEFFREYS, George (1678-1755)
English dramatist CP/2-3,
DNB, GT, TD/1-2
JEFFREYS, Hilda Irish actress
GRB/1
JEFFREYS, Ida (d 1926 [70])
actress BE*, BP/10*, WWT/
14*
JEFFREYS-GOODFRIEND, Ida
see Jeffreys, Ida
JEFFRIES, Emblem Ann (d 1892
[82]) EA/93*
JEFFRIES, Maud (1869-1946)
American actress GRB/1-4,
SR, PP/2, WWS, WWT/1-8
JEFFRIES, W. W. (d 1867) actor
HAS
JEFFRYS, George (d 1755 [77])
dramatist BE*, WWT/14*
JEFFS, Charles William (d 1886
[55]) music-hall singer EA/87*
JEFFS, Elizabeth Walker [Mrs.
Waller Jeffs] (d 1909 [43])
EA/10*
JEFFS, Mrs. Waller see Jeffs,
Elizabeth Walker
JEFTON, J. O. (d 1881) comedian
EA/82*
JEHLINGER, Charles (1866-1952)
American teacher TW/9
JELLICOE, Anne (b 1927) English
dramatist, director AAS, CD,

CH, ES, MH, MWD, PDT, RE,
WWT/14-16
JELLIFFE, Rowena Woodham (b
1892) American executive, di-
rector BE
JELLINECK, Frances see Wil-
liams, Frances
JELLINGS-BLOW, Sydney see
Blow, Sydney
JENKINS, Allen (d 1974 [74]) actor
BP/59*, WWT/16*
JENKINS, Billy (d 1880 [34]) eques-
trian clown EA/81*
JENKINS, Claude (d 1967 [88])
producer/director/choreographer
BP/52*
JENKINS, David (d 1883 [31]) pro-
prietor EA/84*
JENKINS, Emma (d 1909) EA/10*
JENKINS, George (b 1910) American
designer BE, ES, TW/5-8,
WWT/15-16
JENKINS, James George (d 1878
[21]) musician EA/79*
JENKINS, Megs (b 1917) English
actress AAS, WWT/10-16
JENKINS, Patricia American ac-
tress TW/13-14
JENKINS, R. Claud (1878-1967)
English producer, manager
WWT/9-11
JENKINS, Richard Walter see
Burton, Richard
JENKINS, Warren E. C. (b 1905)
English actor, director WWT/
8-16
JENKINS, William K. (d 1968 [77])
executive BP/52*
JENKS, Frank (d 1962) American
actor BE*
JENKS, Fred (1874-1947) American
clown SR
JENKS, Si (d 1970 [93]) performer
BP/54*
JENNENS, Charles (d 1773) editor,
composer CP/2-3, GT, TD/1-2
JENNER, Caryl [Pamela Penelope
Ripman] (1917-73) English di-
rector, manager COC, WWT/
12-15
JENNER, Charles (1737-74) drama-
tist CP/2-3, GT
JENNER, Edwin (d 1909) EA/10*
JENNINGS, Mr. (d 1880 [32])
EA/82*
JENNINGS, Mrs. (fl 1863) English
actress HAS
JENNINGS, Mrs. Charles Herrick

see Auckland, Marie

JENNINGS, Dewitt C. (d 1937) American actor BE*, BP/21*

JENNINGS, Frederick (1890-1947) actor, banjoist SR

JENNINGS, Frederick Summers (b 1872) English manager GRB/1

JENNINGS, George (d 1912) EA/14*

JENNINGS, Gertrude E. (d 1958 [81]) dramatist WWT/3-12, WWW/5

JENNINGS, Hargrave (d 1890) singer? EA/91*

JENNINGS, Harry (d 1910) comic singer, clog dancer EA/11*

JENNINGS, Mrs. J. H. (d 1893) singer EA/94*

JENNINGS, John Charles (d 1887 [27]) equestrian EA/88*

JENNINGS, John Henry (d 1902 [78]) singer, manager CDP

JENNINGS, Thomas (d 1880 [70]) musician EA/81*

JENNINGS, Toney (d 1878 [80]) musician EA/79*

JENNION, Tom (d 1901) EA/02*

JENNISON, John (d 1869 [80]) proprietor EA/70*

JENNYNGES, Giles (fl 1594) actor DA

JENOURE, Aida [Mrs. Howard Cochran] English actress, singer GRB/1-4, WWT/1-7

JENS, Salome (b 1935/36) American actress BE, TW/19-21, 23-26, 28, WWT/15-16

JENSEN, Adolf (d 1879 [41]) composer EA/80*

JENSEN, Howard C. (d 1972 [58]) producer/director/choreographer BP/57*

JENSEN, Petronella see Ella, Miss

JENSEN, Sterling (b 1925) American actor TW/27-28

JEPHSON, Robert (1736-1803?) Irish? dramatist CDP, CP/2-3, DNB, GT, SR, TD/1-2

JEPPE, Mr. (fl 1874?) singer CDP

JEREMY, James (d 1899) musician EA/00*

JERITZA, Maria (b 1887) Czech singer ES

JERNINGHAM, Edward (1727-1812) English dramatist CDP, CP/

2-3, DNB, GT, TD/1-2

JEROME, Ben M. (d 1938 [c. 55]) American composer BE*

JEROME, Mrs. Charles [Ella Jerome] (d 1889 [35]) vaudevillian EA/90*

JEROME, Daisy American actress, variety artist GRB/1-4

JEROME, Edwin (d 1959 [73]) actor BE*, BP/44*

JEROME, Ella see Jerome, Mrs. Charles

JEROME, Helen (b 1883) English dramatist WWT/9-11

JEROME, Jerome K[lapka] (1859-1927) English dramatist COC, DNB, ES, GRB/1-4, HP, MH, MWD, OC/1-3, PDT, WWM, WWS, WWT/1-5, WWW/2

JEROME, Peter (d 1967 [74]) dramatist BP/52*

JEROME, Rowena (b 1889/90) actress WWT/2-5

JEROME, Sadie (1876-1950) American actress GRB/2-4, WWT/1-5

JEROME, William (d 1932 [67]) American lyricist BE*

JERRARD, John Francis (d 1906 [54]) actor EA/07*, WWT/14*

JERROLD, Douglas William (1803-57) English dramatist CDP, COC, DNB, ES, HP, MH, OC/1-3

JERROLD, Evelyn Douglas (d 1885 [34]) EA/86*

JERROLD, Mary (1877-1955) English actress ES, WWT/1-11, WWW/5

JERROLD, Mary Ann (d 1910 [78]) EA/11*

JERROLD, Robert (c. 1755-c. 1818) English actor ES

JERROLD, Samuel (d 1820) English actor, impresario ES

JERROLD, William Blanchard (1826-84) English dramatist DNB, ES, OC/1-3

JERVIS, George F. (1784-1851) English singer, actor HAS

JERVIS, Mrs. St. Vincent see Wadman, Miss

JERWOOD, T. J. (d 1866) lawyer EA/72*

JESON, Thomas (d 1688) actor, dancing master, dramatist GT

JESSE, Fryn[iwyd] Tennyson (1889-1958) dramatist COC, WWT/

4-12, WWW/5

JESSE, Stella (b 1897) English actress WWT/4-6

JESSEL, George (b 1898) American actor, dramatist, producer BE, CB, SR, WWT/6-16

JESSEL, Joseph (b 1859) American dramatist SR

JESSEL, Mrs. Joseph A. see Herndon, Agnes

JESSEL, Patricia (1920-68) English actress BE, TW/11-12, WWT/10-14

JESSEMAN, Caroline (d 1888) EA/90*

JESSEMAN, Tom (d 1873 [29]) EA/74*

JESSNER, Leopold (1878-1945) German director, producer BE*

JESSOP, George H. (d 1915) Irish dramatist SR

JESSOP, Mrs. Henry see Jessop, Maria

JESSOP, Maria [Mrs. Henry Jessop] (d 1880) EA/82*

JESSUP, Stanley (d 1945 [67]) American actor BE*, BP/30*

JETHRO, Phil (b 1947) American actor TW/28-29

JEVON, Thomas (1652-88) English actor, dancer, dramatist COC, CP/1-3, DNB, OC/1-3

JEVONS, Shirley Byron (d 1928) English critic WWW/2

JEWEL, Mr. treasurer TD/1-2

JEWELL, Mrs. (d 1798) actress WWT/14*

JEWELL, Isabel (d 1972 [62]) actress BP/56*, WWT/16*

JEWELL, Izetta [Izetta Kenney] (b 1883) American actress WWS, WWT/1-6

JEWELL, Jacob (d 1884) showman EA/85*

JEWELL, James (d 1975 [69]) producer/director/choreographer BP/60*

JEWELL, James (b 1925) American actor TW/10

JEWELL, James (b 1929) American educator, lighting designer, engineer BE

JEWELL, Jennie (fl 1857) reader HAS

JEWELL, Jesse (d 1909 [62]) performer? EA/10*

JEWETT, Henry (d 1930 [68])

Australian actor PP/2, WWS

JEWETT, Sara (d 1899 [c. 52]) actress CDP

JEWKES, Penny (d 1972 [22]) performer BP/57*

JEWSON, Frederick Bowen (d 1891 [68]) composer, professor of music EA/92*

JEWSON, Solomon (d 1877 [77]) professor of music EA/78*

JILLSON, Franklin F. (d 1892) EA/93*

JILLSON, Joyce (b 1946) American actress TW/22

JIMSON, J. C. (d 1910 [47]) animal trainer EA/11*

JOACHIM, Amelie (d 1899 [60]) singer EA/00*

JOACHIM, Josef (d 1907 [76]) musician, composer EA/08*

JOB, Thomas (1900-47) Welsh dramatist TW/4, WWA/2, WWT/10

JOBIN, Peter (b 1944) Canadian actor TW/25-26

JOBLING, Mrs. M. E. see Cross, Emily

JOCELYN, Mary [Mrs. Calvert Routledge] English actress GRB/1-3

JOCKO, The Brazilian Ape see Magilton, Henry M.

JODRELL, Sir Paul (d 1803) English dramatist CP/2-3, GT

JODRELL, Sir Richard Paul (1745-1831) English dramatist CP/3, DNB

JOE, Nicholas (fl 1509-11) actor DA

JOEL, Clara (b 1890) American actress WWT/5-9

JOEL, Hettie (d 1896) singer EA/97*

JOEL, Michael Joseph (d 1893 [63]) EA/94*

JOFFREY, Robert (b 1930) American choreographer, director, dancer CB

JOHANN, Dalla (b 1944) American actor TW/24-25

JOHANN, John (b 1942) American actor TW/23, 25-26, 28-29

JOHANN, Zita (b 1904) Hungarian actress WWT/7-9

JOHANNET, Miss see Vining, Mrs.

JOHANNOT, Sarah see Hamilton, Mrs. Robert

JOHANNOT, Tony (d 1825) actor CDP

JOHANSEN, Mme. (fl 1856) English singer HAS

JOHANSEN, Aud (b 1930) Norwegian actress, dancer, singer WWT/12

JOHN, Alice (d 1956 [75]) Welsh actress TW/13

JOHN, Errol (b 1924) West Indian dramatist, actor CD, MD, MWD, PDT

JOHN, Evan (1901-53) English actor, dramatist, producer WWT/9-10

JOHN, Graham [Graham John Colmer] (b 1887/89) English dramatist, lyricist WWT/8-11

JOHN, Rosamund [née Nora Rosamund Jones] (b 1913) English actress WWT/11-14

JOHN, Samuel see Johnson, Samuel

JOHN BULL PUNCTURE REPAIR KIT theatre collective CD

JOHNS, Andrew (b 1935) American actor TW/24

JOHNS, Clay (b 1934) American actor TW/26-28

JOHNS, Eric (1907-75) English critic AAS, WWT/11-15

JOHNS, Glynis (b 1923) South African actress AAS, BE, CB, ES, TW/8, 13-15, 19, 29-30, WWT/9-16

JOHNS, Harriette (b 1921) Scottish actress WWT/11-16

JOHNS, John (d 1963 [54]) performer BP/48*

JOHNS, Johnny see Thorogood, John

JOHNS, Mervyn (b 1899) Welsh actor ES, WWT/9-16

JOHNS, William (b c. 1644) dramatist CP/2-3, GT

JOHNSON, Mr. actor CDP

JOHNSON, Mr. (fl 1735) translator CP/2-3, GT

JOHNSON, Mr. (fl 1772) American? actor HAS, SR

JOHNSON, Mr. (fl 1847) singer? actor? HAS

JOHNSON, Prof (d 1877 [38]) "The African Hercules" EA/78*

JOHNSON, Mrs. [née Ford] (fl 1798) English actress TD/1-2

JOHNSON, Adelaide (b 1844) American music-hall performer HAS

JOHNSON, A. E. (d 1909 [35]) musician EA/10*

JOHNSON, Albert (1910-67) American designer, architect, producer, director BE, ES, TW/2, 5-8, 24

JOHNSON, Albert E. (b 1912) American educator, director BE

JOHNSON, Amelia [Mrs. J. G. Johnson] (d 1905) EA/06*

JOHNSON, Arte (b 1931) American actor TW/11

JOHNSON, Bayn (b 1958) American actor TW/24

JOHNSON, Ben (b 1866) American actor WWM

JOHNSON, Benjamin (1665?-1742) actor CDP, DNB

JOHNSON, Bess (d 1975 [73]) performer BP/59*

JOHNSON, Bill (1918-57) American actor, singer TW/2-4, 13, WWT/11

JOHNSON, Bobby (b 1946) American actor TW/26, 29-30

JOHNSON, Bruce Forsyth see Forsyth, Bruce

JOHNSON, Carroll (b 1851) singer, minstrel CDP

JOHNSON, Celia (b 1908) English actress AAS, ES, WWT/7-16

JOHNSON, Charles (1679-1748) dramatist CP/1-3, DNB, GT, TD/1-2

JOHNSON, Charles (d 1865) circus performer HAS

JOHNSON, Charles (d 1879 [68]) music-hall chairman EA/80*

JOHNSON, Charles F. (b 1865) English actor, manager GRB/1

JOHNSON, Chic [né Harold Ogden Johnson] (1891-1962) American actor CB, TW/1-8, 18, WWT/10-13

JOHNSON, Choo Choo American actress TW/1

JOHNSON, Christine actress TW/1

JOHNSON, Clara [Mrs. Frank Johnson] (d 1880) EA/81*

JOHNSON, Clara (d 1912 [55]) equestrienne EA/13*

JOHNSON, Clint (d 1975 [60]) dramatist BP/60*

JOHNSON, David ["The Cruikshank of America"] (fl 1825) American actor? HAS

JOHNSON, Dotts American actor
TW/29
JOHNSON, Edith (d 1901) tank
performer? EA/02*
JOHNSON, Edna (d 1971 [83])
performer BP/56*
JOHNSON, Edward (1880-1959)
Canadian singer, impresario
CB, SR, TW/15
JOHNSON, Elijah (d 1885) circus
proprietor EA/86*
JOHNSON, Elizabeth (fl 1790-1810)
American actress COC, OC/
1-3, WWA/H
JOHNSON, Ellen Augusta see
Hilson, Mrs. Thomas
JOHNSON, Emory (d 1960 [66])
actor, director BE*
JOHNSON, Ethel May (d 1964
[76]) performer, composer
BE*
JOHNSON, Florence (b 1902)
American critic BE
JOHNSON, Florence Osbeck (d
1971 [63]) performer BP/56*
JOHNSON, Frank (fl 1846?) mu-
sician CDP
JOHNSON, Mrs. Frank see
Johnson, Clara
JOHNSON, Fred (b 1899) Irish
actor TW/3
JOHNSON, George (b 1835) Amer-
ican actor HAS
JOHNSON, Gertrude (d 1973
[78]) performer BP/57*
JOHNSON, Gladys (d 1974 [40s])
performer BP/59*
JOHNSON, Greer (d 1974 [54])
dramatist BP/59*
JOHNSON, Hall (1888-1970)
American musician, composer
CB, TW/26
JOHNSON, Harold Ogden see
Johnson, Chic
JOHNSON, Harriet see Field,
Sylvia
JOHNSON, Harry (d 1878) musi-
cian EA/79*
JOHNSON, Harry Whitmarsh
see Meddows, Kenny
JOHNSON, Henry (fl 1576-86)
gatherer DA
JOHNSON, Henry (d 1760) Eng-
lish? translator CP/2-3, GT
JOHNSON, Henry (d 1910 [103])
acrobat EA/11*
JOHNSON, Henry Erskine (d 1840)
Scottish actor HAS

JOHNSON, Howard E. (1888?-1941)
songwriter, musician CB
JOHNSON, Isa (d 1941) actress
BE*, WWT/14*
JOHNSON, Jacob A. (b 1794)
American carpenter HAS
JOHNSON, James Weldon (1871-
1938) American dramatist HJD
JOHNSON, Jane see Cibber,
Mrs. Theophilus, I
JOHNSON, Janet (b 1915) Australian
actress WWT/9-10
JOHNSON, J. E. (fl 1853) comic
singer, actor HAS
JOHNSON, Mrs. J. G. see
Johnson, Amelia
JOHNSON, Mrs. J. H. see
Johnson, Margaret Jane
JOHNSON, John (1759-1819) English
actor HAS, SR
JOHNSON, John (d 1871 [47]) come-
dian EA/72*
JOHNSON, John (d 1894 [59]) pro-
prietor EA/95*
JOHNSON, John see Etherdo
JOHNSON, Mrs. John (d 1830)
English actress HAS, SR
JOHNSON, Joseph Towers (d 1891
[76]) actor WWT/14*
JOHNSON, J. Rosamond (1873-
1954) American actress, com-
poser BE*
JOHNSON, J. T. (b 1815) actor
CDP
JOHNSON, J. W. (d 1917) variety
agent EA/18*
JOHNSON, Karen (b 1939) Ameri-
can actress TW/26-27
JOHNSON, Katie (d 1957 [78])
English actress TW/13
JOHNSON, Kay American actress
TW/2, WWT/7-9
JOHNSON, Kennedy (d 1906 [38])
music-hall assistant manager
EA/07*
JOHNSON, Lamont (b 1922) Amer-
ican director, actor, producer
BE
JOHNSON, Laurence see Nai-
smith, Laurence
JOHNSON, Lilian Clara see St.
John, Lily
JOHNSON, Lonnie (d 1970 [70])
performer BP/55*
JOHNSON, Louisa (fl 1830s) Eng-
lish actress, dancer CDP,
HAS, SR
JOHNSON, Lydia (b 1896) Russian

dancer, singer ES
JOHNSON, Margaret Jane [Mrs.
J. H. Johnson] (d 1905) EA/
06*
JOHNSON, Marguerite see
Angelou, Maya
JOHNSON, Marion Pollock (fl
1900s) American actress WWS
JOHNSON, Mark see Mitchell,
John W.
JOHNSON, Mrs. Mark (d 1887)
music-hall performer EA/88*
JOHNSON, Mary Ann (d 1902
[65]) proprietor EA/03*
JOHNSON, Molly (b 1903) Eng-
lish actress, singer WWT/
10-11
JOHNSON, Nicholas (d 1857)
circus ringmaster HAS, SR
JOHNSON, Olga [Mrs. Richard
Johnson] (d 1886 [42]) EA/87*
JOHNSON, Onni (b 1949) Ameri-
can actress TW/28-29
JOHNSON, Orrin American actor
GRB/3-4, WWT/1-8
JOHNSON, Ottilie (d 1908) per-
former? EA/09*
JOHNSON, Owen (b 1878) Amer-
ican dramatist WWS
JOHNSON, Page (b 1927/30)
American actor TW/9-16,
21-30
JOHNSON, Pamela Hansford (b
1912) English dramatist CB
JOHNSON, Peter (d 1890) swim-
mer EA/91*
JOHNSON, Philip (b 1900) Eng-
lish dramatist WWT/8-11
JOHNSON, Rachel (b 1845)
American actress HAS, SR
JOHNSON, Richard (fl 1633)
actor DA
JOHNSON, Richard (d 1901 [62])
music-hall performer EA/02*
JOHNSON, Richard (b 1927)
English actor AAS, BE, ES,
WWT/12-16
JOHNSON, Mrs. Richard see
Johnson, Olga
JOHNSON, Robert (fl 1626)
musician DNB
JOHNSON, Robert (b 1827)
American actor HAS, SR
JOHNSON, Robert (d 1892)
scene artist EA/94*
JOHNSON, Roma Burton (d 1976)
publicist BP/60*
JOHNSON, Roy L. (1867-1943)

minstrel SR
JOHNSON, Sam (d 1900 [69]) actor
WWT/14*
JOHNSON, Samuel (d 1773) English
dramatist, actor CP/2, GT,
TD/1-2
JOHNSON, Dr. Samuel (1709-84)
English dramatist CDP, COC,
CP/1-3, ES, HP, GT, OC/1-3,
TD/1-2
JOHNSON, Samuel (1821-63) Irish
actor HAS, SR
JOHNSON, Samuel (fl 1853-79)
Scottish actor, manager OAA/2
JOHNSON, Samuel (d 1900 [69])
comedian EA/01*
JOHNSON, Mrs. Samuel (d 1884)
EA/85*
JOHNSON, Samuel D. (1813-63)
American actor HAS, SR
JOHNSON, Sarah A. see Burnett,
Sally
JOHNSON, S. Kenneth, II (d 1974
[62]) performer BP/59*
JOHNSON, Mrs. Spencer J., Jr.
see Beckwith, Linden
JOHNSON, Susan (b 1927) American
singer, actress BE, TW/9,
12-19
JOHNSON, Suzanne American ac-
tress TW/29
JOHNSON, Thomas (fl 1574) actor
DA
JOHNSON, Thomas Baldwin (d 1917)
manager EA/18*
JOHNSON, Travis (d 1970 [64])
performer BP/55*
JOHNSON, Van (b 1916) American
actor BE, CB, TW/19-20, 22-
23, WWT/16
JOHNSON, Virginia (d 1969 [59])
producer/director/choreographer
BP/53*
JOHNSON, Mrs. W. see Martini,
Laura
JOHNSON, Walter (d 1964 [80])
producer/director BP/49*
JOHNSON, W. F. (d 1859) Ameri-
can? actor CDP, HAS, SR
JOHNSON, Dr. W. Gerald (d 1963
[51]) dramatist, director, actor
BE
JOHNSON, William (fl 1572-88)
actor DA
JOHNSON, William (fl 1638?)
dramatist FGF
JOHNSON, William (fl 1640) actor
DA

JOHNSON, William (d 1882)
music-hall proprietor EA/83*
JOHNSON, William (d 1902 [52])
proprietor EA/04*
JOHNSON, William (d 1905) EA/
06*
JOHNSON, William (d 1957 [41])
American actor TW/11-12
JOHNSON, Mrs. William (d 1905)
EA/06*
JOHNSON, Mrs. William (d 1910)
EA/11*
JOHNSON, William Octavius
(1819-58) American actor
HAS, SR
JOHNSRUD, Harold (d 1939 [35])
American actor BE*, BP/24*
JOHNSTON, Arthur James (d
1954 [56]) composer BE*,
WWT/14*
JOHNSTON, Audre (b 1939) Amer-
ican actress TW/18, 29-30
JOHNSTON, Daisy B. (d 1974
[94]) performer BP/58*
JOHNSTON, David Claypoole
(1799-1865) American actor
DAB
JOHNSTON, Denis (b 1901) Irish
dramatist, educator, director,
actor AAS, BE, CD, COC,
ES, MD, MH, MWD, OC/1-3,
PDT, RE, WWT/8-11, 14
JOHNSTON, Gail (b 1943) Amer-
ican actress TW/23, 29
JOHNSTON, Henry Erskine
(1777-1845) Scottish actor
CDP, COC, DNB, GT, OC/
1-3, SR, TD/1-2
JOHNSTON, Mrs. Henry Erskine
[née Parker] (b 1782) English
actress CDP, OX, TD/1-2
JOHNSTON, Jane A. (b 1934)
American actress TW/28
JOHNSTON, Johnny (b 1918)
American actor TW/7-8
JOHNSTON, Justine (b 1899)
American actress, singer
BE, TW/21-22, 27-30, WWT/
4-8
JOHNSTON, Lyell (b 1875) Eng-
lish singer GRB/1
JOHNSTON, Margaret (b 1917/
18) Australian actress WWT/
10-16
JOHNSTON, Moffat (1886-1935)
Scottish actor WWT/7
JOHNSTON, Oliver (d 1966 [78])
actor WWT/15*

JOHNSTON, T. B. (1815-61)
American actor CDP, HAS, SR
JOHNSTON, Mrs. T. B. [Annie
Lee; Mrs. C. L. Stone] (d
1858) actress HAS, SR
JOHNSTON, Mrs. (fl 1797-1804)
actress TD/1-2
JOHNSTONE, Anna Hill (b 1913)
American costume designer BE
JOHNSTONE, A. S. (d 1917 [83])
EA/18*
JOHNSTONE, Clara [Mrs. Robert
Earle] (d 1902) actress EA/03*
JOHNSTONE, Clarence (d 1953)
performer BE*, WWT/14*
JOHNSTONE, Edward F. (d 1919)
composer SR
JOHNSTONE, Eliza (d 1899) ac-
tress EA/00*, WWT/14*
JOHNSTONE, Elizabeth [Mrs.
Owen Johnstone] (d 1876) EA/
77*
JOHNSTONE, Jack (d 1828 [78])
Irish actor EA/72*, WWT/14*
JOHNSTONE, James (fl 1786)
dramatist CP/3
JOHNSTONE, James (b 1817) Eng-
lish actor, stage manager
OAA/1-2
JOHNSTONE, John (d 1874 [41])
gymnast EA/75*
JOHNSTONE, John Beer (d 1891
[88]) dramatist, actor EA/68
JOHNSTONE, John Henry (1749-
1828) Irish actor, singer CDP,
DNB, GT, OX, TD/1-2
JOHNSTONE, Mrs. John Henry
[née Poctier] (d c. 1785) actress
TD/2
JOHNSTONE, Justine see John-
ston, Justine
JOHNSTONE, Keith English drama-
tist, director CD
JOHNSTONE, Madge (d 1913) ac-
tress BE*, WWT/14*
JOHNSTONE, Owen (d 1908) EA/
09*
JOHNSTONE, Mrs. Owen see
Johnstone, Elizabeth
JOHNSTONE, Paul (d 1976 [55])
producer/director/choreographer
BP/60*
JOHNSTONE, Susan [Mrs. James
W. Wallack] (d 1850) actress
CDP
JOHNSTONE, Thomas (d 1970 [81])
composer/lyricist BP/54*
JOHNSTONE, Thomas see Gor-

don, Cecil

JOHNSTONE, W. H. (d 1890 [68]) musical & variety agent EA/92*

JOHNSTONE-SMITH, George (d 1963 [81]) actor, producer BE*

JOINER, Barbara (d 1961 [61]) performer BE*

JO JO (d 1904) "dog-faced man" EA/05*

JOLIVET, Andre (d 1974 [69]) composer/lyricist BP/59*

JOLIVET, Rita American actress WWT/3-5

JOLLY, Edward (b 1876) American vaudevillian WWM

JOLLY, George (fl 1640-73) English actor COC, OC/1-3

JOLLY, John (d 1864 [74]) composer, conductor EA/72*

JOLSON, Al[bert; Asa Yoelson] (1886-1950) American actor CB, CDP, DAB, ES, NTH, SR, TW/3-7, WWA/3, WWT/4-10

JOLSON, Harry (d 1953 [71]) Polish vaudevillian TW/9

JONA, Mrs. see Ambrose, Mrs.

JONAS, Douglas Peter see Dexter, Aubrey

JONAS, Elizabeth (fl 1832) musician CDP

JONAY, Roberta (d 1976 [50s]) performer BP/60*

JONES, Mr. (d 1806) English actor HAS

JONES, Mr. (d 1868 [22]) conductor EA/69*

JONES, Mrs. [née Granger] (1782-1806) English singer HAS, SR

JONES, Mrs. [née Wallack] (d 1860) English actress HAS, SR

JONES, Mrs. (d 1864) see Stickney, Mrs. E. M.

JONES, Miss see Simpson, Mrs. E.

JONES, Al (b 1909) American manager BE

JONES, Ann Courtney [Mrs. M. Jones] (d 1875) EA/76*

JONES, Anne see Moreland, Mrs. Harry

JONES, Avonia Stanhope [Mrs. Gustavus Vaughan Brooke]

(1839-67) American actress CDP, COC, DNB, HAS, SR

JONES, Bambi (b 1961) American actress TW/25

JONES, Barry (b 1893/94) English actor, manager BE, CB, TW/8-15, WWT/7-14

JONES, Bartholomew (fl 1633) actor DA

JONES, Benjamin (d 1878 [41]) musician EA/79*

JONES, Mrs. Benjamin see Jones, Maria B.

JONES, Benjamin M. (fl 1858) American actor? HAS

JONES, B. N. (d 1890) Australian actor EA/91*

JONES, Brooks (b 1934) American producer, director, composer, singer BE

JONES, Buck (d 1942 [53]) American actor BE*

JONES, Carolyn (b 1933) American actress CB

JONES, Carrie B. (d 1904 [21]) music-hall performer EA/05*

JONES, Mrs. Charles F. (1796-1866) English actress CDP, OX

JONES, Charlotte [Mrs. George Jones] (d 1872 [86]) EA/73*

JONES, Charlotte American actress TW/22-30

JONES, Clingan (d 1874) comedian EA/76*

JONES, C. S. actor, manager TD/2

JONES, David (b 1934) English director AAS, WWT/15-16

JONES, Mrs. David H. [Lizzie Mandlebert] (d 1883 [49]) actress EA/84*

JONES, Dean (b 1930/35) American actor BE, TW/16-17, 26

JONES, D. H. (d 1867) actor EA/68*

JONES, Disley (b 1926) English designer WWT/14-16

JONES, Douglas P., Jr. (d 1964 [38]) actor, director BE*

JONES, Dudley (b 1914) English actor WWT/14-16

JONES, Edmund R. (d 1873 [67]) pantomime writer EA/74*

JONES, Edward (d 1917) conductor, composer, musical director WWT/3

JONES, Edward H. (d 1905 [53])

manager EA/06*
JONES, Mrs. E. J. see Jones,
Ellen E.
JONES, Elizabeth (fl early 19th
cent) actress CDP
JONES, Ellen [Mrs. George
Jones] (d 1881) EA/82*
JONES, Ellen E. [Mrs. E. J.
Jones] (d 1916 [75]) EA/17*
JONES, Emrys (1915-72) English
actor AAS, WWT/10-15
JONES, Ersser (d 1877 [71])
actor EA/78*, WWT/14*
JONES, Mrs. Evan see Jones,
Henrietta
JONES, Fanny [Mrs. Samuel
Jones] (d 1878) EA/79*
JONES, Francis (d 1888) scene
artist EA/90*
JONES, Frederick (d 1891 [31])
actor EA/92*
JONES, Frederick Edward (1759-
1834) Irish patentee, manager
DNB, TD/1-2
JONES, Gemma (b 1942) English
actress WWT/15-16
JONES, George (d 1872 [77])
proprietor EA/73*
JONES, George (1810-79) Eng-
lish actor CDP, HAS, SR
JONES, Mrs. George see
Jones, Charlotte
JONES, Mrs. George see
Jones, Ellen
JONES, Griffith (b 1910) English
actor AAS, WWT/8-16
JONES, Hazel (1896-1974) Eng-
lish actress TW/2, 25,
WWT/4-6
JONES, Henrietta [Miss H. Simms;
Mrs. Evan Jones] (d 1887 [45])
actress EA/88*
JONES, Henry (1721-70) Irish
dramatist CP/2-3, DNB, GT
JONES, Henry (fl 18th cent)
dramatist, shoemaker CP/
1-3, TD/1-2
JONES, Henry (d 1890 [86])
dramatic curiosity collector
EA/91*
JONES, Henry (b 1912) American
actor BE, TW/5-8, 10-16
JONES, Henry Arthur (1851-
1929) English dramatist
COC, DNB, ES, GRB/1-4,
HP, MH, MWD, NTH, OC/
1-3, PDT, RE, SR, WWM,
WWS, WWT/1-5, WWW/3

JONES, Mrs. Herbert B. [Elise
Dale] (d 1917) EA/18*
JONES, Howard Mumford (b 1892)
dramatist HJD
JONES, Ifano (1865-1955) Welsh
dramatist WWW/5
JONES, Mrs. Ike see Cushman,
Corlene
JONES, Inigo (1573-1652) English
architect, artist COC, ES,
FGF, HP, NTH, OC/1-3, PDT
JONES, Isham (1894-1956) Ameri-
can composer, musician BE*
JONES, J. see Hart, Josh
JONES, Jack (fl 1602) actor? DA
JONES, James (fl 1623) actor DA
JONES, James (fl 1818) theatre
founder CDP
JONES, James Earl (b 1931) Amer-
ican actor AAS, BE, CB, TW/
18-23, 25-30, WWT/15-16
JONES, Jeff see Warren, Jeff
JONES, Jeffrey Duncan (b 1947)
American actor TW/30
JONES, Cpt. Jenkin (fl 1801)
dramatist CP/3
JONES, Jennifer (b 1919) American
actress BE, CB, ES, SR, TW/
23
JONES, J. Matheson (d 1931 [83])
clown, director BE*, WWT/14*
JONES, Joan Granville (d 1974)
performer BP/58*
JONES, John (fl 1615) actor DA
JONES, John (fl 1635) dramatist
CP/1-3, FGF
JONES, John (1796-1861) English
singer HAS, SR
JONES, John (d 1881 [75]) EA/82*
JONES, John (b 1917) American
educator, designer, director
BE
JONES, Johnny (d 1971 [71]) mana-
ger BP/55*
JONES, John Price (d 1961 [70])
actor, singer TW/17
JONES, Joseph Stevens (1809-77)
American dramatist, actor
COC, DAB, HJD, NTH, OC/1-3,
RJ, SR, WWA/H
JONES, J. S. (fl 1857) actor,
manager HAS
JONES, Julia (d 1847) actress
HAS
JONES, Julia A. see Jones,
Mrs. W. G.
JONES, Julian (d 1930 [57]) con-
ductor WWT/14*

JONES, J. Wilton (d 1897 [43])
dramatist BE*, EA/98*,
WWT/14*
JONES, Mrs. J. Wilton (d 1886
[31]) EA/87*
JONES, Lauren (b 1942) Ameri-
can actress TW/24-25, 28
JONES, Lena Beatrice (d 1895
[15]) variety performer EA/
96*
JONES, Leroi see Baraka,
Imamu Amiri
JONES, Leslie Julian (b 1910)
English composer, librettist
WWT/10-12
JONES, Lillian B. (d 1962 [80])
Canadian monologist BE*
JONES, Lindesius (fl 1755)
dramatist CP/3
JONES, Louise M. (d 1912 [81])
EA/13*
JONES, Mrs. M. see Jones,
Ann Courtney
JONES, Margo (1913-55) Ameri-
can director, producer COC,
ES, NTH, OC/2-3, TW/3-8,
12, WWT/11
JONES, Maria (d 1893) actress
EA/95*, WWT/14*
JONES, Maria B. [Mrs. Francis
Phillips] (d 1873 [27]) actress,
dramatist BE*, EA/74*,
WWT/14*
JONES, Marie [Mrs. Ernest
Munro] English actress GRB/1
JONES, Marjorie Dunn (d 1974
[86]) performer BP/59*
JONES, Mary (b 1915) Welsh
actress WWT/9-16
JONES, Mary Kay (b 1925)
American actress TW/4
JONES, Mary Tupper (d 1964
[86]) performer BP/49*
JONES, Melinda [née Topping]
(1815-75) American actress
CDP, HAS, SR
JONES, Neil (b 1942) American
actor TW/20-28
JONES, Nora Rosamund see
John, Rosamund
JONES, Patty see Astley, Mrs.
Philip
JONES, Paul [né Pond] (b 1942)
English actor TW/27, WWT/
15-16
JONES, Peter (b 1920) English
actor, dramatist WWT/12-16
JONES, Phyllis Ann (d 1962

[24]) performer BE*
JONES, Richard (fl 1590-1615)
English actor DA, OC/1-3
JONES, Richard (1779-1851) Eng-
lish actor, dramatist BS, CDP,
DNB, OX
JONES, Richard de Freyne see
Beasley, Edward
JONES, Richard P. (1826-69)
American minstrel, actor HAS
JONES, Richard William Cattlin
(d 1889 [49]) pantomimist EA/
90*
JONES, Robert (fl 1602) actor DA
JONES, Robert (b 1819) English
actor, prompter HAS
JONES, Robert Edmond (1887-1954)
American designer, producer,
manager AAS, CB, COC, ES,
HJD, NTH, OC/1-3, TW/2-8,
11, WWT/5-11, WWW/5
JONES, Lady Roderick see
Bagnold, Enid
JONES, Rozene Kemper (d 1964
[74]) actress BE*, BP/49*
JONES, Rupel J. (b 1895) Ameri-
can educator BE
JONES, Mrs. Samuel see Jones,
Fanny
JONES, S[amuel] Major (1863-
1952) English actor, stage
manager GRB/1, 3-4, WWT/
3-9
JONES, Mrs. S[amuel] Major see
Stanley, Blanche
JONES, Shirley (b 1934) American
actress, singer BE, CB, ES,
TW/25
JONES, Stanley D. (d 1963 [49])
songwriter, actor BE*
JONES, Stephen (d 1827 [64]) his-
torian WWT/14*
JONES, Sydney (1861/69-1946)
English composer, conductor
GRB/1-4, DNB, ES, WWT/1-9
JONES, T. (fl 1803-05) dramatist
CP/3
JONES, T. (fl 1809) dramatist
CP/3
JONES, T. singer CDP
JONES, T. actor CDP
JONES, T. C. (1920-71) American
female impersonator, actor,
dancer BE, TW/13-15, 28
JONES, Mrs. Theodore see
Mansfield, Ada
JONES, Thomas (d 1893 [77])
EA/94*

JONES, Tom (d 1905 [37]) actor?
EA/06*
JONES, Tom (b 1928) American
dramatist, lyricist, librettist
BE, CD
JONES, Tom Lee (b 1946) Amer-
ican actor TW/26-27, 29-30
JONES, Trefor (1902-65) Welsh
actor, singer WWT/8-13
JONES, W. A. see Oliver,
Roland
JONES, Walter (1868/72-1922)
American actor SR, WWS
JONES, W. G. (1817-53) Ameri-
can actor CDP, HAS, SR
JONES, Mrs. W. G. [Julia A.
Deane] (1829-1907) American
actress CDP, GRB/3, HAS,
PP/2, SR
JONES, Whitworth (b 1873) Eng-
lish actor WWT/4
JONES, Sir William (1746-94)
English dramatist CP/3
JONES, William (d 1828) Cana-
dian clown HAS
JONES, William (1781-1841)
American manager, actor
HAS
JONES, William Andrew see
De Wolfe, Billy
JONES, William H. (d 1883 [39])
lessee EA/84*
JONES, Mrs. Wilton see War-
den, Gertrude
JONES, Winifred Arthur see
Faber, Mrs. Leslie
JONES, W. O. (d 1890 [29])
actor EA/91*
JONES, Dr. W. T. (d 1871
[42]) actor EA/72*
JONES, "Young" (fl 1818-19)
actor CDP
JONG, Frank de (d 1903) manager
WWT/14*
JONGEYANS, George see
Gaynes, George
JONGHMANS, Edward (d 1902)
musical director, composer
EA/03*
JONGMANS, F. (d 1887 [65])
singer CDP
JONNS, Daniel (fl 1586) actor?
DA
JONSON, Ben (1572-1637) Eng-
lish dramatist, actor CDP,
COC, CP/1-3, DA, DNB,
ES, FGF, HP, MH, NTH,
OC/1-3, PDT, RE

JONSON, Benjamin, Jr. (d 1635)
dramatist CP/3, FGF
JONSON, William (d 1972 [51])
producer/director/choreographer
BP/57*
JONSTON, Alexander (d 1775) actor
CDP
JOOSS, Kurt (b 1901) German
dancer, choreographer ES, OC/
2, WWT/9-12
JOPE-SLADE, Christine (d 1942
[49]) dramatist BE*, WWT/14*
JORDAN, Annie see Jordan,
Mrs. George Clifford
JORDAN, Bernard (d 1962 [77])
English performer BE*
JORDAN, Clifford, Jr. (b 1931)
American actor TW/29
JORDAN, Dorothy (1761-1816) Eng-
lish actress CDP, COC, DNB,
ES, GT, HP, NTH, OC/1-3,
OX, TD/1-2
JORDAN, Dorothy (b 1908) Ameri-
can actress WWT/7-8
JORDAN, Elizabeth (1867-1947)
American dramatist WWA/2,
WWM
JORDAN, Frances (b 1890) Ameri-
can actress WWM
JORDAN, George (d 1873 [43])
actor EA/74*
JORDAN, George C. (b 1847)
American actor HAS
JORDAN, George Clifford (1825-73)
English actor CDP, HAS, SR
JORDAN, Mrs. George Clifford
[Annie Walters] (fl 1848-67)
actress CDP, HAS, SR
JORDAN, Glenn R. (d 1975 [56])
producer/director/choreographer
BP/60*
JORDAN, Henry Charles (b 1821)
American actor HAS, SR
JORDAN, Mrs. Henry Charles (fl
1846) English actress HAS, SR
JORDAN, James E. ["Fibber Mc-
Gee"] (b 1898) actor SR
JORDAN, Mrs. James E. [Molly
Driscoll Jordan] actress SR
JORDAN, Joe (d 1971 [89]) com-
poser/lyricist BP/56*
JORDAN, John (b 1923) American
actor TW/3-7
JORDAN, Jules (1850-1927) Amer-
ican singer, composer, con-
ductor CDP, WWA/1
JORDAN, Kate (1862-1926) Irish
dramatist DAB

JORDAN, Louis (d 1975 [66])
performer BP/59*
JORDAN, Mabel (fl 1877) actress
CDP
JORDAN, Marian (1898-1961)
American performer BE*
JORDAN, Marion Driscoll see
Jordan, Mrs. James E.
JORDAN, Richard (b 1938) Amer-
ican actor TW/18, 20-23,
26-27
JORDAN, Thomas (d 1685?) actor,
dramatist CP/2-3, DA, FGF
JORDAN, Walter C. (d 1951
[74]) American literary repre-
sentative, producer BE*,
BP/35*
JORDAN, Dr. Warwick (d 1909
[68]) professor of music
EA/10*
JORDAN, William (fl 1611) Eng-
lish dramatist DNB
JORDAN, William dramatist
CP/3
JORDIN, Russ (d 1972 [43]) per-
former BP/57*
JORDISON, Mrs. H. A. [Nellie
Jordison] (d 1901) EA/02*
JORDISON, Nellie see Jordi-
son, Mrs. H. A.
JORDON, Gaye American ac-
tress TW/15
JORGENSEN, Robert (b 1903)
Danish press representative,
journalist WWT/8-9
JORY, Victor (b 1902) Alaskan
actor, producer BE, TW/
1-3, 6, WWT/10-16
JOSE, Richard J. (b 1869/70)
English actor, singer CDP,
WWM
JOSEFFY, Rafael (b 1853) musi-
cian, composer CDP
JOSEPH, Harry (fl 1867-69)
Scottish actor SR
JOSEPH, Harry (d 1962 [64])
English theatre owner BE*
JOSEPH, Jackie (b 1936) Amer-
ican actress TW/16
JOSEPH, John Charles (d 1871)
patentee, lessee EA/72*
JOSEPH, Marilyn (b 1948) English
actress TW/26
JOSEPH, Robert L. (b 1924)
American producer BE
JOSEPH, Stephen (1921-67) Eng-
lish actor, producer COC,
OC/3

JOSEPH, Will C. (d 1973 [88])
designer BP/58*
JOSEPHS, Fanny (d 1890 [48]) ac-
tress CDP, OAA/1-2
JOSEPHS, Harry (b 1845) Scottish
actor HAS
JOSEPHS, Henry (d 1880) comedian
EA/81*
JOSEPHS, Patti [Mrs. J. H. Fitz-
patrick] (d 1876) actress, singer
EA/77*, WWT/14*
JOSLIN, Howard (d 1975 [67])
performer BP/60*
JOSLYN, Allyn (b 1905) American
actor WWT/9-10
JOSSET, Alfred (d 1878) dancer,
pantomimist EA/79*
JOURDAN, Mons. (d 1879) singer
EA/80*
JOURDAN, Alecia actress, singer
CDP
JOURDAN, Louis (b 1920) French
actor BE, CB, TW/10-15
JOURNET, Marcel (1870-1933)
French singer WWA/1
JOUVET, Louis (1887-1951) French
actor, manager, director CB,
COC, ES, NTH, TW/8, WWT/11
JOWSEY, John Edward (d 1916)
variety agent, director EA/18*
JOY, Mrs. Ernest see Busley,
Jessie
JOY, Job (d 1869) proprietor EA/
70*
JOY, John (b 1937) American actor
TW/24-25
JOY, Leonard W. (d 1961 [65])
producer BE*, BP/46*
JOY, Nicholas (1889-1964) French/
English actor TW/1-9, 13-15,
20, WWT/10-13
JOY, Signa (b 1947) American ac-
tress TW/29
JOY, William (1675?-1734) "Eng-
lish Sampson" CDP, DNB
JOYCE, Alice (1890-1955) Ameri-
can actress TW/12
JOYCE, Archibald (d 1963) com-
poser BE*
JOYCE, Barbara American actress
TW/3
JOYCE, Billy (d 1970 [73]) agent
BP/54*
JOYCE, Elaine (b 1945) American
actress TW/28-29
JOYCE, James (1882-1941) Irish
dramatist AAS, DNB, ES, HP,
MD, MWD, WWW/4

JOYCE, James (d 1974 [53])
performer BP/58*
JOYCE, Laura [née Maskell;
Mrs. James V. Taylor; Mrs.
Digby Bell] (b 1856) actress,
singer CDP
JOYCE, Lind (d 1971 [51]) per-
former BP/55*
JOYCE, Peggy Hopkins (d 1957
[64]) American showgirl
TW/13
JOYCE, Sarah [Mrs. Walter
Joyce] (d 1907 [75]) EA/08*
JOYCE, Stephen (b 1931/33)
American actor TW/22, 24,
26-27, WWT/15-16
JOYCE, Thomas (fl 1849) Cana-
dian actor HAS
JOYCE, Walter (d 1916 [79/81])
actor, manager BE*, EA/
17*, WWT/14*
JOYCE, Mrs. Walter see Joyce,
Sarah
JOYNER, William (d 1706) Eng-
lish dramatist CP/1-3
JOYNSON-POWELL, Queenie (d
1907) actress EA/09*
JUANA [Johanna Jurgens] (b
1916) English/American
dancer ES
JUBA (fl 1848) dancer CDP
JUBY, Edward (fl 1602) drama-
tist, actor CP/3, DA
JUBY, Richard (fl 1600-02)
actor DA
JUBY, [William?] (fl 1599-1602)
sharer DA
JUCH, Emma [Mrs. Francis L.
Wellman] (1863/65-1939)
Austrian/American singer
CDP, WWA/1, WWM
JUDAH, Emanuel (fl 1832) Amer-
ican actor HAS, SR
JUDAH, Mrs. Emanuel see
Judah, Sophia
JUDAH, Samuel Benjamin Hel-
bert (c. 1799-1876) American
actor, dramatist DAB, EAP,
RJ, SR
JUDAH, Sophia (1829-83) Ameri-
can actress CDP, HAS, SR
JUDD-GREEM, Richard A. (d
1909 [32]) music-hall manager
EA/10*
JUDE, Patrick (b 1951) American
actor TW/29
JUDELL, Maxson F. (d 1972
[74]) publicist BP/57*

JUDELS, Charles (b 1881) Dutch
actor TW/3-4
JUDGE, Arline (d 1974 [61])
dancer, actress TW/30
JUDGE, John (d 1917) EA/18*
JUDGE, Lily (d 1911) music-hall
performer EA/13*
JUDGE, William James (d 1903
[54]) animal trainer EA/04*
JUDIC, Anne Marie Louise (1849-
1911) French actress CDP,
GRB/4
JUDITH, Mlle. [Julie Bernat] (d
1912 [85]) actress BE*, WWT/
14*
JUDSON, Edward Z. C. (d 1886
[64]) actor, dramatist CDP
JUGLER, Richard (fl 1550) actor
DA
JUKES, Mrs. W. see Bird,
Miss
JULEENE, H. F. [John Parsons]
(d 1905 [59]) performer? EA/
06*
JULIA, Raul (b 1940) Puerto Rican
actor TW/24-30, WWT/16
JULIAN, Henry (d 1878 [30])
gymnast EA/79*
JULIAN, W. R. (d 1886 [59])
music-hall performer EA/87*
JULIE, Lillian (d 1966) performer
BP/51*
JULIEN, Jay (b 1919) American
producer, attorney BE
JULIEN, Louis Antoine (1812-60)
French composer, conductor
CDP, DNB
JULIEN, Paul [Gus Vaughan] (d
1877 [31]) comic singer EA/78*
JULIET [Juliet Rosenfeld] (1889-
1962?) American impersonator
WWM
JULLIEN, Louis George (1812-60)
actor? HAS
JULLIEN, Paul (fl 1851) violinist
HAS
JULVES, Encarnación López see
Argentinita
JUNCA, Marcel (d 1878) singer
CDP
JUNDELIN, Robert American actor
TW/29
JUNE [June Howard Tripp] (b
1900/01) English actress, singer
WWT/5-11
JUNE, Lewis (d 1888) circus
manager SR
JUNG, Carl (d 1893) musician

EA/94*
JUNG, Paul (d 1965 [65]) per-
former BP/49*
JUNOT, W. E. D. [Edmund
Clifford] (d 1872 [21]) harle-
quin EA/73*
JURGENS, Johanna see Juana
JURMANN, Walter (d 1971 [67])
composer/lyricist BP/56*
JUSTICE, Barry (b 1940) Indian/
English actor TW/20
JUSTICE, James Robertson (d
1975 [70]) actor BP/60*,
WWT/16*
JUSTICE, Jimmy (b 1941) Amer-
ican actor TW/26
JUSTIN, John (b 1917) English
actor WWT/11-16
JUSTIN, Morgan (d 1974 [47])
performer BP/59*
JUVENEAU, John J. (d 1973
[57]) performer BP/57*

- K -

K., F. [Francis Kirkman] (fl
1661) dramatist CP/1-3, GT
KAELRED, Katherine (b 1882)
English actress WWT/2-6
KAESTNER, Erich (d 1974 [75])
dramatist BP/59*
KAFKA, John H. (d 1974 [71])
dramatist BP/58*
KAGAN, Diane American actress
TW/24, 29-30
KAGEN, Sergius (d 1964 [55])
Russian composer BE*
KAHAN, Evelyn K. (d 1976 [72])
performer BP/60*
KAHAN, Judy (b 1948) American
actress TW/29-30
KAHANU, Archie (d 1975 [69])
performer BP/60*
KAHL, Howard (b 1930) Ameri-
can actor TW/23-24, 26-28
KAHN, Carolyn Sally see
Teitel, Carol
KAHN, Florence (1877/78-1951)
American actress COC, OC/
3, WWS, WWT/1-2
KAHN, Gilbert W. (d 1975 [72])
patron BP/60*
KAHN, Gustav Gerson (1886-
1941) German lyricist DAB
KAHN, L. Stanley (d 1964 [66])
American producer BE*,
BP/49*

KAHN, Madeline (b 1942) Ameri-
can actress TW/24, 26-28, 30
KAHN, Marvin (d 1969 [54]) com-
poser/lyricist BP/53*
KAHN, Michael American director
AAS, WWT/15-16
KAHN, Otto Hermann (d 1962
[68]) German/American? patron
BE*, BP/18*
KAIFFER, Mons. (fl 1840) dancer
HAS
KAINZ, Josef (1858-1910) German
actor GRB/2
KAISER, Ardyth American actress
TW/27, 30
KALB, Marie (d 1930 [76]) actress
BE*, WWT/14*
KALCHEIM, Harry (d 1974 [73])
agent BP/59*
KALCHEIM, Lee (b 1938) Ameri-
can dramatist CD
KALEM, Theodore (b 1919) Amer-
ican critic BE
KALICH, Bertha (1874-1939)
Galician actress GRB/3-4,
SR, WWT/1-8
KALICH, Jacob (1891-1975) Polish
director, actor, producer,
dramatist BE
KALIDASA (373-415) dramatist
COC
KALISCH, Alfred (1863-1933) Eng-
lish librettist WWW/3
KALIZ, Armand (d 1941 [49]) ac-
tor, songwriter, singer BE*,
WWT/14*
KALKOVEN, Frederick D'Alton
(d 1894 [70]) music-hall chair-
man EA/95*
KALLAN, Randi (b 1950) American
actress TW/29
KALLESSER, Michael (d 1975
[89]) dramatist BP/59*
KALLMAN, Chester (d 1975 [53])
composer/lyricist BP/59*
KALLMAN, Dick (b 1933) Ameri-
can actor, singer, dancer BE,
TW/8-12, 23
KALMAN, Emmerich (1882-1953)
Hungarian composer TW/10,
WWT/6-11
KALMANOVTICH, Harry (d 1966
[80]) dramatist BP/51*
KALMAR, Bert (d 1947 [66])
American lyricist, librettist,
composer TW/4, WWT/6-10
KALTHOUM, Um (d 1975 [77])
performer BP/59*

KAMINSKA, Ida (b 1899) American actress, producer, director CB, TW/24, 26, WWT/15-16

KAMLOT, Robert (b 1926) Austrian/American actor, manager TW/25-26

KAMMANS, Louise-Philippe (d 1972 [60]) performer BP/57*

KAMMER, Klaus (d 1964 [35]) performer BP/48*

KAMMERER, Mr. (d 1879) musician EA/80*

KAMSLER, Ben (b 1905) American producer, director, actor BE

KANDER, John (b 1927) American composer, musician BE, WWT/15-16

KANE, Charles S. (b 1822) American actor HAS

KANE, Gail (1887-1966) English actress WWT/6-7

KANE, Helen (d 1966 [62]) singer, actress TW/23

KANE, Irving (d 1972 [68]) performer BP/56*

KANE, John Irish actor TD/1-2

KANE, John (b 1920) American actor TW/22

KANE, Joseph (d 1975 [81]) producer/director/choreographer BP/60*

KANE, Richard (b 1938) English actor WWT/16

KANE, Whitford (1881/82-1956) Irish actor TW/1-13, WWM, WWT/4-12

KANER, Ruth (d 1964) American producer, actress BE*

KANIN, Fay American dramatist, actress BE

KANIN, Garson (b 1912) American actor, dramatist, director AAS, BE, CB, CD, ES, HJD, MD, MWD, PDT, SR, TW/2-8, WWT/10-16

KANIN, Michael (b 1910) American dramatist, producer, director BE

KANN, Lily German actress WWT/11-14

KANNER, Alexis (b 1942) French actor WWT/15-16

KANNON, Jackie (d 1974 [54]) performer BP/58*

KANTER, Mitchell (d 1972 [68]) treasurer BP/57*

KAPEC, Michael (b 1944) American actor TW/24

KAPEN, Ben (b 1928) American actor TW/25-26

KAPLAN, Dewitte (fl 1903-10) American dramatist WWM

KAPLAN, Eddie (d 1964 [57]) talent representative BE*

KAPLAN, Harriet (1917-69) American talent representative BE

KAPLAN, Jeanne American actress TW/24-26, 28

KAPLAN, Saul (b 1898) American manager BE

KAPLAN, Sol (b 1919) American composer, musician BE

KAPPEL, Gertrude (1884/93-1971) German singer ES, WWA/5

KAPPELER, Alfred (d 1945 [69]) Swiss actor BE*, BP/30*

KAPP-YOUNG, Louise (fl 1867) singer CDP

KAPRAL, Janet Czech actress TW/27, 30

KAPROW, Allan painter CD

KAPS, Arthur (d 1974 [66]) producer/director/choreographer BP/58*

KARATY, Tommy (b 1940) American actor TW/23-26

KAREN, James (b 1923) American actor TW/26, 28, 30

KARGER, Ann (d 1975 [89]) performer BP/60*

KARISBALIS, Curt (b 1947) American actor TW/29-30

KARIN, Rita (b 1919) Polish actress TW/24-28

KARINSKA, Barbara (b 1886) Russian costume designer BE, CB

KARL, Theodore O. H. (b 1912) American educator, producer, director BE

KARL, Tom (1846-1916) Irish singer CDP, WWA/4

KARLAN, Richard (b 1919) American actor TW/2

KARLIN, Miriam (b 1925) English actress WWT/12-16

KARLOFF, Boris [né William Henry Pratt] (1887-1969) English actor BE, CB, ES, SR, TW/4-8, 12-14, 25, WWA/5, WWT/11-14, WWW/6

KARLWEIS, Oscar (d 1956 [60]) Austrian actor, singer TW/2-8, 12, WWT/10-11

KARM, Michael (b 1941) American

actor TW/27-28
KARNILOVA, Maria (b 1920)
American dancer, actress
BE, TW/19, 21-25, 30, WWT/
15-16
KARNO, Fred (1866-1941) English
manager, producer CB, GRB/
2-3, OC/1-3
KARNO, Mrs. Ted (d 1917) EA/
18*
KARNS, Roscoe (1893-1970)
American actor TW/1
KAROLY, Mons. (d 1879) snake
trainer EA/80*
KARR, Harold (b 1921) American
composer BE
KARR, Patti (b 1932) American
singer, dancer, actress BE,
TW/25-26, 28-30
KARSAVINA, Tamara (b 1885)
Russian dancer ES, WWT/
4-11
KARSON, Kit (d 1940 [65]) per-
former BE*
KARSON, Nat (1910-54) American
scene designer NTH, TW/11
KASCHMANN, Giuseppe (1850-
1925) Italian singer ES
KASE, C. Robert (b 1905) Amer-
ican educator BE
KASHA, Lawrence N. (b 1933)
American producer, director
BE, WWT/15-16
KASON, Corinne American ac-
tress TW/26-30
KASS, Alan (b 1928) American
actor TW/28-29
KASSABIAN, Jack (b 1934)
American actor TW/23
KASZNAR, Kurt S. (b 1913)
Austrian actor BE, TW/4-9,
12-22, WWT/14-16
KATAYEV, Valentin Petrovich
(b 1897) Russian dramatist
COC, OC/1-3
KATES, Bernard (b 1922) Amer-
ican actor TW/7-8, 15, 22
KATOW, Helen De (fl 1865)
musician HAS
KATSELAS, Milton (b 1933)
American director WWT/15-16
KATSMAN, Sam (d 1973 [72])
producer/director/choreographer
BP/58*
KATTERFELTO, Gustavus (d
1799) conjurer DNB
KATZ, Herman (d 1973 [73])
performer BP/58*

KATZ, Raymond American talent
representative BE
KATZELL, William R. (d 1974
[68]) producer TW/5-7
KATZENELSON, Isaac (1886-c.
1941) producer BE*
KATZKA, Emil (d 1966 [69]) backer
BP/50*
KAUFFMAN, Abraham (d 1911 [74])
performer EA/12*
KAUFFMAN, Archie E. (d 1899)
manager EA/00*
KAUFMAN, Alvin S. (d 1973) com-
poser/lyricist BP/58*
KAUFMAN, George Simon (1889-
1961) American dramatist, pro-
ducer AAS, CB, ES, HJD,
MD, MH, MWD, NTH, OC/1-3,
PDT, RE, SR, TW/18, WWT/
5-13, WWW/6
KAUFMAN, Harry A. (d 1944 [57])
director BE*, WWT/14*
KAUFMAN, Irving (d 1976 [85])
performer BP/60*
KAUFMAN, S. Jay (1886-1957)
dramatist, press representative
BE*, BP/42*
KAUFMAN, Wolfe (d 1970 [65])
critic, press agent TW/27
KAUL, Avtar (d 1974 [34]) pro-
ducer/director/choreographer
BP/59*
KAUSER, Alice (d 1945 [73]) Hun-
garian play broker, agent
WWM
KAVANAGH, J. H. (d 1907) vari-
ety performer EA/08*
KAVANAGH, Mary (d 1887) EA/
88*
KAVANAGH, Mike (d 1967 [80])
manager BP/51*
KAVANAGH, Patrick (d 1967 [62])
dramatist BP/52*
KAVANAGH, Seamus (d 1964 [53])
performer BP/48*
KAVANAUGH, Dorrie American
actress TW/27-28
KAY, Arthur composer, musical
director BE
KAY, Beatrice (b c. 1912) come-
dienne CB
KAY, Charles [né Piff] (b 1930)
English actor AAS, WWT/15-16
KAY, Ethel [Mrs. Frank Harrison]
(b 1877) English actress GRB/1
KAY, Hershey (b 1919) American
composer BE, CB
KAY, Jay (d 1970 [48]) dramatist

BP/55*
KAY, Katherine E. (d 1967 [44])
performer BP/52*
KAY, Mary see Barrington,
Pattie
KAY, Richard (b 1937) English
actor WWT/15-16
KAY, Sidney (b 1927) American
actor TW/13
KAY, Virginia (d 1969 [42])
columnist BP/53*
KAYE, Albert Patrick (1878-1946)
English actor SR, TW/3,
WWT/9
KAYE, Alma (b 1925) American
actress TW/1
KAYE, Anne (b 1942) American
actress TW/24-26, 30
KAYE, Benjamin (d 1970 [86])
dramatist BP/54*
KAYE, Carmen (d 1962) perform-
er BE*
KAYE, Danny [né Daniel Komin-
ski] (b 1913) American per-
former, actor BE, CB, COC,
ES, SR, OC/3, TW/27-28,
WWT/10-16
KAYE, Deborah (d 1976 [83])
performer BP/60*
KAYE, Frederick (d 1913 [58])
actor DP, WWT/1
KAYE, Mrs. Frederick see
Kaye, Lucy
KAYE, Gloria (b 1944) American
actress TW/24
KAYE, Joseph (d 1975 [77]?)
journalist BE
KAYE, Lucy [Mrs. Frederick
Kaye] (d 1917) EA/18*
KAYE, Nora (b 1920) American
dancer CB, ES, TW/9
KAYE, Sparky (d 1971 [65])
performer BP/56*
KAYE, Stubby (b 1918) American
comedian, singer BE, TW/
14-15, 30, WWT/16
KAYSER, Kathryn E. (b 1896)
American educator BE
KAZAN, Elia (b 1909) Turkish/
American actor, director
AAS, BE, CB, COC, ES,
HJD, OC/3, PDT, TW/2-8,
WWT/10-15
KAZAN, Molly (1906-63) Amer-
ican dramatist BE, TW/20
KAZNAR, Kurt see Kaszar,
Kurt S.
KCHESSINSKA, Mathilde (d 1971

[99]) dancer BP/56*, WWT/16*
KEACH, Edward F. (1824-63)
American actor HAS
KEACH, Stacy (b 1941) American
actor, director AAS, CB, TW/
25-28, WWT/15-16
KEAL, Anita American actress
TW/29-30
KEALY, Thomas J. (1874-1949)
Irish business manager WWT/
5-10
KEAN (fl 1811) dramatist CP/3
KEAN, Betty (b 1920) American
actress, comedienne BE
KEAN, Charles John (1811-68)
English actor, manager CDP,
COC, DNB, ES, HAS, HP,
NTH, OC/1-3, WWA/H
KEAN, Mrs. Charles John [Ellen
Tree] (1805-80) English actress
CDP, COC, DNB, ES, HAS,
OAA/1-2, OC/1-3, OX, SR
KEAN, Edmund (1787-1833) English
actor BS, CDP, COC, DNB,
ES, HAS, HP, NTH, OC/1-3,
OX, PDT, SR, WWA/H
KEAN, Mrs. Edmund [Mary
Chambers] (c. 1780-1844) actress
COC
KEAN, Ellen see Kean, Mrs.
Charles John
KEAN, Jane (b 1924/28) American
actress, singer BE, TW/2-4
KEAN, J. Harold (d 1975 [79])
critic BP/60*
KEAN, Marie (b 1922) Irish actress
WWT/15-16
KEAN, Moses (fl 1789) imitator
CDP, TD/1-2
KEAN, Norman (b 1934) American
manager, producer, stage
manager BE, WWT/16
KEAN, Thomas (fl mid 18th cent)
English manager, actor COC,
OC/1-3, SR, WWA/H
KEAND, Mrs. Arthur see Talbot,
Evelyn
KEANE, Claire Whitney (d 1969
[79]) performer BP/54*
KEANE, Doris (b 1881/85-1945)
American actress CB, COC,
GRB/3-4, NTH, SR, TW/2,
WWA/2, WWM, WWT/1-9
KEANE, George (b 1917) American
actor TW/2-7
KEANE, John B. (b 1928) Irish
dramatist CD
KEANE, Joseph H. (d 1890 [45])

actor CDP
KEANE, Robert Emmett (b 1883)
American actor WWT/4-9
KEANEY, Patrick (d 1933)
dramatist SR
KEARNEY, Mr. (fl 1875?) come-
dian, singer CDP
KEARNEY, John Joseph (d 1875)
property man EA/76*
KEARNEY, Kate (d 1926 [85])
actress BE*, WWT/14*
KEARNEY, Mary Agnes (d 1881)
EA/82*
KEARNEY, Michael (b 1955) Amer-
ican actor TW/25
KEARNEY, Patrick (d 1933 [36])
American dramatist BE*,
BP/17*
KEARNS, Allen (1893-1956)
Canadian actor TW/1, 12,
WWT/6-9
KEARNS, Elsie Herndon (b 1884)
American actress WWM
KEARNS, Joseph (d 1962 [55])
American actor BE*, BP/46*
KEARNS, Red (d 1971 [64]) per-
former BP/56*
KEARNS, Rosie [Mrs. Alfred H.
Hook] (1878-1917) Irish ac-
tress, singer GRB/1
KEARNS, William Henry (1794-
1846) Irish composer DNB
KEAST, G. V. (d 1905 [56])
pantomime writer EA/06*
KEATE, George (1729/30-97)
English dramatist CP/2-3
KEATHLEY, George (b 1925)
American director BE
KEATING, Charles (b 1941)
English actor WWT/16
KEATING, Dan actor CDP
KEATING, Fred (d 1961 [64])
American magician, actor
TW/18
KEATING, John (1919-68) Amer-
ican critic NTH
KEATING, Joseph (1871-1934)
Welsh dramatist WWW/3
KEATING, Larry (d 1963 [67])
American performer BE*
KEATING, Michael see Shandy,
Tristram
KEATING, Nicholas (d 1903)
music-hall manager EA/04*
KEATON, Buster (1895/96-1966)
American variety performer
ES, WWA/4
KEATON, Georgia (d 1975 [65])

performer BP/60*
KEATS, John (1795-1821) English
dramatist DNB, ES, HP
KEATS, Sydney Carl (d 1908 [24])
EA/09*
KEATS, Thomas (d 1889 [92])
singer EA/90*
KEATS, Viola (b 1911) Scottish
actress WWT/8-16
KEAY, Arthur (d 1895 [32]) music-
hall performer EA/96*
KEBBLE, Nora (d 1917 [37]) come-
dian EA/18*
KECK, Edith see King, Edith
KEDOBRA, Maurice (d 1973 [88])
dramatist BP/58*
KEDROV, Mikhail Nikolayevich
(1893-1972) Russian actor, di-
rector, producer COC, OC/3
KEEBLE, G. Walter (fl 1854-69)
actor HAS
KEEDICK, Lee (1879-1959) Amer-
ican manager WWA/4
KEEDICK, Mabel Ferris (d 1973
[89]) performer BP/57*
KEEFE, Adam (b 1931) American
actor TW/26
KEEFE, Jim (d 1881 [24]) Negro
comedian EA/82*
KEEFE, John (fl 1779-81) actor,
dramatist CP/2
KEEFER, Don (b 1916) American
actor TW/5-9
KEEGAN, Joseph (d 1901 [60])
music-hall comedian EA/02*
KEEL, Howard (b 1919) American
actor, singer BE, TW/29,
WWT/15-16
KEELER, Charles D. (1820-59)
American actor HAS
KEELER, Jane (d 1974 [93]) edu-
cator BP/58*
KEELER, Ralph (1840-73) actor
CDP
KEELER, Ruby (b 1909/10) Cana-
dian actress, dancer AAS, BE,
CB, TW/27-29, WWT/8-10,
15-16
KEELEY, Edward Montague (d
1872 [37]) actor EA/73*
KEELEY, Mrs. E. M. (d 1896
[69]) EA/97*
KEELEY, Louise (1833-77) actress
CDP, OC/3
KEELEY, Louise see Williams,
Mrs. Montague
KEELEY, Mary Ann [Mary Ann
Goward; Mrs. Robert Keeley]

(1806-99) English actress
CDP, COC, DNB, ES, HAS,
OAA/1-2, OC/1-3, OX
KEELEY, Robert (1793-1869)
English actor BS, CDP, COC,
DNB, ES, HAS, OC/1-3, OX,
SR
KEELEY, Mrs. Robert see
Keeley, Mary Ann
KEEN, Elsie (d 1973) actress
TW/30
KEEN, Frederick Grinham see
Kerr, Frederick
KEEN, Geoffrey (b 1916/18)
English actor BE, WWT/9-16
KEEN, Malcolm (1887-1970)
English actor AAS, BE, NTH,
TW/4, 6-9, WWT/4-14
KEENAN, Frank [né James Fran-
cis] (1858-1929) American actor
DAB, WWA/1, WWT/4-5
KEENAN, James Francis see
Keenan, Frank
KEENAN, Sam (d 1895) minstrel
comedian EA/96*
KEENAN, Mrs. Tom (d 1899)
EA/00*
KEENE, Arthur (d 1845) Irish
actor CDP, HAS
KEENE, Donald (b 1922) trans-
lator BE
KEENE, Laura [Mary Moss]
(c. 1820-73) American actress,
manager CDP, COC, DAB,
ES, HAS, NTH, OC/1-3,
SR, WWA/H
KEENE, Richard Wynne ["Dy
Kwynkyn"] (d 1887 [76]) the-
atrical modeller, mask de-
signer EA/88*
KEENE, Theophilus (d 1718)
actor WWT/14*
KEENE, Thomas Wallace [né
Eagleson] (1840-98) American
actor CDP, DAB, HAS,
OC/1-3, SR, WWA/H
KEENE, Tom (d 1963 [65]) Amer-
ican performer BE*
KEES, John David American
actor TW/28-29
KEESE, William Linn (1835-1904)
American writer WWA/1
KEGLEY, Kermit (1918-74)
American director, stage
manager, actor BE, TW/30
KEHL, Mary Anne see Stir-
ling, Fanny
KEIGHLEY, William (b 1893)

American actor, director ES
KEIGHTLEY, Cyril (1875-1929)
Australian actor GRB/2-4,
WWM, WWT/1-5
KEIGWIN, John (1641-1716) English
dramatist CP/3, DNB
KEILING, John (fl 1720) musician
CDP
KEIM, Adelaide (b 1880/85) Amer-
ican actress WWS, WWT/1-2
KEIM, Betty Lou (b 1938/39)
American actress BE, TW/12
KEIM, Buster C. (d 1974 [68])
producer/director/choreographer
BP/59*
KEIPER, Robert (b 1935) American
actor TW/29
KEISER, Kris American actor
TW/24
KEITH, Benjamin Franklin (1846-
1914) American manager COC,
DAB, GRB/3-4, NTH, OC/1-3,
SR, WWA/1, WWS
KEITH, Caroline [Mrs. J. L.
Keith] (d 1900) EA/01*
KEITH, Charles Henry (d 1895 [57])
circus proprietor EA/96*
KEITH, Eliane Muriel (d 1910 [24])
EA/11*
KEITH, Mrs. H. (d 1917) EA/18*
KEITH, Ian (1899-1960) American
actor TW/5-9, 16, WWT/6-12
KEITH, James (d 1970 [68]) per-
former BP/55*
KEITH, J. L. (d 1905) scene artist
EA/06*
KEITH, Mrs. J. L. see Keith,
Caroline
KEITH, Mrs. J. L. see Keith,
Susannah
KEITH, Lawrence (b 1931) Ameri-
can actor TW/28, 30
KEITH, Leslie (d 1908 [32]) actor
EA/09*
KEITH, Maxine (d 1966 [50]) press
agent, critic TW/22
KEITH, Penelope English actress
WWT/16
KEITH, Robert (1898-1966) Ameri-
can dramatist, actor, director,
producer BE, TW/1-8, WWT/
8-12
KEITH, Robert, Jr. (b 1921) Amer-
ican actor TW/7-8
KEITH, Sherwood (d 1972 [59])
performer BP/56*
KEITH, Susannah [Mrs. J. L.
Keith] (d 1873 [30]) EA/74*

KEITH-JOHNSTON, Colin (b 1896) English actor BE, TW/2-15, WWT/6-14

KEL[B]Y, Lydia (fl 1824-31) actress HAS

KELCEY, Herbert (1855/56-1917) English actor GRB/2-4, PP/2, WWA/1, WWM, WWS, WWT/1-3

KELCEY, Mrs. Herbert see Shannon, Effie

KELETY, Julia (d 1972 [85]) actress, singer TW/28

KELF, Mrs. see Ambrose, Miss

KELHAM, Avice (b 1892) English actress, singer WWT/4-5

KELK, Jackie (b 1923) American actor TW/3-4, 9

KELL, Michael (b 1944) American actor TW/30

KELLAR, Harry (1849-1922) American magician CDP, SR, WWA/1, WWM

KELLARD, Ralph (1884/85-1955) American actor TW/11, WWM, WWS

KELLAWAY, Cecil (d 1973 [79]) actor TW/29

KELLEHER, Charles (d 1878 [25]) singer EA/79*

KELLEHER, Louis (1858-98) actor EA/97

KELLER, Mr. (fl 1854) actor HAS

KELLER, Jeff (b 1947) American actor TW/30

KELLER, Jules (d 1906) acrobat, equilibrist EA/07*

KELLER, Lewis (fl 1856) Polish actor CDP, HAS

KELLER, Mrs. Lewis (d 1860) actress CDP, HAS

KELLER, Nan (d 1975) performer BP/60*

KELLER, Nell Clark (d 1965 [89]) performer BP/50*

KELLER, Nina (d 1974 [43]) originator of mini-theatre BP/59*

KELLER, Wilhelmina see Keller, Mrs. Lewis

KELLERD, John E. (1863/66-1929) English actor PP/2, WWM, WWS

KELLEY, Edgar Stillman (1857-1944) American composer DAB

KELLEY, John T. (1852-1922) American minstrel, comedian SR

KELLEY, Lloyd (d 1972 [69]) electrician BP/57*

KELLEY, Peter (b 1925) American actor TW/9-15

KELLEY, Robert F. (d 1975 [75]) publicist BP/60*

KELLIE, Lawrence (1862-1932) English singer WWW/3

KELLIN, Mike (b 1922) American actor BE, TW/5, 9, 12-15, 19, 23-24, 30

KELLIN, Nina C. (d 1963 [44]) performer BP/47*

KELLING, Alfred (d 1893 [68]) clown EA/94*

KELLING, Thomas (d 1886 [49]) acrobat, pantomimist EA/87*

KELLINO, Pamela (b 1917) English actress TW/3

KELLOGG, Mr. (d 1850) actor HAS

KELLOGG, Clara Louise (1842-1916) American singer CDP, DAB, ES, HAS, WWA/1

KELLOGG, Fannie (fl 1881?) actress, singer CDP

KELLOGG, Gertrude reader CDP

KELLOGG, Lynn American actress TW/24

KELLOGG, Nelly (b c. 1855) actress HAS

KELLOGG, Riley (b 1961) American actor TW/28-29

KELLOGG, Shirley (b 1888) actress, singer WWT/4-7

KELLSTROM, Gail (b 1944) American actress TW/27, 29

KELLY, Mr. (fl 1792-1803) English actor TD/2

KELLY, Mr. (d 1876) Negro comedian EA/77*

KELLY, Al (d 1966 [67]) performer BP/51*

KELLY, Alfred Cain (d 1911) variety acting manager EA/12*

KELLY, Miss A. M. see Clavering-Wardell, Anna Maria

KELLY, Ann (d 1852 [103]) actress BE*, WWT/14*

KELLY, Anthony Paul (d 1932 [37]) American dramatist BE*, BP/17*

KELLY, Bob (b 1923) American perruquier, make-up artist BE

KELLY, Cathleen see Cordell,
Cathleen

KELLY, Charles [Charles Clavering Wardell] (1839-85) actor
CDP, COC, OAA/2

KELLY, Charles D. (d 1859)
American actor? HAS

KELLY, Charlotte actress CDP

KELLY, Desmond (b 1884) American actress WWM

KELLY, Dorothy H. (d 1969
[51]) performer BP/54*

KELLY, Edward (fl 1860s) minstrel SR

KELLY, Edwin (1835-98) Irish
singer, actor CDP, HAS

KELLY, E. H. Irish actor
GRB/1-2, WWT/3-4

KELLY, Mrs. E. H. see Boucicault, Nina

KELLY, Emmett (b 1898) American clown CB

KELLY, Eva [Mrs. G. P. Hunt-
ley] (1880-1948) American actress, singer GRB/1-4,
WWT/1-5

KELLY, Fanny see Kelly,
Frances Maria

KELLY, Flo (d 1972 [68]) performer BP/57*

KELLY, Francis Harriet (b
1800/03/05) English actress
BS, CDP, OX

KELLY, Frances Maria (1790-
1882) English actress, singer
BS, CDP, COC, DNB, ES,
OC/1-3, OX

KELLY, Fred (d 1902) pantomimist, acrobat EA/03*

KELLY, Gene (b 1912) American
actor, dancer, choreographer
BE, CB, ES, WWT/10-11

KELLY, George (b 1872) Canadian actor SR

KELLY, George (1887-1974)
American actor, producer,
dramatist BE, COC, ES,
HJD, MD, MH, MWD, NTH,
OC/1-3, SR, WWT/5-11

KELLY, G. M. (b 1841) American acrobat HAS

KELLY, Grace (b 1928/29)
American actress BE, CB,
ES, TW/6-11

KELLY, Grace see Arundale,
Grace

KELLY, Gregory (d 1927 [36])
American actor BE*, BP/12*,

WWT/14*

KELLY, Harry (d 1936 [63]) American comedian WWS

KELLY, Herb (d 1970 [71]) critic
BP/55*

KELLY, Hugh (1739-77) English
dramatist CDP, COC, CP/2-3,
DNB, GT, OC/1-3, SR, TD/1-2

KELLY, Jack American actor
TW/19, 21

KELLY, James (d 1964 [49]) performer BE*

KELLY, James T. (b 1855) actor,
singer CDP

KELLY, Jno (d 1856) HAS

KELLY, John (d 1751 [71]) dramatist CP/1-3, DNB, GT, TD/1-2

KELLY, John T. (1855-1922)
American comedian CDP, WWS

KELLY, Judy (b 1913) Australian
actress WWT/9-11

KELLY, J. W. (1857-96/97) American actor EA/97*, SR

KELLY, Kate [Mrs. Edwin Brown]
(d 1899) variety comedian EA/
01*

KELLY, Mrs. K. B. (d 1904 [78])
manager EA/05*

KELLY, Kevin (b 1930) American
critic BE

KELLY, Kitty (d 1968 [66]) performer BP/53*

KELLY, Lawrence (d 1974 [46])
impresario BP/59*

KELLY, Lew (d 1944 [65]) American actor TW/1

KELLY, Lydia (b 1795) English
actress BS, CDP

KELLY, Margot (d 1976 [82]) performer BP/60*

KELLY, Maurice (d 1974 [59])
performer BP/59*

KELLY, Michael (1764?-1826)
Irish singer, composer, actor
CDP, DNB, ES, GT, TD/1-2

KELLY, Nancy (b 1921) American
actress BE, CB, TW/7-9, 11-
20, 25, WWT/14-16

KELLY, Nolan (d 1893 [34]) American song & dance artist EA/94*

KELLY, Pat (d 1908 [50]) songwriter EA/09*

KELLY, Patsy (b 1910) American
actress, singer TW/27-30,
WWT/16

KELLY, Paul (1899-1956) American
actor ES, TW/2-8, 13, WWA/
3, WWT/9-12

KELLY, Renée (1888-1965) English actress WWT/2-12
KELLY, Robert (d 1949 [74]) American actor BE*, BP/34*
KELLY, Sybil see Arundale, Sybil
KELLY, Toney (d 1883) comic singer EA/84*
KELLY, Walter C. (1873-1939) American actor WWT/8
KELLY, William J. (1875-1949) American actor TW/5
KELLY, W. W. (1853-1933) American manager WWT/1-7
KELLY AND LEON see Kelly, Edward, & Leon, Mr.
KELMAR, Fred (d 1901) ventriloquist EA/02*
KELSEY, Emily [Mrs. Charles R. Stone] (b 1860) English actress GRB/1
KELSEY, Herbert (fl 1880s) English actor SR
KELSEY, Jennie see Hughes, Sarah Jane
KELSEY, Lizzie (d 1888 [36]) actress CDP
KELSEY, Matilda (d 1916) EA/17*
KELSO, Vernon (b 1893) English actor WWT/10-11
KELT, John (d 1935 [70]) actor BE*, WWT/14*
KELTON, Aggie [Mrs. George Hall] (d 1910) singer EA/11*
KELTON, Dorrit American actress TW/19
KELTON, Gene (b 1938) American actor TW/26-29
KELTON, Pert (d 1968 [61]) American actress BE, TW/24-25
KELVIN, James [James Watt Gilchrist] (d 1905 [37]) EA/06*
KEMBLE, Adelaide [Mrs. E. T. Sartoris] (c. 1816/17-79) actress, singer CDP, DNB, ES, NTH, OAA/1-2
KEMBLE, Agnes see Cooper, Mrs. Clifford
KEMBLE, Blanche see Shea, Mrs.
KEMBLE, Charles (1775-1854) English actor, dramatist BS, CDP, CP/3, DNB, ES, GT, HAS, HP, NTH, OC/1-3, OX, SR, TD/1-2
KEMBLE, Eliza [Mrs. Thomas

Kemble] (d 1855) HAS
KEMBLE, Elizabeth [Elizabeth Whitlock] (1761-1836) English actress HAS, OC/1-3, SR, TD/1-2
KEMBLE, Elizabeth [Mrs. Stephen Kemble] (1763?-1841) actress CDP, DNB, ES, TD/1, WWA/H
KEMBLE, Eugenie [Miss Stevens] English actress GRB/1
KEMBLE, Fanny [Fanny Butler] (1809-93) English actress CDP, COC, DAB, DNB, ES, HAS, HJD, HP, NTH, OAA/1-2, OC/1-3, SR, WWA/H
KEMBLE, Frances [Mrs. Twiss] (d 1822 [62]) actress BE*, WWT/14*
KEMBLE, Frances "Frankie" actress CDP
KEMBLE, Frances Anne see Kemble, Fanny
KEMBLE, "Frankie" see Kemble, Frances
KEMBLE, Henry (1848-1907) English actor DNB, EA/96, ES, GRB/1-3, OAA/1-2, OC/1-3
KEMBLE, Mrs. Henry see Kemble, Nina
KEMBLE, Henry Stephen (1789-1836) English actor BS, CDP, DNB, ES, OX
KEMBLE, H. J. [H. J. Green] (b 1861) English actor GRB/1
KEMBLE, John (d 1908) performer EA/09*
KEMBLE, John Mitchell (d 1857 [49]) examiner of plays BE*, WWT/14*
KEMBLE, John Philip (1757-1823) English actor, dramatist, adapter CDP, COC, CP/3, DNB, ES, GT, HP, NTH, OC/1-3, OX, TD/1-2
KEMBLE, Mrs. John Philip [née Hopkins] (1756-1845) actress CDP, DNB, ES, TD/1-2
KEMBLE, Marie-Therese see Kemble, Theresa
KEMBLE, Myra [Mrs. James H. White] (d 1906) Australian actress DP
KEMBLE, Nina [Mrs. Henry Kemble] (d 1904 [33]) EA/05*
KEMBLE, Priscilla see Kemble, Mrs. John Philip
KEMBLE, Roger (1721-1802) English actor, manager CDP,

COC, DNB, ES, GT, NTH,
OC/1-3, TD/1-2

KEMBLE, Mrs. Roger see
Kemble, Sarah

KEMBLE, Sarah (1735-1807)
actress CDP, ES, NTH

KEMBLE, Stephen (1758-1822)
English actor, dramatist
CDP, CP/3, ES, GT, OC/
1-3, OX, TD/1-2

KEMBLE, Mrs. Stephen see
Kemble, Elizabeth (d 1841)

KEMBLE, T. D. (fl 1846) HAS

KEMBLE, Mrs. T. D. (d 1855)
HAS

KEMBLE, Theresa (1773-1838)
English actress, dancer,
dramatist CDP, CP/3, DNB,
ES, GT, OC/1-3

KEMBLE, Mrs. Thomas see
Kemble, Eliza

KEMBLE-BARNETT, Harry (d
1913) EA/14*

KEMP, Annie (fl 1860s) American singer, actress HAS

KEMP, Beatriz [Beatriz Phipps;
Mrs. Maurice F. Kemp] (d
1887) EA/88*

KEMP, Cornelius (d 1887) advance agent EA/88*

KEMP, Everett (b 1873) American monologist WWA/5

KEMP, Isaac (d 1889) music-
hall proprietor EA/90*

KEMP, Mrs. I. T. (d 1874)
EA/75*

KEMP, Jeremy [né Walker] (b
1935) English actor WWT/
15-16

KEMP, John (fl 1601) actor DA

KEMP, John (d 1867 [33])
pantomimist EA/68*

KEMP, Joseph (fl 1809-10)
dramatist CP/3

KEMP, Mrs. Maurice F. see
Kemp, Beatriz

KEMP, Robert (d 1959 [73])
French critic BE*, WWT/14*

KEMP, Roger (b 1931) English
actor TW/24

KEMP, Sally (b 1933) American
actress BE

KEMP, T[homas] C[harles] (1891-
1955) English critic, dramatist
COC, OC/3, WWT/11

KEMPE, William (d 1603) English
clown, actor, dancer, dramatist CDP, COC, CP/3, DA,

DNB, ES, FGF, GT, HP, NTH,
OC/1-3

KEMPER, Colin (1870-1955) American manager GRB/2-4, WWS,
WWT/1-7

KEMPER, Dolly [Charlotte Keogh]
(d 1943) actress SR

KEMPSON, Rachel (b 1910) English
actress COC, WWT/8-16

KEMPSTER, Frederick (d 1881)
actor, elocutionist EA/82*

KEMP-WELCH, Joan (b 1906) English actress, director WWT/
10-16

KENDAL, Doris actress WWT/5-6

KENDAL, Felicity (b 1946) English
actress WWT/15-16

KENDAL, Dame Madge [Margaret]
(1848-1935) English actress,
manager CDP, COC, DNB,
DP, ES, GRB/1-4, NTH, OAA/
1-2, OC/1-3, SR, WWA/4,
WWS, WWT/1-7, WWW/3

KENDAL, William Hunter [Grim-
ston] (1843-1917) English actor,
manager CDP, COC, DNB,
DP, ES, GRB/1-4, OAA/1-2,
OC/1-3, SR, WWA/1, WWS,
WWT/1-3, WWW/2

KENDALL, Mrs. (d 1906 [54])
EA/07*

KENDALL, A. A. (d 1916 [20])
EA/18*

KENDALL, Cricket E. (d 1972
[65]) publicity director BP/56*

KENDALL, Edward P. (1834-75)
American actor, manager, agent
HAS

KENDALL, Ezra Fremont (1861-
1910) American actor, dramatist
GRB/3-4, SR, WWA/1, WWS

KENDALL, Henry (1897-1962)
English actor AAS, WWT/4-13,
WWW/6

KENDALL, Jennie (fl 1858) American actress HAS

KENDALL, John (b 1869) English
dramatist WWT/2-7

KENDALL, Kay (1926-59) English
actress TW/16

KENDALL, Lizzie (fl 1858) American actress HAS

KENDALL, Marie (d 1964 [90])
singer CDP

KENDALL, Richard (fl 1635) actor
DA

KENDALL, Richard (b 1945) Canadian actor TW/25-26

KENDALL, Thomas (d 1608) patentee, manager DA

KENDALL, Will (d 1892) Negro comedian EA/94*

KENDALL, William (fl 1597-1614) actor DA

KENDALL, William (b 1903) English actor WWT/8-16

KENDRICK, Alfred (b 1869) English actor GRB/1-4, WWT/1-7

KENDRICK, Brian (d 1970 [40]) performer BP/54*

KENDRICK, Jackie (d 1917) EA/18*

KENDRICK, Merle T. (d 1968 [71]) composer/lyricist BP/53*

KENDRICK, Richard (b 1910) American actor TW/5-7

KENEDE, Richard (fl 1607) actor DA

KENLEY, John (b 1907) American producer BE

KENMORE, Eddie (b 1940) American actor TW/19-20

KENNA (fl 1785) actor HAS

KENNA, Mrs. (fl 1785) actress HAS

KENNA, Peter (b 1930) Australian dramatist CD

KENNARD, Jane see Kennark, Jane

KENNARD, Willie (d 1910) EA/11*

KENNARK [Or Kennard], Jane (d 1938 [75]) American actress BE*, BP/22*

KENNAWAY, James (d 1968 [40]) dramatist BP/53*

KENNEALLY, Michael (d 1972 [80]) performer BP/56*

KENNEDY, Mr. (d 1786 [66]) actor TD/1-2

KENNEDY, Mrs. (d c. 1788) actress GT, TD/1-2

KENNEDY, Miss (d 1888) actress EA/89*

KENNEDY, Adrienne (b 1931) American dramatist CD, CH

KENNEDY, Anne G. (d 1974 [38]) performer BP/58*

KENNEDY, Arthur (b 1914) American actor AAS, BE, CB, TW/3-15, 24-25, 30, WWT/11-16

KENNEDY, Beulah (d 1964 [71]) American performer BE*

KENNEDY, Bob (d 1974 [41])

performer BP/59*

KENNEDY, Charles E. (b 1867) American actor WWS

KENNEDY, Charles Rann (1871-1950) English dramatist, actor GRB/4, HJD, TW/6, WWA/2, WWT/1-9, WWW/4

KENNEDY, Mrs. Charles Rann see Matthison, Edith Wynne

KENNEDY, Cheryl (b 1947) English actress, singer WWT/15-16

KENNEDY, David (1825-86) Scottish singer CDP, DNB

KENNEDY, Edgar (d 1948 [58]) American actor BE*

KENNEDY, Edmund F. (b 1873) English actor GRB/1-4, WWT/1-5

KENNEDY, Edward J. (b 1844) dancer, minstrel CDP

KENNEDY, Mrs. E. J. (d 1899 [51]) EA/00*

KENNEDY, Elise Marie Dalton (d 1876) actress EA/77*

KENNEDY, Florence [Mrs. James H. Huntley] (c. 1849-87) American actress NYM

KENNEDY, Mrs. H. A. see Lovel, Gertrude

KENNEDY, Harold J. actor, director, dramatist WWT/16

KENNEDY, Harry see Kennedy, William Henry

KENNEDY, Hugh Arthur (d 1905 [50]) dramatist, critic GRB/1

KENNEDY, Mrs. Hugh Arthur see Lovel, Gertrude

KENNEDY, Joe (d 1969 [80]) performer BP/54*

KENNEDY, John (d 1898 [34]) proprietor EA/99*

KENNEDY, John (b 1902) American director BE, TW/3

KENNEDY, Joyce (1898/1900-1943) English actress WWT/5-9

KENNEDY, J. T. (d 1896) actor EA/97*

KENNEDY, Kathleen M. (d 1975 [28]) publicist BP/60*

KENNEDY, Lila (b 1903) American executive, director, actress BE

KENNEDY, Madge (b 1890) American actress TW/22, WWT/4-9

KENNEDY, Margaret (1896-1967) English dramatist ES, MH, MWD, NTH, WWA/4, WWT/8-13, WWW/6

KENNEDY, Margaret see Farrell, Margaret

KENNEDY, Mary (d 1887 [57]) EA/88*

KENNEDY, Mary American actress, dramatist WWT/7-9

KENNEDY, Maurice (d 1962 [51]) manager BE*

KENNEDY, Merna (d 1944 [35]) actress TW/1

KENNEDY, Patricia (b 1917) Australian actress WWT/16

KENNEDY, Mrs. T. (fl 1773) actress CDP

KENNEDY, Thomas (d 1898 [32]) actor EA/99*

KENNEDY, Walter (d 1886) EA/87*

KENNEDY, Warder Howard (1880-1943) actor SR

KENNEDY, William Henry (1855-91) ventriloquist, singer, composer CDP

KENNEDY, Zona American actress TW/23

KENNER, Chris (d 1976 [46]) performer BP/60*

KENNER, Hugh (b 1923) Canadian critic BE

KENNETT, Amelia Sevenoaks (d 1907) actress? EA/09*

KENNETTE (d 1906) aerial wonder EA/07*

KENNEY, Charles Horace (d 1909 [52]) actor EA/10*

KENNEY, Charles Lamb (1821-81) French/English dramatist DNB

KENNEY, Mrs. Charles Lamb see Kenney, Rosa

KENNEY, Ed (b 1933) American actor TW/15

KENNEY, Horace (d 1955 [65]) music-hall performer WWT/14*

KENNEY, Izetta see Jewell, Izetta

KENNEY, Jack (d 1964 [76]) actor BE*

KENNEY, James (1780-1849) Irish dramatist CDP, CP/3, DNB, GT, TD/2

KENNEY, James (b 1930) English actor WWT/12-16

KENNEY, Rosa [Mrs. Charles Lamb Kenney] (d 1900) EA/01*

KENNEY, Rose (d 1905) actress

GRB/1, OAA/2

KENNICOTT, James H. (fl 1830) American dramatist EAP, RJ

KENNINGHAM, Charles (d 1925) actor BE*, WWT/14*

KENNINGTON, Anne (d 1962 [77]) dramatist WWT/14*

KENNION, Rose (d 1912) actress EA/13*

KENNIS, Stanley (d 1897) EA/99*

KENNY, Mr. (fl 1794) actor HAS

KENNY, Mrs. George [Georgiana Harris] (d 1883 [27]) EA/84*

KENNY, James see Kenney, James

KENNY, Nick (d 1975 [80]) songwriter, columnist BP/60*, WWT/16*

KENNY, Sean (1932-73) Irish designer AAS, BE, ES, PDT, WWT/14-15

KENRICK, William (1725?-79) English dramatist CDP, CP/2-3, GT, TD/1-2

KENT, Miss see Da Costa, Mrs.

KENT, Allegra (b 1938) American dancer CB, ES

KENT, Barbara (b 1921) English actress TW/1

KENT, Barry [né Sautereau] (b 1932) English actor WWT/15-16

KENT, Beatrice E. English lyricist GRB/1

KENT, Carl (b 1918) American designer TW/3-5

KENT, Charles (d 1923 [69]) English actor BE*, BP/7*

KENT, Crawford (d 1953 [72]) actor BE*

KENT, Eleanor (b 1879) American singer WWM

KENT, Frederick M. (1829-57) American actor CDP, HAS

KENT, Fred S. American actor HAS

KENT, Mrs. Fred S. [Josephine Tyson] (d 1869 [30]) actress HAS

KENT, Georgia Tyler (1848-1914) actress HAS

KENT, Harry (fl 1897?) singer CDP

KENT, Helen see Herbert, Mrs.

KENT, Herbert (d 1973 [96]) English actor TW/29

KENT, Imogene (b 1838) American actress HAS

KENT, Jean [née Field] (b 1921)

English actress WWT/12-16

KENT, John (d 1830) English actor HAS

KENT, John, Jr. (d 1833) English actor HAS

KENT, Mrs. John [née Yardley] (fl 1824-33) English actress HAS

KENT, Keneth (1892-1963) English actor, producer AAS, WWT/5-13

KENT, Sidney Miller (c. 1861-1948) actor SR

KENT, Thomas M. (d 1898 [58]) actor EA/99*

KENT, Walter composer BE

KENT, Walter Speakman (d 1887 [18]) EA/88*

KENT, Willard (d 1968 [85]) performer BP/53*

KENT, William (b 1811) Scottish dancer HAS

KENT, William (1886-1945) American actor SR, TW/2, WWT/6-9

KENT, Mrs. William [Elizabeth Eberle] (d 1850) American actress, singer HAS

KENTISH, Agatha (b 1897) English actress WWT/5-8

KENTON, Godfrey (b 1902) English actor AAS, WWT/8-16

"KENTUCKY GIANT, The" see Porter, Mr. (fl 1838)

KENWARD, Edith (d 1905) actress, dramatist CDP, GRB/1

KENWAY, George (d 1909 [73]) EA/10*

KENWAY, Rebecca (d 1912 [89]) EA/13*

KENYON, Charles (1878-1961) English actor WWT/2-7

KENYON, Doris (b 1897) American actress WWT/5-9

KENYON, Harry (d 1907 [37]) performer? EA/08*

KENYON, Laura (b 1947) American actress TW/28

KENYON, Neil [Neil McKinnon] (d 1946 [73]) Scottish actor WWT/4-7

KENYON, Taldo (b 1936) American actor TW/23

KEOGH, Mrs. Arthur H. see Keogh, Leah

KEOGH, Charlotte see Kemper, Dolly

KEOGH, John see Stables, Harry

KEOGH, Joseph Augustus (1884-1942) Irish actor, manager GRB/1, SR

KEOGH, Leah [Mrs. Arthur H. Keogh] (d 1876 [24]) EA/77*

KEOGH, William T. (d 1947 [87]) producer, manager BE*, WWT/14*

KEOUGH, Emma (b 1829) English actress, singer HAS

KEOWN, Eric (1904-63) English critic WWT/12-13

KEPLER, Constance (fl 1838) dancer HAS

KEPPELL, W. H. (fl 1880s) actor SR

KER, Paul (d c. 1929 [54]) German singer, actor BP/13*

KERBY, Marion (d 1956 [79]) American actress, singer TW/13

KERCHEVAL, Ken (b 1935) American actor TW/24-29

KERIN, Nora [Mrs. Cyril Michael] (b 1883) English actress GRB/4, WWT/1-7

KERKER, Gustave Adolph (1857-1923) German composer, conductor GRB/3-4, SR, WWA/1, WWM, WWS, WWT/1-4

KERKOW, Herbert (d 1972 [68]) producer/director/choreographer BP/57*

KERMOYAN, Michael (b 1925) American actor, singer BE, TW/22-24, 30

KERN, Jerome David (1885-1945) American composer AAS, CB, DAB, ES, HJD, MH, NTH, PDT, SR, TW/2, WWA/2, WWT/4-9, WWW/4

KERNAN, David (b 1939) English actor WWT/15-16

KERNAN, Joseph Lewis (d 1964 [83]) manager, talent representative BE*

KERNELL, Harry (1853-93) Irish comedian, minstrel CDP

KERNELL, Harry (b 1888) American actor WWM

KERNODLE, George R. (b 1907) American educator, director BE

KERNWOOD, Grace (1863-1943) singer SR

KERR, Miss (fl 1839) actress HAS

KERR, Alexander (d 1876 [50]) scene artist EA/77*

KERR, Dr. Alfred (d 1948 [80])

critic BE*, WWT/14*
KERR, Anne (d 1973 [48]) per-
former BP/58*
KERR, Ann Jeannette see Hunt,
Mrs. Charles
KERR, Bill actor WWT/16
KERR, Charles see Arnold,
Mat
KERR, Deborah (b 1921) Scottish
actress BE, CB, ES, WWT/
10-14, 16
KERR, Elaine (b 1942) American
actress TW/28-29
KERR, Frederick [Frederick
Grinham Keen] (1858-1933)
English actor DP, EA/95,
GRB/1-4, NTH, WWM, WWT/
1-7
KERR, Geoffrey (b 1895) English
actor, dramatist BE, TW/6-
7, WWT/4-14
KERR, Jean (b 1923/24) Ameri-
can dramatist BE, CB, ES,
WWT/14-16
KERR, John (fl 1830?) drama-
tist EAP
KERR, John (b 1931) American
actor BE, TW/9-18, 24
KERR, John George (b 1814)
English actor, dancer HAS
KERR, Marge American talent
representative BE
KERR, Molly (b 1904) English
actress WWT/5-6
KERR, Philip (b 1940) American
actor TW/26-27, 29
KERR, Sophie (1880-1965) Amer-
ican dramatist WWA/4
KERR, Walter F. (b 1913)
American critic, director,
dramatist AAS, BE, CB,
COC, HJD, NTH, WWT/13-16
KERRIDGE, Donald (d 1874)
musical director EA/75*
KERRIDGE, Mary (b 1914) Eng-
lish actress COC, WWT/
11-16
KERRIGAN, J. M. (1885-1964)
Irish actor TW/3, WWT/
2-11
KERRIGAN, J. Warren (1880-
1947) actor BE*
KERRIGAN, T. F. musician,
composer, dancer CDP
KERRY, Norman (d 1956 [66])
actor BE*
KERSANDS, "Billy" actor CDP
KERSHAW, Elinor (d 1971 [86])

performer BP/56*
KERSHAW, Willette (1890-1960)
American actress TW/16,
WWT/4-10
KERT, Larry [né Frederick Law-
rence] (b 1930) American actor,
singer AAS, BE, TW/18-20,
23, 25-30, WWT/15-16
KERZ, Leo (1912-76) German de-
signer, director, producer BE
KESHAN, Fred (d 1890) music-hall
performer EA/91*
KESHAN, John (d 1877) instrument
maker EA/78*
KESSELRING, Charlotte E. (d
1971) dramatist BP/56*
KESSELRING, Joseph D. (1902-67)
American dramatist BE, ES,
MH, MWD, TW/24, WWA/4,
WWT/10-14
KESSLER, David (1860-1920) Rus-
sian dramatist ES
KESSLER, Ferdinand Mozart (d
1888 [38]) conductor EA/89*
KESSLER, Joseph (d 1933 [51])
actor BE*, WWT/14*
KESSLER, Mabel (b 1873) English
singer, musician GRB/1
KESSLER, Phillip (d 1878 [55])
musician EA/79*
KESTELMAN, Sara (b 1944) Eng-
lish actress TW/27, 30,
WWT/16
KESTER, Paul (1870-1933) Ameri-
can dramatist COC, DAB,
GRB/2-4, OC/1-3, WWA/1,
WWM, WWT/1-7
KESTON, C. B. [Charles H. Dun-
can] English actor CDP, GRB/1
KETCHUM, George F. (1837-80)
American actor, stage manager
CDP, HAS
KETCHUM, Robyna Neilson (d
1972) performer BP/57*
KETHRO, Frank (d 1910) musical
director EA/11*
KETTEN, Henry (d 1883 [35]) com-
poser, musician EA/84*
KEY, Kathleen (d 1954 [57]) actress
BE*
KEY, Pat Ann (d 1962) performer
BE*
KEYES, Daniel (b 1914) American
actor TW/22-27, 29-30
KEYMER, Mrs. (d 1882) EA/83*
KEYS, Miss see Lee, Mrs.
KEYS, Miss see Mills, Mrs.
KEYS, Nelson (1886-1939) English

actor WWT/3-8
KEYS, Simon actor TD/1-2
KEYS, Mrs. Simon (fl 1803)
 actress TD/2
KEYSAR, Robert (fl 1605-08)
 lessee DA
KEZER, Glenn (b 1923) American
 actor TW/24-26
KHACIDOVITCH, Tamara see
 Toumanova, Tamara
KHOURY, Edith Leslie (d 1973)
 performer BP/57*
KIALLMARK [or Kilmark],
 George (1781-1835) English
 composer, musician DNB
KIBBEE, Guy (1882-1956) Amer-
 ican actor TW/12
KIDD, Kathleen (d 1961) Cana-
 dian actress BE*, BP/45*,
 WWT/14*
KIDD, Michael [né Milton Green-
 wald] (b 1918/19) American
 dancer, choreographer, di-
 rector AAS, BE, CB, ES,
 WWT/14-16
KIDD, Robert (b 1943) Scottish
 director WWT/15-16
KIDDER, E. E. American
 dramatist SR
KIDDER, Kathryn [Mrs. Louis
 Kaufman Anspacher] (1867-
 1939) American actress CDP,
 GRB/2-4, PP/2, SR, WWA/1,
 WWM, WWS, WWT/1-7
KIDDIE, Polly see Burton, Polly
KIDGER, Mrs. John see
 Kidger, Mary
KIDGER, Mary [Mrs. John Kid-
 ger] (d 1887) acting manager
 EA/88*
KIDWELL, Gene (b 1946) Amer-
 ican actor TW/25-27
KIENZL, Florian (d 1972 [77])
 critic BP/56*
KIEPURA, Jan (1904-66) Polish
 singer, actor BE, CB, SR,
 TW/2-3, 23, WWA/4, WWT/
 10-14
KIERNAN, James (1939-75)
 American actor TW/30
KIESLER, Frederick J. (b 1896)
 Austrian scene designer BE
KIKUME, Al (d 1972 [78]) per-
 former BP/56*
KILBRIDE, Percy (d 1964 [76])
 American actor TW/2-3, 21
KILBURN, Eliza (d 1891) EA/92*
KILBURN, Harry (d 1908 [42])

comedian EA/09*
KILBURN, Terrance (b 1928) Eng-
 lish actor TW/8, 10-14
KILDARE, Tom J. see Gilbey,
 Tom
KILEY, Richard (b 1922) American
 actor, singer BE, CB, TW/9-
 25, 28-30, WWT/14-16
KILFOIL, Thomas F. (b 1922)
 American librarian, curator BE
KILFOY, Tam (d 1874) musician
 EA/75*
KILGALLEN, Dorothy (d 1965 [52])
 journalist BP/50*
KILGOUR, Joseph (1863/72-1933)
 Canadian actor SR, WWM
KILIAN, Victor (b 1891) American
 actor BE, TW/14-15
KILLIAN, Phil American actor
 TW/29-30
KILLICK, C. Egerton (1891/92-
 1967) English manager WWT/5-
 14
KILLIGREW, Charles (1665-1725)
 English manager, Master of the
 Revels DNB, OC/1-3
KILLIGREW, Dr. Henry (1612-1700)
 English dramatist CP/1-3,
 FGF, HP
KILLIGREW, Thomas (1612-83)
 English dramatist, manager,
 Master of the Revels CDP,
 COC, CP/1-3, DNB, FGF, HP,
 NTH, OC/1-3, RE
KILLIGREW, Thomas (1657-1719)
 English dramatist CP/1-3,
 DNB, HP, OC/1-3
KILLIGREW, Sir William (1606-95)
 English dramatist CP/1-3,
 DNB, ES, HP, OC/1-3
KILLINGER, Marion (b 1941) Amer-
 ican actress TW/29
KILLMER, Nancy (b 1936) Ameri-
 can actress TW/26
KILMARK, George see Kiallmark,
 George
KILMOREY, Earl of (d 1915 [73])
 producer, dramatist, manager
 BE*, WWT/14*
KILNER, Naomi (d 1900 [64])
 EA/01*
KILNER, Thomas (1777-1862) Eng-
 lish actor CDP, HAS
KILPACK, Bennett (d 1962 [79])
 English actor BE*
KILPACK, Frank (d 1889 [51])
 acting manager EA/90*
KILPATRICK, Mrs. Edwin E. see

Kilpatrick, Kintchie
KILPATRICK, Jack Frederick (b 1915) American composer, educator BE
KILPATRICK, Kintchie [Mrs. Edwin E. Kilpatrick] (d 1917) EA/18*
KILPATRICK, Thomas (b 1902) American producer, manager, publicist BE
KILTY, Jerome (b 1922) American actor, director, dramatist BE, COC, ES, WWT/14-16
KIM, Christal (b 1916) American actress TW/27-28
KIMBALL, Grace [Mrs. Laurence McGuire] (b 1870) American actress GRB/2-4, SR, WWS, WWT/1-2
KIMBALL, Jennie (1848-96) American actress, manager CDP, HAS, SR
KIMBALL, Louis (1889-1936) American actor WWT/6-7
KIMBALL, Moses (1810-95) manager CDP
KIMBER, J. W. (d 1884) manager EA/86*
KIMBER, Mrs. J. W. (d 1879) EA/80*
KIMBERLEY, Mrs. F. G. (d 1939 [62]) dramatist, producer BE*, WWT/14*
KIMBERLY, E. (fl 1849) actress, reader CDP
KIMBRELL, Marketa (b 1928) Czech actress TW/23
KIMBROUGH, Charles (b 1936) American actor TW/25-28, 30
KIMBROUGH, Clinton (b 1935/36) American actor BE, TW/18-21
KIMM, Anne (d 1911) EA/12*
KIMM, H. Val (b 1873) English business manager GRB/1
KIMMIE, Miss (fl 1851) actress HAS
KIMMINS, Anthony (1901-64) English dramatist AAS, WWT/8-13
KIMMINS, Grace (b 1942) American actress TW/27
KIMMINS, Kenneth (b 1941) American actor TW/28-29
KIMPTON, Robert (fl 1629-32) actor DA
KINDLE, Tom (b 1948) American actor TW/29

KING, Mr. (fl 1801-04) actor, dancer, equestrian TD/1-2
KING, Mrs. see Brookyn, May
KING, Mrs. [née Brett] (fl 1793) actress HAS
KING, Ada (d 1940 [78]) actress WWT/2-8
KING, Adah (fl 1850s) English actress HAS
KING, Alan (b 1927) American actor, producer CB
KING, Alfred George (d 1907) EA/08*
KING, Amelia (d 1900) EA/01*
KING, Archer American talent representative, producer BE
KING, Arthur (fl 1581) actor DA
KING, Bob Brown (d 1970 [33]) performer BP/54*
KING, Cecil (d 1958 [83]) Irish actor, stage manager WWT/4-10
KING, Charles (d 1881) acting manager EA/83*
KING, Charles (1887/89-1944) American actor, singer SR, WWT/7-8
KING, Mrs. Charles see King, Martha
KING, Charles A. (1823-57) American actor? HAS
KING, Clara (d 1879 [29]) actress EA/80*
KING, Clara (d 1884 [46]) ballet mistress, dancer EA/85*
KING, Claude (1876-1941) English actor WWT/2-9
KING, Dennis (1897-1971) English actor, singer, director AAS, BE, TW/1-24, 26-27, WWT/6-15
KING, Dennis, Jr. English actor TW/1, 3-5
KING, Donald W. (d 1886 [74]) actor, singer WWT/14*
KING, Edith (d 1975 [91]) BP/59*
KING, Edith [née Keck] (b 1896/97) American actress BE, TW/1-3, 8, 10-18, 20, WWT/10-15
KING, Ellen Langley (d 1916 [79]) EA/17*
KING, Emmett C. (d 1953 [87]) American actor BE*, BP/37*
KING, George (d 1909 [36]) proprietor EA/10*
KING, Gerard James (d 1889 [53]) comedian EA/90*
KING, Harry (d 1870 [19]) duologue artist EA/71*

KING, Harry (d 1886 [39]) Negro comedian, panorama proprietor EA/87*

KING, Henry (b 1888) American actor ES

KING, Henry James see Martley, Bob

KING, Herbert G. (d 1975 [73]) director of opera club BP/60*

KING, Hetty (d 1972 [89]) music-hall performer BP/57*, WWT/16*

KING, Howard (d 1975 [91]) circus executive BP/60*

KING, James (d 1909 [81]) music-hall manager EA/10*

KING, James Joyce (d 1971 [61]) publicist BP/56*

KING, Jane (d 1971 [75]) vaude-villian, actress TW/27

KING, John-Michael (b 1926/29) American actor, singer BE, TW/12-16, 22-24

KING, Karl L. (d 1971 [80]) composer/lyricist BP/55*

KING, Katty [Mrs. Arthur Lloyd] (d 1891 [39]) actress EA/92*

KING, Lottie [Mrs. Henry Belding] (d 1899) actress EA/00*

KING, Marie see Sutherland, Marie

KING, Martha [Mrs. Charles King] (d 1876) EA/78*

KING, Mary [Mrs. Tom King] (fl 1772?) dancer CDP

KING, Matthias (fl early 19th cent) clown, actor CDP

KING, Murray (b 1874) English actor, manager GRB/2

KING, Nosmo (d 1949 [63]) performer BE*, WWT/14*

KING, Omega J. (d 1973 [81]) performer BP/58*

KING, P. (fl 1805) English composer TD/2

KING, Philip (b 1904) dramatist, actor WWT/10-16

KING, Robert (b 1936) American actor TW/28

KING, Robert A. (1862-1932) American composer BE*

KING, Robert M. (d 1974 [54]) producer/director/choreographer BP/58*

KING, Mrs. T. C. (d 1878) EA/79*

KING, Mrs. T. G. see Richardson, Nell

KING, Thomas (fl 1586-87) actor DA

KING, Thomas (d 1903 [68]) proprietor EA/04*

KING, T[homas] C. (1825-93) English actor CDP, OAA/1-2

KING, Tom (1730-1804) English actor, dramatist CDP, COC, CP/2-3, DNB, GT, OC/1-3, TD/1-2

KING, Tom (b 1835) singer CDP

KING, Mrs. Tom see King, Mary

KING, Vicki Kernan (d 1975 [49]) performer BP/59*

KING, Victor (d 1964 [72]) former BE*

KING, Walter (d 1911 [44]) comic singer EA/12*

KING, Walter Woolf (b 1899) American actor, singer WWT/8-9

KING, Dr. William (1663-1712) English dramatist CP/2-3, GT

KING, William (d 1796) actor HAS

KING, William A. (d 1968 [41]) stage manager BP/53*

KING, Woodie, Jr. (b 1937) American actor TW/25-26

KING, Wright (b 1927) American actor TW/6-8

KING-COBURN, S. (d 1892 [39]) American actor EA/93*

KINGDOM, John M. (d 1876) dramatist WWT/14*

KINGDON, Edith [Mrs. George J. Gould] (1862-1921) American actress CDP

KINGDON, Frank (d 1937 [72]) American actor BE*, BP/21*

KINGDON, John M. (d 1876) dramatist BE*

KINGDON, W. (d 1878 [46]) musician, singer EA/79*

KINGDON-GOULD, Edith Maughan see Kingdon, Edith

KING-HALL, Sir Stephen (1893-1966) dramatist WWT/7-14

KINGHORNE, Mark Alexander Mackenzie (1850/51-1906) English actor DP, EA/96, GRB/1

KING-LLOYD, Mrs. Harry see Lloyd, Margaret Leah

KINGSBURY, Alice (fl 1859-69) American actress HAS

KINGSBURY, Frederick (d 1892 [76]) conductor EA/93*

KINGSFORD, Walter (1881-1959) English actor TW/1-3, 15

KINGSLEY, A. F. actor HAS

KINGSLEY, Mrs. A. F. [née Kate Thornton] actress HAS

KINGSLEY, Cecil (b 1876) Canadian actor GRB/1

KINGSLEY, Edith see Loraine, Mrs. Henry

KINGSLEY, Grace (d 1962 [89]) journalist BE*

KINGSLEY, Mary (d 1936 [74]) actress CDP

KINGSLEY, Omar see Ella Zoyara, Miss

KINGSLEY, Rex (d 1974 [73]) performer BP/59*

KINGSLEY, Sidney (b 1906) American dramatist, actor, director AAS, BE, CB, CD, CH, COC, ES, HJD, MD, MH, MWD, NTH, OC/1-3, PDT, RE, SR, WWT/8-16

KINGSLEY, Walter J. (1878-1929) American press representative WWM

KINGSMAN, Philip (fl 1596-1615) actor DA

KINGSMAN, Robert (fl 1599-1618) actor DA

KINGSMILL, Percy T. F. see Hamilton, Sidney

KINGSTON, Al (d 1975 [72]) agent BP/59*

KINGSTON, Bertha English actress GRB/1

KINGSTON, Gertrude [Mrs. Silver] (1866/68-1937) English actress, manager, producer CDP, COC, DP, EA/95, GRB/1-4, NTH, OC/1-3, WWT/1-8, WWW/3

KINGSTON, Kaye (b 1924) American actress TW/24, 30

KINGSTON, Sam F. (c. 1866-1929) Irish manager SR

KINGSTON, Thomas (1870-1911) actor EA/96

KING-WOOD, David actor TW/13

KINHARVIE, Frances (d 1892) EA/93*

KINKEAD, Cleves (1882-1955) American dramatist WWA/3

KINLOCH, John (d 1873 [63]) acting manager EA/74*

KINLOCK, Eliza (1796-1887) English actress HAS, NYM, SR

KINLOCK, Georgiana (d 1864) actress HAS

KINNAIRD, David (d 1971 [45]) performer BP/55*

KINNAIRD, Helen English actress GRB/2

KINNEAR, De Leon (d 1870 [55]) circus manager EA/71*

KINNEAR, Roy (b 1934) English actor WWT/14-16

KINNELL, Murray (d 1954 [65]) English actor BE*, BP/39*

KINNEY, Ray (d 1972 [71]) performer BP/56*

KINNIAD, Annie singer CDP

KINO, Walter (d 1901 [34]) music-hall comedian CDP

KINROSS, Charles (d 1905 [21]) actor EA/06*

KINSELLA, Kathleen (d 1961 [83]) English actress TW/17

KINSELLA, Polly (d 1910) actress EA/11*

KINSELLA, Walter (d 1975 [74]) performer BP/59*

KINSOLVING, Lee (d 1974 [36]) performer BP/59*

KINTON, Swaine [Mrs. Balsir Chatterton] (d 1897 [32]) actress EA/98*

KINWELLMARSHE, Francis (fl 1575) translator CP/3

KINZIE, Elizabeth Miller (1875-1947) actress SR

KIPNESS, Joseph producer BE, WWT/16

KIPNIS, Alexander (b 1891) Russian/American singer CB, ES

KIRALFY, Amalia [Mrs. Gabriel Bremaure] (d 1917) actress SR

KIRALFY, Arnold (d 1908) dancer GRB/4*

KIRALFY, Bolossy (d 1932 [84]) Hungarian dancer, manager CDP

KIRALFY, Haniola [Mrs. A. L. Parkes] (d 1889) Hungarian dancer CDP

KIRALFY, Imre (1845-1919) Hungarian producer, dramatist CDP, GRB/1-4, SR

KIRALYFY, Johana (fl 1861?) dancer CDP

KIRBY, Mrs. see Stark, Mrs. James

KIRBY, Miss (fl 1844) actress HAS

KIRBY, Elisabeth [Mrs. James Bernard Fagan] English actress GRB/1-2

KIRBY, Hartwell J. (d 1910) EA/11*

KIRBY, Helen DuVall (d 1973 [81]) performer BP/58*

KIRBY, Hudson (1819-48) American actor CDP, DAB, HAS, SR, WWA/H

KIRBY, Mrs. Hudson (d 1896 [74]) actress HAS

KIRBY, James (d 1826) English clown CDP, HAS

KIRBY, J. Hudson see Kirby, Hudson

KIRBY, John (1894-1930) New Zealand actor WWT/6

KIRBY, John (d 1973 [41]) performer BP/58*

KIRBY, Mae Elaine (d 1968 [87]) performer BP/53*

KIRBY, Norman (d 1905 [71]) singer EA/06*

KIRBY, Thomas, Jr. (d 1876 [21]) musical director EA/77*

KIRBY, Tom (d 1884) comic singer EA/85*

KIRCHMAYER, Thomas (1511-63) German dramatist OC/2-3

KIRCHNER, Simplicieus (d 1879) musician EA/80*

KIRCK, John (fl 1579-80) actor DA

KIRK, George (d 1912) actor EA/13*

KIRK, Mrs. Harry see Eversleigh, Flo

KIRK, Helen (d 1871) Scottish singer EA/72*

KIRK, James (fl 1858) actor HAS

KIRK, Jessie [Mrs. Kenneth Black] (d 1905) EA/06*

KIRK, John (d 1948 [86]) American actor, producer, director TW/4

KIRK, Joseph (d 1975 [71]) performer BP/59*

KIRK, Lisa (b 1925) American actress, singer, dancer TW/5-9, 20, WWT/16

KIRK, Neil (d 1972 [79]) booking agent BP/57*

KIRK, Samuel (d 1883 [64]) musician EA/84*

KIRK, Sarah (d 1879) EA/80*

KIRK, William (d 1887 [78]) supermaster EA/88*

KIRK, William T. (d 1974 [65]) producer/director/choreographer BP/58*

KIRKE, John (d 1643) English actor, dramatist CP/1-3, DA, DNB, FGF, OC/1-3

KIRKHAM, Miss singer CDP

KIRKHAM, Edward (fl 1602-06) yeoman of the Revels DA

KIRKHAM, Sam (1923-70) American actor TW/23-24, 26-27

KIRKLAND, Alexander (b 1903/08) Mexican/American actor, director, dramatist BE, NTH, TW/1-6, WWT/8-11

KIRKLAND, Gelsey (b 1952) American dancer CB

KIRKLAND, Hardee (b 1868) American actor WWM

KIRKLAND, Jack (1901-69) American dramatist, producer BE, MD, MH, MWD, TW/25, WWT/9-14

KIRKLAND, Muriel (1903/04-71) American actress BE, TW/25, 28, WWT/7-15

KIRKLAND, Patricia (b 1925) American actress TW/1, 3-4, WWT/11-12

KIRKLAND, Sally (b 1944) American actress TW/24-25, 27-28, WWT/16

KIRKMAN, Francis see K., F.

KIRKWOOD, Gertrude Robinson (d 1962 [71]) actress BE*

KIRKWOOD, Jack (1894-1964) Scottish performer BE*, BP/49*

KIRKWOOD, James (d 1879) proprietor EA/80*

KIRKWOOD, James (d 1963 [80]) performer BP/48*

KIRKWOOD, Mrs. James see Kirkwood, Martha

KIRKWOOD, Jim (b 1925) American actor TW/6-7

KIRKWOOD, Martha [Mrs. James Kirkwood] (d 1879) EA/80*

KIRKWOOD, Pat (b 1921) English actress, singer AAS, WWT/10-16

KIRKWOOD-HACKETT, Eva (d 1968 [91]) performer BP/52*

KIRSCH, Carolyn (b 1942) American actress TW/26-27, 30

KIRSHON, Vladimir Mikhailovich (1902-38) Russian dramatist COC

KIRSTEIN, Lincoln (b 1907) American director CB, ES

KIRSTEN, Dorothy (b 1917) American singer CB

KIRTLAND, Louise (b 1905/10) American actress BE, TW/5, 30, WWT/8-16

KIRTLEY, Mrs. Thomas (d 1897) EA/98*

KIRTLEY, Thomas H. (d 1900) proprietor EA/01*

KIRWAN, Patrick (d 1929 [67]) Irish actor, manager GRB/2-4, WWT/1-5

KISER, Terry (b 1939) American actor TW/23-30

KISER, Virginia (b 1939) American actress TW/25

KISKADDEN, Maude see Adams, Maude

KISSEL, Herman (d 1964 [53]) critic BP/49*

KISSOCK, James Mills (d 1917) manager EA/18*

KISTEMAECHERS, Henry (1872-1938) dramatist BE*, WWT/14*

KITCHELL, Iva (b 1912) American dancer CB

KITCHEN, Dick (d 1907 [47]) EA/08*

KITCHEN, Fred (d 1951 [77]) performer BE*, WWT/14*

KITCHEN, R. H. (d 1910 [80/81]) clown BE*, EA/11*, WWT/14*

KITCHIN, Laurence (b 1913) English critic, actor WWT/16

KITE, Mrs. see Thomas, Mrs.

KITE, John (fl 1508) actor DA

KITT, Eartha (b 1930) American singer, actress, dancer BE, CB, TW/8-9, WWT/15-16

KITTREDGE, George Lyman (1860-1941) American scholar CB, DAB, HJD

KIVER, Hubert W. (d 1917 [23]) performer? EA/18*

KLAFSKY, Katharina (1855-96) Hungarian singer CDP, ES

KLANERT, Mr. (fl 1798) actor TD/1-2

KLANWELL, Marie (d 1911 [58]) singer EA/12*

KLATT, Mme. (fl 1845) equestrienne CDP

KLAUBER, Adolph (1879-1933) American producer, manager, critic WWA/1, WWM,

WWT/4-7

KLAUSNER, Margot (d 1975 [70]) dramatist BP/60*

KLAVUN, Walter (b 1906) American actor, director BE, TW/6, 28-29

KLAW, Alonzo (1886-1944) manager, producer SR

KLAW, Marc (1858-1936) American manager, agent, producer DAB, GRB/2-4, WWA/1, WWS, WWT/1-8

KLEIN, Adelaide (b 1904) American actress BE

KLEIN, Alfred (1864-1904) actor, singer CDP

KLEIN, Arthur (d 1964 [79]) producer/director BP/49*

KLEIN, Cecil (b 1875) American actor GRB/1-2

KLEIN, Charles (1867-1915) English dramatist COC, DAB, GRB/2-4, HJD, OC/1-3, SR, WWA/1, WWM, WWS, WWT/1-2

KLEIN, Deanne A. (d 1975 [40]) critic BP/59*

KLEIN, Gordon D. (d 1972 [58]) performer BP/57*

KLEIN, Jacob (d 1973 [94]) lawyer BP/57*

KLEIN, Joseph (d 1970 [62]) journalist BP/55*

KLEIN, Manuel (1876-1919) English composer, conductor WWA/1, WWM

KLEIN, Miriam Lillian (d 1973 [78]) performer BP/58*

KLEIN, Paul (d 1964 [61]) press representative BE*

KLEIN, Reid (b 1938) American actor TW/24

KLEIN, Robert (b 1942) American actor TW/24-25

KLEIN, Sadie (d 1974 [91]) performer BP/59*

KLENOSKY, William J. (b 1922) American actor TW/24

KLEPER, Sidney H. (d 1974 [58]) manager BP/59*

KLETT, Mr. (d 1834) actor HAS

KLEWER, Leonore N. (b 1912) American manager BE

KLIBAN, Terry (b 1942) American actor TW/26

KLIEGL, Herbert (b 1904) American executive BE

KLIETZ, Valesca (fl 1848) German singer? HAS

KLIMT, George (1861-1942)
American actor SR
KLINE, James C. (1850-1934)
actor SR
KLINE, Kevin (b 1947) American actor TW/29-30
KLINE, Richard (b 1944) American actor TW/28-29
KLINE, Tiny (d 1964 [74]) Hungarian acrobat BE*
KLING, Irene Frances (b 1947) American actress TW/29
KLIPSTEIN, Abner D. (b 1912) American press representative BE
KLOET, Miss see Bostock, Mrs. W. B.
KLOT, Georgia see Brown, Georgia
KLOTZ, Florence American designer WWT/15-16
KLUGMAN, Jack (b 1922) American actor BE, TW/22-23, 25, WWT/15-16
KLUNIS, Tom American actor TW/22, 24, 26, 29
KNAGGES, Richard (fl 1612) actor DA
KNAIZ, Judy (b 1940) American actress TW/28
KNAPP, Betty (d 1973 [72]) performer BP/57*
KNAPP, Edward Lee (d 1896 [59]) EA/97*
KNAPP, Eleanore American actress TW/29
KNAPP, Fred L. (d 1962 [67]) performer BE*
KNAPP, Harry L. (b 1863) American editor, singer, stage manager, actor WWM
KNAPP, Henry (fl 1780-84) dramatist CP/2-3, TD/1-2
KNAPP, S. C. see Chester, S. K.
KNAR, Henry see Knapp, Henry
KNAUB, Richard K. (b 1928) American educator BE
KNEALE, Patricia (b 1925) English actress WWT/11-16
KNEASS, Mrs. [née Sharpe] (d 1857) singer HAS
KNEASS, Nelson (d 1869) American actor CDP, HAS
KNECHT, Karl Kae (d 1972 [88]) journalist BP/57*
KNELL, William? (fl 1580s) actor DA, DNB

KNELLER, James (fl 1623) actor DA
KNEPP, Mary (d 1677) English actress COC, DNB, OC/1-3
KNEVET, Ralph (fl 1631) English? dramatist CP/1-3, FGF
KNICKERBOCKER, Paine (b 1912) American critic BE
KNIGHT (fl 1628) actor DA
KNIGHT (fl 1633) book-keeper DA
KNIGHT, Mr. (fl 1803-09) actor, dramatist CP/3, EA/92
KNIGHT, Mrs. (fl 1749) singer CDP
KNIGHT, Mrs. [née Annie Manton] (d 1876) musician EA/77*
KNIGHT, Anthony (fl 1624) musician? DA
KNIGHT, Augustine (1868-1910) English actor GRB/1
KNIGHT, David [né Mintz] (b 1927) American actor WWT/14-16
KNIGHT, Mrs. E. [née Eliza Povey] (1804-61) English singer, actress HAS
KNIGHT, Edward (fl 1624) musician? DA
KNIGHT, Edward (1774-1826) English actor BS, CDP, DNB, OX
KNIGHT, Mrs. Edward see Knight, Susan
KNIGHT, Esmond (b 1906) English actor, singer AAS, BE, TW/9, WWT/7-16
KNIGHT, Frank (d 1973 [79]) actor TW/30
KNIGHT, Fuzzy (d 1976 [74]) former BP/60*
KNIGHT, George S. (1850-92) actor CDP
KNIGHT, Mrs. George S. [Sophie Worrell] (d 1917) actress CDP, SR
KNIGHT, G. Wilson (b 1897) English educator BE
KNIGHT, H. (d 1839) English actor HAS
KNIGHT, Mrs. H. see Da Costa, Mrs.
KNIGHT, Irene (d 1966) performer BP/50*
KNIGHT, John (d 1964 [64]) American actor BE*
KNIGHT, Joseph (1829-1907) English critic DNB, GRB/1-3, OC/1-3, WWW/1
KNIGHT, Joseph Philip (d 1887 [75]) composer EA/88*

KNIGHT, Julius (1863-1941)
Scottish actor GRB/3-4,
WWT/1-6
KNIGHT, June [née Margaret
Rose Valliquietto] (b 1911)
American actress, dancer
TW/2-3, WWT/8-11
KNIGHT, Lloyd (b 1922) American
actor TW/8
KNIGHT, Percival (d 1923 [50])
comedian, dramatist BE*,
BP/8*, WWT/14*
KNIGHT, Robert (fl 1574) actor
DA
KNIGHT, Shirley (b 1937) Amer-
ican actress TW/22-23, 25,
WWT/16
KNIGHT, Mrs. Stephen see
Hind, Mrs. Thomas James
KNIGHT, Susan [Mrs. Edward
Knight] (1788-1859) actress
CDP
KNIGHT, Thomas (d 1820) actor,
dramatist BE*, WWT/14*
KNIGHT, Thomas (1759-1838)
English actor, proprietor,
dramatist CDP, CP/3, DNB,
GT, TD/1-2
KNIGHT, Mrs. Thomas [née
Farren] (d 1804) actress
TD/1-2
KNIGHT, William (b 1934) Amer-
ican actor TW/27-28, 30
KNIGHTLEY, Winifred Welsh
singer GRB/1
KNILL, C. Edwin manager BE
KNIPE, Charles (fl 1715) drama-
tist CP/1-3
KNIPP, Mrs. (fl 1664-77) ac-
tress WWT/14*
KNIPSCHIELD, Edward Henry
see Captain Eddie
KNITTEL, John Herman Emanuel
(1891-1970) Indian/English
dramatist WWW/6
KNIVETON, Mrs. actress TD/2
KNOBLAUCH [or Knoblock], Ed-
ward (1874-1945) American
dramatist CB, COC, ES,
MWD, NTH, OC/1-3, PDT,
TW/2, WWM, WWT/1-9
KNORR, Ludwig (d 1871) actor
EA/72*
KNOTT, Else (d 1975 [63]) per-
former BP/60*
KNOTT, Frederick English
dramatist AAS, BE
KNOTT, John (d 1878 [61]) musi-

cian EA/79*
KNOTT, Roselle [Agnes Roselle]
(1870-1948) Canadian actress
GRB/3-4, WWM, WWS, WWT/
1-4
KNOTT, W. Frederick (d 1889
[35]) EA/90*
KNOWLES, Alex (1850-1917) Scot-
tish critic, press representative
WWT/1-3
KNOWLES, Charles see Flana-
gan, Charles
KNOWLES, Christopher W. (d 1889
[56]) actor EA/90*
KNOWLES, David (d 1974 [27])
performer BP/59*
KNOWLES, Mrs. E. M. A. M.
see Elphinstone, Emma Marian
Maria
KNOWLES, Mrs. Forrest [née
Annie Manners] (d 1876 [40])
actress EA/77*
KNOWLES, Frederick Milton (b
1877) American dramatist
WWA/5
KNOWLES, George H. (d 1905
[32]) acting manager EA/06*
KNOWLES, James Sheridan (1784-
1862) English dramatist, actor
CDP, COC, DNB, ES, HAS,
HP, MH, OC/1-3, SR
KNOWLES, Mrs. James Sheridan
see Elphinstone, Emma Marian
Maria
KNOWLES, John (d 1880 [69])
manager, lessee EA/81*,
WWT/14*
KNOWLES, Nellie actress HAS
KNOWLES, Richard Brinsley (1820-
82) Scottish dramatist DNB
KNOWLES, Richard George (1858-
1919) Canadian variety artist
CDP, COC, GRB/4, OC/1-3
KNOWLTON, Maude (fl 1900s)
American actress WWS
KNOX, Alexander (b 1907) Cana-
dian actor AAS, BE, TW/6-8,
WWT/9-16
KNOX, Henry (fl 1781-84) drama-
tist GT
KNOX, Mabel [Mrs. Philip F.
Knox] (d 1905 [25]) EA/06*
KNOX, Mrs. Philip F. see
Knox, Mabel
KNUDSEN, Hans (d 1971 [84])
critic BP/55*
KNUST, Valli see Valli, Valli
KNUTSON, Wayne S. (b 1926)

American educator, director
BE
KNYVETT, Mrs. (d 1876) singer
CDP
KNYVETT, Charles, Sr. (1752-
1822) musician CDP
KNYVETT, William (1779-1856)
English singer, composer
CDP, DNB
KOBART, Ruth [née Ruth Maxine
Kohn] (b 1924) American ac-
tress, singer BE, TW/22,
26, WWT/15-16
KOBBE, Gustave (b 1857) Ameri-
can writer WWM
KOBER, Arthur (1900-75) Ameri-
can dramatist, press repre-
sentative, producer BE, MWD
KOBRIN, Leon (1873-1946) Rus-
sian/American dramatist ES
KOCH, Fred, Jr. (b 1911) Amer-
ican educator, director BE
KOCH, Frederick Henry (1877-
1944) American scholar CB,
DAB, ES, OC/1-3
KOCH, Howard dramatist CD
KOCH, Kenneth (b 1925) Ameri-
can dramatist, director CD
KOEHLER, Ted (d 1973 [83])
lyricist WWT/16*
KOENIG, John (1910-63) German
designer BE*, BP/47*
KOENIGSGARTEN, H. F. see
Garten, H. F.
KOERBER, Hilde (d 1969 [63])
performer BP/54*
KOERBER, Lelia see Dres-
sler, Marie
KOETTER, Paul (d 1974 [76])
performer BP/59*
KOHL, John Y. (d 1974 [79])
critic BP/59*
KOHLER, Charles (d 1888 [39])
American actor EA/89*
KOHLER, Donald American actor
TW/1
KOHLER, Estelle (b 1940) South
African actress AAS, WWT/
15-16
KOHLMAR, Lee (d 1946 [73])
actor TW/2
KOHN, Ruth Maxine see Kobart,
Ruth
KOHNER, Susan (b 1936) Ameri-
can actress BE, TW/14
KOLAS, Mary Lynn (b 1950)
American actress TW/28
KOLB, Clarence (d 1964 [90])

vaudevillian TW/21
KOLB, Matt B., Sr. (d 1947)
American producer, actor SR
KOLKER, Henry (1874-1947) Ger-
man actor SR, TW/4, WWM,
WWT/4-9
KOLLMAR, Richard (1910-71)
American actor, manager, pro-
ducer BE, CB, TW/2, 27,
WWT/10-14
KOLTAI, Ralph (b 1924) German
designer AAS, WWT/15-16
KOMEDA, Christopher (d 1969 [36])
composer/lyricist BP/53*
KOMINSKI, Daniel see Kaye,
Danny
KOMISARJEVSKAYA, Vera Fedorovna
(1864-1910) Russian actress,
manager COC, NTH, OC/3
KOMISARJEVSKY, Theodore (1882-
1954) Russian producer, designer
AAS, COC, DNB, NTH, OC/1-3,
PDT, TW/10, WWT/6-11, WWW/
5
KONDOR, R. W. (b 1937) American
producer, business manager BE
KONER, Pauline (b 1912?) Ameri-
can dancer, choreographer CB
KONIG, Marie (fl 1880) German
actress CDP
KONING, Fred Wittop see Wittop,
Freddy
KONOW, Charles (d 1890) variety
proprietor EA/91*
KONSTAM, Anna (b 1914) English
actress WWT/10-11
KONSTAM, Phyllis (1907-76) Eng-
lish actress WWT/6-10
KONSTANTINOV, Vladimir (d 1972
[67]) producer/director/chore-
ographer BP/56*
KONTSKI, Herr (d 1879) musician
EA/80*
KOOK, Edward (b 1903) American
executive, designer of lighting
equipment BE
KOOP, Mary Jane (d 1975 [57])
performer BP/60*
KOOY, Pete (d 1963) actor BE*
KOP, Mila (d 1973 [68]) performer
BP/57*
KOPF, Jack (d 1973 [79]) costumier
BP/57*
KOPIT, Arthur (b 1937/38) Ameri-
can dramatist AAS, BE, CB,
CH, COC, ES, HJD, MD, MH,
MWD, PDT, WWT/15-16
KOPLAN, Harry (d 1973 [53]) pro-

ducer/director/choreographer
BP/57*
KOPP, Rudolph G. (d 1972 [84])
composer/lyricist BP/56*
KOPS, Bernard (b 1920/26/28)
English dramatist AAS, BE,
CD, CH, ES, MD, MWD,
PDT, WWT/15-16
KOPSKI (b 1870) English musician
GRB/1-2
KORALLI, Vera (d 1972 [81])
performer BP/57*
KORDA, Zoltan (1895-1961) Hun-
garian producer, director BE*
KORFF, Arnold (1870-1944) Aus-
trian actor SR, TW/1
KORMAN, Murray (d 1961 [59])
Russian photographer BE*,
BP/46*
KORMAN, Sey (d 1971 [60]) critic
BP/55*
KORNGOLD, Erich Wolfgang (1897-
1957) Moravian composer CB,
WWA/3
KORNMAN, Mary (d 1973 [56])
performer BP/58*
KORNZWEIG, Ben (d 1969 [59])
American press representative
BE, TW/26
KORRIE, Edith [Mrs. Ernest
Korrie] (d 1896) music-hall
performer EA/98*
KORRIE, Mrs. Ernest see
Korrie, Edith
KORRIS, Harry (d 1971 [79]) per-
former BP/56*
KORSINSKI, Mlle. M. (fl 1847)
singer HAS
KORTNER, Fritz (d 1970 [78])
performer BP/55*
KORVIN, Charles (b 1912) Hun-
garian actor, director BE,
TW/22
KOSARIN, Oscar (b 1918) Ger-
man musical director, com-
poser BE
KOSLECK, Martin (b 1914) Ger-
man actor TW/15-16
KOSLOFF, Theodore (d 1956
[74]) Russian dancer, actor
TW/13
KOSMA, Joseph (d 1969 [63])
composer/lyricist BP/54*
KOSOW, Sophia see Sidney,
Sylvia
KOSSOFF, David (b 1919) English
actor WWT/12-16
KOSTA, Tessa (b 1893) American

actress, singer WWT/5-8
KOSTELANETZ, André (b 1901)
Russian/American conductor,
musician CB
KOSTER, John (d 1895) American?
proprietor EA/96*
KOSTRESSEN, Johan (fl 1623) mu-
sician DA
KOTT, Jan (b 1914) Polish critic
CB, COC
KOTTAUN, Anny [Mrs. Celian
Kottaun] (d 1910) EA/11*
KOTTAUN, Mrs. Ceclian see
Kottaun, Anny
KOTTAUN, Mrs. M. M. [Mrs.
Thomas Kottaun] (d 1888) EA/
89*
KOTTAUN, Thomas (d 1885 [57])
musician EA/86*
KOTTAUN, Mrs. Thomas see
Kottaun, Mrs. M. M.
KOTTO, Yaphet (b 1937) American
actor TW/22, 26
KOTZEBUE, August Friedrich
Ferdinand (1761-1819) German
dramatist COC, OC/1-3, SR
KOUN, Karolos (b 1908) Greek
director COC, WWT/14
KOURKOULOS, Nikos (b 1934)
Greek actor TW/23-24
KOUTOUKAS, H. M. Greek/Ameri-
can dramatist, director CD
KOVACS, Ernie (1919-62) American
comedian CB
KOVAL, Francis W. (d 1971 [62])
critic BP/55*
KOVAL, Rene (d 1936 [50]) actor,
singer BE*, WWT/14*
KOVE, Kenneth [John William
Stevenson Bridgewater] (b 1893)
English actor WWT/7-10
KOVENS, Edward (b 1934) Ameri-
can actor TW/27, 29
KOWAL, Mitchell (d 1971 [56])
performer BP/56*
KOZELKA, Paul (b 1909) American
educator BE
KRABER, Karl (b 1935) American
actor TW/25
KRAFFT, John (fl 1579-80) actor
DA
KRAFT, Beatrice American actress
TW/1
KRAFT, Gil (b 1926) American
publisher BE
KRAFT, Hy (1899-1975) American
dramatist BE
KRAFT, Jill (1930-70) American

actress BE, TW/27

KRAFT, Leonard (b 1932) American executive BE

KRAFT, Martin (b 1919) American actor TW/2

KRAKOWER, Arnold (d 1969 [53]) lawyer BP/53*

KRAMER, Amelia (d 1905 [66]) EA/06*

KRAMER, A. Walter (d 1969 [79]) composer/lyricist BP/53*

KRAMER, Joel (b 1943) American actor TW/30

KRAMER, John (b 1938) American actor TW/25-26

KRAMER, Lawrence (d 1975 [66]) performer BP/60*

KRAMER, Lloyd (b 1947) American actor TW/26-27

KRAMER, Marsha (b 1945) American actress TW/29

KRAMER, Phil (d 1972 [72]) performer BP/56*

KRAMER, Wright (d 1941 [71]) American actor BE*, BP/26*, WWT/14*

KRAMM, Joseph (b 1907/08) American dramatist, director, actor BE, CB, HJD, MD, MWD, WWT/12-16

KRANSKE, Violet [Mrs. Ambrose Thorne] (d 1897 [28]) EA/98*

KRANTZ, Milton (b 1912) American executive BE

KRAPP, Herbert J. (d 1973 [86]) architect BP/57*

KRASNA, Norman (b 1909) American dramatist BE, CB, MH, WWT/11-16

KRATOCHVIL, Frantisek (b 1934) Czech actor TW/23

KRATON, Harry (d 1912 [30]) music-hall performer EA/13*

KRATZ, Karl L. (d 1974 [74]) critic BP/59*

KRAUS, Philip (b 1949) American actor TW/29

KRAUS, Ted M. (b 1923) American publisher, editor BE

KRAUSS, Ruth (b 1911) American dramatist CD

KRAUSS, Werner (1884-1959) German actor OC/3, TW/16, WWT/8-11

KRAWFORD, Gary (b 1941) American actor TW/24, 27, 29

KRAWITZ, Seymour (b 1923)

American press representative BE

KRELLING, Joseph (1855-87) proprietor, manager NYM

KREMBSER, Frangott (d 1889 [55]) circus director EA/90*

KREMER, Theodore (b 1873) German dramatist GRB/3-4, WWT/1-2

KRESS, Gladys (d 1969 [67]) performer BP/54*

KRESSEN, Samuel (b 1918) American actor TW/24

KRETLOW, Arthur (d 1968 [73]) producer/director/choreographer BP/53*

KRETZMER, Herbert (b 1925) South African critic, dramatist WWT/15-16

KREUTZER, Leon (d 1868) composer EA/69*

KREYMBORG, Alfred (1883-1966) American dramatist HJD

KRIEGER, Lee (1919-67) American actor TW/4-5, 24

KRIEGER, Lester (d 1975 [71]) executive BP/59*

KRIMSKY, John (b 1906) American producer BE

KRIPS, Josef (1902-74) Austrian conductor CB

KRISS, Fred (d 1964 [76]) magician BE*

KRISTEN, Erik (b 1921) Danish actor TW/4

KRISTEV, George (d 1974 [32]) performer BP/59*

KRISTIN, Karen (b 1939) American actress TW/25

KRITZ, Karl (d 1969) conductor WWA/5

KRIZA, John (1919-75) Czech/American dancer ES

KRIZMAN, Lynne Allen (d 1972 [48]) performer BP/57*

KROEGER, Berry (b 1912) American actor TW/2-3, 7-8

KROLL, Lucy American literary & talent representative BE

KROLLMAN, Gustave (d 1857) musician HAS

KRONE, Gerald (b 1933) American producer, director, actor BE

KRONEMANN, Ludwig (d 1899) acrobat EA/00*

KRONENBERGER, Louis (b 1904) American critic BE, CB, HJD, NTH, WWT/10-16

KROSCHELL, Joan American actress TW/22, 25

KROSS, Ronald (b 1936) American actor TW/25-28

KROT, William (d 1971 [45]) stage manager TW/28

KRUEGER, Bum (d 1971 [65]) performer BP/55*

KRUEGER, Emmy (d 1976 [89]) performer BP/60*

KRUG, Karl (d 1963 [65]) critic BP/48*

KRUGER, Alma (d 1960 [88]) American actress GRB/3-4, TW/16, WWT/1-10

KRUGER, Annie [Mlle. Coradini] German/American actress HAS

KRUGER, Daniel D. (b 1942) American actor TW/30

KRUGER, Fred H. (d 1961 [48]) actor BE*

KRUGER, Hardy (b 1928) German actor TW/22

KRUGER, Hugo German actor, singer CDP

KRUGER, Jaques (d 1910 [69]) actor CDP

KRUGER, Ottilie (b 1926) American actress TW/2-3, 5

KRUGER, Otto (1885-1974) American actor BE, TW/2-7, WWT/4-11

KRUMSCHMIDT, E. A. (b 1904) German actor TW/3-4

KRUPSKA, Dania (b 1923) American dancer, choreographer BE, WWT/15-16

KRUSCHEN, Jack (b 1922) Canadian actor BE, TW/18

KRUTCH, Joseph Wood (1893-1970) American critic BE, CB, COC, ES, HJD, NTH, OC/1-3, WWA/5, WWT/10-14

KUBIAK, Thomas J. (b 1936) American actor TW/26, 30

KUGELL, Joan see Darling, Joan

KUGELMANN, Georges see Benda, Georges K.

KUHL, H. Calvin (d 1973 [66]) producer/director/choreographer BP/58*

KUHN, Sophie Gimber (1838-67) English actress HAS

KUHNER, John (b 1942) American actor TW/24, 26-29

KULUKUNDIS, Eddie (b 1932) English producing manager WWT/15-16

KULUVA, Will (b 1917) American actor TW/7-9, 15

KUMARI, Meena (d 1972 [40]) performer BP/56*

KUMMER, Clare [Clare Rodman Beecher] (d 1958 [85]) American dramatist HJD, SR, WWT/4-12

KUMMER, Frederic Arnold (1873-1943) American dramatist WWT/5-9

KUN, Magda (1912-45) Hungarian actress WWT/8-9

KUNKEL, George (d 1885 [62]) actor, manager CDP

KUNKEL, Jacob composer, publisher CDP

KUNNEKE, Eduard (b 1885) composer WWT/6-9

KUNZ, Raoul de Dreux (d 1906 [37]) EA/07*

KUPCINET, Karyn (d 1963 [22]) performer BP/48*

KUPPERMAN, Alvin (b 1945) American actor TW/26-28

KURENKO, Maria Russian singer CB

KURKAMP, John (d 1914) American actor SR

KURNITZ, Harry (1908-68) American dramatist BE

KURNITZ, Julie (b 1942) American actress TW/30

KURT, Melanie (1880-1941) Austrian singer ES

KURTON, Peggy actress, singer WWT/4-7

KURTY, Hella (d 1954 [48]) Austrian actress, singer WWT/8-10

KURTZ, Efrem (b 1900) Russian conductor CB

KURTZ, Marcia Jean American actress TW/29

KURTZ, Swoosie (b 1944) American actress TW/25-28

KURZ, Laura singer CDP

KURZ, Selma (1874-1933) Austrian singer ES

KUSCHER, Marion North (d 1971 [54]) performer BP/56*

KUSELL, Mrs. Harold (d 1971 [68]) performer BP/55*

KUSS, Richard (b 1927) American actor TW/29

KUSSACK, Elaine American actress TW/26-29

KYASHT, Lydia (1886-1959) Russian

dancer ES, WWT/4-11
KYD, Thomas (1558-94) English
dramatist COC, CP/1-3,
DNB, ES, FGF, HP, MH,
NTH, OC/1-3, PDT, RE
KYDD, Samuel (d 1892 [78])
lawyer EA/94*
KYFFIN, Maurice (fl 1588) trans-
lator CP/1-3
KYLE, Edward musician CDP
KYLE, Howard [Howard Anderson
Vandergrift] (1861-1950) Amer-
ican actor TW/7, WWM
KYNASTON, Edward (c. 1640-
1706) English actor CDP,
DNB, OC/1-3
KYNDER, Philip dramatist FGF
KYRLE, Judith (d 1922) actress
BE*, WWT/14*

- L -

L. , G. (fl 1778) dramatist CP/3
LABAN, Rudolf von (1879-1958)
Hungarian choreographer,
dancer ES
LABATE, Bruno (d 1968 [85])
composer/lyricist BP/53*
LaBELLE, Rupert (d 1972
[72]) performer BP/57*
LABICHE, Eugène (1815-88)
French dramatist COC, NTH,
OC/1-3
LABIS, Attilio (b 1936) French
dancer, choreographer ES
LABLACHE, Fanny (d 1897)
singer WWT/14*
LABLACHE, Fanny Rose Louise
(d 1885) EA/86*
LABLACHE, Frederick (1815-87)
singer DNB
LABLACHE, Louise (fl 1886)
singer CDP
LABLACHE, Luigi (1794-1858)
Italian singer CDP, DNB, ES
LABLACHE, Luigi (d 1914 [64])
actor DP, GRB/3-4, WWT/
1-2
LABLANCHE, Bianca see Daven-
port, Blanche
LABOCHETTA, Sig. D. (fl 1857)
singer CDP
LABORDE, Mons. (fl 1848)
singer HAS
LABORDE, Mme. (fl 1848) singer
HAS
LABOUCHERE, Henry (d 1912

[81]) producer, manager BE*,
WWT/14*
LABOUCHERE, Mrs. Henry see
Hodson, Henrietta
LABOUSE, Charles (d 1889) Amer-
ican aeronaut EA/90*
LABROCA, Mario (d 1973 [76])
composer/lyricist BP/58*
LABURNUM, Walter singer, song-
writer CDP
LACEBY, Arthur (b 1879) English
actor WWM
LACEY, Catherine (b 1904) English
actress AAS, WWT/8-16
LACEY, Charles (d 1909) EA/11*
LACEY, Franklin (b 1917) Canadian
dramatist, lyricist BE
LACEY, Fred (d 1904 [39]) music-
hall performer EA/05*
LACEY, George (d 1896) comic
singer EA/97*
LACEY, Henry see Lacy, Henry
LACEY, Marion (d 1915 [95]) ac-
tress BE*, WWT/14*
LACEY, Paul see Godfrey,
Charles
LACEY, Willoughby (fl 1774-1801)
proprietor GT, TD/1-2
LACHMAN, Harry (d 1975 [88])
producer/director/choreographer
BP/59*
LACHNER, Ignaz (d 1895 [87])
composer, musician EA/96*
LACK, Simon [né Macalpine] (b
1917) Scottish actor WWT/12-16
LACKAYE, Helene [Mrs. H. J.
Ridings] (b 1883) American ac-
tress WWM
LACKAYE, James (1867-1919)
American actor SR
LACKAYE, Wilton (1862-1932)
American actor COC, DAB,
GRB/2-4, OC/1-3, PP/2, SR,
WWA/1, WWS, WWT/1-6
LACKET, Dr. John see Hacket,
Dr. John
LACKEY, Kenneth (d 1976 [74])
performer BP/60*
LACOMBE, Mrs. see Allen,
Clarissa
LA COMPTE, Mons. (fl 1840)
dancer HAS
LA COMPTE, Mme. (fl 1838)
dancer HAS
LA COOMB, Mrs. see Allen,
Clarissa
LACOSTE, Anna (1848-68) Amer-
ican actress, reader HAS

LACY, Mr. (fl 1850) actor HAS
LACY, Mrs. (fl 1850) actress HAS
LACY, Miss (fl 1822) actress BS
LACY, Ernest (1863-1916) American dramatist DAB, HJD
LACY, Frances see Cooper, Frances
LACY, Frank (b 1842) English actor, aeronaut, dancer, tightrope dancer HAS
LACY, Frank (d 1870 [28]) harlequin EA/71*
LACY, Frank (1867-1937) English actor GRB/1-4, WWM, WWT/1-7
LACY, George (b 1904) English actor WWT/10
LACY, Harriette Deborah (1807-74) English actress DNB
LACY, Henry (fl 1586) dramatist CP/3, FGF
LACY, James (1696-1774) patentee CDP
LACY, Jerry (b 1936) American actor TW/25-26
LACY, John (1622-81) English actor, dramatist, dancing master CDP, COC, CP/1-3, DA, DNB, GT, NTH, OC/1-3
LACY, Mrs. John see Bianchi, Mrs. Francesco
LACY, Maria Anne see Lovell, Maria Anne
LACY, Michael Rophino (1795-1867) Spanish musician, composer, actor CDP, DNB, SR
LACY, Robin T. (b 1920) American educator, scene designer BE
LACY, Rophino see Lacy, Michael Rophino
LACY, Sara see Roberts, Sara
LACY, Sarah (d 1868) EA/69*
LACY, Mrs. Sidney see Stalman, Julia
LACY, Thomas Haines (1809-73) actor, dramatist, publisher DNB, SR
LACY, Mrs. Thomas Haines see Cooper, Frances
LACY, Tom (b 1933) American actor TW/23-26, 28-30
LACY, Walter (1809-98) actor CDP, DNB, OAA/2
LACY, Mrs. Walter (d 1874 [67]) actress EA/75*, WWT/14*

LACY, William (1788-1871) singer DNB
LACY, Willoughby (d 1831 [62]) actor, manager WWT/14*
LADD, Alan (1913-64) American actor WWA/4
LADD, Hank American actor TW/4-5, 23
LADD, Margaret (b 1942) American actress TW/22-23, 26
LAFAYETTE [Sigmund Neuburger] (d 1911 [38]) German illusionist SR
LA FEUILLADE, Sarah Elizabeth (d 1887) EA/88*
LAFFAN, Kevin Barry (b 1922) English dramatist CD, WWT/15-16
LAFFAN, Patricia (b 1919) English actress WWT/10-15
LAFFAN, Mrs. Robert Stuart de Courcy (d 1912) English dramatist WWW/1
LAFFAR, Mrs. (d 1885 [73]) EA/87*
LAFFAR, Mrs. William (d 1871) EA/72*
LAFFAR, William Joseph (d 1900 [65]) scene artist EA/01*
LAFFERTY, Wilson (d 1962) performer BE*
LAFFIN, Charles (b 1922) American actor TW/2
LA FOLLE, Mrs. [Mrs. Placide; née Pownall] (d 1823) actress HAS
LA FOLLETTE, Fola (1882-1970) American actress BE, TW/26, WWA/5
LA FOND, Florence (b 1845) American actress HAS
LAFONTAINE, Anna [Mrs. John Lafontaine] (d 1890) EA/91*
LAFONTAINE, Mrs. John see Lafontaine, Anna
LA FORREST, Mr. (fl 1823-30) American actor, circus performer HAS
LA FORREST, Mrs. [Sophia Eberle] (fl 1824) American actress HAS
LA FORREST, Sophia (d 1888 [76]) American actress EA/89*
LAGERFELT, Carolyn French actress TW/27, 29
LAGIER, Suzanne (1833-93) French actress, singer ES
LAGIOIA, John P. (b 1937) Amer-

ican actor TW/26-27

LAGRANGE, Anne-Caroline de (1824-1905) French singer ES

LAGRANGE, Felix (d 1901 [75]) actor BE*, WWT/14*

LAGUERRE, John (d 1748) English scene painter, actor DNB

LA HIFF, Ann see Carroll, Nancy

LAHR, Bert [Irving Lahrheim] (1895-1967) American actor AAS, BE, CB, COC, TW/1-21, 24, WWA/4, WWT/7-14

LAHR, John (b 1941) American critic WWT/16

LAHR, Mercedes (d 1965 [67]) performer BP/49*

LAHRHEIM, Irving see Lahr, Bert

LAHTINEN, Warner H. (d 1968 [58]) performer BP/53*

LAIDLAW, Alexander Hamilton, Jr. (1869-1908) American dramatist WWA/1

LAIDLAW, Clara see Lloyd, Clara

LAIDLAW, Louise (d 1871) actress WWT/14*

LAIDLAW, Louise Caroline see Weston, Louise Caroline

LAIDLER, Francis (1870-1955) English manager WWT/8-11

LAIDMAN, C. H. (d 1874) actor? EA/75*

LAINE, Vicki (d 1972 [41]) performer BP/56*

LAING, Alexander (d 1873 [28]) musician EA/74*

LAING, Hugh (b 1914) West Indian dancer CB, ES

LAING, Peggy (b 1899) English press representative WWT/9

LAIRD, Gus (b 1881) English actor, singer GRB/1

LAIRD, Jenny (b 1917) English actress TW/26, WWT/10-16

LAIRD, Landon (d 1970 [75]) critic BP/55*

LAIRE, Judson actor TW/1, 15

LAISON (fl 1796) circus manager, equestrian HAS

LAIT, Jack (1883-1954) American critic BE*, BP/38*

LAIT, Sarah (d 1917 [68]) EA/18*

LAKE, Mr. (fl 1785) actor HAS

LAKE, Charles H. F. (d 1905 [18]) EA/06*

LAKE, Emma (d 1911) circus performer CDP, SR

LAKE, Ethel Mae (d 1975 [73]) actress, singer BP/59*, WWT/16*

LAKE, Fanny [Mrs. J. Lake, Sr.] (d 1876 [52]) EA/78*

LAKE, Harriette see Sothern, Anne

LAKE, Mrs. J., Sr. see Lake, Fanny

LAKE, Lew (d 1939 [65]) performer, producer BE*, WWT/14*

LAKE, Samuel (d 1859) English dancer, pantomimist, actor HAS

LAKE, Sue (d 1970) performer BP/55*

LAKE, Veronica (d 1973 [53]) actress BP/58*, WWT/16*

LAKE, William (1835-69) circus performer & manager SR

LAKOMSKA, Sylvia Jadviga see Daneel, Sylvia

LaKOTA, Jewel (d 1968 [60]) performer BP/52*

LALLY, Gwen (d 1963 [81]) English actress, producer, pageant master WWT/8-9, WWW/6

LALO, Louise Dorothy [Mrs. Charles Best] (d 1905 [35]) EA/06*

LALOR, Frank (1869-1932) American actor WWT/4-6

LA MAMA EXPERIMENTAL THEATRE CLUB theatre collective CD

LAMAREUX, Augusta (b 1845) American dancer, actress HAS

LAMAREUX, Edith (d 1868) music-hall performer HAS

LA MARR, Barbara (d 1926 [30]) actress BE*

LA MARR, Harry (fl 1887?) singer, songwriter CDP

LAMAS, Fernando (b 1920/23) Argentinian actor, director BE, TW/13

LAMASH, Philip (d 1800) actor TD/1-2

LAMB, Alexander (d 1871) comedian EA/73*

LAMB, Beatrice (b 1866) actress CDP, EA/95, GRB/3-4, WWT/1-5

LAMB, Charles (1775-1834) English critic, dramatist COC, CP/3, DNB, ES, HP, NTH,

OC/1-3

LAMB, Edward (1829-87) American actor CDP, HAS, NYM

LAMB, Florence (d 1966 [82]) performer BP/50*

LAMB, Frank E. (d 1918) actor, director SR

LAMB, George (1784-1834) dramatist DNB

LAMB, Mr. H. (d 1869 [88]) president of the Dover Catch Club EA/70*

LAMB, Henry (d 1888 [77]) music-hall performer? EA/89*

LAMB, Shirley (b 1939) American actress TW/30

LAMB, Sybil (b 1932) American actress TW/14

LAMB, T. (d 1875) pantomimist EA/76*

LAMB, Thomas see Melrose, Tom

LAMBART, Ernest (d 1945 [71]) Irish actor, singer BE*, BP/30*, WWT/14*

LAMBART, Ernest O. C. (1876-1924) English actor SR

LAMBART, Richard (d 1924) actor BE*, WWT/14*

LAMBART, Mrs. Richard F. L. see Spencer-Brunton, Enid

LAMBDIN, John O. (d 1923 [50]) critic BE*, BP/7*

LAMBE, George (fl 1807) dramatist CP/3

LAMBELET, Napoleon (1864-1932) composer, musical director WWT/4-6

LAMBERT, Mr. (b 1816) English actor HAS

LAMBERT, Mrs. (fl 1838-41) English? actress HAS

LAMBERT, Barrowdale (fl 1747) dramatist CP/2-3, GT

LAMBERT, Charles Edward (d 1910) EA/11*

LAMBERT, Constant (1905-51) English composer, conductor, critic DNB, ES, WWT/8-11, WWW/5

LAMBERT, Daniel (1770-1809) fat man CDP

LAMBERT, Daniel, Jr. fat giant CDP

LAMBERT, David (d 1873) singer EA/74*

LAMBERT, E. A. [Mrs. Fal-coner] (d 1901) singer EA/02*

LAMBERT, Edward see Stirling, Edward

LAMBERT, George (1710-65) English scene designer & painter ES

LAMBERT, Harry (d 1879 [38]) Negro comedian EA/80*

LAMBERT, H. S. (d 1935 [68]) treasurer WWT/14*

LAMBERT, Hugh choreographer, dancer BE

LAMBERT, Jack (b 1899) Scottish actor WWT/8-16

LAMBERT, James (d 1880) Negro comedian EA/81*

LAMBERT, John (d 1871 [56]) proprietor EA/72*

LAMBERT, J. W. (b 1917) English critic WWT/14-16

LAMBERT, Lawson (1870-1944) Indian/English business manager GRB/1-3, WWT/6-9

LAMBERT, Louie [Mrs. Walter Lambert] (d 1902) EA/03*

LAMBERT, Mabel [Mrs. John Terry] American actress GRB/1-2

LAMBERT, Richard (b 1870) Irish manager, press representative WWM

LAMBERT, Sammy (b 1907) Russian/American producer TW/4-8

LAMBERT, Spencer (d 1872 [45]) treasurer EA/73*

LAMBERT, Mrs. Walter see Lambert, Louie

LAMBERTI, Prof. (d 1950 [58]) comedian TW/6

LAMBLE, T. B. (d 1917) EA/18*

LAMBORN, Amy English actress GRB/1-2

LAMBOURNE, Harry (d 1891 [31]) musician EA/92*

LAMER, Mrs. (d 1851) HAS

LA MERI (b 1903) American dancer, choreographer ES

LAMOND, Stella (d 1973 [62]) performer BP/58*

LAMONT, Forrest (1885-1937) Canadian singer WWA/1

LAMONT, Robin (b 1950) American actor TW/27-30

LAMOS, Mark (b 1946) American actor TW/28-29

LaMOTTA, Johnny (b 1939) American actor TW/24-26, 28

LAMOURET, Robert (1916-59)
French performer ES
LAMOUREUX, Louise (fl 1857)
dancer CDP
LAMPARD, Edward James (d
1896 [34]) EA/97*
LAMPE, Gus (d 1975 [74]) pro-
ducer/director/choreographer
BP/60*
LAMPE, Isabella (d 1795) singer,
actress WWT/14*
LAMPE, John Frederick (1703?-
51) German? composer DNB
LAMPELL, Millard (b 1919)
American dramatist BE
LAMPERT, Zohra (b 1936)
American actress BE, TW/
14, 18-20, 22-23, 25-26, 28
LAMSLEY (d 1891) conductor
EA/92*
LAMSON, Ernest (d 1908) Amer-
ican actor, dramatist WWS
LAMSON, Gardner American
singer WWM
LAMSON, Gertrude see O'Neill,
Nance
LAMY, Marcel (d 1970 [52])
producer/director/choreographer
BP/55*
LAN, David (b 1952) South Afri-
can dramatist CD
LANA, Agustin (d 1970 [70])
composer/lyricist BP/55*
LANAGAN, Michael J. (d 1879
[45]) American actress EA/80*
LANCASHIRE BELL RINGERS
(fl 1850) HAS
LANCASTER, Ann (d 1970 [50])
performer BP/55*
LANCASTER, Burt (b 1913)
American actor, vaudevillian,
acrobat CB, ES, TW/2-3
LANCASTER, Henry John (d 1892
[72]) scene artist EA/93*
LANCASTER, John (d 1896)
manager, proprietor EA/97*,
WWT/14*
LANCASTER, John (d 1970 [67])
performer BP/54*
LANCASTER, Lucie (b 1907)
American actress TW/24,
26-27, 29-30
LANCASTER, Nora (b 1877/82)
English actress GRB/1-4,
WWT/1-5
LANCASTER, Sylvester (fl 1640)
actor DA
LANCASTER, William (d 1889)

EA/90*
LANCASTER-WALLIS, Ellen (d
1940 [86]) actress, producer,
manager BE*, WWT/14*
LANCE, Leon O. (d 1973 [76])
agent BP/58*
LANCHESTER, Elsa (b 1902) Eng-
lish actress BE, CB, ES,
NTH, WWT/6-11
LANCHESTER, Robert (b 1941)
American actor TW/26-27, 30
LAND, Charles (d 1883 [28]) EA/
84*
LAND, Robert E. (b 1948) Cana-
dian actor TW/26
LANDAU, David (d 1935 [57])
American actor WWT/7
LANDAU, Jack (1925-67) American
director, producer, designer
BE, TW/23
LANDAU, Marty W. (d 1973 [74])
artists' manager BP/57*
LANDEAU, Cecil (b 1906) actor,
producing manager WWT/11-13
LANDECK, Ben (1864-1928) Eng-
lish dramatist WWT/4-5
LANDEN, Dinsdale (b 1932) Eng-
lish actor WWT/15-16
LANDER, Charles Oram (1866-
1934) English actor GRB/2-4
LANDER, Mrs. Frederick W.
see Lander, Jean Margaret
Davenport
LANDER, Harald (d 1972 [66])
producer/director/choreographer
BP/56*
LANDER, Jean Margaret Davenport
(1829-1903) English actress
CDP, COC, DAB, HAS, OC/1-3,
PP/2, WWA/1
LANDESMAN, Jay (b 1919) Ameri-
can producer, dramatist BE
LANDI, Elissa (1904-48) Italian
actress ES, SR, TW/1, 5,
WWT/6-10
LANDI, Erberto (d 1971 [63]) pro-
ducer, publicist BP/56*
LANDICK, Olin (d 1972 [77]) per-
former BP/56*
LANDIN, Hope (d 1973 [80]) ac-
tress BP/57*, WWT/16*
LANDIS, Carole (1919-48) Ameri-
can actress TW/1, 5
LANDIS, Cullen (d 1975 [79]) per-
former BP/60*
LANDIS, Jeanette English actress
TW/28
LANDIS, Jessie Royce (1900/04-

72) American actress BE,
TW/1-15, 21, 24, 28, WWA/
5, WWT/7-15

LANDIS, Joe (d 1966) performer
BP/51*

LANDIS, John (d 1863) minstrel
HAS

LANDIS, William (b 1921) American producer, actor, director
BE

LANDON, Avice (1908/10-76) In-
dian/English actress AAS,
WWT/10-16

LANDRETH, Gertrude Griffith
(d 1969 [72]) performer BP/
54*

LANDSMAN, Jenny (fl 1866-67)
Hungarian/American singer
HAS

LANDSTONE, Charles (b 1891/
97) Austrian business manager, dramatist, administrator
WWT/7-15

LANDWEST, Tom (d 1878 [26])
Negro comedian EA/79*

LANE, Alfred (d 1881) actor?
EA/82*

LANE, Allan (d 1973 [64]) performer BP/57*

LANE, Burton [né Burton Levy]
(b 1912) American composer
BE, CB, WWT/15-16

LANE, Clara [Mrs. J. K. Mur-
ray] (fl 1884-95) American
actress, singer WWS

LANE, Dorothy (b 1889/90)
English actress WWT/4-11

LANE, Genette (b 1940) American actress TW/27

LANE, Grace [Mrs. Kenneth
Douglas] (1876-1956) actress
GRB/1-2, 4, WWT/1-11

LANE, Horace English actor
GRB/2

LANE, Jane (d 1882 [78]) EA/
83*

LANE, Jane [Jenny Elton; Mrs.
W. E. Lane] (d 1883) actress?
EA/84*

LANE, Louisa see Drew, Mrs.
John

LANE, Lucie (d 1901 [20]) burlesque actress EA/02*

LANE, Lupino (1892-1959) English actor, dancer, manager
AAS, COC, DNB, ES, OC/
1-3, TW/16, WWT/4-12,
WWW/5

LANE, Montague (b 1882) English
actor GRB/1

LANE, Pete (d 1858) jig dancer
HAS

LANE, Rosemary (d 1974 [64])
performer BP/59*

LANE, Russell (d 1918) EA/19*

LANE, Rusty (b 1899) American
actor, educator TW/3-6, 11-12

LANE, Sam (1804-71) manager
COC

LANE, Sara (1823-99) English actress, manager CDP, COC,
OC/2-3

LANE, Sherry (d 1974 [55]) performer BP/59*

LANE, Sylvia (b 1934) American
actress TW/3

LANE, Mrs. W. E. see Lane,
Jane

LANE, Willie (b 1879) English actor GRB/1

LANEHAM, John (fl 1572-91) actor
DA

LANERGAN, James W. (1828-86)
actor CDP

LAN-FANG, Mei see Mei Lan-
Fang

LANFIELD, Sidney (d 1972 [74])
performer BP/57*

LANG, Alois (d 1971 [80]) performer BP/56*

LANG, Benjamin Johnson (1837-
1909) American conductor, composer DAB

LANG, Charles (b 1915) American
actor TW/1-6

LANG, Doreen (b 1918) New Zealand actress TW/6-8

LANG, Eva Clara (d 1933 [48])
American actress BE*

LANG, Gertrude (d 1941 [42])
performer BE*

LANG, Gertrude (d 1942) actress
BE*, WWT/14*

LANG, Gertrude (d 1971 [73]) performer BP/56*

LANG, Harold (d 1970) performer
BP/55*

LANG, Harold (b 1920/23) American dancer, actor, singer BE,
TW/2-3, 5-16, 18, 21, WWT/
14-16

LANG, Harry (d 1953 [58]) actor
BE*, WWT/14*

LANG, Howard (d 1941 [65]) actor
WWT/7-8

LANG, Ione (fl 1873?) singer CDP

LANG, Jimmy (d 1970) performer
BP/55*

LANG, Matheson (1879-1948)
Canadian actor, manager,
dramatist AAS, COC, DNB,
ES, GRB/1-4, NTH, OC/1-3,
PDT, TW/4, WWT/1-10,
WWW/4

LANG, Mrs. Matheson see Britton, Hutin

LANG, Pearl (b 1922/25) American choreographer, dancer,
educator BE, CB, TW/6

LANG, Peter (d 1932 [73]) actor,
singer BE*, BP/17*

LANG, Philip J. (b 1911) American composer, educator,
musician BE

LANG, Robert (b 1934) English
actor, director AAS, WWT/
15-16

LANGAN, Glenn (b 1917) American actor TW/5-9

LANGBAINE, Garard (d 1692
[35]) historian WWT/14*

LANGDON, George C. (d 1859)
HAS

LANGDON, Harry (1884-1944)
American actor, vaudevillian
CB, DAB, ES, SR, TW/1

LANGDON, Henry A. (fl 1849-
57) American actor HAS

LANGDON, Mrs. Henry A., I
[Emily Rosalie Reed] (1832-
57) American dancer, singer,
actress HAS

LANGDON, Mrs. Henry A., II
[Annie Senter] (1836-67)
American actress HAS

LANGDON, Sue Ann American
actress TW/24

LANGE, Barbara Pearson (b
1910) American educator
BE

LANGE, Mary (d 1973 [60])
actress TW/29

LANGE, Sven (d 1930 [62])
dramatist BE*, WWT/14*

LANGELLA, Frank (b 1940)
American actor TW/22-23,
25-26, WWT/16

LANGER, Anton (d 1879 [56])
dramatist EA/81*

LANGFORD, Abraham (1711-74)
English dramatist CP/1-3,
DNB, GT, TD/1-2

LANGFORD, Joseph Munt (d
1884 [75]) dramatist, critic

EA/85*

LANGFORD, William (d 1955 [35])
Canadian actor BE*, BP/40*

LANGHAM, Michael (b 1919) English director AAS, BE, CB,
WWT/13-16

LANGHAM, Mrs. W. Clement
see Langham, Winnifred

LANGHAM, Winnifred [Mrs. W.
Clement Langham] (d 1917)
EA/18*

LANGHANS, Edward A. (b 1923)
American director, designer,
historian, educator BE

LANGHORNE, John (d 1779) English dramatist CP/2-3, GT

LANGLEY, Charles [George Budd]
(d 1911) actor EA/12*

LANGLEY, Francis (d 1601) theatre builder DA

LANGLEY, Frank (d 1879) American actor EA/80*

LANGLEY, Georgianna (b 1845)
American actress, dancer HAS

LANGLEY, Kate (d 1886) actress
EA/87*

LANGLEY, Noel (b 1911) South
African dramatist AAS, BE,
WWT/8-15

LANGLEY, Stuart (d 1970 [60])
actor, singer TW/26

LANGLEY, Mrs. Will (d 1897
[53]) music-hall performer
EA/98*

LANGLEY, William (d 1849) circus performer HAS

LANGLOIS, Caroline [Lottie Ellis;
Mrs. H. A. Langlois] (d 1882
[30]) EA/83*

LANGLOIS, Mrs. H. A. see
Langlois, Caroline

LANGNER, Herbert B. (d 1965
[73]) patron BP/50*

LANGNER, Lawrence (1890-1962)
Welsh/American dramatist,
director CB, COC, ES, MWD,
NTH, OC/3, TW/2-8, 19,
WWT/6-13

LANGNER, Philip (b 1926) American producer BE, WWT/16

LANGRISH, John S. (1830-95)
Irish actor, manager SR

LANGSTAFFE, Arthur (d 1904)
musical director EA/05*

LANGTON, Basil C. (b 1912)
English actor, manager, producer TW/24, WWT/10-11

LANGTON, Fred (d 1903 [31])

variety comedian EA/04*

LANGTON, J. D. (d 1918 [60])
EA/19*

LANGTON, Polly (d 1896) music-
hall performer EA/98*

LANGTRY, Edward (d 1897)
EA/98*

LANGTRY, Lily [or Lillie;
Lady de Bathe] (1852-1929)
English actress CDP, COC,
DP, ES, GRB/1-4, HP, NTH,
OC/1-3, PDT, WWA/2, WWS,
WWT/1-5

LANGTRY, Paul [John Dunlop]
(d 1903 [32]) Negro comedian
EA/05*

LANIER, Nicholas (1588-1666)
English composer DNB

LANIER, Thomas see Williams,
Tennessee

LANING, Robert E. (d 1974
[56]) dramatist BP/59*

LANNER, Katti (1831-1908) Austrian dancer CDP, ES, GRB/
1-4

LANNIER, Minnie (fl 1866) actress HAS

LANNING, Jerry (b 1943) American actor TW/23-24, 28-30

LANPHIER, James F. (d 1969
[48]) actor TW/25

LANSBURY, Angela (b 1925)
English actress AAS, BE,
CB, TW/20, 22-26, WWT/15-16

LANSBURY, Edgar (b 1930) English producer, designer BE,
WWT/15-16

LANSCAR, Christine (d 1907
[22]) performer? EA/08*

LANSDALE, Harry Nelson (d
1964 [49]) critic BP/49*

LANSDOWN, Lord see Gran-
ville, George

LANSING, Mr. (fl 1831) actor
HAS

LANSING, Loi (d 1972 [37]) performer BP/57*

LANSING, Robert American actor
BE, TW/29-30

LANTEAU, William (b 1922)
American actor TW/8, 13-
14

LANTZ, Robert (b 1914) German/
American literary & talent
representative, producer,
dramatist BE

LAPARCERIE, Cora [Mme. La-
parcerie-Richepin] French

actress GRB/1, 3-4, WWT/1-3

LAPARCERIE-RICHEPIN, Mme.
see Laparcerie, Cora

LA PLANTE, Laura (b 1904) American actress WWT/8

LAPOINTE, Doris Lilian (d 1917
[19]) EA/18*

LAPORTE, Mons. (fl 1827) actor
CDP

LAPORTE, Miss (d 1880) actress
EA/81*

LAPOTAIRE, Jane (b 1944) English
actress WWT/16

LA PRADE, Ernest (d 1969 [79])
performer BP/53*

LARABEE, Louise American actress TW/9, 22-23

LARDNER, Ring (1885-1933) American dramatist NTH, PDT, SR

LARGAY, Raymond J. (d 1974
[88]) performer BP/59*

LARIMORE, Earle (1899-1947)
American actor TW/4, WWT/7-
10

LARK, Kingsley (d 1948 [58]) actor,
singer WWT/14*

LARKELLE, Lillie [Elizabeth
Eayrs Collins] (d 1898 [26])
burlesque actress EA/99*

LARKELLE, Nellie (fl 1o77) actress CDP

LARKIN, Bob (b 1929) American
actor TW/26

LARKIN, John (d 1965) dramatist
BP/49*

LARKIN, Joseph (d 1908) variety
manager EA/09*

LARKIN, Peter (b 1926) American
designer BE, ES, WWT/14-16

LARKIN, Rhoda actress EA/97

LARKIN, Sophie (d 1903 [70]) actress OAA/2

LARKINS, Mr. (fl 1840) English
actor HAS

LARKINS, Mrs. (d 1880) EA/81*

LARKINS, Mrs. see Coveney,
Jane

LARNED, Mel (1925-55) American
singer TW/11-12

LAROCHE, James (fl 1696-1713)
singer CDP, DNB

LA ROCQUE, Rod (1898-1969)
American actor ES, TW/26

LaROSA, Julius (b 1930) American
actor TW/21

LaROSE, Rose (d 1972 [59]) performer BP/57*

LARPENT, John (1741-1824) inspector of plays DNB

LARRALDE, Rômulo see Brent, Romney

LARRIMORE, Francine (1898-1975) French actress BE, NTH, TW/ 2-8, WWT/4-11

LARSEN, Darrell D. (d 1965 [68]) producer/director BP/50*

LARSEN, Niels (d 1975 [49]) producer/director/choreographer BP/60*

LARSEN, William (b 1927) American actor TW/24-26, 28-29

LARSON, John (b 1914) American actor TW/3-4

LARSON, Paul (b 1918) American actor TW/6, 23, 29

LARSON, Philip (b 1942) American actor TW/28

LARSSEN, Signe see Hasso, Signe

LA RUE, Danny [Daniel Patrick Carroll] (b 1928) Irish female impersonator COC

LA RUE, Grace (1882-1956) American actress, singer TW/12, WWT/4-7

LASCELLES, Miss (fl 1800) actress TD/1-2

LASCELLES, Ernita (d 1972 [87]) English actress, dramatist TW/29

LASCELLES, Mrs. Francis see Catley, Ann

LASCELLES, Frank (d 1934 [58]) English actor, pageant master GRB/1-4

LASCELLES, Vera see Lascelles-Scott, Mrs.

LASCELLES-SCOTT, Mrs. [Vera Lascelles] (d 1885) actress EA/86*

LASCOE, Henry (d 1964 [50]) actor TW/21

LASHANSKA, Hulda (d 1974 [80]) performer BP/58*

LA SHELLE, Kirke (1863-1905) manager BP/2*, WWT/14*

LASHWOOD, George (d 1942 [79]) singer, composer, actor CDP

LASHWOOD, Mrs. George see Williams, Lottie

LASK, George Edwin (b 1865) American director, manager, actor WWM

LASKY, Jesse L. (1880-1958) American manager, producer

WWM, WWW/5

LASKY, Zane (b 1953) American actor TW/29-30

LASLEY, David (b 1947) American actor TW/29

LASLO, Alexander (d 1970 [75]) composer/lyricist BP/55*

LASSALLE, Jean-Louis (1845-1909) French singer ES

LASSER, Louise (b 1940?) American actress CB

LASTFOGEL, Abe (b 1898) American talent representative BE

LASZLO, Miklos (d 1973 [69]) dramatist BP/57*

LATCHAW, Paul (b 1945) American actor TW/29

LATEINER, Joseph (1853-1935) Rumanian dramatist MWD, OC/ 2-3

LATELLE, Cornelius (d 1910 [63]) EA/11*

LATEWARE, Dr. Richard (1560-1601) English writer CP/3

LATHAM, Mr. (fl 1834) actor HAS

LATHAM, Alfred Henry (d 1899 [32]) EA/00*

LATHAM, Cynthia (b 1897) English actress TW/14-15, 26

LATHAM, Daniel (d 1885 [24]) actor, manager EA/86*

LATHAM, Frederick G. (d 1943 [90]) English producer, director, manager SR, WWT/7-9

LATHAM, Mrs. Frederick G. see Brooke, Cynthia

LATHAM, Hope (d 1951 [79]) actress TW/7

LATHAM, Joseph W., Sr. (d 1970 [80]) actor TW/27

LATHAM, W. H. (d 1844) actor, singer CDP

LATHBURY, Stanley (b 1873) English actor GRB/1-2, WWT/5-11

LATHOM, Earl of see Wilbraham, Edward

LATHOM, Francis (1777-1832) English dramatist CP/3

LA THORNE, John (fl 1845-69) American actor, athlete, circus performer, stage manager HAS

LATHRAM, Elizabeth (b 1947) American actress TW/29-30

LATHROP, Elise (fl 1901-07) American translator WWM

LATHROP, George Parsons (1851-

98) Hawaiian composer, writer
WWA/H

LATHROP, Sam American clown
CDP

LATHY, Thomas Pike (b 1771)
English dramatist CP/3,
DNB, EAP

LATIMAR, Mrs. (d 1894) EA/95*

LATIMER, Edyth [Mrs. William
Haviland] (1883-1967) Australian
actress GRB/3-4, WWT/1-5

LATIMER, Henry (d 1963 [86])
performer BE*

LATIMER, Hugh (b 1913) English
actor WWT/11-16

LATIMER, Sally (b 1910) English
actress, producer, manager
WWT/10-14

LATONA, Jen (fl 1911?) singer,
actress CDP

LATOUCHE, John Treville (1917-
56) American dramatist, lyricist CB, MH, TW/13

LATOUR, M. (d 1854) aeronaut
EA/72*

LaTOUR, Babe (d 1973 [79]) performer BP/57*

LATOUR, William (b 1845) Ger-
man/American actor HAS

LATRILHE, Jeanne see Dulac,
Odette

LA TROBE, Charles (1879-1967)
English director, producer
WWT/7-14

LA TROBE, Mrs. Charles see
Addison, Carlotta

LA TROBE, Charles Albert (d
1909 [63]) EA/10*

LATTER, Mary (1725-77) English dramatist CP/2-3, GT

LATTIMER, Miss see Holman,
Mrs. Joseph George

LATTIMORE, Richmond (b 1906)
American educator, translator
BE

LAU, Hurfries de [Josias Flor-
idor] (fl 1635) French actor
DA

LAUB, Ferdinand (d 1875) musician EA/76*

LAUCHLAN, Agnes (b 1905) English actress WWT/8-16

LAUCK, Pierre Ham (d 1899
[42]) gymnast EA/00*

LAUDENBACH, Pierre see
Fresnay, Pierre

LAUDER, Mrs. (d 1905) EA/06*

LAUDER, Sir Harry (1870-1950)

English singer, actor CDP,
COC, DNB, ES, NTH, OC/1-3,
PDT, SR, TW/6, WWA/4,
WWT/4-10

LAUDER, John C. (d 1916) EA/18*

LAUDICINA, Dino (b 1939) American actor TW/24, 26

LAUGHLIN, Anna [Mrs. Dwight
Van Monroe] (1885-1937) American actress CDP, WWS

LAUGHLIN, Sharon actress TW/
26-28, 30

LAUGHTON, Charles (1899-1962)
English actor, director AAS,
CB, ES, NTH, PDT, TW/8-9,
13-15, 19, WWA/4, WWT/6-13,
WWW/6

LAUHER, Bob (d 1973 [42]) performer BP/58*

LAUNDON, Mrs. John Crossley (d
1909 [61]) EA/10*

LAURA, Fraulein see Descombes,
Mrs.

LAUREL, Jane (fl 1900-12) actress
WWM

LAUREL, Lily (d 1897) serio-
comic EA/98*

LAUREL, Mrs. Sid (d 1912 [27])
performer? EA/13*

LAUREL, Stan (b 1890) English
performer ES

LAUREN, Jane (d 1974 [56]) performer BP/59*

LAURENCE, Baby (d 1974 [53])
performer BP/58*

LAURENCE, Charles (d 1896 [62])
property master EA/97*

LAURENCE, Larry (b 1920) Italian
actor TW/2

LAURENCE, Paula (b 1916) American actress, singer BE, TW/
1-16, 20, 22-23, 26, WWT/11-
16

LAURENS, William B. (d 1879
[42]) American actor EA/80*

LAURENT, Mr. (fl 1808) comedian,
harlequin CDP

LAURENT, Ada (fl 1860s) English
actress HAS

LAURENT, Charles Emile (d 1857)
musician EA/72*

LAURENT, Edwin (d 1877) singer?
EA/78*

LAURENT, Henry (d 1861 [26])
musician EA/72*

LAURENT, Marie (d 1904 [78])
actress WWT/14*

LAURENTI, Mario (d 1922) Italian

singer WWA/1

LAURENTS, Arthur (b 1918/20)
American dramatist, director
AAS, BE, CD, ES, GT, MD,
MH, MWD, PDT, WWT/12-16

LAURET, Laryssa (b 1939) Polish
actress TW/26

LAUREYS, Simon W. (c. 1827-
87) Belgian costumier NYM

LAURI, Charles (1833-89) pantomimist, clown CDP

LAURI, Charles, Jr. (d 1904
[56]) pantomimist, animal mimic
CDP, DP

LAURI, Charlotte [Mrs. W. Fos-
ter] (d 1878) singer EA/79*

LAURI, Edward (d 1919) actor,
manager CDP

LAURI, Mrs. Edward (d 1907)
actress EA/08*

LAURI, Ernest (d 1904 [26])
EA/05*

LAURI, George (d 1909) actor
WWT/14*

LAURI, Harry see Lowe,
Albert Henry

LAURI, Joe, Jr. (1892-1954)
American actor BE*

LAURI, John (d 1881 [52]) pantomimist EA/82*

LAURI, Lelia [Mrs. Fred H.
Lowerre] (1856-84) singer
CDP

LAURI, Stella [Mrs. Harry Ulph]
(d 1907 [44]) dancer EA/08*

LAURI, Ted (d 1893) pantomimist
EA/94*

LAURI BROTHERS (fl 1869) English pantomimists HAS

LAURIA, Larri (d 1965 [64])
performer BP/50*

LAURIE, Fannie (d 1885 [37])
performer? EA/86*

LAURIE, Joe, Jr. (1892-1954)
American vaudevillian NTH,
TW/10

LAURIE, John (b 1897) Scottish
actor AAS, WWT/6-16

LAURIE, William Pitcairn (d
1871 [28]) actor EA/72*

LAURIEN, Fanny [Mrs. James
G. Laurien] (d 1884 [34])
EA/86*

LAURIEN, Mrs. James G. see
Laurien, Fanny

LAURIER, Jay (1879-1969) English actor WWT/7-11

LAURILLARD, Edward (b 1870)

Dutch manager WWT/4-8

LAURI-VOLPI, Giacomo (b 1893)
Italian singer ES

LAUTNER, Joe (b 1924) American
actor TW/10

LaVALLEE, Bill (b 1943) American
actor TW/27-30

LAVALLIERE, Eve (d 1929 [61])
Italian/French actress WWT/3-4

LAVENU, E. singer, actress CDP

LAVER, James (1899-1975) English
dramatist, historian BE, COC,
OC/1-3, WWT/8-14

LAVER, Mrs. James H. see
Laverne, Pattie

LA VERE, Earl (d 1962 [71])
performer BE*

LAVERICK, Beryl (b 1919) English
actress WWT/8-9

LA VERNE, Lucille (1875-1945)
American actress TW/1, WWT/
5-9

LAVERNE, Pattie [Mrs. James H.
Laver] (d 1916) English actress
OAA/1-2

LAVERTON, Vyvian see Thomas,
Vyvian

LAVERY, Emmet (b 1902) American writer, dramatist BE, CB,
MD, MWD

LAVERY, Richard (d 1962 [79])
Australian equestrian BE*

LAVIGNE, Mlle. (fl 1852) dancer
HAS

LAVIGNE, Joseph (d 1875) ballet
master, pantomimist EA/76*

LAVIN, Linda (b 1937/39) American actress TW/21-27, 29,
WWT/15-16

LAVINA [Mrs. Joseph Miller] (d
1909 [47]) performer? EA/10*

LAVINE, Miss see Simmons,
Lavinia

LAVIZZO, Valcour (b 1953) American actor TW/28

LAVREN, Christine (b 1944) American actress TW/27

LAW, Arthur (1844-1913) English
dramatist, actor GRB/1-4, SR,
WWT/1, WWW/1

LAW, Fred (d 1902 [57]) singer,
actor, manager CDP

LAW, Mrs. Fred (d 1892) EA/93*

LAW, Jenny Lou (d 1961 [39]) actress TW/17

LAW, John Phillip (b 1937) American actor TW/21

LAW, Mouzon (b 1922) American

educator, director BE
LAWDER, Wallace actor TW/1
LAWES, Henry (1596-1662)
English composer CDP, DNB
LAWES, William (d 1645) English
composer DNB
LAWFORD, Betty (1910-60) Eng-
lish actress WWT/10-11
LAWFORD, Ernest (1870-1940)
English actor CB, WWT/8-9
LAWLER, D. (fl 1808) dramatist
CP/3
LAWLER, Frank (b 1835) Amer-
ican actor, manager HAS, SR
LAWLER, John William (d 1869)
actor EA/70*
LAWLER, Kate (fl 1878) actress
OAA/2
LAWLER, Mike (1828-65) Irish
actor HAS
LAWLER, Ray (b 1921/22) Aus-
tralian actor, dramatist
AAS, BE, CD, COC, MD,
MH, MWD, OC/3, PDT, RE
LAWLER, Richard H., Sr. (d
1969 [67]) designer BP/54*
LAWLER, William (d 1916)
musician EA/17*
LAWLESS, Sue American actress
TW/23, 25-26, 29
LAWLOR, Mr. (fl 1888?) singer,
actor CDP
LAWLOR, Charles B. (d 1925
[73]) Irish performer BE*,
BP/9*
LAWLOR, Mary American ac-
tress, singer WWT/6-8
LAWRENCE, Mrs. (d 1890) EA/
91*
LAWRENCE, Adrian (d 1953 [79])
actor, producer, manager
BE*, WWT/14*
LAWRENCE, Mrs. Arthur [Mary
Campbell] (d 1889) EA/90*
LAWRENCE, Bert (d 1971 [47])
performer BP/56*
LAWRENCE, Boyle (1869-1951)
English dramatist, critic,
lyricist GRB/1-4, WWT/1-9,
WWW/5
LAWRENCE, Carol (b 1932/35)
American dancer, singer,
actress CB, TW/18-19,
WWT/16
LAWRENCE, C. E. (d 1940
[69]) dramatist BE*, WWT/
14*
LAWRENCE, Charles (b 1896)

American actor WWT/5-9
LAWRENCE, Delphi (b 1932) Eng-
lish actress TW/28-29
LAWRENCE, D. H. (1885-1930)
English dramatist AAS, COC,
MD, MWD, WWT/6, WWW/3
LAWRENCE, Dorset William see
D'Orsay, Lawrence
LAWRENCE, Eddie (b 1919) Amer-
ican actor TW/23
LAWRENCE, Elaine (d 1971 [28])
performer BP/55*
LAWRENCE, Eliza Jane [Mrs.
Sidney Lawrence] (d 1869) mu-
sician EA/70*
LAWRENCE, Elliot (b 1926) Amer-
ican musical director, com-
poser BE
LAWRENCE, Emma [Mrs. Joe
Lawrence] (d 1916 [66]) EA/17*
LAWRENCE, Florence (1888-1938)
actress BE*
LAWRENCE, Frederick see
Kert, Larry
LAWRENCE, George A., Jr. (d
1894) musician EA/95*
LAWRENCE, Georgia (d 1923 [46])
actress BE*, BP/7*
LAWRENCE, Gerald (1873-1957)
English actor COC, GRB/1-4,
OC/3, WWS, WWT/1-11
LAWRENCE, Mrs. Gerald see
Davis, Fay
LAWRENCE, Mrs. Gerald see
Braithwaite, Lilian
LAWRENCE, Gertrude (1898-1952)
English actress AAS, CB,
COC, DNB, ES, NTH, OC/3,
SR, TW/2-9, WWA/3, WWT/
5-11, WWW/5
LAWRENCE, Jack (b 1912) Amer-
ican lyricist, composer, pro-
ducer BE
LAWRENCE, James (fl 1799) drama-
tist CP/3
LAWRENCE, Jennie (d 1894) gym-
nast, trapezist EA/95*
LAWRENCE, Jerome (b 1915)
American dramatist, director
BE, CD, MWD, WWT/13-16
LAWRENCE, Joe (d 1909 [60])
singer, actor CDP
LAWRENCE, Mrs. Joe see
Lawrence, Emma
LAWRENCE, J. W. (d 1900 [70])
clown, pantaloon EA/01*
LAWRENCE, J. W. (d 1916 [83])
actor EA/17*

LAWRENCE, Katie (fl 1890s?)
singer, actress CDP
LAWRENCE, Lawrence Shubert
(1894-1965) American executive BE, TW/21
LAWRENCE, Lawrence Shubert,
Jr. (b 1916) American executive BE
LAWRENCE, Lillian (fl 1892-1908) American actress WWS
LAWRENCE, Margaret (1889-1929) American actress HAS,
WWA/1, WWT/4
LAWRENCE, Marjorie (b 1908)
Australian singer CB
LAWRENCE, Nellie [Mrs. Harry
McClelland] (d 1912 [51])
EA/13*
LAWRENCE, Pauline (d 1971
[70]) designer BP/56*
LAWRENCE, Reginald (1900-67)
American dramatist BE,
TW/24
LAWRENCE, Mrs. Sidney see
Lawrence, Eliza Jane
"LAWRENCE, Slingsby" see
Lewes, George Henry
LAWRENCE, Stan make-up artist
BE
LAWRENCE, Steve (b 1935)
American actor, singer BE,
CB, TW/24
LAWRENCE, Sydney Boyle see
Lawrence, Boyle
LAWRENCE, Thomas (d 1896
[78]) portable theatre manager
EA/97*
LAWRENCE, Vincent (b 1896)
English press representative
WWT/6-8
LAWRENCE, Vincent S. (1890-1946) American dramatist
TW/3, WWT/6-10
LAWRENCE, Walter N. (d 1920
[62]) manager BE*, BP/4*,
WWT/14*
LAWRENCE, William (d 1921)
actor BE*, BP/5*
LAWRENCE, William John (1862-1940) Irish historian, critic
GRB/4, WWT/1-9
LAWRENCE, Wingold (b 1874)
English actor GRB/1
LAWRIE, Charles singer, actor
CDP
LAWRIE, Ted (b 1923) American
actor TW/4, 28
LAWRIE, T. T. V. (d 1868

[22]) actor? EA/69*
LAWS, Edmund (d 1852 [48]) actor
WWT/14*
LAWS, Mrs. Edmund (d 1880 [69])
actress WWT/14*
LAWS, Frederick (d 1976 [65])
dramatist BP/60*
LAWS, Jane (d 1880 [69]) actress
EA/81*
LAWS, Jerry (b 1912) American
actor TW/25-26
LAWS, Steve (b 1937) American
actor TW/30
LAWSON, Charles (d 1879 [30])
American musician EA/80*
LAWSON, Lady Edward see
Lawson, Henrietta
LAWSON, Ennis (d 1888 [52]) actor
EA/89*
LAWSON, Henrietta [Lady Edward
Lawson] (d 1897) EA/98*
LAWSON, James (1799-1880) Scottish? American dramatist CDP,
EAP, HJD, RJ
LAWSON, John (d 1920 [55]?) English variety artist GRB/1-3
LAWSON, John Howard (1895-1977)
American dramatist AAS, BE,
CD, HJD, MD, MH, MWD,
NTH, WWT/8-11
LAWSON, Kate (b 1894) American
designer, executive BE
LAWSON, Lee (b 1941) American
actress TW/24-25, 27-30
LAWSON, Lionel (d 1879) proprietor EA/80*
LAWSON, Mary (1910-41) English
actress, singer CB, WWT/6-9
LAWSON, Robb (d 1947 [74]) critic
BE*, WWT/14*
LAWSON, Roger (b 1942) American
actor TW/25-26, 29-30
LAWSON, Wilfred (1900-66) English
actor AAS, WWT/7-14
LAWSON, William E. (d 1897)
musical director EA/98*
LAWSON, Winifred (1894-1961)
English actress, singer WWT/
5-10
LAWTON, Elizabeth Ann (d 1917)
EA/18*
LAWTON, Frank (d 1914) actor,
whistler CDP
LAWTON, Frank (1904-69) English
actor COC, TW/26, WWT/6-14, WWW/6
LAWTON, Thais (1881/82-1956)
American actress TW/13,

WWM, WWT/1-11
LAWTON, Thomas (d 1913 [42])
EA/14*
LAX, Percy (d 1909 [44]) musi-
cal director EA/10*
LAY, Dilys see Laye, Dilys
LAYE, Dilys [née Lay] (b 1934)
English actress WWT/15-16
LAYE, Evelyn (b 1900) English
actress, singer AAS, BE,
COC, ES, WWT/4-16
LAYFIELD, James (d 1877) comic
singer EA/79*
LAYLAND, Edward [E. West-
bourne] (d 1882 [28]) actor?
EA/83*
LAYTON, Joe [né Lichtman] (b
1931) American choreographer,
director BE, CB, WWT/14-16
LAYTON, Thomas (d 1893) con-
ductor EA/94*
LAYTON, William (b 1917) Amer-
ican actor TW/4-6
LAZAR, Irving (b 1907) Ameri-
can literary representative
BE
LAZARUS, Emma (1849-87)
American dramatist WWA/H
LAZARUS, Henry (d 1895) musi-
cian EA/96*
LAZELLO, Bob (d 1909) gym-
nast, acrobat EA/10*
LAZER, Peter (b 1946) Ameri-
can actor BE, TW/13-14,
26-27
LAZZARI, Carolina (1891-1946)
American singer TW/3,
WWA/2
LEA, Albert (d 1863) HAS
LEA, Bruce (b 1949) American
actor TW/29-30
LEA, Fanny Heaslip (1884-1955)
American dramatist WWA/3
LEA, Marion see Mitchell,
Mrs. Langdon Elwyn
LEABO, Loi (b 1938) American
actress TW/22
LEACH, Arthur (d 1887 [22])
advance agent EA/88*
LEACH, Emily Sarah [Mrs.
Gus Leach] (d 1895 [48])
EA/96*
LEACH, Gus (d 1903) comedian,
music-hall manager EA/04*
LEACH, Gus see Leach, Emily
Sarah
LEACH, Harvey (1804-47) Amer-
ican performer CDP, HAS

LEACH, Mrs. Harvey (fl 1841)
actress HAS
LEACH, Hervey [Sig. Hervio Nano]
(1804-47) dwarf CDP
LEACH, Marjorie (b 1902) Ameri-
can actress TW/27
LEACH, Stephen W. (d 1895 [75])
singer, actor, composer HAS
LEACH, Wilford (b 1929) American
educator, dramatist, director
BE
LEACHMAN, Cloris (b 1926?)
American actress CB, TW/8-19
LEACHMAN, Cloris W. (d 1967
[66]) little theatre pioneer BP/
52*
LEACOCK, John (fl c. 1776) drama-
tist EAP
LEADER, John (d 1897) choir
secretary EA/98*
LEADLAY, Edward O. (1884-1951)
Canadian press representative
WWT/5-9
LEAHY, Christine Dobbins (d 1974
[82]) performer BP/59*
LEAHY, Eugene (1883-1967) Irish
actor WWT/6-14
LEAK, Miss (fl 1792) English
singer GT, TD/1-2
LEAK, Elizabeth (b 1777) actress
CDP
LEAK, Thomas [Tom French] (d
1888 [25]) pantomimist EA/89*
LEAKE, James (d 1791 [76])
patentee BE*, WWT/14*
LEAKE, W. H. (b 1832) English
actor, manager HAS
LEAL, Milagros (d 1975 [73])
performer BP/59*
LEAMAN, Felix (d 1899 [36])
musical director EA/00*
LEAMAN, Samuel B. (d 1857 [27])
American actor HAS
LEAMAR, Alice (d 1950 [81])
performer BE*, WWT/14*
LEAMAR, Kate [Mrs. W. Bint]
(d 1893) music-hall singer
EA/94*
LEAMAR SISTERS singers CDP
LEAMING, Chet (b 1925) American
actor TW/12-15, 18, 25
LEAMORE, Florence [Florrie
Palmer; Mrs. Tom Leamore]
(d 1895) EA/96*
LEAMORE, Tom (d 1939 [73])
actor, songwriter, dancer CDP
LEAMORE, Mrs. Tom see
Leamore, Florence

LEAN, Cecil (1878-1935) Canadian actor WWT/4-7

LEAN, Mrs. Francis see Marryat, Florence

LEANDER, Harry (d 1909 [50]) comedian EA/10*

LEANDER, Thomas S. (d 1890 [48]) music-hall performer EA/91*

LEANERD, John (fl 1679-78) dramatist CP/1-3, DNB, GT

LEAPOR, Mary (1722-46) English dramatist CP/2-3, GT

LEAR, Evelyn (b 1929?) American singer CB

LEAR, Joyce (b 1926) American actress TW/7

LEARMONT, John (fl 1791) dramatist CP/3

LEARMOUTH, Mary (d 1913 [46]) EA/14*

LEARY, Miss (fl late 18th cent) singer CDP

LEARY, David (b 1939) American actor TW/25, 27, 29

LEARY, Gilda (d 1927 [31]) English actress BE*, BP/11*

LEASK, George Alfred (1878-1950) English dramatist WWW/4

LEATHEM, Barclay (b 1900) American educator, director BE

LEATHERBEE, Mary American educator BE

LEATHES, Edmund (1847-91) actor DP, OAA/2

LEATITIA, Mme. [Mrs. W. H. Clarke] (d 1880 [27]) equestrienne EA/81*

LEAVER, Philip (b 1903/04) English actor, dramatist WWT/7-14

LEAVETT, Marie see Rose, Marie

LEAVITT, Charles [Max] (b 1905) American actor TW/2

LEAVITT, Michael B. (1843-1935) German/American actor, manager CDP, COC, SR

LE BARGY, Charles Gustave Antoine (1858-1936) French actor GRB/1, 3-4, WWT/1-4

LE BARGY, Simone see Simone, Mme.

LeBARON, Louise (fl 1904-10) American singer, actress

WWM, WWS

LE BARON, William (1883-1958) American dramatist, producer WWA/3, WWT/4-12

LE BARR, Fanny [Mrs. Henry Le Barr] (d 1897) EA/98*

LE BARR, Mrs. Henry see Le Barr, Fanny

LEBEDEFF, Ivan (d 1953 [58]) Russian actor BE*, BP/37*

LEBERWURST, Hans (fl 1613) actor DA

LEBLANC-MAETERLINCK, Georgette (1876-1941) French actress, singer WWT/3-4

LE BLOND, Mr. (fl 1820) French dancer CDP, EA/92

LEBOWSKY, Stanley (b 1926) American conductor, composer, musician BE, TW/28-29

LE BOZEC, Marcel see Varnel, Marcel

LE BRETON, Flora (b 1898) English actress WWT/6-9

LE BRETON, Rev. William Corbet (d 1888 [73]) EA/89*

LEBRUN-DANZI, Franziska (1756-91) German singer ES

LE BRUNN, George (1863-1905) English composer GRB/1

LE BRUNN, Thomas (b 1864) English songwriter GRB/1

LE BUTT, Ada [Mrs. Arthur Brogden] (d 1902) singer EA/03*

LECKIE, William Lloyd (d 1916 [30]) EA/17*

LECKY, Eleazer (b 1903) American educator BE

LeCLAIR, Henry American actor TW/25-28

LE CLAIR, Maggie (d 1923 [65]) American comedienne BE*, BP/7*

LE CLAIR, Shedrach see Smith, Shedrach

LE CLAIR, William (d 1910) dog trainer EA/11*

LE CLERCK, Mme. (fl 1822) dancer CDP

LECLERCQ, Arthur (d 1890) pantomimist, dancer, acting manager EA/91*, WWT/14*

LECLERCQ, Carlotta [Mrs. John Nelson] (1836-93) English actress CDP, DNB, DP, OAA/1-2

LECLERCQ, Charles (1797-1861)

dancer, ballet master CDP
LECLERCQ, Charles (d 1895)
pantomimist, ballet master
EA/96*, WWT/14*
LECLERCQ, Louise (d 1898)
dancer, actress EA/99*,
WWT/14*
LECLERCQ, Pierre (d 1932)
dramatist BE*, WWT/14*
LECLERCQ, Rose (1845?-99)
actress CDP, DNB, DP,
EA/95, OAA/1-2
LE CLERCQ, Tanaquil (b 1929)
American dancer CB, ES
LECLERQ, Mrs. (d 1889 [77])
actress EA/90*
LE CLERQ, Florence (d 1960 [89])
actress BE*, WWT/14*
LE CLERQ, George (1855-1911?)
Irish actor GRB/1
LECOCQ, Charles (d 1918 [86])
EA/19*
LECOMTE, Mons. (fl 1838)
singer CDP
LECOMTE, Mme. (fl 1837)
dancer CDP
LEDBETTER, Robert (fl 1597-
1606) actor DA
LEDERER, Charles (1911-76)
American dramatist, producer,
director BE
LEDERER, Francis (b 1906)
Czech actor, director BE,
NTH, TW/2-9, WWT/7-14
LEDERER, George W. (1861-
1938) American manager
GRB/2-4, SR, WWA/1,
WWT/1-8
LEDERER, George W., Jr. (d
1924 [33]) talent representative
BE*, BP/9*
LEDERER, Gretchen (d 1955
[64]) actress BE*
LEDFORD, Harrison C. (d 1970
[69]) performer BP/55*
LEDGER, Mr. ["Honest Ledger"]
actor TD/1-2
LEDGER, Edward (d 1921) jour-
nalist WWW/1
LEDGER, Frederick (d 1874
[58]) editor, publisher BE*,
EA/75*, WWT/14*
LEDIARD, Thomas (d 1759)
dramatist CP/2-3, GT,
TD/1-2
LEDUC, Claudine (d 1969) BP/
53*
LEE (fl 1798) actor, dramatist

CP/3, GT
LEE, Mr. (fl 1795-98) manager,
actor TD/1-2
LEE, Mr. (fl c. 1850) actor CDP
LEE, Mrs. [née Keys] (fl 1793)
actress TD/1-2
LEE, Ada (d 1902 [35]) actress
EA/03*
LEE, Albert (d 1888) minstrel
EA/90*
LEE, Alexander (d 1851) composer
EA/72*
LEE, Mrs. Alexander (d 1851
[51]) EA/72*
LEE, Alfred (d 1906) composer
EA/07*
LEE, Annie see Johnston, Mrs.
T. B.
LEE, Auriol (1880-1941) English
actress, producer CB, GRB/
3-4, WWT/1-9
LEE, Belinda (d 1961 [26]) English
actress BE*, WWT/14*
LEE, Bernard (b 1908) English ac-
tor AAS, WWT/8-16
LEE, Bert (1880-1946) English
dramatist, composer WWT/7-9
LEE, Bessie [Mrs. F. Cumminger]
(d 1904 [31]) "Coloured Patti"
EA/05*
LEE, Bessie (d 1972 [66]) perform-
er BP/57*
LEE, Big (b 1939) American actor
TW/27
LEE, Bruce (d 1973 [32]) performer
BP/58*
LEE, Bryarly (b 1934/35) American
actress BE, TW/13-15, 30
LEE, Canada [né Leonard Lionel
Cornelius Canegata] (1907-52)
American actor CB, COC, TW/
1-8, WWA/3, WWT/10-11
LEE, Charles (d 1947 [71]) per-
former BE*, WWT/14*
LEE, Clara (d 1899 [74]) actress
EA/00*
LEE, Edgar [William Tasker] (d
1908 [58]) journalist EA/10*
LEE, Elizabeth (d 1905) EA/06*
LEE, Esmé (fl 1881) singer CDP
LEE, Florence (d 1962 [74]) ac-
tress BE*
LEE, Fred (d 1890) comedian
EA/91*
LEE, Mrs. Fred (d 1889) EA/91*
LEE, George (d 1871 [47]) come-
dian EA/72*
LEE, George Alexander (1802-51)

English composer, singer, conductor DNB

LEE, George B. (b 1866) American business manager GRB/1

LEE, George Vandeleur (d 1886 [55]) composer EA/87*

LEE, Gypsy Rose [née Rose Louise Hovick] (1914-70) American actress BE, CB, COC, SR, TW/26, WWA/5, WWT/10-11

LEE, Harriet (1757-1851) English dramatist CP/2-3, DNB, GT

LEE, Harriett [Mrs. Richard Austin Lee] (d 1883 [50]) EA/84*

LEE, Harry A. (d 1919 [76]) American manager BE*, BP/4*

LEE, Henry (1765-1836) English manager, dramatist, actor CP/3, DNB

LEE, Henry (d 1910 [53]) performer BE*, WWT/14*

LEE, Mrs. Henry (d 1874 [63]) actress EA/75*

LEE, Hettie de (b 1849) American actress HAS

LEE, Ida (d 1867) music-hall performer HAS

LEE, James (b 1923) American dramatist BE

LEE, James E. (d 1965 [58]) critic BP/50*

LEE, Jane (d 1957 [45]) performer BE*

LEE, Jean (d 1963) performer BE*

LEE, Jennie (d 1925 [75]) actress BE*, BP/10*, WWT/14*

LEE, Jennie [Mrs. J. P. Burnett] (d 1930 [84]) English actress CDP, DP, GRB/1-4, OAA/1-2, WWT/1-6

LEE, Jenny [Mrs. E. S. Vincent] (d 1893) actress EA/94*

LEE, Jim (d 1866) minstrel HAS

LEE, John (d 1781) actor, dramatist, manager CDP, CP/2-3, DNB, TD/1-2

LEE, John (1795-1881) actor, stage manager CDP

LEE, Johnny see Wardroper, John

LEE, J. Stacey (d 1868 [42])

comic songwriter EA/69*

LEE, Kathryn (b 1926) American actress TW/4-6

LEE, Katie [Mrs. C. Stuart] (d 1916) actress EA/17*

LEE, Lavater (d 1891 [73]) EA/92*

LEE, Lavater (d 1899) performing dog proprietor EA/00*

LEE, Lila (d 1973 [68]) actress TW/30

LEE, Lillie (d 1941 [81]) actress, dancer BE*, WWT/14*

LEE, Madaline (d 1974) performer BP/58*

LEE, Marion (d 1864 [24]) American actress HAS

LEE, Mary Ann see Vanhook, Mrs. W. F.

LEE, Mary Anne (fl 1837-45) American dancer HAS

LEE, Michele (b 1942) American actress, singer, dancer BE, TW/18-19, 29-30

LEE, Ming Cho (b 1930) Chinese designer BE, WWT/15-16

LEE, Moe (d 1966 [81]) performer BP/50*

LEE, Nathaniel (c. 1653-92) English dramatist CDP, COC, CP/1-3, DNB, ES, GT, HP, MH, NTH, OC/1-3, RE

LEE, Nelson (1806-72) English dramatist, manager CDP, EA/68

LEE, Olga (b 1899) American talent representative BE

LEE, Raymond (d 1974 [64]) performer BP/59*

LEE, R. G. (fl 1793) dramatist CP/3

LEE, Richard (d 1905) EA/06*

LEE, Richard Austin (d 1883 [63]) actor EA/84*

LEE, Mrs. Richard Austin see Lee, Harriett

LEE, Richard L. (b 1872) American actor WWS

LEE, Richard Nelson (1806-72) English actor, dramatist DNB

LEE, Robert (fl 1590-1622) dramatist, actor, lessee CP/3, DA

LEE, Robert E. (b 1918) American dramatist, producer, director BE, CD, MWD, WWT/13-16

LEE, Rosa (fl 1872?) actress, singer CDP

LEE, Rowland V. (d 1975 [84]) producer/director/choreographer

BP/60*
LEE, Sammy (d 1968 [78]) pro-
ducer/director/choreographer
BP/52*
LEE, S. L. (d 1906 [49]) pro-
prietor EA/07*
LEE, Sondra (b 1930) American
actress, dancer BE, TW/
11, 13, 20-24
LEE, Sophia (1750-1824) English
dramatist CDP, CP/3, DNB,
TD/1-2
LEE, Thomas (1810-56) Irish
actor CDP
LEE, Tom (d 1971 [61]) designer
BP/56*
LEE, Valerie (d 1975 [52])
American actress TW/26
LEE, Vanessa [née Winifred
Ruby Moule] (b 1920) English
actress, singer WWT/11-16
LEE, Cpt. W. H. (d 1874 [33])
business manager EA/76*
LEE, Will (b 1908) American
actor, teacher, director BE,
TW/23, 29
LEE, William (d 1907 [52])
music-hall performer EA/08*
LEE, William A. (b 1890) Amer-
ican actor, vaudevillian TW/
2-4, 8-9
LEE, William T. (fl 1850) actor
HAS
LEECH, Dempster (b 1942)
American actor TW/29
LEECH, Richard [né Richard
Leeper McClelland] (b 1922)
Irish actor AAS, WWT/11-16
LEECHMAN, Kate [Mrs. Harry
Walker] (d 1909) comedian
EA/10*
LEEDER, Mlle. (fl 1852) dancer
HAS
LEEDS, Mrs. Charles S. see
Glose, Augusta
LEEDS, Florence (d 1970 [75])
performer BP/55*
LEEDS, Phil American actor
BE, TW/23, 26, 29-30
LEEDS, Strelsa (b 1920) Amer-
ican actress TW/2
LEEDY, Harry (d 1975 [67])
artists' manager BP/59*
LEEKE, David (fl 1571) actor
DA
LEE LEWIS, Charles (d 1803
[63]) actor GT, TD/1-2
LEEMAN, Walter H. (d 1903)

business manager EA/04*
LEES, C. Lowell (b 1904) Ameri-
can educator BE
LEES, Mrs. M. (d 1875) EA/76*
LEES, Noah (d 1905 [69]) music-
hall performer? EA/06*
LEES, Thomas (d 1908) variety
performer EA/09*
LEES, Tom (d 1878 [57]) eques-
trian, gymnast EA/79*
LEESON, Dan (d 1903 [42]) variety
performer EA/04*
LEESON, Mrs. Dan see Danvil,
Maud
LEESON, Dan W. (fl 1859-61) actor
HAS
LEESON, Henrietta [Mrs. William
Thomas Lewis] (1751-1826) Eng-
lish actress COC, TD/1-2
LEE-THOMPSON, Jack (b 1914)
English dramatist ES
LE FANU, Alicia (1753-1817)
dramatist DNB
LEFANU, Peter (fl 1778) dramatist
CP/3, DNB
LE FANU, Sheridan (1814-73)
dramatist HP
LEFEAUX, Charles (b 1909) Eng-
lish actor, director WWT/9-15
LE FEUVRE, Guy (1883-1950)
Canadian actor, singer, com-
poser WWT/10
LEFEVRE, Mrs. see Bride,
Elizabeth
LEFFINGWELL, Miron [or Myron]
Winslow (1828-79) American ac-
tor HAS, CDP
LEFFINGWELL, Mrs. Miron [Win-
slow] (b 1836) American actress
HAS
LEFFLER, Adam (1805-57) English
singer CDP, HAS
LEFFLER, Adam (d 1905 [76])
actor EA/06*, WWT/14*
LEFFLER, George (d 1951 [77])
American producer BE*, BP/
36*
LEFFLER, John (1875-1947) mana-
ger, producer SR
LEFKOWITZ, Nat (b 1905) Ameri-
can executive, talent representa-
tive BE
LEFORT, Adrien see Charvay,
Robert
Le FRE, Albert (d 1970 [99]) per-
former BP/54*
LE FRE, Albert William (d 1905
[13]) EA/05*

LE FRE, Elizabeth [Mrs. James Le Fre] (d 1903 [47]) EA/04*

LE FRE, Mrs. James see Le Fre, Elizabeth

LE FRE, William (d 1894 [34]) performer? EA/95*

LEFTLY, Charles (fl 1802) dramatist CP/3

LEFTWICH, Alexander (d 1947 [63]) producer TW/3, WWT/ 6-9

LEFTWICH, Alexander (d 1974 [66]) producer/director/choreographer BP/59*

LEGA, Mons. (d 1868) circus performer? EA/69*

LE GALLIENNE, Eva (b 1899) English actress, producer, director, translator AAS, BE, CB, COC, ES, GT, NTH, OC/1-3, SR, TW/2-22, 24, WWT/4-16

LEGARD, [Charles?] see Delagarde, [Charles?]

LEGARDE, Millie actress, singer CDP, GRB/3-4, WWT/1-5

LEGAT, Nadine (d 1971 [81]) performer BP/55*

LEGAT, Nikolai (1869-1937) Russian dancer, choreographer ES

LEGE, Mr. (fl 1796) actor HAS

LEGE, Mrs. (fl 1796) actress HAS

LEGG, Miss see Duncan, Mrs. Timothy

LEGGATT, Alison Joy (b 1904) English actress AAS, WWT/ 6-16

LEGGATT, Steve (d 1896) music-hall songwriter EA/97*

LEGGE, Lydia Alice see Foote, Lydia

LEGGE, R. G. (b 1864) English manager GRB/1

LEGGE, Thomas (d 1607 [72]) English dramatist CP/1-3, FGF

LEGGETT, Mr. (fl 1826) actor HAS

LEGGETT, Emma Elizabeth [Mrs. R. Leggett] (d 1901) burlesque actress EA/03*

LEGGETT, Mrs. R. see Leggett, Emma Elizabeth

LEGGETT, Richard (d 1906) music-hall comedian EA/07*

LEGHERE, Mrs. Leopold see Naroni, Mlle.

LEGIONAIRE, Robert (b 1926) American actor TW/27

LEGLERE, Alice [Mrs. George Leglere] (d 1896 [35]) acrobat EA/97*

LEGLERE, Artois Leopold (d 1886 [55]) pantomimist EA/87*

LEGLERE, Mrs. George see Leglere, Alice

LEGLERE, Louis (d 1885) EA/86*

LE GRAND, Mlle. [Mrs. F. Galloway] (d 1898) tank performer EA/99*

LEGRAND, Claude Maria Eugent see Dauphin, Claude

LEGRAND, Eugénie [Mrs. Kyrle Bellew] (fl 1882-84) actress CDP

LE GRAND, Phyllis actress, singer WWT/2-7

LE GRYS, Sir Robert (fl 1629-60) dramatist CP/2-3, FGF

LE GUERE, George (d 1947 [66]) American actor TW/4

LEHAR, Franz (1870-1948) Austrian composer GRB/3-4, WWS, WWT/1-2, 9-10

LE HAY, Daisy (b 1883) actress, singer WWT/2-5

LE HAY, John [John Healy] (1854-1926) Irish actor DP, EA/97, GRB/1-4, WWT/1-5

LEHMAN, Adelaide HAS

LEHMAN, Andrew (d 1863 [30]) pantomimist HAS

LEHMAN, Anna (d 1868 [32]) HAS

LEHMAN, Christian (d 1868 [73]) HAS

LEHMAN, Moriz (d 1877 [58]) scene painter EA/78*

LEHMAN, Susan (b 1940) American actress TW/27

LEHMAN, Walter M. (fl 1827-56) American actor, call boy HAS

LEHMAN FAMILY, The HAS

LEHMANN, Beatrix (b 1903) English actress AAS, WWT/7-16

LEHMANN, Carla (b 1917) Canadian actress WWT/10-11

LEHMANN, Caroline (fl 1847) CDP

LEHMANN, Lilli (1848-1929) German singer ES

LEHMANN, Liza [Mrs. Herbert Bedford] (d 1918) singer, composer CDP

LEHMANN, Lotte (1888-1976)

German singer CB, ES
LEHMANN, Maurice (d 1974
[79]) producer/director/
choreographer BP/58*
LEHN, Norma American actress
TW/2
LEHR, Harry (1830-81) minstrel
CDP
LEHR, Wilson (b 1913) American
educator BE
LEHRER, George (d 1966 [77])
performer BP/51*
LEIBER, Fritz (1882/83/84-
1949) American actor DAB,
NTH, TW/6, WWM, WWT/
7-10
LEIBMAN, Ron (b 1937) Ameri-
can actor TW/25-26, WWT/
15-16
LEIBOWITZ, Rene (d 1972 [59])
composer/lyricist BP/57*
LEICESTER, Mr. (fl 1830-37)
American actor, singer CDP,
HAS
LEICESTER, Charles (d 1907)
actor EA/08*
LEICESTER, Ernest (1866-1939)
actor EA/97, GRB/3-4,
WWT/1-6
LEICESTER, George F. (d 1916
[72]) actor BE*, EA/17*,
WWT/14*
LEICESTER, Lillie (d 1884)
singer EA/85*
LEICHNER, Ludwig (b 1836)
singer, inventor of grease
paint COC
LEIDER, Frida (1888-1975) Ger-
man singer ES
LEIGH, Adèle (b 1928) English
singer ES
LEIGH, Andrew George (1887-
1957) English actor, producer
WWT/5-11
LEIGH, Anthony (d 1692) Eng-
lish actor CDP, COC, DNB,
OC/1-3
LEIGH, Carol (b 1933) American
actress TW/10
LEIGH, Carolyn American lyri-
cist BE
LEIGH, Charlotte (b 1907) Eng-
lish actress, singer WWT/
9-10
LEIGH, Dorma (b 1893) English
actress, dancer WWT/4-8
LEIGH, George (d 1909 [76])
actor EA/10*

LEIGH, Georgie (d 1884) singer
EA/85*
LEIGH, Gracie [Mrs. Lionel Mac-
kinder] (d 1950 [75]) actress
GRB/1-4, WWT/1-10
LEIGH, Henry (d 1881 [63]) actor
EA/82*, WWT/14*
LEIGH, Mrs. Henry (d 1915 [90])
actress WWT/14*
LEIGH, Henry Sambrooke (1837-
83) English dramatist DNB
LEIGH, J. H. (d 1934 [75]) pro-
ducer, actor, scholar BE*,
WWT/14*
LEIGH, John (d 1726 [37]) Irish
actor, dramatist CP/1-3, GT,
TD/1-2
LEIGH, Miss Marston [Mrs. James
Carden] (d 1897) actress EA/98*
LEIGH, Mary (1904-43) English
actress, singer WWT/5-7
LEIGH, Philip (d 1935 [55]) actor
BE*, BP/20*, WWT/14*
LEIGH, Richard (fl 1809) dramatist
CP/3
LEIGH, Rowland (1902-63) drama-
tist, lyricist WWT/7-13
LEIGH, Stella [Mrs. George Mal-
lett] English actress GRB/1
LEIGH, Vivien [Vivian Mary Hart-
ley] (1913-67) Indian/English
actress AAS, BE, CB, COC,
ES, OC/2-3, PDT, TW/8-24,
WWA/4, WWT/8-14, WWW/6
LEIGH, Walter (b 1905) English
composer WWT/9
LEIGH-HUNT, Barbara (b 1935)
English actress TW/24
LEIGHTON, Alexes (d 1926) ac-
tress BE*, WWT/14*
LEIGHTON, Bert (d 1964 [87])
performer, songwriter BE*
LEIGHTON, Betty (b 1920) English
actress TW/29
LEIGHTON, Clara [Mrs. E. Lew-
is] (d 1913) EA/14*
LEIGHTON, Frank (1908-62) Aus-
tralian actor WWT/10-13
LEIGHTON, Harry (d 1913 [42])
EA/14*
LEIGHTON, Harry (1866-1926)
American actor WWM
LEIGHTON, Margaret [Mrs. Mar-
garet Alcott] (d 1908 [56]) Welsh
actress CDP, OAA/1-2
LEIGHTON, Margaret (1922-76)
English actress AAS, BE, CB,
COC, ES, OC/3, PDT, TW/2,

13-20, 22, 24, WWT/10-16
LEIGHTON, Queenie (1872-1943)
    actress, singer GRB/1-4,
    WWT/4-6
LEIGHTON, Mrs. W. H. actress
    HAS
LEINSDORF, Erich (b 1912)
    Austrian conductor CB
LEIPZIG, Nate (1873-1939) Swed-
    ish magician DAB
LEISEN, Mitchell (d 1972 [74])
    producer/director/choreographer
    BP/57*
LEISH, Kenneth William (b 1936)
    American critic BE
LEISTER, Frederick (1885-1970)
    English actor WWT/6-14
LEITCH, George (d 1907) actor,
    dramatist EA/08*
LEITCH, William Leighton (1804-
    83) Scottish scene painter
    DNB
LEITZEL, Lillian (1891/93-1931)
    German aerial performer SR
LEIVICK, H. [Leivick Halpern]
    (1888-1962) Russian/American
    dramatist MH, MWD, RE
LEJARS, Mme. (d 1899) eques-
    trienne CDP
LEJEUNE, C. A. (d 1973 [76])
    critic BP/57*
LEKAIN, Henri Louis Cain
    (1728-78) French actor CDP
LELAND, Aaron W. (1761-1833)
    American dramatist EAP
LELAND, Rosa M. [Mrs. Rosa
    St. Clair] (d 1889) actress,
    manager EA/90*
LELOIR, Louis (d 1909 [49])
    actor WWT/14*
LELY, Durward (d 1944 [91])
    actor DP
LE MAIGNEN, Jeanne see
    Brillant, Marie
LEMAIRE, Fred (d 1896) music-
    hall singer EA/97*
LE MAIRE, George (d 1930
    [46]) comedian BE*
LEMAIRE, Harry (d 1896) music-
    hall singer EA/97*
LeMAIRE, Rufus (d 1950 [55])
    American producer BP/35*
LEMAITRE, Antoine-Louis-
    Prosper see Frédérick
LEMAITRE, Frédérick (1800-
    76) French actor ES
LEMAITRE, Jules (1853-1914)
    French dramatist GRB/1, 3-4

LEMARE, Edwin Henry (1866-
    1934) English composer WWA/1
LE MASSENA, William (b 1916)
    American actor BE, TW/6-17,
    19-20, 22, 24-26, 28, WWT/
    15-16
LEMBECK, Harvey (b 1923) Amer-
    ican actor BE, TW/4-8
LEMMENS-SHERRINGTON, Helen
    (1834-1906) singer DNB
LEMMON, Harry see Warde,
    George Henry
LEMMON, Jack (b 1925) American
    actor BE, CB, ES
LEMMON, Priscilla see Warde,
    Mrs. George
LEMMON, Shirley (b 1948) Amer-
    ican actress TW/30
LEMON, Mark (1809-70) English
    dramatist CDP, COC, DNB,
    EA/68, HP, OC/1-3
LEMON, Mrs. Mark (d 1890)
    EA/91*
LEMONT, John (d 1888) American
    acrobat EA/89*
LEMORE, Clara [Mrs. Clara
    Lemore Roberts] (d 1898 [48])
    actress EA/99*
LEMORE, Harry (d 1898) music-
    hall singer EA/99*
LE MOYNE, Sarah Cowell (1859-
    1915) American actress CDP,
    PP/2, WWS, WWT/1-2
LE MOYNE, William J. (1831-
    1905) American actor CDP,
    DAB, PP/2, WWA/1
LENA, Lily [Mrs. Alice Lily New-
    house] (b 1879) English come-
    dian CDP, WWM
LENARD, Mark (b 1927) American
    actor BE
LENDER, Marcelle (d 1926 [64])
    actress BE*, WWT/14*
LE NEVE, Marion (d 1897) music-
    hall performer EA/98*
LENG, Fred G. (d 1878) musical
    director EA/79*
LENGEL, Elijah (fl 1848-68) Amer-
    ican animal tamer CDP, HAS
LENGEL, William C. (d 1965
    [77]) dramatist BP/50*
LENGYEL, Menyhert (1880-1974?)
    Hungarian dramatist NTH
LENIER, A. W. (fl 1855) actor
    HAS
LENIHAN, Brigid (d 1970 [41])
    performer BP/55*
LENIHAN, Burton (d 1974 [96])

performer BP/59*
LENIHAN, Wilfred T. (d 1972
[89]) manager BP/57*
LENIHAN, Winifred (1898-1964)
American actress TW/21,
WWT/5-11
LENN, Robert (b 1914) American
actor TW/4, 24-25
LENNARD, Arthur (d 1954 [86])
singer, actor CDP
LENNARD, Mrs. Arthur T.
see Lennard, Sophia
LENNARD, Horace (d 1920)
dramatist, lyricist BE*,
WWT/14*
LENNARD, Sophia [Mrs. Arthur
T. Lennard] (d 1909 [21])
EA/10*
LENNART, Isobel (d 1971 [55])
dramatist BP/55*
LENNON, John (d 1908) EA/09*
LENNON, Mathilde singer CDP
LENNON, Nestor Forbes Richard-
son (b 1863) American actor
WWS
LENNON, Tom (d 1963 [67])
journalist BE*
LENNON, William (d 1898 [44])
manager EA/99*
LENNOX (d 1889) aeronaut EA/
90*
LENNOX, Charlotte (1720-1804)
American dramatist CDP,
CP/1-3, DAB, GT, HP,
NTH, TD/1-2, WWA/H
LENNOX, Cosmo Gordon see
Stuart, Cosmo
LENNOX, Fred (fl 1878) come-
dian, singer CDP
LENNOX, Frederick (d 1884)
EA/85*
LENNOX, Fred J. [Frederick
Jeans] (d 1916) EA/17*
LENNOX, James [Jem Collins]
(d 1879) comedian EA/80*
LENNOX, Lottie (d 1947 [61])
actress, singer CDP
LENNOX, Thomas F. (d 1849)
Scottish actor HAS
LENNOX, Vera (b 1904) English
actress, singer WWT/5-11
LENNOX, Walter S. (fl 1867)
American actor HAS
LENNOX, Will (d 1884 [24])
comic singer EA/85*
LENNY, Jack American talent
representative, casting di-
rector, producer BE

LENO, Dan [George Galvin] (1860-
1904) English variety artist,
actor CDP, COC, DNB, ES,
GRB/1, OC/1-3, PDT
LENO, Dan, Jr. see Galvin,
Sydney Paul
LE NOIRE, Rosetta [née Burton]
(b 1911) American actress,
singer, dancer BE, TW/1,
15-23, 25, 28-30, WWT/14-16
LENON, Edmund Fitz-Maurice
see Maurice, Edmund
LENORE, Fred [Frederick Smith]
(d 1903) music-hall performer
EA/05*
LENORMAND, Henri-René (1882-
1951) French dramatist COC,
MWD
LENS, Patricia (b 1947) American
actress TW/25-29
LENSCHOW, Charles (d 1890) con-
ductor CDP
LENT, Lewis B. (1813/14-87)
American circus manager CDP,
HAS, NYM, SR
LENTHALL, David (b 1948) Amer-
ican actor TW/29
LENTHALL, Franklyn (b 1919)
American director, producer,
theatre owner, actor BE
LENTO, Mrs. E. [Mrs. Harry
Lento] (d 1891) EA/92*
LENTO, Harry (d 1900 [54]) panto-
mimist EA/01*
LENTO, Mrs. Harry see Lento,
Mrs. E.
LENTON, Harry (d 1884) singer
EA/85*
LENTON, J. (d 1895) ventriloquist
EA/96*
LENTON, Lance (d 1900) variety
performer EA/01*
LENTON, Thomas (d 1878 [47])
gymnast, acrobat, clown, ceil-
ing walker EA/79*
LENTZ, Abraham (d 1975 [64])
writer BP/60*
LENYA, Lotte [née Karoline
Blamauer] (b 1900) Austrian
actress, singer BE, CB, PDT,
TW/1, 10-12, 23-25, WWT/15-
16
LENZ, Rick (b 1939) American
actor TW/23-24, 26
LEO, Beatrice (fl 1884?) singer
CDP
LEO, Frank (d 1940 [66]) com-
poser CDP

LEO, Tom (b 1936) American
actor TW/30

LEON, Mr. (d 1844) minstrel
SR

LEON, Anne (b 1925) English
actress WWT/11-14

LEON, Dan (1826-63) minstrel
HAS

LEON, Francis (b 1840/44)
American dancer, singer,
minstrel manager CDP, HAS

LEON, Frank (d 1909) variety
dancer EA/10*

LEON, Geoff American actor
TW/28-29

LEON, Henry Cecil see Cecil,
Henry

LEON, John see Standing,
John

LEON, Joseph (d 1917 [63])
proprietor, musician EA/18*

LEON, Joseph (b 1923) American
actor TW/28, 30

LEON, W. D. (d 1964 [78]) performer, theatre operator BE*

LEON, William Henry (d 1901
[34]) variety performer
EA/03*

LEONARD, Agnes (d 1890 [38])
actress CDP

LEONARD, Billy (1892/95-1974)
Irish actor BTR/74, WWT/
4-13

LEONARD, Denis (d 1878 [78])
Irish comedian EA/79*

LEONARD, Eddie (1871?/75-
1941) American minstrel,
vaudevillian, comedian, songwriter CB, CDP

LEONARD, Frank (d 1904 [28])
acrobat EA/05*

LEONARD, Frederick see
Lonsdale, Frederick

LEONARD, Georgina (fl 1900s?)
actress, singer CDP

LEONARD, Hugh [né John Keyes
Byrne] (b 1926) Irish dramatist AAS, CD, CH, WWT/
14-16

LEONARD, Mrs. J. A. see
Sefton, Mrs. Joseph

LEONARD, Jack E. (d 1973
[61]) comedian WWT/16*

LEONARD, Joseph A. (b 1830)
American actor HAS

LEONARD, Julie (b 1923) American talent representative,
casting consultant BE

LEONARD, Louise see Russell,
Lillian

LEONARD, Mabel (fl 1876) actress
CDP

LEONARD, Marion (d 1956 [75])
actress BE*

LEONARD, Murray (d 1970 [72])
performer BP/55*

LEONARD, Patricia (b 1916) English actress, singer WWT/9-11

LEONARD, Patrick A. (d 1971
[82]) performer BP/55*

LEONARD, Robert (1889-1948)
actor ES, TW/4, WWT/4-10

LEONARD, Tom (d 1878 [27])
comic singer EA/79*

LEONARD, William Ellery (1876-
1944) American writer HJD

LEONARD-BOYNE, Eva (1883/85-
1960) English actress TW/1,
3, 8, 12-13, WWT/4-12

LEONARDO, Harry (d 1964 [61])
performer BP/49*

LEONARDOS, Urylee American
actress TW/25-26, 30

LEONCAVALLO, Ruggero (1858-
1919) Italian composer ES

LEONE, Henry (d 1922 [64]) actor,
singer BE*, BP/6*

LEONE, Leonard (b 1914) American
educator BE

LEONE, Maude (d 1930 [45]) actress BE*, WWT/14*

LEONI, Mr. (d 1797) singer, actor
CDP, GT, TD/1-2

LEONI, Henri actor, singer CDP

LEONIDOFF, Leon (b 1895) Rumanian producer CB

LEONIE, Annie [Mrs. Edward
Colley] (d 1899) serio-comic
EA/00*

LEONOV, Leonid Maximovich (b
1899) Russian dramatist COC,
OC/3

LEONTINE, Countess (b 1881)
French singer WWM

LEONTOVITCH, Eugenie (b 1894/
1900) Russian actress, director,
dramatist AAS, BE, NTH,
TW/3-8, 14-15, 28-29, WWT/
7-16

LEOPOLD, Bertha (d 1905 [26])
EA/06*

LEOPOLD, George (d 1895) gymnast EA/96*

LEOPOLD, Harry (d 1904) acrobat
EA/05*

LEOPOLD, Lydia [Mrs. William

Leopold] (d 1899 [53]) EA/00*
LEOPOLD, Sid (d 1897 [23])
pantomimist EA/98*
LEOPOLD, William (d 1888) per-
former? EA/89*
LEOPOLD, Mrs. William see
Leopold, Lydia
LEOTARD, Jules (1830-70) French
gymnast HAS, OC/3
LEOTI, Mr. (fl 1848) actor?
HAS
LEOTI, Mrs. (fl 1848) actress?
HAS
LEPIN, Emanuel (d 1972 [55])
composer/lyricist BP/57*
LEPORSKA, Zoya (b 1920) Rus-
sian actress TW/28
LEPRIS, Sig. (d 1893) ballet
master EA/94*
LE RAE, Grace (d 1956 [75])
actress BE*, WWT/14*
LERIGO, Charles (d 1907 [71])
actor EA/08*
LERMAN, Omar K. (b 1927)
American producer, theatre
consultant BE
LERNER, Alan Jay (b 1918)
American dramatist, lyricist
AAS, BE, CB, CD, ES,
HJD, MWD, PDT, WWT/14-16
LERNER, Carl (d 1973 [61])
performer BP/58*
LERNER, Robert (b 1921) Amer-
ican producer BE
LEROUX, Camille (fl 1843)
French equestrienne CDP
LeROUX, Madeleine (b 1946)
American actress TW/27-30
LEROY, Ernie (d 1917) come-
dian EA/18*
LeROY, Gloria American actress
TW/25, 27
LeROY, Ken (b 1927) American
actor, dancer BE, TW/14,
25-29
LeROY, Loretta (d 1975 [77])
performer BP/60*
LE ROY, Warner (b 1935) Amer-
ican producer, director, actor
BE
LESAGE (d 1882) singer EA/83*
LE SAGE, Geraldine (d 1913
[25]) EA/14*
LE SAGE, Stanley (1880-1932)
English business manager
WWT/2-5
LESAN, David E. (d 1974 [64])
producer/director/choreographer

BP/58*
LESBOROUGH, Violet (d 1910) per-
former? EA/11*
LESDERNIER, Emily (fl 1851-54)
reader, actress HAS
LESLEY, Brenda American actress
TW/23
LESLEY, Carole (d 1974 [38])
performer BP/58*
LESLEY, George (fl 1675-76) Scot-
tish? dramatist CP/2-3
LESLIE, Mrs. (d 1887) EA/88*
LESLIE, Alfred (d 1876) comedian
EA/77*
LESLIE, Alfred (b 1875) English
actor GRB/1
LESLIE, Alfred see Lester,
Alfred
LESLIE, Amy (1860-1939) American
critic, actress WWA/4
LESLIE, Arthur (d 1894 [30]) drama-
tist EA/95*
LESLIE, Arthur (d 1970 [68]) per-
former BP/55*
LESLIE, Bethel (b 1929) American
actress TW/7-9, 21-22, 25
LESLIE, Charlotte Jane [Mrs. T.
N. Leslie] (d 1878) EA/79*
LESLIE, Coss (d 1890) musician,
comedian EA/91*
LESLIE, Edgar (d 1976 [90]) lyri-
cist BP/60*, WWT/16*
LESLIE, Edwin (b 1867) English
manager GRB/1
LESLIE, Elsie [Mrs. W. J. Winter]
(1880/81-1966) American actress
PP/1, WWM, WWS
LESLIE, Enid (d 1890 [34]) actress
CDP
LESLIE, Enid (b 1888) English ac-
tress WWT/2-5
LESLIE, Fannie [or Fanny] (1856-
1935) actress, singer CDP
LESLIE, Frank (b 1926) American
actor TW/8-9
LESLIE, Fred [Fred Hobson] (b
1881) English actor WWT/2-7
LESLIE, Fred[erick] (1855-92)
English actor, dramatist, singer
CDP, DNB, DP, NTH
LESLIE, Mrs. Fred (d 1891 [33])
EA/92*
LESLIE, George W. (d 1911 [48])
actor WWT/14*
LESLIE, Grace [Mrs. George S.
Tutton] (1861-87) actress, singer
NYM
LESLIE, Harry (1837-76) American

tight-rope performer, proprietor, minstrel CDP, HAS

LESLIE, Henry (1830-81) English dramatist, actor EA/68

LESLIE, Henry David (d 1896 [74]) composer EA/97*

LESLIE, Henry J. (d 1900) manager, composer CDP

LESLIE, H. L. [Leslie Lovell] (d 1916) singer EA/17*

LESLIE, Ida (b 1844) American actress HAS

LESLIE, James Orr (d 1907 [70]) singer EA/08*

LESLIE, Lew (1886-1963) composer, producer TW/19, WWT/8-10

LESLIE, Lillian (fl 1895?) singer, actress CDP

LESLIE, Marguerite (1884-1958) Swedish actress GRB/4, WWT/1-6

LESLIE, Marie see Coughtrie, Rosa Ann

LESLIE, Mary (d 1945) English actress SR

LESLIE, May (d 1965 [84]) performer BP/50*

LESLIE, Minnie [Mrs. John Cecil] (d 1907 [38]) actress, dancer GRB/3

LESLIE, Noel (1888-1974) English actor TW/4, 15, 30

LESLIE, Scott (d 1975) performer BP/60*

LESLIE, Sid [Leslie Talford Munford] (b 1882) English actor, singer GRB/1

LESLIE, Sylvia (b 1900) English actress, singer WWT/5-11

LESLIE, Mrs. T. N. see Leslie, Charlotte Jane

LESLIE, Tom (d 1964 [68]) performer BE*

LESLIE, Vera actress GRB/1-2

LESLIE, Will [W. W. Pigott] (d 1911 [39]) EA/12*

LESLIE, William minstrel CDP

LESLIE-STUART, May English actress WWT/2-7

LESMERE, Henry [Strangways Churton Collins] (b 1876) English actor GRB/1

LESSAC, Arthur (b 1910) Palestinian voice teacher & therapist BE

LESSANE, Leroy (b 1942) American actor TW/28

LESSER, Amy (fl 1899-1911) American actress WWM

LESSEY, Mrs. George see Abbey, May Evers

LESSEY, Percy (d 1890) actor EA/91*

LESSING, Doris (b 1919/21) South African dramatist CB, CD, CH, MD, MWD, PDT

LESSING, Gotthold Ephraim (1729-81) German dramatist, critic COC, OC/1-3

LESSING, Madge [Mrs. McClellan] English actress, singer GRB/1-4, WWS, WWT/1-8

LESSINGHAM, Jane (d 1774) actress CDP

LESTER, Ada (d 1881) actress EA/82*

LESTER, Alfred [Alfred Leslie] (1872/74-1925) English actor GRB/4, WWT/1-5

LESTER, Annie [Mrs. Leo Lester] (d 1906) EA/07*

LESTER, Barbara (b 1928) English actress TW/26-29

LESTER, Charles H. English actor GRB/1

LESTER, Edwin American producer, executive BE

LESTER, The Great [Maryan Czajowski] (b 1880) Polish ventriloquist WWM

LESTER, Harry (d 1908) secretary EA/09*

LESTER, Kate English actress WWS

LESTER, Keith (b 1904) English dancer, choreographer ES

LESTER, Ketty (b 1938) American actress TW/20

LESTER, Mrs. Leo see Lester, Annie

LESTER, Mark (b 1876) English actor WWT/4-11

LESTER, William (1889-1956) English composer, musician WWA/3

LESTER, Mrs. William see Hart, Annie

LESTOCK, Charles (d 1900) acting manager EA/01*

LESTOCQ, George (d 1924) actor, director BE*, WWT/14*

LESTOCQ, William [Lestocq Boileau Woolridge] (d 1920 [69]) actor, manager DP, GRB/1-4, WWT/1-3

L'ESTRANGE, Mr. (fl 1796) English

actor HAS
L'ESTRANGE, Mrs. (fl 1796)
English actress HAS
L'ESTRANGE, Jules [or Julian]
(1878-1918) actor GRB/3-4,
WWT/1-3
L'ESTRANGE, Mary (d 1885 [25])
EA/86*
L'ESTRANGE, Nellie singer,
actress CDP
LeSTRANGE, Philip (b 1942)
American actor TW/26, 30
LESTREE, Charles (d 1917)
manager EA/18*
LE SUEUR, Charles (b 1879)
English singer GRB/1-3
LeSUEUR, Hal (d 1963 [59])
actor BE*
LETCHFORD, John (d 1874) actor
EA/76*
LETHBRIDGE, J. W. English
acting manager GRB/3-4,
WWT/1-2
LETHCOURT, H. J. [J. H.
Lorimer] (d 1897 [41]) actor
EA/98*, WWT/14*
LE THIERE, Roma Guillon (d
1903) Italian actress OAA/
1-2
LETTERI, Al (d 1975 [47]) per-
former BP/60*
LETTERS, Will (d 1910 [33])
singer, composer CDP
LETTON, Francis (b 1912)
American dramatist, director,
actor BE
LETTS, Pauline (b 1917) English
actress WWT/10-16
LETTY, Frances (d 1918) EA/19*
LeVAKE, Dorothy Jean see
Darling, Jean
LEVAN, Harry (d 1963 [61])
performer BE*
LEVANI, Henry (d 1870 [20])
trapezist EA/71*
LEVANT, Oscar (1906-72) Amer-
ican composer, musician CB
LEVANTINE, Frederick F. (fl
1866) equilibrist CDP
LEVASSEUR, Mons. (d 1871)
singer EA/73*
LEVE, Samuel (b 1910) scene
designer TW/2-4, 6-8
LEVEAUX, Montagu V. (b 1875)
English manager WWT/2-3
L'EVEILLE, Auguste (d 1882
[52]) composer EA/83*
LEVENE, Mrs. George see

Levene, Madeline A.
LEVENE, Madeline A. [Mrs. George
Levene] (d 1890 [31]) EA/91*
LEVENE, Samuel (b 1905/07) Amer-
ican actor BE, TW/2-24, 26-27,
29-30, WWT/9-16
LEVENS, Chrissy see Wardell,
Chrystabel Elizabeth
LEVENS, Eva (d 1900 [30]) singer,
dancer EA/01*
LEVENSTON, Michael (d 1904
[48]) manager EA/05*, WWT/
14*
LE VENT, J. (d 1871) gymnast
EA/72*
LEVENTHAL, Jules (1889-1949)
Russian producer TW/5
LEVER, Lady Arthur Levy (d 1917)
dramatist EA/18*
LEVER, J. W. (d 1975 [62]) drama-
tist BP/60*
LEVERE, Mr. American actor
HAS
LEVERIDGE, Lynn Ann (b 1948)
American actress TW/28-30
LEVERIDGE, Richard (c. 1670-1758)
English dramatist, singer, com-
poser CDP, CP/2-3, DNB
LEVERING, Annie (b 1830) Ameri-
can actress HAS
LEVERSEE, Loretta (b 1928) Amer-
ican actress TW/10-16, 18-19
LEVERTON, George [or Garrett]
H. (d 1949 [52]) American edu-
cator, editor BE*, BP/34*
LEVERTON, Henry Fergus (d 1876
[35]) musical director EA/77*
LEVERTON, W. H. (d 1941 [75])
box-office keeper WWT/14*
LEVESON, John (d 1905 [75]) singer
EA/06*
LEVESON, Robert (fl 1580) actor
DA
LEVETT, George (d 1901 [21])
acrobat EA/03*
LEVETTEZ, Edward Ernest (d
1894) EA/95*
LEVEY, Adèle (fl 1900s?) singer,
actress CDP
LEVEY, Carlotta (fl 1900s?) sing-
er, actress CDP
LEVEY, Charles (b 1877) English
actor GRB/1
LEVEY, Ethel (1881-1955) Ameri-
can actress, singer TW/2-4,
11, WWS, WWT/1-11
LEVEY, Florence (fl 1895) dancer,
singer CDP

LEVEY, Harold A. (d 1967 [73])
composer TW/24
LEVEY, John (d 1891) dramatist,
actor EA/92*
LEVEY, Joseph (d 1899 [44])
circus manager EA/00*
LEVEY, Jules (d 1903) musician
EA/04*
LEVEY, Jules (d 1975 [78]) pro-
ducer/director/choreographer
BP/59*
LEVEY, May Lilian singer CDP
LEVEY, Nellie [Mrs. J. H.
Anderson] (d 1916) EA/17*
LEVEY, R. M. (d 1899) con-
ductor EA/00*
LEVEY, W. C. (d 1894 [57])
composer, conductor EA/95*
LEVI, A. actor? HAS
LEVI, Baruk (b 1947) American
actor TW/28-29
LEVICK, Gustavus (1854-1909)
actor CDP
LEVICK, Halper (1888-1962)
dramatist OC/1-3
LEVICK, Milnes (1825/27-97)
English actor CDP, SR
LEVILLY, Jacques (d 1893)
EA/94*
LEVIN, Bernard critic BE
LEVIN, David (b 1932) American
actor TW/12-15
LEVIN, Harry (d 1972 [68])
ticket broker BP/56*
LEVIN, Herman (b 1907) Amer-
ican producing manager BE,
WWT/11-16
LEVIN, Ira (b 1929) American
dramatist BE
LEVIN, Meyer (b 1905) Ameri-
can dramatist BE, HJD, MD
LEVIN, Michael (b 1932) Amer-
ican actor TW/22-23, 26-27
LEVIN, Philip J. (d 1971 [62])
executive BP/56*
LEVINE, Charles B. (d 1974
[75]) creator of Broadway
displays BP/59*
LEVINE, Elliot (b 1924) American
actor TW/23
LEVINE, James (b 1943) Amer-
ican conductor CB
LEVINE, Joseph (d 1964 [68])
lawyer BE*
LEVINE, Joseph E. (b 1905)
American producer BE
LEVINE, Joseph I. (b 1926)
American producer, lawyer BE

LeVINESS, Carl (d 1964 [79]) per-
former BP/49*
LEVINSON, Barry (b 1932) Ameri-
can talent representative BE
LEVINSON, Leonard Louis (d 1974
[69]) dramatist BP/58*
LEVIS, Dora actress GRB/1
LEVISON, Alfred (d 1907 [46])
circus manager EA/09*
LEVI-TANAI, Sara Israeli director,
composer, choreographer CB
LEVITE, Jessie Nina (d 1883)
EA/85*
LEVITE, Katie (d 1903) EA/04*
LEVITON, Stewart (b 1939) English
lighting designer WWT/16
LEVITT, Paul (b 1926) American
producer BE
LEVITT, Sanford (b 1947) American
actor TW/30
LEVITT, Saul (b 1913) American
dramatist BE
LEVOY, Albert E. (d 1972 [70])
producer/director/choreographer
BP/57*
LEVY, Benn W. (1900-73) English
dramatist AAS, BE, MD, MH,
MWD, NTH, TW/30, WWT/6-15
LEVY, Burton see Lane, Burton
LEVY, Edwin L. (b 1917) American
educator, director BE
LEVY, Helen Marsh (d 1962) Amer-
ican journalist BE*
LEVY, Mrs. J. see Fox, Della
LEVY, Jacques (b 1935) American
director WWT/15-16
LEVY, Jean see Eckart, Jean
LEVY, J. Langley (d 1945 [74])
critic, journalist BE*, WWT/
14*
LEVY, Jonas (d 1894) lawyer EA/
95*
LEVY, José G. (1884-1936) English
manager, dramatist WWT/3-8
LEVY, Leon Ralph (d 1975 [75])
designer BP/60*
LEVY, Marianne see Tearle,
Marianne
LEVY, Sylvan (d 1962 [56]) per-
former BE*
LEWELLEN, Mr. English actor
HAS
LEWELLEN, Mrs. actress HAS
LEWELLEN, Hester (b 1946)
American actress TW/30
LEWES, Charles Lee (1740-1803)
English actor CDP, DNB,
OC/1-3

LEWES, Charles Lee (d 1891)
EA/92*

LEWES, Mrs. Charles Lee (fl 1792) actress CDP

LEWES, George Henry (1817-78) English dramatist, critic COC, DNB, EA/69, ES, OC/1-3, PDT

LEWES, Miriam Russian/English actress GRB/2-4, WWT/1-9

LEWESTEIN, Oscar (b 1917) English manager WWT/14-16

LEWIN, Thomas Herbert F. see Terriss, Tom

LEWINE, Irving I. (d 1965 [84]) theatre owner BP/49*

LEWINE, Richard (b 1910) American composer, producer BE

LEWINSKY, Josef (d 1907 [72]) actor WWT/14*

LEWIS, Abby (b 1910) American actress BE, TW/24, 27

LEWIS, Ada (c. 1875-1925) American actress CDP, SR, WWM, WWS, WWT/4-5

LEWIS, Allan (b 1908) American educator, critic, director BE

LEWIS, Alwyn (d 1893 [29]) acting manager EA/94*

LEWIS, Ann (d 1975 [76]) journalist? BP/59*

LEWIS, Arthur (1846-1930) English actor, manager DAB, SR, WWT/1-6

LEWIS, Arthur (b 1916) American producer, director WWT/14-16

LEWIS, Mrs. Arthur see Terry, Kate

LEWIS, Arthur James (d 1901 [76]) EA/02*

LEWIS, Bertha (b 1831) English actress HAS

LEWIS, Bertha (1887-1931) English actress, singer WWT/4-6

LEWIS, Brenda (b 1921) American singer, actress BE, TW/11

LEWIS, Carole Ann (b 1939) American actress TW/23-24

LEWIS, Catherine (1856-1942) actress, singer CDP

LEWIS, Cathy (d 1968 [50]) performer BP/53*

LEWIS, Charles Bertrand (1842-1924) American dramatist DAB

LEWIS, Charles M. (b 1836) American actor HAS

LEWIS, Curigwen Welsh actress WWT/9-11

LEWIS, Curtis R. (d 1969 [50]) composer/lyricist BP/54*

LEWIS, Dan (fl 1890?) songwriter CDP

LEWIS, Darrelene (d 1975 [18]) performer BP/59*

LEWIS, Dave (1870-1924) American actor WWA/5

LEWIS, David (fl 1727-47) dramatist CP/1-3, GT

LEWIS, David (b 1916) American actor TW/8, 10

LEWIS, Mrs. E. see Leighton, Clara

LEWIS, Edward (fl 1754-69) dramatist CP/2-3, GT

LEWIS, Edward (1866-1922) English actor CDP? EA/97

LEWIS, Emily see Bland, Mrs. Humphrey

LEWIS, Emory (b 1919) American critic BE

LEWIS, Eric [Tuffley] (1855-1935) English actor DP, EA/95, GRB/1-4, WWT/1-7

LEWIS, Estelle Anna Blanche Robinson (1824-80) American dramatist WWA/H

LEWIS, Frank (fl 1850?) minstrel CDP

LEWIS, Frank A. (d 1963 [71]) director BE*

LEWIS, Fred (1860-1927) English actor WWT/1-5

LEWIS, Frederick G. (1873-1946) American actor GRB/3-4, TW/2, WWM, WWS, WWT/1-8

LEWIS, Fred Irving actor TW/1

LEWIS, Mrs. G. [Adelaide Downing] (d 1870) actress EA/72*

LEWIS, George (d 1893) music-hall performer CDP

LEWIS, Mrs. George see Bullen, Julia

LEWIS, George W. (1827-53) American actor, prompter, agent HAS

LEWIS, Gilbert (b 1941) American actor TW/26, 28, 30

LEWIS, Mrs. H. see Terry, Eliza

LEWIS, Hal (d 1934 [61]) business manager WWT/14*

LEWIS, Henrietta see Henderson, Mrs. William
LEWIS, Henry singer, actor CDP
LEWIS, Henry (1803-92) English actor CDP, HAS
LEWIS, Henry (b 1932) American conductor CB
LEWIS, Mrs. Henry [née Harvey] (d 1855) English actress CDP, HAS
LEWIS, Henry Naish (d 1862 [46]) actor WWT/14*
LEWIS, Horace (fl 1869-1900) American actor PP/2
LEWIS, Ida (d 1935 [86]) actress BE*, WWT/14*
LEWIS, Ida T. (d 1879 [24]) dancer EA/80*
LEWIS, James (1837/40-96) American actor CDP, DAB, SR, WWA/H
LEWIS, Jane (d 1907) EA/08*
LEWIS, Jeffreys (c. 1857-1926) English actress CDP, SR
LEWIS, Jerry (b 1926) American comedian CB
LEWIS, Mrs. Joe see Ward, Fanny
LEWIS, Joe E. (d 1971 [69]) performer BP/56*
LEWIS, John (d 1873 [29]) actor EA/74*
LEWIS, John (d 1892) music-hall performer EA/93*
LEWIS, Mrs. John see Baker, Alexina
LEWIS, Larry (d 1974 [106]) performer BP/58*
LEWIS, Leopold David (1828-90) English dramatist DNB
LEWIS, Lillian [Mrs. Lawrence Marsden] (d 1899) American actress WWA/1
LEWIS, Lloyd Downs (1891-1949) American critic, historian, dramatist BE*, BP/33*
LEWIS, Mabel Terry see Terry-Lewis, Mabel
LEWIS, Marcia (b 1938) American actress TW/25-26, 28-29
LEWIS, Martin (1888-1970) English actor WWT/4-13
LEWIS, Mary Sybil (1900-41) American singer CB, WWA/1
LEWIS, Matthew Gregory (1775-1818) English dramatist CDP, COC, CP/3, DNB, GT, HP,

OC/1-3, PDT, TD/1-2
LEWIS, Mel (d 1973 [53]) critic BP/58*
LEWIS, Michael (1930-75) American actor TW/22-24
LEWIS, Mitchell (d 1956 [76]) actor TW/13
LEWIS, Morgan (d 1968 [63]) composer TW/25
LEWIS, Percy (d 1890 [27]) actor EA/92*
LEWIS, Philip (d 1931) musical director BE*, WWT/14*
LEWIS, R. B. (d 1897 [44]) manager EA/98*
LEWIS, Ripple (d 1969 [45]) performer BP/54*
LEWIS, Robert (b 1909) American director, producer, actor BE, TW/3-8, WWT/13-16
LEWIS, Rosie see Haynes, Rosetta
LEWIS, Rudolph (d 1917) actor? singer? EA/18*
LEWIS, Russell (b 1908) American producer BE, TW/3-5, 7
LEWIS, Sam (d 1964) performer BE*
LEWIS, Sarah [Mrs. William Lewis] (d 1886 [68]) EA/87*
LEWIS, Sheldon (1869-1958) American actor TW/14, WWM
LEWIS, Sinclair (1885-1951) American dramatist HJD, MWD, NTH, WWA/3, WWW/5
LEWIS, Sue American actress GRB/1
LEWIS, Susan L. (b 1847) American actress HAS
LEWIS, Ted (1891-1971) American vaudevillian, musician WWA/5
LEWIS, Tim (d 1893 [28]) performer? EA/94*
LEWIS, Tom (d 1927 [63]) Canadian comedian BE*, BP/12*
LEWIS, Tommy (d 1912 [29]) Welsh comedian EA/13*
LEWIS, Violet (b 1885) English actress GRB/1-2
LEWIS, Mrs. W. [Kate Herbert] (d 1873 [21]) EA/74*
LEWIS, Walter (d 1881) EA/82*
LEWIS, William (d 1891 [63]) EA/93*
LEWIS, William (d 1900 [68]) lessee EA/01*
LEWIS, Mrs. William see Lewis, Sarah
LEWIS, William Thomas (1749-

1811) English actor CDP,
COC, DNB, GT, OC/1-3,
TD/1-2
LEWIS, Mrs. William Thomas
see Leeson, Henrietta
LEWIS, Willie (b 1910) American
actor TW/7
LEWIS, Windsor (1918-72) Amer-
ican director, producer BE,
TW/28
LEWISOHN, Alice (fl 1915-59)
American designer, choreog-
rapher, director BE, COC,
OC/3
LEWISOHN, Irene (d 1944) de-
signer, choreographer, di-
rector COC, OC/3
LEWISOHN, Oscar (d 1917)
EA/18*
LEWISOHN, Mrs. Oscar see
May, Edna
LEWISOHN, Victor Max (1897-
1934) English actor WWT/
6-7
LEWITAN, Joseph (d 1976 [82])
critic BP/60*
LEWNS, R. (d 1916) EA/17*
LEXY, Edward (b 1897) English
actor WWT/9-10
LEY, Marie actress COC
LEYBOURNE, George [Joe
Saunders] (1842-84) English
music-hall performer CDP,
COC, OC/1-3
LEYDEN, Leo (b 1929) Irish
actor TW/24, 26-29
LEYEL, Carl F. (1875-1925)
English manager WWT/5
LEYERLE, William American
actor TW/30
LEYRITZ, Mr. G. (d 1869 [48])
professor of music EA/70*
LEYSSAC, Paul (d 1946) Danish
actor, lecturer SR, TW/1, 3
LEYTON, Edgar [Louis T.
Dupuy] (d 1902 [33]) singer
EA/03*
LEYTON, George (d 1948 [84])
performer BE*, WWT/14*
LEYTON, Harry (d 1889) music-
hall performer EA/91*
LEYTON, Helen (d 1913) ac-
tress EA/96
LEYTON, H. Lawrence actor
GRB/1
LEYTON, Sydney (d 1909 [43])
actor EA/10*
LIAGRE, Alfred de, Jr. (b 1904)

American producer, manager
WWT/9-14
LIBBEY, J. Aldrich (1864-1925)
singer, actor CDP
LIBBY, George A. (d 1973 [86])
performer BP/57*
LIBERTO, Don (b 1915) American
actor TW/4, 28
LIBIN, Paul (b 1930) American
producer, theatre operator BE,
WWT/16
LIBOTT, Robert Y. dramatist,
director, producer BE
LIBUSE, Frank American actor
TW/1
LICHINE, David (1909-72) Russian/
American dancer, choreographer
ES, WWT/9-12
LICHNIAVSKAIA, Alexandra (d
1973 [24]) performer BP/57*
LICHT, David (d 1975 [71]) actor,
director BP/60*, WWT/16*
LICHTENSTEIN, Miss (fl 1847)
singer HAS
LICHTENSTEIN, Ethel [Mrs. Fred-
erick Rosse] (d 1908) EA/09*
LICHTENSTEIN, George (d 1893
[70]) musician EA/94*
LICHTERMAN, Marvin (b 1938)
American actor TW/24-27
LICHTMAN, Joe see Layton, Joe
LICKFOLD, Charles see Warner,
Charles
LICKFOLD, James (d 1888) actor
EA/89*
LIDDELL, John (d 1899 [69]) EA/
00*
LIDDELL, Mrs. John see Mark-
ham, Agnes
LIDDON, Amy (d 1896 [52]) actress
EA/97*
LIDDY, Thomas (d 1903 [76]) EA/
04*
LIDEL, Joseph (d 1878) singer,
musician EA/79*
LIDGETT, Dr. Scott (d 1953 [98])
administrator BE*, WWT/14*
LIDINGTON, Alva (d 1917) EA/18*
LIEB, Herman (d 1966 [93]) per-
former BP/50*
LIEBENAU, Henry (fl 1826) artist
CDP
LIEBHART, Louise (1828-99) sing-
er, actress CDP
LIEBLER, Theodore A. (1852/53?-
1941) American manager, pro-
ducer CB, WWM
LIEBLER, Theodore A., Jr. (b

1886) American press repre-
sentative WWM
LIEBLING, George (b 1865)
German composer WWA/4
LIEBLING, Leonard (1874-1945)
American librettist, composer
CB
LIEBLING, William (1895-1969)
Polish/American talent repre-
sentative BE, TW/26
LIEBMAN, Marvin (b 1923)
American producing manager
WWT/15-16
LIEBMAN, Max (b 1902) American
producer, director BE, CB
LIEBOVITZ, David (d 1968 [76])
dramatist BP/52*
LIEURANCE, Thurlow (1878-1963)
American composer WWA/4
LIEVAN, Albert (1906-65) Ger-
man actor WWT/10-11
LIEVEN, Tatiana (b 1910) Rus-
sian actress WWT/10-11
LIFAR, Serge (b 1905) Russian
dancer, choreographer ES,
WWT/9-12
LIFF, Samuel (b 1919) Ameri-
can stage manager, director,
producer BE
LIGERO, Miguel (d 1968 [71])
performer BP/52*
LIGHT, James (d 1964 [69])
American director BE*,
BP/48*
LIGHT, Norman (d 1970 [70])
manager TW/26
LIGHTFOOT, T. R. (d 1893
[48]) comedian EA/94*
LIGHTNER, Rosella (d 1974
[66]) performer BP/59*
LIGHTNER, Winnie [Winnie
Hanson] (1901-71) American
actress, singer TW/27,
WWT/7-8
"LIGHTNING CALCULATOR, The"
see Hutchings, W. S.
LIGON, Tom (b 1945) American
actor TW/26, 28
LIKELEY, Patricia (d 1976
[52]) performer BP/60*
LILBURN, Charles (fl c. 1900?)
singer, actor CDP
LILIAN, Mme. see Pitt, Mrs.
H. M.
LILLEY, Edward Clarke (d 1974
[86]) actor, director TW/30
LILLEY, Mrs. John (d 1887)
EA/88*

LILLEY, Joseph J. (d 1971 [56])
composer/lyricist BP/55*
LILLIBRIDGE, Gardner R. (fl
1824?) dramatist EAP, RJ
LILLIE, Miss [Lizzie Swindlehurst]
(fl 1863) actress CDP, HAS
LILLIE, Beatrice (b 1898) Canadian
actress AAS, BE, CB, COC,
ES, NTH, PDT, TW/1-2, 4-21,
WWT/4-16
LILLIE, George (fl 1628) actor DA
LILLIE, John (fl 1628) actor DA
LILLIE, Muriel (d 1973 [81]) com-
poser/lyricist BP/58*
LILLIES, Leonard (1860-1923)
English business manager GRB/
4, WWT/1-3
LILLO, George (1693-1739) English
dramatist COC, CP/1-3, DNB,
ES, GT, HP, MH, NTH, OC/
1-3, PDT, RE, TD/1-2
LILLY, A. C. (d 1916 [75]) actor
WWT/14*
LILO, Toby [Walter Eginton] (d
1902 [22]) bicyclist EA/03*
LIMBERT, Roy (1893-1954) English
manager, producer WWT/7-11,
WWW/5
LIMERICK, Mona South American
actress COC, WWT/1-8
LIMON, José (1908-72) Mexican
dancer, choreographer CB, ES,
WWA/5
LIMPUS, Alban Brownlow (1878-
1941) English producer, manager
WWT/6-9
LINA, Mme. [Mrs. Cooper] (d
1906) musician EA/08*
LINCOLN, Alpheus (d 1970 [78])
performer BP/54*
LINCOLN, Ann American actress
TW/1
LINCOLN, Elmo (1889-1952) actor
BE*, BP/37*
LINCOLN, Frank (d 1912 [33])
actor EA/13*
LINCOLN, Jean (d 1969 [34]) agent
BP/54*
LINCOLN, Pattie see Wise,
Mrs. John
LIND, Bertha (fl 1870) dancer
CDP
LIND, Eliza see Zilla, Mme.
LIND, Gillian (b 1904) Indian/Eng-
lish actress WWT/6-16
LIND, Jenny (1820-87) Swedish ac-
tress, singer CDP, DNB, ES,
HAS, HP, NTH, NYM, SR,

WWA/H

LIND, Karl acrobat CDP

LIND, Letty [Rudge] (1862-1923) actress, dancer, singer CDP, DP, EA/96, GRB/1-4, WWT/1-4

LIND, Marion English actress GRB/1-2

LINDELHEIM, Johanna Maria see "Baroness, The"

LINDEN, Eric (b 1909) American actor TW/2-3, WWT/8-10

LINDEN, Frank (d 1911) actor, manager SR

LINDEN, Hal [né Harold Lipshitz] (b 1931) American actor, singer BE, TW/19, 21, 24, 27-28, 30, WWT/15-16

LINDEN, Harry (1831-87) American actor CDP, HAS, NYM

LINDEN, Henry see Linden, Harry

LINDEN, Mrs. Henry [Laura Bentley] (fl 1860s) actress HAS

LINDEN, Laura (d 1906 [49]) actress, singer CDP, EA/95

LINDEN, Marie (b 1862) English actress EA/95, WWT/1-9

LINDEN, Marta (b 1910) American actress TW/3-4, 6-9

LINDEN, Robert (b 1912) American stage manager, producer BE

LINDEN, Tommy (d 1969) performer BP/54*

LINDER, Cec (b 1921) Polish actor TW/25-26

LINDER, Jack (b 1896) American producer BE

LINDER, Max (d 1925 [41]) actor BE*, WWT/14*

LINDERMAN, Ed (b 1947) American actor TW/29

LINDFORS, Viveca (b 1920/21) Swedish actress BE, CB, TW/9, 22, 24-25, 27, 30, WWT/15-16

LINDIG, Jillian (b 1944) American actress TW/26-27

LINDLEY, Audra (b 1918) American actress TW/4-5, 22, 24-25, WWT/11

LINDLEY, Henrietta actress EA/96

LINDLEY, Henry (b 1836) Irish actor HAS

LINDLEY, Robert (1776-1855) English musician CDP, DNB

LINDO, Frank (d 1933 [68]) actor, producer, dramatist BE*, WWT/14*

LINDO, Olga (1898-1968) English actress WWT/5-14

LINDOE (fl 1804) actor, dramatist CP/3

LINDON, Agnes (d 1886) singer EA/87*

LINDON, Clarence (d 1862 [37]) actor, manager EA/72*

LINDON, George (d 1883 [28]) EA/84*

LINDON, Isabel (d 1897) music-hall performer EA/98*

LINDON, Louie [Jessie Ferrier] (d 1907 [20]) actress EA/08*

LINDON, Millie (fl 1900s?) singer, actress CDP

LINDON, Tom (d 1888) songwriter EA/89*

LINDROTH, Walter (d 1889 [27]) actor EA/90*

LINDSAY, Mr. (fl 1808) English actor HAS

LINDSAY, Mr. (fl 1836) actor HAS

LINDSAY, Bertha Goulding [Mrs. Charles Mildare] (d 1901) EA/02*

LINDSAY, Sir David (1490-1553/55) Scottish dramatist CP/2-3, HP, PDT

LINDSAY, Howard (1889-1968) American actor, dramatist, producer AAS, BE, CB, COC, ES, MD, MH, MWD, OC/1-3, SR, TW/2-8, 24, WWA/4, WWT/8-14, WWW/6

LINDSAY, Hugh ["Old Hontz, the Clown"] (b 1804) American circus performer HAS

LINDSAY, Jack Graham see Tracy, Douglas

LINDSAY, James (1869-1928) English actor WWT/4-5

LINDSAY, John V. (b 1921) American lawyer BE

LINDSAY, Kevin (d 1975 [51]) performer BP/59*

LINDSAY, Kevin-John (b 1957) American actor TW/26-28

LINDSAY, Lex (d 1971 [69]) actor TW/27

LINDSAY, Philip (b 1924) American actor TW/25-26

LINDSAY, T. (d 1877) Negro comedian EA/78*

LINDSAY, Vera [Vera Poliakoff] (b 1911) Russian actress WWT/9-10

LINDSAY, Mrs. W. see Harvey, Rose

LINDSEY, Gene (b 1936) American actor TW/23, 25, 30

LINDSEY, William (1858-1922) American dramatist DAB

LINDSLEY, A. B. (fl 1809?) dramatist EAP, RJ

LINDSLEY, Guy (d 1923) American actor BE*, BP/7*

LINDSTROM, Carl (b 1938) American actor TW/28-29

LINDSTROM, Erik (d 1974 [68]) performer BP/59*

LING, Ritchie (d 1937 [70]) English actor, singer BE*, BP/21*, WWT/14*

LING, Mrs. Richie see Faust, Lotta

LINGARD, Alice [Mrs. William Horace Lingard] (1847-97) actress CDP, DP

LINGARD, Dickey [Harriet Sarah Dunning] (b 1850) English actress CDP, HAS

LINGARD, George A. (d 1876) actor EA/77*, WWT/14*

LINGARD, George Alexander (d 1871 [32]) minstrel? EA/72*

LINGARD, Horace (d 1927 [89]) producer, actor, singer BE*, WWT/14*

LINGARD, James W. (1823-70) English actor, manager CDP, HAS, WWA/H

LINGARD, Nellie [Mrs. George Beauchamp] (d 1899) serio-comic, actress DP

LINGARD, William Horace (b c. 1840) English actor, manager CDP, HAS, SR

LINGARD, Mrs. William Horace see Lingard, Alice

LINGHAM, Matthew W. (1832-81) American actor CDP, HAS

LINGHAM, Mrs. Randal see Dawson, Jane

LINGRAM, Randall Hopley (d 1907 [83]) actor EA/08*

LINJERIS, George (b 1942) American actor TW/23, 25

LINK, Adolf (d 1933 [81]) Hungarian actor BE*, BP/18*

LINK, Peter (b 1944) American composer WWT/16

LINKLATER, Eric (1899-1974) Scottish dramatist AAS, MD, MWD, PDT

LINLEY, Betty (d 1951 [61]) English actress WWT/7-11

LINLEY, Elizabeth Ann [Mrs. R. B. Sheridan] (1754-92) English singer COC, ES

LINLEY, George (1798-1865) English composer CDP, DNB

LINLEY, Mrs. George (d 1872) EA/74*

LINLEY, Margaret (d 1969 [65]) casting director BP/54*

LINLEY, Maria (1763-84) singer CDP

LINLEY, Thomas, Sr. (1733-95) English musician, composer ES

LINLEY, Thomas (1756-78) English composer, dramatist CDP, DNB, ES, TD/1-2

LINLEY, William (1771-1835) English dramatist, composer CP/3, DNB, ES

LINN, Bambi (b 1926) American dancer, actress BE, TW/1-15, 18-19, WWT/11-15

LINN, Mrs. George (d 1875) EA/77*

LINN, Harry (d 1890 [44]) Scottish singer, songwriter CDP

LINN, John Blair (1777-1804) American dramatist CDP, EAP, RJ

LINN, Margaret (1934-73) American actress TW/24-30

LINNECAR, Richard (fl 1789) dramatist CP/3

LINNET, Mrs. Alfred see North, Ada

LINNEY, Daniel A. (b 1930) American educator BE

LINNIT, S. E. (d 1956 [58]) manager, business manager, agent WWT/9-12

LINNIT AND DUNFEE LTD. producing managers WWT/13-16

LINTON, Mr. (d c. 1802) singer TD/1-2

LINTON, Betty Hyatt (b 1930) American actress TW/25

LINTON, Fred (d 1917 [50]) music-hall proprietor EA/18*

LINTON, William (b 1935) Scottish actor TW/28

LINTOTT, Bernard (d 1903)
stage manager EA/04*
LINUS, Ludwig (d 1900) contor-
tionist EA/02*
LINVILLE, Lawrence (b 1939)
American actor TW/24
LINWOOD, Miss (d 1845 [90])
EA/72*
LINYARD, W. K. [W. R.
Goodwin] (b 1837) English
actor HAS
LION, Leon M. (1879-1947)
English actor, dramatist,
manager GRB/1-4, WWT/
1-10
LIONEL, George A. (d 1898)
actor EA/99*
LIONEL, Jerome (d 1887) clown,
pantomimist EA/88*
LIONEL, Mme. Jerome (d
1869) EA/70*
"LION QUEEN" see Moore,
Eliza
LiPARI, Marjorie (b 1945)
American actress TW/25-28,
30
LIPMAN, Mrs. actress HAS
LIPMAN, Alvah S. (1884-1911)
actor, dramatist CDP, SR
LIPMAN, Ann (d 1972 [32])
publicist BP/57*
LIPMAN, Clara [Mrs. Louis
Mann] (1869-1952) American
actress, dramatist GRB/2-4,
TW/9, WWA/3, WWM, WWS,
WWT/1-9
LIPMAN, Mike (fl 1858) clown,
actor HAS
LIPMAN, Sol J. clown HAS
LIPP, Helen Louise see
Bliss, Helena
LIPPARD, George dramatist RJ
LIPPARD, John B. (b 1919)
American theatre designer
BE
LIPPIN, Renee (b 1946) Ameri-
can actress TW/28
LIPPMAN, Monroe (b 1905)
American educator, director
BE
LIPPMANN, Julie Mathilde
(1864-1952) American drama-
tist, critic WWA/3, WWM
LIPPMANN, Zilla American
executive BE
LIPSCOMB, William Percy (1887-
1958) English dramatist
WWT/8-10

LIPSETT, Marianne see Cald-
well, Marianne
LIPSHITZ, Harold see Linden,
Hal
LIPSIS, Elias (d 1879) stage mana-
ger EA/80*
LIPSKY, David (b 1907) American
press representative BE
LIPSON, Clifford (b 1947) Ameri-
can actor TW/26-29
LIPSON, Paul (b 1913) American
actor TW/26-30
LIPTON, Celia (b 1923) Scottish
actress, singer WWT/10-13
LIPTON, Dan English songwriter
GRB/1
LIPTON, George (d 1962 [45])
singer, actor BE*, BP/46*
LIPTON, James (b 1926) American
actor TW/7-8
LIPTON, Michael (b 1925) Ameri-
can actor TW/11, 22-23, 25-
26, 28
LIPZIN, Kenny (1856-1918) Rus-
sian actor ES
LISA, Luba (d 1972 [31]) American
actress TW/21-22, 26, 28-29
LISBOURNE, John (d 1899 [34])
comedian EA/00*
LISBOURNE, Mrs. John see
Priestly, Kate
LISITZKY, Prof. Ephram E. (d
1962 [77]) Russian educator,
scholar BE*
LISLE, Herbert (d 1917) EA/18*
LISLE, Lucille Australian actress
WWT/8-11
LISLE, Rose (d 1891) actress EA/
92*
LISLEY, Mrs. see Barsanti,
Jane
LIST, Emanuel (1891-1967) Austrian
singer WWA/4
LIST, Kurt (d 1970 [57]) producer/
director/choreographer BP/55*
LISTER, Edward (fl 1612) actor
DA
LISTER, Eve (b 1918) English ac-
tress, singer WWT/11-14
LISTER, Francis (1899-1951) Eng-
lish actor TW/8, WWT/4-11
LISTER, Frank (1868-1917) Eng-
lish actor GRB/1, WWT/1-3
LISTER, Mrs. Frank see
Beaufort, Grace
LISTER, George (d 1893) comedian,
manager EA/95*
LISTER, Lance [Solomon Lancelot

Inglis Watson] (b 1901) actor
WWT/4-10
LISTER, Laurier (b 1904/07)
English actor, manager,
director WWT/9-16
LISTER, Moira (b 1923) South
African actress AAS, WWT/
11-16
LISTER, Thomas Henry (1800-
42) English dramatist DNB
LISTMAN, Ryan (b 1939) Amer-
ican actor TW/24-25
LISTON, Mr. actor TD/2
LISTON, Alice [Mrs. Victor
Liston] (d 1880 [23]) EA/81*
LISTON, Mrs. Andrew (d 1899
[27]) actress EA/00*
LISTON, Effie [Mrs. H. Elmore-
Frith] (d 1904 [42]) actress
EA/05*
LISTON, Eleanor [Mrs. Harry
Liston] (d 1890) EA/91*
LISTON, Harry actor, singer,
songwriter CDP
LISTON, Mrs. Harry see
Liston, Eleanor
LISTON, John (1776-1846) Eng-
lish actor BS, CDP, COC,
DNB, ES, GT, OC/1-3, OX
LISTON, Mrs. John [née Sarah
Tyrer] (c. 1780-1854) English
actress BS, CDP, ES
LISTON, Mary Ann (d 1882
[68]) EA/83*
LISTON, Sarah see Liston,
Mrs. John
LISTON, Victor (1838-1913)
English music-hall comedian
CDP, COC, OC/1-3
LISTON, Mrs. Victor see
Liston, Alice
LISTON, William Henry (d 1876
[46]) acting manager EA/77*,
WWT/14*
LISTON, Mrs. W. H. [Maria
Simpson] (d 1879 [45]) actress,
manager EA/80*, WWT/14*
LITCHFIELD, Edward Carr
(d 1894 [57]) manager EA/95*
LITCHFIELD, Mrs. E[dward]
C[arr] (d 1905 [71]) EA/96*
LITCHFIELD, Harriett [née
Hay] (1777-1854) English ac-
tress CDP, DNB, GT, TD/
1-2
LITEL, John (d 1972 [77]) actor
TW/28
LITHGOW, Arthur W. (b 1915)

actor, director, administrator
BE
LITHGOW, John American actor
TW/30
LITOLFF, Henry (d 1891 [72])
composer EA/92*
LITONIUS, Marian (d 1971 [62])
performer BP/56*
LITT, Isaac (d 1887) manager
NYM
LITT, Jacob (1860-1905) American
manager WWA/1
LITT, Sol (d 1913) American
manager SR
LITTA, Marie (1850-83) singer
CDP
LITTELL, Joseph (1821-56) actor
HAS
LITTELL, Mrs. Joseph see
Florence, Mrs. William Jermyn
LITTELL, Robert (1896-1963)
American critic, dramatist
WWA/4, WWT/6-11
LITTLE, Betty Green (b 1898)
American actress TW/5
LITTLE, Cleavon (b 1939) Ameri-
can actor TW/26-28, 30,
WWT/16
LITTLE, C. P. (d 1914) actor,
journalist BE*, WWT/14*
LITTLE, Mrs. Fred J. (d 1894)
EA/95*
LITTLE, George W. (d 1863 [41])
HAS
LITTLE, Guy S. , Jr. (b 1935)
American producer, director,
manager BE
LITTLE, James F. (d 1969 [62])
performer BP/54*
LITTLE, Lillian (d 1972 [66]) ac-
tress TW/29
LITTLE, Ron Paul (b 1949) Amer-
ican actor TW/29-30
LITTLE, Rose Amelia [Mrs. Tom
E. Little] (d 1910 [33]) EA/11*
LITTLE, Stuart W. (b 1921)
American theatre reporter BE
LITTLE, Terence (b 1920) Amer-
ican stage manager, actor BE
LITTLE, Mrs. Tom E. see
Little, Rose Amelia
"LITTLE CORINNE" see Corinne
LITTLEDALE, Richard (d 1951
[47]) actor BE*, WWT/14*
LITTLEFIELD, Catherine (1904/
05-51) American dancer, chore-
ographer ES, WWT/10-11
LITTLEFIELD, Emma [Mrs. Victor

Frederick Moore] (1883-1934)
American actress WWS

LITTLEFIELD, Lucien (d 1960
[64]) American actor BE*

LITTLE GULLIVER [John
Bromelow] (d 1906 [29]) dwarf
comedian EA/07*

"LITTLE MAC" (1844-90) comedian, minstrel CDP

"LITTLE NELL" see Dauvray,
Helen

LITTLER, Blanche (b 1899) English manager OC/1-2, WWT/
8-13

LITTLER, Emile (b 1903) English manager, producer OC/
1-2, WWT/7-16

LITTLER, F. R. (d 1940 [60])
manager BE*, WWT/14*

LITTLER, Prince (1901-73)
English manager, proprietor
OC/1-2, WWT/7-15

LITTLE SIMMY [William Arthur
Simmons] (d 1908) circus
performer EA/09*

LITTLE TICH see Tich, Little

LITTLEWOOD, Joan (b 1914)
English director, manager
BE, CH, COC, ES, OC/3,
PDT, WWT/13-16

LITTLEWOOD, S[amuel] R[ob-
inson] (1875-1963) English
critic GRB/2-4, OC/1-2,
WWT/1-13, WWW/6

LITTON, Marie [Mrs. Whybrow
Robertson] (1847-84) English
actress CDP, DNB, OAA/2

LITVINNE, Félia (1860-1936)
Russian/French singer ES

LIVANOV, Boris N. (d 1972
[68]) performer BP/57*

LIVELY, William E. (d 1973
[66]) dramatist BP/58*

LIVERIGHT, Horace Brisbin
(1886-1933) American manager, producer, publisher
DAB, OC/2-3, WWT/6-7

LIVERMORE, Charles John (d
1906 [61]) variety theatre
director EA/07*

LIVERMORE, Louis (d 1891)
performer? EA/92*

LIVERT, Richard (b 1944)
American actor TW/30

LIVESEY, Barrie (b 1904) actor
ES, WWT/8-12

LIVESEY, Gustavus Carter (d
1905 [34]) EA/06*

LIVESEY, Jack (1901-61) Welsh
actor ES, TW/14-15, WWT/7-
13

LIVESEY, Joseph (d 1911 [31])
actor EA/12*

LIVESEY, Maggie (d 1913) EA/14*

LIVESEY, Roger (1906-76) Welsh
actor AAS, ES, WWT/8-16

LIVESEY, Sam (1873-1936) Welsh
actor ES, WWT/4-8

LIVESEY, Thomas Carter (d 1890)
EA/91*

LIVINGS, Henry (b 1929) English
dramatist, actor AAS, CD,
CH, ES, MH, MWD, PDT, RE,
WWT/14-16

"LIVING SKELETON, The" see
Edson, Calvin

LIVINGSTON, Deacon (d 1963 [c.
75]) performer BE*

LIVINGSTON, Jay (b 1915) American songwriter, composer BE

LIVINGSTONE, Kay (d 1975 [55])
performer BP/60*

LIVING THEATRE, The theatre
collective CD

LIVIUS, Charles Barham (d 1865
[80]) dramatist EA/72*

LJUNGBERG, Göta (d 1955) Swedish
singer WWW/5

LLEWELYN, Alfred H. (d 1964)
actor BE*

LLEWELLYN, Fewlass (1866-1941)
English actor, manager, pro-
ducer, dramatist GRB/1-4,
WWT/1-9

LLEWELLYN, Richard Welsh
dramatist CB

LLOYD (d c. 1807) actor, dramatist
CP/3

LLOYD, Al (d 1964 [80]) performer
BE*, BP/49*

LLOYD, Alfred (d 1916) EA/17*

LLOYD, Alice [Mrs. T. McNaugh-
ton] (d 1949 [76]) singer, actress CDP, TW/6

LLOYD, Alice Marie (d 1891)
music-hall performer EA/92*

LLOYD, Arthur (1840-1904) English
music-hall performer CDP,
OC/1-2

LLOYD, Mrs. Arthur see King,
Katty

LLOYD, Arthur Watson see
Rigby, Arthur

LLOYD, Charles (d 1889) advance
agent EA/90*

LLOYD, Mrs. Charles F. see

Stafford Smith, Mary
LLOYD, Clara [Clara Laidlaw; Mrs. F. W. Lloyd] (d 1887) actress EA/88*
LLOYD, Delarue (d 1899) comedian EA/00*
LLOYD, Doris (d 1968 [68]) English actress WWT/5-9
LLOYD, Eddie (d 1974 [83]) performer BP/59*
LLOYD, Edward (d 1909 [74]) EA/10*
LLOYD, Eliza [Mrs. F. H. Lloyd] (d 1870 [60]) EA/71*
LLOYD, Mrs. F. H. see Lloyd, Eliza
LLOYD, Florence (b 1876) Welsh actress, singer GRB/4, WWT/1-5
LLOYD, Frederick (d 1962 [75]) manager WWT/14*
LLOYD, Frederick William (1880-1949) English actor WWT/6-10
LLOYD, Fred W. (d 1884) acting manager EA/85*
LLOYD, Mrs. F. W. see Lloyd, Clara
LLOYD, George American actor TW/1
LLOYD, Grace (d 1961 [86]) performer BE*
LLOYD, Hannibal Evans (fl 1799) translator CP/3
LLOYD, Harold (1894-1971) American actor, producer CB
LLOYD, Horatio F. (d 1889) actor, singer CDP
LLOYD, Jack (d 1976 [53]) performer BP/60*
LLOYD, James William (d 1909) performer? EA/10*
LLOYD, John (d 1873 [56]) actor? EA/74*
LLOYD, John (d 1944 [74]) actor BE*, WWT/14*
LLOYD, John (d 1976 [38]) dramatist BP/60*
LLOYD, Mrs. John (d 1886 [40]) EA/87*
LLOYD, John Robert (b 1920) American designer BE, TW/7-8
LLOYD, Margaret Leah [Mrs. Harry King-Lloyd] (d 1904 [30]) EA/05*
LLOYD, Marie [Wood] (1870-

1922) English variety artist CDP, COC, ES, GRB/1-4, OC/1-3, PDT, WWT/4
LLOYD, Mildred Davis (d 1969 [68]) performer BP/54*
LLOYD, Morris (d 1974 [83]) actor, vaudevillian BP/58*, WWT/16*
LLOYD, Myra Mackenzie see Rosalind, Myra
LLOYD, Norman (b 1914) American producer, director, actor BE, TW/10, 13
LLOYD, Ramsey Percy R. (d 1910 [23]) EA/11*
LLOYD, Robert (d 1764) dramatist CP/1-3, GT, TD/1-2
LLOYD, Robert (d 1881 [44]) Scottish comedian EA/83*
LLOYD, Roderick (d 1945 [39]) singer WWT/14*
LLOYD, Rosie (d 1944 [64]) singer, actress CDP
LLOYD, Sam (d 1883 [37]) comedian EA/84*
LLOYD, Theodore (d 1907) showman EA/08*
LLOYD, Tom singer, actor CDP
LLOYD, Violet (b 1879) English actress GRB/1-4, WWT/1-5
LLOYD, William Watkiss (1813-93) scholar DNB
LLOYD-JAMES, Mrs. (d 1911 [28]) actress EA/12*
LLOYDS, Frederick (d 1894) scene artist WWT/14*
LLOYD-WEBBER, Andrew (b 1948) English composer AAS, WWT/16
LOADER, A. McLeod (b 1869) English manager, dramatist WWT/3
LOANE, Mary American actress TW/27
LOBB, Graham see Graham, Ly
LoBIANCO, Tony (b 1936) American actor TW/24-26
LOBLEY, William (d 1883 [65]) mechanist, modeller EA/84*
LOCATILI, Louisa (d 1857) singer HAS
LOCHER, Felix (d 1969 [87]) performer BP/53*
LOCK, J. H. (d 1888) agent EA/89*
LOCK, Mrs. J. H. [Mme. Ramsden] (d 1883 [55]) EA/84*
LOCKARD, Edmond see Duquesne,

Edmond
LOCKE, Mrs. C. H. (d 1910)
EA/11*
LOCKE, Edward (1869-1945)
English dramatist, actor
WWA/2, WWM, WWT/3-7
LOCKE, Fanny see Hatton,
Fanny
LOCKE, Fred (d 1907 [55]) ac-
tor, manager, pantomime
writer GRB/3
LOCKE, George E. (1817-80)
American actor CDP, HAS,
SR
LOCKE, Mrs. George E. (b
1828) American actress
HAS
LOCKE, Katherine (b 1910)
American actress WWT/9-11
LOCKE, Matthew (1632?-77)
English composer CDP,
DNB, ES
LOCKE, Robinson (1856-1920)
American critic NTH
LOCKE, Sam (b 1917) American
dramatist BE
LOCKE, Vivia (b 1917) American
educator BE
LOCKE, Will H. (d 1950 [82])
dramatist BE*, WWT/14*
LOCKE, William John (1863-
1930) West Indian dramatist
GRB/2-4, WWM, WWT/1-6
LOCKE, Yankee (d 1880) Ameri-
can actor EA/81*
LOCKER, Jody (b 1944) Ameri-
can actor TW/24
LOCKERBIE, Beth (d 1968 [53])
performer BP/53*
LOCKETT, Louis (d 1964 [71])
American performer, dancer
BE*, BP/49*
LOCKHART, Alice [Mrs. Sam
Lockhart] (d 1897 [41]) EA/
98*
LOCKHART, Annie see Jack-
son, Mrs. Harry
LOCKHART, Gene (1891/92-
1957) Canadian actor CB,
TW/1, 6-7, 13, WWA/3,
WWT/9-12
LOCKHART, George (d 1904
[54]) animal trainer EA/05*
LOCKHART, June (b 1925)
American actress BE, TW/
4-8, 11-13
LOCKHART, Kathleen actress
TW/1

LOCKHART, Mrs. Sam see
Lockhart, Alice
LOCKHART, Samuel (d 1894 [69])
EA/95*
LOCKMAN, John (d 1771) dramatist
CP/2-3
LOCKRIDGE, Frances D. (d 1963
[66]) dramatist BP/47*
LOCKRIDGE, Richard (b 1898)
American critic, dramatist
CB, NTH, WWT/10-11
LOCKTON, Joan (b 1901) English
actress, singer WWT/6-7
LOCKWOOD, Adolphus (d 1885)
musician EA/86*
LOCKWOOD, Carolyn (b 1932)
American educator, director
BE
LOCKWOOD, Edmund E. P. (d
1911 [55]) manager EA/12*,
WWT/14*
LOCKWOOD, Ernest Raven (d 1897
[57]) singer? EA/98*
LOCKWOOD, Mrs. Fred see
Lockwood, Harriet
LOCKWOOD, Harold (1887-1918)
actor BE*
LOCKWOOD, Harriet [Mrs. Fred
Lockwood] (d 1889) EA/91*
LOCKWOOD, John (d 1891 [61])
bandmaster EA/92*
LOCKWOOD, King (d 1971 [73])
performer BP/55*
LOCKWOOD, Margaret (b 1916)
Indian/English actress AAS,
CB, ES, WWT/8-16
LOCKWOOD, Robert (d 1885 [89])
comedian EA/86*
LOCKYER, Miss see Jefferson,
Mrs. Joseph, I
LODEN, Barbara American actress
BE, TW/15, 20-21, 24
LODER, Basil (b 1885) English
actor WWT/6-8
LODER, Mrs. Basil see Deane,
Barbara
LODER, Charles A. (1858-1949)
actor SR
LODER, Edward James (1813-65)
English conductor, composer
CDP, DNB, HAS
LODER, Mrs. [Edward James]
(d 1855) actress HAS
LODER, Mrs. [Edward James],
II [Emily Neville] (d 1867) HAS
LODER, Mrs. E. J. (d 1880 [67])
singer EA/81*
LODER, George (1816?-68) English

composer DNB

LODER, John (d 1853 [41]) musician EA/72*

LODER, Kathryn (b 1940) American actress TW/30

LODGE, John Davis (b 1903) American actor BE

LODGE, Ruth (b 1914) English actress WWT/9-14

LODGE, Thomas (c. 1558-1625) English dramatist CP/1-3, FGF, HP, NTH, PDT

LODS, Jean (d 1974 [71]) producer/director/choreographer BP/58*

LOEB, John Jacob (d 1970 [60]) composer/lyricist BP/54*

LOEB, Philip (1892/94-1955) American actor, producer TW/1-6, 8-9, 12, WWT/9-11

LOESSER, Frank (1910-69) American composer, lyricist AAS, BE, CB, ES, NTH, TW/26, WWT/14

LOESSER, Lynn producer BE

LOEW, David L. (d 1973 [75]) producer/director/choreographer BP/57*

LOEW, Marcus (1870-1927) American manager DAB, NTH, SR, WWA/1

LOEWE, Frederick (b 1901/04) Austrian/American composer AAS, BE, CB, ES, HJD, PDT, WWT/16

LOEWE, Sophie (1815-66) singer CDP

LOFTHOUSE, Mrs. (d 1872 [29]) music-hall performer? EA/73*

LOFTHOUSE, John Steel (d 1883 [54]) equestrian & variety agent EA/85*

LOFTING, Kitty actress GRB/2

LOFTUS, Cissie [Cissy] see Loftus, Marie Cecilia

LOFTUS, Edgar (d 1891) EA/92*

LOFTUS, John (d 1896) EA/97*

LOFTUS, Kitty [Mrs. P. Warren-Smith] (1867-1927) English actress, singer CDP, GRB/1-4, WWT/1-5

LOFTUS, Marie (d 1940 [83]) singer, actress CDP

LOFTUS, Marie Cecilia [Cissie] (1876-1943) Scottish actress CB, CDP, EA/94, GRB/1-4, NTH, OC/1-3, SR, WWS,

WWT/1-9, WWW/4

LOFTUS-LEYTON, Rosie [Mrs. A. G. Spry] (d 1902 [27]) actress EA/03*, WWT/14*

LOGAN, Miss see Colman, Mary

LOGAN, Celia (fl 1852-68) American actress HAS

LOGAN, Cornelius A. (1806-53) American actor, manager, dramatist CDP, DAB, HAS, HJD, RJ, WWA/H

LOGAN, Eliza (1829/30-72) American actress, lessee CDP, HAS

LOGAN, Ella (1910/13-69) Scottish actress, singer BE, TW/3-15, 25, WWT/11

LOGAN, John (1748-85) Scottish dramatist CP/3

LOGAN, John (d 1972 [48]) performer BP/57*

LOGAN, Joshua (b 1908) American producing manager, dramatist AAS, BE, CB, CD, ES, MWD, PDT, TW/2-8, WWT/11-16

LOGAN, Mary see Colman, Mary

LOGAN, Nedda Harrigan (b c. 1900) American actress BE

LOGAN, Olive (1839/41-1909) American actress CDP, DAB, HAS, WWA/1

LOGAN, Stanley (1885-1953) English actor, producer WWT/4-10

LOGAN, T. D. (d 1854) HAS

LOGGIA, Robert (b 1930) American actor TW/13-15, 21, 25-26, 29-30

LOGIE, Charles Harry Gordon (d 1897 [20]) EA/98*

LoGRIPPO, Joe (b 1939) American actor TW/30

LOGUE, Christopher (b 1926) English dramatist MD, MWD

LOGUE, Mary see Nagle, Mrs. Joseph E.

LOHMAN, Dorothy (d 1973) agent BP/57*

LOHMANN, Otto (b 1921) American actor TW/18

LOHN, Anna (1830-1902) actress CDP

LOHR, Marie (1890-1975) Australian/English actress AAS, ES, GRB/3-4, WWT/1-15

LOHSE, Frau (d 1906 [30]) singer EA/07*

LOISSET, Mr. (fl 1847) acrobat CDP

LOISSET, Emilie (d 1882 [25])

equestrian CDP
LOKER, William A. (d 1965
[74]) performer BP/50*
LOLA, Little (b c.1854) actress
HAS
LOLKES, Mynheer Wylrand (fl
1799) dwarf CDP
LOLLER, Charles P. (d 1908
[28]) conductor EA/09*
LOM, Herbert (b 1917) Czech
actor WWT/12-13
LOMAN, Hal (b 1929) American
actor TW/12
LOMAS, Mr. (fl 1851) actor
HAS
LOMAS, Bert (d 1898) music-
hall performer EA/99*
LOMAS, Herbert (1887-1961)
English actor WWT/3-13,
WWW/6
LOMAS, Richard (b 1877) Eng-
lish animal impersonator
GRB/1
LOMAS, William (d 1881) scene
painter EA/82*
LOMATH, Stuart Scottish actor
GRB/1
LOMATH, Mrs. Stuart see
Owen, Ellen
LOMAX, Dick (d 1889 [36])
comedian EA/90*
LOMAX, Elizabeth [Mrs. Robert
Lomax] (d 1887) EA/88*
LOMAX, Mrs. Fawcett see
Birchenough, Agnes
LOMAX, Felix (b 1858) English
actor GRB/1
LOMAX, John (d 1895 [71]) actor,
manager EA/96*
LOMAX, Mrs. John (d 1891
[80]) actress EA/92*
LOMAX, John A. (d 1974 [67])
performer BP/59*
LOMAX, Mrs. Robert see
Lomax, Elizabeth
LOMAX, Robert Charles (d
1890 [47]) EA/91*
LOMBARD, Harry (d 1963 [74])
performer BE*
LOMBARD, Michael (b 1934)
American actor TW/22-23,
26-27, 30
LOMBARD, Pat (d 1974 [61])
producer/director/choreographer
BP/59*
LOMBARD, Peter (b 1935) Amer-
ican actor TW/28-29
LOMBARDO, Carmen (d 1971

[67]) performer BP/55*
LOMBARDO, Guy (1902-77) Cana-
dian producer, musical director
BE
LOMIER, Charles (fl 1894) singer
CDP
LONDON, Chet (b 1931) American
actor TW/22
LONDON, Ernest A. (d 1964 [85])
performer BE*, BP/49*
LONDON, George (b 1920/21) Cana-
dian/American singer CB, ES
LONDON, Jack (d 1916 [40])
dramatist WWT/14*
LONDON, Marc (b 1930) American
actor TW/21
LONDON, Tom (d 1963 [81]) actor
BE*
LONERGAN, Leonore (b 1928)
American actress TW/1-9
LONERGAN, Lester (d 1931 [62])
Irish actor, director BE*, BP/
16*
LONERGAN, Lester, Jr. (d 1959
[65]) actor BE*, BP/44*
LONERGAN, Mrs. Lester see
Ricard, Amy
LONG, Avon (b 1910) American
actor, singer, dancer, song-
writer BE, TW/2-5, 28-29,
WWT/16
LONG, Charles (d 1906 [49])
architect EA/07*
LONG, Gabrielle (1888-1952)
English dramatist WWW/5
LONG, Harriet C. [Mrs. J. H.
Long; Mrs. Charles Butler]
(1830-98) singer CDP
LONG, Mrs. J. H. see Long,
Harriet C.
LONG, John (d 1897) manager
EA/98*
LONG, John Luther (1861-1927)
American dramatist COC,
DAB, GRB/2-4, HJD, MWD,
OC/3, WWS, WWT/1-5, WWW/2
LONG, Mrs. Johnny see Long,
Norah
LONG, Joseph Sidney (d 1904 [56])
writer EA/05*
LONG, J. P. singer, songwriter
CDP
LONG, Juanita see Hall, Juanita
LONG, Lily Augusta (d 1927)
American writer WWA/1
LONG, Lois (d 1974 [73]) journalist
EA/59*
LONG, Mary Elitch (d 1936 [86])

American theatre owner &
manager BE*, BP/21*

LONG, Nicholas (d 1622) actor,
manager DA

LONG, Nick, Jr. (d 1949 [43])
dancer TW/6

LONG, Norah [Mrs. Johnny Long]
(d 1916) EA/18*

LONG, Ray American actor
TW/6

LONG, Richard (d 1974 [47])
performer BP/59*

LONG, Sam, Big (d 1863) HAS

LONG, Shorty (b 1923) American
actor TW/12-13

LONG, Sumner Arthur (b 1921)
American dramatist BE

LONG, Susan (b 1947) American
actress TW/27

LONG, Tamara (b 1941) American actress TW/25-26,
29-30

LONG, Mrs. V. C. (d 1870
[36]) EA/71*

LONG, Walter (b 1889) American
actor TW/1

LONG, W. Bethell, Jr. (d 1969
[53]) actor TW/26

LONG, Wesley (d 1973 [72])
performer BP/57*

LONGDEN, C. H. (d 1918 [60])
EA/19*

LONGDEN, Mrs. C. H. see
Dottridge, Dolly

LONGDEN, John (b 1900) West
Indian actor WWT/7-9

LONGDON, Terence (b 1922)
English actor WWT/15-16

LONGE, Jeffery (d 1974 [51])
stage manager BP/59*

LONGFELLOW, H. W. American
dramatist RJ

LONGFELLOW, Stephanie (fl
1906-08) actress WWS

LONGFORD, Earl of (1902-61)
English dramatist, manager
COC, MH, OC/1-3, WWT/
9-13

LONGFORD, Lady see Trew,
Christine Patti

LONGO, Peggy (b 1943) American actress TW/26-29

LONGO, Peggy see Atkinson,
Peggy

LONGSTREET, Stephen (b 1907)
American dramatist BE, CD

LONGSTRETH, Marian (b 1906)
executive BE

"LONG TOM COFFIN" see
Scott, John M.

LONGVILLE, Emily Kate (d 1886
[31]) music-hall performer
EA/88*

LONGWORTH, Theresa (d 1881)
public reader & lecturer EA/
82*

LONGWORTH, Thomas Frederick
[Teddy O'Lynn] (d 1883 [31])
performer? EA/84*

LONNEN, Beatrice Helen see
Lonnen, Jessie

LONNEN, Edward Jesse (d 1863-
1901) singer, actor CDP, CP

LONNEN, Ellen Farren see
Lonnen, Nellie

LONNEN, Harriett [Mrs. William
Rooles Lonnen] (d 1892 [67])
EA/93*

LONNEN, Jessie [Beatrice Helen
Lonnen] (b 1886) English actress
GRB/2-4, WWT/1-5

LONNEN, Nellie [Ellen Farren
Lonnen] (b 1887) English actress GRB/2-4, WWT/1-5

LONNEN, Walter (d 1903) actor
EA/05*, WWT/14*

LONNEN, William Rooles see
Champion, William

LONNEN, Mrs. William Rooles
see Lonnen, Harriett

LONNON, Alice (b 1872) American
actress GRB/3-4, WWS, WWT/
1-5

LONSDALE, Ada (d 1889 [16])
variety performer EA/90*

LONSDALE, Annie (fl 1852) English actress CDP, HAS

LONSDALE, Frederick [Frederick
Leonard] (1881-1954) English
dramatist AAS, COC, DNB,
ES, MD, MH, MWD, NTH,
OC/1-3, PDT, TW/10, WWT/
1-11, WWW/5

LONSDALE, H. G. (d 1923) actor
BE*, WWT/14*

LONSDALE, Lillie (d 1880 [39])
actress EA/81*

LONSDALE, M. (fl 1784-94) machinist, dramatist CP/3

LONSDALE, Thomas J. (d 1928)
lyricist BE*, WWT/14*

LONSDALE, T. W. S. (d 1910
[28]) EA/11*

LOOFBOURROW, John G. (d 1964
[61]) American actor BE*

LOOMIS, Deborah (b 1945) American actress TW/29

LOOMIS, Harvey Worthington (1865-1930) American composer WWA/1, WWM

LOOMIS, Rod (b 1942) American actor TW/28-30

LOONE, Mrs. E. [Mrs. Samuel Loone] (d 1870) actress? EA/71*

LOONE, Samuel (d 1878 [59]) portable theatre manager EA/79*

LOONE, Mrs. Samuel see Loone, Mrs. E.

LOOS, Anita (b 1893) American dramatist AAS, BE, CB, ES, HJD, WWT/6-16

LOPER, Don (d 1972 [66]) choreographer, dancer BP/57*, WWT/16*

LOPEZ, Miss (fl 1828-50) American actress, dancer HAS

LOPEZ, Eddie (d 1971 [31]) journalist BP/56*

LOPEZ, Gerald (d 1905 [27]) coloured comedian EA/06*

LOPEZ, Jesus M. (d 1962 [85]) Mexican magician BE*

LOPEZ-CEPERO, Luis American actor TW/26

LOPOKOVA, Lydia (b 1892) Russian dancer, actress WWT/4-12

LOPUKHOV, Fyodor (d 1973 [86]) performer BP/57*

LOQUASTO, Santo designer WWT/16

LORAINE, A. S. English actor, manager GRB/1

LORAINE, Henry (d c. 1857) English actor HAS

LORAINE, Henry (d 1899 [80]) actor BE*, EA/00*, WWT/14*

LORAINE, Mrs. Henry [Edith Kingsley] (d 1895) EA/96*

LORAINE, Robert (1876-1935) English actor, manager AAS, COC, ES, GRB/2-4, OC/1-3, WWM, WWS, WWT/1-7

LORAINE, Violet (1886/87-1956) English actress, singer CDP, DNB, WWT/4-11

LORCA, Federico García (1898-1936) Spanish dramatist COC, NTH, OC/1-3

LORD, Barbara (b 1937) American actress BE

LORD, Basil (b 1913) English actor WWT/12-16

LORD, Charles minstrel CDP

LORD, Jack American actor TW/11-16

LORD, James A. (fl 1860) American actor HAS

LORD, Lucy (d 1969 [70]) performer BP/53*

LORD, Pauline (1890-1950) American actress AAS, DAB, ES, NTH, TW/1-7, WWA/3, WWT/5-10

LORD, Philip (d 1968 [89]) performer BP/53*

LORD, Phillips H. (d 1975 [73]) dramatist BP/60*

LORD, Robert New Zealand dramatist CD

LORD, William (d 1868) pianist EA/69*

LORD, Wilson (d 1880 [41]) musical director EA/81*

LORDE, Athena (d 1973 [57]) performer BP/57*

LORENGAR, Pilar (b 1930) Spanish singer ES

LORENZ, George (d 1972 [52]) performer BP/57*

LORENZ, John A. (d 1972 [85]) performer BP/57*

LORENZ, Max (d 1975 [72]) performer BP/59*

LORENZI, Frank (d 1906) performer? EA/07*

LORENZO, Ange (d 1971 [77]) composer, lyricist BP/55*

LORENZO, Will (d 1880) musichall performer EA/81*

LORIMER, Jack [John G.] (b 1883) Scottish actor, dancer, entertainer CDP, GRB/1

LORIMER, J. H. see Lethcourt, H. J.

LORIMER, Maxwell George see Wall, Max

LORIMER, Wright (1874-1911) American actor, dramatist GRB/3-4, SR, WWA/1, WWS

LORING, Master (b 1790) American actor HAS

LORING, Estelle (b 1925) American actress TW/4-9

LORING, Eugene (b 1914) American choreographer, dancer BE, CB, ES

LORING, Kay (b 1913) American actress TW/2

LORING, Norman (1888-1967) English producer, manager, actor WWT/6-10

LORINI, Sig. Domenico Bragioni (fl 1847-50) singer CDP, HAS

LORINI, Virginia (d 1865 [31]) singer CDP

LORNE, Constable (d 1969 [55]) performer BP/54*

LORNE, Constance (b 1914) Scottish actress WWT/11-16

LORNE, Marion (1888-1968) American actress BE, SR, TW/24, WWA/5, WWT/4-12, WWW/6

LOROS, George (b 1944) American actor TW/24, 27, 29-30

LORRAINE, Emily (d 1944 [66]) English actress TW/1

LORRAINE, Ettie (d 1884) music-hall performer EA/86*

LORRAINE, Lilian [Eulallean de Jacques] (1892-1955) American actress CDP, TW/11, WWT/4-6

LORRAINE, Miss Percy see Boyer, Mrs.

LORREANO, Harry (b 1861) English actor GRB/1

LORRING, Joan (b 1931) actress BE, TW/26

LORTEL, Lucille American producer, actress BE, WWT/15-16

LORTON, John T. (1824-60) American actor, manager HAS

LOS ANGELES, Victoria de (b 1923) Spanish singer ES

LOSCH, Tilly (1907?-75) Austrian dancer, choreographer, actress BE, CB, WWT/7-12

LOSEBY, Constance [Mrs. John Caulfield] (d 1906 [55]) actress, singer OAA/2

LOSEBY, Elizabeth (d 1888 [69]) EA/90*

LOSEE, Frank (1856-1937) American actor PP/2

LOSEE, Mrs. Frank see Elmore, Marion

LOSEY, Joseph (b 1909) American director ES

LOTHAR, Rudolph (b 1865) German dramatist, critic GRB/3-4, WWT/1

LOTINGA, Ernest (1876-1951) English actor WWT/8-11

LOTITO, Louis A. (b 1900) American manager BE

LOTTA [Charlotte Crabtree] (1847-1924) American actress CDP, COC, DAB, ES, HAS, GRB/3-4, HJD, NTH, OC/1-3, PP/1, SR, WWA/1, WWS, WWT/1-4

LOTTO, Alf (d 1912 [34]) trick cyclist EA/13*

LOTTO, Mrs. Jack (d 1904) EA/05*

LOUCHLAMN, Gearold O. (d 1970 [78]) performer BP/55*

LOUDON, Dorothy (b 1933) American actress WWT/15-16

LOUGHEAD, Flora Haines (b 1855) American dramatist WWA/4

LOUIS, Mons. (fl 1826?) French giant CDP

LOUIS, Miss (fl 1829) actress CDP

LOUIS, Anita (d 1970 [53]) performer BP/54*

LOUIS, Murray (b 1926) American dancer, choreographer CB

LOUISE, Mme. [Louise Miller] (d 1892 [81]) dancer EA/93*

LOUISE, Mlle. (fl 1828) French dancer HAS

LOUISE, Tina (b 1937) American actress BE

LOUISETTE, Josephine [Mrs. Josephine Heiskell] (1837-60) American performer HAS

LOU-TELLEGEN (b 1881/85) Dutch/French actor WWT/3-7

LOUTHER, Henry (d 1887) actor EA/88*

LOUTHERBOURG, Philip James de see De Loutherbourg, Philip James

LOUW, Allan (b 1915) American actor TW/23

LOVAT, Nancie (1900-46) English actress, singer WWT/4-8

LOVE, Mr. (fl 1753) actor HAS

LOVE, Mrs. (fl 1753) actress HAS

LOVE, Miss see Love, Emma Sarah

LOVE, Bessie [née Horton] (b 1891/98) American actress BE, ES, WWT/13-16

LOVE, Ellen American actress TW/2-3

LOVE, Emma Sarah [Mrs. Grandby Calcraft] (b 1801) English ac-

tress, singer BS, CDP, OX
LOVE, James see Dance, James
LOVE, John James magician,
  ventriloquist CDP
LOVE, Mabel (1874-1953) English
  actress, dancer DP, EA/94,
  GRB/1-4, WWT/1-10
LOVE, Montagu (1877-1943) Eng-
  lish actor WWT/7-9
LOVE, Phyllis (b 1925/29) Amer-
  ican actress BE, TW/10-17
LOVE, Valentine (fl 1869) per-
  former HAS
LOVE, Mrs. Valentine (fl 1869)
  performer HAS
LOVE, William Edward (1806-67)
  polyphonist CDP
LOVECRAFT, Frederick A. (d
  1893 [42]) manager CDP
LOVEDAY, Mrs. Ely (d 1892
  [92]) actress EA/93*
LOVEDAY, George (d 1887 [54])
  acting manager EA/89*
LOVEDAY, George B. (d 1887)
  manager NYM
LOVEDAY, Henry Joseph (d 1910
  [71]) stage manager GRB/1-4
LOVEDAY, Thomas (fl 1635-67?)
  actor DA
LOVEGROVE, Jane (d 1905 [95])
  actress EA/06*
LOVEGROVE, William (1778-
  1816) actor CDP
LOVEGROVE, William (d 1879
  [63]) actor, manager EA/80*
LOVEJOY, Alexander Frederick
  (d 1896) music-hall proprietor
  EA/97*
LOVEJOY, Mrs. Alexander Fred-
  erick see Lovejoy, Louisa
LOVEJOY, Alfred (d 1891 [41])
  music-hall manager EA/92*
LOVEJOY, Edith (d 1891) EA/
  92*
LOVEJOY, Frank (1914-62)
  American actor TW/19
LOVEJOY, Louisa [Mrs. Alex-
  ander Frederick Lovejoy]
  (d 1895) EA/97*
LOVEJOY, Robin (b 1923) Fijian
  director WWT/16
LOVEKYN, Arthur (fl 1509-13)
  member of the Chapel Royal
  DA
LOVEL, Gertrude [Mrs. H. A.
  Kennedy] (1868-1908) English
  actress GRB/1
LOVELACE, Richard (1618-58)

English dramatist CP/2-3, FGF
LOVELL, Florence (d 1972 [50])
  critic BP/57*
LOVELL, George William (1804-78)
  dramatist DNB, EA/69
LOVELL, Mrs. George William
  see Lovell, Maria Anne
LOVELL, Harold C. (d 1969 [82])
  founder of American Shakespeare
  Festival BP/53*
LOVELL, Henry V. (fl 1853) actor
  HAS
LOVELL, Mrs. Henry V. (fl 1853)
  actress HAS
LOVELL, James (d 1972 [59])
  producer/director/choreographer
  BP/57*
LOVELL, Leslie see Leslie,
  H. L.
LOVELL, Maria Anne [née Lacy]
  (1803-77) English actress,
  dramatist CDP, DNB, OX
LOVELL, Raymond (1900-53) Cana-
  dian actor WWT/8-11
LOVELL, Thomas (fl 1635) actor
  DA
LOVELL, Tom (d 1909) clown
  EA/10*, WWT/14*
LOVELL, W. T. actor GRB/3-4,
  WWT/1-6
LOVELY, Joseph (d 1882 [35])
  minstrel CDP
LOVER, Mr. (fl 1848) actor HAS
LOVER, Samuel (1797-1868) Irish
  dramatist, actor CDP, EA/68,
  SR
LOVESEY, Alfred Frank (d 1908
  [33]) music-hall manager EA/
  09*
LOVETT, Beresford (b 1878) Eng-
  lish actor GRB/1
LOVETT, Robert Irish dramatist
  CP/2-3
LOVETT, Robert Morss (1870-
  1956) American dramatist HJD
LOVETT-JANISON, P. W. (d 1916)
  EA/17*
LOW, Carl (b 1916) American ac-
  tor, designer, director BE
LOW, Samuel (fl 1788) American
  dramatist EAP, RJ
LOWANDE, Martinho equestrian
  CDP
LOWDEN, George D. (d 1876)
  singer EA/77*
LOWE, Albert Henry [Harry Lauri]
  (d 1886 [44]) EA/87*
LOWE, Alva Hovery (d 1972 [80])

LOWE, agent BP/57*

LOWE, Arthur (b 1915) English actor WWT/15-16

LOWE, Caroline (1865-1947) actress SR

LOWE, Christopher (d 1801) English bill distributor TD/1-2

LOWE, David (b 1913) American producer, director TW/6

LOWE, Douglas (b 1882) English business manager WWT/4

LOWE, Edmund (1892-1971) American actor ES, TW/2-3, 27, WWT/7-11

LOWE, Enid (b 1908) English actress, singer WWT/11-15

LOWE, Jane (d 1883 [75]) EA/84*

LOWE, J. J. M. (d 1876 [24]) musician EA/77*

LOWE, John Francis (d 1887 [77]) EA/88*

LOWE, Joshua (d 1945 [72]) journalist BE*, WWT/14*

LOWE, K. Elmo (1899-1971) American executive, director, actor BE, TW/27

LOWE, Nicholas (fl 1628) actor DA

LOWE, Robert (d 1939 [64]) American actor BE*, BP/24*

LOWE, Sophie (d 1903) EA/04*

LOWE, Susanna see Drayton, Mrs. Henry

LOWE, Thomas (d 1783) singer, actor, lessee, manager CDP, DNB, GT, TD/1-2

LOWE, Trevor (d 1910 [32]) actor EA/11*, WWT/14*

LOWE, Mrs. William [Fanny Wallis] (d 1916) actress EA/17*

LOWELL, Cal (d 1967 [45]) stage manager BP/52*

LOWELL, Helen [Helen Lowell Robb] (1866-1937) American actress WWT/7-8

LOWELL, Joan (1902-67) American actress WWA/4

LOWELL, Molly [or Mollie] English actress GRB/1-4, WWT/1-5

LOWELL, Robert (b 1917) American dramatist AAS, CB, CD, CH, ES, MWD

LOWENFELD, Henry (d 1931 [72]) producer, manager BE*, WWT/14*

LOWENS, Curt (b 1925) German actor TW/22

LOWER, Sir William (1600?-62) English dramatist CDP, DNB, CP/1-3, FGF

LOWERRE, Mrs. Fred H. see Lauri, Lelia

LOWERY, Marcella (b 1945/46) American actress TW/25, 28-30

LOWERY, Robert (d 1971 [57]) performer BP/56*

LOWIN, G. (fl 1619) actor DA

LOWIN, John (1576-1653) English actor CDP, COC, DA, DNB, ES, GT, NTH, OC/1-3

LOWN, Bert (d 1962 [59]) composer/lyricist BP/47*

LOWNE, C[harles] M[acready] (d 1941 [78]) actor EA/97, GRB/2-4, WWT/1-8

LOWREY, Annie [Mrs. D. Lowrey] (d 1889 [24]) EA/90*

LOWREY, Mrs. D. see Lowrey, Annie

LOWREY, Dan, Sr. (d 1889 [66]) music-hall proprietor EA/90*

LOWREY, Mrs. Dan (d 1882) EA/83*

LOWREY, Mrs. Dan, Jr. (d 1887 [49]) EA/88*

LOWREY, Daniel (d 1897 [56]) music-hall proprietor EA/98*

LOWREY, Mrs. Mary Anne see Connolly, Maria

LOWREY, W. H. (d 1885 [26]) musical director EA/86*

LOWRIE, Edward (d 1965 [72]) performer BP/50*

LOWRIE, Jeanette [Mrs. Thomas Q. Seabrooke] Welsh/American actress WWS

LOWRY, C. H. equestrian CDP

LOWRY, John (d 1962 [79]) executive BE*

LOWRY, Judith (1890-1976) American actress TW/26-28

LOWRY, Philip W. (d 1969 [75]) lawyer BP/53*

LOWRY, Robert (d 1840) clown HAS

LOWRY, Rudd (d 1965 [73]) performer BP/50*

LOWRY, W. McNeil (b 1913) American executive, journalist BE

LOWTHER, George F. (d 1975 [62]) producer/director/choreographer BP/59*

LOWTHER, J. G. (d 1917) EA/18*

LOXLEY, Violet (b 1914) English actress WWT/9-10

LOY, Myrna (b 1905) American actress TW/22, 29

LOYAL, Leopold (d 1889) circus ringmaster EA/91*

LOYALE, Mme. (d 1863) English equestrienne HAS

LOYO, Caroline (fl 1851) equestrienne CDP

LOZANO, Roy (b 1943) American actor TW/24

LUBBOCK, Sydney Reginald (d 1905) EA/07*

LUBIN, Frederick (fl 1856) magician HAS

LUBIN BROTHERS jugglers CDP

LUBINOFF, A. Russian actor CDP

LUBOTSKY, Charlotte see Rae, Charlotte

LUBY, Edna (b 1884) American actress, mimic WWS

LUCAN, Arthur (d 1954 [67]) performer BE*, WWT/14*

LUCAS, Mr. (d 1824) actor HAS

LUCAS, Arthur Melville (1881-1943) American manager WWA/2

LUCAS, Charles (1808-69) English composer DNB

LUCAS, Mrs. Edward H. see Lucas, May

LUCAS, Henry (fl 1776-95) Irish? dramatist CP/2-3, GT

LUCAS, J. Frank American actor TW/30

LUCAS, John T. (d 1880 [45]) dramatist EA/81*

LUCAS, Jonathan (b 1922) American director, choreographer, producer, actor BE, TW/5-13

LUCAS, Karl (b 1919) American actor TW/8

LUCAS, Louisa (d 1885 [72]) EA/87*

LUCAS, May [Mrs. Edward H. Lucas] (d 1911 [39]) EA/12*

LUCAS, Nellie [Nellie Heitzman] (b 1884) English actress GRB/1

LUCAS, Paul (b 1908) actor SR

LUCAS, Rupert (d 1953 [57]) actor BE*, WWT/14*

LUCAS, Samuel (fl 1878?) songwriter, minstrel CDP

LUCAS, Thomas (d 1917 [78]) EA/18*

LUCAS, William (fl 1809) dramatist CP/3

LUCCA, Helen (d 1895 [29]) actress EA/96*, WWT/14*

LUCCA, Pauline (1841-1908) singer CDP

LUCCHESE, Josephine (d 1974 [78]) performer BP/59*

LUCE, Claire (b 1901/03) American actress BE, NTH, TW/3-20, WWT/6-16

LUCE, Claire Boothe (b 1903) American dramatist BE, CB, HJD

LUCE, Polly [Pauline Marion Luce] (1905-73) American actress WWT/7-9

LUCELLE, Fannie (fl 1869) dancer CDP

LUCELLE, Rose dancer CDP

LUCETTE, Catherine [Mrs. Charles Medwin] (d 1892) English actress CDP, HAS

LUCETTE, Madeline singer CDP

LUCK, Booth P. (d 1962 [52]) actor BE*

LUCKETT, Edith (b 1891) American actress WWM

LUCKHAM, Cyril (b 1907) English actor AAS, WWT/12-16

LUCKINBILL, Laurence George (b 1934/38) American actor TW/21, 24-26, 29, WWT/16

LUCY, Arnold [Walter George Campbell] (1865-1945) English actor GRB/1, 3-4

LUDECUS, Louisa (fl 1860) American actress? singer? HAS

LUDERS, Gustav (1865-1913) German composer GRB/3-4, WWA/1, WWM, WWT/1

LUDGER, C. (fl 1799) translator CP/3

LUDLAM, Charles (b 1943) American actor, dramatist, director, producer CD, WWT/16

LUDLAM, Christine see Zavistowski, Christine

LUDLOW, Charles Lyon (d 1911) actor EA/12*

LUDLOW, Henry (b 1879) English actor GRB/1-2

LUDLOW, Kate (fl 1846) actress HAS

LUDLOW, Noah Miller (1795-
1886) American actor, mana-
ger CDP, COC, DAB, ES,
HAS, OC/1-3, SR, WWA/H
LUDLOW, Patrick (b 1903)
English actor WWT/4-16
LUDLUM, Robert (b 1927) Amer-
ican producer, actor BE
LUDWIG, Christa (b 1932?)
German singer CB, ES
LUDWIG, Karen (b 1942) Amer-
ican actress TW/22, 25
LUDWIG, Salem (b 1915) Amer-
ican actor, director TW/22-
23, 25-26, 28, 30, WWT/
15-16
LUDWIG, W. (fl 1890) actor DP
LUEBBEN, Anita see Gillette,
Anita
LUELLA, Marie (fl 1887) actress
CDP
LUFF, William (b 1872) actor
GRB/1-4
LUFTIG, Charles (d 1975) per-
sonal manager BP/60*
LUGG, Alfred (b 1889) English
actor, executive WWT/4
LUGG, William (1852-1940) Eng-
lish actor GRB/3-4, WWT/
1-7
LUGNE-POË, Aurélien-Marie
(1869/70-1940) French actor,
manager COC, GRB/1, 3-4,
OC/1-3, WWT/1-4
LUGOSI, Bela (1883-1956) Hun-
garian actor TW/13, WWT/
9-11
LUGUET, André (b 1892) French
actor WWT/10
LUHDE, Henry (d 1866) German
musician HAS
LUISI, James (b 1928) American
actor TW/22-25
LUKA, Milo (b 1890) Czech
singer WWA/3
LUKAS, Paul (1891/94/95-1971)
Hungarian actor BE, CB,
ES, TW/28, WWA/5, WWT/
10-13
LUKASHOK, E. David (d 1974
[34]) producer/director/chore-
ographer BP/59*
LUKE, Peter (b 1919) English
dramatist, director AAS, CD
LUKOS, Alex (d 1918) EA/19*
LULLI, Folco (d 1970 [58])
performer BP/55*
"LULU" see Farini

LUM, Alvin (b 1931) American
actor TW/28-30
LUM, Charles N. (d 1966 [88])
performer BP/50*
LUMB, Geoffrey (b 1905) English
actor BE, TW/5-6, 10-15
LUMBARD, Jules G. (fl 1896?)
singer CDP
LUMBY, Ilah R. (b 1911) American
executive BE
LUMET, Baruch (b 1898) Polish
actor, dramatist BE
LUMET, Sidney (b 1924) American
director BE, ES, TW/4
LUMIERE, La Belle (d 1917) elec-
trical dancer EA/18*
LUMIERE AND SON theatre collec-
tive CD
LUMLEY, Benjamin (1811-75)
manager CDP, DNB
LUMLEY, Eliza (fl 1868) English
singer HAS
LUMLEY, Ralph Robert (d 1900
[35]) dramatist BE*, EA/01*,
WWT/14*
LUMLEY, Reginald Hope (d 1917)
dramatist EA/18*
LUMLEY, Terry (b 1945) American
actor TW/28
LUMSDEN, Alexander (d 1890 [35])
singer EA/91*
LUMSDEN, Geoffrey (b 1914) Eng-
lish actor TW/22-23
LUNA, Edelberta (d 1964 [27])
Cuban circus performer BE*
LUND, Art (b 1920) American ac-
tor, singer BE, TW/22-23,
WWT/14-16
LUND, Arthur (d 1917) EA/18*
LUND, Joe (d 1894) Negro come-
dian EA/95*
LUND, Mrs. Joe see Lund,
Rebecca
LUND, John (fl 1777) dramatist
CP/3
LUND, John (b 1913) American
actor TW/1-14
LUND, Rebecca [Mrs. Joe Lund]
(d 1876 [28]) EA/77*
LUNDBERG, Ada [Margaret Ada
Clegg Everard] (d 1899 [49])
music-hall comedian EA/00*
LUNDEL, Kert Fritjof (b 1936)
Swedish designer WWT/16
LUNDELL, Ludovic (d 1867 [48])
equestrian EA/68*
LUNDIGAN, William (d 1975 [61])
actor BP/60*, WWT/16*

LUNDY, Harry (d 1908 [45])
music-hall manager GRB/4
LUNN, Henry C. (d 1894 [76])
professor of music EA/95*
LUNN, Joseph (1784-1863)
dramatist DNB
LUNN, Louise Kirkby (1873-
1930) English singer ES,
WWW/3
LUNN, William Arthur Brown (d
1879) composer EA/80*
LUNNY, Robert (b 1942) American
actor TW/30
LUNT, Alfred (1892/93-1977)
American actor AAS, BE,
CB, COC, ES, HJD, NTH,
OC/1-3, PDT, SR, TW/2-21,
WWT/5-16
LUNT, Mrs. Alfred see Fon-
tanne, Lynn
LUNT, Eleanor (d 1900) EA/01*
LUNT, James (d 1879 [65])
actor EA/80*
LUPINO, Arthur (d 1908 [44])
pantomimist, animal imper-
sonator EA/09*
LUPINO, Barry (1882/84-1962)
English actor, pantomimist,
dancer COC, OC/1-3, TW/
19, WWT/7-13
LUPINO, Florence [Mrs. George
Lupino] (d 1899 [38]) EA/00*
LUPINO, George (d 1903) clown,
pantomimist EA/04*
LUPINO, George (1853-1932)
English pantomimist COC
LUPINO, Mrs. George see
Lupino, Florence
LUPINO, Harry (d 1896 [68])
pantomimist EA/97*
LUPINO, Henry George see
Lane, Lupino
LUPINO, Ida (b 1918) English
actress SR
LUPINO, Lily (d 1912 [20])
EA/13*
LUPINO, Mark (d 1930 [36]) actor
BE*, WWT/14*
LUPINO, Pandora Bronson Amer-
ican actress TW/27
LUPINO, Richard (b 1929) Amer-
ican actor TW/27
LUPINO, Stanley (1893/94-1942)
English actor, dancer CB,
COC, OC/2-3, SR, WWT/
4-9
LUPINO, Wallace (1897-1961)
Scottish actor WWT/7-12

LUPINO FAMILY ES
LUPO, George G. (d 1973 [49])
performer BP/58*
LUPO, Giovanni Batista (d 1868)
dancer HAS
LuPONE, Patti (b 1949) American
actress TW/29-30
LUPRIEL, George see Cox,
George William
LUPTON, Thomas (fl 1578) drama-
tist CP/1-3, FGF
LURIE, Louis (d 1972 [84]) "Broad-
way angel" BP/57*
LURIE, Samuel press representative
BE
LUSBY, William (d 1907) proprietor
EA/08*
LUSBY, Mrs. William (d 1889)
EA/90*
LUSTIK, Marlena (b 1944) American
actress TW/28
LUTHER, Anna (d 1960 [67]) ac-
tress BE*
LUTHER, Lester (d 1962 [74]) actor
BE*
LUTZ, E. O. (b 1919) American
educator, executive BE
LUTZ, H. B. American producer,
dramatist BE
LUTZ, William Aynesley (d 1898)
EA/99*
LUTZ, W. Meyer (1829-1903)
Bavarian composer, conductor
DNB
LUTZER, Jenny (d 1877 [51])
singer EA/78*
LUXMORE, Ada [Mrs. Will Evans]
(d 1897) music-hall performer
EA/98*
LYALL, Charles (d 1911) singer
EA/12*
LYALL, Edna [Ada Ellen Bayly]
(d 1903 [45]) dramatist EA/04*
LYDGATE, John (c. 1370-c. 1451)
English dramatist ES
LYDIARD, Bob (b 1944) American
actor TW/25-27, 30
LYEL, Viola (1900-72) English ac-
tress AAS, WWT/7-15
LYLE, Arthur (d 1903) English ac-
tor OAA/2
LYLE, Cecil (d 1955 [63]) magician
BE*, WWT/14*
LYLE, Kenyon [Marcus Goldberg]
(d 1902 [35]) actor EA/04*
LYLE, Lyston [Edward Gibson]
(1856-1920) actor, manager
GRB/1-4, WWT/1-3

LYLY, John (c. 1554-1606) English dramatist, lessee COC, CP/1-3, DA, DNB, ES, FGF, HP, MH, NTH, OC/1-3, PDT, RE

LYMAN, Debra (b 1940) American actress TW/23, 28-29

LYMAN, Dorothy (b 1947) American actress TW/26

LYMAN, George (1869-1943) actor SR

LYMAN, Peggy (b 1950) American actress TW/28-29

LYMAN, Rose Blaine (d 1974) performer BP/59*

LYMAN, Tommy (d 1964 [73]) singer BE*, BP/48*

LYNCH, Brid (d 1969 [55]) performer BP/54*

LYNCH, Edward D. (b 1880) American actor WWM

LYNCH, Francis (fl 1737) dramatist CP/1-3

LYNCH, Francis composer, minstrel CDP

LYNCH, Fred (d 1968 [59]) publicist BP/52*

LYNCH, Harry (d 1890 [34]) Negro comedian EA/91*

LYNCH, Nell (d 1910) markswoman EA/11*

LYNCH, Richard (b 1940) American actor TW/22, 27, 29

LYNCH, William (d 1861 [78]) pantaloon EA/72*

LYND, Rosa (1884-1922) American actress WWT/4

LYNDE, Flo [Mrs. Charles J. Hoby] (d 1898 [22]) actress EA/99*

LYNDE, Janice (b 1947) American actress TW/26, 28-29

LYNDE, Joseph (d 1905) singer EA/06*

LYNDE, Paul (b 1926) American actor, director BE, CB, TW/8-9

LYNDECK, Edmund (b 1925) American actor TW/25-29

LYNDON, Barré (b 1896) English dramatist WWT/9-11

LYNDON, Harry (d 1916) EA/18*

LYNDSAY, Sir David (1490-c. 1554) Scottish dramatist COC, ES

LYNE, Thomas A. (b 1806)

American actor HAS

LYNHAM, William (d 1881 [42]) lessee EA/82*

LYNILL, Harry (d 1878) actor EA/79*

LYNLEY, Carol (b 1942) American actress ES, TW/13-16

LYNN [Arthur A. Chippendale] American actor, singer GRB/1

LYNN, Charlotte (d 1974) performer BP/58*

LYNN, Dane W. (d 1975 [56]) producer/director/choreographer BP/60*

LYNN, Diana (1926-71) American actress BE, CB, TW/8-12, 28

LYNN, Eleanor (b 1925) American actress TW/6-7

LYNN, Harry (d 1918) EA/19*

LYNN, Iola (b 1922) Welsh actress TW/14

LYNN, Jeffrey (b 1909) American actor BE, TW/8, 23

LYNN, John Westley Symonds (d 1899 [63]) conjuror EA/00*

LYNN, J. Wellesley (b 1875) English actor, entertainer GRB/1

LYNN, Mara (b 1929) American dancer, actress, choreographer BE

LYNN, Natalie (d 1964) performer BP/49*

LYNN, Mrs. Neville see Corri, Ghita

LYNN, Ralph (1882-1962) English actor COC, OC/3, WWT/4-13, WWW/6

LYNN, Regina (b 1938) American actress TW/24

LYNN, Sharon (d 1963 [53]) performer BP/47*

LYNN, William H. (d 1952 [63]) American dancer, actor TW/8

LYNNE, Ada (b 1928) American actress TW/4

LYNNE, Carole [née Helen Violet Carolyn Haymen] (b 1918) English actress, singer WWT/10-12

LYNNE, Frank (d 1916) singer, actor CDP

LYNNE, Gillian English director, choreographer, dancer WWT/16

LYNTON, Ethel (fl 1881?) actress, singer CDP

LYNTON, Mayne (b 1885) English actor WWT/7

LYON, Ben (b 1901) American actor ES, WWT/7-14

LYON, Frank (b 1905) American
actor TW/3
LYON, Herb (d 1968 [49]) jour-
nalist BP/53*
LYON, James S. (d 1897 [72])
theatrical furnisher EA/98*
LYON, John Henry Hobart (d
1961 [83]) scholar BE*,
BP/46*
LYON, Louis see Aldrich, Louis
LYON, Sarah see Allen, Mrs.
C. Leslie
LYON, Thomas (1812-69) actor,
dramatist CDP
LYON, Wanda (b 1897) American
actress WWT/7-8
LYON, William (d 1748) actor,
dramatist CP/2-3, GT, TD/
1-2
LYONNET, William [or Henry]
(d 1933 [80]) historian BE*,
WWT/14*
LYONS, A. Neil (1880-1940)
South African dramatist WWT/
6-7
LYONS, Arthur S. (d 1963 [62])
talent agent BP/48*
LYONS, Edmund (d 1867 [39])
actor WWT/14*
LYONS, E. D. (d 1867 [39])
lessee EA/68*
LYONS, E. D. (d 1880) giant
EA/81*
LYONS, Edmund D. (1851-1906)
Scottish actor OAA/1-2
LYONS, Edward (d 1905 [77])
actor EA/07*
LYONS, Frederick (d 1887)
singer, actor NYM
LYONS, George (d 1911 [38])
dancer EA/12*
LYONS, Gretchen [Mrs. Lucius
Henderson] (fl 1890) English
actress WWS
LYONS, Harry (d 1975) dramatist
BP/59*
LYONS, Sir Joseph (d 1917)
actor, dramatist EA/18*
LYONS, Katharine (1889-1933)
American critic WWA/1
LYONS, Robert (d 1908) actor
GRB/4*
LYONS, Robert Charles (1853-
92) Scottish actor OAA/1-2
LYRIC, Dora (d 1962 [83])
performer BE*
LYSLE, Cora (1861-87) actress
NYM

LYSTER, Frederick (b 1822) Irish
singer HAS
LYSTER, Mrs. Frederick see
Walton, Minnie
LYSTER, Mrs. John Richard Kir-
wan see Barsanti, Jane
LYTELL, Bert (1885/87/90-1954)
American actor TW/2-8, 11,
WWA/3, WWT/7-11
LYTELL, Wilfred (d 1954 [62])
actor TW/11
LYTTLETON, Dame Edith (d 1948
[83]) dramatist WWT/2-7
LYTTON, Miss [née Foote] (d 1890
[27]) EA/91*
LYTTON, Bart (d 1969 [56]) drama-
tist BP/54*
LYTTON, Doris (1893-1953) Eng-
lish actress WWT/2-10
LYTTON, Edward English business
manager, actor GRB/1-4
LYTTON, Mrs. Edward see
Grattan, Kittie
LYTTON, Edward George Earle
Lytton Bulwer-Lytton, Lord
(1803-73) English dramatist
CDP, COC, DNB, EA/68, ES,
HP, MH, NTH, OC/1-3, SR
LYTTON, Elsie Keith [Mrs. Wil-
liam Henry Hart] actress GRB/1
LYTTON, Henry, Jr. [Lord Alva
Lytton] (1904-65) English singer,
actor WWT/6-8
LYTTON, Sir Henry A. (1860/65/
67-1936) English actor DNB,
GRB/1-4, NTH, WWT/1-7,
WWW/3
LYUS, James (d 1885) music-hall
chairman EA/86*
LYVEDEN, Lord [Percy Vernon]
(1857-1926) English actor GRB/1

- M -

M., E. dramatist CP/1-3
M., J. C. (fl 1801?) dramatist
CP/3
M., W. (fl 1697?) dramatist CP/
1-3, FGF
MAARTENS, Maarten [Joost Marius
Willem Van der Poorten-
Schwartz] (b 1858) Dutch drama-
tist WWM
MAAS, Audrey Gellen (d 1975 [40])
dramatist BP/60*
MAAS, Joseph (1847-86) English
singer CDP, DNB

MABBE, James (1569-c. 1642)
English dramatist CP/2-3,
FGF, HP

MABBETT, Ambrose (d 1916)
musical director EA/18*

MABLEY, Edward (b 1906)
American dramatist, educator
BE

MABLEY, Moms (d 1975 [75])
performer BP/59*

MABOU MINES theatre collective
CD

MacADAM, William (b 1943)
American actor TW/24

McADAMS, Stanley (b 1938)
American actor TW/25,
28-29

McADOO, Orpheus M. (d 1900)
minstrel, proprietor EA/01*

McAFEE, Diane (b 1943) American actress TW/25

MACAFERRI, Sig. (fl 1857)
singer CDP

McALEER, Mr. (fl 1851) actor
HAS

McALINNEY, Patrick (d 1913)
Irish actor TW/12

MACALLAME, Anna (b 1615)
bearded woman CDP

MACALLAN, Patrick Robert
see Robertson, Robert

MACALLISTER, Andrew (d 1856)
magician CDP, HAS

MacALLISTER, Mme. L. A.
de (d 1859 [27]) magician
CDP, HAS

McALLISTER, Alister P. see
Wharton, Anthony P.

McALLISTER, William (b 1843)
minstrel, manager CDP

McALLON, Andrew see Mack,
Andrew

MacALPINE, Miss (fl 1815)
actress CDP

MACALPINE, Simon see
Lack, Simon

McANALLY, Ray (b 1926) Irish
actor AAS, WWT/14-16

McANDREWS, J. W. (1835-99)
minstrel SR

McARDLE, Arthur (d 1898)
EA/99*

McARDLE, James (d 1881 [38])
EA/82*

McARDLE, J. F. American
actor WWT/1-5

McARDLE, John F. songwriter
CDP

McARDLE, John Francis (d 1883
[41]) dramatist EA/84*

MACARTE, Adelaide (d 1908) variety performer EA/09*

MACARTE, Dan (d 1873) equestrian
EA/74*

MACARTE, Regina (d 1892) equestrian EA/93*

MACARTHUR, Charles (1895?-1956)
American dramatist AAS, ES,
HJD, MH, MWD, NTH, TW/12,
WWA/3, WWT/6-11

MacARTHUR, Harry (d 1973 [62])
critic BP/58*

MacARTHUR, James (b 1937)
American actor BE

MacARTHUR, Mary (1930-49)
American actress TW/6

McARTHUR, Molly (1900-72) English designer WWT/8-12

MACARTHUR, Samuel (fl 1780)
dramatist CP/3

MACARTHY, Mr. (fl 1848) actor
CDP

MACARTHY, Harry (fl 1869?)
singer, songwriter CDP

MacARTHY, Harry B. (b 1834)
English actor HAS

MacARTHY, Huntley May (d 1866
[51]) manager EA/72*

MacARTHY, Marion (1838-63) English actress, singer CDP, HAS

MACARTNEY, C. L. (fl 1800)
actor, dramatist CP/3, TD/1-2

McASKILL, Angus (d 1863) giant
HAS

McATEE, Ben (d 1961 [58]) actor
BE*

MACAULAY, John (fl 1785) dramatist CP/3

MACAULAY, Joseph (d 1967 [76])
American actor, singer WWT/
9-14

MACAULAY, Rose Kathleen (d
1900) EA/01*

MACAULEY, Mrs. (d 1837 [52])
actress WWT/14*

MACAULEY, Bernard (1837-86)
American actor, manager
CDP, HAS, SR

MACAULEY, Mrs. Bernard see
Macauley, Rachel

MACAULEY, Elizabeth Wright
(1785-1837) English? actress
CDP, OX

MACAULEY, John T. (d 1915 [69])
manager WWT/14*

MACAULEY, Rachel [Mrs. Bernard

Macauley] (1845-98) actress
CDP
MCAULL, John A. (d 1894) mana-
ger WWT/14*
McBAN, Patrick (d 1906) juggler
EA/07*
MACBETH, Allan (d 1910 [54])
composer, conductor EA/11*
MACBETH, Florence (1891-
1966) American singer WWA/4
MACBETH, Helen [Mrs. Frank
Mills] American actress
GRB/1-4, WWT/1-5
McBRIDE, Alex (fl 1853-58) actor
HAS
McBRIDE, Claude E. (d 1973
[36]) composer/lyricist BP/57*
MacBRIDE, Donald (d 1957
[63]) actor BE*
McBRIDE, James (d 1917 [75])
doorkeeper EA/18*
McBRIDE, Jinnie (d 1916) EA/
17*
McBRIDE, John S. (d 1961 [84])
ticket agent BE*
McBRIDE, Mary Margaret (d
1976 [76]) performer BP/60*
McBRIDE, Miss M. C[ecelia]
(d 1846) American dancer
CDP, HAS
McBRIDE, Patricia (b 1942)
American dancer CB, ES
MacBRYDE, John N. (d 1966
[84]) performer BP/51*
McCABE, D. W. (d 1907 [47])
minstrel, manager CDP
MACCABE, Frederick (1831-
1904) ventriloquist, mimic,
musician CDP
MacCABE, James (d 1918) EA/
19*
McCABE, Mary (d 1975 [73])
performer BP/60*
McCABE, May North (d 1949
[76]) actress BE*, BP/34*
MACCABE, Michael (d 1883)
EA/84*
MACCABE, Mike (d 1894 [39])
Irish comedian EA/95*
MACCABE, Joseph (d 1893)
music-hall performer EA/94*
McCAFFREY, Edward (d 1911
[85]) musician EA/12*
MacCAFFREY, George (1870-
1939) Irish critic WWT/8
McCAHEN, Col. J. (fl 1828)
American actor HAS
McCALL, Angela (d 1965 [90])

performer BP/50*
McCALL, Janet (b 1935) American
actress TW/28-30
McCALL, Joan (b 1943) American
actress TW/21
McCALL, Lizzie (d 1942 [84])
actress BE*, WWT/14*
McCALL, Monica English literary
representative BE
McCALLA, Dolly (b 1891) American
actress GRB/1
McCALLIN, Clement (b 1913) Eng-
lish actor AAS, WWT/9-16
McCALLUM, Colin Whitton see
Coborn, Charles
McCALLUM, David (b 1933) Scot-
tish actor TW/25
McCALLUM, John (b 1914/18)
Australian actor, director
WWT/12-16
McCALLUM, Neil (d 1976 [46])
performer BP/60*
McCALMON, George A. (b 1909)
American educator BE
McCAMBRIDGE, Mercedes (b 1918)
American actress BE, CB,
TW/28
McCAMMON, Bessie J. (d 1964
[80]) American actress BE*
McCANDLESS, Stanley (1897-1967)
American educator, lighting de-
signer BE
McCANE, Mabel (fl 1906-12) Amer-
ican actress WWM
MACCANN, Mrs. (d 1896 [59])
musician EA/97*
McCANN, Alfred W., Jr. (d 1972
[64]) performer BP/57*
McCANN, Dora (d 1975 [60]) per-
former BP/60*
McCANN, Frances actress TW/3
McCANN, Mrs. J. H. see Mc-
Cann, Mary Jane
McCANN, Harrison (d 1962 [82])
advertising executive BE*
McCANN, Mary Jane [Mrs. J. H.
McCann] (d 1908) EA/10*
McCANN, Walter E. (fl 1890-1912)
American editor WWM
McCAREY, Leo (d 1969 [71]) pro-
ducer/director/choreographer
BP/54*
McCARROLL, Alexander (d 1876)
musician EA/78*
McCARROLL, James (1814-92)
Irish/Canadian dramatist DAB
McCARTEN, John (1916-74) Amer-
ican critic BE

McCARTHER, Avis (b 1947)
American actress TW/26, 28
McCARTHY, Mrs. (d 1872)
EA/74*
McCARTHY, Bartlett singer,
songwriter CDP
McCARTHY, Charles singer,
songwriter CDP
MACCARTHY, Charlotte (fl
1765?) dramatist CP/2-3
McCARTHY, Daniel musician,
composer, dancer CDP
McCARTHY, Daniel (b 1869)
English actor GRB/4, WWT/
1-5
MacCARTHY, Sir Desmond (1877-
1952) English critic COC,
DNB, ES, GRB/2-4, OC/1-3,
PDT, WWT/1-11, WWW/5
McCARTHY, John (d 1888) circus
rider EA/89*
McCARTHY, Joseph A. (d 1975
[53]) dramatist BP/60*
McCARTHY, Justin (d 1912 [81])
EA/13*
McCARTHY, Justin Huntly (1860-
1936) English dramatist GRB/
1-4, MWD, WWM, WWT/1-7,
WWW/3
McCARTHY, Kevin (b 1914)
American actor BE, TW/2-
12, 14-15, 18, 21, 23, 30,
WWT/11-16
McCARTHY, Lillah (1875-1960)
English actress COC, DNB,
ES, GRB/1-4, NTH, OC/3,
TW/16, WWT/1-11
McCARTHY, Lin American actor
TW/13
McCARTHY, Mary (b 1912)
American critic BE
McCARTHY, Neil S. (d 1972
[84]) lawyer BP/57*
McCARTHY, Mrs. W. H. see
MacNally, Jessie
McCARTY, E. Clayton (b 1901)
American educator, dramatist
BE
McCARTY, Eddie (b 1940) Amer-
ican actor TW/24
McCARTY, Mary (b 1923) Amer-
ican actress, singer TW/5-7,
20, 27-29, WWT/15-16
MacCAULAY, Joseph (d 1967
[76]) actor, singer TW/24
McCAULEY, Jack (b 1900) Amer-
ican actor TW/4-7
McCAULEY, Judith American

actress TW/29-30
MacCAULEY, Mark (b 1948)
American actor TW/26, 28-
30
McCAULL, John A. (d 1894) Amer-
ican manager EA/95*
McCAWLEY, Charles H. (b 1928)
American actor TW/9
McCAY, Peggy (b 1931) American
actress TW/12-13
McCHLERY, Grace (d 1975 [77])
performer BP/59*
McCLAIN, John (1904-67) Amer-
ican critic BE, NTH, TW/
23
McCLANAHAN, Rue American ac-
tress TW/23, 25-26, 28-29,
WWT/16
McCLANE, John E. (d 1972 [50])
publicist BP/57*
McCLANNIN, Robert F. (b 1832)
American actor HAS
McCLARNEY, Pat (b 1925) Amer-
ican actress TW/2
McCLEAN, Mrs. [née Fairfield]
(fl 1828-62) actress HAS
McCLEAN, Jessie (fl 1856-62)
actress HAS
McCLEERY, Albert (d 1972 [60])
producer/director/choreographer
BP/56*
McCLEERY, R. C. (d 1927) scene
artist WWT/14*
McCLELLAN, Mrs. see Les-
sing, Madge
McCLELLAN, John Jasper (1874-
1926) American conductor
WWA/1
McCLELLAND, Allan (b 1917) Irish
actor WWT/12-16
McCLELLAND, Charles actor
TW/1
McCLELLAND, Donald (1903-55)
American actor TW/2, 12
McCLELLAND, Evelyn A. (d 1972
[79]) performer BP/57*
McCLELLAND, Mrs. Harry see
Lawrence, Nellie
McCLELLAND, Richard Leeper
see Leech, Richard
McCLENDON, Ernestine (b 1918)
American actress BE
McCLENDON, Rose (1885-1936)
American actress NTH
McCLINTIC, Guthrie (1893-1961)
American actor, producing
manager, director AAS, CB,
COC, ES, NTH, OC/1-3, SR,

TW/2-8, 18, WWA/4, WWT/
6-12
McCLOSKEY, James R. (b 1918)
American educator, director
BE
McCLOSKY, J. J. (1826-1913)
dramatist, manager, actor
SR
McCLURE, Mrs. (fl 1832-54)
actress HAS
McCLURE, Linda (b 1947) Amer-
ican actress TW/30
McCLURE, Michael (b 1932)
American dramatist CD
MacCLURE, Victor (1887-1963)
Scottish dramatist WWW/6
McCOLE, John (d 1874) actor?
EA/75*
McCOLL, Ewan theatre group
founder COC
MACCOLL, James (d 1956 [44])
actor TW/12
MacCOLL, Virginia Lenore (b
1951) American actress TW/29
McCOLLOM, James [or John]
C. (1838-83) American actor
CDP, HAS
McCOLLOUGH, John (1832-85)
Irish actor, manager SR
McCOLLUM, Thomas (d 1872
[44]) equestrian, circus pro-
prietor CDP
McCOLLUM, Mrs. Thomas (d
1906) EA/08*
McCOMAS, Carroll (1891/94-1962)
American actress TW/6-8,
19, WWT/6-7
McCOMB, H. (d 1971 [90]) per-
former BP/56*
McCOMB, Kate (d 1959 [87])
actress BE*, BP/43*
MACCOMO, Martini (d 1871 [32])
lion tamer EA/72*
McCONNELL, Anna (d 1891
[21]) music-hall performer
EA/93*
McCONNELL, Charles (d 1916)
EA/17*
McCONNELL, C. J. (d 1895
[52]) music-hall singer EA/96*
McCONNELL, Mrs. C. J. see
McConnell, Mary
McCONNELL, Forrest W. (d
1962 [51]) American performer
BE*
McCONNELL, Lulu (d 1962 [80])
American actress TW/19
McCONNELL, Mary [Mrs. C.

J. McConnell] (d 1893 [53])
EA/94*
McCONNELL, Ty (b 1940) Ameri-
can actor TW/25-26, 29-30
McCONNELL, Mr. W. (d 1867
[36]) artist EA/68*
McCORD, J. C. (b 1920) American
actor TW/8
McCORD, Nancy American actress,
singer WWT/8-10
McCORMAC, Esther see Ashley,
Esther Potter
McCORMACK, Benjamin (d 1871)
clown EA/72*
McCORMACK, Frank (d 1941 [65])
American actor BP/25*
MacCORMACK, Franklyn (d 1971
[63]) performer BP/56*
McCORMACK, John (1884-1945)
Irish/American singer CB,
DAB, ES, WWA/2, WWW/4
McCORMACK, Mrs. M. [née
Bramah] (d 1871) ballet mistress
EA/72*
McCORMACK, Patty (b 1945)
American actress BE
McCORMICK, Arthur Langdon (d
1954 [81]) American dramatist
WWM, WWT/4-8
McCORMICK, F. J. (d 1947 [c.
50]) Irish actor TW/3
McCORMICK, John (d 1945 [61])
singer TW/2
McCORMICK, John (d 1975 [82])
theatrical store owner BP/60*
McCORMICK, Langdon (d 1954)
American dramatist WWA/3
McCORMICK, Myron (1906/07/08-
62) American actor CB, TW/
1-15, 19, WWA/4, WWT/9-13
McCORMICK, Nancy (b 1946)
American actress TW/25
McCORMICK, Ruth (b 1913) Amer-
ican actress TW/29
McCORRY, Marion (b 1945) Amer-
ican actress TW/30
McCOURT, Joseph (d 1876 [52])
musician EA/78*
McCOWEN, Alec (b 1925) English
actor AAS, CB, COC, TW/24-
27, WWT/12-16
McCOY, Bessie [Mrs. Richard
Harding Davis] (d 1931 [45])
comedienne BE*, BP/16*,
WWT/14*
McCOY, Frank (d 1947 [58]) pro-
ducer BE*, BP/31*
McCOY, W. [William Greenwood]

(d 1885 [26]) music-hall performer EA/86*

McCRACKEN, Esther (1902-71) English dramatist, actress AAS, PDT, WWT/10-14

McCRACKEN, James (b 1926) American singer CB

McCRACKEN, Joan (1922-61) American actress, singer, dancer CB, TW/1-15, 18, WWT/10-13

McCREE, Junie (b 1866) American actress, writer WWM

McCREERY, Bud (b 1925) American composer, lyricist, performer BE

McCULLERS, Carson (1917-67) American dramatist AAS, BE, MD, MH, MWD, PDT, TW/24

McCULLEY, Johnston (1883-1958) American dramatist WWA/3

McCULLOCH, Andrew [Albert Macolla] (d 1889) musician EA/90*

McCULLOCH, Arthur (b 1860) Scottish actor GRB/1

McCULLOCH, Rose (d 1886) EA/87*

McCULLOUGH, Brien (d 1911) actor, dramatist EA/12*

McCULLOUGH, John (1832-85) Irish/American actor CDP, DAB, ES, HAS, NTH, OC/1-3, WWA/H

McCULLOUGH, Mrs. John see McCullough, Letitia

McCULLOUGH, Letitia [Mrs. John McCullough] (d 1888) EA/89*

McCULLOUGH, Paul (1883-1936) American actor WWT/7-8

McCULLOUGH, Russell H. (d 1972 [76]) director of theatre construction BP/57*

MACCUNN, Hamish (1868-1916) Scottish composer, conductor DNB, GRB/1-4, WWW/2

MacCURDY, James Kyrle (fl 1894) American actor WWS

McCURRY, Jack Howard (d 1970 [94]) performer BP/55*

McCUTCHEON, George Barr (b 1866) American dramatist WWM

McCUTCHEON, Thomas (d 1847) American actor HAS

McCUTCHEON, Wallace (d 1928

[47]) actor BE*, BP/12*

McDANIEL, Hattie (1898-1952) American actress CB

MacDERMOT, Galt composer AAS, WWT/16

MacDERMOT, Robert [Robert MacDermot Barbour] (1910-64) Indian/English dramatist WWT/9-13

MacDERMOTT, The Great [Gilbert Hastings] (1845-1901) actor, stage manager, manager, agent, singer CDP, DNB, OC/1-3

McDERMOTT, Aline (d 1951 [70]) actress TW/7

MacDERMOTT, Gilbert Hastings see MacDermott, The Great

McDERMOTT, Hugh (1908-72) Scottish actor WWT/10-14

McDERMOTT, James (d 1869 [30]) actor? EA/70*

MacDERMOTT, Norman (b 1890) Scottish producer, manager, director COC, OC/3, WWT/4-13

McDERMOTT, Robert Joseph (d 1917 [55]) musical director, composer EA/18*

McDERMOTT, William F. (1891-1958) American critic TW/15, WWA/3

McDEVITT, Ruth [née Shoecraft] (1895-1976) American actress BE, WWT/14-16

MACDONA, Charles (d 1946 [86]) Irish manager WWT/5-10

MACDONA, Henry Edwin (d 1900) EA/01*

MACDONA, William (d 1892) EA/93*

MacDONAGH, Donagh (d 1968 [55]) dramatist BP/52*

McDONALD, Mr. (fl 1802) actor HAS

McDONALD, Mr. (d 1832) clown HAS

McDONALD, Mrs. (d 1883) EA/84*

McDONALD, Albert (d 1900) music-hall manager EA/01*

McDONALD, Andrew (1755?-90) Scottish dramatist CP/3, DNB, GT, TD/1-2

MACDONALD, Ballard (d 1935 [52]) American songwriter BE*, BP/20*

McDONALD, Bella (d 1892) EA/93*

MacDONALD, Brian (b 1928) Canadian choreographer, ballet

director CB
McDONALD, Charles (fl 1818-19)
  clown HAS
MACDONALD, Mrs. Charles
  [Mrs. James Macdonald] (d
  1877 [47]) EA/78*
McDONALD, Christie (1875-1962)
  Canadian actress, singer TW/
  19, WWM, WWS, WWT/1-6
MacDONALD, Cordelia Howard
  (1848-1941) American actress
  CB
MacDONALD, Donald (1898-1959)
  American actor TW/2-3, 16,
  WWT/8-12
MacDONALD, Duncan (fl 1753?)
  Scottish equilibrist CDP
McDONALD, Earl (b 1905) Amer-
  ican actor TW/21, 24
MACDONALD, Emily (d 1889
  [19]) actress? singer? EA/90*
McDONALD, Estelle [Estelle
  Potter] (fl 1842-59) American
  actress HAS
MACDONALD, Eva (b 1886) Aus-
  tralian actress WWM
MacDONALD, Eve March (d 1974)
  performer BP/59*
McDONALD, Flora see Spencer,
  Mrs. George Preston
McDONALD, Francis (d 1968
  [77]) performer BP/53*
McDONALD, Gordon (b 1921)
  American actor TW/2
McDONALD, James (d 1889 [60])
  comedian, lessee EA/90*
McDONALD, James American
  actor TW/24, 27-29
MACDONALD, Mrs. James see
  Macdonald, Mrs. Charles
MacDONALD, James Weatherby
  (d 1962 [63]) actor BE*
MACDONALD, J. C. (d 1895
  [45]) Scottish comedian, singer
  EA/96*
MacDONALD, J. Carlisle (d 1974
  [80]) publicist, journalist BP/
  59*
MacDONALD, Jeanette (1907-65)
  American actress, singer BE,
  TW/21, WWA/4, WWT/7-12
MacDONALD, Jet (b 1927) Amer-
  ican actor TW/3-4
McDONALD, John G. (d 1888)
  American comedian EA/89*
MacDONALD, Katherine (d 1956
  [c. 64]) actress BE*
MACDONALD, Lily see Morelli,

Mrs. Charles
MacDONALD, McGregor (d 1856)
  actor HAS
McDONALD, Marie (d 1965 [42])
  performer BP/50*
McDONALD, Marvin (d 1973 [78])
  producer/director/choreographer
  BP/57*
MacDONALD, Michael Alan (b 1941)
  American actor TW/23
MacDONALD, Murray [Walter Mac-
  Donald Honeyman] (b 1899)
  Scottish producer, director,
  manager, actor AAS, WWT/9-16
McDONALD, Ray (d 1959 [38])
  American dancer TW/15
MACDONALD, Robert (d 1887)
  music-hall Irish comedian EA/
  88*
MacDONALD, Robert (d 1964 [91])
  producer/director BP/49*
MACDONALD, Ronald (1860-1933)
  dramatist WWW/3
McDONALD, Sadie (d 1896) actress
  EA/97*
McDONALD, Samuel ["Big Sam"]
  (1762-1802) giant CDP
McDONALD, Tanny (b 1939) Amer-
  ican actress TW/23, 28-30
MACDONALD, William H. (d 1906)
  American singer WWA/1
MacDONELL, Kathlene (b 1890)
  Canadian actress WWT/7-8
McDONNELL, Frank (d 1905 [49])
  actor EA/06*
MacDONNELL, Rev. George Alcock
  (d 1899 [69]) dramatic reader
  EA/00*
MACDONNELL, Leslie A. (b 1903)
  Welsh manager, producer
  WWT/14-15
MacDONOUGH, Glen (d 1924 [57])
  librettist WWT/4
MACDONOUGH, Glen librettist,
  dramatist GRB/3-4, WWT/1-8
MACDONOUGH, Harry (fl 1880-
  1913) American actor WWM
MACDONOUGH, Harry, Jr. (fl
  1908-13) American actor, ban-
  joist WWM
McDONOUGH, John Edwin (1825-
  82) American actor CDP, HAS,
  SR
MacDONOUGH, Thomas B. (b 1835)
  American actor, business mana-
  ger, manager HAS
McDOUGALL, Gordon (b 1941)
  Scottish director WWT/16

MacDOUGALL, Roger (b 1910) Scottish dramatist, director AAS, BE, CD, PDT, WWT/ 11-16

MacDOUGALL, Ronald (d 1973 [58]) dramatist BP/58*

McDOUGALL, R. W. (b 1819) American actor HAS

MacDOUGALL, Sally (d 1973 [97]) critic BP/57*

McDOWALL, George (d 1879 [35]) EA/80*

McDOWALL, Roddy (b 1928) English actor AAS, BE, CB, TW/9-20, WWT/13-16

McDOWELL, Anderson see Elliot, George

McDOWELL, Claire (d 1966 [88]) performer BP/51*

MACDOWELL, Edward (d 1908 [47]) composer EA/09*

McDOWELL, Fred (d 1972 [68]) performer BP/57*

McDOWELL, J. (fl 1839) actor HAS

McDOWELL, J. (d 1883) manager EA/84*

McDOWELL, John H. (b 1903) American educator BE

McDOWELL, Joseph (d 1888 [44]) comic singer EA/89*

MacDOWELL, Melbourne (1856-1941) American actor PP/2, WWS

McDOWELL, Norman (b 1931) Irish dancer, choreographer, director ES

McDOWELL, Roddy see Mc-Dowall, Roddy

MacDOWELL, William Melbourne (d 1941 [84]) American actor BP/25*

MACE, Harriet see Booth, Mrs. Junius Brutus, Jr., II

MACE, James (1831-1910) circus performer, showman DNB

MACE, Louis L. (d 1965 [71]) critic BP/50*

McEARCHAN, Malcolm (d 1945 [61]) performer BE*, WWT/14*

McELHANY, Thomas J. (d 1966 [75]) performer BP/51*

McELHONE, Eloise (d 1974 [53]) performer BP/59*

McENERY, Peter (b 1940) English actor AAS, WWT/14-16

McENROE, Robert E. dramatist BE

McENTEE, Millicent Evison (d

1970 [93]) performer BP/54*

McETHENREY, Jane see Clare, Ada

McEVOY, Arthur Thompson (d 1891) composer EA/92*

MacEVOY, Charles (fl 1871?) comedian, song composer CDP

McEVOY, Charles (1875/79-1929) English dramatist GRB/4, WWT/1-5, WWW/3

MacEVOY, John lecturer, manager CDP

McEVOY, J. P. (1894/95/97-1958) American dramatist, librettist WWA/3, WWT/7-11

MacEVOY, Mary musician CDP

McEVOY, Nellie [Mrs. Neil Soloman] (d 1882) EA/83*

MacEVOY, Master Spaulding (fl 1868?) singer CDP

McEWAN, Geraldine [née McKeown] (b 1932) English actress AAS, BE, COC, TW/20, WWT/12-16

MacFADDEN, Gertrude (d 1967 [67]) performer BP/52*

McFADYEN, Louisa (d 1870) actress? EA/71*

MacFARLAND, Mr. (fl 1851) actor HAS

McFARLAND, Mr. (fl 1848) vaulter HAS

MCFARLAND, Mrs. see Woodbury, Miss S.

McFARLAND, Beulah (d 1964 [67]) American showgirl BE*, BP/49*

MacFARLAND, Dorothea American actress TW/3-6, 30

McFARLAND, Edith Agnes (d 1892 [17]) EA/93*

McFARLAND, Gary (d 1971 [38]) composer/lyricist BP/56*

McFARLAND, Nan (1916-74) American actress TW/8-9, 12

McFARLAND, Mrs. W. (d 1882 [36]) EA/83*

McFARLAND, William (d 1888) actor SR

McFARLAND, William (d 1898 [61]) lessee EA/99*

MacFARLANE, Bruce (d 1967 [57]) actor TW/1, 24, WWT/9-11

MacFARLANE, Elsa (b 1899) English actress, singer WWT/5-9

McFARLANE, George (d 1932 [55]) Canadian singer BE*, BP/16*

McFARLANE, Lillian C. (d 1975

[73]) producer/director/chore-
ographer BP/59*
McFARLIN, Julius R. (d 1973
[85]) performer BP/57*
MACFARREN, Alice [Mrs. Henry
Anderson] (d 1879 [26]) actress
EA/80*
MACFARREN, Clarina Thalia,
Lady (fl 1849?) singer CDP
MacFARREN, Mme. G. A. (fl
1847) singer HAS
MacFARREN, George (1788-1843)
English dramatist, manager
DNB
MACFARREN, Sir George Alex-
ander (1813-87) English musi-
cian, composer, conductor
CDP, DNB, NYM
MACFARREN, John (d 1901 [83])
EA/02*
MACFARREN, Walter Cecil (d
1905 [79]) composer EA/06*
McFAYDEN, Charles D. (d 1894)
actor EA/95*
McGAVIN, Darren (b 1922)
American actor BE, TW/9-
15, 23
McGAW, Charles (b 1910)
American educator, director
BE
MacGEACHEY, Charles (d 1921
[62]) manager BE*, BP/6*
McGEE, Fibber (b 1896) actor
CB
McGEE, Harold (1899-1955) Amer-
ican actor TW/2
McGEE, Molly (b 1898) actress
CB
McGHEE, Paul A. (d 1964 [64])
educator BE*
McGILL, Everett (b 1945) Amer-
ican actor TW/29
MacGILL, Moyna [Chattie Mc-
Ildowie] (d 1975 [80]) Irish
actress TW/11-12, WWT/4-8
McGILL, R. C. (d 1918) EA/19*
McGILL, Wallace Read (d 1973
[67]) performer BP/58*
McGILVRAY, Laura [Mrs. Frank
Gillmore] American actress
WWS
MAGINLEY, Benjamin R. (d 1888
[51]) American actor EA/89*
McGINLEY, Laurence Joseph (b
1905) American educator BE
MacGINNIS, Niall (b 1913) Irish
actor WWT/9-13
McGINTY, Miss see Clifford,

Elizabeth
McGIVENEY, Owen (d 1967 [83])
performer BP/52*
McGIVER, John (1913-75) American
actor BE, TW/14, 24-26, WWT/
15-16
McGLATHERY, Mr. (fl 1831) Amer-
ican actor HAS
McGLYNN, Frank (1866-1951) Amer-
ican actor TW/7, WWA/3,
WWT/5-8
McGOLRIC, Kate (d 1858) actress
HAS
McGONAGILL, Gerald (b 1925)
American actor TW/20, 23
McGONICLE, Margaret (d 1975
[66]) performer BP/60*
McGOOHAN, Patrick (b 1928)
American actor WWT/12-14
McGOVERN, John actor BE
McGOWAN, J. D. (d 1866) actor
HAS
McGOWAN, John [Jack] (b 1892)
American dramatist, director,
actor BE
McGOWAN, John P. (d 1952 [72])
Australian dramatist, librettist
WWT/7-9
McGOWAN, John W. American
dramatist, librettist WWT/10
MacGOWAN, Kenneth (1888-1963)
American critic, producer,
manager, director COC, ES,
NTH, OC/1-3, TW/19, WWT/
5-11
McGOWAN, Oliver (1907-71) Amer-
ican actor, director BE, TW/28
MacGOWRAN, Jack (1918-73) Irish
actor AAS, TW/27-29, WWT/
14-15
McGRAIL, Walter B. (d 1970 [81])
performer BP/54*
McGRATH, Don (b 1940) American
actor TW/28, 30
McGRATH, Frank (d 1976 [72])
dramatist BP/60*, WWT/16*
MacGRATH, Harold (1871-1932)
American librettist WWA/1
McGRATH, James W. see Mack,
James W.
McGRATH, John (b 1935) English
dramatist, director AAS, CD,
PDT, WWT/15-16
MCGRATH, Katherine (b 1944)
American actress TW/27, 29
MacGRATH, Leueen (b 1914/19)
English actress AAS, BE, TW/
5-16, WWT/10-16

McGRATH, Michael (d 1976) performer BP/60*
McGRATH, Paul (b 1904) American actor BE, TW/1, 3-5, 8-12, 21, 26, WWT/9-16
McGRATH, William P. (d 1971 [45]) performer BP/56*
McGRAW, Bill (b 1920) American actor TW/4
McGRAW, William Ralph (b 1930) American educator BE
McGREEVEY, Annie American actress TW/28, 30
MacGREGOR, Barry (b 1936) Scottish actor TW/26
MacGREGOR, Jock (d 1971 [56]) journalist BP/56*
McGREGOR, Joseph (d 1871) Jacobite singer EA/72*
MacGREGOR, Lynn (b 1945) American actress TW/29
McGREGOR, Malcolm (1892-1945) actor BE*
McGREGOR, Parke (d 1962 [55]) actor BE*
MacGREGOR, Robert M. (1911-74) American editor, publisher BE
McGREW, James (b 1917) American actor TW/2
McGROARTY, John Steven (1862-1944) American dramatist CB
McGUCKIN, Barton (1852/53-1913) Irish singer GRB/1, WWW/1
MACGUFFIE, W. M. see Raymond, Mat
McGUINN, Joseph Ford (d 1971 [67]) performer BP/56*
McGUINNESS, Edward (d 1869 [42]) duologist EA/70*
McGUINNESS, Jack [John D. Cowie] (d 1889 [30]) Irish comedian EA/90*
McGUIRE, Barry (b 1930) American actor TW/12
McGUIRE, Biff [né William J. McGuire] (b 1926) American actor, dramatist BE, TW/6, 12-16, 26-30, WWT/12-16
McGUIRE, Dorothy (b 1918) American actress BE, CB, ES, WWT/10-16
McGUIRE, Mrs. Laurence see Kimball, Grace
McGUIRE, Lavinia (d 1971 [56]) performer BP/56*

McGUIRE, Maeve American actress TW/24-25
McGUIRE, Michael see McGuire, Mitchell
McGUIRE, Mitchell [né Michael] (b 1936) American actor TW/24-29
McGUIRE, William Anthony (1885/87-1940) American dramatist, producing manager CB, WWM, WWT/6-9
McGUIRE, William J. see McGuire, Biff
McGURK, Harriet (d 1975 [72]) performer BP/60*
MACHADO, Lena (d 1974 [70]) performer BP/58*
McHAFFIE, Amelia (d 1868) EA/69*
McHALE, Rosemary (b 1944) English? actress WWT/16
McHATTIE, Stephen [Stephen Smith] Canadian actor TW/25-30
MACHATY, Gustav (d 1963 [63]) director BP/48*
McHENRY, Carrie (d 1881) actress CDP
McHENRY, Don (b 1908) American actor BE, TW/4, 15, 19, 23, 25, 27-28, 30
McHENRY, James (1785-1845) Irish dramatist EAP, RJ
McHENRY, Nellie [Mrs. John Webster] (d 1935 [82]) actress CDP
McHENRY, Tillie actress CDP
MACHIAVELLI, Niccolo di Bernardo dei (1469-1527) Italian writer COC, OC/1-3
MACHIN, Mr. (d 1870 [72]) singer EA/71*
MACHIN, Mrs. Charles E. (d 1898) EA/99*
MACHIN, Lewis (fl 1608) dramatist CP/1-3, FGF
MACHIN, Richard (fl 1600-06) actor DA
MACHIZ, Herbert (1923-76) American director BE, WWT/14-16
MACHRAY, Robert (b 1945) American actor TW/29
MacHUGH, Augustin dramatist, actor WWT/4-7
McHUGH, Edward A. (d 1973 [81]) stage manager BP/58*
McHUGH, Florence (b 1906) Canadian actress, singer WWT/6-8
McHUGH, Frank (b 1898) American actor BE, TW/23

MCHUGH, James Francis (1896-
1967) American composer BE,
TW/25
McHUGH, Mathew (d 1971 [77])
performer BP/55*
McHUGH, Therese Irish press
representative WWT/10-13
McIAN, R. (d 1856 [51]) actor,
artist EA/72*
McILDOWIE, Chattie see Mac-
Gill, Moyna
McILLWAY, John see Jackson,
John
McILRATH, Patricia (b 1917)
American educator, director
BE
MACINDOE, Alexander [Alexander
Dillon] (d 1878 [30]) actor?
EA/79*
McINERNEY, Bernie (b 1936)
American actor TW/30
McINNES, Mrs. (d 1869 [30])
Scottish? singer EA/70*
McINNES, Donald (d 1889) pro-
prietor EA/90*
McINTIRE, Janet (b 1945) Amer-
ican actress TW/26
McINTOSH, Burr (1862-1942)
American actor, dramatist
SR, WWA/2, WWM, WWS
McINTOSH, Madge [Mrs. Graham
Browne] (1875-1950) Indian/
English actress, producer
EA/97, GRB/1-4, WWT/1-9
McINTOSH, Nancy (fl 1895) ac-
tress, singer CDP
McINTYRE, Bill (b 1935) Amer-
ican actor TW/29
McINTYRE, Rev. Duncan (d 1892)
EA/93*
McINTYRE, Duncan (d 1973 [66])
performer BP/58*
McINTYRE, Frank J. (1879-1949)
American actor SR, TW/6,
WWM, WWT/4-10
McINTYRE, James (1857-1937)
American minstrel, comedian
DAB, NTH, SR, WWM, WWS
MacINTYRE, Dr. John see
Brandane, John
McINTYRE, John T. (1871-1951)
American dramatist WWA/3,
WWM
McINTYRE, Leila (d 1953 [71])
actress TW/9
McINTYRE, Marion (d 1975 [90])
performer BP/60*
McINTYRE, Mark Walton (d 1970

[53]) composer/lyricist BP/55*
McINTYRE, Molly (d 1952 [65])
actress TW/8
McINTYRE, William (d 1885) actor
EA/86*, WWT/14*
McINTYRE AND HEATH see
McIntyre, James & Heath, Thomas
McIVER, William (b 1942) American
actor TW/9
MACK, Andrew [Andrew McAloon]
(1863-1931) American actor,
singer CDP, GRB/3-4, SR,
WWA/1, WWS, WWT/1-6
MACK, Annie (d 1935 [85]) actress
BE*, WWT/14*
MACK, Charles E. (d 1934 [46])
American actor SR
MACK, George E. (d 1948 [82])
comedian TW/4
MACK, Harry (d 1909 [69]) variety
performer EA/10*
MACK, Herbert J. (1856-1947)
actor, manager SR
MACK, James W. [né McGrath]
(d 1889 [41]) actor CDP
MACK, John (d 1891 [38]) minstrel
CDP
MACK, Joseph H. (1849-92) mana-
ger CDP
MACK, Lester (d 1972 [66]) actor
TW/29
MACK, Nila (d 1953 [62]) American
actress, producer, director
BE*, BP/37*
MACK, Russell (d 1972 [79]) per-
former BP/57*
MACK, Vantile giant baby CDP
MACK, Wilbur (d 1964 [91]) per-
former BE*, BP/48*
MACK, Willard (1873/78-1934)
American actor, dramatist,
manager SR, WWT/4-7
MACK, William B. (fl 1902-12)
American actor WWM
MACKARNESS, George Fleming
(b 1884) English actor GRB/2
MACKARNESS, Mrs. Henry (d 1881)
writer EA/82*
McKASSON, Molly (b 1947) Ameri-
can actress TW/30
MacKAY, Barry (b 1906) English
actor WWT/8-13
MACKAY, Charles (c. 1785-1857)
Scottish actor CDP, COC, OC/3
MacKAY, Colin (d 1905 [29])
dramatist, actor GRB/1
McKAY, David (d 1884) acting
manager EA/85*

McKAY, David actor TW/1

MacKAY, Elsie (b 1894) Australian actress WWT/4-7

MACKAY, Eric Colin (d 1905 [29]) actor EA/06*

MACKAY, Fenton (d 1929) dramatist BE*, WWT/14*

MacKAY, Frank Findley (1832-1923) Canadian/American actor CDP, PP/2, WWM

McKAY, Frederick E. (1874-1944) agent, manager, critic, producer SR

McKAY, Mrs. Frederick E. see Ring, Blanche

MACKAY, Fulton (b 1922) Scottish actor WWT/15-16

MACKAY, J. L. (b 1867) English actor GRB/3-4, WWT/1-5

MacKAY, John actor TW/26

MACKAY, John A. (d 1891 [c. 40]) American actor CDP

MACKAY, Joseph (d 1889 [39]) dramatist EA/91*

MACKAY, Leonard (d 1929 [53]) actor BE*, WWT/14*

MACKAY, Phoebe (b 1890) English actress TW/11-12

MacKAY, Ruth English actress GRB/1-4, WWT/1-6

McKAY, Scott [Carl Gose] (b 1915/17) American actor BE, TW/2-3, 6-15, 21, 24, 30, WWT/16

McKAY, Mrs. Scott see Morgan, Joan

McKAY, Ted (d 1973 [55]) dramatist BP/58*

McKAY, Tony actor TW/26

MACKAY, W. Gayer (d 1920) actor, dramatist BE*, WWT/14*

MacKAY, Mrs. W. Gayer see "Ord, Robert"

MacKAYE, James Morrison Steele (1842-94) American theatre designer, dramatist, actor, manager CDP, COC, DAB, ES, HJD, MH, NTH, OC/1-3, SR, WWA/H

MacKAYE, Norman (d 1968 [62]) performer BP/52*

MacKAYE, Percy Wallace (1875-1956) American dramatist CDP, COC, ES, GRB/3-4, HJD, MD, MH, MWD, NTH, OC/1-3, RE, TW/13, WWA/3, WWM, WWS, WWT/1-12

MacKAYE, Steel see MacKaye, James Morrison Steele

MACKAYE, W. Payson (d 1889 [21]) actor EA/90*

McKAYLE, Donald (b 1930) American choreographer, dancer BE, CB

McKEAN, R. (d 1885 [36]) music-hall proprietor EA/86*

McKEAN, Thomas (1869-1942) American dramatist WWA/1

McKEAND, Emily (d 1891) actress EA/92*

McKECHNIE, Donna (b 1940/44) American actress, dancer, singer TW/25-28, 30, WWT/16

McKECHNIE, James (1911-64) Scottish actor WWW/6

McKEE, Andy (b 1844) dancer, minstrel CDP

McKEE, Clive R. (b 1883) Canadian manager WWT/4-7

McKEE, Donald (1898-1968) American actor TW/10, 25

McKEE, James W. (fl 1874?) singer, actor CDP

McKEE, John (d 1953 [80+]) Irish actor, director BE*, BP/38*

MACKEEN, Mr. (fl 1821?) actor CDP

McKEEVER, Jacquelyn (b 1934) American actress TW/14-15

McKELLAN, Ian (b 1939) English actor AAS, TW/24, WWT/15-16

MacKELLAR, Helen (b 1891/95) American actress BE, TW/2-7, WWT/4-13

McKELLEN, Ian see McKellan, Ian

MACKEN, Walter (1915-67) Irish actor, dramatist MD, TW/7, 11, 23

McKENNA, Edwin (d 1969 [68]) producer/director/choreographer BP/53*

MACKENNA, John (d 1873) secretary, agent EA/74*

MacKENNA, Kenneth (1899-1962) American actor TW/18, WWT/7-11

McKENNA, Rose (d 1886) EA/87*

McKENNA, Siobhan (b 1922/23) Irish actress AAS, BE, CB, ES, PDT, TW/12-16, 27, 29, WWT/11-16

McKENNA, T. P. (b 1929) Irish actor WWT/15-16

McKENNA, Virginia (b 1931) Eng-

lish actress AAS, ES, WWT/
12-16
McKENNA, William J. (d 1950
[69]) American songwriter
BE*, BP/34*
MACKENZIE (d 1896 [60]) pro-
prietor EA/97*
MacKENZIE, Sir Alexander Camp-
bell (1847-1935) Scottish com-
poser, conductor ES
McKENZIE, Alexander James
see Moore, Alec
MacKENZIE, Charles see Comp-
ton, Henry
MacKENZIE, Compton (d 1972
[89]) dramatist BP/57*
MACKENZIE, Mrs. Compton see
Oliffe, Geraldine
McKENZIE, D. (fl 1811) Scottish
actor HAS
MACKENZIE, Donald (d 1972
[92]) performer BP/57*
McKENZIE, Florence [Mrs. Her-
bert Garland] (d 1909 [35])
actress EA/10*
MacKENZIE, Francis Sidney see
Compton, Francis
MACKENZIE, George (d 1975
[74]) performer BP/60*
MACKENZIE, Hector Kenneth
Leslie (d 1878 [38]) actor
EA/79*
MacKENZIE, Henry (fl 1771-93)
Scottish dramatist CP/2-3
MACKENZIE, Herbert (d 1918
[35]) EA/19*
MacKENZIE, Hetty (d 1845) Amer-
ican actress HAS
McKENZIE, James B. (b 1926)
American producer, manager,
actor BE, WWT/16
MacKENZIE, J. H. (fl 1777-89)
Scottish dramatist GT, TD/1-2
McKENZIE, Joseph (d 1969 [62])
critic BP/54*
MACKENZIE, Katharine see
Compton, Miss
MACKENZIE, Mary (b 1922)
English actress WWT/11-14
MacKENZIE, May (b 1883) Amer-
ican actress WWM
MACKENZIE, Sir Morell (d 1892
[55]) EA/93*
McKENZIE, Richard (b 1930)
American actor TW/26, 29-30
MACKENZIE, Ronald (d 1932
[29]) dramatist BE*, WWT/14*
MACKENZIE, Tandy (1892-1963)

Hawaiian singer WWA/4
MACKENZIE, Will (b 1938) Amer-
ican actor TW/20-24, 26-27,
29-30
McKEON, Thomas [né Blackburn]
(fl 1833-65) English actor, mana-
ger HAS
McKEOWN, Geraldine see Mc-
Ewan, Geraldine
McKERN, Leo (b 1920) Australian
actor, director AAS, WWT/13-
16
McKESSON, Molly (b 1947) Ameri-
can actress TW/27
MACKETT, John (fl 179-) dramatist
CP/3
MACKEY, Colin singer, song com-
poser CDP
MACKEY, F. F. American actor
SR
MACKEY, George William Reay (d
1883 [35]) manager EA/84*
MACKEY, Julie (fl 1896?) singer,
actress CDP
MACKEY, Keith (b 1918) American
actor TW/26
MACKIE, Charles (d 1940) journal-
ist WWW/3-4
MACKIE, Philip dramatist CD
MacKILLOP, T. H. see Ramsay,
Scott
McKIM, Robert Stewart (d 1904
[33]) lessee EA/05*
MacKINDER, Lionel (d 1915 [46])
actor WWT/1-2
MacKINDER, Mrs. Lionel see
Leigh, Gracie
MacKINLAY, Jean Sterling (1882-
1958) English actress COC,
GRB/1-4, OC/1-3, WWT/1-9,
WWW/5
MacKINLAY, Malcolm Sterling (b
1876) actress, singer GRB/1-4
McKINLEY, John (d 1893) EA/94*
McKINLEY, Mrs. W. J. [née
Florence Wilson] (d 1870) music-
hall performer EA/71*
McKINNEL, Norman (1870-1932)
Scottish actor GRB/1-4, WWT/
1-6
McKINNELL, Mrs. Norman see
Scott, Gertrude
McKINNEY, Mr. (fl 1835) actor,
manager HAS
McKINNEY, George W. (b 1923)
American educator, designer
BE
McKINNEY, Mrs. Glennford see

Webster, Jean
McKINNON, Neil see Kenyon,
    Neil
MACKINTOSH, Mrs. (d 1886 [72])
    EA/87*
MACKINTOSH, Elizabeth see
    Daviot, Gordon
MACKINTOSH, Robert (b 1925)
    costume designer BE
MacKINTOSH, William (1855-1929)
    Australian actor DP, GRB/
    1-4, OAA/2, WWT/1-5
McKINZIE, Alexander (fl 1830s)
    American manager, actor? SR
McKISSOCK, John Lawrence (d
    1964 [94]) American magician
    BE*
MACKLIN, Mr. (fl 1846) actor
    HAS
MACKLIN, Charles (c. 1700-97)
    Irish actor, dramatist CDP,
    COC, CP/1-3, DNB, ES, GT,
    HP, NTH, OC/1-3, OX, TD/
    1-2
MACKLIN, Francis Henry (1848-
    1903) English actor DP, OAA/
    1-2
MACKLIN, Mrs. Francis Henry
    [Blanche Henri] (d 1904 [55])
    actress BE*, EA/05*, WWT/
    14*
MACKLIN, Maria (d 1781) actress
    CDP, DNB
MACKNEY, C. H. (d 1886 [65])
    theatrical leader EA/87*
MACKNEY, Mrs. C. H. see
    Mackney, Eliza
MACKNEY, Eliza [Mrs. C. H.
    Mackney] (d 1867) EA/68*
MACKNEY, E. W. (1824/35-
    1909) music-hall performer
    CDP, OC/1-3
McKNIGHT, Mrs. S. C. see
    Randolph, Louise
McKNIGHT, Tom (d 1963 [62])
    producer BE*
MacKRIS, Orestes (d 1975 [75])
    performer BP/59*
MACKWORTH, Patti [Ellie De-
    Courcy] (b 1851) Scottish ac-
    tress HAS
MACLACHLAN, Agnes Bruce
    [Mrs. B. G. Maclachlan] (d
    1911) EA/12*
MACLACHLAN, Mrs. B. G.
    see Maclachlan, Agnes Bruce
MACLACHLAN, Frederic W.
    see Clive, F. Wybert

MACLAGAN, Thomas (d 1902 [75])
    actor, singer CDP
MACLAGAN, Tom, Jr. (d 1889)
    singer, musician EA/90*
MACLAGHLAN, B. G. (d 1916)
    manager EA/17* [see also:
    Maclachlan]
McLAGLEN, Victor (1886-1959)
    English actor BE*, BP/44*
McLAIN, Oscar see Willis, Oscar
MacLAINE, Shirley (b 1934) Amer-
    ican actress, dancer CB, ES
MACLANE, Barton (d 1969 [66])
    actor TW/25
McLANE, Robert (b 1944) American
    actor TW/26, 29
McLANEY, Celestine (d 1894)
    coloured artist EA/95*
McLAREN, Archibald (1755-1826)
    Scottish actor, dramatist CP/
    3, DNB, RJ
MacLAREN, Ian (b 1879) English
    actor WWM, WWT/7-10
MacLAREN, Ivor (d 1962 [58])
    English performer, producer
    BE*
McLAREN, Mary [Mrs. Tom Dil-
    lon] (d 1882) Negro artist EA/
    83*
McLAREN, Neil (d 1889) actor
    EA/90*
MacLARNIE, Thomas (d 1931 [60])
    American actor BE*, BP/16*
McLAUGHLIN, Emily Louisa (d
    1898) elocution teacher EA/99*
McLAUGHLIN, John (d 1968 [71])
    composer/lyricist BP/53*
McLAUGHLIN, Leonard B. (1892-
    1970) American manager BE
McLAUGHLIN, Michael (d 1916)
    EA/17*
McLAUGHLIN, Millicent English
    actress GRB/1-2, WWS
McLAUGHLIN, Robert (d 1973
    [65]) dramatist BP/58*
MacLAURIN, John, Lord Dreghorn
    (1734-96) Scottish dramatist
    CP/3
McLAURIN, Kate (b 1885) Ameri-
    can actress WWS
McLEAN, Miss actress CDP
McLEAN, A. G. (d 1879 [27]) actor
    EA/80*
MacLEAN, Alick Scottish composer,
    conductor GRB/1
MacLEAN, Douglas (d 1967 [77])
    performer BP/52*
MacLEAN, John (1835?-90) English

actor OAA/1-2

McLEAN, Lex (d 1975 [67]) performer BP/59*

MacLEAN, Peter (b 1936) American actor TW/25-27

McLEAN, R. D. [R. D. Shepherd] (1859-1948) American actor SR, WWM, WWT/3-6

McLEAN, Mrs. R. D. see Tyler, Odette

McLEAN, Mrs. Robert D. see Prescott, Marie Victor

MACLEAN, Tom (d 1892 [47]) singer EA/94*

McLEARN, Frank C. (d 1969 [67]) executive BP/53*

McLEAY, Franklin (d 1900) actor EA/01*, WWT/14*

McLEAY, Mrs. Franklin see Warner, Grace

MacLEISH, Archibald (b 1892) American dramatist AAS, BE, CB, CD, CH, COC, ES, HJD, HP, MD, MH, MWD, NTH, OC/3, PDT, WWT/13-16

McLELLAN, C. M. S. ["Hugh Morton"] (1865-1916) American dramatist GRB/1-4, WWS, WWT/1-3, WWW/2

McLELLAN, G. B. (d 1932 [65]) producer BE*, WWT/14*

McLELLAN, R. C. (fl 1839?) dramatist RJ

MACLENNAN, Francis (1879-1935) American singer WWA/1

McLENNAN, K. J. (d 1917 [64]) scene artist EA/18*

McLENNAN, Rodney Australian actor TW/1

MACLEOD, Alexander Burgess (d 1889 [22]) acting manager EA/90*

MacLEOD, Angus (d 1962 [82]) producer, manager BE*, WWT/14*

McLEOD, Archibald (b 1906) Scottish educator, director, producer BE

McLEOD, Helen (d 1964 [40]) actress BE*

MacLEOD, Mary Canadian actress TW/5-6

MACLEOD, Norman (d 1903) manager EA/04*

McLEOD, Norman Z. (d 1964 [68]) director BP/48*

McLEOD, Tex (d 1973 [83]) performer BP/57*

MacLEOD, W. Angus (b 1874) English manager GRB/2-4, WWT/2-13

McLERIE, Allyn Ann (b 1926) Canadian actress, singer, dancer BE, TW/5-20, 23, WWT/15-16

McLIAM, John (b 1920) Canadian actor, dramatist BE

MacLIAMMOIR, Micheál (b 1899) Irish actor, designer, producer, director AAS, BE, COC, ES, MD, MH, MWD, OC/1-3, PDT, TW/4-7, WWT/8-16

MAC LOW, Jackson (b 1922) American dramatist, actor CD

MacMAHON, Aline (b 1899) American actress BE, TW/2-7, 10-18, 23-25, 27-28, WWT/7-16

McMAHON, Charles (d 1917 [55]) Australian executive EA/18*

McMAHON, Charles W., Sr. (d 1973 [93]) agent BP/58*

McMAHON, David (d 1972 [63]) performer BP/56*

McMAHON, Mrs. [Dennis] (fl 1857) actress CDP, HAS

MACMAHON, George (d 1908) boy actor-singer EA/09*

McMAHON, Horace (1907-71) American actor BE, TW/28

McMAHON, Jere dancer TW/1

McMAHON, Tim (d 1916) music-hall comedian EA/17*

McMANNS, Charles A. (d 1888 [59]) American actor EA/90*

McMANUS, C. A. (fl 1865) actor HAS

MacMANUS, Clive (d 1953) English critic, journalist WWT/9

McMANUS, John L. (d 1963 [71]) musical director BE*

MacMANUS, Patrick F. (d 1965 [56]) dramatist BP/50*

MacMANUS, Seumas (1869-1960) Irish dramatist WWA/4, WWW/5

McMARTIN, John American actor TW/22-24, 27-30, WWT/16

McMASTER, Anew (1894-1962) Irish actor, director AAS, COC, OC/3, WWT/8-9

McMATH, Virginia Katherine see Rogers, Ginger

MacMICHAEL, Florence actress TW/1

McMILLAN, Mr. (b 1813) English actor HAS

McMILLAN, Mrs. [Julia Barton] (fl 1847) singer HAS

MACMILLAN, Alick (d 1908 [21])
EA/09*

McMILLAN, Dan (d 1860) actor
HAS

MacMILLAN, Duncan (d 1866
[49]) ventriloquist EA/72*

MacMILLAN, J. T. Scottish actor
GRB/1

MacMILLAN, Kenneth (b 1929)
Scottish dancer, choreographer
ES

McMILLAN, Kenneth (b 1934)
American actor TW/26, 30

McMILLAN, Lida (d 1940 [71])
American actress WWM

McMILLAN, Roddy (b 1923) Scottish actor, dramatist WWT/16

MACMILLAN, Violet [Mrs. John
H. Folger] (1885-1953) Amer-
ican actress TW/10, WWM,
WWS

McMULLAN, Frank (b 1907)
American educator, director
BE

MacMULLEN, Charles see
Munro, C. K.

McMULLEN, Susan (b 1944)
American actress TW/24

McMURDIE, Joseph (d 1878 [85])
EA/80*

McMURRAY, J. S. (fl 1881)
minstrel CDP

McNAIR, Barbara (b 1939) American singer, actress BE, CB

MACNALLY, Jessie (d 1886)
EA/87*

MACNALLY, Jessie [Mrs. W.
H. McCarthy] (d 1903 [35])
serio-comic EA/04*

McNALLY, John J. (d 1931 [76])
American critic, dramatist
BE*, BP/15*, WWT/14*

MacNALLY, J. J. (d 1918) EA/
19*

MACNALLY, J. P. (d 1908 [49])
performer? EA/09*

MacNALLY, Mrs. J. P. see
O'Beirne, Tessie

MacNALLY, Leonard (1752-1820)
Irish dramatist CP/3, GT,
TD/1-2

McNALLY, Terrence (b 1930/39)
American dramatist CD, CH,
MH, WWT/15-16

MACNAMARA, Mrs. (d 1862
[84]) actress EA/72*, WWT/
14*

MACNAMARA, Brinsley [John

Weldon] (1890/91-1963) Irish actor, dramatist COC, MD, MH,
MWD, OC/3

McNAMARA, Daniel I. (d 1962
[76]) press representative, editor
BE*

McNAMARA, Dermot (b 1925) Irish
actor TW/18, 22-23, 26-27

McNAMARA, Edward (1887-1944)
English actor, singer SR, TW/1

McNAMARA, Maggie (b 1928)
American actress TW/7-9

McNAMARA, Rosemary (b 1943)
American actress TW/23

McNAMARA, Tom (d 1964 [78])
performer BE*

McNATTY, Ted (d 1904) music-hall
performer EA/05*

MacNAUGHTON, Alan (b 1920)
Scottish actor AAS, WWT/12-16

MCNAUGHTON, Anne (b 1943)
American actress TW/29

McNAUGHTON, Gus (1884-1969)
English actor WWT/10-11

McNAUGHTON, Harry (d 1967 [70])
actor TW/23

McNAUGHTON, Mrs. T. see
Lloyd, Alice

McNAUGHTON, Tom (1867-1923)
English actor WWT/4

McNAY, Evelyn [Mrs. William Mol-
lison] (d 1944 [73]) actress
BE*, WWT/14*

McNEAR, Howard (d 1969 [64])
performer BP/53*

MACNEE, Patrick (b 1922) English
actor TW/29-30

McNEELEY, Gale (b 1946) American
actress TW/28

MacNEICE, Louis (1907-65) Irish
dramatist NTH, PDT

McNEIL, Claudia (b 1917) American
actress BE, TW/14-20, 24-26,
WWT/14-16

MacNEIL, Cornell (b 1922) American singer CB

McNEILE, Lt.-Col. Cyril see
"Sapper"

McNEILL, Mrs. A. D. see
Ryder, Jessie Henry

McNEILL, Alexander Duncan (d
1884 [55]) lessee EA/85*

McNEILL, Amy New Zealand actress EA/96

McNEILL, Robert Stuart (d 1887
[70]) manager? EA/88*

McNEILL, W. J. see Emmett,
Bobbie

McNICHOL, Eileen American executive BE

McNISH, Francis Edward (1853-1924) American manager, minstrel CDP

McNUTT, Patterson (d 1948 [52]) American producer, dramatist TW/5

MACOLLA, Albert see McCulloch, Andrew

MACOLLUM, Barry Irish actor TW/1, 24

MACOMB, General (fl 1838?) dramatist RJ

MACOSKO, Greg (b 1947) American actor TW/30

MacOWAN, Michael (b 1906) English producer, actor AAS, COC, OC/3, WWT/9-16

MacOWAN, Norman (1877-1961) Scottish actor, dramatist COC, WWT/5-13

McPETERS, Taylor (d 1962 [62]) actor BE*

McPHAIL, Lindsay (d 1965 [70]) composer/lyricist BP/49*

McPHARLIN, Paul (1903-48) puppeteer CB

McPHARLIN, Mrs. Paul see Batchelder, Marjorie

McPHERRIN, John W. (d 1974 [77]) investor BP/59*

McPHERSON, Mr. (fl 1787) actor HAS

McPHERSON, Alexander (d 1883 [36]) actor EA/84*

MACPHERSON, Andrew (d 1913) EA/14*

MACPHERSON, J. (fl 1771) dramatist EAP

McPHERSON, Mervyn (b 1892) English press representative WWT/6-10

MACPHERSON, Quinton (d 1940 [69]) actor BE*, WWT/14*

McPHILLIPS, Edward (b 1925) English actor TW/24-25, 29

McQUADE, Arlene (b 1936) American actress TW/5

McQUEEN, Annie (d 1890) EA/91*

McQUEEN, Butterfly (b 1911) American actress TW/24, 26, WWT/15-16

McQUEEN, Steve (b 1930?) American actor CB, ES

McQUEENEY, Robert American actor TW/11-12

MacQUEEN-POPE, W. James

(1888-1960) English business manager, dramatist, press-manager, historian, manager AAS, COC, DNB, OC/3, WWT/4-12, WWW/5

McQUIGGAN, Jack (b 1935) American producer, actor BE

McQUINN, Robert (d 1975 [92]) designer BP/60*

McQUIRE, Christopher (d 1893 [52]) EA/94*

McQUOID, Percy (1852-1925) designer, painter WWT/4, WWW/2

McQUOID, Rose Lee (d 1962 [75]) actress BE*

McRAE, Anne Buchanan (d 1889 [61]) EA/90*

MacRAE, Arthur (1908-62) English actor, dramatist AAS, WWT/7-13

McRAE, Bruce (1867-1927) Indian/English actor GRB/3-4, WWA/1, WWM, WWS, WWT/1-5

McRAE, Duncan (d 1931) actor, director BE*, WWT/14*

MACRAE, Duncan (1905-67) Scottish actor COC, WWT/14

MACREADY, Mrs. (d 1873) actress CDP, HAS

MACREADY, Caroline [Mrs. Edmund Edmunds] (d 1867 [27]) EA/68*

MACREADY, Cécile Louisa [Mrs. W. C. Macready] (d 1908 [81]) EA/09*

MACREADY, George (d 1973 [63/73]) actor TW/30

MACREADY, Mrs. W. C. see Macready, Cécile Louisa

MacREADY, William (1755-1829) Irish actor, manager, dramatist CDP, CP/3, ES, GT, TD/1-2

MACREADY, William Charles (1793-1873) English actor, manager BS, CDP, COC, DNB, ES, HAS, HJD, HP, NTH, OC/1-3, OX, PDT, SR

MacROE (fl 1784) dramatist CP/3

MacSARIN, Kenneth (d 1967 [55]) press agent BP/51*

McSHANE, Ian (b 1942) English actor WWT/15-16

McSHANE, Kitty (d 1964 [66]) actress BE*

McSORLEY, Lars Michael (d 1972 [41]) publicist BP/56*

McSPADDEN, Joseph W. (b 1874) American writer WWM

McSTAY, Robert (d 1964 [60])
journalist BP/48*
MacSWINEY, Owen (d 1754)
manager WWT/14*
MacTAGGART, James (d 1974
[46]) performer BP/59*
McTERNAN, Agnes M. (d 1974
[56]) editor BP/59*
McTURK, David Harvey (d 1972
[67]) performer BP/57*
McVEY, Patrick (1913-73) Amer-
ican actor TW/11-12, 21-22,
25-27, 30
MacVICARS, Frank (d 1907) actor
GRB/3*
McVICKER, Horace (d 1931 [75])
American manager BE*, BP/
16*, WWT/14*
McVICKER, James Hubert [or
Horace] (1822/24-76) American
actor, manager CDP, DAB,
HAS, SR, WWA/H
McVICKER, Sara (fl 1880s) ac-
tress SR
McWADE, Robert (1835-1913)
Canadian actor CDP, HAS,
SR
McWADE, Robert (d 1938 [56])
American actor WWT/7-8
McWATTERS, Arthur J. (d 1963
[92]) performer BP/48*
McWHINNEY, Michael (d 1970
[39]) composer/lyricist BP/
55*
McWHINNIE, Donald (b 1920) Eng-
lish director AAS, BE, WWT/
14-16
McWILLIAMS, Caroline American
actress TW/28
McWILLIAMS, James (fl 1852)
actor HAS
MACY, Carleton (d 1946 [85])
actor, vaudevillian TW/3
MACY, Gertrude (b 1904) Amer-
ican manager, producer BE,
TW/2, 5-8
MACY, William (b 1922) American
actor TW/23-27
MADACH, Imre (1823-64) Hun-
garian dramatist OC/1
MADDEN, Miss see Hook,
Mrs. James
MADDEN, Archibald American
clown HAS
MADDEN, Cecil (b 1902) English
dramatist WWT/9-14
MADDEN, Ciaran (b 1945) ac-
tress WWT/15-16

MADDEN, Donald (b 1933) Ameri-
can actor BE, TW/16-21, 23-
25, 27, WWT/14-16
MADDEN, Richard (d 1951 [71])
American literary representative
BE*, BP/35*
MADDEN, Dr. Samuel (1686-1765)
Irish dramatist CP/2-3, GT
MADDERN, Emma (fl 1842-69)
American actress HAS
MADDERN, Merle (b 1887) Ameri-
can actress TW/1-7
MADDICK, Mrs. Gordon see
Illington, Marie
MADDOCK, C. B. (d 1974 [93])
producer/director/choreographer
BP/59*
MADDOCKS (fl 1829?) dramatist
EAP
MADDOX, Mrs. (fl 1854) actress
HAS
MADDOX, Anthony (d 1758) equili-
brist CDP
MADDOX, Diana (b 1926) English
actress TW/14
MADDOX, J. M. (d 1861 [72])
manager EA/72*, WWT/14*
MADDOX, Thomas (d 1880) propri-
etor EA/81*
MADEIRA, Humberto (d 1971 [50])
performer BP/56*
MADEIRA, Jean (1924-72) American
singer CB, WWA/5
MADELAINE, Marion (d 1865) ac-
tress HAS
MADELLE-STONE, Charles R.
see Stone, Charles R.
MADERNA, Bruno (d 1973 [53])
composer/lyricist BP/58*
MADIGAN, Eggie (d 1892 [34])
equestrian EA/93*
MADIGAN, Henry P. (1820-62)
American circus manager,
vaulter, equestrian HAS
MADISON, Mrs. see Grattan,
Mrs. Henry P.
MADISON, Cleo (d 1964 [81]) ac-
tress BE*
MADISON, Nathaniel J. (d 1968
[72]) performer BP/52*
MADISON, Noel (d 1975 [77])
performer BP/59*
MAEDER, Frank manager CDP
MAEDER, Frederick G. (d 1891
[50]) American actor, dramatist
HAS, SR
MAEDER, Mrs. Frederick G.
see Maeder, Rena

MAEDER, Mrs. James see
Fisher, Clara
MAEDER, James Gaspard (d 1876
[67]) musician, composer,
director, manager CDP
MAEDER, Maria A. (c. 1839-1916)
actress SR
MAEDER, Rena [Mrs. Frederick
G. Maeder] actress CDP
MAEKEY, James (d 1882) EA/83*
MAETERLINCK, Maurice (1862-
1949) Belgian dramatist COC,
ES, GRB/1-4, MH, NTH,
OC/1-3, RE, WWM, WWT/
1-3, 10, WWW/4
MAETZKER-MERITT, Mrs. (d
1887 [72]) EA/88*
MAFFEI, Scipione (1675-1755)
Italian dramatist OC/1-3
MAFFITT, James Strawbridge
(1832-97) actor, pantomimist
CDP
MAFLIN, Alfred W. (b 1840) Eng-
lish actor WWS
MAGALLANES, Nicholas (1919-77)
Mexican/American dancer CB,
ES
MAGAN, James see Middleton,
James
MAGARSHACK, David (b 1899)
Latvian translator BE
MAGEE, Patrick Irish actor
AAS, WWT/15-16
MAGENON, Mrs. actress CDP
MAGET, Stephen (fl 1596) actor
DA
MAGGART, Brandon (b 1933)
American actor TW/18-20,
24, 26-30
MAGGIORE, Charles (b 1936)
American actor TW/24, 29
MAGILTON, Henry M. [Jocko,
The Brazilian Ape] (d 1901)
acrobat CDP
MAGINLEY, Benjamin R. (1832-
88) American actor, circus
manager, clown CDP, HAS
MAGINN, Bonnie (fl 1903-04)
American actress, dancer
WWS
MAGINN, Dr. William (d 1842
[49]) critic BE*, EA/72*,
WWT/14*
MAGLEY, Guy (d 1971 [79]) per-
former BP/55*
MAGNANI, Anna (d 1973 [65])
actress BP/58*, WWT/16*
MAGNAY, Sir William (d 1917)

dramatist EA/18*
MAGO, William (fl 1624-31) actor
DA
MAGOWAN, Mrs. (fl 1847) actress
HAS
MAGRANE, Thais (d 1957 [79])
American actress WWM
MAGRATH, Charles [Charles Ryland
Magrath] (b 1865) Irish singer
GRB/1-2
MAGUINNIS, Daniel J. (1834-89)
American actor CDP
MAGUIRE, James [J. M. Cooke]
(d 1880) actor? EA/81*
MAGUIRE, James (d 1899) perform-
er EA/00*
MAGUIRE, J. R. (d 1883 [44])
actor EA/84*
MAGUIRE, Kathleen American ac-
tress BE, TW/14, 25
MAHARAM, Joseph (b 1898) Amer-
ican executive BE
MAHARIS, George (b 1928/33)
American actor, singer BE,
TW/15-20
MAHER, James P. (d 1973 [78])
critic BP/57*
MAHER, Joseph (b 1933) Irish actor
TW/23-24, 26, 28, 30
MAHIEU, Charles (d 1964 [70])
performer BP/49*
MAHLER, Gustav (1860-1911) Ger-
man conductor, composer ES,
WWA/4
MAHON, Mrs. (fl 1781?) actress
CDP
MAHON, Miss (fl 1770-89) see
Ambrose, Mrs.
MAHON, Robert (fl 1775) singer
TD/1-2
MAHON, Thomas Raleigh (1827-59)
American actor? singer? musi-
cian? HAS
MAHONEY, Elizabeth Ann Katherine
see Bellwood, Bessie
MAHONEY, Trish (b 1946) Egyptian/
American actress TW/28-29
MAHONEY, Will (1896-1967) Amer-
ican actor TW/23, WWT/7-14
MAHR, Herman Carl (d 1964 [62])
composer BE*
MAIDMAN, Irving (b 1897) Russian/
American theatre owner BE
MAIDWELL, L. (fl 1680) dramatist
CP/1-3, GT
MAILLARD, Alfonso see Dubois,
James
MAILLY, William (1871-1912)

American critic DAB
MAIN, Ann (d 1894) EA/95*
MAIN, Marjorie (1890-1975) ac-
tress CB
MAINBOCHER (b 1890) American
costumier, costume designer
BE
MAINE, Bruno (1896-1962)
Finish designer BE*, BP/47*
MAINSTONE, Gracie (d 1891)
music-hall performer EA/92*
MAINWARING, Ernest (1876-1941)
English actor WWT/2-9
MAIORANO, Gaetano see Caf-
farelli, Sig.
MAIR, George Herbert (1887-
1926) critic WWT/5
MAIRVIN (fl 1635) actor DA
MAIS, Stuart Petre Brodie (1885-
1975) critic WWT/5
MAISELL, Joe (b 1939) American
actor TW/26
MAISEY, E. J. (d 1890) lessee
EA/91*
MAISEY, Elise (fl 1875-78) ac-
tress OAA/2
MAISON, René (d 1962 [67])
Belgian singer TW/19
MAITLAND, Mrs. see Chester,
Marie
MAITLAND, Ada (d 1871) singer
EA/72*
MAITLAND, Charles (d 1892)
actor EA/93*
MAITLAND, Lauderdale (d 1929
[52]) English actor WWT/2-5
MAITLAND, Mrs. Lauderdale
see Valentine, Gertrude
MAITLAND, Mary Ann (d 1875
[59]) actress EA/76*
MAITLAND, Michael (b 1956)
American actor TW/27-28
MAITLAND, Ruth (1880/83-1961)
English actress GRB/2,
WWT/5-13
MAITLAND, Ruth (b 1926) Amer-
ican actress TW/28-29
MAJERONI, Edward (d 1892)
actor CDP
MAJERONI, Mario (d 1931 [61])
actor BE*
MAJILTON, Charles (1849-1931)
pantomimist, dancer CDP
MAJILTON, Flo [Mrs. W. Har-
rison] (d 1906) actress EA/07*
MAJILTON, Frank (fl late 19th
cent) performer CDP
MAJILTON, Marie actress, dancer

CDP
MAJOR, Bessie actress WWT/3-5
MAJOR, Charles (1856-1913) Amer-
ican dramatist WWM
MAJOR, Clare Tree (d 1954 [74])
English producer TW/11
MAJOR, Elizabeth [Mrs. Thomas
Major] (d 1892 [44]) music-hall
singer EA/93*
MAJOR, Frank A. (b 1925) Ameri-
can executive BE
MAJOR, H. A. (d 1902) dramatist
EA/03*
MAJOR, Hannah [Mrs. Tom Major]
(d 1886) EA/87*
MAJOR, H. Lance (d 1876 [25])
songwriter EA/77*
MAJOR, Mrs. Thomas see Major,
Elizabeth
MAJOR, Tom (d 1896) property
master EA/98*
MAJOR, Mrs. Tom see Major,
Hannah
MAKAROVA, Natalia (b 1940) Rus-
sian dancer CB
MAKEATH, Miss see Vandenhoff,
Mrs. George
MAKEHAM, Eliot (1882-1956) Eng-
lish actor TW/12, WWT/6-11
MAKEHAM, Gladys (b 1891) English
actress GRB/1-2
MAKGILL-MAITLAND, Maisie (b
1871) American actress GRB/1
MAKIN, Mrs. (fl 1806) English ac-
tress GT
MAKLETZOVA, Xenia (d 1974
[81]) performer BP/58*
MALBIN, Elaine (b 1932) American
singer CB
MALCOLM, Edith Fisk (d 1976
[67]) performer BP/60*
MALCOLM, John (1906-69) English
actor TW/22-23, 26
MALCOLM, Reginald (d 1966 [82])
performer BP/50*
MALDEN, Herbert John (1882-1966)
English business manager WWT/
9-12
MALDEN, Karl (b 1914) American
actor, director BE, CB, ES,
TW/2-9, 11-15
MALEKOS, Nick (b 1935) Greek
actor TW/25
MALET, Arthur (b 1927) English
actor TW/13-16
MALEY, Denman (d 1927 [50])
American comedian BE*, BP/
11*

MALEY, Peggy American actress
TW/4-6

MALIANDI, Paula (b 1949) American actress TW/29

MALIBRAN, Maria Felicita (1808-36) French singer, actress
CDP, ES, HAS, HP

MALIGNY, Félix Bernier de
see Aristippe

MALINA, Judith (b 1926) German director, producer, actress
BE, COC, WWT/15-16

MALINA, Luba Russian actress
TW/3, 14-15

MALINOFSKY, Max (d 1963 [70]) performer, manager BE*

MALIPIERO, Gian Francesco (d 1973 [91]) composer/lyricist
BP/58*

MALIPIERO, Luigi (d 1975 [74]) producer/director/choreographer
BP/59*

MALIS, Claire (b 1944) American actress TW/25

MALKIN, Beata (d 1973 [82]) performer BP/58*

MALKIN, Benjamin Heath (fl 1804) dramatist CP/3

MALL, Dr. Richard (d 1973 [54]) performer BP/58*

MALLAH, Vivian (b 1924) American actress TW/2

MALLALIEU, Aubrey (1873-1948) English actor WWT/8-10

MALLALIEU, William (d 1927 [81]) actor BE*, WWT/14*

MALLANDAINE, J. (d 1886) musician, conductor EA/87*

MALLESON, Miles (1888-1969) English actor, dramatist AAS, COC, ES, OC/3, PDT, WWT/4-14, WWW/6

MALLET, David (d 1765) Scottish dramatist CP/1-3, GT, TD/1-2

MALLETT, George English actor, stage manager, manager GRB/1-2

MALLETT, Mrs. George see Leigh, Stella

MALLETT, Richard (d 1972 [62]) critic BP/57*

MALLIN, Tom dramatist CD

MALLINGER, Mathilde (b 1847) singer CDP

MALLINSON, Joseph (fl 1811) actor CDP

MALLISON, Marvin Morton see

Ward, William H.

MALLORY, Ben (1829-59) American minstrel, equestrian HAS

MALLORY, Boots (d 1958 [45]) American actress BE*, BP/43*

MALLORY, Burton (d 1962 [79]) performer BE*

MALLORY, Rene (d 1931 [24]) actress BE*, WWT/14*

MALLORY, Victoria (b 1948) American actress TW/25, ·27-30

MALLOY, Marie Louise American critic WWM

MALO, Gina (1909-63) American actress, singer TW/20, WWT/7-10

MALONE, Andrew E. (d 1939) critic BE*, WWT/14*

MALONE, Dudley Field (b 1931) American talent representative BE

MALONE, Edmond (1741-1812) Irish scholar COC, DNB, GT, HP, NTH, OC/1-3, TD/1-2

MALONE, Elizabeth (d 1955 [75]) actress BE*, WWT/14*

MALONE, J. A. E. (d 1929 [69]) Indian/English manager, producer WWT/2-5

MALONE, Mrs. J. A. E. see Moody, Hilda

MALONE, John (b 1854) American actor PP/2

MALONE, Mary (b 1924) American actress TW/5-7

MALONE, Nancy (b 1935) American actress TW/13-15, 27-28

MALONE, Patricia (b 1899) English actress, singer WWT/6-8

MALONE, Pick (d 1962 [69]) performer BE*

MALONE, Ray (d 1970 [44]) actor, dancer TW/26

MALONE, Richard see Raymond, Malone

MALONEY, J. W. (d 1897) manager EA/98*

MALONY, Mrs. (d 1894 [52]) EA/95*

MALTBY, Alfred (d 1901 [59]) actor, dramatist CDP

MALTBY, Harold Constable (d 1892) actor EA/93*

MALTBY, Henry Francis W. (1880-1963) South African actor, dramatist GRB/1-2, WWT/4-13, WWW/6

MALTBY, Mara English actress

GRB/2

MALTBY, Tom (d 1918 [75])
EA/18*

MALTEN, Therese (b 1855)
singer CDP

MALTEN, William (b 1902) actor
TW/2

MALTZ, Albert (b 1908) American
dramatist BE, CB, CD, ES,
HJD, MD, MWD, NTH

MALVERN, Emma (d 1877) actress EA/78*

MALVERN, J. H. (d 1901 [73])
actor EA/02*

MALVERN, Louisa Maud (d 1901
[25]) EA/02*

MALVEY, Harold (d 1975 [70])
performer BP/59*

MAMOULIAN, Rouben (b 1897/98)
Russian/American director
AAS, BE, CB, COC, ES,
NTH, TW/2-8, WWT/7-14

MAN, Henry (1747-99) English
dramatist CP/3

MANA, Archibald (d 1878 [43])
singer EA/80*

MANAHAN, Anna Irish actress
TW/25

MANBY, Dr. Fred (d 1891)
director EA/92*

MANCHESTER, Hannah see Albertine, Hannah

MANCHESTER, Thomas (d 1897
[34]) acting manager EA/99*

MANCINELLI, Luigi (1848-1921)
Italian conductor, composer
ES, WWW/2

MANCINELLI, Marino (d 1894
[52]) composer, conductor
EA/95*

MANCINI, Ric (b 1933) American
actor TW/27-28

MANDAN, Robert (b 1932) American actor TW/13, 25-28

MANDEL, Bebe (d 1975 [50])
booking agent BP/60*

MANDEL, Frank (1884-1958)
American dramatist, librettist,
producer, manager TW/14,
WWT/5-11

MANDEL, Loring (b 1928) American dramatist BE

MANDEL, Mike (d 1963 [69])
stage manager BE*

MANDELL, Israel (d 1962 [60])
performer BE*

MANDELSTAM, Abraham (d 1969
[86]) dramatist BP/54*

MANDERS, Mr. (d 1871) menagerie
proprietor EA/72*

MANDERS, James (d 1907 [74])
menagerie proprietor EA/08*

MANDERS, Louisa (d 1880 [79])
actress EA/81*

MANDERS, Lucy [Mrs. G. Howard
Watson] (d 1894) actress EA/95*

MANDERS, Thomas (d 1859 [61])
actor EA/72*, WWT/14*

MANDEVILLE, Alicia (fl 1859-67)
actress HAS

MANDEVILLE, Frank N. (d 1921)
American conductor BE*, BP/6*

MANDIA, Joe (d 1970 [45]) performer BP/55*

MANDLEBERT, Kate [Mrs. George
Chapman] (d 1899) EA/00*

MANDLEBERT, Lizzie see Jones,
Mrs. David H.

MANEY, Richard (1891-1968) American press representative BE,
CB, TW/25

MANFIELD, A. B. (d 1901) manager EA/02*

MANFRE, Blaise de (b c. 1579)
juggler CDP

MANFRED, Emily see Etherdo,
Mary Ann

MANGAN, Francis A. (d 1971 [86])
producer/director/choreographer
BP/55*

MANGEON, Mrs. (fl 1826-32) English actress HAS

MANGEON, Miss (fl 1816) singer,
actress CDP

MANGER, Itzik (d 1969 [67]) manager BP/53*

MANGES, Carl (d 1874) proprietor
EA/75*

MANGES, John (d 1878 [59]) musician EA/79*

MANGIN, Edward (fl 1810) translator CP/3

MANHILL, James (d 1899 [51])
comedian EA/00*

MANHOFF, Arnold (d 1965 [50])
dramatist BP/49*

MANHOFF, Wilton (d 1974 [54])
dramatist BP/59*

MANIS, James (b 1939) American
actor TW/25

MANKIEWICZ, Herman J. (d 1953
[56]) American dramatist, critic
BE*, BP/37*, WWT/14*

MANKOWITZ, Wolf (b 1924) English
dramatist, producer CD, PDT,
WWT/13-16

MANLEY, Alfred (d 1869) eques-
trian EA/70*
MANLEY, Beatrice (b 1921)
American actress TW/4, 23
MANLEY, Prof. E. (d 1880 [59])
scene artist EA/81*
MANLEY, Mrs. H. see Man-
ley, Martha
MANLEY, Henry (d 1887) circus
proprietor EA/88*
MANLEY, Mrs. Henry (d 1874
[44]) actress EA/75*
MANLEY, Henry Christian (d
1891 [72]) EA/92*
MANLEY, J. H. (d 1917 [78])
actor EA/18*
MANLEY, John (d 1892 [76])
stage manager EA/93*
MANLEY, Martha [Mrs. H. Man-
ley] (d 1872 [55]) EA/74*
MANLEY, Mary de la Riviere
(1663-1724) English dramatist
CP/1-3, DNB, GT
MANLEY, Oliver (d 1878 [38])
musician, composer EA/79*
"MAN MONKEY, The" see
Gouffe, Mons.
MANN, Alice Placide (fl 1855-
61) actress CDP, HAS
MANN, Anthony (1906-67) Amer-
ican director, actor TW/23,
WWA/4
MANN, Billy (d 1974) performer
BP/58*
MANN, Caroline (d 1907 [80])
GRB/3*
MANN, Charlton (1876-1958)
English manager, dramatist
WWT/4-8
MANN, Christopher (b 1903) Eng-
lish press representative
WWT/6-13
MANN, Daniel (b 1912) American
director BE, ES
MANN, David (d 1908) managing
director EA/09*
MANN, Eliza (d 1874) actress
CDP
MANN, Erika (d 1969 [63]) per-
former BP/54*
MANN, Frances (d 1969 [68])
dancer, play doctor BP/54*
MANN, Mrs. H. (d 1878 [70])
EA/80*
MANN, Hannah (d 1881) EA/82*
MANN, Harry (d 1901) manager
EA/02*
MANN, Henry John see Mon-

tague, F. J.
MANN, Iris (b 1939) American ac-
tress TW/9
MANN, Louis (1865-1931) American
actor, dramatist DAB, GRB/
2-4, WWA/1, WWM, WWS,
WWT/1-6
MANN, Mrs. Louis see Lipman,
Clara
MANN, Paul (b 1913/15) American
actor, director BE, TW/8, 13,
21-23
MANN, Ralph (b 1922) American
talent representative BE
MANN, Sam (d 1965 [77]) performer
BP/50*
MANN, Mrs. Sheridan [née Eliza
Placide] (fl 1814-69) actress
HAS
MANN, Theodore [né Goldman] (b
1924) American producer, di-
rector BE, WWT/15-16
MANN, Winifred American actress
TW/24
MANNA, Charlie (1925-71) comedian
CB
MANNERING, Doré Lewin (1879-
1932) Polish/English actor
WWT/4-6
MANNERING, Mary [Mrs. J. K.
Hackett] (1876-1953) English ac-
tress CDP, GRB/2-4, NTH,
PP/2, SR, TW/9, WWM, WWS,
WWT/1-7
MANNERING, Moya [Moya Doyle]
(b 1888) actress, singer WWT/
3-8
MANNERS, Mr. (fl 1839-50) Eng-
lish singer HAS
MANNERS, Annie see Knowles,
Mrs. Forrest
MANNERS, Catherine (d 1890) EA/
91*
MANNERS, Charles [Mansergh]
(1857/58-1935) English singer,
manager GRB/1-4, WWW/3
MANNERS, Mrs. Charles see
Moody, Fanny
MANNERS, David (b 1900/05) Cana-
dian actor SR, TW/2-7, WWT/
11
MANNERS, George (fl 1806) drama-
tist CP/3
MANNERS, Jayne English actress,
manager BE
MANNERS, John Hartley (1870-
1928) Irish/American dramatist,
actor COC, DAB, ES, HJD,

MWD, NTH, OC/1-3, SR,
WWA/1, WWM, WWT/1-5,
WWW/2
MANNERS, Josephine (fl 1856)
English actress HAS
MANNERY, Samuel (fl 1631)
actor DA
MANNES, Florence V. (d 1964
[68]) performer BP/49*
MANNEY, Charles Fonteyn (b
1872) American composer
WWM
MANNHARDT, Renata German ac-
tress TW/27
MANNHEIM, Albert (d 1972 [58])
dramatist BP/58*
MANNHEIM, Lucie (1899/1905-
1976) German actress ES,
WWT/8-14
MANNING, Mrs. (d 1891) EA/92*
MANNING, Ambrose (d 1940 [79])
actor GRB/1-4, WWT/1-9
MANNING, Billy (d 1876) min-
strel SR
MANNING, David (b 1958) Amer-
ican actor TW/24
MANNING, Edward Betts (1874-
1948) Canadian composer
WWA/2
MANNING, Francis (fl 1688-1716)
dramatist CP/1-3
MANNING, Frank (d 1899 [34])
actor EA/00*
MANNING, Hugh Gardner (b 1920)
English actor WWT/15-16
MANNING, Irene [née Inez Har-
vuot] (b 1916/17/18) American
actress, singer BE, TW/2-3,
WWT/11-14
MANNING, Jack (b 1916) Ameri-
can actor, director BE, TW/
1-4, 7-9, 11-16, 21-22, 27
MANNING, John (1850-87) Amer-
ican actor, performer NYM
MANNING, John (d 1890 [64])
actor EA/91*, WWT/14*
MANNING, Marty (d 1971 [55])
actor BP/56*
MANNING, Maybelle (d 1968 [74])
costumier BP/52*
MANNING, Otis (d 1963 [50]) American performer BE*
MANNING, Riccardo (d 1954 [40])
singer WWT/14*
MANNION, Moira (d 1964 [46])
actress BE*
MANNO, Anthony P. (d 1973 [34])
composer/lyricist BP/58*

MANNOCK, Patrick L. (b 1887)
English critic WWT/7-13
MANNON, C. H. (d 1918) EA/
19*
MANNS, Mrs. A. (d 1893) EA/94*
MANNS, Sir August (d 1907 [81])
conductor EA/08*
MANNS, Otto, Jr. (b 1873) Ger-
man musical director, com-
poser GRB/1
MANNY, Charles (d 1962 [71])
performer BE*
MANOLA, Adelaide [Mrs. Rupert
Hughes] (b 1885) Canadian ac-
tress WWM
MANOLA, Marion (d 1914 [48])
performer BE*, WWT/14*
MANON, Sylvia (d 1966 [56]) per-
former BP/51*
MANSEL, Lady [Lily Ernest] (d
1916) comedian EA/17*
MANSEL, Eliza [Mrs. Frederic
Reynolds] (fl 1795-96?) actress
CDP
MANSEL, Sir Richard (d 1892)
EA/93*
MANSELL, Mrs. Ernest see
Wright, Maudie
MANSELL, John (fl 1607) actor
DA
MANSELL, Richard (d 1907) mana-
ger, actor GRB/1-3
MANSELL, William (fl 1784) drama-
tist CP/3
MANSELL, W. L. (d 1893 [48])
EA/94*
MANSERGH, Charles see Man-
ners, Charles
MANSFIELD, Ada [Mrs. Theodore
Jones] (d 1906) actress EA/08*
MANSFIELD, Alfred F. (d 1938
[60]) actor, director BE*,
WWT/14*
MANSFIELD, Alice (d 1938 [80])
actress WWT/4-7
MANSFIELD, Beatrice [Beatrice
Cameron] (1868-1940) American
actress COC, DD, OC/1-3,
SR, WWA/4
MANSFIELD, Fred see Martin,
F. W.
MANSFIELD, Jayne (1933-67) Amer-
ican actress ES, TW/12-15,
22, WWA/4
MANSFIELD, Josephine (b c. 1840)
actress SR
MANSFIELD, Portia (b 1887) Amer-
ican educator BE

MANSFIELD, Richard (1854/57-
1907) American actor, mana-
ger, dramatist CDP, COC,
DAB, DP, ES, GRB/1-3,
HJD, NTH, OC/1-3, PP/2,
SR, WWA/1, WWS, WWW/1
MANSFIELD, Scott (b 1949)
American actor TW/30
MANSON, Alan American actor
TW/24, 26-27, 29
MANSON, Eddy (b 1919) Ameri-
can actor TW/3
MANSON, Edward (d 1969 [77])
public relations BP/54*
MANSOUR, George P., Jr. (b
1949) American actor TW/29
MANTELL, Bruce (d 1933 [24])
American actor BE*
MANTELL, Marianne (b 1929)
German/American executive
BE
MANTELL, Robert Bruce (1854-
1928) Scottish/American actor,
manager COC, DAB, ES,
GRB/2-4, NTH, OC/1-3,
PP/2, SR, WWA/1, WWM,
WWS, WWT/1-5
MANTELL, Mrs. Robert Bruce
see Russell, Marie Booth
MANTELL, Mrs. R[obert]
B[ruce] see Sheldon, Marie
MANTIA, Charles (d 1974 [85])
actor TW/30
MANTIN, Sig. (fl 1847) dancer
HAS
MANTLE, George Hunter (d 1886)
EA/87*
MANTLE, Robert Burns (1873-
1948) American critic CB,
COC, DAB, NTH, OC/1-3,
SR, TW/4, WWT/5-10
MANTON, Annie see Knight,
Mrs.
MANTON, Maria (b 1924) German
actress TW/1
MANTON, Mme. T. (d 1886)
singer EA/87*
MANUCHE, Cosmo (fl 1650-52)
Italian? dramatist CP/1-3,
DNB, FGF
MANUEL, Dean (d 1964 [30])
conductor, manager, musician
BE*
MANUTI, Alfred Joseph (b 1909)
American union executive,
musician BE
MANVERS, Charles W. (d 1874)
singer CDP

MANVERS, Louise [Mrs. David
Honeysett] (d 1891) EA/93*
MANZ, Julia Chandler American
editor WWM
MANZINI, Constanza (fl 1853-54)
singer CDP, HAS
MANZOTTI, Luigi (1835-1905)
Italian choreographer, mimist
ES
MAPES, Victor (1870-1943) Amer-
ican dramatist, manager, di-
rector CB, GRB/3-4, WWA/5,
WWM, WWS, WWT/1-9
MAPHOON and MOUNG-PHOSET (fl
1886?) hairy family CDP
MAPLE, Audrey (d 1971 [72]) ac-
tress TW/27
MAPLESON, Agnes [Mrs. Harry
Mapleson] (d 1892) EA/93*
MAPLESON, Charles (d 1893) act-
ing manager EA/94*
MAPLESON, Mrs. Harry see
Mapleson, Agnes
MAPLESON, Henry (b 1851) English
impresario WWM
MAPLESON, James Henry, Sr.
(d 1869) manager EA/70*,
WWT/14*
MAPLESON, James Henry (1830-
1901) singer, musician, manager
CDP, DNB
MAPLESON, Mrs. James Henry
see Mapleson, Laura
MAPLESON, Laura [Mrs. Arthur
Byron; Mrs. James Henry
Mapleson] (1862-94) singer
CDP
MARA, Mr. (fl 1806-07) Irish GT
MARA, Gertrude Elizabeth [née
Scheneling] (1749-1833) Austrian
singer CDP, DNB, ES, GT,
TD/1-2
MARALTI, E. (fl 1850) singer
CDP
MARAND, Patricia (b 1934) Amer-
ican actress TW/9, 22-23
MARANO, Charles (d 1964 [61])
talent representative BE*
MARASCO, Robert (b 1936) Ameri-
can dramatist WWT/15-16
MARATIER, Florence Tanner (d
1970) performer BP/55*
MARAVAN, Lila (d 1950 [54]) ac-
tress WWT/5-8
MARBECK, Thomas (fl 1602-03)
actor DA
MARBERG, Lili (d 1962 [84]) per-
former BP/46*

MARBLE, Anna [Mrs. Channing Pollock] American press representative WWM

MARBLE, Danforth (1810-49) American actor CDP, COC, DAB, HAS, HJD, OC/1-3, WWA/H

MARBLE, Mrs. Danforth [née Anna Warren] (b 1815) American actress HAS

MARBLE, Emma (1848-1930) American actress SR

MARBLE, John S. (b 1844) actor HAS

MARBLE, Mary (1873-1965) American actress SR, TW/21, WWM, WWS

MARBLE, Scott (fl 1865) actor, dramatist SR

MARBLE, William (d 1912) actor SR

MARBURY, Elizabeth (1856-1933) American agent DAB, OC/1-3

MARCEAU, Felicien (b 1913) Belgian dramatist BE

MARCEAU, Marcel (b 1923) French mimist BE, CB, PDT

MARCEL, Gabriel (d 1973 [83]) dramatist BP/58*

MARCELINE (1873-1927) Spanish clown BE*, WWT/14*

MARCELLA, Marco (d 1962 [53]) performer BE*

MARCELLUS, George W. (d 1921 [80]) actor BE*

MARCH, Ellen (b 1948) American actress TW/30

MARCH, Elspeth English actress WWT/10-16

MARCH, Frederic [Frederick McIntyre Bickel] (1897-1975) American actor AAS, BE, CB, ES, SR, TW/1-21, WWT/7-15

MARCH, Hal (1920-70) American actor BE, TW/26, WWA/5

MARCH, Kendall American actor TW/25-26

MARCH, Lori American actress TW/10

MARCH, Mary Ann Virginia see Gabriel, Virginia

MARCH, Nadine (1898-1944) English actress WWT/5-9

MARCH, Virginia see Gabriel, Virginia

MARCHAND, Alida (d 1876 [107]) dancer EA/78*

MARCHAND, Colette (b 1925) French dancer, actress ES, TW/8

MARCHAND, Floram juggler CDP

MARCHAND, Leopold (d 1952) dramatist WWT/14*

MARCHAND, Nancy (b 1928) American actress AAS, BE, TW/14-18, 22-30, WWT/14-16

MARCHANT, Beatie (d 1892 [19]) music-hall performer EA/93*

MARCHANT, Frank (d 1878 [41]) dramatist BE*, WWT/14*

MARCHANT, Frederick (d 1878 [41]) dramatist, actor EA/80*

MARCHANT, G. F. (fl 1851) English actor HAS

MARCHANT, Mrs. G. F. [née Emeline Raymond] (b 1831) English actress HAS

MARCHANT, Will (d 1885 [38]) sketch artist EA/86*

MARCHANT, William (b 1923) American dramatist BE

MARCHESI, Blanche (fl 1895-1903) French singer WWM

MARCHESI, Mathilde (d 1913) EA/14*

MARCHESI, Salvatore (d 1908) singer EA/08*

MARCHESIO, Antonio (d 1875) musician, composer EA/76*

MARCHINGTON, Maria F. singer CDP

MARCHISO, Barbara (fl 1860) singer CDP

MARCHISO, Carlotta (fl 1860) singer CDP

MARCIN, Max (1879-1948) German/American dramatist, producing manager SR, TW/4, WWT/4-10

MARCIONA, Anthony (b 1961) American actor TW/25

MARCIONA, Suzan (b 1959) American actress TW/25

MARCKWALD, F. V. (fl 1874?) singer CDP

MARCO, Caterina singer CDP

MARCONI, Francesco (d 1916 [60]) EA/17*

MARCOTTE, Don (d 1964 [58]) composer/lyricist BP/49*

MARCUPP, Samuel (fl 1598) actor DA

MARCUS, Albert (d 1873) music-hall chairman EA/74*

MARCUS, Frank (b 1928) German/English dramatist, critic, director, actor AAS, CD, CH, COC, MH, WWT/14-16

MARCUS, Sol (d 1976 [63]) composer/lyricist BP/60*

MARCUSE, Theodore (d 1967 [47]) performer BP/52*

MARCY, George (b 1930) American actor TW/12-13, 23, 25

MARCY, Helen (b 1920) American actress TW/2-3, 8

MARDEN, Mr. (b 1833) American actor HAS

MARDEN, Ben (d 1973 [77]) showman, theatre owner BP/57*

MARDEN, Emma see Morella, Mrs. William

MARDEN, Lillie (fl 1868) English actress HAS

MARDEN, Mary (d 1892 [29]) EA/93*

MARDO, Charles (d 1976 [80]) performer BP/60*

MARDYN, Charlotte (b 1789) Irish actress CDP, OX

MARECHAL, Judith Rutherford (b 1937) American producer BE

MARETZEK, Bertucca (fl 1849-51) singer CDP, HAS

MARETZEK, Max (1821-97) Moravian manager, composer, musical director, conductor CDP, DAB, HAS, WWA/H

MAREY, Jacques (b 1877) French actor GRB/4, WWT/1-3

MARFIELD, Dwight American actor TW/2

MARGETSON, Arthur (1887/97-1951) English actor, singer TW/1-8, WWT/5-11

MARGO [Maria Margharita Bolado] (b 1917/18/19/20) Mexican actress, dancer BE, TW/1, WWT/9-11

MARGOLIN, Janet (b 1943) American actress TW/18-19

MARGOLIS, Henry (b 1909) American producer BE

MARGOT, John David (d 1886 [57]) EA/87*

MARGOT, John David see Mildmay, Frank

MARGUERITES, Julie de (d 1866) French singer, actress? HAS

MARGUERITES, Noemie de (fl 1865) actress, critic HAS

MARGULIES, Virginia M. (d 1969 [53]) performer BP/53*

MARIA, Lisa (b 1948) Polish actress TW/24

MARIAN (d 1884 [48]) Amazon queen EA/85*

MARIAN, Miss (fl 1854) actress HAS

MARIANO, Patti (b 1945) American actress TW/24-26

MARIASSEY, Felix (d 1975 [55]) producer/director/choreographer BP/59*

MARICLE, Leona (b 1905) American actress BE

MARICLE, Marijane (b 1922) American actress TW/8-9, 24

MARIE, Mlle. [Marie Rabineau] (d 1863 [18]) dancer HAS

MARIE, La Belle [Marie Hart; Mrs. Billy Hart] (b 1881) American vaudevillian WWM

MARIE, Julienne (b 1943) American actress TW/20-23

MARIE, Paola (b 1851/52) American dancer, singer CDP, HAS

MARIE-JEANNE (b 1921) American dancer ES

MARIEMMA (b 1912) Spanish dancer, choreographer ES

MARIES, Nance (d 1910) music-hall comedian EA/11*

MARIETTA, Miss (fl 1853-67) American dancer HAS

MARIMON, Marie Ernestine (b 1835) singer CDP

MARINELLI, H. B. (1864-1924) German vaudeville agent BE*, BP/8*

MARINELLI, Mrs. H. B. (d 1908) GRB/4*

MARINI, Ignazio (1811-73) Italian singer CDP, ES, HAS

MARINI, Sofia (fl 1847) singer HAS

MARINO, Louis (d 1965 [75]) costumier BP/50*

MARINOFF, Fania (1890-1971) Russian actress BE, TW/2-8, 28, WWT/5-11

MARIO, Dot [Mrs. Alfred Gibbons] (d 1898) burlesque actress EA/99*

MARIO, Giuseppe (1810-83) Sardinian singer CDP, ES, HAS

MARIO, Minnie (d 1905 [46]) actress, singer CDP, GRB/1

MARIO, Queena (1896-1951) American singer TW/7, WWA/3

MARION, Miss (fl 1848) actress

HAS
MARION, Charles (d 1889 [23])
American vaudevillian EA/90*
MARION, Dave (d 1934 [73])
American dramatist, manager,
actor BE*, BP/19*
MARION, Frances (d 1973 [86])
performer BP/57*
MARION, George (1860-1945)
American actor, producer CB,
WWT/5-9
MARION, George, Jr. (d 1968
[68]) librettist, actor BE,
TW/24, WWT/10-12
MARION, Joan (b 1908) Tasmanian
actress WWT/8-13
MARION, Millie (fl 1889) actress
CDP
MARION, Sid (d 1965 [65]) per-
former BP/50*
MARIUS, Claude [Claude Marius
Duplany] (1850-96) French ac-
tor, singer, stage manager
CDP, DP, OAA/1-2
MARK, Dr. (d 1868 [52]) propri-
etor EA/69*
MARK, Donald (b 1944) American
actor TW/26
MARK, Michael (d 1975 [88]) per-
former BP/59*
MARKAS, Gary (d 1972 [42]) pro-
ducer/director/choreographer
BP/57*
MARKBY, Robert Bremner (d
1908 [66]) actor OAA/2
MARKERT, Gladys (d 1975 [71])
publicist BP/59*
MARKEY, Enid American actress
BE, TW/1-21, 24, WWT/15-16
MARKEY, Melinda (b 1934) Amer-
ican actress TW/9
MARKHAM, Agnes [Mrs. John
Liddell] (d 1889) actress EA/
90*
MARKHAM, Daisy (b 1886) Indian/
English actress WWT/1-8
MARKHAM, David [Peter Basil
Harrison] (b 1913) English ac-
tor WWT/9-16
MARKHAM, Gervase (1568-1637)
dramatist CP/1-3, FGF, HP
MARKHAM, Monte (b 1935)
American actor TW/29
MARKHAM, Pauline (1847-1919)
English actress CDP, HAS,
SR
MARKLIN, Peter (b 1939) Amer-
ican actor TW/26-29

MARKOE, Peter (c. 1752-92) West
Indian dramatist DAB, EAP,
HJD, RJ, WWA/H
MARKOVA, Alicia [Alicia Marks]
(b 1910) English dancer CB,
ES, OC/1-2, TW/1, 3, WWT/
8-12
MARKS, Alfred (b 1921) English
actor WWT/12-16
MARKS, Alicia see Markova,
Alicia
MARKS, Ben (d 1970 [72]) per-
former BP/55*
MARKS, Fred (b 1884) English ac-
tor GRB/1
MARKS, Jeannette (1875-1964)
American dramatist WWA/4
MARKS, Joe E. (1891-1973) Amer-
ican actor TW/6-7, 13-15, 19,
23-24, 30
MARKS, Josephine Preston Peabody
see Peabody, Josephine
MARKS, Mrs. Lionel see Pea-
body, Josephine
MARKS, Sherman (d 1975) pro-
ducer/director/choreographer
BP/59*
MARKUS, Thomas B. (b 1934)
American actor TW/27
MARLATT, Donald (b 1940) Amer-
ican actor TW/23
MARLBOROUGH, Leah (d 1953/54
[85]) actress BE*, WWT/14*
MARLE, Arnold (d 1970 [82]) per-
former BP/54*
MARLER, George F. (d 1902 [68])
singer, manager EA/03*
MARLER, Mrs. George F. (d
1894) EA/95*
MARLER, Maitland (b 1863) English
actor EA/97, GRB/1-2
MARLER, Mrs. Maitland see
Maitland, Mary
MARLER, Mrs. Maitland see
Rawlings, Mabel
MARLER, Mary [Mrs. Maitland
Marler] (d 1898) EA/99*
MARLEY, John (b 1914) American
actor TW/11, 14, 23
MARLIN, Max composer BE
MARLIN, Paul (b 1925) American
actor TW/3
MARLING, Ilse see Marvenga,
Ilse
MARLO, Micki (b 1932) American
actress TW/13
MARLOW, David (b 1945) American
actor TW/29

MARLOW, George (d 1939 [62])
actor BE*, WWT/14*
MARLOW, Harry [Charles Wil-
liam Blomfield] (1880-1957)
English actor GRB/1
MARLOW, John Horatio (d 1893)
marionettist EA/94*
MARLOWE, Alan (d 1975 [40])
performer BP/59*
MARLOWE, Anthony (b 1913)
English actor WWT/11-16
MARLOWE, Christopher (1564-
93) English dramatist COC,
CP/3, DNB, ES, FGF, HP,
MH, NTH, OC/1-3, PDT,
RE, SR
MARLOWE, Ethel (d 1898) ac-
tress CDP
MARLOWE, Frank (d 1964 [60])
actor BE*
MARLOWE, Frederick (d 1964
[61]) producer WWT/14*
MARLOWE, Gloria American
actress TW/9-14
MARLOWE, Hugh [né Hipple]
(b 1911/14) American actor
BE, TW/3-6, 22-25, WWT/
11-12, 15-16
MARLOWE, James C. [né Gurn]
(b 1866) American comedian
WWM
MARLOWE, Joan (b 1920) Amer-
ican publisher, writer BE
MARLOWE, Julia (1866-1950)
English actress CDP, COC,
DAB, ES, GRB/2-4, HJD,
NTH, OC/1-3, PP/2, SR,
TW/7, WWM, WWS, WWT/
1-10
MARLOWE, Marion (b 1930)
American singer, actress,
dancer BE, TW/23-24
MARLOWE, Owen (1830-76) Eng-
lish/American actor CDP,
HAS
MARLOWE, Mrs. Owen [Virginia
Nickinson] (fl 1853-66) Amer-
ican actress HAS
MARMION, Emily M. [née
Trewren; Mrs. Thomas Mar-
mion] (d 1906 [56]) EA/07*
MARMION, Shackerley (c. 1602-
39) English dramatist CP/
1-3, DNB, FGF, HP
MARMION, Thomas (d 1903)
manager EA/05*
MARMION, Mrs. Thomas see
Marmion, Emily M.

MARMONT, Patricia (b 1921/22)
American actress TW/4, 7
MARMONT, Percy (b 1883) English
actor WWT/7-14
MARNAY, Carol E. (b 1942/43)
American actress TW/25, 30
MARNER, Mrs. C. Foster see
Belfry, Venie
MARNEY, Frank (d 1909) comedian,
dancer EA/10*
MARNEY, Lily (fl 1898?) singer
CDP
MAROFF, Robert (b 1934) Ameri-
can actor TW/30
MAROWITZ, Charles (b 1934)
American director, dramatist,
critic AAS, COC, WWT/15-16
MAROZZI, Lorenza (fl 1833) singer
HAS
MARQUERIE, Alfredo (d 1974 [67])
critic BP/59*
MARQUES, René (b 1919) Puerto
Rican dramatist MWD, RE
MARQUET, Louise (d 1890 [58])
dancer, ballet mistress EA/92*
MARQUIS, Don (1878-1937) Amer-
ican dramatist WWA/1, WWT/
6-8
MARQUIS, Marjorie Vonnegut (d
1936 [44]) American actress
BE*, BP/21*
MARR, Joe (b 1916) American ac-
tor TW/4-6
MARR, Paul (d 1976 [71]) booking
agent BP/60*
MARR, Paula American actress
WWT/1-5
MARR, Richard (b 1928) American
actor TW/25-26, 29-30
MARRANT, Edward theatre owner
DA
MARRAS, Giacinto (1810-83) Italian
singer, composer DNB
MARRE, Albert (b 1925) American
director, producer BE, WWT/
15-16
MARRIOT, Mr. (fl 1794) Scottish
actor HAS
MARRIOT, Mrs. (fl 1794) Scottish
actress HAS
MARRIOTT, Miss (fl 1802) actress
CDP, GT, TD/2
MARRIOTT, Miss (fl 1854) actress
EA/96
MARRIOTT, Miss (fl 1850-69) Eng-
lish actress HAS
MARRIOTT, Alice [Mrs. R. Edgar]
(1824-1900) actress CDP, COC,

DP, OAA/1-2
MARRIOTT, Frank (d 1888 [42])
  minstrell proprietor EA/89*
MARRIOTT, G. M. (d 1940 [81])
  actor BE*, WWT/14*
MARRIOTT, J. H. (d 1886 [87])
  EA/87*
MARRIOTT, John (1900-77) Amer-
  ican actor TW/4, 12, 15, 24
MARRIOTT, Moore (d 1949 [64])
  actor BE*, WWT/14*
MARRIOTT, Raymond Bowler (b
  1911) English critic WWT/16
MARRIOTT, Sarah (d 1885) EA/
  86*
MARRIOTT, Thomas Arthur
  see Picardo, Arthur
MARRIOTT-WATSON, Nan (b
  1899) actress, dramatist
  WWT/5-8
MARRIS, Samuel Arthur (d 1906
  [63]) EA/07*
MARRONEY, Peter R. (b 1913)
  American educator, director
  BE
MARRYAT, Florence [Mrs. Fran-
  cis Lean] (1837-99) dramatist,
  actress BE*, EA/00*, WWT/
  14*
MARS, Mons. (d 1892) menagerie
  proprietor EA/93*
MARS, Mme. (d 1892) EA/93*
MARS, Leo (fl 1896-1901) panto-
  mimist, singer WWS
MARS, Marjorie (b 1903) English
  actress WWT/6-13
MARS, Severin (d 1921 [43]) ac-
  tor WWT/14*
MARSDEN, Betty (b 1919) Eng-
  lish actress WWT/12-16
MARSDEN, Fred (d 1888) actor,
  dramatist SR
MARSDEN, Mrs. Lawrence see
  Lewis, Lillian
MARSDENE, Beatrice [Miles]
  Welsh actress GRB/1
MARSDIN, Dorothy Chiffon Eng-
  lish actress GRB/1
MARSH, Mr. (fl 1846-55) actor
  HAS
MARSH, Alec (b 1860) English
  singer DP
MARSH, Alexander (d 1947) ac-
  tor, producer BE*, WWT/14*
MARSH, Alphonso (1648?-92)
  musician DNB
MARSH, Mrs. Arthur H. see
  Marsh, Juliana Phillis

MARSH, Charles (d 1782) dramatist
  CP/1-3, GT
MARSH, Daisy (d 1887) EA/88*
MARSH, Della (d 1973) performer
  BP/57*
MARSH, Ernest W. (d 1917) EA/
  18*
MARSH, Garry (b 1902) English
  actor WWT/7-15
MARSH, George W. (b 1848) actor
  CDP
MARSH, Henry see Marston,
  Henry
MARSH, Howard (d 1969) actor,
  singer TW/26
MARSH, Juliana Phillis [Mrs.
  Arthur H. Marsh] (d 1878 [34])
  EA/79*
MARSH, Leo A. (d 1936 [42]) jour-
  nalist BE*, WWT/14*
MARSH, Linda American actress
  TW/20
MARSH, Lucille (b 1921) American
  actress TW/1-15
MARSH, Mae (d 1968 [72]) per-
  former BP/52*
MARSH, Maria (d 1907 [76]) EA/
  08*
MARSH, Mary (b 1847) actress
  CDP
MARSH, Muriel see Alexander,
  Muriel
MARSH, Richard Henry see
  Marston, Henry
MARSH, Risley Halsey (d 1965
  [38]) performer BP/49*
MARSH, William Henry the infant
  drummer CDP
MARSH, W. Ward (d 1971 [77])
  critic BP/56*
MARSHAK, Samuel (d 1964 [77])
  performer BP/49*
MARSHAL, Alan (d 1961 [52]) actor
  TW/18
MARSHALL, Mr. (fl 1790) drama-
  tist CP/3
MARSHALL, Mr. (fl 1781-90) Eng-
  lish actor TD/1-2
MARSHALL, Mr. (d 1816) English
  actor CDP, HAS
MARSHALL, Mrs. see Wilmot,
  Mrs.
MARSHALL, Miss (fl 1841) singer
  HAS
MARSHALL, Miss see Yeomans,
  Mrs. Thomas
MARSHALL, Alan (d 1961 [52])
  Australian actor BE*

MARSHALL, Armina (b 1900)
American producer, actress
BE, WWT/16
MARSHALL, Charles (fl 1613-16)
actor DA
MARSHALL, Charles (1806-90)
scene painter DNB
MARSHALL, Charles E. (d 1975
[76]) performer BP/59*
MARSHALL, Charles Frederick
(d 1879 [84]) comedian EA/80*
MARSHALL, David (d 1917) elec-
trician EA/18*
MARSHALL, Edward (d 1904 [78])
actor BE*, WWT/14*
MARSHALL, Edward (b 1869)
American dramatist WWM
MARSHALL, Edward (d 1884)
EA/85*
MARSHALL, Edward (d 1904 [78])
comedian EA/05*
MARSHALL, E. G. (b 1910)
American actor BE, ES,
TW/2-6, 9-13, 22, 24-25, 29,
WWT/16
MARSHALL, Ethelbert A. (fl
1838-57) manager HAS
MARSHALL, Everett (b 1901)
American actor, singer WWT/
10
MARSHALL, F. Elmer (d 1971
[89]) performer BP/55*
MARSHALL, Francis Albert
(1840-89) English dramatist
DNB
MARSHALL, Frank (d 1889 [34])
actor EA/90*
MARSHALL, Frank (d 1939
[81]) critic WWT/14*
MARSHALL, Mrs. Frank see
Cavendish, Ada
MARSHALL, Mrs. Frank see
Marshall, Imogene
MARSHALL, Mrs. Fred (d 1884)
EA/85*
MARSHALL, Frederick (1848-86)
Scottish actor OAA/1-2
MARSHALL, Mrs. G. [née
Harding] actress HAS
MARSHALL, George (d 1975 [84])
producer/director/choreographer
BP/59*
MARSHALL, Harry (d 1895)
comedian EA/96*
MARSHALL, Henry (d 1895 [71])
comedian EA/96*
MARSHALL, Herbert (1890-1966)
English actor BE, ES, NTH,

TW/22, WWA/4, WWT/4-11
MARSHALL, Horace (d 1976 [73])
performer BP/60*
MARSHALL, Imogene [Mrs. Frank
Marshall] (d 1885) EA/86*
MARSHALL, Mrs. James see
Marshall, Margaret
MARSHALL, Jane (fl 1772) drama-
tist CP/3
MARSHALL, Joseph (d 1873) ballet
master EA/74*
MARSHALL, Julian J. (d 1889 [27])
actor EA/90*
MARSHALL, Lois (b 1924) Canadian
singer CB
MARSHALL, Louisa (d 1896 [70])
actress EA/97*
MARSHALL, Margaret [Mrs. James
Marshall] (d 1889 [43]) EA/90*
MARSHALL, Mary see St. Clair,
Mme.
MARSHALL, Mort (b 1918) Amer-
ican actor BE, TW/28-29
MARSHALL, Norman (b 1901) In-
dian/English producer, director,
manager AAS, COC, ES, PDT,
WWT/8-16
MARSHALL, Norman Thomas (b
1939) American actor TW/25,
28, 30
MARSHALL, O. (b 1822) American
actor HAS
MARSHALL, Oriana (d 1867) ac-
tress HAS
MARSHALL, Patricia American ac-
tress TW/2-3, 12-15
MARSHALL, Percy F. (1861-1927)
English actor EA/95, GRB/1-4
MARSHALL, Peter L. (b 1930)
American actor TW/22-23
MARSHALL, Polly [Mrs. Zerman]
(1813-78) English actress,
dancer HAS
MARSHALL, Cpt. Robert (1863-
1910) Scottish dramatist GRB/
1-4, WWW/1
MARSHALL, Sarah (b 1933) Amer-
ican actress BE, TW/9-19
MARSHALL, Sid (b 1941) American
actor TW/26, 28
MARSHALL, Tully (1864-1943)
American actor, director CB,
SR, WWA/2, WWM, WWT/1-9
MARSHALL, Mrs. Tully see
Fairfax, Marion
MARSHALL, William (d 1875 [69])
EA/76*
MARSHALL, William (b 1924)

American actor, singer, di-
rector BE, TW/23
MARSHALL, Will Sharpe (b 1947)
American actor TW/29-30
MARSHALL, Wyzeman (1815-96)
actor, manager CDP
MARSHALOV, Boris (d 1967 [65])
Russian/American actor TW/
24
MARSH TROUPE, The (fl 1855)
HAS
MARSON, Aileen (1912-39)
Egyptian/English actress WWT/8
MARSON, Frederick C. (d 1889
[21]) Negro minstrel EA/90*
MARSTON, Beatrice (d 1868 [17])
actress EA/72*
MARSTON, Eleanor Jane [Mrs.
Westland Marston] (d 1870)
EA/71*
MARSTON, E. W. (b 1836) Amer-
ican actor, manager HAS
MARSTON, H. E. (d 1901 [56])
acting manager EA/02*
MARSTON, Henry [Richard Henry
Marsh] (d 1883 [79]) English
actor CDP, OAA/2
MARSTON, Mrs. Henry (1809-
87) English actress CDP,
NYM
MARSTON, Jenny actress CDP
MARSTON, Joel (b 1922) Amer-
ican actor TW/1-3
MARSTON, John (c. 1575-1634)
English dramatist COC, CP/
1-3, DA, DNB, ES, FGF,
HP, MH, NTH, OC/1-3, PDT,
RE
MARSTON, John (d 1962 [72])
actor TW/19
MARSTON, John Westland (1819-
90) English dramatist CDP,
DNB, EA/68, HP, OC/1-3
MARSTON, Philip Bourke (d 1887
[35]) EA/88*
MARSTON, Richard (d 1917 [75])
scene artist WWT/14*
MARSTON, Mrs. Westland see
Marston, Eleanor Jane
MARTAIN, A. J. (fl 1861)
American actor HAS
MARTEL, Flora American execu-
tive BE
MARTEL, Tom (b 1949) American
actor TW/28
MARTEL, William (b 1916) Amer-
ican actor TW/25
MARTELL, Gillian (b 1936) Eng-

lish actress WWT/15-16
MARTELL, Mrs. Harry see
Martell, May
MARTELL, May [Mrs. Harry Mar-
tell] (d 1890) EA/91*
MARTENS, The (fl 1882) vaudevil-
lians CDP
MARTERSTEIG, Dr. Max (b 1853)
German manager GRB/4, WWT/
1-2
MARTIN, Mr. see Booth, Joseph
MARTIN, Mons. (fl 1831) French
animal trainer, actor CDP
MARTIN, Mons. (fl 1839) dancer
HAS
MARTIN, Ada Beatrice [Mrs. Wil-
liam Martin] (d 1905) EA/06*
MARTIN, Allen (b 1936) American
actor TW/6
MARTIN, Angela actress TW/24
MARTIN, Boyd (d 1963 [76]) critic,
director, educator BE*, BP/47*,
WWT/14*
MARTIN, Charles G. (b 1912)
American actor TW/6
MARTIN, Christina (d 1973) dresser
BP/57*
MARTIN, Cye (d 1972 [56]) per-
former BP/56*
MARTIN, Dolphe (d 1974 [81])
composer/lyricist BP/59*
MARTIN, E. (d 1881) secretary
EA/82*
MARTIN, Edgar (d 1900) music-
hall performer EA/01*
MARTIN, Edie (1880-1964) English
actress WWT/9-13
MARTIN, Edward (d 1897) manager
EA/98*
MARTIN, Elliot (b 1924) American
producer, stage manager BE,
WWT/16
MARTIN, Ernest (b 1862) English
actor, dramatist GRB/1
MARTIN, Ernest H. (b 1919) Amer-
ican manager, producer, drama-
tist BE, WWT/12-16
MARTIN, Eugene see Geniat,
Marcelle
MARTIN, Frank (d 1974 [84]) com-
poser/lyricist BP/59*
MARTIN, F. W. [Fred Mansfield]
(d 1881) EA/82*
MARTIN, George William (d 1881
[53]) musician EA/82*
MARTIN, Harry (d 1970 [67]) per-
former BP/54*
MARTIN, Harry J. (d 1975 [82])

promoter, manager BP/60*

MARTIN, Helen American actress BE, TW/26, 29-30

MARTIN, H. Sherwood (b 1877) English manager GRB/1

MARTIN, Hugh composer, lyricist BE

MARTIN, Hugh Whitfield see Martin, Riccardo

MARTIN, Ian (b 1912) Scottish actor TW/29-30

MARTIN, Mrs. Jacques (1863-1936) American actress BE*, BP/21*

MARTIN, James (b 1825) Canadian actor HAS

MARTIN, Jared (b 1943) American actor TW/24

MARTIN, John (d 1764) actor WWT/14*

MARTIN, John E. (1768-1807) American actor CDP, HAS, NTH

MARTIN, John F. X. (d 1973 [46]) performer BP/57*

MARTIN, Joy (b 1944) American actress TW/24

MARTIN, Laura (d 1898 [57]) EA/99*

MARTIN, Leila (b 1932/36) American actress, singer BE, TW/11, 13, 16, 27-29

MARTIN, Lewis (1898-1969) American actor TW/3, 25

MARTIN, Miss M. (d 1889) EA/90*

MARTIN, Martin Adams (d 1878 [38]) professor of music EA/79*

MARTIN, Mary (b 1913/14) American actress, singer AAS, BE, CB, ES, PDT, TW/1-25, WWT/10-16

MARTIN, Mildred Palmer (d 1962 [59]) critic BE*

MARTIN, Millicent (b 1934) English actress, singer AAS, WWT/14-16

MARTIN, Nan (b 1927) American actress BE, TW/8, 16, 21, 23

MARTIN, Nicholas (b 1938) American actor TW/23-25

MARTIN, Owen (d 1960 [71]) actor TW/16

MARTIN, Pam American actress TW/28

MARTIN, Pete (b 1901) journalist

BE

MARTIN, Philip dramatist CD

MARTIN, Philip, Jr. (d 1974 [57]) producer/director/choreographer BP/58*

MARTIN, Riccardo [Hugh Whitfield Martin] (1879-1952) American singer WWA/3, WWM

MARTIN, Robert Jasper (d 1905 [62]) songwriter, journalist EA/06*

MARTIN, Ron (b 1947) American actor TW/27-29

MARTIN, Sarah (d 1879 [71]) EA/80*

MARTIN, T. (d 1890) stage manager EA/91*

MARTIN, Mrs. Theodore see Faucit, Helen

MARTIN, Thomas J. (1842-87) American actor NYM

MARTIN, Mrs. Thomas J. see Fiske, Marian

MARTIN, Tom (d 1962 [58]) artists' representative BE*

MARTIN, Townsend (d 1951 [55]) American writer BE*, BP/36*

MARTIN, Virginia (b 1932) American actress, singer BE, TW/13, 19, 28

MARTIN, Vivian (b 1893) American actress WWT/6-7

MARTIN, Vivienne (b 1936) New Zealand actress WWT/15-16

MARTIN, Walter (d 1916 [19]) actor EA/17*

MARTIN, William (1767-1810) English actor DNB

MARTIN, William (d 1917) EA/18*

MARTIN, Mrs. William see Martin, Ada Beatrice

MARTIN, William Richard see Minton, William Richard

MARTIN, W. T. (b 1947) American actor TW/29-30

MARTINDEL, Edward (d 1955 [80]) actor TW/11

MARTINE, Stella (d 1961 [81]) actress BE*

MARTINEAU, Francis (d 1886 [29]) actor EA/87*

MARTINEC, Lee A. (d 1975 [49]) performer BP/60*

MARTINELLI [?], Angelica (fl 1580?) Italian actress DA

MARTINELLI, Drusiano (d 1606/08) Italian actor COC, DA, OC/2-3

MARTINELLI, Giovanni (1885-1969)

Italian singer CB, ES, TW/
25, WWA/5
MARTINETTE, Albert (d 1898
[33]) variety performer EA/99*
MARTINETTI, Clara (d 1945)
pantomimist BE*, WWT/14*
MARTINETTI, Ignacio actor CDP
MARTINETTI, Julian (1821-84)
acrobat, pantomimist, clown
CDP
MARTINETTI, Paul (d 1924 [73])
American pantomimist, mana-
ger CDP, GRB/2-4
MARTINETTI, Pauline (d 1927
[82]) pantomimist BE*,
WWT/14*
MARTINEZ SIERRA, Gregorio
(1881-1947) Spanish dramatist
COC, OC/1-3
MARTIN-HARVEY, John see
Harvey, John Martin
MARTIN-HARVEY, Muriel (b
1891) English actress WWT/
2-9
MARTINI, Fausto Maria (1886-
1931) Italian dramatist MWD
MARTINI, Laura [Mrs. W. John-
son] (d 1909) variety performer
EA/10*
MARTINO, Mrs. Fred see
Martino, Lydia
MARTINO, Lydia [Mrs. Fred
Martino] (d 1898) circus per-
former EA/99*
MARTINOT, Sadie [Mrs. Louis
F. Nethersole] (1861-1923)
American actress, singer
CDP, GRB/2-4, SR, WWA/4,
WWM, WWS, WWT/1-4
MARTINSON, Joseph B. (b 1911)
American executive BE
MARTLEW, Mary (b 1919) Eng-
lish actress WWT/10-12
MARTLEY, Bob [Henry James
King] (d 1895) performer?
EA/96*
MARTON, Thomas (fl 1601) actor
DA
MARTSON, Beatrice (d 1868 [17])
actress EA/69*
MARTYN, Mr. (fl 1839-40) ac-
tor? singer? HAS
MARTYN, Benjamin (d 1763 [64])
dramatist CP/1-3, GT
MARTYN, Mrs. Charles [Miss
Inverarity] (1813-47) actress?
singer? CDP, DNB, HAS
MARTYN, Edward (1859-1924)

Irish dramatist COC, HP, MD,
MWD, OC/2-3, RE, WWW/2
MARTYN, Eliza (d 1846 [33]) ac-
tress BE*, WWT/14*
MARTYN, Katherine (d 1893 [17])
EA/94*
MARTYN, May [Mrs. Nigel Play-
fair] (1880-1948) English actress
GRB/2-3
MARTYN, William (fl 1569-72) ac-
tor DA
MARTYN-GREEN, William see
Green, Martyn
MARTYR, Margaret [née Thornton]
(d 1807) actress, singer CDP,
GT, TD/1-2
MARUM, John Daily see Dillon,
John
MARUM, Marilyn Harvey (d 1973
[44]) performer BP/57*
MARUNAS, P. Raymond (b 1939)
Lithuanian actor TW/26
MARVEL, Pauline [Pauline Anton]
(b 1918) American actress TW/
24
MARVENGA, Ilse [Ilse Marling]
German actress, singer WWT/
7-9
MARVIN, Charles see Mervin,
Fred
MARVIN, Lee (b 1924) American
actor CB, ES
MARWIG, Carl (fl 1879) CDP
MARX, Chico (1891-1961) American
comedian CB, TW/18
MARX, Groucho (1895-1977) Amer-
ican actor BE, CB
MARX, Gummo (1894-1977) Ameri-
can comedian BE
MARX, Harpo (1893-1964) American
comedian, musician BE, CB,
TW/21
MARX, Marie Simard (d 1974) per-
former BP/58*
MARX, Marvin (d 1975 [50]) drama-
tist BP/60*
MARX, Milton (d 1973 [75]) car-
toonist BP/57*
MARX, Zeppo (b 1901) American
comedian BE
MARY ANGELITA, Sister (b 1912)
American educator BE
MARYE, Donald (b 1905) American
actor TW/22-23, 28
MARY IMMACULATE, Sister
executive BE
MARYON, Alice (d 1883) actress?
EA/84*

MARYOTT, Susan (d 1963 [30])
performer BP/48*
MARZETTI, Joseph (d 1864)
pantomimist CDP, HAS
MARZETTI, Mathilde actress,
dancer CDP
MASCAGNI, Pietro (1863-1945)
Italian composer, conductor
ES, GRB/1, WWM
MASCHWITZ, Eric (1901-69)
English dramatist, composer
AAS, WWT/9-14
MASCOLO, Joseph (b 1935) Amer-
ican actor TW/23, 26-30
MASEFIELD, John (1878-1967)
English dramatist COC, ES,
HP, MH, MWD, NTH, OC/
1-3, WWT/1-14, WWW/6
MASFIRI, Sidi-El-Hadjali-Ben-
Mahomed (d 1895 [80]) acrobat
EA/96*
MASIELL, Joe (b 1939) American
actor TW/25, 27-30
MASINI, Angelo (1844-1926) Italian
singer ES
MASKELL, Mr. (fl 1855) English
actor HAS
MASKELL, Fanny see Baynham,
Mrs. Walter
MASKELL, George K. (d 1881)
comedian EA/82*
MASKELL, Laura see Joyce,
Laura
MASKELL, Virginia (d 1968
[31]) performer BP/52*
MASKELYNE, Elizabeth [Mrs.
John Nevil Maskelyne] (d 1911
[70]) EA/12*
MASKELYNE, John Nevil (1839-
1917) English mechanical &
optical illusionist GRB/1-4
MASKELYNE, Mrs. John Nevil
see Maskelyne, Elizabeth
MASKOVA, Hana (d 1972) per-
former BP/56*
MASKY, Jeanne (b 1926) Amer-
ican actress TW/3
MASON (fl 1515) actor DA
MASON, Mrs. [née Barber]
English actress HAS
MASON, Mrs. [Mrs. Elizabeth;
Mrs. Crooke; Mrs. Entwistle]
(1780-1835) English actress
CDP, HAS
MASON, Miss (fl 1836) Scottish
actress HAS
MASON, Alfred Edward Woodley
(1865-1948) English dramatist,

actor DNB, GRB/4, MH,
WWT/1-10, WWW/4
MASON, Ann (d 1948 [50]) Ameri-
can actress TW/4
MASON, Beryl (b 1921) English ac-
tress WWT/10-16
MASON, Brewster (b 1922) English
actor AAS, WWT/14-16
MASON, Bruce (b 1921) New Zea-
land dramatist CD
MASON, Charles Kemble (1805-75)
English actor CDP, HAS, SR
MASON, Colin (d 1971 [47]) critic
BP/55*
MASON, Dan [Daniel Grassman]
(b 1855) American comedian
WWM
MASON, David (d 1888 [74]) musi-
cian EA/89*
MASON, Edith (d 1973 [80]) per-
former BP/58*
MASON, Edward (d 1916) singer,
songwriter CDP
MASON, Elliot C. (d 1949 [52])
Scottish actress WWT/9-10
MASON, F. R. (d 1904) acting
manager EA/05*
MASON, Fred (d 1895 [27]) comic
singer EA/97*
MASON, Mrs. Fred (d 1899 [34])
EA/00*
MASON, Gladys (b 1886) English
actress GRB/4, WWT/1-8
MASON, Henry J. (d 1901 [38])
music-hall manager EA/02*
MASON, Herbert producer WWT/
5-9
MASON, Homer B. (d 1959 [80])
actor, vaudevillian TW/16
MASON, James (fl 1805) dramatist
CP/3
MASON, James (b 1909) English
actor CB, ES, TW/3, WWT/9-
14
MASON, Mrs. James see
Wheatley, Emma
MASON, Jane (d 1874) singer EA/
75*
MASON, Jennie (d 1909 [72]) EA/
10*
MASON, Mrs. J. J. (d 1881) pro-
prietor EA/82*
MASON, J. M. (d 1871 [27])
musician EA/71*
MASON, John (fl 1606-10) drama-
tist, lessee CP/1-3, DA
MASON, John B. (1857/58-1919)
American actor CDP, DAB,

ES, GRB/2-4, PP/2, WWA/1,
WWM, WWS, WWT/1-3
MASON, John Kemble (fl 1831-
32) Scottish actor CDP, HAS
MASON, John Monck (1726-1809)
Irish scholar DNB
MASON, Joseph B. (d 1897 [67])
actor EA/98*
MASON, Mrs. J. W. see
Mason, Theresa
MASON, Kitty [Mrs. W. E. As-
pinall] (b 1882) English dancer
GRB/1-4, WWT/1-3
MASON, Lawrence (d 1939 [57])
American critic, educator
BE*, WWT/14*
MASON, LeRoy (d 1947 [44])
actor BE*
MASON, Lesley (d 1964 [76])
American press representative,
journalist BE*
MASON, Marjorie (d 1968) per-
former BP/53*
MASON, Marlyn (b 1940) Amer-
ican actress TW/24
MASON, Marsha (b 1942) Amer-
ican actress TW/23-24, 27,
30
MASON, Mary (d 1867 [79])
EA/68*
MASON, Reginald (1882-1962)
American actor TW/1, 4,
9-10, 19, WWT/7-13
MASON, Richard (d 1970 [24])
actor TW/26
MASON, Ruth Fitch (d 1974 [84])
agent, author BP/59*
MASON, Theresa [Mrs. J. W.
Mason] (d 1897 [44]) EA/98*
MASON, Thomas Monk (d 1889
[86]) entrepreneur, musician,
aeronaut EA/90*
MASON, William (1725-77) Eng-
lish dramatist CP/2-3, GT,
TD/1-2
MASS, Joseph E. (d 1974 [62])
performer BP/58*
MASSARIK, Friederike see
Massary, Fritzi
MASSARY, Fritzi [Friederike
Massarik] (1882-1969) Aus-
trian actress, singer ES,
WWT/9-10
MASSEN, Louis F. (d 1925 [67])
French/American actor, di-
rector BE*, BP/9*, WWT/14*
MASSENET, Jules (1842-1912)
French composer GRB/1,

SR, WWM
MASSET, Stephen C. (1820-98)
English actor, singer CDP,
HAS, SR
MASSEY, Mrs. (fl 1778?) actress
CDP
MASSEY, Anna (b 1937) English ac-
tress BE, ES, TW/13-14,
WWT/13-16
MASSEY, Blanche (d 1929 [51])
actress BE*, WWT/14*
MASSEY, Charles (d 1625) English
actor, dramatist CP/3, DA,
OC/1-3
MASSEY, Daniel (b 1933) English
actor BE, TW/14, 19, 30,
WWT/13-16
MASSEY, George (fl 1622) lessee
DA
MASSEY, Ilona (d 1974 [60/62])
actress, singer BP/59*, WWT/
16*
MASSEY, Mary (d 1902 [79]) EA/
03*
MASSEY, Raymond (b 1896) Cana-
dian actor, producer, director
AAS, BE, CB, ES, NTH, TW/
2-16, WWT/6-16
MASSEY, Rose (d 1883 [32]) Eng-
lish actress HAS, OAA/2
MASSI, Bernice American actress
BE, TW/20-22, 24-27, 30,
WWT/15-16
MASSINE, Leonide (b 1896) Rus-
sian/American dancer, chore-
ographer, maître de ballet CB,
ES, WWT/8-12
MASSINGER, Philip (1583-1640)
English dramatist CDP, COC,
CP/1-3, DNB, ES, FGF, HP,
MH, NTH, OC/1-3, PDT, RE
MASSINGHAM, Dorothy (1889-1933)
English actress, dramatist
WWT/5-7
MASSINK, Mr. (d 1789) machinist,
pantomime inventor TD/1-2
MASSOT, Pierre (d 1868) ballet
master EA/69*
MASTEROFF, Joe (b 1919) Amer-
ican dramatist, librettist BE,
CD
MASTERS, Amos (d 1917 [67])
stage manager, carpenter EA/
18*
MASTERS, Benjamin (b 1947)
American actor TW/27-28
MASTERS, E. H. Frank (d 1917)
comedian, manager EA/18*

MASTERS, Harry (d 1974 [79])
performer BP/58*
MASTERS, M. K. (fl 1811)
dramatist CP/3
MASTERS, Ruth (d 1969 [75])
performer TW/26
MASTERSON, C. (fl 180-) drama-
tist CP/3
MASTERSON, Carroll (b 1913)
American producer BE
MASTERSON, Harris (b 1914)
American producer BE
MASTERSON, Peter (b 1936)
American actor TW/24-26
MASUR, Richard (b 1948) Amer-
ican actor TW/29-30
MATACHENA, Oreste (b 1941)
Cuban actor TW/25
MATALON, Vivian (b 1929) Eng-
lish director WWT/14-16
MATALON, Zack (b 1928) English
actor, singer, dancer, pro-
ducer, director BE, TW/18
MATE, Charles (b 1776) actor
TD/2
MATERNA, Amalie (1844-1918)
Austrian singer CDP, ES
MATHER, Aubrey (1885-1958)
English actor TW/1, 3, 6-7,
14, WWT/6-12
MATHER, Donald (b 1900) Eng-
lish actor, singer WWT/7-9
MATHER, Margaret (1859-98)
actress CDP
MATHER, Sydney (d 1925 [49])
English actor BE*, BP/9*
MATHERS, Arthur (d 1878 [34])
musician EA/79*
MATHERS, Edward Powys (1892-
1939) dramatist WWW/3
MATHESON, Murray (b 1912)
Australian actor BE, TW/
10-16
MATHEW, Ann (d 1976 [65])
dancer WWT/16*
MATHEW, Ray (b 1929) Aus-
tralian dramatist CD
MATHEWS, Mr. actor CDP
MATHEWS, Anne (d 1869) writer
CDP
MATHEWS, Carmen (b 1914/18)
American actress BE, TW/
2-9, 13-20, 22-25, 28-29,
WWT/11-16
MATHEWS, Carole (b 1922)
American actress TW/6
MATHEWS, Charles (1776-1835)
English actor BS, CDP,

COC, DNB, ES, GT, HAS,
NTH, OC/1-3, OX, TD/2
MATHEWS, Mrs. Charles (d 1869
[87]) EA/70*
MATHEWS, Mrs. Charles see
Mathews, Eliza Kirkland
MATHEWS, Charles James (1803-
78) English actor, dramatist
CDP, COC, DNB, EA/68, ES,
HAS, NTH, OAA/1-2, OC/1-3,
SR
MATHEWS, Mrs. Charles James
see Vestris, Mme.
MATHEWS, Mrs. Charles James,
II [Lizzie Weston; née Jackson;
Lizzie Davenport] (d 1899)
American actress CDP, HAS,
OAA/1-2, SR
MATHEWS, Chris ["Comical
Chris"] (d 1916) ventriloquist
EA/17*
MATHEWS, Cicely (d 1975 [65])
producer/director/choreographer
BP/60*
MATHEWS, Cornelius (1817-89)
dramatist CDP
MATHEWS, Elizabeth see Math-
ews, Mrs. Charles James, II
MATHEWS, Eliza Kirkland (d 1802)
CDP
MATHEWS, Frances Aymar (d
1923) American dramatist
GRB/3-4, WWA/2, WWM,
WWT/1-2
MATHEWS, George (b 1911) Amer-
ican actor BE, TW/1, 3-9,
11-16, 21-23, 25-26, WWT/11-
16
MATHEWS, Helen (d 1890) actress
EA/91*
MATHEWS, James W. (d 1920
[56]) New Zealand business
manager GRB/3-4, WWT/1-3
MATHEWS, Joyce actress TW/1
MATHEWS, Julia (d 1876 [34]) ac-
tress, singer CDP
MATHEWS, Lizzie Weston see
Mathews, Mrs. Charles James,
II
MATHEWS, Mark (b 1943) Ameri-
can actor TW/27
MATHEWS, Norman American ac-
tor TW/25
MATHEWS, Richard (b 1823) Amer-
ican actor HAS
MATHEWS, Sarah (d 1876 [74])
EA/77*
MATHIAS, Yrca (fl 1853) dancer

CDP
MATHIESEN, Jack (b 1924) American actor TW/3
MATHIS, June (1890/92-1927) American actress ES, WWM
MATHIS, Sherry (b 1949) American actress TW/29-30
MATINEZ, Joseph J. (d 1975 [82]) performer BP/59*
MATLAW, Myron (b 1924) German/American educator, historian BE
MATRON, Miss see Second, Mrs.
MATSON, Norman (d 1965 [72]) dramatist BP/50*
MATSUI, Suisei (d 1973 [73]) performer BP/58*
MATSUSAKA, Tom American actor TW/24, 30
MATT, John (d 1910 [66]) professor of music EA/11*
MATTEI, Tito (1841-1914) Italian conductor, composer WWW/1
MATTESON, Ruth (1909-75) American actress BE, TW/1-3, 6-9, 14-16, WWT/11-15
MATTFELD, Julius (b 1893) American composer BE
MATTFELD, Marie (fl 1890-1912) German singer WWA/5, WWM
MATTHAEI, Konrad American actor TW/25-26, 28-29
MATTHAU, Walter [né Matthow] (b 1920) American actor BE, CB, ES, TW/21, WWT/14-16
MATTHEW, Sir Robert (d 1975 [68]) designer BP/60*
MATTHEW, Ross actor TW/1
MATTHEWS, Miss actress CDP
MATTHEWS, Adelaide (b 1886) dramatist WWT/6-11
MATTHEWS, A[lfred] E[dward] (1869-1960) English actor AAS, COC, DNB, ES, GRB/3-4, OC/3, TW/17, WWM, WWT/1-12, WWW/5
MATTHEWS, Ann (d 1891 [58]) EA/92*
MATTHEWS, Art American actor TW/18, 22-27
MATTHEWS, Bache (1876-1948) English director WWT/6-9
MATTHEWS, Billy (b 1922) American director, stage manager, actor BE
MATTHEWS, Brander see Matthews, James Brander

MATTHEWS, Charles Eli (d 1897 [60]) actor EA/98*
MATTHEWS, Cornelius (d 1889 [71]) American dramatist EA/90*
MATTHEWS, Dakin (b 1940) American actor TW/29
MATTHEWS, Dan (b 1922) American actor TW/8
MATTHEWS, Eliza (d 1879) EA/80*
MATTHEWS, Emma (d 1890) EA/91*
MATTHEWS, Emma Louisa (d 1917) EA/18*
MATTHEWS, Ethel (b 1870) actress DP, GRB/1-4, WWT/1-5
MATTHEWS, Fanny Marie [Mrs. Tom Matthews] (d 1871) EA/72*
MATTHEWS, Frances Aymar see Mathews, Frances Aymar
MATTHEWS, Francis (b 1933) English actor TW/23
MATTHEWS, Frank (d 1871 [64]) actor CDP
MATTHEWS, Mrs. Frank (d 1873 [66]) actress EA/74*, WWT/14*
MATTHEWS, George see Mathews, George
MATTHEWS, Gerry (b 1936) American actor TW/23-24
MATTHEWS, Harry (d 1896) minstrel? EA/97*
MATTHEWS, Helen see Brunton, Mrs. W. H.
MATTHEWS, H. P. singer CDP
MATTHEWS, Inez (b 1917) American singer, actress BE
MATTHEWS, James (d 1879 [55]) actor EA/80*
MATTHEWS, James (d 1880 [60]) prestidigitateur EA/81*
MATTHEWS, James Brander (1852-1929) American dramatist, critic CDP, COC, ES, GRB/3-4, HJD, NTH, OC/1-3, SR, WWA/1, WWM, WWT/1-5, WWW/3
MATTHEWS, Mrs. J. C. see Matthews, Sarah Elizabeth
MATTHEWS, Jessie (b 1907) English actress, dancer AAS, BE, ES, WWT/6-16
MATTHEWS, John Thomas (1805-89) clown CDP
MATTHEWS, Lacy (d 1902) actor EA/04*
MATTHEWS, Lester (b 1900)

English actor WWT/6-9

MATTHEWS, Mary Frances (d 1906 [45]) actress EA/07*

MATTHEWS, Sant (d 1896) actor EA/97*, WWT/14*

MATTHEWS, Sarah Blanche (b 1794) actress CDP

MATTHEWS, Sarah E. [Mrs. Fred Matthews] (d 1891 [31]) EA/92*

MATTHEWS, Sarah Elizabeth [Mrs. J. C. Matthews] (d 1876) EA/77*

MATTHEWS, Sherrie (1868-1921) comedian SR

MATTHEWS, Susannah Elizabeth see Harvey, Susie

MATTHEWS, Theodore (d 1888 [32]) performer? EA/89*

MATTHEWS, Mrs. Theodore see Harvey, Susie

MATTHEWS, Thomas (1805-89) actor, pantomimist DNB

MATTHEWS, Thomas F. (d 1904 [26]) music-hall performer EA/05*

MATTHEWS, Mrs. Tom see Matthews, Fanny Marie

MATTHEWS, Will (d 1892) comedian EA/94*

MATTHEWS, William (d 1906 [70]) minstrel EA/07*

MATTHEWS, William S. (d 1907) dramatic student EA/08*

MATTHEWSON, John (d 1871) actor EA/72*

MATTHISON, Arthur (d 1883 [57]) dramatist, actor BE*, EA/84*, WWT/14*

MATTHISON, Edith Wynne [Mrs. Charles Rann Kennedy] (1875-1955) English actress GRB/1-4, SR, TW/12, WWA/3, WWS, WWT/1-11

MATTHISON, Mrs. H. [Kate Wynne] (d 1912) singer EA/13*

MATTHISON, Henry (d 1905) singer GRB/1

MATTHOW, Walter see Matthau, Walter

MATTIOLI, Lino (b 1853) Italian musician WWA/4

MATTOCKS, George (d 1804) actor CDP

MATTOCKS, Isabella (1746-1826) English actress CDP, COC, DNB, GT, HAS, OC/1-3,

TD/1-2

MATTOX, Matt (b 1921) American dancer, actor, singer, choreographer BE, TW/12-15

MATTSON, Eric (b 1908) American producer, director BE, TW/1

MATURA, Mustapha (b 1939) West Indian dramatist CD, WWT/16

MATURE, Victor (b 1915) American actor ES

MATURIN, Charles Robert (1782-1824) Irish dramatist CDP, DNB

MATURIN, Eric (1883-1957) Indian/English actor WWT/1-12

MATYAS, Maria (d 1963 [57]) singer BE*

MATZ, Walter J. (d 1975 [81]) performer BP/60*

MATZENAUER, Margarete (1881-1963) Hungarian singer ES, TW/19, WWA/4

MAUDAUNT, Frank (b 1841) American actor SR

MAUDE, Charles Raymond (1882-1943) actor COC, GRB/3-4, WWT/1-5

MAUDE, Mrs. Charles Raymond see Price, Nancy

MAUDE, Cyril (1862-1951) English actor, manager CDP, COC, DP, EA/95, ES, GRB/1-4, OC/1-3, SR, TW/7, WWA/3, WWT/1-11, WWW/5

MAUDE, Mrs. Cyril see Emery, Winifred

MAUDE, Elizabeth (b 1912) actress WWT/7-10

MAUDE, Gillian actress WWT/9-10

MAUDE, Joan (b 1908) English actress WWT/5-11

MAUDE, Margery (b 1889) English actress BE, TW/2-3, 8, 25, WWT/1-16

MAUDE, Maude Amy Mannakay (d 1896 [20]) acrobat EA/97*

MAUDE, Robert Henry Ernest (d 1916 [26]) actor EA/17*

MAUDE-ROXBY, Roddy (b 1930) English actor WWT/15-16

MAUDSLEY, Mrs. H. (d 1872 [37]) EA/74*

MAUGHAM, Augustus Freshwater (d 1871 [41]) Negro minstrel EA/72*

MAUGHAM, William Somerset (1874-1965) French/English dramatist AAS, BE, CB, COC,

ES, GRB/2-4, HP, MD, MH,
MWD, NTH, OC/1-3, PDT,
RE, TW/22, WWM, WWT/
1-14, WWW/6

MAUGHAN, Fanny Amelia [Mrs.
John Sheffield Maughan] (d
1879) EA/80*

MAUGHAN, John Sheffield see
Maughan, Fanny Amelia

MAUGIN, Emile (fl 1856) pantomimist CDP

MAULE, Annabel (b 1922/23)
English actress WWT/9-16

MAULE, Donovan (b 1899) English director, manager WWT/
14-16

MAULE, Herbert (b 1873) English actor GRB/1

MAULE, Robin (1924-42) English
actor WWT/9

MAUNDER, Edith (fl 1889) actress CDP

MAUNDER, Henry J. (d 1897
[30]) actor EA/98*

MAUNDY-GREGORY, J. English
manager, dramatist GRB/1-4

MAUNSELL, Charles (d 1968)
performer BP/53*

MAURAN, Carlos see Blood-
good, Harry

MAUREL, Victor (1848-1923)
French singer, actor CDP,
ES, GRB/1-4

MAURER, Peggy (b 1931) American actress TW/13

MAUREY, Max (d 1947 [76])
manager WWT/14*

MAURICE (d 1927 [41]) dancer
BE*, WWT/14*

MAURICE, Edmund [Edmund
Fitz-Maurice Lenon] (d 1928
[65]) actor GRB/1-4, WWT/
1-5

MAURICE, Mrs. Edmund see
Hughes, Annie

MAURICE, George (d 1903)
music-hall comedian EA/04*

MAURICE, Mary (1844-1918)
American actress BE*

MAURICE, Newman (d 1920)
actor, producer BE*, WWT/
14*

MAURICE, Mrs. Newman see
Moncrieff, Rose

MAURICE, Thomas (fl 1779-
1812) dramatist CP/2-3, GT

MAUS, Herr (d 1869 [57]) circus
proprietor EA/70*

MAUS, Arthur (d 1975 [70]) performer BP/60*

MAUS, Louisa (d 1869 [49]) EA/
70*

MAUS DAYTON, Mary [Mrs. O.
Maus Dayton] (d 1910 [31])
EA/11*

MAUS DAYTON, Mrs. O. see
Maus Dayton, Mary

MAVIUS, Arthur Henry (d 1887
[28]) actor EA/88*

MAVOR, Osborne Henry see
Bridie, James

MAWDESLEY, Robert (d 1953 [53])
actor BE*, WWT/14*

MAWER, Irene (d 1962) teacher of
mime & dance WWT/14*

MAWSON, Edward R. (d 1917 [55])
actor BE*, WWT/14*

MAWSON, Harry P. (b 1853) American dramatist WWM

MAX, Edouard Alexandre de (1869-
1925) French actor GRB/1-4,
WWT/1-4

MAXAM, Clara [Mrs. Harry Max-
am] (d 1907 [38]) comic singer
EA/08*

MAXAM, Mrs. Harry see Maxam,
Clara

MAXAM, Louella Modie (d 1970
[74]) performer BP/55*

MAXE, William (fl 1509-13) actor
DA

MAXEY, Paul (d 1963 [55]) American actor BE*

MAXSEY, Gilbert (fl 1554) actor
DA

MAXTONE-GRAHAM, John (b 1929)
American stage manager BE

MAXWELL, Arthur (b 1919) American actor TW/5-10

MAXWELL, Barry (b 1848) actor,
minstrel CDP

MAXWELL, Edwin (d 1948 [58])
Irish actor BE*, BP/33*

MAXWELL, Elsa (1883-1963)
American actress CB, SR

MAXWELL, Frank (b 1916) American actor TW/8

MAXWELL, Gary (b 1939) American actor TW/25

MAXWELL, George (b 1837) American actor, manager HAS

MAXWELL, Gerald (1862-1930)
English actor, critic EA/96,
WWT/3-6

MAXWELL, Guy (d 1918) EA/19*

MAXWELL, John (fl 1740-61)

English dramatist CP/2-3
MAXWELL, Margery (1895-1966)
American singer WWA/4
MAXWELL, Marilyn (d 1972
[49]) actress, singer WWT/
16*
MAXWELL, Meg (d 1955) actress
BE*, WWT/14*
MAXWELL, Robert (d 1971 [61])
producer/director/choreographer
BP/55*
MAXWELL, Vera (d 1950 [58])
actress, dancer TW/6
MAXWELL, Walter (b 1877) Eng-
lish business manager, mana-
ger GRB/4, WWT/1-5
MAXWELL, Mrs. Walter see
Silver, Christine
MAXWELL, Mrs. Walter see
Harrison, Evelyn
MAXWELL, Wayne (b 1939)
American actor TW/23
MAY, Miss actress CDP
MAY, Ada (b 1900) actress,
dancer WWT/7-10
MAY, Akerman (1869-1933) Eng-
lish actor GRB/1-4, WWT/
1-7
MAY, Alice [Mrs. Louis Ray-
mond] (1847-87) English sing-
er, actress NYM
MAY, Alice English actress
GRB/2
MAY, Charles F. (d 1911 [67])
costumier EA/12*
MAY, Edna [Edna Pettie; Mrs.
Oscar Lewisohn] (1878-1948)
American actress, singer
GRB/1-4, SR, TW/4, WWA/
1, WWS, WWT/1-10
MAY, Edward (fl 1494-1503)
actor DA
MAY, Edward (fl 1631-35) actor
DA
MAY, Elaine [née Berlin] (b
1932) actress, dramatist,
director BE, CB, CD,
WWT/15-16
MAY, Eva [Mrs. George Hayes]
(d 1908) EA/09*
MAY, Frances [Mrs. Samuel
May, Jr.] (d 1873) EA/74*
MAY, Frank (1829-96) American
actor, manager SR
MAY, Hans (1891-1959) Austrian
composer, musical director
WWT/11-12
MAY, Harold R. (d 1973 [70])

performer BP/58*
MAY, H. Gomer (b 1865) English
actor GRB/1
MAY, Jack (b 1922) English actor
WWT/16
MAY, Jane French actress, singer
WWT/1-4
MAY, Joe (d 1964 [60]) performer
BP/49*
MAY, John (1816-54) American
circus performer, actor HAS
MAY, Juliana (fl 1857-58) American
singer CDP, HAS
MAY, Martha (d 1868) EA/69*
MAY, Marty (d 1975 [77]) comedian,
singer BP/60*, WWT/16*
MAY, Nathan (fl 1615) actor DA
MAY, Olive [Mrs. John W. Al-
baugh, Jr.] (d 1938 [65]) Amer-
ican actress WWS
MAY, Olive [Countess of Drogheda]
(d 1947) actress WWT/14*
MAY, Pamela (b 1917) West Indian/
English dancer WWT/10-12
MAY, Randolph (b c. 1540) stage-
attendant? DA
MAY, Rose (fl 1851) English sing-
er? HAS
MAY, Samuel (d 1876 [54]) cos-
tumier EA/77*, WWT/14*
MAY, Samuel, Jr. (d 1875 [30])
costumier EA/76*
MAY, Mrs. Samuel, Jr. see
May, Frances
MAY, Thomas (1595-1650) English
dramatist CP/1-3, FGF
MAY, Val[entine] (b 1927) English
director WWT/14-16
MAY, Winston (b 1937) American
actor TW/27-29
MAYAKOVSKY, Vladimir Vladimiro-
vich (1894-1930) Russian drama-
tist COC, OC/3
MAYBRICK, Michael [Stephen Ad-
ams] (1844-1913) singer, com-
poser CDP
MAYCOCK, John Henry (d 1907
[89]) musician EA/08*
MAYCOCKE, William (fl 1594)
actor DA
MAYDESTON, John (fl 1423) actor
DA
MAYE, Bernyce (d 1962 [52])
American performer BE*
MAYE, Geraldine (fl 1875) actress
CDP
MAYEHOFF, Eddie (b 1914) actor
BE

MAYER, Mrs. (fl 1847) actress
HAS
MAYER, Bertie Alexander English
business manager GRB/1
MAYER, Charles (b 1904) actor
TW/30
MAYER, Daniel (1856-1928) agent,
impresario WWT/3-5
MAYER, Dot (d 1964 [68]) per-
former BE*
MAYER, Edwin Justus (1896/97-
1960) American dramatist
MD, MH, MWD, WWT/7-11
MAYER, Gaston (1869-1923) Eng-
lish manager, director GRB/
1-4, WWT/1-4
MAYER, Mrs. Gaston see The-
cla, Maud
MAYER, Jack W. (d 1971 [77])
theatre owner BP/55*
MAYER, Jerome (d 1965 [55])
producer, director TW/21
MAYER, Jerry (b 1941) American
actor TW/24, 27, 29-30
MAYER, Marcus (d 1918 [77])
producer, manager BE*,
WWT/14*
MAYER, Marcus L. (d 1903 [71])
French manager EA/04*,
WWT/14*
MAYER, Renée (b 1900) English
actress, dancer WWT/2-7
MAYER, Sylvain (d 1948 [85])
dramatist BE*, WWT/14*
MAYER, Therese (fl 1885) ac-
tress CDP
MAYER-BOERCKEL, Ferdy
see Mayne, Ferdy
MAYERL, Billy [Joseph W.
Meyer] (1902-59) English con-
ductor, composer WWT/9-12
MAYERS, Wilmette K. (d 1964)
singer BE*
MAYEUR, Eugene F. (1866-1919)
English actor GRB/3-4, WWT/
1-3
MAYFIELD, Cleo [Cleo Empy]
(d 1954 [59]) actress TW/11,
WWT/4-9
MAYHALL, Jerome (d 1964 [70])
musical director BE*
MAYHEW, Augustus S. (d 1875
[49]) dramatist EA/77*
MAYHEW, Charles (b 1908) Eng-
lish actor, singer WWT/8-9
MAYHEW, Edward (d 1868)
manager, actor EA/69*
MAYHEW, H. (d 1834) manager

WWT/14*
MAYHEW, Henry (1812-87) English
dramatist DNB, HP, NYM
MAYHEW, Henry (d 1900 [54])
proprietor EA/01*
MAYHEW, Horace (d 1872 [53])
dramatist BE*, EA/73*, WWT/
14*
MAYHEW, Kate (1853-1944) Amer-
ican actress SR, TW/1
MAYHEW, Stella [née Sadler; Mrs.
Billee Taylor] (1871-1934) Amer-
ican actress SR, WWM
MAYLEAS, Ruth (b 1925) American
executive BE
MAYLER, George (fl 1526-40) actor
DA
MAYNARD, Ambrose [William Hill]
(d 1888 [66]) agent EA/89*
MAYNARD, George (d 1851 [40])
actor EA/72*, WWT/14*
MAYNARD, Gertrude (d 1953 [48])
Canadian actress BE*, BP/37*
MAYNARD, Sir John (fl 1619-24)
dancer, masque writer FGF
MAYNARD, Ken (d 1973 [77]) per-
former BP/57*
MAYNARD, Kermit (d 1971 [73])
performer BP/55*
MAYNARD, Lizzie [Mrs. Henry
Wilson] (b 1865) English dancer,
singer GRB/1
MAYNARD, Richard (d 1944 [70])
business manager WWT/14*
MAYNARD, Ruth (b 1913) American
actress BE
"MAYNARD, Walter" see Beale,
Thomas Willert
MAYNE, Clarice (1886-1966) Eng-
lish actress, singer OC/1-3,
WWT/5-8
MAYNE, Eric (d 1947 [81]) Irish
actor BE*
MAYNE, Ernest (1872-1937) Eng-
lish actor, singer CDP, GRB/1
MAYNE, Ferdy [né Mayer-Boerckel]
(b 1920) actor WWT/15-16
MAYNE, Jasper (1604-72) English
dramatist CP/1-3, FGF
MAYNE, Rutherford (1878-1967)
Irish dramatist COC, OC/1-3,
RE
MAYNE, Will (d 1918 [41]) EA/19*
MAYO, Archie (b 1898) American
actor ES
MAYO, Ella (1862-81) singer CDP
MAYO, Frank (1839-96) American
actor CDP, DAB, HAS, HJD,

WWA/H

MAYO, Frank (d 1963 [74]) actor
BE*, BP/48*

MAYO, Mrs. Frank (d 1896) actress BE*

MAYO, Harry (d 1964 [65]) actor
BE*

MAYO, Joseph Anthony (d 1966
[36]) performer BP/51*

MAYO, Margaret [Lilian Clatten]
(1882-1951) American dramatist, actress NTH, TW/7,
WWM, WWS, WWT/1-9

MAYO, Nannie Nye (fl 1850?)
singer CDP

MAYO, Nick (b 1922) American
producer, director BE

MAYO, Paul (b 1918) English
scene designer ES

MAYO, Sam (d 1938 [63]) comedian, songwriter BE*, WWT/
14*

MAYON, Amy [Mrs. Edwin Mayon]
(d 1904) EA/05*

MAYON, Mrs. Edwin see Mayon, Amy

MAYOR, George (d 1890) property
man EA/91*

MAYORGA, Margaret (b 1894)
American editor, writer BE

MAYR, Richard (b 1877) Austrian
singer ES

MAYRO, Jacqueline (b 1948)
American actress TW/24-25,
27

MAYRSEIDL, Caroline see
Seidl, Lea

MAYVILLE, Harry (d 1912 [37])
marionettist EA/13*

MAYWOOD, Augusta (1825-76?)
American actress CDP, ES,
HAS

MAYWOOD, Martha (1793-c. 1855)
English actress HAS

MAYWOOD, Mary Elizabeth (b
1822) Irish actress, lessee
HAS

MAYWOOD, Robert Campbell
(1786/90-1856) Scottish actor
CDP, HAS, SR

MAZURIER, Mons. (d 1828)
French dancer, pantomimist
CDP

MAZZA, Alfred (b 1946) American actor TW/27

MAZZINGHI, Joseph (1765-1844)
English composer DNB, TD/
1-2

MAZZO, Kay (b 1947) American
dancer CB

MAZZOLA, John W. (b 1928)
American executive BE

MEACHAM, Anne (b 1925) American actress BE, TW/16, 18-20,
23-25, WWT/14-16

MEACHUM, James H. (d 1963 [70])
American performer BP/51*

MEAD (fl 1819?) dramatist EAP

MEAD, Charles (d 1894 [41])
chairman EA/95*

MEAD, Charlotte (d 1906) actress
EA/07*

MEAD, Jessie (d 1901 [18]) actress
EA/02*

MEAD, Robert (1616-52) English
dramatist CP/1-3, FGF

MEAD, Thomas (1819/21-89) English actor, dramatist CDP,
OAA/1-2

MEADE, Gerald (d 1965) performer
BP/49*

MEADE, Mrs. Henry (d 1874 [26])
EA/75*

MEADE, Jacob (fl 1599-1619)
manager? DA

MEADE, James H. (d 1898 [c. 65])
manager CDP

MEADE, Julia (b 1928) American
actress BE, TW/13, 25-26

MEADER, George (1888/90-1963)
American actor, singer BE,
TW/2-3, WWT/8-10

MEADOW, Walter (d 1879 [33])
actor EA/80*

MEADOWS, Mr. (fl 1821) actor
BS

MEADOWS, Connie [Miss Wood]
English actress GRB/1

MEADOWS, Drinkwater (1799-1869)
English actor CDP, DNB, OX

MEADOWS, James (d 1863 [64])
scene artist EA/72*

MEADOWS, Jayne [Jayne Cotter]
(b 1920?/23/26) American actress BE, CB, TW/1-3

MEADOWS, Joseph R. (d 1964 [65])
clown BE*

MEADOWS, Kate see Ryner,
Mrs. H.

MEADOWS, T. (fl 1805) actor,
dramatist CDP, CP/3

MEAGHERSON, Henry George (d
1895) actor EA/96*

MEAKINS, Charles (d 1951 [70])
actor TW/7

MEAKINS, Mrs. Charles see

Bradford, Edith
MEARA, Anne (b 1929) American
   actress TW/12
MEARES, Thomas Charles see
   Melville, Charles
MEARNS, T. (d 1879) actor?
   EA/80*
MEARS, DeAnn American actress
   TW/26-27, 30
MEARS, George (d 1879) actor?
   EA/80*
MEARS, J. H. (d 1956 [78])
   director, lyricist BE*, WWT/
   14*
MEARS, Marion (d 1970 [71])
   performer BP/54*
MEARS, William (d 1902 [67])
   master carpenter EA/03*
MEASE, Peter (fl c. 1618-27)
   dramatist FGF
MEASEY, John see Franconi
MEASOR, Adela (1860/65-1933)
   Irish actress EA/96, GRB/
   2-4, WWT/1-7
MEASOR, Beryl (1908-65) English
   actress TW/13, WWT/9-13
MEATES, Mrs. Arthur E. [Mrs.
   S. A. Emery] (d 1889) EA/91*
MECHANIC, Emaline (d 1971)
   production assistant BP/55*
MEDBOURNE, Matthew (d 1679)
   actor, dramatist CP/1-3,
   DNB, GT
MEDCRAFT, Russell Graham
   (d 1962 [65]) dramatist BE*
MEDDOWS, Kenny [Harry Whit-
   marsh Johnson] (d 1904 [36])
   EA/05*
MEDEIROS, John (b 1944) Amer-
   ican actor TW/25
MEDFORD, Kay [née Regan] (b
   1920) American actress BE,
   TW/12-24, WWT/14-16
MEDICA, Miss (fl 1850) actress
   HAS
MEDINA, Louisa (c. 1795-1838)
   American? dramatist RJ,
   SR
MEDINA, Patricia (b 1923) Eng-
   lish actress BE
MEDLEY, George (d 1898 [44])
   music-hall mimic EA/99*
MEDLEY, Matthew see Aston,
   Anthony
MEDNICK, Murray (b 1939)
   American dramatist, director
   CD
MEDOFF, Mark (b 1940) Amer-

ican dramatist, actor, director
   CD
MEDWALL, Henry (c. 1462-1500)
   English dramatist COC, CP/2-
   3, DNB, ES, MH, OC/1-3
MEDWIN, Mrs. Charles see
   Lucette, Catherine
MEE, Charles Louis, Jr. (b 1938)
   American dramatist BE
MEECH, John H. (1842-1902) Amer-
   ican manager SR
MEEHAN, Danny (b 1933) American
   actor TW/20, 22, 30
MEEHAN, William E. (d 1920 [35])
   American comedian BE*, BP/4*
MEEK, Donald (1880-1946) Scottish
   actor SR, TW/3, WWT/7-10
MEEK, Francis dramatist CP/3
MEEK, John Robert (b 1882) circus
   performer EA/83*
MEEK, Kate (c. 1838-1925) actress
   SR
MEEKER, Ralph [née Rathgeber]
   (b 1920) American actor BE,
   TW/4-16, 18-20, 22, 28, WWT/
   12-16
MEEKER, W. H. (fl 1845-48)
   American actor HAS
MEEN, George (d 1887 [34]) comic
   singer EA/88*
MEES, Arthur (1850-1923) American
   musical director WWA/1
MEGGAS, Joseph J. (d 1971 [53])
   performer BP/55*
MEGGS, Mary (d 1691) English ac-
   tress COC, OC/1-3
MEGIA, F. (fl 1824-25?) dramatist
   EAP
MEGLEY, Macklin (d 1965 [74])
   producer/director BP/49*
MEGNA, John (b 1952) American
   actor BE
MEGRUE, Roi Cooper (1882/83-
   1927) American dramatist DAB,
   SR, WWA/1, WWM, WWT/4-5
MEHAFFEY, Harry (d 1963 [56])
   American actor TW/3
MEHARRY, Houston (d 1911) actor
   EA/12*
MEHTA, Zubin (b 1936) Indian
   conductor CB
MEIER, Dave (d 1912 [35]) music-
   hall performer EA/13*
MEIGHAM, Thaddeus W. (b 1821)
   American actor HAS
MEIGHAN, James E. , Jr. (d 1970
   [66]) actor TW/27
MEIGHAN, Thomas (1879-1936)

American actor ES, WWA/1,
WWT/4-8
MEIGHAN, Mrs. Thomas see
Ring, Frances
MEIKLE, Pat (d 1973 [49]) per-
former BP/57*
MEILAN, Mark Anthony (fl 1771)
dramatist CP/3
MEI LAN-FANG (1894-1961)
Chinese actor COC, NTH,
OC/3, RE, TW/18
MEISER, Edith (b 1898) American
actress, dramatist, director,
producer BE, TW/4-8, 10-
15, 29, WWT/16
MEISLE, Kathryn (1899-1970)
American singer WWA/5
MEISNER, Sanford (b 1905) Amer-
ican teacher, actor, director
BE
MEISSNER, Alfred Austin (d 1885
[63]) dramatist EA/86*
MEISTER, Barbara Ann American
actress, singer BE
MELANCON, Louis (d 1974 [73])
photographer BP/59*
MELBA, Dame, Nellie [Mrs.
Charles Armstrong] (1859/61/
63/66-1931) Australian singer
CDP, DNB, ES, GRB/1-4,
HP, SR, WWA/1, WWS, WWW/3
MELBOURNE, Mr. (fl 1844) actor
CDP
MELBOURNE, Miss (fl 1796)
actress HAS
MELBOURNE, Arthur E. (b 1867)
English acting manager, busi-
ness manager GRB/1
MELBOURNE, Robert Rivers (d
1869 [57]) actor? EA/70*
MELBOURNE, Mrs. Walter [Nina
Anato] (d 1889) EA/90*
MELCHIOR, Lauritz (1890-1973)
Danish singer CB, ES, TW/
29, WWA/5
MELDON, H. Percy (b 1856)
Irish director WWM
MELFI, Leonard (b 1935) Amer-
ican dramatist, actor CD,
WWT/15-16
MELFORD, Austin (1855/60-1908)
English actor, manager EA/
96, GRB/1-4
MELFORD, Austin (1884-1971)
English actor, dramatist, pro-
ducer WWT/2-14
MELFORD, Jack (1899-1972)
English actor WWT/5-14

MELFORD, Jill (b 1934) English
actress WWT/15-16
MELFORD, Mark (d 1914) actor,
producer, dramatist BE*,
WWT/14*
MELHADO, William Henry Hunter
(d 1906) EA/07*
MELIA, Joe English actor WWA/16
MELINGUE, Etienne Marin (1808-
75) French actor CDP
MELLER, Harro (d 1963 [56])
German dramatist, actor BE*
MELLER, Raquel (d 1962 [74])
Spanish diseuse TW/19
MELLING, James Alfred (d 1870)
musician EA/71*
MELLING, T. (d 1878) musical
director EA/79*
MELLISH, Fuller (1865-1936) Eng-
lish actor DP, GRB/2-4,
WWM, WWS, WWT/1-8
MELLISH, Fuller, Jr. (d 1930
[35]) actor BE*, BP/14*,
WWT/14*
MELLISH, Mary (b 1890) American
singer WWA/3
MELLISON, Sarah Ann (d 1878 [64])
performer? EA/79*
MELLON, Ada (d 1914) actress
EA/96
MELLON, Alfred (1820-67) English
composer, conductor, musician
CDP, DNB
MELLON, Alfred (d 1904) EA/05*
MELLON, Mrs. Alfred [Sarah Jane
Woolgar] (1824-1909) English
actress CDP, COC, DNB,
OAA/1-2, OC/1-3
MELLON, Emily (d 1899 [51])
music-hall performer EA/00*
MELLON, Harriot (1777-1837)
English actress CDP, COC,
DNB, GT, OC/1-3, OX, TD/1-2
MELLON, Henry (d 1876) actor
EA/77*
MELLON, Sarah Jane see Mel-
lon, Mrs. Alfred
MELLOR, Henry (d 1889) performer
EA/90*
MELLOR, Mark Moss (d 1897) ac-
tor EA/98*
MELLORS, Arthur (d 1899) acro-
bat, gymnast EA/00*
MELLY, Andrée (b 1932) English
actress WWT/14-16
MELMOTH, Charlotte (1749-1823)
American actress CDP, COC,
HAS, OC/1-3, TD/1-2

MELMOTH, Courtney see Pratt,
S. J.
MELNIKER, William (d 1976 [80])
lawyer BP/60*
MELNITZ, William W. (b 1900)
German educator, director
BE
MELNOTTE, Violet (1856-1935)
English actress, manager
COC, GRB/3-4, OC/1-3,
WWT/1-7
MELONEY, William Brown (d
1971 [69]) producer/director/
choreographer BP/55*
MELROSE, Mr. (b 1799) English
actor CDP, OX
MELROSE, Doris [Mrs. Ernie
Vincent] (d 1916) EA/18*
MELROSE, Tom [Thomas Lamb]
(d 1895 [44]) Negro comedian
EA/96*
MELROY, Clara (d 1966 [68])
performer BP/51*
MELROYD, Frank (b 1879) Eng-
lish actor, dancer GRB/1
MELTON, Miss (fl 1840-61)
English actress HAS
MELTON, Charles (d 1869) music-
hall performer EA/70*
MELTON, Fred (d 1917 [47])
performer? EA/18*
MELTON, James (1904-61)
American singer CB, TW/
17, WWA/4
MELTON, J. Rexton [Francis
Michael Thompson] (d 1900)
actor EA/02*
MELTZER, Charles Henry (d
1936 [83]) English critic,
dramatist GRB/2-4, WWA/1,
WWM, WWS, WWT/1-7
MELVILLE, Miss (fl 1810?)
CDP
MELVILLE, Alan (b 1910) Eng-
lish lyricist, dramatist AAS,
BE, WWT/10-16
MELVILLE, Alice (d 1906 [39])
variety performer EA/07*
MELVILLE, Andrew (d 1896
[43]) manager, proprietor
EA/97*, WWT/14*
MELVILLE, Andrew (d 1938 [52])
producer, director, actor,
dramatist BE*, WWT/14*
MELVILLE, Andrew (b 1912)
English producing manager
WWT/11-14
MELVILLE, Mrs. Andrew (d 1904

[54]) actress EA/05*, WWT/14*
MELVILLE, Mrs. Andrew (d 1927
[46]) actress WWT/14*
MELVILLE, Charles (d 1862) actor
WWT/14*
MELVILLE, Charles [Thomas
Charles Meares] (d 1896 [38])
actor EA/97*
MELVILLE, Charles (d 1901 [65])
manager, agent, minstrel CDP
MELVILLE, Mrs. Charles (d 1893)
EA/94*
MELVILLE, Daisy (d 1895) actress
EA/96*
MELVILLE, Eliza (d 1892 [86])
actress EA/93*
MELVILLE, Emilie (d 1932 [82])
actress BE*, WWT/14*
MELVILLE, Emily (fl 1855-68)
American actress CDP, HAS
MELVILLE, Frederick (1876/79-
1938) Welsh actor, proprietor,
dramatist, manager COC, OC/
1-3, WWT/3-8
MELVILLE, George (d 1898 [74])
actor EA/00*, WWT/14*
MELVILLE, George (d 1900) Aus-
tralian actor EA/01*
MELVILLE, Harry [William Grif-
fith Hart] (d 1898) Irish come-
dian CDP
MELVILLE, James (b 1837) Aus-
tralian equestrian HAS
MELVILLE, Jean-Pierre (d 1973
[55]) producer/director/chore-
ographer BP/58*
MELVILLE, Jennie see Carroll,
Mrs. J. W.
MELVILLE, John (d 1908) EA/09*
MELVILLE, June (1915-70) English
actress, manager OC/1, WWT/
9-13
MELVILLE, M. A. (d 1900) ac-
tress EA/01*
MELVILLE, Nina (d 1966 [56])
performer BP/51*
MELVILLE, Pearl (d 1917) actress
SR
MELVILLE, Richard (d 1873 [35])
composer EA/74*
MELVILLE, Rose (1873-1946)
American actress TW/3, WWA/
2, WWM, WWS, WWT/1-5
MELVILLE, Violet (d 1911 [25])
actress EA/12*
MELVILLE, Walter (1874/75-1937)
English actor, manager COC,
GRB/2-4, OC/1-3, WWT/1-8

MELVILLE, Winifred (d 1950
[40]) actress BE*, WWT/14*
MELVILLE, Winnie (d 1937 [42])
actress, singer WWT/4-8
MELVIN, Mr. (fl 1806) actor
CDP, GT, TD/2
MELVIN, Mrs. A. Douglas [Edith
Ince] (d 1917) EA/18*
MELVIN, Donnie (b 1955) Ameri-
can actor TW/24-25
MELVIN, Duncan (b 1913) Scot-
tish press representative
WWT/13-14
MELVIN, George J. (d 1911 [47])
Scottish entertainer EA/13*
MELVIN, G. S. (d 1946 [69])
comedian BE*, WWT/14*
MELVIN, Murray English actor
WWT/14-16
MELYONEK, John (fl 1483-85)
master of the Chapel Royal?
DA
MEMBRIVES, Lola (d 1969 [86])
performer BP/54*
MEMINGER, Edward Lynn (d
1975 [70]) performer BP/59*
MENAGE, Master (fl 1801)
pantomimist CDP
MENAGE, Bella actress TD/1-2
[see also: Sharp, Mrs. W.]
MENCKEN, Helen actress SR
MENCKEN, Henry Louis (1880-
1956) American critic, drama-
tist ES, HP, NTH, WWA/3
MENDEL, Mr. (d 1905) EA/06*
MENDEL, Hugo S. (b 1877)
manager GRB/1
MENDEL, [James Samuel Smith]
(b 1875) English pianist
GRB/1
MENDELSSOHN, Eleonora (d 1951
[51]) German actress TW/2-
3, 7
MENDES, Catulle (1841-1909)
French dramatist, critic
GRB/1, 3-4
MENDES, Lothar (d 1974 [79])
producer/director/choreographer
BP/58*
MENDEZ, Moses (d 1758) drama-
tist CP/1-3, DNB, GT, TD/
1-2
MENDHAM, James, Jr. (fl 1811)
dramatist CP/3
MENDUM, Georgie Drew (d 1957
[82]) American actress TW/
14, WWM
MENELLY, Lilian (d 1900 [27])

actress EA/01*
MENG, Constance (b 1939) Ameri-
can actress TW/24
MENGES, Herbert (1902-72) English
composer, conductor WWT/8-15
MENGOZZI, Signora Bernardo see
Benimi, Anna
MENJOU, Adolphe Jean (1890-1963)
American actor WWA/4
MENKE, Cpt. Bill (d 1968 [88])
river showboat owner BP/53*
MENKEN, Adah Isaacs [Dolores
Adios Fuertes] (1835-68) Amer-
ican actress CDP, COC, DAB,
DNB, ES, HAS, HJD, NTH,
OC/1-3, SR, WWA/H
MENKEN, Faye (b 1947) American
actress TW/26-29
MENKEN, Helen (1901-66) Ameri-
can actress, producer, executive
BE, NTH, TW/2-3, 22, WWT/
6-14
MENNIN, Peter (b 1923) American
composer BE
MENNINGER, Marion K. (d 1973)
performer BP/57*
MENOTTI, Gian Carlo (b 1911)
Italian composer, librettist BE,
CB, ES, HJD, MH, NTH
MENZIES, Amy see Fawsitt,
Amy
MENZIES, Archie (b 1904) English
dramatist WWT/9-14
MERANDE, Doro (d 1975 [70s])
American actress BE, TW/1,
3-16, 25-26, 29, WWT/15
MERANTE, Louis (d 1887 [58])
dancer, choreographer BE*,
WWT/14*
MERCE, Antonia see Argentina
MERCEDES, Joe (d 1966 [77]) per-
former BP/51*
MERCER, Amelia (d 1890) actress
EA/91*
MERCER, Ben J. (d 1906 [22])
Negro comedian EA/07*
MERCER, Beryl (1882-1939)
Spanish/English actress GRB/4,
WWT/1-8
MERCER, David (b 1928) English
dramatist AAS, CD, CH, COC,
PDT, WWT/15-16
MERCER, Ernestine American ac-
tress TW/25
MERCER, J. (b 1820) actor HAS
MERCER, Johnny (1909-76) Amer-
ican composer, lyricist BE,
CB, WWT/15-16

MERCER, Marian (b 1935) American actress, singer BE, TW/18-19, 22, 24-27, WWT/15-16

MERCER, Thomas, Sr. (b 1796) English actor HAS

MERCER, Thomas, Jr. (b 1817) English actor HAS

MERCER, Tom (d 1916) music-hall singer EA/17*

MERCER, Tony (d 1973 [51]) performer BP/58*

MERCHANT, Thomas see Dibdon, Thomas

MERCHANT, Vivien [né Thomson; Mrs. Harold Pinter] (b 1929) English actress AAS, WWT/14-16

MERCIER, Louis Sébastien (1740-1814) French dramatist OC/1-3

MERCOURI, Melina Greek actress TW/29

MERCUR, William (d 1972 [74]) publicist BP/57*

MEREDITH, Mr. (d 1810) singer CDP

MEREDITH, Burgess (b 1907/08/09) American actor, director AAS, BE, CB, ES, NTH, SR, TW/2-16, 21, WWT/9-16

MEREDITH, Charles H. (d 1964 [70]) performer BP/49*

MEREDITH, George (1828-1909) English dramatist DNB

MEREDITH, Harry C. (d 1898 [68]) actor CDP

MEREDITH, Lee (b 1947) American actor TW/29-30

MERENSKY, John (b 1943) American actor TW/26, 28

MERER, Frederick (d 1911 [61]) actor, manager EA/12*

MERES, Francis (1565-1647) English writer NTH

MEREST, Mrs. J. D. see Hawes, Maria B.

MERETZEK, Max (fl 1848) conductor, impresario SR

MERIC-LALANDE, Mme. (d 1867 [69]) singer EA/68*

MERIN, Eda Reiss American actress TW/25, 27

MERINGTON, Marguerite (d 1951) dramatist WWA/3, WWM

MERITON, Thomas (fl 1658) dramatist CP/1-3, DNB

MERIVALE, Bernard (1882-1939) English dramatist WWT/6-8

MERIVALE, Herman (1839-1906) English dramatist DNB, HP, GRB/1, WWW/1

MERIVALE, Mrs. Herman (d 1932 [85]) dramatist BE*, WWT/14*

MERIVALE, John (b 1917) Canadian actor BE, TW/4-14, 16, 22-23

MERIVALE, Philip (1886-1946) Indian/English actor CB, ES, NTH, TW/2, WWA/2, WWT/2-9

MERKEL, Una (b 1903) American actress BE, WWT/6-14

MERLI, Francesco (b 1887) Italian singer ES

MERLIN, Clarence de (fl 1850) American singer, actress HAS

MERLIN, Frank (d 1968 [76]) Irish/American actor, director, producer TW/24

MERLIN, Joanna (b 1931) American actress BE

MERLIN, Mrs. Max see Merlin, Ray

MERLIN, Ray [Mrs. Max Merlin] (d 1901 [24]) EA/02*

MERLINI (d 1971 [64]) performer BP/55*

MERMAN, Ethel (b 1908/09) American actress, singer AAS, BE, CB, ES, PDT, SR, TW/2-20, 22-23, 26-27, WWT/8-16

MERRALL, Mary (1889/90-1973) English actress AAS, WWT/4-15

MERRICK, David (b 1912) American producing manager AAS, CB, WWT/13-16

MERRICK, Leonard (1864-1939) English dramatist GRB/2-4, WWT/1-8, WWW/3

MERRIDEW, T. J. (d 1895) actor EA/96*

MERRIE, Cecil actor, singer CDP

MERRIGE-ABRAMS, Salway (d 1973 [43]) performer BP/58*

MERRILEES, Andrew (d 1892 [79]) EA/93*

MERRILEES, Andy (d 1904 [63]) comedian EA/05*

MERRILEES, Mrs. Andy see Merrilees, Jessie

MERRILEES, Jane [Mrs. Andy Merrilees] (d 1879) EA/80*

MERRILEES, Jessie [Mrs. Andy Merrilees] (d 1900 [37]) Scottish comedian EA/01*

MERRILL, Alfa (fl 1878) actress

CDP

MERRILL, Beth actress TW/
3-4, 6, WWT/6-7, 10-11

MERRILL, Bob (b 1920) American composer, lyricist BE,
WWT/15-16

MERRILL, Fred R. (d 1976 [87])
performer BP/60*

MERRILL, Gary (b 1915) American actor BE, TW/2-3,
5-6, 23

MERRILL, Louis (d 1963 [52])
performer BE*

MERRILL, Robert (b 1919) American singer CB

MERRILL, Scott (b 1922) American actor TW/10-20

MERRIMAN, Dan (b 1929) American actor TW/23-24, 28

MERRIMAN, Richard (d 1917 [34])
performer? EA/18*

MERRINGTON, Margaret dramatist SR

MERRITON, Annie see Richardson, Annie

MERRITT, Alice see Oates,
Mrs. James A.

MERRITT, George (b 1890) English actor WWT/6-16

MERRITT, Grace (b 1881) actress
WWT/1-5

MERRITT, Guy E. (d 1975 [49])
designer BP/60*

MERRITT, James (d 1908 [57])
music-hall chairman, singer
EA/09*

MERRITT, Kate (fl 1861) actress
HAS

MERRITT, Larry (b 1937) American actor TW/28

MERRITT, Lillie (d 1971 [90])
performer BP/55*

MERRITT, Paul (d 1895) dramatist BE*, WWT/14*

MERRITT, William (1852-87)
American actor NYM

MERRY, Anne see Brunton,
Ann[e]

MERRY, Lydia Ellen (fl 1816)
singer, actress CDP

MERRY, Robert (1755-98) English dramatist CDP, CP/3,
EAP, GT, RJ, TD/1-2

MERRY, Mrs. Robert see
Brunton, Ann[e]

MERRYFIELD, Jerry (1820-62)
English actor HAS

MERRYFIELD, Rose [Rose Cline]

(fl 1850) actress CDP, HAS

MERRYLEES, James (d 1902 [33])
variety comedian EA/03*

MERSON, Billy [William Henry
Thompson] (1881-1947) English
actor, singer COC, OC/1-3,
WWT/4-10

MERSON, Fred (d 1875) comedian,
singer EA/76*

MERTON, Annie [Mrs. Charles
Sennett] (d 1912 [67]) EA/13*

MERTON, Charlie (d 1892) performer? EA/93*

MERTON, Collette (d 1968 [61])
performer BP/53*

MERVIN, Frederick [Charles Mar-
vin] (d 1897) English actor
OAA/2

MERVIN, Will (d 1886 [32]) comic
singer EA/87*

MERVYN, Lee (d 1962 [34]) performer BE*

MERVYN, William [né Pickwoad]
(1912-76) Kenyan/English actor
WWT/15-16

MERWIN, W. S. (b 1927) American
dramatist HJD

MERYELL, Henry (fl 1509-11)
member of the Chapel Royal
DA

MESERVEY, Robert see Preston,
Robert

MESSAGER, André (1853-1929)
French composer, conductor,
manager GRB/4, WWT/1,
WWW/3

MESSEL, Oliver (b 1905) English
designer AAS, BE, COC, ES,
OC/3, PDT, TW/6-8, WWT/7-16

MESSITER, Eric (d 1960 [68]) actor
BE*, WWT/14*

MESTAYER, Anna Maria see
Thorne, Mrs. Charles Robert,
Sr.

MESTAYER, Charles (c. 1820-49)
actor HAS, SR

MESTAYER, Emily see Houpt,
Mrs. Charles J.

MESTAYER, Harry musician HAS

MESTAYER, Henry (fl 1716) dramatist CP/2-3

MESTAYER, John actor HAS

MESTAYER, Mrs. John (d 1860
[74]) actress HAS

MESTAYER, Louis J. (d 1880 [60])
American actor EA/81*

MESTAYER, Louis Joseph (1818-80)
American actor CDP, HAS

MESTAYER, Maria Ann see Thorne, Mrs. Charles Robert, Sr.

MESTAYER, William A. [né William Ayers Haupt] (1844-96) American actor CDP, HAS, SR

MESTAYER, Mrs. William H. see Vaughn, Theresa

MESTEL, Jacob (d 1958 [74]) Polish actor, director BE*, BP/43*

METASTASIO, Abbé (fl 18th cent) dramatist CP/1

METAXA, Georges (1899-1950) Rumanian actor, singer TW/7, WWT/6-9

METCALF, A. (d 1892 [29]) conductor EA/93*

METCALF, Mark American actor TW/30

METCALF, S. (d 1900 [66]) director EA/01*

METCALF, Thomas Edmund see Rosenthal, Edmund

METCALFE, Catharine (d c. 1790?) dramatist CP/3

METCALFE, Ernest (b 1869) English acting manager GRB/1

METCALFE, George Taylor (d 1908 [24]) manager EA/09*

METCALFE, James Stetson (1858-1927) American critic GRB/2-4, WWA/1, WWM, WWT/1-5

METCALFE, Madge [Mrs. Arthur Jefferson] (d 1908) actress EA/10*

METCALFE, Mrs. P. A. see Rochester, Jenny

METEYARD, Eliza (d 1879 [63]) writer EA/80*

METHOT, Mayo (d 1951 [47]) American actress TW/8

METRA, Olivier (d 1889 [58]) composer, conductor EA/90*

METZ, E. (fl 1827) actor HAS

METZ, Lucius Wells (d 1969 [71]) performer BP/53*

METZ, Theodore (1848-1936) German songwriter BE*

METZLER, George Richard (d 1893 [24]) EA/95*

MEURICE, Paul (d 1905 [85]) dramatist WWT/14*

MEUX, Lady [Valerie Reece] actress GRB/1

MEWBURN, Hugh (d 1909 [31]) actor EA/10*

MEWE, Mr. dramatist CP/3, FGF

MEWHA, Sam A. (d 1917) actor EA/18*

MEYER, Mr. actor HAS

MEYER, Bertie Alexander (1877-1967) English business manager GRB/2-4, WWT/1-14

MEYER, Charles (d 1881 [59]) musician EA/82*

MEYER, Ernest (d 1927 [50]) literary representative BE*, WWT/14*

MEYER, Frederic E. (d 1973 [63]) actor, director, stage manager TW/30

MEYER, George W. (1884-1959) American composer BE*

MEYER, Jean (b 1914) French actor, director CB

MEYER, Johannes (d 1976) producer/director/choreographer BP/60*

MEYER, Kerstin (b 1928) Swedish singer ES

MEYER, Leopold de (1816-83) pianist, composer CDP, HAS

MEYER, Lester (d 1965 [91]) producer/director BP/50*

MEYER, Louis (1871-1915) English manager, lessee WWT/2, WWW/1

MEYER, Rudy (d 1969 [67]) producer/director/choreographer BP/54*

MEYER, Torben (d 1975 [90]) performer BP/59*

MEYER, Yale (d 1966 [49]) acting teacher BP/51*

MEYER-FORSTER, Wilhelm (d 1934 [72]) dramatist WWT/14*

MEYERL, Joseph W. see Mayerl, Billy

MEYERS (fl 1792) translator CP/3

MEYERS, Louisa (fl 1865) American actress, singer CDP, HAS

MEYERS, Marsha (b 1946) American actress TW/29

MEYERS, Martin (b 1934) American actor TW/24-25, 27

MEYN, Robert (d 1972 [76]) performer BP/56*

MEYNALL, Percy (d 1900) actor EA/01*

MEYNELL, Claude (1867-1934) English manager, actor WWT/1-7

MEYRICK, Ellen (fl 1874-79)

actress OAA/2
MEYRICK, George (d 1868) EA/
69*
MICHAEL, Mrs. Cyril see
Kerin, Nora
MICHAEL, Edward (d 1950 [97])
business manager GRB/1-3
MICHAEL, Gertrude (1910-64/65)
American actress WWT/8-9
MICHAEL, Kathleen (b 1917) Eng-
lish actress WWT/11-16
MICHAEL, Mary American ac-
tress TW/4, 8
MICHAEL, Meyers (b 1960) Amer-
ican actor TW/27
MICHAEL, Mickie (d 1973 [30])
performer BP/58*
MICHAEL, Ralph [né Ralph Champ-
ion Shotter] (b 1907) English
actor AAS, WWT/10-16
MICHAELIS, Robert (1882/84-
1965) French actor, singer
WWT/2-7
MICHAELS, Bert (b 1943) Ameri-
can actor TW/30
MICHAELS, Frankie (b 1955)
American actor TW/23
MICHAELS, Laura (b 1953) Amer-
ican actress TW/26-29
MICHAELS, Max (d 1968 [70])
manager BP/52*
MICHAELS, Patricia American
actress TW/25
MICHAELS, Raf (b 1928) Ameri-
can actor TW/29
MICHAELS, Sidney (b 1927)
American dramatist MWD
MICHAELS, Stuart (b 1940) Amer-
ican actor TW/28
MICHAELS, Sully (d 1966 [49])
performer BP/50*
MICHAELS, Timmy (b 1963)
American actor TW/26
MICHALESCO, Michael (d 1957
[72]) Russian actor BE*,
WWT/14*
MICHELBORNE, John (fl 1688-
89) dramatist CP/2-3, GT
MICHELENA, Vera (d 1961 [77])
actress, singer TW/18
MICHELL, Agnes see Herbert,
Mrs.
MICHELL, Keith (b 1926/28)
Australian actor AAS, BE,
TW/17, 20, 26-27, WWT/13-16
MICHLIN, Barry (b 1941) Ameri-
can actor TW/30
MICHOT, M. (d 1896 [66]) singer

EA/97*
MICKEY, Jered (b 1934) American
actor TW/27-28
MICKLE, William Julius (1735-88)
Scottish dramatist CP/3
MICKMAN, Mrs. James T. (d
1882) EA/83*
MIDDLEMAS, Henry (d 1918) EA/
19*
MIDDLETON, Alfred (d 1887 [53])
marionettist EA/88*
MIDDLETON, Arthur D. (1880-
1929) American singer WWA/1
MIDDLETON, Edgar (1894-1939)
English dramatist WWT/6-8,
WWW/3
MIDDLETON, Edwin (d 1887 [47])
marionettist EA/88*
MIDDLETON, George (c. 1845-1926)
American manager SR
MIDDLETON, George (1880-1967)
American dramatist BE, WWA/
4, WWM, WWT/4-11
MIDDLETON, Guy (1907-73) English
actor WWT/9-11, 13-14
MIDDLETON, Herman D. (b 1925)
American educator BE
MIDDLETON, James [né Magan]
(c. 1768-99) Irish actor CDP,
GT, TD/1-2
MIDDLETON, James (d 1880 [76])
marionettist EA/81*
MIDDLETON, Mrs. James Alfred
see Middleton, Mary
MIDDLETON, John F. (d 1912
[27]) musician EA/13*
MIDDLETON, Josephine (1886-1971)
American actress WWT/10-14
MIDDLETON, Mary [Mrs. James
Alfred Middleton] (d 1877 [72])
EA/78*
MIDDLETON, Olive (d 1974 [83])
performer BP/59*
MIDDLETON, Ray (b 1907) Ameri-
can actor, singer BE, TW/22-
27, WWT/11-16
MIDDLETON, Robert (1911-77)
American actor TW/10
MIDDLETON, Thomas (c. 1570-
1627) English dramatist CDP,
COC, CP/1-3, DNB, ES, FGF,
GT, HP, MH, NTH, OC/1-3,
PDT, RE
MIDGLEY, Robin (b 1934) English
director WWT/16
MIELL, William (d c. 1796) English
actor TD/2
MIELZINER, Jo (1901-76) French/

American designer AAS, BE,
CB, COC, ES, NTH, OC/1-3,
PDT, TW/2-8, WWT/7-16
MIERS, Charles J. (fl 1869?)
singer, song composer CDP
MIERS, Virgil (d 1967 [42]) critic
BP/52*
MIGATZ, Marshall (d 1973) pro-
ducer/director/choreographer
BP/57*
MIGAUX, Frank (d 1891) singer
EA/92*
MIGDEN, Chester L. (b 1921)
American executive, lawyer
BE
MIGHEL (fl 1619) actor DA
MIGNON, Sara [Mrs. Rollo Bal-
main] English actress GRB/
1-3
MIGNOT, Flore French actress
WWT/2-3
MIHAIL, Alexandra (d 1975 [28])
performer BP/60*
MIHALYI, Judith (b 1944) Amer-
ican actress TW/25
MILAN, Frank American actor
TW/12-16
MILANA, Vincent (b 1939) Amer-
ican actor TW/25, 27, 29-30
MILANO, Mrs. see Sidney,
Minnie
MILANO, Frank (d 1962) American
performer BE*
MILANO, John (d 1874 [49]) har-
lequin, ballet master EA/75*
MILANOV, Zinka (b 1906) Yugo-
slavian singer CB
MILBANK, George (1853-1902)
manager CDP
MILBANK, Mrs. George see
Paine, Lizzie
MILBERT, Seymour (b 1915)
American stage manager BE
MILBURN, J. H. (d 1941 [73])
comedian, singer CDP
MILDARE, Mrs. Charles see
Lindsay, Bertha Goulding
MILDMAY, Frank [John David
Margot] (d 1894 [38]) music-
hall manager EA/95*
MILES, Miss see Fawcett,
Mrs.
MILES, Allan (b 1929) American
dancer notator BE
MILES, Beatrice see Marsdene,
Beatrice
MILES, Sir Bernard (b 1907)
English actor, director,

manager AAS, COC, ES, OC/3,
PDT, WWT/10-16
MILES, Lady Bernard see Wil-
son, Josephine
MILES, Bridget [Mrs. Paddy
Miles] (d 1878 [27]) EA/79*
MILES, Carlton (d 1954 [70+])
American dramatist, talent
representative, critic BE*,
BP/39*
MILES, Edward (1814-1906) English
actor EA/07*, GRB/2*
MILES, Eugene (b 1928) American
actor TW/15
MILES, George (d 1911 [49]) musi-
cian EA/12*
MILES, George Henry (1824-71)
American dramatist DAB, HJD
MILES, Helen Clark (d 1976)
treasurer BP/60*
MILES, Jackie (d 1968 [54]) per-
former BP/52*
MILES, James (d 1882) music-hall
performer EA/83*
MILES, Joanna (b 1940) French/
American actress TW/28
MILES, Joseph (d 1874) musician
EA/75*
MILES, Julia (b 1829) American
actress HAS
MILES, Kate see Munroe, Kate
MILES, Maralyn Canadian actress
TW/25
MILES, Mrs. Paddy see Miles,
Bridget
MILES, Mrs. Patrick see Miles,
Susannah
MILES, Pliny (d 1865) American
lecturer HAS
MILES, Robert E. J. (1834/35-94)
American actor, manager CDP,
HAS, SR
MILES, Sarah actress WWT/15-16
MILES, Sophie [Mrs. S. Shorey]
(d 1891) actress EA/92*, WWT/
14*
MILES, Susannah [Mrs. Patrick
Miles] (d 1886) EA/87*
MILES, Sylvia (b 1932/34) American
actress BE, TW/28-30
MILES, William Augustus (fl 1779-
1812) dramatist CP/2-3, GT,
TD/1-2
MILFORD, Mary see Waller,
Mary
MILGRIM, Lynn (b 1944) American
actress TW/25-27, 29
MILIAN, Tomas (b 1937) Cuban

actor ES
MILJAN, John (d 1960 [67]) Amer-
ician actor BE*
MILL, Paul ["The Whistling Come-
dian"] (d 1916 [53]) entertainer,
singer, composer GRB/1-2
MILL, Robert Reid (d 1906) EA/
08*
MILLAIS, Helena (b 1887) English
actress, singer GRB/1-2
MILLAND, Ray (b 1908) Welsh
actor TW/22-23
MILLAR, Douglas (1875-1943)
Scottish manager WWT/4-7
MILLAR, Gertie [Mrs. Lionel
Monckton] (1879-1952) English
actress COC, DNB, ES,
GRB/1-4, OC/3, TW/8, WWT/
1-11
MILLAR, Mack (d 1962 [57])
press representative BE*
MILLAR, Mary [née Wetton] (b
1936) English actress, singer
WWT/15-16
MILLAR, Robins (1889-1968)
Canadian dramatist, journalist
OC/1-2, WWT/8-10
MILLAR, Ronald (b 1919) English
actor, dramatist AAS, CD,
COC, WWT/10-16
MILLAR, Mrs. S. A. [Miss
Isaacs] (d 1878 [41]) EA/79*
MILLAR, William see Boyd,
Stephen
MILLARD, Edward R. (d 1963)
performer BE*
MILLARD, Evelyn [Mrs. Robert
Porter Coulter] (1869-1941)
English actress, manager EA/
95, GRB/1-4, WWT/1-9,
WWW/4
MILLARD, Harry W. (d 1969 [41])
performer BP/54*
MILLARD, J. (d 1893) professor
of elocution & music EA/94*
MILLARD, Ursula (b 1901) Eng-
lish actress WWT/5-6
MILLAUD, Albert (d 1892 [47])
dramatist EA/93*
MILLAY, Edna St. Vincent (1892-
1950) American dramatist MD,
MH, MWD
MILLAY, George (d 1901) gymnast
EA/02*
MILLER, Mr. (fl 1806?) actor,
singer CDP
MILLER, Mr. (d 1879 [60]) musi-
cian EA/80*

MILLER, Miss (fl 1795?) actress
CDP, TD/1-2
MILLER, Agatha Mary Clarissa
see Christie, Dame Agatha
MILLER, Agnes English actress
WWT/2-5
MILLER, Alice Duer (1874-1942)
American dramatist CB
MILLER, Allan (b 1929) American
actor TW/30
MILLER, Andrew Kennedy (d 1906
[45]) manager EA/07*
MILLER, Ann (b 1919) American
actress, dancer, singer TW/25-
26, WWT/16
MILLER, Art (d 1971 [67]) per-
former BP/55*
MILLER, Arthur (d 1935) drama-
tist BE*, WWT/14*
MILLER, Arthur (b 1915) American
dramatist, director AAS, BE,
CB, CD, CH, COC, ES, HJD,
HP, MD, MH, MWD, OC/2-3,
PDT, RE, WWT/11-16
MILLER, Arthur H. (d 1975 [81])
critic BP/59*
MILLER, Ashley (b 1877) American
actor WWS
MILLER, Barbara (d 1972 [86])
performer BP/56*
MILLER, Benjamin (b 1923) Amer-
ican actor TW/3
MILLER, Betty (b 1925) American
actress TW/22-25, 27, 29
MILLER, Bob (b 1929) American
actor TW/11
MILLER, Buzz (b 1928) American
dancer, actor, choreographer
BE, TW/19-23
MILLER, Clarence (d 1963 [67])
stagehand BE*
MILLER, Clementine (d 1905) EA/
06*
MILLER, David (1871-1933) Scottish
actor, director WWT/4-7
MILLER, David Prince (d 1873
[65]) producer, manager, showman BE*, EA/74*, WWT/14*
MILLER, Drout (b 1942) American
actor TW/26, 28
MILLER, Dutch (b 1927) American
actor TW/24
MILLER, Eddie (d 1971 [80]) performer BP/55*
MILLER, Edith (d 1903) singer,
actress EA/04*, WWT/14*
MILLER, Edward (1735-1807) composer CDP

MILLER, Elizabeth see Baker, Mrs. Thomas

MILLER, Emily (d 1902 [62]) actress WWT/14*

MILLER, Flournoy (d 1971 [84]) comedian TW/27

MILLER, Gary Neil see Dunn, Michael

MILLER, Mr. G. H. (d 1868) EA/69*

MILLER, Gilbert Heron (1884-1969) American producing manager, producer BE, CB, NTH, OC/2-3, TW/2-8, 25, WWA/5, WWT/4-14, WWW/6

MILLER, Harold (b 1935) American actor TW/25, 28

MILLER, Harry M. (b 1934) New Zealand producing manager WWT/16

MILLER, Hattie Brown (fl 1861?) singer CDP

MILLER, Henry (1860-1926) English actor, manager COC, DAB, ES, GRB/2-4, OC/1-3, PP/2, SR, WWA/1, WWM, WWS, WWT/1-5

MILLER, Mrs. Henry [Bijou Heron] (1863-1937) American actress CDP, PP/2

MILLER, Hugh (1889-1976) English actor WWT/8-14

MILLER, Irene Bliss (d 1962 [86]) publicity representative BE*

MILLER, James (1703-44) English dramatist CP/1-3, DNB, GT, TD/1-2

MILLER, James see Wilmot, Fred

MILLER, James Hull (b 1916) American theatre design consultant, scene designer BE

MILLER, Jason (b 1932/39?/40) American dramatist, actor AAS, CB, CD, TW/28-30, WWT/16

MILLER, Mrs. J. Ellis see Mason, Katherine Jane

MILLER, Jennie [Mrs. Kennedy Miller] (d 1899) EA/00*

MILLER, Joan (b 1910) Canadian actress AAS, WWT/11-16

MILLER, Joan Maxine see Copeland, Joan

MILLER, Joaquin (1841-1913) American dramatist SR

MILLER, John D. (b 1771) Amer-ican actor HAS

MILLER, Jonathan (b 1934) English actor, director, dramatist AAS, BE, CB, COC, ES, WWT/14-16

MILLER, Joseph ["Joe"] (1684-1738) English actor CDP, NTH

MILLER, Mrs. Joseph see Lavina

MILLER, Josephine see Clifton, Josephine

MILLER, June (b 1934) American actress TW/24

MILLER, Katherine Jane [Mrs. J. Ellis Miller] (d 1917) EA/18*

MILLER, Kathleen (b 1945) American actress TW/27-29

MILLER, Mrs. Kennedy see Miller, Jennie

MILLER, Leon C. (b 1902) American executive, editor BE

MILLER, Llewellyn (d 1971 [72]) critic BP/56*

MILLER, Louisa Missouri see Missouri, Miss

MILLER, Louise see Louise, Mme.

MILLER, Madeline (b 1945) American actress TW/26

MILLER, Malcolm E. (d 1963 [40]) critic BE*, BP/47*

MILLER, Marilyn (1898-1936) American actress, dancer, singer AAS, ES, NTH, SR, WWT/4-8

MILLER, Martin (1899-1969) Czech actor WWT/10-14

MILLER, Marty (b 1934) American actor TW/2

MILLER, Mary Beth (b 1942) American actress TW/26

MILLER, Max (d 1963 [68]) performer BE*, BP/47*, WWT/14*

MILLER, Maximillian Christopher (1674-1734) German giant CDP

MILLER, Michael (b 1931) American actor TW/27-30

MILLER, Mildred (b 1924) American singer CB

MILLER, Morris (b 1927) American actor TW/9-10, 13

MILLER, Page (b 1947) American actor TW/28

MILLER, Paul Eduard (d 1972 [64]) critic BP/57*

MILLER, R. Mack (b 1937) American actor TW/30

MILLER, Ruby (1889-1976) English actress WWT/4-10

MILLER, Seton I. (d 1974 [71])
dramatist BP/58*
MILLER, Seymour (d 1971 [63])
composer/lyricist BP/56*
MILLER, Sharron (b 1948) Amer-
ican actress TW/29
MILLER, Skedge (b 1918) Amer-
ican actor TW/9-19
MILLER, Sonny (d 1969 [64])
composer/lyricist BP/54*
MILLER, Tod (b 1944) American
actor TW/25, 27
MILLER, Tom (d 1917) secretary
EA/18*
MILLER, Truman (d 1963 [39])
stage manager, actor BE*
MILLER, Walter (1892-1940)
BE*
MILLER, W. Christie (b 1842)
American actor HAS
MILLER, Mrs. W. Christie [née
Towell] (b 1847) Irish actress
HAS
MILLER, William (fl 1819?) im-
personator CDP
MILLER, Wyn (d 1932 [85]) pro-
ducer, dramatist, manager
BE*, WWT/14*
MILLER, Wynne (b 1930/35) Amer-
ican actress, singer BE, TW/
14-19
MILLET, Albert (d 1891) com-
poser EA/92*
MILLETT, Maude [Mrs. Tennant]
(1867-1920) Indian/English ac-
tress DP, GRB/1-4, WWT/
1-3
MILLI, Robert (b 1933) American
actor TW/20, 25-26
MILLICAN, Jane (b 1902) Ameri-
can actress WWT/7-10
MILLIGAN, John Canadian actor
TW/17, 22
MILLIGAN, Spike [Terence Alan]
(b 1918) Indian/English actor,
director, dramatist WWT/14-16
MILLIKEN, Mr. (fl 1835) Ameri-
can actor HAS
MILLIKEN, Col. James Foster
(d 1917) manager, agent SR
MILLIKEN, J. Edwin (d 1884
[35]) actor CDP
MILLIKEN, Sandol [Mrs. Carlos
French Stoddard] (fl 1900-04)
American actress WWS
MILLINGEN (fl 1811) dramatist
CP/3
MILLINGHEN, J. (d 1874 [95])

EA/75*
MILLINGTON, Miss (fl 1850) ac-
tress HAS
MILLINGTON, Rodney (b 1905)
English actor, publisher BE,
WWT/8-16
MILLIS, Fred W. (d 1913 [55])
EA/14*
MILLONS, Thomas (d 1853) Scottish
actor? HAS
MILLS, Mr. (fl 1806) English actor
HAS
MILLS, Mr. (fl 1830-39) English
actor HAS
MILLS, Mrs. [née Keys] (fl 1798-
1804) actress TD/1-2
MILLS, Mrs. (fl 1830-39) English
actress HAS
MILLS, Miss (b c. 1787) actress
TD/2
MILLS, Miss see Brown, Mrs. J.
MILLS, Annette (d 1955 [60]) per-
former, actress BE*, WWT/14*
MILLS, A. W. (d 1889 [22]) music-
hall performer EA/90*
MILLS, Bertram Wagstaff (1873-
1938) English circus proprietor
DNB, ES, WWW/3
MILLS, Carley (d 1962 [65]) com-
poser BE*, BP/47*
MILLS, Mrs. Clifford (d 1933 [70])
dramatist WWT/4-7
MILLS, Donna (b 1943) American
actress TW/23-24
MILLS, Eleanor see Chalmers,
Mrs. James
MILLS, Eliza (d 1857) singer HAS
MILLS, Florence (1895/1901-1927)
American actress, singer
WWT/5
MILLS, Frank [Frank Ransom]
(1870-1921) American actor
GRB/1-4, WWT/1-3
MILLS, Mrs. Frank see Macbeth,
Helen
MILLS, Frederick see Norton,
Fleming
MILLS, Grant (d 1973) actor TW/
30
MILLS, Guy (d 1962 [64]) performer
BE*
MILLS, Mrs. Harry see Doyle,
Lila
MILLS, Hayley (b 1946) English ac-
tress WWT/16
MILLS, Horace (1864-1941) English
actor, dramatist CDP, WWT/2-5
MILLS, Hugh Travers (d 1971)

dramatist BP/56*
MILLS, Jack (d 1974 [88]) circus
owner BP/59*
MILLS, Jake (d 1975 [65]) circus
owner BP/60*
MILLS, James (d 1870 [58]) agent,
stage manager EA/71*
MILLS, James (d 1908) EA/09*
MILLS, John, Sr. (1670-1736)
actor CDP, DNB
MILLS, John (d 1872 [35]) musi-
cian, singer EA/73*
MILLS, Sir John (b 1908) English
actor, singer AAS, BE, CB,
ES, TW/18-19, WWT/8-16
MILLS, Juliet (b 1941) English ac-
tress BE, WWT/14-16
MILLS, Kerry (1869-1948) Amer-
ican composer BE*
MILLS, Martha Norman (d 1906
[78]) EA/07*
MILLS, Mary Louisa [Louie Coote]
(d 1905 [30]) EA/06*
MILLS, Oscar see Barry, Bob
MILLS, R. J. (d 1889 [46]) music-
hall chairman EA/90*
MILLS, Steve (b 1895) American
actor TW/26-27
MILLS, Stratton (d 1916 [45])
actor EA/17*
MILLS, T. E. [T. Mills Edwards]
(fl 1857) English actor CDP,
HAS
MILLS, Tom Norman (d 1917 [55])
clown, comedian EA/18*
MILLS, William (d 1750) actor
TD/1-2
MILLS, Win (d 1971 [63]) columnist
BP/56*
MILLSTEIN, Gilbert writer BE
MILLWARD, Augusta (d 1892)
EA/94*
MILLWARD, Charles (d 1892
[62]) dramatist BE*, EA/93*,
WWT/14*
MILLWARD, F. Aubrey (b 1879)
English actor, singer GRB/2
MILLWARD, Jessie [Mrs. John
Glendinning] (1861-1932) Eng-
lish actress CDP, DP, EA/
95, GRB/1-4, PP/2, SR,
WWM, WWS, WWT/1-6
MILLWARD, John (d 1890) actor
EA/91*
MILMAN, Dean (d 1868 [77])
dramatist BE*, WWT/14*
MILMAN, Rev. Henry Hart (d
1868 [77]) dramatist EA/69*

MILN, Mrs. W. S. see Richards,
Cicely
MILNE (fl 1798) dramatist EAP
MILNE, A[lan] A[lexander] (1882-
1956) English dramatist AAS,
DNB, ES, HP, MD, MH, MWD,
NTH, PDT, TW/12, WWT/4-11,
WWW/5
MILNE, George C. actor CDP
MILNE, Lennox Scottish actor
TW/24
MILNER, Mr. (fl 1839) Canadian
actor HAS
MILNER, Lieut.-Col. (d 1917 [70])
EA/18*
MILNER, Alfred (d 1887 [63]) mu-
sic-hall proprietor EA/89*
MILNER, Annie (b 1836) Scottish
singer HAS
MILNER, Prof. George (d 1907
[84]) performer? EA/08*
MILNER, Martin (b 1931) American
actor TW/24
MILNER, Ron (b 1938) American
dramatist CD
MILNES, Sherrill (b 1935) American
singer CB
MILO, Vic (d 1965 [80]) performer
BP/50*
MILORADOVICH, Milo (d 1972
[71]) performer BP/57*
MILS, Tobias (fl 1583-94?) actor
DA
MILTERN, John E. (d 1937 [67])
American actor WWT/4-8
MILTON, Arthur (d 1918 [61])
EA/19*
MILTON, Mrs. Arthur (d 1936) ac-
tress BE*, WWT/14*
MILTON, Betty Rea (d 1969) per-
former BP/54*
MILTON, Billy (b 1905) English ac-
tor, dancer, lyricist WWT/7-15
MILTON, Charles [Charles Hooper
Wilson] (d 1900 [35]) actor EA/
01*
MILTON, E. C. (d 1906) gymnast
EA/08*
MILTON, Ernest (1890-1974) Amer-
ican actor AAS, BTR/74,
WWT/4-15
MILTON, Frank (b 1918) American
actor TW/3
MILTON, Mrs. Hal (d 1908 [21])
EA/09*
MILTON, Harry (1900-65) English
actor, singer WWT/7-11
MILTON, John (1606-74) English

dramatist CP/1-3, DNB, ES, FGF, GT, HP, NTH, PDT, RE, SR

MILTON, Mark (fl 1896?) actor, singer CDP

MILTON, Maud (1859-1945) English actress CDP, GRB/1-4, WWT/1-9

MILTON, Percy (d 1898) comedian EA/00*

MILTON, Mrs. Percy see Pigot, Elizabeth

MILTON, Robert (d 1956 [70]) Russian producer, director TW/12, WWT/6-10

MILWARD, Dawson (1862/70-1926) English actor GRB/1-4, WWT/1-5

MILWARD, John (d 1742 [40]) actor WWT/14*

MILWARD, William (d 1742) actor WWT/14*

MINCIOTTI, Esther (d 1962 [74]) Italian actress BE*, BP/46*

MINDIL, Philip (b 1874) American press agent, editor WWM

MINELLI, Liza (b 1946) American actress BE, CB, WWT/16

MINELLI, Vincente (b 1908) American designer, director ES

MINEO, Sal (d 1976 [37]) performer BP/60*

MINER, Henry Clay (d 1950 [84]) American manager SR

MINER, Jan (b 1917/19) American actress BE, TW/25, 27-30, WWT/16

MINER, Worthington C. (b 1900) American producer, director BE, WWT/8-10

MINETTI, Maria (d 1971) actress WWT/7-8

MINEVITCH, Borrah (d 1955 [52]) Russian performer TW/12

MINIL, Renée du see Du Minil, Renée

MINION, Samuel (fl 1634) actor DA

MINNER, Kathryn (d 1969 [77]) performer BP/54*

MINNEY, Charles John Cuninghame see Cuninghame, Charles

MINNEY, Rubeigh James (b 1895) Indian/English critic WWT/6-10

MINOR, Philip (b 1927) American actor TW/25

MINOTIS, Alexis (b 1902/06) Greek actor, director BE, COC, OC/3, TW/9

MINOTTA, Duchess of see Sorma, Agnes

MINSHULL, Mrs. George see Minshull, Mary Jane

MINSHULL, George T. (d 1943 [87]) actor, producer, manager DP

MINSHULL, John (fl 1801-05) dramatist EAP

MINSHULL, Mary Jane [Mrs. George Minshull] (d 1879) EA/80*

MINSKY, Abraham Bennet (1881-1949) American producer BE*, BP/34*, WWT/14*

MINSKY, Jack (d 1973 [85]) manager BP/58*

MINSKY, Mollie (d 1964 [69]) American executive BE*

MINSTER, Jack (1901-66) English actor WWT/8-14

MINSTER, Mrs. Robert see Minster, Sybil

MINSTER, Sybil [Mrs. Robert Minster] (d 1909) EA/10*

MINTER, Mary Miles (b 1902) American actress WWT/4-7

MINTO, Dorothy [Mrs. Shiel Barry] (b 1891) English actress GRB/3-4, WWT/1-9

MINTON, William Richard [William Richard Martin] (d 1916) actor? EA/17*

MINTUN, John (b 1941) American actor TW/26, 30

MINTURN, Harry L. (d 1963 [79]) producer, actor BE*

MINTZ, David see Knight, David

MINTZ, Eli (b 1904) Polish actor TW/21-22, 25, 30

MINZESHEIMER, Blanche see Blanche, Belle

MINZEY, Frank (d 1949 [70]) American actor BE*, BP/34*

MIRAMOVA, Elena Russian actress WWT/7-11

MIRAN, Miss actress, singer CDP

MIRANDA, Carmen (1913-55) Brazilian singer, actress CB, TW/12

MIRANDA, David Myers (d 1886 [50]) singer EA/87*

MIRANDOLA, Sig. (fl 1860) singer HAS

MIRATO, Sig. (d 1885) singer

EA/87*

MIRBEAU, Octave (1848-1917) French dramatist COC, GRB/ 1-4, WWT/1-3

MIRREN, Helen (b 1946) actress HAS, WWT/15-16

MISHIMA, Masao (d 1973 [67]) performer BP/58*

MISITA, Michael (b 1947) actor TW/26-30

MISKEL, Caroline [née Scales] (b 1873) actress SR

MISSA, Edmond (d 1910) composer WWT/14*

MISSOURI, Miss [Louisa Missouri Miller] (1821-38) American actress CDP, HAS

MISTALE (fl 1635) actor DA

MISTINGUETT [née Jeanne Bourgeois] (1875-1956) French actress, dancer COC, TW/12, WWT/10-11, WWW/5

MISTRAL, Jorge (d 1972 [49]) performer BP/56*

MITCHEL, Thomas (d 1894 [57]) musician EA/95*

MITCHELHILL, J. P. (1879-1966) English manager, proprietor WWT/9-11

MITCHELL, Abbie (d 1960 [76]) actress, singer TW/16

MITCHELL, Ada (b 1880) American actress WWS

MITCHELL, Adrian (b 1932) English dramatist CD

MITCHELL, Ann American actress TW/20, 28-29

MITCHELL, Arthur (b 1934) American dancer, choreographer CB, ES, TW/25

MITCHELL, Cameron (b 1918) American actor BE, TW/5-9, 27

MITCHELL, Charles, Jr. (d 1917) EA/18*

MITCHELL, Charlotte (fl 1840) English actress HAS

MITCHELL, Colin (d c. 1800) Scottish actor TD/1-2

MITCHELL, Cooper (d 1918 [37]) EA/19*

MITCHELL, David designer WWT/16

MITCHELL, Dodson (1868-1939) American actor, dramatist WWT/7-9

MITCHELL, Doris (fl 1907-13) American actress WWM

MITCHELL, Earle (d 1946 [64]) American actor TW/2

MITCHELL, Edith (1834-68) English actress HAS

MITCHELL, Elihu (b 1861) English singer GRB/1

MITCHELL, Emma (fl 1853-58) actress HAS

MITCHELL, Esther (d 1953 [56]) Australian actress TW/2-3, 10

MITCHELL, Fred (d 1890) comedian EA/91*

MITCHELL, Gary (b 1938) Canadian actor TW/25-27

MITCHELL, George (1905-72) American actor BE, TW/28

MITCHELL, Grant (1874-1957) American actor SR, TW/13, WWM, WWT/5-11

MITCHELL, Grover E. (d 1969 [60]) critic BP/54*

MITCHELL, G. W. (b 1840) American actor HAS

MITCHELL, Ian Priestley (d 1969 [77]) performer BP/54*

MITCHELL, James (b 1920) American actor, dancer BE, TW/3-20, 30

MITCHELL, James I. (d 1969 [78]) performer BP/54*

MITCHELL, Jan (b 1916) Swedish investor, backer BE

MITCHELL, J. F. (d 1888) songwriter EA/89*

MITCHELL, John (d 1856 [57]) actor, manager EA/72*, WWT/14*

MITCHELL, John (d 1874 [68]) manager EA/76*, WWT/14*

MITCHELL, John D. (b 1917) American executive, director BE

MITCHELL, John W. [Mark Johnson] (d 1887) professor of living statuary EA/88*

MITCHELL, Joseph (c. 1684-1738) Scottish? dramatist CP/1-3, GT, TD/1-2

MITCHELL, Julian (d 1926 [72]) director, producer BE*, BP/ 11*, WWT/14*

MITCHELL, Julien (1888-1954) English actor, director SR, WWT/9-11

MITCHELL, Katherine see Corey, Mrs. John

MITCHELL, Ken (b 1944) American actor TW/26, 30

MITCHELL, Kittie (b 1868) American actress SR

MITCHELL, Langdon Elwyn (1862-
1933) American dramatist
DAB, ES, GRB/3-4, HJD, MD,
MH, MWD, OC/1-3, WWA/1,
WWM, WWT/1-7

MITCHELL, Mrs. Langdon Elwyn
[née Marion Lea] (1864-1944)
English actress DP, SR, TW/1

MITCHELL, Lathrop (b 1907)
American actor TW/6-14

MITCHELL, Lee (b 1906) American educator BE

MITCHELL, Leonard (d 1905)
musician EA/06*

MITCHELL, Les (d 1975 [70])
performer BP/59*

MITCHELL, Loften (b 1919) American dramatist, actor BE, CD

MITCHELL, Mae (d 1963 [52])
performer BE*

MITCHELL, Maggie [Margaret
Julia] (1832/37-1918) American
actress CDP, COC, DAB,
HAS, OC/1-3, PP/2, SR,
WWA/1, WWM

MITCHELL, Margaret Julia see
Mitchell, Maggie

MITCHELL, Mary (b 1831) American actress HAS

MITCHELL, Mason (b 1859) American actor WWM

MITCHELL, Maurine American
educator, costume designer
BE

MITCHELL, Millard (1903-53)
Cuban actor TW/1, 3-5, 10

MITCHELL, Norma (d 1967)
dramatist BP/51*

MITCHELL, Mrs. Percival J.
see Van Buskirk, June

MITCHELL, Rhea (d 1957 [63])
actress BE*

MITCHELL, Ronald E. (b 1905)
English educator, director BE

MITCHELL, Ruth (b 1919) American stage manager, producer,
director BE, WWT/16

MITCHELL, Sam (d 1965 [90])
performer BP/49*

MITCHELL, Stephen (b 1901/07)
Scottish manager WWT/10-16

MITCHELL, Theodore (d 1938
[63]) American press representative, critic BE*, BP/22*

MITCHELL, Thomas (1895-1962)
American actor, dramatist
ES, SR, TW/4-9, 19, WWA/4,

WWT/7-13

MITCHELL, Victoria (d 1911) EA/
12*

MITCHELL, Warren (b 1926) English actor WWT/15-16

MITCHELL, William (1798-1856)
English/American manager, actor
CDP, COC, DAB, HAS, OC/1-3,
SR, WWA/H

MITCHELL, William (d 1870 [53])
circus clown EA/71*

MITCHELL, William see Revolti,
Felix

MITCHELL, William C. manager
CDP

MITCHELL, William Henry (d 1901
[51]) manager EA/02*

MITCHELL, Yvonne (b 1925) English actress ES, WWT/11-16

MITCHENSON, William (d 1870
[49]) pantomimist EA/71*

MITE, Mjr. [John Dempster Simp-
son] (d 1902 [30]) midget performer EA/03*

MITE, General Tiny (b 1864) dwarf
CDP

MITFORD, Mary Russell (1787-
1855) English dramatist CDP,
DNB

MITTERWURZER, Friedrich (1844-
97) German actor CDP

MITTLER, William H. (d 1976
[70s]) manager BP/60*

MITTY, Nomi (b 1939) American
actress TW/8

MITZI (b 1891) Hungarian actress
WWT/4-11

MIX, Tom (1880-1940) American
actor DAB, ES

MIXON, Alan (b 1933) American
actor TW/22-24, 28-29

MIZNER, Wilson (1875/76-1933)
American dramatist SR, WWA/
1, WWM

MOBERG, Vilhelm (d 1973 [74])
dramatist BP/58*

MOBERLY, Robert (b 1939) American actor TW/25-26, 28

MOCEK, Henry K. (d 1973) pro-
ducer/director/choreographer
BP/59*

MOCKERITZ, Arnold (d 1857) freak
child HAS

MODENA, Gustavo (1803-61) Italian
actor OC/1-3

MODJESKA, Helena (1844-1909)
Polish actress CDP, COC,
DAB, DP, ES, GRB/1-4, HJD,

NTH, OC/1-3, PDT, PP/2,
SR, WWA/1, WWS, WWW/1
MODLEY, Sidney Allen (d 1976
[73]) performer BP/60*
MOE, Christian H. (b 1929) Amer-
ican dramatist, educator BE
MOELLER, Philip (1880-1958)
American dramatist, producer,
director ES, HJD, MWD,
NTH, TW/14, WWA/3, WWT/
5-10
MOFFAT, Dickson (d 1916) per-
former EA/17*
MOFFAT, Donald (b 1930) English
actor, director AAS, BE,
TW/22-25, 27, WWT/15-16
MOFFAT, Graham (1866-1951)
Scottish actor, dramatist
WWT/2-11, WWW/5
MOFFAT, Mrs. Graham (1873-
1943) Scottish actress WWT/
6-9
MOFFAT, Kate Scottish actress
WWT/2-8
MOFFAT, Margaret (1882-1942)
Scottish actress WWT/5-9
MOFFAT, Winifred (b 1902) Scot-
tish actress WWT/5-8
MOFFATT, Alice (b 1894/90)
German/Scottish actress
WWT/4-7
MOFFATT, Edward (d 1876) eques-
trian, gymnast EA/77*
MOFFATT, Mrs. Edward see
Moffatt, Rebecca
MOFFATT, Henry Howard see
Howard, Henry
MOFFATT, John (b 1922) Eng-
lish actor AAS, BE, TW/14,
WWT/14-16
MOFFATT, Rebecca [Mrs. Ed-
ward Moffatt] (d 1872 [22])
equestrienne EA/73*
MOFFATT, Richard (d 1883 [72])
equestrian EA/84*
MOFFATT, Sanderson (d 1918)
actor BE*, EA/19*, WWT/14*
MOFFET, Harold (b 1892) Amer-
ican actor WWT/8
MOFFET, Sally (b 1931) Ameri-
can actress TW/5
MOFFETT, Cleveland (1863-1926)
American dramatist WWM
MOFFETT, Harold (1892-1938)
American actor BE*, WWT/14*
MOFFIT, James W. (1830-95)
American actor, manager SR
MOFFITT, Harry see Walton,

H. B.
MOFFO, Anna (b 1935?) American
singer CB, ES
MOGUY, Leonide (d 1976 [77]) pro-
ducer/director/choreographer
BP/60*
MOHR, Gerald (d 1968 [54]) per-
former BP/53*
MOHR, Marcia (b 1935) American
actress TW/23, 28
MOHUN, Michael (c. 1620-84) Eng-
lish actor CDP, COC, DA,
DNB, OC/1-3
MOHYEDDIN, Zia (b 1931/33)
Pakistani actor TW/24, WWT/
15-16
MOINAUX, Georges see Courte-
line, Georges
MOIR, Frank L. (d 1904 [53])
composer EA/05*
MOIR, William Wallace (d 1901)
actor EA/02*
MOISEIWITSCH, Tanya (b 1914)
English designer AAS, BE, CB,
COC, ES, PDT, WWT/10-16
MOISEYEV, Igor (b 1906) Russian
choreographer, dancer CB, ES
MOISSI, Alexander (1880-1935)
German actor COC, NTH, OC/
1-3
MOJICA, Jose (d 1974 [78]) per-
former BP/59*
MOK, Michel (d 1961 [72]) Dutch
press agent TW/17
MOKANA [James Mayer Goldston]
(d 1905 [23]) handcuff performer
EA/06*
MOLASSO, Giovanni (1870-1928)
Italian choreographer, dancer,
impresario ES
MOLESWORTH, Ida (d 1951) Indian/
English actress, manager GRB/
2-4, WWT/1-8
MOLIERE (1622-73) French drama-
tist COC, ES, OC/3
MOLIQUE, Bernhardt (d 1869 [75])
musician EA/70*
MOLLENHAUER, Henrietta singer
CDP
MOLLIEN, Roger (b 1931) French
actor TW/15
MOLLISON, Clifford (b 1896/97)
English actor AAS, WWT/5-16
MOLLISON, Henry (b 1905) Scottish
actor WWT/7-13
MOLLISON, William (1862-1911)
Scottish actor GRB/1-4
MOLLISON, William (1893-1955)

English producer WWT/6-11

MOLLISON, Mrs. William see McNay, Evelyn

MOLLOY, Charles (d 1767) Irish dramatist CP/1-3, GT, TD/ 1-2

MOLLOY, James Lynam (1837-1909) Irish composer DNB

MOLLOY, Joseph Fitzgerald (d 1908) author EA/09*

MOLLOY, Michael (b 1917) Irish dramatist CD

MOLNAR, Ferenc (1878-1952) Hungarian dramatist COC, ES, MH, MWD, NTH, OC/ 1-3, PDT, SR, TW/8, WWA/ 3, WWT/10-11

MOLNAR, Lily (d 1950) actress BE*, WWT/14*

MOLYNEUX, Eileen (1893-1962) South African actress WWT/ 4-6

MOMBACH, J. L. (d 1880 [66]) professor of music EA/81*

MOMBER, Harry (d 1917) actor EA/18*

MONACO, Jimmy (1885-1945) Italian composer BE*

MONACO, Mario del (b 1915) Italian singer CB

MONAGHAN, George (d 1889) music-hall performer EA/90*

MONAHAN, Kaspar J. (b 1900) American critic BE

MONCION, Francisco (b c. 1922) American dancer ES

MONCK, Matthews (d 1907 [57]) actor, manager GRB/3*, WWT/14*

MONCK, Nugent (1877-1958) English actor, producer COC, OC/1-3, WWT/5-12, WWW/5

MONCKTON, Lady (d 1920 [83]) English actress CDP, GRB/ 1-4

MONCKTON, Fanny (d 1912 [35]) performer? EA/13*

MONCKTON, Lionel (1862-1924) English composer GRB/1-4, WWT/1-4, WWW/2

MONCKTON, Mrs. Lionel see Millar, Gertie

MONCKTON, Lady Louisa (fl 1858-90) actress DP

MONCRIEFF, Gladys (1893-1976) Australian actress, singer WWT/6-11

MONCRIEFF, John (d c. 1767)

Scottish dramatist CP/1-3, GT, TD/1-2

MONCRIEFF, Murri (d 1949) actor BE*, WWT/14*

MONCRIEFF, Richard (1840-1915) American actor SR

MONCRIEFF, Rose [Mrs. Newman Maurice] (d 1916) actress, singer CDP

MONCRIEFF, R. Scott [Cyril Bowen] (d 1882 [28]) dramatist, acting manager EA/83*

MONCRIEFF, William George Thomas (1794-1857) English dramatist, manager CDP, COC, OC/1-3, SR

MONDOSE, Alex (d 1972 [78]) performer BP/56*

MONEAN, Thomas P. (d 1875 [69]) actor EA/76*

MONEY, Henry (d 1877) musician EA/78*

MONGINI, Sig. (d 1874) singer EA/75*

MONIER, Virginia (fl 1834-41) West Indian actress HAS, SR

MONK, Ada (d 1898 [53]) actress CDP

MONK, Albert P. (d 1905 [30]) musician EA/06*

MONK, C. W. Montague (d 1895) circus performer EA/96*

MONK, John (d 1880) musician EA/81*

MONKE, William (fl 1619) musician DA

MONKHOUSE, Allan (1858-1936) English dramatist, critic, journalist COC, MWD, OC/3, WWT/5-8

MONKHOUSE, Harry (1854-1901) English actor DP, EA/95

MONKMAN, Phyllis (1892-1976) English actress, dancer WWT/ 4-11

MONKS, James (b 1917) American actor TW/3, 5, 13-15, WWT/10

MONKS, John, Jr. (b 1910) American dramatist BE

MONNAI, Mme. singer CDP

MONNIER, Marguerite (d 1883 [19]) dancer EA/84*

MONNOT, Marguerite (d 1961 [58]) composer BP/46*, WWT/14*

MONPLAISIR, Adele (fl 1847) French dancer CDP

MONPLAISIR, Hyppolyte (1821-77) French dancer, choreographer

ES
MONPLAISIR TROUPE see Montplaisir Troupe
MONRO, G. see Graham, John
MONROE, Ann Swinburne (d 1973 [87]) performer BP/58*
MONROE, Dale (b 1930) American actor TW/16
MONROE, Mrs. Dwight Van see Laughlin, Anne
MONROE, Frank (d 1937 [73]) American actor BE*, BP/22*
MONROE, George W. (d 1932 [75]) American actor BE*, WWT/14*
MONROE, Lucy American singer CB
MONROE, Shirley American actress TW/29
MONRO-MORTIMER, Rosa Susannah (d 1913) EA/14*
MONTA, Rudolph (d 1963 [62]) lawyer BE*
MONTAGNANI, William Francis Montague (d 1885) EA/86*
MONTAGU, Arthur (d 1909 [36]) actor EA/10*
MONTAGU, Elizabeth (b 1909) English actress WWT/8-9
MONTAGU, Jane A. [Mrs. Will Montagu] (d 1911) EA/13*
MONTAGU, Mrs. Will see Montagu, Jane A.
MONTAGUE, Mr. see Talbot, Mr.
MONTAGUE, Alicia [Mrs. William Montague] (d 1877) EA/78*
MONTAGUE, Bertram (b 1892) English manager WWT/11-13
MONTAGUE, Charles see Henri, Charles
MONTAGUE, Charles Edward (1867-1928) English journalist, critic ES, OC/1-3, WWT/5
MONTAGUE, Daisy (d 1893 [25]) singer EA/94*
MONTAGUE, Edward John Bruce (d 1876 [25]) actor EA/77*
MONTAGUE, Emmeline (d 1910) actress BE*, WWT/14*
MONTAGUE, F. J. [Henry John Mann] (1843-78) actor SR
MONTAGUE, G. H. (d 1887) marionette manager EA/88*
MONTAGUE, G. L. (d 1901) comedian EA/02*
MONTAGUE, H. (d 1888) minstrel EA/89*

MONTAGUE, Harold [Harold Montague Smith] (b 1874) English actor, entertainer, producer GRB/1-3
MONTAGUE, Harry (d 1927 [83]) actor, songwriter BE*, BP/11*
MONTAGUE, Mrs. Harry see Montague, Margaret Elizabeth
MONTAGUE, Henry (d 1869) actor? EA/70*
MONTAGUE, Henry James (1843/44-78) American actor CDP, COC, DAB, DNB, OC/1-3, WWA/H
MONTAGUE, Lee (b 1927) English actor TW/9, 22, WWT/15-16
MONTAGUE, Louise (1871-1906) performer BE*
MONTAGUE, Louise (1859-1910) actress CDP
MONTAGUE, Margaret Elizabeth [Mrs. Harry Montague] (d 1884) EA/85*
MONTAGUE, Rita (d 1962 [78]) actress, dramatist BE*
MONTAGUE, Susie [Mrs. Walter Lewis] (d 1905) actress EA/07*
MONTAGUE, Walter (d 1669) English dramatist CP/1-3, FGF
MONTAGUE, William (d 1869 [73]) actor WWT/14*
MONTAGUE, William (d 1885) lessee EA/86*
MONTAGUE, William (d 1900 [75]) actor EA/01*
MONTAGUE, Mrs. William see Montague, Alicia
MONTAGUE, Winnetta [Mrs. Walter Montgomery] (d 1877 [26]) American actress EA/78*
MONTAGU-SMITHSON, Mr. (d 1891 [64]) actor EA/92*
MONTAIGNE, Frank (d 1896) EA/97*
MONTALBAN, Ricardo (b 1920) Mexican actor BE, TW/14-15, 29
MONTANO, Delhi (d 1892) lion tamer EA/93*
MONTCHRETIEN, Antoine de (c. 1575-1621) French dramatist COC, OC/1-3
MONTCRIEFF, W. T. (d 1857 [63]) dramatist WWT/14*
MONTEFIORE, Eade (1866-1944) English manager, producer, press representative WWT/2-4, 8-9

MONTEFIORE, Thomas Cecil
(d 1939 [29]) press-representa-
tive, manager WWT/14*
MONTEITH, Benjamin (d 1908)
musician EA/09*
MONTEREY, Carlotta (d 1970
[82]) actress TW/27
MONTEROSSO, Emily Jan Madson
(d 1971 [29]) performer BP/
56*
MONTESOLE, Max (d 1942 [52])
dramatist, director BE*,
WWT/14*
MONTEUX, Pierre (1875-1964)
French conductor ES
MONTEZ, Lola (1818/24-61) Irish
dancer, actress CDP, ES,
HAS, HJD, SR, WWA/H
MONTEZ, Minnie [née Folland]
(fl 1857) actress HAS
MONTFORT, Stanley W. (d 1970
[67]) performer BP/55*
MONTGOMERY, Mr. (fl 1807)
actor CDP
MONTGOMERY, Alfred Augustus
(d 1911 [66]) variety agent
EA/12*
MONTGOMERY, Charles (fl 1850)
actor HAS
MONTGOMERY, Charles (d 1866
[56]) clown EA/72*
MONTGOMERY, Charles (d 1871
[30]) singer EA/72*
MONTGOMERY, Christopher (d
1902 [33]) EA/03*
MONTGOMERY, David Craig
(1870-1917) American actor,
producer BE*, BP/3*, EA/
18*
MONTGOMERY, Douglass (1909-66)
American actor BE, TW/23,
WWT/8-14
MONTGOMERY, Earl (b 1921)
American actor BE, TW/10,
12-13, 15, 19-20, 22-25, 30,
WWT/15-16
MONTGOMERY, Elizabeth (b
1902) English designer BE,
WWT/9-16 [see also: "Motley"]
MONTGOMERY, Elizabeth (b 1933)
American actress ES, TW/
10-15
MONTGOMERY, Florence [Mrs.
George Arliss] (d 1950 [77])
actress BE*, WWT/14*
MONTGOMERY, Harry "Scamp"
(1868-1911) American actor
SR

MONTGOMERY, Henry W. (1842-
1908) actor CDP
MONTGOMERY, Hugh Welsh actor
GRB/1
MONTGOMERY, Jack (d 1962 [70])
actor BE*
MONTGOMERY, James H. (1882-
1966) dramatist, actor SR,
TW/23, WWT/2-11
MONTGOMERY, Marshall (d 1942
[55]) American ventriloquist
BE*, BP/27*
MONTGOMERY, Matthew (d 1906
[61]) proprietor EA/07*
MONTGOMERY, Monty (b 1945)
American actor TW/25
MONTGOMERY, Robert (b 1904)
American actor BE, CB, ES,
WWT/7-10
MONTGOMERY, Robert Humphrey,
Jr. (b 1923) American lawyer
BE
MONTGOMERY, Rose (d 1912) ac-
tress EA/13*
MONTGOMERY, Walter (1827-71)
American/English actor DNB
MONTGOMERY, Mrs. Walter see
Montgomery, Winnetta
MONTGOMERY, William Henry (d
1886 [76]) composer, conductor
EA/87*
MONTGOMMERY, David Craig
(1870-1917) American actor
GRB/3-4, WWT/1-3
MONTHERLANT, Henri de (b 1896)
French dramatist COC, OC/3
MONTI, Mlle. (fl 1851) actress
CDP
MONTI, Gertie [Mrs. Harry Dale]
(d 1910 [45]) variety performer
EA/11*
MONTPLAISIR, Ippolito see
Monplaisir, Hyppolyte
MONTPLAISIR TROUPE, The (fl
1848) HAS
MONTRESOR, Beni (b 1926) Italian
designer CB
MONTRESSOR, George B. (fl 1833)
singer HAS
MONTRESSOR, Giovanni Batta (fl
1832) singer CDP
MONTROSE, Jack [John Thacker]
(d 1916) EA/18*
MONTROSE, Kate (fl 1873?) singer
CDP
MONTROSE, Marie actress EA/96
MONTROSE, Muriel English ac-
tress, dancer WWT/10-11

MONTT, Cristina (d 1969 [72])
performer BP/53*
MOODIE, Douglas (d 1973 [64])
performer BP/58*
MOODIE, George (d 1894) panto-
mimist EA/95*
MOODIE, Louise M. R. (d 1934
[88]) actress CDP, EA/97,
GRB/1-4, OAA/2
MOODNICK, Ronald see Moody,
Ron
MOODY, Catherine Grace Frances
see Gore, Catherine Grace
Frances
MOODY, Fanny [Mrs. Charles
Manners] (1864/66-1945) English
singer CDP, ES, GRB/1-4,
WWW/4
MOODY, Hilda [Mrs. J. A. E.
Malone] English actress GRB/
1-2
MOODY, John (c 1724?-1813)
Irish? actor CDP, DNB, GT,
SR, TD/1-2
MOODY, John (d 1852 [38]) comic
singer EA/72*
MOODY, Mrs. John, II see
Armstrong, Elizabeth
MOODY, Mary [Mrs. Charles
Williams] (d 1910) EA/11*
MOODY, Michaux (d 1970 [78])
manager BP/54*
MOODY, Ralph (d 1971 [84]) per-
former BP/56*
MOODY, Richard (b 1911) Amer-
ican educator, historian BE
MOODY, Ron [né Ronald Mood-
nick] (b 1924) English actor
AAS, WWT/14-16
MOODY, William Vaughn (1869-
1910) American dramatist
COC, DAB, ES, GRB/2-4,
HJD, MH, MWD, NTH, OC/
1-3, RE, SR, WWA/1, WWS
MOON, Nellie (d 1907) music-
hall artist CDP, GRB/3
MOON, Peter (fl 1562) actor
DA
MOON, William H. (d 1889 [27])
EA/90*
MOONEY, Harry (d 1972 [83])
vaudevillian WWT/16*
MOONEY, Rita (d 1973 [69]) ac-
tress, director BP/57*,
WWT/16*
MOONEY, William American ac-
tor TW/23, 26, 29-30
MOOR, Bill (b 1931) American

actor TW/23-26, 29-30
MOORA, Robert L. (d 1971 [58])
critic BP/55*
MOORE, A. C. singer, songwriter
CDP
MOORE, Ada American singer BE
MOORE, Adelaide (b 1865) Irish
actress DP
MOORE, A. E. see Hogarth,
Vladimir
MOORE, Alec [Alexander James
McKenzie] (d 1896 [35]) comic
singer CDP
MOORE, A. P. (b 1906) Irish
manager WWT/9
MOORE, Augustus G. M. (d 1910
[54]) stage manager, dramatist,
journalist EA/12*, WWT/14*
MOORE, Bella (fl 1870) actress,
song composer CDP
MOORE, Bertha [Mrs. Frank Huth]
English singer, actress GRB/
1-4
MOORE, Carlyle (b 1875) American
actor, stage manager WWS
MOORE, Carrie (1882/83-1956)
Australian actress GRB/1-4,
WWT/1-5
MOORE, Carrie Augusta (b 1843)
American actress HAS
MOORE, Carroll (b 1913) American
dramatist BE
MOORE, Charles American actor
TW/24, 26-27
MOORE, Charles J. (d 1962 [84])
American performer BE*
MOORE, Charles Werner (b 1920)
American educator, actor, di-
rector BE
MOORE, Chris (d 1975 [55]) per-
former BP/60*
MOORE, Cleo (d 1973 [44]) per-
former BP/58*
MOORE, Colleen (b 1900) American
actress ES
MOORE, Cornelius (d 1916) car-
penter EA/17*
MOORE, Cullen (d 1975) writer
BP/59*
MOORE, C. W. (d 1895 [32]) scene
artist EA/96*
MOORE, Daniel (d 1873 [54]) come-
dian EA/74*
MOORE, Daniel (d 1874 [27])
Negro artist EA/75*
MOORE, Decima [Mrs. Guggisberg]
(1871-1964) English actress,
singer CDP, DP, EA/94,

GRB/1-4, WWS, WWT/1-8

MOORE, Del (d 1970 [53]) performer BP/55*

MOORE, Dennie (b 1907) American actress BE, TW/1, 12, WWT/10-11

MOORE, Diane (b 1948) American actress TW/25

MOORE, Dick (b 1925) American actor, director, editor BE

MOORE, Douglas (1893-1969) American composer HJD

MOORE, Dudley (b 1935) English actor, composer BE, WWT/15-16

MOORE, Edith (d 1907) singer EA/08*

MOORE, Edward (1712-57) English dramatist CDP, COC, CP/1-3, GT, HP, OC/1-3, TD/1-2

MOORE, Edward (b 1935) American actor TW/24, 26

MOORE, Eileen (d 1902 [22]) actress EA/03*

MOORE, Eleanora [Nelly] (d 1869 [24]) actress DNB

MOORE, Eliza ["Lion Queen"] (fl 1836) dancer, performer HAS

MOORE, Elizabeth [Mrs. G. W. Moore] (d 1882 [50]) EA/84*

MOORE, Elizabeth (d 1904 [80]) EA/05*

MOORE, Elsie actress, singer CDP, WWS

MOORE, Eulabelle (d 1964 [61]) American actress BE, TW/21

MOORE, Eunice singer CDP

MOORE, Eva [Mrs. H. V. Esmond] (1870-1955) English actress COC, EA/95, GRB/1-4, WWT/1-11, WWW/5

MOORE, Fanny see Buckley, Mrs. W. H.

MOORE, F. Frankfort (d 1931 [75]) dramatist BE*, WWT/14*

MOORE, Flora (fl 1893?) actress, singer CDP

MOORE, Florence (d 1935 [49]) actress WWT/4-7

MOORE, Frances see Brooke, Frances

MOORE, Frank F. (b 1880) American comedian WWM

MOORE, Gar (b 1920) American actor TW/4

MOORE, George (fl 1804) dramatist CP/3, TD/2

MOORE, George (1852-1933) Irish dramatist COC, DNB, HP, MWD, NTH, OC/3, RE, WWT/2-7, WWW/3

MOORE, George A. E. (d 1906 [27]) EA/07*

MOORE, George Austin (b 1876) American vaudevillian WWM

MOORE, George F. (d 1890) music-hall performer EA/91*

MOORE, George Washington, Jr. (1820/25-1909) American comedian, manager CDP, HAS

MOORE, Gerald (d 1897) actor EA/96

MOORE, Grace (1901-47) American actress, singer CB, DAB, SR, TW/3, WWA/2, WWT/7-10

MOORE, Mrs. G. W. see Moore, Elizabeth

MOORE, Mrs. G. W., Jr. see Moore, Mrs. Louie

MOORE, Hattie (d 1898) actress CDP

MOORE, Henrietta (d 1973 [50]) performer BP/58*

MOORE, Hilda (d 1929 [42]) actress WWT/2-5

MOORE, Horatio Newton (b 1820?) dramatist RJ

MOORE, Ioma Mae [Dennie Graves] (d 1974 [73]) performer BP/59*

MOORE, Irene (b 1890) American actress WWS

MOORE, Irene (b 1928) French/American actress TW/6

MOORE, Jack (b 1930) American dancer TW/12-14

MOORE, Jennifer (b 1944) South African actress TW/27

MOORE, Jenny (d 1973 [50]) dramatist BP/58*

MOORE, Jessie [Mrs. Cairns James] (d 1910) English actress GRB/2-4

MOORE, John (b 1814) English actor HAS

MOORE, John (fl 1818-25) American actor HAS

MOORE, John Cecil (1907-67) dramatist WWW/6

MOORE, Jonathan (b 1923) American actor TW/25-28

MOORE, Joseph (fl 1st half of 17th cent) English actor DA, OC/1-3

MOORE, Mrs. J. Warwick (d 1893)

EA/94*
MOORE, Laura singer CDP
MOORE, Laurens (b 1919) American actor TW/24
MOORE, Leon (b 1926) American actor TW/9-11
MOORE, Lillian (1911/17-67) American dancer ES, WWA/4
MOORE, Mrs. Louie [Mrs. G. W. Moore, Jr.] (d 1891) EA/92*
MOORE, Louisa (d 1898) English actress HAS
MOORE, Maggie (1847-1926) American actress, singer WWT/5
MOORE, Marshall (b 1861) Scottish director GRB/2-4
MOORE, Mary [Lady Wyndham] (1861/62-1931) English actress CDP, COC, DNB, DP, EA/96, ES, GRB/1-4, OC/1-3, SR, WWT/1-6, WWW/3
MOORE, Mary Alice (b 1923) American actress TW/3, 10
MOORE, Mary Tyler (b 1937) American actress CB
MOORE, Matt (1890-1960) Irish actor BE*
MOORE, Mavor (b 1919) Canadian dramatist, critic, educator, director, actor CD
MOORE, Melba (b 1945) American singer, actress CB, TW/26-27
MOORE, Michael (b 1942) American actor TW/24
MOORE, Monette (d 1961 [50]) performer BE*
MOORE, Nelly see Moore, Eleanora
MOORE, Owen (1886-1939) Irish actor, producer BE*, BP/23*, WWT/14*
MOORE, Patti (d 1972 [71]) performer BP/57*
MOORE, Percy (d 1945 [67]) Canadian actor TW/1
MOORE, Raymond (1897-1940) theatre founder CB
MOORE, Reginald (d 1880 [41]) actor EA/81*
MOORE, Robert (b 1927/30) American actor, director TW/22-24, WWT/15-16
MOORE, Robert Francis (d 1964 [69]) American critic BE*, BP/48*
MOORE, Roger (b 1927?) English

actor CB
MOORE, Mrs. Sheridan see Harris, Flora
MOORE, Sonia Russian/American producer, director BE
MOORE, Stephen (b 1937) English actor WWT/15-16
MOORE, Sir Thomas (d 1735) dramatist CP/1-3, GT
MOORE, Thomas (fl 1801) dramatist CP/3, GT
MOORE, Tom (d 1955 [71]) Irish actor BE*, BP/39*
MOORE, Victor Frederick (1876-1962) American actor AAS, GRB/3-4, SR, TW/1-16, 19, WWA/4-5, WWM, WWS, WWT/1-13
MOORE, Mrs. Victor Frederick see Littlefield, Emma
MOORE, William A. (b 1825) English singer, prompter, business manager, stage manager, manager HAS
MOORE, William Henry (d 1890 [30]) scene artist EA/92*
MOORE, Wyke (d 1884) actor EA/85*
MOOREHEAD, Agnes (1906-74) American actress BE, BTR/74, CB, ES, TW/8, 19, 29-30, WWT/14-16
MOOREHEAD, John (d 1804) Irish composer, musician DNB, TD/1-2
MOORES, Franklin T. (d 1909 [32]) singer EA/10*
MOOREY, Stefa (d 1972 [38]) performer BP/56*
MOORHEAD, Jean (d 1953 [39]) American actress BE*, BP/38*
MOORHOUSE, Mrs. Charles see Wallack, Fanny
MOOR-JONES, Edna (d 1975 [84]) performer BP/60*
MORA [Richard Price] (d 1901 [25]) gymnast EA/02*
MORA, Thomas (d 1908 [37]) performer? EA/09*
MORAHAN, Christopher (b 1929) English director, producing manager WWT/15-16
MORALES, Santos (b 1935) actor TW/30
MORALT, Mrs. John Alvis see Dussek, Mrs. Jan Ladislav
MORAN, Dominick see Murray, Dominick

MORAN, Don American actor
TW/24
MORAN, F. H. J. (d 1916) mu-
sical director, composer
EA/17*
MORAN, George (d 1949 [67])
American performer BE*
MORAN, James (d 1866) musician
HAS
MORAN, Jim (b 1909) American
press representative, per-
former BE
MORAN, Lee (d 1961 [73]) actor
BE*
MORAN, Lois (b 1907) American
actress, singer WWT/7-9
MORAN, Pat (d 1965 [64]) per-
former BP/50*
MORAN, Patsy (d 1968 [63])
performer BP/53*
MORAN, Polly (1885-1952) Amer-
ican actress BE*
MORAND, Mary Catharine (d 1894
[56]) EA/95*
MORAND, M. R. (1860-1922)
English actor GRB/1-4,
WWT/2-4
MORANT, C. Ellen (fl 1857) ac-
tress HAS
MORANT, Fanny (1821-1900)
English actress CDP, HAS
MORATH, Max (b 1927) American
actor TW/25
MORCHEN, Horace (d 1905) black
& white artist, actor EA/06*
MORDANT, Edwin (d 1942 [74])
American actor WWM
MORDANT, Mrs. Edwin see
Atwell, Grace
MORDAUNT, Mrs. Charles see
Peterborough, Anastasia,
Countess of
MORDAUNT, Frank (d 1891 [40])
ventriloquist EA/92*
. MORDAUNT, Frank (1841-1906)
American actor CDP, HAS,
PP/2
MORDAUNT, Mrs. Frank (d
1878) American actress HAS
MORDAUNT, George (d 1890)
comedian EA/91*
MORDAUNT, John (d 1871) actor
EA/72*
MORDAUNT, Louisa Cranstoun
see Nisbett, Louisa Crans-
toun
MORDAUNT, Marian actress
CDP

MORDAUNT, Plessy (fl 1871) ac-
tress CDP
MORDE, Gertie (d 1902) variety
singer EA/04*
MORDEN, Roger (b 1939) American
actor TW/27, 29
MORDEY, Mrs. George, Sr. see
Mordey, Rachel
MORDEY, Rachel [Mrs. George
Mordey, Sr.] (d 1881 [53])
EA/82*
MORDKIN, Mikhail H. (1881?-1944)
Russian? dancer, ballet master
CB, SR
MORE, Miss see Fawcett, Mrs.
John
MORE, George (fl 1554) actor DA
MORE, Hannah (1745-1833) English
dramatist CDP, CP/2-3, DNB,
GT, HP, TD/1-2
MORE, Kenneth (b 1914) English
actor AAS, ES, WWT/12-16
MORE, Roger (fl 1640) actor DA
MORE, Unity (b 1894) Irish ac-
tress, dancer, singer WWT/3-6
MOREAU, Emile (b 1852) French
dramatist WWT/2
MOREHEN, Horace (d 1905) actor
GRB/1
MOREHOUSE, Ward (1897/98/1900-
1966) American critic, drama-
tist BE, CB, COC, NTH, OC/
1-3, TW/23, WWT/10-14
MORELAND, Mr. (fl 1848) actor
CDP
MORELAND, Abraham (d 1875)
actor EA/76*
MORELAND, Frank (d 1884 [62])
actor EA/85*
MORELAND, George Harry (d 1832)
English actor HAS
MORELAND, Harry actor HAS
MORELAND, Mrs. Harry [née Anne
Jones] (d 1866) actress HAS
MORELAND, Mantan (d 1973) per-
former BP/58*
MORELAND, Marjorie (b 1896)
American actress SR
MORELAND, Peg Leg (d 1973 [84])
performer BP/57*
MORELL, André (b 1909) English
actor AAS, WWT/9-16
MORELL, Dollie [Mrs. Bond-Sayers]
(d 1908) comedian EA/09*
MORELL, H. H. see Morrell,
H. H.
MORELL, Dr. Thomas (1701-84)
dramatist CP/2-3

MORELLA, Mrs. William [Emma Marden] (d 1889) vaudevillian EA/90*

MORELLI, Sig. (fl 1856) singer CDP, HAS

MORELLI, Antonio (d 1974 [69]) producer/director/choreographer BP/59*

MORELLI, Carlo (d 1970 [72]) singer TW/26

MORELLI, Mrs. Charles [née Lily Macdonald] (d 1876 [29]) actress EA/77*

MORELLI, Charles Francis (d 1882 [81]) pantomimist, scene painter EA/83*

MORELLI, Fanny [Mrs. Henry Rivers] (d 1901 [75]) actress EA/02*

MORELLI, Giovanni (fl 1790s) singer CDP

MORENO, Antonio (d 1967 [78]) actor TW/23

MORENO, Ascension (d 1972 [86]) performer BP/57*

MORENO, Rita (b 1931) Puerto Rican actress, dancer TW/27, 29, WWT/16

MORETON, J. C. (d 1888) phatoscopic entertainer EA/89*

MORETON, John Pollard [né Pollard] (d 1798) American actor CDP, HAS

MORETON, Lottie see George, Mrs. E.

MORETON, Lydia [Elizabeth Harriman Potier] (d 1897) burlesque actress EA/98*

MORETON, Ursula (b 1903) English dancer ES, WWT/9-12

MORETTI, Eleanor English actress WWS

MOREY, Arthur (b 1941) American actor TW/27, 30

MORFA-HUGHES, Ethel Margaret see Hughes, Morfa

MORFITT, Ada (d 1889) performer? EA/90*

MORFOGEN, George (b 1933) American actor TW/30

MORFORD, Henry (1823-81) American dramatist HJD

MORGAN, Lady (fl 1803?) dwarf CDP

MORGAN, Mrs. [Lizzie Rayner] (d 1882 [35]) actress EA/83*

MORGAN, Miss (fl 1836) actress HAS

MORGAN, Miss (fl 1849) actress HAS

MORGAN, Ada [Ada Mary Copley; Mrs. Walter Copley] (d 1893 [25]) actress EA/94*

MORGAN, Agnes American director BE

MORGAN, Al (b 1920) American dramatist BE

MORGAN, Appleton (1845-1928) American scholar WWA/1, WWM

MORGAN, Armel (d 1898) limelight contractor EA/99*

MORGAN, Beatrice (fl 1895-1913) American actress WWM

MORGAN, Charles (d 1917) EA/18*

MORGAN, Mrs. Charles (d 1903) EA/04*

MORGAN, Charles Langbridge (1894-1958) English critic, dramatist AAS, CH, COC, DNB, ES, HP, MD, MWD, OC/1-3, PDT, WWA/3, WWT/5-12, WWW/5

MORGAN, Charles S., Jr. (d 1950 [75]) American producer, director BE*, BP/35*

MORGAN, Clara (d 1882) dancer EA/83*

MORGAN, Claudia [Claudia Wuppermann] (1912-74) American actress BE, TW/1-3, 8-9, 13-16, WWT/8-15

MORGAN, Clifford (d 1908) advertising manager EA/09*

MORGAN, Mrs. Clifford see Morgan, Norah Louise

MORGAN, Diana (b 1910/13) Welsh dramatist, actress WWT/9-16

MORGAN, Mrs. Edmund Nash (b 1857) American dramatist WWM

MORGAN, Edward (b 1866) English actor GRB/1-2

MORGAN, Edward J. (1871-1906) English actor PP/2

MORGAN, Mrs. Edward J. see Bertram, Helen

MORGAN, E. N. see Bonville, Mr.

MORGAN, Etta singer CDP

MORGAN, Fitzroy (d 1912 [50]) actor EA/13*, WWT/14*

MORGAN, Fluellen (fl 1633) actor? puppeteer? DA

MORGAN, Frank (1890/93-1949) American actor ES, TW/6, WWT/7-10

MORGAN, Gareth (b 1940) Welsh
director, actor WWT/15-16
MORGAN, George (d 1949 [67])
performer TW/6
MORGAN, George (d 1975 [50])
performer BP/60*
MORGAN, Helen (1900-41) Amer-
ican actress, singer DAB,
SR, WWT/7-9
MORGAN, Henry (d 1884 [36])
limelight contractor EA/85*
MORGAN, Henry (d 1906) EA/07*
MORGAN, Jane (d 1972 [91]) per-
former BP/56*
MORGAN, Joan [Mrs. Scott Mc-
Kay] (d 1962 [43]) American
actress BE*, BP/47*
MORGAN, Joan (b 1905) English
actress, dramatist WWT/5-7,
10-16
MORGAN, Mrs. John Hartman
see Halstan, Margaret
MORGAN, Kay Summersby (d
1975 [66]) designer BP/59*
MORGAN, Laura (d 1884) EA/85*
MORGAN, McNamara (d 1762)
Irish dramatist CP/1-3,
DNB, GT, TD/1-2
MORGAN, Matt (d 1890 [54])
scene artist CDP
MORGAN, Merlin (d 1924 [47])
conductor, composer BE*,
WWT/14*
MORGAN, Netty (d 1881) EA/82*
MORGAN, Norah Louise [Mrs.
Clifford Morgan] (d 1905)
EA/06*
MORGAN, Rachel [Mrs. Walter
Morgan] (d 1868 [38]) EA/69*
MORGAN, Ralph (1887/88-1956)
American actor ES, TW/2-4,
6-8, 12, WWT/6-12
MORGAN, Ray (d 1974) performer
BP/59*
MORGAN, Rebekah (d 1898 [69])
EA/99*
MORGAN, R. J. (fl 1863) actor
HAS
MORGAN, Roger (b 1938) Ameri-
can lighting designer, theatre
consultant WWT/16
MORGAN, Swifty (d 1975 [90])
Broadway character BP/60*
MORGAN, Sydney (1885-1931)
Irish actor WWT/6
MORGAN, Thomas (fl 1817-18)
actor WWA/H
MORGAN, Violet [Mrs. Jack

Ford] (d 1909) mimic EA/10*
MORGAN, Walter (d 1885) panto-
mimist EA/86*
MORGAN, Mrs. Walter see
Morgan, Rachel
MORGAN, Wilford (fl 1879) singer
OAA/2
MORGAN, Wilfred R. (d 1912)
singer EA/13*
MORGAN, William (1829-1907)
English manager GRB/3
MORGAN, William (d 1944 [92])
actor BE*, WWT/14*
MORGAN, William A. (d 1888 [33])
American singer EA/89*
MORGAN, William Alton (d 1898
[73]) circus performer EA/99*
MORGANTHAU, Rita Wallach (1880-
1964) American educator BE
MORIARTY, Mr. (fl 1847) actor
HAS
MORIARTY, Joanne (d 1964 [25])
actress BE*
MORIARTY, Michael (b 1941) Amer-
ican actor CB, TW/30, WWT/
16
MORISON, Bradley (b 1924) Amer-
ican press representative BE
MORISON, David (fl 1790) drama-
tist CP/3
MORISON, Patricia (b 1915/19)
American actress, singer AAS,
BE, TW/5-13, 15, 21, WWT/
11-15
MORITZ, Edward (d 1974 [83])
composer/lyricist BP/59*
MORLACCHI, Josephine (d 1886)
dancer CDP, HAS
MORLAY, Gaby (d 1964 [71]) ac-
tress BE*, BP/49*, WWT/14*
MORLEY, Mr. (fl 1839) actor
CDP, HAS
MORLEY, Mrs. actress CDP
MORLEY, Charles (b 1938) Amer-
ican actor TW/23
MORLEY, Charles see Cart-
wright, Charles
MORLEY, Charlotte [Mrs. Joe G.
Scott] (d 1911) EA/12*
MORLEY, Christopher designer
AAS, WWT/15-16
MORLEY, Christopher Darlington
(1890-1957) American dramatist,
manager HJD, WWA/3
MORLEY, D. (d 1894 [72]) jour-
nalist EA/95*
MORLEY, Harry William (d 1953
[82]) actor BE*, WWT/14*

MORLEY, Henry (1822-94) English critic OC/1-3

MORLEY, John (b 1914) Canadian actor TW/6-7

MORLEY, Malcolm (1890-1966) English actor, manager, producer WWT/6-14

MORLEY, Robert (b 1908) English actor, dramatist AAS, BE, CB, COC, OC/3, PDT, TW/5-6, WWT/9-16

MORLEY, Ruth costume designer BE

MORLEY, Thomas (fl 1574) actor DA

MORLEY, Victor (d 1953 [82]) English vaudevillian, actor TW/10

MORNINGSTAR, Carter (d 1964 [53]) American scene designer BE*

MORON, Carmen Unda Y prima donna CDP

MOROSCO, Oliver (1875/76-1945) American manager SR, TW/2, WWA/5, WWM, WWT/3-9

MOROSS, Jerome (b 1913) American composer BE

MOROZOV, Mikhail Mikolaevich (1897-1952) Russian scholar OC/3

MORRA, Sig. (fl 1847) dancer HAS

MORREL (fl 1596?) dramatist FGF

MORRELL, Mr. (fl 1810) actor HAS

MORRELL, H. H. (d 1916) producer, actor DP

MORRELL, Millie [Mrs. Walter Scott] (d 1904) serio-comic EA/05*

MORRELL, Thomas (fl 1722-73) dramatist, translator GT

MORRICE, Norman (b 1931) dancer, choreographer ES

MORRILL, Priscilla (b 1927) American actress BE, TW/23

MORRIS, Miss (fl 1797) actress TD/2

MORRIS, Alfred J. (d 1905 [44]) songwriter, librettist EA/06*

MORRIS, Mrs. Allen see Morris, Madge

MORRIS, Annie (d 1880) trapezist EA/81*

MORRIS, Austin W. (d 1887) American advance agent,
manager NYM

MORRIS, Chauncey (d 1917 [42]) English actor, stage manager, manager GRB/1

MORRIS, Chester (1901-70) American actor BE, TW/17-19, 22, 27, WWT/7-9

MORRIS, Clara [Mrs. F. C. Harriott] (1846/48/49-1925) Canadian actress CDP, COC, DAB, ES, GRB/2-4, NTH, OC/1-3, PP/2, SR, WWA/1, WWM, WWT/1-5

MORRIS, Mrs. Cleze Gill (d 1963 [78]) performer BE*

MORRIS, David E. (d 1842 [72]) manager, proprietor EA/72*, WWT/14*

MORRIS, David L. (d 1879) comedian CDP

MORRIS, Edward (fl 1790-99) dramatist CP/3, GT, TD/1-2

MORRIS, Elizabeth see Morris, Mrs. Owen, II

MORRIS, Felice (fl 1903-13) American actress WWM

MORRIS, Felix (1850-1900) English actor SR, WWA/1

MORRIS, Mrs. Felix (d 1954) American actress BE*, BP/38*

MORRIS, Frederick [Frederick Laroche] (d 1881) actor? EA/82*

MORRIS, F. S. (d 1847) actor HAS

MORRIS, Garrett (b 1944) American actor TW/26-30

MORRIS, George Pope (1802-64) American dramatist CDP, EAP, RJ

MORRIS, Howard (b 1919) American actor TW/2

MORRIS, Ida (b 1895) serio-comic EA/96*

MORRIS, J. (d 1870) actor EA/71*

MORRIS, J. actor, singer CDP

MORRIS, Jack (d 1948 [61]) actor WWT/10

MORRIS, John (b 1926) American composer, conductor BE

MORRIS, Mrs. John see Cantrell, Miss

MORRIS, Johnny (d 1969 [83]) performer BP/54*

MORRIS, Joseph M. (d 1882 [70]) proprietor EA/83*

MORRIS, Leigh E. (b 1934) American community theatre leader BE

MORRIS, Lily (d 1952 [68]) per-

former BE*, WWT/14*
MORRIS, Lon (1830-82) minstrel manager & performer CDP
MORRIS, Lorena A. Adee (d 1967 [83]) performer BP/52*
MORRIS, McKay (1890/91-1955) American actor TW/1-4, 7, 12, WWT/8-11
MORRIS, Madge [Mrs. Allen Morris] (d 1896) EA/97*
MORRIS, Mrs. Maesmore [Gertrude Wilmot] English actress GRB/1-3
MORRIS, Margaret (b 1891) English dancer WWT/4-9
MORRIS, Marty [or Marti] (b 1949) American actress TW/29-30
MORRIS, Mary (1895-1970) American actress AAS, BE, TW/26, WWT/8-14
MORRIS, Mary (b 1915) Fijian/English actress AAS, WWT/10-16
MORRIS, Mathias (fl early 17th cent) actor DA
MORRIS, Maynard (d 1964 [65]) agent TW/20
MORRIS, Mrs. M. C. see Ralph, Julia
MORRIS, Mildred (fl 1902-11) English actress WWM, WWS
MORRIS, Mowbray (d 1911 [63]) critic BE*, WWT/14*
MORRIS, Nat (b 1951) American actor TW/29
MORRIS, Newbold (d 1966) executive BP/50*
MORRIS, Owen (1719-1809) American actor HAS, OC/1-3
MORRIS, Mrs. Owen, I (d 1767) actress HAS
MORRIS, Mrs. Owen, II (1753-1826) American actress CDP, COC, DAB, HAS, OC/1-3, WWA/H
MORRIS, Peter (b 1821) American comic singer CDP, HAS
MORRIS, Phyllis (b 1894) English dramatist, actress WWT/6-16
MORRIS, Richard (b 1924) American dramatist, director BE
MORRIS, Robert (fl 1742) dramatist CP/2-3
MORRIS, Theodore (d 1892 [c. 63]) manager, proprietor CDP
MORRIS, Thomas (d 1894) musician EA/95*

MORRIS, Thomas E. (b 1829) American actor, manager, agent HAS
MORRIS, Wayne (1914-59) American actor TW/14-16
MORRIS, William (1873-1932) German/American manager, agent SR
MORRIS, William (1861-1936) American actor GRB/3-4, WWA/1, WWM, WWS, WWT/1-8
MORRIS, Mrs. William see Terry, Florence
MORRIS, William, Jr. (b 1899) American executive BE
MORRIS, William E. (1831/32-78) American minstrel, manager CDP, HAS
MORRISON, Mr. (fl early 19th cent) actor CDP
MORRISON, Mrs. (d 1917 [79]) EA/18*
MORRISON, Adrienne (1889-1940) American actress CB
MORRISON, Allan (d 1968 [51]) critic BP/52*
MORRISON, Anna Marie (d 1972 [88]) performer BP/57*
MORRISON, Arthur (1863-1945) dramatist WWW/4
MORRISON, Bill dramatist CD
MORRISON, Charles P. (fl 1899?) music-hall singer CDP
MORRISON, Effie (d 1974 [57]) performer BP/59*
MORRISON, George E. (1860-1930) English critic, dramatist, journalist WWT/1-6
MORRISON, George Pete (d 1973 [82]) performer BP/57*
MORRISON, Henrietta Lee (d 1948 [79]) actress BE*, WWT/14*
MORRISON, Hobe (b 1904) American critic BE, WWT/15-16
MORRISON, Howard Priestly (d 1938 [66]) American actor, director, producer BE*, BP/22*
MORRISON, Jack (1887-1948) English actor, singer WWT/4-10
MORRISON, Jack (b 1912) American educator BE
MORRISON, James W. (d 1974 [86]) performer BP/59*
MORRISON, Jim (1944-71) American singer, lyricist WWA/5
MORRISON, John (d 1903 [102]) clown EA/05*
MORRISON, John Clark (1828-87)

American actor NYM

MORRISON, Leo (d 1974 [75])
publicist BP/58*

MORRISON, Lewis (1844/45-1906)
West Indian actor, manager
CDP, HAS, PP/2, SR, WWA/1

MORRISON, Mrs. Lewis see
Roberts, Florence

MORRISON, Mrs. Lewis see
Wood, Rose

MORRISON, Paul (b 1906) American designer BE

MORRISON, Priestly (1871-1938)
American producer WWT/8

MORRISON, Rosabel (1869-1911)
American actress SR

MORRISON, Talmadge H. (d
1974 [82]) photographer BP/59*

MORRISON, William James (d
1901) EA/02*

MORRISS, Mary Ann [Mrs. William Morriss] (d 1885) EA/
86*

MORRISS, Mrs. William see
Morriss, Mary Ann

MORRISSEY, Eamon (b 1943) Irish
actor TW/22-23, 25

MORRISSEY, James W. (d 1917)
Irish dramatist? manager SR,
WWM

MORRISSEY, John F. (d 1941
[58]) actor BE*, WWT/14*

MORRISSEY, John J. (c. 1855-
1925) American actor SR

MORRISSEY, Marguerite (b 1920)
American actress TW/5

MORRISSEY, Will (d 1957 [72])
actor, songwriter, producer
TW/14

MORROS, Boris (d 1963 [c. 70])
Russian musical director, producer BE*

MORROW, Mr. (d 1867) singer
EA/68*

MORROW, Doretta (1928-68)
American actress, singer BE,
TW/5-13, 24, WWT/12-13

MORROW, Karen (b 1936) American actress TW/18-25, 28,
30

MORSE, Mr. (b 1784) American
actor HAS

MORSE, Barry (b 1919) English
actor WWT/10-11

MORSE, Hayward (b 1947) English
actor TW/29

MORSE, John M. (b 1911) American architect BE

MORSE, Richard (b 1927) American
actor TW/11-15, 18-20, 24-30

MORSE, Robert (b 1931) American
actor, singer BE, CB, ES,
TW/12-20, 28-29, WWT/16

MORSE, Salmi (1826?-84) dramatist, manager CDP

MORSE, Theodore F. (1873-1924)
American composer BE*

MORSE, Woolson (1858-97) American composer BE*

MORSELL, Fred A. (b 1940)
American actor TW/27, 29-30

MORSELL, Herndon (fl 1882?) actor, songwriter CDP

MORTIMER, Mr. (fl early 19th
cent) actor CDP

MORTIMER, Miss (fl 1803) actress
TD/2

MORTIMER, Miss (d 1874) music-
hall performer EA/76*

MORTIMER, Allie (d 1866 [8])
actress HAS

MORTIMER, Bella [Mrs. Charles
Dillon] (d 1886 [40]) actress
EA/87*

MORTIMER, C. H. (fl 1852) actor
HAS

MORTIMER, Charles (d 1913 [82])
actor BE*, WWT/14*

MORTIMER, Charles (1885-1964)
actor WWT/9-11

MORTIMER, Mrs. Charles (d 1881)
EA/82*

MORTIMER, Charles Neil (d 1913)
EA/14*

MORTIMER, Dorothy (d 1950 [52])
actress TW/6

MORTIMER, Ellen see Smith,
Mrs.

MORTIMER, Estelle (d 1904 [52])
actress CDP

MORTIMER, George Charles (d
1912 [87]) singer EA/13*

MORTIMER, Henry (b 1882) Canadian actor WWM

MORTIMER, James (1833-1911)
French dramatist GRB/2-4

MORTIMER, John (b 1923) English
dramatist, critic AAS, CD,
CH, COC, MD, MH, MWD,
PDT, RE, WWT/13-16

MORTIMER, John K. (d 1878 [48])
American actor CDP

MORTIMER, John K. (b 1862)
American actor HAS

MORTIMER, Joseph H. (d 1880
[38]) manager EA/81*

MORTIMER, Joseph Parker
Hopwood (d 1884 [36]) EA/86*
MORTIMER, Miss L. (fl 1850)
actress HAS
MORTIMER, Lee (d 1963 [58])
American journalist BE*
MORTIMER, Lillian (d 1941) ac-
tress, dramatist, producer
SR
MORTIMER, Mrs. T. G. see
Saker, Maria
MORTLOCK, Charles Bernard
(1888-1967) English critic
WWT/7-14
MORTON, Mrs. see Chapman,
Charlotte Jane
MORTON, Alfred H. (d 1974
[76]) producer/director/chore-
ographer BP/58*
MORTON, Brooks (b 1932) Amer-
ican actor TW/25-27, 29
MORTON, Charles (1819-1904)
English manager CDP, COC,
OC/1-3, WWW/1
MORTON, Mrs. Charles see
Temple, Henrietta
MORTON, Charles H. (1832-82)
Scottish actor, manager CDP,
HAS
MORTON, Clara (d 1948 [66])
performer TW/4
MORTON, Clive (1904-75) Eng-
lish actor AAS, WWT/8-15
MORTON, E. (fl 1758) dramatist
CP/2-3, GT
MORTON, Mrs. E. see Morton,
Rosamond
MORTON, Edward (d 1922) drama-
tist, critic GRB/1-4, WWT/
1-4, WWW/2
MORTON, E. M. (d 1856) Eng-
lish actor? HAS
MORTON, Mrs. F. [Mrs. R.
Honnor] (d 1870 [61]) actress
EA/71*
MORTON, George (1849-1917)
American actor HAS, SR
MORTON, Mrs. George see
Hawthorne, Louise
MORTON, George W. actor CDP
MORTON, Gregory (b 1911) Amer-
ican actor TW/11
MORTON, Guy Mainwaring see
Traill, Peter
MORTON, Harry K. (d 1956
[67]) vaudevillian, actor TW/
12
"MORTON, Hugh" see McLellan,

C. M. S.
MORTON, James C. (b 1884)
American comedian WWM
MORTON, James J. (1861-1938)
American vaudevillian WWM
MORTON, Jennie (fl 1865) actress
CDP, HAS
MORTON, Joe (b 1947) American
actor TW/30
MORTON, John (d 1907) Negro
comedian EA/08*
MORTON, John (d 1974 [84]) actor
BP/58*, WWT/16*
MORTON, John Henry (d 1911
[62]) proprietor EA/12*
MORTON, John Maddison (1811-91)
English dramatist CDP, DNB,
EA/68, HP, OC/1-3
MORTON, Joseph (d 1884 [29])
actor, minstrel CDP
MORTON, Kitty (d 1927 [65])
American actress BE*, BP/11*
MORTON, Leon (d 1941) actor
WWT/4
MORTON, Louis Russell (d 1917
[68]) advertising agent EA/18*
MORTON, Maggie (d 1939 [82])
actress, producer BE*, WWT/
14*
MORTON, Margaret [Mrs. W. H.
Morton] (d 1899) EA/00*
MORTON, Martha [Mrs. Herman
Conheim] (1870-1925) American
dramatist GRB/2-4, WWM,
WWT/1-5
MORTON, Michael (c. 1863-1931)
English dramatist GRB/2-4,
SR, WWT/1-6, WWW/3
MORTON, Rosamund [Mrs. E.
Morton] (d 1905) dramatist,
critic EA/06*
MORTON, Rosco (d 1887 [42])
conjurer EA/88*
MORTON, Sam (d 1941 [79])
American actor BE*, BP/26*
MORTON, Thomas (c. 1764-1838)
English dramatist CDP, COC,
CP/3, DNB, GT, HP, OC/1-3,
SR, TD/1-2
MORTON, Thomas (d 1879 [76])
dramatist BE*, EA/80*,
WWT/14*
MORTON, Tom J. English actor
GRB/1
MORTON, Mrs. Tom J. see
Bowman, Maggie
MORTON, Tommy (b 1926) Amer-
ican actor TW/5-6, 12

MORTON, W. H. (d 1894 [62])
  actor EA/95*
MORTON, Mrs. W. H. see
  Morton, Margaret
MORTON, Will H. (d 1895) singer,
  minstrel CDP
MORTON, William (b 1829) Eng-
  lish actor HAS
MORTON, William (1838-1938)
  producer, manager BE*,
  WWT/14*
MOSCONA, Nicola (d 1975 [68])
  performer BP/60*
MOSCONI, Charlie (d 1975 [84])
  performer BP/59*
MOSCONI, Louis (d 1969 [74])
  dancer TW/26
MOSCOVITCH, Maurice (1871-1940)
  Russian actor CB, WWT/4-9
MOSCOWITZ, Jennie (d 1953 [85])
  Rumanian actress TW/10
MOSEDALE, Edward (d 1908
  [70]) music-hall performer
  CDP
MOSEL, Tad (b 1922) American
  dramatist BE, CB, CD, ES,
  HJD, MH, MWD
MOSELEY, Hannah (d 1905 [82])
  EA/06*
MOSELEY, Thomas W. (d 1971
  [93]) actor TW/28
MOSELEY, W. B. (d 1907 [50])
  impersonator EA/08*
MOSENTHAL, Solomon Hermann
  (d 1877 [66]) dramatist WWT/
  14*
MOSER, Hans (d 1964 [84]) per-
  former BP/49*
MOSER, Joseph (b 1748) English
  dramatist CP/3
MOSER, Margot (b 1930) Amer-
  ican actress, singer BE,
  TW/24
MOSES, Gilbert, III (b 1942)
  American director WWT/16
MOSES, Harry (d 1937 [64])
  American producer BE*,
  BP/22*, WWT/14*
MOSES, John (d 1967 [60]) agent,
  producer TW/23
MOSES, Montrose Jonas (1878-
  1934) American critic DAB,
  ES, HJD, NTH, OC/1-3,
  WWT/7
MOSES, Robert (b 1888) American
  executive BE
MOSHEIM, Grete (b 1907) German
  actress TW/1, WWT/8-10

MOSKOWITZ, Dr. Henry (d 1936
  [57]) lawyer BE*, WWT/14*
MOSKVIN, Ivan M. (d 1946 [72])
  Russian actor TW/2
MOSLEY, John (d 1869 [62]) mana-
  ger EA/70*
MOSS, Mr. (fl 1786-91) Irish actor
  TD/1-2
MOSS, Amelia Hogue Burgess [Mrs.
  Joseph L. S. Moss] (d 1916)
  EA/17*
MOSS, Arnold (b 1910) American
  actor, director, producer, execu-
  tive BE, TW/1, 3-4, 6-8, 28-
  29, WWT/11-16
MOSS, Clarence H. (d 1975 [75])
  executive BP/60*
MOSS, Sir Edward see Moss,
  Sir Horace Edward
MOSS, Mrs. H. E. (d 1892) EA/
  94*
MOSS, Henry (1729-73) Irish actor
  GT
MOSS, Henry Charles see Borani,
  Charles
MOSS, Sir [Horace] Edward (1852/
  54-1912) English director GRB/
  1-4, OC/1-3, WWT/1
MOSS, Hugh (1855-1926) Indian/
  English stage manager, producer,
  dramatist GRB/1-4
MOSS, Mrs. Hugh see Wallis,
  Bella
MOSS, James (d 1882 [49]) propri-
  etor, comic singer EA/83*
MOSS, James Edward (d 1904 [23])
  EA/05*
MOSS, Joseph Lewis (d 1917 [55])
  proprietor EA/18*
MOSS, Mrs. Joseph L. S. see
  Moss, Amelia Hogue Burgess
MOSS, Little Dot (b 1890) English
  actress GRB/1
MOSS, Mrs. M. (d 1908) EA/09*
MOSS, Maitland (d 1967 [66]) per-
  former BP/52*
MOSS, Marty (d 1973) producer/
  director/choreographer BP/58*
MOSS, Mary see Keene, Laura
MOSS, Paul (d 1950 [70]) American
  producer BE*, BP/34*
MOSS, Sydney (d 1902 [48]) musi-
  cian EA/03*
MOSS, Theophilus (fl 1749) drama-
  tist CP/1-3
MOSS, W. (d 1817) actor CDP
MOSS, W. F. actor, singer CDP
MOSS, W. Keith (1892-1935) Eng-

lish producer, director, journalist WWT/7

MOSSENSON, Yig'al (b 1917) Israeli dramatist RE

MOSSETTI, Carlotta (b 1890) English dancer, ballet mistress WWT/5-8

MOSSOLOVA, Vera (d 1949 [74]) dancer WWT/14*

MOSSOP, George (1814-49) Irish actor, singer HAS, SR

MOSSOP, Henry (1729-74) Irish actor, manager CDP, DNB, OC/1-3, TD/1-2

MOSTEL, Samuel Joel see Mostel, Zero

MOSTEL, Zero [né Samuel Joel] (1915-77) American actor AAS, BE, CB, COC, ES, WWT/14-16

MOSTYN, Annie [Mrs. W. J. Gilbert] (d 1877) actress EA/78*

MOSTYN, George H. (d 1885 [26]) business manager EA/86*

MOSTYN, Hallen actor, singer CDP

MOTE, John Hurden (d 1898) lawyer EA/99*

MOTLEY designers AAS, ES, PDT, TW/2-3, 5-8, WWT/8-16

MOTT, Charles (d 1918) EA/19*

MOTTE, Adelina Sophia (1855-96) American singer SR

MOTTER, Charlotte Kay (b 1922) American educator, director BE

MOTTERAM, John (fl 1600-01) member of the Chapel Royal DA

MOTTEUX, Peter Anthony (1660-1718) French dramatist CP/1-3, DNB, GT

MOTTL, Felix (1856-1911) Austrian conductor, composer ES

MOTTLEY, John (1692-1750) English dramatist CP/1-3, DNB, GT, HP, TD/1-2

MOTYLEFF, Ilya (d 1970 [76]) producer/director/choreographer BP/55*

MOUBRAY, Mr. (fl 1798) dramatist CP/3

MOUBREY, Lilian (d 1970 [95]) performer BP/55*

MOUILLOT, Frederick (1864-1911)

Irish proprietor GRB/1-4

MOUILLOT, Mrs. Frederick see Mouillot, Gertrude

MOUILLOT, Gertrude [Mrs. Frederick Mouillot] (d 1961 [91]) actress GRB/1-4, WWT/1-7

MOUL, Alfred (d 1924) managing director WWT/14*

MOULAN, Frank (1875-1939) American actor, singer WWS, WWT/7-8

MOULAND, Florence (d 1897 [19]) performer? EA/98*

MOULD, Raymond Wesley (b 1905) English press representative WWT/10-11

MOULDER, Walter (1935-67) American actor TW/19-20, 24

MOULE, Winifred Ruby see Lee, Vanessa

MOULT, Rosina see Brandram, Rosina

MOULTON, Arthur E. (fl 1891?) actor, singer CDP

MOULTON, Mrs. Charles (fl 1870s?) singer CDP

MOULTON, Robert (b 1922) American educator, dancer, choreographer, director BE

MOULTRIE, Arthur (d 1893) Negro singer, musician EA/94*

MOULTRU, Rev. (fl 1798) dramatist CP/3

MOUNET-SULLY, Jean (1841-1922) French actor GRB/1-4, WWT/1

MOUNFELD, John (fl 1538) actor DA

MOUNT, Peggy (b 1916) English actress AAS, WWT/12-16

MOUNTAIN, Earl B. (d 1962 [74]) performer BE*

MOUNTAIN, Mrs. Rosoman [née Wilkinson] (c. 1770-1841) English actress, singer CDP, DNB, GT, OX, TD/1-2

MOUNTCASTLE, Fanny [Mrs. Charles H. Thorpe] (d 1887) English actress NYM

MOUNTFIELD, Reginald (d 1911) conductor EA/13*

MOUNTFORD, Mrs. see Vanbruggen, Mrs.

MOUNTFORD, Harry (d 1950 [79]) Irish actor, dramatist BE*, BP/35*

MOUNTFORD, Mrs. Harry see Briscoe, Lottie

MOUNTFORT, Susanna Percival

(1667-1703) English actress
COC, DNB, ES, OC/1-3
MOUNTFORT, William (1664-92)
English actor, dramatist
COC, CP/1-3, DNB, ES,
GT, OC/1-3
MOUNTFORT, Mrs. William see
Mountfort, Susanna Percival
MOUNTIER, Thomas (fl 1719-33)
singer DNB
MOURAVIEF, Mme. (d 1868)
Russian dancer EA/69*
MOUVET, Maurice (d 1927 [40])
Swiss dancer BP/11*
MOVAR, Dunja (d 1963 [23]) per-
former BP/47*
MOVING BEING, The theatre
collective CD
MOWAT, David (b 1943) Egyptian/
English dramatist CD
MOWATT, Anna Cora [Anna Cora
Ogden; Mrs. Ritchie] (1819-70)
American dramatist, actress
CDP, COC, DAB, ES, HAS,
HJD, MH, NTH, OC/1-3, RJ,
SR, WWA/H
MOWBRAY, Mrs. (fl 1854) actress
HAS
MOWBRAY, Alan (d 1969 [72])
English actor, dramatist, di-
rector BE, TW/25
MOWBRAY, Charles (d 1909)
EA/10*
MOWBRAY, Fanny (fl 1849) dancer
HAS
MOWBRAY, Laura (fl 1854) ac-
tress HAS
MOWBRAY, Thomas (d 1900 [77])
actor, dramatist BE*, WWT/
14*
MOWBRAY, Mrs. Thomas (d 1885)
manager EA/86*
MOXON, Constance (fl 1888-91)
actress, singer CDP
MOYA, Natalie (b 1900) Irish
actress WWT/6-11
MOYER, Dot (d 1964 [68]) per-
former BP/49*
MOYER, Irene (d 1975) performer
BP/59*
MOYES, Patricia (b 1923) Irish
dramatist BE
MOYLAN, Mrs. Cecil see
Moylan, Edith Mary
MOYLAN, Edith Mary [Mrs.
Cecil Moylan] (d 1916 [35])
EA/17*
MOYLAN, Mary Ellen (b 1926)

American dancer CB, TW/2
MOYLIN, Mlle. see Cochois,
Mme. Michel
MOZART, George (d 1947 [83])
English performer BE*, WWT/
14*
"MOZART BRITANNICUS" see
Cianchettini, Pio
MOZEEN, Thomas (d 1768) actor,
dramatist CP/1-3, DNB, GT,
TD/1-2
MOZLEY, William Orford [William
Orford] (d 1886) EA/87*
MROZEK, Slawomir (b 1930) Polish
dramatist MH
MUCK, Carl (1859-1940) German
conductor ES
MUDIE, Mrs. (fl 1808) actress
CDP
MUDIE, A. S. (b 1798?) actress
CDP
MUDIE, George (d 1918 [59]) actor
BE*, EA/19*, WWT/14*
MUDIE, Mrs. George see Newton,
Adelaide
MUDIE, Leonard [Leonard Cheetham]
(1883/84-1965) English actor
TW/5, WWT/4-11
MUDIE, T. M. (d 1876) composer,
musician EA/77*
MUECKE, Mrs. see Crossley,
Ada
MUELLER, Mrs. (fl 1848) actress
HAS
MUFFORD, John (fl 1590) actor
DA
MUHLMANN, Adolf (b 1867) Rus-
sian singer WWA/4
MUIR, Emily Margaret (d 1883)
singer EA/84*
MUIR, Florabel (d 1970 [81]) jour-
nalist BP/54*
MUIR, Gavin (d 1972 [62]) performer
BP/56*
MUIR, Jean (b 1911) American ac-
tress WWT/9-10
MUIR, Kenneth (b 1907) English
scholar BE
MULCAHY, Cara (d 1901 [24])
EA/02*
MULCASTER, G. H. (1891-1964)
English actor WWT/4-11
MULCASTER, Richard (fl 1561-
1608) headmaster DA, DNB
MULDENER, Louise (d 1938 [84])
American actress BE*, BP/22*
MULDOON, William (1852-1933)
American wrestler DAB

MULHARE, Edward (b 1923) Irish actor BE, TW/29

MULHERN, Harry (b 1897) manager BE

MULHOLLAND, J. B. (1858-1925) manager GRB/3-4, WWT/1-5

MULHOLLAND, Mrs. J. B. see Nunn, Annette

MULLALLY, Don (d 1933 [48]) American actor, dramatist, director BE*, BP/17*, WWT/14*

MULLANEY, Jack (b 1932) American actor TW/11

MULLE, Ida (1863-1934) American actress SR

MULLEN, Barbara (b 1914) American actress WWT/10-16

MULLEN, Jack (d 1972 [54]) publicist BP/57*

MULLEN, Margaret (b 1910) American actress TW/22

MULLER, Harrison (b 1926) American actor TW/8

MULLER, Maxmillian Christopher (1674-1734) German giant CDP

MULLETT, Ann (d 1906 [77]) EA/07*

MULLETT, C. (d 1888 [46]) waxwork proprietor EA/89*

MULLETT, James (d 1909 [70]) manager EA/10*

MULLIGAN, Eugene (d 1976 [47]) dramatist BP/60*

MULLIGAN, John (1827-73) minstrel, circus performer CDP, HAS

MULLIGAN, Joseph see Freeland, Frank

MULLIGAN, Richard (b 1932) American actor TW/22-23, 27-28, 30, WWT/16

MULLIKIN, Bill (b 1927) American actor TW/8-9, 26

MULLINS, Michael (b 1951) American actor TW/30

MULLIS, George (d 1910 [81]) bootmaker EA/11*

MULREAN, Linda (b 1950) American actress TW/30

MULROY, Steve (d 1972 [80]) performer BP/57*

MULVANEY, Constance (d 1918) EA/19*

MULVANEY, John (d 1976 [45]) performer BP/60*

MULVEY, Walter (d 1899 [30])

actor EA/00*

MUMFORD, Mr. (fl 1826-27) actor HAS

MUMFORD, Dora A. (fl 1847?) dancer CDP

MUMFORD, Ethel Watts (d 1940) dramatist CB

MUNCK, Mme. E. de (d 1889 [49]) singer EA/90*

MUNDAY, Anthony (c. 1553-1633) English actor, dramatist COC, CP/2-3, DA, DNB, ES, FGF, HP, NTH, OC/1-3

MUNDAY, Penelope (b 1926) English actress TW/9

MUNDEN, Joseph Shepherd (1758-1832) English actor BS, CDP, COC, DNB, ES, GT, NTH, OC/1-3, OX, TD/1-2

MUNDIN, Herbert (1898-1939) English actor WWT/5-8

MUNDY, Frank (d 1974 [65]) manager BP/58*

MUNDY, John (d 1971 [85]) composer/lyricist BP/56*

MUNDY, Meg English actress, singer BE, TW/4-16, WWT/11-14

MUNFORD, Leslie Talfourd see Leslie, Sid

MUNFORD, Robert (d 1784) American dramatist DAB, EAP

MUNFORD, William (1775-1825) American dramatist EAP

MUNI, Paul (1895-1967) Austrian/American actor BE, CB, ES, NTH, PDT, TW/5-7, 24, WWT/7-14, WWW/6

MUNK, Kaj (d 1944 [45]) dramatist WWT/14*

MUNKITTRICK, Howard see Talbot, Howard

MUNNINGS, Hilda see Sokolova, Lydia

MUNNINGS, J. S. (fl 1803) dramatist CP/3

MUNOZ, Morayma (d 1975 [30]) performer BP/59*

MUNRO, Billy (d 1969 [76]) composer/lyricist BP/54*

MUNRO, C. K. (1889-1973) Irish dramatist MD, MH, NTH, WWT/5-11

MUNRO, Donald (d 1911) manager EA/12*

MUNRO, Douglas English actor GRB/1-3

MUNRO, Ernest Overton (b 1865)

English actor GRB/1
MUNRO, Mrs. Ernest see
Jones, Marie
MUNRO, George (d 1968 [66])
dramatist BP/52*
MUNRO, James (d 1916) EA/17*
MUNRO, Janet (d 1972 [38]) per-
former BP/57*
MUNRO, Nan (b 1905) South Afri-
can actress AAS, WWT/9-16
MUNROE, Elizabeth Emma [Mrs.
Walter Munroe] (d 1902 [39])
EA/03*
MUNROE, Harry (d 1875 [32])
comic singer EA/76*
MUNROE, J. L. (d 1856?) Amer-
ican actor HAS
MUNROE, Kate [Mrs. Miles]
(1848-87) American singer,
actress CDP, NYM, OAA/
1-2
MUNROE, Katherine see Munroe,
Kate
MUNROE, Walter actor, singer
CDP
MUNSAL, F. A. (b 1822) Ameri-
can actor HAS
MUNSEL, Patrice (b 1925) Amer-
ican actress, singer BE, CB
MUNSELL, J. (b 1825) American
actor HAS
MUNSELL, Jeanette (d 1974 [84])
performer BP/60*
MUNSELL, Warren P. (b 1889)
American executive, director,
manager, actor BE
MUNSELL, Warren P., Jr. (d
1952 [37]) American dramatist,
manager BE*, BP/37*
MUNSHIN, Jules (1915-70) Amer-
ican actor BE, TW/2-3, 7-13,
16-18, 22-23, 26
MUNSON, Ona (1906-55) American
actress, singer TW/11, WWT/
6-11
MUNTO, Mr. (fl 1793) actor HAS
MUNYARD, James Henry (d 1850
[35]) comedian CDP
MURA, Corinna (d 1965 [55]) per-
former BP/50*
MURATORE, Lucien (d 1954)
French singer WWA/3
MURCELL, George (b 1925)
Italian actor, director WWT/
15-16
MURCH, Robert G. (b 1935)
American actor TW/26-30
MURCOYNE, Margaret see

Burke, Mrs. Charles A.
MURDOCH, Daisy Adele (d 1887
[18]) actress, singer CDP
MURDOCH, Frank actor CDP
MURDOCH, Frank Hitchcock (1843-
72) American actor, dramatist
DAB, HJD, OC/1-3
MURDOCH, Harry Stark (1845-76)
actor CDP
MURDOCH, Irene actress CDP
MURDOCH, Iris (b 1919) Irish
dramatist CD
MURDOCH, James Edward (1811-93)
American actor CDP, COC,
DAB, HAS, OC/1-3, SR, WWA/H
MURDOCH, John (fl 1783) dramatist
CP/3
MURDOCH, Mortimer (d 1908 [86])
actor, dramatist GRB/4
MURDOCH, Richard (b 1907) Eng-
lish actor WWT/10-16
MURDOCH, Samuel K. (b 1821)
American actor HAS
MURDOCK, Ann [Irene Coleman]
(b 1890) American actress
WWM, WWT/4-6
MURDOCK, Henry (1902-71) Amer-
ican critic BE, WWA/5
MURDOCK, J. (fl 1795?) dramatist
EAP
MURDOCK, John J. (1865-1949)
American manager SR
MURDOCK, Kermit (b 1908) Amer-
ican actor TW/24
MURDOCK, Mortimer (b 1815) Eng-
lish actor, dramatist SR
MURFIN, Jane (d 1955 [62]) Amer-
ican dramatist WWT/7-8
MURIEL, Will (d 1909 [52]) per-
former? EA/10*
MURIELLE, Constance (d 1887) ac-
tress NYM
MURILLA, Edith actress, singer
CDP
MURPHY, Arthur (1727-1805) Irish
actor, dramatist CDP, COC,
CP/1-3, DNB, GT, HP, OC/1-3,
SR, TD/1-2
MURPHY, Arthur Lister (b 1906)
Canadian dramatist CD
MURPHY, Audie (d 1971 [46]) per-
former BP/55*
MURPHY, Christopher (b 1944)
American actor TW/28
MURPHY, C. W. (d 1913 [38])
English composer GRB/1
MURPHY, Danny (d 1966 [75]) per-
former BP/51*

MURPHY, Delia (d 1971 [68])
performer BP/55*
MURPHY, Donald (b 1920)
American actor TW/1-13
MURPHY, Eliza [Mrs. Bill
Powell] (d 1900 [88]) EA/01*
MURPHY, Ella [Mrs. P. Murphy]
(d 1891 [38]) actress, music-
hall performer CDP
MURPHY, Frank M. (d 1970 [59])
executive BP/55*
MURPHY, Gerry (b 1934) Amer-
ican actor TW/27-28
MURPHY, Guffer (d 1964 [64])
performer BP/49*
MURPHY, James (1725-59) Irish
dramatist DNB
MURPHY, Jennie see Calef,
Jennie
MURPHY, John Daly (1873-1934)
Irish actor SR, WWM
MURPHY, John E. (b 1855)
actor, minstrel CDP
MURPHY, John T. (d 1964 [64])
performer BE*
MURPHY, Joseph (d 1916 [83])
American minstrel, actor,
manager CDP, SR
MURPHY, Juliette (d 1973 [71])
performer BP/58*
MURPHY, Lillian see Calef,
Lillian
MURPHY, Mark (1855-1917)
actor SR
MURPHY, Mary (d 1887) EA/89*
MURPHY, Mrs. P. see Murphy,
Ella
MURPHY, Paddy (d 1917) come-
dian, dancer CDP
MURPHY, Pat (d 1917) comedian,
dancer EA/18*
MURPHY, Pat see Bodie, Jack
MURPHY, Rosemary (b 1927)
German/American actress
AAS, BE, TW/20-21, 23-25,
27, WWT/15-16
MURPHY, Seamus American actor
TW/25
MURPHY, Thomas (b 1935) Irish
dramatist CD
MURPHY, Tim (d 1928 [67])
American actor WWM
MURPHY, W. H. (d 1912 [60])
musician, singer EA/13*
MURRAY, Mrs. [nee Parker]
English actress HAS
MURRAY, Mrs. see Nicholls,
Elizabeth

MURRAY, Miss see Siddons,
Mrs. Henry
MURRAY, Miss (fl 1860?) actress
CDP
MURRAY, Miss (d 1905) EA/06*
MURRAY, Ada (d 1913 [74]) actress
WWT/14*
MURRAY, Alma (1854/55/56-1945)
English actress COC, DP,
GRB/1-4, OAA/1-2, OC/3,
WWT/1-9, WWW/4
MURRAY, Arthur (d 1918 [24])
EA/19*
MURRAY, Arthur B. actor EA/96
MURRAY, Barbara (b 1929) English
actress WWT/15-16
MURRAY, Braham [né Goldstein]
(b 1943) English director WWT/
15-16
MURRAY, Brian [né Bell] (b 1937/
39) South African actor AAS,
TW/25-26, 28-30, WWT/14-16
MURRAY, Charles (1754-1821)
English dramatist, actor CDP,
CP/2-3, DNB, GT, TD/1-2
MURRAY, Mrs. Charles see
Victor, Ethel
MURRAY, Charlie (1872-1941)
American comedian CB
MURRAY, David Christie (1847-
1907) English actor GRB/3,
WWW/1
MURRAY, Dominick [né Moran] (fl
1853-69) Irish actor CDP, HAS,
OAA/2
MURRAY, Don (b 1929) American
actor CB, TW/7-13
MURRAY, Douglas (d 1936 [73])
dramatist WWT/4-8
MURRAY, Edward (d 1878 [49])
acting manager EA/79*
MURRAY, Elizabeth [Mrs. Leigh
Murray] (d 1892 [77]) actress
CDP, DNB, OAA/2
MURRAY, Elizabeth M. (d 1946
[75]) comedienne TW/2
MURRAY, Emma (d 1843) actress
CDP
MURRAY, Esther Jane (d 1875)
actress CDP
MURRAY, Euphemia see Ellsler,
Mrs. John A.
MURRAY, Fanny see Murray,
Mary Frances
MURRAY, Gaston [Garstin Parker
Wilson] (1826-89) English actor
CDP, DNB, OAA/1-2
MURRAY, Mrs. Gaston see

Murray, Mary Frances
MURRAY, George Cecil (b 1851)
Scottish actor GRB/1
MURRAY, George Gilbert Aimé
(1866-1957) Australian drama-
tist, scholar COC, DNB, ES,
GRB/2-4, HP, NTH, OC/3,
WWA/3, WWT/1-12, WWW/5
MURRAY, Gladys (d 1967 [65])
performer BP/52*
MURRAY, G. W. [George Barker]
(d 1878) comic singer EA/80*
MURRAY, Henry Leigh (1820-70)
English actor CDP, DNB
MURRAY, Henry Valentine (d
1963 [71]) performer BE*
MURRAY, Isabel (d 1879) dancer
EA/80*
MURRAY, James (d 1878 [42])
minstrel? EA/79*
MURRAY, J. Harold (1891-1940)
American actor, singer CB,
WWT/7-9
MURRAY, J. K. [George Edward
Sykes] (d 1905 [64]) English
actor, dramatist, manager,
singer GRB/1, WWS
MURRAY, Mrs. J. K. see
Lane, Clara
MURRAY, John (d 1889 [70])
American actor EA/90*
MURRAY, John (b 1906) American
dramatist, lyricist, composer
BE
MURRAY, John H. (1829-81)
circus manager CDP
MURRAY, John J. (d 1924)
clown, manager, performer
BE*, BP/8*
MURRAY, John W. (d 1868 [30])
actor? EA/69*
MURRAY, Julia [Mrs. Samuel
Brandram] (d 1907) actress
WWT/14*
MURRAY, Katherine (d 1974
[80]) performer BP/60*
MURRAY, Kathleen (1932-69)
American actress TW/16, 26
MURRAY, Mrs. Leigh see
Murray, Elizabeth
MURRAY, Lillian [Mrs. T. B.
Brabazon] English actress
GRB/1
MURRAY, Lucy [Finette Raymur]
(d 1880) acrobat EA/81*
MURRAY, Mae (1889-1965)
American actress, dancer
ES, TW/21

MURRAY, Mary Frances [Mrs.
Gaston Murray] (d 1891 [61])
German/English actress DNB,
DP, OAA/1-2
MURRAY, Michael (b 1932) Ameri-
can director BE
MURRAY, Montague (d 1880) Aus-
tralian actor EA/81*
MURRAY, Paul (1885-1949) Irish
manager WWT/6-7
MURRAY, Peg American actress
TW/23-30, WWT/16
MURRAY, Percy [Percival H. T.
Sykes] (b 1870) English actor
GRB/1
MURRAY, Peter (b 1925) English
actor TW/4, WWT/11
MURRAY, Slade actor, singer CDP
MURRAY, Stephen (b 1912) English
actor AAS, WWT/8-16
MURRAY, T[homas] C[ornelius]
(1873-1959) Irish dramatist
COC, MD, MWD, OC/1-3, RE,
WWT/2-10, WWW/5
MURRAY, Thomasina Pringle [Mrs.
W. A. Davies] (d 1896 [27])
EA/98*
MURRAY, Tom (d 1895 [40]) whistler
EA/96*
MURRAY, Walter (fl 18th cent) ac-
tor, manager COC, OC/3, SR
MURRAY, Will (d 1955 [77]) actor,
director, producer BE*, WWT/
14*
MURRAY, William Henry (d 1852
[62]) actor, manager CDP
MURRAY, Wynn (d 1957 [35])
American actress, singer TW/
13
MURREL, Roger E. (d 1973 [86])
vaudeville agent BP/57*
MURTAGH, Thomas (d 1886) EA/
87*
MURTAUGH, James (b 1942) Amer-
ican actor TW/25
MURTON, Henry (d 1876 [34]) actor
EA/77*
MUSANTE, Mrs. John Wilson see
Waring, Bertha
MUSANTE, Tony (b 1936) American
actor TW/23, 28
MUSAPHIA, Joseph (b 1935) New
Zealand dramatist CD
MUSGRAVE, Frank (d 1888 [54])
composer, conductor EA/89*
MUSGRAVE, Frank see Goree,
Frederick
MUSGRAVE, Will (fl 1900?) actor,

singer CDP
MUSGROVE, Cpt. Forbes (d
1906) EA/07*
MUSGROVE, George (1854-1916)
Australian manager GRB/1-3
MUSGROVE, Mrs. George see
Stewart, Nellie
MUSGROVE, Gertrude (b 1912)
English actress, singer WWT/
9-10
MUSGROVE, Stuart (d 1916 [28])
EA/17*
MUSKERRY, William (d 1918)
dramatist BE*, WWT/14*
MUSKERRY-TILSON, W. (d 1918)
EA/19*
MUSSAY, Ethel Gordon see
Batley, Mrs. Ernest G.
MUSSER, Tharon (b 1925) Amer-
ican lighting designer BE,
WWT/16
MUSSET, Alfred de (1810-57)
French dramatist COC, OC/3
MUSSIERE, Lucien (d 1972 [82])
performer BP/57*
MUSSULMO, Mahomet Achmed
Vizaro (fl 1637) Turkish tight-
rope walker CDP
MUTCH, James E. (d 1974 [84])
performer BP/58*
MUZIO, Sig. (fl 1865) musician
HAS
MUZIO, Claudia (1889/92-1936)
Italian singer ES, WWA/1
MUZIO, Emanuele (d 1890 [65])
conductor EA/91*
MUZZY, Charles (d 1852) actor
HAS
MUZZY, Mrs. Charles actress
HAS
MUZZY, Helen see Muzzy,
Mrs. Charles
MUZZY, William American actor?
HAS
MYDELL, Joseph (b 1945) Amer-
ican actor TW/29
MYERBERG, Michael (1906-74)
American producer, agent
BE, TW/30
MYERS, Mr. (d 1859 [85]) actor
HAS
MYERS, Mrs. (d 1853) actress?
HAS
MYERS, Annie see Phillips,
Mrs. J. B.
MYERS, Bessie Allen (d 1964)
American performer BE*
MYERS, Beverly H. (d 1976 [49])

performer BP/60*
MYERS, Cecilia Dora [Mrs. Wil-
liam Myers] (d 1889) EA/90*
MYERS, Frederick S. (1816-48)
American actor HAS
MYERS, Harry C. (1882-1938)
American actor BE*
MYERS, James (d 1855) clown
HAS
MYERS, Mrs. James see Myers,
Rosaltha
MYERS, James Washington (d 1892
[69]) circus proprietor EA/94*
MYERS, John Edgar (d 1885) actor
EA/86*
MYERS, Joseph C. (b 1818) Amer-
ican actor, manager CDP, HAS,
SR
MYERS, J. R. (b 1810) American
minstrel HAS
MYERS, Louis (d 1916 [53]) EA/
17*
MYERS, Louise (fl 1866?) singer
CDP
MYERS, Michaele (d 1974 [49])
American actress TW/25-26
MYERS, Pamela (b 1947) American
actress TW/26-28
MYERS, Paul (b 1917) American
librarian, stage manager, actor
BE
MYERS, Pauline American actress
TW/2, 10
MYERS, Peter (b 1923) English
lyricist, dramatist AAS, WWT/
12-16
MYERS, Richard (b 1901) American
producing manager, composer
BE, TW/2, 4-8, WWT/10-15
MYERS, Rosaltha [Mrs. James
Myers] (d 1907 [63]) EA/08*
MYERS, Samuel (fl 1849) American
actor HAS
MYERS, William (d 1856) American
clown CDP, HAS
MYERS, William (d 1892) actor,
journalist EA/93*
MYERS, Mrs. William see
Myers, Cecilia Dora
MYERS, William H. (d 1860)
American actor HAS
MYHERS, John (b 1924) American
actor, singer, director BE,
TW/16
MYLDEVALE, Thomas (fl 1423)
member of the Chapel Royal
DA
MYLES, Lynda actress TW/24-28

MYLNE, James (1737-c. 90) Scottish dramatist CP/3
MYLONG, John (d 1975 [82])
performer BP/60*
MYNOTT, Mrs. (d 1890 [81])
EA/91*
MYRON, D. (b 1828) American
actor HAS
MYRTIL, Odette (b 1898) French
actress, violinist BE, TW/
2-4, WWT/4-14

- N -

N., L. (fl 1735) dramatist CP/3
N., M. (fl 1706) dramatist CP/
1-3
N., N. (fl 1681) dramatist CP/3
NABBES, Thomas (fl 1637-40)
dramatist CP/1-3, DNB, FGF
NADAJAN (d 1974) performer
BP/59*
NADEL, Norman (b 1915) American critic BE, WWT/15-16
NADIR, Moses (1885-1943) American dramatist OC/1-3
NAGEL, Claire (d 1921 [25])
American actress BE*, BP/6*
NAGEL, Conrad (1897-1970)
American actor, director
BE, ES, SR, TW/1-20, 26,
WWA/5, WWT/8-14
NAGIAH, V. (d 1973 [70]) performer BP/58*
NAGLE, Mrs. see Cramer,
Fanny
NAGLE, Archibald (d 1899) director EA/00*
NAGLE, Joseph E. (b 1828)
actor CDP
NAGLE, Joseph E. (b 1828)
American actor HAS
NAGLE, Mrs. Joseph E. [Mary
Logue] (fl 1847) actress HAS
NAGLE, Kate (fl 1858-59) Irish
actress HAS
NAGLE, Rev. Urban (d 1965
[59]) dramatist BP/49*
NAGLER, A. M. (b 1907) Austrian educator, historian BE
NAGRIN, Daniel (b 1921) American actor TW/6-8, 11-14
NAGY, Bill (d 1973) performer
BP/57*
NAGY, Dr. Elmer (d 1972 [65])
producer/director/choreographer
BP/56*

NAIDOO, Bobby (d 1967 [40]) performer BP/52*
NAIL, Joanne (b 1947) American
actress TW/27, 29-30
NAIL, John (d 1905) EA/07*
NAILER, Miss (fl 1770?) CDP
NAILL, Mahlon (b 1912) American
actor TW/2
NAINBY, Robert (1869-1948) Irish
actor GRB/1-2, WWT/4-9
NAIRN, Ralph (d 1934 [61]) Scottish
comedian BE*, BP/19*
NAISH, J. Carrol (1901-73) American actor BE, CB, TW/29
NAISMITH, Laurence [né Johnson]
(b 1908) English actor BE,
TW/20, 22-23, 25, WWT/12-16
NALDI, Giuseppe (1765-1820)
singer, actor CDP
NALDI, Nita (1899/1900-1961)
American actress ES, TW/9-14,
17
NALOD, Edward (1857-1919) American actor SR
"NANEYS GOWN" see Clark,
Mrs.
NANKEVILLE, William (d 1911)
manager WWT/14*
NANNETTI, Romano (c. 1845-1910)
Italian singer ES
NANO, Sig. Hervio see Leach,
Hervey
NANSEN, Betty (d 1943 [67]) actress BE*, WWT/14*
NANTON, Lewis (d 1871 [31])
dramatist, actor EA/72*
NANTON, Mrs. Lewis [Pauline
Burette] (d 1888) actress EA/
89*
NAPHTALI, Israel (d 1886 [86])
EA/87*
NAPIER, Alan (b 1903) English actor TW/10, 13, WWT/7-13
NAPIER, Frank (d 1949 [45]) actor,
director BE*, WWT/14*
NAPIER, Mrs. Frederick Craig
(d 1912) EA/13*
NAPIER, John (b 1926) American
actor TW/17-19
NAPIER, John (b 1944) English designer WWT/16
NAPIERKOWSKA, Stanislawa Turkish dancer WWT/4
NAPOLI, Joseph (b 1940) American
actor TW/27-29
NARDINO, Gary (b 1935) American
talent & literary representative
BE

NARELLE, Marie (1874?-1941)
Australian singer CB
NARES, Geoffrey (1917-42) English actor, designer WWT/9
NARES, Owen (1888-1943) English actor, producer AAS,
CB, COC, ES, OC/1-3,
WWT/2-9, WWW/4
NARONI, Mlle. [Mrs. Leopold
Leghere] (d 1911 [48]) EA/12*
NARPIER, Mrs. A. B. see
Theodore, Mlle.
NASH, Miss (b 1797) singer CDP
NASH, Miss see Davis, Mrs.
Henry
NASH, Florence (1888-1950) American actress TW/6, WWT/4-8
NASH, George Frederick (1866-1944) American actor SR,
TW/1, WWT/4-9
NASH, Harry (d 1894 [41]) proprietor EA/95*
NASH, John (1828-1901) English
music-hall artist CDP, OC/
1-2
NASH, Louis Joseph (d 1901 [40])
EA/02*
NASH, Mary (1885-1965?) American actress BE, WWT/4-9
NASH, N. Richard (b 1913/16)
American dramatist AAS,
BE, MD, MH, MWD, PDT,
WWT/16
NASH, Ogden (1902-71) American
lyricist BE, CB, HJD, WWA/5
NASHE, Thomas (1567-1601) English dramatist COC, CP/1-3,
DNB, FGF, HP, NTH, OC/
1-3
NASON, Emma (d 1916 [80])
EA/17*
NASSAU, Paul (b 1930) American
composer, lyricist BE
NASSOUR, Edward (d 1962 [45])
American producer, inventor
BE*
NASTASI, Frank (b 1923) American actor TW/24, 27
NATALI, Agnes [née Heron] (fl
1848-60) American actress,
singer CDP, HAS
NATALI, Fanny [née Heron] (fl
1848-60) American actress,
singer CDP, HAS
NATANSON, Jacques dramatist
WWT/9
NATHAN, Baron (d 1856 [63])
master of ceremonies EA/72*

NATHAN, Ben (1857/59-1919) Scottish agent GRB/1-3
NATHAN, Benjamin (d 1892) American manager EA/93*
NATHAN, George Jean (1882-1958)
American critic AAS, CB, COC,
ES, HJD, HP, NTH, OC/1-3,
PDT, TW/14, WWA/3, WWT/4-
12, WWW/5
NATHAN, Rose (d 1872 [43]) actress EA/73*
NATHAN, Vivian (b 1921) American
actress BE, TW/23, 25, 30
NATION, Henry (fl 1574) actor DA
NATION, W. H. C. (1843-1914)
English manager, composer,
dramatist GRB/2-4, WWT/1-2
NATION, William, Jr. (fl 1789)
dramatist CP/3
NATIONAL THEATRE CO. producing
manager WWT/14-15
NATURAL THEATRE, The theatre
collective CD
NATWICK, Mildred (b 1908) American actress AAS, BE, TW/2-21,
26-27, WWT/9-16
NAU, Dolores (1818-91) actress,
singer CDP, HAS
NAUDAIN, May (1880-1923) American actress WWS
NAUDIN, Emilio (1823-90) Italian
singer ES
NAUGHTON, Bill (b 1910) Irish
dramatist AAS, CD, CH, RE,
WWT/14-16
NAUGHTON, Charles (d 1976 [89])
performer BP/60*
NAUGHTON, James (b 1945) American actor TW/27-28
NAVARRO, Mrs. see Zulima,
Mme.
NAVARRO, Carlos (d 1969 [47])
performer BP/53*
NAVARRO, Emilio (d 1903 [57])
circus performer EA/04*
NAVARRO, John (fl 1635) actor
DA
NAVARRO, Mary de see Anderson, Mary
NAYLOR, Henry (d 1879 [61]) actor,
pantomimist, prompter EA/80*
NAYLOR, John (d 1898) showman
EA/99*
NAYLOR, Robert (b 1899) English
actor, singer WWT/7-10
NAYLOR, Sidney (d 1893 [52]) musician EA/94*
NAYLOR, William (d 1888 [76])

stage manager EA/89*

NAYLOR, William Frederick (d 1878 [60]) EA/79*

NAZIMOVA, Alla (1878/79-1945) Russian/American actress AAS, CB, COC, DAB, ES, GRB/3-4, NTH, OC/1-3, PDT, SR, TW/2, WWA/2, WWM, WWS, WWT/1-9

NAZZO, Angelo (b 1939) Indian actor TW/25-26

NEAFIE, Andrew Jackson (1815-92) American actor CDP, HAS

NEAGLE, Dame Anna [Marjorie Robertson] (b 1904) English actress, singer, dancer AAS, BE, CB, COC, ES, WWT/7-16

NEAL, Charles Edward (d 1917) carpenter EA/18*

NEAL, John (1793-1876) American dramatist EAP

NEAL, Patricia (b 1926) American actress BE, CB, ES, TW/3-4, 6, 9-19, WWT/13-14

NEAL, Tom (d 1972 [58/59]) actor BP/57*, WWT/16*

NEAL, Walter (b 1920) American stage manager, actor BE

NEALE, Frederick (d 1856) producer, dramatist, manager BE*, WWT/14*

NEALE, Lille Dillon (d 1889 [4]) gymnast EA/90*

NEALE, Thomas (fl 1637?) dramatist FGF

NEALE, W. Vaughan Greek stage flyer GRB/1

NEALIE, Mary (b 1949) American actress TW/30

NEARY, Sime (d 1971 [77]) performer BP/56*

NEATE, Charles (d 1877 [93]) musician EA/78*

NEATT, Fred see Weston, Harold

NEBIOL, Gary (b 1943) American actor TW/29

NED (fl 1590) actor DA

NED (fl 1592) clown DA

NEDD, Stuart (b 1915) American actor TW/2

NEDELL, Bernard (1897-1972) American actor, producer, director BE, WWT/7-13

NEDERLANDER, David T. (d 1967 [81]) executive BP/52*

NEDERLANDER, James (b 1922)

American theatre owner, producer BE, WWT/16

NEDHAM, Marchmont (1620-78) English dramatist CP/2-3

NEEBE, Fred E. H. (d 1897 [54]) manager EA/98*

NEEDHAM, Vincent Loraine (d 1916) musician EA/17*

NEEDHAM, William (d 1903 [41]) conductor EA/04*

NEEL, Mr. (fl 1851) actor HAS

NEELY, Henry M. (d 1963 [84]) actor, director BE*

NEGRO, Mary-Joan (b 1948) American actress TW/30

NEGRO ENSEMBLE CO. theatre collective CD

NEHRER, John W. (d 1972 [61]) performer BP/56*

NEIDLINGER, William Harold (1863-1924) American composer WWA/1

NEIGHBORS, George American actor TW/17-19

NEIL, Jimmy (d 1976 [58]) performer BP/60*

NEIL, Ross [Isabella Harwood] (d 1888 [48]) dramatist BE*, WWT/14*

NEILAN, Marshall (1891-1958) American director, actor BE*

NEILD, Samuel (d 1873 [54]) comic dwarf EA/74*

NEILE, Rufus W. singer CDP

NEILE, William Cyrus (d 1874 [25]) singer, minstrel EA/75*

NEILL, James (d 1931 [70]) actor BE*, BP/15*

NEILL, James (d 1962 [65]) American actor BE*

NEILL, Mrs. James see Chapman, Edythe

NEILL, Richard R. (d 1970 [94]) performer BP/54*

NEILSON, Ada [Mrs. Allen Thomas] (1846-1905) actress GRB/1

NEILSON, Adelaide (1846-80) English actress CDP, COC, DNB, ES, NTH, OAA/1-2, OC/1-3, SR

NEILSON, Francis (1867-1961) English/American dramatist, director WWT/1-3, WWW/6

NEILSON, Harold V. (1874-1956) English actor, manager WWT/5-10

NEILSON, James Gardner (d 1872 [44]) comedian EA/73*

NEILSON, Julia [Mrs. Fred Terry] (1868/69-1957) English actress COC, DNB, DP, EA/94, ES, GRB/1-4, OC/1-3, WWM, WWT/1-11, WWW/5

NEILSON, Perlita [née Margaret Sowden] (b 1933) English actress WWT/13-16

NEILSON-TERRY, Dennis (1895-1932) English actor ES, WWT/2-6

NEILSON-TERRY, Julia (1868-1957) English actress TW/13

NEILSON-TERRY, Phyllis (1892-1977) English actress AAS, BE, ES, TW/13-15, WWT/1-14

NEIMAN, Adolf (d 1902) EA/03*

NEIMAN, Fred (d 1910 [50]) ventriloquist, variety agent EA/12*

NEIMAN, John M. (b 1935) English press representative WWT/13-14

NeJAME, George (b 1953) American actor TW/24

NELIGAN, Donal (d 1975 [27]) performer BP/60*

NELLIGAN, Kate (b 1951) English actress WWT/16

NELLIS, S. K. G. (1817-65) American freak CDP, HAS

NELMS, Henning (b 1900) American director BE

NELSON, Mr. (fl 1850) American actor HAS

NELSON, Alfred (d 1894 [64]) professor of elocution EA/95*

NELSON, Alice Brainerd (d 1963 [79]) director BE*

NELSON, Annette see Brougham, Mrs. John, I

NELSON, Arthur (d 1860 [49]) clown EA/72*

NELSON, Barry [né Robert Nielson] (b 1925) American actor AAS, BE, TW/6-15, 22-26, 29, WWT/12-16

NELSON, Carrie (d 1916 [80]) actress, singer HAS

NELSON, Christopher (b 1944) American actor TW/28-29

NELSON, Ed (d 1969 [84]) composer/lyricist BP/53*

NELSON, Edith (d 1970 [78]) performer BP/55*

NELSON, Eliza [Mrs. H. T. Craven] (d 1908 [81]) actress GRB/4

NELSON, Florence [Mrs. John A. Atkin] English actress GRB/1

NELSON, Francis Arthur St. George (d 1916 [24]) EA/17*

NELSON, Gail American actress TW/27, 30

NELSON, Gene (b 1920) American actor, dancer, singer, director TW/5-9, 27-30, WWT/16

NELSON, Gordon (d 1956 [58]) actor TW/12

NELSON, Harold (d 1901 [35]) manager EA/02*

NELSON, Mrs. Harry Adair see Nelson, Nellie

NELSON, Harry G. (d 1908) actor EA/09*, WWT/14*

NELSON, Haywood, Jr. (b 1960) American actor TW/30

NELSON, Henry (b 1843) English actor, stage manager GRB/1

NELSON, Herbert (b 1913) American actor TW/29

NELSON, James (d 1794 [83]) English dramatist CP/3

NELSON, Joan (b 1943) American actress TW/28-29

NELSON, John (d 1879 [49]) actor EA/80*, WWT/14*

NELSON, John (d 1972 [74]) performer BP/56*

NELSON, Mrs. John see Leclercq, Carlotta

NELSON, Kenneth (b 1930) American actor BE, TW/8-9, 23-25, 27, WWT/15-16

NELSON, Millie Catherine see Blanche, Mme.

NELSON, Nellie [Mrs. Harry Adair Nelson] (d 1898) manager EA/99*

NELSON, Oliver (d 1975 [43]) performer BP/60*

NELSON, Ozzie (d 1975 [69]) actor BP/60*, WWT/16*

NELSON, Peggy (b 1930) American actress TW/8

NELSON, Raymond (b 1898) American manager, treasurer BE

NELSON, Ruth (b 1905) American actress TW/26, 28, WWT/15-16

NELSON, Sarah (fl 1860-62) actress, singer HAS

NELSON, Sidney (d 1862 [62]) composer EA/72*

NELSON, Mrs. Sidney (d 1880) EA/81*

NELSON, Skip (d 1974 [53]) performer BP/58*

NELSON, Tom (d 1918) EA/19*

NELSON, Violet actress, singer
CDP

NELSON, Virginia Tallent (d
1968 [57]) performer BP/53*

NELSON SISTERS, The (fl 1860-
62) HAS

NELTHORPE, Mrs. A. R. (d
1917) EA/18*

NEMCHINOVA, Vera dancer
WWT/9-11

NEMETZ, Lee (d 1963) producer
BP/47*

NEMIROFF, Robert librettist
CD

NEMIROVITCH-DANTCHENKO,
Vladimir Ivanovich (d 1943
[85]) Russian actor, producer
BP/27*

NENO, George singer, actor
CDP

NERI, Gaetano (1821-52) Italian
actor HAS

NERI, Mme. Gaetano (fl c. 1850)
dancer? actress? HAS

NERINA, Nadia (b 1927) South
African dancer CB, ES

NERREY, Jessie (d 1906) EA/08*

NERVO, Jimmy (d 1975 [78])
music-hall performer BP/
60*, WWT/16*

NESBIT, G. (fl 1733) Scottish
dramatist CP/2-3, GT

NESBITT, Cathleen (b 1888/89)
English actress AAS, BE,
CB, ES, TW/6-19, 29-30,
WWT/2-16

NESBITT, Max (d 1966 [63])
performer BP/50*

NESBITT, Miriam Anne (b 1879/
80) American actress GRB/
3-4, WWM, WWS, WWT/1-5

NESBITT, Robert (b 1906) English dramatist, producer
AAS, WWT/9-16

NESBITT, Tom (1890-1927)
English actor BE*, WWT/14*

NESMITH, Ottola (b 1893) American actress WWT/4-5

NESTEL, Charles W. see
Foote, Commodore

NESTEL, Eliza see Fairy Queen

NESTOR, Mrs. (b 1824) American
dancer HAS

NESTOR, Al (b 1920) American
actor TW/26

NESTOR, George (b 1935) American
actor TW/25

NESTROY, Johann Nepomuk (1801-
62) Austrian actor, dramatist
COC

NESVILLE, Juliette (d 1900 [30])
actress, singer EA/01*, WWT/
14*

NETCHER, Roszika (d 1970 [71])
performer BP/54*

NETHE, John (fl 1550) actor DA

NETHERSALL, John (fl 1550)
actor DA

NETHERSOLE, Louis (d 1936 [71])
producer, press representative,
manager BE*, WWT/14*

NETHERSOLE, Mrs. Louis F.
see Martinot, Sadie

NETHERSOLE, Olga Isabel (1863/
70-1951) English actress DP,
ES, GRB/1-4, OC/3, TW/7,
WWA/3, WWM, WWS, WWT/1-
11, WWW/5

NETTLEFOLD, Archibald (1870-
1944) English manager WWT/6-8

NETTLEFOLD, Frederick John
(1867-1949) English actor, manager WWT/4-8

NETTLETON, John (b 1929) English
actor WWT/15-16

NETTLETON, Lois American actress BE, TW/29-30, WWT/16

NEUBURGER, Sigmund see Lafayette

NEUENDORF, Mme. (1850-1914)
German singer SR

NEUENDORFF, Adolph Heinrich
Anton Magnus (1843-97) German
musician, conductor, impresario
DAB, WWA/H

NEUMAN, H. (fl 1798-99) translator CP/3

NEUMANN, Elisabeth (b 1906)
Austrian actress TW/3

NEUMANN, F. Wight (1851-1924)
German impresario WWA/1

NEVADA, Aimée (d 1903) actress
EA/04*

NEVADA, Emma (1861-1940) American singer CDP, DAB, WWA/5

NEVERE, Norah (d 1891 [21])
music-hall performer EA/92*

NEVERIST, Kate [Mrs. J. C.
Shepherd] (d 1896) actress,
singer EA/97*

NEVILE, Robert (d 1694) dramatist
CP/1-3, DNB, FGF, GT

NEVILL, Alexander (1544-1614)

English dramatist CP/1-3
NEVILLE (fl 1779) dramatist
CP/2-3, GT
NEVILLE, Mr. (fl 1840?) actor
CDP
NEVILLE, Charlotte [Sophie Char-
lotte Garbois; Mrs. W. H.
Garbois] (d 1891) EA/92*
NEVILLE, Emily see Loder,
Mrs. , II
NEVILLE, Fred (d 1899) minstrel
EA/00*
NEVILLE, Harry (d 1945 [77])
actor TW/1
NEVILLE, Henry (d 1694) English
dramatist CP/2-3
NEVILLE, Henry [Henry Gart-
side] (1837-1910) English actor
CDP, DNB, DP, GRB/1-4,
OAA/1-2, OC/1-3, WWW/1
NEVILLE, John (b 1925) English
actor, director, manager AAS,
BE, CB, COC, ES, TW/13-15,
WWT/12-16
NEVILLE, John Gartside (d 1874
[87]) actor, manager EA/75*,
WWT/14*
NEVILLE, Katie (d 1964 [94])
performer BP/49*
NEVILLE, Mary C. H. [Mrs.
George Gartside-Neville] (d
1899 [67]) EA/00*
NEVIN, Arthur Finley (1871-1943)
American composer HJD,
WWA/2, WWM
NEVIN, Gordon Balch (1892-1943)
American composer WWA/2
NEVIN, Hardwick (d 1965 [68])
dramatist BP/50*
NEVIN, P. J. (d 1893) stage
manager EA/94*
NEVINS, Claudette American ac-
tress TW/24-26
NEVIS, Ben (fl 1890s?) actor,
singer CDP
NEVIT, Thomas (d 1873 [36])
chairman EA/74*
NEWALL, Guy (1885-1937) Eng-
lish actor WWT/6-8
NEWARK, William (fl 1493-1509)
master of the Chapel Royal
DA
NEWAY, Patricia (b 1919) Amer-
ican singer, actress AAS,
BE, WWT/15-16
NEWBERRY, Barbara (b 1910)
American actress, dancer
WWT/8

NEWBORN, Abe (b 1920) American
talent representative BE
NEWBURG, Frank (d 1969 [83])
performer BP/54*
NEWBURN, George (d 1918) EA/19*
NEWBURY, Pollie [Mrs. Frederick
Wolstenholme] (d 1891 [27])
music-hall performer EA/92*
NEWBY, John J. (d 1876 [23]) mu-
sician EA/77*
NEWCASTLE, Duchess of see
Cavendish, Margaret
NEWCASTLE, Duke of see Caven-
dish, William
NEWCOMB, Bobby (1847-88) min-
strel CDP
NEWCOMB, George (d 1890 [54])
lion tamer EA/91*
NEWCOMB, Mary (1897-1966)
American actress TW/23, WWT/
6-12
NEWCOMB, William W. (1823/30-
77) American comedian, manager
CDP, HAS
NEWCOMBE, Albert (d 1881 [48])
acting manager, treasurer EA/
82*
NEWCOMBE, Arthur (d 1883 [34])
business manager EA/84*
NEWCOMBE, Caroline (d 1941 [69])
actress BE*, WWT/14*
NEWCOMBE, Effie singer CDP
NEWCOMBE, Jessamine (d 1961)
actress WWT/14*
NEWCOMBE, John Reilly (d 1887
[84]) lessee EA/86*
NEWCOMBE, Mabel [Frances Mabel
D'Erne] (d 1890 [25]) actress
EA/91*
NEWELL, Frank (b 1946) American
actor TW/25
NEWELL, Joan (b 1921) English
actress TW/4
NEWELL, Michael (b 1931) English
actor TW/4
NEWELL, Raymond (b 1894) Eng-
lish actor, singer WWT/7-11
NEWELL, Thomas (d 1899 [61])
actor EA/00*
NEWELL, Tom D. (d 1935 [45])
actor BE*, WWT/14*
NEWELL, William (d 1967 [73])
performer BP/51*
NEWES, Tilly (1886-1970) actress
COC
NEWHALL, Patricia American ac-
tress, director, producer BE
NEWHAM, Rose [Mrs. A. M.

Stuart] (d 1905) actress GRB/1
NEWHAM, Mrs. W. H. (d 1883)
EA/84*
NEWHAM, William (d 1870) come-
dian, pantaloon EA/71*
NEWHOUSE, Alice Lily see
Lena, Lily
NEWHOUSE, Willie (d 1911) trick
bicyclist EA/12*
NEWLAND, David (d 1879) property
master EA/80*
NEWLAND, Mary [Lilian Oldfield]
(b 1905) English actress WWT/
7-8
NEWLAND, Samuel (d 1867) Negro
comedian EA/68*
NEW LAYFAYETTE THEATRE
theatre collective CD
NEWLEY, Anthony (b 1931) Eng-
lish actor, director, composer,
writer, singer AAS, BE, CB,
CD, TW/19, 21-22, WWT/14-
16
NEWMAN, Mjr. A. A. (d 1908)
EA/09*
NEWMAN, Alfred (d 1970 [68])
composer/lyricist BP/54*
NEWMAN, Benjamin (d 1875)
carpenter EA/76*
NEWMAN, Claude (1903/08-74)
English dancer WWT/9-12
NEWMAN, Ellen (b 1950) Amer-
ican actress TW/29-30
NEWMAN, George (d 1871 [48])
comic singer EA/72*
NEWMAN, Greatrex (b 1892) Eng-
lish lyricist, librettist, drama-
tist BE, WWT/6-15
NEWMAN, Joseph J. (d 1967 [80])
ticket broker BP/52*
NEWMAN, Martin (b 1924) Amer-
ican actor TW/8-9, 27
NEWMAN, Paul (b 1925) Ameri-
can actor AAS, BE, CB,
ES, TW/9-21, WWT/13-15
NEWMAN, Phyllis (b 1935)
American actress, singer
BE, TW/15, 18-19, 23-24,
28-30, WWT/16
NEWMAN, Stephen D. (b 1943)
American actor TW/27-30
NEWMAN, Stuart see Ander-
son, Stuart
NEWMAN, Thomas (fl 1627)
translator CP/1-3
NEWMAN, Thomas Edmund see
Wenman, Thomas Edmund
NEWMAN, Mrs. W. see

Ormonde, Nelly
NEWMAN, Will (d 1905 [36]) actor,
singer CDP
NEWMAN, W. S. (d 1897) music-
hall comedian EA/98*
NEWMAR, Julie (b 1935) American
actress, singer, dancer BE,
TW/15
NEWNHAM-DAVIS, Lieut.-Col.
Nathaniel (1854-1917) English
critic, producer, dramatist
GRB/1-4, WWT/1-3
NEWSHAM, Mrs. (fl 1790) white
negress CDP
NEWSOM, Earl (d 1973 [75]) pub-
licist BP/57*
NEWSOME, Carman (d 1974 [62])
performer BP/59*
NEWSOME, James (d 1912 [87])
circus proprietor EA/13*
NEWSOME, Mrs. James see
Newsome, Pauline
NEWSOME, Pauline [Mrs. James
Newsome] (d 1904 [78]) EA/05*
NEWSOME, W. H. (d 1917 [73])
EA/18*
NEWSON-SMITH, Elizabeth [Mrs.
Henry Newson-Smith] (d 1898
[43]) EA/99*
NEWSON-SMITH, Henry (d 1898
[43]) music-hall director EA/99*
NEWSON-SMITH, Mrs. Henry see
Newson-Smith, Elizabeth
NEWTE, Horace Wykeham (d 1949
[80]) dramatist WWW/4
NEWTON, Adelaide [Mrs. George
Mudie] (d 1900) singer, actress
EA/01*, WWT/14*
NEWTON, Amelia [Mrs. Thomas
Thorne] (d 1884) actress WWT/
14*
NEWTON, Eliza (d 1882) Scottish
actress CDP, HAS
NEWTON, Elizabeth Blanche [Mrs.
Charles J. Barber] (d 1893)
EA/94*
NEWTON, George (d 1880) actor
EA/81*
NEWTON, Henry Chance (1854-
1931) English critic, dramatist,
lyricist GRB/1-4, WWT/1-6,
WWW/3
NEWTON, James (fl 1722) drama-
tist CP/2-3
NEWTON, John (d 1625) English
actor DA, OC/1-3
NEWTON, John (d 1872) comedian,
singer EA/73*

NEWTON, John (b 1925) American
actor TW/29-30
NEWTON, Kate (1842-73) actress
CDP, HAS
NEWTON, Kate (d 1940 [94])
actress BE*, WWT/14*
NEWTON, Richard (b 1911) Cana-
dian actor TW/3, 10
NEWTON, Robert (1905-56) Eng-
lish actor ES, TW/12, WWT/
9-11, WWW/5
NEWTON, Theodore (1904-63)
American actor TW/5-7, 19
NEWTON, Thomas (d 1607) Eng-
lish translator CP/1-3
NEY, Marie (b 1895) English ac-
tress AAS, WWT/5-14
NEYLIN, James (b 1920) Irish
actor TW/12-15
NGUGI, James T. (b 1938)
Nigerian dramatist CD
NIBLO, Fred (1874-1948) Amer-
ican actor, entertainer ES,
TW/5, WWM
NIBLO, William (1789-1878)
Irish/American manager CDP,
DAB, WWA/H
NICANDER, Edwin (1876-1951)
American actor TW/7, WWT/7
NICCOLS, [Richard] (b 1584)
dramatist CP/2-3, FGF
NICHOL, Charles (d 1894) actor
EA/95*
NICHOLAS (fl 1626-31) actor DA
NICHOLAS, Denise (d 1944) Amer-
ican actress TW/24
NICHOLAS, Fayard performer
TW/2
NICHOLAS, Harold performer
TW/2
NICHOLAS, Harry (fl 1574?)
dramatist CP/3
NICHOLL, William (d 1902 [50])
singer EA/03*
NICHOLLS, Agnes [Mrs. Hamilton
Harty] English singer GRB/1
NICHOLLS, Allan (b 1945) Cana-
dian actor TW/28-29
NICHOLLS, Anne (1891/96-1966)
American dramatist, producing
manager, actress BE, MH,
MWD, NTH, TW/23, WWA/4,
WWT/5-11
NICHOLLS, Anthony (b 1907)
English actor AAS, WWT/14-16
NICHOLLS, Bernhard Downs (d
1886) musician EA/87*
NICHOLLS, Elizabeth [Mrs. Mur-

ray] (d 1887 [55]) actress EA/
88*
NICHOLLS, Harry (1852-1926) Eng-
lish actor CDP, DP, GRB/1-4,
WWT/1-5, WWW/2
NICHOLLS, Richard (b 1900) Eng-
lish actor TW/25-26
NICHOLLS, W. Dutton (d 1917)
EA/18*
NICHOLS, Anne see Nicholls,
Anne
NICHOLS, Beatrice (d 1970 [78])
actress TW/27
NICHOLS, Beverley (b 1898/99)
composer, critic WWT/6-14
NICHOLS, Emma J. [née Davis]
(b 1841) American singer HAS
NICHOLS, George A. (b 1872)
American musical director
WWM
NICHOLS, Guy (d 1928 [65]) actor
BE*, BP/12*
NICHOLS, Master Horace circus
performer CDP
NICHOLS, Mrs. Horace F. [née
Barker; Mrs. Preston] (fl 1828)
American actress HAS
NICHOLS, Joseph V. (b 1846) glass
blower CDP
NICHOLS, Les (d 1964 [63]) per-
former BP/49*
NICHOLS, Lewis (b 1903) American
critic WWT/10-11
NICHOLS, Marjorie J. (d 1970)
performer BP/55*
NICHOLS, Mike (b 1931) German/
American actor, director AAS,
BE, CB, ES, WWT/14-16
NICHOLS, Noreen (b 1945) Ameri-
can actress TW/26
NICHOLS, Peter (b 1927) English
dramatist, director AAS, CD,
COC, MH, PDT, WWT/15-16
NICHOLS, Robert Malise Bowyer
(1893-1944) English dramatist
WWW/4
NICHOLS, William American actor
TW/4
NICHOLSON, Alfred (d 1870 [48])
musician EA/71*
NICHOLSON, Alfred C. (d 1909
[60]) professor of music EA/10*
NICHOLSON, Anne P. (b 1920)
American manager, dramatist
BE
NICHOLSON, Arthur W. (d 1882)
EA/83*
NICHOLSON, Charles (1795-1837)

musician, composer CDP
NICHOLSON, George (d 1907 [73])
proprietor EA/08*
NICHOLSON, G. W. singer, actor
CDP
NICHOLSON, Henry (d 1907 [83])
musician EA/08*
NICHOLSON, H. O. (b 1868)
Swedish actor WWT/4-9
NICHOLSON, Jack (d 1917) EA/
18*
NICHOLSON, James (d 1972 [56])
producer/director/choreographer
BP/57*
NICHOLSON, John (d 1916) come-
dian EA/17*
NICHOLSON, John (d 1934 [61])
American actor BE*, BP/19*
NICHOLSON, Kenyon (b 1894)
American dramatist BE,
NTH, WWT/6-13
NICHOLSON, Nora (1889/92-1973)
English actress AAS, WWT/
11-15
NICHOLSON, Norman (b 1914)
English dramatist CH
NICHOLSON, Renton (d 1861 [52])
EA/72*
NICHOLSON, Val (d 1898) musi-
cian EA/00*
NICHOLSON, Sir William (d 1949
[77]) designer, artist BE*,
WWT/14*
NICHOLSON, William Henry (d
1875 [28]) musician EA/76*
NICHTERN, Claire (b 1920)
American producer BE
NICK (fl 1590-1603) actor DA
NICKEL, Paul (d 1975 [35]) per-
former BP/60*
NICKERSON, Emily H. (d 1889)
American actress EA/90*
NICKERSON, Shane (b 1964)
American actor TW/29-30
NICKINSON, Charlotte (fl 1858-
64) actress CDP, HAS
NICKINSON, Isabella (1847-1906)
actress BE*
NICKINSON, John (1808-64) Eng-
lish actor, stage manager
CDP, HAS, SR
NICKINSON, Isabella see Wal-
cot, Isabella
NICKINSON, Virginia see
Marlowe, Mrs. Owen
NICKLE, Robert (b 1842) Ameri-
can magician CDP, HAS
NICKLIN, Horace Montgomery

(d 1880 [34]) actor, musician
EA/81*
NICKOLE, Leonidas (b 1929) Amer-
ican educator BE
NICOL, Mrs. (fl 1834) actress
CDP, DNB
NICOL, Alex (b 1919) American
actor, director BE
NICOL, Emma (1801-77) actress
DNB
NICOL, Lesslie Scottish actress
TW/23, 30
NICOLINI, Ernesto (1834-98) French
singer ES
NICOLL, Allardyce (1894-1976)
Scottish historian BE, COC,
ES, NTH, OC/1-3, PDT, WWT/
6-16
NICOLL, Basilius sharer DA
NICOLL, Harry N. (d 1962 [73])
vaudeville agent BE*
NICOLL, Oliver H. (d 1971 [67])
manager BP/56*
NICOLSON, T. Smyth see Beau-
fort, Leslie
NIDORF, Mike (d 1975 [60s]) agent
BP/60*
NIELSEN, Alice [Mrs. Benjamin
Wentwig] (1870/76-1943) Ameri-
can singer CDP, DAB, GRB/
1-4, PP/2, SR, WWA/2, WWM,
WWS, WWT/2-7
NIELSEN, Asta (d 1972 [90]) per-
former BP/57*
NIELSEN, Karl (d 1975 [85]?)
American stage manager BE
NIELSEN, Leslie (b 1926) Canadian
actor TW/9-10
NIELSON, Robert see Nelson,
Barry
NIEMEYER, Joseph H. (d 1965
[78]) performer BP/50*
NIESEN, Claire (d 1963 [40]) per-
former BP/48*
NIESEN, Gertrude (1910/17-75)
American actress, singer TW/
1-8, WWT/9-11
NIGHTINGALE, Alfred (d 1957
[67]) general manager BE*,
WWT/14*
NIGHTINGALE, Joe actor WWT/
4-6
NIGHTINGALE, John William (d
1911 [60]) proprietor EA/12*
NIGHTINGALE, W. H. (d 1841)
imitator EA/72*
NIJINSKA, Bronislava (1891-1972)
Russian dancer, choreographer

ES, WWT/9-11
NIJINSKY, Vaslav (1890-1950)
Russian dancer, choreographer
CB, ES, TW/6, WWA/4,
WWT/4, 10
NIKI, Mariko Japanese actor
TW/10-12
NIKITA, Louise (b 1872) singer
CDP
NIKITINA, Alice (b 1909) Russian
dancer ES, WWT/7-10
NIKOLA, Louis (b 1878) English
prestidigitateur & shadowgraphist
GRB/1
NIKOLAIS, Alwin (b 1912) Amer-
ican choreographer, composer,
designer CB, CD
NILES, Mary Ann (b 1933) Amer-
ican actress TW/21-30
NILES, P. James (1851-82)
singer, dancer CDP
NILL, John (fl 1601) actor DA
NILLO, David (b 1918) American
actor TW/2-3, 15-16, 24
NILLSON, Anna Q. (d 1974 [85])
actress BP/58*, WWT/16*
NILLSON, Carlotta (c. 1878-1951)
Swedish/American actress
GRB/3-4, TW/8, WWS, WWT/
1-5
NILSON, Einar (d 1964 [83]) com-
poser, conductor BE*
NILSON, Loy (b 1918) American
actor TW/2
NILSSON, Anna Q. see Nillson,
Anna Q.
NILSSON, Birgit (b 1918) Swedish
singer CB, ES
NILSSON, Christine (1843-1921)
Swedish singer CDP, ES,
WWW/2
NIMMO, Andrew (d 1872 [54])
agent EA/73*
NIMMO, Derek (b 1932) English
actor AAS, WWT/15-16
NIMS, Letha (b 1917) American
executive BE
NIRDLINGER, Charles Frederic
(d 1940 [77]) dramatist, critic
BE*, WWT/14*
NIRDLINGER, Jane Nixon (d 1971
[80]) performer BP/56*
NISBET, John Ferguson (1851-99)
Scottish critic WWW/1
NISBETT, Louisa Cranstoun
[Louisa Cranstoun Mordaunt]
(1812?-58) actress CDP, DNB
NISBETT, William Walker (d

1905 [83]) EA/06*
NISH, Antony (d 1874 [43]) musical
director EA/75*
NISITA, Giovanni (d 1962 [66])
singer BE*
NISSEN, Brian (b 1927) English ac-
tor WWT/10-13
NISSEN, Greta [Grethe Ruzt-Nissen]
(b 1906) Norwegian dancer, ac-
tress WWT/8-10
NISSEN, Peter (b 1964) American
actor TW/29
NISSEN-SALOMAN, Henrietta (d
1879 [58]) singer EA/80*
NIXEN, Gilbert S. (b 1795) Ameri-
can actor HAS
NIXON, Adelaide (1848-75) Ameri-
can singer, equestrienne, dancer
CDP, HAS
NIXON, Caroline L. (d 1864) Amer-
ican equestrienne HAS
NIXON, Charles Elston (b 1860)
American editor, dramatist
WWA/4
NIXON, Hugh (d 1921 [62]) actor
BE*, BP/5*
NIXON, Rebecca see Sinclair,
Rebecca
NIXON, Samuel F. (b 1848) Amer-
ican manager WWA/4, WWM
NIXON, Thomas (d 1896 [34]) mu-
sic-hall performer EA/97*
NIXON, William Joseph (d 1902
[43]) marionettist EA/03*
NIXON-NIRDLINGER, Fred G. (d
1931 [54]) theatre owner BE*,
BP/15*, WWT/14*
NIX-WEBBER, G. (b 1872) English
actor GRB/1-2
NIZER, Louis (b 1902) English
lawyer, writer BE
NKOSI, Lewis (b 1936) South Afri-
can/English dramatist CD
NOAH, Moredecai Manuel (1785-
1851) American dramatist
CDP, COC, DAB, EAP, HJD,
OC/1-3, RJ, SR
NOAH, Rachel Adine (b 1845)
American actress HAS
NOAKES, Frances [Mrs. J. Noakes]
(d 1895 [56]) EA/96*
NOAKES, Mrs. J. see Noakes,
Frances
NOAKES, Richard John (d 1908
[33]) EA/09*
NOBLE, Mr. (fl 1803-05) actor
GT, TD/2
NOBLE, Monsieur le (fl 1718?)

French dramatist CP/1-3, GT
NOBLE, Dennis (1898-1966) English actor, singer WWT/7-11, WWW/6
NOBLE, Florence (fl 1866-67) actress HAS
NOBLE, James (b 1922) American actor TW/6-8, 23, 25-28
NOBLE, John (d 1875) circus tent master EA/76*
NOBLE, Milner (b 1878) English actor GRB/1
NOBLE, Milton American actor, dramatist SR
NOBLE, Tim (b 1945) American actor TW/28
NOBLE, Vernon (d 1909 [28]) performer? EA/10*
NOBLE, William (b 1921) American dramatist BE
NOBLES, Dolly (d 1930 [67]) American actress BE*, BP/15*
NOBLES, Milton (1847-1924) American actor, dramatist CDP, WWA/1, WWM, WWS
NOBLES, Milton, Jr. (d 1925 [32]) American actor BE*, BP/9*
NOBLET, Lise (fl 1821) French dancer CDP
NOEHDEN, N. H. (fl 1798) translator CP/3
NOEL, Craig R. (b 1915) American producer, director BE
NOEL, Nancy actress CDP
NOEL, Nestor (d 1874 [37]) manager EA/74*
NOEL, Tom (b 1911) American actor TW/23
NOEL, W. H. actor, singer CDP
NOEMI, Lea (d 1973 [90]) actress TW/30
NOKES, James (d 1696) English actor COC, DNB, OC/1-3
NOLA, Mina (fl 1837) musician CDP
NOLAN, Doris (b 1915/16) American actress TW/6-7, WWT/10-12
NOLAN, John Francis (d 1908) actor EA/09*
NOLAN, Kathy [or Kathleen] (b 1933) American actress TW/11-12, 23
NOLAN, Lloyd (b 1902/03) American actor AAS, BE, CB,

ES, TW/10-13, WWT/8-10, 13-14
NOLAN, Mary (d 1904 [68]) EA/05*
NOLAN, Mary (1906-48) actress TW/5
NOLAN, Michael Patrick (d 1909/10 [42]) Irish musician, actor, comedian CDP, EA/11*
NOLAN, Pattie [Mrs. Michael H. Daly; Mrs. Pat Rooney] (d 1907) EA/08*
NOLAN, Robin (b 1945) American actor TW/30
NOLAND, Nancy (b 1912) American actress TW/1
NOLEN, Joyce (b 1949) American actress TW/24, 28
NOLTE, Charles (b 1926) American actor, dramatist BE, TW/6-21
NONELL, Mrs. (fl 1850) actress HAS
NOONAN, Billy performer CDP
NOONAN, John Ford (b 1943) American dramatist, actor, director CD
NOONAN, Tommy (d 1968 [46]) performer BP/52*
NOONE, Bill E. (b 1944) American actor TW/29
NORCROSS, Frank (d 1926 [70]) actor BE*, BP/11*
NORCROSS, Hale (d 1947 [70]) American actor TW/4
NORCROSS, Joseph M. (d 1925 [84]) performer BE*, BP/9*
NORD, Betty (d 1976 [69]) performer BP/60*
NORDICA, Lillian [Mrs. Zoltan Dome] (1859-1914) American singer CDP, DAB, ES, GRB/1, SR, WWA/1, WWS, WWW/1
NORDLI, Ernie (d 1968 [55]) designer BP/52*
NORDSTROM, Clarence (d 1968 [75]) American actor TW/21, 23
NORDSTROM, Frances dramatist WWT/4-7
NORDSTROM, Marie (b 1886) American actress WWS
NORELLI, Jennie Swedish singer WWM
NORFLEET, Cecelia (b 1949) American actress TW/28-30
NORFOLK, Edgar (b 1893) English actor WWT/7-13
NORGATE, W. Matthew (b 1900/01)

English critic WWT/6, 9-16

NORINS, Leslie H. (d 1975 [59])
performer BP/60*

NORMA, Bebe (d 1975 [49]) performer BP/59*

NORMA, Hettie [Janet MacIntyre
Mackenzie Stevenson] (d 1907)
EA/09*

NORMAN, Miss (fl 1850) actress
HAS

NORMAN, A. D. (d 1908) pier
manager EA/09*

NORMAN, Arthur W. (d 1896
[31]) actor EA/97*

NORMAN, Bruce (d 1976 [73])
performer BP/60*

NORMAN, E. B. (d 1930 [77])
actor, producer, director,
manager BE*, WWT/14*

NORMAN, Mrs. E. B. see
Hope, Ethel

NORMAN, Ethel (fl 1866-69) English actress HAS

NORMAN, Frank (b 1930/31)
English dramatist CD, CH,
MWD, PDT

NORMAN, Fred (d 1972 [78])
agent BP/56*

NORMAN, Gertrude (d 1961 [81])
actress WWT/14*

NORMAN, Harry (fl 1867?)
singer, minstrel CDP

NORMAN, Helen (d 1891) singer
EA/92*

NORMAN, Henry (b 1862) singer,
actor CDP

NORMAN, Horace singer CDP

NORMAN, Mrs. James see
Norman, Rhoda

NORMAN, Jessye (b 1945)
American singer CB

NORMAN, Karyl (d 1947 [51])
vaudevillian, female impersonator TW/4

NORMAN, Mabel (d 1930) actress
SR

NORMAN, Maurice (d 1969 [82])
performer BP/54*

NORMAN, May (d 1899 [25])
musician EA/00*

NORMAN, Norman J. (1870-1941)
American manager WWT/5-9

NORMAN, Norman V. (1864-
1943) English actor, manager
GRB/1-4, WWT/4-9

NORMAN, R. (d 1858 [70])
pantaloon CDP

NORMAN, Rhoda [Mrs. James

Norman] (d 1891 [50]) EA/92*

NORMAN, Thyrza (b 1884) English
actress WWT/2-5

NORMAN, Walter English actor
GRB/1

NORMAN-BURT, George Templeman (b 1872) English actor
GRB/1-3

NORMAND, Mabel (1894-1930)
Canadian actress BE*, BP/14*

NORMAUTON, Sara actress, singer
CDP

NORMINGTON, John (b 1937/38)
English actor TW/23, WWT/
15-16

NORREYS, Rose (d 1946 [84])
American/English actress DP

NORRIE, Anna (d 1957 [97]) actress
BE*, WWT/14*

NORRIE, James (fl 1899?) singer,
actor CDP

NORRIE, Russell English actor
GRB/1

NORRIS, Prof. (d 1904 [81]) conjuror EA/05*

NORRIS, Mrs. (fl 1759) actress
HAS

NORRIS, Charles (b 1846) Canadian
actor HAS

NORRIS, Ernest E. (1865-1935)
manager, actor, dramatist
GRB/1-4

MORRIS, Henry (d 1731) actor,
dramatist CP/1-3, GT, TD/1-2

MORRIS, Herbert (d 1950) costume
designer WWW/4

NORRIS, Ida [Ada Sennett] (d 1894
[24]) actress EA/95*

NORRIS, James W. (b 1849) American actor HAS

NORRIS, Jay (b 1917) American
actor TW/2-3

NORRIS, Kathleen (1880-1966)
American dramatist WWA/4

NORRIS, Lee (d 1964 [59]) actress
BE*

NORRIS, Percy (d 1889) actor
EA/90*

NORRIS, Thomas (1741-90) musician, singer CDP

NORRIS, W. H. (d 1910) actor
EA/11*

NORRIS, William [William Norris
Block] (1870/71/72-1929) Amer-
ican actor GRB/2-4, WWA/1,
WWM, WWS, WWT/1-5

NORSA, Hannah (d 1785) actress
CDP

NORTH, Ada [Mrs. Alfred Linnet]
(d 1900) EA/02*
NORTH, Alan (b 1927) American
actor TW/24
NORTH, Alex (b 1910) American
composer BE
NORTH, Bobby (b 1884) American
actor, manager WWM
NORTH, Charles see Smith,
Charles Frederick
NORTH, Corinne F. (d 1966 [69])
performer BP/50*
NORTH, Francis, Earl of Guilford
(b 1761) dramatist CP/3, GT,
TD/1-2
NORTH, Heather (b 1945) Amer-
ican actress TW/24
NORTH, Henry Morley (d 1869
[58]) actor? EA/70*
NORTH, John (d 1891 [39]) con-
ductor EA/92*
NORTH, Levi J. (1814-85) eques-
trian CDP
NORTH, Rex (d 1969 [52]) jour-
nalist BP/54*
NORTH, Sheree (b 1933) Ameri-
can actress TW/9-11, 18-19
NORTH, Wilfred [W. Northcroft]
(fl 1882-1913) English actor,
stage manager WWM
NORTHALL, Julia L. (d 1896)
singer CDP
NORTHALL, William K. drama-
tist CDP
NORTHCOTE, Charles (d 1877)
prompter EA/78*
NORTHCOTE, Thomas Price (d
1904) variety manager EA/05*
NORTHCOTT, John (d 1905 [62])
critic GRB/1
NORTHCOTT, Richard (1871-
1931) English composer,
critic, writer, archivist
WWT/5-6
NORTHCROFT, W. see North,
Wilfred
NORTHEN, Michael (b 1921) Eng-
lish lighting designer WWT/
15-16
NORTHWAY, Alfred [Alfred Ed-
ward Robbins] (b 1876) English
manager, actor GRB/1
NORTON (fl 1696?) dramatist
CP/2-3
NORTON, Mrs. [Miss Gilbert]
(fl 1796) actress TD/1-2
NORTON, Miss (fl 1808?) actress
CDP

NORTON, Mrs. Alfred see Nor-
ton, Sophie
NORTON, Annie Burt actress CDP
NORTON, Barry (d 1956 [51]) Ar-
gentinian/American actor BE*
NORTON, Bruce (d 1861 [43]) actor
EA/72*, WWT/14*
NORTON, C. W. (d 1875 [25]) actor
EA/76*
NORTON, Dean (b 1914) American
actor TW/4-8
NORTON, Elliot (b 1903) American
critic BE, WWT/14-16
NORTON, Fleming [Frederick
Mills] (d 1895 [59]) entertainer
OAA/2
NORTON, Mrs. Fleming see
Norton, Jeannie
NORTON, Frederic (d 1946) English
composer WWT/4-10, WWW/4
NORTON, Frederick Naphtali (d
1882) EA/84*
NORTON, I. T. musician CDP
NORTON, Jack (d 1958 [69]) Amer-
ican actor BE*, BP/43*
NORTON, Jeannie [Mrs. Fleming
Norton] (d 1880) EA/81*
NORTON, John (fl 1827) English
actor HAS
NORTON, John W. (d 1895 [50])
actor, manager CDP, SR
NORTON, Ruby English actress
GRB/1
NORTON, Sophie [Mrs. Alfred
Norton] (d 1902 [44]) EA/03*
NORTON, Thomas (1532-84) English
dramatist COC, CP/1-3, FGF,
MH, OC/1-3
NORTON, Timothy W. (d 1862
[23]) minstrel HAS
NORTON, Washington (b 1839)
American minstrel HAS
NORTON, William Henry (d 1876
[67]) English actor CDP, HAS
NORTON, William Henry [William
Selmore] (d 1884) acrobat EA/
85*
NORVAL, James (fl 1792) drama-
tist CP/3, EAP
NORWICK, Douglas American actor
TW/29
NORWOOD, Edwin P. (1881-1940)
American writer WWA/1
NORWOOD, Eille (1861-1948) Eng-
lish actor GRB/3-4, WWT/1-10
NORWOOD, John (fl 1598) actor
DA
NORWORTH, Jack (1879-1959)

American actor CDP, COC,
OC/3, SR, TW/16, WWT/4-11
NOSILLIE, Lucia (d 1886) singer
EA/87*
NOSSECK, Max (d 1972 [70])
performer BP/57*
NOSSEN, Bram actor TW/1
NOSWORTHY, Frank (d 1892)
actor EA/93*
NOTO, Lore (b 1923) American
producer, actor BE
NOTT, Cicely [Sarah Ann Adams;
Mrs. Sam Adams] (d 1900
[67]) actress, singer BE*,
EA/01*, WWT/14*
NOTT, Rosie see Courtneidge,
Mrs. Robert‾
NOTTEBOHM, Gustav (d 1882
[67]) historian EA/83*
NOURI, Michael (b 1945) Ameri-
can actor TW/27
NOVAK, Norma (b 1937) American
actress TW/26
NOVARA, Franco (d 1899) pro-
fessor of singing EA/00*
NOVARRO, Ramon (1899-1968)
Mexican dancer, actor WWA/5
NOVELLI, Ermete (1851-1919)
Italian actor COC, GRB/3-4,
OC/1-3, WWS, WWT/1-3
NOVELLI, Pedro (fl 1847) singer
HAS
NOVELLO, Clara Anastasia (1818-
1908) singer CDP, DNB, ES
NOVELLO, Ivor (1893-1951)
Welsh actor, manager, drama-
tist, composer AAS, COC,
DNB, ES, MH, MWD, OC/
1-3, PDT, TW/7, WWA/4,
WWT/4-11, WWW/5
NOVELLO, Richard Italian actor
TW/26
NOVELO, Ruben Z. (d 1974 [43])
performer BP/59*
NOVEMBER, Mrs. Norman see
Green, Dorothy
NOVERRE, Jean Georges (1727-
1810) French maître de ballet
ES, OC/1-2
NOVIKOFF, Laurent (d 1956 [68])
Russian dancer TW/13
NOVIS, Donald (d 1966 [60])
singer TW/23
NOVOTNA, Jarmila (b 1911)
Czech singer CB, TW/1
NOVY, Nita (b 1950) American
actress TW/29
NOWAK, Adelaide (fl 1903-10)

American actress WWM
NOWELL, Mrs. Wedgwood see
Colwell, Claire‾
NOWLAN, Patrick (d 1876) Irish
singer, dancer EA/77*
NOYES, Mrs. Frank P. see
Clare, Ada‾
NOYES, Mrs. J. F. (fl 1862) ac-
tress HAS
NOYES, Lilly (b 1944) American
actress TW/29
NOYES, Thomas (b 1922) American
producer, actor BE
NOYLE, Olga Kate (d 1899) actress
EA/00*
"NUBIAN KING, The" see Sung-
ham, Harry‾
NUCE, Thomas (fl 1581) dramatist
CP/1-3
NUCHTERN, Jean (b 1939) Ameri-
can actress TW/27
NUDELL, Sam actor TW/24
NUGENT, Mr. (d 1880) EA/81*
NUGENT, Mrs. (d 1890 [81]) EA/
91*
NUGENT, Charles (d 1876 [67])
actor EA/77*
NUGENT, Claud (d 1901 [33]) com-
poser EA/02*
NUGENT, Eddie (b 1904) American
actor TW/1-2
NUGENT, Elliott (b 1899/1900)
American actor, dramatist, pro-
ducer, director AAS, BE, CB,
CD, ES, MD, MH, MWD, TW/
1-8, WWT/6-15
NUGENT, George William (d 1884)
music-hall proprietor EA/85*
NUGENT, James (d 1917) EA/18*
NUGENT, John Charles (1878-1947)
American actor, dramatist SR,
TW/1, 3, WWT/6-10
NUGENT, Moya (1901-54) actress
WWT/4-11
NUGENT, Nancy (b 1933) American
actress, producer BE
NUNN, Annette [Mrs. J. B. Mul-
holland] (d 1896) actress EA/97*
NUNN, Trevor (b 1940) English
director AAS, COC, WWT/15-
16
NUNO, Jaime (1824-1908) Spanish
conductor, composer, impresario
DAB, WWA/H
NUNS, Mr. (fl 1786) actor, mana-
ger TD/1-2
NUREYEV, Rudolf (b 1938) Rus-
sian/English dancer CB, ES

NUSKAY, Anne see Greene,
Mrs. John
NUTE, Don American actor
TW/29-30
NUTT, Commodore see Nutt,
George Washington M.
NUTT, Mrs. Commodore (d 1878)
dwarf EA/79*
NUTT, George Washington M.
(1844-81) dwarf CDP
NUTTALL, Thomas (d 1887)
singer EA/88*
NUTTER, Edna May see Oliver,
Edna May
NUYEN, France (b 1939) French
actress BE, TW/15
NYBERG, Peter (b 1939) Canadian
actor TW/23, 27
NYCOWLLES, Robert (fl 1595)
actor DA
NYE, Carrie actress BE, TW/
25, 28-29, WWT/15-16
NYE, Carroll (d 1974 [72]) per-
former BP/58*
NYE, Elizabeth Ann see Staun-
ton, Ella
NYE, Gene (b 1939) American
actor TW/23, 27
NYE, Henry (fl 1849) actor CDP
NYE, Mary (d 1879 [70]) EA/80*
NYE, Pat (b 1908) English ac-
tress WWT/11-16
NYE, Tom F. (d 1925 [78]) actor
BE*, WWT/14*
NYITRAY, Emil (d 1922) drama-
tist BE*, BP/6*, WWT/14*
NYLAND, Robert (d 1877) eques-
trian EA/78*
NYPE, Russell (b 1924) American
actor, singer BE, TW/7-8,
12-16, 23-24, 26-27, 29,
WWT/15-16
NYREN, David (d 1973 [47]) the-
atrical agency executive BP/
57*

- O -

OAKDEN, William (d 1876) musician EA/77*
OAKELEY, Sir Herbert Stanley
(d 1903 [73]) composer EA/
04*
OAKER, Jane [Minnie Dorothy
Peper] (b 1880) American
actress WWM, WWS, WWT/
4-7

OAKES, Betty (b 1930) American
actress TW/8, 30
OAKES, Gary (b 1936) American
actor TW/23, 27-28
OAKES, George (d 1966 [69]) per-
former BP/51*
OAKEY, Mr. (d 1845) dancer,
pantomimist HAS
OAKLAND, Si (b 1918) American
actor TW/4, 6, 11-15
OAKLAND, Simon (b 1920) Ameri-
can actor TW/26, 28-29
OAKLAND, Will (1883-1956) Amer-
ican entertainer TW/12
OAKLEY, Ada [Mrs. Walter Cop-
ley] English actress GRB/1
OAKMAN, Wheeler (d 1949 [59])
American actor BE*
OATES, Miss see Delagarde,
Mrs. J.
OATES, Alice see Oates, Mrs.
James A.
OATES, Cicely (d 1934 [45]) ac-
tress BE*, WWT/14*
OATES, James A. (b 1842) Irish
actor, manager HAS
OATES, Mrs. James A. [née
Alice Merritt] (1849-87) Ameri-
can actress, singer CDP, HAS,
NYM, SR
OATES, Henry see Austin, Henry
OATLEY, Julia (fl 1856-57) Amer-
ican actress HAS
OBEE, Lois see Dresdel, Sonia
O'BEIRNE, Calder (d 1917 [69])
singer EA/18*
O'BEIRNE, Tessie [Mrs. J. P.
Macnally] (d 1912) EA/13*
O'BEIRNE, Thomas Lewis (fl 1781)
Irish dramatist CP/2-3, GT,
TD/1-2
OBER, George (1849-1912) Ameri-
can actor SR
OBER, Harold (d 1959 [78]) liter-
ary representative BE*
OBER, Philip (b 1902) American
actor BE, TW/3-7, WWT/9-13
OBER, Robert (1881/89-1950)
American actor TW/2-3, 7,
WWS
OBERDING, Antoine (d 1974 [81])
costumier BP/59*
OBERLE, Thomas (d 1906) actor
BE*, WWT/14*
OBERLIN, Russell (b 1928) Ameri-
can singer CB
OBEY, André (b 1892) French
dramatist COC, MWD, OC/3

OBOLER, Arch (b 1907/09) American dramatist, director, producer BE, MD, MWD, NTH

OBORIN, Lev (d 1973 [66]) performer BP/58*

OBRAZTSOV, Sergei Vladimirovich (b 1901) Russian puppetmaster COC

O'BRIAN, Hugh (b 1925/28) American actor, producer BE, CB, TW/18-19, 23-24, WWT/16

O'BRIAN, John Skenado (b 1753) American actor HAS

O'BRIEN, Barry (1893-1961) English producing manager, agent WWT/8-13

O'BRIEN, Charles (1848-1917) circus performer & manager SR

O'BRIEN, Chet (b 1911) stage manager, performer BE

O'BRIEN, Cornelius A. see Bryant, Neil

O'BRIEN, David (b 1930) English actor WWT/10-15

O'BRIEN, David (b 1935) American actor TW/22-26

O'BRIEN, Dennis (fl 1783) Irish dramatist GT, TD/1-2

O'BRIEN, Donnell (d 1970) actor, singer TW/27

O'BRIEN, E. C. (d 1916 [34]) comedian EA/17*

O'BRIEN, Edmond (b 1915) American actor ES

O'BRIEN, Edward ["Tennyson"] (d 1878 [24]) ventriloquist, music-hall proprietor EA/79*

O'BRIEN, Edward J. (1890-1941) dramatist HJD

O'BRIEN, Fitz-James (c. 1828-62) Irish/American dramatist HJD

O'BRIEN, Frank American actor TW/28-30

O'BRIEN, Havergal (d 1972 [96]) composer BP/57*

O'BRIEN, Henry (d 1878) marionette proprietor EA/79*

O'BRIEN, Jerry see Bryant, Jerry

O'BRIEN, John see Raymond, John T.

O'BRIEN, J. T. (fl 1854) actor HAS

O'BRIEN, Justin (d 1968 [62])

dramatist BP/53*

O'BRIEN, Kate (1897/98-1974) Irish dramatist WWT/6-7, 10-11

O'BRIEN, Liam (b 1913) American dramatist, producer BE

O'BRIEN, Marcia (b 1934) American actress TW/27, 29

O'BRIEN, Marie see Saker, Mrs. Edward

O'BRIEN, Maureen (b 1943) English actress WWT/15-16

O'BRIEN, M. Barry (b 1893) English producer, manager, agent WWT/6-7

O'BRIEN, Neil (d 1909 [55]) actor BE*, WWT/14*

O'BRIEN, Neil (d 1954 [85]) American minstrel performer & manager SR

O'BRIEN, Mrs. Neil see Davenport, Eva

O'BRIEN, Pat (b 1899) American actor BE, CB, ES

O'BRIEN, Patrick see Cotter, Patrick

O'BRIEN, Seamus (b 1932) English actor TW/29

O'BRIEN, Sylvia (b 1924) Irish actress TW/23, 25-27, 29

O'BRIEN, Terence (1887-1970) Irish actor WWT/5-12

O'BRIEN, Thomas Simon (d 1898 [40]) comedian, acrobat EA/99*

O'BRIEN, Timothy (b 1929) Indian/English designer AAS, WWT/15-16

O'BRIEN, Virginia (b 1896) American actress, singer WWT/7-8

O'BRIEN, William (d 1815 [79]) dramatist, actor CDP, CP/2-3, DNB, GT, TD/1-2

O'BRIEN-MOORE, Erin (b 1908) actress TW/3-8, WWT/7-11

O'BRYAN, Miss dancer CDP

O'BRYAN, Daniel Webster see Bryant, Dan

O'BRYAN, Pat (d 1912) comedian EA/13*

O'BRYEN, Dennis (1755-1832) dramatist CP/3, DNB

O'BRYEN, W[ilfrid] J[ames Wheeler] (b 1898) English manager, agent WWT/9-10

O'CALLAGHAN, Daniel J. (d 1900 [84]) EA/01*

O'CALLAGHAN, Delia see Friganza, Trixie

O'CALLAGHAN, Richard (b 1940)

English actor WWT/16
O'CALLAN, Thomas [T. C. Harris] (d 1897 [59]) actor EA/98*
O'CASEY, Sean (1880-1964) Irish dramatist AAS, BE, CB, CH, ES, HP, MD, MH, MWD, NTH, OC/1-3, PDT, RE, TW/21, WWA/4, WWT/6-13, WWW/6
OCASIO, Jose (b 1938) Puerto Rican actor TW/24, 29
OCEANA [Oceana Renz] (d 1895) wire walker EA/96*
OCEANA, La Belle (fl 1846-69) dancer HAS
OCHS, Al (d 1964 [70]) talent representative BE*
OCHS, Lillian (d 1964) talent representative BE*
OCHS, Phil (d 1975 [35]) performer BP/60*
O'CONNELL, Arthur (b 1908) American actor BE, TW/9-15, WWT/16
O'CONNELL, Gerald (b 1904) American manager BE
O'CONNELL, Hugh (1898-1943) American actor CB, SR, WWT/7-9
O'CONNELL, Jerry (d 1969 [64]) manager BP/54*
O'CONNELL, Patricia American actress TW/28, 30
O'CONNELL, Thomas (d 1970 [96]) publicist BP/55*
O'CONNER, James Owen (1839-94) actor CDP
O'CONNOR, Mrs. (d 1886) EA/87*
O'CONNOR, Mrs. (d 1917) EA/18*
O'CONNOR, Bill (b 1919) Canadian singer, actor WWT/12-13
O'CONNOR, Carroll (b 1924) American actor CB
O'CONNOR, Charles William (1878-1955) Irish press agent GRB/1-4, WWT/1-3
O'CONNOR, Donald (b 1925) American comedian, singer, dancer CB
O'CONNOR, Edwin (d 1968) dramatist BP/52*
O'CONNOR, Frank (1903-66) Irish dramatist, director HP, MD, WWA/4, WWW/6
O'CONNOR, Harry M. (d 1971

[98]) performer BP/56*
O'CONNOR, Mrs. J. see Willing, Bella
O'CONNOR, James Francis (1892-1963) American editor WWA/4
O'CONNOR, John [Harry Wilkinson] (d 1883 [29]) performer? EA/84*
O'CONNOR, John (d 1889 [57/59]) scene artist EA/90*, WWT/14*
O'CONNOR, John (d 1897 [58]) variety & circus manager EA/98*
O'CONNOR, John J. (b 1933) American critic WWT/15
O'CONNOR, Kathryn (d 1965 [71]) performer BP/50*
O'CONNOR, Kevin (b 1938) American actor, director, producer TW/23-26, 28-30, WWT/16
O'CONNOR, Richard (d 1975 [59]) performer BP/59*
O'CONNOR, Robert (d 1947) actor TW/3
O'CONNOR, Robert Emmett (d 1962 [77]) American actor BE*
O'CONNOR, Rod (d 1964 [51]) actor BE*
O'CONNOR, Thomas (d 1881 [25]) stage manager EA/82*
O'CONNOR, Thomas [Tom Wilkinson] (d 1881) Irish comedian EA/83*
O'CONNOR, Una (1880/93-1959) Irish actress TW/2-7, 11-13, 15, WWT/6-12
O'CONNOR, William (d 1955 [77]) press representative, journalist WWT/3
O'CONOLLY, Gerald (d 1909) executive? EA/10*
O'CONOR, Joseph (b 1916) Irish actor, dramatist AAS, MH, WWT/11-16
O'DALY, Cormac (d 1949 [55]) dramatist BE*, WWT/14*
O'DAY, Alice (d 1937) actress BE*, WWT/14*
ODDY, George (d 1888 [15]) aerial flight performer EA/89*
O'DEA, Denis (b 1905) Irish actor WWT/11-14
O'DEA, James (1871-1914) Canadian dramatist, librettist SR, WWA/1, WWM
O'DEA, Jimmy (d 1965 [66]) performer BP/49*
O'DEA, John (d 1972 [63]) dramatist

BP/56*
O'DELL, Dell (d 1962) magician
BE*
ODELL, E. J. (d 1928 [93]) actor
BE*, WWT/14*
ODELL, George C. D. (1866-
1949) American historian CB,
DAB, ES, HJD, NTH, WWT/
6-10
ODELL, Maude (d 1937 [65])
American actress BE*, BP/
21*, WWT/14*
ODELL, Thomas (1691-1749)
Master of the Revels, drama-
tist, proprietor CP/1-3,
DNB, GT, TD/1-2
O'DEMPSEY, Brigit (d 1952 [65])
actress BE*, WWT/14*
ODETS, Clifford (1906-63) Amer-
ican actor, dramatist AAS,
CB, CH, COC, ES, HJD, HP,
MD, MH, MWD, NTH, OC/
1-3, PDT, RE, TW/20, WWA/
4, WWT/8-13, WWW/6
ODETS, Mrs. Clifford see
Grayson, Bette
ODETTE, Mary (b 1901) French
actress WWT/4-7
ODINGSELS, Gabriel (1690-1734)
English dramatist CP/1-3,
DNB, GT
ODIVA [Alma Beaumont] (b 1883)
English aquatic entertainer
WWM
ODLUM, Drelincourt (b 1865)
Irish actor GRB/1
O'DOHERTY, Eileen [Anna Walk-
er] (b 1891) Irish actress
WWT/2-7
O'DOHERTY, Mignon (1890-1961)
Australian actress WWT/4-13
O'DONNELL, Anne American
actress TW/27
O'DONNELL, Cathy (d 1970 [45])
performer BP/54*
O'DONNELL, Charles H. (d 1962
[76]) performer BE*
O'DONNELL, Edwin P. (1895-
1943) dramatist CB
O'DONOVAN, Desmond (b 1933)
English director WWT/15-16
O'DONOVAN, Frank (d 1974
[74]) actor BP/59*, WWT/
16*
O'DONOVAN, Fred (1889-1952)
Irish actor WWT/2-11
O'DUFFY, Eimar Ultan (1893-
1935) Irish dramatist WWW/3

ODY, Mel (d 1976 [62]) performer
BP/60*
OELRICHS, Blanche (d 1950 [60])
actress BE*, WWT/14*
OENSLAGER, Donald (1902-75)
American designer BE, CB,
COC, ES, NTH, OC/1-3, TW/
2-8, WWT/8-15
OESTREICHER, Gerard (b 1916)
American producer BE
O'FARRELL, Mary (1892-1968)
English actress WWT/4-8
O'FARRELL, Talbot (d 1952 [72])
performer BE*, WWT/14*
OFFENBACH, Joseph (d 1971 [66])
performer BP/56*
OFFERMAN, George, Jr. (d 1963
[45]) American actor BE*
OFFIN, Phil (d 1974 [70]) agent
BP/58*
OFFLEY, Thomas (fl c. 1509-22)
actor DA
OFFNER, Mortimer (d 1965 [64])
producer/director BP/50*
OFFROY, Auguste see Dianta
OFFROY, Mrs. Auguste see
Offroy, Emily Jane
OFFROY, Emily Jane [Mrs. Au-
guste Offroy] (d 1899) EA/00*
O'FLYNN, Michael (d 1908 [60])
EA/09*
OGBORNE, David (fl 1765?) Eng-
lish dramatist CP/2-3, GT
OGDEN, Anna Cora see Mowatt,
Anna Cora
OGDEN, Grace [Mrs. Nat Ogden]
(d 1873 [37]) EA/74*
OGDEN, Mrs. John see Bullock,
Henrietta Maria
OGDEN, John H. (d 1864 [35])
English comic singer CDP,
HAS
OGDEN, Nat (d 1876 [43]) comic
singer EA/77*
OGDEN, Mrs. Nat see Ogden,
Grace
OGG, Marguerite (d 1972 [64])
agent BP/57*
OGILBY, John (1600-76) Scottish
dramatist CP/3
OGILVIE, Mrs. (fl 1823) actress
BS, CDP
OGILVIE, George (b 1931) Aus-
tralian director, actor WWT/
16
OGILVIE, Glencairn Stuart (1858-
1932) English dramatist GRB/
1-4, WWT/1-6

O'GORMAN, Dave (d 1964 [70])
performer BP/49*
O'GORMAN, Mrs. J. see Cole-
man, Maggie
O'GORMAN, Jane (d 1906 [84])
EA/07*
O'GORMAN, Jessie [Mrs. Joe
O'Gorman] (d 1908 [34]) gym-
nast EA/09*
O'GORMAN, Joe (d 1974 [85])
music-hall performer BTR/
74, CDP
O'GORMAN, Mrs. Joe see
O'Gorman, Jessie
O'GORMAN, William (d 1966
[63]) performer BP/51*
O'GRADY, Mrs. F. [Miss H.
Daly] (d 1889 [33]) actress
EA/90*
O'GRADY, Frank (d 1901) come-
dian EA/01*
O'GRADY, Hubert (d 1899 [58])
dramatist, actor EA/01*
O'GRADY, William (d 1893 [56])
EA/94*
O'GRATH, Mrs. (fl 1836) ac-
tress HAS
OGUS, Joyce see Blair, Joyce
OGUS, Lionel see Blair, Lionel
O'HAFFEY, Thom (d 1971 [53])
journalist BP/56*
O'HAGAN, Mrs. John D. (d 1969
[78]) performer BP/54*
O'HANLON, Redmond L. (d 1964
[48]) Shakespearean authority
BE*
O'HARA, Mrs. Dan Briggs (d
1876) singer EA/77*
O'HARA, Fiske [né George Fiske
Brenen] (1880-1945) American
actor, dramatist SR, TW/2
O'HARA, Frank (1926-66) Amer-
ican dramatist WWA/4
O'HARA, Geoffrey (1882-1967)
Canadian composer WWA/4
O'HARA, Hugh (d 1901) music-hall
comedian EA/02*
O'HARA, Jenny American actress
TW/26-30
O'HARA, Jill (b 1947) American
actress TW/24-28
O'HARA, John (d 1929 [70]) actor
BE*, BP/14*
O'HARA, John (1905-70) American
writer, dramatist BE, CB,
MD, WWW/6
O'HARA, Kane (1714?-82) Irish
dramatist CDP, CP/2-3, DNB,

GT, TD/1-2
O'HARA, Maureen (b 1921) Irish
actress CB
O'HARA, Neal (d 1962 [69]) jour-
nalist BP/47*
O'HARA, Terence (d 1917) EA/18*
O'HEARN, Robert (b 1921) Ameri-
can designer BE
O'HERLIHY, Daniel (b 1919) Irish
actor TW/5
O'HIGGINS, Harvey J. (1876-1929)
Canadian dramatist HJD, WWT/
4-5
OHNET, Georges (1848-1918)
French dramatist COC, GRB/1,
3, OC/1-3, WWT/1
O'HORGAN, Tom (b 1927) American
director, composer CB, WWT/
16
O'KEEFE, Anna American actress
WWA/5
O'KEEFE, Dennis (d 1968 [60])
performer BP/53*
O'KEEFFE, Mrs. actress CDP
O'KEEFFE, John (1747-1833) Irish
dramatist CDP, COC, CP/3,
DNB, ES, GT, HP, OC/1-3,
SR, TD/1-2
O'KELLY, Joseph (d 1885) French
composer EA/86*
O'KELLY, Seumas (1881-1918) Irish
dramatist RE
OKHLOPKOV, Nicolai (1900-67)
Russian actor, director WWT/
13-14
OLAF, Pierre [né Pierre-Olaf
Trivier] (b 1928) French actor
BE, TW/17-21, 23, 25, WWT/
15-16
OLAND, Warner (1880-1938) Swedish
actor WWT/7-8
OLCOTT, Chauncey (1860-1932)
American actor, singer CDP,
DAB, GRB/2-4, SR, WWA/1,
WWM, WWS, WWT/1-6
OLCOTT, Ida Lillian (d 1888 [c. 27])
actress CDP
OLCOTT, Sidney (d 1949 [76])
director, actor BE*
OLD, John (d 1892 [65]) composer
EA/93*
OLD, Mary Ann (d 1874 [83]) ac-
tress EA/75*
OLDAKER, Max (d 1972 [64]) per-
former BP/56*
OLDAKER, Thomas Norris (d 1918)
EA/19*
OLDALE, Marion (d 1876 [17])

dancer EA/77*
OLDENBURG, Claes sculptor CD
OLDFIELD, Miss (fl 1797) actress
HAS
OLDFIELD, Anne (1683-1730)
English actress CDP, COC,
DNB, ES, GT, HP, NTH,
OC/1-3, TD/1-2
OLDFIELD, Lilian see Newland,
Mary
OLDFIELD, Nance (d 1904 [30])
EA/05*
OLDFIELD, Thomas J. (b 1809)
English actor, musical director
HAS
OLDHAM, Derek (1892-1968)
English actor, singer AAS,
WWT/4-14
"OLD JOE" see De La Salle,
Michel Joseph
OLDLAND, Lilian (b 1905) English
actress WWT/6
OLDLAND, Marion (d 1892) EA/
93*
OLDMIXON, Mrs. [Georgina Sidus]
(d 1835) English singer, actress
CDP, COC, HAS, OC/1-3
OLDMIXON, John (1673-1742)
English dramatist CP/1-3,
DNB, GT
OLDMIXON, Sir John (d 1818)
dramatist CDP, CP/3
OLDMIXON, Mrs. John see
Oldmixon, Mrs.
O'LEARY, Bryan (d 1970 [36])
performer BP/54*
O'LEARY, F. L. see Fred-
ericks, Fred
O'LEARY, John (b 1926) Ameri-
can actor TW/23, 29-30
O'LEARY, Kevin (b 1940) Amer-
ican actor TW/25, 30
O'LEARY, Miriam (fl c. 1890?)
actress CDP
O'LEARY, Pat see Tollett,
John
O'LEARY, Willie (d 1973 [69])
performer BP/58*
OLESEN, Oscar (b 1916) English
manager BE
OLESEN, Otto K. (d 1964 [72])
Danish lighting equipment
expert BE*
OLFSON, Ken (b 1937) American
actor TW/24, 30
OLGINI, Olga (b 1846) Polish
singer HAS
OLIFF, Mr. (fl 1810) actor,

prompter HAS
OLIFFE, Geraldine [Mrs. Compton
Mackenzie] actress GRB/1,
WWT/2-5
OLIM, Dorothy (b 1934) American
producer BE
OLINZA, Margaretta (fl 1854)
tight-rope dancer HAS
OLIPHANT, Jack (b 1895) English
press representative WWT/10-
13
OLIPHANT, Julie (d 1969 [60])
performer BP/54*
OLIPHANT, Robert (d 1792) English
dramatist CP/3
OLIPHANT, Thomas (1799-1873)
Scottish composer DNB
OLITZKA, Rosa (d 1949 [76])
singer BE*, WWT/14*
OLIVARI, Francis (fl 1797) Italian
dramatist CP/3
OLIVE, Edyth [Mrs. Arthur Applin]
(d 1956 [84]) English actress
GRB/1-4, WWT/1-6
OLIVE, Kittie [Mrs. Tom Pilbeam]
(d 1913) EA/14*
OLIVE, Lily (d 1909 [34]) actress
EA/10*
OLIVER, Mrs. A. E. (d 1890)
EA/91*
OLIVER, Anthony (b 1923/24) Welsh
actor TW/10, 24, WWT/12-16
OLIVER, Barrie (b 1900) American
actor, dancer WWT/6-8
OLIVER, Bessie [Mrs. Henry Ar-
lington Duncan] (d 1885) actress
EA/86*
OLIVER, C. W. (d 1890) lessee
EA/91*
OLIVER, Eddie (b 1894) American
treasurer, manager BE
OLIVER, Edith [née Goldsmith] (b
1913) American critic BE,
WWT/15-16
OLIVER, Edna May [Edna May
Nutter] (1883/85-1942) American
actress CB, ES, SR, WWA/2,
WWT/7-9
OLIVER, Florence [Mrs. Will Oli-
ver] (d 1902 [40]) EA/03*
OLIVER, Harry (d 1973 [85]) de-
signer BP/58*
OLIVER, Henry (b 1921) American
actor TW/23
OLIVER, J. (fl 1849) actor HAS
OLIVER, Jody (b 1954) American
actor TW/28-29
OLIVER, Larry (d 1973 [93]) actor

TW/29

OLIVER, Maggie (d 1892 [44])
soubrette EA/93*

OLIVER, Martha [Mrs. W. C.
Phillips] (1834-80) English
actress, singer, manager
CDP, DNB

OLIVER, Mary (d 1903 [73]) EA/
04*

OLIVER, Olive (d 1961 [90])
American actress BE*, BP/
46*, WWT/14*

OLIVER, Rochelle (b 1937) American actress BE, TW/25, 30

OLIVER, Roland [W. A. Jones]
(d 1899 [57]) singer EA/00*

OLIVER, Susan (b 1936) American
actress BE, TW/15-16

OLIVER, Vic (1898-1964) Austrian
actor, musician WWT/9-13,
WWW/6

OLIVER, Will (d 1916 [63]) singer,
comedian, agent, composer
CDP

OLIVER, Mrs. Will see Oliver,
Florence

OLIVER, William Ball (d 1907
[71]) EA/08*

OLIVER, William E. (d 1964)
critic BP/49*

OLIVER, William I. (b 1926)
Panamanian educator, dramatist, director BE

OLIVETTE, Nina (d 1971 [63])
singer, actress TW/27

OLIVIER, Mrs. H. C. S. see
Beere, Mrs. Bernard

OLIVIER, Baron Laurence (b
1907) English actor, producer,
director, manager AAS, BE,
CB, COC, ES, NTH, OC/1-3,
PDT, SR, TW/2-20, WWT/6-
16

OLLENDORF, Paul (d 1920) publisher BE*, WWT/14*

OLLIER, J. (fl 1849) American
actor HAS

OLLIFFE, Geraldine see
Oliffe, Geraldine

OLLIVES, Tom (d 1897 [38])
music-hall performer EA/98*

OLMAR, Mons. [James Chadwick]
(d 1885) gymnast EA/86*

OLMSTED, Gertrude (d 1975 [70])
performer BP/59*

OLMSTED, Rem (b 1917) American dancer TW/2

OLNEY, Dorothy McGrayne (d

1973 [73]) producer/director/
choreographer BP/57*

O'LOUGHLIN, Gerald (b 1921)
American actor BE, TW/18-20,
22, 25

OLP, Georgie (d 1970) performer
BP/55*

OLSEN, George (d 1971 [78]) bandleader TW/27

OLSEN, Moroni (d 1954 [65]) American actor, director BE*,
WWT/14*

OLSEN, Ole [né John Siguard Olsen]
(1892-1963) American actor CB,
TW/1, 3-8, 19, WWT/10-13

OLSON, Dale (b 1943) American
actor TW/27

OLSON, James (b 1930) American
actor TW/12-15, 20-23

OLSON, Kay (b 1942) American actress TW/22

OLSON, Murray (b 1932) American
actor TW/24

OLSON, Nancy (b 1928) American
actress BE

OLVENE, Tom (d 1898) gymnast
EA/00*

OLVER, Hal (d 1963 [70]) press
representative BE*, BP/47*

OLWINE, Wayne (d 1862) actor
CDP, HAS

OLWINE, Mrs. Wayne see Daly,
Julia

OLWYNE, Isaac Wayne see Olwine, Wayne

O'LYNN, Teddy see Longworth,
Thomas Frederick

O'MAHONY, Nora English actress
TW/4

O'MALLEY (d 1883 [28]) ventriloquist EA/84*

O'MALLEY, Alice Mary [Mrs.
George Davies] (d 1899) EA/00*

O'MALLEY, Dan (d 1906 [42])
music-hall comedian EA/07*

O'MALLEY, Ellen (d 1961) Irish
actress WWT/1-8

O'MALLEY, Frank Ward (1875-
1932) American dramatist
WWA/1

O'MALLEY, Grania (d 1973 [75])
Irish actress TW/25, 30

O'MALLEY, J. Pat (b 1904) English actor BE, TW/1, 11-12

O'MALLEY, Pat (d 1966 [75]) performer BP/50*

O'MALLEY, Rex (1901-76) English
actor, director BE, TW/1-4,

10-11, 13-15, 19, 21, WWT/
9-15
OMAN, Julia Trevelyan (b 1930)
English designer WWT/15-16
OMAR, Jemela (b 1941) American
actress TW/25
O'MARA (d 1891 [67]) acrobat
EA/92*
O'MARA, Joseph Irish singer
GRB/1-4
O'MARA, Kate (b 1939) English
actress WWT/16
OMENS, Estelle (b 1928) Ameri-
can actress TW/26-28
OMOHUNDRO, John B. (d 1880)
actor CDP
O'MORRISON, Kevin (b 1916)
American actor TW/23
O'NEAL, Frederick (b 1905)
American actor, director,
administrator, lecturer BE,
CB, TW/1, 10-12, 20-23,
26, WWT/12-16
O'NEAL, Patrick (b 1927) Ameri-
can actor TW/18, WWT/14-16
O'NEAL, Ron (b 1937) American
actor TW/25-27
O'NEAL, Zelma (b 1907) Ameri-
can actress, singer WWT/
7-9
ONEGIN, Sigrid (1891-1943)
German singer ES
O'NEIL, Barbara actress TW/1,
3, 11-13
O'NEIL, Billy (b 1834) American
singer, dancer, actor HAS
O'NEIL, Charles (d 1863) come-
dian HAS
O'NEIL, Colette Scottish actress
WWT/16
O'NEIL, George (1898-1940)
American dramatist CB, MD
O'NEIL, J. H. (fl 1871) dancer
CDP
O'NEIL, Kathleen ["Kitty"] (1840-
93) Irish music-hall performer
CDP, HAS
O'NEIL, Nance see O'Neill,
Nance
O'NEIL, Nancy (b 1911) Australian
actress WWT/8-9
O'NEIL, Peggy (1898-1960) Irish
actress TW/16, WWT/4-10
O'NEIL, Standish (d 1969 [75])
producer/director/choreographer
BP/54*
O'NEIL, Tricia (b 1945) American
actress TW/27-28

O'NEIL, William (d 1868 [34])
comedian, singer EA/69*
O'NEILL, Annie (b 1872) Scottish
actress SR
O'NEILL, Carlotta Monterey (d
1970 [82]) performer BP/55*
O'NEILL, Dick (b 1928) American
actor TW/22-28, 30
O'NEILL, Eliza (1791-1872) English
actress CDP, COC, DNB, OC/
1-3, OX
O'NEILL, Eugene F. (d 1972 [84])
performer BP/57*
O'NEILL, Eugene Gladstone (1888-
1953) American dramatist AAS,
CH, COC, ES, HJD, HP, MD,
MH, MWD, NTH, OC/1-3, PDT,
RE, SR, TW/10, WWA/3,
WWT/4-11, WWW/5
O'NEILL, Frank B. (1869-1959)
English business manager
GRB/4, WWT/1-9
O'NEILL, Henry [or Harry] (1891-
1961) American actor TW/17,
WWT/8-10
O'NEILL, James (1849-1920) Irish
actor CDP, DAB, ES, HJD,
GRB/1-4, NTH, PP/2, SR,
WWA/1, WWM, WWS, WWT/1-3
O'NEILL, James, Jr. (d 1923
[43]) actor BE*, BP/8*
O'NEILL, James, Jr. (b 1920)
American critic BE
O'NEILL, Joseph J. (d 1962 [66])
performer BE*
O'NEILL, J. R. [Hugo Vamp] (d
1860 [37]) author EA/72*
O'NEILL, Maire (1887-1952) Irish
actress COC, ES, OC/2-3,
TW/9, WWT/2-11
O'NEILL, Michael English drama-
tist CD
O'NEILL, Nance [Gertrude Lamson]
(1874-1965) American actress
BE, COC, ES, GRB/2-4, WWM,
TW/4-7, 21, WWS, WWT/1-11
O'NEILL, Norman (1875-1934)
English composer, conductor
WWT/4-7, WWW/3
O'NEILL, Mrs. Robert see
Dennett, Eliza
O'NEILL, Sally (d 1968 [55]) per-
former BP/53*
O'NEILL, Sheila (b 1930) English
actress, dancer, choreographer
WWT/15-16
O'NEILL, T. H. (d 1907 [47])
American business manager

GRB/3*

ONETO, Richard (b 1925) American actor TW/11

ONGAR, Ivy (b 1883) English dancer GRB/1

O'NIEL, Colette [Lady Constance Annesley] (1896-1975) Irish actress WWT/4-8

ONODERA, Sho (d 1974 [59]) performer BP/59*

ONOE, Biacho (d 1965 [73]) performer BP/49*

ONRA [Harriet Gilleno Giles] (d 1909 [37]) acrobat EA/10*

ONZALO, Elise [Mrs. Harry Biddle] (d 1889) gymnast EA/90*

ONZALO, William (d 1900 [51]) gymnast, acrobat EA/01*

OPATOSHU, David (b 1918) American actor BE, TW/19, 25, 29

OPENSHAW, Charles Elton dramatist WWT/6-10

OPEN THEATRE theatre collective CD

OPERTI, Le Roi (1895-1971) American actor, singer, director BE, TW/1, 28

OPFERMANN, Arthur Edward (d 1909 [39]) variety acting manager EA/10*

OPIE, Mrs. (b c.1772) English dramatist CP/3

OPP, Julie [Mrs. William Faversham] (1871-1921) American actress GRB/2-4, WWA/1, WWM, WWS, WWT/1-3

OPP, Paul F. (b 1894) American educator BE

OPPENHEIMER, George (1900-77) American critic, dramatist BE

ORAM, Mona K. [Mrs. Arthur Greville] English actress GRB/1, 3-4

O'RAMEY, Georgia (1886-1928) American actress WWM, WWT/4-5

ORBACH, Jerry (b 1935) American actor AAS, BE, CB, TW/21-27, 29, WWT/15-16

ORBASANY, Irma (d 1961 [95]) performer BE*

ORCHARD, Julian (b 1930) English actor TW/22, WWT/16

ORCZY, Baroness Emmusca (d 1947 [80]) Hungarian dramatist

WWT/4-10, WWW/4

ORD, Ralph Jerrold (b 1869) Irish actor GRB/1

"ORD, Robert" [Mrs. W. Gayer MacKay] dramatist WWT/4-7

ORD, Simon (1874-1944) Scottish manager WWT/6-7

ORDZ, Josephine see D'Orme, Josephine

O'REGAN, Kathleen (b 1903) Irish actress WWT/6-11

O'REILLY, General see O'Reilly, Eugene

O'REILLY, Emmie [Mrs. Austin-Leigh] actress GRB/1

O'REILLY, Eugene [General O'Reilly] (d 1873) actor EA/74*

O'REILLY, William see Bailey, William

O'REILLY, Mrs. William see Bailey, Mrs. William

O'REILY, William (fl 1792) Irish actor CDP, TD/1-2 [see also: O'Riley, Mr.]

ORFALY, Alexander (b 1935) American actor TW/24, 26-30

ORFORD, Earl of see Walpole, Horace

ORFORD, Emma Maria (d 1898) actress EA/99*

ORFORD, Emmeline English actress EA/96, GRB/1-2

ORFORD, William see Mozley, William Orford

ORFORD, William Henry (d 1906 [74]) EA/07*

ORGAN, Harriet [Mrs. Selim Bridges] (d 1888) EA/89*

ORGANIC THEATRE theatre collective CD

ORGER, Mrs. Thomas [née Ivers] (1788-1849) English actress BS, CDP, OX

O'RIADA, Sean (d 1971 [40]) Irish? musical director BP/56*

ORIENT, Milt H. (d 1975 [56]) composer/lyricist BP/59*

ORIGLIO, Tony (b 1948) American actor TW/30

O'RILEY, Mr. (fl 1792) Irish actor HAS [see also: O'Reily, William]

ORIN, Renee American actress TW/29

ORKIN, Harvey (d 1975 [57]) performer BP/60*

ORKNEY, Countess of see Gilchrist, Connie

ORLANDI, Felice (b 1925) Italian actress TW/11-12, 21

ORLANDINI, Ernesto (fl 1833) singer HAS

ORLENEV, Pavel Nikolayevich (1869-1932) Russian actor COC, OC/3

ORLOB, Harold (b 1885) American composer, lyricist, dramatist, producer BE

ORLOVA, Lyubov (d 1975) performer BP/59*

ORLOVITZ, Gil (d 1973 [55]) dramatist BP/58*

ORME, Denise [Hon. Mrs. John Yarde-Buller] (1884-1960) actress, singer GRB/1-4, WWT/1-5

ORME, Michael see Greveen, Alice Augusta

ORMEROD, John (d 1896) lessee EA/98*

ORMEROD, John (d 1906 [73]) director EA/07*

ORMISTON, George (b 1939) American actor TW/24

ORMOND, Mr. (d 1870) music-hall chairman EA/71*

ORMOND, Mme. (d 1863) equestrienne HAS

ORMONDE, Dr. (d 1902 [60]) conjuror EA/03*

ORMONDE, Florrie (d 1905 [30]) comedian, dancer EA/06*

ORMONDE, Mabel Irish actress GRB/2

ORMONDE, Nelly [Mrs. W. Newman] (d 1891) EA/92*

ORMONDE, Will (d 1904) music-hall performer EA/05*

ORMS, Howard R. (b 1920) American executive BE

ORMSBY, E. L. (d 1905) lessee EA/06*

ORNBO, Robert (b 1931) English lighting designer WWT/15-16

ORNELLAS, Norman (d 1975 [36]) performer BP/60*

ORNSTEIN, Honora (d 1975 [92]) performer BP/60*

O'RORKE, Brefni (1889-1946) Irish actor WWT/10

O'RORKE, John (d 1899 [76]) actor? EA/00*

O'ROURKE, Edna (b 1925) American actress TW/4

O'ROURKE, Eugene (b 1863) American actor CDP, WWM, WWS

O'ROURKE, J. A. (d 1937 [55]) actor BE*, WWT/14*

O'ROURKE, Tex (d 1963 [77]) American performer BE*

ORR, Charles W. (d 1976 [82]) performer BP/60*

ORR, Christine Grant Millar (d 1963 [63]) dramatist WWW/6

ORR, Forrest (d 1963 [63]) American actor TW/1

ORR, James Morrice see Holmes, Morrice

ORR, Margaret (d 1894 [78]) EA/95*

ORR, Mary (b 1918) American actress, dramatist BE, TW/1-6, WWT/15-16

ORR, William Amory (d 1892) music-hall comedian EA/93*

ORRERY, Lord (1621-79) English dramatist COC, CP/1-3, GT, OC/1-3

ORRIDGE, Miss (d 1883 [26]) singer EA/84*

ORRIN, Edward acrobat CDP

ORRIN, George acrobat CDP

ORRIN, George Frederick (d 1884 [68]) EA/85*

ORRIN, Mrs. George Frederick see Orrin, Zilla Toncliffe

ORRIN, George W. (1846-92) circus manager CDP

ORRIN, Zilla Toncliffe [Mrs. George Frederick Orrin] (d 1884 [58]) EA/85*

ORRY-KELLY (1897-1964) Australian designer WWA/4

ORSKA, Marie (d 1930) actress BE*, WWT/14*

ORT, Izzy (d 1975 [84]) performer BP/60*

ORTEGA, Carlos M. (d 1965 [80]) dramatist BP/50*

ORTEGA, Santos (d 1976 [76]) performer BP/60*

ORTH, Frank (d 1962 [82]) actor BE*

ORTH, Lizette Emma (1858-1913) American composer WWA/1

ORTON, Joe (1933-67) English dramatist AAS, CD, CH, COC, MH, MWD, PDT, RE

ORTON, John Nicholas Colthurst see Overton, Charles

ORTON, Josephine (1843-1926) American actress CDP, HAS

ORY, Edward (d 1973 [86]) composer/lyricist BP/57*

OSATO, Sona (b 1919) American dancer, actress BE, CB, TW/1, 3-5

OSBALDESTONE, Estelle M. see Phelps, Stella

OSBALDISTON, David Webster (1794-1850) actor CDP

OSBORN, E. W. (1860-1930) American critic WWT/6

OSBORN, Laughton (c. 1809-78) American dramatist DAB, WWA/H

OSBORN, Paul (b 1901) American dramatist BE, MD, MH, MWD, NTH, WWT/9-15

OSBORN, Master R. W. dwarf CDP

OSBORNE, Annie [Mrs. Fred G. Latham] (d 1894) actress CDP, EA/95*

OSBORNE, Charles (d 1908 [79]) dramatist EA/09*

OSBORNE, Charles (d 1911) actor EA/12*

OSBORNE, Edward (d 1876 [33]) actor EA/77*

OSBORNE, Mrs. Elizabeth C. Douglas (d 1890 [61]) EA/91*

OSBORNE, Fanny (d 1855) actress HAS

OSBORNE, Fred (d 1888 [35]) minstrel EA/89*

OSBORNE, George Alexander (d 1893 [87]) composer EA/94*

OSBORNE, Georgia Lund (d 1975 [57]) talent agent BP/60*

OSBORNE, Hubert (b 1881) Canadian actor WWM

OSBORNE, James (d 1889 [51]) EA/90*

OSBORNE, Jane see Barry, Mrs. William

OSBORNE, John (b 1929) English dramatist, actor, director AAS, BE, CB, CD, CH, COC, ES, HP, MD, MH, MWD, OC/3, PDT, RE, WWT/14-16

OSBORNE, Kate actress GRB/1

OSBORNE, Kipp (b 1944) American actor TW/27-30, WWT/16

OSBORNE, Lennie (d 1964 [69]) actor BE*

OSBORNE, Theresa [Mrs. Sydney Compton] Indian/English actress GRB/1-2

OSBORNE, Vivienne (b 1900/05) American actress WWT/6-10

OSBORNE, Walter (d 1900 [43]) performer? EA/01*

OSBORN-HANNAH, Jane (d 1943) American singer WWA/3

OSBOURNE, Lloyd (1868-1947) American dramatist HJD

OSCAR, [Mons. ?] (d 1879 [21]) trapezist EA/80*

OSCAR, Henry (1891-1969) English actor, producer WWT/5-14

OSCARD, Fifi (b 1921) American talent representative BE

OSGOOD, Charles (d 1922 [63]) manager BE*, BP/6*

OSGOOD, Helen (fl 1863) actress HAS

OSGOOD, Mrs. J. M. (fl 1874?) singer CDP

OSGOOD, Lawrence (b 1929) American dramatist, director CD

O'SHAUGHNESSY, John (b 1907) American director, actor BE, TW/4-8, 22

O'SHAUGHNESSY, Peter (d 1910) proprietor EA/11*

O'SHEA, John (d 1908 [76]) EA/09*

O'SHEA, Julia (d 1974 [83]) performer BP/59*

O'SHEA, Kevin (b 1915) American actor TW/2-3

O'SHEA, Michael (d 1973 [67]) actor TW/30

O'SHEA, Michael Sean (b 1922) American press representative BE

O'SHEA, Milo (b 1926) Irish actor TW/24-25

O'SHEA, Tessie (b 1918) Welsh actress TW/20, 22-23

OSHEROWITCH, Mendel (d 1965 [78]) dramatist BP/49*

OSHINS, Julie (d 1956 [50]) American performer TW/12

OSHRIN, George (d 1972 [69]) manager BP/57*

OSMAN, Harry (d 1907 [46]) actor EA/08*

OSMAN, William (d 1891) actor EA/92*

OSMOND, Maude see Walton, Mrs. J. K.

OSMONDE, Florrie (d 1905 [30]) English variety artist GRB/1

OSNATH-HALEVY, Sarah (d 1975 [62]) performer BP/60*

OSRANI, Jean (d 1908 [49]) acrobat

EA/09*

OSSORY, Bishop of see Bale, John

OSTERMAN, Jack (d 1939 [37]) American comedian BE*, BP/23*

OSTERMAN, Kathryn (d 1956 [73]) actress TW/13

OSTERMAN, Lester (b 1914) American producer BE, WWT/14-16

OSTERMAN, Rolfe A. (d 1969 [78]) performer BP/54*

OSTERSTOCK, Fred see Forth, Eric

OSTERTAG, Barna (b 1902) American agent, actress BE

OSTERWALD, Bibi (b 1920/21) American actress, singer BE, TW/1, 4-8, 10-15, 26-27, WWT/13-16

OSTLER, William (d 1614) English actor COC, DA, DNB, GT, NTH, OC/1-3

OSTRANDER, Albert A. (d 1964 [61]) designer TW/21

OSTRANDER, Clarence M. (d 1887) singer NYM

OSTRIN, Art (b 1937) American actor TW/22, 25-26

OSTROSKA, George (d 1969 [32]) performer BP/54*

OSTROVSKY, Alexander Nikolaivich (1823-86) Russian dramatist COC, NTH, OC/3

OSTROW, Stuart (b 1932) American producer WWT/15-16

O'SULLIVAN, Denis (1868-1908) American actor, singer GRB/1-4

O'SULLIVAN, James Joseph (d 1872 [37]) Irish comedian EA/73*

O'SULLIVAN, Mairin D. Irish actress TW/22-23, 26

O'SULLIVAN, Maureen (b 1911/17) Irish actress BE, TW/19-22, 26-27, 29, WWT/14-16

O'SULLIVAN, Michael (1934-71) American actor TW/21-24, 26, 28

O'SULLIVAN, Vincent (b 1872) American dramatist WWA/5

OSUNA, Jess (b 1933) American actor TW/23-25

OSWALD, Charlie [Charlie Oswald Young] (d 1898) music-hall comedian EA/99*

OSWALD, Frank (d 1896 [38]) actor EA/97*

OSWALD, Genevieve (b 1923) American librarian BE

OSWALD, John (fl 1783-89) Scottish dramatist CP/3

OSWALD, Virginia (b 1926) American singer, actress BE

OTERO, Caroline (1868/71-1965) Spanish dancer, variety artist GRB/1-4, WWS

OTIS, Elita Proctor (d 1927 [76]) American actress WWS

OTLEY, Charles (b 1850) English actor GRB/1

O'TOOLE, Peter (b 1932/33) Irish actor AAS, CB, ES, WWT/13-16

OTT, Alexander (d 1970 [82]) producer/director/choreographer BP/55*

OTTAWAY, Frank (d 1907) minstrel bone soloist EA/08*

OTTAWAY, James (b 1908) English actor WWT/15-16

OTTENHEIMER, Albert M. (b 1904) American actor TW/22, 29

OTTER, William (d 1896 [38]) Negro comedian EA/97*

OTTINGER, Maurice American actor TW/23

OTTO, Mme. (d 1860/75) actress, singer CDP, HAS, SR

OTTO, Liz American actress TW/26-28

OTTO-ALVSLEBEN, Melitta (1842-93) singer CDP

OTWAY, Grace (d 1935) actress BE*, WWT/14*

OTWAY, Rita (d 1972 [85]) performer BP/57*

OTWAY, Silvester see Oswald, John

OTWAY, Thomas (1652-85) English dramatist CDP, COC, CP/1-3, DNB, ES, GT, HP, MH, NTH, OC/1-3, PDT, RE, SR

OUELLETTE, Paul E. (b 1927) American educator BE

OUGHTERSON, Hugh George (d 1916) EA/17*

OUGHTON, Winifred (1890-1964) English actress WWT/9-13

OUKRAINSKY, Serge (d 1972 [86]) performer BP/57*

OULD, Hermon (1885/86-1951) English dramatist, journalist MD, MWD, WWT/6-11

OULTON, Brian (b 1908) English
actor WWT/12-16
OULTON, Walley Chamberlaine
(d 1820 [50]) Irish dramatist
CP/3, GT, TD/1-2
OUROUSSOW, Eugenie (d 1975
[66]) producer/director/chore-
ographer BP/59*
OURSLER, Fulton (1893-1952)
American dramatist CB
OUSPENSKAYA, Maria (1876-1949)
Russian actress TW/6, WWT/
10
OUSTER, Murray (d 1974 [67])
performer BP/59*
OUTRAM, Leonard S. (d 1901
[45]) actor, dramatist EA/01*,
WWT/14*
OUVILLY, George Gerbier D'
see D'Ouvilly, George Gerbier
OVEREND, Dorothy Australian
actress WWT/5-7
OVERMAN, Lynne (1887-1943)
American actor CB, SR,
WWT/5-9
OVERTON, Charles [John Nicholas
Colthurst Orton] (d 1898 [44])
actor, dramatist EA/99*
OVERTON, Frank (1918-67) Amer-
ican actor BE, TW/10, 14, 23
OVERTON, Hall (d 1972 [52])
composer/lyricist BP/57*
OVERTON, Robert (1859-1924)
dramatist WWW/2
OVETTE, Joseph (d 1946 [61])
Italian/American magician SR
OWEN, Mr. (d 1905 [61]) EA/06*
OWEN, Mrs. (d 1879 [44]) music-
hall proprietor EA/80*
OWEN, Mrs. (d 1905 [57]) EA/
06*
OWEN, Master actor CDP
OWEN, Alun (b 1925/26) Welsh
dramatist, actor, assistant
stage manager AAS, CD, CH,
ES, MH, PDT, WWT/14-16
OWEN, Bill (b 1916) English actor
TW/6, WWT/11-16
OWEN, Catherine Dale (1900-65)
American actress TW/22,
WWT/6-8
OWEN, Charles (d 1912 [38])
music-hall manager EA/13*
OWEN, Charles (d 1917) circus
& variety performer EA/18*
OWEN, Dave (d 1906) singer
EA/07*
OWEN, Ellen [Mrs. Stuart

Lomath] English actress GRB/1
OWEN, Emmie (d 1905 [33]) ac-
tress, singer CDP
OWEN, F. C. (d 1875 [53]) propri-
etor EA/76*
OWEN, Mrs. Fred see Robert-
son, Marie
OWEN, George (d 1882) actor,
manager EA/83*, WWT/14*
OWEN, Mrs. George (d 1907 [81])
EA/08*
OWEN, Harold (1872-1930) English
dramatist WWT/4-6
OWEN, Harrison (1890/91-1966)
Australian dramatist WWT/7-9,
WWW/6
OWEN, Henry C. (d 1916 [75])
EA/17*
OWEN, Jennie (d 1904 [28]) bur-
lesque actress EA/05*
OWEN, John (d 1883 [62]) composer
EA/84*
OWEN, John (d 1911 [64]) comedian
EA/12*
OWEN, Reginald (1887-1972) Eng-
lish actor, dramatist BE,
GRB/4, TW/7-8, 28-29, WWT/
1-14
OWEN, Rich (d 1884 [38]) master
carpenter EA/85*
OWEN, Robert (fl 1696) dramatist
CP/1-3, GT
OWEN, Robert Dale (1801-77) Eng-
lish/American dramatist CDP,
HJD
OWEN, T. James (d 1916) EA/17*
OWEN, Mrs. W. H. see Smith-
ers, Florence
OWEN, William (d 1975 [38]) edu-
cator BP/60*
OWEN, William Florence (1844-
1906) Irish actor CDP, DAB,
HAS, PP/2
OWENS, Elizabeth (b 1938) Ameri-
can actress TW/27-30
OWENS, John Edmond (1823-86)
English/American actor CDP,
COC, DAB, ES, HAS, OC/1-3,
SR, WWA/H
OWENS, John Lennergan Irish actor
TD/1-2
OWENS, Rochelle [née Rochelle
Bass] (b 1936) American drama-
tist CD, CH, WWT/15-16
OWENS, William (d 1926 [63]) actor
BE*, BP/11*
OWENS, William H. (b 1922)
American educator BE

OWENSON, Mr. (fl 1785-1804)
Irish actor TD/1-2
OWENSON, Miss (fl 1807) drama-
tist CP/3
OWENSON, Robert (1744-1812)
Irish actor DNB
OXBERRY, Vincent Wild (d 1881
[44]) acting manager EA/82*
OXBERRY, William (1784-1824)
English actor, publisher BS,
CDP, COC, DNB, OC/1-3
OXBERRY, William Henry (1808-
52) English actor COC, DNB,
OC/1-3
OXENFORD, Edward (d 1929
[82]) dramatist, librettist
BE*, WWT/14*
OXENFORD, John (1812-77) Eng-
lish dramatist CDP, DNB,
EA/68
OXFORD, Mr. ["Hugo"] (d 1871
[18]) trapezist EA/72*
OXFORD, Countess of see
Davenport, Hester
OXLEY, John E. (b c. 1800)
American actor, manager
CDP, HAS, SR
OYA, Ichijiro (d 1972 [78]) per-
former BP/57*
OYRA, Jan (b 1888) Polish
dancer WWT/4-6
OYSHER, Moishe (d 1958 [51])
Bessarabian composer, actor
TW/15
OYSTER, Jim (b 1930) American
actor TW/11-20, 23-25
OZELL, John (d 1743) English
translator CP/1-3, GT

- P -

P., G. (fl 1742) dramatist CP/3
P., P., Mons. (fl 1674) drama-
tist CP/1-3
P., R. (fl 1575) dramatist CP/1-3
P., S. see Pordage, Samuel
P., T. (fl 1663-78) dramatist
CP/1-3
PAAL, Alexander (d 1972 [60s])
producer/director/choreographer
BP/57*
PAALEN, Bella (d 1964 [82])
Austrian singer BE*
PAAP, Simon (fl 1820) Dutch
dwarf CDP
PABLO ["Boston George"] (d
1881) circus performer EA/

82*
PACCHIEROTTI, Gaspare (1740-
1821) Italian singer ES
PACEY, John (d 1873) scene artist,
stage manager EA/74*
PACEY, Tom (b 1863) English vari-
ety artist GRB/1
PACINI, Regina (b 1871) Portuguese
singer ES
PACINO, Al (b 1940) American ac-
tor CB, TW/24-26, WWT/16
PACK, George (fl 1700-24) actor
DNB
PACKARD, Miss see Wilks,
Mrs.
PACKARD, Albert (b 1909) Ameri-
can business manager BE
PACKARD, Edward G. (b 1843)
American actor HAS
PACKARD, Marie singer CDP
PACKER, John Hayman (1730-1806)
actor CDP, DNB, GT, TD/1-2
PACKER, Netta (d 1962 [65]) per-
former BE*
PACKWOOD, Harry (b 1944) Amer-
ican actor TW/25
PACUVIO, Giulio (b 1910) Italian
director ES
PADDOCK, Robert Rowe (b 1914)
American scene designer BE
PADUANI, Virginia (fl 1847) singer
HAS
PADULA, Edward (b 1916) Ameri-
can producer, director BE
PAEZ, Cecelia de [née Saeman]
(fl 1857) French singer HAS
PAGAN, Anna (b 1946) American
actress TW/25
PAGAN, Peter (b 1921) Australian
actor TW/13-15, 22-23
PAGANINI, Niccolo (1784-1840)
musician CDP
PAGDEN, Emma Tanner (d 1899)
EA/00*
PAGDEN, Harry [or Henry] (d
1907) actor EA/08*, WWT/14*
PAGDEN, Leonard (d 1928 [66])
English actor GRB/1-2
PAGE, Ambrose (d 1887 [74])
EA/88*
PAGE, Anthony (b 1935) Indian/
English director AAS, WWT/
15-16
PAGE, Ashley (d 1934 [67]) actor
BE*, WWT/14*
PAGE, Augusta (fl 1862) actress
HAS
PAGE, Austin dramatist WWT/7-11

PAGE, Dr. Byrd (d 1916) con-
jurer EA/17*
PAGE, Charles (d 1898) music-
hall manager EA/99*
PAGE, Mrs. Charles see Tal-
bot, Mrs.
PAGE, Curtis C. (b 1914) Amer-
ican educator BE
PAGE, E. V. manager, song
composer CDP
PAGE, Mrs. E. V. see Page,
Sarah Florence
PAGE, Evelyn American actress
TW/25, 28
PAGE, Geraldine (b 1924) Amer-
ican actress AAS, BE, CB,
ES, TW/9-24, 26-27, 29,
WWT/12-16
PAGE, Henry C. (b 1825) Ameri-
can actor, manager, agent HAS
PAGE, James Augustus [Sydney
Hayes] (d 1888 [30]) actor
EA/89*
PAGE, John (fl c. 1626) actor
DA
PAGE, Kitty see Hargreaves,
Mrs. Albert
PAGE, Nathaniel Clifford (b
1866) American composer
WWA/4, WWM
PAGE, Norman (d 1935 [59])
English actor, stage manager,
producer GRB/2-3, WWT/1-7
PAGE, Oliver (fl 1550) actor
DA
PAGE, Patti (b 1927) American
singer CB
PAGE, Paul (d 1974 [70]) per-
former BP/58*
PAGE, Philip (d 1968 [80]) actor
WWT/15*
PAGE, Philip P. (b 1884/89)
English critic, dramatist
WWT/5-13
PAGE, Reginald Ernest see
Harley, Rex
PAGE, Rita (1906-54) English ac-
tress, singer WWT/7-8
PAGE, Ruth (b 1903?/05) Amer-
ican dancer, choreographer
CB, ES
PAGE, Sarah Florence [Mrs. E.
V. Page] (d 1902 [50]) EA/03*
PAGE, Tilsa (b 1926) English
actress WWT/11-12
PAGE, Will A. (d 1928 [55])
press representative BE*,
BP/13*

PAGE, William J. (d 1870) music-
hall chairman EA/71*
PAGENT, Robert (b 1917) American
actor TW/1-3
PAGE-PHILLIPS, Percy see An-
stey, Percy
PAGET, Lord Alfred (d 1888 [72])
EA/89*
PAGET, Cecil (d 1955) manager
WWT/6-9
PAGET, Mrs. F. M. see Paget,
Martha E.
PAGET, Frederick Maurice (d 1911
[62]) actor EA/12*
PAGET, Martha E. [Mrs. F. M.
Paget] (d 1912 [82]) EA/13*
PAGET, Rose Vernon English ac-
tress GRB/1-2
PAGET, Violet [Vernon Lee] (1856-
1935) dramatist WWW/3
PAGET-BOWMAN, Cicely (b 1910)
English actress WWT/10-16
PAGETT, Nicola (b 1945) Egyptian/
English actress WWT/16
PAGLIA, Gina (b 1955) American
actress TW/28
PAGNOL, Marcel (1895-1974)
French dramatist, director, pro-
ducer BE, CB, ES, MD, MWD,
NTH
PAIGE, Autris (b 1941) American
actor TW/28
PAIGE, Janis [née Donna Mae Jaden]
(b 1922) American actress, singer
BE, CB, TW/8, 10-15, 24-25,
WWT/15-16
PAIGE, Mabel (d 1954 [74]) Ameri-
can actress TW/10
PAIGE, Raymond North (1900-65)
American conductor WWA/4
PAIN, Mr. (fl 1857?) actor CDP
PAINE, Albert Bigelow (1861-1937)
dramatist HJD
PAINE, Ira (d 1889 [53]) marksman
EA/90*
PAINE, John Knowles (1839-1906)
American composer DAB, HJD
PAINE, Lizzie [Mrs. George Mil-
bank] (fl 1888?) songwriter CDP
PAINTER, Eleanor (1890-1947)
American actress, singer TW/
4, WWT/4-7
PAISNER, Dina (b 1963) American
actress TW/27, 29
PAKENHAM, Essie [Mrs. R. J.
Pakenham] (d 1893) EA/94*
PAKENHAM, Henry (d 1875) actor
EA/76*

PAKENHAM, Mrs. R. J. see
Pakenham, Essie
PALANCE, Jack (b 1920) Ameri-
can actor ES, TW/7-14
PALERME, Gina actress, dancer
WWT/4-5
PALERMO, Alex (b 1929) Ameri-
can director, choreographer,
actor BE
PALETTE, Billy (d 1963) English
performer BE*
PALEY, John (d 1918) EA/19*
PALFREY, May Lever [Mrs.
Weedon Grossmith] (1867/73-
1929) English actress CDP,
EA/96, GRB/1-4, WWT/1-6
PALFREYMAN, Thomas (d 1589?)
member of the Chapel Royal
DNB
PALITZ, Morty (d 1962 [53])
composer/lyricist BP/47*
PALLADINO, Emma (1861-1922)
Italian dancer ES
PALLADINO, Joseph Antony see
Faye, Joey
PALLADIO, Andrea (1518-80)
Italian architect COC, OC/
1-3
PALLANT, Robert (fl 1590-1616)
actor DA
PALLANT, Robert, the Younger
(fl 1620s) actor DA
PALLANT, Walter (d 1904 [45])
dramatist, theatre chairman
BE*, EA/05*, WWT/14*
PALLENBERG, Max (d 1934 [57])
actor WWT/14*
PALLERINI, Antonia (1790-1870)
Italian dancer, mimist ES
PALLES, Joseph (d 1895 [45])
music-hall comedian EA/96*
PALLETTE, Eugene (d 1954 [65])
American actor BE*, BP/39*
PALLING, Arthur (d 1916) actor
EA/17*
PALLING, Mrs. Arthur see
Palling, Laura
PALLING, Laura [Mrs. Arthur
Palling] (d 1896) EA/97*
PALLING, Walter (d 1896) actor
EA/97*
PALLISER, Esther (b 1872) ac-
tress, singer CDP, DP
PALMER, Mr. (fl 19th cent)
actor CDP
PALMER, Mr. (d 1833) American
actor CDP, HAS
PALMER, Mrs. see Gee,

Caroline Eliza
PALMER, Miss (fl 1752-53) actress
HAS
PALMER, Ada English actress
GRB/1
PALMER, Albert Marshman (1838-
1905) American manager CDP,
COC, DAB, ES, NTH, OC/1-3,
SR, WWA/1
PALMER, Alexander (d 1888 [74])
comic singer EA/90*
PALMER, Mrs. A. M. (d 1923)
president of the Professional
Women's League BP/7*
PALMER, Anthony (b 1934) Ameri-
can actor TW/26, 29-30
PALMER, Arthur A. see Boswell,
A. P.
PALMER, Barbara (b 1911) English
actress WWT/9
PALMER, Bessie (d 1910 [79])
singer EA/11*
PALMER, Betsy (b 1929) American
actress BE, TW/12, WWT/16
PALMER, Byron (b 1921) American
actor TW/5-16
PALMER, Charles (1869-1920)
critic WWT/2-3
PALMER, Charles (d 1976 [46])
performer BP/60*
PALMER, Charles Edward (d 1878
[75]) actor EA/79*
PALMER, David S. (1826-57) Amer-
ican actor HAS
PALMER, Mrs. David S. [Lizzie
Steele] (1832-58) American ac-
tress HAS
PALMER, Dawson (d 1972 [35]) per-
former BP/57*
PALMER, E. Blanchard (d 1877)
caterer EA/78*
PALMER, Ethelyn (b 1879) Ameri-
can actress WWS
PALMER, F. C. (d 1917) EA/18*
PALMER, F. Grove see Grove,
Fred
PALMER, Florrie see Leamore,
Florence
PALMER, Henry [Harry Siddons]
(d 1886 [41]) actor? EA/87*
PALMER, Henry David (1832-79)
American manager CDP
PALMER, Herbert Edward (1880-
1961) English dramatist WWW/6
PALMER, Jack (d 1976 [75]) com-
poser/lyricist BP/60*
PALMER, James (d 1882 [52])
ceiling walker EA/84*

PALMER, Jay (d 1970 [71]) per-
former BP/55*
PALMER, John (1728-68) English
actor COC, DNB, GT, OC/
1-3, TD/1-2
PALMER, John (1742/45/47-98)
English actor CDP, COC,
DNB, GT, OC/1-3, OX, TD/
1-2
PALMER, John (fl 1791) actor
CDP
PALMER, John (d 1868 [86])
wardrobe keeper EA/69*
PALMER, John (1885-1944) Eng-
lish critic, dramatist CB,
NTH, WWT/2-9, WWW/4
PALMER, Langford H. (d 1894
[28]) comedian EA/96*
PALMER, Leland (b 1945) Amer-
ican actor TW/28-30
PALMER, Lilli (b 1914) Austrian
actress AAS, CB, ES, TW/
5-15, WWT/9-16
PALMER, Lucienne see Hill,
Lucienne
PALMER, Mary see Adcock,
Mrs. William
PALMER, Millicent see Band-
mann-Palmer, Mrs.
PALMER, Minnie (1857/60-
1936) American actress,
singer CDP, DP, GRB/2-4,
PP/2, WWS, WWT/1-8
PALMER, Peter (b 1931) Amer-
ican actor, singer BE, TW/
13-16, 21, 29-30
PALMER, Reginald (d 1964 [74])
performer BP/49*
PALMER, Robert (1754-1817)
English actor COC, GT,
OC/3, TD/2
PALMER, Robert (1757-1805)
actor CDP
PALMER, Samuel (d 1869 [42])
pantomimist EA/70*
PALMER, Samuel S. (fl 1848)
American actor HAS
PALMER, Sarah Annie [Mrs.
William Palmer] (d 1883 [35])
EA/84*
PALMER, Stacy (b 1930) Ameri-
can actor TW/28, 30
PALMER, Thomas (d 1868 [41])
costumier EA/69*
PALMER, Thomas (b 1914) Cana-
dian actor TW/6-7
PALMER, William (d 1797) actor
COC, OC/3, TD/2

PALMER, William (d 1887) music-
hall manager EA/88*
PALMER, Mrs. William see
Palmer, Sarah Annie
PALMER, William Henry [Robert
Heller] (c. 1830-78) English en-
tertainer DAB, WWA/H
PALMERSTON, Minnie [Mrs. Har-
riett Burrows] (d 1904) music-
hall performer EA/05*
PALMERTON, Guy (d 1975 [61])
producer/director/choreographer
BP/59*
PALMIERI, Joseph (b 1939) Amer-
ican actor TW/23-24, 26, 28-30
PALMIERI, Maria (fl 1876) singer
CDP
PALMO, Ferdinand (1785-1869)
Italian manager, singer? CDP,
HAS
PALOTTA, Grace Austrian actress
GRB/2
PALSEN, Mlle. (fl 1852) English
dancer HAS
PALSGRAVE, John (fl 1514-31)
translator CP/1-3
PAMPANINI, Rosetta (1900-73)
Italian singer ES
PANAIEFF, Michel (b 1913) Rus-
sian/American dancer, chore-
ographer ES
PANAMA, Norman (b 1914) Ameri-
can dramatist, producer, di-
rector BE
PANASSIE, Hugues (d 1974 [62])
critic BP/59*
PANDELAKIS, Beatrice (d 1973
[52]) performer BP/58*
PANDOLFI, Frank (d 1975 [73])
performer BP/59*
PANDOLFINI, Francesco (1836-
1916) Italian singer ES
PANE-GASSER, John (1897-1964)
Italian singer WWA/4
PANETTA, George (1915-69) Amer-
ican dramatist BE
PANGBORN, Franklyn (1889-1958)
American actor TW/15, WWM
PANKEY, Aubrey (d 1971 [65]) per-
former BP/55*
PANKHURST, Frank (fl 1869?)
minstrel CDP
PANKIN, Stuart (b 1946) American
actor TW/28-29
PANT, Thomas (fl 1607-10) actor
DA
PANTALEONI, Adriano (1837-1908)
Italian singer ES

PANTER, Joan (b 1909) English actress WWT/9-10

PANTHULU, B. R. (d 1974 [64]) producer/director/choreographer BP/59*

PANVINI, Ron (b 1945) American actor TW/28

PANZER, Paul W. (d 1958 [86]) actor BE*

PAOLIS, Alessio de (d 1964 [71]) Italian singer BE*

PAONE, Marion American actress TW/28

PAPALEO, Anthony see Franciosa, Anthony

PAPANTI, Sig. (fl 1827) actress? singer? HAS

PAPAS, Irene (b 1929) Greek actress TW/29

PAPE, Herr (d 1874) musician EA/75*

PAPE, Joan (b 1944) American actress TW/27, 29-30

PAPE, Willie Barnesmore (b 1854) American pianist CDP, HAS

PAPENDICK, George (fl 1798) translator CP/3

PAPI, Gennaro (1886-1941) Italian conductor CB, WWA/1

PAPINI, Guido (d 1912 [65]) musician EA/13*

PAPIROFSKY, Joseph see Papp, Joseph

PAPP, Joseph [né Papirofsky] (b 1921) American producer, director AAS, BE, CB, COC, ES, OC/3, WWT/14-16

PAPPENHEIM, Eugenie singer CDP

PAQUE, Mons. C. (d 1876 [50]) musician EA/77*

PARADISE, Sophia (d 1906 [63]) EA/07*

PARADO, Eleanore (d 1974) wardrobe mistress BP/58*

PARDAVE, Jose (d 1970 [68]) performer BP/55*

PARDEE, Chester F. (d 1974 [58]) producer/director/choreographer BP/59*

PARDEE, C. W. (d 1975 [90]) performer BP/60*

PARDEY, George (b 1835) English actor HAS

PARDEY, Mrs. George [Josephine Costigan] (b 1852) American actress HAS

PARDEY, H. O. (1808-65) English actor, dramatist HAS, SR

PARDINI, Gaetano (fl 1849) singer CDP

PARDOLL, David (b 1908) American stage manager, production supervisor BE

PARDUE, Henry (d 1917 [34]) EA/18*

PARDY, Laurie Athey (d 1916 [42]) EA/18*

PAREEZER, Barnett (d 1918 [59]) EA/19*

PARELLA, Anthony (b 1915) American producer, director BE

PARENTEAU, Zoel (d 1972 [89]) composer/lyricist BP/57*

PAREPA, Euphrosyne see Rosa, Parepa

PAREPA-ROSA, Euphrosyne see Rosa, Parepa

PARERA, Grace Moore (d 1947) singer WWW/4

PARFITT, Judy English actress AAS, WWT/15-16

PARFRE, Ihan (fl 1512?) dramatist CP/2-3

PARIS, Jackie (b 1961) American actress TW/29

PARIS, Robert Graham (d 1974 [68]) drama coach BP/58*

PARISH, James (1904-74) English dramatist, actor WWT/9-15

PARISH, Michael J. American actor TW/26

PARISH, William (d 1917 [74]) circus proprietor EA/18*

PARISOT, Mlle. (fl 1796-99?) dancer CDP

PARK, Merle (b 1937) Rhodesian dancer CB, ES

PARK, R. (d 1894 [56]) EA/95*

PARK, Tom (d 1891 [32]) actor EA/93*

PARKE, James H. (d 1970) educator BP/55*

PARKE, John (b c. 1750) American dramatist EAP

PARKE, Walter (d 1922) dramatist BE*, WWT/14*

PARKE, William (1873?-1941) actor, manager CB

PARKER, Mr. (fl 1769) actor HAS

PARKER, Mrs. (fl 1700) singer CDP

PARKER, Mrs. (fl 1798) actress TD/1-2

PARKER, Mrs. (d 1893) EA/94*

PARKER, Miss (fl 1863) American
singer HAS
PARKER, Miss see Johnston,
Mrs. Henry Erskine
PARKER, Miss see Murray,
Mrs.
PARKER, Ada see Stetson, Ada
PARKER, Adam (fl 1849) American
actor HAS
PARKER, Albert (d 1974 [87]) pro-
ducer/director/choreographer
BP/59*
PARKER, Amelia (1827-59) Amer-
ican actress HAS
PARKER, Annie [Mrs. Edwin
Drew] (d 1913) EA/14*
PARKER, Annie see Corri,
Mrs. V.
PARKER, Anthony (b 1912) English
producer, manager WWT/11-14
PARKER, Barnett (1889?-1941)
English comedian CB
PARKER, Bob (d 1975) performer
BP/60*
PARKER, Cecil (1897-1971)
English actor TW/7, 27,
WWT/7-14
PARKER, Charles (d 1889) Amer-
ican actor, dancer EA/90*
PARKER, Charles (d 1898) scene
artist EA/99*
PARKER, Clementina (d 1888
[85]) actress EA/89*
PARKER, Dorothy (fl 1910-13)
English actress WWM
PARKER, Dorothy (1893-1967)
American lyricist, dramatist,
critic HJD, WWW/6
PARKER, Eleanor (b 1922) Amer-
ican actress ES
PARKER, Flora (d 1950 [67])
actress, singer TW/7
PARKER, Frank (d 1919) EA/19*
PARKER, Frank (1858/62/64-1926)
stage manager, producer
GRB/1-4, WWT/1-5
PARKER, George (1732-1800)
actor DNB
PARKER, George (d 1910) fire-
man EA/11*
PARKER, George D. (d 1937
[64]) producer, director BE*,
WWT/14*
PARKER, Sir Gilbert (1862-1932)
Canadian dramatist WWW/3
PARKER, Gilbert (b 1927) Amer-
ican talent representative BE
PARKER, Harry L. see Han-

son, Harry L.
PARKER, Henry, Lord Morley (d
1556 [80]) dramatist CP/2-3
PARKER, Henry Taylor (1867-
1934) American critic DAB,
NTH, OC/1-3, WWA/1
PARKER, Horatio William (1863-
1919) American composer DAB,
HJD, WWM, WWA/1
PARKER, Jane (fl 1827) dancer
CDP
PARKER, Jane (d 1908 [74]) EA/
09*
PARKER, Jean (b 1918) American
actress TW/3-8
PARKER, John (d 1858) clown,
ballet master HAS
PARKER, John (d 1892 [31]) pro-
prietor EA/93*
PARKER, John (1875-1952) Ameri-
can critic, historian COC,
DNB, GRB/2-4, OC/1-3, WWA/
3, WWT/1-11, WWW/5
PARKER, Mrs. John (fl 1798-1818)
actress, dancer CDP
PARKER, John Barry (d 1917)
scene artist EA/18*
PARKER, Johnny (d 1893) variety
owner EA/94*
PARKER, John William (b 1909)
American educator BE
PARKER, Joseph (fl 1832-41) Eng-
lish actor HAS
PARKER, Joseph S. (d 1970 [57])
producer/director/choreographer
BP/54*
PARKER, Joy (b 1924) English ac-
tress WWT/11-14
PARKER, Lara (b 1942) American
actress TW/25-26, 28
PARKER, Leonard (b 1932) Ameri-
can actor TW/29
PARKER, Lester (d 1975 [43]) per-
former BP/60*
PARKER, Lew [né Austin Lewis
Jacobs] (1906/10-72) American
actor BE, TW/2-3, 6-7, 11-15,
20, 29, WWT/11-15
PARKER, Lizzie (fl 1861?) singer
CDP
PARKER, Lottie Blair (1858-1937)
American dramatist GRB/3-4,
SR, WWA/1, WWM, WWT/1-8
PARKER, Louise Little (d 1857)
child actress CDP, HAS
PARKER, Louis Napoleon (1852-
1944) French/English dramatist
CB, COC, DNB, ES, GRB/1-4,

MWD, OC/1-3, SR, WWM,
WWS, WWT/1-9, WWW/4
PARKER, Margaret (fl 1850s)
actress HAS
PARKER, Martha Marian (d 1868
[37]) singer EA/69*
PARKER, Mary [Mrs. Stafford
Smith] (d 1910) EA/11*
PARKER, Mary Jennie (fl 1838-
67) American actress HAS
PARKER, Murray (d 1965 [69])
performer BP/50*
PARKER, Rachel (d 1904 [80])
EA/05*
PARKER, Richard (d 1892 [39])
scene artist EA/93*
PARKER, Roger (d 1917) come-
dian EA/18*
PARKER, Ross (d 1974 [59])
composer/lyricist BP/59*
PARKER, Sarah (fl 1827) dancer
CDP
PARKER, Sarah Naomi Jane
[Mrs. Will Parker] (d 1876)
EA/77*
PARKER, Thane (1907-75) English
manager WWT/9-14
PARKER, T. W. (d 1892) actor
EA/93*
PARKER, Warren (b 1909) Amer-
ican actor TW/3
PARKER, W. E. (d 1875 [52])
pantaloon EA/76*
PARKER, Will (d 1886) Negro
comedian EA/87*
PARKER, Mrs. Will see Parker,
Sarah Naomi Jane
PARKER, William (d 1886) sing-
er, composer CDP
PARKER, W. Oren (b 1911) Amer-
ican educator, designer BE
PARKER SISTERS singers,
dancers CDP
PARKES, Mrs. A. L. see Kiral-
fy, Haniola
PARKES, Caroline see Fenton,
Mrs. Charles
PARKES, George (d 1894) actor
CDP
PARKES, George (d 1895 [68])
lessee EA/96*
PARKES, Mrs. George Richmond
see Robins, Elisabeth
PARKES, W. S. (d 1908) EA/09*
PARKHILL, Dale (b 1925) Amer-
ican actor TW/8-10
PARKHIRST, Douglass (1921-64)
American actor TW/13-14, 20

PARKHOUSE, Miss see Cowley,
Mrs. Abraham
PARKHOUSE, Hannah see Cowley,
Hannah
PARKHURST, Edwin R. (b 1848)
English critic WWM
PARKHURST, George A. (d 1890)
American comedian EA/91*
PARKIN, Mrs. Thomas P. (d 1868)
actress? EA/69*
PARKINA, Elizabeth (b 1882) Amer-
ican singer GRB/1-4
PARKINSON, James (d 1894 [46])
actor EA/95*
PARKINSON, Thomas (fl 1769-89)
portrait-painter DNB
PARKINSON, William (d 1891)
cornopean player EA/92*
PARKS, Alonzo [Alonzo Chapman]
(d 1863 [31]) American actor?
HAS
PARKS, Bernice actress TW/3
PARKS, Fanny see Edrian, Fanny
PARKS, George R. (d 1887) actor
NYM
PARKS, Hildy (b 1926) American
actress BE, TW/8-9
PARKS, J. C. (d 1888 [30]) "circus
leader" EA/90*
PARKS, John Gower (1904-55) Eng-
lish designer ES
PARKS, Larry (1914-75) American
actor BE, WWT/15
PARKS, Trina American actress
TW/28
PARLO, Dita (d 1972 [65]) per-
former BP/56*
PARLOWE, Richard see Par-
rowe, Richard
PARMALEE, Barbara (d 1965 [24])
performer BP/50*
PARMALEE, Charles (d 1965 [37])
performer BP/50*
PARNELL, James (1923-61) Amer-
ican actor TW/2-6
PARNELL, Thomas Frederick see
Russell, Fred
PARNELL, Val (1894-1972) English
manager COC, WWT/10-14
PARNES, Nathan (d 1964 [69])
producer/director BP/49*
PARODI, Teresa (b 1827) singer
CDP, HAS
PAROSSI, Napoleon (fl 1848) actor?
singer? HAS
PARR, Miss see Smith, Mrs.
PARR, W. Henry see Furnival,
Henry

PARR, William (fl 1602-20) actor
DA
PARRIS, George John (d 1910
[79]) actor? EA/11*
PARRIS, Steve Greek/American?
actor TW/25
PARRISH, Helen (d 1959 [35])
American actress BE*
PARRISH, Judy (b 1916) American
artists' representative, actress
BE
PARROCK, Eliza (b 1806) actress
CDP
PARROCK, Isabella [Mrs. William
Parrock] (d 1891) EA/92*
PARROCK, Mrs. William see
Parrock, Isabella
PARROWE, Richard (fl 1538-45)
actor DA
PARRY, Alfred (d 1892) EA/93*
PARRY, Alfred W. English drama-
tist GRB/1
PARRY, Sir Edward Abbott (d
1943 [80]) dramatist GRB/1-4,
WWT/1-7
PARRY, Henry (d 1886 [43]) ac-
tor? EA/87*
PARRY, John (1776-1851) musi-
cian, composer, dramatist
CDP, DNB
PARRY, John (d 1877 [67]) actor
EA/78*
PARRY, John (d 1881) comedian,
pantomimist EA/82*
PARRY, Mrs. John actress CDP
PARRY, John Orlando (1810-79)
English actor, singer CDP,
DNB, OAA/1-2
PARRY, Joseph (1841-1903) com-
poser DNB
PARRY, Katharine (b 1880) Eng-
lish actress GRB/1-2
PARRY, Robert (d 1869) musician
EA/70*
PARRY, R. W. (d 1905 [31])
actor EA/06*
PARRY, Sefton Henry (1822-87)
manager, actor DNB, NYM
PARRY, Stella (d 1906) burlesque
actress EA/07*
PARRY, Tom (d 1862 [56]) actor,
dramatist BE*, EA/72*,
WWT/14*
PARRY, W. Haydn (d 1894 [29])
composer EA/95*
PARRY, William (b 1856) English
manager, actor, stage manager
WWS

PARSELLE, John (1820-85) actor
CDP
PARSLEY, Daniel (d 1890) EA/91*
PARSLEY, William (d 1880 [95])
EA/81*
PARSLOE, Charles Thomas (1804-
70) English actor, agent CDP,
HAS
PARSLOE, Charles Thomas, Jr.
(1836-98) American actor CDP,
HAS, SR
PARSLOE, Edmond John (d 1832
[31]) actor, pantomimist CDP,
HAS
PARSLOE, James (d 1847 [48])
actor, prompter EA/72*, WWT/
14*
PARSONAGE, Mr. J. (d 1868 [34])
proprietor EA/69*
PARSONS, Mrs. [née Phelps] (d
1811) dramatist CP/3
PARSONS, Alan (1888-1933) English
critic, journalist COC, WWT/
6-7
PARSONS, Charles Booth (b 1805)
American actor CDP, HAS
PARSONS, Donovan (b 1888) lyricist
WWT/6-9
PARSONS, Eliza (d 1811) dramatist
DNB
PARSONS, Estelle (b 1927) Ameri-
can actress BE, CB, TW/19-28,
30, WWT/15-16
PARSONS, George (b 1873) Ameri-
can actor WWM
PARSONS, Gram (d 1973 [27]) per-
former BP/58*
PARSONS, John see Juleene, H.
F.
PARSONS, Louella (d 1972 [91])
critic BP/57*
PARSONS, Milton (b 1904) American
actor TW/6
PARSONS, Nancie [Lady Mercy
Greville] (b 1904) actress WWT/
6-7
PARSONS, Percy (1878-1944) Amer-
ican actor, singer WWT/5-9
PARSONS, Philip dramatist FGF
PARSONS, Thomas (fl 1599-1602)
actor DA
PARSONS, Thomas A. (1822-57)
American actor HAS
PARSONS, Tom (d 1874 [60]) comic
singer, pantomimist EA/75*
PARSONS, William (1736-95) English
actor CDP, DNB, GT, TD/1-2
PARSONS, Sir William (1746?-

1817) professor of music CDP
PARSONS, William C. (d 1973
[49]) union representative
BP/57*
PARTCH, Harry (d 1974 [73])
composer/lyricist BP/59*
PARTINGTON, Mary (fl 1853)
dancer HAS
PARTINGTON, Sally (fl 1865)
actress CDP
PARTLETON, Henry (d 1893)
actor EA/94*
PARTRIDGE, Bernard see
Gould, Bernard
PARTRIDGE, William see Tit-
bits, Mjr.
PARVER, Michael (b 1936) Amer-
ican producer BE
PASCAL, Ernest (d 1966 [70])
dramatist BP/51*
PASCAL, Gabriel (1894-1954)
Hungarian director BE*
PASCO [John Evans] (d 1902)
music-hall performer EA/03*
PASCO, Richard (b 1926) English
actor AAS, TW/23, WWT/
14-16
PASCOE, Charles Eyre (d 1912
[70]) editor BE*, WWT/14*
PASCOE, James (d 1910 [34])
EA/11*
PASERO, Tancredi (b 1893) Italian
singer ES
PASLE-GREEN, Jeanne American
actress TW/26
PASO, Alfonso (b 1926) Spanish
dramatist MWD
PASQUA, Giuseppina (1855-1930)
Italian singer ES
PASQUIN, Antony see Williams,
John
PASSANTINO, Anthony (b 1945)
American actor TW/26-27
PASSELTINER, Bernie (b 1931)
American actor TW/27-29
PASSEUR, Steve (d 1966 [67])
dramatist BP/51*, WWT/15*
PASSMORE, Mr. (fl 1848) actor
HAS
PASSMORE, Alfred (d 1889)
EA/90*
PASSMORE, James (d 1889)
EA/90*
PASSMORE, Walter (1867-1946)
English actor, singer GRB/
1-4, WWT/1-9
PASSMORE, Mrs. Walter see
Fraser, Agnes

PASTA, Guiditta (1797/98/99-1865)
Italian singer CDP, ES, OX
PASTA, Johnny [John Wilson Wood-
ley] (d 1890) EA/91*
PASTENE, Robert (b 1918) Ameri-
can actor TW/7-9, 19-20, 25
PASTON, Adelaide Clotilda (d
1898 [46]) equestrienne EA/99*
PASTON, George [Emily Morse
Symonds] (d 1936) dramatist
WWT/1-8
PASTOR, Antonio [Tony] (1837-
1908) American manager CDP,
COC, DAB, HAS, HJD, GRB/
3-4, NTH, OC/3, SR, WWS
PASTOR, Billy (fl 1860s) American
vaulter, equestrian, comic singer
HAS
PASTOR, Frank (b 1837) American
equestrian CDP, HAS
PASTOR, G. W. (d 1918) EA/19*
PASTOR, Lizzie (d 1891) circus
performer EA/92*
PASTOR, Stuart (d 1881 [34]) clown
EA/82*
PASTOR, Tony see Pastor, An-
tonio
PASTOR, William H. (1840-77)
actor, acrobat, singer, manager
CDP
PASTRANA, Julia (d 1860) freak
CDP, HAS
PATANIA, Deolia (fl 1855) singer
HAS
PATANIA, Elise (fl 1855) singer
CDP
PATCH, Blanche (d 1966 [87])
secretary BP/51*
PATCH, Julia (d 1872) actress
EA/73*
PATCH, W. (d 1895) actor? EA/
96*
PATCH, Wally (1888-1970) English
actor WWT/10-14
PATE, Emma (d 1884) EA/85*
PATEGG, Max (b 1855) German
actor, manager WWT/2
PATEMAN, Bella [Mrs. Robert
Pateman] (1843-1908) English
actress CDP, GRB/3-4, OAA/
1-2
PATEMAN, Mrs. Charles see
Cosgrove, Marie
PATEMAN, Isabella see Pateman,
Bella
PATEMAN, Robbie (d 1910 [24])
EA/11*
PATEMAN, Robert (1840-1924)

actor GRB/3-4, OAA/1-2,
WWT/1-4
PATEMAN, Mrs. Robert see
Pateman, Bella
PATERSON, William (fl 1740)
Scottish dramatist CP/1-3, GT
PATERSON, William (b 1919)
American actor, director BE,
TW/26
PATESON, William (fl 1584) actor
DA
PATEY, George (d 1893) actor?
EA/95*
PATEY, Janet Monach [Mrs.
John G. Patey] (1842-94) Eng-
lish singer CDP, DNB
PATEY, Mrs. John G. see
Patey, Janet Monach
PATEY, John George (d 1902 [66])
singer EA/03*
PATI, Pramod (d 1975 [42]) pro-
ducer/director/choreographer
BP/59*
PATIERNO, Sig. (d 1877) singer
EA/78*
PATON, Mr. (fl 1780) Scottish
dramatist CP/2-3, GT
PATON, Miss see Paton, Mary
Ann
PATON, Eliza (fl 1829-34?) ac-
tress CDP
PATON, Isabella (fl 1827?) singer
CDP
PATON, Mary Ann (1802-64)
Scottish singer, actress BS,
DNB, OX
PATRICK, Benilde (b 1927)
American educator BE
PATRICK, Dennis [Dennis Har-
rison] (b 1918) American actor
TW/6-15, 23, 28
PATRICK, Edward John Harley
(d 1898) EA/99*
PATRICK, Jerome (d 1923 [40])
New Zealand actor BE*,
BP/8*
PATRICK, John (b 1902/05/06/
07/10) American dramatist
AAS, BE, CD, HJD, MD, MH,
MWD, WWT/11-16
PATRICK, Lee American actress
BE
PATRICK, Leonard stage manager,
actor BE
PATRICK, Nigel (b 1913) English
actor, director AAS, WWT/
9-16
PATRICK, Richard (fl 1607) actor

DA
PATRICK, Robert (b 1937) Ameri-
can dramatist, director, actor
CD
PATRICK, Dr. Samuel (d 1748)
dramatist CP/1-3
PATRICOLA, Tom (1891-1950)
American actor, singer TW/6,
WWT/7-8
PATRICOLO, Angelo Italian com-
poser CDP
PATRIZIO, Count Ernest (fl 1878)
strong man CDP
PATSALL (fl 1773) dramatist CP/3
PATSTON [Or Patson], Doris (1908-
57) English actress, singer
TW/1, 5-6, 8, 13
PATTEN, Dorothy (d 1975 [70])
actress BP/59*, WWT/16*
PATTERSON, Ada (d 1939) Ameri-
can writer, critic WWM
PATTERSON, Albert (b 1911) Amer-
ican actor TW/3
PATTERSON, Bayard see Harri-
son, Bob
PATTERSON, Benjamin performer?
CD
PATTERSON, Burdella (d 1973 [90])
performer BP/57*
PATTERSON, Dick American actor
TW/21
PATTERSON, Elizabeth (1874/82-
1966) American actress BE,
TW/10, 22
PATTERSON, Elma C. (d 1975
[86]) performer BP/60*
PATTERSON, James (1932-72)
American actor TW/22, 24-26,
29
PATTERSON, James Henry see
Sutton, Sambo
PATTERSON, John (d 1889) circus
clown EA/90*
PATTERSON, Mrs. Johnny (d 1886)
EA/87*
PATTERSON, Joseph Medill (1879-
1946) American dramatist WWM
PATTERSON, Lee (d 1967 [49])
critic BP/52*
PATTERSON, Marjorie (d 1948
[61]) actress BE*, WWT/14*
PATTERSON, Neva (b 1922) Amer-
ican actress BE, TW/4-16,
WWT/14
PATTERSON, Phil (b 1952) Ameri-
can actor TW/27
PATTERSON, Tom (b 1920) Cana-
dian journalist, founder of

Stratford Shakespearian festival
of Canada AAS, WWT/13-16
PATTERSON, Troy (d 1975 [49])
performer BP/60*
PATTERSON, Wilbur, Jr. (b 1946)
American actor TW/27-29
PATTERSON, William (d 1907
[76]) marksman EA/08*
PATTERSON, Mrs. William see
Templeton, Fay
PATTI, Adelina [Baroness Ceder-
strom] (1843-1919) Spanish sing-
er CDP, GRB/1-4, ES, HAS,
HP, SR, WWA/1, WWS,
WWW/2
PATTI, Amalia see Strakosch,
Mme.
PATTI, Signora Barilli (fl 1848)
singer HAS
PATTI, Carlotta (1840-89) singer
CDP, DNB, HAS
PATTI, Caterina singer CDP
PATTI, Salvatore (d 1869) Italian
singer CDP, HAS
PATTISON, Mr. see Paterson,
William
PATTISON, Emma (fl 1892?)
singer CDP
PATTISON, Kate (fl 1877-79)
English actress OAA/1-2
PATTMIE? Edward (fl 1574) actor
DA
PATTON, Fred (1888-1951) Amer-
ican singer WWA/3
PATTON, Lucille American ac-
tress TW/23, 25-26, 28-29
PATTON, Phil (d 1972 [61]) pro-
ducer/director/choreographer
BP/57*
PATTON, Willard (1853-1924)
American composer WWA/1
PATTRICK, William (fl 1624-36)
actor DA
PATZAK, Julius (d 1974 [75])
performer BP/58*
PAUKER, Dr. Edmond (d 1962
[74]) Hungarian literary repre-
sentative BE*, BP/46*
PAUL, Ann [Mrs. W. Paul] (d
1891 [71]) EA/92*
PAUL, Betty (b 1921) English
actress BE, WWT/11-14
PAUL, Elliot (b 1942) American
actor TW/24
PAUL, George (fl 1755) drama-
tist CP/3
PAUL, Howard (1830-1905) Amer-
ican entertainer, dramatist,

actor CDP, EA/69, GRB/1,
HAS
PAUL, Mrs. Howard [Isabella
Featherstone] (1833-79) English
actress, singer CDP, DNB,
HAS, OAA/1-2
PAUL, James (d 1891) music-hall
proprietor EA/92*
PAUL, Marie-Rose see Didelot,
Mme. Charles-Louis
PAUL, Rene (b 1914) Swiss actor
TW/6, 13
PAUL, Steven (b 1959) American
actor TW/26-27
PAUL, Mrs. W. see Paul, Ann
PAUL, Wauna (d 1973 [61]) actress,
producer TW/29
PAUL, W. H. (d 1865 [32]) agent
HAS
PAUL, William (d 1882) music-hall
proprietor EA/83*
PAULDING, Frederick (1859-1937)
American actor, dramatist CDP
PAULDING, James Kirke (1779-
1860) American dramatist CDP,
EAP, RJ
PAULETTE, Larry (b 1949) Amer-
ican actor TW/30
PAULINA, Princess (d 1895 [19])
music-hall performer EA/96*
PAULL, Harry Major (1854-1934)
English dramatist GRB/4,
WWT/1-7, WWW/3
PAULLIN, Mr. (fl 1854-64) actor
HAS
PAULLIN, Miss (fl 1864) actress
HAS
PAULLIN, Louise [Mrs. H. B.
Warner] (d 1910) actress, singer
CDP
PAULO, Sig. (d 1835 [48]) clown
CDP
PAULO, James (d 1883) clown,
pantomimist BE*, EA/84*,
WWT/14*
PAULO, Mrs. James see Paulo,
Matilda
PAULO, Matilda [Mrs. James
Paulo] (d 1880 [64]) EA/81*
PAULSEN, Albert (b 1927) actor
TW/28
PAULSEN, Arno (d 1969 [69]) per-
former BP/54*
PAULTON, Edward Antonio (d 1939
[73]) Scottish dramatist, lyricist
BE*, WWT/14*
PAULTON, Harry (1842-1917) Eng-
lish actor, dramatist CDP,

GRB/1-4, OAA/2, WWT/1-3
PAULTON, Joseph (d 1875) actor
EA/76*
PAULTON, Tom (d 1914 [76])
English actor, dramatist
GRB/1-3
PAULY, Rose (b 1894) Austrian
singer ES
PAUMGARTNER, Bernhard (d
1971 [83]) producer/director/
choreographer BP/56*
PAUMIER, Alfred [Alfred G. P.
Hodgson] (1870-1951) English
actor, manager GRB/1,
WWT/4-7
PAUMIER, M. N. (d 1876) actor,
lessee EA/77*
PAUNCEFORT, Claire (d 1924)
actress BE*, WWT/14*
PAUNCEFORT, George (fl 1854-
62) actor HAS
PAUNCEFORT, George (d 1942
[72]) actor BE*, WWT/14*
PAUNCEFORT, Mrs. George
[née Georgiana Edward] (d 1895
[70]) actress HAS, OAA/2
PAUNCEFORT, Georgiana see
Pauncefort, Mrs. George
PAUR, Emil (1855-1932) con-
ductor WWW/3
PAVAROTTI, Luciano (b 1935)
Italian singer CB
PAVEK, Janet (b 1936) American
singer, actress BE
PAVILLIO, Tom (d 1906) acrobat
EA/07*
PAVLOS, Anthony E. (d 1975
[44]) performer BP/60*
PAVLOVA, Anna (1882-1932)
Russian dancer ES, OC/2,
WWT/4-6
PAVLOW, Muriel (b 1921) English
actress WWT/10-16
PAVY, Salathiel [or Salmon]
(1590-1603) English actor
DA, OC/2-3
PAVYE, William (fl 1597-1608)
actor DA
PAWLE, J. Lennox (1872-1936)
English actor GRB/1-4,
WWT/1-8
PAWLEY, Edward (b 1901) Amer-
ican actor CB
PAWLEY, Eric (b 1907) American
educator, architect BE
PAWLEY, Nancy (b 1901) English
actress WWT/9-10
PAWLEY, William (d 1952 [47])

American actor BE*
PAWNEE, Bill [Gordon W. Lily]
(1866-1942) American performer
SR
PAWSON, Hargrave (1902-45) Eng-
lish actor WWT/9
PAXINOU, Katina (1900-73) Greek
actress BE, CB, COC, OC/3,
PDT, TW/1, 3, 9-10, 29,
WWT/10-15
PAXTON, Glenn (b 1931) American
composer BE
PAXTON, Sydney [Sydney Paxton
Hood] (1860-1930) English actor,
manager GRB/1-4, WWT/1-6
PAXTON-HOOD, Lavinia (d 1903)
EA/04*
PAYE, Mrs. Edmund see Paxton,
Emily Saxon
PAYE, Emily Saxon [Mrs. Edmund
Paye] (d 1899) EA/01*
PAYN, Graham (b 1918) South Afri-
can actor, singer TW/4, WWT/
10-16
PAYNE, Ben Iden (1881-1976) Eng-
lish actor, manager, director
AAS, BE, COC, GRB/4, NTH,
OC/3, WWT/1-15
PAYNE, Edmund (1865-1914) actor
GRB/1-4, WWT/1-2
PAYNE, F[anny] Ursula (fl 1894-
1928) American dramatist WWA/
5
PAYNE, Frederick (d 1880 [39])
pantomimist EA/81*, WWT/14*
PAYNE, Mrs. G. A. see Payne,
Mary Ann Misterson
PAYNE, George Adney (1846-1907)
Irish music-hall proprietor,
manager GRB/1-3
PAYNE, George Henry (1876-1945)
American dramatist WWA/2
PAYNE, Harry (d 1895 [63/64])
clown, pantomimist CDP, DP
PAYNE, Henry Neville (fl 1672-
1700) dramatist DNB
PAYNE, John (b 1912) American
actor ES
PAYNE, John Howard (1791-1852)
American actor, dramatist
CDP, COC, DAB, EAP, ES,
HAS, HJD, HP, OC/1-3, RJ,
SR, WWA/H
PAYNE, Laurence (b 1919) English
actor WWT/11-13
PAYNE, Leon (d 1969 [52]) per-
former BP/54*
PAYNE, Louisa (d 1887) actress

PAYNE 734

EA/88*
PAYNE, Mary Ann Misterson
[Mrs. G. A. Payne] (d 1897
[47]) EA/98*
PAYNE, Millie (d 1917) EA/18*
PAYNE, Nevil (fl 1673-75) drama-
tist CP/2-3, GT
PAYNE, Reginald [Reginald
Charles Greenwood] (b 1883)
English actor GRB/1
PAYNE, Robert (fl 1604) patentee
DA
PAYNE, Walter (d 1949 [76])
English director, manager
WWT/5-10
PAYNE, William Henry (1804-
78) actor, pantomimist CDP,
DNB
PAYNE, William J. (d 1900
[33]) bellringer EA/01*
PAYNE, William Louis (d 1953
[80]) American actor TW/10,
WWM, WWS
PAYNE, Willie (d 1889 [23])
skater EA/90*
PAYNE, W. Reuben (d 1909)
actor EA/10*
PAYNE-JENNINGS, Victor (1900-
62) English manager TW/19,
WWT/9-10
PAYNE-TOWNSHEND, Charlotte
Frances see Shaw, Mrs.
George Bernard
PAYNTER, David William (1791-
1823) English dramatist DNB
PAYNTON, Harry (d 1964 [74])
performer BE*, BP/49*
PAYSON, Blanche (d 1964 [83])
actress BE*
PAYSON, William Farquhar (1876-
1939) American dramatist
WWA/1
PAYTON, Adelaide (d 1901 [61])
EA/02*
PAYTON, Adelaide (d 1904)
EA/05*
PAYTON, Corse (1867-1934)
American actor, manager
WWS
PAYTON-WRIGHT, Pamela (b 1941)
American actress TW/1, 24-
29, WWT/16
PEABODY, Josephine [Mrs. Lionel
Marks] (1874-1922) American
dramatist DAB, HJD, MWD,
WWA/1, WWM
PEACH, Mrs. see Carr, Louisa
Maria

PEACH, George R. (d 1908 [52])
actor EA/09*
PEACH, Lawrence Du Garde (d
1974 [94]) dramatist BTR/74
PEACH, Louisa actress EA/97
PEACHEY, Catherine [Mrs. George
Darrell] (d 1892) actress EA/
93*
PEACOCK, Bertram (d 1963 [70/
79]) American actor, singer
TW/19
PEACOCK, Kim (1901-66) English
actor WWT/8-11
PEACOCK, Trevor (b 1931) English
actor, composer, dramatist
WWT/15-16
PEACOCKE, Robert (fl 1550) actor
DA
PEADON, Pamela (b 1947) Ameri-
can actress TW/30
PEAKE, Lewis (d 1917) EA/18*
PEAKE, Mervyn (1911-68) Chinese/
English dramatist WWW/6
PEAKE, Richard Brinsley (1792-
1847) English dramatist DNB
PEAKES, Henry C. actor, singer
CDP
PEAK FAMILY (fl 1850s) bell
ringers SR
PEAL, Gilbert (d 1964 [76]) Lithu-
anian performer BE*
PEAPS, William dramatist CP/1-
3, FGF
PEARCE, Lady [Carrie Coote] (1870-
1907) actress DD, DP, GRB/3
PEARCE, Alice (1917-66) American
actress BE, TW/6-8, 14-18,
22, WWT/14
PEARCE, Edward (fl 1598-1609)
master of the Children of Paul's
DA
PEARCE, Mrs. G. J. (d 1880)
performer? EA/81*
PEARCE, H. Edward (d 1901 [40])
treasurer EA/02*
PEARCE, James (d 1884 [53])
property master EA/86*
PEARCE, John (b 1931) American
actor TW/15, 20
PEARCE, Lizzie [Mrs. Arnold
Burnett] (d 1890) serio-comic
singer EA/92*
PEARCE, Lottie [Mrs. R. J.
Hamer] (d 1916) EA/17*
PEARCE, Sam (1909-71) American
curator BE
PEARCE, S. T. (d 1917 [66]) actor
EA/18*

PEARCE, Vera (d 1966 [70])
Australian actress, singer
WWT/6-13

PEARCE, Walter (b 1878) English
actor GRB/3-4

PEARCE, Mrs. Will see Renetti, Lilian

PEARCE, William (fl 1785-96)
dramatist CP/3, GT, TD/1-2

PEARCE, W. W. (d 1864 [26])
comedian HAS

PEARCE, Mrs. W. W. see
Crapeau, Marion H.

PEARCE, Wynn (b 1929) American
actor TW/14

PEARL, Cora (d 1886) EA/87*

PEARL, Hal (d 1975 [61]) dramatist BP/60*

PEARL, Irwin (b 1945) American
actor TW/24-26

PEARL, Jack (b 1895) American
actor BE, WWT/8-11

PEARLMAN, Steve [or Stephen]
(b 1935) American actor TW/
23, 26, 30

PEARMAN, William (1792-1837)
English singer, actor CDP,
HAS, OX

PEARS, Peter (b 1910) English
singer CB

PEARSON, Alfred (d 1868 [34])
comedian EA/69*

PEARSON, Anne (b 1931) American actress TW/13

PEARSON, Beatrice (b 1920)
American actress TW/1-14,
WWT/11-12

PEARSON, Elizabeth (d 1896 [67])
EA/97*

PEARSON, Harry (1824-84) English actor CDP, HAS

PEARSON, Henry (fl 1826) American actor HAS

PEARSON, Hesketh (1887-1964)
English writer, actor AAS,
WWW/6

PEARSON, James (d 1910) carpenter EA/11*

PEARSON, John Henry (d 1887)
equestrian ring-master EA/
88*

PEARSON, Joshua (d 1870 [42])
stage carpenter EA/71*

PEARSON, Leon Morris (1899-
1963) American critic BE*,
BP/47*

PEARSON, Lloyd (1897-1966)
English actor WWT/9-14

PEARSON, Mary Ann see Croswell, Anne

PEARSON, Molly (d 1959 [83])
Scottish actress TW/15, WWM,
WWT/4-10

PEARSON, Richard (b 1918) Welsh
actor AAS, WWT/15-16

PEARSON, Scott (b 1941) American
actor TW/23, 25-28

PEARSON, Sidney (fl 1836) actor
HAS

PEARSON, Susan G. (b 1941)
American actress TW/26-28

PEARSON, Virginia (1886-1958)
American actress WWM

PEARSON, William C. [William P.
Collins] (d 1881) Negro minstrel
EA/82*

PEARSONS, Lyle (b 1947) American
actor TW/27

PEART, Prof. (d 1896 [23]) high
diver EA/97*

PEASE, Alfred Humphries (1838-
82) musician, composer CDP

PEASE, Charles H. (fl 1866?)
singer, songwriter CDP

PECHEY, Archibald Thomas see
Valentine

PECHNER, Gerhard (d 1969 [66])
singer TW/26

PECK, Mrs. (fl 1797) actress HAS

PECK, Francis (1692-1743) English
dramatist CP/2-3, GT

PECK, Gregory (b 1916) American
actor BE, CB, ES, WWT/10-11

PECK, Jack (d 1974 [72]) performer
BP/58*

PECK, Jon (b 1938) American actor
TW/30

PECKHAM, John (d 1974 [45]) pro-
ducer/director/choreographer
BP/59*

PECKOVER, J. W. (d 1888) music-
hall proprietor EA/89*

PECON, John J. (d 1975 [60]) performer BP/59*

PEDEL, Abraham (fl 1614-23) actor
DA

PEDEL, Jacob (fl 1597-1615) actor
DA

PEDEL, William (fl 1608-39?)
pantomimist, dancer DA

PEDEN, Emily (b 1944) American
actress TW/24

PEDERSON, Michael (b 1947)
American actor TW/24, 30

PEDGRIFT, Frederic Henchman
journalist GRB/2-4, WWT/1

PEDI, Tom (b 1913) American
actor BE, TW/23-24
PEDICORD, Harry W. (b 1912)
American educator BE
PEDINA, Gustave (d 1901 [28])
acrobat EA/02*
PEDRICK, Gale (1905-70) English
critic, journalist WWT/9-11
PEDRO, Little Dick (d 1894)
performer? EA/95*
PEDROTTI, Sig. (fl 1833) singer
HAS
PEDROTTI, Adelaide Varese (fl
1832-33) singer CDP, HAS
PEEL, David (b 1920) English
actor WWT/11
PEEL, Eileen (b 1909) English
actress AAS, WWT/6-16
PEEL, Matt (1830-59) American
minstrel, manager CDP,
HAS
PEEL, Tommy [Thomas Riley]
(d 1869) American jig dancer
HAS
PEELE, George (c. 1558-97) Eng-
lish dramatist COC, CP/1-3,
DNB, ES, FGF, HP, MH,
NTH, OC/1-3, PDT, RE, SR
PEER, William (d 1713) actor
DNB
PEERCE, Jan (b 1904) American
singer, actor CB, TW/28-29
PEERS, Donald (d 1973 [64])
performer BP/58*
PEERS, Edward see Pearce,
Edward
PEERS, Thomas (fl 1607) actor
DA
PEFFER, Crawford A. (d 1961
[94]) booking agent BE*
PEIL, Charles Edward (d 1962
[54]) actor BE*
PEIL, Edward J. (d 1958 [70])
actor BE*
PEILE, Frederick Kinsey (1862-
1934) Indian/English dramatist,
actor GRB/4, WWT/1-7
PEISLEY, Frederick (b 1904)
English actor WWT/5-16
PELBY, Julia see Thomas,
Mrs. Jacob Wonderly, II
PELBY, Ophelia see Anderson,
Ophelia
PELBY, Rosalie see Pelby,
Mrs. William
PELBY, William (1793-1850)
American manager, actor
CDP, HAS

PELBY, Mrs. William (1793-1857)
American actress CDP, HAS
PELHAM, Miss (fl 1834-36) Eng-
lish actress HAS
PELHAM, Dick (1815-76) minstrel
CDP
PELHAM, Harriet (fl 1863?) ac-
tress CDP
PELHAM, Jimmy American actor
TW/25-26, 28, 30
PELHAM, Meta (d 1948 [98]) ac-
tress BE*, WWT/14*
PELHAM, Paul (fl 1899?) singer,
songwriter CDP
PELHAM, Richard Ward (d 1876
[60]) minstrel manager EA/77*
PELHAM, Walter (d 1907 [72])
American actor GRB/3*, WWT/
14*
PELISSIER, Harry Gabriel (1874-
1913) English composer, enter-
tainer COC, DNB, GRB/3-4,
OC/1-3, WWT/1-2
PELL, Abner W. (d 1865 [45])
circus advertiser HAS
PELL, Gilbert Ward (d 1872 [47])
minstrel CDP
PELL, Harry (d 1866) Ethiopian
performer HAS
PELL, Johnny [John A. Davin]
(d 1866 [33]) Ethiopian comedian
HAS
PELLET, Ida (1838-63) actress
CDP
PELLETIER, Gilles (b 1925) Cana-
dian actor TW/21
PELLETIER, Wilfred (b 1896)
Canadian conductor CB
PELLICER, Pina (d 1964 [24])
performer BP/49*
PELLOW, Clifford (b 1928) Amer-
ican actor TW/23-25
PELLY, Ellen (d 1873 [20]) dancer
EA/74*
PELLY, Farrell (d 1963 [72]) Irish
performer BE*, BP/47*
PELMAN, Paul (d 1971 [81]) com-
poser/lyricist BP/55*
PELTON, Walter (d 1887) actor
NYM
PELTZER, William (c. 1832-87)
German actor NYM
PELZER, Catherina Josepha see
Pratten, Mme. Sydney
PEMBER, Ron (b 1934) English
actor WWT/15-16
PEMBERTON, Mr. (fl 1824) Eng-
lish actor HAS

PEMBERTON, Mrs. see Tatnall, Mrs.

PEMBERTON, Brock (1885-1950) American producing manager CB, DAB, NTH, TW/2-6, WWA/2, WWT/6-10

PEMBERTON, Charles Reece (1790-1840) Welsh/English actor DNB

PEMBERTON, Henry W. (d 1952 [77]) actor BE*, BP/37*

PEMBERTON, Mrs. John C. see Fowler, Emily

PEMBERTON, John Wyndham (1883-1947) Indian/English manager WWT/9-10

PEMBERTON, Madge (d 1970 [85]) dramatist BP/55*

PEMBERTON, Sir Max (1863-1950) English dramatist WWT/3-10

PEMBERTON, Reece (b 1913/14) English designer ES, WWT/15-16

PEMBERTON, Thomas Edgar (1849-1905) English dramatist, historian DNB, GRB/1, OC/1-3, WWW/1

PEMBERTON, William (d 1879 [37]) music-hall performer EA/81*

PEMBERTON-BILLING, Robin (b 1929) English director, dramatist WWT/15-16

PEMBROKE, Countess of see Herbert, Mary

PEMBROKE, George see Prud'homme, George

PEMBROKE, Wilson (d 1916) singer EA/17*

PENA, Julio (d 1972 [70]) performer BP/57*

PENBERTHY, Beverly American actress TW/25

PENCO, Rosina (1823/30-94) Italian singer CDP, ES

PENDENNIS, Rose (d 1943) actress BE*, WWT/14*

PENDERED, Mary Lucy (1858-1940) English dramatist WWW/4

PENDLETON, Austin (b 1940) American actor TW/23-24, 26-27, 30, WWT/16

PENDLETON, David (b 1937) American actor TW/30

PENDLETON, Marc J. (d 1892 [43]) actor CDP

PENDLETON, Nat (d 1967 [72])

performer BP/52*

PENDLETON, Mrs. William F. see Blauvett, Lilian

PENDLETON, Wyman (b 1916) American actor TW/22-23, 25-28, WWT/15-16

PENDRY, Charles (fl 1598) actor DA

PENE du BOIS, Raoul (b 1914) American designer BE

PENFOLD, George (d 1896 [40]) actor EA/97*

PENKETHMAN, William (d 1725) English actor COC, OC/1-3, TD/1-2

PENLEY, Mr. (fl 1807-08) actor GT

PENLEY, Mr. (fl 1815) actor BS

PENLEY, Arthur (1881-1954) English business manager WWT/2-7

PENLEY, Belville (d 1893 [84]) actor, manager EA/94*, WWT/14*

PENLEY, Belville S. (d 1940) producer, manager, author BE*, WWT/14*

PENLEY, Sampson (d 1838) actor, dramatist CDP

PENLEY, William (d 1838) actor WWT/14*

PENLEY, William Sydney (1851/52-1912) English actor, manager CDP, COC, DNB, DP, GRB/1-4, OC/1-3, WWT/1, WWW/1

PENLEY, Mrs. W[illiam] S[ydney] (d 1916) EA/17*

PENMAN, Charles (d 1912) carpenter EA/13*

PENMAN, Lea (d 1962 [67]) American actress BE*

PENN, Arthur (b 1922) American director, actor AAS, BE, CB, ES, WWT/13-16

PENN, Arthur A. (1880-1941) English composer, musician CB, WWA/1

PENN, Bill (b 1931) American actor, producer, director TW/12-20, WWT/15

PENN, Edward American actor TW/28-30

PENN, John (fl 1792) dramatist CP/3

PENN, Leo (b 1921) American actor TW/8-18

PENN, William (b c.1592/98) English actor DA, OC/1-3

PENNA, Catherine (d 1879)
singer EA/81*
PENNA, Susanna Elizabeth [Mrs.
William Penna] (d 1885 [25])
EA/86*
PENNA, William (d 1889 [38])
music-hall singer EA/90*
PENNA, Mrs. William see
Penna, Susanna Elizabeth
PENNECUIK, Alexander (fl 1723)
dramatist CP/3
PENNER, Joe (1904-41) Hungarian
comedian CB
PENNER, Ralph (b 1947) American
actor TW/29
PENNICK, Ronald (d 1964 [69])
American actor BE*
PENNIE, John Fitzgerald (1782-
1848) English dramatist DNB
PENNIKET, Thomas (d 1877
[63]) comic singer EA/78*
PENNINGTON, Ann (1892/93/98-
1971) American dancer, ac-
tress BE, TW/28, WWT/6-11
PENNINGTON, Michael (b 1943)
English actor TW/25
PENNINGTON, W. E. actor,
minstrel CDP
PENNINGTON, W. H. (d 1923
[91]) actor BE*, WWT/14*
PENNOCK, Christopher (b 1944)
American actor TW/26-27
PENNOYER, Augustus S. (b
1829) American property man,
carpenter, actor, prompter,
stage manager, treasurer,
manager, business manager,
agent HAS
PENNOYER, Kate (fl 1855) Amer-
ican dancer, pantomimist HAS
PENNY, Anne (d 1784 [53])
dramatist CP/2-3, GT
PENNY, Henry see Carney,
Tom
PENNYCUICKE, Andrew (b 1620)
English dramatist, actor DA,
OC/1-3
"PENNY SHOWMAN, The" see
Richardson, Mr.
PENROSE, Charles (d 1952 [76])
comedian BE*, WWT/14*
PENROSE, Edith (fl 1888) actress
CDP
PENROSE, John (b 1917) English
actor WWT/11-13
PENROSE, John H. R. see
Able, Frank
PENROSE, Mrs. John H. R.

see Anson, Cecile E.
PENROSE, Pearl singer, actress
CDP
PENSON, Mrs. A. W. see Bel-
lamy, Mrs. William Hoare
PENSON, George (d 1833) singer,
actor CDP
PENSON, John Cranmer (d 1874
[73]) actor EA/75*
PENTECOST, George (b 1939)
American actor TW/23, 25-30
PENTITH, Mrs. (d 1900) actress?
EA/01*
PENTLAND, Joseph (fl 1841-68)
clown CDP, HAS
PENTLAND, Nicol actor EA/97
PENTLAND, Young (d 1906) EA/
07*
PENTLAND, Mrs. Young (d 1905)
EA/06*
PENTON, Fabian (fl 1602) actor
DA
PENZNER, Seymour (b 1915) Amer-
ican actor TW/26-29
PEOPLE SHOW, The theatre col-
lective CD
PEPER, Minnie Dorothy see
Oaker, Jane
PEPEREL, Giles (fl c. 1564-65?)
actor DA
PEPI see Brull, Joseph
PEPITA, Señorita (fl 1863) Spanish
dancer HAS
PEPLE, Edward H. (b 1867/69)
American dramatist GRB/2-4,
WWM, WWS, WWT/1-7
PEPOLI, Countess see Alboni,
Marietta
PEPPARD, George (b 1933) Amer-
ican actor CB, TW/13-16
PEPPER, Barbara (d 1969 [57])
performer BP/54*
PEPPER, George (fl 1830-31?)
American? dramatist EAP, RJ
PEPPER, Harry (fl 1890) actor,
songwriter CDP
PEPPER, Harry S. (d 1970 [79])
composer/lyricist BP/55*
PEPPER, Herman (d 1975 [77])
theatregoer BP/59*
PEPPER, John Henry (d 1900 [79])
EA/01*
PEPPIN, Henry Bedford (d 1916)
EA/17*
PEPPIN AND BURSCHARD (fl 1806)
French circus performers HAS
PEPUSCH, John Christopher (1667-
1752) German/English composer

ES
PEPUSCH, Mrs. John Christopher
see De L'Epine, Francesca
Margherita
PEPYS, Samuel (1633-1703) Eng-
lish diarist COC, ES, NTH,
OC/1-3
PERCASSI, Don American actor
TW/30
PERCEVAL-CLARK, Perceval
(1881-1938) English actor
WWT/4-8
PERCIE, Norman (d 1885 [27])
author, composer EA/86*
PERCIVAL, A. E. (d 1898 [39])
actor EA/99*
PERCIVAL, Mrs. A. E. see
Percival, Emily
PERCIVAL, Emily [Mrs. A. E.
Percival] (d 1890 [25]) EA/91*
PERCIVAL, Horace (d 1961 [73/
75]) actor BE*, WWT/14*
PERCIVAL, James Gates (1795-
1856) American dramatist
EAP
PERCIVAL, Percy (d 1909 [58])
music-hall manager EA/10*
PERCIVAL, Susanna see Mount-
fort, Susanna Percival
PERCIVAL, Thomas Purcell (d
1904) actor EA/05*
PERCIVAL, Mrs. W. see
Breeze, Mabel
PERCIVAL, Walter C. (d 1934
[46]) American actor, drama-
tist BE*, BP/18*
PERCIVAL, William (d 1871 [37])
Negro singer & dancer EA/
72*
PERCY, A. C. [Thomas Percy
Carmichael] (d 1905 [45]) actor
GRB/1
PERCY, Arthur Cecil [Thomas
Percy Carmichael] (d 1905
[43]) actor EA/06*
PERCY, Edward (1891-1968)
English dramatist AAS, BE,
WWT/5-14
PERCY, Eileen (d 1973 [72]) per-
former BP/58*
PERCY, Ernest (d 1912 [44])
actor EA/13*
PERCY, Esmé (1887-1957) Eng-
lish actor, producer COC,
ES, GRB/4, OC/3, TW/13,
WWT/1-12, WWW/5
PERCY, George (d 1962 [90])
performer BE*

PERCY, Mrs. H. (d 1875) singer
EA/76*
PERCY, Harry (d 1874 [50]) comic
singer EA/75*
PERCY, Henry (d 1880 [31]) singer,
composer EA/81*
PERCY, Madeleine see Richard-
son, Mrs. L. A.
PERCY, Rita (b 1840) English
singer HAS
PERCY, Robert (fl 1586-87) actor
DA
PERCY, S. Esmé see Percy,
Esmé
PERCY, Thomas (d 1811 [83])
-    dramatist CP/2-3, GT
PERCY, Thomas (d 1878 [35])
actor EA/79*
PERCY, William (fl 1602) dramatist
FGF
PERCY, William Stratford (1872-
1946) Australian actor WWT/4-5
PERCYVAL, T. Wigney (b 1865)
English actor, dramatist EA/
96, GRB/1-4, WWT/4-9
PEREIRA, Louisa see Slater,
Mrs. J. H.
PERELLI, Natole (d 1867) singer
HAS
PERELMAN, Laura (d 1970 [58])
dramatist BP/54*
PERELMAN, S. J. (b 1904) Amer-
ican dramatist, writer BE,
CB, CD, HJD, MH
PEREZ, Lazaro (b 1945) Cuban ac-
tor TW/25, 29
PEREZ, Pepito (d 1975 [79]) per-
former BP/60*
PERFECT, J. R. (d 1912 [77])
manager WWT/14*
PERFECT, William (1740-1809)
English dramatist CP/3
PERFITT, Frank (b 1880) English
actor, singer GRB/1-2
PERFITT, Samuel (d 1872) actor
EA/73*
PERFORMANCE GROUP, The
theatre collective CD
PERHACS, Marylou (b 1944) Amer-
ican actress TW/29
PERHAM, Josiah (1803-68) Ameri-
can showman DAB
PERIER, Jean-Alexis (1869-1954)
French actor, singer ES
PERKIN, John (fl 1572) actor DA
PERKINS, Anthony (b 1932) Amer-
ican actor, director BE, CB,
ES, TW/11-20, 23-24, 27,

WWT/13-16
PERKINS, Berkley (d 1904) actor
EA/05*
PERKINS, Charles (d 1869 [66])
actor? EA/70*
PERKINS, David Fessenden (d
1962 [77]) actor, dramatist
BE*, BP/47*, WWT/14*
PERKINS, Don (b 1928) American
actor TW/26-27
PERKINS, Francis D. (d 1970
[72]) critic BP/55*
PERKINS, Giulio (d 1875) singer
EA/76*
PERKINS, John (b 1927) Ameri-
can actor TW/9, 30
PERKINS, Julius Edson (1845-
75) singer CDP
PERKINS, Osgood (1892-1937)
American actor ES, WWT/
7-8
PERKINS, Richard (1585?-1650)
English actor CDP, DA, OC/
1-3
PERKINS, Rodney Croskey see
Rodney, Frank
PERKINS, Walter Eugene (d 1925
[55]) American actor WWA/5
PERKINS, Will (fl c. 1599?)
actor DA
PERKS, George [George Edward
Reed] (d 1893 [62]) EA/94*
PERKS, John (d 1874) actor?
performer? equestrian? EA/
75*
PERL, Arnold (1914-71) Ameri-
can producer, writer BE
PERL, Lothar (d 1975 [64]) com-
poser/lyricist BP/59*
PERLET, Herman (b 1864)
American conductor, composer
WWM
PERLEY, Frank Lee (b 1859)
American designer GRB/3
PERLMAN, Phyllis American
press representative BE
PERLMAN, William J. (d 1954
[72]) dramatist, director,
producer BE*, BP/39*,
WWT/14*
PERMAIN, Fred W. (d 1933)
actor EA/96
PERONI, Carlo (1889?-1944)
Italian conductor CB
PEROZZI, Luigi (fl 1844) singer
HAS
PERPER, Bob (d 1972) com-
poser/lyricist BP/57*

PERREN, George (1823-1909)
singer, director CDP
PERRETT, Francis L. (d 1972
[73]) publicist BP/57*
PERREY, Mireille French actress,
singer WWT/7-8
PERRIE, Ernestine (b 1912) Amer-
ican director BE
PERRIN, Mrs. [née J. B. Wood-
bury] actress HAS
PERRIN, Ceci (b 1945) American
actress TW/25
PERRINE, Valerie (b 1943) Ameri-
can actress, dancer CB
PERRINER, J. (fl 1839) actor
HAS
PERRING, James Ernest (d 1889
[66]) EA/90*
PERRINI, Signorina (fl 1850) sing-
er? HAS
PERRINI, Alfred Edward (d 1899
[38]) musician EA/00*
PERRINS, Leslie (d 1962 [60])
English actor WWT/5-11
PERRUCCHINI, Sig. (d 1870) com-
poser EA/71*
PERRY, Albert H. (d 1933 [63])
American actor BE*, BP/17*
PERRY, Alf [Alfred Thomas Allan]
(d 1902) minstrel comedian
EA/03*
PERRY, Antoinette (1888-1946)
American actress, manager,
producer, director CB, DAB,
NTH, TW/3, WWA/2, WWT/8-9
PERRY, Charles (d 1969) performer
BP/54*
PERRY, Charlotte (b 1890) Ameri-
can educator, director BE
PERRY, Clara [Mrs. Ben Davies]
(d 1944 [86]) singer BE*,
WWT/14*
PERRY, Elaine (b 1921) American
actress, producer, director BE
PERRY, Elizabeth see Creese,
Mrs. T. A.
PERRY, Florence (d 1949 [80])
actress BE*, WWT/14*
PERRY, Frederick William (d 1917
[81]) musician EA/18*
PERRY, Mrs. Harold see Bran-
don, Florence
PERRY, Harry A. (1826-62) Amer-
ican actor CDP, HAS
PERRY, Mrs. Harry A., I ac-
tress HAS
PERRY, Mrs. Harry A., II [née
Marian Agnes Land Rookes] (b

1843) Australian actress HAS
PERRY, Harry H. (d 1965 [84])
  performer BP/50*
PERRY, Henry (d 1877 [36]) actor
  EA/78*
PERRY, Horatio (d 1876 [29])
  singer EA/77*
PERRY, Irma (d 1955 [79]) ac-
  tress BE*, WWT/14*
PERRY, Joe (d 1904) minstrel?
  EA/05*
PERRY, John (b 1906) Irish
  dramatist, actor WWT/10-14
PERRY, John Bennett (b 1941)
  American actor TW/24-25,
  27, 29
PERRY, Margaret (b 1913) Amer-
  ican actress, director, drama-
  tist BE, WWT/7-11
PERRY, Martha American admin-
  istrator BE
PERRY, Mary (d 1971 [83])
  American actress TW/12-15
PERRY, Robert E. (d 1962 [83])
  actor, director BE*
PERRY, Ronald (d 1963 [53])
  performer BE*
PERRY, Ty (b 1918) American
  actor TW/5
PERRY, Vic (d 1974 [54]) per-
  former BP/59*
PERRY, William (fl 1615-42)
  actor, manager DA
PERRYMAN, Daniel (d 1878 [68])
  manager EA/80*
PERRYMAN, Jill (b 1933) Aus-
  tralian actress WWT/16
PERSIAN DWARF (fl 18th cent)
  CDP
PERSIANI, Sig. (d 1869 [65])
  composer EA/70*
PERSIANI, Fanny (1812-67)
  singer CDP
PERSIAN TWIN SISTERS CDP
PERSINI, Elise singer CDP
PERSIVANI [R. Brown] (d 1890
  [48]) clown, contortionist
  EA/91*
PERSJ, Rupert see Percy,
  Robert
PERSKE, Betty see Bacall,
  Lauren
PERSOFF, Nehemiah (b 1920)
  Israeli actor BE, WWT/14-16
PERSONN, Johann (fl 1579-80)
  actor DA
PERSSON, Frederic J. (d 1966
  [74]) actor, singer TW/23

PERSTEN, Rupert see Percy,
  Robert
PERTOLDI, Ermina (d 1907 [52])
  dancer GRB/3
PERTWEE, Jon (b 1919) English ac-
  tor TW/24, WWT/15-16
PERTWEE, Michael (b 1916) Eng-
  lish dramatist WWT/15-16
PERTWEE, Roland (1885/86-1963)
  English dramatist WWT/5-13,
  WWW/6
PERUGINI, Sig. [John Chatterton]
  (d 1914 [59]) English actor BE*,
  WWT/14*
PERY, Robert (fl 1529-31) member
  of the Chapel Royal DA
PERY, William (fl 1530) member
  of the Chapel Royal DA
PESCHKA-LEUTNER, Minna (1839-
  90) singer CDP
PESSINA, Arturo (1858-1926) Italian
  singer ES
PESTELL, Thomas (fl 1631-45)
  dramatist CP/3, FGF
PETE [Herbert Williams] (d 1909
  [38]) minstrel? EA/10*
"PETER?" (fl early 17th cent) ac-
  tor? DA
PETERBOROUGH, Anastasia, Coun-
  tess of [Mrs. Charles Mordaunt]
  (d 1755) singer CDP, DNB
PETERKIN, Daisy see Dazie,
  Mlle.
PETERS, Miss see Hamilton,
  Mrs.
PETERS, Bernadette (b 1948) Amer-
  ican actress, singer TW/24-28,
  WWT/15-16
PETERS, Brandon (d 1956 [63])
  American actor TW/12
PETERS, Brock (b 1927) American
  actor, singer BE, TW/22-23,
  28
PETERS, Charles (1825-70) English
  actor CDP, HAS
PETERS, Fred (d 1963 [78]) actor
  BE*
PETERS, F. W. (fl 1859) actor
  HAS
PETERS, Gunnar (d 1974) performer
  BP/58*
PETERS, Holly (b 1946) German/
  American? actress TW/27
PETERS, Kay (b 1942) American
  actress TW/25
PETERS, Roberta (b 1930) American
  singer CB, ES
PETERS, Rollo (1892-1967) French

actor, designer, director, producer BE, TW/23, WWT/5-11
PETERS, Stephen [or Stefan] (b 1944) American actor TW/23, 28, 30
PETERS, Susan (d 1952 [31]) American actress BE*, BP/37*
PETERS, Werner (d 1971 [52]) performer BP/55*
PETERS, William (d 1975 [51]) performer BP/59*
PETERSEN, Alfred (d 1911) musical director EA/12*
PETERSEN, Erika (b 1949) American actress TW/26, 28
PETERSEN, Karen (d 1940 [37]) actress BE*, WWT/14*
PETERSILEA, Franz musician CDP
PETERSON, Daniel McCloud (d 1974 [57]) performer BP/59*
PETERSON, Eloise Kimball Walton (d 1971 [69]) publicist BP/56*
PETERSON, Joe (d 1964 [63]) performer BP/49*
PETERSON, Joseph (d 1798) actor, dramatist CP/2-3, GT, TD/1-2
PETERSON, Kurt (b 1948) American actor TW/25-29
PETERSON, Lenka (b 1925) American actress BE, TW/4, 8, 30
PETERSON, Louis (b 1922) American dramatist, actor BE
PETERSON, Margaret (1883-1933) dramatist WWW/2
PETERSON, Marjorie (d 1974 [68]) American actress TW/6-14
PETERSON, May (1889-1952) American singer WWA/3
PETERSON, Wally (b 1919) American actor TW/23
PETHERBRIDGE, Edward (b 1936) English actor AAS, WWT/15-16
PETIE, Mary Ann (d 1884 [30]) EA/85*
PETINA, Irra (b 1900/14) Russian actress, singer BE, TW/1-3, 5-7, 13-15, 22
PETIPA, Marius (1822-1910) dancer, choreographer BE*, WWT/14*
PETIT, Roland (b 1924) French

dancer, choreographer CB, ES, WWT/11-12
PETLEY, E. S. (d 1945 [69]) actor BE*, WWT/14*
PETLEY, Frank E. (1872-1945) English actor WWT/4-9
PETRASS, Sari (1890-1930) Austrian actress, singer WWT/2-6
PETRICOFF, Elaine American actress TW/28-30
PETRIE, Daniel M. (b 1920) Canadian director, actor BE
PETRIE, David Hay (1895-1948) Scottish actor WWT/5-10
PETRIE, Eliza Place (d 1865) actress HAS
PETRIE, George (b 1915) American actor TW/2-3
PETRIE, Howard A. (d 1968 [61]) performer BP/52*
PETRO, Michael (b 1944) American actor TW/27-29
PETRONE, Susan (d 1963 [32]) performer BP/48*
PETRONJ, Egidio [Bernard Sylvester] (d 1882) actor, pantomimist EA/84*
PETROVA, Olga (1886-1977) English actress, dramatist WWT/5-7
PETT dramatist FGF
PETTEBONE, Jean (d 1970 [56]) publicist BP/55*
PETTENGILL, Charlie (d 1870 [27]) minstrel manager & performer CDP
PETTET, Edwin Burr (b 1913) American educator, director BE
PETTET, Joanna (b 1944) English actress TW/21
PETTIE, Edna see May, Edna
PETTIFER, Mary Ann [Mrs. John Bond Ratcliffe] (d 1892 [70]) actress CDP
PETTIGROVE, Richard (d 1902 [70]) showman EA/03*
PETTINGELL, Frank (1891-1966) English actor WWT/7-14
PETTINGTON, Henry (fl 1636) actor DA
PETTIT, Paul Bruce (b 1920) American educator, director BE
PETTITT, Annette [Mrs. Henry Pettitt] (d 1916) EA/17*
PETTITT, Henry (1848-93) English dramatist DNB

PETTITT, Henry (b 1881) English actor, manager, dramatist GRB/1-2

PETTITT, Mrs. Henry see Pettitt, Annette

PETTMAN, Julia (d 1896 [28]) actress EA/97*

PEVERIL, C. H. (d 1875) actor EA/76*

PEW, John (d 1890) conductor EA/91*

PEYRANI, Giovanni (d 1901) animal trainer EA/02*

PFEIFER, Allan Cameron see Dalzell, Allan C.

PFEIFER, Sidney B. (d 1967 [73]) critic BP/52*

PFEIFFER, Oscar (b 1830) Austrian pianist HAS

PFLUGBEIL, August (fl 1614-15) actor DA

PHALEN, Robert (b 1937) American actor TW/23-30

PHARAR, Renée (d 1962 [83]) actress BE*

PHELAN, John A. (b 1842) American actor HAS

PHELPS, Miss see Parsons, Mrs.

PHELPS, A. R. (b 1824) American actor HAS

PHELPS, Charles H. (d 1910) actor EA/11*

PHELPS, Dodie (d 1963 [65]) performer BE*

PHELPS, Edmund (d 1870 [32]) actor EA/71*

PHELPS, Edmund actor OAA/1

PHELPS, Mrs. Edmund (d 1907 [67]) actress GRB/3

PHELPS, Eleanor (d 1882) EA/83*

PHELPS, Eleanor American actress TW/26, 30

PHELPS, Fanny Morgan (fl 1854-67) Irish actress HAS

PHELPS, Frederick (d 1912) music-hall manager EA/13*

PHELPS, George Turner (1867-1920) American writer WWA/1

PHELPS, Leonard P. (d 1924 [73]) American manager BE*, BP/8*

PHELPS, Lucian (d 1973 [65]) performer BP/57*

PHELPS, Lyon (b 1923) American dramatist BE

PHELPS, Pauline (fl 1908-13) American dramatist WWM

PHELPS, Rev. Robert (d 1890 [84]) EA/91*

PHELPS, Samuel (1804-78) English actor CDP, COC, DNB, ES, OAA/1-2, OC/1-3

PHELPS, Mrs. Samuel (d 1867) EA/68*

PHELPS, Stella [Estelle M. Osbaldestone] (d 1918) EA/19*

PHELPS, William Robert (d 1867) EA/68*

PHELPS-LEO, Arthur [Louis H. T. Phelps-Payne] (b 1882) English actor, singer GRB/1

PHELPS-PAYNE, Louis H. T. see Phelps-Leo, Arthur

PHELTON, John, Jr. see Flynn, J. D.

PHETHEAN, David (b 1918) English director, actor WWT/15-16

PHILBIN, Jane Devereux see Dreyfuss, Jane

PHILBRICK, Norman (b 1913) American educator BE

PHILIP (fl 1599?) dramatist FGF

PHILIP, James E. (d 1910 [42]) actor, composer BE*

PHILIP, Robert (fl 1514) member of the Chapel Royal DA

PHILIPE, Gérard (1922-59) French actor COC, OC/3, TW/16

PHILIPP, Adolf (1867-1936) German dramatist, composer, actor, manager, singer WWM

PHILIPPS, Thomas (1774-1881) English singer CDP, DNB

PHILIPS, Ambrose (c. 1671/74-1749) English dramatist CDP, COC, CP/1-3, GT, OC/3, TD/1-2

PHILIPS, Augustus (b 1873) American actor WWS

PHILIPS, F. C. (1849-1921) English dramatist GRB/1-4, WWT/1-3, WWW/2

PHILIPS, John (fl 1716-17) dramatist CP/1-3, GT

PHILIPS, Katherine (1631-64) English dramatist CP/1-3, GT

PHILIPS, Lee (b 1927) American actor, director, writer BE, TW/12-14

PHILIPS, Marie L. (b 1925) American director, administrator, actress BE

PHILIPS, Marvin James (b 1923) American educator BE

PHILIPS, Mary (1901-75) Amer-
ican actress WWT/8-13
PHILIPS, Robert (fl 1543-59?)
musician DNB
PHILIPS, William see Phillips,
William
PHILLIMORE, Mr. actor TD/1-2
PHILLIPP, Peter (fl 1574) actor DA
PHILLIPPE, Robert (fl 1559)
actor DA
PHILLIPS, Mr. (fl 1797) singer
TD/1-2
PHILLIPS, Mr. ["Harlequin Phil-
lips"] (fl 1748-49?) actor CDP
PHILLIPS, Mrs. (d 1906 [65])
EA/07*
PHILLIPS, Mrs. see Rogers,
Mrs.
PHILLIPS, Aaron J. (d 1846)
American actor, manager HAS
PHILLIPS, Acton (d 1899 [69])
proprietor, manager EA/00*,
WWT/14*
PHILLIPS, Acton (d 1940 [86]) pro-
ducer, manager BE*, WWT/14*
PHILLIPS, Adelaide (b 1822)
American actress SR
PHILLIPS, Adelaide (1833-82)
English actress, singer CDP,
HAS
PHILLIPS, Albert (1875-1940)
American actor CB
PHILLIPS, Mrs. Alfred (d 1876
[54]) dramatist, actress BE*,
EA/77*, WWT/14*
PHILLIPS, Alfred S. (d 1888
[34]) comedian EA/89*
PHILLIPS, Andrew (d 1871 [70])
scene artist EA/72*
PHILLIPS, Anna Maria see
Crouch, Mrs. Rawlings Edward
PHILLIPS, Ann Eliza see
Stone, Ann Eliza
PHILLIPS, Augustine (d 1605)
English actor COC, DA,
NTH, OC/1-3
PHILLIPS, Augustus G. (1838-93)
actor CDP
PHILLIPS, Benjamin Woolf (d
1899 [74]) actor? EA/00*
PHILLIPS, Catherine see
Philips, Katherine
PHILLIPS, Charles (1880-1933)
American dramatist WWA/1
PHILLIPS, Charles (d 1974 [25])
performer BP/59*
PHILLIPS, Cyril L. (b 1894)
English manager WWT/8-9

PHILLIPS, David Graham (1867-
1911) American dramatist HJD
PHILLIPS, Diane (b 1945) Ameri-
can actress TW/26
PHILLIPS, Eddie (b 1928) American
actor TW/13-14, 23, 30
PHILLIPS, Edward (fl 1730-39)
dramatist CP/1-3, DNB, GT,
TD/1-2
PHILLIPS, Edwin (b 1911) Ameri-
can actor TW/14-15
PHILLIPS, Eleanor Hyde (d 1975
[94]) performer BP/60*
PHILLIPS, Eliza (fl 1837) actress
CDP
PHILLIPS, Elizabeth [Mrs. Philip
Phillips] (d 1887 [76]) EA/88*
PHILLIPS, Emily (d 1894 [59])
EA/95*
PHILLIPS, Rev. Forbes Alexander
["Athol Forbes"] (b 1866) Eng-
lish dramatist GRB/1-4
PHILLIPS, Mrs. F. R. (d 1899
[70]) music-hall performer EA/
01*
PHILLIPS, Mrs. Francis see
Jones, Maria B.
PHILLIPS, Frederick [Philip Han-
nan] (d 1871) lessee, manager
EA/72*
PHILLIPS, Mrs. Frederick L.
see Daly, Ellen
PHILLIPS, Harriet [née Kate Horn-
by] (d 1873 [24]) singer EA/74*
PHILLIPS, Harriet see Holman,
Mrs. George
PHILLIPS, Harry (d 1891 [58])
showman EA/92*
PHILLIPS, H. B. (b 1819) Ameri-
can actor, stage manager,
manager HAS
PHILLIPS, H. B. (d 1950 [83])
impresario BE*, WWT/14*
PHILLIPS, Mrs. H. B. (d 1867)
English dancer HAS
PHILLIPS, Henry (1801-76) English
singer, actor, musician CDP,
DNB
PHILLIPS, H. I. (d 1965 [75])
dramatist BP/49*
PHILLIPS, Ida English actress
GRB/1
PHILLIPS, Irna (d 1973 [72])
dramatist BP/58*
PHILLIPS, Jack (d 1956 [55]) stage
manager, director BE*, WWT/
14*
PHILLIPS, J. B. (d 1862) stage

manager HAS
PHILLIPS, Mrs. J. B. [Annie Myers] (1833-68) American actress HAS
PHILLIPS, J. O. (fl 1828-30?) dramatist EAP
PHILLIPS, Joe (d 1966 [78]) performer BP/51*
PHILLIPS, Jonas B. (fl 1820s?) dramatist RJ, SR
PHILLIPS, Kate (1856-1931) English actress DP, EA/97, GRB/1-4, OAA/2, WWT/1-6
PHILLIPS, Leslie (b 1924) English actor, director AAS, WWT/12-16
PHILLIPS, Louisa Anne see Salzberg, Mrs.
PHILLIPS, Mabel [Mrs. Polly Fox] (d 1912 [29]) variety performer EA/13*
PHILLIPS, Margaret (b 1923) Welsh actress BE, TW/1, 3-20, 23-24, WWT/11-16
PHILLIPS, Marie Eugenie see Gordon, Marie
PHILLIPS, Mary Bracken (b 1946) American actress TW/26-29
PHILLIPS, Mathilde (1841-1915) actress, singer SR
PHILLIPS, Matilda see Stoddart, Mrs. James Henry
PHILLIPS, Minna (d 1963 [91]) Australian actress TW/19
PHILLIPS, Montague Fawcett (1885-1969) composer WWW/6
PHILLIPS, Norma (1893-1931) American actress BE*, BP/16*
PHILLIPS, Mr. P. (d 1869) music-hall performer EA/70*
PHILLIPS, Paul (b 1947) American actor TW/30
PHILLIPS, Philip (d 1864 [62]) scene artist EA/72*
PHILLIPS, Mrs. Philip see Phillips, Elizabeth
PHILLIPS, R. (fl 1683) dramatist CP/1-3, GT
PHILLIPS, Randy (b 1926) American actor TW/24-26, 29
PHILLIPS, Richard Empson (d 1872 [51]) actor EA/73*
PHILLIPS, Robin (b 1942) English director, actor AAS, WWT/15-16
PHILLIPS, Miss S. see Crouch, Mrs.

PHILLIPS, Siân Welsh actress WWT/14-16
PHILLIPS, Sid (d 1973 [65]) composer/lyricist BP/58*
PHILLIPS, Sidney (d 1973 [82]) producer/director/choreographer BP/58*
PHILLIPS, Sophia (fl 1828) singer CDP
PHILLIPS, Stephen (1864-1915) English dramatist, actor COC, DNB, ES, GRB/1-4, MH, MWD, NTH, OC/1-3, PDT, WWT/1-3, WWW/1
PHILLIPS, T. (1802-41) English actor HAS
PHILLIPS, Thomas (d 1739) dramatist CP/2-3, GT, TD/1-2
PHILLIPS, Mrs. W. A. (d 1867) actor? EA/68*
PHILLIPS, Watts (1825/29-74) English dramatist DNB, EA/68
PHILLIPS, Mrs. Watts (d 1899 [68]) EA/00*
PHILLIPS, Mrs. W. C. see Hastings, Kate
PHILLIPS, Mrs. W. C. see Oliver, Martha
PHILLIPS, Wendell K. (b 1907) American actor, director, designer, dramatist BE, TW/23, 28-29
PHILLIPS, W. H. (d 1887 [28]) comedian EA/88*
PHILLIPS, William (d 1734) Irish? actor, dramatist CDP, CP/1-3, DNB, GT
PHILLIPS, William Lovell (d 1860 [43]) composer EA/72*
PHILLPOTTS, Adelaide (b 1896) dramatist WWT/6-14
PHILLPOTTS, Ambrosine (b 1912) English actress WWT/10-16
PHILLPOTTS, Eden (1862-1960) Indian/English dramatist COC, DNB, ES, OC/1-3, PDT, WWT/3-12, WWW/5
"PHILO-NAUTICUS" see Halloran, L. H.
PHILP, Elizabeth (d 1885) author, composer EA/86*
PHILP, James East (d 1910 [42]) conductor, composer EA/11*, WWT/14*
PHILP, Rowline [Harry Proctor] (d 1887) actor EA/88*
PHINN, C. Mort (d 1965 [75]) performer BP/50*

PHIPP, Sophia Matilda (d 1906
[74]) EA/08*
PHIPP, W. Scott (b 1870) Eng-
lish manager, dramatist, lyri-
cist, composer GRB/1
PHIPPS, Beatriz see Kemp,
Beatriz
PHIPPS, Charles John (d 1897
[62]) architect EA/98*
PHIPPS, Nicholas (b 1913) Eng-
lish actor WWT/11-16
PHIPPS, William Henry (d 1877
[69]) EA/78*
PHISTER, Montgomery (b 1852)
American critic WWA/4
PHOENIX, Walter (fl 1880?)
dancer, singer, songcomposer
CDP
PHYDORA, Joe (d 1896) panto-
mimist EA/97*
PHYDORA, William (d 1909) per-
former? EA/10*
PHYSIOC, Joseph Allen (d 1951
[86]) American scene artist
BE*, BP/36*
PIACENTINI, Anne American ac-
tress TW/27
PIAF, Edith (1915-63) French
singer, actress CB, OC/3,
TW/20
PIATOV, Sascha (1890-1947)
dancer, director SR
PIATTI, Alfredo (d 1901 [79])
musician, composer EA/02*
PIAZZA, Ben (b 1934) American
actor BE, TW/15-20, 24-25,
WWT/14-16
PIAZZA, Dario (d 1974 [70])
costumier BP/59*
PICARD, Louis Baptiste (1769-
1828) French dramatist COC,
OC/2-3
PICARDO, Arthur [Thomas Arthur
Marriott] (d 1900 [31]) music-
hall performer EA/01*
PICAUD, Mrs. (d 1905) EA/06*
PICCAVER, Alfred (1884-1958)
Anglo-Austrian singer ES
PICCOLOMINI, Henry Pontent
(d 1902) composer EA/03*
PICCOLOMINI, Maria (1834-99)
Italian singer CDP, ES, HAS
PICHEL, Irving (d 1954 [63])
American actor, director BE*,
BP/39*, WWT/14*
PICKARD, Helena (1899-1959)
English actress COC, OC/
2-3, WWT/6-12

PICKARD, James (d 1874 [34]) comic
singer EA/75*
PICKARD, Mae (d 1946) actress
BE*, WWT/14*
PICKARD, Margery (b 1911) English
actress WWT/8-11
PICKENS, Miss see Abbott,
Bessie
PICKENS, Jane American singer
CB, TW/8
PICKER, Mlle. (fl 1856) German
singer HAS
PICKERING, Alexander L. (fl 1839)
actor CDP
PICKERING, Andrew (fl 1839) actor
HAS
PICKERING, Mrs. Andrew (d 1837
[19]) actress HAS
PICKERING, Edward A. (b 1871/73)
English actor, acting manager,
business manager GRB/3-4,
WWT/1, 4-7
PICKERING, James (fl 1612) actor
DA
PICKERING, John (fl 1567?) drama-
tist FGF
PICKERING, J. Russell (d 1947
[67]) producer, manager BE*,
WWT/14*
PICKERT, Willis clog dancer CDP
PICKETT, Ingram B. (d 1963 [64])
actor BE*
PICKETT, Jack (b 1935) American
actor TW/23
PICKFORD, Jack (d 1933 [36])
Canadian actor, producer BE*
PICKFORD, James (d 1872) music-
hall proprietor EA/73*
PICKFORD, Lottie (1895-1936)
Canadian actress BE*, BP/21*
PICKFORD, Mary [Gladys Mary
Smith] (b 1893) Canadian actress
CB, ES, NTH, SR, WWT/4-11
PICKLES, Little [John Scott] (d
1895 [32]) circus clown EA/96*
PICKLES, David Joseph (d 1891
[42]) manager EA/92*
PICKLES, James (d 1872 [63])
musician EA/73*
PICKULS, Sarah [Mrs. Stephen
Pickuls] (d 1874) EA/75*
PICKULS, Mrs. Stephen see
Pickuls, Sarah
PICKUP, Mrs. [née Miss Brooks]
(d 1874) actress EA/75*
PICKUP, Ronald (b 1941) English
actor AAS, WWT/15-16
PICKWOAD, William see Mer-

vyn, William
PICO, Rosina (fl 1844) singer
CDP
PICON, Molly (b 1898) American
actress, manager BE, CB,
NTH, TW/5-8, 23-24, 26,
WWT/10-16
PICTON, George (d 1882) EA/84*
PICTON, Sam (d 1893 [34]) comic
singer, manager EA/94*
PIDCOCK, Richard (d 1894 [74])
director EA/95*
PIDDOCK, J. C. (d 1919 [56])
actor, singer BE*, WWT/14*
PIDGEON, Edward Everett (1869-
1941) American editor, critic
WWM
PIDGEON, Walter (b 1897) Cana-
dian actor BE, CB, ES, SR,
TW/23, WWT/15-16
PIDGIN, Charles Felton (1844-
1923) American dramatist
WWA/1, WWM
PIEL, David (b 1946) American
actor TW/25
PIERCE, Earl Horton (1823-59)
American minstrel CDP, HAS
PIERCE, Edward (d 1974 [80])
performer BP/59*
PIERCE, Frank (d 1897) propri-
etor EA/98*
PIERCE, George (d 1964 [70])
performer BP/49*
PIERCE, Grace Adele (d 1923)
American writer WWA/1
PIERCE, Mrs. H. (d 1883 [34])
EA/89*
PIERCE, Jane [Mrs. J. H.
Pierce] (d 1888) EA/89*
PIERCE, J. H. [James Hart
Glen] (d 1895) music-hall per-
former EA/96*
PIERCE, Mrs. J. H. see
Pierce, Jane
PIERCE, Randolph (b 1940)
American actor TW/23
PIERCE, Rik (b 1939) American
actor TW/24
PIERCE, William E. (b 1847)
American actor HAS
PIERCEY, William Edgar see
Austin, Edgar
PIERCY, Samuel W. (1849-82)
actor CDP
PIERLOT, Francis (d 1955 [79])
actor BE*
PIERPOINT, Joseph Charles
Garland (d 1887 [40]) singer

EA/88*
PIERPOINT, Laura (1890-1972)
American actress TW/5-7, 9-
12, 29
PIERRO, Annie (d 1884) EA/85*
PIERS, Edward see Pearce, Ed-
ward
PIERSON, Arthur (d 1975 [73])
actor, director, writer WWT/
16*
PIERSON, Blanche (b 1840) actress
CDP
PIERSON, Ethel [Mrs. Frank E.
Randell] (d 1892) singer, actress
EA/93*
PIERSON, Henry Hugh (d 1873
[58]) composer EA/74*
PIERSON, Rennie (d 1973 [75])
performer BP/58*
PIERSON, Thomas (d 1791) drama-
tist CP/3
PIESEN, Margery Korman (d 1968
[62]) performer BP/53*
PIETER, Ruth Yingling (d 1974
[80]) critic BP/59*
PIETRACK, Irving (d 1972 [70])
composer/lyricist BP/57*
PIETRO, Paul see Tarrant,
George
PIFF, Charles see Kay, Charles
PIFFARD, Frederick (1902-75) In-
dian/English manager WWT/11-
15
PIG, John (fl 1593-99) actor DA
PIGEON, Richard Walter (d 1887
[56]) EA/88*
PIGNIERES, Rene (d 1973 [68])
producer/director/choreographer
BP/58*
PIGOT, Elizabeth [Mrs. Percy
Milton] (d 1899 [44]) EA/00*
PIGOTT, A. S. English business
manager WWT/2-5
PIGOTT, Edward Frederick Smyth
(d 1895 [71]) examiner of plays
EA/96*, WWT/14*
PIGOTT, Howard H. (d 1974 [76])
performer BP/59*
PIGOTT, Tempe (d 1962 [78]) per-
former BE*
PIGOTT, W. W. see Leslie, Will
PIGUE, William W. (d 1970 [62])
journalist, publicist BP/54*
PIGUENIT, D. J. (fl 1774) drama-
tist CP/3
PIHODNA, Gottlieb (d 1969 [61])
critic BP/53*
PIKE, Marshall S. (1818-1901)

American female impersonator
CDP, HAS

PIKE, Maurice B. (b 1837) American actor HAS

PIKE, Richard Jarvis (d 1905) bandmaster EA/06*

PIKE, Robert (d 1974 [56]) manager, press agent BP/59*

PIKE, Samuel N. theatre builder CDP

PIKET, Frederick (d 1974 [71]) composer/lyricist BP/58*

PILARCZYK, Helga (b 1925) German singer ES

PILAR-MORIN, Mme. (fl 1900s) Spanish actress, pantomimist WWM

PILBEAM, Nova (b 1919) English actress WWT/8-11

PILBEAM, Mrs. Tom see Olive, Kittie

PILBROW, Richard (b 1933) English lighting designer, managing director, producer WWT/14-16

PILCER, Harry (d 1961 [75]) American dancer, actor TW/17, WWT/4-7

PILGRIM, James (1825-79) actor, dramatist, manager CDP, HAS

PILKINGTON, Laetitia (1712-50) Irish dramatist CP/1-3, GT

PILLANS, R. S. (d 1878 [34]) Scottish comedian EA/79*

PILLETTS, Edmund see De Mondion, Edmund

PILLING, Mr. (d 1907) musical director EA/08*

PILLING, Harry (d 1910) EA/11*

PILON, Frederick (1750-88) Irish actor, dramatist CP/2-3, DNB, GT, TD/1-2

PILOTTI, Alessandro (d 1875) professor of music EA/76*

PIM, Sgt. (d 1917) EA/18*

PIMBURY, Martha (d 1878 [77]) EA/79*

PIMLEY, John (d 1972 [53]) performer BP/57*

PIMM, Harry S. (d 1965 [75]) performer BP/50*

PIM-PIM [Charles Stuart Hall] (d 1905) circus clown EA/07*

PINACCI, Giovanni Battista see Bagnolesi, Anna

PINANSKI, Sam (d 1971 [77]) pioneer in developing theatres BP/56*

PINANSKY, Sam (d 1966 [77]) performer BP/50*

PINAUD, Charles Phoite (d 1906) performer? EA/07*

PINCHOT, Rosamond (1904-38) American actress BE*, BP/22*

PINCUS, Warren (b 1938) American actor TW/24, 27-29

PINDAR, Peter see Wolcot, John

PINDER, Mrs. (fl 1826-31) English actress HAS

PINDER, Emma (d 1890) performer? EA/91*

PINDER, George (d 1906 [75]) circus proprietor EA/07*

PINDER, Mrs. George see Pinder, Louisa

PINDER, George Ord (d 1912 [43]) circus manager EA/13*

PINDER, James (d 1886 [32]) performer? EA/88*

PINDER, Louisa [Mrs. George Pinder] (d 1892 [57]) EA/93*

PINDER, Powis (d 1941 [68]) actor GRB/3

PINDER, Rebecca [Mrs. William Pinder] (d 1901) EA/02*

PINDER, Mrs. W. (d 1870) EA/71*

PINDER, William (d 1876) carpenter EA/77*

PINDER, Mrs. William see Pinder, Rebecca

PINDER, William Olman (d 1906 [38]) circus director EA/07*

PINE, Phillip (b 1925) American actor TW/8-12

PINERO, Sir Arthur Wing (1855-1934) English dramatist, actor CDP, COC, DNB, ES, GRB/1-4, HP, MH, MWD, NTH, OAA/1-2, OC/1-3, PDT, RE, SR, WWM, WWS, WWT/1-7, WWW/3

PINERO, Lady Arthur Wing see Holme, Myra

PINERO, Lucy (d 1905 [69]) EA/06*

PINI CORSI, Antonio (1858-1918) Italian singer ES

PINK, Wal (d 1922 [60]) English actor, singer, dramatist, writer WWT/4

PINKARD, Maceo (d 1962 [65]) composer BE*, BP/47*

PINKERT, Regina (1869-1931) Polish/Italian singer ES

PINKES, Elijah see Potter, Stanley

PINKETHMAN, William (d 1725)
actor CDP, DNB
PINKETT, Willis (d 1975 [55])
performer BP/59*
PINNER, David (b 1940) English
dramatist, actor CD
PINSKI, David (1872-1959) Rus-
sian dramatist MH, MWD,
RE, WWA/5
PINTER, Emily (d 1965 [65])
performer BP/50*
PINTER, Harold (b 1930) English
dramatist, director, actor
AAS, BE, CB, CD, CH,
COC, ES, MD, MH, MWD,
OC/3, PDT, RE, WWT/13-16
PINTER, Mrs. Harold see
Merchant, Vivien
PINTO, Mrs. see Brent, Char-
lotte
PINTO, Charlotte (d 1802) ac-
tress, singer WWT/14*
PINTO, Effingham (b 1886) Amer-
ican actor WWM
PINTO, Thomas (1710?-73) Eng-
lish musician DNB
PINZA, Carla (b 1942) Puerto
Rican actress TW/28-29
PINZA, Ezio (1892-1957) Italian
singer, actor AAS, CB, ES,
TW/5-8, 11-13, WWA/3
PIPER, John (b 1903) English
scene designer ES
PIPER, Walter H. (d 1903 [28])
proprietor EA/04*
PIPO (d 1970 [68]) performer
BP/55*
PIP SIMMONS THEATRE GROUP
theatre collective CD
PIRANDELLO, Luigi (1867-1936)
Italian dramatist COC, ES,
OC/2-3, RE, WWT/8
PIRANDELLO, Stefano (d 1972
[76]) dramatist BP/56*
PIRO, Phillip (b 1943) American
actor TW/25
PIRSSON, J. P. (fl 19th cent)
dramatist EAP
PISANI, Mme. (fl 1879?) singer
CDP
PISARONI, Benedetta Rosmunda
(1793-1872) Italian singer ES
PISCATOR, Erwin (1893-1966)
German producer, director
BE, CB, CH, COC, ES, OC/
1-3, PDT, TW/22, WWA/4
PISCATOR, Maria Ley [Maria
Ley] Austrian director BE

PISHOU, Jane (d 1864) "fat lady"
HAS
PISTONI, Mario (b 1933) Italian
dancer ES
PITCAIRNE, Dr. Archibald (1652-
1713) Scottish dramatist CP/
2-3, GT
PITHEY, Wensley (b 1914) South
African actor WWT/15-16
PITKIN, William (b 1925) American
designer BE, WWT/15-16
PITMAN, Richard (d 1941 [67])
American actor, talent repre-
sentative BE*, BP/26*
PITOËFF, Georges (1886/87-1939)
Russian actor, manager OC/1-
3, WWT/8-9
PITOËFF, Ludmilla (1896-1951)
Russian actress COC, OC/1-3,
WWT/8-11
PITOT, Genevieve American com-
poser BE
PITOU, Augustus (1843-1915)
American manager, dramatist
GRB/3-4, SR, WWA/1, WWM,
WWT/1-3
PITOU, Mrs. Augustus, Jr. see
Coghlan, Gertrude
PITROT, Antoine Bonaventure (fl
1744-84) French dancer, chore-
ographer ES
PITT, Mrs. (d 1800) English ac-
tress TD/1-2
PITT, Miss actress CDP
PITT, Addison (d 1968 [91]) per-
former BP/52*
PITT, Ann (1720?-99) English ac-
tress CDP, DNB
PITT, Annie [Mrs. Henry Pitt]
(d 1870 [39]) EA/71*
PITT, Archie (1885-1940) actor,
manager COC, WWT/6-9
PITT, Cecil (d 1879 [53]) actor
CDP
PITT, Charles (d 1871) actor EA/
72*
PITT, Mrs. Charles see Pitt,
Ellen
PITT, Charles Dibdin (d 1866 [47])
actor, manager CDP, HAS
PITT, Mrs. Charles Dibdin (fl
1849-50) actress HAS
PITT, Charles Isaac Mungo see
Dibdin, Charles Isaac Mungo
PITT, Dibdin (d 1855 [56]) actor,
dramatist CDP
PITT, Ellen [Mrs. Charles Pitt]
(d 1897 [76]) EA/98*

PITT, Emily Lavinia (fl 1863-
68) singer HAS
PITT, Fanny (d 1898) actress
EA/99*
PITT, Fanny Addison (d 1937
[93]) English actress BE*,
BP/21*, WWT/14*
PITT, Felix (d 1922) actor EA/96
PITT, Mrs. Felix see Arm-
strong, Clara
PITT, Frank J. (b 1878) English
actor GRB/1
PITT, George Dibdin see Pitt,
Dibdin
PITT, Harriet (d 1814) dancer
DNB
PITT, Mrs. Harry see Pitt,
Annie
PITT, Henry Mader (1850-98)
American actor, stage manager
CDP, OAA/1-2
PITT, Mrs. H. M. [Mme. Lilian]
(d 1873) actress EA/75*
PITT, John (d 1871 [46]) propri-
etor EA/72*
PITT, Lottie (d 1885) actress
EA/87*
PITT, Mary (fl 1863-68) English
singer HAS
PITT, Percy (1870-1932) English
composer, conductor WWW/3
PITT, Rose Ellen Dibdin (d 1912
[40]) actress EA/13*
PITT, Samuel (d 1897 [65]) show-
man EA/99*
PITT, Thomas Henry (d 1873
[70]) scene artist EA/74*
PITT, Thomas John see Dib-
din, Thomas John
PITT, Tom (d 1924 [68]) English
business manager WWT/2-4
PITT, W. H. (d 1879 [44]) actor
EA/80*
PITT-HARDACRE, Mrs. J. see
Pitt-Hardacre, Kate Adelaide
PITT-HARDACRE, Kate Adelaide
[Mrs. J. Pitt-Hardacre] (d
1916) EA/17*
PITTMAN, Frank (d 1973 [50s])
producer/director/choreographer
BP/58*
PITTMAN, Josiah (1816-66) mu-
sician, librettist DNB
PITTMAN, W. E. [Will Harris]
(d 1873 [19]) Negro comedian
EA/74*
PITTS, Eliza Susan see Pitts,
ZaSu

PITTS, ZaSu [née Eliza Susan]
(1898/1900-1963) American actress ES, TW/9, 20, WWT/10-
13
PIX, Mary (1666-1720?) English
dramatist CP/1-3, DNB, GT
PIXERECOURT, René Charles
Guilbert de (1773-1844) French
dramatist COC, OC/1-3
PIXLEY, Annie [Mrs. Robert Full-
ford] (1858-93) American ac-
tress CDP, SR
PIXLEY, Frank (1867-1919) Amer-
ican librettist GRB/3-4, SR,
WWA/1, WWM, WWT/1-3
PIXLEY, Gus (d 1923 [58]) come-
dian BE*, WWT/14*
PIZZI, Donna (b 1945) American
actress TW/27
PLACE, Mrs. Robert see Clif-
ton, Josephine
PLACIDE, Mrs. see La Folle,
Mrs.
PLACIDE, Alexandre (d 1812)
French dancer ES, HAS, OC/
1-3, WWA/H
PLACIDE, Mrs. Alexandre (d 1823
[50]) singer, dancer, actress
HAS
PLACIDE, Caroline see Blake,
Mrs. William Rufus
PLACIDE, Eliza see Mann, Mrs.
Sheridan
PLACIDE, Henry (1799-1870) Amer-
ican actor, manager CDP,
COC, DAB, ES, GC, HAS,
OC/1-3, SR, WWA/H
PLACIDE, Jane (1804-35) American
actress HAS
PLACIDE, Thomas (1808-77) Amer-
ican actor, manager CDP, HAS
PLACKETT, Mrs. Isaac see
Plackett, Nellie
PLACKETT, Nellie [Mrs. Isaac
Plackett] (d 1916) EA/17*
PLANCHE, James Robinson (1796-
1880) English dramatist CDP,
COC, DNB, EA/68, ES, HP,
OC/1-3, PDT
PLANCHON, Roger (b 1931) French
producer, actor, dramatist
COC, OC/3, WWT/14
PLANÇON, Paul Henry (1853-1914)
French singer ES
PLANE, Miss see Durang, Mrs.
F.
PLANK, Thomas C. (d 1962 [34])
performer BE*

PLANQUETTE, Robert (d 1903
[54]) composer EA/04*
PLANQUETTE, Mrs. Robert (d
1903) EA/04*
PLANT, Jack (d 1973 [77]) per-
former BP/58*
PLANT, Jimmy (d 1964 [66])
performer BP/49*
PLANTOU, Mr. (fl 1827) actor
HAS
PLATER, Alan (b 1935) English
dramatist AAS, CD, WWT/
15-16
PLATT, Agnes English journalist
WWT/4-6
PLATT, Batt (d 1758) actor CDP
PLATT, Edward (1916-74) Amer-
ican actor TW/14
PLATT, Livingston designer
WWT/8-9
PLATT, Louise (b 1915) Amer-
ican actress TW/5-7
PLATT, Marjorie L. see
Dycke, Marjorie L.
PLATTEZ, Louisa (d 1890 [68])
EA/91*
PLATTS, Mr. (d 1872) band-
master EA/73*
PLATTS, William (d 1875 [33])
perruquier EA/76*
PLATZER, Joseph (d 1877 [36])
composer EA/78*
PLAYFAIR, Arthur (1869-1918)
Indian/English actor GRB/
2-4, WWT/1-3, WWW/2
PLAYFAIR, Mrs. Arthur see
Ashwell, Lena
PLAYFAIR, Sir Nigel (1874-
1934) English actor AAS,
COC, DNB, ES, GRB/2-4,
OC/1-3, PDT, WWT/1-7,
WWW/3
PLAYFAIR, Mrs. Nigel see
Martyn, May
PLAY-HOUSE OF THE RIDI-
CULOUS, The theatre col-
lective CD
PLAYTEN, Alice (b 1947) Amer-
ican actress, singer TW/
24-27, 29-30
PLAYWRIGHTS' COMPANY pro-
ducers TW/2-8
PLEASANT, Richard (d 1962
[52]) American press repre-
sentative BE*, BP/46*
PLEASENCE, Angela English
actress WWT/15-16
PLEASENCE, Donald (b 1919/20/

21) English actor AAS, BE,
CB, TW/18, 21, 28, WWT/12-
16
PLEGE, Nicolo (d 1877 [47])
equestrian EA/78*
PLEON, Harry (d 1911) actor,
singer, composer CDP
PLEON, Harry, Jr. (d 1911 [19])
EA/12*
PLEON, Joseph (d 1884) EA/85*
PLEON, Percy (d 1900 [31]) music-
hall comedian EA/01*
PLEON, Tom (d 1892 [30]) actor,
music-hall performer EA/93*
PLESCHETTE, Suzanne (b 1937)
American actress BE, TW/15
PLESHETTE, John (b 1942) Amer-
ican actor TW/22-24, 27, 29-
30
PLEWS, Arthur Gordon Lane see
Poulton, A. G.
PLEYDELL, George [George P.
Bancroft] (1868-1956) English
dramatist DD, GRB/2-4, WWT/
1-6, WWW/5
PLEYELL, Mme. (d 1875 [64])
musician EA/76*
PLIMMER, Annie [Mrs. James
Yuill, Jr.] (d 1892) EA/94*
PLIMMER, Edward (d 1878 [50])
Negro artist EA/79*
PLIMMER, Walter J. (d 1968 [67])
performer BP/53*
PLIMPTON, C. F. (d 1870 [66])
actor? EA/71*
PLIMPTON, Shelley (b 1947) Amer-
ican actress TW/27
"PLINGE, Walter" actor WWT/12
PLISETSKAYA, Maya (b 1925)
Russian dancer CB
PLOUGHMAN, Miss see Sloan,
Mrs. John T. K.
PLOUX, Edith [Mme. Theisen]
(d 1892 [34]) singer EA/93*
PLOWDEN, Florence [Mrs. Vyner
Robinson] (d 1890 [38]) actress
EA/91*
PLOWDEN, Mrs. Frances (fl 1800)
dramatist GT, TD/1-2
PLOWMAN, Joseph John (d 1898)
lessee EA/99*
PLOWRIGHT, Joan (b 1929) English
actress AAS, BE, CB, COC,
ES, OC/3, PDT, TW/14-18,
WWT/13-16
PLUGGE, Mary Lou (b 1906)
American educator BE
PLUMER, Mr. (fl 1828) singer

CDP
PLUMER, Mrs. see Cramer,
Miss
PLUMFIELD, Thomas (fl 1632)
actor DA
PLUMLEY, Don (b 1934) American
actor TW/26-29
PLUMMER, Christopher (b 1927/
29) Canadian actor AAS, BE,
CB, COC, TW/11-23, 29-30,
WWT/13-16
PLUMMER, John (fl 1444-55)
master of the Chapel Royal
DA
PLUMPTON, Alfred Thomas (d
1902 [61]) musical director
EA/03*
PLUMPTON, Mrs. Alfred Thomas
see Plumpton, Charlotte E.
PLUMPTON, Charlotte E. [Mrs.
Alfred Thomas Plumpton] (d
1902 [54]) EA/03*
PLUMPTON, Josiah singer, song
composer CDP
PLUMPTRE, Anne (1760-1818)
translator CP/3, DNB
PLUMPTRE, Bell (fl 1799) trans-
lator CP/3
PLUMPTRE, James (1770-1832)
dramatist CP/3, DNB
PLUNKETT, Adeline see Plunkett,
Marie Adeline
PLUNKETT, Charles (b 1822)
English actor HAS
PLUNKETT, Mrs. Charles [Eliza
Louisa Canavan] (1835-67) ac-
tress HAS
PLUNKETT, Edward John More-
ton Drax see Dunsany, Lord
PLUNKETT, Marie Adeline (1824-
1910) Belgian dancer CDP,
ES
PLUNKETT, Patricia (b 1926)
English actress WWT/11-13
PLYMPTON, Eben (1853-1915)
American actor CDP, GRB/
3-4, PP/2, WWA/1, WWS,
WWT/1-2
POBER, Leon (d 1971 [51]) com-
poser/lyricist BP/56*
"POCKET SIMS REEVES" see
Collard, Henry
POCKETT, James G. (d 1950
[69]) business manager WWT/
14*
POCKRISS, Lee (b 1927) Ameri-
can composer BE
POCOCK, Isaac (1782-1835) Eng-

lish dramatist COC, DNB, OC/
1-3
POCOCK, J. (fl 1809-10) dramatist
CP/3
POCTIER, Miss see Johnstone,
Mrs. John
PODELL, Rick (b 1946) American
actor TW/28-29
PODGLAZE, Roderick (d 1884)
showman EA/85*
PODMORE, Frederick Vere see
Vere, Fred R.
PODMORE, William (b 1888) Eng-
lish actor TW/11
POE, Aileen (d 1973 [79]) actress
TW/30
POE, David (b 1773) actor SR
POE, Elizabeth Arnold (d 1811)
English actress CDP, WWA/H
POE, Gary (b 1947) American actor
TW/25, 27
POEL, William [Pole] (1852-1934)
English actor, producer COC,
DNB, ES, GRB/1-4, NTH, OC/
1-3, PDT, WWT/1-7, WWW/3
POGANY, Willy (d 1955 [72]) Hun-
garian designer BE*
POGGI, Antonio (1808-75) Italian
singer ES
POGODIN, Nikolai Fedorovich
(1900-62) Russian dramatist
COC, OC/1-3
POHLMAN, Max Edward (d 1971)
dramatist BP/56*
POINTER, Priscilla American ac-
tress TW/22-30
POINTER, Sidney (d 1955) actor,
singer BE*, WWT/14*
POITIER, Sidney (b 1924) Ameri-
can actor BE, CB, ES, WWT/
15-16
POKELEY, Richard (fl 1550) actor
DA
POL, Talitha (d 1971 [31]) per-
former BP/56*
POLACCO, Giorgi (1875-1960)
Italian conductor WWA/4
POLACEK, Louis Vask (1920-63)
American performer BE*, BP/
47*
POLAIRE, Mlle. [Emilie Zouzé]
(1879-1939) French actress
WWT/2-4
POLAK, Jeanie Gertrude (d 1888)
EA/89*
POLAK, John Michael (d 1887 [54])
EA/88*
POLAK, Marie (d 1966 [70]) per-

former BP/50*

POLAN, Barron (b 1914) American talent representative BE

POLAN, Lou (1904/05-76) Russian/American actor BE, TW/4, 11-13, 24, 29, WWT/15-16

POLANSKI, Eugen (d 1912 [62]) musician EA/13*

POLDEN, T. E. (d 1916) theatre chairman EA/17*

POLE (fl 1582) gatekeeper DA

POLE, William see Poel, William

POLERI, David Samuel (1927-67) American singer WWA/4

POLGAR, Alfred (d 1955 [81]) Austrian/American dramatist BP/39*

POLHILL, Cowley see Fiennes, Sydney

POLIAKOFF, David (b 1953) dramatist CD

POLIAKOFF, Nikolai [Coco the Clown] (d 1974 [78]) clown BP/59*

POLIAKOFF, Vera see Lindsay, Vera

POLIKOFF, Benet, Sr. (d 1970 [72]) lawyer BP/55*

POLINI, Emilie (d 1927) English actress GRB/1-2

POLINI, G[iovanni] M[aria] (d 1914 [63]) Italian manager GRB/1-3

POLINI, Marie (d 1960) English actress GRB/1-2, WWT/2-6

POLINI, Mary Ann (d 1886 [58]) EA/87*

POLITO, Philip (b 1944) American actor TW/25-28, 30

POLK, Joseph B. (d 1902 [61]) actor CDP

POLLACK, Lew (d 1946 [50]) American songwriter TW/2

POLLAND, Elizabeth (d 1975 [82]) acting teacher BP/60*

POLLARD, Daphne (b 1890) Australian actress WWT/4-9

POLLARD, Fred (b 1862) English actor GRB/1

POLLARD, Mrs. Fred see Clarke, Marion

POLLARD, Harry (d 1934 [55]) American director, actor BE*

POLLARD, Harry (d 1962 [72]) Australian performer BE*

POLLARD, John (d 1880) box

attendant EA/81*

POLLARD, John see Moreton, John Pollard

POLLARD, Michael J. (b 1939) actor BE

POLLARD, Percival (1869-1911/12) German/English dramatist, critic DAB, WWM

POLLARD, Thomas (fl first half of 17th cent) English actor DA, COC, OC/1-3

POLLER, Rosa Cash (b 1842) Hungarian singer HAS

POLLEY, Mr. minstrel CDP

POLLICK, Teno (b 1935) American actor TW/26-27

POLLINI, Bianca Charitas Bianchi (1858-1947) German singer ES

POLLINI, Hograth (d 1897 [57]) manager EA/98*

POLLITZER, Adolphe (d 1900 [68]) musician EA/01*

POLLOCK, Mrs. (d 1875 [73]) actress, manager EA/76*

POLLOCK, Allan (d 1942 [64]) English actor CB, WWM

POLLOCK, Anna (d 1946 [65]) American press representative, dramatist BE*, BP/30*

POLLOCK, Arthur (b 1886) American critic WWT/9-13

POLLOCK, Channing (1880-1946) American dramatist CB, DAB, GRB/2-4, HJD, MWD, NTH, SR, TW/3, WWA/2, WWM, WWS, WWT/1-9

POLLOCK, Mrs. Channing see Marble, Anna

POLLOCK, Elizabeth (1898-1970) English actress WWT/5-9

POLLOCK, Ellen (b 1903) German/English actress AAS, WWT/7-16

POLLOCK, Frank (b 1878) American singer WWM

POLLOCK, Gordon W. (d 1956 [28]) producer BE*

POLLOCK, Sir John (1878-1963) dramatist WWT/4-7

POLLOCK, Nancy R. [née Reiben] (b 1905/07) American actress BE, TW/12, 20, 24-26, WWT/15-16

POLLOCK, W. H. (d 1877) actor EA/78*

POLLOCK, William (1881-1944) English journalist WWT/5-8

POLO, Eddie (d 1961 [86]) actor,

acrobat BE*
POLONSKY, Joe (d 1974 [81])
publicist BP/59*
POLSON, Edith Mary [Mrs.
George P. Polson] (d 1892)
EA/93*
POLSON, Mrs. George P. see
Polson, Edith Mary
POLUSKI, Miss (d 1888) EA/89*
POLWORTH, Lewis actor CDP
POMERANZ, Joseph see Pom-
eroy, Jay
POMEROY, Jay [né Joseph Pom-
eranz] (1895-1955) Russian di-
rector WWT/10-11
POMEROY, Louise ["Elm Orton"]
(d 1893) actress, dramatist
CDP
PONAZECKI, Joe (b 1934) Amer-
ican actor TW/22-28, 30
PONCHARD, Mme. (d 1873 [81])
singer EA/74*
PONCIN, Marcel (d 1953) actor
BE*, WWT/14*
PONCIONE, John P., Jr. (d 1890
[57]) lawyer EA/92*
PONCIONE, Mrs. John Paul see
Poncione, Sophia
PONCIONE, Sophia [Mrs. John
Paul Poncione] (d 1898 [89])
actress EA/99*
POND, Anson Phelps (1856-1920)
American dramatist WWA/4
POND, Charles Glover (d 1880)
musician, composer EA/81*
POND, Christopher (d 1881 [54])
EA/82*
POND, Helen (b 1924) American
designer WWT/16
POND, John (d 1975 [72]) designer
BP/60*
POND, Paul see Jones, Paul
PONGER, Fred (b 1922) American
actor TW/30
PONIATOWSKI, Prince (d 1873
[56]) composer EA/74*
PONISI, Elizabeth (1818-99) Eng-
lish actress CDP
PONISI, James (fl 1850) English
actor HAS
PONISI, Mrs. James (fl 1848-69)
English actress HAS
PONS, Helene (b 1898) Russian
costume designer BE, ES
PONS, Lily (1904-76) French
singer CB, ES
PONSELLE, Rosa (b 1897) Amer-
ican singer ES

PONSFORD, Phyllis see Cecil,
Phyllis
PONSONBY, Eustace (d 1924) com-
poser, actor BE*, WWT/14*
PONTE, Lorenzo da see Da
Ponte, Lorenzo
PONTERIO, Robin (b 1957) Ameri-
can actor TW/24
PONTOPPIDAN, Clara (d 1975
[80s]) performer BP/59*
POOL, F. C. (d 1944 [69]) business
manager BE*, WWT/14*
POOLE, Mr. (fl 1851) actor HAS
POOLE, Mrs. (d 1883) EA/85*
POOLE, Miss (fl 1839) English ac-
tress HAS
POOLE, Annie [Mrs. Russell Crau-
furd] (d 1895) actress, singer
EA/96*
POOLE, Charles (b 1815) English
actor, manager HAS
POOLE, Charles (d 1877 [54]) EA/
78*
POOLE, C. W. (d 1918 [60]) EA/
19*
POOLE, Elizabeth (1820-1906) ac-
tress, singer CDP
POOLE, Ellen [Mrs. J. J. Poole]
(d 1895 [49]) proprietor EA/96*
POOLE, Ernest (1880-1950) Amer-
ican dramatist WWA/2, WWM
POOLE, Flora (d 1896) music-hall
performer EA/97*
POOLE, Frederick (d 1907) pro-
prietor EA/08*
POOLE, George (d 1898 [25])
myriorama manager EA/99*
POOLE, George Walter (d 1878)
panorama proprietor EA/79*
POOLE, Mrs. Harry (d 1893 [38])
EA/94*
POOLE, Harry Herbert (d 1905
[26]) EA/06*
POOLE, J. J. (d 1882) proprietor
EA/83*
POOLE, Mrs. J. J. see Poole,
Ellen
POOLE, John (1786?/92-1872)
English dramatist CDP, DNB,
EA/69, HP
POOLE, John (d 1889 [71]) EA/90*
POOLE, John Peter (d 1899 [64])
actor EA/00*
POOLE, Joseph (d 1906 [59]) my-
riorama proprietor? EA/07*
POOLE, Joseph J. (d 1895) EA/97*
POOLE, Maria see Dickons,
Maria

POOLE, Matilda (d 1899 [75])
EA/01*
POOLE, Miss M. E. see
Cramer, Mrs. H.
POOLE, Richard Edward (d 1901
[48]) minstrel? EA/02*
POOLE, Roy (b 1924) American
actor TW/14, 19, 21, 25-27
POOLE, Sidney G. E. (d 1905
[28]) EA/06*
POOLE, Sivori (d 1896) EA/97*
POOLE, Tilly see Warde, Mrs.
G. F.
POOLE, Vivien (d 1897 [14])
EA/98*
POOLEY, Olaf English actor,
director WWT/12-15
POORTEN-SCHWARTZ, Joost
Marius Willem van der see
Maartens, Maarten
POPE, Alexander (1688-1744)
English dramatist CDP, CP/
3, HP
POPE, Alexander (1763-1835)
Irish actor, dramatist BS,
CDP, CP/3, DNB, ES, GT,
TD/1-2
POPE, Mrs. Alexander, I [née
Young] (1740-97) English ac-
tress CDP, DNB, ES, GT,
TD/2
POPE, Mrs. Alexander, II see
Campion, Maria Ann
POPE, Charles R. (1829/32-99)
German/American actor,
manager CDP, HAS, SR
POPE, Mrs. Charles R. see
Cunningham, Virginia
POPE, Coleman (d 1868) actor
HAS
POPE, Mrs. Coleman (b 1809)
English actress HAS
POPE, Curtis L. (b 1919) Amer-
ican educator BE
POPE, Elizabeth see Pope,
Mrs. Alexander, I
POPE, Jane (1742-1818) English
actress, dramatist CDP,
COC, CP/3, DNB, ES, GT,
OC/1-3, TD/1-2
POPE, Johanna [Mrs. William
Coleman Pope] (1809-80) ac-
tress CDP
POPE, John (d 1874 [64]) actor
EA/75*
POPE, Dr. Joseph (d 1885 [49])
surgeon EA/86*
POPE, Maria Ann see Campion,

Maria Ann
POPE, Muriel Indian/English ac-
tress WWT/4-7
POPE, Peggy (b 1929) American
actress TW/13, 23-24, 26-28
POPE, Robert (b 1911) American
actor, singer TW/2
POPE, Susan (b 1797) English ac-
tress CDP, OX
POPE, Thomas (d 1604) English
actor DA, COC, GT, OC/1-3
POPE, T. Michael (d 1930 [55])
critic, journalist BE*, WWT/
14*
POPE, William Coleman (d 1868)
actor BE*, WWT/14*
POPE, Mrs. William Coleman see
Pope, Johanna
POPOV, Alexei Dmitrevich (1892-
1961) Russian producer OC/3
POPOV, Oleg (b 1930) Russian
clown CB
POPPER, Hermine I. (d 1968 [53])
editor BP/53*
POPPLE, William (1701-64) English
dramatist CP/1-3, DNB, GT
POPPLEWELL, Jack (b 1911) Eng-
lish dramatist WWT/13-16
PORDAGE, Samuel [P. , S.] (1633-
91?) English dramatist CP/1-3,
DNB
POREL, Paul (d 1917 [73]) manager
WWT/14*
PORRET, Robert (fl 1788) dramatist
CP/3
PORSON, Richard (1759-1808) Eng-
lish translator CP/3
PORT, George (d 1887) musician
EA/88*
PORTAL, Abraham (fl 1758-96)
boxkeeper, dramatist CP/1-3,
DNB, GT
PORTANS, Miss see Shaw, Mrs.
Alfred
PORTEOUS, Gilbert (1868-1928)
English actor GRB/4, WWT/1-5
PORTEOUS, Mrs. Gilbert see
Irving, Ethel
PORTER, Mr. ["Kentucky Giant"]
(fl 1838) actor HAS
PORTER, Mrs. (fl first half of 18th
cent) actress TD/1-2
PORTER, Miss see Baker, Mrs.
J. S.
PORTER, Alexander W. (d 1975
[94]) performer BP/59*
PORTER, Anna Maria (fl 1803)
dramatist CP/3

PORTER, Benjamin C. (1839-79)
actor, stage manager CDP

PORTER, Caleb (1867-1940) English actor WWT/5-9

PORTER, Charles S. (1797-1867) American actor HAS

PORTER, Cole (1892-1964) American composer AAS, BE, CB, ES, MH, NTH, PDT, TW/21, WWA/4, WWT/6-13, WWW/6

PORTER, Don (b 1912) American actor TW/21, 25-26, WWT/15-16

PORTER, Elise see Bartlett, Elise

PORTER, Eric (b 1928) English actor AAS, COC, WWT/13-16

PORTER, Hal (b 1911) Australian dramatist CD

PORTER, Harry A. (d 1920 [52]) actor BE*, BP/5*

PORTER, Henry (fl 1596-99) English dramatist CP/1-3, DNB, FGF, OC/1-3, RE

PORTER, Henry (d 1876 [40]) agent EA/77*

PORTER, James S. (d 1863) actor HAS

PORTER, Jane (1776-1850) dramatist HP

PORTER, J. G. (fl 1834) actor HAS

PORTER, Mrs. J. G. see Duff, Mary

PORTER, Joshua (fl 1837) American actor HAS

PORTER, Mabel Butterworth (d 1970 [85]) performer BP/55*

PORTER, Mary Ann (d 1765) English actress DNB, GT, OC/1-3

PORTER, Neil (1895-1944) English actor, producer WWT/7-9

PORTER, Stan (b 1928) American actor TW/25-28, 30

PORTER, Stephen (fl 1798) translator CP/3

PORTER, Stephen (b 1925) American director, producer WWT/15-16

PORTER, Thomas (1636-80) dramatist CP/1-3, DNB

PORTER, Walsh (d 1809) dramatist CP/3

PORTERFIELD, Robert (1905-71) American actor, director, manager BE, TW/28, WWA/5,

WWT/13-15

PORTIS, Diana see Dane, Clemence

PORTMAN, Eric (1903-69) English actor AAS, BE, CB, COC, ES, TW/15-16, 26, WWA/5, WWT/7-14, WWW/6

POSER, Linda American actress TW/30

POSFORD, George (b 1906) English composer WWT/9-14

POSSART, Ernst Ritter von see Von Possart, Ernest Ritter

POST, Guy Bates (1875-1968) American actor GRB/3-4, NTH, TW/24, WWS, WWT/1-11

POST, Lily (d 1890) actress, singer WWT/14*

POST, Lu Ann (b 1947) American actress TW/29

POST, William, Jr. actor TW/1, 3, 10-11

POST, Wilmarth H. (1867-1930) American dramatist SR

POSTLETHWAITE, Frank (d 1910 [37]) variety agent EA/11*

POSTON, Richard (b 1922) American actor TW/8

POSTON, Tom (b 1921/27) American actor BE, CB, TW/11-12, 25-26, 29, WWT/15-16

POTEL, Victor (d 1947 [57]) comedian TW/3

POTIER, Elizabeth Harriman see Moreton, Lydia

POTT, Joseph Holden (fl 1782) dramatist CP/3

POTTER, Andrew (b 1944) American actor TW/28

POTTER, Mrs. Brown see Potter, Cora Urquhart

POTTER, Cora Urquhart [Mrs. Brown Potter] (1859-1936) American actress CDP, DP, GRB/1-4, NTH, OC/1-3, SR, WWA/1, WWS, WWT/1-8, WWW/3

POTTER, Dennis (b 1935) English dramatist CD, WWT/16

POTTER, Don (b 1932) American actor TW/26-27

POTTER, Elizabeth (d 1887) EA/88*

POTTER, Estelle see McDonald, Estelle

POTTER, Gillie (d 1975 [87]) performer BP/59*

POTTER, H. C. (1904-77) American director, producer BE,

TW/5-8, WWT/11-13
POTTER, Helen impersonator,
reader CDP
POTTER, Henry (fl 1733) drama-
tist CP/2-3, GT
POTTER, John (b 1734) English
composer, critic, dramatist
CP/2-3, DNB, GT
POTTER, John H. (d 1966 [78])
talent manager BP/51*
POTTER, John Hindley (d 1892
[53]) EA/93*
POTTER, John S. (1809-69)
American actor, manager
HAS
POTTER, Joseph (d 1908 [64])
proprietor EA/09*
POTTER, Paul American actor
TW/1
POTTER, Paul Meredith (1853-
1921) English/American drama-
tist DAB, GRB/2-4, HJD,
SR, WWA/1, WWM, WWS,
WWT/1-3
POTTER, Philip Cipriani (d
1871 [78]) principal of the
Royal Academy of Music EA/
72*
POTTER, Reuben (fl 1825?)
dramatist EAP, RJ
POTTER, Robert (1721-1804)
English translator CP/2-3,
DNB
POTTER, Stanley [Elijah Pinkes]
(d 1894 [75]) singer? EA/96*
POTTER, T. H. (d 1887) stage
manager EA/88*
POTTINGER, Israel (fl 1759-61)
dramatist CP/2-3, DNB, GT
POTTLE, Gilbert Emery Bensley
see Emery, Gilbert
POTTS, Harry see Fragson,
Harry
POTTS, Nancy costume designer
WWT/16
POTTS, Sidney (d 1968 [62])
producer/director/choreographer
BP/52*
POTTS, William J. (d 1888
[36]) American manager EA/
89*
POUGARD, Leontine (fl 1852)
French dancer CDP, HAS
POUGIN, Arthur (d 1921 [78])
historian, critic BE*, WWT/
14*
POULAIN, Bernard (b 1934)
French actor TW/24-25

POULTNEY, George (d 1972) union
representative BP/57*
POULTON, A. G. [Arthur Gordon
Lane Plews] (b 1867) English
actor WWT/2-8
POUNDS, Courtice (1862-1927)
English actor, singer CDP, DP,
GRB/1-4, WWT/2-5, WWW/2
POUNDS, Louie English actress
GRB/1-4, WWT/1-8
POVAH, Phyllis American actress
BE, TW/1, 3, 5, 10-12, WWT/
6-13
POVEY, Miss see Povey, Mary
Ann
POVEY, Eliza see Knight, Mrs.
E.
POVEY, John (d 1867 [68]) actor,
agent CDP
POVEY, Mary Ann (1804-61) Eng-
lish singer, actress BS, CDP,
OX
POWEL, Eldred (d 1903) music-hall
comedian EA/04*
POWELL, Mr. (b c. 1768?) actor
BS
POWELL, Mr. (fl 1788-1800) actor
GT, TD/1-2
POWELL, Mr. (fl 1798-1804) actor
TD/1-2
POWELL, Mrs. (fl 1787-94) ac-
tress GT, TD/1-2
POWELL, Alfred Henry (d 1882
[26]) scene artist EA/83*
POWELL, Alfred Thomas (d 1902
[61]) circus manager EA/03*
POWELL, Alma Webster (1874-
1930) American singer DAB
POWELL, Anthony James (d 1882
[52]) circus proprietor EA/83*
POWELL, Arthur W. (d 1885 [63])
prompter EA/86*
POWELL, Bertha T. (b 1895)
American actress TW/3
POWELL, Mrs. B. H. (d 1894)
EA/95*
POWELL, Mrs. Bill see Murphy,
Eliza
POWELL, Charles Anthony (d 1887
[17]) EA/88*
POWELL, Charles Stuart (d 1811
[62]) English actor, manager
HAS, WWA/H
POWELL, Mrs. Charles Stuart (fl
1794) actress HAS
POWELL, Clara (d 1897) actress
EA/98*
POWELL, Mrs. Edward (d 1891)

EA/92*

POWELL, Edward Soldene (b 1865) English actor, stage manager WWS

POWELL, Eleanor (b 1912) American actress, dancer BE, ES, WWT/9-11

POWELL, Eliza Ann [Mrs. William Powell] (d 1885 [70]) EA/87*

POWELL, Elizabeth Jane [Mrs. T. Morton Powell] (d 1891 [24]) EA/92*

POWELL, Ellis (d 1963 [57]) actress BE*

POWELL, Fanny (d 1877) seriocomic, singer EA/79*

POWELL, George (1668-1714) English actor, dramatist CP/1-3, DNB, GT, OC/1-3

POWELL, George Frederick (d 1887 [75]) EA/88*

POWELL, Henry (d 1878) equestrian actor EA/79*

POWELL, J. (d 1836 [82]) actor EA/72*, WWT/14*

POWELL, Jack (d 1976 [75]) performer BP/60*

POWELL, James (fl 1787?) dramatist CP/3

POWELL, James (fl 1805) dramatist CP/3

POWELL, James, Sr. (d 1894 [63]) EA/95*

POWELL, Jane (b 1929) American actress, singer CB

POWELL, John (fl 1798) actor CDP

POWELL, John (d 1873 [22]) EA/74*

POWELL, John (d 1893 [67]) circus performer EA/94*

POWELL, Johnny (d 1897) music-hall performer EA/98*

POWELL, Ken (d 1976 [61]) performer BP/60*

POWELL, Martin (fl 1709-29) English puppeteer, dramatist CP/2-3, DNB, OC/2-3

POWELL, Mary Ann (1761-1831) actress CDP, DNB

POWELL, Maude (d 1920 [51]) musician BE*, BP/4*

POWELL, Maud Morton (d 1969) performer BP/53*

POWELL, Peggy (d 1970 [56]) performer BP/55*

POWELL, Peter (b 1908) English

producer, director WWT/11-14

POWELL, Rebecca (d 1870) EA/71*

POWELL, Robert (fl 18th cent) fire-eater CDP

POWELL, Robert (fl 1710-15) English puppeteer OC/2

POWELL, Robert (b 1944) English actor WWT/16

POWELL, S. Morgan (d 1962 [95]) critic BP/47*

POWELL, Snelling (1758-1821) Welsh actor DAB, HAS, WWA/H

POWELL, Mrs. Snelling [née Harrison] (1774-1843) English actress HAS

POWELL, Thomas (1809-87) English dramatist DAB, WWA/H

POWELL, Mrs. T. Morton see Powell, Elizabeth Jane

POWELL, Tom (d 1961 [79]) minstrel BE*

POWELL, Walter Templer (d 1949) actor, producer, manager BE*, WWT/14*

POWELL, William (1735-69) English actor, manager CDP, DNB, ES, GT, OC/1-3, TD/1-2

POWELL, William (b 1892) American actor CB, ES, WWT/9-10

POWELL, Mrs. William, Sr. see Powell, Eliza Ann

POWELL, William H. (d 1888 [47]) circus manager EA/89*

POWER, Agnes (d 1894) EA/95*

POWER, Alexander (d 1901 [54]) minstrel manager EA/02*

POWER, Caroline Amelia [Mrs. Clavering Power] (d 1911 [71]) EA/12*

POWER, Clavering (1842-1931) English actor OAA/1-2

POWER, Mrs. Clavering see Power, Caroline Amelia

POWER, Mrs. Fred [Maggie Smith] (d 1878 [31]) EA/79*

POWER, Sir George (1848-1928) Irish actor OAA/2

POWER, Harry (d 1898) comedian EA/99*

POWER, Hartley (1894-1966) American actor BE, WWT/6-13

POWER, Henrietta Maria (d 1895 [66]) EA/96*

POWER, James (d 1890 [64]) singer, songcomposer CDP

POWER, John (fl 1846) singer CDP

POWER, Maurice (d 1849) Irish
actor COC, HAS
POWER, Nelly (d 1887 [32])
English music-hall singer
CDP
POWER, R. J. (d 1884) box office
keeper EA/85*
POWER, Robert (d 1875 [36])
pantomimist EA/76*
POWER, Rosine (1840-1932)
English singer, actress BE*,
WWT/14*
POWER, Mrs. S. (d 1909) EA/
10*
POWER, Tyrone (1795-1841) Irish
actor BS, CDP, COC, DNB,
ES, HAS, NTH, OC/1-3, OX,
SR
POWER, Tyrone (1869-1931) Eng-
lish actor COC, DAB, ES,
GRB/3-4, NTH, OC/1-3,
WWM, WWS, WWT/1-6
POWER, Tyrone (1914-58) Amer-
ican actor CB, COC, ES,
NTH, OC/1-3, TW/9-15,
WWA/3, WWT/9-12
POWER, Mrs. Tyrone (d 1876
[81]) EA/77*
POWER, Mrs. Tyrone see
Crane, Edith
POWERS, Arba Eugene (d 1935
[62]) American actor BE*,
BP/19*
POWERS, Chris L. (d 1972 [82])
performer BP/57*
POWERS, Ed (b 1938) American
actor TW/24
POWERS, Eugene (1872-1935)
American actor WWT/7
POWERS, Harry Joseph (1859-
1941) Irish manager WWA/
1-2
POWERS, James T. (1862-1943)
American actor, singer GRB/
2-4, SR, WWA/4, WWS,
WWT/1-9
POWERS, John (b 1935) Aus-
tralian dramatist WWT/16
POWERS, Leona (1896/1900-
1967) American actress BE,
TW/26, WWT/9-11
POWERS, Marie (1913?-73) Amer-
ican actress, singer BE, CB,
TW/30
POWERS, Tom (1890-1955) Amer-
ican actor TW/2-4, 12, WWA/
3, WWT/6-11
POWIER, Robert John (d 1884

[57]) EA/85*
POWLES, William Henry see
Ball, Harry
POWLEY, Bryan (d 1962 [91]) actor
WWT/14*
POWLTON, Thomas (fl 1584) actor
DA
POWNALL, Mrs. (d 1796) English
singer, actress HAS, WWA/H
POWNALL, Miss see La Folle,
Mrs.
POWNALL, John (d 1910) singer
EA/11*
POWRIE, Thomas (d 1868 [44])
actor EA/69*
POWYS, Stephen [Virginia de Lanty]
(b 1907) American dramatist
BE, WWT/9-15
POYNTER, Mrs. (d 1898 [81]) ac-
tress EA/99*, WWT/14*
POYNTER, Beulah (b 1886) Ameri-
can actress WWM
POYNTER, Richard (d 1882 [72])
actor EA/83*
POYNTON, Frank (d 1895) comic
singer EA/96*
POZZOLINI, Gasparo (fl 1853)
singer CDP
PRAEGER, Ferdinand (d 1891 [76])
musician EA/92*
PRAGER, Bernard (d 1969 [71])
executive BP/54*
PRAGER, Gerhard (d 1975 [55])
producer/director/choreographer
BP/60*
PRAGER, Stanley (1917-72) Amer-
ican actor, director, producer
BE, TW/28
PRATESI, Signorina (fl 1860)
dancer HAS
PRATESI SISTERS (fl 1857) dancers
CDP
PRATT, Mrs. (fl 1848) actress
HAS
PRATT, Charles Edward James
Blyth manager GRB/2-4
PRATT, G. (d 1881 [56]) EA/82*
PRATT, G. H. ["Yankee" Pratt]
(d 1867) comedian HAS
PRATT, Judson (b 1916) American
actor TW/11-12
PRATT, Mike (d 1976 [45]) actor
WWT/16*
PRATT, Muriel (d 1945 [54]) Eng-
lish actress WWT/4-7
PRATT, Robert (fl 1774-90) actor,
dramatist TD/1-2
PRATT, Silas Gamaliel (1846-1916)

American composer DAB,
WWA/1, WWM
PRATT, S. J. [Courtney Melmoth]
(1749-1814) English actor,
dramatist CP/2-3, DNB, GT
PRATT, William Henry see
Karloff, Boris
PRATT, W. W. (fl 1821-64)
actor, dramatist, musician,
manager, lecturer, preacher
HAS
PRATTEN, R. Sidney (d 1868)
musician EA/69*
PRATTEN, Mme. Sidney [Cath-
erina Josepha Pelzer] (d 1895)
musician EA/96*
PRAXY, Raoul (d 1967 [75])
dramatist BP/52*
PRAY, Anna (d 1878) EA/79*
PRAY, Anna M. (d 1971 [80])
performer BP/56*
PRAY, Isaac Clark (1813-69)
American producer, drama-
tist, critic, actor, manager
DAB, HAS, WWA/H
PRAY, Louisa (fl 1849) dancer
HAS
PRAY, Malvina see Florence,
Mrs. William Jermyn
PRAY, Maria see Williams,
Mrs. Barney
PREBLE, Ed (b 1919) American
actor TW/26
PREDOVIC, Dennis (b 1950)
American actor TW/30
PREECE, Josephine (d 1909)
actress EA/10*
PREECE, Richard (d 1918 [85])
EA/19*
PREECE, Tim (b 1938) English
actor TW/23, WWT/15-16
PREEDY, George R. [Gabrielle
Margaret Vere Campbell]
(1888-1952) English dramatist
WWT/8-11
PREISCH, J. Allen singer CDP
PREISSER, Cherry (d 1964
[46]) acrobatic dancer TW/21
PREMICE, Josephine (b 1926)
American actress, dancer,
singer BE, TW/12, 14-15,
23-24, 29-30
PREMINGER, Marion (d 1972 [58])
performer BP/56*
PREMINGER, Otto (b 1906) Aus-
trian producer, director BE,
CB, ES
PRENDERGAST, John (d 1869)

comedian HAS
PRENDERGAST, Thomas B. (d
1869) minstrel CDP, HAS
PRENSKY, Lester American lawyer
BE
PRENTICE, Aleck see Prentice,
John
PRENTICE, Charles W. ["Jock"]
(b 1898) Scottish musical di-
rector, composer WWT/9-14
PRENTICE, Herbert M. (b 1890)
English producer, designer
WWT/8-13
PRENTICE, John (1829-67) actor
HAS
PRENTICE, Lena (fl 1866-68) ac-
tress HAS
PRENTISS, Alvin Stewart (1826-65)
American agent HAS
PRENTISS, Lewis (d 1967 [62])
performer BP/52*
PRESANO, Rita (d 1935 [70]) ac-
tress BE*, WWT/14*
PRESBREY, Eugene Wyley (1853-
1931) American dramatist DAB,
GRB/2-4, WWA/1, WWM,
WWT/3-6
PRESCOTT, Marie Victor [Mrs.
Robert D. McLean] (1853-93)
actress CDP
PRESCOTT, Norman (d 1973 [81])
performer BP/58*
PRESCOTT, Norman see Pres-
cott-Davies, N.
PRESCOTT, Walter [Ernest Charles
Coverdale] (d 1903 [50]) actor
EA/05*
PRESCOTT-DAVIES, N. [Norman
Prescott] (1862-1915) English
dramatist WWW/1
PRESLEY-EMERY, Mary Jane (d
1905) EA/06*
PRESNELL, Harve (b 1933) Amer-
ican actor TW/17, 22
PRESSMAN, David (b 1913) Rus-
sian/American director, educa-
tor, actor BE
PRESSMAN, Lawrence (b 1939)
American actor TW/20, 25
PRESTBURY, Sarah see Roberts,
Sarah
PRESTIGE, Fanny (b 1846) English
actress CDP, HAS
PRESTON, Mr. (fl 1750) actor,
dramatist CP/3
PRESTON, Mrs. see Nichols,
Mrs. Horace F.
PRESTON, Amy see Sheridan,

Amy
PRESTON, Barry (b 1945) American actor TW/23
PRESTON, Christopher (d 1902) EA/03*
PRESTON, Edna (b 1892) American actress TW/8-15
PRESTON, Ellen Washington see Grey, Marie de
PRESTON, Georgina actress, dancer, singer CDP
PRESTON, Henry W. (d 1859) actor, manager HAS
PRESTON, Isabella (fl 1845) actress HAS
PRESTON, J. B. (d 1886 [50]) actor EA/87*
PRESTON, Jessie (d 1928 [51]) actress, dancer, singer CDP
PRESTON, Robert [né Meservey] (b 1913/18) American actor BE, CB, TW/8-24, WWT/13-16
PRESTON, Thomas (1537-98) English dramatist COC, CP/1-3, FGF, HP, MH, OC/1-3
PRESTON, Tom (d 1899 [26]) comedian EA/00*
PRESTON, William (1753-1807) Irish dramatist CP/3, DNB
PRESTON, William (fl 1794?) American? dramatist EAP, RJ
PRESTON, William (b 1921) American actor TW/30
PRESTON, William C. (d 1963) HAS
PRESTWICH, Edmund (fl 1650-51) dramatist CP/1-3
PREVIN, André (b 1929) German/American composer, conductor CB, ES
PREVIN, Charles (d 1973 [86]) producer/director/choreographer BP/58*
PREVOST, Eugene-Prosper (1809-72) French conductor WWA/H
PREWETT, Eda Valerga (d 1964 [81]) singer, dancer BE*
PREY, Hermann (b 1929) German singer CB, ES
PRICE, Mr. equestrian CDP
PRICE, Mr. (d 1842) HAS
PRICE, Mrs. [née Warren; Mrs. Clifford] actress HAS
PRICE, Albert Guy (b 1885) Canadian editor WWM

PRICE, Annie (d 1889 [47]) fat woman EA/90*
PRICE, Dennis (1915-73) English actor BE, WWT/10-15
PRICE, E. D. (1849-1935) American manager, dramatist GRB/3, WWM
PRICE, Edward (b 1847) Canadian actor HAS
PRICE, Edward (d 1895 [55]) actor EA/96*
PRICE, Mrs. Edward see Ryder, Emma
PRICE, Edwin H. (d 1907) American manager GRB/3
PRICE, Eleazer D. (d 1935 [86]) American manager, press agent BP/19*
PRICE, Evadne [Helen Zenna Smith] (b 1896) actress WWT/9-11
PRICE, Fanny Bayard (b 1847) American actress HAS
PRICE, Frank (d 1885) scene artist EA/86*
PRICE, George (1900-64) American vaudevillian, actor TW/20
PRICE, George N. (d 1962 [86]) performer BE*
PRICE, Georgie see Price, George
PRICE, Gerald (b 1921) American actor TW/10-15
PRICE, Gilbert (b 1942) American actor TW/20-22, 26-28
PRICE, Graham (d 1916) English actor GRB/1-2
PRICE, H. E. (d 1892) American actor EA/93*
PRICE, Mrs. Henry Ernest see Price, Mary Ann
PRICE, Henry P. (d 1908) EA/09*
PRICE, James (1761-1805) English dancer ES
PRICE, James (1801-65) English dancer ES
PRICE, Mrs. James see Price, Jane
PRICE, Jane [Mrs. James Price] (d 1881 [66]) EA/82*
PRICE, J. B. (fl 1842) actor HAS
PRICE, Jesse (d 1974 [64]) performer BP/58*
PRICE, John (fl 1609-29) musician DA
PRICE, John (fl 1795) dramatist CP/3
PRICE, John Adolph (1805-90) dancer ES

PRICE, John Edward (d 1863
[45]) manager EA/72*
PRICE, John L. , Jr. (b 1920)
American producer, actor,
director BE
PRICE, Joseph Percy (b 1822)
Irish actor HAS
PRICE, Kate (1873-1943) Irish
actress BE*
PRICE, Leontyne (b 1927) Amer-
ican singer, actress BE,
CB, ES
PRICE, Lillah [Mrs. Parke Hunter]
(d 1910) performer? EA/11*
PRICE, Lizzie (b 1842) American
actress CDP, HAS
PRICE, Lorain M. (d 1963 [53])
performer BE*
PRICE, Maire (d 1958) Irish ac-
tress COC, OC/3
PRICE, Mary Ann [Mrs. Henry
Ernest Price] (d 1887) EA/88*
PRICE, Morton [Horton Rhys] (d
1876 [52]) actor, lessee CDP,
HAS
PRICE, Nancy [Mrs. Charles
Maude] (1880-1970) English
actress, manager COC, GRB/
2-4, OC/1-3, WWT/1-14,
WWW/6
PRICE, Paul B. (b 1933) Ameri-
can actor TW/26-27, 29
PRICE, Richard (fl 1600) actor
DA
PRICE, Richard (fl 1612-27)
actor DA
PRICE, Richard see Mora
PRICE, Roger (b 1920) American
actor TW/6-7
PRICE, Cpt. Spencer Cosby (d
1892 [72]) EA/93*
PRICE, Stanley (d 1955 [55]) ac-
tor TW/12
PRICE, Stephen (1782/83-1840)
American manager CDP,
COC, DAB, OC/1-3, WWA/H
PRICE, Stuart Banner (d 1917
[39]) EA/18*
PRICE, Thomas (d 1863 [52])
actor, prompter HAS
PRICE, Tom (d 1901) actor?
EA/02*
PRICE, Vincent (b 1911) Ameri-
can actor BE, CB, TW/10-
15, 24, WWT/8-16
PRICE, Will (d 1962 [49]) director
BE*
PRICE, William (d 1873) actor

EA/75*
PRICE, William Thompson (1846-
1920) American dramatist DAB
PRICE-DRURY, Lt. -Col. W. (d
1949 [87]) dramatist BE*,
WWT/14*
PRICKETT, Oliver B. (b 1905)
American manager, producer,
actor BE
PRIDE, Malcolm (b 1930) English
designer AAS, ES, WWT/14-16
PRIDE, Sam (d 1871) musician
EA/72*
PRIDE, Ted (d 1963) performer
BE*
PRIDEAUX, Miss (fl 1789) actress
TD/1-2
PRIDEAUX, James (d 1887 [44])
musician EA/89*
PRIDEAUX, Tom editor BE
PRIEST, Dan (b 1924) American
actor TW/23-26
PRIEST, Janet (b 1881) American
actress WWM, WWS
PRIEST, Josias (d 1734) dancer,
choreographer ES
PRIEST, Sophia (d 1874 [32]) EA/
75*
PRIESTLEY, J[ohn] B[oynton] (b
1894) English dramatist, director
AAS, BE, CB, CD, CH, COC,
ES, HP, MD, MH, MWD, NTH,
OC/1-3, PDT, WWT/8-16
PRIESTLEY, Kate [Mrs. John Lis-
bourne] (d 1891) EA/92*
PRIEUR, Don (b 1942) American
actor TW/26
PRIGMORE, Mrs. (fl 1793) English
actress HAS
PRIMAVESI, Herbert (d 1917) EA/
18*
PRIMROSE, "The Spotted Indian"
(fl 1789) CDP
PRIMROSE, Alek (b 1934) American
actor TW/25-26, 28-29
PRIMROSE, Dorothy (b 1916) Scot-
tish actress WWT/11-16
PRIMROSE, George H. (1852-1919)
Canadian minstrel CDP, WWM
PRIMROSE, Jenny [Mrs. J. E.
Marshall] (d 1910) actress EA/
12*
PRIMUS, Barry (b 1938) American
actor TW/21, 25-26, 29-30
PRIMUS, Pearl (b 1919) West In-
dian dancer CB, ES
PRINCE, Adelaide [Mrs. Creston
Clarke] (1866-1941) English

actress, dramatist CDP,
GRB/3-4, WWM, WWS, WWT/
1-7
PRINCE, Arthur (d 1948 [66])
ventriloquist BE*, WWT/14*
PRINCE, Mrs. Arthur (d 1904)
EA/06*
PRINCE, Elsie (b 1902) English
actress, singer WWT/6-9
PRINCE, Harold S. (b 1928)
American producer, director
AAS, BE, CB, WWT/14-16
PRINCE, Jessie (d 1903 [36])
serio-comic EA/04*
PRINCE, Lillian (d 1962 [68])
actress BE*
PRINCE, Rebecca (d 1886) EA/
87*
PRINCE, William (b 1913) Amer-
ican actor BE, TW/3-16,
18-19, 24, 26, 30, WWT/11-16
PRINCEP, Valentine Cameron
(d 1904) dramatist EA/05*
PRINDLE, Johnnie (fl 1880?)
comedian CDP
PRINE, Andrew American actor
BE
PRINELLA, Joe (d 1909 [31])
acrobat EA/10*
PRING, Edward H. (d 1887) Eng-
lish agent NYM
PRINGLE, Lemprière (d 1914)
actor, singer WWT/14*
PRINGLE, Thomas (d 1869 [28])
actor? EA/70*
PRINSEP, Anthony Leyland (1888-
1942) English manager WWT/
5-9, WWW/4
PRINSEP, Val (d 1904 [66])
dramatist WWT/14*
PRINTEMPS, Yvonne (1894/95-
1977) French actress, singer
BE, COC, ES, OC/3, WWT/
4, 8-14
PRIOLO, Susan (b 1957) American
actress TW/22
PRIOR, Allan actor, singer WWT/
6-9
PRIOR, Anna Louise (b 1854)
American actress HAS
PRIOR, George Bertram (d
1897 [39]) comedian EA/98*
PRIOR, James J. (1823-75)
English actor CDP, HAS
PRIOR, Mrs. James J. [Louisa
Young] (1830-83) American
actress CDP, HAS
PRIOR, Louisa see Prior, Mrs.

James J.
PRIOR, Lulu (b 1854) actress CDP
PRITCHARD, Mr. (fl 1736) drama-
tist CP/2-3
PRITCHARD, Mrs. (fl 1832-36)
English actress HAS
PRITCHARD, Miss (d 1781) actress
CDP
PRITCHARD, David actor TD/2
PRITCHARD, Dick (d 1963 [58])
manager BE*
PRITCHARD, Hannah (1711-68)
English actress CDP, COC,
DNB, ES, GT, OC/1-3, TD/1-2
PRITCHARD, Irving J. (d 1975
[93]) photographer BP/59*
PRITCHARD, James (d 1823) Eng-
lish actor HAS
PRITCHARD, Johanna actress
CDP
PRITCHARD, John (d 1868 [38])
actor EA/69*, WWT/14*
PRITCHARD, John Langford (1799-
1850) actor CDP, DNB
PRITCHARD, Maria (fl 1863) ac-
tress HAS
PRITCHARD, Marie [Mrs. Fred-
erick Archer] (d 1910) actress
EA/11*
PRITCHARD, R. (d 1876 [39]) mu-
sician EA/77*
PRITCHARD, Richard Valentine (d
1973 [79]) performer BP/58*
PRITCHARD, Ted (b 1936) Ameri-
can actor TW/30
PRITCHARD, Val (d 1898) Negro
comedian EA/99*
PRITCHARD, William (d 1763)
treasurer COC
PRITCHARD, William (d 1892 [35])
EA/93*
PRITCHETT, Lizabeth (b 1920)
American actress TW/28-29
PRITECA, B. Marcus (d 1971 [81])
architect BP/56*
PRITT, Stephen (b 1873) English
manager, dramatist GRB/1
PROBY, David (d 1964) actor BE*
PROBY, John Joshua, Earl of
Carysfort (b 1751) dramatist
CP/3
PROCTER, Arthur Wyman (1889-
1961) American dramatist
WWA/4
PROCTER, Ivis Goulding (d 1973
[67]) performer BP/57*
PROCTER, Lionel Claude Race
see Dunrobin, L. Race

PROCTOR (fl c. 1599?) actor?
DA

PROCTOR, Bryan Walter [Barry Cornwall] (1787-1874) dramatist CDP

PROCTOR, Catherine (b 1879) Canadian actress TW/1, WWS

PROCTOR, Cecil Vernon (b 1878) English actor GRB/1

PROCTOR, Charles (b 1925) American actor TW/8-14

PROCTOR, David (b 1878) American? actor WWS

PROCTOR, Frederick Francis (1851/56-1929) American actor, manager COC, DAB, GRB/3-4, OC/1-3, SR, WWS

PROCTOR, Harry see Philp, Rowline

PROCTOR, James D. (b 1907) American press representative BE

PROCTOR, Jessie (d 1975 [102]) performer BP/60*

PROCTOR, Joseph (b c. 1798) actor, manager HAS, SR

PROCTOR, Joseph (1816-97) American actor, manager CDP, DAB, WWA/H

PROCTOR, Mrs. Joseph [Hester Warren; Mrs. Willis] (1810-41) American actress HAS

PROCTOR, Maria [Mrs. Robert Proctor] (d 1906 [69]) EA/07*

PROCTOR, Philip (b 1940) American actor TW/20, 22-23

PROCTOR, Robert (d 1888 [56]) circus proprietor EA/89*

PROCTOR, Mrs. Robert see Proctor, Maria

PROFANATO, Gene (b 1964) American actor TW/27

PROFEIT, Leopold (d 1917) actor EA/18*, WWT/14*

PROKOFIEV, Serge (1891-1953) Russian composer, conductor CB, ES

PROSER, Monte (d 1973 [69]) English producer BE

PROSPER, Eugénie (fl 1844?) singer CDP

PROTHERO, May [Mrs. H. Athol Forde] (d 1900) actress EA/97

PROUT, Dr. Ebenezer (d 1909 [74]) professor of music EA/11*

PROUTY, Charles (d 1974 [64]) scholar BP/58*

PROUTY, Jed (d 1956 [77]) American actor TW/12

PROVAN, Lizzie (d 1867) tight-rope performer EA/68*

PROVO, Frank (d 1975 [62]) dramatist BP/60*

PROVOL [Nathan Provolsky] (b 1882) American vaudevillian WWM

PROVOLSKY, Nathan see Provol

PROVOST, Mary [Mrs. J. P. Addams] (b 1835) American actress CDP, HAS

PRUD'HOMME, Cameron (1892-1967) American actor, director BE, TW/13-15, 24

PRUD'HOMME, George [George Pembroke] (d 1972 [71]) actor TW/29

PRUD'HOMME, June American actress TW/26

PRUDOM, Miss (fl 1781?) actress, singer CDP

PRUETTE, William American actor, singer WWS

PRUN, Peter de (fl 1594) actor DA

PRUNIERE, M. (d 1878) contortionist EA/79*

PRUSSING, Louise (b 1897) American actress WWT/6-11

PRYCE, Catharine Gompertz [Kitty Turner] (d 1889 [15]) actress EA/90*

PRYCE, Richard (d 1942 [79]) French/English dramatist WWT/1-9, WWW/4

PRYCE-JONES, Alan (b 1908) English critic, dramatist BE

PRYDE, Peggy (fl 1891?) actress, dancer, singer CDP

PRYNCE, Richard (fl 1554) actor DA

PRYNNE, William (1600-69) writer CDP

PRYOR, Ainslie (b 1921) American actor TW/10-13

PRYOR, Arthur W. (1870-1942) American composer DAB

PRYOR, C. E. (fl 1862) American actor HAS

PRYOR, Maureen (b 1924) Irish actress TW/24

PRYOR, Nicholas (b 1935) American actor BE, TW/14-15, 23, 26, 30

PRYOR, Roger (1901/03-74) American actor TW/3, 30, WWT/7-11

PRYORE, Rychard see Price, Richard

PRYSE, Hugh (1910-55) English actor WWT/11

PRYTHERCH, Harriet [Mme. Gerard Coventry] (d 1882 [33]) musician EA/83*

PSACHAROPOULOS, Nikos (b 1928) Greek educator, director BE

PUCCINI, Giacomo (1858-1924) Italian composer ES, GRB/1, WWM

PUCCIO, Mae Crane (d 1969 [44]) performer BP/53*

PUCK, Harry (d 1964 [71]) performer, songwriter BE*

PUDSEY, Edward (fl 1628-40) actor DA

PUENTE, Giuseppe del (1841-1900) Italian singer WWA/H

PUGH, Mrs. J. (d 1887 [41]) wardrobe mistress EA/88*

PUGH, John (d 1886 [34]) equestrian EA/87*

PUGH, Ted (b 1937) American actor TW/23-26, 29-30

PUGH, Winnifred (d 1881) EA/82*

PUGLIA, Frank (d 1975 [83]) actor BP/60*, WWT/16*

PUGLIESE, Rudolph E. (b 1918) American educator BE

PUGNANI, Gaetano (1728-98) composer, musician CDP

PUGNI, Sig. (d 1869) composer EA/70*

PULASKI, Jack (d 1948) American theatrical reporter, editor, critic BE*, BP/33*, WWT/14*

PULHAM, George (d c. 1612) sharer DA

PULITZER, Margaret Leech (d 1974 [80]) dramatist BP/58*

PULLAN, Henry (d 1903 [86]) proprietor EA/04*

PULLAN, James (d 1894 [45]) music-hall lessee EA/95*

PULLEN, Master actor CDP

PULLY, B. S. (1910-72) American actor TW/28, WWA/5

PULOS, Virginia (b 1947) American actress TW/29-30

PUMA, Marie American actress TW/26

PUMAREJO, Gaspar (d 1975 [61]) producer/director/choreographer BP/59*

PURCELL, Charles (1883-1962) American actor, singer TW/3-4, 18, WWT/7-11

PURCELL, Gertrude (d 1963 [67]) performer, dramatist BE*, BP/47*

PURCELL, Harold (b 1907) English dramatist, librettist, lyricist WWT/10-14

PURCELL, Henry (1658?-95) English composer CDP, DNB, ES, HP

PURCELL, Irene (1903-72) American actress TW/29, WWT/7-10

PURCELL, Tom (d 1892) mimic, entertainer EA/93*

PURCHASE, Andrew (d 1879 [78]) wax-work proprietor EA/81*

PURDELL, Reginald (1896-1953) English actor WWT/8-11

PURDOM, C. B. (1883-1965) English critic, general secretary of British actors' Equity BE, WWT/9-13, WWW/6

PURDOM, Edmund (b 1926) English actor ES

PURDY, Alexander H. (d 1862) manager, proprietor CDP, HAS

PURDY, Richard American actor TW/8-9

PURDY, Richard Augustus (1863-1925) American dramatist, lecturer WWA/1, WWWM

PURDY, S. S. (b 1836) American comedian HAS

PURKIS, J., Jr. (b 1781) musician CDP

PURKISS, M. A. [Mrs. W. T. Purkiss] (d 1905 [72]) EA/06*

PURKISS, William (d 1894) EA/95*

PURKISS, Cpt. W. S. (d 1899 [75]) music-hall proprietor EA/01*

PURKISS, Mrs. W. T. see Purkiss, M. A.

PURNELL, Louise (b 1942) English actress AAS, WWT/15-16

PURNELL, Roger (b 1943) American actor TW/27-28

PURNELL, Thomas (d 1889) journalist EA/91*

PURSSORD, Walter (d 1896 [39]) conjurer EA/97*

PURTON, John C. (d 1876 [66]) musician EA/77*

PURVIANCE, Edna (1895-1958) American actress BE*

PURVIS, Mrs. Billy (d 1880
[94]) EA/81*
PURVIS, Walter (b 1870) Welsh
actor GRB/1
PURVIS, Walter (d 1912 [45])
actor EA/13*
PURVIS, William Frederick (b
1870) English critic GRB/2-4
PUSEY, Arthur actor WWT/4-11
PUSSER, Buford (d 1974 [36]) per-
former BP/59*
PUTNAM, Boyd (d 1908) actor
GRB/4*
PUTNAM, Katie (b 1852) Ameri-
can actress, singer CDP,
HAS
PUTNAM, William James (d
1897) musician EA/98*
PUTTENHAM, George (fl 1589)
dramatist CP/2-3, FGF
PUZZI, Sig. (d 1876 [84]) musi-
cian EA/77*
PUZZI, Giacinta (d 1889 [81])
singer EA/90*
PYAT, Félix (d 1889 [79]) drama-
tist, singer EA/90*
PYE, Henry James (d 1813 [58])
English dramatist CP/3, GT,
TD/1-2
PYE, Mrs. Henry James (d
1796) dramatist CP/3
PYE, John (fl 1559) actor DA
PYE, Merrill (d 1975 [73]) de-
signer BP/60*
PYGE, John see Pig, John
PYK, John see Pig, John
PYKMAN, Phillip (fl 1600-01)
member of the Chapel Royal
DA
PYLE, Thomas F. (d 1976 [58])
performer BP/60*
PYM, Miss see Cromwell,
Cecil
PYMER, James (d 1898 [79])
clown EA/00*
PYMER, Mrs. James see
Pymer, Matilda
PYMER, Matilda [Mrs. James
Pymer] (d 1881 [64]) EA/82*
PYNE, Mr. singer, actor BS
PYNE, George (d 1877 [87]) mu-
sician, singer EA/78*
PYNE, J. (d 1857) singer EA/
72*
PYNE, Louisa Fanny [Louisa
Fanny Bodda] (1835-1904) Eng-
lish singer CDP, DNB, HAS
PYNE, Rena (d 1889) music-hall

singer EA/90*
PYNE, Susan [Mrs. F. H. Celli]
(d 1886) singer EA/87*
PYNES, Thomas see Sanford,
Jim
PYTCHER, Carolus (fl 1598) actor
DA

- Q -

QUAGLIENI, Amalia Gasperini
[Mrs. Antonio Quaglieni] (d
1882 [63]) EA/84*
QUAGLIENI, Antonio (d 1892)
equestrian, circus director EA/
93*
QUAGLIENI, Mrs. Antonio see
Quaglieni, Amalia Gasperini
QUAGLIENI, Georgina [Mrs. Romeo
Quaglieni] (d 1895 [47]) EA/96*
QUAGLIENI, Mrs. Romeo see
Quaglieni, Georgina
QUALCH, Mr. (fl 1759-61) actor
HAS
QUALTERS, Tot (d 1974 [79]) ac-
tress, singer TW/30
QUAM, Mylo (b 1942) American
actor TW/22-24
QUARLES, Francis (1592-1665)
English dramatist CP/1-3,
DNB, FGF
QUARREL, William Thomas see
Thomas, William
QUARRY, Richard (b 1944) Ameri-
can actor TW/26, 28-30
QUARRY, Robert (b 1924) American
actor TW/6-9
QUARTERMAINE, Charles (1877-
1958) English actor COC, GRB/
4, OC/1-3, WWT/1-11
QUARTERMAINE, Leon (1876-1967)
English actor BE, COC, OC/
1-3, WWT/1-11, WWW/6
QUAYLE, Anna (b 1936/37) English
actress BE, TW/19, WWT/15-
16
QUAYLE, Anthony (b 1913) English
actor, producer, director AAS,
BE, CB, COC, ES, OC/1-3,
PDT, TW/23-24, 27-30, WWT/
9-16
QUAYLE, Calvin (b 1927) American
educator, scene designer, director BE
QUAYLE, Charles (d 1901) Irish
comedian EA/02*
QUAYLE, Peter (fl 1834-38) Amer-

ican singer HAS

QUEDENS, Eunice see Arden, Eve

QUEEN, Ellery (b 1905) American dramatist CB

QUEEN, John (1843-84) dancer, minstrel CDP

QUEEN, Richard (d 1870) EA/71*

QUEEN ELIZABETH I translator CP/1-3

"QUEEN'S JESTER" see Croueste, Harry

QUELER, Eve (b 1936) American conductor, musician CB

QUENOT, Mons. (fl 1794) French actor HAS

QUESTEL, Mae (b 1910) American actress BE

QUICK, Mrs. Charles (d 1887) EA/88*

QUICK, Charles E. (d 1888) actor EA/89*

QUICK, Charles M. (d 1886) scene artist EA/87*

QUICK, Gerard C. (1811-69) American circus proprietor HAS

QUICK, John (1748-1831) English actor CDP, COC, DNB, ES, GT, OC/1-3, TD/1-2

QUICK, John William see Jean, Jess

QUIDANT, Alfred (d 1893 [79]) composer, musician EA/94*

QUIGLEY, Jennie dwarf CDP

QUIGLEY, Thomas see Seabrooke, Thomas Q.

QUILLEY, Denis (b 1927) English actor, singer AAS, WWT/14-16

QUILTER, Roger (1877-1953) English composer WWW/5

QUIMBY, Harriet (1884-1938) American critic WWA/1

QUIN, Edward (fl 1790) Irish dramatist GT

QUIN, James (1693-1766) English actor CDP, COC, DNB, ES, GT, HP, OC/1-3, TD/1-2

QUIN, Thomas H. (d 1832) English actor HAS

QUINBY, George H. (b 1901) American educator, director BE

QUINE, Richard (b 1920) American actor ES

QUINLAN, Gertrude (1875-1963) American actress, singer

GRB/4, WWM, WWS, WWT/1-5

QUINLAN, John C. (d 1954 [62]) New Zealand actor, singer TW/11

QUINLAN, Mark (b 1846) Irish actor HAS

QUINLIVAN, Charles (d 1974 [50]) performer BP/59*

QUINN, Anna Maria (b 1845) actress HAS

QUINN, Anthony (b 1915) Mexican actor BE, CB, ES, WWT/16

QUINN, Arthur Hobson (1875-1960) American critic, historian ES, HJD, NTH

QUINN, Billy (d 1863) Negro performer HAS

QUINN, Billy (b 1945) American actor TW/13

QUINN, Joe (d 1971 [54]) toastmaster, publicist BP/55*

QUINN, Joe (d 1974 [75]) actor TW/30

QUINN, Mary see Digges, Mary

QUINN, Miriam (d 1970 [71]) performer BP/55*

QUINN, Tony (1899-1967) Irish actor WWT/9-14

QUINNEY, Maureen (b 1931) English actress TW/15

QUINTERO, Joaquin Alvarez see Alvarez Quintero, Joaquin

QUINTERO, José (b 1924) Panamanian/American director AAS, BE, CB, COC, ES, PDT, WWT/14-16

QUINTERO, Lamar C. (b 1863) Mexican critic WWM

QUINTERO, Serafin Alvarez see Alvarez Quintero, Serafin

QUINTON, Mark (d 1891 [32]) dramatist, actor BE*, EA/92*, WWT/14*

QUIRK, Margaret C. (d 1971 [70]) performer BP/55*

QUITAK, Oscar (b 1926) English actor TW/22

QUITTNER, Joseph (d 1971 [83]) lawyer BP/55*

QUIVE, Grace see Van Studdiford, Grace

QUONG, Rose Lanu (d 1972 [93]) performer BP/57*

- R -

R. , C. (fl 1769) dramatist CP/3

R. 768

R. , J. dramatist CP/1-3
R. , T. dramatist CP/1-3
R. , W. dramatist CP/1-2
RAB, Phyllis talent representative
BE
RABB, Ellis (b 1930) American
actor, director, producer
AAS, TW/15-16, 23-25,
WWT/15-16
RABE, David (b 1940) American
dramatist CB, CD, WWT/16
RABEL, A. dancing master
CDP
RABINEAU, Augusta see Au-
gusta, Mlle.
RABINEAU, Marie see Marie,
Mlle.
RABINOFF, Max (1877-1966)
Russian impresario WWA/4,
WWM
RABORN, George (d 1974 [50])
critic BP/59*
RABY, Roger Allan (b 1939)
American actor TW/25-26
RACHEL [Elisa Félix] (1820-
58) French actress CDP,
COC, ES, HAS, NTH, OC/
1-3, PDT, SR, WWA/H
RACHEL, Lydia (d 1915) actress
WWT/14*
RACHELLE, Bernie (b 1939)
American actor TW/24, 29
RACHINS, Alan (b 1942) Ameri-
can actor TW/24-29
RACIMO, Victoria (b 1945) Amer-
ican actress TW/28
RACINE, Jean (1639-99) French
dramatist COC, ES, OC/1-3
RACIOPPI, James (b 1946)
American actor TW/26
RACKERBY, Don (b 1926) Amer-
ican actor TW/11
RACKIN, Martin Lee (d 1976
[58]) producer/director/chore-
ographer BP/60*
RACKSTRAW, Mary J. (d 1907)
EA/08*
RADBOURNE, Caroline (d 1890
[80]) EA/91*
RADCLIFF, Ralph (1519?-59)
English dramatist CP/2-3,
DNB
RADCLIFFE, J. (d 1875) actor
EA/76*
RADCLIFFE, John (d 1917 [75])
musician EA/18*
RADCLIFFE, Mat (d 1874 [30])
actor EA/75*

RADCLIFFE, Minnie (d 1918) ac-
tress SR
RADCLIFFE, Thomas B. (1812-66)
English actor HAS
RADCLIFFE, Thornton (d 1909)
EA/10*
RADCLIFFE, Mrs. Walter Thorn-
ton see Watson, Henrietta
RADD, Ronald (1929-76) English
actor TW/22-23, 27, WWT/
15-16
RADECKE, Luise Moore (b 1847)
singer CDP
RADFORD, Basil (1897-1952) Eng-
lish actor WWT/9-11, WWW/5
RADFORD, Robert (1874-1933)
English singer WWW/3
RADICATI, Teresa (b 1778) singer
CDP
RADILAK, Charles H. (d 1972
[65]) performer BP/57*
RADO, James librettist CD
RADSTONE, John (fl 1550) actor
DA
RAE, Alexander (1782-1820) English
actor CDP, DNB, GT, OX
RAE, Bob (d 1899 [33]) singer
CDP
RAE, Charlotte [née Lubotsky] (b
1926) American actress, singer
BE, TW/8, 12-15, 19, 22, 25-
26, 29-30, WWT/15-16
RAE, Mrs. E. J. S. see Rae,
Finaretta
RAE, Eric (b 1899) English actor
WWT/2-3
RAE, Finarette [Mrs. E. J. S.
Rae] (d 1899) EA/00*
RAE, J. B. (d 1891) comedian
EA/92*
RAE, Kenneth (b 1901) English ad-
ministrator BE, WWT/14-15
RAE, Melba (d 1971 [49]) perform-
er BP/56*
RAE, Peter (d 1870 [70]) actor
EA/71*
RAE, Robert (d 1899 [33]) singer
EA/00*
RAE, Sheilah (b 1946) American
actress TW/28
RAEBURN, Henzie (1900-73) Eng-
lish actress COC, WWT/12-15
RAEBURN, Sam [George Ellis] (d
1890 [25]) minstrel? EA/91*
RAEDLER, Dorothy (b 1917) Amer-
ican director, producer, mana-
ger BE, CB, WWT/15-16
RAEVSKY, Iosif Moiseevich (b

1900) Russian director WWT/ 13-14

RAFAEL, Al (d 1897 [16]) acrobat EA/98*

RAFF, Joachim (d 1882 [58]) composer EA/83*

RAFFERTY, Chips (d 1971 [62]) performer BP/55*

RAFFERTY, Emily [Mrs. Pat Rafferty] (d 1906) music-hall singer EA/07*

RAFFERTY, Pat (d 1952 [91]) actor, songwriter, singer CDP

RAFFERTY, Mrs. Pat see Rafferty, Emily

RAFILLE, Mr. (fl 1834-41) actor HAS

RAFT, George (b 1903) American actor ES

RAFT, Tommy Moe (d 1974 [59]) performer BP/58*

RAFTERY, Edward C. (d 1967 [69]) lawyer BP/51*

RAGLAN, James [Thomas James Raglan Cornewall-Walker] (1901-61) English actor WWT/ 8-13

RAGLAND, Rags (1905?-46) American comedian CB, TW/3

RAGNI, Gerome librettist CD

RAGNO, Joseph (b 1936) American actor TW/28-30

RAGOTZY, Jack (b 1921) American director, producer, actor BE

RAHERE (d 1144) jester COC, OC/1-3

RAHN, Muriel (d 1961 [50]) American singer TW/18

RAHN, Patsy (b 1950) American actress TW/28

RAHT, Katharine (b 1904) American actress TW/4, 13-14, 20

RAIMUND, Ferdinand (d 1836 [46]) actor, manager WWT/ 14*

RAIN, Douglas Canadian actor AAS, WWT/13-16

RAINBIRD, Marie [Mrs. Fred Danvers] (d 1904 [30]) actress EA/05*

RAINBOW, Frank (b 1913) English press representative WWT/ 14-16

RAINBOW, J. G. (d 1893) proprietor EA/94*

RAINBOW, John (d 1892 [79]) EA/93*

RAINE, Bessie [Elizabeth Rowlands] (d 1901/02) actress EA/03*, EA/04*

RAINE, Gillian Ceylonese actress TW/20

RAINE, Jack (b 1897/98) English actor BE, WWT/6-15

RAINER, J. C. see Buckley, R. Bishop

RAINER, Luise (b 1912) Austrian actress WWT/9-11

RAINES, Walter (b 1940) American actor TW/24

RAINESCROFTE, Thomas (fl 1598) actor DA

RAINEY, Ford (b 1908) American actor BE

RAINEY, William S. (d 1964 [70]) producer/director BP/49*

RAINFORD, James H. (d 1900 [53]) actor, stage manager EA/ 01*

RAINFORD, Louis minstrel CDP

RAINFORD, Tom H. (d 1906 [75]) singer EA/07*

RAINFORTH, Elizabeth (1814-77) singer CDP, DNB

RAINFORTH, John (d 1888 [28]) actor EA/89*

RAINGER, Ralph (1901-42) American composer BE*

RAINIERT, Teresa (fl 1847) singer HAS

RAINOLDI, Paul pantomime master CDP

RAINS, Claude (1889-1967) English actor AAS, BE, CB, ES, NTH, TW/7-9, 13-16, 23, WWA/4, WWT/4-14

RAINS, Leon (1870-1954) American singer WWA/3, WWM

RAINSFORD, Louis (d 1873) singer EA/74*

RAISA, Rosa (1893-1963) Russian singer ES, TW/20, WWA/4

RAITT, John (b 1917) American actor, singer BE, TW/1-9, 12-16, 22-24, WWT/12-16

RAJAH, Raboid (d 1962) performer BE*

RAKE, J. (d 1876) comic singer EA/78*

RALEIGH, Cecil [Rowlands] (1856-1914) GRB/1-4, SR, WWT/1-2, WWW/1

RALEIGH, Mrs. Cecil [Isabel Ellissen] (1866-1923) actress GRB/1-4, WWT/1-4

RALEIGH, Desmond Mountjoy [W. M. Chapman-Huston] (b 1881) Irish manager, writer GRB/2-3

RALEIGH, Saba see Raleigh, Mrs. Cecil

RALF, Emily [Mrs. Tony Griffin] (d 1892 [25]) EA/93*

RALL, Tommy (b 1929) American dancer, singer, actor, choreographer BE, TW/26

RALLAND, Bertie (b 1883) English manager GRB/1

RALLAND, Clarissa (d 1899) EA/01*

RALLAND, Herbert (d 1942 [82]) business manager WWT/14*

RALLAND, Mrs. Herbert see Clifton, Ethel

RALLI, Richard (d 1913) EA/14*

RALPH, Francis (d 1887 [40]) musician EA/88*

RALPH, James (1695/c. 1705-1762) American? dramatist CP/1-3, GT, HJD, WWA/H

RALPH, Jessie (d 1944 [79]) American actress BE*, BP/28*

RALPH, Julia [Mrs. M. C. Morris] (b 1876) American actress WWM

RALSTON, Teri (b 1943) American actress TW/26-30

RAM, Jerry (b 1946) Indian actor TW/24

RAMAGE, Cecil B. (b 1895) Scottish actor WWT/7-12

RAMA RAU, Santha (b 1923) Indian dramatist BE, CB

RAMBAL, Enrique (d 1971 [47]) performer BP/56*

RAMBAUD, Mme. George Gibier see Gerville-Reache, Jeanne

RAMBEAU, Marjorie (1889-1970) American actress TW/27, WWA/5, WWT/4-11

RAMBERT, Marie [Mrs. Ashley Dukes] (b 1888) Polish choreographer, ballet teacher ES, OC/1-2, WWT/8-12

RAMIN, Sid (b 1924) American composer, conductor BE

RAMIREZ, Ray (b 1939) American actor TW/23

RAMKINS, William (fl 1598-1600) dramatist CP/3

RAMM, Matilde (d 1877) actress EA/78*

RAMOS, Signorina (fl 1857) singer HAS

RAMOS, Carlos (d 1969 [62]) performer BP/54*

RAMOS, Richard (b 1941) American actor TW/25, 28, 30

RAMSAY, Allan (1686-1758) Scottish dramatist CDP, COC, CP/1-3, DNB, GT

RAMSAY, Ernest actor, composer GRB/1

RAMSAY, John Nelson (d 1892 [53]) EA/93*

RAMSAY, Nelson (d 1929 [66]) actor WWT/14*

RAMSAY, Remak (b 1937) American actor TW/26-30, WWT/16

RAMSAY, Scott [T. H. MacKillop] (d 1871) actor EA/72*

RAMSAY, Thomas (d 1896) lessee EA/97*

RAMSDALE, Alice [Alice Fisher] (b 1877) English actress GRB/1

RAMSDALE, Edwin (d 1909 [40]) manager EA/10*

RAMSDALE, Fred (b 1879) English actor GRB/1

RAMSDALE, Isabella Fisher (d 1911 [75]) EA/12*

RAMSDALE, James (d 1891 [69]) touring manager EA/92*

RAMSDALE, Lilian [Lilian May Fisher] actress GRB/1

RAMSDALE, William N. (d 1909) actor? EA/10*

RAMSDEN, Mme. see Lock, Mrs. J. H.

RAMSDEN, Dennis (b 1918) English actor, director WWT/15-16

RAMSDEN, Newton (d 1896 [43]) actor EA/97*

RAMSEL, Gina (b 1950) American actress TW/30

RAMSEY, Alicia (d 1933) English dramatist GRB/3-4, WWT/1-3, 6-7, WWW/3

RAMSEY, Cecil (d 1814) actor WWT/14*

RAMSEY, Cecil actor EA/97

RAMSEY, Charles Ernest (d 1905 [33]) advance agent EA/06*

RAMSEY, James (b 1928) American actor TW/6

RAMSEY, John (b 1940) American actor TW/30

RAMSEY, Johnnie (d 1962 [86]) magician BE*

RAMSEY, Logan (b 1921) American

actor BE, TW/7-8, 13, 22
RAMSEY, Marion (b 1947)
American actress TW/27-28,
30
RAMSEY, Mary E. (d 1972) performer BP/57*
RAMSEY, Nelson (d 1929 [66])
actor BE*
RAMSEY, Owen (d 1878) actor
EA/79*
RAMZA, Frank W. (d 1889) minstrel comedian EA/90*
RANALLI, Ralph (d 1974 [53])
performer BP/59*
RANALOW, Frederick Baring
(1873-1953) Irish actor, singer
WWT/5-11, WWW/5
RAND, Bill (d 1961) performer
BE*
RAND, L. F. (fl 1852-59) American actor HAS
RAND, Mrs. L. F. (fl 1855)
American actress HAS
RAND, Olivia (fl 1867-69) American actress HAS
RAND, Rosa (fl 1868) American
actress HAS
RAND, Mrs. William W., Jr.
(b 1927) American director
BE
RANDALL, Adelaide actress, singer
CDP
RANDALL, Annie (d 1913) EA/
14*
RANDALL, Beard (b 1880) English actor, stage manager
GRB/1
RANDALL, Billy (d 1898) comedian
EA/99*
RANDALL, Bob librettist CD
RANDALL, Brett (d 1963 [79])
Australian actor, director
WWT/14*
RANDALL, Carl (d 1965 [67])
American dancer, producer
WWT/8-10
RANDALL, Charles (b 1923) American actor TW/24, 28
RANDALL, Harry (1860-1932)
English actor, music-hall performer CDP, COC, GRB/
1-4, OC/1-3, WWW/3
RANDALL, Joe (d 1876 [31])
Negro comedian EA/77*
RANDALL, John (fl 1732) dramatist CP/2-3, GT
RANDALL, Leslie (b 1924) English actor, comedian WWT/

13-15
RANDALL, Maria (d 1887 [29])
music-hall performer EA/88*
RANDALL, Martha American actress TW/9
RANDALL, Paul E. (b 1902) American educator, director, actor
BE
RANDALL, Peter (d 1971 [55]) producer/director/choreographer
BP/56*
RANDALL, Pollie [Mrs. Walter
Burnet] (d 1910 [57]) burlesque
performer CDP
RANDALL, Richard (1736-1828)
singer CDP
RANDALL, Samuel (1778-1864)
American dramatist DAB
RANDALL, Susann (b 1943) American actress TW/25
RANDALL, Thomas (fl 1660) dramatist CP/3
RANDALL, Tony (b 1920/24) American actor BE, CB, ES, TW/4,
6, 14-15, 22, WWT/16
RANDALL, W. [Billy Forbes] (d
1917) EA/18*
RANDALL, Mrs. W. (d 1888) EA/
89*
RANDALL, William (fl 1584-1603)
musician DNB
RANDALL, William (d 1917) actor,
singer CDP
RANDALLE, Willie (d 1901) acrobat
EA/02*
RANDEGGER, Alberto (1832-1911)
Italian conductor, composer
DNB, GRB/1, WWW/1
RANDEGGER, Giuseppe Aldo (b
1874) Italian composer WWM
RANDELL, Mrs. Frank E. see
Pierson, Ethel
RANDELL, Ron (b 1920/23) Australian actor BE, TW/6-8, 15-
16, WWT/14-16
RANDLE, Percy E. (d 1918) EA/
19*
RANDOLPH, Amanda (d 1967 [65])
actress TW/24
RANDOLPH, Clemence (d 1970 [81])
dramatist BP/55*
RANDOLPH, Donald South African
actor TW/3
RANDOLPH, Miss E. (d 1847) English actress HAS
RANDOLPH, Elsie (b 1904) English
actress, singer WWT/6-16
RANDOLPH, Eva (d 1927 [64])

actress BE*, BP/12*

RANDOLPH, Isabel (d 1973 [83])
actress TW/29

RANDOLPH, John (b 1915) American actor, dramatist, producer BE, TW/4, 6-7, 9-
10, 19, 22-24, 26-27, 29-30

RANDOLPH, Louise [Mrs. S.
C. McKnight] (d 1953 [83])
American actress WWM,
WWS

RANDOLPH, Mimi (b 1922) Canadian actress TW/27-29

RANDOLPH, Robert [or Thomas]
(b 1926) American designer
BE, WWT/15-16

RANDOLPH, Thomas (1605-35)
English dramatist CP/1-3,
DNB, FGF, RE

RANDOLPH, Thomas see Ran-
dolph, Robert

RANDOLPH, Virginia (b 1882)
American actress WWS

RANDS, Harry actor, singer
CDP

RANEVSKY, Boris (b 1891) Russian actor WWT/6-10

RANGER, Mr. (fl 1840) actor
HAS

RANGER, George (d 1917) EA/
18*

RANKEN, Frederick W. (d 1905
[36]) American librettist,
lyricist BE*

RANKIN, Mrs. (fl 1791) actress
HAS

RANKIN, Arthur (d 1947 [51])
American actor TW/3

RANKIN, Arthur McKee (1841-
1914) Canadian actor, manager
CDP, COC, DAB, GRB/2-4,
OC/1-3, PP/3, SR, WWS,
WWT/1-2

RANKIN, Mrs. Arthur McKee
see Blanchard, Kitty

RANKIN, Doris [Mrs. Lionel
Barrymore] (c. 1880-c. 1946)
actress BE*

RANKIN, Gladys (d 1914 [40])
actress BE*, WWT/14*

RANKIN, Linda (b 1945) American actress TW/25

RANKIN, Maud see Burton,
Maud

RANKIN, Molly Scottish actress
WWT/9-10

RANKIN, Phyllis [Mrs. Harry
Davenport] (1874-1934) Amer-

ican actress, singer GRB/2-4,
WWS, WWT/1-6

RANKIN, Thomas (1862-1944) Canadian showman SR

RANKINS, William (fl 1587-1601)
dramatist DNB, FGF

RANKL, Karl (1898-1968) conductor
WWW/6

RANKLEY, Caroline (d 1846 [29])
actress WWT/14*

RANNEY, Frank (b 1863) American
actor WWS

RANNIE, John (fl 1806) dramatist
CP/3

RANOE, Miss see Barrett, Mrs.
Giles Linnett

RANOE, Cecilia see Burnand,
Mrs. F. C.

RANOE, James (d 1877 [69]) actor
EA/78*

RANSFORD, Edwin (1805-76) English actor, singer CDP, DNB

RANSFORD, Mrs. Edwin see
Ransford, Hannah

RANSFORD, George (d 1910) performer? EA/11*

RANSFORD, Hannah [Mrs. Edwin
Ransford] (d 1876 [71]) EA/77*

RANSFORD, Mary Elizabeth CDP

RANSLEY, Peter (b 1931) English
dramatist CD

RANSOM, Mrs. Charles B. (fl
1859?) CDP

RANSOM, Frank see Mills, Frank

RANSOME, John W. (1860-1929)
actor CDP, SR

RANSON, Blanche [Mrs. Sam Ran-
son] (d 1892 [36]) music-hall
performer EA/93*

RANSON, Herbert (1889-1970) English actor WWT/8-14

RANSON, Sam (d 1893) performer
EA/94*

RANSON, Mrs. Sam see Ranson,
Blanche

RANSONE, John W. see Ran-
some, John W.

RAPETTI, Michele (fl 1832) conductor, musician CDP

RAPHAEL, Miss see Ruskin,
Sybil

RAPHAEL, Bette-Jane (b 1943)
American actress TW/25

RAPHAEL, Enid (d 1964) actress
BE*

RAPHAEL, Frederic dramatist CD

RAPHAEL, Gerrianne (b 1935) American actress TW/17, 22-24, 29

RAPHAEL, John N. (1868-1917)
dramatist GRB/3-4, SR,
WWT/1-3, WWW/2
RAPHAEL, William (b 1858)
Scottish scene artist WWT/3-7
RAPHAELSON, Samson (b 1896/
99) American dramatist, di-
rector BE, MH, WWT/8-13
RAPOPORT, Gene W. (d 1975
[36]) agent BP/60*
RAPP, Charles (d 1974 [71])
agent BP/59*
RAPP, William J. (1895-1942)
American dramatist CB,
WWA/2
RAPPOLD, Marie (d 1957 [80])
American singer TW/13,
WWA/3
RAPPOPORT, Salomov see
Ansky
RASBACH, Oscar (d 1975 [86])
performer BP/59*
RASCH, Albertina (1896-1967)
Austrian maîtresse de ballet BE,
TW/24, WWA/4, WWT/8-13
RASCOE, Burton (1892-1957)
American critic WWT/10-12
RASKIN, Judith (b 1928) Ameri-
can singer CB
RASPE, R. E. (fl 1781) drama-
tist CP/2-3
RASTALL, John see Rastell,
John
RASTELL, John (c. 1475-1536) English
dramatist COC, CP/2-3, ES,
OC/1-3
RASTELL, William (d 1608)
manager DA
RASUMNY, Mikhail (1896-1956)
Russian actor TW/10
RATCLIFFE, Annie (d 1899 [31])
EA/00*
RATCLIFFE, E. J. (fl 1860s)
actor SR
RATCLIFFE, Mrs. John Bond
see Pettifer, Mary Ann
RATCLIFFE, Samuel D. (b 1945)
American actor TW/26-29
RATHBONE, Basil (1892-1967)
South African actor AAS,
BE, CB, ES, TW/3-16, 24,
WWA/4, WWT/4-14, WWW/6
RATHBONE, George (d 1972
[77]) performer BP/56*
RATHBONE, Guy B. (1884-1916)
English actor WWT/2-3
RATHBONE, Ouida (b 1887)
Spanish/American dramatist,

designer BE
RATHBUN, Janet (d 1975) perform-
er BP/59*
RATHBURN, Roger (b 1940) Amer-
ican actor TW/27-29
RATHGEBER, Ralph see Meeker,
Ralph
RATNER, Anna (d 1967 [75]) per-
former BP/52*
RATNER, Herbert (b 1912) Ameri-
can actor TW/7
RATOFF, Gregory (1893/97-1960)
Russian actor CB, SR, TW/17,
WWA/4, WWT/7-12
RATTIGAN, Sir Terence (1911-77)
English dramatist AAS, BE,
CB, CD, CH, COC, ES, MD,
MH, MWD, NTH, OC/2-3,
PDT, WWT/9-16
RAUCH, Greta (d 1976 [74]) publi-
cist BP/60*
RAUH, Ida (d 1970 [92]) founder of
the Provincetown Players BP/
54*
RAUSCHENBERG, Robert (b 1925)
American designer CD, ES
RAUZZINI, Matteo (1754-91) singer
DNB
RAUZZINI, Venanzio (1747-1810)
Italian composer, singer CDP,
DNB
RAVEL, Antoine (b 1812) French
performer CDP, HAS
RAVEL, François (1823-81) actor
CDP
RAVEL, Gabriel (1810-82) French
acrobat CDP, HAS, SR
RAVEL, Jerome (1814-90) French
performer CDP, HAS
RAVEL, Marietta (b 1847) French
dancer, tight-rope performer,
actress CDP, HAS
RAVEL FAMILY (fl 1832) HAS
RAVEN, David (d 1971 [58]) per-
former BP/56*
RAVEN, Elsa (b 1929) American
actress TW/26, 28, 30
RAVENOT, Adrie (fl 1828) French
dancer HAS
RAVENSCROFT, Edward (fl 1671-
97) English dramatist COC,
CP/1-3, DNB, GT, OC/1-3
RAVENSCROFT, Ernest (d 1897)
acting manager EA/98*
RAVIK, Michael (d 1971 [40])
performer BP/56*
RAWLING, Sylvester (d 1921 [63])
English critic BE*, BP/5*

RAWLINGS, Francis (d 1887
[65]) lessee, manager EA/88*
RAWLINGS, Mabel [Mrs. Mait-
land Marler] (d 1894 [26])
EA/95*
RAWLINGS, Margaret (b 1906)
Japanese/English actress AAS,
WWT/7-16
RAWLINS, Lester (b 1924) Amer-
ican actor BE, TW/18, 21-
22, 25-26, 28, WWT/15-16
RAWLINS, Thomas (1620?-70)
dramatist CP/1-3, DNB,
FGF, GT
RAWLINS, W. H. (d 1927) actor
BE*, WWT/14*
RAWLINSON, A. R. (b 1894)
English dramatist WWT/11-14
RAWLINSON, Herbert (d 1953
[67]) English actor TW/10
RAWLINSON, John (d 1875 [36])
minstrel CDP
RAWLINSON, Priscilla see
Abbott, Annie
RAWLINSON, William (d 1884
[72]) EA/86*
RAWLS, Eugenia (b 1916) Amer-
ican actress BE, TW/1-2,
24, WWT/16
RAWLSTON, Zelma (d 1915)
German?/American? actress,
singer SR, WWS
RAWLYNS, John (fl 1550) actor
DA
RAWORTH, Mr. (fl 1767) English
actor HAS
RAWSON, Graham (1890-1955)
English dramatist WWT/8-11
RAWSON, Sarah Ellen (d 1916
[67]) EA/17*
RAWSON, Thomas William (b
1867) English actor GRB/1
RAWSON, Mrs. Thomas William
see Bertram, Lily
RAWSON, Tristan (1888-1974)
English actor, dramatist
AAS, BTR/74, WWT/5-14
RAY, Alfred (d 1868) actor EA/
69*
RAY, Andrew (b 1939) English
actor BE
RAY, Charles (1891-1943) Ameri-
can actor ES
RAY, Ellen American choreog-
rapher, dancer, singer, ac-
tress BE
RAY, Estelle Goulding (d 1970
[82]) performer BP/55*

RAY, Gabrielle (1883-1973) English
actress, dancer GRB/3-4,
WWT/1-6
RAY, Helen (d 1965 [86]) vaudevil-
lian, actress TW/22
RAY, Isaac (d 1876 [71]) minstrel?
EA/77*
RAY, Jack (d 1975 [58]) performer
BP/60*
RAY, James (d 1901 [36]) perform-
er? EA/02*
RAY, James (b 1932) American
actor BE, TW/25-27, WWT/15-16
RAY, J. H. (d 1875) actor EA/
76*, WWT/14*
RAY, John (d 1873 [42]) Negro
comedian EA/74*
RAY, John William (d 1871 [64])
actor, dramatist BE*, EA/72*,
WWT/14*
RAY, Johnny (d 1927 [68]) Welsh
comedian BE*, BP/12*
RAY, Martha (d 1779) singer DNB
RAY, Naomi (d 1966 [73]) perform-
er BP/50*
RAY, Nicholas (b 1911) American
actor, producer, director ES
RAY, Phil (d 1918 [46]?) singer,
composer CDP
RAY, René [René Creese] (b 1912)
English actress WWT/9-14
RAY, Ruby (fl 1905-07) Brazilian/
English? actress, dancer WWS
RAYBURN, Kittie (fl 1900?) ac-
tress, singer CDP
RAYE, Carol [née Kathleen Mary
Corkrey] (b 1923) English ac-
tress WWT/10-13
RAYE, Martha [née Margaret
Theresa Yvonne Reed] (b 1916)
American actress, singer BE,
CB, TW/23, 29, WWT/15-16
RAYE, Ralph (fl 1594) actor? DA
RAYE, Thelma (fl 1907-08) Bra-
zilian/English? actress WWS
RAYFIELD, Fred (d 1972 [49])
critic BP/57*
RAYM, Maxmilian E. (d 1974
[71]) publicist BP/58*
RAYMON, Rubee (d 1971 [77]) per-
former BP/56*
RAYMOND, Mr. actor CDP
RAYMOND, Mrs. (d 1875 [57])
actress CDP
RAYMOND, Agnes (fl 1850) actress
HAS
RAYMOND, Alfred G. (d 1888
[36]) EA/87*

RAYMOND, Charles (d 1911) dramatist BE*, WWT/14*

RAYMOND, Charles Reeves (d 1903 [42]) dancer EA/04*

RAYMOND, Cyril (d 1973) actor AAS, WWT/5-15

RAYMOND, Dorothy American actress TW/22

RAYMOND, Emeline see Marchant, Mrs. G. F.

RAYMOND, Florence (d 1886) EA/87*

RAYMOND, Gene [Raymond Guion] (b 1908) American actor, producer, director BE, ES, TW/14-15, WWT/7-16

RAYMOND, Helen (d 1965 [76]) American actress BE, TW/22, WWT/4-11

RAYMOND, James (d 1854) circus manager HAS

RAYMOND, James Grant (1771-1817) Scottish?/Irish? actor CDP, GT, TD/1-2

RAYMOND, John T. (1836-87) American actor CDP, COC, DAB, HAS, NTH, NYM, OC/1-3, SR, WWA/H

RAYMOND, Mrs. John T. see Gordon, Marie

RAYMOND, Kate [Mrs. O. B. Collins] (1840/44-79) French/American actress CDP, HAS

RAYMOND, Mrs. Louis see May, Alice

RAYMOND, Malone [né Richard Malone] (d 1862 [64]) Irish? actor? HAS

RAYMOND, Mark (d 1875) performer? EA/76*

RAYMOND, Mat [W. M. Macguffie] (d 1879) comedian, stage manager EA/80*

RAYMOND, Maud (d 1961 [89]) American actress WWS

RAYMOND, Maurice (1878-1948) magician SR, TW/4

RAYMOND, Moore (d 1965 [62]) critic BP/50*

RAYMOND, Ned (d c. 1827) actor HAS

RAYMOND, O. B. (d 1851) American actor HAS

RAYMOND, Richard Malone (d 1862 [62]) EA/72*

RAYMOND, Mrs. W. (d 1880) EA/81*

RAYMOND, Walter (1852-1931) English dramatist WWW/3

RAYMOND, William (fl 1900s) American actor WWM

RAYMOND, William Giddens (d 1905) lessee EA/06*

RAYMONDE, Frankie (b 1874) American actress WWS

RAYMUND, Carl (d 1966 [50]) editor TW/22

RAYMUR, Finette see Murray, Lucy

RAYNAUD, Fernand (d 1973) performer BP/59*

RAYNE, Mrs. Henry E. see Rayne, Mary

RAYNE, John Charles Lin (d 1886 [47]) actor EA/87*

RAYNE, Leonard (1869-1925) actor, manager WWT/4-5

RAYNE, Mrs. Leonard see Grace, Amy

RAYNE, Lin (d 1886 [47]) Indian/English actor OAA/2

RAYNE, Mary [Mrs. Henry E. Rayne] (d 1911) EA/12*

RAYNER, Alfred (d 1898 [75]) actor BE*, EA/99*, WWT/14*

RAYNER, Mrs. Alfred see Rayner, Martha

RAYNER, Lionel Benjamin (1787/88?-1855) English actor BS, CDP, DNB, OX

RAYNER, Lizzie see Morgan, Mrs.

RAYNER, Martha [Mrs. Alfred Rayner] (d 1893 [55]) EA/94*

RAYNER, Minnie Gray [Mrs. Frederic Jacques] (1869-1941) English actress, singer GRB/1, WWT/6-9

RAYNER, Sarah (d 1871 [50]) actress EA/72*

RAYNER, William John (d 1894 [50]) EA/95*

RAYNHAM, Miss (d 1871 [27]) actress EA/72*, WWT/14*

RAYNHAM, Carry (d 1874) dancer EA/75*

RAYNHAM, Kate actress, singer CDP

RAYNOR, Charles (d 1896 [47]) music-hall performer EA/97*

RAYNOR, Mrs. Charles (d 1896 [38]) EA/97*

RAYNOR, Mrs. Charles see St. Ledger, Clara

RAYNOR, Clarice (b 1878) English singer GRB/1

RAYNOR, George see Rea, George James

RAYNOR, Harry (d 1890 [45])
Negro comedian, performer
EA/91*
RAYNOR, Mrs. Jack see
Simpson, Catherine Raynor
RAYNOR, Joseph Napoleon (d
1901 [81]) EA/02*
RAYNOR, J. W. (1823-1900) min-
strel manager, performer
CDP
RAYNOR, Thomas (d 1873) comic
singer EA/74*
RAYNOR, William (d 1904 [30])
music-hall performer EA/05*
RAYNORE, Katherine (fl 1897-
1907) American actress WWS
RAYSON, Benjamin American
actor TW/29-30
RAYTON, Velma (d 1974 [81])
actress WWT/16*
RAZAF, Andy (d 1973 [77]) com-
poser, lyricist TW/29
REA, Alec L. (1878-1953) Eng-
lish manager WWT/4-11
REA, Frank E. (1819-87) Amer-
ican actor, singer NYM
REA, George James [George
Raynor] (d 1864 [44]) minstrel
HAS
REA, Oliver (b 1923) American
executive, producer BE
REA, William J. (1884-1932)
Irish actor WWT/4-6
REACH, Angus B. (d 1856 [35])
dramatist BE*, EA/72*,
WWT/14*
REACH, James (d 1970 [60])
dramatist BP/54*
READ, Alvin A. (1830-64) Amer-
ican actor HAS
READ, Grace see Arthur,
Mrs. John, II
READ, Henrietta Fanning (fl 1848)
actress HAS
READ, Henry (d 1898 [57]) lessee
EA/99*
READ, John (fl 1885?) singer,
composer, chairman of Col-
lins's Music Hall CDP
READ, Opie (b 1852) American
writer WWM
READ, Theophilus (d 1906 [59])
EA/07*
READE, Charles (1814-84) Eng-
lish dramatist CDP, COC,
DNB, EA/68, ES, HP, OC/
1-3
READE, Emanuel (fl 1613-20)

actor DA
READE, John (fl 1600-08) actor
DA
READE, Timothy (fl 1626-47) Eng-
lish actor COC, DA, OC/1-3
READER, Ralph (b 1903/04) English
actor, producer, director BE,
WWT/7-16
READING, Beatrice (b 1933) Amer-
ican actress TW/15
READING, Hazel (d 1966) performer
BP/51*
READING, William (d 1563) actor
DA
READY, Eddie (d 1974) performer
BP/59*
REAMS, Lee Roy (b 1942) American
actor TW/26-30
REANEY, James (b 1926) Canadian
dramatist, director, actor CD,
MH, RE
REANO, Archie (d 1903) acrobat,
gymnast EA/04*
REARDON, Catherine (d 1884 [49])
EA/85*
REARDON, Dennis J. (b 1944)
American dramatist CD
REARDON, Edward (d 1894) actor
EA/95*
REARDON, Mrs. Edward see
Reardon, Rosalind Becket
REARDON, Eleanor (d 1903) actress
EA/04*
REARDON, John (b 1930) American
actor, singer BE, CB, TW/17-
19
REARDON, Leo F. (d 1965 [73])
dramatist BP/50*
REARDON, Nancy (b 1942) Ameri-
can actress TW/24-25, 27
REARDON, Rosalind Becket [Mrs.
Edward Reardon] (d 1893) EA/
94*
REASON, Gilbert (fl 1610-25) actor
DA
REAY, George Campbell (d 1899
[28]) proprietor EA/00*
RECKORD, Barry (b 1952) Jamaican
dramatist, director CD
REDD, Cora (d 1968 [c. 70]) per-
former BP/52*
REDDEN, Eliza [Mrs. Sam Redden]
(d 1875) EA/77*
REDDEN, Mrs. Sam (d 1880) singer
EA/81*
REDDEN, Mrs. Sam see Redden,
Eliza
REDDICK, Walter (d 1971 [65])

performer BP/56*

REDDIN, Kenneth S. (d 1967 [72]) dramatist BP/52*

REDDING, Eugene (b 1870) Canadian actor WWS

REDDISH, Samuel (1735-85) English actor CDP, DNB, GT, TD/1-2

REDDISH, Mrs. Samuel, II see Canning, Mrs. George

REDDY, Max (d 1973 [59]) performer BP/58*

REDE, Leman Thomas Tertius (1799-1832) English actor COC, DNB, OC/1-3

REDE, William Leman (1802-47) English dramatist CDP, DNB, OC/1-3

REDFERN, Mrs. (d 1905 [49]) EA/06*

REDFERN, Lilian English singer GRB/1

REDFERN, Sam singer, composer CDP

REDFERN, W. B. (d 1923 [83]) producer, manager BE*, WWT/14*

REDFIELD, Billy see Redfield, William

REDFIELD, William (1927-76) American actor BE, TW/1, 3, 5-15, 18-19, 24, 28-29, WWT/14-16

REDFORD, George Alexander (d 1916) Lord Chamberlain's examiner of plays GRB/1-4, WWW/2

REDFORD, John (fl c. 1540) master of the Children of Paul's, dramatist DA, DNB

REDFORD, Leslie (b 1929) American actor TW/23-24

REDFORD, Robert (b 1937) American actor BE, CB, TW/20-21

RED FOX, Chief William (d 1976 [105]) performer BP/60*

REDGATE, William (d 1874 [66]) musician EA/75*

REDGRAVE, Corin (b 1939) English actor PDT, TW/20, WWT/15-16

REDGRAVE, Lynn (b 1943/44) English actress CB, PDT, TW/23, 30, WWT/14-16

REDGRAVE, Sir Michael Scudamore (b 1908) English actor, dramatist, director AAS, BE,

CB, COC, ES, OC/2-3, PDT, TW/4-7, 12-21, 30, WWT/9-16

REDGRAVE, Vanessa (b 1937) English actress AAS, CB, COC, ES, PDT, WWT/13-16

REDHEAD, Joseph William see Reed, Howard

RED LADDER THEATRE theatre collective CD

REDMAN, Mr. (fl 1751-55) actor CDP

REDMAN, Ben Ray (1896-1961/62) American critic BE*, BP/46*

REDMAN, John (d 1893) singer EA/94*

REDMAN, Joyce (b 1918/19) Irish actress AAS, BE, TW/2-8, WWT/9-16

REDMAN, William E. see Emerson, William P.

REDMOND, Billy see Emerson, Billy

REDMOND, Charles (fl 1880?) dancer, singer CDP

REDMOND, George E. (d 1893 [38]) actor? EA/95*

REDMOND, Liam (b 1913) Irish actor AAS, TW/23-24, WWT/11-16

REDMOND, Moira actress WWT/15-16

REDMOND, T. C. (d 1937 [80]) actor BE*, WWT/14*

REDMUND, Clara S. [Mrs. Thomas Barry; Mrs. William Redmund] (1840-1905) actress CDP

REDMUND, William (1850-1915) English actor CDP, OAA/2, PP/3

REDMUND, Mrs. William see Redmund, Clara S.

REDNER, Frederick August (d 1899 [61]) musical director EA/00*

REDPATH, James (1833-91) Scottish booking agent WWA/H

REDPATH, William Seyton (d 1881 [59]) dramatist EA/82*

REDSTONE, Willy (d 1949 [66]) composer, musical director BE*, WWT/14*

REDWOOD, Arthur (d 1887) comedian EA/88*

REDWOOD, John Henry (b 1942) American actor TW/27-28

REECE, Arthur (fl 1890s) music-hall singer CDP

REECE, Mrs. Arthur see Sullivan, Rose

REECE, Brian (1913-62) English actor WWT/11-13

REECE, Louisa [Mrs. Robert
Reece] (d 1900) EA/01*
REECE, Robert (1838-91) West
Indian/English dramatist DNB,
EA/68
REECE, Mrs. Robert see Reece,
Louisa
REECE, Valerie see Meux,
Lady
REED, Mr. (fl 1759-61) actor
HAS
REED (d 1891 [83]) actor, stage-
door keeper EA/92*
REED, Alexander (b 1916) Amer-
ican actor TW/28, 30
REED, Alfred German (1847-95)
actor DNB
REED, Billy (d 1974 [60]) dancer,
choreographer TW/30
REED, Carl D. (d 1962 [79])
producer BE*
REED, Carol (1906-70) English
actor, director WWT/7, 10-11
REED, Charles (d 1889) assistant
stage manager EA/90*
REED, Clara (b 1840) American
singer, actress HAS
REED, Dan[iel] (b 1892) American
actor TW/4, 6-9, 15
REED, Daniel (d 1836) American
actor HAS
REED, Dave (1830-1906) minstrel
manager & performer CDP
REED, E. dwarf CDP
REED, Emily Rosalie see Lang-
don, Mrs. Henry A., I
REED, Flora [Florence Matilda
McNiven] (1844-68) Irish dancer,
music-hall performer HAS
REED, Florence (1883-1967)
American actress BE, TW/
1-17, 24, WWA/4, WWM,
WWT/4-14
REED, Frank Arthur (d 1912 [56])
musician EA/13*
REED, George Edward see
Perks, George
REED, Mrs. German see Reed,
Priscilla
REED, Gus (d 1965 [85]) perform-
er BP/50*
REED, Henry dramatist CD
REED, Henry Dore (d 1897 [56])
manager EA/98*
REED, Howard [Joseph William
Redhead] (d 1899) manager
EA/00*
REED, Isaac (1742-1807) English

critic, historian CDP, DNB
REED, Janet (b 1920) American
dancer ES
REED, Jared (d 1962 [38]) Amer-
ican actor, singer TW/19
REED, Jennings (d 1918) EA/19*
REED, Mrs. Jerrold E. (d 1916)
EA/17*
REED, John (d 1880 [74]) music-
hall manager EA/81*
REED, John (d 1898) manager
EA/99*
REED, John (d 1971 [66]) lawyer
BP/56*
REED, John Roland (1808-91)
American actor CDP, HAS
REED, Joseph (1723/25-87) English
dramatist CDP, CP/2-3, DNB,
GT, TD/1-2
REED, Joseph Verner, Sr. (1902-
73) French/American producer
BE, TW/30, WWT/15
REED, Julian (b 1860) American
actor, dancer HAS
REED, Laura (b 1850) actress?
HAS
REED, Lewis (d 1976 [80]) per-
former BP/60*
REED, Lydia (b 1944) American
actress TW/8-9
REED, Margaret Theresa Yvonne
see Raye, Martha
REED, Mark (b 1890/93) American
dramatist BE, MH, WWT/9-11
REED, Peter Hugh (d 1969 [77])
critic BP/54*
REED, Priscilla [née Horton; Mrs.
Thomas German Reed] (1818-95)
English actress CDP, DNB,
OAA/1-2
REED, Robert (d 1873) musician
EA/74*
REED, Mrs. Roland see Hastings,
Alice
REED, Roland Lewis (1852-1901)
American actor CDP, HAS,
PP/3, WWA/1
REED, T. (d 1871 [76]) musician
EA/72*
REED, Thomas German (1817-88)
English actor, singer, musician
CDP, DNB
REED, Mrs. Thomas German see
Reed, Priscilla
REED, Vernon minstrel CDP
REED, William (d 1889 [46]) musi-
cian EA/90*
REED, William Albert (d 1892 [38])

EA/93*
REED, William Francis (d 1898
[78]) EA/99*
REED, William Henry (1831-60)
American dancer, prompter
HAS
REED, Wilton (b 1866) English
actor, business manager
GRB/1
REEDER, George (b 1931) Amer-
ican actor TW/24
REEDER, Louisa (1837-59) Amer-
ican actress HAS
REEKIE, A. L. (d 1917) EA/18*
REES, Mr. actor, mimic TD/
1-2
REES, Mr. (d 1843) English actor
HAS
REES, Alice [Mrs. Matthew
Brodie] (d 1906 [36]) EA/07*
REES, David (d 1843 [49]) come-
dian EA/72*, WWT/14*
REES, Edward (d 1976 [57]) pro-
ducer/director/choreographer
BP/60*
REES, Ernest (d 1916) actor,
singer CDP
REES, James (1802-85) critic,
dramatist CDP, RJ
REES, Les (d 1973 [84]) Variety
stringer BP/57*
REES, Llewellyn (b 1901) Eng-
lish actor, executive, manager
WWT/10-16
REES, Roger (b 1944) Welsh actor
WWT/16
REES, Rosemary New Zealand
actress GRB/1-2
REES, T. D. (fl 1795) dramatist
CP/3
REESE, James W. (d 1960 [62])
American actor BE*, BP/44*
REESE, J. Mark (d 1974 [31])
agent BP/59*
REEVE, Ada [Mrs. Wilfred Cot-
ton] (1876-1966) English actress
CDP, GRB/1-4, WWT/1-14,
WWW/6
REEVE, Alex (b 1900) English
educator, director BE
REEVE, Charles (d 1906 [63])
actor EA/07*
REEVE, Emma Louisa [Mrs.
Robert Wardell] (d 1868 [44])
EA/69*
REEVE, George (d 1871) musician
EA/72*
REEVE, Mrs. James [née Sey-

mour] (d 1825) actress HAS
REEVE, Joey [Mrs. James Horn]
(d 1898) serio-comic EA/99*
REEVE, John (1799-1838) English
actor BS, CDP, DNB, HAS,
OX, SR
REEVE, Ralph (fl 1603-11) actor
DA
REEVE, William (1757-1815) Eng-
lish composer, actor CDP,
DNB, ES, TD/1-2
REEVE, Wybert (1831-1906) English
actor, dramatist CDP, OAA/1-2
REEVES, Arnold [Aubrey Ruggles]
(fl 1891-1913) Canadian dramatist
WWM
REEVES, Emma [Mrs. Sims
Reeves] (d 1895 [74]) EA/96*
REEVES, Fanny [Mrs. Elliot Galer]
(d 1897) singer EA/98*
REEVES, Fanny (d 1917) actress
SR
REEVES, Geoffrey (b 1939) English
director WWT/15-16
REEVES, George (d 1959 [45])
American actor BE*
REEVES, Jackie (d 1917) EA/18*
REEVES, Jim (d 1959 [45]) Ameri-
can singer, actor BE*
REEVES, John (fl 1842) Irish actor
HAS
REEVES, John (d 1890 [57]) acting
manager EA/91*
REEVES, John Sims (1818/22-1900)
English musician, singer CDP,
DNB, ES, WWW/1
REEVES, Joseph (fl 1794) translator
CP/3
REEVES, Kynaston (1893-1971/72)
English actor AAS, WWT/9-15
REEVES, Mrs. Sims see Reeves,
Emma
REEVES, Steve (b 1928) American
actor TW/10-11
REEVES, Theodore (1910-73) drama-
tist BE
REEVES, W. H. (d 1857 [36]) singer
CDP, HAS
REEVES, William Sheridan (d 1925
[40]) comedian BE*, BP/9*
REEVES-SMITH, Mrs. G. (d 1898
[57]) EA/99*
REEVES-SMITH, George (d 1897
[67]) manager EA/98*
REEVES-SMITH, H. see Smith,
H. Reeves
REEVES-SMITH, Olive (1894-1972)
English actress, singer BE,

TW/2-3, 12-17, 29
REGAN, Daniel T. (d 1975 [60s])
performer BP/60*
REGAN, Kay see Medford, Kay
REGAN, Sylvia (b 1908) Ameri-
can dramatist, actress BE
REGAS, Pedro (d 1974 [82])
performer BP/59*
REGENT, Ernest (d 1917) EA/
18*
REGNAL, Ferdinand see Er-
langer, Frederic
REGNIER, Martha (b 1880)
French actress WWT/1-4
REHAN, Ada [Ada Crehan]
(1860-1916) Irish/American
actress CDP, COC, DAB,
DP, ES, GRB/1-4, HJD,
NTH, OC/1-3, PP/3, SR,
WWA/1, WWM, WWS, WWT/
1-3, WWW/2
REHAN, Mary (d 1963 [76])
American actress BE*
REHAN, Meg [Mrs. Fred Dun-
ville] (d 1904) comedienne
EA/05*
REIBEN, Nancy R. see Pollock,
Nancy R.
REICH, George (b 1926) American
actor TW/10-14
REICH, John (b 1906) Austrian/
American director, producer,
educator BE
REICHARDT, Alexander (1825-85)
singer CDP
REICHER, Emmanuel (1849-1924)
actor, director BE*
REICHER, Frank (1875-1965) Ger-
man actor, producer WWM,
WWT/6-9
REICHER, Hedwig (b 1884) Ger-
man actress WWM
REICHER-KINDERMANN, Mme.
(d 1883 [30]) singer EA/84*
REICHMAN, Thomas (d 1974
[30]) producer/director/choreo-
ographer BP/59*
REICHMANN, Theodore (1849-
1903) German singer ES
REID, Beryl (b 1920) English
actress AAS, WWT/14-16
REID, Carl Benton (1893-1973)
American actor TW/6, 29
REID, Mrs. Charles H. see
Henley, Josephine
REID, Elliott (b 1920) American
actor BE, TW/4-6, 8-9, 16
REID, Frances (b 1918) Ameri-

can actress BE, TW/2-3, 5-10,
WWT/11
REID, Francis Ellison (d 1933
[67]) American press representa-
tive BE*, BP/18*
REID, Hal (d 1920 [60]) American
dramatist GRB/2-4, WWT/1-4
REID, Henry (d 1868 [65]) armourer
EA/69*
REID, Henry E. (d 1910 [83]) pro-
prietor EA/11*
REID, Ian (d 1969 [51]) agent
BP/54*
REID, James Halleck actor SR
REID, James MacArthur (d 1970
[70]) critic BP/55*
REID, Kate (b 1930) English actress
BE, TW/22, 24-25, 30, WWT/
14-16
REID, Margaret (fl 1892) singer
CDP
REID, Marita (b 1895) Spanish ac-
tress TW/10
REID, Mayne (1818-83) Irish actor,
dramatist HJD
REID, Patricia see Stanley, Kim
REID, S. (d 1878 [70]) actor?
EA/79*
REID, Trevor (d 1965 [56]) per-
former BP/49*
REID, Wallace (b 1891) American
actor WWT/4
REIDY, Kitty (b 1902) Australian
actress, singer WWT/6-11
REIF, Keith (d 1976 [33]) performer
BP/60*
REIFFARTH, Jennie (b 1848) Amer-
ican actress WWS [see also:
Reiforth, Jennie]
REIFORTH, Jennie (1848-1913)
actress, singer SR [see also:
Reiffarth, Jennie]
REIFSNEIDER, Robert (b 1912)
American educator BE
REIGNOLDS, F. S. (fl 1858)
prompter HAS
REIGNOLDS, Kate (d 1911 [75])
English actress CDP, HAS,
PP/3
REILEY, Orrin (b 1946) American
actor TW/26-30
REILLY, Anastasia (d 1961 [58])
performer BE*
REILLY, Charles Nelson (b 1931)
American actor BE, TW/21-23,
WWT/15-16
REILLY, Daniel (b 1833) American
actor HAS

REILLY, Frederick Freame (d
1876 [70]) professor of singing
EA/77*
REILLY, James F. (d 1967 [80])
executive BP/52*
REILLY, John (fl 1876?) actor,
singer CDP
REILLY, William W. (d 1975
[53]) producer/director/chore-
ographer BP/59*
REINAGLE, Alexander (1756-1809)
American musician, impresario
DAB, SR, WWA/H
REINAGLE, Hugh (d 1834) Amer-
ican actor? HAS
REINER, Carl (b 1922) American
actor, producer BE, CB
REINER, Ethel Linder (d 1971
[65]) producer BE, TW/27
REINER, Fritz (1888-1963) Hun-
garian conductor CB, ES,
WWA/4
REINHARDT, Lizzie (d 1872 [34])
actress EA/73*
REINHARDT, Max [né Goldmann]
(1873-1943) German actor,
manager, director CB, COC,
ES, NTH, OC/1-3, PDT, SR,
WWA/2, WWT/1-2, 7-9,
WWW/4
REINHARDT, Mrs. Max see
Thimig, Helene
REINHARDT, Stephen (b 1947)
American actor TW/25-26
REINHEIMER, Howard E. (1899-
1970) American lawyer BE
REINHOLD, Mr. (fl 1776-84)
actor TD/1-2
REINHOLD, Charles Frederick
(1737-1815) English singer,
actor DNB
REINHOLD, Conny (d 1974 [42])
producer/director/choreographer
BP/59*
REINHOLD, Thomas (1690?-1751)
German singer DNB
REINHOLT, George (b 1940)
American actor TW/24-25
REINKING, Ann (b 1949) Ameri-
can actress TW/30
REIS, Irving (d 1953 [47]) Amer-
ican director BE*
REISER, Robert (b 1946) Amer-
ican actor TW/26
REISNER, Robert (d 1974 [53])
critic BP/58*
REJANE, Gabrielle [Charlotte
Reju] (1857-1920) French ac-

tress COC, GRB/1-4, NTH,
OC/1-3, PDT, WWM, WWT/1-3
REJU, Charlotte see Réjane,
Gabrielle
RELF, Robert S. (d 1905 [41])
EA/06*
RELPH, George (1888-1960) English
actor AAS, TW/2, 16, WWT/
3-12
RELPH, Harry see Tich, Little
RELPH, Michael (b 1915) English
scene designer WWT/10-13
RELPH, Phyllis (b 1888) actress
WWT/3-13
REMENYI, Eduard (1830-98) musi-
cian CDP
REMER, Helen see Ware, Helen
REMICK, Lee (b 1935) American
actress BE, CB, TW/9, 22-23
REMINGTON, Earle American
vaudevillian WWM
REMME, John (b 1935) American
actor TW/28
REMMELSBURG, Betty (fl 1867)
dancer CDP
REMMELSBURG, Sophie (fl 1867)
dancer CDP
REMOND, Fritz (d 1976 [73]) pro-
ducer/director/choreographer
BP/60*
REMUS, Jorie (b 1929) American
actress TW/18
REMUSAT, Jean (d 1880 [65]) mu-
sician EA/81*
RENAD, Mrs. Charles see
Renad, Jeanne Juliette
RENAD, Frederick (d 1939 [73])
actor BE*, WWT/14*
RENAD, Mrs. Frederick see
Emmerson, Aggie
RENAD, Jeanne Juliette [Mrs.
Charles Renad] (d 1895 [34])
EA/96*
RENARD, David (d 1973 [52]) per-
former BP/58*
RENARD, Jules (1864-1910) French
dramatist MWD
RENAUD, Madeleine (b 1900) French
actress BE, WWT/14
RENAUD, Maurice (1862-1933)
French singer ES
RENAUD, May (d 1910) actress
EA/12*
RENAULT, Francis (d 1955 [62])
female impersonator TW/11
RENAULT, Paul (b 1945) actor
TW/25
RENDER, Dr. William (fl 1798)

translator CP/3

RENDLE, John (d 1882 [66]) musical director EA/83*

RENDLE, Thomas McDonald (1856-1926) English critic WWT/4-5

RENDLE, William Edgecumbe (d 1881 [61]) lessee EA/82*

RENETTI, Lilian [Mrs. Will Pearce] (d 1904) serio-comic singer EA/05*

RENEVANT, Georges (d 1969 [75]) actor TW/25

RENFRO, Rennie (d 1962 [69]) animal trainer BE*

RENNELL, Charles (d 1882) actor EA/83*

RENNERT, Günther (b 1911) German director, producer, opera director CB

RENNIE, Hugh (d 1953 [50]) English actor, director TW/10

RENNIE, James (1890-1965) Canadian actor BE, TW/2-9, 14-15, 22, WWT/5-13

RENNIE, John (d 1952 [77]) actor BE*, WWT/14*

RENNIE, Margaret (d 1903 [84]) EA/04*

RENNIE, Michael (1909-71) English/American actor, director BE, TW/28

RENNON, "Tilda" (d 1916 [24]) EA/17*

RENO, Doris (d 1973) critic BP/57*

RENOUF, Henry (d 1913 [53]) actor BE*, EA/14*, WWT/14*

RENSHAW, Edyth (b 1901) American educator, director BE

RENTZ, Master (b 1844) American singer CDP, HAS

RENZ, Herr (d 1892) circus proprietor EA/93*

RENZ, Oceana see Oceana

REPP, Stafford (d 1974 [56]) performer BP/59*

REPTON, H. (fl 1804) dramatist CP/3

RESDAN, Rita [Flo Windsor] (d 1912) burlesque performer EA/13*

RESNICK, Muriel dramatist BE

RESNICK, Regina (b 1922) American singer CB

RESOR, Stanley Burnet (d 1962 [83]) American executive BE*

RESS, Regina American actress TW/29

RESSLER, Benton Crews (d 1963) performer BE*

RESTER (fl c. 1602) actor DA

RESTIFO, Gary (b 1948) American actor TW/27

RESZKE, Josephine see De Retzske, Josefina

RETFORD, Ella (d 1962 [76]) Irish actress, singer WWT/5-13

RETHBERG, Elisabeth (1894-1976) German singer ES

RETTICH, Julie (b 1810) actress CDP

RETZSKE see De Retzske

REVAL, Rosie (d 1909 [19]) variety performer EA/10*

REVEL, Harry (1905-58) English composer BE*

REVELL, Dorothy (1879-1908) American actress WWS

REVELL, Lilian M. English actress GRB/1-2

REVELLE, Arthur Hamilton [Arthur Hamilton Engström] (1872-1958) English actor GRB/3-4, TW/15, WWS, WWT/1-6

REVERE, Anne (b 1903/06) American actress BE, TW/23, WWT/9-10

REVET, Edward (fl 1671) dramatist CP/1-3

REVILL, Clive (b 1930) New Zealand actor AAS, BE, TW/9, 19, 23, 28, WWT/13-16

REVILL, Frederick William (d 1892 [35]) EA/93*

REVILL, Juliet [Mrs. W. Revill] (d 1885) EA/86*

REVILL, Mrs. W. see Revill, Juliet

REVILL, Wallace (d 1898 [40]) proprietor, manager EA/00*

REVILL, Mrs. Wallace (d 1899 [36]) proprietor EA/00*

REVILL, Mrs. Wallace Ann [Mrs. William Revill] (d 1871 [35]) EA/72*

REVILL, Mrs. William see Revill, Mrs. Wallace Ann

REVILL, William John (d 1897) proprietor EA/98*

REVILL, William Wallace (d 1898 [16]) EA/00*

REVILLE, Robert [Robert Reville Barrett] (d 1893) actor BE*, EA/94*, WWT/14*

REVNER, Katherine Howard (d 1964)

performer BP/49*

REVOLTI, Felix [William Mitchell] (d 1879 [50]) equestrian director CDP

REVY, Aurelie Hungarian actress, singer GRB/1-3

REX, Charles (d 1903) actor EA/04*

REX, Harry (d 1917) EA/18*

REXROAD, David (b 1950) American actor TW/30

REXROTH, Kenneth (b 1905) American dramatist CD

REY, Antonia (b 1927) Cuban actress TW/25-30

REY, Roberto (d 1972 [67]) performer BP/57*

REYMOND, Charles Aguri (d 1902) actor EA/03*

REYMOND, Phil singer CDP

REYNOLDS (fl 1797) dramatist CP/3

REYNOLDS, Miss see Brampton, Lady

REYNOLDS, Adeline de Walt (1862-1961) American actress BE*

REYNOLDS, A. E. (d 1879 [81]) actor EA/80*

REYNOLDS, Alfred (d 1901) musician EA/02*

REYNOLDS, Alfred (1884-1969) English composer, conductor WWT/8-14, WWW/6

REYNOLDS, Alfred John (d 1895 [72]) waxworks exhibitor EA/96*

REYNOLDS, Barney actor CDP

REYNOLDS, Burt (b 1936) American actor CB, TW/18

REYNOLDS, Carrie [Mrs. Charles F. Tingay] (d 1893) EA/95*

REYNOLDS, Charles (d 1918 [69]) EA/19*

REYNOLDS, Charles H. (d 1874) acting manager EA/75*

REYNOLDS, Craig (1907-49) American actor BE*

REYNOLDS, Dale (b 1944) American actor TW/25

REYNOLDS, Debbie (b 1932) American actress TW/29-30

REYNOLDS, Dorothy (b 1913) English actress, dramatist AAS, WWT/13-16

REYNOLDS, Ellis (d 1868 [65]) musician EA/69*

REYNOLDS, Emma [Mrs. R. G. Reynolds] (d 1887 [35]) EA/88*

REYNOLDS, Eugene (b 1944) American actor TW/26

REYNOLDS, E. Vivian (1866-1952) English actor, stage manager GRB/2-4, WWT/1-9

REYNOLDS, Frank E. (d 1962 [57]) director, producer, actor BE*

REYNOLDS, Fred (d 1970) agent BP/55*

REYNOLDS, Frederic (1764-1841) English dramatist CDP, COC, CP/3, DNB, GT, OC/1-3, SR, TD/1-2

REYNOLDS, Mrs. Frederic see Mansel, Eliza

REYNOLDS, George (d 1897) comedian EA/99*

REYNOLDS, George Francis (b 1880) English manager WWT/7-12

REYNOLDS, Harold (d 1973 [76]) performer BP/57*

REYNOLDS, Howard (d 1898 [49]) musician EA/99*

REYNOLDS, James (1891-1957) American designer ES

REYNOLDS, James J. (d 1894 [46]) EA/95*

REYNOLDS, Jane (fl 1839-46) English actress HAS

REYNOLDS, Jane Louisa [Baroness Brampton] (1824-1907) actress, singer CDP

REYNOLDS, John (fl 1628) translator CP/2-3

REYNOLDS, John (d 1871 [29]) Irish comedian EA/72*

REYNOLDS, Jonathan (b 1942) American actor TW/24

REYNOLDS, Joseph (d 1887 [69]) actor EA/88*

REYNOLDS, Joseph (d 1917) musician EA/18*

REYNOLDS, Lydia (fl 1886) music-hall performer COC

REYNOLDS, Patrick J. (d 1972 [59]) director BP/57*

REYNOLDS, Mrs. R. G. see Reynolds, Emma

REYNOLDS, Robert (fl 1610-40) English actor COC, DA, OC/1-3

REYNOLDS, Thomas (d 1947 [67]) producer, director WWT/7-9

REYNOLDS, Tom (1866-1942) Eng-

lish actor, producer WWT/
4-9
REYNOLDS, Vera (d 1962 [61])
actress BE*
REYNOLDS, Walter (d 1941 [89])
dramatist, producer BE*,
WWT/14*
REYNOLDS, Mrs. Walter (d 1901)
EA/02*
REYNOLDS, Mrs. Walter see
Wallis, Ellen Lancaster
REYNOLDS, William (fl c. 1630)
actor DA
REYNOLDS, William H. (d 1863)
actor CDP, HAS
REYNOLDSON, T. H. (d 1883
[75]) dramatist, singer EA/84*
REYNOLDSON, T. H. (d 1888
[80]) actor, dramatist BE*,
WWT/14*
REYNOR, Tom (d 1893) musician,
singer, dancer EA/94*
REZENE, Mrs. Charles see
Cusick, Polly
REZZUTO, Tom (b 1929) Ameri-
can educator, designer, di-
rector BE
RHEA, Hortense (1844-99) Belgian
actress CDP, WWA/1
RHO, Stella (b 1886) English ac-
tress WWT/4-9
RHODES, Bill (d 1967 [72]) per-
former BP/52*
RHODES, Enoch (d 1880 [43])
actor EA/81*
RHODES, Erik (b 1906) American
actor, singer, director BE,
TW/9-15, 25, 27
RHODES, George Ambrose (fl
1806) dramatist CP/3
RHODES, Harrison (1871-1929)
American dramatist WWM,
WWT/4-6
RHODES, Helen (d 1936) French
singer WWW/3
RHODES, James (d 1904 [81])
proprietor EA/05*
RHODES, John (c. 1606-68?)
English bookseller, prompter,
manager COC, DA, NTH,
OC/1-3
RHODES, John (d 1850) proprietor
EA/72*
RHODES, Marie [Mrs. J. H.
Savile] (d 1891) actress EA/
92*
RHODES, Marjorie (b 1903) Eng-
lish actress WWT/10-16

RHODES, Percy William (d 1956
[85]) actor BE*, WWT/14*
RHODES, Pollie [Mrs. Arthur For-
rest] (d 1901 [43]) music-hall
singer EA/02*
RHODES, Raymond Crompton (1887-
1935) English critic, dramatist
WWT/6-7
RHODES, Richard (d 1668) English?
dramatist CP/1-3, DNB, GT
RHODES, Ruth (d 1975 [79]) per-
former BP/60*
RHODES, Thomas (fl 1789) drama-
tist CP/3
RHODES, Thomas Stanley (d 1911)
EA/12*
RHODES, William Barnes (1772-
1826) English dramatist CP/3,
DNB
RHYNSBURGER, H. Donovan (b
1903) American educator BE
RHYS, Horton see Price, Morton
RHYS, William (b 1945) American
actor TW/29-30
RHYS-JONES, Dilys see Watling,
Dilys
RIABOUCHINSKA, Tatiana (b 1916)
Russian dancer TW/2, WWT/
9-12
RIAL, Louise (d 1940 [90]) actress
BE*, BP/25*, WWT/14*
RIANO, Renie (d 1971) actress
TW/28
RIBAS, Mrs. (fl 1847) actress
HAS
RIBBON, Miss see Conduit,
Mrs. Mauvaise
RIBBON, William (d 1875 [29])
equestrian EA/77*
RIBMAN, Ronald (b 1932) American
dramatist CD, CH, WWT/15-16
RIBNER, Irving (1921-72) American
scholar BE
RICARD, Amy [Mrs. Lester Lon-
ergan] (b 1880) American ac-
tress WWM
RICARDEL, Molly (d 1963 [56])
dramatist, actress BE*
RICARDO, Henry (d 1886 [66])
acrobat, pantomimist EA/87*
RICCI, Nora (d 1976 [51]) per-
former BP/60*
RICCI, Rosalin (b 1948) American
actress TW/29
RICCOBONI, Antonio (fl 1675-95)
Italian actor OC/1-3
RICE, Alice Hegan [Mrs. Cale
Young Rice] (fl 1900s) American

dramatist WWM

RICE, Andy (d 1963 [82]) performer BE*

RICE, Cale Young (1872-1943) American dramatist WWA/2, WWM, WWW/4

RICE, Mrs. Cale Young see Rice, Alice Hegan

RICE, Charles (d 1880 [60]) actor, producer, manager BE*, EA/ 81*, WWT/14*

RICE, Mrs. Charles see Rice, Harriot

RICE, Charles P. (d 1944) dramatist SR

RICE, Charles William (d 1879) menagerie proprietor EA/80*

RICE, Cy (d 1971 [58]) writer BP/56*

RICE, Dan (d 1881) equestrian clown EA/82*

RICE, Dan (1822/23-1900) American clown, manager CDP, DAB, HAS, HJD, WWA/H

RICE, Decius (fl 1833) English actor HAS

RICE, Mrs. Dominic see Cuyler, Margaret

RICE, Edward Everett (1848-1924) American manager, dramatist, composer CDP, GRB/ 3-4, WWM, WWS, WWT/1-4

RICE, Elmer E. (1892-1967) American dramatist AAS, BE, CB, COC, ES, HJD, HP, MD, MH, MWD, NTH, OC/ 1-3, PDT, RE, SR, TW/23, WWA/4, WWT/4-14, WWW/6

RICE, Mrs. E. Roberts (d 1891) EA/92*

RICE, Fanny (d 1936 [77]) American actress BE*, BP/21*, WWT/14*

RICE, Felix (b 1946) American actor TW/25

RICE, Florence (d 1974 [67]) actress TW/30

RICE, Gitz (d 1947 [56]) songwriter TW/4

RICE, Harriot [Mrs. Charles Rice] (d 1887) EA/88*

RICE, John (b c. 1596) English actor COC, DA, GT, NTH, OC/1-3

RICE, John (d 1887) Negro comedian EA/88*

RICE, John B. (1809-74) American actor, manager CDP,

HAS, SR

RICE, Mrs. John B. [née Mary Ann Warren] (fl 1837-39) American actress HAS

RICE, J. R. (d 1860 [52]) performer EA/72*

RICE, Myron B. (b 1864) American manager WWS

RICE, Peter (b 1928) Indian/English designer AAS, ES, WWT/15-16

RICE, Roy (d 1966 [79]) performer BP/51*

RICE, Thomas Dartmouth (1808-60) American vaudevillian CDP, COC, HAS, HJD, OC/1-3, SR, WWA/H

RICE, Tim (b 1944) English lyricist CD, WWT/16

RICE, Vernon (d 1954 [46]) American editor TW/10

RICE-KNOX, Florence actress CDP

RICH, Charles J. (1855-1921) American manager BE*, BP/5*

RICH, Christopher (d 1714) English manager COC, DNB, NTH, OC/1-3

RICH, Doris (b 1905) American actress TW/4-7, 12, 21-23, 28

RICH, Eddie (b 1926) American producer BE

RICH, Helen (d 1963 [66]) performer BE*, BP/48*

RICH, Irene (b 1895) American actress TW/5-6

RICH, Isaac B. (1827-1908) American manager GRB/3-4, SR

RICH, J. C. actor, singer CDP

RICH, John (c. 1682-1761) English manager, actor CDP, COC, DNB, ES, GT, HP, OC/1-3, TD/1-2

RICH, Lillian (d 1954) actress BE*

RICH, Lucius C. [Bozo Kelly] (d 1975 [61]) performer BP/59*

RICH, Ron (b 1938) American actor TW/26

RICH, Roy (b 1909) English manager WWT/9-14

RICH, Sally see Jacobs, Sally

RICHARD, Charles (d 1888) singer EA/89*

RICHARD, Don (d 1967 [22]) performer BP/52*

RICHARD, George N. (b 1892) executive BE

RICHARD, Georges (d 1891 [60])

actor, producer, dramatist,
manager BE*, WWT/14*
RICHARD, Houston (d 1965 [79])
performer BP/50*
RICHARDS (fl 1777) dramatist
CP/2-3, GT
RICHARDS, Mr. actor CDP
RICHARDS, Mr. (fl 1794) Irish
actor HAS
RICHARDS, Mrs. [Mrs. Thomas
Greenhill] (d 1917) EA/18*
RICHARDS, Addison (d 1964 [61])
actor BE*
RICHARDS, Alfred Bate (1820-
76) English dramatist, producer
EA/69
RICHARDS, Angela (b 1944) ac-
tress WWT/16
RICHARDS, Archie (d 1901)
music-hall serio EA/02*
RICHARDS, Beah American ac-
tress BE, TW/24
RICHARDS, Brinley (d 1885 [66])
composer, musician EA/86*
RICHARDS, Cicely [Mrs. W. S.
Miln] (d 1933 [83]) English ac-
tress GRB/3-4, OAA/2,
WWT/1-7
RICHARDS, Davis (d 1867) Amer-
ican equestrian HAS
RICHARDS, Donald (1919-53)
American actor TW/3-7, 10,
WWA/3
RICHARDS, Elizabeth Rebecca
see Edwin, Elizabeth Rebecca
RICHARDS, Ernest H. (d 1917
[20]) EA/18*
RICHARDS, George (fl 1791-1804)
dramatist CP/3
RICHARDS, George (fl 1854)
comedian, minstrel CDP
RICHARDS, Gordon (1893-1964)
English actor TW/7
RICHARDS, Grant (d 1963 [47])
performer BP/48*
RICHARDS, Huston (d 1965 [79])
actor TW/22
RICHARDS, Janet (d 1909) EA/
10*
RICHARDS, Jean American ac-
tress TW/26
RICHARDS, Jennifer (b 1948)
American actress TW/29-30
RICHARDS, Jess (b 1943) Amer-
ican actor TW/28-29
RICHARDS, John (d 1810) scene
artist WWT/14*
RICHARDS, John Frederick (d

1884 [35]) music-hall performer
EA/85*
RICHARDS, Johnny (d 1968 [56])
composer/lyricist BP/53*
RICHARDS, Jon American actor
TW/27-29
RICHARDS, Kurt American actor
TW/2, 9
RICHARDS, Lex American actor
TW/4
RICHARDS, Lloyd Canadian director,
educator, actor BE, TW/14
RICHARDS, Louis Arthur (d 1906)
actor EA/07*
RICHARDS, Marie (d 1903 [60])
actress EA/04*
RICHARDS, Nathaniel (d 1652)
dramatist CP/1-3, DNB, FGF
RICHARDS, Neil A. (b 1879) Welsh
singer GRB/1
RICHARDS, Nellie actress, singer
CDP
RICHARDS, Paul (d 1974 [50]) per-
former BP/59*
RICHARDS, Paul (b 1934) American
actor TW/25-28
RICHARDS, Paul E. (b 1924) Amer-
ican actor TW/10-12, 15
RICHARDS, Penelope (b 1948) Amer-
ican actress TW/29
RICHARDS, Richard R. (d 1925
[52]) press representative BE*,
BP/9*
RICHARDS, Sam (fl 1902?) song
composer CDP
RICHARDS, Susan (b 1898) Welsh
actress WWT/10-14
RICHARDS, Thomas (fl 1560?)
dramatist FGF
RICHARDS, Tom (d 1893) song-
writer EA/94*
RICHARDSON, Mr. (fl 1790) English
actor, singer CDP, TD/1-2
RICHARDSON, Mr. ["Penny Show-
man"] (d 1836) American actor
CDP, HAS
RICHARDSON, Mr. (d 1856) actor,
property man HAS
RICHARDSON, Miss (fl 1852) ac-
tress HAS
RICHARDSON, Miss see Vickery,
Mrs. J. G.
RICHARDSON, Annie [née Merriton]
(d 1868 [30]) actress? EA/69*
RICHARDSON, Mrs. Augustus see
Chapman, Elizabeth
RICHARDSON, Bella (d 1910 [56])
actress EA/11*

RICHARDSON, Billy (d 1913)
EA/14*
RICHARDSON, Mrs. Billy see
Richardson, Mary
RICHARDSON, Dorothy (d 1955)
American press representative
WWA/3
RICHARDSON, Elizabeth (d 1779)
dramatist CP/2-3, GT, TD/
1-2
RICHARDSON, Elizabeth (1813-
53) American singer, actress
HAS
RICHARDSON, Ernest (d 1917
[24]) EA/18*
RICHARDSON, Foster (d 1942
[52]) singer WWW/4
RICHARDSON, Frank (1871-1917)
English dramatist, critic
GRB/4, WWT/1-3
RICHARDSON, Frankie (d 1962
[63]) performer BE*
RICHARDSON, Mrs. F. R. Gwyn
see Harlington, Grace
RICHARDSON, Gwyn (b 1879)
English actor GRB/1
RICHARDSON, Harry (d 1910)
actor EA/12*
RICHARDSON, Mrs. Harry see
Richardson, Minnie
RICHARDSON, Henry Royston
(d 1873) circus manager EA/
74*
RICHARDSON, Howard (b 1917)
American dramatist, actor,
director, educator, producer
BE, MH
RICHARDSON, Ian (b 1934) Scot-
tish actor AAS, WWT/14-16
RICHARDSON, Jack (b 1935)
American dramatist, critic
BE, CD, CH, ES, MD, MH,
MWD, RE
RICHARDSON, John (d 1837 [76])
showman CDP
RICHARDSON, John (d 1889 [34])
musician EA/90*
RICHARDSON, Joseph (c. 1756-
1803) English dramatist CDP,
CP/3, GT, TD/1-2
RICHARDSON, Joseph (d 1862)
musician EA/72*
RICHARDSON, Mrs. Joseph
patentee, dramatist CP/3
RICHARDSON, Mrs. L. A. [née
Madeleine Percy] (d 1870)
actress EA/71*
RICHARDSON, Leander (1856-

1918) American dramatist, jour-
nalist GRB/3-4, WWM, WWT/
1-3
RICHARDSON, Leander B. (d 1852)
comedian HAS
RICHARDSON, Lee (b 1926) Amer-
ican actor BE
RICHARDSON, Mary [Mrs. Billy
Richardson] (d 1882) EA/83*
RICHARDSON, Minnie [Mrs. Harry
Richardson] (d 1916) EA/18*
RICHARDSON, Myrtle English ac-
tress WWT/9-10
RICHARDSON, Nell [Mrs. T. G.
King] (d 1908) actress, singer
EA/09*
RICHARDSON, Sir Ralph David
(b 1902) English actor AAS,
BE, CB, COC, ES, OC/1-3,
PDT, TW/2-17, 27, WWT/7-16
RICHARDSON, Susanna see
Collis, Mrs. [Francis?]
RICHARDSON, Tony (b 1928) Eng-
lish director, producer AAS,
BE, CB, COC, ES, PDT,
WWT/13-16
RICHARDSON, W. E. actor EA/97
RICHARDSON, Wells American ac-
tor TW/11-14
RICHARDSON, William (1743-1814)
Scottish dramatist, writer
CDP, CP/3
RICHARDSON, William (d 1890
[56]) EA/91*
RICHARDSON, William Thomas (d
1896 [53]) comedian EA/97*
RICHEPIN, Jean (1849-1926) Al-
gerian/French dramatist GRB/
1-4, WWT/1
RICHEUX, Jules (d 1911) lessee
EA/12*
RICHINGS, Caroline Mary (d 1882)
English pianist, actress, mana-
ger HAS
RICHINGS, Peter (1797/98-1871)
English singer, dancer, mana-
ger, actor CDP, DAB, HAS,
SR, WWA/H
RICHINGS-BERNARD, Caroline (d
1882) musician, singer CDP
RICHMAN, Arthur (1886-1944)
American dramatist NTH, SR,
WWA/2, WWT/5-9
RICHMAN, Charles J. (1870-1940)
American actor CB, GRB/2-4,
WWM, WWS, WWT/1-9
RICHMAN, Harry (1895-1972)
American actor, singer BE,

TW/29, WWT/7-11
RICHMAN, Henry John (d 1868
[39]) music-hall performer?
EA/69*
RICHMAN, Lou (d 1970 [84])
performer BP/55*
RICHMAN, Mark (b 1927) Amer-
ican actor BE, TW/10-12
RICHMOND, Mrs. (d 1883) EA/
85*
RICHMOND, Adah actress, singer
CDP
RICHMOND, Harry G. (d 1885)
actor, dancer, singer CDP
RICHMOND, Henry (d 1902) ac-
tor EA/03*
RICHMOND, Mrs. James see
Richmond, Winifred
RICHMOND, Jane (d 1962 [47])
performer BP/47*
RICHMOND, Lizzie see Col-
son, Lizzie
RICHMOND, Susan (1894-1959)
English actress WWT/8-12
RICHMOND, Winifred [Mrs.
James Richmond] (d 1881)
EA/82*
RICHMOND SISTERS dancers,
singers CDP
RICHTER, George (d 1905 [48])
EA/06*
RICHTER, Hans (1843-1916)
Austrian conductor ES
RICHTER, Hans (d 1976 [87])
producer/director/choreographer
BP/60*
RICKARD, Al (d 1962 [69]) talent
representative, performer BE*
RICKARD, Ellen (d 1917) EA/
18*
RICKARDS, Harry (d 1911 [63])
manager, singer CDP, GRB/
2-3
RICKARDS, J. H. (fl 1857) actor
CDP
RICKARDS, W. E. (d 1879 [50])
music-hall proprietor EA/80*
RICKER, Elswyth Thane see
Thane, Elswyth
RICKETS, J. (fl 1570?) drama-
tist FGF
RICKETTS, Arthur (b 1845)
American actor GRB/1
RICKETTS, Charles (1866-1931)
Swiss/English designer OC/
2-3, WWT/6
RICKETTS, Harry (d 1896 [45])
pantomimist EA/97*

RICKETTS, John (d 1873 [43]) pan-
tomimist EA/74*
RICKETTS, John (d 1899 [61]) the-
atre chairman EA/00*
RICKETTS, John Bill (fl 1793) cir-
cus manager & proprietor CDP
RICKETTS, Richard (d 1883 [29])
pantomimist EA/84*
RICKETTS, Mrs. Samuel see
Allingham, Maria Caroline
RICKS, James (d 1974 [49]) per-
former BP/59*
RICKS, Nellie [Mrs. Pat J. Ricks]
(d 1898 [31]) EA/99*
RICKS, Mrs. Pat J. see Ricks,
Nellie
RICKS, William R. (d 1880) treas-
urer EA/81*
RIDDELL, George (d 1944 [80])
actor BE*, WWT/14*
RIDDICK, Margaret see Bennett,
Faith
RIDDLE, Miss see Sedley-Smith,
Mrs. William Henry
RIDDLE, Cordelia (fl 1834) actress
HAS
RIDDLE, Eliza (fl 1835) American
actress HAS
RIDDLE, Fred (d 1892 [52]) con-
ductor, musician EA/93*
RIDDLE, George (1851/53-1910)
American actor, reader CDP,
DAB, PP/3
RIDDLE, George (b 1937) American
actor TW/25
RIDEOUT, Percy Rodney (1862-
1956) English composer WWW/5
RIDER, William (fl 1613) dramatist
CP/1-3, FGF
RIDER-KELSEY, Corinne (b 1881)
American singer WWM
RIDER-NOBLE, Mrs. Charles
see Belton, Phoebe
RIDGELY, John (d 1968 [59]) per-
former BP/52*
RIDGES, Stanley (d 1951 [59]) Eng-
lish actor TW/7
RIDGEWAY, Peter (d 1938 [44])
actor, producer BE*, WWT/14*
RIDGEWAY, Philip (1891-1954)
English producing manager
WWT/6-7
RIDGEWAY, Philip (b 1920) English
press-representative, producer,
writer WWT/12-14
RIDGEWELL, Audrey (d 1968 [64])
performer BP/53*
RIDGLEY, Cleo (d 1962 [68]) ac-

tress BE*
RIDGWAY, Charles (d 1893 [82])
actor CDP
RIDGWAY, Mrs. Charles (d 1881
[62]) EA/83*
RIDGWAY, Mrs. Charles see
Ridgway, Elizabeth
RIDGWAY, Elizabeth [Mrs. Charles
Ridgway] (d 1897) EA/98*
RIDGWAY, Graziella (fl 1872?)
singer CDP
RIDGWAY, John (d 1907 [62])
EA/08*
RIDGWAY, Nellie (d 1904 [51])
music-hall performer EA/05*
RIDGWAY, T. (fl 1829?) actor
CDP
RIDGWAY, Thomas (d 1880 [37])
acrobat EA/81*
RIDGWELL, Charles (d 1916)
writer EA/17*
RIDICULOUS THEATRE CO.
theatre collective CD
RIDINGS, Mrs. H. J. see
Lackaye, Helene
RIDLER, Anne (b 1912) English
dramatist CD
RIDLEY, Arnold (b 1896) English
dramatist WWT/6-16
RIDLEY, Elizabeth see Bowtell,
Mrs. Barnaby
RIDLEY, Dr. Gloster (1702-74)
English dramatist CP/2-3
RIDLEY, Mrs. James see Rid-
ley, Mary Ann
RIDLEY, John (d 1899) comedian
EA/00*
RIDLEY, Joseph (d 1868) acrobat
EA/69*
RIDLEY, Mary Ann [Mrs. James
Ridley] (d 1882) EA/83*
RIDOUT, Mr. (d c. 1760/61) actor
TD/2
RIDYARD, William Henry (d 1879
[45]) comedian EA/80*
RIEDEL, Karl Heinrich (1879-
1946) Austrian conductor
WWA/2
RIEGER, W. H. songwriter CDP
RIESENFELD, Hugo (1884/85-
1939) Austrian conductor,
composer WWA/1, WWW/3
RIETTI, Victor (1888-1963)
Italian actor, producer, trans-
lator WWT/12-13
RIETTY, Robert (b 1923) English
actor, dramatist, translator,
director WWT/11-16

RIFFE, Bessie Tons (d 1976 [93])
wardrobe mistress BP/60*
RIFKIN, Ron (b 1939) American
actor TW/28
RIGA, Nadine (d 1968 [59]) per-
former BP/53*
RIGAUT, Mme. (d 1883 [86]) singer
EA/84*
RIGBY, Mr. (fl 1752-53) English?
actor HAS
RIGBY, Mrs. (fl 1752-53) English?
actress HAS
RIGBY, Arthur [Arthur Watson
Lloyd] (d 1894 [36]) actor EA/
96*
RIGBY, Arthur [William Turner]
(1870-1944) English dramatist,
actor, singer WWT/8-9
RIGBY, Arthur, Jr. [Arthur Turn-
er] (1900-71) English actor
WWT/8-16
RIGBY, Edward [Edward Coke]
(1879-1951) English actor GRB/
1-4, WWT/4-11
RIGBY, Frank J. (d 1963 [100])
musician BE*
RIGBY, Lionel (d 1891) actor EA/
92*
RIGDEN, Maud [Mrs. Sydney L.
Hallows] (d 1904) EA/05*
RIGER, John (d 1874 [40]) profes-
sor of music EA/75*
RIGG, Diana (b 1938) English ac-
tress AAS, CB, WWT/14-16
RIGGS, Elizabeth see Brent,
Evelyn
RIGGS, Mrs. George C. see
Wiggin, Kate Douglas
RIGGS, Glenn E. (d 1975 [68])
performer BP/60*
RIGGS, Katherine Witchie (d 1967
[80]) dancer, vaudevillian TW/
23
RIGGS, Lynn (1899-1954) American
dramatist AAS, HJD, MD,
MH, MWD, NTH, TW/11,
WWT/9-11
RIGGS, Ralph (d 1951 [66]) Ameri-
can actor, singer, dancer TW/8
RIGGS, Thomas Grattan (1835-99)
American actor CDP, HAS
RIGGS, Mrs. Thomas Grattan (fl
1866?) actress CDP
RIGHTON, Edward ["Corrie Burns"]
(1838-99) English actor, drama-
tist CDP, DP, HAS, OAA/2,
WWW/1
RIGHTON, J. H. (d 1873) musician

EA/74*
RIGHTON, Mary (d 1913) EA/14*
RIGL, Emily (fl 1866) actress,
    dancer CDP
RIGNALL, Lionel see Rignold,
    Lionel
RIGNALL, Walter Lionel see
    Rignold, Walter Lionel
RIGNOLD, Emily (d 1913) EA/14*
RIGNOLD, George (d 1912 [76])
    English actor, manager CDP,
    GRB/3-4, OAA/2, WWT/1
RIGNOLD, Mrs. George see
    Henderson, Marie
RIGNOLD, Henry (1813?-73)
    actor CDP
RIGNOLD, Kate [Mrs. Caroline
    Mary Hayward] (d 1897) EA/
    98*
RIGNOLD, Lilian [Mrs. James
    Salter] (b 1883) English ac-
    tress GRB/1
RIGNOLD, Lionel [Lionel Rignall]
    (d 1919 [69]) English actor
    DP, EA/95, GRB/1-4, WWT/
    1-3
RIGNOLD, Mrs. Lionel see
    Daltra, Marie
RIGNOLD, Marie see Daltra,
    Marie
RIGNOLD, Patience Blaxland (d
    1888 [88]) actress EA/89*
RIGNOLD, Stanley (1868-1943)
    actor SR
RIGNOLD, Susan (d 1895) actress
    OAA/2
RIGNOLD, Walter Lionel [Rignall]
    (b 1875) English actor GRB/
    1-2
RIGNOLD, William (d 1904 [68])
    actor BE*, EA/06*, WWT/14*
RIGNOLD, William Henry Rignall
    (1836/38-1910) English actor
    DP, OAA/2
RIGNOLD, William Ross (d 1883
    [79]) actor EA/85*
RIKER, Franklin Wing (1876-
    1958) American singer WWA/
    3, WWM
RILEY, Ed (b 1933) American
    actor TW/25-26
RILEY, Edna Goldsmith (d 1962
    [82]) dramatist BE*
RILEY, Eliza [Mrs. H. Hessle-
    grave] (d 1899) EA/00*
RILEY, Fanny L. see Goodall,
    Mrs. William R.
RILEY, Fred (d 1909 [55]) music-

hall singer EA/10*
RILEY, George (d 1972 [72]) per-
    former BP/57*
RILEY, Henry D. (d 1970 [71])
    circus agent BP/55*
RILEY, Henry J. (1801-41) English
    actor HAS, SR
RILEY, James (d 1869 [52]) EA/
    70*
RILEY, Janet (b 1930) American
    actress TW/11-12
RILEY, John (d 1897 [47]) manager
    EA/98*
RILEY, Lawrence (1891-1975)
    American dramatist BE
RILEY, Madeline Lucette see
    Ryley, Madeleine Lucette
RILEY, Pat (d 1894 [37]) Irish
    comedian, dancer EA/95*
RILEY, Ritter William (d 1904
    [31]) actor EA/05*
RILEY, Thomas see Peel, Tom-
    my
RILEY, W. H. (1833-67) American
    actor HAS
RILEY, Mrs. W. H. [née Katie
    L. Woodbury] (fl 1856) actress
    HAS
RILEY, William (d 1897 [52])
    manager, music-hall singer
    CDP
RILL, Eli (b 1926) American actor,
    director, dramatist BE
RILLEY, James (b 1947) American
    actor TW/27
RIMBAULT (d 1890) assistant stage
    manager EA/91*
RIMBAULT, Dr. E. F. (d 1876
    [60]) antiquarian EA/77*
RIMINI, Giacomo (d 1952) Italian
    singer WWA/3
RIMMA, Fritz (d 1904 [44]) actor
    EA/05*, WWT/14*
RINALDI, Joy American actress
    TW/25, 30
RINALDINI, Sig. (d 1875) singer
    EA/76*
RINALDO, Mrs. Nicholas see
    Dale, Margie
RIND, Kathleen English actress
    GRB/1-2
RINDLER, Milton (b 1898) Ameri-
    can accountant, treasurer BE
RINEHART, Mary Roberts (1876-
    1958) American dramatist
    MWD, NTH, WWA/3, WWM,
    WWT/4-11
RING, Barbara T. (1879-1941)

dramatist CB
RING, Blanche [Mrs. Frederick
E. McKay] (1877-1961) American actress, singer GRB/
2-4, SR, TW/2-3, 5-7, 17,
WWA/4, WWS, WWT/1-11
RING, Cyril (d 1967 [74]) performer BP/52*
RING, Frances [Mrs. Thomas
Meighan] (1882-1951) American
actress GRB/3-4, TW/7,
WWM, WWS, WWT/1-7
RING, James H. (fl 1848) English
actor HAS
RINGGOLD, Benjamin T. (b 1835)
American actor PP/3
RINGLE, Dave (d 1965 [71]) composer/lyricist BP/50*
RINGLING, Albert (1858-1916)
American circus proprietor
ES
RINGLING, Alfred (1861-1919)
American circus proprietor
ES
RINGLING, August (d 1918) American circus proprietor ES
RINGLING, Charles (1863-1926)
American circus proprietor
ES, WWA/H, 4
RINGLING, Henry (d 1918) American circus proprietor ES
RINGLING, John (1866-1936)
American circus proprietor
ES, WWA/1
RINGLING, Otto (1851-1911)
actor, circus manager ES,
SR
RINGLING, Robert E. (1897-1950)
American circus executive,
singer CB, WWA/2
RINGLING BROTHERS circus
managers SR
RIORDAN, Naomi (b 1926) American actress TW/6-7
RIOS, Lalo (d 1973 [46]) performer BP/57*
"RIP" [George Thenon] (d 1941)
revue author WWT/14*
RIPLEY, Gladys (1908-55) singer
WWW/5
RIPLEY, Patricia see Ripley,
Trescott
RIPLEY, Trescott [Patricia]
(b 1926) American actress
BE, TW/22-23
RIPMAN, Pamela Penelope see
Jenner, Caryl
RIPON, George (d 1908) actor,

singer CDP
RIPON, Mrs. George [Elizabeth
Collins] (d 1883) EA/84*
RIPON, John Scott see Byerley,
John Scott
RIPPON, Mrs. S. A. (d 1892)
EA/93*
RISCOE, Arthur (1896-1954) English
actor WWT/7-11
RISDON, Elizabeth (1887-1958)
English actress TW/15, WWT/
6-10
RISKIN, Robert (1897-1955) American dramatist ES
RISLEY, Prof. (d 1874) manager,
athlete, musician CDP
RISLEY, Miss L. (d 1892) singer
EA/93*
RISQUE, W. H. (d 1916) librettist,
lyricist BE*, EA/17*, WWT/
14*
RISS, Dan (d 1970 [60]) performer
BP/55*
RISTORI, Adelaide (1822-1906)
Italian actress CDP, COC,
ES, HAS, NTH, OC/1-3, SR,
WWW/1
RITCHARD, Cyril (1898-1977)
Australian actor, director AAS,
BE, CB, TW/5-22, 25, 28-29,
WWT/6-16
RITCHER, Rene see Collier,
Patience
RITCHEY, Buck (d 1973 [58]) composer/lyricist BP/58*
RITCHIE, Mrs. see Mowatt,
Anna Cora
RITCHIE, Adele (1874-1930) American actress, singer GRB/3-4,
SR, WWA/1, WWM, WWS,
WWT/1-6
RITCHIE, Alice Jane (d 1893) EA/
94*
RITCHIE, Camilla (b 1945) American actress TW/26
RITCHIE, Carl (d 1974 [64]) performer BP/58*
RITCHIE, Estelle American actress
TW/15
RITCHIE, June actress WWT/16
RITCHIE, Robert (d 1912 [24])
EA/13*
RITCHIE, Mrs. W. E. (d 1901
[21]) EA/02*
RITELLI, Harry (d 1901 [59]) pantomimist EA/03*
RITMAN, William designer WWT/
16

RITT, Martin (b 1920) American
actor, director BE, ES
RITTENBERG, Arnold (d 1974
[78]) showman BP/58*
RITTENBERG, Barbara (d 1973
[42]) dramatist BP/58*
RITTENHOUSE, David (fl 1798?)
dramatist EAP, RJ
RITTENHOUSE, Florence (d 1929
[35]) American actress BE*,
BP/13*
RITTENHOUSE, Mae (d 1972 [88])
performer BP/57*
RITTER, Blake (d 1973 [58])
singer, actress TW/30
RITTER, John P. (d 1920 [62])
dramatist BE*, BP/5*
RITTER, Kathryn (b 1948) Amer-
ican actress TW/30
RITTER, Tex (d 1974 [67]) per-
former BP/58*
RITTER, Thelma (1905-1969)
American actress BE, CB,
TW/22, 25, WWA/5
RITTER, Theodore (1841-86) mu-
sician CDP
RITTMAN, Trude German com-
poser BE
RITWISE, John (fl 1507-22) Eng-
lish dramatist CP/2-3
RITZ, Al (d 1965 [62]) comedian
TW/22
RIVALLI [John Watkins] (d 1900)
"The Fire Prince" EA/01*
RIVE, Caroline (d 1882 [60])
singer CDP
RIVE-KING, Julie (b 1857) musi-
cian, composer CDP
RIVERA, Chita [née Concita del
Rivero] (b 1933/34) American
actress, singer, dancer AAS,
BE, TW/21-22, WWT/14-16
RIVERO, Julian (d 1976 [85])
performer BP/60*
RIVERS, Mr. (fl 1635) dramatist
CP/1-3, FGF
RIVERS, Mr. (d 1889) EA/90*
RIVERS, Mrs. see Barnett,
Mrs. Giles Linnett
RIVERS, Miss (fl 1827) actress
HAS
RIVERS, Albert singer CDP
RIVERS, Alfred (d 1955 [88])
actor BE*, WWT/14*
RIVERS, Basil George (d 1870
[54]) actor EA/71*
RIVERS, Harry (fl 1862) Ameri-
can actor, singer CDP, HAS

RIVERS, Henry (d 1901 [82]) actor
EA/03*
RIVERS, Mrs. Henry see Mor-
elli, Fanny
RIVERS, Joan (b 1935?) American
comedienne CB
RIVERS, Laurence see Stebbins,
Rowland
RIVERS, Pamela (b 1926) American
actress TW/2
RIVERS, R. (d 1889 [22]) advance
agent EA/90*
RIVES, Amélie (1863-1945) Amer-
ican dramatist HJD, WWW/4
RIVIERE, Anna see Bishop,
Anna
RIVINGTON, Reginald (b 1869)
English actor GRB/3-4
RIX, Brian (b 1924) English actor,
manager WWT/12-16
RIX, John [Charles Clements] (d
1874 [28]) comic singer EA/75*
RIZARELI, Virginia [Virginia Bur-
goyne] (d 1891 [26]) EA/93*
ROACH, James Conner actor CDP
ROACH, Thomas A. (d 1962 [51])
performer BE*
ROACHE, Viola (1885-1961) English
actress TW/1-7, 12-17, WWT/
9-13
ROAD, Michael (b 1915) American
actor TW/3
ROBARDS, Jason, Sr. (d 1963
[70]) American actor TW/19
ROBARDS, Jason, Jr. (b 1922)
American actor AAS, BE,
CB, ES, TW/13-22, 25, 28,
WWT/13-16
ROBARTS, Mrs. Carl see Bra-
ham, Amelia Georgina
ROBB, Helen Lowell see Lowell,
Helen
ROBB, Lotus (d 1969) actress
TW/1, 26
ROBB, Miriam G. [née Goodenow]
(d 1856) performer CDP, HAS
ROBBINS, Alfred Edward see
Northway, Alfred
ROBBINS, Sir Alfred Farthing
(1856-1931) English dramatist,
critic GRB/2-4, WWT/1-6
ROBBINS, Archie (d 1975 [62])
performer BP/60*
ROBBINS, Carrie Fishbein (b 1943)
American costume designer
WWT/16
ROBBINS, Edward E. (b 1930)
American talent representative

BE
ROBBINS, Herbert (d 1918) EA/
18*
ROBBINS, Jane Kiser (d 1974
[53]) performer BP/59*
ROBBINS, Jane Marla (b 1943)
American actress TW/24-25
ROBBINS, Jerome (b 1918) American director, choreographer,
dancer AAS, BE, CB, ES,
NTH, PDT, TW/2-8, WWT/
13-16
ROBBINS, Marla Jane (b 1944)
American actress TW/30
ROBBINS, Rex (b 1939) American
actor TW/26-27, 29
ROBBINS, Richard (d 1969 [50])
actor TW/26
ROBBINS, Rose J. [Mrs. Wal
Rose] (d 1908) EA/09*
ROBBINS, Mrs. Wal see Robbins, Rose J.
ROBE, Annie (d 1922) actress
BE*, WWT/14*
ROBE, [Miss?] J. (fl 1723) dramatist CP/2-3, GT
ROBE, James Banks (d 1880
[38]) scene artist EA/81*
ROBER, Richard (1906-52) American actor TW/1-3, 8
ROBERDEAU, John Peter (d 1815
[60]) dramatist CP/3
ROBERT, Eugene (b 1877) Hungarian producer, manager
WWT/9
ROBERT-HOUDIN, Jean Eugène
(1805-71) magician CDP
ROBERTI, Lyda (1909-38) Polish
actress WWT/8
ROBERTS, Mr. (fl 1767) actor
HAS
ROBERTS, Miss see Bernard,
Mrs. John, I
ROBERTS, Anthony (b 1939)
American actor TW/23-27
ROBERTS, Arthur (1852-1933)
English actor CDP, COC,
DP, ES, GRB/1-4, OC/1-3,
WWS, WWT/1-7, WWW/3
ROBERTS, Arthur (b 1938) American actor TW/26, 28-29
ROBERTS, Beverly (b 1914/17)
American actress, director,
executive BE, TW/1
ROBERTS, Carrie (d 1895) seriocomic EA/96*
ROBERTS, Charles (d 1869)
actor? EA/70*

ROBERTS, Charles (d 1897) agent
EA/98*
ROBERTS, Clara Lemore see
Lemore, Clara
ROBERTS, Cledge (d 1957 [52])
actor, director TW/13
ROBERTS, David (d 1864 [68])
scene artist EA/72*, WWT/14*
ROBERTS, Davis (b 1917) American actor TW/27-28
ROBERTS, Dennis (b 1950) American actor TW/29
ROBERTS, Doris (b 1930) American
actress TW/26-27, 29-30,
WWT/16
ROBERTS, Edward Barry (d 1972
[71]) performer BP/57*
ROBERTS, Ellis (d 1873) musician
EA/74*
ROBERTS, Mrs. Ellis see
Roberts, Isabel
ROBERTS, Evelyn (1886-1962) English actor WWT/7-13
ROBERTS, Ewan (b 1914) Scottish
actor WWT/11-16
ROBERTS, Florence [Mrs. Frederick Vogeling] (d 1927 [56])
American actress BE*, BP/
12*, WWT/14*
ROBERTS, Florence [Mrs. Lewis
Morrison] (1871-1940) American
actress CB, GRB/3-4, WWA/
1, WWM, WWS, WWT/1-5
ROBERTS, Florence Smythe (d
1925 [47]) actress BE*
ROBERTS, Frank (d 1907 [58])
American actor GRB/3*
ROBERTS, Mrs. Franklyn see
Wainright, Marie
ROBERTS, George [Robert Walters]
(b 1832) English dramatist EA/
69
ROBERTS, Hans (d 1954 [80]) actor
TW/10
ROBERTS, H. R. Indian/English
actor GRB/2
ROBERTS, Isabel [Mrs. Ellis
Roberts] (d 1868 [41]) EA/69*
ROBERTS, Jack (d 1899 [25])
EA/01*
ROBERTS, James (fl 1564-1606)
printer DNB
ROBERTS, James (fl 1794) dramatist CP/3
ROBERTS, James (1798/99-1833)
Scottish actor, circus performer
CDP, HAS
ROBERTS, James (d 1892 [56])

scene artist EA/93*
ROBERTS, James Booth (1815/
18-1901) American actor
CDP, HAS, PP/3
ROBERTS, J. H. (fl 1867) English
comedian, minstrel HAS
ROBERTS, J. H. (1884-1961)
English actor WWT/4-13
ROBERTS, Jimmy (d 1962 [60])
American performer BE*
ROBERTS, Joan (b 1918/20/22)
American actress, singer BE,
TW/2-5, WWT/10-12
ROBERTS, John (1916-72) English
producing manager, actor
WWT/15-16
ROBERTS, Joseph L. (d 1970
[61]) public relations BP/54*
ROBERTS, J. St. Clair see
Bayfield, St. Clair
ROBERTS, Marilyn (b 1939)
American actress TW/24-26
ROBERTS, Mark (b 1921) Amer-
ican actor TW/8-9
ROBERTS, Meade (b 1930)
American dramatist BE
ROBERTS, Morley (1857-1942)
English dramatist WWW/4
ROBERTS, Nancy (d 1962 [70])
actress BE*
ROBERTS, N. D. manager CDP
ROBERTS, Owen (d 1911 [52])
singer EA/12*
ROBERTS, Paddy (d 1975 [65])
composer/lyricist BP/60*
ROBERTS, Peter editor AAS
ROBERTS, R. (d 1873) comedian
EA/74*
ROBERTS, Miss R. (fl 1779)
dramatist CP/2-3
ROBERTS, R. A. (b 1870) Eng-
lish actor GRB/1-3, WWM
ROBERTS, Rachel (b 1927)
Welsh actress AAS, ES,
TW/30, WWT/14-16
ROBERTS, Ralph (d 1944 [75])
Indian/English actor WWT/
8-9
ROBERTS, Ralph (b 1918) Amer-
ican actor TW/4-16, 20,
28-29
ROBERTS, Mrs. Ralph see
Caryllon, Ethel L.
ROBERTS, Sir Randall (d 1899
[62]) actor, producer, drama-
tist BE*, EA/00*, WWT/14*
ROBERTS, R. J. (d 1884 [34])
comedian EA/85*

ROBERTS, Robert (d 1888) minstrel
EA/89*
ROBERTS, Rose [Mrs. Louis Cal-
vert] English actress EA/96,
GRB/1-3
ROBERTS, Roy (d 1975 [69]) per-
former BP/60*
ROBERTS, Sara [Sara Lacy; Mrs.
Valentine Roberts] (d 1881 [59])
EA/82*
ROBERTS, Sarah [Sarah Prestbury]
(d 1873) actress, singer EA/75*
ROBERTS, Sara Jane (d 1968 [44])
performer BP/53*
ROBERTS, Stephen (b 1917) Amer-
ican actor TW/3
ROBERTS, Theodore (1861-1928)
American actor DAB, GRB/4,
WWA/1, WWS, WWT/1-5
ROBERTS, Thomas (d 1876 [44])
acting manager EA/77*
ROBERTS, Mrs. Thomas see
Isaacs, Rebecca
ROBERTS, T. M. (d 1885 [75])
scene artist EA/86*
ROBERTS, Tony (b 1939) American
actor TW/28-29, WWT/16
ROBERTS, Mrs. Valentine see
Roberts, Sara
ROBERTS, Vera Mowry (b 1918)
American educator, director
BE
ROBERTS, Wallace (d 1890) mana-
ger EA/91*
ROBERTS, Walter (d 1917 [83])
EA/18*
ROBERTS, William (fl 1770-82)
dramatist CP/3
ROBERTS, William (fl 1791) dram-
atist CP/3
ROBERTS, William (d 1888) acting
manager EA/89*
ROBERTSHAW, Jerrold (1866-1941)
English actor GRB/1-4, WWT/
1-9
ROBERTSON, Mr. (fl 1778-90)
dramatist CP/3
ROBERTSON, Mrs. (fl 1800) ac-
tress, dramatist CP/3
ROBERTSON, Miss actress HAS
ROBERTSON, Agnes Kelly see
Boucicault, Mrs. Dion
ROBERTSON, Alex (d 1964 [64])
Scottish dramatist BE*, BP/49*
ROBERTSON, Alexander (d 1885
[20]) scene artist EA/86*
ROBERTSON, Mrs. Brougham [née
Tanner] (1820-65) English ac-

tress, manager CDP, HAS
ROBERTSON, Cliff (b 1925)
American actor, director BE,
CB, ES, TW/11-16
ROBERTSON, Craven (d 1879
[33]) actor, manager EA/80*,
WWT/14*
ROBERTSON, Donald (1860-1926)
Scottish actor SR, WWA/1,
WWM, WWS
ROBERTSON, E. [Mrs. W.
Robertson] (d 1876) EA/78*
ROBERTSON, East (d 1916) ac-
tress BE*, WWT/14*
ROBERTSON, Edward Shafto (d
1871 [27]) actor EA/72*
ROBERTSON, E. T. (d 1890
[30]) EA/91*
ROBERTSON, G. Douglas see
Douglas, G. R.
ROBERTSON, Guy (b 1892) Amer-
ican actor, singer TW/2-3,
6-7, WWT/7-11
ROBERTSON, Hamish (b 1943)
Scottish actor TW/28
ROBERTSON, Cpt. Henry (d
1885) EA/86*
ROBERTSON, Hermine (d 1962
[61]) actress BE*
ROBERTSON, Hopkins (d 1819
[40]) actor HAS
ROBERTSON, Ian [Ian Forbes-
Robertson] (1858-1936) English
actor, stage manager GRB/
3-4, OC/1-3, WWT/1-8
ROBERTSON, Jack [J. G.] Peru-
vian/English actor, singer
GRB/1-3
ROBERTSON, James (1714-95)
actor CDP
ROBERTSON, Jane (b 1948)
American actress TW/27-28
ROBERTSON, Jerome (d 1962
[62]) performer BE*
ROBERTSON, J. G. see Robert-
son, Jack
ROBERTSON, John (d 1908 [46])
variety agent EA/09*
ROBERTSON, John (d 1962 [35])
scene designer BE*
ROBERTSON, John S. (b 1878)
Canadian actor ES
ROBERTSON, Johnston Forbes
see Forbes-Robertson, Johnston
ROBERTSON, John Wylie see
Watson, Wylie
ROBERTSON, Kate (d 1868) lessee
EA/69*

ROBERTSON, Mrs. Lionel [née
Edith Tinsley] (d 1876) EA/77*
ROBERTSON, Louisa see Dorn-
ton, Louisa
ROBERTSON, Malcolm (b 1933)
Australian director, actor
WWT/16
ROBERTSON, Margaret see
Kendal, Mrs.
ROBERTSON, Maria (d 1892 [91])
EA/93*
ROBERTSON, Marie [Mrs. Fred
Owen] (d 1889 [26]) actress
EA/90*
ROBERTSON, Marjorie see
Neagle, Anna
ROBERTSON, Maud (d 1930) actress
BE*, WWT/14*
ROBERTSON, Orie O. (d 1964 [83])
actor, stunt man BE*
ROBERTSON, Pax (d 1948) actress,
director BE*, WWT/14*
ROBERTSON, Peter (1847-1911)
Scottish dramatist, critic WWA/
1, WWM
ROBERTSON, Robert [Patrick
Robert Macallan] (d 1894 [49])
actor EA/95*
ROBERTSON, Mrs. T. (fl 1796)
dramatist CP/3
ROBERTSON, Mrs. Thomas (d 1855
[87]) actress, producer BE*,
WWT/14*
ROBERTSON, Thomas William
(1829-71) English dramatist,
actor CDP, COC, DNB, EA/
68, ES, HP, MH, NTH, OC/1-3,
PDT
ROBERTSON, Thomas William
Shafto (d 1895 [37]) actor, pro-
ducer, manager BE*, EA/96*,
WWT/14*
ROBERTSON, Toby (b 1928) English
director AAS, WWT/15-16
ROBERTSON, Tom (d 1916) EA/17*
ROBERTSON, Mrs. T. W. see
Rodwell, Mrs. John
ROBERTSON, W. (d 1836) American
actor HAS
ROBERTSON, Mrs. W. see
Robertson, E.
ROBERTSON, W. Graham (1867-
1948) English dramatist WWT/
4-10, WWW/4
ROBERTSON, Mrs. Whybrow see
Litton, Marie
ROBERTSON, William (d 1872 [73])
actor EA/74*, WWT/14*

ROBERTSON, William (b 1908)
American actor TW/26-27,
29-30

ROBERTSON, Mrs. William (d
1876 [71]) actress WWT/14*

ROBERTSON, Sir William Tindal
(d 1889) EA/90*

ROBESON, Paul (1898-1976) Amer-
ican actor, singer AAS, BE,
CB, COC, ES, HJD, NTH,
OC/1-3, PDT, SR, TW/1-3,
WWT/6-14

ROBEY, Don D. (d 1975 [71])
entertainment pioneer BP/60*

ROBEY, Sir George [George Ed-
ward Wade] (1869-1954) Eng-
lish variety artist AAS, CDP,
COC, DNB, GRB/1-4, OC/1-3,
PDT, TW/11, WWT/4-11,
WWW/5

ROBIN, Leo (b 1899) American
lyricist BE

ROBINA, Fanny (d 1927 [65]) actress, singer BE*, WWT/14*

ROBINA, Florrie (d 1953 [86])
actress, singer CDP

ROBINA, Lilian [Mrs. Joe Ed-
wards] (d 1903) serio-comic
EA/04*

ROBINI, Mrs. Alf [Maud Cuthbert]
(d 1905) EA/06*

ROBINS, Miss see Clifford,
Mrs.

ROBINS, Adolph (d 1950 [64])
Austrian/American comedian,
clown TW/7

ROBINS, Edward H. (1880/81-
1955) American actor TW/12,
WWT/5-11

ROBINS, Elisabeth [or Elizabeth;
Mrs. George Richmond Parkes]
(1862/65-1952) American ac-
tress COC, EA/95, GRB/1-4,
HJD, OC/1-3, WWT/1-8,
WWW/5

ROBINS, Gertrude L. [Mrs.
Charles Dawson] (d 1917 [30/
31]) actress, dramatist WWT/
2-3

ROBINS, J. F. (d 1890) EA/91*

ROBINS, Joseph (d 1878 [52])
actor CDP

ROBINS, Mrs. Joseph (d 1894)
comedian EA/95*

ROBINS, William (d 1645?) actor
DA

ROBINS, William A. (d 1948 [81])
Australian conductor, composer

GRB/1-4

ROBINS, William Robert (d 1911
[87]) actor EA/12*

ROBINSON, Mr. (fl 1738) dramatist
CP/3, GT

ROBINSON, Mr. (fl 1787) dramatist
CP/3

ROBINSON, Mr. (fl 1793) actor,
dramatist CP/3

ROBINSON, Mrs. [Polly Sinclair]
(d 1880 [28]) actress? EA/81*

ROBINSON, Alexander (c. 1812-87)
American circus manager NYM

ROBINSON, Anastasia see Peterborough, Anastasia, Countess of

ROBINSON, Andy (b 1942) American
actor TW/25-28

ROBINSON, Anna [Lady Rosslyn] (d
1917 [47]) American actress
GRB/1

ROBINSON, Bartlett (b 1912) American actor TW/3, 5, 8-10

ROBINSON, Bertrand (d 1959 [70])
American actor, dramatist BE*,
BP/43*

ROBINSON, Bill (1878-1949) American dancer, singer CB, DAB,
SR, TW/6, WWA/2, WWT/10

ROBINSON, Charles American actor
TW/16

ROBINSON, Charles (b 1909) American dramatist BE

ROBINSON, Charles see Chapman,
Barnet

ROBINSON, David (1868-1913)
American manager WWM

ROBINSON, Edward G. (1893-1973)
Rumanian/American actor BE,
CB, ES, TW/29, WWA/5,
WWT/7-14

ROBINSON, Edwin Arlington (1869-
1935) American dramatist HJD,
WWA/1

ROBINSON, Ethan M. (d 1919 [47])
vaudeville manager BE*, BP/4*

ROBINSON, Fayette Lodawick
["Yankee Robinson"] (1818-84)
American actor, circus propri-
etor CDP, HAS

ROBINSON, Forrest (1859-1924)
actor SR

ROBINSON, Dr. Francis (d 1872)
composer EA/73*

ROBINSON, Frederic C. P. (1832-
1912) English actor CDP, HAS,
PP/3

ROBINSON, Mrs. G. see Billings, Mary

ROBINSON, Gad (fl 1883?) song
composer CDP
ROBINSON, Geoffrey see Chater,
Geoffrey
ROBINSON, George (d 1857 [57])
singer CDP
ROBINSON, Gil circus performer
SR
ROBINSON, Gladys L. (d 1971
[75]) performer BP/56*
ROBINSON, Hal American actor
TW/30
ROBINSON, Harry [Harry W.
Bishop] (d 1889 [55]) American
minstrel manager EA/90*
ROBINSON, Henry (d 1879 [28])
dramatist EA/80*
ROBINSON, Horace (b 1909)
American educator, director
BE
ROBINSON, Hubbell (d 1974 [68])
producer/director/choreographer
BP/59*
ROBINSON, J. (fl 1791-1806)
English actor HAS
ROBINSON, J. (fl 1792?) actor,
dramatist EAP, RJ
ROBINSON, Jack (d 1975 [65])
dramatist BP/60*
ROBINSON, James (fl 1600) mana-
ger DA
ROBINSON, James American cir-
cus performer SR
ROBINSON, James [Michael Fitz-
gerald] (b 1835) American
equestrian CDP, HAS, SR
ROBINSON, James Hall (d 1862)
American actor HAS
ROBINSON, Jay (b 1930) Ameri-
can actor BE, TW/8
ROBINSON, Jethro T. (d 1878)
architect EA/79*
ROBINSON, John (d 1641) actor
DA
ROBINSON, John (1801-88) Amer-
ican circus performer, mana-
ger CDP, SR
ROBINSON, John (b 1908) English
actor AAS, WWT/11-16
ROBINSON, J. Russel (d 1963
[71]) American composer,
lyricist, performer BE*,
BP/48*
ROBINSON, Judith (b 1937) Amer-
ican actress TW/14
ROBINSON, Kathleen (b 1909)
Australian actress, manager
WWT/9-11

ROBINSON, Larry (b 1929) Ameri-
can actor TW/9
ROBINSON, Lennox (1886-1958)
Irish manager, dramatist, pro-
ducer, actor, critic COC,
DNB, ES, HP, MD, MH, MWD,
OC/1-3, PDT, RE, TW/15,
WWA/3, WWT/2-12, WWW/5
ROBINSON, Leslie (b 1940) Ameri-
can actor TW/26
ROBINSON, Lily (d 1893 [21]) mid-
get EA/94*
ROBINSON, Mrs. Lottie see
Walton, Lottie
ROBINSON, Madeleine (b 1908) Eng-
lish actress WWT/4-6
ROBINSON, Marie (d 1903 [80])
lion tamer EA/04*
ROBINSON, Mary [Mary Darby;
"Perdita"] (1758-1800) English
actress, dramatist CDP, COC,
CP/2-3, DNB, GT, OC/1-3,
TD/1-2
ROBINSON, Matthew, Lord Rokeby
(1713-1800) English dramatist
CP/3
ROBINSON, Norah (b 1901) actress
WWT/5-9
ROBINSON, Percy (1889-1967) Irish
dramatist, actor WWT/6-14
ROBINSON, Perdita see Robinson,
Mary
ROBINSON, Raisbeck Welford (d
1889 [42]) EA/90*
ROBINSON, Richard (d 1648) Eng-
lish actor COC, DA, GT, NTH,
OC/1-3
ROBINSON, Richard Clare see
Clare, Dickie
ROBINSON, Riddell (d 1913) EA/
14*
ROBINSON, Cpt. Robert Dansey
(d 1894) EA/95*
ROBINSON, Roger (b 1941) Ameri-
can actor TW/23-25, 28-29
ROBINSON, Stuart (b 1936) Ameri-
can literary representative BE
ROBINSON, Susan E. (d 1916)
singer SR
ROBINSON, Thomas (fl 1627-28)
actor DA
ROBINSON, Thomas (d 1891 [36])
EA/92*
ROBINSON, Tom (d 1875 [37]) mu-
sician EA/76*
ROBINSON, Mrs. Vyner see
Plowden, Florence
ROBINSON, Walter W. (d 1974

ROBINSON 798

[46]) writer, publicist BP/59*
ROBINSON, Wayne (b 1916) American editor BE
ROBINSON, Will E. see Ching Ling Loo
ROBINSON, William (d 1875 [58]) scene artist EA/77*
ROBINSON, William see Robins, William
ROBINSON, William Ellesworth see Chung Ling Soo
ROBINSON-DUFF, Frances (d 1951 [74]) American actress BE*, BP/36*
ROBLES, Rud (d 1970 [60]) performer BP/55*
ROBSON, Eleanor Elise (b 1879) English actress GRB/2-4, NTH, SR, WWS, WWT/2-8
ROBSON, E. M. (1855-1932) English actor GRB/4, OAA/1-2, WWT/1-6
ROBSON, Emily Maria [Mrs. Mat Robson] (d 1909) EA/10*
ROBSON, Ernest singer CDP
ROBSON, Evelyn Stuart [Mrs. W. S. Stevenson] (b 1874) English actress GRB/1
ROBSON, Dame Flora (b 1902) English actress AAS, BE, CB, COC, ES, OC/1-3, PDT, TW/2-19, WWT/7-16
ROBSON, Frederick [Thomas Robson Brownbill] (1821-64) English actor CDP, COC, DNB, ES, NTH, OC/1-3
ROBSON, Frederick (d 1919 [72]) actor BE*, WWT/14*
ROBSON, Mrs. Frederick see Robson, Rosetta Frances
ROBSON, Horatio (fl 1784-93) dramatist CP/3
ROBSON, John (d 1917) comedian, dancer EA/18*
ROBSON, June (d 1972 [50]) performer BP/56*
ROBSON, Mary (b 1893) English actress WWT/4-7
ROBSON, Mat (d 1899 [69]) actor, singer CDP
ROBSON, Mrs. Mat see Robson, Emily Maria
ROBSON, May [Mrs. A. H. Brown] (1858/65-1942) Australian actress CB, CDP, DAB, ES, GRB/3-4, PP/3, SR, WWA/1, WWM, WWS, WWT/1-9

ROBSON, Rosetta Frances [Mrs. Frederick Robson] (d 1899 [77]) EA/00*
ROBSON, Stuart [Henry Robson Stuart] (1836-1903) American actor COC, DAB, HAS, OC/1-3, PP/3, SR, WWA/1
ROBSON, Stuart, Jr. (d 1946) actor BE*
ROBSON, Mrs. Stuart [May Waldron] (d 1924 [56]) actress BE*, BP/9*, WWT/14*
ROBSON, Thomas (d 1893) musician EA/94*
ROBSON, Tom (d 1892 [50]) Negro comedian EA/93*
ROBSON, William (d 1863 [78]) writer EA/72*, WWT/14*
ROBSON, William see Robins, William
ROBY, Henry Greatrex (d 1875) comedian EA/76*
ROBY, Mrs. Henry Greatrex (d 1880) EA/81*
ROBYN (fl 1518) member of the Chapel Royal DA
ROBYN, Alfred George (1860-1935) American composer WWA/1, WWM
ROCCO, Luigi (fl 1853) singer CDP
ROCH, Madeleine (d 1930 [46]) French actress BE*, WWT/14*
ROCHE, Emeline American costume designer TW/4-8
ROCHE, Eugene (b 1928) American actor TW/24
ROCHE, Eugenius (fl 1808) dramatist CP/3
ROCHE, Mrs. R. (d 1874 [34]) EA/75*
ROCHEAD, Mrs. Charles J. see Rochead, Maggie
ROCHEAD, Maggie [Mrs. Charles J. Rochead] (d 1878) EA/80*
ROCHELLE, Edward (d 1908 [56]) actor BE*, EA/09*, WWT/14*
ROCHELLE, Lisa (b 1959) American actress TW/30
ROCHELLE, Sandy (b 1942) American actress TW/24
ROCHESTER, Jenny [Mrs. P. A. Metcalfe] (d 1900) EA/01*
ROCHESTER, John Wilmot, Earl of see Wilmot, John
ROCHETTE, J. B. (d 1866 [41]) clown, cannon-ball performer HAS

ROCHEZ, Mr. (fl 1846) bottle
equilibrist CDP
ROCHIN, Paul (d 1964 [75])
actor BE*
ROCK, Mr. (fl 1790s-1800s) Irish
actor GT, TD/1-2
ROCK, Charles [Arthur Charles
Rock de Fabeck] (1866-1919)
Indian/English actor GRB/
1-4, WWT/1-3
ROCK, Mrs. Charles see Wynne,
Cybel
ROCK, Edward Anthony (d 1815)
actor CDP
ROCK, Mrs. Edward Anthony (fl
1785-91) actress CDP
ROCK, Mary (d 1883) actress
CDP
ROCK, William (d 1922 [53])
comedian, dancer BE*, BP/7*
ROCKEFELLER, John D., III (b
1906) American executive BE
ROCKHILL, Mr. (fl 1838) actor
HAS
ROCKMORE, Robert (d 1963 [60])
lawyer BP/47*
ROCKSTRO, William S. (d 1895)
composer, musician EA/96*
ROCKWELL, Charles Henry (d
1883 [40]) actor CDP
ROCKWELL, Donald S. (d 1974
[75]) composer/lyricist BP/58*
ROCKWELL, Florence (1880/82-
1964) American actress TW/
20, WWM, WWS
ROCOMORA, Susanne (fl 1900s)
German actress WWM
RODALE, J. I. (d 1971 [72])
dramatist BP/56*
RODD, Marcia (b 1940) American
actress, singer TW/23-24,
26-27, 29, WWT/15-16
RODD, Thomas (fl 1800) trans-
lator CP/3
RODDICK, John (b 1944) Aus-
tralian actor TW/30
RODEN, Eric John (b 1966)
American actor TW/29
RODEN, Frank (d 1896 [45]) mu-
sic-hall singer EA/97*
RODGER-REID, Paul (b 1938)
American actor TW/26
RODGERS, Cpt. (d 1907) propri-
etor, manager EA/08*, WWT/
14*
RODGERS, Anton (b 1933) English
actor, director WWT/15-16
RODGERS, Bob (b 1924) American

dramatist, actor, director BE
RODGERS, Carrie (d 1961 [59])
talent representative BE*
RODGERS, Eileen (b 1933) Ameri-
can actress, singer BE, TW/
16-18
RODGERS, Enid (b 1924) English
actress TW/26, 29-30
RODGERS, Gaby German/American?
actress TW/12-19
RODGERS, James (d 1890 [74])
producer, proprietor, manager
BE*, EA/91*, WWT/14*
RODGERS, Jerry (b 1941) American
actor TW/27
RODGERS, Jimmy (1897-1933)
American performer BE*
RODGERS, Katherine (d 1892) ac-
tress EA/93*
RODGERS, Lou (b 1935) actor
TW/23-24, 26
RODGERS, Mary (b 1931) American
composer BE
RODGERS, Richard (b 1902) Amer-
ican composer, producer, lyri-
cist AAS, BE, CB, ES, HJD,
MH, NTH, PDT, TW/2-8,
WWT/6-16
RODGERS, Shev (b 1928) American
actor TW/22-25, 28-30
RODGERS, Mrs. T. J. (d 1872
[35]) EA/73*
RODIN, Gil (d 1974 [64]) producer/
director/choreographer BP/59*
RODNEY, Arthur (d 1918) EA/19*
RODNEY, Mrs. Arthur see
Gwynne, Jennie
RODNEY, Babette [Mrs. George
Bowles] actress CDP
RODNEY, Mrs. Charles see
Bell, Eva
RODNEY, Mrs. C. M. see
Settle, Nellie
RODNEY, Frank [Rodney Croskey
Perkins] (d 1902 [43]) English
actor EA/97
RODNEY, John (b 1914) American
actor TW/8
RODNEY, Stratton (d 1932 [67])
actor BE*, WWT/14*
RODRIGUES, Diana (d 1968 [25])
performer BP/52*
RODRIGUEZ, Charlie J. (b 1944)
Puerto Rican actor TW/29-30
RODRIQUEZ, Tito (d 1973 [50])
performer BP/57*
RODWAY, Norman (b 1929) Irish
actor AAS, WWT/14-16

RODWAY, Philip (d 1932 [55])
producer, manager BE*,
WWT/14*
RODWELL, George Herbert Buon-
aparte (1800-52) English musi-
cal director, composer, pro-
prietor DNB
RODWELL, Mrs. John [Mrs. T.
W. Robertson] (d 1912) EA/13*
ROE, Mrs. Alfred see Roe,
Mrs. R.
ROE, Bassett (1860-1934) English
actor DP, EA/95, GRB/1-4,
WWT/1-7
ROE, Dan F. (b 1879) actor
GRB/1
ROE, John E. (d 1871 [33]) pan-
tomime writer EA/72*
ROE, Patricia (b 1932) American
actress BE, TW/18-20, 24-26
ROE, Mrs. R. (d 1871 [35])
EA/72*
ROE, William (fl 1640) actor DA
ROEBLING, Paul (b 1934) Amer-
ican actor BE, TW/11-20, 24,
WWT/15-16
ROEBUCK, Cpt. Disney (d 1885
[66]) actor, producer, manager
BE*, EA/86*, WWT/14*
ROEBUCK, Cpt. Francis Algernon
Disney see Roebuck, Cpt.
Disney
ROEBURT, John (d 1972 [63])
dramatist BP/56*
ROECKEL, Herr (d 1870) singer
EA/71*
ROECKER, Edward O. (d 1975
[65]) performer BP/59*
ROEDER, Benjamin F. (d 1943
[77]) American producer,
manager BE*, BP/27*,
WWT/14*
ROEHRICH, William see
Roerick, William
ROELAND, Augusta American ac-
tress TW/9-11
ROELS, Marcel (d 1973 [80])
performer BP/58*
ROERICK, William [né Roehrich]
(b 1912) American actor TW/
2-4, 10, 22-25, 27, 30, WWT/
15-16
ROEWADE, Paul (d 1976 [39])
producer/director/choreographer
BP/60*
ROFFMAN, Rose actress TW/25
ROGAN, Peter (b 1939) Irish
actor TW/28-29

ROGELL, Sid (d 1973 [73]) pro-
ducer/director/choreographer
BP/58*
ROGER BROTHERS (fl 1885) vari-
ety performers SR
ROGERS, Mr. (fl 1857) English
actor HAS
ROGERS, Mrs. [Mrs. Phillips]
(d 1850) English actress HAS
ROGERS, Miss (b 1821) actress
CDP
ROGERS, Alfred R. (d 1891) EA/
92*
ROGERS, Anne (b 1933) English ac-
tress, singer AAS, BE, TW/
23, WWT/13-16
ROGERS, Arthur (d 1894) EA/95*
ROGERS, Ben G. (d 1895 [75])
American actor CDP, HAS
ROGERS, Mrs. Ben G. [née Mar-
garet Downs] (d 1852) actress
HAS
ROGERS, Bernard (1893-1968)
American composer WWA/5
ROGERS, Bob (d 1974) performer
BP/59*
ROGERS, Budd (d 1975 [84]) pro-
ducer/director/choreographer
BP/60*
ROGERS, Charles (d 1899) drama-
tist EA/00*
ROGERS, Charles J. (fl 1845)
equestrian manager, equestrian
HAS
ROGERS, Charles R. (d 1957 [64])
producer BE*
ROGERS, Charles S. (d 1888)
American actor EA/90*
ROGERS, Charles S. (1845-90)
actor CDP, HAS
ROGERS, Clara Kathleen ["Clara
Doria"] (1844-1931) English
singer DAB, WWA/1, WWM
ROGERS, Cynthia (1912-71) Amer-
ican actress TW/6, 27
ROGERS, Daniel (fl 1818?) drama-
tist EAP
ROGERS, E. [né Frazer] (fl 1850)
Scottish actor HAS
ROGERS, Edmund (d 1889 [33])
journalist EA/90*
ROGERS, Edward (fl 1626) actor
DA
ROGERS, Emmett (1915-65) Amer-
ican producer, director, actor
BE, TW/2-8, 22
ROGERS, E. W. (d 1913 [49])
EA/14*

ROGERS, Felix (fl 1863-69)
English comedian HAS
ROGERS, Genevieve (1859-89)
actress CDP
ROGERS, G. H. (d 1872 [54])
Australian comedian EA/73*
ROGERS, Gil (b 1934) American
actor TW/25-26, 29-30
ROGERS, Ginger [Virginia Kath-
erine McMath] (b 1911) Amer-
ican actress, dancer BE,
CB, ES, SR, TW/22-24,
WWT/8-10, 16
ROGERS, Gus (1869-1908) actor
GRB/3-4, WWS
ROGERS, H. (d 1909 [42])
manager EA/10*
ROGERS, Harry (d 1889 [40])
musician EA/90*
ROGERS, Helen Augusta (d 1890
[23]) actress EA/91*
ROGERS, Henry (d 1896) music-
hall chairman EA/97*
ROGERS, Herbert (d 1912 [33])
EA/13*
ROGERS, Mrs. J. [née Minne
Shemelds] (d 1878 [28]) serio-
comic EA/79*
ROGERS, James (d 1877 [78])
American? actor EA/78*
ROGERS, Mrs. James see
Rogers, Sarah Ann
ROGERS, James G. (1822-63)
English comedian, singer
CDP, HAS
ROGERS, Jane see Bullock,
Mrs. Christopher
ROGERS, John (d 1905 [65])
EA/06*
ROGERS, John R. (d 1932 [92])
American press representative,
manager BE*, BP/17*,
WWT/14*
ROGERS, Jonathan (d 1880 [68])
musician EA/81*
ROGERS, Katherine (d 1891)
actress CDP
ROGERS, Laura (d 1948 [74])
actress TW/5
ROGERS, Louise Mackintosh (d
1933 [68]) actress BE*,
BP/18*
ROGERS, Maggie [née Margaret
Stowell; Mrs. John Crean]
(1818-87) Canadian actress
NYM
ROGERS, Max [Max Solomon] (d
1932 [59]) American actor

GRB/3-4, WWA/1, WWS, WWT/
1-5
ROGERS, Mildred (d 1973 [74])
performer BP/57*
ROGERS, Oliver (b 1873) English
actor GRB/1
ROGERS, Paul (b 1917) English ac-
tor AAS, BE, CB, ES, TW/
24, 28-30, WWT/12-16
ROGERS, Robert (1727-98) Ameri-
can dramatist CP/2-3, EAP,
GT
ROGERS, Robert Emmons (1888-
1941) American dramatist
WWA/1
ROGERS, Robert John (d 1871
[34]) manager EA/72*
ROGERS, Sarah Ann [Mrs. James
Rogers] (d 1917 [68]) EA/18*
ROGERS, Stuart actor, impersona-
tor CDP
ROGERS, Suzanne (b 1947) Ameri-
can actress TW/26
ROGERS, W. actor, singer CDP
ROGERS, Will (1879-1935) Ameri-
can actor COC, DAB, ES,
OC/1-3, SR, WWT/7, WWW/3
ROGERS, William (fl 1628) actor
DA
ROGERS, William (d 1876 [70])
actor EA/77*, WWT/14*
ROGERSON, Anne [Mrs. J. Roger-
son] (d 1868 [58]) EA/69*
ROGERSON, Budd (b 1927) Ameri-
can actor TW/5-6
ROGERSON, Mrs. J. see Roger-
son, Anne
ROGERSON, James B. (d 1876
[68]) actor EA/77*
ROGERSON, J. B. (d 1879 [32])
actor EA/80*
ROGERSON, Tom W. (d 1889 [53])
EA/90*
ROGERSON, Whit (d 1906 [63])
comedian EA/07*
ROGERSON, Mrs. Whit [Edith
Sandford] (d 1889 [52]) eques-
trian actress EA/90*
ROGIER, Frank (b 1918) American
actor TW/3, 9
ROGNAN, Lorraine (d 1969 [57])
performer BP/54*
ROGOFF, Gordon (b 1931) Ameri-
can critic, educator, producer
BE
ROHLFS, Anna K. G. see
Green, Anna Katherine
ROHMER, Sax [Arthur Sarsfield

Ward] (1886-1959) English
dramatist, composer WWT/
6-11, WWW/5
ROKEBY, Lord see Robinson,
Matthew
ROLAND, Frank (d 1882 [42])
comedian EA/83*
ROLAND, Ida (1881-1951) Aus-
trian actress BE*, WWT/14*
ROLAND, Ruth (1893-1937)
American actress BE*
ROLAND, Will (d 1973 [63]) pro-
ducer/director/choreographer
BP/57*
ROLF, Frederick (b 1926) German
actor, director BE, TW/14-
15, 22-23
ROLFE, Arthur Collins actor
GRB/1
ROLFE, Fourness (d 1891 [69])
actor, singer EA/92*
ROLFE, William James (1827-
1910) American scholar WWA/1
ROLIN, Judi (b 1946) American
actress TW/26
ROLL, John (d 1539) actor DA
ROLLA, Kate (b 1865) singer
CDP
ROLLA, Theresa (b 1837) dancer
CDP, HAS
ROLLAND, Caroline (fl 1871)
equestrienne CDP
ROLLAND, Romain (d 1944 [78])
dramatist, critic, historian
WWT/14*
ROLLAND, William E. (d 1890)
clown EA/91*
ROLLAND, Little Willie (d 1879
[15]) equestrian, acrobat EA/
80*
ROLLASON, Ellen Elizabeth see
Chart, Ellen Elizabeth
ROLLASON, John (d 1879 [79])
EA/80*
ROLLE, Esther American actress
TW/22-23, 25-29, WWT/16
ROLLI, Paolo Antonio (fl 1744)
Italian dramatist? manager,
composer? CP/1
ROLLINE, Mr. (fl 1833) actor
HAS
ROLLINS, Jack personal manager,
producer BE
ROLLINS, Walter E. (d 1973
[66]) composer/lyricist BP/
57*
ROLLINSON (fl 1596?) dramatist
FGF

ROLLITT, Joe (d 1917 [38]) EA/
18*
ROLLO, Billy (d 1964 [40]) actor,
stage manager BE*
ROLLS, Mrs. Alexander see
Barry, Helen
ROLLY, Jeanne (d 1929 [70]) ac-
tress BE*, WWT/14*
ROLPH, Mr. (d 1917) EA/18*
ROLSTON, William (d 1964) actor,
director, stage manager BE*
ROLT, Bernard (1874-1937) com-
poser, lyricist WWW/3
ROLT, Richard (1724/25-70) Eng-
lish dramatist CP/2-3, GT,
TD/1-2
ROLYAT, Dan [Herbert Taylor]
(1872-1927) English actor GRB/
2-4, WWT/1-5
ROMA, Caro (b 1869) American
singer, composer WWM, WWS
ROMA, Willy (d 1902 [25]) acro-
bat, gymnast EA/03*
ROMAH, Lou (d 1918) EA/19*
ROMAINE, Annie (d 1893) EA/94*
ROMAINE, Charles (d 1896) panto-
mimist EA/97*
ROMAINE, Mrs. Charles see
Bernarto, Mlle.
ROMAINE, Claire (1873/77-1964)
English actress, singer WWT/
4-8
ROMAINE, Doug (d 1971 [56]) per-
former BP/56*
ROMAINE, Edith (d 1974 [87]) per-
former BP/59*
ROMAINE, Martin (d 1917) per-
former? EA/18*
ROMAINS, Jules (1885-1972)
French dramatist COC, OC/3
ROMAN, Joseph (b 1927) American
actor TW/8
ROMAN, Lawrence (b 1921) Amer-
ican dramatist BE
ROMANI, Maria Theresa Catherine
see Bland, Mrs. George
ROMANINI, Mme. (fl 1841) rope
dancer CDP
ROMANO, Charles (d 1937 [38])
English actor BE*, BP/22*
ROMANO, Jane (d 1962 [33])
American actress TW/19
ROMANO, Nicolino (d 1901 [56])
proprietor EA/02*
ROMANOV, Boris Georgievik (1891-
1957) Russian/American dancer,
choreographer ES
ROMANZINI, Maria Theresa see

Bland, Maria Theresa Romanzini
ROMANZINI, Maria Theresa Catherine see Bland, Mrs. George
ROMBERG, Bernard (1767-1841) composer, conductor, musician CDP
ROMBERG, Sigmund (1887-1951) Hungarian/American composer AAS, CB, ES, NTH, PDT, TW/8, WWA/3, WWT/4-11
ROME, Harold (b 1908) American composer, lyricist AAS, BE, CB
ROMEO, Gene (b 1944) American actor TW/25
ROMER, Mr. (d 1886 [64]) minstrel singer EA/87*
ROMER, Alec [Alex Haines Woodman] (d 1909 [37]) EA/10*
ROMER, Anne [Mrs. William Brough] (d 1852 [23]) actress BE*, WWT/14*
ROMER, Carrie see Stokes, Caroline Ann
ROMER, Emma see Almond, Emma
ROMER, Frank (d 1889) composer EA/90*
ROMER, Robert (d 1874 [66]) actor BE*, EA/75*, WWT/14*
ROMER, Tomi (d 1969 [45]) actress TW/26
ROMER, Violet (b 1895) American dancer WWM
ROMEYN, Jane (d 1963 [62]) actress BE*
ROMNEY, Edana (b 1919) South African actress WWT/9-10
ROMOFF, Woody (b 1918) American actor BE
ROMONDO, George eccentric mimic CDP
RONALD, Sir Landon (1873-1938) English composer, conductor GRB/1-4, WWT/1-8, WWW/3
RONAN, Robert (b 1938) American actor TW/24-28
RONCA, Frank (d 1886) concerthall chairman EA/87*
RONCONI, Sig. (d 1875) composer EA/76*
RONCONI, Giorgio (d 1890) singer HAS
RONDIRIS, Dimitrios (b 1899) Greek director BE, COC
RONELL, Ann composer, lyricist,

librettist BE
RONNER, John (fl 1550) actor DA
RONZANI, Domenico (1800-68) Italian maître de ballet HAS
ROO, John see Roll, John
ROODS, John theatre owner DA
ROOKE, Arthur Leonard (d 1892) singer EA/93*
ROOKE, Irene (1878-1958) English actress COC, GRB/3-4, OC/3, WWT/1-8
ROOKE, Valentine (b 1912) English actor WWT/8-10
ROOKE, William Michael (1794-1847) Irish composer, musician, director? CDP, DNB
ROOKES, Marian Agnes Land see Booth, Agnes, & Perry, Mrs. Harry A., II
ROOME, Edward (d 1729) dramatist CP/1-3, DNB, GT
ROON, Al (d 1976 [73]) dance trainer BP/60*
ROONEY, James C. (d 1889 [33]) vaudevillian EA/90*
ROONEY, J. P. (d 1870) comic singer, dancer EA/71*
ROONEY, Mickey [Joe Yule] (b 1920) American actor SR
ROONEY, Pat, Sr. (1880-1962) American actor TW/7-14, 19
ROONEY, Mrs. Pat see Bent, Marion
ROONEY, Mrs. Pat see Nolan, Pattie
ROONEY, Patrick (1844-92) Irish actor, dancer CDP
ROONEY, William (b 1945) American actor TW/26
ROOP, Reno Estonian actor TW/29-30
ROOS, Joanna (b 1901) American actress BE, WWT/7-9
ROOS, Patricia (b 1945) American actress TW/29-30
ROOSE, Olwen (b 1900) English actress WWT/5-9
ROOSE-EVANS, James (b 1927) English director AAS, WWT/14-16
ROOSEVELT, Blanche (d 1898) composer, singer CDP
ROOT, Arabella (fl 1881?) singer, song composer CDP
ROOT, Mrs. E. B. see Root, Ivy Ashton
ROOT, George Frederick (1820-95) American songwriter BE*

ROOT, Ivy Ashton [Mrs. E. B.
Root] (b 1872) American dram-
atist WWM
ROOT, John (b 1904) American
scene designer ES, TW/2,
5-8
ROOT, Lynn (b 1905) American
dramatist, actor BE
ROPER, Mrs. (d 1835) actress
HAS
ROPER, Eric (d 1916) revue
comedian EA/17*
ROPER, Samuel Henry (d 1890)
performer? EA/91*
ROPER, Susannah (d 1908 [67])
EA/09*
ROPES, Arthur Reed see Ross,
Adrian
ROPES, Bradford (d 1966 [60])
performer BP/51*
ROQUEMORE, Henry (1890-1943)
actor SR
ROQUEVERT, Noel (d 1973 [81])
performer BP/58*
ROREM, Ned (b 1923) American
composer CB
RORIE, Yvonne (1907-59) Scot-
tish actress WWT/6-11
RORKE, Cecilia (d 1877 [17])
actress EA/78*, WWT/14*
RORKE, John (d 1908) EA/09*
RORKE, John (d 1957 [65]) actor
BE*, WWT/14*
RORKE, Kate [Mrs. Douglas
Cree] (1866-1945) English ac-
tress CDP, COC, DP, EA/
95, GRB/1-4, OC/1-3, WWT/
1-9, WWW/4
RORKE, Margaret Hayden (d
1969 [85]) performer BP/53*
RORKE, Mary [Mrs. Frank St.
Aubyn] (1858-1938) English
actress DP, EA/96, GRB/
1-4, OAA/2, WWT/1-8
ROSA, Mme. de (d 1897) dancer
EA/98*
ROSA, Carl (1843-89) German
conductor, musician CDP,
DNB, ES
ROSA, Mrs. Carl see Rosa,
Parepa
ROSA, H. C. (d 1917) EA/18*
ROSA, Madeline [Mrs. Frank
Travis] (d 1907) ventriloquist
EA/08*
ROSA, Nera (d 1920 [80]) actress
BE*, BP/5*
ROSA, Parepa [née Euphrosyne

Parepa; Mrs. Carl Rosa] (1836-
74) Scottish actress, singer
CDP, DNB, HAS
ROSA, Patti (d 1894) actress, sing-
er CDP
ROSALIND, Myra [Myra MacKenzie
Lloyd] (d 1908 [49]) actress
EA/09*
ROSAR, Annie (d 1963 [75]) per-
former BE*
ROSATI, Carolina (1826-1905)
Italian dancer, mimist ES
ROSAY, Françoise (1891-1974)
French actress BE, BTR/74,
ES, WWT/11-15
ROSCOW, Eleanor [Mrs. George
B. Roscoe] (d 1899) EA/91*
ROSCOW, G. B. (d 1904) agent
EA/05*
ROSCOW, Mrs. George B. see
Roscow, Eleanor
ROSE, Mr. (fl 1612) actor DA
ROSE, Mr. (fl 1839) English actor
HAS
ROSE (d 1893) gymnast EA/94*
ROSE, Miss (fl 1770?) actress
CDP
ROSE, Miss (fl 1854) actress HAS
ROSE, Mlle. [Mrs. E. Harris]
(d 1887 [29]) EA/88*
ROSE, Annie [Mrs. Frederick
Bond] (d 1892 [48]) actress
EA/93*
ROSE, Annie (d 1902 [58]) actress
EA/97*
ROSE, Arthur see Rose, Clarkson
ROSE, Betty Clarke (d 1947) ac-
tress BE*
ROSE, Billy [né William Samuel
Rosenberg] (1899-1966) American
actor, producer BE, CB,
COC, NTH, SR, TW/2-8, 22,
WWA/4, WWT/10-14
ROSE, Mrs. Cecil see Thomas,
Dorothy
ROSE, Clark (1838-87) American
actor? circus performer? circus
proprietor NYM
ROSE, Clarkson (1890-1968) Eng-
lish actor COC, OC/3, WWT/
9-14
ROSE, Clifford (b 1929) English
actor TW/22-23
ROSE, Edward (1849-1904) English
dramatist WWW/1
ROSE, Edward Everett (1862-1939)
Canadian dramatist, director
GRB/3-4, WWA/1, WWM,

WWT/1-7
ROSE, Francis A. (b 1849) American actor, prompter HAS
ROSE, George (b 1920) English actor AAS, BE, TW/22-30, WWT/12-16
ROSE, George see Sketchley, Arthur
ROSE, George Thomas (d 1893) EA/94*
ROSE, Harry (d 1962 [70]) performer BE*, BP/47*
ROSE, Heloise Durant (fl 1890-1921) American dramatist WWA/5
ROSE, Henry (d 1971 [61]) performer BP/55*
ROSE, Jane American actress BE, TW/9, 13, 15, 23-24, 29
ROSE, Rev. John (fl 1788-93) dramatist CP/3
ROSE, Kathleen Mary ["Dolores"] (d 1975 [83]) Ziegfeld girl WWT/16*
ROSE, L. Arthur (1887-1958) Scottish dramatist WWT/10-12
ROSE, Lieut. Manfred (d 1908) manager EA/09*
ROSE, Marie [Marie Leavett] (1856-1919) actress SR
ROSE, Nancie (d 1917) EA/18*
ROSE, Norman (b 1917) American actor TW/9, 23, 25
ROSE, Patrick Latham (d 1896) actress EA/97*
ROSE, Peter librettist CD
ROSE, Philip [né Rosenberg] (b 1921) American producer BE, WWT/15-16
ROSE, Mrs. P. L. see Boone, Lizzie
ROSE, Reginald (b 1920) American dramatist BE
ROSE, Reva (b 1940) American actress TW/23-24
ROSE, Rufus C. (d 1975 [70]) marionettist BP/60*
ROSE, Tom (d 1976 [51]) dramatist BP/60*
ROSEAU, Emé (fl 1870s?) singer CDP
ROSEBERY, Arthur (d 1928) producer, dramatist, manager BE*, WWT/14*
ROSELIE, William (1882-1945) actor SR
ROSELLA, Mlle. (d 1906 [19])

gymnast EA/08*
ROSELLE, Agnes see Knott, Roselle
ROSELLE, Amy [Mrs. Arthur Dacre] (1854-95) English actress CDP, DP, OAA/2
ROSELLE, Emily [Mrs. Gustave Roselle] (d 1882) EA/83*
ROSELLE, Mrs. Gustave see Roselle, Emily
ROSELLE, Julia (fl 1871-78) actress OAA/2
ROSELLE, Percy (b 1856) actor CDP
ROSELLE, W. H. [William Hawkins] (d 1878) actor? EA/80*
ROSELLE, William (d 1945 [67]) American actor BE*, BP/29*
ROSEMONT, Walter (d 1969 [91]) composer/lyricist BP/53*
ROSEN, Abigail (b 1946) Swiss/American actress TW/25
ROSEN, Albert H. (d 1974 [82]) manager BP/59*
ROSEN, Frederick (d 1912 [46]) music-hall agent EA/13*
ROSEN, Irwin (b 1936) American actor TW/26
ROSEN, Jerry M. (d 1972 [60]) agent BP/56*
ROSENBAUM, Edward, Sr. (d 1927 [72]) manager BE*, BP/12*
ROSENBERG, George (d 1969) agent BP/53*
ROSENBERG, Marvin (b 1912) American educator BE
ROSENBERG, Michel (d 1972 [71]) performer BP/57*
ROSENBERG, Philip see Rose, Philip
ROSENBERG, Sarah (d 1964 [90]) actress BE*
ROSENBERG, William Samuel see Rose, Billy
ROSENBLOOM, Maxie (d 1976 [71]) performer BP/60*
ROSENBLUM, M. Edgar (b 1932) American producer, manager BE
ROSENBURGH, Carleton F. (d 1974 [69]) theatre construction BP/59*
ROSENE, Charles F. (b 1844) American actor HAS
ROSENFELD, Jay C. (d 1975 [80]) critic BP/60*
ROSENFELD, Jerome M. producer,

publisher, executive BE
ROSENFELD, John, Jr. (d 1966
[66]) critic BP/51*
ROSENFELD, Juliet see Juliet
ROSENFELD, Sydney (1855-1931)
American dramatist GRB/2-4,
WWA/1, WWM, WWS, WWT/
1-6
ROSENGREN, Frank Duane see
Duane, Frank
ROSENHAIN, Jacob (d 1894 [81])
composer, musician EA/95*
ROSENSTOCK, Joseph (b 1895)
Polish conductor, composer
CB
ROSENSTOCK, Milton (b 1917)
American musical director
BE
ROSENTHAL, Andrew (b 1917)
American dramatist, com-
poser BE
ROSENTHAL, Edmund [Thomas
Edmund Metcalf] (d 1902 [77])
singer EA/03*
ROSENTHAL, Harry (d 1953 [60])
Irish composer, musician,
actor BE*, BP/37*
ROSENTHAL, Jean (1912-69)
American lighting designer
BE, TW/25, WWA/5
ROSENTHAL, J. J. (d 1923 [60])
American manager, talent
representative BE*, BP/8*
ROSENTHAL, Laurence (b 1926)
American composer BE
ROSENTHAL, Moriz (1863-1946)
Polish pianist SR
ROSENTHAL, Steven (b 1946)
American actor TW/28
ROSETTI, Marie (fl 1872) singer
CDP
ROSEWALD, Julie (b 1850)
singer CDP
ROSHANARA (d 1926) Indian
dancer BE*, BP/11*
ROSICH, Sig. (fl 1825) singer
HAS
ROSICH, Signora (fl 1825) singer
HAS
ROSIER, Mlle. (fl 1837?) dancer
CDP
ROSIER, Fitz William (fl 1881?)
musician CDP
ROSIER, Jack (d 1909) actor
EA/10*
ROSIERE, J. G. (d 1870) actor
WWT/14*
ROSING, Vladimir (1890-1963)

Russian singer, director WWA/4
ROSINI, Victor (d 1910 [56]) variety
performer EA/11*
ROSKAM, Cathryn (b 1943) Ameri-
can actress TW/27
ROSMER, Milton (1881/82-1971)
English actor, producer, direc-
tor AAS, WWT/2-14
ROSQUI, Tom (b 1928) American
actor BE, TW/22-24, 26-29
ROSS, Adelaide [Mrs. T. W.
Ford] (b 1842) English actress
GRB/1
ROSS, Adrian [Arthur Reed Ropes]
(1859-1933) English dramatist,
lyricist, librettist DNB, GRB/
1-4, WWT/1-7, WWW/3
ROSS, Alan (b 1920) American actor
TW/5-6
ROSS, Anna see Brunton, Mrs.
John
ROSS, Ann Boothby American ac-
tress TW/27
ROSS, Annie (b 1930) English ac-
tress, singer WWT/16
ROSS, Anthony (1906-55) American
actor TW/1-12, WWT/11-12
ROSS, Babs (d 1973 [62]) performer
BP/58*
ROSS, Bertie (d 1905 [30]) panto-
mimist EA/06*
ROSS, Bill (b 1915) American stage
manager, director BE
ROSS, Charles [Charles Edward
Cobb] (b 1880) English actor,
singer GRB/1
ROSS, Charles Cowper (b 1929)
English actor, director, pro-
ducing manager WWT/15-16
ROSS, Charles H. [Charles H.
Thornton] (b 1882) English actor,
pantomimist GRB/1
ROSS, Charles Henry (d 1897)
dramatist CDP
ROSS, Charles J. (1859-1918)
Canadian actor SR, WWM,
WWS
ROSS, Charlie [William George
Gant] (d 1893) actor EA/95*
ROSS, Chris (d 1970 [24]) per-
former BP/54*
ROSS, Corinne Heath Sumner (d
1965 [86]) performer BP/50*
ROSS, Danny (d 1976 [45]) per-
former BP/60*
ROSS, David (1723/28-90) English
actor CDP, DNB, GT, TD/1-2
ROSS, David (1922/24-66) American

director, producer, actor BE,
TW/13-18, 22
ROSS, Mrs. David see Ross,
Frances
ROSS, Dorothy (b 1912) American
press representative BE
ROSS, Elizabeth (b 1926/28)
American actress BE, TW/
2-3, 10
ROSS, Eva Florence (d 1887) ac-
tress NYM
ROSS, F. Clure (1874-1942) Eng-
lish actor, stage manager
GRB/1
ROSS, Frances (d 1770?) actress?
CDP
ROSS, Frederick (b 1879) English
actor WWT/1-7
ROSS, Fred Q. (1858-1942) actor
SR
ROSS, George (b 1911) American
producer, dramatist, press
representative BE
ROSS, George A. (d 1916 [42])
EA/17*
ROSS, George I. (b 1907) South
African dramatist AAS, WWT/
14-16
ROSS, Gertrude Mary see Gitana,
Gertie
ROSS, Harriet (fl 1900s) American
actress WWM
ROSS, Henry (b 1913) English ac-
tor WWT/10-14
ROSS, Hector (b 1915) English
actor WWT/11
ROSS, Helen (b 1914) American
actress TW/23, 26, 29
ROSS, Herbert [Herbert Tait]
(1865-1934) Indian/English
actor WWT/2-7
ROSS, Herbert (b 1927) American
choreographer, director, dancer
BE, ES
ROSS, Irene English actress
GRB/1-2
ROSS, Isabel (d 1881 [24]) EA/
83*
ROSS, Jack [Jack Snyder] Amer-
ican actor, dancer GRB/1
ROSS, James (d 1873) strolling
player & showman EA/74*
ROSS, Jamie (b 1939) Scottish
actor TW/27-30
ROSS, Jan (b 1948) American
actress TW/28
ROSS, Jerry (1926-56) American
librettist, composer TW/12

ROSS, John E. (d 1859 [54]) Eng-
lish actor HAS
ROSS, John Wilson (d 1887 [69])
dramatist EA/88*
ROSS, Justin (b 1954) American
actor TW/30
ROSS, Kate see Windley, Mrs.
John
ROSS, Katherine (b 1930) American
actress TW/13
ROSS, Larry (d 1973 [65]) per-
former BP/57*
ROSS, Larry (b 1945) American
actor TW/26-27
ROSS, Lenny (d 1976 [71]) per-
former BP/60*
ROSS, Mabel Fenton (d 1931 [63])
American actress BE*, BP/15*
ROSS, Marion (d 1966 [68]) per-
former BP/51*
ROSS, Martin (b 1938) American
actor TW/24-25, 27
ROSS, Minnie (d 1892 [25]) ac-
tress? EA/94*
ROSS, Oriel [Muriel Swinstead]
(b 1907) actress WWT/8-13
ROSS, Robert (d 1954 [52]) Cana-
dian actor, director TW/10
ROSS, Robert (d 1974 [65]) per-
former BP/59*
ROSS, Ronnie (d 1965 [25]) per-
former BP/50*
ROSS, Rosalind (b 1934) English
actress TW/26
ROSS, Roy Irving (d 1968 [56])
composer/lyricist BP/53*
ROSS, Shirley (d 1975 [62]) per-
former BP/59*
ROSS, Steven (b 1941) American
actor TW/25
ROSS, Thomas W. (1875/78-1959)
American actor GRB/2-4, TW/
16, WWM, WWS, WWT/1-11
ROSS, T. J. (d 1975 [81]) public
relations BP/59*
ROSS, Weedon (b 1878) English
actor GRB/1
ROSS, W. G. actor CDP
ROSS, Lieut. William (fl 1790)
dramatist CP/3
ROSS, William (d 1963 [38]) per-
former BE*, BP/47*
ROSS, Mrs. William see Brown,
Mrs. J.
ROSSBOROUGH, H. T. (d 1887)
music-hall proprietor EA/88*
ROSS-CATTANACH, William see
Windsor, Albert C.

ROSS-CLARKE, Betty American
actress WWT/6-7
ROSSE, Frederick (d 1940 [73])
composer BE*, WWT/14*
ROSSE, Mrs. Frederick see
Lichtenstein, Ethel
ROSSE, Herman (d 1965 [78])
designer TW/21
ROSSE, Matthew Russell (d 1910)
manager EA/11*
ROSSE, Russell (d 1910) actor,
producer, manager BE*,
WWT/14*
ROSSEN, Carol American actress
TW/18, 20
ROSSEN, Robert (1908-66) Amer-
ican director, dramatist
WWA/4
ROSSET, Barney (b 1922) Amer-
ican editor BE
ROSSETER, Philip (c. 1575-1623)
English musician, lessee,
composer COC, DA, OC/1-3
ROSSI, Ernesto Fortunato Giovanni
Maria (1827/29-96) Italian actor
CDP, COC, ES, OC/1-3
ROSSI, Gloria (b 1946) American
actress TW/30
ROSSI, Settimio (d 1864) Italian
singer HAS
ROSSI LEMENI, Nicola (b 1920)
Italian singer ES
ROSSILL (fl 1597) actor? DA
ROSSIN, Alfred A. (d 1976 [57])
producer/director/choreographer
BP/60*
ROSSITER, Leonard (b 1926) Eng-
lish actor AAS, TW/20,
WWT/15-16
ROSSLYN, Earl of [James Fran-
cis Harry St. Clair-Erskine]
(1869-1939) English actor
GRB/1-2
ROSSLYN, Lady see Robinson,
Anna
ROSSLYN, Elaine (d 1964) per-
former BE*
ROSSMAN, Edward (d 1876 [36])
musician EA/77*
ROSS-SELWICKE, Ethel (d 1906)
actress, dancer EA/07*,
WWT/14*
ROSTAND, Edmond (1868-1918)
French dramatist COC, GRB/
1-4, MWD, OC/3, SR, WWT/1
ROSTAND, Maurice (d 1968 [76])
performer BP/52*
ROSTEN, Norman (b 1914) Amer-

ican dramatist BE, CB
ROSTOVA, Mira (b 1919) Russian
actress TW/10
ROTCHLEY, Minnie [Sarah Ann
Woollams] (d 1902 [46]) actress
EA/03*
ROTH, Al (d 1972 [68]) musical
director BP/57*
ROTH, Albert A. (d 1969 [71])
performer BP/54*
ROTH, Ann costume designer
WWT/16
ROTH, Carl Heins (d 1972 [62])
producer/director/choreographer
BP/56*
ROTH, Lillian (b 1910) American
actress, singer BE, TW/18,
22, 27, WWT/7-8, 16
ROTH, Wolfgang (b 1910) German
designer TW/3-8
ROTHA, Wanda Austrian actress
WWT/9-16
ROTHAFEL, Samuel Lionel (1881-
1936) American showman DAB,
WWA/H, 4
ROTHE, Anita (d 1944 [77]) Amer-
ican actress BE*, BP/28*,
WWT/14*
ROTHENBERG, David (b 1933)
American press representative
BE
ROTHENSTEIN, Albert Daniel (b
1883) English designer WWT/4
ROTHIER, Leon (1874-1951) French
singer TW/8, WWA/5
ROTHMAN, Benjamin (d 1973 [76])
producer, manager BP/58*,
WWT/16*
ROTHMAN, Lawrence (b 1934)
American manager, producer
BE
ROTHSCHILD, Alfred (d 1972 [83])
editor BP/57*
ROTHWELL, Joan Dorothy see
Benesh, Joan Dorothy
ROTTER, Fritz Austrian dramatist
BE
ROUDENKO, Lobov Russian dancer
TW/2
ROUGH, William (fl 1797) drama-
tist CP/3
ROUGHWOOD, Owen (1876-1947)
English actor GRB/4, WWT/
1-8
ROUKE, Andy (d 1881 [31]) min-
strel EA/83*
ROUND, Henry (d 1905 [66]) com-
poser EA/06*

ROUNDS, David (b 1938) Amer-
ican actor TW/26-30
ROUNSEVILLE, Robert (1914/19-
74) American actor, singer
BE, TW/9-10, 13-15, 22-29,
WWT/12-16
ROURKE, E. (d 1878 [71]) come-
dian EA/79*
ROURKE, Georgiana (d 1870
[42]) EA/71*
ROUS, Helen [Miss Shaw] (d
1934 [71]) Irish actress
GRB/1-4, WWT/1-7
ROUSBEY, Arthur (d 1899) singer
EA/00*, WWT/14*
ROUSBEY, Mrs. Arthur see
Rousbey, Margaret
ROUSBEY, Margaret [Mrs. Arthur
Rousbey] (d 1895 [48]) EA/96*
ROUSBY, Alfred (d 1905 [50])
actor EA/06*
ROUSBY, Alice [Mrs. Walter]
(d 1883 [24]) actress EA/84*
ROUSBY, Clara Marion Jessie
(1852-79) English actress
CDP, DNB, OAA/1-2
ROUSBY, Mrs. Walter see
Rousby, Alice
ROUSBY, Wybert (1835-1907)
actor, manager DNB, GRB/
3, OAA/1-2
ROUSE, Mrs. [Sarah Ann Gale;
Mrs. William Charles Gale]
(d 1893 [53]) actress EA/94*
ROUSE, Fanny Denham (1837-
1912) English actress SR
ROUSE, John (d 1891?) actor,
singer CDP
ROUSE, John Frederick Taylor
(d 1902) music-hall chairman
EA/03*
ROUSE, Thomas (d 1852 [68])
actor EA/72*, WWT/14*
ROUSILLION, W. see Hatt, W.
ROUSSEAU, Gladys (d 1975 [76])
designer BP/59*
ROUSSET SISTERS, The (fl 1851)
dancers HAS
ROUSSIN, André (b 1911) French
dramatist BE, MWD
ROUTLEDGE, Calvert (1869-
1916) English actor, manager
GRB/1-3
ROUTLEDGE, Mrs. Calvert see
Jocelyn, Mary
ROUTLEDGE, Edmund J. P. (d
1899 [56]) actor EA/00*
ROUTLEDGE, Patricia (b 1929)

English actress AAS, TW/23-
24, WWT/14-16
ROUTLEDGE, Mrs. William see
Schofield, Laura
ROUVAUN (d 1975 [36]) performer
BP/60*
ROUVEROL, Mrs. Aurania (d 1955
[69]) American dramatist BE*,
BP/40*
ROVERE, Sig. (d 1865 [60]) singer
HAS
ROVIN, Robert H. American actor
TW/27
ROWAN, Lansing (1881-1912) ac-
tress SR
ROWBOTHAM, Mrs. see Hamil-
ton, Mrs. Robert
ROWBOTHAM, H. H. (d 1837)
English actor, manager CDP,
HAS
ROWBOTHAM, Mrs. H. H. ac-
tress CDP
ROWCROFT, Emma (fl 1860) ac-
tress? singer? HAS
ROWDEN, Elizabeth (d 1908) EA/
09*
ROWDON, George (d 1917) athlete,
trick performer EA/18*
ROWE, Alice E. (d 1916) EA/17*
ROWE, Earl (b 1920) American
actor TW/7-8
ROWE, Frances [or Fanny] (b 1913)
English actress TW/4-6, WWT/
10-14
ROWE, George (fl 1826) American
actor HAS
ROWE, George Fawcett (1834-89)
American actor, dramatist
CDP, COC, HAS, OC/1-3, SR
ROWE, Mrs. George Fawcett
see Girard, Kate
ROWE, George T. (d 1880 [81])
American comedian EA/81*
ROWE, Hansford (b 1924) American
actor TW/25, 28-29
ROWE, Harry (1726-1800) English
puppeteer, commentator, drama-
tist CDP, CP/3, DNB
ROWE, Harry [James Rowe] (d
1891 [39]) comedian EA/92*
ROWE, James see Rowe, Harry
ROWE, Louisa (b 1805) American
actress HAS
ROWE, Mary Alice (1851-87) Eng-
lish actress NYM
ROWE, Nicholas (1674-1718) Eng-
lish dramatist CDP, COC,
CP/1-3, DNB, ES, GT, HP,

MH, NTH, OC/1-3, PDT, RE,
SR, TD/1-2
ROWE, Sir Reginald (d 1945
[75]) executive BE*, WWT/
14*
ROWE, Mr. W. (d 1867) scene
artist EA/68*
ROWELLA, William (d 1896)
pantomimist EA/97*
ROWLAND (fl 1631) actor DA
ROWLAND, H. W. (d 1937 [70])
producer BE*, WWT/14*
ROWLAND, Mabel (d 1943 [61])
American actress BE*, BP/
27*
ROWLAND, Margery (1910-45)
English critic WWT/9
ROWLAND, Richard (d 1880 [21])
musician EA/81*
ROWLAND, Samuel (fl 1615)
dramatist CP/3
ROWLAND, Toby (b 1916) Amer-
ican producing manager
WWT/15-16
ROWLAND, William (d 1905 [62])
EA/06*
ROWLANDS, Cecil see Raleigh,
Cecil
ROWLANDS, Elizabeth see
Raine, Bessie
ROWLANDS, Gaynor (d 1906)
actress, dancer BE*, EA/
07*, WWT/14*
ROWLANDS, Gena (b 1936?)
American actress BE, CB,
TW/12-15
ROWLANDS, Patsy (b 1935)
English actress WWT/15-16
ROWLES, Polly (b 1914) Amer-
ican actress BE, TW/7-20,
23, 25-26, 28-29, WWT/14-16
ROWLEY, Cpt. [William Duncan]
(d 1910) lion tamer EA/12*
ROWLEY, Alec (1892-1958)
English composer WWW/5
ROWLEY, Anne [Mrs. J. W.
Rowley] (d 1874 [27]) EA/75*
ROWLEY, Joseph [Sig. Eurardo]
(d 1871 [26]) spiral ascen-
sionist EA/72*
ROWLEY, J. W. (d 1925 [78])
actor, singer CDP
ROWLEY, Mrs. J. W. see
Rowley, Anne
ROWLEY, Samuel (c. 1575-1624)
English actor, dramatist
COC, CP/1-3, DA, DNB,
FGF, HP, OC/1-3, RE

ROWLEY, Thomas (fl 1602) actor
DA
ROWLEY, William (c. 1585-1637/
42?) English actor, dramatist
COC, CP/1-3, DA, DNB, FGF,
HP, MH, NTH, OC/1-3, PDT,
RE
ROWNTREE, Mrs. Bert see
Rowntree, Edna
ROWNTREE, Edna [Mrs. Bert
Rowntree] (d 1916) EA/17*
ROWSELL, Mary Catharine (fl
1884-1911) English dramatist
WWW/2
ROWSON, Mr. (fl 1794) actor HAS
ROWSON, Miss (b 1787) English
singer HAS
ROWSON, Jane see Crowe, Mrs.
William
ROWSON, Susanna H. (1761?/62-
1824) English actress, dramatist
CDP, DAB, EAP, HAS, HJD,
RJ, SR, WWA/H
ROX, John Jefferson (d 1957 [50])
lyricist, composer BE*
ROXBOROUGH, Picton [Picton
Gaunt] (1875-1932) English actor
GRB/1-4
ROXBURY, Mrs. Harry see
Fenton, Kitty
ROXBY, Robert (d 1866 [58]) actor,
stage manager EA/72*, WWT/
14*
ROXBY, Samuel (d 1863 [58]) ac-
tor, manager EA/72*, WWT/
14*
ROXBY, Wilfred see Collett,
Thomas George
ROXBY, William, Jr. (1814-89)
English designer ES
ROY, Agnese (d 1964 [69]) dancer
BE*
ROY, Herbert (b 1880) English
actor, singer GRB/1
ROY, John (d 1975 [77]) performer
BP/60*
ROY, Renee (b 1935) American ac-
tress TW/26
ROYAARDS, William (d 1929 [62])
actor, director BE*, WWT/14*
ROYAL, Creed (d 1876 [68]) musi-
cian EA/77*
ROYAL, Harry (d 1903) circus
performer EA/04*
ROYAL, Harry (d 1904) comedian
EA/05*
ROYAL, Ted (b 1904) American
composer BE

ROYAL BALLET ES
ROYAL-DAWSON, O. S. (d 1917
[32]) dramatist, manager EA/
18 *
ROYALE, Harry M. (d 1963 [88])
performer BE *
"ROYAL PUNCH MAN, The" see
Dean, Thomas
ROYAL SHAKESPEARE CO. pro-
ducing manager WWT/14
ROYCE, Brigham (d 1933 [69])
American actor BE *, BP/17 *
ROYCE, Edward (1870-1964) Eng-
lish stage manager, producer
WWT/3-11
ROYCE, Edward William (1841-
1926) English actor, stage
manager OAA/1-2, WWT/2-5
ROYCE, Julian [Julian Gardener]
(1870-1946) English actor
WWT/1-8
ROYCE, Mrs. Julian see Day,
Nora
ROYCE, Virginia (d 1962 [30])
actress BE *
ROYCE, Mrs. W. [née Emily
Watson] (d 1871 [22]) actress
EA/73 *
ROYDE, Frank (b 1882) English
actor WWT/6-14
ROYDE-SMITH, Naomi (d 1964
[89]) English dramatist WWT/
8-9
ROYELLE, Charles [E. O.
Bauemann] (d 1894) EA/95 *
ROYLE, Edwin Milton (1862-
1942) American actor, drama-
tist CB, GRB/2-4, HJD,
MH, PP/3, WWA/2, WWM,
WWS, WWT/1-9
ROYLE, Frederick Powis (d
1884) EA/85 *
ROYLE, Josephine American
actress WWT/7-8
ROYLE, Selena (b 1904) Ameri-
can actress WWT/7-10
ROYLE, Selena Fetter [née
Selena Fetter] (d 1955 [95])
American actress PP/3,
TW/11
ROYS, Lyman P. (b 1815) Amer-
ican actor HAS
ROYSTON, Viscount see Yorke,
Philip
ROYSTON, Laura Eugenie [Mrs.
Frank Jefferson] (d 1884 [27])
EA/85 *
ROYSTON, Roy [Roy Crowden]

(1899-1976) English actor WWT/
4-13
ROYSTON, Thomas (d 1889 [19])
actor EA/90 *
ROYTON, Helen [Mrs. Walter G.
Douglas] (fl 1900s) Irish ac-
tress, singer WWM
ROYTON, Velma (d 1974 [81]) per-
former BP/59 *
ROZAKIS, Gregory (b 1943) Amer-
ican actor TW/22-25, 27
ROZANT, Ina [Theodora Zorn]
American actress, singer
GRB/1-4
ROZE, Eliza Barker (d 1912)
EA/13 *
ROZE, Marie (1846/50-1926)
French singer CDP, ES, GRB/1
ROZE, Raymond (1875-1920) Eng-
lish composer, conductor
WWT/3
ROZEWICZ, Tadeusz (b 1921)
Polish dramatist MWD
ROZIER, Mlle. (fl 1830?) dancer
CDP
ROZOV, Victor (b 1913) Russian
dramatist PDT
RUBBER, Violla (b 1910) producer,
personal manager BE
RUBEN, José (1886-1969) Belgian
actor, director, dramatist
TW/25, WWT/4-11
RUBEN, Neal (d 1969 [38]) writer,
producer BP/54 *
RUBENS, Alma (1898-1931) Ameri-
can actress BE *
RUBENS, Maurie [or Maury] (d
1948 [55]) American composer
BE *
RUBENS, Paul A. (1875/76-1917)
librettist, composer GRB/1-4,
WWT/1-3, WWW/2
RUBIE, Jennie [Mrs. Tom Fan-
court] (d 1910) comedian EA/11 *
RUBIN, Joel E. (b 1928) illuminat-
ing engineer BE
RUBIN, Menachem (d 1962 [67])
Polish actor, director BE *
RUBINI, Adelaide (d 1874 [79])
EA/75 *
RUBINI-SCALISI, Mme. (d 1871)
singer CDP
RUBINSTEIN, Harold F. (1891/92-
1975) dramatist WWT/4-10
RUBINSTEIN, Ida (d 1960) dancer,
actress WWT/8-11
RUBINSTEIN, John (b 1946) Amer-
ican actor TW/29-30

RUBINSTEIN, Leon J. (d 1972
[83]) publicist BP/56*
RUBY, Harry (1895-1974) Amer-
ican composer, lyricist BE,
TW/30, WWT/6-11
RUBY, Thelma [née Wigoder]
(b 1925) English actress
WWT/14-16
RUCKER, Sim G. (d 1865) Amer-
ican actor? HAS
RUDD, Henry (d 1872 [50]) con-
ductor EA/73*
RUDD, Paul (b 1940) American
actor TW/25-26, 30
RUDD, Sam (d 1905) comedian
EA/06*
RUDDOCK, John (b 1897) Peru-
vian/English actor WWT/11-16
RUDEL, Julius (b 1921) Austrian
musical director BE, CB
RUDERSDORFF, Hermine (1822-
82) Ukranian singer CDP,
WWA/H
RUDGE, Albert (d 1892 [25])
manager EA/93*
RUDGE, J. F. (d 1873) acting
manager EA/74*
RUDGE, Letty see Lind, Letty
RUDGE, William (d 1893) music-
hall proprietor EA/94*
RUDICH, Nathan M. (d 1975
[56]) executive, publicist
BP/60*
RUDKIN, David (b 1936) English
dramatist CD, CH, MH, RE,
WWT/16
RUDMAN, Michael (b 1939)
American director, stage
manager WWT/16
RUDNER, Reta (b 1953) American
actress TW/30
RUDNEY, Edward (b 1939) Amer-
ican actor TW/23, 25
RUDY, Martin (b 1915) American
actor TW/3, 8, 25
RUFFO, Titta (1877-1953) Italian
singer ES
RUGE, Williams acrobat CDP
RUGG, William Augustus see
Conway, William Augustus
RUGGERI, Ruggero (1871-1953)
Italian actor COC, OC/3
RUGGLE, George (1575-1622)
English dramatist COC, CP/
1-3, FGF, OC/1-3
RUGGLES, Miss (fl 1890?)
dancer CDP
RUGGLES, Aubrey see Reeves,

Arnold
RUGGLES, Carl (d 1971) com-
poser/lyricist BP/56*
RUGGLES, Charles (1892-1970)
American actor BE, ES, TW/
27, WWA/5, WWT/6-11
RUHL, Arthur Brown (d 1935 [58])
American critic BE*, BP/19*,
WWT/14*
RUHLAND, Stanley see Gaige,
Truman
RUICK, Barbara (d 1974 [42]) per-
former BP/58*
RUICK, Melville (b 1898) American
actor TW/5, 8
RUISINGER, Thomas (b 1930)
American actor TW/29
RUIZ, Enrique (d 1975 [67]) per-
former BP/60*
RULE, Charles (b 1928) American
actor TW/24-26
RULE, Janice (b 1931) American
actress BE, TW/11-12, 27,
WWT/16
RULE, John (fl 1766) dramatist
CP/2-3, GT
RUMANN, Sig. (d 1967 [82]) Ger-
man actor TW/23
RUMFORD, Kennerley (b 1871)
English singer GRB/1
RUMFORD, Mrs. Kennerley see
Butt, Clara
RUMLEY, Edward actor HAS
RUMLEY, Jerry (b 1930) American
educator, choreographer, di-
rector BE
RUMMELL, Joseph (d 1880 [62])
professor of music EA/81*
RUMSEY, Charles Ernest (d 1905
[33]) advance agent EA/06*
RUNCIE, Constance Fauntleroy
(1836-1911) American composer
WWA/1
RUNNEL, Albert F. (d 1974 [82])
performer BP/58*
RUNNELS, Bonnie (1857-84) come-
dian, circus performer CDP
RUNNELLS, Burnett American cir-
cus performer SR
RUNYON, Damon (1884-1946)
American dramatist MWD,
NTH, SR, WWA/2
RUPERT, Mike (b 1951) American
actor TW/24
RUPP, Elmer Kohler (b 1871)
American critic WWM
RUSCHENBERGER, Mrs. dramatist
RJ

RUSH, Bert [John A. G. Sims]
(b 1883) English actor, variety
artist GRB/1
RUSH, Cecile (fl 1856-59) actress
HAS
RUSH, Edward F. (b 1864) Aus-
trian manager WWM
RUSHBURY, W. T. (d 1909)
manager EA/10*
RUSHFORTH, Elizabeth [Mrs.
Willie Rushforth] (d 1907) EA/
08*
RUSHFORTH, Mrs. Willie see
Rushforth, Elizabeth
RUSHTON, Lucy [Mary Wilde]
(1844-1909) actress, manager
CDP, COC, HAS
RUSKIN, Leonard (d 1973 [51])
producer TW/30
RUSKIN, Shimen (1907-76) Polish
actor TW/25-26, 28
RUSKIN, Sybil [Miss Raphael]
(1880-1940) English actress
GRB/1-4
RUSS, Giannina (1878-1951) Italian
singer ES
RUSS, Mrs. L. J. see Russ,
Meta Anderson
RUSS, Meta Anderson [Mrs. L.
J. Russ] (d 1905 [28]) EA/06*
RUSS, William R. see Har-
land, Fred
RUSSAK, Gerard (b 1927) Ameri-
can actor TW/23, 25, 30
RUSSEL, Mark (b 1948) American
actor TW/27
RUSSEL, William (1746-94) Scot-
tish dramatist CP/3
"RUSSELL" see Craythorne,
James
RUSSELL, Mr. circus performer?
HAS
RUSSELL, Master (fl 1831) actor
CDP
RUSSELL, Countess (d 1908 [37])
actress GRB/4
RUSSELL, Mrs. [Grace Hamilton]
(d 1883) pantomimist EA/85*
RUSSELL, Miss singer CDP
RUSSELL, Agnes [Mrs. C. W.
Somerset] (d 1947 [73]) actress
BE*, WWT/14*
RUSSELL, Andy (d 1867) Negro
performer EA/68*
RUSSELL, Ann see Bullock,
Mrs. Hildebrand
RUSSELL, Anna [Anna Claudia
Russell-Brown] (b 1911/13)

English performer BE, CB,
COC, OC/3, TW/10
RUSSELL, Annie [Mrs. Oswald
Yorke] (1864-1936) English ac-
tress COC, DAB, GRB/2-4,
OC/1-3, PP/3, WWA/1, WWM,
WWS, WWT/1-8
RUSSELL, Bernard (d 1910 [34])
actor, singer CDP
RUSSELL, Billy (d 1971) performer
BP/56*
RUSSELL, Byron (d 1963 [79])
Irish actor BE*, BP/48*
RUSSELL, Charlotte (d 1901 [64])
singer EA/02*
RUSSELL, David Forbes (d 1969
[77]) performer BP/54*
RUSSELL, Diarmuid (d 1973 [71])
agent BP/58*
RUSSELL, Dorothy (b 1881) Ameri-
can actress WWS
RUSSELL, Edd X. (d 1966 [88])
performer BP/51*
RUSSELL, Edith [Mrs. Irton] (d
1897 [27]) actress, lessee EA/
98*
RUSSELL, Edward Haslingden (d
1906 [46]) EA/07*
RUSSELL, Sir Edward Richard
(1834-1920) English critic
GRB/3-4, WWT/1-3
RUSSELL, Ella [Countess di Rhigini]
American actress CDP, GRB/1
RUSSELL, Ethel English actress
GRB/1
RUSSELL, Evelyn (d 1976 [49]?)
American actress TW/29
RUSSELL, Frank (d 1883) comedian
EA/84*
RUSSELL, Fred [Thomas Frederick
Parnell] (1862-1957) ventriloquist
COC, OC/3
RUSSELL, Fred H. (d 1974 [73])
critic BP/59*
RUSSELL, F. W. see Barry,
H. C.
RUSSELL, Gail (d 1961 [36]) Amer-
ican actress BE*, BP/46*
RUSSELL, George (d 1896 [78])
equestrian EA/97*
RUSSELL, George Henry (fl 1857?)
CDP
RUSSELL, George William see
A. E.
RUSSELL, Harold (fl 1884-1908)
American actor WWS
RUSSELL, Mrs. Harold see
Dwyer, Ada

RUSSELL, Harriet Ellis (d 1912
[66]) actress, proprietor EA/
13*
RUSSELL, Henry (d 1874) musi-
cian EA/75*
RUSSELL, Henry [Henry Falconer]
(d 1887 [49]) actor? EA/88*
RUSSELL, Henry (1812-1899/1900)
American singer, composer
CDP, DNB, HAS
RUSSELL, Henry (d 1900 [87]?)
English actor, composer EA/
02*, HAS
RUSSELL, Henry (fl 1900s) Eng-
lish opera director WWM
RUSSELL, Henry (d 1909) stage
manager EA/10*
RUSSELL, Herbert M. (d 1907)
singer EA/08*
RUSSELL, Howard (1835-1914)
English actor OAA/1-2
RUSSELL, Mrs. Howard (d 1880
[30]) EA/81*
RUSSELL, H. Scott (1868-1949)
English actor, singer WWT/
6-10
RUSSELL, Irene (b 1899/1901)
Tasmanian actress, singer
WWT/6-8
RUSSELL, Iris (b 1922) English
actress WWT/11-16
RUSSELL, J. (fl 1846) actor
HAS
RUSSELL, James (d 1845 [79])
EA/72*
RUSSELL, James (1789-1859)
English actor CDP, OX
RUSSELL, James Howell (d 1909)
scene painter EA/10*
RUSSELL, Jane (b 1921) Amer-
ican actress TW/27-28
RUSSELL, Jay (d 1970 [57])
publicist BP/55*
RUSSELL, J. Fritz Scottish actor
GRB/2
RUSSELL, Jim (b 1927) American
actor TW/13
RUSSELL, John (fl 1617-19)
gatherer DA
RUSSELL, John (d 1925 [69])
comedian BE*, BP/9*
RUSSELL, Mrs. John see
Fanchette, Kate
RUSSELL, Mrs. John see
Huddart, Fanny
RUSSELL, Kathleen actress
GRB/1-2
RUSSELL, Kenna (d 1907) ac-

tress EA/08*
RUSSELL, Lewis (d 1961 [76])
actor BE*
RUSSELL, Lillian [Louise Leonard]
(1861-1922) American actress,
singer CDP, ES, GRB/2-4,
HJD, NTH, OC/1-3, SR, WWA/
1, WWM, WWS, WWT/1-4
RUSSELL, Mabel (d 1908 [36])
actress GRB/4*, WWT/14*
RUSSELL, Mabel (1887-1951) ac-
tress, dancer WWT/2-9
RUSSELL, Maria (d 1905 [77])
EA/06*
RUSSELL, Marian (b 1929) Amer-
ican actress TW/7-8
RUSSELL, Marie (d 1969 [86])
performer BP/53*
RUSSELL, Marie Booth [Mrs. R.
B. Mantell] (d 1911) American
actress GRB/3-4
RUSSELL, Mary (d 1891) EA/93*
RUSSELL, Mary Ann see Far-
ren, Mrs. George Percy
RUSSELL, R. (d 1849) English ac-
tor, manager HAS
RUSSELL, Robert (b 1912) Ameri-
can dramatist BE
RUSSELL, Rosalind (1911/12-76)
American actress AAS, BE,
CB, ES, SR, TW/13, WWT/
13-16
RUSSELL, Samuel Thomas (1769?-
1845) English actor CDP, DNB,
GT, OX, TD/1-2
RUSSELL, Sol Smith (1848-1902)
American actor, manager CDP,
DAB, NTH, OC/1-3, PP/3,
SR, WWA/1
RUSSELL, Thomas (d 1891 [49])
proprietor EA/92*
RUSSELL, Tom H. (d 1892) music-
hall comedian EA/93*
RUSSELL, Violet actress DP
RUSSELL, Walter actor GRB/1
RUSSELL, William (1777-1813)
English composer DNB
RUSSELL, William (1884-1929)
actor, director BE*
RUSSELL, William Clark (d 1911
[67]) writer BE*, WWT/14*
RUSSELL, William H. (d 1871
[49]) stage manager EA/72*
RUSSELL-BROWN, Anna Claudia
see Russell, Anna
RUSSELL-DAVIS, Arthur (d 1917)
EA/18*
RUSSO, Sarett Rude (d 1976 [58])

dramatist BP/60*
RUSSOM, Leon (b 1941) American actor TW/25-28
RUSSON, Joseph (d 1911) minstrel EA/12*
RUST, Alan American actor TW/30
RUST, Gordon A. (1908-77) American executive BE
RUSTON, Ernest (b 1864) English actor GRB/1
RUTH, Jack (b 1921) American actor TW/5, 10
RUTH, Josephine see Taylor, Mrs. J. G.
RUTHERFORD, Mr. (fl 1807) actor HAS
RUTHERFORD, John [Mrs. Evelyn Greenleaf Sutherland] (d 1909) dramatist EA/10*
RUTHERFORD, Dame Margaret (1892-1972) English actress AAS, BE, CB, COC, ES, OC/3, PDT, TW/3, 28, WWA/5, WWT/8-15
RUTHERFORD, Mary (b 1945) Canadian actress WWT/16
RUTHERFORD, Tom (d 1973) actor TW/29
RUTHERSTON, Albert Daniel (1881/83-1953) English designer ES, WWT/5-9
RUTHVEN, Edgar (d 1909 [22]) actor EA/10*
RUTLAND, Ruth [Mrs. W. H. Crosland] (d 1892) actress EA/93*, WWT/14*
RUTLEY, Henry (d 1874 [58]) lessee EA/75*
RUTT, Mrs. Fred see Hayes, Blanche
RUTTER, Grace see Elliston, Grace
RUTTER, Joseph (fl 1635-40) dramatist CP/1-3, FGF
RUTTER, William (fl 1503) actor DA
RUTTLEDGE, Annie (d 1894) EA/95*
RUTTLEDGE, Frances [Mrs. F. Lumsden Hare] English actress GRB/1-3
RUTTY, Herbert Waring see Waring, Herbert
RUYMEN, Ayn (b 1947) American actress TW/27
RUZT-NISSEN, Grethe see Nissen, Greta

RYAN, Mr. (fl 1787) actor HAS
RYAN, Mr. (fl 1850) American actor HAS
RYAN, Belvil (d 1878 [48]) comedian EA/80*
RYAN, Ben (d 1968) performer BP/53*
RYAN, Cecil (b 1886) New Zealand actor, singer WWM
RYAN, Charlene American actress TW/26-29
RYAN, Charles V. (b 1913) American talent representative BE
RYAN, Conny (d 1963 [62]) performer BE*, BP/47*
RYAN, Dennis (d 1786) Irish actor, manager WWA/H
RYAN, Desmond (d 1868 [54]) critic EA/69*
RYAN, Dick (d 1969 [72]) performer BP/54*
RYAN, Edmon (b 1910) American actor TW/7-9, 14-15
RYAN, Grace M. (d 1972 [82]) performer BP/57*
RYAN, Herbert (d 1898 [22]) actor EA/99*
RYAN, Herbert Henry (b 1875) American editor WWM
RYAN, Irene (d 1973 [70]) actress TW/29
RYAN, Jack (d 1850 [53]) prompter, lessee EA/72*
RYAN, James (d 1875 [76]) circus proprietor EA/76*
RYAN, James E. (d 1976 [35]) performer BP/60*
RYAN, John P. (b 1938) American actor TW/26, 28-29
RYAN, Kate (d 1922 [65]) American actress BE*, BP/7*
RYAN, Lacy (1694-1760) English actor, dramatist COC, CP/1-3, DNB, GT, OC/1-3, TD/1-2
RYAN, Madge (b 1919) Australian actress WWT/14-16
RYAN, Mary (1885-1948) American actress SR, TW/5, WWT/4-6
RYAN, Michael (b 1929) American actor TW/19
RYAN, Redmond (d 1855) Irish comedian HAS
RYAN, Richard Nesbitt (d 1865 [46]) actor, manager EA/72*
RYAN, Robert (1909/13-73) American actor AAS, BE, ES, TW/10, 19, 25-27, 30, WWT/14-15
RYAN, Mrs. Robert see Cad-

walader, Jessica
RYAN, Samuel (b 1834) American actor, stage manager HAS
RYAN, Sheila (d 1975 [54]) performer BP/60*
RYAN, Sophie see Eyre, Sophie
RYAN, Sue American actress TW/1
RYAN, T. E. (d 1920) scene artist BE*, WWT/14*
RYAN, Thomas (d 1928 [73]) comedian CDP
RYBNER, Martin Cornelius (1853-1929) Danish composer DAB
RYDE, Will (d 1917) EA/18*
RYDELL, Charles (b 1931) American actor TW/21, 23
RYDER, Alfred [né Alfred Jacob Corn] (d 1919) American actor, director BE, TW/3, 7-13, WWT/15-16
RYDER, Arthur W. (d 1938 [61]) American educator, translator BE*
RYDER, Emma [Mrs. Edward Price] (d 1889) actress EA/90*
RYDER, G. V. M. (fl 1844-61) American actor HAS
RYDER, Jessie Henry [Mrs. A. D. McNeill] (d 1904 [70]) lessee EA/05*
RYDER, John (1814-85) English actor CDP, DNB, OAA/1-2
RYDER, Mrs. John (d 1874) EA/75*
RYDER, T. (d 1872 [61]) actor EA/74*
RYDER, Thomas (1735-1790/91) English actor, dramatist CDP, CP/3, DNB, GT, TD/1-2
RYDER, William (d 1871 [24]) musician EA/72*
RYDER, William John (d 1917) EA/18*
RYDER, Willie (d 1899 [27]) music-hall comedian EA/00*
RYDON, Nita [Mrs. John Villiers] (d 1899) actress EA/00*
RYE, Mr. (fl 1834) property man CDP
RYE, Daphne (b 1916) English producer WWT/11-12
RYER, George (fl 1847-63) American actor, stage manager CDP, HAS

RYERSON, Florence (b 1892) American dramatist BE
RYERSON, Margaret see Arlington, Maggie
RYES, Elizabeth (d 1797) dramatist CP/2-3, GT
RYGA, George (b 1932) Canadian dramatist CD
RYKEN, Mabel (d 1968 [77]) performer BP/53*
RYLAND, Ann (d 1907 [74]) EA/08*
RYLAND, Cliff (fl 1895?) actor, singer CDP
RYLAND, Jack (b 1935) American actor TW/22, 24, 26, 29
RYLANDS, George (b 1902) English producer, director AAS, COC, WWT/10-16
RYLESTON, Mrs. Edward A. see Forde, Emmie
RYLEY, Charles (d 1897) actor, singer EA/98*
RYLEY, J. H. (d 1922 [81]) actor BE*, WWT/14*
RYLEY, J. T. (d 1876 [49]) performer? EA/77*
RYLEY, Madeleine Lucette (1865-1934) English actress, dramatist, singer GRB/1-4, SR, WWS, WWT/1-7, WWW/3
RYLEY, Samuel William (1759-1837) English dramatist CDP, CP/3
RYMAN, Add (d 1896 [55/59]) American minstrel manager & performer CDP
RYMER, Thomas (1641-1713) English dramatist CDP, CP/1-3, GT, HP, NTH
RYNER, Mrs. H. [née Kate Meadows] (fl 1835) actress HAS
RYSANEK, Leonie (b 1926/28) Austrian singer CB, ES
RYSKIND, Morrie (b 1895) American librettist, dramatist BE, CD, MWD, NTH, WWT/8-11
RYVES, Elizabeth see Ryes, Elizabeth

- S -

S., Mr. see Still, John
S., E. (fl 1607) dramatist CP/1-3
S., J. dramatist CP/1-3, FGF
S., S. (fl 1616) dramatist CP/2-3, FGF

S., T. (fl 1671-80) dramatist
CP/3
S., W. (fl 1619) dramatist FGF
SAAL, Alfred P. (d 1962 [70])
magician BE*
SAARI, Charles (b 1944/47)
American actor BE, TW/14
SAARINEN, Aline B. (d 1972
[58]) critic BP/57*
SABATINI, Rafael (1875-1950)
Italian/English dramatist
NTH, WWT/5-10, WWW/4
SABEL, Josephine (d 1945 [79])
American actress, singer
WWS
SABIN, David (b 1937) American
actor TW/24-26, 29
SABIN, Robert (d 1969 [57])
critic BP/53*
SABINE, Martin (b 1876) English
manager, producer WWT/8-9
SABINSON, Harvey B. (b 1924)
American press representative
BE
SABINSON, Lee (b 1911) Ameri-
can producing manager BE,
TW/2-8, WWT/11-12
SABLON, Jean (b 1909) French
singer, composer BE
SABOL, Dick (b 1937) American
actor TW/22
SABU (d 1963 [39]) Indian actor
BE*
SACCHETTI, Lorenzo (1759-1830)
Italian scene artist ES
SACCOMANI, Signora (fl 1833)
actress HAS
SACCONI, Rosalinda musician
CDP
SACHEVERELL, Mrs. John see
Charke, Mrs. Richard
SACHS, Ann (b 1948) American
actress TW/30
SACHS, Arthur L. (b 1913) Amer-
ican actor TW/3
SACHS, Leonard (b 1909) South
African actor, producer, di-
rector WWT/11-16
SACHS, Mary P. K. (d 1973
[91]) dramatist BP/58*
SACK, Nathaniel (d 1966 [84])
actor TW/23
SACK, Penelope American ac-
tress TW/4
SACKETT, Millie (b 1842) Amer-
ican actress HAS
SACKLER, Howard (b 1929)
American dramatist, director

CD, MH
SACKS, Joseph Leopold (1881-1952)
Russian/English manager WWT/
4-11
SACKVILLE, Thomas (1536-1608)
English dramatist COC, CP/
1-3, DNB, FGF, HP, MH, OC/
1-3
SACKVILLE, Thomas (d 1628) actor
DA
SADAKICHI, Thomatzu (fl 1867)
acrobat CDP
SADDLER, Donald (b 1920) Ameri-
can choreographer, director,
dancer BE, TW/7, WWT/16
SADLER, Anthony (c. 1610-c. 80)
English dramatist CP/1-3
SADLER, Dudley (b 1918) American
actor TW/1, 3
SADLER, Frank (d 1873) performer
EA/74*
SADLER, Ian (d 1971 [69]) per-
former BP/56*
SADLER, J. (fl 1640) dramatist
CP/2-3, FGF
SADLER, James (d 1828) aeronaut
CDP
SADLER, Mary Ann [Mrs. Thomas
Sadler] (d 1890 [54]) EA/91*
SADLER, Michael dramatist CD
SADLER, Stella see Mayhew,
Stella
SADLER, Thomas (fl 1766) drama-
tist CP/3
SADLER, Mrs. Thomas see
Sadler, Mary Ann
SADLER, Thomas H. (d 1893)
American comedian EA/95*
SADOFF, Fred E. (b 1926) Ameri-
can actor, director, producer
BE
SAEMAN, Cecelia see Paez,
Cecelia de
SAENGER, Oscar (b 1868) American
singer, teacher WWM
SAFIER, Gloria (b 1921) American
talent representative BE
SAGAL, Sara Macon (d 1975 [47])
producer/director/choreographer
BP/60*
SAGAN, Leontine (1889/95-1974)
Austrian actress, producer
BTR/74, WWT/8-11
SAGE, Mons. (fl 1859) actor HAS
SAGE, Edward (d 1969 [41]) per-
former BP/54*
SAGE, John Sylvester (d 1908 [55])
gymnast EA/09*

SAGE, Letitia Anne aeronaut
CDP
SAGER, Max (d 1975 [82]) BP/
60*
SAHARA, Tilly (d 1884) American
singer EA/86*
SAHL, Mort (b 1927) Canadian
comedian CB
SAIDY, Fred (b 1907) American
dramatist, director, lyricist
BE
SAINER, Arthur (b 1924) Ameri-
can dramatist, director, actor
CD
SAINT, Eva Marie (b 1924/29)
American actress BE, ES,
TW/10-15, 29
ST. ALBIN, Mr. (fl 1826?)
dancer CDP
ST. ALBYN, Alfred (d 1871)
singer CDP
ST. ALBYN, E. (d 1872) actor?
EA/73*
ST. ANGE, Josephine (d 1892)
actress, singer CDP, DP
ST. AUBIN, Mrs. (d 1895) EA/
96*
ST. AUBYN, Cpt. (d 1917 [29])
EA/18*
ST. AUBYN, Mrs. Frank see
Rorke, Mary
ST. AUBYN, Harry (d 1906)
EA/07*
ST. AUDRIE, Stella (d 1925
[49]) actress BE*, WWT/14*
ST. CASSE, Clara (b 1841)
singer CDP
ST. CLAIR, Mme. [Mary Mar-
shall] (d 1884 [42]) actress,
manager EA/85*
ST. CLAIR, F. V. (fl 1895?)
singer, composer CDP
ST. CLAIR, Ivy (d 1916) EA/17*
ST. CLAIR, Lydia (d 1970) ac-
tress TW/26
ST. CLAIR, Maurice (d 1970
[67]) performer BP/54*
ST. CLAIR, Norman (d 1910
[44]) actor EA/11*
ST. CLAIR, Robert (d 1967 [57])
dramatist BP/52*
ST. CLAIR, Rosa see Leland,
Rosa
ST. CLAIR, Sallie (1831-67)
English dancer HAS
ST. CLAIR, Stuart (d 1907 [57])
actor EA/08*
ST. CLAIR, Yvonne (d 1971

[57]) performer BP/56*
ST. CLAIR-ERSKINE, James Fran-
cis Harry see Rosslyn, Earl
of
ST. CLARE, Edith (d 1917) pro-
prietor, actress, performer
EA/18*
ST. CYR, Lillian Red Wing (d
1974 [90]) performer BP/58*
ST. CYR, Mimi (fl 1896?) singer
CDP
SAINT-DENIS, Michel (1897-1971)
French actor, dramatist, pro-
ducer AAS, BE, COC, ES,
OC/1-3, PDT, WWA/5, WWT/
8-15
ST. DENIS, Ruth [née Ruth Denis]
(1878-1968) American dancer,
choreographer CB, ES, TW/
25, WWA/5
ST. DENIS, Teddie [June Catherine
Church Denham] (b 1909) Scot-
tish actress, singer WWT/9-10
ST. GEORGE, Julia (d 1903 [79])
actress CDP
ST. GEORGE, Rosie (d 1901) ac-
tress EA/02*
ST. HELIER, Ivy [Ivy Aitchison]
(d 1971) English actress, singer
WWT/3-12
SAINTHILL, Loudon (1919-69) Tas-
manian designer COC, ES,
PDT, WWT/13-14, WWW/6
ST. JOHN, Al (d 1963 [70]) actor
BE*
ST. JOHN, Beatrice (d 1974 [60s])
performer BP/59*
ST. JOHN, Betta (b 1929) American
actress TW/5-8
ST. JOHN, Christopher Marie (d
1960) dramatist GRB/2-4,
WWT/1-12
ST. JOHN, Florence [Florence
Greig] (1854-1912) English ac-
tress, singer CDP, DP, GRB/
1-4, OAA/2, WWT/1
ST. JOHN, George Keller see
Campbell, J. C.
SAINT JOHN, Hon. Henry (fl 1789)
dramatist GT, TD/1-2
ST. JOHN, Herbert [W. H. St.
John Walter] English actor
GRB/1
ST. JOHN, Howard (1905-74)
American actor BE, TW/3,
8-14, 30, WWT/11-15
ST. JOHN, Miss J. [Mrs. J.
Dwight] (d 1897) variety per-

former EA/98*
ST. JOHN, John (d 1793) drama-
tist CP/3
ST. JOHN, Lily [Lilian Clara
Johnson] (b 1895) English ac-
tress, singer WWT/4-7
ST. JOHN, Marco (b 1939)
American actor TW/21, 23-
26, 28
ST. JOHN, Margaret Florence
see St. John, Florence
ST. JOHN, Marguerite (d 1940
[79]) English actress BE*,
WWT/14*
ST. JOHN, Nelson B. (b c. 1865)
manager SR
ST. JOHN, Norah (d 1962 [58])
performer BE*
ST. LEDGER, Annie (d 1891
[43]) EA/92*
ST. LEDGER, Catherine M. [née
Williams] (fl 1799-1802) Irish
actress CDP, GT, TD/1-2
ST. LEDGER, Harry (d 1906)
EA/07*
ST. LEGER, Clara [Mrs. Charles
Raynor] (d 1896 [38]) EA/97*
ST. LEON, Arthur M. (1821-70)
French dancer, ballet master,
musician CDP, ES
ST. LEON, Mr. W. (d 1867)
bottle equilibrist, pantomimist
EA/68*
ST. LEONARD, Florence (fl 1901-
13) Canadian actress WWM
ST. LUKE, Mr. (d 1850) Eng-
lish actor HAS
ST. LUKE, Miss (fl 1837) ac-
tress HAS
ST. MARIE, Blanche (fl 1900?)
actress, singer CDP
ST. MAUR, John (d 1888 [40])
manager EA/89*
ST. ODY, M. (fl 1853) English
dancer HAS
SAINTON, Charlotte Helen (1821-
85) singer CDP, DNB
SAINTON-DOLBY, Charlotte
Helen see Sainton, Char-
lotte Helen
ST. PIERRE, Louis (d 1971
[82]) designer BP/56*
SAINT-SAENS, Camille (1836-
1921) French composer GRB/
1, WWM
SAINTSBURY, H. A. (1869-1939)
English actor, dramatist
WWT/2-8

ST. SERFE, Sir Thomas (fl 1668)
Scottish dramatist CP/1-3, GT
SAINT-SUBBER, Arnold (b 1918)
American producer BE, WWT/
13-16
ST. VINCENT, Arthur music-hall
singer CDP
SAIVI, Sig. (fl 1850) singer HAS
SAKALL, S. Z. (d 1955 [67]) Hun-
garian actor BE*, BP/39*
SAKAROFF, Clothide (d 1974 [80])
performer BP/58*
SAKER, Mr. actor CDP
SAKER, Ann [Mrs. Horatio Saker]
(d 1885 [58]) EA/86*
SAKER, Annie (1882-1932) Scottish
actress GRB/1-4, WWT/1-6
SAKER, Master C. R. (fl 1836?)
actor CDP
SAKER, Edward (1831-83) English
actor, manager CDP, DNB
SAKER, Mrs. Edward [Marie
O'Brien] (1847-1912) Irish ac-
tress, dramatist, manager CDP,
GRB/4, WWT/1
SAKER, Horace (d 1861 [34]) actor
BE*, WWT/14*
SAKER, Horatio (d 1902 [54]) actor
DNB
SAKER, Mrs. Horatio see Saker,
Ann
SAKER, Maria [Mrs. T. G. Morti-
mer] (d 1902) actress BE*,
EA/03*, WWT/14*
SAKER, Marie see Saker, Mrs.
Edward
SAKER, Richard Henry (d 1870
[28]) actor, producer BE*,
EA/71*, WWT/14*
SAKER, Rose [Mrs. Charles Hay]
(d 1923) English actress DP
SAKER, William (d 1849 [59])
actor BE*, WWT/14*
SAKER, Mrs. William (d 1877 [77])
EA/78*
SAKREN, Jared (b 1950) American
actor TW/29
SAKS, Gene (b 1921) American ac-
tor, director BE, WWT/15-16
SALA, Mme. (d 1860 [67]) singer
CDP
SALA, Mrs. George A. (d 1885)
EA/87*
SALA, George Augustus (d 1895
[67]) dramatist, journalist, critic
BE*, EA/97*, WWT/14*
SALACROU, Armand (b 1899) French
dramatist COC, OC/2-3

SALAMAN, Charles Kensington (d 1901 [87]) musician, composer EA/02*
SALAMAN, Malcolm C. (d 1940 [84]) critic BE*, WWT/14*
SALBERG, Derek S. (b 1912/22) English manager, stage manager AAS, WWT/14-16
SALBERG, Leon (d 1937 [62]) producer, manager BE*, WWT/14*
SALBERG, Valérie French actress GRB/2
SALE, Charles (1885-1936) American actor WWA/1, WWT/7-8
SALE, Sara [Mrs. Frank Pacey Buck] (d 1899 [30]) singer EA/00*
SALES, Sammy (d 1967 [61]) performer BP/51*
SALIG, Louis (d 1876 [25]) acting manager EA/77*
SALINGER, Conrad (d 1962 [59]) composer BE*
SALISBURY, Charles (1821-64) American actor HAS
SALISBURY, Leah (d 1975) American literary representative BE
SALKIND, Michel (d 1974 [83]) producer/director/choreographer BP/58*
SALLE, Marie (1707/10-56) French dancer ES, OC/1-2
SALLERT, Ulla Swedish actress TW/21
SALLIS, Peter (b 1921) English actor AAS, TW/22, WWT/13-16
SALMAGGI, Alfredo (d 1975 [89]) producer/director/choreographer BP/60*
SALMI, Albert (b 1928) American actor BE, TW/25
SALMON, Eliza (1787-1849) English singer DNB
SALMON, Scotty (b 1943) American actor TW/24, 28
SALMON, T. H. (d 1867 [54]) band leader EA/68*
SALMOND, Norman (1858-1914) English singer, actor GRB/2-4
SALOMON, Johann Peter (1745-1815) German/English musician CDP, DNB, ES
SALSBURY, Nathan (1846-1902) American actor, manager,

showman CDP
SALT, Charles H. (d 1904) acrobat EA/05*
SALT, Jennifer (b 1944) American actress TW/26-27
SALT, Samuel (d 1890) equestrian EA/91*
SALTER, Mr. (fl 1818) actor CDP
SALTER, Henry (d 1892 [51]) variety theatre proprietor EA/93*
SALTER, Mrs. James see Rignold, Lilian
SALTERNE, George dramatist FGF
SALTIKOV-SHCHEDRIN, Mikhail Evgrafovich (1826-89) Russian dramatist OC/3
SALTOUN, Walter (d 1965 [84]) dramatist, manager, critic WWT/14*
SALTZBERG, Geraldine (d 1972 [80]) critic BP/57*
SALVI, Mlle. singer CDP
SALVI, Lorenzo (1810-79) Italian singer CDP, ES
SALVINI, Mme. (d 1868 [37]) Italian actress EA/69*
SALVINI, Alexander (1861-96) Italian actor CDP
SALVINI, Gustavo (d 1930) actor WWT/14*
SALVINI, Tommaso (1829-1916) Italian actor CDP, COC, ES, GRB/1-4, NTH, OC/1-3, SR, WWT/1-3
SALVIO, Robert (b 1942) American actor TW/23-26
SALVIONI, Sig. (fl 1855) singer HAS
SALVIONI, Enrichetta (fl 1833) singer HAS
SALZBERG, Louisa Ann [Miss L. A. Phillips] (b 1812) English actress CDP, HAS
SALZER, Eugene (d 1964 [c. 80]) musical director, conductor BE*
SAM (fl 1590?) actor DA
SAMARY, Jeanne (d 1890 [33]) actress BE*, WWT/14*
SAMARY, Marie (d 1941 [93]) actress WWT/14*
SAMEGO-BRUGNOLI, Amalia (fl early 19th cent) Italian dancer, mimist ES
SAMINSKY, Lazare (1882-1959) Russian composer WWA/3

SAMMARCO, Mario (1868/73/74-
1930) Italian singer ES,
WWA/5, WWM, WWW/3
SAMMIS, George W. (d 1927
[72]) manager BE*, BP/11*
SAMMON, Matilda (d 1898 [34])
wardrobe mistress EA/99*
SAMOILOFF, L. S. (b 1877)
Russian singer, teacher WWM
SAMPLE, Forrest (d 1975 [76])
performer BP/60*
SAMPSON, Selma (d 1965 [53])
performer BP/49*
SAMPSON, William (1590?-1636?)
dramatist CP/1-3, DNB,
FGF
SAMPSON, William (d 1922 [63])
actor BE*, BP/6*
SAMROCK, Victor (b 1907) Amer-
ican manager, producer BE
SAMS, William Raymond (d 1872
[52]) actor? EA/73*
SAMSON, George see Alex-
ander, Sir George
SAMSON, Ivan (1894-1963) Eng-
lish actor WWT/7-13
SAMUEL, Mrs. Emanuel see
Davies, Anna
SAMUEL, Joe (d 1868 [32]) dram-
atic & equestrian agent EA/
69*
SAMUEL, Leopold (d 1975 [92])
composer/lyricist BP/59*
SAMUELL, L. L. (d 1893 [35])
music-hall lessee EA/94*
SAMUELL, W. J. (d 1916) singer
EA/17*
SAMUELLS, Alexander R. mana-
ger CDP
SAMUELS, Maurice Victor (1873-
1945) American dramatist
WWA/2, WWM
SAMUELSON, Julian see Wylie,
Julian
SAMUELSON, Morris Laurence
see Wylie, Lauri
SAMWELL, W. equestrian CDP
SAMWELLS, John (d 1883 [63])
equestrian EA/84*
SAMWELLS, Mrs. John (d 1907
[95]) performer? EA/08*
SAMWELLS, Roland (d 1908 [49])
ringmaster, scene artist
EA/10*
SAMWORTH, Mrs. see Bride,
Elizabeth
SANCHEZ, Jaime (b 1938) Puerto
Rican actor TW/22, 24, 30

SANCHIOLI, Mlle. singer CDP
SAND, Inge (d 1974 [45]) performer
BP/58*
SAND, Paul (b 1935) American ac-
tor TW/20-23, 27, WWT/16
SAND, Tom Hughes (b 1927) West
Indian actor TW/8
SANDE, Walter (d 1971 [63]) per-
former BP/56*
SANDEEN, Darrell (b 1930) Amer-
ican actor TW/17, 25
SANDEMAN, Christopher (1882-
1951) dramatist WWW/5
SANDEMAN, Eleanor Brady (d 1971
[73]) performer BP/55*
SANDER, Ian American actor
TW/28
SANDERS, Albert (b 1943) Ameri-
can actor TW/25, 29-30
SANDERS, Alfred (d 1876) musician
EA/77*
SANDERS, Betty (d 1975 [53]) per-
former BP/60*
SANDERS, Byron (b 1927) Ameri-
can actor TW/12-18, 21
SANDERS, Charlotte (fl 1797)
dramatist CP/3
SANDERS, Dirk actor TW/15-18
SANDERS, Donna American actress
TW/26
SANDERS, Edward S. see Ab-
bott, Edward S.
SANDERS, Felicia (d 1975 [53])
performer BP/59*
SANDERS, George (1906-72) Rus-
sian/English actor CB, ES
SANDERS, Henry Charles (d 1879
[43]) professor of music EA/81*
SANDERS, Honey (b 1928) Ameri-
can actress TW/24, 28
SANDERS, John (d 1865 [66]) actor
EA/72*
SANDERS, Mary (fl 1885-1901)
American actress PP/3
SANDERS, Richard (b 1940) Amer-
ican actor TW/30
SANDERS, Scott (d 1956 [68]) mu-
sic-hall comedian BE*, WWT/
14*
SANDERS, William (fl 1624) actor
DA
SANDERSON, Mr. (fl 1805) actor
HAS
SANDERSON, Mrs. (d 1872) singer
EA/73*
SANDERSON, George (fl 1640) actor
DA
SANDERSON, Gregory (fl c. 1619)

SANDERSON 822

actor DA
SANDERSON, Harry S. actor
CDP
SANDERSON, James (1769?-1841?)
musician DNB
SANDERSON, Julia [Mrs. J. T.
Sloan] (1887-1975) American
actress, singer BE, GRB/
3-4, WWM, WWS, WWT/1-8
SANDERSON, Mary see Better-
ton, Mrs. Thomas
SANDERSON, Sibyl (1865-1903)
American singer CDP, DAB,
SR, WWA/1, WWW/1
SANDFORD, Mr. actor, manager
TD/2
SANDFORD, Mr. (fl 1724) dram-
atist CP/2-3
SANDFORD, Mr. (fl 1812) Eng-
lish actor HAS
SANDFORD, Charles J. (d 1917)
actor EA/18*
SANDFORD, Charles V. (d 1917)
actor EA/18*
SANDFORD, Charles W. (1796-
1878) proprietor, lawyer
CDP
SANDFORD, Mrs. C. W. see
Holman, Mrs. Joseph George
SANDFORD, E. (b 1825) Ameri-
can actor HAS
SANDFORD, Edith see Roger-
son, Mrs. Whit
SANDFORD, Joseph J. (d 1879)
gymnast EA/80*
SANDFORD, Marjorie (b 1910)
English actress, singer WWT/
10-13
SANDFORD, Samuel (fl 1660-99)
English actor DNB, OC/1-3
SANDILANDS, George Sommerville
(1889-1961) Scottish dramatist
WWW/6
SANDILANDS, W. S. (fl 1881?)
singer CDP
SANDISON, Gordon (1913-58)
English executive WWT/11-
12
SANDLE, Floyd (b 1913) Ameri-
can educator BE
SANDLER, Jacob Koppel (1856-
1931) Russian/American com-
poser, conductor DAB
SANDLER, Jesse (d 1975 [57])
producer/director/choreographer
BP/59*
SANDOE, Alfred (d 1911 [46])
actor EA/12*

SANDONI, Signora Pietro Giuseppe
see Cuzzoni, Francesca
SANDOR, Alfred (b 1918) Hungari-
an/American actor BE, TW/
23-25
SANDOW, Eugene (d 1925 [58])
Prussian athlete GRB/1
SANDROCK, Adele (d 1937 [73])
German actress CDP
SANDS, Diana (1934-73) American
actress AAS, BE, ES, TW/19-
22, 24-25, 28, 30, WWT/15
SANDS, Dick (1840-1900) English
clog dancer CDP, HAS
SANDS, Dorothy (b 1893/1900)
American actress, director
BE, TW/2-3, 9-17, 20, 24-26,
WWT/13-16
SANDS, Edward (d 1887) American
actor NYM
SANDS, George E. (d 1887) Amer-
ican manager EA/88*
SANDS, James (fl 1605-17) actor
DA
SANDS, Larry (d 1974 [42]) pro-
ducer/director/choreographer
BP/59*
SANDS, Leslie (b 1921) English
actor, dramatist WWT/15-16
SANDS, Richard (1814-61) Ameri-
can circus performer CDP,
HAS
SANDS, Thomas (fl 1635) actor
DA
SANDT, Bernhardt (fl 1600) actor
DA
SANDY, Little [Alexander Coleman]
(d 1903 [53]) circus clown EA/
04*
SANDYS, George (1577-1643) Eng-
lish dramatist CP/1-3
SANFORD, Jane (b 1943) Ameri-
can actress TW/26, 30
SANFORD, Jim [Thomas Pynes]
(d 1891) minstrel EA/93*
SANFORD, John L. (fl 1866)
comedian HAS
SANFORD, Robert (1904-71) Amer-
ican talent representative BE
SANFORD, Samuel S. (1821-1905)
American singer, minstrel, cir-
cus clown CDP, HAS
SAN FRANCISCO DANCERS' WORK-
SHOP CD
SAN FRANCISCO MIME TROUPE
CD
SANG, Leonard B. (b 1904) Amer-
ican manager BE

SANGALLI, Rita (b 1849) Italian
dancer CDP, HAS
SANGER, Alfred (d 1880 [60])
stage manager EA/81*
SANGER, Mrs. Alfred (d 1889
[69]) EA/90*
SANGER, Elizabeth [Mrs. John
Sanger] (d 1893 [67]) EA/94*
SANGER, Ellen [Mrs. George
Sanger] (d 1899 [67]) EA/00*
SANGER, Eugene (fl 1881) actor
CDP
SANGER, Frank W. (d 1904)
manager EA/05*, WWT/14*
SANGER, Fred (d 1923 [72]) per-
former BE*
SANGER, George (1825/26-1911)
English circus manager, per-
former DNB, SR
SANGER, Mrs. George see
Sanger, Ellen
SANGER, John (1816-89) English
circus proprietor DNB, HP
SANGER, Mrs. John see Sang-
er, Elizabeth
SANGER, Rachel [Mrs. James
Scanlan] (d 1884 [34]) actress,
singer CDP
SANGER, Rachel Mary (fl 1851-
79) English actress OAA/2
SANGER, William (d 1901 [74])
circus proprietor EA/02*
SANGER, Mrs. William (d 1893)
EA/95*
SANGIOVANNI, A. (fl 1852)
singer CDP
SANGSTER, Alfred (1880-1972)
English actor, dramatist
WWT/8-11
SANNA, Johnny (d 1965 [64]) per-
former BP/50*
SANSBURY, Vernon J. (d 1913)
EA/14*
SANSOM, Mrs. Charles (d 1871)
singer EA/72*
SANSONE, Charles (d 1968 [63])
composer/lyricist BP/52*
SANTANGELO, Melody (b 1946)
American actress TW/28-29
SANTE, Mrs. (d 1912 [86])
EA/13*
SANTE, George Testo (d 1916
[58]) proprietor, circus &
music-hall performer, gym-
nast EA/17*
SANTELL, Marie American ac-
tress TW/26-27, 30
SANTINI, Gabriele (b 1886)

Italian conductor ES
SANTLEY, Sir Charles (1834-1922)
English singer CDP, DNB,
ES, GRB/1-4, WWW/2
SANTLEY, Frederic (1887-1953)
American actor, singer TW/9,
WWT/7-8
SANTLEY, H. R. (d 1888) advance
agent EA/89*
SANTLEY, Joseph (1889-1971)
American actor, producer TW/
28, WWT/3-10
SANTLEY, Kate (d 1923 [86])
American actress, singer,
manager CDP, GRB/1-4,
OAA/1-2, WWT/1-4
SANTLEY, Mabel (fl 1879) actress
CDP
SANTLEY, Marie [Marie Elizabeth
Day] (d 1898) actress EA/99*
SANTLEY, William (d 1891 [82])
musician EA/92*
SANTLOW, Hester see Booth,
Mrs. Barton, II
SANTLY, Joseph H. (1886-1962)
American performer, songwriter
BE*, BP/47*
SANTORO, Dean (b 1938) American
actor TW/25-27
SANYEAH, Mme. (d 1910 [68])
gymnast CDP
SAPHRINI, Mrs. see Bower,
Miss E.
SAPIGNOLI, Francesco (fl 1833)
singer HAS
SAPIO, Antonio (d 1868 [64]) pro-
fessor of music EA/69*
SAPIO, Lewis (1792-1851) English
actor CDP, OX
SAPORITI, Mme. see Codesaca,
Mme.
"SAPPER" [Lieut.-Col. Cyril Mc-
Neile] (d 1937 [48]) dramatist
BE*, WWT/14*
SAPPINGTON, Fay (b 1906) Amer-
ican actress TW/8, 22, 24, 28
SAPPINGTON, Margo (b 1947)
American actress TW/26-27
SAPPIR, Gerald (b 1939) American
actor TW/25
SAQUI, Mme. (d 1866 [80]) rope
dancer CDP
SARACCO, Prof. inventor, dancer,
teacher CDP
SARAGO, Theo (d 1970 [33]) per-
former BP/55*
SARANDON, Chris (b 1942) Amer-
ican actor TW/27-29

SARANDON, Susan (b 1946) American actress TW/28

SARANOFF, Jules (d 1967 [80]) BP/52*

SARCIUT, Mrs. see Victor, Mary Ann

SARDI, Vincent, Sr. (d 1969 [83]) restauranteur BP/54*

SARDI, Vincent, Jr. (b 1915) American restauranteur, actor BE

SARDOU, Victorien (1831-1908) French dramatist COC, GRB/ 1-4, MWD, NTH, OC/1-3

SARG, Tony (1880/82/83-1942) English marionettist CB, DAB, SR

SARGANO [John Holloway Bright] (d 1892) EA/94*

SARGEANTSON, Kate see Serjeantson, Kate

SARGENT, Mrs. (d 1889) EA/90*

SARGENT, Brent (b 1914) American actor TW/5-7

SARGENT, Epes (1813/14-80) American dramatist CDP, DAB, HJD, RJ, SR, WWA/H

SARGENT, Franklin Haven (1856-1923) American director GRB/ 3, WWM

SARGENT, Frederic[k] (b 1879) English actor GRB/1-2, WWT/ 4-8

SARGENT, Herbert C. (b 1873) English dramatist WWT/6-8

SARGENT, H. J. (1843-96) actor, manager, magician CDP

SARGENT, John (fl 1785) dramatist CP/3

SARGENT, Sir Malcolm (1895-1967) English conductor CB

SARGENT, Margherita (d 1964 [81]) actress TW/21

SARGENT, Mary American actress TW/1

SARGOOD, James J. (b 1875) English conductor, pianist GRB/1

SARIDIS, Angelo (b 1932) Greek actor TW/25

SARINA, Mrs. (d 1883 [21]) EA/84*

SARL, Ernest James [Ernest Sutton] (d 1887 [33]) actor EA/88*

SARL, Sydney Claude (d 1916) EA/17*

SARMENT, Jean (b 1897) French actor, dramatist MWD

SARNER, Alexander (1892-1948) English actor WWT/8-10

SARNO, James (d 1972 [62]) publicist BP/57*

SARNOFF, Dorothy (b 1919) American singer, actress BE, TW/ 5-13

SARONI [William Frederick Short] (d 1888 [38]) musical clown EA/90*

SARONI, Rose [Rose Bell] (d 1881 [29]) EA/82*

SARONY, Leslie (b 1897) English actor, singer WWT/6-10

SARONY, Oliver (d 1879) proprietor, photographer EA/80*

SAROYAN, Lucy American actress TW/26

SAROYAN, William (b 1908) American dramatist, director AAS, BE, CB, CD, COC, ES, HJD, MD, MH, MWD, NTH, OC/1-3, PDT, RE, WWT/10-16

SARRACINI, Gerald (d 1957 [30]) actor TW/14

SARRATT, Mrs. Jacob Henry see Dufour, Camilla

SARTLEE Hottentot Venus CDP

SARTORIS, Mrs. E. T. see Kemble, Adelaide

SARTRE, Jean-Paul Charles Aymard (b 1905) French dramatist BE, CB, COC, OC/2-3

SARZEDAS, Mr. (fl 1827) actor, stage manager HAS

SASS, Edward (d 1916 [58]) actor, manager GRB/1-4, WWT/1-3

SASS, Mrs. Edward see Gwynne, Emma

SASS, Enid (1889-1959) English actress WWT/4-8

SATCHELL, Catherine Mary see Duill, Mrs. John Lewis

SATCHELL, Susanna see Benson, Mrs. Robert

SATTER, Gustav (b 1832) Austrian pianist HAS

SATTIN, Lonnie American actor, singer BE

SATZ, Lillie (d 1974 [78]) performer BP/58*

SAUBERE, Mr. (fl 1805) actor HAS

SAUERS, Patricia (b 1941) American actress TW/23-24

SAUMAREZ, Cissie [Mrs. Arthur

Whitby] English actress, singer GRB/1-3

SAUNDERS, Mrs. (d 1875) singer EA/76*

SAUNDERS, Master (fl 1801?) equestrian CDP

SAUNDERS, Ann see Matthew, Ann

SAUNDERS, C. H. dramatist RJ

SAUNDERS, Charles (fl 1681) dramatist CP/1-3, GT

SAUNDERS, Charles H. (1818-57) American actor HAS

SAUNDERS, Charlotte (d 1899 [73]) English actress OAA/2

SAUNDERS, Clara Verrinder (d 1909 [47]) EA/10*

SAUNDERS, Dan (d 1883) music-hall manager EA/85*

SAUNDERS, Edward (d 1876) comedian EA/77*

SAUNDERS, E. G. (d 1913 [51]) producer BE*, EA/14*, WWT/14*

SAUNDERS, Elizabeth (d 1909 [90]) actress WWT/14*

SAUNDERS, Emily see Don, Lady Emilia Eliza

SAUNDERS, F. J. (d 1917) EA/18*

SAUNDERS, Florence (1890-1926) Chilean/English actress WWT/4-5

SAUNDERS, George (d 1871) comedian EA/72*

SAUNDERS, George Lemon (d 1870 [53]) dramatist EA/71*

SAUNDERS, Mrs. Heath see Hayden, Maud

SAUNDERS, Henry Hooper (d 1905 [49]) circus clown EA/06*

SAUNDERS, Henry Martin (fl 1794) dramatist CP/3

SAUNDERS, James (b 1925) English dramatist AAS, CD, CH, COC, MH, PDT, WWT/14-16

SAUNDERS, Joe see Leybourne, George

SAUNDERS, John (d 1879 [62]) comedian EA/80*

SAUNDERS, John (d 1895 [84]) dramatist BE*, EA/96*, WWT/14*

SAUNDERS, Joseph George (d 1882 [55]) dramatist EA/83*

SAUNDERS, Lanna (b 1941)

American actress TW/28-29

SAUNDERS, Madge (1894-1967) South African actress, singer WWT/4-8

SAUNDERS, Margaret (b 1686) actress DNB

SAUNDERS, Marie [Mrs. Sam Saunders] (d 1894) EA/95*

SAUNDERS, Marilyn (b 1948) American actress TW/26-29

SAUNDERS, Nicholas (b 1914) Russian actor TW/2, 26

SAUNDERS, Peter (b 1911) English producing manager BE, WWT/11-16

SAUNDERS, Sam (d 1893) EA/94*

SAUNDERS, Mrs. Sam (d 1884) EA/85*

SAUNDERS, Mrs. Sam see Saunders, Marie

SAUNDERS, William (fl c. 1517) member of the Chapel Royal DA

SAUNDERSON, Mary see Betterton, Mrs. Thomas

SAURIN, Bernard Joseph (1706-81) French dramatist OC/1-3

SAUSS, Everhart (fl 1592) actor DA

SAUTEREAU, Barry see Kent, Barry

SAVAGE, Miss (fl 1851) actress HAS

SAVAGE, Amelia Jane (d 1887) EA/88*

SAVAGE, Courtenay (1890-1946) American dramatist WWA/2

SAVAGE, David D. (d 1975 [62]) producer/director/choreographer BP/60*

SAVAGE, Mrs. E. G. see Gilbert, Lizzie

SAVAGE, George (b 1904) American educator, dramatist BE

SAVAGE, Henry Wilson (1859/65-1927) American manager DAB, SR, WWA/1, WWM, WWT/2-5

SAVAGE, J. (fl 1707) translator CP/3

SAVAGE, Jerome (fl 1575-79) actor DA

SAVAGE, John (1792-1834) West Indian actor HAS

SAVAGE, John (1828-88) Irish dramatist WWA/H

SAVAGE, Mrs. John [Elizabeth White] actress HAS

SAVAGE, John Dawson (d 1879

[66]) custodian EA/80*
SAVAGE, Rafe DA
SAVAGE, Richard (1697-1743)
English dramatist CP/1-3,
DNB, GT, HP
SAVALAS, Telly (b 1924?) Amer-
ican actor CB
SAVAN, Bruce (b 1927) American
talent representative BE
SAVELLA, Marcia (b 1947) Amer-
ican actress TW/30
SAVEREY, Abraham (fl 1604-06)
actor DA
SAVERY, Marion Castleray (d
1967 [62]) performer BP/52*
SAVIGNY, Mr. (fl 1770) actor
CDP
SAVILE, Geoffrey (d 1969 [87])
performer BP/54*
SAVILE, Mrs. J. H. see
Rhodes, Marie
SAVILL, Arthur (fl 1631) actor
DA
SAVILL, Ethel actress GRB/1
SAVILLE, Alfred (d 1885 [72])
actor EA/86*
SAVILLE, Edmund Faucit (1811-
57) actor CDP
SAVILLE, Mrs. E. Faucit [Miss
Grant] (d 1879) actress, pro-
ducer BE*, EA/80*, WWT/
14*
SAVILLE, Eliza Helena (fl 1870-
79) actress OAA/2
SAVILLE, Helena see Faucit,
Helen
SAVILLE, Henry Faucit (d 1871
[26]) dramatist EA/72*
SAVILLE, J. F. (d 1853 [70])
manager, dramatist EA/72*
SAVILLE, J. Faucit (d 1855
[48]) actor BE*, WWT/14*
SAVILLE, Mrs. J. Faucit (d
1889 [77]) actress, producer,
manager BE*, EA/90*,
WWT/14*
SAVILLE, John (fl 1603) drama-
tist CP/3, FGF
SAVILLE, Kate (d 1922) actress
OAA/2
SAVILLE, May (b 1846) Canadian
actress HAS
SAVILLE, T. G. (d 1934 [31])
actor BE*, WWT/14*
SAVINA, Maria (d 1915 [61])
actress BE*, WWT/14*
SAVINO, Domenico (d 1973 [91])
composer/lyricist BP/58*

SAVINO, Frank (b 1936) American
actor TW/26
SAVO, Jimmy (1895-1960) American
actor TW/2-12, 17, WWT/9-11
SAVOIR, Alfred (d 1934 [51]) dra-
matist WWT/14*
SAVORY, Gerald (b 1909) English
actor, dramatist AAS, MD,
PDT, WWT/9-16
SAVORY, Kenneth see Douglas,
Kenneth
SAVOY, Bert (d 1923 [35]) Ameri-
can comedian BE*, BP/8*
SAVOY, Harry (d 1974 [76]) per-
former BP/59*
SAWFORD, Mr. (b 1818) actor
CDP
SAWFORD, Samuel (d 1891 [81])
EA/92*
SAWIN, George Arthur (b 1842)
American actor, prompter HAS
SAWIN, Mrs. George Arthur [Katie
Gardner] (b 1845) American ac-
tress, dancer HAS
SAWYER, Carl (b 1921) American
producer, manager BE
SAWYER, Charles P. (d 1935 [80])
American critic BE*, BP/19*
SAWYER, Dorie (b 1897) English
actress WWT/6-8
SAWYER, Frank (d 1895 [32]) vari-
ety performer EA/96*
SAWYER, Ivy (b 1896/97) English
actress, singer WWT/4-8
SAWYER, Jeanette (d 1971) publi-
cist BP/56*
SAWYER, Laura (d 1970 [85]) per-
former BP/55*
SAWYER, Lemuel (d 1844) Ameri-
can dramatist EAP, RJ
SAWYER, William (b 1828) English
dramatist EA/68
SAWYER, William Kingston (d
1882 [54]) dramatist EA/83*
SAXE, Serge (d 1967 [67]) com-
poser/lyricist BP/52*
SAXE, Templer [or Templar]
(1866/68-1935) English singer,
actor WWM, WWS
SAXE, Thomas, Jr. (d 1975 [72])
actor? executive? BP/60*
SAXON, Kate (d 1863 [36]) lecturer,
actress CDP, HAS
SAXON, Marie (d 1941 [37]) American actress BE*, BP/26*
SAXON, Thomas A. [Thomas Ell-
more] (fl 1867-69) actor HAS
SAXTON, Luther (b 1916) American

actor TW/1-3
SAYAO, Bidu (b 1906?) Brazilian
singer CB
SAYERS, Dorothy L. (1893-1957)
English dramatist DNB, ES,
HP, MD, MWD, WWA/3,
WWT/9-12, WWW/5
SAYERS, Frank (fl 1790) drama-
tist CP/3
SAYERS, Harry (d 1934 [77])
producer, songwriter BE*
SAYERS, Tom (1826-65) clown,
pugilist CDP
SAYLER, Oliver Martin (1887-
1958) American critic TW/
15, WWA/3, WWT/5-11
SAYLOR, Sid (d 1962 [67]) per-
former BE*
SAYRE, Jeffrey (d 1974 [73]) per-
former BP/59*
SAYRE, Theodore Burt (1874-
1954) American dramatist
GRB/2-4, WWA/3, WWS,
WWT/1-7
SBRIGLIA, Giovanni (fl 1859)
singer CDP
SCACCIATI, Bianca (1894-1948)
Italian singer ES
SCAIFE, Gillian (d 1976) Turkish/
English actress WWT/3-11
SCALA, Gia (d 1972 [38]) per-
former BP/56*
SCALCHI, Sofia (1850-1922)
Italian singer CDP, ES
SCALES, Caroline see Miskel,
Caroline
SCALES, Prunella [née Illing-
worth] (b 1932) English ac-
tress WWT/15-16
SCALLAN, Miss see Stoneall,
Mrs.
SCAMMELL, Terence (b 1937)
English actor TW/21, 24
SCANLAN, James (d 1909 [76])
manager, singer EA/10*,
WWT/14*
SCANLAN, Mrs. James see
Sanger, Rachel
SCANLAN, James C. (d 1897)
actor, stage manager EA/98*
SCANLAN, James F. (d 1973
[51]) publicist BP/58*
SCANLAN, John (b 1924) Amer-
ican actor TW/24-25
SCANLAN, William J. (1856-98)
American actor, singer, song-
writer CDP, SR
SCANLON, William J. see

Scanlan, William J.
SCAPILLON freak CDP
SCARBOROUGH, Earl of (d 1969
[72]) former Lord Chamberlain
BP/54*
SCARBOROUGH, George (b 1875)
American dramatist WWA/5,
WWT/4-11
SCARDINO, Don (b 1949) American
actor TW/30
SCARDON, Paul (d 1954 [79]) ac-
tor, director BE*
SCARIA, Emil (1838-86) Austrian
singer ES
SCARISBRICK, Mrs. [née M. Whit-
nall] (d 1874 [45]) singer EA/
75*
SCARISBRICK, Alice Mary (d 1912)
actress EA/13*
SCARISBRICK, C. J. (d 1918)
EA/19*
SCARLETT, John (fl 1605) actor
DA
SCARLETT, Kathleen (b 1943)
American actress TW/24
SCARLETT, Richard (d 1609) actor
DA
SCARPINATI, Nicholas (b 1944)
American actor TW/30
SCATES, Fred L. (d 1900 [45])
actor EA/01*
SCATES, Joseph (d 1899 [80]) pro-
fessor of music EA/01*
SCAWEN, John (fl 1773-90) drama-
tist CP/3, GT, TD/1-2
SCHAAF, Helen (fl 1851) musi-
cian? HAS
SCHAAL, Richard American actor
TW/23, 27
SCHACHT, Sam (b 1936) American
actor TW/25-27, 29-30
SCHACHTER, Leon (d 1974 [74])
performer BP/59*
SCHADER, Freddie (d 1962 [77])
press representative, journalist
BE*
SCHADLEUTNER, Sebastian (fl
1623) actor DA
SCHAEFER, George (b 1920)
American director, producer
BE, CB, WWT/14-16
SCHAEFER, Louis (b 1931) Amer-
ican actor TW/29-30
SCHÄFER, Mrs. Albert see
Schäfer, Lily
SCHAFER, John K. (d 1970 [51])
composer/lyricist BP/55*
SCHÄFER, Lily [Mrs. Albert

Schäfer] (d 1903 [22]) EA/04*
SCHAFER, Milton (b 1920) Amer-
ican composer, lyricist BE
SCHAFER, Natalie (b 1912)
American actress BE, TW/
14-19, 24, 30, WWT/10-11
SCHALK, Franz (1863-1931)
Austrian conductor ES
SCHALKENBACH, J. B. (d 1910
[85]) inventor of electric or-
chestra EA/11*
SCHALLERT, William (b 1925)
American actor TW/27
SCHALLMAN, Sidney M. (d 1972
[82]) agent BP/57*
SCHARF, Erwin (d 1972 [71])
designer BP/56*
SCHARF, Henry (1822-87) English
actor HAS, NYM
SCHARF, Herman (d 1963 [62])
performer BE*
SCHARY, Doré (b 1905) American
dramatist, director, producer,
actor AAS, BE, CD, MWD,
WWT/13-16
SCHATTNER, Meyer (b 1911)
American publisher BE
SCHATZ, Johanna (fl 1888) Ger-
man actress CDP
SCHAUFFLER, Elsie T. (d 1935
[47]) American dramatist
BE*, BP/20*, WWT/14*
SCHEAR, Robert (b 1936) Amer-
ican stage manager BE
SCHECHNER, Richard (b 1934)
American producer, director,
scholar BE, WWT/15-16
SCHECHTMAN, Saul (b 1924)
American musical director,
composer BE
SCHEERER, Bob (b 1928) Amer-
ican actor TW/5-15
SCHEERER, Maud (d 1961 [80])
American actress TW/13-15,
18
SCHEFF, Fritzi [Baroness
Fritz von Bardeleben] (1879/
80-1954) Austrian actress,
singer GRB/2-4, SR, TW/1,
3-10, WWA/3, WWM, WWS,
WWT/1-8
SCHEIDEMANTEL, Karl (1859-
1923) German singer ES
SCHEIDER, Roy R. (b 1935)
American actor TW/22, 25,
27
SCHEINFELD, Lou (d 1974 [72])
lawyer BP/59*

SCHELL, Maximilian (b 1930)
Austrian actor BE, CB, TW/26
SCHELLER, Marie (fl 1858-64)
German actress HAS
SCHELLOW, Erich (b 1915) Ger-
man actor WWT/14
SCHENCK, Joseph (1892-1930)
American variety performer,
actor SR
SCHENCK, Nicholas (d 1969) Rus-
sian/American? executive
WWA/5
SCHENELING, Gertrude Elizabeth
see Mara, Gertrude Elizabeth
SCHENK, Frances Victoria see
Day, Frances
SCHENK, Al (d 1966 [61]) per-
former BP/51*
SCHENKER, Joel (b 1903) Ameri-
can producer BE
SCHEPARD, Eric talent represent-
ative BE
SCHERER, Susan (b 1948) Ameri-
can actress TW/30
SCHERTZINGER, Victor (d 1941
[52]) composer, conductor
WWT/14*
SCHEUER, Philip (b 1902) Ameri-
can critic, editor BE
SCHEVILL, James (b 1920) Amer-
ican dramatist CD
SCHIAPARELLI, Elsa (d 1973 [83])
designer BP/58*
SCHIESKE, Alfred (d 1970 [61])
performer BP/55*
SCHIFF, David (d 1917) actor,
minstrel SR
SCHIFFMAN, Frank (d 1974 [80])
operator BP/58*
SCHILDKRAUT, Joseph (1895/96-
1964) Austrian actor AAS, BE,
CB, ES, NTH, TW/2-18, 20,
WWA/4, WWT/5-13
SCHILDKRAUT, Rudolf (1862-1930)
German actor ES, SR, WWT/2
SCHILLER, Friedrich von (1759-
1805) German dramatist COC
SCHILLER, Leon (1887-1954)
Polish director COC
SCHILLER, Mrs. Max see
Guilbert, Yvette
SCHILLING, Berthe-Agnès-Lisette
see Bréval, Lucienne
SCHINDLER, Ellen (b 1942) Amer-
ican actress TW/28-29
SCHINDLER, Kurt (1882-1935)
German composer, conductor
DAB

SCHINHAN, Jan Philip (d 1975
[87]) composer/lyricist BP/
59*
SCHINK, A. (fl 1798) translator
CP/3
SCHINOTTI, Mr. actor HAS
SCHINOTTI, Mrs. (d 1829 [22])
actress HAS
SCHIOTZ, Aksel (1906-75) Danish
singer CB
SCHIPA, Tito (1888-1965) Italian
singer ES, WWA/4
SCHIPPERS, Thomas (1930-77)
American conductor CB, ES
SCHIRMER, Albert (b 1790)
German actor CDP
SCHIRMER, Gus, Jr. (b 1918)
American director, talent
representative BE
SCHISGAL, Murray (b 1926)
American dramatist BE, CB,
CD, CH, ES, MH, MWD,
PDT, WWT/15-16
SCHLAMME, Martha (b 1930?)
Austrian actress, singer CB
SCHLANGER, Ben (1904-71)
American architect, lecturer
BE
SCHLEE, Robert (b 1938) Amer-
ican actor TW/29
SCHLENTER, Dr. Paul (d 1916
[62]) producer, actor, manager
BE*, WWT/14*
SCHLESINGER, Florence Augusta
(d 1906) EA/07*
SCHLESINGER, John (b 1926)
English director CB, WWT/
15-16
SCHLESINGER, Isidore (d 1949
[78]) theatre owner & manager
WWT/14*
SCHLETTER, Annie (d 1944) ac-
tress BE*, WWT/14*
SCHLISSEL, Jack (b 1922) Amer-
ican manager BE
SCHMEISSER, Martin (d 1878
[29]) musician EA/79*
SCHMELING, Walter B. (d 1973
[73]) performer BP/58*
SCHMERTS, Robert W. (d 1975
[77]) composer/lyricist BP/
60*
SCHMIDT, Art (d 1969 [68])
public relations BP/54*
SCHMIDT, Charles A. (b 1923)
American educator BE
SCHMIDT, Douglas W. (b 1942)
American designer WWT/

15-16
SCHMIDT, Harvey (b 1939) Ameri-
can composer BE
SCHMUCK, A. (d 1871) musical
director EA/72*
SCHNABEL, Stephan (b 1912) Ger-
man actor TW/9, 11-15, 22,
25-26, 28-29, WWT/16
SCHNEE, Charles (d 1962 [46])
dramatist BP/47*
SCHNEE, Thelma actress WWT/
10-12
SCHNEEMANN, Carolee kinetic
theatre works CD
SCHNEIDEMAN, Robert Ivan (b
1926) American educator, di-
rector BE
SCHNEIDER, Alan (b 1917) Rus-
sian/American actor AAS, BE,
CB, ES, WWT/14-16
SCHNEIDER, Gunther see Ar-
nold, Edward
SCHNEIDER, Hortense (1833-1920)
French singer ES
SCHNEIDER, Stanley (d 1975 [45])
producer/director/choreographer
BP/59*
SCHNIEBER, Dolph J. (fl 1873?)
composer, actor, singer CDP
SCHNITZER, Robert (b 1906) ad-
ministrator, educator, actor
BE
SCHNITZLER, Arthur (d 1931
[69]) Austrian dramatist BP/
16*, WWT/14*
SCHOEFFEL, John B. (d 1918)
impresario SR
SCHOEN, Judy (b 1941) American
actress TW/25, 29-30
SCHOENFELD, William C. (d 1969
[75]) composer/lyricist BP/53*
SCHOFIELD, Alfred (d 1906 [37])
musician EA/07*
SCHOFIELD, Dick (d 1903 [48])
music-hall performer EA/04*
SCHOFIELD, James A. (d 1903)
contortionist EA/05*
SCHOFIELD, Johnny (d 1921 [65])
actor, minstrel BE*, WWT/
14*
SCHOFIELD, Laura [Mrs. William
Routledge] (d 1894) music-hall
performer EA/95*
SCHOFIELD, Robert W. (d 1970
[69]) manager BP/55*
SCHOFIELD, William (d 1901 [40])
EA/02*
SCHOLES, Charles Henry [Charles

Henry Duval] (d 1883 [52])
lessee EA/84*
SCHOLEY, Anne see Hield,
Anne
SCHOLL, Danny (b 1921) Ameri-
can actor TW/2-3, 6
SCHOMBERG, Ralph (d 1792 [78])
dramatist CP/2-3
SCHOMER, Nahum Meir (1849-
1905) Russian/American dram-
atist DAB
SCHONBERG, Rosalyn (d 1973
[60]) critic BP/58*
SCHONCEIT, Louis (d 1970 [74])
ticket agent BP/54*
SCHONTHAN, Franz von (d 1913)
German dramatist SR
SCHOOLCRAFT, Alfreda see
Chippendale, Alfreda
SCHOOLCRAFT, Luke (1847-93)
minstrel CDP
SCHOOLER, Lee (d 1975 [52])
publicist BP/60*
SCHOPRGER, James (d 1884
[56]) actor EA/85*
SCHORR, Friedrich (1888-1953)
Hungarian singer CB, ES,
WWW/5
SCHOTT, Angie actress, drama-
tist CDP
SCHOTT, Helena Cecile see
Ernstone, Helena Cecile
SCHRADER, Frederick Franklin
(1857/59-1943) German/Amer-
ican critic, dramatist WWA/
2, WWM, WWS, WWT/3
SCHRATT, Katharina (d 1940
[84]) Austrian actress CDP,
SR
SCHREINER, Wilfred P. (d 1901
[28]) music-hall agent EA/02*
SCHRIFT, Shirley see Winters,
Shelley
SCHROCK, Robert (b 1945)
American actor TW/27-28
SCHRODER, Friedrich (d 1972
[62]) composer/lyricist BP/
57*
SCHRODER, Friedrich Ludwig
(1744-1816) German actor
OC/1-3
SCHRODER-DEVRIENT, Wil-
helmine (1804-60) German
singer ES
SCHROEDER, Mme. (d 1868
[87]) German actress EA/
69*
SCHROEDER, Michael (b 1943)

Australian actor TW/24
SCHROER, Joseph (b 1943) Ameri-
can actor TW/25
SCHROTT, Eugene (d 1973 [62])
publicist BP/58*
SCHUBERT, Georgina (d 1878)
singer EA/80*
SCHUBERT, Vivian Curtis (d 1967
[75]) performer BP/52*
SCHUDY, Frank (d 1963 [59])
manager BE*
SCHUENZEL, Reinhold (d 1954
[68]) German actor, director
TW/11
SCHULBERG, B. P. (1892-1957)
American producer BE*
SCHULBERG, Budd (b 1914) Amer-
ican dramatist, producer, li-
brettist BE, CD, ES
SCHULMAN, Arnold (b 1925) Amer-
ican dramatist BE
SCHULMAN, Max (d 1964 [65])
performer BP/49*
SCHULT, Minnie (fl 1886?) singer
CDP
SCHULTZ, Cecelia (d 1971 [92])
impresario BP/55*
SCHULTZ, Jack (b 1936) American
actor TW/29-30
SCHULTZ, Michael A. (b 1938)
American director WWT/15-16
SCHULTZ, William H. (d 1889)
American actor EA/90*
SCHULZ, Fritz (d 1972 [76]) Ger-
man actor BP/57*, WWT/16*
SCHULZE, Herr (d 1876) enter-
tainer EA/77*
SCHUMAN, William Howard (b
1910) American composer, edu-
cator BE, ES
SCHUMANN, Elisabeth (1888-1952)
German/American singer ES,
WWW/5
SCHUMANN, Joseph (d 1870) ac-
tor? EA/71*
SCHUMANN, Walter (1913-58)
American composer, conductor
BE*
SCHUMANN-HEINK, Ernestine
(1861-1936) Austrian/American
singer DAB, ES, WWA/1,
WWM, WWS
SCHUMANN-HEINK, Henry (b
1886) German actor WWM
SCHUMER, Henry (b 1914) Amer-
ican hauler, producer BE
SCHUMER, Yvette (b 1921) Ameri-
can manager, producer BE

SCHUNZEL, Reinhold (b 1886)
German actor TW/3, 5-6
SCHUSTER, Milton (d 1975 [92])
booking agent BP/60*
SCHUTTE, Ethel see Shutta,
Ethel
SCHUYLER, Philip (b 1921) Amer-
ican actor TW/6
SCHWAB, Laurence (1893-1951)
American dramatist, producing
manager TW/7, WWT/6-11
SCHWANNECKE, Ellen (d 1972)
performer BP/57*
SCHWARTZ, Abe (d 1963 [75])
composer, conductor BE*
SCHWARTZ, Arthur (b 1900/02)
American composer, producer
BE, WWT/7-16
SCHWARTZ, Delmore (1913-66)
American dramatist WWA/4
SCHWARTZ, Evgeny Lvovich
see Shwartz, Evgeny Lvovich
SCHWARTZ, Ida (d 1976 [80s])
performer BP/60*
SCHWARTZ, Jean (1878-1956)
Hungarian/American composer
WWT/6-11
SCHWARTZ, Maurice (1888/89/
90-1960) Russian/American
actor, manager, director, pro-
ducer COC, CB, ES, NTH,
OC/1-3, TW/16, WWA/4,
WWT/6-12
SCHWARTZ, Oscar see Shaw,
Oscar
SCHWARTZ, Phil (d 1964 [74])
composer/lyricist BP/49*
SCHWARTZ, Ruth (b 1908) Amer-
ican executive, lecturer BE
SCHWARTZ, Stephen L. (b 1948)
American composer WWT/16
SCHWARTZ, Wendie Lee (d 1968
[45]) performer BP/53*
SCHWARZ, Emil (1880-1946)
American impresario ES
SCHWARZKOPF, Elisabeth (b
1915) Polish/English singer
CB, ES
SCHWEID, Mark (d 1969 [78])
actor TW/26
SCHWEIGHOFER, Felix (fl 1900)
German actor CDP
SCHWEYER, Emil (1880-1947)
showman SR
SCHWEZOFF, Igor (b 1904)
Russian dancer, choreographer
ES
SCHYMACHER, Eli (d 1975 [87])

theatrical mover BP/59*
SCIORTINO, Pat (b 1951) American
actor TW/28
SCOBIE, Lizzie [Mrs. J. B. Gor-
don] (d 1912) actress EA/13*
SCOFIELD, Paul (b 1922) English
actor AAS, BE, CB, COC,
ES, OC/2-3, PDT, TW/20,
WWT/11-16
SCOGIN, Robert (b 1937) American
actor TW/26
SCOGNAMIGLIO, Vincent see
Gardenia, Vincent
SCORDLEY, Jack (d 1973 [59])
performer BP/58*
SCOTT, Miss (fl 1829) actress
CDP
SCOTT, Mrs. A. see Ethair,
Emily
SCOTT, A. C. (b 1909) English
educator, writer BE
SCOTT, Agnes Elliot (fl 1900s)
actress WWM, WWS
SCOTT, Allan (b 1909) American
dramatist, producer BE
SCOTT, Arthur (d 1968 [66])
secretary BP/52*
SCOTT, Bonnie (b 1941) American
actress, singer, dancer BE
SCOTT, Bruce (b 1947) American
actor TW/25, 27
SCOTT, Mrs. Clement see
Scott, Isabel
SCOTT, Clement William (1841-
1904) English critic, dramatist
COC, DNB, ES, GRB/1, OC/
1-3, WWW/1
SCOTT, Clifford B. see Bruce,
Clifford
SCOTT, Cyril (1866-1946) Irish
actor GRB/2-4, TW/2, WWM,
WWS, WWT/1-9
SCOTT, Dorothy [Griffiths] (b
1884) English actress GRB/1-2
SCOTT, Ellen Jane [Mrs. William
Scott] (d 1905 [65]) EA/06*
SCOTT, Eric English actor GRB/
1-3
SCOTT, Frances Emily [Mrs.
Walter Egerton] (d 1893) EA/
94*
SCOTT, George (d 1909) English
manager GRB/1-4
SCOTT, George C. (b 1927) Amer-
ican actor AAS, BE, CB, ES,
TW/14-20, 24-25, 29-30, WWT/
14-16
SCOTT, George Henry (d 1910

[29]) EA/11*

SCOTT, Gertrude [Mrs. Norman McKinnell] (d 1951) English actress GRB/3-4, WWT/1-5

SCOTT, Hal (d 1969 [73]) performer BP/54*

SCOTT, Harold (1891-1964) English actor WWT/5-13

SCOTT, Harold (b 1935) American actor BE, TW/24-25, 27

SCOTT, Harry (d 1947 [67]) English actor GRB/1-3

SCOTT, Hazel (b 1920) West Indian singer CB

SCOTT, Helena American actress, singer BE

SCOTT, Henri (1876-1942) American singer WWA/2

SCOTT, Isabel [Mrs. Clement Scott] (d 1890) EA/91*

SCOTT, Ivy (d 1947 [61]) actress TW/1, 3

SCOTT, Mrs. James see Scott, May

SCOTT, James M. (d 1849) actor, manager CDP

SCOTT, Jane (d 1899) EA/00*

SCOTT, Jay Hutchinson (b 1924) English designer ES, WWT/15-16

SCOTT, Jeannie see Ford, Mrs. Martin

SCOTT, Mrs. Joe G. see Morley, Charlotte

SCOTT, John (fl 1503-28) actor DA

SCOTT, John (d 1912 [57]) circus proprietor EA/13*

SCOTT, Mrs. John see Scott, Nellie

SCOTT, John see Pickles, Little

SCOTT, John M. ["Long Tom Coffin"] (d 1849) American actor HAS

SCOTT, John Randolph (1808-56) American actor CDP, HAS, WWA/H

SCOTT, Mrs. John R[andolph] (fl 1851) American actress HAS

SCOTT, Joshua (d 1893 [46]) music-hall proprietor EA/94*

SCOTT, Kay (d 1971 [43]) composer/lyricist BP/55*

SCOTT, Kevin (b 1928) American actor TW/10-13

SCOTT, Lea American actress

TW/28

SCOTT, Leslie (d 1969 [48]) performer BP/54*

SCOTT, Louie [Mrs. Frank S. Strickland] (d 1908 [42]) actress EA/09*

SCOTT, Malcolm (d 1929 [57]) comedian BE*, WWT/14*

SCOTT, Margaret Clement actress GRB/3-4, WWT/1

SCOTT, Margaretta (b 1912) English actress AAS, WWT/7-16

SCOTT, Martha (b 1914) American actress BE, ES, TW/1-8, 10-22, WWT/10-16

SCOTT, May [Mrs. James Scott] (d 1884 [64]) EA/85*

SCOTT, Nan (d 1970 [72]) performer BP/55*

SCOTT, Nellie [Mrs. George Elliott] (d 1890 [33]) music-hall singer EA/91*

SCOTT, Nellie [Mrs. John Scott] (d 1906 [47]) EA/07*

SCOTT, Noel (1889/90-1956) English dramatist WWT/6-12, WWW/5

SCOTT, Norman (1928-68) American singer WWA/5

SCOTT, Peter (b 1932) English actor WWT/11

SCOTT, Pippa (b 1935) American actress BE, TW/13-16

SCOTT, Richard L. (d 1962 [36]) performer BE*

SCOTT, Robert (d 1871 [36]) clown EA/72*

SCOTT, Robert Adrian (d 1972 [61]) producer/director/choreographer BP/57*

SCOTT, Rosemary (b 1914) English actress WWT/9-14

SCOTT, Sam (d 1841 [27]) American diver EA/72*

SCOTT, Seret (b 1949) American actress TW/30

SCOTT, Stephen (b 1928) English actor TW/26, 28

SCOTT, Steve (b 1949) American actor TW/29-30

SCOTT, Thomas (fl 1696-97) dramatist CP/1-3, GT

SCOTT, Thomas (fl 1793) dramatist CP/3

SCOTT, Tom (b 1912) American singer, composer CB

SCOTT, Mrs. W. (d 1907) EA/08*

SCOTT, Walter (fl 1799) Scottish

translator CP/3
SCOTT, Sir Walter (1771-1832)
Scottish dramatist HP, SR
SCOTT, Walter (d 1909 [66])
circus proprietor EA/10*
SCOTT, Mrs. Walter see Mor-
rell, Millie
SCOTT, Walter, Jr. (d 1896
[15]) EA/97*
SCOTT, Cpt. W. E. (d 1893 [25])
EA/94*
SCOTT, Mrs. William see
Scott, Ellen Jane
SCOTT, William Hamilton (d
1886 [36]) musician EA/87*
SCOTT, Winnie (b 1883) English
actress, dancer GRB/1
SCOTT, W. T. (d 1899 [58]) mu-
sician EA/00*
SCOTT, Zachary (1914-65) Amer-
ican actor TW/15-16, 22
SCOTT-DALGLEISH, Mrs. D.
see Brooke, Marie
SCOTT-FISHE, Mr. (d 1898) ac-
tor, singer EA/99*
SCOTT-GATTY, Sir A. (d 1918
[71]) EA/19*
SCOTT-GATTY, Alexander (1876-
1937) English actor WWM,
WWT/2-8
SCOTTI, Antonio (1866/68-1936)
Italian singer ES, WWA/1
SCOTTI, Joe (d 1972 [57]) per-
former BP/56*
SCOTT-SIDDONS, Mary Frances
(1844-96) Indian/English ac-
tress CDP, HAS, OAA/2
SCOTT-SIDDONS, Sarah (d 1896)
actress OAA/1, SR
SCOTT-SMITH, Peter (b 1932)
English actor TW/6
SCOTT-WARING, Mrs. see
Esten, Harriet Pye
SCOULER, Willie (d 1892 [36])
EA/93*
SCOURBY, Alexander (b 1913)
American actor BE, CB,
TW/23, 28, WWT/15-16
SCOVEL, Chevalier (b 1852)
American singer, actor DP
SCOVILLE, William H. (d 1858)
actor HAS
SCRACE, Miss (fl 1784) actress
CDP
SCRAGGS, William Beckwith (d
1886) music-hall proprietor
EA/87*
SCRASE, Patty Ann see Bates,

Mrs. James
SCRIBE, Eugène (1791-1861) French
dramatist COC, OC/3
SCRIBNER, Samuel A. (d 1941 [82])
American manager BE*, BP/
26*
SCROPPO, Dennis (b 1940) Italian
actor TW/17
SCRYMGEOUR, Lizzie (d 1878)
musician EA/80*
SCUDAMORE, Frank A. (d 1904
[56]) dramatist, actor BE*,
EA/05*, WWT/14*
SCUDAMORE, Margaret (1884-1958)
English actress WWT/5-12
SCUDDER, John proprietor CDP
SCUDERY, Georges de (1601-67)
French dramatist OC/3
SCULLION, James H. J. (d 1920)
treasurer BE*, BP/5*
SCULLY, Barbara singer, actress
TW/1
SCULLY, Frank (d 1964 [72])
columnist BP/49*
SCULLY, Tim (d 1897) music-hall
performer EA/98*
SCULTHORPE, F. (d 1916) musi-
cian EA/17*
SCUTT, Charles E. (b 1868) Eng-
lish business manager, actor
GRB/1
SEABERT, Charles F. (c. 1836-87)
actor NYM
SEABROOK, Jeremy (b 1939) Eng-
lish dramatist CD
SEABROOKE, Thomas (fl 1629)
actor DA
SEABROOKE, Thomas Q. [Thomas
Quigley] (1860-1913) American
actor, singer CDP, GRB/2-4,
SR, WWA/1, WWS, WWT/1
SEABROOKE, Mrs. Thomas Q.
see Crox, Elvia
SEABROOKE, Mrs. Thomas Q.
see Lowrie, Jeanette
SEABURY, Ynez (d 1973 [65])
performer BP/57*
SEACOMBE, Dorothy (b 1905) Eng-
lish actress WWT/6-9
SEADER, Richard (b 1923) Ameri-
can manager, musician BE
SEAFORTH, Harriet, Countess of
(d 1779) actress CDP
SEAGLE, Oscar (1877-1945) Amer-
ican singer WWA/2
SEAGRAM, Wilfrid (1884-1938)
English actor WWT/5-8
SEAL, Miss see Bellamy, Mrs.

SEAL, David Abbey (d 1898)
circus jester EA/99*
SEAL, Elizabeth (b 1933) Italian/
English actress, dancer,
singer AAS, BE, WWT/13-16
SEALBY, Mabel (b 1885) English
actress, singer WWT/3-8
SEALBY, Walter (d 1904 [43])
actor, manager EA/05*,
WWT/14*
SEALBY, Mrs. Walter see
Taylor, Agnes
SEALE, Douglas (b 1913) English
director, actor AAS, BE,
WWT/12-16
SEALE, Kenneth (b 1916) English
newspaper executive WWT/16
SEALLY, John (b c. 1747) Eng-
lish dramatist CP/3
SEAMAN, Isaac (d 1923 [88])
critic BE*, WWT/14*
SEAMAN, Julia (1837-1909) ac-
tress CDP
SEAMAN, Sir Owen (1861-1936)
critic GRB/2-4, WWT/1-8
SEAMAN, William (d 1883 [74])
actor EA/85*
SEAMAN, Mrs. William (d
1906 [94]) actress EA/07*
SEAMON, Helen (b 1929) Ameri-
can actress TW/6
SEAMORE, T. F. see Sneath,
Thomas F.
SEARELLE, Luscombe (d 1907
[47]) actor, singer, dramatist
GRB/3
SEARLE, Caroline (b 1799) Eng-
lish actress, dancer CDP,
OX
SEARLE, Mrs. C. F. (d 1880)
actress? EA/81*
SEARLE, Cyril (1840-87) Eng-
lish actor CDP, NYM
SEARLE, Mrs. Cyril see Ey-
tinge, Rose
SEARLE, Eliza [Mrs. William
Searle] (d 1886) EA/87*
SEARLE, Kate [Mrs. Harry
Fischer] (d 1892) actress EA/
93*
SEARLE, Louise actress, singer
CDP
SEARLE, Townley [W. F. D.
Townley-Searle] (b 1882)
English actor GRB/1
SEARLE, Walter (d 1885) come-
dian EA/86*
SEARLE, William (d 1864 [49])

comedian EA/72*, WWT/14*
SEARLE, Willis (b 1857) English
actor EA/97, GRB/1
SEARS, Heather (b 1935) English
actress WWT/15-16
SEARS, Zelda (1873-1935) Ameri-
can actress WWA/1, WWM,
WWT/1-7
SEATON, John (d 1875) master of
ceremonies EA/76*
SEATON, Mrs. R. J. see
Clifford, Marie
SEATON, Scott (d 1968 [97]) per-
former BP/53*
SEAWELL, Donald R. American
producer, publisher WWT/15-16
SEBASTIAN (b 1837) Italian circus
performer HAS
SEBASTIAN, Dorothy (d 1957 [52])
American actress BE*, BP/41*
SEBASTIAN, Paul (b 1943) Ameri-
can actor TW/27
SEBECK, Henry (fl 1617) actor
DA
SEBRING, Paul E. (d 1974 [84])
performer BP/59*
SECOMBE, Harry (b 1921) Welsh
actor, singer AAS, TW/22,
WWT/14-16
SECOND, Mrs. [née Matron] (fl
1796) singer TD/1-2
SECRETAN, Lance (b 1939) English
actor WWT/12-13
SECUNDA, Sholom (d 1974 [79])
composer BP/59*, WWT/16*
SEDDON, W. Payne English actor,
manager GRB/1-3
SEDGER, Horace (d 1917 [63/64])
lessee EA/18*, WWT/14*
SEDGER, Mrs. Horace see
Harris, Nelly
SEDGWICK, Mr. (d 1803) singer
TD/2
SEDGWICK, Mrs. (d 1868 [79])
EA/69*
SEDGWICK, Amy [Mrs. Charles
Goostry] (1830/35-97) actress
CDP, DNB, OAA/1-2
SEDGWICK, Edie (d 1971 [28])
performer BP/56*
SEDGWICK, Ellen (d 1894) EA/95*
SEDGWICK, Josephine (d 1964 [92])
performer BP/49*
SEDGWICK, Josie (d 1973 [75])
performer BP/57*
SEDGWICK, Ruth (d 1974 [82])
journalist BP/58*
SEDGWICK, Mrs. Sam (d 1877)

EA/78*

SEDLEY, Sir Charles (c. 1639-
1701) English dramatist COC,
CP/1-3, DNB, GT, HP, OC/
1-3

SEDLEY, Henry (fl 1855-61)
American actor HAS

SEDLEY, William Henry see
Sedley-Smith, William Henry

SEDLEY-SMITH, William Henry
(1806-72) English/American
actor CDP, COC, DAB,
HAS, OC/1-3, WWA/H

SEDLEY-SMITH, Mrs. William
Henry [née Riddle] (d 1861)
American actress HAS

SEEBERG, Harry (d 1975 [61])
composer/lyricist BP/60*

SEEBOHM, E. V. (d 1888) dramatist BE*, EA/88*, WWT/
14*

SEEBOLD, Mrs. Jack see
Dent, Lizzie

SEED, Phil (d 1971 [70]) performer BP/56*

SEEFRIED, Irmgard (b 1919)
Bavarian singer CB, ES

SEEL, Charles [Frederick
Charles Brown] (d 1903) music-hall comedian CDP

SEELEN, Arthur (b 1923)
American bookseller, actor
BE

SEELEY, Blossom (d 1974 [82])
singer, vaudevillian TW/30

SEELEY, Frank (d 1913) actor,
singer CDP

SEELEY, James L. (d 1943
[76]) American actor BE*,
BP/27*

SEELIN, Elpha (d 1975 [62])
dramatist BP/60*

SEETZ, George (1888-1944)
American actor, dramatist
SR

SEFF, Manuel (d 1969 [74])
critic BP/54*

SEFF, Richard (b 1927) American talent representative,
actor BE, TW/7

SEFTON, Angela (b 1840) American actress HAS

SEFTON, Annie see Sefton,
Mrs. Joseph

SEFTON, Ernest (d 1954 [71])
actor BE*, WWT/14*

SEFTON, John (1805-68) English
actor, dancer CDP, HAS

SEFTON, Mrs. John [Miss Wells]
(fl 1827-31) English actress
HAS

SEFTON, Joseph (fl 1836) English
actor HAS

SEFTON, Joseph (d 1881) actor,
manager CDP

SEFTON, Mrs. Joseph [Mrs. J.
A. Leonard; Annie Eberle]
(1833-74) American actress
CDP, HAS

SEFTON, Mrs. John [Mrs. Watts]
(1810-95) English actress HAS

SEFTON, L. J. (d 1876 [45])
lessee EA/77*

SEFTON, Marion see Sefton,
Mrs. John

SEFTON, Philip (d 1917 [48]) actor, singer EA/18*

SEFTON, William (1810/13-39)
English actor HAS, SR

SEFTON, William (d 1866 [25])
scene artist HAS

SEFTON, Mrs. William see
Wallack, Mrs. James William

SEGAL, Alex (1915-77) American
director BE, ES

SEGAL, George (b 1936) American
actor CB

SEGAL, Vivienne (b 1897) American actress, singer BE, TW/
2-9, WWT/4-13

SEGALL, Harry (d 1975 [78])
dramatist BP/60*

SEGER, Lucia Backus (d 1962
[88]) actress BE*

SEGUIN, Ann see Seguin, Mrs.
Arthur Edward Sheldon

SEGUIN, Arthur Edward Sheldon
(1809-52) English singer CDP,
DNB, HAS, SR

SEGUIN, Mrs. Arthur Edward
Sheldon [née Ann Child] (1814-
88) English singer CDP, DNB,
HAS

SEGUIN, Edward (1836-79) American singer CDP, HAS

SEGUIN-WALLACE, Zelda (fl 1876-
83) singer CDP

SEHAIS, Jehan (fl 1598) actor DA

SEIDEL, Tom (b 1917) American
actor TW/1-3

SEIDEN, Stanley (b 1922) American
producer, press representative
BE

SEIDENBERG, Mrs. Edgar see
James, Millie

SEIDL, Anton (1850-98) Hungarian

conductor DAB, ES, WWA/H
SEIDL, Lea [Caroline Mayrseidl]
(b 1902) Austrian actress,
singer WWT/7-11
SEIDMAN, J. S. (b 1901) American investor BE
SEIGER, Marvin L. (b 1924)
American educator, dramatist,
director BE
SEITZ, Dran (b 1928) American
actress, singer, director,
producer BE
SEITZ, Tani (b 1928) American
actress BE, TW/12
SEITZ, Wayne T. (b 1932) American costume designer, executive BE
SEJOUR, Victor (1817-74) American dramatist DAB
SEKI, Hoshin (b 1941) American
actor TW/27-28
SELBERT, Marianne (b 1946)
American actress TW/25
SELBOURNE, David (b 1937)
English dramatist CD
SELBY, Charles (1802?-63) actor,
dramatist DNB
SELBY, Mrs. Charles see Selby, Clara
SELBY, Clara [Mrs. Charles
Selby] (d 1873 [76]) actress
CDP
SELBY, Henry C. (d 1903 [49])
actor EA/04*
SELBY, Nicholas (b 1925) English
actor AAS, WWT/15-16
SELBY, Percival M. (1886-1955)
English actor, executive
WWT/10-12, WWW/5
SELBY, Tony (b 1938) English
actor WWT/15-16
SELBY, Wilton J. (d 1906) actor
EA/07*
SELDEN, Albert (b 1922) American producer, composer, lyricist BE
SELDEN, Almira (fl 1820?)
dramatist EAP
SELDEN, Samuel (b 1899)
Chinese/American educator,
director, actor BE
SELDES, Gilbert (1893-1970)
American dramatist, critic
BE, NTH
SELDES, Marian (b 1928) American actress BE, TW/7-12,
23-24, 26-27, 30, WWT/14-
16

SELDON, George (d 1894 [28])
actor EA/96*
SELIG, William N. (1864-1948)
American magician, minstrel
TW/5
SELIGER, Mrs. Madison see
Beveridge, Ray
SELIGMAN, Marjorie (1900-74)
American dramatist, bookseller,
editor BE
SELIGMAN, Minnie (1869-1919)
American actress SR
SELIGMANN, Lilias Hazewell MacLane (d 1964 [71]) dancer BE*
SELIGMANN, Prosper (d 1882 [65])
musician EA/83*
SELKIRK, William (d 1911 [79])
EA/12*
SELL, Janie (b 1941) American
actress, singer TW/26, 29-30,
WWT/16
SELLAR, Robert J. B. (d 1960
[67]) dramatist BE*, WWT/14*
SELLARS, Elizabeth (b 1923) Scottish actress WWT/12-16
SELLERS, Arthur D. (b 1945)
American actor TW/26, 29
SELLERS, Peter (b 1925) English
actor CB
SELLERS, Virginia (d 1973 [51])
performer BP/57*
SELLMAN, Hunton D. (b 1900)
American educator, director
BE
SELLS, Lewis (d 1907 [65]) American manager GRB/3*, WWT/
14*
SELMAN, Linda American actress
TW/26
SELMORE, William see Norton,
William Henry
SELOUS, Angiolo Robson (d 1883
[71]) dramatist EA/84*
SELOUS, H. Courtney (d 1890
[87]) painter EA/91*
SELTEN, Morton [Morton Richard
Stubbs] (1860-1939) actor WWT/
5-8
SELWART, Tonio (b 1896/1906)
German actor BE, TW/3-9,
13-16, WWT/9-15
SELWICKE, Ethel Ross actress
EA/97
SELWOOD, Ethel (d 1916) EA/17*
SELWYN, Archibald (d 1959 [82])
Canadian producing manager
TW/15, WWT/6-11
SELWYN, Edgar (1875-1944) Amer-

ican actor, dramatist CB,
ES, GRB/2-4, SR, WWA/2,
WWM, WWS, WWT/1-9
SELWYN, John H. (1836-73) English actor, manager, scene
artist CDP, HAS
SELWYN, Ruth (d 1954 [49]) producer, actress BE*, BP/39*
SELZNICK, Irene Meyer (b 1910/
11) American producer BE,
TW/5-8
SELZNICK, Myron (d 1944 [45])
American talent representative
BE*
SEMBRICH, Marcella (1858-1935)
Polish singer CDP, DAB,
ES, WWA/1
SEMES, Renee (b 1947) American
actress TW/30
SEMPER, Gottfried (d 1879) architect EA/80*
SEMPLE, Robert (fl 1570-71)
dramatist CP/3
SENDELBECK, Annie see Boudinot, Annie
SENECA, Lucius Annaeus (c. 4
B. C. -65 A. D.) Roman dramatist COC, ES, OC/3, PDT
SENN, Herbert (b 1924) American
designer WWT/16
SENN, Ken (d 1973 [51]) performer BP/58*
SENNETT, Ada see Norris, Ida
SENNETT, Blanche (d 1896)
EA/97*
SENNETT, Charles (d 1905 [73])
actor CDP
SENNETT, Mrs. Charles see
Merton, Annie
SENNETT, Edwin (d 1891 [51])
actor EA/92*
SENNETT, Mack (1880-1960)
Canadian actor TW/17
SENNETT, Thomas (d 1897 [54])
actor EA/98*
SENNETT, Mrs. Thomas [née
Blanche Ford] (d 1875 [32])
actress EA/76*
SENNETT, W. H. (d 1871) comedian, lessee EA/72*
SENNETT, William (d 1875 [76])
actor EA/76*, WWT/14*
SENNETT, Mrs. William (d 1876
[69]) EA/77*
SENSENDERFER, Robert E. P.
(d 1957 [73]) American critic
BE*, BP/41*
SENTER, Annie see Langdon,

Mrs. Henry A. , II
SENZ, Edward (d 1973 [74]) make-up man BP/58*
SERABIAN, Lorraine (b 1945)
American actress TW/21, 25,
29
SERAFIN, Tullio (b 1878) Italian
conductor ES
SERBAGI, Roger Omar (b 1937)
American actor TW/26, 30
SERGAVA, Katharine (b 1918)
Russian dancer TW/1-4
SERGEANT, Mrs. (fl 1847) actress
HAS
SERGENT, John W. (d 1920) magician BE*, BP/5*
SERGINE, Vera (d 1946 [62])
French actress WWT/3-4
SERGUEEFF, Nicholas Grigorievich
(1876-1951) Russian dancer,
ballet master ES
SERJEANT, Will (d 1912 [60]) music-hall manager EA/13*
SERJEANTSON, Kate (d 1918) actress GRB/3-4, WWT/1-3
SERLE, Thomas James (1798-1889)
English dramatist, actor, acting
manager CDP, EA/69
SERLIN, Edward (d 1968 [56]) publicist BP/52*
SERLIN, Oscar (1901-71) Russian/
American producing manager
BE, CB, TW/2-8, 27, WWA/5,
WWT/10-13
SERLING, Rod (d 1975 [50]) dramatist BP/60*
SERNEAU, Gunther (d 1976 [51])
producer/director/choreographer
BP/60*
SEROFF, Muni (b 1905) Russian
actor TW/23-24, 26
SERON, Orie (b 1945) American
actress? TW/27
SERRANO, Lupe (b 1931) Mexican
dancer ES
SERRANO, Vincent (1870-1935)
American actor WWM, WWT/
4-7
SERRES, Olivia (fl 1805) dramatist
CP/3
SERVAIS, Jean (d 1976 [65]) performer BP/60*
SERVAIS, Joseph (d 1885 [35])
musician EA/86*
SERVANDONY, Jean-Nicholas
(1695-1766) French scene artist
COC
SERVOSS, Mary (d 1968 [80])

American actress BE, TW/
2-7, 25, WWT/7-13
SESSI, Mathilde (fl 1815) singer
CDP
SESSIONS, Almira (d 1974 [85])
actress BP/59*, WWT/16*
SESSIONS, Roger (b 1896) Amer-
ican composer CB, ES, HJD
SESTINI, [Giovana] (fl 1783)
singer CDP, TD/1-2
SETCHELL, Daniel (1831-66)
American actor, manager
CDP, HAS, SR
SETH, Will (d 1964) performer
BE*
SETON, Bruce (d 1969 [60]) per-
former BP/54*
SETTERBERG, Carl Douglas (d
1973 [54]) performer BP/57*
SETTI, Corrodi (fl 1850) singer
HAS
SETTI, Giulio (1869-1938) Italian
conductor WWA/2
SETTIMIO, Al (b 1945) American
actor TW/24
SETTLE, Elkanah (1648-1724)
English dramatist COC, CP/
1-3, DNB, GT, HP, OC/1-3
SETTLE, Maurice (b 1912) Amer-
ican executive BE
SETTLE, Nellie [Mrs. C. M.
Rodney] (d 1891) actress EA/
92*
SEURAT, Claude A. (b 1798)
freak CDP
SEVAREID, Michael (b 1940)
French actor TW/19, 25
SEVENING, Dora (b 1883) ac-
tress, secretary of Royal
Academy of Dramatic Art
WWT/8-10
SEVENING, Nina English actress
WWT/1-5
SEVERIN-MARS, Mons. (d 1921)
actor WWT/14*
SEVERI, Juan B. (fl 1847)
singer HAS
SEVERN, A. [Herr Hengler] (d
1916 [79]) conjurer EA/17*
SEVERN, Gerry (d 1974) pro-
ducer/director/choreographer
BP/59*
SEVIER, Clara Driscoll (b 1881)
American composer WWM
SEVRA, Robert (b 1945) Ameri-
can actor TW/28
SEWALL, Jonathan Mitchell
(1748-1808) American drama-

tist EAP
SEWARD, Billy (d 1899 [46]) Negro
comedian EA/00*
SEWARD, Emily [Mrs. E. M.
Holland] actress CDP
SEWARD, John (d 1884) EA/85*
SEWELL, Mrs. (fl 1785) actress
HAS
SEWELL, Charles (b 1878) English
actor GRB/1
SEWELL, E. J. (d 1916) EA/18*
SEWELL, Dr. George (d 1726)
dramatist CP/1-3, DNB, GT
SEWELL, Hetty Jane (d 1961)
American dramatist BE*
SEYLER, Athene (b 1889) English
actress AAS, COC, ES, OC/
3, WWT/1-16
SEYMOUR, Mr. (fl 1797-98) actor
HAS
SEYMOUR, Mr. (fl 1803) actor
TD/2
SEYMOUR, Mrs. (fl 1717-23) ac-
tress DNB
SEYMOUR, Mrs. (fl 1797-98) ac-
tress HAS
SEYMOUR, Mrs. [née Allison] (b
1819) English actress HAS
SEYMOUR, Miss see Reeve,
Mrs. James
SEYMOUR, Alan (b 1927) Australian
dramatist, director CD
SEYMOUR, Anne (b 1909) American
actress BE, TW/14-21
SEYMOUR, Charles Guilfoyle (d
1904) actor EA/05*
SEYMOUR, Clarine (1900-19) ac-
tress BE*
SEYMOUR, Cy (d 1973 [70]) per-
former BP/57*
SEYMOUR, Frank (d 1891) come-
dian EA/92*
SEYMOUR, Fred (d 1968 [68])
producer/director/choreographer
BP/52*
SEYMOUR, George actor CDP
SEYMOUR, Mrs. Guilfoyle [née
Harriet Hunter] (d 1875 [20])
actress EA/76*
SEYMOUR, Harry (1821-83) actor,
costumier CDP, HAS
SEYMOUR, Harry (d 1877) musi-
cian EA/78*
SEYMOUR, Harry (d 1967 [77])
composer/lyricist BP/52*
SEYMOUR, Henry (d 1868) stage
manager EA/69*
SEYMOUR, James [James Cun-

ningham] (1823-64) Irish actor
COC, HAS, OC/1-3
SEYMOUR, James (d 1976 [80])
dramatist BP/60*
SEYMOUR, James (b 1948) Amer-
ican actor TW/30
SEYMOUR, Jane (d 1956 [64])
Canadian actress TW/12
SEYMOUR, John D. (b 1897)
American actor BE, TW/4-
20, 24, 29
SEYMOUR, Katie [Katherine Phoebe
Mary Athol] (d 1903 [33]) ac-
tress, dancer EA/04*, WWT/
14*
SEYMOUR, Laura (d 1879 [59])
actress, producer, manager
BE*, EA/80*, WWT/14*
SEYMOUR, Linda (d 1877 [18])
music teacher EA/78*
SEYMOUR, Lynn (b 1939) Cana-
dian dancer ES
SEYMOUR, Madeline (b 1891)
English actress WWT/3-9
SEYMOUR, May Davenport (1883-
1967) American actress, cura-
tor BE, TW/24
SEYMOUR, Milly see Fuell,
Emelia
SEYMOUR, Mollie [Mrs. Sim-
mons] (b 1884) English actress,
dancer GRB/1
SEYMOUR, Nelse (1835-75) min-
strel CDP
SEYMOUR, Phoebe (d 1912 [75])
EA/13*
SEYMOUR, Robert William (d
1877 [77]) musician EA/78*
SEYMOUR, Thomas Orlando (d
1909) EA/10*
SEYMOUR, Will actor, singer
CDP
SEYMOUR, William Gorman (1855-
1933) American actor, stage
manager, director COC,
DAB, GRB/3-4, OC/1-3, PP/
3, WWA/1, WWM, WWS,
WWT/1-7
SEYMOUR, W. J. see Birchell,
William John
SEYTON, Charles (d 1894) actor
WWT/14*
SEYTON, Clara dramatic reader,
singer CDP
SEYTON, John C. (d 1867 [45])
comedian, manager EA/68*
SHACKELL, Frank (d 1917)
musician EA/18*

SHACKLETON, Robert (d 1956
[42]) American actor TW/7-8
SHADE, Ellen (b 1945) American
actress TW/24
SHADE, Lillian (d 1962 [51]) per-
former BE*
SHADWELL, Charles (d 1726)
dramatist CP/1-3, DNB, GT
SHADWELL, Thomas (c. 1642-92)
English dramatist CDP, COC,
CP/1-3, DNB, ES, GT, HP,
MH, NTH, OC/1-3, PDT, RE
SHAFER, Robert American actor
TW/1
SHAFF, Monty American producer,
manager BE
SHAFFER, Anthony (b 1926) Eng-
lish dramatist AAS, CB, CD,
COC, WWT/15-16
SHAFFER, Oscar (fl 1876?) singer
CDP
SHAFFER, Peter Levin (b 1926)
English dramatist AAS, BE,
CD, CH, COC, ES, MD, MH,
MWD, PDT, RE, WWT/14-16
SHAHN, Ben (b 1898) American
designer ES
SHAINMARK, Lou (d 1976 [75])
producer/director/choreographer
BP/60*
SHAIRP, Alexander Mordaunt
(1887-1939) English dramatist
MWD, NTH, WWT/6-8
SHAKAR, Martin (b 1940) American
actor TW/23, 25-30
SHAKERLEY, Edward (fl 1620s)
actor DA
SHAKESPEARE, Edmund (d 1607)
actor DA
SHAKESPEARE, Edward (d 1607)
actor DA
SHAKESPEARE, William (1564-1616)
English dramatist, actor CDP,
COC, CP/1-3, DA, DNB, ES,
FGF, HP, MH, NTH, OC/1-3,
PDT, RE, SR
SHAKSHAFTE, William (fl 1581)
actor DA
SHALDERS, Charles William (d
1862 [43]) scene artist, actor
EA/72*, WWT/14*
SHALDERS, William (d 1872 [72])
manager EA/73*
SHALE, T. A. (1867-1953) English
actor WWT/3-9
SHALEK, Bertha (b 1884) American
actress, singer WWS
SHALER, Anna (b 1940) American

SHANAHAN

840

actor TW/29
SHANAHAN, Elva (d 1973 [48])
performer BP/58*
SHANAHAN, James A. , Sr. (d
1970 [82]) performer BP/55*
SHANBROOKE, John (d 1618)
actor DA
SHANCKE, John see Shank,
John
SHAND, Ernest (fl 1900-04?) ac-
tor, singer CDP
SHAND, John (1901-55) English
critic, journalist WWT/8-10
SHAND, Phyllis (b 1894) English
actress WWT/9-10
SHANDY, Tristram [Michael
Keating] (d 1895) manager
EA/96*
SHANE, Jerry (d 1974 [42]) per-
former BP/58*
SHANE, Peggy (d 1965 [69]) dra-
matist BP/50*
SHANK, John (d 1636) English
actor, dramatist COC, CP/
3, DA, DNB, FGF, NTH,
OC/1-3
SHANK, John, the Younger (fl
1630-42) actor DA
SHANK, Theodore J. (b 1929)
American educator, director
BE
SHANKS, Alec (b 1904) English
director WWT/12-16
SHANNON, Effie [Mrs. Herbert
Kelcey] (1867-1954) American
actress ES, GRB/2-4, PP/3,
SR, TW/2-6, 11, WWA/3,
WWM, WWS, WWT/1-11
SHANNON, Frank (d 1959 [83])
Irish actor WWT/6-10
SHANNON, Harry (d 1964 [74])
performer BP/49*
SHANNON, Mark (b 1948) Amer-
ican actor TW/26
SHANNON, Michael (b 1943)
American actor TW/28-30
SHANNON, Nance (d 1965) per-
former BP/50*
SHANNON, Peggy (1907-41)
American actress CB, WWT/
7-9
SHANNON, Ray (d 1971 [76])
comedian TW/27
SHANNON, Wayne (b 1948) Amer-
ican actor TW/29
SHANNON, William J. (d 1973
[62]) performer BP/57*
SHANNON, Winona (d 1950

[76]) American actress TW/7
SHAPIRO, Herman (b 1898) Amer-
ican stage manager BE
SHAPTER, Mr. (fl 1802) actor
HAS
SHARAFF, Irene (b 1908) Ameri-
can designer BE, ES, TW/2,
4-8, WWT/10-16
SHARKEY, Susan (b 1943) Ameri-
can actress TW/27-29
SHARLAND, Reginald (1886-1944)
English actor, singer WWT/
5-8
SHARMA, Barbara (b 1942) actress
TW/24-25, 27
SHARON, Fran (b 1939) American
actress TW/19
SHARON, Muriel (b 1920) Ameri-
can director, educator, drama-
tist, actress BE
SHARP (d 1894 [72]) music-hall
performer EA/95*
SHARP, Anthony (b 1915) English
actor, director, dramatist
WWT/12-16
SHARP, Arabella (fl 1793) actress
CDP
SHARP, Eileen (b 1900) English
actress, singer WWT/5-8
SHARP, F. B. J. (b 1874) English
actor WWT/4-7
SHARP, Henry (1889-1964) Latvian
actor TW/2, 10
SHARP, Janet Achurch see
Achurch, Janet
SHARP, John W. (d 1856 [38])
singer, musical director CDP
SHARP, Margery (b 1905) drama-
tist WWT/10-14
SHARP, Oliver (d 1969 [38]) pro-
ducer/director/choreographer
BP/54*
SHARP, Richard (fl 1618-29) actor
DA
SHARP, Theodore (d 1882) librarian
EA/83*
SHARP, Mrs. W. [née Bella Men-
age] dancer GT
SHARP, William (b 1924) American
educator, director BE
SHARPE, Mrs. [née Le Sugg] (d
1863) English actress CDP,
HAS
SHARPE, Miss see Kneass,
Mrs.
SHARPE, Miss actress CDP
SHARPE, Albert (b 1885) Irish
actor TW/3-4

SHARPE, A. N. (d 1865 [24])
actor HAS
SHARPE, Belle (d 1913 [40])
EA/14*
SHARPE, Don (d 1975) producer/
director/choreographer BP/
60*
SHARPE, Edith (b 1894) English
actress WWT/7-15
SHARPE, Gyda (d 1973 [65])
performer BP/57*
SHARPE, John (fl 1791) drama-
tist CP/3
SHARPE, John (b 1932) American
actor TW/8, 11-13, 22-24
SHARPE, J. W. (d 1856) comic
singer HAS
SHARPE, L. [Launcelot Sharpe
Abram] (d 1891) musician EA/
92*
SHARPE, Lewis (fl 1640) drama-
tist CP/1-3, FGF, GT
SHARPE, Lizzie see Thomp-
son, Eliza
SHARPE, Louisa (d 1801) musi-
cian CDP
SHARPE, Richard (c. 1602-32)
English actor COC, OC/1-3
SHARPHAM, Edward (d 1608
[32]?) dramatist CP/1-3,
DNB, FGF, GT
SHARPLES, William (d 1876
[56]) juggler, cannon-ball per-
former EA/78*
SHARPLEY, Sam (1831-75)
American Ethiopian comedian,
minstrel manager CDP, HAS
SHARPMAN, Edward see
Sharpham, Edward
SHATNER, William (b 1931)
Canadian actor BE, TW/12-
20, WWT/16
SHATTERELL, Edward (fl
c. 1640-54) English actor
COC, OC/2-3
SHATTERELL, Robert (d c. 1684)
English actor COC, DA,
OC/2-3
SHATTUCK, Charles F. (d 1905
[69]) minstrel CDP
SHATTUCK, Ethel (d 1963 [73])
performer BE*
SHATTUCK, Robert (b 1940)
American actor TW/24-26
SHATTUCK, Truly [Mrs. Stephen
A. Douglas] (1876-1954)
American actress, singer
GRB/3-4, WWM, WWS,

WWT/1-7
SHAUB, Edna E. (d 1975 [98])
performer BP/60*
SHAVER, Bob (b 1932) American
actor TW/13
SHAVER, C. L. (b 1905) American
educator BE
SHAW, Mr. (fl 1786) musician,
conductor CDP
SHAW, Mr. (b 1794) dwarf CDP
SHAW, Mrs. (fl 1800) actress
HAS
SHAW, Mrs. [née Eliza Marian
Trewar; Mrs. Thomas Sowerby
Hamblin, IV] (fl 1817-39) ac-
tress SR
SHAW, Miss (b 1790) dwarf CDP
SHAW, Miss see Rous, Helen
SHAW, Mrs. Alfred [née Mary
Portans] (1814-76) English singer
CDP, DNB
SHAW, Annie Isabel [Mrs. Tom
Shaw] (d 1900 [23]) EA/01*
SHAW, Anthony (b 1897) actor
WWT/8-13
SHAW, Arthur (d 1946 [65]) Amer-
ican actor TW/2
SHAW, Miss C. (fl 1846) actress
HAS
SHAW, Charles (d 1879 [33]) EA/
80*
SHAW, Charles A. (b 1835) show-
man HAS
SHAW, Charlotte (fl 1842) actress
CDP
SHAW, Claude [David Macgregor
Shaw] (d 1891) business manager
EA/92*
SHAW, David Macgregor see
Shaw, Claude
SHAW, Dennis (d 1970 [50]) per-
former BP/55*
SHAW, Dora (fl 1849-63) American
actress HAS
SHAW, E. J. (fl 1839-51) Irish
actor HAS
SHAW, F. W. (d 1901 [47]) singer
EA/03*
SHAW, George Bernard (1856-1950)
Irish dramatist, critic AAS,
CB, COC, DNB, ES, GRB/1-4,
HP, MD, MH, MWD, NTH,
OC/1-3, PDT, RE, TW/7,
WWA/3, WWM, WWS, WWT/1-
10, WWW/4
SHAW, Mrs. George Bernard [née
Charlotte Frances Payne-Town-
shend] (1857-1943) Irish drama-

tist   BE*, WWT/14*
SHAW, Gerald (b 1950) American
  actor   TW/30
SHAW, Glen Byam (b 1904) Eng-
  lish actor, director AAS,
  BE, COC, ES, OC/3, WWT/
  7-16
SHAW, G. Tito (b 1943) Ameri-
  can actor   TW/24
SHAW, Harry E. (d 1903) Amer-
  ican minstrel comedian EA/
  04*
SHAW, Henry W.   see Billings,
  "Josh"
SHAW, Irwin (b 1913) American
  dramatist, producer AAS,
  BE, CB, CD, ES, HJD,
  MD, MH, MWD, NTH,
  WWT/10-16
SHAW, J. A. (d 1880) actor?
  EA/81*
SHAW, Jack (d 1970 [88]) per-
  former   BP/54*
SHAW, Joe (d 1898 [29]) actor?
  EA/00*
SHAW, John (d 1867 [85]) actor?
  EA/68*
SHAW, John (d 1886) proprietor,
  manager   EA/87*
SHAW, John (d 1890) professor
  of music EA/91*
SHAW, Joseph English actor
  TW/24
SHAW, Josephine see Hoey,
  Mrs. John
SHAW, Lewis (b 1910) English
  actor   WWT/6-10
SHAW, Mary [Mrs. T. S. Ham-
  blin?] (d 1873 [56]?) actress,
  singer CDP, HAS
SHAW, Mary (d 1894) actress,
  singer CDP
SHAW, Mary (1854-1929) Amer-
  ican actress DAB, ES,
  GRB/3-4, PP/3, WWA/1,
  WWS, WWT/1-5
SHAW, Montague (d 1968 [85])
  performer BP/52*
SHAW, Oscar [Oscar Schwartz]
  (1889-1967) American actor,
  singer TW/23, WWT/6-9
SHAW, Mrs. Oscar see Givler,
  Mary Louise
SHAW, Paula (b 1941) American
  actress TW/22-23, 25
SHAW, Ray (b 1926) American
  actor   TW/11
SHAW, Reta (b 1912) American

actress TW/9-15
SHAW, Robert (fl 1597-1602) actor
  DA
SHAW, Robert (d 1908 [55]) actor
  EA/09*
SHAW, Robert (b 1927) English
  actor, dramatist AAS, BE,
  CB, CD, CH, MH, TW/18,
  21, 26, 28, 30, WWT/13-16
SHAW, Robert Gould (d 1931 [80])
  curator BE*, WWT/14*
SHAW, Rosina see Watkins,
  Mrs. Harry
SHAW, Sala (d 1972 [66]) performer
  BP/57*
SHAW, Sam (d 1968 [50]) critic
  BP/52*
SHAW, Samuel (1635-96) English
  dramatist CP/1-3
SHAW, Sebastian (b 1905) English
  actor AAS, WWT/7-16
SHAW, Sidney (d 1969 [45]) com-
  poser/lyricist BP/54*
SHAW, Sydney (d 1910 [45]) com-
  poser, conductor EA/11*
SHAW, Tom (d 1912 [45]) English
  agent GRB/1
SHAW, Mrs. Tom see Shaw,
  Annie Isabel
SHAW, W. B. (d 1880) musician
  EA/81*
SHAWE, Robert (fl 1602) dramatist
  CP/3
SHAWHAN, April (b 1940) Ameri-
  can actress TW/23-26, 29-30
SHAWLEY, Robert (b 1932) Amer-
  ican actor TW/7-9
SHAWN, Dick American actor
  TW/24, 27, WWT/16
SHAWN, Michael (b 1944) American
  actor TW/25-28
SHAWN, Ted (1891-1972) American
  dancer, choreographer CB, ES
SHAWN, Wallace (b 1943) Ameri-
  can dramatist, director CD
SHAYNE, Al (d 1969 [82]) per-
  former BP/54*
SHAYNE, Alan (b 1925) American
  actor TW/6-16
SHEA, Mrs. [née Blanche Kemble]
  (d 1851) actress HAS
SHEA, Jack (d 1970 [70]) performer
  BP/55*
SHEA, Joe (d 1970 [72]) publicist
  BP/55*
SHEA, Patrick (b 1946) American
  actor TW/26-27
SHEA, Thomas E. (d 1940 [79])

American actor, dramatist
BE*, BP/24*, WWT/14*
SHEAHAN, John J. (d 1952
[60]) American actor BP/36*
SHEALDEN (fl 1594) actor DA
SHEAN, Al (1868-1949) German/
American actor DAB, TW/
1, 4, 6, WWT/9-10
SHEARD, Charles Henry (d 1913
[60]) EA/14*
SHEARER, Mrs. (d 1872) propri-
etor EA/73*
SHEARER, Denny (b 1941) Amer-
ican actor TW/25
SHEARER, James (d 1868) pro-
prietor EA/69*
SHEARER, Juanita (b 1919)
American educator, director
BE
SHEARER, Moira (b 1926) Scot-
tish dancer, actress CB,
ES, WWT/11-14
SHEE, Sir Martin Archer (1769-
1850) Irish dramatist DNB
SHEEAN, Vincent (d 1975 [75])
writer BP/59*
SHEEHAN, Bailie (d 1975 [74])
producer/director/choreographer
BP/59*
SHEEHAN, Jack (1890-1952)
American actor TW/8
SHEEHAN, Jack (d 1958 [67])
actor TW/1, 15
SHEEHAN, Jack (d 1973 [53])
performer BP/58*
SHEEHAN, Joseph F. (fl 1892-
1907) American singer WWS
SHEEHAN, Margaret Flavin (d
1969 [88]) Welsh actress
TW/25
SHEEHY, T. J. M. (d 1974
[56]) critic BP/59*
SHEEN, Martin [né Ramon Es-
tevez] (b 1940) American
actor TW/20-24, 26, WWT/
15-16
SHEEN, Pauline (d 1909) variety
performer EA/10*
SHEERING, James (d 1906 [86])
boxkeeper EA/07*
SHEFFIELD, Flora (b 1902)
English actress WWT/6-9
SHEFFIELD, John, Duke of
Buckingham (1649-1720) dram-
atist CP/2-3
SHEFFIELD, Leo (1873-1951)
English actor, singer WWT/
4-11

SHEFFIELD, Nellie (d 1957 [84])
actress BE*, WWT/14*
SHEFFIELD, Reginald (1900/01-
57) English actor WWT/3-9
SHEFFIELD, Thorpe [Robert
Thorpe Wilson] (d 1908 [42])
actor, singer EA/09*
SHEFFIELD, Wilson (d 1903 [38])
actor, singer EA/04*
SHEIL, Richard Lalor (1791-1851)
Irish dramatist CDP, DNB
SHELASKY, George Irving see
Irving, George S.
SHELBY, Daniel manager CDP
SHELBY, Jeanne (d 1964 [71])
performer BP/49*
SHELDON, A. H. (b 1847) Ameri-
can actor HAS
SHELDON, Charles (d 1870 [28])
musician EA/71*
SHELDON, David (b 1931) Ameri-
can producer, director, drama-
tist, actor BE
SHELDON, Edward (d 1878 [58])
bill poster EA/79*
SHELDON, Edward Brewster (1886-
1946) American dramatist CB,
COC, ES, MD, MH, MWD,
NTH, OC/1-3, RE, TW/2,
WWA/2, WWT/1-9
SHELDON, Georg (b 1864) English
actor, musician, stage mana-
ger, producer, dramatist
GRB/2
SHELDON, Herb (d 1964) American
performer BE*
SHELDON, H. Sophus (d 1940
[63]) Danish dramatist WWT/
6-9
SHELDON, Jerome (d 1962 [71])
actor BE*
SHELDON, Jerry (d 1962 [61])
actor BE*
SHELDON, Lechmere (d 1907
[29]) EA/08*
SHELDON, Marie [Mrs. R. B.
Mantell] (d 1939 [83]) Scottish
actress BE*, WWT/14*
SHELDON, Sidney (b 1917) Amer-
ican dramatist, director, pro-
ducer BE
SHELDON, Suzanne [Mrs. Henry
Ainley] (1875-1924) American
actress GRB/1-4, WWS,
WWT/1-4
SHELLE, Lori (b 1955) American
actress TW/25
SHELLEY, Master (fl 1847) actor

HAS
SHELLEY, Carole (b 1939) English actress TW/23-27, WWT/15-16
SHELLEY, Evelyn (d 1918) EA/19*
SHELLEY, Herbert (d 1921 [50]) actor, producer, manager BE*, WWT/14*
SHELLEY, Joshua (b 1920) American producer, director, actor BE, TW/3-4, 6-8, 10-12
SHELLEY, Percy Bysshe (1792-1822) English dramatist CDP, COC, DNB, ES, HP, MH, NTH, OC/1-3, PDT, RE
SHELLY, Norman (b 1921) American actor TW/6, 25-28
SHELTON, Benjamin (d 1885 [73]) EA/86*
SHELTON, Bertie (d 1920) stage manager, actor WWT/14*
SHELTON, George (1852/53-1932) English actor GRB/1-4, WWT/1-6
SHELTON, George (d 1971 [87]) comedian TW/27
SHELTON, Mrs. George (d 1908) GRB/4*
SHELTON, James (d 1975 [62]) performer BP/60*
SHELTON, Kenneth E. (d 1962 [37]) performer BE*
SHELTON, Laura Blanche [Mrs. Tom Diacoff] (d 1917 [40]) EA/18*
SHELTON, Reid (b 1924) American actor TW/23, 25, 28-30
SHELTON, Sloane (b 1934) American actor TW/23-24, 27-28, 30
SHELVING, Paul (1888-1968) English designer ES, WWT/6-11
SHEMELDS, Minnie see Rogers, Mrs. J.
SHENAR, Paul (b 1936) American actor TW/26
SHENBURN, Archibald A. (1905-54) English manager WWT/10
SHENSTON, E. (d 1885 [46]) EA/86*
SHENTON, J. W. (d 1886 [34]) dramatist EA/87*
SHENTON, Thomas Bartlett (d 1887 [74]) actor EA/88*
SHEPARD (fl 1582) doorkeeper DA

SHEPARD, Burt (d 1913 [58]) singer CDP
SHEPARD, Frank (d 1899) American comedian EA/01*
SHEPARD, Grove Burt (d 1913 [58]) EA/14*
SHEPARD, Joan (b 1933) American actress TW/1, 3, 23
SHEPARD, Red American actor TW/27-28
SHEPARD, Sam (b 1943) American dramatist, musician, actor CD, WWT/16
SHEPARD, William J. (d 1965 [74]) performer BP/50*
SHEPEARD, Jean (b 1904) English actress WWT/6-11
SHEPERD, Mr. (fl 1810?) actor CDP
SHEPERD, Mrs. actress CDP
SHEPHARD, Firth (1891-1949) English dramatist, producing manager TW/5, WWT/6-10, WWW/4
SHEPHARD, Rensselaer Albert (1832-54) American actor HAS
SHEPHERD, Mrs. [Mrs. Pope] (d 1862 [65]) actress EA/72*
SHEPHERD, Edward (c. 1670-1747) English architect COC, OC/1-3
SHEPHERD, Elizabeth (b 1936) English actress TW/26-27
SHEPHERD, Henry (fl 1800) dramatist CP/3
SHEPHERD, Jack (b 1940) English actor WWT/15-16
SHEPHERD, Mrs. J. C. see Neverist, Kate
SHEPHERD, Joseph (d 1887 [71]) musician EA/88*
SHEPHERD, Leonard (b 1872) English actor WWS, WWT/4-11
SHEPHERD, R. D. see McLean, R. D.
SHEPHERD, Richard (fl 1757-72) dramatist CP/2-3
SHEPHERD, Richard (d 1886 [76]) actor, manager EA/87*, WWT/14*
SHEPHERD, William Walton (d 1891 [41]) actor EA/92*
SHEPLEY, Ida (d 1975) performer BP/59*
SHEPLEY, Michael (1907-61) English actor WWT/8-13
SHEPLEY, Ruth (1889/92-1951) American actress TW/8, WWT/4-10

SHEPMAN, Louis Evan see
Shipman, Louis Evan
SHEPPARD, Miss see Cowell,
Mrs.
SHEPPARD, Billy (d 1872) min-
strel CDP
SHEPPARD, E. (d 1892) musi-
cian EA/93*
SHEPPARD, Edwin James (d
1908 [76]) actor GRB/4*
SHEPPARD, Guy (b 1912) Eng-
lish designer ES
SHEPPARD, Hattie see Hallam,
Mrs.
SHEPPARD, S. (fl 1647) drama-
tist CP/1-3
SHEPPARD, Sarah Amelia [Mrs.
W. C. Sheppard] (d 1880)
EA/81*
SHEPPARD, Mrs. W. C. see
Sheppard, Sarah Amelia
SHEPPARD, William (fl 1602)
actor DA
SHERAR, John [Sam Honey] (d
1888) EA/89*
SHERBROOKE, Michael (1874-
1957) actor GRB/2-4, WWT/1-
8
SHERBURNE, Sir Edward (b
1616) English translator CP/
1-3
SHERBURNE, Ernest O. (1878-
1952) American critic WWA/3
SHERBURNE, Col. John B.
(fl 1844?) dramatist RJ
SHEREK, Henry (1900-67) Eng-
lish manager, producer AAS,
BE, WWT/9-14, WWW/6
SHERIDAN, Mr. actor TD/2
SHERIDAN, Miss (fl 1781) dram-
atist CP/3
SHERIDAN, Amy [Mrs. Preston]
(d 1878 [39]) burlesque ac-
tress CDP
SHERIDAN, Ann (1915-67) Amer-
ican actress ES
SHERIDAN, Brinsley (d 1890
[55]) comedian, proprietor
EA/91*
SHERIDAN, Dinah (b 1920) Eng-
lish actress WWT/16
SHERIDAN, Elizabeth Ann see
Linley, Elizabeth Ann
SHERIDAN, Elizabeth Francis
[Mrs. Henry Brinsley Sheri-
dan] (d 1893) EA/94*
SHERIDAN, Emily Brinsley Eng-
lish actress EA/97

SHERIDAN, Emma V. (b 1864)
American actress PP/3
SHERIDAN, Esther Jane [Mrs.
Richard Brinsley Sheridan, II]
(1776-1817) CDP
SHERIDAN, Frances [née Chamber-
laine] (c. 1724-66) Irish drama-
tist CDP, CP/1-3, DNB, GT
SHERIDAN, Frank (1869-1943)
American actor SR
SHERIDAN, Helen Selina (1807-
77) dramatist, songwriter DNB
SHERIDAN, Henry Brinsley (d
1907) actor GRB/2*
SHERIDAN, Mrs. Henry Brinsley
see Sheridan, Elizabeth Francis
SHERIDAN, Mrs. J. see Sheri-
dan, Zoe Simeon
SHERIDAN, John (d 1869 [29])
property man EA/70*
SHERIDAN, John (d 1911 [69])
manager EA/12*
SHERIDAN, John Francis (d 1908
[64]) actor, manager CDP,
GRB/4
SHERIDAN, J. T. (d 1906 [34])
electrician EA/07*
SHERIDAN, Margaret (1889-1958)
Irish singer ES
SHERIDAN, Mark (d 1917) English
music-hall performer CDP,
COC, OC/1-3
SHERIDAN, Mary [Daphne Graham]
(b 1903) English actress WWT/
7-10
SHERIDAN, Richard Brinsley
(1751-1816) English dramatist,
manager CDP, COC, CP/2-3,
DNB, ES, GT, HP, MH, NTH,
OC/1-3, PDT, RE, SR, TD/1-2
SHERIDAN, Mrs. Richard Brins-
ley, I see Linley, Elizabeth
Ann
SHERIDAN, Mrs. Richard Brins-
ley, II see Sheridan, Esther
Jane
SHERIDAN, Dr. Thomas (c. 1684-
1738) Irish translator CP/2-3,
DNB
SHERIDAN, Thomas (1719/21-88)
Irish manager, dramatist CDP,
CP/1-3, DNB, ES, GT, TD/
1-2
SHERIDAN, Mrs. Thomas see
Sheridan, Frances
SHERIDAN, William Edward (1839/
40-87) American actor CDP,
COC, HAS, NYM, OC/1-3

SHERIDAN, Mrs. William Edward actress COC
SHERIDAN, Zoe Simeon [Mrs. J. Sheridan] (d 1909 [67]) EA/10*
SHERIFF, Jane see Sherriff, Jane
SHERIN, Edwin (b 1930/32) American actor, director TW/19, WWT/16
SHERINGHAM, George (1885-1937) English designer WWT/6-8
SHERK, Theresa (fl 1868) actress HAS
SHERLOCK, William (fl first half of 17th cent) English actor DA, OC/1-3
SHERMAN, Allan (d 1973 [49]) performer BP/58*
SHERMAN, Allan (d 1973 [76]) composer/lyricist BP/58*
SHERMAN, Frederick (d 1969 [64]) actor TW/25
SHERMAN, Geraldine English actress TW/29
SHERMAN, Henry (fl 1840) American singer HAS
SHERMAN, Hiram (b 1908) American actor BE, TW/3-19, 22, 24, WWT/11-16
SHERMAN, James B. (d 1975 [67]) composer/lyricist BP/60*
SHERMAN, Joe (d 1970 [76]) performer BP/55*
SHERMAN, John K. (1898-1969) American critic BE
SHERMAN, Lowell J. (1885-1934) American actor SR, WWT/4-7
SHERMAN, Margaret American executive BE
SHERMAN, Maud (d 1900) American singer EA/01*
SHERMAN, Noel (d 1972 [41]) composer/lyricist BP/57*
SHERMAN, William (b 1924) American educator, scene designer BE
SHERRATT, Mrs. William (d 1877) EA/78*
SHERRIFF, Jane (fl 1831-39) English singer, actress HAS, SR
SHERRIFF, Robert Cedric (1896-1975) English dramatist AAS, BE, CH, COC, ES, HP, MD, MH, MWD, NTH, OC/2-3,

PDT, WWT/6-15
SHERRIN, Ned (b 1931) English producer, director, dramatist CD, WWT/15-16
SHERRINGTON, Mme. Lemmens (1834-1906) English singer CDP
SHERRINGTON, Louie actress, singer CDP
SHERRY, Miss (d c. 1800?) actress TD/1-2
SHERRY, Katherine (d 1782) actress CDP
SHERWELL, Yvonne (b 1934) American actress TW/26
SHERWIN, Amy (d 1935 [81]) Tasmanian singer WWW/3
SHERWIN, Jeanette (d 1936 [42]) actress WWT/6-7
SHERWIN, Louis (b 1880) German/American critic WWM
SHERWIN, Mrs. Louis F. see Fealy, Maude
SHERWIN, Maude (1903-74) American composer WWT/10-14
SHERWIN, Ralph (1799-1830) English actor BS, CDP, DNB, OX
SHERWOOD, Mrs. (d 1917) proprietor EA/18*
SHERWOOD, Charles E. (b 1825) American actor, circus performer HAS
SHERWOOD, Mrs. Charles E. [Virginia] (1832-88) Irish equestrienne CDP, HAS
SHERWOOD, Garrison P. (1902-63) American actor, historian, journalist WWT/10-13
SHERWOOD, Henry (d 1967 [83]) actor TW/24
SHERWOOD, Henry (b 1931) English presenting manager WWT/15-16
SHERWOOD, James (b 1927) American actor TW/4
SHERWOOD, James Peter (1894-1973) English presenting manager WWT/15
SHERWOOD, Josephine (fl 1906-07) American actress WWS
SHERWOOD, Josephine see Hull, Josephine
SHERWOOD, Lydia (b 1906) English actress WWT/6-13
SHERWOOD, Madeleine [née Thornton] (b 1926) Canadian actress TW/9, 11-12, 21-22, 27-30,

WWT/14-16
SHERWOOD, Robert Emmet (1896-1955) American dramatist AAS, CB, COC, ES, HJD, MD, MH, MWD, NTH, OC/1-3, PDT, RE, TW/12, WWA/3, WWT/6-11, WWW/5
SHERWOOD, Virginia see Sherwood, Mrs. Charles E.
SHERWOOD, Wayne American actor TW/25, 27-28
SHERWOOD, William American actor TW/26
SHESGREEN, James (fl 1890-1913) Canadian press representative WWM
SHEVELOVE, Burt (b 1915) American director, dramatist, librettist BE, CD, WWT/15-16
SHEWELL, Livingston Robert (1833-1904) American actor CDP, HAS
SHEWELL, Mrs. L. R., I [née Henrietta Wilks] (1838-57) American dancer HAS
SHEWELL, Mrs. L. R., II [née Rose Skerrett] (b 1840) American actress HAS
SHIEL, Julia Lalor (d 1902) actress EA/04*
SHIEL, Lalor (b 1869) Canadian actress EA/97
SHIELD, Harry (d 1875 [38]) dramatist EA/76*
SHIELD, William (1748-1829) English composer, musician CDP, DNB, ES, TD/1-2
SHIELDS, Albert Charles (d 1870) advance agent EA/71*
SHIELDS, Arthur (1900-70) Irish actor WWT/9-11
SHIELDS, Ella (d 1952 [73]) American music-hall performer TW/9
SHIELDS, Helen (d 1963) actress BE*, BP/48*
SHIELDS, Robin Neilance (b 1872) Scottish actor GRB/1
SHIELDS, Rose (d 1916) EA/17*
SHIELDS, Sydney (d 1960 [72]) American actress TW/17
SHIELDS, William Joseph see Fitzgerald, Barry
SHIELS, George (1886-1949) Irish dramatist COC, MWD, MH, OC/1-3, RE, WWT/9-10
SHIFFRIN, Helen (d 1975 [55])

performer BP/59*
SHIFRIN, Nisson Abramovich (1892-1959) Russian designer COC
SHILKRET, Jack (d 1964 [67]) American composer, bandleader BE*, BP/49*
SHILLEN, Joseph P. (d 1971 [55]) performer BP/55*
SHILLING, Ivy Australian dancer WWT/4-7
SHILLITO, Charles (fl 1789) dramatist CP/3
SHIMIZU, Dana (b 1958) American actor TW/27
SHIMIZU, Keenan (b 1956) American actor TW/30
SHIMONO, Sab American actor TW/25-27, 30
SHINDELL, Dario (d 1974 [67]) performer BP/59*
SHINE, Bill [né Wilfred William Dennis] (b 1911) English actor WWT/10-16
SHINE, Giles (1860-1912) American actor SR
SHINE, Harry comedian GRB/2
SHINE, J. Myer (d 1971 [78]) theatre owner BP/55*
SHINE, Joe (d 1973 [70]) performer BP/57*
SHINE, John L. (1854-1930) actor CDP, DP, EA/96, GRB/1-4, WWT/1-6
SHINE, Wilfred E. (1864-1939) English actor GRB/1-4, WWT/1-8
SHINE, Wilfred William Dennis see Shine, Bill
SHINE, William H. (d 1909 [40]) EA/10*
SHINER, Ronald (1903-66) English actor AAS, WWT/10-14, WWW/6
SHINGLER, Helen (b 1919) English actress WWT/11-14
SHINTON, John (b 1870) English actor GRB/1
SHIPLEY, Joseph T. (b 1893) American critic NTH, WWT/11-16
SHIPLEY, Mrs. Sam see Worth, Beatrice
SHIPMAN, Ernest (b 1871) Canadian/American manager GRB/3-4, WWT/1-2
SHIPMAN, Louis Evan (1869-1933) American dramatist GRB/2-4, WWA/1, WWM, WWS, WWT/

1-7, WWW/3
SHIPMAN, Samuel (1883-1937)
American dramatist WWA/1,
WWT/4-8
SHIPMAN, Thomas (d c. 1691)
dramatist CP/1-3, GT
SHIPP, Cameron (d 1961 [57])
American writer BE*
SHIPP, Edward (d 1945) circus
manager, performer SR
SHIPP, Julia Lowande (d 1962
[81]) performer BE*
SHIPSTAD, Roy (d 1975 [64])
co-founder of Ice Follies
BP/59*
SHIRA, Jerry (d 1973 [28]) critic
BP/58*
SHIREBURN, Frances see
Cross, Mrs. Richard
SHIRLEY, Mr. (fl 1858) actor
HAS
SHIRLEY, Arthur (1853-1925)
English actor, dramatist
GRB/1-4, WWT/1-5
SHIRLEY, Bill (b 1921) American
actor, singer BE
SHIRLEY, Florence actress TW/1
SHIRLEY, Henry (fl 1638-53)
dramatist CP/1-3, FGF
SHIRLEY, James (1596-1666)
English dramatist CDP, COC,
CP/1-3, DNB, ES, FGF,
GT, HP, MH, NTH, OC/
1-3, PDT, RE
SHIRLEY, James Elliott (d 1892
[61]) EA/93*
SHIRLEY, Madge actress, musi-
cian, singer CDP
SHIRLEY, Nellie (d 1882) Eng-
lish actress GRB/1-2
SHIRLEY, Peg American actress
TW/28
SHIRLEY, Thomas P. (d 1962
[62]) actor BE*, BP/46*
SHIRLEY, Walter, Sr. (d 1963
[67]) performer BE*
SHIRLEY, William (fl 1739-80)
dramatist CP/1-3, DNB, GT
SHIRLING, Jack (d 1916) EA/17*
SHIRO, James A. (d 1975) per-
former BP/60*
SHIRRA, Edmunston (d 1861) ac-
tor BE*, WWT/14*
SHIRREFF, Jane [Mrs. Thomas
Walcott] (1811-83) singer CDP
SHIRREFS, Andrew (fl 1790-96)
dramatist CP/3
SHIRVELL, James (1902-62)

English manager WWT/10-14
SHOECRAFT, Ruth see McDevitt,
Ruth
SHOEMAKER, Ann (b 1891) Amer-
ican actress BE, WWT/13-16
SHOLEM ALEICHEM (1859-1916)
Russian dramatist MH, MWD,
RE
SHONE, Minnie Marion [Mrs.
Robert V. Shone] (d 1898 [33])
EA/99*
SHONE, Robert V[ictor] (d 1901
[45]) manager, agent, business
manager EA/02*, WWT/14*
SHONE, Mrs. Robert V[ictor]
see Shone, Minnie Marion
SHONE, W. (fl 1810) editor CP/3
SHOR, Miriam Craig (d 1971
[54]) performer BP/55*
SHORE, Dinah (b 1917) American
singer CB
SHORE, J. G. [James Gregory
McLoughlin] (d 1885 [58]) actor
OAA/1-2
SHORE, Katherine see Cibber,
Mrs. Colley
SHORT, Antrim (d 1972 [72]) per-
former BP/57*
SHORT, Bobby (b 1924) American
performer CB
SHORT, Ernest (1875-1959) Aus-
tralian writer WWW/5
SHORT, Frank Lea (d 1949 [75])
American actor, director
BE*, BP/34*
SHORT, Hassard (1877-1956) Eng-
lish producer, director, actor
CB, TW/2-8, 13, WWT/5-12
SHORT, Joe (d 1974 [91]) per-
former BP/59*
SHORT, Sarah (d 1970 [95]) per-
former BP/55*
SHORT, Sylvia (b 1927) American
actress, singer BE, TW/11-12
SHORT, William Frederick see
Saroni
SHORT, William Saroni (d 1886)
musical clown EA/87*
SHOSHANO, Rose (d 1968 [73])
performer BP/53*
SHOTTER, Ralph Champion see
Michael, Ralph
SHOTTER, Winifred (b 1904) Eng-
lish actress WWT/6-14
SHOTWELL, Marie (d 1934) Amer-
ican actress WWS
SHOWALTER, Edna Blanche (b
1888) American singer WWM

SHOWALTER, Max [Casey Adams]
(b 1917) American actor TW/
3-5, 22-24, 28
SHOWERISKEY, Ivan slack-rope
dancer HAS
SHRADER, Frederick Franklin
(1859-1943) German/American
dramatist, critic GRB/3-4,
WWT/1-2
SHRAPTER, Thomas (fl 1790)
dramatist CP/3
SHREVE, Tiffany (d 1964 [31])
actress BE*
SHRINER, Herb (1918-70) Amer-
ican humorist, monologist,
musician BE, TW/26
SHRIVAL, Mr. (fl 1843) singer
HAS
SHUARD, Amy (1924-75) English
singer ES
SHUBERT, Jacob J. (1880-1963)
American manager AAS,
COC, ES, NTH, OC/2-3,
SR, TW/2-8, 20, WWA/4,
WWM, WWT/3-13
SHUBERT, John (1908-62) Amer-
ican executive TW/19
SHUBERT, Lee (1875-1953)
American manager AAS,
COC, GRB/2-4, ES, NTH,
OC/2-3, SR, TW/2-8, WWA/
3, WWS, WWT/1-11
SHUBERT, Milton (d 1967 [66])
producer TW/23
SHUBERT, Sam S. (1876-1905)
American manager AAS,
COC, ES, GRB/1, NTH,
OC/2-3
SHUCKBOROUGH, Charles (fl
1740) English? dramatist
CP/2-3
SHUKSHIN, Vasily (d 1974 [75])
producer/director/choreographer
BP/59*
SHULL, Leo (b 1913) American
publisher, producer, journalist
BE, WWT/15-16
SHULL, Richard B. (b 1929)
American actor TW/26
SHULMAN, Max (b 1919) Ameri-
can dramatist BE, CB
SHULMAN, Milton (b 1913) Cana-
dian critic, dramatist AAS,
WWT/14-16
SHULMAN, Thomas (d 1971)
writer? BP/56*
SHUMAN, Roy (d 1973 [48]) actor
TW/30

SHUMER, Harry (d 1965) theatrical
haulier BP/50*
SHUMLIN, Carmen (d 1970) per-
former BP/55*
SHUMLIN, Herman E. (b 1896/98)
American producing manager
BE, CB, ES, NTH, TW/2-8,
WWT/8-16
SHUNMUGHAM, T. K. (d 1973
[61]) performer BP/57*
SHURR, Lester H. (d 1971) talent
agent BP/55*
SHURR, Louis (d 1967) talent
representative BE, TW/24
SHURTLEFF, Michael American
dramatist, casting director BE
SHUTER, Mr. actor TD/2
SHUTER, Edward (1728-76) English
actor CDP, COC, DNB, ES,
GT, OC/1-2, TD/1-2
SHUTTA, Ethel [née Schutte] (1896-
1976) American actress, singer
TW/20, 27-29, WWT/15
SHUTTLEWORTH, Miss (fl 1805)
actress TD/2
SHWARTZ, Evgenyi Lvovich (1896-
1961) Russian dramatist COC
SHWARTZ, Martin (b 1923) Amer-
ican press representative BE
SHY, Gus (d 1945 [51]) comedian
TW/2
SHYRE, Paul (b 1926/29) American
director, producer, dramatist,
actor BE, TW/13-14, 21, 27,
WWT/15-16
SIAMESE TWINS, The (1810/11-74)
freaks CDP, HAS
SIBBS, John (d 1886) Negro come-
dian EA/87*
SIBLEY, Antoinette (b 1939) Eng-
lish dancer CB, ES
SIBLEY, Lucy [Mrs. Edgar Smart]
(d 1945) English actress EA/
96, GRB/1
SIBONI, Erik (d 1892 [63]) com-
poser EA/93*
SIBTHORPE, Edward (fl 1608)
share-holder DA
SICARD, Clara (d 1876) reader
EA/77*
SICARI, Joseph R. (b 1939) Amer-
ican actor TW/24-26, 29
SICKELMORE, Richard (fl 1797-
1805) dramatist CP/3
SICKERT, Walter Richard (d 1942
[81]) actor BE*, WWT/14*
SIDAY, Eric (d 1976 [71]) com-
poser/lyricist BP/60*

SIDDLE, S. B. (d 1889) music-hall proprietor EA/90*
SIDDONS, Harriett see Siddons, Mrs. Henry
SIDDONS, Harry see Palmer, Henry
SIDDONS, Henry (1774-1815) English actor, manager, dramatist CP/3, DNB, ES, GT, TD/1-2
SIDDONS, Mrs. Henry [née Murray] (c. 1783-1844) actress CDP, DNB, TD/1-2
SIDDONS, Sarah (1755-1831) English actress CDP, COC, DNB, ES, GT, HP, NTH, OC/1-3, OX, PDT, TD/1-2
SIDDONS, William J. (d 1890 [59]) musician EA/91*
SIDELLE, Mr. singer, change artist CDP
SIDGWICK, Ethel (1877-1970) English dramatist WWW/6
SIDNEY, Mr. actor CDP
SIDNEY, Miss (d 1833) actress CDP
SIDNEY, Fred W. (d 1910) English actor, dramatist, stage manager WWS
SIDNEY, George (1876/78-1945) American actor ES, SR, TW/1
SIDNEY, H. C. (d 1890) actor EA/91*
SIDNEY, Irene (d 1970) performer BP/55*
SIDNEY, Mabel (d 1969 [85]) performer BP/54*
SIDNEY, Minnie [Mrs. Milano] (d 1873) actress EA/74*
SIDNEY, Sir Philip (1554-86) English writer DNB, ES, FGF, NTH
SIDNEY, P. Jay (b 1934) actor TW/22
SIDNEY, Suzan (b 1946) American actress TW/25, 27
SIDNEY, Sylvia [Sophia Kosow] (b 1910) American actress AAS, BE, ES, TW/22-24, WWT/7-16
SIDNEY, William (d 1895) stage manager EA/96*
SIDUS, Georgina see Mrs. Oldmixon
SIEBERT, Charles (b 1938) American actor TW/25, 27-30
SIEBERT, Ronald H. American actor TW/29-30

SIEDENBERG, Mme. (fl 1852) singer CDP
SIEGEL, Arthur (b 1923) American composer, musician, actor BE
SIEGEL, Harvey (b 1945) American actor TW/28
SIEGEL, Mark (b 1947) American actor TW/29
SIEGEL, Max (d 1958 [57]) producer BE*, BP/43*
SIEGEL, William (d 1966 [73]) dramatist BP/50*
SIEGLER, Ivy American actress TW/27
SIEGMEISTER, Elie (b 1909) American composer, musical director, educator BE
SIEGRIST AND LEVANION acrobats CDP
SIENKIEWICZ, Henry (1846-1916) Polish actor SR
SIEPI, Cesare (b 1922/23) Italian singer BE, CB, TW/19
SIERRA, Gregorio Martinez (d 1947 [66]) Spanish dramatist BP/32*, WWT/14*
SIERRA, Margarita (d 1963 [26]) performer BP/48*
SIEVEKING, Margot English actress WWT/8
SIEVIER, Mary Jane [Mrs. W. R. Sievier] (d 1868 [22]) EA/69*
SIEVIER, Mrs. W. R. see Sievier, Mary Jane
SIFACE (1653-97) Italian singer ES
SIFF, Ira (b 1946) American actor TW/30
SIFTON, Paul (1898-1972) American dramatist MD, MWD
SIGGINS, Jeff (b 1943) American actor TW/22-24
SIGNORET, Gabriel (1878-1937) French actor WWT/4
SIKS, Geraldine B. (b 1912) American educator, director BE
SILBER, Don (b 1936) American actor TW/23-24, 26
SILBERT, Lisa (d 1965 [85]) performer BP/50*, WWT/14*
SILBON, Cornelius (d 1891) performer? EA/92*
SILBON, Fred [Little Ebor] (d 1876) gymnast EA/77*
SILBON, Minnie [Mrs. Walter Silbon] (d 1905 [34]) EA/06*
SILBON, Walter (d 1903 [37]) acrobat EA/04*

SILBON, Mrs. Walter see
Silbon, Minnie
SILBURNE, Edward (d 1888 [48])
actor EA/89*
SILETTI, Mario (b 1935) Amer-
ican actor TW/27
SILETTI, Mario G. (d 1964 [60])
actor BE*
SILL, William Raymond (1869-
1922) American press repre-
sentative, manager WWM,
WWS
SILLMAN, Leonard (b 1908)
American producer, actor,
director BE, TW/24, 26,
WWT/15-16
SILLS, Beverly (b 1929) Ameri-
can singer CB
SILLS, Gladys Wynne (d 1964
[78]) performer BP/49*
SILLS, Milton (1882-1930) Amer-
ican actor DAB, ES, WWA/1,
WWM
SILLS, Pawnee American actress
TW/25, 30
SILLWARD, Edward (d 1930)
actor BE*, WWT/14*
SILLY, Lea French singer CDP
SILSBEE, Joshua S. (1813/15-53)
American actor CDP, HAS,
SR
SILSBEE, Mrs. Josiah see
Chapman, Mrs. William A.
SILVA, Nina de see De Silva,
Nina
SILVAIN, Mons. (d 1856 [50])
dancer EA/72*
SILVANO, Mme. Alfonso (d 1917)
EA/18*
SILVANO, Jack (d 1917) EA/18*
SIL-VARA, G. (d 1938 [62])
dramatist WWT/14*
SILVER, Mrs. see Kingston,
Gertrude
SILVER, Christine [Mrs. Walter
Maxwell] (1883/84-1960) Eng-
lish actress GRB/4, WWT/
1-12
SILVER, Joe (b 1922) American
actor BE, TW/22-24, 27-28,
30
SILVER, Monty (b 1933) Ameri-
can talent representative BE
SILVER, Ronald (b 1946) Amer-
ican actor TW/30
SILVER, Stuart (b 1947) Ameri-
can actor TW/29
SILVERA, Frank (1914-70)

Jamaican actor, director BE,
TW/27, WWA/5
SILVERBLATT, Howard see Da
Silva, Howard
SILVERMAN, Harriet (d 1975
[100]) columnist WWT/16*
SILVERMAN, Jack (d 1974 [86])
restaurateur BP/59*
SILVERMAN, Sid (1898-1950)
American publisher BE*, BP/
34*
SILVERMAN, Sime (1872-1933)
American editor, publisher
BE*, BP/18*, WWT/14*
SILVERMAN, Syd (b 1932) Ameri-
can newspaper publisher BE
SILVERS, Louis (d 1954 [64])
American composer BE*, BP/
38*
SILVERS, Phil (b 1911/12) Ameri-
can actor BE, CB, ES, TW/
4-5, 8-20, 27-29, WWT/16
SILVERSTONE, Jonas T. (b 1906)
American attorney, producer
BE
SILVESTER (fl 1625) actor DA
SILVESTER, Mr. (fl 1788) drama-
tist CP/3
SILVIA, Leslie (b 1958) American
actress TW/26-27
SILVO, William (d 1880 [17])
gymnast EA/81*
SIM, Alastair (1900-76) Scottish
actor AAS, ES, WWT/9-16
SIM, Henry Edward Clulow (d 1901
[29]) EA/03*
SIM, Millie (b 1895) English ac-
tress WWT/6-9
SIM, Sheila (b 1922) English ac-
tress WWT/11-13
SIM, William (d 1885) musical
director EA/86*
SIMANEK, Otto (d 1967 [66]) per-
former BP/52*
SIMEON, Mrs. J. H. see
Simeon, Mrs. L.
SIMEON, Mrs. L. [Mrs. J. H.
Simeon] (d 1886) EA/87*
SIMEON, Louisa see Chatterley,
Louisa
SIMEONS (fl 1802) dramatist CP/3
SIMIONATO, Giulietta (b 1910/16)
Italian singer CB, ES
SIMKINS, William (d 1870) actor
EA/71*
SIMMONDS, Benjamin (d 1910
[84]) musician EA/11*
SIMMONDS, James (d 1882 [98])

EA/83*
SIMMONDS, John (d 1874 [45])
actor EA/75*
SIMMONDS, J. Rewe (d 1886)
treasurer EA/87*
SIMMONDS, Morris (1836-96)
American agent, manager SR
SIMMONDS, Stanley (b 1907)
American actor TW/24-26
SIMMONS, Mr. (fl c. 1802-04)
actor OX, TD/1-2
SIMMONS, Mrs. see Seymour,
Molly
SIMMONS, Charles (d 1872 [71])
musician, composer EA/73*
SIMMONS, Connie (b 1952)
American actress TW/24-25
SIMMONS, Ernest Romaine (d
1954 [80+]) casting director,
dance director, business
manager, musician BP/38*
SIMMONS, Georgia (b 1884)
American actress TW/23
SIMMONS, James Wright (fl
early 19th cent [68]) Ameri-
can dramatist EAP, RJ
SIMMONS, Joseph (d 1875 [50])
music-hall proprietor EA/
76*
SIMMONS, Keith (b 1955) Amer-
ican actor TW/30
SIMMONS, Lavinia [Miss Lavine]
(d 1872) actress EA/73*
SIMMONS, Lew (1838-1908)
minstrel manager, actor
CDP
SIMMONS, Nat (b 1936) Ameri-
can actor TW/22-24
SIMMONS, Samuel (1777?-1819)
English actor CDP, DNB,
EA/92, GT
SIMMONS, Viola Bowers see
Bowers, Viola
SIMMONS, William Arthur see
Little Simmy
SIMMS, Mrs. C. H. (d 1885)
EA/86*
SIMMS, Don[ald] (b 1934) Amer-
ican actor TW/26, 28
SIMMS, Henrietta (d 1887) ac-
tress WWT/14*
SIMMS, Hilda (b 1920) American
actress BE, CB, TW/1-3,
26, WWT/11-16
SIMMS, John (d 1885) marionette
proprietor EA/86*
SIMMS, Lizzie (d 1886) dancer
EA/87*

SIMMS, Sheryl American actress
TW/30
SIMMS, Willard (fl 1900-06) Amer-
ican actor WWS
SIMMS, William Gilmore (1806-70)
dramatist CDP
SIMON dramatist CP/3, FGF
SIMON, Mme. actress CDP
SIMON, Bernard (1904-77) Ameri-
can press representative BE
SIMON, Charles (d 1910 [60])
dramatist BE*, WWT/14*
SIMON, Harry (d 1976 [87]) in-
surer BP/60*
SIMON, Henrietta (fl 1858) singer
HAS
SIMON, Henry W. (d 1970 [68])
critic BP/55*
SIMON, Herb (b 1946) American
actor TW/27
SIMON, Herb see Braha, Herb
SIMON, Joan Baim (d 1973 [41])
performer BP/58*
SIMON, John (b 1925) Jugoslav/
American BE, WWT/15-16
SIMON, Joseph (1594-1671) English
dramatist OC/3
SIMON, Leila (b 1876) American
reader WWM
SIMON, Louis M. (b 1906) Ameri-
can stage manager, executive
WWT/11-16
SIMON, Michel (d 1975 [80]) actor
BP/59*, WWT/16*
SIMON, Neil (b 1927) American
dramatist AAS, BE, CB, CD,
COC, ES, MH, MWD, WWT/
15-16
SIMON, William J. (d 1971 [80s])
composer/lyricist BP/56*
SIMONE, Mme. [Simone Le Bargy]
(b 1880) French actress GRB/
1-4, WWM, WWT/1-4
SIMONET, Mme. (fl 1781?) dancer
CDP
SIMONET, Miss (fl 1796?) ac-
tress, aeronaut CDP
SIMONIAN, Ronald (b 1948) Amer-
ican actor TW/28
SIMONOV, Konstantin Mikhailovich
(b 1915) Russian dramatist OC/
1-3
SIMONOV, Ruben (d 1968 [69])
performer BP/53*
SIMONS, Beverley (b 1938) Canadian dramatist CD
SIMONS, Eva H. (d 1974 [77])
producer/director/choreographer

BP/59*
SIMONS, Lucy American singer
HAS
SIMONS, Seymour (d 1949 [53])
songwriter TW/5
SIMONSEN, Fanny (d 1896 [61])
Australian singer EA/97*
SIMONSENS, Christie see
Farthing, Maud
SIMONSON, Lee (1888-1967)
American designer, executive
BE, CB, COC, ES, NTH,
OC/1-3, TW/3-8, 23, WWA/
4, WWT/7-14, WWW/6
SIMPLE, Pete (b 1908) circus
clown EA/09*
SIMPSON, Mr. (d 1827) Ameri-
can actor HAS
SIMPSON, Mr. (fl 1796-97)
actor HAS
SIMPSON, Mr. ["Irish Simpson"]
(fl 1797) actor HAS
SIMPSON, Mrs. see Thomas,
Mrs.
SIMPSON, Mrs. (d 1832) actress
HAS
SIMPSON, Mrs. [née Louisa
Dalby] (d 1872 [34]) singer
EA/73*
SIMPSON, Catherine Raynor
[Mrs. Jack Raynor] (d 1912)
EA/13*
SIMPSON, C. H. (1771-1835)
master of ceremonies CDP
SIMPSON, Charles (d 1879 [27])
variety artist EA/80*
SIMPSON, Charles (d 1894 [80])
pantomimist EA/95*
SIMPSON, Mrs. Charles see
Simpson, Emma Ann
SIMPSON, Cheridah (d 1922 [58])
American singer, actress
SR
SIMPSON, Christopher (fl 1610-
12) actor DA
SIMPSON, Clifford (d 1906
[35]) performer? EA/07*
SIMPSON, Cuthbert (fl 1616)
actor DA
SIMPSON, Dennis (b 1950) West
Indian actor TW/29-30
SIMPSON, Mrs. E. [née Jones]
(fl 1809-22) actress HAS
SIMPSON, Edmund Shaw (1784-
1848) American actor, mana-
ger CDP, COC, DAB,
HAS, OC/1-3, SR, WWA/H
SIMPSON, Edward (d 1868) pro-

prietor EA/69*
SIMPSON, Elizabeth see Inch-
bald, Elizabeth
SIMPSON, Emma Ann [Mrs.
Charles Simpson] (d 1881) EA/
82*
SIMPSON, Harold lyricist, libret-
tist WWT/5-11
SIMPSON, Harry (d 1872) actor?
EA/73*
SIMPSON, Ivan (1875-1951) English
actor TW/1-8
SIMPSON, James (d 1877) music-
hall proprietor EA/78*
SIMPSON, John (fl 1616) actor
DA
SIMPSON, John Dempster see
Mite, Mjr.
SIMPSON, John Henry (d 1878
[37]) comedian EA/79*
SIMPSON, John Palgrave (1807-87)
English dramatist CDP, EA/
68, NYM
SIMPSON, Joseph (fl 1785) drama-
tist CP/3
SIMPSON, Joseph (d 1869 [69])
actor? EA/70*
SIMPSON, Mrs. L. [née Woodling]
(d 1873 [26]) EA/74*
SIMPSON, Maria see Liston,
Mrs. W. H.
SIMPSON, Marion (d 1913 [56])
EA/14*
SIMPSON, Mercer Hampson (d
1902 [66]) lessee, manager
EA/03*, WWT/14*
SIMPSON, N[orman] F[rederick]
(b 1919) English dramatist
AAS, BE, CD, CH, COC, ES,
MH, MWD, PDT, WWT/14-16
SIMPSON, Pamela English actress
TW/8
SIMPSON, Peggy (b 1913) English
actress WWT/10-14
SIMPSON, Reginald (d 1964 [68])
performer BP/49*
SIMPSON, Richard (fl 1616) actor
DA
SIMPSON, Robert (fl 1616) actor
DA
SIMPSON, Ronald (1896-1957)
English actor WWT/7-12
SIMPSON, Russell (d 1959 [81])
actor BE*
SIMPSON, Sean (b 1944) American
actor TW/25
SIMPSON, Sloan American actor
TW/13

SIMPSON, Steve (b 1947) American actor TW/29-30
SIMPSON, Thomas Bartlett (d 1872 [66]) proprietor EA/73*
SIMPSON, Timothy Ogilvie (d 1880 [22]) comedian EA/81*
SIMPSON, T. P. (d 1877 [64]) proprietor EA/78*
SIMPSON, Mrs. T. P. (d 1885 [76]) proprietor EA/86*
SIMPSON, T. W. (d 1875) actor EA/76*
SIMPSON, Mrs. William (d 1877 [37]) EA/78*
SIMPSON, William Robert (d 1878 [33]) stage manager EA/79*
SIMS, Mrs. (d 1892) EA/93*
SIMS, Miss (fl 1797) actress TD/1-2
SIMS, Christine (d 1878) dancer EA/79*
SIMS, Mrs. Fred see Taylor, Ada
SIMS, Mrs. George see Clifford, Mrs.
SIMS, George R[obert] (1847-1922) English dramatist CDP, GRB/1-4, WWS, WWT/1-4, WWW/2
SIMS, Mrs. George R[obert] see Sims, Sarah Elizabeth
SIMS, Joan (b 1930) English actress WWT/13-16
SIMS, John A. G. see Rush, Bert
SIMS, Mamie see Williams, Mrs. Alan
SIMS, Marley (b 1948) American actor TW/29-30
SIMS, S. (fl 1797) actress CDP
SIMS, Sarah Elizabeth [Mrs. George R. Sims] (d 1886 [36]) EA/88*
SIMS, Violet (b 1883) English actress GRB/3
SIMS, William (d 1841 [53]) agent EA/72*
SIMS REEVES, Constance Emma (d 1901) EA/02*
SINATRA, Frank (b 1917) American singer CB
SINCKLER, William (fl 1629) musician DA
SINCLAIR, Anna (fl 1846) actress HAS
SINCLAIR, Arthur (1883-1951) Irish actor COC, ES, OC/1-3, TW/8, WWT/2-11

SINCLAIR, Barry (b 1911) English actor, singer WWT/10-16
SINCLAIR, Betty (b 1907) English actress TW/4, 9, 11-14, 22-23, 28
SINCLAIR, Caroline N. [Mrs. Edwin Forrest] (d 1891 [74]) American actress EA/92*
SINCLAIR, Catherine (fl 1837-59) American actress HAS, SR
SINCLAIR, Prof. Charles (d 1890 [63]) ventriloquist EA/91*
SINCLAIR, Mrs. Charles see Sinclair, Eliza
SINCLAIR, Eliza [Mrs. Charles Sinclair] (d 1887 [63]) EA/88*
SINCLAIR, Eric (b 1922) American actor TW/8-17
SINCLAIR, E. V. (d 1887) EA/88*
SINCLAIR, George (b 1858) English agent, composer GRB/1
SINCLAIR, H. (d 1886) actor EA/87*
SINCLAIR, Mrs. Harry [Fanny Vernon] (d 1887 [34]) EA/88*
SINCLAIR, Henry (b 1834) actor OAA/1-2
SINCLAIR, Henry (d 1879 [50]) actor EA/81*, WWT/14*
SINCLAIR, Hugh (1903-62) English actor AAS, TW/19, WWT/7-13
SINCLAIR, Sir John (b 1754) Scottish? dramatist CP/3
SINCLAIR, John (1790/91/93-1857) Scottish singer BS, CDP, DNB, HAS, SR
SINCLAIR, J. P. (d 1871) singer EA/72*
SINCLAIR, Mabel (d 1916 [36]) ventriloquist EA/17*
SINCLAIR, Moray (d 1964 [63]) Canadian actor, press representative BE*
SINCLAIR, Nellie (d 1897) actress EA/98*
SINCLAIR, Polly see Robinson, Mrs.
SINCLAIR, Rebecca [Mrs. Nixon] (d 1875) actress EA/76*
SINCLAIR, Robert B. (1905-70) American director, actor BE, TW/26
SINCLAIR, Tom (b 1941) American actor TW/25, 30
SINCLAIR, Upton (1878-1968) American dramatist CB, HJD
SINCLAIR-HILL, Gerald Arthur Lewin see Hill, Sinclair

SINCLER, John (fl 1590-1604)
actor DA
SINDEN, Burt (d 1911) comedian,
dancer EA/12*
SINDEN, Donald (b 1923) English
actor AAS, WWT/13-16
SINDEN, Topsy (b 1878) actress,
singer, dancer GRB/1-4,
WWT/1-6
SINGER, Arthur R. (d 1967 [66])
manager BP/52*
SINGER, Campbell (1909-76)
English actor, dramatist
WWT/14-16
SINGER, Israel J. (1893-1944)
dramatist CB
SINGER, John (fl 1598-1602)
dramatist, actor CP/3, DA,
DNB, FGF
SINGER, Teresina (1850-1928)
Moravian singer CDP, ES
SINGERMAN, Bernard (d 1973
[61]) performer BP/58*
SINGHER, Martial (b 1904)
French singer CB, ES
SINGLETON, Mr. (fl 1752-53)
English actor HAS
SINGLETON, Mr. (fl 1826) actor
HAS
SINGLETON, Catherine (d 1969
[65]) performer BP/54*
SINGLETON, Charles W. (d
1880) EA/81*
SINGLETON, Miss E. (fl 1839)
actress HAS
SINGLETON, Kate (fl 1864) ac-
tress HAS
SINGLETON, Sam (b 1940)
American actor TW/26-27
SINGLETON, Rev. Thomas (fl
1656-83) dramatist CP/3
SINNOTT, Catherine (d 1911)
EA/12*
SIODMAK, Robert (d 1973 [72])
producer/director/choreographer
BP/57*
SIPLE, S. M. (d 1854) actor
HAS
SIPPERLEY, Ralph (d 1928 [38])
actor BE*, BP/12*
SIPPLE, John James (d 1905)
music-hall comedian EA/06*
SIPPLE, Rosina [Mrs. George
Aytoun] (d 1906 [47]) EA/07*
SIRCOM, Arthur R. (b 1899)
American director, actor
BE, TW/2
SIRE, Henry B. (d 1917) pro-

ducer, manager BE*, WWT/14*
SIRKIN, Stephen (d 1974 [30])
dramatist BP/58*
SIROLA, Joseph (b 1929) American
actor TW/24
SISSLE, Noble (d 1975 [86]) com-
poser WWT/16*
SITES, G. (fl 1829) American actor
HAS
SITGREAVES, Beverley (1867-1943)
American actress CB, WWM,
WWS, WWT/4-9
SIVADO, Robert (d 1908) music-
hall performer EA/09*
SIVRONI, Amy (d 1910 [39]) per-
former? EA/11*
SIVY, Michael (b 1921) American
actor TW/3
SIZEMORE, Asher (d 1975 [69])
performer BP/60*
SIZOVA, Alla (b 1939) Russian
dancer ES
SKAIFE, William (d 1892) acting
manager, actor EA/93*
SKALA, Lilia Austrian actress
TW/7-8, 25, 27, WWT/16
SKEAF, Joseph (d 1884 [46]) pro-
fessor of music EA/85*
SKEAPING, Mary (fl 1925-59)
English dancer ES
SKEFFINGTON, Sir Lumley St.
George (1771/78-1850) English
dramatist CDP, CP/3, DNB,
GT, HP
SKEGGS, Matthew (d 1773) actor
CDP
SKEIN, Farmer (b 1877) actor
GRB/1
SKELLEY, Henry (d 1904 [49])
property master EA/05*
SKELLEY, Joseph Harold see
Skelly, Hal
SKELLY, Hal [Joseph Harold
Skelley] (1891-1934) American
actor WWT/7
SKELLY, James (d 1969 [33])
performer BP/53*
SKELLY, Madge (b 1904) American
actress, producer, director,
educator BE
SKELTON, Herbert Sleath see
Sleath, Herbert
SKELTON, Mrs. Herbert Sleath
see Jeffreys, Ellis
SKELTON, John (c. 1460-1529)
English dramatist COC, CP/
2-3, DNB, HP, MH, OC/2-3
SKELTON, Red (b 1913) American

comedian CB, ES

SKELTON, Thomas lighting designer, stage manager WWT/16

SKEMP, Arthur Rowland (1882-1918) English dramatist, educator WWW/2

SKERRETT, Emma see Skerrett, Mrs. George

SKERRETT, Fanny (b 1849) American actress HAS

SKERRETT, George (1810-55) English actor CDP, HAS

SKERRETT, Mrs. George [Emma; Mrs. Henry L. Bascomb] (1817-87) Scottish actress CDP, HAS, NYM

SKERRETT, Rose see Shewell, Mrs. L. R., II

SKETCHLEY, Arthur [George Rose] (d 1882 [64]) English dramatist, actor CDP, DNB, EA/68, HAS

SKIBINE, George (b 1920) Russian/American dancer, choreographer ES

SKIKNE, Laurence see Harvey, Laurence

SKILES, Steve (b 1945) American actor TW/24

SKILLAN, George (b 1893) English actor WWT/6-14

SKINNER, Cornelia Otis (b 1901) American actress AAS, BE, CB, COC, ES, HJD, NTH, OC/1-3, TW/1-17, WWT/7-16

SKINNER, Edith Warman (b 1904) Canadian educator, acting coach BE

SKINNER, Edna (b 1922) American actress TW/1

SKINNER, Frank (d 1968 [69]) composer/lyricist BP/53*

SKINNER, George (d 1896) actor EA/97*

SKINNER, Harold Otis (d 1922 [33]) actor BE*, BP/7*

SKINNER, Howard K. (d 1971) American executive WWA/5

SKINNER, Mrs. H. R. see Zimmer, Maggie

SKINNER, Maud Durbin (b 1873) American actress GRB/3-4

SKINNER, Otis (1858-1942) American actor CB, CDP, COC, DAB, ES, GRB/2-4, HJD, NTH, OC/1-3, PP/3, SR,

WWA/1, WWM, WWS, WWT/1-9

SKINNER, Mrs. Otis see Durbin, Maud

SKINNER, Richard (fl 1547-59) actor DA

SKINNER, Richard (1900-71) American producer, manager, actor BE, TW/28

SKINNER, Mrs. Robert see Bristow, Mrs.

SKINNER, Ted (b 1911) American educator BE

SKINNER, W. (d 1906) music-hall stage manager EA/07*

SKIPITARIS, Loukas Greek actor TW/25

SKIPPER, Bill (b 1922) American actor, dancer? TW/2-6, 12

SKIPWORTH, Alison (1863-1952) English actress TW/9, WWS, WWT/8-11

SKIRPAN, Stephen J. (b 1930) American equipment designer, lighting consultant, inventor BE

SKLAR, George (b 1908) American dramatist BE, MH, MWD, NTH

SKLAR, Michael (b 1944) American actor TW/28

SKOURAS, George P. (d 1964 [68]) Greek executive BE*

SKOURATOFF, Vladimir (b 1925) French dancer ES

SKRINE, Mary Nesta see Farrell, M. J.

SKULNIK, Menashe (1894/98-1970) Polish actor BE, TW/11-20, 22-23, 27, WWA/5, WWT/13-14

SLACK, Ben (b 1937) American actor TW/28-29

SLADE, Alfred George (d 1907) circus manager EA/08*

SLADE, John (d 1760) dramatist CP/2-3

SLADE, Julian (b 1930) English composer, dramatist, actor AAS, PDT, WWT/13-16

SLADE, Olga (d 1949) actress BE*, WWT/14*

SLANE, Eva Weith (b 1929) German talent representative BE

SLATE, Henry (b 1915) American actor TW/5-6

SLATE, Syd (d 1976 [68]) performer BP/60*

SLATER, Mr. actor HAS

SLATER, Arthur [Arthur Stewart] actor, variety artist GRB/1

SLATER, C. Dundas (d 1912
[60]) manager WWT/14*
SLATER, Chris (d 1880) music-
hall chairman & manager
EA/81*
SLATER, Daphne (b 1928) English
actress AAS, WWT/11-14
SLATER, Elizabeth [Mrs. Thomas
Slater] (d 1870) EA/71*
SLATER, George M. (d 1949
[79]) actor, producer, mana-
ger BE*, WWT/14*
SLATER, Hartley (d 1964 [63])
performer BE*
SLATER, Mrs. J. H. [Louisa
Pereira] (d 1885 [39]) actress
EA/87*
SLATER, John (d 1886 [43])
stage manager EA/87*
SLATER, John (1916-75) English
actor WWT/12-15
SLATER, Martin (d 1625?) ac-
tor, dramatist CP/3, DA
SLATER, Samuel (fl 1679) dra-
matist CP/3
SLATER, Mrs. Thomas see
Slater, Elizabeth
SLATKIN, Felix (d 1963 [47])
composer, conductor BE*
SLATTERY, Daniel G. (d 1964
[91]) manager BE*
SLATTERY, James (d 1974
[26]) performer BP/58*
SLAUGHTER, Harriet (b 1937)
American actress TW/26-29
SLAUGHTER, Henry (d 1882
[38]) manager EA/83*
SLAUGHTER, Martin see Slater,
Martin
SLAUGHTER, N. Carter (1885-
1956) English actor, manager
WWT/6-11
SLAUGHTER, Ted see Slaughter,
N. Carter
SLAUGHTER, Walter (1860-1908)
English composer, conductor
GRB/1-3
"SLAUGHTER, William" actor
DA
SLAVENSKA, Mia (b 1914/17)
Yugoslav dancer, choreographer
CB, ES
SLAVIN, John C. (d 1940 [71])
American actor BE*, BP/
25*, WWT/14*
SLAVIN, Susan American actress
TW/26
SLEAP, Ellen Caroline [Mme.

Helena; Mrs. William S. Sleap]
(d 1884) EA/85*
SLEAP, Mrs. William S. see
Sleap, Ellen Caroline
SLEATH, Herbert [Herbert Sleath
Skelton] (1870-1921) English
actor, producer GRB/1-4,
WWM, WWS, WWT/1-5
SLEE, John (fl 1537-40) actor DA
SLEEPER, Martha (b 1910/11)
American actress BE, TW/1-3,
WWT/9-11
SLEIGH, J. P. (d 1905 [54]) actor
GRB/1
SLEIGH, Louise Elizabeth [Mrs.
W. H. Sleigh] (d 1869 [24])
EA/70*
SLEIGH, Mrs. W. H. see Sleigh,
Louise Elizabeth
SLEMONS, Frederica (d 1964 [90])
performer BP/49*
SLEZAK, Leo (1873-1946) Austrian
singer ES, TW/3, WWA/2
SLEZAK, Walter (b 1902) Austrian
actor, singer AAS, BE, CB,
ES, TW/15-16, WWT/8-10, 15-
16
SLINGSBY, Mary (d 1694) actress
DNB
SLINGSBY, Simon (fl 1758-85)
English dancer ES
SLITER, Dick (d 1861) jig dancer
HAS
SLOAN, Fern (b 1940) American
actress TW/29
SLOAN, John T. K. (1832-61) Eng-
lish actor, manager HAS
SLOAN, Mrs. John T. K. [née
Ploughman] (fl 1849-68) English
actress HAS
SLOAN, Mrs. J. T. see Sander-
son, Julia
SLOAN, Mimi American actress
TW/24
SLOANE, Alfred Baldwin (1872-
1924) American composer GRB/
3-4, WWA/1, WWM, WWS,
WWT/1-5
SLOANE, Everett (1909-65) Ameri-
can actor CB, TW/22
SLOANE, Olive (1894/96-1963) ac-
tress WWT/5-13
SLOCUM, Edwin N. (1836-95)
minstrel, minstrel manager
CDP
SLOMAN, Charles (1808-70) English
music-hall performer COC,
OC/1-3

SLOMAN, Henry (d 1869 [72])
machinist EA/71*
SLOMAN, Henry (d 1873 [80])
comedian EA/74*, WWT/
14*
SLOMAN, John (d 1873 [79])
English comic singer CDP,
HAS
SLOMAN, Mrs. John [née
Whitaker; Mrs. H. Darton]
(d 1858 [59]) English actress
CDP, HAS, OX
SLONIMSKY, Nicolas (b 1894)
Russian composer, conductor
CB
SLOPER, Edward Hugh Lindsay
(1826-87) composer, musician
CDP
SLOPER, Lindsay see Sloper,
Edward Hugh Lindsay
SLOSSER, Pauline Hall (d 1974
[83]) performer BP/59*
SLOUS, A. R. (d 1883 [71])
dramatist EA/68
SLOWACKI, Juliusz (1809-49)
Polish dramatist COC
SLY, William (d 1608) English
actor DA, ES, GT, NTH,
OC/1-3
SLYE, Thomas actor DA
SMALE, Mrs. T. E. see El-
liott, Charlotte
SMALE, Thomas E. (d 1890)
acting manager, business
manager EA/91*, WWT/14*
SMALE, Mrs. Tom see Elliott,
Charlotte
SMALL, Dick (d 1972 [58]) per-
former BP/56*
SMALL, Jack (d 1962 [52]) Amer-
ican manager BE*, BP/46*
SMALL, Lillian Schary (d 1961
[60]) talent representative
BE*
SMALL, Michael (b 1939) Amer-
ican manager BE
SMALL, Neva (b 1952) American
actress TW/22-28, 30
SMALL, Paul (d 1954 [45]) Amer-
ican talent representative
BE*
SMALL, Seldon (d 1974 [72])
costume supplier BP/58*
SMALL, William (d 1969 [84])
secretary BP/54*
SMALLENS, Alexander (1889-1972)
Russian/American conductor
CB, WWA/5

SMALLEY, Eugene B. (d 1968
[46]) composer/lyricist BP/53*
SMALLEY, John (d 1881 [61])
actor? EA/82*
SMALLS, Ed (d 1974 [92]) showman
BP/59*
SMALLWOOD, Mr. (fl 1786) actor
HAS
SMALLWOOD, Ernest Edward
see Wood, Ernest
SMALLWOOD, William (d 1897)
composer EA/98*
SMART, Christopher (1722-71)
English dramatist CP/2-3,
DNB
SMART, Dick (b 1915) Hawaiian
actor TW/3, 5-6
SMART, Edgar (d 1896 [47]) EA/
97*
SMART, Mrs. Edgar see Sibley,
Lucy
SMART, Sir George Thomas (1776-
1867) English conductor, com-
poser CDP, DNB
SMART, Henry (d 1879 [66]) com-
poser, musician EA/80*
SMART, Henry Edward (d 1894
[50]) EA/95*
SMART, Mary (d 1869) EA/70*
SMEAD, Mr. (fl 1850) actor HAS
SMEATON, Mary (d 1893) EA/94*
SMEDLEY, Arnold (d 1908 [28])
actor EA/09*
SMEDLEY, Constance (1881-1941)
dramatist CB
SMEDLEY, Morgan T. (d 1964
[46]) American actor BE*,
BP/48*
SMEDLEY, William Ellis (d 1916)
actor SR
SMILEY, Brenda (b 1947) Ameri-
can actress TW/24-25
SMILEY, Ralph (b 1916) American
actor TW/2
SMILEY, Red (d 1972 [47]) per-
former BP/56*
SMITH, Mr. actor TD/2
SMITH (fl 1798) dramatist CP/3
SMITH, Dr. dramatist CP/2-3
SMITH, Mrs. [née Parr] (fl 1831)
Welsh dancer HAS
SMITH, Mrs. [née Ellen Mortimer]
(d 1874) actress EA/75*
SMITH, Mrs. see Dixon, Clara
Ann
SMITH, A. B. (d 1896) acting
manager EA/97*
SMITH, Adam (fl 1776) actor,

singer, dramatist CP/3
SMITH, Albert (1816-60) English
dramatist, actor CDP, COC,
DNB, OC/1-3
SMITH, Mrs. Albert see Smith,
Mary Lucy
SMITH, Alexis (b 1921) Canadian
actress TW/27-29, WWT/16
SMITH, Alf E. (d 1917) EA/18*
SMITH, Alfred (d 1870 [19])
acrobat EA/71*
SMITH, A. Montem (d 1891 [73])
singer EA/92*
SMITH, Anthony (fl 1616-28)
actor DA
SMITH, Archie American actor
TW/6-10
SMITH, Art (d 1973 [73]) actor
TW/29
SMITH, Arthur Corbett (d 1945
[65]) dramatist, composer
BE*, WWT/14*
SMITH, Arthur W. W. (1825-61)
English entertainer DNB
SMITH, Sir Aubrey see Smith,
Sir C. Aubrey
SMITH, Barrey American per-
former TW/30
SMITH, Beasley (d 1968 [67])
composer/lyricist BP/52*
SMITH, Betty (1904/06-72) Amer-
ican dramatist, educator BE,
CB, HJD
SMITH, Betty Jane (d 1973 [49])
performer BP/57*
SMITH, Billie see Bard, Wilkie
SMITH, Billy (d 1963 [60]) per-
former BE*
SMITH, Bruce (d 1942 [87])
scene artist BE*, WWT/14*
SMITH, Sir C. Aubrey (1863-
1948) English actor CB,
GRB/1-4, TW/5, WWS, WWT/
1-9
SMITH, C. F. (1813-64) Ameri-
can manager HAS
SMITH, Charles (1786-1856) Eng-
lish dramatist, singer CP/3,
DNB, EAP, RJ
SMITH, Charles F. (d 1894 [43])
secretary of Guildhall School
of Music EA/95*
SMITH, Charles Frederick
[Charles North] (d 1889 [29])
EA/90*
SMITH, Charles T. (1817-69)
English actor, manager HAS
SMITH, Charles W. (d 1971

[74]) performer BP/56*
SMITH, Chris (1879-1949) Ameri-
can composer BE*
SMITH, Christopher John (d 1888
[80]) pantomimist EA/89*
SMITH, C. J. (fl 1851) actor HAS
SMITH, Clara (fl 1803) actress
TD/2
SMITH, Clay (b 1885) American
actor WWT/4-7
SMITH, Constance M. see
Grafton, Cecil
SMITH, Cyril (1892-1963) Scottish
actor WWT/7-13
SMITH, Delos V., Jr. (b 1906)
American actor TW/24, 26
SMITH, Dodie [C. L. Anthony]
(b 1896) English dramatist, ac-
tress, director AAS, BE, CD,
ES, MH, NTH, PDT, WWT/7-
16
SMITH, Doyle R. (b 1924) Ameri-
can producer, director, actor,
educator BE
SMITH, E. dramatist CP/3
SMITH, Eddie (d 1964 [70]) talent
representative BE*
SMITH, Edgar McPhail (1857-1938)
American librettist GRB/3-4,
WWA/1, WWS, WWT/1-8
SMITH, Mrs. Edith see French,
Edie
SMITH, Edmund (1668/72-1710)
dramatist CP/1-3, DNB, GT
SMITH, Edward A. (d 1974 [85])
manager BP/58*
SMITH, Edward Tyrrell (1804-77)
English manager CDP, COC,
OC/1-3
SMITH, Elihu Hubbard (1771-98)
American dramatist CDP,
CP/3, EAP, HJD, RJ
SMITH, Eliza (d 1913 [58]) EA/14*
SMITH, Eliza see Groves, Eliza
SMITH, Elizabeth [Mrs. Sol Smith]
(d 1887 [75]) EA/88*
SMITH, Elizabeth see Arnold,
Mrs. Henry
SMITH, Elmer (d 1963 [71]) per-
former BE*
SMITH, Elsie Linehan (d 1964
[86]) actress BE*
SMITH, Mrs. Ernest J. (d 1975
[77]) dramatist BP/59*
SMITH, Fanny see Higginbottom,
Frances Ann
SMITH, F. H. (d 1869) acting
manager EA/70*

SMITH, Frank L. (d 1953 [67])
American press representa-
tive, manager BE*, BP/37*,
WWT/14*

SMITH, Frank M. (d 1976 [70])
composer/lyricist BP/60*

SMITH, Frederica (d 1910 [28])
EA/11*

SMITH, Frederica C. (d 1911)
lady superintendent of Guildhall School of Music EA/12*

SMITH, Frederick Wilson (d
1944 [64]) actor TW/1

SMITH, F. W. (d 1917) acting
manager EA/18*

SMITH, G. Albert (1898-1959)
American actor TW/2-3, 16

SMITH, Garnett (b 1937) American actor TW/25, 29-30

SMITH, Geddeth (b 1934) American actor TW/23

SMITH, George American actor
HAS

SMITH, George (1777-1836) English actor, singer BS, CDP,
EA/92

SMITH, George (d 1877 [78])
actor? EA/79*

SMITH, George Frederick (fl
1821) American actor HAS

SMITH, George T. (d 1947
[45]) producer, manager BE*,
WWT/14*

SMITH, George Totten (b 1871)
American dramatist WWM

SMITH, George W. (fl 1849)
maître de ballet HAS

SMITH, Gerald (d 1974 [81])
performer BP/59*

SMITH, Gladys Mary see Pickford, Mary

SMITH, Harold Montague see
Montague, Harold

SMITH, Harry Bache (1860-1936)
American librettist, dramatist
DAB, GRB/3-4, NTH, SR,
WWA/1, WWM, WWS, WWT/
1-7

SMITH, Harry James (1880-1918)
American dramatist DAB

SMITH, Harvey (b 1904) American teacher of stage lighting,
theatre consultant BE

SMITH, Helen S. (b 1909) American educator BE

SMITH, Helen Zenna see Price,
Evadne

SMITH, Henry (fl 1699) drama-

tist CP/1-3, GT

SMITH, Mrs. Henry B. see
Bentley, Irene

SMITH, Henry Oscar (d 1882)
EA/83*

SMITH, Henry Richard (b
1861) English manager
GRB/4

SMITH, Howard (1894/95-1968)
American actor, director BE,
TW/1-3, 5-14, 23-24, WWT/
11-14

SMITH, H. Reeves (1862-1938)
English actor EA/95, GRB/3-4,
WWT/1-8

SMITH, Hugh (d 1874) music-hall
lessee EA/75*

SMITH, Jack (1898-1950) American
vaudevillian TW/6

SMITH, James (fl 1796) dramatist
CP/3

SMITH, James (d 1876 [29]) musician EA/77*

SMITH, James Samuel see
Mendel

SMITH, J. C. (d 1888 [80]) American actor HAS

SMITH, J. C. (d 1889 [58]) stage
manager EA/90*

SMITH, Mrs. J. C. see Burchell, Clara

SMITH, Jenny (d 1865) dancer
HAS

SMITH, Jim see Dale, Jim

SMITH, Joe (d 1952) performer
BE*

SMITH, John (fl 1547-80) actor
DA

SMITH, John (fl 1609) actor
DA

SMITH, John (fl 1677) dramatist
CP/1-3

SMITH, John (d 1909) manager
EA/10*

SMITH, John Christopher (1712-95)
musician, composer CDP

SMITH, John N. (fl 1840) dramatist RJ

SMITH, John P. (d 1897 [65])
manager CDP

SMITH, John Washington (1815-77)
American minstrel, minstrel
manager CDP

SMITH, Jonathan S. (fl 1823?)
dramatist EAP

SMITH, Joseph (fl 1834-50) American actor HAS

SMITH, Joseph (d 1871 [42])

acrobat EA/72*
SMITH, Joseph (d 1903 [59])
music-hall managing director
EA/04*
SMITH, J. Rawson (1813-64)
American scene painter HAS
SMITH, J. Sebastian (1869-1948)
English actor WWT/5-10
SMITH, J. Sidney (d 1865)
manager HAS
SMITH, J. Stanley (d 1974 [69])
performer BP/58*
SMITH, Julia actress CDP
SMITH, J. W. (d 1864) Ethiopian
comedian HAS
SMITH, Kate (fl 1879) singer SR
SMITH, Kate (b 1909) American
singer, actress CB
SMITH, Kent (b 1907) American
actor BE, TW/3-13, WWT/
9-16
SMITH, Lemuel (d 1832) actor
HAS
SMITH, Len, Jr. (b 1925) Amer-
ican actor TW/4-6
SMITH, Leonard (fl 1640) actor
DA
SMITH, Lester (d 1970 [77])
publicist BP/55*
SMITH, Lewis Worthington (1866-
1947) American dramatist
WWA/2
SMITH, Lillian (b 1897) American
dramatist HJD
SMITH, Mrs. Lillian Boardman
see Boardman, Lillian
SMITH, Lois (b 1930) American
actress BE, TW/12-13, 27,
29-30, WWT/16
SMITH, Loring (b 1895) American
actor BE, TW/8-15, 20,
WWT/14-15
SMITH, Maggie (b 1934) English
actress AAS, CB, COC, ES,
WWT/13-16
SMITH, Maggie see Power,
Mrs. Fred
SMITH, Marcus see Smith,
Mark
SMITH, Margaret Armstrong (d
1971 [73]) composer/lyricist
BP/55*
SMITH, Mark (1829-74) American
actor CDP, COC, DAB, HAS,
OC/1-3, WWA/H
SMITH, Mark (b 1855) American
actor PP/3
SMITH, Mark (b 1877) American

comedian WWM
SMITH, Mark, III (d 1944 [57])
American actor BE*, BP/28*
SMITH, Mary Lucy [Mrs. Albert
Smith] (d 1870 [39]) EA/71*
SMITH, Mary Sedley [Mrs. Sol
Smith, Jr.] (d 1917 [87]) ac-
tress CDP
SMITH, Matthew (fl 1631-38) actor
DA
SMITH, Matthew (d 1875 [36]) les-
see EA/76*
SMITH, Maybelle (d 1972 [48])
performer BP/56*
SMITH, Mrs. M. E. (d 1867 [27])
EA/68*
SMITH, Mrs. M. E. [Mrs. George
Smith] (d 1880 [70]) EA/81*
SMITH, Merritt (b 1920) American
actor TW/23
SMITH, Michael (b 1935) American
dramatist, director CD
SMITH, Mildred Joanne (b 1923)
American actress TW/3, 5-6
SMITH, Millicent Granville see
Granville, Millicent
SMITH, Milton (b 1890) American
educator, director BE
SMITH, Moses (d 1964 [63]) writer
BE*
SMITH, Muriel (b 1923) American
actress, singer BE, TW/1-6,
12
SMITH, Nicholas (b 1934) English
actor TW/24
SMITH, Norwood (b 1915) American
actor, singer BE, TW/27, 30
"SMITH, O." see Smith, Richard
John
SMITH, Oliver (b 1918) American
designer, producer BE, CB,
ES, PDT, TW/2-8, WWT/13-16
SMITH, Oscar (d 1971 [74]) critic
BP/55*
SMITH, Patricia (b 1930) American
actress BE, TW/8-9, 14
SMITH, Paul (b 1939) American
actor TW/15
SMITH, Paul Gerard (1894-1968)
American librettist, dramatist,
actor, director WWT/7-9
SMITH, Queenie (b 1898/1902)
American actress, singer,
dancer TW/2, 6-8, WWT/6-10
SMITH, Ralph Errolle see
Errolle, Ralph
SMITH, R. F. (d 1881) actor,
lessee, manager EA/82*

SMITH, Richard (d 1884) singer
EA/86*
SMITH, Richard John (1786-1855)
English actor CDP, DNB
SMITH, Richard Penn (1799-1854)
American dramatist CDP,
COC, DAB, EAP, HJD, OC/
1-3, RJ, SR
SMITH, Robert (b 1912) American
actor TW/8, 10, 13-15
SMITH, Robert B. (d 1951 [76])
American librettist WWT/
2-9
SMITH, Robert Paul (b 1915)
American dramatist BE
SMITH, Robinson (d 1966 [54])
producer TW/23
SMITH, Roger bell-ringer CDP
SMITH, Ross Alexander see
Alexander, Ross
SMITH, Ross Johnstone see
Austin, George
SMITH, Rufus (b 1917) American
actor TW/24
SMITH, Sammy (b 1904) American
actor TW/11, 22, 25, 30
SMITH, Samuel Morgan (d 1882
[49]) actor EA/83*
SMITH, Sandra (b 1940) Ameri-
can actress TW/22-23
SMITH, Sarah [Mrs. W. H.
Smith] (1811-61) actress CDP
SMITH, Sarah (d 1905 [53])
EA/06*
SMITH, Sarah see Bartley,
Mrs. George
SMITH, Sarah Jane American ac-
tress TW/24-25
SMITH, Sebastian English actor
GRB/2
SMITH, Seymour (d 1905 [69])
entertainer, songcomposer
CDP
SMITH, Shedrach [Shedrach Le
Clair] (d 1884 [33]) EA/85*
SMITH, Sheila (b 1933) American
actress TW/23-29
SMITH, Sidney (d 1889) Ameri-
can actor EA/90*
SMITH, Sidney director, business
manager, treasurer GRB/1-4,
WWT/1-3
SMITH, Mrs. Sidney (d 1911)
EA/13*
SMITH, Sol[omon Franklin] (1801-
69) American actor, manager
CDP, COC, DAB, ES, HAS,
HJD, OC/1-3, SR, WWA/H

SMITH, Mrs. Sol see Smith,
Elizabeth
SMITH, Mrs. Sol, Jr. see
Smith, Mary Sedley
SMITH, Mrs. Stafford see
Parker, Mary
SMITH, Stephen (d 1871 [69]) actor
EA/72*
SMITH, Stephen see McHattie,
Stephen
SMITH, Susan (d 1975 [34]) pro-
ducer/director/choreographer
BP/60*
SMITH, Sydney (d 1889 [49]) com-
poser EA/90*
SMITH, Sydney (d 1935 [80]) busi-
ness manager, director WWT/3
SMITH, Mrs. Sydney see Hol-
man, Gertrude
SMITH, Mrs. T. H. see Hast-
ings, Helen
SMITH, Thomas (d 1909) EA/10*
SMITH, Thomas see Fisher,
Thomas Alexander
SMITH, Tom (d 1976 [84]) per-
former BP/60*
SMITH, T. Sebastian English actor
GRB/1
SMITH, Vere (d 1910 [26]) per-
former? EA/11*
SMITH, Wallace (b 1923) American
educator, director BE
SMITH, W. C. (d 1870) acting
manager EA/71*
SMITH, Wentworth (fl 1602-23)
dramatist CP/3, DNB, FGF
SMITH, Mrs. W. H. see Smith,
Sarah
SMITH, Will (b 1869) Scottish ac-
tor, manager GRB/1
SMITH, Mrs. Will see Webb,
Alice
SMITH, William (fl 1615) dramatist
CP/1-3, FGF, GT
SMITH, William (d 1696) English
actor COC, DNB, ES, OC/1-3
SMITH, William (1730-1819) Eng-
lish actor CDP, COC, DNB,
ES, GT, OC/1-3, TD/1-2
SMITH, William (fl 1844) English
actor HAS
SMITH, William (d 1847 [49])
comedian EA/72*
SMITH, William (d 1867 [33])
manager EA/68*
SMITH, William (d 1911 [77])
superintendent EA/11*
SMITH, William Henry see

Sedley-Smith, William Henry
SMITH, Mrs. William Henry
see Sedley-Smith, Mrs.
William Henry
SMITH, William N. (d 1869)
bone soloist HAS
SMITH, Winchell (1871/72-1933)
American actor, dramatist,
manager, director DAB, ES,
GRB/3-4, HJD, MD, MWD,
SR, WWA/1, WWT/1-7
SMITH, Wingate (d 1974 [79])
producer/director/choreographer
BP/59*
SMITH, Winifred (d 1967 [88])
educator BP/52*
SMITH, W. R. dramatist RJ
SMITHERS, Charles (d 1879
[46]) scene artist EA/81*
SMITHERS, Emily (d 1887 [27])
music-hall performer EA/88*
SMITHERS, Florence [Mrs. W.
H. Owen] English actress
GRB/1-3
SMITHERS, William (b 1927)
American actor TW/7-16, 20
SMITHSON, Florence (1884-1936)
English actress, singer GRB/
1-4, WWT/1-8
SMITHSON, Frank (d 1949 [88])
Irish actor, director BE*,
WWT/14*
SMITHSON, Frederick (d 1892
[68]) actor EA/93*
SMITHSON, Georgie (d 1899)
actress EA/00*
SMITHSON, Harriet Constance
(1800-54) English actress
BS, CDP, COC, DNB, EA/
92, OC/1-3, OX
SMITHSON, Laura (1885-1963)
English actress WWT/5-11
SMITHSON, Will (d 1927 [67])
producer, manager BE*,
WWT/14*
SMITH-THOMAS, Eleanor Mary
Tydfil see Fayre, Eleanor
SMOLKO, John (b 1928) Ameri-
can actor TW/14, 22-23
SMOLLETT, Tobias (1720/21-71)
Scottish dramatist CDP,
CP/1-3, DNB, GT, HP,
TD/1-2
SMYCH, J. Anthony (d 1966 [80])
performer BP/50*
SMYGHT, William (fl 1595) actor
DA
SMYTH, Dame Ethel Mary (1858-

1944) English composer DNB,
ES, WWW/4
SMYTH, John (1662-1717) English
dramatist CP/3, DNB, GT
SMYTH, Mrs. W. G. see
Armstrong, Sydney
SMYTHE, George (fl 1796) drama-
tist CP/3
SMYTHE, George see Davies,
George
SMYTHE, James Moore (1702-34)
English dramatist CP/1-3,
DNB
SMYTHE, Paul (d 1961 [79]) di-
rector WWT/14*
SMYTHE, William G. (d 1921 [66])
producer, manager BE*, BP/6*
SMYTH-PIGGOTT, A. (d 1936
[73]) manager WWT/14*
SMYTHSON, George (d 1883 [70])
actor EA/84*
SMYTHSON, Miss Montague [Amelia
Jane James; Mrs. P. R.
James] (d 1891) EA/92*
"SNAPDRAGON, Hector" (fl 1813?)
dramatist EAP
SNAPE, Fred A. (d 1900 [41])
actor EA/01*
SNAPE, Mrs. George (d 1878)
EA/79*
SNAPE, Louis (d 1899) actor
EA/00*
SNAZELLE, Annie T. [Mrs.
George H. Snazelle] (d 1911
[50]) EA/13*
SNAZELLE, George H. (d 1912
[63]) singer, entertainer, actor
EA/13*, WWT/14*
SNAZELLE, Mrs. George H. see
Snazelle, Annie T.
SNAZELLE, Lionel James (d 1907
[33]) EA/08*
SNEATH, Thomas F. [T. F. Sea-
more] (d 1875 [28]) actor EA/
76*
SNELL, David (b 1942) American
actor TW/30
SNELLING, Thomas (fl 1651)
dramatist CP/3
SNOW, Amanda (d 1972 [67]) per-
former BP/56*
SNOW, C[harles] P[ercy] (b 1909)
English dramatist PDT
SNOW, Davis (d 1975 [62]) drama-
tist BP/60*
SNOW, Ellen Rebecca (d 1912)
EA/13*
SNOW, Harry David (b 1928)

American actor TW/15-16,
21
SNOW, Marguerite (d 1958 [69])
actress BE*
SNOW, Norman (b 1950) Ameri-
can actor TW/30
SNOW, Ross (1868-1947) come-
dian SR
SNOW, Sophia see Baddeley,
Sophia
SNOW, Ted (d 1903) minstrel
CDP
SNOW, Valaida see Valaida
SNOWDEN, Mrs. (fl 1800) ac-
tress HAS
SNOWDON, Launcelot Marshall
(d 1902 [44]) lessee EA/03*
SNOWDON, Mary J. see Chip-
pendale, Mary J.
SNOWDON, Walter (d 1912 [50])
music-hall performer EA/
13*
SNYDER, Agnes Tilton (d 1974
[90s]) composer/lyricist
BP/58*
SNYDER, Arlen Dean (b 1933)
American actor TW/25-29
SNYDER, Bert N. (d 1975) per-
former BP/60*
SNYDER, Denton (b 1915) Amer-
ican educator, director, de-
signer BE
SNYDER, Drew (b 1946) Ameri-
can actor TW/25, 27-30
SNYDER, Gene (d 1953 [45])
American dance director
BE*, BP/37*
SNYDER, Glyde (d 1972) per-
former BP/56*
SNYDER, Harold (d 1974) mana-
ger BP/59*
SNYDER, William (b 1929)
American dramatist, educator
CD
SOANE, George (d 1860 [69])
dramatist BE*, EA/72*,
WWT/14*
SOARES, Frank (d 1868) actor?
EA/69*
SOBEL, Bernard (1887/90-1964)
American dramatist, critic
BE, NTH, TW/20, WWA/4,
WWT/9-13
SOBOL, Edward (d 1962 [70])
producer BE*
SOBOLEWSKI, J. Friedrich Edu-
ard (1808-72) Prussian con-
ductor, composer DAB

SOBOLOFF, Arnold (b 1930) Amer-
ican actor, singer BE, TW/
22-26, 29-30, WWT/16
SOBOTKA, Ruth (d 1967 [42]) de-
signer BP/52*
SODEN, Mrs. John see Forrest,
Ella
SODERO, Cesare (1886-1947)
Italian conductor, composer
CB
SÖDERSTRÖM, Elisabeth (b 1927)
Swedish singer ES
SODI, Pietro (c. 1716-c. 75) Italian
dancer, choreographer ES
SOFAER, Abraham (b 1896) Bur-
mese/English actor AAS,
WWT/7-16
SOHLKE, Gus (1865-1924) pro-
ducer, director WWT/4
SOKOLOFF, Vladimir (1889-1962)
Russian actor TW/4-6, 18
SOKOLOVA, Lydia [Hilda Munnings]
(1896-1974) English dancer, ac-
tress BTR/74, ES, WWT/9-12
SOKOLOVA, Natasha (b 1917)
Brazilian actress, dancer
WWT/10-11
SOKOLOW, Anna (b 1912/15)
American choreographer BE,
CB
SOLANO, Solita (d 1975 [86]) critic
BP/60*
SOLAR, Willie (d 1956 [65]) come-
dian, dancer BE*, WWT/14*
SOLDENE, Emily (1840/44-1912)
English actress, singer CDP,
COC, GRB/1-4, OC/1-3,
WWW/1
SOLEE, Mr. (fl 1797) French
manager HAS
SOLEM, Delmar E. (b 1915) Amer-
ican educator BE
SOLEN, Paul (b 1941) American
actor TW/29-30
SOLER, Antonio Ruiz see Antonio
SOLIN, Harvey American actor
TW/29
SOLOMAN, Mrs. Neil see Mc-
Evoy, Nellie
SOLOMON, Charles (d 1890 [71])
composer EA/91*
SOLOMON, Edward (d 1895 [36])
musical director, composer
CDP
SOLOMON, Edward (d 1976 [64])
publicist BP/60*
SOLOMON, Max see Rogers,
Max

SOLOMON, Neal (d 1917) comedian EA/18*

SOLOMON, Solomon [Cpt. F. Athya] (d 1886 [44]) actor? EA/87*

SOLOMON, Steve (d 1972 [24]) agent BP/56*

SOLOTAIRE, George (d 1965 [62]) ticket broker BP/49*

SOLOV, Zachary (b 1923) American actor TW/5

SOLOVYOV, Vladimir Aleksandrovich (b 1907) Russian dramatist MWD

SOLOWAY, Leonard (b 1928) American manager BE

SOLTERS, Lee (b 1919) American press representative BE

SOLTI, Sir Georg (b 1912) Hungarian conductor CB, ES

SOMACK, Jack (b 1918) American actor TW/23, 25, 27, 30

SOMAN, Claude (1897-1960) English manager WWT/10-12

SOMERBY, Rufus (b 1833) American showman HAS

SOMERFIELD, Fred C. (d 1910 [39]) actor EA/11*

SOMERFIELD, Tom (d 1918 [59]) EA/19*

SOMERS, Brett (b 1927) Canadian actress TW/14

SOMERS, Dalton actor EA/97

SOMERS, Jimsey (b 1937) American actor TW/2

SOMERS, John Isaac (d 1899 [44]) music-hall agency manager EA/00*

SOMERSET, C. W. (1847-1929) actor EA/97, GRB/2-4, WWT/1-5

SOMERSET, Mrs. C. W. see Russell, Agnes

SOMERSET, Mrs. C. W. see Somerset, Fanny

SOMERSET, Fanny [Mrs. C. W. Somerset] (d 1900) EA/01*

SOMERSET, Patrick (b 1897) English actor WWT/4-8

SOMERSETT, George (fl 1600-24) actor DA

SOMERVILE, William (d 1743) English translator CP/2-3

SOMERVILLE, Mr. English singer HAS

SOMERVILLE, Henry (d 1884) reciter EA/85*

SOMERVILLE, Mrs. Henry (d 1867) EA/68*

SOMERVILLE, John Baxter (1907-63) English manager WWT/8-13

SOMERVILLE, Margaret Agnes see Bunn, Margaret Agnes Somerville

SOMERVILLE, Marjorie (d 1916 [19]) EA/18*

SOMERVILLE, Randolph (1891-1958) American director WWA/3

SOMES, Michael (b 1917) English dancer CB, ES, WWT/11-12

SOMLO, Josef (d 1973 [89]) producer/director/choreographer BP/58*

SOMLYO, Roy A. (b 1925) American manager BE

SOMMER, Edith dramatist BE

SOMMER, Henry (fl 1740) dramatist CP/1-3, GT

SOMMER, Josef (b 1934) German actor TW/27-30

SOMMERLAD, A. (d 1909 [46]) conductor EA/10*

SOMMERS, Ben (b 1906) American executive BE

SOMMERS, Harry G. (1870-1953) American dramatist, manager, treasurer SR

SOMNES, George (d 1956 [68]) American director, producer, actor TW/12

SONDERGAARD, Edith Holm see Sondergaard, Gale

SONDERGAARD, Gale [née Edith Holm] (b 1901) American actress BE, TW/23, WWT/15-16

SONDHEIM, Stephen (b 1930) American composer, lyricist AAS, BE, CB, ES, WWT/14-16

SONDHEIMER, Hans (b 1901) German stage manager, lighting director BE

SONNEMANN, Emmy (d 1973 [80]) performer BP/58*

SONNENTHAL, Adolf Ritter von see Von Sonnenthal, Adolf Ritter

SONNEVELD, Wim (d 1974 [56]) performer BP/58*

SONTAG, Carl (d 1900) actor WWT/14*

SONTAG, Henrietta (1805-64) German singer CDP, ES, HAS

SONTAG, Nina (fl 1829?) singer CDP

SOO, Kim Yen (d 1963 [72]) magi-

cian BE*
SOPER, Paul (b 1906) American
educator BE
SOPHOCLES (c. 497-406 B. C.)
Greek dramatist ES
SORAKICHI, Motsada (d 1891
[32]) Japanese wrestler EA/
92*
SOREL, Cecile (d 1966 [92])
performer BP/51*
SOREL, Felicia (d 1972 [66])
American choreographer,
dancer TW/3-4
SOREL, Sonia (b 1921) American
actress TW/3, 8
SORELL, Doris (d 1971) drama-
tist BP/56*
SORIN, Louis (1893-1961) Amer-
ican actor TW/4
SORMA, Agnes [Duchess of
Minotta] (1865-1927) German
actress ES, GRB/4, OC/1-3,
WWT/1-2
SOROKIN, Rachel (d 1969 [84])
performer BP/54*
SORVINO, Paul (b 1939) American
actor WWT/16
SOTHEBY, William (fl 1790-1802)
dramatist CP/3, GT, TD/2
SOTHERDEN, Betsy see Ver-
non, Flo
SOTHERN, Ann (b 1909/12)
American actress, singer,
producer CB, WWT/8-10
SOTHERN, Mrs. E. A. (d 1882)
EA/83*
SOTHERN, Edward Askew (1826-
81) English actor CDP, COC,
DAB, DNB, ES, HAS, HJD,
NTH, OAA/1-2, OC/1-3,
WWA/H
SOTHERN, Edward Hugh (1859-
1933) American actor, drama-
tist CDP, COC, DAB, ES,
GRB/2-4, HJD, NTH, OAA/2,
OC/1-3, PP/3, WWA/1,
WWM, WWT/1-7, WWW/3
SOTHERN, Mrs. Edward Hugh
see Harned, Virginia
SOTHERN, Harry (1883/84-1957)
English actor ES, TW/2-3,
13
SOTHERN, Hugh [Roy Sutherland]
(d 1947 [65]) actor BE*,
WWT/14*
SOTHERN, Janet Evelyn English
actress WWM, WWT/1-5
SOTHERN, Jean (d 1964) actress

BE*
SOTHERN, Lytton Edward (1851/56-
87) American actor CDP, DNB,
NYM
SOTHERN, Sam [George Evelyn
Augustus T. Sothern] (1870-1920)
English actor ES, GRB/1-4,
WWT/1-3
SOTHERNE, David (fl 1538) actor
DA
SOTO, Senorita (fl 1852) dancer
CDP, HAS
SOTO, Luchy (d 1970 [50]) per-
former BP/55*
SOUDEIKINE, Serge (d 1946 [60])
Russian designer TW/3
SOULE, Robert (b 1926) American
designer BE
SOUPER, G. Kay (d 1947) actor
BE*, WWT/14*
SOURAY, Eleanor (1880-1931) Eng-
lish actress GRB/1-3
SOURIS, Andre (d 1970 [70]) com-
poser/lyricist BP/54*
SOUSA, John Philip (1854-1932)
American composer, conductor
DAB, ES, GRB/1-4, HJD, SR,
WWS, WWT/1-6, WWW/3
SOUSSANIN, Nicholas (d 1975 [86])
actor BP/59*, WWT/16*
SOUTAR, Andrew (d 1941 [61])
dramatist BE*, WWT/14*
SOUTAR, J. Farren (1870/74-1962)
English actor GRB/1-4, WWT/
1-9
SOUTAR, Robert (1827-1908) Eng-
lish dramatist, actor, stage
manager COC, EA/69, GRB/4,
OAA/1-2
SOUTAR, Mrs. Robert see
Farren, Ellen
SOUTH, Barbara (d 1975 [45])
producer/director/choreographer
BP/60*
SOUTH, Eddie (1904-62) American
musician BE*, BP/46*
SOUTH, Richard W. (d 1892 [48])
actor, entertainer EA/93*
SOUTHALL, Carrie see Aldridge,
Carrie
SOUTHAMPTON, Henry Wriothes-
ley, Third Earl of (1573-1624)
English patron NTH
SOUTHARD, Lucien H. (1827-81)
American composer DAB
SOUTHBY, Mr. (fl 1835?) actor
CDP
SOUTHERN, Colette (d 1965 [73])

performer BP/50*

SOUTHERN, John (d 1893) manager WWT/5-7

SOUTHERNE, Thomas (1660-1746) Irish dramatist CDP, COC, CP/1-3, DNB, ES, GT, HP, NTH, OC/1-3, PDT

SOUTHEY, Thomas (fl 1547-56) actor DA

SOUTHGATE, Howard S. (d 1971 [76]) performer BP/56*

SOUTHWELL, Henry (d 1841) Irish actor HAS

SOUTHWELL, Maria (fl 1828) Irish actress HAS

SOUTHWORTH, Robert (d 1870 [59]) musician EA/71*

SOUTHWORTH, S. S. dramatist RJ

SOUTHYN, Robert (fl 1550) actor DA

SOUTTEN, Mme. [Millie Barnett] (d 1883 [77]) actress EA/84*

SOUTTEN, Ben professor of dancing GRB/3

SOUTTER, Lillie (fl 1903?) actress, singer CDP

SOUZAY, Gérard (b 1920) French singer CB

SOVEY, Raymond (1895/97-1966) American designer actor BE, ES, TW/2-8, 23, WWT/7-14

SOWARDS, Len (d 1962 [69]) actor BE*

SOWDEN, Margaret see Neilson, Perlita

SOWDON, Thomas (d 1789) Irish actor CDP

SOWELL, Ione M. (d 1975 [62]) performer BP/60*

SOWERBY, Ann (d 1883) EA/84*

SOWERBY, F. (d 1849) English actor HAS

SOWERBY, Katherine Githa English dramatist NTH, WWT/2-7

SOWERBY, Leo (d 1968 [73]) composer/lyricist BP/53*

SOWINSKI, Albert (d 1880 [74]) musician EA/81*

SOYINKA, Wole (b 1934) Nigerian dramatist, director CB, CD, COC, MWD

SOYLES, William (fl 1636) actor DA

SPACHNER, Leon (d 1971 [87]) manager BP/55*

SPAIN, Elsie (d 1970 [91]) actress WWT/1-5

SPAIN, Katharine Stewart see Stewart, Katharine

SPAISMAN, Zipora (b 1920) Polish actress TW/29-30

SPALDING, Gilbert R. (d 1880 [68]) circus manager & proprietor CDP

SPAMER, Richard (1856-1938) American critic WWA/1

SPANISH DANCERS, Troupe of (fl 1855) HAS

SPAR, Herbert (d 1976 [35]) agent BP/60*

SPARER, Paul actor WWT/16

SPARK, Dr. William (d 1897 [71]) musician EA/98*

SPARKES, Thomas (fl 1622) lessee DA

SPARKS, Mrs. (d 1837 [83]?) actress GT, TD/1-2

SPARKS, Charles actor CDP

SPARKS, Hugh (d 1816 [64]) actor WWT/14*

SPARKS, Isaac (d 1776) Irish actor CDP, TD/1-2

SPARKS, John G. (d 1922 [70]) comedian BE*, BP/6*

SPARKS, Joseph M. (b 1856) American actor WWS

SPARKS, Luke (d 1768 [57]) actor TD/2

SPARKS, Ned (d 1957 [73]) Canadian comedian TW/13

SPARROW, Fanny (d 1903 [76]) EA/04*

SPARROW, Frank (d 1888 [42]) American actor EA/89*

SPARROW, G. (d 1878 [74]) actor EA/79*

SPARROW, Jesse (b 1849) English music-hall singer GRB/1-4

SPARROW, John William (d 1898 [72]) EA/99*

SPATEMAN, Thomas (fl 1742) dramatist CP/2-3

SPAULDING, Georgie Dean [née Georgie Dean] (b 1845) American musician HAS

SPAULDING, George Lawson (1864-1921) American composer WWA/1

SPAULDING, John F. (b 1833) American musician, musical director HAS

SPAULDING, Kim American actor TW/1

SPAULDING, William P. (1836-

87?) American musician HAS, NYM

SPAULL, Guy (b 1904) American actor TW/30

SPEACHLEY, John (d 1869) musician EA/70*

SPEAIGHT, James (d 1874) performer CDP

SPEAIGHT, Robert (1904-76) English actor AAS, ES, WWT/7-16

SPEAKMAN, James T. (d 1908) EA/09*

SPEAKMAN, Walter (d 1886 [42]) actor CDP

SPEAKS, Oley (1874-1948) American songwriter TW/5

SPEAR, Felix P. (1836-69) American actor, property man HAS

SPEAR, George Gaines (1809-87) American actor HAS, NYM

SPEAR, Harry (d 1969 [56]) performer BP/53*

SPEARE, Dorothy (d 1951) American dramatist WWA/3

SPEARS, Anna Maria [Mrs. Tom Spears] (d 1897) EA/98*

SPEARS, Margaret (d 1892 [73]) EA/93*

SPEARS, Sammy (d 1966) performer BP/50*

SPEARS, Mrs. Tom see Spears, Anna Maria

SPECTOR, Edward (d 1974 [73]) American producer BE, TW/30

SPECTOR, Joel producer BE

SPEECHLEY, Billy (b 1911) English actor WWT/6-7

SPEED, John (d 1640) English dramatist CP/2-3, FGF

SPEEDY, George (d 1880) music-hall proprietor EA/81*

SPEEDY, Henry (d 1883) music-hall performer? EA/84*

SPEICHER, Ann Drew (d 1974 [83]) performer BP/58*

SPEIGHT, Fred (d 1916) EA/18*

SPEIGHT, Johnny (b 1921/22) English dramatist CD, MH

SPELMAN, Leon (b 1945) American actor TW/29

"SPELVIN, George" BE, NTH

SPENCE, Beatrice [Mrs. Frank Cooton] (d 1908 [44]) EA/09*

SPENCE, Edward F. (1860-1932) English critic GRB/2-4, WWT/1-6

SPENCE, Harry (d 1898) Negro comedian EA/99*

SPENCE, Henry (d 1902 [58]) variety performer EA/03*

SPENCE, James William (d 1873) music-hall proprietor EA/74*

SPENCE, Margaret (d 1881 [73]) EA/82*

SPENCE, Ralph (d 1949 [59]) director, producer BE*, WWT/14*

SPENCE, Tom [Tom Dillon] (d 1884) Negro comedian EA/85*

SPENCER, Mr. (d 1804) actor TD/2

SPENCER, Mr. (d c. 1836) English actor HAS

SPENCER, Mrs. (fl 1794) actress HAS

SPENCER, Bob (b 1938) American actor TW/27, 29-30

SPENCER, Mrs. Clarence S. see Ashley, Helen

SPENCER, Colin (b 1933) English dramatist CD

SPENCER, Edmund (fl 1798) dramatist CP/3

SPENCER, Franz (d 1971) dramatist BP/56*

SPENCER, Gabriel (d 1598) English actor COC, DA, OC/1-3

SPENCER, George (d 1906) musician EA/07*

SPENCER, George (d 1907) proprietor EA/08*

SPENCER, Mrs. George (d 1876) actress EA/78*

SPENCER, Mrs. George Preston [Flora McDonald] (d 1916 [65]) singer EA/17*

SPENCER, Helen (b 1903) English actress WWT/5-8

SPENCER, Mrs. Herbert H. see Conway, Helen

SPENCER, Isabella (d 1911) performer? EA/12*

SPENCER, Jessica (b 1919) English actress WWT/10-14

SPENCER, John (fl early 17th cent) English actor COC, DA, OC/1-3

SPENCER, Kenneth (d 1964 [51]) American singer BE*, BP/48*

SPENCER, Lillian (fl 1880) actress CDP

SPENCER, Lou (d 1972 [56]) performer BP/57*

SPENCER, Lucy (b 1884) American actress, dramatist WWS
SPENCER, Mabel (fl 1907) American actress WWS
SPENCER, Marian (b 1905) English actress WWT/10-16
SPENCER, Willard (1852-1933) American composer BE*
SPENCER, William (fl 1589) payee DA
SPENCER, William (d 1880 [56]) bill inspector EA/81*
SPENCER, William Robert (fl 1796-1802) dramatist CP/3
SPENCER-BRUNTON, Enid [Mrs. Richard F. L. Lambart] English actress GRB/1-2, 4
SPENDER, Stephen (b 1909) English dramatist CB, ES, HP, MD, MWD, NTH
SPENS, Andrew William (d 1917 [45]) EA/18*
SPENSE (fl 1592?) dramatist FGF
SPERANZA, Adelina (fl 1859) singer HAS
SPESSIVTZENA, Olga (b 1895) Russian dancer ES
SPEWACK, Bella (b 1899) Hungarian/American dramatist, librettist AAS, BE, CD, MD, MH, MWD, NTH, WWT/9-14
SPEWACK, Samuel (1899-1971) Russian/American dramatist AAS, BE, MD, MH, MWD, NTH, WWA/5, WWT/9-14
SPEYSER, Paul J., III (b 1941) American actor TW/24
SPIEGAL, Barbara American actress TW/26
SPIEGEL, Henry (d 1971 [61]) publicity director BP/56*
SPIELBERG, David (b 1940) American actor TW/27-28, 30
SPIER, William H. (d 1973 [66]) producer/director/choreographer BP/57*
SPIERS, Mrs. (d 1893) EA/94*
SPIERS, Harry F. (d 1902 [30]) manager EA/04*
SPIERS, Helen Bateson [Mrs. J. H. Spiers] (d 1878) EA/80*
SPIERS, Mrs. J. H. see Spiers, Helen Bateson
SPIGELGASS, Leonard (b 1908)

American dramatist BE, WWT/15-16
SPIKER, Ray (d 1964 [62]) actor BE*
SPILLANE, Dan (d 1884) musical director EA/85*
SPILLER, Mr. (fl 1811) actor CDP
SPILLER, Mr. (d 1826) English actor HAS
SPILLER, Anne (d 1906 [72]) EA/07*
SPILLER, Emily (d 1941 [81]) actress BE*, WWT/14*
SPILLER, Isaac (d 1905 [77]) EA/06*
SPILLER, James (1692-1727/30) English? actor CDP, DNB
SPILLER, James, Jr. (d 1871) musician EA/72*
SPILSBURY, Percy (d 1895 [25]) actor EA/96*
SPINACUTA, Sig. animal trainer? CDP
SPINELLI, Andree (b 1891) French actress WWT/4
SPINETTI, Victor (b 1933) Welsh actor AAS, TW/21-22, 27, WWT/14-16
SPINK, Beatrice Mary see Bertoldi, Ena
SPIRA, Francoise (d 1965 [30s]) performer BP/49*
SPIRES, James (d 1887) EA/88*
SPITZ, Mrs. Leo (d 1974 [72]) performer BP/58*
SPIVAK, Alice (b 1935) American actress TW/26, 28, 30
SPIVAK, Irene Daye (d 1971 [53]) performer BP/56*
SPIVY (d 1971 [64]) performer BP/55*
SPLANE, Elza K. (d 1968 [63]) performer BP/52*
SPLATT, W. F. (d 1893 [83]) licensee EA/94*
SPOFFORD, Charles M. (b 1902) American executive BE
SPOFFORTH, Reginald (1770-1827) English composer, musician DNB
SPONG, Hilda (1875-1955) Australian actress CDP, GRB/1-4, PP/3, TW/11, WWM, WWS, WWT/1-9
SPONG, W. B. (d 1929 [79]) scene artist BE*, WWT/14*
SPONSELLER, Howard L., Jr. (b

1945) American actor TW/30
SPOONER, Cecil American actress WWT/1-5
SPOONER, Edna May (d 1953 [78]) American actress TW/10, WWT/1-4
SPOONER, Mary G. (d 1940 [87]) manager WWT/14*
SPORLE, Nathan James (d 1853 [42]) composer EA/72*
SPOTTSWOOD, James (1882-1940) American actor CB
SPRACHER, Dwight L. (1903-70) American executive WWA/5
SPRAGG, John C. (d 1886 [56]) musician EA/87*
SPRAGUE, Mrs. see Drummond, Dolores
SPRAGUE, H. N. (1818-58) American actor HAS
SPRAGUE, Mrs. H. N. (b 1833) Irish actress HAS
SPRAKE, Charlotte Amelia [Mrs. Herbert Sprake] (d 1898 [42]) EA/99*
SPRAKE, Frederick (d 1887 [78]) EA/88*
SPRAKE, Herbert (d 1904) music-hall proprietor EA/06*
SPRAKE, Mrs. Herbert see Sprake, Charlotte Amelia
SPRAKE, Herbert Arthur (d 1917) music-hall assistant manager EA/18*
SPRAKE, Thomas (d 1877) musician EA/78*
SPRANGE, Adnam (d 1919) English actor, business manager, stage manager GRB/1
SPRAY, William actor GRB/1-3
SPRIGGE, Elizabeth (1900-74) English translator, director, producer BE
SPRIGGS, Elizabeth (b 1929) actress AAS, WWT/16
SPRIGGS, Mrs. James see Brangin, Rhoda
SPRIGHTLY, William (fl 1780) musician CDP
SPRING, Samuel (d 1839 [62]) box book-keeper EA/72*
SPRINGER, J. H. (fl 1854) actor HAS
SPRINGETT, Freddie (b 1915) English actor WWT/7
SPRINGMEYER, Charles see Durand, Charles
SPROULES, Edwin (d 1873 [42])

actor? EA/74*
SPRUNG, Sandy (b 1937) American actor TW/25, 27
SPRY, Mrs. A. G. see Loftus-Leyton, Rosie
SPRY, Henry (d 1904 [69]) dramatist, manager BE*, EA/05*, WWT/14*
SPRY, Mrs. Henry see Claremont, Lizzie
SPURIN-CALLEIA, Joseph see Calleia, Joseph
SPURLING, John (b 1936) Kenyan/English dramatist CD
SPURR, Mel B. (d 1904) entertainer EA/05*
SPURR, Mrs. Mel B. (d 1910 [59]) EA/11*
SPURWAY, Thomas see Hatton, Walter
SPURWAY, William (d 1890 [79]) EA/91*
SQUIBB, June (b 1935) American actress BE, TW/24
SQUIRE, J. C. (1884-1958) English dramatist, writer MWD
SQUIRE, John (fl 1620) dramatist CP/3, FGF
SQUIRE, Katherine (b 1903) American actress BE, TW/19, 23, 25, WWT/14-16
SQUIRE, Lawrence (fl 1486-93) master of the Chapel Royal DA
SQUIRE, Ronald (1886-1958) English actor AAS, TW/15, WWT/3-12, WWW/5
SQUIRE, Tom (d 1891) actor, singer CDP
SQUIRE, William (b 1920) Welsh actor AAS, BE, WWT/13-16
SQUIRES, Mr. (fl 1827?) actor CDP
SQUIRES, John (d 1889 [49]) musician EA/90*
SRNEC, Jiri (b 1931) Czech actor TW/23
STABILE, Mariano (b 1888) Italian singer ES
STABLES, Harry [John Keogh] (d 1878 [35]) comic singer EA/80*
STACEY, Alexander (d 1897 [63]) proprietor EA/98*
STACEY, R. F. W. (d 1916 [38]) EA/17*
STACEY, Walter [Thomas Wick] (d 1877) comedian, singer EA/78*

STACK, James (d 1973 [65])
performer BP/57*
STACK, William (b 1882) Amer-
ican actor WWT/4-8
STADLEN, Lewis J. (b 1947)
American actor TW/26-27,
29-30, WWT/16
STAFFORD, Alfred (d 1906)
EA/07*
STAFFORD, Altona (d 1965 [78])
actress BP/49*, WWT/14*
STAFFORD, C. (fl 1837) English
actor HAS
STAFFORD, Emily [Mrs. Albert
Bernard] (d 1907 [59]) actress
GRB/3*
STAFFORD, Grey (b 1920) Eng-
lish actor TW/2
STAFFORD, Hanley (d 1968 [69])
performer BP/52*
STAFFORD, John Gascoigne (d
1917 [66]) printer EA/18*
STAFFORD, William (d 1897
[37]) actor CDP
STAFFORD-CLARK, Max (b 1941)
English director WWT/15-16
STAFFORD SMITH, Mary [Mrs.
Charles F. Lloyd] (d 1917
[34]) actress EA/18*
STAGG, Charles (d 1735) Eng-
lish/American actor COC,
OC/1-3, WWA/H
STAGG, Mary (fl early 18th cent)
American actress OC/1-3
STAGNO, Sig. (d 1879) singer
EA/80*
STAHL, Herbert M. (b 1914)
American educator, director
BE
STAHL, Max theatre owner BE
STAHL, Rose (1873-1955) Amer-
ican actress CDP, GRB/3-4,
SR, TW/12, WWM, WWS,
WWT/1-7
STAHL, Stanley theatre owner
BE
STAIGER, Libi (b 1928) Ameri-
can actress, singer BE
STAINES, Thomas (d 1870)
master carpenter EA/71*
STAINFORTH, Frank (d 1899)
dramatist, songwriter EA/01*
STAINSTREET, James (d 1874)
musician EA/75*
STAINTON, Philip (1908-61) Eng-
lish actor WWT/11-13
STAKHOUSE, Roger (fl 1554)
actor DA

STALEY, George actor, singer
CDP
STALEY, James (b 1948) American
actor TW/28-30
STALLING, Carl W. (d 1972 [84])
performer BP/57*
STALLINGS, Laurence (1894-1968)
American dramatist, librettist
BE, HJD, MH, MWD, NTH,
SR, WWT/6-11
STALMAN, Julia [Mrs. Sidney
Lacy] (d 1898) actress EA/99*
STAMFORD, Annie [Mrs. John
Stamford] (d 1878) EA/79*
STAMFORD, Mrs. John see
Stamford, Annie
STAMFORD, John J. (d 1899 [50])
music-hall manager EA/00*
STAMMERS, Blanche see Garner,
Mrs. Arthur
STAMMERS, Frank (d 1921) com-
poser BE*, BP/6*
STAMMERS, Joseph (d 1871) im-
presario EA/72*
STAMPER, Dave (1883-1963) Amer-
ican composer WWT/6-10
STAMPER, F. Pope (1880-1950)
English actor WWT/3-8
STAMPER, Francis (fl 1751) dram-
atist CP/3
STAMP-TAYLOR, Enid (b 1904)
English actress, singer WWT/
6-7
STANDER, Hollice (b 1944) Ameri-
can actress TW/24
STANDER, Lionel (b 1908) Ameri-
can actor, producer BE
STANDIDGE, John (d 1890 [74])
EA/91*
STANDING, Charles Wyndham (b
1880) English actor WWT/4-5
STANDING, Ellen (d 1906 [50])
actress EA/07*, GRB/2*,
WWT/14*
STANDING, Emily (d 1899) actress
BE*, EA/00*, WWT/14*
STANDING, Sir Guy (1873-1937)
English actor GRB/2-4, WWS,
WWT/1-8
STANDING, Mrs. Guy see
Urquhart, Isabelle
STANDING, Herbert [Crellin] (1846-
1923) English actor DP, GRB/
1-4, OAA/2, WWS, WWT/1-4
STANDING, Herbert (d 1955 [71])
English actor TW/12
STANDING, Mrs. Herbert (d 1887)
EA/88*

STANDING, Jack (d 1917) EA/
18*
STANDING, John [né Leon] (b
1934) English actor WWT/
15-16
STANDING, Michael (b 1939)
English actor TW/20
STANDING, Mrs. Percy Cross
see Wright, Ellen
STANDISH, Pamela (b 1920) Eng-
lish actress WWT/9-10
STANDISH, Walter (d 1888 [35])
American actor EA/90*
STANDON, Harriet (b 1886)
American singer, actress
WWM
STANDREN, Charles (d 1891
[40]) musician, musical di-
rector EA/92*
STANFIELD, Agnes see Clare,
Ada
STANFIELD, Alfred D'Arcy (d
1902 [41]) actor EA/03*
STANFIELD, Clarkson (1793-
1867) English scene designer
COC, OC/1-3
STANFIELD, James Field (d
1824) Irish dramatist, actor
CP/3, DNB
STANFORD, Arthur (b 1878)
American actor WWM
STANFORD, Sir Charles Villiers
(1852-1924) Irish composer
DNB, ES
STANFORD, Henry B. (1872-
1921) Egyptian/English actor
GRB/1-4, WWM, WWT/1-3
STANFORD, Mrs. H[enry] B.
see Burt, Laura
STANFORD, Henry (b 1872)
Egyptian/English actor WWS
STANFORD, Jack (d 1968 [67])
performer BP/52*
STANG, Arnold (b 1925) Ameri-
can actor BE, TW/25-26
STANGE, Stanislaus (1861-1917)
English actor, dramatist
GRB/2-4, SR, WWT/1-3
STANHOPE, Adeline [Mrs. Amory
Sullivan] (fl 1872-79) actress
OAA/2
STANHOPE, Frederick [Frederick
Stanhope Counter] (b 1875)
English manager, producer
GRB/1
STANHOPE, O. H. Butler (d
1917) EA/18*
STANHOPE, Robert Butler (d

1917) EA/18*
STANILAND, Albert (d 1973 [71])
theatre operator BP/58*
STANISLAUS, Frederick (d 1891
[47]) composer, conductor BE*,
EA/92*, WWT/14*
STANISLAVSKY, Konstantin Sergei-
vich (1863-1938) Russian actor,
director, acting teacher COC,
NTH
STANLEY, Mr. (fl 1823) actor
CDP
STANLEY, Mr. (d 1841) actor
HAS
STANLEY, Mrs. [née Wattle; Mrs.
Twistleton] (d c. 1808/09) ac-
tress CDP, HAS, TD/1-2
STANLEY, Mrs. (d 1834) see
Hill, Mrs.
STANLEY, Mrs. (1796?-1861)
see Fleming, Miss
STANLEY, Mrs. (fl early 19th
cent) actress CDP
STANLEY, Miss (b 1795) actress
CDP
STANLEY, Adelaide (b 1906) ac-
tress, singer WWT/9-10
STANLEY, Alma (1854-1931) Eng-
lish actress, dancer DP, EA/
96, OAA/2, WWT/6
STANLEY, Bessie [Mrs. E. T.
Stanley] (d 1880 [39]) EA/82*
STANLEY, Blanche [Mrs. S. Major
Jones] English actress GRB/1-2
STANLEY, Charles (b 1851) Ameri-
can actor PP/3
STANLEY, Charles actor, singer
CDP
STANLEY, Charlotte Mary actress
CDP
STANLEY, Edward (fl 1790) drama-
tist CP/3
STANLEY, Emma (1823-81) English
actress CDP, HAS
STANLEY, Eric (b 1884) English
actor WWT/8-9
STANLEY, Mrs. E. T. see
Stanley, Bessie
STANLEY, Flora Middleton see
Alleyne, Muriel
STANLEY, Florence American ac-
tress TW/26-30, WWT/16
STANLEY, Frederic Arthur manager
GRB/2-3
STANLEY, F. W. (d 1917) EA/18*
STANLEY, Gase (d 1965 [75]) per-
former BP/50*
STANLEY, George (b 1786) English

actor BS, CDP

STANLEY, George (d 1820) English actor HAS

STANLEY, George (d 1898 [75]) actor, manager EA/99*

STANLEY, Mrs. George (fl 1806-20) English actress HAS

STANLEY, George B. (d 1850) stage manager HAS

STANLEY, Gladys B. (d 1971) performer BP/56*

STANLEY, Gwladys (d 1974) actress BTR/74

STANLEY, Harry (d 1896) manager EA/97*

STANLEY, Harry (d 1901) actor EA/02*

STANLEY, Helen (1889-1966) American singer WWA/4

STANLEY, Hodson [Charles Henry Hodson] (d 1885 [42]) actor, music-hall singer EA/86*

STANLEY, Hubert Rudolph Gordon (d 1916) EA/17*

STANLEY, Jack (d 1916 [30]) EA/17*

STANLEY, Jean [Joseph Haynes] (d 1904 [52]) music-hall performer EA/05*

STANLEY, Jean see Hosmer, Jean

STANLEY, Jocelyn (d 1883 [32]) singer EA/84*

STANLEY, John (1714-86) English musician DNB

STANLEY, Kim [née Patricia Reid] (b 1921/25) American actress AAS, BE, CB, TW/8-21, WWT/13-16

STANLEY, Laura [Mrs. S. E. Bernard] (d 1893) EA/94*

STANLEY, Lilian M. [Mrs. Charles Vernon] (d 1943 [65]) English actress GRB/1

STANLEY, Marion (fl 1903-07) American actress WWS

STANLEY, Martha (b 1879) American dramatist WWT/6-9

STANLEY, Montague (1809-44) Scottish actor DNB

STANLEY, Nelly [Mrs. Harry Diamond] (d 1902) EA/03*

STANLEY, Pamela (b 1909) English actress WWT/8-11

STANLEY, Pat (b 1931) American actress, dancer, singer BE, TW/15

STANLEY, Phyllis (b 1914) English actress, singer, dancer WWT/9-11

STANLEY, Raymond (d 1973 [54]) performer BP/57*

STANLEY, Rose [Mrs. Fred H. Constable] (d 1899 [38]) EA/00*

STANLEY, Samuel (d 1870 [77]) EA/71*

STANLEY, S. Victor (1892-1939) English actor WWT/7-8

STANLEY, Thomas (d 1678) English dramatist CP/2-3

STANLEY, Walter (fl 1902?) actor, singer CDP

STANLEY, William (fl 1599) dramatist FGF

STANMORE, Frank (1878-1943) English actor GRB/1, 4, WWT/1-4

STANMORE, James (d 1901 [87]) actor EA/02*

STANNARD, Miss see Lewis, Mrs. John

STANNARD, Mrs. Arthur see Winter, John Strange

STANNARD, Heather (b 1928) actress WWT/11-13

STANNARD, Rachel (b 1800) English actress HAS

STANNARD, Sarah (fl 1827) English actress HAS

STANNARD, Will (d 1905 [26]) music-hall performer EA/06*

STANNERS, J. H. (d 1917) actor EA/18*

STANNUS, Edris see De Valois, Ninette

STANSBURY, George (d 1846 [50]) composer EA/72*

STANSBURY, Hope (b 1945) actress TW/23

STANSFIELD, Mrs. (d 1907) EA/08*

STANSFIELD, Agnes see Clare, Ada

STANSFIELD, Grace see Fields, Gracie

STANSFIELD, Mrs. W. (d 1916) EA/17*

STANTLEY, Ralph (d 1964 [67]) actor BE*

STANTLEY, Ralph (d 1972 [58]) actor TW/28

STANTON, Alfred (d 1918) EA/19*

STANTON, Charlotte see Goodall, Charlotte

STANTON, Frank (b 1908) American executive BE

STANTON, Kate (d 1865) jig dancer HAS

STANTON, William (d 1875) actor EA/76*

STANWELL, Mrs. (fl 1804) actress GT

STANWOOD, Moody (fl 1847?) minstrel CDP

STANWYCK, Barbara [Ruby Stevens] (b 1907) American actress, dancer BE, CB, ES, SR, WWT/7-10

STANWYCK, Jay (d 1967 [58]) producer TW/24

STANYON, Brian (b 1941) English actor TW/20

STAPELTON, Ray (d 1974 [52]) performer BP/59*

STAPLES, Arthur Durnford (d 1917) EA/18*

STAPLES, George (d 1898) music-hall stage manager EA/99*

STAPLETON, Jean (b 1923) American actress BE, CB, TW/10-15, 20-21, WWT/16

STAPLETON, Maureen (b 1925) American actress AAS, BE, CB, TW/6-30, WWT/13-16

STAPLETON, Sir Robert see Stapylton, Sir Robert

STAPLETON, Vivian see Blaine, Vivian

STAPLETON, Zoë Margaret see Gail, Zoë

STAPYLTON, Sir Robert (d 1669) dramatist CDP, CP/1-3, DNB, FGF, GT

STARBUCK, James American choreographer, director, actor, dancer BE

STARK, Douglas (b 1916) actor TW/24

STARK, Harold W. (d 1975 [61]) performer BP/60*

STARK, James (d 1875 [57]) actor CDP, HAS

STARK, Mrs. James [Mrs. Kirby] (fl 1850-58) manager, actress HAS

STARK, Joy (b 1952) American actress TW/25

STARK, Molly American actress TW/30

STARK, Ray (b 1915) producer, literary agent BE

STARK, Sally (b 1938) American actress TW/25-27

STARKAND, Martin American actor TW/26

STARKE, Mariana (1762?-1838) dramatist CP/3, DNB, TD/1-2

STARKEY, Walter (b 1921) American actor TW/2-4

STARKIE, Martin (b 1925) English director, dramatist, presenting manager WWT/15-16

STARKWEATHER, A. (fl 1859) actor HAS

STARKWEATHER, David (b 1935) American dramatist, director CD

STARLING, Lynn (1891-1955) American dramatist WWT/6-10

STARMER, Richard (d 1870 [85]) actor EA/71*

STARMER, Mrs. Richard (d 1874 [85]) actress EA/75*

STARR, Bill American actor TW/28-29

STARR, Frances Grant (1886-1973) American actress BE, ES, GRB/3-4, SR, TW/5-19, 30, WWM, WWS, WWT/1-13

STARR, Mrs. Harry see Danbury, Ethel

STARR, Muriel (1888-1950) Canadian actress TW/6, WWT/4-10

STARR, Stanley (fl 1890?) singer, songwriter CDP

STARR, Sylvia (b 1879) American actress WWS

STASHEFF, Edward (b 1909) American educator, writer BE

STATHAM, Jonathan (d 1895 [42]) acting manager EA/96*

STATHER, Frank [H. Stather-Dunn] (b 1869) manager GRB/3

STATHER-DUNN, H. see Stather, Frank

STATTEL, Robert (b 1937) American actor TW/24-26, 29-30

STAUFFER, Ivan Rex (d 1974 [72]) publicist BP/58*

STAUNTON, Alexander (d 1878) Irish comedian, singer, dancer EA/80*

STAUNTON, Alice see Tyrrell, Ruby

STAUNTON, Bernard (d 1888 [34]) EA/89*

STAUNTON, Ella [Elizabeth Ann Nye] (d 1896 [57]) actress EA/98*

STAUNTON, Howard (1810-74) scholar DNB

STAVIS, Barrie (b 1906) American dramatist BE, CD

STAW, Sala (d 1972 [66]) Polish actress TW/29

STAYLEY, George (1727-79?/ 80) English dramatist, actor CP/2-3, DNB, GT

STAYTON, Frank (1874-1951) English dramatist WWT/2-7

STEAD, James Henry (d 1886) English music-hall performer CDP, COC, OC/1-3

STEAD, James Hurst (d 1886) music-hall singer EA/87*

STEADMAN, Walter (d 1900 [45]) actor EA/01*, WWT/14*

STEAGLES, Mr. (d 1867) actor? EA/68*

STEARNS, Charles (1753-1826) American dramatist EAP

STEARNS, Edith Bond (d 1961 [77]) producer BE*

STEARNS, Kate Palmer (d 1900) EA/01*

STEARNS, Myron Morris (d 1963 [78]) writer, producer BE*

STEARNS, Theodore (1880-1935) American composer WWA/1

STEARNS, William H. (1828-61) American actor HAS

STEBBING, Robert (d 1830) actor CDP

STEBBINS, Rowland [Laurence Rivers] (1882-1948) American producer TW/5

STEBBINS, Walter C. (d 1969 [70]) executive BP/54*

STEBER, Eleanor (b 1916) American singer CB

STECK, Olga (d 1935 [38]) American singer BE*, BP/20*

STEDMAN, Lincoln (d 1948 [41]) actor, producer BE*

STEDMAN, Myrtle (1888-1938) American actress BE*

STEEL, Edward (d 1965 [68]) performer BP/50*

STEEL, John (d 1971 [71]) singer TW/28

STEEL, Susan (1906-59) American actress TW/10, 16

STEEL, Vernon (1882-1955) Chilean actor WWT/2-8

STEEL, Willis (b 1866) American dramatist GRB/3

STEELE, Albert (d 1887) actor, music-hall manager NYM

STEELE, Mrs. Albert Richard see Steele, Ellen

STEELE, Archibald (fl 1789) Scottish? dramatist CP/3

STEELE, Barbara (b 1938) English actress ES

STEELE, Bill American actor TW/25

STEELE, Blanche (d 1944 [80]) actress BE*, WWT/14*

STEELE, David (b 1944) American actor TW/27

STEELE, Dora Gordon singer CDP

STEELE, Ellen [Mrs. Albert Richard Steele] (d 1881) EA/82*

STEELE, Mrs. J. B. see Bowering, Adelaide

STEELE, Lizzie see Palmer, Mrs. David S.

STEELE, Marjorie American actress TW/13-15

STEELE, Michael (b 1921) American actor TW/10-12

STEELE, Sir Richard (1672-1729) English dramatist CDP, COC, CP/1-3, DNB, ES, GT, HP, MH, NTH, OC/1-3, RE, SR, TD/1-2

STEELE, Richard (d 1887 [51]) actor, music-hall singer EA/89*

STEELE, Mrs. R. P. (d 1888) EA/89*

STEELE, Sarah Maria (b 1837) American actress HAS

STEELE, Silas S. (b 1812) American actor, dramatist HAS, RJ

STEELE, Tommy [né Hicks] (b 1936) English actor TW/20, 22, WWT/14-16

STEELE, Vernon (1882-1955) American actor TW/12

STEELE, Vickie (d 1975 [28]) performer BP/60*

STEELE, Wilbur Daniel (1886-1970) American dramatist HJD

STEELL, Willis (1859?-1941) American dramatist CB, WWA/1-2

STEEN, Marguerite (d 1975 [81]) English dramatist, actress CB

STEET, Alban Thomas see Carrick, Tom

STEEVENS, George (1736-1800) English commentator CDP, DNB, GT, HP, TD/1-2

STEFAN, Virginia (d 1964 [38])
actress BE*
STEFFANI, Sig. (fl 1859) singer
CDP
STEFFANONE, Balbina (fl 1850)
singer CDP, HAS
STEGER, Julius (1870-1959) Aus-
trian/American actor, stage
manager WWA/3, WWM,
WWS
STEGGALL, Charles (d 1905 [79])
musician EA/06*
STEGMEYER, William J. (d 1968
[51]) composer/lyricist BP/
53*
STEHLI, Edgar (1884-1973)
French/American actor BE,
TW/6-9, 13-15, 22-23, 30
STEHMAN, Jacques (d 1975 [62])
critic BP/59*
STEIGER, Rod (b 1925) American
actor BE, CB, ES, TW/9
STEIN, Ann R. (d 1970 [72])
lawyer BP/55*
STEIN, Carl (d 1890 [57]) lessee
EA/91*
STEIN, Gertrude (1874-1947)
American dramatist CB,
DAB, ES, HJD, MD, MWD,
PDT, WWW/4
STEIN, Joseph (b 1912) American
dramatist, librettist BE, CD,
WWT/15-16
STEIN, Michael (b 1933) American
actor TW/25-26
STEINBECK, John (1902-68)
American dramatist AAS,
BE, CB, COC, ES, HJD,
MD, MH, MWD, NTH, OC/
1-3, WWT/9-14
STEINBERG, Amy (d 1920 [70])
actress BE*, WWT/14*
STEINBERG, William (b 1899)
German/American conductor
CB
STEINER, George (d 1967 [67])
composer/lyricist BP/52*
STEINER, Ira (b c. 1915) talent
representative BE
STEINER, Max (1888-1971)
Austrian composer WWA/5
STEINFIRST, Donald S. (d 1972
[68]) critic BP/57*
STEININGER, Franz (d 1974
[69]) composer, conductor
BP/60*, WWT/16*
STEINKE, Hans (d 1971 [78])
performer BP/56*

STEINMAN, Harold (d 1975 [70])
producer/director/choreographer
BP/60*
STEINMAN, Morris W. (d 1976
[65]) publicist BP/60*
STEINMETZ, Joseph S. (d 1913)
EA/14*
STELLA, Antonietta (b 1929) Italian
singer CB, ES
STELLA, Nina [Marie Nina de
Harven Duval] (b 1886) New
Zealand actress GRB/1
STELOFF, Frances (b 1887) Amer-
ican bookseller BE
STEMBRIDGE-RAY, Mr. (d 1893)
EA/94*
STENBORG, Helen (b 1925) Ameri-
can actress TW/23, 28-30
STENDER, Doug (b 1942) American
actor TW/29-30
STEPAN, Carl (d 1887) singer
NYM
STEPAN, Celeste (d 1909 [85])
dancer EA/10*
STEPANEK, Karel (b 1899) Czech
actor WWT/10-15
STEPHAN, Mlle. (fl 1839) actress
HAS
STEPHAN, Petit (fl 1843) dancer
CDP
STEPHAN, Celeste (d 1909 [85])
dancer WWT/14*
STEPHEN, John (d 1974 [62]) actor
TW/30
STEPHEN, Stainless (d 1971 [79])
performer BP/55*
STEPHENS (d 1901) dramatist, ac-
tor EA/02*
STEPHENS, Mrs. [née Elizabeth
Taft] (d 1858) English circus
performer, actress HAS
STEPHENS, Miss (b 1794) English
singer, actress BS
STEPHENS, Miss (fl 1798-1801)
actress TD/1-2
STEPHENS, Miss (d 1882) see
Stephens, Catherine
STEPHENS, Alfred (d 1900) musi-
cal director EA/01*
STEPHENS, Alfred George Gower
(d 1933) Australian dramatist
WWW/3
STEPHENS, Ann Sophia (1813-86)
dramatist CDP
STEPHENS, Mrs. B. N. (d 1970
[78]) performer BP/55*
STEPHENS, Catherine, Countess of
Essex (1794-1882) English

singer, actress CDP, DNB
STEPHENS, C. E. (d 1892 [71])
composer EA/93*
STEPHENS, E. B. (d 1884 [31])
manager EA/85*
STEPHENS, Frances (b 1906)
English critic WWT/11-14
STEPHENS, Francis John (d
1917) EA/18*
STEPHENS, Fred W. (fl 1893?)
actor, singer CDP
STEPHENS, Garn American ac-
tress TW/28-30
STEPHENS, George (1800-51)
English dramatist DNB
STEPHENS, Harvey (b 1902)
American actor TW/1, 3,
5-9
STEPHENS, Henry (d 1892 [77])
EA/93*
STEPHENS, Henry Pottinger (d
1903) dramatist BE*, EA/04*,
WWT/14*
STEPHENS, Jane (1813?-96)
actress DNB, OAA/2
STEPHENS, J. Frank (d 1950
[72]) executive TW/6
STEPHENS, John (fl 1613) dram-
atist CP/1-3, FGF
STEPHENS, Kitty see Stephens,
Catherine
STEPHENS, Mrs. Lyne see
Duvernay, Pauline Yolande
Marie Louise
STEPHENS, Olga Worth (d 1964
[75]) performer BP/49*
STEPHENS, Peter (d 1872) circus
proprietor EA/73*
STEPHENS, Richard (1817-69)
English actor HAS
STEPHENS, Robert (b 1931)
English actor, director AAS,
COC, WWT/14-16
STEPHENS, Stephanie (b 1900)
actress WWT/6-8
STEPHENS, Mrs. W. H. (d 1896
[83]) actress BE*, WWT/14*
STEPHENS, William Henry (d
1888) English actor HAS,
OAA/2
STEPHENS, Yorke (1856/60/62-
1937) English actor DP, EA/
97, GRB/1-4, WWT/1-8
STEPHENSON, B. C. (d 1906
[67]) dramatist WWT/14*
STEPHENSON, Charles A. (b
1879) English actor GRB/1
STEPHENSON, Charles Henry

(d 1905 [82]) actor GRB/1
STEPHENSON, Charlotte (d 1905
[54]) EA/06*
STEPHENSON, Frank (d 1890 [31])
actor EA/91*
STEPHENSON, Henry (1874-1956)
English actor TW/12, WWT/
7-11
STEPHENSON, James (1898/1900-
1941) English actor CB, WWA/2
STEPHENSON, Jane (d 1893 [89])
EA/94*
STEPHENSON, John (d 1963 [74])
performer, producer BE*
STEPHENSON, Orlistus Bell (b
1867) American manager
WWA/4
STEPHENSON, Robert (d 1887)
manager EA/88*
STEPHENSON, Robert Robinson
(d 1970 [69]) performer BP/55*
STEPHENSON, William (d 1891
[65]) "spotted man" EA/92*
STEPPAT, Ilse (d 1969 [52]) per-
former BP/54*
STEPT, Sammy (d 1964 [67]) com-
poser/lyricist BP/49*
STERICKER, Hilda (d 1916 [41])
EA/17*
STERLING, Mrs. see Dixon,
Clara Ann
STERLING, Antoinette (1843/50-
1904) American singer CDP,
DNB
STERLING, Edyth (d 1962 [75])
actress BE*
STERLING, Ella [Emma Sophia
Homfray] (d 1898 [38]) actress
EA/99*
STERLING, Ford (c. 1884-1939)
American actor BE*, WWT/14*
STERLING, Frank B. (d 1970
[84]) performer BP/55*
STERLING, James (1701?-63) Irish
dramatist CP/1-3, DNB, GT,
HJD
STERLING, Jan (b 1923) American
actress BE, SR, TW/2-3, 5,
13, 19-20, 26, WWT/16
STERLING, John (d 1916) EA/17*
STERLING, Philip (b 1922) Amer-
ican actor TW/23-24, 28-29
STERLING, Richard (1880-1959)
American actor TW/1, 3, 15,
WWT/6-12
STERLING, Robert (b 1917) Ameri-
can actor BE, TW/7-8
STERLING, Roy (b 1933) American

actor TW/2

STERN, Ernest (1876-1954)
Rumanian designer ES, WWT/
10-11

STERN, G[ladys] B[ertha] (b
1890) English dramatist
WWT/7-11

STERN, Harold (d 1972 [65])
lawyer BP/57*

STERN, Harold S. (d 1976 [53])
critic BP/60*

STERN, Henry R. (d 1966 [91])
producer/director BP/50*

STERN, Jean (d 1974 [84]) performer BP/59*

STERN, Joseph (b 1940) American
actor TW/28, 30

STERN, Joseph William (1870-
1934) American songwriter
DAB

STERNBERG, Ann (d 1975 [42])
composer/lyricist BP/60*

STERNDALE-BENNETT, T. C.
(d 1944) composer, performer
BE*, WWT/14*

STERNE, Eleanor (d 1873) singer
EA/74*

STERNE, Morgan (b 1926) American actor BE, TW/16

STERNE, Richard (b 1942) American actor TW/24, 30

STERNER, Ernest (d 1891 [21])
actor EA/92*

STERNFELD, Tommy (d 1974
[65]) producer/director/chore-
ographer BP/59*

STERNHAGEN, Frances (b 1930/
32) American actress BE,
TW/15, 20, 22-23, 25, 27-
30, WWT/15-16

STERNHEIM, Carl (1878-1943)
German dramatist COC,
OC/3

STERNROYD, Vincent (1857-1948)
English actor WWT/1-10

STETSON, Ada [née Parker] (fl
1847) actress HAS

STETSON, E. T. (b 1836)
American actor CDP, HAS

STETSON, John (d 1892 [96])
manager WWT/14*

STETSON, John (1830/35-95)
American actor, manager,
dramatist? CDP, SR

STETSON, Mrs. John [née Kate
Stokes] (d 1896) actress,
equestrienne CDP, SR

STETTHEIMER, Florine (d 1944)

designer BE*

STETTITH, Olive (d 1937) actress
BE*, WWT/14*

STEVENS, Mr. (fl 1834?) dramatist RJ

STEVENS, Miss see Kemble,
Eugenie

STEVENS, Miss see Stavart,
Mrs. H. E.

STEVENS, Alfred Peck see
Vance, Alfred Glenville

STEVENS, Ashton (1872-1951)
American critic NTH, TW/8,
WWA/3, WWM, WWT/10-11

STEVENS, Charles (d 1964 [71])
actor BE*

STEVENS, Charles E. (d 1910)
actor EA/11*

STEVENS, Clifford (b 1936) American talent representative BE

STEVENS, Connie (b 1938) American actress TW/23

STEVENS, Constance Vera see
Gray, Sally

STEVENS, Craig American actor
BE, TW/20

STEVENS, Edwin (b 1860) American
actor GRB/3-4, WWM, WWT/
1-6

STEVENS, Emily (1882-1928)
American actress DAB, WWM,
WWT/4-5

STEVENS, Mrs. Ernest see
Deering, Rebekah

STEVENS, Ferriss Percival (d
1917 [50]) actor EA/18*,
WWT/14*

STEVENS, Fran American actress
TW/24-26, 28-30

STEVENS, Frank R. (d 1887) actor
NYM

STEVENS, Frank S. (d 1966 [43])
performer BP/51*

STEVENS, George see Steevens,
George

STEVENS, George (d 1889 [32])
elephant keeper EA/91*

STEVENS, George (d 1975 [70])
producer/director/choreographer
BP/59*

STEVENS, George Alexander (d
1784 [49]) English actor, dramatist CDP, CP/1-3, GT, TD/1-2

STEVENS, H. C. G. (1892-1967)
English press representative,
composer WWT/5-14

STEVENS, Henry Edmund (1814-54)
English actor, stage manager

HAS
STEVENS, Inger (1934-70) Swedish
actress BE, TW/26, WWA/5
STEVENS, Jenny (d 1897) actress
CDP
STEVENS, Jeremy (b 1938)
American actor TW/25
STEVENS, John (fl 1744) drama-
tist CP/1-3
STEVENS, Cpt. John (d 1726)
dramatist CP/1-3, GT
STEVENS, John A. (d 1916 [73])
actor, dramatist, manager
CDP
STEVENS, Jon (b 1946) American
actor TW/26
STEVENS, Julia Warren (d 1903)
actress EA/04*
STEVENS, Katherine (b 1794)
English actress, singer OX
STEVENS, K. T. (b 1919) Amer-
ican actress TW/4, WWT/11
STEVENS, Leith (d 1970 [60])
composer/lyricist BP/55*
STEVENS, Leon B. (b 1926)
American actor TW/23
STEVENS, Leslie (b 1924) Amer-
ican dramatist, director, pro-
ducer BE
STEVENS, Marie (d 1881 [24])
music-hall performer EA/83*
STEVENS, Mark (b 1922) Amer-
ican actor TW/9
STEVENS, Morton L. (d 1959
[69]) actor TW/16
STEVENS, Nan (b 1921) Ameri-
can owner of theatrical secre-
tarial service BE
STEVENS, Onslow [Onslow Ford
Stevenson] (1906-77) American
actor, director BE, TW/4,
WWT/9-14
STEVENS, Pat American actress
TW/27-28
STEVENS, Paul (b 1924) Ameri-
can actor BE, TW/9, 15,
19-20, 22, 24
STEVENS, Risë (b 1913) Ameri-
can singer CB
STEVENS, Robert (d 1963 [83])
actor, director BE*
STEVENS, Robert E. (1838-1918)
American manager SR
STEVENS, Roger (b 1938) Amer-
ican actor TW/10-12
STEVENS, Roger L. (b 1910)
American producer AAS, BE,
CB, WWT/13-16

STEVENS, Ronnie (b 1925) English
actor WWT/15-16
STEVENS, Rose (d 1887) actress
NYM
STEVENS, Rowena (d 1975 [68])
producer/director/choreographer
BP/59*
STEVENS, Ruby see Stanwyck,
Barbara
STEVENS, Sara [Mrs. John C.
Heenan] (d 1904 [70]) American
actress CDP, HAS, PP/3
STEVENS, Sydney (d 1888) EA/89*
STEVENS, Mrs. T. see Alzar,
Mme.
STEVENS, Thomas (fl 1586-87)
actor DA
STEVENS, Thomas Wood (1880-
1942) American producer, coach
SR
STEVENS, Tony (b 1948) American
actor TW/26-28
STEVENS, Ursula (b 1936) German/
American actress TW/15
STEVENS, Victor (d 1925 [72])
actor, dramatist BE*, WWT/
14*
STEVENS, Wallace (1879-1955)
American dramatist HJD
STEVENS, Walter (d 1887 [62])
musician EA/88*
STEVENSON, Mr. (fl 1824-52)
English actor HAS
STEVENSON, Miss (fl 1819?) ac-
tress CDP
STEVENSON, Charles Alexander
(1851-1929) Irish actor CDP,
PP/3, SR
STEVENSON, Douglas (d 1934 [52])
American actor BE*, BP/19*
STEVENSON, Ebenezer (d 1886
[56]) manager EA/87*
STEVENSON, Edward (d 1968 [62])
designer BP/53*
STEVENSON, George Alexander
(d 1869) manager EA/70*
STEVENSON, Hugh (1910-56) Eng-
lish designer ES
STEVENSON, James (d 1894 [27])
variety performer EA/95*
STEVENSON, Mrs. James see
Stevenson, Julia
STEVENSON, Janet MacIntyre Mac-
Kenzie see Norma, Hettie
STEVENSON, John Andrew Irish
composer TD/1-2
STEVENSON, Julia [Mrs. James
Stevenson] (d 1896) EA/97*

STEVENSON, Margot (b 1914/18)
American actress BE, TW/
5-6, 12, 22-23, WWT/9-16
STEVENSON, Onslow Fred see
Stevens, Onslow
STEVENSON, Percy Malcolm
(d 1909 [26]) actor EA/10*
STEVENSON, Robert Louis (1850-
94) Scottish dramatist DNB,
HP
STEVENSON, William (d 1575)
English dramatist COC, MH,
OC/1-3
STEVENSON, W. S. (b 1867)
Scottish actor GRB/1
STEVENSON, Mrs. W. S. see
Robson, Evelyn Stuart
STEWART, Mr. comedian CDP
STEWART, Alfred (b 1843) Eng-
lish actor, singer HAS
STEWART, Anita (d 1961 [65])
American actress BE*
STEWART, Anna Bird American
actress, writer CB
STEWART, Arthur see Slater,
Arthur
STEWART, Athole (1879-1940)
English actor, producer GRB/
1-4, WWT/1-9
STEWART, Caroline (d 1863)
actress HAS
STEWART, Carolyn Hill Ameri-
can actress TW/2
STEWART, Charles (b 1887)
American manager BE
STEWART, Charlotte (d 1855)
actress HAS
STEWART, Clare [Mrs. James
Stewart] (d 1907) EA/08*
STEWART, Danny (d 1962 [55])
actor, musician, composer
BE*
STEWART, David J. (1918-66)
American actor BE, TW/2,
4, 8, 10-15, 18-23
STEWART, David Ogilvie (d 1870
[57]) comedian EA/71*
STEWART, Don (b 1935) Ameri-
can actor TW/20-21
STEWART, Donald Ogden (b
1894) American actor BE,
WWT/7-14
STEWART, Douglas (fl 1852)
actor HAS
STEWART, Douglas (b 1913)
Australian/New Zealand drama-
tist CD
STEWART, Mrs. E. F. [Mrs.

Woodward] (fl 1851) actress
HAS
STEWART, Ellen American pro-
ducer, manager, director CB,
WWT/16
STEWART, Emily (fl 1855?) dancer
CDP
STEWART, Emma (b 1849) English
actress HAS
STEWART, Ernie (d 1974 [61])
composer/lyricist BP/59*
STEWART, Florence Lenora see
Carleton, Billie
STEWART, Fred (1906-70) Ameri-
can actor, director AAS, BE,
TW/4, 9, 11-13, 23-24, 26-27,
WWA/5, WWT/14-15
STEWART, Grant (1866-1929) Eng-
lish actor, dramatist SR, WWS
STEWART, Gwen actress GRB/1
STEWART, Mrs. H. E. [Miss
Stevens] (b 1820) English actress
HAS
STEWART, Henry (b 1842) English
actor HAS
STEWART, Henry E. (d 1917 [22])
EA/18*
STEWART, Hilda (b 1881) Aus-
tralian actress GRB/1-4
STEWART, Humphrey John (1854/
56-1932) English musician, com-
poser DAB, WWM
STEWART, James (fl 1774-79)
dramatist CP/2-3, GT
STEWART, James (d 1881 [61])
music-hall performer? EA/82*
STEWART, James (b 1908/11)
American actor BE, CB, ES,
SR, WWT/9-16
STEWART, Mrs. James see
Stewart, Clare
STEWART, James Lablache see
Granger, Stewart
STEWART, Jean-Pierre (b 1946)
American actor TW/25-26, 30
STEWART, Job (b 1934) South Af-
rican actor TW/23
STEWART, John (d 1957 [58]) di-
rector OC/3
STEWART, John[ny] (b 1934) Amer-
ican actor TW/8-19, 23, 29-30
STEWART, Julia (b 1862) English
actress OAA/2
STEWART, Katharine [Katharine
Stewart Spain] (d 1949 [81])
English actress GRB/1-3,
TW/5
STEWART, Maggie (d 1903) ac-

tress EA/04*
STEWART, Mary (d 1916) actress SR
STEWART, Maud (d 1892 [18])
actress EA/93*
STEWART, Melville (b 1869)
English singer, actor WWM
STEWART, Michael (b 1929)
American dramatist, librettist
BE, CD, ES, WWT/16
STEWART, Nancye (b 1893) English actress WWT/7
STEWART, Nellie [Mrs. George
Musgrove] (1860-1931) Australian actress GRB/1-4,
WWT/1-6
STEWART, Patrick (b 1940)
English actor AAS, TW/27,
WWT/15-16
STEWART, Paula (b 1933) American actress, singer BE
STEWART, Ray (b 1932) American actor TW/23-26, 28, 30
STEWART, Richard (d 1902 [75])
actor, manager WWT/14*
STEWART, Rowland (d 1907)
manager EA/08*
STEWART, Sophie (b 1908) Scottish actress AAS, WWT/8-16
STEWART, Thomas (fl 1772)
dramatist CP/3, GT
STEWART, Thomas (b 1928)
American singer CB
STEWART, William G. (1869-1941) American singer, producer, manager CB, WWS
STEWER, Jan [né A. J. Coles]
actor, dramatist WWT/8
STEYNE, Adele [Mrs. Charles
Steyne] (d 1893) EA/94*
STEYNE, Charles (d 1897 [65])
actor EA/98*
STEYNE, Mrs. Charles see
Steyne, Adele
STEYNE, E. T. (d 1912) stage
manager, producer, actor
EA/13*, WWT/14*
STEYNE, Nelson [Richard Nelson
Sutcliffe] (d 1901 [80]) actor
EA/03*
STICH RANDALL, Teresa (b
1930) American singer ES
STICKNEY, Mr. (d 1840) American actor HAS
STICKNEY, Mrs. see Buttersby, Mrs.
STICKNEY, Benjamin (d 1860
[40]) equestrian EA/72*

STICKNEY, Dorothy (b 1900/03)
American actress BE, CB,
TW/2-21, 24, 26, 29-30, WWT/
7-16
STICKNEY, Mrs. E. M. [Mrs.
Jones] (d 1864 [58]) English actress HAS
STICKNEY, Robert (b 1846) American equestrian CDP, HAS
STICKNEY, Sallie (fl 1861-69)
American equestrienne HAS
STICKNEY, Samuel P. (1808-77)
equestrian CDP
STIEFEL, Milton (b 1900) American
director, producer, actor BE
STIERS, David Ogden (b 1942)
American actor TW/30
STIGANT, Arthur (b 1871) English
actor GRB/1
STIGELLI, Sig. (fl 1859) singer?
HAS
STIGNANI, Ebe (b 1907) Italian
singer CB
STILES, Leslie (b 1876) English
actor, dramatist, composer,
producer WWT/1-8
STILES, Mrs. Leslie (d 1913) EA/
14*
STILL, John (d 1607 [63]) English
dramatist COC, CP/1-3, FGF,
OC/3
STILL, John A. (d 1849) actor?
singer? HAS
STILLINGFLEET, Benjamin (1700-
71) dramatist CP/2-3, GT
STILLMAN, David B. (d 1963 [57])
attorney BP/47*
STILLMAN, Marsha (d 1962 [23])
actress BE*, BP/47*
STILLSBURY, Agnes (fl 1858) English
actress HAS
STILT, Richard (d 1878 [59]) pantomimist EA/79*
STIMSON, Fred J. (d 1884 [27])
actor EA/85*
STINCHCOMBE, William Campbell
(d 1886 [48]) costumier EA/88*
STINE, Lawrence (b 1912) American
educator BE
STINNETT, Ray J. (d 1974 [92])
theatre owner BP/58*
STINTON, Mrs. (d 1894) EA/95*
STINTON, John Arthur (d 1876
[22]) musician EA/77*
STIRLING, Mr. actor CDP
STIRLING, Earl of see Alexander,
William
STIRLING, Mrs. [Fanny Clifton;

Lady Charles Gregory] (1816-95) English actress CDP, OAA/1

STIRLING, Mrs. actress CDP

STIRLING, Alfred (d 1872 [22]) actor EA/73*

STIRLING, Arthur (d 1898 [71]) actor OAA/2

STIRLING, Mrs. Arthur [née Cleveland] (d 1902) actress OAA/2

STIRLING, Charles [Charles Davies] (b 1878) English actor GRB/1

STIRLING, Edward [Edward Lambert] (1809/11-94) English dramatist, actor CDP, EA/68, OC/1-3

STIRLING, Edward see Stirling, W. Edward

STIRLING, Fanny [Mary Anne Kehl] (1813/15-95) English actress CDP, COC, DNB, DP, OAA/1-2, OC/1-3

STIRLING, Fanny (fl 1860-61) actress OAA/2

STIRLING, W. Edward (1891-1948) English actor, manager, dramatist WWT/5-10, WWW/4

STIRLING, William Alexander see Alexander, William

STIRLING, William Fitzgerald (d 1917) EA/18*

STITH, Calvert G. (b 1883) American editor WWM

STITT, Jesse (d 1971 [67]) play sponsor BP/56*

STIX, John (b 1920) American director BE

STIX, Thomas L. (d 1974 [78]) agent BP/59*

STOCK, Charles (d 1891 [68]) steam circus proprietor EA/92*

STOCK, Frederick A. (1872-1942) German conductor WWA/2

STOCK, Jack (d 1954 [60]) actor BE*, WWT/14*

STOCK, Nigel (b 1919) Maltese/English actor AAS, WWT/9-16

STOCK, Thomas dramatist EAP, RJ

STOCKDALE, Ann (b 1943) American actress TW/23

STOCKDALE, Rev. Percival (1736-1811) translator CP/2-3, GT

STOCKEN, Agnes (d 1909) EA/10*

STOCKER, Nannette dwarf CDP

STOCKFIELD, Betty (1905-66) Australian actress WWT/6-13

STOCKHAUSEN, Mons. (d 1868) musician EA/69*

STOCKHAUSEN, Mme. (d 1877) EA/78*

STOCKHOFF, Walter C. (d 1968 [91]) composer/lyricist BP/52*

STOCKING, Robert (b 1941) American actor TW/28

STOCKTON, Fanny (1844-70) American singer CDP, HAS

STOCKTON, Martha Hughes see Brush, Mrs. Clinton E.

STOCKTON, Reginald (d 1898) actor EA/99*

STOCKWELL, Miss see Barrett, Mrs. George Horton

STOCKWELL, Harry American actor TW/1-3

STOCKWELL, Jeremy American actor TW/26, 28

STOCKWELL, L. R. (1851-1912) actor, manager CDP

STOCKWELL, Martha [Mrs. Walter Stockwell] (d 1910) EA/11*

STOCKWELL, Walter (fl 1894?) actor, singer CDP

STOCKWELL, Mrs. Walter see Stockwell, Martha

STOCQUELER, Fanny (b 1847) English actress CDP, HAS

STODARE, Col. (d 1866 [35]) illusionist EA/72*

STODDARD, Mrs. Carlos French see Milliken, Sandol

STODDARD, George (1875-1944) librettist SR

STODDARD, Mrs. George (1832-1911) English actress SR

STODDARD, George D. (b 1897) American educator BE

STODDARD, George William (1826-88) actor CDP

STODDARD, Haila (b 1913/14) American actress, producer, director BE, TW/2-16, WWT/11-16

STODDART, Alexandra (b 1947) American actress TW/28

STODDART, George (fl 1850s) English actor HAS

STODDART, Mrs. George (fl 1850s) English actress HAS

STODDART, J. (fl 1798) translator CP/3

STODDART, James Henry (d
1867 [71]) actor EA/68*
STODDART, James Henry (1827-
1907) English actor CDP,
DAB, HAS, PP/3, SR, WWA/1
STODDART, Mrs. James Henry
[Matilda Phillips] (fl 1856-61)
actress CDP, HAS
STODDART, Marie Scottish ac-
tress GRB/1
STODDART, Mary [Mrs. Richard
D. Stoddart] (d 1892) EA/93*
STODDART, Mrs. Richard D.
see Stoddart, Mary
STOEPEL, Robert [or Richard]
(1821-87) German/American
musician, composer NYM
STOESSEL, Albert Frederic
(1894-1943) American con-
ductor DAB
STOGEL, Syd (d 1974 [60]) pub-
licist BP/58*
STOKEDALE, Edmund (fl 1550)
actor DA
STOKER, Mrs. (d 1885 [84]) ac-
tress EA/86*
STOKER, Bram (1858-1912)
Irish manager, secretary
GRB/1-4, WWW/1
STOKER, Hew Gordon Dacre
(1885-1966) Irish actor WWT/
5-13
STOKER, Willard [né William
Richard] (b 1905) English ac-
tor, producer, director
WWT/11-16
STOKER, William Richard see
Stoker, Willard
STOKES, Ann (d 1894) EA/95*
STOKES, Annie Elizabeth (d
1891 [49]) EA/92*
STOKES, Caroline Ann [Carrie
Romer; Mrs. W. S. Hardy
Stokes] (d 1883) singer? EA/
84*
STOKES, Emma equestrienne
CDP
STOKES, Ernest L. (d 1964
[57]) actor BE*
STOKES, Mrs. Fred see
Ethlo, Maggie
STOKES, Mrs. Henry see
Stokes, Laura Adelaide
STOKES, J. (fl c. 1820) drama-
tist EAP
STOKES, James (d 1833) slack-
rope vaulter HAS
STOKES, John (d 1877) dancer

EA/78*
STOKES, Kate see Stetson, Mrs.
John
STOKES, Laura Adelaide [Mrs.
Henry Stokes] (d 1882) EA/83*
STOKES, Sewell (b 1902) English
dramatist WWT/9-11
STOKES, Thomas (d 1900 [35])
dancer EA/01*
STOKES, Mrs. W. S. Hardy see
Stokes, Caroline Ann
STOLBER, Dean (b 1944) American
actor TW/28
STOLL, Blanche [Mrs. Brukerwich]
(d 1896) EA/97*
STOLL, Harriet [Mrs. Oswald
Stoll] (d 1902 [27]) EA/03*
STOLL, Sir Oswald (1866-1942)
Australian managing director
COC, DNB, GRB/1-4, OC/1-3,
WWT/4-9, WWW/4
STOLL, Mrs. Oswald see Stoll,
Harriet
STOLL, Roderick (d 1890) variety
agent EA/91*
STOLTZ, Rosine (d 1903) singer
EA/04*
STOLZ, Don (b 1919) American
producer, director BE
STOLZ, Robert (1880/86-1975)
Austrian composer, conductor
BE, CB, WWT/10-14
STONE, Alix (b 1918) English de-
signer ES, WWT/15-16
STONE, Amelia (b 1879) American
actress, singer WWS
STONE, Amy actress CDP
STONE, Ann Eliza [née Phillips]
(b 1830) American actress HAS
STONE, Barton (b 1920) American
actor TW/24
STONE, Bentley (b c. 1908) Ameri-
can dancer, choreographer,
costume designer ES
STONE, Carol (b 1915/16) Ameri-
can actress, director BE, TW/
1, 5-19, WWT/10-14
STONE, Charles actor WWT/6-8
STONE, Charles R. [Madelle
Stone] (b 1859) English actor,
producer, stage manager
GRB/1
STONE, Mrs. Charles R. see
Kelsey, Emily
STONE, Christopher Lucius (b
1819) American actor HAS
STONE, Mrs. C[hristopher] L[ucius]
see Drew, Mrs. Frank Melson

STONE, Mrs. C[hristopher]
L[ucius] see Johnston, Mrs.
T. B.

STONE, Dorothy (1905-74) American actress, singer BE,
TW/1-7, WWT/6-11

STONE, Eaton (b 1818) American
equestrian CDP, HAS

STONE, Edward Durell (b 1902)
American architect, educator
BE

STONE, Emma (d 1910) EA/11*

STONE, Ezra (b 1917) American
director, actor, producer,
writer BE

STONE, Florence Oakley [Mrs.
Lewis Stone] (d 1956 [65])
actress BE*, WWT/14*

STONE, Fred Andrew (1873-1959)
American actor GRB/3-4,
SR, TW/1-7, 15, WWA/3,
WWT/1-11

STONE, George (d 1889 [32])
comedian EA/90*, WWT/14*

STONE, George (b 1861) English manager GRB/1

STONE, George E. (d 1967
[64]) performer BP/51*

STONE, Harvey (d 1974 [61])
comedian TW/30

STONE, H. F. (fl 1851) American actor HAS

STONE, Isabel Diaz (d 1924)
singer CDP

STONE, John Augustus (1801-34)
American dramatist, actor
CDP, COC, DAB, EAP, HAS,
HJD, OC/1-3, RJ, WWA/H

STONE, Leonard (b 1923) American actor TW/14-15

STONE, Lewis (1878/79-1953)
American actor TW/10,
WWA/3, WWT/7-10

STONE, Mrs. Lewis see
Stone, Florence Oakley

STONE, Louis H. (d 1972 [76])
producer/director/choreographer
BP/57*

STONE, Mary Anne (d 1883 [58])
EA/84*

STONE, Maxine (d 1964 [54])
performer BP/49*

STONE, Paddy (b 1924/25)
Canadian dancer, choreographer, director AAS, WWT/14-
16

STONE, Paula (b 1916) American
producer, actress BE,

WWT/12-14

STONE, Peter H. (b 1930) American dramatist, librettist BE,
CD, WWT/15-16

STONE, Phil (d 1863 [65]) property
man CDP

STONE, Philip (fl c. 1612-13) lessee DA

STONE, Robinson (b 1919) American actor TW/2, 4

STONE, Sarah see Elliston,
Louise

STONE, Thomas Frederick (d
1895) EA/96*

STONE, William Pidcock (d 1912)
EA/14*

STONEALL, Mrs. [née Scallan]
(fl 1839-49) actress HAS

STONEBURNER, Sam (b 1934)
American actor TW/28

STONEHAM, Adelaide (d 1890
[68]) actress EA/92*

STONEHOUSE, Ruth (1894-1941)
actress BE*

STONER, Mrs. Joe see Stoner,
Marion

STONER, Joseph (d 1889) singer
EA/90*

STONER, Marion [Mrs. Joe Stoner]
(d 1882) EA/84*

STONETTE, Alfred (d 1874 [30])
clown EA/75*

STONETTE, Tom (d 1873) pantomimist EA/74*

STOODLEY, Charles (d 1888)
equestrian EA/89*

STOODLEY, Mrs. G. (d 1878
[37]) EA/79*

STOODLEY, George (d 1903 [69])
circus proprietor EA/04*

STOPPARD, Tom [né Straussler]
(b 1937) Czech/English dramatist, director AAS, CB, CD,
CH, COC, MH, MWD, PDT,
WWT/15-16

STORACE, Anna Selina (1766-
1817) English singer, actress
CDP, DNB, ES, GT, TD/1-2

STORACE, Stephen (1763-96) English musician, proprietor, dramatist, translator CP/2-3,
DNB, ES, TD/1-2

STORCH, Arthur (b 1925) American actor, director TW/10,
12-15, 29, WWT/15-16

STORCH, Larry (b 1923) American
actor BE, TW/12, 14

STORDAHL, Axel (d 1963 [50])

American composer, conductor
BE*
STORER, Mrs. (fl 1760) singer,
actress TD/2
STORER, Miss see Henry,
Mrs. John, I
STORER, Ann see Hogg, Mrs.
John
STORER, Maria (c. 1760-95) ac-
tress COC
STOREY, David [Malcolm] (b
1933) English dramatist AAS,
CB, CD, CH, COC, WWT/
15-16
STOREY, Fred (1861-1917) Eng-
lish actor, dancer, scene
painter DP, GRB/1-4, WWT/
1-3
STOREY, F. T. (d 1892) circus
performer? EA/93*
STOREY, John (d 1870 [21])
equestrian EA/71*
STOREY, John (d 1885 [47])
EA/86*
STOREY, Sylvia Lilian (d 1947)
English actress BE*, WWT/
14*
STOREY, Wilson see Bolero
STORM, Howard (b 1939) Amer-
ican actor TW/28
STORM, Lesley (1903-75) Scot-
tish dramatist BE, WWT/
9-15
STORM, Violet (d 1911) per-
former? EA/12*
STORMONT, Leo (d 1923) actor
BE*, WWT/14*
STORRI, Sadrenne (d 1918 [19])
EA/19*
STORRS, Caryl B. (b 1870)
American editor WWM
STORY, Aubrey (d 1963 [c. 75])
literary representative BE*
STORY, Bob (d 1973 [47]) per-
former BP/57*
STORY, Mrs. Julian see
Eames, Emma
STORY, Robert (d 1973 [47])
actor TW/29
STORY, Ted (b 1942) American
actor TW/26
STORY, William (d 1870 [86])
actor EA/71*
STORY-GOFTON, Edward English
actor, producer GRB/2-3
STOSSEL, Ludwig (d 1973 [89])
Austrian/American actor
BP/57*, WWT/16*

STOTHART, Herbert P. (d 1949
[64]) American composer WWT/
6-10
STOTT, Judith (b 1929) English ac-
tress AAS, WWT/13-15
STOTT, Mike (b 1944) English
dramatist, stage manager CD
STOVALL, Babe (d 1974 [66])
performer BP/59*
STOVALL, Count (b 1946) American
actor TW/30
STOWE, Carl F. (d 1964 [90]) per-
former BP/49*
STOWELL, Margaret see Rogers,
Maggie
STOYLE, James D. (d 1880 [49])
comedian EA/82*, WWT/14*
STRACCIARI, Riccardo (1875-1955)
Italian singer ES
STRACHAN, Alan (b 1946) Scottish
director WWT/16
STRACHEY, Jack (1894-1972) Eng-
lish composer WWT/11-14
STRADNER, Rose (1913-58) Austrian
actress BE*
STRAHAN, C. G. (fl 1853) actor
HAS
STRAIGHT, Beatrice (b 1918)
American actress, producer
BE, TW/4-15, 24, 29, WWT/
11-16
STRAKER, John Robert (d 1898)
manager EA/99*
STRAKOSCH, Mme. [née Amalia
Patti] (fl 1848) singer HAS
STRAKOSCH, Charles G. (d 1965
[82]) assistant manager, manager
BP/50*
STRAKOSCH, Maurice (1825?-87)
Moravian musician, composer,
manager CDP, ES, HAS, NYM
STRAKOSCH, Max (1835-92) mana-
ger CDP
STRANACK, Wallace (d 1950 [78])
actor, business manager BE*,
WWT/14*
STRANGE, Frederick (d 1878 [51])
manager EA/79*
STRANGE, Glenn (d 1973 [74])
performer BP/58*
STRANGE, Michael (1890-1950)
American actress DAB, TW/7,
WWA/3
STRANGE, Robert (d 1975 [61])
actor WWT/7-10
STRASBERG, Lee (b 1901) Ameri-
can director, actor, producer,
coach AAS, BE, CB, COC,

ES, NTH, PDT, WWT/15-16
STRASBERG, Paula (d 1966 [55])
American actress, director,
coach BE, TW/22
STRASBERG, Susan (b 1938)
American actress BE, CB,
ES, TW/12-20
STRASSBERG, Max (d 1968 [55])
performer BP/53*
STRASSBERG, Morris (1897-1974)
actor TW/26, 30
STRASSER, Ilona (d 1976 [55])
performer BP/60*
STRASSER, Robin (b 1945)
American actress TW/23,
29
STRATEN, Mary M. (b 1940)
American actress TW/29
STRATER, Christopher (b 1943)
American actor TW/23
STRATFORD, Dr. (fl 1784) Irish?
dramatist CP/3
STRATFORD, Robert (fl 1631)
actor DA
STRATFORD, William (d 1625)
actor DA
STRATHMORE, Countess of
see Bowes, Mary Eleanor
STRATTON, Charles see
"Thumb, Tom"
STRATTON, Chester (1915-70)
American actor TW/4-8, 27
STRATTON, Eugene (1861-1918)
American variety artist CDP,
COC, GRB/1-4, OC/1-3
STRATTON, John (b 1925) Eng-
lish actor WWT/11-16
STRATTON, John American
actor TW/28
STRATTON, Lottie (d 1907)
EA/08*
STRATTON, Nellie (fl 1900?)
singer CDP
STRATTON, Sam (d 1967 [80])
publicist BP/52*
STRAUS, Oskar (1870-1954)
Austrian composer CB, ES,
TW/10, WWA/3
STRAUS, Sylvie (b 1923) Amer-
ican actress TW/26
STRAUSBAUGH, Warren L. (b
1909) American educator BE
STRAUSBERG, Morris O. (d
1974 [62]) executive BP/58*
STRAUSS, Helen American lit-
erary representative BE
STRAUSS, John (b 1920) Amer-
ican composer, conductor,

musician BE
STRAUSS, Joseph (d 1870 [42])
composer EA/71*, WWT/14*
STRAUSS, Richard (1864-1949)
German composer CB, ES,
WWM
STRAUSS, Robert (1913-75) Amer-
ican actor BE
STRAUSSLER, Tom see Stoppard,
Tom
STRAVINSKY, Igor (1882-1971)
Russian composer, conductor
CB, ES
STRAYCOCK, J. (fl 1804) drama-
tist CP/3
STREAMER, Volney (b 1853) Amer-
ican actor WWM
STREATER, Robert (1624-80) Eng-
lish painter COC, OC/1-3
STREDHELER, Josephine (b 1847)
English dancer HAS
STREET, Ann see Barry, Mrs.
Spranger
STREET, Mrs. Fred see Cousins,
Rosie
STREET, George Slythe (1867-
1936) English examiner of plays
WWT/3-8, WWW/3
STREETER, F. (fl 1778) dramatist
CP/3
STREETER, George Wellington (d
1921) circus proprietor WWA/4
STREIFORD, Hobart A. (d 1974
[63]) performer BP/59*
STREISAND, Barbra (b 1942)
American actress, singer AAS,
BE, CB, ES, TW/18-22, WWT/
14-16
STREIT, Pierre (d 1975 [52]) pro-
ducer/director/choreographer
BP/60*
STRENGTH, William T. (d 1973
[45]) performer BP/58*
STRETCH, John (fl 1635) actor
DA
STRETTON, George (fl 1835) singer
CDP
STRICKLAND, Cowles (d 1971
[68]) director TW/28
STRICKLAND, Enfield (d 1964
[94]) performer BE*, BP/49*
STRICKLAND, Mrs. Frank S.
see Scott, Louie
STRICKLAND, Helen (d 1938 [75])
American actress BE*, BP/22*
STRICKLAND, Robert (d 1845 [47])
actor CDP
STRICKLER, Jerry (b 1939) Amer-

actor BE, TW/19, 22, 24
STRICKLYN, Ray (b 1930)
American actor TW/9-16
STRIDE, James (d 1891 [74])
box office keeper EA/92*
STRIDE, John (b 1936) English
actor TW/18-20, WWT/14-16
STRIDEL, Gene (d 1973 [46])
performer BP/57*
STRIKER, Joseph (d 1974 [74])
actor TW/30
STRIKER, Richard (d 1974 [42])
performer BP/59*
STRIMPEL, Stephen (b 1937)
American actor TW/18-20,
25-26
STRINDBERG, August (1849-
1912) Swedish dramatist
COC, GRB/1-4, OC/3, WWT/1
STRINGER, Emma [Mrs. John
H. Stringer] (d 1877) EA/78*
STRINGER, Mrs. John H. see
Stringer, Emma
STRINGER, John Henry (d 1890
[40]) manager EA/91*
STRINGER, Richard (d 1897
[78]) manager EA/98*
STRINGFIELD, Lamar (1897-
1959) American composer
WWA/3
STRINGHAM, Edwin (d 1974 [83])
composer/lyricist BP/59*
STRINI, Severo (fl 1848) actor?
singer? HAS
STRITCH, Elaine (b 1925/26)
American actress, singer
AAS, BE, TW/4, 11-15,
23-24, 26-28, WWT/14-16
STROBEL, Heinrich (d 1970
[72]) critic BP/55*
STRODE, Warren Chetham (1897-
1974) English dramatist BTR/
74, WWT/10
STRODE, Dr. William (1602-45)
English dramatist CP/1-3,
FGF
STROLLO, Angie (d 1964) cos-
tumier BE*
STROMBERG, John (1853-1902)
composer BE*
STRONG, Austin (1881-1952)
American dramatist HJD,
MWD, TW/9, WWA/3, WWM,
WWT/1-11, WWW/5
STRONG, Henry C. (1842-87)
actor NYM
STRONG, Henry K. (fl 1823?)
dramatist EAP, RJ

STRONG, Jay (d 1953 [57]) actor,
director, producer BE*, BP/
38*
STRONG, Michael (b 1918/23)
American actor TW/3, 5-6, 9,
12, 21, 27
STRONG, Rudolph H. (c. 1847-77)
English actor NYM
STROOCK, Bianca (b 1896) Ameri-
can costume designer BE, TW/
3, 6-8
STROOCK, Geraldine (b 1925)
American actress TW/2
STROOCK, James E. (1891-1965)
American executive BE, TW/22
STROUD, Mrs. (d 1872) actress?
EA/73*
STROUD, Clarence G., Sr. (d
1973 [66]) performer BP/58*
STROUD, Gregory (b 1892) English
actor, singer WWT/5-9
STROUD, Henry Charles (d 1888
[61]) singer EA/89*
STROUDE, Mr. (fl 1662-71?)
dramatist CP/2-3
STROUSE, Charles (b 1928) Ameri-
can composer AAS, BE, ES,
WWT/15-16
STROWDEWIKE, Edmund (fl 1559-
68) actor DA
STROZZI, Kay American actress
WWT/7-9
STRUDWICK, Shepperd (b 1907)
American actor BE, TW/3,
9-16, 22-23, 25, 28, 30, WWT/
14-16
STRUGNELL, W. J. (d 1888)
musician EA/89*
STRUTHERS, Robert (b 1837) Scot-
tish actor HAS
STRUTHERS, Sally (b 1948) Ameri-
can actress CB
STRUTT, Joseph (d 1802 [55])
dramatist CP/3
STUART, Mrs. (fl 1800) actress
HAS
STUART, Mrs. [née Vos] (1815-54)
actress HAS
STUART, Mrs. A. B. [Mrs. R.
B. Stuart] (d 1889 [39]) EA/90*
STUART, Aimée (d 1890) Scottish
dramatist WWT/6-14
STUART, Alexander (d 1877) actor
EA/78*
STUART, Alexander (d 1909) stage
manager EA/11*
STUART, Alexander fat boy CDP
STUART, Alicia A. (d 1889 [83])

EA/90*

STUART, Mrs. A. M. see Newham, Rose

STUART, Ann (d 1809) actress CDP

STUART, Barney (d 1913 [41]) EA/14*

STUART, Mrs. C. see Lee, Katie

STUART, C. Douglas (b 1864) English secretary of music-hall artists' railway association GRB/1-3

STUART, Charles (fl 1777-91) Scottish dramatist CP/3, GT, TD/1-2

STUART, Charles (d 1882) music-hall manager EA/83*

STUART, Charles fat boy CDP

STUART, Colin (b 1825) Canadian actor HAS

STUART, Cora (d 1940 [83]) actress BE*, WWT/14*

STUART, Cosmo [Cosmo Stuart Charles Gordon-Lennox] (1869-1921) actor, dramatist COC, DD, GRB/1-4, WWS, WWT/1-3, WWW/1

STUART, Donald (d 1972 [52]) producer BP/56*

STUART, Donald Clive (1881-1943) American dramatist WWA/3

STUART, Dora [Dora Bradford] (d 1887) American actress NYM

STUART, Edward Patrick [James Gray] (b 1867) Scottish dancer GRB/1

STUART, Eliza (d 1877 [74]) actress WWT/14*

STUART, Ella (d 1902) gymnast, trapezist EA/03*

STUART, Frank (d 1917 [54]) EA/18*

STUART, Harry [Harry Stuart Hawkins] (b 1880) English actor GRB/1

STUART, Henri (d 1891 [46]) actor WWT/14*

STUART, Henry Robson see Robson, Stuart

STUART, Ian John (b 1940) English actor TW/28

STUART, James (d 1901 [36]) conjuror EA/02*

STUART, Jay American actor TW/30

STUART, Jeanne (b 1908) English actress WWT/7-11

STUART, Joel (b 1938) American actor TW/23

STUART, John (b 1804) actor CDP

STUART, John (b 1898) Scottish actor WWT/8-16

STUART, Laura (b 1938) American actress TW/25-28

STUART, Leslie [T. A. Barrett] (1864/66-1928) English composer GRB/1-4, WWT/1-5

STUART, Louisa (d 1867) actress? equestrienne? EA/68*

STUART, Lynne American actress TW/29

STUART, Madge (b 1897) actress WWT/6-7

STUART, Maggie (d 1897 [23]) actress EA/98*

STUART, Nick (d 1973 [69]) performer BP/57*

STUART, Otho [Otto Stuart Andreae] (1865-1930) manager, actor GRB/2-4, WWT/1-6

STUART, Philip (1887-1936) Indian/English dramatist WWT/6-8

STUART, Ralph (1860-1910) actor, dramatist SR

STUART, Mrs. R. B. see Stuart, Mrs. A. B.

STUART, Thomas (d 1878 [76]) actor EA/79*, WWT/14*

STUART, William (1821-86) manager, critic CDP

STUBBE, Mr. (fl 1632) dramatist CP/3, FGF

STUBBS, Morton Richard see Selten, Morton

STUBBS, Una actress, dancer WWT/16

STUBBS, William (d 1877) conductor EA/78*

STUCKEY, Phyllis actress WWT/4-7

STUCKMANN, Eugene (b 1917) American actor TW/3-4, 10, 26, 28

STUDHOLME, Marie (1875-1930) English actress GRB/1-4, WWT/1-6

STUDLEY, John B. (1831-1910) American actor HAS

STUDLY, John (d 1587) translator CP/1-3

STUDT, John Peter (d 1912) amusement caterer EA/13*

STUDT, Katherine see Broxup, Katherine

STUDT, Mary Ann (d 1917) EA/ 18*

STURANI, Giuseppe (1877-1940) Italian conductor WWA/1

STURCKEN, Frank W. (b 1929) American educator BE

STURGES, Charley (fl 1871?) dancer, singer CDP

STURGES, Preston (1898-1959) American dramatist ES, MWD, SR, TW/16, WWA/3, WWT/7-12

STURGESS, Arthur (d 1931) librettist, dramatist BE*, WWT/14*

STURGIS, Julian (1848-1904) American dramatist, librettist WWW/1

STURM, Justin (1899-1967) American dramatist, producer WWA/4

STURMY, John (fl 1722-28) dramatist CP/2-3, GT

STUTCHKOFF, Nahum (d 1965 [73]) dramatist BP/50*

STUTFIELD, George (fl 1632-35) actor DA

STUTHMAN, Fred (b 1919) American actor TW/28-30

STUTZ, Dick (d 1969 [60]) composer/lyricist BP/54*

STYLER, Alan (d 1970 [44]) performer BP/55*

STYLER, Charlotte (d 1971 [75]) performer BP/56*

STYLES, Edwin (1899-1960) English actor WWT/8-12

STYNE, Jule (b 1905) English composer, producer AAS, BE, ES, WWT/12-16

STYRES, Earle E. (d 1966 [69]) performer BP/51*

SUBTEL, Walter (d 1918 [37]) EA/19*

SUCHER, Joseph (1844-1908) conductor CDP

SUCHER, Mrs. Joseph see Sucher, Rosa

SUCHER, Rosa [Mrs. Joseph Sucher] (1849-1927) German singer CDP, ES

SUCKLING, Sir John (1609-42) English dramatist CP/1-3, DNB, FGF, HP, OC/3, RE

SUCKLING, John see Wyckham, John

SUCKLING, Robert see Chetwyn, Robert

SUDBURY, Thomas (d 1546) actor DA

SUDERMANN, Hermann (1857-1928) German dramatist COC, GRB/ 1-4, OC/3, WWT/1

SUDLOW, Bessie (d 1928 [78]) singer, actress CDP

SUDLOW, Eliza (d 1906 [87]) EA/ 07*

SUDLOW, Joan (d 1970 [78]) performer BP/54*

SUES, Leonard (d 1971 [50]) performer BP/56*

SUETT, Richard (1755-1805) English actor CDP, COC, DNB, GT, OC/1-3, OX, TD/1-2

SUGARMAN, Harry (d 1972 [72]) theatre owner BP/56*

SUGDEN, Charles (1850-1921) English actor DP, GRB/1-4, OAA/1-2, WWT/1-3, WWW/2

SUGDEN, Mrs. Charles [Helen Vane] (d 1940 [79]) actress WWT/2-4

SUGG, Catharine Lee see Hackett, Mrs. James Henry

SUGG, Lee (d 1831 [85]) ventriloquist EA/72*

SUGRUE, Frank (b 1927) American producer BE

SULKA, Elaine American actress TW/30

SULLAVAN, Margaret (1911-60) American actress CB, COC, ES, OC/3, TW/5-6, 9-12, 16, WWA/3, WWT/8-12

SULLIVAN, Mr. see Sylvian, Mons.

SULLIVAN, Mrs. (d 1882) EA/83*

SULLIVAN, Mrs. Amory see Stanhope, Adeline

SULLIVAN, Annette Kellerman (d 1975 [87]) performer BP/60*

SULLIVAN, Sir Arthur (1842-1900) English composer CDP, DNB, ES, HP, PDT, WWW/1

SULLIVAN, Barry (1821-91) Irish actor CDP, COC, DNB, HAS, OAA/1-2, OC/1-3

SULLIVAN, Barry (b 1912) American actor BE

SULLIVAN, Mrs. Barry see Sullivan, Mary

SULLIVAN, Brian (1919-69) American singer, actor CB, TW/2-3, 6, 26

SULLIVAN, Charles see Gas-
coigne, Charles
SULLIVAN, Mrs. Charles see
D'Alton, Marion
SULLIVAN, Deirdre (b 1925)
American actress TW/24
SULLIVAN, D. J. see Sullivan,
Jeremiah
SULLIVAN, Ed (d 1974 [73])
critic BP/59*
SULLIVAN, Rev. Edward S. (d
1970 [72]) circus priest BP/
54*
SULLIVAN, Elliott (1907-74)
American actor, director,
producer BE, TW/3
SULLIVAN, Francis L. (1903-56)
English actor TW/4, 6, 11-
13, WWA/3, WWT/7-12,
WWW/5
SULLIVAN, Frederic (d 1877
[39]) actor, singer CDP
SULLIVAN, Gael (1904-56) Amer-
ican executive WWA/3
SULLIVAN, George (d 1971) de-
signer BP/55*
SULLIVAN, James see Carney,
Pat
SULLIVAN, James E. (d 1931
[67]) American actor CDP,
GRB/2-4, WWT/1
SULLIVAN, James Francis (b
1880) American actor WWS
SULLIVAN, James W. (d 1974
[65]) designer BP/59*
SULLIVAN, Jeremiah [D. J.
Sullivan] (b 1937) American
actor TW/17-20, 23, 25-28
SULLIVAN, J. F. (d 1866 [25])
balladist HAS
SULLIVAN, Mrs. J. F. see
Clarke, Della
SULLIVAN, Jo American actress,
singer BE, TW/12-16
SULLIVAN, John A. (d 1964
[75+]) ticket broker BE*,
BP/49*
SULLIVAN, John Amory (d 1897)
actor EA/98*
SULLIVAN, John Florence see
Allen, Fred
SULLIVAN, John J. (d 1882)
actor CDP
SULLIVAN, Joseph ["Yankee"
Sullivan] (d 1917 [100]) show-
man, musician, clown, music-
hall proprietor EA/18*
SULLIVAN, Joseph (b 1918)

American actor TW/7, 11, 21-
24, 26-29
SULLIVAN, Kate (d 1912 [56])
burlesque actress EA/13*
SULLIVAN, Liam (b 1923) Ameri-
can actor TW/8-9, 24, 28-29
SULLIVAN, Mary [Mrs. Barry
Sullivan] (d 1908) EA/09*
SULLIVAN, Mella (d 1963 [87])
voice-drama coach BE*
SULLIVAN, Mike (d 1895 [40])
music-hall performer EA/97*
SULLIVAN, Pamela W. (d 1969
[30]) dramatist BP/53*
SULLIVAN, Patrick (b 1848) Eng-
lish actor HAS
SULLIVAN, Richard (d 1877) Irish
comedian EA/78*
SULLIVAN, Rose [Mrs. Arthur
Reece] (d 1895 [32]) Irish singer
EA/97*
SULLIVAN, Thomas Russell (1849-
1916) dramatist BE*
SULLIVAN, Master Tim (d 1904
[13]) actor EA/05*
SULLIVAN, William Francis (fl
1792-97) actor, dramatist TD/2
SULLON, Paul (d 1975 [55]) per-
former BP/60*
SULLY, Daniel [Daniel Sullivan]
(1855-1910) American actor,
dramatist CDP, GRB/3-4,
WWA/1, WWS
SULLY, Frank (d 1975 [67]) actor
BP/60*, WWT/16*
SULLY, Mariette (b 1878) French
actress, singer WWT/1-4
SULLY, Mathew (d 1812) English
actor HAS
SULLY, Robert (b 1918) American
actor TW/2-3
SULLY, Ruby (d 1971 [51]) drama-
tist BP/55*
SULLY, Thomas F. (fl 1870?)
dancer, singer CDP
SULLY, William (d 1969) performer
BP/54*
SULZER, Elmer G. (d 1976 [72])
educator, publicist BP/60*
SUMAC, Yma (b 1927) Peruvian
singer CB, TW/8
SUMMERFIELD, Eleanor (b 1921)
English actress WWT/11-14
SUMMERS, Ann (d 1974 [54]) per-
former BP/58*
SUMMERS, Arthur (d 1969 [59])
agent BP/53*
SUMMERS, Mrs. Charles see

Summers, Emily Jane
SUMMERS, David (b 1952) American actor TW/30
SUMMERS, Dorothy (d 1964 [70]) actress BE*
SUMMERS, Emily Jane [Mrs. Charles Summers] (d 1882) actress EA/84*
SUMMERS, J. W. (d 1893) American comedian EA/94*
SUMMERS, Louisa (d 1879 [42]) burlesque actress EA/80*
SUMMERS, Madlyn Jane American actress, dancer WWS
SUMMERS, Montague (1880-1946/48) English critic, historian COC, OC/1-3, WWT/5-10
SUMMERS, Oliver (d 1878) comedian, buffo singer EA/79*
SUMMERS, Peter (d 1888 [47]) EA/89*
SUMMERS, Styles Joseph (d 1917 [69]) musician EA/18*
SUMMERS, Vikki American actress TW/26
SUMMERS, Walter (d 1905 [38]) dramatist GRB/1
SUMMERSON, James Henry (d 1875 [36]) music-hall performer EA/76*
SUMMERTON, Peter (d 1969 [40]) producer/director/choreographer BP/54*
SUMMERVILLE, Amelia (d 1934 [71]) Irish actress, singer WWA/1, WWM, WWS
SUMMERVILLE, Annie actress CDP
SUMMERVILLE, Hamilton S. [James H. Drew] (d 1888) Negro minstrel EA/89*
SUMMERVILLE, Slim (d 1946 [54]) American actor BE*
SUMNER, Geoffrey (b 1908) English actor WWT/15-16
SUMNER, John (d 1651) actor DA
SUMNER, John (b 1924) English director WWT/16
SUMNER, Mary (1888-1956) English actress WWT/4-7
SUMNER, Reginald (d 1897 [46]) manager EA/98*
SUMNER, Stanley (d 1971 [81]) manager BP/56*
SUNDBERG, Clinton (b 1906) American actor BE, TW/12

SUNDERLAND, Nan (d 1973) actress TW/30
SUNDERLAND, Scott (b 1883) English actor WWT/5-11
SUNDGAARD, Arnold (b 1909) American dramatist BE
SUNDSTEN, Lani (b 1949) American actress TW/30
SUNDSTROM, Florence (b 1918) American actress BE, TW/3
SUNDSTROM, Frank Swedish? actor TW/2
SUNGHAM, Harry ["The Nubian King"] (d 1893) Negro comedian EA/94*
SUNSHINE, Marion (d 1963 [66]) actress, singer TW/19
SURATT, Valeska (fl 1900s) American vaudevillian WWM
SURMAN, Joseph (d 1871 [66]) singer? EA/72*
SUROVY, Nicholas (b 1944) American actor TW/21, 30
SUSANN, Jacqueline (1921-74) American actress CB
SUSINI [Agostino Guillano] (d 1883 [60]) singer HAS
SUSINI, Isabella (d 1862) singer CDP
SUSSKIND, David (b 1920) American producer BE, CB
SUTCLIFFE, Mrs. Alfred (d 1910 [34]) EA/11*
SUTCLIFFE, Richard Nelson see Steyne, Nelson
SUTER, Frederick (d 1896 [21]) actor EA/97*
SUTER, W. E. (d 1882 [70]) dramatist, comedian BE*, EA/83*, WWT/14*
SUTER, William see Suter, W. E.
SUTHERD, Mrs. Arthur (d 1888) singer EA/89*
SUTHERLAND, A. Edward (d 1974 [77]) performer BP/58*
SUTHERLAND, Agnes M. (fl 1857) English singer HAS
SUTHERLAND, Alec (d 1973 [35]) designer BP/57*
SUTHERLAND, Annie [Mrs. Charles Harding] (1867-1942/43) American actress GRB/3-4, WWA/2, WWT/1-9
SUTHERLAND, Birdie (d 1955 [81]) actress BE*, WWT/14*
SUTHERLAND, Efua (b 1924) Ghanaian dramatist CD

SUTHERLAND, Evelyn Greenleaf (1855-1908) American dramatist GRB/2-4, WWS

SUTHERLAND, Mrs. Evelyn Greenleaf see Rutherford, John

SUTHERLAND, Frank (d 1894 [57]) acting manager EA/95*

SUTHERLAND, Fred [Fred Anderson] (d 1889) acrobat EA/90*

SUTHERLAND, Joan (b 1926) Australian singer CB, ES

SUTHERLAND, Marie [Marie King] (d 1898) actress EA/99*

SUTHERLAND, Robert C. (d 1962 [79]) theatre operator BE*

SUTHERLAND, Roy see Sothern, Hugh

SUTHERLAND, Victor (1894-1968) American actor TW/4, 25

SUTHERLAND, Will see Belasco, Will

SUTHERLAND, William A. (d 1969 [52]) performer BP/54*

SUTHERLAND, W. R. (d 1904 [50]) actor EA/97

SUTORIUS, James L. (b 1944) American actor TW/26, 28-30

SUTRO, Alfred (1863-1933) English dramatist DNB, ES, GRB/1-4, MH, MWD, WWS, WWT/1-7, WWW/3

SUTTON, Mrs. (fl 1841-45) singer HAS

SUTTON, Charles [H. Bunth] (d 1904) performer? EA/05*

SUTTON, Dolores American actress TW/28

SUTTON, Dudley (b 1933) English actor TW/22

SUTTON, Emily (fl 1841) singer CDP

SUTTON, Ernest see Sarl, Ernest James

SUTTON, Frank (d 1908 [42]) actor EA/09*

SUTTON, Frank (d 1974 [51]) performer BP/59*

SUTTON, Henry (d 1911) managing director EA/12*

SUTTON, Henry (b 1926) American actor TW/30

SUTTON, John P. (d 1887) actor NYM

SUTTON, Paul (d 1970 [58]) performer BP/54*

SUTTON, Robert (fl 1550) actor DA

SUTTON, Sam (d 1896 [58]) music-hall chairman EA/97*

SUTTON, Sambo [James Henry Patterson] (d 1902) Negro comedian EA/03*

SUTTON, Tom (b 1874) English conductor, composer, pianist GRB/1

SUTTON, Will (d 1907) performer? EA/08*

SUTTON-VANE, Frank (d 1913) EA/14*

SUTTON-VANE, Vane (1888-1963) actor, dramatist, stage manager WWT/4-8

SUZMAN, Janet (b 1939) South African actress AAS, CB, WWT/15-16

SUZUKI, Pat (b 1930?/34) American singer CB, TW/14, 16, 30

SVANHOLM, Set (1904-64) Swedish singer, director CB, WWA/4

SVELTO (d 1895 [13]) musician EA/96*

SVENDSEN, Olaf (d 1888 [56]) musician EA/89*

SVERDLIN, Lev (d 1969 [57]) performer BP/54*

SVOBODA, Josef (b 1920) Czech scene designer COC, WWT/16

SWAFFER, Hannen (1879-1962) English critic, journalist WWT/5-13, WWW/6

SWAIN, Elizabeth (b 1941) English actress TW/25, 27, 30

SWAINE, G. B. (fl 1849) actor, singer CDP

SWALLOW, Fred (d 1900) circus performer EA/01*

SWALLOW, John (d 1895 [76]) circus performer EA/96*

SWALLOW, J. T. (d 1871) concert speculator EA/73*

SWALLOW, Margaret (1896-1932) English actress WWT/6

SWALLOW, William Charles (d 1900 [22]) EA/01*

SWAN, Bradford F. (d 1976 [68]) critic BP/60*

SWAN, Charles (d 1908 [80]) actor EA/09*

SWAN, John (d 1861) actor WWT/14*

SWAN, Lew (d 1964 [69]) performer BE*

SWAN, Mark Elbert (1871-1942)

American dramatist WWT/
4-9

SWAN, Paul (d 1972 [88]) American dancer, actor WWA/5

SWANBOROUGH, Ada (d 1893
[48]) English actress CDP,
OAA/1-2

SWANBOROUGH, Arthur (d 1895
[58]) manager EA/97*, WWT/
14*

SWANBOROUGH, Mrs. Arthur
see Bufton, Eleanor

SWANBOROUGH, Edward (d 1908
[67]) music-hall manager
GRB/4*

SWANBOROUGH, Fanny [Fanny
Hughes] (d 1888 [45]) actress
EA/89*

SWANBOROUGH, Louisa (fl 1856)
actress CDP

SWANBOROUGH, Mary Ann (d
1889 [85]) lessee, actress
EA/90*, WWT/14*

SWANBOROUGH, William Henry
(d 1886 [56/57]) actor, manager EA/88*, WWT/14*

SWANN, Caroline Burke (d 1964
[51]) American producer, director, dramatist, actress
BE, TW/21

SWANN, Donald [Ibrahim] (b
1923) English composer, songwriter, entertainer AAS, BE,
CB, COC, ES, OC/3, TW/
23, WWT/13-16

SWANN, Elaine American actress
TW/20-21

SWANN, Francis (b 1913) American dramatist, director BE

SWANN, William (d 1872 [15])
gymnast EA/73*

SWANSEN, Larry (b 1930) American actor TW/30

SWANSON, Britt (b 1947) American dancer, actress? TW/
29-30

SWANSON, Gloria (b 1899) American actress BE, ES, TW/1,
8, 28-29, WWT/16

SWANSON, Larry (b 1930) American actor TW/25-26, 28

SWANSON, Marcella (d 1973
[80s]) performer BP/58*

SWANSTON, Eliard [or Hilliard]
(d 1651) English actor COC,
DA, OC/1-3

SWANTON, John G. (d 1886 [48])
actor EA/87*

SWANTON, Mary (d 1918 [76])
EA/19*

SWANWICK, Anna (1813-99) English
translator DNB

SWARTHOUT, Gladys (1904-69)
American singer CB, TW/26,
WWA/5

SWARTOUT, Norman Lee (b 1879)
American dramatist WWM

SWASH, Bob (b 1929) English producing manager WWT/16

SWAYNE, Eleanor American actress TW/2

SWEARINGEN, John (b 1935) American actor TW/26-27

SWEARS, Herbert (d 1946 [77])
dramatist BE*, WWT/14*

SWEASEY, John Samuel (d 1890)
music-hall performer? EA/91*

SWEATMAN, Willis P. (1864-1930)
American minstrel, actor, minstrel manager CDP, SR

SWEENEY, Andrew (d 1892) cannon-ball performer EA/93*

SWEENEY, Claire see Degener,
Claire S.

SWEENEY, John J. (d 1892 [28])
music-hall performer EA/93*

SWEENY, Joel Walker (1813-60)
actor, musician, minstrel
manager CDP

SWEENY, J. W. (d 1900) Irish
comedian EA/01*

SWEET, Blanche (b 1896) American
actress BE, TW/2-3, 6

SWEET, Dolph (b 1920) American
actor, director BE, TW/22-26,
28, 30

SWEET, Mrs. H. see Howard,
Carrie

SWEET, Sam (d 1948 [27]) actor
TW/4

SWEETEN, Robert G. (d 1972
[59]) publicist BP/57*

SWEETLAND, Reynolds (d 1970
[79]) critic BP/54*

SWEETMAN, Robert (d 1892 [57])
actor EA/93*

SWEETMAN, Mrs. Robert (d 1886)
actress EA/87*

SWEETMAN, Mrs. Robert see
Sweetman, Rose

SWEETMAN, Rose [Mrs. Robert
Sweetman] (d 1871) EA/72*

SWEIGARD, Lulu E. (d 1974) dance
educator? BP/59*

SWENDALL, Mr. (fl 1790-1803)
actor, manager TD/1-2

SWENSON, Alfred G. (1883-1941) actor CB

SWENSON, Inga (b 1932/34) American actress, singer BE, TW/13-17, 20-22, 25, WWT/14-16

SWENSON, Karl actor TW/1

SWENSON, Linda (b 1945) American actress TW/29

SWENSON, Swen (b 1932/34) American actor, singer, dancer BE, TW/16-20, 23, 30, WWT/14-16

SWERLING, Jo (b 1897) Russian/American dramatist BE

SWETE, E. Lyall (1865-1930) English actor, dramatist, producer GRB/1-4, WWT/1-6

SWIFT, Mr. (fl 1806) dramatist CP/3

SWIFT, Mr. (fl 1869) singer EA/70*

SWIFT, Alexandra see Carlisle, Alexandra

SWIFT, Clive (b 1936) English actor WWT/15-16

SWIFT, Eva (d 1901 [24]) EA/02*

SWIFT, Jonathan (1667-1745) Irish author CP/2-3

SWIFT, Joseph (d 1869) singer CDP

SWIFT, Joseph (d 1888 [37]) EA/89*

SWINARSKI, Konrad (d 1975 [46]) Polish director WWT/16*

SWINBOURNE, Mr. (fl 1858-59) English actor HAS

SWINBOURNE, Ann Elizabeth [Mrs. Thomas Swinbourne] (d 1886 [57]) EA/87*

SWINBOURNE, Charlotte Elizabeth see Vandenhoff, Charlotte Elizabeth

SWINBOURNE, Harriett (d 1883 [79]) EA/84*

SWINBOURNE, Thomas (d 1895 [72]) English actor OAA/1-2

SWINBOURNE, Mrs. Thomas see Swinbourne, Ann Elizabeth

SWINBURNE, Algernon Charles (1837-1909) English dramatist DNB, HP, NTH, WWW/1

SWINBURNE, John [J. P. Edwards] (fl 1868) English actor HAS

SWINBURNE, Mercia (b 1900) Australian actress WWT/6-11

SWINBURNE, Nora (b 1902) English actress WWT/5-16

SWINBURNE, Thomas (d 1895 [72]) actor CDP

SWINDEN, Edward (d 1887 [77]) EA/88*

SWINDLEHURST, Lizzie see Lillie, Miss

SWINERD, Esther (d 1899 [67]) EA/00*

SWINERD, Henry (d 1909 [57]) manager EA/11*

SWINERD, Mrs. Henry (d 1906 [51]) EA/07*

SWINEY, J. M. dramatist CP/3

SWINEY, Owen (c. 1675-1754) Irish actor, manager COC, CP/1-3, DNB, GT, OC/1-3, TD/1-2

SWINGLER, Randall (d 1967 [58]) dramatist BP/52*

SWINHOE, Gilbert (fl 1658) English dramatist CP/1-3, FGF

SWINLEY, E. Ion (1891-1937) English actor AAS, WWT/2-8

SWINNERTON, Abel (fl 1628) actor DA

SWINNERTON, Thomas (fl 1603-28) actor DA

SWINNY, Owen Mac (d 1754) manager CDP

SWINSTEAD, Joan (b 1903) English actress WWT/9-13

SWINSTEAD, Muriel see Ross, Oriel

SWINY, Owen Mac see Swiney, Owen

SWIRE, Willard (b 1910) American actor TW/4

SWITZER, Carl (d 1959 [33]) actor BE*

SWOPE, Herbert Bayard, Jr. American director, producer BE

SWOPE, Tracy Brooks (b 1952) American actress TW/25

SWOR, Burt (1873-1947) American minstrel SR

SWOR, John (d 1965 [87]) performer BP/50*

SYDENHAM, Ernest (d 1875 [25]) comic singer EA/76*

SYDENHAM, George English manager, actor GRB/1

SYDNEY, Basil (1894-1968) English actor AAS, BE, TW/24, WWT/4-14

SYDNEY, Harry (d 1870 [45]) singer, composer, songwriter CDP
SYDNEY, Lewis (d 1941) comedian BE*, WWT/14*
SYDNEY, Sir Philip (1554-86) English dramatist CP/1-3
SYDNEY, Vernon (fl 1874?) minstrel, singer CDP
SYDOW, Jack (b 1921) American director, dramatist BE
SYERS, Morris Robert (d 1876 [58]) music-hall proprietor EA/77*
SYFERWESTE, Richard (fl 1602) actor DA
SYKES, Mrs. Arthur see Ganthony, Nellie
SYKES, George Edward see Murray, J. K.
SYKES, Jerome H. (d 1903 [35]) American singer, comedian WWA/1
SYKES, Percival H. T. see Murray, Percy
SYLOS, Frank Paul (d 1976 [75]) designer BP/60*
SYLVA, Eloi (fl 1885) Russian singer CDP
SYLVA, Ilena (b 1916) English actress WWT/10
SYLVA, Marguerite (d 1957 [81]) Belgian singer TW/13, WWA/3
SYLVA, Vesta (b 1907) English actress WWT/5-7
SYLVAIN, Mons. (fl 1840) dancer CDP
SYLVAIN, Eugène (d 1930 [79]) actor WWT/14*
SYLVAIN, Louise (d 1930 [56]) actress BE*, WWT/14*
SYLVAINE, Vernon (1897-1957) English actor AAS, WWT/6-12, WWW/5
SYLVESTER, A. B. (d 1878 [37]) Negro comedian EA/79*
SYLVESTER, Bernard see Petronj, Egidio
SYLVESTER, Bob (d 1975 [68]) columnist WWT/16*
SYLVESTER, Frank see Franks, Sydney
SYLVESTER, Louisa (b 1851) American singer, actress CDP, HAS
SYLVESTER, Robert (d 1975 [68]) critic BP/59*

SYLVESTER, William (b 1922) American actor TW/12-13, WWT/11-15
SYLVESTER, William George (d 1916) caterer EA/17*
SYLVESTRE, Cleo English actress TW/30
SYLVIA, Estrella (d 1895) dancer EA/96*
SYLVIAN, Mons. [Sullivan] (fl 1833-40) dancer HAS
SYLVIE (d 1970 [88]) performer BP/54*
SYMCOCKES (fl 1604-05) actor DA
SYMINGTON, Donald (b 1925) American actor TW/10-13, 24, 27-29
SYMMONDS, Rev. Charles (fl 1796) dramatist CP/3
SYMMONS (fl 1800) dramatist CP/3
SYMNS, Thomas Kelly (d 1873 [52]) comedian, comic singer EA/74*
SYMONDS, Emily Morse see Paston, George
SYMONDS, Margaret see Davey, Nuna
SYMONDS, Robert (b 1926) American actor, director, producer BE, TW/22-30, WWT/15-16
SYMONS, Arthur William (1865-1945) Welsh dramatist, critic DNB
SYMONS, Beatrice [Mrs. David Symons] (d 1905) EA/06*
SYMONS, Daniel (fl 1865-69) manager, actor, business manager HAS
SYMONS, Mrs. David see Symons, Beatrice
SYMONS, John (fl 1583-99) tumbler DA
SYMPSON, Tony (b 1906) English actor WWT/12-16
SYMS, Algernon [Syms-Wilcox] (d 1915 [71]) English actor GRB/1-3
SYMS, Mrs. Algernon see Syms, Rosina
SYMS, Robert John (d 1895) EA/96*
SYMS, Rosina [Mrs. Algernon Syms] (d 1901) EA/02*
SYMS, Sylvia English actress ES
SYMS, Sylvia (b 1920) American actress TW/15, 26
SYMS, Walter (d 1903) EA/04*

SYMS-WILCOX, Algernon see
Syms, Algernon
SYNGE, Mrs. see Granville,
Charlotte
SYNGE, John Millington (1871-
1909) Irish dramatist COC,
DNB, ES, HP, MD, MH,
MWD, NTH, OC/1-3, PDT,
RE, WWW/1
SYPHER, Willie (b 1905) Amer-
ican educator BE
SYRUS, Napoleon [James Syrus
Tully] (d 1891 [63]) comic
singer EA/92*
SYSE, Glenna (b 1927) Canadian
critic BE
SZABO, Sandor (b 1915) Hungarian
actor BE
SZELL, George (1897-1970) Hun-
garian conductor CB

- T -

T., J. (fl 1662) dramatist CP/3
T., R. (fl 1619) actor DA
TAAFF, Joseph Pierce (d 1890
[56]) music-hall performer
EA/91*
TAAFF, Mrs. J. P. (d 1867)
singer? EA/68*
TABACHNIK, Abraham Ber (d
1970 [68]) critic BP/55*
TABBERT, William (1921-74)
American actor, singer BE,
TW/2-17, WWT/11-14
TABELAK, John-Michael librett-
tist CD
TABER, Richard (1891-1957)
American actor TW/3, 5-6,
14
TABER, Robert (1865-1904)
American actor PDT, SR
TABOR, Disiree (d 1957 [57])
actress, singer TW/13
TABOR, Ethel F. (d 1972 [70s])
costumier BP/56*
TABOR, Joan (d 1968 [35]) per-
former BP/53*
TABORI, George (b 1914) Hun-
garian dramatist, director
BE, CD, WWT/15-16
TABORI, Kristoffer (b 1952)
American actor TW/25-26,
30
TABRAR, Joseph (1857-1931)
English composer WWW/3
TABRAR, Tom (d 1904 [50])

music-hall comedian EA/05*
TACAGNI, Benedict (d 1880 [6])
actor EA/81*
TACCHINARDI, Nicola (1772-1859)
singer CDP
TACKABERRY, John (d 1969 [55])
dramatist BP/54*
TACKNEY, Stanley (b 1909) Amer-
ican actor, director, producer
BE
TACKOVA, Jarmilla (d 1971 [59])
performer BP/56*
TADEMA, Sir Laurence Alma see
Alma-Tadema, Sir Laurence
TADLOCK, Renee (b 1949) Ameri-
can actress TW/30
TADOLINI, Eugenia (b 1810) singer
CDP
TAFLER, Sidney (b 1916) English
actor TW/2
TAFT, Elizabeth see Stephens,
Mrs.
TAFT, James Gordon (d 1971 [42])
lawyer BP/56*
TAGG, Alan (b 1928) English de-
signer AAS, ES, WWT/15-16
TAGGART, Hal (d 1971 [79]) per-
former BP/56*
TAGGER, Theodor see Bruckner,
Friedrich
TAGLIAVINI, Ferruccio (b 1913)
Italian singer CB
TAGLIONI, Mons. (d 1868) EA/69*
TAGLIONI, Amalie see Taglioni,
Mme. Paul
TAGLIONI, Filippo (d 1871 [94])
dancer, choreographer WWT/14*
TAGLIONI, Louise dancer CDP
TAGLIONI, Luigia (d 1893 [70])
dancer EA/94*
TAGLIONI, Marie (1804/09-84)
Swedish dancer CDP, DNB, ES
TAGLIONI, Marie P. dancer CDP
TAGLIONI, Paul (1808-84) dancer
CDP, HAS
TAGLIONI, Mme. Paul (d 1881)
dancer CDP, HAS
TAHSE, Martin (b 1930) American
producer BE
TAILLADE, Paul (d 1898 [72]) actor
BE*, WWT/14*
TAILOR, Robert (fl 1597-1601)
actor DA
TAILOR, Robert (fl 1614) dramatist
CP/1-3, DNB, FGF
TAIT, Annie (d 1886) composer
EA/87*
TAIT, Edward J. (c. 1879-1947)

Australian producer SR
TAIT, Sir Frank (d 1965 [81])
Australian manager WWT/14*
TAIT, Herbert see Ross,
Herbert
TAIT, James N. (d 1961 [85])
Australian manager WWT/14*
TAJIRI, Larry S. (b 1914) Amer-
ican editor, critic BE
TAJO, Halo (b 1915) Italian
singer ES
TALBERT, Rose Hershfield (d
1975 [91]) performer BP/59*
TALBOT, Mr. [Mr. Montague]
(fl 1800) actor TD/1-2
TALBOT, Mr. (fl 1820) Irish ac-
tor HAS
TALBOT, Mrs. [Mrs. Charles
Page] (d 1838) Irish actress
HAS
TALBOT, Mrs. see Clifford,
Miss E.
TALBOT, Miss (d 1865 [39]) ac-
tress EA/72*, WWT/14*
TALBOT, Charles (fl 1827?)
dramatist EAP, RJ
TALBOT, Evelyn [Mrs. Arthur
Keand] (d 1910) EA/11*
TALBOT, Hayden (b 1882)
American dramatist WWM
TALBOT, Henry (d 1894 [61])
actor, architect EA/95*
TALBOT, Howard [Howard Mun-
kittrick] (1865-1928) American
composer, conductor GRB/
1-4, WWA/1, WWT/1-5,
WWW/2
TALBOT, Mrs. Howard see
Bellamy, Ada
TALBOT, J. (fl 1686?) trans-
lator CP/2-3
TALBOT, John (d 1831) Irish
manager EA/72*
TALBOT, Lyle (b 1902) American
actor, director BE
TALBOT, Montague (1774-1831)
American/English actor,
manager CDP, DNB
TALBOT, Nita (b 1930) Ameri-
can actress TW/8-13, 25
TALBOT, Rupert (d 1917) singer
EA/18*
TALBOT, Slim (d 1973 [77])
stand-in BP/57*
TALBOT, William C. (d 1866
[27]) manager HAS
TALCOTT, Michael (b 1939)
American actor TW/26

TALENT, Bill (d 1974 [81]) per-
former BP/59*
TALFOURD, Francis (1828-62)
English? dramatist DNB
TALFOURD, Sir Thomas Noon
(1795-1854) English dramatist
CDP, COC, DNB, HP, NTH,
OC/1-3, SR
TALIAFERRO, Edith (1892/93-
1958) American actress ES,
TW/14, WWM, WWT/1-10
TALIAFERRO, Mabel (b 1887)
American actress BE, ES,
TW/1-9, WWM, WWS, WWT/
1-13
TALLCHIEF, Maria (b 1925) Amer-
ican dancer CB, ES, WWT/11-
12
TALLEY, William Edgar (d 1975
[64]) executive BP/60*
TALLIOTT, James (d 1877) ring
master EA/79*
TALLIS, Sir George (1867-1948)
manager WWT/5-9
TALLMAN, Ellen (d 1963 [73])
performer BE*
TALLMER, Jerry (b 1920) Ameri-
can critic, journalist BE
TALLON, Annie [Mrs. William
Tallon] (d 1897) EA/98*
TALLON, William (d 1910 [66])
actor EA/12*
TALLON, Mrs. William see
Tallon, Annie
TALMA, Charlotte (1771-1861)
actress CDP
TALMA, François-Joseph (1763-
1826) French actor CDP, COC,
OC/3, OX
TALMADGE, Constance (d 1973
[73]) actress BP/58*, WWT/16*
TALMADGE, Natalie (d 1969 [70])
performer BP/54*
TALMADGE, Norma (1897-1957)
American actress BE*
TALMAN, William (d 1968 [53])
performer BP/53*
TALMON-GROS, Walter (d 1973
[62]) performer BP/58*
TALOT, Alex (d 1861) actor HAS
TALVA, Galina (1930-68) American
actress TW/7-8, 25
TAMAGNO, Francesco (1850-1905)
Italian singer ES
TAMANTI, Mme. Bastatelli (d
1869 [100]) singer EA/70*
TAMANY, Mary (1856-1918) Amer-
ican comedienne SR

TAMARA [Tamara Drasin] (1907-43) Russian/American actress WWT/9-10

TAMBERLIK, Enrico (1820-89) Italian singer CDP, ES

TAMBURINI, Antonio (1800-76) Italian singer ES

TAMIRIS, Helen (1905-66) American choreographer, dancer BE, ES, TW/2-8, 23, WWA/4, WWT/11-14

TAMIROFF, Akim (1901-72) Russian actor BE, TW/29

TAMKIN, David (d 1975 [68]) composer/lyricist BP/60*

TAMS, Arthur W. (b 1848) American musical director WWM

TANDY, Jessica (b 1909) English/American actress AAS, BE, CB, ES, TW/4, 6-23, 26-27, 29-30, WWT/7-16

TANDY, Valerie (1921-65) English actress, singer WWT/11-12

TANGUAY, Eva (1878-1947) Canadian actress, singer DAB, GRB/3-4, SR, TW/3, WWS, WWT/1-5

TANNEHILL, Frances actress TW/1

TANNEN, Don (d 1974 [60s]) performer BP/58*

TANNEN, Julius (d 1965 [84]) performer BP/49*

TANNER, Miss see Robertson, Mrs. Brougham

TANNER, Annie Louise (d 1921 [65]) singer BE*, BP/5*

TANNER, Beatrice Stella see Campbell, Mrs. Patrick

TANNER, Carolyn (b 1927) American actress TW/4

TANNER, Cora (fl 1880-98) actress CDP, PP/3

TANNER, George (d 1870) pantaloon EA/71*

TANNER, Gordon (b 1918) Canadian actor TW/12

TANNER, James T. (d 1915 [56]) librettist WWT/2

TANNER, Jill (b 1943) English actress TW/29

TANNER, Tony (b 1932) English actor TW/22-23, 26-27, 29

TANNETT, Mrs. A. [Mrs. Charles S. Tanner] (d 1888 [38]) EA/89*

TANNETT, Mrs. B. (d 1882) actress EA/84*

TANNETT, Mrs. Charles S. see Tannett, Mrs. A.

TANNETT, Edward Harley (d 1875 [52]) songwriter EA/76*

TANNYHILL, Francis A. (b c. 1830) American actor HAS

TANNYHILL, Mrs. Francis A. [née Ella Clayton] (fl 1855) American actress HAS

TANSLEY, Derek (b 1917) English actor TW/9

TANSWELL, Bertram (b 1908) English director, actor BE

TAPLEY, Douglas (d 1916 [14]) EA/17*

TAPLEY, Joseph (fl 1885-90) actor DP

TAPLEY, Mrs. Joseph see Varley, Violet

TAPLIN, Mrs. William see Chambers, Harriet

TAPLINGER, Robert (d 1975 [66]) publicist BP/60*

TAPPING, Mrs. A. see Tapping, Lavinia

TAPPING, Alfred (d 1880) actor EA/82*, WWT/14*

TAPPING, Alfred B. (d 1928 [77]) actor, stage manager WWT/3-5

TAPPING, Mrs. Alfred B. [Florence Cowell] (1852-1926) actress EA/95, ES, OC/1-3, WWT/3-5

TAPPING, Lavinia [Mrs. A. Tapping] (d 1873) EA/74*

TARA, Sheila (d 1969 [81]) performer BP/54*

TARAS, John (b 1919) American choreographer, dancer ES

TARASOVA, Alla Konstantinovna (1898-1973) Russian actress WWT/13-14

TARBOCK, John (fl 1610) patentee DA

TARBUCK, Barbara (b 1942) American actress TW/26-27, 30

TARIOL-BAUGE, Anna (b 1872) French actress, singer WWT/1-4

TARJAN, George (d 1973 [63]) performer BP/58*

TARKINGTON, Newton Booth (1869-1946) American dramatist CB, COC, DAB, ES, GRB/3-4, HJD, HP, MH, MWD, NTH, OC/1-3, SR, TW/2, WWA/2, WWM, WWT/1-9, WWW/4

TARKINGTON, William O. (d 1962

[89]) talent representative, manager BE*

TARLETON, Diane American actress TW/29

TARLETON, Richard (1530-88) English clown, dramatist CDP, COC, CP/2-3, DA, DNB, ES, FGF, GT, NTH, OC/1-3

TARLOW, Florence (b 1929) American actress TW/24-29

TARN, Adam (d 1975 [73]) dramatist BP/60*

TARPEY, Tom (b 1943) American actor TW/26-27, 29-30

TARR, Edward Sinclair (b 1842) American actor HAS

TARRANT, George [Paul Pietro] (d 1880) clown EA/81*

TARRANT, L. Newell (b 1911) American director, manager, actor BE

TARRI, Suzette (d 1955 [74]) performer BE*, WWT/14*

TARTEL, Michael (b 1936) American actor TW/26

TASHMAN, Lilyan (1899-1934) American actress WWT/7

TASISTRO, Fitzgerald (fl 1841) actor HAS

TASK, Maggie American actress TW/24, 26, 28

TASKER, William (1740-1800) English dramatist CP/3

TASKER, William see Lee, Edgar

TASSEL, Hazel Mae (d 1973 [80]) performer BP/57*

TATE, Alfred (d 1908) EA/09*

TATE, Dennis (b 1938) American actor TW/24, 26-27, 29

TATE, Harry [Ronald Macdonald Hutchison] (1872-1940) Scottish actor COC, ES, OC/1-3, PDT, WWT/4-9

TATE, James W. (1875-1922) English composer, manager WWT/4

TATE, Margaret see Teyte, Maggie

TATE, Nahum (1652-1715) English dramatist COC, CP/1-3, DNB, GT, HP, NTH, OC/1-3

TATE, Reginald (1896-1955) English actress WWT/7-11

TATE, Mrs. Thomas C. see Busch, Mae

TATE, William Henry Gilbert (d 1900 [50]) agent EA/01*

TATHAM, John (fl 1632-64) dramatist CP/1-3, DNB, FGF

TATIN, Mons. (fl 1822) pantomimist HAS

TATNALL, Mrs. [Mrs. Pemberton] (fl 1822) actress HAS

TATTERDELL, Hugh (fl 1629) actor DA

TAUBE, Evert (d 1976 [85]) composer/lyricist BP/60*

TAUBENHAUS, Eugene see Doyle, Gene

TAUBER, Richard (1890/91/93-1948) Austrian/English actor, singer, composer, conductor ES, TW/4, WWA/2, WWT/7-10

TAUBIN, Amy (b 1939) American actress TW/23-24, 29

TAUBMAN, Howard (b 1907) American critic AAS, BE, WWT/14-15

TAUBMAN, Matthew (fl 1685-89) dramatist CP/3

TAULEE, Gladys (d 1975) performer BP/60*

TAUPIER, Gerald (b 1941) American actor TW/26

TAVARIS, Eric (b 1939) American actor TW/29

TAVARY, Mme. (d 1893 [34]) singer EA/94*

TAVEL, Ronald (b 1941) American dramatist, lyricist, director, actor CD, WWT/15-16

TAVERNER, William (d 1731) dramatist CP/1-3, DNB, GT, TD/1-2

TAWDE, George (b 1883) Scottish actor WWT/4-9

TAWYER, William (d 1625?) actor DA

TAYLEURE, Miss (fl 1842) actress, dancer HAS

TAYLEURE, Clifton W. (1830/31/32-1887/91) American actor, manager CDP, HAS, NTH

TAYLEURE, Harriet [Mrs. Joseph Tayleure] (d 1891 [50]) EA/92*

TAYLEURE, Jane (fl 1834?) actress CDP

TAYLEURE, John (1782-1861) actor CDP

TAYLEURE, Joseph (d 1894) EA/95*

TAYLEURE, Mrs. Joseph see Tayleure, Harriet

TAYLOR dramatist RJ
TAYLOR (fl early 17th cent)
actor DA
TAYLOR, Mr. (b 1777) English
singer, actor BS, GT
TAYLOR [of Norwich] (fl 1793-
1805) dramatist CP/3
TAYLOR, Mr. (fl 1794-1837)
actor HAS
TAYLOR, Mrs. [nee Valentine]
(fl 1789) actress TD/1-2
TAYLOR, Miss (d 1857) dancer
HAS
TAYLOR, Ada (d 1890 [17])
EA/91*
TAYLOR, Ada [Mrs. Fred Sims]
(d 1900) actress EA/01*
TAYLOR, Agnes [Mrs. Walter
Sealby] (d 1898) actress EA/
99*
TAYLOR, Alfred (d 1906 [61])
doorkeeper EA/07*
TAYLOR, Alma (d 1974 [79])
performer BP/58*
TAYLOR, Annie [Mrs. E. C.
Corlesse] (d 1896 [48]) actress
EA/97*
TAYLOR, Ashworth (d 1917)
musical director EA/18*
TAYLOR, Ben (d 1901) music-
hall comedian EA/02*
TAYLOR, Bianchi (d 1876) mu-
sician EA/77*
TAYLOR, Mrs. Billee see
Mayhew, Stella
TAYLOR, Cecil P. (b 1929)
Scottish dramatist CD, WWT/
15-16
TAYLOR, Charles (1781-1847)
English actor CDP, TD/2
TAYLOR, Charles (fl 1865) actor
HAS
TAYLOR, Charles (b 1940)
American actor TW/10
TAYLOR, Mrs. Charles [née
Herbert] (fl 1804) actress
TD/2
TAYLOR, Charles A. (1864-1942)
American producer, dramatist
CB, DAB
TAYLOR, Charles H. (d 1907
[46]) lyricist, dramatist
GRB/3
TAYLOR, Charles Western (fl
1819) English actor HAS
TAYLOR, Christopher (d 1913)
EA/14*
TAYLOR, Clarice (b 1927) Amer-

ican actress TW/25-30, WWT/
16
TAYLOR, Mrs. C. R. [née Nellie
Browne] (d 1864) actress HAS
TAYLOR, C. W. (b 1845) English
actor HAS
TAYLOR, David Joseph (d 1917)
EA/18*
TAYLOR, Deems (1885-1966)
American composer ES, HJD,
TW/23, WWA/4, WWT/8-10
TAYLOR, Don (b 1920) American
actor TW/11-12
TAYLOR, Don dramatist CD
TAYLOR, Dwight (b 1902) Ameri-
can dramatist BE
TAYLOR, Edward Fenton (b 1817)
English actor HAS
TAYLOR, Elizabeth (d 1874) per-
former? EA/75*
TAYLOR, Elizabeth see Bayzand,
Mrs. William
TAYLOR, Emma Elizabeth (1838-
63) American actress CDP,
HAS
TAYLOR, Enid Stamp (1904-46)
English actress, singer WWT/
8-9
TAYLOR, Estelle (1899-1958)
American actress BE*, BP/42*,
WWT/14*
TAYLOR, Ethel S. (d 1975 [80])
dramatist BP/59*
TAYLOR, Florence [Mrs. Herbert
Taylor] (d 1911 [34]) EA/12*
TAYLOR, Frederica (fl 1869-76)
American/English actress
OAA/1-2
TAYLOR, Frederick see Bush,
Fred
TAYLOR, Frederick Gray (d 1889
[45]) comic singer EA/90*
TAYLOR, G. Bartholomew (d 1890
[36]) director EA/91*
TAYLOR, Geoffrey (b 1945) Amer-
ican actor TW/27-28
TAYLOR, George (b 1930) English
actor TW/29-30
TAYLOR, George Henry (d 1876)
musician EA/77*
TAYLOR, Gerhard (b 1827) musi-
cian CDP
TAYLOR, Greene (d 1907) actor,
singer EA/08*
TAYLOR, Harriet D. [Mrs. Walter
Lacy] (1808-74) actress CDP
TAYLOR, Harry (d 1889) comedian,
singer CDP

TAYLOR, Harvey (d 1975 [63])
critic BP/59*

TAYLOR, Helen Marie American actress, director, educator
BE

TAYLOR, Sir Henry (1800-86)
dramatist HP

TAYLOR, Mrs. Henry see
Taylor, Margaret

TAYLOR, Henry J. P. (d 1910
[67]) proprietor EA/11*

TAYLOR, Herbert see Rolyat,
Dan

TAYLOR, Mrs. Herbert see
Taylor, Florence

TAYLOR, H. J. (d 1917) manager
EA/18*

TAYLOR, Holland (b 1943) American actress TW/24-26, 29-30

TAYLOR, Howard P. (b 1851)
dramatist SR

TAYLOR, Isaac (d 1880) musician EA/81*

TAYLOR, James (fl 1868) English comic singer HAS

TAYLOR, James (d 1872 [31])
"second-sighted youth" EA/73*

TAYLOR, James (d 1889) conjuror EA/90*

TAYLOR, James (d 1895) musichall comedian EA/96*

TAYLOR, James Goulde (d 1904
[67]) English actor OAA/2

TAYLOR, James H. (d 1884)
lessee EA/85*

TAYLOR, James H. (1825-97)
American actor CDP, HAS

TAYLOR, Mrs. James V. see
Joyce, Laura

TAYLOR, Jennie see Edgar,
Mrs. Richard

TAYLOR, Mrs. J. G. [née
Josephine Ruth] (d 1877) EA/
78*

TAYLOR, John (fl 1561-57)
choirmaster DA

TAYLOR, John (1580-1654) English dramatist CP/3, FGF,
GT, HP

TAYLOR, John (fl 1594-98) actor
DA

TAYLOR, John (fl 1599?) actor
DA

TAYLOR, John actor TD/2

TAYLOR, John (1757-1832) critic
CDP

TAYLOR, Mrs. John, I see
Duill, Mrs. John Lewis

TAYLOR, John Russell (b 1935)
English critic AAS, WWT/15-16

TAYLOR, Joseph (c. 1585-1652)
English actor COC, DA, DNB,
GT, NTH, OC/1-3

TAYLOR, June (b 1918) American choreographer BE

TAYLOR, Kate (fl 1852) actress
HAS

TAYLOR, Laurette [Laurette
Cooney] (1884-1946) American
actress AAS, CB, COC, DAB,
ES, NTH, OC/1-3, PDT, TW/
1-3, WWA/2, WWT/3-10

TAYLOR, Louise (d 1965 [57])
performer BP/49*

TAYLOR, Louise (d 1974 [89])
performer BP/58*

TAYLOR, Mabel (d 1970) actress
TW/27

TAYLOR, Madeline (d 1870 [19])
actress EA/71*

TAYLOR, Margaret (fl 1815-19)
actress CDP

TAYLOR, Margaret [Mrs. Henry
Taylor] (d 1901) EA/03*

TAYLOR, Mary [Cecilia] (1825-66)
American actress, singer CDP,
HAS, SR

TAYLOR, Maude (d 1886) actress
EA/87*

TAYLOR, Mitch (b 1936) American
actor TW/25

TAYLOR, Nellie (1894-1932) English actress, singer WWT/4-6

TAYLOR, Noel (b 1917) American
designer BE, WWT/15-16

TAYLOR, Pat (b 1918) English actress, singer WWT/10-11

TAYLOR, Paul (b 1930) American
dancer, choreographer CB, ES

TAYLOR, Raynor (c. 1747-1825)
English musician, composer,
musical director DAB, WWA/H

TAYLOR, Robert (d 1969 [57])
performer BP/54*

TAYLOR, Mrs. Robinson actress,
manager TD/2

TAYLOR, Sam (d 1958 [62]) director BE*

TAYLOR, Samuel (d 1888 [42])
EA/89*

TAYLOR, Samuel (b 1912) American dramatist AAS, BE, CD,
ES, MH, WWT/14-16

TAYLOR, Sylvia (d 1973 [50])
producer/director/choreographer
BP/57*

TAYLOR, Tom (1817-80) English dramatist CDP, COC, DNB, EA/68, HP, MH, NTH, OC/1-3, SR

TAYLOR, Tom (d 1911 [28]) musician EA/12*

TAYLOR, V. (fl 1819?) dramatist EAP

TAYLOR, Valerie (b 1902) English actress AAS, WWT/6-16

TAYLOR, Vaughn (b 1911) American actor TW/11-12

TAYLOR, Walter W. (d 1896) actor EA/97*

TAYLOR, Weston (d 1975 [47]) critic BP/60*

TAYLOR, William (d 1836 [70]) critic BE*, WWT/14*

TAYLOR, William (d 1898) equestrian business manager EA/99*

TAYLOR, William (d 1901 [60]) music-hall proprietor EA/02*

TAYLOR, William G. (d 1859) actor, costumier HAS

TAYLOR, William S. (b 1925) American manager, director BE

TAYLOR-PLATT, E. (d 1946 [75]) business manager WWT/14*

TAZEWELL, Charles (d 1972 [72]) actor TW/29

TCHERNICHEVA, Lubov (b 1890) Russian dancer ES

TEAGARDEN, Jack (d 1964 [58]) American musician BE*, BP/48*

TEAGUE, Anthony (b 1940) American actor TW/28-29

TEAGUE, Brian (d 1970 [33]) performer BP/55*

TEAGUE, Terri (b 1946) American actress TW/25

TEAL, Ben (d 1917 [55]) stage manager, director, producer BE*, WWT/14*

TEAL, Ray (d 1976 [74]) performer BP/60*

TEARLE, Conway (1878-1938) American actor ES, WWT/2-8

TEARLE, Edmund (1856-1913) English actor, producer, manager BE*, EA/14*, WWT/14*

TEARLE, George (d 1896 [73]) EA/98*

TEARLE, Mrs. George Osmond see Tearle, Mary Alice

TEARLE, Sir Godfrey (1884-1953) English actor AAS, COC, DNB, ES, OC/1-3, TW/4-8, 10, WWT/1-11

TEARLE, Malcolm (d 1935 [47]) actor BE*, WWT/14*

TEARLE, Marianne [Marianne Levy; Marianne Conway] (1854-96) English actress CDP, OC/1-3

TEARLE, Mary Alice [Mrs. George Osmond Tearle] (d 1887 [37]) EA/88*

TEARLE, Osmond (1852-1901) English actor CDP, COC, DNB, EA/96, OAA/1-2, OC/1-3

TEARLE, Mrs. Osmond see Conway, Marianne

TEASDALE, Verrée (b 1906) American actress WWT/7-10

TEATRO CAMPESINO, El theatre collective CD

TEBALDI, Renata (b 1922) Italian singer CB, ES

TEBBUTT, Joseph (d 1901 [56]) manager EA/03*

TECOSKY, Morton see Da Costa, Morton

TEDDER, Aynscomb (d 1897 [38]) actor EA/98*

TEDDER, George (d 1896 [77]) singer EA/97*

TEDESCO, Fortunata (fl 1847) singer CDP, HAS

TEED, John (b 1911) English actor WWT/8-10

TEEGE, Joachim (d 1969 [44]) performer BP/54*

TEER, Barbara Ann (b 1937) American actress TW/23

TEESDALE, Henry Robert (b 1841) English actor OAA/1-2

TEICHMANN, Howard (b 1916) American dramatist, educator BE, MH

TEITEL, Carol [née Carolyn Sally Kahn] (b 1929) American actress BE, TW/14-20, 23-24, 26, 30, WWT/15-16

TEIXEIRA DE MATTOS, Alexander Louis (1865-1921) Dutch dramatist, translator WWT/1-3, WWW/2

TELBIN, Rose (d 1849 [22]) English actress CDP, HAS

TELBIN, William (1813-73) English scene painter COC, OC/1-3

TELBIN, William Lewis (1846-1931) English scene painter

COC, OC/1-3
TELESHOVA, Elizabeth (d 1943)
actress WWT/14*
TELFORD, Richard (d 1912)
actor EA/13*
TELFORD, Robert S. (b 1923)
American director BE
TELL, Alma (1892-1937) American actress WWT/5-8
TELL, Olive (1894-1951) American actress TW/8, WWT/
4-8
TELLEGAN, Lou (1881-1934)
Dutch actor? SR
TELLET, Clara Anne (d 1887
[67]) actress CDP
TELLINGS, Mr. (fl 1847) actor
HAS
TELVA, Marion (1897-1962)
American singer TW/19,
WWA/4
TEMPEST, Amy [Mrs. Charles
Darrell] (1860-1908) English
actress GRB/1
TEMPEST, Florence (b 1873) actress GRB/1-4
TEMPEST, Mabel Emily (d 1899
[23]) actress EA/00*, WWT/
14*
TEMPEST, Dame Marie Susan
[Mrs. C. Cosmo Gordon-
Lennox] (1864-1942) English
actress AAS, CB, CDP,
COC, DNB, DP, ES, GRB/
1-4, NTH, OC/1-3, PDT, SR,
WWA/2, WWM, WWS, WWT/
1-8, WWW/4
TEMPLE, Clarence (d 1911 [42])
actor EA/12*
TEMPLE, Edward P. (d 1921
[60]) American director BE*,
BP/6*
TEMPLE, Mrs. Edward P. see
Temple, Mary
TEMPLE, Mrs. Fred see
Graham, Gertrude
TEMPLE, G. (fl 1872) actor
CDP
TEMPLE, Helen (b 1894) English
actress WWT/4-7
TEMPLE, Henrietta [Mrs. Charles
Morton] (d 1890) actress EA/
91*
TEMPLE, Joan (d 1965 [78])
English dramatist, actress
WWT/6-13
TEMPLE, Madge (d 1943) actress,
singer BE*, WWT/14*

TEMPLE, Mary [Mrs. Edward P.
Temple] (d 1883 [22]) EA/84*
TEMPLE, Nora see Turner,
Florence
TEMPLE, Richard [Richard Cobb]
(1847-1912) English actor,
singer DP, EA/97, GRB/1-4,
OAA/2, WWT/1
TEMPLE, Mrs. Richard see
Emmett, Bessie
TEMPLE, Mrs. Richard, Jr. see
Greene, Evie
TEMPLE, Rose [Mrs. John Donald]
English actress GRB/1-3
TEMPLE, William Clarence (d
1870) comedian EA/71*
TEMPLEMAN, Samuel (d 1867
[27]) comedian, harlequin EA/
68*
TEMPLETON, Mr. (fl 1831) Scottish singer HAS
TEMPLETON (d 1888) stage manager EA/89*
TEMPLETON, Alec Andrew (1910-
63) Welsh composer, performer,
musician BE*, BP/47*
TEMPLETON, Andrew (d 1896)
music-hall comedian EA/97*
TEMPLETON, C. Mercer (d 1973
[83]) performer BP/57*
TEMPLETON, Fay [Mrs. William
Patterson] (1865-1939) American
actress, singer CDP, GRB/2-
4, NTH, SR, WWA/1, WWS,
WWT/1-9
TEMPLETON, Harry (d 1890 [62])
singer CDP
TEMPLETON, Isabella [Mrs.
Robert Templeton] (d 1879)
EA/80*
TEMPLETON, James (fl 1801)
dramatist CP/3
TEMPLETON, John (1802-86) Scottish singer CDP, DNB
TEMPLETON, John (d 1907 [69])
American actor, manager
CDP, GRB/3
TEMPLETON, Robert (d 1892
[60]) music-hall performer
EA/93*
TEMPLETON, Mrs. Robert see
Templeton, Isabella
TEMPLETON, Robert Williamson
(d 1883 [82]) proprietor EA/84*
TEMPLETON, William (d 1868)
comedian, pantomimist EA/69*
TEMPLETON, Willie (d 1886 [43])
circus clown EA/87*

TEMPLETON, W. P. (b 1913/15)
Scottish dramatist BE, WWT/
11-13
TEN BROECK, May singer, song-
writer CDP
TENDUCCI, Giusto Ferdinado
(1736?-90) singer, dramatist
CDP, CP/3
TENNANT, Mrs. see Millett,
Maude
TENNANT, Dorothy (fl 1900s)
American actress WWM
TENNANT, Edmund H. (d 1916)
EA/17*
TENNANT, Francis (d 1907 [67])
EA/08*
TENNANT, Philip (d 1916) EA/
17*
TENNENT, Hector Norman (d
1904 [62]) director EA/05*
TENNENT, Henry M. (1879/87-
1941) English manager WWT/
8-9
TENNENT LTD., H. M. pro-
ducing managers WWT/10-16
TENNEY, Caryl Jeanne Ameri-
can actress TW/24, 28, 30
TENNY, Marion H. (d 1964 [73])
performer, actress BE*
TENNYCK, Egbert Fairchild
[Tom E. Egbert] (d 1888 [50])
American actor EA/89*
"TENNYSON" see O'Brien,
Edward
TENNYSON, Alfred Lord (1809-
92) English dramatist COC,
ES, HP, MH, NTH, OC/1-3,
PDT, RE
TENNYSON, Ann (d 1887 [68])
EA/88*
TENNYSON, Joe (fl 1903?) singer
CDP
TENNYSON, Thomas (d 1887
[80]) EA/88*
TEODOR, Jacob (fl 1627-28)
actor DA
TERAN, Fernando Arrabal see
Arrabal, Fernando
TER-ARUTUNIAN, Rouben (b
1920) Russian/American de-
signer BE, CB, ES, WWT/
13-16
TERENCE (c. 190-159 B.C.)
Roman dramatist COC
TERES, T. (fl 1769?) translator
CP/2-3, GT
TERESIA, Mme. ["The Corsican
Fairy"] (b 1743) dwarf CDP

TERHUNE, Albert Payson (b 1872)
American dramatist WWM
TERHUNE, Anice (d 1964) Ameri-
can composer WWA/4
TERHUNE, Max (d 1973 [82]) per-
former BP/58*
TERMINI, Joe (d 1964 [72]) per-
former BE*
TERNAN, Fanny (b 1837) American
actress HAS
TERNAN, Frances Eleanor see
Ternan, Mrs. Thomas
TERNAN, Thomas (1804-46) Irish
actor HAS
TERNAN, Mrs. Thomas [Frances
Eleanor Jarman] (1805-73) Eng-
lish actress CDP, DNB, HAS,
OX
TERNINA, Milka (1864-1941)
Croatian singer ES
TERRANOVA, Dino (d 1969 [65])
actor TW/25
TERRAUX, L. H. du (d 1878)
dramatist WWT/14*
TERRELL, St. John (b 1916)
American producer, actor, the-
atre owner BE, CB
TERRIS, Malcolm (b 1941) English
actor TW/25
TERRIS, Norma (b 1904) American
actress, singer WWT/7-12
TERRISS, Ellaline [Mrs. Seymour
Hicks] (1871-1971) English ac-
tress COC, EA/94, ES, GRB/
1-4, OC/1-3, TW/27, WWT/1-
11
TERRISS, Tom [Thomas Herbert
F. Lewin] (1874-1964) English
actor ES, GRB/4, WWT/1-8
TERRISS, W. (d 1916) EA/17*
TERRISS, William (1847-97) Eng-
lish actor CDP, COC, DNB,
DP, OAA/1-2, OC/1-3, WWW/1
TERRISS, Mrs. William see
Fellowes, Amy
TERROTT, William Mulready (d
1899 [74]) EA/00*
TERRY, Mrs. (d 1892) EA/93*
TERRY, Alice (b c. 1896) American
actress ES
TERRY, Beatrice (b 1890) English
actress COC, GRB/2-4, OC/3,
WWT/1-11
TERRY, Benjamin (1818-96) Eng-
lish actor COC, ES, OC/1-3
TERRY, Mrs. Benjamin see
Terry, Sarah Ballard
TERRY, Charles (1857-1933)

manager COC

TERRY, Daniel (1789-1829) English actor, manager, dramatist BS, CDP, COC, DNB, HAS, OC/1-3, OX

TERRY, Dennis (1895-1932) English actor OC/1-3

TERRY, Mrs. Edward see Terry, Ellen

TERRY, Edward O'Connor (1844-1912) English actor, manager CDP, COC, DP, EA/95, GRB/1-4, OAA/1-2, OC/1-3, SR, WWM, WWS, WWT/1, WWW/1

TERRY, Eliza [Mrs. H. Lewis] (d 1878 [61]) actress BE*, EA/80*, WWT/14*

TERRY, Ellen [Mrs. Edward Terry] (d 1897) EA/98*

TERRY, Dame Ellen Alice (1847-1928) English actress CDP, COC, DNB, DP, ES, GRB/1-4, NTH, OAA/1-2, OC/1-3, PDT, SR, WWA/1, WWM, WWS, WWT/1-5, WWW/2

TERRY, Ethelind (b 1900) American actress, singer WWT/6-10

TERRY, Florence [Mrs. William Morris] (1854-96) English actress CDP, COC, ES, OAA/1-2, OC/1-3

TERRY, Fred (1863-1933) English actor COC, DNB, DP, ES, GRB/1-4, OC/1-3, WWM, WWS, WWT/1-7, WWW/3

TERRY, Mrs. Fred see Neilson, Julia

TERRY, George (1850-1928) manager COC

TERRY, George (b 1938) American actor TW/25

TERRY, Hazel (1918-74) English actress BTR/74, ES, WWT/9-14

TERRY, Herbert E. (b 1875) English actor, manager, dramatist GRB/1-2

TERRY, J. E. Harold (1885-1939) English dramatist WWT/3-8

TERRY, Mrs. John see Lambert, Mabel

TERRY, John S. (b 1870) English actor GRB/1-2

TERRY, Kate [Mrs. Arthur Lewis] (1844-1924) English actress

COC, ES, GRB/1-4, OAA/1-2, OC/1-3, SR, WWS, WWT/1-4

TERRY, Mabel (1872-1957) actress ES

TERRY, Marian (d 1904 [63]) EA/06*

TERRY, Marion (1852/56-1930) English actress CDP, COC, DP, EA/95, ES, GRB/1-4, OAA/1-2, OC/1-3, WWS, WWT/1-6, WWW/3

TERRY, Megan (b 1932) American dramatist, actress, director CD, CH, WWT/16

TERRY, Minnie [Mrs. Edmund Gwenn] (1882-1964) English actress COC, DP, GRB/2-4, OC/3, WWT/1-8

TERRY, Muriel (d 1947 [62]) singer WWT/14*

TERRY, Olive (b 1884) English actress GRB/2-4, WWT/1-5

TERRY, Phyllis (b 1892) English actress OC/1-3

TERRY, Sarah Ballard [Mrs. Benjamin Terry] (1819-92) English actress COC, OC/1-3

TERRY, Teresa (fl 1856) actress HAS

TERRY, Walter (d 1932) editor BE*, WWT/14*

TERRY, Walter (b 1913) critic NTH

TERRY, Mrs. Warwick (d 1913) EA/14*

TERRY, W. Benson (b 1927) American actor TW/25

TERRY, William (b 1914) American actor TW/2-3

TERRY-LEWIS, Mabel [Mrs. R. C. Batley] (1872-1957) English actress COC, GRB/1-4, OC/1-6, WWT/1-11, WWW/5

TERRY-THOMAS (b 1911) English performer ES

TERSHAY, Joe (d 1970) performer BP/55*

TERSI, Maria Theresa Catherine see Bland, Mrs. George

TERSON, Peter [Peter Patterson] (b 1932) English dramatist AAS, CD, CH, COC, PDT, RE, WWT/16

TESTER, Desmond (b 1919) English actor WWT/8-13

TESTO, Charles (d 1872 [54]) equestrian director EA/73*

TETHERINGTON, Mrs. see

Collet, Catherine
TETLEY, Dorothy Argentinian
actress WWT/4-8
TETLEY, Glen (b 1926) American
dancer, choreographer CB,
ES
TETLEY, Walter (d 1975 [60])
performer BP/60*
TETRAZZINI, Louisa [or Luisa]
(1871/74-1940) Italian singer
CB, ES, SR, WWA/1
TETRAZZINI CAMPANINI, Eva
(1862-1938) Italian singer ES
TETU, Princess (d 1971 [79])
circus performer BP/56*
TETZEL, Joan (1921-77) Ameri-
can actress BE, TW/4-8,
10-11, WWT/10-16
TEXAS, Temple (b 1925) Ameri-
can actress TW/3
TEYTE, Maggie [Margaret Tate]
(1889-1976) English actress,
singer CB, WWT/4-13
THACKER, John see Montrose,
Jack
THACKER, Rusty [or Russ] (b
1946) American actor TW/
24-25, 28-30
THALBERG, Franceska (d 1895
[84]) EA/96*
THALBERG, Sigismund (1812-71)
Swiss musician CDP, HAS
THALBERG, T. B. (1864-1947)
English actor EA/96, GRB/
3-4, WWT/1-4
THALIN, Vivien Parker (d 1974
[77]) performer BP/58*
THALL, Al (d 1973 [63]) publicist
BP/58*
THANE, Adele (b 1904) American
actress, dramatist, director,
educator BE
THANE, Elswyth [Elswyth Thane
Ricker] dramatist WWT/8-10
THARE, John (fl 1602-03) actor
DA
THARP, Twyla (b 1941?) Ameri-
can dancer, choreographer
CB
THARPE, Rosetta (d 1973 [57])
performer BP/58*
THATCHER, Billy (d 1964 [43])
performer BP/49*
THATCHER, George (1846/49-
1913) American minstrel
CDP, SR
THATCHER, Heather English ac-
tress, singer WWT/4-14

THATCHER, Torin (b 1905) Indian/
English actor AAS, BE, TW/
5-8, 14-16, WWT/10-15
THAW, Evelyn Nesbit (1884-1967
[82]) American showgirl TW/
23, WWA/4
THAW, John (b 1942) English actor
WWT/15-16
THAXTER, Phyllis (b 1920) Amer-
ican actress BE, TW/18-19,
WWT/14-16
THAXTER, Phyllis Schuyler (d
1966 [74]) performer BP/51*
THAYER, Miss see Walstein,
Mrs. Westervelt
THAYER, Agnes (d 1873) actress
CDP
THAYER, Ambrose A. (d 1863/64)
minstrel CDP, HAS
THAYER, Amidon L. (d 1864
[41]) manager, minstrel CDP,
HAS
THAYER, Mrs. Edward [Mrs.
Palmer Fisher] (fl 1824) Eng-
lish actress HAS
THAYER, Edward Niles (b 1798)
American actor CDP, HAS
THAYER, Tiffany Ellsworth (1902-
59) American actor WWA/3
THAYER, William (fl 1594-98)
actor DA
THEAKER, John (d 1870 [45])
EA/71*
THEARLE, Nellie [Mrs. Stanley
Hope] (d 1910) actress EA/11*
THEATRE GUILD, The TW/2-8
THEATRE INCORPORATED TW/
2-5
THEATRE WORKSHOP theatre
collective CD
THEBOM, Blanche American singer
CB
THECLA, Maud [Mrs. Gaston
Mayer] American singer GRB/
1-3
THEILADE, Nini (b 1915) Dutch
dancer, choreographer ES,
WWT/8-9
THEILMANN, Helen (d 1956 [41])
actress BE*, WWT/14*
THEISE, Mortimer M. (b 1866)
American manager WWS
THEISEN, Mme. see Ploux,
Edith
THELWALL, John (fl 1794-1802)
dramatist CP/3
THENON, George see "Rip"
THEOBALD, John (d 1760) trans-

lator CP/2-3
THEOBALD, Lewis (1688-1744)
English dramatist, editor CP/
1-3, DNB, GT, HP, TD/1-2
THEODORE, Mme. see D'Aub-
erval, Mme. Jean
THEODORE, Mlle. [Mrs. A. B.
Narpier] (fl 1851) dancer HAS
THEOHAROUS, Ted (b 1930)
American actor TW/29
THERESA, Mlle. (b 1837) ac-
tress, singer CDP
THESIGER, Ernest (1879-1961)
English actor AAS, ES, TW/
6, 14-15, 17, WWT/4-13,
WWW/6
THIDBLAD, Inga (d 1975 [73])
performer BP/60*
THIEL, Mrs. Leonard see
Welling, Nellie
THIELE, William J. (d 1975
[85]) producer/director/chore-
ographer BP/60*
THILLON, Anna (1812/13/19-
1903) English singer CDP,
HAS, SR
THIMIG, Helene [Mrs. Max Rein-
hardt] (d 1974 [85]) actress
BP/59*, WWT/16*
THIMM, Daisy English actress
WWT/2-5
THIODON, Alfred Aspinall (d
1902 [48]) music-hall manager
EA/03*
THIRER, Irene (d 1964 [59])
critic BP/48*
THIRLWALL, Annie [Mrs. E.
Dussek Corri] (d 1881 [51])
EA/82*
THIRLWALL, John (d 1887 [42])
musician EA/88*
THIRLWALL, John Wade (d 1876
[67]) musician EA/77*
THIRWALL, Connop (1797-1875)
critic, historian, musician
CDP
THOM, Richie (d 1902) music-
hall manager EA/03*
THOMA, Carl (b 1947) American
actor TW/26-28
THOMA, Mike (b 1926) American
director, stage manager, actor
BE
THOMAN, Jacob Wonderly (b 1816)
American actor HAS
THOMAN, Mrs. Jacob Wonderly,
I [Elizabeth Anderson] (b 1818)
American actress HAS

THOMAN, Mrs. Jacob Wonderly,
II [Julia Pelby] (1832-66) Amer-
ican actress HAS
THOMAS, Mrs. [Mrs. Simpson]
(d 1802) actress TD/2
THOMAS, Mrs. [Mrs. Kite] (d
1879 [57]) equestrienne EA/80*
THOMAS, Miss see Jefferson,
Mrs. Joseph
THOMAS, A. E. see Thomas,
Albert E.
THOMAS, Agnes actress WWT/
2-7
THOMAS, A. Goring (d 1892 [40])
composer BE*, EA/93*,
WWT/14*
THOMAS, Mrs. A. K. see
Brophy, Annie
THOMAS, Albert E. (1872-1947)
American dramatist NTH, SR,
TW/4, WWA/2, WWM, WWT/
4-10
THOMAS, Mrs. Alex see
Thomas, Emily
THOMAS, Mrs. Allen see Neil-
son, Ada
THOMAS, Ambroise (1811-96)
French composer CDP
THOMAS, Ann (b 1920) American
actress TW/2-15, 30
THOMAS, Annie (d 1905) EA/06*
THOMAS, Arthur Goring see
Thomas, A. Goring
THOMAS, Augustus (1857-1934)
American dramatist COC,
DAB, ES, GRB/2-4, HJD, MH,
MWD, NTH, OC/1-3, RE, SR,
WWA/1, WWS, WWT/1-7,
WWW/3
THOMAS, Basil (1912-57) English
dramatist WWT/12
THOMAS, Berte (b 1863) actor
WWT/2-3
THOMAS, Brandon (1856-1914)
English actor, dramatist CDP,
COC, DP, EA/97, ES, GRB/
1-4, MH, MWD, OC/3, PDT,
SR, WWT/1-2, WWW/1
THOMAS, Buddy (d 1967 [55])
producer/director/choreographer
BP/52*
THOMAS, Calvin (d 1964 [79])
American actor TW/1, 11-13,
21
THOMAS, Charles Henry (d 1941
[76]) business manager BE*,
WWT/14*
THOMAS, Christian Friedrich

Theodore (1835-1905) German
conductor DAB

THOMAS, Clara Amelia (d 1899)
EA/01*

THOMAS, Mrs. Dan see Dare,
Dulcie

THOMAS, Danny (b 1914) American actor CB

THOMAS, Dick (d 1910 [37])
quick-change sketch artist
EA/11*

THOMAS, Dorothy [Mrs. Cecil
Rose] (b 1882) English actress
GRB/3-4, WWS, WWT/1-7

THOMAS, Dylan (1914-53) Welsh
dramatist DNB, ES, HP,
MD, MH, MWD, WWW/5

THOMAS, E. (d 1893) secretary
EA/94*

THOMAS, Edna (d 1974 [88])
actress BP/59*, WWT/16*

THOMAS, Mrs. Edward (d 1871)
dramatist EA/72*

THOMAS, Elizabeth (fl 1762)
dramatist CP/3

THOMAS, Emily [Mrs. Alex
Thomas] (d 1886) EA/88*

THOMAS, Emily [Mrs. W. P.
Thomas] (d 1893) EA/95*

THOMAS, Evan (b 1891) Canadian actor TW/3, 24-25,
WWT/5-14

THOMAS, E. W. (d 1892) musician EA/93*

THOMAS, Frank, Jr. (b 1926)
American actor, producer,
director, writer BE

THOMAS, Frank M. (b 1890)
American actor TW/2-3,
10-13

THOMAS, Fred (d 1909 [75])
actor EA/10*

THOMAS, Freyda-Ann (b 1943)
American actress TW/30

THOMAS, Gwyn (b 1913) Welsh
dramatist CD, CH, WWT/
14-16

THOMAS, Harding (b 1861) Welsh
actor, manager GRB/1

THOMAS, Henry (d 1872 [49])
singer EA/73*

THOMAS, Herbert (b 1868) actor
WWT/4-6

THOMAS, Hilda (fl 1885?) actress, singer CDP

THOMAS, Jamieson (d 1939 [45])
actor BE*, WWT/14*

THOMAS, Jess (b 1927) American

singer CB

THOMAS, Joel (b 1919) American
actor TW/6-9

THOMAS, John (d 1877 [56]) lessee
EA/78*

THOMAS, John (d 1913) EA/14*

THOMAS, John Charles (1887/91?-
1960) American actor, singer
CB, SR, WWA/4

THOMAS, J. R. (b 1830) Welsh
singer, composer HAS

THOMAS, J. W. (d 1878) publisher,
editor, journalist BE*, EA/
79*, WWT/14*

THOMAS, Les (d 1967 [71]) business manager BP/52*

THOMAS, Lewis (d 1896 [70])
singer, critic EA/97*

THOMAS, Lily (d 1916) EA/17*

THOMAS, L. S. dramatist RJ

THOMAS, Marlo (b 1938) American
actress TW/30

THOMAS, Minna L. [Mrs. Theodore Thomas] (d 1889 [50])
EA/90*

THOMAS, Olive (1898?-1920) actress BE*, BP/5*

THOMAS, Philip M. (b 1949) American actor TW/28

THOMAS, Phyllis (b 1904) English
actress WWT/7-11

THOMAS, Rhys Arthur D. (d 1917)
EA/18*

THOMAS, Richard (b 1951) American actor CB, TW/22-24

THOMAS, Ruth (d 1970 [59]) performer BP/54*

THOMAS, Sandra (d 1972) founder
of stage mothers' club BP/56*

THOMAS, Stephen (d 1961 [63])
director of drama, British
Council BE*, WWT/14*

THOMAS, Theodore (1835-1905)
German/American conductor,
musician CDP, GRB/1, SR,
WWW/1

THOMAS, Mrs. Theodore see
Theodore, Minna L.

THOMAS, Tony American actor
TW/26-27, 29

THOMAS, Vyvian [Vyvian Laverton]
English actor GRB/1

THOMAS, Wally (d 1864 [26])
minstrel HAS

THOMAS, William (d 1870) music-
hall proprietor EA/71*

THOMAS, William (d 1872 [74])
musician EA/73*

THOMAS, William [William Thomas Quarrel] (d 1891) music-hall manager EA/92*

THOMAS, William, Jr. American actor TW/29-30

THOMAS, William Freeman (d 1898 [54]) EA/99*

THOMAS, W. Moy (d 1910 [81]) critic BE*, WWT/14*

THOMAS, W. P. (d 1882 [47]) Negro comedian EA/83*

THOMAS, Mrs. W. P. see Thomas, Emily

THOMASHEFSKY, Bessie (d 1962 [88]) actress WWT/14*

THOMASHEFSKY, Boris (d 1939 [71/75]) Russian actor, producer, impresario BP/24*, WWT/14*

THOMASSIN, Jeanne French actress WWT/1-4

THOME, Francis (d 1909 [59]) composer BE*, WWT/14*

THOMKINS, John (fl 1598) actor DA

THOMMEN, Edward director, actor BE

THOMPSON, Mr. (fl c. 1800?) actor BS

THOMPSON, Mjr. (d 1900) EA/01*

THOMPSON, A. (fl 1799) dramatist CP/3

THOMPSON, Alexander M. (1861-1948) dramatist WWT/2-10

THOMPSON, Alfred (d 1895) dramatist, designer BE*, WWT/14*

THOMPSON, Augusta (d 1877 [36]) actress WWT/14*

THOMPSON, A. W. (b 1878) Scottish actor, stage manager GRB/1

THOMPSON, Benjamin (1776?-1816) translator, dramatist CDP, CP/3, DNB

THOMPSON, C. dancer CDP

THOMPSON, Charles (d 1869 [86]) actor, dramatist EA/70*

THOMPSON, Charles H. (d 1867 [28]) minstrel EA/68*

THOMPSON, Charles H. (d 1871) acting manager EA/72*

THOMPSON, Mrs. Charlie see Thompson, Sarah

THOMPSON, Charlotte (1843-98) English actress CDP, HAS

THOMPSON, Charlotte American

dramatist WWM

THOMPSON, Clisbia (d 1868 [c. 100]) actress HAS

THOMPSON, Creighton (b 1889) American actor TW/3

THOMPSON, Denman (1833-1911) American actor, dramatist CDP, DAB, GRB/2-3, HJD, MWD, PP/3, SR, WWA/1, WWS

THOMPSON, Edward (d 1786) English dramatist CP/2-3, GT, TD/1-2

THOMPSON, Edward (1817-65) American actor HAS

THOMPSON, Mrs. Edward (b 1817) American actress HAS

THOMPSON, Eliza [née Lizzie Sharpe] (d 1875 [35]) singer EA/76*

THOMPSON, Emma see Fox, Emma

THOMPSON, Emma Janet [Mrs. W. Thompson] (d 1877) EA/78*

THOMPSON, Ephraim (d 1909) animal trainer EA/10*

THOMPSON, Eric (b 1929) English actor, director WWT/16

THOMPSON, Evan (b 1931) American actor TW/26-27

THOMPSON, Foster D. (d 1976 [63]) production manager BP/60*

THOMPSON, Francis Michael see Melton, J. Rexton

THOMPSON, Frank costume designer WWT/16

THOMPSON, Fred (1884-1949) English dramatist WWT/3-10, WWW/4

THOMPSON, Frederick W. (1872-1919) American manager WWT/1-3

THOMPSON, George (d 1889 [75]) music-hall singer? EA/90*

THOMPSON, George W. (1838-1901) American actor, dramatist, manager CDP, HAS

THOMPSON, Gerald Marr (1856-1938) English/Australian critic GRB/2-4, WWT/1-3, 5-8

THOMPSON, H. (fl 1852) actor HAS

THOMPSON, Harlan (d 1966 [76]) writer, director TW/23

THOMPSON, Harry (d 1873 [44]) comedian EA/74*

THOMPSON, Henry O'Neil J. (b

1866) Australian press manager
GRB/2-3

THOMPSON, Jack (d 1966 [59])
critic BP/50*

THOMPSON, James E. (d 1900
[34]) actor EA/01*

THOMPSON, Jay (b 1927) American dramatist, composer,
lyricist BE

THOMPSON, Jean M. (b 1867)
American juvenile dramatist
WWA/5

THOMPSON, J. Lee (b 1914)
English dramatist WWT/10-13

THOMPSON, John (c. 1600-34)
English actor COC, DA,
OC/1-3

THOMPSON, Lydia [Mrs. Alex-
ander Henderson] (1836-1908)
English actress CDP, COC,
DNB, DP, GRB/1-4, HAS,
NTH, OAA/1-2, OC/1-3

THOMPSON, Lysander (d 1892)
American actor EA/93*,
WWT/14*

THOMPSON, Lysander Steel
(1817-54) English actor CDP,
HAS

THOMPSON, Marshall (b 1925)
American actor TW/10

THOMPSON, Mary (b 1844)
American actress HAS

THOMPSON, Palmer (d 1969
[51]) producer/director/chore-
ographer BP/54*

THOMPSON, Percy Harry see
Honri, Percy

THOMPSON, Peter American
actor TW/27, 30

THOMPSON, Rebecca (b 1942)
American actress TW/26-27

THOMPSON, Rex (b 1942) American actor TW/10, 18, 27-28

THOMPSON, Richard D. (b 1933)
American lighting consultant
BE

THOMPSON, Ronnie (b 1941)
American actor TW/26

THOMPSON, Sada (b 1929) American actress AAS, BE, CB,
TW/24-29, WWT/15-16

THOMPSON, Sam (d 1965 [48])
performer BP/49*

THOMPSON, Sarah [Mrs. Charlie
Thompson] (d 1890 [35]) EA/
92*

THOMPSON, Tazewell (b 1948)
American actor TW/24

THOMPSON, Thomas J. (d 1881)
actor EA/82*

THOMPSON, Vance (1863-1925)
dramatist WWA/1

THOMPSON, Venie actress CDP

THOMPSON, W. (d 1891 [93])
EA/92*

THOMPSON, Mrs. W. see
Thompson, Emma Janet

THOMPSON, Mrs. Walter see
Carsoni, Marie

THOMPSON, William (fl 1738-51)
dramatist CP/1-3

THOMPSON, William (d 1869)
music-hall chairman EA/70*

THOMPSON, William (d 1881 [32])
musician EA/82*

THOMPSON, William (d 1894)
EA/95*

THOMPSON, William (d 1971 [58])
performer BP/56*

THOMPSON, William A. (fl 1832-
61) American actor HAS

THOMPSON, William C. (d 1868)
actor, manager HAS

THOMPSON, W[illiam] H. (1852-
1923) Scottish/American actor
CDP, GRB/2-4, SR, WWM,
WWT/1-3

THOMPSON, Mrs. W[illiam] H.
see Irving, Isabel

THOMPSON, William Henry see
Merson, Billy

THOMPSON, Woodman (1889-1955)
American designer ES

THOMPSON, W. T. (d 1940) actor
BE*, WWT/14*

THOMS, Virginia American manager BE

THOMSON, Adam (fl 1738) dramatist CP/3

THOMSON, Alexander (fl 1791)
dramatist CP/3

THOMSON, Augusta (d 1877 [36])
actress, singer EA/78*

THOMSON, Barry American actor
TW/2-4

THOMSON, Beatrix (b 1900) English actress WWT/6-13

THOMSON, Brenda (b 1944) American actress TW/28

THOMSON, Mrs. George (d 1870
[70]) actress? EA/71*

THOMSON, James (1700-48) Eng-
lish dramatist CDP, COC,
CP/1-3, GT, HP, OC/1-3,
TD/1-2

THOMSON, Jane Elizabeth see

Vezin, Jane Elizabeth
THOMSON, John (d 1877 [33])
  critic EA/79*
THOMSON, Lesly (d 1902) actor
  EA/03*
THOMSON, Lysander (d 1854
  [37]) comedian EA/72*
THOMSON, R. H. (b 1947) Cana-
  dian actor TW/30
THOMSON, Thomas (fl 1668)
  dramatist CP/1-3
THOMSON, Virgil (b 1896) Amer-
  ican composer, musical di-
  rector BE, CB, ES
THOMSON, Vivien see Merchant,
  Vivien
THOR, Jerome P. (b 1915) Amer-
  ican actor TW/1-3
THOR, Larry (d 1976 [59]) per-
  former BP/60*
THORBORG, Kerstin (1897?/
  1906-1970) Swedish singer
  CB, TW/26, WWA/5
THORBURN, H. M. (1884-1924)
  English business manager
  WWT/4
THORN, Geoffrey see Town-
  ley, Charles
THORNBURY, Cecil H. actor
  EA/97*
THORNDIKE, Arthur Russell
  see Thorndike, Russell
THORNDIKE, Eileen (1891-1953)
  English actress COC, OC/
  1-3, WWT/7-11
THORNDIKE, Frank (d 1917
  [23]) actor EA/18*
THORNDIKE, Louise [Mrs. Dion
  Boucicault, II; Mrs. Fred G.
  Calhoun] actress CDP
THORNDIKE, Russell (1885-
  1972) English actor, drama-
  tist AAS, COC, OC/1-3,
  WWT/4-14
THORNDIKE, Dame Sybil (1882-
  1976) English actress, mana-
  ger AAS, BE, CB, COC,
  ES, NTH, OC/1-3, PDT,
  TW/13-15, WWT/2-16
THORNE, Alice [Mrs. Crayford]
  (d 1896 [40]) actress EA/97*
THORNE, Mrs. Ambrose see
  Kranske, Violet
THORNE, Amelia see Newton,
  Amelia
THORNE, Ann Maria [née Mestay-
  er] (d 1881 [69]) American
  actress CDP, OC/1-3

THORNE, Charles (d 1893 [70])
  actor WWT/14*
THORNE, Charles R. (d 1882)
  American actor EA/83*
THORNE, Charles Robert, Sr.
  (c. 1814-93) American actor,
  manager CDP, DAB, HAS,
  OC/1-3, SR, WWA/H
THORNE, Mrs. Charles Robert,
  Sr. [Maria Ann Mestayer] (d
  1881) American actress, singer
  HAS
THORNE, Charles Robert, Jr.
  (1840-83) American actor CDP,
  COC, DAB, OC/1-3, WWA/H
THORNE, Clara (d 1915 [63]) ac-
  tress BE*, WWT/14*
THORNE, Edwin F. (b 1845)
  American actor HAS
THORNE, Emily (d 1907) actress
  CDP, GRB/3, HAS, OAA/2, SR
THORNE, Eric (d 1922 [60]) actor
  BE*, WWT/14*
THORNE, Frances [Mrs. J.
  Thorne] (d 1874 [42]) EA/75*
THORNE, George (1856-1922)
  English actor DP, GRB/1-4,
  OC/1-3
THORNE, Ivy Ellaline (b 1888)
  English actress GRB/1
THORNE, Mrs. J. see Thorne,
  Frances
THORNE, James (d 1843) English
  actor, singer CDP, HAS
THORNE, James (d 1882 [60])
  pantomimist, scene artist EA/
  83*
THORNE, John N., Jr. (d 1972
  [56]) journalist BP/56*
THORNE, J. W. (d 1860) actor?
  HAS
THORNE, Marguerite (d 1917)
  EA/18*
THORNE, Mary English actress
  GRB/2
THORNE, Maude actress GRB/2
THORNE, May [Mrs. Clifton Ald-
  erson] (d 1898) actress EA/99*
THORNE, Raymond (b 1934) Amer-
  ican actor TW/23, 26, 29
THORNE, Richard (d 1873 [34])
  actor EA/74*, WWT/14*
THORNE, Richard (d 1891 [61])
  musician EA/92*
THORNE, Richard Samuel (d 1875
  [62]) actor, manager WWT/14*
THORNE, Mrs. Richard Samuel
  (d 1896) EA/97*

THORNE, Robert (d 1965 [84])
actor TW/22
THORNE, Sarah (1837-99) English actress, manager COC,
OAA/1-2, OC/1-3
THORNE, Sylvia (d 1922 [55])
singer BE*, BP/6*
THORNE, Thomas (d 1864) actor
HAS
THORNE, Thomas (1841-1918)
English actor CDP, DP,
GRB/1-4, OAA/1-2, OC/1-3,
WWT/1-3
THORNE, Mrs. Thomas see
Newton, Amelia
THORNE, Thomas Wilson (d
1879 [25]) actor OAA/1
THORNE, W. S. (d 1868 [64])
actor? EA/69*
THORNTON, Miss see Martyr,
Margaret
THORNTON, Angela English actress TW/22-23, 29
THORNTON, Arthur J. (d 1967)
performer BP/51*
THORNTON, Bonnell (c. 1726-
68) English dramatist, translator CP/2-3, DNB
THORNTON, Bonnie (d 1920
[47]) American comedian BE*,
BP/4*
THORNTON, Charles (d 1881 [60])
music-hall proprietor EA/82*
THORNTON, Charles H. see
Ross, Charles H.
THORNTON, Edna (d 1964) English singer WWW/6
THORNTON, Ellen (d 1900 [83])
actress EA/01*
THORNTON, Emma [Mrs. R.
Thornton] (d 1869 [24]) EA/
70*
THORNTON, Emma (d 1882)
singer EA/83*
THORNTON, Frank (d 1918 [73])
English actor, manager CDP,
SR
THORNTON, Frank [né Ball] (b
1921) English actor WWT/
15-16
THORNTON, George (d 1880)
actor EA/81*
THORNTON, Harry (d 1918)
EA/19*
THORNTON, Henry manager,
actor TD/1-2
THORNTON, James (1861-1938)
English vaudevillian WWM

THORNTON, Kate see Kingsley,
Mrs. A. F.
THORNTON, L. M. (d 1888) EA/
89*
THORNTON, Louis Edmund (d 1908)
EA/09*
THORNTON, Madeleine see Sherwood, Madeleine
THORNTON, Margaret see
Martyr, Margaret
THORNTON, Percy (d 1891 [37])
journalist EA/92*
THORNTON, Mrs. R. (d 1893 [49])
EA/94*
THORNTON, Mrs. R. see
Thornton, Emma
THOROGOOD, John [Johnny Johns]
(d 1872 [21]) clown EA/73*
THORP, Mrs. J. see Edgar,
Alice
THORP, Joseph Peter (1873-1962)
English critic WWT/2-8
THORPE, Mrs. Charles H. see
Mountcastle, Fanny
THORPE, Clinton (d 1916) EA/17*
THORPE, George (1891-1961) English actor WWT/10-13
THORPE, Henry (d 1884 [37])
equestrian EA/85*
THORPE, Henry see Alvo, Henry
THORPE, Richard (b 1896) American actor ES
THORPE, Thomas (1570?-1635?)
English publisher DNB
THORPE, Thomas (d 1871) amusement caterer EA/72*
THORPE-BATES, Peggy (b 1914)
English actress WWT/12-16
THOURLBY, William (b 1924)
American actor TW/10-15
THRASHER, Ethelyn (b 1912)
American producer BE
THRELKELD, Budge (b 1922)
American educator BE
THROCKMORTON, Cleon (1897-
1965) American designer BE,
CB, NTH, TW/22, WWA/4,
WWT/8-10
THROPP, Clara (1875-1960) American actress SR, WWM
THULIN, Ingrid (b 1929) Swedish
actress TW/23
"THUMB, Tom" [Charles Stratton]
(1832/37/38-83) American midget
CDP, HAS, SR, WWA/H
"THUMB, Mrs. Tom" [Lavinia
Warren] (b 1842) HAS
THURBER, James (1894-1961)

American dramatist ES, HJD, MH

THURBURN, Gwynneth (b 1899) Argentinian/English educator WWT/14-16

THURE, Hanson (d 1871) ceiling walker EA/72*

THURLOW, Lady see Bolton, Mary

THURLOW, James Edgar (d 1903 [50]) actor EA/04*

THURMOND, John (fl 1724-49) dancing master, dramatist CP/2-3, GT, TD/1-2

THURMOND, Mrs. John [née Lewis] (fl 1715-37) actress DNB

THURNER, Georges (d 1910 [32]) dramatist BE*, WWT/14*

THURNHILL, Fred Raymond (d 1875 [40]) comic singer EA/76*

THURRELL, Frederick (d 1869) trapezist EA/70*

THURSBY, Emma Cecilia (1845/57-1931) American singer CDP, DAB, WWM

THURSTON, Ernest Temple (1879-1933) Irish dramatist WWT/3-7

THURSTON, Fred (b 1920) American actor TW/23

THURSTON, Harry (d 1955 [81]) English actor BE*, BP/40*, WWT/14*

THURSTON, Howard (1869-1936) American magician DAB, SR, WWA/1

THURSTON, Ted (b 1920) American actor TW/25-26, 28-29

THURTON, John Robert (d 1886 [54]) performer? EA/87*

THURTON, Mrs. Robert see Thurton, Susan

THURTON, Susan [Mrs. Robert Thurton] (d 1880 [57]) EA/81*

THURY, Ilona (d 1953 [77]) Hungarian actress BE*, BP/37*

TIANO, Lou (b 1935) American actor TW/26, 30

TIBBALS, Seymour Selden (1869-1949) American dramatist WWA/3

TIBBETT, Lawrence (1896-1960) American actor, singer CB, ES, TW/17, WWA/4, WWT/7-9

TIBBITTS, Mrs. (d 1888) EA/89*

TIBBITTS, James (d 1890) EA/91*

TIBERINI, Sig. (1807-85) singer CDP, HAS

TICEHURST, James (d 1889) musician EA/90*

TICEHURST, John (d 1871 [76]) musician EA/72*

TICH, Little [Harry Relph] (1868-1928) English variety artist COC, ES, GRB/1-4, OC/1-3, PDT

TICHBOURNE, S. W. L. (d 1879) secretary EA/80*

TICHENOR, Tom (b 1923) American puppeteer, dramatist, actor, director, composer, designer BE

TICKELL, Richard (d 1793) dramatist CP/3, GT, TD/1-2

TICKLE, Frank (1893-1955) English actor WWT/10-11

TICKTON, Dick (d 1907 [58]) topical singer EA/08*

TIDD, John Dunstone (d 1900 [76]) secretary EA/01*

TIDEN, Fritz (d 1931 [54]) actor BE*, BP/16*

TIDMARSH, T. U. (d 1866) circus advertizer HAS

TIDMARSH, Vivian (1896-1941) English dramatist, critic WWT/9

TIDSWELL, [Charlotte?] (d c. 1846) English actress TD/1-2

TIECK, Ludwig (1778-1853) dramatist, director, critic BE*, EA/72*

TIERNEY, Agnes (d 1975 [60s]) performer BP/60*

TIERNEY, Eliza (d 1912 [80]) housekeeper EA/13*

TIERNEY, Harry (1890/94-1965) American composer BE, WWA/4, WWT/5-10

TIERNEY, John T. (1863-1913) American comedian SR

TIERNEY, William A. (d 1974) performer BP/59*

TIETJENS, Paul (d 1943 [66]) American composer, conductor BE*, WWT/14*

TIETJENS, Therese (1831/34-77) Hungarian singer CDP, DNB, ES

TIFFANY, Annie Ward [Mrs. Charles C. Greene] actress CDP

TIFFIN, Pamela (b 1942) American

actress TW/23
TIGAR, Ken (b 1942) American
actor TW/29-30
TIGHE, Edward (fl 1786-88)
dramatist CP/3
TIGHE, Harry (d 1935 [50])
American actor BE*, BP/19*
TIGHE, James (d 1893 [40])
stage manager EA/94*
TIHMAR, David (1918-71) Amer-
ican actor, dancer, director
TW/2, 27
TILBERY, John (fl 1405) mem-
ber of the Children of the
Chapel Royal DA
TILBURY, William Harries (1806-
64) actor CDP
TILBURY, Zeffie [Mrs. L. D.
Woodthorpe] (1862/63-1950)
English actress GRB/2-4,
WWT/1-10
TILDEN, Miss (fl 1824-52) ac-
tress HAS
TILDEN, Miss see Bernard,
Mrs. Charles
TILDEN, Bill (1893-1953) Ger-
man actor BE*, BP/38*
TILDEN, Milano C. (d 1951
[73]) French performer BE*,
BP/36*
TILDSLEY, Peter (d 1962 [64])
performer, manager BE*
TILKIN, John see Caryll,
Ivan
TILL, John (d 1910) marionettist
EA/11*
TILL, John (d 1963 [77]) Amer-
ican puppeteer BE*
TILLBROOK, Oscar (d 1872)
actor EA/73*
TILLER, John (d 1925 [73]) Eng-
lish dancing master, director,
designer BE*
TILLEY, John (d 1935 [35]) actor
BE*, WWT/14*
TILLEY, Vesta [Mrs. Walter de
Frece] (1864-1952) English
variety artist CDP, COC,
DNB, ES, GRB/1-4, OC/1-3,
PDT, TW/9, WWS, WWT/
4-11, WWW/5
TILLINGER, John (b 1938) Iranian
actor TW/23-27, 29
TILLSTROM, Burr (b 1917)
American puppeteer CB
TILNEY, Sir Edmund (d 1610)
master of the Revels COC,
DNB, OC/3

TILSTON, Jennifer (b 1947) English
actress TW/23-24, 26
TILSTON, Kate (b 1851) American
dancer HAS
TILTMAN, Nan (d 1912 [38]) EA/
13*
TILTON, Edward Lafayette (1824-
87) American actor, manager
CDP, HAS, NYM
TILTON, James F. (b 1937) Amer-
ican designer WWT/15-16
TILTON, Webb (b 1915) American
actor, singer BE
TILZER, Albert von (d 1956 [78])
producer, songwriter WWT/14*
TIMBLIN, Slim (d 1962 [70]) per-
former BE*
TIMM, Henry Christian (1811-92)
German/American musician,
conductor, composer CDP,
DAB, WWA/H
TIMM, Sarah H. (d 1854) actress
CDP
TIMMONS, Mary see Hawthorne,
Louise
TINDALL, Loren (d 1973 [52])
performer BP/57*
TINGAY, Mrs. Charles F. see
Reynolds, Carrie
TINGAY, Mrs. Charles S. see
Gray, Ada
TINNEY, Frank (1878-1940) Amer-
ican actor CB, WWA/1, WWT/
4-9
TINNEY, Henry James (d 1896
[50]) conductor, musician EA/
98*
TINSLEY, Arthur (d 1894 [29])
comedian EA/95*
TINSLEY, Edith see Robertson,
Mrs. Lionel
TINSLEY, Tom (1853-1910) English
music-hall manager, comedian
GRB/1
TIPPETT, Sir Michael (b 1905)
English composer CB, ES
TIPPING, Frank Blamphin (d
1917) musician EA/18*
TIPPIT, Wayne (b 1932) American
actor TW/25-26
TISDALE, Benjamin (d 1888 [64])
EA/89*
TISSIER, Jean (d 1973 [77]) per-
former BP/57*
TISSOT, Alice (d 1971 [81]) French
actress BP/55*, WWT/16*
TISSOT, Mme. Jules (d 1898 [38])
EA/99*

TITBITS, Mjr. [William Partridge] (d 1898 [31]) dwarf comedian EA/99*

TITHERADGE, Dion (1889-1934) Australian dramatist, actor WWT/4-7

TITHERADGE, George S[utton] (1848-1916) English actor GRB/1-4, OAA/1-2, WWT/1-3

TITHERADGE, Lily (d 1937) actress BE*, WWT/14*

TITHERADGE, Madge (1887-1961) Australian actress AAS, COC, GRB/3-4, TW/18, WWT/1-11, WWW/6

TITHERINGTON, Ellis (d 1908) conductor EA/10*

TITHERINGTON, Lilian (d 1894 [23]) EA/95*

TITMAN, Mrs. S. A. (d 1897 [54]) proprietor EA/98*

TITMUSS, Phyllis (1900-46) English actress, singer WWT/4-8

TITTELL, Charlotte (d 1941 [60]) actress BE*, WWT/14*

TITTERTON, Frank (1882-1956) English singer WWW/5

TITTERTON, William Richard (1876-1963) English critic, press representative WWT/5-7

TITUS, Lydia Yeamans (d 1929 [63]) comedian BE*, BP/14*

TITUS, Tracy (c. 1846-87) American ticket-seller, actor? NYM

TOBANI, Theodore Moses (1855-1933) German/American composer, musician DAB

TOBIAS, George (d 1970 [72]) composer/lyricist BP/55*

TOBIN, Genevieve (b 1901/02) American actress WWT/5-11

TOBIN, John (1770-1804) English dramatist CP/3, DNB, GT

TOBIN, Matthew (b 1933) American actor TW/26-28, 30

TOBIN, Vivian (b 1903/04) American actress WWT/5-9

TOBYE, Edward (fl 1623) actor DA

TOCH, Ernst (1887-1964) Austrian/American composer WWA/4

TOCHE, Raoul (d 1895 [45]) dramatist WWT/14*

TODD, Little acrobat CDP

TODD, Ann (b 1909/10) English actress BE, ES, TW/14-15, WWT/7-16

TODD, F. C. (d 1877 [32]) secretary EA/78*

TODD, Rev. Henry John (fl 1798) editor CP/3

TODD, James actor TW/1

TODD, J. Garrett business manager WWT/4-7

TODD, Michael [né Goldbogen] (1907/09-58) American producing manager CB, TW/2-8, 14, WWA/3, WWT/10-12

TODD, Richard (b 1919) Irish actor, producing manager CB, ES, WWT/16

TODD, Thelma (1905-35) actress BE*

TODD-STEWART, James (d 1916) EA/17*

TODHUNTER, Dr. John (1839-1916) Irish dramatist WWW/2

TOFT, William (d 1904 [44]) roundabout proprietor EA/05*

TOFTS, Katherine (d 1756 [76]) actress, singer WWT/14*

TOGURI, David Canadian dancer, director, choreographer WWT/16

TOKELY, James (d 1819 [29]) actor CDP

TOLAN, Michael American actor BE, TW/14-15, 22-23, 28

TOLAND, John (b 1926) American actor TW/23

TOLANO, Raphael (d 1896) Australian lessee EA/97*

TOLER, Sidney (1874-1947) American actor, dramatist SR, TW/3, WWM, WWT/7-16

TOLHURST, G. W. (d 1877) musician EA/78*

TOLKEIN, Alfred [Boleno Marsh] (d 1867 [32]) clown EA/68*

TOLL, David (b 1943) American actor TW/26, 30

TOLLER, Ernst (1893-1939) German dramatist COC, MWD, NTH, OC/1-3, WWA/4

TOLLER, James (b 1795) giant CDP

TOLLER, Rosalie (b 1885) actress WWT/1-5

TOLLET, Elizabeth (1694-1755) dramatist CP/2-3

TOLLET, George (1725-79) English? critic DNB

TOLLETT, Henrietta Maria see Crisp, Mrs. Samuel

TOLLETT, John [Pat O'Leary] (d 1882) EA/83*

TOLLINGER, Ned (d 1972 [69]) performer BP/56*

TOLSON, Francis (d 1745/46) dramatist CP/1-3, GT

TOLSTOY, Count Leo Nikolaevich (1828-1910) Russian dramatist COC

TOM, Blind (b c. 1848) American musician CDP, HAS

TOMACK, Sid (d 1962) American performer BE*

TOMKINS, Gregory C. (d 1895) lessee EA/96*

TOMKINS, Gregory Styles (d 1893 [63]) journalist EA/94*

TOMKI[N]S, John see Tomkis, Thomas

TOMKINS, Robert (d 1897) proprietor EA/98*

TOMKINSON, Annie (d 1908 [57]) EA/09*

TOMKIS, Thomas (fl 1594-1615?) dramatist CP/2-3, DNB, FGF, HP

TOMLIN, Blanche (b 1889) English actress, singer WWT/4-8

TOMLIN, Felicity see Douglas, Felicity

TOMLINS, Frederick Guest (d 1867 [63]) critic, journalist, dramatist BE*, EA/68*, WWT/14*

TOMLINSON, Mr. (fl 1759-61) actor HAS

TOMLINSON, Miss (fl 1829?) actress CDP

TOMLINSON, David (b 1917) English actor AAS, WWT/12-16

TOMLINSON, John (fl 1792) dramatist CP/3

TOMLINSON, Kellom (fl 1754?) dancing master CDP

TOMPKINS, Eugene (1850-1909) manager, proprietor CDP

TOMPKINS, Toby (b 1942) American performer TW/29

TOMS, Mr. (fl 1796) actor CDP, GT, TD/1-2

TOMS, Carl (b 1927) English designer WWT/15-16

TOMS, Edward (d c. 1779) drama-

tist CP/2-3

TOMSON, Sam (fl early 17th cent) actor DA

TOMSONE, John (fl 1598) actor DA

TONDESILLA, Jesus (d 1973 [80]) Spanish actor WWT/16*

TONE, Franchot (1905/06-68) American actor BE, CB, SR, TW/1-20, 24-25, WWA/5, WWT/7-14

TONER, Tom (b 1928) American actor TW/29

TONGE, H. Asheton (d 1927 [55]) actor BE*, WWT/14*

TONGE, Philip (1892-1959) English actor GRB/3-4, TW/4-16, 15, WWT/1-12

TONKS, John (d 1867 [48]) EA/68*

TONSON, Jacob (d 1736 [80]) publisher BE*, WWT/14*

TONY, Little (d 1918 [43]) EA/19*

TONY, Will (fl late 16th cent) actor DA

TOOHEY, John Latham (1916-75) American press representative BE

TOOHEY, John Peter (d 1947 [66]) American press representative BE*, BP/31*

TOOKER, Guy (d 1975 [83]) performer BP/60*

TOOKER, Joseph Henry (1830-96) manager CDP

TOOKEY, William see Vol Becque, William

TOOLE, Mrs. Alec see Toole, Maggie

TOOLE, Florence Mabel (d 1888 [22]) EA/89*

TOOLE, Frank (d 1889 [70]) EA/90*

TOOLE, Frank Laurence (d 1879 [23]) EA/80*

TOOLE, Harry (d 1892 [23]) EA/93*

TOOLE, J. E. (fl 1872-86) American actor SR

TOOLE, Mrs. John L. see Toole, Susan

TOOLE, John Lawrence (1830-1906) English actor, manager CDP, COC, DNB, DP, ES, GRB/1, OAA/1-2, OC/1-3, WWW/1

TOOLE, Kate (d 1903) music-hall singer EA/04*

TOOLE, Maggie [Mrs. Alec Toole] (d 1917) EA/18*

TOOLE, Susan [Mrs. John L. Toole] (d 1889) EA/90*
TOOLEY, Nicholas [né Wilkinson] (c. 1575-1623) English actor COC, DA, GT, NTH, OC/1-3
TOOMER, Mr. actor HAS
TOONE, Geoffrey (b 1910) Irish actor WWT/10-16
TOOSEY, George Philip (d 1795) dramatist CP/2-3, GT
TOOTLE, Milton (c. 1824-87) manager NYM
TOPA, John A. (b 1909) American actor TW/24
TOPAZ, Murial (b 1932) American dancer, choreographer BE
TOPHAM, Edward (1751-1820) dramatist CDP, CP/3, DNB, GT, TD/1-2
TOPHAM, Frederic (1858-1908) English actor GRB/1-3
TOPHAM, Thomas (1710?-49) strong man CDP, DNB
TOPHOFFS, Mons. (d 1865) ballet master HAS
TOPOL, Chaim (b 1934) Israeli actor COC
TOPPING, Melinda see Jones, Melinda
TORDESILLA, Jesus (d 1973 [80]) performer BP/57*
TORETZKA, Ludmilla (b 1903) Russian actress TW/9
TORMEY, John (b 1937) American actor TW/23-24, 26
TORN, Elmore Rual see Torn, Rip
TORN, Rip [né Elmore Rual Torn] (b 1931) American actor, director BE, TW/20, 23, 25-27, 30, WWT/15-16
TORNATORE, Michael (d 1973 [53]) performer BP/58*
TORR, Clara music-hall singer CDP
TORR, Sam (d 1899 [53]) music-hall singer & manager CDP
TORR, Mrs. Sam (d 1899 [53]) proprietor EA/00*
TORRE, Della (fl 1887?) singer, songwriter CDP
TORREN, Frank (b 1939) American actor TW/26
TORRENCE, David (b 1870) Scottish actor WWT/7-9
TORRENCE, Ernest (1878-1933) Scottish actor, singer WWT/7

TORRENCE, Frederick Ridgely (1874-1950) American dramatist DAB, HJD
TORRENCE, Marietta S. (b 1813) HAS
TORRES, Andy (b 1945) Puerto Rican actor TW/29-30
TORREY, Susan (d 1968 [61]) actress TW/24
TORRIANI, Aimee (d 1963 [73]) performer BP/48*, WWT/14*
TORRIANI, Astava (fl 1874) singer CDP
TORRIANI, Charles (1852-98) musician CDP
TOSCANINI, Arturo (1867-1957) Italian conductor CB, ES, TW/13, WWA/3, WWW/5
TOSEDALL, Roger (fl 1635) actor DA
TOSTI, Sir Paolo (d 1916 [70]) composer EA/18*
TOTHEROH, Dan (1894/95/98-1976) American dramatist HJD, MD, MWD, WWT/9-11
TOTIEN, Henry (d 1878 [63]) actor EA/79*
TOTTEN, Mrs. Henry (d 1889 [73]) EA/90*
TOTTEN, John J. (d 1969 [83]) executive BP/53*
TOTTEN, Joseph Byron (1875-1946) American dramatist, director WWA/2
TOTTEN, Mrs. Joseph Byron see Bingham, Leslie
TOTTERTON CDP
TOTTNELL, Harry (d 1593?) actor DA
TOUBEL, Philippe see Alcidor
TOULIATOS, George (b 1929) American director, manager BE
TOULMOUCHE, Frederic (d 1909 [58]) composer WWT/14*
TOUMANOVA, Tamara [Tamara Khacidovitch] (b 1917) Russian dancer WWT/9-12
TOURBUTTS, Richard (d 1905) conductor EA/06*
TOUREL, Jennie (1910-73) Canadian/French singer CB
TOURNEUR, Cyril (1575-1626) English dramatist COC, CP/1-3, DNB, ES, FGF, HP, MH, NTH, OC/1-3, PDT, RE
TOURNEY, Minna (fl 1854) French singer? musician? HAS

TOURNIAIRE, Benoit (d 1865)
circus performer? CDP, HAS
TOURNIAIRE, Louise (fl 1851)
equestrienne CDP
TOURNOUR, Millie (fl 1868)
aerial bar performer CDP
TOURS, Frank E. (1877-1963)
English musical director,
composer GRB/4, WWT/1-
11, WWW/6
TOUSSAINT, Marie American ac-
tress TW/25-26
TOUSSARD, E. J. (fl 1897?)
music-hall singer CDP
TOUTAIN, Blanche (d 1932)
French actress WWT/2-4
TOVATT, Ellen American ac-
tress TW/29-30
TOVEY, Sir Donald Francis
(1875-1940) English composer
DNB
TOVEY, Henry (d 1885) assistant
stage manager EA/86*
TOVSTONOGOV, Georgyi Alex-
androvich (b 1915) Russian
producer COC
TOWB, Harry (b 1925) Irish actor
TW/23, WWT/15-16
TOWBER, Chaim (d 1972 [70])
dramatist BP/56*
TOWBIN, Beryl (b 1938) Amer-
ican actress TW/24, 26
TOWELL, Miss see Miller,
Mrs. W. Christie
TOWELL, George (d 1894 [21])
musical director, musician
EA/95*
TOWER, Allen (d 1963) American
performer BE*
TOWER, W. C. (fl 1881?) singer,
songwriter CDP
TOWERS, Constance (b 1933)
American actress, singer
TW/22-24, 26-28, WWT/16
TOWERS, Edward (d 1918 [76])
EA/19*
TOWERS, Harry (fl 1897?) singer
CDP
TOWERS, Harry P. (b 1873)
English business manager
WWT/2, 5-7
TOWERS, John (b 1836) English
writer WWM
TOWERS, Johnson (d 1891 [78])
dramatist, manager, actor
BE*, EA/92*, WWT/14*
TOWERS, Susan (b 1948) Ameri-
can actress TW/23

TOWNE, Charles Hanson (1877-
1949) American editor, actor,
writer BE*, BP/33*
TOWNE, Edward Owings (b 1869)
American dramatist WWA/1,
WWM, WWS
TOWNE, John (fl 1583-97) actor
DA
TOWNE, Thomas (d 1612?) actor
DA
TOWNES, Harry (b 1918) American
actor TW/6-9, 25-26
TOWNE'S BOY (fl 1600-01) actor
DA
TOWNLEY, Charles [Geoffrey
Thorn] (d 1905 [62]) pantomime
writer, dramatist BE*, EA/
06*, WWT/14*
TOWNLEY, Rev. James (1714-78)
English dramatist CDP, CP/3
TOWNLEY, James (d 1882 [66])
EA/83*
TOWNLEY, Richard Thomas (d
1889 [31]) EA/90*
TOWNLEY, William (d 1894 [65])
singer EA/95*
TOWNLEY-SEARLE, W. F. D.
see Searle, Townley
TOWNLY, Charles (fl 1760) drama-
tist CP/3
TOWNSEND, Mr. actor, singer
TD/1-2
TOWNSEND, Mrs. (fl 1796) actress
CDP
TOWNSEND, Alice (1860-90) singer
CDP
TOWNSEND, Aurelian (fl 1601-43)
dramatist CP/3, FGF
TOWNSEND, Barbara American
actress TW/23
TOWNSEND, C. (d 1909 [41])
property master EA/10*
TOWNSEND, Daniel E. (b 1823)
American actor HAS
TOWNSEND, Mrs. E. (d 1908)
EA/09*
TOWNSEND, Horace (1859-1922)
English dramatist WWA/1
TOWNSEND, J. E. (d 1899 [44])
actor? EA/00*
TOWNSEND, John (fl 1611-34) ac-
tor DA
TOWNSEND, John Frederick (d
1888) music-hall performer
EA/89*
TOWNSEND, Sarah [Mrs. William
Thompson Townsend] (d 1885)
EA/86*

TOWNSEND, Mrs. Stephen see
Burnett, Frances Hodgson
TOWNSEND, Thompson (d 1870
[64]) dramatist EA/71*,
WWT/14*
TOWNSEND, Mrs. William Thompson see Townsend, Sarah
TOWNWAY, Mrs. George see
Herbert, Annie
TOWSE, John Rankin (1845-1927)
English/American critic COC,
OC/1-3, WWA/1
TOY (fl 1592) actor DA
TOY, Agnes (d 1899) EA/01*
TOY, Beatrice (d 1938 [64]) actress BE*, WWT/14*
TOYE, Geoffrey Edward (b 1889)
conductor WWT/4-9
TOYE, Wendy (b 1917) English
actress, dancer, director
AAS, WWT/8-16
TOYNE, Gabriel (1905-63) English actor, producer WWT/
8-13
TOZER, Annie [Mrs. Henry
Tozer] (d 1899 [47]) EA/01*
TOZER, Sir Henry (d 1918 [67])
EA/19*
TOZER, Mrs. Henry see
Tozer, Annie
TOZER, J. B. (fl 1850s) comedian HAS
TOZERE, Frederic (1901-72)
American actor BE, TW/1-4,
8-9, 16, 26, 29, WWA/5,
WWT/10-15
TOZZI, Giorgio (b 1923) American singer CB
TRACEY, Andrew (b 1936) South
African actor TW/22-23
TRACEY, Herbert (b 1877) English singer GRB/1
TRACEY, Paul (b 1939) South
African actor TW/22-23,
27-28
TRACEY, Sid (d 1970 [70])
performer TW/27
TRACEY, Thomas F. (d 1961
[86]) Irish actor BE*, BP/
46*
TRACT, Jo (b 1939) American
actress TW/21, 25-26
TRACY, Agnes Ethel (fl 1868-75)
actress PP/3
TRACY, Douglas [Jack Graham
Lindsay] (d 1895 [38]) manager
EA/96*
TRACY, Helen (fl 1870-1908)

American actress WWS
TRACY, Hettie [Mrs. Jesse Williams] (d 1907) actress EA/08*
TRACY, John (d 1735) dramatist
CP/1-3
TRACY, John (b 1938) American
actor TW/20
TRACY, Lee (1898-1968) American
actor BE, TW/5-8, 22, 25,
WWA/5, WWT/7-14
TRACY, Lisa (b 1945) American
actress TW/26
TRACY, Spencer (1900-67) American actor BE, CB, ES, SR,
TW/24, WWA/4, WWT/7-11,
WWW/6
TRACY, Virginia (d 1946 [72])
American actress BE*, BP/
30*, WWT/14*
TRACY, William (d 1967 [48]) performer BP/52*
TRADER, Mrs. George Henry see
Augarde, Gertrude
TRAHAN, Al (d 1966 [69]) comedian
TW/23
TRAILL, George (b 1853) Scottish
actor GRB/1
TRAILL, Peter [Guy Mainwaring
Morton] (1896-1968) English
dramatist WWT/6-8
TRAIN, Arthur (1875-1945) American dramatist WWA/2, WWW/4
TRAJETTA, Philip (c. 1776-1854)
Italian/American composer,
manager DAB, WWA/H
TRANSFIELD, Cpt. (d 1887) performer? EA/89*
TRANSFIELD, Mrs. (d 1907 [75])
EA/08*
TRANSFIELD, Bellamina [Mrs. T.
G. Transfield] (d 1899 [39])
EA/00*
TRANSFIELD, Mrs. T. G. see
Transfield, Bellamina
TRANSFIELD, Thomas George (d
1911 [54]) circus proprietor
EA/12*
TRANSFIELD, Tilly (d 1890) EA/
91*
TRANUM, Charles B. (b 1916)
American talent representative
BE
TRAPANI, Lou (b 1947) American
actor TW/28-30
TRAPIDO, Joel (b 1913) American
educator, director BE
TRAPP, Dr. Joseph (1679-1747)
English dramatist CP/1-3, GT

TRASK, Franklin (b 1907) American producer, actor, educator BE

TRASK, Kate Nichols (d 1922) American dramatist WWA/1

TRAUBE, Shepard (b 1907) American manager, producer, director BE, WWT/10-16

TRAUBEL, Helen (1899/1903-1972) American singer, actress CB, ES, TW/12, 29, WWA/5

TRAUTMAN, William E. (d 1973 [75]) critic BP/58*

TRAUX, Sarah [Mrs. C. S. Albert] (b 1877) American actress GRB/3-4, WWT/1

TRAVER, Julia Merrick (fl 1900s) American editor WWM

TRAVER, Lee (d 1975 [70]) performer BP/60*

TRAVER, Sharry (b 1922) American actress TW/4

TRAVERS, Ben (b 1886) English dramatist AAS, BE, CD, CH, COC, MH, PDT, WWT/6-16

TRAVERS, Bill (b 1922) English actor TW/18-20

TRAVERS, Eliza see Brent, Bessie

TRAVERS, Ernest (d 1891) actor EA/92*

TRAVERS, Henry (1874-1965) English actor WWT/7-11

TRAVERS, Linden (b 1913) English actress WWT/10-11

TRAVERS, Nat (fl 1902?) music-hall singer CDP

TRAVERS, Roland (d 1970 [88]) performer BP/54*

TRAVERS, William (d 1880) English actor, dramatist EA/69

TRAVERS, Mrs. W. M. see Walsh, Blanche

TRAVERSE, Madlaine (d 1964 [88]) American actress BE*

TRAVIS, Mrs. Frank see Rosa, Madeline

TRAVIS, Jan R. (d 1975 [23]) performer BP/60*

TRAVIS, Joe (d 1879 [46]) manager EA/80*

TRAVIS, Michael (b 1928) American costume designer BE

TRAVOLTA, John (b 1954) American actor TW/28-30

TRAYLOR, William (b 1930) American actor TW/14-15, 23

TRAYNOR, Edward (d 1886 [31]) actor EA/87*

TRAYNOR, Tom (d 1907) variety comedian EA/08*

TREACHER, Arthur (1894-1975) English actor BE

TREACY, Emerson (d 1967 [66]) performer BP/51*

TREADWAY, Charlotte (d 1963 [68]) actress BE*

TREADWAY, Sophie (1890-1970) American dramatist MD, MH, MWD

TREBELLI, Zelia (1838-92) singer CDP

TREBLE, Sepha (b 1908) English actress, dancer WWT/9-10

TRECHMAN [or Treckman], Emma (b 1909) English actress WWT/9-13

TRECKMAN, Emma see Trechman, Emma

TREE, Miss (fl 1821?) dancer CDP

TREE, Anne (fl 1823) actress CDP

TREE, Ann Maria see Bradshaw, Ann Maria

TREE, David (b 1915) English actor WWT/9-11

TREE, Ellen see Kean, Mrs. Charles

TREE, Sir Herbert Beerbohm (1853-1917) English actor, manager CDP, COC, DNB, DP, ES, GRB/1-4, NTH, OC/1-3, PDT, SR, WWA/1, WWM, WWS, WWT/1-3, WWW/2

TREE, Iris (d 1968) dramatist BP/52*

TREE, Maria see Bradshaw, Ann Maria

TREE, Maud Beerbohm [Maud Holt] (1863-1937) English actress CDP, COC, DP, ES, GRB/1-4, NTH, OC/1-3, WWT/1-8, WWW/3

TREE, Viola (1884-1938) English actress ES, GRB/1-4, NTH, OC/1-3, WWT/1-8

TREES, Amanda American actress TW/25

TREFFZ, Henriette (fl 1850?) singer CDP

TREFOURET, Jeanne Alfredine see Hading, Jane

TREGETOUR, Prof. (d 1899 [32]) juggler, shadowgraphist EA/00*

TREGETOUR, Mrs. C. see

Tregetour, Mary
TREGETOUR, Mary [Mrs. C.
Tregetour] (d 1890 [31]) EA/
91*
TREGRE, George P. (b 1939)
American actor TW/25
TREHERNE, Bernard [Herbert
B. Cooper] (d 1898 [34]) actor
EA/99*
TRELAWNEY, R. S. [Thomas
Reid Strachan Hicks] actor
GRB/1
TREMAINE, Mr. (fl 1759) actor
HAS
TREMAINE, Annie see Amadi,
Mme.
TREMAINE, John (b 1946) Amer-
ican actor TW/30
TREMAYNE, Bella [Mrs. Henry
J. Butler] (d 1900) actress
EA/01*
TREMAYNE, Les (b 1913) Eng-
lish actor TW/7
TREMAYNE, Maude English ac-
tress GRB/1
TRENAMAN, John (b 1932) Aus-
tralian actor TW/25
TRENCH, Herbert (1865-1923)
Irish director, dramatist
DNB, WWT/1-4
TRENCH, Mrs. Ormsby (d 1902)
EA/03*
TRENCHARD, Sarah (1864-87)
actress NYM
TRENHOLME, Helen (1911-62)
Canadian actress WWT/9-11
TRENT, Bruce English actor,
singer WWT/12-16
TRENT, Edie (d 1888) dancer
EA/89*
TRENT, Sheila (d 1954 [46])
actress TW/10
TRENTINI, Emma (d 1959 [74])
Italian actress, singer TW/
15, WWT/4-5
TRESAHAR, John (d 1936 [76])
actor GRB/1-4, WWT/1-5
TRESCOTT, Virginia Drew (d
1911 [41]) American actress
SR
TRESKO, Elsa Austrian actress
TW/30
TRESMAND, Ivy (b 1898) Eng-
lish actress, singer WWT/
4-11
TRESSIDDER (d 1890) stage mana-
ger EA/91*
TRESSIDDER, Mrs. Arthur (d

1889) EA/91*
TRESSIDER, John Arthur (d 1894
[33]) manager EA/95*
TRETYAKOV, Sergei Mikhailovich
(1892-1939) Russian dramatist
COC
TREVANION, Edward (d 1887 [38])
lessee, proprietor EA/88*
TREVANION, Harry (d 1917 [58])
manager, actor EA/18*
TREVELL, William (fl 1608-21)
share-holder DA
TREVELYAN (d 1892 [25]) EA/93*
TREVELYAN, Florence see
Brough, Mrs. Robert
TREVELYAN, Hilda [née Tucker]
(1877/79/80-1959) English ac-
tress COC, DNB, GRB/1-4,
OC/3, WWT/1-11, WWW/5
TREVILLE, Roger (b 1903) French
actor, singer WWT/9
TREVISAN, Vittorio (b 1868) Italian
singer WWA/4
TREVOR, Ann [Annie Trilnick]
(1899-1970) actress WWT/4-9
TREVOR, Austin (b 1897) Irish ac-
tor AAS, WWT/6-15
TREVOR, Claire (b 1909) American
actress ES, WWT/8-11
TREVOR, Enid (d 1965) actress
BP/49*, WWT/14*
TREVOR, Francis (b 1827) English
singer HAS
TREVOR, Leo (d 1927 [62]) drama-
tist GRB/4, WWT/1-5
TREVOR, Norman (1877-1929) In-
dian/English actor WWT/1-6
TREVOR, Spencer (1875-1945)
French/English actor WWT/1-9
TREVOR, Theodore [Herbert Theo-
dore Garland] (d 1909 [56]) EA/
10*
TREVOR, Vaughan (b 1880) English
actor WWM
TREVOR, William [William Trevor
Cox] (b 1928) Irish dramatist
CD
TREVORI, Sig. (d 1916 [89]) per-
former, conjuror, ventriloquist,
musician EA/18*
TREW, Christine Patti [Lady Long-
ford] (fl 1933-40) dramatist,
translator COC
TREWAR, Eliza Marian see
Shaw, Mrs.
TREWIN, John Courtenay (b 1908)
English critic AAS, COC,
PDT, WWT/10-16

TREWREN, Emily M. see
Marmion, Emily M.
TRIANA, Rafael (b 1947) Ameri-
can actor TW/27
TRIBUSH, Nancy (b 1940) Amer-
ican actress TW/26-29
TRIEGLE, Norman (d 1975 [47])
performer BP/59*
TRIEVE, Richard Ernest (d 1916)
EA/17*
TRIGG, William (fl first half of
17th cent) actor COC, DA,
OC/3
TRIGGER, Ian J. (b 1942) Eng-
lish actor TW/30
TRIGGS, Alfred Standen (d 1910
[62]) EA/11*
TRILLING, Ossia (b 1913) Eng-
lish actor, director, stage
manager, critic WWT/13-16
TRILNICK, Annie see Trevor,
Ann
TRIMBLE, Byron A. (d 1976
[61]) executive BP/60*
TRIMBLE, Jessie (d 1957 [83])
American dramatist BE*,
BP/41*
TRIMBLE, Lawrence (d 1954
[69]) director BE*
TRIMMER, Sarah (1741-1810)
English dramatist CDP, CP/3
TRIMMINGHAM, Ernest (d 1942
[63]) actor BE*, WWT/14*
TRINDER, Tommy (b 1909)
English comedian WWT/10-16
TRIPLETT, Erna La Quer
(d 1964 [66]) equestrian BE*
TRIPP, Emily (d 1893 [70])
EA/95*
TRIPP, Frederick (d 1968 [76])
performer BP/53*
TRIPP, June Howard see June
TRIPP, Susan fat girl CDP
TRIPPAS, Henry (d 1874) music-
hall manager EA/75*
TRIPPELLO, Sig. see Good-
liffe, John Herbert
TRIQUET, M. , Jr. (d 1876)
aeronaut EA/77*
TRITSCHLER, Conrad (d 1939
[71]) scene artist WWT/14*
TRITSCHLER, Henry Joseph (d
1917 [19]) EA/18*
TRITTIPO, James (d 1971 [43])
designer TW/28
TRIVIER, Pierre-Olaf see
Olaf, Pierre
TRIX, Helen (d 1951 [59]) actress

BE*, WWT/14*
TROCHON, Marie see Aimée,
Marie
TROLLOPE, Fred James (d 1910)
EA/11*
TRONTO, Rudy (b 1928) American
actor TW/21, 27-29
TROOBNICK, Eugene (b 1926)
American actor TW/24, 26,
28, WWT/16
TROTERE, H. (d 1912) composer
EA/13*
TROTMAN, William C. (b 1930)
American administrative director
BE
TROTTER, Catharine see Cock-
burn, Catharine
TROTTER, Thomas actor, manager
TD/2
TROUBAT, Francis dramatist RJ
TROUGHTON, Adolphus Charles
English dramatist EA/69
TROUNCER, Cecil (1898-1953)
English actor COC, OC/3,
WWT/9-11, WWW/5
TROUTMAN, Ivy (b 1883) American
actress WWM, WWS, WWT/4-
11
TROW, William (d 1973 [82]) per-
former BP/58*
TROWBRIDGE, Mr. (d 1838) mana-
ger, actor HAS
TROWBRIDGE, Mrs. see Chap-
man, Mrs. William A.
TROWBRIDGE, Annie (d 1886 [21])
singer EA/87*
TROWBRIDGE, Hester (d 1890)
music-hall performer EA/91*
TROWBRIDGE, Will (d 1911 [74])
music-hall performer EA/13*
TROWER, Carlos (d 1889 [40])
"African Blondin" EA/90*
TROY, Hector (b 1941) American
actor TW/25-26
TROY, John J. (d 1975 [56]) per-
former BP/60*
TROY, Louise American actress,
singer BE, WWT/15-16
TROY, Rachel Finney see Denvil,
Rachel
TRUAX, Sarah (b 1877) American
actress WWM, WWS, WWT/2-6
TRUE, Oswald (d 1899) manager
EA/00*
TRUEBA, Don (d 1835) dramatist
BE*, WWT/14*
TRUEMAN, Mr. actor TD/1-2
TRUEMAN, Paula (b 1907) Ameri-

can actress BE, TW/1, 8,
12-13, 20, 23-24, 26, WWT/
15-16
TRUESDELL, Frederick (d 1937
[64]) actor BE*, BP/21*
TRUESDELL, Mrs. Frederick
see Hall, Laura Nelson
TRUEX, Ernest (1889/90-1973)
American actor BE, CB,
SR, TW/1-19, 22, 30, WWT/
4-15
TRUEX, Philip (b 1911) American
actor TW/2-5
TRUFFI, Teresa (fl 1848) singer
CDP, HAS
TRUMBO, Dalton dramatist CD
TRUMBO, Nancy (b 1945) Amer-
ican actress TW/29
TRUSSELL, Alvery (fl 1600-01)
actor DA
TRUSSELL, Fred (1858-1923)
English manager, conductor
GRB/1-4
TRZCINSKI, Edmund (b 1921)
American dramatist, director,
actor BE
TSEGAYE GABRE-MEDHIN (b
1936) Ethiopian dramatist,
director CD
TSIANG, H. T. (d 1971 [72])
performer BP/56*
TSOUTSOUVAS, Sam (b 1948)
American actor TW/29-30
TUBBS, Arthur Lewis (1867-
1946) American dramatist
WWA/2, WWM
TUBBS, Mrs. Charles see
Arnold, Mrs. Henry
TUCCI, Maria (b 1941) Italian
actress TW/22-27, WWT/16
TUCHIN, John see Tutchin,
John
TUCK, Mrs. Albert see
Cullen, Rose
TUCKER, Mr. (d 1874) musician
EA/75*
TUCKER, Forrest (b 1919)
American actor, writer BE,
TW/20, 30
TUCKER, Frederick C. (d 1917
[40]) managing director EA/
18*
TUCKER, George Loane (d 1921
[49]) American actor, director
BE*, BP/6*
TUCKER, Hilda see Trevelyan,
Hilda
TUCKER, Ian (b 1946) American

actor TW/30
TUCKER, Johnny (d 1971 [73])
composer/lyricist BP/55*
TUCKER, Richard (1913-75) Ameri-
can singer CB, ES
TUCKER, Sophie [Sophie Abuza]
(1884-1966) American actress,
singer BE, CB, ES, NTH,
TW/2-7, 18-19, 22, WWA/4,
WWT/7-14
TUCKER, William T. (d 1881
[32]) EA/82*
TUCKERMAN, Maury (1905-66)
American director, stage mana-
ger, actor BE
TUCKETT, Harvey (d 1854) English
actor HAS
TUCKETT, Mrs. Harvey (fl 1850s)
English actress, manager HAS
TUCKETT, Margaret see Tuckett,
Mrs. Harvey
TUCKFEILD, Thomas (fl 1624)
actor DA
TUDOR, Alice (d 1876 [29]) eques-
trienne EA/77*
TUDOR, Annie (1855-87) English
actress NYM
TUDOR, Anthony (b 1909) English
dancer, choreographer BE,
CB, ES, WWT/10-12
TUDOR, Carry (d 1879) actress
EA/80*
TUDOR, Rowan (b 1905) American
actor, singer, director BE
TUDOR, Valerie (b 1910) Welsh
actress WWT/9-10
TUERK, John (d 1951 [62]) Ameri-
can producer TW/7
TUESKI, Sophie H. (d 1892 [46])
musician EA/93*
TUFFLEY, Eric see Lewis, Eric
TUFTS, Sonny (d 1970 [59]) per-
former BP/55*
TUKE, Miss see Hallam, Mrs.
Lewis
TUKE, Richard (fl 1672) dramatist
CP/1-3
TUKE, Sir Samuel (d 1674) English
dramatist CDP, CP/1-3, GT,
OC/1-3
TULA, John (d 1906 [58]) gymnast
EA/07*
TULL, Patrick (b 1941) English
actor TW/23
TULLETT, Fred (d 1889) EA/90*
TULLOCK, William (d 1899) EA/
00*
TULLOCK, William, Jr. (d 1886

[23]) musician EA/87*

TULLY, Emily Jane (d 1887 [58]) EA/88*

TULLY, Ethel (d 1968 [70]) performer BP/53*

TULLY, George F. (1876-1930) Irish actor GRB/1, WWT/3-6

TULLY, James H. (d 1868 [53]) musical director EA/69*

TULLY, James Syrus see Syrus, Napoleon

TULLY, May (1884-1924) Canadian actress, dancer SR

TULLY, Richard Walton (1877-1945) American dramatist, producer HJD, WWA/2, WWT/4-9

TUMARIN, Boris [né Tumarinson] (b 1910) Latvian actor, director, teacher BE, TW/24-25, WWT/15-16

TUMARINSON, Boris see Tumarin, Boris

TUNBRIDGE, Joseph A. (1886-1961) English composer, conductor WWT/8-11

TUNE, Tommy (b 1939) American actor TW/29-30

TUNNELL, George N. (d 1975 [62]) performer BP/59*

TUNSTALL, Catherine (1796-1846) actress, singer CDP

TUNSTALL, James (fl 1583-97) actor DA

TUPLIN, Lily [Mrs. T. A. Edge] (d 1898) actress EA/99*

TUPOU, Manu (b 1935/39) Fijian actor TW/26, 28, WWT/16

TUPPER, Martin Farquhar (d 1889 [78]) dramatist EA/90*

TUPPER, Mary (d 1964 [86]) American actress BE*

TURBUTT, Mr. (d 1746) actor CDP

TURGENEV, Ivan Sergeivich (1818-83) Russian dramatist COC, OC/3

TURGEON, Peter (b 1919) American actor, director, writer BE

TURKISH ROPEDANCER CDP

TURLE (d 1882 [80]) musician EA/83*

TURLEIGH, Veronica (1903-71) Irish actress COC, WWT/6-14

TURNBULL, Mr. (fl 1799) actor HAS

TURNBULL, Miss C. (fl 1826) American actress HAS

TURNBULL, Dixon (d 1917) EA/18*

TURNBULL, Jill (b 1963) American actress TW/30

TURNBULL, John (1880-1956) Scottish actor, stage manager WWT/9-11

TURNBULL, John D. (fl 1799?) dramatist EAP, RJ

TURNBULL, Julia (1822?-87) American actress HAS, NYM

TURNBULL, Julia (d 1887 [65]) dancer CDP

TURNBULL, Margaret (d 1942) Scottish dramatist WWA/2

TURNBULL, Stanley (d 1924) English actor WWT/4

TURNER, Aidan (1908/16-68) Indian actor TW/4

TURNER, Alfred (1870-1941) English manager GRB/4, WWT/1-9

TURNER, Annie [Mrs. H. J. Turner] (d 1872) EA/73*

TURNER, Anthony (fl 1st half of 17th cent) English actor COC, DA, OC/1-3

TURNER, Arthur see Rigby, Arthur, Jr.

TURNER, Bob (b 1922) American actor TW/4

TURNER, Bridget English actress WWT/16

TURNER, Carrie (d 1897) actress WWT/14*

TURNER, Charles (d 1894) singer EA/95*

TURNER, Cicely [Mrs. W. H. Leverton] (d 1940) actress BE*, WWT/14*

TURNER, Claramae American actress, singer BE

TURNER, David (b 1927) English dramatist AAS, CD, CH, ES, MH, PDT, WWT/15-16

TURNER, Dorothy (1895-1969) actress WWT/6-9

TURNER, Douglas (b 1930) American actor TW/22-26

TURNER, Drewe (fl 1633) actor DA

TURNER, Eardley (d 1929) actor, journalist BE*, WWT/14*

TURNER, Ella (fl 1866) actress HAS

TURNER, Ellen (d 1872) American

actress HAS
TURNER, Florence [Nora Temple]
(d 1917) EA/18*
TURNER, Florence (1887/88-
1946) American actress ES,
TW/3
TURNER, George (b 1902) Eng-
lish actor BE, TW/13, 22
TURNER, George (d 1968) per-
former BP/53*
TURNER, G. G. (1844-69) Amer-
ican actor HAS
TURNER, Harold (1909-62) Eng-
lish dancer WWT/9-12
TURNER, Harry (d 1916) music-
hall singer CDP
TURNER, Helena [Hélène Cros-
mond] (d 1888 [35]) singer
EA/89*
TURNER, H. J. (d 1891 [85])
actor EA/92*, WWT/14*
TURNER, H. J. (d 1898 [36])
EA/00*
TURNER, Mrs. H. J. see
Turner, Annie
TURNER, Jim (b 1947) American
actor TW/29
TURNER, John (d 1881) actor
EA/82*
TURNER, Mrs. John (d 1881)
actress EA/82*
TURNER, John Hastings (1892-
1956) English dramatist,
producer WWT/4-11, WWW/5
TURNER, Julia (fl 1832) actress
HAS
TURNER, J. W. (d 1913 [68])
singer, producer, manager
BE*, WWT/14*
TURNER, Kitty see Pryce,
Catharine Gompertz
TURNER, Leon (d 1900) musi-
cal director EA/01*
TURNER, Maidel (d 1953 [72])
American actress TW/1-6,
9
TURNER, Margaret (fl 1790)
translator? CP/3
TURNER, Marion actress GRB/
1-2
TURNER, Maurice Clark (1878-
1953) American manager
WWA/3
TURNER, Michael (b 1921) South
African actor WWT/15-16
TURNER, Montague [Raymond
Dudley] (d 1917) EA/18*
TURNER, Percy M. (d 1971)

performer BP/55*
TURNER, Richard J. (d 1857)
American singer CDP, HAS
TURNER, Robert (d 1970) performer
BP/55*
TURNER, Terry (d 1971 [79])
publicist BP/56*
TURNER, W. (d 1872) minstrel
EA/73*
TURNER, William see Rigby,
Arthur
TURNER, William A. (fl 1810)
English actor HAS
TURNER, Mrs. William A. (fl
1810) English actress HAS
TURNER, Willis Lloyd (b 1927)
American educator, director
BE
TURNER, W. J. (1889-1946) Eng-
lish dramatist MD
TURNEY, Catherine (b 1906) Amer-
ican dramatist BE
TURNEY, John (d 1853) HAS
TURPIN, Mr. actor TD/2
TURPIN, Miss (fl 1837) actress
HAS
TURPIN, Ben (1868/69/74-1940)
American vaudevillian ES,
WWA/4
TURPIN, George (d 1872 [60])
box book-keeper EA/73*
TURPIN, Mrs. George see Tur-
pin, Isabella
TURPIN, Isabella [Mrs. George
Turpin] (d 1872 [59]) EA/73*
TURPIN, Maria see Wallack,
Mrs. Henry John
TURPIN, S. Hart (d 1899 [62])
scene artist EA/00*
TURQUE, Mimi (b 1939) American
actress TW/22-24
TURRELL, Thomas Edward (d
1903) musical director EA/04*
TURTON-BROWNE, Margaret ac-
tress GRB/1
TUSHINGHAM, Rita (b 1942) Eng-
lish actress CB, ES, WWT/
15-16
TUSON, Isabella [Miss George] (d
1870 [25]) actress EA/71*
TUSSAUD, Mme. (d 1850 [90])
wax-work, exhibitor EA/72*
TUSSAUD, Dorothy Allen (d 1897)
EA/98*
TUSSAUD, Francis (d 1873 [73])
waxwork exhibitor? EA/74*
TUSSAUD, Joseph (d 1892 [61])
EA/93*

TUSSER, Thomas (fl c. 1540)
actor DA
TUSTIN, John T. (d 1886 [40])
musician EA/87*
TUTCHIN, John (d 1707 [47])
dramatist CP/1-3, GT
TUTE, Agnes Clare [Mrs.
James T. Tute] (d 1886 [33])
EA/88*
TUTE, James (d 1870) proprietor
EA/71*
TUTE, Mrs. James T. see
Tute, Agnes Clare
TUTE, John (d 1885) musician
EA/86*
TUTE, Mrs. John see Tute,
Mrs. M. M.
TUTE, Mary Elizabeth [Mrs.
Sam Tute] (d 1894) EA/95*
TUTE, Mrs. M. M. [Mrs. John
Tute] (d 1876 [26]) EA/77*
TUTE, Mrs. Sam see Tute,
Mary Elizabeth
TUTHILL, Harry (d 1863) Irish
actor HAS
TUTIN, Dorothy (b 1930) English
actress AAS, BE, ES, PDT,
TW/24, WWT/12-16
TUTON, E. S. (d 1867 [64]) pro-
prietor EA/68*
TUTTLE, Day (b 1902) American
director, actor, dramatist,
educator BE
TUTTON, Mrs. George S. see
Leslie, Grace
TWAIN, Mark (1835-1910) Amer-
ican dramatist ES, NTH
TWAIN, Michael (b 1936) Amer-
ican actor TW/25
TWAIN, Norman (b 1930) Amer-
ican producer, director BE
TWAITS, William (c. 1770-1814)
English actor COC, OC/1-3,
SR
TWAITS, William (1781-1814)
English actor CDP, HAS
TWAITS, Mrs. William [Miss
E. A. Westray; Mrs. Villiers]
(1787-1813) English actress
HAS
TWEDDELL, Frank (1895-1971)
Indian actor TW/5, 7, 28
TWEDDELL, Oliver L. (d 1898)
scene artist EA/99*
TWEED, Tommy (d 1971 [64])
performer BP/56*
TWEEDALE, Harold (d 1909)
manager EA/10*

TWELVETREES, Helen (d 1958
[49]) actress TW/14
TWIBELL, Mrs. (d 1893) EA/94*
TWIBELL, Miss (fl 1842) American
actress HAS
TWIBELL, William (d 1890 [56])
EA/91*
TWIGG, Lieut. James (d 1884 [66])
business manager EA/85*
TWINBERROW, William Henry
see Wolston, Henry
TWINEM, Leo L. (d 1968 [78])
performer BP/53*
TWISS, Mrs. see Kemble,
Frances
TWIST, John (d 1976 [77]) producer/
director/choreographer BP/60*
TWISTLETON, Mrs. (d c. 1808/09)
see Stanley, Mrs.
TWOMEY, John (b 1948) American
actor TW/28
TWYBELL, Miss see Flynn,
Mrs. Thomas
TWYFORD, J. Henry (b 1880) Eng-
lish actor, stage manager
GRB/1-2
TWYFORD, Warner (d 1968 [57])
critic BP/52*
TYARS, Frank (1848-1918/19) Eng-
lish actor GRB/3-4, OAA/1-2,
WWT/1-3
TYERS, Jonathan (d 1767) propri-
etor DNB
TYLER, Mr. (d 1851) actress
HAS
TYLER, Charles (d 1972 [32])
performer BP/57*
TYLER, Elizabeth Priscilla see
Tyler, Mrs. Robert
TYLER, George (d 1878) musician
EA/79*
TYLER, George Crouse (1867-
1946) American producing mana-
ger DAB, GRB/2-4, NTH,
TW/2, WWA/2, WWM, WWS,
WWT/1-9
TYLER, George H. (d 1884) actor,
manager CDP
TYLER, Gladys (d 1972 [79]) per-
former BP/56*
TYLER, Janet American actress
TW/1
TYLER, Joseph (1751-1823) actor
HAS
TYLER, Joseph (d 1883) musician
EA/84*
TYLER, Joseph (d 1904 [93]) musi-
cal director EA/05*

TYLER, Mrs. Joseph (fl 1795-96) English actress HAS
TYLER, Joseph Saunders (b 1811) actor CDP
TYLER, Judy (d 1957 [24]) actress TW/14
TYLER, Leslie (d 1912 [48]) singer EA/13*
TYLER, Marie [Mrs. Leo Dryden] (d 1905 [30]) burlesque actress EA/06*
TYLER, Odette [Mrs. R. D. McLean] (1869-1936) American actress GRB/3-4, SR, WWA/2, WWS, WWT/1-5
TYLER, Parker (d 1974 [70]) critic BP/59*
TYLER, Richard (b 1932) American actor TW/3
TYLER, Mrs. Robert (1816-89) actress CDP, SR
TYLER, Royall (1757-1826) American dramatist CDP, COC, DAB, EAP, ES, HJD, MH, NTH, OC/1-3, RE, RJ, SR, WWA/H
TYLER, Thomas (1826-1902) English scholar DNB
TYLER, Tom (d 1954 [50]) actor BE*
TYLER, T. Texas (d 1972 [55]) composer/lyricist BP/56*
TYLER, William (d 1864 [65]) EA/72*
TYNAN, Brandon (1879-1967) Irish/American actor, dramatist TW/23, WWT/4-10
TYNAN, Kenneth [Peacock] (b 1927) English critic AAS, BE, CB, CH, COC, NTH, PDT, WWT/13-16
TYNDALL, Kate (d 1919) actress BE*, WWT/14*
TYNE, George (b 1917) American actor TW/2, 13-15
TYRA, Dan (b 1936) American actor TW/24-25
TYREE, Bessie (b 1870) American actress WWM
TYREE, Elizabeth (fl 1889-1907) American actress PP/3, WWS
TYRER, Miss (fl 1800-05) singer TD/1-2
TYRER, Sarah see Liston, Mrs. John
TYRREL, Mrs. M. A. (b 1815) English actress HAS

TYRREL, Thomas Moore (fl 1852) English actor HAS
TYRRELL, Brad (b 1943) American actor TW/30
TYRRELL, David (b 1916) American actor TW/3
TYRRELL, Henry (b 1865/66) American dramatist GRB/3, WWM
TYRRELL, Mrs. H. F. see Holt, Issy
TYRRELL, Mrs. Joseph see Tyrrell, Lucy Alice
TYRRELL, Kittie [Mrs. Harry Ewins] (d 1894 [35]) actress EA/96*
TYRRELL, Lucy Alice [Mrs. Joseph Tyrrell] (d 1869) EA/70*
TYRRELL, Rose (d 1934 [75]) dancer BE*, WWT/14*
TYRRELL, Ruby [Alice Staunton] (d 1895) actress EA/96*
TYRRELL, Susan American actress TW/26
TYSALL, Harriett (d 1881 [21]) singer EA/82*
TYSON, Caroline (fl 1854-56) American actress HAS
TYSON, Cicely (b 1939?) American actress CB, TW/24, WWT/16
TYSON, Davey (d 1976 [73]) performer BP/60*
TYSON, Josephine see Kent, Mrs. Fred S.
TYSON, Ruth M. (d 1971 [58]) producer/director/choreographer BP/56*
TYSON, Tara American actress TW/27
TYZACK, Margaret actress WWT/15-16

- U -

UBALDINI, Petruccio (fl 1576) Italian actor DA
UDALL, Charles (d 1884) proprietor EA/85*
UDALL, Nicholas (1505-56) English dramatist COC, CP/2-3, DNB, ES, FGF, HP, MH, NTH, OC/1-3, PDT
UDELL, Peter lyricist CD
UFFNER, Frank manager CDP
UGARTE, Floro M. (d 1975 [91]) composer/lyricist BP/60*

UGGAMS, Eloise (d 1972 [75])
performer BP/57*
UGGAMS, Leslie (b 1943) Amer-
ican singer, actress CB,
TW/23-25
UHDE, Hermann (1914-65) Ger-
man singer WWA/4
UHL, May see Buckley, May
ULANOVA, Galina (b 1910)
Russian dancer CB
ULLENDORF, Jacquie (b 1945)
American actress TW/29
ULLMAN, Bernard manager
CDP
ULLMAN, James Ramsey (d 1971
[63]) dramatist BP/56*
ULLMAN, Robert (b 1928) Amer-
ican press representative BE
ULLMAN, S. George (d 1975
[82]) agent BP/60*
ULMANN, Doris (d 1972 [56])
performer BP/57*
ULMAR, Geraldine (1862-1932)
American actress, singer
CDP, DP, WWT/6
ULMER, Edgar G. (d 1972 [68])
producer/director/choreographer
BP/57*
ULMER, Lizzie May actress CDP
ULMER, Roch (d 1975) producer/
director/choreographer BP/
59*
ULPH, Mrs. Harry see Lauri,
Stella
ULPH, Henry (d 1897 [37]) pro-
prietor EA/98*
ULRIC, Lenore (1892/94-1970)
American actress BE, TW/
3-13, 27, WWT/4-11
ULRICH, Charles (1859?-1941)
dramatist CB
ULRICH, Pauline (b 1835) actress
CDP
ULRICO, Pietro (d 1888 [40])
musician EA/89*
UMANN, Olga (d 1972 [57]) per-
former BP/57*
UMEKO, Miyoshi (b 1929) Japan-
ese actress BE
UNDERELL (fl 1602) actor DA
UNDERHILL, Cave (c. 1634-
c. 1710) English actor CDP,
COC, DNB, OC/1-3
UNDERHILL, Edward (d 1964
[65]) actor BE*
UNDERHILL, John Garrett (1876-
1946) American dramatist,
critic, producer WWA/2

UNDERHILL, Nicholas (fl 1624)
actor DA
UNDERWOOD, Cecil (d 1906) actor
EA/07*
UNDERWOOD, Frank (d 1917)
actor EA/18*
UNDERWOOD, Franklyn (d 1940
[63]) American actor BE*,
BP/25*
UNDERWOOD, Grace see Barry,
Christine
UNDERWOOD, Isabelle (fl 1895-
1907) American actress, singer
WWS
UNDERWOOD, John (c. 1590-1624)
English actor COC, DA, GT,
NTH, OC/1-3
UNDERWOOD, T. (fl 1782) drama-
tist CP/3
UNGER, Gladys B. [Gladys B.
Goodman] (d 1940 [55]) Ameri-
can dramatist GRB/4, WWM,
WWT/1-9, WWW/3
UNGER, Stella (d 1970 [65]) dram-
atist BP/54*
UNRUH, Walther (1898-1973) Ger-
man theatre technician, educator
BE
UNSWORTH, Evelyn [Mrs. J. B.
Ashley] (d 1892 [26]) actress
EA/93*
UNSWORTH, James (1838-75) Eng-
lish minstrel HAS
UNWIN, George actor, manager
GRB/1
UPSHER, Peter (d 1963 [70]) per-
former BE*
UPTON, Frances (d 1975 [71])
performer BP/60*
UPTON, Leonard (b 1901) English
actor WWT/6-9
UPTON, Robert (fl 1750-52) English
actor, manager WWA/H
UPTON, Robert Michael Garbois
(d 1891 [16]) musician, com-
poser EA/92*
URBAN, Joseph (1872-1933) Aus-
trian/American architect, de-
signer COC, DAB, ES, NTH,
OC/1-3
URE, Mary (1933-75) Scottish ac-
tress BE, ES, TW/28, WWT/
12-15
URICH, John (1849-1939) West In-
dian composer WWW/3
URICH, Tom Canadian actor TW/
23, 26-28
URQUHART, Isabelle [Mrs. Guy

Standing] (1865-1907) American
actress CDP, WWS
URQUHART, Mary Sinclair see
Urquhart, Molly
URQUHART, Molly [née Mary
Sinclair Urquhart] (d 1977)
Scottish actress WWT/11-14
URSO, Camilla (1842-1902) musi-
cian CDP
USCO CD
USERA, Ramon (d 1972 [67])
composer/lyricist BP/57*
USHER, Dora (d 1881 [27]) ac-
tress EA/82*
USHER, Graham (d 1975 [36])
performer BP/59*
USHER, Lancelot (d 1916 [44])
EA/17*
USHER, Luke (d 1815) American
actor, manager HAS, WWA/H
USHER, Noble B. (b c. 1770)
actor SR
USHER, Richard (1785-1843)
pantomimist, clown CDP,
DNB
USTINOV, Peter [Alexander] (b
1921) English actor, dramatist,
producer, director AAS, BE,
CB, CD, CH, COC, ES, MD,
MH, MWD, OC/2-3, PDT,
TW/14-19, WWT/10-16
USTINOV, Tamara English ac-
tress TW/30

- V -

VACCARO, Brenda (b 1939) Amer-
ican actress BE, TW/18-20,
22-25, 27, WWT/15-16
VACHE, William A. (d 1849)
American actor HAS
VACHELL, Horace Annesley
(1861-1955) English dramatist
GRB/3, WWT/3-11, WWW/5
VAGUE, Vera (d 1974) actress
BP/59*, WWT/16*
VAHANIAN, Marc (b 1956) Amer-
ican actor TW/26
VAIDIS, Lizzie [Mrs. J. H. Al-
len] (d 1911 [46]) trapezist
EA/12*
VAIL, Mr. American circus
performer HAS
VAIL, Lester (d 1959 [59])
American actor, director
WWT/7-8
VAILE, Amy see Fanchette,

Amy
VAILLAND, Roger (d 1965 [57])
dramatist BP/49*
VAJDA, Ernest (1887-1954) Hun-
garian dramatist TW/10, WWT/
8-11
VAL, Mons. (fl 1796) English actor
HAS
VAL, Mme. (fl 1796) English ac-
tress HAS
VAL, Paul (d 1962 [75]) actor,
producer BE*
VALAIDA [Valaida Snow] American
actress, singer WWT/8-10
VALASCO, David see Belasco,
David
VALDARE, Sunny Jim (d 1962
[88]) American performer BE*
VALDO, Mrs. H. see Chadwick,
Sophia
VALDO, Harry (d 1917) EA/18*
VALDO, Pat (d 1970 [89]) circus
director BP/55*
VALE, Michael (b 1922) American
actor TW/22-26, 28-29
VALE, Samuel (1797-1848) English
actor CDP, OX
VALE, Mrs. W. (d 1882 [42])
EA/83*
VALE, Will (d 1889) music-hall
acting manager EA/90*
VALENCEY, Miss (fl 1812?)
dancer CDP
VALENCY, Maurice (b 1903) Amer-
ican educator, dramatist BE
VALENTI, Michael (d 1943) Amer-
ican actor TW/24-26
VALENTIA, George, Lord Viscount
(b 1769) dramatist CP/3
VALENTINE, Miss (fl 1789) see
Taylor, Mrs.
VALENTINE [Archibald Thomas
Pechey] (b 1876) lyricist, dram-
atist WWT/5-8
"VALENTINE" see D'Iffanger,
Thomas Howard Paul
VALENTINE, Dickie (d 1971 [41])
performer BP/55*
VALENTINE, Gertrude [Mrs.
Lauderdale Maitland] (d 1907
[26]) actress EA/08*
VALENTINE, Grace (1884/91-1964)
American actress TW/3, 5-12,
21, WWT/6-13
VALENTINE, James (b 1933)
American actor TW/18
VALENTINE, James see Balen-
tyne, James

VALENTINE, Paul (d 1924 [85])
dancer, ballet master BE*,
WWT/14*
VALENTINE, Paul (b 1919) Amer-
ican actor, dancer, choreog-
rapher BE, TW/1-3, 9-12,
14-16
VALENTINE, Sidney [or Sydney]
(1865-1919) actor EA/95,
GRB/1-4, WWT/1-3
VALENTINE, T. C. (d 1909)
actor WWT/14*
VALENTINE, Thomas (d 1878
[87]) composer EA/79*
VALENTINE, Dr. William (d
1865/66) actor CDP, HAS
VALENTINI, Eliza (fl 1856?)
CDP
VALENTINO, Rudolph (1895-
1926) Italian dancer, actor
WWA/1
VALENTINOFF, Val see Val-
entine, Paul
VALENTY, Lili Polish actress
TW/2
VALERIO, Theresa (d 1964
[70+]) performer BE*
VALERO, Fernando (1854/57-
1914) Spanish singer ES
VALERIUS, John (fl 1819?)
freak CDP
VALINOTE, Merrick D. (d
1976 [78]) conductor BP/60*
VALK, Frederick (d 1956 [55])
German/Czech actor AAS,
WWT/10-11
VALLANCE, W. S. (d 1903)
teacher of elocution EA/05*
VALLEE, Henrietta see
De Bar, Mrs. Benedict
VALLEE, Rudy (d 1901) Amer-
ican actor, singer, musician,
composer BE, CB
VALLEE SISTERS, The (fl 1836)
American actress HAS
VALLENTINE, Benjamin Benna-
ton (1843-1926) English/
American dramatist DAB,
WWA/2
VALLERIA, Alwina Lohmann (b
1848) singer CDP
VALLETTI, Cesare (b 1922)
Italian singer ES
VALLI, Valli [Valli Knust] (1882-
1927) German actress GRB/
4, WWM, WWT/1-5
VALLI, Virginia (d 1968 [70])
performer BP/53*

VALLIERE, Florence actress CDP
VALLIN, Ninon (d 1961 [75]) singer
BE*
VALLIQUIETTO, Margaret Rose
see Knight, June
VALLO, Domenico (b 1803) musi-
cian, writer CDP
VALLON, Michael (b 1897) Ameri-
can actor TW/2
VALOIS, Ninette de see De
Valois, Ninette
VALOR, Henrietta American ac-
tress TW/29-30
VALPY, Richard (fl 1795-1803)
dramatist CP/3
VALROSE, Lizzie singer, actress
CDP
VAMP, Hugo see O'Neill, J. R.
VAN, Billy (d 1973 [61]) performer
BP/58*
VAN, Billy B. (1870-1950) Ameri-
can actor SR, TW/7, WWA/3,
WWT/5-7
VAN, Bobby (b 1930/32) American
dancer, singer, actor TW/27-
29, WWT/15-16
VAN, Charley (d 1963 [80]) per-
former BE*
VAN, Gus (1887-1968) American
actor TW/3, 24
VAN, Samye (d 1972 [61]) performer
BP/57*
VAN, Shirley (b 1927) American
actress TW/3
VAN AKEN, Gretchen (b 1940)
American actress TW/23,
28-29
VAN ALSTYNE, Egbert Aanson
(1882-1951) American songwriter
BE*, BP/36*
VAN AMBURGH, Isaac A. (1812-
65) American actor CDP, HAS,
ES
VAN ARK, Joan (b 1943) American
actress TW/27
VAN BEERS, Stanley (1911-61)
English actor WWT/12-13
VAN BENSCHOTEN, Stephen (b
1943) American actor TW/28,
30
VAN BEUREN, Mrs. A. H. see
Bernard, Dorothy
VAN BEUREN, Archbold (d 1974
[68]) publisher BP/59*
VAN BIENE, Auguste (1850-1913)
Dutch actor, composer GRB/
1-4, WWM, WWT/1
VANBRUGGEN, Mrs. [Mrs. Mount-

ford] actress GT, TD/2

VANBRUGH, Dame Irene [Mrs. Dion G. Boucicault] (1872-1949) English actress AAS, CDP, COC, DNB, EA/95, ES, GRB/1-4, OC/1-3, TW/6, WWT/1-10, WWW/4

VANBRUGH, Sir John (1664-1726) English dramatist, architect CDP, COC, CP/1-3, DNB, ES, GT, HP, MH, NTH, OC/1-3, PDT, RE, SR, TD/1-2

VANBRUGH, Prudence (b 1902) English actress WWT/5-7

VANBRUGH, Violet [Mrs. Arthur Bourchier] (1867-1942) English actress CB, CDP, COC, DNB, DP, EA/96, ES, GRB/1-4, OC/1-3, SR, WWS, WWT/1-9, WWW/4

VAN BUREN, A. H. (1879-1965) American actor TW/22, WWM

VAN BUREN, Mabel (d 1947 [69]) actress TW/4

VAN BUSKIRK, June [Mrs. Percival J. Mitchell] (b 1880/82) American actress GRB/2-4, WWS, WWT/1-5

VANCE, Alfred Glenville [Alfred Peck Stevens] (d 1888 [49/50]) comic singer EA/90*, WWT/14*

VANCE, Charles [né Goldblatt] (b 1929) Irish actor, director, producing manager WWT/15-16

VANCE, Eunice singer, dancer CDP

VANCE, The Great (1839-88) English music-hall performer COC, OC/1-3

VANCE, Kate [née Warwick] (1840-67) French actress HAS

VANCE, Nina American producer, director BE

VANCE, Thomas (d 1889 [57]) pantomimist, singer EA/90*

VANCE, Vivian (b 1914) American actress TW/4

VAN CLEAVE, Nathan (d 1970 [60]) composer/lyricist BP/55*

VAN CLEVE, Edith (b 1903) American talent representative, actress, director BE

VANDAMM, Florence (d 1966 [83]) English photographer TW/22

VAN DAMM, Vivian (d 1960 [71]) manager BE*, WWT/14*

VANDEGRIFT, B. F. (d 1888) aeronaut EA/89*

VANDENBURGH, Theodore H. [Jack Bunsby] (d 1869 [33]) actor HAS

VANDENHOFF, Charles H. (d 1890) English actor BE*, EA/91*

VANDENHOFF, Charlotte Elizabeth (1818-60) English actress CDP, COC, DNB, ES, HAS, OC/1-3

VANDENHOFF, George (b 1839) English actor HAS

VANDENHOFF, Mrs. George [née Makeath] (1835-85) actress CDP, HAS

VANDENHOFF, George Charles (1813-85) English actor CDP, COC, DAB, ES, OC/1-3, SR, WWA/H

VANDENHOFF, Mrs. H. (d 1870) actress EA/71*

VANDENHOFF, Henry (d 1888) English actor SR

VANDENHOFF, Mrs. Henry (d 1870) actress BE*, WWT/14*

VANDENHOFF, John M. (1790-1861) English actor CDP, COC, DNB, ES, HAS, OC/1-3

VANDENHOFF, Kate (d 1942 [73]) actress BE*, WWT/14*

VANDENHOFF, Mary E. see Vandenhoff, Mrs. George

VANDERBILT, Cornelius, Jr. (d 1974 [76]) journalist BP/59*

VANDERBILT, Gertrude (d 1960 [70]) American actress, singer TW/16

VANDERBILT, Gloria (b 1924) American actress, writer BE, TW/11

VANDERBILT, Jeanne Murray American actress TW/24

VANDERCOOK, John W. (d 1963 [60]) English writer BE*

VANDERFELT, E. H. (d 1900) actor EA/02*, WWT/14*

VANDERGRIFT, Howard Anderson see Kyle, Howard

VANDERMERE, John Byron (d 1786 [43]) actor TD/1-2

VANDERPOOL, Frederick W. (1877/86-1947) American actor, composer, singer SR, WWA/2

VANDERSTOP, Cornelius (fl
1777) dramatist CP/3
VAN der VLIS, Diana (b 1935)
Canadian actress BE, TW/
15, 30
VANDERVORT, Philip (b 1945)
American actor TW/22-23
VAN-DE-VELDE (d 1890 [36])
acrobat, clown EA/91*
VANDEVER, Michael American
actor TW/16
VAN DEVERE, Trish (b 1947)
American actress TW/23
VANDIS, Titos (b 1917) Greek
actor TW/22-24, 26-29
VAN DOREN, Mark (1894-1972)
American dramatist BE
VAN DREELEN, John (b 1922)
Dutch actor TW/7
VAN DRESSER, Marcia (d 1937
[60]) American singer WWA/1
VAN DRUTEN, John (1901-57)
English/American dramatist
AAS, CB, COC, ES, HJD,
MD, MH, MWD, NTH, OC/
1-3, PDT, TW/5-8, 14,
WWA/3, WWT/6-12, WWW/5
VAN DYCK, Ernest (1861-1923)
Belgian singer CDP, ES,
WWA/3
VAN DYKE, Dick (b 1925) Amer-
ican actor, comedian CB, ES
VAN DYKE, Marcia American
actress TW/7-12
VANE, Daphne (d 1966 [49])
dancer TW/23
VANE, Dorothy (d 1947 [76])
actress, singer BE*, WWT/
14*
VANE, Helen see Sugden, Mrs.
Charles
VANE, Richard Scottish actor
GRB/1
VANE, Sutton (1880/85-1963)
English dramatist, actor ES,
MH, MWD, NTH
VANE, W. H. [James Doran]
(d 1891 [33]) banjoist EA/92*
VANE-TEMPEST, Francis Adolphus
(1863-1932) actor GRB/1-4,
WWT/1-5
VAN EYCK, Peter (d 1969 [56])
performer BP/54*
VAN FLEET, Jo (b 1922) Amer-
ican actor AAS, BE, ES,
TW/22, WWT/13-16
VAN GORDON, Cyrena (d 1964
[67]) American singer TW/20,

WWA/4
VAN GRIETHUYSEN, Ted [né
Theodore André] (b 1934) Amer-
ican actor, director, designer
BE, TW/22-23, 25-26, 29,
WWT/15-16
VAN GYSEGHEM, André (b 1906)
English actor, producer, director
WWT/7-16
VAN HAGEN, Peter Albrecht (fl
1774-1800) Dutch composer
WWA/H
VAN HEUSEN, James [né Edward
Chester Babcock] (b 1913) Amer-
ican composer, producer BE,
CB, WWT/15-16
VANHOOK, Mrs. W. F. [née Mary
Ann Lee] (fl 1847) dancer
CDP, ES, HAS
VAN HORN, Rollin (1882-1964)
American costumier, designer,
director BE
VANINI, Francesca see Boschi,
Signora Giuseppe Maria
VANISON, Dolores (b 1942) Ameri-
can actress TW/27-28
VAN ITALLIE, Jean-Claude (b 1936)
Belgian/American dramatist,
director CD, CH, MH, MWD,
WWT/15-16
VAN LEER, Arnold (d 1975 [80])
performer BP/60*
VANLEER, Jay (b 1931) American
actor TW/28-29
VAN LENNEP, William (1906-62)
American curator, scholar BE*
VANLOO, Albert (d 1920) drama-
tist BE*, WWT/14*
VAN MILL, Arnold (b 1921) Dutch
singer ES
VANN, Al (d 1973 [73]) composer/
lyricist BP/58*
VANNE, Marda (d 1970) South Afri-
can actress WWT/6-14
VAN NOORDEN, P. E. (d 1896
[70]) EA/97*
VAN NOORDEN, Walter (d 1916
[50]) managing director EA/17*
VAN NOSTRAND, Morris Abbott (b
1911) American publisher, liter-
ary representative BE
VANNUYS, Ed (b 1930) American
actor TW/25-26, 28, 30
VAN NUYS, Eric (b 1933) American
actor TW/18
VANONI, Marie (fl 1892?) dancer,
singer CDP
VAN ORDEN, Charles (d 1918)

EA/19*
VAN ORE, Harry (b 1944) American actor TW/26
VAN PARYS, Georges (d 1971 [68]) composer/lyricist BP/55*
VAN PATTEN, Dick (b 1928) American actor BE, TW/2-4, 25-26, 30, WWT/11-16
VAN PATTEN, Joyce (b 1934) American actress BE, TW/2-4, 12-13, 20, WWT/15-16
VAN PEEBLES, Melvin actor, dramatist, composer, lyricist, director, producer CD, WWT/16
VAN PELT, Homer (d 1973) photographer BP/58*
VAN ROOTEN, Luis (1906-73) Mexican actor BE, TW/30
VAN ROOY, Anton (d 1932 [62]) Dutch singer BE*, BP/17*
VAN ROSEM, Robert E. (b 1904) Russian/American designer ES
VAN SABER, Mrs. Lilla Alexander (d 1968 [56]) performer BP/53*
VAN SCOTT, Glory actress TW/24-27
VAN SCOYK, Robert (b 1928) American writer BE
VAN SICKLE, Raymond (d 1964 [79]) American actor, dramatist TW/3, 8, 21
VANSITTART, Sir Robert G. (b 1881) dramatist WWT/3-4, 9
VAN SLOAN, Edward (d 1964 [82]) American actor BE*
VANSTAVOREN, Jackson P. (fl 1836) American call boy, actor? HAS
VANSTAVOREN, Joseph (d 1852) American call boy, actor HAS
VAN STUDDIFORD, Grace [Grace Quive] (1873-1927) American actress, singer SR, WWT/1-5
VAN THAL, Dennis (b 1909) English composer, conductor WWT/8-10
VAN TULY, Helen (d 1964 [73]) actress, educator BE*
VAN VECHTEN, Carl (1880-1964) American critic HJD
VAN VOLKENBURG, Ellen

American actress, producer WWT/7-9
VAN VOOREN, Monique (b 1933) Belgian actress, singer BE
VAN WILDER, Philip (fl 1550) musician DA
VAN ZANDT, Mrs. [Jenny Elitz] (fl 1863-67) singer HAS
VAN ZANDT, Marie (1858/61-1918/19) American singer ES, WWA/1
VAN ZANDT, Porter (b 1923) American stage manager, director, actor BE
VAN ZILE, Edward S. (b 1863) American dramatist WWM
VANZINI, Jenny Van Zandt (fl 1864) singer CDP [see also: Van Zandt, Mrs.]
VARDEN, Dorothy [Mrs. James Dallas] (d 1913) EA/14*
VARDEN, Evelyn (1893/95-1958) American actress TW/2-13, 15, WWT/9-12
VARELA, Nina (b 1917) American actress TW/23
VARENNES, Julie de (fl 1821-23) dancer CDP
VARESI, Gilda (b 1887) Italian actress WWT/4-9
VARLEY, Louisa Rose (d 1908 [75]) actress EA/09*
VARLEY, Nelson (d 1883 [39]) actor? singer? EA/85*
VARLEY, Tom F. (d 1895 [49]) actor? EA/96*
VARLEY, Violet [Mrs. Joseph Tapley] (d 1895) actress EA/96*
VARNA, Elizabeth (d 1895) EA/96*
VARNAY, Astrid (b 1918) American singer CB, ES
VARNEL, Marcel [né Marcel Le-Bozec] (1894-1947) French producer, director WWT/10
VARNEY, Louis (d 1908) American composer ES
VARRATO, Edmond (b 1919) American actor TW/28-29
VARREY, Edwin (d 1907 [80]) American actor BE*, GRB/3*, WWT/14*
VARVARO, Gloria (d 1976 [61]) performer BP/60*
VASCO [E. A. Bedford] (b 1869) English vaudevillian WWM
VASNICK, Andrew (b 1926) American actor TW/25-26

VASQUEZ, Manuel (d 1970 [19])
performer BP/54*
VASQUEZ, Myrna (d 1975 [40])
performer BP/59*
VASSAR, Queenie (d 1960 [89])
Scottish actress, singer
TW/17
VASSEUX, Jean-Claude (b 1940)
Venezuelan actor TW/25
VATSKE, Roberta (b 1945) Amer-
ican actress TW/25
VATTELLINA, Sig. (fl 1847)
singer HAS
VATTEMARE, Alexander see
Alexandre
VAUGHAN, Miss see Christian,
Mrs.
VAUGHAN, Ada [Edith Donnahey]
(d 1893) burlesque actress
EA/94*
VAUGHAN, Arthur C. (d 1900
[45]) actor EA/01*
VAUGHAN, Blanche (1859-1919)
American actress SR
VAUGHAN, David (b 1924) Eng-
lish actor TW/14-16, 25-27
VAUGHAN, Gladys American
director BE
VAUGHAN, Gus see Julien,
Paul
VAUGHAN, Henry (d 1779) actor
COC
VAUGHAN, Henry (d 1881 [37])
actor EA/82*
VAUGHAN, Herbert (d 1896
[27]) music-hall performer
EA/97*
VAUGHAN, Hilda Welsh dramatist
WWT/9-13
VAUGHAN, James Jones (d 1871
[59]) comic singer EA/72*
VAUGHAN, Kate [Catherine
Candelon] (c. 1852-1903) Eng-
lish actress CDP, COC,
DNB, DP, OAA/2, OC/1-3
VAUGHAN, Olea Bull (d 1911)
actress SR
VAUGHAN, Sarah (b 1924) Amer-
ican singer CB
VAUGHAN, Stuart (b 1925) Amer-
ican director, actor, drama-
tist AAS, BE, WWT/14-16
VAUGHAN, Susie [Susan Mary
Charlotte Candelin] (1853-
1950) English actress DP,
EA/96, WWT/3-10
VAUGHAN, T. B. (d 1928) pro-
ducer, manager BE*, WWT/

14*
VAUGHAN, Thomas (fl 1772-1820)
dramatist CP/2-3, DNB, GT,
TD/1-2
VAUGHAN, William Russell see
Vaun, Russell
VAUGHAN WILLIAMS, Ralph (1872-
1958) English composer CB,
DNB, ES, WWA/3, WWW/5
VAUGHN, Heidi American actress
TW/24
VAUGHN, Hilda (d 1957 [60])
American actress TW/3-8, 14
VAUGHN, Theresa [Mrs. William
H. Mestayer] (d 1903 [43])
comedienne CDP
VAUGHT, George (d 1975 [46])
producer/director/choreographer
BP/59*
VAUL, Polly [Mrs. F. Fredericks]
(d 1894) actress EA/95*
VAUN, Russell [William Russell
Vaughan] (b 1872) English actor,
dramatist GRB/1-4
VAZ DIAS, Selma (b 1911) Dutch
actress WWT/8-15
VAZQUEZ, Vicente (b 1975 [60])
performer BP/60*
VEAL, George see Collier, Joel
VEBER, Pierre (b 1869) French
dramatist, critic WWT/4
VEDOVELLI, Umberto (b 1972
[60]) conductor BP/57*
VEDRENNE, John E. (1867-1930)
English manager AAS, COC,
ES, GRB/1-4, OC/1-3, WWT/
1-6, WWW/3
VEDRENNE, Mrs. John E. see
Blair, Phyllis
VEGA, Jose (b 1920) American
manager, producer, director
BE
VEGERIUS, Paul (fl 1693) translator
CP/1-3
VEIDT, Conrad (1893-1943) German
actor BE*, WWT/14*
VEIDT, Lily Hungarian talent
representative BE
VEILLER, Anthony (b 1903) Ameri-
can manager ES
VEILLER, Bayard (1869/71-1943)
American dramatist CB, ES,
WWT/4-9
VEJAR, Harry (b 1968 [78]) per-
former BP/52*
VELANCHE, Harry [G. H. Wills]
(d 1916 [38]) animal trainer
EA/17*

VELAZQUEZ, Conchita (d 1974)
performer BP/58*
VELEX, Lupe [Guadeloupe Velez
de Villabos] (1909-44) Mexican
actress, dancer TW/1,
WWT/9
VELIE, Jay (b 1892) American
actor TW/7-8, 23-24, 27, 30
VENABLE, Reginald (d 1974
[48]) performer BP/59*
VENABLES, Ann see Arne,
Mrs. Michael, III
VENAFRA, M. (fl 1836) actor
CDP
VENARD, Celeste (d 1909) dancer
EA/10*
VENDOME, Sidney (d 1907) per-
former? EA/08*
VENESS, Amy (d 1960 [84]) ac-
tress BE*, WWT/14*
VENN, Topsy (d 1897) actress
CDP
VENNARD [or Vennar], Richard
(fl 1602) dramatist FGF
VENNE, Lottie (1852-1928)
English actress CDP, COC,
DP, GRB/1-4, OAA/2, OC/
1-3, WWT/1-5
VENNING, Kate (d 1917) critic
EA/18*
VENNING, Una (b 1893) English
actress WWT/5-14
VENOI, Jeannie [Jeannie Elliott]
(d 1892) music-hall singer
EA/93*
VENORA, Lee (b 1932) American
singer, actress BE, TW/22
VENTANTONIO, John (b 1943)
American actor TW/26-27
VENTH, Carl (1860-1938) Ger-
man composer WWA/1
VENTO, Harry (d 1899 [66])
ventriloquist EA/00*
VENTO, Lillie (d 1918) EA/19*
VENTON, F. W. (d 1918) EA/
19*
VENTURA, Dick (d 1973 [80s])
performer BP/58*
VENUA, Frederic Marc Antoine
(d 1872 [86]) composer EA/
73*
VENUTA, Benay [née Venuta Rose
Crooke] (b 1911/12) American
actress, singer BE, TW/9,
14-15, 22-23, 29, WWT/15-16
VERA, Mme. (d 1867 [83])
singer CDP
VERA-ELLEN (b 1926) American

dancer, actress CB
VERBRUGGEN, John (d 1708) actor
DNB
VERBRUGGEN, Mrs. John see
Mountfort, Susanna Percival
VERCHININA, Nina dancer WWT/
9-12
VERDI, Ruby (d 1918) actress
GRB/1
VERDON, Gwen (b 1925/26) Ameri-
can actress, singer, dancer
AAS, BE, CB, TW/9-20, 22-23,
28, WWT/14-16
VERDY, Violette (b 1933) French
dancer CB
VERE, Charles (d 1876) actor
EA/77*
VERE, Edward, Earl of Oxford
dramatist FGF
VERE, Fred R. [Frederick Vere
Podmore] (d 1897) actor EA/98*
VEREEN, Ben (b 1946) American
actor, singer, dancer TW/28-
30, WWT/16
VERGA, Giovanni (1840-1922) Italian
dramatist COC
VERGERIUS, Paul (fl 1693) see
Vegerius, Paul
VERHOEVEN, Paul (d 1975 [74])
performer BP/59*
VERITY, Agnes actress CDP
VERITY, Sarah (d 1850) American
actress HAS
VERITY, Mrs. William (d 1890)
EA/91*
VERLINO, Charles [George
Brookes] (d 1906 [64]) harlequin
EA/07*
VERMILYE, Kate Jordan (d 1926)
Irish dramatist WWA/1
VERMILYEA, Harold (1889-1958)
American actor TW/2-3, 14,
WWT/9-11
VERNE, Arthur (d 1912 [48]) come-
dian EA/13*
VERNE, Fred (d 1902) comedian
EA/03*
VERNE, Jules (d 1905) French
writer GRB/1
VERNER, Charles (d 1869 [39])
actor EA/70*, WWT/14*
VERNER, Charles Erin (fl 1887)
Irish comedian, singer SR
VERNER, Linda (d 1892) actress?
singer? EA/93*
VERNER, Thomas (d 1900) actor
EA/01*
VERNEUIL, Louis (1893-1952)

French dramatist, actor, manager TW/9, WWT/4, 8-11, WWW/5

VERNEY, Guy (d 1970) performer BP/55*

VERNO, Jerry (1895-1975) English actor WWT/7-15

VERNO, Jess (d 1908 [38]) variety performer EA/09*

VERNON, Mr. (d c. 1800?) actor TD/1-2

VERNON, Mr. (fl 1827-49) actor HAS

VERNON, Anne [Mrs. W. H. Vernon] (d 1912 [77]) EA/13*

VERNON, Anne (b 1926) French actress TW/10

VERNON, Charles [George E. J. Williams] (b 1875) English actor GRB/1

VERNON, Mrs. Charles see Stanley, Lilian M.

VERNON, Clari singer, actress CDP

VERNON, Mrs. Darville see Vernon, Louie

VERNON, E. R. (d 1880) actor EA/81*

VERNON, Fanny see Sinclair, Mrs. Harry

VERNON, Flo [Betsy Sotherden] (d 1912 [34]) variety performer EA/13*

VERNON, Frank (1875-1940) Indian/English actor, director, producer WWT/2-9, WWW/3

VERNON, George (fl 1624-29) actor DA

VERNON, George (d 1830 [33]) manager, actor HAS

VERNON, Mrs. George [née Jane Marchant] (1796-1869) English actress CDP, HAS

VERNON, Mrs. George see Fisher, Jane

VERNON, Harriet (d 1923 [71]) actress, singer CDP

VERNON, Harry J. (d 1902) actor EA/03*

VERNON, Harry M. (b 1878) American dramatist WWT/3-9

VERNON, Harvey (b 1927) American actor TW/28

VERNON, Hilary (d 1973 [52]) performer BP/57*

VERNON, Ida (1843-1923) American actress CDP, HAS,

WWS

VERNON, Jane Marchant see Vernon, Mrs. George

VERNON, John H. (d 1893) sketch artist EA/94*

VERNON, John William (d 1913 [25]) EA/14*

VERNON, Joseph (1738?-82) English actor, singer CDP, DNB

VERNON, Kate Olga (d 1939 [71]) actress BE*, WWT/14*

VERNON, Louie [Mrs. Darville Vernon] (d 1906) EA/07*

VERNON, Percy see Lyveden, Lord

VERNON, Richard (b 1925) English actor WWT/15-16

VERNON, Virginia [Virginia Fox Brooks] (b 1893) American actress, singer, dramatist WWT/4-9

VERNON, Wally (d 1970 [64]) performer BP/54*

VERNON, Walter (d 1884) comedian EA/85*

VERNON, W. H. (d 1905 [71]) actor EA/07*, WWT/14*

VERNON, Mrs. W. H. see Vernon, Anne

VERRECKE, Mons. (b 1834) Belgian circus performer? HAS

VERREN, Milner (d 1908 [34]) singer EA/09*

VERRETT, Shirley (b 1933?) American singer CB

VERT, Henirato (d 1893) acting manager EA/94*

VERT, N. (d 1905 [62]) impresario EA/06*

VERTES, Marcel (d 1961 [66]) scene designer BP/46*

VERTIPRACH, Vietti (fl 1856) singer HAS

VESEY, Clara dancer CDP

VESEY, Katie (b 1883) English actress, singer, dancer GRB/2

VESSELLA, Oreste (b 1877) Italian composer WWA/5

VESTOFF, Floria (d 1963 [c. 43]) Russian choreographer, dancer BE*

VESTOFF, Valodja (d 1947 [45]) Russian dancer TW/4

VESTOFF, Virginia (b 1940) American actress TW/22-29

VESTRIS, Mme. [Lucia Elizabeth Bartolozzi; Mrs. Charles James Mathews] (1797-1856)

Italian actress, manager BS, CDP, COC, DNB, ES, HAS, OC/1-3, OX, PDT, SR

VESTRIS, Armand (1788-1825) Italian dancer OC/1-2

VESTRIS, Caroline Mary Theresa (b 1802) dancer CDP

VESTRIS, Gaetano Apollino (1729-1808) ballet master CDP

VESTRIS, Marie Jean Augustin (1760-1842) Italian dancer CDP, OC/1-2

VESTVALI, Felicita (1839-80) singer CDP, HAS

VESTVALI, Henry (d 1863) HAS

VEZIN, Arthur (b 1878) English actor WWT/2-8

VEZIN, Hermann (1829-1910) American actor CDP, COC, DAB, DNB, DP, EA/97, ES, GRB/1-4, HAS, OAA/1-2, OC/1-3, WWW/1

VEZIN, Mrs. Hermann see Vezin, Jane Elizabeth

VEZIN, Jane Elizabeth [Mrs. Charles Young; Mrs. Hermann Vezin] (1827-1902) American actress COC, DNB, HAS, OAA/1-2, OC/1-3

VIALETTI, Sig. (d 1870) singer EA/71*

VIAN, Boris (1920-59) French dramatist COC

VIARDOT-GARCIA, Pauline (1821-1910) singer CDP

VIBART, Henry (1863-1939) Scottish actor EA/96, GRB/3-4, SR, WWT/1-9

VICKERS, Henry (d 1871 [64]) comic singer EA/73*

VICKERS, Jon (b 1927?) Canadian singer CB, ES

VICKERS, Martha (d 1971 [46]) performer BP/56*

VICKERS, Mrs. W. G. (d 1880) EA/81*

VICKERY, Mrs. J. G. [née Richardson] (fl 1850-52) actress HAS

VICOTT, Connie (d 1903 [39]) actress EA/04*

VICTOR, Benjamin (d 1778) dramatist, manager CP/1-3, DNB, GT, TD/1-2

VICTOR, Charles (1896-1965) English actor WWT/11-14

VICTOR, C. Leonard (d 1974 [94]) producer/director/choreographer BP/59*

VICTOR, Elizabeth (d 1893) EA/95*

VICTOR, Emma actress EA/96

VICTOR, Eric Swiss actor TW/4-6

VICTOR, Ethel [Mrs. Charles Murray] (d 1902 [45]) serio-comic singer EA/03*

VICTOR, Ethel actress, singer CDP

VICTOR, Frederick [Frederick Clarke] (b 1869) actor GRB/1

VICTOR, Josephine (b 1885) Hungarian/American actress WWS, WWT/5-10

VICTOR, Lionel (d 1940) actor BE*, WWT/14*

VICTOR, Lucia American stage manager, director, dramatist BE

VICTOR, M[ary] A[nn] [Mrs. Sarciut] (d 1907 [67/76]) actress GRB/3

VICTORELLI, John (d 1902) acrobat EA/03*

VICTORELLI, William (d 1897 [52]) acrobat EA/99*

VICTORIA (b 1874) aerial velocipedist CDP

VICTORIA, Vesta (d 1951 [77]) English variety artist CDP, GRB/1-3, WWS

VIDAL, Gore (b 1925) American dramatist AAS, BE, CB, CD, CH, ES, HJD, MD, MH, MWD, PDT, WWT/14-16

VIDAL, Henri (d 1959 [40]) actor WWT/14*

VIDAL, Leonard (d 1906 [45]) acting manager EA/07*

VIE, Florence (d 1939 [63]) actress BE*, WWT/14*

VIEHMAN, Theodore (1889-1970) American director, educator BE

VIEHOEVER, Joseph (d 1973 [47]) producer/director/choreographer BP/58*

VIELLER, Bayard (1869-1943) American dramatist SR

VIENNOISE, The Children (fl 1847) dancers HAS

VIERI, Sig. (fl 1857) musician? HAS

VIETTI, Sig. (fl 1850) singer HAS

VIEUXTEMPS, Mme. (d 1868 [52]) EA/69*

VIEUXTEMPS, Henry (1820-81)

musician HAS
VIEUXTEMPS, Jules Joseph Ernest
(d 1896 [64]) musician EA/97*
VIGNA, Arturo (1863-1927) Italian
conductor ES
VIGNOLA, Robert G. (d 1953
[71]) Italian actor, director
BE*
VIGODA, Abe (b 1921) American
actor TW/23, 25-26, 28
VILAR, Jean (1912-71) French
actor, manager, director,
producer BE, TW/27, WWT/
13-14
VILDRAC, Charles Messager
(b 1882) French dramatist
COC, NTH
VILES, H. A. (d 1894 [78])
EA/95*
VILLA, Alba (d 1976 [55]) per-
former BP/60*
VILLA, Danny (b 1934) American
actor TW/29-30
VILLECHAIZE, Herve (b 1943)
French actor TW/27-28
VILLELLA, Edward (b 1936/37)
American dancer CB, ES,
TW/24
VILLENEUVE, Le Blanc de (fl
1753?) dramatist EAP
VILLETARD, Edmond (d 1890
[78]) dramatist WWT/14*
VILLIERS, Mr. (d 1805) English
actor HAS
VILLIERS, Mrs. (1787-1813)
see Twaits, Mrs. William
VILLIERS, Edwin (d 1904 [73])
actor, music-hall manager
WWT/14*
VILLIERS, Ernest E. (d 1891)
business manager EA/92*
VILLIERS, Frederick (d 1885
[59]) actor EA/86*
VILLIERS, George see Buck-
ingham, Duke of
VILLIERS, Mrs. George see
Flange, Dora
VILLIERS, Harry (d 1906)
music-hall performer EA/07*
VILLIERS, James (d 1863 [76])
actor EA/72*, WWT/14*
VILLIERS, James (b 1933) Eng-
lish actor WWT/15-16
VILLIERS, J. C. (fl 1789) dram-
atist CP/3
VILLIERS, Mrs. John see
Rydon, Nita
VILLIERS, Lizzie [Elizabeth

Villiers Bullock] (d 1901 [41])
music-hall dancer EA/02*
VILLIERS, Lyon (fl 1812) actor
CDP
VILLIERS, Mavis (d 1976) Aus-
tralian actress TW/22-23
VILLIERS, R. Edwin (d 1904 [73])
music-hall proprietor EA/05*
VILLION, Lizzie [Mrs. V. Villion]
(d 1895) EA/96*
VILLION, Mrs. W. see Villion,
Lizzie
VILNER, David (b 1941) American
actor TW/24
VINAVER, Steven (d 1968 [31])
producer/director/choreographer
BP/53*
VINCENT (fl 1590) musician DA
VINCENT, Mrs. [née Birchill] (d
1802) actress TD/1-2
VINCENT, Miss CDP
VINCENT, Charles (fl 1777) actor
CDP
VINCENT, Charles see Viner,
Charles Penrucker
VINCENT, Charles T. (1858-1935)
English actor, dramatist WWM
VINCENT, Eliza [Mrs. Benjamin
Crowther] (1815-56) actress,
manager CDP
VINCENT, Ellen Harriet [Mrs. G.
A. Vincent] (d 1876 [43]) EA/
77*
VINCENT, Mrs. Ernie see Mel-
rose, Doris
VINCENT, E. S. (d 1907 [53])
actor EA/08*, WWT/14*
VINCENT, Mrs. E. S. see
Lee, Jenny
VINCENT, Eva (1849-1914) actress
SR
VINCENT, Felix A. (1831-1912)
English actor CDP, HAS, SR
VINCENT, Fred (d 1904 [54])
manager EA/06*
VINCENT, Mrs. G. A. see
Ellen, Harriet
VINCENT, Gene (d 1971 [36]) per-
former BP/56*
VINCENT, George (d 1876) actor
EA/77*
VINCENT, Henry (d 1873 [23])
actor EA/74*
VINCENT, Henry Bethuel (d 1941)
American composer WWA/1
VINCENT, H. H. (1848-1913) Eng-
lish actor, stage manager EA/
97

VINCENT, Isabella (d 1802 [67])
actress, singer WWT/14*
VINCENT, James (d 1957 [74])
American actor, director
BE*, BP/42*
VINCENT, James R. (d 1850)
actor CDP, HAS
VINCENT, Mrs. J[ames] R.
[née Mary Ann Farley] (1818-
87) English/American actress
CDP, COC, DAB, HAS, NYM,
OC/1-3, WWA/H
VINCENT, Larry (d 1975 [50])
performer BP/59*
VINCENT, Leon John (d 1925
[91]) actor CDP
VINCENT, Madge (b 1884) Eng-
lish actress, singer WWT/
1-6
VINCENT, Mary Ann see Vin-
cent, Mrs. James R.
VINCENT, Naomi (1816-33)
American actress CDP, HAS
VINCENT, Nellie [Mrs. George
Barrett] (d 1886) actress
EA/87*
VINCENT, Romo (b 1909/12)
American actor TW/2, 15
VINCENT, Ruth [Mrs. John
Fraser] (1877-1955) English
actress, singer GRB/1-4,
WWS, WWT/1-8
VINCENT, Thomas (fl c. 1600)
prompter DA
VINCENT, Thomas (fl 1627)
dramatist CP/3, FGF
VINCENT, Virginia (b 1924)
American actress TW/8
VINCENT, Mr. W. (d 1869 [28])
pantomimist EA/70*
VINCENT, Walter (1868-1959)
American actor, producer,
writer TW/15
VINEER, Edmund John (d 1889)
EA/90*
VINER, Charles Penrucker (d
1868 [45]) actor? EA/69*
VINES, Margaret (b 1910) Eng-
lish actress WWT/7-14
VINING, Mr. (d 1881) EA/83*
VINING, Mrs. [née Johannet]
(fl 1820) English actress,
dancer BS, OX
VINING, Mrs. (d 1868) actress?
EA/69*
VINING, Mrs. A. [Rose Bella]
(d 1876) music-hall performer
EA/77*

VINING, Amelia see Wilde,
Amelia
VINING, Arthur (d 1895) music-
hall performer EA/96*
VINING, Charles William (fl 1819)
actor CDP
VINING, Fanny Elizabeth see
Davenport, Fanny Elizabeth
VINING, Frederick (1790-1871)
actor BS, CDP, DNB
VINING, Mrs. Frederick (d 1853
[61]) actress WWT/14*
VINING, George James (1823/24-
75) actor, manager CDP, DNB
VINING, Mrs. Henry (d 1874 [69])
actress EA/76*, WWT/14*
VINING, James (d 1870 [74]) EA/
72*
VINING, James (1795-1870) actor
DNB
VINING, Johannot (fl 1813) actress,
dancer CDP
VINING, Louisa actress CDP
VINING, Matilda Charlotte see
Wood, Mrs. John
VINING, William (d 1861 [78])
actor EA/72*, WWT/14*
VINSON, Helen (b 1907) American
actress WWT/8-10
VINT, Mrs. Leon (d 1917 [40])
EA/18*
VINTNER, Gilbert (d 1969 [60])
composer BP/54*
VINTON, Arthur R. (d 1963)
American actor BE*
VINTON, Stanley (d 1976 [63])
conductor BP/60*
VIOLETTI, Eva Maria CDP
VIOLINSKY [Sol Ginsberg] (1888-
1963) Russian musician, vaude-
villian WWM
VIPOND, Neil (b 1929) Canadian
actor TW/12
VIRNIUS, Johann Friedrich (fl
1615) actor DA
VIRSKY, Pavel (d 1975 [70]) Rus-
sian choreographer BP/60*,
WWT/16*
VIRTO, Albert (d 1890 [29]) EA/
91*
VISCONTI, Luchino (1906-76)
Italian director, designer CB,
ES, PDT
VISHNEVSKAYA, Galina (b 1926)
Russian singer CB
VISSCHER, William Lightfoot (1842-
1924) American actor DAB
VITA, Luis (fl 1847) singer HAS

VITA, Signora Luis (fl 1847) singer HAS

VITA, Michael (b 1941) American actor TW/28

VITALE, Joseph actor TW/1

VITELO see Cryer, Charles Henry

VITU, Auguste (d 1891 [67]) critic EA/92*

VIVIAN, Anthony Crespigny Claud (b 1906) English press representative, producing manager WWT/8-12

VIVIAN, Charles Algernon (b c. 1830) English actor SR

VIVIAN, Edward (d 1900) actor EA/01*

VIVIAN, George (d 1970 [85]) performer BP/54*

VIVIAN, Percival (d 1961 [70]) English actor, director BE*

VIVIAN, Robert (d 1944 [85]) English actor BE*, BP/28*, WWT/14*

VIVIAN, Ruth (d 1949 [60]) English actress BE*, BP/34*, TW/6, WWT/14*

VIVIAN, Violet (d 1960 [74]) English actress BE*, BP/45*

VIVIAN-REES, Joan Welsh actress WWT/5-8

VIOLETTI, Eva Maria [Mrs. David Garrick] (1724-1822) dancer COC

VITRAC, Roger (1899-1952) French dramatist COC, OC/3

VIVASH, Henry (d 1879) actor EA/80*

VIVASH, Sarah see Buchanan, Mrs. J.

VIZARD, Harold (b 1871) English actor WWM, WWS

VLADIMIROFF, Pierre (d 1970 [77]) performer BP/55*

VOELLER, Emmeline (fl 1865) actress HAS

VOELLER, Will H. (d 1975 [75]) producer/director/choreographer BP/59*

VOELPEL, Fred designer WWT/16

VOGEL, Eleanore (d 1973 [70]) performer BP/58*

VOGEL, Henry (d 1925 [60]) actor BE*, BP/10*

VOGEL, John W. (1862-1951) American minstrel, manager SR

VOGELING, Mrs. Frederick see Roberts, Florence

VOGHT, Alexander (fl 1854) actor? HAS

VOGL, Heinrich (1845-1900) German singer ES

VOGRICH, Max Wilhelm Karl (1852-1916) composer DAB

VOGT, Gustav (d 1870 [90]) musician EA/71*

VOIGHT, Jon (b 1938) American actor CB, TW/23, WWT/16

VOKES, Fawdon (d 1890) actor CDP, OAA/2

VOKES, F. M. T. (d 1890 [74]) pantomimist, dancer BE*, EA/91*, WWT/14*

VOKES, Frederick Mortimer (1846-88) English actor COC, DNB, OAA/1-2, OC/1-3

VOKES, George (d 1895 [43]) comedian EA/96*

VOKES, George Henry (d 1910 [32]) EA/11*

VOKES, Harry (d 1922 [56]) comedian BE*, BP/6*

VOKES, Jessie [Mrs. Neddy Vokes] (d 1912 [33]) EA/13*

VOKES, Jessie Catherine (1851-84) English actress, dancer CDP, COC, DNB, OAA/1-2, OC/1-3

VOKES, John Russell (d 1924 [52]) Australian vaudevillian BE*, BP/8*

VOKES, May (d 1957 [70+]) comedienne TW/14

VOKES, Neddy see Vokes, Jessie

VOKES, Robert (d 1912 [56]) pantomimist, dancer BE*, EA/13*, WWT/14*

VOKES, Rosina [Mrs. Cecil Clay] (1854-94) actress CDP, COC, DNB, OAA/1-2, OC/1-3

VOKES, Victoria (1853-94) English actress, singer CDP, COC, DNB, OAA/1-2, OC/1-3

VOKES, Walter [né Fawdon] (d 1904) English actor COC, OAA/1, OC/1-3

VOKES, William (d 1894 [83]) circus agent EA/95*

VOLA, Vicki American actress BE

VOL BECQUE, William [William Tookey] (d 1892 [40]) EA/93*

VOLIER, Frank (d 1893) gymnast

EA/94*
VOLKERT, Erie T. (b 1913)
American educator, director
BE
VOLKMAN, Ivan (d 1972) mana-
ger, director BP/57*
VOLKOVA, Vera (d 1975 [71])
ballet teacher BP/59*
VOLLAIRE, Harry (d 1897 [42])
actor EA/98*
VOLLAIRE, John (1820-89)
English actor OAA/2
VOLLAND, Virginia (b 1909)
American costume designer
BE
VOLLMER, Lula (1898-1955)
American dramatist ES, HJD,
MD, MWD, TW/11, WWA/3,
WWT/5-11
VOLMOELLER, Karl (d 1948
[69]) German dramatist BP/
33*, WWT/14*
VOLPE, Frederick (1865-1932)
English actor GRB/1-4,
WWT/1-6
VOLTA, Charlotte E. M. [Mrs.
Edwin Volta] (d 1910 [51])
EA/11*
VOLTA, Mrs. Edwin see
Volta, Charlotte E. M.
VOLTAIRE, Jeanne (d 1970 [70])
performer BP/54*
VOLTAIRE, Nellie (d 1905)
music-hall performer EA/06*
VOLTERRA, Leon (d 1949 [61])
manager, producer WWT/14*
VOLTYNE, Edwin (d 1895) gym-
nast? EA/96*
VON BARDELEBEN, Baroness
Fritz see Scheff, Fritzi
VON BERKEL, Mme. (fl 1856-
57) German singer HAS
VON BERLIN, Ivan Emanuel
Julian see Berlyn, Ivan
VON BONHORST, Julius A. (d
1869) banjo player HAS
VON BUSING, Fritzi (d 1948
[64]) American actress, singer
TW/4
VON DER FINCK, Herman see
Finck, Herman
VONE, William (fl 1807) drama-
tist CP/3
VON ELTZ, Theodore (d 1964
[70]) performer BP/49*
VON FIELITZ, Andrew (b 1860)
German conductor WWA/4
VON FURSTENBERG, Betsy (b

1931/35) German/American ac-
tress BE, TW/7-10, 12-19,
23-24, 27, WWT/15-16
VON HATZFELDT, Olga [Mrs.
Irving Brooks] (b 1884) Ameri-
can actress WWM
VONLEER, Sarah [Mrs. J. M.
Hardie] (d 1916) actress, mana-
ger SR
VON MEYERINCK, Herbert (d 1971
[74]) performer BP/55*
VONNEGUT, Kurt, Jr. (b 1922)
American dramatist CD
VONNEGUT, Walter (d 1940 [56])
American actor, director BE*,
BP/25*
VON NIESSEN-STONE, Matja (b
1870) Russian singer WWM
VON OSTFELDEN, Maria (d 1971
[75]) producer/director/chore-
ographer BP/55*
VON POSSART, Ernst Ritter (1841-
1921) German actor, manager
GRB/4, OC/1-3, WWT/1-2
VON REINHOLD, Calvin (b 1927)
Canadian dancer, choreographer,
singer, actor BE
VON SCHERLER, Sasha (b 1939)
American actress TW/22-24,
26-28, WWT/15-16
VON SONNENTHAL, Adolf Ritter
(1834-1909) German actor,
manager GRB/4
VON STERNBERG, Josef (d 1969
[75]) producer/director/chore-
ographer BP/54*
VON STROHEIM, Erich (1885-1957)
Austrian/American actor WWA/3
VON TILZER, Albert (1878-1956)
American composer, performer
TW/13
VON TILZER, Harry (1873-1946)
American vaudevillian, lyricist
CB, DAB
VON TILZER, Jules (b 1869)
American vaudevillian WWM
VON TWARDOWSKI, Hans Heinrich
(d 1958 [60]) German actor,
director BP/43*
VON UNRUH, Fritz (d 1970 [85])
dramatist BP/55*
VON WITT, Joseph (1843-87)
Bohemian singer NYM
VON ZERNECK, Peter (b 1908)
Hungarian actor TW/1, 3
VOORHEES, Donald (b 1903)
American conductor, musical
director CB

VORSTIUS, Louisa Ann (d 1893
[46]) EA/95*
VOS, Miss (1815-54) see Stuart,
Mrs.
VOSBURGH, David (b 1938) Amer-
ican actor TW/25
VOSE, Val [Thomas Davis Eaton]
(d 1887) ventriloquist CDP
VOSKOVEC, George (b 1905)
Czech actor, producer, di-
rector BE, MD, TW/10, 12,
18-27, 30, WWT/14-16
VOSOFF, Hellen Howes (d 1975
[79]) playhouse founder BP/
59*
VOSPER, Frank (1899-1937)
English actor, dramatist
AAS, ES, WWT/6-8
VOSS, Stephanie (b 1936) English
actress, singer WWT/13-16
VOTION, Jack (d 1975 [75]) pro-
ducer/director/choreographer
BP/60*
VOTIPKA, Thelma (1898-1972)
American singer WWA/5
VOULLAIRE, Andrew Leonard
[A. V. Campbell] (d 1870
[80]) actor EA/71*
VOUSDEN, Francis Valentine
(d 1905 [43]) musician EA/
06*
VOWLES, Mrs. J. (d 1890)
EA/91*
VOX, Horace (d 1881 [28]) come-
dian EA/82*
VOY, Lawrance (d 1868 [42])
Negro comedian EA/69*
VROOM, Lodewick (d 1950 [66])
Canadian producer, press
representative BE*, BP/35*
VROOM, Paul (b 1917) American
producer, manager BE
VYE, Murvyn (1913-76) Ameri-
can actor TW/1-8, 22-23
VYNER, R. G. (d 1918) EA/19*
VYVYAN, Jennifer (d 1974 [49])
performer BP/58*

- W -

W., J. (fl 1637) dramatist
CP/3, FGF
W., J. (fl 1743-50) dramatist
CP/3
W., L. (fl 1658) dramatist CP/
3, FGF
W., M. (fl 1662) dramatist

CP/3, FGF
W., R. (fl c. 1548?) dramatist
CP/3
W., R. (fl 1680) dramatist CP/3
W., T. (fl 1662?) dramatist FGF
WACHTEL, Theodor (1823-93)
singer CDP
WADBROOK, Mrs. (d 1889) EA/90*
WADDINGTON, Patrick (b 1901/03)
English actor, singer BE,
WWT/7-16
WADDINGTON, Mrs. W. H. (d
1892 [29]) EA/93*
WADDS, Elijah (d 1875 [68]) box-
office keeper EA/77*
WADDY, Mr. (fl 1798-1802) Irish
actor GT, TD/1-2
WADE, Mrs. (d 1888) EA/89*
WADE, Allan (1881-1954) English
business manager, producer,
actor, manager COC, OC/1-3,
WWT/5-11
WADE, Cecily (d 1916) actress
EA/17*
WADE, Florence (d 1896) actress
EA/97*
WADE, Gene (d 1917) comedian
EA/18*
WADE, George Edward see
Robey, George
WADE, John P. (b 1876) American
actor WWM
WADE, Joseph Augustine (1796?-1845)
Irish composer, conductor DNB
WADE, Julia see Harwood, Mrs.
WADE, Peter J. (b 1850) Irish
actor HAS
WADE, Philip (d 1950 [54]) actor
BE*, WWT/14*
WADE, Samuel (d 1878 [67]) musi-
cian EA/79*
WADE, Thomas (1805-75) English
dramatist DNB
WADE, Tom (d 1908 [47]) music-
hall performer EA/09*
WADE, Walter (d 1963 [52]) per-
former, songwriter BE*
WADE, Warren (d 1973 [76]) actor,
director BP/57*, WWT/16*
WADESON, Antony (fl 1601) drama-
tist CP/3, DNB, FGF
WADKAR, Hansa (d 1971 [47]) per-
former BP/56*
WADMAN, Miss (fl 1878-90) ac-
tress DP, OAA/2
WADMAN, Miss [Mrs. St. Vincent
Jervis] (d 1892) singer EA/94*
WADMORE, Mr. (d 1878) singer

EA/79*
WADSWORTH, Handel (d 1964)
English director BE*
WADSWORTH, Henry (d 1974
[72]) actor BP/59*, WWT/
16*
WADSWORTH, Jessie (d 1973
[81]) talent agent BP/57*
WAGENHALS, Lincoln A. (1869-
1931) American producing
manager GRB/2-4, WWT/1-6
WAGER, Lewis (fl 1567) dramatist
CP/1-3, FGF
WAGER, Michael [né Emanuel
Weisgal] (b 1925) American
actor, director BE, TW/7,
23, 25, 27-28, 30, WWT/
15-16
WAGER, W. (fl Elizabethan
period) dramatist CP/2-3
WAGHORN, William (d 1883)
theatrical laceman EA/84*
WAGNER, Arthur (b 1923) American educator BE
WAGNER, Calvin (b 1840) American comedian HAS
WAGNER, Carl (b 1865) German
actor WWT/2
WAGNER, Rev. C. Everett (d
1969 [73]) BP/54*
WAGNER, Charles L. (d 1956
[87]) American producing
manager TW/12, WWA/3,
WWT/6-7
WAGNER, Frank American choreographer, director BE
WAGNER, Harold (b 1885) English actor GRB/1
WAGNER, Jack (d 1965 [68])
performer BP/49*
WAGNER, Johanna (1828-94)
singer CDP
WAGNER, Joseph (d 1974 [74])
composer/lyricist BP/59*
WAGNER, Joseph (b 1913) American educator BE
WAGNER, Leopold (b 1858) English actor, dramatist GRB/1
WAGNER, Nathaniel M. (d 1961
[65]) actor, singer TW/18
WAGNER, Richard Cyril (d
1916 [23]) actor EA/17*
WAGNER, Robin (b 1933) Amer-
ican designer BE, WWT/
15-16
WAGNER, William (d 1964 [79])
actor BE*, WWT/14*
WAHL, Walter Dare (d 1974

[78]) performer BP/59*
WAINRIGHT, Hope (d 1972 [30])
performer BP/56*
WAINWRIGHT, Dr. (fl 1801) drama-
tist CP/3
WAINWRIGHT, Miss (fl 1767-69)
English actress HAS
WAINWRIGHT, Jane [Mrs. John
Wainwright] (d 1888) EA/89*
WAINWRIGHT, John (d 1911 [69])
actor, producer, manager BE*,
EA/12*, WWT/14*
WAINWRIGHT, Mrs. John see
Wainwright, Jane
WAINWRIGHT, Marie [Mrs. Frank-
lyn Roberts] (1853-1923) Ameri-
can actress CDP, COC, GRB/
2-4, PP/3, SR, WWA/1, WWS,
WWT/1-4
WAITE, Annie (b 1843) American
actress HAS
WAITE, Edward Willoughby (d 1906)
musician EA/07*
WAITE, Harriett [Mrs. Harry
Waite] (d 1886) EA/88*
WAITE, Harry (d 1900 [71]) EA/01*
WAITE, Mrs. Harry see Waite,
Harriett
WAITE, Margaret [Mrs. William
Waite] (d 1880) EA/81*
WAITE, Salome B. (d 1890) EA/91*
WAITE, Mrs. William see
Waite, Margaret
WAKE, Ada Eliza (d 1903) actress
EA/04*
WAKE, Maria [Mrs. Richard Wake]
(d 1911) EA/13*
WAKE, Richard (d 1918) EA/19*
WAKE, Mrs. Richard see Wake,
Maria
WAKEFIELD, Ann (b 1931) English
actress TW/11-12
WAKEFIELD, Douglas (1899-1951)
English actor WWT/7-10
WAKEFIELD, Edward (fl 1597-1602)
actor DA
WAKEFIELD, Gilbert Edward (1892-
1963) English dramatist WWT/
6-13
WAKEFIELD, Henrietta (d 1974
[96]) performer BP/59*
WAKEFIELD, Hugh (1888-1971)
English actor WWT/5-14
WAKEFIELD, J. H. (d 1900) music-
hall comedian, lessee EA/01*
WAKEFIELD, Willa Holt American
entertainer WWM
WAKELIN, Sarah see Baker, Sarah

WAKELING, Mrs. A. C. see
Wakeling, Emma
WAKELING, Emma [Mrs. A.
C. Wakeling] (d 1878) EA/79*
WAKEMAN, Annie (fl 1867) ac-
tress CDP
WAKEMAN, Antoinette von Hoesen
(b 1856) American dramatist
WWA/4
WAKEMAN, Emily [Mrs. Randolph
Hartley] (fl 1900s) American
actress WWM
WAKEMAN, Keith (1866-1933)
American actress EA/96,
WWA/1, WWT/2-5
WAKER, Mr. actor CDP
WAKER, Joseph (fl 1785) drama-
tist CP/3
WAKLEY, Ronald Ford (d 1918
[27]) EA/19*
WALBERG, Betty (b 1921) Amer-
ican composer, dance arranger,
educator, musician BE
WALBOURN, William H. (fl
1821) actor CDP
WALBOURNE, Mr. (fl 1837-40)
English actor HAS
WALBRAN, Kate (d 1916) actress
EA/18*
WALBROOK, Anton [Adolph Anton
Wilhelm Wohlbrück] (1900-66)
Austrian actor WWT/9-14,
WWW/6
WALBROOK, Henry Mackinnon
(1863-1941) Irish dramatist,
critic WWT/1-9, WWW/4
WALBURN, Raymond (1887-1969)
American actor BE, TW/22,
26
WALCOT, Mrs. (fl 1797) actress
TD/1-2
WALCOT, Charles Melton (1816-
68) English/American actor,
dramatist CDP, COC, DAB,
HAS, OC/1-3, SR, WWA/H
WALCOT, Charles Melton [or
Melcot] (1840-1921) American
actor COC, DAB, HAS,
OC/1-3, PP/3, WWS
WALCOT, Isabella [née Nickinson]
(1847-1906) American actress
COC, HAS, OC/1-3, PP/3
WALCOT, Mrs. see Shirreff,
Miss
WALCOTT, Alexander (1887-
1943) actor SR
WALCOTT, Derek (b 1930) West
Indian dramatist CD

WALCOTT, Mrs. Thomas see
Shirreff, Jane
WALDECK, Elise von (d 1898 [60])
EA/99*
WALDEGRAVE, Cecile (d 1838)
dancer, actress HAS
WALDEGRAVE, Lilias actress
GRB/2-4, WWT/1-6
WALDEGRAVE, Robert [Robert
James Penny Wilson] (d 1894
[37]) EA/95*
WALDEN, Harry (1875-1921) Ger-
man actor BE*, WWT/14*
WALDEN, Robert (b 1944) Ameri-
can actor TW/25
WALDIS, Otto (d 1974 [68]) per-
former BP/58*
WALDMANN, Antoinette (d 1892
[75]) singer EA/93*
WALDO, Fullerton Leonard (b
1877) American dramatist
WWA/5
WALDO, Helen (fl 1900s) American
entertainer WWM
WALDON, Mrs. (d 1886) EA/87*
WALDON, Charles see Escamo
WALDORF, Wilella Louise (1899-
1945) American critic TW/2,
WWA/2
WALDRON, Mr. (fl c. 1839?) actor
CDP
WALDRON, Charles D. (1874-
1946) American actor TW/2,
WWT/7-9
WALDRON, Daniel Gilman (b 1833)
American manager HAS
WALDRON, Fanny see Christian,
Frances Ann
WALDRON, Francis Godolphin
(1744-1818) actor, manager,
dramatist, prompter CDP,
CP/2-3, DNB, GT, TD/1-2
WALDRON, Mrs. Francis G. see
Harlowe, Sarah
WALDRON, Georgia [Mrs. Edward
Emery] (1872-1950) American
actress BE*, WWT/14*
WALDRON, Jack (1893-1969) Amer-
ican actor, comedian BE,
TW/26
WALDRON, James A. (d 1931 [79])
editor BE*, WWT/14*
WALDRON, Isabel see Waldron,
Georgia
WALDRON, May see Robson,
Mrs. Stuart
WALDRON, William R. (d 1910
[88]) manager EA/11*

WALDROP, Gid (b 1919) Amer-
ican educator, conductor,
composer BE
WALENN, Cecil see Barth,
Cecil
WALENN, Charles R. (d 1948)
actor BE*, WWT/14*
WALENN, James Farquharson
(d 1884) conductor EA/85*
WALES, Gary American actor
TW/25
WALFORD, Ann (b 1928) Indian/
English actress WWT/12-14
WALFORD, Marie Henry (d
1906 [21]) EA/07*
WALFORD-HENRY, Marie (d
1912 [23]) EA/13*
WALKEN, Christopher [Ronald
Walken] (b 1943) American
actor TW/19, 22-30, WWT/16
WALKEN, Ronald see Walken,
Christopher
WALKER, Alfred actor, singer
CDP
WALKER, Alice Johnstone (b
1871) American dramatist
WWA/5
WALKER, Allan (d 1970) per-
former BP/55*
WALKER, Anna see O'Doherty,
Eileen
WALKER, Arlene (d 1973 [54])
actress, casting director
TW/29
WALKER, Benjamin (d 1910
[72]) EA/11*
WALKER, Mrs. Benjamin see
Walker, Sarah Ann
WALKER, Betty (d 1976 [81])
performer BP/60*
WALKER, Bob (1918-51) Amer-
ican actor BE*
WALKER, Charles (d 1882) scene
artist EA/83*
WALKER, Charlotte [Mrs. Eugene
Walter] (1878-1958) American
actress GRB/3-4, TW/14,
WWM, WWS, WWT/1-11
WALKER, Danton (d 1960 [61])
columnist TW/17
WALKER, Diana (b 1942) Amer-
ican actress TW/23-26, 30
WALKER, Don (b 1907) American
composer, conductor BE
WALKER, Dorothy Casson see
Christie, Dorothy
WALKER, Elizabeth (b 1947)
American actress TW/26

WALKER, Eva (d 1889) EA/90*
WALKER, F. S. (d 1917) EA/18*
WALKER, George F. (b 1947)
Canadian dramatist CD
WALKER, Hal (d 1972 [76]) pro-
ducer/director/choreographer
BP/57*
WALKER, Harry (d 1896 [65]) actor
EA/97*
WALKER, Mrs. Harry see
Leechman, Katie
WALKER, Heather Eulalie see
Walker, Polly
WALKER, James J. (d 1946) song-
writer SR
WALKER, Jeremy see Kemp,
Jeremy
WALKER, John (1732-1807) actor
CDP
WALKER, John (d 1889 [26]) EA/
90*
WALKER, John (d 1890 [61]) musi-
cian EA/91*
WALKER, John (d 1910) roundabout
proprietor EA/11*
WALKER, John A. (b 1916) Ameri-
can educator BE
WALKER, John Henry (d 1883 [31])
equestrian EA/84*
WALKER, Johnny (1894-1949) actor
BE*
WALKER, Joseph A. American
dramatist, director CD
WALKER, June (1899/1904-1966)
American actress BE, ES,
TW/1-8, 10-16, 22, WWT/5-14
WALKER, Kathryn American ac-
tress TW/29-30
WALKER, Laura English actress
GRB/1
WALKER, Laura (d 1951 [57]) ac-
tress, dramatist TW/7
WALKER, Lillian (d 1975 [88])
actress BP/60*, WWT/16*
WALKER, Martin (1901-55) English
actor WWT/7-11
WALKER, Maynard Chamberlain
(fl 1771) dramatist CP/3
WALKER, Muriel see Ashwynne,
Muriel
WALKER, Nancy (b 1921/22)
American actress, singer BE,
CB, TW/2-6, 15, 17-19, 25,
WWT/10-16
WALKER, Norman (1907-63) Eng-
lish singer WWW/6
WALKER, Polly [Heather Eulalie
Walker] (b 1908) American

actress, singer WWT/7-9
WALKER, Rhoderick (b 1920)
English actor TW/4
WALKER, Robert Francis (d
1906 [29]) EA/07*
WALKER, Sarah Ann [Mrs.
Benjamin Walker] (d 1873)
EA/74*
WALKER, Sidney see Walker,
William Sidney
WALKER, Stanley (d 1962 [64])
journalist BP/47*
WALKER, Stuart (1880/86/88-
1941) American actor, di-
rector, manager, dramatist
CB, DAB, NTH, WWA/1,
WWT/7-9
WALKER, Syd (1886-1945) Eng-
lish actor WWT/7-9
WALKER, Sydney (b 1921) Amer-
ican actor TW/22-30, WWT/
16
WALKER, T. (fl 1705) dramatist
CP/2-3, GT
WALKER, T-Bone (d 1975 [64])
performer BP/59*
WALKER, Thomas (1693/98-
1744) English actor, dramatist
CDP, CP/1-3, DNB, GT,
TD/1-2
WALKER, Thomas ["Whimsical
Walker"] (d 1934 [84]) clown
BE*, WWT/14*
WALKER, Thomas Henry (d 1901
[41]) musical director EA/02*
WALKER, Wally (d 1975 [74])
performer BP/60*
"WALKER, Whimsical" see
Walker, Thomas
WALKER, William (d 1726) West
Indian dramatist CP/1-3, GT
WALKER, William Sidney (1795-
1846) Welsh critic DNB
WALKER, Dr. W. Miller (d
1881 [47]) actor EA/82*
WALKER, Zena (b 1934) English
actress TW/24, WWT/15-16
WALKES, W[illiam] R[obert] (d
1913 [59]) dramatist BE*,
EA/14*, WWT/14*
WALKINGTON, John Augustus
(d 1916 [77]) entertainer
EA/18*
WALKLEY, Arthur Bingham
(1855-1926) English critic
COC, DNB, GRB/1-4, OC/
1-3, PDT, WWT/1-5, WWW/2
WALKUP, Fairfax Proudfit (b

1887) American educator, cos-
tumier BE
WALL, Mr. (fl 1767) actor HAS
WALL, Prof. (d 1906) EA/07*
WALL, Mrs. (fl 1767) actress
HAS
WALL, Geraldine (d 1970 [57]) ac-
tress TW/27
WALL, Mrs. H. see Adams,
Annie
WALL, Harry (b 1838) American
actor CDP, HAS
WALL, Harry (1886-1966) English
dramatist WWT/5-10
WALL, Mrs. Harry [née Louisa
Clarkson] (1846-67) American
actress HAS
WALL, Horace (1837-99) actor,
manager, agent CDP
WALL, Joe (d 1895 [29]) phanto-
scope proprietor EA/96*
WALL, Max [né Maxwell George
Lorimer] (b 1908) English actor,
dancer WWT/10-16
WALLACE, Agnes (b 1851) English
dancer HAS
WALLACE, Agnes (b 1851) actress
CDP
WALLACE, Alfred E. (d 1866
[33]) comedian EA/72*
WALLACE, Annie Adelaide [Mrs.
Fitzroy Wallace] (d 1881 [45])
EA/83*
WALLACE, Art (b 1935) American
actor TW/23-25, 28-29
WALLACE, Charles (d 1903) Negro
comedian EA/04*
WALLACE, Mrs. Claude see
Belmore, Lily
WALLACE, David (d 1955 [66])
American dramatist BE*,
BP/40*
WALLACE, Mrs. Edgar (d 1933
[36]) producer, manager BE*,
WWT/14*
WALLACE, Edgar Horatio (1875-
1932) English dramatist AAS,
COC, DNB, ES, HP, OC/1-3,
PDT, WWT/6
WALLACE, Lady Eglantine (d 1803)
dramatist DNB, GT
WALLACE, Eustace (d 1916 [40])
EA/17*
WALLACE, Fitzroy (d 1883 [45])
actor, manager EA/84*
WALLACE, Mrs. Fitzroy see
Wallace, Annie Adelaide
WALLACE, Frank (d 1966 [73])

performer BP/51*
WALLACE, George (d 1883 [49])
EA/84*
WALLACE, George (b 1917/24)
American actor, singer BE,
TW/27
WALLACE, George Carlton actor
GRB/1
WALLACE, Harry (d 1920) mana-
ger BP/5*
WALLACE, Hazel Vincent (b
1919) English managing director
WWT/15-16
WALLACE, J. (fl 1835) American
actor HAS
WALLACE, James actor HAS
WALLACE, Lady James [née
Maxwell] (fl 1780s) dramatist
CP/3, TD/1-2
WALLACE, James S. (fl 1833-38?)
dramatist RJ
WALLACE, Jenny (b 1852) English
dancer CDP, HAS
WALLACE, John (fl 1802) drama-
tist CP/3
WALLACE, John J. (1831-92)
American actor HAS
WALLACE, Lee (b 1930) American
actor TW/27, 29-30
WALLACE, Gen. Lew (1827-1905)
American dramatist GRB/1
WALLACE, Lionel [Lionel Saund-
ers] (b 1872) English actor,
agent GRB/1
WALLACE, Louise Chapman (d
1962 [80]) actress BE*
WALLACE, Marcia (b 1942)
American actress TW/26
WALLACE, Marie (b 1939)
American actress TW/22, 29
WALLACE, Mike (b 1918) Amer-
ican actor TW/11
WALLACE, Minnie actress CDP
WALLACE, Mrs. M. M. (d 1889)
EA/90*
WALLACE, Morgan (d 1953 [72])
American actor BE*, BP/38*
WALLACE, Nat (d 1891) come-
dian EA/92*
WALLACE, Nellie (1870/82-
1948) Scottish actress, singer
COC, OC/1-3, PDT, WWT/
5-10
WALLACE, Paul (b 1938) Amer-
ican actor, dancer, singer
BE
WALLACE, Percy (d 1916) EA/
17*

WALLACE, Regina American ac-
tress BE
WALLACE, Rosa (d 1904) EA/05*
WALLACE, Ruby Ann see Dee,
Ruby
WALLACE, Vincent (d 1865 [51])
composer EA/72*
WALLACE, William Henry (d 1893
[28]) EA/94*
WALLACE, William Vincent (1814-
65) Irish composer, musician
CDP, DNB
WALLACE SISTERS, The HAS
WALLACH, Edgar (d 1953 [68])
American manager BE*, BP/
37*
WALLACH, Eli (b 1915) American
actor AAS, BE, CB, ES, TW/
2, 4, 7-22, 24, 28, 30, WWT/
12-16
WALLACH, Ira (b 1913) American
dramatist, lyricist BE
WALLACH, Joseph (d 1974 [62])
stage manager BP/59*
WALLACK, Miss see Jones,
Mrs.
WALLACK, Ann Duff see Wallack,
Mrs. James William
WALLACK, Arthur J. (d 1940
[91]) manager BE*, WWT/14*
WALLACK, Elizabeth [Mrs. Wil-
liam Wallack] (d 1850 [90]) ac-
tress CDP, ES
WALLACK, Fanny [Mrs. Charles
Moorhouse] (d 1856 [34]) actress
CDP, ES
WALLACK, George actor CDP
WALLACK, George Gordon (fl 1858)
actor HAS
WALLACK, Mrs. Henry (d 1845)
English actress HAS
WALLACK, Henry John (1790-1870)
English actor BS, CDP, COC,
DAB, DNB, ES, HAS, HJD,
OC/1-3, WWA/H
WALLACK, Mrs. Henry John [née
Turpin] (d 1860) English actress
CDP, HAS
WALLACK, James H. (d 1908
[64]) actor, manager GRB/4*
WALLACK, Mrs. James W. see
Johnstone, Susan
WALLACK, James William (1791-
1864) English actor, manager
CDP, COC, DAB, DNB, ES,
HAS, OC/1-3, OX, WWA/H
WALLACK, James William (1818-
73) English actor CDP, COC,

DAB, ES, HAS, OC/1-3, SR, WWA/H

WALLACK, Mrs. James William [Mrs. William Sefton; née Ann Waring] (d 1879 [64]) American actress CDP, HAS

WALLACK, Julia see Harland, Julia

WALLACK, Lester [John Johnstone Wallack] (1820-88) English/American actor, stage manager, manager CDP, COC, DAB, DNB, ES, HAS, NTH, OC/1-3, SR, WWA/H

WALLACK, Mrs. Lester (d 1909 [84]) actress BE*, WWT/14*

WALLACK, William (d 1805) actor CDP

WALLACK, Mrs. William see Wallack, Elizabeth

WALLACK, William H. W. (1760-1850) actor ES

WALLENDA, Yetta (d 1963 [42]) performer BE*

WALLER, Alma see Waller, Maggie

WALLER, Arthur (d 1898 [35]) actor EA/99*

WALLER, Mrs. Arthur see Cawthorn, Lily

WALLER, Carl (d 1900 [28]) pantomimist EA/01*

WALLER, Mrs. Carl see Waller, Mary

WALLER, Daniel Wilmarth (d 1882 [58]) actor, manager CDP

WALLER, David (b 1920) English actor AAS, WWT/15-16

WALLER, D. W. (d 1882 [58]) American actor HAS

WALLER, Mrs. D. W. see Waller, Emma

WALLER, Edmund (1605-87) English dramatist CP/1-3, GT

WALLER, Edmund Lewis (b 1884) English actor GRB/3-4, WWT/1-8

WALLER, Mrs. Edmund [Lewis] see Warwick, Ethel

WALLER, Emma (1820-99) American actress CDP, COC, DAB, HAS, OC/2-3, WWA/H

WALLER, Guy (d 1907 [34]) actor EA/08*

WALLER, Henry (b 1864) Scottish composer, conductor WWA/4

WALLER, Jack (1885-1957) English producing manager, composer, actor WWT/6-12

WALLER, John (d 1908 [59]) manager EA/09*

WALLER, J. Wallet (d 1951 [69]) director BE*, WWT/14*

WALLER, Lee (d 1974 [59]) producer/director/choreographer BP/59*

WALLER, Lewis (1860-1915) Spanish/English actor CDP, COC, DNB, EA/97, ES, GRB/1-4, OC/1-3, SR, WWA/1, WWM, WWT/1-3, WWW/1

WALLER, Mrs. Lewis [Florence West] (1862-1913) actress EA/97, GRB/1-4, OC/2-3, WWT/1

WALLER, Maggie [Alma Waller] (d 1909) EA/10*

WALLER, Mary [née Mary Milford; Mrs. Carl Waller] (d 1876) EA/77*

WALLER, Pauline (d 1907) EA/08*

WALLETT, Mrs. (d 1872 [84]) EA/73*

WALLETT, Edgar (d 1906 [23]) EA/07*

WALLETT, John (d 1869 [79]) EA/70*

WALLETT, Russell (d 1912 [44]) comedian EA/13*

WALLETT, William Frederick (1808-92) English clown CDP, HAS

WALLFORD, W. C. P. (d 1866) Yankee comedian HAS

WALLICK, John M. actor, manager SR

WALLING, Roy (d 1964 [75]) American dramatist, actor BE*

WALLINGTON, James S. (d 1972 [65]) performer BP/57*

WALLIS, Miss see Campbell, Mrs.

WALLIS, Bella [Mrs. Hugh Moss] (d 1960) actress BE*, WWT/14*

WALLIS, Bertram (1874-1952) English actor, singer GRB/4, WWT/1-11

WALLIS, Ellen (d 1895) EA/96*

WALLIS, Ellen Lancaster [Mrs. Walter Reynolds] (1856-1940) actress CDP, DP, GRB/1-4, OAA/1-2, WWT/1-8

WALLIS, Fanny see Lowe, Mrs.

William
WALLIS, Fritz (d 1900 [71])
scene artist EA/01*
WALLIS, Mrs. Fritz see
Wallis, Sabina
WALLIS, Dr. George (1740-1802)
English dramatist CP/2-3,
GT
WALLIS, George Ambrose (d 1895)
director EA/97*
WALLIS, Gladys (b c. 1772) ac-
tress SR
WALLIS, Gladys (d 1953 [80])
American actress TW/10
WALLIS, Mrs. H. see Water-
house, Mrs. John
WALLIS, Mrs. Hal see Fazenda,
Louise
WALLIS, Joseph L. (d 1860)
American actor HAS
WALLIS, Sabina [Mrs. Fritz
Wallis] (d 1910 [83]) EA/11*
WALLIS, Samuel H. (d 1890)
EA/91*
WALLIS, Shani (b 1933) English
actress, singer WWT/12-15
WALLIS, Walter (fl 1901?)
actor, singer CDP
WALLIS, William H. (b 1825)
English actor HAS
WALLMAN, Lawrence A. (b
1902) American educator BE
WALLNER, Agnes (1824-1901)
actress CDP
WALLON, T. E. see Dunville,
T. E.
WALLOP, Douglass (b 1920)
American dramatist BE
WALLS, Tom (1883-1949) Eng-
lish actor, manager, producer
AAS, COC, DNB, WWT/3-10
WALLY, Gus (d 1966 [62]) per-
former BP/50*
WALMISLEY, Blanche [Mrs.
Frank Williams] (d 1888)
actress EA/89*
WALPOLE, Mr. actor CDP
WALPOLE, Frances (fl 1616-17)
actor DA
WALPOLE, Horace, Earl of
Orford (c. 1717-97) English
author CDP, CP/2-3, DNB,
GT
WALPOLE, Sir Hugh (1884-1941)
New Zealand dramatist CB,
WWT/8-9
WALSH, Bill (d 1975 [61]) pro-
ducer/director/choreographer

BP/59*
WALSH, Blanche [Mrs. W. M.
Travers] (1873-1915) American
actress DAB, GRB/2-4, PP/3,
SR, WWA/1, WWM, WWS,
WWT/1-3
WALSH, Eliza see Breyer, Mrs.
J. E.
WALSH, Ellen (d 1917) EA/18*
WALSH, Emmet (b 1935) American
actor TW/25, 30
WALSH, Flora see Hoyt, Mrs.
Charles Hale
WALSH, Frederick G. (b 1915)
American educator, dramatist,
director BE
WALSH, Harry (b 1875) Irish actor,
stage manager, singer GRB/1
WALSH, John (d 1736) Irish? editor
ES
WALSH, John (d 1868 [28]) come-
dian, dancer EA/69*
WALSH, Joseph F. (d 1972 [76])
performer BP/56*
WALSH, Kate (d 1903) variety per-
former EA/04*
WALSH, Katherine actress SR
WALSH, Lionel (1876-1916) English
actor WWS
WALSH, Michael (d 1866 [27])
banjoist HAS
WALSH, Michael (d 1917) EA/18*
WALSH, Michael (d 1974 [70])
British stage manager BP/59*
WALSH, Miriam Cooper (d 1976
[84]) performer BP/60*
WALSH, Sam (d 1920 [42]) actor
BE*, WWT/14*
WALSH, Sean J. (b 1938) American
actor TW/25-26
WALSH, Shelford (b 1862) English
producer GRB/1
WALSH, Thomas H. (d 1925 [62])
actor BE*, BP/9*
WALSH, Thomas J. (d 1962 [59])
executive BE*
WALSH, Tom (b 1926) American
actor TW/4, 10
WALSH, Tom Hector see Hector,
"Little"
WALSH, William Thomas (1891-
1949) American dramatist
WWA/2
WALSHAM, Henry (d 1898) singer
EA/99*
WALSHE, William Sesnan (d 1910
[50]) EA/11*
WALSINGER, Bertha singer SR

WALSTEIN, Eliza (d 1833) actress CDP
WALSTEIN, Westervelt (d 1836) American actor HAS
WALSTEIN, Mrs. Westervelt [née Thayer] (d 1856) actress HAS
WALSTON, Ray (b 1917/18/19) American actor, director AAS, BE, TW/8-17, 23, WWT/15-16
WALTER, Mrs. see Bellamy, Mrs.
WALTER, Bruno (1876-1962) German conductor CB, ES, TW/18, WWA/4, WWW/6
WALTER, Charles (d 1883) acting manager, treasurer EA/84*
WALTER, Edwin (d 1953 [82]) American actor TW/10
WALTER, Emilie singer CDP
WALTER, Eugene (1874-1941) American dramatist, actor, manager CB, COC, DAB, ES, HJD, MH, MWD, NTH, OC/1-3, SR, WWA/1, WWM, WWT/1-9
WALTER, Mrs. Eugene see Walker, Charlotte
WALTER, Nancy (b 1939) American dramatist CD
WALTER, Olive (b 1898) English actress, manager WWT/8-13
WALTER, Tracey (b 1950) American actor TW/29
WALTER, W. H. St. John see St. John, Herbert
WALTER, Wilfrid (1882-1958) English actor WWT/5-12
WALTER, Wilmer (1884-1941) actor CB
WALTER-BRIANT, Fredda (b 1912) American wardrobe supervisor BE
WALTER-ELLIS, Desmond (b 1914) English actor WWT/11-16
WALTERS, Mr. (fl 1836) actor HAS
WALTERS, Annie see Jordan, Mrs. George
WALTERS, A. S. (d 1903 [47]) director EA/04*
WALTERS, Bessie see Cooke, Mrs. James
WALTERS, Casey (b 1916) American actor TW/4
WALTERS, Charles American

actor, dancer, choreographer ES
WALTERS, Clara (fl 1859) actress HAS
WALTERS, Henry Arnold (d 1872 [13]) gymnast EA/73*
WALTERS, Maud see Walters, Polly
WALTERS, Patricia Wheeler (d 1967) performer BP/52*
WALTERS, Polly [née Maud] (b 1910) American actress, dancer WWT/8-10
WALTERS, Robert see Roberts, George
WALTERS, Thorley (b 1913) English actor TW/4-6, WWT/11-16
WALTERS, Walter H. (b 1917) American educator BE
WALTERS, W. H. (d 1880 [50]) comedian EA/81*
WALTERS, Mrs. W. H. [Ellen Bertram] (d 1867) dancer EA/68*
WALTERS, Wilmarth (fl 1851) American actor HAS
WALTERS-CRAWFORD, William (d 1916) EA/18*
WALTHALL, Henry Brazeal (1878-1936) American actor DAB
WALTHER, Gretchen (b 1938) American actress TW/19
WALTON, Mr. (fl 1827) English actor, stage manager HAS
WALTON, Douglas (d 1961 [51]) Canadian actor BE*
WALTON, Edith (d 1975 [71]) critic BP/59*
WALTON, Elsie [Miss Hemming] (b 1888) English actress GRB/1
WALTON, Eugene A. (d 1967 [76]) theatrical haulier BP/52*
WALTON, Fred (d 1886 [57]) stage manager EA/87*
WALTON, Fred (d 1903 [52]) juggler EA/04*
WALTON, Fred (d 1936 [71]) actor BE*, WWT/14*
WALTON, George (d 1903) comedian EA/04*
WALTON, George Everett (d 1917) EA/18*
WALTON, H. B. [Harry Moffitt] (d 1917) manager EA/18*
WALTON, Henry Everett (d 1917) EA/18*
WALTON, Herbert (d 1954 [74]) actor BE*, WWT/14*

WALTON, J. K. (d 1928 [79])
actor BE*, WWT/14*

WALTON, Mrs. J. K. [Maude
Osmond] (d 1917) EA/18*

WALTON, Mrs. J. K. see
Walton, Sarah Ann

WALTON, John (d 1847) actor,
singer WWT/14*

WALTON, Lottie [Mrs. Robin-
son] (d 1904 [27]) EA/05*

WALTON, Mary (fl 1845) actress
HAS

WALTON, Minnie [Mrs. Frederick
Lyster] (d 1879) actress,
singer CDP

WALTON, Sarah Ann [Mrs. J.
K. Walton] (d 1888 [37])
EA/89*

WALTON, Tony (b 1934) English
designer, producer BE,
WWT/14-16

WALTON, Vera (d 1965 [74])
actress TW/22

WALTON, Mrs. W. see
Craston, Annie

WALTON, Welmouth (fl 1852)
actor HAS

WALTON, William (d 1878 [23])
music-hall performer? EA/
79*

WALTON, William (d 1904 [44])
EA/05*

WALTON, Sir William (b 1902)
English composer ES, HP

WALTON-HEMMING, Mrs. Richard
see Walton-Hemming, Sarah

WALTON-HEMMING, Sarah [Mrs.
Richard Walton-Hemming] (d
1910) EA/11*

WALTZER, Jack (b 1936) American actor TW/29

WALWYN, B. (b 1750) English
dramatist CP/3

WAMBOLD, David (1836-1889)
American minstrel CDP, HAS,
SR

WAMBUS, Francis (fl 1611-24)
actor DA

WANAMAKER, Sam (b 1919)
American actor, director,
producer AAS, BE, PDT,
TW/2-8, WWT/11-16

WANDESFORD, Osborne Sydney
(fl 1730) dramatist CP/2-3,
GT

WANDREY, Donna (b 1947)
American actress TW/26

WANGER, Walter (1894-1968)

American producer ES

WAPUL, George (fl 1576) dramatist
CP/1-3, FGF

WARAM, Percy (d 1961 [80]) English actor TW/1, 3-4, 9, 11-
13, 18, WWT/9-13

WARBOYS, Thomas (fl 1770-77)
actor, dramatist CP/2-3, GT

WARBURTON, A. Hornby (d 1910)
actor? EA/11*

WARBURTON, Charles M. (1887-
1952) English actor WWT/4-7

WARBURTON, Edward A. (b 1867)
Irish actor GRB/1-2

WARD, Mrs. [née Hoare] actress
GT, TD/1-2

WARD, Mrs. (d c. 1770) actress
TD/1-2

WARD, Miss see Guerrabella,
Mme.

WARD, Albert (b 1869) English
actor GRB/1

WARD, Albert (d 1956 [86]) actor
BE*, WWT/14*

WARD, Alfred William (d 1894)
tank performer EA/96*

WARD, Annie (fl 1867) actress
HAS

WARD, Annie [Mrs. James Moor
Ward] (d 1910) EA/11*

WARD, Annie (d 1918 [72]) actress
BE*, WWT/14*

WARD, Anthony (fl 1603) actor
DA

"WARD, Artemus" see Browne,
Charles Farrar

WARD, Arthur Sarsfield see
Rohmer, Sax

WARD, Sir A. W. (d 1924 [86])
historian BE*, WWT/14*

WARD, Bedelia [Mrs. John Ward]
(d 1879) EA/80*

WARD, Betty Australian actress
WWT/4-7

WARD, Charles (b 1761) property
man HAS

WARD, Clara (d 1973 [48]) performer BP/57*

WARD, Dolph (d 1891 [41]) EA/92*

WARD, Dorothy (b 1890) English
actress, singer COC, OC/3,
WWT/3-13

WARD, Douglas Turner (b 1930)
American actor, dramatist,
director, producer CB, CD,
TW/28-30, WWT/15-16

WARD, E. D. (d 1889 [36]) actor
CDP

WARD, Edgar (d 1901) musical
director EA/02*
WARD, Edward ["Ned"] (1667-
1731) English dramatist CP/
1-3, GT
WARD, E. L. (d 1916) EA/17*
WARD, Ethel (d 1955 [75]) actress
BE*, WWT/14*
WARD, Evelyn (d 1895 [32])
EA/96*
WARD, Fanny [or Fannie; Mrs.
Joe Lewis] (1872/75-1952)
American actress COC,
GRB/1-4, OC/3, TW/8,
WWM, WWS, WWT/1-11
WARD, Fleming (d 1962 [75])
actor TW/1, 19
WARD, Dame Geneviève [Countess
de Guerbel] (1838-1922) Amer-
ican actress CDP, COC, DP,
ES, GRB/1-4, OAA/1-2, OC/
1-3, WWA/1, WWM, WWS,
WWT/1-4, WWW/2
WARD, Hap (d 1944 [76]) Amer-
ican performer, producer
BE*, BP/28*
WARD, Henry (fl 1736) actor,
dramatist CP/1-3, GT
WARD, Henry [Arthur W. Dud-
ley] (1868-1913) American
minstrel, manager SR
WARD, Henry Rohadehouse (d
1886) EA/87*
WARD, Hettie (d 1892 [12]) ac-
tress EA/93*
WARD, Hugh J. (1871-1941)
American manager WWT/
3-8
WARD, Mrs. Humphrey (1851-
1920) Tasmanian dramatist
WWW/2
WARD, James M. (d 1892 [41])
actor EA/93*
WARD, Mrs. James Moor see
Ward, Annie
WARD, Jane [Mrs. Tom Ward]
(d 1892 [56]) EA/93*
WARD, Janet American actress
BE, TW/14-17, 22-23, 26-29
WARD, John (d 1893) EA/95*
WARD, Mrs. John see Ward,
Bedelia
WARD, Mrs. John see Ward,
Sarah
WARD, Joseph (1867-1946) actor,
minstrel, vaudevillian SR
WARD, Kate (d 1872) actress
EA/73*

WARD, Lem (1907-42) director
CB
WARD, Lewis J. (d 1903) actor
EA/05*
WARD, Mrs. Lewis J. (d 1893
[30]) EA/94*
WARD, Mackenzie (b 1903) English
actor WWT/8-12
WARD, Mary (d 1966 [78]) Ameri-
can press representative, ac-
tress BE, TW/22
WARD, Ned see Ward, Edward
WARD, Penelope Dudley (b 1914)
English actress TW/3-4, WWT/
9-11
WARD, Polly (b 1909) English ac-
tress WWT/9-11
WARD, Richard (b 1915) American
actor TW/25, 30
WARD, Richard H. (d 1970 [59])
producer/director/choreographer
BP/54*
WARD, Ronald (b 1901) English
actor WWT/8-14
WARD, Samuel actor HAS
WARD, Col. Samuel (d 1879 [70])
EA/80*
WARD, Sarah (d 1771 [39]) actress
WWT/14*
WARD, Sarah [Mrs. John Ward]
(d 1786) actress CDP
WARD, Simon (b 1941) English ac-
tor WWT/15-16
WARD, Solly (1891-1942) actor SR
WARD, Sydney (d 1902) musical
director EA/03*
WARD, Thomas (b 1799) English
actor HAS
WARD, Thomas (1807-73) American
composer, dramatist CDP,
DAB
WARD, Thomas H. (d 1886 [35])
clog dancer EA/87*
WARD, Mrs. Tom see Ward,
Jane
WARD, W. (fl 1785) dramatist
CP/3
WARD, William (d 1972 [62]) per-
former BP/56*
WARD, William H. [Marvin Morton
Mallison] (b 1852) minstrel,
comedian CDP
WARD, William Melmoth (b 1822)
English actor HAS
WARD, Winifred (d 1975 [95])
music-hall performer, male
impersonator BP/60*, WWT/
16*

WARD, W. M. (d 1879) American pantomimist EA/80*

WARDALE, R. (d 1904) lessee EA/05*

WARDE, Annie [Mrs. John Warde] (d 1876) EA/77*

WARDE, Anthony (d 1975 [66]) performer BP/59*

WARDE, Eleanor [Mrs. John Warde] (d 1881 [69]) EA/82*

WARDE, Ernest C. (d 1923 [49]) actor, stage manager BE*, BP/8*

WARDE, Frederick Barkham (1851-1935) English actor, manager CDP, COC, DAB, GRB/2-4, OC/1-3, PP/3, SR, WWA/1, WWM, WWS, WWT/1-7

WARDE, George (d 1917 [80]) actor EA/97

WARDE, Mrs. George [née Priscilla Lemmon] (d 1877) actress EA/78*

WARDE, George Faulkner (d 1898 [41]) scene artist EA/99*

WARDE, George Henry [Harry Lemmon] (d 1888) actor EA/89*

WARDE, Mrs. G. F. [Tilly Poole] (d 1884) EA/85*

WARDE, James Prescott (1792-1840) English actor CDP, DNB, OX

WARDE, J. G. (d 1887 [85]) EA/88*

WARDE, Mrs. John see Warde, Annie

WARDE, Mrs. John see Warde, Eleanor

WARDE, Johnny (d 1892) music-hall comedian EA/93*

WARDE, Trevor (d 1899 [36]) EA/00*

WARDE, William (fl 1756) dramatist CP/2-3

WARDE, William (d 1859 [48]) comic singer EA/72*

WARDE, Willie (1857-1943) English actor, dancer CDP, GRB/1-4, WWT/2-8

WARDE, W. Lemmon (b 1870) English actor GRB/1

WARDELL, Charles see Kelly, Charles

WARDELL, Charles Clavering see Kelly, Charles

WARDELL, Chrystabel Elizabeth [Chrissy Levens] (d 1888 [16]) music-hall performer EA/89*

WARDELL, Mrs. Robert see Reeve, Emma Louisa

WARDEN, Mrs. (d 1884) EA/85*

WARDEN, Edward Adams (b 1822) English singer, actor HAS

WARDEN, Edwin Adams (d 1880 [60]) minstrel EA/81*

WARDEN, Fred W. (d 1929 [68]) actor, producer, manager BE*, WWT/14*

WARDEN, Gertrude [Mrs. Wilton Jones] (b 1862) English actress CDP, EA/96, GRB/1-3

WARDEN, Jack (b 1920) American actor BE, TW/10, 12-15, 25

WARDEN, Jenny [Mrs. J. F. Warden] (d 1912) EA/13*

WARDEN, J. F. (1836-98) English actor, managing director OAA/2

WARDEN, Mrs. J. F. [née Jenny Bellair] (b 1837) English actress OAA/2

WARDEN, Mrs. J. F. see Warden, Jenny

WARDEN, Samuel (d 1884 [18]) EA/85*

WARDEN, Sydney (d 1901) actor EA/02*

WARDEN-REED, Frank [Fritz E. A. Weiste] (b 1879) English actor GRB/1

WARDHAUGH, Mathew (d 1888 [75]) actor EA/89*

WARDLE, Irving (b 1929) English critic AAS, WWT/15-16

WARDROPER, Henry (d 1910) EA/11*

WARDROPER, John [Johnny Lee] (d 1880) Scottish comedian EA/81*

WARDWELL, Geoffrey (1900-55) English actor, director WWT/10-11

WARDWELL, John American actor TW/30

WARE, Dr. dramatist RJ

WARE, Albert see Cartini, Albert

WARE, Bill (b 1943) American actor TW/28

WARE, Charles (fl 1858) actor HAS

WARE, Courtney (d 1878) manager EA/79*

WARE, Mrs. Courtney see Willmore, Lizzie

WARE, George (d 1895 [66])
singer, agent EA/97*
WARE, Harriet (d 1962 [84])
American composer WWA/4
WARE, Helen [Helen Remer]
(1877/79-1939) American ac-
tress GRB/3-4, WWA/1,
WWM, WWT/1-8
WARE, Irene [Mrs. J. F. Cli-
burn] (d 1909) EA/10*
WARE, Nettee (d 1913 [29])
EA/14*
WARE, William Hibbert (d 1908
[36]) EA/09*
WAREING, Alfred (1876-1942)
English business manager,
manager, producer, librarian
GRB/3, WWT/2-9
WAREING, Lesley (b 1913) Eng-
lish actress WWT/8-12
WAREING, Robert (d 1888 [39])
proprietor EA/89*
WARFAZ, Georges de (1889?-
1959) Belgian actor BE*
WARFIELD, David (1866-1951)
American actor CDP, COC,
ES, GRB/2-4, HJD, NTH,
OC/1-3, SR, TW/8, WWA/3,
WWM, WWS, WWT/1-11
WARFIELD, Joel (b 1937) Amer-
ican actor TW/19, 25
WARFIELD, Marlene (b 1941)
American actress TW/25-26
WARFIELD, William (b 1920)
American singer, actor BE,
TW/22-23
WARIK, Josef American actor
TW/26-27
WARING, Mrs. (fl 1822-24)
English actress HAS
WARING, Ann see Wallack,
Mrs. James William
WARING, Barbara (b 1912) Eng-
lish actress WWT/10-11
WARING, Bertha [Mrs. John
Wilson Musante] (d 1904)
EA/05*
WARING, Claire (b 1917) Ameri-
can actress TW/25
WARING, Dorothy May Graham
(b 1895) English actress,
singer WWT/3-6
WARING, Herbert [Herbert War-
ing Rutty] (1857-1932) English
actor EA/95, GRB/1-4,
WWT/1-6, WWW/3
WARING, James (d 1975 [53])
producer/director/choreographer

BP/60*
WARING, Leigh (d 1817) English
actor, stage manager HAS
WARING, Mary (d 1964 [72]) ac-
tress BE*
WARING, Noel E. (d 1854) circus
manager HAS
WARING, Richard (b 1912) English
actor BE, TW/3-11, 13-19,
24, WWT/10-16
WARLEY, May English actress
GRB/2-4
WARMINGTON, Stanley J. (1884-
1941) English actor WWT/6-9
WARMINGTON, William (fl 1880)
actor CDP
WARNE, George (d 1868 [71])
musician EA/69*
WARNE, Harry (d 1884) equestrian
clown EA/85*
WARNE, Thomas B. (d 1891 [39])
EA/93*
WARNER, Mrs. see Warner,
Mary Amelia
WARNER, Andrew J. (d 1965 [81])
critic BP/50*
WARNER, Anne [Anne Warner
French] (1869-1913) American
dramatist WWM, WWS
WARNER, Charles (d 1865 [34])
circus showman HAS
WARNER, Charles [Charles Lick-
fold] (1846-1909) English actor
CDP, COC, DNB, DP, GRB/
1-4, OAA/2, OC/1-3
WARNER, David (b 1941) English
actor AAS, WWT/14-16
WARNER, Elizabeth [Mrs. Richard
Warner] (d 1884 [29]) EA/85*
WARNER, Ernest A. (b 1882)
English agent GRB/1
WARNER, Fred (d 1900) EA/01*
WARNER, George Frederick (d
1867 [32]) comic singer EA/68*
WARNER, Grace [Mrs. Franklin
McLeay] (1873-1925) English
actress, manager GRB/1-4,
WWT/1-5
WARNER, Mrs. H. [Emmie d'Este]
(d 1874 [29]) burlesque actress
EA/75*
WARNER, Harry (d 1908) scene
artist EA/09*
WARNER, Henry Byron (1876-1958)
English actor ES, GRB/1-4,
SR, TW/15, WWA/5, WWM,
WWS, WWT/1-11
WARNER, Mrs. H[enry] B[yron]

see Paullin, Louise
WARNER, Hugh L. (d 1894
[41]) EA/95*
WARNER, Jemmy (fl 1777?) clown
CDP
WARNER, Jennie (fl 1858) HAS
WARNER, J. L. (d 1871 [26])
actor EA/72*
WARNER, Kate L. (d 1899 [70])
EA/00*
WARNER, Marsha (b 1949) Amer-
ican actress TW/29
WARNER, Mary Amelia [née
Huddart] (1797/1804-1854)
Irish actress CDP, DNB,
HAS, SR
WARNER, Neil (d 1901 [71])
Australian actor HAS
WARNER, Richard (d 1775) trans-
lator CP/2-3
WARNER, Mrs. Richard see
Warner, Elizabeth
WARNER, Rick (b 1943) American
actor TW/30
WARNER, W. A. (b 1826) Amer-
ican actor HAS
WARNER, William (d 1608/09)
dramatist, translator CP/3
WARNICK, Clay (b 1915) Amer-
ican composer, musical di-
rector, producer BE
WARNOW, Helen (d 1970 [46])
performer BP/55*
WARRAL, Mrs. (fl 1777) singer
CDP
WARRE, Michael (b 1922) English
actor, designer AAS, TW/
2-3, WWT/10-16
WARRELL, Master (fl 1793-1812)
Scottish actor HAS
WARRELL, Mrs. (fl 1790) ac-
tress TD/1-2
WARRELL, Eliza see Atkins,
Mrs. William
WARREN, Mr. actor CDP
WARREN, Mrs. (fl 1786?) ac-
tress CDP
WARREN, Miss see Price,
Mrs.
WARREN, Albert H. (fl 1876-79)
actor OAA/1-2
WARREN, Anna see Marble,
Mrs. Danforth
WARREN, Betty [Babette Hilda
Hogan] (b 1905) English ac-
tress, singer WWT/9-14
WARREN, Bob (d 1892) circus
performer EA/93*

WARREN, Brett (b 1910) American
director BE
WARREN, C. Denier (1889-1971)
American actor WWT/4-15
WARREN, Mrs. Charles see
Fish, Marguerite
WARREN, Mrs. Duane (fl 1866)
actress HAS
WARREN, Edward Alyn (d 1974
[54]) manager BP/59*
WARREN, Ella (fl 1850) dancer
HAS
WARREN, Ernest (d 1887 [45])
dramatist NYM
WARREN, F. Brooke (d 1950 [83])
actor BE*, WWT/14*
WARREN, Georgiana [Mrs. Philip
Warren] (1829-96) actress CDP
WARREN, Harry (b 1893) American
composer BE, CB
WARREN, Hester see Proctor,
Mrs. Joseph
WARREN, Mrs. H. L. see
Frost, Edith
WARREN, Iris (d 1963) speech
teacher WWT/14*
WARREN, James (d 1876) comedian
EA/77*
WARREN, Jeff [né Jones] (b 1921)
American actor, director, singer
BE, WWT/12-16
WARREN, Jennifer (b 1941) Amer-
ican actress TW/29
WARREN, Jimmy (d 1972 [50])
performer BP/57*
WARREN, John Byrne Leicester
(1835-95) dramatist HP
WARREN, Joseph (b 1916) Ameri-
can actor TW/22-24, 26, 29
WARREN, J. V. (fl 1848) actor
HAS
WARREN, Kenneth J. (1929-73)
Australian actor TW/20,
WWT/15-16
WARREN, Lavinia see "Thumb,
Mrs. Tom"
WARREN, Leonard (1911-60)
American singer CB, ES,
TW/16, WWA/3
WARREN, Lesley Ann (b 1946)
American actress TW/20, 22,
30
WARREN, Mary Ann see Rice,
Mrs. John B.
WARREN, Mercy Otis (1728-1814)
American dramatist CP/3,
DAB, EAP, HJD, NTH, RJ
WARREN, Minnie (fl 1877?) dwarf

CDP
WARREN, Mirian Howell (d 1972
[72]) agent BP/56*
WARREN, Mrs. Philip see
Warren, Georgiana
WARREN, Richard Henry (1859-
1933) American composer
DAB, WWA/1, WWM
WARREN, Robert Penn (b 1905)
American dramatist MD,
MWD
WARREN, Suzanne Le Mesurier
(d 1969 [75]) performer BP/
54*
WARREN, T. Gideon (d 1919
[65]) actor, dramatist BE*,
WWT/14*
WARREN, Wade (d 1973 [76])
actor, director TW/29
WARREN, W. H. (d 1878 [35])
circus stud groom EA/79*
WARREN, William (1767-1832)
English/American actor CDP,
COC, DAB, HAS, OC/1-3,
SR, WWA/H
WARREN, William (d 1878 [32])
musician EA/79*
WARREN, William (1812-88)
American actor CDP, DAB,
HAS, OC/1-3, WWA/H
WARREN, Mrs. William see
Brunton, Anne
WARREN, William Henry see
Atom, Willie
WARRENDER, Harold (1903-53)
English actor WWT/7-11
WARRENER, Warren (d 1961
[73]) actor BE*
WARREN-SMITH, Mrs. P. see
Loftus, Kitty
WARRICK, Elizabeth (d 1974
[60]) performer BP/59*
WARRICK, Ruth (b 1915) Amer-
ican actress BE, TW/27-30,
WWT/16
WARRILOW, John (d 1906 [70])
comedian EA/07*
WARRINER, Annie (d 1900 [44])
EA/01*
WARRINER, Frederic (b 1916)
American actor TW/7-8,
11-15, 22-25, 27-28, WWT/
14-16
WARRINGTON, Ann [Mary L.
Woods] (fl 1895-1909) Amer-
ican actress WWM
WARRINGTON, William (d 1887
[44]) music-hall performer

EA/88*
WARRISS, G. A. (d 1893 [52])
journalist EA/94*
WARTENBERG, P. (b 1867) Dutch
acrobat GRB/1
WARTENBERG, W. (b 1871) Dutch
acrobat GRB/1
WARTON, Elizabeth Hines (d 1971
[76]) performer BP/55*
WARWICK, Ethel [Mrs. Edmund
Waller] (1882-1951) English ac-
tress GRB/1-4, WWT/1-9
WARWICK, Giulia (d 1904 [47])
singer, actress DP
WARWICK, J. H. (fl 1847-57) Eng-
lish actor HAS
WARWICK, John (d 1972 [67])
performer BP/56*
WARWICK, Kate see Vance,
Kate
WARWICK, Robert (d 1964 [85])
actor WWT/14*
WARWICK, Robert [Robert Taylor
Bien] (1878-1964) American ac-
tor TW/21, WWM, WWT/4-11
WARWICK, Rev. Thomas (fl 1784)
dramatist CP/3
WARWICK-MOORE, J. (b 1868)
English musical director, com-
poser GRB/1
WASE, Christopher (d c. 1690)
translator CP/2-3
WASHBOURNE, Mona (b 1903)
English actress AAS, TW/14-
15, 27, WWT/13-16
WASHBURN, Bryant (1889-1963)
American actor BE*, BP/47*
WASHBURN, Charles (d 1972 [82])
dramatist BP/56*
WASHBURN, Jack (b 1927) Ameri-
can singer, actor BE, TW/19
WASHER, Ben (b 1906) American
press representative BE
WASHINGTON, Dinah (d 1963 [39])
performer BP/48*
WASHINGTON, Florence (d 1872)
dancer EA/73*
WASHINGTON, Lamont (d 1969
[24]) actor, singer TW/25
WASHINGTON, Vernon (b 1927)
American actor TW/24-25
WASSERMAN, Dale (b 1917) Amer-
ican dramatist, librettist BE,
CD
WATERFIELD, Charles singer,
composer CDP
WATERHOUSE, Mr. singer TD/
1-2

WATERHOUSE, Frederick G.
(d 1904) EA/05*
WATERHOUSE, Mrs. John [Mrs.
H. Wallis] (d 1871) actress
EA/72*
WATERHOUSE, Keith (b 1929)
English dramatist CD, CH,
WWT/14-16
WATERLOW, Marjorie (1888-
1921) English actress WWT/
2-3
WATERMAN, Dennis (b 1948)
English actor WWT/15-16
WATERMAN, Ida (d 1941 [89])
actress BE*, WWT/14*
WATERMAN, Willard (b 1914)
American actor TW/23-26,
30
WATEROUS, Allen H. (d 1965
[61]) performer BP/50*
WATEROUS, Herbert L. (1868-
1947) American singer TW/4,
WWM
WATERS, Ethel (1900-77) Amer-
ican actress, singer BE,
CB, COC, OC/3, TW/1,
3-20, WWT/9-16
WATERS, James (d 1923 [68])
critic WWT/1-4, WWW/2
WATERS, James R. (d 1945)
Hungarian/American comedian
CB
WATERS, Jan (b 1937) English
actress, singer WWT/15-16
WATERS, Paulette (b 1947)
American actress TW/22-23
WATERS, T. Hadley (d 1964
[67]) dramatist BP/49*
WATERS, Thomas (fl 1607) actor
DA
WATERSON, J. (d 1893) band-
master EA/94*
WATERSON, Samuel A. (b 1940)
American actor TW/24-30,
WWT/15-16
WATERSTREET, Edmund (b 1943)
American actor TW/25-26
WATFORD, Gwen (b 1927) Eng-
lish actress WWT/15-16
WATHALL, Alfred G. (d 1938
[58]) English composer BE*,
BP/23*
WATHEN, Mr. (fl c. 1792?) actor
CDP, GT, TD/1-2
WATKIN, Alexander see Afrique
WATKIN, Pierre (d 1960) actor
BE*
WATKINS, Catherine (d 1916

[72]) EA/17*
WATKINS, Charles (d 1882) photog-
rapher EA/83*
WATKINS, Mrs. Charles A. see
Gray, Ada
WATKINS, Charles W. (d 1892)
EA/93*
WATKINS, Dick (d 1864 [36]) comic
singer, comedian HAS
WATKINS, Elizabeth [Mrs. Pio
Watkins] (d 1894) EA/95*
WATKINS, Harry (1825-94) Ameri-
can actor, manager CDP, HAS
WATKINS, Mrs. Harry [Mrs.
Charles Howard; née Rosina
Shaw] (1829-1904) English ac-
tress CDP, HAS
WATKINS, Helen W. (d 1972 [84])
performer BP/56*
WATKINS, Henry (d 1875 [38])
singer EA/76*
WATKINS, John (d 1905 [68]) EA/
06*
WATKINS, John see Rivalli
WATKINS, Linda (1908/14-76)
American actress TW/2-4,
WWT/7-11
WATKINS, Maurine (d 1968 [68])
dramatist BP/54*
WATKINS, Perry R. (d 1974 [67])
producer/director/choreographer
BP/59*
WATKINS, Mrs. Pio see Watkins,
Elizabeth
WATKINS, Rosina see Watkins,
Mrs. Harry
WATKINS, Thomas (d 1911) EA/12*
WATKINS, William (fl 1802) drama-
tist CP/3
WATKYN, Arthur (1907-65) Welsh
dramatist WWT/12-14
WATKYN-WYNNE, Nora (d 1908)
EA/09*
WATLING, Dilys [née Rhys-Jones]
(b 1946) English actress WWT/
15-16
WATLING, Jack (b 1923) English
actor WWT/11-16
WATLING, Peter (d 1961 [40])
dramatist WWT/14*
WATSON, Mrs. [Mrs. Dodge] (fl
1835-36) actress HAS
WATSON, Mrs. (d 1871) actress?
EA/72*
WATSON, Mrs. (d 1883) EA/84*
WATSON, Miss actress CDP
WATSON, Miss see Bailey, Mrs.
WATSON, Miss see Brooks, Mrs.

WATSON, Alfred Edward Thomas (1849-1922) critic GRB/2-4

WATSON, Alfred R. (d 1903 [58]) musical director, composer EA/04*

WATSON, Ann [née Wells] (d 1854) actress? HAS

WATSON, Mrs. Barney see Watson, Kate

WATSON, Betty Jane (b 1926/28) American actress, singer BE, TW/5-6, WWT/11

WATSON, Billy (d 1945 [78]) American performer, producer BE*, BP/29*

WATSON, Bobby (d 1965 [77]) performer BP/49*

WATSON, Charles (d 1851) American actor HAS

WATSON, Charlotte see Bailey, Mrs. Thomas

WATSON, David Scott [D. W. Servius] (d 1889 [51]) music-hall performer EA/90*

WATSON, Douglas [or Douglass] (b 1921) American actor AAS, BE, TW/4-21, 23-24, 28-30, WWT/12-16

WATSON, E. Bradlee (d 1961 [82]) American educator, editor BE*

WATSON, Eleanor (fl 1861) singer HAS

WATSON, Elizabeth (d 1931) Scottish actress WWT/5-6

WATSON, Elizabeth see Boman, Mrs. John

WATSON, Ellen Maria see Williams, Nelly

WATSON, Emily see Royce, Mrs. W.

WATSON, Fanny (d 1970 [80]) vaudevillian BP/54*

WATSON, Fanny Mary (d 1874 [92]) manager EA/75*

WATSON, F. Groves (d 1907 [53]) comedian EA/08*

WATSON, F. H. (d 1882 [50]) acting manager EA/83*

WATSON, Florence English actress, singer GRB/1

WATSON, Frederick (d 1874 [21]) pantomimist EA/76*

WATSON, George (fl 1795) dramatist CP/3

WATSON, George (d 1896) registrar & secretary of Royal College of Music EA/97*

WATSON, George M. (d 1971 [51]) publicist BP/55*

WATSON, G. Howard see Manders, Lucy

WATSON, G. L. (d 1872 [46]) music-hall proprietor EA/73*

WATSON, Harry actor CDP

WATSON, Henrietta [Mrs. Walter Thornton Radcliffe] (1873-1964) Scottish actress EA/96, GRB/1-4, WWT/1-12

WATSON, Horace (1867-1934) English manager WWT/4-6

WATSON, Master I. L. Z. juvenile prodigy CDP

WATSON, Ivan Vernon (d 1904 [48]) actor EA/05*

WATSON, Jack Bowles (d 1906 [36]) EA/07*

WATSON, Mrs. J. B. (d 1892) actress EA/93*

WATSON, Dr. J. C. (d 1889) EA/90*

WATSON, John (1520-83) English dramatist CP/2-3, FGF

WATSON, John (d 1867 [63]) stage manager EA/68*

WATSON, John (d 1889 [55]) proprietor EA/90*

WATSON, Mrs. John (fl 1835) actress, singer CDP

WATSON, John Boel (d 1881 [43]) comedian EA/82*

WATSON, John Bowles (d 1804) manager TD/1-2

WATSON, J. R. (d 1887) architect EA/88*

WATSON, Kate [Mrs. Barney Watson] (d 1894 [45]) EA/95*

WATSON, Kitty (d 1967 [80]) performer BP/51*

WATSON, Lee (b 1926) American lighting designer BE

WATSON, Leona (fl 1900s) American actress, singer WWM

WATSON, Lucille (1879-1962) Canadian actress CB, TW/2-11, 19, WWT/7-13

WATSON, Malcolm (1853/57-1929) Scottish critic, dramatist GRB/2-4, WWT/1-5

WATSON, Margaret (d 1940 [65]) actress WWT/4-9

WATSON, Margaret Sarah (d 1913) EA/14*

WATSON, Maria (d 1869 [66]) costumier EA/70*

WATSON, Michael (d 1889) composer EA/90*

WATSON, Minor (1889-1965) American actor TW/2-4, 22, WWT/6-11

WATSON, Moray (b 1930) English actor TW/20

WATSON, Paddy (d 1908 [62]) comedian, circus clown EA/10*

WATSON, Ralph Haines see Granville, Fred

WATSON, Rosabel (d 1959 [94]) conductor WWT/14*

WATSON, Rosabel Grace (d 1940 [65]) actress BE*

WATSON, Sammy (b 1854) Irish animal trainer WWM

WATSON, Solomon Lancelot Inglis see Lister, Lance

WATSON, Stuart (d 1956 [64]) producer, lessee, manager BE*, WWT/14*

WATSON, Susan (b 1938) American actress, singer, dancer BE, TW/21-23, 25-29

WATSON, Thomas (d 1886 [81]) actor? EA/87*

WATSON, Thomas (d 1896 [49]) comedian EA/97*

WATSON, Thomas M. (d 1963 [62]) dramatist, critic BE*

WATSON, Tilly (d 1898) serio-comic EA/99*

WATSON, Tom (d 1860) English circus clown HAS

WATSON, Tony (d 1913 [23]) EA/14*

WATSON, Vernon (d 1949 [62]) performer BE*, WWT/14*

WATSON, William (fl c. 1782?) dramatist CP/3

WATSON, Wylie [John Wylie Robertson] (1899-1966) Scottish actor WWT/8-10

WATSON-SCOTT, Mr. (d 1909) EA/10*

WATT, Billie Lou (b 1924) American actress TW/2-3, 28

WATT, Hannah (d 1969) performer BP/54*

WATTERS, George Manker (d 1943 [52]) American dramatist, producer BE*, WWT/14*

WATTERS, Hal (b 1943) American actor TW/25, 27, 29

WATTERSON, George (1783-1854) American dramatist EAP

WATTIS, Richard (1912-75) Eng-

lish actor WWT/12-15

WATTLE, Miss see Stanley, Mrs.

WATTS, Mrs. (d 1876 [45]) EA/77*

WATTS, Mrs. see Sefton, Mrs. John

WATTS, Charles (d 1883) comedian EA/84*

WATTS, Charles (d 1966) actor TW/23

WATTS, Dodo (b 1910) English actress WWT/7-9

WATTS, Elizabeth (d 1967 [79]) actress, singer TW/24

WATTS, Francis Walter [Frank Clifford] (d 1874) actor EA/75*

WATTS, Henry (d 1881 [70]) music-hall proprietor EA/82*

WATTS, John see Hanson, John

WATTS, Jonathan (b 1934) American dancer ES

WATTS, Joseph Albert (d 1881 [29]) musician EA/82*

WATTS, Norman (d 1891) actor EA/92*

WATTS, Peter (d 1972 [72]) producer/director/choreographer BP/57*

WATTS, Richard, Jr. (b 1898) American critic AAS, BE, NTH, OC/1-3, WWT/9-16

WATTS, Stephen (b 1910) Scottish critic WWT/11-16

WATTS, Weldon (d 1902 [45]) proprietor, director EA/03*

WATTS-PHILLIPS, Mrs. Basil see Watts, Sophie

WATTS-PHILLIPS, John Edward (1894-1960) Welsh manager WWT/9-11

WATTS-PHILLIPS, Sophie [Mrs. Basil Watts-Phillips] (d 1894) EA/95*

WAUGH, Amelia (1836-87) American actress NYM

WAUGH, Mrs. De Witt (fl 1843) actress HAS

WAVER, Robert see Wever, Robert

WAXMAN, Arthur (b 1921) American manager, producer BE

WAXMAN, Morris D. (d 1931 [55]) actor BE*, WWT/14*

WAY, Mrs. (fl 1843) actress HAS

WAYBURN, Ned (1874-1942) American director, producer WWA/2, WWT/7-9

WAYER, William (fl 1598-1605) dramatist CP/1-3

WAYHO, Jack (d 1917) variety
performer EA/18*
WAYLETT, Harriet (1798-1851)
English actress, singer BS,
CDP, DNB, OX
WAYNE, Burt (d 1879) minstrel,
songcomposer CDP
WAYNE, David (b 1914) American
actor AAS, BE, CB, TW/3-
6, 10-24, WWT/11-16
WAYNE, Fredd (b 1923) American
actor TW/6-8
WAYNE, Horace Stokes (b 1858)
American dramatist WWM
WAYNE, Naunton (1901-70)
Welsh actor, entertainer
AAS, WWT/9-14, WWW/6
WAYNE, Paula (b 1937) Ameri-
can actress, singer BE
WAYNE, Rollo (1899-1954) Amer-
ican scene designer WWT/
7-10
WAYNE, Thomas (d 1971 [31])
performer BP/56*
WAYT, Lizzie (b 1841) American
lecturer HAS
WEAD, Frank W. (1894-1947)
dramatist SR
WEADOCK, Mrs. Louis see
Bergere, Ouida
WEADON, Percy (d 1939 [79])
American producer, press
representative BE*, BP/23*
WEALES, Gerald (b 1925) Amer-
ican educator BE
WEAR, Millard (d 1970 [73])
journalist BP/55*
WEATHERBURN, Elizabeth (d
1905 [63]) EA/06*
WEATHERBURN, William (d
1886 [32]) pantomimist EA/
87*
WEATHERHEAD, Elizabeth K.
(d 1892) EA/93*
WEATHERLEY, Alec (1874-1910)
English business manager,
stage manager GRB/1-2
WEATHERLY, Alec see Weather-
ley, Alec
WEATHERS, Roscoe (d 1976 [55])
composer/lyricist BP/60*
WEATHERSBY, Eliza [Mrs. Nat
C. Goodwin] (1849-87) English
actress CDP, HAS, NYM,
SR
WEATHERSBY, Eliza Jane (d
1904 [67]) actress EA/05*
WEATHERSBY, Miss Ernie (d

1884 [22]) actress EA/85*
WEATHERSBY, Frank (b 1870) Eng-
lish agent, manager GRB/1-3
WEATHERSBY, George (d 1911
[81]) actor EA/13*
WEATHERSBY, Helen (d 1943 [80])
actress BE*, WWT/14*
WEATHERSBY, Jennie actress
CDP
WEAVER, Affie (1855-1940) actress
CB
WEAVER, "Doddles" (b 1914)
American actor TW/2-3
WEAVER, Fritz (b 1926) American
actor BE, CB, TW/12-22, 25-
27, WWT/14-16
WEAVER, Henry A. , Sr. (b 1832)
English actor PP/3
WEAVER, Henry A. , Jr. (b 1858)
American actor PP/3
WEAVER, John (1673-1760) English
dancing-master, dramatist COC,
CP/1-3, DNB, ES, GT, OC/3,
TD/1-2
WEAVER, Mrs. John (d 1916)
EA/17*
WEAVER, John H. (fl 1833) Amer-
ican actor HAS
WEAVER, John V. A. (1893-1938)
American dramatist, critic HJD
WEAVER, Paul Fred see Ford,
Paul
WEBB, Mr. (fl 1822) actor CDP
WEBB, Mrs. [née Child] (d 1793)
English actress CDP, GT,
TD/1-2
WEBB, Mrs. (fl 1808?) actress
CDP
WEBB, Mrs. A. (d 1905) EA/06*
WEBB, Ada (b 1845) American ac-
tress CDP, HAS
WEBB, Alan (b 1906) English actor,
director AAS, BE, TW/4, 8-9,
14, 18, 20, 22-24, WWT/8-16
WEBB, Alfred (d 1899) EA/00*
WEBB, Alfred (d 1901 [48]) come-
dian EA/02*
WEBB, Alice [Mrs. Will Smith]
(d 1904) swimmer EA/05*
WEBB, Alyce Elizabeth (b 1934)
American actress TW/26-27,
29-30
WEBB, Arthur Cecil (d 1907) actor
EA/08*
WEBB, Charles (d 1851) American
actor HAS
WEBB, Charles (d 1889) actor,
manager CDP

WEBB, Charles (d 1906) actor,
scene artist EA/08*
WEBB, Clifton (1891/93/94-
1966) American actor, singer
CB, ES, SR, TW/2-6, 23,
WWA/4, WWT/7-11
WEBB, Constance (d 1872 [31])
singer EA/72*
WEBB, Edmund (d 1899) jour-
nalist EA/00*
WEBB, Elizabeth [Mrs. J. J.
Webb] (d 1906) EA/07*
WEBB, Emma (b 1843) American
actress CDP, HAS
WEBB, Ernest Henry (d 1868
[16]) EA/69*
WEBB, George John (d 1911 [74])
musician EA/12*
WEBB, Harry [or Henry] (1814-
67) actor CDP
WEBB, Harry (d 1903) advance
agent EA/04*
WEBB, Henry Berry (d 1867
[52]) comedian EA/68*
WEBB, Jack (d 1954 [65]) mana-
ger BE*, WWT/14*
WEBB, James A. (d 1859) actor
HAS
WEBB, James Curtois (d 1893)
EA/94*
WEBB, James Watson (1802-84)
critic CDP
WEBB, Mrs. J. J. see Webb,
Elizabeth
WEBB, John (1611-72) English
scene painter, scene designer
COC, ES, NTH, OC/1-3
WEBB, John (d 1913 [49]) actor
EA/14*, WWT/14*
WEBB, Joseph James (d 1917)
EA/18*
WEBB, Kenneth Seymour (1885-
1966) American dramatist
WWA/4
WEBB, Leonard (b 1930) English
dramatist, actor CD
WEBB, Lizabeth (b 1926) English
actress, singer WWT/11-12
WEBB, Lizzie see Fraser-
Brunner, Queenie
WEBB, Mary (fl 1881) actress,
singer CDP
WEBB, Nella (d 1954 [78]) Amer-
ican actress, singer TW/11,
WWS
WEBB, Ruth (b 1923) American
talent representative, singer,
actress BE

WEBB, Sidney F. (d 1956 [64])
producer BE*, WWT/14*
WEBB, William (d 1903) scene
artist EA/04*
WEBB, Little Willie (d 1878 [6])
actor EA/79*
WEBBE, Samuel (1740-1816) com-
poser CDP
WEBBER, Carrie actress SR
WEBBER, Charles (d 1954 [79])
conductor BE*, WWT/14*
WEBBER, Eliza [Mrs. Arthur
Wood] (d 1896) actress EA/97*
WEBBER, John F. (b 1867) Amer-
ican actor WWM
WEBBER, Lisa (c. 1842-87) English
actress NYM
WEBBER, M. (d 1893 [57]) manager
EA/94*
WEBBER, Mrs. M. A. (d 1893)
EA/94*
WEBBER, Robert American actor
BE, TW/12-18
WEBB SISTERS, The HAS
WEBER, Carl Maria von (1786-
1826) German composer ES
WEBER, Edmund (d 1885) musician,
composer EA/86*
WEBER, Edwin J. (d 1968 [75])
composer/lyricist BP/53*
WEBER, Fredricka (b 1940) Amer-
ican actress TW/26-27
WEBER, Henry William (1783-1818)
Russian?/English editor DNB
WEBER, Mrs. Joe [Lillian Fried-
man] (d 1951 [76]) actress
BE*, BP/36*
WEBER, Joseph (1867-1942) Amer-
ican actor, manager COC,
DAB, ES, GRB/3-4, NTH, OC/
3, SR, WWA/2, WWM, WWS,
WWT/1-9
WEBER, Karl (b 1916) American
actor TW/4-6
WEBER, Leonard S. (d 1973 [45])
producer/director/choreographer
BP/58*
WEBER, Liza [Mrs. Robert Brit-
ton] (d 1887 [45]) actress CDP
WEBER, L. Lawrence (1872-1940)
American producing manager
CB, WWT/6-9
WEBER, William (b 1915) American
actor TW/2-3
WEBER AND FIELDS COC, OC/3
WEBERN, Anton von (1883-1945)
Austrian composer, conductor
ES

WEBLEY, John (d 1971 [24])
performer BP/56*
WEBSTER, Mr. actor HAS
WEBSTER, Mr. (d c. 1784)
actor TD/1-2
WEBSTER, Anthony (d c. 1785)
actor CDP
WEBSTER, Mrs. Anthony see
Davies, Elizabeth
WEBSTER, Ben (1864-1947)
English actor COC, DNB,
EA/95, ES, GRB/1-4, OC/
1-3, TW/3, WWT/1-10, WWW/4
WEBSTER, Mrs. Ben see
Whitty, May
WEBSTER, Benjamin Nottingham
(1797-1882) English dramatist,
actor, manager CDP, COC,
DNB, EA/68, OAA/1-2, OC/
1-3
WEBSTER, Byron (b 1933) Eng-
lish actor TW/23, 25, 27
WEBSTER, Clara (1821/23-44)
English dancer CDP, ES
WEBSTER, Florence (d 1893
[28]) EA/94*
WEBSTER, Florence Ann (1860-
99) English actress, dancer
COC, OC/1-3
WEBSTER, Frederick (1802-78)
English stage manager COC,
OC/1-3
WEBSTER, George (fl 1598-
1603) actor DA
WEBSTER, Henry Kitchell (1875-
1932) American dramatist
WWA/1
WEBSTER, Jean [Mrs. Glennford
McKinney] (1876-1916) Amer-
ican dramatist WWA/1
WEBSTER, John (c. 1580-1634)
English dramatist COC, CP/
1-3, DNB, ES, FGF, HP,
MH, NTH, OC/1-3, PDT,
RE
WEBSTER, John (fl 1596) actor
DA
WEBSTER, John (b 1813) actor
CDP
WEBSTER, John actor CDP
WEBSTER, Mrs. John see
McHenry, Nellie
WEBSTER, Lizzie (fl 1878) ac-
tress CDP
WEBSTER, Margaret (1905-72)
American actress, producer,
director AAS, BE, CB, COC,
ES, OC/1-3, SR, TW/2-8,

23, 29, WWA/5, WWT/7-16
WEBSTER, Margaret Davies Eng-
lish actress GRB/1-3
WEBSTER, Marion Litonius (d
1971 [62]) performer BP/56*
WEBSTER, Paul Francis (b 1907)
American lyricist BE
WEBSTER, Thomas (d 1913 [80])
EA/14*
WEBSTER, Mrs. W. H. see
Greville, Mabel
WEBSTER, Wilfred H. Irish actor
GRB/1
WEBSTER-GLEASON, Lucile (1888-
1947) American actress WWT/
6-8
WEBSTER-POWELL, Alma Hall
(b 1874) American singer WWM
WECKER, Gero (d 1974 [51]) pro-
ducer/director/choreographer
BP/59*
WEDDELL (fl 1737-42) dramatist
CP/3
WEDDELL, George Hill (d 1867
[35]) drummer EA/68*
WEDEKIND, Frank (1864-1918)
German dramatist, actor COC,
ES, NTH, OC/3, PDT
WEDGEWORTH, Ann American ac-
tress TW/20-22, 27, 30
WEDWER, William (fl 1627-40)
actor DA
WEED, Leland T. (d 1975 [74])
performer BP/60*
WEEDE, Robert (1903-72) American
actor, singer BE, CB, TW/12-
13, 26, 29
WEEDEN, Evelyn (d 1961 [86])
English actress WWT/2-5
WEEKES, H. (d 1838) comedian
EA/72*, WWT/14*
WEEKES, James Eyre (fl 1743)
dramatist CP/3
WEEKES, Richard (fl 1629-36)
manager, actor DA
WEEKS, Barbara (d 1954 [47])
American actress BE*, BP/39*
WEEKS, Charles [Butler Wentworth]
(fl 1850-59) actor CDP, HAS
WEEKS, Frank (d 1906 [56]) mana-
ger EA/07*
WEEKS, James Ayre (fl 1791)
dramatist CP/3
WEEKS, James Ray (b 1942) Amer-
ican actor TW/29-30
WEEKS, Marion (1887?/1903-68)
American actress TW/4, 24
WEEKS, William J. (d 1972 [71])

composer/lyricist BP/57*

WEEMS, Nancy (b 1948) American actress TW/28

WEEMS, Ted (d 1963) conductor BP/47*

WEGENER, Paul (d 1948 [73]) actor WWT/14*

WEGUELIN, Thomas N. (b 1885) English actor WWT/2-8

WEHLE, Billy (d 1968 [73]) performer BP/52*

WEHLEN, Emmy (b 1887) German actress, singer CDP, WWT/1-5

WEHLI, James M. (fl 1865) pianist CDP, HAS

WEHLING, Will (d 1975 [47]) producer/director/choreographer BP/59*

WEICHSEL, Elizabeth see Billington, Mrs. James

WEICHSEL, Frederica (d 1786) singer CDP

WEIDLER, Virginia (b 1927) American actress TW/2

WEIDMAN, Charles (1901-75) American dancer, choreographer BE, CB, ES

WEIDMAN, Jerome (b 1913) American dramatist, librettist BE, CD, HJD, WWT/15-16

WEIGEL, Helene (1900-71) Austrian actress WWT/14

WEIGELT, Lizzie (d 1910) EA/11*

WEIGHELL, Christopher William (d 1897) music-hall manager EA/98*

WEIGHELL, R. (d 1893) proprietor EA/94*

WEIGHT, Hannah Louisa (d 1908 [56]) actress? EA/09*

WEIGHT, Michael (1906-73) South African designer WWT/11-14

WEIGHTMAN, John Albert (d 1884 [23]) acrobat EA/85*

WEIGHTON, Louis English actor, acting manager GRB/1

WEIL, Harry (d 1974 [84]) performer BP/59*

WEIL, Joe (d 1974 [57]) performer BP/59*

WEIL, Mrs. Leonard (d 1963 [62]) theatre operator, puppet collector BE*

WEIL, Oscar (b 1840) American composer WWA/4

WEIL, Robert E. (b 1914) American actor TW/26-30

WEILER, Berenice (b 1927) American producer, manager, director BE

WEILER, Constance (d 1965 [47]) performer BP/50*

WEILL, Kurt (1900-50) German composer CB, DAB, ES, NTH, PDT, TW/6, WWA/3, WWT/9-10

WEIMAN, Ruth [or Rita] (d 1954) American dramatist WWA/3

WEINBERG, Gus (d 1952 [86]) American actor GRB/3-4, WWT/1-5

WEINBERG, Myron K. (d 1971 [43]) manager BP/56*

WEINER, Ann (b 1931) American actor TW/23, 29

WEINER, Lawrence A. (d 1961 [62]) advertising executive BE*, BP/46*

WEINER, Robert American producer BE

WEINGARTEN, Lawrence (d 1975 [77]) producer/director/choreographer BP/59*

WEININGER, Lloyd (d 1971 [78]) scene designer, teacher BP/56*

WEINRIB, Leonard (b 1935) American actor TW/16

WEINSTEIN, Arnold (b 1927) American dramatist, lyricist, director, educator BE, CD

WEINSTOCK, Herbert (d 1971 [65]) critic BP/56*

WEINSTOCK, Jack (1909-69) American dramatist BE, TW/25

WEINTRAUB, Frances (d 1963 [62]) treasurer BE*

WEINTRAUB, Milton (b 1897) American manager BE

WEIPPERT, Mr. (fl 1797?) musician? CDP

WEIPPERT, John Charles (d 1867 [44]) musician EA/68*

WEIR, Charles (d 1916) actor EA/17*

WEIR, George R. (d 1909 [56]) actor BE*, EA/10*, WWT/14*

WEIR, Milton R. (d 1973 [75]) lawyer BP/58*

WEIR, Walter (d 1876 [54]) scene artist EA/77*

WEIR, Walter V. (d 1887 [27]) scene artist EA/88*

WEIRE, Sylvester (d 1970 [60]) performer BP/55*

WEISBERG, Sylvia (d 1962) actress BE*

WEISER, Grethe (d 1970 [67]) performer BP/55*

WEISFELD, Zelma H. (b 1931) American costume designer, educator BE

WEISGAL, Emanuel see Wager, Michael

WEISMAN, Rita (d 1954 [71]) dramatist TW/11

WEISS, Karl (d 1911) manager WWT/14*

WEISS, Kenneth (b 1947) American actor TW/28

WEISS, Paul (b 1933) American actor TW/2

WEISS, Peter (b 1916) German dramatist CB, COC, MWD, PDT, RE, WWT/14-16

WEISS, Willoughby Hunter (d 1867 [47]) singer EA/68*, WWT/14*

WEISSBERGER, L. Arnold (b 1907) American lawyer BE

WEISSMAN, Dora (d 1974) actress TW/30

WEISSMULLER, Don (b 1923) American actor TW/1, 3

WEISTE, Fritz E. A. see Warden-Reed, Frank

WEISZ, Herbert see Wise, Herbert

WEITZEL, Thomas (d 1975 [50]) producer/director/choreographer BP/60*

WEITZENKORN, Louis (1893-1943) American dramatist BE*, WWT/14*

WELBES, George M. (1934-74) American actor TW/26-29

WELCH, Ben (d 1926) comedian BE*, BP/11*

WELCH, Charles (b 1921) American actor TW/24-25, 27-30

WELCH, Constance American educator BE

WELCH, Deshler (d 1920 [65]) critic BE*, BP/4*

WELCH, Elisabeth (b 1904/08/09) American actress, singer BE, WWT/8-16

WELCH, Harry Foster (d 1973 [74]) performer BP/58*

WELCH, James (1865-1917) English actor GRB/1-4, WWT/1-3, WWW/2

WELCH, Mrs. James see Ford, Audrey

WELCH, James B. (d 1965 [54]) producer/director BP/50*

WELCH, John Bacon (d 1887 [47]) professor of singing EA/88*

WELCH, Lew (d 1952 [67]) actor TW/9

WELCH, Loren (b 1923) American actress TW/4

WELCH, Mary (d 1958 [35]) American actress TW/10-14

WELCH, Robert Gilbert (d 1924 [45]) critic BE*, BP/9*

WELCH, Rufus (1800-65) American circus performer HAS

WELCH, William (1849-87) minstrel CDP, NYM

WELCH, William Addams (d 1976 [61]) dramatist BP/60*

WELCHMAN, Harry (1886-1966) English actor, singer AAS, WWT/2-13

WELD, Arthur Cyril Gordon (1862-1914) American musician, composer, conductor DAB

WELDEN, Ben (b 1901) American actor WWT/7-10

WELDON, Ann (b 1938) American actress TW/26

WELDON, Charles (b 1940) American actor TW/26-29

WELDON, Duncan Clark (b 1941) English producing manager WWT/16

WELDON, Fay dramatist CD

WELDON, John see MacNamara, Brinsley

WELDON, Miss P. see Clifton, Lina

WELFARE STATE theatre collective CD

WELFORD, Dallas (1874-1946) English actor GRB/4, TW/3, WWS, WWT/1-7

WELITSCH, Ljuba (b 1913) Bulgarian singer CB

WELLAND, Colin actor, dramatist CD

WELLBY, William George (d 1879 [34]) musician EA/80*

WELLER, Miss (fl 1778) actress CDP

WELLER, Bernard (1870-1943) English critic GRB/2-4, WWT/1-9, WWW/4

WELLER, Carrie (d 1954 [84]) American actress TW/11

WELLER, Michael (b 1942) American dramatist CD

WELLER, Peter (b 1947) American actor TW/30

WELLER, Sam (d 1907 [47]) stage manager EA/08*

WELLES, Orson (b 1915) American actor, producer, director AAS, BE, CB, COC, ES, NTH, PDT, TW/2-6, WWT/ 9-15

WELLES, Violet American press representative BE

WELLESLEY, Arthur (d 1906) actor EA/07*

WELLESLEY, Arthur (b 1890) English actor WWT/5-8

WELLESZ, Egon (d 1974 [89]) composer/lyricist BP/59*

WELLING, Nellie [Mrs. Leonard Thiel] (d 1907 [27]) EA/08*

WELLING, Sylvia (b 1901) English actress, singer WWT/ 10-11

WELLMAN, Emily Ann [Mrs. H. W. Wellman] (d 1946) English actress TW/2, WWM

WELLMAN, Mrs. Francis L. see Juch, Emma

WELLMAN, Mrs. H. W. see Wellman, Emily Ann

WELLMAN, Pearl see Argyle, Pearl

WELLMAN, William A. (d 1975 [79]) producer/director/choreographer BP/60*

WELLS, Mme. (d 1885) singer EA/86*

WELLS, Miss see Sefton, Mrs. John

WELLS, Albert (d 1909) equestrian EA/10*

WELLS, Amelia see Butler, Mrs. Robert

WELLS, Amos (d 1911 [50]) musician EA/12*

WELLS, Ann see Watson, Ann

WELLS, Benjamin (d 1899 [73]) EA/00*

WELLS, Mrs. Benjamin see Wells, Elizabeth

WELLS, Charles B. (d 1924 [73]) actor BE*, BP/9*

WELLS, Miss Clarence (fl 1839) actress HAS

WELLS, Deering (1896-1961) English actor WWT/7-8

WELLS, Doreen (b 1937) English

dancer ES

WELLS, Elizabeth [Mrs. Benjamin Wells] (d 1893 [66]) EA/94*

WELLS, H. (fl 1856) actor HAS

WELLS, Harriet Emma [Mrs. John Wells] (d 1886 [64]) EA/ 88*

WELLS, Herbert (b 1859) actor SR

WELLS, John (d 1880) equestrian manager EA/81*

WELLS, Mrs. John see Wells, Harriet Emma

WELLS, John Grimaldi (d 1852) circus clown HAS

WELLS, Julia Elizabeth see Andrews, Julie

WELLS, Louisa (b 1927) English actress HAS

WELLS, Malcolm (d 1970 [51]) dramatist BP/55*

WELLS, Marie (d 1949 [55]) actress TW/6

WELLS, Mary [née Davis] (d 1826?) English actress CDP, DNB, GT, TD/1-2

WELLS, Mary (1829-78) English actress CDP, HAS, SR

WELLS, Mary K. American actress TW/24, 26-27

WELLS, Minnie (fl 1872?) "Lion Queen" CDP

WELLS, Roxanna (d 1964 [70]) executive, agent BE*

WELLS, Samuel (d 1864 [38]) comedian HAS

WELLS, Tony (b 1940) American actor TW/29

WELLS, T. W. (d 1902) EA/03*

WELLS, Victor Thaddeus (d 1905 [50]) equestrian EA/06*

WELLS, William (d 1956 [72]) American actor, writer BE*

WELLS, William G. (d 1841) English dancer CDP, HAS

WELLS, Wilmot (fl 1801) manager, actor TD/1-2

WELMHURST, Anne see Howard, Anne

WELSH, Edward see Edwards, Welsh

WELSH, Jane (b 1905) English actress WWT/6-14

WELSH, Thomas (1781-1848) English singer DNB

WELSH, Mrs. Thomas see Wilson, Mary Ann

WELSH, Violet [Mrs. Harold

Clements] (b 1884) English ac-
tress GRB/1
WELSON, Mr. [né Bland] (fl 1802)
English actor HAS
WELSTED, Leonard (d 1747)
dramatist CP/1-3, GT
WELTON, Mrs. James see
Cavanna, Elise
WEMMS, Joe (d 1899) music-hall
comedian EA/00*
WEMYSS, Catherine (b 1821)
actress CDP
WEMYSS, Francis Courtney (1797-
1859) English actor, manager
CDP, COC, DAB, HAS, OC/
1-3, RJ, WWA/H
WEMYSS, Kate see Duffield,
Kate
WEMYSS, Thomas Courtney (b
1831) American actor HAS
WEMYSS, W. C. (b 1841) Amer-
ican actor HAS
WENBURN, Mrs. Harry see
Haynes, Jennie
WEND, John (fl 1627-40) actor
DA
WENDELL, Howard David (d 1975
[67]) performer BP/60*
WENDELL, Jacob (b 1868) actor
SR
WENDLING, Charles (d 1971
[72]) talent agent BP/55*
WENDLING, Pete (d 1974 [85])
performer BP/58*
WENGRAF, John E. (1907-74)
Austrian actor, director TW/
2-3, 5-6, 30
WENHAM, Jane [née Figgins]
English actress WWT/15-16
WENMAN, Henry N. (1875-
1953) English actor WWT/
4-10
WENMAN, Thomas Edmund
[Thomas Edmund Newman]
(1844-92) English actor OAA/2
WENNING, Thomas H. (1903-62)
American critic NTH
WENRICH, Percy (1887-1952)
American composer, per-
former BE*, BP/36*
WENSLEY, Emma (b 1799) ac-
tress CDP
WENSLEY, Frank (d 1889 [22])
singer EA/91*
WENTWIG, Mrs. Benjamin see
Nielsen, Alice
WENTWORTH, Bessie (d 1901
[27]) actress, singer CDP

WENTWORTH, Butler see Weeks,
Charles
WENTWORTH, Clayton (d 1969
[62]) performer BP/54*
WENTWORTH, Fanny (d 1930 [70])
English entertainer CDP, GRB/
1-4
WENTWORTH, Maude (d 1889)
American actress EA/90*
WENTWORTH, Stephen (d 1935)
actor BE*, WWT/14*
WENTZ, John K. (d 1964 [40])
educator, critic BE*
WERBA, Louis F. (d 1942) pro-
ducer, director BE*, WWT/14*
WERDON, George (d 1882 [32])
EA/83*
WERFEL, Franz (1890-1945) Aus-
trian dramatist CB, COC,
MWD, NTH, OC/1-3, WWA/2
WERRENRATH, George (d 1898)
singer EA/99*
WERRENRATH, Reinald (1883-1953)
American singer WWA/3
WERY, Carl (d 1975 [77]) per-
former BP/59*
WESFORD, Susan [79] American
actress BE*
WESKER, Arnold (b 1932) English
dramatist, director AAS, BE,
CB, CD, CH, COC, ES, MD,
MH, MWD, OC/3, PDT, RE,
WWT/13-16
WESNER, Ella actress CDP
WESS, Richard (d 1973 [43]) com-
poser/lyricist BP/57*
WESSEL, Richard (d 1965 [52])
performer BP/49*
WESSELS, Florence (d 1971 [72])
performer BP/56*
WESSON, Gene (d 1975 [54]) per-
former BP/60*
WEST, Mr. (fl 1816) equestrian
manager HAS
WEST, Miss (fl 1848) actress HAS
WEST, Algernon (b 1886) English
actor WWT/7-8
WEST, Arthur (d 1894 [30]?)
singer, song composer CDP
WEST, Bernard [or Bernie] (b 1918)
American actor BE, TW/26
WEST, Billy (d 1975 [82]) performer
BP/60*
WEST, Buster (d 1966 [64]) per-
former BP/50*
WEST, Christopher (1915-67) Eng-
lish director, actor, producer
WWW/6

WEST, Con (b 1891) English librettist, dramatist WWT/6-13

WEST, Edna Rhys (d 1963 [76]) American performer BE*, BP/47*

WEST, Florence see Waller, Mrs. Lewis

WEST, Florrie (d 1908) burlesque actress EA/09*

WEST, Gilbert (b 1706) dramatist CP/2-3

WEST, Henry St. Barbe (1880-1935) English actor WWT/6-7

WEST, Mrs. H. G. see West, Sarah

WEST, J. (fl 1809) English? HAS

WEST, Jane (1758-1852) English dramatist CP/3, DNB

WEST, Jennifer (b 1939) American actress TW/20-21, 23-24

WEST, John (d 1871 [52]) actor? EA/72*

WEST, Lillie [Amy Leslie] actress, writer CDP

WEST, Lockwood (b 1905) English actor WWT/14-16

WEST, Mae (b 1892/93) American actress, dramatist BE, CB, COC, ES, MWD, NTH, SR, TW/1-13, WWT/6-16

WEST, Rev. Matthew (fl 1769-1803) dramatist CP/2-3, GT

WEST, Olive [Althea Olive Bowman] (b 1871) American actress WWM

WEST, Paul (1871-1918) American dramatist GRB/3-4, WWA/1, WWM, WWS

WEST, Paul (d 1965 [75]) performer BP/50*

WEST, Richard (d 1726) dramatist CP/2-3, DNB

WEST, Sarah [Mrs. William West] (1790-1876) English actress BS, CDP, DNB, OX

WEST, Sarah [Mrs. H. G. West] (d 1886) EA/88*

WEST, Timothy (b 1934) English actor WWT/15-16

WEST, Mrs. W. (d 1876 [86]) actress EA/78*, WWT/14*

WEST, W. H. C. (d 1876) comedian, songwriter EA/77*

WEST, Will (1867-1922) actor WWT/4

WEST, William (1796-1888) English actor BS, CDP, DNB

WEST, William (d 1890 [77]) EA/91*

WEST, Mrs. William see West, Sarah

WEST, William C. (1837-1913) English minstrel CDP, SR

WEST, William H. (1855-1902) minstrel, dancer CDP, SR

WEST, William W. (d 1902 [48]) minstrel EA/03*

WESTBOURNE, E. see Layland, Edward

WESTBROOK, John (b 1922) English actor AAS, WWT/11-16

WESTCOTT, Emily (d 1903 [59]) EA/04*

WESTCOTT, John Smith (d 1908) EA/09*

WESTCOTT, Lynda (b 1942) American actress TW/25-26, 28

WESTCOTT, Netta (d 1953 [60]) English actress WWT/10-11

WESTCOTT, Sebastian (fl 1557-82) Master of the Children of Paul's DA

WESTE, Humphrey (fl 1594) actor DA

WESTE, Thomas (fl 1594) actor DA

WESTERFIELD, James (1916-71) American actor TW/12, 28

WESTERN, George (d 1969 [74]) performer BP/54*

WESTERN, Helen (1844-68) American actress CDP, COC, HAS, OC/1-3, SR

WESTERN, Kenneth (d 1963 [62]) performer BE*

WESTERN, Lucille (1843-77) American actress CDP, COC, DAB, HAS, OC/1-3, SR, WWA/H

WESTERTON, Frank H. (d 1923) English actor BE*, BP/8*, WWT/14*

WESTFORD, Owen (d 1908) actor GRB/4*

WESTFORD, Susanne (1865-1944) American actress, singer BE*, BP/28*, WWT/14*

WESTGATE, Rebecca see Clofullia, Josephine Fortune

WESTLAND, Henry (1838-1906) English actor OAA/1-2

WESTLEY, Helen (1875/79-1942) American actress CB, DAB, ES, WWT/7-9

WESTLEY, John (d 1948 [70]) actor TW/5

WESTMAN, Lolita Ann (d 1965
[65]) performer BP/50*
WESTMAN, Nydia (1902/07-70)
American actress BE, TW/1,
3-7, 9-10, 13-19, 26, WWT/
7-14
WESTMAN, Theodore (d 1927
[24]) actor BP/12*
WESTMORE, George (d 1973 [55])
makeup man BP/58*
WESTMORE, Walter J. (d 1973
[57]) makeup man BP/58*
WESTMORELAND, Miss M. B.
(fl 1856) actress HAS
WESTON, Mr. (fl 1803-04) actor
TD/2
WESTON, Mrs. [Mrs. Edmund
Falconer] (d 1864) actress
EA/72*
WESTON, Ada [Mrs. Arthur
Weston] (d 1909 [44]) EA/10*
WESTON, Arthur see Boz,
Sig.
WESTON, Mrs. Arthur see
Weston, Ada
WESTON, Charles (d 1870) musi-
cal director EA/71*
WESTON, Charles H. (d 1904)
music-hall performer EA/06*
WESTON, Eddie (b 1925) Ameri-
can actor, dancer, singer BE
WESTON, Edward (d 1874 [54])
music-hall proprietor EA/75*
WESTON, Ellen (b 1939) Ameri-
can actress BE
WESTON, Emmeline Montague
Falconer [Mrs. T. W. Ben-
son] (d 1887) EA/88*
WESTON, Ferdinand Fullerton
(fl 1808) dramatist CP/3
WESTON, Frank (b 1849) actor
CDP
WESTON, George (d 1857) come-
dian HAS
WESTON, George Howarth (d
1901 [58]) EA/02*
WESTON, Graham (b 1944) Eng-
lish actor TW/27
WESTON, Harold [Fred Neatt]
(d 1917 [36]) performer? EA/
18*
WESTON, Jack actor WWT/16
WESTON, James [or Jim] (b
1942) American actor TW/
25, 27-30
WESTON, James Pitney (d 1902)
lessee EA/03*
WESTON, Mrs. James Pitney

see Weston, Marian
WESTON, John (fl 1667) dramatist
CP/1-3
WESTON, Joseph J. (d 1972 [84])
performer BP/56*
WESTON, Julia see Blake, Mrs.
Orlando
WESTON, Mrs. J. W. (fl 1877-
80?) singer CDP
WESTON, Lizzie see Mathews,
Mrs. Charles James
WESTON, Lottie [Mrs. John P.
Cooke] (d 1877 [35]) EA/78*
WESTON, Louise Caroline [née
Laidlaw] (d 1871 [23]) actress
EA/72*
WESTON, Marian [Mrs. James
Pitney Weston] (d 1884) EA/85*
WESTON, Robert P. (1878-1936)
English dramatist, lyricist,
composer WWT/7-8
WESTON, Ruth (1908/11-55) Amer-
ican actress TW/1, 3-6, 12,
WWT/10-11
WESTON, Thomas (1737-76) English
actor CDP, COC, DNB, GT,
OC/1-3, TD/1-2
WESTOVER, Robert (d 1916) actor
BE*
WESTOVER, William H. (d 1905
[58]) musician EA/07*
WESTRAY, Mrs. Anthony (d 1836)
actress COC, OC/3
WESTRAY, Miss E. A. see
Twaits, Mrs. William
WESTRAY, Ellen see Darley,
Mrs.
WESTRAY, Juliana see Wood,
Mrs. William Burke
WESTRUP, Jack A. (d 1975 [70])
critic BP/59*
WESTWOOD, Ellen [Mrs. W. H.
Westwood] (d 1917) EA/18*
WESTWOOD, Mrs. W. H. see
Westwood, Ellen
WESTWOOD, William Henry (d
1918 [67]) EA/19*
WESTZEL, Charles (d 1970 [79])
producer/director/choreographer
BP/55*
WETHERALL, Frances (d 1923)
English actress WWT/4
WETHERBY, Eliza see Weathers-
by, Eliza
WETHERBY, James (fl 1730) dram-
atist CP/1-3
WETHERELL, E. G. (d 1889)
EA/90*

WETHERELL, Joseph (d 1884
[57]) printer EA/85*
WETMORE, Alphonso dramatist
EAP, RJ
WETMORE, Joan (b 1911) Aus-
tralian actress BE, TW/1,
7, 10-11, 22, WWT/10-15
WETTACH, Adrien see Grock
WETTON, Mary see Millar,
Mary
WEVER, Robert (fl 1561?) dram-
atist CP/1-3
WEWITZER, Miss (fl 1772-89)
actress CDP, DNB
WEWITZER, Ralph (1748-1825)
actor, manager, dramatist
CP/3, DNB, GT, TD/1-2
WEXLER, Peter (b 1936) Amer-
ican designer WWT/16
WEXLEY, John (b 1902/07)
American dramatist, actor
HJD, MD, MWD, NTH,
WWT/8-9
WEYAND, Roland (b 1929) Amer-
ican actor TW/14, 23-25
WEYMARK, James (d 1882 [34])
comedian EA/83*
WEYMER, Marguerite-Joséphine
see George, Mlle.
WHAITE, Henry (d 1890) marion-
ettist? EA/91*
WHAITE, John (d 1892 [53])
artist EA/93*
WHAITE, Septimus (d 1892 [84])
scene artist EA/93*
WHALE, James (1896-1957)
English actor, producer, de-
signer ES, WWT/6-12
WHALE, W. dancer CDP
WHALEN, David Barry (d 1967
[58]) publicist BP/52*
WHALEN, Michael (1899-1974)
American actor TW/1
WHALING, Harry (d 1896) comic
singer EA/97*
WHALLEY, Caroline see
Barclay, Caroline
WHALLEY, J. S. (fl 1799)
dramatist TD/1-2
WHALLEY, Norma Australian
actress WWT/2-6
WHALLEY, Rev. Thomas Sedg-
wick (fl 1799) dramatist
CP/3
WHALLEY, W. H. (b 1837)
Irish actor HAS
WHAMBOULT, Leo (d 1917
[62]) EA/18*

WHAREHAM, William (d 1849)
HAS
WHARTON, Anne (d 1685) drama-
tist CP/2-3
WHARTON, Anthony P. [Alister
P. McAllister] (1877-1943) Irish
dramatist GRB/3-4, WWT/1-7
WHARTON, Carly [Mrs. John F.
Wharton] American producer
TW/2
WHARTON, Mrs. Charles (d 1881
[67]) actress EA/82*
WHARTON, John F. (1894-1977)
American lawyer BE
WHARTON, Mrs. John F. see
Wharton, Carly
WHARTON, Philip, Duke of (1699-
1731) dramatist CP/2-3
WHARTON, Thomas Edmond see
Edmonds, T. W.
WHATFORD, William Starr (d 1887
[94]) comedian EA/88*
WHATMORE, A. R. (1889-1960)
English actor, producer AAS,
WWT/7-12
WHATTON, W. (d 1878 [33]) actor
EA/79*
WHAUTKINS, Pio (d 1879 [50])
juggler EA/80*
WHEAT, Laurance (b 1876) Amer-
ican actor WWM
WHEATCROFT, Adeline Stanhope
(1856-1935) French/English ac-
tress GRB/3-4
WHEATCROFT, Nelson (1852-97)
English actor SR
WHEATLEIGH, Charles (fl 1848-
65) English actor HAS, SR
WHEATLEY, Miss (fl 1796) ac-
tress, singer TD/1-2
WHEATLEY, Alan (b 1907) English
actor WWT/9-16
WHEATLEY, Emma [Mrs. James
Mason] (1822-54) American ac-
tress CDP, COC, HAS, OC/1-3
WHEATLEY, Frederick (d 1836)
Irish entertainer COC, HAS,
OC/1-3
WHEATLEY, Horace English come-
dian GRB/2
WHEATLEY, Jane (1881-1935)
American actress WWT/4-7
WHEATLEY, Mrs. S. (fl 1815)
Irish actress HAS
WHEATLEY, Sarah Ross (1790-
1872) Irish/American actress
COC, HAS, OC/1-3
WHEATLEY, William (1816-76)

American actor, manager CDP, COC, DAB, HAS, OC/1-3, WWA/H

WHEATON, Anna (d 1961 [65]) actress, singer TW/18

WHEATON, Elizabeth (fl 1627) gatherer DA

WHEEL, Patricia (b 1925) American actress TW/6, 8-10, 24, 27-29

WHEELER, Mrs. (d 1893) EA/95*

WHEELER, Miss (b 1781) English actress, singer TD/1-2

WHEELER, Mrs. Andrew C. see Wheeler, Anna

WHEELER, Andrew Carpenter (d 1903 [67]) critic BE*, WWT/14*

WHEELER, Anna [Mrs. Andrew C. Wheeler] (d 1888) EA/89*

WHEELER, Arthur (d 1907) acting manager EA/08*

WHEELER, Benjamin F. (d 1934 [74]) producer, manager BE*, WWT/14*

WHEELER, Benjamin H. (d 1908 [73]) manager EA/09*

WHEELER, Bert (1895-1968) American actor, vaudevillian BE, TW/24

WHEELER, Charles (d 1894) EA/95*

WHEELER, Desmondoe (d 1966 [67]) performer BP/51*

WHEELER, Fanny (fl 1840-49) American actress HAS

WHEELER, H. (d 1895) lessee EA/96*

WHEELER, Hugh (b 1912/16) English/American dramatist BE, CD, WWT/16

WHEELER, Jimmy (d 1973 [63]) performer BP/58*

WHEELER, Lois (b 1920/22) American actress BE, TW/ 1, 3, 9-11, WWT/11-14

WHEELER, Mark (d 1899) living statue EA/00*

WHEELER, Mary Ann (d 1898 [53]) living statue EA/99*

WHEELOCK, Mrs. J. F. [Anna France] (d 1866) actress HAS

WHEELOCK, Joseph (1839-1908) actor CDP, GRB/4

WHEELOCK, Joseph, Jr. (d 1910 [38]) American actor GRB/3-4

WHEELWRIGHT, Rev. C. A. (fl

1810) translator CP/3

WHELAN, Albert (1875-1961) English music-hall performer COC, OC/1-3

WHELAN, Tim (d 1957 [63]) American actor BE*

WHELEN, Frederick (b 1867) English secretary GRB/3-4, WWT/ 1-6

WHERRY, John (d 1876 [34]) singer EA/77*

WHETSTONE, George (1544?-87?) dramatist, actor CP/2-3, DA, FGF, HP

WHIFFIN, Blanche [Mrs. Thomas Whiffin] (1845-1936) English actress CDP, GRB/3-4, PP/3, SR, WWA/4, WWM, WWS, WWT/1-8, WWA/H

WHIFFIN, Thomas (1845-97) English actor SR

WHIFFIN, Mrs. Thomas see Whiffin, Blanche

WHILEY, Manning (b 1915) English actor WWT/10-11

WHINCOP, Thomas (d 1730) dramatist CP/1-3

WHIPPER, Leigh (d 1975 [98]) performer BP/60*

WHIPPLE, Sidney Beaumont (1888-1975) American critic NTH, WWT/9

WHISENANT, Elijah (d 1973 [62]) manager BP/57*

WHISTLER, Rex (1905-44) English designer ES, WWT/9

"WHISTLING COMEDIAN, The" see Mill, Paul

WHISTON, J. W. humorist CDP

WHITAKER, Miss see Sloman, Mrs. John

WHITAKER, Grenna (b 1948) American actress TW/29-30

WHITAKER, Sam (d 1890) actor EA/91*

WHITAKER, Willette [Mrs. F. Wilbur Hill] American musician, singer WWM

WHITAKER, William (fl 1680) dramatist CP/1-3

WHITBECK, Frank L. (d 1963 [81]) press representative BE*

WHITBREAD, Isabel Louisa (d 1916) EA/17*

WHITBREAD, J. W. (d 1916 [68]) dramatist BE*, EA/17*, WWT/ 14*

WHITBREAD, Samuel (1758-1815)

executive CDP
WHITBY, Miss (fl 1856) actress
    HAS
WHITBY, Arthur (1869-1922)
    English actor GRB/1-4,
    WWT/1-4
WHITBY, Mrs. Arthur see
    Saumarez, Cissie
WHITBY, Elsie (d 1911) actress
    EA/12*
WHITBY, Gwynne (b 1903) Eng-
    lish actress WWT/5-16
WHITE, Alfred H. (d 1972 [89])
    actor TW/29
WHITE, Archie (1847-1912)
    minstrel SR
WHITE, Beatrice [Beatrice Cur-
    tis] (d 1963 [62]) performer
    BE*
WHITE, Bertie actor GRB/1
WHITE, Bradford (b 1912) Amer-
    ican educator, director, de-
    signer BE
WHITE, Miss C. (fl 1836-39)
    American actress HAS
WHITE, Caroline [Mrs. Harold
    White] (d 1893 [58]) EA/95*
WHITE, Charles (1821-91) Amer-
    ican comedian, manager,
    minstrel CDP, HAS
WHITE, Charles (d 1897) come-
    dian EA/98*
WHITE, Charles (b 1920) Amer-
    ican actor TW/25-26, 29
WHITE, Charles A. (d 1892
    [62]) American composer,
    publisher EA/93*
WHITE, Charles O. (d 1889)
    manager EA/90*
WHITE, Christine (b 1926) Amer-
    ican actress TW/8
WHITE, Clarence Cameron (1880-
    1960) American composer
    WWA/4
WHITE, Clement (d 1873) singer
    EA/74*
WHITE, Cool (1821-91) actor
    CDP, HAS
WHITE, Mrs. Cool [née Eliza
    F. Bonnet; Mrs. W. M.
    Foster] (d 1887) American
    actress HAS, NYM
WHITE, Dana (b 1930) American
    actor TW/14
WHITE, Danny (d 1974 [67]) talent
    agent BP/59*
WHITE, Donald (b 1925) American
    actor TW/2, 5-6

WHITE, Edgar Charles (d 1909)
    EA/10*
WHITE, Edward J. (d 1973 [76])
    producer/director/choreographer
    BP/58*
WHITE, Elizabeth see Hartley,
    Elizabeth
WHITE, Elizabeth see Savage,
    Mrs. John
WHITE, Ellen F. (d 1900) manager
    EA/01*
WHITE, Elmore (d 1964 [75]) per-
    former, songwriter BE*
WHITE, F. B. (1817-68) American
    actor HAS
WHITE, Frances (d 1969 [71]) ac-
    tress, singer, vaudevillian
    TW/25
WHITE, Fred (d 1872) harlequin
    EA/73*
WHITE, George (d 1876 [38]) actor?
    EA/77*
WHITE, George (d 1905 [54])
    comedian EA/06*
WHITE, George (1890-1968) Cana-
    dian actor, producer, dancer,
    dramatist BE, COC, ES, NTH,
    PDT, TW/25, WWT/6-11
WHITE, George W. (1816-86) sing-
    er, minstrel CDP, HAS
WHITE, Mrs. Harold see White,
    Caroline
WHITE, Harry (d 1898) actor EA/
    99*
WHITE, Henry (d 1900 [88]) pub-
    lisher EA/01*
WHITE, J. (d 1871 [72]) comedian
    EA/72*
WHITE, James (fl 1759-61) trans-
    lator CP/2-3
WHITE, Rev. James (d 1862 [77])
    dramatist BE*, WWT/14*
WHITE, James (d 1882) EA/83*
WHITE, James (d 1927 [49]) mana-
    ger WWT/5
WHITE, Mrs. James H. see
    Kemble, Myra
WHITE, Jane (b 1922) American
    actress BE, TW/2-3, 9-10,
    15-18, 20-21, 25, 28, WWT/15-
    16
WHITE, Jenny (d 1897) actress
    EA/98*
WHITE, Jesse (b 1918/19) Ameri-
    can actor, comedian BE, TW/
    4-6, 21, 25-26
WHITE, J. Fisher (1865-1945)
    English actor GRB/1-4, WWT/

1-9

WHITE, Joan (b 1909) Egyptian/
English actress, producer,
director, teacher BE, TW/
24, WWT/8-16

WHITE, Joan (d 1975 [43]) performer BP/59*

WHITE, John (d 1910 [76]) showman EA/11*

WHITE, John (b 1919) American
dramatist, actor CD

WHITE, John Blake (1781/83-
1859) American dramatist
CDP, DAB, EAP, RJ, SR,
WWA/H

WHITE, John J. (fl 1830) actor
HAS

WHITE, Josh (1908/15-69) American actor TW/6, 26

WHITE, Josias (fl 1628) actor
DA

WHITE, J. W. (d 1898) music-
hall proprietor EA/99*

WHITE, Kitty see Burden,
Kitty

WHITE, Laura [Mrs. Leonard
White] (d 1895 [24]) EA/96*

WHITE, Lee (1886-1927) American actress, singer WWT/4-5

WHITE, Lemuel G. (b 1792)
American actor HAS

WHITE, Leonard (b 1916) English actor TW/8

WHITE, Mrs. Leonard see
White, Laura

WHITE, Mary see Durang,
Mrs. Charles

WHITE, Mary Ann (d 1860) actress HAS

WHITE, Melvin R. (b 1911)
American educator, director
BE

WHITE, Michael Simon (b 1936)
Scottish producing manager
AAS, WWT/15-16

WHITE, Miles (b 1914/17/20)
American costume designer
BE, ES, TW/3-8, WWT/15-16

WHITE, Mrs. M. J. see Hyde,
Marion

WHITE, M. M. dramatist RJ

WHITE, Onna Canadian dancer,
choreographer, director BE,
WWT/15-16

WHITE, Patrick (b 1912) Eng-
lish/Australian dramatist
CD, ES

WHITE, Paul T. (d 1973 [77])

composer/lyricist BP/58*

WHITE, Penny American actress
TW/27

WHITE, Princess (d 1976 [95])
performer BP/60*

WHITE, R. B. (d 1872) musician
EA/73*

WHITE, Rebecca (d 1911) actress?
EA/12*

WHITE, Robert (fl 1617?) dramatist
FGF

WHITE, Robert (b 1926) American
actor TW/5-6

WHITE, Robert, Jr. (d 1881 [30])
EA/82*

WHITE, Ruth (d 1969 [55]) American actress BE, TW/22-26

WHITE, Sammy (1896-1960) American actor TW/3, 16

WHITE, Sidney see Drew, Sidney

WHITE, Tom (d 1900 [42]) music-
hall comedian EA/01*

WHITE, Tommy (b 1943) American
actor TW/13

WHITE, Valerie (1915-75) South
African actress TW/4, WWT/
10-16

WHITE, Watson (b 1888) American
actor TW/3

WHITE, Wilfred Hyde (b 1903) English actor TW/8, 13-14, WWT/
10-13

WHITE, William Charles (fl 1797-
1806) American actor, dramatist
CDP, EAP, HAS, RJ

WHITE, William Henry (d 1911
[57]) treasurer EA/12*

WHITE, Willoughby (d 1917) actor
EA/18*

WHITEBREAD, Mr. (d 1875) EA/
76*

WHITECAR, W. A. actor SR

WHITEHALL, Clarence (1871-
1932) American singer DAB,
WWA/1, WWW/3

WHITEHEAD, Allen (b 1921) American producer BE

WHITEHEAD, Charles (1804-62)
dramatist DNB, HP

WHITEHEAD, Douglass (d 1968
[93]) drama instructor BP/52*

WHITEHEAD, E. A. (b 1933) English dramatist AAS, CD, WWT/
16

WHITEHEAD, James (d 1885) musician EA/86*

WHITEHEAD, John (d 1962 [89])
actor BE*

WHITEHEAD, Paxton English actor
TW/26

WHITEHEAD, Robert (b 1916)
Canadian producer BE, TW/
6-8, WWT/14-16

WHITEHEAD, Robert M. (d 1880
[33]) actor EA/81*

WHITEHEAD, Virginia (d 1965
[84]) executive BP/49*

WHITEHEAD, Virginia Bolen (d
1965 [49]) designer BP/50*

WHITEHEAD, William (1714/15-
85) English dramatist CDP,
CP/1-3, GT, TD/1-2

WHITEHEAD, William (d 1867
[32]) musician EA/68*

WHITEHILL, Jane American actress TW/25, 28

WHITEHOUSE, Mrs. C. (d 1887
[46]) EA/88*

WHITEHOUSE, Esther (d 1946
[51]) actress BE*, WWT/14*

WHITEHOUSE, Florence Brooks
(fl 1894-1904) American dramatist WWA/5

WHITEHOUSE, Freeman H. (d
1865) singer HAS

WHITEHOUSE, William J. (d
1887 [28]) regisseur EA/88*

WHITELAMB, Kelham (fl 1787)
dwarf CDP

WHITELAW, Arthur producer
WWT/16

WHITELAW, Billie English actress AAS, WWT/14-16

WHITELEY, A. (d 1909 [36])
carpenter EA/10*

WHITELEY, James see Whitley,
James Augustus

WHITELEY, John Allen (d 1888
[45]) equestrian EA/89*

WHITELEY, Larry (b 1936)
American actor TW/27

WHITELEY, Leonora C. (d 1969
[93]) performer BP/54*

WHITELOCKE, James actor DA

WHITELY, James see Whitley,
James Augustus

WHITEMAN, George Frederick
Carl see Carroll, Sydney
W.

WHITEMAN, Paul (1890-1967)
American performer BE,
TW/24

WHITESIDE, Ann American actress TW/12, 26-27

WHITESIDE, Walker (1869-1942)
American actor CDP, SR,

WWA/2, WWM, WWT/1-9

WHITFIELD, Mr. (fl 1776) actor
CDP, TD/1-2

WHITFIELD, Howard (b 1914)
American stage manager, director, actor BE

WHITFIELD, James (d 1880) musician EA/81*

WHITFIELD, Joseph (d 1916 [69])
EA/17*

WHITFIELD, Louise (fl 1865) actress HAS

WHITFIELD, Walter W. (d 1966
[78]) performer BP/50*

WHITFORD, Annabelle (d 1961
[83]) actress, singer TW/18

WHITHAM, George (d 1883) circus
performer EA/84*

WHITHORNE, Emerson (b 1884)
American composer HJD

WHITING, Charles (d 1903 [36])
proprietor EA/04*

WHITING, David (1811-81) actor
CDP

WHITING, Edward (fl 1633) actor
DA

WHITING, Frank M. (b 1907)
American educator, director,
designer BE

WHITING, George Elbridge (1842-
1923) American composer DAB,
WWA/1

WHITING, Jack (1901-61) American
actor, singer TW/2-15, 17,
WWT/8-12

WHITING, John (1917-63) English
dramatist, actor AAS, CD,
CH, COC, ES, MD, MH,
MWD, OC/3, PDT, RE, WWT/
13, WWW/6

WHITING, Joseph (fl 1852) American
actor HAS

WHITING, Joseph E. (1842-1910)
American actor CDP, PP/3

WHITING, Richard (fl 1633) actor
DA

WHITING, Richard A. (1891-1938)
American composer BE*

WHITING, Sadie Burt (d 1966)
performer BP/51*

WHITLEY, Bert American actor
TW/3-4

WHITLEY, Clifford (b 1894) English
producing manager WWT/6-10

WHITLEY, James Augustus (c. 1724-
81) Irish manager, dramatist
COC, CP/3, GT, TD/2

WHITLEY, Larry (b 1936) American

actor TW/25
WHITLING, Townsend (1869-1952)
English actor WWT/5-11
WHITLOCK, Mr. (d 1812) English actor HAS
WHITLOCK, Billy (d 1951 [76])
composer, performer BE*
WHITLOCK, E. Clyde (d 1970
[84]) critic BP/55*
WHITLOCK, Elizabeth see
Kemble, Elizabeth
WHITLOCK, Henry (b 1787)
English actor HAS
WHITLOCK, William M. (1813-78) minstrel CDP
WHITMAN, Chance Halliday (d
1974 [39]) performer BP/59*
WHITMAN, Essie (d 1963 [81])
performer BE*
WHITMAN, Estelle (d 1970)
performer BP/55*
WHITMAN, Frank (1826-62)
English actor? HAS
WHITMAN, John P. (d 1963
[91]) performer BE*
WHITMAN, Robert painter,
sculptor CD
WHITMAN, Stuart (b 1929)
American actor ES
WHITMAN, William (b 1925)
American actor TW/8-12,
15
WHITMEE, Mrs. Alfred see
Whitmee, Clara B.
WHITMEE, Clara B. [Mrs. Alfred Whitmee] (d 1912) EA/
13*
WHITMORE, Mr. (d 1916) EA/
17*
WHITMORE, James (b 1921/22)
American actor BE, CB,
TW/4-5, 26, 30, WWT/16
WHITNALL, Miss M. see
Scarisbrick, Mrs.
WHITNER, Edwin (d 1962 [53])
actor BE*, BP/46*
WHITNEY, Mr. (fl 1839) actor,
lecturer HAS
WHITNEY, Art (d 1972 [60])
stage manager, booking agent
BP/57*
WHITNEY, Bert C. (1869-1929)
American producer, manager
SR
WHITNEY, Clark J. (b 1832)
American manager SR
WHITNEY, Fred C. (1865-1930)
American manager, producer

WWT/1-5
WHITNEY, Iris American actress
TW/22
WHITNEY, Myron W. (1835-1910)
American singer CDP, DAB,
WWA/1
WHITNEY, Peter (d 1972 [55])
performer BP/56*
WHITROW, Benjamin (b 1937)
English actor WWT/16
WHITSUN-JONES, Paul (1923-74)
Welsh actor BTR/74, TW/14
WHITTAKER, Arthur (d 1914) producer, manager BE*, WWT/14*
WHITTAKER, Francis Warren
(1818-87) American circus performer, actor? NYM
WHITTAKER, Herbert (b 1911)
Canadian critic WWT/13-16
WHITTAKER, Jack (d 1847) equestrian HAS
WHITTAKER, James (d 1964 [73])
journalist, critic BE*, BP/48*
WHITTAKER, Patrick (d 1826) circus performer HAS
WHITTAKER, William H. B. (d
1888 [50]) American manager
EA/89*
WHITTINGHAM, John (d 1875 [26])
comic singer EA/77*
WHITTLE, Charles R. (d 1947
[73]) English music-hall performer OC/1-3
WHITTLE, James (b 1939) American actor TW/24-25, 29
WHITTLE, Margaret (d 1917 [11])
EA/18*
WHITTLESEY, White (d 1940 [79])
American actor PP/3, WWS
WHITTON, Leon (d 1899 [42])
"Canadian colossus" EA/00*
WHITTON, Peggy (b 1950) American actress TW/29
WHITTY, J. Edward Irish actor,
manager, proprietor GRB/1
WHITTY, Dame May [Mrs. Ben
Webster] (1865-1948) English
actress CB, COC, DP, EA/96,
ES, GRB/1-4, OC/1-3, TW/2-4,
WWA/2, WWT/1-10, WWW/4
WHITWORTH, Geoffrey (1883-1951)
English secretary of the British
Drama League COC, DNB,
OC/1-3, WWT/7-11
WHOMES, Frederick (d 1878) professor of music EA/79*
WHORF, Richard (1906/07-66)
American actor BE, TW/4-13,

23, WWA/4, WWT/9-14
WHYATT, Mrs. George Goddard
see Willmore, Jenny
WHYLEY, William (d 1893 [53])
proprietor EA/94*
WHYTAL, Russ (1860-1930)
American actor, dramatist
WWT/2-6
WHYTAL, Mrs. Russ [Mary Adelaide] American actress WWT/
1-7
WHYTE (fl 1779) dramatist CP/3
WHYTE, Bettina F. (d 1974 [87])
critic BP/59*
WHYTE, Mrs. Carl (d 1907)
EA/08*
WHYTE, Donn (b 1941) American
actor TW/26-29
WHYTE, Frederic (d 1941 [74])
dramatist WWW/4
WHYTE, George (d 1888 [44])
comedian EA/90*
WHYTE, Harold (d 1919 [73])
dramatist, actor BE*,
WWT/14*
WHYTE, Jerome (1908-74) American stage manager BE
WHYTE, Robert, Jr. (1874-1916)
English actor GRB/4, WWT/
1-3
WHYTE, Stirling (d 1911 [72])
actor EA/12*
WIBURNE, D. (fl 1597?) dramatist FGF
WICK, Thomas see Stacey,
Walter
WICKER, Ireene (b 1905) American actress CB
WICKES, Mary (b 1916) American
actress TW/1-3, 5-8, WWT/
11
WICKHAM, Florence (fl 1900s)
American singer WWM
WICKHAM, Glynne (b 1922) South
African director, scholar BE,
WWT/15-16
WICKHAM, Tony [Anthony Wickham-Jones] (1922-48) English
actor WWT/9-10
WICKHAM-JONES, Anthony see
Wickham, Tony
WICKMAN, Sally (d 1963 [49])
American dancer, choreographer, producer BE*
WICKWIRE, Nancy (1925-74)
American actress AAS, BE,
TW/11-21, 24, WWT/14-16
WIDDECOMB, Wallace (b 1878)

English actor TW/2
WIDDECOME, Wallace (d 1969
[100]) actor TW/26
WIDDELL, Mrs. Tessy see
Hilton, Tessy
WIDDELL, Joseph (d 1896) actor
EA/97*
WIDDICOMB, Harry [or Henry]
(1813-68) actor CDP, DNB
WIDDICOMB, Jarvis (d 1898 [43])
comedian EA/99*
WIDDICOMB, John Esdale (d 1854
[66]) pantomimist, actor BE*,
WWT/14*
WIDDICOMBE, R. H. (d 1854 [67])
actor EA/72*, WWT/14*
WIDDICOMBE, Victor (d 1912)
English actor GRB/3
WIDDOES, Kathleen (b 1939) American actress BE, TW/14, 22-
23, 25, 28-30, WWT/15-16
WIDEMAN, Julia see Hache,
Mlle.
WIDERMAN, Robert see Clary,
Robert
WIDMARK, Richard (b 1914/15)
American actor CB, ES, TW/
1-3
WIDNER, Randell C. (d 1971 [47])
managing director BP/56*
WIDOM, Leonard (d 1976 [58])
performer BP/60*
WIEBEN, Michael (b 1944) American actor TW/28
WIEHE, Charlotte [Mrs. Henry
Bereny] (b 1875) Danish dancer,
actress, pantomimist GRB/1-4
WIEHE, Dagmar Indian/English actress WWT/1-3
WIELAND, Adelaide see Zaeo
WIELAND, Clara (fl 1900?) actress, singer CDP
WIELAND, George (1810-47) actor
CDP, HAS
WIELAND, H. W. (d 1922 [80])
pantomimist, dancer BE*,
WWT/14*
WIELAND, Mrs. H. W. see
Zaeo
WIELAND, James (d 1890 [43])
actor, musical artist EA/92*
WIELAND, W. H. (d 1866 [35])
Negro singer EA/72*
WIELEPP, Kurt O. (d 1962 [80])
German performer BE*
WIEMAN, Mathias (d 1969 [67])
performer BP/54*
WIER, Mrs. (b c. 1724) actress

TD/1-2

WIESE, Henry William (1903-74) American talent representative BE

WIEST, Stan (b 1943) American actor TW/27

WIETH, Mogens (1920-62) Danish actor COC, OC/3

WIETHOFF, Mons. (fl 1848) dancer HAS

WIGAN, Mrs. Alfred see Wigan, Leonora

WIGAN, Alfred Sidney (1818-78) English dramatist, actor CDP, DNB, EA/68, ES, OAA/1-2

WIGAN, Horace (1818?-85) actor, dramatist DNB, OAA/1-2

WIGAN, Leonora [Mrs. Alfred Wigan] (1805-84) actress, stage manager CDP, DNB, ES, OAA/2

WIGGIN, Kate Douglas [Mrs. George C. Riggs] (1856/59-1923) American writer HJD, WWM

WIGGLESWORTH, Hugh (d 1908 [44]) manager EA/09*

WIGGLESWORTH, Mrs. Hugh see Wigglesworth, Mary G.

WIGGLESWORTH, Mary G. [Mrs. Hugh Wigglesworth] (d 1895 [28]) EA/96*

WIGHT, Frederick Coit (1859-1933) American musician, composer DAB

WIGHTMAN, Mr. actor CDP

WIGHTMAN, T. C. (d 1874) equestrian EA/75*

WIGHTON, David see Devant, David

WIGLEY, Alfred (d 1916) stage manager, actor EA/17*, WWT/14*

WIGMAN, Mary (1886-1973) German dancer, choreographer CB

WIGNELL, J. (d 1774) actor, dramatist CP/2-3, GT, TD/1-2

WIGNELL, Thomas (1753-1803) American actor, manager CDP, COC, DAB, HAS, OC/1-3, SR, WWA/H

WIGODER, Thelma see Ruby, Thelma

WIGPITT, Thomas (fl 1622) lessee DA

WIKLIN, Stan (b 1938) American actor TW/30

WILBER, Mabel [Mrs. Madison Corey] (b 1882) American singer WWM

WILBRAHAM, Alfred (d 1875 [46]) carpenter EA/76*

WILBRAHAM, Edward [Earl of Lathom] (1895-1930) English dramatist WWT/6

WILBRAHAM, Tilly see Bramhall, Mrs. Walter

WILBRAHAM, William (fl 1635-40) actor DA

WILBUR, Mrs. (fl 1861) actress HAS

WILBUR, Claire American actress TW/27

WILBUR, Crane (1889-1973) American actor, dramatist, producer TW/30, WWT/6-10

WILBUR, Richard (b 1921) American critic, translator, teacher BE, HJD, WWT/15-16

WILCOX, Art (d 1974 [50]) publicist BP/59*

WILCOX, Barbara (b 1906) English actress WWT/7-10

WILCOX, Collin (b 1935) American actress BE, TW/15-16, 18-19, 21

WILCOX, Frank (d 1974 [66]) actor TW/30

WILCOX, Ralph (b 1951) American actor TW/28-30

WILCOX, Richard (d 1889) minstrel EA/90*

WILCOX, Robert (d 1955 [44]) American actor TW/12

WILCOX, R. Turner (b 1888) American costumier BE

WILCOXON, Henry (b 1905) West Indian/English actor TW/4-6, WWT/8-10

WILD, George (1805-56) actor, manager CDP

WILD, George (d 1894) EA/95*

WILD, Harold (d 1917) musical director EA/18*

WILD, James (d 1801 [52]) prompter, dramatist, actor CP/3, TD/1-2

WILD, James (fl 1804) translator, dramatist CP/3

WILD, James (d 1867 [57]) equestrian clown EA/68*

WILD, John (1843-98) minstrel CDP

WILD, Louisa (d 1874 [56])
actress EA/75*
WILD, Dr. Robert (fl 1689)
dramatist CP/1-3
WILDBERG, John J. (1902-59)
American producing manager
TW/2, 6-8, WWT/11
WILDE, Al (d 1970 [60]) personal
manager BP/55*
WILDE, Amelia [née Vining] (d
1869) EA/70*
WILDE, Cornel (b 1915/18)
American actor, director,
producer BE, ES
WILDE, Edwin (d 1909) actor
EA/10*
WILDE, George (b 1609) English
dramatist CP/2-3, FGF
WILDE, Hagar (d 1971 [67])
dramatist BE
WILDE, Henry J. (d 1911) Eng-
lish business manager, acting
manager GRB/1
WILDE, Lilla (b 1865) English
actress GRB/1
WILDE, Mary see Rushton,
Lucy
WILDE, Oscar Fingal O'Flahertie
Wills (1854-1900) Irish drama-
tist CDP, COC, DNB, ES,
HP, MD, MH, MWD, NTH,
OC/1-3, PDT, RE, SR
WILDE, Patricia (b 1928) Cana-
dian dancer, choreographer
CB, ES
WILDE, Percival (1887-1953)
American dramatist NTH,
WWA/3
WILDE, W. J. (d 1868 [45])
treasurer EA/69*
WILDER, Alec (b 1907) American
composer BE
WILDER, Clinton (b 1920) Amer-
ican producer, stage manager
BE, WWT/14-16
WILDER, David (b 1936) Amer-
ican actor TW/25, 28-29
WILDER, Gene (b 1934) Amer-
ican actor BE
WILDER, Ian (b 1939) American
actor TW/27
WILDER, James (fl 1750-c. 1810)
actor, dramatist CDP, CP/
1-3, GT, TD/1-2
WILDER, Mrs. Jay L. (d 1975
[82]) promoter BP/60*
WILDER, John C. (1826-69)
American showman HAS

WILDER, Joseph (d 1871) pyrotech-
nist EA/73*
WILDER, Lilyan American actress
TW/25
WILDER, Marshall Pinckney (1859-
1915) American entertainer
GRB/3-4, SR, WWA/1, WWM
WILDER, Robert (d 1974 [73])
dramatist BP/59*
WILDER, Sophia [Mrs. William
Wilder] (d 1884 [28]) EA/85*
WILDER, Thornton Niven (1897-
1975) American dramatist, actor
AAS, BE, CB, CD, CH, COC,
ES, HJD, MD, MH, MWD,
NTH, OC/1-3, PDT, RE, WWT/
6-15
WILDER, Mrs. William see
Wilder, Sophia
WILDING, Michael (b 1912) English
actor ES, WWT/10-11
WILDISH, Charles Henry (d 1874
[27]) property man EA/75*
WILDMAN, Clara (fl 1875?) singer
CDP
WILDMAN, Edward (d 1886) EA/
87*
WILDMAN, Mrs. F. J. (d 1867
[32]) actress HAS
WILEY, Dora [Mrs. Richard
Golden] (d 1924 [71]) actress,
singer CDP
WILEY, John A. (d 1962 [78])
actor BE*
WILEY, Lee (d 1975 [60]) per-
former BP/60*
WILEY, Major American actor
TW/23
WILFORD, Miss A. J. (d 1865)
actress HAS
WILFORD, Charles see Dukes,
Charles William
WILFORD, Isabel New Zealand ac-
tress WWT/7-8
WILFORD, Mary see Bulkley,
Mrs. George
WILHELM, C. (1858-1925) English
designer, ballet-inventor ES,
WWT/4
WILHELM, Theodore (d 1971 [62])
performer BP/56*
WILHORST, Cora de [née Withers]
American singer HAS
WILKE, C. actor CDP
WILKE, Hubert (d 1940 [85]) Ger-
man singer, actor BE*, BP/
25*
WILKERSON, Arnold (b 1943)

American actor TW/24-25,
28-30

WILKERSON, Guy (d 1971 [70])
performer BP/56*

WILKERSON, William R. (d 1962
[72]) American publisher BE*

WILKES, Sarah (d 1881) EA/83*

WILKES, Thomas Egerton (d 1854
[42]) dramatist BE*, EA/72*,
WWT/14*

WILKIE, Allan (1878-1970) English actor, manager WWT/7-8

WILKINS, George (fl 1607) dramatist CP/1-3, DNB, FGF

WILKINS, John (d 1853 [26])
actor, dramatist BE*, WWT/
14*

WILKINS, Margaret (d 1886 [68])
EA/88*

WILKINS, Marie (d 1883 [70])
English actress CDP, HAS

WILKINS, Mrs. Sidney (d 1878)
American actress EA/79*

WILKINSON, Mr. equestrian
CDP

WILKINSON, Mrs. (fl early 19th
cent) actress CDP

WILKINSON, Mrs. see Allen,
Marie

WILKINSON, Miss see Moun-
tain, Mrs.

WILKINSON, Anna see Carteret,
Anna

WILKINSON, Arthur John (d 1894
[34]) actor EA/95*

WILKINSON, Charles De Witt
Clinton (1830-88) American
actor, stage manager CDP,
HAS

WILKINSON, Christopher (b 1941)
British dramatist, director
CD

WILKINSON, Flossie see Heriot,
Mrs. Wilton

WILKINSON, Harry see O'Connor, John

WILKINSON, Henry Spencer (1853-
1937) English critic GRB/2-
4, WWT/1-3

WILKINSON, James Pimbury (b
1787) English actor BS, CDP,
HAS, OX

WILKINSON, Jan see Holden,
Jan

WILKINSON, J. Benjamin (d 1891
[37]) manager EA/92*

WILKINSON, John Edward (d
1910 [50]) EA/11*

WILKINSON, Kate American actress TW/26-30

WILKINSON, Leslie (d 1971 [72])
performer BP/56*

WILKINSON, Lillie [Mrs. Charles
De Witt Wilkinson] (d 1920?)
English? actress CDP

WILKINSON, Lillie M. (d 1971
[90]) performer BP/55*

WILKINSON, Marc (b 1929) French
composer, conductor WWT/15-
16

WILKINSON, Marcus (d 1892) music-
hall comedian EA/93*

WILKINSON, Marguerite Ogden
Bigelow (1883-1928) Canadian
dramatist WWA/1

WILKINSON, Nicholas see
Tooley, Nicholas

WILKINSON, Norman (1882-1934)
English artist, designer COC,
DNB, OC/1-3, WWT/4-7

WILKINSON, Richard (fl 1703)
dramatist CP/2-3

WILKINSON, Sarah Scott (d 1894
[55]) EA/95*

WILKINSON, Tate (1739-1803) English actor, manager CDP, COC,
DNB, ES, GT, OC/1-3, TD/1-2

WILKINSON, Tom see O'Connor,
Thomas

WILKINSON, William (fl 1699)
dramatist CP/1

WILKS, Mrs. [née Packard] (fl
1834-57) American dancer, actress HAS

WILKS, Annie (1840-63) American
actress HAS

WILKS, Benjamin G. S. (fl 1836)
English actor, musician HAS

WILKS, Henrietta see Shewell,
Mrs. L. R., I

WILKS, Robert (1665-1732) English
actor CDP, COC, DNB, ES,
GT, OC/1-3, TD/1-2

WILKS, Thomas Egerton see
Wilkes, Thomas Egerton

WILKS, William (fl 1717-23) actor
DNB

WILL (fl c. 1590) actor DA

WILL (fl 1597) actor DA

WILLA, Suzanne (d 1951 [58]) actress TW/7

WILLAN, Healey (d 1968 [87])
composer/lyricist BP/52*

WILLAN, Leonard (fl 1651) dramatist CP/1-3, FGF

WILLARD, Catherine Livingston

(1895-1954) American actress
TW/1-3, 5-6, 8, 11, WWT/
4-7, 10-12

WILLARD, Edmund (1884-1956)
English actor COC, OC/3,
WWT/5-12

WILLARD, E[dward] S[mith]
(1853-1915) English actor
CDP, COC, DP, EA/95,
GRB/1-4, OC/1-3, SR,
WWA/1, WWM, WWS, WWT/
1-3, WWW/1

WILLARD, Fred American actor
TW/25-26

WILLARD, George Owen (d 1893
[61]) journalist, historian CDP

WILLARD, Harry Francis (d
1970 [74]) performer BP/55*

WILLARD, Helen D. (b 1905)
American curator BE

WILLARD, Henry E. (1802-78)
American? manager CDP

WILLARD, James (b 1871) English actor, manager GRB/
1-3

WILLARD, John (1885-1942) American dramatist WWT/5-9

WILLAT, Irvin V. (d 1976 [84])
producer/director/choreographer
BP/60*

WILLEMETZ, Albert (d 1964
[77]) composer/lyricist BP/
49*

WILLEMS, Miss see Greene,
Mrs.

WILLEMS, Elizabeth see Addison, Mrs. John

WILLENENS, Mme. (d 1871)
EA/72*

WILLERBY, Arthur [Arthur
Gostling Eggington] (d 1911)
actor EA/12*

WILLES, Louise [Mrs. B. Gray
Heald] (d 1889) American actress OAA/1-2

WILLET, Thomas (fl 1778) dramatist CP/2-3

WILLETT, Joseph M. (d 1864)
performer HAS

WILLETT, Mittens (1864-93)
actress CDP

WILLETT, Miss W. [Mrs. H.
Aveling] (d 1893 [29]) American actress EA/94*

WILLEY, Olive (d 1968 [80])
performer BP/52*

WILLEY, Robert (b 1920) American actor TW/3

WILLIAM, David [né Williams] (b
1926) English actor, director
AAS, WWT/14-16

WILLIAM, Earl (b 1924) American
actor TW/6-9

WILLIAM, Robert (d 1931 [34])
American actor BE*

WILLIAM, Warren (1895-1948)
American actor TW/5, WWT/
7-10

WILLIAMES, Mr. [Matthew?] (d
1801) Welsh actor TD/1-2

WILLIAMS, Mr. Welsh actor TD/
1-2

WILLIAMS, Mr. (fl early 19th
cent) actor CDP

WILLIAMS, Mr. (d 1878) musician
EA/79*

WILLIAMS, Mrs. [Fanny Wright]
(d 1883 [43]) singer, dancer,
actress EA/84*

WILLIAMS, Master (fl 1813) singer
CDP

WILLIAMS, Miss see Brougham,
Mrs. John, II

WILLIAMS, Miss see Davis, Mrs.

WILLIAMS, Miss see St. Ledger,
Mrs.

WILLIAMS, A. B. (d 1964 [67])
performer BE*, BP/49*

WILLIAMS, Agnes [Mrs. Alfred
Williams] (d 1894) EA/95*

WILLIAMS, Mrs. Alan [Mamie
Sims] (d 1917) EA/18*

WILLIAMS, Alf (d 1904) ghost
illusion proprietor EA/05*

WILLIAMS, Mrs. Alfred see
Williams, Agnes

WILLIAMS, Ann (b 1935) American
actress BE

WILLIAMS, Anna (d 1783) translator CP/2-3

WILLIAMS, Annabelle Rucker (d
1967 [63]) performer BP/52*

WILLIAMS, Annie (d 1890) singer
EA/91*

WILLIAMS, Arthur (d 1893 [41])
pantomimist EA/94*

WILLIAMS, Arthur (1844-1915)
English actor CDP, DP, GRB/
1-4, WWT/1-3

WILLIAMS, Audrey (d 1975) performer BP/60*

WILLIAMS, Avril see Elgar,
Avril

WILLIAMS, Barbara American actress TW/20, 28

WILLIAMS, Barney (1823-76)

American actor CDP, COC, DAB, HAS, OC/1-3, SR, WWA/H

WILLIAMS, Mrs. Barney [née Maria Pray] (1826-1911) American dancer, actress CDP, COC, HAS, PP/3, SR

WILLIAMS, Bernie (d 1971 [60]) publicist BP/56*

WILLIAMS, Bert A. (c. 1876-1922) West Indian/American performer CDP, COC, DAB, ES, SR, WWA/4

WILLIAMS, Betty (d 1967) performer BP/51*

WILLIAMS, Billy (d 1972 [62]) performer BP/57*

WILLIAMS, Billy Dee (b 1937/38) American actor BE, TW/17, 24-26, WWT/15-16

WILLIAMS, Bransby (1870-1961) English actor, mimic COC, GRB/1-4, OC/1-3, WWT/4-13

WILLIAMS, Camilla (b c. 1922?) American singer CB

WILLIAMS, Campbell (b 1906) English producing manager WWT/13

WILLIAMS, Celeste (b 1830) American dancer HAS

WILLIAMS, Charles (d 1877 [33]) comedian EA/78*

WILLIAMS, Charles [Charles Thomas Howard] (d 1880 [27]) topical singer EA/81*

WILLIAMS, Charles (1815-83) actor CDP

WILLIAMS, Mrs. Charles see Moody, Mary

WILLIAMS, Charles B. (1829-1915) American actor SR

WILLIAMS, Charles Walter Stansby (1886-1945) English dramatist HP, MWD

WILLIAMS, Clarence, III (b 1939) American actor TW/21-24, WWT/15-16

WILLIAMS, Clark American actor TW/7

WILLIAMS, Claud (d 1972 [81]) performer BP/57*

WILLIAMS, C. Leonard (b 1943) American actor TW/24

WILLIAMS, Clifford (b 1926) Welsh director AAS, ES, WWT/14-16

WILLIAMS, Clyde American actor TW/22

WILLIAMS, Mrs. Daniel see Arthur, Mrs. John, II

WILLIAMS, Daniel James (d 1871 [55]) actor EA/72*

WILLIAMS, David see William, David

WILLIAMS, Derek (b 1910) English actor WWT/9-10

WILLIAMS, Dick (d 1962 [46]) journalist, editor BE*

WILLIAMS, Dick (b 1926) American actor TW/14

WILLIAMS, Dick Anthony (b 1938) American actor, director, producer TW/25, 28-30, WWT/16

WILLIAMS, Dorian American actor TW/29

WILLIAMS, Dorothy Trilby (d 1901) EA/02*

WILLIAMS, Earle (1880-1927) American actor BE*, BP/11*

WILLIAMS, E. B. [né Adam Brock] (1824-67) American actor HAS

WILLIAMS, Edward (d 1908 [64]) musical director EA/09*

WILLIAMS, Edwin (d 1880 [56]) music-hall proprietor EA/81*

WILLIAMS, Egbert Austin (c. 1876-1922) actor OC/1-3

WILLIAMS, E. Harcourt (1880-1957) English actor, producer AAS, COC, GRB/1-4, OC/1-3, WWT/1-12, WWW/5

WILLIAMS, Miss E. L. (fl 1857) Welsh singer CDP, HAS

WILLIAMS, Elizabeth (d 1869) EA/70*

WILLIAMS, Ellwoodson (b 1937) American actor TW/28-30

WILLIAMS, Emlyn (b 1905) Welsh actor, dramatist, producer AAS, BE, CB, CD, CH, COC, ES, MD, MH, MWD, NTH, OC/1-3, PDT, SR, TW/8-15, 18-21, 27, WWT/7-16

WILLIAMS, Emma [Mrs. Henry D. Burton] (d 1890) EA/91*

WILLIAMS, Espy (1852-1908) American dramatist WWA/1

WILLIAMS, Evelyn M. (d 1959 [63]) executive of British Drama Council BE*, WWT/14*

WILLIAMS, Fanny (d 1909) performer? EA/10*

WILLIAMS, Florence (b 1912) American actress WWT/9-11

WILLIAMS, F. Osborne (d 1890) professor of music EA/91*

WILLIAMS, Frances [Frances Jellineck] (1903-59) American actress, singer TW/15, WWT/9-11

WILLIAMS, Frank see Hepton, William Thomas

WILLIAMS, Mrs. Frank see Walmisley, Blanche

WILLIAMS, Fred (d 1916) music-hall performer, actor EA/17*

WILLIAMS, Mrs. Fred (d 1890) EA/91*

WILLIAMS, Fritz (1865-1930) American actor PP/3, SR, WWT/1-6

WILLIAMS, George (fl 1629-35) actor DA

WILLIAMS, George (d 1890) musician EA/91*

WILLIAMS, George E. J. see Vernon, Charles

WILLIAMS, Guinn (d 1962 [62]) American actor BE*

WILLIAMS, Gus (1847-1915) American actor, singer CDP, SR

WILLIAMS, Gwen (d 1962) performer BE*

WILLIAMS, H. A. (fl 1817) actor HAS

WILLIAMS, Harcourt see Williams, E. Harcourt

WILLIAMS, Harry (fl 1860s) manager, actor SR

WILLIAMS, Harry (d 1886 [53]) actor EA/87*

WILLIAMS, Hattie (1874-1942) American actress, singer GRB/3-4, SR, WWM, WWT/1-5

WILLIAMS, H. B. (fl 1868-69) English clown CDP, HAS

WILLIAMS, Heathcote (b 1941) English dramatist AAS, CD

WILLIAMS, Henry (d 1891) EA/92*

WILLIAMS, Herb (d 1936 [52]) American comedian BE*, BP/21*, WWT/14*

WILLIAMS, Herbert (d 1876) clown EA/77*

WILLIAMS, Herbert see Pete

WILLIAMS, Herschel (b 1909) American dramatist, director BE

WILLIAMS, Hope (b 1901) Amer-

ican actress WWT/7-9

WILLIAMS, Hugh (1904-69) English actor AAS, MH, TW/26, WWT/7-14, WWW/6

WILLIAMS, Ina (d 1962 [65]) Australian performer BE*

WILLIAMS, I. R. (fl early 19th cent) actor CDP

WILLIAMS, Irene (d 1970 [38]) performer BP/55*

WILLIAMS, Jennifer American actress TW/25, 27

WILLIAMS, Mrs. Jesse see Tracy, Hettie

WILLIAMS, Jesse Lynch (1871-1929) American dramatist DAB, ES, GRB/3-4, HJD, MD, MH, MWD, NTH, WWA/1, WWT/5-6

WILLIAMS, Joey (fl 1822) circus performer HAS

WILLIAMS, John (fl 1509-11) member of the Chapel Royal DA

WILLIAMS, John (fl 1723) dramatist CP/2-3

WILLIAMS, John (fl 1784) dramatist CP/3

WILLIAMS, John [Antony Pasquin] (1761/65-1818) English dramatist CDP, CP/3, EAP

WILLIAMS, John (fl 1885?) dancer, singer CDP

WILLIAMS, John (d 1887 [58]) actor EA/88*

WILLIAMS, John (b 1903) English actor AAS, BE, TW/8-13, 18-20, 27, WWT/4-16

WILLIAMS, John D. (1886?-1941) American producing manager CB, WWT/6-7

WILLIAMS, Joseph (fl 1673-1700) actor DNB, GT

WILLIAMS, Joseph (fl 1694) dramatist CP/3

WILLIAMS, Joseph (d 1875 [79]) musician EA/76*

WILLIAMS, Kate (fl 1869?) actress, singer CDP

WILLIAMS, Kathlyn (d 1960 [72]) actress TW/17

WILLIAMS, Kenneth (b 1926) English actor AAS, WWT/13-16

WILLIAMS, Le Roy A. (d 1962 [70]) American performer BE*

WILLIAMS, Lottie [Mrs. George Lashwood] (d 1907) EA/08*

WILLIAMS, Louise (d 1872) actress EA/73*

WILLIAMS, Lucas translator CP/3

WILLIAMS, Mack (d 1965 [58])
performer BP/50*
WILLIAMS, Malcolm (d 1937
[67]) American actor BE*,
BP/21*, WWT/14*
WILLIAMS, Maria Kathleen
see Williams, Mrs. Barney
WILLIAMS, Marie (d 1891) burlesque
actress CDP
WILLIAMS, Marjorie (d 1975
[92]) producer/director/chore-
ographer BP/59*
WILLIAMS, Mattie [Mattie Wood]
(c. 1862-87) actress NYM
WILLIAMS, Michael (b 1935) English
actor TW/20, WWT/15-16
WILLIAMS, Minnie (d 1878) ac-
tress EA/79*
WILLIAMS, Miss M. J. (d 1873
[79]) Welsh singer EA/74*
WILLIAMS, Molly (d 1967) per-
former BP/52*
WILLIAMS, Montague (1835-92)
actor, dramatist CDP
WILLIAMS, Mrs. Montague [née
Louise Keeley] (d 1877 [41])
actress EA/78*
WILLIAMS, Nellie (d 1906 [41])
music-hall comedian EA/07*
WILLIAMS, Nellie see Dauvray,
Helen
WILLIAMS, Nelly [Ellen Maria
Watson] (d 1897) actress EA/98*
WILLIAMS, Noel (b 1919) Irish
actor TW/8
WILLIAMS, Norman (d 1938
[57]) singer WWT/14*
WILLIAMS, Odell (d 1902) Amer-
ican actor EA/03*
WILLIAMS, O. T. (d 1976 [68])
performer BP/60*
WILLIAMS, P. (d 1873) actor,
stage manager EA/74*
WILLIAMS, Paul (d 1973 [34])
performer BP/58*
WILLIAMS, Percy (1857-1923)
American actor, manager SR
WILLIAMS, Peter (b 1915) Amer-
ican actor TW/7
WILLIAMS, Randall (d 1898
[50]) showman EA/99*
WILLIAMS, Rex (b 1914) Ameri-
can actor TW/2, 6
WILLIAMS, Rhys (1897-1969)
Welsh actor, dancer, producer
TW/1-3, 5-6, 25, WWT/10-11
WILLIAMS, Richard see Earle
WILLIAMS, Rico (b 1963) Amer-

ican actor TW/27
WILLIAMS, Rita (d 1971 [51]) per-
former BP/56*
WILLIAMS, Robert (fl 1837) actor?
HAS
WILLIAMS, Robert (d 1901) show-
man EA/02*
WILLIAMS, Robert (d 1931 [34])
American actor BE*, BP/16*,
WWT/14*
WILLIAMS, Robert N. American
educator BE
WILLIAMS, R. S. (d 1880) come-
dian EA/81*
WILLIAMS, Ruth (d 1897 [85]) wax-
work proprietor EA/98*
WILLIAMS, Sailor see Winshurst,
George
WILLIAMS, Sonia (b 1926) English
actress WWT/12-13
WILLIAMS, Stephen (1900-57) Eng-
lish critic WWT/8-12
WILLIAMS, Tennessee [Thomas
Lanier] (b 1914) American dram-
atist, actor AAS, BE, CB,
CD, CH, COC, ES, HJD, HP,
MD, MH, MWD, NTH, OC/1-3,
PDT, RE, TW/28-29, WWT/11-
16
WILLIAMS, Thomas (d 1881 [56])
mechanical exhibition proprietor
EA/82*
WILLIAMS, Thomas H. (d 1888)
American circus performer
EA/89*
WILLIAMS, Thomas J. (1824-74)
English dramatist EA/68
WILLIAMS, Tom (d 1910) stage
manager EA/11*
WILLIAMS, Tony (d 1891) American
actor SR
WILLIAMS, Vanilla (d 1973 [35])
performer BP/58*
WILLIAMS, Walter (d 1882 [68])
actor EA/83*
WILLIAMS, Walter (1887-1940)
English actor, singer WWT/4-9
WILLIAMS, William A. (b 1893)
American actor, singer, director
BE
WILLIAMS, William Carlos (1883-
1963) American dramatist MD,
MWD
WILLIAMS, William Henry (1797-
1846) English actor, magician
CDP, HAS, OX, SR
WILLIAMS, William Henry see
Williams, John

WILLIAMS, William T. (d 1906
[72]) musical director EA/07*
WILLIAMSON, Mr. (fl 1783)
actor, dramatist CP/3, TD/
1-2
WILLIAMSON, Mr. actor CDP
WILLIAMSON, Mr. (fl 1795-97)
English actor HAS
WILLIAMSON, Miss see Bart-
ley, Mrs. George
WILLIAMSON, A. J. (fl 1800?)
dramatist EAP
WILLIAMSON, Audrey (b 1913)
critic AAS
WILLIAMSON, David Irish actor,
prompter TD/2
WILLIAMSON, David (b 1942)
Australian dramatist CD,
WWT/16
WILLIAMSON, Henry William
(d 1899 [60]) dramatist EA/
00*
WILLIAMSON, Hugh Ross (b 1901)
English dramatist BE, WWT/
9-14
WILLIAMSON, James (d 1881 [67])
musician EA/82*
WILLIAMSON, J[ames] C[assius]
(1845-1913) American actor,
manager CDP, GRB/1-4,
HAS, SR, WWT/1-2
WILLIAMSON, Mrs. James Cas-
sius see Williamson, Maggie
WILLIAMSON, J. Brown (d 1802)
actor HAS
WILLIAMSON, Mrs. J. Brown
[née Fontenelle] (d 1799) ac-
tress CDP, HAS, TD/1-2
WILLIAMSON, L. B. (fl 1800?)
dramatist RJ
WILLIAMSON, Maggie [Mrs.
James Cassius Williamson]
(1847-1926) actress CDP
WILLIAMSON, Nicol (b 1937/38)
English actor AAS, CB, PDT,
TW/29-30, WWT/14-16
WILLIAMSON, William Charles
(d 1872 [33]) Negro singer
EA/73*
WILLIARD, Carol (b 1947) Amer-
ican actress TW/29
WILLIG, Steven (d 1975 [30])
producer/director/choreographer
BP/60*
WILLING, Mr. actor CDP
WILLING, Bella [Mrs. J. O'Con-
nor] (d 1894) music-hall per-
former EA/95*

WILLING, James (d 1915 [77])
dramatist BE*, WWT/14*
WILLINGHAM, Calder (b 1922)
American dramatist BE, MD
WILLIS, Prof. (d 1901) comical
conjuror EA/02*
WILLIS, Mrs. see Proctor, Mrs.
Joseph
WILLIS, Constance (d 1940) singer
WWT/14*
WILLIS, Daniel (d 1901) music-hall
comedian EA/02*
WILLIS, Dave (d 1973 [78]) vaude-
villian BP/57*, WWT/16*
WILLIS, H. O. (d 1972) performer
BP/57*
WILLIS, Horton (b 1946) American
actor TW/26
WILLIS, Kirk (d 1966 [60]) director,
actor TW/23
WILLIS, Nathaniel Parker (1806-
67) American dramatist, critic
CDP, DAB, ES, HP, MH, NTH,
OC/3, RJ, SR
WILLIS, Oscar [né McLain] (b
1843) American banjoist, come-
dian HAS
WILLIS, Richard (fl 1628) actor
DA
WILLIS, Sally (b 1948) Welsh ac-
tress TW/29-30
WILLIS, Sam (d 1879 [58]) duologue
artist EA/81*
WILLIS, Susan American actress
TW/24-25
WILLIS, Ted [Baron Willis of
Chislehurst] (b 1914/18) English
dramatist, director CD, COC,
PDT, WWT/14-16
WILLIS-CROFT, Stanley (d 1969)
producer/director/choreographer
BP/53*
WILLISON, James (d 1888) music-
hall singer EA/89*
WILLISON, Walter (b 1947) Ameri-
can actor TW/26-30
WILLMAN, Noel (b 1918) Irish
actor, producer BE, WWT/
11-16
WILLMORE, Ernest (d 1892 [17])
music-hall performer EA/93*
WILLMORE, Jenny [Mrs. George
Goddard Whyatt] (d 1894) English
actress HAS
WILLMORE, Lizzie [Mrs. Courtney
Ware] (d 1877 [29]) actress
EA/78*, WWT/14*
WILLMORE, Lizzie (d 1894) English

actress CDP, HAS
WILLMORE, William (d 1876)
actor EA/77*
WILLMOTT, W. C. (d 1894 [53])
stage manager EA/95*
WILLNER, A. M. (d 1929 [71])
librettist BE*, WWT/14*
WILLOTT, William (d 1870 [53])
lessee EA/71*
WILLOUGHBY, Mr. actor TD/2
WILLOUGHBY, Mrs. Digby (d
1891) actress EA/93*
WILLOUGHBY, Hugh (b 1891)
English designer WWT/4-10
WILLOUGHBY, J. M. (d 1872)
actor? EA/73*
WILLOUGHBY, Kathleen Indian/
English actress GRB/1
WILLS, Betty Chappele (d 1971
[63]) performer BP/56*
WILLS, Beverly (d 1963 [29])
actress BE*, BP/48*
WILLS, Bob (d 1975 [70]) per-
former BP/59*
WILLS, Brember (d 1948 [65])
English actor WWT/4-9
WILLS, Drusilla (1884-1951)
English actress WWT/5-11
WILLS, Rev. Freeman Irish
dramatist GRB/1-3
WILLS, G. H. see Velanche,
Harry
WILLS, Harry (d 1879 [33])
comic singer EA/80*
WILLS, Ivah see Coburn, Ivah
WILLS, James (d 1839) Ameri-
can actor CDP, HAS
WILLS, John S. (1862-1943)
actor, manager SR
WILLS, Lou, Jr. actor TW/2
WILLS, Lou (b 1928) American
actor TW/27
WILLS, Nat M. (1873-1917)
American performer BE*
WILLS, Tommy (d 1962 [59])
performer BE*
WILLS, Walter (d 1967 [86])
performer BP/51*
WILLS, W. G. (1828-91) Irish
dramatist DNB, EA/69
WILLSON, Henry (d 1883)
music-hall proprietor EA/84*
WILLSON, Meredith (b 1902)
American composer, lyricist,
comedian AAS, BE, CB,
CD, NTH
WILLSON, Osmund (b 1896) Eng-
lish actor WWT/6-14

WILLSON, Rini Zarova (d 1966
[54]) Russian/American actress,
singer TW/23
WILLY, J. H. (d 1869) professor
of music EA/70*
WILLYAMS, Walter (fl 1635) actor
DA
WILMER, Douglas (b 1920) English
actor WWT/13-16
WILMER, Lambert A. (1805-63)
American dramatist EAP, RJ
WILMER, Sydney actor, dramatist,
manager SR
WILMER-BROWN, Maisie (d 1973
[80]) performer BP/57*
WILMORE, Ernest see Woollams,
Ernest
WILMOT, Mrs. [Mrs. Marshall]
(fl 1793) English actress HAS
WILMOT, Annie see Hastings,
Annie
WILMOT, Charles (d 1896 [57])
actor, producer, proprietor
BE*, EA/97*, WWT/14*
WILMOT, Fred [James Miller] (d
1917 [50]) performer, managing
director EA/18*
WILMOT, Mrs. George (d 1890)
actress? singer? EA/92*
WILMOT, John, Earl of Rochester
(1648-80) English dramatist
CDP, CP/1-3, GT
WILMOT, John (d 1911) showman
EA/12*
WILMOT, Lottie (d 1903) EA/04*
WILMOT, Maurice (b 1883) English
actor, variety artist GRB/1
WILMOT, Robert (fl 1568-1608)
dramatist CP/1-3, DNB, FGF,
HP
WILMOTT, Charles (d 1955 [95])
songwriter BE*, WWT/14*
WILMOTT, Uriah [J. W. Duriah]
(d 1873 [44]) comic singer
EA/74*
WILSHERE, Austin M. (d 1918)
EA/19*
WILSHIN, Sunday (b 1905) English
actress WWT/6-10
WILSON, Mr. actor GT
WILSON, Mr. (b 1801) Scottish
singer HAS
WILSON, Mrs. [née Adcock] (d
1786) actress DNB
WILSON, Mrs. (fl 1773-91) actress
CDP
WILSON, Mrs. see Davenport,
Ruth

WILSON, Miss (fl 1814) actress
HAS
WILSON, Ada (d 1908) EA/09*
WILSON, Al (d 1964 [76]) per-
former BP/49*
WILSON, Albert C. (d 1974
[98]) performer BP/59*
WILSON, Albert Edward (1885-
1960) English critic, journalist
WWT/5-12
WILSON, Alexander (d 1854)
actor, manager CDP, HAS
WILSON, Mrs. Alexander [née
Brobston] (d 1855) American
actress HAS
WILSON, Rev. Alex M. (d 1895
[51]) professor of music
EA/96*
WILSON, Al H. (b 1868) Ameri-
can singing comedian WWM
WILSON, Ann (fl 1783) dramatist
CP/3
WILSON, Ann (d 1902 [84])
EA/03*
WILSON, A. R. (d 1875) musician
EA/76*
WILSON, Arthur (1595-1652)
English dramatist CP/2-3,
DNB, FGF
WILSON, Beatrice (d 1943 [63])
Indian/English actress, pro-
ducer GRB/1-3, WWT/4-9
WILSON, Billy (d 1887 [29])
Negro comedian EA/88*
WILSON, Carrie (b 1944) Amer-
ican actress TW/26
WILSON, Mrs. C. Baron (d
1846 [49]) dramatist BE*,
WWT/14*
WILSON, Cecil Frank Petch
(b 1909) English critic
WWT/11-13
WILSON, Charles (d 1909 [49])
stage manager, producer,
maître de ballet GRB/2-4
WILSON, Charles Henry (d 1808
[52]) Irish? translator CP/3
WILSON, Charles Hooper see
Milton, Charles
WILSON, Christopher (d 1919
[43]) composer, conductor
BE*, WWT/14*
WILSON, David (d 1917) EA/18*
WILSON, Demond (b 1946) Amer-
ican actor TW/27
WILSON, Diana (1897-1937) Eng-
lish actress WWT/5-8
WILSON, Dooley (b 1895) Amer-

ican actor TW/1
WILSON, Mrs. E. see Wilson,
Mary Elizabeth
WILSON, Earl, Jr. (b 1942) Amer-
ican actor TW/27
WILSON, Edith American actress,
singer WWT/8-9
WILSON, Edmund (1895-1972)
American critic, dramatist BE,
CB, MD, MWD, WWA/5
WILSON, Mrs. Edward (d 1877
[90]) equestrian EA/78*
WILSON, Edwin L. (fl 1900s)
American singer WWM
WILSON, Eleanor American actress
TW/3, 11, 24
WILSON, Elizabeth (b 1925) Amer-
ican actress TW/12-13, 23,
25-30, WWT/16
WILSON, Florence see McKinley,
Mrs. W. J.
WILSON, Frances Annie [Mrs.
Robert Wilson] (d 1885 [45])
EA/86*
WILSON, Francis (1854-1935)
American actor, manager, dram-
atist CDP, COC, DAB, GRB/
2-4, OC/1-3, PP/3, SR, WWA/
1, WWM, WWT/1-7
WILSON, Frank (1890/91-1956)
American actor, dramatist
TW/5-6, 12, WWT/9-11
WILSON, Fred (b 1827) minstrel,
manager CDP
WILSON, Fred C. see Fax, Max
WILSON, Garstin Parker see
Murray, Gaston
WILSON, Gene A. (b 1920) Ameri-
can educator, director BE
WILSON, George (d 1874 [21])
musician, composer EA/75*
WILSON, George (d 1876 [22])
musician EA/77*
WILSON, George W. (1844/49-1930)
American actor, minstrel CDP,
PP/3, SR
WILSON, Germaine (fl 1594) actor
DA
WILSON, G. J. minstrel CDP
WILSON, Grace (b 1903) Scottish
actress WWT/6-8
WILSON, Mrs. Harry (d 1888)
EA/89*
WILSON, Harry Leon (1867-1939)
American dramatist DAB,
HJD, MWD, WWA/1, WWM,
WWT/1-8, WWW/3
WILSON, Harry T. (d 1890) advance

agent EA/91*

WILSON, Harvey L. (d 1972 [72])
performer BP/57*

WILSON, Henry (fl 1624) actor
DA

WILSON, Mrs. Henry see Maynard, Lizzie

WILSON, Mrs. H. F. see Wilson, Ruth

WILSON, Hilda (d 1918) EA/19*

WILSON, Jack (b 1876) American
comedian WWM

WILSON, Jack (d 1966 [49]) performer BP/51*

WILSON, Jack (d 1970 [76]) performer BP/55*

WILSON, Jane dramatist RJ

WILSON, Jessie (d 1867 [52])
actress EA/68*

WILSON, Joe (d 1875 [33]) writer,
singer EA/76*

WILSON, John (1585-1641?) English actor DA, COC, OC/1-3

WILSON, John (1627?-96) Irish?
dramatist CP/1-3, DNB, GT,
HP

WILSON, John (1800/01-49) Scottish actor, singer CDP,
DNB, SR

WILSON, John (d 1885) circus
director EA/86*

WILSON, John see Hill, John
Henry

WILSON, John C. (1899-1961)
American manager, producer,
director TW/2-8, 18, WWT/
8-13

WILSON, John Crawford (b 1826)
Irish dramatist EA/69

WILSON, John Dover (1881-1969)
English scholar BE, WWW/6

WILSON, John Henry (d 1913)
EA/14*

WILSON, John S. (b 1913) American critic BE

WILSON, Joseph (1858-1940)
Irish actor, manager, singer
GRB/1-4, WWT/2-6

WILSON, Josephine [Lady Bernard
Miles] actress COC

WILSON, Joseph Maria (1872-
1933) designer NTH

WILSON, Julia (b 1860) actress,
singer CDP

WILSON, Katherine (b 1904)
American actress WWT/7-9

WILSON, Lanford (b 1937) American dramatist, director, actor

CD, WWT/15-16

WILSON, Lee (b 1948) American
actress TW/27-28

WILSON, Leigh singer CDP

WILSON, Leigh see Cockram,
William Edward

WILSON, Lillian Brown (d 1969 [83])
performer BP/54*

WILSON, Lionel (b 1924) American
actor TW/1-4, 11-12

WILSON, Lisle (b 1943) American
actor TW/24-26

WILSON, Lois (b 1898/1900) American actress BE, TW/2-4, 6-7,
26

WILSON, Lucy (b 1876) actress
WWT/3-6

WILSON, Marie (d 1972 [54/56])
actress BP/57*, WWT/16*

WILSON, Mary Anne [Mrs. Thomas
Welsh] (1802-67) singer CDP,
DNB

WILSON, Mary Elizabeth [Mrs. E.
Wilson] (d 1877) EA/78*

WILSON, Mary Louise (b 1936)
American actress TW/25-30

WILSON, Matthew (d 1886) actor
EA/87*

WILSON, Nellie (fl 1896?) actress,
singer CDP

WILSON, "Old" (d 1853 [102]) actor
EA/72*

WILSON, Paul (b 1873) English actor, variety artist GRB/1

WILSON, Perry (b 1916) American
actress TW/1, 3-4, 10-11,
WWT/10-13

WILSON, Ray (d 1963 [56]) director,
producer BE*

WILSON, Richard (d 1796/c. 1802)
actor, dramatist CDP, CP/3,
DNB, TD/2

WILSON, Mrs. Richard (fl 1773-86)
actress WWT/14*

WILSON, Robert (d c. 1600) English
actor, dramatist COC, CP/1,
3, DA, DNB, FGF, NTH, OC/
1-3

WILSON, Robert (1579-1610) dramatist DNB, FGF

WILSON, Mrs. Robert see Wilson,
Frances Annie

WILSON, Roberta (d 1972 [68]) performer BP/56*

WILSON, Robert James Penny see
Waldegrave, Robert

WILSON, Robert M. [Byrd Hoffman]
(b 1944) American dramatist,

director, designer CD
WILSON, Robert Thorpe see
Sheffield, Thorpe
WILSON, Ruth [Mrs. H. F. Wil-
son] (d 1906) EA/07*
WILSON, Samuel T. (d 1971 [71])
critic BP/55*
WILSON, Sandy (b 1924) English
dramatist, composer AAS,
BE, CD, PDT, WWT/12-16
WILSON, Snoo (b 1948) English
dramatist, director, actor
CD, WWT/16
WILSON, T. H. (d 1879) music-
hall manager EA/80*
WILSON, Theodore (b 1943)
American actor TW/25
WILSON, Thomas (d 1882 [49])
musician EA/83*
WILSON, Thomas (d 1887 [73])
EA/88*
WILSON, Tom (d 1887) actor
EA/88*
WILSON, Tom (d 1905) EA/06*
WILSON, Ural (b 1930) American
dancer, singer TW/24
WILSON, Virginia de Luce see
De Luce, Virginia
WILSON, Mr. W. (d 1867) musi-
cal director EA/68*
WILSON, Walter M. (d 1926
[52]) actor, director BE*,
BP/11*
WILSON, Wayne (d 1970 [71])
actor TW/26
WILSON, W. Cronin (d 1934)
actor WWT/4-7
WILSON, William (fl 1617) actor?
DA
WILSON, William (d 1875) musi-
cian EA/77*
WILSON, William (d 1916 [44])
EA/17*
WILSON, William J. (d 1936
[62]) Scottish director WWT/
4-8
WILSON, William John (d 1909
[73]) scene artist EA/10*
WILSON, William Woodrow (d
1972 [60]) performer BP/57*
WILSTACH, Frank Jenners (1865-
1933) American manager
WWA/1
WILSTACH, Paul (1870-1952)
American dramatist, business
manager GRB/3-4, WWT/1-9
WILT, Marie (1833-91) Austrian
singer ES

WILTON (fl 1789) dramatist CP/3
WILTON, Amelia [Mrs. F. Wilton]
(d 1873) stage manager EA/74*
WILTON, Augusta (d 1926) actress
BE*, WWT/14*
WILTON, Clara Goldsby see
Hundon, Mrs. T. J.
WILTON, Edwin (d 1879 [29]) actor?
EA/80*
WILTON, Ellie [Mrs. Thomas C.
Doremus] (d 1902 [50]) actress
CDP
WILTON, Mrs. F. see Wilton,
Amelia
WILTON, Mrs. Frank see Wilton,
Kate
WILTON, Fred (d 1890 [30]) topical
singer EA/92*
WILTON, Fred C. J. (d 1889 [87])
stage manager EA/90*
WILTON, Henry Dolan (d 1871 [28])
agent EA/72*
WILTON, Jenny [Mrs. Louis Bat-
ten] (d 1890) music-hall per-
former EA/91*
WILTON, J. Hall (d 1862 [50])
agent CDP, HAS
WILTON, John (d 1881) music-hall
proprietor EA/82*
WILTON, Kate [Mrs. Frank Wilton]
(d 1888 [27]) EA/89*
WILTON, Marie (fl 1899?) actress,
singer CDP
WILTON, Marie Effie see Ban-
croft, Lady
WILTON, Robb (d 1957 [75]) Eng-
lish music-hall comedian BE*,
WWT/14*
WILTON, Robert Pleydell (d 1873
[75]) actor EA/74*, WWT/14*
WIMAN, Anna Deere (1924-63)
American producer, manager
WWT/13
WIMAN, Dwight Deere (1895-1951)
American producing manager
CB, NTH, TW/3-7, WWT/6-11
WIMPERIS, Arthur (1874/76-1953)
English dramatist, lyricist
WWT/2-11, WWW/5
WINANS, John (1817-59) American
actor CDP, HAS, SR
WINANS, Mrs. John (fl 1843)
actress HAS
WINANS, John, Jr. (d 1861) come-
dian HAS
WINANT, Forrest (1888-1928)
American actor WWM, WWT/
4-5

WINANT, Haim (b 1927) American actor TW/8-12

WINCELBERG, Shimon (b 1924) German writer BE

WINCHELL, Mr. (fl 1841) entertainer CDP

WINCHELL, Walter (1897-1972) American critic, journalist, vaudevillian CB, NTH, TW/28, WWT/7-14

WINCHELL, Mrs. Walter [June Magee] (d 1970 [64]) performer BP/54*

WINCHESTER, Barbara (d 1968 [70s]) performer BP/52*

WINCHILSEA, Countess of see Finch, Anne

WINCOTT, Mrs. Charles see Bridges, Gertrude Agnes

WINDE, Beatrice American actress TW/28-29

WINDEATT, George (1901-59) English musical director, composer WWT/9-10

WINDEL, Lina dancer CDP

WINDER, E. (d 1893 [75]) music-hall proprietor EA/94*

WINDER, Mrs. Edwin see Winder, Mrs. E. S. Bovey

WINDER, Mrs. E. S. Bovey [Mrs. Edwin Winder] (d 1887 [66]) EA/88*

WINDERMERE, Charles [Charles F. Todd] (1872-1955) English actor, dramatist, manager GRB/1-3, WWT/4-8

WINDGASSEN, Wolfgang (d 1974 [60]) performer BP/59*

WINDHAM, Donald (b 1920) American dramatist BE

WINDLEY, Emily [Mrs. John Windley] (d 1876 [37]) EA/77*

WINDLEY, John (d 1901 [67]) lessee EA/02*

WINDLEY, Mrs. John [Kate Ross] (d 1913) EA/14*

WINDLEY, Mrs. John see Windley, Emily

WINDOM, William (b 1923) American actor BE, TW/3, 10-12

WINDOW, Muriel (d 1965) performer BP/50*

WINDSOR, Mrs. see Daniels, Alicia

WINDSOR, Albert C. [William Ross-Cattanach] (d 1908 [58]) EA/09*

WINDSOR, Barbara [née Deeks]

(b 1937) English actress WWT/15-16

WINDSOR, Claire (1898-1972) American actress TW/2

WINDSOR, Flo see Resdan, Rita

WINDSOR, John Peter (d 1976 [60]) composer/lyricist BP/60*

WINDSOR, Lilly (b 1924) American singer SR

WINDUST, Bretaigne (1906-60) French director CB, TW/2-4, 16, WWT/11-12

WINDUST, Penelope American actress TW/24, 28

WINELL, Mr. (fl 1752) English actor HAS

WINES, Christopher (b 1939) American actor TW/25

WINFREE, Richard (d 1975 [76]) composer/lyricist BP/59*

WING, Dan (d 1969 [46]) performer BP/54*

WINGARD, Prof. (d 1912) EA/14*

WINGETT, Edwin see Wingett, Harry

WINGETT, Harry [Edwin Wingett] (d 1905 [60]) comic singer EA/06*

WINGFIELD, Conway (d 1948 [81]) actor TW/4

WINGFIELD, Lewis Strange (1842-91) actor, designer DNB

WINGFIELD, M. (fl 1631) dramatist CP/3, FGF

WINGHAM, Thomas (d 1893 [47]) composer EA/94*

WINIK, Edna Mae (d 1971) performer BP/56*

WINIK, Leslie (d 1975 [72]) producer/director/choreographer BP/59*

WINKELMANN, Hermann (1845-1912) singer CDP

WINKELMEIER, Herr (d 1887 [20]) Austrian giant CDP

WINKLER, Frank (d 1964 [64]) performer BE*

WINKLER, Henry (b 1945) American actor CB

WINKWORTH, Mark J. (b 1948) American actor TW/29-30

WINN, Anona Australian actress, singer WWT/11-12

WINN, Florence singer CDP

WINN, Godfrey (1906-71) English actor WWT/6

WINN, H. (d 1880) EA/81*

WINN, Kitty (b 1944) American

actress TW/28-29

WINNEMORE, Tony (fl 1846)
actor HAS

WINNER, Septimus (1827-1902)
American songwriter BE*

WINNETT, Thomas (1851-1912)
American minstrel, agent SR

WINNING, Mrs. Lawrence see
Winning, Marie

WINNING, Marie [Mrs. Lawrence
Winning] (d 1890 [24]) EA/91*

WINNINGER, Charles (1884-
1969) American actor BE,
SR, TW/25, WWT/4-10

WINOGRADSKY, Barnet see
Delfont, Bernard

WINPENNY, Mabel see Audre,
Olga

WINROW, Samuel (d 1969 [89])
performer BP/54*

WINSCOTT, Dudley A. (d 1972
[70]) manager BP/57*

WINSHIP, George (b 1830) American comedian HAS

WINSHIP, Loren (b 1904) American educator, director BE

WINSHURST, George [Sailor
Williams] (d 1873 [48]) nautical
singer & dancer EA/74*

WINSLOW, A. H. (fl 1852) actor
HAS

WINSLOW, Catherine Mary (d
1911) English actress WWA/1

WINSLOW, Herbert Hall (1865-
1930) American actor, dramatist SR, WWM

WINSLOW, Kate Reignolds [Mrs.
Harry Farren] (b 1814) actress WWA/H

WINSTANLEY, Mr. dramatist
RJ

WINSTANLEY, Mrs. (d 1899 [84])
EA/00*

WINSTANLEY, A. N. [Mrs. J.
A. Winstanley] (d 1908 [42])
EA/10*

WINSTANLEY, Eliza (fl 1849)
actress CDP, HAS

WINSTANLEY, Mrs. J. A.
see Winstanley, A. N.

WINSTON, Mr. actor, manager
TD/2

WINSTON, C. Bruce (1879-1946)
English actor, designer WWT/
4-9

WINSTON, Hattie (b 1945) American actress TW/24, 26-30

WINSTON, Helen (d 1972 [40])

performer BP/57*

WINSTON, Helene Canadian actress
TW/26

WINSTON, Jackie (d 1971 [56])
performer BP/56*

WINSTON, James (1773-1843) English actor, manager CDP, GT

WINSTON, Jane (d 1959 [51]) actress BE*

WINSTON, Jeannie (fl 1876) singer
CDP

WINSTONE, Eric (d 1974 [61]) performer BP/58*

WINSTONE, Richard (d 1788) actor
GT, TD/1-2

WINTER, Banks (1857-1936) minstrel, songwriter CDP

WINTER, Mrs. E. C. (fl 1863-69)
actress HAS

WINTER, Edward (b 1937) American
actor TW/22-29

WINTER, Jessie (1885-1971) English
actress WWT/2-9

WINTER, John Strange [Mrs. Arthur
Stannard] (d 1911) writer EA/13*

WINTER, Joseph P. (fl 1865) actor
CDP

WINTER, Keith (b 1906) Welsh
dramatist WWT/8-11

WINTER, Percy (1861-1928) Canadian
actor, stage manager PP/3

WINTER, Richard (fl 1571) actor?
DA

WINTER, Rose Hélène see
Hélène

WINTER, Tom (d 1876) singer
EA/77*

WINTER, Wenonah Gordon (1888-
1940) American actress, singer
GRB/1

WINTER, William (1836-1917)
American critic CDP, COC,
DAB, ES, GRB/2-4, HJD, NTH,
OC/1-3, WWA/1, WWM, WWT/
1-3, WWW/2

WINTER, Winona see Winter,
Wenonah Gordon

WINTER, Mrs. W. J. see Leslie, Elsie

WINTERBOTTOM, W. (d 1889)
bandmaster, composer EA/90*

WINTERFELD, M. see Gilbert,
Jean

WINTERS, Banks (fl 1880s) actor,
singer, songwriter SR

WINTERS, David (b 1939) English
actor TW/18

WINTERS, Lawrence (1915-65)

American actor TW/2-3, 10-11, 22

WINTERS, Marian (b 1924) American actress, dramatist BE, TW/8-20, 22, WWT/14-16

WINTERS, Roland (b 1904) American actor BE, TW/18-19, 26, 28

WINTERS, Shelley [née Shirley Schrift] (b 1922/23) American actress AAS, BE, CB, ES, TW/23, 26, WWT/14-16

WINTERSEL, William see Wintershall, William

WINTERSHALL, William (d 1679) actor DA, DNB

WINTERSOLE, Bill (b 1931) American actor TW/30

WINTHROP, Adelaide (d 1923 [32]) actress BE*, BP/8*

WINTHROP, Robert see Flanagan, Bud

WINTON, Ethel Alice see Balfour, Ethel

WINTOUR, Ernest (d 1907) actor EA/08*

WINWOOD, Estelle (b 1883) English actress AAS, BE, SR, TW/1-16, 22, WWT/3-15

WIRES, Rodney S. (d 1887) advance agent NYM

WIRGES, William (d 1971 [77]) composer/lyricist BP/56*

WISDOM, Norman (b 1920) English actor, comedian ES, WWT/12-16

WISE, Edward J. (b 1876) English composer, agent GRB/1

WISE, Herbert [né Weisz] (b 1924) Austrian director, actor WWT/15-16

WISE, James Peter (d 1889) acrobat EA/90*

WISE, Mrs. John [née Pattie Lincoln] (d 1879 [27]) music-hall performer EA/80*

WISE, Joseph (fl 1766-79) dramatist CP/3, GT

WISE, Patricia Doyle (d 1975 [60]) performer BP/60*

WISE, Thomas A. (1862/65-1928) English actor DAB, SR, WWA/1, WWM, WWT/1-5

WISEMAN, Charles (d 1916) EA/17*

WISEMAN, Emily (fl 1870?) actress, singer CDP

WISEMAN, Jane (fl 1702) drama-

tist CP/1-3, GT

WISEMAN, Joseph (b 1918) Canadian actor AAS, BE, TW/3-9, 12-13, 21, 25-26, 28-29, WWT/14-16

WISEMAN, Robert (d 1917) EA/18*

WISHENGRAD, Morton (d 1963 [50]) American dramatist BE*, BP/47*

WISSLER, Anna (fl 1860) American actress HAS

WISTER, Owen (b 1860) American dramatist WWM

WITCHETT, Hawkins see Cowell, Joseph Leathley

WITCOVER, Walt (b 1924) American director, actor BE

WITHALL, Mrs. C. see Fitzwilliam, Kathleen Mary

WITHALL, Charles Edward (d 1886 [65]) lawyer EA/87*

WITHAM, Miss (b 1801) actress CDP

WITHAM, John (b 1947) American actor TW/28-29

WITHAM, Marjorie Alexandra see Aubrey, Madge

WITHEE, Mabel (d 1952 [55]) American singer, actress TW/9

WITHERS, Charles (d 1947 [58]) American vaudevillian TW/4

WITHERS, Googie (b 1917) Indian/ English actress AAS, WWT/10-16

WITHERS, Grant (d 1959 [55]) American actor BE*

WITHERS, Henry (d 1879 [27]) clown EA/81*

WITHERS, Iva (b 1917) Canadian actress, singer BE, TW/25-27, WWT/11-16

WITHERSPOON, Cora (1890-1957) American actress TW/14, WWT/8-11

WITHERSPOON, Herbert (1873-1935) American singer, manager DAB, WWA/1

WITMARK, Edward (fl 1891) singer CDP

WITMARK, Frank (fl 1891) singer CDP

WITMARK, Isidore (1869-1941) American publisher, composer DAB

WITMARK, Julius P. (d 1929 [58]) actor, singer CDP

WITMARK, Marcus (d 1910 [76]) publisher EA/11*

WITT, Max Siegfried (1871-1914)
German composer WWA/1,
WWM

WITT, Peter (b 1911) German
talent representative BE

WITTENBERG, Philip (b 1895)
American executive, lawyer,
writer BE

WITTOP, Freddy [né Fred Wittop Koning] (b 1921) Dutch designer, dancer BE, WWT/
15-16

WITTSTEIN, Ed (b 1929) American
designer BE, WWT/15-16

WIZARD OF THE NORTH see
Anderson, John Henry

WIZIARDE, Lou (d 1973 [83])
performer BP/58*

WODEHOUSE, Sir Pelham Granville (1881-1975) English dramatist AAS, BE, CB, ES, HP,
MH, NTH, PDT, SR, WWT/4-11

WODERAM, Richard (fl 1586-87)
actor? DA

WODHULL, Michael (fl 1782)
translator CP/3

WOFFINGTON, Peg [Margaret]
(c. 1714-60) English actress
CDP, COC, DNB, ES, GT,
HP, NTH, OC/1-3, PDT,
TD/1-2

WOHLBRUCK, Adolph Anton Wilhelm see Walbrook, Anton

WOHLMUTH, Alois (b 1852)
German actress WWT/2

WOIZIKOVSKY, Leon (b 1897)
dancer WWT/9-12

WOLCOT, John [Peter Pindar]
(fl 1778-82) English? dramatist CP/3

WOLF, Gerd (d 1973 [50]) pro-
ducer/director/choreographer
BP/58*

WOLF, Jack (d 1965 [56]) performer BP/50*

WOLF, Jay (b 1929) American
talent representative BE

WOLF, Lawrence (b 1934) American actor TW/28

WOLF, Louis J. (d 1972 [67])
critic BP/57*

WOLF, Rennold (1874-1922)
American dramatist, journalist
SR, WWA/1, WWM, WWT/3-4

WOLF, Mrs. Rennold see
Booth, Hope

WOLF, Thomas E. (d 1864)
actor HAS

WOLF, Van (d 1972 [44]) producer/
director/choreographer BP/56*

WOLFE, Mr. (d 1877) Australian
actor EA/78*

WOLFE, Clarence (d 1963 [75])
performer BE*

WOLFE, Humbert (1886-1940)
Italian dramatist BE*, WWT/14*

WOLFE, Joel (b 1936) American
actor TW/26, 28

WOLFE, Karin (b 1944) American
actress TW/23, 30

WOLFE, R. Driskill (d 1973 [72])
performer BP/58*

WOLFE, Thomas (1900-38) American dramatist MWD

WOLFENDEN, Joseph (d 1883 [34])
actor EA/84*

WOLFF, Albert (d 1891 [64]) critic
EA/93*

WOLFF, Edward (d 1880 [64])
musician EA/81*

WOLFF, Frank (d 1971 [43]) performer BP/56*

WOLFF, Laura Sawyer (d 1970
[85]) performer BP/55*

WOLFF, William (1858-1936) German performer BE*

WOLFINGTON, Iggie (b 1920)
American actor BE

WOLFIT, Sir Donald (1902-68) English actor, manager AAS, CB,
COC, ES, OC/2-3, PDT, TW/
3-4, 21, 24, WWA/4, WWT/7-
14, WWW/6

WOLFOWSKY, Boris (d 1910)
dancer? EA/11*

WOLFSON, Abraham (d 1973 [65])
agent BP/58*

WOLFSON, Billy (d 1973 [75]) performer BP/57*

WOLFSON, Martin (1904-73) American actor BE, TW/4-13, 15,
26, 30

WOLFSON, Victor (b 1910) American dramatist BE

WOLHEIM, Louis Robert (1881-
1931) American actor AAS,
DAB, OC/1-3, SR

WOLKIND, Phoebe see Ephron,
Phoebe

WOLLHEIM, Eric (1879-1948) impresario WWT/7-10

WOLPE, Stefan (d 1972 [69]) com-
poser/lyricist BP/56*

WOLPER, David (1901-64) American producer TW/2

WOLSELEY-COX, Garnet (d 1904

[32]) composer WWT/14*
WOLSK, Eugene V. (b 1928)
American producer WWT/16
WOLSTENHOLME, Frederick
see Newbury, Pollie
WOLSTON, Henry [William Henry
Twinberrow] (b 1877) English
actor WWT/7-8
WOLVERIDGE, Carol (b 1940)
English actress WWT/12-13
WOMACK, George (d 1912 [30])
stage manager EA/13*
WOMACK, Joyce see Ebert,
Joyce
WOMBLE, Andre (b 1940) Amer-
ican actor TW/24-27
WOMBWELL, Miss see Bostock,
Mrs.
WOMBWELL, George (d 1909)
circus showman EA/10*
WOMBWELL, Jeremiah (1780-
1850) menagerie manager CDP
WOMEN'S THEATRE GROUP
theatre collective CD
WONDER, The Little see
Fraser, Kate
WONDER, Tommy American actor
TW/6-9
WONG, Anna May (1908-61) Amer-
ican actress TW/17, WWT/
6-9
WONTNER, Arthur (1875-1960)
English actor AAS, WWT/
1-12, WWW/5
WOOD, Mrs. dramatist EAP, RJ
WOOD, Miss see Meadows,
Connie
WOOD, Alfred (d 1876 [46]) Negro
comedian EA/77*
WOOD, Annie (d 1905 [64]) ac-
tress CDP
WOOD, Arthur (1875-1953)
English conductor, composer
WWT/4-11
WOOD, Mrs. Arthur see Webber,
Eliza
WOOD, Arthur Augustus (d 1907
[83]) actor GRB/3
WOOD, Arthur O. (d 1908) EA/
09*
WOOD, Audrey (b 1905) American
literary representative BE
WOOD, Britt (d 1965 [70]) per-
former BP/49*
WOOD, Charles (d 1902 [68])
manager EA/03*
WOOD, Charles (d 1917) scene
artist EA/18*

WOOD, Charles (b 1932/33) English
dramatist AAS, CD, CH, COC,
PDT, RE, WWT/16
WOOD, Mrs. Charles (b 1840) Eng-
lish actress GRB/1
WOOD, Mrs. Charles see Wood,
Clara
WOOD, Charles Octavius (d 1887
[21]) scene artist EA/88*
WOOD, Clara [Mrs. Charles Wood]
(d 1879) actress EA/80*
WOOD, David (b 1944) English ac-
tor, dramatist WWT/15-16
WOOD, David James (d 1889 [31])
musical director EA/90*
WOOD, Edna (b 1918) English ac-
tress, singer WWT/10-11
WOOD, Elizabeth (fl 1839) American
actress HAS
WOOD, Elizabeth E. [Mrs. W. H.
Wood] (d 1883 [37]) EA/84*
WOOD, Ernest [Ernest Edward
Smallwood] (d 1897 [37]) actor
EA/99*
WOOD, Eugene R. (1903-71) Amer-
ican actor TW/18-19, 21-23,
25-27
WOOD, Florence [Mrs. Ralph R.
Lumley] English actress GRB/
1-4, WWT/1-9
WOOD, Frank (fl 1866?) dancer,
singer CDP
WOOD, Frank (d 1876) actor EA/
77*
WOOD, Frank Motley (d 1919 [75])
actor BE*, WWT/14*
WOOD, Frank Percy (d 1912) EA/
13*
WOOD, Fred W. (d 1913 [57])
EA/14*
WOOD, G. (fl 1845) Irish comedian
HAS
WOOD, G. (b 1919) American actor
TW/23, 26
WOOD, George (d 1886 [63]) mana-
ger CDP
WOOD, George (d 1963 [63]) agent
BP/48*
WOOD, George (d 1970) performer
BP/55*
WOOD, Master H. (fl 1863?) singer
CDP
WOOD, Harry H. (b 1845) English
actor, ballet master HAS
WOOD, Helen (b 1933/35) American
actress TW/8-9, 13
WOOD, Henry minstrel manager
CDP

WOOD, Henry J. (b 1870) English
conductor GRB/1
WOOD, Mrs. Henry J. see
Wood, Olga
WOOD, Herbert (d 1916) adver-
tising manager EA/17*
WOOD, H. J. (d 1910) EA/11*
WOOD, Jane (b 1886) English
actress WWT/6-9
WOOD, J. C. (d 1871 [49]) actor
EA/72*
WOOD, Col. J. H. (d 1900)
manager, proprietor CDP
WOOD, J. H. (d 1906 [64]) music-
hall manager EA/07*
WOOD, J. Hickory (d 1913 [54])
dramatist BE*, EA/14*,
WWT/14*
WOOD, John (d 1863) English
actor CDP, HAS
WOOD, John English actor AAS,
WWT/16
WOOD, Mrs. John [Matilda Char-
lotte Vining] (1831/33/45-1915)
English actress, manager
CDP, COC, DP, GRB/1-4,
HAS, OC/1-3, OAA/2, WWT/
1-2
WOOD, Mrs. John D. (d 1865)
actress HAS
WOOD, John S. (d 1911 [80])
actor EA/12*
WOOD, Joseph (1801-90) English
actor, singer CDP, SR
WOOD, Mrs. Joseph [Mary Ann
Wood; Mary Ann Paton]
(1802-64) Scottish actress,
singer CDP, HAS, SR
WOOD, Juliana see Wood, Mrs.
William Burke
WOOD, Kelly (b 1943) American
actress TW/28, 30
WOOD, Lizzie (fl 1846-65) Amer-
ican dancer HAS
WOOD, Marie see Lloyd, Marie
WOOD, Marjorie (1887-1955)
English actress TW/12
WOOD, Mary see Clarke, Mary
WOOD, Mary Ann see Wood,
Mrs. Joseph
WOOD, Mattie see Williams,
Mattie
WOOD, Metcalfe dramatist, actor
WWT/1-8
WOOD, Rev. Nathaniel (fl 1581?)
dramatist CP/1-2
WOOD, Norma Jean (b 1942)
American actress TW/26

WOOD, N. S. (fl 1876) actor CDP
WOOD, Olga [Mrs. Henry J. Wood]
(d 1909) singer EA/11*
WOOD, Mrs. Paddy see Bennett,
Lily
WOOD, Peggy (b 1892/94) American
actress, singer AAS, BE, CB,
TW/2-16, 20-21, 24, 26-27,
WWT/4-16
WOOD, Peter (b 1927) English di-
rector AAS, WWT/13-16
WOOD, Philip (1895-1940) actor,
dramatist CB
WOOD, Ralph dramatist CP/3
WOOD, Richard (fl 1613) actor
DA
WOOD, Roland (d 1966 [70]) actor
TW/23
WOOD, Rosabel (b 1845) American
dancer, actress HAS
WOOD, Rose [Mrs. Lewis Morri-
son] actress CDP
WOOD, Stuart Craig (b 1945) Amer-
ican actor TW/27, 29
WOOD, Thomas (d 1913) EA/14*
WOOD, Tom (d 1898 [27]) comedian
EA/99*
WOOD, Victor (b 1914) actor TW/8
WOOD, W. H. (d 1882) minstrel
EA/83*
WOOD, Mrs. W. H. see Wood,
Elizabeth E.
WOOD, William (fl 1615) actor DA
WOOD, William (d 1855) English
actor CDP, HAS
WOOD, William A. (1833-62) Eng-
lish actor HAS
WOOD, William Burke (1779-1861)
American actor, manager CDP,
COC, DAB, HAS, OC/1-3, SR,
WWA/H
WOOD, Mrs. William Burke [née
Juliana Westray] (d 1836) ac-
tress CDP, HAS
WOOD, Zilpha Barnes (b 1871)
American teacher, musician,
conductor WWM
WOODALL, Doris (d 1954 [76])
singer WWT/14*
WOODALL-BIRD, John (d 1917)
actor EA/18*, WWT/14*
WOODBRIDGE, George (1907-73)
English actor WWT/9-13
WOODBRIDGE, James (d 1893 [41])
EA/94*
WOODBRIDGE, Robert (fl 1793)
dramatist CP/3
WOODBURN, James (1888-1948)

Scottish actor WWT/10

WOODBURY, Mr. (fl 1838) actor
HAS

WOODBURY, Clare (d 1949 [69])
American actress TW/5

WOODBURY, Miss J. B. see
Perrin, Mrs.

WOODBURY, Katie L. see
Riley, Mrs. W. H.

WOODBURY, Lael J. (b 1927)
American director, producer,
educator BE

WOODBURY, Miss S. [Mrs. Mc-
Farland] (fl 1853) actress HAS

WOODES, Nathaniel (fl 1581)
dramatist CP/3, FGF

WOODFALL, Miss (fl 1804) actress TD/2

WOODFALL, Henry Sampson
dramatist CP/3

WOODFALL, Mrs. Thomas see
Collins, Clementina

WOODFALL, William (1746-1803)
dramatist, critic CP/3, DNB,
TD/1-2

WOODFORD, Francis D. (d 1892)
scene artist EA/93*

WOODFORD, J. C. (d 1873 [56])
scene artist EA/74*

WOODFORD, Jennie (b 1940)
actress TW/25

WOODFORD, John (d 1878 [51])
musician EA/79*

WOODFORD, Margaretta (d 1913)
EA/14*

WOODFORD, Thomas (fl 1600-
20) lessee DA

WOODGER, Ben (d 1918) EA/19*

WOODGER, Harry (d 1890 [54])
EA/91*

WOODHAM, Mr. (fl 1806-16)
actor HAS

WOODHAM, Mrs. (1743-1803)
singer, actress DNB

WOODHAM, Mrs. Charles Somerset see Daniel, Mrs.
William

WOODHEAD, John (d 1891) EA/
92*

WOODHEAD, Mrs. William (d
1886) EA/87*

WOODHEAD, W. W. (d 1910
[74]) musician EA/11*

WOODHOUSE, J. H. (d 1906)
comedian EA/07*

WOODHOUSE, Vernon (1874-1936)
English dramatist, critic,
journalist WWT/5-8, WWW/3

WOODHULL, Clara (d 1837) actress
SR

WOODHULL, Fred [William Blanch]
(b 1843) English actor HAS

WOODHULL, Jacob (d 1832 [40])
American actor, manager HAS

WOODHULL, John (d 1838) American actor HAS

WOODHULL, Victoria C. actress
CDP

WOODHULL, Zula Maud American
dramatist WWA/5

WOODIN, William Samuel (d 1882
[62]) entertainer CDP

WOODLEY, Jane see Hill, Jenny

WOODLEY, John Wilson see
Pasta, Johnny

WOODLING, Miss see Simpson,
Mrs. L.

WOODMAN, Alex Haines see
Romer, Alec

WOODROFFE, S. H. see Woodroffe-Boyce, S.

WOODROFFE-BOYCE, S. [S. H.
Woodroffe] (b 1877) English actor, singer GRB/1

WOODRUFF, Edna (d 1947 [73])
actress BE*, WWT/14*

WOODRUFFE, Henry Mygatt (1869/
70-1916) American actor GRB/
3-4, PP/3, SR, WWA/1, WWT/
1-3

WOODS, Albert Herman (1870-1951)
American producing manager,
proprietor NTH, SR, TW/7,
WWT/4-11

WOODS, Allie (b 1940) American
actor TW/25-27

WOODS, Annie Louise (d 1917)
EA/18*

WOODS, Aubrey librettist CD

WOODS, Donald Canadian actor
BE, TW/21

WOODS, Col. George H. (fl 1865-
71) manager SR

WOODS, Graham (d 1918 [44])
EA/19*

WOODS, Harry L. (d 1968 [79])
performer BP/53*

WOODS, Harry M. (d 1970 [73])
composer/lyricist BP/54*

WOODS, Henry (d 1889 [29]) comic
singer EA/90*

WOODS, James (d 1947) American
actor TW/26-29

WOODS, J. M. (fl 1884?) singer
CDP

WOODS, John (fl 1604) actor DA

WOODS, Lesley American actress TW/18-19

WOODS, Maria (d 1909) EA/10*

WOODS, Mary L. see Warrington, Ann

WOODS, Richard (b 1930) American actor TW/21-30

WOODS, Robert stage manager BE

WOODS, Rupert (d 1893 [42]) EA/94*

WOODS, William (1760-1802) actor, dramatist CDP, CP/3, TD/2

WOODS, William (d 1909) property master EA/10*

WOODTHORPE, Peter (b 1931) English actor AAS, WWT/14-16

WOODTHROPE, Mrs. L. D. see Tilbury, Zeffie

WOODVILLE, W. F. (d 1875) actor EA/76*

WOODVINE, John (b 1929) English actor AAS, WWT/15-16

WOODWARD, Mrs. (d 1869 [43]) singer EA/70*

WOODWARD, Mrs. see Stewart, Mrs. E. F.

WOODWARD, Charles, Jr. producer WWT/16

WOODWARD, Charles E. (d 1904 [38]) actor EA/05*

WOODWARD, Edward (b 1930) English actor AAS, BE, WWT/14-16

WOODWARD, Mrs. Eugene Lindeman (1859-1947) actress SR

WOODWARD, Grace [Mrs. Warner Hagen] (d 1907) actress EA/08*

WOODWARD, Harry [or Henry] (1714/17-77) English actor, dramatist CDP, COC, CP/2-3, DNB, ES, GT, OC/1-3, TD/1-2

WOODWARD, Horace L. (d 1973 [68]) producer/director/choreographer BP/57*

WOODWARD, Joanne (b 1930/31?) American actress BE, CB, ES

WOODWARD, Mary S. (b 1819) actress HAS

WOODWARD, Milton (d 1964) magician BE*

WOODWARD, Robert (d 1972 [63]) performer BP/56*

WOODWARD, William Jarman (d 1903 [27]) animal trainer EA/04*

WOODWORTH, Samuel (1785-1842) American dramatist COC, DAB, EAP, MH, OC/1-3, RJ, SR

WOOLAND, Norman German/English actor WWT/16

WOOLCOTT, May (fl 1884-88) actress CDP

WOOLDRIDGE, Mrs. (d 1887 [67]) actress EA/88*

WOOLER, John Pratt (d 1868 [44]) dramatist BE*, EA/69*, WWT/14*

WOOLERY, Miss (fl 1784-66) actress TD/1-2

WOOLF, Barney (d 1972 [95]) performer BP/56*

WOOLF, Benjamin Edward (1836-1901) English/American critic, dramatist, musician CDP, DAB

WOOLF, Edgar Allan (1881-1943) American dramatist, actor SR, WWT/4-9

WOOLF, Jack (d 1918) EA/19*

WOOLF, Kitty (d 1944 [73]) actress BE*, WWT/14*

WOOLF, M. actress CDP

WOOLF, Michael Angelo (1837-99) actor CDP

WOOLF, Stanley (d 1959 [59]) producer, performer BE*, BP/43*

WOOLF, Walter (b 1899) American actor, singer WWT/7

WOOLFENDEN, Guy Anthony (b 1937) English musical director, composer WWT/15-16

WOOLFORD, Louise [Mrs. Andrew Ducrow] (d 1901 [86]) rope dancer, equestrienne CDP

WOOLGAR, Elizabeth [Mrs. W. Woolgar] (d 1883) EA/84*

WOOLGAR, Ellen (d 1875 [24]) actress EA/76*

WOOLGAR, Sarah Jane see Mellon, Mrs. Alfred

WOOLGAR, Mrs. W. see Woolgar, Elizabeth

WOOLGAR, William (d 1885 [84]) actor EA/87*

WOOLLAMS, Ernest [Ernest Wilmore] (d 1887 [38]) actor? EA/88*

WOOLLAMS, Sarah Ann see Rotchley, Minnie

WOOLLARD, Robert (d 1971 [83]) performer BP/55*

WOOLLCOTT, Alexander (1887-1943) American critic, actor AAS, CB, COC, DAB, ES, HJD, MWD, NTH, OC/1-3, WWT/5-9, WWW/4

WOOLLEY, Monty (1888-1963) American actor, producer BE, CB, SR, TW/19, WWA/4, WWT/10-11

WOOLLIDGE, Mrs. (d 1863 [63]) actress WWT/14*

WOOLRICH, Cornell (d 1968 [64]) dramatist BP/53*

WOOLRIDGE, Lestocq Boileau see Lestocq, William

WOOLS, Stephen (1729-99) English actor HAS, SR

WOOLSEY, Robert (1889-1938) American actor WWT/7-8

WOOTTWELL, Thomas (fl 1900?) actor, singer, song composer CDP

WORBOYS, William (d 1877 [48]) comedian EA/79*

WORDSWORTH, Richard (b 1915) English actor AAS, WWT/11-16

WORDSWORTH, William (1770-1850) English dramatist HP

WORDSWORTH, William Derrick (b 1912) English press representative WWT/10-13

WORGAN, T. D. (fl 1808) dramatist CP/3

WORK, Henry Clay (1832-84) American songwriter BE*

WORK, William (b 1923) American executive, educator, director BE

WORKMAN, Miss (fl 1828) English actress HAS

WORKMAN, C. Herbert (1873-1923) English actor, singer GRB/4, WWT/1-4

WORKMAN, Gertrude (d 1972 [87]) performer BP/56*

WORKMAN, James (fl 1803) dramatist EAP, RJ

WORKMAN, John William (d 1895) acrobat EA/96*

WORLAND, Jerry (d 1864 [32]) circus performer HAS

WORLEY, Jo Anne (b 1937) American actress, singer BE, TW/22-23

WORLOCK, Frederick G. (1886-1973) English actor BE, TW/8-12, 30, WWT/4-15

WORLOCK, Kitty Ann see Armstrong, Elizabeth

WORLOOU, Lambros see Guetary, Georges

WORLOW, Percy (d 1918) EA/19*

WORM, A. Toxen (d 1922 [55]) Danish producer, press representative BE*, BP/6*, WWT/14*

WORMSER, Andre (d 1926 [75]) composer BE*, WWT/14*

WORONOV, Mary (b 1946) American actress TW/30

WORRALL, Lechmere (b 1874/75) English dramatist WWT/2-11

WORRELL, Irene (b 1849) actress CDP

WORRELL, Jennie (1850-99) actress CDP

WORRELL, Sophia see Knight, Mrs. George S.

WORRELL, Thomas J. (fl 1848) American actor HAS

WORRELL, William (fl 1851) clown HAS

WORRELL SISTERS, The (fl 1848-68) American dancers HAS

WORRENBERGH, Hans (b 1650) Swiss dwarf CDP

WORSDALE, James (d 1767) dramatist, composer, singer CP/1-3, GT

WORSLEY, Bruce (b 1899) English manager WWT/9-14

WORSLEY, T. C. (b 1907) critic AAS

WORSTER, Howett (b 1882) English actor, singer WWT/6-8

WORSWICK, Alfred (d 1917) EA/18*

WORSWICK, James (d 1903) conductor EA/05*

WORSWICK, John (d 1906 [66]) proprietor EA/07*

WORSWICK, Mrs. John (d 1911) EA/12*

WORTH, Beatrice [Mrs. Sam Shipley] (d 1907) variety performer EA/08*

WORTH, Billie (b 1917) American actress BE, TW/8-12

WORTH, Ellis (fl 1615-35) actor DA

WORTH, Irene (b 1916) American actress AAS, BE, CB, ES, TW/21, WWT/11-16

WORTHING, Frank (1866-1910) Scottish actor GRB/2-4

WORTHING, Helen Lee (d 1948
  [43]) American actress BE*,
  BP/33*
WORTHINGTON, Mrs. actress
  TD/2
WORTHINGTON, Thomas (d 1868
  [25]) star diver EA/69*
WORTHINGTON, William (d 1966
  [69]) performer BP/50*
WORTMAN, Don A. (b 1927)
  American talent representative,
  actor, director, producer BE
WORTON, Mrs. Erskine [Mrs.
  Israel Worton] (d 1886) EA/
  87*
WORTON, Mrs. Israel see
  Worton, Mrs. Erskine
WOTTON, Sir Henry (1568-1639)
  English dramatist CP/2-3,
  FGF
WOTY, William (d 1791) drama-
  tist CP/3
WOUK, Herman (b 1915) American
  dramatist BE, CH, ES, HJD,
  MD, MWD
WRANGHAM, Rev. Francis (fl
  1792-1801) dramatist CP/3
WRAY, Ada English singer
  CDP, HAS
WRAY, Edward A. (d 1866 [27])
  comedian HAS
WRAY, Fay (b 1907) Canadian
  actress ES
WRAY, George (d 1900 [60]) actor
  EA/01*
WRAY, John (1888-1940) American
  actor CB, WWT/7-9
WRAY, Louisa Payne (b 1835)
  English singer, performer
  HAS
WRAY, Maxwell (1898-1972) Eng-
  lish producer, actor WWT/
  7-15
WRAY, Samuel (d 1886) Negro
  comedian EA/87*
WRAY, William A. American
  comedian HAS
WREGHITT, George (d 1884 [36])
  manager EA/85*
WREN, Alice (d 1880) actress,
  singer EA/81*
WREN, Sir Christopher (1631-
  1723) English architect, de-
  signer NTH, OC/1-3
WREN, Fred R. (1848-1917)
  American actor SR
WREN, George (b 1837) English
  actor HAS

WREN, Harry (d 1973 [57]) show-
  man BP/58*
WREN, Sam (d 1962 [65]) American
  actor, director BE*
WRENCH, Benjamin (1778-1843)
  English actor BS, CDP, DNB,
  OX
WRENCH, James (d 1884) actor
  EA/85*
WRIGHT, Mr. (fl 1736) actor CDP
WRIGHT, Mr. (fl 1834-69) Ameri-
  can actor HAS
WRIGHT, Mrs. Alex see Wright,
  Margaret
WRIGHT, Alexander (d 1878) musi-
  cian EA/79*
WRIGHT, Alexander (d 1902 [75])
  manager EA/03*
WRIGHT, Alice (d 1892 [59]?)
  actress, singer CDP, EA/93*
WRIGHT, Amanda (d 1968 [78])
  performer BP/52*
WRIGHT, Belinda (b 1929) English
  dancer ES
WRIGHT, Bob (b 1911) American
  actor TW/23, 25-28
WRIGHT, Brittain (d 1877 [40])
  actor CDP
WRIGHT, Catherine (b 1948) Amer-
  ican actress TW/26
WRIGHT, C. B. (d 1892) treasurer
  EA/93*
WRIGHT, Charlotte see Blanchard,
  Mrs. Thomas
WRIGHT, Cowley (1889-1923) Eng-
  lish actor WWT/4
WRIGHT, David (b 1941) English
  dramatist, director WWT/15-16
WRIGHT, Edward (1813-59) actor
  CDP, DNB
WRIGHT, Mrs. Edward see
  Wright, Rose Olivia
WRIGHT, Edwin (d 1916 [60]) EA/
  17*
WRIGHT, E. H. (b 1950) American
  actor TW/29
WRIGHT, Elizabeth see Arne,
  Mrs. Michael, II
WRIGHT, Ellen (fl 1865) actress
  HAS
WRIGHT, Ellen [Mrs. Percy Cross
  Standing] (d 1904) composer
  EA/05*
WRIGHT, Ethel (b 1886) Canadian
  actress WWM
WRIGHT, Fanny (d 1954) actress
  BE*, WWT/14*
WRIGHT, Fanny see Williams,

Mrs.
WRIGHT, Frances (1795-1852)
Scottish/American dramatist
EAP, RJ
WRIGHT, Fred, Sr. (1826-1911)
English actor, manager GRB/
1-4
WRIGHT, Mrs. Fred [Sr. ?] (d
1919 [72]) actress BE*,
WWT/14*
WRIGHT, Fred, Jr. (1871-1928)
English actor EA/97, GRB/
3-4, WWM, WWT/1-5
WRIGHT, George see Wright-
man, George
WRIGHT, George Edward see
Bealby, George
WRIGHT, Georgie (d 1937 [79])
English actress BE*, WWT/
14*
WRIGHT, G. Harry (b 1901)
American educator, director
BE
WRIGHT, Haidée (1868-1943) Eng-
lish actress GRB/2-4, WWM,
WWT/1-9
WRIGHT, Harold Bell (1878-1944)
writer SR
WRIGHT, Harry (d 1877) panto-
mimist EA/78*
WRIGHT, Hazel (d 1971 [70s])
performer BP/56*
WRIGHT, Henry (fl 1900?) actor,
singer CDP
WRIGHT, Henry (d 1905) EA/06*
WRIGHT, Horace (b 1876) English
actor, singer WWM
WRIGHT, Hugh E. (1879-1940)
French actor, dramatist
WWT/4-9
WRIGHT, Huntley (1869-1941/43)
English actor CB, GRB/1-4,
WWT/1-9, WWW/4
WRIGHT, Jack (d 1917) EA/18*
WRIGHT, Jane (d 1905) EA/07*
WRIGHT, John (fl 1631) actor
DA
WRIGHT, John (fl 1674) drama-
tist CP/1-3
WRIGHT, John (d 1890) musician
EA/91*
WRIGHT, John (d 1900) variety
comedian EA/01*
WRIGHT, John B. (b 1814) Amer-
ican call boy, stage manager
HAS
WRIGHT, Mrs. John B. (d 1857)
American actress? HAS

WRIGHT, John W. (b 1899) Amer-
ican educator, director BE
WRIGHT, Jonas S. (d 1874 [35])
manager EA/75*
WRIGHT, Lawrence (d 1964 [76])
publisher, songwriter BE*
WRIGHT, Mrs. Leonard see
Wright, Minnie
WRIGHT, Lloyd, Jr. (d 1964 [65])
lawyer BE*
WRIGHT, Louis B. (b 1899) Amer-
ican educator, library director
BE
WRIGHT, Margaret [Mrs. Alex
Wright] (d 1899) EA/00*
WRIGHT, Marie (d 1949 [87]) ac-
tress BE*, WWT/14*
WRIGHT, Martha (b 1926) American
actress, singer BE, CB, TW/
4-10
WRIGHT, Mary Ann (d 1902 [64])
EA/03*
WRIGHT, Maudie [Mrs. Ernest
Mansell] (d 1911 [28]) actress
EA/12*
WRIGHT, Minnie [Mrs. Leonard
Wright] (d 1906) EA/08*
WRIGHT, Nelly [Mrs. Alfred Baker]
(d 1888 [26]) actress EA/89*
WRIGHT, Nicholas (b 1940) South
African director WWT/16
WRIGHT, Richard (d 1891) EA/92*
WRIGHT, Richard (1908-60) Amer-
ican dramatist BE*
WRIGHT, Robert (b 1911) American
actor, singer BE
WRIGHT, Robert (b 1914) American
lyricist, composer BE
WRIGHT, Roger (d 1786) actor
TD/1-2
WRIGHT, Rose Olivia [Mrs. Ed-
ward Wright] (d 1888 [61]) EA/
89*
WRIGHT, Teresa (b 1918/19) Amer-
ican actress BE, CB, ES, TW/
24, 26-27, 29, WWT/15-16
WRIGHT, Mrs. Theodore (d 1922)
actress GRB/3-4, WWT/1-4
WRIGHT, Thomas (fl 1693) ma-
chinist, dramatist CP/1-3
WRIGHT, Will (d 1962 [68]) American actor BE*, BP/47*
WRIGHT, William Aldis (1831-1914)
scholar DNB
WRIGHT, William W. (d 1885 [56])
journalist EA/86*
WRIGHT, Wynn (d 1965 [68]) performer BP/49*

WRIGHTEN, Miss (fl 1848?) actress CDP

WRIGHTEN, James (d 1793) prompter GT, TD/1-2

WRIGHTEN, Mrs. James see Wrighten, Mary Ann

WRIGHTEN, Mary Ann [Mrs. James Wrighten] (d 1796 [40]) actress CDP

WRIGHTMAN, George [né Wright] (d 1866) comedian HAS

WRIGHTON, Norman H. F. (d 1917) actor EA/18*

WRIGHTON, W. T. (d 1880 [83]) composer, musician EA/81*

WRIGHTON, Frank Henry see Wrighton, Norman

WRIGHTON, Norman [Frank Henry Wrighton] (b 1887) English actor GRB/1-2

WRIGHTSON, Earl actor TW/1

WRIGLEY, H. C. (d 1918) EA/19*

WRIXON-BECHER, Lady Eliza see O'Neill, Eliza

WROTHE, Edwin Lee (d 1922 [54]) American comedian BE*, BP/7*

WROUGHTON, Richard (1748-1822) English actor, manager CDP, DNB, GT, TD/1-2

WRUBEL, Allie (d 1973 [68]) composer/lyricist BP/58*

WUELLNER, Ludwig (b 1858) German musician, singer WWM

WULFRIES, Mrs. [née Gunn] (fl 1843) English actress HAS

WUNDERLICH, Fritz (1930-66) German singer WWA/4

WUPPERMANN, Claudia see Morgan, Claudia

WUTKE, Louis M. (d 1974) theatre equipment specialist BP/59*

WYATT, Agnes (d 1932) actress, singer BE*, WWT/14*

WYATT, E. actress, singer CDP

WYATT, Euphemia van Rensselaer (b 1884) American critic BE

WYATT, Frances (d 1897) actress EA/98*

WYATT, Frank, Jr. (1890-1933) producer, manager BE*, WWT/14*

WYATT, Frank Gunning (1852-1926) actor, manager COC, DP, EA/95, GRB/1-4, WWT/1-5

WYATT, George H. (d 1860) actor CDP

WYATT, George W. (d 1860) actor HAS

WYATT, Jane (b 1912) American actress BE, CB, WWT/8-15

WYBERT, Charles (d 1906 [60]) actor EA/07*

WYBROW, Mrs. (fl 1808?-13) actress, dancer CDP

WYBROW, Waller actress, singer CDP

WYCHERLEY, William (1640-1716) English dramatist CDP, COC, CP/1-3, DNB, ES, GT, HP, MH, NTH, OC/1-3, PDT, RE

WYCHERLY, Margaret (1881-1956) English actress GRB/3-4, ES, TW/2-7, 10-12, WWT/1-12

WYCKHAM, John [né Suckling] (b 1926) English lighting designer, theatre consultant WWT/15-16

WYCKOFF, Evelyn (b 1917) American actress, singer TW/1, WWT/10-15

WYCKOFF, Robert Fletcher see Fletcher, Robert

WYES, William (d 1903 [46]) actor BE*, EA/04*, WWT/14*

WYETTE, Charlotte (fl 1858) actress HAS

WYKE, Byam (d 1944 [84]) dramatist BE*, WWT/14*

WYLDE, Dr. Henry (d 1890 [68]) conductor, professor EA/91*

WYLE, Edwin A. (d 1964 [86]) manager, press representative BE*

WYLE, Larry (d 1975 [53]) performer BP/59*

WYLER, Gretchen (b 1932) American dancer, singer, actress BE, TW/11-12

WYLER, Hillary (b 1946) American actress TW/28

WYLER, James (b 1922) American actor TW/8

WYLEY, George (b 1879) English actor GRB/1

WYLIE, Arthur (d 1903) music-hall comedian EA/04*

WYLIE, David B. (d 1868) Scottish singer HAS

WYLIE, James (d 1941 [65]) critic BE*, WWT/14*

WYLIE, Julian [Julian Samuelson]
(1878-1934) English producer,
manager COC, OC/1-3,
WWT/4-7

WYLIE, Lauri [Morris Laurence
Samuelson] (b 1880) English
dramatist, librettist WWT/6-8

WYLIE, Max (d 1975 [71]) dramatist BP/60*

WYLIE, William (d 1973 [44])
general manager BP/57*

WYLKYNSON, John (fl 1549) DA

WYLLYAMS, Adeline (d 1880 [22])
actress EA/81*

WYMAN, Prof. (d 1904 [40]) illusionist EA/05*

WYMAN, John (fl 1854?) magician
CDP

WYMARK, Olwen [Mrs. Patrick
Wymark] American dramatist
CD

WYMARK, Patrick (1926-70) English actor WWT/14, WWW/6

WYMARK, Mrs. Patrick see
Wymark, Olwen

WYMETAL, William (d 1970 [80])
producer/director/choreographer
BP/55*

WYMORE, Patricia [or Patrice]
(b 1927) American dancer
TW/4-8

WYN, Marjery (b 1909) English
actress, singer WWT/7-9

WYNDGARDE, Peter French/English
actor, director WWT/16

WYNDHAM (d 1911 [34]) wire performer EA/12*

WYNDHAM, Lady see Moore,
Mary

WYNDHAM, Arthur (d 1888 [47])
dramatic sketch artist EA/89*

WYNDHAM, Sir Charles (1837-
1919) English actor, manager
CDP, COC, DNB, DP, EA/
97, ES, GRB/1-4, HAS, OAA/
1-2, OC/1-3, SR, WWM,
WWT/1-3, WWW/2

WYNDHAM, Lady Charles see
Moore, Mary

WYNDHAM, Dennis (b 1887)
South African actor WWT/4-13

WYNDHAM, Fanny (fl 1838?) actress, singer CDP

WYNDHAM, Fred W. (d 1930
[77]) producer, manager BE*,
WWT/14*

WYNDHAM, Gwen actress WWT/
6-9

WYNDHAM, Horace (d 1878 [17])
EA/80*

WYNDHAM, Howard (1865-1947)
English manager, actor OC/2-3,
SR, WWT/8-10

WYNDHAM, Louise Isabella (d 1942)
actress BE*, WWT/14*

WYNDHAM, Olive (b 1886) American actress WWM, WWT/2-9

WYNDHAM, R[obert] H[enry] (1814/
17-94) Scottish manager, actor
COC, DNB

WYNDHAM, Mrs. R[obert] H[enry]
(d 1901 [82]) EA/02*

WYNN, Ed (1886-1966) American
actor, producer BE, CB, NTH,
TW/2-7, 23, WWA/4, WWT/5-11

WYNN, Henry S. (d 1890) proprietor, manager EA/91*

WYNN, Kennan (b 1916) American
actor BE

WYNN, Mabel Emily Swinton (d
1916) EA/17*

WYNN, Nan (d 1971 [55]) actress
TW/27

WYNN, W. S. (d 1899) manager
EA/00*

WYNNE, Mr. (fl 1836) English actor HAS

WYNNE, Augusta see Angelelli,
Augusta

WYNNE, Cybel [Mrs. Charles
Rock] English actress GRB/1-2

WYNNE, Edith (d 1897 [55]) singer
EA/98*

WYNNE, Evelyne [Lotta Brightling]
(d 1887) EA/88*

WYNNE, George (d 1846) actor
CDP

WYNNE, Jane [Mrs. Johnny Wynne]
(d 1892 [38]) EA/93*

WYNNE, Mrs. Johnny see Wynne,
Jane

WYNNE, Kate see Matthison,
Mrs. H.

WYNNE, Watkin Wyatt see De
Glorion, William

WYNNE, Wish (1882-1931) English
actress WWT/2-6

WYNTER, Amy [Mrs. George Hark-
er] (d 1906) actress EA/08*

WYNTER, Edyth (d 1910) musician
EA/11*

WYNTER, Florrie [Mrs. Charles E.
Derwood] (d 1894) EA/95*

WYNTOUR, Bernard (d 1908 [27])
actor EA/09*

WYN WEAVER, A. E. (b 1872)

English actor GRB/1
WYNYARD, Diana [Dorothy Isobel
Cox] (1906-64) English ac-
tress AAS, COC, ES, OC/3,
TW/20, WWT/7-13, WWW/6
WYNYARD, John (b 1915) English
actor TW/3, WWT/11-16
WYSE, John (b 1904) English ac-
tor WWT/7-16
WYVLLE, Amber English singer
GRB/1

- X -

XIFO, Ray (b 1942) American
actor TW/30

- Y -

YAHNE, Mlle. [Marie Léonie
Eugénie Jahn] French actress
GRB/1-4
YAKKO, Sada Japanese actress
GRB/2-4, WWT/1-4
YAKOBSON, Leonid (d 1975 [71])
producer/director/choreographer
BP/60*
YALE, Charles H. (d 1920 [64])
actor, manager SR
YAMAMOTO, Kajiro (d 1974 [72])
producer/director/choreographer
BP/59*
YANKOWITZ, Susan (b 1941)
American dramatist CD
YANNIS, Michael (b 1922) Greek
actor WWT/11-12
YAPP, Cecil (b 1879) Canadian/
American actor WWM, WWT/
7-8
YARBOROUGH, Bertram (d 1962
[58]) director BE*, BP/47*
YARDE, Margaret (1878-1944)
English actress WWT/5-9
YARDE-BULLER, Mrs. John
see Orme, Denise
YARDLEY, Miss see Kent,
Mrs. John
YARDLEY, William (d 1900 [51])
dramatist, critic BE*, EA/
01*, WWT/14*
YARMOUTH, Earl of [Eric
Hope] (b 1871) English actor
GRB/1
YARNELL, Bruce (1935-73)
American actor, singer TW/
17-19, 22-23, 26, 30

YARNOLD, Mrs. [née Grove] (fl
1836) actress HAS
YARNOLD, Anna Maria [Mrs.
George Yarnold] (d 1895 [80])
EA/96*
YARNOLD, Edwin (d 1848 [58])
actor EA/72*, WWT/14*
YARNOLD, Mrs. Edwin [Emma
Yarnold] (1822-67) CDP
YARNOLD, Emma see Yarnold,
Mrs. Edwin
YARNOLD, G. (b 1817) actor CDP
YARNOLD, C. B. (d 1891 [41])
scene artist EA/92*
YARNOLD, George (d 1878 [63])
comedian EA/80*
YARNOLD, Mrs. George see
Yarnold, Anna Maria
YARRINGTON, Robert (fl 1601)
dramatist CP/1-3, DNB, FGF
YARROW, Duncan (b 1884) English
actor WWT/10
YARROW, Joseph (fl 1742) actor,
dramatist CP/2-3, GT
YARROW, Susannah see Davies,
Mrs. Thomas
YARWOOD, George Julian (d 1909)
musical director EA/10*
YASSIN, Ismail (d 1972 [60])
Egyptian actor BP/57*, WWT/
16*
YATES, Anna Maria see Yates,
Mary Ann
YATES, Benjamin (d 1891 [74])
English/American actor, dancer,
manager CDP
YATES, Edmund Hodgson (1831/32-
94) English dramatist, journalist
CDP, DNB, EA/68, OC/1-3
YATES, Elizabeth [Mrs. Frederick
Henry Yates; Elizabeth Brunton]
(1799-1860) English actress
CDP, DNB, ES, OX
YATES, Ellen [née Benson] (d 1890
[26]) EA/91*
YATES, Frederick Henry (1795-
1842) English actor BS, CDP,
COC, DNB, ES, OC/1-3, OX
YATES, Mrs. Frederick Henry
see Yates, Elizabeth
YATES, George [William Cleghorn]
(d 1907 [81]) actor EA/08*,
WWT/14*
YATES, Irving (d 1969 [75]) vaude-
ville booker BP/54*
YATES, John Lowndes (d 1889
[34]) EA/90*
YATES, Miss M. dancer CDP

YATES, Mark (d 1885) treasurer, acting manager EA/86*

YATES, Mary Ann [née Graham] (1728-87) English actress CDP, COC, DNB, ES, GT, OC/1-3, TD/1-2

YATES, Peter B. (d 1976 [66]) critic BP/60*

YATES, Richard (1706-96) English actor CDP, COC, DNB, ES, GT, OC/1-3, TD/1-2

YATES, Mrs. Richard see Yates, Mary Ann

YATES, Stephen (d 1972 [43]) agent BP/57*

YATES, Theodosia (d 1904 [89]) actress BE*, WWT/14*

YAVORSKA, Lydia (1874-1921) Russian actress WWT/1-3

YAW, Ellen Beach (1869-1947) American singer SR, WWA/2

YAZINSKY, Jean (d 1973 [81]) performer BP/57*

YEAGER, Robert (d 1976 [64]) publicist BP/60*

YEAMAN, George (d 1827) Scottish equestrian? HAS

YEAMANS, Annie (1835-1912) English actress CDP, GRB/ 3-4, PP/3, SR, WWT/1

YEAMANS, Jennie (1862-1906) Australian actress CDP

YEARSLEY, Anne (d 1806) dramatist CP/3

YEARSLEY, Claude Blakesley (1885-1961) manager, composer WWT/4-5

YEATON, Kelly (b 1911) American educator, director BE

YEATS, Jack B. (1871-1957) Irish dramatist MD, WWW/5

YEATS, Murray F. (d 1975 [65]) performer BP/59*

YEATS, William Butler (1865-1939) Irish dramatist AAS, COC, DNB, ES, GRB/3-4, HP, MD, MH, MWD, NTH, OC/1-3, PDT, RE, WWM, WWT/1-8, WWW/3

YELDING, Harry (d 1918 [50]) EA/19*

YELDING, John (d 1892) EA/93*

YELDING, Mrs. John (d 1903 [80]) circus performer? EA/04*

YELLAND, Estelle D'Arcy [Estelle D'Arcy Bodenham] (d 1871 [27]) actress EA/72*

YELLAND, Willie [George D'Arcy] (d 1886) dramatist EA/87*

YELLEN, Jack (b 1892) Polish lyricist, dramatist BE

YELVINGTON, Ramsey (d 1973 [60]) dramatist BP/58*

YEO (fl 1790) dramatist CP/3

YEOLAND, Edith (d 1901) actress EA/02*

YEOLAND, Ida (d 1901) actress EA/02*

YEOMANS, Thomas (1826-55) American call boy, actor? HAS

YEOMANS, Mrs. Thomas [Miss Marshall; Mrs. Edmonds] HAS

YEZBAK, John J. (d 1965 [53]) dramatist BP/49*

YOELSON, Asa see Jolson, Albert

YOHE, May (1869-1938) American actress, singer EA/94, GRB/1, WWT/2-8

YOHN, Erica American actress TW/25, 27-29

YOKEL, Alexander (1887/89-1947) American producing manager TW/4, WWT/9-10

YONGE, Sir William (fl 1731) dramatist CP/3

YORDAN, Phillip (b c. 1914) American dramatist BE

YORK, Cecil Morton (b 1864) English actor EA/95

YORK, Dick (b 1928) American actor ES

YORK, Elizabeth (d 1909 [90]) EA/ 10*

YORK, Elizabeth (d 1969 [46]) performer BP/53*

YORK, Michael (b 1942) English actor CB, TW/29

YORK, Richard (b 1930) American producer, actor, dancer, singer BE

YORKE, Alan see Feinstein, Alan

YORKE, Augustus (d 1939 [79]) actor WWT/4-9

YORKE, Augustus see Danemore, A.

YORKE, Dallas (d 1963) performer BE*

YORKE, Harry singer CDP

YORKE, Oswald (1885?-1943) English actor CB, EA/96, GRB/ 3-4, WWT/1-9

YORKE, Mrs. Oswald see Russell, Annie

YORKE, Philip, Viscount Royston (1784-1808) English translator

CP/3
YORKE, Philip English manager,
agent GRB/1-4
YORKE, Tommy (d 1965 [73])
performer BP/49*
YOST, Agnes Scott American ac-
tress TW/1
YOST, Herbert A. (d 1945 [65])
American actor TW/2
YOUDAN, Thomas (d 1876 [60])
proprietor EA/77*
YOUENS, Cpt. John Henry (d
1879 [33]) aeronaut EA/80*
YOULL, Jim (d 1962) stage
manager BE*
YOUMANS, Vincent (1898-1946)
American composer, producer
AAS, CB, DAB, ES, PDT,
TW/2, WWT/6-9
YOUNG, Mr. (fl 1792-1800)
actor, dramatist CP/3
YOUNG, Mr. (fl 1801) dramatist
CP/3
YOUNG, Mrs. see Hughes,
Mrs.
YOUNG, Miss (fl 1849) actress
HAS
YOUNG, A. tight-rope walker
CDP
YOUNG, Alfred (d 1883 [54])
manager EA/84*
YOUNG, Alfred W. (d 1876)
actor EA/77*
YOUNG, Anne (b 1773/75) Eng-
lish actress CDP, GT, TD/2
YOUNG, Arthur (d 1917) come-
dian EA/18*
YOUNG, Arthur (1898-1959)
English actor WWT/9-11
YOUNG, Aston S. (b 1930) Amer-
ican actor TW/26, 28-29
YOUNG, Benjamin (fl 1838-50)
American actor HAS
YOUNG, Bertram Alfred (b 1912)
English critic WWT/15-16
YOUNG, Bryan (b 1945) Ameri-
can actor TW/26
YOUNG, Carleton G. (d 1971
[64]) performer BP/56*
YOUNG, Cecilia see Arne,
Mrs. Thomas Augustine
YOUNG, Charles (b 1854) min-
strel CDP
YOUNG, Charles (d 1874) Amer-
ican actor COC, HAS, OC/
1-3
YOUNG, Mrs. Charles [née
Foster] (d 1831) actress HAS

YOUNG, Mrs. Charles see
Vezin, Jane Elizabeth
YOUNG, Charles Frederick (d 1874)
comedian EA/75*
YOUNG, Sir Charles Lawrence
(1839-87) dramatist NYM
YOUNG, Charles Mayne (1777-1856)
English actor BS, CDP, COC,
DNB, ES, GT, OC/1-3, OX
YOUNG, Mrs. Charles Wayne see
Grimani, Julia
YOUNG, Charlie Oswald see
Oswald, Charlie
YOUNG, Charlotte Elizabeth see
Hope, Charlotte
YOUNG, Christopher B. (d 1975
[67]) producer/director/chore-
ographer BP/60*
YOUNG, Clara (1890-1960) Ameri-
can actress ES, TW/17, WWA/4
YOUNG, Daniel (d 1888) EA/89*
YOUNG, David R. (1832-1918)
American actor SR
YOUNG, D. B. [D. B. Buchan]
Scottish actor, singer GRB/1
YOUNG, Edgar Berryhill (b 1908)
American executive BE
YOUNG, Dr. Edward (1681/83-
1765) English dramatist CDP,
CP/1-3, GT, HP, TD/1-2
YOUNG, Elizabeth see Dorman,
Mrs. Ridley
YOUNG, F. (d 1867 [45]) actor?
EA/68*
YOUNG, Felix (d 1976 [80]) pro-
ducer/director/choreographer
BP/60*
YOUNG, Florence (d 1920) actress,
singer BE*, WWT/14*
YOUNG, Francis Brett (1884-1954)
English dramatist WWW/5
YOUNG, Frank (d 1968 [56]) press
agent BP/53*
YOUNG, George (d 1896 [30]) actor
EA/97*
YOUNG, Mrs. George (d 1917)
EA/18*
YOUNG, George Ralph (d 1894 [58])
property man, actor EA/95*
YOUNG, Gig [né Byron Ellsworth
Barr] (b 1917) American actor
BE, TW/10-15, 17-19, 24,
WWT/15-16
YOUNG, Gilbert (d 1874) actor
EA/75*
YOUNG, Gladys (d 1975 [70]) per-
former BP/60*
YOUNG, Harry L. (b 1910) Ameri-

can stage manager, actor,
director BE

YOUNG, Henry (d 1890 [76]) actor
EA/91*

YOUNG, Mrs. H. F. see Henderson, Bessie

YOUNG, Howard Irving (b 1893)
American dramatist WWT/8-11

YOUNG, Howard L. (b 1911)
American producing manager
BE, TW/3-6, WWT/11-12

YOUNG, H. Richard (b 1930)
American actor TW/30

YOUNG, Mrs. H. Wilmot see
Adams, Margie

YOUNG, Isabella Jane (d 1901)
EA/02*

YOUNG, James, Jr. American
actor WWM

YOUNG, James (b 1878) American actor ES

YOUNG, James (d 1974 [51])
performer BP/59*

YOUNG, James L. (d 1975 [58])
performer BP/60*

YOUNG, Janis American actress
TW/24

YOUNG, J. Arthur (d 1943 [63])
American actor BE*, BP/28*

YOUNG, Mrs. J. F. (d 1886)
EA/87*

YOUNG, J. Falconer (d 1887)
actor NYM

YOUNG, Joan (b 1903) English
actress WWT/11-16

YOUNG, Joe (b 1905) American
actor TW/25, 29-30

YOUNG, John (fl 1537-70) actor
DA

YOUNG, John (fl 1626-35) actor
DA

YOUNG, John (d 1909) EA/10*

YOUNG, John Wray (b 1909)
American director, educator
BE

YOUNG, La Monte composer
CD

YOUNG, Louisa see Prior,
Mrs. James J.

YOUNG, Madonna American actress TW/28

YOUNG, Margaret (d 1969 [69])
performer BP/53*

YOUNG, Margaret Mary (b 1911)
American designer, director
BE

YOUNG, Mary Marsden (d 1971
[92]) actress TW/28

YOUNG, Noel American actor
TW/29

YOUNG, Ollie (b 1876) American
vaudevillian WWM

YOUNG, Percival (d 1917) EA/18*

YOUNG, Ralph (b 1923) American
actor TW/15

YOUNG, Richard (d 1846 [55]) actor
CDP

YOUNG, Richard (d 1869 [31])
comic singer EA/70*

YOUNG, Richard W. (d 1887 [65])
actor EA/88*

YOUNG, Rida Johnson (1875-1926)
American dramatist SR, WWA/
1, WWM, WWT/1-5

YOUNG, Robert (b 1907) American
actor CB

YOUNG, Roland (1887-1953) English
actor AAS, ES, TW/10, WWA/
3, WWT/6-11

YOUNG, Ron[ald] (b 1941) American
actor TW/22-24, 28

YOUNG, Sophie (fl 1869-79) actress OAA/2

YOUNG, Stanley (1906-75) American
dramatist, executive BE

YOUNG, Stark (1881-1963) American
dramatist, critic, director
COC, ES, HJD, NTH, OC/1-3,
PDT, WWA/4, WWT/5-13

YOUNG, T. B. (d 1918) EA/19*

YOUNG, Thomas actor TD/2

YOUNG, Victor (1900-56) American
composer, musical director
WWA/3

YOUNG, Victor (d 1968 [79]) composer/lyricist BP/53*

YOUNG, William (1847-1920) American dramatist GRB/3-4,
WWA/1, WWM

YOUNG, Winifred (d 1964 [86])
actor BE*

YOUNGE, A. (b 1806) actor CDP

YOUNGE, Fred (d 1870 [45]) actor,
manager EA/71*, WWT/14*

YOUNGE, Margaret [Mrs. Richard
W. Younge] (d 1883) EA/84*

YOUNGE, Richard (d 1846 [55])
actor EA/72*, WWT/14*

YOUNGE, Mrs. Richard W. see
Younge, Margaret

YOUNGE, R. W. (1822-87) English
actor NYM

YOUNGE, William (d 1897 [39])
actor, author EA/98*

YOUNGER, Elizabeth (1699?-1762)
actress DNB

YOUNGER, Joseph (fl 1774)
   prompter, manager TD/1-2
YOUNGER, Thomas actor CDP
YOUNGSON, Robert (d 1974 [56])
   producer/director/choreographer
   BP/58*
"YOUNG SWEENEY" see Buckley,
   George Swayne
YOUSKEVITCH, Igor (b 1912)
   Russian dancer CB
YOW, Joe (d 1964 [70]) American
   performer BE*
YUILL, Mrs. James, Jr. see
   Plimmer, Annie
YULE, Joe see Rooney, Mickey
YULIN, Harris (b 1937) American
   actor TW/25
YURGEV, Yuri (d 1948 [77]) ac-
   tor WWT/14*
YURIKO (b 1920) American dancer,
   choreographer BE
YURKA, Blanche (1893-1974)
   American actress, director
   AAS, BE, BTR/74, COC,
   TW/3-7, 12-16, 18-20, 23,
   26, WWT/4-15

- Z -

ZABELLE, Flora (d 1968 [88])
   Turkish actress, singer TW/
   25, WWT/1-8
ZACCHINI, Ernest (d 1975 [83])
   performer BP/59*
ZACCHINI, Hugo (d 1975 [77])
   performer BP/60*
ZACCHINI, Ildebrando (d 1948
   [79]) circus performer BP/33*
ZAEO [Adelaide Wieland; Mrs.
   H. W. Wieland] (d 1906 [43])
   gymnast EA/07*
ZAHL, Eda (b 1948) American
   actress TW/28
ZAHL, Ephraim (d 1975 [48])
   agent BP/60*
ZAINNCZEK, Mr. (fl 1853) Polish
   actor HAS
ZAKOWSKI, Rita (d 1974 [43])
   agent BP/58*
ZAKS, Jerry (b 1946) German/
   American actor TW/30
ZALA, Nancy (b 1936) American
   actress TW/29
ZALOOM, Joe (b 1944) American
   actor TW/28
ZALTZBERG, Charlotte Singer (d
   1974 [49]) writer of musicals

CD, TW/30
ZALUD, Sam (d 1963 [77]) designer
   BE*
ZAMBRA [John Buxton] (d 1898)
   acrobat EA/99*
ZAMEZOU, Mons. [Thomas Jame-
   son] (d 1885 [66]) equestrian
   EA/86*
ZAMPI (d 1905 [49]) one-legged
   gymnast EA/06*
ZANFRETTA, Josephine [née Josie
   Dupree] (fl 1863) dancer HAS
ZANFRETTA, Marietta (fl 1858)
   French tight-rope dancer CDP,
   HAS
ZANFRETTA, Rosita (fl 1863)
   tight-rope dancer HAS
ZANFRETTI, Francesca (d 1952
   [90]) dancer BE*, WWT/14*
ZANG, Edward (b 1934) American
   actor TW/24-28, 30
ZANGWILL, Israel (1864-1926)
   English dramatist CDP, COC,
   DNB, ES, GRB/1-4, HP, MWD,
   NTH, OC/1-3, SR, WWM,
   WWT/1-5, WWW/2
ZANTE, Mme. (d 1890) pantomimist,
   dancer EA/91*
ZARATE, Lucia (1864-90) dwarf
   CDP
ZARAZA, Mme. [Mrs. George
   Helton] (d 1898) rifle shot EA/
   99*
ZARIT, Pam (b 1944) American
   actress TW/26-28
ZAVADSKY, Yuri Alexeivich (1894-
   1977) Russian actor, director
   COC
ZAVISTOWSKI, Mons. (fl 1848)
   dancer CDP
ZAVISTOWSKI, Alice (b 1851)
   American dancer HAS
ZAVISTOWSKI, Christine [née
   Ludlam] (fl 1848-69) English
   dancer, actress CDP, HAS
ZAVISTOWSKI, Emeline (b 1850)
   American dancer HAS
ZAVISTOWSKI SISTERS, The (fl
   1850-69) American dancers HAS
ZEANI, Virginia (b 1928) singer
   ES
ZEDORA, Adèle (d 1902 [32]) acro-
   bat EA/03*
ZEFFIRELLI, Franco (b 1923)
   Italian director, scene designer
   BE, CB, COC, ES, OC/3,
   PDT, WWT/14-16
ZEIGER, Mme. see Alboni,

Marietta
ZEIGLER, Clara see Ziegler,
Clara
ZEISLER, Peter (b 1923) Amer-
ican managing director BE
ZEITZ, Daisy (d 1974 [67]) per-
former BP/58*
ZELLER, Mark (b 1932) Ameri-
can actor TW/27, 30
ZEMACH, Nahum L. (1887-1939)
Russian producer, director
BE*
ZENATELLO, Giovanni (1876-1949)
Italian singer ES
ZENIDA, Mme. (d 1891 [28])
lion tamer EA/92*
"ZENO" see Cook, Francis
Edward
ZENTO (d 1894 [48]) bicyclist
EA/95*
ZERBINI, Mrs. (d 1884) EA/85*
ZERBINI, Carlotta [Mrs. John
Harvey] (d 1912 [69]) English
actress, singer GRB/1-4
ZERMAN, Mrs. see Marshall,
Polly
ZERR, Anna (1822-81) singer
CDP
ZERRAHN, Carl (1826-1909)
German/American conductor
CDP
ZETTERLING, Mai (b 1925)
Swedish actress WWT/11-14
ZIBORAN, George (b 1931) Amer-
ican actor TW/11
ZIDES, Max (d 1975 [70]) per-
former BP/59*
ZIEGFELD, Florenz, Jr. (1867-
1932) American manager
AAS, COC, DAB, ES, GRB/4,
HJD, NTH, OC/1-3, PDT,
SR, WWA/1, WWM, WWT/1-6
ZIEGFELD, Mrs. Florenz see
Held, Anna
ZIEGLER, Anne [née Irene Fran-
ces Eastwood] (b 1910) English
actress, singer WWT/10-13
ZIEGLER, Clara (1844-1909) ac-
tress, dramatist BE*, WWT/
14*
ZIEGLER, Edward (1870-1947)
American manager BE*,
BP/32*
ZIEGLER, Jules (b 1900) Amer-
ican talent representative,
manager BE
ZIEGLER, Larry (d 1974 [27])
assistant stage manager

TW/30
ZIGA, Casey (d 1974 [56]) per-
former BP/58*
ZILAHY, Lajos (b 1891) Hungarian
dramatist MD
ZILLA, Mme. [Eliza Lind] (d 1900
[49]) clairvoyant EA/01*
ZIMBALIST, Al (d 1975 [59]) pro-
ducer/director/choreographer
BP/60*
ZIMBALIST, Efrem, Jr. (b 1913/
23?) American actor, producer,
composer BE, CB
ZIMBALIST, Sam (d 1958 [54])
producer BE*
ZIMMER, Dolph M. (d 1975 [75])
producer/director/choreographer
BP/60*
ZIMMER, Maggie [Mrs. H. R.
Skinner] (d 1893) EA/94*
ZIMMERL, Christl (d 1976 [36])
performer BP/60*
ZIMMERMAN, Mlle. [née Anchutz]
(fl 1858) actress HAS
ZIMMERMAN, J. Fred (d 1925 [84])
manager BE*, WWT/14*
ZIMMERMAN, J. Fred, Jr. (d 1948
[77]) director, producer BE*,
WWT/14*
ZIMMERMANN, Ed (1935-72) Amer-
ican actor TW/22-24, 26-27, 29
ZIMMERMANN, Jacob F. (d 1877)
treasurer CDP
ZINDEL, Paul (b 1936) American
dramatist CB, CD, MH, WWT/
15-16
ZINKEISEN, Doris Clare Scottish
designer WWT/7-14
ZIPPRODT, Patricia costume de-
signer WWT/16
ZISKE, Carol Anne (b 1946) Amer-
ican actress TW/28
ZOBOLI, Alessandro (d 1896 [68])
singer EA/97*
ZOE, Marie (1840-86) Cuban
dancer, pantomimist CDP, HAS
ZOELLER, Carli (d 1889 [49])
bandmaster EA/90*
ZOELLNER, Peter Lee (d 1971)
dramatist BP/56*
ZOFF, Otto (b 1890) Austrian
dramatist MD
ZOFFANY, John (1733/35-1810)
Bohemian painter COC, OC/1-3
ZOHN, Chester E. (d 1975 [71])
performer BP/59*
ZOLA, Miss (d 1901) gymnast
EA/02*

ZOLA, Emile-Edouard-Charles-
Antoine (1840-1902) French
dramatist COC, OC/3
ZONIS, Stuart Michael see
Damon, Stuart
ZORICH, Louis (b 1924) American
actor TW/22-23, 25-26, 28-29
ZORINA, Vera [Brigitta Hartwig]
(b 1917) German/American ac-
tress, dancer AAS, BE, CB,
TW/1-7, WWT/9-16
ZORN, Fritz (b 1871) English
dramatist GRB/2-3
ZORN, Theodora see Rozant,
Ina
ZORRAN (d 1976 [60s]) performer
BP/60*
ZOUCH, R. (fl 1631-38?) drama-
tist FGF
ZOUZE, Emilie see Polaire,
Mlle.
ZOYARA, Ella see Ella Zoyara,
Miss
ZUCCHINI, Giovanni (d 1892)
singer EA/93*
ZUCCO, George (1886-1960) Eng-
lish actor WWT/6-11
ZUCKERBERG, Regina (d 1964
[76]) performer BP/49*

ZUCKMAŸER, Carl (1896-1977)
German dramatist COC, NTH,
OC/3, WWT/14-16
ZULIMA, Mme. [Mrs. Navarro]
(d 1903 [52]) circus performer
EA/04*
ZUNSER, Jesse (b 1898) American
critic BE
ZUSSIN, Victoria (b 1927) Amer-
ican actress TW/24
ZWAR, Charles (b 1914) Aus-
tralian composer, lyricist
AAS, WWT/11-16
ZWEIBELSHARF, David see
Dank, David
ZWEIG, Stefan (d 1942 [60])
Austrian dramatist BP/26*,
WWT/14*
ZWERDLING, Allen (b 1922)
American publisher, director
BE
ZWERLING, Darrell American
actor TW/26
ZWICK, Joel (b 1942) American
actor TW/23, 28
ZWISSIG, William (b 1905) Amer-
ican manager, producer BE
ZYLBERCWEIG, Zalmen (d 1972
[77]) historian BP/57*